The Norton Anthology of Modern and Contemporary Poetry

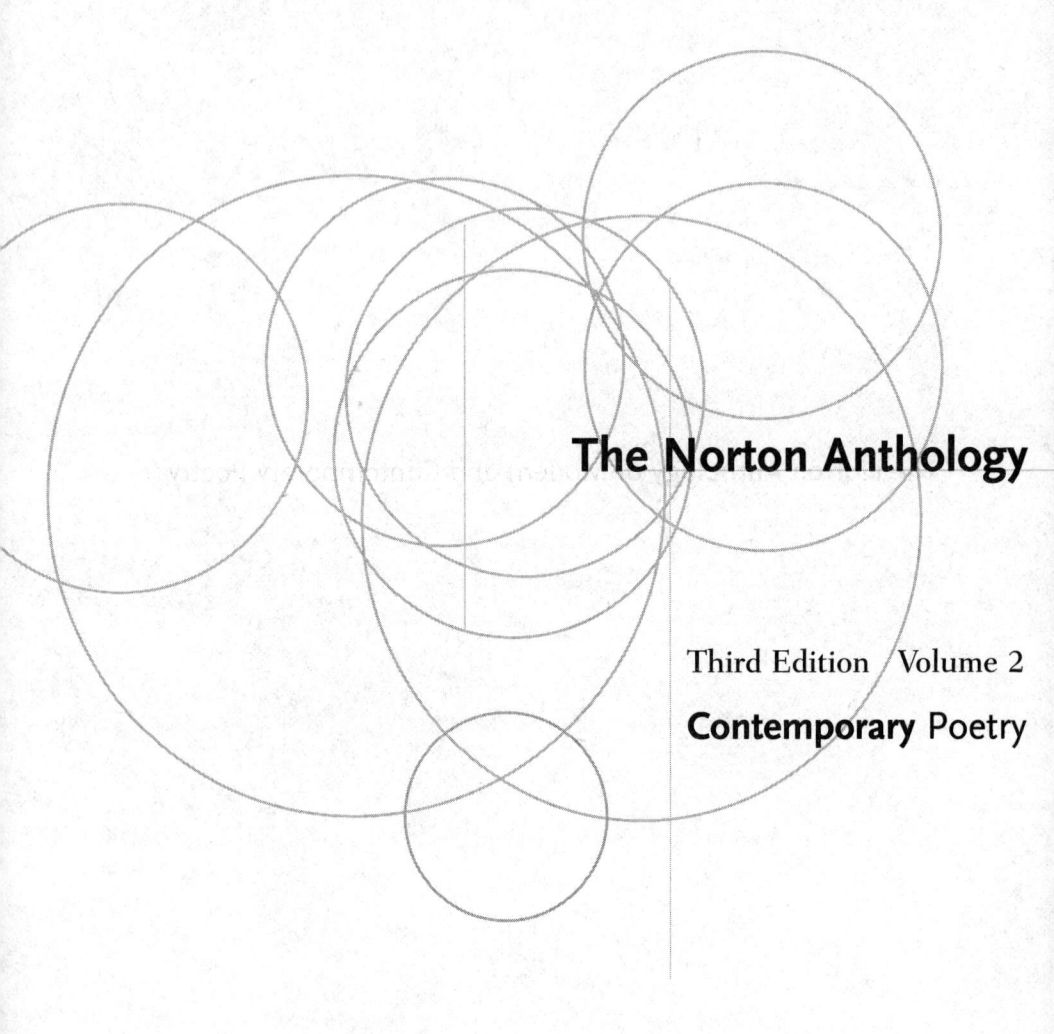

The Norton Anthology

Third Edition Volume 2

Contemporary Poetry

of Modern and Contemporary Poetry

edited by

Jahan Ramazani
EDGAR F. SHANNON PROFESSOR,
UNIVERSITY OF VIRGINIA

Richard Ellmann
LATE GOLDSMITHS' PROFESSOR EMERITUS,
OXFORD UNIVERSITY

Robert O'Clair
LATE OF MANHATTANVILLE COLLEGE

W · W · **Norton** & Company · New York · London

Previous editions published as THE NORTON ANTHOLOGY OF MODERN POETRY

Editor: Julia Reidhead
Developmental Editor: Kurt Wildermuth
Production Manager: Diane O'Connor
Manuscript Editor: Kate Lovelady
Project Editors: Lory Frenkel, Sarah Chamberlin
Editorial Assistants: Brian Baker, Carey Schwaber
Permissions Manager and Associate: Nancy Rodwan, Margaret Gorenstein
Managing Editor: Marian Johnson
Book Designer: Antonina Krass
Cover Designer: Joan Greenfield
Art Researcher: Ruth Mandel

Library of Congress Cataloging-in-Publication Data

The Norton anthology of modern and contemporary poetry / edited by Jahan Ramazani, Richard Ellmann, Robert O'Clair. — 3rd ed.
p. cm.
Rev. ed. of: The Norton anthology of modern poetry. 2nd ed. New York : Norton, c1988.
Includes bibliographical references and index.
Contents: v. 1. Modern poetry — v. 2. Contemporary poetry.

ISBN 0-393-97791-9 (v. 1 : pbk.) — ISBN 0-393-97792-7 (v. 2 : pbk.)

1. American poetry—20th century. 2. English poetry—20th century. 3. American poetry—19th century. 4. English poetry—19th century. I. Ramazani, Jahan, 1960– II. Ellmann, Richard, 1918– III. O'Clair, Robert. IV. Norton anthology of modern poetry.

PS613 .N67 2003
821.008—dc21 2002037990

W. W. Norton & Company, Inc., 500 Fifth Avenue, New York, N.Y. 10110
www.wwnorton.com

W. W. Norton & Company Ltd., Castle House, 75/76 Wells Street, London W1T 3QT

4 5 6 7 8 9 0

Contents

Preface to the Third Edition

Thirty years ago, in their preface to the First Edition, Richard Ellmann and Robert O'Clair set forth this anthology's aims and assumptions: "The most acute rendering of an era's sensibility is its poetry. In the twentieth century, probably in reaction to its horrors, poets have created new and powerful consolidations of the imaginative life. Some writers have accepted the discipline of the literary tradition, others have flouted it. During the last seventy-five [now, over a hundred] years in the English-speaking nations, many poets of consequence have written well in an unprecedented range of styles and subjects. This book aspires to present their best work, and also to delineate the many different tendencies of modern poetry in English."

In revising the anthology created by my predecessors, I have sought to preserve its strong conceptual core, while renewing the text for current use. Two prominent changes signal and respond to recent developments in the field: where the 1973 and 1988 editions were entitled *The Norton Anthology of Modern Poetry,* with this Third Edition, the anthology becomes *The Norton Anthology of Modern and Contemporary Poetry,* and the single volume now becomes two, Volume 1, *Modern Poetry,* and Volume 2, *Contemporary Poetry*. With the close of the twentieth century, it has become increasingly difficult to stretch the term "modern" to encompass all innovative poetry in English since the late nineteenth century, and critics and teachers have recently sharpened the term's more narrow historical use for the literature centered in the early twentieth century. College curricula embody this distinction in courses on poetry variously distinguished as "modern" and "contemporary," "modern" and "postmodern," or "pre–" and "post–World War II." Since the First Edition was published, more poetry-writing courses emphasizing postwar poetic models have also contributed to this shift. Because of the continuities between pre- and postwar poetry—poets, forms, and trends extending across the divide—this anthology still embraces both, but the two periods are made available in separate volumes for teachers and readers who wish to focus on one at a time.

The boundary between "modern" and "contemporary" is inevitably somewhat arbitrary, but poets who came to maturity on either side of World War II have broad generational affinities. Volume 1, *Modern Poetry,* begins with the precursors Walt Whitman, Emily Dickinson, and Gerard Manley Hopkins. At its center are the innovations and consolidations of the first-generation modern poets, from W. B. Yeats and Gertrude Stein to Marianne Moore and T. S. Eliot. The volume ends with the second generation of modern poets—most of them born in the final decade of the nineteenth century and the first of the twentieth—which includes the Fugitives, the Harlem Renaissance poets, the Objectivists, and the Auden circle. (Because Keith

Douglas was killed in World War II, he appears, in an exception to birth order, last in Volume 1.)

Contemporary Poetry opens with two towering presences in contemporary poetry, Charles Olson and Elizabeth Bishop. Born in and around the 1910s and 1920s, the first generation of postwar poets is "contemporary" in that it created many of the paradigms and fomented many of the debates that still inform poetry writing today. This generation and the next, born largely in the 1930s and 1940s, founded a host of new schools and movements in the 1950s and 1960s: in the United States, the Black Mountain school, Beat poetry, confessional poetry, the New York school, Deep Image poetry, and the Black Arts Movement; in Britain, the New Apocalypse and the Movement. Poets of these generations also developed distinctive poetries in the older nations of the British Commonwealth, such as Canada and Australia, and postcolonial poetry in the newer nations of the so-called Third World, such as Jamaica, Nigeria, and India.

Since its first publication, this anthology has presented an international vision of modern and contemporary poetry in English. Confounding national classification, many key poets of the twentieth century led migratory lives, including such modern expatriates as T. S. Eliot (U.S./U.K.), Gertrude Stein (U.S./France), Ezra Pound (U.S./U.K./Italy), H. D. (U.S./U.K./Switzerland), Mina Loy (U.S./U.K.), Claude McKay (Jamaica/U.S./Europe), Laura Riding (U.S./U.K./Spain), and W. H. Auden (U.K./U.S./Europe), and such contemporaries as Denise Levertov (U.K./U.S.), Sylvia Plath (U.S./U.K.), Thom Gunn (U.K./U.S.), A. K. Ramanujan (India/U.S.), Agha Shahid Ali (India/U.S.), and Grace Nichols (Guyana/U.K.). Other poets have lived much of their lives outside their natal countries—W. B. Yeats, Elizabeth Bishop, Gary Snyder, Derek Walcott, Kamau Brathwaite, Seamus Heaney, Paul Muldoon, Eavan Boland, Wole Soyinka, and Lorna Goodison, to mention but a few. Like these transnational lives, literary influence has, especially since the start of the twentieth century, continually crossed national boundaries, so that much modern poetry is transatlantic, and much contemporary poetry is in its bearings global. Not that this anthology aims to give equal representation to every anglophone nation. Produced in the United States, its center of gravity is American. But its selection extends well beyond the borders of the United States, since modern poetry in English is impossible to understand without reading poets such as Thomas Hardy, Gerard Manley Hopkins, W. B. Yeats, D. H. Lawrence, Wilfred Owen, Stevie Smith, and W. H. Auden, as is contemporary poetry without engaging poets such as Dylan Thomas, Philip Larkin, Derek Walcott, Seamus Heaney, Agha Shahid Ali, Les Murray, Eavan Boland, Tony Harrison, Paul Muldoon, Derek Mahon, and Anne Carson.

Reshaping the anthology's selections, I have been guided by some general aims. One priority has been to expand the selections of some of the most influential, most frequently taught poets already in the Second Edition, so that they can be read and studied in greater depth. In *Modern Poetry,* more space has been devoted to selections by Gertrude Stein, Wallace Stevens, Ezra Pound, H. D., Marianne Moore, T. S. Eliot, Claude McKay, Wilfred Owen, Hart Crane, Langston Hughes, W. H. Auden, and Theodore Roethke; in *Contemporary Poetry,* by Charles Olson, Elizabeth Bishop, Robert Hayden, Robert Lowell, Amy Clampitt, Philip Larkin, A. R. Ammons, Allen Ginsberg, Frank O'Hara, John Ashbery, Adrienne Rich, Derek Walcott, Sylvia Plath, Tony Harrison, Seamus Heaney, Louise Glück, Paul Muldoon, and Rita Dove.

Another priority has been to welcome into the anthology what John Ashbery has called an "other tradition"—experimental poetry by modern avant-garde writers, such as Mina Loy and Laura Riding, and the Objectivists Charles Reznikoff, Louis Zukofsky, Lorine Niedecker, and George Oppen, extending to the contemporary avant-garde of Language poetry by Susan Howe, Lyn Hejinian, Michael Palmer, and Charles Bernstein.

I have also tried to represent the accelerated globalization of English-language poetry in the second half of the twentieth century, particularly in the work of postcolonial poets who creatively hybridize indigenous traditions with British and American influences. Along with Walcott and Michael Ondaatje, in the Second Edition, Caribbean poets Louise Bennett, Kamau Brathwaite, Grace Nichols, and Lorna Goodison have been included, as have African poets Christopher Okigbo, Wole Soyinka, and Okot p'Bitek, and Indian poets A. K. Ramanujan, Eunice de Souza, and Agha Shahid Ali.

Another aim has been to add significant longer poems and poetic sequences, including Kipling's "Epitaphs of the War," Yeats's "Nineteen Hundred and Nineteen," Stein's "Sacred Emily," Moore's "An Octopus," Hart Crane's *The Bridge,* Theodore Roethke's "The Lost Son," Robert Hayden's "Middle Passage" and "Elegies for Paradise Valley," Allen Ginsberg's "Howl," Adrienne Rich's *Twenty-One Love Poems,* Derek Walcott's "The Schooner *Flight,*" John Ashbery's "Self-Portrait in a Convex Mirror," Seamus Heaney's "Clearances," Frank Bidart's "Ellen West," Amy Clampitt's "A Procession at Candlemas," Tony Harrison's *v.*, Jorie Graham's "The Dream of the Unified Field," James Merrill's "Self-Portrait in Tyvek(TM) Windbreaker," Richard Howard's " 'Man Who Beat Up Homosexuals Reported to Have AIDS Virus,' " and Susan Howe's "Rückenfigur."

A final, and perhaps obvious, priority has been to present various modern and contemporary poets who have only recently emerged into prominence, including poets of the Harlem Renaissance and African American modernism, such as James Weldon Johnson, Sterling Brown, and Melvin Tolson, and their contemporary inheritors Lucille Clifton, Yusef Komunyakaa, and Thylias Moss; female modern poets such as Amy Lowell, Elinor Wylie, Dorothy Parker, and their contemporary counterparts May Swenson, Mary Oliver, Sharon Olds, Jorie Graham, Anne Carson, and Carol Ann Duffy; poets of ethnic American minorities, such as Joy Harjo, Dionisio D. Martínez, Li-Young Lee, and Sherman Alexie; poets of Ireland and Northern Ireland, such as Michael Longley, Derek Mahon, Eavan Boland, and Medbh McGuckian; poets of gay experience, such as Mark Doty and Henri Cole; poets influenced by European surrealism and East Asian literature, such as Charles Simic, Charles Wright, and Robert Hass; an influential poet of World War I, Ivor Gurney; and an eminent Australian, Les Murray.

My overriding aim has been to gather some of the most influential, imaginative, and aesthetically accomplished modern and contemporary poems. Aesthetic criteria are notoriously impossible to pin down, but this edition's have included—to catalog them baldly—creative daring, figurative reach, verbal dexterity, formal skill, historical responsiveness, social significance, psychological complexity, emotional richness, and the inventive engagement with, and revision of, literary and extraliterary genres and discourses. I have looked for poems that seem not merely representative or illustrative—of trends, schools, or identities—but among the best of their kind. Trying to be as open as possible to advice and suggestion, I have hoped to capture, where possible, something like a current critical consensus, while tentatively outlining some newly emerging areas, such as those mentioned above. But because the canons of modern and especially contemporary poetry are still being formed, such choices must be provisional. Since no anthology can be boundlessly inclusive, additions have meant, inevitably, excisions. A publisher's survey of college teachers, showing which texts were taught least often, provided some guidance in the painful task of removing poets and poems to make space for new texts. The anthology's selections are necessarily constrained by page limits, by permissions fees, and by my taste and the taste of colleagues I have consulted.

In addition to poems, the Third Edition also includes, for the first time, a Poetics section at the end of each volume. Poets' explanatory statements help illuminate poems, schools, and movements, as well as the intellectual and social forces that shaped them. As poetry became more difficult, as poets founded new styles, as groups of poets competed for attention, such statements enjoyed an unprecedented boom, with especially large concentrations accompanying the creative ferment of the 1910s and 1920s and again of the 1950s and 1960s. Some of these documents became manifestos for movements and schools, such as Langston Hughes's "The Negro Artist and the Racial Mountain" for the Harlem Renaissance and Charles Olson's "Projective Verse" for the Black Mountain school. Many have also become standard reference points for poets learning their trade—for example, Ezra Pound's famous series of "don'ts" and the aphorisms of Robert Frost, Wallace Stevens, and W. H. Auden. Some are of great interest in themselves, from the typographic experimentation of *Blast* and of Mina Loy's "Feminist Manifesto" to Derek Walcott's meditation on cross-cultural mixture in the Caribbean. Others include revelatory self-analyses and self-explications, such as the statements by Gerard Manley Hopkins, T. S. Eliot, Hart Crane, Gertrude Stein, Dylan Thomas, Philip Larkin, Adrienne Rich, Allen Ginsberg, and Seamus Heaney. Some echo and revise each other, such as Frank O'Hara's parodic engagement with the multitudinous manifestos of the 1950s and A. K. Ramanujan's indigenization of Eliot's "Tradition and the Individual Talent." Though not every poet has published a poetics, and though theory sometimes aligns imperfectly with practice, these primary materials have become an integral part of the history of modern and contemporary poetry.

Also to help in understanding poems, the anthology's editorial features—period introductions, headnotes, annotations, bibliographies—have been substantially revised. These features are designed to enrich the engagement of readers, students, and teachers with the poems; they are meant to reduce spadework and thus to help focus attention on the vital and creative task of interpreting the poetry. Many headnotes are new, others have been tightened or rewritten in light of recent scholarship and of unfolding poetic careers. They seek to distill each poet's formal and thematic preoccupations, to place each poet in a literary historical context, to encapsulate essential biographical and historical information, and to suggest possible lines of analysis. Attentive to how poets see their own contributions, the headnotes frequently quote poets' letters, interviews, and essays. A general introduction to each volume surveys the interconnected movements and key developments in the poetry of the period. Modern and contemporary poems often demand specialized knowledge, and the annotations are meant to meet this need while being concise and minimally interpretive. The bibliographies have been rewritten from scratch; for the first time, they include entries on movements and schools, and on ethnic, national, and regional poetries.

A final note on the texts: in presenting major modern poets who revised their early work at much later stages of their careers, such as Yeats, Pound, Moore, Hughes, and Auden, the Third Edition often gives preference to early versions or early revisions of their texts, since their historical and literary development is of special interest and is sometimes obscured by their later revisions. Throughout the anthology, the date that appears at the bottom right of a poem is its publication date. When there are two dates at the bottom right, the first is the date of first publication, the second the date of the revision or of the poem's inclusion in a volume of poetry. A date provided on the bottom left of a poem is its composition date.

Acknowledgments

The making of this edition was a collaborative venture from start to finish. My first debt is to the late editors of this anthology, Richard Ellmann and Robert O'Clair, whose generosity of spirit, shrewdness of insight, and breadth of vision live on in this edition's introductions, notes, and selections. As a former student of Ellmann's, I am especially glad for the example of his humane sensibility and of his elegant, wit-brimming prose.

For wise counsel on selections and brilliant advice on editorial apparatus, I have turned repeatedly to scholars elsewhere who have been, in effect, an informal advisory group: Paul Breslin (Northwestern University), Langdon Hammer (Yale University), Henry Hart (College of William and Mary), Nicholas Jenkins (Stanford University), Lucy McDiarmid (Villanova University), Mervyn Morris (University of the West Indies, Jamaica), Michael North (University of California, Los Angeles), Marjorie Perloff (Stanford University), Vincent Sherry (Villanova University), Willard Spiegelman (Southern Methodist University), and Helen Vendler (Harvard University). In this group, Bonnie Costello (Boston University) wrote a marvelously astute commissioned review of the Second Edition, as did Charles Berger (University of Utah), Paul Hoover (Columbia College), and Mark Jeffreys (University of Alabama, Birmingham).

I have also sought and gratefully received incisive help and sage suggestions from Calvin Bedient (University of California, Los Angeles), Harold Bloom (Yale University), George Bornstein (University of Michigan), David Bromwich (Yale University), Reed Way Dasenbrock (New Mexico State University, Las Cruces), Ian Duncan (University of California, Berkeley), Sascha Feinstein (Lycoming College), Oren Izenberg (Harvard University), David Kadlec (Georgetown University), Bruce King (independent scholar), Alan Golding (University of Louisville), Elizabeth Gregory (University of Houston), Christopher MacGowan (College of William and Mary), Douglas Mao (Harvard University), Steven Meyer (Washington University), Paul Morrison (Brandeis University), Charles Pollard (Calvin College), Alison Rieke (University of Cincinnati), Neil Roberts (University of Sheffield), William Rushton (University of Alabama, Birmingham), John Whittier-Ferguson (University of Michigan), and David Wyatt (University of Maryland). Peter Quartermain (University of British Columbia) provided several excellent corrections, and thoughtful advice also came from William Packard (New School for Social Research).

Teachers who patiently filled out a questionnaire that provided sound and precise guidance include Leonard Adame (Butte College), Barry Ahearn (Tulane University), Joel Brouwer (University of Alabama), Luke Carson (University of Victoria), Christopher Collins (New York University), Michael J. Coulombe (University of Wisconsin, La Crosse), Joanne Craig (Bishop's University), Paul J. Dolan (SUNY, Stony Brook), Sharm Dolin (formerly at

Cooper Union), P. E. Firchow (University of Minnesota at Minneapolis), Karen J. Ford (University of Oregon), J. T. French III (Coker College), Philip Furia (University of North Carolina, Wilmington), R. F. Gish (California Polytechnic Institute), Albert G. Glover (St. Lawrence University), Beverly Gross (Queens College), Michael Harris (formerly at Dawson College), Louise Harrison (Boston University), Sarah K. Inman (formerly at New York University), Bill Johnsen (Michigan State University), Anthony Low (New York University), Sara Lundquist (University of Toledo), David Mason (Colorado College), David Middleton (Nicholls State University), Pat Moran (University of Wisconsin, Green Bay), James Persoon (Grand Valley State University), Deborah Sarbin (Clarion University of Pennsylvania), J. D. Scrimgeous (Salem State College), Kenith Simmons (University of Hawaii, Hilo), R. Sullivan (University of Wisconsin, La Crosse), John H. Timmerman (Calvin College), Mary Turnbell (University of Puget Sound), Michael Webster (Grand Valley State University), B. H. Wang (formerly at Florida International University at Miami), Marianne Werner (Butte College), and Don Wood (Langara College).

Also truly helpful in advancing this edition were the respondents to a subsequent, shorter questionnaire, including Bruce Bond (University of North Texas), Samuel Lee Cohen (Bernard Baruch College), Michael Collier (University of Maryland at College Park), Joanne Craig (Bishop's University), Richard K. Cross (University of Maryland at College Park), Anne Herzog (West Chester University), Jonathan Hufstader (University of Connecticut at Storrs), Donald W. Markos (California State University at Hayward), Paul D. McGlynn (Eastern Michigan University), Eliza Richards (Boston University), David St. John (University of Southern California), Dennis Taylor (Boston College), Daniel Thurber (Concordia University), Jonathan Warren (York University), Laura Lee Washburn (Pittsburg State University), and Nancy M. Whitt (Samford University).

Poets who graciously responded to personal queries include the late Agha Shahid Ali, Amiri Baraka, Frank Bidart, Kamau Brathwaite, Rita Dove, Carolyn Forché, Lorna Goodison, Robert Hass, Seamus Heaney, John Hollander, Susan Howe, the late Kenneth Koch, Yusef Komunyakaa, Paul Muldoon, Robert Pinsky, and Charles Wright.

Though not granted for this purpose, fellowships from the John Simon Guggenheim Memorial Foundation and the Virginia Foundation for the Humanities helped get this edition off the ground while I was completing another book. At the Virginia Foundation for the Humanities, Robert Vaughan, Roberta Culbertson, Andrew Wyndham, and Kevin McFadden provided kind encouragement, as did my colleagues in residence Jean Maria Arrigo, Paul Harvey, Anne Goodwyn Jones, Ralph Luker, and Carlos Pereda. I am also grateful for the support of the Richard A. and Sarah Page Mayo NEH Distinguished Teaching Professorship at the University of Virginia.

For their unstinting readiness to furnish much-needed assistance and to share immense reserves of knowledge and insight, I thank the colleagues at the University of Virginia I frequently imposed on, including Stephen Cushman, Victor Luftig, Jerome McGann, Raymond Nelson, Marlon Ross, and Herbert Tucker, and I thank Marva Barnett, Alison Booth, Daniel Ehnbom, Jessica Feldman, David Gies, Jeffrey Grossman, Robert Hueckstedt, Dell Hymes, Michael Levenson, Eric Lott, Debra Nystrom, Peter Onuf, Gregory Orr, Lisa Russ-Spaar, and Patricia Spacks. Librarians at special collections, reference, interlibrary loan, and library express have been forthcoming and efficient; Gary Treadway and Bryson Clevenger kindly answered numerous queries, and Karen Marshall speedily acquired needed volumes. At ITC, Nancy Hopkins designed a most useful spreadsheet. Students in my classes on modern and contemporary poetry have motivated and schooled me. I heartily thank the graduate assistants I worked with, whether for a few hours or much longer: at various early stages, James Parr, Joy Asekun, Kevin Seidel, and Nicole Gharda gathered criticism, texts, and page tallies; in the last stretch, Lauryl Hicks, Kate Nash, and Hallie Smith helped greatly with proofreading and with demanding research; and for over a year, Brian Glavey labored with diligence and keen intelligence to help draft many annotations and compile the bibliographies.

At Norton, Julia Reidhead has been a tremendously energetic and inspiring collaborator. I feel especially fortunate to have worked closely and intensively with her and with Kurt Wildermuth, who edited at a brisk pace while remaining always meticulous and sensitive. For scrupulous copyediting of standing editorial materials, I thank Kate Lovelady; for equally scrupulous work on proofs, I thank Lory Frenkel and Sarah Chamberlin. Marian Johnson and Diane O'Connor kept a close watch on a tight schedule. Nancy Rodwan and Margaret Gorenstein were great allies in permissions, even through some painful cuts. Toni Krass brought elegance to the task of book design. And Brian Baker and Carey Schwaber were efficient and helpful points of contact.

My last and best thanks go to my ever-sustaining parents, Nesta and Ruhi; to my dear children, Cyrus and Gabriel, whose early-morning laughter and end-of-day exuberance renewed me; and to Caroline Rody, who has been wondrously responsive and indefatigably supportive, especially through the last challenging year of this project.

Introduction

The poetry of our own time is characterized by its pluralism, by its welter and crosscurrents. No longer can any single group or individual claim centrality, since contemporary poets in English have proliferated a vast array of idioms, forms, and movements. They have sometimes competed noisily, at other times forged surprising alliances across boundaries of ethnicity, nationality, and aesthetics. They have offered irreconcilable visions of what it means to be contemporary, have deployed many different kinds of English, and have drawn on their unique historical and geographic experiences. But while listening to their own muses, they have also heard one another's voices in the raucous babel of the contemporary—the transnational literary village after World War II.

This volume's point of departure is the generation of poets who published their first books largely after World War II, since poetry today grows out of the debates, innovations, and consolidations of this first postwar generation (roughly, born in the 1910s and 1920s) and the second (born in and around the 1930s and 1940s). Some of these immediately postwar poets are still active; others wrote poems that can be still considered "contemporary" because vitally present as models and antagonists for emerging poets. Even though World War II did not completely divide the poetry written before it from that written after, it is a useful historical marker for the period's beginnings. Other events and trends were also formative for poets born after 1910—the Great Depression, the political polarization of the 1930s, the increasing economic and political might of the United States, the cold war, the weakening and eventual disintegration of the British Empire. But the war had perhaps the greatest aggregate influence. More than twice the number of Americans were killed in it (292,000) than in World War I (117,000). Although fewer than a third the number of British combatants died than in World War I (264,000), the war came home in the Nazi bombing of English cities. Altogether, World War II resulted in the highest death toll of any war—between forty and fifty million. Its destruction was cataclysmic, its scope was international, and its aftershocks reverberated long afterward.

World War II haunts the work even of poets not directly involved. In her 1941 meditation "Roosters," Elizabeth Bishop vividly, if somewhat obliquely, evokes aerial combat, which played a far greater role in this war than in any before: "Now in mid-air / by twos they fight each other," and when one bomberlike rooster falls, "his torn-out, bloodied feathers drift down." Sylvia Plath, a young adolescent when planes dropped atomic bombs on Japanese cities, takes "Hiroshima ash" as an integral part of her psychic experience ("Fever 103°"). In "Poem," Muriel Rukeyser declares her time: "I lived in the first century of world wars." Indeed, the first of the century's world wars had a comparable, defining effect on first-generation modern poets, including those not at the Western Front; Ezra Pound had famously lamented, "There died a myriad / And of the best, among them."

Many more American poets served directly in World War II than in World War I, and a brief survey of their participation in the armed forces indicates the broad impact of World War II on men of the first contemporary generation. Randall Jarrell was a celestial navigation tower operator, William Meredith a naval aviator; Howard Nemerov was in the Royal Canadian Air Force and then, like James Dickey and Alan Dugan, in the U.S. Army Air Corps; Karl Shapiro, Richard Wilbur, and Anthony Hecht were all in the U.S. Army. Louis Simpson served in an army tank corps and then as a combat infantryman, Kenneth Koch as an army rifleman; and Richard Hugo flew thirty-five missions as an army bombardier. Toward the end of the war, W. D. Snodgrass, A. R. Ammons, David Wagoner, Frank O'Hara, Robert Bly, and Galway Kinnell served in the American navy, James Merrill and James Wright in the army. After the war, many of these veterans, with millions of others, were able to attend college thanks to the educational subsidies of the 1944 GI Bill of Rights, which helped turn soldiers into poets. In Britain, Kingsley Amis served in the army, Donald Davie in the navy. The war was, perhaps unsurprisingly, the first muse for a number of these budding writers. "Men wash their hands, in blood, as best they can," writes Jarrell in "Eighth Air Force," suggesting that the war stains everything in the combatants' lives. The war also conspicuously affected the lives of men who didn't serve. A conscientious objector, William Stafford worked in public service camps, where pacifists performed nonmilitary work under civilian direction, and Robert Lowell, another conscientious objector, spent six months in a federal prison in 1943–44, after he wrote a "manic statement, / telling off the state and president," condemning the bombing of German civilians and American demands for Germany's unconditional surrender. Robert Duncan was discharged from the army in 1941 as, in his ironic words, "an officially certified fag."

Of all the devastating wartime events that affected poetry—the massive bombing of London and firebombing of Dresden, the nuclear annihilation of Hiroshima and Nagasaki—the horrors of the Holocaust cast the longest shadow. The German philosopher and social critic Theodor Adorno declared it barbaric to write poetry after the Holocaust, and, indeed, in much post-Holocaust verse, poets worry about the ethics of beauty in an age of mass murder, about how to evoke industrialized genocide without exploiting it or dishonoring the dead. They imprint art with the disfiguring marks of the times. In caustically self-ironizing poems, Geoffrey Hill addresses victims of the Nazis while acknowledging the unavoidable failure of such address: "Undesirable you may have been, untouchable / you were not" ("September Song"). In Plath's "Daddy," an American daughter's address to her German father is warped and fractured by the knowledge of the concentration camps: "I never could talk to you. / The tongue stuck in my jaw. / / It stuck in a barb wire snare." Poets cannot fall entirely silent and still be poets, of course, but post-Holocaust poets such as Hill and Plath, Anthony Hecht and Derek Walcott embed within their poetry an intensified skepticism about the redemptive capacities of language and art.

Modern and Contemporary

Postwar poets were acutely conscious of coming after the modern poets. The major achievements of the first-generation moderns—W. B. Yeats, Gertrude

Stein, Robert Frost, Wallace Stevens, William Carlos Williams, Ezra Pound, Marianne Moore, T. S. Eliot—loomed like a massive edifice over postwar poets, who sometimes worried that all routes to innovation had already been explored and exhausted. As they looked back on the groundbreaking works of the 1910s and 1920s, postwar poets were apt to see as fixed what was once experimental. They sought out areas of creativity and awareness, both commonplace and exotic, neglected by their predecessors, and in the process launched a series of iconoclastic movements. Meanwhile, Stevens, Williams, Pound, and Moore continued to publish important new collections of poetry into the 1950s and 1960s, seeming at once titans who dominated the earth in the distant past and contemporary rivals extending their reign into the present.

Contemporary poetry is often distinguished from modern poetry according to general tendencies, and these distinctions help reveal broad similarities and differences among poets, schools, and movements. As such, they are worth stating at the outset, though individual poets often work against or outside these trends, though the periods are profoundly interwoven, and though these differences can also be found within the periods.

Contemporary poetry is generally seen as more personal than modern poetry. According to T. S. Eliot's famous modernist doctrine, the "emotion of art is impersonal." The first-generation modernists, in reaction against what they saw as the slushy, self-expressive Romanticism of the nineteenth century, often ironized, allusively contextualized, or symbolically transmuted their most personal feelings. By contrast, many of the best-known poets after World War II reclaimed a fiercely personal poetry for the late 1950s and the 1960s. Reflecting the pervasive influence of psychoanalysis in elite and mass culture, many a poet explored the formation of personal identity within the matrix of the family, writing candidly about childhood trauma, guilt, and desire. "They fuck you up, your mum and dad," Philip Larkin wryly summarized ("This Be The Verse"). It would be difficult to imagine Eliot or Pound, Yeats or Moore writing poems about childhood anger toward a weak father, as did Robert Lowell, or incestuous desire for a father, as did Anne Sexton, or combined desire and revulsion toward a mother's naked body, as did Allen Ginsberg. Sylvia Plath's explosive line "Daddy, daddy, you bastard, I'm through" does not express the sort of impersonal emotion that Eliot had in mind. Even Charles Olson, though protesting egocentric poetry, remembers his mother and father as "the precessions / / of me, the generation of those facts / which are my words" ("Maximus to Gloucester, Letter 27 *[Withheld]*"). Chafing against the conformist and consumerist ethos of what Lowell called the "tranquillized *Fifties,*" perhaps fearing the quashing of individuality by massive organizations, bureaucracies, laboratories, and businesses spawned by the war and by postwar prosperity, these writers made poetry not a space for "the extinction of personality," as Eliot put it, but for its passionate expression.

Even so, this distinction between modern and contemporary can be overdrawn. Critics have increasingly seen Eliot's supposedly "impersonal" art as steeped in personal losses—*The Waste Land* as an elegy for his failed marriage, his dead father, and his close friend Jean Verdenal, killed in World War I. Modernism's Romantic literary roots have likewise been increasingly exposed, including Eliot's debts to the nineteenth-century poets he sternly repudiated in prose, such as Percy Bysshe Shelley and Walt Whitman. Nor do poets such as Olson, Lowell, and Plath spring free from their modernist inheritances: they deliberately mediate their experiences through the artifice of personae, myth, archetype, irony, and other such modernist devices. Plath said poets, instead of offering mere "cries from the heart," must "control and manipulate experiences." In "The Colossus," she presents herself and her father through classical archetypes; in "Cut," she metaphorically transforms physical pain; and in "Lady Lazarus," she ironizes her poetic marketing of suffering: "There is a charge / / For the eyeing of my scars." Some contemporary poets, such as Richard Wilbur and Geoffrey Hill, are even more mistrustful of personal self-expression, or, such as Michael Palmer and Lyn Hejinian, deconstruct notions of personal subjectivity altogether.

At least until recently, the dominant formal trend in contemporary poetry has been toward looser, more discrete, more organic kinds of aesthetic structure, and so contemporary poetry is often said to be more "open" than modern poetry. Contemporary poets have wanted to make their forms more responsive to accident, flux, and history, less inwardly molded and self-enclosed. Instead of plotting an inner trajectory toward finality in meaning, form, and emotion, their lyrics often end raggedly, in irresolution or distraction. Their long poems, instead of unfolding sequentially toward a destination, are often organized serially, in modular units that have a tentative relation to one another. Prose genres such as the diary or notebook are the model for many such poems, sometimes dated to indicate their contingency, their immersion in history. The contemporary poem places itself within—not above or outside or beyond—the open-ended course of everyday experience. Instead of aspiring to be a single, coherent utterance, a contemporary poem may be a collage of disjointed discourses or perceptions. Contemporary poets, typically refusing regimentation and overt order, have often patterned their poems on the natural rhythms of personal experience and the body. They have sought to mirror the unpredictable process of composition, as exemplified by what Frank O'Hara called his "I do this I do that" poems. Taking as his motto "First thought, best thought," Ginsberg also epitomized this premium on "spontaneous improvisation": "I really don't know what I'm doing when I sit down to write. I figure it out as I go along (and revise as little as possible)" ("Poetics: Mind Is Shapely, Art Is Shapely").

But statements about this trend also need to be qualified, since it is far from monolithic. Even Ginsberg, as the manuscripts of "Howl" and "Kaddish" reveal, carefully revised and refashioned his major poems for years before publishing them. Moreover, the scattered and extemporized structures of modernist works such as Ezra Pound's *Cantos,* William Carlos Williams's *Spring and All,* and Gertrude Stein's *Tender Buttons* have provided strong precedents for contemporary poets interested in further opening up poetic form. And whereas some modern poets, such as Williams, inveighed against the prototypically "closed" form of the sonnet, some contemporary poets, such as James Merrill, Thom Gunn, Anthony Hecht, Marilyn Hacker, and Agha Shahid Ali, have written brilliantly in this fixed form and others—the sestina, the villanelle, the canzone, the ghazal, even the heroic couplet.

Contemporary poets are often said to write poems less hierarchical in outlook, form, or ideology than are modern poems. Most postwar poets take a democratic view of language and of poetry's function in society, and they are open to a variety of discourses and even popular genres. By contrast, Yeats, Eliot, Pound, and H. D. see the poet as playing an almost priestly or ritualistic role in society, amalgamating and creating myths, purifying and renovating the verbal icon. Eliot and Pound often satirize less cultivated genres and uses of language. The difference is stark between modernism at its most sacramental and contemporary poetry at its most egalitarian—the deliberately flat, campy, and self-parodic poetry written, for example, by O'Hara and James Tate. Contemporary poets seem to feel little of Yeats's or Eliot's revulsion toward the urban, the popular, the utterly heterogeneous. In A. R. Ammons's sequence *Garbage,* about an enormous trash heap seen from an interstate highway, poetry and garbage come to seem inextricable. A further contrast with modern poetry's transcendent thrust is with contemporary poetry's frequent politicizing and historicizing of art. Witness such forcefully political contemporary poems as Amiri Baraka's "Poem for Black Hearts," Carolyn Forché's "The Colonel," Mark Doty's "Homo Will Not Inherit," and Margaret Atwood's "Footnote to the Amnesty Report on Torture," in which a man cleans the floor of a torture chamber: "every morning the same vomit, / the same shed teeth, the same / piss and liquid shit, the same panic."

But here, too, the difference should not be overstated. Modern poets also wrote poems immersed in the particulars of politics and history. Claude McKay, Jean Toomer, Langston Hughes, and—perhaps surprisingly, given his southern agrarian affiliations—Allen Tate all wrote searing poems about lynchings. And some of the most resonant and rust-proof twentieth-century political poetry is Yeats's about the Easter Rising of 1916, Wilfred Owen's about World War I, and W. H. Auden's about the Spanish Civil War. Furthermore, contemporary poets in revolt against a belief in art as transcendent and hierarchical have been able to look to modern precursors, such as Marianne Moore, who welcomed travel guides and science into her poems, and Langston Hughes, who turned to the then-disreputable forms of jazz and the blues as poetic models. Nor is all contemporary poetry antihierarchical. Seeking the aesthetic, even visionary power afforded by exacting uses of language and form, some contemporary poets, including Ammons, Jorie Graham, James Merrill, Philip Larkin, Derek Walcott, Louise Glück, Rita Dove, and Anne Carson, have extended traditions of high-art lyricism, even if such traditions run counter to the temper of the times.

Less ambiguous are the changes in poetry brought about by postwar demographic trends, such as globalization, ethnicization, and feminization. After World War II, as national self-consciousness increased in anglophone areas of the globe outside American and British centers of power, more poets wrote distinctive poetry in the former white settler colonies or "dominions," such as Australia and Canada, and in the decolonizing British outposts in the "underdeveloped world," such as Barbados, Uganda, and India. In the last few decades of the twentieth century, the range of poets in the United States and elsewhere in the so-called First World became more ethnically diverse, including non-European immigrants and their descendents. And as educational access increased across gender lines, more women throughout the anglophone world published poetry after 1945 than in the fifty years before. Writers who identified with national, ethnic, or sexual groups not formerly part of the literary mainstream were inspired by identity-centered political movements, such as, in the 1950s and 1960s, the civil rights movement and, in the 1960s and 1970s, the movements for women's rights, gay rights, and political rights and cultural recognition for Latinos, Native Americans, and Asian Americans.

THE NEW CRITICISM AND POETRY

One form in which modernism survived World War II was the New Criticism—a movement initiated in the 1920s and 1930s by, in America, poet-critics such as John Crowe Ransom, Allen Tate, Robert Penn Warren, and

Yvor Winters, and, in Britain, by I. A. Richards and William Empson. The New Criticism, which consolidated and complicated the ideal of the well-wrought poem, shaped the dominant style in American poetry at mid-century. Drawing heavily on T. S. Eliot's critical essays, the movement enshrined certain complex literary values: paradox irreducible to logical paraphrase; irony too intricate to permit strong commitments; metaphysical wit (as exemplified by John Donne) that yoked together opposites; impersonality that regulated strong feelings; and self-conscious technique of great dexterity. These aspects of modernism lent themselves to the New Criticism's more rigorous classroom teaching of literature. New Critical pedogogy in turn created audiences receptive to this institutionalized form of modernism; it also fostered writers eager to write economical, internally coherent poems that rewarded New Criticism's signature strategy of close reading. In a 1961 interview, Robert Lowell indicated the influence of the New Criticism on poetry, saying that when he was learning to write poetry, the New Critics "were very much news. You waited for their essays, and when a good critical essay came out it had the excitement of a new imaginative work." At the same time, the poets in the New Critical style often set aside less readily assimilated aspects of modernism—formal fragmentation, cross-cultural syncretism, polyglot assemblage, and ambitious mythmaking. Many of the major American poets of the time—Lowell, Plath, Anne Sexton, Adrienne Rich, John Berryman, W. S. Merwin, and Gwendolyn Brooks—began to write in accordance with New Critical principles, though they were violating them in earnest by the late 1950s and the 1960s.

But not all the poets who began within this framework discarded it. The verse of Randall Jarrell, William Stafford, Richard Wilbur, Howard Nemerov, Anthony Hecht, and John Hollander exemplifies the wry, cultivated qualities associated with the New Criticism. Their work displays fertility and deftness in its imagery and phrases; it is unsentimental and yet alive to the senses and sympathies, well made and careful not to become repetitive or predictable. And it enriches individual utterance with traditional poetic resources such as meter and rhyme, stanzaic forms and rhetorical patterning. "I am for wit and wakefulness," announces the speaker of Wilbur's "Ceremony," adding, "What's lightly hid is deepest understood." These learned, polished poets gravitated to careers as critics and college teachers, and partly as a result their work was often disparaged as "academic." Formally and psychologically extending the range of such tightly controlled verse, Elizabeth Bishop, Robert Hayden, May Swenson, Donald Justice, Amy Clampitt, and James Merrill also shared broad affinities with the restraint, compression, and formal discipline favored by the New Criticism.

The Black Mountain School

In contrast to the postwar formalists, American proponents of the most revolutionary aesthetic movements of the 1950s and 1960s rejected the legacy of T. S. Eliot and the New Critics. Not that the rebels dispensed altogether with first-generation modernism: they affiliated themselves with the more subversive and at that time less academically respectable work of William Carlos Williams and Ezra Pound. Williams continued to live the life of a doctor in Rutherford, New Jersey, and was the object of pilgrimages by young poets including A. R. Ammons and Allen Ginsberg. Pound, under indictment for treason because of his wartime radio broadcasts from Fascist Rome, was extradited to the United States in 1945, bringing with him the manuscript of *The Pisan Cantos*. Found mentally incompetent to stand trial, he was committed to a Washington sanatorium, and until his release (as incurably insane but harmless) twelve years later, he attracted younger American poets who sought in his work an immersion in the welter of experience that they found lacking in the poetry of Eliot, John Crowe Ransom, and their followers. Drawing strength from their association with the old impresario of experimental verse and the even older physician in Rutherford, they preferred "open" to "closed" poetic forms, agreeing with Robert Creeley that "Form is never more than an extension of content."

Creeley was one of the poets who gathered around Charles Olson at Black Mountain College, an experimental and unaccredited school in North Carolina that was to become one of the centers of new American poetry. Olson's essay "Projective Verse" (1950) provided the theoretical manifesto for the Black Mountain poets and for others with similar aims: in it, he offers a conception of "open-field" form and champions a dynamism like that of Pound's Vorticist doctrine of heightened energy in the arts. Here, and in his *Maximus Poems* of the 1960s, Olson cast himself as the heir of Pound and Williams. Like Williams, he emphasized the breath, rather than the iamb, as the basis of rhythm. Like Pound, he mixed colloquialism and farflung learning, and made poems out of juxtapositions. Against subjective verse, Olson offered what he called "objectism," a form of verse in which the ego is washed away and the poet "fronts to the whole of reality." The poet is wholly immersed in and energized by the surrounding environment. "I, Maximus," declares his central character, "a metal hot from boiling water."

After joining the faculty of Black Mountain College, Creeley edited *The Black Mountain Review;* during its short run of seven issues (1954–57), it was a major outlet for the anti-academic verse that was to explode into prominence in the late 1950s. In 1956, Robert Duncan came from San Francisco to join the college staff, and though she never joined the faculty, Denise Levertov published in the *Review*. Her influential essay "Notes on Organic Form" conceives of form not as a predetermined shape arbitrarily imposed on experience but as a coherent whole that closely reflects the inner distinctiveness of an experience. A. R. Ammons's poetry has much in common with the organic form, environmentalism, typographic experimentation, and prosodic velocity of "projective verse." The leader of the Black Arts Movement, Amiri Baraka acknowledged the fundamental influence of Olson on his poetry, as did Adrienne Rich, the preeminent feminist poet after World War II.

The Raw and the Cooked

In the 1950s and 1960s, the central divide in American poetry was between the formalists in the New Critical style and poets in "open" forms, including the Black Mountain poets, the Beats, and the New York poets. Accepting the 1960 National Book Award for *Life Studies*, Robert Lowell most famously encapsulated the situation in a wryly anthropological distinction: "Two poetries are now competing, a cooked and a raw. The cooked, marvelously expert, often seems laboriously concocted to be tasted and digested by a graduate seminar. The raw, huge blood-dripping gobbets of unseasoned experience are dished up for midnight listeners. There is a poetry that can only be studied, and a poetry that can only be declaimed, a poetry of pedantry, and a poetry of scandal." Although Lowell admitted to some exaggeration, this competition among poets for recognition, influence, and publication was intense; one of its early manifestations was the so-called battle of the anthologies. In *New Poets of England and America* (1957), American poets Donald Hall, Robert Pack, and Louis Simpson gathered formalist poets whose work—most of it in rhymed and metered stanzas—could be understood largely within New Critical terms, including Richard Wilbur and the early Lowell, as well as English poets of the Movement, such as Philip Larkin, Donald Davie, and Thom Gunn. The American critic Donald Allen included none of the same poets in the anthology widely seen as a response, *The New American Poetry* (1960), which influentially grouped and distinguished anti-academic American poets, including the Black Mountain school, the New York school, and the Beats. Ensuing anthologies took sides with the "raw" or the "cooked," or attempted to bridge the distance, but in either case could not ignore the rift.

To clarify this postwar divide in American poetry, it may be useful to focus comparatively on the first two poets in this volume. Charles Olson and Elizabeth Bishop became fountainheads of these very different kinds of contemporary poetry. Born just six weeks after Olson, Bishop is nearly his opposite in matters of form and taste. If he is the first major postwar exponent of "open" form, she masters and remakes inherited poetic models. Though not a disciple of the New Criticism, Bishop created an outstanding example of a body of poetry consonant with New Critical principles. In the 1950s and 1960s, she was less influential than other formalist poets, but her eminence mounted after her death, and her verse remains a strong model for emerging poets attentive to studied craft, precise description, personal memory, and understated but intense lyric feeling. If Olson hectors and proclaims, Bishop speaks in a steely whisper. Intent on kinetics and propulsion, Olson practices a mobile and shaggy giganticism; Bishop, an exacting and exquisite miniaturist, is more interested in the still life. While Olson thinks of poetry as breathing, Bishop conceives of it as looking. Olson's cascading free verse and rhapsodic vistas can be traced back to Walt Whitman; the nineteenth-century foremother of Bishop's controlled measures and pain-stubbed lines is Emily Dickinson. The more immediate, modernist legacy that Olson transmits is that of the fragmentary long poems of Pound and Williams; Bishop extends instead, in poems such as "The Fish," the precise physical descriptions and poetic self-reflections of Marianne Moore (who wrote a poem with the same title):

> I looked into his eyes
> which were far larger than mine
> but shallower, and yellowed,
> the irises backed and packed
> with tarnished tinfoil
> seen through the lenses
> of old scratched isinglass.

But for all their differences, both Bishop and Olson develop permutations of modernism, respond energetically to their environments, and expand the geography of American verse into South and Central America. Distinctions between the "raw" and the "cooked," the "open" and the "closed," provide a basic framework for understanding postwar poetry, but that framework extends only so far, since contemporary poets from Gwendolyn Brooks and

Adrienne Rich to Susan Howe and Henri Cole have straddled the gulf. Major poets such as John Ashbery and Seamus Heaney have written as skillfully in free as in metered verse, in organic as in inherited forms. Indeed, at the time he gave his acceptance speech, Lowell was formally somewhere between the "raw" and the "cooked," having uncoiled his densely wrought New Critical style through the influence of Williams and the Beats.

THE BEATS AND THE NEW YORK SCHOOL

The Beat poets, like the Black Mountain poets, aligned themselves with the "open" prosody of Pound and especially of Williams, who wrote an introduction for Allen Ginsberg's *"Howl" and Other Poems* (1956). The Beats were featured in the last issue of the *Black Mountain Review,* of which Ginsberg was a contributing editor. They tended, however, to dismiss the Black Mountain poets as too much at ease with authority figures; their own consistent opposition to authority made their poetry the most notorious and conspicuous of the 1950s. They rejected the stuffy majority culture, the anticommunist inquisitions, and the formalist poetry of the times, and decided to drop out and create among themselves a counterculture based on inspired improvisation, whether through jazz, drugs, or East Asian mysticism. Ginsberg and Lawrence Ferlinghetti, exiles from New York, found a congenial milieu in San Francisco, where a poetic renaissance had already been fomented within "the alternative society," as Kenneth Rexroth, doyen of the San Francisco poets, called it. Robert Duncan returned to the San Francisco scene after Black Mountain College collapsed in 1956; Gary Snyder returned to his birthplace after years in the lumber camps of Oregon and more years studying Zen Buddhism in a Japanese monastery.

Following Whitman's example, Beat writers such as Ginsberg shaped their public utterances out of the private experiences that some of their first readers found shameful and appalling, others thrilling and liberating. They presented, often as visionary experiences, confidences that were once uttered only to priest, doctor, or closest friend. Ginsberg, for example, in one of the rhapsodic long lines of "Howl," writes of those "who let themselves be fucked in the ass by saintly motorcyclists, and screamed with joy."

Another major force behind the opening of poetic form was the so-called New York school of poets. It included Frank O'Hara, John Ashbery, and Kenneth Koch, who had met at Harvard University and were associated with the Poets' Theatre, an experimental drama group of the early 1950s. Inspired by the paintings of abstract expressionists such as Jackson Pollock and Willem de Kooning, they went to New York City and immersed themselves in contemporary art—Ashbery and O'Hara wrote for *Art News* and O'Hara worked for the Museum of Modern Art. Like the abstract expressionists, they represented art not as a finished product but as a process. In a 1980 interview, Ashbery credited the influences of "the simultaneity of Cubism" and "the Abstract Expressionist idea that the work is a sort of record of its own coming-into-existence; it has an 'anti-referential sensuousness.' " The New York poets practiced in their sometimes montagelike verse a calculated diffidence and discontinuity of perception. Unlike other pioneers of "open" form—such as the Beats and the Black Mountain poets—they spoke not in prophetic or religiously ecstatic tones but through layers of irony. Their work, as Ashbery writes in "Self-Portrait in a Convex Mirror," is "pure / Affirmation that doesn't affirm anything." "All we know," he says in the same poem,

> Is that we are a little early, that
> Today has that special, lapidary
> Todayness that the sunlight reproduces
> Faithfully in casting twig-shadows on blithe
> Sidewalks. No previous day would have been like this.

Highspirited but knowing, these poets celebrated New York and recorded its landscape, as when O'Hara, characteristically looking from the window of an art gallery, says that "the warm traffic going by is my natural scenery." Partly because of his early death, O'Hara was the first of these poets to become famous. By the 1970s, Ashbery had become the most prominent member of the group, poetically manipulating reality and fantasy, humor and intricate perceptions, and in the process rapidly assuming different selves. No other contemporary poet has been such a strong influence on both "experimental" poets, most interested in his collagelike structures and decentered consciousness, and "mainstream" poets, impressed by his unsentimental lyricism, quick shifts of tone and sense, and dreamlike vividness.

Deep Image Poetry and Confessional Poetry

Surrealism, a mode that uses the unconscious and its distortion of reality, had until the 1960s been more common to the visual arts, and to European and South American writing, than to Anglo-American poetry. Now, this changed: French surrealism was among the influences on the irrational sequences of images in the poetry of the New York school. Along with French surrealism, Spanish surrealism was an even more central influence on another group of American poets, known as the Deep Image poets (a term coined by Robert Kelly in his 1961 essay "Notes on the Poetry of the Deep Image"). They drew on surrealism to compose elemental, psychologically archetypal poems. Robert Bly's magazine *The Fifties* (subsequently renamed for successive decades) made available new translations of surrealist poets including the South Americans Pablo Neruda and César Vallejo, and his poems helped establish a "new surrealism," as did those of James Wright, W. S. Merwin, Philip Levine, Louis Simpson, Galway Kinnell, Mark Strand, and Charles Simic. Others, such as Charles Wright, Robert Hass, and Louise Glück, were also periodically attracted to the surrealist dislocation of sense and image. In "Fork," Simic reimagines a fork as the foot of a bird, its head "large, bald, beakless, and blind." "The dead," says Charles Wright in his "Homage to Paul Cézanne, "are constant in / The white lips of the sea." The reader is invited to experience such visions without the effort of logical construction. In Strand's work, the very mysteriousness of what is going on contributes to a mounting effect of uncanny power.

In the late 1950s and early 1960s, another group of poets became interested in writing deeply psychological verse, though they relied less on psychic archetypes than on self-analysis. They came to be known as the "confessional" poets—a term that the reviewer M. L. Rosenthal first applied to Robert Lowell's *Life Studies* (1959) and that eventually became a general label for intensely personal poetry about once-taboo subjects. As a young man, Lowell had left Harvard to study at Kenyon College with John Crowe Ransom; Lowell and his older friend Allen Tate, like Ransom a leading New Critic and poet, became Roman Catholics at the same time. Lowell's Pulitzer Prize–

winning second book, *Lord Weary's Castle* (1946), showed technical mastery of rhyme, meter, and complex symbolism, and established his eminent place among young poets. Lowell fused the New Critical tradition of elaborate structure and the Whitmanesque tradition of radical contact with subject. Then, teaching at the University of Iowa, Lowell was struck by the unabashed self-revelations and open form of Beat poetry, and by the self-exploration in the poetry of one of his students, W. D. Snodgrass. Lowell had come to feel that poetry written under the influence of the New Criticism, as he said in a 1961 interview, "can't handle much experience. It's become a craft, purely a craft, and there must be some breakthrough back into life." Although Lowell's loosening of form and psychic self-excavations in *Life Studies* at first made it seem as if he might be becoming a Beat, his verse remained meticulously controlled, his tone still marked by the wit and irony preferred by the New Criticism. If, as he says in *History*, "imperfection is the language of art," his constant revisions showed his lingering allegiance to the well-made poem.

Other poets who wrote in this intensely autobiographical vein, such as Snodgrass, John Berryman (who invented an "anti-sonnet" of three six-line stanzas for his *Dream Songs*), Sylvia Plath, Anne Sexton, and Adrienne Rich, either played against conventional form or wrote free verse in a peculiarly unrelaxed way. These poets wrote about key moments of revelatory pain more often than of pleasure, and they saw such moments as epitomizing the general condition of their time. As they turned against New Critical norms of impersonality and formal regulation, Plath, Sexton, and Rich increasingly rooted their poetry in female bodily and psychic existence. Rich reflects in her essay "When We Dead Awaken: Writing as Re-Vision": "In the late fifties I was able to write, for the first time, directly about experiencing myself as a woman. . . . Until then I had tried very much *not* to identify myself as a female poet." Rich, Sexton, and Plath harnessed the confessional mode to express feelings and insights that violated literary and social strictures on American women. They presented their lusts, hatreds, and suicidal urges in extraordinarily charged and intimate terms. In "Ariel," Plath strips herself of mundane responsibilities and ecstatically rides her horse into the sunrise:

> The child's cry
>
> Melts in the wall.
> And I
> Am the arrow,
>
> The dew that flies
> Suicidal, at one with the drive
> Into the red
>
> Eye, the cauldron of morning.

Such writing sometimes came at a high personal cost: three of the confessionals—Plath, Berryman, and Sexton—committed suicide; others, Lowell included, endured repeated breakdowns, hospitalizations, addictions, which led to early deaths. But Rich, who publicly denounced female self-destructiveness after Sexton's death, attested to the energizing potential of poetry in which "at last the woman in the poem and the woman writing the poem become the same person," in which women "are speaking to and of women . . . out of a newly released courage to name." Women, gay and lesbian, and "ethnic" American poets—previously impeded from naming their experiences in their own literary voices—thus turned so-called personal or confessional poetry into a tool of collective self-definition and liberation.

The Black Arts Movement and Later African American Poetry

From the mid-1960s through the early 1970s, poets of the Black Arts Movement also focused their poems on agony, rage, and love, but these emotions had a stronger political dimension in their openly polemical, politically revolutionary work. These African American poets were inspired by the Black Power movement, whose leaders had grown impatient with the integrationist, nonviolent ethos of the civil rights movement and emphasized instead black nationalism, economic power, and self-determination. "Black Art," wrote the exponent Larry Neal in "The Black Arts Movement" (1968), "is the aesthetic and spiritual sister of the Black Power concept." Amiri Baraka, at that time called LeRoi Jones, gave the movement its name when he coined the term *Black Arts,* founding in 1965 the Black Arts Repertory Theater. Having absorbed the improvisatory aesthetics of the Beat and Black Mountain poets, Baraka left the white avant-garde during the 1960s to move toward a distinctively black aesthetic, which insisted on a commitment to the needs of the African American community and to the discovery of artistic resources in it. In "The Myth of a 'Negro Literature' " (1963), Baraka ridiculed black artists who were "content to imperfectly imitate the bad poetry of the ruined minds of Europe." Proposing the blues and jazz as alternatives to Euro-American forms, he modeled his poems on the explosive energy and polyphonic voicing of post-bebop jazz.

In keeping with the Black Arts Movement, Audre Lorde, Lucille Clifton, and June Jordan, all born, like Baraka, in the 1930s, also wrote poems inveighing against racial injustice and drawing on black experience and poetic tradition, poems steeped in the speech rhythms and rhetorical verve of the black vernacular. But resisting the masculinist tenor of the Black Arts Movement, they put the black female body and their personal emotional histories at the center of their art. Theirs are poems about social identity as seen from within the experiences of storytelling, erotic passion, and physical loss. Clifton writes homages to her hips, her uterus, her last period; childbirth is Lorde's subject in "Now that I Am Forever with Child": "I bore you one morning just before spring— / My head rang like a firey piston / My legs were towers between which / A new world was passing."

Meanwhile, older African American poets, born in the 1910s, were forced to choose sides by the Black Arts Movement. Gwendolyn Brooks had already been writing poems such as "The Last Quatrain of the Ballad of Emmett Till," about an African American teenager murdered for whistling at a white woman: Emmett's mother "sits in a red room, / drinking black coffee. / She kisses her killed boy. / And she is sorry. / Chaos in windy grays / through a red prairie." Deeply impressed by the radical younger generation, Brooks shifted in the 1960s from such understated, tightly controlled poetry to "wild, raw, ragged free verse," as she called it. She dated her transformation to the Second Fisk University Black Writers' Conference, in 1967. A year earlier, at the first of these conferences, Robert Hayden found himself sidelined and spurned by black nationalists. Still, he kept to his universalist Baha'i faith and international modernist affinities, and later African American poets have championed his indirect, dramatic approach to black history and social injustice. In the sequence "Middle Passage," for example, he ironically adopts the voices of white slave-ship officers to evoke the atrocities of the slave trade.

Since the Black Arts Movement broke up in 1974, splintering into nationalist, Marxist, and Pan-Africanist factions, many African American poets have departed from its nationalism, but the movement's emphasis on African American oral, literary, and musical genres has remained influential. African American poets such as Michael S. Harper and Yusef Komunyakaa have continued to draw sustenance from African American musical forms, capturing in their verse the melancholy starkness of the blues or the abrupt shifts and syncopations of jazz. Whereas the Black Arts Movement sought cultural self-sufficiency, they hybridize indigenous models in surprising ways with forms adapted from other cultural sources. Thylias Moss invokes the black preacher's technique of "making text" by meditating on a central concept—rapture, slavery, God—but she gives the strategy a new strangeness by combining it with surrealist profusions of discontinuous images. Rita Dove reenters moments of violation and injustice in the history of African Americans, but she makes them haunting, ironically, by adapting such European fixed forms as the sestina and the villanelle, in her poem "Parsley," or such "mainstream" American modes as confessional lyricism and semi-dramatic, semipersonal portraiture, as in the sequence *Thomas and Beulah.*

THE NEW APOCALYPSE AND THE MOVEMENT

During World War II, a number of British poets emerged whose response to the "age of anxiety," as W. H. Auden called it, was vehement and extreme. Among the poets of this late Romantic movement sometimes called the New Apocalypse, Dylan Thomas was the major figure. In opposition to the analytic understatement of W. H. Auden and his British circle of the 1930s, Thomas reintroduced openly expressed emotion and rhetoric into English verse, with the most spectacular display of language since Hart Crane. In ordinary situations the Welsh poet heard extraordinary reverberations, and like William Wordsworth, William Blake, and Samuel Taylor Coleridge, he tried to restore a radiance lost to English nature poetry since the seventeenth century.

Reacting against this apocalyptic mode was a loose association of university poets who, in the 1950s, came to be known as the Movement. Its leading figures were Philip Larkin, Kingsley Amis, Donald Davie, and Thom Gunn, all included in Robert Conquest's *New Lines* (1956), an anthology that put them on Britain's literary map. The Movement had affinities with developments in the other British arts, in fiction, in the "kitchen-sink" school of painting, in "ordinary language" philosophy, and in plays by "angry young men" such as John Osborne. While objecting to what they saw as the Romantic excesses of the New Apocalypse, the poets of the Movement also rejected Yeats's symbolism and Pound and Eliot's high modernism, and favored wit over prophecy and extravagance, urban and suburban realities over myth-making. "A neutral tone is nowadays preferred," as Davie summarized in "Remembering the 'Thirties." These poets tried to reclaim a native English line of civil, rational, and accessible poetry that bypassed the complexities of a supposedly imported modernism and went back through Robert Graves and William Empson to Thomas Hardy, A. E. Housman, and the Georgian pastoralists of the 1910s. "Poetry is an affair of sanity, of seeing things as they are," Larkin said, implicitly contrasting his work with the supposed "insanity" of the modernist Pound and the confessionals Lowell and Plath.

Through deliberately deflated language, the Movement poets aimed to consolidate the achievements of the Auden circle, without its leftist political commitments, to write a poetry that in its diction and tone, subjects and regular meters, would express rather than overthrow the restrictions of ordinary life. Even so, their poetry sometimes quietly bridges the distance between the mundane and the sublime, as in Larkin's "Sad Steps," which begins, "Groping back to bed after a piss / I part thick curtains, and am startled by / The rapid clouds, the moon's cleanliness."

British Poetry after the Movement

Not everyone in Britain followed the lead of Larkin and the Movement. Although Charles Tomlinson resembled Movement poets in rejecting Dylan Thomas's apocalyptic Romanticism, and though he also prized precision and clarity, his points of reference in crafting a poetry respectful of the world as other, as irreducible to human symbols, included the American modernists and the Objectivists. Other British poets rejected the Movement's notion of a limited, rationalist, polished poetics. In the late 1950s and the 1960s, Ted Hughes began to write poems in which he presented the world as a Darwinian world of violent struggle and himself as having a savage role to fill. He found emblems of violence in the outer world of animals, weather, and his physical work as a sheep and cattle farmer. Also in contrast to the Movement, Geoffrey Hill saw a rationalist humanism as inadequate to the atrocities of twentieth-century war and genocide; he has investigated political, religious, and personal turmoil in a style knotted with allusions and fierce in its demands, its strenuous language recalling both the high modernist tradition and Metaphysical poetry.

Stylistically closer to the reserve of the Movement, another group of British poets nevertheless sought to dislocate normal habits of perception, presenting the familiar world through the defamiliarizing lens of an alien or an anthropologist. Craig Raine's "The Martian Sends a Postcard Home," in which an alien invader describes ordinary life in an English home, was this group's signature poem; its title was adapted for fellow poets who were called the Martian school. Casting his net beyond the domestic world, James Fenton adapts the Martian strategy in a poem such as "Dead Soldiers," in which the Cambodian wars he witnessed as a journalist are presented in terms of a battlefield dinner party.

Since the 1980s, the spectrum of Britain's poets has become more diverse in class, ethnicity, gender, and region than ever before, bringing new voices into the English literary tradition. Born in the Northern industrial city of Leeds, Tony Harrison often writes as a "remembering exile" from his working-class origins; in "Turns," he says that his poet persona is that of a street entertainer for "the class that broke" his working-class father. His long poem *v.* synthesizes traditional verse—Thomas Gray's "Elegy Written in a Country Churchyard" is the obvious precursor poem—with a local vernacular, the oral energy and resonance of Harrison's Yorkshire idiom and rhythms exploding on the page. Born in Scotland to an Irish mother in a left-wing, working-class Catholic family, Carol Ann Duffy grew up amid Irish, Scottish, and Standard varieties of English, and this youthful experience helped equip her to speak in different voices in dramatic monologues. Having moved from Guyana to England in her twenties, Grace Nichols, code-switching between West Indian Creole and Standard English, celebrates the erotic energy and force of the black female body. Like other "Black British" poets from England's former colonies, she has helped bring into British poetry a vibrant new imagery, diction, and cultural sensibility.

POETRY OF IRELAND AND NORTHERN IRELAND

In the early 1960s, a group of aspiring young writers, all of them born and brought up in Northern Ireland, began to meet in the apartment of Philip Hobsbaum, then a Lecturer at Queen's University, in Belfast. Some of them were Catholic by background, others Protestant; all agreed that the endless guerilla warfare between religiously and politically divided populations in Ulster should not divert them from their writing or become their sole subject. If the Troubles in Northern Ireland were to be treated in poems, they felt, it must be by indirection. Seamus Heaney, who became a Nobel laureate in 1995, is the oldest among these poets. Between his birth, in 1939, and Paul Muldoon's, in 1951, Ulster produced an extraordinary number of strong poets for its small population. Viewing bloodshed through the obliquities of metaphor, myth, allusion, and strict formal pattern, they created one of the most significant bodies of poetry about political violence in the English-speaking world.

"I grew up in between," writes Heaney in "Terminus," and the consciousness of intercultural strife and yet cross-cultural abundance has helped to fuel his poetry and the poetry of other Ulster writers. Seen by many as the most gifted English-language poet of his generation, Heaney has said that Irish poets cannot hate the English, because without them they would not have their language, a poet's chief resource; indeed, he has ransacked the English literary tradition from *Beowulf* to William Wordsworth, Gerard Manley Hopkins, and Ted Hughes. Heaney welds this inheritance from centuries of English rule to indigenous Irish genres (such as the *aisling*, or vision poem), Irish sonorities (gutturals, alliterations, assonances of Gaelic), and an Irish sensibility (an earthy, rural, tough-mindedness combined with an almost mystical sense of the unseen). In his poetry about the violence in Northern Ireland, he grapples courageously with the ethics of representation—how to write about public suffering without appropriating, simplifying, or aestheticizing it.

Unlike Heaney, who is a Catholic by background, his near-contemporaries Derek Mahon and Michael Longley came, like Yeats, from Protestant families. Out of the tension between a sense of participation in, and alienation from, the island's predominantly Catholic culture, they have forged poetry that is tonally complex, formally accomplished, and unfailingly elegant. Medbh McGuckian and Paul Muldoon, both of Catholic origins, were among Heaney's students. McGuckian's poetry is the most dreamlike and evocative to come out of Ireland since Yeats's. Muldoon's influential poetry displays great skill in eerily distorted fixed forms, multiple screens of irony, numerological patterning, and a combination of experimental zaniness with formal reserve. Born in the Irish Republic, Eavan Boland has centered her career on making a space within the largely male tradition of Irish verse—with its standard, mythical emblems of femininity—for Irish women's historical experiences of survival and suffering, even including the "scream of beaten women."

Canadian and Australian Poetry

After World War II, the geographical contours of poetry written in English began to change more than at any time since the first publication of American poets, three centuries earlier. One shift of the literary center of gravity was from England to America, a shift that Auden and Denise Levertov seemed to confirm when—in a reversal of the expatriation of Stein, Pound, and Eliot to Europe a generation earlier—they came to the United States. Another was the emergence of new literatures in English from the dominions of the British Empire, such as Canada and Australia. With a few exceptions, such as the Australian A. D. Hope, earlier writers of the British Commonwealth wrote poems derivative of metropolitan fashion. While still drawing on their English inheritances, these writers now began to assert the terms of their own literatures. One of the changes came with greater fidelity to locale. Though indebted to Auden, the Canadian poet P. K. Page strongly roots her imagistic verse in the local landscape. Thus rooted, too, is the work of contemporary Australian poet Judith Wright, which is haunted by the absent presence of a partly destroyed Aboriginal civilization. The Australian poet Les Murray adapts Aboriginal song techniques in his poetry, fusing them with the witty defamiliarizing strategy of the Martian school. Self-conscious about being at the margins of the former empire, Murray fashions a brash, playful, overbrimming poetry that mines the British and classical traditions while remaking them in what he styles his "redneck," Australian manner.

In her introduction to *The New Oxford Book of Canadian Verse in English* (1982), Margaret Atwood observes that in Canada "the modern movement took some time to build a following . . . [because] puritanism and the colonial worship of imports still restricted taste." Atwood writes of isolation and survival as distinguishing preoccupations of Canadian literature, and her poems display a divided vision—both attachment to the Canadian landscape and the sense of being estranged from it. "We are all immigrants to this place even if we were born here," remarks one of her characters. Even as Canadian poetry has become increasingly independent, it has continued a dialogue with its British literary origins. Anne Carson, for example, imaginatively engages the British Victorian writers Charlotte and Emily Brontë in her poem "The Glass Essay," transplanting their voices to a Canadian landscape. But Carson, like Atwood, also illustrates a heightened interest in U.S. poetry and popular culture, reflecting Canada's postwar shift in political and cultural orientation from Britain to the United States. Indeed, she brings into the literary mix influences that range from ancient Greek poetry to Pound and Plath, television and video. This diversity of inheritances can also be seen in the work of other Canadian poets. Reflecting the increasing multiculturalism of Canada due to the large-scale immigration that began in 1948, Michael Ondaatje fuses the American confessional mode adapted from Robert Lowell with his classical Sri Lankan inheritance of verse cut in spare, imagistic lines.

Postcolonial Poetry of Africa, India, and the Caribbean

The most dramatic geographic shift in literary activity after World War II was the rise of new literatures from the former colonies of the British Empire in the so-called Third World, particularly in Africa, India, and the Caribbean.

Britain had the largest, most powerful, best organized of the modern European empires, and had expropriated enormous quantities of land, raw materials, and labor from its widely scattered overseas territories. The emergence of new literatures in English coincided loosely with the wave of decolonization that began after World War II: India and Pakistan became independent in 1947; Ghana in 1957, Nigeria in 1960, and Uganda in 1962; Jamaica and Trinidad and Tobago in 1962, Barbados and Guyana in 1966, and Saint Lucia in 1979. Unlike the literatures of the former white settler colonies, which extended and adapted the British literary inheritance to new settings, postcolonial literatures brought together more disparate traditions of colonizer and colonized, European and native. Born under British rule and undergoing a colonial education that repressed or denigrated native languages and traditions, these poets grew up with an acute awareness of the riches of their own cultural inheritances. Searching through oral histories and personal memories, postcolonial poets sought to give voice to a cultural past that colonialism had degraded and gagged. They expanded the range of possibilities in English-language poetry by hybridizing it with their indigenous images and speech rhythms, creoles and genres.

In the middle of the twentieth century, when colonial prejudices still branded West Indian English, or Creole, a backward language, a "corruption" of English, the Afro-Jamaican poet Louise Bennett claimed its wit, vibrancy, and proverbial richness for poetry. In the late 1960s, the Barbadian Kamau Brathwaite (then Edward Brathwaite) wrote the three long sequences, gathered as *The Arrivants,* that revalue the linguistic, musical, and mythic survivals of Africa in the Caribbean—resources long repressed because of colonial attitudes. Whereas Bennett and Brathwaite have emphasized Afro-Caribbean inheritances, the most eminent West Indian poet, Nobel laureate Derek Walcott, has drawn largely on British, American, and classical European models. But in poems such as "The Schooner *Flight*" and *Omeros,* he, like Bennett and Brathwaite, creolizes the rhythms, diction, and sensibility of English-language poetry. "I have Dutch, nigger, and English in me," declares the mulatto hero of "The Schooner *Flight,* "and either I'm nobody, or I'm a nation." A leading West Indian poet of the next generation, the Jamaican Lorna Goodison sinuously interweaves Creole and Standard English, Afro-Caribbean and European cultural resources, exclaiming, "It all belongs to me."

In poetry as well as fiction, Nigeria was the most prolific anglophone African nation around the time of independence, said to be the "golden age" of letters in sub-Saharan Africa. In musically cadenced verse, Christopher Okigbo synthesized Igbo myth and imagery with the Anglo-modernist allusive strategies of Pound and Eliot. Another Nigerian, Wole Soyinka, later the first black African to win the Nobel Prize, stretched English syntax and figurative language in poems dense with Yoruba-inspired wordplay and myth. Okot p'Bitek, the preeminent East African poet after independence, Africanized English with literally rendered Acoli images, metaphors, and idioms; his long poem *Song of Lawino* (1966) embodied the conflict between westernization and nativism in an Acoli village woman's boisterous attacks on her Europeanized husband. Working in a language imposed by missionaries and governments that considered them culturally and racially inferior, these African poets transform a tool of oppression into a vehicle for voicing and exploring their rich cultural identities.

Poets from India have brought its great variety of indigenous cultures into

English-language poetry. A. K. Ramanujan drew primarily on traditions of the Hindu majority in sharply etched poems that interfuse Anglo-modernist principles with the south Indian legacies of Tamil and Kannada poetry. Of the Shi'a Muslim minority, the Kashmiri poet Agha Shahid Ali, who like Ramanujan emigrated to the United States for graduate study, interwove first Eliot's modernism, then James Merrill's formalism, with the music, tonality, and fixed forms of Urdu poetry. A poet from the Catholic community in the former Portuguese colony of Goa, whose speech rhythms and diction she echoes, Eunice de Souza employs the confessional mode to explore the often painful experience of growing up female in a patriarchal society. All of these poets respond with emotional ambivalence and linguistic versatility to the experience of living after colonialism, between non-Western traditions and modernity, in a period of explosive change in the relation between Western and "native" cultures.

Postconfessional Poetry, New Formalism, and Language Poetry

In the United States, the late 1970s were marked by the deaths of Elizabeth Bishop and Robert Lowell, two towering figures in the older generation of contemporaries; and by the early deaths of James Wright and Richard Hugo. But other prominent post-1945 writers continued to develop and change. John Ashbery wrote daring long poems and lyrics, employing not only free verse but also fixed forms, such as the sestina and couplet. A. R. Ammons blended his descriptive and meditative modes with more personal introspections in works that meditate on landscape, ecology, and poetry. James Merrill, in *The Changing Light at Sandover,* produced an American cosmological epic unlike anything before him. Adrienne Rich, continuing to forge afresh her "dream of a common language," wrote poems about collective experience, especially that of women, while probing the ethics and meaning of intimate relationships with family, friends, and lovers. Amy Clampitt, an unknown contemporary of the confessionals, began publishing in 1983 some of the most finely embroidered and verbally dazzling poetry of the late twentieth century.

During this period, the postwar movement of American poetry into the academy accelerated. In the first postwar generation, poets such as Robert Lowell and John Berryman took temporary posts as itinerant writers in residence and competed for grants. The next generation's entry into graduate education and university employment was more permanent and pervasive. With few exceptions, American poets born from the 1930s on have received some training in creative-writing programs. Charles Wright, Mark Strand, James Tate, and Jorie Graham, for example, all studied with Donald Justice at the Iowa Writers' Workshop, and they, like most of their contemporaries, went on to teach creative writing. Similarly, a group of teacher-poets of the Pacific northwest had all studied with Theodore Roethke, whether at Pennsylvania State University (David Wagoner) or at the University of Washington (James Wright and Richard Hugo). A sign of the changing relation of poetry to the academy was the routinization of the campus poetry reading in the 1980s as a social activity, in contrast to the 1970s, when it had been a psychedelic or revolutionary event.

After the late 1970s, American poetry splintered anew, this time into several distinct factions. As in the 1960s, these factions continued to be bridged by some poets, such as John Ashbery and Jorie Graham, whose work can be seen as both "experimental" and "personal," "avant-garde" and "formal." At the center, attacked by both literary conservatives and radicals, is the dominant mode in M.F.A. programs, anthologies, publishing houses, national awards, and magazines such as *American Poetry Review:* a modified form of confessional free verse, sometimes called "postconfessional" or "neoconfessional," though in an age of relentless confession on radio, television, and the Internet, the personal revelations tend to be less shocking to today's readers than those of the first-wave confessionals and Beats were to their early audiences. At its best, the mode's introspective lyricism is complicated and enriched. Exploring personal guilt, ambivalence, and psychic distress, Graham often puzzles out personal feelings through deliberately strained comparisons between her inner states and public history—the Holocaust, imperialism, and so forth. Charles Wright also enlarges the postconfessional mode, his Deep Image background widening the scope of personal references, his grids of syllable and line count binding his free verse, and his postreligious melancholy casting the natural world in shadow. Robert Hass has brought to the personal lyric the discipline of the East Asian haiku. Louise Glück has deepened the mode through the use of archetypes and myths. Poets of gay experience, such as Mark Doty and Henri Cole, redeploy confessionalism to resist the humiliations of homophobia, mourn the collective ravages of AIDS, and probe marginal sexual identities. And Sharon Olds, perhaps the clearest example of a late confessionalist, writes poetry so erotically vehement, psychologically intent, and metaphorically rich that she, too, exceeds the bounds of the merely personal.

In reaction against what they see as the slackness of free verse lyricism, a group of poets known as the New Formalists, who published anthologies and manifestos largely in the 1980s, has championed a return to meter and rhyme, which they believe have the potential to restore the tattered social contract between poet and common reader. Their first anthology, Philip Dacey and David Jauss's anthology *Strong Measures: Contemporary American Poetry in Traditional Forms* (1985), recalled the formalist collections in the "battle of the anthologies" twenty-five years earlier. Because their agenda is recuperative, insistent on the virtues of narrative and stanzaic structure, the New Formalists are often assumed to be neoconservatives in politics as well as form. But this is not so. Marilyn Hacker, belatedly adopted into the group, plays the "nontraditional" content of her lesbian feminism within and against forms such as the sestina, the rondeau, the villanelle, and the sonnet, forms renewed by her respectful skewing of prosodic and stanzaic strictures. Other noted poets associated with the group include Gjertrud Schnackenberg, Dana Gioia, Brad Leithauser, and Vikram Seth. During the emergence of the New Formalists, some of the preeminent formalists of the earlier generation—James Merrill, Richard Wilbur, Donald Justice, Anthony Hecht, John Hollander—continued to produce masterful poetry in "closed" verse forms, setting a high standard for such poetry. Within an international context, many contemporary poets have also exemplified formal brilliance and skill in meter and rhyme, including Northern Irish poets such as Seamus Heaney, Derek Mahon, and Michael Longley, English poets such as Tony Harrison, James Fenton, and Carol Ann Duffy, and such postcolonial poets as Louise Bennett, Derek Walcott, and Agha Shahid Ali.

From the opposite end of the aesthetic spectrum arose another prominent challenge to "official verse culture," as Charles Bernstein calls the lyrical "mainstream." In rejecting postconfessional free verse, the New

Formalists buttoned up form in strict patterns, whereas the Language poets scattered it wildly. The Language poets emerged in the 1970s and burst into full view in the 1980s with manifestos and magazines such as *L=A=N=G=U=A=G=E,* which Bernstein coedited with Bruce Andrews. They centered their critique on the notion that poetry expresses lyric feeling and subjectivity. In their writing, they enact the poststructuralist view that the coherent self is an ideological illusion. "Various *selves*" create a poem, according to Michael Palmer, and Lyn Hejinian states that writing begins "not in the self but in language," in "the not-I." Taking the Marxist view that normative syntax and grammar enforce political oppression, these poets try to make visible the contradictory discourses hidden within language and the restrictive norms that threaten to homogenize speech. Rejecting rationalist transparency in communication, they foreground the materiality of language—its sounds, shapes, and structures, the look of words on the page. A poem, in Susan Howe's view, is not a seamless discursive unity but a collage-like assemblage, and its sutures should be left frayed and exposed. For her, as for other Language poets, the linear or narrative flow of language needs to be interrupted, even garbled, to reveal its multiple vectors, its hidden multiplicity, fractures, and instability. Despite their radicalism and iconoclasm, the Language poets—many now in university positions, some in the Academy of American Poets—build on long-standing practices and theories of "open" form, including avant-garde modernism, surrealism, Dada, Objectivism, the Black Mountain school, and the New York school, as well as the Russian formalist theory of "defamiliarization."

Latino, Native American, and Asian American Poetries

Another development in English-language poetry beginning in the wake of identity-centered political movements of the 1960s and 1970s and intensifying since the 1980s has been the rise of various poetries by ethnic American minorities. Some of these poetries emerged initially from specific regions. Chicano and Chicana literature is centered in the American southwest, where vast Mexican territories were ceded to the United States in 1848—what became California, Texas, Arizona, Nevada, New Mexico, Utah, and western Colorado. The Mexican American residents in these areas officially became American citizens, but the "Anglo" majority shunted them into ghettos called *barrios.* Other Mexicans made their way north in search of economic opportunity. The descendents of these immigrants and natives came to be known by the word *Chicano* in 1954 and, for women, *Chicana* in 1967. In the 1960s, as a result of heightened political and ethnic self-consciousness after the civil rights movement, the nationalist Chicano movement, *La Causa,* urged greater rights for the Mexican American minority. A protest literature developed, which prepared the way in turn for various kinds of Chicano poetry to emerge in the late 1970s. In his early work, for example, Gary Soto vividly details the often grim circumstances of migrant life and manual labor in the San Joaquin Valley. His later work centers on the intimate life of the Chicano family.

Perhaps the most striking linguistic feature of Latino poetry—which includes poetry by Chicanos and others descended from Spanish-speaking nations in the Americas—is its direct or indirect incorporation of Spanish. This linguistic hybridization at once enriches contemporary poetry and challenges the norm of American poetry written exclusively in English. In her poems, Chicana writer Lorna Dee Cervantes intersplices Spanish words and phrases with English, echoing the bilingual texture of Latino life in the United States. Other poets, such as Alberto Ríos, absorb Spanish less directly into their poetry, capturing in their use of English the music, oral rhythms, and rhetorical forms of Spanish. Ríos and other Latino poets also draw on the Latin American literary tradition of magical realism, blurring boundaries between fantasy and fact. In his "A Man Then Suddenly Stops Moving," an old man spits out a plum, only to watch it metamorphose into a younger version of himself: the old man "puts him onto his finger / like a parakeet / and sits him on the shelf / with the pictures." Not all Latino poets thematize ethnic experience. Dionisio D. Martínez, for example, an immigrant from Cuba, avails himself of the traditions of European surrealism, American abstract expressionism, and the New York school. But he, too, obliquely refers to questions of ethnic identity in his frequent images of displacement and dispossession. The sense of being between languages, between cultures, between identities informs the work of all these poets.

Native American poetry in English originates in the American west, where numerous regional tribes flourished, each with its own rich set of tales, traditions, and ways of seeing the world. While there were earlier twentieth-century precursors, the flowering of Native American poetry in English dates to the 1960s and 1970s, a period of renewed cultural self-expression, new publishing opportunities, and intense political activism—led by the American Indian Movement (AIM), a militant civil rights organization (1968–78) that worked to restore tribal lands and revitalize traditional cultures. As in Latino poetry, questions of cultural in-betweenness also pervade Native American poetry. Sherman Alexie, a Spokane/Coeur d'Alene Indian who grew up on a reservation in eastern Washington, has said that the sense of "living in both worlds"—that of the dominant Euro-American culture and a minority culture—is "part of who I am." His poems juxtapose, always ironically, popular American icons such as Marilyn Monroe with Native American practices such as the ritual use of the sweat lodge. Louise Erdrich, partly of Chippewa descent, switches back and forth between Roman Catholic and Native American points of reference. The poetry of Joy Harjo (Creek) and Leslie Marmon Silko (Laguna Pueblo) leaps the gap between "dream time" and the sordid present, between narrative realism and an elemental mysticism. Acutely aware of the colonial devastation of their indigenous languages and cultures, Native American poets vividly detail the grim circumstances—poverty, alcoholism, unemployment—of contemporary life on the reservation. But their poetry aesthetically recuperates and revitalizes elements of Native American culture, such as storytelling, tricksterism, animism, and cyclical time consciousness. For all their similarities, these poets belong to different indigenous populations and reflect different fusions of Native and Euro-American cultures, inflected by their individual sensibilities. Alexie, for example, continually recalls the Native American trickster aesthetic in his wily poems, while Harjo is more of a seer; his skeptical poems are like caustic banter, hers more like supplications or blessings, centered on the sacred, the mythical, and the natural.

American poets of the East Asian diaspora also fuse and juxtapose their divergent cultural inheritances. The number and variety of Americans of East Asian descent increased dramatically after the 1965 Immigration and Nationality Act abolished quotas favoring immigrants from northern Europe. In the wake of this watershed legislation and of the civil rights movement, a large population of East Asian Americans in the 1970s began to search for ways to embody poetically their complex cultural identities. Indonesian-born poet Li-Young Lee, who immigrated to the United States as a grown boy in 1964, writes about the painful childhood experience of being in between Mandarin Chinese and English, at home in neither. Yet his poetry brings together the imagistic influence of Tang dynasty poetry and the psychological drama of American confessional poetry. Another East Asian immigrant, born in Hong Kong, Marilyn Chin incorporates traditions such as the Chinese quatrain into a brashly American feminist neoconfessionalism. Her blunt irreverence—toward both Chinese and American culture—contrasts sharply with Lee's more elegiac sensibility, as also with Cathy Song's more delicately lyrical poetry. Of both Korean and Chinese descent, Song explores intercultural perception in economical poems that draw on her Asian cultural inheritances without idealizing or exoticizing them. Born to a Japanese father and a mother of African American, Native American, and European descent, Ai—who is especially skilled in the use of dramatic monologue—exemplifies the difficulty of ethnically defining contemporary poets, many of whom cross boundaries of race, ethnicity, and nation, whether in their familial or cultural inheritances.

Transnational and Cross-Ethnic Poetry

There are good reasons for reading postwar poets in national or ethnic clusters. Many of these poets have taken their first cultural bearings from ethnic movements and national experiences. Their sensibilities and uses of the English language have been enriched and formed by distinctive cultural styles, political histories, and educations. Moreover, the gap between English and American poetry is often said to have widened after World War II, in contrast to the earlier transatlantic modernism of Pound, Eliot, Stein, Mina Loy, the Objectivists, Auden, and others. American poets of "open" form—the Black Mountain poets, the Beats, the New York poets—had no equivalent in Great Britain or Ireland during the late 1950s or the 1960s. "Ethnic" poets gained a strong foothold in American poetry much earlier than in British.

But in their lives and literary influences, contemporary poets have continually crossed lines of nationality and ethnicity. Strong linkages exist, for example, across the transatlantic divide. Reflecting a general postwar mood of exhaustion with the extremist politics that had devastated much of the world, American poets in the New Critical style had much in common with British poets of the Movement. Both groups rejected sharply political poetry; both refused the self-revelatory and utopian drives of late Romanticism; both privileged irony and understatement; both preferred well-made poems in rhyme, meter, and stanzaic patterns; and both adhered to a rational syntax and grammar. Although the leading figure of the Movement, Philip Larkin, was a self-declared English nativist, he took an American musical form—jazz—as his model of all that was best (traditional jazz) and worst (bebop and free jazz) in poetry and art. He and other Movement poets wanted to reestablish a "native" English line of poetry that went back to Thomas Hardy and the Georgians of the 1910s. But their willful provincialism can be understood only in a transnational context—that of reaction and resistance to the supposedly "alien" modernism of Yeats, Eliot, and Pound. Similarly, American poets of "open" form, such as Charles Olson, Allen Ginsberg, Robert Duncan, and Amiri Baraka, cannot be understood outside the transnational context of the "closed" forms that they, like Williams before them, associated with a British imperial legacy in America and that they were trying to supplant, even while reclaiming prophetic English poets such as William Blake.

A number of English, Irish, and American poets crossed the Atlantic after World War II, in the process cross-pollinating poetic forms and idioms. Having moved to the United States just before the outbreak of the war, Auden, who presided over the Yale Series of Younger Poets, became one of the strongest influences on a generation of form-hungry American poets, including Robert Hayden, Adrienne Rich, James Merrill, John Ashbery, and Anthony Hecht. Even without moving to England or Ireland, Robert Lowell influenced key poets such as Geoffrey Hill and Seamus Heaney, who muscled up their style after reading him. Sometimes postwar British poetry is presented as if no British poet were reading American verse, but Charles Tomlinson, who traveled to the United States, took Wallace Stevens, Marianne Moore, and the Objectivists as his models. Donald Davie, originally a poet of the Movement, and one of Tomlinson's students, migrated to the United States and complicated the rationalist Movement paradigm with asymmetries drawn from Pound's aesthetic. Thom Gunn, who also began as a Movement poet, decamped to California, where he studied with Yvor Winters and later wrote some of the best poetry about the effects of AIDS in the American homosexual community. Geoffrey Hill, later a migrant to the United States, took some of his first cues from the tonal, linguistic, and ethical complexity of the American New Critical poet Allen Tate. One of the most eminent poets of the Black Mountain group, British-born Denise Levertov, was a migrant from English forms to an American organicism that recuperated and updated, ironically, an English Romantic conception of poetry. Sylvia Plath, who settled in England, wrote poetry influenced by the violent primitivism of verse by her husband, Ted Hughes, England's future poet laureate. She, along with other American women poets whose work reflects what became an international women's movement, had a strong liberating influence on Irish poets such as Eavan Boland, who now teaches at Stanford University, and Indian poets such as Eunice de Souza. Among later Euro-American poets, Charles Simic, born in the former Yugoslavia, arrived in the United States at sixteen, and Jorie Graham, who grew up in Italy and France, moved to New York in her twenties. Many postwar American poets lived for long periods in Europe or other parts of the world, such as Elizabeth Bishop in Brazil, Gary Snyder in Japan, John Ashbery and Marilyn Hacker in France. Many more traveled widely and regularly. All of this physical mobility has echoed the increasing globalization of film, print, video, telecommunications, computers, and other such technologies, which, flowing across national boundaries, have exposed contemporary poets to an accelerated circulation of images, words, and experiences from around the world.

Although Irish poetry is often said to be more "conservative" than American poetry, the two national streams have frequently come together in the contemporary period. After a year at the University of California, Berkeley, Seamus Heaney wrote his important volume about Ulster's violence, *North,* in the short-lined free verse he discovered in American poets such as Robert Creeley and William Carlos Williams—a tubular style that subsequently disseminated widely in British and Irish verse. Even his earliest poetry does not flow from an exclusively Irish origin: he has credited Ted Hughes with being a key initial influence in helping him find his voice. While Heaney has spent part of many years at Harvard University, his former student Paul Muldoon has been teaching at Princeton University, both poets absorbing and returning American influences. Having lived much of his mature life in New York and London, and feeling inherently awkward in relation to Ireland because of his Protestant background, the poet Derek Mahon questions—as might perhaps all these contemporary poets—"what is meant by home" ("Afterlives"). The ample record of transatlantic crossings, migrations, and entanglements should remind us that, even if we cannot abandon altogether conceptions of contemporary poetry as "British," "Irish," or "American," we should at least qualify and complicate what is meant by home.

Postcolonial poets are even less possible to understand within strictly limited identity- or nation-based paradigms, since their lives, histories, and poetry have persistently crossed such boundaries. Growing up in the interstices of indigenous and imposed colonial cultures, most of the prominent first- and second-generation postcolonial poets had British educations at home and then ventured to the imperial "motherland" or to the United States for higher education, even including the "nativist" poets who put the strongest emphasis on their local cultural resources: Jamaican poet Louise Bennett, though writing almost entirely in West Indian English, studied at the Royal Academy of Dramatic Art, in London; the most influential Afro-Caribbean-centered poet, Kamau Brathwaite, studied at Cambridge University and the University of Sussex; and Okot p'Bitek, though reclaiming the idioms, tales, and perspectives of East African village culture, was trained as an anthropologist at Oxford University. A. K. Ramanujan, who completed a dissertation at Indiana University, wryly noted that Indology was a Western invention. Those who stayed at home for higher education, such as Derek Walcott and Christopher Okigbo, were, paradoxically, among the most internationalist in their poetry, Walcott drawing on the Elizabethan and modernist traditions, Okigbo intermingling high modernist strategies with Igbo praise songs. Because of the economic imbalance between the First World and their homelands, many postcolonial poets have lived, taught, and written for long periods in Britain—Grace Nichols and Wole Soyinka—and/or in North America—Brathwaite, Ramanujan, Walcott, Michael Ondaatje, Lorna Goodison, and Agha Shahid Ali. The ironies of postcolonial literary influence reveal the limitations of a nationalist approach to contemporary poetry: the High Church royalist T. S. Eliot was, for example, one of the strongest early influences on Brathwaite, Walcott, and Ali, helping free them from the dead hand of Victorian colonial models. Although many contemporary American and British poets have seen Anglo-modernism as compromised by the reactionary politics of its leading figures, poets of the formerly colonized world have often embraced it as profoundly enabling and subversive, borrowing modernist principles such as juxtaposition, montage, compression, allusion, and psychic ambivalence to fashion their own hybrid art.

Finally, "ethnic" American poetries are by definition cross-cultural, as poetries of national, ethnic, and linguistic in-betweenness. Many Latino and East Asian American poets were born abroad, such as Dionisio D. Martínez, Li-Young Lee, and Marilyn Chin. Still more of these "ethnic" poets are the children of parents who spoke another language at home, including Spanish, Chinese, Japanese, Korean, and Native American languages. Arising out of this interlingual and intercultural matrix, the cross-cultural texture of this poetry, interweaving indigenous and Anglo-American traditions, has much in common with the hybridity of postcolonial and of African American poetry. While the strongest impulse in "ethnic" American poetries has been to reclaim indigenous cultural resources, these poetries are also, in turn, closely interlinked with one another and with the dominant Euro-American traditions in English-language poetry. An Asian American poet such as Chin clearly draws on the African American feminist poetics of June Jordan and others who came out of the Black Arts Movement, and African American poets have drawn, in turn, on other ethnic traditions—Thylias Moss, for example, on the neosurrealist style Simic made partly out of Serbian and Slovene sources. The neoconfessional mode that seems to have lost much of its force for Anglo-American poets has been renewed and adapted by poets such as Lee, Alberto Ríos, and Joy Harjo, who write poems that straddle the introspection of confessional poetry and the communal reach of "identity poetry." We can only anticipate with excitement the new intercultural forms and connections that the next generation of poets will forge in an increasingly transnational and cross-ethnic world.

Charles Olson
1910–1970

Charles Olson is a pivotal figure in the development of American poetry after World War II. His combination of an intense personal dynamism with experimentation in form, primitivism in sensibility, and responsiveness to the environment helped propel into being new kinds of poetry. His improvisatory poetics inspired avant-garde writers as different as the then-Beat poet LeRoi Jones (later Amiri Baraka) and the Language poet Susan Howe. Conceiving of poetry as "projective" or "open," he helped set in motion an aesthetic of sprawling energy, loosened structures, and unpredictable didacticism, all of which ran counter to the New Critical principles of unity, balance, and subtle indirection.

Olson was the dominant and senior figure in a group that included Robert Creeley, Denise Levertov, Robert Duncan, and other writers centered at Black Mountain College, an experimental school in North Carolina where he was first instructor and later rector, or head. He had a gift for prophetic exhortation that combined the plainest language with bursts of obscure information about Neolithic humans and the Pleistocene age or Hittite poems and Mayan inscriptions.

Olson worked, as he proudly indicated, in the same vein as Ezra Pound and William Carlos Williams, and he was particularly impressed by *The Cantos* and by *Paterson*. Pound's work he found "ego-dominated," however, and lacking "flow" (*Mayan Letters*), and in a pamphlet titled *Proprioception* ("one's own perception") he urged writers: "Wash the ego out." In Williams, he saw the ego as happily eradicated, but he objected to *Paterson*'s limitation to one city's history. Nonetheless, Olson's own epic effort, *The Maximus Poems*, resembles *The Cantos* in its free verse assemblage of heterogeneous incidents, characters, and scenes, and it resembles *Paterson* in centering on a specific town, Gloucester, Massachusetts. Instead of calling his representative man Gloucester, Olson names him Maximus. The name might seem to bear a relation to Olson's height of six feet seven or eight inches, but it is more closely related to his theory of the writer as maximally here, living in the moment, resuming in the psychological self past and present, and always constituting, as well, a function of the environment. "I, Maximus / metal hot from boiling water" ("I, Maximus of Gloucester, to You").

Olson was born on December 27, 1910, in Worcester, Massachusetts, to a Swedish father and an Irish American mother. He speaks of his parents as his "definers": "the work of each of us is to find out the true lineaments of ourselves by facing up to the primal features of these founders who lie buried in us—that this is us, the Double-Backed Beast" (*Twentieth-Century Authors*, First Supplement, ed. Stanley Kunitz). He seeks in effect a juncture of his own past with a mythological past, "the hinges of civilization to be put back on the door" (*Proprioception*). The necessary mythology he discovers as much among the Sumerians and Mayans as among Americans, and so he can say in *The Maximus Poems*, "Just last week / 300,000,000 years ago" ("Song 4").

Though well-read, Olson was not bookish and would have nothing to do with T. S. Eliot's theory, in "Tradition and the Individual Talent," of mere "literary antecedence" (*A Bibliography of America for Edward Dorn*). He found it "awkward to call myself a poet or a writer. If there are no walls there are no names. This is the morning, after the dispersion, and the work of the morning is methodology: how to use oneself, and on what. That is my profession. I am an archeologist of morning" (Kunitz). He preferred, among writers, Homer and those before Homer, and, in later time, visionary outsiders, such as Herman Melville, Fyodor Dostoyevsky, Arthur Rimbaud, and D. H. Lawrence.

The prophetic writers William Blake, Walt Whitman, and Friedrich Nietzsche are also implicated in his thought.

Olson believed that his age took its fundamental character from being posthumanist, posthistoric, and postmodern (he inaugurated the latter term's use for poetry). A letter to Cid Corman, editor of *Origin* (an important magazine of the 1950s), celebrates "ENERGY" over "humanism," a leaping "NATURE" over "progress, accumulation, succession, tradition" (*Letters for Origin, 1950–1956*, ed. Albert Glover). Against reason and the art of comparison, Olson offers direct perception and contraries. In *Proprioception*, he speaks forcefully if vaguely of "the data of depth sensibility." In a letter of May 1959, Olson wrote that he would replace "the Classical-representational by the *primitive-abstract*" (*Selected Writings*). Accordingly, he does not so much try to persuade as to confront and overwhelm.

Olson's first book, *Call Me Ishmael*, was an attempt to read Melville viscerally rather than critically. It was published in 1947, by which time Olson was thirty-seven. Up to then, his life is somewhat obscured by his own random accounts of it. He was "uneducated" at Wesleyan, Yale, and Harvard Universities: "I have had to learn the simplest things / last," he says in "Maximus, to Himself." From Wesleyan, he received a B.A. in 1932 and an M.A. the following year. He taught first at Clark University, in Worcester, then, from 1936 to 1939, at Harvard. For the next nine years he had various occupations, which came to a focus in the publication of his Melville book. The following year, 1948, he took the place of his friend the novelist Edward Dahlberg at Black Mountain College. Many of its teachers and students became important figures in painting, music, and dance as well as in literature. In 1951, Olson became rector of the college, and he stayed in this position until 1956. He was to teach later, in his own dynamic, unpredictable fashion, at the State University of New York at Buffalo, and then (briefly) at the University of Connecticut.

Though some of them were written earlier, Olson's poems became known and were collected in the 1960s. He had been struggling to phrase his aesthetic position and, in 1950, succeeded in formulating his essay on "Projective Verse." This became the manifesto for a number of writers; indeed, William Carlos Williams was so impressed that he quoted much of it in his *Autobiography*. In place of inherited line, stanza, formal pattern—all that Olson calls "closed form" or "verse that print bred"—Olson offers "composition by field," open form. Perhaps with William Blake's dictum in mind that "energy is eternal delight," Olson says: "A poem is energy transferred from where the poet got it (he will have some several causations), by way of the poem itself to, all the way over to, the reader. Okay. Then the poem itself must, at all points, be a high energy-construct and, at all points, an energy-discharge." For this poetry, "Form is never more than an extension of content," a quotation from Robert Creeley that Olson incorporates in his poem "A B Cs." The form is somehow to be the product of the breath rather than of literary tradition. "Who knows what a poem ought to sound like? until it's thar?" This new verse, he insists, "involves a stance toward reality outside a poem as well as a new stance towards the reality of a poem itself." Olson rejects the humanizing of the external world and extols "objectism"—by which he means "getting rid of the lyrical interference of the individual as ego, of the 'subject' and his soul." He abolishes the poet as observer, or commentator, in favor of the poem as the necessary expression of a confluence with the poet in and out of space and time, archaically rooted but totally present.

Pacific Lament

In memory of William Hickey, a member of the crew of the U.S.S. *Growler*, lost at sea in February, 1944.

Black at that depth
turn, golden boy no more
white bone to bone, turn
hear who bore you weep
hear him who made you
deep there on ocean's floor
turn
as waters stir;
turn, bone of man

Cold as a planet is
cold, beat of blood no more
the salt sea's course
along the bone jaw white
stir, boy, stir
motion without motion
stir, and hear
love come down.

Down as you fell
sidewise, stair to green stair
without breath, down
the tumble of ocean
to find you, bone
cold and new among the ships
and men and fish askew.

You alone o golden boy no more
turn now and sleep
washed white by water
sleep in your black deep
by water out of which man came
to find his legs, arms, love, pain.
Sleep, boy, sleep
in older arms than hers,
rocked by an older father;
toss no more,
love;
sleep.

1946

The Thing Was Moving

It's so beautiful, life, goddamn death
that we have to die, only the mind knows
what lies next the heart or a five-petaled flower
restores the fringed gentians[1] I used to so love
I'd lie amongst them in the meadow near the house
which was later covered by a dump to make an athletic field
and the brook was gone to which we tried to speed our sleds
from the hill the house stood on and which the dump
was meant to join, the loss punctuated by the shooting
my father taught me with the rifle he gave me from the back porch
of the three-decker, the rats living among the cans and peat
as the dump came closer, and I hated
all of it (the same porch the chameleon he had bought me
escaped from, from the cage I'd made it
of old screen when we brought it home from the circus

the smoke from the dump-fires all the time the thing was moving
toward us, covering the meadow, coming from the hill
(where we had had the single cable swing had broke
that day i was alone there and i had flown
out over all that space, and my glasses
beyond me, and my back to this day . . . and i groping
not to tell my parents, and to find the glasses
to find my way back. The fire-engines
in the evening dousing—and no flames but the littlest, all
smoke turning into steam there, but the excitement . . .

the concrete sections, when the dump began to reach
the brook, to put it under, like hoops we could not roll
in which—they were so high—we lost ourselves
like tunnels, or took it we were five-figured forms
fit to fill a circle and be acrobats, our heads
wedged but no movement of those sections even
when we pried them and were unknowingly in such danger
as when we built the club-house of railroad ties
on the edge of another flat, the swamp where the man
and his horse and team went down in the quicksand, and we
did not know until after the cops had broken down the structure
and even later when the auto showrooms covered it, and piles
had to be driven . . . the hunting, of each other, before the brook
was let in and only way above, or below at Chandler Street
was it any more where I had sunk in, where the irises were,
where I had seen my first turtle, or further up, where
girls had swum naked that day I had tittupped
from the piano lesson, seeking my friends, and suddenly,
coming on the pool, had heard the voices first, and slowed

1. Flowering plants.

so that I saw them from the bushes (the older woman
turning me back . . . the invasion

or the ford[2] (below Dick Marsden's house) horses crossed
and we sailed boats, or made dams, the wonder
of the way the hill sloped up there, the gradual way
before it became a suburb and was still the West
(the trench we were sure had been emplacements
of King Phillip's Wars[3] ended before the ford, before
the whole brook system got transverse to what it was below
near where I lived, Hill's Farm getting its fields
from the change of the direction of its flow,
and the topography
                                        the flowers (as well as the ball field)
were located, in my space, by this curving
from west to south, the farm marking the change
and running against the foot of my house, the brick wall
on which all the wood stood which shook
when the wind bellied down that valley and struck
the broad back of the house and I used to think
why the whipping of the house on that third-floor
didn't throw it down, and only that the storm
was not like marching men on a bridge, was out of step
was irregular as men are, and as multiple, the times we are
and our materials are so much more numerous
than any such thing as the heart's flow
or the sun's coming up, why
man is man's delight, and there is no backward
except his, how far it goes, as far
as any thing he's made, dug up or lighted
by a flare in some such cave as I never knew
except as that concrete hid my brook and I was as large
(before they put the pieces in below ground) inside any one hoop
as any pentamerous thing, this figwort[4]
which provokes me
and I study
bract thallus involucre whorl[5]
of all my life, of torus[6] I am, holding
all I shall be, hungry
that it should never end, that my throat
which has no longer thymus and all that went with it
might speak forever the glory of
what it is to live, so bashful as man is
bare

1952   1987

2. Shallow portion where a body of water can be more easily crossed.
3. War between Native Americans and British settlers in New England (1675–76).
4. Plant of the snapdragon family. *Pentamerous:* having five parts.
5. Technical descriptions of parts of flowers.
6. Ring-shaped surface.

From The Maximus Poems

I, Maximus of Gloucester,[7] to You

Off-shore, by islands hidden in the blood
jewels & miracles, I, Maximus
a metal hot from boiling water, tell you
what is a lance, who obeys the figures of
the present dance

1

the thing you're after
may lie around the bend
of the nest (second, time slain, the bird! the bird![8]

And there! (strong) thrust, the mast! flight
(of the bird
o kylix,[9] o
Antony of Padua[1]
sweep low, o bless

the roofs, the old ones, the gentle steep ones
on whose ridge-poles the gulls sit, from which they depart,

And the flake-racks[2]
of my city!

2

love is form, and cannot be without
important substance (the weight
say, 58 carats each one of us, perforce
our goldsmith's scale

feather to feather added
(and what is mineral, what
is curling hair, the string
you carry in your nervous beak, these

make bulk, these, in the end, are
the sum

(o my lady of good voyage[3]
in whose arm, whose left arm rests

7. Gloucester, Massachusetts, is a fishing town northeast of Boston founded in 1623. Olson, or Maximus, peoples the town with historic and invented figures, and with people he knew when he lived there as a boy and as a young man.
8. Throughout his writing, Olson used unclosed parentheses to signify birth and a receptive consciousness.
9. A shallow drinking bowl of classical Greece.
1. Thirteenth-century Franciscan monk and teacher. He preached a famous sermon to the fishes in the Brenta River, near Padua.
2. Used for drying fish.
3. The Virgin Mary, depicted on the roof of a church in Gloucester, My Lady of Good Voyage, as holding a schooner.

no boy[4] but a carefully carved wood, a painted face, a schooner!
a delicate mast, as bow-sprit for

forwarding

3

the underpart is, though stemmed, uncertain
is, as sex is, as moneys are, facts!
facts, to be dealt with, as the sea is, the demand
that they be played by, that they only can be, that they must
be played by, said he, coldly, the
ear!

By ear, he sd.
But that which matters, that which insists, that which will last,
that! o my people, where shall you find it, how, where, where shall you
listen
when all is become billboards, when, all, even silence, is spray-gunned?

when even our bird, my roofs,
cannot be heard

when even you, when sound itself is neoned in?

when, on the hill, over the water
where she who used to sing,
when the water glowed,
black, gold, the tide
outward, at evening

when bells came like boats
over the oil-slicks, milkweed
hulls

And a man slumped,
attentionless,
against pink shingles

o sea city)

4

one loves only form,
and form only comes
into existence when
the thing is born

born of yourself, born
of hay and cotton struts,

4. As in conventional representations of Mary with the baby Jesus.

of street-pickings, wharves, weeds
you carry in, my bird

of a bone of a fish
of a straw, or will
of a color, of a bell
of yourself, torn

5

love is not easy
but how shall you know,
New England, now
that pejorocracy[5] is here, how
that street-cars, o Oregon, twitter
in the afternoon, offend
a black-gold loin?

how shall you strike,
o swordsman, the blue-red black
when, last night, your aim
was mu-sick, mu-sick, mu-sick
And not the cribbage game?

(o Gloucester-man,
weave
your birds and fingers
new, your roof-tops,
clean shit upon racks
sunned on
American
braid
with others like you, such
extricable surface
as faun and oral,
satyr lesbos[6] vase

o kill kill kill kill kill[7]
those
who advertise you
out)

6

in! in! the bow-sprit, bird, the beak
in, the bend is, in, goes in, the form
that which you make, what holds, which is

5. "Worsening rule"; Ezra Pound's term for the increasing insincerity he saw in art and culture.
6. The island of Lesbos, near Greece, was home to the sixth-century B.C.E. lyric poet Sappho. Fauns and satyrs were minor classical deities of the fields and forests.
7. Cf. Shakespeare's *King Lear* 4.6.181: "Then, kill, kill, kill, kill, kill, kill!"

the law of object, strut after strut, what you are, what you must be, what
the force can throw up, can, right now hereinafter erect,
the mast, the mast, the tender
mast!

The nest, I say, to you, I Maximus, say
under the hand, as I see it, over the waters
from this place where I am, where I hear,
can still hear

from where I carry you a feather
as though, sharp, I picked up,
in the afternoon delivered you
a jewel,
it flashing more than a wing,
than any old romantic thing,
than memory, than place,
than anything other than that which you carry

than that which is,
call it a nest, around the head of, call it
the next second

than that which you
can do!

1953

Maximus, to Himself

I have had to learn the simplest things
last. Which made for difficulties.
Even at sea I was slow, to get the hand out, or to cross
a wet deck.
The sea was not, finally, my trade.
But even my trade, at it, I stood estranged
from that which was most familiar.[8] Was delayed,
and not content with the man's argument
that such postponement
is now the nature of
obedience,
that we are all late
in a slow time,
that we grow up many
And the single
is not easily
known

8. Cf. Greek philosopher Heracleitus (c. 540–c. 480 B.C.E.): "We are estranged from that with which we are most familiar."

It could be, though the sharpness (the *achiote*[9])
I note in others,
makes more sense
than my own distances. The agilities

they show daily
who do the world's
businesses
And who do nature's
as I have no sense
I have done either

I have made dialogues,
have discussed ancient texts,
have thrown what light I could, offered
what pleasures
doceat[1] allows

But the known?
This, I have had to be given,
a life, love, and from one man
the world

Tokens.
But sitting here
I look out as a wind
and water man, testing
And missing
some proof

I know the quarters
of the weather, where it comes from,
where it goes. But the stem of me,
this I took from their welcome,
or their rejection, of me

And my arrogance
was neither diminished
nor increased,
by the communication

2

It is undone business
I speak of, this morning,

9. Seed crushed to make a dye with a color like that of red pepper (hence, sharp).
1. That he teach (Latin); one of the traditional functions of a poet, as later emphasized by Ezra Pound.

with the sea
stretching out
from my feet

1960

Maximus, to Gloucester, Letter 19 (A Pastoral Letter

relating
to the care of souls,
it says)

He had smiled at us,
each time we were in town, inquired
how the baby was, had two cents
for the weather, wore
(besides his automobile)
good clothes.
And a pink face.

It was yesterday
it all came out. The gambit
(as he crossed the street,
after us): "I don't believe
I know your name." Given.
How do you do,
how do you do. And then:
"Pardon me, but
what church
do you belong to,
may I ask?"

And the whole street, the town, the cities, the nation
blinked, in the afternoon sun, at the gun
was held at them. And I wavered
in the thought.

I sd, you may, sir.
He sd, what, sir.
I sd, none,
sir.

And the light was back.

For I am no merchant.
Nor so young I need to take a stance
to a loaded
smile.

I have known the face
of God.
And turned away,
turned
as He did,
his backside

2

And now it is noon
of a cloudy sunday.
And a bird sings
loudly

And my daughter, naked
on the porch, sings
as best she can, and loudly,
back

She wears her own face
as we do not,
until we cease to wear
the clouds
of all confusion,

of all confusers
who wear the false face
He never wore, Whose
is terrible. Is
perfection

1960

Maximus to Gloucester, Letter 27 *[Withheld]*

I come back to the geography of it,
the land falling off to the left
where my father shot his scabby golf
and the rest of us played baseball
into the summer darkness until no flies
could be seen and we came home
to our various piazzas where the women
buzzed

To the left the land fell to the city,
to the right, it fell to the sea

I was so young my first memory
is of a tent spread to feed lobsters

to Rexall[2] conventioneers, and my father,
a man for kicks, came out of the tent roaring
with a bread-knife in his teeth to take care of
a druggist they'd told him had made a pass at
my mother, she laughing, so sure, as round
as her face, Hines[3] pink and apple,
under one of those frame hats women then

This is no bare incoming
of novel abstract form, this

is no welter or the forms
of those events, this,

Greeks, is the stopping
of the battle

        It is the imposing
of all those antecedent predecessions, the precessions

of me, the generation of those facts
which are my words, it is coming

from all that I no longer am, yet am,
the slow westward motion of

more than I am

There is no strict personal order

for my inheritance.

        No Greek will be able

to discriminate my body.

        An American

is a complex of occasions,

themselves a geometry

of spatial nature.

        I have this sense,

2. American drug company.
3. Duncan Hines, maker of cake mixes and other food products.

that I am one

with my skin

Plus this—plus this:

that forever the geography

which leans in

on me I compell

backwards I compell Gloucester

to yield, to

change

Polis

is this

1968

[Sun / Right in My Eye]

Sun
right in my eye
4 PM December 2nd arrived
at my kitchen
window blazing
at me full in the
face approaching
the hill it sets
behind glaring
in its burst of late
heat right on me
and as orange and hot
as sun at noonday practically
can be. Only this one
is straight at me like a
beam shot to hit me
It feels like
enforcing itself
on me giving me its
message that it is sliding
under the hill and
that I better
hear it say

be hot man
be hot
be hot and orange
like I am
I am
sending you
this message as
I slip exactly to
West I am burning you man
as I leave I'm even stronger
now just as I
go I am already
cooled that much but still
I turn on you
and flare
as I start to
go. But still
hot and red now blaring
on the south slope of my disappearance
point.
Now I begin to
go hear me I
have sent you
the message I am
gone

1975

ELIZABETH BISHOP
1911–1979

Elizabeth Bishop, whose fame and influence have mounted steadily since her death, is one of the central progenitors of contemporary poetry. She masters and remakes inherited lyric models perhaps as successfully as any poet of her generation. Her controlled artifice contrasts with the "open" form espoused by postwar poets such as Charles Olson, the author of long, declamatory, ramshackle poems indebted to Ezra Pound and William Carlos Williams. Instead, she takes her cue from Marianne Moore, who remarked, "Elizabeth Bishop is spectacular in being unspectacular," and who praised Bishop's technique for being "cold, sober," "accurate and modest" (*The Complete Prose of Marianne Moore*).

Bishop is an exacting and exquisite miniaturist. Her poetry is precise in its descriptive language and rigorous in its discretion. Her fastidious eye inspects with luminous intensity the physical world. "Watch it closely," she says in "The Monument." What she observes takes form and gathers itself, as if nature were being brought to a boil: under her eye, "The Fish" and all around it turn to "rainbow, rainbow, rainbow."

Bishop was born on February 8, 1911, in Worcester, Massachusetts. An only child, she suffered the first of many calamitous losses at only eight months, when her father died. Her mother, greatly afflicted by his death, was in and out of hospitals and mental institutions for the next few years, until she was diagnosed as insane and permanently institutionalized. Bishop was five when this happened, and though her mother lived another eighteen years, she never saw her again. Bishop was taken in by her maternal grandparents in Great Village, Nova Scotia, where she would subsequently return for summers; but she was soon uprooted once again ("kidnapped" was her word) by her father's wealthy family, which took her first to its mansion in Worcester, Massachusetts, then to live with her mother's sister Maud, near Boston. She spent much of her childhood in bed suffering from asthma and various allergies, but also memorizing poetry. "In the Waiting Room," "Sestina," "First Death in Nova Scotia," and the autobiographical prose piece "In the Village" are among her writings about her youth. After a few years in high school, Bishop attended Vassar College, where she made important literary friendships, the most important with Moore. But Bishop's life would continue to be plagued by asthma, depression, and alcoholism. Living off a modest income from her father's estate, she spent some years in New York City and Key West, Florida. In 1947, she met and became lifelong friends with Robert Lowell, who helped her secure a year-long stint as the consultant in poetry to the Library of Congress (1949–50).

In 1951, depressed, lonely, and fearing for her health, Bishop sailed to Brazil on a planned trip around the world. She fell ill after eating fruit from a Brazilian cashew tree and then fell in love with the person who was taking care of her, Lota de Macedo Soares, a wealthy Brazilian aristocrat she had known at Vassar. Bishop stayed on in Soares's Brazilian villa for the next fifteen years. Little wonder that travel and exile should be steady themes in her work; in "Questions of Travel," she asks, "Should we have stayed at home, / wherever that may be?" Bishop returned to the United States after Lota Soares's health deteriorated in 1967, and Soares joined her in New York, only to commit suicide. In 1970, Bishop began teaching at Harvard University; she died in Cambridge at sixty-eight. She had won the Pulitzer Prize in 1956, the National Book Award in 1970, the Neustadt International Prize and the National Book Critics Circle Award in 1976.

A perfectionist, Bishop published relatively few poems. Many of them, especially early on, begin with a found object, often nondescript (e.g., the misprinted word "Man-Moth"; "the monument") yet capable of being contemplated with passion and so imaginatively transfigured. In contrast to the confessional poetry written by her contemporaries, which she found distasteful, her poems typically deflect or distill autobiographical content. Emotion is often attributed to rather distant others, as in "Songs for a Colored Singer," a poem about Billie Holiday that contains the wry promise "I'm going to go and take the bus / and find someone monogamous." At times, she seems determinedly reticent, as if to suggest that her life inheres in the way she observes external phenomena, not in any private events. But Bishop is clearly capable of writing poetry as intensely personal and erotic as anything since Sappho. Not published until the year 2000, long after her death, "Vague Poem" ends:

> Just now, when I saw you naked again,
> I thought the same words: rose-rock, rock-rose . . .
> Rose, trying, working, to show itself,
> forming, folding over,
> unimaginable connections, unseen, shining edges.
> Rose-rock, unformed, flesh beginning, crystal by crystal,
> clear pink breasts and darker, crystalline nipples,
> rose-rock, rose-quartz, roses, roses, roses,
> exacting roses from the body,
> and the even darker, accurate, rose of sex—

But Bishop left such works unpublished in her lifetime, and this poem, if astounding in its imagistic crisscrossing of stone and flesh, its rhapsodic rhythms, and its transformation of the blason (lyric inventory of the beloved's parts), is unfinished.

The posthumous appearance of clearly autobiographical material has helped readers appreciate more fully the personal dimension of Bishop's verse. Grief, tenderness, terror, desire—such feelings are vividly present within Bishop's rhythms, metaphors, and forms. The late poem "One Art," with its repeated line "The art of losing isn't hard to master," exemplifies the fusion of passionate self-expression and precise self-control in Bishop's poetry. The speaker returns obsessively to losses that range from the trivial ("door keys") to the unbearably large ("two cities," "a continent," perhaps even "you"); but Bishop's use of the insistently repetitive form of the villanelle, and her tonal blending of antic self-mockery with melancholy, enable her both to contain and to display overwhelming feelings of fear and grief. In "Crusoe in England," Bishop sees in the speaker's grief over displacement and lost same-sex companionship the image of her own experience: "—And Friday, my dear Friday, died of measles / seventeen years ago come March." Autobiography is unmistakable in "In the Waiting Room," a poem in which Bishop even names herself: "But I felt: you are an *I*, / you are an *Elizabeth*." Yet the poem throws into doubt the very contours of identity—"Why should I be my aunt, / or me, or anyone?" At once personal and objective, self-expressive and self-effacing, Bishop's poetry confounds such distinctions.

One way to take the measure of Bishop's achievement is to notice how many different forms and genres she wrote in, each time seeming to transform the template permanently. She composed in both metered and free verse, in each case keeping the stresses muted. She used fixed forms with strict requirements, such as the sestina and the villanelle, as well as long verse paragraphs of varying lengths. She wrote in perfect rhyme, off-rhyme, and unrhymed verse. While she produced poems of unparalleled lucidity about nature and landscape, she also fashioned self-referring poems about art, language, and representation, such as "The Monument" and "Poem." Some works, such as "The Fish," manage to be both kinds of poems at once. Bishop is famed for her understatement and restraint, her unpretentious diction of the everyday and the domestic; and yet in "At the Fishhouses" she summons a visionary rhetoric, moving at the end from a description of cold seawater to a meditation on knowledge as "dark, salt, clear, moving, utterly free." As this example suggests, she humanized the natural world through anthropomorphic language, but she also criticized attempts to personify and prettify the nonhuman: *"Too pretty, dreamlike mimicry!"* calls out the speaker of "The Armadillo." Bishop is a realist and a surrealist, a poet of place and of displacement. That she succeeds so completely in all these modes and styles, while remaining unmistakably herself, ensures her reputation as a poet, and her use as a model for future poets, for many years to come.

The Map

Land lies in water; it is shadowed green.
Shadows, or are they shallows, at its edges
showing the line of long sea-weeded ledges
where weeds hang to the simple blue from green.
Or does the land lean down to lift the sea from under,
drawing it unperturbed around itself?
Along the fine tan sandy shelf
is the land tugging at the sea from under?

The shadow of Newfoundland lies flat and still.
Labrador's[1] yellow, where the moony Eskimo
has oiled it. We can stroke these lovely bays,

1. Northeastern portion of the Canadian mainland in the province of Newfoundland.

under a glass as if they were expected to blossom,
or as if to provide a clean cage for invisible fish.
The names of seashore towns run out to sea,
the names of cities cross the neighboring mountains
—the printer here experiencing the same excitement
as when emotion too far exceeds its cause.
These peninsulas take the water between thumb and finger
like women feeling for the smoothness of yard-goods.

Mapped waters are more quiet than the land is,
lending the land their waves' own conformation:
and Norway's hare runs south in agitation,
profiles investigate the sea, where land is.
Are they assigned, or can the countries pick their colors?
—What suits the character or the native waters best.
Topography displays no favorites; North's as near as West.
More delicate than the historians' are the map-makers' colors.

1935, 1946

The Man-Moth[2]

Here, above,
cracks in the buildings are filled with battered moonlight.
The whole shadow of Man is only as big as his hat.
It lies at his feet like a circle for a doll to stand on,
and he makes an inverted pin, the point magnetized to the moon.
He does not see the moon; he observes only her vast properties,
feeling the queer light on his hands, neither warm nor cold,
of a temperature impossible to record in thermometers.

But when the Man-Moth
pays his rare, although occasional, visits to the surface,
the moon looks rather different to him. He emerges
from an opening under the edge of one of the sidewalks
and nervously begins to scale the faces of the buildings.
He thinks the moon is a small hole at the top of the sky,
proving the sky quite useless for protection.
He trembles, but must investigate as high as he can climb.

Up the façades,
his shadow dragging like a photographer's cloth behind him,
he climbs fearfully, thinking that this time he will manage
to push his small head through that round clean opening
and be forced through, as from a tube, in black scrolls on the light.
(Man, standing below him, has no such illusions.)
But what the Man-Moth fears most he must do, although
he fails, of course, and falls back scared but quite unhurt.

2. "Newspaper misprint for 'mammoth' " [Bishop's note].

Then he returns
to the pale subways of cement he calls his home. He flits,
he flutters, and cannot get aboard the silent trains
fast enough to suit him. The doors close swiftly.
The Man-Moth always seats himself facing the wrong way
and the train starts at once at its full, terrible speed,
without a shift in gears or a gradation of any sort.
He cannot tell the rate at which he travels backwards.

Each night he must
be carried through artificial tunnels and dream recurrent dreams.
Just as the ties recur beneath his train, these underlie
his rushing brain. He does not dare look out the window,
for the third rail, the unbroken draught of poison,
runs there beside him. He regards it as a disease
he has inherited the susceptibility to. He has to keep
his hands in his pockets, as others must wear mufflers.

If you catch him,
hold up a flashlight to his eye. It's all dark pupil,
an entire night itself, whose haired horizon tightens
as he stares back, and closes up the eye. Then from the lids
one tear, his only possession, like the bee's sting, slips.
Slyly he palms it, and if you're not paying attention
he'll swallow it. However, if you watch, he'll hand it over,
cool as from underground springs and pure enough to drink.

1936, 1946

The Monument

Now can you see the monument? It is of wood
built somewhat like a box. No. Built
like several boxes in descending sizes
one above the other.
Each is turned half-way round so that
its corners point toward the sides
of the one below and the angles alternate.
Then on the topmost cube is set
a sort of fleur-de-lys of weathered wood,
long petals of board, pierced with odd holes,
four-sided, stiff, ecclesiastical.
From it four thin, warped poles spring out,
(slanted like fishing-poles or flag-poles)
and from them jig-saw work hangs down,
four lines of vaguely whittled ornament
over the edges of the boxes
to the ground.
The monument is one-third set against
a sea; two-thirds against a sky.

The view is geared
(that is, the view's perspective)
so low there is no "far away,"
and we are far away within the view.
A sea of narrow, horizontal boards
lies out behind our lonely monument,
its long grains alternating right and left
like floor-boards—spotted, swarming-still,
and motionless. A sky runs parallel,
and it is palings, coarser than the sea's:
splintery sunlight and long-fibred clouds.
"Why does that strange sea make no sound?
Is it because we're far away?
Where are we? Are we in Asia Minor,
or in Mongolia?"
An ancient promontory,
an ancient principality whose artist-prince
might have wanted to build a monument
to mark a tomb or boundary, or make
a melancholy or romantic scene of it . . .
"But that queer sea looks made of wood,
half-shining, like a driftwood sea.
And the sky looks wooden, grained with cloud.
It's like a stage-set; it is all so flat!
Those clouds are full of glistening splinters!
What is that?"
It is the monument.
"It's piled-up boxes,
outlined with shoddy fret-work, half-fallen off,
cracked and unpainted. It looks old."
—The strong sunlight, the wind from the sea,
all the conditions of its existence,
may have flaked off the paint, if ever it was painted,
and made it homelier than it was.
"Why did you bring me here to see it?
A temple of crates in cramped and crated scenery,
what can it prove?
I am tired of breathing this eroded air,
this dryness in which the monument is cracking."

It is an artifact
of wood. Wood holds together better
than sea or cloud or sand could by itself,
much better than real sea or sand or cloud.
It chose that way to grow and not to move.
The monument's an object, yet those decorations,
carelessly nailed, looking like nothing at all,
give it away as having life, and wishing;
wanting to be a monument, to cherish something.
The crudest scroll-work says "commemorate,"
while once each day the light goes around it
like a prowling animal,

or the rain falls on it, or the wind blows into it.
It may be solid, may be hollow.
The bones of the artist-prince may be inside
or far away on even drier soil.
But roughly but adequately it can shelter
what is within (which after all
cannot have been intended to be seen).
It is the beginning of a painting,
a piece of sculpture, or poem, or monument,
and all of wood. Watch it closely.

1939, 1946

The Fish

I caught a tremendous fish
and held him beside the boat
half out of water, with my hook
fast in the corner of his mouth.
He didn't fight.
He hadn't fought at all.
He hung a grunting weight,
battered and venerable
and homely. Here and there
his brown skin hung in strips
like ancient wallpaper,
and its pattern of darker brown
was like wallpaper:
shapes like full-blown roses
stained and lost through age.
He was speckled with barnacles,
fine rosettes of lime,
and infested
with tiny white sea-lice,
and underneath two or three
rags of green weed hung down.
While his gills were breathing in
the terrible oxygen
—the frightening gills,
fresh and crisp with blood,
that can cut so badly—
I thought of the coarse white flesh
packed in like feathers,
the big bones and the little bones,
the dramatic reds and blacks
of his shiny entrails,
and the pink swim-bladder
like a big peony.
I looked into his eyes
which were far larger than mine

but shallower, and yellowed,
the irises backed and packed
with tarnished tinfoil
seen through the lenses
of old scratched isinglass.[3]
They shifted a little, but not
to return my stare.
—It was more like the tipping
of an object toward the light.
I admired his sullen face,
the mechanism of his jaw,
and then I saw
that from his lower lip
—if you could call it a lip—
grim, wet, and weaponlike,
hung five old pieces of fish-line,
or four and a wire leader[4]
with the swivel still attached,
with all their five big hooks
grown firmly in his mouth.
A green line, frayed at the end
where he broke it, two heavier lines,
and a fine black thread
still crimped from the strain and snap
when it broke and he got away.
Like medals with their ribbons
frayed and wavering,
a five-haired beard of wisdom
trailing from his aching jaw.
I stared and stared
and victory filled up
the little rented boat,
from the pool of bilge
where oil had spread a rainbow
around the rusted engine
to the bailer rusted orange,
the sun-cracked thwarts,
the oarlocks on their strings,
the gunnels[5]—until everything
was rainbow, rainbow, rainbow!
And I let the fish go.

1940, 1946

3. Mica; whitish, semitransparent substance from the air bladders of fish, used for windows.
4. Short piece of wire connecting fishhook and fishline.
5. Upper edges of the boat. *Bailer*: bucket for bailing water out of the boat. *Thwarts:* rowers' seats or benches. *Oarlocks:* metal devices to hold the oars, attached by a "string" to the boat itself.

Roosters

At four o'clock
in the gun-metal blue dark
we hear the first crow of the first cock

just below
the gun-metal blue window
and immediately there is an echo

off in the distance,
then one from the backyard fence,
then one, with horrible insistence,

grates like a wet match
from the broccoli patch,
flares, and all over town begins to catch.

Cries galore
come from the water-closet door,
from the dropping-plastered henhouse floor,

where in the blue blur
their rustling wives admire,
the roosters brace their cruel feet and glare

with stupid eyes
while from their beaks there rise
the uncontrolled, traditional cries.

Deep from protruding chests
in green-gold medals dressed,
planned to command and terrorize the rest,

the many wives
who lead hens' lives
of being courted and despised;

deep from raw throats
a senseless order floats
all over town. A rooster gloats

over our beds
from rusty iron sheds
and fences made from old bedsteads,

over our churches
where the tin rooster perches,
over our little wooden northern houses,

making sallies
from all the muddy alleys,
marking out maps like Rand McNally's.[6]

glass-headed pins,
oil-golds and copper greens
anthracite blues, alizarins,[7]

each one an active
displacement in perspective;
each screaming, "This is where I live!"

Each screaming
"Get up! Stop dreaming!"
Roosters, what are you projecting?

You, whom the Greeks elected
to shoot at on a post, who struggled
when sacrificed, you whom they labeled

"Very combative . . ."[8]
what right have you to give
commands and tell us how to live,

cry "Here!" and "Here!"
and wake us here where are
unwanted love, conceit and war?

The crown of red
set on your little head
is charged with all your fighting blood.

Yes, that excrescence
makes a most virile presence,
plus all that vulgar beauty of iridescence.

Now in mid-air
by twos they fight each other.
Down comes a first flame-feather,

and one is flying,
with raging heroism defying
even the sensation of dying.

And one has fallen,
but still above the town
his torn-out, bloodied feathers drift down;

6. American map-making company.
7. Various shades of red.
8. The ancient Greeks used roosters for target practice, sacrifice, and cockfighting.

and what he sung
no matter. He is flung
on the gray ash-heap, lies in dung

with his dead wives
with open, bloody eyes,
while those metallic feathers oxidize.

St. Peter's sin
was worse than that of Magdalen
whose sin was of the flesh alone;[9]

of spirit, Peter's,
falling, beneath the flares,
among the "servants and officers."

Old holy sculpture[1]
could set it all together
in one small scene, past and future:

Christ stands amazed,
Peter, two fingers raised
to surprised lips, both as if dazed.

But in between
a little cock is seen
carved on a dim column in the travertine,[2]

explained by *gallus canit;*
flet Petrus[3] underneath it.
There is inescapable hope, the pivot;

yes, and there Peter's tears
run down our chanticleer's[4]
sides and gem his spurs.

Tear-encrusted thick
as a medieval relic
he waits. Poor Peter, heart-sick,

still cannot guess
those cock-a-doodles yet might bless,
his dreadful rooster come to mean forgiveness,

9. Mary Magdalen, as a prostitute, committed sins of the flesh. Peter denied his relationship with Jesus as a rooster crowed three times. He later took a leading role in the Christian Church.
1. Carved c. 400 C.E. and now in the Vatican, Rome.
2. Marble. The iconography of Jesus and Peter standing beside a cock on a column's capital is frequent in early Christian art.
3. The cock crows; Peter weeps (Latin). Cf. Matthew 26.75.
4. That is, rooster's.

a new weathervane
on basilica and barn,
and that outside the Lateran[5]

there would always be
a bronze cock on a porphyry[6]
pillar so the people and the Pope might see

that even the Prince
of the Apostles long since
had been forgiven, and to convince

all the assembly
that "Deny deny deny"
is not all the roosters cry.

In the morning
a low light is floating
in the backyard, and gilding

from underneath
the broccoli, leaf by leaf;
how could the night have come to grief?

gilding the tiny
floating swallow's belly
and lines of pink cloud in the sky,

the day's preamble
like wandering lines in marble.
The cocks are now almost inaudible.

The sun climbs in,
following "to see the end,"
faithful as enemy, or friend.

1941, 1946

At the Fishhouses

Although it is a cold evening,
down by one of the fishhouses
an old man sits netting,
his net, in the gloaming almost invisible,
a dark purple-brown,
and his shuttle worn and polished.
The air smells so strong of codfish
it makes one's nose run and one's eyes water.

5. Cathedral in Rome where the Pope presides. *Basilica*: church.

6. Type of stone.

The five fishhouses have steeply peaked roofs
and narrow, cleated gangplanks slant up
to storerooms in the gables
for the wheelbarrows to be pushed up and down on.
All is silver: the heavy surface of the sea,
swelling slowly as if considering spilling over,
is opaque, but the silver of the benches,
the lobster pots, and masts, scattered
among the wild jagged rocks,
is of an apparent translucence
like the small old buildings with an emerald moss
growing on their shoreward walls.
The big fish tubs are completely lined
with layers of beautiful herring scales
and the wheelbarrows are similarly plastered
with creamy iridescent coats of mail,
with small iridescent flies crawling on them.
Up on the little slope behind the houses,
set in the sparse bright sprinkle of grass,
is an ancient wooden capstan,[7]
cracked, with two long bleached handles
and some melancholy stains, like dried blood,
where the ironwork has rusted.
The old man accepts a Lucky Strike.[8]
He was a friend of my grandfather.
We talk of the decline in the population
and of codfish and herring
while he waits for a herring boat to come in.
There are sequins on his vest and on his thumb.
He has scraped the scales, the principal beauty,
from unnumbered fish with that black old knife,
the blade of which is almost worn away.

Down at the water's edge, at the place
where they haul up the boats, up the long ramp
descending into the water, thin silver
tree trunks are laid horizontally
across the gray stones, down and down
at intervals of four or five feet.

Cold dark deep and absolutely clear,
element bearable to no mortal,
to fish and to seals . . . One seal particularly
I have seen here evening after evening.
He was curious about me. He was interested in music;
like me a believer in total immersion,[9]
so I used to sing him Baptist hymns.
I also sang "A Mighty Fortress Is Our God."

7. Rotating drum wound with rope used for hauling heavy items.
8. Brand of cigarette.
9. Baptist belief that a person being baptized must be wholly submerged under water.

He stood up in the water and regarded me
steadily, moving his head a little.
Then he would disappear, then suddenly emerge
almost in the same spot, with a sort of shrug
as if it were against his better judgment.
Cold dark deep and absolutely clear,
the clear gray icy water . . . Back, behind us,
the dignified tall firs begin.
Bluish, associating with their shadows,
a million Christmas trees stand
waiting for Christmas. The water seems suspended
above the rounded gray and blue-gray stones.
I have seen it over and over, the same sea, the same,
slightly, indifferently swinging above the stones,
icily free above the stones,
above the stones and then the world.
If you should dip your hand in,
your wrist would ache immediately,
your bones would begin to ache and your hand would burn
as if the water were a transmutation of fire
that feeds on stones and burns with a dark gray flame.
If you tasted it, it would first taste bitter,
then briny, then surely burn your tongue.
It is like what we imagine knowledge to be:
dark, salt, clear, moving, utterly free,
drawn from the cold hard mouth
of the world, derived from the rocky breasts
forever, flowing and drawn, and since
our knowledge is historical, flowing, and flown.

1947, 1955

Over 2,000 Illustrations and a Complete Concordance[1]

Thus should have been our travels:
serious, engravable.
The Seven Wonders of the World are tired
and a touch familiar, but the other scenes,
innumerable, though equally sad and still,
are foreign. Often the squatting Arab,
or group of Arabs, plotting, probably,
against our Christian Empire,
while one apart, with outstretched arm and hand
points to the Tomb, the Pit, the Sepulcher.[2]
The branches of the date-palms look like files.
The cobbled courtyard, where the Well is dry,

1. Part of the title page of an old edition of the Bible described in the opening lines. It advertises itself as containing "over 2,000 illustrations"—engravings of the Holy Land—and a concordance (a guide to occurrences of words and proper names in a book, often found in Bibles).

2. The burial place of Jesus depicted (along with other places associated with his life, such as the Well where he preached to a Samaritan woman in John 4) among the "2,000 illustrations."

is like a diagram, the brickwork conduits
are vast and obvious, the human figure
far gone in history or theology,
gone with its camel or its faithful horse.
Always the silence, the gesture, the specks of birds
suspended on invisible threads above the Site,
or the smoke rising solemnly, pulled by threads.
Granted a page alone or a page made up
of several scenes arranged in cattycornered[3] rectangles
or circles set on stippled gray,
granted a grim lunette,[4]
caught in the toils of an initial letter,
when dwelt upon, they all resolve themselves.
The eye drops, weighted, through the lines
the burin[5] made, the lines that move apart
like ripples above sand,
dispersing storms, God's spreading fingerprint,
and painfully, finally, that ignite
in watery prismatic white-and-blue.

Entering the Narrows at St. Johns[6]
the touching bleat of goats reached to the ship.
We glimpsed them, reddish, leaping up the cliffs
among the fog-soaked weeds and butter-and-eggs.
And at St. Peter's[7] the wind blew and the sun shone madly.
Rapidly, purposefully, the Collegians[8] marched in lines,
crisscrossing the great square with black, like ants.
In Mexico the dead man lay
in a blue arcade; the dead volcanoes
glistened like Easter lilies.
The jukebox went on playing "Ay, Jalisco!"
And at Volubilis[9] there were beautiful poppies
splitting the mosaics; the fat old guide made eyes.
In Dingle[1] harbor a golden length of evening
the rotting hulks held up their dripping plush.
The Englishwoman poured tea, informing us
that the Duchess was going to have a baby.
And in the brothels of Marrakesh[2]
the little pockmarked prostitutes
balanced their tea-trays on their heads
and did their belly-dances; flung themselves
naked and giggling against our knees,
asking for cigarettes. It was somewhere near there
I saw what frightened me most of all:
A holy grave, not looking particularly holy,
one of a group under a keyhole-arched stone baldaquin[3]

3. Placed on a diagonal.
4. The oval, often a segment of an enlarged initial letter, framing an illustration.
5. Engraver's tool.
6. City in Newfoundland, on the Atlantic Ocean.
7. The great cathedral in Rome. *Butter-and-eggs:* common name for narcissus flowers.
8. That is, members of the College of Cardinals in the Vatican, Rome.
9. Ruined Roman city in Morocco.
1. Town in southwest Ireland.
2. City in Morocco.
3. Architectual canopy.

open to every wind from the pink desert.
An open, gritty, marble trough, carved solid
with exhortation, yellowed
as scattered cattle-teeth;
half-filled with dust, not even the dust
of the poor prophet paynim[4] who once lay there.
In a smart burnoose[5] Khadour looked on amused.

Everything only connected by "and" and "and."
Open the book. (The gilt rubs off the edges
of the pages and pollinates the fingertips.)
Open the heavy book. Why couldn't we have seen
this old Nativity while we were at it?
—the dark ajar, the rocks breaking with light,
an undisturbed, unbreathing flame,
colorless, sparkless, freely fed on straw,
and, lulled within, a family with pets,
—and looked and looked our infant sight away.

1948, 1955

Sestina

September rain falls on the house.
In the failing light, the old grandmother
sits in the kitchen with the child
beside the Little Marvel Stove,[6]
reading the jokes from the almanac,
laughing and talking to hide her tears.

She thinks that her equinoctial tears
and the rain that beats on the roof of the house
were both foretold by the almanac,
but only known to a grandmother.
The iron kettle sings on the stove.
She cuts some bread and says to the child,

It's time for tea now; but the child
is watching the teakettle's small hard tears
dance like mad on the hot black stove,
the way the rain must dance on the house.
Tidying up, the old grandmother
hangs up the clever almanac

on its string. Birdlike, the almanac
hovers half open above the child,
hovers above the old grandmother

4. Archaic literary word for pagan, especially Muslim.

5. One-piece hooded cloak, worn by some Arabs.

6. Wood- or coal-burning stove.

and her teacup full of dark brown tears.
She shivers and says she thinks the house
feels chilly, and puts more wood in the stove.

It was to be, says the Marvel Stove.
I know what I know, says the almanac.
With crayons the child draws a rigid house
and a winding pathway. Then the child
puts in a man with buttons like tears
and shows it proudly to the grandmother.

But secretly, while the grandmother
busies herself about the stove,
the little moons fall down like tears
from between the pages of the almanac
into the flower bed the child
has carefully placed in the front of the house.

Time to plant tears, says the almanac.
The grandmother sings to the marvellous stove
and the child draws another inscrutable house.

1956, 1965

The Armadillo

For Robert Lowell[7]

This is the time of year
when almost every night
the frail, illegal fire balloons appear.
Climbing the mountain height,

rising toward a saint
still honored in these parts,
the paper chambers flush and fill with light
that comes and goes, like hearts.

Once up against the sky it's hard
to tell them from the stars—
planets, that is—the tinted ones:
Venus going down, or Mars,

or the pale green one. With a wind,
they flare and falter, wobble and toss;
but if it's still they steer between
the kite sticks of the Southern Cross,[8]

7. American poet (1917–1977).
8. A constellation visible only from the Southern Hemisphere. The balloons were for St. John's Eve.

receding, dwindling, solemnly
and steadily forsaking us,
or, in the downdraft from a peak,
suddenly turning dangerous.

Last night another big one fell.
It splattered like an egg of fire
against the cliff behind the house.
The flame ran down. We saw the pair

of owls who nest there flying up
and up, their whirling black-and-white
stained bright pink underneath, until
they shrieked up out of sight.

The ancient owls' nest must have burned.
Hastily, all alone,
a glistening armadillo left the scene,
rose-flecked, head down, tail down,

and then a baby rabbit jumped out,
short-eared, to our surprise.
So soft!—a handful of intangible ash
with fixed, ignited eyes.

Too pretty, dreamlike mimicry!
O falling fire and piercing cry
and panic, and a weak mailed fist
clenched ignorant against the sky!

1957, 1965

Brazil, January 1, 1502

. . . embroidered nature . . . tapestried landscape.
—*Landscape Into Art*, by Sir Kenneth Clark[9]

Januaries, Nature greets our eyes
exactly as she must have greeted theirs:
every square inch filling in with foliage—
big leaves, little leaves, and giant leaves,
blue, blue-green, and olive,
with occasional lighter veins and edges,
or a satin underleaf turned over;
monster ferns
in silver-gray relief,

9. British art historian (1903–1983); the phrases are from the chapter "Landscape of Symbols," about medieval depictions of a garden enclosing the Virgin, or *Hortus Conclusis*, in his 1949 book.

and flowers, too, like giant water lilies
up in the air—up, rather, in the leaves—
purple, yellow, two yellows, pink,
rust red and greenish white;
solid but airy; fresh as if just finished
and taken off the frame.

A blue-white sky, a simple web,
backing for feathery detail:
brief arcs, a pale-green broken wheel,
a few palms, swarthy, squat, but delicate;
and perching there in profile, beaks agape,
the big symbolic birds keep quiet,
each showing only half his puffed and padded,
pure-colored or spotted breast.
Still in the foreground there is Sin:
five sooty dragons near some massy rocks.
The rocks are worked with lichens, gray moonbursts
splattered and overlapping,
threatened from underneath by moss
in lovely hell-green flames,
attacked above
by scaling-ladder vines, oblique and neat,
"one leaf yes and one leaf no" (in Portuguese).
The lizards scarcely breathe; all eyes
are on the smaller, female one, back-to,
her wicked tail straight up and over,
red as a red-hot wire.

Just so the Christians, hard as nails,
tiny as nails, and glinting,
in creaking armor, came and found it all,
not unfamiliar:
no lovers' walks, no bowers,
no cherries to be picked, no lute music,
but corresponding, nevertheless,
to an old dream of wealth and luxury
already out of style when they left home—
wealth, plus a brand-new pleasure.
Directly after Mass, humming perhaps
L'Homme armé[1] or some such tune,
they ripped away into the hanging fabric,
each out to catch an Indian for himself—
those maddening little women who kept calling,
calling to each other (or had the birds waked up?)
and retreating, always retreating, behind it.

1960, 1965

1. The armed man (French); an old French song whose melody was often used in medieval settings of the Mass.

In the Waiting Room

In Worcester, Massachusetts,
I went with Aunt Consuelo
to keep her dentist's appointment
and sat and waited for her
in the dentist's waiting room.
It was winter. It got dark
early. The waiting room
was full of grown-up people,
arctics and overcoats,
lamps and magazines.
My aunt was inside
what seemed like a long time
and while I waited I read
the *National Geographic*
(I could read) and carefully
studied the photographs:
the inside of a volcano,
black, and full of ashes;
then it was spilling over
in rivulets of fire.
Osa and Martin Johnson[2]
dressed in riding breeches,
laced boots, and pith helmets.
A dead man slung on a pole
—"Long Pig,"[3] the caption said.
Babies with pointed heads
wound round and round with string;
black, naked women with necks
wound round and round with wire
like the necks of light bulbs.
Their breasts were horrifying.
I read it right straight through.
I was too shy to stop.
And then I looked at the cover:
the yellow margins, the date.

Suddenly, from inside,
came an *oh!* of pain
—Aunt Consuelo's voice—
not very loud or long.
I wasn't at all surprised;
even then I knew she was
a foolish, timid woman.
I might have been embarrassed,
but wasn't. What took me

2. Then-popular husband-and-wife team of explorers and naturalists.

3. Translation of cannibals' name for a human carcass.

completely by surprise
was that it was *me:*
my voice, in my mouth.
Without thinking at all
I was my foolish aunt,
I—we—were falling, falling,
our eyes glued to the cover
of the *National Geographic*,
February, 1918.

I said to myself: three days
and you'll be seven years old.
I was saying it to stop
the sensation of falling off
the round, turning world
into cold, blue-black space.
But I felt: you are an *I*,
you are an *Elizabeth*,
you are one of *them*.
Why should you be one, too?
I scarcely dared to look
to see what it was I was.
I gave a sidelong glance
—I couldn't look any higher—
at shadowy gray knees,
trousers and skirts and boots
and different pairs of hands
lying under the lamps.
I knew that nothing stranger
had ever happened, that nothing
stranger could ever happen.
Why should I be my aunt,
or me, or anyone?
What similarities—
boots, hands, the family voice
I felt in my throat, or even
the *National Geographic*
and those awful hanging breasts—
held us all together
or made us all just one?
How—I didn't know any
word for it—how "unlikely" . . .
How had I come to be here,
like them, and overhear
a cry of pain that could have
got loud and worse but hadn't?

The waiting room was bright
and too hot. It was sliding
beneath a big black wave,
another, and another.

Then I was back in it.
The War[4] was on. Outside,
in Worcester, Massachusetts,
were night and slush and cold,
and it was still the fifth
of February, 1918.

1971, 1976

Crusoe in England[5]

A new volcano has erupted,
the papers say, and last week I was reading
where some ship saw an island being born:
at first a breath of steam, ten miles away;
and then a black fleck—basalt, probably—
rose in the mate's binoculars
and caught on the horizon like a fly.
They named it. But my poor old island's still
un-rediscovered, un-renamable.
None of the books has ever got it right.

Well, I had fifty-two
miserable, small volcanoes I could climb
with a few slithery strides—
volcanoes dead as ash heaps.
I used to sit on the edge of the highest one
and count the others standing up,
naked and leaden, with their heads blown off.
I'd think that if they were the size
I thought volcanoes should be, then I had
become a giant;
and if I had become a giant,
I couldn't bear to think what size
the goats and turtles were,
or the gulls, or the overlapping rollers
—a glittering hexagon of rollers
closing and closing in, but never quite,
glittering and glittering, though the sky
was mostly overcast.

My island seemed to be
a sort of cloud-dump. All the hemisphere's
left-over clouds arrived and hung
above the craters—their parched throats
were hot to touch.

4. World War I.
5. Shipwrecked hero of *Robinson Crusoe* (1719), by Daniel Defoe (1660–1731).

Was that why it rained so much?
And why sometimes the whole place hissed?
The turtles lumbered by, high-domed,
hissing like teakettles.
(And I'd have given years, or taken a few,
for any sort of kettle, of course.)
The folds of lava, running out to sea,
would hiss. I'd turn. And then they'd prove
to be more turtles.
The beaches were all lava, variegated,
black, red, and white, and gray;
the marbled colors made a fine display.
And I had waterspouts. Oh,
half a dozen at a time, far out,
they'd come and go, advancing and retreating,
their heads in cloud, their feet in moving patches
of scuffed-up white.
Glass chimneys, flexible, attenuated,
sacerdotal[6] beings of glass . . . I watched
the water spiral up in them like smoke.
Beautiful, yes, but not much company.

I often gave way to self-pity.
"Do I deserve this? I suppose I must.
I wouldn't be here otherwise. Was there
a moment when I actually chose this?
I don't remember, but there could have been."
What's wrong about self-pity, anyway?
With my legs dangling down familiarly
over a crater's edge, I told myself
"Pity should begin at home." So the more
pity I felt, the more I felt at home.

The sun set in the sea; the same odd sun
rose from the sea,
and there was one of it and one of me.
The island had one kind of everything:
one tree snail, a bright violet-blue
with a thin shell, crept over everything,
over the one variety of tree,
a sooty, scrub affair.
Snail shells lay under these in drifts
and, at a distance,
you'd swear that they were beds of irises.
There was one kind of berry, a dark red.
I tried it, one by one, and hours apart.
Sub-acid, and not bad, no ill effects;
and so I made home-brew. I'd drink
the awful, fizzy, stinging stuff

6. Priestly.

that went straight to my head
and play my home-made flute
(I think it had the weirdest scale on earth)
and, dizzy, whoop and dance among the goats.
Home-made, home-made! But aren't we all?
I felt a deep affection for
the smallest of my island industries.
No, not exactly, since the smallest was
a miserable philosophy.

Because I didn't know enough.
Why didn't I know enough of something?
Greek drama or astronomy? The books
I'd read were full of blanks;
the poems—well, I tried
reciting to my iris-beds,
"They flash upon that inward eye,
which is the bliss . . ."[7] The bliss of what?
One of the first things that I did
when I got back was look it up.

The island smelled of goat and guano.[8]
The goats were white, so were the gulls,
and both too tame, or else they thought
I was a goat, too, or a gull.
Baa, baa, baa and *shriek, shriek, shriek,*
baa . . . shriek . . . baa . . . I still can't shake
them from my ears; they're hurting now.
The questioning shrieks, the equivocal replies
over a ground of hissing rain
and hissing, ambulating turtles
got on my nerves.

When all the gulls flew up at once, they sounded
like a big tree in a strong wind, its leaves.
I'd shut my eyes and think about a tree,
an oak, say, with real shade, somewhere.
I'd heard of cattle getting island-sick.
I thought the goats were.
One billy-goat would stand on the volcano
I'd christened *Mont d'Espoir*[9] or *Mount Despair*
(I'd time enough to play with names),
and bleat and bleat, and sniff the air.
I'd grab his beard and look at him.
His pupils, horizontal, narrowed up
and expressed nothing, or a little malice.
I got so tired of the very colors!
One day I dyed a baby goat bright red

7. From "I Wandered Lonely as a Cloud" (1807), by William Wordsworth (1770–1850): "They flash upon that inward eye / Which is the bliss of solitude."
8. Bird excrement.
9. Mount Hope (French).

with my red berries, just to see
something a little different.
And then his mother wouldn't recognize him.

Dreams were the worst. Of course I dreamed of food
and love, but they were pleasant rather
than otherwise. But then I'd dream of things
like slitting a baby's throat, mistaking it
for a baby goat. I'd have
nightmares of other islands
stretching away from mine, infinities
of islands, islands spawning islands,
like frogs' eggs turning into polliwogs
of islands, knowing that I had to live
on each and every one, eventually,
for ages, registering their flora,
their fauna, their geography.

Just when I thought I couldn't stand it
another minute longer, Friday[1] came.
(Accounts of that have everything all wrong.)
Friday was nice.
Friday was nice, and we were friends.
If only he had been a woman!
I wanted to propagate my kind,
and so did he, I think, poor boy.
He'd pet the baby goats sometimes,
and race with them, or carry one around.
—Pretty to watch; he had a pretty body.

And then one day they came and took us off.

Now I live here, another island,[2]
that doesn't seem like one, but who decides?
My blood was full of them; my brain
bred islands. But that archipelago
has petered out. I'm old.
I'm bored, too, drinking my real tea,
surrounded by uninteresting lumber.
The knife there on the shelf—
it reeked of meaning, like a crucifix.
It lived. How many years did I
beg it, implore it, not to break?
I knew each nick and scratch by heart,
the bluish blade, the broken tip,
the lines of wood-grain on the handle . . .
Now it won't look at me at all.
The living soul has dribbled away.
My eyes rest on it and pass on.

1. Crusoe's native companion.

2. Crusoe ultimately returned to England.

The local museum's asked me to
leave everything to them:
the flute, the knife, the shrivelled shoes,
my shedding goatskin trousers
(moths have got in the fur),
the parasol that took me such a time
remembering the way the ribs should go.
It still will work but, folded up,
looks like a plucked and skinny fowl.
How can anyone want such things?
—And Friday, my dear Friday, died of measles
seventeen years ago come March.

1971, 1976

Poem

About the size of an old-style dollar bill,
American or Canadian,
mostly the same whites, gray greens, and steel grays
—this little painting (a sketch for a larger one?)
has never earned any money in its life.
Useless and free, it has spent seventy years
as a minor family relic
handed along collaterally[3] to owners
who looked at it sometimes, or didn't bother to.

It must be Nova Scotia; only there
does one see gabled wooden houses
painted that awful shade of brown.
The other houses, the bits that show, are white.
Elm trees, low hills, a thin church steeple
—that gray-blue wisp—or is it? In the foreground
a water meadow with some tiny cows,
two brushstrokes each, but confidently cows;
two minuscule white geese in the blue water,
back-to-back, feeding, and a slanting stick.
Up closer, a wild iris, white and yellow,
fresh-squiggled from the tube.
The air is fresh and cold; cold early spring
clear as gray glass; a half inch of blue sky
below the steel-gray storm clouds.
(They were the artist's specialty.)
A specklike bird is flying to the left.
Or is it a flyspeck looking like a bird?

Heavens, I recognize the place, I know it!
It's behind—I can almost remember the farmer's name.

3. That is, indirectly.

His barn backed on that meadow. There it is,
titanium white,[4] one dab. The hint of steeple,
filaments of brush-hairs, barely there,
must be the Presbyterian church.
Would that be Miss Gillespie's house?
Those particular geese and cows
are naturally before my time.

A sketch done in an hour, "in one breath,"
once taken from a trunk and handed over.
Would you like this? I'll probably never
have room to hang these things again.
Your Uncle George, no, mine, my Uncle George,
he'd be your great-uncle, left them all with Mother
when he went back to England.
You know, he was quite famous, an R.A.[5] *. . .*

I never knew him. We both knew this place,
apparently, this literal small backwater,
looked at it long enough to memorize it,
our years apart. How strange. And it's still loved,
or its memory is (it must have changed a lot).
Our visions coincided—"visions" is
too serious a word—our looks, two looks:
art "copying from life" and life itself,
life and the memory of it so compressed
they've turned into each other. Which is which?
Life and the memory of it cramped,
dim, on a piece of Bristol board,[6]
dim, but how live, how touching in detail
—the little that we get for free,
the little of our earthly trust. Not much.
About the size of our abidance
along with theirs: the munching cows,
the iris, crisp and shivering, the water
still standing from spring freshets,
the yet-to-be-dismantled elms, the geese.

1972, 1976

The End of March

For John Malcolm Brinnin and Bill Read: Duxbury[7]

It was cold and windy, scarcely the day
to take a walk on that long beach.

4. A very bright white pigment.
5. Member of the Royal Academy of Arts, in England.
6. Cardboard with a smooth surface.
7. John Malcolm Brinnin (b. 1916): American poet; Bill Read (b. 1917): American scholar. Bishop often visited their home at Duxbury, on the Massachusetts coast.

Everything was withdrawn as far as possible,
indrawn: the tide far out, the ocean shrunken,
seabirds in ones or twos.
The rackety, icy, offshore wind
numbed our faces on one side;
disrupted the formation
of a lone flight of Canada geese;
and blew back the low, inaudible rollers
in upright, steely mist.

The sky was darker than the water
—*it* was the color of mutton-fat jade.
Along the wet sand, in rubber boots, we followed
a track of big dog-prints (so big
they were more like lion-prints). Then we came on
lengths and lengths, endless, of wet white string,
looping up to the tide-line, down to the water,
over and over. Finally, they did end:
a thick white snarl, man-size, awash,
rising on every wave, a sodden ghost,
falling back, sodden, giving up the ghost. . . .
A kite string?—But no kite.

I wanted to get as far as my proto-dream-house,
my crypto-dream-house, that crooked box
set up on pilings, shingled green,
a sort of artichoke of a house, but greener
(boiled with bicarbonate of soda?),[8]
protected from spring tides by a palisade
of—are they railroad ties?
(Many things about this place are dubious.)
I'd like to retire there and do *nothing*,
or nothing much, forever, in two bare rooms:
look through binoculars, read boring books,
old, long, long books, and write down useless notes,
talk to myself, and, foggy days,
watch the droplets slipping, heavy with light.
At night, a *grog à l'américaine*.[9]
I'd blaze it with a kitchen match
and lovely diaphanous blue flame
would waver, doubled in the window.
There must be a stove; there *is* a chimney,
askew, but braced with wires,
and electricity, possibly
—at least, at the back another wire
limply leashes the whole affair
to something off behind the dunes.
A light to read by—perfect! But—impossible.

8. That is, as though boiled with baking soda, an old trick to preserve the color of green vegetables.

9. Alcoholic drink.

And that day the wind was much too cold
even to get that far,
and of course the house was boarded up.

On the way back our faces froze on the other side.
The sun came out for just a minute.
For just a minute, set in their bezels[1] of sand,
the drab, damp, scattered stones
were multi-colored,
and all those high enough threw out long shadows,
individual shadows, then pulled them in again.
They could have been teasing the lion sun,
except that now he was behind them
—a sun who'd walked the beach the last low tide,
making those big, majestic paw-prints,
who perhaps had batted a kite out of the sky to play with.

1975, 1976

One Art

The art of losing isn't hard to master;
so many things seem filled with the intent
to be lost that their loss is no disaster.

Lose something every day. Accept the fluster
of lost door keys, the hour badly spent.
The art of losing isn't hard to master.

Then practice losing farther, losing faster:
places, and names, and where it was you meant
to travel. None of these will bring disaster.

I lost my mother's watch. And look! my last, or
next-to-last, of three loved houses went.
The art of losing isn't hard to master.

I lost two cities, lovely ones. And, vaster,
some realms I owned, two rivers, a continent.
I miss them, but it wasn't a disaster.

—Even losing you (the joking voice, a gesture
I love) I shan't have lied. It's evident
the art of losing's not too hard to master
though it may look like (*Write* it!) like disaster.

1976

1. Rims, usually on jewelry or pocket watches.

North Haven

In memoriam: Robert Lowell[2]

I can make out the rigging of a schooner
a mile off; I can count
the new cones on the spruce. It is so still
the pale bay wears a milky skin, the sky
no clouds, except for one long, carded horse's-tail.

The islands haven't shifted since last summer,
even if I like to pretend they have
—drifting, in a dreamy sort of way,
a little north, a little south or sidewise,
and that they're free within the blue frontiers of bay.

This month, our favorite one is full of flowers:
Buttercups, Red Clover, Purple Vetch,
Hawkweed still burning, Daisies pied, Eyebright,
the Fragrant Bedstraw's incandescent stars,
and more, returned, to paint the meadows with delight.

The Goldfinches are back, or others like them,
and the White-throated Sparrow's five-note song,
pleading and pleading, brings tears to the eyes.
Nature repeats herself, or almost does:
repeat, repeat, repeat; revise, revise, revise.

Years ago, you told me it was here
(in 1932?) you first "discovered *girls*"
and learned to sail, and learned to kiss.
You had "such fun," you said, that classic summer.
("Fun"—it always seemed to leave you at a loss . . .)

You left North Haven, anchored in its rock,
afloat in mystic blue . . . And now—you've left
for good. You can't derange, or re-arrange,
your poems again. (But the Sparrows can their song.)
The words won't change again. Sad friend, you cannot change.

1978, 1979

2. American poet (1917–1977).

May Swenson
1913–1989

May Swenson is a difficult poet to classify. She writes about conventional lyric subjects, such as love, death, nature, and youthful pleasures. Yet her approach to such topics is quirky and unconventional. In a poem about the physical and emotional transfusions of love, "In Love Made Visible," for example, Swenson borrows from traditional love poetry the notion of the eye as window to the soul, but she also recasts stock heterosexual images, presenting both lovers, by poem's end, as cups or vials: "We are released / and flow into each other's cup / Our two frail vials pierced / drink each other up." By contrast to this celebration of lesbian communion, Swenson's "A Couple" is less sanguine about the seemingly heterosexual meeting of a bullet-shaped bee and a bowl-like flower: "When he's done his honey-thieving / at her matrix, whirs free, leaving, / she closes, still tall, chill, / unrumpled on her stem." Lyrical, steeped in tradition, Swenson's love poems are nevertheless wryly revisionist, if less erotically explicit than those of some of her contemporaries.

Similarly, Swenson's interest in manipulating the typographical layout of words can seem experimental, recalling early modernist attention to spatial form and pointing ahead to the contemporary avant-garde; but her shape poems, or "iconographs," such as her lyric in the form of a butterfly, "Unconscious Came a Beauty," also recall an older poetic tradition, the *carmen figuratum*, that extends from the ancient Greeks through George Herbert and beyond. Exemplifying Swenson's playful use of typography, this poem refrains from naming the "butterfly," as if not to duplicate visual through verbal naming. When the butterfly's shadow merges with her "hand's ghost," Swenson wittily figures the shape of the poem as a shadow of the butterfly, the words as a ghostly trace of the poet's hand. Modest and oblique, she wants to evoke the butterfly without trapping it in a name or a word picture.

Although Swenson is well known for her shape poems, typographic play is but one device in her large array of techniques. Often, she appeals less to the eye than to the ear, employing the sonic echoes and twists of internal rhyme, alliteration, assonance, consonance, and onomatopoeia. Words resonate, invert, and play off one another in lines such as "when Body my good / bright dog is dead" ("Question"). Her feel for rhythm and narrative pacing is strong. In "The Centaur," the speaker recalls using a willow as an imaginary pony when she was a ten-year-old child. This imaginative transformation culminates when "I was the horse and the rider," rhapsodically cadenced in lines such as "I shied and skittered and reared." A friend of Elizabeth Bishop's, Swenson recalls the visual exactitude and exquisite restraint of her near-contemporary. Like Marianne Moore, too, Swenson crafts highly particularized descriptions of nature. A butterfly's "thin-as-paper wings, near black, / were edged on the seam side poppy orange, / as were its spots" ("Unconscious Came a Beauty"). Her figurative language is precise: the same butterfly "bent its tongue long as / a leg / black on my skin," a simile heightened by the syntactic deferral of "black."

Like Moore, Bishop, and Emily Dickinson, Swenson avoids overt self-disclosure. In this, she differs from the so-called confessional poets, and her poem "Strawberrying" is a reply to Sylvia Plath's "Blackberrying." Even so, Swenson's distinctive kind of self-effacement allows for considerable intimacy, examining and distilling emotion. Her poems about death and loss, such as "Staring at the Sea on the Day of the Death of Another" and "Last Day," are taut with affect. Imagining the sea as a mausoleum and a shaft of light as a coffin, Swenson quietly but powerfully evokes the menace of mortality.

Swenson was born on May 28, 1913, in Logan, Utah, to a devout Mormon family. She attended Utah State Agricultural College (1930–34). Escaping to New York during the Depression, she worked with the Writers' Project of the Works Progress Administration (WPA). Struggling for some years to make a living, she was eventually employed by New Directions Press, where she was for twelve years a manuscript reader. After she left New Directions in 1966, she held visiting professorships at various universities. In 1981, she won the Bollingen Prize; in 1987, a MacArthur Fellowship. Having long suffered from high blood pressure and asthma, she died at the age of seventy-six.

Question

Body my house
my horse my hound
what will I do
when you are fallen

Where will I sleep
How will I ride
What will I hunt

Where can I go
without my mount
all eager and quick
How will I know
in thicket ahead
is danger or treasure
when Body my good
bright dog is dead

How will it be
to lie in the sky
without roof or door
and wind for an eye

With cloud for shift
how will I hide?

1954

The Centaur[1]

The summer that I was ten—
Can it be there was only one
summer that I was ten? It must

1. Half-horse, half-human creature of Greek mythology.

have been a long one then—
each day I'd go out to choose
a fresh horse from my stable

which was a willow grove
down by the old canal.
I'd go on my two bare feet.

But when, with my brother's jack-knife,
I had cut me a long limber horse
with a good thick knob for a head,

and peeled him slick and clean
except a few leaves for the tail,
and cinched my brother's belt

around his head for a rein,
I'd straddle and canter him fast
up the grass bank to the path,

trot along in the lovely dust
that talcumed over his hoofs,
hiding my toes, and turning

his feet to swift half-moons.
The willow knob with the strap
jouncing between my thighs

was the pommel and yet the poll[2]
of my nickering pony's head.
My head and my neck were mine,

yet they were shaped like a horse.
My hair flopped to the side
like the mane of a horse in the wind.

My forelock swung in my eyes,
my neck arched and I snorted.
I shied and skittered and reared,

stopped and raised my knees,
pawed at the ground and quivered.
My teeth bared as we wheeled

and swished through the dust again.
I was the horse and the rider,
and the leather I slapped to his rump

2. Top of the head. *Pommel:* bulge at the front of a saddle.

spanked my own behind.
Doubled, my two hoofs beat
a gallop along the bank,

the wind twanged in my mane,
my mouth squared to the bit.
And yet I sat on my steed

quiet, negligent riding,
my toes standing the stirrups,
my thighs hugging his ribs.

At a walk we drew up to the porch.
I tethered him to a paling.
Dismounting, I smoothed my skirt

and entered the dusky hall.
My feet on the clean linoleum
left ghostly toes in the hall.

Where have you been? said my mother.
Been riding, I said from the sink,
and filled me a glass of water.

What's that in your pocket? she said.
Just my knife. It weighted my pocket
and stretched my dress awry.

Go tie back your hair, said my mother,
and *Why is your mouth all green?*
Rob Roy, he[3] *pulled some clover*
as we crossed the field, I told her.

1954

A Couple

A bee rolls in the yellow rose.
Does she invite his hairy rub?
He scrubs himself in her creamy folds.
A bullet soft imposes her spiral
and, spinning, burrows
to her dewy shadows.
The gold grooves almost match
the yellow bowl.
Does his touch please or scratch?
When he's done his honey-thieving
at her matrix, whirs free, leaving,

3. The speaker's imaginary horse. Rob Roy (1671–1734) was a celebrated Scottish outlaw.

she closes, still tall, chill,
unrumpled on her stem.

1958

Unconscious Came a Beauty

Unconscious
came a beauty to my
wrist
and stopped my pencil,
merged its shadow profile with
my hand's ghost
on the page:
Red Spotted Purple or else Mourning
Cloak,
paired thin-as-paper wings, near black,
were edged on the seam side poppy orange,
as were its spots.

I sat arrested, for its soot-haired
body's worm
shone in the sun.
It bent its tongue long as
a leg
black on my skin
and clung without my
feeling,
while its tomb-stained
duplicate parts of
a window opened.
And then I
moved.

1970

Staring at the Sea on the Day of the Death of Another

The long body of the water fills its hollow,
slowly rolls upon its side,
and in the swaddlings of the waves,
their shadowed hollows falling forward with the tide,

like folds of Grecian garments molded to cling
around some classic immemorial marble thing,
I see the vanished bodies of friends who have died.

Each form is furled into its hollow,
white in the dark curl,
the sea a mausoleum, with countless shelves,
cradling the prone effigies of our unearthly selves,

some of the hollows empty, long niches in the tide.
One of them is mine
and gliding forward, gaping wide.

1972

Last Day

I'm having a sunbath on the rug
alone in a large house facing south.
A tall window admits a golden trough
the length of a coffin in which I lie
in December, the last day of the year.
Sky in the window perfectly empty.
Naked tree limbs without wind.
No sounds reach my ears except their
ringing, and heart's thud hollow and
slow. Uncomplicated peace. Scarcely
a motion. Except a shadow that un-
detected creeps. On the table a clay pot,
a clump of narcissus lengthens its stems.
Blue buds sip the sun. Works of the clock
circle their ratchets.[4] There is nothing
to wish for. Nothing to will.
What if this day is endless? No *new*
year to follow. Alteration done with.
A golden moment frozen, clenched.

1986

Strawberrying

My hands are murder-red. Many a plump head
drops on the heap in the basket. Or, ripe
to bursting, they might be hearts, matching
the blackbird's wing-fleck. Gripped to a reed
he shrieks his ko-ka-ree in the next field.
He's left his peck in some juicy cheeks, when
at first blush and mostly white, they showed
streaks of sweetness to the marauder.

We're picking near the shore, the morning
sunny, a slight wind moving rough-veined leaves
our hands rumple among. Fingers find by feel
the ready fruit in clusters. Here and there,
their squishy wounds. . . . Flesh was perfect

4. The teeth on a gear.

yesterday. . . . June was for gorging. . . .
sweet hearts young and firm before decay.

"Take only the biggest, and not too ripe,"
a mother calls to her girl and boy, barefoot
in the furrows. "Don't step on any. Don't
change rows. Don't eat too many." Mesmerized
by the largesse, the children squat and pull
and pick handfuls of rich scarlets, half
for the baskets, half for avid mouths.
Soon, whole faces are stained.

A crop this thick begs for plunder. Ripeness
wants to be ravished, as udders of cows when hard,
the blue-veined bags distended, ache to be stripped.
Hunkered in mud between the rows, sun burning
the backs of our necks, we grope for, and rip loose
soft nippled heads. If they bleed—too soft—
let them stay. Let them rot in the heat.

When, hidden away in a damp hollow under moldy
leaves, I come upon a clump of heart-shapes
once red, now spiderspit-gray, intact but empty,
still attached to their dead stems—
families smothered as at Pompeii[5]—I rise
and stretch. I eat one more big ripe lopped
head. Red-handed, I leave the field.

1987

In Love Made Visible

In love are we made visible
As in a magic bath
are unpeeled
to the sharp pit
so long concealed

With love's alertness
we recognize
the soundless whimper
of the soul
behind the eyes
A shaft opens
and the timid thing
at last leaps to surface
with full-spread wing

5. Italian city destroyed by the eruption of Mt. Vesuvius in 79 C.E.

The fingertips of love discover
more than the body's smoothness
They uncover a hidden conduit
for the transfusion
of empathies that circumvent
the mind's intrusion

In love are we set free
Objective bone
and flesh no longer insulate us
to ourselves alone
We are released
and flow into each other's cup
Our two frail vials pierced
drink each other up

1991

ROBERT HAYDEN
1913–1980

A poet of elegance and restraint, Robert Hayden nevertheless wrote about such emotionally fraught subjects as the lynching of African Americans during the civil rights movement, the transport of slaves from Africa to the New World, and his own pained perplexity as a youth raised in a Detroit slum called Paradise Valley. Exploring the difficult personal and historical experiences of African Americans and others, Hayden's poetry condenses and evokes feelings and ideas in intricate sonic textures—resonant vowel and consonant patterns and carefully modulated rhythms. Embodying history, his vivid characters include hypocritical slavers, brutal lynchmen, awe-inspiring singers, a stern foster father, an overlubricated preacher, and an "AfroIndian" fortune-teller with "silver crucifix / and manycolored beads" ("Elegies for Paradise Valley" IV). In monologue and direct narrative verse, they are defined through an accumulation of sharply apprehended detail and rendered with precision and style.

Hayden often approaches highly charged subjects indirectly. He even risks adopting the voices of victimizers, as if to emphasize the furious silence of the oppressed. In the long sequence "Middle Passage," Hayden brilliantly presents the slave trade from the point of view of slave-ship officers, his own anger and grief apparent in the ironic gaps between the vicious practices of slavery and ships named after Jesus, Hope, and Mercy, between the slavers' cruelty and their Christian prayers. Similarly, a poem written from the perspective of a white family long engaged in the practice of racial lynching, "Night, Death, Mississippi," incorporates the nostalgic, if revolting, reminiscences of an old man who fondly recalls earlier lynchings and emasculations, and it thus leaves the reader to infer a response:

> Time was. Time was.
> White robes like moonlight
>
> In the sweetgum dark.
> Unbucked that one then

and him squealing bloody Jesus
as we cut it off.

One of the leading African American poets of the twentieth century, Hayden synthesizes both African American and European American literary traditions, and he has been both celebrated and denounced for his literary dexterity. In 1966, he was honored for his contribution to the literature of Africa and the African diaspora, winning the Grand Prize for anglophone poetry at the Third World Festival of Negro Arts in Dakar, Senegal. Back home at the First Black Writers' Conference at Fisk University, he was criticized by African American cultural nationalists as a traitor to the race. In the heyday of the Black Arts Movement, which proclaimed that poetry was to be didactic, propagandistic, and revolutionary, Hayden found himself spurned, even by some of his own students, as an "Uncle Tom."

Hayden's influence on the next generation of African American poets, including Michael S. Harper, Yusef Komunyakaa, and Rita Dove, has helped vindicate his reputation as a poet who wrote vividly and movingly about the African American experience. His poetic sequences, such as the early "Middle Passage" and the late "Elegies for Paradise Valley," which subtly weave together a variety of perspectives, characters, and discourses, have cast a long shadow. His poetry is imbued with African American literary legacies, including the Harlem Renaissance innovations of Langston Hughes, Countee Cullen, Jean Toomer, and Claude McKay. Like his precursors, Hayden adapts the rich oral and musical legacies of the blues, jazz, and spirituals ("Homage to the Empress of the Blues," "Mourning Poem for the Queen of Sunday"), and he reimagines crucial episodes in African American history, having researched slavery and the Civil War for the Federal Writers' Project from 1936 to 1940.

Hayden rejected, however, a self-segregating outlook or poetics, and he became a Baha'i in 1943, embracing a religion that teaches the unity of all faiths and peoples. Availing himself of the resources of European and Anglo-American poetry, Hayden put to powerful use such modernist aesthetic principles as concision, allusion, juxtaposition, collage, symbolism, multiple personae, psychic ambivalence, and generic heterogeneity. His "Middle Passage" recalls Eliot's *Waste Land* as it abruptly shifts among voices, echoes Shakespeare's lines about a drowned man ("Full fathom five thy father lies"), and pastes together such diverse forms as hymns, prayers, diaries, and legal depositions. Yet unlike Eliot's spiritual and literary waste land, Hayden's is that of a specific, traumatic episode in African American history.

Born on August 4, 1913, in Detroit, to a couple whose relationship soon dissolved, Hayden was raised, with his mother's help, by a foster family next door. Though poor and uneducated, his guardians nevertheless encouraged the bookish child. Struggling with severe nearsightedness, Hayden early showed an interest in writing. After high school, he could not afford to go on immediately to college. Reading on his own, he discovered American poets such as Cullen, Edna St. Vincent Millay, and Carl Sandburg, as well as the English classics. At Detroit City College (now Wayne State University), Hayden majored in foreign languages, with an emphasis on Spanish. After college, he worked at several government-sponsored historical projects, and he was the part-time drama and music critic for a Detroit newspaper. In 1940, he married, published his first book, and spent a short time in New York City.

Hayden returned to the midwest to take an M.A. (1944) at the University of Michigan. Among his teachers was W. H. Auden, whom Hayden greatly admired: the older poet was an inventive teacher, incisive in his judgments, and his influence may be seen in the technical pith of Hayden's verse. Once his graduate studies were complete, Hayden taught briefly at the University of Michigan, and for the rest of his life made his living by teaching, writing poems as time allowed. In 1946, Hayden moved south to

Nashville, Tennessee, where he joined the faculty of Fisk University. More than twenty years later, in 1969, he returned to the University of Michigan, where he taught until his death.

Middle Passage[1]

I

Jesús, Estrella, Esperanza, Mercy:[2]

Sails flashing to the wind like weapons,
sharks following the moans the fever and the dying;
horror the corposant and compass rose.[3]

Middle Passage:
voyage through death
to life upon these shores.

"10 April 1800—
Blacks rebellious. Crew uneasy. Our linguist says
their moaning is a prayer for death,
ours and their own. Some try to starve themselves.
Lost three this morning leaped with crazy laughter
to the waiting sharks, sang as they went under."

Desire, Adventure, Tartar, Ann:

Standing to America, bringing home
black gold, black ivory, black seed.

Deep in the festering hold thy father lies,
of his bones New England pews are made,
those are altar lights that were his eyes.[4]

Jesus Saviour Pilot Me[5]
Over Life's Tempestuous Sea

We pray that Thou wilt grant, O Lord,
safe passage to our vessels bringing
heathen souls unto Thy chastening.

Jesus Saviour

1. The journey of slaves across the Atlantic from Africa to the Americas, in perilously overcrowded ships.
2. Slave ships. *Estrella:* star (Spanish). *Esperanza:* hope (Spanish).
3. Circle on a map showing compass directions. *Corposant:* eerie light sometimes seen during an electrical storm; also called St. Elmo's Fire.
4. Cf. the song from Shakespeare's *Tempest* in which Ariel explains the transformation of Ferdinand's father after his apparent death by drowning: "Full fathom five thy father lies, / Of his bones are coral made; / These are pearls that were his eyes" (1.2.400–402).
5. From a Protestant hymn.

"8 bells. I cannot sleep, for I am sick
with fear, but writing eases fear a little
since still my eyes can see these words take shape
upon the page & so I write, as one
would turn to exorcism. 4 days scudding,[6]
but now the sea is calm again. Misfortune
follows in our wake like sharks (our grinning
tutelary[7] gods). Which one of us
has killed an albatross?[8] A plague among
our blacks—Ophthalmia: blindness—& we
have jettisoned the blind to no avail.
It spreads, the terrifying sickness spreads.
Its claws have scratched sight from the Capt.'s eyes
& there is blindness in the fo'c'sle[9]
& we must sail 3 weeks before we come
to port."

What port awaits us, Davy Jones'[1]
or home? I've heard of slavers drifting, drifting,
playthings of wind and storm and chance, their crews
gone blind, the jungle hatred
crawling up on deck.

Thou Who Walked On Galilee[2]

"Deponent[3] further sayeth *The Bella J*
left the Guinea Coast[4]
with cargo of five hundred blacks and odd
for the barracoons[5] of Florida:

"That there was hardly room 'tween-decks for half
the sweltering cattle stowed spoon-fashion there;
that some went mad of thirst and tore their flesh
and sucked the blood:

"That Crew and Captain lusted with the comeliest
of the savage girls kept naked in the cabins;
that there was one they called The Guinea Rose
and they cast lots and fought to lie with her:

"That when the Bo's'n piped all hands,[6] the flames
spreading from starboard already were beyond

6. Running before a strong wind.
7. Guardian.
8. Seabird that sailors believed would, if slain, bring bad luck. In "The Rime of the Ancient Mariner," by Samuel Taylor Coleridge (1772–1834), a sailor who kills an albatross is doomed to wear it around his neck and forever tell his tale.
9. That is, forecastle; the forward part of a ship, under the deck, where the crew lives.

1. Davy Jones's locker, where sailors go after they drown.
2. Matthew 14 recounts Jesus' walking on the water.
3. Someone offering evidence.
4. Region of West Africa.
5. Slave quarters.
6. The boatswain (officer in charge of riggings and sails) summoned the crew.

control, the negroes howling and their chains
entangled with the flames:

"That the burning blacks could not be reached,
that the Crew abandoned ship,
leaving their shrieking negresses behind,
that the Captain perished drunken with the wenches:

"Further Deponent sayeth not."

Pilot Oh Pilot Me

II

Aye, lad, and I have seen those factories,
Gambia, Rio Pongo, Calabar;[7]
have watched the artful mongos[8] baiting traps
of war wherein the victor and the vanquished

Were caught as prizes for our barracoons.
Have seen the nigger kings whose vanity
and greed turned wild black hides of Fellatah,
Mandingo, Ibo, Kru[9] to gold for us.

And there was one—King Anthracite[1] we named him—
fetish face beneath French parasols
of brass and orange velvet, impudent mouth
whose cups were carven skulls of enemies:

He'd honor us with drum and feast and conjo[2]
and palm-oil-glistening wenches deft in love,
and for tin crowns that shone with paste,
red calico and German-silver trinkets

Would have the drums talk war and send
his warriors to burn the sleeping villages
and kill the sick and old and lead the young
in coffles to our factories.

Twenty years a trader, twenty years,
for there was wealth aplenty to be harvested
from those black fields, and I'd be trading still
but for the fevers melting down my bones.

III

Shuttles in the rocking loom of history,
the dark ships move, the dark ships move,

7. Nigerian city. *Gambia:* country in West Africa. *Rio Pongo:* East African river.
8. Bantu-speaking people of Zaire, East Africa.
9. African tribes.
1. Variety of coal.
2. Dance.

their bright ironical names
like jests of kindness on a murderer's mouth;
plough through thrashing glister toward
fata morgana's[3] lucent melting shore,
weave toward New World littorals[4] that are
mirage and myth and actual shore.

Voyage through death,
                    voyage whose chartings are unlove.

A charnel stench, effluvium of living death
spreads outward from the hold,
where the living and the dead, the horribly dying,
lie interlocked, lie foul with blood and excrement.

Deep in the festering hold thy father lies,
the corpse of mercy rots with him,
rats eat love's rotten gelid eyes.

But, oh, the living look at you
with human eyes whose suffering accuses you,
whose hatred reaches through the swill of dark,
to strike you like a leper's claw.

You cannot stare that hatred down
or chain the fear that stalks the watches
and breathes on you its fetid scorching breath;
cannot kill the deep immortal human wish,
the timeless will.

"But for the storm that flung up barriers
of wind and wave, *The Amistad*[5] señores,
would have reached the port of Príncipe in two,
three days at most; but for the storm we should
have been prepared for what befell.
Swift as the puma's leap it came. There was
that interval of moonless calm filled only
with the water's and the rigging's usual sounds,
then sudden movement, blows and snarling cries
and they had fallen on us with machete
and marlinspike. It was as though the very
air, the night itself were striking us.
Exhausted by the rigors of the storm,
we were no match for them. Our men went down

3. Mirage's.
4. Shores.
5. "Part III follows in the main the account of the *Amistad* mutiny given by Muriel Rukeyser [1913–1980, American poet] in her biography of Willard Gibbs [1839–1903, American physicist]" [Hayden's note]. In July 1839, Cinquez, or Cinqué, led fifty-three slaves in a mutiny aboard the *Amistad*, a Spanish slave ship. The captain, the mate, and the captain's slave Celestino were all killed. After drifting for two months, the ship was seized off Long Island and the mutineers arrested. The owners, who had been onboard and spared, demanded that the surviving slaves be extradited to Cuba to stand trial for murder. During the ensuing Supreme Court trial, however, John Quincy Adams successfully convinced the court to acquit the mutineers. The thirty-seven survivors were released to Africa.

before the murderous Africans. Our loyal
Celestino ran from below with gun
and lantern and I saw, before the cane-
knife's wounding flash, Cinquez,
that surly brute who calls himself a prince,
directing, urging on the ghastly work.
He hacked the poor mulatto down, and then
he turned on me. The decks were slippery
when daylight finally came. It sickens me
to think of what I saw, of how these apes
threw overboard the butchered bodies of
our men, true Christians all, like so much jetsam.
Enough, enough. The rest is quickly told:
Cinquez was forced to spare the two of us
you see to steer the ship to Africa,
and we like phantoms doomed to rove the sea
voyaged east by day and west by night,
deceiving them, hoping for rescue,
prisoners on our own vessel, till
at length we drifted to the shores of this
your land, America, where we were freed
from our unspeakable misery. Now we
demand, good sirs, the extradition of
Cinquez and his accomplices to La
Havana. And it distresses us to know
there are so many here who seem inclined
to justify the mutiny of these blacks.
We find it paradoxical indeed
that you whose wealth, whose tree of liberty
are rooted in the labor of your slaves
should suffer the august John Quincy Adams
to speak with so much passion of the right
of chattel slaves to kill their lawful masters
and with his Roman rhetoric weave a hero's
garland for Cinquez. I tell you that
we are determined to return to Cuba
with our slaves and there see justice done.
    Cinquez—
or let us say 'the Prince'—Cinquez shall die."

The deep immortal human wish,
the timeless will:

Cinquez its deathless primaveral[6] image,
life that transfigures many lives.

Voyage through death
                    to life upon these shores.

1945, 1962

6. Earliest springtime.

Homage to the Empress of the Blues[7]

Because there was a man somewhere in a candystripe silk shirt,
gracile and dangerous as a jaguar and because a woman moaned
for him in sixty-watt gloom and mourned him Faithless Love
Twotiming Love Oh Love Oh Careless Aggravating Love,

She came out on the stage in yards of pearls, emerging like
a favorite scenic view, flashed her golden smile and sang.

Because grey laths began somewhere to show from underneath
torn hurdygurdy lithographs of dollfaced heaven;
and because there were those who feared alarming fists of snow
on the door and those who feared the riot-squad of statistics,

She came out on the stage in ostrich feathers, beaded satin,
and shone that smile on us and sang.

1948

Mourning Poem for the Queen of Sunday

Lord's lost Him His mockingbird,
His fancy warbler;
Satan sweet-talked her,
four bullets hushed her.
Who would have thought
she'd end that way?

Four bullets hushed her. And the world a-clang with evil.
Who's going to make old hardened sinner men tremble now
and the righteous rock?
Oh who and oh who will sing Jesus down
to help with struggling and doing without and being colored
all through blue Monday?
Till way next Sunday?

All those angels
in their cretonne[8] clouds and finery
the true believer saw
when she rared back her head and sang,
all those angels are surely weeping.
Who would have thought
she'd end that way?

Four holes in her heart. The gold works wrecked.
But she looks so natural in her big bronze coffin

7. Bessie Smith (1895–1937), a great blues singer of the 1920s and 1930s, was known as the Empress of the Blues.
8. Cotton or linen fabric.

among the Broken Hearts and Gates-Ajar,
it's as if any moment she'd lift her head
from its pillow of chill gardenias
and turn this quiet into shouting Sunday
and make folks forget what she did on Monday.

Oh, Satan sweet-talked her,
and four bullets hushed her.
Lord's lost Him His diva,
His fancy warbler's gone.
Who would have thought,
who would have thought she'd end that way?

1949, 1962

Witch Doctor[9]

I

He dines alone surrounded by reflections
of himself. Then after sleep and benzedrine
descends the Cinquecento[1] stair his magic
wrought from hypochondria of the well-
to-do and nagging deathwish of the poor;
swirls on smiling genuflections of
his liveried chauffeur into a crested
lilac limousine, the cynosure[2]
of mousey neighbors tittering behind
Venetian blinds and half afraid of him
and half admiring his outrageous flair.

II

Meanwhile his mother, priestess in gold lamé,
precedes him to the quondam[3] theater
now Israel Temple of the Highest Alpha,
where the bored, the sick, the alien, the tired
await euphoria. With deadly vigor
she prepares the way for mystery
and lucre. Shouts in blues-contralto, "He's
God's dictaphone of all-redeeming truth.
Oh he's the holyweight champeen who's come
to give the knockout lick to your bad luck;
say he's the holyweight champeen who's here
to deal a knockout punch to your hard luck."

9. The Rev. James F. (Prophet) Jones (1907–1971) founded the Church of Universal Triumph, the Dominion of God Inc., in 1938 in Detroit. He lived in an opulent chateau, held services in a luxurious redecorated theater, and preached for five or six hours at a time dressed in velvet, silk, and jewels.
1. Sixteenth century (Italian); more specifically, a style of Renaissance Italian art and architecture.
2. Someone who attracts attention.
3. Former.

III

Reposing on cushions of black leopard skin,
he telephones instructions for a long
slow drive across the park that burgeons now
with spring and sailors. Peers questingly
into the green fountainous twilight, sighs
and turns the gold-plate dial to Music For
Your Dining-Dancing Pleasure. Smoking Egyptian
cigarettes rehearses in his mind
a new device that he must use tonight.

IV

Approaching Israel Temple, mask in place,
he hears ragtime allegros of a "Song
of Zion" that becomes when he appears
a hallelujah wave for him to walk.
His mother and a rainbow-surpliced cordon[4]
conduct him choiring to the altar-stage,
and there he kneels and seems to pray before
a lighted Jesus painted sealskin-brown.
Then with a glittering flourish he arises,
turns, gracefully extends his draperied arms:
"Israelites, true Jews, O found lost tribe
of Israel, receive my blessing now.
Selah, selah."[5] He feels them yearn toward him
as toward a lover, exults before the image
of himself their trust gives back. Stands as though
in meditation, letting their eyes caress
his garments jewelled and chatoyant,[6] cut
to fall, to flow from his tall figure
dramatically just so. Then all at once
he sways, quivers, gesticulates as if
to ward off blows or kisses, and when he speaks
again he utters wildering vocables,[7]
hypnotic no-words planned (and never failing)
to enmesh his flock in theopathic tension.
Cries of eudaemonic[8] pain attest
his artistry. Behind the mask he smiles.
And now in subtly altering light he chants
and sinuously trembles, chants and trembles
while convulsive energies of eager faith
surcharge the theater with power of
their own, a power he has counted on

4. Group surrounding him, wearing many-colored surplices, or robes.
5. Hebrew word, often found in the Psalms, believed to mean "lift up your voices."
6. Changing in color.
7. Meaningless words that bewilder. Jones would chant in an "unknown tongue" that included phrases such as "the lubritorium of lubrimentality."
8. Producing happiness. *Theopathic:* intensely absorbed in worship.

and for a space allows to carry him.
Dishevelled antiphons[9] proclaim the moment
his followers all day have hungered for,
but which is his alone.
He signals: tambourines begin, frenetic
drumbeat and glissando. He dances from the altar,
robes hissing, flaring, shimmering; down aisles
where mantled guardsmen intercept wild hands
that arduously strain to clutch his vestments,
he dances, dances, ensorcelled and aloof,
the fervid juba[1] of God as lover, healer,
conjurer. And of himself as God.

1962

Those Winter Sundays

Sundays too my father got up early
and put his clothes on in the blueblack cold,
then with cracked hands that ached
from labor in the weekday weather made
banked fires blaze. No one ever thanked him.

I'd wake and hear the cold splintering, breaking.
When the rooms were warm, he'd call,
and slowly I would rise and dress,
fearing the chronic angers of that house,

Speaking indifferently to him,
who had driven out the cold
and polished my good shoes as well.
What did I know, what did I know
of love's austere and lonely offices?

1962

Night, Death, Mississippi[2]

I

A quavering cry. Screech-owl?
Or one of them?

9. Choruses sung responsively.
1. A Haitian dance for the dead; also, a complicated dance that used to be performed by blacks in the deep south. *Ensorcelled:* bewitched.
2. Written in response to the murder of civil rights activists Michael Schwerner, Andrew Goodman, and James Earl Chaney by Klansmen and police deputies in Philadelphia, Mississippi, in 1964. Schwerner, Goodman, and Chaney were working to register black voters during Freedom Summer of 1964.

The old man in his reek
and gauntness laughs—

One of them, I bet—
and turns out the kitchen lamp,
limping to the porch to listen
in the windowless night.

Be there with Boy and the rest
if I was well again.
Time was. Time was.
White robes like moonlight

In the sweetgum dark.
Unbucked that one then
and him squealing bloody Jesus
as we cut it off.

Time was. A cry?
A cry all right.
He hawks and spits,
fevered as by groinfire.

Have us a bottle,
Boy and me—
he's earned him a bottle—
when he gets home.

II

Then we beat them, he said,
beat them till our arms was tired
and the big old chains
messy and red.

O Jesus burning on the lily cross

Christ, it was better
than hunting bear
which don't know why
you want him dead.

O night, rawhead and bloodybones night

You kids fetch Paw
some water now so's he
can wash that blood
off him, she said.

O night betrayed by darkness not its own

1966

Elegies for Paradise Valley[3]

I

My shared bedroom's window
opened on alley stench.
A junkie died in maggots there.
I saw his body shoved into a van.
I saw the hatred for our kind
glistening like tears
in the policemen's eyes.

II

No place for Pestalozzi's
fiorelli.[4] No time of starched
and ironed innocence. Godfearing
elders, even Godless grifters, tried
as best they could to shelter
us. Rats fighting in their walls.

III

Waxwork Uncle Henry
(murdered Uncle Crip)
lay among floral pieces
in the front room where
the Christmas tree had stood.

Mister Hong of the
Chinese Lantern (there
Auntie as waitress queened it
nights) brought freesias, wept
beside the coffin.

Beautiful, our neighbors
murmured; he would be proud.
Is it mahogany?
Mahogany—I'd heard
the victrola[5] voice of

dead Bert Williams[6]
talk-sing that word as macabre
music played, chilling
me. Uncle Crip
had laughed and laughed.

3. Nickname for St. Antoine, a Detroit slum.
4. Little flowers (Italian). Johann Heinrich Pestalozzi (1746–1827), Swiss educational reformer and advocate for education of the poor.
5. Phonograph.
6. Popular, American vaudeville comedian (1876–1922) from the West Indies, who often played the stereotype of the bumbling, black minstrel character.

IV

Whom now do you guide, Madam Artelia?
Who nowadays can summon you to speak
from the spirit place your ghostly home
of the oh-riental wonders there—
of the fate, luck, surprises, gifts

awaiting us out here? Oh, Madam,
part Seminole and confidante
("Born with a veil over my face")
of all our dead, how clearly you
materialize before the eye

of memory—your AfroIndian features,
Gypsy dress, your silver crucifix
and manycolored beads. I see
again your waitingroom, with its wax
bouquets, its plaster Jesus of the Sacred Heart.

I watch blue smoke of incense curl
from a Buddha's lap as I wait with Ma
and Auntie among your nervous clients.
You greet us, smiling, lay your hand
in blessing on my head, then lead

the others into a candlelit room
I may not enter. She went into a trance,
Auntie said afterward, and spirits
talked, changing her voice to suit
their own. And Crip came.

Happy yes I am happy here,
he told us; dying's not death. Do not grieve.
Remembering, Auntie began to cry
and poured herself a glass of gin.
Didn't sound a bit like Crip, Ma snapped.

V

And Belle the classy dresser, where is she,
who changed her frocks three times a day?
    Where's Nora, with her laugh, her comic flair,
    stagestruck Nora waiting for her chance?
Where's fast Iola, who so loved to dance
she left her sickbed one last time to whirl
in silver at The Palace till she fell?
    Where's mad Miss Alice, who ate from garbage cans?
    Where's snuffdipping Lucy, who played us 'chunes'
on her guitar? Where's Hattie? Where's Melissabelle?
    Let vanished rooms, let dead streets tell.

Where's Jim, Watusi[7] prince and Good Old Boy,
who with a joke went off to fight in France?
    Where's Tump the defeated artist, for meals or booze
    daubing with quarrelsome reds, disconsolate blues?
Where's Les the huntsman? Tough Kid Chocolate, where
is he? Where's dapper Jess? Where's Stomp the shell-
shocked, clowning for us in parodies of war?
    Where's taunted Christopher, sad queen of night?
    And Ray, who cursing crossed the color line?
Where's gentle Brother Davis? Where's dopefiend Mel?
    Let vanished rooms, let dead streets tell.

VI

Of death. Of loving too:
Oh sweet sweet jellyroll:
so the sinful hymned it while
the churchfolk loured.

I scrounged for crumbs:
I yearned to touch the choirlady's hair,
I wanted Uncle Crip

to kiss me, but he danced
with me instead;
we Balled-the-Jack
to Jellyroll

Morton's[8] brimstone
piano on the phonograph,
laughing, shaking the gasolier
a later stillness dimmed.

VII

Our parents warned us: Gypsies
kidnap you. And we must never play
with Gypsy children: Gypsies
all got lice in their hair.

Their queen was dark as Cleopatra
in the Negro History Book. Their king's
sinister arrogance flashed fire
like the diamonds on his dirty hands.

Quite suddenly he was dead,
his tribe clamoring in grief.

7. Alternate name of Tutsi people of Central Africa.
8. American jazz pianist, composer, and bandleader (1885–1941). Ballin'-the-Jack was a dance step popularized by a ragtime song of the same name in the 1910s.

They take on bad as Colored Folks,
Uncle Crip allowed. Die like us too.

Zingaros: Tzigeune: Gitanos:[9] Gypsies:
pornographers of gaudy otherness:
aliens among the alien: thieves,
carriers of sickness: like us like us.

VIII

Of death, of loving,
of sin and hellfire too.
Unsaved, old Christians
gossiped; pitched

from the gamblingtable—
Lord have mercy on
his wicked soul—
face foremost into hell.

We'd dance there, Uncle
Crip and I,
for though I spoke
my pieces well in Sunday School,

I knew myself (precocious
in the ways of guilt
and secret pain)
the devil's own rag babydoll.

1978

Bone-Flower Elegy

In the dream I enter the house
wander vast rooms that are
catacombs midnight subway
cavernous ruined movie-palace
where presences in vulture masks
play scenes of erotic violence
on a scaffold stage   I want
to stay and watch but know somehow
I must not linger and come to the funeral
chamber   in its icy nonlight see
a naked corpse
turning with sensual movements
on its coffin-bed

9. Synonyms for "Gypsies."

I have wept for you many times
I whisper but shrink from the arms
that would embrace me
and treading water reach
arched portals opening on a desert
groves of enormous nameless flowers
twist up from firegold sand
skull flowers flowers of sawtooth bone
their leaves and petals interlock
caging me for you beastangel
raging toward me
angelbeast shining come
to rend me and redeem

1985

Karl Shapiro
1913–2000

Karl Shapiro was a stubbornly independent presence in twentieth-century poetry; he pursued his own way with a conspicuous disregard of some compelling poetic models. He began to write in the mid-1930s and thus unavoidably grew up "in the shadow of T. S. Eliot" (*In Defense of Ignorance*). Long before it became fashionable to attack modernism, Shapiro criticized Eliot for being too formalist and contrived; together with Ezra Pound and W. B. Yeats, he had attempted "to arrest the forms of poetry via the amazing stratagem of arresting the forms of society." Shapiro's antipathy toward modernism came to a head in 1948, when he voted against awarding the first Bollingen Prize to Pound; he felt the older poet's social and political views, in particular his anti-Semitism, marred his poetry.

Shapiro's first two important books were published while he was in the U.S. Army. The poems, many concerning army life, were an immediate popular success; *V-Letter* won the Pulitzer Prize in 1945. Shapiro named William Carlos Williams and Hart Crane as his first heroes among modern poets, but their influence on his early poems, which are formally traditional, is not obvious. These verses are sharply observed, carefully organized, and openly emotional. After the war, Shapiro used his poetry to search for personal identity. Celebrating "Jewish consciousness," he courageously wrote about Jewishness at a time when it was unpopular to do so (e.g., "The First Time"). His other surprising subjects included masturbation and sexual initiation. He was amused by the anomaly of being a "bourgeois poet," a visionary with a mortgage. In the face of such contradictions, he tried to express "cosmic consciousness," a sense of the unity of all life—a term he borrowed from Walt Whitman. Shapiro was drawn to the poetry of Whitman and the Beats, finding in them the inclusiveness from which Eliot shrank.

Shapiro was born on November 10, 1913, in Baltimore, Maryland. After graduating from high school there, he enrolled at the University of Virginia, but he soon withdrew to devote himself to writing. After working for a time in Baltimore and studying on his own, Shapiro resumed his education at Johns Hopkins University, but he was inducted into the army before receiving his degree and served in the South Pacific through World War II. While overseas, Shapiro continued to write poetry, which his fiancée, Evelyn

Katz (whom he married in 1945), sought successfully to get published. When he returned to civilian life, he was well known in American letters, and he served for a year as poetry consultant to the Library of Congress; he then taught at Johns Hopkins. He edited *Poetry* magazine from 1950 to 1956, after which he joined the faculty of the University of Nebraska and edited *Prairie Schooner,* resigning in 1966 because the university refused, he said, to allow him to publish a short story involving a homosexual. From 1968 to 1984, he taught at the University of California at Davis. He died in New York City.

The Fly

O hideous little bat, the size of snot,
With polyhedral eye and shabby clothes,
To populate the stinking cat you walk
The promontory of the dead man's nose,
Climb with the fine leg of a Duncan-Phyfe[1]
  The smoking mountains of my food
    And in a comic mood
  In mid-air take to bed a wife.

Riding and riding with your filth of hair
On gluey foot or wing, forever coy,
Hot from the compost and green sweet decay,
Sounding your buzzer like an urchin toy—
You dot all whiteness with diminutive stool,
  In the tight belly of the dead
    Burrow with hungry head
  And inlay maggots like a jewel.

At your approach the great horse stomps and paws
Bringing the hurricane of his heavy tail;
Shod in disease you dare to kiss my hand
Which sweeps against you like an angry flail;
Still you return, return, trusting your wing
  To draw you from the hunter's reach
    That learns to kill to teach
  Disorder to the tinier thing.

My peace is your disaster. For your death
Children like spiders cup their pretty hands
And wives resort to chemistry of war.
In fens of sticky paper and quicksands
You glue yourself to death. Where you are stuck
  You struggle hideously and beg,
    You amputate your leg
  Imbedded in the amber muck.

But I, a man, must swat you with my hate,
Slap you across the air and crush your flight,

1. Duncan Phyfe (c. 1768–1854), U.S. furniture maker whose early style was delicate.

Must mangle with my shoe and smear your blood,
Expose your little guts pasty and white,
Knock your head sidewise like a drunkard's hat,
Pin your wings under like a crow's,
Tear off your flimsy clothes
And beat you as one beats a rat.

Then like Gargantua[2] I stride among
The corpses strewn like raisins in the dust,
The broken bodies of the narrow dead
That catch the throat with fingers of disgust.
I sweep. One gyrates like a top and falls
And stunned, stone blind, and deaf
Buzzes its frightful F
And dies between three cannibals.

1942

The First Time

Behind shut doors, in shadowy quarantine,
There shines the lamp of iodine and rose
That stains all love with its medicinal bloom.
This boy, who is no more than seventeen,
Not knowing what to do, takes off his clothes
As one might in a doctor's anteroom.

Then in a cross-draft of fear and shame
Feels love hysterically burn away,
A candle swimming down to nothingness
Put out by its own wetted gusts of flame,
And he stands smooth as uncarved ivory
Heavily curved for some expert caress.

And finally sees the always open door
That is invisible till the time has come,
And half falls through as through a rotten wall
To where chairs twist with dragons from the floor
And the great bed drugged with its own perfume
Spreads its carnivorous flower-mouth for all.

The girl is sitting with her back to him;
She wears a black thing and she rakes her hair,
Hauling her round face upward like moonrise;
She is younger than he, her angled arms are slim
And like a country girl her feet are bare.
She watches him behind her with old eyes,

2. Giant of medieval legend adopted by the French writer François Rabelais (1483–1553) in *Gargantua and Pantagruel* (1532). One of his exploits was to swallow five pilgrims, with their staves, in a salad.

Transfixing him in space like some grotesque,
Far, far from her where he is still alone
And being here is more and more untrue.
Then she turns round, as one turns at a desk,
And looks at him, too naked and too soon,
And almost gently asks: *Are you a Jew?*

1958

Manhole Covers

The beauty of manhole covers—what of that?
Like medals struck by a great savage khan,
Like Mayan calendar stones,[3] unliftable, indecipherable,
Not like the old electrum, chased and scored,[4]
Mottoed and sculptured to a turn,
But notched and whelked[5] and pocked and smashed
With the great company names
(Gentle Bethlehem, smiling United States[6]).
This rustproof artifact of my street,
Long after roads are melted away will lie
Sidewise in the grave of the iron-old world,
Bitten at the edges,
Strong with its cryptic American,
Its dated beauty.

1968

The Piano Tuner's Wife

That note comes clear, like water running clear,
Then the next higher note, and up and up
And more and more, with now and then a chord,
The highest notes like tapping a tile with a hammer,
Now and again an arpeggio,[7] a theme,
As if the keyboard spoke to the one key,
Saying, No interval is exactly true,
And the note whines slightly and then truly sings.

She sits on the sofa reading a book she has brought,
A ray of sunlight on her white hair.
She is here because he is blind. She drives.
It is almost a platitude to say
That she leads him from piano to piano.

3. Large round stones fashioned by the ancient Mayas of Central America, inscribed with symbols denoting their calendar. *Khan:* medieval Asian ruler.
4. Amber, ornamented and marked with lines.
5. Ridged.
6. A reference to the logos of the companies that made them.
7. Tones of a chord played in succession.

And this continues for about an hour,
Building bridges from both sides of the void,
Coasting the chasms of the harmonies.

And in conclusion,
When there is no more audible dissent,
He plays his comprehensive keyboard song,
The loud proud paradigm,
The one work of art without content.

1976

Delmore Schwartz
1913–1966

In his essay "The Isolation of Modern Poetry" (1941), Delmore Schwartz argues that, in the twentieth century, the "only life available to the man of culture has been the cultivation of his own sensibility, that is the only subject available to him, if we may assume that a poet can only write about subjects of which he has an absorbing experience in every sense." Schwartz's poems explore divisions within his own consciousness and divisions between the apprehending self and the baffling exterior world with which the self must come to terms. They enact simultaneously a drama of ideas and a conflict of deeply personal interests.

In his early poems, Schwartz incarnates traditional philosophical dichotomies. Thus "The Heavy Bear Who Goes with Me" is an animal fable about the relationship between mind and body. The first line of "In the Naked Bed, in Plato's Cave" forces us to consider each detail of this early-morning meditation in the light of Plato's great allegory of the dualism of appearance and reality. Schwartz called his last collection *Summer Knowledge* (1959, rev. 1967), and the poems' longer lines and more relaxed syntax are a stylistic change of direction. The poet now hopes—prays, even, since the poems are often beseeching—that he can settle his argument with himself by substituting for the warfare of philosophical concepts the healing rhythms of nature. In the volume, Schwartz strives for a certain American insouciance in the face of irreconcilable conflicts and sometimes presents this metaphysical casualness comically.

Schwartz was born on December 8, 1913, in Brooklyn, New York, to a middle-class Romanian Jewish family. He was educated at the University of Wisconsin, Madison, New York University (B.A., 1935), and Harvard University, where he studied philosophy with Alfred North Whitehead. In 1938, he published his first book, *In Dreams Begin Responsibilities*. Apart from writing poems, stories, plays, and criticism, Schwartz found outlets for his intellectual energies in teaching writing at six colleges and selecting poetry for the *Partisan Review* and *The New Republic*. He was also a brilliant talker and followed Dylan Thomas as "house poet" of the White Horse Tavern, in New York's Greenwich Village. Exhilarated by the life of the mind whether expressed in social theory, classical philosophy, or popular culture, he also entertained listeners for hours with improbable stories and dialogues in which he played both himself and T. S. Eliot ("from whom," he wrote, "I've learned the little I know about literature").

When awarded the Bollingen Prize in 1959 for *Selected Poems: Summer Knowledge,* Schwartz was the youngest poet to have received this prestigious award. Instead of being encouraged, however, he grew increasingly dissatisfied with the quality of his work and published only a handful of poems during the rest of his life—nothing at all after 1963—though he continued to write copiously. One reason may have been the depredations of mental illness; since the late 1940s, he had been in and out of sanatoriums. In the grip of paranoid obsessions, he denounced all his old friends, resigned as visiting professor at Syracuse University in 1965, and dropped out of sight for over a year. His last months were spent alone in a Times Square hotel, still writing; it was not until three days after his death, by heart attack, that someone was found to claim his body from a morgue.

In the Naked Bed, in Plato's Cave[1]

In the naked bed, in Plato's cave,
Reflected headlights slowly slid the wall,
Carpenters hammered under the shaded window,
Wind troubled the window curtains all night long,
A fleet of trucks strained uphill, grinding,
Their freights covered, as usual.
The ceiling lightened again, the slanting diagram
Slid slowly forth.
                Hearing the milkman's chop,
His striving up the stair, the bottle's chink,
I rose from bed, lit a cigarette,
And walked to the window. The stony street
Displayed the stillness in which buildings stand,
The street-lamp's vigil and the horse's patience.
The winter sky's pure capital
Turned me back to bed with exhausted eyes.

Strangeness grew in the motionless air. The loose
Film grayed. Shaking wagons, hooves' waterfalls,
Sounded far off, increasing, louder and nearer.
A car coughed, starting. Morning, softly
Melting the air, lifted the half-covered chair
From underseas, kindled the looking-glass,
Distinguished the dresser and the white wall.
The bird called tentatively, whistled, called,
Bubbled and whistled, so! Perplexed, still wet
With sleep, affectionate, hungry and cold. So, so,
O son of man,[2] the ignorant night, the travail
Of early morning, the mystery of beginning
Again and again,
                while History is unforgiven.

1938

1. In the ancient Greek philosopher Plato's famous allegory of the cave, the humanly perceivable world is only a projected image of a realer world of ideal forms, as if humans are sitting in a cave and can see the outside world only as shadows on the cave's walls.

2. The words used by God in addressing the prophet Ezekiel in the Valley of the Dry Bones, in which the bones rise up, put on flesh, and live (Ezekiel 37). See also T. S. Eliot's *Waste Land*, line 20.

The Heavy Bear Who Goes with Me

"the withness of the body"[3]

The heavy bear who goes with me,
A manifold honey to smear his face,
Clumsy and lumbering here and there,
The central ton of every place,
The hungry beating brutish one
In love with candy, anger, and sleep,
Crazy factotum, dishevelling all,
Climbs the building, kicks the football,
Boxes his brother in the hate-ridden city.

Breathing at my side, that heavy animal,
That heavy bear who sleeps with me,
Howls in his sleep for a world of sugar,
A sweetness intimate as the water's clasp,
Howls in his sleep because the tight-rope
Trembles and shows the darkness beneath.
—The strutting show-off is terrified,
Dressed in his dress-suit, bulging his pants,
Trembles to think that his quivering meat
Must finally wince to nothing at all.

That inescapable animal walks with me,
Has followed me since the black womb held,
Moves where I move, distorting my gesture,
A caricature, a swollen shadow,
A stupid clown of the spirit's motive,
Perplexes and affronts with his own darkness,
The secret life of belly and bone,
Opaque, too near, my private, yet unknown,
Stretches to embrace the very dear
With whom I would walk without him near,
Touches her grossly, although a word
Would bare my heart and make me clear,
Stumbles, flounders, and strives to be fed
Dragging me with him in his mouthing care,
Amid the hundred million of his kind,
The scrimmage of appetite everywhere.

1938

The Mind Is an Ancient and Famous Capital

The mind is a city like London,
Smoky and populous: it is a capital

3. From *Process and Reality* (1929), by English philosopher Alfred North Whitehead (1861–1947).

Like Rome, ruined and eternal,
Marked by the monuments which no one
Now remembers. For the mind, like Rome, contains
Catacombs, aqueducts, amphitheatres, palaces,
Churches and equestrian statues, fallen, broken or soiled.
The mind possesses and is possessed by all the ruins
Of every haunted, hunted generation's celebration.

"Call us what you will: we are made such by love."[4]
We are such studs as dreams are made on, and
Our little lives are ruled by the gods, by Pan,[5]
Piping of all, seeking to grasp or grasping
All of the grapes; and by the bow-and-arrow god,
Cupid, piercing the heart through, suddenly and forever.

Dusk we are, to dusk returning,[6] after the burbing,
After the gold fall, the fallen ash, the bronze,
Scattered and rotten, after the white null statues which
Are winter, sleep, and nothingness: when
Will the houselights of the universe
Light up and blaze?
                    For it is not the sea
Which murmurs in a shell,
And it is not only heart, at harp o'clock,
It is the dread terror of the uncontrollable
Horses of the apocalypse,[7] running in wild dread
Toward Arcturus[8]—and returning as suddenly . . .

1959

4. Quoted from "The Canonization," line 19, by John Donne (1572–1631).
5. Cf. Shakespeare's *Tempest* 4.1.156–58: "We are such stuff / As dreams are made on, and our little life / Is rounded with a sleep." Pan is a fertility god in classical mythology.
6. "You are dust, and to dust you will return" (Genesis 3.19).
7. In the biblical vision of the world's end (Revelation), the agents of destruction are the horsemen Conquest, Slaughter, Famine, and Death.
8. A star in the constellation Ursa Major (the Great Bear).

MURIEL RUKEYSER
1913–1980

To be absolutely contemporary was Muriel Rukeyser's aim. Left-wing politics played a considerable part in her life, as did science. She could vividly detail both the suffering of miners carelessly exposed to deadly silica dust ("The Book of the Dead") and the microscopic exchanges of genetic material between single-celled organisms ("The Conjugation of the Paramecium"). Her prize-winning first volume, *Theory of Flight* (1935), displayed her knowledge of aviation, gained as a student at Roosevelt Aviation School; she also wrote a biography of the nineteenth-century mathematician Willard Gibbs (which included information about a slave-ship mutiny that poet Robert Hayden adapted in his sequence "Middle Passage"). As the editor of a student newspaper she took part in the social activism of the Great Depression and was arrested in Alabama for protesting the second Scottsboro trial, in which nine black youths were accused of raping two white women. She sided with the Loyalists during the Spanish Civil War. Later, she was jailed for protesting the Vietnam War on the steps of the U.S. Capitol. Her poetry declares her time: "I lived in the first century of world wars," she writes in "Poem," and the present-day metropolis, with its garbage, its violence, and its vagabondage, plays a large role in her imagery.

A poet of idealism and intensity, Rukeyser was an ardent participant in the Old Left activism of the Depression and the New Left radicalism of the 1960s. In her 1930s poetry, she adapts techniques of modernism—collage, multiple voices, arcane allusions—for leftist political purposes. In her long poetic sequence "The Book of the Dead," she interweaves congressional testimony on the outbreak of lung disease in West Virginia with the ancient spells of the Egyptian *Book of the Dead*. Her documentary techniques link her to W. H. Auden; her use of archaic materials, to T. S. Eliot and Ezra Pound. In the less oblique poetry of her later career, she recalls Walt Whitman's prophetic voice, collectivist stance, and Bible-imbued rhetoric. Although she never officially described herself as a feminist, her 1960s proclamation "No more masks! No more mythologies!" became a *cri de coeur* for liberation from gender-based constraints on expression ("The Poem as Mask"). Her willingness to use an engaged, visionary rhetoric was not always welcomed, but her fusion of passionate advocacy with technical sophistication and intimate awareness inspired such poets as Adrienne Rich and Anne Sexton.

Immersing herself in the present, Rukeyser freely denounced the past: "We focus on our times, destroying you, fathers/in the long ground: you have given strange birth / to us who turn against you in our blood" ("The Blood Is Justified"). In "Poem out of Childhood," she makes her position even clearer: "Not Sappho, Sacco. / Rebellion pioneering among our lives." (Nicola Sacco, an anarchist executed for murder, was thought to be innocent by the Left.) Her revolutionary ardor underlies much of her poetry, but in her later work her attention is also directed to traditional lyric problems of love, sympathy, and death. She imagines her poems as arising naturally from her body: "Breathe-in experience, breathe-out poetry" ("Poem out of Childhood").

Rukeyser was born on December 15, 1913, in New York City, the daughter of middle-class Jewish parents. She attended Vassar College and Columbia University from 1930 to 1932. After World War II, she taught at Sarah Lawrence College and the California Labor School in Berkeley, and she raised a child as a single parent. Along with poetry, she also wrote plays, translations, and children's books.

From THE BOOK OF THE DEAD[1]

Absalom[2]

I first discovered what was killing these men.
I had three sons who worked with their father in the tunnel:
Cecil, aged 23, Owen, aged 21, Shirley, aged 17.

1. A twenty-one poem sequence (1938), in which Rukeyser explores an outbreak in the early 1930s of silicosis, a fatal lung disease caused by inhaling silica dust, that afflicted two thousand miners of the Hawk's Nest tunneling project, in Gauley Bridge, West Virginia. The disaster became the subject of a congressional investigation and was widely publicized. Rukeyser traveled to Gauley Bridge in 1936 to interview survivors and perform the research that she was to synthesize in the sequence. *The Book of the Dead* is an ancient Egyptian collection of spells placed in tombs to offer protection and aid to the deceased in the afterlife.

2. The name of King David's youngest son, who rebelled against his father and was consequently

They used to work in a coal mine, not steady work
for the mines were not going much of the time.
A power Co. foreman learned that we made home brew,
he formed a habit of dropping in evenings to drink,
persuading the boys and my husband—
give up their jobs and take this other work.
It would pay them better.
Shirley was my youngest son; the boy.
He went into the tunnel.

My heart   my mother   my heart   my mother
My heart   my coming into being.

My husband is not able to work.
He has it, according to the doctor.
We have been having a very hard time making a living since
this trouble came to us.
I saw the dust in the bottom of the tub.
The boy worked there about eighteen months,
came home one evening with a shortness of breath.
He said, "Mother, I cannot get my breath."
Shirley was sick about three months.
I would carry him from his bed to the table,
from his bed to the porch, in my arms.

My heart is mine in the place of hearts,
They gave me back my heart, it lies in me.

When they took sick, right at the start, I saw a doctor.
I tried to get Dr. Harless to X-ray the boys.
He was the only man I had any confidence in,
the company doctor in the Kopper's mine,
but he would not see Shirley.
He did not know where his money was coming from.
I promised him half if he'd work to get compensation,
but even then he would not do anything.
I went on the road and begged the X-ray money,
the Charleston hospital made the lung pictures,
he took the case after the pictures were made.
And two or three doctors said the same thing.
The youngest boy did not get to go down there with me,
he lay and said, "Mother, when I die,
"I want you to have them open me up and
"see if that dust killed me.
"Try to get compensation,
"you will not have any way of making your living
"when we are gone,
"and the rest are going too."

killed (2 Samuel 13–19). The monologue is spoken in the voice of Mrs. Dora Jones, a member of the Gauley Bridge community's defense committee, which undertook lawsuits against the companies responsible for the disaster. Rukeyser combines the testimony of various survivors. The italicized passages adapt and translate excerpts from the Egyptian *Book of the Dead*.

I have gained mastery over my heart
I have gained mastery over my two hands
I have gained mastery over the waters
I have gained mastery over the river.

The case of my son was the first of the line of lawsuits.
They sent the lawyers down and the doctors down;
they closed the electric sockets in the camps.
There was Shirley, and Cecil, Jeffrey and Oren,
Raymond Johnson, Clev and Oscar Anders,
Frank Lynch, Henry Palf, Mr. Pitch, a foreman;
a slim fellow who carried steel with my boys,
his name was Darnell, I believe. There were many others,
the towns of Glen Ferris, Alloy, where the white rock lies,
six miles away; Vanetta, Gauley Bridge,
Gamoca, Lockwood, the gullies,
the whole valley is witness.
I hitchhike eighteen miles, they make checks out.
They asked me how I keep the cow on $2.
I said one week, feed for the cow, one week, the children's flour.
The oldest son was twenty-three.
The next son was twenty-one.
The youngest son was eighteen.
They called it pneumonia at first.
They would pronounce it fever.
Shirley asked that we try to find out.
That's how they learned what the trouble was.

I open out a way, they have covered my sky with crystal
I came forth by day, I am born a second time,
I force a way through, and I know the gate
I shall journey over the earth among the living.

He shall not be diminished, never;
I shall give a mouth to my son.

Alloy

This is the most audacious landscape. The gangster's
stance with his gun smoking and out is not so
vicious as this commercial field, its hill of glass.

Sloping as gracefully as thighs, the foothills
narrow to this, clouds over every town
finally indicate the stored destruction.

Crystalline hill: a blinded field of white
murdering snow, seamed by convergent tracks;
the travelling cranes reach for the silica.

And down the track, the overhead conveyor
slides on its cable to the feet of chimneys.
Smoke rises, not white enough, not so barbaric.

Here the severe flame speaks from the brick throat,
electric furnaces produce this precious, this clean,
annealing[3] the crystals, fusing at last alloys.

Hottest for silicon, blast furnaces raise flames,
spill fire, spill steel, quench the new shape to freeze,
tempering it to perfected metal.

Forced through this crucible, a million men.
Above this pasture, the highway passes those
who curse the air, breathing their fear again.

The roaring flowers of the chimney-stacks
less poison, at their lips in fire, than this
dust that is blown from off the field of glass;

blows and will blow, rising over the mills,
crystallized and beyond the fierce corrosion
disintegrated angel on these hills.

1938

Boy with His Hair Cut Short

Sunday shuts down on this twentieth-century evening.
The El[4] passes. Twilight and bulb define
the brown room, the overstuffed plum sofa,
the boy, and the girl's thin hands above his head.
A neighbor radio sings stocks, news, serenade.

He sits at the table, head down, the young clear neck exposed,
watching the drugstore sign from the tail of his eye;
tattoo, neon, until the eye blears, while his
solicitous tall sister, simple in blue, bending
behind him, cuts his hair with her cheap shears.

The arrow's electric red always reaches its mark,
successful neon! He coughs, impressed by that precision.
His child's forehead, forever protected by his cap,
is bleached against the lamplight as he turns head
and steadies to let the snippets drop.

Erasing the failure of weeks with level fingers,
she sleeks the fine hair, combing: "You'll look fine tomorrow!

3. Heating and cooling.
4. The elevated railway that ran above Third Avenue in New York City; it was dismantled in the 1930s.

You'll surely find something, they can't keep turning you down;
the finest gentleman's not so trim as you!" Smiling, he raises
the adolescent forehead wrinkling ironic now.

He sees his decent suit laid out, new-pressed,
his carfare on the shelf. He lets his head fall, meeting
her earnest hopeless look, seeing the sharp blades splitting,
the darkened room, the impersonal sign, her motion,
the blue vein, bright on her temple, pitifully beating.

1938

Night Feeding

Deeper than sleep but not so deep as death
I lay there sleeping and my magic head
remembered and forgot. On first cry I
remembered and forgot and did believe.
I knew love and I knew evil:
woke to the burning song and the tree burning blind,
despair of our days and the calm milk-giver who
knows sleep, knows growth, the sex of fire and grass,
and the black snake with gold bones.

Black sleeps, gold burns; on second cry I woke
fully and gave to feed and fed on feeding.
Gold seed, green pain, my wizards in the earth
walked through the house, black in the morning dark.
Shadows grew in my veins, my bright belief,
my head of dreams deeper than night and sleep.
Voices of all black animals crying to drink,
cries of all birth arise, simple as we,
found in the leaves, in clouds and dark, in dream,
deep as this hour, ready again to sleep.

1951

The Conjugation of the Paramecium[5]

This has nothing
to do with
propagating

5. The paramecium is a microscopic, single-celled organism that reproduces asexually through binary fission, splitting itself in two. But without the genetic reorganization and cross-fertilization achieved through conjugation, in which two paramecia temporarily unite, the paramecium will age and eventually die.

The species
is continued
as so many are
(among the smaller creatures)
by fission

(and this species
is very small
next in order to
the amoeba, the beginning one)

The paramecium
achieves, then,
immortality
by dividing

But when
the paramecium
desires renewal
strength   another joy
this is what
the paramecium does:

The paramecium
lies down beside
another
paramecium

Slowly   inexplicably
the exchange
takes place
in which
some bits
of the nucleus of each
are exchanged

for some bits
of the nucleus
of the other

This is called
the conjugation of the paramecium.

1968

The Poem as Mask

Orpheus[6]

When I wrote of the women in their dances and wildness, it was a mask,
on their mountain, gold-hunting, singing, in orgy,
it was a mask; when I wrote of the god,
fragmented, exiled from himself, his life, the love gone down with song,
it was myself, split open, unable to speak, in exile from myself.

There is no mountain, there is no god, there is memory
of my torn life, myself split open in sleep, the rescued child
beside me among the doctors, and a word
of rescue from the great eyes.

No more masks! No more mythologies!

Now, for the first time, the god lifts his hand,
the fragments join in me with their own music.

1968

Poem

I lived in the first century of world wars.
Most mornings I would be more or less insane,
The newspapers would arrive with their careless stories,
The news would pour out of various devices
Interrupted by attempts to sell products to the unseen.
I would call my friends on other devices;
They would be more or less mad for similar reasons.
Slowly I would get to pen and paper,
Make my poems for others unseen and unborn.
In the day I would be reminded of those men and women
Brave, setting up signals across vast distances,
Considering a nameless way of living, of almost unimagined values.
As the lights darkened, as the lights of night brightened,
We would try to imagine them, try to find each other.
To construct peace, to make love, to reconcile
Waking with sleeping, ourselves with each other,
Ourselves with ourselves. We would try by any means
To reach the limits of ourselves, to reach beyond ourselves,
To let go the means, to wake.

I lived in the first century of these wars.

1968

6. In Greek mythology, a musician whose songs enchanted all creatures; who descended into the underworld and tried to rescue his wife, Eurydice; and who was torn apart and killed in an orgy by the women of Thrace.

William Stafford
1914–1993

Some poets rebel against the world, against society, against matter, against time, and get their power from such rebelliousness. William Stafford saw no necessity for this. "Your job is to find what the world is trying to be," his father tells him in "Vocation," and this aptly characterizes Stafford's aim. He accepted life's terms: "Even the flaws were good—," he remarks in "At the Fair." In his writing, he sees the world with the eyes of someone who feels most at home in the sparsely populated countryside. "In scenery I like flat country. / In life I don't like much to happen" ("Passing Remark"). The sense of belonging has in his poetry the place that the sense of alienation has in others'. He is content with his "Aunt Mabel," content that "There are Aunt Mabels all over the world."

In poems of memory and mystical awe before nature, Stafford fashioned a quiet, lucid, conversational idiom that helped make him one of the most frequently read American poets in the post–World War II period. There is no seeking after grandeur; his poetry, he said, is "much like talk, with some enhancement." Nor does he often seek a radiant view of creation. Instead, he allies himself with Thomas Hardy, who, he said, "is my most congenial landmark" and has the same strong sense of place (*Contemporary Poets*, ed. Rosalie Murphy, 1970). (He has little, however, of Hardy's irony.) In what seems to be an undistorted view of the world, some oddity always catches Stafford's eye, and unobtrusively yet slyly he brings it forth.

Stafford was born on January 17, 1914, in Hutchinson, Kansas. After taking two degrees at the University of Kansas, he received his doctorate from the University of Iowa. His generally accepting attitude did not prevent his being a conscientious objector during World War II. Although he didn't publish his first book until he was forty-six, he published frequently after that. Stafford lived by a lake in Oregon and, like Richard Hugo and David Wagoner, fellow poets of the Pacific northwest, he set most of his poems in a nonurban locale. He taught at Lewis and Clark College, in Portland, and was Oregon's poet laureate from 1975 until his death. In 1963, he won the National Book Award for *Traveling through the Dark*.

Traveling through the Dark

Traveling through the dark I found a deer
dead on the edge of the Wilson River road.
It is usually best to roll them into the canyon:
that road is narrow; to swerve might make more dead.

By glow of the tail-light I stumbled back of the car
and stood by the heap, a doe, a recent killing;
she had stiffened already, almost cold.
I dragged her off; she was large in the belly.

My fingers touching her side brought me the reason—
her side was warm; her fawn lay there waiting,
alive, still, never to be born.
Beside that mountain road I hesitated.

The car aimed ahead its lowered parking lights;
under the hood purred the steady engine.
I stood in the glare of the warm exhaust turning red;
around our group I could hear the wilderness listen.

I thought hard for us all—my only swerving—,
then pushed her over the edge into the river.

1960

At the Bomb Testing Site

At noon in the desert a panting lizard
waited for history, its elbows tense,
watching the curve of a particular road
as if something might happen.

It was looking for something farther off
than people could see, an important scene
acted in stone for little selves
at the flute end of consequences.

There was just a continent without much on it
under a sky that never cared less.
Ready for a change, the elbows waited.
The hands gripped hard on the desert.

1966

For the Grave of Daniel Boone[1]

The farther he went the farther home grew.
Kentucky became another room;
the mansion arched over the Mississippi;
flowers were spread all over the floor.
He traced ahead a deepening home,
and better, with goldenrod:

Leaving the snakeskin of place after place,
going on—after the trees
the grass, a bird flying after a song.
Rifle so level, sighting so well
his picture freezes down to now,
a story-picture for children.

They go over the velvet falls
into the tapestry of his time,

1. American frontier explorer and folk hero (1734–1820), who helped establish the first settlement in Kentucky.

heirs to the landscape, feeling no jar:
it is like evening; they are the quail
surrounding his fire, coming in for the kill;
their little feet move sacred sand.

Children, we live in a barbwire time
but like to follow the old hands back—
the ring in the light, the knuckle, the palm,
all the way to Daniel Boone,
hunting our own kind of deepening home.
From the land that was his I heft this rock.

Here on his grave I put it down.

1966

RANDALL JARRELL
1914–1965

After Randall Jarrell's death, his friend Robert Lowell described him as the most "heart-breaking" poet of his generation. Many of Jarrell's early poems were written out of his experience of World War II. They are about the losses of war, about young men made childlike by the nearness of death and by their obligations as killers. Many of Jarrell's later poems are dramatic monologues in the voices of women. Written in a plain style, they express the painful transformations of life and our desire to be changed into something that we once were or that we ache to become.

Jarrell was born on May 16, 1914, in Nashville, Tennessee. His family soon moved to California, and his parents divorced. He returned to Nashville, where he spent a somewhat drab childhood during the Great Depression. His refuge was books and the local public library. Jarrell studied at Vanderbilt University, moving from psychology to English. In 1937–39, he taught at Kenyon College, and his friends there—John Crowe Ransom, Robert Lowell, and the novelist Peter Taylor—all wrote of his gaiety, learning, and bright assurance. In 1942, he published his first book of poems, *Blood for a Stranger*, and enlisted in the army air corps. He washed out as a pilot, then served as a control tower operator working with B-29 crews.

The poet Robert Fitzgerald described Jarrell as "practically the only American poet able to cope with the Second Great War" (*Randall Jarrell, 1914–1965*, ed. Robert Lowell et al). The war poems, which often reflect W. H. Auden's influence, are found in two books, *Little Friend, Little Friend* (1945) and *Losses* (1948). Jarrell explores the murderous mechanisms of war and the diminished, helpless men who operate them. In the poem "Eighth Air Force," the soldiers "wash their hands, in blood, as best they can." Moved to cleanse themselves, they can find nothing untainted by their humanity. Though murderers, Jarrell's soldiers also seem passive and innocent before the technology of modern war. In another poem, an aerial gunner is killed in his womb-shaped ball turret and thus born into his own death.

After the war, in 1946, Jarrell taught at Sarah Lawrence College and served as acting literary editor of *The Nation*. He had, according to Lowell, a "deadly hand for killing what he despised" (*Randall Jarrell*). His reviews were hortatory, sometimes cruel, spattered with allusions, full of memorable epigrams and wisecracks. His most influential critical essays, such as those on Walt Whitman and Robert Frost, are richly documented, passionately argued appeals to readers to pay attention to poets who were neglected or improperly appreciated. From 1947 until his death, after being struck by a car, Jarrell taught at the Women's College of the University of North Carolina at Greensboro. In addition to his poetry and criticism, he published a novel and several children's books. His last book of poems, *The Lost World*, was published in 1965.

"Dramatic monologue," Jarrell writes in *Poetry and the Age* (1953), "which once had depended for its effect upon being a departure from the norm," has now become "in one form or another the norm." Certainly, it became the norm for Jarrell's later poetry. He seems to have tried to bring into his poems some of the qualities of the prose he admired: a strong sense of character and particular circumstance, the expressive fluctuations of language, the aura of implication that surrounds dramatic speech. Jarrell usually touches his characters at a moment of private anguish. Repeatedly in Jarrell's later poems we encounter the figure of an aging woman who mourns for a world she has lost or never more than dreamed of. The last poem of Jarrell's last book, "Thinking of the Lost World," is a meditation on what mortals can regain from the past by an act of loving memory. Jarrell begins the poem in imitation of novelist Marcel Proust, whom he called the "greatest of the writers of this century." A spoonful of chocolate tapioca replaces the madeleine that induced Proust's remembrance of the past. The poem concludes: "I hold in my own hands, in happiness, / Nothing: the nothing for which there's no reward." The recollected past is, of course, nothing: "Back in Los Angeles, we missed / Los Angeles." But the nothing recollected, by a final transformation, survives in the happiness of the poet and the eloquence of his poem.

90 North[1]

At home, in my flannel gown, like a bear to its floe,
I clambered to bed; up the globe's impossible sides
I sailed all night—till at last, with my black beard,
My furs and my dogs, I stood at the northern pole.

There in the childish night my companions lay frozen,
The stiff furs knocked at my starveling throat,
And I gave my great sigh: the flakes came huddling,
Were they really my end? In the darkness I turned to my rest.

—Here, the flag snaps in the glare and silence
Of the unbroken ice. I stand here,
The dogs bark, my beard is black, and I stare
At the North Pole . . .
                                        And now what? Why, go back.

Turn as I please, my step is to the south.
The world—my world spins on this final point
Of cold and wretchedness: all lines, all winds
End in this whirlpool I at last discover.

And it is meaningless. In the child's bed
After the night's voyage, in that warm world

1. Ninety north latitude; that is, the North Pole.

Where people work and suffer for the end
That crowns the pain—in that Cloud-Cuckoo-Land[2]

I reached my North and it had meaning.
Here at the actual pole of my existence,
Where all that I have done is meaningless,
Where I die or live by accident alone—

Where, living or dying, I am still alone;
Here where North, the night, the berg of death
Crowd me out of the ignorant darkness,
I see at last that all the knowledge

I wrung from the darkness—that the darkness flung me—
Is worthless as ignorance: nothing comes from nothing,[3]
The darkness from the darkness. Pain comes from the darkness
And we call it wisdom. It is pain.

1942

The Death of the Ball Turret Gunner[4]

From my mother's sleep I fell into the State,
And I hunched in its belly till my wet fur froze.
Six miles from earth, loosed from its dream of life,
I woke to black flak and the nightmare fighters.
When I died they washed me out of the turret with a hose.

1945

Eighth Air Force[5]

If, in an odd angle of the hutment,
A puppy laps the water from a can
Of flowers, and the drunk sergeant shaving
Whistles *O Paradiso!*[6]—shall I say that man
Is not as men have said: a wolf to man?

The other murderers troop in yawning;
Three of them play Pitch,[7] one sleeps, and one

2. In *The Birds,* by Aristophanes (c. 450–c. 388 B.C.E.), Greek dramatist, an imaginary city built in the clouds by the cuckoos; hence, any fantastic, illusory world.
3. Cf. Shakespeare's *King Lear* 1.1.89: "Nothing will come of nothing" (an Aristotelian maxim).
4. "A ball turret was a plexiglass sphere set into the belly of a B-17 or B-24, and inhabited by two .50 caliber machine-guns and one man, a short small man. When this gunner tracked with his machine guns a fighter attacking his bomber from below, he revolved with the turret; hunched upside-down in his little sphere, he looked like the foetus in the womb. The fighters which attacked him were armed with cannon firing explosive shells. The hose was a steam hose" [Jarrell's note].
5. " 'Eighth Air Force' is a poem about the air force which bombed the continent from England. The man who lies counting missions has one to go before being sent home. The phrases from the Gospels compare such criminals and scapegoats as these with that earlier criminal and scapegoat about whom the Gospels were written" [Jarrell's note]. Later, Jarrell remarked: " 'Eighth Air Force' expresses better than any other of the poems I wrote about the war what I felt about the war."
6. An operatic aria.
7. Card game.

Lies counting missions, lies there sweating
Till even his heart beats: One; One; One.
O murderers! . . . Still, this is how it's done:

This is a war. . . . But since these play, before they die,
Like puppies with their puppy; since, a man,
I did as these have done, but did not die—
I will content the people as I can
And give up these to them: Behold the man![8]

I have suffered, in a dream, because of him,
Many things;[9] for this last saviour, man,
I have lied as I lie now. But what is lying?
Men wash their hands, in blood, as best they can:
I find no fault in this just man.

1948

Next Day

Moving from Cheer to Joy, from Joy to All,[1]
I take a box
And add it to my wild rice, my Cornish game hens.
The slacked or shorted, basketed, identical
Food-gathering flocks
Are selves I overlook. Wisdom, said William James,

Is learning what to overlook.[2] And I am wise
If that is wisdom.
Yet somehow, as I buy All from these shelves
And the boy takes it to my station wagon,
What I've become
Troubles me even if I shut my eyes.

When I was young and miserable and pretty
And poor, I'd wish
What all girls wish: to have a husband,
A house and children. Now that I'm old, my wish
Is womanish:
That the boy putting groceries in my car

8. Pilate offered the Jews their choice whether Jesus or Barabbas should be released, and the people chose Barabbas. "Pilate therefore went forth again, and said to them, Behold, I bring him forth to you, that you may know that I find no fault in him. Then came Jesus forth, wearing the crown of thorns, and the purple robe. And Pilate said unto them, Behold the man!" (John 19.4–5).

9. Just before asking the Jews to decide between Jesus and Barabbas, Pilate received a message from his wife: "Have nothing to do with that just man: for I have suffered many things this day in a dream because of him" (Matthew 27.19).

1. Names of detergents.

2. William James (1842–1910), American philosopher and psychologist; the quotation, slightly paraphrased, is from *The Principles of Psychology* (1890).

See me. It bewilders me he doesn't see me.
For so many years
I was good enough to eat: the world looked at me
And its mouth watered. How often they have undressed me,
The eyes of strangers!
And, holding their flesh within my flesh, their vile

Imaginings within my imagining,
I too have taken
The chance of life. Now the boy pats my dog
And we start home. Now I am good.
The last mistaken,
Ecstatic, accidental bliss, the blind

Happiness that, bursting, leaves upon the palm
Some soap and water—
It was so long ago, back in some Gay
Twenties, Nineties, I don't know . . . Today I miss
My lovely daughter
Away at school, my sons away at school,

My husband away at work—I wish for them.
The dog, the maid,
And I go through the sure unvarying days
At home in them. As I look at my life,
I am afraid
Only that it will change, as I am changing:

I am afraid, this morning, of my face.
It looks at me
From the rear-view mirror, with the eyes I hate,
The smile I hate. Its plain, lined look
Of gray discovery
Repeats to me: "You're old." That's all, I'm old.

And yet I'm afraid, as I was at the funeral
I went to yesterday.
My friend's cold made-up face, granite among its flowers,
Her undressed, operated-on, dressed body
Were my face and body.
As I think of her I hear her telling me

How young I seem; I *am* exceptional;
I think of all I have.
But really no one is exceptional,
No one has anything, I'm anybody,
I stand beside my grave
Confused with my life, that is commonplace and solitary.

1965

Thinking of the Lost World

This spoonful of chocolate tapioca
Tastes like—like peanut butter, like the vanilla
Extract Mama told me not to drink.
Swallowing the spoonful, I have already traveled
Through time to my childhood. It puzzles me
That age is like it.
                    Come back to that calm country
Through which the stream of my life first meandered,
My wife, our cat, and I sit here and see
Squirrels quarreling in the feeder, a mockingbird
Copying our chipmunk, as our end copies
Its beginning.
                Back in Los Angeles, we missed
Los Angeles. The sunshine of the Land
Of Sunshine is a gray mist now, the atmosphere
Of some factory planet: when you stand and look
You see a block or two, and your eyes water.
The orange groves are all cut down . . . My bow
Is lost, all my arrows are lost or broken,
My knife is sunk in the eucalyptus tree
Too far for even Pop to get it out,
And the tree's sawed down. It and the stair-sticks
And the planks of the tree house are all firewood
Burned long ago; its gray smoke smells of Vicks.

Twenty Years After, thirty-five years after,
Is as good as ever—better than ever,
Now that D'Artagnan[3] is no longer old—
Except that it is unbelievable.
I say to my old self: "I believe. Help thou
Mine unbelief."[4]
                I believe the dinosaur
Or pterodactyl's married the pink sphinx
And lives with those Indians in the undiscovered
Country[5] between California and Arizona
That the mad girl told me she was princess of—
Looking at me with the eyes of a lion,
Big, golden, without human understanding,
As she threw paper-wads from the back seat
Of the car in which I drove her with her mother
From the jail in Waycross to the hospital
In Daytona.[6] If I took my eyes from the road
And looked back into her eyes, the car would—I'd be—

3. The most daring of the musketeers in *The Three Musketeers* and its sequel, *Twenty Years After*, by Alexandre Dumas (1824–1895), French novelist and dramatist.
4. Spoken by the father of an epileptic child whom Jesus miraculously cured (Mark 9.24).
5. Cf. Shakespeare's *Hamlet* 3.1.81–82: "The undiscovered country from whose bourn no traveller returns."
6. From a small town in southeastern Georgia to the east-central coast of Florida.

Or if only I could find a crystal set
Sometimes, surely, I could still hear their chief
Reading to them from Dumas or *Amazing Stories;*[7]
If I could find in some Museum of Cars
Mama's dark blue Buick, Lucky's electric,
Couldn't I be driven there? Hold out to them
The paraffin half picked out, Tawny's dewclaw—
And have walk to me from among their wigwams
My tall brown aunt, to whisper to me: "Dead?
They told you I was dead?"
As if you could die!
If I never saw you, never again
Wrote to you, even, after a few years,
How often you've visited me, having put on,
As a mermaid puts on her sealskin, another face
And voice, that don't fool me for a minute—
That are yours for good . . . All of them are gone
Except for me; and for me nothing is gone—
The chicken's body is still going round
And round in widening circles, a satellite
From which, as the sun sets, the scientist bends
A look of evil on the unsuspecting earth.
Mama and Pop and Dandeen are still there
In the Gay Twenties.
The Gay Twenties! You say
The Gay Nineties . . . But it's all right: they *were* gay,
O so gay! A certain number of years after,
Any time is Gay, to the new ones who ask:
"Was that the first World War or the second?"
Moving between the first world and the second,
I hear a boy call, now that my beard's gray:
"Santa Claus! Hi, Santa Claus!" It *is* miraculous
To have the children call you Santa Claus.
I wave back. When my hand drops to the wheel,
It is brown and spotted, and its nails are ridged
Like Mama's. Where's my own hand? My smooth
White bitten-fingernailed one? I seem to see
A shape in tennis shoes and khaki riding-pants
Standing there empty-handed; I reach out to it
Empty-handed, my hand comes back empty,
And yet my emptiness is traded for its emptiness,
I have found that Lost World in the Lost and Found
Columns whose gray illegible advertisements
My soul has memorized world after world:
LOST—NOTHING. STRAYED FROM NOWHERE. NO REWARD.
I hold in my own hands, in happiness,
Nothing: the nothing for which there's no reward.

1965

7. A science fiction magazine of the 1940s.

John Berryman
1914–1972

John Berryman's poetry has an air of authority although it is often extremely eccentric. He succeeded in making his elusive, moody self seem momentous and fascinating, in part by gyrating between farcical humor and exaggerated despondency. Like Robert Lowell, Sylvia Plath, and other so-called confessional poets of the middle generation, he wrote intensely personal poetry, though his style of self-expression was especially theatrical.

Berryman was born John Smith on October 25, 1914, in McAlester, Oklahoma. He lived until the age of ten in Anadarko, a nearby town where his father was a banker and his mother a schoolteacher. Then the family moved to Tampa, Florida, where his parents' quarrels, furious for years, ended when his father shot himself outside John's window. "That mad drive wiped out my childhood," Berryman later reflected in Dream Song 143. After his father's death, his mother brought John and a younger son to Gloucester, Massachusetts, and then to New York City, where she married another banker, John Berryman, whose name the children took. The couple soon divorced, but the stepfather remained kind to the children. He sent John to a private school in Connecticut (South Kent School), and then to Columbia University. Berryman received a B.A. in 1936 and then attended Clare College, Cambridge, on a fellowship. When he returned to the United States, he taught at several universities: for a year at Wayne (now Wayne State), then from 1940 to 1943 at Harvard, and following that, off and on from 1943 to 1951 at Princeton. From 1955 until his death, he taught at the University of Minnesota. A nervous, tense man prone to overdrinking, Berryman lived turbulently. He was married three times. In later life, he returned to Roman Catholicism, the faith of his childhood, yet his last book, *Delusions, Etc.* (1972), continues to debate faith with God. On January 7, 1972, he threw himself from a bridge in Minneapolis to end his life.

Berryman's early work formed part of the volume *Five Young American Poets* (1940). The influence of W. B. Yeats, W. H. Auden, Gerard Manley Hopkins, Hart Crane, and Ezra Pound on him was strong, and Berryman's own voice—by turns nerve-racked and sportive—took time to be heard. His voice was always an amalgam, first of other poets but later of Berryman's various selves. In his lyrics, he unexpectedly jumps from educated language to wild dialect, and before he finishes a statement he begins to question and sometimes to mock it. These characteristics, expressed in contorted syntax, give the poetry an air of painful self-involvement. A sense of agony pervades Berryman's work, even when, as often happens, it is funny. He noted as a defect in Wallace Stevens, whom he otherwise admired, Stevens's failure to wound ("So Long? Stevens"). Berryman's poetry wounds and is itself wounded; in *His Toy, His Dream, His Rest* (1968), the second volume of Dream Songs, he both celebrates and attacks dead friends and poets. His father's death, which he regarded as the defining trauma of his life, looms larger than any of these losses, the poet struggling ever more violently with this incomprehensible tragedy. The first of his Dream Songs refers obliquely to "a departure," but the penultimate poem in Berryman's sequence describes a visit to his father's grave and comments, with unmitigated bitterness, "I spit upon this dreadful banker's grave / who shot his heart out in a Florida dawn" (Dream Song 384).

Berryman gradually saw the autobiographical element in his poems as all-important. Interviewed for the *Harvard Advocate* (Spring 1969), he insisted that T. S. Eliot's theory of the impersonality of poetry was wrong. He called his own verse personal, as some of it ostentatiously is. About his long poem on the early American poet Anne Bradstreet,

Homage to Mistress Bradstreet (1956), Berryman said that, despite disliking her work, he "fell in love with her; and wrote about her, putting myself in it." Although there may be some dialogue between the old poet and the new, the poem's shifting moods and syntax are far more Berryman than Bradstreet.

His major work was a series of 385 Dream Songs that appeared in two separate volumes. They form a poetic journal and represent, half phantasmagorically, the changes in Berryman's mood and attitude. Or as he puts it more grandly in No. 366, they are meant "to terrify and comfort." The tone is often wildly humorous, but turns quickly toward melancholy again. Because the first volume, *77 Dream Songs* (1964), was misinterpreted as simply autobiography, Berryman wrote in a prefatory note to the sequel, "The poem then, whatever its cast of characters, is essentially about an imaginary character (not the poet, not me) named Henry, a white American in early middle age sometimes in blackface, who has suffered an irreversible loss and talks about himself sometimes in the first person, sometimes in the third, sometimes even in the second; he has a friend, never named, who addresses himself as Mr. Bones and variants thereof." (Mr. Bones is a name from the minstrel-show circuit.) When Berryman was asked about the sequence's seeming lack of unity, he insisted that it "has a plot. Its plot is the personality of Henry as he moves on in the world," from ages forty-one to fifty-one. Domestic difficulties, the deaths of friends, and personal anxieties are fused into verse that thrives on brief asides, knowing winks, and interruptions in syntax. These sustained irregularities are balanced against a surprisingly strict six-line stanza (borrowed, as Berryman said, from Yeats), in which lines 1, 2, 4, and 5 are in pentameter, lines 3 and 6 in trimeter. Each Dream Song is eighteen lines long. The motif of the father's death by suicide, returned to near the end of each book, also helps give structure to the emotive sprawl.

Though Berryman insisted that he and Henry were not the same, and some stylization has certainly occurred, Berryman's traits are still easily recognizable. The poetry is confessional and neurotic, but also learned, both in mobilizing traditional literary resources and in savoring all the resources of contemporary diction. Berryman was well versed in English and American literature; he wrote a biography of Stephen Crane (1950) in which he attempted to analyze Crane's psychology as he analyzed his own. What seems likely to survive of his poetry is its pungent and many-leveled portrait of a complex personality that, for all its eccentricity, was close to the center of the intellectual and emotional life of the mid-twentieth century.

From The Dream Songs

1

Huffy Henry hid   the day,
unappeasable Henry sulked.
I see his point,—a trying to put things over.
It was the thought that they thought
they could *do* it made Henry wicked & away.
But he should have come out and talked.

All the world like a woolen lover
once did seem on Henry's side.
Then came a departure.

Thereafter nothing fell out as it might or ought.
I don't see how Henry, pried
open for all the world to see, survived.

What he has now to say is a long
wonder the world can bear & be.
Once in a sycamore I was glad
all at the top, and I sang.
Hard on the land wears the strong sea
and empty grows every bed.

1964

4

Filling her compact & delicious body
with chicken páprika, she glanced at me
twice.
Fainting with interest, I hungered back
and only the fact of her husband & four other people
kept me from springing on her

or falling at her little feet and crying
'You are the hottest one for years of night
Henry's dazed eyes
have enjoyed, Brilliance.' I advanced upon
(despairing) my spumoni. —Sir Bones: is stuffed,
de world, wif feeding girls.

—Black hair, complexion Latin, jewelled eyes
downcast . . . The slob beside her feasts . . . What wonders is
she sitting on, over there?
The restaurant buzzes. She might as well be on Mars.
Where did it all go wrong? There ought to be a law against Henry.
—Mr. Bones: there is.

1964

14

Life, friends, is boring. We must not say so.
After all, the sky flashes, the great sea yearns,
we ourselves flash and yearn,
and moreover my mother told me as a boy
(repeatingly) 'Ever to confess you're bored
means you have no

Inner Resources.' I conclude now I have no
inner resources, because I am heavy bored.

Peoples bore me,
literature bores me, especially great literature,
Henry bores me, with his plights & gripes
as bad as achilles,[1]

who loves people and valiant art, which bores me.
And the tranquil hills, & gin, look like a drag
and somehow a dog
has taken itself & its tail considerably away
into mountains or sea or sky, leaving
behind: me, wag.

1964

29

There sat down, once, a thing on Henry's heart
só heavy, if he had a hundred years
& more, & weeping, sleepless, in all them time
Henry could not make good.
Starts again always in Henry's ears
the little cough somewhere, an odour, a chime.

And there is another thing he has in mind
like a grave Sienese face[2] a thousand years
would fail to blur the still profiled reproach of. Ghastly,
with open eyes, he attends, blind.
All the bells say: too late. This is not for tears;
thinking.

But never did Henry, as he thought he did,
end anyone and hacks her body up
and hide the pieces, where they may be found.
He knows: he went over everyone, & nobody's missing.
Often he reckons, in the dawn, them up.
Nobody is ever missing.

1964

37

Three around the Old Gentleman

His malice was a pimple down his good
big face, with its sly eyes. I must be sorry
Mr Frost[3] has left:

1. In Homer's *Iliad*, the Greek warrior Achilles withdrew from fighting over a slight from the Greeks' general, King Agamemnon.
2. That is, like the somber religious portraits painted in thirteenth- and fourteenth-century Siena.
3. Robert Frost (1874–1963), American poet.

I like it so less I don't understood—
he couldn't hear or see well—all we sift—
but this is a *bad* story.

He had fine stories and was another man
in private; difficult, always. Courteous,
on the whole, in private.
He apologize to Henry, off & on,
for two blue slanders; which was good of him.
I don't know how he made it.

Quickly, off stage with all but kindness, now.
I can't say what I have in mind. Bless Frost,
any odd god around.
Gentle his shift, I decussate[4] & command,
stoic deity. For a while here we possessed
an unusual man.

1964

76

Henry's Confession

Nothin very bad happen to me lately.
How you explain that? —I explain that, Mr Bones,
terms o' your bafflin odd sobriety.
Sober as man can get, no girls, no telephones,
what could happen bad to Mr Bones?
—*If* life is a handkerchief sandwich,

in a modesty of death I join my father
who dared so long agone leave me.
A bullet on a concrete stoop
close by a smothering southern sea
spreadeagled on an island, by my knee.
—You is from hunger, Mr Bones,

I offers you this handkerchief, now set
your left foot by my right foot,
shoulder to shoulder, all that jazz,
arm in arm, by the beautiful sea,[5]
hum a little, Mr Bones.
—I saw nobody coming, so I went instead.

1964

4. Cross (myself).

5. A popular song of 1914.

145

Also I love him: me he's done no wrong
for going on forty years—forgiveness time—
I touch now his despair,
he felt as bad as Whitman on his tower[6]
but he did not swim out with me or my brother
as he threatened—

a powerful swimmer, to take one of us along
as company in the defeat sublime,
freezing my helpless mother:
he only, very early in the morning,
rose with his gun and went outdoors by my window
and did what was needed.

I cannot read that wretched mind, so strong
& so undone. I've always tried. I—I'm
trying to forgive
whose frantic passage, when he could not live
an instant longer, in the summer dawn
left Henry to live on.

1968

149

This world is gradually becoming a place
where I do not care to be any more. Can Delmore die?[7]
I don't suppose
in all them years a day went ever by
without a loving thought for him. Welladay.[8]
In the brightness of his promise,

unstained, I saw him thro' the mist of the actual
blazing with insight, warm with gossip
thro' all our Harvard years
when both of us were just becoming known
I got him out of a police-station once, in Washington, the world is *tref*[9]
and grief too astray for tears.

6. Charles Whitman gunned down dozens of people from the top of a tower at the University of Texas at Austin on August 1, 1966. News accounts quoted his fearful and suicidal notes. He is compared to the poet's father on the verge of suicide.
7. Delmore Schwartz (1913–1966), American poet, was a close friend of Berryman's and, in 1940, helped him get his first teaching job, at Harvard. *His Toy, His Dream, His Rest*, the second book of Berryman's Dream Songs (in which this poem appears) is in part dedicated "to the sacred memory of Delmore Schwartz."
8. Alas.
9. Ritually unclean, according to Jewish law.

I imagine you have heard the terrible news,
that Delmore Schwartz is dead, miserably & alone,
in New York: he sang me a song
'I am the Brooklyn poet Delmore Schwartz
Harms & the child I sing, two parents' torts'[1]
when he was young & gift-strong.

1968

153

I'm cross with god who has wrecked this generation.
First he seized Ted, then Richard, Randall, and now Delmore.
In between he gorged on Sylvia Plath.
That was a first rate haul. He left alive
fools I could number like a kitchen knife
but Lowell[2] he did not touch.

Somewhere the enterprise continues, not—
yellow the sun lies on the baby's blouse—
in Henry's staggered thought.
I suppose the word would be, we must submit.
Later.
I hang, and I will not be part of it.

A friend of Henry's[3] contrasted God's career
with Mozart's, leaving Henry with nothing to say
but praise for a word so apt.
We suffer on, a day, a day, a day.
And never again can come, like a man slapped,
news like this

1968

219

So Long? Stevens[4]

He lifted up, among the actuaries,
a grandee crow. Ah ha & he crowed good.
That funny money-man.
Mutter we all must as well as we can.

1. Torments. A parody of the opening words of Virgil's *Aeneid*, "Of arms and the man I sing."
2. Robert Lowell (1917–1977), American poet, like the other people named in this stanza. Theodore Roethke (1908–1963) died after problems with depression. "Richard" is R. P. Blackmur (1904–1965). Randall Jarrell (1914–1965) was struck by a car in a suspicious accident. Delmore Schwartz (1913–1966) died alone after years of mental illness. Sylvia Plath (1932–1963) committed suicide.
3. Howard Nemerov (1920–1991), American poet; in *Journal of the Fictive Life* (1965), he wrote that "Mozart's life and work express a purer and more efficacious benevolence to mankind than the life and work of God."
4. Wallace Stevens (1879–1955), American poet and insurance company vice president. Berryman alludes to "Thirteen Ways of Looking at a Blackbird," "Sunday Morning," and other poems by Stevens.

He mutter spiffy. He make wonder Henry's
wits, though, with a odd

. . . something . . . something . . . not there in his flourishing art.
O veteran of death, you will not mind
a counter-mutter.
What was it missing, then, at the man's heart
so that he does not wound? It is our kind
to wound, as well as utter

a fact of happy world. That metaphysics
he hefted up until we could not breathe
the physics. *On our side,*
monotonous (or ever-fresh)—it sticks
in Henry's throat to judge—brilliant, he seethe;
better than us; less wide.

1968

312

I have moved to Dublin to have it out with you,
majestic Shade,[5] You whom I read so well
so many years ago,
did I read your lesson right? did I see through
your phases to the real? your heaven, your hell
did I enquire properly into?

For years then I forgot you, I put you down,
ingratitude is the necessary curse
of making things new:[6]
I brought my family to see me through,
I brought my homage & my soft remorse,
I brought a book or two

only, including in the end your last
strange poems made under the shadow of death
Your high figures float
again across my mind and all your past
fills my walled garden with your honey breath
wherein I move, a mote.

1968

5. W. B. Yeats (1865–1939), Irish poet, whom Berryman called his first and last influence. In 1936, while a student at Clare College, Cambridge University, Berryman had tea with Yeats, an event celebrated in Dream Song 215.
6. An adaptation of Ezra Pound's famous slogan, "make it new."

384

The marker slants, flowerless, day's almost done,
I stand above my father's grave with rage,
often, often before
I've made this awful pilgrimage to one
who cannot visit me, who tore his page
out: I come back for more,

I spit upon this dreadful banker's grave
who shot his heart out in a Florida dawn
O ho alas alas
When will indifference come, I moan & rave
I'd like to scrabble till I got right down
away down under the grass

and ax the casket open ha to see
just how he's taking it, which he sought so hard
we'll tear apart
the mouldering grave clothes ha & then Henry
will heft the ax once more, his final card,
and fell it on the start.

1969

Henry's Understanding

He was reading late, at Richard's, down in Maine,
aged 32? Richard & Helen long in bed,
my good wife long in bed.
All I had to do was strip & get into my bed,
putting the marker in the book, & sleep,
& wake to a hot breakfast.

Off the coast was an island, P'tit Manaan,
the bluff from Richard's lawn was almost sheer.
A chill at four o'clock.
It only takes a few minutes to make a man.
A concentration upon now & here.
Suddenly, unlike Bach,

& horribly, unlike Bach, it occurred to me
that *one* night, instead of warm pajamas,
I'd take off all my clothes
& cross the damp cold lawn & down the bluff
into the terrible water & walk forever
under it out toward the island.

1972

Dylan Thomas 1914–1953

Dylan Thomas used to say in his American readings that his poems had to be read either very soft or very loud, and it is true that he has none of the middle style of Thomas Hardy or W. H. Auden. A Romantic visionary, he is comparable to Hart Crane, though less interested than Crane in the ineffable ecstasies beyond verbal expression. He liked to speak of his poems as narratives, as in his reply to a questionnaire in 1934: "Poetry is the rhythmic, inevitably narrative, movement from an overclothed blindness to a naked vision that depends in its intensity on the strength of the labour put into the creation of the poetry. My poetry is, or should be, useful to me for one reason: it is the record of my individual struggle from darkness towards some measure of light." Each poem, he said, was to be "a formally watertight compartment of words, preferably with a main moving column (i.e. narrative) to hold a little of the real causes and forces of the creative brain and body."

At the root of his poetry is a sense of doubleness, of womb and tomb, of the worm as penis and as death, which he embodied in one of his earliest published poems, "The Force That through the Green Fuse Drives the Flower." He built poems out of such paradoxes: as he wrote in a letter, "I make one image—though 'make' is not the word; I let, perhaps, an image be 'made' emotionally in me and then apply to it what intellectual and critical forces I possess—let it breed another, let that image contradict the first, make, of the third image bred out of the other two together, a fourth contradictory image, and let them all, within my imposed formal limits, conflict. Each image holds within it the seed of its own destruction, and my dialectical method, as I understand it, is a constant building up and breaking down of the images that come out of the central seed, which is itself destructive and constructive at the same time. . . . Out of the inevitable conflict of images— . . . the womb of war—I try to make that momentary peace which is a poem" (*Dylan Thomas,* ed. Henry Treece, 1936).

His view of life coincided with the Christian, but perhaps only because Christianity offered the necessary symbols for his imagery of death-in-life and life-in-death. Certainly, Thomas's is a different form of Christianity from T. S. Eliot's, in that it is so radiantly aware of the sweetness of living, especially before the child learns an adult sense of time and death. His poems about adults are more somber. Yet he insisted, in a note to his *Collected Poems* (1952): "These poems, with all their crudities, doubts, and confusions, are written for the love of Man and in praise of God, and I'd be a damn fool if they weren't."

Thomas was born on October 27, 1914, in Swansea, Wales, which he described bitterly as "the smug darkness of a provincial town." He was educated at the Swansea Grammar School, which he left in 1931. His father, a schoolteacher, urged him to go to a university, but Thomas followed the example of the Irish playwright Bernard Shaw and attempted to become a writer at once. His style, in fact, was formed by the time he was seventeen. At twenty, he published his first book, *18 Poems* (1934), which won ecstatic praise from Edith Sitwell and others, and went to live in London. In 1936, he met Caitlin Macnamara, a young Irishwoman whose temperament was as turbulent as his own; they married the following year and subsequently had three children. Thomas also wrote short stories, plays, and film scripts. The most successful was *Under Milk Wood* (1954), a radio play depicting the residents of a small Welsh town by the sea from the middle of one night to the middle of the next. He supported himself in his last years in part with long lecture tours of the United States, during which—drunk or sober—he gave magnificent readings of poems (mostly by other writers) on dozens of college campuses. His extravagant drinking gradually usurped most of his time, and chronic alcoholism helped bring about his early death, in New York City.

Thomas appears in twentieth-century poetry with the air of a mystic rhapsodist. He knew no Welsh, but he accepted the traditional role of the Welsh bard and was depicted by painter Augustus John as wild and inspired. In fact, his verse played its bravura of language against tight verse forms and was always subjected to stern intellectual ordering. Nonetheless, his full-throated rhetoric, so different from the usual understatement of Auden and other poets of the 1930s, was attacked by some critics as masking a paucity of ideas. (In the 1950s, the Movement of Philip Larkin and others was a reaction against Thomas.) A modest man, Thomas could berate himself as a "freak user of words, not a poet," but he usually felt that his verbal mannerisms were justified: "I am a painstaking, conscientious, involved and devious craftsman in words, however unsuccessful the result so often appears, and to whatever wrong uses I may apply my technical paraphernalia." He lists his poetic devices and adds: "Poets have got to enjoy themselves sometimes, and the twistings and convolutions of words, the inventions and contrivances, are all part of the joy that is part of the painful, voluntary work" ("Poetic Manifesto").

The Force That through the Green Fuse Drives the Flower

The force that through the green fuse drives the flower
Drives my green age; that blasts the roots of trees
Is my destroyer.
And I am dumb to tell the crooked rose
My youth is bent by the same wintry fever.

The force that drives the water through the rocks
Drives my red blood; that dries the mouthing streams
Turns mine to wax.
And I am dumb to mouth unto my veins
How at the mountain spring the same mouth sucks.

The hand that whirls the water in the pool
Stirs the quicksand; that ropes the blowing wind
Hauls my shroud sail.
And I am dumb to tell the hanging man
How of my clay is made the hangman's lime.[1]

The lips of time leech to the fountain head;
Love drips and gathers, but the fallen blood
Shall calm her sores.
And I am dumb to tell a weather's wind
How time has ticked a heaven round the stars.

And I am dumb to tell the lover's tomb
How at my sheet[2] goes the same crooked worm.

1933 1934

1. Quicklime poured in the graves of victims of the public hangman, to quicken decomposition.

2. Winding sheet (for a corpse).

And Death Shall Have No Dominion[3]

And death shall have no dominion.
Dead men naked they shall be one
With the man in the wind and the west moon;
When their bones are picked clean and the clean bones gone,
They shall have stars at elbow and foot;
Though they go mad they shall be sane,
Though they sink through the sea they shall rise again;
Though lovers be lost love shall not;
And death shall have no dominion.

And death shall have no dominion.
Under the windings of the sea
They lying long shall not die windily;
Twisting on racks when sinews give way,
Strapped to a wheel, yet they shall not break;
Faith in their hands shall snap in two,
And the unicorn evils run them through;
Split all ends up they shan't crack;
And death shall have no dominion.

And death shall have no dominion.
No more may gulls cry at their ears
Or waves break loud on the seashores;
Where blew a flower may a flower no more
Lift its head to the blows of the rain;
Though they be mad and dead as nails,
Heads of the characters hammer through daisies;
Break in the sun till the sun breaks down,
And death shall have no dominion.

1933 1936

The Hand That Signed the Paper[4]

The hand that signed the paper felled a city;
Five sovereign fingers taxed the breath,
Doubled the globe of dead and halved a country;
These five kings did a king to death.

The mighty hand leads to a sloping shoulder,
The finger joints are cramped with chalk;
A goose's quill has put an end to murder
That put an end to talk.

3. "Death hath no more dominion" (Romans 6.19). This was the first poem Thomas published after his school poems—though not in his first book.
4. Likely an allusion to the 1919 Treaty of Versailles, signed by Britain, France, Italy, Japan, and the United States (though never ratified by the U.S. Congress). The treaty imposed heavy reparations on Germany and was seen as precipitating later diplomatic crises.

The hand that signed the treaty bred a fever,
And famine grew, and locusts came;
Great is the hand that holds dominion over
Man by a scribbled name.

The five kings count the dead but do not soften
The crusted wound nor stroke the brow;
A hand rules pity as a hand rules heaven;
Hands have no tears to flow.

1933 1936

When All My Five and Country Senses See

When all my five and country senses see,
The fingers will forget green thumbs and mark
How, through the halfmoon's vegetable eye,
Husk of young stars and handfull zodiac,
Love in the frost is pared and wintered by,
The whispering ears will watch love drummed away
Down breeze and shell to a discordant beach,
And, lashed to syllables, the lynx tongue cry
That her fond wounds are mended bitterly.
My nostrils see her breath burn like a bush.

My one and noble heart has witnesses
In all love's countries, that will grope awake;
And when blind sleep drops on the spying senses,
The heart is sensual, though five eyes break.

1938 1939

Twenty-Four Years

Twenty-four years remind the tears of my eyes.
(Bury the dead for fear that they walk to the grave in labour.)
In the groin of the natural doorway I crouched like a tailor
Sewing a shroud for a journey
By the light of the meat-eating sun.
Dressed to die, the sensual strut begun,
With my red veins full of money,
In the final direction of the elementary town
I advance for as long as forever is.

1939 1939

The Hunchback in the Park[5]

The hunchback in the park
A solitary mister
Propped between trees and water
From the opening of the garden lock
That lets the trees and water enter
Until the Sunday sombre bell at dark[6]

Eating bread from a newspaper
Drinking water from the chained cup
That the children filled with gravel
In the fountain basin where I sailed my ship
Slept at night in a dog kennel
But nobody chained him up.

Like the park birds he came early
Like the water he sat down
And Mister they called Hey mister
The truant boys from the town
Running when he had heard them clearly
On out of sound

Past lake and rockery[7]
Laughing when he shook his paper
Hunchbacked in mockery
Through the loud zoo of the willow groves
Dodging the park keeper
With his stick that picked up leaves.

And the old dog sleeper
Alone between nurses and swans
While the boys among willows
Made the tigers jump out of their eyes
To roar on the rockery stones
And the groves were blue with sailors

Made all day until bell time
A woman figure without fault
Straight as a young elm
Straight and tall from his crooked bones

5. "Though the details in this poem . . . could apply to almost any park, this particular park is undoubtedly Cwmdonkin, not far from the Thomas house. There was, indeed, a hunchback who seemed to have nowhere else to go, who stayed from the moment the park opened until it closed. Cwmdonkin Park was a favourite haunt of truants from Swansea Grammar School, because it was bordered on one side by a road that led directly to the school, but sometimes didn't. Thomas and I often met there to read poems to one another or write them, when, perhaps, we should have been learning Geography. But usually our amusements were more boisterous and less 'cultured' " (*The Poems of Dylan Thomas*, ed. David Jones, 1971). Jones was a lifelong friend of Thomas's.

6. The bell that signals the closing of the park at night.

7. Rock garden.

That she might stand in the night
After the locks and chains

All night in the unmade park
After the railings and shrubberies
The birds the grass the trees the lake
And the wild boys innocent as strawberries
Had followed the hunchback
To his kennel in the dark.

1941 1946

Poem in October

It was my thirtieth year to heaven
Woke to my hearing from harbour and neighbour wood
And the mussel pooled and the heron
Priested shore
The morning beckon
With water praying and call of seagull and rook[8]
And the knock of sailing boats on the net webbed wall
Myself to set foot
That second
In the still sleeping town and set forth.

My birthday began with the water-
Birds and the birds of the winged trees flying my name
Above the farms and the white horses
And I rose
In the rainy autumn
And walked abroad in a shower of all my days.
High tide and the heron dived when I took the road
Over the border
And the gates
Of the town closed as the town awoke.

A springful of larks in a rolling
Cloud and the roadside bushes brimming with whistling
Blackbirds and the sun of October
Summery
On the hill's shoulder,
Here were fond climates and sweet singers suddenly
Come in the morning where I wandered and listened
To the rain wringing
Wind blow cold
In the wood faraway under me.

Pale rain over the dwindling harbour
And over the sea wet church the size of a snail

8. Crow.

With its horns through mist and the castle
Brown as owls
But all the gardens
Of spring and summer were blooming in the tall tales
Beyond the border and under the lark full cloud.
There could I marvel
My birthday
Away but the weather turned around.

It turned away from the blithe country
And down the other air and the blue altered sky
Streamed again a wonder of summer
With apples
Pears and red currants
And I saw in the turning so clearly a child's
Forgotten mornings when he walked with his mother
Through the parables
Of sun light
And the legends of the green chapels

And the twice told fields of infancy
That his tears burned my cheeks and his heart moved in mine.
These were the woods the river and sea
Where a boy
In the listening
Summertime of the dead whispered the truth of his joy
To the trees and the stones and the fish in the tide.
And the mystery
Sang alive
Still in the water and singingbirds.

And there could I marvel my birthday
Away but the weather turned around. And the true
Joy of the long dead child sang burning
In the sun.
It was my thirtieth
Year to heaven stood there then in the summer noon
Though the town below lay leaved with October blood.
O may my heart's truth
Still be sung
On this high hill in a year's turning.

1944 1946

A Refusal to Mourn the Death, by Fire, of a Child in London

Never until the mankind making
Bird beast and flower
Fathering and all humbling darkness
Tells with silence the last light breaking

And the still hour
Is come of the sea tumbling in harness

And I must enter again the round
Zion[9] of the water bead
And the synagogue of the ear of corn
Shall I let pray the shadow of a sound
Or sow my salt seed
In the least valley of sackcloth to mourn

The majesty and burning of the child's death.
I shall not murder
The mankind of her going with a grave truth
Nor blaspheme down the stations of the breath
With any further
Elegy of innocence and youth.

Deep with the first dead lies London's daughter,
Robed in the long friends,
The grains beyond age, the dark veins of her mother,
Secret by the unmourning water
Of the riding Thames.[1]
After the first death, there is no other.

1945 1946

Fern Hill[2]

Now as I was young and easy under the apple boughs
About the lilting house and happy as the grass was green,
The night above the dingle[3] starry,
Time let me hail and climb
Golden in the heydays of his eyes,
And honoured among wagons I was prince of the apple towns
And once below a time I lordly had the trees and leaves
Trail with daisies and barley
Down the rivers of the windfall light.

And as I was green and carefree, famous among the barns
About the happy yard and singing as the farm was home,
In the sun that is young once only,
Time let me play and be
Golden in the mercy of his means,
And green and golden I was huntsman and herdsman, the calves
Sang to my horn, the foxes on the hills barked clear and cold,

9. City of God.
1. River that flows through London.
2. A country house where the poet's aunt lived, and where he spent summer holidays as a boy.
3. Small wooded valley.

    And the sabbath rang slowly
  In the pebbles of the holy streams.

All the sun long it was running, it was lovely, the hay
Fields high as the house, the tunes from the chimneys, it was air
  And playing, lovely and watery
    And fire green as grass.
  And nightly under the simple stars
As I rode to sleep the owls were bearing the farm away,
All the moon long I heard, blessed among stables, the nightjars
  Flying with the ricks,[4] and the horses
    Flashing into the dark.

And then to awake, and the farm, like a wanderer white
With the dew, come back, the cock on his shoulder: it was all
  Shining, it was Adam and maiden,
    The sky gathered again
  And the sun grew round that very day.
So it must have been after the birth of the simple light
In the first, spinning place, the spellbound horses walking warm
  Out of the whinnying green stable
    On to the fields of praise.

And honoured among foxes and pheasants by the gay house
Under the new made clouds and happy as the heart was long,
  In the sun born over and over,
    I ran my heedless ways,
  My wishes raced through the house high hay
And nothing I cared, at my sky blue trades, that time allows
In all his tuneful turning so few and such morning songs
  Before the children green and golden
    Follow him out of grace,

Nothing I cared, in the lamb white days, that time would take me
Up to the swallow thronged loft by the shadow of my hand,
  In the moon that is always rising,
    Nor that riding to sleep
  I should hear him fly with the high fields
And wake to the farm forever fled from the childless land.
Oh as I was young and easy in the mercy of his means,
    Time held me green and dying
  Though I sang in my chains like the sea.

1945 1946

4. Stacks of hay. *Nightjars:* nocturnal birds.

In My Craft or Sullen Art

In my craft or sullen art
Exercised in the still night
When only the moon rages
And the lovers lie abed
With all their griefs in their arms,
I labour by singing light
Not for ambition or bread
Or the strut and trade of charms
On the ivory stages
But for the common wages
Of their most secret heart.

Not for the proud man apart
From the raging moon I write
On these spindrift[5] pages
Nor for the towering dead
With their nightingales and psalms
But for the lovers, their arms
Round the griefs of the ages,
Who pay no praise or wages
Nor heed my craft or art.

1945 1946

Do Not Go Gentle into That Good Night[6]

Do not go gentle into that good night,
Old age should burn and rave at close of day;
Rage, rage against the dying of the light.

Though wise men at their end know dark is right,
Because their words had forked no lightning they
Do not go gentle into that good night.

Good men, the last wave by, crying how bright
Their frail deeds might have danced in a green bay,
Rage, rage against the dying of the light.

5. Driven, like sea spray, by the wind.
6. Thomas wrote at the time, "The only person I can't show the little enclosed poem to is, of course, my father, who doesn't know he's dying." Quoted by Jones, who goes on to add that Thomas's father "lingered for more than a year after this, and died on 15th December 1952. . . . It is significant that for this subject and on this occasion, Thomas deliberately chose to discipline himself by the use of a strict form, the villanelle" (*The Poems of Dylan Thomas*).

Wild men who caught and sang the sun in flight,
And learn, too late, they grieved it on its way,
Do not go gentle into that good night.

Grave men, near death, who see with blinding sight
Blind eyes could blaze like meteors and be gay,
Rage, rage against the dying of the light.

And you, my father, there on the sad height,
Curse, bless, me now with your fierce tears, I pray.
Do not go gentle into that good night.
Rage, rage against the dying of the light.

1951 1952

Judith Wright
1915–2000

Some qualities of Judith Wright's verse derive from her childhood, in a rural region of New South Wales, Australia. Living far from the nearest school, she was educated until age twelve through a correspondence course organized by the Department of Education. Later, she attended the University of Sydney and chose to take English literature alone rather than the usual variety of courses. She had grown up loving the land and wild animals, and her marriage to philosopher J. P. McKinney introduced her to a philosophy confirming her intimations that the time had arrived for humans to reject mere intellectual analysis and embrace an intuitive or emotional bond with the world. She became an impassioned advocate for the natural environment and Aboriginal rights.

Her poems convey at times a radiant sense of oneness with Australia, particularly the eastern part known as the New England Plateau. In "The Moving Image," Wright identifies the poet with Tom of Bedlam, the seeming madman whose madness is the ultimate sanity. The sense of the poet as a convergence of outer and inner becomes explicit in "The Maker": "into myself I took / all living things that are," and in "For New England": "Many roads meet here / in me, the traveller and the ways I travel." She laments the death of the wild country and the dying out of Aboriginal civilization in "Bora Ring," though she suggests that the Aboriginal past still haunts the present and curses it. The dingoes' cry in "Drought Year" reminds us of the unseen world that remains a part of us. Of herself, in old age, she wrote, "In my last quarter let me be hag, but poet" ("Easter Moon and Owl").

Wright was born on May 31, 1915, in Armidale, New South Wales. She received many awards for her verse. Besides many books of verse, her writings include memoirs, essays, short stories, and children's books, and she edited several anthologies of Australian poetry.

Bora Ring[1]

The song is gone; the dance
is secret with the dancers in the earth,
the ritual useless, and the tribal story
lost in an alien tale.

Only the grass stands up
to mark the dancing-ring: the apple-gums
posture and mime a past corroboree,[2]
murmur a broken chant.

The hunter is gone: the spear
is splintered underground; the painted bodies
a dream the world breathed sleeping and forgot.
The nomad feet are still.

Only the rider's heart
halts at a sightless shadow, an unsaid word
that fastens in the blood the ancient curse,
the fear as old as Cain.[3]

1946

Drought Year

That time of drought the embered air
burned to the roots of timber and grass.
The crackling lime-scrub would not bear
and Mooni Creek was sand that year.
The dingoes' cry was strange to hear.

I heard the dingoes cry
in the whipstick scrub on the Thirty-mile Dry.
I saw the wagtail[4] take his fill
perching in the seething skull.
I saw the eel wither where he curled
in the last blood-drop of a spent world.

I heard the bone whisper in the hide
of the big red horse that lay where he died.
Prop that horse up, make him stand,
hoofs turned down in the bitter sand—
make him stand at the gate of the Thirty-mile Dry.

1. Site of initiation ceremonies held by Australian Aborigines.
2. Nighttime ceremony held by the Aborigines. *Apple-gums*: Australian timber trees.
3. Son of Adam and Eve, who, in killing his brother, Abel, committed the first murder (Genesis 4.1–16); "the ancient curse" is the curse of God upon Cain.
4. Australian bird.

Turn this way and you will die—
and strange and loud was the dingoes' cry.

1953

Flood Year

Walking up the driftwood beach at day's end
I saw it, thrust up out of a hillock of sand—
a frail bleached clench of fingers dried by wind—
the dead child's hand.

And they are mourning there still, though I forget,
the year of flood, the scoured ruined land,
the herds gone down the current, the farms drowned,
and the child never found.

When I was there the thick hurling waters
had gone back to the river, the farms were almost drained.
Banished half-dead cattle searched the dunes; it rained;
river and sea met with a wild sound.

Oh with a wild sound water flung into air
where sea met river; all the country round
no heart was quiet. I walked on the driftwood sand
and saw the pale crab crouched, and came to a stand
thinking, A child's hand. The child's hand.

1953

Ishtar[5]

When I first saw a woman after childbirth
the room was full of your glance who had just gone away.
And when the mare was bearing her foal
you were with her but I did not see your face.

When in fear I became a woman
I first felt your hand.
When the shadow of the future first fell across me
it was your shadow, my grave and hooded attendant.

It is all one whether I deny or affirm you;
it is not my mind you are concerned with.
It is no matter whether I submit or rebel;
the event will still happen.

5. One of the great mother-goddesses of the ancient Near East; the goddess of both fertility and war in the Babylonian and Assyrian religions.

You neither know nor care for the truth of my heart;
but the truth of my body has all to do with you.
You have no need of my thoughts or my hopes,
living in the realm of the absolute event.

Then why is it that when I at last see your face
under that hood of slate-blue, so calm and dark,
so worn with the burden of an inexpressible knowledge—
why is that I begin to worship you with tears?

1953

Request to a Year

If the year is meditating a suitable gift,
I should like it to be the attitude
of my great-great-grandmother,
legendary devotee of the arts,

who, having had eight children
and little opportunity for painting pictures,
sat one day on a high rock
beside a river in Switzerland

and from a difficult distance viewed
her second son, balanced on a small ice-floe,
drift down the current towards a waterfall
that struck rock-bottom eighty feet below,

while her second daughter, impeded,
no doubt, by the petticoats of the day,
stretched out a last-hope alpenstock[6]
(which luckily later caught him on his way).

Nothing, it was evident, could be done;
and with the artist's isolating eye
my great-great-grandmother hastily sketched the scene.
The sketch survives to prove the story by.

Year, if you have no Mother's day present planned;
reach back and bring me the firmness of her hand.

1953

"Dove—Love"

The dove purrs—over and over the dove
purrs its declaration. The wind's tone
changes from tree to tree, the creek on stone

6. Staff used in mountain-climbing.

alters its sob and fall, but still the dove
goes insistently on, telling its love
        "I could eat you."

And in captivity, they say, doves do.
Gentle, methodical, starting with the feet
(the ham-pink succulent toes
on their thin stems of rose),
baring feather by feather the wincing meat:
        "I could eat you."

That neat suburban head, that suit of grey,
watchful conventional eye and manicured claw—
these also rhyme with us. The doves play
on one repetitive note that plucks the raw
helpless nerve, their soft "I do. I do.
        I could eat you."

1962

P. K. PAGE
1916–2010

Many of P. K. Page's poems transport the reader to a world of snow, ice, and bright sunlight, a white and glittering world in which the visionary poet transcends ordinary social concerns and behavior. Margaret Atwood, another Canadian poet, describes Page as often appearing as a "tranced observer who verges on mysticism" (*The New Oxford Book of Canadian Verse in English*, 1982). The word "mysticism," as applied to Page, should suggest not a separation of body and spirit, but rather a vision in which the senses are liberated from immediacies of time and place.

Page's earliest poems, written under the influence of W. H. Auden and his circle, occasionally echo the young Auden's social concerns and rhetoric. One poem is called "Bank Strike"; others, "Offices" and "Typists": "Crowded together typists touch / softly as ducks." The women in "The Stenographers" represent many office workers, living regimented lives and emotionally dispossessed to the point of madness. Page's later poems are packed with vivid visual images. The winter landscape of "Stories of Snow" is ultimately sinister, though it beguiles us as a welcome alternative to tropical lushness. In "Photos of a Salt Mine," the mine, a world of salt, seems beautiful only at first. The poem concludes with an abrupt change of perspective; now the mine, peopled by the damned, is one of the circles of Hell.

Patricia Kathleen Page was born on November 23, 1916, in Dorset, England; she emigrated to Canada when she was a very young child. She received her formal education at St. Hilda's School, in Calgary, Alberta, and at the Art Students League and Pratt Institute, in New York City. She devoted her life to a variety of arts: she worked as a radio actress and a script writer, and she was widely known as a painter and printmaker. In addition to her poems, she wrote fiction, essays, and children's stories.

The Stenographers

After the brief bivouac[1] of Sunday,
their eyes, in the forced march of Monday to Saturday,
hoist the white flag, flutter in the snowstorm of paper,
haul it down and crack in the midsun of temper.

In the pause between the first draft and the carbon
they glimpse the smooth hours when they were children—
the ride in the ice-cart, the ice-man's name,
the end of the route and the long walk home;

remember the sea where floats at high tide
were sea marrows[2] growing on the scatter-green vine
or spools of grey toffee, or wasps' nests on water;
remember the sand and the leaves of the country.

Bell rings and they go and the voice draws their pencil[3]
like a sled across snow; when its runners are frozen
rope snaps and the voice then is pulling no burden
but runs like a dog on the winter of paper.

Their climates are winter and summer—no wind
for the kites of their hearts—no wind for a flight;
a breeze at the most, to tumble them over
and leave them like rubbish—the boy-friends of blood.

In the inch of the noon as they move they are stagnant.
The terrible calm of the noon is their anguish;
the lip of the counter, the shapes of the straws
like icicles breaking their tongues are invaders.

Their beds are their oceans—salt water of weeping
the waves that they know—the tide before sleep;
and fighting to drown they assemble their sheep
in columns and watch them leap desks for their fences
and stare at them with their own mirror-worn faces.

In the felt of the morning the calico-minded,
sufficiently starched, insert papers, hit keys,
efficient and sure as their adding machines;
yet they weep in the vault, they are taut as net curtains
stretched upon frames. In their eyes I have seen
the pin men[4] of madness in marathon trim
race round the track of the stadium pupil.

1946

1. Temporary army encampment in the open.
2. That is, the "floats" (buoys) looked like sea vegetables.
3. That is, when they take dictation.
4. "Stick figures, such as children draw" [Page's note].

Photos of a Salt Mine

How innocent their lives look,
how like a child's
dream of caves and winter, both combined:
the steep descent to whiteness
and the stope
with its striated walls[5]
their folds all leaning as if pointing to
the greater whiteness still,
that great white bank
with its decisive front,
that seam upon a slope,
salt's lovely ice.

And wonderful underfoot the snow of salt,
the fine
particles a broom could sweep,
one thinks
muckers[6] might make angels in its drifts,
as children do in snow,
lovers in sheets,
lie down and leave imprinted where they lay
a feathered creature holier than they.

And in the outworked stopes
with lamps and ropes
up miniature Matterhorns[7]
the miners climb,
probe with their lights
the ancient folds of rock—
syncline, anticline[8]—
and scoop from darkness an Aladdin's cave:
rubies and opals glitter from its walls.

But hoses douse the brilliance of these jewels,
melt fire to brine.
Salt's bitter water trickles thin and forms
slow fathoms down
a lake within a cave
lacquered with jet—
white's opposite.
There grey on black the boating miners float
to mend the stays and struts of that old stope
and deeply underground
their words resound,

5. With parallel grooves. *Stope:* steplike excavation in a mine.
6. Laborers who, or machines that, remove muck.
7. The Matterhorn is a mountain peak in the Alps.
8. A "syncline" is a trough of stratified rock (here, salt) in which the beds of ore (here again, salt) tip toward each other; an "anticline" is the reverse: an arch, with the beds tipping away from each other.

are multiplied by echo, swell and grow
and make a climate of a miner's voice.

So all the photographs like children's wishes
are filled with caves or winter,
innocence
has acted as a filter,
selected only beauty from the mine.
Except in the last picture, shot
from an acute high angle. In a pit
figures the size of pins are strangely lit
and might be dancing but you know they're not.
Like Dante's vision of the nether hell[9]
men struggle with the bright cold fires of salt
locked in the black inferno of the rock:
the filter here, not innocence but guilt.

1967

Deaf-Mute in the Pear Tree

His clumsy body is a golden fruit
pendulous in the pear tree

Blunt fingers among the multitudinous buds

Adriatic[1] blue the sky above and through
the forking twigs

Sun ruddying tree's trunk, his trunk
his massive head thick-nobbed with burnished curls
tight-clenched in bud

(Painting by Generalić.[2] Primitive.)

I watch him prune with silent secateurs[3]

Boots in the crotch of branches shift their weight
heavily as oxen in a stall

Hear small inarticulate mews from his locked mouth
a kitten in a box

Pear clippings fall
soundlessly on the ground

9. In Dante's *Inferno*, the innermost circle of Hell is made of ice.
1. As of the Adriatic Sea, part of the Mediterranean.
2. Ivan Generalić (1914–1992), considered the founder of Croatian naive art.
3. Pruning shears.

Spring finches sing
                                soundlessly in the leaves

A stone. A stone in ears and on his tongue

Through palm and fingertip he knows the tree's
quick springtime pulse

Smells in its sap the sweet incipient pears

Pale sunlight's choppy water glistens on
his mutely snipping blades

and flags and scraps of blue
above him make regatta of the day

But when he sees his wife's foreshortened shape
sudden and silent in the grass below
uptilt its face to him

then air is kisses, kisses

stone dissolves

his locked throat finds a little door

and through it feathered joy
flies screaming like a jay

1985

ROBERT LOWELL
1917–1977

Robert Lowell presented himself in his poetry as a gnarled, knotty, unwieldy figure—almost a gargoyle. This portrait is not what might be anticipated from a member of a patrician New England family, with James Russell Lowell a great-great-uncle and Amy Lowell a distant cousin. Lowell insisted on his own version of the family history. In the prose autobiography that forms a large part of his book *Life Studies* (1959), as in his unflattering elegies, he shows little indulgence toward his domineering mother and ineffectual father, and he relentlessly recalls their lifelong dialogue as that of a shrew and a wobbler: " *'Weelawaugh, we-ee-eeelawaugh, weelawaugh,'* shrilled Mother's high voice. *'But-and, but-and, but and!'* Father's low mumble would drone in answer." With other ancestors whom he presented more attractively, Lowell constructed a new family for himself from dead writers such as Milton, Jonathan Edwards, Nathaniel Hawthorne, T. S. Eliot, John Berryman, and Ezra Pound—patricians not of blood but of tortured talent.

Whether he was discussing the intricacies of the Puritan conscience, or writing as a Catholic or an agnostic, Lowell was, like the title character in his translation of Jean

Racine's *Phaedra,* "Always, always agonized." He beat against what he called awkwardly "blind alleys of our rooms." A deliberate awkwardness jackets many of his poems. Attacking himself, his parents, his Puritan forebears, even language itself, Lowell fashioned an elegant yet explosive style of poetry, dense with conflicting impulses and images. In his preface to a book of translated poems, *Imitations,* he declared that "the dark and against the grain" primarily interested him.

He was born on March 1, 1917, in "this planned / Babel of Boston where our money talks" ("As a Plane Tree by the Water"). He spent his early years there, except for several periods in Washington and Philadelphia, where his father, a naval officer, was stationed. In "Commander Lowell" and other poems in *Life Studies,* Lowell offers a chilly, relentless picture of his father, who died in 1950. Lowell attended St. Mark's School and soon began to prepare himself deliberately for a poet's life. He enrolled at Harvard University and immersed himself in English literature, but after two years, he abruptly transferred to Kenyon College to study with the New Critic and poet John Crowe Ransom. After graduation in 1940, Lowell attended Louisiana State University, where he studied with two other leaders of the New Criticism, Robert Penn Warren and Cleanth Brooks. At the same time, he formed a close friendship with another, Allen Tate. He was greatly influenced by the predilection of these poets and critics for "formal, difficult poems."

While at Kenyon, Lowell experimented in the most divergent styles, but he found congenial models in Hart Crane, Dylan Thomas, and Tate, as well as in the examples cited and elaborately explained by William Empson in *Seven Types of Ambiguity* (1930, rev. 1947). Lowell's poems became increasingly ambiguous, to the point that Ransom found them forbidding and clotted. Lowell was also dissatisfied with them, though he did not renounce his dense details or jagged syntax. Upon graduating from Kenyon, Lowell married the novelist Jean Stafford. (They were divorced in 1948, and he married his second wife, Elizabeth Hardwick, in 1949. Lowell and Hardwick were divorced in 1972.) He also, like Tate, converted to Catholicism, and he found an intense vantage point in the change from his family's Episcopalianism. In his first book, *Land of Unlikeness* (1944), and later, Lowell wrote scathingly of the modern world as a Babylon or a wasteland, "where the landless blood of Cain / Is burning, burning the unburied grain" ("Children of Light"), and he prophesied the death of "our mighty merchants" ("Rebellion"). Like the historian R. H. Tawney, he connected the Puritan tradition with the rise of predatory capitalism.

Lowell was greatly disturbed by the advent of World War II. At first he tried, unsuccessfully, to enlist. Then in 1943, as his apocalyptic view sharpened, he grew horrified, particularly by the bombing of civilians, and declared himself a conscientious objector. As he wrote in "Memories of West Street and Lepke," with some humor, "I was a fire-breathing Catholic C.O., / and made my manic statement, . . . / Given a year, / I walked on the roof of the West Street Jail." He was released after six months and afterward lived for a time in Black Rock, near Bridgeport, Connecticut, where he found imagery for some of his best poems, reflecting the acute distress he then felt, for the world and himself.

Like many poets of the twentieth century, Lowell attempted in middle age to break through his own formality and obscurity, to write at once more intimately of his own experience and more publicly. The change was marked by a looser meter and form, beginning with *Life Studies,* one of the most influential books of post–World War II American poetry, written in part under the influence of the more "open" poetry of Allen Ginsberg and other Beats, as well as William Carlos Williams. Lowell also altered his symbolism: he gave up the Christian symbols of his early work, made his manner less forbidding, and presented details less viscously, with more individual sharpness.

Lowell confronted important events with courage and conviction. He protested the Vietnam War, both through poems and by public action. In June 1965, he formally refused an invitation to the White House Festival of the Arts from President Lyndon

B. Johnson, as a statement against the war. During the Democratic primary campaign for the presidency in 1968, Lowell accompanied Senator Eugene McCarthy, whose antiwar platform he supported. In 1970, he withdrew from the political scene by moving to England, where he married writer Caroline Blackwood two years later. The strain of his episodes of mania and depression was more than she could bear, and he was on his way back to his second wife and daughter when he died in a taxi from New York's Kennedy Airport.

As if caught between formality and informality, Lowell's later work includes unrhymed sonnets. Not as savage as his earlier work, and with an awareness of those around him—wife, daughter, friends—these poems still kept what Lowell called his "surrealism," by which he meant the grotesquerie that was always his brand and distinction. In *History* (1973), he insisted that "imperfection is the language of art" ("Last Things, Black Pines at 4 a.m."). His work was imperfect, as his own persistent revisions of it suggested, but it touched the nerve of the time.

The confessional aspect of Lowell's poetry, and his impingement on crucial events in the world, brought him as close to being central in then-contemporary verse as the fragmented literary scene allowed. Because of his sense of himself, his impressive personality, and his wit, intelligence, and talent, he throned it over his rivals from about 1950 to 1970. Although in recent decades his reputation has taken on more modest proportions, he remains one of the dominant voices of the latter half of the twentieth century.

The Quaker Graveyard in Nantucket

(For Warren Winslow,[1] Dead at Sea)

> Let man have dominion over the fishes of the sea and the fowls of the air and the beasts of the whole earth, and every creeping creature that moveth upon the earth.[2]

I

A brackish reach of shoal off Madaket[3]—
The sea was still breaking violently and night
Had steamed into our North Atlantic Fleet,
When the drowned sailor clutched the drag-net. Light
Flashed from his matted head and marble feet,
He grappled at the net
With the coiled, hurdling muscles of his thighs:
The corpse was bloodless, a botch of reds and whites,
Its open, staring eyes
Were lusterless dead-lights
Or cabin-window on a stranded hulk
Heavy with sand.[4] We weight the body, close

1. A cousin of Lowell's, who died in New York Harbor when his naval vessel exploded in World War II.
2. Slightly paraphrased from Genesis 1.26.
3. Fishing village on the west end of Nantucket Island.
4. The imagery of these lines is largely borrowed from Henry David Thoreau's *Cape Cod* (Boston, 1898): "The brig *St. John,* from Galway, Ireland, laden with emigrants, was wrecked on Sunday morning; it was not Tuesday morning, and the sea was still breaking violently on the rocks. . . . I saw many marble feet and matted heads as the clothes were raised, and one livid, swollen, and mangled body of a drowned girl . . . ; the coiled-up wreck of a human hulk, gashed by the rocks or fishes, so that the bone and muscle were exposed, but quite bloodless,—merely red and white,—with wide-open and staring eyes, yet lusterless, dead-lights; or like the cabin windows of a stranded vessel, filled with sand."

Its eyes and heave it seaward whence it came,
Where the heel-headed dogfish barks its nose
On Ahab's void and forehead;[5] and the name
Is blocked in yellow chalk.
Sailors, who pitch this portent at the sea
Where dreadnaughts shall confess
Its hell-bent deity,
When you are powerless
To sand-bag this Atlantic bulwark, faced
By the earth-shaker, green, unwearied, chaste
In his steel scales: ask for no Orphean lute
To pluck life back.[6] The guns of the steeled fleet
Recoil and then repeat
The hoarse salute.

II

Whenever winds are moving and their breath
Heaves at the roped-in bulwarks of this pier,
The terns and sea-gulls tremble at your death
In these home waters. Sailor, can you hear
The Pequod's[7] sea wings, beating landward, fall
Headlong and break on our Atlantic wall
Off 'Sconset, where the yawing S-boats[8] splash
The bellbuoy, with ballooning spinnakers,
As the entangled, screeching mainsheet clears
The blocks: off Madaket, where lubbers[9] lash
The heavy surf and throw their long lead squids
For blue-fish? Sea-gulls blink their heavy lids
Seaward. The winds' wings beat upon the stones,
Cousin, and scream for you and the claws rush
At the sea's throat and wring it in the slush
Of this old Quaker graveyard[1] where the bones
Cry out in the long night for the hurt beast
Bobbing by Ahab's whaleboats in the East.

III

All you recovered from Poseidon died
With you, my cousin, and the harrowed brine
Is fruitless on the blue beard of the god,
Stretching beyond us to the castles in Spain,
Nantucket's westward haven. To Cape Cod
Guns, cradled on the tide,
Blast the eelgrass about a waterclock

5. Ahab is the monomaniacal hunter of the white whale in *Moby-Dick*, by Herman Melville (1819–1891).
6. Orpheus went to Hades and with his music persuaded Persephone to let his wife, Eurydice, return to Earth. *Earth-shaker:* epithet for Poseidon, Greek god of the sea.
7. Ahab's ship, which the whale Moby-Dick destroyed.
8. Large racing sailboats once popular in New England. *'Sconset:* Siasconset, on eastern Nantucket.
9. Landlubbers.
1. A Quaker cemetery in Madaket. In the nineteenth century, Nantucket had a large Quaker population, including many whalers.

Of bilge and backwash, roil the salt and sand
Lashing earth's scaffold, rock
Our warships in the hand
Of the great God, where time's contrition blues
Whatever it was there Quaker sailors lost
In the mad scramble of their lives. They died
When time was open-eyed,
Wooden and childish; only bones abide
There, in the nowhere, where their boats were tossed
Sky-high, where mariners had fabled news
Of IS,[2] the whited monster. What it cost
Them is their secret. In the sperm-whale's slick
I see the Quakers drown and hear their cry:
"If God himself had not been on our side,
If God himself had not been on our side,
When the Atlantic rose against us, why,
Then it had swallowed us up quick."

IV

This is the end of the whaleroad[3] and the whale
Who spewed Nantucket bones on the thrashed swell
And stirred the troubled waters to whirlpools
To send the Pequod packing off to hell:
This is the end of them, three-quarters fools,
Snatching at straws to sail
Seaward and seaward on the turntail whale,
Spouting out blood and water as it rolls,
Sick as a dog to these Atlantic shoals:
Clamavimus,[4] O depths. Let the sea-gulls wail

For water, for the deep where the high tide
Mutters to its hurt self, mutters and ebbs.
Waves wallow in their wash, go out and out,
Leave only the death-rattle of the crabs,
The beach increasing, its enormous snout
Sucking the ocean's side.
This is the end of running on the waves;
We are poured out like water. Who will dance
The mast-lashed master of Leviathans[5]
Up from this field of Quakers in their unstoned graves?

V

When the whale's viscera go and the roll
Of its corruption overruns this world
Beyond tree-swept Nantucket and Woods Hole[6]

2. Cf. God's naming of himself to Moses as "I AM" (Exodus 3.14).
3. An Old English kenning (or epithet) for the sea.
4. We have cried (Latin). Cf. Psalm 130.1: "Out of the depths have I cried unto thee, O Lord."
5. Leviathan is an Old Testament serpent-monster from the sea.
6. The closest point on the mainland of Massachusetts to Martha's Vineyard, an island near Nantucket.

And Martha's Vineyard, Sailor, will your sword
Whistle and fall and sink into the fat?
In the great ash-pit of Jehoshaphat[7]
The bones cry for the blood of the white whale,
The fat flukes arch and whack about its ears,
The death-lance churns into the sanctuary, tears
The gun-blue swingle, heaving like a flail,
And hacks the coiling life out: it works and drags
And rips the sperm-whale's midriff into rags,
Gobbets of blubber spill to wind and weather,
Sailor, and gulls go round the stoven timbers
Where the morning stars sing out together
And thunder shakes the white surf and dismembers
The red flag hammered in the mast-head.[8] Hide,
Our steel, Jonas Messias,[9] in Thy side.

VI

OUR LADY OF WALSINGHAM[1]

There once the penitents took off their shoes
And then walked barefoot the remaining mile;
And the small trees, a stream and hedgerows file
Slowly along the munching English lane,
Like cows to the old shrine, until you lose
Track of your dragging pain.
The stream flows down under the druid tree,
Shiloah's whirlpools gurgle and make glad
The castle of God. Sailor, you were glad
And whistled Sion[2] by that stream. But see:

Our Lady, too small for her canopy,
Sits near the altar. There's no comeliness
At all or charm in that expressionless
Face with its heavy eyelids. As before,
This face, for centuries a memory,

7. "The valley of judgment. The world, according to some prophets and scientists, will end in fire" (Lowell writing to Kimon Friar and John Malcolm Brinnin). Jehoshaphat, biblical king of Judah, was persuaded by Ahab (king of Israel) to go to war (Joel 3.12).
8. At the end of *Moby-Dick,* as the *Pequod* is sinking, the American Indian Tashtego's arm rises from the water to nail Ahab's flag to the sinking mast.
9. Jonah (in the New Testament, Jonas) is identified with the Messiah because Lowell imagines the whaler's harpoon penetrating the whale, and Jonah within it, the way the centurion's spear pierced Jesus' side, and also because Jonah, like Jesus, emerged after a three-day "burial."
1. Adapted, Lowell said, from E. I. Watkins's *Catholic Art and Culture* (London, 1947): "For centuries the shrine of Our Lady of Walsingham has been an historical memory. Now once again pilgrims visit her image erected in a mediaeval chapel, where, it is said, they took off their shoes to walk barefoot the remaining mile to the shrine. . . . The road to the chapel is a quiet country lane shaded with trees, and lined on one side by a hedgerow. On the other, a stream flows beneath the trees, the water symbol of the Holy Spirit, 'the waters of Shiloah that go softly,' the 'flow of the river making glad the city of God.' Within the chapel, an attractive example of Decorated architecture, near an altar of medieval fashion, is seated Our Lady's image. It is too small for its canopy, and is not superficially beautiful. 'Non est species neque decor,' there is no comeliness or charm in that expressionless face with heavy eyelids. But let us look carefully. . . . We become aware of an inner beauty more impressive than outward grace. That expressionless countenance expresses what is beyond expression. . . . Mary is beyond joy and sorrow. . . . No longer the Mother of Sorrows nor yet of the human joy of the crib, she understands the secret counsel of God to whose accomplishment Calvary and Bethlehem alike ministered."
2. Or Zion. Cf. Isaiah 51.11: "Therefore the redeemed of the Lord shall return, and come with singing unto Zion."

Non est species, neque decor,
Expressionless, expresses God: it goes
Past castled Sion. She knows what God knows,
Not Calvary's Cross nor crib at Bethlehem
Now, and the world shall come to Walsingham.

VII

The empty winds are creaking and the oak
Splatters and splatters on the cenotaph,[3]
The boughs are trembling and a gaff
Bobs on the untimely stroke
Of the greased wash exploding on a shoal-bell[4]
In the old mouth of the Atlantic. It's well;
Atlantic, you are fouled with the blue sailors,
Sea-monsters, upward angel, downward fish:
Unmarried and corroding, spare of flesh
Mart once of supercilious, wing'd clippers,
Atlantic, where your bell-trap guts its spoil
You could cut the brackish winds with a knife
Here in Nantucket, and cast up the time
When the Lord God formed man from the sea's slime
And breathed into his face the breath of life,
And blue-lung'd combers lumbered to the kill.
The Lord survives the rainbow of His will.

1946

After the Surprising Conversions[5]

September twenty-second, Sir: today
I answer. In the latter part of May,
Hard on our Lord's Ascension, it began
To be more sensible.[6] A gentleman
Of more than common understanding, strict
In morals, pious in behavior, kicked
Against our goad. A man of some renown,
An useful, honored person in the town,
He came of melancholy parents; prone
To secret spells, for years they kept alone—
His uncle, I believe, was killed of it:
Good people, but of too much or little wit.
I preached one Sabbath on a text from Kings;
He showed concernment for his soul. Some things

3. Tomb for someone whose remains are elsewhere.
4. A bell buoy marking shallow waters.
5. Based on the "Faithful Narrative of the Surprising Work of God in the Conversion of Many Hundred Souls in Northampton" (1737), an account by the American preacher and theologian Jonathan Edwards (1703–1758) of the spectacular revival in 1734–35 of Christian faith in his Massachusetts parish. Lowell also uses earlier letters by Edwards describing the same phenomenon entitled "A Narrative of Surprising Conversions."
6. "It began to be very sensible [apparent] that the spirit of God was gradually withdrawing from us" (Edwards's letter of May 30, 1735. See lines 37–38).

In his experience were hopeful. He
Would sit and watch the wind knocking a tree
And praise this countryside our Lord has made.
Once when a poor man's heifer died, he laid
A shilling on the doorsill; though a thirst
For loving shook him like a snake, he durst
Not entertain much hope of his estate
In heaven. Once we saw him sitting late
Behind his attic window by a light
That guttered on his Bible; through that night
He meditated terror, and he seemed
Beyond advice or reason, for he dreamed
That he was called to trumpet Judgment Day
To Concord. In the latter part of May
He cut his throat.[7] And though the coroner
Judged him delirious, soon a noisome stir
Palsied our village. At Jehovah's nod
Satan seemed more let loose amongst us: God
Abandoned us to Satan, and he pressed
Us hard, until we thought we could not rest
Till we had done with life. Content was gone.
All the good work was quashed. We were undone.
The breath of God had carried out a planned
And sensible withdrawal from this land;
The multitude, once unconcerned with doubt,
Once neither callous, curious nor devout,
Jumped at broad noon, as though some peddler groaned
At it in its familiar twang: "My friend,
Cut your own throat. Cut your own throat. Now! Now!"
September twenty-second, Sir, the bough
Cracks with the unpicked apples, and at dawn
The small-mouth bass breaks water, gorged with spawn.

1946

Grandparents

They're altogether otherworldly now,
those adults champing for their ritual Friday spin
to pharmacist and five-and-ten in Brockton.[8]
Back in my throw-away and shaggy span
of adolescence, Grandpa still waves his stick
like a policeman;
Grandmother, like a Mohammedan,[9] still wears her thick

7. Edwards describes the suicide of his uncle Joseph Hawley, on June 1, 1735: "My Uncle Hawley, the last Sabbath morning, laid violent hands on himself, by cutting his own throat. He had been for a considerable time greatly concerned about the condition of his soul; by the ordering of Providence he was suffered to fall into a deep melancholy, a distemper that the family are very prone to; the devil took the advantage and drove him into despairing thoughts." This event caused a setback to the religious revival, as the remainder of Lowell's poem tells.
8. Just south of Boston.
9. Muslim.

lavender mourning and touring veil;
the Pierce Arrow clears its throat in a horse stall.
Then the dry road dust rises to whiten
the fatigued elm leaves—
the nineteenth century, tired of children, is gone.
They're all gone into a world of light;[1] the farm's my own.

The farm's my own!
Back there alone,
I keep indoors, and spoil another season.
I hear the rattly little country gramophone
racking its five foot horn:
"O Summer Time!"
Even at noon here the formidable
Ancien Régime[2] still keeps nature at a distance. Five
green shaded light bulbs spider the billiards-table;
no field is greener than its cloth,
where Grandpa, dipping sugar for us both,
once spilled his demitasse.[3]
His favorite ball, the number three,
still hides the coffee stain.
Never again
to walk there, chalk our cues,
insist on shooting for us both.
Grandpa! Have me, hold me, cherish me!
Tears smut my fingers. There
half my life-lease later,
I hold an *Illustrated London News*—;
disloyal still,
I doodle handlebar
mustaches on the last Russian Czar.

1959

Commander Lowell[4]

1887–1950

There were no undesirables or girls in my set,
when I was a boy at Mattapoisett[5]—
only Mother, still her Father's daughter.
Her voice was still electric
with a hysterical, unmarried panic,
when she read to me from the Napoleon book.[6]
Long-nosed Marie Louise
Hapsburg[7] in the frontispiece

1. Adapted from first line of poem by English religious poet Henry Vaughan (1621 or 1622–1695). *Pierce Arrow*: type of automobile.
2. Old rule (French); from the political system of France before the 1789 revolution.
3. Small cup of black coffee.
4. The poet's father.
5. Massachusetts resort town.
6. *Memoirs of Emperor Napoleon from Ajaccio to Waterloo*, by Laure Junot (1784–1838), duchess d'Abrantès.
7. Archduchess Marie-Louise (1791–1847), second wife of Napoleon Bonaparte (1769–1821).

had a downright Boston bashfulness,
where she groveled to Bonaparte, who scratched his navel,
and bolted his food—just my seven years tall!
And I, bristling and manic,
skulked in the attic,
and got two hundred French generals by name,
from *A* to *V*—from Augereau to Vandamme.[8]
I used to dope myself asleep,
naming those unpronounceables like sheep.

Having a naval officer
for my Father was nothing to shout
about to the summer colony at "Matt."
He wasn't at all "serious,"
when he showed up on the golf course,
wearing a blue serge jacket and numbly cut
white ducks[9] he'd bought
at a Pearl Harbor commissariat . . .
and took four shots with his putter to sink his putt.
"Bob," they said, "golf's a game you really ought to know how to play,
if you play at all."
They wrote him off as "naval,"
naturally supposed his sport was sailing.
Poor Father, his training was engineering!
Cheerful and cowed
among the seadogs at the Sunday yacht club,
he was never one of the crowd.

"Anchors aweigh," Daddy boomed in his bathtub,
"Anchors aweigh,"
when Lever Brothers[1] offered to pay
him double what the Navy paid.
I nagged for his dress sword with gold braid,
and cringed because Mother, new
caps on all her teeth, was born anew
at forty. With seamanlike celerity,
Father left the Navy,
and deeded Mother his property.

He was soon fired. Year after year,
he still hummed "Anchors aweigh" in the tub—
whenever he left a job,
he bought a smarter car.
Father's last employer
was Scudder, Stevens and Clark, Investment Advisors,
himself his only client.
While Mother dragged to bed alone,
read Menninger,[2]

8. Military officers under Napoleon.
9. Trousers.
1. Soap manufacturers.
2. Karl Augustus Menninger (1893–1990), American psychiatrist.

and grew more and more suspicious,
he grew defiant.
Night after night,
à la clarté déserte de sa lampe,[3]
he slid his ivory Annapolis slide rule
across a pad of graphs—
piker[4] speculations! In three years
he squandered sixty thousand dollars.

Smiling on all,
Father was once successful enough to be lost
in the mob of ruling-class Bostonians.
As early as 1928,
he owned a house converted to oil,[5]
and redecorated by the architect
of St. Mark's School[6] . . . Its main effect
was a drawing room, "longitudinal as Versailles,[7]"
its ceiling, roughened with oatmeal, was blue as the sea.
And once
nineteen, the youngest ensign in his class,
he was "the old man" of a gunboat on the Yangtze.[8]

1959

Waking in the Blue

The night attendant, a B.U.[9] sophomore,
rouses from the mare's-nest of his drowsy head
propped on *The Meaning of Meaning.*[1]
He catwalks down our corridor.
Azure day
makes my agonized blue window bleaker.
Crows maunder on the petrified fairway.
Absence! My heart grows tense
as though a harpoon were sparring for the kill.
(This is the house for the "mentally ill.")

What use is my sense of humor?
I grin at Stanley, now sunk in his sixties,
once a Harvard all-American fullback
(if such were possible!),
still hoarding the build of a boy in his twenties,
as he soaks, a ramrod
with the muscle of a seal
in his long tub,

3. By the empty brilliance of his lamp (French); from "Brise Marine," by French poet Stéphane Mallarmé (1842–1898).
4. Cheap gambler.
5. That is, updated to have oil heating.
6. Massachusetts boarding school.
7. Palace built for Louis XII and XIV, southwest of Paris.
8. Chinese river.
9. Boston University.
1. Philosophical work (1923) by C. K. Ogden and I. A. Richards.

vaguely urinous from the Victorian plumbing.
A kingly granite profile in a crimson golf cap,
worn all day, all night,
he thinks only of his figure,
of slimming on sherbet and ginger ale—
more cut off from words than a seal.

This is the way day breaks in Bowditch Hall at McLean's;[2]
the hooded night lights bring out "Bobbie,"
Porcellian[3] '29
a replica of Louis XVI[4]
without the wig—
redolent and roly-poly as a sperm whale,
as he swashbuckles about in his birthday suit
and horses at chairs.
These victorious figures of bravado ossified young.

In between the limits of day,
hours and hours go by under the crew haircuts
and slightly too little nonsensical bachelor twinkle
of the Roman Catholic attendants.
(There are no Mayflower
screwballs in the Catholic Church.)

After a hearty New England breakfast,
I weigh two hundred pounds
this morning. Cock of the walk,
I strut in my turtle-necked French sailor's jersey
before the metal shaving mirrors,
and see the shaky future grow familiar
in the pinched, indigenous faces
of these thoroughbred mental cases,
twice my age and half my weight.
We are all old-timers,
each of us holds a locked razor.

1959

Memories of West Street and Lepke[5]

Only teaching on Tuesdays, book-worming
in pajamas fresh from the washer each morning,
I hog a whole house on Boston's
"hardly passionate Marlborough Street,"[6]
where even the man

2. McLean Hospital, outside Boston.
3. Exclusive club at Harvard University.
4. French king (1754–1793).
5. In 1943, Lowell was sentenced to a year in New York's West Street jail for his refusal to serve in the army. Among the other prisoners was Lepke Buchalter, head of Murder, Inc., an organized crime syndicate, who had been convicted of murder.
6. William James's phrase for a street in the elegant Back Bay section of Boston, where Lowell lived in the 1950s.

scavenging filth in the back alley trash cans,
has two children, a beach wagon, a helpmate,
and is a "young Republican."
I have a nine months' daughter,
young enough to be my granddaughter.
Like the sun she rises in her flame-flamingo infants' wear.

These are the tranquillized *Fifties,*
and I am forty. Ought I to regret my seedtime?
I was a fire-breathing Catholic C.O.,[7]
and made my manic statement,
telling off the state and president, and then
sat waiting sentence in the bull pen
beside a Negro boy with curlicues
of marijuana in his hair.

Given a year,
I walked on the roof of the West Street Jail, a short
enclosure like my school soccer court,
and saw the Hudson River once a day
through sooty clothesline entanglements
and bleaching khaki tenements.
Strolling, I yammered metaphysics with Abramowitz,
a jaundice-yellow ("it's really tan")
and fly-weight pacifist,
so vegetarian,
he wore rope shoes and preferred fallen fruit.
He tried to convert Bioff and Brown,
the Hollywood pimps, to his diet.
Hairy, muscular, suburban,
wearing chocolate double-breasted suits,
they blew their tops and beat him black and blue.

I was so out of things, I'd never heard
of the Jehovah's Witnesses.[8]
"Are you a C.O.?" I asked a fellow jailbird.
"No," he answered, "I'm a J.W."
He taught me the "hospital tuck,"[9]
and pointed out the T-shirted back
of *Murder Incorporated's* Czar Lepke,
there piling towels on a rack,
or dawdling off to his little segregated cell full
of things forbidden the common man:
a portable radio, a dresser, two toy American
flags tied together with a ribbon of Easter palm.
Flabby, bald, lobotomized,
he drifted in a sheepish calm,
where no agonizing reappraisal

7. Conscientious objector (to war).
8. Christian evangelist sect that opposes war and forbids its members to have any secular political involvement.
9. Standard way of making beds in a hospital.

jarred his concentration on the electric chair—
hanging like an oasis in his air
of lost connections. . . .

1959

"To Speak of Woe That Is in Marriage"[1]

"It is the future generation that presses into being by means of these exuberant feelings and supersensible soap bubbles of ours."
—Schopenhauer[2]

"The hot night makes us keep our bedroom windows open.
Our magnolia blossoms. Life begins to happen.
My hopped up husband drops his home disputes,
and hits the streets to cruise for prostitutes,
free-lancing out along the razor's edge.
This screwball might kill his wife, then take the pledge.
Oh the monotonous meanness of his lust. . . .
It's the injustice . . . he is so unjust—
whiskey-blind, swaggering home at five.
My only thought is how to keep alive.
What makes him tick? Each night now I tie
ten dollars and his car key to my thigh. . . .
Gored by the climacteric of his want,
he stalls above me like an elephant."

1959

Skunk Hour[3]

(For Elizabeth Bishop)[4]

Nautilus Island's hermit
heiress still lives through winter in her Spartan cottage;
her sheep still graze above the sea.
Her son's a bishop. Her farmer
is first selectman in our village;
she's in her dotage.

1. In *The Canterbury Tales,* by Geoffrey Chaucer (1340?–1400), the Wife of Bath begins to tell of her several marriages with this line.
2. Arthur Schopenhauer (1788–1860), pessimistic German philosopher.
3. The scene is Castine, Maine, where Lowell had a summer house. As he writes, "The first four stanzas are meant to give a dawdling more or less amiable picture of a declining Maine sea town. I move from the ocean inland. Sterility howls through the scenery, but I try to give a tone of tolerance, humor, and randomness to the sad prospect" (*The Contemporary Poet as Artist and Critic,* ed. Anthony Ostroff).
4. "The dedication is to Elizabeth Bishop, because re-reading her suggested a way of breaking through the shell of my old manner. . . . 'Skunk Hour' is modelled on Miss Bishop's 'The Armadillo.' . . . Both . . . use short line stanzas, start with drifting description and end with a single animal" [Lowell's note].

Thirsting for
the hierarchic privacy
of Queen Victoria's century,
she buys up all
the eyesores facing her shore,
and lets them fall.

The season's ill—
we've lost our summer millionaire,
who seemed to leap from an L. L. Bean
catalogue. His nine-knot yawl
was auctioned off to lobstermen.
A red fox stain covers Blue Hill.[5]

And now our fairy
decorator brightens his shop for fall;
his fishnet's filled with orange cork,
orange, his cobbler's bench and awl;
there is no money in his work,
he'd rather marry.

One dark night,[6]
my Tudor Ford climbed the hill's skull;
I watched for love-cars. Lights turned down,
they lay together, hull to hull,
where the graveyard shelves on the town. . . .
My mind's not right.

A car radio bleats,
"Love, O careless Love. . . ."[7] I hear
my ill-spirit sob in each blood cell,
as if my hand were at its throat. . . .
I myself am hell;[8]
nobody's here—

only skunks, that search
in the moonlight for a bite to eat.
They march on their soles up Main Street:
white stripes, moonstruck eyes' red fire
under the chalk-dry and spar spire
of the Trinitarian Church.

I stand on top
of our back steps and breathe the rich air—
a mother skunk with her column of kittens swills the garbage pail.
She jabs her wedge-head in a cup

5. "Meant to describe the rusty reddish color of autumn on Blue Hill, a Maine mountain near where we were living" [Lowell's note].
6. A reference, Lowell said, to *The Dark Night of the Soul* of St. John of the Cross.
7. A popular song of the time, "Careless Love," contains the lines "Now you see what careless love will do . . . / Make you kill yourself and your sweetheart too."
8. An adaption of Lucifer's line from Milton's *Paradise Lost* 4.75: "Which way I fly is Hell; myself am Hell."

of sour cream, drops her ostrich tail,
and will not scare.[9]

1959

For the Union Dead[1]

"Relinquunt Omnia Servare Rem Publicam."[2]

The old South Boston Aquarium stands
in a Sahara of snow now. Its broken windows are boarded.
The bronze weathervane cod has lost half its scales.
The airy tanks are dry.

Once my nose crawled like a snail on the glass;
my hand tingled
to burst the bubbles
drifting from the noses of the cowed, compliant fish.

My hand draws back. I often sigh still
for the dark downward and vegetating kingdom
of the fish and reptile. One morning last March,
I pressed against the new barbed and galvanized

fence on the Boston Common. Behind their cage,
yellow dinosaur steamshovels were grunting
as they cropped up tons of mush and grass
to gouge their underworld garage.

Parking spaces luxuriate like civic
sandpiles in the heart of Boston.
A girdle of orange, Puritan-pumpkin colored girders
braces the tingling Statehouse,

shaking over the excavations, as it faces Colonel Shaw
and his bell-cheeked Negro infantry
on St. Gaudens' shaking Civil War relief,
propped by a plank splint against the garage's earthquake.

Two months after marching through Boston,
half the regiment was dead;
at the dedication,
William James[3] could almost hear the bronze Negroes breathe.

9. "The skunks," according to Lowell, "are both quixotic and barbarously absurd, hence the tone of amusement and defiance."

1. First published with the title "Colonel Shaw and the Massachusetts 54th." The monument it describes is a bronze relief by Augustus Saint-Gaudens (1848–1907) depicting Robert Gould Shaw (1837–1863), commander of the first African American regiment organized in a free state, who was killed in the assault his troops led against Fort Wagner, South Carolina. The relief, dedicated in 1897, stands on Boston Common opposite the Massachusetts State House.

2. They give up everything to serve the Republic (Latin); slightly modified from the relief, which reads, "He gives up. . . ."

3. American philosopher and psychologist (1842–1910), who taught at Harvard.

Their monument sticks like a fishbone
in the city's throat.
Its Colonel is as lean
as a compass-needle.

He has an angry wrenlike vigilance,
a greyhound's gentle tautness;
he seems to wince at pleasure,
and suffocate for privacy.

He is out of bounds now. He rejoices in man's lovely,
peculiar power to choose life and die—
when he leads his black soldiers to death,
he cannot bend his back.

On a thousand small town New England greens,
the old white churches hold their air
of sparse, sincere rebellion; frayed flags
quilt the graveyards of the Grand Army of the Republic.

The stone statues of the abstract Union Soldier
grow slimmer and younger each year—
wasp-waisted, they doze over muskets
and muse through their sideburns . . .

Shaw's father wanted no monument
except the ditch,
where his son's body was thrown[4]
and lost with his "niggers."

The ditch is nearer.
There are no statues for the last war[5] here;
on Boylston Street,[6] a commercial photograph
shows Hiroshima boiling

over a Mosler Safe, the "Rock of Ages"
that survived the blast. Space is nearer.
When I crouch to my television set,
the drained faces of Negro school-children rise like balloons.

Colonel Shaw
is riding on his bubble,
he waits
for the blessèd break.

The Aquarium is gone. Everywhere,
giant finned cars nose forward like fish;
a savage servility
slides by on grease.

1959

4. By the Confederate soldiers at Fort Wagner.
5. That is, World War II.
6. In downtown Boston

Waking Early Sunday Morning

O to break loose, like the chinook
salmon jumping and falling back,
nosing up to the impossible
stone and bone-crushing waterfall—
raw-jawed, weak-fleshed there, stopped by ten
steps of the roaring ladder, and then
to clear the top on the last try,
alive enough to spawn and die.

Stop, back off. The salmon breaks
water, and now my body wakes
to feel the unpolluted joy
and criminal leisure of a boy—
no rainbow smashing a dry fly
in the white run is free as I,
here squatting like a dragon on
time's hoard before the day's begun!

Vermin run for their unstopped holes;
in some dark nook a fieldmouse rolls
a marble, hours on end, then stops;
the termite in the woodwork sleeps—
listen, the creatures of the night
obsessive, casual, sure of foot,
go on grinding, while the sun's
daily remorseful blackout dawns.

Fierce, fireless mind, running downhill.
Look up and see the harbor fill:
business as usual in eclipse
goes down to the sea in ships—
wake of refuse, dacron rope,
bound for Bermuda or Good Hope,
all bright before the morning watch
the wine-dark hulls of yawl and ketch.[7]

I watched a glass of water wet
with a fine fuzz of icy sweat,
silvery colors touched with sky,
serene in their neutrality—
yet if I shift, or change my mood,
I see some object made of wood,
background behind it of brown grain,
to darken it, but not to stain.

O that the spirit could remain
tinged but untarnished by its strain!

7. Types of boats. *Wine-dark:* epithet for the sea in Homer's *Odyssey.*

Better dressed and stacking birch,
or lost with the Faithful at Church—
anywhere, but somewhere else!
And now the new electric bells,
clearly chiming, "Faith of our fathers,"[8]
and now the congregation gathers.

O Bible chopped and crucified
in hymns we hear but do not read,
none of the milder subtleties
of grace or art will sweeten these
stiff quatrains shoveled out four-square—
they sing of peace, and preach despair;
yet they gave darkness some control,
and left a loophole for the soul.

No, put old clothes on, and explore
the corners of the woodshed for
its dregs and dreck: tools with no handle,
ten candle-ends not worth a candle,
old lumber banished from the Temple,
damned by Paul's precept and example,
cast from the kingdom, banned in Israel,
the wordless sign, the tinkling cymbal.

When will we see Him face to face?
Each day, He shines through darker glass.
In this small town where everything
is known, I see His vanishing
emblems, His white spire and flag-
pole sticking out above the fog,
like old white china doorknobs, sad,
slight, useless things to calm the mad.

Hammering military splendor,
top-heavy Goliath in full armor—
little redemption in the mass
liquidations of their brass,
elephant and phalanx moving
with the times and still improving,
when that kingdom hit the crash:
a million foreskins stacked like trash[9] . . .

Sing softer! But what if a new
diminuendo[1] brings no true
tenderness, only restlessness,
excess, the hunger for success,
sanity of self-deception

8. Protestant hymn.
9. 1 Samuel 17–18 describes David's early military exploits, such as defeating the giant Goliath and bringing back the foreskins of hundreds of defeated Philistine soldiers.
1. Gradual decrease in volume (musical instruction in Italian).

fixed and kicked by reckless caution,
while we listen to the bells—
anywhere, but somewhere else!

O to break loose. All life's grandeur
is something with a girl in summer . . .
elated as the President
girdled by his establishment
this Sunday morning, free to chaff
his own thoughts with his bear-cuffed staff,
swimming nude, unbuttoned, sick
of his ghost-written rhetoric!

No weekends for the gods now. Wars
flicker, earth licks its open sores,
fresh breakage, fresh promotions, chance
assassinations, no advance.
Only man thinning out his kind
sounds through the Sabbath noon, the blind
swipe of the pruner and his knife
busy about the tree of life . . .

Pity the planet, all joy gone
from this sweet volcanic cone;
peace to our children when they fall
in small war on the heels of small
war—until the end of time
to police the earth, a ghost
orbiting forever lost
in our monotonous sublime.

1967

Reading Myself

Like thousands, I took just pride and more than just,
struck matches that brought my blood to a boil;
I memorized the tricks to set the river on fire—
somehow never wrote something to go back to.
Can I suppose I am finished with wax flowers
and have earned my grass on the minor slopes of Parnassus.[2] . . .
No honeycomb is built without a bee
adding circle to circle, cell to cell,
the wax and honey of a mausoleum—
this round dome proves its maker is alive;
the corpse of the insect lives embalmed in honey,
prays that its perishable work live long

2. Greek mountain sacred to Apollo and the Muses.

enough for the sweet-tooth bear to desecrate—
this open book . . . my open coffin.

1973

Dolphin

My Dolphin,[3] you only guide me by surprise,
captive as Racine, the man of craft,
drawn through his maze of iron composition
by the incomparable wandering voice of Phèdre.[4]
When I was troubled in mind, you made for my body
caught in its hangman's-knot of sinking lines,
the glassy bowing and scraping of my will. . . .
I have sat and listened to too many
words of the collaborating muse,
and plotted perhaps too freely with my life,
not avoiding injury to others,
not avoiding injury to myself—
to ask compassion . . . this book, half fiction,
an eelnet made by man for the eel fighting—

my eyes have seen what my hand did.

1973

Epilogue[5]

Those blessèd structures, plot and rhyme—
why are they no help to me now
I want to make
something imagined, not recalled?
I hear the noise of my own voice:
The painter's vision is not a lens,
it trembles to caress the light.
But sometimes everything I write
with the threadbare art of my eye
seems a snapshot,
lurid, rapid, garish, grouped,
heightened from life,
yet paralyzed by fact.
All's misalliance.
Yet why not say what happened?
Pray for the grace of accuracy

3. According to legend, the dolphin saves drowning sailors. Lowell called his third wife, Caroline Blackwood, his "dolphin," saying that she had saved his life.
4. Heroine of 1677 tragedy by French dramatist Jean Racine (1639–1699), a play Lowell translated in 1961.
5. The last poem (excluding a few translations) in Lowell's final book, *Day by Day* (1977).

Vermeer[6] gave to the sun's illumination
stealing like the tide across a map
to his girl solid with yearning.
We are poor passing facts,
warned by that to give
each figure in the photograph
his living name.

1977

6. Jan Vermeer (1632–1675), Dutch painter noted for his subtle handling of the effects of light.

Gwendolyn Brooks
1917–2000

Gwendolyn Brooks is perhaps best known for the poem "We Real Cool," memorable for its depiction of young, black, urban men and its skillful use of syncopated rhythms, enjambment, alliteration, rhyme, caesura, ellipsis, and tonal complexity. Much of her best work is in compressed short poems that display both formal mastery and keen social insight. The central subject of her verse is the black inner city. Like Edgar Lee Masters (another Illinois poet) in *Spoon River Anthology,* Brooks often presents the "characters" of local people, whether the preacher or the gangster, the dreamy young girl or the madam of a brothel. Her miniaturized narratives reveal a life story in a few quick strokes.

Brooks learned the hard discipline of compression from two sources. The modernists famously demanded that superfluities be eliminated, that every word be made to count (*le mot juste*), and this seems to have been the guiding principle of the Chicago poetry workshop she attended in the early 1940s, in which she read T. S. Eliot, Ezra Pound, and E. E. Cummings. Brooks also learned this lesson from the spare, hard, stripped-down idiom of the blues, which Langston Hughes urged her to study. Like the authors of the blues, she uses insistent rhymes and terse simplicity, and she can be at once understated and robust. Despite Brook's reputation for directness, her poetry, like the blues and other African American oral traditions, evinces a sly and ironic indirection.

In presenting her vivid characters, Brooks knows what to put into her poems and what to keep out. Her laconic but exuberant poems reflect the mixture of irreverence and control she portrays in her character Annie Allen, a girl who, pleased to be "rid" of a "relative beneath the coffin lid," instead of affecting solemnity when no one is near, "stuck her tongue out; slid" ("old relative"). Eliding pronouns and articles, suspending the verb "slid" at the end of the line, Brooks says more by saying less. Even when responding to emotionally and politically violent events, Brooks practices restraint. In "The Last Quatrain of the Ballad of Emmett Till," written after the fourteen-year-old was murdered, in 1955, for whistling at a white woman, Brooks holds back from venting grief directly. She locates it instead in the violent, unresolved tensions between tightly woven oppositions of color ("red," "black"), size ("red room," "red prairie,"), and feeling ("kisses," "killed"). "And she is sorry," Brooks writes of the mother's searing grief and rage. Here, as elsewhere, Brooks mixes colloquial black speech ("a pretty-faced thing," "black coffee") with high poetic discourse ("Chaos in windy grays"). Brooks dexterously moves among various rhetorical registers and forms: her poems range from the formal to the vernacular, from ballads and perfectly rhymed sonnets (especially early in her career) to what she called, at Chapman College, the "wild, raw, ragged free verse" of her later work.

Determined to represent the everyday lives of African American city dwellers, especially women, Brooks lights up the most ordinary details with a sudden rhythm, passionate observation, or exciting refrain. As she says in "A Street in Bronzeville," she would like to have "a dream send up through onion fumes / Its white and violet, fight with fried potatoes / And yesterday's garbage ripening in the hall." She prefers wild girls to safe ones ("Sadie and Maud") and endorses all that is "luminously indiscreet" ("The Sermon on the Warpland"). She seems to agree with the title character of "Big Bessie Throws Her Son into the Street": "Hunt out your own or make your own alone. / Go down the street." She is for gumption, for independence of spirit, not for compromise.

In 1967, Brooks had an experience that changed the temper of her poetry. Attending the Second Fisk University Black Writers' Conference, she met some of the younger poets espousing a new black cultural nationalism, notably Amiri Baraka (then LeRoi Jones). Brooks felt she had awakened "in some inscrutable and uncomfortable wonderland." She was later to write: "Until 1967 my own blackness did not confront me with a shrill spelling of itself" (*Report from Part One*). On her return to Chicago, she organized a poetry workshop for young African Americans, including a teenage gang called the Blackstone Rangers. She assisted in community programs and tirelessly worked to inspire younger black poets.

Brooks was born on June 17, 1917, in Topeka, Kansas, but she grew up in Chicago, was educated at Englewood High School and Wilson Junior College there, and identified herself with that city. After her graduation in 1936, she worked for a quack "spiritual advisor" who sold potions and charms to the needy, her job being to write hundreds of letters to prospective patients. Her office was in the Mecca Building on South State Street, where many poor families and derelicts lived. At the end of what she said was the worst period of her life, Brooks refused to take on the duties of "Assistant Pastor" and was honorably fired. Her book *In the Mecca* (1968) draws much of its material from this experience.

Attending a poetry workshop at the South Side Community Art Center, Brooks displayed extraordinary talent. She won contests sponsored by *Poetry* magazine and various organizations and was able to publish her first book in 1945. In 1950, she became the first African American writer to win the Pulitzer Prize, awarded for her book *Annie Allen.* She was appointed poet laureate of Illinois, a post in which she succeeded Carl Sandburg. She traveled in East Africa and in the former Soviet Union. At sixty-eight, she became the first African American woman to be appointed poetry consultant to the Library of Congress. Of her awards, perhaps the most agreeable to the poet was the 1981 dedication of the Gwendolyn Brooks Junior High School in Harvey, Illinois. She was married to Henry Blakely and had a son and a daughter.

A Song in the Front Yard

I've stayed in the front yard all my life.
I want to peek at the back
Where it's rough and untended and hungry weed grows.
A girl gets sick of a rose.

I want to go in the back yard now
And maybe down the alley,

To where the charity children play.
I want a good time today.

They do some wonderful things.
They have some wonderful fun.
My mother sneers, but I say it's fine
How they don't have to go in at quarter to nine.
My mother, she tells me that Johnnie Mae
Will grow up to be a bad woman.
That George'll be taken to Jail soon or late
(On account of last winter he sold our back gate).

But I say it's fine. Honest, I do.
And I'd like to be a bad woman, too,
And wear the brave stockings of night-black lace
And strut down the streets with paint on my face.

1945

Sadie and Maud

Maud went to college.
Sadie stayed at home.
Sadie scraped life
With a fine-tooth comb.

She didn't leave a tangle in.
Her comb found every strand.
Sadie was one of the livingest chits
In all the land.

Sadie bore two babies
Under her maiden name.
Maud and Ma and Papa
Nearly died of shame.
Every one but Sadie
Nearly died of shame.

When Sadie said her last so-long
Her girls struck out from home.
(Sadie had left as heritage
Her fine-tooth comb.)

Maud, who went to college,
Is a thin brown mouse.
She is living all alone
In this old house.

1945

Of De Witt Williams on His Way to Lincoln Cemetery[1]

He was born in Alabama.
He was bred in Illinois.
He was nothing but a
Plain black boy.

Swing low swing low sweet sweet chariot.[2]
Nothing but a plain black boy.

Drive him past the Pool Hall.
Drive him past the Show.
Blind within his casket,
But maybe he will know.

Down through Forty-seventh Street:[3]
Underneath the L,[4]
And—Northwest Corner, Prairie,
That he loved so well.

Don't forget the Dance Halls—
Warwick and Savoy,
Where he picked his women, where
He drank his liquid joy.

Born in Alabama.
Bred in Illinois.
He was nothing but a
Plain black boy.

Swing low swing low sweet sweet chariot.
Nothing but a plain black boy.

1945

The Vacant Lot

Mrs. Coley's three-flat brick
Isn't here any more.
All done with seeing her fat little form
Burst out of the basement door;
And with seeing her African son-in-law
(Rightful heir to the throne)
With his great white strong cold squares of teeth
And his little eyes of stone;
And with seeing the squat fat daughter

1. African American cemetery in Chicago.
2. A line from a spiritual.
3. The main street of Bronzeville, Chicago's black ghetto.
4. Elevated railway.

Letting in the men
When majesty has gone for the day—
And letting them out again.

1945

The Rites for Cousin Vit

Carried her unprotesting out the door.
Kicked back the casket-stand. But it can't hold her,
That stuff and satin aiming to enfold her,
The lid's contrition nor the bolts before.
Oh oh. Too much. Too much. Even now, surmise,
She rises in the sunshine. There she goes,
Back to the bars she knew and the repose
In love-rooms and the things in people's eyes.
Too vital and too squeaking. Must emerge.
Even now she does the snake-hips with a hiss,
Slops the bad wine across her shantung,[5] talks
Of pregnancy, guitars and bridgework, walks
In parks or alleys, comes haply on the verge
Of happiness, haply hysterics. Is.

1949

The Bean Eaters

They eat beans mostly, this old yellow pair.
Dinner is a casual affair.
Plain chipware on a plain and creaking wood,
Tin flatware.

Two who are Mostly Good.
Two who have lived their day,
But keep on putting on their clothes
And putting things away.

And remembering . . .
Remembering, with twinklings and twinges,
As they lean over the beans in their rented back room that is full of beads
and receipts and dolls and cloths, tobacco crumbs, vases and fringes.

1960

5. Fabric with irregular surface.

We Real Cool

THE POOL PLAYERS.
SEVEN AT THE GOLDEN SHOVEL.

We real cool. We
Left school. We

Lurk late. We
Strike straight. We

Sing sin. We
Thin gin. We

Jazz June. We
Die soon.

1960

The Last Quatrain of the Ballad of Emmett Till[6]

AFTER THE MURDER,
AFTER THE BURIAL

Emmett's mother is a pretty-faced thing;
    the tint of pulled taffy.
She sits in a red room,
    drinking black coffee.
She kisses her killed boy.
    And she is sorry.
Chaos in windy grays
    through a red prairie.

1960

Boy Breaking Glass

To Marc Crawford[7]
from whom the commission

Whose broken window is a cry of art
(success, that winks aware
as elegance, as a treasonable faith)
is raw: is sonic: is old-eyed première.

6. Fourteen-year-old African American murdered in Mississippi, in 1955, for whistling at a white woman.

7. The writer and editor who suggested Brooks write a poem on the survival of inner-city African Americans.

Our beautiful flaw and terrible ornament.
Our barbarous and metal little man.

"I shall create! If not a note, a hole.
If not an overture, a desecration."

Full of pepper and light
and Salt and night and cargoes.

"Don't go down the plank
if you see there's no extension.
Each to his grief, each to
his loneliness and fidgety revenge.

Nobody knew where I was and now I am no longer there."

The only sanity is a cup of tea.
The music is in minors.

Each one other
is having different weather.

"It was you, it was you who threw away my name!
And this is everything I have for me."

Who has not Congress, lobster, love, luau,
the Regency Room, the Statue of Liberty,
runs. A sloppy amalgamation.
A mistake.
A cliff.
A hymn, a snare, and an exceeding sun.

1968

The Blackstone Rangers[8]

I
As Seen by Disciplines[9]

There they are.
Thirty at the corner.
Black, raw, ready.
Sores in the city
that do not want to heal.

8. A tough Chicago street gang. Blackstone Street is the eastern boundary of Chicago's black ghetto.
9. That is, law enforcers. "Vexed by some who misread this first section as her own condemnation, Brooks insists that, in any reprinting, the entire poem be published as a unit" (D. H. Melhem, *Gwendolyn Brooks: Poetry and the Heroic Voice*, 1987).

II
The Leaders

Jeff. Gene. Geronimo. And Bop.[1]
They cancel, cure and curry.
Hardly the dupes of the downtown thing
the cold bonbon,
the rhinestone thing. And hardly
in a hurry.
Hardly Belafonte, King,
Black Jesus, Stokely, Malcolm X or Rap.[2]
Bungled trophies.
Their country is a Nation on no map.

Jeff, Gene, Geronimo and Bop
in the passionate noon,
in bewitching night
are the detailed men, the copious men.
They curry, cure,
they cancel, cancelled images whose Concerts
are not divine, vivacious; the different tins
are intense last entries; pagan argument;
translations of the night.

The Blackstone bitter bureaus
(bureaucracy is footloose) edit, fuse
unfashionable damnations and descent;
and exulting, monstrous hand on monstrous hand,
construct, strangely, a monstrous pearl or grace.

III
Gang Girls

A RANGERETTE

Gang Girls are sweet exotics.
Mary Ann
uses the nutrients of her orient,
but sometimes sighs for Cities of blue and jewel
beyond her Ranger rim of Cottage Grove.[3]
(Bowery Boys, Disciplines, Whip-Birds will
dissolve no margins, stop no savory sanctities.)

Mary is
a rose in a whiskey glass.

1. Kind of jazz. *Geronimo*: Apache Indian chief who led raids against the whites in Arizona.
2. H. Rap Brown (b. 1943): black nationalist leader. Harry Belafonte (b. 1927): American singer and activist. Martin Luther King (1929–1968): American civil rights leader. Stokely Carmichael (1941–1998): black nationalist leader. Malcolm X (1925–1965): black nationalist leader.
3. Street of overcrowded tenements in the black ghetto.

Mary's
Februaries shudder and are gone. Aprils
fret frankly, lilac hurries on.
Summer is a hard irregular ridge.
October looks away.
And that's the Year!
          Save for her bugle-love.
Save for the bleat of not-obese devotion.
Save for Somebody Terribly Dying, under
the philanthropy of robins. Save for her Ranger
bringing
man amount of rainbow in a string-drawn bag.
"Where did you get the diamond?" Do not ask:
but swallow, straight, the spirals of his flask
and assist him at your zipper; pet his lips
and help him clutch you.

Love's another departure.
Will there be any arrivals, confirmations?
Will there be gleaning?

Mary, the Shakedancer's child
from the rooming-flat, pants carefully, peers at
her laboring lover. . . .
          Mary! Mary Ann!
Settle for sandwiches! settle for stocking caps!
for sudden blood, aborted carnival,
the props and niceties of non-loneliness—
the rhymes of Leaning.

1968

The Boy Died in My Alley[4]

Without my having known.
Policeman said, next morning,
"Apparently died Alone."
"You heard a shot?" Policeman said.
Shots I hear and Shots I hear.
I never see the dead.

The Shot that killed him yes I heard
as I heard the Thousand shots before;
careening tinnily down the nights
across my years and arteries.

4. Brooks said the poem fuses two separate incidents involving an honors student, Kenneth Alexander, killed running from a policeman, and a boy Brooks saw running in Ghana in 1974.

Policeman pounded on my door.
"Who is it?" "POLICE!" Policeman yelled.
"A Boy was dying in your alley.
A Boy is dead, and in your alley.
And have you known this Boy before?"

I have known this Boy before.
I have known this Boy before, who
ornaments my alley.
I never saw his face at all.
I never saw his futurefall.
But I have known this Boy.

I have always heard him deal with death.
I have always heard the shout, the volley.
I have closed my heart-ears late and early.
And I have killed him ever.

I joined the Wild and killed him
with knowledgeable unknowing.
I saw where he was going.
I saw him Crossed. And seeing,
I did not take him down.

He cried not only "Father!"
but "Mother!
Sister!
Brother."
The cry climbed up the alley.
It went up to the wind.
It hung upon the heaven
for a long
stretch-strain of Moment.

The red floor of my alley
is a special speech to me.

1973, 1981

Robert Duncan
1919–1988

Among the diverse writers associated with Charles Olson at Black Mountain College, in North Carolina, Robert Creeley and Denise Levertov developed their art in sudden, short-lived lyrical insights, but Robert Duncan developed a mystical aesthetic. Olson did not meet him until 1947, but at once praised him as "a beautiful poet," with "ancient, permanent wings of Eros—& of Orphism." Much of Olson's reading was in the sciences, but Duncan was primarily interested in metaphysics, or rather, in philosophy and poetry that implied or recognized a "secret doctrine." He was erudite in this literature, unlike Creeley or Levertov, and became an exponent of it in prose as well as in verse. With Kenneth Rexroth, Duncan helped make the San Francisco Bay area a major center of poetic activity in the United States.

Duncan considered himself a wanderer, both in geographical terms and in "areas of being" (*The Years as Catches*). Born on January 7, 1919, in Oakland, California, to a mother who died in childbirth and a father who was a day laborer, he was adopted at six months by a family named Symmes; his early poetry was signed with that name. His adoptive family adhered to theosophy and other occult beliefs that would influence his visionary poetics. His homosexuality was also important in his life and in his work. Of it, he wrote: "Perhaps the sexual irregularity underlay and led to the poetic; neither as homosexual nor as poet could one take over readily the accepted paradigms of the Protestant ethic" (*The Years as Catches*). He dropped out of the University of California at Berkeley during his sophomore year, to follow a lover east. Subsequently, he spent some time in the army but, in 1941, was granted a psychiatric discharge because of his homosexuality. Editing various magazines, he taught sporadically at universities, notably Berkeley from 1948 to 1950 and with Olson at Black Mountain College in 1956.

In his early period, Duncan eagerly embraced the influences of many poets in the Romantic tradition. Under the sway of Walt Whitman, H. D., and "demi-surrealists" such as Dylan Thomas, Duncan considered poetry a mode of rhetoric, as far-reaching as possible. At the end of "The Years as Catches," he pronounced his mature intention: "Catch from the years the line of joy, / impatient & repeated day, / my heart, break, Eye / break open and set free / His world, my ecstasy." He sought a dithyrambic verse and learned a good deal not only from poetic visionaries, but also from the discontinuous and unportentous verse of William Carlos Williams and Ezra Pound. He regarded himself, however, as an isolated writer until he read Denise Levertov's "The Shifting" in 1952, Robert Creeley's "The Gold Diggers" in 1954, and Olson's *Maximus Poems* in the 1950s.

For Duncan, poetry was ultimately magical. "Every moment of life is an attempt to come to life," he said (*The New American Poetry*, ed. Donald M. Allen, 1960). His collage-based, syncretic poetry is a melee of reading and mother wit, adulthood and childishness, all "higglety-pigglety." He learned from one of his teachers to regard "poetry not as a cultural commodity or an exercise to improve sensibility, but as a vital process of the spirit" (*New American Poetry*). The making of a poem is the exercise of his "faculties at large," which some achieve by making war or love. In this making, as he learned from another teacher, "to form is to transform." This transformation meant the discovery of "an immediate correspondence between inner being and outer world, a metaphysical aura, that remains for me the sign of the poem." The pursuit of this multitudinous radiance is his quest in his poems, but it is also their subject.

In the 1960s, Duncan was outraged by the Vietnam War and began to introduce political events into his work. His method was based on William Blake's Prophetic

Books; like Blake writing about the French Revolution or about battles in the mind, Duncan wrote of President Lyndon Johnson, in "Up Rising, Passages 25": "Now Johnson would go up to join the great simulacra of men, / Hitler and Stalin, to work his fame / with planes roaring out from Guam over Asia." Johnson becomes, like Blake's Urizen, an antipoetic principle of mythical proportions. Duncan carries this difficult maneuver off with considerable adroitness. During the 1970s, in contrast with his earlier prolific work, Duncan published little, but he returned to print in the 1980s with *Ground Work* (1984).

In general, Duncan's poems either surge against the confines of consciousness or stand as integrations of experience. They seek a state in which there is "no duality but the variety of the one" (*The Years as Catches*). Duncan's work plays off structural looseness against thematic intensities. It achieves concentration in images of fire, music, dancing, possession, greenness, light, opening, and speech itself. Ultimately, the poems, which often have love as their subject, seek to illumine as with love the entire poetic situation. Duncan moves toward the vividness of revelation, the wonder of the "first day" ("Passages 13").

Often I Am Permitted to Return to a Meadow

as if it were a scene made-up by the mind,
that is not mine, but is a made place,

that is mine, it is so near to the heart,
an eternal pasture folded in all thought
so that there is a hall therein

that is a made place, created by light
wherefrom the shadows that are forms fall.

Wherefrom fall all architectures I am
I say are likeness of the First Beloved
whose flowers are flames lit to the Lady.

She it is Queen Under The Hill[1]
whose hosts are a disturbance of words within words
that is a field folded.

It is only a dream of the grass blowing
east against the source of the sun
in an hour before the sun's going down

whose secret we see in a children's game
of ring a round of roses told.

1. Cf. Persephone, queen of the underworld in Greek mythology. Gathering flowers in a field, she was kidnapped by Hades. She had to spend part of every year with him, part in the upper world with her mother, Demeter, goddess of agriculture.

Often I am permitted to return to a meadow
as if it were a given property of the mind
that certain bounds hold against chaos,

that is a place of first permission,
everlasting omen of what is.

1960

Poetry, a Natural Thing

Neither our vices nor our virtues
further the poem. "They came up
and died
just like they do every year
on the rocks."

The poem
feeds upon thought, feeling, impulse,
to breed itself,
a spiritual urgency at the dark ladders leaping.

This beauty is an inner persistence
toward the source
striving against (within) down-rushet of the river,
a call we heard and answer
in the lateness of the world
primordial bellowings
from which the youngest world might spring,

salmon not in the well where the
hazelnut falls
but at the falls battling, inarticulate,
blindly making it.

This is one picture apt for the mind.

A second: a moose painted by Stubbs,[2]
where last year's extravagant antlers
lie on the ground.
The forlorn moosey-faced poem wears
new antler-buds,
the same,

"a little heavy, a little contrived",

his only beauty to be
all moose.

1960

2. George Stubbs (1724–1806), English painter of animals.

Passage over Water

We have gone out in boats upon the sea at night,
lost, and the vast waters close traps of fear about us.
The boats are driven apart, and we are alone at last
under the incalculable sky, listless, diseased with stars.

Let the oars be idle, my love, and forget at this time
our love like a knife between us
defining the boundaries that we can never cross
nor destroy as we drift into the heart of our dream,
cutting the silence, slyly, the bitter rain in our mouths
and the dark wound closed in behind us.

Forget depth-bombs, death and promises we made,
gardens laid waste, and, over the wastelands westward,
the rooms where we had come together bombd.

But even as we leave, your love turns back. I feel
your absence like the ringing of bells silenced. And salt
over your eyes and the scales of salt between us. Now,
you pass with ease into the destructive world.
There is a dry crash of cement. The light fails,
falls into the ruins of cities upon the distant shore
and within the indestructible night I am alone.

1966

What I Saw

The white peacock roosting
might have been Christ,

featherd robe of Osiris,[3]

the radiant bird, a sword-flash,

percht in the tree •

and the other, the fumed-glass slide

—were like night and day,

3. The Egyptian god of the underworld.

the slit of an eye opening in

time

vertical to the horizon

•

1968

Up Rising Passages 25

Now Johnson[4] would go up to join the great simulacra of men,
Hitler and Stalin, to work his fame
with planes roaring out from Guam[5] over Asia,
all America become a sea of toiling men
stirrd at his will, which would be a bloated thing,
drawing from the underbelly of the nation
such blood and dreams as swell the idiot psyche
out of its courses into an elemental thing
until his name stinks with burning meat and heapt honors

And men wake to see that they are used like things
spent in a great potlach,[6] this Texas barbecue
of Asia, Africa, and all the Americas,
And the professional military behind him, thinking
to use him as they thought to use Hitler
without losing control of their business of war,

But the mania, the ravening eagle of America
as Lawrence saw him "bird of men that are masters,
lifting the rabbit-blood of the myriads up into . . ."[7]
into something terrible, gone beyond bounds, or
As Blake saw America in figures of fire and blood raging,
. . . in what image?[8] the ominous roar in the air,
the omnipotent wings, the all-American boy in the cockpit
loosing his flow of napalm,[9] below in the jungles
"any life at all or sign of life" his target, drawing now
not with crayons in his secret room
the burning of homes and the torture of mothers and fathers and children,
their hair a-flame, screaming in agony, but
in the line of duty, for the might and enduring fame
of Johnson, for the victory of American will over its victims,
releasing his store of destruction over the enemy,

4. Lyndon B. Johnson, U.S. president from 1963 to 1969, originally from Texas; he dramatically escalated the Vietnam War.
5. U.S. territory in the West Pacific.
6. Native American word for the showy distribution of gifts at a festival.
7. From the poem "The American Eagle" (1923), by English writer D. H. Lawrence (1885–1930).
8. Cf. the 1793 poem "Preludium (to 'America')," by English Romantic William Blake (1757–1827); he characterizes the spirit of freedom that inspired the American Revolution: "A quiver with its burning stores, a bow like that of night, / When pestilence is shot from heaven: no other arms she need!"
9. Jellied gasoline used by the U.S. military in the Vietnam War to incinerate trees and vegetation in which the Viet Cong could hide.

in terror and hatred of all communal things, of communion,
of communism •

has raised from the private rooms of small-town bosses and business-men,
from the council chambers of the gangs that run the great cities,
swollen with the votes of millions,[1]
from the fearful hearts of good people in the suburbs turning the
savory meat over the charcoal burners and heaping their barbecue
plates with more than they can eat,
from the closed meeting-rooms of regents of universities and sessions of
profiteers

—back of the scene: the atomic stockpile; the vials of synthesized
diseases eager biologists have developt over half a century dreaming
of the bodies of mothers and fathers and children and hated rivals
swollen with new plagues, measles grown enormous, influenzas
perfected; and the gasses of despair, confusion of the senses, mania,
inducing terror of the universe, coma, existential wounds, that
chemists we have met at cocktail parties, passt daily and with a
happy "Good Day" on the way to classes or work, have workt to
make war too terrible for men to wage—

raised this secret entity of America's hatred of Europe, of Africa, of Asia,
the deep hatred for the old world that had driven generations of America
out of itself,
and for the alien world, the new world about him, that might have been
Paradise
but was before his eyes already cleard back in a holocaust of burning
Indians, trees and grasslands,
reduced to his real estate, his projects of exploitation and profitable
wastes,

this specter that in the beginning Adams and Jefferson feard and knew
would corrupt the very body of the nation
and all our sense of our common humanity,[2]
this black bile of old evils arisen anew,
takes over the vanity of Johnson;
and the very glint of Satan's eyes from the pit of the hell of
America's unacknowledged, unrepented crimes that I saw in
Goldwater's[3] eyes
now shines from the eyes of the President
in the swollen head of the nation.

1968

1. John F. Kennedy won the 1960 presidential election when, under the direction of Chicago mayor Richard Daley, his votes were augmented by the ballots of dead citizens. Voter fraud also occurred in Texas, home of Kennedy's running mate, Lyndon Johnson.
2. Thomas Jefferson (1743–1826), third U.S. president, predicted a time when "[o]ur rulers will become corrupt, our people careless. A single zealot may become persecutor, and better men become his victims" (*Notes on Virginia*). John Adams (1735–1826), second U.S. president, foresaw the terror and despotism of the French Revolution and feared the encroachment of such tyranny in the United States.
3. Barry Goldwater (1909–1998), the unsuccessful Republican candidate for president in 1964; an ardent anticommunist, he supported American military intervention in Vietnam.

Childhood's Retreat

It's in the perilous boughs of the tree
out of blue sky   the wind
sings loudest surrounding me.

And solitude,   a wild solitude
's reveald,   fearfully,   high   I'd climb
into the shaking uncertainties,

part out of longing, part   daring my self,
part to see that
widening of the world,   part

to find my own, my secret
hiding sense and place, where from afar
all voices and scenes come back

—the barking of a dog,   autumnal burnings,
far calls,   close calls—   the boy I was
calls out to me
here the man where I am   "Look!

I've been where you

most fear to be."

1984

From Rites of Passage

II

Something is taking place.
Horns thrust upward from the brow.
Hooves beat impatient where feet once were.
My son, youth grows alarming in your face.
Your innocent regard is cruelly charming to me now.
You bristle where my fond hand would stir
to stroke your cheek.   I do not dare.

Irregular meters beat between your heart and mine.
Snuffling the air you take the heat and scan
the lines you take in going as if I were or were not there
and overtake me.
   And where it seems but yesterday I spilld the wine,
you too grow beastly to become a man.

Peace, peace.   I've had enough.   What can I say
when song's demanded?   —I've had my fill of song?
My longing to sing grows full.   Time's emptied me.

And where my youth was, now the Sun in you grows hot, your day
is young, my place you take triumphantly. All along
it's been for you, for this lowering of your horns in challenge, She
had her will of me and will not

let my struggling spirit in itself be free.

1984

A Little Language

I know a little language of my cat, though Dante says
that animals have no need of speech and Nature
abhors the superfluous.[4] My cat is fluent. He
converses when he wants with me. To speak

is natural. And whales and wolves I've heard
in choral soundings of the sea and air
know harmony and have an eloquence that stirs
my mind and heart—they touch the soul. Here

Dante's religion that would set Man apart
damns the effluence of our life from us
to build therein its powerhouse.

It's in his animal communication Man is
      true, immediate, and
in immediacy, Man is all animal.

His senses quicken in the thick of the symphony,
      old circuits of animal rapture and alarm,
attentions and arousals in which an identity rearrives.
      He hears
particular voices among
      the concert, the slightest
rustle in the undertones,
      rehearsing a nervous aptitude
yet to prove *his*. He sees the flick
      of significant red within the rushing mass
of ruddy wilderness and catches the glow
      of a green shirt
to delite him in a glowing field of green
      —it *speaks* to him—
and in the arc of the spectrum color
      speaks to color.
The rainbow articulates
      a promise he remembers

4. Italian poet Dante Alighieri (1265–1321) said this in his essay *De Vulgari Eloquentia* (Latin for "of the vulgar [i.e., common] speech").

he but imitates
    in noises that he makes,

this speech in every sense
    the world surrounding him.

He picks up on the fugitive tang of mace[5]
    amidst the savory mass,
and taste in evolution is an everlasting key.
    There is a pun of scents in what makes sense.

    Myrrh[6] it may have been,
the odor of the announcement that filld the house.

    He wakes from deepest sleep

upon a distant signal and waits

    as if crouching, springs

    to life.

1984

5. A highly aromatic spice.
6. Bitter gum resin found in North Africa and Arabia.

William Meredith
1919–2007

With wry humor and deft understatement, William Meredith captures the ambivalence we often feel as both children and parents. "Parents," he writes in a poem by that title, "get wrinkles where it is better / smooth, odd coughs, and smells. / / It is grotesque how they go on / loving us, we go on loving them." This poem, like his well-crafted homages to Robert Lowell and Sigmund Freud, illustrates Meredith's abilities as a psychologically astute observer; yet he does not parade his innermost feelings or impose his insights on the reader. A modest writer, he distills intimate experience in calm, elegant verses, which are formally patterned even when unmetered and unrhymed.

In the world of Meredith's poems, creatures and objects are separated from one another and yet engaged in a silent, composed relationship. In one of his war poems, "Battle Problem," he describes a convoy of battleships as moving with the ceremonious, processional beauty of the stars above them: "A company of vessels on the sea / Running in darkness, like a company / Of stars." Such couplings of the human with the natural induce a momentary serenity. Isolated as people are, we communicate, Meredith suggests, in recognition of our common solitude and the rituals we invent to make it tolerable. The poet reminds us that "all go to the grave several ways / and compose themselves elaborately as for an end."

Meredith was born on January 9, 1919, in New York City. He attended the Lenox

School, in Massachusetts, and earned a B.A. from Princeton University in 1940. Meredith then spent five years in the service, most of it as a naval aviator in the Pacific theater. After his release from active duty in 1946, Meredith became a Woodrow Wilson Fellow at Princeton, then a Resident Fellow in creative writing. He reenlisted to fly missions in the Korean War in 1952. From 1955 until 1983, he taught at Connecticut College. In 1978–80, he served as poetry consultant to the Library of Congress, and in 1988, he won the Pulitzer Prize for *Partial Accounts: New and Selected Poems.*

Last Things

For Robert Lowell[1]

I

In the tunnel of woods, as the road
Winds up through the freckled light, a porcupine,
Larger than life, crosses the road.
He moves with the difficulty of relics—
Possum, armadillo, horseshoe crab.
To us they seem creatures arthritic with time,
Winding joylessly down like burnt-out galaxies.
In all their slowness we see no dignity,
Only a want of scale.
Having crossed the road oblivious, he falls off
Deliberately and without grace into the ferns.

II

In another state are hills as choppy as lake water
And, on a hillside there,
Is a junkyard of old cars, kept for the parts—
Fenders and chassis and the engine blocks
Right there in the field, smaller parts in bins
In a shed by the side of the road. Cows graze
Among the widely spaced rows,
Which are irregular only as an old orchard is,
Following the contours of the hill.
The tops of the cars are bright colors still
And as pretty as bottles hung on a bare tree
Or painted cinder blocks in a garden.
Cars the same age are parked on the road like cannibals.

III

At the edge of a harbor, in a field
That faces the ocean they came by and left by,
Statues of soldiers and governors and their queen
Lie where the Africans put them.
Unbewildered, not without understanding,

1. American poet (1917–1977).

The marble countenances look at the green
Continent; they did their best; plunderers
Were fewer among them than men of honor.
But no one comes for them, though they have been offered.
With chipped extremities, in a chipped regalia
They lie at angles of unaccustomed ease.
In the parks and squares of England are set up
Bolder, more dreadful shapes of the ego,
While African lichen confers an antique grandeur
On these, from whom men have withheld it.

IV

At the edge of the Greek world, I think, was a cliff
To which fallen gods were chained, immortal.[2]
Time is without forgiveness, but intermittently
He sends the old, sentimental, hungry
Vulture compassion to gnaw on the stone
Vitals of each of us, even the young, as if
To ready each of us, even the old, for an unthinkable
Event he foresees for each of us—a reckoning, our own.

1970

Parents

For Vanessa Meredith and Samuel Wolf Gezari

What it must be like to be an angel
or a squirrel, we can imagine sooner.

The last time we go to bed good,
they are there, lying about darkness.

They dandle us once too often,
these friends who become our enemies.

Suddenly one day, their juniors
are as old as we yearn to be.

They get wrinkles where it is better
smooth, odd coughs, and smells.

It is grotesque how they go on
loving us, we go on loving them.

The effrontery, barely imaginable,
of having caused us. And of how.

2. For example, the titan Prometheus, for his crime against the Greek gods in teaching humans about fire, was chained to a mountain in the Caucasus. By day a vulture gnawed at his liver, which was restored during the succeeding night.

Their lives: surely
we can do better than that.

This goes on for a long time. Everything
they do is wrong, and the worst thing,

they all do it, is to die,
taking with them the last explanation,

how we came out of the wet sea
or wherever they got us from,

taking the last link
of that chain with them.

Father, mother, we cry, wrinkling,
to our uncomprehending children and grandchildren.

1980

Dying Away

Homage to Sigmund Freud[3]

'Toward the person who has died
we adopt a special attitude:
something like admiration
for someone who has accomplished
a very difficult task,' he said,

and now hospitals and rest-homes
are filled with heroes and heroines
in smocks, at their out-sized, unwonted tasks,
now the second date on tombstones is a saint's day[4]
and there is no craven in any graveyard,

no malingerer there, no trivial person.
It is you and I, still milling around,
who evade our callings, incestuous
in our love for the enduring trees and the snowfall,
for brook-noise and coins, songs, appetites.

And with the one we love most,
the mated one we lose track of ourselves in—
who's giving, who's taking that fleshy pleasure?—
we call those calmings-away, those ecstasies
dyings,[5] we see them as diligent rehearsals.

3. Austrian founder of psychoanalysis (1856–1939). The ensuing quotation is from his "Thoughts for the Times on War and Death" (1915).

4. Day in the Church calendar on which a saint is commemorated.

5. In the seventeenth century, poetic term for sexual intercourse.

The love of living disturbs me,
I am wracked like a puritan by eros and health,
almost undone by brotherhood, rages
of happiness seize me, the world, the fair world,
and I call on the name of the dark healer, Freud.

His appetites, songs, orgasms died away,
his young brother, his daughter, his huge father,
until he saw that the aim of life was death.
But a man cannot learn heroism from another,
he owes the world some death of his own invention.

Then he said, 'My dear Schur,[6] you certainly remember
our first talk. You promised me then not to forsake me
when my time came. Now it is nothing but torture
and makes no sense any more.'
Schur gave him two centigrams of morphine.

At what cost he said it, so diligent of life,
so curious, we can't guess
who are still his conjurings. He told us
it is impossible to imagine our own deaths,
he told us, this may be the secret of heroism.

1980

6. Max Schur (1897–1969), Freud's doctor. The quotation translates Freud's last words.

Lawrence Ferlinghetti
b. 1919

Although Allen Ginsberg was the most famous Beat poet, Lawrence Ferlinghetti was the group's leading proponent, organizer, and publisher, as well as its oldest member. His influences ranging from Walt Whitman to E. E. Cummings, Ferlinghetti combines satiric wit with visionary Romanticism, surrealism with earnest chanting. His poems command our attention both on and off the page. Visually, the words are often scattered across the page, defying the norms of the stanza break and the justified left-hand margin. Aurally, the poems recall the darting rhythms and surprising leaps of musical improvisation—Ferlinghetti sometimes performed them to jazz accompaniment.

Ferlinghetti was born on March 24, 1919, in Yonkers, New York. Shortly before his birth, his Italian-immigrant father died suddenly; soon, his Portuguese Jewish mother had a nervous breakdown and was institutionalized. Ferlinghetti's aunt took him to live with her in France from 1920 to 1924. On their return, she took a job as French governess in a wealthy family; she later disappeared, and the family kept Ferlinghetti with them in Bronxville. He did not learn to speak English until he was five. Ferlinghetti later studied journalism at the University of North Carolina (B.A., 1941). When war broke out, he entered the navy, eventually commanding a ship in the Normandy invasion. After the war, he resumed his education, taking an M.A. at Columbia (1948), then a Doctorat de l'Université at the Sorbonne in 1950.

In the 1950s, Ferlinghetti played a major role in catalyzing the Beat movement in San Francisco, the city that would eventually make him its first poet laureate, in 1998. In 1953, with Peter D. Martin he founded the first all-paperback bookstore in the country, City Lights Bookstore, a key site of avant-garde literary activity. He also founded the City Lights imprint in 1955. As the publisher of Ginsberg's *"Howl" and Other Poems* (1956), he aroused international attention when, with the help of the American Civil Liberties Union, he defended himself in court against charges of printing lewd and indecent material.

Ferlinghetti also issued a mimeographed magazine that he called "Beatitude," in reference to the beatific side, the "renaissance of wonder" ("I Am Waiting"), of Beat poetry. This equivocal name also alluded to being "beat" in the sense of being exhausted. He pursued euphoria by various means: one was Eastern religion (Zen Buddhism being preferred). Another was love, and many of his poems are love poems. Still another was circus antics; he borrowed from Henry Miller the title for *A Coney Island of the Mind* (1958), which became a best-seller in poetry. The final means was drugs. All were ways of finding one's uniqueness. At times, he defined himself against something, flouting and satirizing the establishment institutions of U.S. capitalism, politics, and academia. "A poet, by definition," he said, "has to be an enemy of the State" (*The Independent* [London], May 17, 1998). Accordingly, Ferlinghetti wrote poems of political high jinks, such as "Tentative Description of a Dinner to Promote the Impeachment of President Eisenhower." In other poems, he objects to billboards and to car-addicted America. "Who stole America?" he asks in "Starting from San Francisco." In "Junkman's Obbligato," he espouses "walking anarchy"—perhaps something like the organized chaos, ambling irreverence, and risk-taking energy of his poems.

[In Goya's Greatest Scenes We Seem to See]

In Goya's greatest scenes[1] we seem to see
                                        the people of the world
    exactly at the moment when
         they first attained the title of
                                                'suffering humanity'
      They writhe upon the page
                                      in a veritable rage
                                                      of adversity
      Heaped up
              groaning with babies and bayonets
                                                under cement skies
        in an abstract landscape of blasted trees
            bent statues bats wings and beaks
                    slippery gibbets
            cadavers and carnivorous cocks
        and all the final hollering monsters
              of the
                    'imagination of disaster'
      they are so bloody real
                                  it is as if they really still existed

1. Francisco Goya y Lucientes (1746–1828), Spanish painter and etcher, did a series of etchings, "Disasters of War" (1810–13), that express his outrage at a world at war.

And they do
Only the landscape is changed

They still are ranged along the roads
plagued by legionnaires
false windmills and demented roosters

They are the same people
only further from home
on freeways fifty lanes wide
on a concrete continent
spaced with bland billboards
illustrating imbecile illusions of happiness

The scene shows fewer tumbrils
but more strung-out citizens
in painted cars
and they have strange license plates
and engines
that devour America

1958

Dog

The dog trots freely in the street
and sees reality
and the things he sees
are bigger than himself
and the things he sees
are his reality
Drunks in doorways
Moons on trees
The dog trots freely thru the street
and the things he sees
are smaller than himself
Fish on newsprint
Ants in holes
Chickens in Chinatown windows
their heads a block away
The dog trots freely in the street
and the things he smells
smell something like himself
The dog trots freely in the street
past puddles and babies
cats and cigars
poolrooms and policemen
He doesn't hate cops
He merely has no use for them

and he goes past them
and past the dead cows hung up whole
in front of the San Francisco Meat Market
He would rather eat a tender cow
than a tough policeman
though either might do
And he goes past the Romeo Ravioli Factory
and past Coit's Tower
and past Congressman Doyle of the Unamerican Committee[2]
He's afraid of Coit's Tower
but he's not afraid of Congressman Doyle
although what he hears is very discouraging
very depressing
very absurd
to a sad young dog like himself
to a serious dog like himself
But he has his own free world to live in
His own fleas to eat
He will not be muzzled
Congressman Doyle is just another
fire hydrant
to him
The dog trots freely in the street
and has his own dog's life to live
and to think about
and to reflect upon
touching and tasting and testing everything
investigating everything
without benefit of perjury
a real realist
with a real tale to tell
and a real tail to tell it with
a real live
            barking
                        democratic dog
engaged in real
                        free enterprise
with something to say
                              about ontology
something to say
                        about reality
                                    and how to see it
                                                and how to hear it
with his head cocked sideways
                                    at streetcorners
as if he is just about to have
                                    his picture taken
                                                for Victor Records

2. Clyde Doyle (1887–1963), California congressman and member of the House of Representatives' Un-American Activities Committee, which mounted witch-hunts against communists and others it considered subversive.

listening for
His Master's Voice
and looking
like a living questionmark
into the
great gramophone
of puzzling existence
with its wondrous hollow horn
which always seems
just about to spout forth
some Victorious answer
to everything

1958

Retired Ballerinas, Central Park West[3]

Retired ballerinas on winter afternoons
walking their dogs
in Central Park West
(or their cats on leashes—
the cats themselves old highwire artists)
The ballerinas
leap and pirouette
through Columbus Circle
while winos on park benches
(laid back like drunken Goudonovs)[4]
hear the taxis trumpet together
like horsemen of the apocalypse
in the dusk of the gods
It is the final witching hour
when swains are full of swan songs
And all return through the dark dusk
to their bright cells
in glass highrises
or sit down to oval cigarettes and cakes
in the Russian Tea Room[5]
or climb four flights to back rooms
in Westside brownstones
where faded playbill photos
fall peeling from their frames
like last year's autumn leaves

1981

3. Fashionable avenue on New York City's Upper West Side, overlooking Central Park, just above Columbus Circle (line 8).
4. Boris Godunov, a czar of Russia, is the hero of an 1874 opera by the Russian composer Modest Petrovich Mussorgsky (1839–1881).
5. Expensive restaurant near Columbus Circle.

LOUISE BENNETT
1919–2006

Once thought of as a mere entertainer, Jamaican writer Louise Bennett emerged as the preeminent West Indian poet of Creole verse. Varieties of Creole, everyday speech in the West Indies, were forged by Caribbean slaves in the seventeenth and eighteenth centuries from English dialects, other European languages, and African languages such as Twi and Ewe. Early in life, Bennett chose to write and perform poetry in Creole, even though both the British who colonized Jamaica from 1655 to 1962 and middle-class Jamaicans saw it as a corruption of Standard English.

Bennett was not recognized as a poet until the late 1960s because she worked in Jamaican English. The Jamaican Poetry League excluded her from its meetings, and editors failed to include her in anthologies. Now acknowledged as a crucial precursor for a wide range of Caribbean poets—from "literary" poets such as Kamau Brathwaite and Lorna Goodison to "dub," or performance, poets—Bennett "persisted writing in dialect in spite of all the opposition," as she told an interviewer, "because nobody else was doing so and there was such rich material in the dialect that I felt I wanted to put on paper some of the wonderful things that people say in dialect. You could never say 'look here' as vividly as 'kuyah.' " Creole allowed her to "express" herself "so much more strongly and vividly than in Standard English"; it seemed "rich in wit and humour" because the "nature of Jamaican dialect is the nature of comedy" ("Bennett on Bennett"). Since Bennett's use of this oral language can at first present foreign readers with difficulties, she has been seen as a more "local" poet than, say, fellow West Indian Derek Walcott. But her vital characters, humorous situations, and robust imagination help overcome these barriers.

Bennett brilliantly manipulates the humor of Creole, the ironic possibilities of dramatic monologue, and the symmetrical contrasts and inversions afforded by the ballad stanza. She enriches English-language poetry with the phonemic wit and play of Creole words such as *boonoonoonoos* for "pretty" and *boogooyagga* for "worthless." Some of her poems directly address problems of non-Standard language and status, as when the wry speaker of "Dry-Foot Bwoy" deflates the pretensions of a Jamaican boy who tries to mimic British English. This situation is reversed in the dramatic monologue "No Lickle Twang," which directs irony toward its speaker: because she wishes he had returned from his stay in the United States with symbols of an improved status, including Standard English, a mother absurdly asks her son to call his father by what she imagines is a Standard English word, "Poo."

Bennett wrote many poems from the perspective of the trickster. Indeed, she likened herself to a major trickster of the West Indies, the spider-hero Anancy, whose wily ways in language and deed often land him in trouble, but also help him fool his adversaries. Like the crafty "Jamaica Oman [Woman]" and "South Parade Peddler" celebrated in two of her funniest poems, Bennett's typically female tricksters cunningly subvert the hierarchies that would rob them of power. No one is safe from Bennett's all-encompassing irony. She irreverently mocks British imperialists and Jamaicans, nationalists and antinationalists. "Pass fi White," a poem built around multiple puns on the word *pass*, ridicules both imperialist racial hierarchies and a Jamaican's foolish entrapment within them. In "Colonization in Reverse," Bennett ironically inverts Britain's xenophobic apprehension at the influx of Jamaican migrants, while also wondering if some Jamaicans on welfare are exploiting the British even as they were once exploited. At the crucial moment of Jamaican independence, Bennett pokes fun at the commodification of nationalist symbols and the inflated hopes and pretensions of Jamaica's proud new citizens, in such poems as "Independence Dignity" and "Independance." She celebrates the Jamaican nation not through solemn encomium; instead, she embodies its carnivalesque capacity for mockery and self-mockery.

Bennett was born on September 7, 1919, in Kingston. Her mother was a dressmaker, her father a baker who died when she was seven. While still in high school, she began to perform her Creole poetry, making her debut performance at nineteen. Bennett brought out her first book of poetry, *Dialect Verses*, in 1942, and the next year, she began to publish poetry on a weekly basis in Jamaica's national newspaper, the *Gleaner*. After studying journalism, social work, and local folklore in Jamaica, she attended the Royal Academy of Dramatic Art, in London, on a British Council scholarship from 1945 to 1947, returning homesick to Jamaica to teach high school drama for two years. She went back to Britain to resume her acting career and her work on a special Caribbean program for the BBC, then lived in the United States from 1953 to 1955, performing on radio and the stage in New York and its environs. She married her longtime associate Eric Coverley in 1954, and the couple returned to Jamaica the following year. While writing and performing her poetry, she also gathered Jamaican folklore, traveled extensively in her work as drama specialist for the Jamaican Social Welfare Commission (1955–63), and lectured on folklore and drama for the extramural department of the University of the West Indies (1959–61).

Bennett also created her own regular radio show, "Miss Lou's Views" (1966–82), and a children's television program, "Ring Ding" (1970–82). Building a mass audience in Jamaica for performance genres, "Miss Lou" regularly delivered dramatic renditions of plays, folk songs, and pantomime, sometimes before tens of thousands. Jamaican schoolchildren have often recited competitively her dramatic monologues, sometimes with Bennett serving as judge. She received many awards, including the Order of Jamaica (1974) and the Musgrave Gold Medal of the Institute of Jamaica (1978). In the early 1980s, she moved to North America, and she lived in Toronto, Canada, until her death.

South Parade Peddler

Hairnet! Scissors! Fine-teet comb!
—Whe de nice lady deh?
Buy a scissors from me, no, lady?
Hair pin? Tootpase? Go weh!
Me seh go-weh aready, ef
Yuh doan like it, see me.
Yuh dah swell like bombin plane fun[1]—
Yuh soon bus up like Graf Spee.[2]

Yuh favour—Shoeslace! Powder puff!
Clothes hanger! Belt! Pen knife!
Buy something, no, nice young man?
Buy a hairnet fi yuh wife.
Buy someting wid de change, no, sah,
An meck de Lawd bless yuh!
Me no sell farden[3] hair curler, sah!
Yuh fas an facety to![4]

1. Fund. Many of the ensuing notes are indebted to Mervyn Morris's annotations in Louise Bennett, *Selected Poems* (Kingston, 1983).
2. German battleship blown up by its own captain in 1939.
3. Farthing.
4. Fast and rude, too.

Teck yuh han outa me box!
Pudung[5] me razor blade!
Yuh no got no use fi it, for yuh
Dah suffer from hair raid![6]
Nice boonoonoonoos[7] lady, come,
Me precious, come dis way.
Hair pin? Yes, mah, tank yuh, yuh is
De bes one fi de day.

Toot-brush? Ah beg yuh pardon, sah—
Me never see yuh mout:
Dem torpedo yuh teet, sah, or
Yuh female lick dem out?
No bodder pick me up, yaw, sah!
Yuh face look like a seh
Yuh draw it outa lucky box.
No bodder me—go weh!

One police man dah come, but me
Dah try get one more sale.
Shoeslace! Tootpase! Buy quick, no, sah!
Yuh waan me go a jail?
Ef dah police ever ketch we, Lize,
We peddler career done.
Pick up yuh foot eena yuh han.
Hair pin! Hair curler! Run!

1942

Pass fi White

Miss Jane jus hear from Merica—
Her daughter proudly write
Fi seh[8] she fail her exam, but
She passin dere fi white!

She seh fi tell de trute she know
Her brain part not so bright—
She couldn pass tru college
So she try fi pass fi white.

She passin wid her work-mate-dem,
She passin wid her boss,
An a nice white bwoy she love dah gwan
Wid her like seh she pass![9]

5. Put down.
6. Pun on *air raid*.
7. Pretty; term of endearment.
8. To say.
9. She's passing with her coworkers, passing with her boss, and passing with a nice boy she loves who's going along with her as though she had passed.

But sometime she get fretful and
Her heart start gallop fas
An she bruck out eena cole-sweat
Jussa wonder ef she pass!

Jane get bex[1] seh she sen de gal
Fi learn bout edication,
It look like seh de gal gawn weh
Gawn work pon her complexion.

She no haffi tan a foreign[2]
Under dat deh strain an fright
For plenty copper-colour gal
Deh home yah[3] dah play white.

Her fambily is nayga,[4] but
Dem pedigree is right—
She hope de gal no gawn an tun
No boogooyagga[5] white.

De gal puppa[6] dah laugh an seh
It serve Merica right—
Five year back dem Jim-Crow him, now
Dem pass him pickney white.[7]

Him dah boast[8] all bout de distric
How him daughter is fus-class,
How she smarter dan American
An over deh dah pass!

Some people tink she pass B.A.,
Some tink she pass D.R.—
Wait till dem fine out seh she ongle
Pass de colour bar.[9]

1949, 1966

No Lickle[1] Twang

Me glad fi see yuh come back, bwoy,
But lawd, yuh let me dung;
Me shame a yuh so till all a
Me proudness drop a grung.[2]

1. Vexed.
2. She doesn't have to stay abroad.
3. Here.
4. Negro (pejorative in Jamaican Creole).
5. Low-class; worthless.
6. Papa.
7. Five years ago they persecuted him with racist Jim Crow laws, but now they pass his child as white.
8. Boasts.
9. Wait until they find out she only passed the color bar.

1. Little.
2. Ground. *Dung:* down.

Yuh mean yuh go dah Merica
An spen six whole mont deh,
An come back not a piece better
Dan how yuh did go weh?

Bwoy, yuh no shame? Is so yuh come?
After yuh tan so lang!
Not even lickle language, bwoy?
Not even lickle twang?

An yuh sister what work ongle[3]
One week wid Merican
She talk so nice now dat we have
De jooce[4] fi understan?

Bwoy, yuh couldn improve yuhself!
An yuh get so much pay?
Yuh spen six mont a foreign, an
Come back ugly same way?

Not even a drapes trousiz,[5] or
A pass de riddim coat?
Bwoy, not even a gole teet[6] or
A gole chain roun yuh troat?

Suppose me laas me pass[7] go introjooce
Yuh to a stranger
As me lamented son what lately
Come from Merica!

Dem hooda laugh after me, bwoy!
Me couldn tell dem so!
Dem hooda seh me lie, yuh wasa
Spen time back a Mocho![8]

No back-answer me, bwoy—yuh talk
Too bad! Shet up yuh mout!
Ah doan know how yuh an yuh puppa[9]
Gwine to meck it out.

Ef yuh waan please him, meck him tink
Yuh bring back someting new.
Yuh always call him 'Pa'—dis evenin
When him come, seh 'Poo'.[1]

1949

3. Only.
4. Deuce.
5. Style of trousers popular in the 1940s.
6. Gold tooth. *Pass de riddim coat:* a coat that comes down past (pass) the rhythm section (riddim)—that is, buttocks. Many Jamaican farmers returning from the United States wore such coats.
7. Lose my path; become lost.
8. Back at Mocho. Mocho is a name used to indicate a place of extreme backwardness.
9. Papa.
1. A version of *Papa;* part of a street vendor's cry; baby word for feces. Since Jamaican Creole often turns Standard English *o* sounds into *a* sounds, the speaker is hypercorrecting. "Pa," she seems to think, must be a Creole usage to be corrected.

Dry-Foot Bwoy[2]

Wha wrong wid Mary dry-foot bwoy?
Dem gal got him fi mock,[3]
An when me meet him tarra night
De bwoy gi me a shock!

Me tell him seh him auntie an
Him cousin dem sen howdy[4]
An ask him how him getting awn.
Him seh, 'Oh, jolley, jolley!'

Me start fi feel so sorry fi
De po bad-lucky soul,
Me tink him come a foreign lan
Come ketch bad foreign cole!

Me tink him got a bad sore-troat,
But as him chat-chat gwan
Me fine out seh is foreign twang
De bwoy wasa put awn![5]

For me notice dat him answer
To nearly all me seh
Was 'Actually', 'What', 'Oh deah!'
An all dem sinting deh.[6]

Me gi a joke, de gal dem laugh;
But hear de bwoy, 'Haw-haw!
I'm sure you got that bally-dash[7]
Out of the cinema!'

Same time me laas me temper, an
Me holler, 'Bwoy, kirout![8]
No chat to me wid no hot pittata
Eena yuh mout!'

Him tan[9] up like him stunted, den
Hear him no, 'How silley!
I don't think that I really
Understand you, actually.'

Me seh, 'Yuh understan me, yaw!
No yuh name Cudjoe Scoop?
Always visit Nana kitchen an
Gi laugh fi gungoo soup![1]

2. Thin-legged (inexperienced) boy.
3. The girls are mocking him.
4. I told him that his auntie and his cousins sent [or send] greetings.
5. But as he kept talking I realized his foreign accent was put on.
6. And all them things there.
7. Nonsense; balderdash.
8. Clear out.
9. Stand.
1. Chastising the boy for his pretensions, the speaker reminds him that he is Afro-Jamaican.

'An now all yuh can seh is "actually"?
Bwoy, but tap!
Wha happen to dem sweet Jamaica
Joke yuh use fi pop?'

Him get bex[2] and walk tru de door,
Him head eena de air;
De gal-dem bawl out affa him,[3]
'Not going? What! Oh deah!'

An from dat night till tedeh, mah,
Dem all got him fi mock.
Miss Mary dry-foot bwoy!
Cyaan get over de shock!

1957

Colonization in Reverse

What a joyful news, Miss Mattie;
Ah feel like me heart gwine burs—
Jamaica people colonizin
Englan in reverse.[4]

By de hundred, by de tousan,
From country an from town,
By de ship-load, by de plane-load,
Jamaica is Englan boun.

Dem a pour out a Jamaica;
Everybody future plan
Is fi get a big-time job
An settle in de motherlan.

What a islan! What a people!
Man an woman, ole an young
Jussa pack dem bag an baggage
An tun history upside dung![5]

Some people doan like travel,
But fi show dem loyalty
Dem all a open up cheap-fare-
To-Englan agency;

An week by week dem shippin off
Dem countryman like fire

Cudjoe and *Nana:* African names used in Jamaica. *Gungoo:* congo pea.
2. Vexed.
3. The girls went crying after him.
4. Encouraged by the postwar labor shortage in England and the scarcity of work at home, three hundred thousand Jamaicans migrated to Britain from 1948 to 1962.
5. Down.

Fi immigrate an populate
De seat a de Empire.

Oonoo[6] se how life is funny,
Oonoo see de tunabout?
Jamaica live fi box bread
Out a English people mout.

For when dem catch a Englan
An start play dem different role
Some will settle down to work
An some will settle fi de dole.[7]

Jane seh de dole is not too bad
Because dey payin she
Two pounds a week fi seek a job
Dat suit her dignity.

Me seh Jane will never fine work
At de rate how she dah look
For all day she stay pon Aunt Fan couch
An read love-story book.

What a devilment a Englan!
Dem face war an brave de worse;
But ah wonderin how dem gwine stan
Colonizin in reverse.

1957

Independance

Independance wid a vengeance!
Independance raisin Cain!
Jamaica start grow beard, ah hope
We chin can stan de strain!

When dawg marga him head big, an
When puss hungry him nose clean;[8]
But every puss an dog no know
What Independance mean.

Mattie seh it mean we facety,[9]
Stan up pon we dignity,
An we don't allow nobody
Fi teck liberty wid we.

6. You (plural).
7. For unemployment benefits.
8. Jamaican proverbs: "When the dog is meager his head is big (i.e., proud)," and "when the cat is hungry his sense of smell is keen (the cat will have to get his nose dirty to survive)."
9. Proud; impudent.

Independance is we nature
Born an bred in all we do,
An she glad fi see dat Government
Tun independant to.

She hope dem caution worl-map
Fi stop draw Jamaica small,
For de lickle speck cyaan show[1]
We independantness at all!

Moresomever we must tell map dat
We don't like we position—
Please kindly teck we out a sea
An draw we in de ocean.

What a crosses! Independance
Woulda never have a chance
Wid so much boogooyagga[2]
Dah expose dem ignorance.

Dog wag him tail fi suit him size
An match him stamina—
Jamaica people need a
Independance formula!

No easy-come-by freeness tings,[3]
Nuff labour, some privation,
Not much of dis an less of dat
An plenty studiration.[4]

Independance wid a vengeance!
Wonder how we gwine to cope?
Jamaica start smoke pipe, ah hope
We got nuff jackass rope![5]

1961

Independence Dignity

Dear Cousin Min, yuh miss sinting,[6]
Yuh should be over yah[7]
Fi see Independence Celebration
Capture Jamaica.

Yuh waan see how Jamaica people
Rise to de occasion
An deestant[8] up demself fi greet
De birt a dem new nation!

1. The little speck can't show.
2. Backward people.
3. Things gotten for free.
4. Studying.
5. Local tobacco.
6. Something.
7. Here.
8. Decent.

Not a stone was fling, not a samfie[9] sting,
Not a soul gwan bad an lowrated;[1]
Not a fight bruck out, not a bad-wud shout
As Independence was celebrated.

Concert outa street an lane an park
Wid big-time acs performin,
An we dance outa street
From night till soon a mornin.

Fi de whole long mont a Augus
Independence was in prime;
Everyting was Independence ting
Roun Independence time.

Independence pen an pencil,
Cup an saucer, glass an tray;
Down to Independence baby bawn
Pon Independence Day.

An de Independence light-dem
Jussa pretty up de night-dem
An a sweeten up de crowd fi
Look an wonder at de sight.

Dere was functions by de tousan
An we crowd up every one;
From Packy Piece to Macka Town
De behaviour was gran.

Yuh waan see Jane unruly an
Unmannasable gal
Dah stan up straight an sing out
'Teach us true respec for all!'[2]

Fan lazy bwoy who spen him time
A cotch up[3] Joe shop wall
Serious up him face an holler
'Stir response to duty's call!'

Teet[4] an tongue was all united,
Heart an soul was hans an glove,
Fenky-fenky[5] voice gain vigour
Pon 'Jamaica, land we love'.[6]

It was a sight fi cure sore yeye,
A time fi live fi see:

9. Con artist.
1. Badly behaved.
2. Beginning of the Jamaican national anthem's second verse.
3. Leaning on.
4. Teeth.
5. Puny.
6. From the end of the national anthem.

Jamaica Independence
Celebration dignity.

1966

Jamaica Oman[7]

Jamaica oman cunny, sah![8]
Is how dem jinnal so?[9]
Look how long dem liberated
An de man dem never know!

Look how long Jamaica oman
—Modder, sister, wife, sweetheart—
Outa road an eena yard[1] deh pon
A dominate her part!

From Maroon Nanny[2] teck her body
Bounce bullet back pon man,
To when nowadays gal-pickney[3] tun
Spellin-Bee champion.

From de grass root to de hill-top,
In profession, skill an trade,
Jamaica oman teck her time
Dah mount an meck de grade.

Some backa man a push, some side-a
Man a hole him han,
Some a lick sense eena man head,
Some a guide him pon him plan!

Neck an neck an foot an foot wid man
She buckle hole[4] her own;
While man a call her 'so-so rib'
Oman a tun backbone![5]

An long before Oman Lib[6] bruck out
Over foreign lan
Jamaica female wasa work
Her liberated plan!

Jamaica oman know she strong,
She know she tallawah,[7]

7. Woman.
8. Cunning, sir.
9. How are they so tricky?
1. Home.
2. Jamaican national hero who led the Maroons, fugitive slaves, in battle during the eighteenth century. Bullets reputedly ricocheted off her and killed her enemies.
3. Girl-child.
4. Take hold.
5. Eve is said to have come from Adam's rib (Genesis 2.21–22).
6. Women's Liberation Movement.
7. Sturdy.

But she no want her pickney-dem
Fi start call her 'Puppa'.[8]

So de cunny Jamma[9] oman
Gwan like pants-suit is a style,
An Jamaica man no know she wear
De trousiz all de while!

So Jamaica oman coaxin
Fambly budget from explode
A so Jamaica man a sing
'Oman a heaby load!'[1]

But de cunny Jamma oman
Ban her belly,[2] bite her tongue,
Ketch water, put pot pon fire
An jus dig her toe a grung.[3]

For 'Oman luck deh a dungle',[4]
Some rooted more dan some,
But as long as fowl a scratch dungle heap
Oman luck mus come!

Lickle by lickle man start praise her,
Day by day de praise a grow;
So him praise her, so it sweet her,
For she wonder if him know.

1975

8. Papa. *Pickney:* children.
9. Jamaican.
1. A folk song often sung while working in the fields.
2. Binds her belly (a practice associated with grief; also a suggestion of belt tightening, as in hunger).
3. And just digs her toes into the ground.
4. That is, woman's luck will be rediscovered (proverbial). *Dungle:* garbage dump.

Howard Nemerov
1920–1991

"Immediate and mutual lust" is what pornography promises, and yet in reality, Howard Nemerov wryly concludes, "We think about sex obsessively except / During the act, when our minds tend to wander" ("Reading Pornography in Old Age"). Nemerov builds his elegantly crafted poems around sly ironies and unexpected convergences, such as the lovers and the grinning death's head of "The Goose Fish." He approaches his subjects obliquely, taking his readers a little by surprise and upsetting conventional ways of seeing things. Though often formally metered and rhymed, his poems move sinuously and combat fixities. He deplores any kind of idolatry, any institution or cliché that blinds our appreciation of the free and lively movements of life.

Nemerov grew up in a literary atmosphere dominated by T. S. Eliot, W. B. Yeats, and W. H. Auden, and he began by imitating them, but his own poetry moved steadily away from modernist ambiguity toward lucidity and precision. Nemerov came to regard "simplicity and the appearance of ease in the measure as primary values" ("Attentiveness and Obedience"). He was committed to wit—to seeing relationships among disparate phenomena and creating metaphors. For him, poetry was the art of "combination, or discovering the secret valences which the most widely differing things have for one another" (*Poets in Progress,* ed. Edward Hungerford, 1967). Nemerov's new combinations of experience often emerge as jokes, and one of the pleasures of reading his poems is watching the shifts in his comic sense. The tone of Nemerov's later poems is casual yet elegant and precise, familiar without condescension, clear yet lively and provocative. Their melancholy is never ponderous. He valued "[s]eriousness, but not solemnity" (*Washington Post,* October 4, 1988).

Nemerov was born on March 1, 1920, into a Jewish family in New York City, where he lived until 1937. He received his A.B. from Harvard University in 1941, "in nice time for a summer vacation before entering the war" (*Twentieth Century Authors,* First Supplement, 1955), then enlisted in the Royal Canadian Air Force and became a pilot, flying combat missions against German shipping in the North Sea; he joined the U.S. Army Air Corps for the last two years of the war. Married in 1944, Nemerov became a professor at several college campuses, including Bennington College (1948–66) and Washington University (1976–91). He served as poetry consultant to the Library of Congress in 1963–64 and again in 1988–90, when the post had been retitled poet laureate. In 1978, he won the Pulitzer Prize and the National Book Award for his *Collected Poems*; in 1981, he won the Bollingen Prize. When awarded the National Medal of Arts in 1987, he said, with characteristic self-mockery, that he was pleased to be honored by a country "where poets are, for the most part, an impertinence, like birds at an airport" (*St. Louis Post-Dispatch,* July 9, 1991).

The Goose Fish

On the long shore, lit by the moon
To show them properly alone,
Two lovers suddenly embraced
So that their shadows were as one.
The ordinary night was graced
For them by the swift tide of blood
That silently they took at flood,
And for a little time they prized
   Themselves emparadised.

Then, as if shaken by stage-fright
Beneath the hard moon's bony light,
They stood together on the sand
Embarrassed in each other's sight
But still conspiring hand in hand,
Until they saw, there underfoot,
As though the world had found them out,
The goose fish turning up, though dead,
   His hugely grinning head.

There in the china light he lay,
Most ancient and corrupt and grey
They hesitated at his smile,
Wondering what it seemed to say
To lovers who a little while
Before had thought to understand,
By violence upon the sand,
The only way that could be known
To make a world their own.

It was a wide and moony grin
Together peaceful and obscene;
They knew not what he would express,
So finished a comedian
He might mean failure or success,
But took it for an emblem of
Their sudden, new and guilty love
To be observed by, when they kissed,
That rigid optimist.

So he became their patriarch,
Dreadfully mild in the half-dark.
His throat that the sand seemed to choke,
His picket teeth, these left their mark
But never did explain the joke
That so amused him, lying there
While the moon went down to disappear
Along the still and tilted track
That bears the zodiac.

1955

The Icehouse in Summer

see Amos, 3:15[1]

A door sunk in a hillside, with a bolt
thick as the boy's arm, and behind that door
the walls of ice, melting a blue, faint light,
an air of cedar branches, sawdust, fern:
decaying seasons keeping from decay.

A summer guest, the boy had never seen
(a servant told him of it) how the lake
froze three foot thick, how farmers came with teams,
with axe and saw, to cut great blocks of ice,
translucid, marbled, glittering in the sun,

1. " 'I will smite the winter house with the summer house; and the houses of ivory shall perish, and the great houses shall come to an end,' says the Lord." Amos, a shepherd and prophet, was warning the Israelites of God's retribution for their transgressions.

load them on sleds and drag them up the hill
to be manhandled down the narrow path
and set in courses for the summer's keeping,
the kitchen uses and luxuriousness
of the great houses. And he heard how once
a team and driver drowned in the break of spring:
the man's cry melting from the ice that summer
frightened the sherbet-eaters off the terrace.

Dust of the cedar, lost and evergreen
among the slowly blunting water walls
where the blade edge melted and the steel saw's bite
was rounded out, and the horse and rider drowned
in the red sea's blood,[2] I was the silly child
who dreamed that riderless cry, and saw the guests
run from a ghostly wall, so long before
the winter house fell with the summer house,
and the houses, Egypt, the great houses, had an end.

1960

Snowflakes

Not slowly wrought, nor treasured for their form
In heaven, but by the blind self of the storm
Spun off, each driven individual
Perfected in the moment of his fall.

1973

Gyroscope[3]

This admirable gadget, when it is
Wound on a string and spun with steady force,
Maintains its balance on most any smooth
Surface, pleasantly humming as it goes.
It is whirled not on a constant course, but still
Stands in unshivering integrity
For quite some time, meaning nothing perhaps
But being something agreeable to watch,
A silver nearly silence gleaning a still-
ness out of speed, composing unity
From spin, so that its hollow spaces seem
Solids of light, until it wobbles and

2. Alludes to the Israelites' escape from Egypt through the miraculously parted Red Sea, which then rejoined, destroying Pharoah's horsemen.

3. A wheel mounted in a set of rings so that its axis of rotation is free to turn in any direction.

Begins to whine, and then with an odd lunge
Eccentric and reckless, it skids away
And drops dead into its own skeleton.

1975

Reading Pornography in Old Age

Unbridled licentiousness with no holds barred,
Immediate and mutual lust, satisfiable
In the heat, upon demand, aroused again
And satisfied again, lechery unlimited.

Till space runs out at the bottom of the page
And another pair of lovers, forever young,
Prepotent,[4] endlessly receptive, renews
The daylong, nightlong, interminable grind.

How decent it is, and how unlike our lives
Where "fuck you" is a term of vengeful scorn
And the murmur of "sorry, partner" as often heard
As ever in mixed doubles or at bridge.

Though I suspect the stuff is written by
Elderly homosexuals manacled to their
Machines, it's mildly touching all the same,
A reminiscence of the life that was in Eden

Before the Fall, when we were beautiful
And shameless, and untouched by memory:
Before we were driven out to the laboring world
Of the money and the garbage and the kids

In which we read this nonsense and are moved
At all that was always lost for good, in which
We think about sex obsessively except
During the act, when our minds tend to wander.

1984

4. Having exceptional power; very potent.

Amy Clampitt
1920–1994

Years after Sylvia Plath, John Berryman, Anne Sexton, and Robert Lowell had died, an unknown contemporary of theirs came to prominence. In 1983, at sixty-three, Amy Clampitt published her first full-length book of poetry, *The Kingfisher* (she had previously published two chapbooks). Although her career proved that the energy of her literary generation was not spent, Clampitt was a very different kind of poet from the confessionals. Whereas agonized rebellion fuels much of their poetry, Clampitt is more affiliative. She, too, writes ambivalent elegies for her mother ("A Procession at Candlemas") and father ("Beethoven, Opus 111"), but without the self-dramatizing violence of rejection. Journeying "down the long-unentered nave of childhood" to recover her maternal origins, to stitch up "the lost connection" between mother and daughter, Clampitt honors the interwovenness of each life with its maternal source—hence her images of layering, wrapping, knotting, quilting, and threading. Through bold comparisons of her father, an Iowa farmer, with Beethoven, she commemorates her parent as an unwitting artist of the earthly sublime.

Clampitt was also on more peaceful terms with her literary parents, openly declaring her debts to older poets. From Gerard Manley Hopkins she borrows the epigraph for *The Kingfisher* ("As kingfishers catch fire, dragonflies draw flame . . ."), as well as his hyphenated compounds and dense sonic clusters. She dedicates a sequence of biographical poems to John Keats, as well as to George Eliot and William and Dorothy Wordsworth, and Keats's luxurious sensuousness also inspires her verse. Few postwar American poets are as comfortable with their British literary inheritance. And like the American modernist Marianne Moore, she often creates odd assortments, poems that ponder and transform the quotidian world observed by science.

At a time when some American writers were seeking to make poetry ever more elemental, self-sufficient, and stripped down, Clampitt sprawled in lush fields of diction and allusion. Her language dilates in multiple directions, taking in works of music and visual art as well as scientific disciplines such as botany, geology, and ornithology. "For the ocean," she writes in "Beach Glass," "nothing / is beneath consideration"; everything is continually reshuffled and recycled, from geological formations to the debris of driftwood and bottles to the great stained-glass windows of cathedrals that derive from sand and must ultimately return to it. Similarly, the poet's erudite and multilayered descriptions take up and turn over and over everything within reach, keeping an inventory of the worn out and cast away, as well as the "permutations of novelty."

Clampitt's background might seem unpromising for such a wondrous delight in the arts. Having grown up on Depression-era farms in Iowa, she remembers the high-art world of music and painting as a luxury and a distraction: "High art / with a stiff neck," "harpstrings and fripperies of air / congealed into an object nailed against the wall" ("Beethoven, Opus 111"). From Clampitt's late Romantic perspective, great art is born of suffering, deprivation, and grief. Clampitt affirms poetic art as a precise tool for understanding losses, inheritances, loves, and our abundant, ever-shifting world. "What is real except // what's fabricated?" she asks in "A Procession at Candlemas." She fabricates with abandon, spinning out diaphanous texts that combine imaginative pleasure with scrupulous observation.

Clampitt's formal structures include long-lined tercets and short-lined verse paragraphs. Her descriptive language is expansive, proliferating adjectives and metaphors with sustained energy. Patterns of alliteration, assonance, and rhythmic parallelism bind together her words. Her syntax is complex, often building a sinuous momentum in extended sentences. It moves forward only to twist back on itself, hesitate, embroider, rush headlong, break off, and start again, all the while threading together long trains of association, feeling, and observation. Her poems often evoke complex resemblances between seemingly incongruous subjects—the ocean and the poet's mind, her father and Beethoven, her mother and the goddess Athena. Clampitt's poetry conveys both intellectual alertness and imaginative fecundity. Steeped in a wide-ranging knowledge of the past, it also reacquaints us, vividly, with our present.

A Quaker by background, Clampitt was born on June 15, 1920, in New Providence, Iowa. In 1941, she completed her B.A. at Grinnell College, and she did some graduate work at Columbia University before becoming a secretary at Oxford University Press. From 1952 to 1959, she was a reference librarian for the National Audubon Society, and indeed her poems keenly observe bird life. She then became a freelance writer, editor, and researcher. During the Vietnam War, she joined the antiwar movement, and in 1982, she turned full time to poetry writing. Living in New York, she summered and wrote in Maine. She died of ovarian cancer.

Beach Glass

While you walk the water's edge,
turning over concepts
I can't envision, the honking buoy
serves notice that at any time
the wind may change,
the reef-bell clatters
its treble monotone, deaf as Cassandra
to any note but warning.[1] The ocean,
cumbered by no business more urgent
than keeping open old accounts
that never balanced,
goes on shuffling its millenniums
of quartz, granite, and basalt.
                                        It behaves
toward the permutations of novelty—
driftwood and shipwreck, last night's
beer cans, spilt oil, the coughed-up
residue of plastic—with random
impartiality, playing catch or tag
or touch-last like a terrier,
turning the same thing over and over,
over and over. For the ocean, nothing
is beneath consideration.
                                        The houses
of so many mussels and periwinkles[2]
have been abandoned here, it's hopeless
to know which to salvage. Instead
I keep a lookout for beach glass—

1. The "reef-bell" warns ships about a reef of rocks or sand beneath the surface of the water. In Homer's *Iliad,* Cassandra prophesied the fall of Troy, but because of Apollo's curse, no one believed her.

2. Varieties of shellfish.

amber of Budweiser, chrysoprase
of Almadén and Gallo, lapis[3]
by way of (no getting around it,
I'm afraid) Phillips'
Milk of Magnesia, with now and then a rare
translucent turquoise or blurred amethyst
of no known origin.
The process
goes on forever: they came from sand,
they go back to gravel,
along with the treasuries
of Murano, the buttressed
astonishments of Chartres,[4]
which even now are readying
for being turned over and over as gravely
and gradually as an intellect
engaged in the hazardous
redefinition of structures
no one has yet looked at.

1983

Meridian

First daylight on the bittersweet-hung
sleeping porch at high summer : dew
all over the lawn, sowing diamond-
point-highlighted shadows :
the hired man's shadow revolving
along the walk, a flash of milkpails
passing : no threat in sight, no hint
anywhere in the universe, of that

apathy at the meridian, the noon
of absolute boredom : flies
crooning black lullabies in the kitchen,
milk-soured crocks, cream separator
still unwashed : what is there to life
but chores and more chores, dishwater,
fatigue, unwanted children : nothing
to stir the longueur of afternoon

except possibly thunderheads :
climbing, livid, turreted alabaster
lit up from within by splendor and terror
—forked lightning's
split-second disaster.

1983

3. Or lapis lazuli, a rich, sky-blue color (and the name of a semiprecious stone). *Chrysoprase:* apple-green color (also a semiprecious stone).

4. Chartres Cathedral, in France, is noted for the beauty of its stained-glass windows. Murano, in Italy, is famous for its glasswork.

A Procession at Candlemas[5]

I

Moving on or going back to where you came from,
bad news is what you mainly travel with:
a breakup or a breakdown, someone running off

or walking out, called up or called home:
death in the family. Nudged from their stanchions
outside the terminal, anonymous of purpose

as a flock of birds, the bison of the highway
funnel westward onto Route 80, mirroring
an entity that cannot look into itself and know

what makes it what it is. Sooner or later
every trek becomes a funeral procession.
The mother curtained in Intensive Care—

a scene the mind leaves blank, fleeing instead
toward scenes of transhumance, the belled sheep
moving up the Pyrenees,[6] red-tasseled pack llamas

footing velvet-green precipices, the Kurdish
women, jingling with bangles, gorgeous
on their rug-piled mounts—already lying dead,

bereavement altering the moving lights
to a processional, a feast of Candlemas.
Change as child-bearing, birth as a kind

of shucking off: out of what began
as a Mosaic[7] insult—such a loathing
of the common origin, even a virgin,

having given birth, needs purifying—
to carry fire as though it were a flower,
the terror and the loveliness entrusted

into naked hands, supposing God might have,
might actually need a mother: people have
at times found this a way of being happy.

A Candlemas of moving lights along Route 80;
lighted candles in a corridor from Arlington
over the Potomac, for every carried flame

5. Feast of the purification of the Virgin Mary and presentation of the infant Jesus in the temple, commemorated by candlelight on February 2.
6. Mountain chain in southwestern Europe. *Transhumance:* seasonal transfer of livestock to different pastures.
7. Related to Moses and the ancient Hebraic law.

the name of a dead soldier: an element
fragile as ego, frightening as parturition,
necessary and intractable as dreaming.

The lapped, wheelborne integument,[8] layer
within layer, at the core a dream of
something precious, ripped: Where are we?

The sleepers groan, stir, rewrap themselves
about the self's imponderable substance,
or clamber down, numb-footed, half in a drowse

of freezing dark, through a Stonehenge
of fuel pumps, the bison hulks slantwise
beside them, drinking. What is real except

what's fabricated? The jellies glitter
cream-capped in the cafeteria showcase;
gumball globes, Life Savers cinctured

in parcel gilt, plop from their housings
perfect, like miracles. Comb, nail clipper,
lip rouge, mirrors and emollients[9] embody,

niched into the washroom wall case,
the pristine seductiveness of money.
Absently, without inhabitants, this

nowhere oasis wears the place name
of Indian Meadows. The westward-trekking
transhumance, once only, of a people who,

in losing everything they had, lost even
the names they went by, stumbling past
like caribou, perhaps camped here. Who

can assign a trade-in value to that sorrow?
The monk in sheepskin over tucked-up saffron
intoning to a drum becomes the metronome

of one more straggle up Pennsylvania Avenue[1]
in falling snow, a whirl of tenderly
remorseless corpuscles, street gangs

amok among magnolias' pregnant wands,
a stillness at the heart of so much whirling:
beyond the torn integument of childbirth,

8. Skin.
9. Softeners.

1. Street in Washington, D.C., on which the White House is located.

sometimes, wrapped like a papoose into a grief
not merely of the ego, you rediscover almost
the rest-in-peace of the placental coracle.[2]

II

Of what the dead were, living, one knows
so little as barely to recognize
the fabric of the backward-ramifying

antecedents, half-noted presences
in darkened rooms: the old, the feared,
the hallowed. Never the same river[3]

drowns the unalterable doorsill. An effigy
in olive wood or pear wood, dank
with the sweat of age, walled in the dark

at Brauron, Argos, Samos: even the unwed
Athene, who had no mother, born—it's declared—
of some man's brain like every other pure idea,

had her own wizened cult object, kept
out of sight like the incontinent whimperer
in the backstairs bedroom, where no child

ever goes—to whom, year after year,
the fair linen of the sacred peplos[4]
was brought in ceremonial procession—

flutes and stringed instruments, wildflower-
hung cattle, nubile Athenian girls, young men
praised for the beauty of their bodies. Who

can unpeel the layers of that seasonal
returning to the dark where memory fails,
as birds re-enter the ancestral flyway?

Daylight, snow falling, knotting of gears:
Chicago. Soot, the rotting backsides
of tenements, grimed trollshapes of ice

2. Small wicker boat. *Papoose:* Native American word for young child.
3. Pre-Socratic Greek philosopher Heracleitus (c. 540–c. 480 B.C.E.) declared the impossibility of stepping twice into the same river.
4. In ancient Greece, an embroidered shawl or robe, woven and presented in a great procession every four years as a gift to Athena; the frieze of the Parthenon depicts this procession. Although a monumental statue of Athena was in the Parthenon, Clampitt cites in a note a statement that the sacred peplos was ritually offered to the older, wooden, doll-like image kept in the Erechtheum. "Similar wooden images were central to the worship of Artemis at Brauron, and of Hera at Argos and Samos" [Clampitt's note]. *Brauron, Argos:* Greek cities. *Samos:* Greek island. Athena, Greek goddess of wisdom and war, was not born but sprang fully armed from Zeus's skull.

underneath the bridges, the tunnel heaving
like a birth canal. Disgorged, the infant
howling in the restroom; steam-table cereal,

pale coffee; wall-eyed TV receivers, armchairs
of molded plastic: the squalor of the day
resumed, the orphaned litter taken up again

unloved, the spawn of botched intentions,
grief a mere hardening of the gut,
a set piece of what can't be avoided:

parents by the tens of thousands living
unthanked, unpaid but in the sour coin
of resentment. Midmorning gray as zinc

along Route 80, corn-stubble quilting
the underside of snowdrifts, the cadaverous
belvedere[5] of windmills, the sullen stare

of feedlot cattle; black creeks puncturing
white terrain, the frozen bottomland
a mush of willow tops; dragnetted in ice,

the Mississippi. Westward toward the dark,
the undertow of scenes come back to, fright
riddling the structures of interior history:

Where is it? Where, in the shucked-off
bundle, the hampered obscurity that has been
for centuries the mumbling lot of women,

did the thread of fire, too frail
ever to discover what it meant, to risk
even the taking of a shape, relinquish

the seed of possibility, unguessed-at
as a dream of something precious? Memory,
that exquisite blunderer, stumbling

like a migrant bird that finds the flyway
it hardly knew it knew except by instinct,
down the long-unentered nave of childhood,

late on a midwinter afternoon, alone
among the snow-hung hollows of the windbreak
on the far side of the orchard, encounters

5. Structure designed to command a view.

sheltering among the evergreens, a small
stilled bird, its cap of clear yellow
slit by a thread of scarlet—the untouched

nucleus of fire, the lost connection
hallowing the wizened effigy, the mother
curtained in Intensive Care: a Candlemas

of moving lights along Route 80, at nightfall,
in falling snow, the stillness and the sorrow
of things moving back to where they came from.

1983

Beethoven, Opus 111

For Norman Carey

> There are epochs . . . when mankind, not content with the present, longing for time's deeper layers, like the plowman, thirsts for the virgin soil of time.
>
> OSIP MANDELSTAM[6]

—Or, conversely, hungers
for the levitations of the concert hall:
the hands like rafts of *putti*[7]
out of a region where the dolorous stars
are fixed in glassy cerements of Art;
the *ancien régime*'s[8] diaphanous plash
athwart the mounting throb of hobnails—
shod squadrons of vibration
mining the air, its struck ores hardening
into a plowshare, a downward wandering
disrupting every formal symmetry:
from the supine harp-case, the strung-foot
tendons under the mahogany, the bulldozer
in the bass unearths a Piranesian[9]
catacomb: Beethoven ventilating,
with a sound he cannot hear, the cave-in
of recurring rage.
In the tornado country
of mid-America, my father
might have been his twin—a farmer
hacking at sourdock, at the strangle-

6. Russian poet and critic (1891–1938). Ludwig van Beethoven (1770–1827), German composer whose work both crowned the classical period and helped initiate the Romantic period in European music. Beethoven was already deaf when he composed the Sonata No. 32 in C minor, Op. 111, in 1821–22.

7. Stylized infant cherubs (Italian).

8. Of the political and social system before the French Revolution of 1789 (French). *Cerements:* grave-clothes, usually made of wax.

9. Giovanni Battista Piranesi (1720–1778), Italian architect and artist.

roots of thistles and wild morning glories,
setting out rashly, one October,
to rid the fencerows of poison ivy:
livid seed-globs turreted
in trinities of glitter, ripe
with the malefic glee no farmer doubts
lives deep down things.[1] My father
was naïve enough—by nature
revolutionary, though he'd have
disowned the label—to suppose he might
in some way, minor but radical, disrupt
the givens of existence: set
his neighbors' thinking straight, undo
the stranglehold of reasons nations
send their boys off to war. That fall,
after the oily fireworks had cooled down
to trellises of hairy wicks,
he dug them up, rootstocks and all,
and burned them. Do-gooder!
The well-meant holocaust[2] became
a mist of venom, sowing itself along
the sculptured hollows of his overalls,
braceleting wrists and collarbone—
a mesh of blisters spreading to a shirt
worn like a curse. For weeks
he writhed inside it. Awful.
High art
with a stiff neck: an upright Steinway
bought in Chicago; a chromo of a Hobbema
tree-avenue, or of Millet's[3] imagined peasant,
the lark she listens to invisible, perhaps
irrelevant: harpstrings and fripperies of air
congealed into an object nailed against the wall,
its sole ironic function (if it has any)
to demonstrate that one, though he may
grunt and sweat at work, is not a clod.
Beethoven might declare the air
his domicile, the winds kin,[4] the tornado
a kind of second cousin; here,
his labor merely shimmers—a deracinated
album leaf, a bagatelle, the "Moonlight"
rendered with a dying fall[5] (the chords

1. Cf. "God's Grandeur," by English poet Gerard Manley Hopkins (1844–1889): "There lives the dearest freshness deep down things." *Malefic:* baleful, ominous.
2. Sacrifice completely consumed by fire.
3. Jean-François Millet (1814–1875): French painter renowned for his peasant subjects, in particular an often-imitated picture of a peasant pausing from her work to listen to an invisible lark. The European skylark sings only in flight, often too high to be seen, and its invisible song is often, as in Percy Bysshe Shelley's (1792–1822) "To a Sky-Lark," a Romantic symbol. *Chromo:* chromolithograph; a type of reproduced print. Meindhart Hobbema (1638–1709): Dutch Baroque landscape painter.
4. "In a letter to Count Brunswick dated February 13, 1814, Beethoven wrote: 'As regards me, great heavens! my dominion is in the air; the tones whirl like the wind, and often there is a whirl in my soul'" [from Clampitt's note].
5. Cf. the beginning of Shakespeare's *Twelfth Night:* "If music be the food of love, play on . . .

subside, disintegrate, regroup
in climbing sequences *con brio*[6]); there's
no dwelling on the sweet past here,
there being no past to speak of
other than the setbacks: typhoid
in the wells, half the first settlers
dead of it before a year was out;
diphtheria and scarlet fever
every winter; drought, the Depression,
a mortgage on the mortgage. High art
as a susurrus,[7] the silk and perfume
of unsullied hands. Those hands!—
driving the impressionable wild with anguish
for another life entirely: the Lyceum[8] circuit,
the doomed diving bell of Art.
                                        Beethoven
in his workroom: ear trumpet,
conversation book and pencil, candlestick,
broken crockery, the Graf piano
wrecked by repeated efforts to hear himself—
out of a humdrum squalor the levitations,
the shakes and triplets, the *Adagio*
molto semplice e cantabile, the Arietta[9]
a disintegrating surf of blossom
opening along the keyboard, along the fencerows
the astonishment of sweetness. My father,
driving somewhere in Kansas or Colorado,
in dustbowl country, stopped the car
to dig up by the roots a flower
he'd never seen before—a kind
of prickly poppy most likely, its luminousness
wounding the blank plains like desire.
He mentioned in a letter the disappointment
of his having hoped it might transplant—
an episode that brings me near tears,
still, as even his dying does not—
that awful dying, months-long, hunkered,
irascible. From a clod no plowshare
could deliver, a groan for someone
(because he didn't want to look
at anything) to take away the flowers,
a bawling as of slaughterhouses, slogans
of a general uprising: *Freiheit!*[1]
Beethoven, shut up with the four walls
of his deafness, rehearsing the unhearable
semplice e cantabile, somehow reconstituting
the blister shirt of the intolerable

that strain again! It had a dying fall" (1.1.1, 4). *Moonlight:* Beethoven's *Moonlight* Sonata.
6. With vigor (musical instruction in Italian).
7. Whisper.
8. Building used for cultural activities.
9. Short song or instrumental piece. *Adagio molto semplice e cantabile:* slowly, very simply and singingly (musical instruction in Italian).
1. Freedom (German).

into these shakes and triplets, a hurrying
into flowering along the fencerows: dying,
for my father, came to be like that
finally—in its messages the levitation
of serenity, as though the spirit might
aspire, in its last act,
                    to walk on air.

1983

Hispaniola[2]

Note how the bear
though armed and dangerous
caring not at all for
dignity, undaintily
snacks on fat white things
paws strawberry meadows
lunges swinging smeared
through blackberry canebrakes
maps a constellated
dream of bee trees
snoring galaxies
the primum mobile[3]
twanging the gulfs
of slumber   beatific
on the tongue
the kiss of honey :
or so we imagine
a hulking innocence
child's-play bedfellow
to the sapient
omnivorous
prehensile
raptor   world-class
bully : the rumor
brought to Alexander[4]
of, in India, a reed
that brought forth honey
sans the help of bees
began it   a topography
of monoculture
blackening the Indus
Tigris-Euphrates[5]

2. Island of the West Indies divided into Haiti in the west and the Dominican Republic in the east. In a note, Clampitt quotes a newsmagazine article stating that Columbus planned from the start to establish a sugar industry on Hispaniola, like the ones on the Canary and Madeira Islands.

3. Prime mover (Latin); in the medieval, Ptolemaic astronomical system, the outer sphere of the heavens that provided the energy for all other motion.

4. Macedonian emperor (356–323 B.C.E.).

5. River system of southwest Asia; considered the cradle of civilization. *Indus:* Trans-Himalayan river of south Asia.

westward-spreading
molasses stain
island plantations
off the coast of
Africa leapfrogging
the Atlantic
Hispaniola
Spanish Mexico
Peru   Paraguay
along the Amazon
the Portuguese
the Dutch   the British
Barbados Antigua Montserrat[6]
Jamaica   huger and huger
deforestations
making way for
raising cane   to be
holed   planted   cut
crushed   boiled
fermented or
reduced to crystalline
appeasement of mammalian
cravings   slave ships
whip-wielding
overseers   world-class
indignity   the bubbling
hellhole of molasses pits
the bear's
(or if not his, whose?)
nightmare

1994

Syrinx[7]

Like the foghorn that's all lung,
the wind chime that's all percussion,
like the wind itself, that's merely air
in a terrible fret, without so much
as a finger to articulate
what ails it, the aeolian
syrinx, that reed
in the throat of a bird,
when it comes to the shaping of
what we call consonants, is
too imprecise for consensus
about what it even seems to

6. Islands of the West Indies.
7. Vocal organ of birds, named after a Greek nymph who was turned into a reed to protect her chastity from Pan. Pan made the panpipe, or syrinx, from that reed.

be saying: is it *o-ka-lee*
or *con-ka-ree,* is it really *jug jug,*
is it *cuckoo* for that matter?—
much less whether a bird's call
means anything in
particular, or at all.

Syntax comes last, there can be
no doubt of it: came last,
can be thought of (is
thought of by some) as a
higher form of expression:
is, in extremity, first to
be jettisoned: as the diva
onstage, all soaring
pectoral breathwork,
takes off, pure vowel
breaking free of the dry,
the merely fricative
husk of the particular, rises
past saying anything, any
more than the wind in
the trees, waves breaking,
or Homer's gibbering
Thespesiae iachē:[8]

those last-chance vestiges
above the threshold, the all-
but dispossessed of breath.

1994

8. Unearthly cry (Greek); emitted by the spirits of the dead crowding around Odysseus (Homer, *Odyssey* 10.34–43).

RICHARD WILBUR
b. 1921

In the pantheon of post–World War II poetry, Richard Wilbur is, like the early Robert Lowell, a master of formal verse. He has inspired many younger poets, such as the New Formalists, who have championed a return to meter and rhyme. But Wilbur has remained faithful to the New Critical formalism that Lowell abandoned for confessional free verse. Wilbur centers his work in the achievement of illuminated, controlled moments, but he is not merely measured and self-possessed. He is alive to inner challenges, and though his mode of expression is deftly sedate, it begins in cross-purposes and cross-sympathies before it culminates in intimations of an earthly paradise.

"I am for wit and wakefulness," Wilbur announces in "Ceremony." But behind his neat stanzas and cheerful optimism lurk encounters with chaos and death. His serious attempts to write poetry arose out of war: "It was not until World War II took me to

Cassino, Anzio and the Siegfried Line that I began to versify in earnest. One does not use poetry for its major purposes, as a means of organizing oneself and the world, until one's world somehow gets out of hand. A general cataclysm is not required; the disorder must be personal and may be wholly so, but poetry, to be vital, does seem to need a periodic acquaintance with the threat of Chaos" (*Twentieth Century Authors,* First Supplement, 1955). Wilbur endorses organization without wanting it to be easy: in "The Beacon," he salutes a human artifact ("sighted ship / Assembles all the sea"), whereas in "Caserta Garden," he cautions, in speaking of the "garden of the world," that "Its shapes escape our simpler symmetries."

He seeks complex symmetries, which he composes with "ceremony." Wilbur's formal dexterity—evident in perfect rhymes, unfaltering meters, expertly placed verbs, and elegantly woven syntax—is a necessary part of his self-expression. He has defended the use of strict poetic forms, traditional or invented, as being "like the use of framing and composition in painting: both serve to limit the work of art, and to declare its artificiality: they say, 'This is not the world, but a pattern imposed upon the world or found in it; this is a partial and provisional attempt to establish relations between things.' " He adds, "There are other less metaphysical reasons for preferring strictness of form: the fact, for example, that subtle variation is unrecognizable without the pre-existence of a norm; or the fact that form, in showing and complicating the writing-process, calls out the poet's full talents, and thereby insures a greater care and cleverness in the choice and disposition of words. In general, I would say that limitation makes for power: the strength of the genie comes of his being confined in a bottle" (*Mid-Century American Poets,* ed. John Ciardi, 1950). For the most part, he declines the themes of dispossession and disintegration, as he has the poetics of fragmentation and "open" form, that occupy many modern and contemporary poets, making his verse an artfully controlled evocation, over difficulties, of desirable experience.

Wilbur was born on March 1, 1921, in New York City. His father was an artist; Wilbur's poem "My Father Paints the Summer" praises him for disregarding the actual rain to paint a perfect summer's day, "always an imagined time." Wilbur's mother came from a family prominent in journalism, a direction he followed briefly. Two years after his birth, the family moved to a very old house in North Caldwell, New Jersey, where he developed his taste for country things; he has written a poem about the potato and writes brilliantly, as in "Seed Leaves," of plant growth—"the doom of taking shape." At Amherst College, he was encouraged by his English courses to develop Horatian poems—that is, poems chiseled in form and rural in setting. After the war, he received an M.A. at Harvard University, teaching there (1950–54), at Wellesley College (1955–57), and at Wesleyan University (1957–77). In 1987, he left his position as writer-in-residence at Smith College to become poet laureate of the United States, succeeding Robert Penn Warren. Besides books of verse, Wilbur has made splendid translations of the verse plays of Molière, Racine, and Voltaire, finding kinship in the wit and form of the French originals. He has twice won the Bollingen Prize and twice the Pulitzer.

The Death of a Toad

A toad the power mower caught,
Chewed and clipped of a leg, with a hobbling hop has got
To the garden verge, and sanctuaried him
Under the cineraria leaves, in the shade
Of the ashen heartshaped leaves, in a dim,
Low, and a final glade.

The rare original heartsblood goes,
Spends on the earthen hide, in the folds and wizenings, flows
In the gutters of the banked and staring eyes. He lies
As still as if he would return to stone,
And soundlessly attending, dies
Toward some deep monotone,

Toward misted and ebullient seas
And cooling shores, toward lost Amphibia's emperies.[1]
Day dwindles, drowning, and at length is gone
In the wide and antique eyes, which still appear
To watch, across the castrate lawn,
The haggard daylight steer.

1950

Ceremony

A striped blouse in a clearing by Bazille[2]
Is, you may say, a patroness of boughs
Too queenly kind toward nature to be kin.
But ceremony never did conceal,
Save to the silly eye, which all allows,
How much we are the woods we wander in.

Let her be some Sabrina[3] fresh from stream,
Lucent as shallows slowed by wading sun,
Bedded on fern, the flowers' cynosure:
Then nymph and wood must nod and strive to dream
That she is airy earth, the trees, undone,
Must ape her languor natural and pure.

Ho-hum. I am for wit and wakefulness,
And love this feigning lady by Bazille.
What's lightly hid is deepest understood,
And when with social smile and formal dress
She teaches leaves to curtsey and quadrille,
I think there are most tigers in the wood.

1950

Boy at the Window

Seeing the snowman standing all alone
In dusk and cold is more than he can bear.
The small boy weeps to hear the wind prepare
A night of gnashings and enormous moan.

1. Amphibia is imagined as the presiding spirit of the toad's (and of all amphibians') universe.
2. Frédéric Bazille (1841–1871), French painter associated with the Impressionists. Most of his paintings show figures in close relation to a landscape.
3. The nymph of the river Severn, in Milton's *Comus*, but here identified with thoughtless, unceremonious nature, and contrasted with Bazille's lady.

His tearful sight can hardly reach to where
The pale-faced figure with bitumen[4] eyes
Returns him such a god-forsaken stare
As outcast Adam gave to Paradise.

The man of snow is, nonetheless, content,
Having no wish to go inside and die.
Still, he is moved to see the youngster cry.
Though frozen water is his element,
He melts enough to drop from one soft eye
A trickle of the purest rain, a tear
For the child at the bright pane surrounded by
Such warmth, such light, such love, and so much fear.

1956

Love Calls Us to the Things of This World[5]

The eyes open to a cry of pulleys,
And spirited from sleep, the astounded soul
Hangs for a moment bodiless and simple
As false dawn.
Outside the open window
The morning air is all awash with angels.

Some are in bed-sheets, some are in blouses,
Some are in smocks: but truly there they are.
Now they are rising together in calm swells
Of halcyon feeling, filling whatever they wear
With the deep joy of their impersonal breathing;

Now they are flying in place, conveying
The terrible speed of their omnipresence, moving
And staying like white water; and now of a sudden
They swoon down into so rapt a quiet
That nobody seems to be there.
The soul shrinks

From all that it is about to remember,
From the punctual rape of every blessèd day,
And cries,
"Oh, let there be nothing on earth but laundry,

4. Asphalt or tar.
5. Quoted from St. Augustine. Wilbur has said, "You must imagine the poem as occurring at perhaps seven-thirty in the morning; the scene is a bedroom high up in a city apartment building; outside the bedroom window, the first laundry of the day is being yanked across the sky and one has been awakened by the squeaking pulleys of the laundry-line."

Nothing but rosy hands in the rising steam
And clear dances done in the sight of heaven."

Yet, as the sun acknowledges
With a warm look the world's hunks and colors,
The soul descends once more in bitter love
To accept the waking body, saying now
In a changed voice as the man yawns and rises,

"Bring them down from their ruddy gallows;
Let there be clean linen for the backs of thieves;
Let lovers go fresh and sweet to be undone,
And the heaviest nuns walk in a pure floating
Of dark habits,
keeping their difficult balance."

1956

Playboy

High on his stockroom ladder like a dunce
The stock-boy sits, and studies like a sage
The subject matter of one glossy page,
As lost in curves as Archimedes[6] once.

Sometimes, without a glance, he feeds himself.
The left hand, like a mother-bird in flight,
Brings him a sandwich for a sidelong bite,
And then returns it to a dusty shelf.

What so engrosses him? The wild décor
Of this pink-papered alcove into which
A naked girl has stumbled, with its rich
Welter of pelts and pillows on the floor,

Amidst which, kneeling in a supple pose,
She lifts a goblet in her father hand,
As if about to toast a flower-stand
Above which hovers an exploding rose

Fired from a long-necked crystal vase that rests
Upon a tasseled and vermillion cloth
One taste of which would shrivel up a moth?
Or is he pondering her perfect breasts?

Nothing escapes him of her body's grace
Or of her floodlit skin, so sleek and warm

6. Greek mathematician and inventor (c. 287–212 B.C.E.).

And yet so strangely like a uniform,
But what now grips his fancy is her face,

And how the cunning picture holds her still
At just that smiling instant when her soul,
Grown sweetly faint, and swept beyond control,
Consents to his inexorable will.

1969

The Writer

In her room at the prow of the house
Where light breaks, and the windows are tossed with linden,
My daughter is writing a story.

I pause in the stairwell, hearing
From her shut door a commotion of typewriter-keys
Like a chain hauled over a gunwale.[7]

Young as she is, the stuff
Of her life is a great cargo, and some of it heavy:
I wish her a lucky passage.

But now it is she who pauses,
As if to reject my thought and its easy figure.
A stillness greatens, in which

The whole house seems to be thinking,
And then she is at it again with a bunched clamor
Of strokes, and again is silent.

I remember the dazed starling
Which was trapped in that very room, two years ago;[8]
How we stole in, lifted a sash

And retreated, not to affright it;
And how for a helpless hour, through the crack of the door,
We watched the sleek, wild, dark

And iridescent creature
Batter against the brilliance, drop like a glove
To the hard floor, or the desk-top,

And wait then, humped and bloody,
For the wits to try it again; and how our spirits
Rose when, suddenly sure,

7. Upper edge of a boat's side.
8. A bird trapped in a house portends a death, according to New England superstition.

It lifted off from a chair-back,
Beating a smooth course for the right window
And clearing the sill of the world.

It is always a matter, my darling,
Of life or death, as I had forgotten. I wish
What I wished you before, but harder.

1976

A Finished Man

Of the four louts who threw him off the dock
Three are now dead, and so more faintly mock
The way he choked and splashed and was afraid.
His memory of the fourth begins to fade.

It was himself whom he could not forgive;
Yet it has been a comfort to outlive
That woman, stunned by his appalling gaffe,
Who with a napkin half-suppressed her laugh,

Or that grey colleague, surely gone by now,
Who, turning toward the window, raised his brow,
Embarrassed to have caught him in a lie.
All witness darkens, eye by dimming eye.

Thus he can walk today with heart at ease
Through the old quad, escorted by trustees.
To dedicate the monumental gym
A grateful college means to name for him.

Seated, he feels the warm sun sculpt his cheek
As the young president gets up to speak.
If the dead die, if he can but forget,
If money talks, he may be perfect yet.

1987

A Barred Owl

The warping night air having brought the boom
Of an owl's voice into her darkened room,
We tell the wakened child that all she heard
Was an odd question from a forest bird,
Asking of us, if rightly listened to,
"Who cooks for you?" and then "Who cooks for you?"

Words, which can make our terrors bravely clear,
Can also thus domesticate a fear,
And send a small child back to sleep at night
Not listening for the sound of stealthy flight
Or dreaming of some small thing in a claw
Borne up to some dark branch and eaten raw.

2000

Kingsley Amis
1922–1995

Kingsley Amis was poetically, as he was politically, conservative. He disliked mawkishness and found it allied with general disorder of emotions and lives. He was also impatient with parochialism, as with excess in whatever form. With his friend Philip Larkin, Amis was a member of the Movement, a 1950s group that praised craft and modesty while debunking grandiloquence. Despite his obvious political difference, W. H. Auden also had a discernible impact. But Amis rejected Dylan Thomas as a baleful influence. As Amis announces in the poem "Against Romanticism," he prefers "a temperate zone" to a "voluble swooning wilderness." The unkempt displeases him, as does the pallid. His poems are small wars of ironies, expressed with great deftness, and covert pleas for what is, as opposed to what might be. His heroes are often all dressed up with no place to go. His poems—sad, comic, and thus wry—frequently catch a man at his most ridiculous: when he searches for love.

Amis was born on April 16, 1922, to a lower-middle-class family in London. He attended the City of London School, then served in the army from 1942 to 1945. After the war, he studied English literature at Oxford University, where he befriended Larkin. He taught at University College, Swansea, for twelve years, long enough to publish two volumes of poetry and gather the material for his much-praised satirical novel *Lucky Jim* (1954). He then went to teach at Cambridge University, but was happy to extricate himself by writing fiction. His later novels proceeded from the comedy of sex to the even more comic situation of old age, dying, and death. He also continued to write poetry. A winner of the Booker Prize, he was honored as a C.B.E. (Commander of the British Empire) in 1981 and knighted in 1990.

Against Romanticism

A traveller who walks a temperate zone
　—Woods devoid of beasts, roads that please the foot—
Finds that its decent surface grows too thin:
　Something unperceived fumbles at his nerves.
To please an ingrown taste for anarchy
　Torrid images circle in the wood,
And sweat for recognition up the road,
　Cramming close the air with their bookish cries.
All senses then are glad to gasp: the eye
　Smeared with garish paints, tickled up with ghosts

That brandish warnings or an abstract noun;
  Melodies from shards, memories from coal,
Or saws from powdered tombstones thump the ear;
  Bodies rich with heat wriggle to the touch,
And verbal scents made real spellbind the nose;
  Incense, frankincense; legendary the taste
Of drinks or fruits or tongues laid on the tongue.
  Over all, a grand meaning fills the scene,
And sets the brain raging with prophecy,
  Raging to discard real time and place,
Raging to build a better time and place
  Than the ones which give prophecy its field
To work, the calm material for its rage,
  And the context which makes its prophecy.
Better, of course, if images were plain,
  Warnings clearly said, shapes put down quite still
Within the fingers' reach, or else nowhere;
  But complexities crowd the simplest thing,
And flaw the surface that they cannot break.
  Let us make at least visions that we need:
Let mine be pallid, so that it cannot
  Force a single glance, form a single word;
An afternoon long-drawn and silent, with
  Buildings free from all grime of history,
The people total strangers, the grass cut,
  Not long, voluble swooning wilderness,
And green, not parched or soured by frantic suns
  Doubling the commands of a rout of gods,
Nor trampled by the havering[1] unicorn;
  Let the sky be clean of officious birds
Punctiliously flying on the left;[2]
  Let there be a path leading out of sight,
And at its other end a temperate zone:
  Woods devoid of beasts, roads that please the foot.

1957

An Ever-Fixed Mark[3]

Years ago, at a private school
Run on traditional lines,
One fellow used to perform
Prodigious feats in the dorm;
His quite undevious designs
Found many a willing tool.

1. Nonsense-talking.
2. A bad omen.
3. Quoted from Shakespeare's Sonnet 116: "Love is not love / Which alters when it alteration finds, / Or bends with the remover to remove: / O no! it is an ever-fixed mark, / That looks on tempests and is never shaken."

On the rugger[4] field, in the gym,
Buck marked down at his leisure
The likeliest bits of stuff;
The notion, familiar enough,
Of 'using somebody for pleasure'
Seemed handy and harmless to him.

But another chap was above
The diversions of such a lout;
Seven years in the place
And he never got to first base
With the kid he followed about:
What interested Ralph was love.

He did the whole thing in style—
Letters three times a week,
Sonnet-sequences, Sunday walks;
Then, during one of their talks,
The youngster caressed his cheek,
And that made it all worth while.

These days, for a quid pro quo,
Ralph's chum is all for romance;
Buck's playmates, family men,
Eye a Boy Scout now and then.
Sex stops when you pull up your pants,
Love never lets you go.

1967

Science Fiction

What makes us rove that starlit corridor
May be the impulse to meet face to face
Our vice and folly shaped into a thing,
And so at last ourselves; what lures us there
Is simpler versions of disaster:
A web that shuffles time and space,
A sentence to perpetual journeying,
A world of ocean without shore,
And simplest, flapping down the poisoned air,
A ten-clawed monster.

In him, perhaps, we see the general ogre
Who rode our ancestors to nightmare,
And in his habitat their maps of hell.[5]

4. Colloquial for rugby.
5. Amis's study of science fiction is *New Maps of Hell* (1960).

But climates and geographies soon change,
Spawning mutations none can quell
With silver sword or necromancer's[6] ring.
Worse than their sires, of wider range,
And much more durable.

1967

6. Magician's.

DONALD DAVIE
1922–1995

Donald Davie is one of a group of English poets (along with Philip Larkin, Kingsley Amis, and Thom Gunn) known as the Movement. Writing in the 1950s, they registered by precept and example their impatience with poetry that (like Dylan Thomas's, in their view) gratuitously inflates its subject matter. They also expressed a preference for understatement over grandiosity and a fondness for cleansing irony and traditional meters. Davie advocated the preservation of metrical and other "rules which have governed ninety percent of English poetry for more than 500 years" (*Delta* 8, 1956). He believed that poets who violate the rules of syntax contribute to a breakdown in civilization. In his *Purity of Diction in English Verse* (1953), which is both literary criticism and a manifesto, Davie warned that "it is impossible not to trace a connection between the laws of syntax and the laws of society. . . . One would almost say, on this showing, that to dislocate syntax in poetry is to threaten the rule of law in the civilized community." Surely not since Plato have greater responsibilities been placed on the poet, though Davie realized he was fighting for a lost cause with a fervor that may have seemed a little ridiculous.

As an antidote to the poetry of excess, impure diction, and confused syntax, Davie recommended reading eighteenth-century English poets and shunning modernist writers. Yet in his many later critical works and collections of poems Davie modified his views, making more room in his aesthetic theory and practice for the asymmetries of Thomas Hardy and Ezra Pound. He continued to demand artistic control from himself and others, however, convinced that though the subject of a poem may be disorder, the poem itself should embody order and intelligibility.

Davie was born on July 17, 1922, in Barnsley, Yorkshire. He attended the local grammar school, then studied at Cambridge University, where, coming under the influence of the critic F. R. Leavis, he received a Ph.D in 1951. His education was interrupted by service in the Royal Navy from 1941 to 1946. He then returned to Cambridge to study, teach, and write. Davie also taught at Trinity College, Dublin, and the University of Sussex. When he emigrated to the United States and took a position at Stanford University (1968–78), he succeeded another poet-critic who influenced him, Yvor Winters. Davie taught another ten years at Vanderbilt University (1978–88) before returning after retirement to England.

Remembering the 'Thirties

1

Hearing one saga, we enact the next.
We please our elders when we sit enthralled;
But then they're puzzled; and at last they're vexed
To have their youth so avidly recalled.

It dawns upon the veterans after all
That what for them were agonies, for us
Are high-brow thrillers, though historical;
And all their feats quite strictly fabulous.

This novel written fifteen years ago,
Set in my boyhood and my boyhood home,
These poems about 'abandoned workings', show
Worlds more remote than Ithaca[1] or Rome.

The Anschluss, Guernica[2]—all the names
At which those poets thrilled or were afraid
For me mean schools and schoolmasters and games;
And in the process some-one is betrayed.

Ourselves perhaps. The Devil for a joke
Might carve his own initials on our desk,
And yet we'd miss the point because he spoke
An idiom too dated, Audenesque.[3]

Ralegh's Guiana also killed his son.[4]
A pretty pickle if we came to see
The tallest story really packed a gun,
The Telemachiad[5] an Odyssey.

2

Even to them the tales were not so true
As not to be ridiculous as well;
The ironmaster met his Waterloo,
But Rider Haggard[6] rode along the fell.

1. Greek island; home of Odysseus.

2. City in the Basque region of northern Spain that was heavily bombed by German planes in 1937. The event inspired a famous painting by Spanish expatriate artist Pablo Picasso (1881–1973). *Anschluss:* union (German); the annexation of Austria by Nazi Germany, in 1938.

3. W. H. Auden (1907–1973), one of the most influential poets of the 1930s.

4. The eldest son of English author and explorer Sir Walter Ralegh (1554?–1618) was killed while with his father on an expedition in Guiana. Ralegh's popular account of his earlier explorations of Guiana, *The Discovery of the Large, Rich, and Beautiful Empire of Guiana* (1596), was accused by many of his contemporaries as being full of lies and exaggerations.

5. The first four books of Homer's *Odyssey,* which center on Odysseus's son, Telemachus.

6. British novelist (1856–1925), famous for adventure novels such as *King Solomon's Mines* (1885). *Waterloo:* Belgian city where Napoleon's military career ended with his defeat in 1815.

'Leave for Cape Wrath tonight!' They lounged away
On Fleming's trek or Isherwood's ascent.[7]
England expected every man that day
To show his motives were ambivalent.

They played the fool, not to appear as fools
In time's long glass. A deprecating air
Disarmed, they thought, the jeers of later schools;
Yet irony itself is doctrinaire,

And curiously, nothing now betrays
Their type to time's derision like this coy
Insistence on the quizzical, their craze
For showing Hector[8] was a mother's boy.

A neutral tone is nowadays preferred.
And yet it may be better, if we must,
To praise a stance impressive and absurd
Than not to see the hero for the dust.

For courage is the vegetable king,
The sprig of all ontologies, the weed
That beards the slag-heap with his hectoring,
Whose green adventure is to run to seed.

1955

Across the Bay[9]

A queer thing about those waters: there are no
Birds there, or hardly any.
I did not miss them, I do not remember
Missing them, or thinking it uncanny.

The beach so-called was a blinding splinter of limestone,
A quarry outraged by hulls.
We took pleasure in that: the emptiness, the hardness
Of the light, the silence, and the water's stillness.

But this was the setting for one of our murderous scenes.
This hurt, and goes on hurting:
The venomous soft jelly, the undersides.
We could stand the world if it were hard all over.

1964

7. Christopher Isherwood (1904–1986), Anglo-American novelist and playwright, collaborated with Auden on a number of plays, including *The Ascent of F6* (1936), and a travel book, *Journey to a War* (1939), about their trip to China, where they met the British travel writer Peter Fleming (1907–1971). *Cape Wrath:* the northernmost point of mainland Scotland. The quoted line comes from Auden's early poem "Missing" (1929).
8. In the *Iliad*, the great warrior of Troy.
9. San Francisco Bay.

In California

Chemicals ripen the citrus;
There are rattlesnakes in the mountains,
And on the shoreline
Hygiene, unhuman caution.

Beef in cellophane
Tall as giraffes,
The orange-rancher's daughters
Crop their own groves, mistrustful.

Perpetual summer seems
Precarious on the littoral.[1] We drive
Inland to prove
The risk we sense. At once

Winter claps-to like a shutter
High over the Ojai valley, and discloses
A double crisis,
Winter and Drought.

Ranges on mountain-ranges,
Empty, unwatered, crumbling,
Hot colours come at the eye.
It is too cold

For picnics at the trestle-tables. Claypit
Yellow burns on the distance.
The phantom walks
Everywhere, of intolerable heat.

At Ventucopa,[2] elevation
Two-eight-nine-six, the water hydrant frozen,
Deserted or broken settlements,
Gasoline stations closed and boarded.

By nightfall, to the snows;
And over the mile on tilted
Mile of the mountain park
The bright cars hazarded.

1964

1. Coastal region.

2. A small community in Santa Barbara County.

From In the Stopping Train[3]

* * *

The things he has been spared . . .
'Gross egotist!' Why don't
his wife, his daughter, shrill
that in his face?

Love and pity seem
the likeliest explanations;
another occurs to him—
despair too would be quiet.

•

Time and again he gave battle,
furious, mostly effective;
nobody counts the wear
and tear of rebuttal.

Time and again he rose
to the flagrantly offered occasion;
nobody's hanged for a slow
murder by provocation.

Time and again he applauded
the stand he had taken; how much
it mattered, or to what
assize,[4] is not recorded.

Time and again he hardened
his heart and his perceptions;
nobody knows just how
truths turn into deceptions.

Time and again, oh time and
that stopping train!
Who knows when it comes to a stand,
and will not start again?

1977

3. Davie explained that his long poem "In the Stopping Train" derived from a miserable train ride from Tours to Paris and back through the pouring rain, on a failed attempt to meet with Irish poet John Montague (b. 1929). The poem is often read as an autobiographical parable.
4. Judicial inquest; court.

Philip Larkin
1922–1985

Philip Larkin's tone is that of a man who has lost opportunities, failed to get the lover he wanted and got another instead (that not lasting either), and always found life less than it might have been. As an undergraduate at Oxford University, Larkin belonged to the group that came to be known as the Movement, its revolt being against rhetorical excess and cosmic portentousness. They sought a more accurate, conversational idiom. Among these poets, included in an anthology called *New Lines* (1956), Larkin, Donald Davie, and Thom Gunn have proved the most important.

Larkin's first book, *The North Ship* (1945), was strongly influenced by W. B. Yeats. Although this influence persisted in the English poet's qualified affirmations and prosodic agility, Larkin began to read Thomas Hardy seriously after World War II, and Hardy's rugged language, local settings, and ironic vision helped counter Yeats's influence. "After that," Larkin said, "Yeats came to seem so artificial—all that crap about masks and Crazy Jane and all the rest. It all rang so completely unreal" (*The Guardian*, May 20, 1965). Larkin inherited some of Hardy's toughness and dourness. Just as Hardy in "The Oxen" half wishes that he might believe a tradition out of Christian folklore, so Larkin in "Church Going" leaves the little country church with the sense that something precious, something in which he can no longer believe, has been lost. Interweaving skepticism and nostalgia, the poem creates a verbal space where, in Larkin's words, "all our compulsions meet." Larkin is perhaps gentler and funnier than Hardy, more amused by ineptitude, more affectionate toward his readers.

Larkin was no friend to the so-called high or international modernists. In a 1964 interview ("Four Conversations"), he summarized his discontent with modernism:

> The poetry I've enjoyed has been the kind of poetry you'd associate with me—Hardy pre-eminently, Wilfred Owen, Auden, Christina Rossetti, William Barnes; on the whole, people to whom technique seems to matter less than content, people who accept the forms they have inherited but use them to express their own content. . . .
>
> What I do feel a bit rebellious about is that poetry seems to have got into the hands of a critical industry which is concerned with culture in the abstract, and this I do rather lay at the door of Eliot and Pound. . . . I think a lot of this myth-kitty business has grown out of that, because first of all you have to be terribly educated, you have to read everything to know these things, and secondly you've got somehow to work them in to show that you are working them in. But to me the whole of the ancient world, the whole of classical and biblical mythology means very little, and I think that using them today not only fills poems full of dead spots but dodges the writer's duty to be original.

Ezra Pound's eclecticism is not for Larkin; indeed, parts of *The Cantos* may seem like a tour of an ethnographic museum led by a sporadically demented guide. Rejecting the polyglot discourse, fragmentary syntax, and intimidating ambition of modernism, Larkin reclaims a more direct, personal, formally regular model of poetry. As a music critic, Larkin attacked avant-garde jazz for the same modernist alienation of the audience. And yet he is not so thoroughly antimodernist as he proclaims, as evidenced by his imagist precision and his solitary, death-obsessed personae, his tonal blending of melancholy with astringent irony, his commingling of poetry and secularized religion.

Larkin was born on August 9, 1922, in Coventry, Warwickshire. He depicts his miseries as a student at Oxford University in *Jill* (1946), the first of his two novels. After taking his B.A. at St. John's College, Oxford, in 1943, he worked as a librarian, mostly at the University of Hull (his poem "Here" evokes the city of Hull). In contrast to his rather sequestered career and his offensive remarks on race and gender voiced in letters, Larkin's poetry sparkles. He published only a few small books of verse. Because their manner is quiet, and because their matter is often melancholy contemplation, Larkin repelled critics looking for radical novelty in technique and for urgent responses to the present.

But Larkin spins out of his disillusionment some of the most emotionally complex, rhythmically polished, and intricately rhymed poems of the second half of the twentieth century. If he paraded no great truths, he offered things that were "almost true," such as the statement of love and fidelity in "An Arundel Tomb": "What will survive of us is love." His acceptance of defeat, in a poem such as "Toads Revisited" ("Give me your arm, old toad; / Help me down Cemetery Road"), cannot be read without recognizing the witty exaggeration of the poet's plight. "Poetry is an affair of sanity, of seeing things as they are," he said ("Big Victims"); "I don't want to transcend the commonplace, I love the commonplace life. Everyday things are lovely to me" (*Viewpoints: Poets in Conversation with John Haffenden,* 1981). The reverse of grandiose or straining, Larkin's poetry is so evidently integral with its author, and so witty and deft, that it speaks with singular authority and aplomb.

Larkin was not the poet to celebrate poetry, but his verse finds affection even in love's failure, creative possibilities in loneliness, humility blossoming from unsuccess. In spite of his affirmations of mundane existence, the interplay between the ordinary and the sublime frequently energizes his work. He is attracted to a sense of what "unfenced existence" might be ("Here"). He recognizes what brilliance passing images have before they dissipate or diminish, as when he notes, with complex feelings, the unrealizable aspirations of "The Whitsun Weddings." In "Solar," the poet beholds, without flinching, the radiant sublimity of the sun. Sometimes, such glimpses are of utter vacancy. In "Aubade," the poet encounters the terrifying blankness of death—"the total emptiness for ever, / The sure extinction that we travel to." "High Windows" suggests both radiant presence and total absence in its final vision of sunlit glass: "And beyond it, the deep blue air, that shows / Nothing, and is nowhere, and is endless."

When Sir John Betjeman died, in 1984, it was widely thought that Larkin might succeed him as poet laureate of England, and it is humorous to imagine a Royal Birthday Ode from the man who wrote the striking first lines of "This Be The Verse" and "High Windows." But a year before he died (after surgery for throat cancer), Larkin was offered and turned down the prestigious post.

Reasons for Attendance

The trumpet's voice, loud and authoritative,
Draws me a moment to the lighted glass
To watch the dancers—all under twenty-five—
Shifting intently, face to flushed face,
Solemnly on the beat of happiness.

—Or so I fancy, sensing the smoke and sweat,
The wonderful feel of girls. Why be out here?
But then, why be in there? Sex, yes, but what
Is sex? Surely, to think the lion's share
Of happiness is found by couples—sheer

Inaccuracy, as far as I'm concerned.
What calls me is that lifted, rough-tongued bell
(Art, if you like) whose individual sound
Insists I too am individual.
It speaks; I hear; others may hear as well,

But not for me, nor I for them; and so
With happiness. Therefore I stay outside,
Believing this; and they maul to and fro,
Believing that; and both are satisfied,
If no one has misjudged himself. Or lied.

December 30, 1953 1955

Water

If I were called in
To construct a religion
I should make use of water.

Going to church
Would entail a fording
To dry, different clothes;

My liturgy would employ
Images of sousing,
A furious devout drench,

And I should raise in the east
A glass of water
Where any-angled light
Would congregate endlessly.

April 6, 1954 1964

Church Going

Once I am sure there's nothing going on
I step inside, letting the door thud shut.
Another church: matting, seats, and stone,
And little books; sprawlings of flowers, cut
For Sunday, brownish now; some brass and stuff
Up at the holy end; the small neat organ;
And a tense, musty, unignorable silence,
Brewed God knows how long. Hatless, I take off
My cycle-clips[1] in awkward reverence,

1. Accessories worn below the knee to protect trousers from getting entangled in the bicycle chain.

Move forward, run my hand around the font.
From where I stand, the roof looks almost new—
Cleaned, or restored? Someone would know: I don't.
Mounting the lectern, I peruse a few
Hectoring large-scale verses,[2] and pronounce
'Here endeth' much more loudly than I'd meant.
The echoes snigger briefly. Back at the door
I sign the book, donate an Irish sixpence.[3]
Reflect the place was not worth stopping for.

Yet stop I did: in fact I often do,
And always end much at a loss like this,
Wondering what to look for; wondering, too,
When churches fall completely out of use
What we shall turn them into, if we shall keep
A few cathedrals chronically on show,
Their parchment, plate and pyx[4] in locked cases,
And let the rest rent-free to rain and sheep.
Shall we avoid them as unlucky places?

Or, after dark, will dubious women come
To make their children touch a particular stone;
Pick simples[5] for a cancer; or on some
Advised night see walking a dead one?
Power of some sort or other will go on
In games, in riddles, seemingly at random;
But superstition, like belief, must die,
And what remains when disbelief has gone?
Grass, weedy pavement, brambles, buttress, sky,

A shape less recognisable each week,
A purpose more obscure. I wonder who
Will be the last, the very last, to seek
This place for what it was; one of the crew
That tap and jot and know what rood-lofts[6] were?
Some ruin-bibber, randy for antique,
Or Christmas-addict, counting on a whiff
Of gown-and-bands and organ-pipes and myrrh?[7]
Or will he be my representative,

Bored, uninformed, knowing the ghostly silt
Dispersed, yet tending to this cross of ground[8]
Through suburb scrub because it held unspilt
So long and equably what since is found

2. That is, verses from a Bible printed in large type for reading aloud.
3. Of no value in England.
4. Box, often made of gold or silver, in which communion wafers are kept.
5. Medicinal herbs.
6. A loft or gallery above the rood screen, which, in an old church, separates the nave, or main hall, from the chancel, which contains the altar; the rood-loft properly holds a rood, or cross.
7. A bitter, aromatic gum used in, among other things, making incense. *Gown-and-bands:* the dress of an old-fashioned clergyman, consisting of a long, black gown or robe and a set of narrow, white strips of cloth at the neck.
8. Churches were usually built in the form of a cross.

Only in separation—marriage, and birth,
And death, and thoughts of these—for which was built
This special shell? For, though I've no idea
What this accoutred frowsty barn is worth,
It pleases me to stand in silence here;

A serious house on serious earth it is,
In whose blent air all our compulsions meet,
Are recognised, and robed as destinies.
And that much never can be obsolete,
Since someone will forever be surprising
A hunger in himself to be more serious,
And gravitating with it to this ground,
Which, he once heard, was proper to grow wise in,
If only that so many dead lie round.

July 28, 1954 1955

An Arundel Tomb[9]

Side by side, their faces blurred,
The earl and countess lie in stone,
Their proper habits[1] vaguely shown
As jointed armour, stiffened pleat,
And that faint hint of the absurd—
The little dogs under their feet.

Such plainness of the pre-baroque
Hardly involves the eye, until
It meets his left-hand gauntlet, still
Clasped empty in the other; and
One sees, with a sharp tender shock,
His hand withdrawn, holding her hand.

They would not think to lie so long.
Such faithfulness in effigy
Was just a detail friends would see:
A sculptor's sweet commissioned grace
Thrown off in helping to prolong
The Latin names around the base.

They would not guess how early in
Their supine stationary voyage
The air would change to soundless damage,
Turn the old tenantry away;
How soon succeeding eyes begin
To look, not read. Rigidly they

Persisted, linked, through lengths and breadths
Of time. Snow fell, undated. Light

9. Tomb of the earl of Arundel and his wife, in Chichester Cathedral, Sussex.

1. Clothing.

Each summer thronged the glass. A bright
Litter of birdcalls strewed the same
Bone-riddled ground. And up the paths
The endless altered people came,

Washing at their identity.
Now, helpless in the hollow of
An unarmorial age, a trough
Of smoke in slow suspended skeins
Above their scrap of history,
Only an attitude remains:

Time has transfigured them into
Untruth. The stone fidelity
They hardly meant has come to be
Their final blazon,[2] and to prove
Our almost-instinct almost true:
What will survive of us is love.

February 20, 1956 1964

The Whitsun[3] Weddings

That Whitsun, I was late getting away:
    Not till about
One-twenty on the sunlit Saturday
Did my three-quarters-empty train pull out,
All windows down, all cushions hot, all sense
Of being in a hurry gone. We ran
Behind the backs of houses, crossed a street
Of blinding windscreens, smelt the fish-dock; thence
The river's level drifting breadth began,
Where sky and Lincolnshire and water meet.

All afternoon, through the tall heat that slept
    For miles inland,
A slow and stopping curve southwards we kept.
Wide farms went by, short-shadowed cattle, and
Canals with floatings of industrial froth;
A hothouse flashed uniquely: hedges dipped
And rose: and now and then a smell of grass
Displaced the reek of buttoned carriage-cloth
Until the next town, new and nondescript,
Approached with acres of dismantled cars.

At first, I didn't notice what a noise
    The weddings made

2. Record of virtue.
3. Or Whitsunday, the seventh Sunday after Easter, one of the six British bank holidays. British tax law in the 1950s made it a financially beneficial weekend to be married.

Each station that we stopped at: sun destroys
The interest of what's happening in the shade,
And down the long cool platforms whoops and skirls
I took for porters larking with the mails,
And went on reading. Once we started, though,
We passed them, grinning and pomaded, girls
In parodies of fashion, heels and veils,
All posed irresolutely, watching us go,

As if out on the end of an event
        Waving goodbye
To something that survived it. Struck, I leant
More promptly out next time, more curiously,
And saw it all again in different terms:
The fathers with broad belts under their suits
And seamy foreheads; mothers loud and fat;
An uncle shouting smut; and then the perms,
The nylon gloves and jewellery-substitutes,
The lemons, mauves, and olive-ochres that

Marked off the girls unreally from the rest.
        Yes, from cafés
And banquet-halls up yards, and bunting-dressed
Coach-party annexes, the wedding-days
Were coming to an end. All down the line
Fresh couples climbed aboard: the rest stood round;
The last confetti and advice were thrown,
And, as we moved, each face seemed to define
Just what it saw departing: children frowned
At something dull; fathers had never known

Success so huge and wholly farcical;
        The women shared
The secret like a happy funeral;
While girls, gripping their handbags tighter, stared
At a religious wounding. Free at last,
And loaded with the sum of all they saw,
We hurried towards London, shuffling gouts of steam.
Now fields were building-plots, and poplars cast
Long shadows over major roads, and for
Some fifty minutes, that in time would seem

Just long enough to settle hats and say
        I nearly died,
A dozen marriages got under way.
They watched the landscape, sitting side by side
—An Odeon[4] went past, a cooling tower,
And someone running up to bowl[5]—and none
Thought of the others they would never meet
Or how their lives would all contain this hour.

4. One of a chain of English movie houses.
5. In the sport of cricket, to pitch the ball to the batsperson.

I thought of London spread out in the sun,
Its postal districts packed like squares of wheat:

There we were aimed. And as we raced across
Bright knots of rail
Past standing Pullmans, walls of blackened moss
Came close, and it was nearly done, this frail
Travelling coincidence; and what it held
Stood ready to be loosed with all the power
That being changed can give. We slowed again,
And as the tightened brakes took hold, there swelled
A sense of falling, like an arrow-shower
Sent out of sight, somewhere becoming rain.

October 18, 1958 1964

Faith Healing

Slowly the women file to where he stands
Upright in rimless glasses, silver hair,
Dark suit, white collar. Stewards tirelessly
Persuade them onwards to his voice and hands,
Within whose warm spring rain of loving care
Each dwells some twenty seconds. *Now, dear child,*
What's wrong, the deep American voice demands,
And, scarcely pausing, goes into a prayer
Directing God about this eye, that knee.
Their heads are clasped abruptly; then, exiled

Like losing thoughts, they go in silence; some
Sheepishly stray, not back into their lives
Just yet; but some stay stiff, twitching and loud
With deep hoarse tears, as if a kind of dumb
And idiot child within them still survives
To re-awake at kindness, thinking a voice
At last calls them alone, that hands have come
To lift and lighten; and such joy arrives
Their thick tongues blort, their eyes squeeze grief, a crowd
Of huge unheard answers jam and rejoice—

What's wrong! Moustached in flowered frocks they shake:
By now, all's wrong. In everyone there sleeps
A sense of life lived according to love.
To some it means the difference they could make
By loving others, but across most it sweeps
As all they might have done had they been loved.
That nothing cures. An immense slackening ache,
As when, thawing, the rigid landscape weeps,
Spreads slowly through them—that, and the voice above
Saying *Dear child,* and all time has disproved.

May 10, 1960 1964

MCMXIV[6]

Those long uneven lines
Standing as patiently
As if they were stretched outside
The Oval or Villa Park,[7]
The crowns of hats, the sun
On moustached archaic faces
Grinning as if it were all
An August Bank Holiday lark;

And the shut shops, the bleached
Established names on the sunblinds,
The farthings and sovereigns,[8]
And dark-clothed children at play
Called after kings and queens,
The tin advertisements
For cocoa and twist, and the pubs
Wide open all day;[9]

And the countryside not caring:
The place-names all hazed over
With flowering grasses, and fields
Shadowing Domesday lines[1]
Under wheat's restless silence;
The differently-dressed servants
With tiny rooms in huge houses,
The dust behind limousines;

Never such innocence,
Never before or since,
As changed itself to past
Without a word—the men
Leaving the gardens tidy,
The thousands of marriages
Lasting a little while longer:
Never such innocence again.

May 17, 1960 — 1964

Talking in Bed

Talking in bed ought to be easiest,
Lying together there goes back so far,
An emblem of two people being honest.

6. The poem envisions England in 1914, at the outbreak of World War I.
7. That is, outside a cricket ground or a professional soccer field; the men are waiting in line to enlist in the army.
8. British coins, both now obsolete; a farthing was worth one-fourth of a penny; a sovereign was worth a little more than a pound.
9. That is, before a law in 1915 restricted taverns' business hours. *Twist:* tobacco.
1. Lines demarcating property, as listed in the Domesday Book, drawn up by William the Conqueror in 1085–86.

Yet more and more time passes silently.
Outside, the wind's incomplete unrest
Builds and disperses clouds about the sky,

And dark towns heap up on the horizon.
None of this cares for us. Nothing shows why
At this unique distance from isolation

It becomes still more difficult to find
Words at once true and kind,
Or not untrue and not unkind.

August 10, 1960 1964

Here

Swerving east, from rich industrial shadows
And traffic all night north; swerving through fields
Too thin and thistled to be called meadows,
And now and then a harsh-named halt, that shields
Workmen at dawn; swerving to solitude
Of skies and scarecrows, haystacks, hares and pheasants,
And the widening river's slow presence,
The piled gold clouds, the shining gull-marked mud,

Gathers to the surprise of a large town:
Here domes and statues, spires and cranes cluster
Beside grain-scattered streets, barge-crowded water,
And residents from raw estates, brought down
The dead straight miles by stealing flat-faced trolleys,
Push through plate-glass swing doors to their desires—
Cheap suits, red kitchen-ware, sharp shoes, iced lollies,
Electric mixers, toasters, washers, driers—

A cut-price crowd, urban yet simple, dwelling
Where only salesmen and relations come
Within a terminate and fishy-smelling
Pastoral of ships up streets, the slave museum,
Tattoo-shops, consulates, grim head-scarfed wives;
And out beyond its mortgaged half-built edges
Fast-shadowed wheat-fields, running high as hedges,
Isolate villages, where removed lives

Loneliness clarifies. Here silence stands
Like heat. Here leaves unnoticed thicken,
Hidden weeds flower, neglected waters quicken,
Luminously-peopled air ascends;
And past the poppies bluish neutral distance
Ends the land suddenly beyond a beach
Of shapes and shingle. Here is unfenced existence:
Facing the sun, untalkative, out of reach.

October 8, 1961 1964

Sunny Prestatyn[2]

Come to Sunny Prestatyn
Laughed the girl on the poster,
Kneeling up on the sand
In tautened white satin.
Behind her, a hunk of coast, a
Hotel with palms
Seemed to expand from her thighs and
Spread breast-lifting arms.

She was slapped up one day in March.
A couple of weeks, and her face
Was snaggle-toothed and boss-eyed;
Huge tits and a fissured crotch
Were scored well in, and the space
Between her legs held scrawls
That set her fairly astride
A tuberous cock and balls

Autographed *Titch Thomas,* while
Someone had used a knife
Or something to stab right through
The moustached lips of her smile.
She was too good for this life.
Very soon, a great transverse tear
Left only a hand and some blue.
Now *Fight Cancer* is there.

October ?, 1962 1964

Solar

Suspended lion face
Spilling at the centre
Of an unfurnished sky
How still you stand,
And how unaided
Single stalkless flower
You pour unrecompensed.

The eye sees you
Simplified by distance
Into an origin,
Your petalled head of flames
Continuously exploding.
Heat is the echo of your
Gold.

2. A seaside resort in north Wales; it is not inevitably sunny.

Coined there among
Lonely horizontals
You exist openly.
Our needs hourly
Climb and return like angels.
Unclosing like a hand,
You give for ever.

November 4, 1964 1974

High Windows

When I see a couple of kids
And guess he's fucking her and she's
Taking pills or wearing a diaphragm,
I know this is paradise

Everyone old has dreamed of all their lives—
Bonds and gestures pushed to one side
Like an outdated combine harvester,[3]
And everyone young going down the long slide

To happiness, endlessly. I wonder if
Anyone looked at me, forty years back,
And thought, *That'll be the life;*
No God any more, or sweating in the dark

About hell and that, or having to hide
What you think of the priest. He
And his lot will all go down the long slide
Like free bloody birds. And immediately

Rather than words comes the thought of high windows:
The sun-comprehending glass,
And beyond it, the deep blue air, that shows
Nothing, and is nowhere, and is endless.

February 12, 1967 1974

Sad Steps[4]

Groping back to bed after a piss
I part thick curtains, and am startled by
The rapid clouds, the moon's cleanliness.

3. Farm machine for harvesting grain.
4. Cf. Sir Philip Sidney's *Astrophil and Stella* (1591), Sonnet 31: "With how sad steps, O moon, thou climb'st the skies."

Four o'clock: wedge-shadowed gardens lie
Under a cavernous, a wind-picked sky.
There's something laughable about this,

The way the moon dashes through clouds that blow
Loosely as cannon-smoke to stand apart
(Stone-coloured light sharpening the roofs below)

High and preposterous and separate—
Lozenge[5] of love! Medallion of art!
O wolves of memory! Immensements! No,

One shivers slightly, looking up there.
The hardness and the brightness and the plain
Far-reaching singleness of that wide stare

Is a reminder of the strength and pain
Of being young; that it can't come again,
But is for others undiminished somewhere.

April 24, 1968 1974

Homage to a Government

Next year we are to bring the soldiers home
For lack of money, and it is all right.
Places they guarded, or kept orderly,
Must guard themselves, and keep themselves orderly.
We want the money for ourselves at home
Instead of working. And this is all right.

It's hard to say who wanted it to happen,
But now it's been decided nobody minds.
The places are a long way off, not here,
Which is all right, and from what we hear
The soldiers there only made trouble happen.
Next year we shall be easier in our minds.

Next year we shall be living in a country
That brought its soldiers home for lack of money.
The statues will be standing in the same
Tree-muffled squares, and look nearly the same.
Our children will not know it's a different country.
All we can hope to leave them now is money.

January 10, 1969 1974

5. Diamond-shaped pattern.

The Explosion

On the day of the explosion
Shadows pointed towards the pithead:
In the sun the slagheap[6] slept.

Down the lane came men in pitboots
Coughing oath-edged talk and pipe-smoke,
Shouldering off the freshened silence.

One chased after rabbits; lost them;
Came back with a nest of lark's eggs;
Showed them; lodged them in the grasses.

So they passed in beards and moleskins,[7]
Fathers, brothers, nicknames, laughter,
Through the tall gates standing open.

At noon, there came a tremor; cows
Stopped chewing for a second; sun,
Scarfed as in a heat-haze, dimmed.

The dead go on before us, they
Are sitting in God's house in comfort,
We shall see them face to face—

Plain as lettering in the chapels
It was said, and for a second
Wives saw men of the explosion

Larger than in life they managed—
Gold as on a coin, or walking
Somehow from the sun towards them,

One showing the eggs unbroken.

January 5, 1970 1974

This Be The Verse[8]

They fuck you up, your mum and dad.
They may not mean to, but they do.
They fill you with the faults they had
And add some extra, just for you.

6. Pile of scrap, refuse. *Pithead*: entrance to a coal mine.
7. Clothes made of a heavy, industrial fabric.
8. Cf. the elegy "Requiem," by Robert Louis Stevenson (1850–1894), of which the final verse reads, "This be the verse you grave for me: / *Here he lies where he longed to be, / Home is the sailor, home from sea, / And the hunter home from the hill.*"

But they were fucked up in their turn
 By fools in old-style hats and coats,
Who half the time were soppy-stern
 And half at one another's throats.

Man hands on misery to man.
 It deepens like a coastal shelf.[9]
Get out as early as you can,
 And don't have any kids yourself.

April ?, 1971 1974

Forget What Did

Stopping the diary
Was a stun to memory,
Was a blank starting,

One no longer cicatrized[1]
By such words, such actions
As bleakened waking.

I wanted them over,
Hurried to burial
And looked back on

Like the wars and winters
Missing behind the windows
Of an opaque childhood.

And the empty pages?
Should they ever be filled
Let it be with observed

Celestial recurrences,
The day the flowers come,
And when the birds go.

August 6, 1971 1974

Going, Going[2]

I thought it would last my time—
The sense that, beyond the town,
There would always be fields and farms,
Where the village louts could climb

9. Underwater land off a coast.
1. Covered with scar tissue.
2. Cf. the auctioneer's cry "Going, going, gone!"

Such trees as were not cut down;
I knew there'd be false alarms

In the papers about old streets
And split-level shopping,[3] but some
Have always been left so far;
And when the old part retreats
As the bleak high-risers come
We can always escape in the car.

Things are tougher than we are, just
As earth will always respond
However we mess it about;
Chuck filth in the sea, if you must:
The tides will be clean beyond.
—But what do I feel now? Doubt?

Or age, simply? The crowd
Is young in the M1 café;[4]
Their kids are screaming for more—
More houses, more parking allowed,
More caravan sites,[5] more pay.
On the Business Page, a score

Of spectacled grins approve
Some takeover bid that entails
Five per cent profit (and ten
Per cent more in the estuaries): move
Your works to the unspoilt dales
(Grey area grants)![6] And when

You try to get near the sea
In summer . . .
                    It seems, just now,
To be happening so very fast;
Despite all the land left free
For the first time I feel somehow
That it isn't going to last,

That before I snuff it, the whole
Boiling[7] will be bricked in
Except for the tourist parts—
First slum of Europe: a role
It won't be so hard to win,
With a cast of crooks and tarts.

3. In old-fashioned shops, the store was on the ground floor, the owner's living quarters above.
4. Restaurants along a highway; in England, major freeways are denoted by the letter *M* and a number.
5. Trailer parks.
6. Building areas are zoned, on English maps, by colors. *Works*: factories.
7. That is, the whole boiling mess.

And that will be England gone,
The shadows, the meadows, the lanes,
The guildhalls,[8] the carved choirs.
There'll be books; it will linger on
In galleries; but all that remains
For us will be concrete and tyres.

Most things are never meant.
This won't be, most likely: but greeds
And garbage are too thick-strewn
To be swept up now, or invent
Excuses that make them all needs.
I just think it will happen, soon.

January 25, 1972 1974

Aubade[9]

I work all day, and get half-drunk at night.
Waking at four to soundless dark, I stare.
In time the curtain-edges will grow light.
Till then I see what's really always there:
Unresting death, a whole day nearer now,
Making all thought impossible but how
And where and when I shall myself die.
Arid interrogation: yet the dread
Of dying, and being dead,
Flashes afresh to hold and horrify.

The mind blanks at the glare. Not in remorse
—The good not done, the love not given, time
Torn off unused—nor wretchedly because
An only life can take so long to climb
Clear of its wrong beginnings, and may never;
But at the total emptiness for ever,
The sure extinction that we travel to
And shall be lost in always. Not to be here,
Not to be anywhere,
And soon; nothing more terrible, nothing more true.

This is a special way of being afraid
No trick dispels. Religion used to try,
That vast moth-eaten musical brocade
Created to pretend we never die,
And specious stuff that says *No rational being*
Can fear a thing it will not feel, not seeing
That this is what we fear—no sight, no sound,
No touch or taste or smell, nothing to think with,

8. That is, town halls (in this case old).

9. Song or poem announcing dawn.

Nothing to love or link with,
The anaesthetic from which none come round.

And so it stays just on the edge of vision,
A small unfocused blur, a standing chill
That slows each impulse down to indecision.
Most things may never happen: this one will,
And realisation of it rages out
In furnace-fear when we are caught without
People or drink. Courage is no good:
It means not scaring others. Being brave
Lets no one off the grave.
Death is no different whined at than withstood.

Slowly light strengthens, and the room takes shape.
It stands plain as a wardrobe, what we know,
Have always known, know that we can't escape,
Yet can't accept. One side will have to go.
Meanwhile telephones crouch, getting ready to ring
In locked-up offices, and all the uncaring
Intricate rented world begins to rouse.
The sky is white as clay, with no sun.
Work has to be done.
Postmen like doctors go from house to house.

November 9, 1977 1977

ANTHONY HECHT
1923–2004

Anthony Hecht's first poems, published in *A Summoning of Stones* (1954), are extraordinarily accomplished; he develops his themes with a baroque profusion, finding a place for seemingly every improbable detail. Hecht pleases by his erudition, his skill in attaching one bit of information to another, his power to sustain a long, periodic sentence, and his ability to maintain a quality of improvisation while meeting the requirements of a daunting verse form. For connoisseurs of rhyming, nuanced rhythms, rhetorical patterning, sustained syntax, and other technical ingenuities, Hecht proves endlessly rewarding. He resembles Andrew Marvell in his deftness, his civility, and his preference for gardens over the wilderness or the city.

In his later volumes, Hecht surrenders to his obsessions. His poems, as he described them, "are about things that had an enormous emotional importance to me; I was prepared to attack them, whether they came out technically perfect or not." Without betraying his craft, Hecht endeavored to confront experience on its own painful terms. He knew the "grotesqueness of modern life," the incongruities between life as it is fabled for his children on the television screen and as it really is—or as it might have been. His mainstay is irony, which, in Hecht's own words, "provides a way of stating very powerful and positive emotions and of taking, as it were, the heaviest possible stance towards some catastrophe." His subjects include the Nazi Holocaust, the Algerian war, and more private subjects, such as the love of parents and children and the imperfect wedding of flesh and spirit.

Hecht was born on January 16, 1923, in New York City. He graduated from Bard College in 1944 and immediately entered the army, with which he served in Europe and Japan; he has called "the cumulative sense" of his wartime years "grotesque beyond anything I could possibly write." After his release from the army Hecht taught briefly at several universities while working for his M.A. at Columbia University (1950); he later taught at the University of Rochester (1967–85) and Georgetown University (1985–93). The author of books of criticism as well as numerous volumes of poetry, he won the Pulitzer Prize in 1968 and the Bollingen Prize in 1983. From 1982 to 1984, he served as poetry consultant to the Library of Congress.

Birdwatchers of America

> I suffer now continually from vertigo, and today, 23rd of January, 1862, I received a singular warning: I felt the wind of the wing of madness pass over me.
>
> —Baudelaire, *Journals*[1]

It's all very well to dream of a dove that saves,
Picasso's or the Pope's,
The one that annually coos in Our Lady's ear
Half the world's hopes,[2]
And the other one that shall cunningly engineer
The retirement of all businessmen to their graves,
And when this is brought about
Make us the loving brothers of every lout—

But in our part of the country a false dusk
Lingers for hours; it steams
From the soaked hay, wades in the cloudy woods,
Engendering other dreams.
Formless and soft beyond the fence it broods
Or rises as a faint and rotten musk
Out of a broken stalk.
There are some things of which we seldom talk;

For instance, the woman next door, whom we hear at night,
Claims that when she was small
She found a man stone dead near the cedar trees
After the first snowfall.
The air was clear. He seemed in ultimate peace
Except that he had no eyes. Rigid and bright
Upon the forehead, furred
With a light frost, crouched an outrageous bird.

1967

1. Charles Baudelaire (1821–1867), French poet, spent his last years in a struggle against insanity following his addiction to drugs. The journal of those years is called *My Heart Laid Bare*.

2. Pablo Picasso (1881–1973), Spanish expatriate artist, often drew the dove of peace; in Christian symbolism, the dove represents the descent of the Holy Spirit at baptism; in flight, it symbolizes the ascension of Christ and the entry into glory of the martyrs and saints.

A Hill

In Italy, where this sort of thing can occur,
I had a vision once—though you understand
It was nothing at all like Dante's,[3] or the visions of saints,
And perhaps not a vision at all. I was with some friends,
Picking my way through a warm sunlit piazza
In the early morning. A clear fretwork of shadows
From huge umbrellas littered the pavement and made
A sort of lucent shallows in which was moored
A small navy of carts. Books, coins, old maps,
Cheap landscapes and ugly religious prints
Were all on sale. The colors and noise
Like the flying hands were gestures of exultation,
So that even the bargaining
Rose to the ear like a voluble godliness.
And then, when it happened, the noises suddenly stopped,
And it got darker; pushcarts and people dissolved
And even the great Farnese Palace[4] itself
Was gone, for all its marble; in its place
Was a hill, mole-colored and bare. It was very cold,
Close to freezing, with a promise of snow.
The trees were like old ironwork gathered for scrap
Outside a factory wall. There was no wind,
And the only sound for a while was the little click
Of ice as it broke in the mud under my feet.
I saw a piece of ribbon snagged on a hedge,
But no other sign of life. And then I heard
What seemed the crack of a rifle. A hunter, I guessed;
At least I was not alone. But just after that
Came the soft and papery crash
Of a great branch somewhere unseen falling to earth.

And that was all, except for the cold and silence
That promised to last forever, like the hill.

Then prices came through, and fingers, and I was restored
To the sunlight and my friends. But for more than a week
I was scared by the plain bitterness of what I had seen.
All this happened about ten years ago,
And it hasn't troubled me since, but at last, today,
I remembered that hill; it lies just to the left
Of the road north of Poughkeepsie;[5] and as a boy
I stood before it for hours in wintertime.

1967

3. Dante Alighieri (1265–1321), Italian poet, author of *The Divine Comedy*.

4. In Rome.

5. City in upstate New York.

"It Out-Herods Herod. Pray You, Avoid It."[6]

Tonight my children hunch
Toward their Western, and are glad
As, with a Sunday punch,
The Good casts out the Bad.

And in their fairy tales
The warty giant and witch
Get sealed in doorless jails
And the match-girl strikes it rich.

I've made myself a drink.
The giant and witch are set
To bust out of the clink
When my children have gone to bed.

All frequencies are loud
With signals of despair;
In flash and morse they crowd
The rondure of the air.

For the wicked have grown strong,
Their numbers mock at death,
Their cow brings forth its young,
Their bull engendereth.

Their very fund of strength,
Satan, bestrides the globe;
He stalks its breadth and length
And finds out even Job.[7]

Yet by quite other laws
My children make their case;
Half God, half Santa Claus,
But with my voice and face,

A hero comes to save
The poorman, beggarman, thief
And make the world behave
And put an end to grief.

And that their sleep be sound
I say this childermas[8]
Who could not, at one time,
Have saved them from the gas.

1967

6. From Hamlet's instructions to the actors (*Hamlet* 3.2), requesting them not to rant like the character Herod in medieval mystery plays.
7. In the Bible, God's most devout servant, and therefore prosperous; God allowed Satan to destroy Job's wealth and family as a test of his faith.
8. The festival of the Holy Innocents, commemorating the slaughter of Hebrew children by Herod in his effort to counter the prophecy that Jesus was to become king of the Jews (Matthew 2.16).

The Deodand[9]

What are these women up to? They've gone and strung
Drapes over the windows, cutting out light
And the slightest hope of a breeze here in mid-August.
Can this be simply to avoid being seen
By some prying *femme-de-chambre*[1] across the boulevard
Who has stepped out on a balcony to disburse
Her dustmop gleanings on the summer air?
And what of these rugs and pillows, all haphazard,
Here in what might be someone's living room
In the swank, high-toned sixteenth *arrondissement?*[2]
What would their fathers, husbands, *fiancés,*
Those pillars of the old *haute-bourgeoisie,*[3]
Think of the strange charade now in the making?
Swathed in exotic finery, in loose silks,
Gauzy organzas[4] with metallic threads,
Intricate Arab vests, brass ornaments
At wrist and ankle, those small sexual fetters,
Tight little silver chains, and bangled gold
Suspended like a coarse barbarian treasure
From soft earlobes pierced through symbolically,
They are preparing some *tableau vivant.*[5]
One girl, consulting the authority
Of a painting, perhaps by Ingres or Delacroix,[6]
Is reporting over her shoulder on the use
Of kohl[7] to lend its dark, savage allurements.
Another, playing the slave-artisan's role,
Almost completely naked, brush in hand,
Attends to these instructions as she prepares
To complete the seductive shadowing of the eyes
Of the blonde girl who appears the harem favorite,
And who is now admiring these effects
In a mirror held by a fourth, a well-clad servant.
The scene simmers with Paris and women in heat,
Darkened and airless, perhaps with a faint hum
Of trapped flies, and a strong odor of musk.
For whom do they play at this hot indolence
And languorous vassalage?[8] They are alone
With fantasies of jasmine and brass lamps,
Melons and dates and bowls of rose-water,

9. "Deodand is defined as 'A thing forfeited or to be given to God; *spec.* in *Eng. Law,* a personal chattel which, having been the immediate occasion of the death of a human being, was given to God as an expiatory offering, i.e. forfeited to the Crown to be applied to pious uses. . . . ' The poem is based on a painting by Pierre-Auguste Renoir [1841–1919] called *Parisians Dressed in Algerian Costume,* in the National Museum of Western Art, Tokyo" [Hecht's note].
1. Chambermaid (French).
2. District in Paris.
3. Upper middle class.
4. Sheer silk fabrics.
5. Literally, "living picture," in which the participants, appropriately costumed, pose to represent a painting.
6. Nineteenth-century French painters, both of whom painted pictures of Middle Eastern subjects.
7. Dark eye makeup used in the Middle East.
8. Slavery.

A courtyard fountain's firework blaze of prisms,
Its basin sown with stars and *poissons d'or,*[9]
And a rude stable smell of animal strength,
Of leather thongs, hinting of violations,
Swooning lubricities and lassitudes.
What is all this but crude imperial pride,
Feminized, scented and attenuated,
The exploitation of the primitive,
Homages of romantic self-deception,
Mimes of submission glamorized as lust?
Have they no intimation, no recall
Of the once queen who liked to play at milkmaid,
And the fierce butcher-reckoning that followed
Her innocent, unthinking masquerade?[1]
Those who will not be taught by history
Have as their curse the office to repeat it,[2]
And for this little spiritual debauch
(Reported here with warm, exacting care
By Pierre Renoir in 1872—
Apparently unnoticed by the girls,
An invisible voyeur, like you and me)
Exactions shall be made, an expiation,
A forfeiture. Though it take ninety years,
All the retributive iron of Racine[3]
Shall answer from the raging heat of the desert.

In the final months of the Algerian war
They captured a very young French Legionnaire.[4]
They shaved his head, decked him in a blonde wig,
Carmined his lips grotesquely, fitted him out
With long, theatrical false eyelashes
And a bright, loose-fitting skirt of calico,
And cut off all the fingers of both hands.
He had to eat from a fork held by his captors.
Thus costumed, he was taken from town to town,
Encampment to encampment, on a leash,
And forced to beg for his food with a special verse
Sung to a popular show tune of those days:
"Donnez moi à manger de vos mains
Car c'est pour vous que je fais ma petite danse;
Car je suis Madeleine, la putain,
Et je m'en vais le lendemain matin,
Car je suis La Belle France."[5]

1980

9. Goldfish.
1. Marie Antoinette, queen of France, one of whose hobbies was dressing up as a milkmaid, was guillotined in 1793, during the French Revolution.
2. "Those who cannot remember the past are condemned to repeat it" (George Santayana, *Life of Reason*). *Office*: duty.
3. Jean Racine (1639–1699), French playwright, most of whose plays were tragedies of revenge.
4. Member of the French foreign legion, an army of volunteers originally founded to control the French colony of Algiers (northern Africa); Algiers (now Algeria) fought for its independence from 1954 to 1962 and won.
5. "The concluding lines in French may be rendered:
'Let me be given nourishment at your hands / Since it's for you I perform my little dance. / For

The Book of Yolek

Wir haben ein Gesetz,
Und nach dem Gesetz soll er sterben.[6]

The dowsed coals fume and hiss after your meal
Of grilled brook trout, and you saunter off for a walk
Down the fern trail, it doesn't matter where to,
Just so you're weeks and worlds away from home,
And among midsummer hills have set up camp
In the deep bronze glories of declining day.

You remember, peacefully, an earlier day
In childhood, remember a quite specific meal:
A corn roast and bonfire in summer camp.
That summer you got lost on a Nature Walk;
More than you dared admit, you thought of home;
No one else knows where the mind wanders to.

The fifth of August, 1942.
It was morning and very hot. It was the day
They came at dawn with rifles to The Home
For Jewish Children, cutting short the meal
Of bread and soup, lining them up to walk
In close formation off to a special camp.

How often you have thought about that camp,
As though in some strange way you were driven to,
And about the children, and how they were made to walk,
Yolek who had bad lungs, who wasn't a day
Over five years old, commanded to leave his meal
And shamble between armed guards to his long home.

We're approaching August again. It will drive home
The regulation torments of that camp
Yolek was sent to, his small, unfinished meal,
The electric fences, the numeral tattoo,
The quite extraordinary heat of the day
They all were forced to take that terrible walk.

Whether on a silent, solitary walk
Or among crowds, far off or safe at home,
You will remember, helplessly, that day,
And the smell of smoke, and the loudspeakers of the camp.
Wherever you are, Yolek will be there, too.
His unuttered name will interrupt your meal.

I am the street-walker, Magdalen, / And come the dawn I'll be on my way again, / The beauty queen, Miss France" [Hecht's note].

6. We have a law, and by that law he ought to die (German). From a translation of John 19.7 by theologian Martin Luther (1483–1546), leader of the Protestant Reformation in Germany. Hecht's poem is inspired by "Yanosz Korczak's Last Walk," by Polish poet Hanna Mortkowicz Olczakowa (1905–1968).

Prepare to receive him in your home some day.
Though they killed him in the camp they sent him to,
He will walk in as you're sitting down to a meal.

1990

JAMES DICKEY
1923–1997

James Dickey insisted, as Oscar Wilde did, that art is the fashioning of illusions and "lies." Once his imagination took hold of some strange, often monstrous event, he pursued it relentlessly. "As Longinus points out," he said in 1970, "there's a razor's edge between sublimity and absurdity. And that's the edge I try to walk. Sometimes *both* sides are ludicrous! . . . But I don't think you can get to sublimity without courting the ridiculous" (*Self-Interviews*). Dickey is a gothic poet, whether he domesticates the monstrous or allows his monsters to range freely.

Dickey spent six of his mature years in advertising. In between producing copy for Coca-Cola and other companies in Atlanta, he composed some of his best poems. He has in his verse a purposefulness and insistence, a demand for attention and for recognition, that is perhaps not so much an echo of his days in advertising as an indication of why he was good at it. He wanted to be an "intensified man" or a "totally responsive man."

Born on February 2, 1923, in a suburb of Atlanta, Dickey became a high school football star. In 1941, he went to Clemson A&M College (later University), in South Carolina, but left after a semester to enlist in the army air corps. Although he claimed to have flown a hundred combat missions, he washed out during flight training and instead operated radar equipment during flights in the Pacific. Awakened to a love of literature by the war, he read books between missions, including an anthology of modern poets such as Dylan Thomas. On his return from the war Dickey attended Vanderbilt University, a center of modern southern poetry, where he worked with an older student's zeal. A friendly professor, Monroe K. Spears, encouraged him to write more poetry and urged him to write as the poem, rather than the real-life experience, necessitated. "That idea was the bursting of a dam for me," said Dickey. He stayed on at Vanderbilt for his M.A. and then taught at Rice Institute (later University), in Texas. The air force recalled him to active service for the Korean War, during which he taught radar operation at U.S. bases. In 1955, after a year in Europe, he began teaching at the University of Florida, where a dispute arose over the propriety of remarks he made to a group of women writers. He abruptly resigned in April 1956 and worked in advertising until 1961. After a year on a Guggenheim Fellowship in Europe, he returned to the United States to teach, lecture, and write. From 1966 to 1968, he served as poetry consultant to the Library of Congress; from 1969, he held a teaching position at the University of South Carolina. In 1970, he published his first novel, *Deliverance,* the film version of which brought him fame, which fueled his debilitating alcoholism.

Dickey's poetry is arresting and powerful. It is characterized more by force than by grace, more by conceptual intricacy than by wit. Part of its pleasure lies in its sense of abundance and confidence. "I don't believe in the kind of cool diffidence people nowadays affect," he said (*Self-Interviews*). Taken with the views of the agrarians as a young man at Vanderbilt, Dickey wished to be on intimate terms with the regenerative forces of nature. He had a keen sense of an archetypal world underlying the real one, accessible at unusual moments, and this deepening or descent from level to level was often his theme. Most of his poems are in the first person, but the "I" is rather impersonal, even if based on actual experience, because it is on its way to becoming "an inspired outline of myself" ("Chenille").

The Hospital Window

I have just come down from my father.
Higher and higher he lies
Above me in a blue light
Shed by a tinted window.
I drop through six white floors
And then step out onto pavement.

Still feeling my father ascend,
I start to cross the firm street,
My shoulder blades shining with all
The glass the huge building can raise.
Now I must turn round and face it,
And know his one pane from the others.

Each window possesses the sun
As though it burned there on a wick.
I wave, like a man catching fire.
All the deep-dyed windowpanes flash,
And, behind them, all the white rooms
They turn to the color of Heaven.

Ceremoniously, gravely, and weakly,
Dozens of pale hands are waving
Back, from inside their flames.
Yet one pure pane among these
Is the bright, erased blankness of nothing.
I know that my father is there,

In the shape of his death still living.
The traffic increases around me
Like a madness called down on my head.
The horns blast at me like shotguns,
And drivers lean out, driven crazy—
But now my propped-up father

Lifts his arm out of stillness at last.
The light from the window strikes me
And I turn as blue as a soul,
As the moment when I was born.
I am not afraid for my father—
Look! He is grinning; he is not

Afraid for my life, either,
As the wild engines stand at my knees
Shredding their gears and roaring,
And I hold each car in its place
For miles, inciting its horn
To blow down the walls of the world

That the dying may float without fear
In the bold blue gaze of my father.
Slowly I move to the sidewalk
With my pin-tingling hand half dead
At the end of my bloodless arm.
I carry it off in amazement,

High, still higher, still waving,
My recognized face fully mortal,
Yet not; not at all, in the pale,
Drained, otherworldly, stricken,
Created hue of stained glass.
I have just come down from my father.

1962

The Heaven of Animals

Here they are. The soft eyes open.
If they have lived in a wood
It is a wood.
If they have lived on plains
It is grass rolling
Under their feet forever.

Having no souls, they have come,
Anyway, beyond their knowing.
Their instincts wholly bloom
And they rise.
The soft eyes open.

To match them, the landscape flowers,
Outdoing, desperately
Outdoing what is required:
The richest wood,
The deepest field.

For some of these,
It could not be the place
It is, without blood.
These hunt, as they have done,
But with claws and teeth grown perfect,

More deadly than they can believe.
They stalk more silently,

And crouch on the limbs of trees,
And their descent
Upon the bright backs of their prey

May take years
In a sovereign floating of joy.
And those that are hunted
Know this as their life,
Their reward: to walk

Under such trees in full knowledge
Of what is in glory above them,
And to feel no fear,
But acceptance, compliance.
Fulfilling themselves without pain

At the cycle's center,
They tremble, they walk
Under the tree,
They fall, they are torn,
They rise, they walk again.

1962

Buckdancer's Choice[1]

So I would hear out those lungs,
The air split into nine levels,
Some gift of tongues of the whistler

In the invalid's bed: my mother,
Warbling all day to herself
The thousand variations of one song;

It is called Buckdancer's Choice.
For years, they have all been dying
Out, the classic buck-and-wing men

Of traveling minstrel shows;
With them also an old woman
Was dying of breathless angina,

Yet still found breath enough
To whistle up in my head
A sight like a one-man band,

Freed black, with cymbals at heel,
An ex-slave who thrivingly danced
To the ring of his own clashing light

1. A buckdancer does the buck-and-wing, a tap dance often performed in wooden shoes.

Through the thousand variations of one song
All day to my mother's prone music,
The invalid's warbler's note,

While I crept close to the wall
Sock-footed, to hear the sounds alter,
Her tongue like a mockingbird's break

Through stratum after stratum of a tone
Proclaiming what choices there are
For the last dancers of their kind,

For ill women and for all slaves
Of death, and children enchanted at walls
With a brass-beating glow underfoot,

Not dancing but nearly risen
Through barnlike, theatrelike houses
On the wings of the buck and wing.

1965

The Sheep Child

Farm boys wild to couple
With anything   with soft-wooded trees
With mounds of earth   mounds
Of pinestraw   will keep themselves off
Animals by legends of their own:
In the hay-tunnel dark
And dung of barns, they will
Say   I have heard tell

That in a museum in Atlanta
Way back in a corner somewhere
There's this thing that's only half
Sheep   like a woolly baby
Pickled in alcohol   because
Those things can't live   his eyes
Are open   but you can't stand to look
I heard from somebody who . . .

But this is now almost all
Gone. The boys have taken
Their own true wives in the city,
The sheep are safe in the west hill
Pasture   but we who were born there
Still are not sure. Are we,

Because we remember, remembered
In the terrible dust of museums?

Merely with his eyes, the sheep-child may

Be saying   saying

I am here, in my father's house.
I who am half of your world, came deeply
To my mother in the long grass
Of the west pasture, where she stood like moonlight
Listening for foxes. It was something like love
From another world that seized her
From behind, and she gave, not lifting her head
Out of dew, without ever looking, her best
Self to that great need. Turned loose, she dipped her face
Farther into the chill of the earth, and in a sound
Of sobbing   of something stumbling
Away, began, as she must do,
To carry me. I woke, dying,

In the summer sun of the hillside, with my eyes
Far more than human. I saw for a blazing moment
The great grassy world from both sides,
Man and beast in the round of their need,
And the hill wind stirred in my wool,
My hoof and my hand clasped each other,
I ate my one meal
Of milk, and died
Staring. From dark grass I came straight

To my father's house, whose dust
Whirls up in the halls for no reason
When no one comes   piling deep in a hellish mild corner,
And, through my immortal waters
I meet the sun's grains eye
To eye, and they fail at my closet of glass.
Dead, I am most surely living
In the minds of farm boys: I am he who drives
Them like wolves from the hound bitch and calf
And from the chaste ewe in the wind.
They go into woods   into bean fields   they go
Deep into their known right hands. Dreaming of me,
They groan   they wait   they suffer
Themselves, they marry, they raise their kind.

1967

Alan Dugan
1923–2003

Alan Dugan was conspicuously unaffiliated—to other poets, to an affirmative creed, to life itself. One poem is partly titled "from an Alienated Point of View," and this description applies to all his work. The final poem of his first book speaks of "prisoners of this world," and Dugan wrote as a prisoner, confident that there was no escape and that come what may the future would be as bad as the present. To Dugan, America is the land not of promise but of decadence and of various despairs. Not that the rest of the universe is any better.

Bluntness, ironic rage, and a ferocious sense of comedy form Dugan's responses to experience. At moments he sounds like a church father denouncing existence; St. Augustine's statement "Nascimur inter faeces et urinas" ("We are born between the feces and the urine") might seem to be his text. Dugan's despair differs from that of others, such as Jonathan Swift, in being anarchic, endless, a cherished anguish. Yet his caustic attacks on comforting hopes are so adroit that one reads him with wincing amusement. He was the clown of nihilism. Heroism, victory, patience, nature, family, even his own art—all are mercilessly felled by his rhetorical ax. Terse and vivid, his satiric poems are tightly constructed and emotionally intense.

Born on February 12, 1923, in Brooklyn, New York, Dugan was a left-wing "anti-fascist" (his term) and served in the army air force during World War II. After the war, he worked for an advertising agency, a staple factory, and a payroll office, eventually making physiological models in plastic. He received a B.A. from Mexico City College. He had published very little poetry until his first book was accepted for the Yale Series of Younger Poets and published in 1961. The resultant praise, and two prizes he won later, the Pulitzer Prize and the National Book Award, allowed him to devote himself to writing. He taught for most of his career at the Fine Arts Work Center in Provincetown, Massachusetts. He won the National Book Award a second time in 2001.

Love Song: I and Thou

Nothing is plumb, level or square:
   the studs are bowed, the joists
are shaky by nature, no piece fits
   any other piece without a gap
or pinch, and bent nails
   dance all over the surfacing
like maggots. By Christ
   I am no carpenter. I built
the roof for myself, the walls
   for myself, the floors
for myself, and got
   hung up in it myself. I
danced with a purple thumb
   at this house-warming, drunk
with my prime whiskey: rage.
   Oh I spat rage's nails

into the frame-up of my work:
  it held. It settled plumb,
level, solid, square and true
  for that great moment. Then
it screamed and went on through,
  skewing as wrong the other way.
God damned it. This is hell,
  but I planned it, I sawed it,
I nailed it, and I
  will live in it until it kills me.
I can nail my left palm
  to the left-hand crosspiece but
I can't do everything myself.
  I need a hand to nail the right,
a help, a love, a you, a wife.

1961

Fabrication of Ancestors

For old Billy Dugan, shot in the ass in
the Civil War, my father said.

The old wound in my ass
has opened up again, but I
am past the prodigies
of youth's campaigns, and weep
where I used to laugh
in war's red humors, half
in love with silly-assed pains
and half not feeling them.
I have to sit up with
an indoor unsittable itch
before I go down late
and weeping to the storm-
cellar on a dirty night
and go to bed with the worms.
So pull the dirt up over me
and make a family joke
for Old Billy Blue Balls,
the oldest private in the world
with two ass-holes and no
place more to go to for a laugh
except the last one. Say:
The North won the Civil War
without much help from me
although I wear a proof
of the war's obscenity.

1963

On Being a Householder

I live inside of a machine
or machines. Every time one
goes off another starts. Why
don't I go outside and sleep
on the ground. It is because
I'm scared of the open night
and stars looking down at me
as God's eyes, full of questions;
and when I do sleep out alone
I wake up soaking wet
with the dew-fall and am
being snuffed at by a female fox
who stinks from being skunked.
Also there are carrion insects
climbing my private parts. Therefore
I would find shelter in houses,
rented or owned. Anything that money
can build or buy is better than
the nothing of the sky at night,
the stars being the visible past.

1974

Internal Migration: On Being on Tour

As an American traveler I have
to remember not to get actionably[1] mad
about the way things are around here.
Tomorrow I'll be a thousand miles away
from the way it is around here. I will
keep my temper, I will not kill the dog
next door, nor will I kill the next-door wife,
both of whom are crazy and aggressive
and think they live at the center of culture
like everyone else in this college town.
This is because I'm leaving, I'm taking off
by car, by light plane, by jet, by taxicab,
for some place else a thousand miles away,
so I caution myself: control your rage,
even if it causes a slight heart attack.
Stay out of jail tonight before you leave,
and don't get obstreperous in transit tomorrow
so as to stay out of jail on arrival tomorrow night.
Think: the new handcuffs are sharp inside
and meant to cut the wrists. You're not too old

1. Affording grounds for a lawsuit.

to be raped in their filthy overcrowded jails
and you'll lose your glasses and false teeth.
How would you eat, study and be
a traveling lecturer if you got out alive and sane?
So remember to leave this place peacefully,
it's only Asshole State University at Nowheresville,
and remember to get to the next place peacefully,
it's only Nowhere State University at Assholeville
and you must travel from place to place for food and shelter.

1983

For Euthanasia and Pain-Killing Drugs

As my father died of cancer of the asshole
the doctor wouldn't give him habit-forming drugs
for fear of making him a hopeless addict
so it took two men to hold him down to die.
I ran around like crazy to the bars that day.
When I got back that night they said he died at noon,
so I squeezed out two tears because they said I should.
Look at what happened to your Uncle John they said.
He couldn't cry when Grandpa died
so he went nuts and tried to kill the priest.
We had to have him put away for life
but you are blessed, you cried, a good son,
you are saved, oh you are not your father's asshole,
may you never rot in shit, God bless your come.

2001

LOUIS SIMPSON
1923–2012

Louis Simpson's early verse, especially his war poetry, explores what he calls "the other side of glory" ("The Legend of Success, the Salesman's Story"). It incongruously frames in fluent meters and rhymed stanzas bitter encounters with death on the battlefield. After his second book of poetry, Simpson abandoned this grim realism, inspired by his participation in the Battle of the Bulge and other armed conflicts of World War II. Instead, his poetry combines a consciousness of how things occur with an awareness of far-flung possibilities, only attainable in dreams. He came to regard his verse as joined to a literary tradition that he traced from symbolism to imagism to surrealism, "rejecting on the one hand the clichés of the rational mind, and on the other, a mere projection of irrational images"; the poet should "reveal the drama and narrative of the subconscious. The images move, with the logic of dreams" (*The Distinctive Voice*, ed. William Martz, 1966). Although his verse is conspicuously formal, it is dotted by dream images. "American poetry," he said (in a poem by that title), "must swim for miles through the desert / Uttering cries that are almost human." With grace, Simpson's verse incorporates fantastic and commonplace material alike, binds physics and metaphysics. Like many American poets, Simpson turned to free verse in the 1960s. His later narrative poetry retains his earlier polish, but it achieves the simplicity of old stories and proverbs, as he writes with wry humor about incidents in his own life.

Simpson was born on March 27, 1923, in Kingston, Jamaica. He emigrated to the United States at seventeen. In his verse, he contemplates the United States with detachment; he is sympathetic, but offers no panegyrics. The Vietnam War in particular alienated him. Simpson's father was a second-generation Jamaican of Scots descent, his mother a Russian Jew. "I most of all wanted to be an American," he said (*Current Biography*, ed. Charles Moritz, 1964). In 1943, he left Columbia University for the American army, serving first with a tank corps, then as a combat infantryman with the 101st Airborne Division; he won the Bronze Star and Purple Heart. His health broke down late in the war; after his recovery, he returned to Columbia for undergraduate and graduate studies. While completing his doctorate, Simpson taught for a time at Columbia and worked briefly in publishing and in export trade. But he reverted to teaching, at the New School for Social Research (1955–59), the University of California at Berkeley (1959–67), and the State University of New York at Stony Brook (1967–93). In addition to books of poetry, he published fiction, plays, essays, an autobiography, and award-winning translations of French poetry.

The Battle

Helmet and rifle, pack and overcoat
Marched through a forest. Somewhere up ahead
Guns thudded. Like the circle of a throat
The night on every side was turning red.

They halted and they dug. They sank like moles
Into the clammy earth between the trees.
And soon the sentries, standing in their holes,
Felt the first snow. Their feet began to freeze.

At dawn the first shell landed with a crack.
Then shells and bullets swept the icy woods.
This lasted many days. The snow was black.
The corpses stiffened in their scarlet hoods.

Most clearly of that battle I remember
The tiredness in eyes, how hands looked thin
Around a cigarette, and the bright ember
Would pulse with all the life there was within.

1955

My Father in the Night Commanding No

My father in the night commanding No
Has work to do. Smoke issues from his lips;
He reads in silence.
The frogs are croaking and the streetlamps glow.

And then my mother winds the gramophone;
The Bride of Lammermoor begins to shriek—[1]
Or reads a story
About a prince, a castle, and a dragon.

The moon is glittering above the hill.
I stand before the gateposts of the King—
So runs the story—
Of Thule,[2] at midnight when the mice are still.

And I have been in Thule! It has come true—
The journey and the danger of the world,
All that there is
To bear and to enjoy, endure and do.

Landscapes, seascapes . . . where have I been led?
The names of cities—Paris, Venice, Rome—
Held out their arms.
A feathered god, seductive, went ahead.

Here is my house. Under a red rose tree
A child is swinging; another gravely plays.
They are not surprised
That I am here; they were expecting me.

And yet my father sits and reads in silence,
My mother sheds a tear, the moon is still,
And the dark wind
Is murmuring that nothing ever happens.

Beyond his jurisdiction as I move
Do I not prove him wrong? And yet, it's true
They will not change
There, on the stage of terror and of love.

The actors in that playhouse always sit
In fixed positions—father, mother, child
With painted eyes.
How sad it is to be a little puppet!

1. The record is probably of the mad scene from the opera *Lucia di Lammermoor*, by Gaetano Donizetti (1797–1848).

2. The name given to an island discovered in the far north by ancient Greek sailors; it symbolizes the explorer's ultimate quest.

Their heads are wooden. And you once pretended
To understand them! Shake them as you will,
They cannot speak.
Do what you will, the comedy is ended.[3]

Father, why did you work? Why did you weep,
Mother? Was the story so important?
"*Listen!*" the wind
Said to the children, and they fell asleep.

1963

American Poetry

Whatever it is, it must have
A stomach that can digest
Rubber, coal, uranium, moons, poems.

Like the shark, it contains a shoe.
It must swim for miles through the desert
Uttering cries that are almost human.

1963

White Oxen

A man walks beside them
with a whip that he cracks.
The cart they draw is painted
with Saracens and Crusaders,[4]
fierce eyes and ranks of spears.

They are on the steep road
that goes up the mountain.
Their neat-stepping hoofs
appear to be flickering
in the sun, raising dust.

They are higher than the roofs
on which striped gourds and melons
lie ripening. They move
among the dark green olives
that grow on the rocks.

3. This line's second half ends the opera *Pagliacci*, by Neapolitan composer Ruggero Leoncavallo (1857/58–1919). The audience, thinking it is watching a play, witnesses a double murder committed by the jealous husband who speaks the line.
4. That is, the Muslims and the European Crusaders who fought them for recovery of the Holy Land, in the Middle Ages.

They dwindle as they climb . . .
vanish around a corner
and reappear walking on the edge
of a precipice. They enter
the region of mist and darkness.

I think I can see them still:
a pair of yoked oxen
the color of ivory
or smoke, with red tassels,
in the gathering dusk.

1987

DENISE LEVERTOV
1923–1997

Denise Levertov writes a poetry of secrets, in which the poet uncovers something hidden, like a physicist plumbing the atom. This something is recognized with such joyful force that it seems to palpitate or shudder at being known. Her work has close connections, as she realized, with that of Black Mountain poets Robert Duncan and Robert Creeley, though it is less mystical than Duncan's, more ecstatic than Creeley's. She regarded these men as "the chief poets among my contemporaries" (*The Poet in the World*). Ezra Pound, William Carlos Williams, and H. D. are among her modernist influences, commemorated in the poem "September 1961." Levertov liked to burst through the trivial, and in "A Common Ground" she speaks of "poems stirred / into paper coffee-cups, eaten / with petals on rye in the / sun . . . entering / human lives forever, / unobserved." In rhapsodic rhythms and incantatory syntax, the poet conveys awe before nature and human relationships. Conifers hold their cones up for the light's blessing in a "festive rite" ("Celebration"), and vine leaves exchange mysterious whispers ("Aware"). Love, desire, and grief are among the emotional resources that flood the poems. In elegies for her sister, she mourns the memory of Olga at sixteen with "breasts / round, round, and / dark-nippled—," now "bones and tatters of flesh in earth."

Written in England, Levertov's first book was in regular stanzas, but her subsequent books, written in the United States, are in free verse. Her sense of pace and climax follows principles outlined in Charles Olson's "Projective Verse" and her "Notes on Organic Form," such as form as a revelation of content, verbal simulation of propulsive movement, avoidance of the iamb, composition to the rhythm of breathing, and conflation of the mundane with the mystical. Her effects are precisely calculated: "I believe every space and comma is a living part of the poem and has its function, just as every muscle and pore of the body has its function. And the way the lines are broken is a functioning part essential to the poem's life" (*The Poet in the World*).

Judeo-Christian in religious background and Anglo-American in nationality, Levertov lived transnationally and cross-culturally. She proudly claimed connection with mystics of the past. Her father was descended from a Russian rabbi, Schneour Zaimon, who was renowned as a Hasid, a member of a Jewish mystical movement that began in the eighteenth century and found a glory in everyday occurrences. Her mother was descended from a Welsh tailor and mystic, Angel Jones of Mold (a town in Wales).

Although her father was born Jewish, he converted to Christianity and became an Anglican priest, with a lifelong hope of uniting the two religions. Born on October 24, 1923, in Ilford, Essex, Levertov went to neither school nor college. "As a child," she writes, "I 'did lessons' at home under the tutelage of my mother and listened to the BBC Schools Programs. For French, piano, and art I was sent to various teachers for private lessons" ("The Untaught Teacher," *The Poet in the World*).

In 1948, when she was twenty-five years old, Levertov moved to the United States with her American husband, the author Mitchell Goodman, who introduced her to Creeley and Duncan. She became a U.S. citizen in 1955. Beginning in the 1960s, Levertov became a war protester and in poetry passionately denounced the Vietnam War, the nuclear arms race, and U.S. policy in El Salvador. Seen by some as "prophetic," by others as "preachy," these poems reflect a change in Levertov's view on the relation of poetry to politics. In 1959, she had stated, "I do not believe that a violent imitation of the horrors of our times is the concern of poetry"; but by 1965, she declared that the poem "has a social *effect* of some kind whether or not the poet wills that it have. It has kinetic force, it sets in motion . . . elements in the reader that would otherwise be stagnant" ("A Testament and a Postscript," *The Poet in the World*).

In her later volumes, Levertov returned to a more intimate kind of poetry. Meanwhile, she had taught at a large number of universities and colleges, remaining from 1981 at Stanford University. She became a Roman Catholic a few years before dying from lymphoma.

Pleasures

I like to find
what's not found
at once, but lies

within something of another nature,
in repose, distinct.
Gull feathers of glass, hidden

in white pulp: the bones of squid
which I pull out and lay
blade by blade on the draining board—

        tapered as if for swiftness, to pierce
        the heart, but fragile, substance
        belying design.   Or a fruit, *mamey*,

cased in rough brown peel, the flesh
rose-amber, and the seed:
the seed a stone of wood, carved and

polished, walnut-colored, formed
like a brazilnut, but large,
large enough to fill
the hungry palm of a hand.

I like the juicy stem of grass that grows
within the coarser leaf folded round,
and the butteryellow glow
in the narrow flute from which the morning-glory
opens blue and cool on a hot morning.

1959

The Dog of Art

That dog with daisies for eyes
who flashes forth
flame of his very self at every bark
is the Dog of Art.
Worked in wool, his blind eyes
look inward to caverns and jewels
which they see perfectly,
and his voice
measures forth the treasure
in music sharp and loud,
sharp and bright,
bright flaming barks,
and growling smoky soft, the Dog
of Art turns to the world
the quietness of his eyes.

1959

Song for Ishtar[1]

The moon is a sow
and grunts in my throat
Her great shining shines through me
so the mud of my hollow gleams
and breaks in silver bubbles

She is a sow
and I a pig and a poet

When she opens her white
lips to devour me I bite back
and laughter rocks the moon

In the black of desire
we rock and grunt, grunt and
shine

1964

1. Life-giving mother-goddess of the ancient Babylonians.

The Ache of Marriage

The ache of marriage:

thigh and tongue, beloved,
are heavy with it,
it throbs in the teeth

We look for communion
and are turned away, beloved,
each and each

It is leviathan[2] and we
in its belly
looking for joy, some joy
not to be known outside it

two by two in the ark of
the ache of it.

1964

September 1961

This is the year the old ones,
the old great ones
leave us alone on the road.

The road leads to the sea.
We have the words in our pockets,
obscure directions. The old ones

have taken away the light of their presence,
we see it moving away over a hill
off to one side.

They are not dying,
they are withdrawn
into a painful privacy

learning to live without words.
E.P. "It looks like dying"—Williams: "I can't
describe to you what has been

happening to me"—
H.D. "unable to speak."[3]
The darkness

2. The great seamonster of the Bible, often identified as a whale, such as swallowed Jonah.

3. American poet H. D. (Hilda Doolittle, b. 1886) died on September 27, 1961. Also that year, Wil-

twists itself in the wind, the stars
are small, the horizon
ringed with confused urban light-haze.

They have told us
the road leads to the sea,
and given

the language into our hands.
We hear
our footsteps each time a truck

has dazzled past us and gone
leaving us new silence.
One can't reach

the sea on this endless
road to the sea unless
one turns aside at the end, it seems,

follows
the owl that silently glides above it
aslant, back and forth,

and away into deep woods.

But for us the road
unfurls itself, we count the
words in our pockets, we wonder

how it will be without them, we don't
stop walking, we know
there is far to go, sometimes

we think the night wind carries
a smell of the sea . . .

1964

Olga Poems

(Olga Levertoff, 1914–1964)[4]

i

By the gas-fire, kneeling
to undress,
scorching luxuriously, raking

liam Carlos Williams (1883–1963) suffered a stroke and Ezra Pound (1885–1972) fell into a silence that lasted until his death.

4. The poet's sister.

her nails over olive sides, the red
waistband ring—

(And the little sister
beady-eyed in the bed—
or drowsy, was I? My head
a camera—)

Sixteen. Her breasts
round, round, and
dark-nippled—

who now these two months long
is bones and tatters of flesh in earth.

iv

On your hospital bed you lay
in love, the hatreds
that had followed you, a
comet's tail, burned out

as your disasters bred of love
burned out,
while pain and drugs
quarreled like sisters in you—

lay afloat on a sea
of love and pain—how you always
loved that cadence, 'Underneath
are the everlasting arms'—[5]

all history
burned out, down
to the sick bone, save for

that kind candle.

vi

Your eyes were the brown gold of pebbles under water.
I never crossed the bridge over the Roding, dividing
the open field of the present from the mysteries,
the wraiths and shifts of time-sense Wanstead Park held suspended,
without remembering your eyes. Even when we were estranged
and my own eyes smarted in pain and anger at the thought of you.
And by other streams in other countries; anywhere where the light
reaches down through shallows to gold gravel. Olga's
brown eyes. One rainy summer, down in the New Forest,[6]
when we could hardly breathe for ennui and the low sky,

5. Deuteronomy 33.27.

6. A district in southern England.

you turned savagely to the piano and sightread
straight through all the Beethoven sonatas, day after day—
weeks, it seemed to me. I would turn the pages some of the time,
go out to ride my bike, return—you were enduring in the
falls and rapids of the music, the arpeggios rang out, the rectory
trembled, our parents seemed effaced.
I think of your eyes in that photo, six years before I was born,
the fear in them. What did you do with your fear,
later? Through the years of humiliation,
of paranoia and blackmail and near-starvation, losing
the love of those you loved, one after another,
parents, lovers, children, idolized friends, what kept
compassion's candle alight in you, that lit you
clear into another chapter (but the same book) 'a clearing
in the selva oscura,[7]
a house whose door
swings open, a hand beckons
in welcome'?
                I cross
so many brooks in the world, there is so much light
dancing on so many stones, so many questions my eyes
smart to ask of your eyes, gold brown eyes,
the lashes short but the lids
arched as if carved out of olivewood, eyes with some vision
of festive goodness in back of their hard, or veiled, or shining,
unknowable gaze . . .

May–August, 1964 1966

A Time Past

The old wooden steps to the front door
where I was sitting that fall morning
when you came downstairs, just awake,
and my joy at sight of you (emerging
into golden day—
                the dew almost frost)
pulled me to my feet to tell you
how much I loved you:

those wooden steps
are gone now, decayed
replaced with granite,
hard, gray, and handsome.
The old steps live
only in me:
my feet and thighs

7. "The quoted lines in the sixth section are an adaptation of some lines in 'Selva Oscura' by the late Louis MacNiece [1907–1963], a poem much loved by my sister" [Levertov's note]. *Selva oscura*: dark wood (Italian); from the opening lines of Dante's *Divine Comedy*.

remember them, and my hands
still feel their splinters.

Everything else about and around that house
brings memories of others—of marriage,
of my son. And the steps do too: I recall
sitting there with my friend and her little son who died,
or was it the second one who lives and thrives?
And sitting there 'in my life,' often, alone or with my husband.
Yet that one instant,
your cheerful, unafraid, youthful, 'I love you too,'
the quiet broken by no bird, no cricket, gold leaves
spinning in silence down without
any breeze to blow them,
                                        is what twines itself
in my head and body across those slabs of wood
that were warm, ancient, and now
wait somewhere to be burnt.

1975

Caedmon[8]

All others talked as if
talk were a dance.
Clodhopper I, with clumsy feet
would break the gliding ring.
Early I learned to
hunch myself
close by the door:
then when the talk began
I'd wipe my
mouth and wend
unnoticed back to the barn
to be with the warm beasts,
dumb among body sounds
of the simple ones.
I'd see by a twist
of lit rush[9] the motes
of gold moving
from shadow to shadow
slow in the wake
of deep untroubled sighs.
The cows
munched or stirred or were still. I
was at home and lonely,

8. "The story comes, of course, from the venerable Bede's *History of the English Church and People*, but I first read it as a child in John Richard Green's *History of the English People*, 1855" [Levertov's note]. Caedmon (fl. 658–80), according to the story, was an illiterate cowherd employed by a monastery; one night he received a divine call to sing verses in praise of God. He is the earliest known English Christian poet.

9. The piths of rush plants were used for candlewicks.

both in good measure. Until
the sudden angel affrighted me—light effacing
my feeble beam,
a forest of torches, feathers of flame, sparks upflying:
but the cows as before
were calm, and nothing was burning,
            nothing but I, as that hand of fire
touched my lips and scorched my tongue
and pulled my voice
                        into the ring of the dance.

1987

Celebration

Brilliant, this day—a young virtuoso of a day.
Morning shadows cut by sharpest scissors,
deft hands. And every prodigy of green—
whether it's ferns or lichen or needles
or impatient points of bud on spindly bushes—
greener than ever before.
                              And the way the conifers
hold new cones to the light for blessing,
a festive rite, and sing the oceanic chant the wind
transcribes for them!
A day that shines in the cold
like a first-prize brass band swinging along the street
of a coal-dusty village, wholly at odds
with the claims of reasonable gloom.

1999

[Scraps of Moon]

Scraps of moon
bobbing discarded on broken water

but sky-moon
complete, transcending

all violation.

1999

Aware

When I opened the door
I found the vine leaves
speaking among themselves in abundant
whispers.

My presence made them
hush their green breath,
embarrassed, the way
humans stand up, buttoning their jackets,
acting as if they were leaving anyway, as if
the conversations had ended
just before you arrived.
I liked
the glimpse I had, though,
of their obscure
gestures. I liked the sound
of such private voices. Next time
I'll move like cautious sunlight, open
the door by fractions, eavesdrop
peacefully.

1999

Richard Hugo
1923–1982

In 1973, the poet James Wright remarked that Richard Hugo's poetry shows us the "special and secret details of places" ("Hugo: Secrets of the Inner Landscape"). Hugo's poems take place, for the most part, in the Pacific northwest, where he lived, but he developed a complex relationship between his region and his fictions. "The place triggers the mind to create the place," he wrote; "the imagination can take off from" known reality "and if necessary return" (*The Triggering Town*). Dying towns and desolate landscapes haunt Hugo's imagination. He is a poet of elegiac remembrance, reclaiming the vacant, the abandoned, and the dead through descriptive detail and second-person address. Often speaking as the lonely outsider, he gives palpable presence to scenes of failure, poverty, and loss. His diction and syntax are spare and straightforward, and he artfully balances these qualities with richly textured images, melancholy tonalities, and pentameter rhythms.

Hugo's mother, a teenager, was forced to abandon him after his birth (on December 21, 1923) to the care of his maternal grandparents, working-class people of German descent who lived in the tough neighborhood of White Center, south of Seattle. Starved of affection, Hugo grew up lonely, shy, and terrified of relationships with women; he admired the local bullies and sought macho friendships with other boys: "By the time I was a young man I was a mess" (*The Real West Marginal Way*). After high school, facing the draft like other men of his generation, he joined the army air force and flew thirty-five missions as a bombardier in Italy. Returning to complete his studies at the University of Washington, he took courses in poetry with Theodore Roethke, who, in teaching modern poets, was "passionately committed to their rhythms and tonalities" (*Triggering Town*). Hugo then went to work for Boeing aircraft, writing poems slowly on the side, marrying for the first time in 1951, and publishing his first book at thirty-seven. After a trip to Italy in 1963, he began teaching at the University of Montana.

Still prey to loneliness and alcohol, Hugo suffered a "minor-league breakdown" in 1971. He married again in 1974, and a Guggenheim Fellowship enabled a visit to, and poems about, the remote island of Skye, off the northern coast of Scotland. Hugo died of leukemia.

The Lady in Kicking Horse Reservoir[1]

Not my hands but green across you now.
Green tons hold you down, and ten bass curve
teasing in your hair. Summer slime
will pile deep on your breast. Four months of ice
will keep you firm. I hope each spring
to find you tangled in those pads
pulled not quite loose by the spillway pour,
stars in dead reflection off your teeth.

Lie there lily still. The spillway's closed.
Two feet down most lakes are common gray.
This lake is dark from the black blue Mission range
climbing sky like music dying Indians once wailed.
On ocean beaches, mystery fish
are offered to the moon. Your jaws go blue.
Your hands start waving every wind.
Wave to the ocean where we crushed a mile of foam.

We still love there in thundering foam
and love. Whales fall in love with gulls
and tide reclaims the Dolly skeletons[2]
gone with a blast of aching horns to China.
Landlocked in Montana here
the end is limited by light, the final note
will trail off at the farthest point we see,
already faded, lover, where you bloat.

All girls should be nicer. Arrows rain
above us in the Indian wind. My future
should be full of windy gems, my past
will stop this roaring in my dreams.
Sorry. Sorry. Sorry. But the arrows sing:
no way to float her up. The dead sink
from dead weight. The Mission range
turns this water black late afternoons.

1. Both Kicking Horse Reservoir and the Mission mountain range (line 11) are on the Flathead Native American reservation, in Montana.

2. Here, skeletons of the Dolly Varden trout (but see also line 54).

One boy slapped the other. Hard.
The slapped boy talked until his dignity
dissolved, screamed a single 'stop'
and went down sobbing in the company pond.
I swam for him all night. My only suit
got wet and factory hands went home.
No one cared the coward disappeared.
Morning then: cold music I had never heard.

Loners like work best on second shift.
No one liked our product and the factory closed.
Off south, the bison multiply so fast
a slaughter's mandatory every spring
and every spring the creeks get fat
and Kicking Horse fills up. My hope is vague.
The far blur of your bones in May
may be nourished by the snow.

The spillway's open and you spill out
into weather, lover down the bright canal
and mother, irrigating crops
dead Indians forgot to plant.
I'm sailing west with arrows to dissolving foam
where waves strand naked Dollys.
Their eyes are white as oriental mountains
and their tongues are teasing oil from whales.

1973

Degrees of Gray in Philipsburg[3]

You might come here Sunday on a whim.
Say your life broke down. The last good kiss
you had was years ago. You walk these streets
laid out by the insane, past hotels
that didn't last, bars that did, the tortured try
of local drivers to accelerate their lives.
Only churches are kept up. The jail
turned 70 this year. The only prisoner
is always in, not knowing what he's done.

The principal supporting business now
is rage. Hatred of the various grays
the mountain sends, hatred of the mill,
The Silver Bill repeal, the best liked girls
who leave each year for Butte.[4] One good
restaurant and bars can't wipe the boredom out.

3. Small town in Montana, which in the early twentieth century was a thriving community supported by a silver-processing mill.

4. City in Montana. *Silver Bill:* law enacted in 1934 empowering the federal government to buy silver.

The 1907 boom, eight going silver mines,
a dance floor built on springs—
all memory resolves itself in gaze,
in panoramic green you know the cattle eat
or two stacks high above the town,
two dead kilns, the huge mill in collapse
for fifty years that won't fall finally down.

Isn't this your life? That ancient kiss
still burning out your eyes? Isn't this defeat
so accurate, the church bell simply seems
a pure announcement: ring and no one comes?
Don't empty houses ring? Are magnesium
and scorn sufficient to support a town,
not just Philipsburg, but towns
of towering blondes, good jazz and booze
the world will never let you have
until the town you came from dies inside?

Say no to yourself. The old man, twenty
when the jail was built, still laughs
although his lips collapse. Someday soon,
he says, I'll go to sleep and not wake up.
You tell him no. You're talking to yourself.
The car that brought you here still runs.
The money you buy lunch with,
no matter where it's mined, is silver
and the girl who serves your food
is slender and her red hair lights the wall.

1973

White Center[5]

Town or poem, I don't care how it looks. Old woman
take my hand and we'll walk one more time these streets
I believed marked me weak beneath catcalling clouds.
Long ago, the swamp behind the single row of stores
was filled and seeded. Roses today where Toughy Hassin
slapped my face to the grinning delight of his gang.
I didn't cry or run. Had I fought him
I'd have been beaten and come home bloody in tears
and you'd have told me I shouldn't be fighting.

Wasn't it all degrading, mean Mr. Kyte sweeping
the streets for no pay, believing what he'd learned
as a boy in England: 'This is your community'?

5. Suburb of Seattle.

I taunted him to rage, then ran. Is this the day
we call bad mothers out of the taverns and point them
sobbing for home, or issue costumes to posturing clowns
in the streets, make fun of drunk barbers, and hope
someone who left and made it returns, vowed
to buy more neon and give these people some class?

The Dugans aren't worth a dime, dirty Irish, nor days
you offered a penny for every fly I killed.
You were blind to my cheating. I saw my future certain—
that drunk who lived across the street and fell
in our garden reaching for the hoe you dropped.
All he got was our laughter. I helped him often home
when you weren't looking. I loved some terrible way
he lived in his mind and tried to be decent to others.
I loved the way we loved him behind our disdain.

Clouds. What glorious floating. They always move on
like I should have early. But your odd love and a war
taught me the world's gone evil past the first check point
and that's First Avenue South. I fell asleep each night
safe in love with my murder. The neighbor girl
plotted to tease every tomorrow and watch me turn
again to the woods and games too young for my age.
We never could account for the python cousin Warren
found half starved in the basement of Safeway.

It all comes back but in bites. I am the man
you beat to perversion. That was the drugstore MacCameron
flipped out in early one morning, waltzing
on his soda fountain. The siren married his shrieking.
His wife said, "We'll try again, in Des Moines."
You drove a better man into himself where he found tunes
he had no need to share. It's all beginning to blur
as it forms. Men cracking up or retreating.
Resolute women deep in hard prayer.

And it isn't the same this time. I hoped forty years
I'd write and would not write this poem. This town would die
and your grave never reopen. Or mine. Because I'm married
and happy, and across the street a foster child
from a cruel past is safe and need no longer crawl
for his meals, I walk this past with you, ghost in any field
of good crops, certain I remember everything wrong.
If not, why is this road lined thick with fern
and why do I feel no shame kicking the loose gravel home?

1980

Kenneth Koch
1925–2002

Not to be pompous, not to be oracular, above all not to be dull: these were the commandments of the short-lived, so-called New York school of poets, of which Kenneth Koch was a founding member. The positive program of this school—modernist and surrealist in origin, urban in wit, abstract expressionist in painterly affiliation—can perhaps best be described by Koch's term "formulalessness." Koch had an eye for the incongruous image and generated tension out of the anarchic profusion of such images. He also had an ear for the lyrical possibilities of seemingly unusable material. The effect was often comic, surprising, even childlike, and indeed Koch recorded in two delightful books his experiences of teaching children to write poetry.

Koch was born on February 27, 1925, in Cincinnati, Ohio. His verse writing began at age five, but became serious at seventeen, when he read John Dos Passos and struggled to represent the stream of consciousness—another key interest of the New York school. At eighteen, he went into the army for three years, serving in the Pacific theater as a rifleman. On his return, he earned a B.A. (in 1948) at Harvard University, where his classmates included John Ashbery and Frank O'Hara. In 1959, he received his doctorate at Columbia University, with a dissertation on doctors as characters in literature, and began a long teaching career at Columbia, the location befitting his metropolitan muse. During three years abroad he discovered the work of the European surrealists. As he writes in "The Art of Poetry": "As for 'surrealistic' methods and techniques, they have become a / Natural part of writing."

A master of parody and pastiche, Koch satirized earlier esteemed poets such as Robert Frost and William Carlos Williams, as well as poets more generally, and did not spare even himself. "Now comes the poet," he writes in "The Stones of Time," "wrapped in a huge white towel, with his head full of imagery." Fast-paced, exhilarated, gleefully shifting in direction, Koch's poetry is a high-spirited romp that delights in its sonic resourcefulness and allusiveness. It risks playfulness and whimsy even when pursuing central questions about contemporary aesthetics. It is by turns intimate and extravagant, self-reflexive and frivolous, drawing energy from the momentum of its own language. Koch's many experiments in varied genres and forms gave him an enviable technical facility that served his more serious poems as well. In "The Art of Poetry," he sums up the desired effect of his poetry: "A reader should put your work down puzzled, / Distressed and illuminated, ready to believe / It is curious to be alive."

Mending Sump[1]

"Hiram, I think the sump is backing up.
The bathroom floor boards for above two weeks
Have seemed soaked through. A little bird, I think
Has wandered in the pipes, and all's gone wrong."
"Something there is that doesn't hump a sump,"
He said; and through his head she saw a cloud
That seemed to twinkle. "Hiram, well," she said,
"Smith is come home! I saw his face just now

1. Cf. Robert Frost's "Mending Wall."

While looking through your head. He's come to die
Or else to laugh, for hay is dried-up grass
When you're alone." He rose, and sniffed the air.
"We'd better leave him in the sump," he said.

1960

Geography

1

In the blue hubbub of the same-through-wealth sky
Amba grew to health and fifteenth year among the jungle scrubbery.
The hate-bird sang on a lower wing of the birch-nut tree
And Amba heard him sing, and in his health he too
Began to sing, but then stopped. Along the lower Congo
There are such high plants of what there is there, when
At morning Amba heard their pink music as gentlemanly
As if he had been in civilization. When morning stank
Over the ridge of coconuts and bald fronds, with agility
Amba climbed the permanent nut trees, and will often sing
To the shining birds, and the pets in their stealth
Are each other among, also, whether it be blue (thhhh) feathers
Or green slumber. Africa in Amba's mind was those white mornings he sang
(thhhh) high trala to the nougat birds, and after
The trenches had all been dug for the day, Amba
Would dream at the edge of some stained and stinking pond
Of the afternight music, as blue pets came to him in his dreams.
From the orange coconuts he would extract some stained milk,
Underneath his feet roots, tangled and filthy green. At night
The moon (zzzzzz) shining down on Amba's sweet mocked sleep.

2

In Chicago Louis walked the morning's rounds with agility.
A boy of seventeen and already recognized as a fast milkman!
The whizz and burr of dead chimes oppressed the
Holocaustic unison of Frank's brain, a young outlaw
Destined to meet dishonor and truth in a same instant,
Crossing Louis' path gently in the street, the great secret unknown.

3

The fur rhubarb did not please Daisy. "Freddie," she called,
"Our fruit's gang mouldy." Daisy, white cheeks with a spot of red
In them, like apples grown in paper bags, smiled
Gently at the fresh new kitchen; and, then, depressed,
She began to cover the rhubarb with her hands.

4

In the crushy green ice and snow Baba ran up and around with exuberance!
Today, no doubt, Father and Uncle Dad would come, and together they three would chase the whale!
Baba stared down through the green crusty ice at the world of fish
And closed his eyes and began to imagine the sweet trip
Over the musky waters, when Daddy would spear the whale, and the wind
Blow "Crad, crad!" through Uncle Dad's fur, and the sweet end
Of the day where they would smile at one another over the smoking blubber
And Uncle Dad would tell tales of his adventures past the shadow bar
Chasing the white snow-eagle. Baba ran
Into the perfect igloo screaming with impatience, and Malmal,
His mother, kissed him and dressed him with loving care for the icy trip.

5

Ten Ko sprinted over the rice paddies. Slush, slosh, sloosh!
His brother, Wan Kai, would soon be returned from the village
Where he had gone . . . (Blue desire! . . .)

6

Roon startled her parents by appearing perfectly dressed
In a little white collar and gown.
Angebor lifted himself up so he might stare in the window at the pretty girl.
His little hands unclenched and dropped the coins he had saved for the *oona*.[2]
He opened wide his eyes, then blinked at the pretty girl. He had never seen anything like that.
That evening, when it whitened in the sky, and a green
Clearness was there, Maggia, and Angebor had no *oona*.
But Angebor talked with excitement of what he had seen, and Maggia drank *zee'th*.

7

The little prisoner wept and wailed, telling of his life in the sand
And the burning sun over the desert. And one night it was cool
And dark, and he stole away over the green sand to search for his parents.
And he went to their tent, and they kissed him and covered him with loving-kindness.

2. Like *zee'th* (line 53), a word invented by Koch.

And the new morning sun shone like a pink rose in the heavens.
And the family prayed, the desert wind scorching their cool skin.

8

Amba arose. Thhhhhhh! went the birds, and clink clank cleck went
The leaves under the monkeys' feet, and Amba went to search for water
Speaking quietly with his fresh voice as he went toward Gorilla Lake
To all the beasts. Wan Kai lifted his body from the rice mat
When his brother Ten Ko came running in. "They have agreed in the village,"
He said. Win Tei brought them tea. Outside the rain
Fell. Plop, plop. Daisy felt something stir inside her.
She went to the window and looked out at the snow. Louis came up the stairs
With the milk. "Roon has bronchitis," said the American doctor,
"She will have to stay inside for ten days during this rain." Amba
Sneaked away, and wanted to go there again, but Maggia said he could not go again in this rain
And would be sure to lose the money for the *oona*. Baba stared
At the green and black sea. Uncle Dad stood up in the boat, while Baba
Watched Father plunge his harpoon three times in the whale. Daisy turned
Dreamily around, her hand on her cheek. Frank's boot
Kicked in the door. Amba wept; Ahna the deer was dead; she lay amid her puzzled young.
The sweet forms of the apple blossoms bent down to Wehtukai.
The boat split. Sun streamed into the apartment. Amba, Amba!
The lake was covered with gloom. Enna plunged into it screaming.

1962

Variations on a Theme by William Carlos Williams[3]

1

I chopped down the house that you had been saving to live in next summer.
I am sorry, but it was morning, and I had nothing to do
and its wooden beams were so inviting.

2

We laughed at the hollyhocks together
and then I sprayed them with lye.
Forgive me. I simply do not know what I am doing.

3. Cf. William Carlos Williams's "This Is Just to Say."

3

I gave away the money that you had been saving to live on for the next
ten years.
The man who asked for it was shabby
and the firm March wind on the porch was so juicy and cold.

4

Last evening we went dancing and I broke your leg.
Forgive me. I was clumsy, and
I wanted you here in the wards, where I am the doctor![4]

1962

From Days and Nights

2. *The Stones of Time*

The bathtub is white and full of strips
And stripes of red and blue and green and white
Where the painter has taken a bath! Now comes the poet
Wrapped in a huge white towel, with his head full of imagery.

Try being really attentive to your life
Instead of to your writing for a change once in a while
Sometimes one day one hour one minute oh I've done that
What happened? I got married and was in a good mood.

We wrote so much that we thought it couldn't be any good
Till we read it over and then thought how amazing it was!

Athena gave Popeye a Butterfinger[5] filled with stars
Is the kind of poetry Z and I used to stuff in jars

When we took a walk he was afraid
Of the dogs who came in parade
To sniffle at the feet
Of two of the greatest poets of the age.

The stars came out
And I was still writing
My God where's dinner
Here's dinner
My wife! I love you
Do you remember in Paris
When I was thinner
And the sun came through the shutters like a knife?

4. Williams was a doctor.
5. A candy bar. *Athena:* the Greek goddess of wisdom.

I said to so many people once, "I write poetry."
They said, "Oh, so you are a poet." Or they said,
"What kind of poetry do you write? modern poetry?"
Or "My brother-in-law is a poet also."
Now if I say, "I am the poet Kenneth Koch," they say, "I think I've heard of you"
Or "I'm sorry but that doesn't ring a bell" or
"Would you please move out of the way? You're blocking my view
Of that enormous piece of meat that they are lowering into the Bay
Of Pigs."[6] What? Or "What kind of poetry do you write?"

"Taste," I said to J and he said
"What else is there?" but he was looking around.

"All the same, she isn't made like that,"
Marguerite said, upon meeting Janice,[7]
To her husband Eddie, and since
Janice was pregnant this had a clear meaning
Like the poetry of Robert Burns.[8]

You must learn to write in form first, said the dumb poet.
After several years of that you can write in free verse.
But of course no verse is really "free," said the dumb poet.
Thank you, I said. It's been great talking to you!

Sweet are the uses of adversity[9]
Became Sweetheart cabooses of diversity
And Sweet art cow papooses at the university
And Sea bar Calpurnia[1] flower havens' re-noosed knees

A book came out, and then another book
Which was unlike the first,
Which was unlike the love
And the nightmares and the fisticuffs that inspired it
And the other poets, with their egos and their works,
Which I sometimes read reluctantly and sometimes with great delight
When I was writing so much myself
I wasn't afraid that what they wrote would bother me
And might even give me ideas.

I walked through the spring fountain of spring
Air fountain knowing finally that poetry was everything:
Sleep, silence, darkness, cool white air, and language.

1982

6. On the west coast of Cuba, site of an unsuccessful U.S.-sponsored invasion in 1961 against the Communist government of Fidel Castro.
7. Koch's wife.
8. Scottish poet (1759–1796).
9. Shakespeare's *As You Like It* 2.1.12.
1. The name of Caesar's wife in Shakespeare's *Julius Caesar*.

One Train May Hide Another

(sign at a railroad crossing in Kenya)

In a poem, one line may hide another line,
As at a crossing, one train may hide another train.
That is, if you are waiting to cross
The tracks, wait to do it for one moment at
Least after the first train is gone. And so when you read
Wait until you have read the next line—
Then it is safe to go on reading.
In a family one sister may conceal another,
So, when you are courting, it's best to have them all in view
Otherwise in coming to find one you may love another.
One father or one brother may hide the man,
If you are a woman, whom you have been waiting to love.
So always standing in front of something the other
As words stand in front of objects, feelings, and ideas.
One wish may hide another. And one person's reputation may hide
The reputation of another. One dog may conceal another
On a lawn, so if you escape the first one you're not necessarily safe;
One lilac may hide another and then a lot of lilacs and on the Appia
Antica[2] one tomb
May hide a number of other tombs. In love, one reproach may hide
another,
One small complaint may hide a great one.
One injustice may hide another—one colonial may hide another,
One blaring red uniform another, and another, a whole column. One bath
may hide another bath
As when, after bathing, one walks out into the rain.
One idea may hide another: Life is simple
Hide Life is incredibly complex, as in the prose of Gertrude Stein[3]
One sentence hides another and is another as well. And in the laboratory
One invention may hide another invention,
One evening may hide another, one shadow, a nest of shadows.
One dark red, or one blue, or one purple—this is a painting
By someone after Matisse.[4] One waits at the tracks until they pass,
These hidden doubles or, sometimes, likenesses. One identical twin
May hide the other. And there may be even more in there! The
obstetrician
Gazes at the Valley of the Var.[5] We used to live there, my wife and I, but
One life hid another life. And now she is gone and I am here.
A vivacious mother hides a gawky daughter. The daughter hides
Her own vivacious daughter in turn. They are in
A railway station and the daughter is holding a bag
Bigger than her mother's bag and successfully hides it.

2. Major Roman road with monumental tombs.
3. Modernist writer (1874–1946), who stated, "After all my only thought is a complicated simplicity. I like a thing simple, but it must be simple through complication" ("A Transatlantic Interview").
4. Henri Matisse (1869–1954), French Fauvist painter who juxtaposes vivid colors.
5. Scenic region near Provence, in southern France.

In offering to pick up the daughter's bag one finds oneself confronted by the mother's
And has to carry that one, too. So one hitchhiker
May deliberately hide another and one cup of coffee
Another, too, until one is over-excited. One love may hide another love or the same love
As when "I love you" suddenly rings false and one discovers
The better love lingering behind, as when "I'm full of doubts"
Hides "I'm certain about something and it is that"
And one dream may hide another as is well known, always, too. In the Garden of Eden
Adam and Eve may hide the real Adam and Eve.
Jerusalem may hide another Jerusalem.
When you come to something, stop to let it pass
So you can see what else is there. At home, no matter where,
Internal tracks pose dangers, too: one memory
Certainly hides another, that being what memory is all about,
The eternal reverse succession of contemplated entities. Reading *A Sentimental Journey* look around
When you have finished, for *Tristram Shandy*,[6] to see
If it is standing there, it should be, stronger
And more profound and theretofore hidden as Santa Maria Maggiore
May be hidden by similar churches inside Rome. One sidewalk
May hide another, as when you're asleep there, and
One song hide another song; a pounding upstairs
Hide the beating of drums. One friend may hide another, you sit at the foot of a tree
With one and when you get up to leave there is another
Whom you'd have preferred to talk to all along. One teacher,
One doctor, one ecstasy, one illness, one woman, one man
May hide another. Pause to let the first one pass.
You think, Now it is safe to cross and you are hit by the next one. It can be important
To have waited at least a moment to see what was already there.

1994

To the Roman Forum

After my daughter Katherine was born
I was terribly excited
I think I would have been measured at the twenty-five-espresso mark
We—Janice, now Katherine, and I—were in Rome
(Janice gave birth at the international hospital on top of Trastevere[7])
I went down and sat and looked at the ruins of you
I gazed at them, gleaming in the half-night

6. Formally complex novel written (1759–67), like the shorter *A Sentimental Journey* (1768), by Irish-born English novelist Laurence Sterne (1713–1768).
7. Quarter of Rome.

And thought, Oh my, My God, My goodness, a child, a wife.
While I was sitting there, a friend, a sculptor, came by
I just had a baby, I said. I mean Janice did. I'm—
I thought I'd look at some very old great things
To match up with this new one. Oh, Adya said,
I guess you'd like to be alone, then. Congratulations. Goodnight.
Thank you. Goodnight, I said. Adya departed.
Next day I saw Janice and Katherine.
Here they are again and have nothing to do with you
A pure force swept through me another time
I am here, they are here, this has happened.
It is happening now, it happened then.

2000

MAXINE KUMIN
1925–2014

Maxine Kumin's poems aim to give a sense of skin and bone, of what it is to live in a body, especially a woman's body. In them, she imparts the experience of being a daughter and mother and lover, of being "a restless Jewish agnostic," living on a farm, participating in the cyclical processes of nature. She had an extraordinary eye for the lives of bears, woodchucks, even stones, and for the deaths of small animals. In "The Excrement Poem," she writes, "It is done by us all." The rural aspects of her verse came from living on a farm in Warner, New Hampshire, where she grew vegetables and bred horses, but Kumin was more than a "nature poet." Much of her work is about intense personal relationships, as in her emotionally intricate poems for a dead friend, a dead mother, a living daughter. Elegizing a friend dead by suicide, she ponders, as she wears the friend's jacket, her nearness to that anguish ("How It Is"). In some poems, she ventures further into history, but always by bringing the past into sharp collision with the present. Both critical and self-critical, she probes religious self-sacrifice and yet also questions her own lack of transcendental belief ("In the Absence of Bliss").

Although her technique is not showy, Kumin was skilled both in free verse and in rhymed and metered stanzas. She mediates between colloquial openness and formal rigor, as also between autobiographical utterance and restraint. Precisely observed, her imagery and figurative language are evocative, as when she compares an airport's blue landing lights to "nail holes in the dark" ("Our Ground Time Here Will Be Brief") or, in a more sustained metaphor, when she likens the quiver of a gong to "the deep nicker the mare makes / swiveling her neck / watching the foal swim / out of her body" ("Bangkok Gong"). In this poem about an object given her by her daughter, Kumin's birthing trope is apt and resonant.

Kumin was born on June 6, 1925, in Philadelphia. She earned B.A. and M.A. degrees at Radcliffe College. In 1973, she won the Pulitzer Prize for *Up Country*, and she was consultant in poetry to the Library of Congress (1981–82) and the poet laureate of New Hampshire (1989–94). She is often associated with Anne Sexton, who collaborated with her on several children's books, but she has less rage and a more buoyant and even humorous sensibility.

How It Is

Shall I say how it is in your clothes?
A month after your death I wear your blue jacket.
The dog at the center of my life recognizes
you've come to visit, he's ecstatic.
In the left pocket, a hole.
In the right, a parking ticket
delivered up last August on Bay State Road.
In my heart, a scatter like milkweed,
a flinging from the pods of the soul.
My skin presses your old outline.
It is hot and dry inside.

I think of the last day of your life,
old friend, how I would unwind it, paste
it together in a different collage,
back from the death car idling in the garage,
back up the stairs, your praying hands unlaced,
reassembling the bits of bread and tuna fish
into a ceremony of sandwich,
running the home movie backward to a space
we could be easy in, a kitchen place
with vodka and ice, our words like living meat.

Dear friend, you have excited crowds
with your example. They swell
like wine bags, straining at your seams.
I will be years gathering up our words,
fishing out letters, snapshots, stains,
leaning my ribs against this durable cloth
to put on the dumb blue blazer of your death.

1982

Our Ground Time Here Will Be Brief

Blue landing lights make
nail holes in the dark.
A fine snow falls. We sit
on the tarmac taking on
the mail, quick freight,
trays of laboratory mice,
coffee and Danish for
the passengers.

Wherever we're going
is Monday morning.
Wherever we're coming from

is Mother's lap.
On the cloud-pack above, strewn
as loosely as parsnip
or celery seeds, lie
the souls of the unborn:

my children's children's
children and their father.
We gather speed for the last run
and lift off into the weather.

1982

In the Absence of Bliss

Museum of the Diaspora,[1] Tel Aviv

The roasting alive of rabbis
in the ardor of the Crusades
went unremarked in *Europe from*
the Holy Roman Empire to 1918,
open without prerequisite
when I was an undergraduate.

While reciting the Sh'ma[2] in full
expectation that their souls
would waft up to the bosom
of the Almighty the rabbis burned,
pious past the humming extremes
of pain. And their loved ones with them.
Whole communities tortured and set aflame
in Christ's name
while chanting Hear, O Israel.

Why?
Why couldn't the rabbis recant,
kiss the Cross, pretend?
Is God so simple that He can't
sort out real from sham?
Did He want
these fanatic autos-da-fé,[3] admire
the eyeballs popping,
the corpses shrinking in the fire?

We live in an orderly
universe of discoverable laws,
writes an intelligent alumna
in *Harvard Magazine.*
Bliss is belief,

1. The settling of Jewish colonies outside Israel.
2. First word ("hear") of the often-recited prayer in which Jews proclaim their faith.
3. Ritual burnings of heretics.

agnostics always say
a little condescendingly
as befits mandarins who function
on a higher moral plane.

Consider our contemporary
Muslim kamikazes
hurling their explosives-
packed trucks through barriers.
Isn't it all the same?
They too die cherishing the fond
certitude of a better life beyond.

We walk away from twenty-two
graphic centuries of kill-the-jew
and hail, of all things, a Mercedes
taxi. The driver is Yemeni,
loves rock music and hangs
each son's picture—three so far—
on tassels from his rearview mirror.

I do not tell him that in Yemen
Jewish men, like women, were forbidden
to ride their donkeys astride,
having just seen this humiliation
illustrated on the Museum screen.

When his parents came
to the Promised Land, they entered
the belly of an enormous
silver bird, not knowing whether
they would live or die.
No matter. As it was written,
the Messiah had drawn nigh.

I do not ask, who tied
the leaping ram inside the thicket?
Who polished, then blighted the apple?
Who loosed pigs in the Temple,
set tribe against tribe
and nailed man in His pocket?[4]

But ask myself, what would
I die for and reciting what?
Not for Yahweh, Allah, Christ,
those patriarchal fists
in the face. But would
I die to save a child?

4. The "ram inside the thicket" is in Genesis 22: God commands Abraham, as a test of his faith, to sacrifice his son Isaac; God then orders the boy spared and provides, instead, a ram, found tangled in a thicket. The "apple" is that of the tree of the knowledge of good and evil. According to Jewish law, pigs are the most unclean animals. "Nailed man" may refer to Jesus' crucifixion.

Rescue my lover? Would
I run into the fiery barn
to release animals,
singed and panicked, from their stalls?

Bliss is belief, but where's
the higher moral plane I roost on?
This narrow plank given to splinters.
No answers. Only questions.

1985

The Bangkok Gong

Home for a visit, you brought me
a circle of hammered brass
reworked from an engine part
into this curio
to be struck with a wad of cotton
pasted onto a stick.
Third World ingenuity
you said, reminds you
of Yankee thrift.

The tone of this gong
is gentle, haunting, but
hard struck three times
can call out as far
as the back fields
to say Supper
or, drummed darkly,
Blood everywhere!
Come quick.

When barely touched it imitates
the deep nicker the mare makes
swiveling her neck
watching the foal swim
out of her body.
She speaks to it even as
she pushes the hindlegs clear.
Come to me is her message
as they curl to reach each other.

Now that you are
back on the border
numbering the lucky ones
whose visas let them
leave everything behind
except nightmares, I hang

the gong on my doorpost.
Some days I
barely touch it.

1989

From Letters

Your laugh, your scarves, the gloss of your makeup,
shallow and vain. I wore your lips, your hair,
even the lift of my eyebrows was yours
but nothing of you could please me, bitten so deep
by the fox of scorn. Like you, I married young
but chose animals, wood heat, hard hours
instead of Sheffield silver, freshcut flowers,
your life of privilege and porcelain.
My children came, the rigorous bond of blood.
Little by little our lives pulled up, pulled even.
A sprinkle here and there of approbation:
we both agreed that what I'd birthed was good.
How did I come to soften? How did you?
Goggy is what my little ones called you.

1996

Donald Justice
1925–2004

Like Richard Wilbur and James Merrill, Donald Justice was an American formalist poet who came to maturity after World War II. Among his models were W. H. Auden and Wallace Stevens, and he was celebrated by the later twentieth-century New Formalists for his mastery of traditional meter and rhyme in such genres as the sonnet, the sestina, the villanelle, and the ballad. Received forms and texts are to him what personal passions are to the confessional poets. He often built poems around an earlier writer's evocative line or phrase, as evidenced by titles such as "Variations on a Text by Vallejo" and "After a Phrase Abandoned by Wallace Stevens." In Justice's adaptations, the previous text or form, to quote Shakespeare's Ariel, "doth suffer a sea-change / Into something rich and strange."

A poet of restraint, Justice comes upon us softly and meditatively. "No house of Atreus ours," he cautions in "Tales from a Family Album," though he then goes on to claim a different sort of doom for his family and himself. Within the air of decorum and quiet tone of his verse, Justice has his heights and abysses, his intimacy and impersonality. Mourning the past, he would re-create that hour "When all things to the eye / Their early splendors wore" (dedication to *The Summer Anniversaries*). An elegist and self-elegist, he clung to forgotten beauty as to dead friends and kinsmen. And like his "Women in Love," he wished in his art "To fasten and not let go." Yet his verse contains another, darker perspective. In their understated way, some poems suggest menace. The cold stares and blank faces in poems such as "The Grandfathers" and "The Tourist from Syracuse" help create a mood of tension and fear.

Sometimes seen as a southern poet, Justice was born in Miami, Florida, on August 12, 1925. He earned a B.A. at Miami University, an M.A. at the University of North Carolina, Chapel Hill, and a Ph.D. at the University of Iowa. He also spent a year at Stanford University studying meter under Yvor Winters. He taught for many years at the University of Iowa (1957–66, 1971–82) and at the University of Florida (1982–92). He won the Lamont, Pulitzer, and Bollingen Prizes for poetry. Among his many students were the poets Mark Strand, Charles Wright, James Tate, and Jorie Graham.

On the Death of Friends in Childhood

We shall not ever meet them bearded in heaven,
Nor sunning themselves among the bald of hell;
If anywhere, in the deserted schoolyard at twilight,
Forming a ring, perhaps, or joining hands
In games whose very names we have forgotten.
Come, memory, let us seek them there in the shadows.

1960

The Grandfathers

Why will they never sleep?
JOHN PEALE BISHOP[1]

Why will they never sleep,
The old ones, the grandfathers?
Always you find them sitting
On ruined porches, deep
In the back country, at dusk,
Hawking and spitting.
They might have sat there forever,
Tapping their sticks,
Peevish, discredited gods.
Ask the lost traveler how,
At road-end, they will fix
You maybe with the cold
Eye of a snake or a bird
And answer not a word,
Only these blank, oracular
Headshakes or headnods.

1967

1. American poet, novelist, and critic (1892–1944), associated with the "lost generation." The phrase is from his "Ode."

After a Phrase Abandoned by Wallace Stevens[2]

The alp at the end of the street
—STEVENS' NOTEBOOKS

The alp at the end of the street
Occurs in the dreams of the town.
Over burgher and shopkeeper,
Massive, he broods,
A snowy-headed father
Upon whose knees his children
No longer climb;
Or is reflected
In the cool, unruffled lakes of
Their minds, at evening,
After their day in the shops,
As shadow only, shapeless
As a wind that has stopped blowing.

Grandeur, it seems,
Comes down to this in the end—
A street of shops
With white shutters
Open for business . . .

1967

The Tourist from Syracuse

One of those men who can be a car salesman or a tourist from Syracuse or a hired assassin.
—JOHN D. MACDONALD[3]

You would not recognize me.
Mine is the face which blooms in
The dank mirrors of washrooms
As you grope for the light switch.

My eyes have the expression
Of the cold eyes of statues
Watching their pigeons return
From the feed you have scattered,

And I stand on my corner
With the same marble patience.
If I move at all, it is
At the same pace precisely

2. American poet (1879–1955). The poem also alludes to several of Stevens's poems, including "To an Old Philosopher in Rome" ("It is a kind of total grandeur at the end") and "The Death of a Soldier" ("the wind stops"), and to a poem by W. H. Auden that begins "Fish in the unruffled lakes."
3. American writer of thrillers (1916–1986).

As the shade of the awning
Under which I stand waiting
And with whose blackness it seems
I am already blended.

I speak seldom, and always
In a murmur as quiet
As that of crowds which surround
The victims of accidents.

Shall I confess who I am?
My name is all names and none.
I am the used-car salesman,
The tourist from Syracuse,

The hired assassin, waiting.
I will stand here forever
Like one who has missed his bus—
Familiar, anonymous—

On my usual corner,
The corner at which you turn
To approach that place where now
You must not hope to arrive.

1967

Men at Forty

Men at forty
Learn to close softly
The doors to rooms they will not be
Coming back to.

At rest on a stair landing,
They feel it moving
Beneath them now like the deck of a ship,
Though the swell is gentle.

And deep in mirrors
They rediscover
The face of the boy as he practices tying
His father's tie there in secret

And the face of that father,
Still warm with the mystery of lather.
They are more fathers than sons themselves now.
Something is filling them, something

That is like the twilight sound
Of the crickets, immense,
Filling the woods at the foot of the slope
Behind their mortgaged houses.

1967

Variations on a Text by Vallejo[4]

Me moriré en París con aguacero . . .

I will die in Miami in the sun,
On a day when the sun is very bright,
A day like the days I remember, a day like other days,
A day that nobody knows or remembers yet,
And the sun will be bright then on the dark glasses of strangers
And in the eyes of a few friends from my childhood
And of the surviving cousins by the graveside,
While the diggers, standing apart, in the still shade of the palms,
Rest on their shovels, and smoke,
Speaking in Spanish softly, out of respect.

I think it will be on a Sunday like today,
Except that the sun will be out, the rain will have stopped,
And the wind that today made all the little shrubs kneel down;
And I think it will be a Sunday because today,
When I took out this paper and began to write,
Never before had anything looked so blank,
My life, these words, the paper, the gray Sunday;
And my dog, quivering under a table because of the storm,
Looked up at me, not understanding,
And my son read on without speaking, and my wife slept.

Donald Justice is dead. One Sunday the sun came out,
It shone on the bay, it shone on the white buildings,
The cars moved down the street slowly as always, so many,
Some with their headlights on in spite of the sun,
And after awhile the diggers with their shovels
Walked back to the graveside through the sunlight,
And one of them put his blade into the earth
To lift a few clods of dirt, the black marl[5] of Miami,
And scattered the dirt, and spat,
Turning away abruptly, out of respect.

1973

4. César Vallejo (1892–1939), Peruvian poet. The epigraph is translated "I will die in Paris in a rainstorm."
5. Clay, earth.

In Memory of the Unknown Poet, Robert Boardman Vaughn[6]

But the essential advantage for a poet is not, to have a beautiful world with which to deal: it is to be able to see beneath both beauty and ugliness; to see the boredom, and the horror, and the glory.

—T. S. ELIOT

It was his story. It would always be his story.
It followed him; it overtook him finally—
The boredom, and the horror, and the glory.

Probably at the end he was not yet sorry,
Even as the boots were brutalizing him in the alley.
It was his story. It would always be his story,

Blown on a blue horn, full of sound and fury,[7]
But signifying, O signifying magnificently
The boredom, and the horror, and the glory.

I picture the snow as falling without hurry
To cover the cobbles and the toppled ashcans completely.
It was his story. It would always be his story.

Lately he had wandered between St. Mark's Place and the Bowery,[8]
Already half a spirit, mumbling and muttering sadly.
O the boredom, and the horror, and the glory.

All done now. But I remember the fiery
Hypnotic eye and the raised voice blazing with poetry.
It was his story and would always be his story—
The boredom, and the horror, and the glory.

1987

Nostalgia and Complaint of the Grandparents

Les morts
C'est sous terre;
Ça n'en sort
Guère.

LAFORGUE[9]

Our diaries squatted, toadlike,
On dark closet ledges.
Forget-me-not and thistle
Decalcomaned[1] the pages.
But where, where are they now,

6. The poem is a villanelle.
7. Cf. Shakespeare's *Macbeth:* life is "full of sound and fury, / Signifying nothing" (5.5.16–27).
8. On New York City's Lower East Side.
9. Jules Laforgue (1860–1887), French poet. The first lines of the epigraph are translated "The dead are under the ground"; Justice translates the last two lines at the end of each stanza.
1. "Decalcomania" is the process of transferring pictures from specially prepared paper to other surfaces.

All the sad squalors
Of those between-wars[2] parlors?—
Cut flowers; and the sunlight spilt like soda
On torporous[3] rugs; the photo
Albums all outspread . . .
The dead
Don't get around much anymore.

There was an hour when daughters
Practiced arpeggios;[4]
Their mothers, awkward and proud,
Would listen, smoothing their hose—
Sundays, half-past five!
Do you recall
How the sun used to loll,
Lazily, just beyond the roof,
Bloodshot and aloof?
We thought it would never set.
The dead don't get
Around much anymore.

Eternity resembles
One long Sunday afternoon.
No traffic passes; the cigar smoke
Coils in a blue cocoon.
Children, have you nothing
For our cold sakes?
No tea? No little tea cakes?
Sometimes now the rains disturb
Even our remote suburb.
There's a dampness underground.
The dead don't get around
Much anymore.

1987

2. That is, in the 1920s and 1930s, between World Wars I and II.
3. That is, torpor-inducing, sluggish-making.
4. Notes of chords, played in succession.

W. D. Snodgrass
1926–2009

W. D. Snodgrass spoke of his poems as exercises in self-discovery; for him, the writing of verse was a discipline in sincerity. "[O]ur only hope as artists," he proposed, "is to continually ask ourselves, 'Am I writing what I really think?' . . . for I believe that the only reality that a man can ever surely know is that self he cannot help being, though he will only know that self through its interactions with the world around us" ("Finding a Poem"). In the poem "Orpheus," Snodgrass has the arch-poet say, "And I went on / rich in the loss of all I sing." Snodgrass does often seem rich in his losses. He sees life slipping away—his marriage dissolves, his little daughter visits him less frequently, some of his contemporaries are more successful than he—yet Snodgrass's poems look for compensation. The careful syllabics, the ingratiating rhythms, and the wry jokes do not qualify the pathos, but coexist with it to produce a particular sweet and sour flavor. Snodgrass's misfortunes were the lode of poetic material that childhood has been for other poets.

William Dewitt Snodgrass was born on January 5, 1926, in Wilkinsburg, Pennsylvania. He grew up in Beaver Falls, Pennsylvania, where he graduated from high school and attended Geneva College, though his studies were soon interrupted by service in the navy during the last years of World War II. In 1947, he went to the State University of Iowa, at whose famous writers' workshop he studied under Robert Lowell. He and Lowell together developed a new confessional mode for poetry. Snodgrass also studied with John Berryman and said that an early version of "A Flat One" "was written as a result of Berryman's asking us to write a stanzaic poem about a death. I wrote about one of the patients at the hospital I was working in [as an aide], something it wouldn't have occurred to me to do without that assignment" (interview with Philip Hoy). The poem's technical fluency counterbalances the speaker's harsh emotional disclosures and frank details. Although the tone switches suddenly to tenderness at the end, the speaker's address to the dead old veteran is bracingly unsentimental: "You seem to be all finished, so / We'll plug your old recalcitrant anus / And tie up your discouraged penis / In a great, snow-white bow of gauze."

In 1959, also the year of Lowell's *Life Studies*, Snodgrass published his first book, *Heart's Needle.* The title is taken from the old Irish saying "An only daughter is the needle of the heart," and it refers specifically to a sequence of poems in which the poet ruefully celebrates his encounters with his young daughter, the only child of a broken marriage. Snodgrass was showered with awards for the book, including the Pulitzer Prize. In his subsequent books, he tried to move beyond personal confession to more "social and philosophical subjects" (*Contemporary Poets of the English Language*, ed. R. Murphy, 1971). In a series of poems called *The Führer Bunker*, written in the voices of Adolf Hitler and his Nazi associates in the last days of World War II, he used the resources of dramatic monologue to arouse in his readers a conflict between open moral censure and sneaking sympathy.

April Inventory

The green catalpa tree has turned
All white; the cherry blossoms once more.
In one whole year I haven't learned
A blessed thing they pay you for.
The blossoms snow down in my hair;
The trees and I will soon be bare.

The trees have more than I to spare.
The sleek, expensive girls I teach,
Younger and pinker every year,
Bloom gradually out of reach.
The pear tree lets its petals drop
Like dandruff on a tabletop.

The girls have grown so young by now
I have to nudge myself to stare.

This year they smile and mind me how
My teeth are falling with my hair.
In thirty years I may not get
Younger, shrewder, or out of debt.

The tenth time, just a year ago,
I made myself a little list
Of all the things I'd ought to know,
Then told my parents, analyst,
And everyone who's trusted me
I'd be substantial, presently.

I haven't read one book about
A book or memorized one plot.
Or found a mind I did not doubt.
I learned one date. And then forgot.
And one by one the solid scholars
Get the degrees, the jobs, the dollars.

And smile above their starchy collars.
I taught my classes Whitehead's[1] notions;
One lovely girl, a song of Mahler's.[2]
Lacking a source-book or promotions,
I showed one child the colors of
A luna moth and how to love.

I taught myself to name my name,
To bark back, loosen love and crying;
To ease my woman so she came,
To ease an old man who was dying.
I have not learned how often I
Can win, can love, but choose to die.

I have not learned there is a lie
Love shall be blonder, slimmer, younger;
That my equivocating eye
Loves only by my body's hunger;
That I have forces, true to feel,
Or that the lovely world is real.

While scholars speak authority
And wear their ulcers on their sleeves,
My eyes in spectacles shall see
These trees procure and spend their leaves.
There is a value underneath
The gold and silver in my teeth.

Though trees turn bare and girls turn wives,
We shall afford our costly seasons;

1. Alfred North Whitehead (1861–1947), English philosopher.

2. Gustav Mahler (1860–1911), Austrian composer.

There is a gentleness survives
That will outspeak and has its reasons.
There is a loveliness exists,
Preserves us, not for specialists.

1959

From Heart's Needle

3

The child between them on the street
Comes to a puddle, lifts his feet
   And hangs on their hands. They start
At the live weight and lurch together,
Recoil to swing him through the weather,
   Stiffen and pull apart.

We read of cold war soldiers that
Never gained ground, gave none, but sat
   Tight in their chill trenches.
Pain seeps up from some cavity
Through the ranked teeth in sympathy;
   The whole jaw grinds and clenches

Till something somewhere has to give.
It's better the poor soldiers live
   In someone else's hands
Than drop where helpless powers fall
On crops and barns, on towns were all
   Will burn. And no man stands.

For good, they sever and divide
Their won and lost land. On each side
   Prisoners are returned
Excepting a few unknown names.
The peasant plods back and reclaims
   His fields that strangers burned

And nobody seems very pleased.
It's best. Still, what must not be seized
   Clenches the empty fist.
I tugged your hand, once, when I hated
Things less: a mere game dislocated
   The radius of your wrist.

Love's wishbone, child, although I've gone
As men must and let you be drawn
   Off to appease another,
It may help that a Chinese play

Or Solomon himself might say
I am your real mother.[3]

8

I thumped on you the best I could
which was no use;
you would not tolerate your food
until the sweet, fresh milk was soured
with lemon juice

That puffed you up like a fine yeast.
The first June in your yard
like some squat Nero[4] at a feast
you sat and chewed on white, sweet clover.
That is over.

When you were old enough to walk
we went to feed
the rabbits in the park milkweed;
saw the paired monkeys, under lock,
consume each other's salt.

Going home we watched the slow
stars follow us down Heaven's vault.
You said, let's catch one that comes low,
pull off its skin
and cook it for our dinner.

As absentee bread-winner,
I seldom got you such cuisine;
we ate in local restaurants
or brought what lunches we could pack
in a brown sack

with stale, dry bread to toss for ducks
on the green-scummed lagoons,
crackers for porcupine and fox,
life-savers for the footpad coons
to scour and rinse,

snatch after in their muddy pail
and stare into their paws.
When I moved next door to the jail
I learned to fry
omelettes and griddlecakes so I

could set you supper at my table.
As I built back from helplessness,

3. Faced with two mothers claiming to be the mother of a child, wise King Solomon identified the rightful one (1 Kings 3:16–28).

4. Nero Claudius Caesar (37–68 C.E.), Roman emperor.

when I grew able,
the only possible answer was
you had to come here less.

This Hallowe'en you come one week.
You masquerade
as a vermilion, sleek,
fat, crosseyed fox in the parade
or, where grim jackolanterns leer,

go with your bag from door to door
foraging for treats. How queer:
when you take off your mask
my neighbors must forget and ask
whose child you are.

Of course you lose your appetite,
whine and won't touch your plate;
as local law
I set your place on an orange crate
in your own room for days. At night

you lie asleep there on the bed
and grate your jaw.
Assuredly your father's crimes
are visited
on you. You visit me sometimes.

The time's up. Now our pumpkin sees
me bringing your suitcase.
He holds his grin;
the forehead shrivels, sinking in.
You break this year's first crust of snow

off the runningboard to eat.
We manage, though for days
I crave sweets when you leave and know
they rot my teeth. Indeed our sweet,
foods leave us cavities.

1959

A Flat One

Old Fritz, on this rotating bed
For seven wasted months you lay
Unfit to move, shrunken, gray,
No good to yourself or anyone
But to be babied—changed and bathed and fed.
At long last, that's all done.

Before each meal, twice every night,
We set pads on your bedsores, shut
Your catheter tube off, then brought
The second canvas-and-black-iron
Bedframe and clamped you in between them, tight,
Scared, so we could turn

You over. We washed you, covered you,
Cut up each bite of meat you ate;
We watched your lean jaws masticate
As ravenously your useless food
As thieves at hard labor in their chains chew
Or insects in the wood.

Such pious sacrifice to give
You all you could demand of pain:
Receive this haddock's body, slain
For you, old tyrant; take this blood
Of a tomato, shed that you might live.
You had that costly food.

You seem to be all finished, so
We'll plug your old recalcitrant anus
And tie up your discouraged penis
In a great, snow-white bow of gauze.
We wrap you, pin you, and cart you down below,
Below, below, because

Your credit has finally run out.
On our steel table, trussed and carved,
You'll find this world's hardworking, starved
Teeth working in your precious skin.
The earth turns, in the end, by turn about
And opens to take you in.

Seven months gone down the drain; thank God
That's through. Throw out the four-by-fours,
Swabsticks, the thick salve for bedsores,
Throw out the diaper pads and drug
Containers, pile the bedclothes in a wad,
And rinse the cider jug

Half-filled with the last urine. Then
Empty out the cotton cans,
Autoclave[5] the bowls and spit pans,
Unhook the pumps and all the red
Tubes—catheter, suction, oxygen;
Next, wash the empty bed.

—All this Dark Age machinery
On which we had tormented you

5. Sterilize.

To life. Last, we collect the few
Belongings: snapshots, some odd bills,
Your mail, and half a pack of Luckies we
Won't light you after meals.

Old man, these seven months you've lain
Determined—not that you would live—
Just to not die. No one would give
You one chance you could ever wake
From that first night, much less go well again,
Much less go home and make

Your living; how could you hope to find
A place for yourself in all creation?—
Pain was your only occupation.
And pain that should content and will
A man to give it up, nerved you to grind
Your clenched teeth, breathing, till

Your skin broke down, your calves went flat
And your legs lost all sensation. Still,
You took enough morphine to kill
A strong man. Finally, nitrogen
Mustard:[6] you could last two months after that;
It would kill you then.

Even then you wouldn't quit.
Old soldier, yet you must have known
Inside the animal had grown
Sick of the world, made up its mind
To stop. Your mind ground on its separate
Way, merciless and blind,

Into these last weeks when the breath
Would only come in fits and starts
That puffed out your sections like the parts
Of some enormous, damaged bug.
You waited, not for life, not for your death,
Just for the deadening drug

That made your life seem bearable.
You still whispered you would not die.
Yet in the nights I heard you cry
Like a whipped child; in fierce old age
You whimpered, tears stood on your gun-metal
Blue cheeks shaking with rage

And terror. So much pain would fill
Your room that when I left I'd pray
That if I came back the next day
I'd find you gone. You stayed for me—

6. Drug used to fight cancer.

Nailed to your own rapacious, stiff self-will.
You've shook loose, finally.

They'd say this was a worthwhile job
Unless they tried it. It is mad
To throw our good lives after bad;
Waste time, drugs, and our minds, while strong
Men starve. How many young men did we rob
To keep you hanging on?

I can't think we did *you* much good.
Well, when you died, none of us wept.
You killed for us, and so we kept
You, because we need to earn our pay.
No. We'd still have to help you try. We would
Have killed for you today.

1967

A. R. Ammons
1926–2001

In A. R. Ammons's poetry, a group of possibilities formulated earlier in the century achieves a fresh and unified expression. The perception of human ambiguities and abstract possibilities in homely bits of nature may have originated in Robert Frost; the attention to the intricacies of poetry as a "supreme fiction" has ties with Wallace Stevens; elements of Ammons's technique, such as the short, lightly punctuated lines and metrical innovations, unite him with William Carlos Williams. Like Charles Olson, Ammons wrote his poems on a typewriter and attended to the spatial layout of words on the page.

Ammons comes on with disarming casualness; he presents himself directly, unfazed, wry when necessary, quick to see symbolic possibilities in ordinary landscapes. Often, his poems are minor journeys that gradually become momentous: an automobile trip deepens into a journey into the past and the passions; a walk releases him from old forms; disjointed maneuvers of the mind move suddenly "towards divine, terrible love" ("Prodigal"). Observed facts, he says in the poem "The Misfit," tear us into questionings, push us toward the edges of order, of being. The sense of long, meditative preparation for writing is imparted by his poems, however unexpected and seemingly impromptu their phrasing, or digressive and self-mocking their manner.

Ammons writes poetry of motion, process, movement. In "Tombstones," he states, "the things of earth are not objects" but "pools of energy cooled into place." The natural world is continuously cooling, radiating, shrinking, mutating, decaying, and reassembling, never in stasis. This vision finds its organic analogue in the loose formal shape and colloquial manner of his poems. Like the mind and like the world, the poem must move and twist and flow. It would be a mistake to try to halt this motion by punctuating its language with end-stopped lines or periods, by impeding it with abstract organization or syntactic closure. Ammons lets his syntax course forward through colons and commas, his enjambed lines, ideas, images, and clauses tumbling over one another. Because "there is no finality of vision," as he says in "Corsons Inlet," the poet should "make / no form of / formlessness," "no forcing of image, plan, / or thought: / no propaganda, no humbling of reality to precept." In his voluble longer poems and sequences, Ammons wants "to fasten into order enlarging grasps of disorder, widening / scope."

In his shorter poems, by converse, Ammons often seeks "narrow order, limited tightness," the "focused beam" of a poem such as "Laser." In these carefully chiseled lyrics, the poet's mind concentrates fiercely. Perceptions are clarified; multiple perspectives narrowly converge. Like the boulders that, in "Motion's Holdings," are said to "take in and give / off heat, adjust nearby to / geomagnetic fields," Ammons's short poems force together the macrocosmic and the microcosmic, observing cosmic process in the tiniest detail.

Ammons continually reflects on the relations among the movements of mind, the world, and the poem, and he often writes in the mode of *ars poetica,* or self-description. As in the Romantic tradition that he assumes, extending from William Wordsworth, Ralph Waldo Emerson, and Walt Whitman to Frost and Stevens, the natural world is read partly for itself, partly as a mirror for the motions of the mind and the poem. When, in 1987, Ammons drove past an enormous Florida landfill on interstate I-95, he saw in it, among other things, a figure for the endless process of linguistic decay and transformation in poetry. He writes in the long poem *Garbage* (1993): "there is a mound, // too, in the poet's mind dead language is hauled / off to and burned down on, the energy held and // shaped into new turns and clusters, the mind / strengthened by what it strengthens."

Earlier, in his *Collected Poems: 1951–1971,* Ammons included a long *ars poetica,* "Essay on Poetics," that powerfully expresses his view of the interlocking of nature and art. For Ammons, Williams's slogan "no ideas but in things" is too limited and must be supplemented by "no things but in ideas," "no ideas but in ideas," and "no things but in things." The possibilities of poems are not to be numbered. More central than any one slogan is the complementary blending of art and nature. With great dexterity and humor, Ammons investigates the relationship between nature and poetry in what are sometimes long experiments in poetic form. He typed his early *Tape for the Turn of the Year* (1965) on a roll of adding-machine tape, not as a joke but as a serious experiment in making a poem adapt to something outside itself. The tape determined both how long the lines are and when the poem ends. Ammons writes about an *ecology* of nature and art, a word he used long before it became commonplace.

Archie Randolph Ammons was born on February 18, 1926, in Whiteville, North Carolina. His early interests were scientific, and he earned a B.S. at Wake Forest College in 1949, having served in the navy at the end of World War II. He later attended the University of California at Berkeley for two years. Still uncertain of his direction, he became principal of an elementary school in his home state, and then for a decade an executive in a biological glass-making firm. Ammons remained loyal to science as well as to literature, his poetry embodying both. The title of his first book, *Ommateum* (1955), means "compound eye," as of an insect or a crustacean, an apt metaphor for his multivisioned approach to the world. After the volume's obscure publication in Philadelphia, he waited nine years to publish a second book. In 1964, he accepted a teaching position at Cornell University, and in seven years he progressed from instructor to full professor. In 1973, his *Collected Poems: 1951–1971* won the National Book Award; in 1975, *Sphere* won the Bollingen Prize; in 1982, *A Coast of Trees* won the National Book Critics Circle Award; and in 1993, *Garbage* won a second National Book Award. Ammons was one of the first recipients of a MacArthur Fellowship, and he received the Tanning Prize in 1998. He died of cancer at seventy-five.

So I Said I Am Ezra[1]

So I said I am Ezra
and the wind whipped my throat
gaming for the sounds of my voice
 I listened to the wind
go over my head and up into the night
Turning to the sea I said
  I am Ezra
but there were no echoes from the waves
The words were swallowed up
 in the voice of the surf
or leaping over the swells
lost themselves oceanward
 Over the bleached and broken fields
I moved my feet and turning from the wind
 that ripped sheets of sand
 from the beach and threw them
 like seamists across the dunes
swayed as if the wind were taking me away
and said
  I am Ezra
As a word too much repeated
falls out of being
so I Ezra went out into the night
like a drift of sand
and splashed among the windy oats
that clutch the dunes
of unremembered seas

1955

Corsons Inlet[2]

I went for a walk over the dunes again this morning
to the sea,
then turned right along
 the surf
  rounded a naked headland
  and returned

 along the inlet shore:

it was muggy sunny, the wind from the sea steady and high,
crisp in the running sand,
 some breakthroughs of sun
 but after a bit

1. Prophet whose return to Jerusalem from exile is described in the biblical book named for him. In Islamic tradition, the prophet Ezra (Uzair) announces, "I am Ezra," when no one recognizes him on his return after one hundred years.
2. In southeast New Jersey.

continuous overcast:

the walk liberating, I was released from forms,
from the perpendiculars
      straight lines, blocks, boxes, binds
of thought
into the hues, shadings, rises, flowing bends and blends
            of sight:

                        I allow myself eddies of meaning:
yield to a direction of significance
running
like a stream through the geography of my work:
   you can find
in my sayings
                        swerves of action
                        like the inlet's cutting edge:
            there are dunes of motion,
organizations of grass, white sandy paths of remembrance
in the overall wandering of mirroring mind:

but Overall is beyond me: is the sum of these events
I cannot draw, the ledger I cannot keep, the accounting
beyond the account:

in nature there are few sharp lines: there are areas of
primrose
      more or less dispersed;
disorderly orders of bayberry; between the rows
of dunes,
irregular swamps of reeds,
though not reeds alone, but grass, bayberry, yarrow, all . . .
predominantly reeds:

I have reached no conclusions, have erected no boundaries,
shutting out and shutting in, separating inside
         from outside: I have
         drawn no lines:
         as

manifold events of sand
change the dune's shape that will not be the same shape
tomorrow,

so I am willing to go along, to accept
the becoming
thought, to stake off no beginnings or ends, establish
         no walls:

by transitions the land falls from grassy dunes to creek
to undercreek: but there are no lines, though
      change in that transition is clear
      as any sharpness: but "sharpness" spread out,

allowed to occur over a wider range
than mental lines can keep:

the moon was full last night: today, low tide was low:
black shoals of mussels exposed to the risk
of air
and, earlier, of sun,
waved in and out with the waterline, waterline inexact,
caught always in the event of change:
    a young mottled gull stood free on the shoals
    and ate
to vomiting: another gull, squawking possession, cracked a crab,
picked out the entrails, swallowed the soft-shelled legs, a ruddy
turnstone running in to snatch leftover bits:

risk is full: every living thing in
siege: the demand is life, to keep life: the small
white blacklegged egret, how beautiful, quietly stalks and spears
        the shallows, darts to shore
                to stab—what? I couldn't
    see against the black mudflats—a frightened
    fiddler crab?

        the news to my left over the dunes and
reeds and bayberry clumps was
        fall: thousands of tree swallows
        gathering for flight:
        an order held
        in constant change: a congregation
rich with entropy: nevertheless, separable, noticeable
      as one event,
               not chaos: preparations for
flight from winter,
cheet, cheet, cheet, cheet, wings rifling the green clumps,
beaks
at the bayberries
  a perception full of wind, flight, curve,
  sound:
  the possibility of rule as the sum of rulelessness:
the "field" of action
with moving, incalculable center:

in the smaller view, order tight with shape:
blue tiny flowers on a leafless weed: carapace of crab:
snail shell:
      pulsations of order
      in the bellies of minnows: orders swallowed,
broken down, transferred through membranes
to strengthen larger orders: but in the large view, no
lines or changeless shapes: the working in and out, together
      and against, of millions of events: this,
               so that I make

no form of
formlessness:

orders as summaries, as outcomes of actions override
or in some way result, not predictably (seeing me gain
the top of a dune,
the swallows
could take flight—some other fields of bayberry
could enter fall
berryless) and there is serenity:

no arranged terror: no forcing of image, plan,
or thought:
no propaganda, no humbling of reality to precept:

terror pervades but is not arranged, all possibilities
of escape open: no route shut, except in
the sudden loss of all routes:

I see narrow orders, limited tightness, but will
not run to that easy victory:
still around the looser, wider forces work:
I will try
to fasten into order enlarging grasps of disorder, widening
scope, but enjoying the freedom that
Scope eludes my grasp, that there is no finality of vision,
that I have perceived nothing completely,
that tomorrow a new walk is a new walk.

1965

Gravelly Run

I don't know somehow it seems sufficient
to see and hear whatever coming and going is,
losing the self to the victory
of stones and trees,
of bending sandpit lakes, crescent
round groves of dwarf pine:

for it is not so much to know the self
as to know it as it is known
by galaxy and cedar cone,
as if birth had never found it
and death could never end it:

the swamp's slow water comes
down Gravelly Run fanning the long
stone-held algal

hair and narrowing roils between
the shoulders of the highway bridge:

holly grows on the banks in the woods there,
and the cedars' gothic-clustered
  spires could make
green religion in winter bones:

so I look and reflect, but the air's glass
jail seals each thing in its entity:

no use to make any philosophies here:
  I see no
god in the holly, hear no song from
the snowbroken weeds: Hegel[3] is not the winter
yellow in the pines: the sunlight has never
heard of trees: surrendered self among
  unwelcoming forms: stranger,
hoist your burdens, get on down the road.

1965

Laser

An image comes
and the mind's light, confused
as that on surf
or ocean shelves,
gathers up,
parallelizes, focuses
and in a rigid beam illuminates the image:

the head seeks in itself
fragments of left-over light
to cast a new
direction,
any direction,
to strike and fix
a random, contradicting image:

but any found image falls
back to darkness or
the lesser beams splinter and
go out:
the mind tries to
dream of diversity, of mountain
rapids shattered with sound and light,

3. George Wilhelm Friedrich Hegel (1770–1831), German philosopher, who believed that reason is the spirit of humankind and that everything is a manifestation of Absolute Spirit.

of wind fracturing brush or
bursting out of order against a mountain
range: but the focused beam
folds all energy in:
the image glares filling all space:
the head falls and
hangs and cannot wake itself.

1970

Love Song

Like the hills under dusk you
fall away from the light:
you deepen: the green
light darkens
and you are nearly lost:
only so much light as
stars keep
manifests your face:
the total night in
myself raves
for the light along your lips.

1970

Small Song

The reeds give
way to the

wind and give
the wind away

1970

The City Limits

When you consider the radiance, that it does not withhold
itself but pours its abundance without selection into every
nook and cranny not overhung or hidden; when you consider

that birds' bones make no awful noise against the light but
lie low in the light as in a high testimony; when you consider
the radiance, that it will look into the guiltiest

swervings of the weaving heart and bear itself upon them,
not flinching into disguise or darkening; when you consider
the abundance of such resource as illuminates the glow-blue

bodies and gold-skeined wings of flies swarming the dumped
guts of a natural slaughter or the coil of shit and in no
way winces from its storms of generosity; when you consider

that air or vacuum, snow or shale, squid or wolf, rose or lichen,
each is accepted into as much light as it will take, then
the heart moves roomier, the man stands and looks about, the

leaf does not increase itself above the grass, and the dark
work of the deepest cells is of a tune with May bushes
and fear lit by the breadth of such calmly turns to praise.

1971

Easter Morning

I have a life that did not become,
that turned aside and stopped,
astonished:
I hold it in me like a pregnancy or
as on my lap a child
not to grow or grow old but dwell on

it is to his grave I most
frequently return and return
to ask what is wrong, what was
wrong, to see it all by
the light of a different necessity
but the grave will not heal
and the child,
stirring, must share my grave
with me, an old man having
gotten by on what was left

when I go back to my home country in these
fresh far-away days, it's convenient to visit
everybody, aunts and uncles, those who used to say,
look how he's shooting up, and the
trinket aunts who always had a little
something in their pocketbooks, cinnamon bark
or a penny or nickel, and uncles who
were the rumored fathers of cousins
who whispered of them as of great, if
troubled, presences, and school
teachers, just about everybody older
(and some younger) collected in one place

waiting, particularly, but not for
me, mother and father there, too, and others
close, close as burrowing
under skin, all in the graveyard
assembled, done for, the world they
used to wield, have trouble and joy
in, gone

the child in me that could not become
was not ready for others to go,
to go on into change, blessings and
horrors, but stands there by the road
where the mishap occurred, crying out for
help, come and fix this or we
can't get by, but the great ones who
were to return, they could not or did
not hear and went on in a flurry and
now, I say in the graveyard, here
lies the flurry, now it can't come
back with help or helpful asides, now
we all buy the bitter
incompletions, pick up the knots of
horror, silently raving, and go on
crashing into empty ends not
completions, not rondures the fullness
has come into and spent itself from
I stand on the stump
of a child, whether myself
or my little brother who died, and
yell as far as I can, I cannot leave this place, for
for me it is the dearest and the worst,
it is life nearest to life which is
life lost: it is my place where
I must stand and fail,
calling attention with tears
to the branches not lofting
boughs into space, to the barren
air that holds the world that was my world

though the incompletions
(& completions) burn out
standing in the flash high-burn
momentary structure of ash, still it
is a picture-book, letter-perfect
Easter morning: I have been for a
walk: the wind is tranquil: the brook
works without flashing in an abundant
tranquility: the birds are lively with
voice: I saw something I had
never seen before: two great birds,
maybe eagles, blackwinged, whitenecked
and -headed, came from the south oaring

the great wings steadily; they went
directly over me, high up, and kept on
due north: but then one bird,
the one behind, veered a little to the
left and the other bird kept on seeming
not to notice for a minute: the first
began to circle as if looking for
something, coasting, resting its wings
on the down side of some of the circles:
the other bird came back and they both
circled, looking perhaps for a draft;
they turned a few more times, possibly
rising—at least, clearly resting—
then flew on falling into distance till
they broke across the local bush and
trees: it was a sight of bountiful
majesty and integrity: the having
patterns and routes, breaking
from them to explore other patterns or
better ways to routes, and then the
return: a dance sacred as the sap in
the trees, permanent in its descriptions
as the ripples round the brook's
ripplestone: fresh as this particular
flood of burn breaking across us now
from the sun.

1981

Motion's Holdings

The filled out gourd rots, the
ridge rises in a wave
height cracks into peaks, the peaks

wear down to low undoings whose undertowing
throws other waves up: the branch
of honeysuckle leaves arcs outward

into its becoming motion but,
completion's precision done, gives
over riddling free to other

motions: boulders, their green and white
moss-molds, high-held in moist
hill woods, stir, hum with

stall and spill, take in and give
off heat, adjust nearby to
geomagnetic fields, tip liquid with

change should a trunk or rock loosen
to let rollers roll, or they loll
inwardly with earth's lie

in space, oxidize at their surfaces
exchanges with fungal thread and rain:
things are slowed motion that,

slowed too far, falls loose, freeing debris:
but in the ongoing warps, the butterfly
amaryllis crowds its bowl with bulbs.

1987

From Tombstones

1

the chisel, chipping in,
finds names the
wind can't blow away

11

the grooves fill with moss,
though, that spring
speaks green
and fall burns out with cold
into winter's black writing

19

the things of earth are not objects,
there is no nature,
no nature of stones and brooks, stumps, and ditches,

for these are pools of energy cooled into place,
or they are starlight pressed
to store,

or they are speeding light held still:
the woods are a fire green-slow
and the pathway of solid earthwork

is just light concentrated blind

27

a flock of
gulls flew
by I thought but

it was a
hillside of stones

29

the letters,
holding what they can, hold
in the stone

but holding flakes or
mists away—a
grainweight of memory

or a rememberer goes:
in so many hundred years,
the names

will be light enough
and as if balloons
will rise out of stone

1987

From Garbage

2

garbage has to be the poem of our time because
garbage is spiritual, believable enough

to get our attention, getting in the way, piling
up, stinking, turning brooks brownish and

creamy white: what else deflects us from the
errors of our illusionary ways, not a temptation

to trashlessness, that is too far off, and,
anyway, unimaginable, unrealistic: I'm a

hole puncher or hole plugger: stick a finger
in the dame (*dam,* damn, dike), hold back the issue

of creativity's flood, the forthcoming, futuristic,
the origins feeding trash: down by I-95 in

Florida where flatland's ocean- and gulf-flat,
mounds of disposal rise (for if you dug

something up to make room for something to put
in, what about the something dug up, as with graves:)

the garbage trucks crawl as if in obeisance,
as if up ziggurats[4] toward the high places gulls

and garbage keep alive, offerings to the gods
of garbage, of retribution, of realistic

expectation, the deities of unpleasant
necessities: refined, young earthworms,

drowned up in macadam[5] pools by spring rains, moisten
out white in a day or so and, round spots,

look like sputum[6] or creamy-rich, broken-up cold
clams: if this is not the best poem of the

century, can it be about the worst poem of the
century: it comes, at least, toward the end,

so a long tracing of bad stuff can swell
under its measure: but there on the heights

a small smoke wafts the sacrificial bounty
day and night to layer the sky brown, shut us

in as into a lidded kettle, the everlasting
flame these acres-deep of tendance keep: a

free offering of a crippled plastic chair:
a played-out sports outfit: a hill-myna[7]

print stained with jelly: how to write this
poem, should it be short, a small popping of

duplexes, or long, hunting wide, coming home
late, losing the trail and recovering it:

should it act itself out, illustrations,
examples, colors, clothes or intensify

reductively into statement, bones any corpus
would do to surround, or should it be nothing

at all unless it finds itself: the poem,
which is about the pre-socratic idea of the

dispositional axis from stone to wind, wind
to stone (with my elaborations, if any)

is complete before it begins, so I needn't
myself hurry into brevity, though a weary reader

4. Pyramidal temples.
5. Type of pavement.
6. Material coughed up from the lungs.
7. Species of tropical bird.

might briefly be done: the axis will be clear
enough daubed here and there with a little ink

or fined out into every shade and form of its
revelation: this is a scientific poem,

asserting that nature models values, that we
have invented little (copied), reflections of

possibilities already here, this where we came
to and how we came: a priestly director behind the

black-chuffing dozer leans the gleanings and
reads the birds, millions of loners circling

a common height, alighting to the meaty streaks
and puffy muffins (puffins?): there is a mound,

too, in the poet's mind dead language is hauled
off to and burned down on, the energy held and

shaped into new turns and clusters, the mind
strengthened by what it strengthens: for

where but in the very asshole of comedown is
redemption: as where but brought low, where

but in the grief of failure, loss, error do we
discern the savage afflictions that turn us around:

where but in the arrangements love crawls us
through, not a thing left in our self-display

unhumiliated, do we find the sweet seed of
new routes: but we are natural: nature, not

we, gave rise to us: we are not, though, though
natural, divorced from higher, finer configurations:

tissues and holograms of energy circulate in
us and seek and find representations of themselves

outside us, so that we can participate in
celebrations high and know reaches of feeling

and sight and thought that penetrate (really
penetrate) far, far beyond these our wet cells,

right on up past our stories, the planets, moons,
and other bodies locally to the other end of

the pole where matter's forms diffuse and
energy loses all means to express itself except

as spirit, there, oh, yes, in the abiding where
mind but nothing else abides, the eternal,

until it turns into another pear or sunfish,
that momentary glint in the fisheye having

been there so long, coming and going, it's
eternity's glint: it all wraps back round,

into and out of form, palpable and impalpable,
and in one phase, the one of grief and love,

we know the other, where everlastingness comes to
sway, okay and smooth: the heaven we mostly

want, though, is this jet-hoveled hell back,
heaven's daunting asshole: one must write and

rewrite till one writes it right: if I'm in
touch, she said, then I've got an edge: what

the hell kind of talk is that: I can't believe
I'm merely an old person: whose mother is dead,

whose father is gone and many of whose
friends and associates have wended away to the

ground, which is only heavy wind, or to ashes,
a lighter breeze: but it was all quite frankly

to be expected and not looked forward to: even
old trees, I remember some of them, where they

used to stand: pictures taken by some of them:
and old dogs, specially one imperial black one,

quad dogs with their hier*archies* (another *archie*)
one succeeding another, the barking and romping

sliding away like slides from a projector: what
were they then that are what they are now:

1992

From Strip

43

sometimes I get the feeling I've never
lived here at all, and 31 years seem

no more than nothing: I have to stop
and think, oh, yeah, there was the

kid, so much anguish over his allergy,
and there was the year we moved to

another house, and oh, yes, I remember
the lilies we planted near that

siberian elm, and there was the year
they made me a professor, and the

year, right in the middle of a long
poem, when I got blood poisoning from

an ingrown toenail not operated on
right: but a wave slices through,

canceling everything, and the space
with nothing to fill it shrinks and

time collapses, so that nothing happened,
and I didn't exist, and existence

itself seems like a wayward temporizing,
an illusion nonexistence sometimes

stumbles into: keep your mind open,
something might crawl in: which

reminds me of my greatest saying:
old poets never die, they just scrawl

away: and then I think of my friends
who may have longed for me, and I say

oh, I'll be here the next time
around: alas, the next time will

not come next: so what am I to say
to friends who know I'm not here and

won't be back: I'm sorry I missed
you guys: but even with the little

I know I loved you a lot, a lot more
than I said: our mountains here are

so old they're hills: they've been
around around 300 million years but

indifference in all that time broke
itself only to wear them out: my

indifference is just like theirs: it
wipes itself clear: surely, I will have

another chance: surely, nothing is
let go till trouble free: when

I come back I'm going to be there
every time: and then the wave that

comes to blank me out will be set
edgy and jiggling with my recalcitrance

and my consciousness will take on weight

1997

JAMES MERRILL
1926–1995

James Merrill's first poems show none of the clumsiness and uncertainty of apprentice work. They are calm and collected, highly finished works of art that are often about other works of art. The subject matter is international, and Merrill's detached connoisseurship often reminds one of novelists Marcel Proust and Henry James. Merrill had a talent for Metaphysical wit. In his mature poems, the earlier exquisite, meditative style is combined with a new interest in narrative and personal experience. The poems are longer, more relaxed, and the wit is more humane. "The Broken Home" is about the relationship between the speaker and his wealthy, energetic father. It begins with Merrill's characteristic opulence:

> Crossing the street,
> I saw the parents and the child
> At their window, gleaming like fruit
> With evening's mild gold leaf.

—but the recollection of the father is at once both offhand and moving.

> Each thirteenth year he married. When he died
> There were already several chilled wives
> In sable orbit—rings, cars, permanent waves.
> We'd felt him warming up for a green bride.

Like other 1960s depictions of fathers, this one is vexed, but the poet's feelings are implied, distilled, metaphorized. In "Lost in Translation"—also about the poet's broken childhood home—a picture puzzle becomes a metaphor for piecing together memory. Various forms of linguistic and artistic translation interweave to suggest what survives and what is lost in time.

Disgruntlement with his father, distress over his parents' divorce, melancholy over emotional and erotic losses, crushes on other boys acting in a play—these are the sorts of personal experiences one might expect in confessional poetry, but Merrill's verse is personal without being confessional. His formal framing of the autobiographical carefully transmutes the raw material of experience into art. Pain, desire, hurt vanity, grief, pathos—such feelings exist, even when unstated, in the cadences, sonorities, images, and settings of Merrill's both musical and painterly verse. "The point about music and song," Merrill said in a 1967 interview, "is that there is the sound of sheer feeling—as opposed to that of sense, of verbal sense. To combine the two is worth dreaming about."

Merrill's mastery of various lyric verse forms is unmatched since W. H. Auden; he writes effortlessly and cleverly in rhymed, slant-rhymed, and unrhymed verse; in syllabics, stressed verse, and free verse; in sonnets, ballad stanzas, and sestinas. He often slips in and out of these forms within the same poem, which may start unrhymed, then rhyme regularly, then rapidly shift stanza pattern, producing subtle changes in cadence, tempo, and tone. Line endings play on half-rhyme and consonance (e.g., "or vote" / "invite" in "The Broken Home," "grooves' bare groves" / "grave's" / "gramophone" in "The Victor Dog"). Wordplay and wit are everywhere, from clever enjambments ("the Home, / Work of " in "Lost in Translation"), to puns ("His forebears lacked, to say the least, forbearance" in "The Victor Dog"), to plays on clichés ("time was money" but "money was not time" in "The Broken Home"). The figurative language and imagery are inventive, luminous ("The green-gold room throbbed like a bruise"; "An avocado in a glass of water—/ Roots pallid, gemmed with air" in "The Broken Home"). His tone often fuses irony and wistfulness, camp and the elegiac. Autobiographical directness coexists with arch, all-knowing deflection. The multileveled diction of a poem such as "Self-Portrait in Tyvek(TM) Windbreaker" encompasses everything from the high literary to the line "Prayer breakfasts. Pay-phone sex. 'Ring up as meat.' " Merrill's style blends an expansive and ornate richness with an aphoristic terseness that makes many individual lines memorable.

With the publication of *Divine Comedies* (1976), Merrill's work took a surprising, even outrageous turn. With the help of his longtime partner David Jackson, an accommodating Ouija board, friends (most of them dead), fellow poets, scientists, and a galaxy of guardians from the spirit world, Merrill assembled over a period of more than twenty years an epic poem that from time to time resembles such different works as W. B. Yeats's *A Vision* and the epic poems of Dante, William Blake, William Wordsworth, and Walt Whitman, as well as the prose narratives of Proust and James. The completed work, eventually called *The Changing Light at Sandover,* is a witty, gracious, genial poem, comforting in its assurance that our friends are never lost to us, and that, thanks to the transmigration of souls, human beings slip, rather comically, from one existence to another.

Merrill was born on March 3, 1926, in New York City, the son of Charles E. Merrill, cofounder of the Merrill Lynch brokerage firm. When he was twelve, his parents divorced, his beloved Prussian English governess was dismissed, and he was sent to boarding school. His undergraduate education was interrupted by army service at the end of World War II, but he received his B.A. from Amherst College in 1947 after writing a thesis on Proust. Much of his adult life he wintered in Greece (later Key West, Florida) and summered in the northeastern United States, sharing houses with David Jackson. He published many volumes of poetry and won the National Book Award

(1967, 1979), the Bollingen Prize (1973), the Pulitzer Prize (1977), and the National Book Critics Circle Award (1983). He created the Ingram Merrill Foundation to support the work of writers and painters. He died of a heart attack just as his volume *A Scattering of Salts* was being published.

The Broken Home

Crossing the street,
I saw the parents and the child
At their window, gleaming like fruit
With evening's mild gold leaf.

In a room on the floor below,
Sunless, cooler—a brimming
Saucer of wax, marbly and dim—
I have lit what's left of my life.

I have thrown out yesterday's milk
And opened a book of maxims.
The flame quickens. The word stirs.

Tell me, tongue of fire,
That you and I are as real
At least as the people upstairs.

•

My father,[1] who had flown in World War I,
Might have continued to invest his life
In cloud banks well above Wall Street and wife.
But the race was run below, and the point was to win.

Too late now, I make out in his blue gaze
(Through the smoked glass of being thirty-six)
The soul eclipsed by twin black pupils, sex
And business; time was money in those days.

Each thirteenth year he married. When he died
There were already several chilled wives
In sable orbit—rings, cars, permanent waves.
We'd felt him warming up for a green bride.

He could afford it. He was "in his prime"
At three score ten. But money was not time.

•

When my parents were younger this was a popular act:
A veiled woman would leap from an electric, wine-dark car
To the steps of no matter what—the Senate or the Ritz Bar—
And bodily, at newsreel speed, attack

1. Charles E. Merrill, a founding partner of the investment firm Merrill Lynch, Pierce, Fenner & Smith.

No matter whom—Al Smith or José Maria Sert
Or Clemenceau[2]—veins standing out on her throat
As she yelled *War mongerer! Pig! Give us the vote!*,
And would have to be hauled away in her hobble skirt.[3]

What had the man done? Oh, made history.
Her business (he had implied) was giving birth,
Tending the house, mending the socks.

Always that same old story—
Father Time and Mother Earth,
A marriage on the rocks.

•

One afternoon, red, satyr-thighed
Michael, the Irish setter, head
Passionately lowered, led
The child I was to a shut door. Inside,

Blinds beat sun from the bed.
The green-gold room throbbed like a bruise.
Under a sheet, clad in taboos
Lay whom we sought, her hair undone, outspread,

And of a blackness found, if ever now, in old
Engravings where the acid bit.
I must have needed to touch it
Or the whiteness—was she dead?
Her eyes flew open, startled strange and cold.
The dog slumped to the floor. She reached for me. I fled.

•

Tonight they have stepped out onto the gravel.
The party is over. It's the fall
Of 1931. They love each other still.

She: Charlie, I can't stand the pace.
He: Come on, honey—why, you'll bury us all!

A lead soldier guards my windowsill:
Khaki rifle, uniform, and face.
Something in me grows heavy, silvery, pliable.

How intensely people used to feel!
Like metal poured at the close of a proletarian novel,
Refined and glowing from the crucible,
I see those two hearts, I'm afraid,

2. Georges Clemenceau (1841–1929): premier of France during World War I; visited the United States in 1922. Alfred E. Smith (1873–1944): governor of New York and a 1928 candidate for the U.S. presidency. José María Sert (1876–1945): Spanish painter who decorated the lobby of New York's Waldorf Astoria Hotel in 1930.
3. A long, straight skirt.

Still. Cool here in the graveyard of good and evil,
They are even so to be honored and obeyed.

•

. . . Obeyed, at least, inversely. Thus
I rarely buy a newspaper, or vote.
To do so, I have learned, is to invite
The tread of a stone guest within my house.[4]

Shooting this rusted bolt, though, against him,
I trust I am no less time's child than some
Who on the heath impersonate Poor Tom[5]
Or on the barricades risk life and limb.

Nor do I try to keep a garden, only
An avocado in a glass of water—
Roots pallid, gemmed with air. And later,

When the small gilt leaves have grown
Fleshy and green, I let them die, yes, yes,
And start another. I am earth's no less.

•

A child, a red dog roam the corridors,
Still, of the broken home. No sound. The brilliant
Rag runners halt before wide-open doors.
My old room! Its wallpaper—cream, medallioned
With pink and brown—brings back the first nightmares,
Long summer colds, and Emma, sepia-faced,
Perspiring over broth carried upstairs
Aswim with golden fats I could not taste.

The real house became a boarding school.
Under the ballroom ceiling's allegory
Someone at last may actually be allowed
To learn something; or, from my window, cool
With the unstiflement of the entire story,
Watch a red setter stretch and sink in cloud.

1966

Days of 1964

Houses, an embassy, the hospital,
Our neighborhood sun-cured if trembling still
In pools of the night's rain . . .

4. In *The Stone Feast,* by French dramatist Jean-Baptiste Molière (1622–1673), the stone statue of the commander of Seville visits his murderer, Don Juan, and drags him off to Hell. Mozart's opera *Don Giovanni* (1787) presents a version of this story.

5. In Shakespeare's *King Lear,* Edgar, disowned by his father, wanders the heath disguised as a madman and calling himself Poor Tom.

Across the street that led to the center of town
A steep hill kept one company part way
Or could be climbed in twenty minutes
For some literally breathtaking views,
Framed by umbrella pines, of city and sea.
Underfoot, cyclamen, autumn crocus grew
Spangled as with fine sweat among the relics
Of good times had by all. If not Olympus,[6]
An out-of-earshot, year-round hillside revel.

I brought home flowers from my climbs.
Kyria Kleo who cleans for us
Put them in water, sighing *Virgin, Virgin.*
Her legs hurt. She wore brown, was fat, past fifty,
And looked like a Palmyra matron
Copied in lard and horsehair.[7] How she loved
You, me, loved us all, the bird, the cat!
I think now she *was* love. She sighed and glistened
All day with it, or pain, or both.
(We did not notably communicate.)
She lived nearby with her pious mother
And wastrel[8] son. She called me her real son.

I paid her generously, I dare say.
Love makes one generous. Look at us. We'd known
Each other so briefly that instead of sleeping
We lay whole nights, open, in the lamplight,
And gazed, or traded stories.

One hour comes back—you gasping in my arms
With love, or laughter, or both,
I having just remembered and told you
What I'd looked up to see on my way downtown at noon:
Poor old Kleo, her aching legs,
Trudging into the pines. I called,
Called three times before she turned.
Above a tight, skyblue sweater, her face
Was painted. Yes. Her face was painted
Clown-white, white of the moon by daylight,
Lidded with pearl, mouth a poinsettia leaf,
Eat me, pay me—the erotic mask
Worn the world over by illusion
To weddings of itself and simple need.

Startled mute, we had stared—was love illusion?—
And gone our ways. Next, I was crossing a square
In which a moveable outdoor market's

6. Mountain in northern Greece that was considered the home of the gods.
7. A horsehair paintbrush. *Palmyra:* ancient city in central Syria. *Lard:* traditionally, mixed with powdered pigment for paint.
8. A loafer.

Vegetables, chickens, pottery kept materializing
Through a dream-press of hagglers each at heart
Leery lest he be taken, plucked,
The bird, the flower of that November mildness,
Self lost up soft clay paths, or found, foothold,
Where the bud throbs awake
The better to be nipped, self on its knees in mud—
Here I stopped cold, for both our sakes;

And calmer on my way home bought us fruit.

Forgive me if you read this. (And may Kyria Kleo,
Should someone ever put it into Greek
And read it aloud to her, forgive me, too.)
I had gone so long without loving,
I hardly knew what I was thinking.

Where I hid my face, your touch, quick, merciful,
Blindfolded me. A god breathed from my lips.
If that was illusion, I wanted it to last long;
To dwell, for its daily pittance, with us there,
Cleaning and watering, sighing with love or pain.
I hoped it would climb when it needed to the heights
Even of degradation, as I for one
Seemed, those days, to be always climbing
Into a world of wild
Flowers, feasting, tears—or was I falling, legs
Buckling, heights, depths,
Into a pool of each night's rain?
But you were everywhere beside me, masked,
As who was not, in laughter, pain, and love.

1966

The Victor Dog[9]

for Elizabeth Bishop[1]

Bix to Buxtehude to Boulez,
The little white dog on the Victor label
Listens long and hard as he is able.
It's all in a day's work, whatever plays.

9. The old trademark for RCA Victor Records showed a small dog listening intently to an old-fashioned gramophone, with the title "His Master's Voice." The poem alludes to a number of musicians and composers: the jazz trumpeter Bix Beiderbecke; the eighteenth-century composers Dietrich Buxtehude, Johann Sebastian Bach, and George Frideric Handel; and the nineteenth-century composers Franz Schubert and Robert Schumann; and the modernists Pierre Boulez, Ernest Bloch, and Maurice Ravel.

1. American poet (1911–1979) and longtime friend of Merrill's.

From judgment, it would seem, he has refrained.
He even listens earnestly to Bloch,
Then builds a church upon our acid rock.[2]
He's man's—no—he's the Leiermann's best friend,[3]

Or would be if hearing and listening were the same.
Does he hear? I fancy he rather smells
Those lemon-gold arpeggios in Ravel's
"Les jets d'eau du palais de ceux qui s'aiment."[4]

He ponders the Schumann Concerto's tall willow hit
By lightning, and stays put. When he surmises
Through one of Bach's eternal boxwood mazes[5]
The oboe pungent as a bitch in heat,

Or when the calypso decants its raw bay rum
Or the moon in *Wozzeck*[6] reddens ripe for murder,
He doesn't sneeze or howl; just listens harder.
Adamant[7] needles bear down on him from

Whirling of outer space, too black, too near—
But he was taught as a puppy not to flinch,
Much less to imitate his bête noire Blanche
Who barked, fat foolish creature, at King Lear.[8]

Still others fought in the road's filth over Jezebel,[9]
Slavered on hearths of horned and pelted barons.
His forebears lacked, to say the least, forbearance.
Can nature change in him? Nothing's impossible.

The last chord fades. The night is cold and fine.
His master's voice rasps through the grooves' bare groves.
Obediently, in silence like the grave's
He sleeps there on the still-warm gramophone

Only to dream he is at the première of a Handel
Opera long thought lost—*Il Cane Minore.*[1]
Its allegorical subject is his story!
A little dog revolving round a spindle

2. In Matthew 16.18, Jesus says to Peter, "Upon this rock I will build my church."
3. In Schubert's song "Der Leiermann" ("The Organ-Grinder"), an old man cranks his barrel organ in the winter cold to an audience of snarling dogs.
4. The fountains of the palace of those who are in love with each other (French).
5. The German composer's variations on musical themes are compared to the boxwoods often planted to form mazes in formal, eighteenth-century gardens.
6. Opera by Alban Berg (1885–1935), in which the protagonist murders his unfaithful wife under a rising moon.
7. Diamond; unyielding.
8. During the storm scene, Shakespeare's Lear says, "The little dogs and all / Tray, Blanch, and Sweet-heart, see, they bark at me" (3.6.57–58). *Bête noire:* something to be feared or avoided; literally, a black beast, whereas *blanche* means white.
9. Jezebel's body was thrown into the street as punishment for her evil deeds. When it was recovered for burial, dogs had eaten most of it (1 Kings 21ff.).
1. The little dog (Italian).

Gives rise to harmonies beyond belief,
A cast of stars. . . . Is there in Victor's heart
No honey for the vanquished? Art is art.
The life it asks of us is a dog's life.

1972

Lost in Translation

for Richard Howard[2]

Diese Tage, die leer dir scheinen
und wertlos für das All,
haben Wurzeln zwischen den Steinen
und trinken dort überall.[3]

A card table in the library stands ready
To receive the puzzle which keeps never coming.
Daylight shines in or lamplight down
Upon the tense oasis of green felt.
Full of unfulfillment, life goes on,
Mirage arisen from time's trickling sands
Or fallen piecemeal into place:
German lesson, picnic, see-saw, walk
With the collie who "did everything but talk"—
Sour windfalls of the orchard back of us.
A summer without parents is the puzzle,
Or should be. But the boy, day after day,
Writes in his Line-a-Day[4] *No puzzle.*

He's in love, at least. His French Mademoiselle,
In real life a widow since Verdun,
Is stout, plain, carrot-haired, devout.
She prays for him, as does a curé[5] in Alsace,
Sews costumes for his marionettes,
Helps him to keep behind the scene
Whose sidelit goosegirl, speaking with his voice,
Plays Guinevere[6] as well as Gunmoll Jean.
Or else at bedtime in his tight embrace
Tells him her own French hopes, her German fears,
Her—but what more is there to tell?
Having known grief and hardship, Mademoiselle
Knows little more. Her languages. Her place.
Noon coffee. Mail. The watch that also waited
Pinned to her heart, poor gold, throws up its hands—
No puzzle! Steaming bitterness

2. American poet (b. 1929).
3. Part of a translation by the Austrian poet Rainer Maria Rilke (1875–1926) of "Palme," by the French poet Paul Valéry (1871–1945; see lines 32–33): "These days, which seem empty and entirely fruitless to you, have roots between the stones and drink from everywhere."
4. That is, diary.
5. French priest. *Mademoiselle:* the poet's French-speaking governess. *Verdun:* site of World War I battle.
6. Wife of the legendary King Arthur.

Her sugars draw pops back into his mouth, translated:
"Patience, chéri. Geduld, mein Schatz."[7]
(Thus, reading Valéry the other evening
And seeming to recall a Rilke version of "Palme,"
That sunlit paradigm whereby the tree
Taps a sweet wellspring of authority,
The hour came back. Patience dans l'azur.
Geduld im . . . Himmelblau? Mademoiselle.)

Out of the blue, as promised, of a New York
Puzzle-rental shop the puzzle comes—
A superior one, containing a thousand hand-sawn,
Sandal-scented[8] pieces. Many take
Shapes known already—the craftsman's repertoire
Nice in its limitation—from other puzzles:
Witch on broomstick, ostrich, hourglass,
Even (surely not just in retrospect)
An inchling, innocently branching palm.
These can be put aside, made stories of
While mademoiselle spreads out the rest face-up,
Herself excited as a child; or questioned
Like incoherent faces in a crowd,
Each with its scrap of highly colored
Evidence the Law must piece together.
Sky-blue ostrich? Likely story.
Mauve of the witch's cloak white, severed fingers
Pluck? Detain her. The plot thickens
As all at once two pieces interlock.

Mademoiselle does borders—(Not so fast.
A London dusk, December last.
Chatter silenced in the library
This grown man reenters, wearing grey.
A medium. All except him have seen
Panel slid back, recess explored,
An object at once unique and common
Displayed, planted in a plain tole
Casket the subject now considers
Through shut eyes, saying in effect:
"Even as voices reach me vaguely
A dry saw-shriek drowns them out,
Some loud machinery—a lumber mill?
Far uphill in the fir forest
Trees tower, tense with shock,
Groaning and cracking as they crash groundward.
But hidden here is a freak fragment
Of a pattern complex in appearance only.
What it seems to show is superficial

7. Have patience, my dear (French and German). In the next lines, these phrases remind the speaker of a line in Valéry's "Palme" and Rilke's translation, "Patience in the blue"—a way of characterizing the slow nature of the palm tree. *Paradigm:* pattern.

8. That is, sandalwood-scented.

Next to that long-term lamination
Of hazard and craft, the karma[9] that has
Made it matter in the first place.
Plywood, Piece of a puzzle." Applause
Acknowledged by an opening of lids
Upon the thing itself. A sudden dread—
But to go back. All this lay years ahead.)

Mademoiselle does borders. Straight-edge pieces
Align themselves with earth or sky
In twos and threes, naive cosmogonists[1]
Whose views clash. Nomad inlanders meanwhile
Begin to cluster where the totem
Of a certain vibrant egg-yolk yellow
Or pelt of what emerging animal
Acts on the straggler like a trumpet call
To form a more sophisticated unit.
By suppertime two ragged wooden clouds
Have formed. In one, a Sheik with beard
And flashing sword hilt (he is all but finished)
Steps forward on a tiger skin. A piece
Snaps shut, and fangs gnash out at us!
In the second cloud—they gaze from cloud to cloud
With marked if undecipherable feeling—
Most of a dark-eyed woman veiled in mauve
Is being helped down from her camel (kneeling)
By a small backward-looking slave or page-boy
(Her son, thinks Mademoiselle mistakenly)
Whose feet have not been found. But lucky finds
In the last minutes before bed
Anchor both factions to the scene's limits
And, by so doing, orient
Them eye to eye across the green abyss.
The yellow promises, oh bliss,
To be in time a sumptuous tent.

Puzzle begun I write in the day's space,
Then, while she bathes, peek at Mademoiselle's
Page to the curé: ". . . cette innocente mère,
Ce pauvre enfant, que deviendront-ils?"[2]
Her azure script is curlicued like pieces
Of the puzzle she will be telling him about.
(Fearful incuriosity of childhood!
"Tu as l'accent allemand,"[3] said Dominique.
Indeed. Mademoiselle was only French by marriage.
Child of an English mother, a remote
Descendant of the great explorer Speke,[4]
And Prussian father. No one knew. I heard it

9. Roughly, fate.
1. Theorists about the origins of the universe.
2. This innocent mother, this poor child, what will become of them? (French).
3. You have a German accent (French).
4. Nineteenth-century English explorer in Africa.

Long afterwards from her nephew, a UN
Interpreter. His matter-of-fact account
Touched old strings. My poor Mademoiselle,
With 1939[5] about to shake
This world where "each was the enemy, each the friend"
To it foundations, kept, though signed in blood,
Her peace a shameful secret to the end.)
"Schlaf wohl, chéri."[6] Her kiss. Her thumb
Crossing my brow against the dreams to come.

This World that shifts like sand, its unforeseen
Consolidations and elate routine,
Whose Potentate had lacked a retinue?
Lo! it assembles on the shrinking Green.

Gunmetal-skinned or pale, all plumes and scars,
Of Vassalage the noblest avatars—
The very coffee-bearer in his vair[7]
Vest is a swart Highness, next to ours.

Kef[8] easing Boredom, and iced syrups, thirst,
In guessed-at glooms old wives who know the worst
Outsweat that virile fiction of the New:
"Insh'Allah,[9] he will tire—" "—or kill her first!"

(Hardly a proper subject for the Home,
Work of—dear Richard, I shall let *you* comb
Archives and learned journals for his name—
A minor lion attending on Gérôme.)[1]

While, thick as Thebes[2] whose presently complete
Gates close behind them, Houri and Afreet[3]
Both claim the Page. He wonders whom to serve,
And what his duties are, and where his feet,

And if we'll find, as some before us did,
That piece of Distance deep in which lies hid
Your tiny apex sugary with sun,
Eternal Triangle, Great Pyramid!

Then Sky alone is left, a hundred blue
Fragments in revolution, with no clue
To where a Niche will open. Quite a task,
Putting together Heaven, yet we do.

5. That is, the outbreak of World War II.
6. Sleep well, darling (German and French).
7. Trimmed with fur. *Avatars*: that is, incarnations of slavery.
8. Narcotic made from hemp.
9. As Allah wills (Arabic).
1. Nineteenth-century French Orientalist painter; cf. also Saint Jerome, said to have pulled a thorn from the paw of a lion and tamed him.
2. Ancient capital of Upper Egypt; cf. also the expression "thick as thieves."
3. Evil demon in Arabic mythology. *Houri*: one of the beautiful maidens living with the blessed in the Islamic paradise.

It's done. Here under the table all along
Were those missing feet. It's done.

The dog's tail thumping. Mademoiselle sketching
Costumes for a coming harem drama
To star the goosegirl. All too soon the swift
Dismantling. Lifted by two corners,
The puzzle hung together—and did not.
Irresistibly a populace
Unstitched of its attachments, rattled down.
Power went to pieces as the witch
Slithered easily from Virtue's gown.
The blue held out for time, but crumbled, too.
The city had long fallen, and the tent,
A separating sauce mousseline,[4]
Been swept away. Remained the green
On which the grown-ups gambled. A green dusk.
First lightning bugs. Last glow of west
Green in the false eyes of (coincidence)
Our mangy tiger safe on his bared hearth.

Before the puzzle was boxed and readdressed
To the puzzle shop in the mid-Sixties,[5]
Something tells me that one piece contrived
To stay in the boy's pocket. How do I know?
I know because so many later puzzles
Had missing pieces—Maggie Teyte's[6] high notes
Gone at the war's end, end of the vogue for collies,
A house torn down; and hadn't Mademoiselle
Kept back her pitiful bit of truth as well?
I've spent the last days, furthermore,
Ransacking Athens for that translation of "Palme."
Neither the Goethehaus nor the National Library
Seems able to unearth it. Yet I can't
Just be imagining. I've seen it. Know
How much of the sun-ripe original
Felicity Rilke made himself forego
(Who loved French words—verger, mûr, parfumer)[7]
In order to render its underlying sense.
Know already in that tongue of his
What Pains, what monolithic Truths
Shadow stanza to stanza's symmetrical
Rhyme-rutted pavement. Know that ground plan left
Sublime and barren, where the warm Romance
Stone by stone faded, cooled; the fluted nouns
Made taller, lonelier than life
By leaf-carved capitals in the afterglow.
The owlet umlaut[8] peeps and hoots

4. A creamy sauce.
5. That is, on New York City's Upper East Side.
6. English soprano (1888–1976), famous for her singing of French opera and songs.
7. Orchard, ripe, to scent (French).
8. German accent mark (¨).

Above the open vowel. And after rain
A deep reverberation fills with stars.

Lost, is it, buried? One more missing piece?

But nothing's lost. Or else: all is translation
And every bit of us is lost in it
(Or found—I wander through the ruin of S[9]
Now and then, wondering at the peacefulness)
And in that loss a self-effacing tree,
Color of context, imperceptibly
Rustling with its angel,[1] turns the waste
To shade and fiber, milk and memory.

1976

From The Changing Light at Sandover

From The Book of Ephraim[2]

Zero hour. Waiting yet again
For someone to fix the furnace. Zero week
Of the year's end. Bed that keeps restlessly
Making itself anew from lamé[3] drifts.
Mercury dropping. Cost of living high.
Night has fallen in the glass studio
Upstairs. The fire we huddle with our drinks by
Pops and snaps. Throughout the empty house
(Tenants away until the New Year) taps
Glumly trickling keep the pipes from freezing.
Summers ago this whole room was a garden—
Orange tree, plumbago, fuchsia, palm;
One of us at the piano playing his
Gymnopédie,[4] the other entering
Stunned by hot news from the sundeck. Now
The plants, the sorry few that linger, scatter
Leaflets advocating euthanasia.
Windows and sliding doors are wadded shut.
A blind raised here and there, what walls us in
Trembles with dim slides, transparencies
Of our least motion foisted on a thereby
Realer—falser?—night. Whichever term

9. Initial of former lover.
1. Cf. the phrase "wrestling with its angel."
2. The first book of Merrill's epic trilogy, *The Changing Light at Sandover.* Its twenty-six sections follow the letters of the alphabet on the Ouija board, which Merrill and David Jackson (DJ) used supposedly to communicate with spirits.
3. Metallic fabric.
4. Composition by French composer Erik Satie (1866–1925).

Adds its note of tension and relief.
Downstairs, doors are locked against the thief:
Night before last, returning from a dinner,
We found my bedroom ransacked, lights on, loud
Tick of alarm, the mirror off its hook
Looking daggers at the ceiling fixture.
A burglar here in the Enchanted Village—
Unheard of! Not that he took anything.
We had no television, he no taste
For Siamese bronze or Greek embroidery.
Except perhaps some loose change on the bureau
Nothing we can recollect is missing.
"Lucky boys," declared the chief of police
Risking a wise look at our curios.
The threat remains, though, of there still being
A presence in our midst, unknown, unseen,
Unscrupulous to take what he can get.
Next morning in my study—stranger yet—
I found a dusty carton out of place.
Had it been rummaged through? What could he fancy
Lay buried here among these—oh my dear,
Letters scrawled by my own hand unable
To keep pace with the tempest in the cup—[5]
These old love-letters from the other world.
We've set them down at last beside the fire.
Are they for burning, now that the affair
Has ended? (Has it ended?) Any day
It's them or the piano, says DJ.
Who'll ever read them over? Take this one.
Limp, chill, it shivers in the glow, as when
The tenor having braved orchestral fog
First sees Brünnhilde[6] sleeping like a log.
Laid on the fire, it would hesitate,
Trying to think, to feel—then the elate
Burst of satori,[7] plucking final sense
Boldly from inconclusive evidence.
And that (unless it floated, spangled ash,
Outward, upward, one lone carp aflash
Languorously through its habitat
For crumbs that once upon a . . .) would be that.
So, do we burn the— Wait the phone is ringing:
Bad connection; babble of distant talk;
No getting through. We must improve the line
In every sense, for life. Again at nine
Sharp above the village clock, *ring-ring*.
It's Bob the furnace man. He's on his way.
Will find, if not an easy-to-repair

5. Merrill and Jackson used a teacup as the pointer for the Ouija board. Also, a play on the expression "a tempest in a teacup."
6. Character from the opera cycle *Der Ring des Nibelungen*, by German composer Richard Wagner (1813–1883).
7. State of enlightenment sought in Zen Buddhism.

Short circuit, then the failure long foreseen
As total, of our period machine.
Let's be downstairs, leave all this, put the light out.
Fix a screen to the proscenium[8]
Still flickering. Let that carton be. Too much
Already, here below, has met its match.
Yet nothing's gone, or nothing we recall.
And look, the stars have wound in filigree[9]
The ancient, ageless woman of the world.
She's seen us. She is not particular—
Everyone gets her injured, musical
"Why do you no longer come to me?"
To which there's no reply. For here we are.

1976

b o d y

Look closely at the letters. Can you see,
entering (stage right), then floating full,
then heading off—so soon—
how like a little kohl-rimmed[1] moon
o plots her course from *b* to *d*

—as *y*, unanswered, knocks at the stage door?
Looked at too long, words fail,
phase out. Ask, now that *body* shines
no longer, by what light you learn these lines
and what the *b* and *d* stood for.

1995

Self-Portrait in Tyvek(™) Windbreaker[2]

The windbreaker is white with a world map.
DuPont contributed the seeming-frail,
Unrippable stuff first used for Priority Mail.
Weightless as shores reflected in deep water,
The countries are violet, orange, yellow, green;
Names of the principal towns and rivers, black.
A zipper's hiss, and the Atlantic Ocean closes
Over my blood-red T-shirt from the Gap.

I found it in one of those vaguely imbecile
Emporia catering to the collective unconscious

8. Area of the theater between the curtain and the orchestra.
9. Delicate ornamentation.
1. *Kohl:* dark eye makeup used in the Middle East.
2. Tyvek is a synthetic fabric manufactured by the DuPont company, also used to strengthen envelopes and packages.

Of our time and place. This one featured crystals,
Cassettes of whalesong and rain-forest whistles,
Barometers, herbal cosmetics, pillows like puffins,
Recycled notebooks, mechanized lucite[3] coffins
For sapphire waves that crest, break, and recede,
As they presumably do in nature still.

Sweat-panted and Reeboked, I wear it to the gym.
My terry-cloth headband is green as laurel.[4]
A yellow plastic Walkman at my hip
Sends shiny yellow tendrils to either ear.
All us street people got our types on tape,
Turn ourselves on with a sly fingertip.
Today I felt like Songs of Yesteryear
Sung by Roberto Murolo.[5] Heard of him?

Well, back before animal species began to become
Extinct, a dictator named Mussolini[6] banned
The street-singers of Naples. One smart kid
Learned their repertoire by heart, and hid.
Emerging after the war with his guitar,
He alone bearing the old songs of the land
Into the nuclear age sang with a charm,
A perfect naturalness that thawed the numb

Survivors and reinspired the Underground.
From love to grief to gaiety his art
Modulates effortlessly, like a young man's heart,
Tonic to dominant[7]—the frets so few
And change so strummed into the life of things
That Nature's lamps burn brighter when he sings
Nannetta's fickleness, or chocolate,
Snow on a flower, the moon, the seasons' round.

I picked his tape in lieu of something grosser
Or loftier, say the Dead or Arvo Pärt,[8]
On the hazy premise that what fills the mind
Shows on the face. My face, as a small part
Of nature, hopes this musical sunscreen
Will keep the wilderness within it green,
Yet looks uneasy, drawn. I detect behind
My neighbor's grin the oncoming bulldozer

And cannot stop it. Ecosaints—their karma
To be Earth's latest, maybe terminal, fruits—
Are slow to ripen. Even this dumb jacket

3. Transparent plastic.
4. In ancient Greece, victorious athletes and distinguished poets were crowned with laurel wreaths.
5. Singer (b. 1912), widely seen as the twentieth-century master of Neapolitan song; he continued to record albums in old age.
6. Benito Mussolini (1883–1945), Italian Fascist dictator before and during World War II.
7. That is, from the first to the fifth note of an octave.
8. Estonian avant-garde composer (b. 1935). *The Dead:* American psychedelic rock band the Grateful Dead.

Probably still believes in Human Rights,
Thinks in terms of "nations," urban centers,
Cares less (can Tyvek breathe?) for oxygen
Than for the innocents evicted when
Ford bites the dust and Big Mac buys the farm.

Hah. As if greed and savagery weren't the tongues
We've spoken since the beginning. My point is, those
Prior people, fresh from scarifying
Their young and feasting in triumph on their foes,
Honored the gods of Air and Land and Sea.
We, though . . . Cut to dead forests, filthy beaches,
The can of hairspray, oil-benighted creatures,
A star-scarred x-ray of the North Wind's lungs.

Still, not to paint a picture wholly black
Some social highlights: Dead white males in malls.
Prayer breakfasts. Pay-phone sex. "Ring up as meat."
Oprah. The GNP.[9] The contour sheet.
The painless death of History. The stick
Figures on Capitol Hill. Their rhetoric,
Gladly—no, rapturously (on Prozac) suffered!
Gay studies. Right to Lifers. The laugh track.

And clothes. Americans, blithe as the last straw,
Shrug off accountability by dressing
Younger than their kids—jeans, ski-pants, sneakers,
A baseball cap, a happy-face T-shirt . . .
Like first-graders we "love" our mother Earth,
Know she's been sick, and mean to care for her
When we grow up. Seeing my windbreaker,
People hail me with nostalgic awe.

"Great jacket!" strangers on streetcorners impart.
The Albanian doorman pats it: "Where you buy?"
Over his ear-splitting drill a hunky guy
Yells, "Hey, you'll always know where you are, right?"
"Ever the fashionable cosmopolite,"
Beams Ray. And "Voilà mon pays"[1]—the carrot-haired
Girl in the bakery, touching with her finger
The little orange France above my heart.

Everyman, c'est moi,[2] the whole world's pal!
The pity is how soon such feelings sour.
As I leave the gym a smiling-as-if-I-should-know-her
Teenager—oh but I *mean,* she's wearing "our"
Windbreaker, and assumes . . . Yet I return her wave
Like an accomplice. For while all humans aren't

9. Gross National Product.
1. Here is my country (French).
2. It is I (French); a variation on the phrase "L'Etat, c'est moi" (I am the State), by Louis XIV (1638–1715).

Countable as equals, we must behave
As if they were, or the spirit dies (Pascal).[3]

"We"? A few hundred decades of relative
Lucidity glinted-through by minnow schools
Between us and the red genetic muck—
Everyman's underpainting. We look up, shy
Creatures, from our trembling pool of sky.
Caught wet-lipped in light's brushwork, fleet but sure,
Flash on shudder, folk of the first fuck,
Likeness breeds likeness, fights for breath—*I live*—

Where the crush thickens. And by season's end,
The swells of fashion cresting to collapse
In breaker upon breaker on the beach,
Who wants to be caught dead in this cliché
Of mere "involvement"? Time to put under wraps
Its corporate synthetic global pitch;
Not throwing out motley once reveled in,
Just learning to live down the wrinkled friend.

Face it, reproduction of any kind leaves us colder
Though airtight-warmer (greenhouse effect)[4] each year.
Remember the figleaf's lesson. Styles betray
Some guilty knowledge. What to dress ours in—
A seer's blind gaze, an infant's tender skin?
All that's been seen through. The eloquence to come
Will be precisely what we cannot say
Until it parts the lips. But as one grows older

—I should confess before that last coat dries—
The wry recall of thunder does for rage.
Erotic torrents flash on screens instead
Of drenching us. Exclusively in dream,
These nights, does a grandsire rear his saurian[5] head,
And childhood's inexhaustible brain-forest teems
With jewel-bright lives. No way now to restage
Their sacred pageant under our new skies'

Irradiated lucite. What then to wear
When—hush, it's no dream! It's my windbreaker
In black, with starry longitudes, Archer, Goat,[6]
Clothing an earphoned archangel of Space,
Who hasn't read Pascal, and doesn't wave . . .
What far-out twitterings he learns by rote,
What looks they'd wake upon a human face,
Don't ask, Roberto. Sing our final air:

3. Blaise Pascal (1623–1662), French mathematician, writer, and scientist.
4. Phenomenon considered the cause of global warming.
5. Lizardlike.
6. The archer and the goat represent the astrological signs Sagittarius and Capricorn.

Love, grief etc. * * * * for good reason.
Now only * * * * * * * STOP signs.
Meanwhile * * * * * if you or I've ex-
ceeded our [?] * * * ~~more than time~~ was needed
To fit a text airless and * * as Tyvek
With breathing spaces and between the lines
Days brilliantly recurring, as once *we* did,
To keep the blue wave dancing in its prison.

1995

An Upward Look

O heart green acre   sown with salt
by the departing   occupier

lay down your gallant   spears of wheat
Salt of the earth   each stellar pinch

flung in blind   defiance backwards
now takes its toll   Up from his quieted

quarry the lover   colder and wiser
hauling himself   finds the world turning

toys triumphs   toxins into
this vast facility   the living come
dearest to die in   How did it happen

In bright alternation   minutely mirrored
within the thinking   of each and every

mortal creature   halves of a clue
approach the earthlights   Morning star

evening star   salt of the sky
First the grave   dissolving into dawn

then the crucial   recrystallizing
from inmost depths   of clear dark blue

1995

Robert Creeley
1926–2005

Robert Creeley's poetry is immediately likable. He has no interest in pompous or oracular utterance, but offers an instantaneous intimacy. He belongs to the Black Mountain school of Charles Olson, but if Olson is Maximus, Creeley is Minimus. His poems are usually short—in total length, in the length of each line, even in title—and always unassuming. He reports brief passages of feeling as minutely as he can, remaining surrounded by a situation rather than entering and leaving it. Citing Olson's concepts of "projective verse" and "composition by field" in an interview, Creeley puts the emphasis on allowing the experience to play upon the poet instead of accepting an imposed shape (*Cottonwood Review,* 1968). As a young man, Creeley says, he "was very intent on [William Carlos] Williams's sense of how you get the thing stated in its own particulars rather than your assumption of those particulars." Like Williams and Olson, Creeley reveres immediate sensation. In reaction to poetry that is "too dry and too intellectually articulate," he wants to create, instead, "a more resonant echo of the subconscious or inner experience."

In his preface to *For Love: Poems 1950–1960,* Creeley disavows lofty occasions for writing. "Wherever it is one stumbles (to get to wherever) at least some way will exist, so to speak, as and when a man takes this or that step—for which, god bless him." His poems are such ways, stumbled into. Avoiding contrivance and closure, they follow a logic that is elliptical and unresolved. What Creeley wants to evoke is often small, and he is prepared to defend smallness: "something small / but infinite / and quiet" ("A Prayer"), or "insistent particularity" ("Listless"). A day-to-day mysticism informs many of Creeley's experiential moments, and in an interview in the *Paris Review,* he speaks of poetry as "a kind of absolute seizure." The effect must be personal; it should be "identity singing." But for all its personal quality, the poem must be made of *relationships*—a word he is fond of—because relationships serve "a common need, for survival and growth." Not surprisingly, love or loss is often Creeley's subject.

Although Creeley rejects traditional meters and rhymes, he develops his own rhythms, often catchy and distinct, as well as quiet internal rhymes, assonances, and idiosyncratic enjambments. "It is all a rhythm, / from the shutting / door, to the window / opening," he insists in "The Rhythm." Possibly his most famous statement on aesthetics is that which Charles Olson continually quoted from him, "Form is never more than an extension of content." Creeley would agree with D. H. Lawrence that every experience has a potential and unique form. Yet as he says in the title poem of *The Finger* (1968): "The forms shift / before we know, / before we thought / to know it." The danger comes from imposition of abstract idea: "The *world,* / dad, is where you / live unless you've for- / gotten it through that / incredible means called / efficacy *or* understanding / *or* superior lines of / *or, or* something else." The form may be obscured, and the poem lost, by making the end of the poem a "*descriptive* act, I mean any act which leaves the attention outside the poem." This defect he finds in poets who subordinate inner form to external content, such as Kenneth Fearing or Karl Shapiro; their poems "argue images of living to which the content of their poems points." They make the poem a means to recognition, rather than "a structure of 'recognition' or—better—cognition itself" (*The New American Poetry,* ed. Donald Allen, 1960). While Creeley's later poetry remains characterized by terseness, reticence, and dramatic pauses, the emotions are often more sharply outlined and conclusive than in his earlier work. Memory plays a stronger role, and aging and death cast a longer shadow.

Creeley's life seemed to flow from his theories of poetry, as he stumbled from one place to another. He was born on May 21, 1926, in Arlington, Massachusetts. Before he was five, he lost his father, a doctor, as well as the use of his left eye. After attending Holderness School, in Plymouth, New Hampshire, Creeley entered Harvard University, but soon left, in 1944, to join the American Field Service in India and Burma. To escape from boredom, he took drugs, and some of his poems describe hallucinatory experiences. He came back to Harvard a year later, but with one term left before receiving a degree dropped out again. He and his wife lived on Cape Cod, then spent three years on a farm in New Hampshire; from there they went to Aix-en-Provence and then to Majorca, where Creeley started the Divers Press. In 1954, Olson invited him to join the faculty of Black Mountain College, and Creeley founded and edited the *Black Mountain Review*. In 1955, his marriage collapsed, and he left the college. He moved west in 1956, just in time to become associated with the flowering of Beat poetry. Domestic life is a preoccupation of his work, and, indeed, Creeley married again in 1957; after a second divorce in 1976, he married for the third time in 1977. From 1956 to 1959, he taught in a boys' school in Albuquerque, and he received an M.A. from the University of New Mexico in 1960. He went to Guatemala and taught, from 1959 to 1961, on a coffee plantation. He had many visiting posts, but from 1966 he was a professor at the State University of New York at Buffalo. He was the New York State poet from 1989 to 1991, and he won the Bollingen Prize in 1999.

Naughty Boy

When he brings home a whale
she laughs and says, that's not for real.

And if he won the Irish sweepstakes,
she would say, where were you last night?

Where are you now, for that matter? Am
I always (she says) to be looking

at you? She says,
if I thought it would get any better I

would shoot you, you
nut, you. Then pats her hair

into place, and waits
for Uncle Jim's deep-fired, all-fat, real gone

whale steaks.

1959

A Wicker Basket

Comes the time when it's later
and onto your table the headwaiter
puts the bill, and very soon after
rings out the sound of lively laughter—

Picking up change, hands like a walrus,
and a face like a barndoor's,
and a head without any apparent size,
nothing but two eyes—

So that's you, man,
or me. I make it as I can,
I pick up, I go
faster than they know—

Out the door, the street like a night,
any night, and no one in sight,
but then, well, there she is,
old friend Liz—

And she opens the door of her cadillac,
I step in back,
and we're gone.
She turns me on—

There are very huge stars, man, in the sky,
and from somewhere very far off someone hands me a slice of apple pie,
with a gob of white, white ice cream on top of it,
and I eat it—

Slowly. And while certainly
they are laughing at me, and all around me is racket
of these cats not making it, I make it

in my wicker basket. 1959

The Door

for Robert Duncan[1]

It is hard going to the door
cut so small in the wall where
the vision which echoes loneliness
brings a scent of wild flowers in the wood.

1. American poet (1919–1988), who was, like Creeley, a teacher at Black Mountain College during the mid-1950s.

What I understood, I understand.
My mind is sometime torment,
sometimes good and filled with livelihood,
and feels the ground.

But I see the door,
and knew the wall, and wanted the wood,
and would get there if I could
with my feet and hands and mind.

Lady, do not banish me
for digressions. My nature
is a quagmire of unresolved
confessions. Lady, I follow.

I walked away from myself,
I left the room, I found the garden,
I knew the woman
in it, together we lay down.

Dead night remembers. In December
we change, not multiplied but dispersed,
sneaked out of childhood,
the ritual of dismemberment.

Mighty magic is a mother,
in her there is another issue
of fixture, repeated form, the race renewal,
the charge of the command.

The garden echoes across the room.
It is fixed in the wall like a mirror
that faces a window behind you
and reflects the shadows.

May I go now?
Am I allowed to bow myself down
in the ridiculous posture of renewal,
of the insistence of which I am the virtue?

Nothing for You is untoward.
Inside You would also be tall,
more tall, more beautiful.
Come toward me from the wall, I want to be with You.

So I screamed to You,
who hears as the wind, and changes
multiply, invariably,
changes in the mind.

Running to the door, I ran down
as a clock runs down. Walked backwards,

stumbled, sat down
hard on the floor near the wall.

Where were You.
How absurd, how vicious.
There is nothing to do but get up.
My knees were iron, I rusted in worship, of You.

For that one sings, one
writes the spring poem, one goes on walking.
The Lady has always moved to the next town
and you stumble on after Her.

The door in the wall leads to the garden
where in the sunlight sit
the Graces[2] in long Victorian dresses,
of which my grandmother had spoken.

History sings in their faces.
They are young, they are obtainable,
and you follow after them also
in the service of God and Truth.

But the Lady is indefinable,
she will be the door in the wall
to the garden in sunlight.
I will go on talking forever.

I will never get there.
Oh Lady, remember me
who in Your service grows older
not wiser, no more than before.

How can I die alone.
Where will I be then who am now alone,
what groans so pathetically
in this room where I am alone?

I will go to the garden.
I will be a romantic. I will sell
myself in hell,
in heaven also I will be.

In my mind I see the door,
I see the sunlight before me across the floor
beckon to me, as the Lady's skirt
moves small beyond it.

1959

2. In classical mythology, the three daughters of Zeus, personifying beauty, charm, and grace.

I Know a Man

As I sd to my
friend, because I am
always talking,—John, I

sd, which was not his
name, the darkness sur-
rounds us, what

can we do against
it, or else, shall we &
why not, buy a goddamn big car,

drive, he sd, for
christ's sake, look
out where yr going.

1962

For Love

for Bobbie[3]

Yesterday I wanted to
speak of it, that sense above
the others to me
important because all

that I know derives
from what it teaches me.
Today, what is it that
is finally so helpless,

different, despairs of its own
statement, wants to
turn away, endlessly
to turn away.

If the moon did not . . .
no, if you did not
I wouldn't either, but
what would I not

do, what prevention, what
thing so quickly stopped.

3. Bobbie Hoeck, Creeley's second wife.

That is love yesterday
or tomorrow, not

now. Can I eat
what you give me. I
have not earned it. Must
I think of everything

as earned. Now love also
becomes a reward so
remote from me I have
only made it with my mind.

Here is tedium,
despair, a painful
sense of isolation and
whimsical if pompous

self-regard. But that image
is only of the mind's
vague structure, vague to me
because it is my own.

Love, what do I think
to say. I cannot say it.
What have you become to ask,
what have I made you into,

companion, good company,
crossed legs with skirt, or
soft body under
the bones of the bed.

Nothing says anything
but that which it wishes
would come true, fears
what else might happen in

some other place, some
other time not this one.
A voice in my place, an
echo of that only in yours.

Let me stumble into
not the confession but
the obsession I begin with
now. For you

also (also)
some time beyond place, or
place beyond time, no
mind left to

say anything at all,
that face gone, now.
Into the company of love
it all returns.

1962

"I Keep to Myself Such Measures . . ."

I keep to myself such
measures as I care for,
daily the rocks
accumulate position.

There is nothing
but what thinking makes
it less tangible.[4] The mind,
fast as it goes, loses

pace, puts in place of it
like rocks simple markers,
for a way only to
hopefully come back to

where it cannot. All
forgets. My mind sinks.
I hold in both hands such weight
it is my only description.

1969

Again

One more day gone,
done, found in
the form of days.

It began, it
ended—was
forward, backward,

slow, fast, a
sun shone, clouds,
high in the air I was

for awhile with others,
then came down
on the ground again.

4. Cf. "there is nothing either good or bad but thinking makes it so" (*Hamlet* 2.2.244–45).

No moon. A room in
a hotel—to begin
again.

1969

Mother's Voice

In these few years
since her death I hear
mother's voice say
under my own, I won't

want any more of that.
My cheekbones resonate
with her emphasis. Nothing
of not wanting only

but the distance there from
common fact of others
frightens me. I look out
at all this demanding world

and try to put it quietly back,
from me, say, thank you,
I've already had some
though I haven't

and would like to
but I've said no, she has,
it's not my own voice anymore.
It's higher as hers was

and accommodates too simply
its frustrations when
I at least think I want more
and must have it.

1983

From Life & Death

[*The Long Road of It All*]

The long road of it all
is an echo,
a sound like an image
expanding, frames growing
one after one in ascending

or descending order, all
of us a rising, falling
thought, an explosion
of emptiness soon forgotten.

[*When It Comes*]

When it comes,
it loses edge,
has nothing around it,
no place now present
but impulse not one's own,
and so empties into a river
which will flow on
into a white cloud
and be gone.

1998

ALLEN GINSBERG
1926–1997

Allen Ginsberg wrote in a Romantic tradition that honors William Blake and Walt Whitman as its distinguished pioneers. He resembled the two earlier poets in his confidence as a prophet-poet, in his disregard for distinctions between poetry and religion, and in his eclecticism. He distrusted abstractions and the antiseptically cerebral, and he wanted to compose poetry that invites a complete emotional and physical participation by the audience. For some, the publication of Ginsberg's *"Howl" and Other Poems* (1956) was the beginning of a mindless and mercifully short-lived poetic fad, a cult of slovenly verse that encouraged dangerously slovenly behavior. For others, it was a fortunate and revolutionary change in the direction of American poetry. Like all poetic innovators, Ginsberg seemed to claim for poetry new areas of experience and new cultural situations. "Howl" is a panoramic vision of the dark side of the complacent Eisenhower years; it discovered for literature an anticommunity of waifs and strays, dope addicts and homosexual drifters. Ginsberg's poetry presented an alternative to the tightly organized, well-mannered poetry written under the influence of the New Criticism; it was emotionally explosive, unashamedly self-preoccupied, and metrically expansive, and it helped create in the 1960s an audience for influential books of psychic rebellion and revelation, such as Robert Lowell's *Life Studies*, Norman Mailer's *Advertisements for Myself*, and Norman O. Brown's *Life against Death*.

Ginsberg was born on June 3, 1926, in Newark, New Jersey. His father, Louis Ginsberg, a high school teacher, wrote conventional verse. His mother, Naomi, a Russian Jewish immigrant and a communist, encouraged her son in his radical bias. She spent the latter part of her life in Pilgrim State Hospital, and Ginsberg, who saw her spontaneity and emotional intensity as important qualities in his own character, was haunted for much of his life by guilt because he had authorized her institutionalization and lobotomy—recommended by her doctor to cure her paranoid delusions. Her death, in 1956, is the occasion for Ginsberg's long poem "Kaddish"—a fusion of the elegy, the blues, and the ritual Kaddish, or Jewish prayer of mourning and remembrance for the dead—in which graphic descriptions of his mother's madness, her scarred body, and his ambivalent attraction and repulsion break taboos on the representation of the dead.

Ginsberg was educated in the public schools of Paterson, New Jersey. One of his earliest friends in the arts was Paterson's most famous man of letters, William Carlos Williams, who later wrote the introduction to *"Howl" and Other Poems*. Williams instructed Ginsberg according to his dictum, "No ideas but in things." "Before I met Williams," Ginsberg told one of his biographers, "I was all hung up on cats like Wyatt, Surrey, and Donne. I would read them and then copy down what I thought poetry like theirs would be. Then I sent some of those poems to Williams, and he thought that they were terrible. Like they showed some promise, but they were phony, unnatural. He told me, 'Listen to the rhythm of your own voice. Proceed intuitively by ear' " (*The New Yorker*, August 24, 1968).

From Paterson, Ginsberg went to Columbia University. In 1945, he was temporarily suspended, and William Burroughs, whose interest in sex and drugs is recorded in experimental novels such as *Naked Lunch* and *Wild Boys*, took over Ginsberg's literary education. Ginsberg received a B.A. from Columbia in 1948, and in the summer of that year he underwent an extraordinary experience that always figures in accounts of his spiritual development. Feeling cut off from his friends and uncertain as to his vocation, he heard a voice, which he took to be that of the poet himself, reciting William Blake's "Ah Sun-Flower" and "The Sick Rose." The auditory hallucination was accompanied by a feeling of participation in a universal harmony. In one account of the experience, to the *Paris Review*, Ginsberg recalls that "looking out at the window, through the window at the sky, suddenly it seemed that I saw into the depths of the universe, by looking simply into the ancient sky. The sky suddenly seemed very *ancient*. And this was the very ancient place that he [Blake] was talking about, the sweet golden clime. I suddenly realized that *this* existence was *it!*" Although Ginsberg eventually freed himself from a dependence on this remembered moment, he continued to believe it was a personal revelation of a quality common to all high poetry.

In 1954, bearing a letter of introduction to Kenneth Rexroth from Williams, Ginsberg went to San Francisco. He already knew Burroughs, Jack Kerouac, and Gregory Corso, all writers who would be identified with the Beat movement. At different times in his life, Ginsberg had sexual relationships with both Burroughs and Kerouac. Another friend and sometime lover was Neal Cassady, a railway brakeman with literary interests, who inspired the figure of Dean Moriarty in Kerouac's novel *On the Road*. Having settled around the corner from Lawrence Ferlinghetti's City Lights Bookstore, which would become the publisher of *"Howl" and Other Poems* and other Beat writing, Ginsberg worked for a time as a market researcher and attempted to follow a heterosexual life-style, but he was dissatisfied and restless. In talks with a psychiatrist, he found the courage to give up his job and to accept his sexuality. He met Peter Orlovsky, who became his longtime companion, and he finished the first part of "Howl."

Among the liberating influences on his poetry, Ginsberg mentioned with particular gratitude the prose of Jack Kerouac. From him, Ginsberg learned the sanctity of the uncorrected first draft ("First thought, best thought" became Ginsberg's motto, though he actually revised and reshaped the initial material for "Howl" and "Kaddish") and to make his writing an extension of his personal relationships. Assuming that "Howl" would never be published, Ginsberg wrote it for himself and his friends; he insisted that live poetry must not make a distinction between "what you tell your friends and what you tell your Muse" (*Paris Review*). Whether he wrote in long, rhapsodic lines or short and easily chantable ones, his ideal was a living speech and an organic metric that expresses the poet's physiological state at the time of composition. Thus the recurrences in "Howl"—the incantatory repetitions of "who," the surrealistically conflated images, the long lines to be read aloud without a pause—express the poet's physical state and induce a similar state in the reader or hearer.

The first edition of *"Howl" and Other Poems* was printed in England and published in October 1956. In March 1957, U.S. Customs intercepted a second printing. A long trial ensued, and after hearing expert testimony from writers and critics, Judge Clayton Horn decided that "Howl" had "redeeming social importance." The publicity made "Howl" an extraordinary popular success—in 1967, there were 146,000 copies in print—and drew public attention to Ginsberg and his friends. A particularly sensational aspect of their lives was their drug use. Although Ginsberg's drug use was more circumspect and less frequent than his detractors claimed, he admitted to what he called "pious investigations" of hallucinogens. Part II of "Howl" recalls a peyote vision—under the influence of the drug, Ginsberg saw the facade of the Sir Francis Drake Hotel, in San Francisco, as the grinning face of Moloch—and he drafted "Kaddish" a day after he took morphine and methamphetamine.

Ginsberg, who once described himself as a Buddhist Jew with attachments to Krishna, Siva, Allah, Coyote, and the Sacred Heart, was a spiritual adventurer. He spent the early 1960s traveling, for the most part in the East, speaking with the wise of all persuasions and endeavoring to find means other than drugs to explore consciousness. One of the people he consulted was the Jewish philosopher Martin Buber, who advised him to turn to relationships between human beings rather than relationships between the human and the nonhuman. From Indian holy men, Ginsberg learned the same lesson, the importance of "living in and inhabiting the human form." As indicated by his poem "The Change," Ginsberg's emphasis shifted from drug use to disciplined meditation and chanting in the effort to expand the mind and unite it with the body: "This is my spirit and / physical shape I inhabit."

In 1965, Ginsberg returned from the East. He was crowned the king of May in Prague and then thrown out of Czechoslovakia as a subversive. Back in the United States, he successfully applied for a Guggenheim Fellowship and, with Orlovsky, began a tour of American colleges and universities. He chanted his poems to students, talked with them endlessly and patiently, and gave sound practical advice; eventually, the institutions he visited gratefully supplied him with classrooms and office space. Ginsberg was not bothered by charges that he had been taken over by the Establishment. At poetry readings, peace demonstrations, love-ins and be-ins, before Senate committees and in courtrooms, he expressed his strongly held radical convictions in a good-humored and disarming way. In the later 1960s, Ginsberg became a vivid presence in American life: his face was familiar to those who had never read a line of poetry, and increasingly his poems were lost in a large, genial public impression. That Ginsberg advertised his poems as fragments of a great confession should not obscure the individual exuberance and daring of much of his work.

In his later years, Ginsberg maintained his role as the most earthy and lovable of prophets, denouncing war and commercialization and preaching the transforming powers of the self. His work comprises a history of youth movements, political upheavals, oppressions and aspirations, and technological changes. Always, Ginsberg was searching for a paradisal self in a paradisal world, and the search gave purpose to his pilgrimage to all points of the geographical and spiritual compass.

Howl[1]

For Carl Solomon

I

I saw the best minds of my generation destroyed by madness, starving hysterical naked,
dragging themselves through the negro streets at dawn looking for an angry fix,
angelheaded hipsters burning for the ancient heavenly connection to the starry dynamo in the machinery of night,
who poverty and tatters and hollow-eyed and high sat up smoking in the supernatural darkness of cold-water flats floating across the tops of cities contemplating jazz,
who bared their brains to Heaven under the El[2] and saw Mohammedan angels staggering on tenement roofs illuminated,
who passed through universities with radiant cool eyes hallucinating Arkansas and Blake-light tragedy[3] among the scholars of war,
who were expelled from the academies for crazy & publishing obscene odes on the windows of the skull,
who cowered in unshaven rooms in underwear, burning their money in wastebaskets and listening to the Terror through the wall,
who got busted in their pubic beards returning through Laredo[4] with a belt of marijuana for New York,
who ate fire in paint hotels or drank turpentine in Paradise Alley,[5] death, or purgatoried their torsos night after night
with dreams, with drugs, with waking nightmares, alcohol and cock and endless balls,
incomparable blind streets of shuddering cloud and lightning in the mind leaping toward poles of Canada & Paterson,[6] illuminating all the motionless world of Time between,

1. This poem is a chronicle, and also one of the most famous artifacts, of the Beat counterculture of the 1950s. It alludes to the experiences of the Beats, especially Carl Solomon, to whom it is dedicated, and Ginsberg himself; they met as patients at the Columbia Psychiatric Institute in 1949; Solomon, whom Ginsberg calls an "intuitive Bronx dadaist and prose-poet," was an inmate of various mental hospitals, undergoing insulin and electroshock therapy, during the 1950s. Others mentioned but not named are William S. Burroughs (1914–1997), whose first book, *Junkie* (1953), was published through Solomon's efforts; Herbert E. Huncke (1915–1996), a down-and-out intellectual, Times Square con artist, petty thief, and hipster who, like his friend Burroughs, was a drug addict, and who appears in *Junkie*; and Neal Cassady (1926–1968), a hipster from Denver, whose travels around the country with Jack Kerouac (1927–1969) were recorded by the latter in *On the Road* (1957), in which the two appear as Dean Moriarty and Sal Paradise. Line 66 and much else in "Howl" evidently derive from Solomon's "apocryphal history of my adventures," which he told to Ginsberg in 1949 and later, but in *More Mishaps* (1968), he describes this account as "compounded partly of truth, but for the most raving self-justification, crypto-bohemian boasting . . . effeminate prancing and esoteric aphorisms." Line 7 refers to Ginsberg's two suspensions from Columbia University, in 1945 for scraping obscene pictures and phrases on the grimy windows of his dormitory room to provoke the cleaning woman into cleaning it, and in 1948 when, in danger of conviction as an accessory to Huncke's burglaries, he volunteered for psychiatric treatment; line 45 describes Huncke's arrival, fresh from jail, at Ginsberg's Lower East Side apartment in 1948. A number of the incidents recalled in the poem happened to more than one of the Beats.

2. Elevated railway in New York City and Hebrew for God.

3. In 1948, Ginsberg hallucinated the English poet William Blake (1757–1827) reciting Blake's poems "Ah Sun-Flower" and "The Sick Rose."

4. A city in Texas, on the Mexican border.

5. In New York's Lower East Side; the setting of Kerouac's novel *The Subterraneans* (1958).

6. In New Jersey, where Ginsberg grew up.

Peyote solidities of halls, backyard green tree cemetery dawns, wine drunkenness over the rooftops, storefront boroughs of teahead joy-ride neon blinking traffic light, sun and moon and tree vibrations in the roaring winter dusks of Brooklyn, ashcan rantings and kind king light of mind,
who chained themselves to subways for the endless ride from Battery to holy Bronx[7] on benzedrine until the noise of wheels and children brought them down shuddering mouth-wracked and battered bleak of brain all drained of brilliance in the drear light of Zoo,[8]
who sank all night in submarine light of Bickford's[9] floated out and sat through the stale beer afternoon in desolate Fugazzi's,[1] listening to the crack of doom on the hydrogen jukebox,
who talked continuously seventy hours from park to pad to bar to Bellevue[2] to museum to the Brooklyn Bridge,
a lost battalion of platonic conversationalists jumping down the stoops off fire escapes off windowsills off Empire State out of the moon,
yacketayakking screaming vomiting whispering facts and memories and anecdotes and eyeball kicks and shocks of hospitals and jails and wars,
whole intellects disgorged in total recall for seven days and nights with brilliant eyes, meat for the Synagogue cast on the pavement,
who vanished into nowhere Zen New Jersey leaving a trail of ambiguous picture postcards of Atlantic City Hall,
suffering Eastern sweats and Tangerian bone-grindings and migraines of China under junk-withdrawal in Newark's bleak furnished room,
who wandered around and around at midnight in the railroad yard wondering where to go, and went, leaving no broken hearts,
who lit cigarettes in boxcars boxcars boxcars racketing through snow toward lonesome farms in grandfather night,
who studied Plotinus Poe St. John of the Cross[3] telepathy and bop kabbalah[4] because the cosmos instinctively vibrated at their feet in Kansas,
who loned it through the streets of Idaho seeking visionary indian angels who were visionary indian angels,
who thought they were only mad when Baltimore gleamed in supernatural ecstasy,
who jumped in limousines with the Chinaman of Oklahoma on the impulse of winter midnight streetlight smalltown rain,
who lounged hungry and lonesome through Houston seeking jazz or sex or soup, and followed the brilliant Spaniard to converse about America and Eternity, a hopeless task, and so took ship to Africa,
who disappeared into the volcanoes of Mexico leaving behind nothing but

7. The southern and northern ends of a New York City subway line.
8. The Bronx Zoo.
9. One of a chain of all-night cafeterias, where Ginsberg mopped floors and washed dishes during his college years.
1. A bar north of New York City's then-bohemian Greenwich Village.
2. Public hospital in New York City with a psychiatric clinic.
3. Ginsberg had studied these writers while in college and perhaps treasured them for their visionary and mystical insights. After hearing the voice of Blake, he immediately reread passages from St. John of the Cross and Plotinus to help him interpret the experience.
4. "Bop" is a style of modern jazz especially influential during the 1940s and 1950s; the Kaballa is a Hebraic system of mystical interpretation of the scriptures, which asserts the supremacy of the spirit over bodily desires.

the shadow of dungarees and the lava and ash of poetry scattered in fireplace Chicago,
who reappeared on the West Coast investigating the FBI in beards and shorts with big pacifist eyes sexy in their dark skin passing out incomprehensible leaflets,
who burned cigarette holes in their arms protesting the narcotic tobacco haze of Capitalism,
who distributed Supercommunist pamphlets in Union Square[5] weeping and undressing while the sirens of Los Alamos[6] wailed them down, and wailed down Wall,[7] and the Staten Island ferry also wailed,
who broke down crying in white gymnasiums naked and trembling before the machinery of other skeletons,
who bit detectives in the neck and shrieked with delight in policecars for committing no crime but their own wild cooking pederasty and intoxication,
who howled on their knees in the subway and were dragged off the roof waving genitals and manuscripts,
who let themselves be fucked in the ass by saintly motorcyclists, and screamed with joy,
who blew and were blown by those human seraphim, the sailors, caresses of Atlantic and Caribbean love,
who balled in the morning in the evenings in rosegardens and the grass of public parks and cemeteries scattering their semen freely to whomever come who may,
who hiccupped endlessly trying to giggle but wound up with a sob behind a partition in a Turkish Bath when the blond & naked angel came to pierce them with a sword,
who lost their loveboys to the three old shrews of fate the one eyed shrew of the heterosexual dollar the one eyed shrew that winks out of the womb and the one eyed shrew that does nothing but sit on her ass and snip the intellectual golden threads of the craftsman's loom,
who copulated ecstatic and insatiate with a bottle of beer a sweetheart a package of cigarettes a candle and fell off the bed, and continued along the floor and down the hall and ended fainting on the wall with a vision of ultimate cunt and come eluding the last gyzym of consciousness,
who sweetened the snatches of a million girls trembling in the sunset, and were red eyed in the morning but prepared to sweeten the snatch of the sunrise, flashing buttocks under barns and naked in the lake,
who went out whoring through Colorado in myriad stolen night-cars, N.C.,[8] secret hero of these poems, cocksman and Adonis of Denver—joy to the memory of his innumerable lays of girls in empty lots & diner backyards, moviehouses' rickety rows, on mountaintops in caves or with gaunt waitresses in familiar roadside lonely petticoat upliftings & especially secret gas-station solipsisms of johns, & hometown alleys too,

5. In New York City; it was a center for radical speeches and demonstrations during the 1930s.
6. In New Mexico; the site of the laboratory at which the development of the atomic bomb was completed.
7. Wall Street, in New York, but perhaps also the Wailing Wall, in Jerusalem, where Jews lament their losses and seek consolation.
8. Neal Cassady.

who faded out in vast sordid movies, were shifted in dreams, woke on a sudden Manhattan, and picked themselves up out of basements hung-over with heartless Tokay and horrors of Third Avenue iron dreams & stumbled to unemployment offices,
who walked all night with their shoes full of blood on the snowbank docks waiting for a door in the East River to open to a room full of steam-heat and opium,
who created great suicidal dramas on the apartment cliff-banks of the Hudson under the wartime blue floodlight of the moon & their heads shall be crowned with laurel in oblivion,
who ate the lamb stew of the imagination or digested the crab at the muddy bottom of the rivers of Bowery,[9]
who wept at the romance of the streets with their pushcarts full of onions and bad music,
who sat in boxes breathing in the darkness under the bridge, and rose up to build harpsichords in their lofts,
who coughed on the sixth floor of Harlem crowned with flame under the tubercular sky surrounded by orange crates of theology,
who scribbled all night rocking and rolling over lofty incantations which in the yellow morning were stanzas of gibberish,
who cooked rotten animals lung heart feet tail borsht & tortillas dreaming of the pure vegetable kingdom,
who plunged themselves under meat trucks looking for an egg,
who threw their watches off the roof to cast their ballot for Eternity outside of Time, & alarm clocks fell on their heads every day for the next decade,
who cut their wrists three times successively unsuccessfully, gave up and were forced to open antique stores where they thought they were growing old and cried,
who were burned alive in their innocent flannel suits on Madison Avenue[1] amid blasts of leaden verse & the tanked-up clatter of the iron regiments of fashion & the nitroglycerine shrieks of the fairies of advertising & the mustard gas of sinister intelligent editors, or were run down by the drunken taxicabs of Absolute Reality,
who jumped off the Brooklyn Bridge this actually happened and walked away unknown and forgotten into the ghostly daze of Chinatown soup alleyways & firetrucks, not even one free beer,
who sang out of their windows in despair, fell out of the subway window, jumped in the filthy Passaic,[2] leaped on negroes, cried all over the street, danced on broken wineglasses barefoot smashed phonograph records of nostalgic European 1930s German jazz finished the whiskey and threw up groaning into the bloody toilet, moans in their ears and the blast of colossal steam-whistles,
who barreled down the highways of the past journeying to each other's hotrod-Golgotha[3] jail-solitude watch or Birmingham jazz incarnation,
who drove crosscountry seventytwo hours to find out if I had a vision or you had a vision or he had a vision to find out Eternity.

9. The lower part of Third Avenue in New York, famous as the haunt of alcoholics and derelicts.
1. The center of the advertising industry in New York. Burroughs had worked for a year as a copy writer during the 1930s.
2. The river that flows past Paterson, New Jersey.
3. In the Bible, Golgotha, or "the place of skulls," is the hill near Jerusalem where Jesus was crucified.

who journeyed to Denver, who died in Denver, who came back to Denver & waited in vain, who watched over Denver & brooded & loned in Denver and finally went away to find out the Time, & now Denver is lonesome for her heroes,
who fell on their knees in hopeless cathedrals praying for each other's salvation and light and breasts, until the soul illuminated its hair for a second,
who crashed through their minds in jail waiting for impossible criminals with golden heads and the charm of reality in their hearts who sang sweet blues to Alcatraz,
who retired to Mexico to cultivate a habit,[4] or Rocky Mount to tender Buddha[5] or Tangiers[6] to boys or Southern Pacific to the black locomotive[7] or Harvard to Narcissus to Woodlawn[8] to the daisychain or grave,
who demanded sanity trials accusing the radio of hypnotism & were left with their insanity & their hands & a hung jury,
who threw potato salad at CCNY lecturers on Dadaism[9] and subsequently presented themselves on the granite steps of the madhouse with shaven heads and harlequin speech of suicide, demanding instantaneous lobotomy,
and who were given instead the concrete void of insulin Metrazol electricity hydrotherapy psychotherapy occupational therapy pingpong & amnesia,
who in humorless protest overturned only one symbolic pingpong table, resting briefly in catatonia,
returning years later truly bald except for a wig of blood, and tears and fingers, to the visible madman doom of the wards of the madtowns of the East,
Pilgrim State's Rockland's and Greystone's[1] foetid halls, bickering with the echoes of the soul, rocking and rolling in the midnight solitude-bench dolmen-realms of love, dream of life a nightmare, bodies turned to stone as heavy as the moon,
with mother finally ******,[2] and the last fantastic book flung out of the tenement window, and the last door closed at 4 A.M. and the last telephone slammed at the wall in reply and the last furnished room emptied down to the last piece of mental furniture, a yellow paper rose twisted on a wire hanger in the closet, and even that imaginary, nothing but a hopeful little bit of hallucination—
ah, Carl, while you are not safe I am not safe, and now you're really in the total animal soup of time—
and who therefore ran through the icy streets obsessed with a sudden flash of the alchemy of the use of the ellipse the catalog the meter & the vibrating plane,
who dreamt and made incarnate gaps in Time & Space through images

4. Burroughs.
5. Kerouac, who was then living in Rocky Mount, North Carolina.
6. Both Burroughs and Ginsberg lived in Tangiers for a time.
7. Neal Cassady, who worked as a brakeman for the Southern Pacific Railroad.
8. A cemetery in the Bronx.
9. An artistic movement (c. 1916–20) based on absurdity and accident. *CCNY:* City College of New York.
1. Three mental hospitals near New York. Carl Solomon was an inmate at Pilgrim State and Rockland Hospitals; Ginsberg's mother was a patient at Greystone Hospital from the late 1940s.
2. Ginsberg's draft reads "mother finally fucked"; his note says: "Author replaced letters with asterisks in final draft of poem to introduce appropriate level of uncertainty."

juxtaposed, and trapped the archangel of the soul between 2 visual images and joined the elemental verbs and set the noun and dash of consciousness together jumping with sensation of Pater Omnipotens Aeterna Deus[3]
to recreate the syntax and measure of poor human prose and stand before you speechless and intelligent and shaking with shame, rejected yet confessing out the soul to conform to the rhythm of thought in his naked and endless head,
the madman bum and angel beat in Time, unknown, yet putting down here what might be left to say in time come after death,
and rose reincarnate in the ghostly clothes of jazz in the goldhorn shadow of the band and blew the suffering of America's naked mind for love into an eli eli lamma lamma sabacthani[4] saxophone cry that shivered the cities down to the last radio
with the absolute heart of the poem of life butchered out of their own bodies good to eat a thousand years.

II

What sphinx[5] of cement and aluminum bashed open their skulls and ate up their brains and imagination?
Moloch![6] Solitude! Filth! Ugliness! Ashcans and unobtainable dollars! Children screaming under the stairways! Boys sobbing in armies! Old men weeping in the parks!
Moloch! Moloch! Nightmare of Moloch! Moloch the loveless! Mental Moloch! Moloch the heavy judger of men!
Moloch the incomprehensible prison! Moloch the crossbone soulless jailhouse and Congress of sorrows! Moloch whose buildings are judgment! Moloch the vast stone of war! Moloch the stunned governments!
Moloch whose mind is pure machinery! Moloch whose blood is running money! Moloch whose fingers are ten armies! Moloch whose breast is a cannibal dynamo! Moloch whose ear is a smoking tomb!
Moloch whose eyes are a thousand blind windows! Moloch whose skyscrapers stand in the long streets like endless Jehovahs![7] Moloch whose factories dream and croak in the fog! Moloch whose smokestacks and antennae crown the cities!
Moloch whose love is endless oil and stone! Moloch whose soul is electricity and banks! Moloch whose poverty is the specter of genius!

3. All-powerful Father, eternal God (Latin). The phrase was used by Paul Cézanne (1839–1906), French Impressionist painter, in a letter of 1904 to Emile Bernard, to describe the sensations he received from observing and registering the appearance of the natural world. "The last part of 'Howl' was really an homage to art but also in specific terms an homage to Cézanne's method. . . . Just as Cézanne doesn't use perspective lines to create space, but it's a juxtaposition of one color against another color (that's one element of his space), so, I had the idea, perhaps over-refined, that by the unexplainable, unexplained nonperspective line, that is, juxtaposition of one *word* against another, . . . there'd be a *gap* between the two words which the mind would fill in with the sensation of existence. . . . So, I was trying to do similar things with juxtapositions like 'hydrogen jukebox' or 'winter midnight smalltown streetlight rain.' . . . like: jazz, jukebox and all that, and we have the jukebox from that; politics, hydrogen bomb, and we have the hydrogen of that, you see 'hydrogen jukebox.' [line 15] And that actually compresses in one instant like a whole series of things" (*Writers at Work*, Third Series, 1967).

4. Jesus' words from the Cross (Matthew 26.46, Mark 15.33): "My God, my God, why have you forsaken me?"

5. Mythological creature that kills those incapable of answering its riddle.

6. In the Bible, Semitic god to whom children were sacrificed.

7. Modern reconstruction of YHWH, the Hebrew name of God.

Moloch whose fate is a cloud of sexless hydrogen! Moloch whose name is the Mind!
Moloch in whom I sit lonely! Moloch in whom I dream Angels! Crazy in Moloch! Cocksucker in Moloch! Lacklove and manless in Moloch!
Moloch who entered my soul early! Moloch in whom I am a consciousness without a body! Moloch who frightened me out of my natural ecstasy! Moloch whom I abandon! Wake up in Moloch! Light streaming out of the sky!
Moloch! Moloch! Robot apartments! invisible suburbs! skeleton treasuries! blind capitals! demonic industries! spectral nations! invincible madhouses! granite cocks! monstrous bombs!
They broke their backs lifting Moloch to Heaven! Pavements, trees, radios, tons! lifting the city to Heaven which exists and is everywhere about us!
Visions! omens! hallucinations! miracles! ecstasies! gone down the American river!
Dreams! adorations! illuminations! religions! the whole boatload of sensitive bullshit!
Breakthroughs! over the river! flips and crucifixions! gone down the flood! Highs! Epiphanies! Despairs! Ten years' animal screams and suicides! Minds! New loves! Mad generation! down on the rocks of Time!
Real holy laughter in the river! They saw it all! the wild eyes! the holy yells! They bade farewell! They jumped off the roof! to solitude! waving! carrying flowers! Down to the river! into the street!

III

Carl Solomon! I'm with you in Rockland[8]
where you're madder than I am
I'm with you in Rockland
where you must feel very strange
I'm with you in Rockland
where you imitate the shade of my mother
I'm with you in Rockland
where you've murdered your twelve secretaries
I'm with you in Rockland
where you laugh at this invisible humor
I'm with you in Rockland
where we are great writers on the same dreadful typewriter
I'm with you in Rockland
where your condition has become serious and is reported on the radio
I'm with you in Rockland
where the faculties of the skull no longer admit the worms of the senses
I'm with you in Rockland
where you drink the tea of the breasts of the spinsters of Utica[9]
I'm with you in Rockland
where you pun on the bodies of your nurses the harpies of the Bronx
I'm with you in Rockland
where you scream in a straightjacket that you're losing the game

8. Mental hospital near New York City.

9. Town in central New York.

of the actual pingpong of the abyss
I'm with you in Rockland
where you bang on the catatonic piano the soul is innocent and immortal it should never die ungodly in an armed madhouse
I'm with you in Rockland
where fifty more shocks will never return your soul to its body again from its pilgrimage to a cross in the void
I'm with you in Rockland
where you accuse your doctors of insanity and plot the Hebrew socialist revolution against the fascist national Golgotha[1]
I'm with you in Rockland
where you will split the heavens of Long Island and resurrect your living human Jesus from the superhuman tomb
I'm with you in Rockland
where there are twentyfive thousand mad comrades all together singing the final stanzas of the Internationale[2]
I'm with you in Rockland
where we hug and kiss the United States under our bedsheets the United States that coughs all night and won't let us sleep
I'm with you in Rockland
where we wake up electrified out of the coma by our own souls' airplanes roaring over the roof they've come to drop angelic bombs the hospital illuminates itself imaginary walls collapse O skinny legions run outside O starry-spangled shock of mercy the eternal war is here O victory forget your underwear we're free
I'm with you in Rockland
in my dreams you walk dripping from a sea-journey on the highway across America in tears to the door of my cottage in the Western night

San Francisco, 1955–1956

1956

A Supermarket in California

What thoughts I have of you tonight, Walt Whitman,[3] for I walked down the sidestreets under the trees with a headache self-conscious looking at the full moon.

In my hungry fatigue, and shopping for images, I went into the neon fruit supermarket, dreaming of your enumerations!

What peaches and what penumbras![4] Whole families shopping at night! Aisles full of husbands! Wives in the avocados, babies in the tomatoes!—and you, García Lorca,[5] what were you doing down by the watermelons?

1. Site of Jesus' crucifixion.
2. Anthem of the socialist movement and, until 1944, the national anthem of the Soviet Union.
3. American poet (1819–1892).
4. Partial shadows.
5. Federico García Lorca (1898–1936), Spanish poet and dramatist; like Ginsberg and Whitman, a homosexual.

I saw you, Walt Whitman, childless, lonely old grubber, poking among the meats in the refrigerator and eyeing the grocery boys.
I heard you asking questions of each: Who killed the pork chops? What price bananas? Are you my Angel?
I wandered in and out of the brilliant stacks of cans following you, and followed in my imagination by the store detective.
We strode down the open corridors together in our solitary fancy tasting artichokes, possessing every frozen delicacy, and never passing the cashier.

Where are we going, Walt Whitman? The doors close in an hour. Which way does your beard point tonight?
(I touch your book and dream of our odyssey in the supermarket and feel absurd.)
Will we walk all night through solitary streets? The trees add shade to shade, lights out in the houses, we'll both be lonely.
Will we stroll dreaming of the lost America of love past blue automobiles in driveways, home to our silent cottage?
Ah, dear father, graybeard, lonely old courage-teacher, what America did you have when Charon quit poling his ferry and you got out on a smoking bank and stood watching the boat disappear on the black waters of Lethe?[6]

1956

Sunflower Sutra[7]

I walked on the banks of the tincan banana dock and sat down under the huge shade of a Southern Pacific locomotive to look at the sunset over the box house hills and cry.
Jack Kerouac[8] sat beside me on a busted rusty iron pole, companion, we thought the same thoughts of the soul, bleak and blue and sad-eyed, surrounded by the gnarled steel roots of trees of machinery.
The oily water on the river mirrored the red sky, sun sank on top of final Frisco[9] peaks, no fish in that stream, no hermit in those mounts, just ourselves rheumy-eyed and hung-over like old bums on the riverbank, tired and wily.
Look at the Sunflower, he said, there was a dead gray shadow against the sky, big as a man, sitting dry on top of a pile of ancient sawdust—
—I rushed up enchanted—it was my first sunflower, memories of Blake[1]—my visions—Harlem
and Hells of the Eastern rivers, bridges clanking Joes Greasy Sandwiches, dead baby carriages, black treadless tires forgotten and unretreaded, the poem of the riverbank, condoms & pots, steel knives, nothing

6. One of the rivers of Hades (it means "forgetfulness"), across which Charon ferried the dead.
7. Buddhist or Hindu teachings; from the Sanskrit word for thread.
8. American writer (1922–1969) and icon of the Beat generation.
9. San Francisco.
1. In Harlem in 1948, Ginsberg hallucinated the English poet William Blake (1757–1827) reciting Blake's poems "Ah Sun-Flower" and "The Sick Rose."

stainless, only the dank muck and the razor-sharp artifacts passing into the past—
and the gray Sunflower poised against the sunset, crackly bleak and dusty with the smut and smog and smoke of olden locomotives in its eye—
corolla[2] of bleary spikes pushed down and broken like a battered crown, seeds fallen out of its face, soon-to-be-toothless mouth of sunny air, sunrays obliterated on its hairy head like a dried wire spiderweb,
leaves stuck out like arms out of the stem, gestures from the sawdust root, broke pieces of plaster fallen out of the black twigs, a dead fly in its ear,
Unholy battered old thing you were, my sunflower O my soul, I loved you then!
The grime was no man's grime but death and human locomotives,
all that dress of dust, that veil of darkened railroad skin, that smog of cheek, that eyelid of black mis'ry, that sooty hand or phallus or protuberance of artificial worse-than-dirt—industrial—modern—all that civilization spotting your crazy golden crown—
and those blear thoughts of death and dusty loveless eyes and ends and withered roots below, in the home-pile of sand and sawdust, rubber dollar bills, skin of machinery, the guts and innards of the weeping coughing car, the empty lonely tincans with their rusty tongues alack, what more could I name, the smoked ashes of some cock cigar, the cunts of wheelbarrows and the milky breasts of cars, wornout asses out of chairs & sphincters of dynamos—all these
entangled in your mummied roots—and you there standing before me in the sunset, all your glory in your form!
A perfect beauty of a sunflower! a perfect excellent lovely sunflower existence! a sweet natural eye to the new hip moon, woke up alive and excited grasping in the sunset shadow sunrise golden monthly breeze!
How many flies buzzed round you innocent of your grime, while you cursed the heavens of the railroad and your flower soul?
Poor dead flower? when did you forget you were a flower? when did you look at your skin and decide you were an impotent dirty old locomotive? the ghost of a locomotive? the specter and shade of a once powerful mad American locomotive?
You were never no locomotive, Sunflower, you were a sunflower!
And you Locomotive, you are a locomotive, forget me not!
So I grabbed up the skeleton thick sunflower and stuck it at my side like a scepter,
and deliver my sermon to my soul, and Jack's soul too, and anyone who'll listen,
—We're not our skin of grime, we're not dread bleak dusty imageless locomotives, we're golden sunflowers inside, blessed by our own seed & hairy naked accomplishment-bodies growing into mad black formal sunflowers in the sunset, spied on by our own eyes under the shadow of the mad locomotive riverbank sunset Frisco hilly tincan evening sitdown vision.

Berkeley, 1955 — 1956

2. Inner envelope of a flower.

America[3]

America I've given you all and now I'm nothing.
American two dollars and twentyseven cents January 17, 1956.
I can't stand my own mind.
America when will we end the human war?
Go fuck yourself with your atom bomb.
I don't feel good don't bother me.
I won't write my poem till I'm in my right mind.
America when will you be angelic?
When will you take off your clothes?
When will you look at yourself through the grave?
When will you be worthy of your million Trotskyites?
America why are your libraries full of tears?
America when will you send your eggs to India?
I'm sick of your insane demands.
When can I go into the supermarket and buy what I need with my good
looks?
America after all it is you and I who are perfect not the next world.
Your machinery is too much for me.
You made me want to be a saint.
There must be some other way to settle this argument.
Burroughs[4] is in Tangiers I don't think he'll come back it's sinister.
Are you being sinister or is this some form of practical joke?
I'm trying to come to the point.
I refuse to give up my obsession.
America stop pushing I know what I'm doing.
America the plum blossoms are falling.
I haven't read the newspapers for months, everyday somebody goes on
trial for murder.
America I feel sentimental about the Wobblies.
America I used to be a communist when I was a kid I'm not sorry.
I smoke marijuana every chance I get.
I sit in my house for days on end and stare at the roses in the closet.
When I go to Chinatown I get drunk and never get laid.
My mind is made up there's going to be trouble.
You should have seen me reading Marx.

3. By 1956, Senator Joseph McCarthy had been discredited, but the memory of his anticommunist witch-hunts stifled political dissent, and Ginsberg's publication of this poem was a courageous act. He alludes to the repressive 1920s and the liberal 1930s, his view colored by that of his mother, a Russian immigrant and a fervent member of the Communist Party. The Trotskyites (line 11) were militant American Communists. The Wobblies (line 27) were members of the Industrial Workers of the World, a radical labor organization active from 1905 to 1930, many of whose members were imprisoned during the "Red scare" of 1919–21. Tom Mooney (1882–1942) (line 57), a labor organizer, was condemned to death on perjured evidence that he had exploded a bomb during a San Francisco parade; he escaped the electric chair and was freed after 23 years in prison, but anarchists Nicola Sacco and Bartholomeo Vanzetti (line 59) were executed in 1927 after what amounted to a political trial. During the 1930s, the American Communist Party was able to take part openly in political campaigns and organized support for Tom Mooney, for the Scottsboro boys (line 60—eight blacks condemned to death after a sensational and unfair rape trial in Scottsboro, Alabama), and for the Loyalists (line 58) who fought in support of the Socialist government of Republican Spain against the Fascist revolution led by General Francisco Franco.

4. William Burroughs (1914–1997), author of *Naked Lunch* (1959), was a heroin addict for fifteen years, until 1957; in 1950, he left the United States for Mexico, and then for Tangiers, to avoid prosecution.

My psychoanalyst thinks I'm perfectly right.
I won't say the Lord's Prayer.
I have mystical visions and cosmic vibrations.

America I still haven't told you what you did to Uncle Max after he came over from Russia.
I'm addressing you.
Are you going to let your emotional life be run by Time Magazine?
I'm obsessed by Time Magazine.
I read it every week.
Its cover stares at me every time I slink past the corner candystore.
I read it in the basement of the Berkeley Public Library.
It's always telling me about responsibility. Businessmen are serious. Movie producers are serious. Everybody's serious but me.
It occurs to me that I am America.
I am talking to myself again.

Asia is rising against me.
I haven't got a chinaman's chance.
I'd better consider my national resources.
My national resources consist of two joints of marijuana millions of genitals an unpublishable private literature that jetplanes 1400 miles an hour and twentyfive-thousand mental institutions.
I say nothing about my prisons nor the millions of underprivileged who live in my flowerpots under the light of five hundred suns.
I have abolished the whorehouses of France, Tangiers is the next to go.
My ambition is to be President despite the fact that I'm a Catholic.[5]

America how can I write a holy litany in your silly mood?
I will continue like Henry Ford my strophes[6] are as individual as his automobiles more so they're all different sexes.
America I will sell you strophes $2500 apiece $500 down on your old strophe
America free Tom Mooney
America save the Spanish Loyalists
America Sacco & Vanzetti must not die
America I am the Scottsboro boys.
America when I was seven momma took me to Communist Cell meetings they sold us garbanzos a handful per ticket a ticket costs a nickel and the speeches were free everybody was angelic and sentimental about the workers it was all so sincere you have no idea what a good thing the party was in 1835 Scott Nearing was a grand old man a real mensch Mother Bloor the Silk-strikers' Ewig-Weibliche made me cry I once saw the Yiddish orator Israel Amter plain.[7] Everybody must have been a spy.
America you don't really want to go to war.
America it's them bad Russians.

5. An allusion to Al Smith (1873–1944), a New York governor who was the first Roman Catholic candidate for U.S. president, in 1928.
6. That is, stanzas.
7. Scott Nearing, a radical economist and socialist who left the Communist Party in 1930. Ella Reeve Bloor and Israel Amter were Party leaders in the New York area. Compare Robert Browning's line, "Ah, did you once see Shelley plain?"

Them Russians them Russians and them Chinamen. And them Russians.
The Russia wants to eat us alive. The Russia's power mad. She wants to take our cars from out our garages.
Her wants to grab Chicago. Her needs a Red *Readers' Digest*. Her wants our auto plants in Siberia. Him big bureaucracy running our filling-stations.
That no good. Ugh. Him make Indians learn read. Him need big black niggers. Hah. Her make us all work sixteen hours a day. Help.
America this is quite serious.
America this is the impression I get from looking in the television set.
America is this correct?
I'd better get right down to the job.
It's true I don't want to join the Army or turn lathes in precision parts factories, I'm nearsighted and psychopathic anyway.
America I'm putting my queer shoulder to the wheel.

Berkeley January 17, 1956

1956

From Kaddish

For Naomi Ginsberg, 1894–1956[8]

* * *

Your last night in the darkness of the Bronx—I phonecalled—thru hospital to secret police
that came, when you and I were alone, shrieking at Elanor[9] in my ear—who breathed hard in her own bed, got thin—
Nor will forget, the doorknock, at your fright of spies,—Law advancing, on my honor—Eternity entering the room—you running to the bathroom undressed, hiding in protest from the last heroic fate—
staring at my eyes, betrayed—the final cops of madness rescuing me—from your foot against the broken heart of Elanor,
your voice at Edie weary of Gimbels coming home to broken radio—and Louis needing a poor divorce, he wants to get married soon—Eugene[1] dreaming, hiding at 125 St., suing negroes for money on crud furniture, defending black girls—
Protests from the bathroom—Said you were sane—dressing in a cotton robe, your shoes, then new, your purse and newspaper clippings—no—your honesty—
as you vainly made your lips more real with lipstick, looking in the mirror to see if the Insanity was Me or a carful of police.
or Grandma spying at 78—Your vision—Her climbing over the walls of the cemetery with political kidnapper's bag—or what you saw on the walls of the Bronx, in pink nightgown at midnight, staring out the window on the empty lot—
Ah Rochambeau Ave.—Playground of Phantoms—last apartment in the

8. The poet's mother, who suffered from mental illness most of her life; she was institutionalized from 1948 until 1956, when she died in Greystone Hospital. *Kaddish:* Jewish prayer of mourning and remembrance for the dead.
9. Naomi's sister.
1. Ginsberg's brother. Louis: Ginsberg's father.

Bronx for spies—last home for Elanor or Naomi, here these communist sisters lost their revolution—
'All right—put on your coat Mrs.—let's go—We have the wagon downstairs—you want to come with her to the station?'
The ride then—held Naomi's hand, and held her head to my breast, I'm taller—kissed her and said I did it for the best—Elanor sick—and Max[2] with heart condition—Needs—
To me—'Why did you do this?'—'Yes Mrs., your son will have to leave you in an hour'—The Ambulance
came in a few hours—drove off at 4 A.M. to some Bellevue[3] in the night downtown—gone to the hospital forever. I saw her led away—she waved, tears in her eyes.

Two years, after a trip to Mexico—bleak in the flat plain near Brentwood,[4] scrub brush and grass around the unused RR train track to the crazyhouse—
new brick 20 story central building—lost on the vast lawns of madtown on Long Island—huge cities of the moon.
Asylum spreads out giant wings above the path to a minute black hole—the door—entrance thru crotch—
I went in—smelt funny—the halls again—up elevator—to a glass door on a Women's Ward—to Naomi—Two nurses buxom white—They led her out, Naomi stared—and I gaspt—She'd had a stroke—
Too thin, shrunk on her bones—age come to Naomi—now broken into white hair—loose dress on her skeleton—face sunk, old! withered—cheek of crone—
One hand stiff—heaviness of forties & menopause reduced by one heart stroke, lame now—wrinkles—a scar on her head, the lobotomy[5]—ruin, the hand dipping downwards to death—

O Russian faced, woman on the grass, your long black hair is crowned with flowers, the mandolin is on your knees—
Communist beauty, sit here married in the summer among daisies, promised happiness at hand—
holy mother, now you smile on your love, your world is born anew, children run naked in the field spotted with dandelions,
they eat in the plum tree grove at the end of the meadow and find a cabin where a white-haired negro teaches the mystery of his rainbarrel—
blessed daughter come to America, I long to hear your voice again, remembering your mother's music, in the Song of the Natural Front—
O glorious muse that bore me from the womb, gave suck first mystic life & taught me talk and music, from whose pained head I first took Vision—
Tortured and beaten in the skull—What mad hallucinations of the damned that drive me out of my own skull to seek Eternity till I find Peace for Thee, O Poetry—and for all humankind call on the Origin
Death which is the mother of the universe!—Now wear your nakedness

2. Elanor's husband.
3. Psychiatric hospital.
4. Town on Long Island, east of New York City; site of the former Pilgrim State mental institution.
5. Surgical procedure once thought to alleviate mental illness by severing the frontal lobes of the brain from the thalamus.

forever, white flowers in your hair, your marriage sealed behind the sky—no revolution might destroy that maidenhood—
O beautiful Garbo[6] of my Karma—all photographs from 1920 in Camp Nicht-Gedeiget[7] here unchanged—with all the teachers from Newark—Nor Elanor be gone, nor Max await his specter—nor Louis retire from this High School—

Back! You! Naomi! Skull on you! Gaunt immortality and revolution come—small broken woman—the ashen indoor eyes of hospitals, ward grayness on skin—
'Are you a spy?' I sat at the sour table, eyes filling with tears—'Who are you? Did Louis send you?—The wires—'
in her hair, as she beat on her head—'I'm not a bad girl—don't murder me!—I hear the ceiling—I raised two children—'
Two years since I'd been there—I started to cry—She stared—nurse broke up the meeting a moment—I went into the bathroom to hide, against the toilet white walls
'The Horror' I weeping—to see her again—'The Horror'—as if she were dead thru funeral rot in—'The Horror!'[8]
I came back she yelled more—they led her away—'You're not Allen—' I watched her face—but she passed by me, not looking—
Opened the door to the ward,—she went thru without a glance back, quiet suddenly—I stared out—she looked old—the verge of the grave—'All the Horror!'

Another year, I left N.Y.—on West Coast in Berkeley cottage dreamed of her soul—that, thru life, in what form it stood in that body, ashen or manic, gone beyond joy—
near its death—with eyes—was my own love in its form, the Naomi, my mother on earth still—sent her long letter—& wrote hymns to the mad—Work of the merciful Lord of Poetry.
that causes the broken grass to be green, or the rock to break in grass—or the Sun to be constant to earth—Sun of all sunflowers and days on bright iron bridges—what shines on old hospitals—as on my yard—
Returning from San Francisco one night, Orlovsky in my room—Whalen[9] in his peaceful chair—a telegram from Gene, Naomi dead—
Outside I bent my head to the ground under the bushes near the garage—knew she was better—
at last—not left to look on Earth alone—2 years of solitude—no one, at age nearing 60—old woman of skulls—once long-tressed Naomi of Bible—
or Ruth who wept in America—Rebecca aged in Newark—David remembering his Harp, now lawyer at Yale
or Srul Avrum—Israel Abraham—myself[1]—to sing in the wilderness

6. Greta Garbo (1905–1990), American film star.
7. No worry (Yiddish); the name of a communist summer camp near Lake Monroe in upstate New York, attended by the Ginsberg family; Naomi Ginsberg was especially happy there.
8. Dying words of Kurtz in the novella *Heart of Darkness* (1902), by Joseph Conrad (1857–1924).
9. Philip Whalen (1923–2002): American Beat poet. Peter Orlovsky (b. 1933): Ginsberg's lover.
1. Ginsberg was named after his paternal great-grandfather, S'rul Avram Ginsberg. *S'rul* is Yiddish for Israel, *Avram* Yiddish for Abraham. Naomi, David, Rebecca, Ruth, Israel, and Abraham are all important figures in the Hebrew Bible.

toward God—O Elohim![2]—so to the end—2 days after her death I got her letter—
Strange Prophecies anew! She wrote—'The key is in the window, the key is in the sunlight at the window—I have the key—Get married Allen don't take drugs—the key is in the bars, in the sunlight in the window.
Love,
your mother'
which is Naomi—

Paris, December 1957–New York, 1959 1961

To Aunt Rose

Aunt Rose—now—might I see you
with your thin face and buck tooth smile and pain
of rheumatism—and a long black heavy shoe
for your bony left leg
limping down the long hall in Newark on the running carpet
past the black grand piano
in the day room
where the parties were
and I sang Spanish loyalist[3] songs
in a high squeaky voice
(hysterical) the committee listening
while you limped around the room
collected the money—
Aunt Honey, Uncle Sam, a stranger with a cloth arm
in his pocket
and huge young bald head
of Abraham Lincoln Brigade[4]

—your long sad face
your tears of sexual frustration
(what smothered sobs and bony hips
under the pillows of Osborne Terrace)
—the time I stood on the toilet seat naked
and you powdered my thighs with calamine
against the poison ivy—my tender
and shamed first black curled hairs
what were you thinking in secret heart then
knowing me a man already—
and I an ignorant girl of family silence on the thin pedestal
of my legs in the bathroom—Museum of Newark.

Aunt Rose
Hitler is dead, Hitler is in Eternity; Hitler is with
Tamburlane and Emily Brontë[5]

2. Lord (Hebrew).
3. During the Spanish Civil War (1936–39), many left-wing Americans—among them Ginsberg's Newark relatives—sympathized with the Spanish Loyalists.
4. A group of American volunteers who fought with the loyalists in the Spanish Civil War.
5. English poet and novelist (1818–1848), author of *Wuthering Heights*. Tamburlaine was the twelfth-century Mideastern "scourge" and conqueror (hero of Christopher Marlowe's *Tamburlaine*, 1588).

Though I see you walking still, a ghost on Osborne Terrace
down the long dark hall to the front door
limping a little with a pinched smile
in what must have been a silken
flower dress
welcoming my father, the Poet, on his visit to Newark
—see you arriving in the living room
dancing on your crippled leg
and clapping hands his book
had been accepted by Liveright[6]

Hitler is dead and Liveright's gone out of business
The Attic of the Past and *Everlasting Minute* are out of print
Uncle Harry sold his last silk stocking
Claire quit interpretive dancing school
Buba sits a wrinkled monument in Old
Ladies Home blinking at new babies

last time I saw you was the hospital
pale skull protruding under ashen skin
blue veined unconscious girl
in an oxygen tent
the war in Spain has ended long ago
Aunt Rose

Paris, June 1958 1961

Last Night in Calcutta

Still night. The old clock Ticks,
half past two. A ringing of crickets
awake in the ceiling. The gate is locked
on the street outside—sleepers, mustaches,
nakedness, but no desire. A few mosquitoes
waken the itch, the fan turns slowly—
a car thunders along the black asphalt,
a bull snorts, something is expected—
Time sits solid in the four yellow walls.
No one is here, emptiness filled with train
whistles & dog barks, answered a block away.
Pushkin[7] sits on the bookshelf, Shakespeare's
complete works as well as Blake's unread—
O Spirit of Poetry, no use calling on you
babbling in this emptiness furnished with beds
under the bright oval mirror—perfect
night for sleepers to dissolve in tranquil
blackness, and rest there eight hours

6. This leading American publisher of the 1920s and 1930s (now a subsidiary of W. W. Norton & Company) published *The Everlasting Minute* (1937), poems by Allen Ginsberg's father, Louis, whose first book was *The Attic of the Past* (Boston, 1920).
7. Alexander Pushkin (1799–1837), Russian poet.

—Waking to stained fingers, bitter mouth
and lung gripped by cigarette hunger,
what to do with this big toe, this arm
this eye in the starving skeleton-filled
sore horse tramcar-heated Calcutta in
Eternity—sweating and teeth rotted away—
Rilke[8] at least could dream about lovers,
the old breast excitement and trembling belly,
is that it? And the vast starry space—
If the brain changes matter breathes
fearfully back on man—But now
the great crash of building and planets
breaks thru the walls of language and drowns
me under its Ganges[9] heaviness forever.
No escape but thru Bangkok and New York death.
Skin is sufficient to be skin, that's all
it ever could be, tho screams of pain in the kidney
make it sick of itself, a wavy dream
dying to finish its all too famous misery
—Leave immortality for another to suffer like a fool,
not get stuck in the corner of the universe
sticking morphine in the arm and eating meat.

May 22, 1963 1968

Mugging

I

Tonite I walked out of my red apartment door on East tenth street's[1] dusk—
Walked out of my home ten years, walked out in my honking neighborhood
Tonite at seven walked out past garbage cans chained to concrete anchors
Walked under black painted fire escapes, giant castiron plate covering a hole in ground
—Crossed the street, traffic lite red, thirteen bus roaring by liquor store,
past corner pharmacy iron grated, past Coca Cola & Mylai[2] posters fading scraped on brick
Past Chinese Laundry wood door'd, & broken cement stoop steps For Rent hall painted green & purple Puerto Rican style
Along E. 10th's glass splattered pavement, kid blacks & Spanish oiled hair adolescents' crowded house fronts—
Ah, tonite I walked out on my block NY City under humid summer sky Halloween,
thinking what happened Timothy Leary[3] joining brain police for a season?

8. Rainer Maria Rilke (1875–1926), German poet, author of the *Duino Elegies*, which celebrate angels and lovers as figures of immortal power.
9. The sacred river of India.
1. On New York City's Lower East Side.
2. Scene of a massacre by American troops during the Vietnam War.
3. Nineteen-sixties counterculture figure (1920–1996), who advocated LSD use.

thinking what's all this Weathermen,[4] secrecy & selfrightousness beyond reason—F.B.I. plots?
Walked past a taxicab controlling the bottle strewn curb—
past young fellows with their umbrella handles & canes leaning against a ravaged Buick
—and as I looked at the crowd of kids on the stoop—a boy stepped up, put his arm around my neck
tenderly I thought for a moment, squeezed harder, his umbrella handle against my skull,
and his friends took my arm, a young brown companion tripped his foot 'gainst my ankle—
as I went down shouting Om Ah Hūṃ[5] to gangs of lovers on the stoop watching
slowly appreciating, why this is a raid, these strangers mean strange business
with what—my pockets, bald head, broken-healed-bone leg, my softshoes, my heart—
Have they knives? Om Ah Hūṃ—Have they sharp metal wood to shove in eye ear ass? Om Ah Hūṃ
& slowly reclined on the pavement, struggling to keep my woolen bag of poetry address calendar & Leary-lawyer notes hung from my shoulder
dragged in my neat orlon shirt over the crossbar of a broken metal door
dragged slowly onto the fire-soiled floor an abandoned store, laundry candy counter 1929—
now a mess of papers & pillows & plastic car seat covers cracked cockroach-corpsed ground—
my wallet back pocket passed over the iron foot step guard
and fell out, stole by God Muggers' lost fingers, Strange—
Couldn't tell—snakeskin wallet actually plastic, 70 dollars my bank money for a week,
old broken wallet—and dreary plastic contents—Amex card & Manf. Hanover Trust Credit too—business card from Mr. Spears British Home Minister Drug Squad—my draft card—membership ACLU & Naropa Institute[6] Instructor's identification
Om Ah Hūṃ I continued chanting Om Ah Hūṃ
Putting my palm on the neck of an 18 year old boy fingering my back pocket crying "Where's the money"
"Oh Am Hūṃ there isn't any"
My card Chief Boo-Hoo Neo American Church New Jersey & Lower East Side
Om Ah Hūṃ—what not forgotten crowded wallet—Mobil Credit, Shell? old lovers addresses on cardboard pieces, booksellers calling cards—
—"Shut up or we'll murder you"—"Om Ah Hūṃ take it easy"
Lying on the floor shall I shout more loud?—the metal door closed on blackness
one boy felt my broken healed ankle, looking for hundred dollar bills behind my stocking weren't even there—a third boy untied my Seiko

4. Radical group of student protesters during the 1960s.
5. Buddhist mantra, or chant.
6. Ginsberg's school for the study of poetry and mysticism in Boulder, Colorado.

Hong Kong watch rough from right wrist leaving a clasp-prick skin tiny bruise
"Shut up and we'll get out of here"—and so they left,
as I rose from the cardboard mattress thinking Om Ah Hūṃ didn't stop em enough,
the tone of voice too loud—my shoulder bag with 10,000 dollars full of poetry left on the broken floor—

November 2, 1974

II

Went out the door dim eyed, bent down & picked up my glasses from step edge I placed them while dragged in the store—looked out—
Whole street a bombed-out face, building rows' eyes & teeth missing
burned apartments half the long block, gutted cellars, hallways' charred beams
hanging over trash plaster mounded entrances, couches & bedsprings rusty after sunset
Nobody home, but scattered stoopfuls of scared kids frozen in black hair
chatted giggling at house doors in black shoes, families cooked For Rent some six story houses mid the street's wreckage
Nextdoor Bodega,[7] a phone, the police? "I just got mugged" I said
to the man's face under fluorescent grocery light tin ceiling—
puffy, eyes blank & watery, sickness of beer kidney and language tongue
thick lips stunned as my own eyes, poor drunken Uncle minding the store!
O hopeless city of idiots empty eyed staring afraid, red beam top'd car at street curb arrived—
"Hey maybe my wallet's still on the ground got a flashlight?"
Back into the burnt-doored cave, & the policeman's gray flashlight broken no eyebeam—
"My partner all he wants is sit in the car never gets out Hey Joe bring your flashlight—"
a tiny throwaway beam, dim as a match in the criminal dark
"No I can't see anything here" . . . "Fill out this form"
Neighborhood street crowd behind a car "We didn't see nothing"
Stoop young girls, kids laughing "Listen man last time I messed with them see this—"
rolled up his skinny arm shirt, a white knife scar on his brown shoulder
"Besides we help you the cops come don't know anybody we all get arrested
go to jail I never help no more mind my business everytime"
"Agh!" upstreet think "Gee I don't know anybody here ten years lived half block crost Avenue C[8]
and who knows who?"—passing empty apartments, old lady with frayed paper bags
sitting in the tin-boarded doorframe of a dead house.

December 10, 1974 1977

7. Corner grocer (Spanish).

8. Which runs at right angles to East 10th Street.

Sphincter[9]

I hope my good old asshole holds out
60 years it's been mostly OK
Tho in Bolivia a fissure operation
    survived the *altiplano*[1] hospital—
a little blood, no polyps, occasionally
    a small hemorrhoid
active, eager, receptive to phallus
    coke bottle, candle, carrot
    banana & fingers—
Now AIDS makes it shy, but still
    eager to serve—
out with the dumps, in with the condom'd
    orgasmic friend—
still rubbery muscular,
    unashamed wide open for joy
But another 20 years who knows,
    old folks got troubles everywhere—
necks, prostates, stomachs, joints—
    Hope the old hole stays young
    till death, relax

March 15, 1986, 1:00 P.M. 1994

Personals Ad

"I will send a picture too
if you will send me one of you"
—R. CREELEY[2]

Poet professor in autumn years
seeks helpmate companion protector friend
young lover w/empty compassionate soul
exuberant spirit, straightforward handsome
athletic physique & boundless mind, courageous
warrior who may also like women & girls, no problem,
to share bed meditation apartment Lower East Side,
help inspire mankind conquer world anger & guilt,
empowered by Whitman Blake Rimbaud Ma Rainey & Vivaldi,[3]
familiar respecting Art's primordial majesty, priapic[4] carefree
playful harmless slave or master, mortally tender passing swift time,
photographer, musician, painter, poet, yuppie or scholar—
Find me here in New York alone with the Alone
going to lady psychiatrist who says Make time in your life

9. Ringlike muscle that maintains constriction of an orifice, such as the anus.
1. Andean plateau.
2. American poet (b. 1926), from his poem "The Conspiracy."
3. Antonio Vivaldi (1678–1741): Italian composer. Walt Whitman (1819–1892): American poet. William Blake (1757–1827): British poet. Arthur Rimbaud (1854–1891): French poet. Ma Rainey (1886–1936): American blues singer.
4. Relating to the penis.

for someone you can call darling, honey, who holds you dear
can get excited & lay his head on your heart in peace.

October 8, 1987 1994

David Wagoner
b. 1926

Born on June 5, 1926, in the small Ohio town of Massillon, David Wagoner as a child was taken by his parents to live in Whiting, Indiana, a heavily industrialized suburb of Chicago. He served in the navy toward the end of World War II. The great event of his education occurred when, as a student at Pennsylvania State University, he took a course taught by Theodore Roethke. They shared a keen interest in nature, and when Roethke moved to the University of Washington in Seattle, he encouraged Wagoner to join him. Wagoner did so, and the natural beauty he found in the Pacific northwest struck him with awe.

Wagoner is the principal, though modest, character in most of his poems. By turns affectionate, sober, and gently humorous, he uses metaphor, pacing, and accumulated detail to create convincing character sketches, such as his father-as-handyman or a girl pouring water from a pitcher. He loves wildernesses and rivers and writes deftly of natural things, often small, such as ferns, a tuft of thistledown, a goldfinch, a dragonfly, in each of which he finds a relevance to human life. His quiet, descriptively astute poems help revitalize the pastoral tradition, bridging the gap between humans and nature without attempting to eliminate it. His response to the destruction of nature is angrily mournful, as in his "Elegy for a Forest Clear-Cut by the Weyerhaeuser Company." Through repetition he reproduces the downing of trees and his own agitated feelings: "You fell and fell again and went on falling / And falling and always falling." Similarly, a one-sentence syntactic tumble summons the natural cascade of "By a Waterfall." In addition to poetry, Wagoner has published numerous novels and prose writings, including a book on the myths and tales of the Northwest Coast and Plateau Indians.

The Man of the House

My father, looking for trouble, would find it
On his hands and knees by hammering on walls
Between the joists or drilling through baseboards
Or crawling into the attic where insulation
Lay under the leaks like sleeping-bags.

It would be something simple as a rule
To be ingenious for, in overalls;
And he would kneel beside it, pouring sweat
Down his red cheeks, glad of a useful day
With something wrong unknown to the landlord.

At those odd times when everything seemed to work
All right, suspiciously all right like silence
In concrete shelters, he'd test whatever hung
Over our heads: such afternoons meant ladders,
Nails in the mouth, flashing and shaking roofs.

In safety shoes going down basement stairs,
He'd flick his rewired rearrangement of lights
And chase all shadows into the coalbin
Where they could watch him, blinking at his glare.
If shadows hadn't worked, he would have made them.

With hands turning to horn against the stone
He'd think on all fours, hunch as if to drink
If his cold chisel broke the cold foundation
And brought dark water pulsing out of clay.
Wrenching at rows of pipes like his cage-bars,

He made them creak in sockets and give way,
But rammed them back, putting his house in order.
Moonlight or rain, after the evening paper,
His mouth lay open under the perfect plaster
To catch the first sweet drop, but none came down.

1966

Elegy for a Forest Clear-Cut by the Weyerhaeuser Company

Five months after your death, I come like the others
Among the slash and stumps, across the cratered
Three square miles of your graveyard:
Nettles and groundsel first out of the jumble,
Then fireweed and bracken
Have come to light where you, for ninety years,
Had kept your shadows.

The creek has gone as thin as my wrist, nearly dead
To the world at the dead end of summer,
Guttering to a pool where the tracks of an earth-mover
Showed it the way to falter underground.
Now pearly everlasting
Has grown to honor the deep dead cast of your roots
For a bitter season.

Those water- and earth-led roots decay for winter
Below my feet, below the fir seedlings
Planted in your place (one out of ten alive
In the summer drought),

Below the small green struggle of the weeds
For their own ends, below grasshoppers,
The only singers now.

The chains and cables and steel teeth have left
Nothing of what you were:
I hold my hands over a stump and remember
A hundred and fifty feet above me branches
No longer holding sway. In the pitched battle
You fell and fell again and went on falling
And falling and always falling.

Out in the open where nothing was left standing
(The immoral equivalent of a forest fire),
I sit with my anger. The creek will move again,
Come rain and snow, gnawing at raw defiles,
Clear-cutting its own gullies.
As selective as reapers stalking through wheatfields,
Selective loggers go where the roots go.

1974

A Young Girl with a Pitcher Full of Water

She carries it unsteadily, warily
Off balance on bare feet across the room,
Believing wholeheartedly in what she carries
And knowing where she is going carefully
Through the narrow doorway into the sunlight,
Holding by handle and lip what she begins
To pour so seriously and slowly now, she leans
That way as if to pour herself. She grows
More and more light. She lightens. She sees it flowing
Away from her to fill her earth to the brim.
Then she stands still, smiling above flowers.

1983

By a Waterfall

Over the sheer stone cliff-face, over springs and star clusters
Of maidenhair giving in and in to the spray
Through thorn-clawed crookshanks
And gnarled root ends like vines where the sun has never from dawn
To noon or dusk come spilling its cascades,
The stream is falling, at the brink
Blue-green but whitening and churning to pale rain
And falling farther, neither as rain nor mist
But both now, pouring

And changing as it must, exchanging all for all over all
Around and past your shape to a dark-green pool
Below, where it tumbles
Over another verge to become a stream once more
Downstream in curving slopes under a constant
Cloud of what it was
And will be, and beside it, sharing the storm of its arrival,
Your voice and all your words are disappearing
Into this water falling.

1996

FRANK O'HARA
1926–1966

Frank O'Hara's strategies as a poet, and as a sponsor of other people's poetry, are summed up in characteristically offhand fashion in the essay "Personism: A Manifesto." He begins by putting poetry in its place as one among many legitimate human amusements. "Too many poets," he protests, "act like a middle-aged mother trying to get her kids to eat too much cooked meat, and potatoes with drippings (tears). I don't give a damn whether they eat or not. Forced feeding leads to excessive thinness (effete). Nobody should experience anything they don't need to, if they don't need poetry bully for them. I like the movies too. And after all, only Whitman and [Hart] Crane and [William Carlos] Williams, of the American poets, are better than the movies." Though it reads like a parody of Charles Olson's manifesto "Projective Verse," O'Hara's essay is illustrated by his own practice. He objects to "abstraction in poetry," which he obliquely defines as the absence of the artist's personal voice or style from his or her work; this is not to be confused with abstractness in painting, because even in the work of abstract expressionists such as Jackson Pollock and Willem de Kooning, one can still feel the presence of a personal style. O'Hara wants poetry to avoid "philosophy," or abstract speculation, but while he is frank about his sexual identity as a gay man, he doesn't opt for "personality or intimacy" either. Once when writing a poem, he says, "I was realizing that if I wanted to I could use the telephone instead of writing the poem" (*Collected Poems,* 1971). This spur-of-the-moment spontaneity pervades his poems and guarantees O'Hara's animating presence in them.

O'Hara was born on June 27, 1926, in Baltimore, Maryland, and grew up in Grafton, a suburb of Worcester, Massachusetts. After serving in the navy during World War II, he received his B.A. from Harvard University, where he helped found the Poets' Theatre, and received his M.A. from the University of Michigan. In 1951, he settled in New York, where he worked for *Art News* and joined the staff of the Museum of Modern Art, eventually becoming associate curator of exhibitions of painting and sculpture. During the 1960s, he became a leading figure in a group of young poets (John Ashbery, Kenneth Koch, and James Schuyler among them) who came to be known as the New York poets. By their own testimony, they derived inspiration from paintings by Pollock, de Kooning, Franz Kline, and others, many of whom were O'Hara's friends. As Schuyler puts it, "New York poets, except I suppose the color blind, are affected most by the floods of paint in whose crashing surf we all scramble. . . . In New York the art world is a painters' world; writers and musicians are in the boat, but they don't steer" (*The*

New American Poetry: 1945–1960, 1960). A direct connection between O'Hara's poetry and the paintings he admired is not obvious, though he says a description in one of his poems was influenced by a de Kooning painting, and his poems, like the paintings, emphasize the process of creation and the materiality of the artistic medium. Some of his poems express a genial appreciation for the neon lights, posters, and other objects that litter the New York landscape (and that received similar attention from the Pop artists). In addition, the dreamlike, irrational sequences of images in some of his poems may have been inspired by surrealist painting and film, the rapid flurry of images dramatizing the dispersal and distraction of postmodern consciousness.

O'Hara's poems are crammed with the discontinuous sights, names, and places of metropolitan experience, traversing media from advertising and film to high art and music, representing encounters with diverse social classes, ethnicities, and nationalities. His "I-do-this I-do-that" poems, such as "The Day Lady Died" and "A Step Away from Them," record in colloquial, sometimes campy, often erudite language the quick turns in the poet's perceptions, showing us what it feels like to live in immediate contact with both the inner and outer worlds. Alert and energetically responsive, the poems stay close to the moment of their inspiration, even narrating the experiences and interruptions that went into their composition. As if mirroring O'Hara's poetics, the personified sun, sounding somewhat like Whitman, instructs the poet in "A True Account of Talking to the Sun at Fire Island": "And / always embrace things, people earth / sky stars, as I do, freely and with / the appropriate sense of space." Yet O'Hara's elegant poems are not purely random in structure; their narrative pacing, for example, is brilliant. The seemingly extraneous details piled one upon another in the "The Day Lady Died," like the poem's paratactic syntax ("and . . . and . . . and"), contribute to the climactic encounter with death at the end, in which the everyday world vanishes and the poet is lost in memory and grief.

O'Hara wrote many of his poems in spare moments snatched from an increasingly busy life in the art world; most were left around his apartment or sent in letters to friends, and the six books of poems he published between 1952 and 1965 gave little idea of his abundance. After O'Hara's death (he was hit by a dune buggy on Fire Island), the editor Donald Allen assembled hundreds of manuscripts to make up O'Hara's *Collected Poems* (1971).

Poem

The eager note on my door said "Call me,
call when you get in!" so I quickly threw
a few tangerines into my overnight bag,
straightened my eyelids and shoulders, and

headed straight for the door. It was autumn
by the time I got around the corner, oh all
unwilling to be either pertinent or bemused, but
the leaves were brighter than grass on the sidewalk!

Funny, I thought, that the lights are on this late
and the hall door open; still up at this hour, a
champion jai-alai player like himself? Oh fie!
for shame! What a host, so zealous! And he was

there in the hall, flat on a sheet of blood that
ran down the stairs. I did appreciate it. There are few
hosts who so thoroughly prepare to greet a guest
only casually invited, and that several months ago.

1952

Poem

At night Chinamen jump
on Asia with a thump

while in our willful way
we, in secret, play

affectionate games and bruise
our knees like China's shoes.

The birds push apples through
grass the moon turns blue,

these apples roll beneath
our buttocks like a heath

full of Chinese thrushes
flushed from China's bushes.

As we love at night
birds sing out of sight,

Chinese rhythms beat
through us in our heat,

the apples and the birds
move us like soft words,

we couple in the grace
of that mysterious race.

1952

Why I Am Not a Painter

I am not a painter, I am a poet.
Why? I think I would rather be
a painter, but I am not. Well,

for instance, Mike Goldberg[1]
is starting a painting. I drop in.
"Sit down and have a drink" he
says. I drink; we drink. I look
up. "You have SARDINES in it."
"Yes, it needed something there."
"Oh." I go and the days go by
and I drop in again. The painting
is going on, and I go, and the days
go by. I drop in. The painting is
finished. "Where's SARDINES?"
All that's left is just
letters, "It was too much," Mike says.

But me? One day I am thinking of
a color: orange. I write a line
about orange. Pretty soon it is a
whole page of words, not lines.
Then another page. There should be
so much more, not of orange, of
words, of how terrible orange is
and life. Days go by. It is even in
prose, I am a real poet. My poem
is finished and I haven't mentioned
orange yet. It's twelve poems, I call
it ORANGES. And one day in a gallery
I see Mike's painting, called SARDINES.

1957

A Step Away from Them

It's my lunch hour, so I go
for a walk among the hum-colored
cabs. First, down the sidewalk
where laborers feed their dirty
glistening torsos sandwiches
and Coca-Cola, with yellow helmets
on. They protect them from falling
bricks, I guess. Then onto the
avenue where skirts are flipping
above heels and blow up over
grates. The sun is hot, but the
cabs stir up the air. I look
at bargains in wristwatches. There
are cats playing in sawdust.
On

1. New York artist (b. 1924), who provided silk-screen prints for O'Hara's *Odes* (1960) and painted *Sardines* (1955).

to Times Square, where the sign
blows smoke over my head,[2] and higher
the waterfall pours lightly. A
Negro stands in a doorway with a
toothpick, languorously agitating.
A blonde chorus girl clicks: he
smiles and rubs his chin. Everything
suddenly honks: it is 12:40 of
a Thursday.
        Neon in daylight is a
great pleasure, as Edwin Denby[3] would
write, as are light bulbs in daylight.
I stop for a cheeseburger at JULIET'S
CORNER. Giulietta Masina, wife of
Federico Fellini, *è bell' attrice*[4]
And chocolate malted. A lady in
foxes on such a day puts her poodle
in a cab.
        There are several Puerto
Ricans on the avenue today, which
makes it beautiful and warm. First
Bunny died, then John Latouche,
then Jackson Pollock.[5] But is the
earth as full as life was full, of them?
And one has eaten and one walks,
past the magazines with nudes
and the posters for BULLFIGHT and
the Manhattan Storage Warehouse,
which they'll soon tear down. I
used to think they had the Armory
Show[6] there.
        A glass of papaya juice
and back to work. My heart is in my
pocket, it is Poems by Pierre Reverdy.[7]

1957

The Day Lady Died

It is 12:20 in New York a Friday
three days after Bastille day,[8] yes
it is 1959 and I go get a shoeshine

2. A famous billboard advertised cigarettes by puffing steam.
3. American poet and dance critic (1903–1983).
4. Is a beautiful actress (Italian). Masina (1920–1994) was married to Italian film director Fellini (1920–1993).
5. American abstract expressionist painter (1912–1956). V. R. "Bunny" Lang (1924–1956): poet and director, who produced several of O'Hara's plays. John Latouche (1917–1956): lyricist. All three were friends of O'Hara's and died tragically.
6. Famous 1913 exhibition that introduced many Americans to modern art.
7. French surrealist poet (1899–1960).
8. July 14, French Independence Day.

because I will get off the 4:19 in Easthampton[9]
at 7:15 and then go straight to dinner
and I don't know the people who will feed me

I walk up the muggy street beginning to sun
and have a hamburger and a malted and buy
an ugly NEW WORLD WRITING to see what the poets
in Ghana are doing these days
I go on to the bank
and Miss Stillwagon (first name Linda I once heard)
doesn't even look up my balance for once in her life
and in the GOLDEN GRIFFIN I get a little Verlaine
for Patsy with drawings by Bonnard[1] although I do
think of Hesiod,[2] trans. Richmond Lattimore or
Brendan Behan's new play[3] or *Le Balcon* or *Les Nègres*
of Genet,[4] but I don't, I stick with Verlaine
after practically going to sleep with quandariness

and for Mike I just stroll into the PARK LANE
Liquor Store and ask for a bottle of Strega and
then I go back where I came from to 6th Avenue
and the tobacconist in the Ziegfeld Theatre and
casually ask for a carton of Gauloises and a carton
of Picayunes, and a NEW YORK POST with her[5] face on it

and I am sweating a lot by now and thinking of
leaning on the john door in the 5 SPOT
while she whispered a song along the keyboard
to Mal Waldron[6] and everyone and I stopped breathing

1964

Rhapsody[7]

515 Madison Avenue[8]
door to heaven? portal
stopped realities and eternal licentiousness
or at least the jungle of impossible eagerness
your marble is bronze and your lianas[9] elevator cables

9. A town on eastern Long Island.
1. An edition of the poems of Paul Verlaine (1844–1896), French poet, with illustrations by Pierre Bonnard (1867–1947).
2. Greek poet (eighth century B.C.E.), author of *Work and Days*.
3. Probably *The Quare Fellow* (1956) or *The Hostage* (1958).
4. Jean Genet (1910–1986), French writer, author of the plays *The Balcony* (1956) and *The Blacks* (1958).
5. Billie Holiday (1915–1959), or "Lady Day," jazz singer.
6. Pianist (died 2002); Billie Holiday's accompanist from 1957 until her death.
7. Also the title of a 1954 movie starring Elizabeth Taylor and John Ericson, alluded to in lines 18–19.
8. "515 is 'off' Madison on 53rd; Frank would have passed it every day to and from the Museum [of Modern Art]. Its door façade is very beautiful" (Bill Berkson, quoted in O'Hara's *Collected Poems*).
9. Climbing plants.

swinging from the myth of ascending
I would join
or declining the challenge of racial attractions
they zing on (into the lynch, dear friends)[1]
while everywhere love is breathing draftily
like a doorway linking 53rd with 54th
the east-bound with the west-bound traffic by 8,000,000s
o midtown tunnels and the tunnels, too, of Holland[2]

where is the summit where all aims are clear
the pin-point light upon a fear of lust
as agony's needlework grows up around the unicorn
and fences him for milk- and yoghurt-work
when I see Gianni[3] I know he's thinking of John Ericson
playing the Rachmaninoff 2nd or Elizabeth Taylor
taking sleeping-pills and Jane thinks of Manderley
and Irkutsk[4] while I cough lightly in the smog of desire
and my eyes water achingly imitating the true blue

a sight of Manahatta[5] in the towering needle
multi-faceted insight of the fly in the stringless labyrinth[6]
Canada plans a higher place than the Empire State Building
I am getting into a cab at 9th Street and 1st Avenue
and the Negro driver tells me about a $120 apartment
"where you can't walk across the floor after 10 at night
not even to pee, cause it keeps them awake downstairs"
no, I don't like that "well, I didn't take it"
perfect in the hot humid morning on my way to work
a little supper-club conversation for the mill of the gods

you were there always and you know all about these things
as indifferent as an encyclopedia with your calm brown eyes
it isn't enough to smile when you run the gauntlet
you've got to spit like Niagara Falls on everybody or
Victoria Falls or at least the beautiful urban fountains of Madrid
as the Niger joins the Gulf of Guinea near the Menemsha Bar[7]
that is what you learned in the early morning passing Madison Avenue
where you've never spent any time and stores eat up light

I have always wanted to be near it
though the day is long (and I don't mean Madison Avenue)

1. Cf. Shakespeare's *Henry V* 3.1.1: "Once more unto the breach, dear friends, once more."
2. The Midtown Tunnel and the Holland Tunnel connect Manhattan respectively with Long Island and New Jersey.
3. Gianni Bates, a pianist and friend of O'Hara's. The movie *Rhapsody* stars Elizabeth Taylor as a beautiful, rich, spoiled woman whose love affair with a talented pianist, played by John Ericson, keeps him from his art. She repents, and at the climax of the movie Ericson gives a triumphant performance of Sergei Rachmaninoff's Second Piano Concerto.
4. City in Russia. Jane Freilicher (b. 1924), New York painter. Manderley is the great house in Daphne du Maurier's novel *Rebecca* (made into a movie by Alfred Hitchcock).
5. Native American name for Manhattan, often used by Walt Whitman.
6. In Greek myth, Theseus rescued Ariadne from the Minotaur's labyrinth by following a string he laid down on the way in.
7. Near the Museum of Modern Art. The river Niger flows through West Africa into the Gulf of Guinea.

lying in a hammock on St. Mark's Place[8] sorting my poems
in the rancid nourishment of this mountainous island
they are coming and we holy ones must go
is Tibet historically a part of China? as I historically
belong to the enormous bliss of American death

1964

A True Account of Talking to the Sun at Fire Island[9]

The Sun woke me this morning loud
and clear, saying "Hey! I've been
trying to wake you up for fifteen
minutes. Don't be so rude, you are
only the second poet I've ever chosen
to speak to personally
so why
aren't you more attentive? If I could
burn you through the window I would
to wake you up. I can't hang around
here all day."
"Sorry, Sun, I stayed
up late last night talking to Hal."

"When I woke up Mayakovsky[1] he was
a lot more prompt" the Sun said
petulantly. "Most people are up
already waiting to see if I'm going
to put in an appearance."
I tried
to apologize "I missed you yesterday."
"That's better" he said. "I didn't
know you'd come out." "You may be
wondering why I've come so close?"
"Yes" I said beginning to feel hot
wondering if maybe he wasn't burning me
anyway.
"Frankly I wanted to tell you
I like your poetry. I see a lot
on my rounds and you're okay. You may
not be the greatest thing on earth, but
you're different. Now, I've heard some
say you're crazy, they being excessively
calm themselves to my mind, and other
crazy poets think that you're a boring
reactionary. Not me.
Just keep on

8. A street on the Lower East Side of New York City.
9. Resort area outside New York City.
1. O'Hara's poem is inspired by "An Extraordinary Adventure which Befell Vladimir Mayakovsky in a Summer Cottage," in which the Russian avant-garde poet (1893–1930) describes his own conversation with the sun.

like I do and pay no attention. You'll
find that people always will complain
about the atmosphere, either too hot
or too cold too bright or too dark, days
too short or too long.
                              If you don't appear
at all one day they think you're lazy
or dead. Just keep right on, I like it.

And don't worry about your lineage
poetic or natural. The Sun shines on
the jungle, you know, on the tundra
the sea, the ghetto. Wherever you were
I knew it and saw you moving. I was waiting
for you to get to work.

                              And now that you
are making your own days, so to speak,
even if no one reads you but me
you won't be depressed. Not
everyone can look up, even at me. It
hurts their eyes."
                    "Oh Sun, I'm so grateful to you!"

"Thanks and remember I'm watching. It's
easier for me to speak to you out
here. I don't have to slide down
between buildings to get your ear.
I know you love Manhattan, but
you ought to look up more often.
                                        And
always embrace things, people earth
sky stars, as I do, freely and with
the appropriate sense of space. That
is your inclination, known in the heavens
and you should follow it to hell, if
necessary, which I doubt.
                              Maybe we'll
speak again in Africa, of which I too
am specially fond. Go back to sleep now
Frank, and I may leave a tiny poem
in that brain of yours as my farewell."

"Sun, don't go!" I was awake
at last. "No, go I must, they're calling
me."
    "Who are they?"
                              Rising he said "Some
day you'll know. They're calling to you
too." Darkly he rose, and then I slept.

1968

Les Luths[2]

Ah nuts! It's boring reading French newspapers
in New York as if I were a Colonial waiting for my gin
somewhere beyond this roof a jet is making a sketch of the sky
where is Gary Snyder[3] I wonder if he's reading under a dwarf pine
stretched out so his book and his head fit under the lowest branch
while the sun of the Orient rolls calmly not getting through to him
not caring particularly because the light in Japan respects poets

while in Paris Monsieur Martory and his brother Jean the poet
are reading a piece by Matthieu Galey and preparing to send a *pneu*[4]
everybody here is running around after dull pleasantries and
wondering if *The Hotel Wentley Poems*[5] is as great as I say it is
and I am feeling particularly testy at being separated from
the one I love by the most dreary of practical exigencies money
when I want only to lean on my elbow and stare into space feeling
the one warm beautiful thing in the world breathing upon my right rib

what are lutes they make ugly twangs and rest on knees in cafés
I want to hear only your light voice running on about Florida
as we pass the changing traffic light and buy grapes for wherever
we will end up praising the mattressless sleigh-bed and the
Mexican egg and the clock that will not make me know how to leave you

1971

2. The lutes (French). In a letter of October 6, 1959, to Pierre Martory (line 8), O'Hara enclosed this poem, saying, "Here is a little poem which you appear in so I am sending it regardless of its soupiness (it was inspired by *Arts* du 16 au 22 Sept which had a picture of a rather boring lute on the back page)."
3. American poet (b. 1930), who was then in Japan.
4. Short for *pneumatique*, a form of rapid communication by which written messages are passed in containers through enclosed pipes by air pressure.
5. First book by Beat poet John Wieners (1934–2002).

Robert Bly
b. 1926

Robert Bly is a prime mover of what came to be known as the Deep Image school, neosurrealists who used images to gain access to unconscious or spiritual levels of experience. Bly speaks of the "underground image"; his poetry can be thought of as an underground or, better, a mystical imagism. In a matter-of-fact tone, shunning grandeur and emphasis, he uses simple diction to describe external landscapes of his beloved, native Minnesota, and landscapes of the mind as well; the objects specified are given a strange, fantastic presentness. The outward and inward aspects of things often coincide, as when, in "Awakening," the poet speaks of "the chestnut blossoms in the mind." This neosurrealism draws on the magical realism of South American poets such as Pablo Neruda; it has connections also with the European poets Federico García Lorca, Georg

Trakl, and Rainer Maria Rilke, as well as the American Wallace Stevens and the Irishman W. B. Yeats, this last poet's work having first impelled Bly to write poetry.

Building visionary poems around the associative processes of the unconscious, Bly has shunned formalism and what he sees as the dry, contrived, cerebral poetry of the American academy. Confessional poetry, such as Robert Lowell's, is too personal to suit his mysticism: "I have risen to a body / Not yet born, / Existing like a light around the body" ("Looking into a Face"). Light and darkness are two versions of the same ultimate reality for Bly, representing a purified, secret existence. The darkness of death is beneficent, and he welcomes what he calls in various poems "the sea of death," "The death we love," and "the black earth of silence." The sense of humanity as grounded, or underground, animates him, in "Evolution from the Fish," to call the human creature "this grandson of fishes," "this nephew of snails."

Bly's poems often begin in a homely setting, such as on a farm or on a trip, into which meaning is infused so that the final effect is surreal. Much of his poetry has a political aspect, especially poems written in the wake of the Vietnam War, but it is politics as William Blake conceived it. Bly made this clear in an essay, "Leaping Up into Political Poetry," in which he states that "the political poem comes out of the deepest privacy." Echoing Yeats's claim that we make out of "the quarrel with ourselves, poetry," Bly writes: "A true political poem is a quarrel with ourselves. . . . The true political poem does not order us either to take any specific acts: like the personal poem, it moves to deepen awareness." Through great leaps of the imagination, the political poet, Bly says in an early version of the essay, "entangles" in language the "half-visible psychic life" of a nation.

Bly was born on December 23, 1926, in Madison, Minnesota. He is of Norwegian descent and remembers it in his verse. He served in the navy during World War II and then entered St. Olaf's College, in Minnesota. After a year, he transferred to Harvard University, from which he graduated in 1950. For several years, he lived in New York, then enrolled in the Writers' Workshop at the University of Iowa before spending a year in Norway. He returned to Minnesota, first living on a farm and then in the small town of Moose Lake, in the eastern part of the state. During the Vietnam War, he was one of the first poet-protesters, founding in 1966 American Writers against the Vietnam War. Earlier, he began to edit a journal called *The Fifties* (later renamed for each successive decade), the purpose of which was to publish new translations. Bly has translated a great number of writers, including not only Neruda, Rilke, and Lorca but also the thirteenth-century Persian-language Sufi poet Jalal al-Din Rumi, whose lyrical intensity is compelling even in translation, and the fifteenth-century Indian mystic Kabir, whose work embodies the "leaps of imagination" Bly has championed. Bly reached his widest audience after the publication of *Iron John: A Book About Men* (1990), which sought to reclaim an archetypal masculinity of wisdom, strength, and courage.

Johnson's Cabinet[1] Watched by Ants

I

It is a clearing deep in a forest: overhanging boughs
Make a low place. Here the citizens we know during the day,
The ministers, the department heads,

1. Presidential cabinet of Lyndon B. Johnson (1908–1973).

Appear changed: the stockholders of large steel companies
In small wooden shoes: here are the generals dressed as gamboling lambs.

II

Tonight they burn the rice-supplies; tomorrow
They lecture on Thoreau;[2] tonight they move around the trees;
Tomorrow they pick the twigs from their clothes;
Tonight they throw the firebombs; tomorrow
They read the Declaration of Independence; tomorrow they are in church.

III

Ants are gathered around an old tree.
In a choir they sing, in harsh and gravelly voices,
Old Etruscan[3] songs on tyranny.
Toads nearby clap their small hands, and join
The fiery songs, their five long toes trembling in the soaked earth.

1967

The Great Society[4]

Dentists continue to water their lawns even in the rain;
Hands developed with terrible labor by apes
Hang from the sleeves of evangelists;
There are murdered kings in the light-bulbs outside movie theaters;
The coffins of the poor are hibernating in piles of new tires.

The janitor sits troubled by the boiler,
And the hotel keeper shuffles the cards of insanity.
The President dreams of invading Cuba.
Bushes are growing over the outdoor grills,
Vines over the yachts and the leather seats.

The city broods over ash cans and darkening mortar.
On the far shore, at Coney Island,[5] dark children
Play on the chilling beach: a sprig of black seaweed,
Shells, a skyful of birds,
While the mayor sits with his head in his hands.

1967

2. Henry David Thoreau (1817–1862), American philosopher and essayist.
3. An early Italian people who preceded the Romans.
4. The keynote slogan of Lyndon B. Johnson's presidential campaign in 1964.
5. Part of New York City.

My Father's Wedding

1924

Today, lonely for my father, I saw
a log, or branch,
long, bent, ragged, bark gone.
I felt lonely for my father when I saw it.
It was the log
that lay near my uncle's old milk wagon.

Some men live with a limp they don't hide,
stagger, or drag
a leg. Their sons often are angry.
Only recently I thought:
Doing what you want . . .
Is that like limping? Tracks of it show in sand.

Have you seen those giant bird-
men of Bhutan?[6]
Men in bird masks, with pig noses, dancing,
teeth like a dog's, sometimes
dancing on one bad leg!
They do what they want, the dog's teeth say that.

But I grew up without dog's teeth,
showed a whole body,
left only clear tracks in sand.
I learned to walk swiftly, easily,
no trace of a limp.
I even leaped a little. Guess where my defect is!

Then what? If a man, cautious,
hides his limp,
somebody has to limp it. Things
do it; the surroundings limp.
House walls get scars,
the car breaks down; matter, in drudgery, takes it up.

On my father's wedding day,
no one was there
to hold him. Noble loneliness
held him. Since he never asked for pity
his friends thought he
was whole. Walking alone he could carry it.

He came in limping. It was a simple
wedding, three
or four people. The man in black,
lifting the book, called for order.

6. Country between Tibet and India.

And the invisible bride
stepped forward, before his own bride.

He married the invisible bride, not his own.
In her left
breast she carried the three drops
that wound and kill. He already had
his bark-like skin then,
made rough especially to repel the sympathy

he longed for, didn't need, and wouldn't accept.
So the Bible's
words are read. The man in black
speaks the sentence. When the service
is over, I hold him
in my arms for the first time and the last.

After that he was alone
and I was alone.
Few friends came; he invited few.
His two-story house he turned
into a forest,
where both he and I are the hunters.

1981

Kneeling Down to Peer into a Culvert[7]

I kneel down to peer into a culvert.
The other end seems far away.
One cone of light floats in the shadowed water.
This is how our children will look when we are dead.

I kneel near floating shadowy water.
On my knees, I am half inside the tunnel—
blue sky widens the far end—
darkened by the shadowy insides of the steel.

Are they all born? I walk on farther;
out in the plowing I see a lake newly made.
I have seen this lake before. . . . It is a lake
I return to each time my children are grown.

I have fathered so many children and returned
to that lake—grayish flat slate banks,
low arctic bushes. I am a water-serpent throwing water drops
off my head. My gray loops trail behind me.

How long I live there alone! For a thousand years
I am alone, with no duties, living as I live.

7. Drain under a road.

Then one morning a head like mine pokes from the water.
I fight—it's time, it's right—and am torn to pieces fighting.

1981

A Week after Your Death

I dreamt last night you
Lived nearby, not
Dead at all, but safe
In a blacksmith's storage room,
With bolts and nails in bins
From floor to ceiling.

You came and brought me
An ivory jar,
Holding a precious fluid,
Which I took. I knew it meant
The time had come,
But I let you leave.

Later a man pushed open
The door and threw
Your body down, a wizened,
Astonishingly small body—
Rope still tied
Around the neck.

I woke and cried to my wife:
"He didn't die
That way! There was no rope!
All that is wrong!" She
Said, "In
Your dream he did."

1994

CHARLES TOMLINSON
b. 1927

Charles Tomlinson read his poem "Swimming Chenango Lake" at a Phi Beta Kappa celebration, and some remarks he made on that occasion are relevant to much of his other work: "The poem tries to celebrate the fact that the help we gain from alien phenomena—even from water, in which (after all) we can't live—the help is towards relation, towards grasp, towards awareness of all that which we are not, yet of relationship with it. It is a help that teaches us not to try merely to reduce objects to our own image, but to respect their otherness and yet find our way into contact with that otherness" (*The Poem as Initiation*). Tomlinson's relationship with the objects and atmospheres he writes about is urgent but respectful. As he writes in "Poem": "this script that untangles itself / out of wind, briars, stars unseen, / keeps telling me what I mean / is theirs, not mine." A poet of exquisite clarity and detachment, he wishes to suppress "the preconceptions of the too conscious mind" (*Eden*) and admires in the painter Paul Cézanne "the entire absence of self-regard." "You cease to impose and you discover," he says in an intentional echo of Wallace Stevens. He quotes the phenomenologist Maurice Merleau-Ponty: "Things have an internal equivalent in me; they arouse in me a carnal formula of their presence." Some of his best poems are about the people and landscapes of the United States; they develop an exciting relationship with phenomena that have at the start for Tomlinson an impervious foreignness.

He began as a painter, and his first experiments in writing were film scripts. An early influence was the nineteenth-century writer John Ruskin, who fostered Tomlinson's interest in pictorial surfaces, in details that change with every slight readjustment of perspective. Tomlinson's respect for the integrity of the environment explains his rejection of the apocalyptic ideas of Dylan Thomas. Tomlinson did not want everything outside the poet swallowed up and converted into a single vision. Instead of large declarations he wanted precise interrelationships. As an alternative to Thomas, Tomlinson turned to American models—Stevens, Marianne Moore, and Elizabeth Bishop. The Objectivists Louis Zukofsky, George Oppen, and William Carlos Williams also became influences. "One of the destined themes of future British poetry," he says, "will be something in the nature of a dialogue with the spirit of the United States." His sense of nature's "otherness" owes something to the English tradition of Thomas Hardy, though where Hardy tends to find a grim neutrality Tomlinson emphasizes "the paradisal aspect of the visual" (*Eden*).

Tomlinson was born on January 8, 1927, in Stoke-on-Trent, England. In 1948, he received his B.A. from Queen's College, Cambridge, where he studied with Donald Davie. During the next few years, he taught in a London elementary school and was a private secretary in northern Italy. He then resumed his studies at the University of London, from which he received an M.A. in 1955. From 1957 until his retirement, he taught English literature at the University of Bristol. He came to the United States as a visiting professor at several universities. Besides many books of verse, the earliest dating from 1951, Tomlinson has published critical essays and translations of poems of Fyodor Tyutchev, Antonio Machado y Ruiz, César Vallejo, and Octavio Paz.

Cézanne at Aix[1]

And the mountain: each day
Immobile like fruit. Unlike, also
—Because irreducible, because
Neither a component of the delicious
And therefore questionable,
Nor distracted (as the sitter)
By his own pose and, therefore,
Doubly to be questioned: it is not
Posed. It is. Untaught
Unalterable, a stone bridgehead

1. French Postimpressionist painter Paul Cézanne (1839–1906) spent much of his life in Aix-en-Provence, a city in southern France, where he painted his famous landscapes of Mt. Saint-Victoire.

To that which is tangible
Because unfelt before. There
In its weathered weight
Its silence silences, a presence
Which does not present itself.

1958

Mr Brodsky

I had heard
before, of an
American who would have preferred
to be an Indian;
but not
until Mr Brodsky, of one
whose professed and long
pondered-on passion
was to become a Scot,
who even sent for haggis and oatcakes[2]
across continent.
Having read him
in Cambridge English
a verse or two
from McDiarmid,[3]
I was invited
to repeat the reading
before a Burns Night Gathering[4]
where the Balmoral Pipers
of Albuquerque would
play in the haggis
out of its New York tin.
Of course, I said
No. No. I could *not* go
and then
half-regretted I had not been.
But to console
and cure the wish, came
Mr Brodsky, bringing
his pipes and played
until the immense, distended
bladder of leather seemed
it could barely contain its water—
tears (idle
tears)[5] for the bridal of Annie Laurie

2. Scottish foods, the former a mixture of herbs, oatmeal, and a sheep's internal organs cooked in its stomach. At a Scottish banquet, the haggis was ceremonially brought to the table to the accompaniment of bagpipes (lines 19–22).
3. Hugh MacDiarmid (1892–1978), Scottish poet.
4. Meetings of devotees of Scottish culture are often called Burns Nights, after the Scottish poet Robert Burns (1759–1796).
5. The first words of a song from the narrative poem "The Princess," by Alfred, Lord Tennyson (1809–1892).

and Morton J. Brodsky.
A bagpipe in a dwelling is
a resonant instrument
and there he stood
lost in the gorse
the heather or whatever
six thousand
miles and more
from the infection's source,
in our neo–New Mexican parlour
where I had heard
before of an
American who would have preferred
to be merely an Indian.

1966

Two Views of Two Ghost Towns

I

Why speak of memory and death
on ghost ground? Absences
relieve, release. Speak
of the life that uselessness
has unconstrained. Rusting
to its rails, the vast obese
company engine that will draw
no more, will draw no more:
Keep Off
the warning says, and all
the mob of objects, freed
under the brightly hard
displacement of the desert light
repeat it: the unaxled wheels,
doorless doors and windowless
regard of space. Clear
of the weight of human
meanings, human need,
gradually
houses splinter to the ground
in white and red, two
rotting parallels beneath
the sombre slag-mound.

II

How dry the ghosts
of dryness are. The air
here, tastes of sparseness
and the graveyard stones

are undecorated. To the left
the sea and, right, the shadows
hump and slide, climbing
the mountainside as clouds go over.
The town has moved away,
leaving a bitten hill
where the minehead's visible. Brambles
detain the foot. Ketchum,
Clay, Shoemake, Jebez O'Haskill
and Judge H. Vennigerholz
all (save for the judge's
modest obelisk) marked
by a metal cross; and there are four
crosses of wood, three
wooden stakes (unnamed)
that the sun, the frost, the sea-
wind shred alternately
in sapless scars. How dry
the ghosts of dryness are.

1966

Swimming Chenango Lake[6]

Winter will bar the swimmer soon.
He reads the water's autumnal hesitations
A wealth of ways: it is jarred,
It is astir already despite its steadiness,
Where the first leaves at the first
Tremor of the morning air have dropped
Anticipating him, launching their imprints
Outwards in eccentric, overlapping circles.
There is a geometry of water, for this
Squares off the clouds' redundances
And sets them floating in a nether atmosphere
All angles and elongations: every tree
Appears a cypress as it stretches there
And every bush that shows the season,
A shaft of fire. It is a geometry and not
A fantasia of distorting forms, but each
Liquid variation answerable to the theme
It makes away from, plays before:
It is a consistency, the grain of the pulsating flow.

6. A lake near the campus of Colgate University, where Tomlinson taught in 1967. In his discussion of this poem, Tomlinson cites Claude Levi-Strauss's anthropological study *The Savage Mind*: "Now, the Pawnee Indians have a ceremony called the Hako, for the crossing of a stream. A poetic invocation is the essence of this ceremony. The invocation is divided, we are told, 'into several parts which correspond respectively to the moment when the travelers put their feet in water, the moment when they move them and the moment when the water completely covers their feet.' All these stages are celebrated and differentiated. I borrow this instance of the crossing of the water because it seems to correspond with the way of working of a poem like 'Swimming Chenango Lake' " (*The Poem as Initiation*, 1968).

But he has looked long enough, and now
Body must recall the eye to its dependence
As he scissors the waterscape apart
And sways it to tatters. Its coldness
Holding him to itself, he grants the grasp,
For to swim is also to take hold
On water's meaning, to move in its embrace
And to be, between grasp and grasping, free.
He reaches in-and-through to that space
The body is heir to, making a where
In water, a possession to be relinquished
Willingly at each stroke. The image he has torn
Flows-to behind him, healing itself,
Lifting and lengthening, splayed like the feathers
Down an immense wing whose darkened spread
Shadows his solitariness: alone, he is unnamed
By this baptism, where only Chenango bears a name
In a lost language he begins to construe—
A speech of densities and derisions, of half-
Replies to the questions his body must frame
Frogwise across the all but penetrable element.
Human, he fronts it and, human, he draws back
From the interior cold, the mercilessness
That yet shows a kind of mercy sustaining him.
The last sun of the year is drying his skin
Above a surface a mere mosaic of tiny shatterings,
Where a wind is unscaping[7] all images in the flowing obsidian,
The going-elsewhere of ripples incessantly shaping.

1968

Snapshot

for Yoshikazu Uehata

Your camera
has caught it all, the lit
angle where ceiling and wall
create their corner, the flame
in the grate, the light
down the window frame
and along the hair
of the girl seated there, her face
not quite in focus—that
is as it should be, too,
for, once seen, Eden
is in flight from you, and yet

7. That is, unlandscaping or unseascaping (Tomlinson's invention).

you have set it down complete
with the asymmetries
of journal, cushion, cup,
all we might then have missed
in that gone moment when
we were living it.

1995

Galway Kinnell
b. 1927

Galway Kinnell is one of those postwar poets who, like Robert Lowell, began his career writing in traditional forms and suddenly felt compelled to find looser ones. Under Walt Whitman's influence, Kinnell learned to shrug off regular meters, capture strong cadences, repeat, chant responsively to the world, and extend his lines, which sometimes vary wildly in length. The compulsion to strip away civilizing norms and dwell in the rough of nature is already evident in such neatly rhymed poems as "First Song," in which a boy's "first song of his happiness" awakens his "heart to the darkness and into the sadness of joy." For Kinnell, poetry is about the "sadness of joy," about the deaths and losses that haunt happiness. Even so, his many elegiac poems for dead family members and friends often convey, paradoxically, physical exuberance and strength. In "On the Oregon Coast," he dryly mentions in one line the recent deaths of two fellow poets, and in the next he recovers something of the wild power and recursive movement of the ocean: "James Wright went back to the end. So did Richard Hugo. / The waves coming in burst up through their crests and fly very brilliant back out to sea. / The log gets up yet again, goes rolling and bouncing down the beach, plunges as though for good into the water." Loss continually reawakens Kinnell to the world's vitality. The earthy pleasures of sex, love, and family life are also among his subjects, and he engages domestic themes with tenderness and humor in "After Making Love We Hear Footsteps."

Kinnell was born on February 1, 1927, in Providence, Rhode Island, the son of immigrants from Ireland (his mother) and Scotland (his father). After serving in the navy during World War II, he received a B.A. at Princeton University, where he exchanged poetry with his contemporary W. S. Merwin, and an M.A. at the University of Rochester; but the process of writing poetry has been for him largely a process of de-educating himself, so as to come closer to a world whose existence he at first only suspected. In the 1960s, he took odd jobs, worked as a member of CORE (Congress of Racial Equality) to register southern black voters, and demonstrated against the Vietnam War. He has taught at more than twenty colleges and universities in the United States and other parts of the world; since 1981, at New York University. His poetry has won various awards, among them the Pulitzer Prize for *Selected Poems* (1983). In 1984, he received a MacArthur Fellowship.

First Song

Then it was dusk in Illinois, the small boy
After an afternoon of carting dung
Hung on the rail fence, a sapped thing
Weary to crying. Dark was growing tall
And he began to hear the pond frogs all
Calling on his ear with what seemed their joy.

Soon their sound was pleasant for a boy
Listening in the smoky dusk and the nightfall
Of Illinois, and from the fields two small
Boys came bearing cornstalk violins
And they rubbed the cornstalk bows with resins
And the three sat there scraping of their joy.

It was now fine music the frogs and the boys
Did in the towering Illinois twilight make
And into dark in spite of a shoulder's ache
A boy's hunched body loved out of a stalk
The first song of his happiness, and the song woke
His heart to the darkness and into the sadness of joy.

1960

After Making Love We Hear Footsteps

For I can snore like a bullhorn
or play loud music
or sit up talking with any reasonably sober Irishman
and Fergus will only sink deeper
into his dreamless sleep, which goes by all in one flash,
but let there be that heavy breathing
or a stifled come-cry anywhere in the house
and he will wrench himself awake
and make for it on the run—as now, we lie together,
after making love, quiet, touching along the length of our bodies,
familiar touch of the long-married,
and he appears—in his baseball pajamas, it happens,
the neck opening so small
he has to screw them on, which one day may make him wonder
about the mental capacity of baseball players—
and flops down between us and hugs us and snuggles himself to sleep,
his face gleaming with satisfaction at being this very child.

In the half darkness we look at each other
and smile
and touch arms across his little, startlingly muscled body—
this one whom habit of memory propels to the ground of his making,

sleeper only the mortal sounds can sing awake,
this blessing love gives again into our arms.

1980

On the Oregon Coast

In memoriam Richard Hugo[1]

Six or seven rows of waves struggle landward.
The wind batters a pewtery sheen on the water between them.
As each wave makes its way in, most of it gets blown back out to sea, subverting even necessity.
The bass rumble of sea stones, audible when the waves flee all broken back out to sea, itself blows out to sea.
Now a log maybe thirty feet long and six across gets up and trundles down the beach.
Like a dog fetching a stick it flops unhesitatingly into the water.
An enormous wave at once sends it wallowing back up the beach again.
It lies among other driftwood, almost panting. Sure enough, after a few minutes it gets up, trundles down the beach, throws itself into the water again.
The last time I was on this coast Richard Hugo and I had dinner together just north of here, in a restaurant overlooking the sea.
The conversation came around to personification.
We agreed that eighteenth- and nineteenth-century poets almost *had* to personify, it was like mouth-to-mouth resuscitation, the only way they could imagine to keep the world from turning into dead matter.
And that as post-Darwinians[2] it was up to us to anthropomorphize the world less and animalize, vegetable-ize, and mineralize ourselves more.
We doubted that pre-Darwinian language would let us.
Our talk turned to James Wright,[3] how his kinship with salamanders, spiders, and mosquitoes allowed him to drift his way back through the evolutionary stages.
When a group of people gets up from a table, the table doesn't know which way any of them will go.
James Wright went back to the end. So did Richard Hugo.
The waves coming in burst up through their crests and fly very brilliant back out to sea.
The log gets up yet again, goes rolling and bouncing down the beach, plunges as though for good into the water.

1985

1. American poet (1923–1982).
2. That is, after Charles Darwin (1809–1882), the naturalist responsible for the theory of evolution.
3. American poet (1927–1980).

Sheffield Ghazal[4] 4: Driving West

A tractor-trailer carrying two dozen crushed automobiles overtakes a
 tractor-trailer carrying a dozen new.
Oil is a form of waiting.
The internal combustion engine converts the stasis of millennia into
 motion.
Cars howl on rain-wetted roads.
Airplanes rise through the downpour and throw us through the blue
 sky.
The idea of the airplane subverts earthly life.
Computers can deliver nuclear explosions to precisely anywhere on
 earth.
A lightning bolt is made entirely of error.
Erratic Mercurys and errant Cavaliers wander the highways.
A girl puts her head on a boy's shoulder; they are driving west.
The windshield wipers wipe, homesickness one way, wanderlust the
 other, back and forth.
This happened to your father and to you, Galway—sick to stay, longing
 to come up against the ends of the earth, and climb over.

1994

4. Lyric genre of Persian and Arabic poetry dating back to the seventh century. Among its requirements are thematic discontinuity and the appearance of the poet's name in the penultimate line.

JOHN ASHBERY
b. 1927

John Ashbery, once set aside as bizarre, is one of the central American poets of the latter half of the twentieth century. Perhaps no postwar writer has influenced so many different kinds of poets, whether identified with formalism or antiformalism, with neo-confessionalism or the avant-garde. His work is written in seemingly antithetical modes, from fragmentary free verse and prose poetry to traditional verse forms such as sonnets, sestinas, and blank verse. It spans a variety of styles, from the early, collage-based experimentalism of *The Tennis Court Oath* (1962) to the poignant lyricism of his middle work. Ashbery had many associations with the New York school, especially with Kenneth Koch and Frank O'Hara (whom he met at Harvard University), and he uses equally wild and witty imagery. Because of his exploration of inner experience, Ashbery has also been linked with the Romantic tradition, from Percy Bysshe Shelley to Wallace Stevens. Because of his poetics of collage, multiple identities, and verbal games, he has been seen, too, as an important precursor to Language poets such as Charles Bernstein. And yet, for all these associations, Ashbery has a unique manner—characteristically mixing surrealist tomfoolery and elegant reserve—that is convincing, though one cannot always fathom what one is being convinced of. Often, Ashbery appears to be writing on the basis of postulates that are firm but never divulged. A dreamlike quality ensues, and Ashbery would like to "reproduce the power dreams have of persuading you that a certain event has a meaning not logically connected with it, or that there is a hidden relation among disparate objects" (quoted in Richard Howard, *Alone with America*). The strangeness and authority of his poetry have drawn readers despite the hiddenness of many of its relations.

In Ashbery's poetry, the self is elusive, multiple, and fractious, shot through with competing discourses, always dissolving into the past and into parody. Similarly, the so-called real world is forever mutating and slipping away, receding from view, vanishing into hints and reflections. Ashbery responds to this postmodern condition of flux and disjunctiveness with a mixture of elegiac pathos and whimsical pleasure. As he suggests in "Soonest Mended," his poetics is "a kind of fence-sitting / Raised to the level of an esthetic ideal." His poems mourn various losses while romping riotously in free associations. They walk the knife's edge between the personal and the impersonal, evoking both inner experience and yet also a strange objectification of subjectivity, often disguising, abstracting, or fragmenting the autobiographical subject. "Most of my poems are about the experience of experience," Ashbery said in a 1981 interview. "I'm trying to set down a generalized transcript of what's really going on in our minds all day long."

Ashbery's poems are resolutely contrary to fact or tangential to it. "Worsening Situation" ends: "My wife / Thinks I'm in Oslo—Oslo, France, that is." Since there is no Oslo, France, the speaker's wife is twice deluded. But delusion and imagination go together. In a more accessible poem, "The Instruction Manual," the poet procrastinates by conjuring up a journey to Guadalajara, which he describes like some archetypal traveler, although he admits he has never been there. Ashbery presents reality as do some modern painters, organizing details to create nature rather than to imitate it. Old bonding techniques between people, their surroundings, and divinity no longer work. "You can't say it that way any more," he declares in "And *Ut Pictura Poesis* Is Her Name." Sometimes, as with action painters, the process of poeticizing obsesses him; he describes it amusingly yet seriously too in the same poem: "The extreme austerity of an almost empty mind / Colliding with the lush, Rousseau-like foliage of its desire to communicate / Something between breaths." In "What Is Poetry," he asks whether poetry is beautiful images, or the attempt "to avoid / Ideas, as in this poem." Or do we "Go back to them as to a wife, leaving / The mistress we desire?" The series of questions is never answered, but his poems do have ideas as well as images, though these ideas are given provisional status only, dependent on a reality that resists summary and analysis. He is endlessly resourceful in propounding this dilemma. In "Self-Portrait in a Convex Mirror," a masterpiece based on a painting by Parmigianino, Ashbery plays with the distorting effect of such a mirror held up to nature. He seems to defend his own work when he says, "But your eyes proclaim / That everything is surface. The surface is what's there / And nothing can exist except what's there." Then he adds, "it is not / Superficial but a visible core."

Sequence and causality are both in jeopardy in Ashbery's work; he is fond of unexpected juxtapositions, such as of the divine sepulcher and Cohen's Drug Store. Sentences fragment or run on, narrative proceeds by non sequiturs, and pronouns ambiguously crisscross. Images and ideas melt into one another. Contemporary jargons of business, journalism, bureaucracy, and advertising are absorbed and parodied. Levels of diction are manipulated along with places. Clichés are echoed and transformed. Ashbery seems to ask his readers to put aside their presuppositions about reading and about experiencing, and instead to observe collisions of images and ideas without asking for logical paraphrases. The tenor of his work is "pure / Affirmation that doesn't affirm anything" ("Self-Portrait in a Convex Mirror"). The world is strange, opaque, and mercurial. Wit and circumspection are the means to write about it.

Ashbery was born on July 28, 1927, in Rochester, New York, and grew up on a fruit farm in upstate New York near Lake Ontario. He received his B.A. from Harvard University in 1949 with a thesis on W. H. Auden, who chose and introduced Ashbery's first book, *Some Trees,* for the Yale Series of Younger Poets in 1956. In 1951, Ashbery completed an M.A. thesis at Columbia University on Henry Green, the witty, impersonal English novelist. During the Korean War, he was exempted from military service only after going on government record as a homosexual. Ashbery found the McCarthy era frightening and depressing; he went to France as a Fulbright Scholar (1955–57) and embarked on a book on Raymond Roussel, a writer who declared his books had been composed not out of experience but out of verbal games. Ashbery returned to France in 1958 and stayed until 1965, writing art criticism for the European edition of the *New York Herald Tribune* and for *Art News.* Returning to New York in 1965, he edited *Art News* until 1972, and he was later the art critic for *Newsweek.* He taught at Brooklyn College from 1974 to 1990 and, since 1990, has taught at Bard College. Among the many books he has published and the many awards he has received, *Self-Portrait in a Convex Mirror* notably won the three major poetry prizes of 1976—the Pulitzer Prize, the National Book Award, and the National Book Critics Circle Award.

Though many literary predecessors have been proposed for him, Ashbery has cited the early Auden, Laura Riding, and Wallace Stevens as "the writers who most formed my language as a poet" (quoted in *The New York School Poets,* ed. John Bernard Myers, 1969). To be tough, incisive, and mellifluous was perhaps the lesson he derived from these three writers. The musical aspect of his verse has always been important to him: "What I like about music is its ability of being convincing, of carrying an argument through successfully to the finish, though the terms of this argument remain unknown quantities. What remains is the structure, the architecture of the argument, scene or story. I would like to do this in poetry" (biographical note in *A Controversy of Poets,* 1965).

Some Trees

These are amazing: each
Joining a neighbor, as though speech
Were a still performance.
Arranging by chance

To meet as far this morning
From the world as agreeing
With it, you and I
Are suddenly what the trees try

To tell us we are:
That their merely being there
Means something; that soon
We may touch, love, explain.

And glad not to have invented
Such comeliness, we are surrounded:
A silence already filled with noises,
A canvas on which emerges

A chorus of smiles, a winter morning.
Placed in a puzzling light, and moving,
Our days put on such reticence
These accents seem their own defense.

1956

The Instruction Manual

As I sit looking out of a window of the building
I wish I did not have to write the instruction manual on the uses of a new metal.
I look down into the street and see people, each walking with an inner peace,
And envy them—they are so far away from me!
Not one of them has to worry about getting out this manual on schedule.
And, as my way is, I begin to dream, resting my elbows on the desk and leaning out of the window a little,
Of dim Guadalajara! City of rose-colored flowers!
City I wanted most to see, and most did not see, in Mexico!
But I fancy I see, under the press of having to write the instruction manual,
Your public square, city, with its elaborate little bandstand!
The band is playing *Scheherazade* by Rimsky-Korsakov.[1]
Around stand the flower girls, handing out rose- and lemon-colored flowers,
Each attractive in her rose-and-blue striped dress (Oh! such shades of rose and blue),
And nearby is the little white booth where women in green serve you green and yellow fruit.
The couples are parading; everyone is in a holiday mood.
First, leading the parade, is a dapper fellow
Clothed in deep blue. On his head sits a white hat
And he wears a mustache, which has been trimmed for the occasion.
His dear one, his wife, is young and pretty; her shawl is rose, pink, and white.
Her slippers are patent leather, in the American fashion,
And she carries a fan, for she is modest, and does not want the crowd to see her face too often.
But everybody is so busy with his wife or loved one
I doubt they would notice the mustachioed man's wife.
Here come the boys! They are skipping and throwing little things on the sidewalk
Which is made of gray tile. One of them, a little older, has a toothpick in his teeth.
He is silenter than the rest, and affects not to notice the pretty young girls in white.
But his friends notice them, and shout their jeers at the laughing girls.

1. Russian composer (1844–1908).

Yet soon all this will cease, with the deepening of their years,
And love bring each to the parade grounds for another reason.
But I have lost sight of the young fellow with the toothpick.
Wait—there he is—on the other side of the bandstand,
Secluded from his friends, in earnest talk with a young girl
Of fourteen or fifteen. I try to hear what they are saying
But it seems they are just mumbling something—shy words of love, probably.
She is slightly taller than he, and looks quietly down into his sincere eyes.
She is wearing white. The breeze ruffles her long fine black hair against her olive cheek.
Obviously she is in love. The boy, the young boy with the toothpick, he is in love too;
His eyes show it. Turning from this couple,
I see there is an intermission in the concert.
The paraders are resting and sipping drinks through straws
(The drinks are dispensed from a large glass crock by a lady in dark blue),
And the musicians mingle among them, in their creamy white uniforms, and talk
About the weather, perhaps, or how their kids are doing at school.

Let us take this opportunity to tiptoe into one of the side streets.
Here you may see one of those white houses with green trim
That are so popular here. Look—I told you!
It is cool and dim inside, but the patio is sunny.
An old woman in gray sits there, fanning herself with a palm leaf fan.
She welcomes us to her patio, and offers us a cooling drink.
"My son is in Mexico City," she says. "He would welcome you too
If he were here. But his job is with a bank there.
Look, here is a photograph of him."
And a dark-skinned lad with pearly teeth grins out at us from the worn leather frame.
We thank her for her hospitality, for it is getting late
And we must catch a view of the city, before we leave, from a good high place.
That church tower will do—the faded pink one, there against the fierce blue of the sky. Slowly we enter.
The caretaker, an old man dressed in brown and gray, asks us how long we have been in the city, and how we like it here.
His daughter is scrubbing the steps—she nods to us as we pass into the tower.
Soon we have reached the top, and the whole network of the city extends before us.
There is the rich quarter, with its houses of pink and white, and its crumbling, leafy terraces.
There is the poorer quarter, its homes a deep blue.
There is the market, where men are selling hats and swatting flies
And there is the public library, painted several shades of pale green and beige.
Look! There is the square we just came from, with the promenaders.
There are fewer of them, now that the heat of the day has increased,
But the young boy and girl still lurk in the shadows of the bandstand.

And there is the home of the little old lady—
She is still sitting in the patio, fanning herself.
How limited, but how complete withal, has been our experience of
Guadalajara!
We have seen young love, married love, and the love of an aged mother
for her son.
We have heard the music, tasted the drinks, and looked at colored houses.
What more is there to do, except stay? And that we cannot do.
And as a last breeze freshens the top of the weathered old tower, I turn
my gaze
Back to the instruction manual which has made me dream of Guadalajara.

1956

The Tennis Court Oath[2]

What had you been thinking about
the face studiously bloodied
heaven blotted region
I go on loving you like water but
there is a terrible breath in the way all of this
You were not elected president, yet won the race
All the way through fog and drizzle
When you read it was sincere the coasts
stammered with unintentional villages the
horse strains fatigued I guess . . . the calls . . .
I worry

the water beetle head
why of course reflecting all
then you redid you were breathing
I thought going down to mail this
of the kettle you jabbered as easily in the yard
you come through but
are incomparable the lovely tent
mystery you don't want surrounded the real
you dance
in the spring there was clouds

The mulatress[3] approached in the hall—the
lettering easily visible along the edge of the *Times*
in a moment the bell would ring but there was time
for the carnation laughed here are a couple of "other"

to one in yon house

2. During the first days of the French Revolution, on June 20, 1789, the commoners (Third Estate) were barred from a regular meeting of the Estates General. They retired to a nearby indoor tennis court and took an oath to stand together until the Constitution was reformed. The oath is the subject of a painting by French painter Jacques-Louis David (1748–1825).

3. Female mulatto (person of mixed white and black ancestry).

The doctor and Philip had come over the road
Turning in toward the corner of the wall his hat on
reading it carelessly as if to tell you your fears were justified
the blood shifted you know those walls
wind off the earth had made him shrink
undeniably an oboe now the young
were there there was candy
to decide the sharp edge of the garment
like a particular cry not intervening called the dog "he's coming! he's
 coming" with an emotion felt it sink into peace
there was no turning back but the end was in sight
he chose this moment to ask her in detail about her family and the
 others
The person. pleaded—"have more of these
not stripes on the tunic—or the porch chairs
will teach you about men—what it means"
to be one in a million pink stripe
and now could go away the three approached the doghouse
the reef. Your daughter's
dream of my son understand prejudice
darkness in the hole
the patient finished
They could all go home now the hole was dark
lilacs blowing across his face glad he brought you

1962

These Lacustrine[4] Cities

These lacustrine cities grew out of loathing
Into something forgetful, although angry with history.
They are the product of an idea : that man is horrible, for instance,
Though this is only one example.

They emerged until a tower
Controlled the sky, and with artifice dipped back
Into the past for swans and tapering branches,
Burning, until all that hate was transformed into useless love.

Then you are left with an idea of yourself
And the feeling of ascending emptiness of the afternoon
Which must be charged to the embarrassment of others
Who fly by you like beacons.

The night is a sentinel.
Much of your time has been occupied by creative games
Until now, but we have all-inclusive plans for you.
We had thought, for instance, of sending you to the middle of the desert,

4. Having to do with lakes.

To a violent sea, or of having the closeness of the others be air
To you, pressing you back into a startled dream
As sea-breezes greet a child's face.
But the past is already here, and you are nursing some private project.

The worst is not over, yet I know
You will be happy here. Because of the logic
Of your situation, which is something no climate can outsmart.
Tender and insouciant by turns, you see

You have built a mountain of something,
Thoughtfully pouring all your energy into this single monument,
Whose wind is desire starching a petal,
Whose disappointment broke into a rainbow of tears.

1966

Soonest Mended[5]

Barely tolerated, living on the margin
In our technological society, we were always having to be rescued
On the brink of destruction, like heroines in *Orlando Furioso*
Before it was time to start all over again.
There would be thunder in the bushes, a rustling of coils,
And Angelica, in the Ingres painting,[6] was considering
The colorful but small monster near her toe, as though wondering whether forgetting
The whole thing might not, in the end, be the only solution.
And then there always came a time when
Happy Hooligan[7] in his rusted green automobile
Came plowing down the course, just to make sure everything was O.K.,
Only by that time we were in another chapter and confused
About how to receive this latest piece of information.
Was it information? Weren't we rather acting this out
For someone else's benefit, thoughts in a mind
With room enough and to spare for our little problems (so they began to seem),
Our daily quandary about food and the rent and bills to be paid?
To reduce all this to a small variant,
To step free at last, minuscule on the gigantic plateau—
This was our ambition: to be small and clear and free.
Alas, the summer's energy wanes quickly,
A moment and it is gone. And no longer
May we make the necessary arrangements, simple as they are.
Our star was brighter perhaps when it had water in it.
Now there is no question even of that, but only

5. From the proverb "Least said, soonest mended."
6. *Roger Delivering Angelica,* by French painter Jean-Auguste Dominique Ingres (1780–1867), depicts a scene from *Orlando Furioso,* a fantastic epic by Italian author Ludovico Ariosto (1474–1533). The heroine is often rescued from monsters, ogres, and other perils.
7. Character from a newspaper comic strip.

Of holding on to the hard earth so as not to get thrown off,
With an occasional dream, a vision: a robin flies across
The upper corner of the window, you brush your hair away
And cannot quite see, or a wound will flash
Against the sweet faces of the others, something like:
This is what you wanted to hear, so why
Did you think of listening to something else? We are all talkers
It is true, but underneath the talk lies
The moving and not wanting to be moved, the loose
Meaning, untidy and simple like a threshing floor.

These then were some hazards of the course,
Yet though we knew the course *was* hazards and nothing else
It was still a shock when, almost a quarter of a century later,
The clarity of the rules dawned on you for the first time.
They were the players, and we who had struggled at the game
Were merely spectators, though subject to its vicissitudes
And moving with it out of the tearful stadium, borne on shoulders, at last.
Night after night this message returns, repeated
In the flickering bulbs of the sky, raised past us, taken away from us,
Yet ours over and over until the end that is past truth,
The being of our sentences, in the climate that fostered them,
Not ours to own, like a book, but to be with, and sometimes
To be without, alone and desperate.
But the fantasy makes it ours, a kind of fence-sitting
Raised to the level of an esthetic ideal. These were moments, years,
Solid with reality, faces, namable events, kisses, heroic acts,
But like the friendly beginning of a geometrical progression
Not too reassuring, as though meaning could be cast aside some day
When it had been outgrown. Better, you said, to stay cowering
Like this in the early lessons, since the promise of learning
Is a delusion, and I agreed, adding that
Tomorrow would alter the sense of what had already been learned,
That the learning process is extended in this way, so that from this standpoint
None of us ever graduates from college,
For time is an emulsion, and probably thinking not to grow up
Is the brightest kind of maturity for us, right now at any rate.
And you see, both of us were right, though nothing
Has somehow come to nothing; the avatars[8]
Of our conforming to the rules and living
Around the home have made—well, in a sense, "good citizens" of us,
Brushing the teeth and all that, and learning to accept
The charity of the hard moments as they are doled out,
For this is action, this not being sure, this careless
Preparing, sowing the seeds crooked in the furrow,
Making ready to forget, and always coming back
To the mooring of starting out, that day so long ago.

1970

8. Incarnations.

Farm Implements and Rutabagas in a Landscape[9]

The first of the undecoded messages read: "Popeye[1] sits in thunder,
Unthought of. From that shoebox of an apartment,
From livid curtain's hue, a tangram[2] emerges: a country."
Meanwhile the Sea Hag was relaxing on a green couch: "How pleasant
To spend one's vacation *en la casa de Popeye*,"[3] she scratched
Her cleft chin's solitary hair. She remembered spinach

And was going to ask Wimpy if he had bought any spinach.
"M'love," he intercepted, "the plains are decked out in thunder
Today, and it shall be as you wish." He scratched
The part of his head under his hat. The apartment
Seemed to grow smaller. "But what if no pleasant
Inspiration plunge us now to the stars? *For this is my country.*"

Suddenly they remembered how it was cheaper in the country.
Wimpy was thoughtfully cutting open a number 2 can of spinach
When the door opened and Swee'pea crept in. "How pleasant!"
But Swee'pea looked morose. A note was pinned to his bib. "Thunder
And tears are unavailing," it read. "Henceforth shall Popeye's apartment
Be but remembered space, toxic or salubrious, whole or scratched."

Olive came hurtling through the window; its geraniums scratched
Her long thigh. "I have news!" she gasped. "Popeye, forced as you know to flee the country
One musty gusty evening, by the schemes of his wizened, duplicate father, jealous of the apartment
And all that it contains, myself and spinach
In particular, heaves bolts of loving thunder
At his own astonished becoming, rupturing the pleasant

Arpeggio[4] of our years. No more shall pleasant
Rays of the sun refresh your sense of growing old, nor the scratched
Tree-trunks and mossy foliage, only immaculate darkness and thunder."
She grabbed Swee'pea. "I'm taking the brat to the country."
"But you can't do that—he hasn't even finished his spinach,"
Urged the Sea Hag, looking fearfully around at the apartment.

But Olive was already out of earshot. Now the apartment
Succumbed to a strange new hush. "Actually it's quite pleasant
Here," thought the Sea Hag. "If this is all we need fear from spinach
Then I don't mind so much. Perhaps we could invite Alice the Goon over"—she scratched

9. Play on the title of the painting *Farm Implements and Vegetables in a Landscape*, by Dutch landscape painter Jacob van Ruysdael (1628–1682).
1. The popular American comic-strip characters Popeye, Olive Oyl, Swee'pea, and Wimpy were created by E. C. Segar (1894–1938) in 1929. When Ashbery wrote the poem, the strip *Popeye the Sailor* appeared in New York City only in the Spanish-language newspaper *El Diario*.
2. Geometric puzzle.
3. In Popeye's house (Spanish).
4. Notes of a chord played in succession.

One dug pensively—"but Wimpy is such a country
Bumpkin, always burping like that." Minute at first, the thunder

Soon filled the apartment. It was domestic thunder,
The color of spinach. Popeye chuckled and scratched
His balls: it sure was pleasant to spend a day in the country.

1970

As One Put Drunk into the Packet-Boat[5]

I tried each thing, only some were immortal and free.
Elsewhere we are as sitting in a place where sunlight
Filters down, a little at a time,
Waiting for someone to come. Harsh words are spoken,
As the sun yellows the green of the maple tree. . . .

So this was all, but obscurely
I felt the stirrings of new breath in the pages
Which all winter long had smelled like an old catalogue.
New sentences were starting up. But the summer
Was well along, not yet past the mid-point
But full and dark with the promise of that fullness,
That time when one can no longer wander away
And even the least attentive fall silent
To watch the thing that is prepared to happen.

A look of glass stops you
And you walk on shaken: was I the perceived?
Did they notice me, this time, as I am,
Or is it postponed again? The children
Still at their games, clouds that arise with a swift
Impatience in the afternoon sky, then dissipate
As limpid, dense twilight comes.
Only in that tooting of a horn
Down there, for a moment, I thought
The great, formal affair was beginning, orchestrated,
Its colors concentrated in a glance, a ballade
That takes in the whole world, now, but lightly,
Still lightly, but with wide authority and tact.

The prevalence of those gray flakes falling?
They are sun motes. You have slept in the sun
Longer than the sphinx,[6] and are none the wiser for it.
Come in. And I thought a shadow fell across the door
But it was only her come to ask once more
If I was coming in, and not to hurry in case I wasn't.

5. The title of Ashbery's poem is the first line of the poem "Tom May's Death," by English poet Andrew Marvell (1621–1678).

6. Mythical creature with a human head and lion's body. In Greek legend, it kills those who fail to answer its riddle. At Giza, Egypt, is the colossal statue of the recumbent sphinx.

The night sheen takes over. A moon of cistercian[7] pallor
Has climbed to the center of heaven, installed,
Finally involved with the business of darkness.
And a sigh heaves from all the small things on earth,
The books, the papers, the old garters and union-suit buttons
Kept in a white cardboard box somewhere, and all the lower
Versions of cities flattened under the equalizing night.
The summer demands and takes away too much,
But night, the reserved, the reticent, gives more than it takes.

1975

Self-Portrait in a Convex Mirror

As Parmigianino[8] did it, the right hand
Bigger than the head, thrust at the viewer
And swerving easily away, as though to protect
What it advertises. A few leaded panes, old beams,
Fur, pleated muslin, a coral ring run together
In a movement supporting the face, which swims
Toward and away like the hand
Except that it is in repose. It is what is
Sequestered. Vasari says, "Francesco one day set himself
To take his own portrait, looking at himself for that purpose
In a convex mirror, such as is used by barbers . . .
He accordingly caused a ball of wood to be made
By a turner, and having divided it in half and
Brought it to the size of the mirror, he set himself
With great art to copy all that he saw in the glass,"[9]
Chiefly his reflection, of which the portrait
Is the reflection once removed.
The glass chose to reflect only what he saw
Which was enough for his purpose: his image
Glazed, embalmed, projected at a 180-degree angle.
The time of day or the density of the light
Adhering to the face keeps it
Lively and intact in a recurring wave
Of arrival. The soul establishes itself.
But how far can it swim out through the eyes
And still return safely to its nest? The surface
Of the mirror being convex, the distance increases
Significantly; that is, enough to make the point
That the soul is a captive, treated humanely, kept
In suspension, unable to advance much farther
Than your look as it intercepts the picture.

7. Ascetic monastic order; that is, somber and subdued.
8. Parmigianino (Girolamo Francesco Mazzola, 1503–1540) is the Italian Mannerist artist who painted *Self-Portrait in a Convex Mirror* (c. 1524).
9. Quotation from *Lives of the Most Eminent Italian Painters, Sculptors, and Architects* (1550), by Italian artist and historian Giorgio Vasari (1511–1574), as translated by Mrs. Jonathan Foster.

Pope Clement[1] and his court were "stupefied"
By it, according to Vasari, and promised a commission
That never materialized. The soul has to stay where it is,
Even though restless, hearing raindrops at the pane,
The sighing of autumn leaves thrashed by the wind,
Longing to be free, outside, but it must stay
Posing in this place. It must move
As little as possible. This is what the portrait says.
But there is in that gaze a combination
Of tenderness, amusement and regret, so powerful
In its restraint that one cannot look for long.
The secret is too plain. The pity of it smarts,
Makes hot tears spurt: that the soul is not a soul,
Has no secret, is small, and it fits
Its hollow perfectly: its room, our moment of attention.
That is the tune but there are no words.
The words are only speculation
(From the Latin *speculum*, mirror):
They seek and cannot find the meaning of the music.
We see only postures of the dream,
Riders of the motion that swings the face
Into view under evening skies, with no
False disarray as proof of authenticity.
But it is life englobed.
One would like to stick one's hand
Out of the globe, but its dimension,
What carries it, will not allow it.
No doubt it is this, not the reflex
To hide something, which makes the hand loom large
As it retreats slightly. There is no way
To build it flat like a section of wall:
It must join the segment of a circle,
Roving back to the body of which it seems
So unlikely a part, to fence in and shore up the face
On which the effort of this condition reads
Like a pinpoint of a smile, a spark
Or star one is not sure of having seen
As darkness resumes. A perverse light whose
Imperative of subtlety dooms in advance its
Conceit to light up: unimportant but meant.
Francesco, your hand is big enough
To wreck the sphere, and too big,
One would think, to weave delicate meshes
That only argue its further detention.
(Big, but not coarse, merely on another scale,
Like a dozing whale on the sea bottom
In relation to the tiny, self-important ship
On the surface.) But your eyes proclaim
That everything is surface. The surface is what's there
And nothing can exist except what's there.

1. Pope Clement VII (1478–1534).

There are no recesses in the room, only alcoves,
And the window doesn't matter much, or that
Sliver of window or mirror on the right, even
As a gauge of the weather, which in French is
Le temps, the word for time, and which
Follows a course wherein changes are merely
Features of the whole. The whole is stable within
Instability, a globe like ours, resting
On a pedestal of vacuum, a ping-pong ball
Secure on its jet of water.
And just as there are no words for the surface, that is,
No words to say what it really is, that it is not
Superficial but a visible core, then there is
No way out of the problem of pathos vs. experience.
You will stay on, restive, serene in
Your gesture which is neither embrace nor warning
But which holds something of both in pure
Affirmation that doesn't affirm anything.

The balloon pops, the attention
Turns dully away. Clouds
In the puddle stir up into sawtoothed fragments.
I think of the friends
Who came to see me, of what yesterday
Was like. A peculiar slant
Of memory that intrudes on the dreaming model
In the silence of the studio as he considers
Lifting the pencil to the self-portrait.
How many people came and stayed a certain time,
Uttered light or dark speech that became part of you
Like light behind windblown fog and sand,
Filtered and influenced by it, until no part
Remains that is surely you. Those voices in the dusk
Have told you all and still the tale goes on
In the form of memories deposited in irregular
Clumps of crystals. Whose curved hand controls,
Francesco, the turning seasons and the thoughts
That peel off and fly away at breathless speeds
Like the last stubborn leaves ripped
From wet branches? I see in this only the chaos
Of your round mirror which organizes everything
Around the polestar of your eyes which are empty,
Know nothing, dream but reveal nothing.
I feel the carousel starting slowly
And going faster and faster: desk, papers, books,
Photographs of friends, the window and the trees
Merging in one neutral band that surrounds
Me on all sides, everywhere I look.
And I cannot explain the action of leveling,
Why it should all boil down to one
Uniform substance, a magma of interiors.
My guide in these matters is your self,

Firm, oblique, accepting everything with the same
Wraith of a smile, and as time speeds up so that it is soon
Much later, I can know only the straight way out,
The distance between us. Long ago
The strewn evidence meant something,
The small accidents and pleasures
Of the day as it moved gracelessly on,
A housewife doing chores. Impossible now
To restore those properties in the silver blur that is
The record of what you accomplished by sitting down
"With great art to copy all that you saw in the glass"
So as to perfect and rule out the extraneous
Forever. In the circle of your intentions certain spars
Remain that perpetuate the enchantment of self with self:
Eyebeams, muslin, coral. It doesn't matter
Because these are things as they are today
Before one's shadow ever grew
Out of the field into thoughts of tomorrow.

Tomorrow is easy, but today is uncharted,
Desolate, reluctant as any landscape
To yield what are laws of perspective
After all only to the painter's deep
Mistrust, a weak instrument though
Necessary. Of course some things
Are possible, it knows, but it doesn't know
Which ones. Some day we will try
To do as many things as are possible
And perhaps we shall succeed at a handful
Of them, but this will not have anything
To do with what is promised today, our
Landscape sweeping out from us to disappear
On the horizon. Today enough of a cover burnishes
To keep the supposition of promises together
In one piece of surface, letting one ramble
Back home from them so that these
Even stronger possibilities can remain
Whole without being tested. Actually
The skin of the bubble-chamber's as tough as
Reptile eggs; everything gets "programmed" there
In due course: more keeps getting included
Without adding to the sum, and just as one
Gets accustomed to a noise that
Kept one awake but now no longer does,
So the room contains this flow like an hourglass
Without varying in climate or quality
(Except perhaps to brighten bleakly and almost
Invisibly, in a focus of sharpening toward death—more
Of this later). What should be the vacuum of a dream
Becomes continually replete as the source of dreams
Is being tapped so that this one dream
May wax, flourish like a cabbage rose,

Defying sumptuary laws,[2] leaving us
To awake and try to begin living in what
Has now become a slum. Sydney Freedberg in his
Parmigianino says of it: "Realism in this portrait
No longer produces an objective truth, but a *bizarria*[3] . . .
However its distortion does not create
A feeling of disharmony. . . . The forms retain
A strong measure of ideal beauty," because
Fed by our dreams, so inconsequential until one day
We notice the hole they left. Now their importance
If not their meaning is plain. They were to nourish
A dream which includes them all, as they are
Finally reversed in the accumulating mirror.
They seemed strange because we couldn't actually see them.
And we realize this only at a point where they lapse
Like a wave breaking on a rock, giving up
Its shape in a gesture which expresses that shape.
The forms retain a strong measure of ideal beauty
As they forage in secret on our idea of distortion.
Why be unhappy with this arrangement, since
Dreams prolong us as they are absorbed?
Something like living occurs, a movement
Out of the dream into its codification.

As I start to forget it
It presents its stereotype again
But it is an unfamiliar stereotype, the face
Riding at anchor, issued from hazards, soon
To accost others, "rather angel than man" (Vasari).
Perhaps an angel looks like everything
We have forgotten, I mean forgotten
Things that don't seem familiar when
We meet them again, lost beyond telling
Which were ours once. This would be the point
Of invading the privacy of this man who
"Dabbled in alchemy, but whose wish
Here was not to examine the subtleties of art
In a detached, scientific spirit: he wished through them
To impart the sense of novelty and amazement to the spectator"
(Freedberg). Later portraits such as the Uffizi
"Gentleman," the Borghese "Young Prelate" and
The Naples "Antea" issue from Mannerist[4]
Tensions, but here, as Freedberg points out,
The surprise, the tension are in the concept
Rather than its realization.
The consonance of the High Renaissance
Is present, though distorted by the mirror.

2. Designed to regulate excess.
3. Eccentricity (Italian). Sydney Freedberg (1913–1997), American art historian, author of *Parmigianino: His Works in Painting* (1950).
4. Mannerism, a style of art that Parmigianino helped pioneer in the 1520s and 1530s, responded to the classical harmony of the High Renaissance by distorting space and scale and emphasizing style over content. *Uffizi* and *Borghese:* galleries in Florence and Rome, respectively.

What is novel is the extreme care in rendering
The velleities[5] of the rounded reflecting surface
(It is the first mirror portrait),
So that you could be fooled for a moment
Before you realize the reflection
Isn't yours. You feel then like one of those
Hoffmann[6] characters who have been deprived
Of a reflection, except that the whole of me
Is seen to be supplanted by the strict
Otherness of the painter in his
Other room. We have surprised him
At work, but no, he has surprised us
As he works. The picture is almost finished,
The surprise almost over, as when one looks out,
Startled by a snowfall which even now is
Ending in specks and sparkles of snow.
It happened while you were inside, asleep,
And there is no reason why you should have
Been awake for it, except that the day
Is ending and it will be hard for you
To get to sleep tonight, at least until late.

The shadow of the city injects its own
Urgency: Rome where Francesco
Was at work during the Sack:[7] his inventions
Amazed the soldiers who burst in on him;
They decided to spare his life, but he left soon after;
Vienna where the painting is today, where
I saw it with Pierre in the summer of 1959; New York
Where I am now, which is a logarithm
Of other cities. Our landscape
Is alive with filiations, shuttlings;
Business is carried on by look, gesture,
Hearsay. It is another life to the city,
The backing of the looking glass of the
Unidentified but precisely sketched studio. It wants
To siphon off the life of the studio, deflate
Its mapped space to enactments, island it.
That operation has been temporarily stalled
But something new is on the way, a new preciosity
In the wind. Can you stand it,
Francesco? Are you strong enough for it?
This wind brings what it knows not, is
Self-propelled, blind, has no notion
Of itself. It is inertia that once
Acknowledged saps all activity, secret or public:
Whispers of the word that can't be understood
But can be felt, a chill, a blight

5. Faint wishes or unrealized inclinations.
6. E. T. A. Hoffmann (1776–1822), German author of supernatural tales.
7. Parmigianino fled Rome after it was sacked by the army of the Hapsburg emperor Charles V in 1527.

Moving outward along the capes and peninsulas
Of your nervures[8] and so to the archipelagoes
And to the bathed, aired secrecy of the open sea.
This is its negative side. Its positive side is
Making you notice life and the stresses
That only seemed to go away, but now,
As this new mode questions, are seen to be
Hastening out of style. If they are to become classics
They must decide which side they are on.
Their reticence has undermined
The urban scenery, made its ambiguities
Look willful and tired, the games of an old man.
What we need now is this unlikely
Challenger pounding on the gates of an amazed
Castle. Your argument, Francesco,
Had begun to grow stale as no answer
Or answers were forthcoming. If it dissolves now
Into dust, that only means its time had come
Some time ago, but look now, and listen:
It may be that another life is stocked there
In recesses no one knew of; that it,
Not we, are the change; that we are in fact it
If we could get back to it, relive some of the way
It looked, turn our faces to the globe as it sets
And still be coming out all right:
Nerves normal, breath normal. Since it is a metaphor
Made to include us, we are a part of it and
Can live in it as in fact we have done,
Only leaving our minds bare for questioning
We now see will not take place at random
But in an orderly way that means to menace
Nobody—the normal way things are done,
Like the concentric growing up of days
Around a life: correctly, if you think about it.

A breeze like the turning of a page
Brings back your face: the moment
Takes such a big bite out of the haze
Of pleasant intuition it comes after.
The locking into place is "death itself,"
As Berg said of a phrase in Mahler's Ninth;[9]
Or, to quote Imogen in *Cymbeline*, "There cannot
Be a pinch in death more sharp than this,"[1] for,
Though only exercise or tactic, it carries
The momentum of a conviction that had been building.
Mere forgetfulness cannot remove it
Nor wishing bring it back, as long as it remains
The white precipitate of its dream

8. Veins, as on a leaf or an insect's wing.
9. *Symphony No. 9* by Gustav Mahler (1860–1911), as described by fellow Austrian composer Alban Berg (1885–1935).
1. Shakespeare, *Cymbeline* 1.1.131–32.

In the climate of sighs flung across our world,
A cloth over a birdcage. But it is certain that
What is beautiful seems so only in relation to a specific
Life, experienced or not, channeled into some form
Steeped in the nostalgia of a collective past.
The light sinks today with an enthusiasm
I have known elsewhere, and known why
It seemed meaningful, that others felt this way
Years ago. I go on consulting
This mirror that is no longer mine
For as much brisk vacancy as is to be
My portion this time. And the vase is always full
Because there is only just so much room
And it accommodates everything. The sample
One sees is not to be taken as
Merely that, but as everything as it
May be imagined outside time—not as a gesture
But as all, in the refined, assimilable state.
But what is this universe the porch of
As it veers in and out, back and forth,
Refusing to surround us and still the only
Thing we can see? Love once
Tipped the scales but now is shadowed, invisible,
Though mysteriously present, around somewhere.
But we know it cannot be sandwiched
Between two adjacent moments, that its windings
Lead nowhere except to further tributaries
And that these empty themselves into a vague
Sense of something that can never be known
Even though it seems likely that each of us
Knows what it is and is capable of
Communicating it to the other. But the look
Some wear as a sign makes one want to
Push forward ignoring the apparent
Naïveté of the attempt, not caring
That no one is listening, since the light
Has been lit once and for all in their eyes
And is present, unimpaired, a permanent anomaly,
Awake and silent. On the surface of it
There seems no special reason why that light
Should be focused by love, or why
The city falling with its beautiful suburbs
Into space always less clear, less defined,
Should read as the support of its progress,
The easel upon which the drama unfolded
To its own satisfaction and to the end
Of our dreaming, as we had never imagined
It would end, in worn daylight with the painted
Promise showing through as a gage, a bond.
This nondescript, never-to-be defined daytime is
The secret of where it takes place
And we can no longer return to the various

Conflicting statements gathered, lapses of memory
Of the principal witnesses. All we know
Is that we are a little early, that
Today has that special, lapidary[2]
Todayness that the sunlight reproduces
Faithfully in casting twig-shadows on blithe
Sidewalks. No previous day would have been like this.
I used to think they were all alike,
That the present always looked the same to everybody
But this confusion drains away as one
Is always cresting into one's present.
Yet the "poetic," straw-colored space
Of the long corridor that leads back to the painting,
Its darkening opposite—is this
Some figment of "art," not to be imagined
As real, let alone special? Hasn't it too its lair
In the present we are always escaping from
And falling back into, as the waterwheel of days
Pursues its uneventful, even serene course?
I think it is trying to say it is today
And we must get out of it even as the public
Is pushing through the museum now so as to
Be out by closing time. You can't live there.
The gray glaze of the past attacks all know-how:
Secrets of wash and finish that took a lifetime
To learn and are reduced to the status of
Black-and-white illustrations in a book where colorplates
Are rare. That is, all time
Reduces to no special time. No one
Alludes to the change; to do so might
Involve calling attention to oneself
Which would augment the dread of not getting out
Before having seen the whole collection
(Except for the sculptures in the basement:
They are where they belong).
Our time gets to be veiled, compromised
By the portrait's will to endure. It hints at
Our own, which we were hoping to keep hidden.
We don't need paintings or
Doggerel written by mature poets when
The explosion is so precise, so fine.
Is there any point even in acknowledging
The existence of all that? Does it
Exist? Certainly the leisure to
Indulge stately pastimes doesn't,
Any more. Today has no margins, the event arrives
Flush with its edges, is of the same substance,
Indistinguishable. "Play" is something else;
It exists, in a society specifically
Organized as a demonstration of itself.

2. Carved in stone; concise or condensed.

There is no other way, and those assholes
Who would confuse everything with their mirror games
Which seem to multiply stakes and possibilities, or
At least confuse issues by means of an investing
Aura that would corrode the architecture
Of the whole in a haze of suppressed mockery,
Are beside the point. They are out of the game,
Which doesn't exist until they are out of it.
It seems like a very hostile universe
But as the principle of each individual thing is
Hostile to, exists at the expense of all the others
As philosophers have often pointed out, at least
This thing, the mute, undivided present,
Has the justification of logic, which
In this instance isn't a bad thing
Or wouldn't be, if the way of telling
Didn't somehow intrude, twisting the end result
Into a caricature of itself. This always
Happens, as in the game where
A whispered phrase passed around the room
Ends up as something completely different.
It is the principle that makes works of art so unlike
What the artist intended. Often he finds
He has omitted the thing he started out to say
In the first place. Seduced by flowers,
Explicit pleasures, he blames himself (though
Secretly satisfied with the result), imagining
He had a say in the matter and exercised
An option of which he was hardly conscious,
Unaware that necessity circumvents such resolutions
So as to create something new
For itself, that there is no other way,
That the history of creation proceeds according to
Stringent laws, and that things
Do get done in this way, but never the things
We set out to accomplish and wanted so desperately
To see come into being. Parmigianino
Must have realized this as he worked at his
Life-obstructing task. One is forced to read
The perfectly plausible accomplishment of a purpose
Into the smooth, perhaps even bland (but so
Enigmatic) finish. Is there anything
To be serious about beyond this otherness
That gets included in the most ordinary
Forms of daily activity, changing everything
Slightly and profoundly, and tearing the matter
Of creation, any creation, not just artistic creation
Out of our hands, to install it on some monstrous, near
Peak, too close to ignore, too far
For one to intervene? This otherness, this
"Not-being-us" is all there is to look at
In the mirror, though no one can say

How it came to be this way. A ship
Flying unknown colors has entered the harbor.
You are allowing extraneous matters
To break up your day, cloud the focus
Of the crystal ball. Its scene drifts away
Like vapor scattered on the wind. The fertile
Thought-associations that until now came
So easily, appear no more, or rarely. Their
Colorings are less intense, washed out
By autumn rains and winds, spoiled, muddied,
Given back to you because they are worthless.
Yet we are such creatures of habit that their
Implications are still around *en permanence,* confusing
Issues. To be serious only about sex
Is perhaps one way, but the sands are hissing
As they approach the beginning of the big slide
Into what happened. This past
Is now here: the painter's
Reflected face, in which we linger, receiving
Dreams and inspirations on an unassigned
Frequency, but the hues have turned metallic,
The curves and edges are not so rich. Each person
Has one big theory to explain the universe
But it doesn't tell the whole story
And in the end it is what is outside him
That matters, to him and especially to us
Who have been given no help whatever
In decoding our own man-size quotient and must rely
On second-hand knowledge. Yet I know
That no one else's taste is going to be
Any help, and might as well be ignored.
Once it seemed so perfect—gloss on the fine
Freckled skin, lips moistened as though about to part
Releasing speech, and the familiar look
Of clothes and furniture that one forgets.
This could have been our paradise: exotic
Refuge within an exhausted world, but that wasn't
In the cards, because it couldn't have been
The point. Aping naturalness may be the first step
Toward achieving an inner calm
But it is the first step only, and often
Remains a frozen gesture of welcome etched
On the air materializing behind it,
A convention. And we have really
No time for these, except to use them
For kindling. The sooner they are burnt up
The better for the roles we have to play.
Therefore I beseech you, withdraw that hand,
Offer it no longer as shield or greeting,
The shield of a greeting, Francesco:
There is room for one bullet in the chamber:
Our looking through the wrong end

Of the telescope as you fall back at a speed
Faster than that of light to flatten ultimately
Among the features of the room, an invitation
Never mailed, the "it was all a dream"
Syndrome, though the "all" tells tersely
Enough how it wasn't. Its existence
Was real, though troubled, and the ache
Of this waking dream can never drown out
The diagram still sketched on the wind,
Chosen, meant for me and materialized
In the disguising radiance of my room.
We have seen the city; it is the gibbous[3]
Mirrored eye of an insect. All things happen
On its balcony and are resumed within,
But the action is the cold, syrupy flow
Of a pageant. One feels too confined,
Sifting the April sunlight for clues,
In the mere stillness of the ease of its
Parameter. The hand holds no chalk
And each part of the whole falls off
And cannot know it knew, except
Here and there, in cold pockets
Of remembrance, whispers out of time.

1975

Wet Casements

When Eduard Raban, coming along the passage, walked into the open doorway, he saw that it was raining. It was not raining much.
—KAFKA, *Wedding Preparations in the Country*[4]

The concept is interesting: to see, as though reflected
In streaming windowpanes, the look of others through
Their own eyes. A digest of their correct impressions of
Their self-analytical attitudes overlaid by your
Ghostly transparent face. You in falbalas[5]
Of some distant but not too distant era, the cosmetics,
The shoes perfectly pointed, drifting (how long you
Have been drifting; how long I have too for that matter)
Like a bottle-imp toward a surface which can never be approached,
Never pierced through into the timeless energy of a present
Which would have its own opinions on these matters,
Are an epistemological snapshot of the processes
That first mentioned your name at some crowded cocktail
Party long ago, and someone (not the person addressed)
Overheard it and carried that name around in his wallet
For years as the wallet crumbled and bills slid in
And out of it. I want that information very much today,

3. Convex.
4. An early story about the isolated character Raban, by German-language writer Franz Kafka (1883–1924).
5. Frilled trim on a dress or petticoat.

Can't have it, and this makes me angry.
I shall use my anger to build a bridge like that
Of Avignon[6] on which people may dance for the feeling
Of dancing on a bridge. I shall at last see my complete face
Reflected not in the water but in the worn stone floor of my bridge.

I shall keep to myself.
I shall not repeat others' comments about me.

1977

Paradoxes and Oxymorons

This poem is concerned with language on a very plain level.
Look at it talking to you. You look out a window
Or pretend to fidget. You have it but you don't have it.
You miss it, it misses you. You miss each other.

The poem is sad because it wants to be yours, and cannot.
What's a plain level? It is that and other things,
Bringing a system of them into play. Play?
Well, actually, yes, but I consider play to be

A deeper outside thing, a dreamed role-pattern,
As in the division of grace these long August days
Without proof. Open-ended. And before you know
It gets lost in the steam and chatter of typewriters.

It has been played once more. I think you exist only
To tease me into doing it, on your level, and then you aren't there
Or have adopted a different attitude. And the poem
Has set me softly down beside you. The poem is you.

1981

At North Farm[7]

Somewhere someone is traveling furiously toward you,
At incredible speed, traveling day and night,
Through blizzards and desert heat, across torrents, through narrow passes.
But will he know where to find you,
Recognize you when he sees you,
Give you the thing he has for you?

Hardly anything grows here,
Yet the granaries are bursting with meal,

6. French city celebrated in the folksong "On the Bridge at Avignon."
7. In *The Kalevala*, a collection of Finnish epic poems, North Farm is a region near Hell where heroes search for wives.

The sacks of meal piled to the rafters.
The streams run with sweetness, fattening fish;
Birds darken the sky. Is it enough
That the dish of milk is set out at night,
That we think of him sometimes,
Sometimes and always, with mixed feelings?

1984

Of the Light

That watery light, so undervalued
except when evaluated, which never happens
much, perhaps even not at all—I intend to conserve it
somehow, in a book, in a dish, even at night,
like an insect in a light bulb.

Yes, day may just be breaking. The importance isn't there
but in the beautiful flights of the trees
accepting their own flaccid destiny,
or the tightrope of seasons.
We get scared when we look at them up close
but the king doesn't mind. He has the tides to worry about,

and how fitting is the new mood of contentment
and how long it will wear thin.

I looked forward to seeing you so much
I have dragged the king from his lair: There,
take that, you old wizard. Wizard enough, he replies,
but this isn't going to save us from the light
of breakfast, or mend the hole in your stocking.
"Now wait"—and yet another day has consumed itself,
brisk with passion and grief, crisp as an illustration in a magazine
from the thirties, when we and this light were all that mattered.

2000

W. S. Merwin
b. 1927

W. S. Merwin was twenty-four when his first book, *A Mask for Janus* (1952), was chosen by W. H. Auden for the Yale Series of Younger Poets, and Merwin has published regularly and prolifically since. Those first poems, technically very accomplished, show Merwin not only "trained . . . thoroughly in the mechanics of verse," as Auden observed, but interested in playing with conventional forms—ballads, sonnets, sestinas, odes, carols, roundels. Merwin has remained on good terms with the poets of the past; his later poem "Lament for the Makers" is a pious roll call of dead poets. His earliest subjects were often mythical or legendary, and many of the poems are about the sea and animals, which he invests with an emblematic quality. With growing intensity through the years, Merwin has revered nature and condemned its poisoning and destruction.

The Drunk in the Furnace (1960) represented a change in direction from Merwin's early neoclassicism. His subjects became more local and personal, and whereas his first poems showed clearly the influence of Wallace Stevens, his work in this volume captures some of Robert Frost's shifting colloquialism and even his oracular quality. The title poem, which depicts an old drunk in a furnace as Orpheus in a new and wonderful form, demonstrates how successfully Merwin absorbed his new influences. The metrical irregularities create a new tone closer to speech ("Where he gets his spirits / It's a mystery. But the stuff keeps him musical"); the straight-faced puns add to the buoyancy and complexity of the poem ("spirits" meaning both liquor and good humor). Merwin finds a new way to praise the unconscious and outrageous forces that disconcert society but make poetry possible.

In the 1960s, Merwin, like many of his contemporaries among American poets, made increasingly daring experiments in metrical irregularity and thematic disorganization. Written during the escalation of the Vietnam War, his collection *The Lice* (1967), perhaps his most powerful, seeks out elemental and archetypal forms of experience in the midst of despair, chaos, and violence. In melancholy poems tinged with surrealism, Merwin opens a hushed space for the irrational, the dead, and the dying to be heard. Both elegiac and prophetic, Merwin once again tries to write a poetry that is closer to its imaginative energies than what he has done before, and he sees traditional form as an obstacle to poetry's "naked condition, where it touches on all that is unrealized" ("On Open Form"). He seeks to achieve in poetry "something that would be like an echo except that it is repeating no sound. Something that always belonged to it: its sense and its conformation before it entered words." This means that his poems resist intellectual interpretation; they are written out of experiences into which the reader may be drawn as by a charm.

Merwin's most influential verse is deliberately bare and meditative, shorn of all punctuation, all detail except an occasional vivid simile or image. The busy, fertile world is excluded in favor of simplicity; things, people, and words become shadows. Absence, silence, and brevity are at the core of his poetics. He avoids mannerisms and decorations as if they were childish things to be put aside in favor of an enigmatic yet exposed reality. Elusive and multifaceted, changing from one volume to the next, Merwin's poetry has been associated with various trends and movements, most often the Deep Image school, but also neoformalism, neosurrealism, ecopoetry, and existentialism.

William Stanley Merwin was born on September 30, 1927, in New York City, and grew up in Union, New Jersey, and Scranton, Pennsylvania; his father was a Presbyterian minister, and Merwin recalls, "I started writing hymns for my father almost as soon as I could write at all" (*Contemporary Authors,* 1966). In 1947, he received his B.A. from Princeton University, where he encountered John Berryman, who taught creative writing, and the poet and critic R. P. Blackmur, to whom he dedicated *The Moving Target* (1963). After a year of graduate work there, during which he continued the study of foreign languages that was to equip him to make excellent translations from Latin, Spanish, and French, he left the United States to live in England, France, and Portugal. In 1950, he tutored Robert Graves's son on Majorca. From 1951 to 1954, he was in London, supporting himself primarily by translating French and Spanish literature for broadcast by the BBC, while his first two books of poetry were published in the United States. He returned briefly to America to be a playwright-in-residence at the Poet's Theatre in Cambridge, Massachusetts (1956) and the poetry editor of *The Nation* (1961–63). Since 1968, he has lived in the United States, moving in the late 1970s to an old pineapple plantation in Hawaii, which he has been restoring to rainforest. He has received the Pulitzer Prize (1970) and the Bollingen Prize (1978). After publishing *Travels* (1993), he won the Lenore Marshall Poetry Prize and became the first recipient of the Tanning Prize.

The Drunk in the Furnace

For a good decade
The furnace stood in the naked gully, fireless
And vacant as any hat. Then when it was
No more to them than a hulking black fossil
To erode unnoticed with the rest of the junk-hill
By the poisonous creek, and rapidly to be added
To their ignorance,

They were afterwards astonished
To confirm, one morning, a twist of smoke like a pale
Resurrection, staggering out of its chewed hole,
And to remark then other tokens that someone,
Cosily bolted behind the eye-holed iron
Door of the drafty burner, had there established
His bad castle.

Where he gets his spirits
It's a mystery. But the stuff keeps him musical:
Hammer-and-anvilling with poker and bottle
To his jugged bellowings, till the last groaning clang
As he collapses onto the rioting
Springs of a litter of car-seats ranged on the grates,
To sleep like an iron pig.[1]

In their tar-paper church
On a text about stoke-holes[2] that are sated never
Their Reverend lingers. They nod and hate trespassers.
When the furnace wakes, though, all afternoon
Their witless offspring flock like piped rats[3] to its siren
Crescendo, and agape on the crumbling ridge
Stand in a row and learn.

1960

1. "Pig iron" is crude iron.
2. Furnace mouths.
3. The Pied Piper of Hamelin's piping lured rats from the town; when he was not paid, he lured away the children as well.

The Hydra[4]

No no the dead have no brothers

The Hydra calls me but I am used to it
It calls me Everybody
But I know my name and do not answer

And you the dead
You know your names as I do not
But at moments you have just finished speaking

The snow stirs in its wrappings
Every season comes from a new place

Like your voice with its resemblances

A long time ago the lightning was practising
Something I thought was easy

I was young and the dead were in other
Ages
As the grass had its own language

Now I forget where the difference falls

One thing about the living sometimes a piece of us
Can stop dying for a moment
But you the dead

Once you go into those names you go on you never
Hesitate
You go on

1967

Some Last Questions

What is the head
A. Ash
What are the eyes
A. The wells have fallen in and have
Inhabitants
What are the feet
A. Thumbs left after the auction
No what are the feet
A. Under them the impossible road is moving

4. In Greek legend, a monster with many heads, slain by Hercules.

Down which the broken necked mice push
Balls of blood with their noses
What is the tongue
A. The black coat that fell off the wall
With sleeves trying to say something
What are the hands
A. Paid
No what are the hands
A. Climbing back down the museum wall
To their ancestors the extinct shrews that will
Have left a message
What is the silence
A. As though it had a right to more
Who are the compatriots
A. They make the stars of bone

1967

For the Anniversary of My Death

Every year without knowing it I have passed the day
When the last fires will wave to me
And the silence will set out
Tireless traveller
Like the beam of a lightless star

Then I will no longer
Find myself in life as in a strange garment
Surprised at the earth
And the love of one woman
And the shamelessness of men
As today writing after three days of rain
Hearing the wren sing and the falling cease
And bowing not knowing to what

1967

The Asians Dying

When the forests have been destroyed their darkness
remains
The ash the great walker follows the possessors
Forever
Nothing they will come to is real
Nor for long
Over the watercourses
Like ducks in the time of the ducks
The ghosts of the villages trail in the sky
Making a new twilight

Rain falls into the open eyes of the dead
Again again with its pointless sound
When the moon finds them they are the color of everything

The nights disappear like bruises but nothing is healed
The dead go away like bruises
The blood vanishes into the poisoned farmlands
Pain the horizon
Remains
Overhead the seasons rock
They are paper bells
Calling to nothing living

The possessors move everywhere under Death their star
Like columns of smoke they advance into the shadows
Like thin flames with no light
They with no past
And fire their only future

1967

For a Coming Extinction

Gray whale
Now that we are sending you to The End
That great god
Tell him
That we who follow you invented forgiveness
And forgive nothing

I write as though you could understand
And I could say it
One must always pretend something
Among the dying
When you have left the seas nodding on their stalks
Empty of you
Tell him that we were made
On another day

The bewilderment will diminish like an echo
Winding along your inner mountains
Unheard by us
And find its way out
Leaving behind it the future
Dead
And ours

When you will not see again
The whale calves trying the light
Consider what you will find in the black garden

And its court
The sea cows the Great Auks[5] the gorillas
The irreplaceable hosts ranged countless
And fore-ordaining as stars
Our sacrifices
Join your word to theirs
Tell him
That it is we who are important

1967

A Given Day

When I wake I find it is late in the autumn
 the hard rain has passed and the sunlight has not yet reached
the tips of the dark leaves that are their own shadows still
 and I am home it is coming back to me I am
remembering the gradual sweetness of morning
 the clear spring of being here as it rises one by one
in silence and without a pause and is the only one
 then one at a time I remember without understanding
some that have gone and arise only not to be here
 an afternoon walking on a bridge thinking of a friend
when she was still alive while a door from a building
 being demolished sailed down through the passing city
my mother half my age at a window long since removed
 friends in the same rooms and the words dreaming between us
the eyes of animals upon me they are all here
 in the clearness of the morning in the first light
that remembers its way now to the flowers of winter

1996

5. Extinct, large, flightless sea birds. *Sea cows:* endangered, walruslike animals.

James Wright
1927–1980

Of the poems in his first two books, James Wright said, "I have tried very hard to write in the mode of Edwin Arlington Robinson and Robert Frost," surprising models for a man whose first books were published in the late 1950s. What Wright seems to have admired in these older poets—and in Thomas Hardy as well—is their seriousness. Wright, as he said on a 1957 dust jacket, "wanted to make the poems say something humanly important instead of just showing off with language." The poems are typically about men and women who find themselves outside society—a convict escaped from prison, a lesbian whose love has been discovered by her neighbors, an old countryman whose wife has just died, even Judas Iscariot. Wright's tone is distinct and powerful. One poem, dedicated to a convicted murderer awaiting his execution, concludes with a prayer: "God, God have pity if he wake, / Have mercy on man who dreamed apart. / God, God have pity on man apart" ("American Twilights, 1957").

Wright's most characteristic first subjects were people not only "apart," but poor. Like his friend Richard Hugo, Wright came from a poor family and grew up in a small town in the depths of the Great Depression. As Hugo later wrote, "Jim had seen his father enslaved to a lousy factory job during the depression and knew what terrible fears bind people to jobs" ("James Wright"). Wright himself said, "Hundreds of times I must have heard a man returning home after a long day's futile search for work, any kind of work at all, and dispiritedly [saying] in his baffled loneliness, 'I ain't got a pot to piss in or a window to throw it out of' " (*American Poets in 1976*, ed. William Heyen). Wright once told Hugo that he and his first wife had married "to escape Martins Ferry"—his hometown and the gritty, industrial "triggering town" of a number of his poems, such as "Autumn Begins in Martins Ferry, Ohio" ("James Wright").

Sometime after the publication of his second collection, Wright set about changing—or renewing—his style, commenting, "I have changed the way I've written, when it seemed appropriate, and continue to do so" (*Contemporary Poets,* 1985). He published translations of the South American poets Pablo Neruda and César Vallejo and the Austrian poet Georg Trakl, all of whom use series of discontinuous images, and Wright—like the "Deep Image" poets Robert Bly and W. S. Merwin—adapted their surrealism for his own poetry. He kept his compassionate interest in social outcasts and an increasing confidence in the transforming beauty of nature—a specifically American nature. What was new was a looser form, a greater personal openness—he was now less interested in creating characters—and an emphasis on deeply felt social concerns. "I wonder," he writes in "The Minneapolis Poem," "how many old men last winter / Hungry and frightened by namelessness prowled / The Mississippi shore / Lashed blind by the wind, dreaming / Of suicide in the river." In 1970, Wright commented: "I try and speak of the beauty and again of the ugliness in the lives of the poor and neglected."

In 1971, he published *Collected Poems,* which won the Pulitzer Prize. It contained most of his first book, all of his second, his translations, and the two books that followed, *The Branch Will Not Break* and *Shall We Gather at the River.* Many of its poems are about the marginal, the hopeless, and the dead, although they occasionally glimpse possibilities of imaginative transformation. The image of humankind in "A Secret Gratitude"—"Man's heart is the rotten yolk of a blacksnake egg / Corroding, as it is just born, in a pile of dead / Horse dung"—is only slightly alleviated by the sound of "a small waterfall" at the end of the poem. The ferocious clarity of Wright's images, compelling and coherent even when disjointed, achieves a visceral effect.

Wright was born on December 13, 1927, in Martins Ferry, Ohio, and served with the U.S. Army in Japan during the American occupation. In 1952, he received his B.A. from Kenyon College, where he studied with John Crowe Ransom, whom he credited with teaching him the classical ideal of a poem "put together so carefully that it does produce a single unifying effect" (*American Poetry Review* 9.3, 1980). After going to Vienna on a Fulbright Scholarship, he earned an M.A. in creative writing and, in 1959, a Ph.D. in English at the University of Washington, where he studied under Theodore Roethke and befriended Hugo. He taught at the University of Minnesota (1957–64) but, after he was denied tenure, took positions at Macalester College, in St. Paul (1963–65), and Hunter College, in New York City (1966–80). After years of struggling with alcoholism and depression, he died of cancer of the tongue. Hugo wrote of him: "No one carried his life more vividly inside him, or simultaneously in plain and in eloquent ways used the pain of his life to better advantage" ("James Wright").

Saint Judas[1]

When I went out to kill myself, I caught
A pack of hoodlums beating up a man.
Running to spare his suffering, I forgot
My name, my number, how my day began,
How soldiers milled around the garden stone
And sang amusing songs; how all that day
Their javelins measured crowds; how I alone
Bargained the proper coins, and slipped away.

Banished from heaven, I found this victim beaten,
Stripped, kneed, and left to cry. Dropping my rope
Aside, I ran, ignored the uniforms:
Then I remembered bread my flesh had eaten,
The kiss that ate my flesh.[2] Flayed without hope,
I held the man for nothing in my arms.

1959

Autumn Begins in Martins Ferry, Ohio

In the Shreve High football stadium,
I think of Polacks nursing long beers in Tiltonsville,
And gray faces of Negroes in the blast furnace at Benwood,
And the ruptured night watchman of Wheeling Steel,
Dreaming of heroes.

All the proud fathers are ashamed to go home.
Their women cluck like starved pullets,[3]
Dying for love.

Therefore,
Their sons grow suicidally beautiful
At the beginning of October,
And gallop terribly against each other's bodies.

1963

1. Judas Iscariot, apostle who betrayed Jesus with a kiss that signaled Roman soldiers to capture him. Matthew 27 recounts Judas' suicide.
2. During the Last Supper, after revealing that one of the disciples would betray him, Jesus distributed bread, saying, "Take, eat; this is my body" (Matthew 26.26)
3. Chickens.

Lying in a Hammock at William Duffy's Farm in Pine Island, Minnesota

Over my head, I see the bronze butterfly,
Asleep on the black trunk,
Blowing like a leaf in green shadow.
Down the ravine behind the empty house,
The cowbells follow one another
Into the distances of the afternoon.
To my right,
In a field of sunlight between two pines,
The droppings of last year's horses
Blaze up into golden stones.
I lean back, as the evening darkens and comes on.
A chicken hawk floats over, looking for home.
I have wasted my life.

1963

A Blessing

Just off the highway to Rochester, Minnesota,
Twilight bounds softly forth on the grass.
And the eyes of those two Indian ponies
Darken with kindness.
They have come gladly out of the willows
To welcome my friend and me.
We step over the barbed wire into the pasture
Where they have been grazing all day, alone.
They ripple tensely, they can hardly contain their happiness
That we have come.
They bow shyly as wet swans. They love each other.
There is no loneliness like theirs.
At home once more,
They begin munching the young tufts of spring in the darkness.
I would like to hold the slenderer one in my arms,
For she has walked over to me
And nuzzled my left hand.
She is black and white,
Her mane falls wild on her forehead,
And the light breeze moves me to caress her long ear
That is delicate as the skin over a girl's wrist.
Suddenly I realize
That if I stepped out of my body I would break
Into blossom.

1953

The Minneapolis Poem[4]

1

I wonder how many old men last winter
Hungry and frightened by namelessness prowled
The Mississippi shore
Lashed blind by the wind, dreaming
Of suicide in the river.
The police remove their cadavers by daybreak
And turn them in somewhere.
Where?
How does the city keep lists of its fathers
Who have no names?
By Nicollet Island I gaze down at the dark water
So beautifully slow.
And I wish my brothers good luck
And a warm grave.

2

The Chippewa young men
Stab one another shrieking
Jesus Christ.
Split-lipped homosexuals limp in terror of assault.
High school backfields search under benches
Near the Post Office. Their faces are the rich
Raw bacon without eyes.
The Walker Art Center crowd stare
At the Guthrie Theater.

3

Tall Negro girls from Chicago
Listen to light songs.
They know when the supposed patron
Is a plainclothesman.
A cop's palm
Is a roach dangling down the scorched fangs
Of a light bulb.
The soul of a cop's eyes
Is an eternity of Sunday daybreak in the suburbs
Of Juárez, Mexico.

4. Nicollet Island, the Walker Art Center, and the Tyrone Guthrie Repertory Theater, mentioned in the poem, are all Minneapolis landmarks.

4

The legless beggars are gone, carried away
By white birds.
The Artificial Limbs Exchange is gutted
And sown with lime.
The whalebone crutches and hand-me-down trusses
Huddle together dreaming in a desolation
Of dry groins.
I think of poor men astonished to waken
Exposed in broad daylight by the blade
Of a strange plough.

5

All over the walls of comb cells
Automobiles perfumed and blindered
Consent with a mutter of high good humor
To take their two naps a day.
Without sound windows glide back
Into dusk.
The sockets of a thousand blind bee graves tier upon tier
Tower not quite toppling.
There are men in this city who labor dawn after dawn
To sell me my death.

6

But I could not bear
To allow my poor brother my body to die
In Minneapolis.
The old man Walt Whitman our countryman
Is now in America our country
Dead.
But he was not buried in Minneapolis
At least.
And no more may I be
Please God.

7

I want to be lifted up
By some great white bird unknown to the police,
And soar for a thousand miles and be carefully hidden
Modest and golden as one last corn grain,
Stored with the secrets of the wheat and the mysterious lives
Of the unnamed poor.

1968

In Response to a Rumor That the Oldest Whorehouse in Wheeling, West Virginia, Has Been Condemned

I will grieve alone,
As I strolled alone, years ago, down along
The Ohio shore.
I hid in the hobo jungle[5] weeds
Upstream from the sewer main,
Pondering, gazing.

I saw, down river,
At Twenty-third and Water Streets
By the vinegar works,
The doors open in early evening.
Swinging their purses, the women
Poured down the long street to the river
And into the river.

I do not know how it was
They could drown every evening.
What time near dawn did they climb up the other shore,
Drying their wings?

For the river at Wheeling, West Virginia,
Has only two shores:
The one in hell, the other
In Bridgeport, Ohio.

And nobody would commit suicide, only
To find beyond death
Bridgeport, Ohio.

1968

Small Frogs Killed on the Highway

Still,
I would leap too
Into the light,
If I had the chance.
It is everything, the wet green stalk of the field
On the other side of the road.
They crouch there, too, faltering in terror
And take strange wing. Many
Of the dead never moved, but many
Of the dead are alive forever in the split second
Auto headlights more sudden
Than their drivers know.

5. Camp made by hoboes or tramps, in this case on the shore of the Ohio River.

The drivers burrow backward into dank pools
Where nothing begets
Nothing.

Across the road, tadpoles are dancing
On the quarter thumbnail
Of the moon. They can't see,
Not yet.

1971

A Centenary Ode: Inscribed to Little Crow, Leader of the Sioux Rebellion in Minnesota, 1862[6]

I had nothing to do with it. I was not here.
I was not born.
In 1862, when your hotheads
Raised hell from here to South Dakota,
My own fathers scattered into West Virginia
And southern Ohio.
My family fought the Confederacy
And fought the Union.
None of them got killed.
But for all that, it was not my fathers
Who murdered you.
Not much.

I don't know
Where the fathers of Minneapolis finalized
Your flayed carcass.
Little Crow, true father
Of my dark America,
When I close my eyes I lose you among
Old lonelinesses.
My family were a lot of singing drunks and good carpenters.
We had brothers who loved one another no matter what they did.
And they did plenty.

I think they would have run like hell from your Sioux.
And when you caught them you all would have run like hell
From the Confederacy and from the Union
Into the hills and hunted for a few things,
Some bull-cat under the stones, a gar[7] maybe,
If you were hungry, and if you were happy,
Sunfish and corn.

If only I knew where to mourn you,
I would surely mourn.

6. The sixty-year-old Little Crow led a failed rebellion in response to the threat of starvation inflicted on the Sioux when the U.S. government forced them off their lands and onto a small reservation.
7. A type of fish.

But I don't know.

I did not come here only to grieve
For my people's defeat.
The troops of the Union, who won,
Still outnumber us.
Old Paddy Beck, my great-uncle, is dead
At the old soldiers' home near Tiffen, Ohio.
He got away with every last stitch
Of his uniform, save only
The dress trousers.

Oh all around us,
The hobo jungles of America grow wild again.
The pick handles bloom like your skinned spine.
I don't even know where
My own grave is.

1971

Philip Levine
b. 1928

Working in the auto plants of Detroit in the 1950s, Philip Levine resolved "to find a voice for the voiceless"—the unsung factory workers of America, blue-collar laborers on assembly lines (*Contemporary Authors*). Uncovering, like Walt Whitman, nobility in the struggle against poverty, defeat, and dispossession, Levine works with elemental themes—father and son, the deaths of relatives, war—and infuses them with a melancholy luster. His poems, he says, "mostly record my discovery of the people, places, and animals I am not, the ones who live at all cost and come back for more, and who if they bore tattoos—a gesture they don't need—would have them say, 'Don't tread on me' or 'Once more with feeling' or 'no pasaran' or 'Not this pig' " (*Not This Pig*, 1968). In "You Can Have It," Levine records the bitter strength in exhaustion of his young brother, his hands "yellowed and cracked" by work in an ice plant, his body "hard / and furious, with wide shoulders and a curse / for God." Levine's poems celebrate the failed, the peripheral, and the uncooperative—as he says in "Silent in America,"

> . . . the ugly
> who had no chance
>
> the beautiful in
> body, the used and the unused,
> those who had courage
> and those who quit.

A gritty realist and yet a Romantic, Levine is true in poems such as "Belle Isle, 1949" to both the ugly and the beautiful—to industrial debris ("car parts, dead fish, stolen bicycles") and to the pleasures of life (a boy and girl strip and "baptize" themselves with an ecstatic swim in a cold river). "Drum" presents mud, metal scraps, and oil drums, but also radiance: "The light diamonds / last night's rain." "They Feed They Lion"—written in response to the 1967 Detroit riots—absorbs the minutiae of urban squalor while also evoking the prophetic in its use of symbolism, strong rhythms, and syntactic parallelism. Levine is a master of sensual detail, colloquial diction, propulsive rhythms, and narrative realism imbued with imaginative hope. His authoritative tone balances the elegiac with wry restraint and humor, and the result is often bizarre but powerful.

Born in Detroit to Russian Jewish immigrant parents on January 10, 1928, Levine remained there to study at Wayne State University. In 1957, he received an M.F.A. from the University of Iowa, where his teachers included John Berryman. The next year, he joined the faculty of California State University, Fresno, where he spent most of his career, with much travel in Spain. He acknowledges the importance to him of Spanish and Latin American surrealist poets and of their American advocate Robert Bly, as well as the influence of Kenneth Rexroth and the San Francisco poets, who, he says, "opened me up." His many books include translations of Spanish poetry, interviews, and memoirs. Among his many awards for books of poetry are the National Book Critics Circle Award (1980), the National Book Award (1991), and the Pulitzer Prize (1995).

They Feed They Lion

Out of burlap sacks, out of bearing butter,
Out of black bean and wet slate bread,
Out of the acids of rage, the candor of tar,
Out of creosote, gasoline, drive shafts, wooden dollies,
They Lion grow.
                    Out of the gray hills
Of industrial barns, out of rain, out of bus ride,
West Virginia to Kiss My Ass, out of buried aunties,
Mothers hardening like pounded stumps, out of stumps,
Out of the bones' need to sharpen and the muscles' to stretch,
They Lion grow.
                    Earth is eating trees, fence posts,
Gutted cars, earth is calling in her little ones,
"Come home, Come home!" From pig balls,
From the ferocity of pig driven to holiness,
From the furred ear and the full jowl come
The repose of the hung belly, from the purpose
They Lion grow.
                    From the sweet glues of the trotters[1]
Come the sweet kinks of the fist, from the full flower
Of the hams the thorax[2] of caves,
From "Bow Down" come "Rise Up,"
Come they Lion from the reeds of shovels,
The grained arm that pulls the hands,
They Lion grow.
                    From my five arms and all my hands,
From all my white sins forgiven, they feed,
From my car passing under the stars,
They Lion, from my children inherit,

1. Cooked pigs' feet.

2. That is, chest cavity.

From the oak turned to a wall, they Lion,
From they sack and they belly opened
And all that was hidden burning on the oil-stained earth
They feed they Lion and he comes.

1972

Belle Isle,[3] 1949

We stripped in the first warm spring night
and ran down into the Detroit River
to baptize ourselves in the brine
of car parts, dead fish, stolen bicycles,
melted snow. I remember going under
hand in hand with a Polish highschool girl
I'd never seen before, and the cries
our breath made caught at the same time
on the cold, and rising through the layers
of darkness into the final moonless atmosphere
that was this world, the girl breaking
the surface after me and swimming out
on the starless waters towards the lights
of Jefferson Ave. and the stacks
of the old stove factory unwinking.
Turning at last to see no island at all
but a perfect calm dark as far
as there was sight, and then a light
and another riding low out ahead
to bring us home, ore boats maybe, or smokers
walking alone. Back panting
to the gray coarse beach we didn't dare
fall on, the damp piles of clothes,
and dressing side by side in silence
to go back where we came from.

1978

You Can Have It

My brother comes home from work
and climbs the stairs to our room.
I can hear the bed groan and his shoes drop
one by one. You can have it, he says.

The moonlight streams in the window
and his unshaven face is whitened

3. Island and public park in Detroit, Michigan.

like the face of the moon. He will sleep
long after noon and waken to find me gone.

Thirty years will pass before I remember
that moment when suddenly I knew each man
has one brother who dies when he sleeps
and sleeps when he rises to face this life,

and that together they are only one man
sharing a heart that always labors, hands
yellowed and cracked, a mouth that gasps
for breath and asks, Am I gonna make it?

All night at the ice plant he had fed
the chute its silvery blocks, and then I
stacked cases of orange soda for the children
of Kentucky, one gray box-car at a time

with always two more waiting. We were twenty
for such a short time and always in
the wrong clothes, crusted with dirt
and sweat. I think now we were never twenty.

In 1948 in the city of Detroit, founded
by de la Mothe Cadillac for the distant purposes
of Henry Ford,[4] no one wakened or died,
no one walked the streets or stoked a furnace,

for there was no such year, and now
that year has fallen off all the old newspapers,
calendars, doctors' appointments, bonds,
wedding certificates, drivers licenses.

The city slept. The snow turned to ice.
The ice to standing pools or rivers
racing in the gutters. Then bright grass rose
between the thousands of cracked squares,

and that grass died. I give you back 1948.
I give you all the years from then
to the coming one. Give me back the moon
with its frail light falling across a face.

Give me back my young brother, hard
and furious, with wide shoulders and a curse
for God and burning eyes that look upon
all creation and say, You can have it.

1979

4. American automobile manufacturer (1863–1947). Antoine Laumet de la Mothe Cadillac (1658–1730), for whom the automobiles are named, founded the fur-trade post that eventually became Detroit.

Drum

Leo's Tool & Die, 1950

In the early morning before the shop
opens, men standing out in the yard
on pine planks over the umber mud.
The oil drum, squat, brooding, brimmed
with metal scraps, three-armed crosses,
silver shavings whitened with milky oil,
drill bits bitten off. The light diamonds
last night's rain; inside a buzzer purrs.
The overhead door stammers upward
to reveal the scene of our day.
We sit
for lunch on crates before the open door.
Bobeck, the boss's nephew, squats to hug
the overflowing drum, gasps and lifts. Rain
comes down in sheets staining his gun-metal
covert suit. A stake truck sloshes off
as the sun returns through a low sky.
By four the office help has driven off. We
sweep, wash up, punch out, collect outside
for a final smoke. The great door crashes
down at last.
In the darkness the scents
of mint, apples, asters. In the darkness
this could be a Carthaginian[5] outpost sent
to guard the waters of the West, those mounds
could be elephants at rest, the acrid half light
the haze of stars striking armor if stars were out.
On the galvanized tin roof the tunes of sudden rain.
The slow light of Friday morning in Michigan,
the one we waited for, shows seven hills
of scraped earth topped with crab grass,
weeds, a black oil drum empty, glistening
at the exact center of the modern world.

1999

5. Carthage was an ancient city on the north coast of Africa.

Thomas Kinsella
b. 1928

Despite his nationality and religion, Thomas Kinsella (whose last name is accented on the first syllable) describes his poetry as an expression of "my own full personality judging and collecting my experiences. . . . I find myself eschewing Catholic subjects and Irish subjects as being limited in themselves." Kinsella's earliest poems were love poems, and his later work explores the satisfactions, pain, and riskiness of married love. His other preoccupations are, as he says, the passage of time and the mysteries of artistic creation. Kinsella's poems on these subjects are restrained, elegant, and introspective. "Mirror in February," for example, is a meditation on that daily first look at oneself in the mirror. The poem concludes with characteristic stoicism, a resolve to go on in spite of all odds: "In slow distaste / I fold my towel with what grace I can, / Not young and not renewable, but man." "Baggot Street Deserta" is a meditation at the end of day; once again alone, the poet muses over the passage of time and the difficulties and satisfactions of his art. The rhetoric suggests that he is somewhat proud of having maintained his integrity: his sacrifices, doubts, and vanities "All feed a single stream, impassioned / Now with obsessed honesty, / A tugging scruple that can keep / Clear eyes staring down the mile, / The thousand fathoms, into sleep." In his later poems, Kinsella achieves a purified diction and an unusual strangeness of imagery and progressions.

Kinsella was born on May 4, 1928, in Dublin. From 1946 until 1956, he worked for the Irish Civil Service, eventually becoming the assistant principal officer in the Department of Finance. In 1956, he published his first book, *Poems,* with the Dolmen Press, of which he later became a director; two years later, his second book, *Another September,* won the Guinness Poetry Award. In 1965, he left Ireland to become writer-in-residence at Southern Illinois University, where he became a professor of English two years later. From 1970 to 1990, he was a professor at Temple University. He has published many books of poems and English translations of the important Irish verse epic *The Táin* (1969) and of other writings in Irish.

Baggot Street Deserta[1]

Lulled, at silence, the spent attack.
The will to work is laid aside.
The breaking-cry, the strain of the rack,
Yield, are at peace. The window is wide
On a crawling arch of stars, and the night
Reacts faintly to the mathematic
Passion of a cello suite
Plotting the quiet of my attic.
A mile away the river toils
Its buttressed fathoms out to sea;
Tucked in the mountains, many miles
Away from its roaring outcome, a shy

1. Abandoned, deserted; Baggot Street is in Dublin.

Gasp of waters in the gorse[2]
Is sonneting origins. Dreamers' heads
Lie mesmerised in Dublin's beds
Flashing with images, Adam's morse.[3]

A cigarette, the moon, a sigh
Of educated boredom, greet
A curlew's[4] lingering threadbare cry
Of common loss. Compassionate,
I add my call of exile, half-
Buried longing, half-serious
Anger and the rueful laugh.
We fly into our risk, the spurious.

Versing, like an exile, makes
A virtuoso of the heart,
Interpreting the old mistakes
And discords in a work of Art
For the One, a private masterpiece
Of doctored recollections. Truth
Concedes, before the dew, its place
In the spray of dried forgettings Youth
Collected when they were a single
Furious undissected bloom.
A voice clarifies when the tingle
Dies out of the nerves of time:
Endure and let the present punish.
Looking backward, all is lost;
The Past becomes a fairy bog
Alive with fancies, double crossed
By pad of owl and hoot of dog,
Where shaven, serious-minded men
Appear with lucid theses, after
Which they don the mists again
With trackless, cotton-silly laughter;
Secretly a swollen Burke
Assists a decomposing Hare[5]
To cart a body of good work
With midnight mutterings off somewhere;
The goddess who had light for thighs
Grows feet of dung and takes to bed,
Affronting horror-stricken eyes,
The marsh bird that children dread.

I nonetheless inflict, endure,
Tedium, intracordal[6] hurt,

2. Spiny evergreen shrub.
3. Morse code.
4. Migratory bird's.
5. In the early nineteenth century, the Irish criminals William Burke and William Hare robbed graves in Scotland of cadavers to sell to medical schools, then turned to murder to increase their stock.
6. That is, within a nerve.

The sting of memory's quick, the drear
Uprooting, burying, prising apart
Of loves a strident adolescent
Spent in doubt and vanity.
All feed a single stream, impassioned
Now with obsessed honesty,
A tugging scruple that can keep
Clear eyes staring down the mile,
The thousand fathoms, into sleep.

Fingers cold against the sill
Feel, below the stress of flight,
The slow implosion of my pulse
In a wrist with poet's cramp, a tight
Beat tapping out endless calls
Into the dark, as the alien
Garrison in my own blood
Keeps constant contact with the main
Mystery, not to be understood.
Out where imagination arches
Chilly points of light transact
The business of the border-marches
Of the Real, and I—a fact
That may be countered or may not—
Find their privacy complete.

My quarter-inch of cigarette
Goes flaring down to Baggot Street.

1961

Je t'adore[7]

The other props are gone.
Sighing in one another's
Iron arms, propped above nothing,
We praise Love the limiter.

1967

Mirror in February

The day dawns with scent of must and rain,
Of opened soil, dark trees, dry bedroom air.
Under the fading lamp, half dressed—my brain
Idling on some compulsive fantasy—

7. I adore you (French).

I towel my shaven jaw and stop, and stare,
Riveted by a dark exhausted eye,
A dry downturning mouth.

It seems again that it is time to learn,
In this untiring, crumbling place of growth
To which, for the time being, I return.
Now plainly in the mirror of my soul
I read that I have looked my last on youth
And little more; for they are not made whole
That reach the age of Christ.[8]

Below my window the awakening trees,
Hacked clean for better bearing, stand defaced
Suffering their brute necessities,
And how should the flesh not quail that span for span
Is mutilated more? In slow distaste
I fold my towel with what grace I can,
Not young and not renewable, but man.

1967

From Songs of the Psyche

1

A character, indistinct, entered,
looked about him, and began:

Why had I to wait until I am graceless,
unsightly, and a little nervous of stooping
until I could see

through those clear eyes I had once?
It is time. And I am
shivering as in stupid youth.

Who have stood where I was born
and snapped my bitten fingers!

1986

8. According to the Bible, Jesus was thirty-three at his crucifixion.

Anne Sexton
1928–1974

The attempt to utter raw feeling before time, contemplation, or conventional reassurance have alleviated it is at the heart of Anne Sexton's work. Poetry, she said in an interview, "should be a shock to the senses. It should almost hurt" (*Hudson Review* 18, 1965–66). As an epigraph for her second volume of poetry, *All My Pretty Ones* (1962), she chose a sentence from one of Franz Kafka's letters: "a book should serve as the ax for the frozen sea within us," should "make us suffer like the death of someone we love more than ourselves." What she finds in that frozen sea, and what she hopes to evoke in the reader, are deep and even repressed emotions—anguish, guilt, grief, hatred, and forbidden desires for sex and self-extinction. "Poetry," she said in a 1968 interview, "milks the unconscious." She often explores difficult and once taboo subjects, such as masturbation, sibling rivalry, surgery, menstruation, mental illness, drug abuse, and suicide.

She studied with Robert Lowell in the same seminar as Sylvia Plath, who became a friend and rival. Sexton is often labeled a member of the "confessional school," which is said to have begun with Lowell's sudden shift toward autobiography in *Life Studies* (1959). But her first influence, she said, was W. D. Snodgrass; his poem "Heart's Needle," she told him, "walked out at me and grew like a bone inside my heart" (letter of March 11, 1959). His verse is also informed by psychoanalytic theory and vivifies emotional stress; as such, it "kind of gave me permission," she said in a 1965 interview, to write intensely personal poetry. Sexton's first book, *To Bedlam and Part Way Back* (1960), includes many poems written in Lowell's workshop and centers on themes of mental collapse and partial recovery. Sexton's work became, in turn, an important resource for other poets. Plath, for example, said that Sexton's "are wonderfully craftsman-like poems and yet they have a kind of emotional and psychological depth which I think is something perhaps quite new, quite exciting" (BBC, 1962). Plath's "Daddy" borrows rhymes and themes from an early poem of Sexton's. Both poets were articulating in verse feelings that violated the social strictures placed on American women at mid-century. Sexton's poetry is strongly rooted in her bodily and psychic existence as a woman. It is, as she said, "intensely physical" (*Hudson Review*). The witch in "Her Kind," who is likened to the poet, claims powers of movement and magic traditionally forbidden to women, even if this means being burned at the stake.

In other poems, Sexton transgresses conventions governing responses to the dead. Although "The Truth the Dead Know" is dedicated to Sexton's parents, the poet refuses ceremony—"the stiff procession to the grave"—and flaunts her indifference toward the dead. In another anti-elegiac elegy, "All My Pretty Ones," the speaker guiltily worries about having possibly caused her father's death and yet sternly refuses to invest with affection the objects he has left behind. The father is remembered as involuntarily revealing incestuous desire for his daughter in the later poem "The Death of the Fathers." Other poems describe suicidal longings. The refrain of "The Starry Night" is "This is how / I want to die."

But as Sexton insisted, her interest was not in direct confession, even though her subject matter is so intimate: "I can be deeply personal, but often I'm not being personal about myself." Although Sexton valued most the "emotional content of a poem," her interest in feeling should not obscure her craft (quoted in Diane Middlebrook, *Anne Sexton*). Through the mid-1960s, she wrote verses skillfully constructed around patterns of rhyme and near-rhyme, assonance and alliteration, rhythms and pauses. They balance violent feeling against a restrained and understated tone. After Sexton's turn to free verse, her imagery—strange, evocative, sometimes surreal—increasingly becomes the most vital aesthetic element in her work. She said, "I prefer to think of myself as an imagist who deals with reality and its hard facts" (*Contemporary Poets of the English Language,* ed. R. Murphy, 1970). Poems such as "The Death Baby" and "The Room of My Life" include catalogs of astonishing metaphors and similes—caviar turning into lava, typewriter keys into eyeballs, and "doors opening and closing like sea clams." "Images are the heart of poetry," said Sexton. "And this is not tricks. Images come from the unconscious" ("Craft Interview," 1970).

Sexton was born Anne Gray Harvey, on November 9, 1928, in Newton, Massachusetts. She was educated at Garland Junior College, then married and had two daughters. Repeated suicide attempts led to hospitalizations, particularly after the birth of her second child. With the encouragement of her psychiatrist, Sexton began to write poetry as a part of her therapy in December 1956. In 1961, she was appointed as a scholar at Radcliffe Institute, and she soon achieved wide acclaim; among many other awards, she won the Pulitzer Prize in 1967. She was in heavy demand as a reader of her poetry and, in 1968, formed a "chamber rock" group, Anne Sexton and Her Kind. In 1970, she accepted a teaching position in creative writing at Boston University. A few years later, at forty-five, after bouts of depression and substance abuse, she committed suicide by idling her car in a closed garage. After Plath's suicide, Sexton was envious that Plath had crawled "down alone / into the death I wanted so badly and for so long" ("Sylvia's Death"). But after Sexton's suicide, leading women poets responded differently, for fear of the dangerous pattern that was being set. While speaking "in Anne's honor and memory," Adrienne Rich said: "We have had enough suicidal women poets, enough suicidal women, enough of self-destructiveness as the sole form of violence permitted to women" (*On Lies, Secrets, and Silence*). In Sexton's obituary, Denise Levertov wrote: "We who are alive must make clear, as she could not, the distinction between creativity and self-destruction" ("Light Up the Cave").

Her Kind

I have gone out, a possessed witch,
haunting the black air, braver at night;
dreaming evil, I have done my hitch
over the plain houses, light by light:
lonely thing, twelve-fingered,[1] out of mind.
A woman like that is not a woman, quite.
I have been her kind.

I have found the warm caves in the woods,
filled them with skillets, carvings, shelves,
closets, silks, innumerable goods;
fixed the suppers for the worms and the elves:
whining, rearranging the disaligned.
A woman like that is misunderstood.
I have been her kind.

I have ridden in your cart, driver,
waved my nude arms at villages going by,

1. Witches were traditionally believed to have six fingers on each hand.

learning the last bright routes, survivor
where your flames still bite my thigh
and my ribs crack where your wheels wind.
A woman like that is not ashamed to die.
I have been her kind.

1960

The Truth the Dead Know

For my mother, born March 1902, died March 1959
and my father, born February 1900, died June 1959

Gone, I say and walk from church,
refusing the stiff procession to the grave,
letting the dead ride alone in the hearse.
It is June. I am tired of being brave.

We drive to the Cape. I cultivate
myself where the sun gutters from the sky,
where the sea swings in like an iron gate
and we touch. In another country people die.

My darling, the wind falls in like stones
from the whitehearted water and when we touch
we enter touch entirely. No one's alone.
Men kill for this, or for as much.

And what of the dead? They lie without shoes
in their stone boats. They are more like stone
than the sea would be if it stopped. They refuse
to be blessed, throat, eye and knucklebone.

1962

All My Pretty Ones

All my pretty ones?
Did you say all? O hell-kite! All?
What! all my pretty chickens and their dam
At one fell swoop? . . .
I cannot but remember such things were,
That were most precious to me.
—Macbeth[2]

Father, this year's jinx rides us apart
where you followed our mother to her cold slumber;
a second shock boiling its stone to your heart,

2. Macduff's lament on learning that Macbeth has had his wife and children brutally murdered (*Macbeth* 4.3.217–25).

leaving me here to shuffle and disencumber
you from the residence you could not afford:
a gold key, your half of a woolen mill,
twenty suits from Dunne's, an English Ford,
the love and legal verbiage of another will,
boxes of pictures of people I do not know.
I touch their cardboard faces. They must go.

But the eyes, as thick as wood in this album,
hold me. I stop here, where a small boy
waits in a ruffled dress for someone to come . . .
for this soldier who holds his bugle like a toy
or for this velvet lady who cannot smile.
Is this your father's father, this commodore
in a mailman suit? My father, time meanwhile
has made it unimportant who you are looking for.
I'll never know what these faces are all about.
I lock them into their book and throw them out.

This is the yellow scrapbook that you began
the year I was born; as crackling now and wrinkly
as tobacco leaves: clippings where Hoover outran
the Democrats,[3] wiggling his dry finger at me
and Prohibition; news where the *Hindenburg* went
down[4] and recent years where you went flush
on war. This year, solvent but sick, you meant
to marry that pretty widow in a one-month rush.
But before you had that second chance, I cried
on your fat shoulder. Three days later you died.

These are the snapshots of marriage, stopped in places.
Side by side at the rail toward Nassau[5] now;
here, with the winner's cup at the speedboat races,
here, in tails at the Cotillion, you take a bow,
here, by our kennel of dogs with their pink eyes,
running like show-bred pigs in their chain-link pen;
here, at the horseshow where my sister wins a prize;
and here, standing like a duke among groups of men.
Now I fold you down, my drunkard, my navigator,
my first lost keeper, to love or look at later.

I hold a five-year diary that my mother kept
for three years, telling all she does not say
of your alcoholic tendency. You overslept,
she writes. My God, father, each Christmas Day
with your blood, will I drink down your glass
of wine? The diary of your hurly-burly years
goes to my shelf to wait for my age to pass.
Only in this hoarded span will love persevere.

3. In the presidential election of 1928.
4. The German airship *Hindenburg* was destroyed by fire, at Lakeville, N.J., in 1936.
5. In the Bahamas.

Whether you are pretty or not, I outlive you,
bend down my strange face to yours and forgive you.

1962

The Starry Night

That does not keep me from having a terrible need of—shall I say the word—religion. Then I go out at night to paint the stars.
—Vincent Van Gogh[6] in a letter to his brother

The town does not exist
except where one black-haired tree slips
up like a drowned woman into the hot sky.
The town is silent. The night boils with eleven stars.
Oh starry starry night! This is how
I want to die.

It moves. They are all alive.
Even the moon bulges in its orange irons
to push children, like a god, from its eye.
The old unseen serpent swallows up the stars.
Oh starry starry night! This is how
I want to die:

into that rushing beast of the night,
sucked up by that great dragon, to split
from my life with no flag,
no belly,
no cry.

1962

From The Death of the Fathers

2. *How We Danced*

The night of my cousin's wedding
I wore blue.
I was nineteen
and we danced, Father, we orbited.
We moved like angels washing themselves.
We moved like two birds on fire.
Then we moved like the sea in a jar,
slower and slower.
The orchestra played
"Oh how we danced on the night we were wed."

6. Dutch painter (1853–1890); in his thirties, he became insane and finally committed suicide. His brother was his only confidant; this letter was written to him in September 1888 from Arles, France. At this time, Van Gogh was painting *Starry Night on the Rhône*.

And you waltzed me like a lazy Susan
and we were dear,
very dear.
Now that you are laid out,
useless as a blind dog,
now that you no longer lurk,
the song rings in my head.
Pure oxygen was the champagne we drank
and clicked our glasses, one to one.
The champagne breathed like a skin diver
and the glasses were crystal and the bride
and groom gripped each other in sleep
like nineteen-thirty marathon dancers.
Mother was a belle and danced with twenty men.
You danced with me never saying a word.
Instead the serpent spoke as you held me close.
The serpent, that mocker, woke up and pressed against me
like a great god and we bent together
like two lonely swans.

1972

From The Death Baby

1. Dreams

I was an ice baby.
I turned to sky blue.
My tears became two glass beads.
My mouth stiffened into a dumb howl.
They say it was a dream
but I remember that hardening.

My sister at six
dreamt nightly of my death:
"The baby turned to ice.
Someone put her in the refrigerator
and she turned as hard as a Popsicle."

I remember the stink of the liverwurst.
How I was put on a platter and laid
between the mayonnaise and the bacon.
The rhythm of the refrigerator
had been disturbed.
The milk bottle hissed like a snake.
The tomatoes vomited up their stomachs.
The caviar turned to lava.
The pimentos kissed like cupids.
I moved like a lobster,
slower and slower.

The air was tiny.
The air would not do.

•

I was at the dogs' party.
I was their bone.
I had been laid out in their kennel
like a fresh turkey.

This was my sister's dream
but I remember that quartering;
I remember the sickbed smell
of the sawdust floor, the pink eyes,
the pink tongues and the teeth, those nails.
I had been carried out like Moses[7]
and hidden by the paws
of ten Boston bull terriers,
ten angry bulls
jumping like enormous roaches.
At first I was lapped,
rough as sandpaper.
I became very clean.
Then my arm was missing.
I was coming apart.
They loved me until
I was gone.

1974

The Room of My Life

Here,
in the room of my life
the objects keep changing.
Ashtrays to cry into,
the suffering brother of the wood walls,
the forty-eight keys of the typewriter
each an eyeball that is never shut,
the books, each a contestant in a beauty contest,
the black chair, a dog coffin made of Naugahyde,
the sockets on the wall
waiting like a cave of bees,
the gold rug
a conversation of heels and toes,
the fireplace
a knife waiting for someone to pick it up,
the sofa, exhausted with the exertion of a whore,
the phone

7. According to tradition, Moses' parents hid him for three months and then set him afloat in a basket on the Nile River to avoid an Egyptian edict that all newborn, male Hebrews were to be killed.

two flowers taking root in its crotch,
the doors
opening and closing like sea clams,
the lights
poking at me,
lighting up both the soil and the laugh.
The windows,
the starving windows
that drive the trees like nails into my heart.
Each day I feed the world out there
although birds explode
right and left.
I feed the world in here too,
offering the desk puppy biscuits.
However, nothing is just what it seems to be.
My objects dream and wear new costumes,
compelled to, it seems, by all the words in my hands
and the sea that bangs in my throat.

1975

A. K. Ramanujan
1929–1993

The most distinguished English-language Indian poet of the twentieth century, Attipat Krishnaswami Ramanujan wrote a body of poetry that—in its crosscultural texture and subject matter—is witness to the complex cultural intermingling within India and across much of the contemporary world. Born in Mysore to a Tamil Brahman family, he grew up in Karnataka and moved among different languages. Downstairs in the family home, he spoke Tamil with his mother. Upstairs, he spoke English with his father, a mathematics professor at Mysore University. On the terrace at night, he learned from his father—also an astronomer and astrologist—the English and Sanskrit names of the stars. Outside, Kannada was the language of the streets. These became the languages of his life's work as poet, translator, and linguist.

Having moved to the United States in 1959, Ramanujan often quipped that he was "the hyphen in Indian-American." The paradoxes of his life, lived among multiple cultures and languages, are many. Though rooted in south Indian Brahman culture, he wrote primarily in English and drew on such modern poets as W. B. Yeats, Ezra Pound, William Carlos Williams, and Wallace Stevens. Far from being an apologist for an essential "Indianness," he criticized Sanskrit-based Indology, Hindu zealotry, and Indian revivalism. Resisting the "monism" and even "cultural imperialism" of proponents of a single "pan-Indian Sanskritic Great Tradition," he brought attention to neglected literatures of south India such as the Dravidian. He affirmed that "cultural traditions in India are indissolubly plural and often conflicting" ("Where Mirrors Are Windows: Towards an Anthology of Reflections"). "India does not have one past," he emphasized, "but many pasts" ("Classics Lost and Found").

Though an English-language poet in the United States, Ramanujan devoted his life to South Asian studies, wrote primarily about India, drew inspiration from Dravidian literatures, and often seemed clinically detached from the English language he worked in. Best known in the West for his crystalline translations of classical and medieval Tamil and Kannada verse, Ramanujan draws on many features of these older literatures in his own anglophone poetry: the strikingly vivid and structural use of metaphor, the intensification of one image by another, "montage" and "dissolve" effects, streams of association, flowing syntax, spare diction, avoidance of heavily stressed rhythms, delight in irony and paradox, precise observation of both interior (*akam*) and exterior (*puṟam*) worlds, and reliance not on metaphysical abstraction but on physical detail for complex thinking. Ramanujan's indigenous models complement Anglo-modernist principles of concision, economy, and nondecorative use of metaphor.

His eye a "rainbow bubble," Ramanujan would, as he rhymes in "Mythologies 2," "see all things double." Straddling the divide between East and West, First World and Third, his work fuses ancient Dravidian poetics with modern forms. At the heart of his poetry are ironic, if plangent, meditations on cultural transfer and loss between East and West, on survivals and disappearances between past and present. His delight in metaphorical resemblance helps him leap the gap between these worlds, even as he skeptically measures the distance between them. Questing after his genetic, psychological, and cultural origins in the wittily entitled "Elements of Composition," as in "Drafts," Ramanujan acknowledges that our mixed and irrecuperable pasts must change the moment we look for them. His depiction of the self resembles a traditional Indian vision of identity as embedded in endlessly fluid, concentrically arranged contexts (as in the concept of *samsara*). At the same time, it can also seem compatible with a postmodern vision of the self as decentered, composite, and provisional.

The family—with its multiple reflections and opacities in relation to the self—is frequently the locus of Ramanujan's poetic acts of self-definition. In poems such as "Self-Portrait" and "Extended Family," the poet defines himself by sorting through his resemblances with his grandparents, parents, and children. Located in dislocation, he puzzles over the ironic connections and differences between himself in Chicago and his grandfather in India, as between a modern Western lightbulb and the ancient Vedic sun.

After receiving a B.A. in English literature from Mysore University in 1949, Ramanujan taught English in Indian schools and became fascinated with Indian folklore. He began to study linguistics at Deccan College and continued on a Fulbright grant at Indiana University in 1959, completing his dissertation in 1963. In 1961, he taught for the first time at the University of Chicago, where he gave classes in linguistics, South Asian languages and civilizations, and creative writing until his death. In 1976, Ramanujan was honored by the Indian government with the Padma Shri, awarded for distinguished service to the nation; in 1983, he received a MacArthur Fellowship.

Self-Portrait

I resemble everyone
but myself, and sometimes see
in shop-windows,
    despite the well-known laws
    of optics,
the portrait of a stranger,
date unknown,
often signed in a corner
by my father.

1966

Elements of Composition

Composed as I am, like others,
of elements on certain well-known lists,
father's seed and mother's egg

gathering earth, air, fire, mostly
water, into a mulberry mass,
moulding calcium,

carbon, even gold, magnesium and such,
into a chattering self tangled
in love and work,

scary dreams, capable of eyes that can see,
only by moving constantly,
the constancy of things

like Stonehenge or cherry trees;

add uncle's eleven fingers
making shadow-plays of rajas[1]
and cats, hissing,

becoming fingers again, the look
of panic on sister's face
an hour before

her wedding, a dated newspaper map
of a place one has never seen, maybe
no longer there

after the riots, downtown Nairobi,[2]
that a friend carried in his passport
as others would

a woman's picture in their wallets;

add the lepers of Madurai,[3]
male, female, married,
with children,

lion faces, crabs for claws,
clotted on their shadows
under the stone-eyed

1. Indian kings or princes.
2. Capital of Kenya.
3. City in south India where leprosy is a continuing problem.

goddesses of dance, mere pillars,
   moving as nothing on earth
can move—

I pass through them
   as they pass through me
taking and leaving

affections, seeds, skeletons,

millennia of fossil records
   of insects that do not last
a day,

body-prints of mayflies,
   a legend half-heard
in a train

of the half-man searching
   for an ever-fleeing
other half[4]

through Muharram[5] tigers,
   hyacinths in crocodile waters,
and the sweet

twisted lives of epileptic saints,

and even as I add,
   I lose, decompose
into my elements,

into other names and forms,
   past, and passing, tenses
without time,

caterpillar on a leaf, eating,
   being eaten.[6]

1986

4. Elsewhere, Ramanujan compares the Hindu myth of the god that "splits himself into male and female" to "the androgynous figure in Plato's *Symposium*, halved into male and female segments which forever seek each other and crave union" ("Some Thoughts on 'Non-Western' Classics, with Indian Examples").

5. During the first month of the Islamic calendar, Muharram processions, often including dancers in tiger masks, commemorate the martyrdom of Muhammad's grandson, Husein.

6. According to the *Taittiriya Upanishad*, "What eats is eaten, / and what's eaten, eats / in turn" (Ramanujan's translation).

Alien

A foetus in an acrobat's womb,
   ignorant yet of barbed wire
and dotted lines,

hanger-on in terror of the fall
   while the mother-world turns somersaults,
whirling on the single bar,

as her body shapes under water
   a fish with gills into a baby
with a face

getting ready to make faces,
   and hands that will soon feel the powder touch
of monarch butterflies,

the tin and silver of nickel and dime,
   and learn right and left to staple, fold
and mutilate

a paper world in search of identity cards.

1986

Drafts

1

A rough draft, getting rougher:
   a struggle in the crowd to see
the well-known

but half-seen Hyde Park[7] rapist's face
   half-seen perhaps only by another,
unseen

because seen too often; now towards,
   now away from what one thought
one always knew

without the help of policemen's
   drawings, a trayful of noses
and cruel lips.

7. Neighborhood on the south side of Chicago in which the University of Chicago is located.

2

Itself a copy of lost events,
   the original is nowhere, of which things,
even these hands,

seem but copies, garbled by a ciphered
   script, opaque as the Indus,[8]
to be refigured

from broken seals, headless bodies,
   mere fingers, of merchants and dancers
in a charred city

with sewers, bath houses, a horned god
   of beasts among real homebodies,
family quarrels,

itches, clogs in the drain, the latter
   too ordinary to be figured
in the classic seals.

3

And we have originals, clay tigers
   that aboriginals drown after each small-
pox ritual,

or dinosaur smells, that leave no copies;
   and copies with displaced originals
like these words,

adopted daughters researching parents
   through maiden names in changing languages,
telephone books,

and familiar grins in railway stations.

4

The DNA leaves copies in me and mine
   of grandfather's violins, and programmes
of much older music;

the epilepsies go to an uncle
   to fill him with hymns and twitches,
bypassing me for now;

8. River in India before 1947; after, in Pakistan.

mother's migraines translate, I guess,
into allergies, a fear of black cats,
and a daughter's passion

for bitter gourd and Dostoevsky;[9]
mother's almond eyes mix with my wife's
ancestral hazel

to give my son green flecks in a painter's eye,
but the troubled look is all his own.

1986

Extended Family

Yet like grandfather
I bathe before the village crow

the dry chlorine water
my only Ganges[1]

the naked Chicago bulb
a cousin of the Vedic sun[2]

slap soap on my back
like father

and think
in proverbs

like me
I wipe myself dry

with an unwashed
Sears turkish towel

like mother
I hear faint morning song

(though here it sounds
Japanese)

9. Fyodor Dostoyevsky (1821–1881), Russian novelist.
1. Indian river considered sacred in Hinduism; many make pilgrimages to bathe in its holy waters.
2. The Vedas—the holy texts of Hinduism—portray the sun as various gods and the divine source of all knowledge.

and three clear strings
nextdoor

through kitchen
clatter

like my little daughter
I play shy

hand over crotch
my body not yet full

of thoughts novels
and children

I hold my peepee
like my little son

play garden hose
in and out
the bathtub

like my grandson
I look up

unborn
at myself

like my great
great-grandson

I am not yet
may never be

my future
dependent

on several
people

yet
to come

1986

Chicago Zen

i

Now tidy your house,
dust especially your living room

and do not forget to name
all your children.

ii

Watch your step. Sight may strike you
blind in unexpected places.

The traffic light turns orange
on 57th and Dorchester,[3] and you stumble,

you fall into a vision of forest fires,
enter a frothing Himalayan river,

rapid, silent.

On the 14th floor,
Lake Michigan crawls and crawls

in the window. Your thumbnail
cracks a lobster louse on the windowpane

from your daughter's hair
and you drown, eyes open,

towards the Indies, the antipodes.[4]
And you, always so perfectly sane.

iii

Now you know what you always knew:
the country cannot be reached

by jet. Nor by boat on jungle river,
hashish behind the Monkey-temple,

nor moonshot to the cratered Sea
of Tranquility, slim circus girls

3. Fifty-seventh Street and Dorchester Avenue, near the University of Chicago.

4. The place on the surface of the earth directly opposite one's current location.

on a tightrope between tree and tree
with white parasols, or the one

and only blue guitar.[5]

Nor by any
other means of transport,

migrating with a clean valid passport,
no, not even by transmigrating

without any passport at all,
but only by answering ordinary

black telephones, questions
walls and small children ask,

and answering all calls of nature.

iv

Watch your step, watch it, I say,
especially at the first high
threshold,

and the sudden low
one near the end
of the flight
of stairs,

and watch
for the last
step that's never there.

1986

Foundlings in the Yukon

In the Yukon[6] the other day
miners found the skeleton
of a lemming
curled around some seeds
in a burrow:
sealed off by a landslide
in Pleistocene times.[7]

5. Cf. Wallace Stevens, "The Man with the Blue Guitar."
6. Mountainous territory in northwestern Canada.
7. The Great Ice Age.

Six grains were whole,
unbroken: picked and planted
ten thousand
years after their time,
they took root
within forty-eight hours
and sprouted
a candelabra of eight small leaves.

A modern Alaskan lupine,[8]
I'm told, waits three years to come
to flower, but these
upstarts drank up sun
and unfurled early
with the crocuses of March
as if long deep
burial had made them hasty

for birth and season, for names,
genes, for passing on:
like the kick
and shift of an intra-uterine
memory, like
this morning's dream of being
born in an eagle's
nest with speckled eggs and the screech

of nestlings, like a pent-up
centenarian's sudden burst
of lust, or maybe
just elegies in Duino[9] unbound
from the dark,
these new aborigines biding
their time
for the miner's night-light

to bring them their dawn,
these infants compact with age,
older than the oldest
things alive, having skipped
a million falls
and the registry of tree-rings,
suddenly younger
by an accident of flowering

than all their timely descendants.

1995

8. Alaskan wildflower.
9. Rainer Maria Rilke (1875–1926), Austro-German poet, overcame thirteen years of writer's block in Duino Castle (near Trieste), where he wrote a famous series of elegies.

Richard Howard
b. 1929

Since Gustave Flaubert, certainly since James Joyce, poetry has seemed to lose ground to the novel, which in the twentieth century appropriated many of the techniques of language once reserved for poetry. Yet a number of postwar American poets, most notably Robert Lowell and Randall Jarrell, have attempted to recapture for poetry lost areas of dramatic interest and psychological complexity. So too has Richard Howard, particularly in his dramatic monologues. Howard's inspiration was certainly Robert Browning, and the late nineteenth century, among other historical periods, often provides Howard with subjects and ambience. Using memoirs, letters, and newspapers, he re-creates a gallery of men and women, gives them life, and lets them have their say. In his later books, particularly in the wake of the AIDS epidemic, Howard has written memorable poems depicting contemporary gay, urban life, such as "My Last Hustler." In " 'Man Who Beat Up Homosexuals Reported to Have AIDS Virus,' " he juxtaposes the dramatic voices of an assailant's sister-in-law and one of his victims, who has suffered injuries and yet remains, like many of Howard's characters, intellectually robust. Howard brings to these late poems his considerable skills in narrative, dramatic voice, and wordplay.

Howard's poems are characterized by great variety and vivacity. They are bookish and learned; like Marianne Moore, Howard seems to squirrel away odd facts and quotations for which he will someday find a poetic use. He is a critic and translator, an addict of language, fascinated by minute instances of its powers to connect and disguise, and pleased with his own virtuosity in using it. In his poetry, the language accumulates closely woven details in a molecular fashion.

Howard was born on May 13, 1929, in Cleveland, Ohio. He was educated at Columbia University and at the Sorbonne. He lived abroad for a time, but he found the expatriate's life uncomfortable and moved to New York, where he now teaches at Columbia. Besides many collections of poems (the first published in 1962) and critical studies of postwar American poetry, Howard has published more than 150 translations from French, ranging from the works of Alain Robbe-Grillet and Roland Barthes to the memoirs of General Charles de Gaulle. He has won many prizes and awards, including the Pulitzer Prize in 1970 for *Untitled Subjects.*

"Man Who Beat Up Homosexuals Reported to Have AIDS Virus"

—The New York Times, *March 8, 1991*

to the memory of Alan Barnett

To *The New York Times:* Your health editor
may not print this; my social-worker says
   it will do me good
to write it anyway, and in my case
the terminal treatment has to be truth.
   Not much else, by now,
can "do me good": the hospital routine
laboriously contends with new bouts

of pneumocystis,[1]
thereby bestowing leisure to survey
my escalating KS[2] lesions—caught
red-handed . . . Last week
you ran an article about a man
whose name you withhold, though his age agrees
with his appearance
when I was in his hands, and he in mine.
This was years ago, long before there was
a reason to think
such handling was red, or led to being dead!
I can identify him all the same,
though all different
from actions in which he says he took part.

—If he took part, then which of us took all?
For all was taken,
as you report: I am one of the "many
gay men beaten in the 1980's
by a truck-driver
in the New York area," and I owe
myself whatever account I can give
of that episode.
It is not the reason I am here, nor
is my being here the result of it—
but it represents
one dimension of the life I am in
a final position (no evasions!)
to evaluate . . .

Maureen, it's Jane. Did you get the clipping? If you read it through, you realize why I had *to call . . . No, now. We need to talk. You put things off, they just get right back on and ride you worse. It has to be Jack, Sis,* your husband and the father of your girls! *Everything fits. First of all about the life-insurance screening—what a way to learn he has that terrible disease! And then that part about "the large amounts of victims' blood on himself" . . . Remember how hard it was—well,* I *can remember your complaining about it all the time—getting those stains out of his jeans* each week! *It was hard because that was blood—and not from lugging pork-bellies out of his truck! . . . I don't care what he told you, do you think I believe what Henry tells me? Of course you're not infected. How could you be if he hasn't . . . The paper said it's been ten years . . . Honey, I know: we're middle-aged, thank God! You don't imagine that Henry and I . . . ? Maureen, you've got to get it through your head there's something wrong with Jack. And I don't mean his getting sick now—wrong all the way back. Dumb of me to think the girls would tell you . . . Sis, do you understand how men get AIDS?*

1. Form of pneumonia that often accompanies the later stages of AIDS.
2. Kaposi's sarcoma, skin disease characterized by reddish lesions, commonly afflicting AIDS sufferers.

My social-worker says "we have to be
downright" (she invariably says
"we" when she means me)
and goes on to assure me that *God is
in the details*—she doubtless heard the phrase
in her Crisis-Class
("Depression and Dying") only last week.
It could be true, for all I know; there's not
much hope of finding
Him in the Master Plan. So let's pray
she's right. Herewith the (divine) specifics:
maybe five years back
I met Mr. X one Saturday night
—more likely it was a Sunday morning—
as I came around
the corner of Washington and Bethune:[3]
a vision! He was playing with himself
in the open cab
of a pork-butcher's van—such diversions
are often met with in the meat-market,
appropriately,
since he asked, when I started cruising him,
if I wanted some. Meat. (I know you won't
run any of this,
but I'm being downright.) So I went down
on him in the back of his truck. Dark there,
hard to see—you have
to feel your way on such occasions—but
I found it easy enough to do that . . .
I found it easy.

Why would *he tell you . . . why tell anyone? A married man with three daughters: Maureen, he must have known people would never think . . . Did* he *ever think . . . ? And that would make it easy for him to do the things he did—easier: he was their dad, whatever else he was . . . When did it start? Probably once you and he . . . stopped. Being in New York must have made a difference too. Because New York is different . . . from Nebraska, anyway. I'm not trying to be funny—you always said you hated living there, right up to when they transferred him back here . . . Maybe you knew why, even if there was no way for you to know . . . The paper said he went out looking for . . . the other kind (maybe they weren't so "other" after all) several times a week—you must have thought* something *even if you wanted not to. Maureen, the paper said "too many times to count"—no,* "to remember." *And it said the other drivers went out with him too. Does that sound right to you? Sis, when did Jack do things* with *others? Even beat up queers?*

Once he was through, or I was—hard to tell
who it is completes such actions, who is

3. Intersection in lower Manhattan.

active, as they say,
and who is passive (even a woman
is never really passive, I suppose)—
once our thing was done,
he began talking to me in the dark—
till then, of course, he hadn't breathed a word,
just breathed, and after
a while of breathing, the usual moan . . .
Maybe my downright talent made him feel
he could shoot the works . . .
He asked, was that all I wanted to do,
and if it was, would I do something else
for him. Something more.
He moved around, I knew what he wanted—
it was easy to tell by the clatter
his belt-buckle made
against the floor. I started to explain
about my "proclivities" (not doing
what my father did),
and as if, right then, something about *him*
had been exposed, something unbearably
humiliating,
he began to yell and lash out at me
with that belt. If it was too dark for me
to guess that my *not*
doing what he needed would enrage him,
it was also too dark for him to see
where the hell I was:
I managed to slither out of *harm's way*
during the mayhem, and to haul myself
eventually
out of the *van,* but not before we both
were something of a mess. That was my clue
to my "assailant"—
there must have been blood, my blood, all over
the place, just as *The Times* reported it.
All in a night's work.

He claims he hasn't done it in three years: maybe he doesn't need to do it now, but maybe he will. Maybe he has *to. Maureen, you've got to trust your own sister: are there times when he takes it out on you? No one talks about beating, but I know it happens in a lot of "happy homes." I'm trying to help you. Listen to me! It could be years before Jack ever shows signs he has this thing—he may keep his strength for quite a while . . . I know you want to take care of him when he's not able to . . . when he needs help. It's a damn good thing you do—at this point I can't see why anyone else would: Maureen, he likes to hurt people! But you've got to take care of yourself first. If it passed into* his *blood from someone he beat up, what about yours? I suppose that's the only way it could happen now . . . Keep away from him if he—Sis, you know what I mean: if he can't go out for it, what's to keep him from beginning at home, like charity? I'm not joking, Maureen, I just want you to recognize the truth . . . If men are more devious than women it must be because they have more to hide.*

But I doubt—being downright—if my man
had much to fear from me—certainly not
   from any of my
blood in any cuts of his, as he told
the Nebraska medical officers.
   I suspected—being
downright and outright—his dose could be traced
to an administration of the same
   bodily fluids
as those I was punished for declining
to provide. Not every faggot who climbs
   into a meat-truck
has my limitations, I know plenty
who would be pleased (*and* able) to oblige
   by humping a hunk . . .
Furthermore—being down and out—I couldn't
care less. I lie here wondering (most days,
   my only life-sign,
unless you count reading *The New York Times*
as a sign of life—and you would, although
   the *Living* section
is sometimes too much for me) . . . Wondering
is what my time is good for—good times! and
   what I wonder is
if the life I have always lived ("always"
being the last 20 years, who could know
   they would be the last?)
was mine at all, my choice—unless it was
just the life I could never acknowledge
   to *The New York Times*
(of course I'm using you as a symbol),
a life so sexually myopic[4]
   I knew only those
faces I had kissed—and not always those!
Is this what it comes to? A tribal tale
   of A Thousand Nights
and a Night, except that this Scheherazade
gets herself 86'd[5] . . . Sex turns out like
   reading (believe me
I know whereof I speak—in my corner
the comparison is anything but idle)
   because it gives you
somewhere to get to when you have to stay
where you are. But life is used up, if it's
   used, spent, or wasted . . .

4. Short-sighted.
5. Killed. In *A Thousand and One Nights* (fourteenth century), the condemned Scheherazade keeps herself alive by telling stories each night.

Mama always used to tell us you get what you pay for. Maureen, that was a crock! I've learned better, and so have you, by now: you pay for what you get. *Jack has to pay, so do you and the girls, Henry and I. The hard thing is to understand just what he got. Not Henry, Jack! Sis, don't be dumb . . . I know he got this disease, what I mean is, what did he get out of what he did that has to be paid for by getting AIDS? Damn right it's a judgment—isn't everything? I'm not saying he doesn't deserve it, it's just that if you're going to see him through to the end, you'd better understand the satisfaction—no, it's more than that: the rush, the thrill, or whatever it is doing things like that to other men could give him. If AIDS is so awful, then* that *has to have been so good. Do you see? You have to realize the joy of it if you're going to reckon up the pain. Think about it, Maureen. I'll call you back once Henry's gone to bed. We'll talk some more.*

The Times keeps referring to a *life-style*
as having consequences. That is why
  I've made this gesture:
not to dispute your claim, but to insist
the consequences are *not* a judgment!
  This sickness I got
is no sentence passed on my wickedness—
recalling which "wickedness" makes up,
  now as before, most
of what I have lived for. Not died for,
I'm grateful, even to Mr. X . . .
  Why should his actions
incur a verdict, any more than mine?
By the time he reaches whatever wards
  Nebraska affords
(social-worker or not), I hope he can
summon up, as I did, the impulse that
  brought us together
and remembers me. That is what it comes
down to: a matter of remembering
  certain encounters,
certain moments entirely free of time.
I am no longer able to excite
  myself (is that verb
fit to print?), my visions are purely that,
just visions, endless reruns of the scenes
  I have collected.
Remembering is not even the word:
making comes closer. Where understanding
  fails, a word will come
to take its place. Making is my word,
my enterprise. Believe me, I lived through
  such episodes as
the sad one I have described for the sake
of . . . what? Of whatever was exchanged there
  in the dark meat-van

before the end . . . The second half of joy,
somebody said, is shorter than the first,
and that gets it right.
Whatever's left of my life, I am *making*,
the way I made it happen all along
—I replay the scenes
from that movie The Past, starring not
Mr. X playing opposite myself
but Endymion,
Narcissus, Patroclus,[6] all the fellows
I have welcomed to the tiny duchy[7]
of my bed—the world's
only country entirely covered by
its flag. I thank you for "covering"
as well as you could
the story to which I have provided
such a lengthy follow-up—gay men do
go in for length, or
at least go out for it; that is part of
our mythology. And now, perhaps, you
know another part . . .
The nurse has just come in with another
delicious concoction. The social-worker
awaits . . . (Name Withheld).

1994

My Last Hustler

. . . all smiles stopped[8]

When "Brad" is lying naked, or rather naked is lying
in wait for whatever those he refers to as clients require
by way of what *they* refer to as satisfaction, denying
himself the distraction of alcohol or amyl,[9] there appears
in his eyes no flicker of shame, no flare of shameless desire,
and what tribute he is paid finds him neither tender nor fierce.

On a bed above suspicion, creases in obviously fresh
linen still mapping a surface only a little creamier than
the creaseless hills and hollows of his compliant flesh,
Brad will extend himself (as the graphic saying goes)
and the upper hand—always his—will push into place *the man*
who happens to be there till happening comes to blows

6. In Homer's *Iliad,* Achilles' companion, whose death he mourns bitterly. The other two names are from Greek mythology. *Endymion:* beautiful young man loved by the moon and put to sleep forever by Zeus. *Narcissus:* young man condemned to fall in love with his own reflection.

7. Domain of a duke; special territory.

8. From "My Last Duchess," a dramatic monologue by English poet Robert Browning (1812–1889).

9. Amyl nitrate, a powerful stimulant believed to be an aphrodisiac.

(another saying you now more fully grasp): full-blown,
Brad will prepare himself, though not precipitately,
for the grateful-kisses stage; he offers cheek and chin
but objects to undergoing your accolade on his mouth:
he has endured such homage too early, too often, too lately,
and for all his boyish ways Brad is not wholly a youth.

Routines on some arduous rigging, however, can restore
him to himself in mirrors, every which way surrounded
by no more than what he seems and mercifully *by no more.*
Booked by a merciless Service for a thousand afternoons,
Brad will become the needs of his "regulars" confounded
by his indifferent regard, by his regardless expense . . .

Take him—young faithful!—there and then. Marvel! praise!
Fond though your touch may be and truly feeling your tact,
yet a mocking echo returns—remote, vague, blasé—
of Every Future Caress, so very like your own!
However entranced the scene you make (the two of you act
as one to all appearance, but one is always alone),

derision will come to mind, or to matter over mind:
the folly, in carnal collusion, of mere presented *skill.*
Undone, played out, discharged, one insight you will have gained
which cannot for all these ardent lapses be gainsaid
—even his murmured subsidence an exercise of will—
is the sudden absolute knowledge Brad would rather be dead.

1999

Adrienne Rich
1929–2012

Adrienne Rich was the leading feminist poet of the twentieth century. Her poetry and prose writings confound distinctions between the private inner world of emotions and the public sphere. "*The moment when a feeling enters the body,*" she wrote, "is political" ("The Blue Ghazals"). Even so, one way to take the measure of her contribution to contemporary poetry is to place her work in the dual contexts of the intensely personal poetry that came out of the so-called confessional school and the resonantly public, even prophetic poetry that extends from Walt Whitman to H. D., Muriel Rukeyser, and Allen Ginsberg. Adapting Whitman's poetics of multiple identification, Rich assimilated women and men of various times and places into her poetry. She crossed divisions of ethnicity, nationality, and class in her sympathies, daring to help dream into existence noncoercive forms of social affiliation. The visionary breadth and ethical force of her poetry are stirring, even though she questioned the possibility of using poetic language to reach beyond self to community.

In seeking to transcend private verse, Rich populated her poems with emblematic female figures. When she wrote about the lives of women in "Snapshots of a Daughter-in-Law" and "Diving into the Wreck," the central figures allegorize the entrapment of women within limiting patriarchal norms and the feminist quest for a revisionary understanding of history and identity. As a public poet, Rich defied the modernist injunctions against abstraction and allegory, in search of "a common language" that will describe shared historical experience.

Rich's descriptions of both herself and others are compelling, however, because they straddle the general and the particular. Her protagonists, if emblematic, are also vividly imagined. "Snapshots of a Daughter-in-Law," inverting traditional norms of female beauty, compares the gleam of a woman's shaved legs to "petrified mammoth-tusk"; the speaker of "Diving into the Wreck" dons flippers, mask, and "the body-armor of black rubber" to descend into the shipwreck of history. "Power," about Marie Curie and her experiments with radiation, ends with the memorable claim that "her wounds came from the same source as her power." This assertion is effective in part because earlier in the poem Rich has drawn Curie's portrait in painful detail—"the cracked and suppurating skin of her finger-ends." Similarly, Rich's self-conception was that of a poet, in her own words, "neither unique nor universal, but a person in history, a woman and not a man, a white and also Jewish inheritor of a particular Western consciousness, from the making of which most women have been excluded" (foreword to *The Fact of a Doorframe*).

In writing about personal feeling and family experience, Rich was influenced by such contemporaries as Robert Lowell, Sylvia Plath, and Anne Sexton. Like them, she understood emotions to be complex and ambivalent—"Poetry," she said, "is a way of expressing unclear feeling" (quoted in Joyce Greenberg, "By Woman Taught," *Parnassus* 7 [1979])—and she wrote about her vexed relationship with her father to understand the formation of her identity, which was early on, by her own accounting, male identified. Her father was an authoritarian figure who harshly supervised her schoolwork and early poetry writing, but she also credited him with teaching her "to believe in hard work," ideas, and language ("Split at the Root: An Essay on Jewish Identity"). In the long poem *Sources*, she reactivates her rage toward him, while also seeing behind his facade of "power and arrogance . . . the suffering of the Jew, the alien stamp you bore." Rich's use of apostrophe, here as elsewhere, both animates her strong but conflicted voice and vivifies the presence of her addressee. She speaks in tenderness and rage, empathy and resistance. In her brilliant book on motherhood, *Of Woman Born* (1976), she affirms such complexity of feeling: "Love and anger *can* exist concurrently." When she addresses her "Grandmothers," in a poem of that title, she describes both the unsatisfying compromises they lived and her own lingering mixed feelings toward them. She writes in an essay, "my gentile grandmother and my mother were also frustrated artists and intellectuals, a lost writer and a lost composer between them" ("Split at the Root").

Rich was also one of the most well-known contemporary love poets. In her groundbreaking series *Twenty-One Love Poems*, first published in a limited edition of 1976, she conjures the erotic passions and daily experiences of a lesbian relationship, recalling only to undermine the Elizabethan sonnet sequences written by men to an impossibly idealized ladylove. Here, as in her family poetry, the relationship is both celebrated and, given its ultimate failure, lamented. Rich said that "poetry can break open locked chambers of possibility, restore numbed zones to feeling, recharge desire" (preface to *What Is Found There*). Although some critics look on her work as doctrinal, it is tonally ambiguous, shot through with emotional contradictions, startlingly clear about the murkiest feelings. And as she self-mockingly suggests in a late poem about a heterosexual relationship, one's feelings—like the poems in which they are embedded—do not always conform to one's theories: "An idea declared itself between us / clear as a washed wineglass / that we'd love / regardless of manifestos I wrote or signed" ("Regardless"). In this poem and in "Seven Skins," Rich's career as love poet takes an unexpected turn, when she reconsiders—with tenderness, self-criticism, and wry humor—her early heterosexual experience.

For Rich, personal feelings could never be completely separated from politics. To reject the tyranny of the voice of the father, for example, was a hard-won political act; Rich had internalized that censorious voice and been taught as a girl that anger was a "dark, wicked blotch" to be avoided (*Of Woman Born*). She suggested that for women the rejection of the fathers is an essential first step in a process that must culminate in the reaffirmation of "woman-identified experience" ("Compulsory Heterosexuality and Lesbian Existence"). "I had been looking for the Women's Liberation Movement since the 1950s. I came into it in 1970," Rich wrote in the 1986 foreword to a collection of essays. "I identified myself as a radical feminist, and soon after—not as a political act but out of powerful and unmistakable feelings—as a lesbian" (*Blood, Bread, and Poetry*). Rich declared her lesbian identity in 1976; from that time, her companion was the Jamaican-born writer Michelle Cliff, best known for her novel *No Telephone to Heaven*. Writing about what she has called the "lesbian continuum," Rich expanded the meaning of the word *lesbian* to mean "a primary intensity between women, an intensity" that the world at large has "trivialized, caricatured, or invested with evil. . . . I believe it is the lesbian in every woman who is compelled by female energy. . . . It is the lesbian in us who drives us to feel imaginatively, render in language, grasp, the full connection between woman and woman. It is the lesbian in us who is creative, for the dutiful daughter of the fathers is only a hack" ("It Is the Lesbian in Us . . .").

Rich was born, "white and middle-class," the elder of two sisters, in Baltimore, Maryland, on May 16, 1929. She graduated from Radcliffe College in 1951, the same year W. H. Auden chose her first volume, *A Change of World*, for the Yale Series of Younger Poets. In his preface, Auden wrote, with condescending approval: "The poems a reader will encounter in this book are neatly and modestly dressed, speak quietly but do not mumble, respect their elders but are not cowed by them, and do not tell fibs." Rich was writing under the influence of male poets—by her reckoning, "Frost, Dylan Thomas, Donne, Auden, MacNeice, Stevens, Yeats"—and in the impersonal, formally tight, exacting style fostered by the New Criticism. But even an early poem such as "Aunt Jennifer's Tigers" evokes the stirrings of gender critique, as Rich suggested in her outline of her early development in the influential essay "When We Dead Awaken: Writing as Re-Vision." Determined to prove that she could be a poet and "have what was then defined as a 'full' woman's life," she married in her twenties and had three sons before she was thirty. Under these circumstances, the 1950s were desperate years for her, in which she began "to feel that politics was not something 'out there' but something 'in here' and of the essence of my condition." Then, in the late 1950s, she "was able to write, for the first time, directly about experiencing myself as a woman," in the poem "Snapshots of a Daughter-in-Law." Later, in "Planetarium," written in 1968, she reached a further synthesis, as in it "at last the woman in the poem and the woman writing the poem become the same person."

In the late 1960s, when Rich's husband accepted a teaching post at the City College of New York, they both became involved in radical politics, especially in opposition to the Vietnam War. Staying on in New York after their separation and his death by suicide in 1970, Rich also taught inner-city, minority young people. These new concerns entered the poems of *Diving into the Wreck* and *A Will to Change*. The language in these books became more urgent and fragmented, the images starker, the prosody more jagged. Punctuation is relinquished, lines are heavily enjambed and cut up by blank spaces, initial letters are infrequently capitalized, rhymes are used sparingly, and speech rhythms are more urgent. Poems often reach to become letters, throwaway leaflets, photographs, shooting scripts. Moreover, after "Snapshots," Rich dated her poems, as if to underline their provisional or journal-entry nature. Her later poetry, while still committed to a radical feminist and lesbian vision, expanded its range of concerns, encompassing global, historical, and ecological issues. It also, perhaps surprisingly, became increasingly lyrical—"the music always ran ahead of the words" ("Late Ghazal"). Rich's later poetry is compressed, imagistic, and intensely self-questioning. "Fox," for example, is a self-lacerating apostrophe to a prerational, instinctual, animal self. The title of Rich's 1971 collection, *The Will to Change*, is taken from Charles Olson's declaration in "The Kingfishers": "What does not change / is the will to change." Indeed, the will to change both herself and her world was the constant in Rich's extraordinary career.

Rich was signally honored for her poetry. In 1974, she won the National Book Award. In 1986, she was the first winner of the Ruth Lilly Poetry Prize; she also won the Lenore Marshall Prize (1992), a MacArthur Fellowship (1994), and the Tanning Prize (1996). She taught at many universities and colleges, including Stanford University (1986–93).

Aunt Jennifer's Tigers[1]

Aunt Jennifer's tigers prance across a screen,
Bright topaz denizens of a world of green.
They do not fear the men beneath the tree;
They pace in sleek chivalric certainty.

Aunt Jennifer's fingers fluttering through her wool
Find even the ivory needle hard to pull.
The massive weight of Uncle's wedding band
Sits heavily upon Aunt Jennifer's hand.

When Aunt is dead, her terrified hands will lie
Still ringed with ordeals she was mastered by.
The tigers in the panel that she made
Will go on prancing, proud and unafraid.

1951

Snapshots of a Daughter-in-Law

1

You, once a belle in Shreveport,
with henna-colored hair,[2] skin like a peachbud,
still have your dresses copied from that time,
and play a Chopin prelude
called by Cortot: "*Delicious recollections*
float like perfume through the memory."[3]

1. See Rich's discussion of this poem in "When We Dead Awaken: Writing as Re-Vision," on p. 1086 of this volume.
2. That is, red; henna is a hair dye. *Shreveport:* city in Louisiana.
3. Remark made by French pianist Alfred Cortot in his book *Chopin: 24 Preludes* (1930); he is referring specifically to Prelude No. 7 by Frédéric Chopin (1810–1849), Polish composer and pianist, who settled in Paris in 1831.

Your mind now, moldering like wedding-cake,
heavy with useless experience, rich
with suspicion, rumor, fantasy,
crumbling to pieces under the knife-edge
of mere fact. In the prime of your life.

Nervy, glowering, your daughter
wipes the teaspoons, grows another way.

2

Banging the coffee-pot into the sink
she hears the angels chiding, and looks out
past the raked gardens to the sloppy sky.
Only a week since They said: *Have no patience.*

The next time it was: *Be insatiable.*
Then: *Save yourself; others you cannot save.*
Sometimes she's let the tapstream scald her arm,
a match burn to her thumbnail,

or held her hand above the kettle's snout
right in the woolly steam. They are probably angels,
since nothing hurts her any more, except
each morning's grit blowing into her eyes.

3

A thinking woman sleeps with monsters.
The beak that grips her, she becomes. And Nature,
that sprung-lidded, still commodious
steamer-trunk of *tempora* and *mores*[4]
gets stuffed with it all: the mildewed orange-flowers,
the female pills, the terrible breasts
of Boadicea[5] beneath flat foxes' heads and orchids.

Two handsome women, gripped in argument,
each proud, acute, subtle, I hear scream
across the cut glass and majolica
like Furies[6] cornered from their prey:
The argument *ad feminam,*[7] all the old knives
that have rusted in my back, I drive in yours,
ma semblable, ma soeur![8]

4. Literally, times and customs—alluding to the protest by Roman orator Cicero (106–43 B.C.E.), "O tempora! O mores!": Alas for the degeneracy of our times and the low standards of our morals! (Latin).

5. British queen (d. 60 C.E.), who led her people in a strong but ultimately unsuccessful revolt against Roman rule. *Female pills*: remedies for menstrual pain.

6. Greek goddesses of vengeance. *Cut glass and majolica*: expensive glassware and earthenware.

7. Feminine version of the phrase *ad hominem* (to the man), referring to an argument directed not to reason but to personal prejudices and emotions.

8. The last line of "Au Lecteur" ("To the Reader"), by French poet Charles Baudelaire (1821–1867), addresses "Hypocrite lecteur!—mon semblable—mon frère!" (Hypocrite reader—like me—my brother!); Rich substitutes *ma soeur* (my sister). See also T. S. Eliot's *Waste Land*, line 76.

4

Knowing themselves too well in one another:
their gifts no pure fruition, but a thorn,
the prick filed sharp against a hint of scorn . . .
Reading while waiting
for the iron to heat,
writing, *My Life had stood—a Loaded Gun*[9]—
in that Amherst pantry while the jellies boil and scum,
or, more often,
iron-eyed and beaked and purposed as a bird,
dusting everything on the whatnot every day of life.

5

Dulce ridens, dulce loquens,[1]
she shaves her legs until they gleam
like petrified mammoth-tusk.

6

When to her lute Corinna sings[2]
neither words nor music are her own;
only the long hair dipping
over her cheek, only the song
of silk against her knees
and these
adjusted in reflections of an eye.

Poised, trembling and unsatisfied, before
an unlocked door, that cage of cages,
tell us, you bird, you tragical machine—
is this *fertilisante douleur?*[3] Pinned down
by love, for you the only natural action,
are you edged more keen
to prise the secrets of the vault? has Nature shown
her household books to you, daughter-in-law,
that her sons never saw?

7

*"To have in this uncertain world some stay
which cannot be undermined, is
of the utmost consequence."*[4]

9. Rich's note to this line refers to T. H. Johnson's *Emily Dickinson, Complete Poems* (1960); this is the poem numbered 764 in that edition. Dickinson (1830–1886) lived her entire life in Amherst, Massachusetts.
1. Sweetly laughing, sweetly speaking (Latin), from Horace's Ode XXII.
2. First line of a poem by the English poet Thomas Campion (1567–1620); Corinna is a generic name for a female shepherd.
3. Fertilizing (life-giving) sorrow (French).
4. "From Mary Wollstonecraft, *Thoughts on the Education of Daughters,* London, 1787" [Rich's note]. Wollstonecraft (1759–1797), one of the first feminist thinkers, is best-known for her *Vindication of the Rights of Woman* (1792).

Thus wrote
a woman, partly brave and partly good,
who fought with what she partly understood.
Few men about her would or could do more,
hence she was labelled harpy, shrew and whore.

8

"You all die at fifteen," said Diderot,[5]
and turn part legend, part convention.
Still, eyes inaccurately dream
behind closed windows blankening with steam.
Deliciously, all that we might have been,
all that we were—fire, tears,
wit, taste, martyred ambition—
stirs like the memory of refused adultery
the drained and flagging bosom of our middle years.

9

Not that it is done well, but
that it is done at all?[6] Yes, think
of the odds! or shrug them off forever.
This luxury of the precocious child,
Time's precious chronic invalid,—
would we, darlings, resign it if we could?
Our blight has been our sinecure:
mere talent was enough for us—
glitter in fragments and rough drafts.

Sigh no more, ladies.
Time is male
and in his cups[7] drinks to the fair.
Bemused by gallantry, we hear
our mediocrities over-praised,
indolence read as abnegation,
slattern[8] thought styled intuition,
every lapse forgiven, our crime
only to cast too bold a shadow
or smash the mould straight off.

For that, solitary confinement,
tear gas, attrition shelling.[9]
Few applicants for that honor.

5. Denis Diderot (1713–1784), French philosopher and writer. Rich's note to this line says that it is quoted from the *Lettres à Sophie Volland* in the influential *Le Deuxième Sexe,* by Simone de Beauvoir (1908–1986), vol. 2, pp. 123–24 (cited in French by Rich).

6. "Sir, a woman's preaching is like a dog's walking on his hinder legs. It is not done well; but you are surprised to find it done at all": Samuel Johnson (1709–1784), English writer, to James Boswell in Boswell's *Life.*

7. While drinking. "Sigh no more, ladies, sigh no more, / Men were deceivers ever": Shakespeare's *Much Ado About Nothing* 2.3.56–57.

8. Unkempt, disorderly.

9. That is, bombing.

10

Well,

she's long about her coming, who must be
more merciless to herself than history.
Her mind full to the wind, I see her plunge
breasted and glancing through the currents,
taking the light upon her
at least as beautiful as any boy
or helicopter,[1]
poised, still coming,
her fine blades making the air wince
but her cargo
no promise then:
delivered
palpable
ours.

1958–60 1963

Face to Face

Never to be lonely like that—
the Early American figure on the beach
in black coat and knee-breeches
scanning the didactic storm in privacy,

never to hear the prairie wolves
in their lunar hilarity
circling one's little all, one's claim
to be Law and Prophets[2]

for all that lawlessness,
never to whet the appetite
weeks early, for a face, a hand
longed-for and dreaded—

How people used to meet!
starved, intense, the old
Christmas gifts saved up till spring,
and the old plain words,

and each with his God-given secret,
spelled out through months of snow and silence,

1. "She comes down from the remoteness of ages, from Thebes, from Crete, from Chichén-Itzá; and she is also the totem set deep in the African jungle; she is a helicopter and she is a bird; and there is this, the greatest wonder of all: under her tinted hair the forest murmur becomes a thought, and words issue from her breasts" (Simone de Beauvoir, *The Second Sex,* tr. H. M. Parshlev [New York, 1953], p. 729; a translation of the passage from *Le Deuxième Sexe,* vol. 2, p. 574).
2. That is, righteous. See Matthew 7.12: "Therefore all things whatsoever ye would that men should do unto you, do ye even so to them: for this is the law and the prophets."

burning under the bleached scalp; behind dry lips
a loaded gun.[3]

1965 1966

Orion[4]

Far back when I went zig-zagging
through tamarack pastures
you were my genius, you
my cast-iron Viking, my helmed
lion-heart king in prison.[5]
Years later now you're young

my fierce half-brother, staring
down from that simplified west
your breast open, your belt dragged down
by an oldfashioned thing, a sword
the last bravado you won't give over
though it weighs you down as you stride

and the stars in it are dim
and maybe have stopped burning.
But you burn, and I know it;
as I throw back my head to take you in
an old transfusion happens again:
divine astronomy is nothing to it.

Indoors I bruise and blunder,
break faith, leave ill enough
alone, a dead child born in the dark,
Night cracks up over the chimney,
pieces of time, frozen geodes
come showering down in the grate.

A man reaches behind my eyes
and finds them empty
a woman's head turns away
from my head in the mirror
children are dying my death
and eating crumbs of my life.

Pity is not your forte.
Calmly you ache up there
pinned aloft in your crow's nest,
my speechless pirate!

3. Cf. Emily Dickinson's poem numbered 1754, "My Life had stood—a Loaded Gun"; see also "Snapshots of a Daughter-in-Law," above, line 45.
4. A constellation named for the giant hunter of Greek mythology, who at his death was placed among the stars by the gods. (See Rich's essay "When We Dead Awaken," p. 1086 of this volume.)
5. Like Richard I of England (1157–1199), called "the lion-hearted," who on his return from a Crusade was briefly imprisoned in Austria.

You take it all for granted
and when I look you back

it's with a starlike eye
shooting its cold and egotistical spear
where it can do least damage.
Breathe deep! No hurt, no pardon
out here in the cold with you
you with your back to the wall.

1965 1969

Planetarium

Thinking of Caroline Herschel,[6] 1750–1848, astronomer, sister of William; and others.

A woman in the shape of a monster
a monster in the shape of a woman
the skies are full of them

a woman 'in the snow
among the Clocks and instruments
or measuring the ground with poles'

in her 98 years to discover
8 comets

she whom the moon ruled
like us
levitating into the night sky
riding the polished lenses

Galaxies of women, there
doing penance for impetuousness
ribs chilled
in those spaces of the mind

An eye,
'virile, precise and absolutely certain'
from the mad webs of Uranusborg[7]
encountering the NOVA

every impulse of light exploding
from the core
as life flies out of us

6. German-born British astronomer. In 1786, she became the first woman to discover a comet, detecting seven more by 1797, including Comet Enckle; she also discovered nebulae. With her help, William Herschel (1738–1822), astronomer to King George III, discovered the first non-naked-eye planet, eventually named Uranus. (See Rich's essay "When We Dead Awaken," p. 1086 of this volume.)
7. Actually Uraniborg, or castle of the heavens (Dutch), the name of the great observatory built by Tycho Brahe (1546–1601), Danish astronomer, famous for his studies of comets.

Tycho whispering at last
'Let me not seem to have lived in vain'

What we see, we see
and seeing is changing

the light that shrivels a mountain
and leaves a man alive

Heartbeat of the pulsar
heart sweating through my body

The radio impulse
pouring in from Taurus[8]

I am bombarded yet I stand

I have been standing all my life in the
direct path of a battery of signals
the most accurately transmitted most
untranslateable language in the universe
I am a galactic cloud so deep so invo-
luted that a light wave could take 15
years to travel through me And has
taken I am an instrument in the shape
of a woman trying to translate pulsations
into images for the relief of the body
and the reconstruction of the mind.

1968 1971

A Valediction Forbidding Mourning[9]

My swirling wants. Your frozen lips.
The grammar turned and attacked me.
Themes, written under duress.
Emptiness of the notations.

They gave me a drug that slowed the healing of wounds.

I want you to see this before I leave:
the experience of repetition as death
the failure of criticism to locate the pain
the poster in the bus that said:
my bleeding is under control.

A red plant in a cemetery of plastic wreaths.

8. The constellation "the Bull."
9. The title of a poem by John Donne (1572–1631), in which the poet assures his beloved that his departure is not dangerous to their love, which has purified and united their souls.

A last attempt: the language is a dialect called metaphor.
These images go unglossed: hair, glacier, flashlight.
When I think of a landscape I am thinking of a time.
When I talk of taking a trip I mean forever.
I could say: those mountains have a meaning
but further than that I could not say.

To do something very common, in my own way.

1970 1971

Diving into the Wreck

First having read the book of myths,
and loaded the camera,
and checked the edge of the knife-blade,
I put on
the body-armor of black rubber
the absurd flippers
the grave and awkward mask.
I am having to do this
not like Cousteau[1] with his
assiduous team
aboard the sun-flooded schooner
but here alone.

There is a ladder.
The ladder is always there
hanging innocently
close to the side of the schooner.
We know what it is for,
we who have used it.
Otherwise
it's a piece of maritime floss
some sundry equipment.

I go down.
Rung after rung and still
the oxygen immerses me
the blue light
the clear atoms
of our human air.
I go down.
My flippers cripple me,
I crawl like an insect down the ladder
and there is no one
to tell me when the ocean
will begin.

1. Jacques-Yves Cousteau (1910–1997), French underwater explorer and writer.

First the air is blue and then
it is bluer and then green and then
black I am blacking out and yet
my mask is powerful
it pumps my blood with power
the sea is another story
the sea is not a question of power
I have to learn alone
to turn my body without force
in the deep element.

And now: it is easy to forget
what I came for
among so many who have always
lived here
swaying their crenellated[2] fans
between the reefs
and besides
you breathe differently down here.

I came to explore the wreck.
The words are purposes.
The words are maps.
I came to see the damage that was done
and the treasures that prevail.
I stroke the beam of my lamp
slowly along the flank
of something more permanent
than fish or weed

the thing I came for:
the wreck and not the story of the wreck
the thing itself and not the myth
the drowned face[3] always staring
toward the sun
the evidence of damage
worn by salt and sway into this threadbare beauty
the ribs of the disaster
curving their assertion
among the tentative haunters.

This is the place.
And I am here, the mermaid whose dark hair
streams black, the merman in his armored body.
We circle silently
about the wreck
we dive into the hold.
I am she: I am he

2. With repeated indentations.
3. Of the ornamental female figurehead that formed the prow of old sailing ships.

whose drowned face sleeps with open eyes
whose breasts still bear the stress
whose silver, copper, vermeil[4] cargo lies
obscurely inside barrels
half-wedged and left to rot
we are the half-destroyed instruments
that once held to a course
the water-eaten log
the fouled compass

We are, I am, you are
by cowardice or courage
the one who find our way
back to this scene
carrying a knife, a camera
a book of myths
in which
our names do not appear.

1972

1973

Power

Living   in the earth-deposits   of our history

Today a backhoe divulged   out of a crumbling flank of earth
one bottle   amber   perfect   a hundred-year-old
cure for fever   or melancholy   a tonic
for living on this earth   in the winters of this climate

Today I was reading about Marie Curie:[5]
she must have known she suffered   from radiation sickness
her body bombarded for years   by the element
she had purified
It seems she denied to the end
the source of the cataracts on her eyes
the cracked and suppurating skin   of her finger-ends
till she could no longer hold   a test-tube or a pencil

She died   a famous woman   denying
her wounds
denying
her wounds   came   from the same source as her power

1974

1978

4. Gilded silver or bronze.
5. Polish-born French physicist (1867–1934), who died from exposure to radiation she experienced in the process of discovering radium and studying radioactivity.

Twenty-One Love Poems

I

Wherever in this city, screens flicker
with pornography, with science-fiction vampires,
victimized hirelings bending to the lash,
we also have to walk . . . if simply as we walk
through the rainsoaked garbage, the tabloid cruelties
of our own neighborhoods.
We need to grasp our lives inseparable
from those rancid dreams, that blurt of metal, those disgraces,
and the red begonia perilously flashing
from a tenement sill six stories high,
or the long-legged young girls playing ball
in the junior highschool playground.
No one has imagined us. We want to live like trees,
sycamores blazing through the sulfuric air,
dappled with scars, still exuberantly budding,
our animal passion rooted in the city.

II

I wake up in your bed. I know I have been dreaming.
Much earlier, the alarm broke us from each other,
you've been at your desk for hours. I know what I dreamed:
our friend the poet comes into my room
where I've been writing for days,
drafts, carbons, poems are scattered everywhere,
and I want to show her one poem
which is the poem of my life. But I hesitate,
and wake. You've kissed my hair
to wake me. *I dreamed you were a poem,*
I say, *a poem I wanted to show someone* . . .
and I laugh and fall dreaming again
of the desire to show you to everyone I love,
to move openly together
in the pull of gravity, which is not simple,
which carries the feathered grass a long way down the upbreathing air.

III

Since we're not young, weeks have to do time
for years of missing each other. Yet only this odd warp
in time tells me we're not young.
Did I ever walk the morning streets at twenty,

my limbs streaming with a purer joy?
did I lean from any window over the city
listening for the future
as I listen here with nerves tuned for your ring?
And you, you move toward me with the same tempo.
Your eyes are everlasting, the green spark
of the blue-eyed grass of early summer,
the green-blue wild cress[6] washed by the spring.
At twenty, yes: we thought we'd live forever.
At forty-five, I want to know even our limits.
I touch you knowing we weren't born tomorrow,
and somehow, each of us will help the other live,
and somewhere, each of us must help the other die.

IV

I come home from you through the early light of spring
flashing off ordinary walls, the Pez Dorado,[7]
the Discount Wares, the shoe-store. . . . I'm lugging my sack
of groceries, I dash for the elevator
where a man, taut, elderly, carefully composed
lets the door almost close on me.—*For god's sake hold it!*
I croak at him. —*Hysterical,*—he breathes my way.
I let myself into the kitchen, unload my bundles,
make coffee, open the window, put on Nina Simone[8]
singing *Here comes the sun.* . . . I open the mail,
drinking delicious coffee, delicious music,
my body still both light and heavy with you. The mail
lets fall a Xerox of something written by a man
aged 27, a hostage, tortured in prison:
My genitals have been the object of such a sadistic display
they keep me constantly awake with the pain . . .
Do whatever you can to survive.
You know, I think that men love wars . . .
And my incurable anger, my unmendable wounds
break open further with tears, I am crying helplessly,
and they still control the world, and you are not in my arms.

V

This apartment full of books could crack open
to the thick jaws, the bulging eyes
of monsters, easily: Once open the books, you have to face
the underside of everything you've loved—

6. Plant, as in watercress.
7. El Pez Dorado is a Puerto Rican restaurant in Brooklyn.
8. American jazz vocalist and pianist (b. 1933), known as the High Priestess of Soul.

the rack and pincers held in readiness, the gag
even the best voices have had to mumble through,
the silence burying unwanted children—
women, deviants, witnesses—in desert sand.
Kenneth tells me he's been arranging his books
so he can look at Blake and Kafka while he types;
yes; and we still have to reckon with Swift[9]
loathing the woman's flesh while praising her mind,
Goethe's dread of the Mothers, Claudel vilifying Gide,[1]
and the ghosts—their hands clasped for centuries—
of artists dying in childbirth, wise-women charred at the stake,
centuries of books unwritten piled behind these shelves;
and we still have to stare into the absence
of men who would not, women who could not, speak
to our life—this still unexcavated hole
called civilization, this act of translation, this half-world.

VI

Your small hands, precisely equal to my own—
only the thumb is larger, longer—in these hands
I could trust the world, or in many hands like these,
handling power-tools or steering-wheel
or touching a human face. . . . Such hands could turn
the unborn child rightways in the birth canal
or pilot the exploratory rescue-ship
through icebergs, or piece together
the fine, needle-like sherds of a great krater-cup[2]
bearing on its sides
figures of esctatic women striding
to the sibyl's den or the Eleusinian cave[3]—
such hands might carry out an unavoidable violence
with such restraint, with such a grasp
of the range and limits of violence
that violence ever after would be obsolete.

9. Cf. the "dressing-room poems" of Anglo-Irish writer Jonathan Swift (1667–1745): in "The Lady's Dressing Room" (1730), "Disgusted Strephon" is horrified to learn that "Celia shits!" and in "Stella's Birthday" (1721), the speaker contrasts Stella's physical aging with her "Angel's Mind."

1. André Gide (1869–1951), French writer, critic, and spokesman for homosexual rights, whom French poet and playwright Paul Claudel (1868–1955) tried unsuccessfully to convert to Catholicism. In *Faust*, by German writer Johann Wolfgang von Goethe (1749–1832), Faust responds to mention of the mothers "with a shudder" and exclaims "The Mothers! Still strikes a shock of fear, / What is this word that I am loath to hear?" (2.1.6265–66).

2. *Krater:* ancient Greek jar with a broad (usually decorated) body and two handles, used for mixing water and wine.

3. In ancient Greece, the sanctuary of Demeter, goddess of Earth and fertility. *Sibyl:* female, usually cave-dwelling prophet. Initiates celebrated ecstatic religious rites at Eleusis, known as the Eleusinian Mysteries and centered on the story of Demeter's life.

VII

What kind of beast would turn its life into words?
What atonement is this all about?
—and yet, writing words like these, I'm also living.
Is all this close to the wolverines' howled signals,
that modulated cantata of the wild?
or, when away from you I try to create you in words,
am I simply using you, like a river or a war?
And how have I used rivers, how have I used wars
to escape writing of the worst thing of all—
not the crimes of others, not even our own death,
but the failure to want our freedom passionately enough
so that blighted elms, sick rivers, massacres would seem
mere emblems of that desecration of ourselves?

VIII

I can see myself years back at Sunion,[4]
hurting with an infected foot, Philoctetes[5]
in woman's form, limping the long path,
lying on a headland over the dark sea,
looking down the red rocks to where a soundless curl
of white told me a wave had struck,
imagining the pull of that water from that height,
knowing deliberate suicide wasn't my métier,
yet all the time nursing, measuring that wound.
Well, that's finished. The woman who cherished
her suffering is dead. I am her descendant.
I love the scar-tissue she handed on to me,
but I want to go on from here with you
fighting the temptation to make a career of pain.

IX

Your silence today is a pond where drowned things live
I want to see raised dripping and brought into the sun.
It's not my own face I see there, but other faces,
even your face at another age.
Whatever's lost there is needed by both of us—
a watch of old gold, a water-blurred fever chart,
a key. . . . Even the silt and pebbles of the bottom
deserve their glint of recognition. I fear this silence,

4. Cape Sunion, in Greece.
5. Legendary Greek hero wounded on the foot by a snake and abandoned on an island by his shipmates to suffer great pain. Cf. Sophocles' play named after him.

this inarticulate life. I'm waiting
for a wind that will gently open this sheeted water
for once, and show me what I can do
for you, who have often made the unnameable
nameable for others, even for me.

X

Your dog, tranquil and innocent, dozes through
our cries, our murmured dawn conspiracies
our telephone calls. She knows—what can she know?
If in my human arrogance I claim to read
her eyes, I find there only my own animal thoughts:
that creatures must find each other for bodily comfort,
that voices of the psyche drive through the flesh
further than the dense brain could have foretold,
that the planetary nights are growing cold for those
on the same journey, who want to touch
one creature-traveler clear to the end;
that without tenderness, we are in hell.

XI

Every peak is a crater. This is the law of volcanoes,
making them eternally and visibly female.
No height without depth, without a burning core,
though our straw soles shred on the hardened lava.
I want to travel with you to every sacred mountain
smoking within like the sibyl stooped over his tripod,[6]
I want to reach for your hand as we scale the path,
to feel your arteries glowing in my clasp,
never failing to note the small, jewel-like flower
unfamiliar to us, nameless till we rename her,
that clings to the slowly altering rock—
that detail outside ourselves that brings us to ourselves,
was here before us, knew we would come, and sees beyond us.

XII

Sleeping, turning in turn like planets
rotating in their midnight meadow:
a touch is enough to let us know
we're not alone in the universe, even in sleep:

6. A tripod over a fissure in the earth provided a safe place for the sibyl at the Delphic oracle, who breathed in smoke or gases and made prophecies.

the dream-ghosts of two worlds
walking their ghost-towns, almost address each other.
I've wakened to your muttered words
spoken light- or dark-years away
as if my own voice had spoken.
But we have different voices, even in sleep,
and our bodies, so alike, are yet so different
and the past echoing through our bloodstreams
is freighted with different language, different meanings—
though in any chronicle of the world we share
it could be written with new meaning
we were two lovers of one gender,
we were two women of one generation.

XIII

The rules break like a thermometer,
quicksilver[7] spills across the charted systems,
we're out in a country that has no language
no laws, we're chasing the raven and the wren
through gorges unexplored since dawn
whatever we do together is pure invention
the maps they gave us were out of date
by years . . . we're driving through the desert
wondering if the water will hold out
the hallucinations turn to simple villages
the music on the radio comes clear—
neither *Rosenkavalier* nor *Götterdämmerung*[8]
but a woman's voice singing old songs
with new words, with a quiet bass, a flute
plucked and fingered by women outside the law.

XIV

It was your vision of the pilot
confirmed my vision of you: you said, *He keeps*
on steering headlong into the waves, on purpose
while we crouched in the open hatchway
vomiting into plastic bags
for three hours between St. Pierre and Miquelon.[9]
I never felt closer to you.
In the close cabin where the honeymoon couples

7. Mercury, used in glass thermometers.
8. "Twilight of the Gods," by Richard Wagner (1813–1883), German composer whose anti-Semitism was admired by Hitler. *Der Rosenkavalier*: "The Knight of the Rose" (1911), a comic opera by German Romantic composer Richard Strauss (1864–1949), who was recruited by Joseph Goebbels (1897–1945), Hitler's minister of propaganda, to head up a group searching for a Nazi musical ethos.
9. French islands about fifteen miles south of Newfoundland.

huddled in each other's laps and arms
I put my hand on your thigh
to comfort both of us, your hand came over mine,
we stayed that way, suffering together
in our bodies, as if all suffering
were physical, we touched so in the presence
of strangers who knew nothing and cared less
vomiting their private pain
as if all suffering were physical.

(The Floating Poem, Unnumbered)

Whatever happens with us, your body
will haunt mine—tender, delicate
your lovemaking, like the half-curled frond
of the fiddlehead fern[1] in forests
just washed by sun. Your traveled, generous thighs
between which my whole face has come and come—
the innocence and wisdom of the place my tongue has found there—
the live, insatiate dance of your nipples in my mouth—
your touch on me, firm, protective, searching
me out, your strong tongue and slender fingers
reaching where I had been waiting years for you
in my rose-wet cave—whatever happens, this is.

XV

If I lay on that beach with you
white, empty, pure green water warmed by the Gulf Stream
and lying on that beach we could not stay
because the wind drove fine sand against us
as if it were against us
if we tried to withstand it and we failed—
if we drove to another place
to sleep in each other's arms
and the beds were narrow like prisoners' cots
and we were tired and did not sleep together
and this was what we found, so this is what we did—
was the failure ours?
If I cling to circumstances I could feel
not responsible. Only she who says
she did not choose, is the loser in the end.

1. A young, edible, tightly coiled fern frond that resembles the spiral end of a violin (fiddle). Its shoots are in their coiled form for only about two weeks before they unfurl.

XVI

Across a city from you, I'm with you,
just as an August night
moony, inlet-warm, seabathed, I watched you sleep,
the scrubbed, sheenless wood of the dressing-table
cluttered with our brushes, books, vials in the moonlight—
or a salt-mist orchard, lying at your side
watching red sunset through the screendoor of the cabin,
G minor Mozart on the tape-recorder,
falling asleep to the music of the sea.
This island of Manhattan is wide enough
for both of us, and narrow:
I can hear your breath tonight, I know how your face
lies upturned, the halflight tracing
your generous, delicate mouth
where grief and laughter sleep together.

XVII

No one's fated or doomed to love anyone.
The accidents happen, we're not heroines,
they happen in our lives like car crashes,
books that change us, neighborhoods
we move into and come to love.
Tristan und Isolde[2] is scarcely the story,
women at least should know the difference
between love and death. No poison cup,
no penance. Merely a notion that the tape-recorder
should have caught some ghost of us: that tape-recorder
not merely played but should have listened to us,
and could instruct those after us:
this we were, this is how we tried to love,
and these are the forces they had ranged against us,
and these are the forces we had ranged within us,
within us and against us, against us and within us.

XVIII

Rain on the West Side Highway,
red light at Riverside:[3]
the more I live the more I think

2. Wagner's 1865 opera about the doomed love affair between a Christian knight and a Pagan princess.

3. Riverside Drive; like the West Side Highway, in Manhattan.

two people together is a miracle.
You're telling the story of your life
for once, a tremor breaks the surface of your words.
The story of our lives becomes our lives.
Now you're in fugue across what some I'm sure
Victorian poet called the *salt estranging sea.*[4]
Those are the words that come to mind.
I feel estrangement, yes. As I've felt dawn
pushing toward daybreak. Something: a cleft of light—?
Close between grief and anger, a space opens
where I am Adrienne alone. And growing colder.

XIX

Can it be growing colder when I begin
to touch myself again, adhesions pull away?
When slowly the naked face turns from staring backward
and looks into the present,
the eye of winter, city, anger, poverty, and death
and the lips part and say: *I mean to go on living?*
Am I speaking coldly when I tell you in a dream
or in this poem, *There are no miracles?*
(I told you from the first I wanted daily life,
this island of Manhattan was island enough for me.)
If I could let you know—
two women together is a work
nothing in civilization has made simple,
two people together is a work
heroic in its ordinariness,
the slow-picked, halting traverse of a pitch
where the fiercest attention becomes routine
—look at the faces of those who have chosen it.

XX

That conversation we were always on the edge
of having, runs on in my head,
at night the Hudson trembles in New Jersey[5] light
polluted water yet reflecting even
sometimes the moon
and I discern a woman
I loved, drowning in secrets, fear wound round her throat
and choking her like hair. And this is she
with whom I tried to speak, whose hurt, expressive head
turning aside from pain, is dragged down deeper

4. English poet Matthew Arnold (1822–1888) concluded his 1857 poem "To Marguerite" with "The unplumb'd, salt, estranging sea."

5. Across the Hudson River from New York City's West Side.

where it cannot hear me,
and soon I shall know I was talking to my own soul.

XXI

The dark lintels,[6] the blue and foreign stones
of the great round rippled by stone implements
the midsummer night light rising from beneath
the horizon—when I said "a cleft of light"
I meant this. And this is not Stonehenge
simply nor any place but the mind
casting back to where her solitude,
shared, could be chosen without loneliness,
not easily nor without pains to stake out
the circle, the heavy shadows, the great light.
I choose to be a figure in that light,
half-blotted by darkness, something moving
across that space, the color of stone
greeting the moon, yet more than stone:
a woman. I choose to walk here. And to draw this circle.

1974–76 1978

Grandmothers

1. *Mary Gravely Jones*

We had no petnames, no diminutives for you,
always the formal guest under my father's roof:
you were "Grandmother Jones" and you visited rarely.
I see you walking up and down the garden,
restless, southern-accented, reserved, you did not seem
my mother's mother or anyone's grandmother.
You were Mary, widow of William, and no matriarch,
yet smoldering to the end with frustrate life,
ideas nobody listened to, least of all my father.
One summer night you sat with my sister and me
in the wooden glider[7] long after twilight,
holding us there with streams of pent-up words.
You could quote every poet I had ever heard of,
had read *The Opium Eater,* Amiel and Bernard Shaw,[8]
your green eyes looked clenched against opposition.
You married straight out of the convent school,
your background was country, you left an unperformed
typescript of a play about Burr and Hamilton,[9]

6. Horizontal crosspieces over the two larger supporting stones at Stonehenge, the prehistoric circle of great standing stones on Salisbury Plain, England.
7. Porch swing.
8. George Bernard Shaw (1856–1950): Irish playwright and socialist. *Confessions of an English Opium-Eater* (1821) is by the English essayist Thomas de Quincey. Henri Fréderic Amiel (1821–1881): Swiss poet and philosopher.
9. Aaron Burr (1756–1836), a flamboyant early U.S. vice president, killed Alexander Hamilton

you were impotent and brilliant, no one cared
about your mind, you might have ended
elsewhere than in that glider
reciting your unwritten novels to the children.

2. *Hattie Rice Rich*

Your sweetness of soul was a mystery to me,
you who slip-covered chairs, glued broken china,
lived out of a wardrobe trunk in our guestroom
summer and fall, then took the Pullman train[1]
in your darkblue dress and straw hat, to Alabama,
shuttling half-yearly between your son and daughter.
Your sweetness of soul was a convenience for everyone,
how you rose with the birds and children, boiled your own egg,
fished for hours on a pier, your umbrella spread,
took the street-car downtown shopping
endlessly for your son's whims, the whims of genius,
kept your accounts in ledgers, wrote letters daily.
All through World War Two the forbidden word
Jewish was barely uttered in your son's house;
your anger flared over inscrutable things.
Once I saw you crouched on the guestroom bed,
knuckles blue-white around the bedpost, sobbing
your one brief memorable scene of rebellion:
you didn't want to go back South that year.
You were never "Grandmother Rich" but "Anana";
you had money of your own but you were homeless,
Hattie, widow of Samuel, and no matriarch,
dispersed among the children and grandchildren.

3. *Granddaughter*

Easier to encapsulate your lives
in a slide-show of impressions given and taken,
to play the child or victim, the projectionist,
easier to invent a script for each of you,
myself still at the center,
than to write words in which you might have found
yourselves, looked up at me and said
"Yes, I was like that; but I was something more. . . ."
Danville, Virginia; Vicksburg, Mississippi;
the "war between the states" a living memory[2]
its aftermath the plague-town closing
its gates, trying to cure itself with poisons.
I can almost touch that little town. . . .
a little white town rimmed with Negroes,
making a deep shadow on the whiteness.[3]

(1755–1804), who had been instrumental in defeating Burr's candidacy for president.

1. Railroad passenger car with sleeping accommodations.

2. The Civil War ended in 1865.

3. Italicized lines (58–60, 64) are from *Killers of the Dream* (1949, rev. 1963), Lillian Smith's (1897–1966) autobiographical critique of white culture and racial segreation in the American south.

Born a white woman, Jewish or of curious mind
—twice an outsider, still believing in inclusion—
in those defended hamlets of half-truth
broken in two by one strange idea,
"blood" the all-powerful, awful theme—
what were the lessons to be learned? If I believe
the daughter of one of you—Amnesia was the answer.

1980 1981

Seven Skins

1

Walk along back of the library
in 1952
someone's there to catch your eye
Vic Greenberg in his wheelchair
paraplegic GI—
Bill of Rights[4] Jew
graduate student going in
by the only elevator route
up into the great stacks where
all knowledge should and is
and shall be stored like sacred grain
while the loneliest of lonely
American decades goes aground
on the postwar rock
and some unlikely
shipmates found ourselves
stuck amid so many smiles

Dating Vic Greenberg you date
crutches and a chair
a cool wit an outrageous form:
"—just back from a paraplegics' conference,
guess what the biggest meeting was about—
Sex with a Paraplegic!—for the wives—"
In and out of cabs his chair
opening and closing round his
electrical monologue the air
furiously calm around him
as he transfers to the crutches

But first you go for cocktails
in his room at Harvard
he mixes the usual martinis, plays Billie Holiday
talks about Melville's[5] vision of evil

4. After World War II, the GI Bill of Rights subsidized veterans' educations.
5. Herman Melville (1819–1891), American writer best-known for his novel *Moby-Dick*. Billie Holiday (1915–1959): American jazz singer.

and the question of the postwar moment:
Is there an American civilization?
In the bathroom huge
grips and suction-cupped
rubber mats long-handled sponges
the reaching tools a veteran's benefits
in plainest sight

And this is only memory, no more
so this is how you remember

Vic Greenberg takes you to the best restaurant
which happens to have no stairs
for talk about movies, professors, food
Vic orders wine and tastes it
you have lobster, he Beef Wellington
the famous dessert is baked alaska
ice cream singed in a flowerpot
from the oven, a live tulip inserted there

Chair to crutches, crutches to cab
chair in the cab and back to Cambridge
memory shooting its handheld frames
Shall I drop you, he says, or shall
we go back to the room for a drink?
It's the usual question
a man has to ask it
a woman has to answer
you don't even think

2

What a girl I was then what a body
ready for breaking open like a lobster
what a little provincial village
what a hermit crab seeking nobler shells
what a beach of rattling stones what an offshore raincloud
what a gone-and-come tidepool

what a look into eternity I took and did not return it
what a book I made myself
what a quicksilver study
bright little bloodstain
liquid pouches escaping

What a girl pelican-skimming over fear what a mica lump splitting
into tiny sharp-edged mirrors through which
the sun's eclipse could seem normal
what a sac of eggs what a drifting flask
eager to sink   to be found
to disembody   what a mass of swimmy legs

3

Vic into what shoulder could I have pushed your face
laying hands first on your head
onto whose thighs pulled down your head
which fear of mine would have wound itself
around which of yours could we have taken it nakedness
without sperm in what insurrectionary
convulsion would we have done it mouth to mouth
mouth-tongue to vulva-tongue to anus earlobe to nipple
what seven skins each have to molt what seven shifts
what tears boil up through sweat to bathe
what humiliatoriums what layers of imposture

What heroic tremor
released into pure moisture
might have soaked our shape two-headed avid
into your heretic
linen-service
sheets?

1997 1999

Fox

I needed fox Badly I needed
a vixen for the long time none had come near me
I needed recognition from a
triangulated face burnt-yellow eyes
fronting the long body the fierce and sacrificial tail
I needed history of fox briars of legend it was said she had run through
I was in want of fox

And the truth of briars she had to have run through
I craved to feel on her pelt if my hands could even slide
past or her body slide between them sharp truth distressing surfaces of fur
lacerated skin calling legend to account
a vixen's courage in vixen terms

For a human animal to call for help
on another animal
is the most riven the most revolted cry on earth
come a long way down
Go back far enough it means tearing and torn endless and sudden
back far enough it blurts
into the birth-yell of the yet-to-be human child
pushed out of a female the yet-to-be woman

1998 2001

Thom Gunn
1929–2004

Thom Gunn was one of the youngest members of the Movement—English poets who began to publish during the 1950s and constituted themselves as a third force in the development of contemporary English poetry. They rejected what seemed to them the Romantic excesses of the New Apocalypse (whose most prominent exponent was Dylan Thomas), and they were equally dissatisfied with the modernist revolution led by Ezra Pound and T. S. Eliot, who, Gunn contended, abandoned important traditional resources of poetry by deciding "to strengthen the images while either banishing concepts or, where they couldn't avoid them, treating them to the same free association as images" (*Yale Review* 53). The Movement sought greater concreteness and a less high-flown diction for poetry. Gunn praised the example of Thomas Hardy, whose terse irony and bleakness he recalls, and of Mina Loy—"tough, cerebral and largely untouched by Imagism" (*TLS*, August 30, 1996). And yet Gunn, unlike other poets of the Movement, was never cautious. "I was wilder than they were," he said. "They were a very sober group of people" (*Gay & Lesbian Review*, Summer 2000). Nor does Gunn's poetry seem especially English. By the time of his inclusion in *New Lines* (1956), the anthology that announced the Movement to the world, he was living in California, studying at Stanford University with Yvor Winters.

Skilled in traditional English forms, Gunn turned to syllabics, after moving to California, then to free verse in the 1960s; but unlike most poets who made this transition, he later wrote poems in both free and metered forms. His subject matter is often nontraditional and includes psychotropic drug use, serial killers, and gay sex. In his signature style, Gunn holds this "wild" content in tension with the tight grid of intricate patterns of rhyme and meter. "In dealing with the experience of the infinite," he said, "I needed to filter it through a finite form, otherwise the whole thing would just drift away" (*Gay & Lesbian Review*). In the heroic couplets of "Moly," for example, he impersonates with almost hallucinatory vividness one of Odysseus's shipmates at the moment of realization that he has been metamorphosed by the female enchanter Circe and is now "buried in swine." "Based on drug experience," in Gunn's words, the early book of which this is the title poem presents a number of experiences of mind expansion as part of the counterculture of his adopted home, San Francisco. Paradoxically, tight forms helped Gunn write "about untenable experiences, experiences beyond the ordinary, hallucinatory things." Gunn often finds his subjects in extreme situations, whether of death or love. Yet as he said of Yvor Winters: "You keep both Rule and Energy in view" ("To Yvor Winters, 1955"). Gunn registered both agitation and the urge to contain it. Like the lover recalled in "The Problem," Gunn's poetry is "disorderly and ordered," balancing "math" against "Passion."

The ultimate test of Gunn's ordering sense of form was the death of many friends in San Francisco during the height of the AIDS crisis, or "plague," as he calls it in the bleak sequence of elegies that closes *The Man with Night Sweats* (1992). Although poems such as "Still Life," "The Missing," and "A Blank" engage intimate and emotionally wrenching subjects, Gunn's acid skepticism and formal control fend off sentimentality. In these poems, some of the best written about the ravages of AIDS, he recalls the slow dying of friends hooked to machines and traces the circulation of their remains in nature; he eyes his own skeleton-haunted frame and mocks his mind's longing for security.

Thomson William Gunn was born on August 29, 1929, in Gravesend, Kent. His parents were journalists. In youth, he endured their divorce and his mother's death. He served for two years in the British army, then received his B.A. from Trinity College, Cambridge University, in 1953.

After following an American lover to California, he entered Stanford University as a graduate student. From that time, Gunn lived most of his life in San Francisco. From 1958 to 1966, he taught at the University of California, Berkeley; from 1975 until his retirement, he taught there one semester a year. Gunn won a MacArthur Fellowship (1993), the Lenore Marshall Prize (1993), and the Lambda Literary Award for Gay Men's Poetry for *Collected Poems* (1995).

My Sad Captains

One by one they appear in
the darkness: a few friends, and
a few with historical
names. How late they start to shine!
but before they fade they stand
perfectly embodied, all

the past lapping them like a
cloak of chaos. They were men
who, I thought, lived only to
renew the wasteful force they
spent with each hot convulsion.
They remind me, distant now.

True, they are not at rest yet,
but now that they are indeed
apart, winnowed from failures,
they withdraw to an orbit
and turn with disinterested
hard energy, like the stars.

1961

Moly[1]

Nightmare of beasthood, snorting, how to wake.
I woke. What beasthood skin she made me take?

Leathery toad that ruts for days on end,
Or cringing dribbling dog, man's servile friend,

Or cat that prettily pounces on its meat,
Tortures it hours, then does not care to eat:

1. A magic herb of Greek mythology. Circe transformed Odysseus's shipmates into swine; Odysseus, protected by the herb moly, which he had been given by the gods' messenger, Hermes, compelled her to restore them to human shape.

Parrot, moth, shark, wolf, crocodile, ass, flea.
What germs, what jostling mobs there were in me.

These seem like bristles, and the hide is tough.
No claw or web here: each foot ends in hoof.

Into what bulk has method disappeared?
Like ham, streaked. I am gross—grey, gross, flap-eared.

The pale-lashed eyes my only human feature.
My teeth tear, tear. I am the snouted creature

That bites through anything, root, wire, or can.
If I was not afraid I'd eat a man.

Oh a man's flesh already is in mine.
Hand and foot poised for risk. Buried in swine.

I root and root, you think that it is greed,
It is, but I seek out a plant I need.

Direct me gods, whose changes are all holy,
To where it flickers deep in grass, the moly:

Cool flesh of magic in each leaf and shoot,
From milky flower to the black forked root.

From this fat dungeon I could rise to skin
And human title, putting pig within.

I push my big grey wet snout through the green,
Dreaming the flower I have never seen.

1971

Still Life

I shall not soon forget
The greyish-yellow skin
To which the face had set:
Lids tight: nothing of his,
No tremor from within,
Played on the surfaces.

He still found breath, and yet
It was an obscure knack.
I shall not soon forget
The angle of his head,
Arrested and reared back
On the crisp field of bed,

Back from what he could neither
Accept, as one opposed,
Nor, as a life-long breather,
Consentingly let go,
The tube his mouth enclosed
In an astonished O.

1992

The Missing

Now as I watch the progress of the plague,[2]
The friends surrounding me fall sick, grow thin,
And drop away. Bared, is my shape less vague
—Sharply exposed and with a sculpted skin?

I do not like the statue's chill contour,
Not nowadays. The warmth investing me
Led outward through mind, limb, feeling, and more
In an involved increasing family.

Contact of friend led to another friend,
Supple entwinement through the living mass
Which for all that I knew might have no end,
Image of an unlimited embrace.

I did not just feel ease, though comfortable:
Aggressive as in some ideal of sport,
With ceaseless movement thrilling through the whole,
Their push kept me as firm as their support.

But death—Their deaths have left me less defined:
It was their pulsing presence made me clear.
I borrowed from it, I was unconfined,
Who tonight balance unsupported here,

Eyes glaring from raw marble, in a pose
Languorously part-buried in the block,
Shins perfect and no calves, as if I froze
Between potential and a finished work.

—Abandoned incomplete, shape of a shape,
In which exact detail shows the more strange,
Trapped in unwholeness, I find no escape
Back to the play of constant give and change.

August 1987 1992

2. AIDS.

A Blank

The year of griefs being through, they had to merge
In one last grief, with one last property:
To view itself like loosened cloud lose edge,
And pull apart, and leave a voided sky.

Watching Victorian porches through the glass,
From the 6 bus, I caught sight of a friend
Stopped on a corner-kerb to let us pass,
A four-year-old blond child tugging his hand,
Which tug he held against with a slight smile.
I knew the smile from certain passages
Two years ago, thus did not know him well,
Since they took place in my bedroom and his.

A sturdy-looking admirable young man.
He said 'I chose to do this with my life.'
Casually met he said it of the plan
He undertook without a friend or wife.

Now visibly tugged upon by his decision,
Wayward and eager. So this was his son!
What I admired about his self-permission
Was that he turned from nothing he had done,
Or was, or had been, even while he transposed
The expectations he took out at dark
—Of Eros[3] playing, features undisclosed—
Into another pitch, where he might work
With the same melody, and opted so
To educate, permit, guide, feed, keep warm,
And love a child to be adopted, though
The child was still a blank then on a form.

The blank was flesh now, running on its nerve,
This fair-topped organism dense with charm,
Its braided muscle grabbing what would serve,
His countering pull, his own devoted arm.

1992

3. Greek god of love, usually depicted as a small, blond boy.

The Problem

Close to the top
Of an encrusted dark
Converted brownstone West of Central Park
(For this was 1961)
In his room that,
                a narrow hutch,
Was sliced from some once-cavernous flat,
Where now a window took a whole wall up
And tints were bleached-out by the sun
Of many a summer day,
We lay
        upon his hard thin bed.

He seemed all body, such
As normally you couldn't touch,
Reckless and rough,
One of Boss Cupid's red-
                        haired errand boys
Who couldn't get there fast enough.
Almost like fighting . . .
We forgot about the noise,
But feeling turned so self-delighting
That hurry soon gave way
To give-and-take,
Till each contested, for the other's sake,
To end up not in winning and defeat
But in a draw.

Meanwhile beyond the aureate[4] hair
I saw
A scrap of blackboard with its groove for chalk,
Nailed to a strip of lath
That had half-broken through,
The problem drafted there
                        still incomplete.
After, I found out in the talk
Companion to a cigarette,
That he, turning the problem over yet
In his disorderly and ordered head,
Attended graduate school to teach
And study math,
                his true
Passion cyphered in chalk beyond my reach.

2000

4. Golden.

John Hollander
1929–2013

John Hollander and Allen Ginsberg attended Columbia University at the same time, and they testified to their friendship by mentioning each other in their poems. But in many ways they were each other's antitype: Hollander's poems are as finished as Ginsberg's are unfinished, and they offer subtle modulations instead of what Ginsberg insisted were "angelical ravings." Hollander accepted the formal and societal rules that Ginsberg overreached. Yet Hollander's formalism is individualistic and against the grain.

An instance of Hollander's elaborateness of mind and form is his addiction to phenomenal plays on words. With Anthony Hecht, he originated a new kind of poem, like the limerick but much harder to write, called the "double dactyl." In *Types of Shape* (1969, 1991), he revisited the ancient tradition of pattern poetry and wrote poems in the shape of a key, an umbrella, a swan, a crescent moon—feats that few other contemporaries could or would attempt. The learned author of numerous critical studies of prosody, Hollander mastered and revitalized an array of formal verse structures. Many of his poems recast seventeenth-century models, some written for music. "I suppose Mr. Hollander must be called a 'literary' poet," wrote W. H. Auden in the introduction to Hollander's first book, *A Crackling of Thorns* (1958). Allusive, aphoristic, and demanding, Hollander has been a severe critic of what he calls the "cheesy sentimentality" and "easy flabbiness of a ubiquitous form of short-line free verse" ("The Work of Poetry," 1997).

Although he presents experience with style, Hollander recognized a necessity for being more than stylish, and his later verse betrays ever deepening concerns with intimate questions of love, loss, and mortality. He admits in "Helicon," as if to emphasize his special concern, that "opening up at all is harder than meeting a measure." He usually begins with homely objects or incidents and develops them with verbal ingenuity and philosophical know-how. In "Under Cancer," Hollander—a less jovial poet than he at first appears—finds in tanning an instance of aging and decay. His poems balance their poised form with something like despair or acute skepticism, their charming polish and intricacy with the plangent harmonies of grief.

Hollander was born on October 28, 1929, in New York City. He received B.A. and M.A. degrees from Columbia, in 1950 and 1952, and then began work on a doctorate at Indiana University. He was elected a Junior Fellow in the Society of Fellows at Harvard University and taught for a time there. In 1959, he received his doctoral degree from Indiana. He also taught at Connecticut and Hunter Colleges and for the remainder of his career was a professor at Yale University. Among his many awards were the Bollingen Prize (1983) and a MacArthur Fellowship (1990). Hollander was also a respected editor, anthologist, and critic.

Under Cancer

On the Memorial building's
Terrace the sun has been buzzing
Unbearably, all the while
The white baking happens
To the shadow of the table's
White-painted iron. It darkens,
Meaning that the sun is stronger,

That I am invisibly darkening
Too, the while I whiten.
And only after the stretching
And getting up, still sweating,
My shirt striped like an awning
Drawn on over airlessness;
After the cool shades
(As if of a long arcade
Where footsteps echo gravely)
Have devoured the light;
Only after the cold of
Plunge and shower, the pale
Scent of deodorant stick
Smelling like gin and limes,
And another stripy shirt
Can come, homing in at last,
The buzzing of having been burnt.
Only then, intimations
Of tossing, hot in the dark
Night, where all the long while
Silently, along edges,
There is flaking away.

In this short while of light
My shadow darkens without
Lengthening ever, ever.

1971

Adam's Task

And Adam gave names to all cattle, and to the fowl of the air, and to every beast of the field . . .

—Gen. 2.20

Thou, paw-paw-paw; thou, glurd; thou, spotted
  Glurd; thou, whitestap, lurching through
The high-grown brush; thou, pliant-footed,
  Implex; thou, awagabu.

Every burrower, each flier
  Came for the name he had to give:
Gay, first work, ever to be prior,
  Not yet sunk to primitive.

Thou, verdle; thou, McFleery's pomma;
  Thou; thou; thou—three types of grawl;
Thou, flisket; thou, kabasch; thou, comma-
  Eared mashawk; thou, all; thou, all.

Were, in a fire of becoming,
  Laboring to be burned away,

Then work, half-measuring, half-humming,
Would be as serious as play.

Thou, pambler; thou, rivarn; thou, greater
Wherret, and thou, lesser one;
Thou, sproal; thou, zant; thou, lily-eater.
Naming's over. Day is done.

1971

Back to Town[1]

These labor days, when shirking hardly looks like working
Yet sounds far too much like it . . . standing idle, I muse
On which of us two helpmeets, when we weave together,
Is the worker, which, unwittingly, the noisy drone.[2]
Warp might contend with weft[3] for priority, wrecking
The whole frame, wrenching the time into a travesty
Of a day of rest. Were the hum of our shuttling song
Stilled for long, the thin lines strung across the workaday
Loom would sag or snap. But back-and-forth breeds up-and-down:
The figures develop in the field, growing under
The sole working light of our attentiveness. Where would
I be without you? Who ever see you save through me?
United we stand and shake the chains heard round the world.

1983

Variations on a Fragment by Trumbull Stickney[4]

I hear a river thro' the valley wander
Whose water runs, the song alone remaining.
A rainbow stands and summer passes under,

Flowing like silence in the light of wonder.
In the near distances it is still raining
Where now the valley fills again with thunder,

Where now the river in her wide meander,
Losing at each loop what she had been gaining,
Moves into what one might as well call yonder.

1. Poem numbered 98 in *Powers of Thirteen.*
2. Male, nonworking bee.
3. Weaving terms: the "warp" is the lengthwise threads on a loom; the "weft," the threads that cross the warp.
4. American poet (1874–1904). Lines 1–3 comprise Stickney's Fragment IX.

The way of the dark water is to ponder
The way the light sings as of something waning.
The far-off waterfall can sound asunder

Stillness of distances, as if in blunder,
Tumbling over the rim of all explaining.
Water proves nothing, but can only maunder.

Shadows show nothing, but can only launder
The lovely land that sunset had been staining,
Long fields of which the falling light grows fonder.

Here summer stands while all its songs pass under,
A riverbank still time runs by, remaining.
I will remember rainbows as I wander.

1993

By Heart

The songs come at us first; and then the rhymed
Verses like speech that half-sings; then the tunes
Of summer evening—the train whistle's sigh
Westering, fading, as I lay in bed
Sunset still creeping past the lowered shade;
The gossip of swallows; the faint, radioed
Reed section of a dance band through an open
Window down at the far end of the street;
And then the strings of digits that we learn
To keep like bunched keys ready to unlock
All the boxes we get assigned to us
By the uncaring sheriffs of life itself.
We play by ear, but learn the words by heart;
(Visions we have by head); yet even when
The sight of the remembered page has dimmed
The jingles that we gleaned from it remain
Lodged with us, useful, sometimes, for the work
Of getting a grip on certain fragile things.
We are ourselves from birth committed to
Memory, to broad access to a past
Framing and filling any presentness
Of self that we could really call our own.
We grasp the world by ear, by heart, by head,
And keep it in a soft continuingness
That we first learned to get by soul, or something.

2000

Derek Walcott
b. 1930

Derek Walcott, the preeminent Caribbean poet writing in English, was born on January 23, 1930, on Saint Lucia, one of the four Windward Islands. Although he has been a constant and fortunate (his word) traveler, the center of his affections and allegiances, the landscape of his memory and his imagination, remains his natal island, in the eastern Caribbean. Despite his devotion to Caribbean culture, Walcott's account of his early years suggests he was somewhat of an outsider. He was reared a Methodist in a society that was largely Roman Catholic; his father, a talented amateur painter, died before Walcott was a year old; his mother, the head teacher at a Methodist nursery school, had a collection of the English classics, which she encouraged her son to read. Walcott's background is racially and culturally mixed. His grandmothers were of African descent; his grandfathers were white, a Dutchman and an Englishman. Schooled in the Standard English that is the official language of Saint Lucia, Walcott also grew up speaking the predominantly French Creole (or patois) that is the primary language of everyday life (Saint Lucia had traded hands fourteen times in colonial wars between the British and the French).

In "A Far Cry from Africa," Walcott, self-consciously "divided to the vein," dramatizes the conflict between his loyalties to his African ancestry and to the "English tongue I love." He has self-mockingly referred to his divided allegiances as those of a "schizophrenic," a "mongrel," a "mulatto of style" ("What the Twilight Says: An Overture"). Sometimes his cross-cultural inheritance is the source of pain and ambivalence, as when he refers to himself as being "poisoned with the blood of both." At other times, it fuels a celebratory integration of multiple forms, visions, and energies, as in parts of his epic poem *Omeros* (1990). With varying degrees of discomfort and elation, Walcott tries to embrace all his cultural influences—European, American, African, and the creolized culture of the West Indies. At the end of his seminal essay "The Muse of History" (1974), he movingly recalls the violent past he carries within his body, addressing a white forefather—"slave seller and slave buyer"—and a black forefather "in the filth-ridden gut of the slave ship." But the scars left by the slavemaster's whip are transformed in Walcott's magnificent image for his and the Caribbean's fusion of black and white skins, of Northern and Southern Hemispheres: "the monumental groaning and soldering of two great worlds, like the halves of a fruit seamed by its own bitter juice."

Even as a schoolboy, Walcott knew he wasn't alone in his effort to sort through his vexed postcolonial affiliations. From a young age, he felt a special "intimacy with the Irish poets" as "colonials with the same kind of problems that existed in the Caribbean." He continues, provocatively: "They were the niggers of Britain" (1977 interview). Various English and American writers—T. S. Eliot, Ezra Pound, Hart Crane, W. H. Auden, and Robert Lowell—have also been strong influences on Walcott. But the young poet passionately identified with W. B. Yeats, James Joyce, and J. M. Synge, knowing he shared their conflicted responses to the cultural inheritances of the British Empire—its literature, religion, and language. At school, Walcott recalls, Joyce's Stephen Dedalus was his "hero": "Like him, I was a knot of paradoxes," among other things "learning to hate England as I worshipped her language." Struck anew in *Omeros* by the shared postcolonial problem of a complex linguistic and literary inheritance, he memorably declares Ireland "a nation / split by a glottal scream." Also recognizing this affinity, Seamus Heaney, Walcott's near-contemporary from Northern Ireland, writes of the Saint Lucian: "I imagine he has done for the Caribbean what Synge did for Ireland, found a language woven out of dialect and literature, neither folksy nor condescending, a singular idiom evolved out of one man's inherited divisions and obsessions" ("The Murmur of Malvern").

Walcott asks time and again how the postcolonial poet can both grieve the agonizing harm of British colonialism and appreciate the empire's literary gift. Without forgetting what he calls in "A Far Cry from Africa" "the drunken officer of British rule," Walcott nevertheless celebrates his British colonial education as "the greatest bequest the Empire made. The grounding was rigid—Latin, Greek, and the essential masterpieces, but there was this elation of discovery. Shakespeare, Marlowe, Horace, Vergil—these writers weren't jaded but immediate experiences." Indeed, "precisely because of their limitations our early education must have ranked with the finest in the world" ("Meanings"). It followed the standard British curriculum: "the writers of my generation were natural assimilators. We knew the literature of Empires, Greek, Roman, British, through their essential classics; and both the patois of the street and the language of the classroom." With this grounding, Walcott was determined to make a poetry "legitimately prolonging the mighty line of Marlowe, of Milton" ("Twilight").

In spite of his affinity for a literature bequeathed by empire, Walcott insists that the copiousness and opulence of his verse reflect his Caribbean inheritance. In a tribute to the West Indies, he said to an interviewer: "I come from a place that likes grandeur; it likes large gestures; it is not inhibited by flourish; it is a rhetorical society; it is a society of physical performance; it is a society of style. . . . Modesty is not possible in performance in the Caribbean, and that's wonderful. It is better to be large and make huge gestures than to be modest and do tiptoeing types of presentations of oneself" ("The Art of Poetry"). Walcott is a no less "authentically" West Indian poet than Louise Bennett, Kamau Brathwaite, Lorna Goodison, or Grace Nichols, though he is often seen as the most Eurocentric of the leading Caribbean poets. A shamelessly hybridizing writer, he resembles the hero Shabine of "The Schooner *Flight*," the character's name itself Creole for "mulatto": "I have Dutch, nigger, and English in me, / and either I'm nobody, or I'm a nation." When in *Omeros* the Saint Lucian hero Achille imaginatively returns to his ancestors in Africa, he uncovers a vital source of identity, while also learning that centuries of creolized life in the West Indies have made it impossible for him to merge with his African heritage.

Over the course of his prolific career, Walcott has adapted various literary archetypes (e.g., the Greek characters Philoctetes and Achilles) and forms (epic, quatrains, hexameters, terza rima). He has related his interest in craft to his religious upbringing: "There is," he has said in an interview, "a very strong sense of carpentry in Protestantism, in making things simply and in a utilitarian way. . . . I think of myself in a way as a carpenter, as one making frames simply and well" (1977 interview). From the 1950s to the 1990s, he moved from the Yeatsian lyric ambivalence in the loosely pentameter lines of "A Far Cry from Africa" to the epic near-hexameters in the anglicized terza rima of *Omeros*. Although much of his poetry is in a rhetorically elevated Standard English, Walcott adapts the calypso rhythms of a lightly creolized English in "The Schooner *Flight*," and he braids together West Indian English, Standard English, and French patois in *Omeros*.

Walcott has a great passion for metaphor, and he delights in weaving figurative connections across cultural and racial boundaries. The Middle Passage's brutal "amnesiac blow," the transatlantic slave journey mourned in "Laventille" and remembered in "The Sea Is History," returns in the metaphor of the wound as the central symbol of Afro-Caribbean historical suffering in *Omeros*; in that poem, Walcott caribbeanizes a Greek hero and classical emblem of suffering, the wounded Philoctetes. This intercultural appropriation is emblematic of Walcott's "mulatto aesthetics": with acute irony, Walcott borrows the classical Philoctetes from what he calls a European "culture of slavery," to memorialize the harm inflicted on Afro-Caribbeans by their European enslavers. Such deft intercultural weaving and cross-cultural negotiation also distinguish "The Schooner *Flight*" and "The Fortunate Traveller."

Walcott's prodigious talent was evident early in his life, despite the seeming modesty of his upbringing in a colonial backwater. At fifteen, he published a poem in the local newspaper, drawing a sharp rebuke in rhyme from a Catholic priest for his heretical pantheism and animism. A few years later, he borrowed money from his mother to print a booklet of twenty-five poems, hawking it on the streets to earn the money back. This book and his first major play, *Henri Christophe,* also met with disapprobation from the Catholic Church. In 1950, he left Saint Lucia to enter the University of the West Indies in Mona, Jamaica, where he was a vibrant literary figure among the university's first graduating class in liberal arts. He received a B.A. in 1953. Staying on in Jamaica, he made his living through teaching and journalism. He moved to Trinidad in 1958, still working as a reviewer and art critic, but pouring energy into directing and writing plays for the Trinidad Theatre Workshop until 1976. His poetry began to receive international attention when *In a Green Night* (1962) was published in England. His plays, which have been performed in New York and London as well as in the Caribbean, are about the history and culture of the West Indies, many of them written in West Indian English. Since 1981, Walcott has taught regularly at Boston University. In the 1990s, he built a home on the northwest coast of Saint Lucia, where he paints and writes. He received the Nobel Prize in Literature in 1992.

A Far Cry from Africa

A wind is ruffling the tawny pelt
Of Africa. Kikuyu,[1] quick as flies,
Batten upon the bloodstreams of the veldt.[2]
Corpses are scattered through a paradise.
Only the worm, colonel of carrion, cries:
"Waste no compassion on these separate dead!"
Statistics justify and scholars seize
The salients of colonial policy.
What is that to the white child hacked in bed?
To savages, expendable as Jews?

Threshed out by beaters,[3] the long rushes break
In a white dust of ibises whose cries
Have wheeled since civilization's dawn
From the parched river or beast-teeming plain.
The violence of beast on beast is read
As natural law, but upright man
Seeks his divinity by inflicting pain.
Delirious as these worried beasts, his wars
Dance to the tightened carcass of a drum,
While he calls courage still that native dread
Of the white peace contracted by the dead.

1. Largest ethnic group in Kenya, whose members, as Mau Mau fighters, conducted a campaign of violent resistance against British colonial settlers in the 1950s.

2. Grassy plain, savannah. *Batten upon:* feed upon gluttonously.

3. In African game hunting, people are hired to beat the brush, chasing birds and animals from their hiding places.

Again brutish necessity wipes its hands
Upon the napkin of a dirty cause, again
A waste of our compassion, as with Spain,[4]
The gorilla wrestles with the superman.
I who am poisoned with the blood of both,
Where shall I turn, divided to the vein?
I who have cursed
The drunken officer of British rule, how choose
Between this Africa and the English tongue I love?
Betray them both, or give back what they give?
How can I face such slaughter and be cool?
How can I turn from Africa and live?

1956, 1962

Laventille

[for V. S. Naipaul]

To find the Western Path
Through the Gates of Wrath—
—BLAKE[5]

It huddled there
steel tinkling its blue painted metal air,
tempered in violence, like Rio's favelas,[6]

with snaking, perilous streets whose edges fell as
its Episcopal turkey-buzzards fall
from its miraculous hilltop

shrine,
down the impossible drop
to Belmont, Woodbrook, Maraval, St. Clair[7]

that shine
like peddlers' tin trinkets in the sun.
From a harsh

shower, its gutters growled and gargled wash
past the Youth Centre, past the water catchment,[8]
a rigid children's carousel of cement;

4. Perhaps a reference to the massacres inflicted on both sides during the Spanish Civil War of 1936–39.
5. From "Morning," by English Romantic poet and visionary William Blake (1757–1827). *Laventille:* hillside slum outside Port of Spain, the capital of Trinidad and Tobago. Our Lady of Laventille, the shrine at the top of the hill, can be seen throughout the city. V. S. Naipaul (b. 1932): Trinidad-born writer, noted for pessimistic examinations of postcolonial life in Third World countries.
6. Shantytowns on the steep hills surrounding Rio de Janeiro, Brazil.
7. Other towns in Trinidad.
8. Basin for collecting rainwater.

we climbed where lank electric
lines and tension cables linked its raw brick
hovels like a complex feud,

where the inheritors of the middle passage[9] stewed,
five to a room, still clamped below their hatch,
breeding like felonies,

whose lives revolve round prison, graveyard, church.
Below bent breadfruit trees
in the flat, coloured city, class

escalated into structures still,
merchant, middleman, magistrate, knight. To go downhill
from here was to ascend.

The middle passage never guessed its end.
This is the height of poverty
for the desperate and black;

climbing, we could look back
with widening memory
on the hot, corrugated-iron sea
whose horrors we all

shared. The salt blood knew it well,
you, me, Samuel's daughter, Samuel,
and those ancestors clamped below its grate.

And climbing steeply past the wild
gutters, it shrilled
in the blood, for those who suffered, who were killed,

and who survive.
What other gift was there to give
as the godparents of his unnamed child?

Yet outside the brown annex of the church, the
stifling odour of bay rum and talc, the particular,
neat sweetness of the crowd distressed

that sense. The black, fawning verger,[1]
his bow tie akimbo, grinning, the clown-gloved
fashionable wear of those I deeply loved

once, made me look on with hopelessness and rage
at their new, apish habits, their excess
and fear, the possessed, the self-possessed;

9. The journey by which African slaves were transported across the Atlantic Ocean to the Americas in morbidly overcrowded ships.

1. Church attendant.

their perfume shrivelled to a childhood fear
of Sabbath graveyards, christenings, marriages,
that muggy, steaming, self-assuring air

of tropical Sabbath afternoons. And in
the church, eyes prickling with rage,
the children rescued from original sin

by their Godfather since the middle passage,
the supercilious brown curate, who intones,
healing the guilt in these rachitic[2] bones,
twisting my love within me like a knife:
"across the troubled waters of this life . . ."

Which of us cares to walk
even if God wished
those retching waters where our souls were fished

for this new world? Afterwards, we talk
in whispers, close to death
among these stones planted on alien earth.

Afterwards,
the ceremony, the careful photograph
moved out of range before the patient tombs,

we dare a laugh,
ritual, desperate words,
born like these children from habitual wombs,

from lives fixed in the unalterable groove
of grinding poverty. I stand out on a balcony
and watch the sun pave its flat, golden path

across the roofs, the aerials, cranes, the tops
of fruit trees crawling downward to the city.
Something inside is laid wide like a wound,

some open passage that has cleft the brain,
some deep, amnesiac blow. We left
somewhere a life we never found,

customs and gods that are not born again,
some crib, some grille of light
clanged shut on us in bondage, and withheld

us from that world below us and beyond,
and in its swaddling cerements[3] we're still bound.

1965

2. Rickety.

3. Burial clothes.

The Sea Is History

Where are your monuments, your battles, martyrs?
Where is your tribal memory? Sirs,
in that grey vault. The sea. The sea
has locked them up. The sea is History.

First, there was the heaving oil,
heavy as chaos;
then, like a light at the end of a tunnel,

the lantern of a caravel,[4]
and that was Genesis.
Then there were the packed cries,
the shit, the moaning:

Exodus.[5]
Bone soldered by coral to bone,
mosaics
mantled by the benediction of the shark's shadow,

that was the Ark of the Covenant.[6]
Then came from the plucked wires
of sunlight on the sea floor

the plangent harps of the Babylonian bondage,[7]
as the white cowries clustered like manacles
on the drowned women,

and those were the ivory bracelets
of the Song of Solomon,[8]
but the ocean kept turning blank pages

looking for History.
Then came the men with eyes heavy as anchors
who sank without tombs,

brigands who barbecued cattle,[9]
leaving their charred ribs like palm leaves on the shore,
then the foaming, rabid maw

4. Ship of the fifteenth and sixteenth centuries.
5. Second book of the Hebrew Bible (Old Testament), Exodus describes the Israelites' escape from Egyptian captivity.
6. In the Bible, the sacred chest that contained the two tablets bearing the Ten Commandments.
7. The period from the fall of Jerusalem (586 B.C.E.) to the reconstruction in Palestine of a new Jewish state (after 538 B.C.E.), during which time the Jews were exiled to Mesopotamia by the conquering Babylonians.
8. Book of the Bible consisting of a series of erotic poems.
9. In Homer's *Odyssey,* Odysseus's men are punished for eating the cattle of the sun god, Helios.

of the tidal wave swallowing Port Royal,
and that was Jonah,[1]
but where is your Renaissance?

Sir, it is locked in them sea-sands
out there past the reef's moiling shelf,
where the men-o'-war floated down;

strop on these goggles, I'll guide you there myself.
It's all subtle and submarine,
through colonnades of coral,

past the gothic windows of sea-fans
to where the crusty grouper, onyx-eyed,
blinks, weighted by its jewels, like a bald queen;

and these groined caves with barnacles
pitted like stone
are our cathedrals,

and the furnace before the hurricanes:
Gomorrah.[2] Bones ground by windmills
into marl and cornmeal,

and that was Lamentations[3]—
that was just Lamentations,
it was not History;

then came, like scum on the river's drying lip,
the brown reeds of villages
mantling and congealing into towns,

and at evening, the midges'[4] choirs,
and above them, the spires
lancing the side of God[5]

as His son set, and that was the New Testament.

Then came the white sisters clapping
to the waves' progress,
and that was Emancipation[6]—

jubilation, O jubilation—
vanishing swiftly
as the sea's lace dries in the sun,

1. Biblical prophet swallowed by a great fish. *Port Royal:* once a major harbor town on the southern coast of Jamaica, it was destroyed by an earthquake in 1692.
2. City destroyed by God along with Sodom in Genesis 19.
3. Book of the Hebrew Bible (Old Testament) that laments the destruction of Judah, Jerusalem, and the Temple by the Babylonians.
4. Tiny flies'.
5. According to the Bible, Jesus' side was lanced during his crucifixion.
6. In the 1830s, slavery was abolished in the British West Indies.

but that was not History,
that was only faith,
and then each rock broke into its own nation;

then came the synod[7] of flies,
then came the secretarial heron,
then came the bullfrog bellowing for a vote,

fireflies with bright ideas
and bats like jetting ambassadors
and the mantis, like khaki police,

and the furred caterpillars of judges
examining each case closely,
and then in the dark ears of ferns

and in the salt chuckle of rocks
with their sea pools, there was the sound
like a rumour without any echo

of History, really beginning.

1979

The Schooner *Flight*

1. *Adios, Carenage*[8]

In idle August, while the sea soft,
and leaves of brown islands stick to the rim
of this Caribbean, I blow out the light
by the dreamless face of Maria Concepcion
to ship as a seaman on the schooner *Flight*.
Out in the yard turning grey in the dawn,
I stood like a stone and nothing else move
but the cold sea rippling like galvanize
and the nail holes of stars in the sky roof,
till a wind start to interfere with the trees.
I pass me dry neighbour sweeping she yard
as I went downhill, and I nearly said:
"Sweep soft, you witch, 'cause she don't sleep hard,"
but the bitch look through me like I was dead.
A route taxi pull up, park-lights still on.
The driver size up my bags with a grin:
"This time, Shabine, like you really gone!"
I ain't answer the ass, I simply pile in
the back seat and watch the sky burn
above Laventille[9] pink as the gown

7. A meeting of bishops or other church officials to decide administrative and theological issues.
8. Waterfront where island schooner ships are cleaned and repaired. *Adios:* goodbye (Spanish).
9. Hillside slum outside Port of Spain, Trinidad.

in which the woman I left was sleeping,
and I look in the rearview and see a man
exactly like me, and the man was weeping
for the houses, the streets, that whole fucking island.

Christ have mercy on all sleeping things!
From that dog rotting down Wrightson Road
to when I was a dog on these streets;
if loving these islands must be my load,
out of corruption my soul takes wings,
But they had started to poison my soul
with their big house, big car, big-time bohbohl,[1]
coolie, nigger, Syrian, and French Creole,
so I leave it for them and their carnival—
I taking a sea-bath, I gone down the road.
I know these islands from Monos to Nassau,[2]
a rusty head sailor with sea-green eyes
that they nickname Shabine, the patois[3] for
any red nigger, and I, Shabine, saw
when these slums of empire was paradise.
I'm just a red nigger who love the sea,
I had a sound colonial education,
I have Dutch, nigger, and English in me,
and either I'm nobody, or I'm a nation.

But Maria Concepcion was all my thought
watching the sea heaving up and down
as the port side of dories, schooners, and yachts
was painted afresh by the strokes of the sun
signing her name with every reflection;
I knew when dark-haired evening put on
her bright silk at sunset, and, folding the sea,
sidled under the sheet with her starry laugh,
that there'd be no rest, there'd be no forgetting.
Is like telling mourners round the graveside
about resurrection, they want the dead back,
so I smile to myself as the bow rope untied
and the *Flight* swing seaward: "Is no use repeating
that the sea have more fish. I ain't want her
dressed in the sexless light of a seraph,
I want those round brown eyes like a marmoset,[4] and
till the day when I can lean back and laugh,
those claws that tickled my back on sweating
Sunday afternoons, like a crab on wet sand."
As I worked, watching the rotting waves come
past the bow that scissor the sea like silk,
I swear to you all, by my mother's milk,
by the stars that shall fly from tonight's furnace,

1. Or *bobol:* corrupt practices or fraud, organized by people in positions of privilege or authority (Eastern Caribbean English).
2. Capital of the Bahamas. *Monos:* island off the northwest coast of Trinidad.
3. Spoken dialect, such as French-based Creole.
4. South American monkey. *Seraph:* angel.

that I loved them, my children, my wife, my home;
I loved them as poets love the poetry
that kills them, as drowned sailors the sea.

You ever look up from some lonely beach
and see a far schooner? Well, when I write
this poem, each phrase go be soaked in salt;
I go draw and knot every line as tight
as ropes in this rigging; in simple speech
my common language go be the wind,
my pages the sails of the schooner *Flight*.
But let me tell you how this business begin.

2. *Raptures of the Deep*

Smuggled Scotch for O'Hara, big government man,
between Cedros and the Main,[5] so the Coast Guard couldn't touch us,
and the Spanish pirogues[6] always met us halfway,
but a voice kept saying: "Shabine, see this business
of playing pirate?" Well, so said, so done!
That whole racket crash. And I for a woman,
for her laces and silks, Maria Concepcion.
Ay, ay! Next thing I hear, some Commission of Enquiry
was being organized to conduct a big quiz,
with himself as chairman investigating himself.
Well, I knew damn well who the suckers would be,
not that shark in shark skin, but his pilot fish,[7]
khaki-pants red niggers like you and me.
What worse, I fighting with Maria Concepcion,
plates flying and thing, so I swear: "Not again!"
It was mashing up my house and my family.
I was so broke all I needed was shades and a cup
or four shades and four cups in four-cup Port of Spain;
all the silver I had was the coins on the sea.

You saw them ministers in *The Express*,
guardians of the poor—one hand at their back,
and one set o' police only guarding their house,
and the Scotch pouring in through the back door.
As for that minister-monster who smuggled the booze,
that half-Syrian saurian,[8] I got so vex to see
that face thick with powder, the warts, the stone lids
like a dinosaur caked with primordial ooze
by the lightning of flashbulbs sinking in wealth,
that I said: "Shabine, this is shit, understand!"
But he get somebody to kick my crutch out his office
like I was some artist! That bitch was so grand,
couldn't get off his high horse and kick me himself.

5. The South American mainland. The Cedros peninsula is on the sparsely populated southwest tip of Trinidad, across a small channel from Venezuela.
6. Canoelike boats.
7. Fish that follows sharks to catch food scraps.
8. Lizard.

I have seen things that would make a slave sick
in this Trinidad, the Limers' Republic.[9]

I couldn't shake the sea noise out of my head,
the shell of my ears sang Maria Concepcion,
so I start salvage diving with a crazy Mick,
name O'Shaughnessy, and a limey[1] named Head;
but this Caribbean so choke with the dead
that when I would melt in emerald water,
whose ceiling rippled like a silk tent,
I saw them corals: brain, fire, sea-fans,
dead-men's-fingers, and then, the dead men.
I saw that the powdery sand was their bones
ground white from Senegal to San Salvador,[2]
so, I panic third dive, and surface for a month
in the Seamen's Hostel. Fish broth and sermons.
When I thought of the woe I had brought my wife,
when I saw my worries with that other woman,
I wept under water, salt seeking salt,
for her beauty had fallen on me like a sword
cleaving me from my children, flesh of my flesh!

There was this barge from St. Vincent,[3] but she was too deep
to float her again. When we drank, the limey
got tired of my sobbing for Maria Concepcion.
He said he was getting the bends. Good for him!
The pain in my heart for Maria Concepcion,
the hurt I had done to my wife and children,
was worse than the bends. In the rapturous deep
there was no cleft rock where my soul could hide
like the boobies[4] each sunset, no sandbar of light
where I could rest, like the pelicans know,
so I got raptures once, and I saw God
like a harpooned grouper bleeding, and a far
voice was rumbling, "Shabine, if you leave her,
if you leave her, I shall give you the morning star."
When I left the madhouse I tried other women
but, once they stripped naked, their spiky cunts
bristled like sea-eggs and I couldn't dive.
The chaplain came round. I paid him no mind.
Where is my rest place, Jesus? Where is my harbour?
Where is the pillow I will not have to pay for,
and the window I can look from that frames my life?

9. *Limers:* people who loaf or spend time idly (West Indian English).
1. Derogatory term for an English person. *Mick:* derogatory term for an Irish person.
2. That is, from Senegal, a country in West Africa, to San Salvador, in Central America, where Columbus first landed in the Americas. Approximately one third of slaves died en route from Africa to the Americas.
3. Island in the eastern Caribbean.
4. Tropical seabirds.

3. *Shabine Leaves the Republic*

I had no nation now but the imagination.
After the white man, the niggers didn't want me
when the power swing to their side.
The first chain my hands and apologize, "History";
the next said I wasn't black enough for their pride.
Tell me, what power, on these unknown rocks—
a spray-plane Air Force, the Fire Brigade,
the Red Cross, the Regiment, two, three police dogs
that pass before you finish bawling "Parade!"?
I met History once, but he ain't recognize me,
a parchment Creole,[5] with warts
like an old sea-bottle, crawling like a crab
through the holes of shadow cast by the net
of a grille balcony; cream linen, cream hat.
I confront him and shout, "Sir, is Shabine!
They say I'se your grandson. You remember Grandma,
your black cook, at all?" The bitch[6] hawk and spat.
A spit like that worth any number of words.
But that's all them bastards have left us: words.

I no longer believed in the revolution.
I was losing faith in the love of my woman.
I had seen that moment Aleksandr Blok[7]
crystallize in *The Twelve*. Was between
the Police Marine Branch and Hotel Venezuelana
one Sunday at noon. Young men without flags
using shirts, their chests waiting for holes.
They kept marching into the mountains, and
their noise ceased as foam sinks into sand.
They sank in the bright hills like rain, every one
with his own nimbus, leaving shirts in the street,
and the echo of power at the end of the street.[8]
Propeller-blade fans turn over the Senate;
the judges, they say, still sweat in carmine,[9]
on Frederick Street the idlers all marching
by standing still, the Budget turns a new leaf.
In the 12:30 movies the projectors best
not break down, or you go see revolution. Aleksandr Blok
enters and sits in the third row of pit eating choc-
olate cone, waiting for a spaghetti West-
ern with Clint Eastwood and featuring Lee Van Cleef.[1]

5. Here, a white descendant of European settlers in the Caribbean.
6. That is, the "Creole," or "History."
7. Russian symbolist (1880–1921), who celebrated the Russian Revolution in his epic poem *The Twelve* (1918).
8. Walcott alludes to the 1970 Black Power revolt in Trinidad, which included street marches and violence in Port of Spain, where he was living. Parts of the army sided with the revolutionaries, and the government was threatened with collapse.
9. Crimson.
1. Like Eastwood (b. 1930), an American actor (1925–1989) who starred in many "spaghetti" westerns produced by Italian and other European filmmakers.

4. *The* Flight, *Passing Blanchisseuse*[2]

Dusk. The *Flight* passing Blanchisseuse.
Gulls wheel like from a gun again,
and foam gone amber that was white,
lighthouse and star start making friends,
down every beach the long day ends,
and there, on that last stretch of sand,
on a beach bare of all but light,
dark hands start pulling in the seine[3]
of the dark sea, deep, deep inland.

5. *Shabine Encounters the Middle Passage*[4]

Man, I brisk in the galley first thing next dawn,
brewing li'l coffee; fog coil from the sea
like the kettle steaming when I put it down
slow, slow, 'cause I couldn't believe what I see:
where the horizon was one silver haze,
the fog swirl and swell into sails, so close
that I saw it was sails, my hair grip my skull,
it was horrors, but it was beautiful.
We float through a rustling forest of ships
with sails dry like paper, behind the glass
I saw men with rusty eyeholes like cannons,
and whenever their half-naked crews cross the sun,
right through their tissue, you traced their bones
like leaves against the sunlight; frigates, barkentines,[5]
the backward-moving current swept them on,
and high on their decks I saw great admirals,
Rodney, Nelson, de Grasse,[6] I heard the hoarse orders
they gave those Shabines, and the forest
of masts sail right through the *Flight*,
and all you could hear was the ghostly sound
of waves rustling like grass in a low wind
and the hissing weeds they trailed from the stern;
slowly they heaved past from east to west
like this round world was some cranked water wheel,
every ship pouring like a wooden bucket
dredged from the deep; my memory revolve
on all sailors before me, then the sun
heat the horizon's ring and they was mist.

2. Village on the north coast of Trinidad. Its name is French for washerwoman.
3. Large fishing net.
4. The route across the Atlantic Ocean by which slaves were transported from Africa to the New World, suffering starvation and disease in morbidly overcrowded ships.
5. Small ships. *Frigates:* warships of the eighteenth and early nineteenth centuries.
6. Admiral George Brydges Rodney (1718–1792) led British naval forces in a decisive defeat over the French warships of François-Joseph-Paul, Count de Grasse (1722–1788) in the 1782 Battle of the Saints, named after a small group of islands between Guadeloupe and Dominica. Before his famous victory at Trafalgar in the Napoleonic Wars, Horatio Nelson (1758–1805), another British admiral, also served extensively in the Caribbean.

Next we pass slave ships. Flags of all nations,
our fathers below deck too deep, I suppose,
to hear us shouting. So we stop shouting. Who knows
who his grandfather is, much less his name?
Tomorrow our landfall will be the Barbados.

6. *The Sailor Sings Back to the Casuarinas*[7]

You see them on the low hills of Barbados
bracing like windbreaks, needles for hurricanes,
trailing, like masts, the cirrus[8] of torn sails;
when I was green like them, I used to think
those cypresses, leaning against the sea,
that take the sea-noise up into their branches,
are not real cypresses but casuarinas.
Now captain just call them Canadian cedars.
But cedars, cypresses, or casuarinas,
whoever called them so had a good cause,
watching their bending bodies wail like women
after a storm, when some schooner came home
with news of one more sailor drowned again.
Once the sound "cypress" used to make more sense
than the green "casuarinas," though, to the wind
whatever grief bent them was all the same,
since they were trees with nothing else in mind
but heavenly leaping or to guard a grave;
but we live like our names and you would have
to be colonial to know the difference,
to know the pain of history words contain,
to love those trees with an inferior love,
and to believe: "Those casuarinas bend
like cypresses, their hair hangs down in rain
like sailors' wives. They're classic trees, and we,
if we live like the names our masters please,
by careful mimicry might become men."

7. *The* Flight *Anchors in Castries*[9] *Harbor*

When the stars self were young over Castries,
I loved you alone and I loved the whole world.
What does it matter that our lives are different?
Burdened with the loves of our different children?
When I think of your young face washed by the wind
and your voice that chuckles in the slap of the sea?
The lights are out on La Toc promontory,
except for the hospital. Across at Vigie[1]
the marina arcs keep vigil. I have kept my own
promise, to leave you the one thing I own,

7. Pinelike trees. Southeast of Saint Lucia, Barbados is the easternmost island of the Caribbean.
8. Wispy cloud.
9. Capital of Saint Lucia.
1. Just north of Castries.

you whom I loved first: my poetry.
We here for one night. Tomorrow, the *Flight* will be gone.

8. *Fight with the Crew*

It had one bitch on board, like he had me mark—
that was the cook, some Vincentian arse
with a skin like a gommier tree,[2] red peeling bark,
and wash-out blue eyes; he wouldn't give me a ease,
like he feel he was white. Had an exercise book,
this same one here, that I was using to write
my poetry, so one day this man snatch it
from my hand, and start throwing it left and right
to the rest of the crew, bawling out, "Catch it,"
and start mincing me like I was some hen
because of the poems. Some case is for fist,
some case is for tholing pin,[3] some is for knife—
this one was for knife. Well, I beg him first,
but he keep reading, "O my children, my wife,"
and playing he crying, to make the crew laugh;
it move like a flying fish, the silver knife
that catch him right in the plump of his calf,
and he faint so slowly, and he turn more white
than he thought he was. I suppose among men
you need that sort of thing. It ain't right
but that's how it is. There wasn't much pain,
just plenty blood, and Vincie and me best friend,
but none of them go fuck with my poetry again.

9. *Maria Concepcion & the Book of Dreams*

The jet that was screeching over the *Flight*
was opening a curtain into the past.
"Dominica ahead!"
"It still have Caribs[4] there."
"One day go be planes only, no more boat."
"Vince, God ain't make nigger to fly through the air."
"Progress, Shabine, that's what it's all about.
Progress leaving all we small islands behind."
I was at the wheel, Vince sitting next to me
gaffing.[5] Crisp, bracing day. A high-running sea.
"Progress is something to ask Caribs about.
They kill them by millions, some in war,
some by forced labour dying in the mines
looking for silver, after that niggers;[6] more

2. Gum tree, one of the largest and most common trees of the Caribbean rain forests. *Vincentian:* from Saint Vincent.
3. Pin in the side of a boat that acts as a fulcrum for an oar.
4. Indigenous people of the Lesser Antilles nearly exterminated by the European conquest. *Dominica:* pronounced *DOM-in-EE-ka;* mountainous, forested island north of Saint Lucia and Martinique.
5. Catching fish with a hooked spear, or gaff.
6. Beginning in the sixteenth century, Europeans imported African slaves to the West Indies to replace the labor force of the largely exterminated indigenous peoples.

progress. Until I see definite signs
that mankind change, Vince, I ain't want to hear.
Progress is history's dirty joke.
Ask that sad green island getting nearer."
Green islands, like mangoes pickled in brine.
In such fierce salt let my wound be healed,
me, in my freshness as a seafarer.

That night, with the sky sparks frosty with fire,
I ran like a Carib through Dominica,
my nose holes choked with memory of smoke;
I heard the screams of my burning children,
I ate the brains of mushrooms, the fungi
of devil's parasols under white, leprous rocks;
my breakfast was leaf mould in leaking forests,
with leaves big as maps, and when I heard noise
of the soldiers' progress through the thick leaves,
though my heart was bursting, I get up and ran
through the blades of balisier[7] sharper than spears;
with the blood of my race, I ran, boy, I ran
with moss-footed speed like a painted bird;
then I fall, but I fall by an icy stream under
cool fountains of fern, and a screaming parrot
catch the dry branches and I drowned at last
in big breakers of smoke; then when that ocean
of black smoke pass, and the sky turn white,
there was nothing but Progress, if Progress is
an iguana as still as a young leaf in sunlight.
I bawl for Maria, and her *Book of Dreams.*

It anchored her sleep, that insomniac's Bible,
a soiled orange booklet with a cyclops' eye
center, from the Dominican Republic.[8]
Its coarse pages were black with the usual
symbols of prophecy, in excited Spanish;
an open palm upright, sectioned and numbered
like a butcher chart, delivered the future.
One night, in a fever, radiantly ill,
she say, "Bring me the book, the end has come."
She said: "I dreamt of whales and a storm,"
but for that dream, the book had no answer.
A next night I dreamed of three old women
featureless as silkworms, stitching my fate,[9]
and I scream at them to come out my house,
and I try beating them away with a broom,
but as they go out, so they crawl back again,
until I start screaming and crying, my flesh
raining with sweat, and she ravage the book

7. Wild, flowering plant.
8. On the island of Hispaniola, in the Greater Antilles (as distinct from Dominica, in the Lesser Antilles).
9. In Greek mythology, the three Fates spin, measure, and cut the thread of life.

for the dream meaning, and there was nothing;
my nerves melt like a jellyfish—that was when I broke—
they found me round the Savannah,[1] screaming:

All you see me talking to the wind, so you think I mad.
Well, Shabine has bridled the horses of the sea;
you see me watching the sun till my eyeballs seared,
so all you mad people feel Shabine crazy,
but all you ain't know my strength, hear? The coconuts
standing by in their regiments in yellow khaki,
they waiting for Shabine to take over these islands,
and all you best dread the day I am healed
of being a human. All you fate in my hand,
ministers, businessmen, Shabine have you, friend,
I shall scatter your lives like a handful of sand,
I who have no weapon but poetry and
the lances of palms and the sea's shining shield!

10. *Out of the Depths*

Next day, dark sea. A arse-aching dawn.
"Damn wind shift sudden as a woman mind."
The slow swell start cresting like some mountain range
with snow on the top.
"Ay, Skipper, sky dark!"
"This ain't right for August."
"This light damn strange,
this season, sky should be clear as a field."

A stingray steeplechase across the sea,
tail whipping water, the high man-o'-wars[2]
start reeling inland, quick, quick an archery
of flying fish miss us! Vince say: "You notice?"
and a black-mane squall pounce on the sail
like a dog on a pigeon, and it snap the neck
of the *Flight* and shake it from head to tail.
"Be Jesus, I never see sea get so rough
so fast! That wind come from God back pocket!"
"Where Cap'n headin? Like the man gone blind!"
"If we's to drong, we go drong, Vince, fock-it!"
"Shabine, say your prayers, if life leave you any!"

I have not loved those that I loved enough.
Worse than the mule kick of Kick-'Em-Jenny[3]
Channel, rain start to pelt the *Flight* between
mountains of water. If I was frighten?
The tent poles of water spouts bracing the sky
start wobbling, clouds unstitch at the seams
and sky water drench us, and I hear myself cry,

1. Large park in Port of Spain.
2. Jellyfish; also, warships.
3. Small islet north of Grenada.

"I'm the drowned sailor in her *Book of Dreams*."
I remembered them ghost ships, I saw me corkscrewing
to the sea-bed of sea-worms, fathom pass fathom,
my jaw clench like a fist, and only one thing
hold me, trembling, how my family safe home.
Then a strength like it seize me and the strength said:
"I from backward people who still fear God."
Let Him, in His might, heave Leviathan[4] upward
by the winch of His will, the beast pouring lace
from his sea-bottom bed; and that was the faith
that had fade from a child in the Methodist chapel
in Chisel Street, Castries, when the whale-bell
sang service and, in hard pews ribbed like the whale,
proud with despair, we sang how our race
survive the sea's maw, our history, our peril,
and now I was ready for whatever death will.
But if that storm had strength, was in Cap'n face,
beard beading with spray, tears salting the eyes,
crucify to his post, that nigger hold fast
to that wheel, man, like the cross held Jesus,
and the wounds of his eyes like they crying for us,
and I feeding him white rum, while every crest
with Leviathan-lash make the *Flight* quail
like two criminal. Whole night, with no rest,
till red-eyed like dawn, we watch our travail
subsiding, subside, and there was no more storm.
And the noon sea get calm as Thy Kingdom come.

11. *After the Storm*

There's a fresh light that follows a storm
while the whole sea still havoc; in its bright wake
I saw the veiled face of Maria Concepcion
marrying the ocean, then drifting away
in the widening lace of her bridal train
with white gulls her bridesmaids, till she was gone.
I wanted nothing after that day.
Across my own face, like the face of the sun,
a light rain was falling, with the sea calm.

Fall gently, rain, on the sea's upturned face
like a girl showering; make these islands fresh
as Shabine once knew them! Let every trace,
every hot road, smell like clothes she just press
and sprinkle with drizzle. I finish dream;
whatever the rain wash and the sun iron:
the white clouds, the sea and sky with one seam,
is clothes enough for my nakedness.

4. Enormous seamonster of Jewish mythology, often represented as a whale.

Though my *Flight* never pass the incoming tide
of this inland sea beyond the loud reefs
of the final Bahamas, I am satisfied
if my hand gave voice to one people's grief.
Open the map. More islands there, man,
than peas on a tin plate, all different size,
one thousand in the Bahamas alone,
from mountains to low scrub with coral keys,
and from the bowsprit,[5] I bless every town,
the blue smell of smoke in hills behind them,
and the one small road winding down them like twine
to the roofs below; I have only one theme:

The bowsprit, the arrow, the longing, the lunging heart—
the flight to a target whose aim we'll never know,
vain search for one island that heals with its harbour
and a guiltless horizon, where the almond's[6] shadow
doesn't injure the sand. There are so many islands!
As many islands as the stars at night
on that branched tree from which meteors are shaken
like falling fruit around the schooner *Flight*.
But things must fall, and so it always was,
on one hand Venus, on the other Mars;[7]
fall, and are one, just as this earth is one
island in archipelagoes of stars.
My first friend was the sea. Now, is my last.
I stop talking now. I work, then I read,
cotching[8] under a lantern hooked to the mast.
I try to forget what happiness was,
and when that don't work, I study the stars.
Sometimes is just me, and the soft-scissored foam
as the deck turn white and the moon open
a cloud like a door, and the light over me
is a road in white moonlight taking me home.
Shabine sang to you from the depths of the sea.

1979

5. Spar or boom extending from the stem of a ship.
6. That is, the sea almond tree's.
7. Planets appearing as if stars, named after Roman gods of love and war, respectively.
8. Sitting for a while (West Indian English).

The Fortunate Traveller

(For Susan Sontag)[9]

And I heard a voice in the midst of the four beasts say,
A measure of wheat for a penny,
and three measures of barley for a penny;
and see thou hurt not the oil and the wine.
—REVELATION 6.6[1]

I

It was in winter. Steeples, spires
congealed like holy candles. Rotting snow
flaked from Europe's ceiling. A compact man,
I crossed the canal in a grey overcoat,
on one lapel a crimson buttonhole
for the cold ecstasy of the assassin.
In the square coffin manacled to my wrist:
small countries pleaded through the mesh of graphs,
in treble-spaced, Xeroxed forms to the World Bank[2]
on which I had scrawled the one word, MERCY;

I sat on a cold bench
under some skeletal lindens.[3]
Two other gentlemen, black skins gone grey
as their identical, belted overcoats,
crossed the white river.
They spoke the stilted French
of their dark river,
whose hooked worm, multiplying its pale sickle,
could thin the harvest of the winter streets.[4]
"Then we can depend on you to get us those tractors?"
"I gave my word."
"May my country ask you why you are doing this, sir?"
Silence.
"You know if you betray us, you cannot hide?"
A tug. Smoke trailing its dark cry.

At the window in Haiti, I remember
a gekko[5] pressed against the hotel glass,
with white palms, concentrating head.
With a child's hands. Mercy, monsieur. Mercy.
Famine sighs like a scythe
across the field of statistics and the desert

9. American philosopher and writer (b. 1933). Cf. the title of the picaresque tale by Thomas Nashe, *The Unfortunate Traveller* (1593).
1. The narrator of this apocalyptic biblical book hears this voice after the Lamb of God has broken the fourth of six seals, and after he has seen the third of four horses, "a black horse, and he that sat on him had a pair of balances in his hand" (Revelation 6.5). This horseman may symbolize famine.
2. An international loan association.
3. Large, European trees, used for city and street planting.
4. "Sickle" refers both to the crescent-shaped farming tool used for cutting grain and to sickle-cell anemia, a disease most common among blacks, in which red blood cells become crescent shaped.
5. Small, tropical lizard, with feet that look somewhat like human palms.

is a moving mouth. In the hold of this earth
10,000,000 shoreless souls are drifting.
Somalia:[6] 765,000, their skeletons will go under the tidal sand.
"We'll meet you in Bristol[7] to conclude the agreement?"
Steeples like tribal lances, through congealing fog
the cries of wounded church bells wrapped in cotton,
grey mist enfolding the conspirator
like a sealed envelope next to its heart.

No one will look up now to see the jet
fade like a weevil[8] through a cloud of flour.
One flies first-class, one is so fortunate.
Like a telescope reversed, the traveller's eye
swiftly screws down the individual sorrow
to an oval nest of antic numerals,
and the iris, interlocking with this globe,
condenses it to zero, then a cloud.
Beetle-black taxi from Heathrow to my flat.[9]
We are roaches,
riddling the state cabinets, entering the dark holes
of power, carapaced in topcoats,[1]
scuttling around columns, signalling for taxis,
with frantic antennae, to other huddles with roaches;
we infect with optimism, and when
the cabinets crack, we are the first
to scuttle, radiating separately
back to Geneva, Bonn, Washington, London.

Under the dripping planes of Hampstead Heath,[2]
I read her letter again, watching the drizzle
disfigure its pleading like mascara. Margo,
I cannot bear to watch the nations cry.
Then the phone: "We will pay you in Bristol."
Days in fetid bedclothes swallowing cold tea,
the phone stifled by the pillow. The telly
a blue storm with soundless snow.
I'd light the gas and see a tiger's tongue.
I was rehearsing the ecstasies of starvation
for what I had to do. *And have not charity.*[3]

I found my pity, desperately researching
the origins of history, from reed-built communes
by sacred lakes, turning with the first sprocketed
water-driven wheels. I smelled imagination
among bestial hides by the gleam of fat,
seeking in all races a common ingenuity.

6. East African republic, site of frequent famines.
7. Industrial and shipping city in southwestern England.
8. Insect whose larvae eat grain and flour.
9. Apartment (British usage). *Heathrow:* London's major airport.
1. The coats are compared to the hard outer shells of insects.
2. Park in the London suburb of Hampstead. *Planes:* plane trees, common in cities.
3. "Though I speak with the tongues of men and of angels, and have not charity, I am become as sounding brass, or a tinkling cymbal" (1 Corinthians 13.1).

I envisaged an African flooded with such light
as alchemized the first fields of emmer wheat[4] and barley,
when we savages dyed our pale dead with ochre,
and bordered our temples
with the ceremonial vulva of the conch
in the grey epoch of the obsidian adze.[5]
I sowed the Sahara with rippling cereals,[6]
my charity fertilized these aridities.

What was my field? Late sixteenth century.
My field was a dank acre. A Sussex don,
I taught the Jacobean anxieties: *The White Devil.*[7]
Flamineo's torch startles the brooding yews.
The drawn end comes in strides. I loved my Duchess,[8]
the white flame of her soul blown out between
the smoking cypresses. Then I saw children pounce
on green meat with a rat's ferocity.

I called them up and took the train to Bristol,
my blood the Severn's[9] dregs and silver.
On Severn's estuary the pieces flash,
Iscariot's salary,[1] patron saint of spies.
I thought, who cares how many million starve?
Their rising souls will lighten the world's weight
and level its gull-glittering waterline;
we left at sunset down the estuary.

England recedes. The forked white gull
screeches, circling back.
Even the birds are pulled back by their orbit,
even mercy has its magnetic field.
Back in the cabin,
I uncap the whisky, the porthole
mists with glaucoma.[2] By the time I'm pissed,
England, England will be
that pale serrated indigo on the sea-line.
"You are so fortunate, you get to see the world—"
Indeed, indeed, sirs, I have seen the world.
Spray splashes the portholes and vision blurs.

Leaning on the hot rail, watching the hot sea,
I saw them far off, kneeling on hot sand

4. A hard, red wheat. *Alchemized:* that is, transmuted.
5. Primitive cutting tool made of volcanic glass. *Ochre:* red or yellow clay. *Bordered . . . conch:* that is, decorated our temples with the innermost parts of conch shells.
6. That is, planted grain.
7. Dark revenge tragedy by John Webster (c. 1580–c. 1625), written in the early seventeenth century ("Jacobean"), a pessimistic time by contrast with the Elizabethan age. *Don:* British university teacher.
8. Flamineo is the Machiavellian villain in *The White Devil;* "the Duchess" is Vittoria Corombona, its heroine. *Yews:* evergreen trees; they are often associated with grief, as are "cypresses" (line 89).
9. The Severn is a river that flows past Bristol.
1. That is, the thirty pieces of silver that Judas Iscariot received for betraying Jesus (Matthew 26.14–16).
2. As one's eyes would mist if one had glaucoma.

in the pious genuflections of the locust,
as Ponce's armored knees crush Florida[3]
to the funeral fragrance of white lilies.

II

Now I have to come to where the phantoms live,
I have no fear of phantoms, but of the real.
The sabbath benedictions[4] of the islands.
Treble clef of the snail on the scored leaf,
the Tantum Ergo[5] of black choristers
soars through the organ pipes of coconuts.
Across the dirty beach surpliced[6] with lace,
they pass a brown lagoon behind the priest,
pale and unshaven in his frayed soutane,
into the concrete church at Canaries;[7]
as Albert Schweitzer moves to the harmonium[8]
of morning, and to the pluming chimneys,
the groundswell lifts *Lebensraum, Lebensraum.*[9]

Black faces sprinkled with continual dew—
dew on the speckled croton, dew
on the hard leaf of the knotted plum tree,
dew on the elephant ears of the dasheen.[1]
Through Kurtz's teeth, white skull in elephant grass,
the imperial fiction sings. Sunday
wrinkles downriver from the Heart of Darkness.[2]
The heart of darkness is not Africa.
The heart of darkness is the core of fire
in the white center of the holocaust.
The heart of darkness is the rubber claw
selecting a scalpel in antiseptic light,
the hills of children's shoes outside the chimneys,
the tinkling nickel instruments on the white altar;
Jacob,[3] in his last card, sent me these verses:
"Think of a God who doesn't lose His sleep
if trees burst into tears or glaciers weep.
So, aping His indifference, I write now,
not Anno Domini: After Dachau."[4]

3. Juan Ponce de Leon (1460–1521), Spanish explorer, discovered Florida in 1513 and attempted to conquer the Native Americans there in 1521.
4. That is, holy-day blessings.
5. So much therefore (from a Latin mass).
6. As though covered by a white ecclesiastical overgarment.
7. Town on west coast of Santa Lucia. *Soutane:* priest's robe.
8. Schweitzer (1875–1965) was a musician and organist who became a medical missionary in Africa in 1913; in the jungle, his instrument was the harmonium, a small reed organ.
9. Living space (German); term used most prominently for Hitler's attempt to enlarge Germany by occupying other countries.
1. Starchy, edible plant of the tropics. *Croton:* castor-oil plant.
2. Title of novella (1902) by the Polish-English novelist Joseph Conrad (1857–1924); Kurtz, the man who is the goal of the narrator's search in the Congo, is finally depicted as having seen into the depth of corruption.
3. Very likely Jacob Timmerman, Argentinian journalist and editor imprisoned and tortured for antigovernment writings.
4. Concentration camp operated by the Nazis, liberated in 1945.

III

The night maid brings a lamp and draws the blinds.
I stay out on the veranda with the stars.
Breakfast congealed to supper on its plate.

There is no sea as restless as my mind.
The promontories snore. They snore like whales.
Cetus, the whale, was Christ.[5]
The ember dies, the sky smokes like an ash heap.
Reeds wash their hands of guilt and the lagoon
is stained. Louder, since it rained,
a gauze of sand flies hisses from the marsh.

Since God is dead, and these are not His stars,
but man-lit, sulphurous, sanctuary lamps,
it's in the heart of darkness of this earth
that backward tribes keep vigil of His Body,[6]
in deya, lampion,[7] and this bedside lamp.
Keep the news from their blissful ignorance.
Like lice, like lice, the hungry of this earth
swarm to the tree of life. If those who starve
like these rain-flies who shed glazed wings in light
grew from sharp shoulder blades their brittle vans
and soared toward that tree, how it would seethe—
ah, Justice! But fires
drench them like vermin, quotas
prevent them, and they remain
compassionate fodder for the travel book,
its paragraphs like windows from a train,
for everywhere that earth shows its rib cage
and the moon goggles with the eyes of children,
we turn away to read. Rimbaud learned that.
                                        Rimbaud, at dusk,
idling his wrist in water past temples
the plumed dates still protect in Roman file,[8]
knew that we cared less for one human face
than for the scrolls in Alexandria's ashes,[9]
that the bright water could not dye his hand
any more than poetry. The dhow's[1] silhouette
moved through the blinding coinage of the river
that, endlessly, until we pay one debt,
shrouds, every night, an ordinary secret.

5. Cetus, Latin for whale, is a constellation. A classical seamonster, Cetus is associated with the biblical story of Jonah, who is said to prefigure Jesus, often symbolized by a fish.
6. *Sanctuary lamps:* refers to the practice in High Catholic churches of keeping a lamp lit above the altar (i.e., "sanctuary") when a consecrated wafer is present; since in Holy Communion the wafer represents Jesus' body, this practice is a "vigil of His Body."
7. Small lamp. *Deya:* small clay lamp, many of which are lit for the major Hindu religious festival of Diwali, which honors Laksmi, the goddess of wealth.
8. Single file. Arthur Rimbaud (1854–1891), French poet, spent the last ten years of his life in North Africa.
9. Many of the scrolls in the great Alexandrian Library (in Egypt) were destroyed by fire in 47 B.C.E.
1. Arab boat's.

IV

The drawn sword comes in strides.
It stretches for the length of the empty beach;
the fishermen's huts shut their eyes tight.
A frisson[2] shakes the palm trees,
and sweats on the traveller's tree.
They've found out my sanctuary. Philippe, last night:
"It had two gentlemen in the village yesterday, sir,
asking for you while you was in town.
I tell them you was in town. They send to tell you,
there is no hurry. They will be coming back."

In loaves of cloud, *and have not charity,*
the weevil will make a sahara of Kansas,
the ant shall eat Russia.
Their soft teeth shall make, *and have not charity,*
the harvest's desolation,
and the brown globe crack like a begging bowl,
and though you fire oceans of surplus grain,
and have not charity,

still, through thin stalks,
the smoking stubble, stalks
grasshopper: third horseman,
the leather-helmed locust.[3]

1981

The Season of Phantasmal Peace

Then all the nations of birds lifted together
the huge net of the shadows of this earth
in multitudinous dialects, twittering tongues,
stitching and crossing it. They lifted up
the shadow of long pines down trackless slopes,
the shadows of glass-faced towers down evening streets,
the shadow of a frail plant on a city sill—
the net rising soundless as night, the birds' cries soundless, until
there was no longer dusk, or season, decline, or weather,
only this passage of phantasmal light
that not the narrowest shadow dared to sever.

And men could not see, looking up, what the wild geese drew,
what the ospreys trailed behind them in silvery ropes
that flashed in the icy sunlight; they could not hear
battalions of starlings waging peaceful cries,
bearing the net higher, covering this world

2. Shiver.
3. Predatory insect, compared to the third horseman of the Apocalypse, famine. Cf. the epigraph and note 1.

like the vines of an orchard, or a mother drawing
the trembling gauze over the trembling eyes
of a child fluttering to sleep;
                                            it was the light
that you will see at evening on the side of a hill
in yellow October, and no one hearing knew
what change had brought into the raven's cawing,
the killdeer's screech, the ember-circling chough[4]
such an immense, soundless, and high concern
for the fields and cities where the birds belong,
except it was their seasonal passing, Love,
made seasonless, or, from the high privilege of their birth,
something brighter than pity for the wingless ones
below them who shared dark holes in windows and in houses,
and higher they lifted the net with soundless voices
above all change, betrayals of falling suns,
and this season lasted one moment, like the pause
between dusk and darkness, between fury and peace,
but, for such as our earth is now, it lasted long.

1981

From Omeros[5]

Book One

Chapter 1

I

"This is how, one sunrise, we cut down them canoes."
Philoctete[6] smiles for the tourists, who try taking
his soul with their cameras. "Once wind bring the news

to the *laurier-cannelles*,[7] their leaves start shaking
the minute the axe of sunlight hit the cedars,
because they could see the axes in our own eyes.

Wind lift the ferns. They sound like the sea that feed us
fishermen all our life, and the ferns nodded 'Yes,
the trees have to die.' So, fists jam in our jacket,

4. Bird in the crow family.
5. Modern Greek version of the name Homer. Homer's *Iliad* and *Odyssey* are, along with Dante's *Divine Comedy,* from which Walcott adapts the terza rima stanza, and James Joyce's *Ulysses* (1922), major influences on this Caribbean epic, which moves across centuries and geographies, from Saint Lucia to Africa to Ireland.
6. Pronounced *fee-lock-TET;* a name shared with Philoctetes, who, in the *Iliad* and Sophocles' eponymous play, is abandoned on an island on the way to the Trojan War after receiving a snakebite. The wound never heals and continually torments Philoctetes, who moans uncontrollably. Later, the gods decide that the war cannot be won without him, and the Greek soldiers have to go back to the island and beg him to return with them to battle.
7. Type of tree.

cause the heights was cold and our breath making feathers
like the mist, we pass the rum. When it came back, it
give us the spirit to turn into murderers.

I lift up the axe and pray for strength in my hands
to wound the first cedar. Dew was filling my eyes,
but I fire one more white rum. Then we advance."

For some extra silver, under a sea-almond,
he shows them a scar made by a rusted anchor,
rolling one trouser-leg up with the rising moan

of a conch. It has puckered like the corolla
of a sea-urchin. He does not explain its cure.
"It have some things"—he smiles—"worth more than a dollar."

He has left it to a garrulous waterfall
to pour out his secret down La Sorcière,[8] since
the tall laurels fell, for the ground-dove's mating call

to pass on its note to the blue, tacit mountains
whose talkative brooks, carrying it to the sea,
turn into idle pools where the clear minnows shoot

and an egret stalks the reeds with one rusted cry
as it stabs and stabs the mud with one lifting foot.
Then silence is sawn in half by a dragonfly

as eels sign their names along the clear bottom-sand,
when the sunrise brightens the river's memory
and waves of huge ferns are nodding to the sea's sound.

Although smoke forgets the earth from which it ascends,
and nettles guard the holes where the laurels were killed,
an iguana hears the axes, clouding each lens

over its lost name, when the hunched island was called
"Iounalao," "Where the iguana is found."
But, taking its own time, the iguana will scale

the rigging of vines in a year, its dewlap fanned,
its elbows akimbo, its deliberate tail
moving with the island. The slit pods of its eyes

ripened in a pause that lasted for centuries,
that rose with the Aruacs'[9] smoke till a new race
unknown to the lizard stood measuring the trees.

8. The sorceress (French); a mountain on Saint Lucia.
9. A people native to the Caribbean who were driven out and killed by the Caribs and the Spanish.

These were their pillars that fell, leaving a blue space
for a single God where the old gods stood before.
The first god was a gommier.[1] The generator

began with a whine, and a shark, with sidewise jaw,
sent the chips flying like mackerel over water
into trembling weeds. Now they cut off the saw,

still hot and shaking, to examine the wound it
had made. They scraped off its gangrenous moss, then ripped
the wound clear of the net of vines that still bound it

to this earth, and nodded. The generator whipped
back to its work, and the chips flew much faster as
the shark's teeth gnawed evenly. They covered their eyes

from the splintering nest. Now, over the pastures
of bananas, the island lifted its horns. Sunrise
trickled down its valleys, blood splashed on the cedars,

and the grove flooded with the light of sacrifice.
A gommier was cracking. Its leaves an enormous
tarpaulin with the ridgepole gone. The creaking sound

made the fishermen leap back as the angling mast
leant slowly towards the troughs of ferns; then the ground
shuddered under the feet in waves, then the waves passed.

Chapter III

III

"Mais qui ça qui rivait-'ous, Philoctete?"
                                        "Moin blessé."[2]
"But what is wrong wif you, Philoctete?"
                                        "I am blest

wif this wound, Ma Kilman,[3] *qui pas ka guérir pièce.*

Which will never heal."
                              "Well, you must take it easy.
Go home and lie down, give the foot a lickle rest."
Philoctete, his trouser-legs rolled, stares out to sea

from the worn rumshop window. The itch in the sore
tingles like the tendrils of the anemone,
and the puffed blister of Portuguese man-o'-war.[4]

1. Gum tree.
2. French patois translated below (though *blessé* actually means "wounded").
3. The owner of the No Pain Café, Ma Kilman serves in the poem as a sybil (female prophet) and an obeah woman (one practicing a kind of West Indian sorcery).
4. Jellyfish (from a term for warship).

He believed the swelling came from the chained ankles
of his grandfathers. Or else why was there no cure?
That the cross he carried was not only the anchor's

but that of his race, for a village black and poor
as the pigs that rooted in its burning garbage,
then were hooked on the anchors of the abattoir.[5]

Ma Kilman was sewing. She looked up and saw his face
squinting from the white of the street. He was waiting
to pass out on the table. This went on for days.

The ice turned to warm water near the self-hating
gesture of clenching his head tight in both hands. She
heard the boys in blue uniforms, going to school,

screaming at his elbow: "Pheeloh! Pheelosophee!"
A mummy embalmed in Vaseline and alcohol.
In the Egyptian silence she muttered softly:

"It have a flower somewhere, a medicine, and ways
my grandmother would boil it. I used to watch ants
climbing her white flower-pot. But, God, in which place?"

Where was this root? What senna, what tepid tisanes,[6]
could clean the branched river of his corrupted blood,
whose sap was a wounded cedar's? What did it mean,

this name that felt like a fever? Well, one good heft
of his garden-cutlass would slice the damned name clean
from its rotting yam. He said, *"Merci."*[7] Then he left.

Chapter IX

III

The Cyclone, howling because one of the lances
of a flinging palm has narrowly grazed his one eye,[8]
wades knee-deep in troughs. As he blindly advances,

Lightning, his stilt-walking messenger, jiggers the sky
with his forked stride, or he crackles over the troughs
like a split electric wishbone. His wife, Ma Rain,

hurls buckets from the balcony of her upstairs house.
She shakes the sodden mops of the palms and once again
changes her furniture, the cloud-sofas' grumbling casters

5. Slaughterhouse.
6. Medicinal beverages. *Senna:* medicinal herb.
7. Thank you (French).
8. Cf. the episode in book 9 of Homer's *Odyssey* in which Odysseus and his men escape by blinding the drunken Cyclops, Polyphemos, with a sharp stick. Polyphemos is the son of Poseidon (Roman, Neptune), the Greek sea god.

not waking the Sun. The Sun had been working all day
and would sleep through it all. After their disasters
it was he who cleaned up after their goddamned party.

So he went straight to bed at the first sign of a drizzle.
Now, like a large coalpot with headlands for its handles,
the Sea cooks up a storm, raindrops start to sizzle

like grease, there is a brisk business in candles
in Ma Kilman's shop. Candles, nails, a sudden increase in
the faithful, and a mark-up on matches and bread.

In the grey vertical forest of the hurricane season,
when the dirty sea returns the wreaths of the dead,
all the village could do was listen to the gods in session,

playing any instruments that came into their craniums,
the harp-sighing ripple of a hither-and-zithering sea,
the knucklebone pebbles, the abrupt Shango[9] drums

made Neptune rock in the caves. Fête start! Erzulie
rattling her ra-ra; Ogun, the blacksmith, feeling
No Pain; Damballa[1] winding like a zandoli

lizard,[2] as their huge feet thudded on the ceiling,
as the sea-god, drunk, lurched from wall to wall, saying:
"Mama, this music so loud, I going in seine,"[3]

then throwing up at his pun. People were praying,
but then the gods, who were tired, were throwing a fête,
and their fêtes went on for days, and their music ranged

from polkas of rain to waves dancing La Comète,[4]
and the surf clapped hands whenever the patterns changed.
For the gods aren't men, they get on well together,

holding a hurricane-party in their cloud-house,
and what brings the gods close is the thunderous weather,
where Ogun can fire one with his partner Zeus.[5]

Achille in his shack heard chac-chac and violin
in the telephone wires, a sound like Helen
moaning, or Seven Seas,[6] blind as a sail in rain.

9. Afro-Caribbean god of thunder, drums, and dance, originally from West Africa (Yoruba); he is often depicted in images of thunder and lighting. *Zither*: stringed instrument.

1. Afro-Caribbean snake god that lives in trees and springs. *Neptune:* cave-dwelling Roman god of the sea. *Fête:* party (French). *Erzulie:* Haitian goddess of love and elemental forces, thought to have origins in West Africa. *Ra-ra:* rattle (West Indian English). *Ogun:* Afro-Caribbean and West African (Yoruba) god of iron, thunder, roads, war, creation, and destruction; he is often depicted as a blacksmith.

2. Small, Antillean lizard.

3. Fishing net.

4. The comet (French).

5. King of the Greek gods.

6. Poet figure in *Omeros. Achille:* pronounced *ah-SHEEL* in the island patois; in the *Iliad,* Achilles is the greatest Greek warrior and the slayer of Hec-

In the devastated valleys, crumpling brown water
at their prows,[7] headlights on, passenger-vans floated
slowly up roads that were rivers, through the slaughter

of the year's banana-crop, past stiff cows bloated
from engorging mud as the antlers of trees tossed
past the banks like migrating elk. It was as if

the rivers, envying the sea, tired of being crossed
in one leap, had joined in a power so massive
that it made islands of villages, made bridges

the sieves of a force that shouldered culverts aside.
The rain passed, but people looked up to the ridges
fraying with its return, and the flood, in its pride,

entered the sea; then Achille could hear the tunnels
of brown water roaring in the mangroves; its tide
hid the keels of the canoes, and their wet gunwales[8]

were high with rainwater that could warp them rotten
if they were not bailed. The river was satisfied.
It was a god too. Too much had been forgotten.

Then, a mouse after a fête, its claws curled like moss,
nosing the dew as the lighthouse opened its eye,
the sunlight peeped out, and people surveyed the loss

that the gods had made under a clearing-up sky.
Candles shortened and died. The big yellow tractors
tossed up the salad of trees, in yellow jackets

men straightened the chairs of dead poles, the contractors
in white helmets and slickers heard the castanets
of the waves going up the islands, moving on

from here to Guadeloupe,[9] the beaded wires were still.
They saw the mess the gods made in one night alone,
as Lightning lifted his stilts over the last hill.

Achille bailed out his canoe under an almond
that shuddered with rain. There would be brilliant days still,
till the next storm, and their freshness was wonderful.

tor. *Chac-chac:* maracas. *Helen:* Achille's lover, who, in this scene, has recently left him. Achille and Hector feud over Helen, recalling their namesakes and the Trojan War in Homer's *Iliad.* Saint Lucia, which traded hands fourteen times in battles between the French and the British, is also referred to as the "Helen of the West Indies."

7. Front parts.
8. Upper edges of their sides.
9. Island third to the north of Saint Lucia.

Chapter XIII

II

"Walk me down to the wharf."[1]
At the corner of Bridge
Street, we saw the liner as white as a mirage,
its hull bright as paper, preening with privilege.

"Measure the days you have left. Do just that labour
which marries your heart to your right hand: simplify
your life to one emblem, a sail leaving harbour

and a sail coming in. All corruption will cry
to be taken aboard. Fame is that white liner
at the end of your street, a city to itself,

taller than the Fire Station, and much finer,
with its brass-ringed portholes, mounting shelf after shelf,
than anything Castries[2] could ever hope to build."

The immaculate hull insulted the tin roofs
beneath it, its pursers were milk, even the bilge
bubbling from its stern in quietly muttering troughs

and its humming engines spewed expensive garbage
where boys balanced on logs or, riding old tires,
shouted up past the hull to tourists on the rails

to throw down coins, as cameras caught their black cries,
then jackknife or swan-dive—their somersaulting tails
like fishes flipped backwards—as the coins grew in size

in the wobbling depth; then, when they surfaced, fights
for possession, their heads butting like porpoises,
all, like a city leaving a city, the lights

blazed in its moving rooms, and the liner would glide
over its own phosphorus, and wash hit the wharves
long after stewards had set the service inside

the swaying chandeliered salons, and the black waves
settle down to their level. The stars would renew
their studded diagrams over Achille's canoe.

From here, in his boyhood, he had seen women climb
like ants up a white flower-pot, baskets of coal
balanced on their torchoned[3] heads, without touching them,

1. In this chapter, the narrator listens to the ghost of his father. A conversation with a ghost or shade from the underworld is a common device of epic poetry.

2. Capital city of Saint Lucia; under British rule, it became the principal coal port in the region.

3. Wrapped in cloth.

up the black pyramids, each spine straight as a pole,
and with a strength that never altered its rhythm.
He spoke for those Helens from an earlier time:

"Hell was built on those hills. In that country of coal
without fire, that inferno the same colour
as their skins and shadows, every labouring soul

climbed with her hundredweight basket, every load for
one copper penny, balanced erect on their necks
that were tight as the liner's hawsers[4] from the weight.

The carriers were women, not the fair, gentler sex.
Instead, they were darker and stronger, and their gait
was made beautiful by balance, in their ascending

the narrow wooden ramp built steeply to the hull
of a liner tall as a cloud, the unending
line crossing like ants without touching for the whole

day. That was one section of the wharf, opposite
your grandmother's house where I watched the silhouettes
of these women, while every hundredweight basket

was ticked by two tally clerks in their white pith-helmets,
and the endless repetition as they climbed the
infernal anthracite hills showed you hell, early."

III

"Along this coal-blackened wharf, what Time decided
to do with my treacherous body after this,"
he said, watching the women, "will stay in your head

as long as a question you have no right to ask,
only to doubt, not hate our infuriating
silence. I am only the shadow of that task

as much as their work, your pose of a question waiting,
as you crouch with a writing lamp over a desk,
remains in the darkness after the light has gone,

and whether night is palpable between dawn and dusk
is not for the living; so you mind your business,
which is life and work, like theirs, but I will say this:

O Thou, my Zero, is an impossible prayer,
utter extinction is still a doubtful conceit.
Though we pray to nothing, nothing cannot be there.

4. Thick ropes.

Kneel to your load, then balance your staggering feet
and walk up that coal ladder as they do in time,
one bare foot after the next in ancestral rhyme.

Because Rhyme remains the parentheses of palms
shielding a candle's tongue, it is the language's
desire to enclose the loved world in its arms;

or heft a coal-basket; only by its stages
like those groaning women will you achieve that height
whose wooden planks in couplets lift your pages

higher than those hills of infernal anthracite.
There, like ants or angels, they see their native town,
unknown, raw, insignificant. They walk, you write;

keep to that narrow causeway without looking down,
climbing in their footsteps, that slow, ancestral beat
of those used to climbing roads; your own work owes them

because the couplet of those multiplying feet
made your first rhymes. Look, they climb, and no one knows them;
they take their copper pittances, and your duty

from the time you watched them from your grandmother's house
as a child wounded by their power and beauty
is the chance you now have, to give those feet a voice."

We stood in the hot afternoon. My father took
his fob-watch from its pocket, replaced it, then said,
lightly gripping my arm,
"He enjoys a good talk,

a serious trim, and I myself look ahead
to our appointment." He kissed me. I watched him walk
through a pillared balcony's alternating shade.

Book Three

Chapter XXV

II

He[5] remembered this sunburnt river with its spindly
stakes and the peaked huts platformed above the spindles
where thin, naked figures as he rowed past looked unkindly

or kindly in their silence. The silence an old fence kindles
in a boy's heart. They walked with his homecoming
canoe past bonfires in a scorched clearing near the edge

5. Achille, suffering from sunstroke, is hallucinating a return to the Congo River, in Africa.

of the soft-lipped shallows whose noise hurt his drumming
heart as the pirogue[6] slid its raw, painted wedge
towards the crazed sticks of a vine-fastened pier.

The river was sloughing its old skin like a snake
in wrinkling sunshine; the sun resumed its empire
over this branch of the Congo; the prow found its stake

in the river and nuzzled it the way that a piglet
finds its favourite dug in the sweet-grunting sow,
and now each cheek ran with its own clear rivulet

of tears, as Achille, weeping, fastened the bow
of the dugout, wiped his eyes with one dry palm,
and felt a hard hand help him up the shaking pier.

Half of me was with him. One half with the midshipman
by a Dutch canal. But now, neither was happier
or unhappier than the other. An old man put an arm

around Achille, and the crowd, chattering, followed both.
They touched his trousers, his undershirt, their hands
scrabbling the texture, as a kitten does with cloth,

till they stood before an open hut. The sun stands
with expectant silence. The river stops talking,
the way silence sometimes suddenly turns off a market.

The wind squatted low in the grass. A man kept walking
steadily towards him, and he knew by that walk it
was himself in his father, the white teeth, the widening hands.

III

He sought his own features in those of their life-giver,
and saw two worlds mirrored there: the hair was surf
curling round a sea-rock, the forehead a frowning river,

as they swirled in the estuary of a bewildered love,
and Time stood between them. The only interpreter
of their lips' joined babble, the river with the foam,

and the chuckles of water under the sticks of the pier,
where the tribe stood like sticks themselves, reversed
by reflection. Then they walked up to the settlement,

and it seemed, as they chattered, everything was rehearsed
for ages before this. He could predict the intent
of his father's gestures; he was moving with the dead.

6. Canoelike boat.

Women paused at their work, then smiled at the warrior
returning from his battle with smoke, from the kingdom
where he had been captured, they cried and were happy.

Then the fishermen sat near a large tree under whose dome
stones sat in a circle. His father said:
"Afo-la-be,"
touching his own heart.
"In the place you have come from

what do they call you?"
Time translates.
Tapping his chest,
the son answers:
"Achille." The tribe rustles, "Achille."
Then, like cedars at sunrise, the mutterings settle.

AFOLABE

Achille. What does the name mean? I have forgotten the one
that I gave you. But it was, it seems, many years ago.
What does it mean?

ACHILLE

Well, I too have forgotten.

Everything was forgotten. You also. I do not know.
The deaf sea has changed around every name that you gave
us; trees, men, we yearn for a sound that is missing.

AFOLABE

A name means something. The qualities desired in a son,
and even a girl-child; so even the shadows who called
you expected one virtue, since every name is a blessing,

since I am remembering the hope I had for you as a child.
Unless the sound means nothing. Then you would be nothing.
Did they think you were nothing in that other kingdom?

ACHILLE

I do not know what the name means. It means something,
maybe. What's the difference? In the world I come from
we accept the sounds we were given. Men, trees, water.

AFOLABE

And therefore, Achille, if I pointed and I said, There
is the name of that man, that tree, and this father,
would every sound be a shadow that crossed your ear,

without the shape of a man or a tree? What would it be?
(And just as branches sway in the dusk from their fear
of amnesia, of oblivion, the tribe began to grieve.)

ACHILLE

What would it be? I can only tell you what I believe,
or had to believe. It was prediction, and memory,
to bear myself back, to be carried here by a swift,

or the shadow of a swift making its cross on water,
with the same sign I was blessed with, with the gift
of this sound whose meaning I still do not care to know.

AFOLABE

No man loses his shadow except it is in the night,
and even then his shadow is hidden, not lost. At the glow
of sunrise, he stands on his own name in that light.

When he walks down to the river with the other fishermen
his shadow stretches in the morning, and yawns, but you,
if you're content with not knowing what our names mean,

then I am not Afolabe, your father, and you look through
my body as the light looks through a leaf. I am not here
or a shadow. And you, nameless son, are only the ghost

of a name. Why did I never miss you until you returned?
Why haven't I missed you, my son, until you were lost?
Are you the smoke from a fire that never burned?

There was no answer to this, as in life. Achille nodded,
the tears glazing his eyes, where the past was reflected
as well as the future. The white foam lowered its head.

Book Six

Chapter XLIX

I

She bathed him in the brew of the root.[7] The basin
was one of those cauldrons from the old sugar-mill,
with its charred pillars, rock pasture, and one grazing

horse, looking like helmets that have tumbled downhill
from an infantry charge. Children rang them with stones.
Wildflowers sprung in them when the dirt found a seam.

She had one in her back yard, close to the crotons,[8]
agape in its crusted, agonized O: the scream
of centuries. She scraped its rusted scabs, she scoured

7. Ma Kilman is bathing Philoctete to heal his wound.

8. Type of tree and shrub.

the mouth of the cauldron, then fed a crackling pyre
with palms and banana-trash. In the scream she poured
tin after kerosene tin, its base black from fire,

of seawater and sulphur. Into this she then fed
the bubbling root and leaves. She led Philoctete
to the gurgling lava. Trembling, he entered

his bath like a boy. The lime leaves leeched to his wet
knuckled spine like islands that cling to the basin
of the rusted Caribbean. An icy sweat

glazed his scalp, but he could feel the putrescent shin
drain in the seethe like sucked marrow, he felt it drag
the slime from his shame. She rammed him back to his place

as he tried climbing out with: *"Not yet!"* With a rag
sogged in a basin of ice she rubbed his squeezed face
the way boys enjoy their mother's ritual rage,

and as he surrendered to her, the foul flower
on his shin whitened and puckered, the corolla
closed its thorns like the sea-egg. What else did it cure?

II

The bow leapt back to the palm of the warrior.
The yoke of the wrong name lifted from his shoulders.
His muscles loosened like those of a brown river

that was damned with silt, and then silkens its boulders
with refreshing strength. His ribs thudded like a horse
cantering on a beach that bursts into full gallop

while a boy yanks at its rein with terrified "Whoas!"
The white foam unlocked his coffles, his ribbed shallop
broke from its anchor, and the water, which he swirled

like a child, steered his brow into the right current,
as calm as *In God We Troust*[9] to that other world,
and his flexed palm enclosed an oar with the ident-

ical closure of a mouth around its own name,
the way a sea-anemone closes slyly
into a secrecy many mistake for shame.

Centuries weigh down the head of the swamp-lily,
its tribal burden arches the sea-almond's spine,
in barracoon[1] back yards the soul-smoke still passes,

9. Near the poem's beginning, Achille chisels this misspelled phrase into his canoe and then decides, "Leave it! Is God' spelling and mine" (1.1.2).

1. Barracks for housing convicts or slaves.

but the wound has found her own cure. The soft days spin
the spittle of the spider in webbed glasses,
as she drenches the burning trash to its last flame,

and the embers steam and hiss to the schoolboys' cries
when he'd weep in the window for their tribal shame.
A shame for the loss of words, and a language tired

of accepting that loss, and then all accepted.
That was why the sea stank from the frothing urine
of surf, and fish-guts reeked from the government shed,

and why God pissed on the village for months of rain.
But now, quite clearly the tears trickled down his face
like rainwater down a cracked carafe from Choiseul,[2]

as he stood like a boy in his bath with the first clay's
innocent prick! So she threw Adam a towel.
And the yard was Eden. And its light the first day's.

Book Seven

Chapter LXIV

I

I sang of quiet Achille, Afolabe's son,[3]
who never ascended in an elevator,
who had no passport, since the horizon needs none,

never begged nor borrowed, was nobody's waiter,
whose end, when it comes, will be a death by water[4]
(which is not for this book, which will remain unknown

and unread by him). I sang the only slaughter
that brought him delight, and that from necessity—
of fish, sang the channels of his back in the sun.

I sang our wide country, the Caribbean Sea.
Who hated shoes, whose soles were as cracked as a stone,
who was gentle with ropes, who had one suit alone,

whom no man dared insult and who insulted no one,
whose grin was a white breaker cresting, but whose frown
was a growing thunderhead, whose fist of iron

would do me a greater honour if it held on
to my casket's oarlocks than mine lifting his own
when both anchors are lowered in the one island,

2. A village in Saint Lucia.
3. From the poem's final chapter; this line echoes and revises the famous openings of the *Iliad* and of Virgil's *Aeneid*.
4. Cf. part 4 of T. S. Eliot's *Waste Land*.

but now the idyll dies, the goblet is broken,
and rainwater trickles down the brown cheek of a jar
from the clay of Choiseul. So much left unspoken

by my chirping nib! And my earth-door lies ajar.
I lie wrapped in a flour-sack sail. The clods thud
on my rope-lowered canoe. Rasping shovels scrape

a dry rain of dirt on its hold, but turn your head
when the sea-almond rattles or the rust-leaved grape
from the shells of my unpharaonic pyramid

towards paper shredded by the wind and scattered
like white gulls that separate their names from the foam
and nod to a fisherman with his khaki dog

that skitters from the wave-crash, then frown at his form
for one swift second. In its earth-trough, my pirogue
with its brass-handled oarlocks is sailing. Not from

but with them, with Hector, with Maud[5] in the rhythm
of her beds trowelled over, with a swirling log
lifting its mossed head from the swell; let the deep hymn

of the Caribbean continue my epilogue;
may waves remove their shawls as my mourners walk home
to their rusted villages, good shoes in one hand,

passing a boy who walked through the ignorant foam,
and saw a sail going out or else coming in,
and watched asterisks of rain puckering the sand.

1990

5. The Irish wife of the British officer Plunkett.

Gary Snyder
b. 1930

In the summer of 1948, after he had finished his freshman year at college, Gary Snyder shipped out of New York as an ordinary seaman. "Going to sea," he has said, "was part of a long growth and extension of my sympathies and sensibilities outside simply one area and to many classes and kinds of people and many parts of the world so that now I feel at home everywhere" (in Dan Kherdian, *Six San Francisco Poets,* 1969). The notion of life as an odyssey and of his poems as progress reports, entries in the explorer's journal, is essential to Snyder. His goal is a poise of mind that will allow him to stand serenely in the midst of conflicting perspectives.

Though rooted in the natural landscape of the Pacific northwest, Snyder has managed to "feel at home everywhere," not only by visiting foreign places, by investigating other cultures and submitting himself to their initiatory rituals, but also by imaginatively investigating the recesses of our common human past. "As poet," Snyder writes, "I hold the most archaic values on earth. They go back to the late Paleolithic: the fertility of the soil, the magic of animals, the power-vision in solitude, the terrifying initiation and re-birth, the love and ecstasy of the dance, the common work of the tribe. I try to hold both history and wilderness in mind, that my poems may approach the true measure of things and stand against the unbalance and ignorance of our times" (*Six*). In Zen Buddhism, Snyder found a way to get back to the preverbal experiences that unite humankind. With characteristic evenhandedness, he grants that the poet faces in two directions: "one is to the world of people and language and society, and the other is to the nonhuman, nonverbal world, which is nature as nature is itself; and the world of human nature—the inner world—as it is itself, before language, before customs, before culture. There's no words in that world. There aren't any rules that we know and that's the area that Buddhism studies" (*Six*).

Snyder's is not a superficial acquaintance with East Asian religion and culture; from 1965 to 1968, he studied with a Zen master in Japan. From these studies, and also from Ezra Pound, William Carlos Williams, and Charles Olson, Snyder found direction in his search for the wordless "world of human nature," and he takes delight in the bright, particular grains of experience of nature "as nature is itself." His relaxed, often cheerful acceptance of a pluralistic world of fragments contrasts markedly with T. S. Eliot's juxtaposition of cultures to point up catastrophe in *The Waste Land*. Snyder does not force nature to provide symbols of his private experience, and he is aware of that temptation. In "T-2 Tanker Blues," he hopes eventually to "dig the / universe as playful, cool and infinitely blank." "Blank" does not here suggest any Romantic forlornness, but rather an appreciation of companionable *otherness*, a peaceful coexistence.

Although Snyder wholeheartedly rejects postwar American society, particularly its ecological devastation, he does not sentimentally reject society as such. He has worked at a variety of trades and occupations, writes his poetry out of these experiences, and relates the rhythm of poetic sequences with the rhythms of particular occupations. Tutored by Zen meditation in alert and egoless attention to the world, he writes in seemingly spontaneous lines and simple diction about nature, sex, family, and the body. His chiseled lines and concrete images often seem surrounded by silence, by negative space in which they shine brightly with an inner presence.

Snyder was born on May 8, 1930, in San Francisco, and was brought up in Oregon and Washington. He received his B.A. in anthropology from Reed College in 1951. He worked as a logger and a fire lookout in the Pacific northwest, then returned to California to study East Asian languages at the University of California, Berkeley from 1953 to 1956. During this time, he also joined Allen Ginsberg, Jack Kerouac, and others in what turned into the Beat movement and wrote the poems later published as *Myths and Texts* (1960). (Kerouac used Snyder as a central character in his novel *The Dharma Bums*.) Though Snyder shares the spontaneity and East Asian interests of the Beats, his ecological priorities contrast with their urban sensibilities. From 1956 until 1964, he lived mainly in Japan, though he visited India for a year and also worked as a hand on an American tanker in the Indian and South Pacific Oceans. He returned to the United States in 1964 to teach at Berkeley, then returned to Japan to study Buddhism of the Mahayana-Vajrayana school; he recounts some of his experiences in the prose book *Earth House Hold* (1969), which is written in the Japanese form of the poetic travel journal. In 1986, he joined the faculty of the University of California, Davis. His many books of poems include a number of translations from ancient and modern Japanese. In 1975, he was awarded the Pulitzer Prize; in 1997, the Bollingen Prize.

Milton[1] by Firelight

Piute Creek, August 1955

"O hell, what do mine eyes
    with grief behold?"[2]
Working with an old
Singlejack[3] miner, who can sense
The vein and cleavage
In the very guts of rock, can
Blast granite, build
Switchbacks[4] that last for years
Under the beat of snow, thaw, mule-hooves.
What use, Milton, a silly story
Of our lost general parents,
    eaters of fruit?

The Indian, the chainsaw boy,
And a string of six mules
Came riding down to camp
Hungry for tomatoes and green apples.
Sleeping in saddle-blankets
Under a bright night-sky
Han River slantwise by morning.
Jays squall
Coffee boils

In ten thousand years the Sierras
Will be dry and dead, home of the scorpion.
Ice-scratched slabs and bent trees.
No paradise, no fall,
Only the weathering land
The wheeling sky,
Man, with his Satan
Scouring the chaos of the mind.
Oh Hell!

Fire down
Too dark to read, miles from a road
The bell-mare clangs in the meadow
That packed dirt for a fill-in
Scrambling through loose rocks
On an old trail
All of a summer's day.[5]

1959

1. John Milton (1608–1674), English poet, author of *Paradise Lost.*
2. Satan speaks these words in *Paradise Lost* (4.358) upon first seeing Adam and Eve in the Garden of Eden.
3. Hammer for percussive hand-drilling by one person.
4. Steep, zigzagging roads or trails.
5. Cf. Milton's epic simile describing Satan's fall: "From morn / to noon he fell, from noon to dewy eve, / A summer's day" (*Paradise Lost* 1.742–44).

Above Pate Valley[6]

We finished clearing the last
Section of trail by noon,
High on the ridge-side
Two thousand feet above the creek
Reached the pass, went on
Beyond the white pine groves,
Granite shoulders, to a small
Green meadow watered by the snow,
Edged with Aspen—sun
Straight high and blazing
But the air was cool.
Ate a cold fried trout in the
Trembling shadows. I spied
A glitter, and found a flake
Black volcanic glass—obsidian—
By a flower. Hands and knees
Pushing the Bear grass, thousands
Of arrowhead leavings over a
Hundred yards. Not one good
Head, just razor flakes
On a hill snowed all but summer,
A land of fat summer deer,
They came to camp. On their
Own trails. I followed my own
Trail here. Picked up the cold-drill,
Pick, singlejack,[7] and sack
Of dynamite.
Ten thousand years.

1959

Riprap[8]

Lay down these words
Before your mind like rocks.
            placed solid, by hands
In choice of place, set
Before the body of the mind
            in space and time:
Solidity of bark, leaf, or wall
            riprap of things:

6. In Yosemite National Park.
7. Hammer for percussive hand-drilling by one person.
8. "A cobble of stone laid on steep slick rock to make a trail for horses in the mountains" [Snyder's note].

Cobble of milky way,
        straying planets,
These poems, people,
        lost ponies with
Dragging saddles
        and rocky sure-foot trails.
The worlds like an endless
        four-dimensional
Game of *Go*.[9]
        ants and pebbles
In the thin loam, each rock a word
        a creek-washed stone
Granite: ingrained
        with torment of fire and weight
Crystal and sediment linked hot
        all change, in thoughts,
As well as things.

1959

Burning the Small Dead

Burning the small dead
    branches
broke from beneath
  thick spreading
      whitebark pine.

      a hundred summers
snowmelt   rock   and air

hiss in a twisted bough.

  sierra granite;
      Mt. Ritter—[1]
      black rock twice as old.

Deneb, Altair[2]

windy fire

1968

9. Ancient Japanese game played with black and white stones, placed one after the other on a checkered board.

1. Peak south of Yosemite National Park, in California.
2. Two of the brightest stars.

The Wild Edge

Curve of the two steel spring-up prongs on
the back of the Hermes
typewriter—paper holders—the same
Curve as the arched wing of a gull:

(sails through the
sides of the eyes by white-stained cliffs
car-park lots and scattered
pop-top beer tabs in the gravel)

Birds sail away and back.

Sudden flurry and buzz of flies in the corner sun.
Heavy beetle drags stiff legs through moss

Caravans of ants bound for the Wall
wandering backward—

Harsh Thrush shrieks in the cherries.
a murmur in the kitchen
Kai[3] wakes and cries—

1970

The Bath

Washing Kai in the sauna,
The kerosene lantern set on a box
outside the ground-level window,
Lights up the edge of the iron stove and the
washtub down on the slab
Steaming air and crackle of waterdrops
brushed by on the pile of rocks on top
He stands in warm water
Soap all over the smooth of his thigh and stomach
"Gary don't soap my hair!"
—his eye-sting fear—
the soapy hand feeling
through and around the globes and curves of his body
up in the crotch,
And washing-tickling out the scrotum, little anus,
his penis curving up and getting hard
as I pull back skin and try to wash it
Laughing and jumping, flinging arms around,
I squat all naked too,
is this our body?

3. Snyder's son.

Sweating and panting in the stove-steam hot-stone
      cedar-planking wooden bucket water-splashing
      kerosene lantern-flicker wind-in-the-pines-out
      sierra forest ridges night—
Masa comes in, letting fresh cool air
      sweep down from the door
      a deep sweet breath
And she tips him over gripping neatly, one knee down
      her hair falling hiding one whole side of
      shoulder, breast, and belly,
Washes deftly Kai's head-hair
      as he gets mad and yells—
The body of my lady, the winding valley spine,
      the space between the thighs I reach through,
      cup her curving vulva arch and hold it from behind,
      a soapy tickle   a hand of grail
The gates of Awe
That open back a turning double-mirror world of
      wombs in wombs, in rings,
      that start in music,
                                        is this our body?

The hidden place of seed
The veins net flow across the ribs, that gathers
      milk and peaks up in a nipple—fits
      our mouth—
The sucking milk from this our body sends through
      jolts of light; the son, the father,
      sharing mother's joy
That brings a softness to the flower of the awesome
      open curling lotus gate I cup and kiss
As Kai laughs at his mother's breast he now is weaned
      from, we
      wash each other,
                                        this our body

Kai's little scrotum up close to his groin,
      the seed still tucked away, that moved from us to him
In flows that lifted with the same joys forces
      as his nursing Masa later,
      playing with her breast,
Or me within her,
Or him emerging,
                                        this is our body:

Clean, and rinsed, and sweating more, we stretch
      out on the redwood benches hearts all beating
Quiet to the simmer of the stove,
      the scent of cedar
And then turn over,

murmuring gossip of the grasses,
talking firewood,
Wondering how Gen's napping, how to bring him in
soon wash him too—
These boys who love their mother
who loves men, who passes on
her sons to other women;

The cloud across the sky. The windy pines.
the trickle gurgle in the swampy meadow

this is our body.

Fire inside and boiling water on the stove
We sigh and slide ourselves down from the benches
wrap the babies, step outside,

black night & all the stars.

Pour cold water on the back and thighs
Go in the house—stand steaming by the center fire
Kai scampers on the sheepskin
Gen standing hanging on and shouting,

"Bao! bao! bao! bao! bao!"

This is our body. Drawn up crosslegged by the flames
drinking icy water
hugging babies, kissing bellies,

Laughing on the Great Earth

Come out from the bath.

1972

Axe Handles

One afternoon the last week in April
Showing Kai how to throw a hatchet
One-half turn and it sticks in a stump.
He recalls the hatchet-head
Without a handle, in the shop
And go gets it, and wants it for his own.
A broken-off axe handle behind the door
Is long enough for a hatchet,
We cut it to length and take it
With the hatchet head
And working hatchet, to the wood block.
There I begin to shape the old handle

With the hatchet, and the phrase
First learned from Ezra Pound[4]
Rings in my ears!
"When making an axe handle
the pattern is not far off."
And I say this to Kai
"Look: We'll shape the handle
By checking the handle
Of the axe we cut with—"
And he sees. And I hear it again:
It's in Lu Ji's *Wên Fu,* fourth century
A.D. "Essay on Literature"—in the
Preface: "In making the handle
Of an axe
By cutting wood with an axe
The model is indeed near at hand."
My teacher Shih-hsiang Chen
Translated that and taught it years ago
And I see: Pound was an axe,
Chen was an axe, I am an axe
And my son a handle, soon
To be shaping again, model
And tool, craft of culture,
How we go on.

1983

4. American poet (1885–1972).

Kamau Brathwaite
b. 1930

The Barbadian poet and historian Kamau Brathwaite has sought to recover and re-value the ignored, concealed, and despised African inheritance in the Caribbean. Through most of the twentieth century, this inheritance was considered embarrassing or taboo in the English-speaking West Indies, despite the survival of African gods in West Indian religions, the sedimentation of African languages in West Indian Creole, and the persistence of African social customs and practices throughout the Caribbean. Educated as British subjects, Afro-Caribbeans, Brathwaite observes, knew more about English kings and queens than about the history of slavery that their own ancestors endured and resisted. As for landscape, they were more comfortable writing about the falling of snow—an "imported alien experience" encountered only in British poems—than about their hurricanes (*History of the Voice*). Brathwaite explores the resultant anguish of deracination and dispossession in the West Indies. "Where then is the nigger's / home?" he asks in the first part of his influential epic, *The Arrivants: A New World Trilogy* (1973), which gathers *Rights of Passage* (1967), *Masks* (1968), and *Islands* (1969). Uprooted by slavery, debased by the master, degraded by impoverishment, Africans in the New World are doomed to conspire in their own futility and despair, unless they repossess themselves by repossessing their hidden past.

For Brathwaite, what he calls "nation language," which includes West Indian Creole, is a crucial tool for recuperating Afro-Caribbean history and experience, because "nation language . . . is the *submerged* area of that dialect which is much more closely allied to the African aspect of experience in the Caribbean," saturated with African words, rhythms, even grammar (*History of the Voice*). In this regard, the Creole poet Louise Bennett is Brathwaite's most significant precursor. Brathwaite tries harder than Bennett to break the "tyranny" of British meters and of the ballad stanza, but Bennett's writing is more thoroughly creolized in diction than Brathwaite's. In Brathwaite's view, through the use of non-Standard English idioms, sounds, and syncopations poets can reclaim linguistic elements that survived the Middle Passage, the terrible voyage in slave ships across the Atlantic. Likewise, in Brathwaite's poem "Ogun," named after an African god who, like Anancy and Shango, is reborn in the New World, a craftsman who carves in nonstandard forms reconnects with ancestral Africa.

The pattern of Brathwaite's career helps explain why he became a compelling West Indian spokesman for what he calls "*the literature of reconnection*" ("The African Presence in Caribbean Literature"). He was born Lawson Edward Brathwaite on May 11, 1930, in Bridgetown, Barbados, at the eastern edge of the West Indies. (He legally changed his name in 1987, adopting the African [Kikuyu] name Kamau.) Barbados had an especially strong British colonial presence; yet as Brathwaite was fond of pointing out, it was also the Caribbean island closest to Africa. Having grown up in a middle-class family, Brathwaite went on a scholarship to Cambridge University, where he earned his B.A. in history in 1953, followed later by a D.Phil. at the University of Sussex in 1968. Like other Caribbean intellectuals, he journeyed for his education to the imperial "motherland," but in an unusual twist, he also traveled to the ancestral "mother" continent, working as an education officer for the Ministry of Education in Ghana from 1955 to 1962. After returning to the West Indies, where he was for many years a professional historian before taking a position in comparative literature at New York University in 1991, Brathwaite viewed Afro-Caribbean culture through the clarifying prism of his dual experiences in Europe and Africa—key sources of West Indian culture.

In his historical research and his poetry, Brathwaite interprets the West Indies through the powerful concept of "creolization," an idea he develops to describe the complex interchange, transformation, and resistance between the cultures of black and white, slave and master, in the Caribbean. Yet he emphasizes the African elements in this intercultural process, because of their marginality in traditional accounts of the West Indies. Analyzing one of the most important kinds of creolization, Brathwaite writes in *The Development of Creole Society in Jamaica*: "It was in language that the slave was perhaps most successfully imprisoned by his master, and it was in his (mis-) use of it that he perhaps most effectively rebelled." For Brathwaite, as for other West Indian writers, the figure of Caliban from Shakespeare's *Tempest* is the model for this transformative appropriation of the master's tools. Despite material impoverishment, the Rastafarian in "Wings of a Dove" remakes English through his distinctive diction, rhythms, and phonetics, cursing the master in a remastered version of the master's language. Translating calypso into the trochees of "Calypso" ("Steel drum steel drum / hit the hot calypso dancing"), Brathwaite syncopates literary English as a medium for West Indian identity, as the steel drummer turns the cast-off oil barrel into a Caribbean musical instrument. Like most West Indians, schooled in Standard English but speaking varieties of Creole on the street and in the yard, Brathwaite nimbly switches codes between different linguistic registers, sometimes even breaking into musical concatenations of nonsense syllables. Into this linguistic callaloo he mixes varieties of music from the African diaspora—worksongs, ska, jazz, the blues, calypso, limbo, and reggae.

Brathwaite has often been contrasted with his fellow Caribbean poet Derek Walcott.

Brathwaite works more from the oral and musical forms of the common people, Walcott from the high-literary forms of lyric and epic. Brathwaite emphasizes the African, Walcott the European ingredients in West Indian culture. Walcott accommodates the Western heritage, while Brathwaite angrily resists it. If these are useful points of departure, the contrasts nevertheless oversimplify. Walcott also searches out African survivals in the West Indies and uses Caribbean speech and song. Brathwaite is no less an inheritor of high modernist literary strategies. He has openly admitted his debt to the supremely canonical Anglo-American poet T. S. Eliot. Eliot's influence, especially when blended with that of Louise Bennett's folk-based Creole verse, helped free Brathwaite from the dead hand of Victorian colonial models. Like Eliot, Brathwaite incorporates jazz and other musical forms; shifts rapidly in tone, speaker, and cultural reference; fuses overlapping characters in overarching personae; bridges lyric despair and epic collectivity; and tries to reassemble a usable inheritance out of the shards of the cultural past. In an irony of twentieth-century literary history, a poet sometimes seen as an elitist, racist, High Church reactionary enables the career of one of the most resistant, perhaps even revolutionary poets of the African diaspora.

From The Arrivants

Wings of a Dove[1]

1

Brother Man the Rasta[2]
man, beard full of lichens
brain full of lice
watched the mice
come up through the floor-
boards of his down-
town, shanty-town kitchen,
and smiled. Blessed are the poor[3]
in health, he mumbled,
that they should inherit this
wealth. Blessed are the meek
hearted, he grumbled,
for theirs is this stealth.

Brother Man the Rasta
man, hair full of lichens
head hot as ice
watched the mice
walk into his poor
hole, reached for his peace
and the pipe of his ganja[4]

1. From *Rights of Passage* (1967), the first book of *The Arrivants* (1973).
2. Rastafarian. Rastafari, or Rastafarianism, is an Afro-Caribbean religion that posits an ultimate return to Africa and the divinity of Haile Selassie I, a former emperor of Ethiopia.
3. A revision of the beatitudes of the New Testament: "Blessed are the poor in spirit: for theirs is the kingdom of heaven" (Matthew 5.3).
4. Marijuana; used ritually and socially by Rastafarians.

and smiled how the mice
eyes, hot pumice
pieces, glowed into his room
like ruby, like rhinestone
and suddenly startled like
diamond.

And I
Rastafar-I
in Babylon's[5] boom
town, crazed by the moon
and the peace of this chalice, I
prophet and singer, scourge
of the gutter, guardian
Trench Town, the Dungle and Young's
Town,[6] rise and walk through the now silent
streets of affliction, hawk's eyes
hard with fear, with
affection, and hear my people
cry, my people
shout:

Down down
white
man, con
man, brown
man, down
down full
man, frown-
ing fat
man, that
white black
man that
lives in
the town.

Rise rise
locks-
man, Solo-
man[7] wise
man, rise
rise rise
leh we
laugh
dem, mock
dem, stop
dem, kill

5. Rastafarian term for the power structure that has suppressed blacks for centuries; originally, an ancient Mesopotamian city devoted to sensual and material values.
6. Apparently, an invention, by analogy with Trench Town (a working-class district in Kingston). *The Dungle:* Kingston slum on a garbage dump, demolished in the 1960s.
7. Pun on wise biblical King Solomon.

dem an' go
back back
to the black
man lan'
back back
to Af-
rica.

2

Them doan mean it, yuh know,
them cahn help it
but them clean-face browns[8] in
Babylon town is who I most fear

an' who fears most I.
Watch de vulture dem a-fly-
in', hear de crow a-dem crow
see what them money a-buy?

Caw caw caw caw.
Ol' crow, ol' crow, cruel ol'
ol' crow, that's all them got
to show.

Crow fly flip flop
hip hop
pun de ground; na[9]
feet feel firm

pun de firm stones; na
good pickney[1] born
from de flesh
o' dem bones;

naw naw naw naw.

3

So beat dem drums
dem, spread

dem wings dem,
watch dem fly

dem, soar dem
high dem,

8. Light-skinned bourgeoisie. *Cahn:* can't (Jamaican English).

9. Not any (Jamaican English).

1. Children.

clear in the glory of the Lord.

Watch dem ship dem
come to town dem

full o' silk dem
full o' food dem

an' dem 'plane dem
come to groun' dem

full o' flash dem
full o' cash dem

silk dem food dem
shoe dem wine dem

that dem drink dem
an' consume dem

praisin' the glory of the Lord.

So beat dem burn
dem, learn

dem that dem[2]
got dem nothin'

but dem
bright bright baubles

that will burst dem
when the flame dem

from on high dem
raze an' roar dem

an' de poor dem
rise an' rage dem

in de glory of the Lord.

1967

2. That is, teach them that they.

Calypso[3]

1

The stone had skidded arc'd and bloomed into islands:
Cuba and San Domingo
Jamaica and Puerto Rico
Grenada Guadeloupe Bonaire[4]

curved stone hissed into reef
wave teeth fanged into clay
white splash flashed into spray
Bathsheba Montego Bay[5]

bloom of the arcing summers . . .

2

The islands roared into green plantations
ruled by silver sugar cane
sweat and profit
cutlass profit
islands ruled by sugar cane

And of course it was a wonderful time
a profitable hospitable well-worth-your-time
when captains carried receipts for rices
letters spices wigs
opera glasses swaggering asses
debtors vices pigs

O it was a wonderful time
an elegant benevolent redolent time—
and young Mrs. P.'s quick irrelevant crime
at four o'clock in the morning . . .

3

But what of black Sam
with the big splayed toes
and the shoe black shiny skin?

He carries bucketfulls of water
'cause his Ma's just had another daughter.

And what of John with the European name
who went to school and dreamt of fame

3. Type of folk song originating in Trinidad, often involving commentary on current events and improvised wordplay with syncopated rhythms. This poem is from *Rights of Passage*.
4. Islands in the Caribbean. The first two stanzas refer to a creation myth in which the islands are formed in a rock-skipping game called ducks and drakes.
5. Jamaican city and tourist resort. *Bathsheba:* seaside resort in Barbados.

his boss one day called him a fool
and the boss hadn't even been to school . . .

4

Steel drum steel drum
hit the hot calypso dancing
hot rum hot rum
who goin' stop this bacchanalling?[6]

For we glance the banjo
dance the limbo
grow our crops by maljo[7]

have loose morals
gather corals
father our neighbour's quarrels

perhaps when they come
with their cameras and straw
hats: sacred pink tourists from the frozen Nawth

we should get down to those
white beaches
where if we don't wear breeches

it becomes an island dance
Some people doin' well
while others are catchin' hell

o the boss gave our Johnny the sack
though we beg him please
please to take 'im back

so the boy now nigratin' overseas . . .

1967

Ogun[8]

My uncle made chairs, tables, balanced doors on, dug out
coffins, smoothing the white wood out

with plane and quick sandpaper until
it shone like his short-sighted glasses.

6. From *Bacchanalia:* festival of Bacchus, the Roman god of wine, celebrated with song, dancing, and revelry.
7. Evil eye.

8. West African and West Indian god of iron, thunder, roads, war, creation, and destruction. The poem is from *Islands* (1969), the third and last book of *The Arrivants* (1973).

The knuckles of his hands were sil-
vered knobs of nails hit, hurt and flat-

tened out with blast of heavy hammer. He was knock-knee'd, flat-
footed and his clip clop sandals slapped across the concrete

flooring of his little shop where canefield mulemen and a fleet
of Bedford lorry drivers dropped in to scratch themselves and talk.

There was no shock of wood, no beam
of light mahogany his saw teeth couldn't handle.

When shaping squares for locks, a key hole
care tapped rat tat tat upon the handle

of his humpbacked chisel. Cold
world of wood caught fire as he whittled: rectangle

window frames, the intersecting x of fold-
ing chairs, triangle

trellises, the donkey
box-cart in its squeaking square.

But he was poor and most days he was hungry.
Imported cabinets with mirrors, formica table

tops, spine-curving chairs made up of tubes, with hollow
steel-like bird bones that sat on rubber ploughs,

thin beds, stretched not on boards, but blue high-tensioned cables,
were what the world preferred.

And yet he had a block of wood that would have baffled them.
With knife and gimlet care he worked away at this on Sundays,

explored its knotted hurts, cutting his way
along its yellow whorls until his hands could feel

how it had swelled and shivered, breathing air,
its weathered green burning to rings of time,

its contoured grain still tuned to roots and water.
And as he cut, he heard the creak of forests:

green lizard faces gulped, grey memories with moth
eyes watched him from their shadows, soft

liquid tendrils leaked among the flowers
and a black rigid thunder he had never heard within his hammer

came stomping up the trunks. And as he worked within his shattered
Sunday shop, the wood took shape: dry shuttered

eyes, slack anciently everted lips, flat
ruined face, eaten by pox, ravaged by rat

and woodworm, dry cistern mouth, cracked
gullet crying for the desert, the heavy black

enduring jaw; lost pain, lost iron;
emerging woodwork image of his anger.

1969

Trane[9]

Propped against the crowded bar
he pours into the curved and silver horn
his old unhappy longing for a home

the dancers twist and turn
he leans and wishes he could burn
his memories to ashes like some old notorious emperor

of rome. but no stars blazed across the sky when he was born
no wise men found his hovel. this crowded bar
where dancers twist and turn

holds all the fame and recognition he will ever earn
on earth or heaven. he leans against the bar
and pours his old unhappy longing in the saxophone

1977

Stone

(for Mikey Smith)[1]

When the stone fall that morning out of the johncrow[2] sky
it was not dark at first . that opening on to the red sea sky
but something in my mouth like feathers . blue like bubbles and light
carrying signals & planets & the sliding curve of the world like a water
    picture
in a raindrop when the pressure drop

9. Nickname of jazz saxophonist John Coltrane (1926–1967).

1. Michael Smith (1954–1983), a charismatic "dub," or performance, poet, was stoned to death on Stony Hill, Jamaica, by thugs a day after he spoke out at a political rally during Jamaican elections.

2. Turkey vulture (Jamaican English). Commonly seen as omen of a person's imminent death.

When the stone fall that morning i
couldn't cry out because my mouth was full of beast & plunder
as if i was gnashing badwords among tombstones
as if angry water was beating up against the curbstones of the palisadoes[3]
as if that road up Stony Hill round the bend by the churchyard on the way to the

post office was a bad bad dream and the dream was on fire all the way past the
white houses higher up the hill and the ogogs[4] bark
ing all teeth & furnace and my mother like she upside down up a tree like
she was screaming and nobody i could hear could hear a word i shouting
even though there were so many poems left and the tape was switched on & running
and the green light was red and they was standing up everywhere in London
& Amsterdam & at UNESCO[5] in Paris & in West Berlin & clapping & clapping &
clapping & not a soul on Stony Hill to even say amen . and yet it was happening happening
the fences began to crack in my skull and there were loud *boodooooongs* like
guns going off them ole time magnums or like fireworks where I dreadlocks were in fire
and the gaps where the river coming down and the dry gully where my teeth used to be
smiling and my tuff gong tongue that used to press against them & parade pronounciation
now unannounce and like a black wick in i head & dead
and it was like a heavy heavy riddim low down in i belly bleeding dub
and there was like this heavy black dog thumping in i chest & pumping murdererrrrrrrr

and my throat like dem tie like dem tie a tight tie around it . twist
ing my neck quick crick quick crick and a never wear neck
tie yet and a laughing more blood and spittin out lawwwwwwwwwwwd
and i two eye lock to the sun and the two sun staring back bright from the grass and i

bline to de butterfly flittin . but i hear de tread of my heart
the heavy flux of the blood in my veins silver tambourines
closer & closer . st joseph[6] band crashing &
closer & bom sicai sica boom ship bell &
closer & bom sicai sica boom ship bell &
when the saints . . .

3. A finger of land on which Kingston's international airport is situated.
4. Wordplay on *dogs* and *Ogog* (evil power prophesied in Revelation 20 and in other Christian and Jewish apocalyptic literature).
5. United Nations Educational, Scientific and Cultural Organization, created to foster world peace through international collaboration.
6. Joseph the Patriarch, husband of the Virgin Mary; his saint's day is celebrated with parades.

•

and it was like a wave on Stony Hill caught in a crust of sunlight
and it was like a broken schooner into harbour muffled in the silence of its wound
and it was like the blue of peace was filling up the heavens with its thunder
and it was like the wind was growing skin the skin had hard hairs hardering
it was like Marcus Garvey[7] rising from his coin . stepping towards his people
crying dark . and every mighty word he trod the ground fell dark & hole behind
him like it was a scream i did not know and yet it was a scream . my ears were bleeding
sound. and i was quiet now because i had become that sound

the sunlit morning washed the coral limestone harsh against the soft volcanic ash
i was & it was slipping past me into water & it was slipping past me into root
i was & it was slipping past me into flower & it was ripping upward into shoot
while every tongue in town was lashing me with spit & cutrass[8] wit & ivy whip &
wrinkle jumbimum[9] . it was like warthog grunting in the ground . and children run
ning down the hill run right on through the splashes
that my breathing made when it was howl & red & bubble and sparrow

twits pluck tic & tapeworm from the grass
as if i-man did never have no face as if i-man did never in this place

When the stone fell that morning out of the johncrow sky
i could not hold it back or black it back or block it off or limp away
or roll it from me into memory or light or rock it steady into night be
cause it builds me now and fills my blood with deaf my bone with dumb &

lawwwwwwwwwwwwwwwwwwwwwwwwwwwwwwwwwwwwwwwwwwwd

i am the stone that kills me.

1986

7. Jamaican national hero (1887–1940), who championed racial uplift and the return of blacks to Africa; his face appears on the Jamaican twenty-five-cent coin.
8. Pun on *cutlass* and *rass*, vulgar term for buttocks and exclamation of scorn or anger (Jamican English).
9. Author's coinage for a Caribbean plant or root with secret power. From *jumbi* (spirit) and *mum* (secret or silent, as in "mum's the word"), by analogy with West Indian words such as *jumbie-coffee* and *jumbie-chocho*.

Irae

dies irae[1] dreadful day
when the world shall pass away
so the priests & showmen say

what gaunt phantoms shall affront me
mi lai sharpville wounded knee
arthur[2] kissorcallatme

to what judgement meekly led
shall men gather trumpeted
by louis armstrong[3] from the dead

life & death shall here be voice
less rising from their moist
interment hoist

ing all their flags before them
poniard poison rocket bomb
nations of the earth shall come

and his record page on page
forever building he shall scan & give each age
sentences of righteous rage[4]

if the pious then shall shake me
what reply can merchants make me
what defences can they fake?

mighty & majestic god
head saviour of the broken herd
heal me nanny cuffee cudjoe[5]
grant me mercy at thy word

day of fire dreadful day
day for which all sufferers pray
grant me patience with thy plenty
grant me vengeance with thy sword

1992

1. Day of wrath (Latin); the opening words (and thus the title) of a thirteenth-century hymn based on Zephaniah 1.14–16. A meditation on the last judgment, once part of the liturgies of the Mass of the Dead and the Office of the Dead, it begins: "That day of wrath, that dreadful day, / shall heaven and earth in ashes lay, / as David and the Sybil say. / / What horror must invade the mind / when the approaching Judge shall find / and sift the deeds of all mankind! / / The mighty trumpet's wondrous tone / shall rend each tomb's sepulchral stone / and summon all before the Throne."

2. Legendary king of Britain. *Mi Lai*: Vietnamese hamlet where American soldiers massacred civilians in 1968. *Sharpville:* South African township where anti-apartheid demonstrators were shot down by the police in 1960. *Wounded Knee*: site of battle in which over two hundred Sioux men and women were massacred by U.S. troops in 1890.

3. Jazz trumpeter and vocalist (1901–1971).

4. Cf. "Dies Irae": "Then shall with universal dread / the Book of Consciences be read / to judge the lives of all the dead."

5. Three leaders of the Maroons, ex-slave rebel warriors.

Christopher Okigbo
1930?–1967

Born on August 16, 1930 (or 1932, according to some scholars), in Ojoto, eastern Nigeria, Christopher Okigbo was killed in the Nigerian Civil War. Before volunteering on the secessionist Biafran side in the first of many internal conflicts to tear apart postcolonial Africa, Okigbo had been a student (B.A. 1956 from the University of Ibadan), an athlete, a teacher, a librarian, a bureaucrat, and a traveling press representative. The poetry he produced in his short career influenced and impressed writers across anglophone Africa, such as fellow Nigerian Wole Soyinka, as well as Western poets, such as Geoffrey Hill and Jay Wright. Okigbo was a leading figure during the so-called golden age of postcolonial anglophone letters in Africa—the period just before and after formal independence. Resistant to the identity politics of negritude, which asserted and valued an essential blackness, he also refused the bald "platform poetry" (his phrase in a 1965 interview) practiced by many of his contemporaries, writing instead poems that are psychologically inward and insistently musical.

Indebted to W. B. Yeats, Ezra Pound, and T. S. Eliot, as well as Igbo praise songs and other oral genres, Okigbo intricately layers public and private meanings and myths in allusive, richly patterned verse. Like the modernists but in an entirely different cultural setting, Okigbo treats poetry as a literary rite. He conceives of his poetry as almost priestly: "My creative activity is in fact one way of performing those functions in a different manner. Every time I write a poem, I am in fact offering a sacrifice" (*Journal of Commonwealth Literature*, 1970). But no single code of belief structures his work. After all, he was brought up in Igbo village ritual, attended Catholic school, taught Latin and the classics, and knew intimately the modernist canon.

Okigbo's first major poetic sequence, *Heavensgate* (1962, rev. 1964), melds these disparate sources in a poetic rite of sacrifice and renewal, charted in the section titles: "The Passage," "Initiations," "Watermaid," "Lustra," and "Newcomer." In his introductory comments on the sequence, Okigbo says the poet, as an Igbo supplicant, undergoes "a complete self-surrender to the water spirit that nurtures all creation," in particular the ancestral river goddess Idoto. With one eye on another set of cultural bearings, he also says "the celebrant, a personage like Orpheus, is about to begin a journey," that is, is setting out to fashion the very poem we read. The sequence is thus both a priestly offering to a local African goddess and an Orphic exploration of poetic creativity. In one of the sequence's many intercultural ironies, the first poem also calls the poet-protagonist the biblical "prodigal" son. How does the poet return to the native religion he abandoned for Christianity? Curiously enough, by way of Christian parable. Prodigal son, Orphic poet, Igbo supplicant—the protagonist synthesizes these various paradigms. Similarly, the goddess invoked by the poet, reappearing in the guises of lioness and "watermaid," is at once Igbo river deity, muse, maternal culture, Eurydice, the beloved, and so forth. Okigbo's rich sensibility enables him to hold in solution these diverse cultural elements.

The notorious "obscurity" of Okigbo's poetry arises from its cross-cultural allusions, its compression, its psychospiritual questing, and its spare, indeterminate settings. Recycling primal images of light, water, and earth, the poet varies his simple palette with carefully paced cadences, alliterations, puns, striking images ("Rainbow . . . arched like boa bent to kill"), and surprising collocations ("armpit-dazzle"). In the late poem "Come Thunder," about the worrisome events preceding the Nigerian Civil War, Okigbo's poetic ambiguity turns nightmarish, recalling Yeats's poems nearly half a century earlier about the civil strife in Ireland. Pondering a violent but still unknowable future, Okigbo skillfully yokes precise details ("The smell of blood already floats in the lavender-mist of the afternoon") with terrifying abstractions ("a great fearful thing already tugs at the cables of the open air"). It is difficult not to see in this poem something of the power of prophecy.

From Heavensgate

[Before You, Mother Idoto]

Before you, mother Idoto[1]
naked I stand;
before your watery presence,
a prodigal

leaning on an oilbean,
lost in your legend.

Under your power wait I
on barefoot,
watchman for the watchword
at *Heavensgate*;

out of the depths my cry:
give ear and hearken . . .

[Dark Waters of the Beginning.]

Dark waters of the beginning.

Rays, violet and short, piercing the gloom,
foreshadow the fire that is dreamed of.

Rainbow on far side, arched like boa bent to kill,
foreshadows the rain that is dreamed of.

Me to the orangery[2]
solitude invites,
a wagtail, to tell
the tangled-wood-tale;
a sunbird, to mourn
a mother on a spray.

1. "A village stream. The oilbean, the tortoise and the python are totems for her worship" [Okigbo's note]. The poet also writes, in his 1965 introduction to the volume: "*Heavensgate* was originally conceived as an Easter sequence. It later grew into a ceremony of innocence, something like a mass, an offering to Idoto, the village stream of which I drank, in which I washed, as a child." The first two excerpts are from a section titled "The Passage"; the next is from "Watermaid"; the last from "Newcomer," at the end of the sequence.
2. Site where orange trees are cultivated.

Rain and sun in single combat;
on one leg standing,
in silence at the passage,
the young bird at the passage.

[Bright]

Bright
with the armpit-dazzle of a lioness,
she answers,

wearing white light about her;

and the waves escort her,
my lioness,
crowned with moonlight.

So brief her presence—
match-flare in wind's breath—
so brief with mirrors around me.

Downward . . .
the waves distil her;
gold crop
sinking ungathered.

Watermaid of the salt-emptiness,
grown are the ears of the secret.

[I Am Standing above the Noontide]

I am standing above the noontide,
Above the bridgehead;

Listening to the laughter of waters
  that do not know why:

Listening to incense—

I am standing above the noontide
  with my head above it;

Under my feet float the waters
Tide blows them under . . .

1962, 1964

Come Thunder

Now that the triumphant march has entered the last street corners,
Remember, O dancers, the thunder among the clouds . . .

Now that laughter, broken in two, hangs tremulous between the teeth,
Remember, O dancers, the lightning beyond the earth . . .

The smell of blood already floats in the lavender-mist of the afternoon.
The death sentence lies in ambush along the corridors of power;
And a great fearful thing already tugs at the cables of the open air,
A nebula immense and immeasurable, a night of deep waters—
An iron dream unnamed and unprintable, a path of stone.

The drowsy heads of the pods in barren farmlands witness it,
The homesteads abandoned in this century's brush fire witness it:
The myriad eyes of deserted corn cobs in burning barns witness it:
Magic birds with the miracle of lightning flash on their feathers . . .

The arrows of God tremble at the gates of light,
The drums of curfew pander to a dance of death;

And the secret thing in its heaving
Threatens with iron mask
The last lighted torch of the century . . .

1967

Ted Hughes
1930–1998

Ted Hughes's subject matter is often violence, and his acknowledged talent in this area has evoked uneasy admiration. He was prone to depicting brutal acts, whether of classical or modern violence, as in his adaptation of Seneca's bloody version of *Oedipus* or poems such as "Out," about his father's World War I experience. When he looked at nature, he found predators and victims; when he showed nature looking at humanity, as in "Crow's First Lesson," the same dynamic appeared. The poet's imagination whirls with increasing wildness, until some readers long for modulations of this baleful glare. Such ferocity, however, is so rare in English poetry, and Hughes was so effective as its exponent, that he gripped a considerable audience. He could not have done so by subject alone: his compression, his daring vocabulary, and his jarring rhythms all contributed. In contrast to the rational lucidity and buttoned-up form of his English contemporaries in the Movement, such as Philip Larkin and Donald Davie, Hughes fashions a mythical consciousness in his poems, embodied in violent metaphors, blunt syntax, harsh alliterative clusters, bunched stresses, incantatory repetitions, insistent assonances, and a dark, brooding tone. Exemplary phrases include "sudden sharp hot stink of fox" ("The Thought-Fox") and "crackle open under a blue-black pressure"

("Thistles"). Though drawing on Shakespeare, Gerard Manley Hopkins, Wilfred Owen, D. H. Lawrence, and Robert Lowell, his primitivist vision and strenuous, muscular language are very much his own.

Such a poet might seem as far from childlike as could be, but children are fond of monstrosity, and Hughes wrote a new kind of children's poem, in which his saturnine consciousness is caught in buoyant accents. Perhaps because, as he said, he collected animals, birds, and fish as a boy, he "thinks of poems as a sort of animal" (*Poetry in the Making*). *Moortown* (1979), a notebook kept on a farm, displays an extraordinary intimacy with animals and insects. He particularly liked things that "have a vivid life of their own, outside mine." That life, as he wrote about it, is anarchic and savage. So also with human enterprises; all his lovers are demon lovers, and hatred sometimes takes over. The image of the poet that Hughes offers is in keeping with this temper of his work; in "Famous Poet," "the demeanour is of mouse, / Yet is he monster," and he speaks of "the world-shouldering, monstrous 'I' " in "The Man Seeking Experience Enquires His Way of a Drop of Water." An index to Hughes's own aspirations appears in his introduction to *A Choice of Emily Dickinson's Verse,* in which he speaks with great approval of "her frightening vision," the sense of an "icy chill," and "the conflagration within her." A blend of fire and ice is the ideal mixture sought in his poems. In Hughes's dualistic vision, darkness usually overcomes light.

Hughes was born on August 17, 1930, in Mytholmroyd, Yorkshire. His father, a carpenter, was one of a handful of survivors of a regiment that perished in the disastrous Gallipoli campaign of World War I. Hughes took a B.A. at Cambridge University, where after first studying English literature he turned to archeology and anthropology. There he met the American poet Sylvia Plath, who was on a Fulbright Scholarship. They married in 1956, at first living in the United States, then settling in England. They had two children, but their marriage was troubled, Hughes had a notorious affair, and they had separated at the time of Plath's suicide, in 1963. As poets, they both dealt in raw sensation and lacerated nerves, though Plath's work centered on the plight of the victim as her husband's centered on the consciousness of the predator. Public anger over Plath's suicide, as well as over Hughes's destruction of the journals Plath wrote when at the peak of her literary powers, followed Hughes the rest of his life; his name was repeatedly defaced from Plath's tombstone. Hughes published a series of verse letters to Plath in *The Birthday Letters* (1998), but they are slack and defensive, lacking the concentration of his earlier verse. By the time of his death, Hughes had been poet laureate of England for nearly a decade and a half (succeeding John Betjeman in 1984), a post he accepted because he thought of England, he said, as a tribe for whose chiefs he could write tribal songs.

The Horses

I climbed through woods in the hour-before-dawn dark.
Evil air, a frost-making stillness,

Not a leaf, not a bird—
A world cast in frost. I came out above the wood

Where my breath left tortuous statues in the iron light.
But the valleys were draining the darkness

Till the moorline—blackening dregs of the brightening grey—
Halved the sky ahead. And I saw the horses:

Huge in the dense grey—ten together—
Megalith-still.[1] They breathed, making no move,

With draped manes and tilted hind-hooves,
Making no sound.

I passed: not one snorted or jerked its head.
Grey silent fragments

Of a grey silent world.

I listened in emptiness on the moor-ridge.
The curlew's[2] tear turned its edge on the silence.

Slowly detail leafed from the darkness. Then the sun
Orange, red, red, erupted

Silently, and splitting to its core tore and flung cloud,
Shook the gulf open, showed blue,

And the big planets hanging.
I turned,

Stumbling in the fever of a dream, down towards
The dark woods, from the kindling tops,

And came to the horses.
                                        There, still they stood,
But now steaming and glistening under the flow of light,

Their draped stone manes, their tilted hind-hooves
Stirring under a thaw while all around them

The frost showed its fires. But still they made no sound.
Not one snorted or stamped,

Their hung heads patient as the horizons,
High over valleys, in the red levelling rays—

In din of the crowded streets, going among the years, the faces,
May I still meet my memory in so lonely a place

Between the streams and the red clouds, hearing curlews,
Hearing the horizons endure.

1957

1. That is, still as the great stones at, for example, Stonehenge.

2. Migratory bird's.

The Thought-Fox

I imagine this midnight moment's forest:
Something else is alive
Beside the clock's loneliness
And this blank page where my fingers move.

Through the window I see no star:
Something more near
Though deeper within darkness
Is entering the loneliness:

Cold, delicately as the dark snow
A fox's nose touches twig, leaf;
Two eyes serve a movement, that now
And again now, and now, and now

Sets neat prints into the snow
Between trees, and warily a lame
Shadow lags by stump and in hollow
Of a body that is bold to come

Across clearings, an eye,
A widening deepening greenness,
Brilliantly, concentratedly,
Coming about its own business

Till, with a sudden sharp hot stink of fox,
It enters the dark hole of the head.
The window is starless still; the clock ticks,
The page is printed.

1957

An Otter

I

Underwater eyes, an eel's
Oil of water body, neither fish nor beast is the otter:
Four-legged yet water-gifted, to outfish fish;
With webbed feet and long ruddering tail
And a round head like an old tomcat.

Brings the legend of himself
From before wars or burials, in spite of hounds and vermin-poles;
Does not take root like the badger. Wanders, cries;
Gallops along land he no longer belongs to;
Re-enters the water by melting.

Of neither water nor land. Seeking
Some world lost when first he dived, that he cannot come at since,
Takes his changed body into the holes of lakes;
As if blind, cleaves the stream's push till he licks
The pebbles of the source; from sea

To sea crosses in three nights
Like a king in hiding. Crying to the old shape of the starlit land,
Over sunken farms where the bats go round,
Without answer. Till light and birdsong come
Walloping up roads with the milk wagon.

II

The hunt's lost him. Pads on mud,
Among sedges, nostrils a surface bead,
The otter remains, hours. The air,
Circling the globe, tainted and necessary,

Mingling tobacco-smoke, hounds and parsley,
Comes carefully to the sunk lungs.
So the self under the eye lies,
Attendant and withdrawn. The otter belongs

In double robbery and concealment—
From water that nourishes and drowns, and from land
That gave him his length and the mouth of the hound.
He keeps fat in the limpid integument[3]

Reflections live on. The heart beats thick,
Big trout muscle out of the dead cold;
Blood is the belly of logic; he will lick
The fishbone bare. And can take stolen hold

On a bitch otter in a field full
Of nervous horses, but linger nowhere.
Yanked above hounds, reverts to nothing at all,
To this long pelt over the back of a chair.

1960

Pike[4]

Pike, three inches long, perfect
Pike in all parts, green tigering the gold.
Killers from the egg: the malevolent aged grin.
They dance on the surface among the flies.

3. Surface, skin (that is, water).

4. Voracious freshwater fish.

Or move, stunned by their own grandeur
Over a bed of emerald, silhouette
Of submarine delicacy and horror.
A hundred feet long in their world.

In ponds, under the heat-struck lily pads—
Gloom of their stillness:
Logged on last year's black leaves, watching upwards.
Or hung in an amber cavern of weeds

The jaws' hooked clamp and fangs
Not to be changed at this date;
A life subdued to its instrument;
The gills kneading quietly, and the pectorals.

Three we kept behind glass,
Jungled in weed: three inches, four,
And four and a half: fed fry[5] to them—
Suddenly there were two. Finally one.

With a sag belly and the grin it was born with.
And indeed they spare nobody.
Two, six pounds each, over two feet long,
High and dry and dead in the willow-herb—

One jammed past its gills down the other's gullet:
The outside eye stared: as a vice locks—
The same iron in this eye
Though its film shrank in death.

A pond I fished, fifty yards across,
Whose lilies and muscular tench[6]
Had outlasted every visible stone
Of the monastery that planted them—

Stilled legendary depth:
It was as deep as England. It held
Pike too immense to stir, so immense and old
That past nightfall I dared not cast

But silently cast and fished
With the hair frozen on my head
For what might move, for what eye might move.
The still splashes on the dark pond,

Owls hushing the floating woods
Frail on my ear against the dream
Darkness beneath night's darkness had freed,
That rose slowly towards me, watching.

1960

5. Young fishes.

6. Variety of freshwater fish.

Thistles

Against the rubber tongues of cows and the hoeing hands of men
Thistles spike the summer air
Or crackle open under a blue-black pressure.

Every one a revengeful burst
Of resurrection, a grasped fistful
Of splintered weapons and Icelandic frost thrust up

From the underground stain of a decayed Viking.
They are like pale hair and the gutturals of dialects.
Every one manages a plume of blood.

Then they grow grey, like men.
Mown down, it is a feud. Their sons appear,
Stiff with weapons, fighting back over the same ground.

1967

Second Glance at a Jaguar

Skinful of bowls, he bowls them,
The hip going in and out of joint, dropping the spine
With the urgency of his hurry
Like a cat going along under thrown stones, under cover,
Glancing sideways, running
Under his spine. A terrible, stump-legged waddle
Like a thick Aztec disemboweller,[7]
Club-swinging, trying to grind some square
Socket between his hind legs round,
Carrying his head like a brazier of spilling embers,
And the black bit of his mouth, he takes it
Between his back teeth, he has to wear his skin out,
He swipes a lap at the water-trough as he turns,
Swivelling the ball of his heel on the polished spot,
Showing his belly like a butterfly,
At every stride he has to turn a corner
In himself and correct it. His head
Is like the worn-down stump of another whole jaguar,
His body is just the engine shoving it forward,
Lifting the air up and shoving on under,
The weight of his fangs hanging the mouth open,
Bottom jaw combing the ground. A gorged look,
Gangster, club-tail lumped along behind gracelessly,
He's wearing himself to heavy ovals,

7. The Aztecs, an Indian nation of central Mexico (where the jaguar is native) at the time of the Spanish Conquest, practiced human sacrifice.

Muttering some mantra, some drum-song of murder
To keep his rage brightening, making his skin
Intolerable, spurred by the rosettes, the cain-brands,
Wearing the spots off from the inside,
Rounding some revenge. Going like a prayer-wheel,
The head dragging forward, the body keeping up,
The hind legs lagging. He coils, he flourishes
The blackjack tail as if looking for a target,
Hurrying through the underworld, soundless.

1967

Gog[8]

I woke to a shout: "I am Alpha and Omega."[9]
Rocks and a few trees trembled
Deep in their own country.
I ran and an absence bounded beside me.

The dog's god is a scrap dropped from the table.
The mouse's savior is a ripe wheat grain.
Hearing the Messiah cry
My mouth widens in adoration.

How fat are the lichens!
They cushion themselves on the silence.
The air wants for nothing.
The dust, too, is replete.

What was my error? My skull has sealed it out.
My great bones are massed in me.
They pound on the earth, my song excites them.
I do not look at the rocks and trees, I am frightened of what they see.

I listen to the song jarring my mouth
Where the skull-rooted teeth are in possession.
I am massive on earth. My feetbones beat on the earth
Over the sounds of motherly weeping. . . .

Afterwards I drink at a pool quietly.
The horizon bears the rocks and trees away into twilight.
I lie down. I become darkness.

Darkness that all night sings and circles stamping.

1967

8. Satanic spirit prophesized by the Book of Revelation.
9. The words of Jesus as reported by John in Revelation 1.8: "I am Alpha and Omega, the beginning and the ending." Alpha and omega are the first and last letters, respectively, of the Greek alphabet.

Out

1. The Dream Time

My father sat in his chair recovering
From the four-year mastication[1] by gunfire and mud,
Body buffeted wordless, estranged by long soaking
In the colors of mutilation.
His outer perforations
Were valiantly healed, but he and the hearth-fire, its blood-flicker
On biscuit-bowl and piano and table leg,
Moved into strong and stronger possession
Of minute after minute, as the clock's tiny cog
Labored and on the thread of his listening
Dragged him bodily from under
The mortised[2] four-year strata of dead Englishmen
He belonged with. He felt his limbs clearing
With every slight, gingerish movement. While I, small and four,
Lay on the carpet as his luckless double,
His memory's buried, immovable anchor,
Among jawbones and blown-off boots, tree-stumps, shell-cases and
craters,
Under rain that goes on drumming its rods and thickening
Its kingdom, which the sun has abandoned, and where nobody
Can ever again move from shelter.

2

The dead man in his cave beginning to sweat;
The melting bronze visor of flesh
Of the mother in the baby-furnace—

Nobody believes, it
Could be nothing, all
Undergo smiling at
The lulling of blood in
Their ears, their ears, their ears, their eyes
Are only drops of water and even the dead man suddenly
Sits up and sneezes—Atishoo!
Then the nurse wraps him up, smiling,
And, though faintly, the mother is smiling,
And it's just another baby.

As after being blasted to bits
The reassembled infantryman
Tentatively totters out, gazing around with the eyes
Of an exhausted clerk.

1. Grinding or chewing.

2. Firmly fixed.

3. *Remembrance Day*[3]

The poppy is a wound, the poppy is the mouth
Of the grave, maybe of the womb searching—

A canvas-beauty puppet on a wire
Today whoring everywhere. It is years since I wore one.

It is more years
The shrapnel that shattered my father's paybook

Gripped me, and all his dead
Gripped him to a time

He no more than they could outgrow, but, cast into one, like iron,
Hung deeper than refreshing of ploughs

In the woe-dark under my mother's eye—
One anchor

Holding my juvenile neck bowed to the dunkings of the Atlantic.
So goodbye to that bloody-minded flower.

You dead bury your dead.
Goodbye to the cenotaphs[4] on my mother's breasts.

Goodbye to all the remaindered charms of my father's survival.
Let England close. Let the green sea-anemone close.

1967

Wodwo[5]

What am I? Nosing here, turning leaves over
Following a faint stain on the air to the river's edge
I enter water. What am I to split
The glassy grain of water looking upward I see the bed
Of the river above me upside down very clear
What am I doing here in mid-air? Why do I find
this frog so interesting as I inspect its most secret
interior and make it my own? Do these weeds
know me and name me to each other have they
seen me before, do I fit in their world? I seem

3. Holiday (November 11) commemorating soldiers who lost their lives in battle. The practice of wearing red poppies in honor of lost soldiers recalls John McCrae's poem "In Flanders Fields" (1915), which depicts the flowers growing between the graves on a battlefield.
4. Empty tombs.
5. Wild man of the woods, or wood demon (Middle English); from line 721 of the anonymous fourteenth-century poem *Sir Gawain and the Green Knight.* Hughes uses lines from this poem as the epigraph for the book of which "Wodwo" is the title poem: "Now with serpents he wars, now with savage wolves, / Now with wild men of the woods, that watched from the rocks" (translation by Marie Borroff).

separate from the ground and not rooted but dropped
out of nothing casually I've no threads
fastening me to anything I can go anywhere
I seem to have been given the freedom
of this place what am I then? And picking
bits of bark off this rotten stump gives me
no pleasure and it's no use so why do I do it
me and doing that have coincided very queerly
But what shall I be called am I the first
have I an owner what shape am I what
shape am I am I huge if I go
to the end on this way past these trees and past these trees
till I get tired that's touching one wall of me
for the moment if I sit still how everything
stops to watch me I suppose I am the exact centre
but there's all this what is it roots
roots roots roots and here's the water
again very queer but I'll go on looking

1967

Crow's First Lesson

God tried to teach Crow how to talk.
"Love," said God. "Say, Love."
Crow gaped, and the white shark crashed into the sea
And went rolling downwards, discovering its own depth.

"No, no," said God, "Say Love. Now try it. LOVE."
Crow gaped, and a bluefly, a tsetse,[6] a mosquito
Zoomed out and down
To their sundry flesh-pots.

"A final try," said God. "Now, LOVE."
Crow convulsed, gaped, retched and
Man's bodiless prodigious head
Bulbed out onto the earth, with swiveling eyes,
Jabbering protest—

And Crow retched again, before God could stop him.
And woman's vulva dropped over man's neck and tightened.
The two struggled together on the grass.
God struggled to part them, cursed, wept—

Crow flew guiltily off.

1970

6. African fly that carries the sleeping-sickness disease.

Roe Deer[7]

In the dawn-dirty light, in the biggest snow of the year
Two blue-dark deer stood in the road, alerted.

They had happened into my dimension
The moment I was arriving just there.

They planted their two or three years of secret deerhood
Clear on my snow-screen vision of the abnormal

And hesitated in the all-way disintegration
And stared at me. And so for some lasting seconds

I could think the deer were waiting for me
To remember the password and sign

That the curtain had blown aside for a moment
And there where the trees were no longer trees, nor the road a road

The deer had come for me.

Then they ducked through the hedge, and upright they rode their legs
Away downhill over a snow-lonely field

Toward tree-dark—finally
Seeming to eddy and glide and fly away up

Into the boil[8] of big flakes.
The snow took them and soon their nearby hoofprints as well

Revising its dawn inspiration
Back to the ordinary.

1979

Orf[9]

Because his nose and face were one festering sore
That no treatment persuaded, month after month,
And his feet four sores, the same,
Which could only stand and no more,

Because his sickness was converting his growth
Simply to strengthening sickness

7. Small European and Asiatic deer, known for their nimbleness and grace.

8. Agitation.

9. Sore mouth, a contagious disease of sheep.

While his breath wheezed through a mask of flies
No stuff could rid him of

I shot the lamb.
I shot him while he was looking the other way.
I shot him between the ears.

He lay down.
His machinery adjusted itself
And his blood escaped, without loyalty.

But the lamb life in my care
Left him where he lay, and stood up in front of me

Asking to be banished,
Asking for permission to be extinct,
For permission to wait, at least,

Inside my head
In the radioactive space
From which the meteorite had removed his body.

1979

From Orts[1]

17. *Buzz in the Window*

Buzz frantic
And prolonged. Fly down near the corner,
The cemetery den. A big bluefly
Is trying to drag a plough, too deep
In earth too stony, immovable. Then the fly
Buzzing its full revs forward, budges backward.
Clings. Deadlock.
The spider has gripped its anus. Slender talons
Test the blue armor gently, the head
Buried in the big game. He tugs
Tigerish, half the size of his prey. A pounding
Glory time for the spider. For the other
A darkening summary of some circumstances
In the window corner, with a dead bee,
Wing-petals, husks of insect-armor, a brambled[2]
Glade of dusty web. It buzzes less
As the drug argues deeper and deeper.
In fluttery soundless tremors it tries to keep
A hold on the air. The north sky
Slides northward. The blossom is clinging
To its hopes, refurnishing the constant

1. Leavings, scraps.

2. As if a thicket.

Of ignorant life. The bluefly,
Without changing expression, only adjusting
Its leg stance, as if to more comfort,
Undergoes ultimate ghastliness. Finally agrees to it.
The spider tugs, retreating. The fly
Is going to let it do everything. Something is stuck.
The fly is fouled in web. Intelligence, the spider,
Comes round to look and patiently, joyfully,
Starts cutting the mesh. Frees it. Returns
To the haul—homeward in that exhausted ecstasy
The loaded hunters of the Pleistocene[3]
Never recorded either.

1979

3. The Ice Age.

OKOT P'BITEK
1931–1982

The Ugandan poet Okot p'Bitek wrote the most significant and widely read poem of anglophone East Africa, *Song of Lawino* (1966). This long poem—witty, lively, satiric—presents the boisterous voice of a traditional African woman from an Acoli village in rural Uganda. Proud of her native culture and her skills in song, dance, and cooking, Lawino furiously upbraids her husband for abandoning Acoli ways. *Song of Lawino* dramatizes as a husband-and-wife quarrel the conflicts between modernization and traditionalism, between Eurocentrism and Afrocentrism.

Although Okot drafted much of the poem in Acoli, it was first published in his English-language version, parts of which did not exist in the earlier Acoli text. African writers have hailed *Song of Lawino* as "possibly the best rounded single work of African poetry in English today," and American critics have concurred, both groups citing the poem's indigenous African imagery, rhetorical devices, and ideas; critics have often contrasted it with the more cosmopolitan work of so-called Euro-modernists such as Wole Soyinka and Christopher Okigbo. This view owes much to Lawino's energetic defense of traditional African ways. Adapting an Acoli proverb, she repeatedly warns her husband, Ocol, against uprooting the pumpkin, symbol of the household and tradition. She berates him for being intoxicated with Western clock time and ballroom dance. For her, Western cuisine seems soft and "slimy like mucus," book learning seems emasculating, Christianity seems abstract and contradictory. Worst of all, Ocol is infatuated with the Western conception of feminine beauty, as exemplified by Lawino's rival, a second wife humorously named Clementine and nicknamed Tina. Mimicking white women, Tina applies ghostly white face powder and blood-red lipstick; slims her waist like a hornet's; even fries, pulls, and stretches her hair to straighten it: "And the vigorous and healthy hair / Curly, springy and thick / That glistens in the sunshine / Is left listless and dead / Like the elephant grass / Scorched brown by the fierce / February sun. / It lies lifeless / Like the sad and dying banana leaves / On a hot and windless afternoon."

Initially engaging the reader through the dramatic tension of this triangular relationship, *Song of Lawino* sustains interest through lively imagery and figurative language that defamiliarize Western values and practices. When Lawino encounters Christian communion for the first time, she sees it as a bizarre, cannibalistic rite. For her, Western kissing is a revolting custom: "You kiss her open-sore lips / As white people do, / You suck slimy saliva / From each other's mouths / As white people do." From the face of the insistent Western clock dangles "a large single testicle," which "goes this way and that way / Like a sausage-fruit / In a windy storm." Lawino reaches for a dizzying variety of similes and metaphors to describe the unfamiliar Western world embraced by her husband. Indeed, the acuity of her figurative language disproves her husband's view of her as stupid. Okot's poem enriches anglophone verse through its figurative profusion, greatly indebted to Acoli proverbs and idioms. *Song of Lawino* is written in an emphatically Africanized English, frequently incorporating Acoli words and literally rendering Acoli phrases.

The view that *Song of Lawino* is purely "native" or "homebred" needs to be modified, however, to allow for the poem's culturally complex texture and influences. As director of the Uganda National Cultural Centre (1966–68) before being forced out for political reasons, Okot advocated a balanced cultural perspective, saying the Centre "must not be reactionary like some old men who reject all foreign art forms, nor must it reflect the bigoted ideas of some miseducated men who despise all things African" (*Africa's Cultural Revolution*). Okot repeatedly cited Longfellow's *Song of Hiawatha* and the biblical Song of Solomon among the precursor texts for *Song of Lawino.* He created something distinctive and new when he hybridized the oral traditions of Acoli song and speech with Western literary traditions, such as the long dramatic monologue.

Song of Lawino also embodies Okot's ambivalence toward the Western academic discipline of anthropology. Having gone to Britain as a member of the Uganda national soccer team that played barefoot at the Summer Olympics of 1956, Okot studied from 1960 to 1963 at Oxford University's acclaimed Institute of Social Anthropology, headed by the social anthropologist E. E. Evans-Pritchard. Plunged into British anthropology during some of its headiest days, Okot was deeply offended by its Eurocentrism and Christian bias. At Oxford, he wrote a thesis in social anthropology, "Oral Literature and Its Social Background Among the Acoli and Lang'o" (1964), which provided the basis for his books of anthropology and his collections of folk songs and folktales. He later wrote a searching critique of Western anthropology, *African Religions in Western Scholarship* (1970). In *Song of Lawino,* he implicitly contests the discipline's assumptions about voice, perspective, and power, even as he incorporates its categories of knowledge in chapters organized around time, religion, and other central Western concepts.

Okot p'Bitek was born in 1931, in Gulu, Uganda. His father was a Protestant schoolteacher but also an accomplished dancer and storyteller from the Patiko chiefdom; his mother, known as Lawino among other names, was a famous composer of songs and a dancer. He attended Gulu High School, King's College, Budo, and the Mbara Teachers Training College. In 1953, he published his first book, a novel in Acoli entitled *Lak tar,* later translated as *White Teeth*; in 1956, an early Acoli version of *Wer pa Lawino* was rejected by a publisher's agent. In Britain, Okot first studied education at the University of Bristol and then received a law degree at the University of Wales, Aberystwyth, in 1960 before going on to Oxford. In the wake of Ugandan independence in 1962, Okot returned to teach in the extramural department at Makerere University in Kampala in 1963. During eleven years of enforced exile from Uganda, he taught African studies, sociology, and literature at the University of Nairobi, Kenya, with brief visiting appointments at the University of Texas and the University of Iowa's writing program. In the last few years of his life, he taught at the University of Ife, Nigeria, and at Makerere University.

FROM SONG OF LAWINO

1. My Husband's Tongue Is Bitter

Husband, now you despise me
Now you treat me with spite
And say I have inherited the stupidity of my aunt;
Son of the Chief,
Now you compare me
With the rubbish in the rubbish pit,
You say you no longer want me
Because I am like the things left behind
In the deserted homestead.
You insult me
You laugh at me
You say I do not know the letter A
Because I have not been to school
And I have not been baptized

You compare me with a little dog,
A puppy.

My friend, age-mate of my brother,
Take care,
Take care of your tongue,
Be careful what your lips say.

First take a deep look, brother,
You are now a man
You are not a dead fruit!
To behave like a child does not befit you!

Listen Ocol, you are the son of a Chief,
Leave foolish behavior to little children,
It is not right that you should be laughed at in a song!
Songs about you should be songs of praise!

Stop despising people
As if you were a little foolish man.
Stop treating me like salt-less ash,[1]
Become barren of insults and stupidity;
Who has ever uprooted the Pumpkin?[2]

•

My clansmen, I cry
Listen to my voice:

1. "Salt is extracted from the ash of certain plants, and also from the ash of the dung of domestic animals. The ash is put in a container with small holes in its bottom, water is then poured on the ash, and the salty water is collected in another container placed below. The useless saltless ash is then thrown on the pathway and people tread on it" [Okot p'Bitek's note].

2. From Acoli proverb about the importance of preserving the household and tradition.

The insults of my man
Are painful beyond bearing.

My husband abuses me together with my parents;
He says terrible things about my mother
And I am so ashamed!

He abuses me in English
And he is so arrogant.

He says I am rubbish,
He no longer wants me!
In cruel jokes, he laughs at me,
He says I am primitive
Because I cannot play the guitar,
He says my eyes are dead
And I cannot read,
He says my ears are blocked
And cannot hear a single foreign word,
That I cannot count the coins.

He says I am like sheep,
The fool.

Ocol treats me
As if I am no longer a person,
He says I am silly
Like the *ojuu* insects that sit on the beer pot.

My husband treats me roughly.
The insults:
Words cut more painfully than sticks!
He says my mother is a witch,
That my clansmen are fools
Because they eat rats,
He says we are all Kaffirs.[3]
We do not know the ways of God,
We sit in deep darkness
And do not know the Gospel,
He says my mother hides her charms
In her necklace
And that we are all sorcerers.

My husband's tongue
Is bitter like the roots of the *lyonno* lily,
It is hot like the penis of the bee,
Like the sting of the *kalang!*[4]
Ocol's tongue is fierce like the arrow of the scorpion,

3. Derived from the Arabic word for infidel, *Kaffir* is both the name of the Xhosa-speaking tribes of South Africa and a derogatory term for any black person.
4. Large fruit bat (Acoli).

Deadly like the spear of the buffalo-hornet.
It is ferocious
Like the poison of a barren woman
And corrosive like the juice of the gourd.

•

My husband pours scorn
On Black People,
He behaves like a hen
That eats its own eggs
A hen that should be imprisoned under a basket.

His eyes grow large
Deep black eyes
Ocol's eyes resemble those of the Nile Perch!
He becomes fierce
Like a lioness with cubs,
He begins to behave like a mad hyena.

He says Black People are primitive
And their ways are utterly harmful,
Their dances are mortal sins
They are ignorant, poor and diseased!

Ocol says he is a modern man,
A progressive and civilized man,
He says he has read extensively and widely
And he can no longer live with a thing like me
Who cannot distinguish between good and bad,

He says I am just a village woman,
I am of the old type,
And no longer attractive.

He says I am blocking his progress,
My head, he says,
Is as big as that of an elephant
But it is only bones,
There is no brain in it,
He says I am only wasting his time.

2. The Woman with Whom I Share My Husband

Ocol rejects the old type.
He is in love with a modern woman,
He is in love with a beautiful girl
Who speaks English.

But only recently
We would sit close together, touching each other!

Only recently I would play
On my bow-harp[5]
Singing praises to my beloved.
Only recently he promised
That he trusted me completely.
I used to admire him speaking in English.

•

Ocol is no longer in love with the old type.
He is in love with a modern girl;
The name of the beautiful one
Is Clementine.

Brother, when you see Clementine!
The beautiful one aspires
To look like a white woman;

Her lips are red-hot
Like glowing charcoal,
She resembles the wild cat
That has dipped its mouth in blood,
Her mouth is like raw yaws[6]
It looks like an open ulcer,
Like the mouth of a fiend!
Tina dusts powder on her face
And it looks so pale;
She resembles the wizard
Getting ready for the midnight dance;

She dusts the ash-dirt all over her face
And when little sweat
Begins to appear on her body
She looks like the guinea fowl!

The smell of carbolic soap
Makes me sick,
And the smell of powder
Provokes the ghosts in my head;
It is then necessary to fetch a goat
From my mother's brother.
The sacrifice over
The ghost-dance drum must sound
The ghost be laid
And my peace restored.

I do not like dusting myself with powder.
The thing is good on pink skin
Because it is already pale,
But when a black woman has used it

5. West African stringed instrument.
6. Infectious tropical disease marked by ulcerating lesions.

She looks as if she has dysentery;
Tina looks sickly
And she is slow moving,
She is a piteous sight.

Some medicine has eaten up Tina's face;
The skin on her face is gone
And it is all raw and red,
The face of the beautiful one
Is tender like the skin of a newly born baby!

And she believes
That this is beautiful
Because it resembles the face of a white woman!
Her body resembles
The ugly coat of the hyena;
Her neck and arms
Have real human skins!
She looks as if she has been struck
By lightning;
Or burnt like the kongoni[7]
In a fire hunt.

And her lips look like bleeding,
Her hair is long,
Her head is huge like that of the owl,
She looks like a witch,
Like someone who has lost her head
And should be taken
To the clan shrine!
Her neck is rope-like,
Thin, long and skinny
And her face sickly pale.

•

Forgive me, brother,
Do not think I am insulting
The woman with whom I share my husband!
Do not think my tongue
Is being sharpened by jealousy.
It is the sight of Tina
That provokes sympathy from my heart.

I do not deny
I am a little jealous.
It is no good lying,
We all suffer from a little jealousy.
It catches you unawares
Like the ghosts that bring fevers;
It surprises people

7. Large, African antelope.

Like earth tremors:
But when you see the beautiful woman
With whom I share my husband
You feel a little pity for her!

Her breasts are completely shrivelled up,
They are all folded dry skins,
They have made nests of cotton wool
And she folds the bits of cow-hide
In the nests
And call them breasts!

O! my clansmen
How aged modern women
Pretend to be young girls!

They mould the tips of the cotton nests
So that they are sharp
And with these they prick
The chests of their men!
And the men believe
They are holding the waists
Of young girls that have just shot up!
The modern type sleep with their nests
Tied firmly on their chests.

How many kids
Has this woman sucked?
The empty bags on her chest
Are completely flattened, dried.
Perhaps she has aborted many!
Perhaps she has thrown her twins
In the pit latrine!

Is it the vengeance ghosts
Of the many smashed eggs
That have captured her head?
How young is this age-mate of my mother?

•

The woman with whom I share my husband
Walks as if her shadow
Has been captured,
You can never hear
Her footsteps;

She looks as if
She has been ill for a long time!
Actually she is starving
She does not eat
She says she fears getting fat,
That the doctor has prevented her

From eating,
She says a beautiful woman
Must be slim like a white woman;

And when she walks
You hear her bones rattling,
Her waist resembles that of the hornet.
The beautiful one is dead dry
Like a stump,
She is meatless
Like a shell
On a dry river bed.

•

But my husband despises me,
He laughs at me,
He says he is too good
To be my husband.

Ocol says he is not
The age-mate of my grandfather
To live with someone like me
Who has not been to school.

He speaks with arrogance,
Ocol is bold;
He says these things in broad daylight.
He says there is no difference
Between me and my grandmother
Who covers herself with animal skins.

•

I am not unfair to my husband,
I do not complain
Because he wants another woman
Whether she is young or aged!
Who has ever prevented men
From wanting women?

Who has discovered the medicine for thirst?
The medicines for hunger
And anger and enmity
Who has discovered them?
In the dry season the sun shines
And rain falls in the wet season.
Women hunt for men
And men want women!

When I have another woman
With whom I share my husband,
I am glad.
A woman who is jealous

Of another, with whom she shares a man,
Is jealous because she is slow,
Lazy and shy,
Because she is cold, weak, clumsy!

The competition for a man's love
Is fought at the cooking place
When he returns from the field
Or from the hunt,

You win him with a hot bath
And sour porridge.
The wife who brings her meal first
Whose food is good to eat,
Whose dish is hot
Whose face is bright
And whose heart is clean
And whose eyes are not dark
Like the shadows:

The wife who jokes freely
Who eats in the open
Not in the bed room,
One who is not dull
Like stale beer,
Such is the woman who becomes
The head-dress keeper.

I do not block my husband's path
From his new wife.
If he likes, let him build for her
An iron roofed house on the hill!
I do not complain,
My grass thatched house is enough for me.

I am not angry
With the woman with whom
I share my husband,
I do not fear to compete with her.

All I ask
Is that my husband should stop the insults,
My husband should refrain
From heaping abuses on my head.
He should stop being half-crazy,
And saying terrible things about my mother.
Listen Ocol, my old friend,
The ways of your ancestors
Are good,
Their customs are solid
And not hollow
They are not thin, not easily breakable

They cannot be blown away
By the winds
Because their roots reach deep into the soil.

I do not understand
The ways of foreigners
But I do not despise their customs.
Why should you despise yours?

Listen, my husband,
You are the son of a Chief.
The pumpkin in the old homestead
Must not be uprooted!

1966

GEOFFREY HILL
b. 1932

Geoffrey Hill is a dominant and enigmatic presence in English poetry after World War II. He is by nature reticent, sardonic, and unyielding, though his verse presents intense feelings that crisscross. Everything he writes is conscious of itself and ultimately intelligible, though the "drama of reason," as he puts it, is compatible with his admiration for mystics such as Robert Southwell and St. John of the Cross. Hill's strenuously paradoxical language evidences his religious yet skeptical sensibility. He writes short poems and poetic sequences of compressed violence on large and painful subjects such as Nazi concentration camps and the Wars of the Roses. He evokes the terror of nightmare and then controls it through changes in perspective and by sporadic lyrical grace. His poems exhibit a clenched decision to face the worst life has to offer. Though they fix their eyes on misery, they purify it through their indignant terseness.

Many of the poems are on religious subjects, and Christianity sometimes appears, very tentatively, as a healing presence. He asks, in the late long poem *The Triumph of Love* (1998), "So what is faith if it is not / inescapable endurance?" In an early poem, "Ovid in the Third Reich," the poet Ovid sings with seeming impropriety of love in a world of murderers, yet he is no more out of place in Nazi Germany than are the damned in the divine order. Hill's poems on the Holocaust are among the best in English. Memorializing a victim of a Nazi concentration camp in "September Song," Hill vigilantly prevents his rhetoric from drifting toward easy solace or identification. Freighting every phrase with grim ironies or double meanings ("Undesirable you may have been, untouchable / you were not"), he tweaks himself with constant verbal reminders of the dead child's inaccessibility to him, despite their having been born one day apart. Even as he elegizes the victims of genocide, Hill worries that his poetry, like other memorials, helps make "their long death / Documented and safe" ("Two Formal Elegies"). In a characteristic paradox, Hill wonders if memorials distance atrocity by making it accessible, by converting senseless violence into rational understanding and aesthetic pleasure. Such ethical self-questioning is at the heart of his poetry, which is—in the modernist tradition—densely allusive, syntactically oblique, and unapologetically demanding.

Some of Hill's works purport to be history and biography. *Mercian Hymns,* regarded by some as his masterpiece, is written in a kind of chanting prose and returns to the eighth century, when Offa was king of Mercia—a large part of England. In describing Offa, Hill appears also to describe early national life, with some autobiographical elements. He pictures Offa as now hero, now antihero. (Seamus Heaney's poems about Sweeney have some of the same effect.) In *The Mystery of the Charity of Charles Péguy,* Hill presents as a martyr this twentieth-century poet, who died leading troops into battle at the Marne, yet he also subjects Péguy's Christianity, socialism, and other characteristics to severe criticism. Here again, Hill scrutinizes the ethics of language, asking whether a poet's metaphors risk not only figurative but worldly violence. Daring, occasionally witty, linguistically exciting, he seeks "those rare moments in which the inertia of language, which is also the coercive force of language, seems to have been overcome" ("Poetry as Menace and Atonement"). The sense of agonized struggle is inseparable from his achievement.

Hill was born on June 18, 1932, in Bromsgrove, Worcestershire, the only child of a police constable and his wife. He attended local schools and then Keble College of Oxford University. In 1952, while still an undergraduate, he published his first book of poems. He was a professor at the University of Leeds, then at Cambridge University, before moving to the United States in 1988. He teaches at Boston University.

In Memory of Jane Fraser

When snow like sheep lay in the fold[1]
And winds went begging at each door,
And the far hills were blue with cold,
And a cold shroud lay on the moor,

She kept the siege. And every day
We watched her brooding over death
Like a strong bird above its prey.
The room filled with the kettle's breath.

Damp curtains glued against the pane
Sealed time away. Her body froze
As if to freeze us all, and chain
Creation to a stunned repose.

She died before the world could stir.
In March the ice unloosed the brook
And water ruffled the sun's hair.
Dead cones upon the alder shook.

1959

1. Shelter for sheep.

Two Formal Elegies

For the Jews in Europe

1

Knowing the dead, and how some are disposed:
Subdued under rubble, water, in sand graves,
In clenched cinders not yielding their abused
Bodies and bonds to those whom war's chance saves
Without the law: we grasp, roughly, the song.
Arrogant acceptance from which song derives
Is bedded with their blood, makes flourish young
Roots in ashes. The wilderness revives,

Deceives with sweetness harshness. Still beneath
Live skin stone breathes, about which fires but play,
Fierce heart that is the iced brain's to command
To judgment—studied reflex, contained breath—
Their best of worlds since, on the ordained day,
This world went spinning from Jehovah's hand.

2

For all that must be gone through, their long death
Documented and safe, we have enough
Witnesses (our world being witness-proof).
The sea flickers, roars, in its wide hearth.
Here, yearly, the pushing midlanders stand
To warm themselves; men brawny with life,
Women who expect life. They relieve
Their thickening bodies, settle on scraped sand.

Is it good to remind them, on a brief screen,
Of what they have witnessed and not seen?
(Deaths of the city that persistently dies. . . ?)
To put up stones ensures some sacrifice.
Sufficient men confer, carry their weight.
(At whose door does the sacrifice stand or start?)

1959

Ovid in the Third Reich[2]

non peccat, quaecumque potest peccasse negare,
solaque famosam culpa professa facit.
—(Amores, III, xiv)[3]

I love my work and my children. God
Is distant, difficult. Things happen.
Too near the ancient troughs of blood
Innocence is no earthly weapon.

I have learned one thing: not to look down
So much upon the damned. They, in their sphere,
Harmonize strangely with the divine
Love. I, in mine, celebrate the love-choir.

1968

September Song

born 19.6.32–deported 24.9.42

Undesirable you may have been, untouchable
you were not. Not forgotten
or passed over at the proper time.

As estimated, you died. Things marched,
sufficient, to that end.
Just so much Zyklon[4] and leather, patented
terror, so many routine cries.

(I have made
an elegy for myself it
is true)[5]

September fattens on vines. Roses
flake from the wall. The smoke
of harmless fires drifts to my eyes.

This is plenty. This is more than enough.

1968

2. Ovid (43 B.C.E.–17 C.E.) was exiled from Rome by the Emperor Augustus, perhaps as a result of his poems about love.
3. Any woman is innocent who denies having sinned, and only a confession of guilt makes her guilty (Latin). These lines support Ovid's plea to his adulterous wife that she hide her doings and deny her guilt even if caught in the act; he promises to believe her.
4. Poisonous gas used in Nazi death camps.
5. Hill was born on June 18, 1932 (18.6.32, English style).

From Funeral Music[6]

William de la Pole, Duke of Suffolk: beheaded 1450
John Tiptoft, Earl of Worcester: beheaded 1470
Anthony Woodville, Earl Rivers: beheaded 1483[7]

6

My little son, when you could command marvels
Without mercy, outstare the wearisome
Dragon of sleep, I rejoiced above all—
A stranger well-received in your kingdom.
On those pristine fields I saw humankind
As it was named by the Father; fabulous
Beasts rearing in stillness to be blessed.
The world's real cries reached there, turbulence
From remote storms, rumour of solitudes,
A composed mystery. And so it ends.
Some parch for what they were; others are made
Blind to all but one vision, their necessity
To be reconciled. I believe in my
Abandonment, since it is what I have.

8

Not as we are but as we must appear,
Contractual ghosts of pity; not as we
Desire life but as they would have us live,
Set apart in timeless colloquy.
So it is required; so we bear witness,
Despite ourselves, to what is beyond us,
Each distant sphere of harmony forever
Poised, unanswerable. If it is without
Consequence when we vaunt and suffer, or
If it is not, all echoes are the same

6. "In this sequence I was attempting a florid grim music broken by grunts and shrieks. . . . *Funeral Music* could be called a commination [denunciation] and an alleluia [that is, song of praise] for the period popularly but inexactly known as the Wars of the Roses [1455–85, for the English throne, between the noble houses of York and Lancaster]. It is now customary to play down the violence of the Wars of the Roses and to present them as dynastic skirmishes fatal, perhaps, to the old aristocracy but generally of small concern to the common people. . . . In the accounts of the contemporary chroniclers it was a holocaust" (from Hill's essay on "Funeral Music").

7. "['Funeral Music'] bears an oblique dedication. In the case of Suffolk the word 'beheaded' is a retrospective aggrandisement; he was in fact butchered across the gunwale of a skiff. Tiptoft enjoyed a degree of ritual, commanding that he should be decapitated in three strokes 'in honour of the Trinity.' This was a nice compounding of orthodox humility and unorthodox arrogance. . . . The Woodville clan invites irritated dismissal: pushful, time-serving, it was really not its business to produce a man like Earl Rivers, who was something of a religious mystic. . . . Suffolk and Rivers were poets, though quite tame. Tiptoft, patron of humanist scholars, was known as the Butcher of England because of his pleasure in varying the accepted postures of judicial death" (from Hill's essay).

In such eternity. Then tell me, love,
How that should comfort us—or anyone
Dragged half-unnerved out of this worldly place,
Crying to the end 'I have not finished'.

1968

From Mercian Hymns[8]

I

King of the perennial holly-groves, the riven sand-
stone: overlord of the M5:[9] architect of the his-
toric rampart and ditch, the citadel at Tamworth,
the summer hermitage in Holy Cross: guardian of
the Welsh Bridge and the Iron Bridge:[1] contractor
to the desirable new estates: saltmaster: money-
changer: commissioner for oaths: martyrologist:
the friend of Charlemagne.[2]

'I liked that,' said Offa, 'sing it again.'

II

A pet-name, a common name.[3] Best-selling brand, curt
graffito. A laugh; a cough. A syndicate. A specious
gift. Scoffed-at horned phonograph.[4]

The starting-cry of a race. A name to conjure with.

8. "The historical King Offa reigned over Mercia (and the greater part of England south of the Humber) in the years AD 757–796. During early medieval times he was already becoming a creature of legend. The Offa who figures in this sequence might perhaps most usefully be regarded as the presiding genius of the West Midlands, his dominion enduring from the middle of the eighth century until the middle of the twentieth (and possibly beyond). The indication of such a timespan will, I trust, explain and to some extent justify a number of anachronisms" [Hill's note].

9. Superhighway in Britain that runs through what was once Offa's kingdom.

1. Where the first iron bridge was built in England, in 1774. *Rampart:* broad mound of earth as a fortification. *Citadel at Tamworth:* fortress, at an ancient town where the historical Offa had a palace. *Summer hermitage:* summer retreat.

2. First-century king of the Franks (a confederation of German tribes) and later emperor of the West. *Saltmaster:* collector of duties paid for importing salt, earlier a valuable commodity. *Commissioner for oaths:* official in charge of agreements and contracts. *Martyrologist:* a specialist in or writer on the lives of the Christian martyrs.

3. "Cf. W. F. Bolton, *A History of Anglo-Latin Literature 597–1066*, Princeton (1967), I, p. 191: 'But Offa is a common name' " [Hill's note].

4. Old-fashioned phonographs had large horns to amplify the sound.

IV

I was invested in mother-earth,[5] the crypt of roots and endings. Child's-play. I abode there, bided my time: where the mole

shouldered the clogged wheel, his gold solidus; where dry-dust badgers thronged the Roman flues,[6] the long-unlooked-for mansions of our tribe.

V

So much for the elves' wergild,[7] the true governance of England, the gaunt warrior-gospel armoured in engraved stone. I wormed my way heavenward for ages amid barbaric ivy, scrollwork of fern.

Exile or pilgrim set me once more upon that ground: my rich and desolate childhood. Dreamy, smug-faced, sick on outings—I who was taken to be a king of some kind, a prodigy, a maimed one.

VI

The princes of Mercia were badger and raven. Thrall[8] to their freedom, I dug and hoarded. Orchards fruited above clefts. I drank from honeycombs of chill sandstone.

'A boy at odds in the house, lonely among brothers.' But I, who had none, fostered a strangeness; gave myself to unattainable toys.

Candles of gnarled resin, apple-branches, the tacky mistletoe. 'Look' they said and again 'look.' But I ran slowly; the landscape flowed away, back to its source.

5. "To the best of my recollection, the expression 'to invest in mother-earth' was the felicitous (and correct) definition of 'yird' given by Mr. Michael Hordern in the programme *Call My Bluff* televised on BBC 2 on Thursday January 29th 1970" [Hill's note]. *Yird:* a Scots word meaning, more literally, to bury in the earth.

6. Passageways for air, as in chimneys. *Solidus:* ancient gold coin.

7. " 'The price set upon a man according to his rank' (O.E.D.)" [Hill's note]; the money was paid to his family or overlord if he was slain, or exacted from him as a fine for a criminal act.

8. Slave.

In the schoolyard, in the cloakrooms, the children boasted their scars of dried snot; wrists and knees garnished with impetigo.[9]

VII

Gasholders, russet among fields. Milldams, marlpools[1] that lay unstirring. Eel-swarms. Coagulations of frogs; once, with branches and half-bricks, he battered a ditchful; then sidled away from the stillness and silence.

Ceolred[2] was his friend and remained so, even after the day of the lost fighter: a biplane, already obsolete and irreplaceable, two inches of heavy snub silver. Ceolred let it spin through a hole in the classroom-floorboards, softly, into the rat-droppings and coins.

After school he lured Ceolred, who was sniggering with fright, down to the old quarries, and flayed him. Then, leaving Ceolred, he journeyed for hours, calm and alone, in his private derelict sandlorry named *Albion.*[3]

X

He adored the desk, its brown-oak inlaid with ebony, assorted prize pens, the seals of gold and base metal into which he had sunk his name.

It was there that he drew upon grievances from the people; attended to signatures and retributions; forgave the death-howls of his rival. And there he exchanged gifts with the Muse of History.[4]

What should a man make of remorse, that it might profit his soul? Tell me. Tell everything to Mother, darling, and God bless.

9. Skin disease.
1. Pools in deposits of crumbling clay and chalk. *Gasholders:* large metal receptacles for gas.
2. A ninth-century bishop of Leicester, but the name is used here as a characteristic Anglo-Saxon Mercian name.
3. Old Celtic name for England, as well as the brand name of a famous make of British truck. *Sandlorry:* sandtruck.
4. One of the nine Muses, ancient Greek goddesses of literature and the arts.

He swayed in sunlight, in mild dreams. He tested the little pears. He smeared catmint on his palm for his cat Smut to lick. He wept, attempting to master *ancilla* and *servus*.[5]

XI

Coins handsome as Nero's; of good substance and weight. *Offa Rex*[6] resonant in silver, and the names of his moneyers. They struck[7] with accountable tact. They could alter the king's face.

Exactness of design was to deter imitation; mutilation if that failed. Exemplary metal, ripe for commerce. Value from a sparse people, scrapers of salt-pans and byres.[8]

Swathed bodies in the long ditch; one eye upstaring. It is safe to presume, here, the king's anger. He reigned forty years. Seasons touched and retouched the soil.

Heathland, new-made watermeadow. Charlock, marsh-marigold. Crepitant[9] oak forest where the boar furrowed black mould, his snout intimate with worms and leaves.

XVI

Clash of salutation. As keels thrust into shingle.[1] Ambassadors, pilgrims. What is carried over? The Frankish gift,[2] two-edged, regaled with slaughter.

The sword is in the king's hands; the crux[3] a craftsman's triumph. Metal effusing its own fragrance, a variety of balm.[4] And other miracles, other exchanges.

Shafts from the winter sun homing upon earth's rim. Christ's mass: in the thick of a snowy forest the flickering evergreen fissured with light.

5. Maidservant and manservant; also slave (Latin).
6. King Offa (Latin). Nero was emperor of Rome from 54 to 68 C.E.
7. Made coins, minted.
8. Stables for cows. *Salt-pans:* hollows near the ocean where the water has evaporated, leaving salt deposits.
9. Rattling, as of dead leaves.
1. Coarse gravel on the seashore.
2. The Franks formed the Frankish Empire in the early Middle Ages. See also note 2 to stanza 1 above.
3. Hilt.
4. Aromatic, restorative preparation.

Attributes assumed, retribution entertained. What is borne amongst them? Too much or too little. Indulgences of bartered acclaim; an expenditure, a hissing. Wine, urine and ashes.

XXV

Brooding on the eightieth letter of *Fors Clavigera,*[5] I speak this in memory of my grandmother, whose childhood and prime womanhood were spent in the nailer's darg.[6]

The nailshop stood back of the cottage, by the fold. It reeked stale mineral sweat. Sparks had furred its low roof. In dawn-light the troughed water floated a damson-bloom of dust—

not to be shaken by posthumous clamour. It is one thing to celebrate the 'quick forge', another to cradle a face hare-lipped by the searing wire.

Brooding on the eightieth letter of *Fors Clavigera,* I speak this in memory of my grandmother, whose childhood and prime womanhood were spent in the nailer's darg.

XXIX

'Not strangeness, but strange likeness. Obstinate, outclassed forefathers, I too concede, I am your staggeringly-gifted child.'

So, murmurous, he withdrew from them. Gran[7] lit the gas, his dice whirred in the ludo-cup,[8] he entered into the last dream of Offa the King.

XXX

And it seemed, while we waited, he began to walk towards us.   he vanished

he left behind coins, for his lodging, and traces of red mud.

1971

5. Series of "Letters to the Workmen and Labourers of Great Britain" published regularly between 1871 and 1884 in which the English essayist, critic, and reformer John Ruskin (1819–1900) mingled personal experience, moralization, and correspondence from his readers in a critique of the capitalist economy.

6. A day's work. Hill's maternal grandmother worked in the nail-making industry.

7. Grandmother (British diminutive).

8. *Ludo:* British form of the board game pachisi.

FROM THE MYSTERY OF THE CHARITY OF CHARLES PÉGUY[9]

1

Crack of a starting-pistol. Jean Jaurès[1]
dies in a wine-puddle. Who or what stares
through the café-window crêped in powder-smoke?
The bill for the new farce reads *Sleepers Awake.*[2]

History commands the stage wielding a toy gun,
rehearsing another scene. It has raged so before,
countless times; and will do, countless times more,
in the guise of supreme clown, dire tragedian.

In Brutus'[3] name martyr and mountebank
ghost Caesar's ghost, his wounds of air and ink
painlessly spouting. Jaurès' blood lies stiff
on menu-card, shirt-front and handkerchief.

Did Péguy kill Jaurès? Did he incite
the assassin? Must men stand by what they write
as by their camp-beds or their weaponry
or shell-shocked comrades while they sag and cry?

Would Péguy answer—stubbornly on guard
among the *Cahiers,*[4] with his army cape
and steely pince-nez and his hermit's beard,
brooding on conscience and embattled hope?

Truth's pedagogue, braving an entrenched class
of fools and scoundrels, children of the world,
his eyes caged and hostile behind glass—
still Péguy said that Hope is a little child.

Violent contrariety of men and days; calm
juddery bombardment of a silent film
showing such things: its canvas slashed with rain
and St Elmo's fire.[5] Victory of the machine!

The brisk celluloid clatters through the gate;
the cortège of the century dances in the street;

9. These stanzas open a hundred-quatrain tribute to Charles Péguy (1873–1914), French poet, philosopher, and socialist killed in World War I.
1. In a biographical note at the end of the poem, Hill explains that during the Dreyfus Affair, in which France was politically divided over the case of a Jewish man falsely convicted of treason, Péguy was a great admirer of the pro-Dreyfus socialist leader Jean Jaurès (1859–1914). However, Hill notes, "by 1914 he was calling for his blood: figuratively, it must be said; though a young madman, who may or may not have been over-susceptible to metaphor, almost immediately shot Jaurès through the head." The assassin believed that Jaurès's pacifism left France in danger of encroachment by imperial Germany.
2. Also a famous portion of J. S. Bach's Cantata 140.
3. Friend and coassassin of Julius Caesar.
4. Péguy founded the journal *Les Cahiers de la Quinzaine* in 1900.
5. Luminosity accompanying discharges of atmospheric electricity.

and over and over the jolly cartoon
armies of France go reeling towards Verdun.[6]

1983

To the High Court of Parliament

November 1994[7]

Where's probity in this—
the slither-frisk
to lordship of a kind
as rats to a bird-table?

England—now of genius
the eidolon[8]—
unsubstantial yet voiding
substance like quicklime:[9]

privatize to the dead
her memory:
let her wounds weep
into the lens of oblivion.

1997

From The Triumph of Love[1]

CXXI

So what is faith if it is not
inescapable endurance? Unrevisited, the ferns
are breast-high, head-high, the days
lustrous, with their hinterlands of thunder.
Light is this instant, far-seeing
into itself, its own
signature on things that recognize
salvation. I
am an old man, a child, the horizon
is Traherne's country.[2]

1998

6. Town in France where, in 1916, the longest battle of World War I was fought.
7. Date when Tory members of Parliament allegedly accepted bribes and a Westminster City Council graveyard was sold.
8. Phantom.
9. Caustic chemical compound.
1. Also title of a 1681 French ballet.
2. Thomas Traherne (1637–1674), mystic poet and religious writer, is the author of *The Centuries*, considered English literature's first convincing depiction of childhood experience.

Sylvia Plath
1932–1963

"Death is the mother of beauty," declares Wallace Stevens, and this certainly holds true for Sylvia Plath. She follows a long and distinguished line of poets who make luminous art out of the final darkness, from John Keats and Emily Dickinson to W. B. Yeats, T. S. Eliot, and Stevie Smith. Unavailable as a direct experience, death is for Plath a rich imaginative resource, an ultimate horizon for intensifying and defining poetic subjectivity. Her fascination with death is rooted in her father's, in 1940, when she was only eight. In her journals, Plath refers to her father as "the buried male muse and god-creator" and the "father-sea-god muse." She wrestles with this traumatic loss in poems such as "The Colossus" and "Daddy." Plath's father was a first-generation Prussian immigrant from Grabów, Poland. As an adult, he taught biology and German at Boston University and wrote a treatise on bees. A diabetic, he died after an infected toe became gangrenous and his leg had to be amputated. Through psychoanalysis, Plath became ever more aware that her feelings for her father were intensely ambivalent: "He was an autocrat," she told Nancy Hunter Steiner. "I adored and despised him, and I probably wished many times that he were dead. When he obliged me and died, I imagined that I had killed him" (*A Closer Look at Ariel*). Plath's poems about her father are the first in English to explore such explosive, suicidal grief and rage toward a dead parent, shattering the boundaries of domestic poetry.

Like Robert Lowell, Anne Sexton, and other poets of the "confessional school," Plath centers much of her poetry on intensely personal and forbidden subjects, such as death, suicide, female rage, and ambivalent mourning. "I've been very excited by what I feel is the new breakthrough that came with, say, Robert Lowell's *Life Studies,*" Plath said in a 1962 interview, "this intense breakthrough into very serious, very personal, emotional experience which I feel has been partly taboo" (*The Poet Speaks,* 1966). Her poetry reaches into the recesses of unconscious feeling—hatred, desire, masochism, melancholia. Her work exemplifies the agonizing and yet creative relationship between pain and creativity. Courting emotional disaster, she discovered within herself areas of trauma, confusion, and heartbreak that she transmuted into some of the twentieth century's most distinguished works of art.

Yet Plath cautioned that her poetry isn't reducible to the personal experience that fueled it. Poets must refashion and remake private material, as she said in an interview (*The Poet Speaks*):

> I think my poems immediately come out of the sensuous and emotional experiences I have, but I must say I cannot sympathize with these cries from the heart that are informed by nothing except a needle or a knife, or whatever it is. I believe that one should be able to control and manipulate experiences, even the most terrifying, like madness, being tortured, this sort of experience, and one should be able to manipulate these experiences with an informed and an intelligent mind. I think that personal experience is very important, but certainly it shouldn't be a kind of shut box and mirror-looking, narcissistic experience. I believe it should be *relevant,* and relevant to the larger things, the bigger things such things as Hiroshima and Dachau and so on.

Plath is well aware that in representing her dead father as a "Fascist," "devil," and "vampire" in the poem "Daddy," she is mythologizing him, connecting her feelings with those of other victims of human aggression, which, for Plath, reached its most extreme form in the Nazi Holocaust. In a picture, the professor "stands at the blackboard," and

Plath represents herself as transfiguring this harmless image into a cleft-chin "devil." In juxtapositions that are deliberately jarring, she boldly interweaves this Gothic imagery with language from nursery rhyme, light verse, elegy, and love poetry.

The father in "Daddy," like the overbearing male figure in "Fever 103°" and "Lady Lazarus," is German, and Plath was uneasily conscious that her background was Germanic on both sides of her family, heightening her sense of connection with the horrific events of the Holocaust. Her mother, a second-generation Austrian immigrant, grew up speaking German at home. Plath's ambivalence toward her mother is at the center of one of her finest early poems, "The Disquieting Muses," an unnerving blend of the real and the fantastic, in which the mother floats off on a balloon of illusions while the daughter is tutored by grim, blank muses of death and oblivion.

Born on October 27, 1932, in Boston, and growing up in Winthrop, Massachusetts, Plath was already conscious at seventeen of the conflict between her powerful ambitions—"I want to be free—I want, I think, to be omniscient. . . . I think I would like to call myself 'The girl who wanted to be God' "—and the limiting expectations for postwar American women: "I am afraid of getting married. Spare me from cooking three meals a day—spare me from the relentless cage of routine and rote" (*Letters Home*). In the semiautobiographical figure of Esther Greenwood in the novel *The Bell Jar* (1963), Plath presents a young woman paralyzed between seemingly irreconcilable social roles: "a wonderful future beckoned and winked" as wife with "a happy home and children," or as "a famous poet," or as "a brilliant professor," or as "the amazing editor," and so forth.

Writing and publishing from an early age, Plath won a scholarship at Smith College and graduated summa cum laude. Among the poets she read most intently were Yeats, Dylan Thomas, and W. H. Auden. But after her junior year, having spent a month as guest college editor at *Mademoiselle,* Plath suffered a breakdown, attempted to kill herself, and was hospitalized at length—events fictionalized in *The Bell Jar.* Later, she spent two years on a Fulbright Scholarship at Cambridge University. In 1956, she married the English poet Ted Hughes. The couple lived in the United States for more than a year, and she taught at Smith, also enrolling in a poetry seminar given by Lowell at Boston University in which she befriended Sexton. But the reading of students' papers at Smith consumed all her energy, and after a short time in Boston, the couple returned to England, where Plath intended to spend the rest of her life. She published a volume of poems, *The Colossus,* in 1960. She and Hughes had two children, a girl in 1960 and a boy in 1962. In the summer of 1962, Plath learned that her husband was having an affair, and they separated a few months later, in October. By the end of 1962, Plath had moved back alone to London from the family home in Devon and brought the children with her.

Plath's final months were a period of extraordinary creativity, during which she wrote as many as three poems a day while contending with depression, small children, and the coldest winter in England in a century and a half. These poems were, she said in notes for a BBC program, "all written at about four in the morning—that still, blue, almost eternal hour before cockcrow, before the baby's cry, before the glassy music of the milkman, settling his bottles." On the morning of February 11, 1963, Plath laid out food and milk for her children, sealed the kitchen door, and put her head in the gas oven. This tragic life story is so affecting that it risks overshadowing the poetry. But the suicide the last poems seem to foretell was not inevitable. Plath seems to have wanted to be saved: she had tried to get herself committed to a psychiatric hospital (the beds were full), had arranged for an au pair to arrive the morning of the suicide (the door was locked), and had left a note with the doctor's name and telephone number.

Far from being mere symptoms in a personal pathology, Plath's poems are works of great aesthetic accomplishment and psychological insight. She transmutes experiences both everyday and extreme with imaginative daring. In "Cut," the mundane experience of accidentally cutting the tip of her thumb instead of an onion undergoes an astonishing series of metamorphoses. A household event becomes the occasion for an imaginative outpouring, the poem mimicking the intensified consciousness of the body in pain by leaping from one increasingly extravagant image to the next. In "The Applicant," a salesman's arrival at the door turns into a savage meditation on the objectification of women in traditional marriage. In "Fever 103°," Plath transforms a high temperature into a meditation on death, lust, fire, and imaginative liberation of the female body from dependence on men. The movement of a horse in "Ariel" becomes the ecstatic drive of the poetic "I" to fuse with the sublime "eye" of Being.

Plath's final style represents a major achievement, especially compared with the overwrought, highly formal artifice of her early poems, written in the arch, New Critical style of the 1950s. Even so, a poem such as "The Colossus" begins to hint at the eruption of something less smooth and deliberate, especially in its juxtapositions of the formal with the colloquial, the mythic with the mundane ("A blue sky out of the Oresteia" but also "pails of Lysol" and the contemptuous remark "It's worse than a barnyard"). The poems written in Plath's last year are wildly heterogeneous, yoking together extremes of Gothicism and gaiety, rage and tenderness. They leap from one metaphor to the next without explicit connections, riding the relentless velocity of short, incantatory, free verse lines. She said they were written, unlike earlier ones, "to be read aloud" (BBC interview). The persona in these poems is volcanic in energy, mercurial in affect, by turns mournful, sardonic, aggressive, visionary, and ruthlessly self-mocking.

The emotional ambivalence of Plath's poetry widened the affective range of lyric poetry in English. Here, motherhood is not all sugar and sweetness, but includes the "stink of fat and baby crap" ("Lesbos"). A grieving daughter can adore her father, but also rage at him: "Daddy, daddy, you bastard, I'm through." A husband may be a "vampire." Nor does the poet spare herself the same tumultuous mix of emotions. Plath even scorns her own supposedly confessional hawking of her inner emotional life for money: "There is a charge," proclaims Lady Lazarus, "For the eyeing of my scars."

Plath's example was not lost on a poet such as John Berryman, one of whose Dream Songs has him splitting open his father's casket and tearing apart his grave clothes. But for a host of women poets, including the Americans Sexton, Adrienne Rich, Maxine Kumin, and Sharon Olds, as well as the Irish Eavan Boland, the British Carol Ann Duffy, and the Indian Eunice de Souza, Plath's example has been fundamental, as evidenced by their poems of fury against fathers and mothers, of suicidal longing and triumphant rebirth, of ferocious self-definition and self-assertion. Plath created a style equal to her keen awareness of her psychic life. Venting repressed feeling, examining it with an icy calm, Plath delivered to us our inner tumult, conflict, but also power.

The Disquieting Muses[1]

Mother, mother, what illbred aunt
Or what disfigured and unsightly
Cousin did you so unwisely keep
Unasked to my christening,[2] that she

1. In a BBC radio program, Plath commented on this poem: "It borrows its title from the painting by Giorgio de Chirico—*The Disquieting Muses.* All through the poem I have in mind the enigmatic figures in this painting—three terrible faceless dressmaker's dummies in classical gowns, seated and standing in a weird, clear light that casts the long strong shadows characteristic of de Chirico's early work. The dummies suggest a twentieth-century version of other sinister trios of women—the Three Fates, the witches in *Macbeth,* [Thomas] De Quincey's sisters of madness."

2. Cf. the fairy tale of Sleeping Beauty: a fairy, angry over not being invited to the christening of the newborn princess, curses her to die on her fifteenth year, by pricking her finger on a spindle.

Sent these ladies in her stead
With heads like darning-eggs to nod
And nod and nod at foot and head
And at the left side of my crib?

Mother, who made to order stories
Of Mixie Blackshort the heroic bear,
Mother, whose witches always, always
Got baked into gingerbread, I wonder
Whether you saw them, whether you said
Words to rid me of those three ladies
Nodding by night around my bed,
Mouthless, eyeless, with stitched bald head.

In the hurricane, when father's twelve
Study windows bellied in
Like bubbles about to break, you fed
My brother and me cookies and Ovaltine
And helped the two of us to choir:
'Thor[3] is angry: boom boom boom!
Thor is angry: we don't care!'
But those ladies broke the panes.

When on tiptoe the schoolgirls danced,
Blinking flashlights like fireflies
And singing the glowworm song, I could
Not lift a foot in the twinkle-dress
But, heavy-footed, stood aside
In the shadow cast by my dismal-headed
Godmothers, and you cried and cried:
And the shadow stretched, the lights went out.

Mother, you sent me to piano lessons
And praised my arabesques[4] and trills
Although each teacher found my touch
Oddly wooden in spite of scales
And the hours of practicing, my ear
Tone-deaf and yes, unteachable.
I learned, I learned, I learned elsewhere,
From muses unhired by you, dear mother.

I woke one day to see you, mother,
Floating above me in bluest air
On a green balloon bright with a million
Flowers and bluebirds that never were
Never, never, found anywhere.
But the little planet bobbed away
Like a soap-bubble as you called: Come here!
And I faced my traveling companions.

3. Norse god of thunder.

4. Musical embellishments.

Day now, night now, at head, side, feet,
They stand their vigil in gowns of stone,
Faces blank as the day I was born,
Their shadows long in the setting sun
That never brightens or goes down.
And this is the kingdom you bore me to,
Mother, mother. But no frown of mine
Will betray the company I keep.

1959

Metaphors

I'm a riddle in nine syllables,
An elephant, a ponderous house,
A melon strolling on two tendrils.
O red fruit, ivory, fine timbers!
This loaf's big with its yeasty rising.
Money's new-minted in this fat purse.
I'm a means, a stage, a cow in calf.
I've eaten a bag of green apples,
Boarded the train there's no getting off.

March 20, 1959

1960

The Colossus

I shall never get you put together entirely,
Pieced, glued, and properly jointed.
Mule-bray, pig-grunt and bawdy cackles
Proceed from your great lips.
It's worse than a barnyard.

Perhaps you consider yourself an oracle,
Mouthpiece of the dead, or of some god or other.
Thirty years now I have labored
To dredge the silt from your throat.
I am none the wiser.

Scaling little ladders with gluepots and pails of Lysol
I crawl like an ant in mourning
Over the weedy acres of your brow
To mend the immense skull-plates and clear
The bald, white tumuli[5] of your eyes.

A blue sky out of the Oresteia[6]
Arches above us. O father, all by yourself

5. Burial mounds.
6. Trilogy by Greek playwright Aeschylus (525–456 B.C.E.), in which the murder of King Agamemnon by his wife, Clytemnestra, is avenged by their children, Elektra and Orestes.

You are pithy and historical as the Roman Forum.
I open my lunch on a hill of black cypress.
Your fluted bones and acanthine[7] hair are littered

In their old anarchy to the horizon-line.
It would take more than a lightning-stroke
To create such a ruin.
Nights, I squat in the cornucopia
Of your left ear, out of the wind,

Counting the red stars and those of plum-color.
The sun rises under the pillar of your tongue.
My hours are married to shadow.
No longer do I listen for the scrape of a keel
On the blank stones of the landing.

1960

Morning Song

Love set you going like a fat gold watch.
The midwife slapped your footsoles, and your bald cry
Took its place among the elements.

Our voices echo, magnifying your arrival. New statue.
In a drafty museum, your nakedness
Shadows our safety. We stand round blankly as walls.

I'm no more your mother
Than the cloud that distills a mirror to reflect its own slow
Effacement at the wind's hand.

All night your moth-breath
Flickers among the flat pink roses. I wake to listen:
A far sea moves in my ear.

One cry, and I stumble from bed, cow-heavy and floral
In my Victorian nightgown.
Your mouth opens clean as a cat's. The window square

Whitens and swallows its dull stars. And now you try
Your handful of notes;
The clear vowels rise like balloons.

February 19, 1961 1965

7. Like the acanthus leaf used atop ornate, Corinthian columns.

In Plaster

I shall never get out of this! There are two of me now:
This new absolutely white person and the old yellow one,
And the white person is certainly the superior one.
She doesn't need food, she is one of the real saints.
At the beginning I hated her, she had no personality—
She lay in bed with me like a dead body
And I was scared, because she was shaped just the way I was

Only much whiter and unbreakable and with no complaints.
I couldn't sleep for a week, she was so cold.
I blamed her for everything, but she didn't answer.
I couldn't understand her stupid behavior!
When I hit her she held still, like a true pacifist.
Then I realized what she wanted was for me to love her:
She began to warm up, and I saw her advantages.

Without me, she wouldn't exist, so of course she was grateful.
I gave her a soul, I bloomed out of her as a rose
Blooms out of a vase of not very valuable porcelain,
And it was I who attracted everybody's attention,
Not her whiteness and beauty, as I had at first supposed.
I patronized her a little, and she lapped it up—
You could tell almost at once she had a slave mentality.

I didn't mind her waiting on me, and she adored it.
In the morning she woke me early, reflecting the sun
From her amazingly white torso, and I couldn't help but notice
Her tidiness and her calmness and her patience:
She humored my weakness like the best of nurses,
Holding my bones in place so they would mend properly.
In time our relationship grew more intense.

She stopped fitting me so closely and seemed offish.
I felt her criticizing me in spite of herself,
As if my habits offended her in some way.
She let in the drafts and became more and more absent-minded.
And my skin itched and flaked away in soft pieces
Simply because she looked after me so badly.
Then I saw what the trouble was: she thought she was immortal.

She wanted to leave me, she thought she was superior,
And I'd been keeping her in the dark, and she was resentful—
Wasting her days waiting on a half-corpse!
And secretly she began to hope I'd die.
Then she could cover my mouth and eyes, cover me entirely,
And wear my painted face the way a mummy-case
Wears the face of a pharaoh, though it's made of mud and water.

I wasn't in any position to get rid of her.
She'd supported me for so long I was quite limp—
I had even forgotten how to walk or sit,
So I was careful not to upset her in any way
Or brag ahead of time how I'd avenge myself.
Living with her was like living with my own coffin:
Yet I still depended on her, though I did it regretfully.

I used to think we might make a go of it together—
After all, it was a kind of marriage, being so close.
Now I see it must be one or the other of us.
She may be a saint, and I may be ugly and hairy,
But she'll soon find out that that doesn't matter a bit.
I'm collecting my strength; one day I shall manage without her,
And she'll perish with emptiness then, and begin to miss me.

March 18, 1961 1962

Tulips

The tulips are too excitable, it is winter here.
Look how white everything is, how quiet, how snowed-in.
I am learning peacefulness, lying by myself quietly
As the light lies on these white walls, this bed, these hands.
I am nobody; I have nothing to do with explosions.
I have given my name and my day-clothes up to the nurses
And my history to the anesthetist and my body to surgeons.

They have propped my head between the pillow and the sheet-cuff
Like an eye between two white lids that will not shut.
Stupid pupil, it has to take everything in.
The nurses pass and pass, they are no trouble,
They pass the way gulls pass inland in their white caps,
Doing things with their hands, one just the same as another,
So it is impossible to tell how many there are.

My body is a pebble to them, they tend it as water
Tends to the pebbles it must run over, smoothing them gently.
They bring me numbness in their bright needles, they bring me sleep.
Now I have lost myself I am sick of baggage——
My patent leather overnight case like a black pillbox,
My husband and child smiling out of the family photo;
Their smiles catch onto my skin, little smiling hooks.

I have let things slip, a thirty-year-old cargo boat
Stubbornly hanging on to my name and address.
They have swabbed me clear of my loving associations.
Scared and bare on the green plastic-pillowed trolley
I watched my teaset, my bureaus of linen, my books

Sink out of sight, and the water went over my head.
I am a nun now, I have never been so pure.

I didn't want any flowers, I only wanted
To lie with my hands turned up and be utterly empty.
How free it is, you have no idea how free——
The peacefulness is so big it dazes you,
And it asks nothing, a name tag, a few trinkets.
It is what the dead close on, finally; I imagine them
Shutting their mouths on it, like a Communion tablet.

The tulips are too red in the first place, they hurt me.
Even through the gift paper I could hear them breathe
Lightly, through their white swaddling, like an awful baby.
Their redness talks to my wound, it corresponds.
They are subtle: they seem to float, though they weigh me down,
Upsetting me with their sudden tongues and their color,
A dozen red lead sinkers round my neck.

Nobody watched me before, now I am watched.
The tulips turn to me, and the window behind me
Where once a day the light slowly widens and slowly thins,
And I see myself, flat, ridiculous, a cut-paper shadow
Between the eye of the sun and the eyes of the tulips,
And I have no face, I have wanted to efface myself.
The vivid tulips eat my oxygen.

Before they came the air was calm enough,
Coming and going, breath by breath, without any fuss.
Then the tulips filled it up like a loud noise.
Now the air snags and eddies round them the way a river
Snags and eddies round a sunken rust-red engine.
They concentrate my attention, that was happy
Playing and resting without committing itself.

The walls, also, seem to be warming themselves.
The tulips should be behind bars like dangerous animals;
They are opening like the mouth of some great African cat,
And I am aware of my heart: it opens and closes
Its bowl of red blooms out of sheer love of me.
The water I taste is warm and salt, like the sea,
And comes from a country far away as health.

March 18, 1961

1962

Blackberrying

Nobody in the lane, and nothing, nothing but blackberries,
Blackberries on either side, though on the right mainly,
A blackberry alley, going down in hooks, and a sea
Somewhere at the end of it, heaving. Blackberries
Big as the ball of my thumb, and dumb as eyes
Ebon[8] in the hedges, fat
With blue-red juices. These they squander on my fingers.
I had not asked for such a blood sisterhood; they must love me.
They accommodate themselves to my milkbottle, flattening their sides.

Overhead go the choughs[9] in black, cacophonous flocks—
Bits of burnt paper wheeling in a blown sky.
Theirs is the only voice, protesting, protesting.
I do not think the sea will appear at all.
The high, green meadows are glowing, as if lit from within.
I come to one bush of berries so ripe it is a bush of flies,
Hanging their bluegreen bellies and their wing panes in a Chinese screen.
The honey-feast of the berries has stunned them; they believe in heaven.
One more hook, and the berries and bushes end.

The only thing to come now is the sea.
From between two hills a sudden wind funnels at me,
Slapping its phantom laundry in my face.
These hills are too green and sweet to have tasted salt.
I follow the sheep path between them. A last hook brings me
To the hills' northern face, and the face is orange rock
That looks out on nothing, nothing but a great space
Of white and pewter lights, and a din like silversmiths
Beating and beating at an intractable metal.

September 23, 1961 — 1962, 1965

Elm

For Ruth Fainlight[1]

I know the bottom, she says. I know it with my great tap root:[2]
It is what you fear.
I do not fear it: I have been there.

Is it the sea you hear in me,
Its dissatisfactions?
Or the voice of nothing, that was your madness?

8. Black.
9. Crows.
1. American poet (b. 1931), who lives in England.
2. Primary root; hence, anything that has a central position in a line of development.

Love is a shadow.
How you lie and cry after it
Listen: these are its hooves: it has gone off, like a horse.

All night I shall gallop thus, impetuously,
Till your head is a stone, your pillow a little turf,
Echoing, echoing.

Or shall I bring you the sound of poisons?
This is rain now, this big hush.
And this is the fruit of it: tin-white, like arsenic.

I have suffered the atrocity of sunsets.
Scorched to the root
My red filaments burn and stand, a hand of wires.

Now I break up in pieces that fly about like clubs.
A wind of such violence
Will tolerate no bystanding: I must shriek.

The moon, also, is merciless: she would drag me
Cruelly, being barren.
Her radiance scathes me. Or perhaps I have caught her.

I let her go. I let her go
Diminished and flat, as after radical surgery.
How your bad dreams possess and endow me.

I am inhabited by a cry.
Nightly it flaps out
Looking, with its hooks, for something to love.

I am terrified by this dark thing
That sleeps in me;
All day I feel its soft, feathery turnings, its malignity.

Clouds pass and disperse.
Are those the faces of love, those pale irretrievables?
Is it for such I agitate my heart?

I am incapable of more knowledge.
What is this, this face
So murderous in its strangle of branches?——

Its snaky acids kiss.
It petrifies the will. These are the isolate, slow faults
That kill, that kill, that kill.

April 19, 1962

1963, 1965

The Arrival of the Bee Box

I ordered this, this clean wood box
Square as a chair and almost too heavy to lift.
I would say it was the coffin of a midget
Or a square baby
Were there not such a din in it.

The box is locked, it is dangerous.
I have to live with it overnight
And I can't keep away from it.
There are no windows, so I can't see what is in there.
There is only a little grid, no exit.

I put my eye to the grid.
It is dark, dark,
With the swarmy feeling of African hands
Minute and shrunk for export,
Black on black, angrily clambering.

How can I let them out?
It is the noise that appalls me most of all,
The unintelligible syllables.
It is like a Roman mob,
Small, taken one by one, but my god, together!

I lay my ear to furious Latin.
I am not a Caesar.
I have simply ordered a box of maniacs.
They can be sent back.
They can die, I need feed them nothing, I am the owner.

I wonder how hungry they are.
I wonder if they would forget me
If I just undid the locks and stood back and turned into a tree.
There is the laburnum,[3] its blond colonnades,
And the petticoats of the cherry.

They might ignore me immediately
In my moon suit and funeral veil.
I am no source of honey
So why should they turn on me?
Tomorrow I will be sweet God, I will set them free.

The box is only temporary.

October 4, 1962 1963

3. Type of tree.

The Applicant

First, are you our sort of a person?
Do you wear
A glass eye, false teeth or a crutch,
A brace or a hook,
Rubber breasts or a rubber crotch,

Stitches to show something's missing? No, no? Then
How can we give you a thing?
Stop crying.
Open your hand.
Empty? Empty. Here is a hand

To fill it and willing
To bring teacups and roll away headaches
And do whatever you tell it.
Will you marry it?
It is guaranteed

To thumb shut your eyes at the end
And dissolve of sorrow.
We make new stock from the salt.
I notice you are stark naked.
How about this suit——

Black and stiff, but not a bad fit.
Will you marry it?
It is waterproof, shatterproof, proof
Against fire and bombs through the roof.
Believe me, they'll bury you in it.

Now your head, excuse me, is empty.
I have the ticket for that.
Come here, sweetie, out of the closet.
Well, what do you think of *that?*
Naked as paper to start

But in twenty-five years she'll be silver,
In fifty, gold.
A living doll, everywhere you look.
It can sew, it can cook,
It can talk, talk, talk.

It works, there is nothing wrong with it.
You have a hole, it's a poultice.[4]
You have an eye, it's an image.

4. Cloth applied to wounds.

My boy, it's your last resort.
Will you marry it, marry it, marry it.

October 11, 1962 1963

Daddy

You do not do, you do not do
Any more, black shoe
In which I have lived like a foot
For thirty years, poor and white,
Barely daring to breathe or Achoo.

Daddy, I have had to kill you.
You died before I had time——
Marble-heavy, a bag full of God,
Ghastly statue with one grey toe
Big as a Frisco seal

And a head in the freakish Atlantic
Where it pours bean green over blue
In the waters off beautiful Nauset.
I used to pray to recover you.
Ach, du.[5]

In the German tongue, in the Polish town[6]
Scraped flat by the roller
Of wars, wars, wars.
But the name of the town is common.
My Polack friend

Says there are a dozen or two.
So I never could tell where you
Put your foot, your root,
I never could talk to you.
The tongue stuck in my jaw.

It stuck in a barb wire snare.
Ich, ich, ich, ich,[7]
I could hardly speak.
I thought every German was you.
And the language obscene

An engine, an engine
Chuffing me off like a Jew.
A Jew to Dachau, Auschwitz, Belsen.

5. Ah, you (German).
6. Perhaps modeled on Grabów, birthplace of the poet's father, Otto Plath.
7. I, I, I, I (German).

I began to talk like a Jew.
I think I may well be a Jew.

The snows of the Tyrol, the clear beer of Vienna
Are not very pure or true.
With my gypsy ancestress and my weird luck
And my Taroc pack and my Taroc pack
I may be a bit of a Jew.

I have always been scared of *you*,
With your Luftwaffe,[8] your gobbledygoo.
And your neat mustache
And your Aryan eye, bright blue.
Panzer-man, panzer-man, O You——

Not God but a swastika
So black no sky could squeak through.
Every woman adores a Fascist,
The boot in the face, the brute
Brute heart of a brute like you.

You stand at the blackboard, daddy,
In the picture I have of you,
A cleft in your chin instead of your foot
But no less a devil for that, no not
Any less the black man who

Bit my pretty red heart in two.
I was ten when they buried you.
At twenty I tried to die
And get back, back, back to you.
I thought even the bones would do.

But they pulled me out of the sack,
And they stuck me together with glue.
And then I knew what to do.
I made a model of you,
A man in black with a Meinkampf[9] look

And a love of the rack and the screw.
And I said I do, I do.
So daddy, I'm finally through.
The black telephone's off at the root,
The voices just can't worm through.

If I've killed one man, I've killed two——
The vampire who said he was you
And drank my blood for a year,

8. Air force (German).
9. *Mein Kampf* (German for "my battle"), the political autobiography of Adolf Hitler (1889–1945).

Seven years, if you want to know.
Daddy, you can lie back now.

There's a stake in your fat black heart
And the villagers never liked you.
They are dancing and stamping on you.
They always *knew* it was you.
Daddy, daddy, you bastard, I'm through.

October 12, 1962 1963

Fever 103°

Pure? What does it mean?
The tongues of hell
Are dull, dull as the triple

Tongues of dull, fat Cerberus[1]
Who wheezes at the gate. Incapable
Of licking clean

The aguey tendon, the sin, the sin.
The tinder cries.
The indelible smell

Of a snuffed candle!
Love, love, the low smokes roll
From me like Isadora's scarves, I'm in a fright

One scarf will catch and anchor in the wheel.[2]
Such yellow sullen smokes
Make their own element. They will not rise,

But trundle round the globe
Choking the aged and the meek,
The weak

Hothouse baby in its crib,
The ghastly orchid
Hanging its hanging garden in the air,

Devilish leopard!
Radiation turned it white
And killed it in an hour.

1. In Greek mythology, three-headed dog that guarded the gate of Hades.
2. Isadora Duncan (1877–1927), American dancer, broke her neck and died when her scarf caught in the open-spoked wheel of her car.

Greasing the bodies of adulterers
Like Hiroshima ash and eating in.
The sin. The sin.

Darling, all night
I have been flickering, off, on, off, on.
The sheets grow heavy as a lecher's kiss.

Three days. Three nights.
Lemon water, chicken
Water, water make me retch.

I am too pure for you or anyone.
Your body
Hurts me as the world hurts God. I am a lantern——

My head a moon
Of Japanese paper, my gold beaten skin
Infinitely delicate and infinitely expensive.

Does not my heat astound you. And my light.
All by myself I am a huge camellia
Glowing and coming and going, flush on flush.

I think I am going up,
I think I may rise——
The beads of hot metal fly, and I, love, I

Am a pure acetylene
Virgin
Attended by roses,

By kisses, by cherubim,
By whatever these pink things mean.
Not you, nor him

Not him, nor him
(My selves dissolving, old whore petticoats)——
To Paradise.

October 20, 1962 1963, 1965

Cut

For Susan O'Neill Roe

What a thrill——
My thumb instead of an onion.
The top quite gone
Except for a sort of a hinge

Of skin,
A flap like a hat,
Dead white.
Then that red plush.

Little pilgrim,
The Indian's axed your scalp.
Your turkey wattle
Carpet rolls

Straight from the heart.
I step on it,
Clutching my bottle
Of pink fizz.

A celebration, this is.
Out of a gap
A million soldiers run,
Redcoats, every one.

Whose side are they on?
O my
Homunculus,[3] I am ill.
I have taken a pill to kill

The thin
Papery feeling.
Saboteur,
Kamikaze man——

The stain on your
Gauze Ku Klux Klan
Babushka[4]
Darkens and tarnishes and when

The balled
Pulp of your heart
Confronts its small
Mill of silence

How you jump——
Trepanned[5] veteran,
Dirty girl,
Thumb stump.

October 24, 1962 — 1963, 1965

3. Miniature person said to exist in the mind or in the spermatozoon or egg.

4. Headkerchief.

5. With the skull removed.

Poppies in October

Even the sun-clouds this morning cannot manage such skirts.
Nor the woman in the ambulance
Whose red heart blooms through her coat so astoundingly——

A gift, a love gift
Utterly unasked for
By a sky

Palely and flamily
Igniting its carbon monoxides, by eyes
Dulled to a halt under bowlers.

O my God, what am I
That these late mouths should cry open
In a forest of frost, in dawn of cornflowers.

October 27, 1962 1963, 1965

Ariel[6]

Stasis in darkness.
Then the substanceless blue
Pour of tor[7] and distances.

God's lioness,
How one we grow,
Pivot of heels and knees!—The furrow

Splits and passes, sister to
The brown arc
Of the neck I cannot catch,

Nigger-eye
Berries cast dark
Hooks——

Black sweet blood mouthfuls,
Shadows.
Something else

Hauls me through air——
Thighs, hair;
Flakes from my heels.

6. Lion of God (Hebrew); the airy spirit in Shakespeare's *Tempest;* also, the name of a horse Plath used to ride.
7. High, rocky hill.

White
Godiva, I unpeel—
Dead hands, dead stringencies.

And now I
Foam to wheat, a glitter of seas.
The child's cry

Melts in the wall.
And I
Am the arrow,

The dew that flies
Suicidal, at one with the drive
Into the red

Eye, the cauldron of morning.

October 27, 1962 — 1963, 1965

Lady Lazarus[8]

I have done it again.
One year in every ten
I manage it—

A sort of walking miracle, my skin
Bright as a Nazi lampshade,[9]
My right foot

A paperweight,
My face a featureless, fine
Jew linen.

Peel off the napkin
O my enemy.
Do I terrify?—

The nose, the eye pits, the full set of teeth?
The sour breath
Will vanish in a day.

Soon, soon the flesh
The grave cave ate will be
At home on me

8. Lazarus was raised from the dead by Jesus (John 11.44).
9. The skins of some Jewish victims of the Nazis were supposedly used to make lampshades. The Nazis also stole gold fillings (line 78) from their victims' remains.

And I a smiling woman.
I am only thirty.
And like the cat I have nine times to die.

This is Number Three.
What a trash
To annihilate each decade.

What a million filaments.
The peanut-crunching crowd
Shoves in to see

Them unwrap me hand and foot——
The big strip tease.
Gentleman, ladies

These are my hands
My knees.
I may be skin and bone,

Nevertheless, I am the same, identical woman.
The first time it happened I was ten.
It was an accident.

The second time I meant
To last it out and not come back at all.
I rocked shut

As a seashell.
They had to call and call
And pick the worms off me like sticky pearls.

Dying
Is an art, like everything else.
I do it exceptionally well.

I do it so it feels like hell.
I do it so it feels real.
I guess you could say I've a call.

It's easy enough to do it in a cell.
It's easy enough to do it and stay put.
It's the theatrical

Comeback in broad day
To the same place, the same face, the same brute
Amused shout:

'A miracle!'
That knocks me out.
There is a charge

For the eyeing of my scars, there is a charge
For the hearing of my heart——
It really goes.

And there is a charge, a very large charge
For a word or a touch
Or a bit of blood

Or a piece of my hair or my clothes.
So, so, Herr Doktor.
So, Herr Enemy.

I am your opus,
I am your valuable,
The pure gold baby

That melts to a shriek.
I turn and burn.
Do not think I underestimate your great concern.

Ash, ash——
You poke and stir.
Flesh, bone, there is nothing there——

A cake of soap,
A wedding ring,
A gold filling.

Herr God, Herr Lucifer,
Beware
Beware.

Out of the ash
I rise with my red hair
And I eat men like air.

October 23–29, 1962 1963

Edge

The woman is perfected.
Her dead

Body wears the smile of accomplishment,
The illusion of a Greek necessity

Flows in the scrolls of her toga,
Her bare

Feet seem to be saying:
We have come so far, it is over.

Each dead child coiled, a white serpent,
One at each little

Pitcher of milk, now empty.
She has folded

Them back into her body as petals
Of a rose close when the garden

Stiffens and odors bleed
From the sweet, deep throats of the night flower.

The moon has nothing to be sad about,
Staring from her hood of bone.

She is used to this sort of thing.
Her blacks crackle and drag.

February 5, 1963 — 1963

AUDRE LORDE
1934–1992

There was more than one Audre Lorde. "I am not one piece of myself," she wrote. "I cannot be simply a Black person, and not be a woman, too, nor can I be a woman without being a lesbian." Lorde contained multitudes, and these different voices survive and affirm themselves through her poetry. "When I say myself, I mean not only the Audre who inhabits my body but all those *feisty, incorrigible Black women* who insist on standing up and saying *I am,* and you can't wipe me out, no matter how irritating I am" ("My Words Will Be There").

Lorde's "biomythography," *Zami: A New Spelling of My Name,* is a fictionalized memoir of her coming-of-age as a lesbian, but it is also about the formation of her racial identity. She describes her vexed effort to learn from the example of her mother—a black woman defensively identifying with white norms. In "Hanging Fire" and other poems, Lorde explores this ambivalent relation to her mother's racial splitting. "I bear two women upon my back"—one black, the other white—says the speaker of "From the House of Yemanjá." The passions articulated in Lorde's poetry are potent and varied. She credited African writers with teaching her how to transmute rage and pain into poetry (her second book was entitled *Cables to Rage*). Love is also, she said, "very important because it is a source of tremendous power," and yet women "have not been taught to respect the erotic urge, the place that is uniquely female" ("My Words"). Describing lesbian eros, the vivid language of "Love Poem" combines vast archetypal landscapes—mountains, valleys, forests—with the particulars of the female body. "Some words," Lorde writes in "Coal," "are open like a diamond / on glass windows." Her best poetry is diamonded with such words, as when she describes being taught to swim in "A Question of Climate" ("cannons of salt   exploding / my nostrils' rage") or giving birth in "Now that I Am Forever with Child" ("My head rang like a fiery piston / My legs were towers between which / A new world was passing").

Lorde was born on February 18, 1934, to West Indian parents living in Harlem. She began writing poetry at twelve or thirteen. "I was very inarticulate as a youngster," she recalled. "I used to speak in poetry. I would read poems, and I would memorize them. People would say, well, what do you think, Audre. What happened to you yesterday? And I would recite a poem and somewhere in that poem there would be a line or a feeling I would be sharing. . . . And when I couldn't find the poems to express the things I was feeling, that's what started me writing poetry" ("My Words"). She received her B.A. from Hunter College in 1959, her Master of Library Science degree from Columbia University in 1961. She married in 1962 and divorced in 1970. Having worked as a librarian, taught school, and spent a year as poet-in-residence at Tougaloo College, in Mississippi, she taught at colleges in New York City including the John Jay College of Criminal Justice. In 1981, she became professor of English at Hunter College. In *The Cancer Journals* (1980), she described her battle with the cancer that ultimately would cause her death.

Coal

I
is the total black, being spoken
from the earth's inside.
There are many kinds of open
how a diamond comes into a knot of flame
how sound comes into a word, coloured
by who pays what for speaking.

Some words are open like a diamond
on glass windows
singing out within the passing crash of sun
Then there are words like stapled wagers
in a perforated book,—buy and sign and tear apart—
and come whatever wills all chances
the stub remains
and ill-pulled tooth with a ragged edge.
Some words live in my throat
breeding like adders. Others know sun
seeking like gypsies over my tongue
to explode through my lips
like young sparrows bursting from shell.
Some words
bedevil me.

Love is a word, another kind of open.
As the diamond comes into a knot of flame
I am Black because I come from the earth's inside
now take my word for jewel in the open light.

1968, 1976

Now that I Am Forever with Child

How the days went
While you were blooming within me
I remember each upon each—
The swelling changed planes of my body—
And how you first fluttered, then jumped
And I thought it was my heart.

How the days wound down
And the turning of winter
I recall, with you growing heavy
Against the wind. I thought
Now her hands
Are formed, and her hair
Has started to curl
Now her teeth are done
Now she sneezes.
Then the seed opened.
I bore you one morning just before spring—
My head rang like a firey piston
My legs were towers between which
A new world was passing.

From then
I can only distinguish
One thread within running hours
You . . . flowing through selves
Toward you.

1968

Love Poem

Speak earth and bless me with what is richest
make sky flow honey out of my hips
rigid as mountains
spread over a valley
carved out by the mouth of rain.

And I knew when I entered her I was
high wind in her forests hollow
fingers whispering sound
honey flowed
from the split cup
impaled on a lance of tongues
on the tips of her breasts on her navel
and my breath

howling into her entrances
through lungs of pain.

Greedy as herring-gulls
or a child
I swing out over the earth
over and over
again.

1974

From the House of Yemanjá[1]

My mother had two faces and a frying pot
where she cooked up her daughters
into girls
before she fixed our dinner.
My mother had two faces
and a broken pot
where she hid out a perfect daughter
who was not me
I am the sun and moon and forever hungry
for her eyes.

I bear two women upon my back
one dark and rich and hidden
in the ivory hungers of the other
mother
pale as a witch
yet steady and familiar
brings me bread and terror
in my sleep
her breasts are huge exciting anchors
in the midnight storm.

All this has been
before
in my mother's bed
time has no sense
I have no brothers
and my sisters are cruel.

Mother I need
mother I need
mother I need your blackness now
as the august earth needs rain.

1. "Mother of the other *Orisha* [gods and goddesses of the Yoruba people, Western Nigeria], Yemanjá is also the goddess of oceans. Rivers are said to flow from her breasts. . . . Those who please her are blessed with many children" (from Lorde's glossary to her volume *The Black Unicorn*).

I am
the sun and moon and forever hungry
and sharpened edge
where day and night shall meet
and not be
one.

1978

Hanging Fire[2]

I am fourteen
and my skin has betrayed me
the boy I cannot live without
still sucks his thumb
in secret
how come my knees are
always so ashy
what if I die
before morning
and momma's in the bedroom
with the door closed.

I have to learn how to dance
in time for the next party
my room is too small for me
suppose I die before graduation
they will sing sad melodies
but finally
tell the truth about me
There is nothing I want to do
and too much
that has to be done
and momma's in the bedroom
with the door closed.

Nobody even stops to think
about my side of it
I should have been on Math Team
my marks were better than his
why do I have to be
the one
wearing braces
I have nothing to wear tomorrow
will I live long enough
to grow up

2. Hesitating, delaying.

and momma's in the bedroom
with the door closed.

1978

A Question of Climate

I learned to be honest
the way I learned to swim
dropped into the inevitable
my father's thumbs in my hairless armpits
about to give way
I am trying
to surface carefully
remembering
the water's shadow-legged musk
cannons of salt exploding
my nostrils' rage
and for years
my powerful breast stroke
was a declaration of war.

1986

Mark Strand
b. 1934

Mark Strand's poems are filled with a terrible strangeness, recorded in stunningly precise language. As in dreams, the laws that govern our waking lives no longer obtain, and the most extraordinary things happen. The speaker in Strand's poems often suffers from a psychic split, a process of self-alienation: "Wherever I am / I am what is missing" ("Keeping Things Whole"). Identity is an inscrutable "absence." Many of Strand's poems resonate with the last lines of Wallace Stevens's "The Snow Man," as well as that poem's frigid, windy setting: the listener, "nothing himself, beholds / Nothing that is not there and the nothing that is." Strand is drawn not to the sensual exuberance but to the darker, colder side of Stevens. Strand's free verse is spare and elemental, stripped down to stark reflections on the absence that is the self, the absence that surrounds the self, and the final absence that awaits the self.

Unlike surrealist paintings or writing, whose mysterious discontinuities they suggest, Strand's mature poems do not rebel against sense; they are unsettlingly clear and coherent. The poems smell of the fear of death, even when defiantly titled "Recovery" and "Not Dying," for as Strand remarks in "The Dance": "And who doesn't have one foot in the grave?" The expectation of rebirth, which figures in several poems, cannot relieve the psychic pressure of this fear, even though the poet hopes that "If a man fears death, / he shall be saved by his poems" ("The New Poetry Handbook"). For all their strangeness, then, his poems explore emotions and experiences that are widespread but rarely communicated, and one reads Strand's best work with a sense of surprised and fearful recognition. Anguished yet ascetic, mournful yet antic, Strand's poetry has the power to haunt, even as it seems haunted by the ghostly negations of language, loss, and death.

Strand was born on April 11, 1934, to American parents in Summerside, Prince Edward Island, Canada. He received his B.A. from Antioch College, then went to Yale University for a B.F.A. He studied under Donald Justice at the University of Iowa, spent a year in Italy on a Fulbright Scholarship, then completed his M.A. in 1962 and stayed on at Iowa as an instructor for three years. In 1965, he went to Rio de Janeiro as Fulbright Lecturer at the University of Brazil; since then, he has taught at a number of American universities, including Utah, Johns Hopkins, and Chicago. The author of short narratives, children's books, and art criticism, he has also edited a wide variety of anthologies, including volumes of European, Mexican, and South American writers. The winner of a MacArthur Fellowship in 1987, the Bollingen Prize in 1993, and the Pulitzer Prize in 1999, he was the U.S. poet laureate in 1990–91.

Keeping Things Whole

In a field
I am the absence
of field.
This is
always the case.
Wherever I am
I am what is missing.

When I walk
I part the air
and always
the air moves in
to fill the spaces
where my body's been.

We all have reasons
for moving.
I move
to keep things whole.

1964

Eating Poetry

Ink runs from the corners of my mouth.
There is no happiness like mine.
I have been eating poetry.

The librarian does not believe what she sees.
Her eyes are sad
and she walks with her hands in her dress.

The poems are gone.
The light is dim.
The dogs are on the basement stairs and coming up.

Their eyeballs roll,
their blond legs burn like brush.
The poor librarian begins to stamp her feet and weep.

She does not understand.
When I get on my knees and lick her hand,
she screams.

I am a new man.
I snarl at her and bark.
I romp with joy in the bookish dark.

1968

The Prediction

That night the moon drifted over the pond,
turning the water to milk, and under
the boughs of the trees, the blue trees,
a young woman walked, and for an instant

the future came to her:
rain falling on her husband's grave, rain falling
on the lawns of her children, her own mouth
filling with cold air, strangers moving into her house,

a man in her room writing a poem, the moon drifting into it,
a woman strolling under its trees, thinking of death,
thinking of him thinking of her, and the wind rising
and taking the moon and leaving the paper dark.

1970

In Celebration

You sit in a chair, touched by nothing, feeling
the old self become the older self, imagining
only the patience of water, the boredom of stone.
You think that silence is the extra page,
you think that nothing is good or bad, not even
the darkness that fills the house while you sit watching
it happen. You've seen it happen before. Your friends
move past the window, their faces soiled with regret.
You want to wave but cannot raise your hand.

You sit in a chair. You turn to the nightshade[1] spreading
a poisonous net around the house. You taste
the honey of absence. It is the same wherever
you are, the same if the voice rots before
the body, or the body rots before the voice.
You know that desire leads only to sorrow, that sorrow
leads to achievement which leads to emptiness.
You know that this is different, that this
is the celebration, the only celebration,
that by giving yourself over to nothing,
you shall be healed. You know there is joy in feeling
your lungs prepare themselves for an ashen future,
so you wait, you stare and you wait, and the dust settles
and the miraculous hours of childhood wander in darkness.

1973

From Elegy for My Father

(Robert Strand 1908–1968)

6. The New Year

It is winter and the new year.
Nobody knows you.
Away from the stars, from the rain of light,
You lie under the weather of stones.
There is no thread to lead you back.
Your friends doze in the dark
Of pleasure and cannot remember.
Nobody knows you. You are the neighbour of nothing.
You do not see the rain falling and the man walking away,
The soiled wind blowing its ashes across the city.
You do not see the sun dragging, the moon like an echo.
You do not see the bruised heart go up in flames,
The skulls of the innocent turn into smoke.
You do not see the scars of plenty, the eyes without light.
It is over. It is winter and the new year.
The meek are hauling their skins into heaven.
The hopeless are suffering the cold with those who have nothing to hide.
It is over and nobody knows you.
There is starlight drifting on the black water.
There are stones in the sea no one has seen.
There is a shore and people are waiting.
And nothing comes back.

1. Or deadly nightshade, a poisonous plant.

Because it is over.
Because there is silence instead of a name.
Because it is winter and the new year.

1973

Poor North

It is cold, the snow is deep,
the wind beats around in its cage of trees,
clouds have the look of rags torn and soiled with use,
and starlings peck at the ice.
It is north, poor north. Nothing goes right.

The man of the house has gone to work,
selling chairs and sofas in a failing store.
His wife stays home and stares from the window into the trees,
trying to recall the life she lost, though it wasn't much.
White flowers of frost build up on the glass.

It is late in the day. Brants and Canada geese are asleep
on the waters of St Margaret's Bay.
The man and his wife are out for a walk; see how they lean
into the wind; they turn up their collars
and the small puffs of their breath are carried away.

1978

The Idea

for Nolan Miller[2]

For us, too, there was a wish to possess
Something beyond the world we knew, beyond ourselves,
Beyond our power to imagine, something nevertheless
In which we might see ourselves; and this desire
Came always in passing, in waning light, and in such cold
That ice on the valley's lakes cracked and rolled,
And blowing snow covered what earth we saw,
And scenes from the past, when they surfaced again,
Looked not as they had, but ghostly and white
Among false curves and hidden erasures;
And never once did we feel we were close
Until the night wind said, 'Why do this,
Especially now? Go back to the place you belong';
And there appeared, with its windows glowing, small,

2. American editor and college professor (b. 1912), who inspired Strand to begin writing poetry.

In the distance, in the frozen reaches, a cabin;
And we stood before it, amazed at its being there,
And would have gone forward and opened the door,
And stepped into the glow and warmed ourselves there,
But that it was ours by not being ours,
And should remain empty. That was the idea.

1990

From Dark Harbor

XX

Is it you standing among the olive trees
Beyond my courtyard? You in the sunlight
Waving me closer with one hand while the other

Shields your eyes from the brightness that turns
All that is not you dead white? Is it you
Around whom the leaves scatter like foam?

You in the murmuring night that is scented
With mint and lit by the distant wilderness
Of stars? Is it you? Is it really you

Rising from the script of waves, the length
Of your body casting a sudden shadow over my hand
So that I feel how cold it is as it moves

Over the page? You leaning down and putting
Your mouth against mine so I should know
That a kiss is only the beginning

Of what until now we could only imagine?
Is it you or the long compassionate wind
That whispers in my ear: alas, alas?

XXX

There is a road through the canyon,
A river beside the road, a forest
If there is more, I haven't seen it yet.

Still, it is possible to say this has been
An amazing century for fashion if for nothing else;
The way brave models held back their tears

When thinking of the millions of Jews and Serbs
That Hitler killed, and how the photographer
Steadied his hand when he considered

The Muzhiks[3] that Stalin took care of.
The way skirts went up and down; how breasts
Were in, then out; and the long and the short of hair.

But the road that winds through the canyon
Is covered with snow, and the river flows
Under the ice. Cross-country skiers are moving

Like secrets between the trees of the glassed-in forest.
The day has made a fabulous cage of cold around
My face. Whenever I take a breath I hear cracking.

1993

3. Russian peasants, millions of whom died as the result of the brutal policies of Russian dictator Joseph Stalin (1879–1953).

Wole Soyinka
b. 1934

Born on July 13, 1934, in Abeokuta, near Ibadan, in western Nigeria, Wole Soyinka became in 1986 the first black African writer to receive the Nobel Prize in Literature. His major work has been in theater, but early in his career he published two richly textured volumes of poetry, *Idanre & Other Poems* (1967) and *The Shuttle in the Crypt* (1972), with *Mandela's Earth* coming later (1988). Poet, playwright, director, actor, novelist, and essayist, Soyinka has been passionate and eloquent in denouncing both the degradations of Western imperialism and the more recent, internal colonization of Africa by indigenous dictators and thugs. His courage has landed him repeatedly in Nigerian jails, with periods of solitary confinement. As early as the critical moment of Nigeria's independence celebrations, Soyinka was willing to ask skeptical questions about the postcolonial fate of sub-Saharan Africa. His pessimism about Africa's self-torment and carnage has deepened in recent decades.

Repressive regimes are not alone in being irked by Soyinka's independence of mind. Among fellow African writers, he has been criticized for nearly opposite reasons. Nativists have seen him as a "cultural mulatto," overly indebted to Western models; they remember that he was an early detractor of the Afrocentrist movement called negritude. At the same time, Marxist and feminist critics have attacked him for, as they see it, irresponsibly championing aesthetics over politics, as well as for celebrating a native Yoruba culture that is said to be feudal and sexist. For many Nigerian critics, Soyinka's writing isn't political enough, while it is often too political for metropolitan tastes. In the West, his work, like that of other postcolonial writers, has not always been welcomed within the traditionally Eurocentric curriculum of English departments. At Cambridge University in 1973–74, Soyinka found himself delivering a series of lectures through the department of anthropology instead of English, which was apparently unable to, as he put it, "believe in any such mythical beast as 'African Literature' " (*Myth, Literature and the African World*). Yet amid all the insults, attacks, and provocations, Soyinka has remained stubbornly, perhaps heroically faithful to his own idiom and vision.

In its citation for the Nobel Prize, the Swedish Academy observed that Soyinka "has his roots in the Yoruba people's myths, rites and cultural patterns, which in their turn have historical links to the Mediterranean region. Through his education in his native land and in Europe he has also acquired deep familiarity with western culture." Soyinka's primary achievement in poetry has been to find a compelling way of hybridizing English literary paradigms with Yoruba oral traditions. His diction and rhetorical strategies draw on Elizabethan and Jacobean dramatic models—high flown, flamboyant, and exuberant. Especially in his early work, he loads individual lines with a verbal extravagance and density that recall the language of the English Renaissance. The influence of Anglo-modernist poets can also be seen in Soyinka's deliberate opacity, gnarled compression, satiric grotesquerie, tonal instability, mythic archetypalism, and delight in incongruous, even violent juxtapositions.

But it would be wrong to see Soyinka's literary language as merely recuperating archaic English models or recapitulating Anglo-modernism. The syntactic elasticity of Yoruba exerts considerable pressure on his early English-language poetry. These are often difficult poems to puzzle out, in part because of the intercultural effect of Soyinka's hybridization of two syntactic systems. In his frequent inversions of word order, he sometimes delays the introduction of his main verb or subject, forcing English syntax to stretch beyond its normal breaking point. His energetic wordplay likewise owes much to Yoruba speech practices. He splits and extends puns until they refract a rich array of meanings. His Africanization of the English language finds its macrocosmic equivalent in Soyinka's yoking together of Yoruba cosmologies—particularly such mythological figures in the Yoruba pantheon as Ogun (god of iron, thunder, roads, war, creation, and destruction)—with the experience of modernization and Western technology.

After attending Government College and University College, in Ibadan, where the poet Christopher Okigbo was among his classmates, Soyinka continued his studies on a scholarship at the University of Leeds, in England, earning an undergraduate degree in 1958 and a doctorate in 1973. He founded a national theater in Nigeria in 1960. Having attempted to mediate between the sides in the Nigerian Civil War, Soyinka was imprisoned for two years (1967–69) for supposedly conspiring with Igbo rebels to form a new secessionist state of Biafra. Forced into exile after the war, he endured a second exile from 1994 to 1998 under the brutal dictatorship of Sani Abacha. He has taught at universities in Ibadan and Ife, as well as at Cambridge, Yale, Cornell, and Emory.

Telephone Conversation

The price seemed reasonable, location
Indifferent. The landlady swore she lived
Off premises. Nothing remained
But self-confession. 'Madam', I warned,
'I hate a wasted journey—I am African.'
Silence. Silenced transmission of
Pressurised good-breeding. Voice, when it came,
Lip-stick coated, long gold-rolled
Cigarette-holder pipped. Caught I was, foully.

'HOW DARK?' . . . I had not misheard . . . 'ARE YOU LIGHT
'OR VERY DARK?' Button B. Button A.[1] Stench
Of rancid breath of public hide-and-speak.
Red booth. Red pillar-box.[2] Red double-tiered
Omnibus[3] squelching tar. It *was* real! Shamed
By ill-mannered silence, surrender
Pushed dumbfoundment to beg simplification.
Considerate she was, varying the emphasis—

'ARE YOU DARK? OR VERY LIGHT?' Revelation came.
'You mean—like plain or milk chocolate?'
Her assent was clinical, crushing in its light
Impersonality. Rapidly, wave-length adjusted,
I chose. 'West African sepia'[4]—and as afterthought,
'Down in my passport.' Silence for spectroscopic[5]
Flight of fancy, till truthfulness clanged her accent
Hard on the mouthpiece. 'WHAT'S THAT?' conceding
'DON'T KNOW WHAT THAT IS.' 'Like brunette.'

'THAT'S DARK, ISN'T IT?' 'Not altogether.
'Facially, I am brunette, but madam, you should see
'The rest of me. Palm of my hand, soles of my feet
'Are a peroxide blonde. Friction, caused—
'Foolishly madam—by sitting down, has turned
'My bottom raven black—One moment madam'—sensing
Her receiver rearing on the thunderclap
About my ears—'Madam', I pleaded, 'Wouldn't you rather
'See for yourself?'

1960, 1962

Death in the Dawn

Driving to Lagos[6] one morning a white cockerel flew out of the dusk and smashed itself against my windscreen. A mile further I came across a motor accident and a freshly dead man in the smash.

Traveller, you must set out
At dawn. And wipe your feet upon
The dog-nose wetness of earth.

Let sunrise quench your lamps, and watch
Faint brush pricklings in the sky light
Cottoned feet to break the early earthworm
On the hoe. Now shadows stretch with sap
Not twilight's death and sad prostration

1. Buttons on old British telephones.
2. Mailbox.
3. Double-decker bus.
4. Reddish brown.
5. Related to study of the spectrum.
6. Largest city in Nigeria.

This soft kindling, soft receding breeds
Racing joys and apprehensions for
A naked day, burdened hulks retract,
Stoop to the mist in faceless throng
To wake the silent markets—swift, mute
Processions on grey byways. . . .

On this
Counterpane, it was—
Sudden winter at the death
Of dawn's lone trumpeter, cascades
Of white feather-flakes, but it proved
A futile rite. Propitiation sped
Grimly on, before.

The right foot for joy, the left, dread
And the mother prayed, Child
May you never walk
When the road waits, famished.[7]

Traveller you must set forth
At dawn
I promise marvels of the holy hour
Presages as the white cock's flapped
Perverse impalement—as who would dare
The wrathful wings of man's Progression. . . .

But such another Wraith! Brother,
Silenced in the startled hug of
Your invention—is this mocked grimace
This closed contortion—I?

1967

Around Us, Dawning

Jet flight

This beast was fashioned well; it prowls
The rare selective heights
And spurns companionship with bird

Wings are tipped in sulphurs
Scouring grey recesses of the void
To a linear flare of dawns

Red haloes through the ports wreathe us
Passive martyrs, bound to a will of rotors

7. African proverb.

Yielding ours,
To the alien mote
The hidden ache . . . when
Death makes a swift descent

The mountains range in spire on spire
Lances at the bold carbuncle[8]
On the still night air. I am light honed

To a still point in the incandescent
Onrush, a fine ash in the beast's sudden
Dessication when the sun explodes.

1967

Massacre, October '66

Written in Tegel[9]

Shards of sunlight touch me here
Shredded in willows. Through stained-glass
Fragments on the lake I sought to reach
A mind at silt-bed

The lake stayed cold
I swam in an October flush of dying leaves
The gardener's labour flew in seasoned scrolls
Lettering the wind

Swept from painted craft
A mockery of waves remarked this idyll sham
I trod on acorns; each shell's detonation
Aped the skull's uniqueness.

Came sharper reckoning—
This favoured food of hogs cannot number high
As heads still harshly crop to whirlwinds
I have briefly fled

The oak rains a hundred more
A kind confusion to arithmetics of death:
Time to watch autumn the removal man
Dust down rare canvases

8. Skin inflammation.
9. Amidst the political turmoil preceding the Nigerian Civil War, thousands of members of the Igbo ethnic group were slaughtered in northern Nigeria by the Hausa army between July and October 1966. Tegel is in Germany.

To let a loud resolve of passion
Fly to a squirrel, burnished light and copper fur
A distant stance without the lake's churchwindows
And for a stranger, love.

A host of acorns fell, silent
As they are silenced all, whose laughter
Rose from such indifferent paths, oh God
They are not strangers all

Whose desecration mocks the word
Of peace—*salaam aleikun*[1]—not strangers any
Brain of thousands pressed asleep to pig fodder—
Shun pork the unholy—cries the priest.

I borrow seasons of an alien land
In brotherhood of ill, pride of race around me
Strewn in sunlit shards. I borrow alien lands
To stay the season of a mind.

1967

Dragonfly at My Windowpane

So when I offer me, a medium as
The windowpane, you beat upon it
Frantic wings against unyielding tolerance?

Yet did I envy this, the unambiguous pane
And thought it clarity enough. But you must
War upon it, wings of frosted light,

And charge in thunderclaps? Each dive
Yields proof enough; your parchment shavings read:
Even clarity masks stubborn substance.

And shall this image I present not stay
Its own determined shield? Much dross
Much stone, much jeweled earth and fire

Have fed the stressing of my wall of light.
Let it content you how in me
I yield a stark view of the world, and trust

No inner warp but smudges left
By probing hands, dust of faith-flimsy wings
Distort true vision.

1. Peace be with you (Arabic); a common Islamic greeting. The Hausa ethnic group is predominantly Muslim.

When darkness gathers I may dance
The world in fey[2] reflections; or splay its truths
In a shadow play of doubts.

1988

2. Visionary.

Amiri Baraka
1934–2014

"Let my poems be a graph of me," Amiri Baraka (then LeRoi Jones) wrote in an early poem, "Balboa, the Entertainer," and his first poems find joy in the liberty of art, in the fashioning of works that make their own rules. In 1959, he wrote, in accordance with Charles Olson's concepts of projective verse and field composition, "There cannot be anything I must *fit* the poem into. Everything must be made to fit into the poem. There must not be any preconceived notion or *design* for what the poem ought to be" ("How You Sound??"). Baraka's early poems, which have affinities with Black Mountain and Beat poetry, are personal and questioning. They explore domestic tenderness and satisfaction, though the poet frequently returns to thoughts of his own death.

A transformative visit to Cuba, in 1960, led Baraka to conclude that most of American life was socially useless and that trying to create a multiracial society was pointless. He began to forsake the individualist Beat aesthetic for black nationalism. In *Blues People* (1963), a powerful book about the abiding influence of the blues and the creation of black music in white America, he describes his progressive alienation: "To understand that you are black in a society where black is an extreme liability is one thing, but to understand that it is the *society* that is lacking and impossibly deformed, and not *yourself,* isolates you even more."

Baraka condemned what he called the "superstructure of filth Americans call their way of life" and exhorted his fellow blacks to abandon the American way of life and to work to destroy it ("An Exploration of the Work"). He had once described art as the "most beautiful resolution of energies that in another context might be violent to myself or anyone else," and for a time he wrote his poems to make a life for himself within a hostile society (*San Francisco Chronicle,* August 23, 1964). From the 1960s on, he no longer sought an alternative to violence, and his social passion and his poetry fused. Yet for all the changes in Baraka's political and aesthetic philosophy, his mature poetry displays the improvisatory energy and spontaneity that jazz achieves in music. In their bold leaps of figuration, abrupt tonal shifts from the sardonic to the explosive, rapid runs of stresses, compression of high diction and the vernacular, wild scattering of lines across the page, erratic punctuation, polyphonic voicing, chants and rants and calls, his poems approach the emotional intensity, humor, and resistant anger of post-bebop jazz.

Baraka was born Leroy (later changed to Leroi) Jones on October 7, 1934, in Newark, New Jersey. He was clearly precocious and completed high school two years early. He then entered Howard University, where the poet Sterling Brown was among his teachers. After flunking out of school, he spent two years as a weatherman and gunner in the U. S. Air Force, until he was dishonorably discharged, in 1957, because of his suspected communism. "The Howard thing," Baraka said in a 1964 interview, "let me understand the Negro sickness. They teach you how to pretend to be white. But the

Air Force made me understand the white sickness. It shocked me into realizing what was happening to me and others. By oppressing Negroes, the whites have become oppressors, twisted in that sense of doing bad things to people and justifying them finally, convincing themselves they are right, as people have always convinced themselves."

In 1957, Baraka moved to New York City and joined the bohemian life of lower Manhattan, where his associates included Frank O'Hara and Allen Ginsberg, writers who shared his interest in people living on the edge of American society. An active figure in the New York literary underground, he and his first wife, the Jewish Beat writer Hettie Cohen, published *Yugen,* a poetry magazine; he was coeditor of a literary newsletter called *Floating Bear*; and in 1961, he helped found the American Theatre for Poets. He was also a brilliant and iconoclastic jazz reviewer, publishing in *Kulchur* and other magazines. Bebop was still vital in New York, but the "new music" of Ornette Coleman, John Coltrane, and other musicians was radically transforming the harmonies and rhythms of jazz. (Later, Baraka performed and recorded his poetry with leading jazz musicians.)

Baraka was searching for indigenous artistic models in African American jazz and blues, and he sharply criticized black poets who turned to Euro-American models instead of the emotionally charged music of Bessie Smith, Billie Holiday, or Ray Charles ("The Myth of a Negro Literature"). In the mid-1960s, he began to make his reputation as a dramatist. His short play *Dutchman,* an encounter in a subway between a young African American and a white woman that ends in a surprising murder, had a long run off-Broadway. In 1965, deeply disturbed by the assassination of Malcolm X, whose death is mourned in "A Poem for Black Hearts," Baraka left his mixed-race family and Greenwich Village and moved uptown to Harlem. Eager to find a focus for a black community that would use the arts, Baraka founded the Black Arts Repertory Theater/School. In 1966, he moved again, this time to the Newark slums, where he set up a community called Spirit House. In 1967, he adopted the Bantuized Muslim name Imamu ("spiritual leader") Ameer ("blessed") Baraka ("prince"), shortened and modified in the early 1970s to Amiri Baraka. During the Newark riots in the summer of 1967, Baraka was beaten by police, arrested, and charged with carrying a concealed weapon; he was convicted, and to justify the unusually heavy sentence, the judge quoted lines from the prose poem "Black People!": "We must make our own World, man, our own world, and we can not do this unless the white man is dead. Let's get together and kill him my man, let's get to gather the fruit of the sun."

Jailed for contempt, Baraka was eventually acquitted in a retrial. In 1968, he founded the Black Community Development and Defense Organization, a group then composed of a hundred men and fifty women; they wore traditional African dress, spoke Swahili as well as English, and practiced Islam. He played an increasingly important role in Newark's politics, in national black politics, and in relations between the African American community and the newly independent nations of sub-Saharan Africa. In 1974, he denounced black nationalism as racist and embraced Third World socialism. From 1979 to 1999, he taught in the Department of Africana Studies at the State University of New York, Stony Brook. He lived for the remainder of his life in Newark. Central to the Black Arts Movement of the 1960s, he continued to write fiercely witty poems, such as the epigrammatic series *Wise, Why's, Y's,* as well as increasingly elegiac and allusive jazz poems, such as "Monk's World"—a tribute to an idiosyncratic genius and to the music that inspired Baraka throughout his career.

An Agony. As Now

I am inside someone
who hates me. I look
out from his eyes. Smell
what fouled tunes come in
to his breath. Love his
wretched women.

Slits in the metal, for sun. Where
my eyes sit turning, at the cool air
the glance of light, or hard flesh
rubbed against me, a woman, a man,
without shadow, or voice, or meaning.

This is the enclosure (flesh,
where innocence is a weapon. An
abstraction. Touch. (Not mine.
Or yours, if you are the soul I had
and abandoned when I was blind and had
my enemies carry me as a dead man
(if he is beautiful, or pitied.

It can be pain. (As now, as all his
flesh hurts me.) It can be that. Or
pain. As when she ran from me into
that forest.
                    Or pain, the mind
silver spiraled whirled against the
sun, higher than even old men thought
God would be. Or pain. And the other. The
yes. (Inside his books, his fingers. They
are withered yellow flowers and were never
beautiful.) The yes. You will, lost soul, say
'beauty.' Beauty, practiced, as the tree. The
slow river. A white sun in its wet sentences.

Or, the cold men in their gale. Ecstasy. Flesh
or soul. The yes. (Their robes blown. Their bowls
empty. They chant at my heels, not at yours.) Flesh
or soul, as corrupt. Where the answer moves too quickly.
Where the God is a self, after all.)

Cold air blown through narrow blind eyes. Flesh,
white hot metal. Glows as the day with its sun.
It is a human love, I live inside. A bony skeleton
you recognize as words or simple feeling.

But it has no feeling. As the metal, is hot, it is not,
given to love.

It burns the thing
inside it. And that thing
screams.

1964

A Poem for Speculative Hipsters

He had got, finally,
to the forest
of motives. There were no
owls, or hunters. No Connie Chatterleys[1]
resting beautifully
on their backs, having casually
brought socialism
to England.
Only ideas,
and their opposites.
Like,
he was *really*
nowhere.

1964

A Poem for Black Hearts

For Malcolm's[2] eyes, when they broke
the face of some dumb white man, For
Malcolm's hands raised to bless us
all black and strong in his image
of ourselves, For Malcolm's words
fire darts, the victor's tireless
thrusts, words hung above the world
change as it may, he said it, and
for this he was killed, for saying,
and feeling, and being/change, all
collected hot in his heart, For Malcolm's
heart, raising us above our filthy cities,
for his stride, and his beat, and his address
to the grey monsters of the world, For Malcolm's
pleas for your dignity, black men, for your life,
black man, for the filling of your minds
with righteousness. For all of him dead and
gone and vanished from us, and all of him which
clings to our speech black god of our time.

1. The heroine of *Lady Chatterley's Lover,* by the English writer D. H. Lawrence (1885–1930); married to an impotent aristocrat, she finds sexual and spiritual salvation with a working-class lover.

2. Malcolm X (1925–1965), African American leader assassinated by members of the Nation of Islam, an American Muslim organization that Malcolm X had left in 1964.

For all of him, and all of yourself, look up,
black man, quit stuttering and shuffling, look up,
black man, quit whining and stooping, for all of him,
For Great Malcolm a prince of the earth, let nothing in us rest
until we avenge ourselves for his death, stupid animals
that killed him, let us never breathe a pure breath if
we fail, and white men call us faggots till the end of
the earth.

1969

Legacy

(For Blues People)

In the south, sleeping against
the drugstore, growling under
the trucks and stoves, stumbling
through and over the cluttered eyes
of early mysterious night. Frowning
drunk waving moving a hand or lash.
Dancing kneeling reaching out, letting
a hand rest in shadows. Squatting
to drink or pee. Stretching to climb
pulling themselves onto horses near
where there was sea (the old songs
lead you to believe). Riding out
from this town, to another, where
it is also black. Down a road
where people are asleep. Towards
the moon or the shadows of houses.
Towards the songs' pretended sea.

1969

A New Reality Is Better Than a New Movie!

How will it go, crumbling earthquake, towering inferno, juggernaut,[3] volcano, smashup,
in reality, other than the feverish nearreal fantasy of the capitalist flunky film hacks
tho they sense its reality breathing a quake inferno scar on their throat even snorts of
100% pure cocaine cant cancel the cold cut of impending death to this society. On all the

3. Massive force or vehicle that moves forward irresistibly and crushes anything in its path. *The Towering Inferno* is Irwin Allen and John Guillermin's 1974 movie about a skyscraper on fire.

screens of america, the joint blows up every hour and a half for two dollars an fifty cents.
They have taken the niggers out to lunch, for a minute, made us partners (nigger charlie) or
surrogates (boss nigger) for their horror. But just as superafrikan mobutu cannot leopardskinhat his
way out of responsibility for lumumba's death,[4] nor even with his incredible billions rockefeller
cannot even save his pale ho's titties in the crushing weight of things as they really are.
How will it go, does it reach you, getting up, sitting on the side of the bed, getting ready
to go to work. Hypnotized by the machine, and the cement floor, the jungle treachery of trying
to survive with no money in a money world, of making the boss 100,000 for every 200 dollars
you get, and then having his brother get you for the rent, and if you want to buy the car you
helped build, your downpayment paid for it, the rest goes to buy his old lady a foam rubber
rhinestone set of boobies for special occasions when kissinger drunkenly fumbles with
her blouse, forgetting himself.[5]
If you dont like it, what you gonna do about it. That was the question we asked each other, &
still right regularly need to ask. You dont like it? Whatcha gonna do, about it??
The real terror of nature is humanity enraged, the true technicolor spectacle that hollywood
cant record. They cant even show you how you look when you go to work, or when you come back.
They cant even show you thinking or demanding the new socialist reality, its the ultimate tidal
wave. When all over the planet, men and women, with heat in their hands, demand that society
be planned to include the lives and self determination of all the people ever to live. That is
the scalding scenario with a cast of just under two billion that they dare not even whisper.
Its called, "We Want It All . . . The Whole World!"

1976

4. Patrice Lumumba, a leader in the bloody struggle for power that followed the independence of Zaire (formerly the Belgian Congo) was murdered, probably by Belgian operatives, in 1961; the strong-arm president Sese Seko Mobutu was placed in power by the American CIA to restore order.

5. Henry Kissinger (b. 1923), secretary of state under Richard Nixon, was often photographed with attractive women.

FROM WISE, WHY'S, Y'S

Wise I

WHYS (Nobody Knows
The Trouble I Seen)[6]
Trad.

If you ever find
yourself, some where
lost and surrounded
by enemies
who won't let you
speak in your own language
who destroy your statues
& instruments, who ban
your omm bomm ba boom
then you are in trouble
deep trouble
they ban your
own boom ba boom
you in deep deep
trouble

humph!

probably take you several hundred years
to get
out!

Y The Link Will Not Always Be "Missing" #40

The Wise One
Trane[7]

Think of Slavery
as
Educational!

1995

6. African American spiritual.
7. John Coltrane (1926–1967), American jazz musician.

In the Funk World

If Elvis Presley/ is
      King
Who is James Brown,[8]
      God?

1996

Monk's World

'Round Midnight[9]

That street where midnight
is round, the moon flat
& blue, where fire engines solo
& cats stand around & look
is Monk's world

When I last saw him, turning around
      high from 78 RPM,[1] growling
      a landscape of spaced funk

When I last spoke to him, coming out
      the Vanguard,[2] he hipped me to
      my own secrets, like Nat[3]
      he dug the numbers & letters
      blowing through the grass
      initials & invocations of the past

All the questions I asked Monk He
      answered first
      in a beret. Why was
      a high priest[4] staring
      Why were the black keys
      signifying.[5] And who was
      wrapped in common magic
      like a street empty of everything
      except weird birds

The last time Monk smiled I read
      the piano's diary. His fingers
      where he collected yr feelings

8. African American singer (b. 1933), sometimes called the Godfather of Soul. Elvis Presley (1935–1977), white American singer sometimes called the King of Rock and Roll.
9. Composition by American jazz composer and pianist Thelonious Monk (1917–1982).
1. Revolutions per minute, the standard record-playing speed early in Monk's career.
2. The Village Vanguard, a Manhattan jazz club.
3. According to Baraka, Nat Turner (1800–1831), American slave insurrectionist.
4. In the 1940s, Monk was called the High Priest of Bebop.
5. Boasting, playing on (African American vernacular), in addition to standard meanings.

The Bar he circled to underscore
the anonymous laughter of smoke
& posters.

Monk carried equations he danced at you.
What's happening?" We said, as he dipped &
spun. "What's happening?"

"Everything. All the time.
Every googoplex[6]
of a second."

Like a door, he opened, not disappearing
but remaining a distant profile
of intimate revelation.

Oh, man! Monk was digging Trane[7] now
w/o a chaser[8] he drank himself
in. & Trane reported from
the 6th or 7th planet[9] deep in

the Theloniuscape.

Where fire engines screamed the blues
& night had a shiny mouth
& scatted flying things.

1996

6. An immense quantity.
7. John Coltrane (1926–1967), American jazz musician.
8. "Straight, No Chaser" is one of Monk's compositions.
9. Five months before his death, Coltrane recorded compositions named after the planets, on *Interstellar Space*.

Charles Wright
b. 1935

In lines from his volume *Black Zodiac* (1997), which won the Pulitzer Prize and the National Book Critics Circle Award, Charles Wright summarizes the central preoccupations of his career: death, memory, landscape, language, and God. "Out of any two thoughts I have, one is devoted to death," he declares, with perhaps some exaggeration ("Meditation on Form and Measure"). Although sly humor often deflects or mutes such thoughts, Wright broods over death, dying, and the dead almost with religious intensity. In "Homage to Paul Cézanne," he adapts the Postimpressionist painter's obsessive focus and layered images as a strategy for meditating from multiple perspectives on the omnipresent and invisible dead: "The dead are with us to stay. / Their shadows rock in the back yard, so pure, so black, / Between the oak tree and the porch." The dead are in the backyard, in the night sky, under our feet, in our clothes. "Their sighs," he writes memorably, "are gaps in the wind."

"I think of landscape incessantly," Wright announces in "Disjecta Membra," but for this landscape poet, the natural world is not a thing in itself but an epitaph of absent presences. It clamors with dead people he has known, dead poets he has read, dead selves he has been in the past, and a dead God he can neither recover nor surrender. Gazing upon the Italian, Appalachian, and Californian landscapes where he has lived, Wright is visited by the ghostly lines of earlier poets—Dante, Emily Dickinson, Gerard Manley Hopkins, Ezra Pound, and T. S. Eliot. Like the Romantics, he also sees this landscape as a tomb for his past. "Memory is a cemetery / I've visited once or twice," he notes with self-deprecating understatement ("Meditation on Form and Measure"). "Journal and landscape," he states more boldly in "Apologia Pro Vita Sua," "I tried to resuscitate both, breath and blood, / making them whole again // Through language." Making dazzling use of the pathetic fallacy and other forms of anthropomorphism and metaphor, Wright weaves together the outer world and the memory-studded river of interior consciousness. Scrutinizing the visible world for traces, signs, emblems not only of his past selves but of the God that once animated it, he writes about the withdrawal of divinity with a mixture of eschatological yearning and postreligious melancholy. If Wright's poems resemble journals, recording the quicksilver flow of his innermost thoughts, they are also what he called in a 1983 interview "little prayer wheels" and "wafers." They mournfully summon the divinity that once inhabited nature but now seems to have left it an empty husk.

Wright was born on August 25, 1935, in Pickwick Dam, Tennessee, where his father worked as a civil engineer for the Tennessee Valley Authority. Growing up in east Tennessee and west North Carolina, he attended Episcopal schools in North Carolina as a teenager, but abandoned orthodox religion after graduation. Evangelical Christianity, hymns, and country music were among his formative experiences. He graduated from Davidson College in 1957 and then served in the U.S. Army's Intelligence Service from 1957 to 1961, three years of which he spent in Verona, Italy. Reading Pound's poetry for the first time in 1959 in the context of its Italian settings inspired Wright to begin to write poetry. Pound's richly sonorous free verse, dropped lines, juxtapositions of images, East Asian interests, and lapidary compression—especially in the hauntingly elegiac *Pisan Cantos*—became abiding influences. Attending the University of Iowa's Writers' Workshop from 1961 to 1963, Wright studied with Donald Justice, befriended Mark Strand, and began to translate Italian poetry, in particular the work of Eugenio Montale. Early in his career, he was associated with the Deep Image poetry of Robert Bly, W. S. Merwin, and James Wright, and he shared the surrealist proclivity of other leading American poets born in the 1930s, including Strand and Charles Simic. After a few more years of study and teaching in Italy and Iowa, he taught at the University of California at Irvine for more than twenty years; he took a position at the University of Virginia in 1983.

Wright's work straddles the divide between the concision of haiku and the rambling openness of the long poem. It has the intensity of lyric and the unstructured freedom of a journal, the impersonality of aphorism and the inward expressiveness of a diary. Pithy, compressed, and musical, individual lines are crafted with jewel-like precision, as if to stand as nearly self-sufficient units. Though balanced and epigrammatic, they are embedded within poems that radiate outward, expanding to encompass great stretches of consciousness and observation, tonal highs and lows, and varying levels of diction, from the colloquial to the sublime. "A kind of American sprawl of a poem," Wright commented to the *Paris Review*, acknowledging his poetry's omnivorous, loose-limbed appearance, but "with a succession of sufficient checks and balances. Epiphanic and oceanic, at once. Intensive and extensive."

Since Wright eschews fixed meter and rhyme, the organizing principles behind his porous yet tightly structured poetry are not immediately self-evident. He has referred to the seven-syllable line as his "ur-line," and most of his lines have an odd number of syllables (he counts a dropped line as part of the same line). The numerological patterning of his work extends from this micro level of syllable count to the number of lines within stanzas, the number of stanzas or sections within poems, the mirror relations among poems within a volume, and even the ordering of books across the career. Thinking of each three of his books as a trilogy, which in turn becomes part of a "trilogy of trilogies," Wright adapts the inferno-purgatorio-paradiso structure of Dante's *Divine Comedy*.

Wright uses such architectonics as scaffolding. With its sensuous details, rich sonic patterning, and quick turns of phrase, his poetry is anything but a sterile exercise in numerology. His rhythms are strongly cadenced, including Hopkins-like spondees, sometimes in hyphenated compounds ("side-kick," "dream-light," "jump-start"), often followed by a rapid rush of unaccented syllables. His writing is highly metaphorical, deliberately artificial, even baroque, sublimating narrative and overt reference. His figurative language has a hallucinatory power and clarity, from his early description of twilight as flaring "like a white disease" ("Blackwater Mountain") to his later evocation of a dogwood's roots as his "mother's hair" ("Apologia Pro Vita Sua"). As if effortlessly, Wright can shift linguistic registers from biblical repetition, ecclesiastical diction, and transcendental abstraction to the down-home, deadpan, folksy interjection, and back again. "The meat of the sacrament is invisible meat and a ghostly substance. / I'll say. / Like any visible thing, / I'm always attracted downward, and soon to be killed and assimilated" ("Apologia Pro Vita Sua").

Blackwater Mountain

That time of evening, weightless and disparate,
When the loon cries, when the small bass
Jostle the lake's reflections, when
The green of the oak begins
To open its robes to the dark, the green
Of water to offer itself to the flames,
When lily and lily pad
Husband the last light
Which flares like a white disease, then disappears:
This is what I remember. And this:

The slap of the jacklight[1] on the cove;
The freeze-frame of ducks
Below us; your shots; the wounded flop
And skid of one bird to the thick brush;
The moon of your face in the fire's glow;
The cold; the darkness. Young,
Wanting approval, what else could I do?
And did, for two hours, waist-deep in the lake,
The thicket as black as death,
Without success or reprieve, try.

The stars over Blackwater Mountain
Still dangle and flash like hooks, and ducks

1. Light used for hunting or fishing at night.

Coast on the evening water;
The foliage is like applause.
I stand where we stood before and aim
My flashlight down to the lake. A black duck
Explodes to my right, hangs, and is gone.
He shows me the way to you;
He shows me the way to a different fire
Where you, black moon, warm your hands.

1973

Stone Canyon Nocturne

Ancient of Days, old friend, no one believes you'll come back.
No one believes in his own life anymore.

The moon, like a dead heart, cold and unstartable, hangs by a thread
At the earth's edge,
Unfaithful at last, splotching the ferns and the pink shrubs.

In the other world, children undo the knots in their tally strings.
They sing songs, and their fingers blear.

And here, where the swan hums in his socket, where bloodroot
And belladonna insist on our comforting,
Where the fox in the canyon wall empties our hands, ecstatic for
more,

Like a bead of clear oil the Healer revolves through the night wind,
Part eye, part tear, unwilling to recognize us.

1977

Clear Night

Clear night, thumb-top of a moon, a back-lit sky.
Moon-fingers lay down their same routine
On the side deck and the threshold, the white keys and the black keys.
Bird hush and bird song. A cassia flower falls.

I want to be bruised by God.
I want to be strung up in a strong light and singled out.
I want to be stretched, like music wrung from a dropped seed.
I want to be entered and picked clean.

And the wind says "What?" to me.
And the castor beans, with their little earrings of death, say "What?"
to me.

And the stars start out on their cold slide through the dark.
And the gears notch and the engines wheel.

1977

Homage to Paul Cézanne[2]

At night, in the fish-light of the moon, the dead wear our white shirts
To stay warm, and litter the fields.
We pick them up in the mornings, dewy pieces of paper and scraps of
cloth.
Like us, they refract themselves. Like us,
They keep on saying the same thing, trying to get it right.
Like us, the water unsettles their names.

Sometimes they lie like leaves in their little arks, and curl up at the edges.
Sometimes they come inside, wearing our shoes, and walk
From mirror to mirror.
Or lie in our beds with their gloves off
And touch our bodies. Or talk
In a corner. Or wait like envelopes on a desk.

They reach up from the ice plant.
They shuttle their messengers through the oat grass.
Their answers rise like rust on the stalks and the spidery leaves.

We rub them off our hands.

•

Each year the dead grow less dead, and nudge
Close to the surface of all things.
They start to remember the silence that brought them there.
They start to recount the gain in their soiled hands.

Their glasses let loose, and grain by grain return to the river bank.
They point to their favorite words
Growing around them, revealed as themselves for the first time:
They stand close to the meanings and take them in.

They stand there, vague and without pain,
Under their fingernails an unreturnable dirt.
They stand there and it comes back,
The music of everything, syllable after syllable

2. French Postimpressionist painter (1839–1906).

Out of the burning chair, out of the beings of light.
It all comes back.
And what they repeat to themselves, and what they repeat to themselves,
Is the song that our fathers sing.

•

In steeps and sighs,
The ocean explains itself, backing and filling
What spaces it can't avoid, spaces
In black shoes, their hands clasped, their eyes teared at the edges:
We watch from the high hillside,
The ocean swelling and flattening, the spaces
Filling and emptying, horizon blade
Flashing the early afternoon sun.

The dead are constant in
The white lips of the sea.
Over and over, through clenched teeth, they tell
Their story, the story each knows by heart:
Remember me, speak my name.
When the moon tugs at my sleeve,
When the body of water is raised and becomes the body of light,
Remember me, speak my name.

•

The dead are a cadmium blue.[3]
We spread them with palette knives in broad blocks and planes.

We layer them stroke by stroke
In steps and ascending mass, in verticals raised from the earth.

We choose, and layer them in,
Blue and a blue and a breath,

Circle and smudge, cross-beak and buttonhook,
We layer them in. We squint hard and terrace them line by line.

And so we are come between, and cry out,
And stare up at the sky and its cloudy panes,

And finger the cypress twists.
The dead understand all this, and keep in touch,

Rustle of hand to hand in the lemon trees,
Flags, and the great sifts of anger

3. Nonexistent shade of paint; Wright's coinage, by analogy with compounds such as cadmium red and cadmium yellow.

To powder and nothingness.
The dead are a cadmium blue, and they understand.

•

The dead are with us to stay.
Their shadows rock in the back yard, so pure, so black,
Between the oak tree and the porch.

Over our heads they're huge in the night sky.
In the tall grass they turn with the zodiac.
Under our feet they're white with the snows of a thousand years.

They carry their colored threads and baskets of silk
To mend our clothes, making us look right,
Altering, stitching, replacing a button, closing a tear.
They lie like tucks in our loose sleeves, they hold us together.

They blow the last leaves away.
They slide like an overflow into the river of heaven.
Everywhere they are flying.

The dead are a sleight and a fade
We fall for, like flowering plums, like white coins from the rain.
Their sighs are gaps in the wind.

•

The dead are waiting for us in our rooms,
Little globules of light
In one of the far corners, and close to the ceiling, hovering, thinking our
thoughts.

Often they'll reach a hand down,
Or offer a word, and ease us out of our bodies to join them in theirs.
We look back at our other selves on the bed.

We look back and we don't care and we go.

And thus we become what we've longed for,
past tense and otherwise,
A BB, a disc of light,
song without words.
And refer to ourselves
In the third person, seeing that other arm
Still raised from the bed, fingers like licks and flames in the boned air.

Only to hear that it's not time.
Only to hear that we must re-enter and lie still, our arms at rest at our sides,
The voices rising around us like mist

And dew, *it's all right, it's all right, it's all right . . .*

•

The dead fall around us like rain.
They come down from the last clouds in the late light for the last time
And slip through the sod.

They lean uphill and face north.
Like grass,
They bend toward the sea, they break toward the setting sun.

We filigree[4] and we baste.
But what do the dead care for the fringe of words,
Safe in their suits of milk?
What do they care for the honk and flash of a new style?

And who is to say if the inch of snow in our hearts
Is rectitude enough?

Spring picks the locks of the wind.
High in the night sky the mirror is hauled up and unsheeted.
In it we twist like stars.

Ahead of us, through the dark, the dead
Are beating their drums and stirring the yellow leaves.

•

We're out here, our feet in the soil, our heads craned up at the sky,
The stars streaming and bursting behind the trees.

At dawn, as the clouds gather, we watch
The mountain glide from the east on the valley floor,
Coming together in starts and jumps.
Behind their curtain, the bears
Amble across the heavens, serene as black coffee . . .

Whose unction can intercede for the dead?
Whose tongue is toothless enough to speak their piece?

What we are given in dreams we write as blue paint,
Or messages to the clouds.
At evening we wait for the rain to fall and the sky to clear.
Our words are words for the clay, uttered in undertones,
Our gestures salve for the wind.

We sit out on the earth and stretch our limbs,
Hoarding the little mounds of sorrow laid up in our hearts.

1981

4. Embellish.

Laguna Blues

It's Saturday afternoon at the edge of the world.
White pages lift in the wind and fall.
Dust threads, cut loose from the heart, float up and fall.
Something's off-key in my mind.
Whatever it is, it bothers me all the time.

It's hot, and the wind blows on what I have had to say.
I'm dancing a little dance.
The crows pick up a thermal that angles away from the sea.
I'm singing a little song.
Whatever it is, it bothers me all the time.

It's Saturday afternoon and the crows glide down,
Black pages that lift and fall.
The castor beans and the pepper plant trundle their weary heads.
Something's off-key and unkind.
Whatever it is, it bothers me all the time.

1981

From Apologia Pro Vita Sua[5]

I

How soon we come to road's end—
Failure, our two-dimensional side-kick, flat dream-light,
Won't jump-start or burn us in,

Dogwood insidious in its constellations of part-charred cross points,
Spring's via Dolorosa[6]
                                        flashed out in a dread profusion,
Nowhere to go but up, nowhere to turn, dead world-weight,

They've gone and done it again,
                                                    dogwood,
Spring's sap-crippled, arthritic, winter-weathered, myth limb,
Whose roots are my mother's hair.

Landscape's a lever of transcendence—
                                                            jack-wedge it here,
Or here, and step back,
Heave, and a light, a little light, will nimbus your going forth:

5. A defense of his life (Latin). Title of famous 1864 autobiography by theologian Cardinal John Henry Newman (1801–1890).

6. Way of suffering (Latin). Street in Jerusalem said to follow the path along which Jesus carried the cross.

The dew bead, terminal bead, opens out
onto a great radiance,
Sun's square on magnolia leaf
Offers us entrance—
who among us will step forward,

Camellia brown boutonnieres
Under his feet, plum branches under his feet, white sky, white noon,
Church bells like monk's mouths tonguing the hymn?

Journal and landscape
—Discredited form, discredited subject matter—
I tried to resuscitate both, breath and blood,
making them whole again

Through language, strict attention—
Verona mi fe', disfecemi Verona,[7] the song goes.
I've hummed it, I've bridged the break

To no avail.
April. The year begins beyond words,
Beyond myself and the image of myself, beyond
Moon's ice and summer's thunder. All that.

The meat of the sacrament is invisible meat and a ghostly substance.
I'll say.
Like any visible thing,
I'm always attracted downward, and soon to be killed and assimilated.

Vessel of life, it's said, vessel of life, brought to naught,
Then gathered back to what's visible.
That's it, fragrance of spring like lust in the blossom-starred orchard,

The shapeless shape of darkness starting to seep through and emerge,
The seen world starting to tilt,
Where I sit the still, unwavering point
under that world's waves.

How like the past the clouds are,
Building and disappearing along the horizon,
Inflecting the mountains,
laying their shadows under our feet

7. Verona made me, Verona undid me (Italian). Cf. Dante's *Purgatorio* 5.133, in which two different cities play the formative roles in the speaker's life story: "Siena mi fe', disfecemi Maremma." Pound's *Hugh Selwyn Mauberley* (1920) quotes and Eliot's *Waste Land* (1922) alludes to this line from Dante.

For us to cross over on.
Out of their insides fire falls, ice falls,
What we remember that still remembers us, earth and air fall.

Neither, however, can resurrect or redeem us,
Moving, as both must, ever away toward opposite corners.
Neither has been where we're going,
                    bereft of an attitude.

Amethyst,[8] crystal transparency,
                    Maya and Pharaoh ring,
Malocchio, set against witchcraft,
Lightning and hailstorm, birthstone, savior from drunkenness.

Purple, color of insight, clear sight,
Color of memory—
                    violet, that's for remembering,[9]
Star-crystals scattered across the penumbra,[1] hard stars.

Who can distinguish darkness from the dark, light from light,
Subject matter from story line,
                    the part from the whole
When whole is part of the part and part is all of it?

Lonesomeness. Morandi, Cézanne, it's all about lonesomeness.
And Rothko. Especially Rothko.[2]
Separation from what heals us
                    beyond painting, beyond art.

Words and paint, black notes, white notes.
Music and landscape; music, landscape and sentences.
Gestures for which there is no balm, no intercession.

Two tone fields, horizon a line between abysses,
Generally white, always speechless.
Rothko could choose either one to disappear into. And did.

Perch'io no spero di tornar giammai, ballatetta, in Toscana,[3]
Not as we were the first time,
                    not as we'll ever be again.
Such snowflakes of memory, they fall nowhere but there.

8. Lines 57–60 describe properties and uses of amethyst, a semiprecious stone thought to ward off evil and drunkenness. *Maya:* indigenous people of southern Mexico and Central America. *Malocchio:* evil eye (Italian).
9. Cf. Ophelia's final appearance in *Hamlet* 4.5: "There's rosemary, that's for remembrance."
1. Shaded area of Earth or the moon experiencing partial phase of an eclipse.
2. Mark Rothko (1903–1970): American abstract expressionist painter noted for works consisting of large fields of color. Giorgio Morandi (1890–1964): Italian still-life painter. Paul Cézanne (1839–1906): French Postimpressionist painter.
3. Because I never hope to return, ballatetta, to Toscana (Italian); a line from the Italian poet Guido di Cavalcanti (c. 1255–1300). *Ballatetta:* small ballet. Eliot echoes this line in his "Ash Wednesday": "Because I do not hope to turn again."

Absorbed in remembering, we cannot remember—
Exile's anthem, O stiff heart,
Thingless we came into the world and thingless we leave.

Every important act is wordless—
to slip from the right way,
To fail, still accomplishes something.
Even a good thing remembered, however, is not as good as not remembering at all.

Time is the source of all good,
time the engenderer
Of entropy and decay.
Time the destroyer, our only-begetter and advocate.

For instance, my fingernail,
so pink, so amplified,
In the half-dark, for instance,
These force-fed dogwood blossoms, green-leafed, defused,
limp on their long branches.

St. Stone,[4] say a little prayer for me,
grackles and jay in the black gum,
Drowse of the peony head,
Dandelion globes luminous in the last light, more work to be done . . .

1997

Stray Paragraphs in February, Year of the Rat[5]

East of town, the countryside unwrinkles and smooths out
Unctuously toward the tidewater and gruff Atlantic.
A love of landscape's a true affection for regret, I've found,
Forever joined, forever apart,
outside us yet ourselves.

Renunciation, it's hard to learn, is now our ecstasy.
However, if God were still around,
he'd swallow our sighs in his nothingness.

The dregs of the absolute are slow sift in my blood,
Dead branches down after high winds, dead yard grass and undergrowth—
The sure accumulation of all that's not revealed
Rises like snow in my bare places,
cross-whipped and openmouthed.

4. In Matthew 16.18, Jesus gives Simon the name Peter because he will form the foundation of the Church (*petra* is Latin for stone).
5. Year of the Chinese calendar.

Our lives can't be lived in flames.
Our lives can't be lit like saints' hearts,
seared between heaven and earth.

February, old head-turner, cut us some slack, grind of bone
On bone, such melancholy music.
Lift up that far corner of landscape,
there, toward the west.
Let some of the deep light in, the arterial kind.

1998

Mary Oliver
b. 1935

"When it's over," Mary Oliver writes, projecting from beyond the grave, "I want to say: all my life / I was a bride married to amazement. / I was the bridegroom, taking the world into my arms" ("When Death Comes"). An ecstatic admirer of nature, Oliver celebrates flora and fauna—berries and goldenrods, snakes and egrets—with the ardor of a mystic. In an age of irony, when an arch, postmodern knowingness marks much contemporary poetry, Oliver's is an earnest and impassioned voice, hymning the multiplicitous life force, "the light at the center of every cell" ("The Black Snake").

Oliver renews the Romantic and Transcendentalist impulse to inhabit nature as an invisible observer, Ralph Waldo Emerson's "transparent eyeball," or what she calls a "rich / lens of attention" ("Entering the Kingdom"). Sometimes, she seems to want to incorporate nature within her body and identity, devouring and becoming its otherness, as she devours the blackberries in the poem "August." Her reverence for nature doesn't deter her from anthropomorphism, and so a hawk becomes "an admiral, / its profile / distinguished with sideburns" ("Hawk"). Her wager is that apt metaphors for nature—the black snake as "an old bicycle tire"—renew our attention to its beauty and particularity ("The Black Snake"). Through various forms of figurative language (personification, metaphor, the pathetic fallacy), Oliver humanizes the natural and yet also animalizes the human, her poems poised on the borderline between these worlds.

Born on September 10, 1935, in Cleveland, Ohio, educated at Ohio State University and Vassar College, Oliver settled in New England, the cradle of American nature writing. She won the Pulitzer Prize in 1984 and the National Book Award in 1992. Her literary lineage can be traced back to the New England nature poetry of Robert Frost, the animal poetry of Marianne Moore and Elizabeth Bishop, the rhapsodies of Edna St. Vincent Millay and Walt Whitman, ultimately to the naive visionary stances of William Blake and William Wordsworth. Seeking immediacy, she describes nature with spare diction, free (but skillfully enjambed) verse in regular stanzas, and verbs in the present tense or present participles ("coiling and flowing"). Modulating rhythm and syntax to build to an often climactic ending, Oliver would lead us into nature's energy, cycles, and flux—human animals fused with a nonhuman world.

The Black Snake

When the black snake
flashed onto the morning road,
and the truck could not swerve—
death, that is how it happens.

Now he lies looped and useless
as an old bicycle tire.
I stop the car
and carry him into the bushes.

He is as cool and gleaming
as a braided whip, he is as beautiful and quiet
as a dead brother.
I leave him under the leaves

and drive on, thinking
about *death:* its suddenness,
its terrible weight,
its certain coming. Yet under

reason burns a brighter fire, which the bones
have always preferred.
It is the story of endless good fortune.
It says to oblivion: not me!

It is the light at the center of every cell.
It is what sent the snake coiling and flowing forward
happily all spring through the green leaves before
he came to the road.

1979

August

When the blackberries hang
swollen in the woods, in the brambles
nobody owns, I spend

all day among the high
branches, reaching
my ripped arms, thinking

of nothing, cramming
the black honey of summer
into my mouth; all day my body

accepts what it is. In the dark
creeks that run by there is
this thick paw of my life darting among

the black bells, the leaves; there is
this happy tongue.

1983

Hawk

This morning
the hawk
rose up
out of the meadow's browse[1]

and swung over the lake—
it settled
on the small black dome
of a dead pine,

alert as an admiral,
its profile
distinguished with sideburns
the color of smoke,

and I said: remember
this is not something
of the red fire, this is
heaven's fistful

of death and destruction,
and the hawk hooked
one exquisite foot
onto a last twig

to look deeper
into the yellow reeds
along the edges of the water
and I said: remember

the tree, the cave,
the white lily of resurrection,[2]
and that's when it simply lifted
its golden feet and floated

1. Tender shoots and twigs of shrubbery that are food for animals.

2. Symbols of Jesus' crucifixion ("the tree"), burial ("the cave"), and resurrection ("the white lily").

into the wind, belly-first,
  and then it cruised along the lake—
    all the time its eyes fastened
      harder than love on some

unimportant rustling in the
  yellow reeds—and then it
    seemed to crouch high in the air, and then it
      turned into a white blade, which fell.

1992

MARGE PIERCY
b. 1936

Indignation and rage prompted Marge Piercy into poetry. She was a determined participant in the succession of political movements that defined her generation—the civil rights movement, the antiwar movement, and the feminist movement. For Piercy, as for many of her contemporaries, the personal and the political were inseparable. An exemplary early work, "Learning Experience," is as poetically effective as it is overtly political, recounting a teacher's observations of a boy on the verge of being drafted. Repeated words and phrases, trademark strategies of Piercy's, help create a mood of futility, boredom, and doom ("in Gary," "in Gary," "in Gary"). Characteristically vivid similes further realize the atmosphere: "in boredom thick and greasy as vegetable shortening." Her simple diction, blunt syntax, and colloquial speech ("I am supposed / to teach him to think a little on demand") draw the reader in before she whips out the poem's stinger: "tomorrow he will try and fail his license to live."

Piercy's feminism is well served by her sardonic wit. In "The Cast Off," a paean to various kinds of openings, from can-openers to zippers, Piercy humorously lists the many clothes that a Victorian lady must shed to make love, exclaiming at the end that the lady "still wants to!" Many of Piercy's poems celebrate nature and love. Like Walt Whitman, she rhapsodically hymns sexual desire and rebirth, as in such poems as "Moonburn" and "The Sky Changes." Female lust, embraced and affirmed, generates a litany of vivid images, which she has called "the rich suggestive stuff of poems." Piercy is unsentimental yet tender.

She was born on March 31, 1936, into a working-class family in Detroit. Proud of her Jewish heritage, she has written liturgy used in Reconstructionist and Reform congregations. Although she often takes an antiacademic stance, Piercy received a B.A. from the University of Michigan and an M.A. from Northwestern University, and she has held various teaching positions. In addition to numerous volumes of poetry, she has published many novels, her best-known the utopian-feminist *Woman on the Edge of Time* (1976). When she writes poetry, she has said, she feels her ordinary life fall away: "I may be dealing with my own anger, my humiliation, my passion, my pleasure; but once I am working with it in a poem, it becomes molten ore. It becomes 'not me.' " Writing poetry is, thus, "so strangely personal and so impersonal at once" (*New York Times,* December 20, 1999).

The Cyclist

Eleven-thirty and hot.
Cotton air.
Dry hands cupped.
The shadow of an empty chandelier
swings on a refrigerator door.
In the street a voice is screaming.
Your head scurries with ants.
Anyone's arms drip with your sweat,
anyone's pliant belly
absorbs your gymnastic thrusts
as your fury subsides into butter.
You are always in combat with questionnaires.
You are always boxing headless dolls
of cherry pudding.
You are the tedious marksman in a forest of thighs,
you with tomcat's shrapnel memory
and irritable eyes.
Tenderness is a mosquito on your arm.
Your hands are calloused with careless touch.
You believe in luck and a quick leap forward
that does not move you.
You rub your sore pride into moist bodies
and pedal off, slightly displeased.

1969

Learning Experience

The boy sits in the classroom
in Gary, in the United States, in NATO, in SEATO[1]
in the thing-gorged belly of the sociobeast
in fluorescent light in slowly moving time
in boredom thick and greasy as vegetable shortening.
The classroom has green boards and ivory blinds,
the desks are new and the teachers not so old.
I have come out on the train from Chicago to talk
about dangling participles. I am supposed
to teach him to think a little on demand.
The time of tomorrow's draft exam[2] is written on the board.
The boy yawns and does not want to be in the classroom in Gary
where the furnaces that consumed his father seethe rusty smoke
and pour cascades of nerve-bright steel
while the slag goes out in little dumpcars smoking,

1. Gary, Indiana, is a large, steel-producing city; NATO and SEATO are the North Atlantic Treaty Organization and Southeast Asia Treaty Organization; the United States is a signatory to both treaties. SEATO was disbanded in 1977.
2. Examination that will exempt him from being drafted into the army.

but even less does he want to be in Today's Action Army
in Vietnam, in the Dominican Republic, in Guatemala,
in death that hurts.
In him are lectures on small groups, Jacksonian democracy,
French irregular verbs, the names of friends
around him in the classroom in Gary in the pillshaped afternoon
where tomorrow he will try and fail his license to live.

1969

The Cast Off

This is a day to celebrate can-
openers, those lantern-jawed long-tailed
humping tools that cut through what keeps
us from what we need: a can of beans
trapped in its armor taunts the nails
and teeth of a hungry woman.

Today let us hear hurrahs for zippers,
those small shark teeth that part
politely to let us at what we want;
the tape on packages that unlock
us birthday presents; envelopes
we slit to thaw the frozen
words on the tundra[3] of paper.

Today let us praise the small
rebirths, the emerging groundhog
from the sodden burrow; the nut
picked from the broken fortress of walnut
shell, itself pried from the oily fruit
shaken from the high turreted
city of the tree.

Today let us honor the safe whose door
hangs ajar; the champagne bottle
with its cork bounced off the ceiling
and into the soup tureen; the Victorian lady
in love who has removed her hood, her cloak,
her laced boots, her stockings, her overdress,
her underdress, her wool petticoat, her linen
petticoats, her silk petticoats, her whalebone
corset, her bustle, her chemise, her drawers, and
who still wants to! Today let us praise the cast
that finally opens, slit neatly in two
like a dinosaur egg, and out at last
comes somewhat hairier, powdered in dead skin

3. Arctic or subarctic treeless plain.

but still beautiful, the lost for months
body of my love.

1980

Moonburn

I stayed under the moon too long.
I am silvered with lust.

Dreams flick like minnows through my eyes.
My voice is trees tossing in the wind.

I loose myself like a flock of blackbirds
storming into your face.

My lightest touch leaves blue prints,
bruises on your mind.

Desire sandpapers your skin
so thin I read the veins and arteries

maps of routes I will travel
till I lodge in your spine.

The night is our fur.
We curl inside it licking.

1997

Lucille Clifton
1936–2010

In her many books of poetry, essays, autobiography, and children's stories, Lucille Clifton affirms and resists. She celebrated African American culture, especially black womanhood, and she protested the injustices and degradations inflicted on it by the larger culture. As a poet, she braved the difficulties of personal loss, of racial and cultural intolerance, yet her poetry hums with prophetic assurance, vision, and candor. It is by turns humorous, angry, elegiac, and radiantly hopeful. Delighting in the wonders of everyday experience in the present, Clifton listened for the silences and absences in official chronicles of the African American past, which she assimilated to her personal, even bodily experience. "History doesn't go away," she declared in an interview with Bill Moyers. "The past isn't back there, the past is *here* too." Intensely personal and yet collectivist, Clifton's poetry bridges the gap between what is sometimes classified as "confessional poetry" (poetry of intimate disclosure) and "identity poetry" (poetry about sociocultural group experience). In poems that recall Walt Whitman in their metaphysical exuberance, Clifton embraces the interwovenness of all things, whether food, bodies, rivers, or family histories.

Like such precursors as Langston Hughes and Gwendolyn Brooks, Clifton wrote in a spare, economical style that conceals its artistry and complexity. Her colloquial language resonates with the rhetorical patterns, cadences, and diction of the Bible and those of African American speech, oratory, and song. Poems such as "at the cemetery, walnut grove plantation, south carolina, 1989" are carefully structured around a series of alternations—between shorter and longer lines, shorter and longer verse paragraphs, repeated and varied phrases—that invoke African American call and response, building cadences that sound like prayer. Clifton's figurative language is vivid and often playful, as when she apostrophizes her uterus as "my estrogen kitchen, / my black bag of desire" ("poem to my uterus"), or her menstrual period as a "hussy" in a "red dress" who has caused much trouble but seems splendid in retrospect ("to my last period"). Clifton's poetry is terse, but rich with meaning.

Thelma Lucille Sayles was born in Depew, New York, where her father worked in the steel mills and her mother in a laundry. She was educated at Howard University and Fredonia State Teachers College. She married Fred Clifton in 1958; worked as a claims clerk in Buffalo, New York; and served as a literature assistant in the U.S. Office of Education, in Washington, D.C. She published her first collection of poems in 1969. Honored as Maryland's poet laureate (1976–85), she taught at Coppin State College, in Baltimore; Columbia University; the University of California, Santa Cruz; and St. Mary's College of Maryland. In her family history, two female ancestors were of great significance to Clifton: her great-great-grandmother Caroline, a Dahomey, or west-central African, girl kidnapped by slave traders, and her great-grandmother Lucille, her namesake and the first woman legally hanged in Virginia (she had murdered the white father of her only son). Clifton wrote frankly about being an incest survivor. She raised six children, whom she credited with inspiring her books of children's stories. In 2000, she won the National Book Award for poetry.

[still]

still
it was nice
when the scissors man come round
running his wheel
rolling his wheel
and the sparks shooting
out in the dark
across the lot
and over to the white folks' section

still
it was nice
in the light of maizie's store
to watch the wheel
and catch the wheel—
fire spinning in the air

and our edges
and our points
sharpening good as anybody's

1969

cutting greens

curling them around
i hold their bodies in obscene embrace
thinking of everything but kinship.
collards and kale
strain against each strange other
away from my kissmaking hand and
the iron bedpot.
the pot is black,
the cutting board is black,
my hand,
and just for a minute
the greens roll black under the knife,
and the kitchen twists dark on its spine
and i taste in my natural appetite
the bond of live things everywhere.

1974

homage to my hips

these hips are big hips
they need space to
move around in.
they don't fit into little
petty places. these hips
are free hips.
they don't like to be held back.
these hips have never been enslaved,
they go where they want to go
they do what they want to do.
these hips are mighty hips.
these hips are magic hips.
i have known them
to put a spell on a man and
spin him like a top!

1980

[i am accused of tending to the past]

i am accused of tending to the past
as if i made it,
as if i sculpted it
with my own hands. i did not.
this past was waiting for me
when i came,
a monstrous unnamed baby,
and i with my mother's itch
took it to breast
and named it
History.
she is more human now,
learning language everyday,
remembering faces, names and dates.
when she is strong enough to travel
on her own, beware, she will.

1991

at the cemetery, walnut grove plantation, south carolina, 1989

among the rocks
at walnut grove
your silence drumming
in my bones,
tell me your names.

nobody mentioned slaves
and yet the curious tools
shine with your fingerprints.
nobody mentioned slaves
but somebody did this work
who had no guide, no stone,
who moulders under rock.

tell me your names,
tell me your bashful names
and i will testify.

the inventory lists ten slaves
but only men were recognized.

among the rocks
at walnut grove
some of these honored dead
were dark
some of these dark
were slaves
some of these slaves
were women
some of them did this
honored work.
tell me your names
foremothers, brothers,
tell me your dishonored names.
here lies
here lies
here lies
here lies
hear

1991

poem to my uterus

you uterus
you have been patient
as a sock
while i have slippered into you
my dead and living children
now
they want to cut you out
stocking i will not need
where i am going
where am i going
old girl
without you
uterus
my bloody print
my estrogen kitchen
my black bag of desire
where can i go
barefoot
without you
where can you go
without me

1991

to my last period

well girl, goodbye,
after thirty-eight years.
thirty-eight years and you
never arrived
splendid in your red dress
without trouble for me
somewhere, somehow.

now it is done,
and i feel just like
the grandmothers who,
after the hussy has gone,
sit holding her photograph
and sighing, *wasn't she*
beautiful? wasn't she beautiful?

1991

cain[1]

so this is what it means
to be an old man;
every member of my body
limp and unsatisfied,
father to sons who never knew
my father, husband to the
sister of the east,
and all night, in the rocky
land of nod,
listening to the thunderous
roll of voices,
unable to tell them where
my brother is.

1993

leda[2] 3

a personal note (re: visitations)

always pyrotechnics;
stars spinning into phalluses
of light, serpents promising
sweetness, their forked tongues
thick and erect, patriarchs of bird

1. First son of Adam and Eve, Cain murdered his younger brother Abel and was exiled to the land of Nod (Genesis 4).

2. In Greek legend, Leda is impregnated by Zeus, who comes to her in the shape of a swan.

exposing themselves in the air.
this skin is sick with loneliness.
You want what a man wants,
next time come as a man
or don't come.

1993

the mississippi river empties into the gulf

and the gulf enters the sea and so forth,
none of them emptying anything,
all of them carrying yesterday
forever on their white tipped backs,
all of them dragging forward tomorrow.
it is the great circulation
of the earth's body, like the blood
of the gods, this river in which the past
is always flowing. every water
is the same water coming round.
everyday someone is standing on the edge
of this river, staring into time,
whispering mistakenly:
only here. only now.

1996

JUNE JORDAN
1936–2002

"Listen to this white man; he is so weird!" exclaims June Jordan, approving Walt Whitman's grand design for a "people's poetry" of the New World, a poetry that affirms "the pride and dignity of the common people." "I too am a descendant of Walt Whitman," she states, his voice "intimate and direct at once," and she goes on to align herself also with other New World poets, such as the Chilean poets Pablo Neruda and Gabriela Mistral and the African American poets Langston Hughes and Margaret Walker (*Passion*). In the introductory poem to *Things That I Do in the Dark,* Jordan writes that her poems are "reaching for you / whoever you are / and / are you ready?" Her lines "are desperate arms for my longing and love," and longing and love are among Jordan's primary subjects.

Jordan came out of the Black Arts Movement, which emphasized address to a black audience, nationalist self-sufficiency, and the fusion of politics and art. The women's movement of the 1960s and 1970s was another early, central influence. In some poems, Jordan is unabashedly polemical and rails against racial, gender, and other forms of oppression across the globe. In others, her approach is less direct, more humorous, though no less biting. In the dramatic monologue "Notes on the Peanut," she impersonates George Washington Carver, comically mocking his monomania through exaggeration, repetition, and the ironic intermingling of the jargons of technology, sales, art, medicine, and social theory. Jordan rejected as disempowering an exclusionary norm of Standard English, and the rhythms and rhetoric of Black English are forcefully alive in a poem such as "The Reception," which closes with the wish for "a true gut-funky blues to make her really dance." Another of Jordan's most effective strategies is the character portrait, and DeLiza, who appears in "DeLiza Spend the Day in the City," is a spunky, streetwise, comic creation: in "A Runaway Lil Bit Poem," DeLiza holds out for the "last drink to close the bars she / holler kissey lips she laugh she let / you walk yourself away." As indicated by her elegy for Buck, Jordan also delights in language's expressive sonorities—onomatopoeia ("ratatat-tat-zap"), staccato rhythms ("shrink back / jump up / cock ears / shake head"), and devices of repetition such as anaphora and rhyme.

Jordan was born on July 9, 1936, to Jamaican immigrants in New York City's Harlem. At school and at Barnard College, she said, "I diligently followed orthodox directions from *The Canterbury Tales* right through *The Waste Land*"; like Adrienne Rich, then, she began with "the poetry of the fathers" until she began to carve her own. She held teaching positions at, among other schools, Sarah Lawrence College (1969–74), the State University of New York, Stony Brook (1978–89), and, from 1989, the University of California, Berkeley. In addition to her volumes of poetry, she published fiction, plays, essays, and books for children. She died of breast cancer, after fighting it for a decade.

Notes on the Peanut

For the Poet David Henderson[1]

Hi there. My name is George
Washington
Carver.[2]
If you will bear with me
for a few minutes I
will share with you
a few
of the 30,117 uses to which
the lowly peanut has been put
by me
since yesterday afternoon.
If you will look at my feet you will notice
my sensible shoelaces made from unadulterated
peanut leaf composition that is biodegradable
in the extreme.
To your left you can observe the lovely Renoir
masterpiece reproduction that I have cleverly
pieced together from several million peanut
shell chips painted painstakingly so as to
accurately represent the colors of the original!
Overhead you will spot a squadron of Peanut B-52

1. American poet (b. 1942)
2. African American chemist (ca. 1864–1943), who developed over three hundred derivative products from the peanut.

Bombers flying due west.
I would extend my hands to greet you
at this time
except for the fact that I am holding a reserve
supply of high energy dry roasted peanuts
guaranteed to accelerate protein assimilation
precisely documented by my pocket peanut calculator;
May I ask when did you last contemplate the relationship
between the expanding peanut products' industry
and the development of post-Marxian economic theory
which (Let me emphasize) need not exclude moral attrition
of prepuberty
polymorphic
prehensible[3] skills within the population age sectors
of 8 to 15?
I hope you will excuse me if I appear to be staring at you
through these functional yet high fashion and prescriptive
peanut contact lenses providing for the most
minute observation of your physical response to all of this
ultimately nutritional information.
Peanut butter peanut soap peanut margarine peanut
brick houses and house and field peanuts *per se* well
illustrate the diversified
potential of this lowly leguminous[4] plant
to which you may correctly refer
also
as the goober the pindar the groundnut
and ground pea/let me
interrupt to take your name down on my
pocket peanut writing pad complete with matching
peanut pencil that only 3 or 4
chewing motions of the jaws will sharpen
into pyrotechnical utility
and no sweat.
Please:
Speak right into the peanut!

Your name?

1980

July 4, 1984: For Buck

April 7, 1978–June 16, 1984

You would shrink back/jump up
cock ears/shake head
tonight
at this bloody idea of a birthday

3. Capable of being grasped. *Polymorphic:* able to exist in several forms without relation to sex.

4. Botanical family of peas and beans.

represented by smackajack explosions
of percussive lunacy and downright
(blowawayavillage) boom boom
ratatat-tat-zap

Otherwise any threat would make you stand
quivering perfect as a story
no amount of repetition could hope to ruin
perfect as the kangaroo boogie you concocted
with a towel in your jaws and your tail
tucked under and your paws
speeding around the ecstatic circle
of your refutation of the rain
outdoors

And mostly you would lunge electrical
and verge into the night
ears practically on flat alert
nostrils on the agitated sniff
(for falling rawhide meteors) and laugh
at compliments galore and then
teach me to love you
by hand
teach me to love you
by heart

as I do now

1985

DeLiza Spend the Day in the City

DeLiza drive the car to fetch Alexis
running from she building past the pickets
make she gap tooth laugh why don't
they think up something new they picket now
for three months soon it be too cold
to care

Opposite the Thrift Shop
Alexis ask to stop at the Botanica[5]
St. Jacques Majeur find oil to heal she
sister lying in the hospital from lymphoma[6]
and much western drug agenda

DeLiza stop. Alexis running back
with oil and myrrh and frankincense[7] and coal
to burn these odors free the myrrh like rocks

5. Shop selling herbs and magical charms.
6. A tumor.
7. Two kinds of aromatic gum resins anciently used in cures; the Magi brought "gold, and frankincense, and myrrh" as gifts to the baby Jesus (Matthew 2.11).

a baby break to pieces fit inside the palm
of long or short lifelines

DeLiza driving and Alexis
point out Nyabinghi's African emporium
of gems and cloth and Kwanza cards and clay:
DeLiza look.

Alexis opening the envelope to give DeLiza
faint gray copies of she article on refugees
from Haiti and some other thing on one white
male one
David Mayer
sixty-six
a second world war veteran
who want America to stop atomic arms
who want America to live without the nuclear death
who want it bad enough to say he'll blow
the Washington
D.C. Monument into the southside of the White House
where the First White Lady counting up she
$209,000. dollar china plates and cups and bowls
but cops blow him away
blow him/he David Mayer
man of peace
away
Alexis saying, "Shit.
He could be Jesus. Died to save you,
didn't he?"
DeLiza nod she head.
God do not seem entirely to be dead.

1985

The Reception

Doretha wore the short blue lace last night
and William watched her drinking so she fight
with him in flying collar slim-jim orange
tie and alligator belt below the navel pants uptight

'I flirt. You hear me? Yes I flirt.
Been on my pretty knees all week
to clean the rich white downtown dirt
the greedy garbage money reek.

I flirt. Damned right. You look at me.'
But William watched her carefully
his mustache shaky she could see
him jealous, 'which is how he always be

at parties.' Clementine and Wilhelmina
looked at trouble in the light blue lace
and held to George while Roosevelt Senior
circled by the yella high and bitterly light blue face

He liked because she worked
the crowded room like clay like molding men
from dust to muscle jerked
the arms and shoulders moving when
she moved.

The Lord Almighty Seagrams[8]
bless
Doretha in her short blue dress
and Roosevelt waiting for his chance:
a true gut-funky blues to make her really dance.

1994

8. Brand of gin.

TONY HARRISON
b. 1937

Tony Harrison was born on April 30, 1937, in the large industrial city of Leeds, England. The city itself is a child of the nineteenth-century Industrial Revolution; it grew prosperous, and ugly, thanks to coal, cotton, and manufacturing of many sorts, but it has been in a state of economic decline since the Great Depression. Harrison's family was working class; his poems often recollect his mother and father (a baker) with love and with a certain remorse. They took great, often uncomprehending, pride in their poet son, who by dint of his energy and education followed a path that veered from their own. In his turn, the poet fears he has lost touch with his working-class roots, lost the regional Yorkshire dialect that he learned from his mother. Harrison's poems embody—in their rich interplay between the literary and the oral, between learned allusion and raw directness, between Standard English and working-class Yorkshire speech—the tension and yearned-for synthesis of the classically educated son and his humble origins.

A collector of languages, Harrison treasures speech, but he also treasures the silence that is the context of speech, the eloquence of the inarticulate. He knows that "Silence and poetry have their own reserves," that the "mute inglorious Miltons" sometimes achieve a force and dignity that are the special property of those for whom words are a hard-won achievement. Harrison praises James Murray, the Scottish lexicographer of rural farm origins who assembled the great *Oxford English Dictionary,* for his hospitable invitation to all words, aristocratic and low-born alike, to join his dictionary. Harrison's characteristic tone, which may have been influenced by William Empson's, is wry and self-deprecating; and sharing James Murray's benevolence toward all words regardless of their social status, delighting in their diversity, recognizing their friction, Harrison takes a similarly wry but benevolent view of human contradictions and contrasts.

Harrison's triumph has been to bring the sensual power, vigor, wit, and immediacy of working-class Yorkshire speech into an exciting amalgam with literary English. He attributes to working-class speech of the north of England a "richer engagement, a more sensual engagement, with language" (*The Economist,* January 23, 1993). Like African American poets, Latino poets, Afro-Caribbean poets, Irish poets, Scottish poets, and others, he has hybridized Standard English with nonstandard oral sounds (e.g., the "glottals" recalled in "On Not Being Milton"), as well as the diction, syntax, and grammar of his regional speech. This is not a harmonious compound but an unstable, sometimes explosive one. The deliberate tension between the sixteen-line sonnet form in the ongoing series *The School of Eloquence* and the poem's unsonnetlike language resembles the struggle between the poet and his skinhead alter ego in the powerful long poem *v.* The *v.* for *versus* signals the poem's preoccupation with oppositions of class, language, and region, but it also, through puns on *versus* and Winston Churchill's *v* sign for *victory,* suggests some hope for mediating these conflicts. One of the most significant British long poems since World War II, *v.* brought Harrison to the notice of a wider audience when a televised version of it aired in 1987, stirring public controversy and charges of obscenity. Since then, he has written on a variety of political subjects, including the Persian Gulf War.

When he was eleven, Tony Harrison was uprooted from his social origins by a scholarship that allowed him to attend the prestigious Leeds Grammar School. Told he would have to learn to speak "properly," he was forbidden, because of his working-class accent, to read his poetry aloud in the classroom. He received a B.A. in classics from the University of Leeds in 1958. After teaching in Nigeria from 1962 to 1966, he taught for a year in Czechoslovakia. In addition to poems, he has written many verse plays, among them versions of Molière's *The Misanthrope* (1973), Racine's *Phaedra Britannica* (1975), and Aeschylus's *Oresteia* (1981). At England's National Theatre, he rendered into an effective dialectal modern English the texts of a number of medieval mystery plays, as *The Mysteries* (1985). This, given what he called the "the plays' Northern character," was a task admirably suited to his genius. He has also translated opera libretti.

From The School of Eloquence[1]

'In 1799 special legislation was introduced "utterly suppressing and prohibiting" by name the London Corresponding Society and the United Englishmen.[2] Even the indefatigable conspirator, John Binns, felt that further national organization was hopeless . . . When arrested he was found in possession of a ticket which was perhaps one of the last "covers"[3] for the old LCS: *Admit for the Season to the School of Eloquence.*'

(E. P. Thompson, *The Making of the English Working Class*)

Nunc mea Pierios cupiam per pectora fontes
Irriguas torquere vias, totumque per ora
Volvere laxatum gemino de vertice rivum;
Ut, tenues oblita sonos, audacibus alis
Surgat in officium venerandi Musa parentis.
Hoc utcunque tibi gratum, pater optime, carmen
Exiguum meditatur opus, nec novimus ipsi
Aptius a nobis quae possint munera donis
Respondere tuis, quamvis nec maxima possint

1. A sequence of sixteen-line "sonnets," from which the rest of this volume's selections except *v.* are taken.

2. Eighteenth-century English workingmen's radical societies.

3. That is, masking device.

Respondere tuis, nedum ut par gratia donis
Esse queat, vacuis quae redditur arida verbis . . .

Si modo perpetuos sperare audebitis annos,
Et domini superesse rogo, lucemque tueri,
Nec spisso rapient oblivia nigra sub Orco,
Forsitan has laudes, decantatumque parentis
Nomen, ad exemplum, servo servabitis aevo.
(John Milton, 1637)[4]

Heredity

How you became a poet's a mystery!
Wherever did you get your talent from?
I say: I had two uncles, Joe and Harry—
one was a stammerer, the other dumb.

1981

On Not Being Milton[5]

for Sergio Vieira & Armando Guebuza (Frelimo)[6]

Read and committed to the flames, I call
these sixteen lines that go back to my roots
my *Cahier d'un retour au pays natal,*
my growing black enough to fit my boots.[7]

The stutter of the scold out of the branks
of condescension, class and counter-class
thickens with glottals to a lumpen mass
of Ludding morphemes[8] closing up their ranks.
Each swung cast-iron Enoch of Leeds stress[9]

4. The first eleven and the last five lines of a Latin poem, *"Ad Patrem"*—"To (My) Father"—by the seventeenth-century English poet. In Douglas Bush's translation the lines read: "Now I wish that the Pierian waters [of a spring on Mt. Olympus sacred to the Muses] would wind their refreshing way through my breast, and that the whole stream flowing from the twin peaks [of Mt. Parnassus; one sacred to Apollo, god of song, one sacred to Dionysis, god of wine and inspiration] would pour over my lips, so that my Muse, forgetting trivial strains, might rise on bold wings to pay tribute to my revered father. The poem she is meditating is a small effort, and perhaps not very pleasing to you, my dear father; yet I do not know what I can more fitly offer in return for your gifts to me, though my greatest gifts could never match yours, much less can yours be equalled by the barren gratitude expressed in mere words. . . . if only you [that is, my youthful poems] dare hope to enjoy lasting life and survive your master's pyre and see the light, and dark oblivion does not carry you down to crowded Orcus [the underworld of the dead], perhaps these praises, and the name of the father they celebrate, you will preserve as an example to a distant age" (*The Complete Poetical Works of John Milton,* ed. Douglas Bush, 1965). In the poem, Milton first ascribes the traditional high qualities to poetry and song and then goes on to thank his father for the extensive education he provided for him.

5. See note to the Latin epigraph above.

6. Mozambique's independence party, of which both are members.

7. Cf. the proverb "He's as black as his boot." The "sixteen lines" may refer to Harrison's own attempted translation, since burned, of the sixteen Latin lines by Milton quoted in the epigraph. The French phrase means "Notebook of a return to the native country" and is the title of a work by Aimé Césaire (b. 1913), Martinican writer and a leader of Negritude, a movement asserting black identity.

8. Smallest meaningful units of language. *Branks:* that is, struttings, airs. *Glottals:* that is, glottal stops, or constrictions in the vocal cords, common to north-of-England speech. *Lumpen:* lower-class. *Ludding:* early nineteenth-century workers' protests were called "Luddite riots," after a mythical King Ludd, avenger of worker's wrongs.

9. Strong syllable in a poetic line. "[A]n 'Enoch' is an iron sledge-hammer used by the Luddites to smash the frames [used for weaving] which were

clangs a forged music on the frames of Art,
the looms of owned language smashed apart!

Three cheers for mute ingloriousness![1]

Articulation is the tongue-tied's fighting.
In the silence round all poetry we quote
Tidd the Cato Street conspirator who wrote:

Sir, I Ham a very Bad Hand at Righting.[2]

1981

Book Ends

I

Baked the day she suddenly dropped dead
we chew it slowly that last apple pie.

Shocked into sleeplessness you're scared of bed.
We never could talk much, and now don't try.

You're like book ends, the pair of you, she'd say,
Hog that grate, say nothing, sit, sleep, stare . . .

The 'scholar' me, you, worn out on poor pay,
only our silence made us seem a pair.

Not as good for staring in, blue gas,
too regular each bud, each yellow spike.[3]

A night you need my company to pass
and she not here to tell us we're alike!

Your life's all shattered into smithereens.

Back in our silences and sullen looks,
for all the Scotch we drink, what's still between 's
not the thirty or so years, but books, books, books.

II

The stone's too full. The wording must be terse.
There's scarcely room to carve the FLORENCE on it—

also made by the same Enoch Taylor of Marsden. The cry was: 'Enoch made them, Enoch shall break them!' " [Harrison's note].

1. Cf. "some mute inglorious Milton" in "Elegy Written in a Country Churchyard," by English poet Thomas Gray (1716–1771).

2. The "Cato Street conspiracy" (1820) was a failed radical plot to kill members of the king's cabinet.

3. Flames from the gas fire, common in lower-class English homes; it is often manufactured to resemble a log, but its flames are more "regular" than those of a real fire.

Come on, it's not as if we're wanting verse.
It's not as if we're wanting a whole sonnet!

After tumblers of neat *Johnny Walker*[4]
(I think that both of us we're on our third)
you said you'd always been a clumsy talker
and couldn't find another, shorter word
for 'beloved' or for 'wife' in the inscription,
but not too clumsy that you can't still cut:

You're supposed to be the bright boy at description
and you can't tell them what the fuck to put!

I've got to find the right words on my own.

I've got the envelope that he'd been scrawling,
mis-spelt, mawkish, stylistically appalling
but I can't squeeze more love into their stone.

1981

Turns

I thought it made me look more 'working class'
(as if a bit of chequered cloth could bridge that gap!)
I did a turn in it before the glass.
My mother said: *It suits you, your dad's cap.*[5]
(She preferred me to wear suits and part my hair:
You're every bit as good as that lot are!)

All the pension queue[6] came out to stare.
Dad was sprawled beside the postbox (still VR),[7]
his cap turned inside up beside his head,
smudged H A H in purple Indian ink
and Brylcreem[8] slicks displayed so folk might think
he wanted charity for dropping dead.

He never begged. For nowt![9] Death's reticence
crowns his life's, and *me,* I'm opening my trap
to busk the class that broke him for the pence
that splash like brackish tears into our cap.[1]

1981

4. Brand of Scotch whiskey.
5. Soft cloth cap with a visor, commonly worn by, as the poem says, members of the "working class."
6. Line of retired people waiting for their pension (that is, social security) checks.
7. Sidewalk mailbox dating from the time of Queen Victoria and bearing her name and Latin title, *Victoria Regina.*
8. Hair oil.
9. Nothing (northern dialect).
1. "Buskers" perform in the street, in train stations, and so on, collecting money in a cap.

Marked with D.[2]

When the chilled dough of his flesh went in an oven[3]
not unlike those he fuelled all his life,
I thought of his cataracts[4] ablaze with Heaven
and radiant with the sight of his dead wife,
light streaming from his mouth to shape her name,
'not Florence and not Flo but always Florrie'.
I thought how his cold tongue burst into flame
but only literally, which makes me sorry,
sorry for his sake there's no Heaven to reach.
I get it all from Earth my daily bread
but he hungered for release from mortal speech
that kept him down, the tongue that weighed like lead.

The baker's man that no one will see rise
and England made to feel like some dull oaf
is smoke, enough to sting one person's eyes
and ash (not unlike flour) for one small loaf.

1981

Timer

Gold survives the fire that's hot enough
to make you ashes in a standard urn.
An envelope of coarse official buff[5]
contains your wedding ring which wouldn't burn.

Dad told me I'd to tell them at St James's[6]
that the ring should go in the incinerator.
That 'eternity' inscribed with both their names is
his surety that they'd be together, 'later'.

I signed for the parcelled clothing as the son,
the cardy,[7] apron, pants, bra, dress—

the clerk phoned down: *6-8-8-3-1?*
Has she still her ring on? (Slight pause) *Yes!*

It's on my warm palm now, your burnished ring!

2. Cf. the nursery rhyme "Pat-a-cake, pat-a-cake baker's man, / Bake me a cake as fast as you can; / Pat it and prick it and mark it with a D [or whatever the baby's initial is], / And put it in the oven for baby and me."
3. His father is being cremated.
4. Clouding of the eyes' lenses.
5. Yellowish; the color of official forms in England.
6. Presumably, the crematorium.
7. Cardigan.

I feel your ashes, head, arms, breasts, womb, legs,
sift through its circle slowly, like that thing
you used to let me watch to time the eggs.[8]

1981

Self Justification

Me a poet! My daughter with maimed limb
became a more than tolerable sprinter.
And Uncle Joe. Impediment spurred him,
the worst stammerer I've known, to be a printer.

He handset type much faster than he spoke.
Those cruel consonants, *ms*, *ps*, and *bs*
on which his jaws and spirit almost broke
flicked into order with sadistic ease.

It seems right that Uncle Joe, 'b-buckshee
from the works',[9] supplied those scribble pads
on which I stammered my first poetry
that made me seem a cissy[1] to the lads.

Their aggro[2] towards me, my need of them 's
what keeps my would-be mobile tongue still tied—

aggression, struggle, loss, blank printer's ems
by which all   eloquence   gets justified.[3]

1981

History Classes

Past scenic laybys and stag warning signs[4]
the British borderlands roll into view.

They read: *Beware of Unexploded Mines!*[5]
I tell my children that was World War II.

They want to walk or swim. We pick up speed.
My children boo the flash of each NO ENTRY:

8. Egg-timer that works like a miniature hourglass.
9. That is, free from the factory.
1. Sissy.
2. Initially short for "aggravation," it now means mindless violence (British slang).
3. (1) Proven to be right; (2) printer's term: to justify is to space lines of type so that the right-hand margins are even. In handset type and linotype, a "blank em" is a small square of metal that leaves a blank space the width of the letter *M*; here, the spaces before and after "eloquence" are "2-em spaces."
4. That is, "deer crossing" signs. *Laybys:* widenings in a highway for parking.
5. Buried underground against possible German attack.

High seas, and shooting, uniform or tweed,
Ministry of Defence, or landed gentry.[6]

Danger flags from valley mills that throve,
after a fashion, on the Empire's needs.

Their own clothes spun in India they wove
the Colonel's khaki and the blue blood's tweeds.

Mill angelus, and church tower twice as high.
One foundry[7] cast the work- and rest-day bells—

the same red cotton 's in the flags that fly
for ranges, revolutions, and rough swells.[8]

1978, 1981

v.

'My father still reads the dictionary every day. He says your life depends on your power to master words.'

—ARTHUR SCARGILL[9]
The Sunday Times, 10 Jan. 1982

Next millennium you'll have to search quite hard
to find my slab behind the family dead,
butcher, publican[1] and baker, now me, bard
adding poetry to their beef, beer and bread.

With Byron three graves on I'll not go short
of company, and Wordsworth's[2] opposite.
That's two peers already, of a sort,
and we'll all be thrown together if the pit,

whose galleries[3] once ran beneath this plot,
causes the distinguished dead to drop
into the rabblement of bone and rot,
shored slack, crushed shale, smashed prop.[4]

Wordsworth built church organs, Byron tanned
luggage cowhide in the age of steam,

6. That is, "NO ENTRY" into army encampments or private estates.
7. Metal-casting factory. *Angelus:* bell announcing a Roman Catholic devotion, used here for the mill's bell.
8. (1) Crude, pompous leaders; (2) stormy ocean. *Ranges:* army firing ranges, where red flags are used as signals.
9. Head (b. 1938) of the British National Union of Mineworkers (N.U.M.), who led the national miner's strike of 1984–85.
1. Keeper of a pub.
2. Here, workers (lines 13–14) with the same last names as William Wordsworth (1770–1850) and George Gordon, Lord Byron (1788–1824), English poets.
3. Underground mine passages. *Pit:* mine shaft.
4. Support beam. *Slack:* small bits of coal.

and knew their place of rest before the land
caves in on the lowest worked-out seam.[5]

This graveyard on the brink of Beeston Hill 's
the place I may well rest if there 's a spot
under the rose roots and the daffodils
by which Dad dignified the family plot.

If buried ashes saw then I'd survey
the places I learned Latin, and learned Greek,
and left, the ground where Leeds United[6] play
but disappoint their fans week after week,

which makes them lose their sense of self-esteem
and taking a shortcut home through these graves here
they reassert the glory of their team
by spraying words on tombstones, pissed[7] on beer.

This graveyard stands above a worked-out pit.
Subsidence makes the obelisks all list.
One leaning left 's marked FUCK, one right 's marked SHIT
sprayed by some peeved supporter who was pissed.

Farsighted for his family's future dead,
but for his wife, this banker 's still alone
on his long obelisk, and doomed to head
a blackened dynasty of unclaimed stone,

now graffitied with a crude four-letter word.
His children and grandchildren went away
and never came back home to be interred
so left a lot of space for skins[8] to spray.

The language of this graveyard ranges from
a bit of Latin for a former mayor
or those who laid their lives down at the Somme,[9]
the hymnal fragments and the gilded prayer,

how people 'fell asleep in the Good Lord,'
brief chisellable bits from the good book
and rhymes whatever length they could afford
to CUNT, PISS, SHIT and (mostly) FUCK!

or, more expansively, there's LEEDS v.
the opponent of last week, this week, or next,
and a repertoire of blunt four-letter curses
on the team or race that makes the sprayer vexed.

5. Layer of coal.
6. Football (soccer) team. *Leeds:* an industrial area in West Yorkshire, in the north of England.
7. Drunk.
8. Skinheads.
9. Site in northern France of costly battles during World War I.

Then, rushed for time, or fleeing some observer,
dodging between tall family vaults and trees,
like his team's best-ever winger, dribbler, swerver,[1]
fills every space he finds with versus Vs.

Vs sprayed on the run at such a lick,
the sprayer master of his flourished tool,
get short-armed on the left like that red tick
they never marked his work much with at school.

Half this skinhead's age but with approval
I helped whitewash a V on a brick wall.
No one clamoured in the press for its removal
or thought the sign, in wartime, rude at all.[2]

These Vs are all the versuses of life
from LEEDS V. DERBY, Black/White
and (as I've known to my cost) man v. wife,
Communist v. Fascist, Left v. Right,

class v. class as bitter as before,
the unending violence of US and THEM,
personified in 1984
by Coal Board MacGregor[3] and the N.U.M.,

Hindu/Sikh, soul/body, heart v. mind,
East/West, male/female, and the ground
these fixtures are fought out on 's Man, resigned
to hope from his future what his past never found.

The prospects for the present aren't too grand
when a swastika with NF (National Front)[4] 's
sprayed on a grave, to which another hand
has added, in a reddish colour, CUNTS.

Which is, I grant, the word that springs to mind
when, going to clear the weeds and rubbish thrown
on the family grave by football fans, I find
UNITED graffitied on my parents' stone.

How many British graveyards now this May
are strewn with rubbish and choked up with weeds
since families and friends have gone away
for work or fuller lives, like me, from Leeds?

When I first came here 40 years ago
with my dad to 'see' my grandma I was 7.

1. Player who moves in the wing, dribbles (moves the ball forward with short kicks), or swerves.
2. During World War II, *V* represented *victory*.
3. Sir Ian MacGregor (1912–1998), head of the National Coal Board, which, as part of the Conservative government of Prime Minister Margaret Thatcher (b. 1925), defeated an N.U.M. strike in 1984–85.
4. Fascist group.

I helped Dad with the flowers. He let me know
she'd gone to join my granddad up in Heaven.

My dad who came each week to bring fresh flowers
came home with clay stains on his trouser knees.
Since my parents' deaths I've spent 2 hours
made up of odd 10 minutes such as these,

Flying visits once or twice a year,
and though I'm horrified, just who's to blame
that I find instead of flowers cans of beer
and more than one grave sprayed with some skin's name?

Where there were flower urns and troughs of water
and mesh receptacles for withered flowers
are the HARP[5] tins of some skinhead Leeds supporter.
It isn't all his fault, though. Much is ours.

5 kids, with one in goal, play 2-a-side.
When the ball bangs on the hawthorn that's one post
and petals fall they hum 'Here Comes the Bride'
though not so loud they'd want to rouse a ghost.

They boot the ball on purpose at the trunk
and make the tree shed showers of shrivelled may.[6]
I look at this word graffitied by some drunk
and I'm in half a mind to let it stay.

(Though honesty demands that I say *if*
I'd wanted to take the necessary pains
to scrub the skin's inscription off
I only had an hour between trains.

So the feelings that I had as I stood gazing
and the significance I saw could be a sham,
mere excuses for not patiently erasing
the word sprayed on the grave of Dad and Mam.)

This pen 's all I have of magic wand.
I know this world's so torn but want no other
except for Dad who'd hoped from 'the Beyond'
a better life than this one *with* my mother.

Though I don't believe in afterlife at all
and know it's cheating, it's hard not to make
a sort of furtive prayer from this skin's scrawl,
his UNITED means 'in Heaven' for their sake,

an accident of meaning to redeem
an act intended as mere desecration

5. Brand of beer.

6. Blossoms of the hawthorn tree.

and make the thoughtless spraying of his team
apply to higher things, and to the nation.

Some, where kids use aerosols, use giant signs
to let the people know who's forged their fetters
like PRI CE O WALES above West Yorkshire mines
(no prizes for who nicked the missing letters!)

The big blue star for booze, tobacco ads,
the magnate's monogram, the royal crest,
insignia in neon dwarf the lads
who spray a few odd FUCKS when they're depressed.

Letters of transparent tubes and gas
in Dusseldorf are blue and flash out KRUPP.[7]
Arms are hoisted for the British ruling class
and clandestine, genteel aggro[8] keeps them up.

And there's HARRISON on some Leeds building sites
I've taken in fun as blazoning my name,
which I've also seen on books, in Broadway lights,
so why can't skins with spray cans do the same?

But why inscribe these *graves* with CUNT and SHIT?
Why choose neglected tombstones to disfigure?
This pitman's of last century daubed PAKI GIT,[9]
this grocer Broadbent's aerosoled with NIGGER?

They're there to shock the living, not arouse
the dead from their deep peace to lend support
for any cause skins' spray cans could espouse.
The dead would want their desecrators caught!

Jobless though they are how can these kids,
even though their team 's lost one more game,
believe that the 'Pakis,' 'Niggers,' even 'Yids'[1]
sprayed on the tombstones here should take the blame?

What is it that these crude words are revealing?
What is it that this aggro act implies?
Giving the dead their xenophobic feeling
or just a *cri-de-coeur*[2] because Man dies.

So what's a cri-de-coeur, *cunt? Can't yer speak*
the language that yer mam spoke? Think of 'er!
Can yer only get yer tongue round fucking Greek?
Go and fuck yerself with cri-de-coeur!

7. German company manufacturing industrial machinery. *Düsseldorf:* city in western Germany.
8. British slang for "aggravation," typically implying a threat of violence.
9. *Paki:* derogatory term for Pakistani. *Git:* worthless person.
1. Derogatory term for Jews.
2. Cry from the heart (French).

'She didn't talk like you do for a start!'
I shouted, turning where I thought the voice had been.
She didn't understand yer fucking art!
She thought yer fucking poetry obscene!

I wish on this skin's word deep aspirations,
first the prayer for my parents I can't make,
then a call to Britain and to all the nations
made in the name of love for peace's sake.

Aspirations, cunt! Folk on t' fucking dole[3]
'ave got about as much scope to aspire
above the shit they're dumped in, cunt, as coal
aspires to be chucked on t' fucking fire.

O.K., forget the aspirations! Look, I know
United's losing gets you fans incensed
and how far the HARP inside you makes you go
but all these Vs: against! against! against!

Ah'll tell yer then what really riles a bloke.
It's reading on their graves the jobs they did—
butcher, publican and baker. Me, I'll croak
doing t' same nowt ah do now as a kid.

'ard birth ah wor, mi mam says, almost killed 'er.
Death after life on t' dole won't seem as 'ard!
Look at this cunt, Wordsworth, organ builder,
this fucking 'aberdasher,[4] *Appleyard!*

If mi mam's up there, don't want to meet 'er
listening to me list mi dirty deeds
and 'ave to pipe up to St. fucking Peter[5]
ah've been on t' dole all mi life in fucking Leeds.

Then t' Alleluias stick in t' angels' gobs.
When dole-wallahs[6] *fuck off to the void*
what'll t' mason carve up for their *jobs?*
The cunts who lieth 'ere wor unemployed?

This lot worked at one job all life through.
Byron, 'Tanner,' Lieth 'ere interred!
They'll chisel fucking poet when they do you
and that, yer cunt, 's a crude four-letter word.

'Listen, cunt!' *I* said, 'before you start your jeering,
the reason why I want this in a book

3. Unemployment benefits.
4. Dealer in hats, fabrics, ribbons, and so on. *Nowt:* nothing.
5. St. Peter is often represented as the holder of the keys to the Christian Heaven.
6. People receiving unemployment. *Wallah:* British slang for person, from the Hindi suffix *wala,* meaning "one in charge of." *Gobs:* mouths (northern English).

's to give ungrateful cunts like you a hearing!'
A book, yer stupid cunt, 's not worth a fuck!

'The only reason why I write this poem at all
on yobs[7] like you who do the dirt on death
's to give some higher meaning to your scrawl!'
Don't fucking bother, cunt! Don't waste your breath!

'You piss-artist skinhead cunt, you wouldn't know
and it doesn't fucking matter if you do,
the skin and poet united fucking Rimbaud[8]
but the *autre* that *je est* is fucking you.'

Ah've told yer, no more Greek. That's yer last warning!
Ah'll boot yer fucking balls to Kingdom Come.
They'll find yer cold on t' grave tomorrer morning.
So don't speak Greek. Don't treat me like I'm dumb.

'I've done my bits of mindless aggro too
not half a mile from where we're standing now.'
Yeah, ah bet yer wrote a poem, yer wanker you!
'No, shut yer gob awhile. Ah'll tell yer 'ow . . .

'Herman Darewski's[9] band played operetta
with a wobbly soprano warbling. Just why
I made my mind up that I'd got to get her
with the fire hose I can't say, but I'll try.

'It wasn't just the singing angered me.
At the same time half a crowd was jeering
as the smooth Hugh Gaitskell, our MP,[1]
made promises the other half was cheering.

'What I hated in those high soprano ranges
was uplift beyond all reason and control
and in a world where you say nothing changes
it seemed a sort of prick-tease of the soul.

'I tell you when I heard high notes that rose
above Hugh Gaitskell's cool electioneering
straight from the warbling throat right up my nose,
I had all your aggro in *my* jeering.

'And I hit the fire extinguisher ON knob
and covered orchestra and audience with spray.
I could run as fast as you then. A good job!
They yelled 'Damned vandal' after me that day . . .'

7. Thugs.
8. French Symbolist poet Arthur Rimbaud (1854–1891) once wrote "Je est un autre" ("I is another").
9. British band leader (1883–1947), music publisher, and composer of popular war songs.
1. Member of Parliament. Hugh Gaitskell (1906–1963), leader of the Labour Party from 1955 until his death.

And then yer saw the light and gave up 'eavy
And knew a man's not 'ow much 'e can sup[2] *. . .*
Yer reward for growing up's this super-bevvy,
*a meths and champagne punch in t'*FA *Cup.*[3]

Ah've 'eard all that from old farts past their prime.
'ow now yer live wi' all yer once detested . . .
Old farts wi' not much left'll give me time.
Fuckers like that get folk like me arrested.

Covet not thy neighbour's wife, thy neighbour's riches.
Vicar and cop who say, to save our souls:
Get thee behind me, Satan![4] *drop their breeches*
and get the Devil's dick right up their 'oles!

It was more a working marriage that I'd meant,
a blend of masculine and feminine.
Ignoring me, he started looking, bent
on some more aerosoling, for his tin.

'It was more a working marriage that I mean!'
Fuck, and save mi soul, eh? That suits me.
Then as if I'd egged him on to be obscene
he added a middle slit to one daubed V.

Don't talk to me of fucking representing
the class yer were born into anymore.
Yer going to get 'urt and start resenting
it's not poetry we need in this class war.

Yer've given yerself toffee, cunt. Who needs
yer fucking poufy words. Ah write mi own.
Ah've got mi work on show all over Leeds
like this UNITED *'ere on some sod's stone.*

'O.K.!' (thinking I had him trapped). 'O.K.!'
'If you're so proud of it then sign your name
when next you're full of HARP and armed with spray,
next time you take this shortcut from the game.'

He took the can, contemptuous, unhurried,
and cleared the nozzle and prepared to sign
the UNITED sprayed where Mam and Dad were buried.
He aerosoled his name, and it was mine.

The boy footballers bawl 'Here Comes the Bride'
and drifting blossoms fall onto my head.

2. Drink. *'Eavy:* that is, heavy bitter (beer).
3. Prize awarded to the winner of the Football Association's annual Challenge Cup series. *Bevvy:* beverage. *Meths:* methylated spirits.
4. Jesus' response both to Peter's objection to the intimations of his ensuing sacrifice (Matthew 16.23, Mark 8.33) and to the temptations of the devil (Luke 4.8).

One half of me 's alive but one half died
when the skin half sprayed my name among the dead.

Half versus half, the enemies within
the heart that can't be whole till they unite.
As I stoop to grab the crushed HARP lager tin
the day 's already dusk, half dark, half light.

The UNITED that I'd wished onto the nation
or as reunion for dead parents soon recedes.
The word 's once more a mindless desecration
by some HARPoholic yob supporting Leeds.

Almost the time for ghosts. I'd better scram.
Though not give much to fears of spooky scaring
I don't fancy an encounter with mi mam
playing Hamlet with me for this swearing.[5]

Though I've a train to catch my step is slow.
I walk on the grass and graves with wary tread
over the subsidences, these shifts below
the life of Leeds supported by the dead.

Further underneath 's that cavernous hollow
that makes the gravestones lean towards the town.
A matter of mere time and it will swallow
this place of rest and all the resters down.

I tell myself I've got, say, 30 years.
At 75 this place will suit me fine.
I've never feared the grave but what I fear 's
that great worked-out black hollow under mine.

Not train departure time and not Town Hall
with the great white clock face I can see,
coal, that began, with no man here at all,
as 300-million-year-old plant debris.

5 kids still play at making blossoms fall
and humming as they do 'Here Comes the Bride.'
They never seem to tire of their ball
though I hear a woman's voice call one inside.

2 larking boys play bawdy bride and groom.
3 boys in Leeds strip la-la *Lohengrin*.[6]
I hear them as I go through growing gloom
still years away from being skald[7] or skin.

5. In Shakespeare's *Hamlet*, the prince is haunted by the ghost of his father.
6. "Here Comes the Bride" comes from *Lohengrin*, an opera by German composer Richard Wagner (1813–1883).
7. Bard.

The ground 's carpeted with petals as I throw
the aerosol, the HARP can, the cleared weeds
on top of Dad's dead daffodils, then go,
with not one glance behind away from Leeds.

The bus to the station 's still the No. 1
but goes by routes that I don't recognize.
I look out for known landmarks as the sun
reddens the swabs of cloud in darkening skies.

Home, home, home, to my woman as the red
darkens from a fresh blood to a dried.
Home, home to my woman, home to bed
where opposites are sometimes unified.

A pensioner in turban taps his stick
along the pavement past the corner shop,
that sells samosas now not beer on tick,[8]
to the Kashmir Muslim Club that was the Co-op.

House after house FOR SALE where we'd played cricket
with white roses[9] cut from flour sacks on our caps,
with stumps chalked on the coal grate for our wicket,
and every one bought now by 'coloured chaps,'

Dad's most liberal label as he felt
squeezed by the unfamiliar, and fear
of foreign food and faces, when he smelt
curry in the shop where he'd bought beer.

And growing frailer, 'wobbly on his pins,'[1]
the shops he felt familiar with withdrew
which meant much longer tiring treks for tins
that had a label on them that he knew.

And as the shops that stocked his favourites receded
whereas he'd fancied beans and popped next door,
he found that four long treks a week were needed
till he wondered what he bothered eating for.

The supermarket made him feel embarrassed.
Where people bought whole lambs for family freezers
he bought baked beans from checkout girls too harassed
to smile or swap a joke with sad old geezers.

But when he bought his cigs he'd have a chat,
his week's one conversation, truth to tell,
but time also came and put a stop to that
when old Wattsy got bought out by M. Patel.

8. Credit.
9. The emblem of Yorkshire and its cricket team.
1. Legs.

And there, 'Time like an ever-rolling stream' 's[2]
what I once trilled behind that boarded front.
A 1000 ages made coal-bearing seams
and even more the hand that sprayed this CUNT

on both Methodist and C of E[3] billboards
once divided in their fight for local souls.
Whichever house more truly was the Lord's
both's pews are filled with cut-price toilet rolls.

Home, home to my woman, never to return
till sexton or survivor has to cram
the bits of clinker[4] scooped out of my urn
down through the rose roots to my dad and mam.

Home, home to my woman, where the fire 's lit
these still-chilly mid-May evenings, home to you,
and perished vegetation from the pit
escaping insubstantial up the flue.

Listening to *Lulu,*[5] in our hearth we burn,
as we hear the high Cs rise in stereo,
what was lush swamp club moss and tree fern
at least 300 million years ago.

Shilbottle cobbles,[6] Alban Berg high D
lifted from a source that bears your name,
the one we hear decay, the one we see,
the fern from the foetid forest, as brief flame.

This world, with far too many people in,
starts on the TV logo as a taw,[7]
then ping-pong, tennis, football; then one spin
to show us all, then shots of the Gulf War.[8]

As the coal with reddish dust cools in the grate
on the late-night national news we see
police v. pickets at a coke[9] plant gate,
old violence and old disunity.

The map that's colour-coded Ulster/Eire[1] 's
flashed on again, as almost every night.
Behind a tiny coffin with two bearers
men in masks with arms show off their might.

The day's last images recede to first a glow
and then a ball that shrinks back to blank screen.

2. From the hymn "O God, our help in ages past."
3. Church of England.
4. Remnants of combustion.
5. Opera by avant-garde Austrian composer Alban Berg (1885–1935).
6. Coal.
7. Marble.
8. War between Iran and Iraq (1980–90).
9. Fuel made from coal.
1. Northern Ireland (Orange) and the Republic of Ireland (Green).

Turning to love, and sleep's oblivion, I know
what the UNITED that the skin sprayed *has* to mean.

Hanging my clothes up, from my parka hood
may and apple petals, brown and creased,
fall onto the carpet and bring back the flood
of feelings their first falling had released.

I hear like ghosts from all Leeds matches humming
with one concerted voice the bride, the bride
I feel united to, *my* bride is coming
into the bedroom, naked, to my side.

The ones we choose to love become our anchor
when the hawser[2] of the blood tie 's hacked or frays.
But a voice that scorns chorales is yelling: *Wanker!*
It's the aerosoling skin I met today's.

My alter ego wouldn't want to know it,
his aerosol vocab would balk at LOVE,
the skin's UNITED underwrites the poet,
the measures carved below the ones above.

I doubt if 30 years of bleak Leeds weather
and 30 falls of apple and of may
will erode the UNITED binding us together.
And now it's your decision. Does it stay?

Next millennium you'll have to search quite hard
to find out where I'm buried, but I'm near
the grave of haberdasher Appleyard,
the pile of HARPS, or some new neoned beer.

Find Byron, Wordsworth, or turn left between
one grave marked Broadbent, one marked Richardson.
Bring some solution with you that can clean
whatever new crude words have been sprayed on.

If love of art, or love, gives you affront
that the grave I'm in 's graffitied, then, maybe,
erase the more offensive FUCK and CUNT
but leave, with the worn UNITED, one small *v.*

victory? For vast, slow, coal-creating forces
that hew the body's seams to get the soul.
Will earth run out of her 'diurnal courses'[3]
before repeating her creation of black coal?

2. Rope used for securing a ship.
3. Cf. Wordsworth's poem "A Slumber Did My Spirit Seal," in which the speaker's spirit "neither hears nor sees; / Rolled round in earth's diurnal course, / With rocks, and stones, and trees."

But choose a day like I chose in mid-May
or earlier when apple and hawthorn tree,
no matter if boys boot their ball all day,
cling to their blossoms and won't shake them free—

if, having come this far, somebody reads
these verses, and he/she wants to understand,
face this grave on Beeston Hill, your back to Leeds,
and read the chiselled epitaph I've planned:

Beneath your feet 's a poet, then a pit.
Poetry supporter, if you're here to find
how poems can grow from (beat you to it!) SHIT
find the beef, the beer, the bread, then look behind.

1985, 1989

Susan Howe
b. 1937

Susan Howe was born on June 10, 1937, in Boston. Her mother was an Irish actress and playwright, her father a law professor at Harvard with a strong interest in American colonial history. Howe remarked in a 1994 interview that her mother "had the ear as a writer," and elsewhere she has said that for her as a poet, "sound creates meaning. Sound is the core" (*The Difficulties*). Her father "was obsessed by footnotes," and Howe refers to at least one of her poems as "one huge footnote" (1994 interview). Her poetry mediates between the archival and the musical, between rigorous historicism and aesthetic abandon. It fuses the Calvinistic severity she associates with her father's New England and the verbal play and performance she associates with her mother's Ireland. After high school, Howe spent two years as an apprentice in acting at the Gate Theatre in Dublin—in her view, "an irrevocable mistake" (*The Difficulties*). Returning to the United States, she majored in painting at the School of the Museum of Fine Arts, Boston, graduating in 1961. As a visual artist, she first became interested in collage and quotation—techniques that would characterize her poetry. In the poetic series "Rückenfigur," she draws on the subgenre of paintings in which spectators are represented with their backs to the viewer. In poems such as "Thorow" (a phonetic misspelling of Thoreau), Howe makes striking use of the visual appearance of poetry on the page, printing lines at angles, upside down, or superimposed on each other. She published her first book of poetry, *Hinge Picture*, in 1974. Having worked as a radio producer and bookseller as well as an artist, she began to teach in the English Department at the State University of New York, Buffalo, in 1988.

Because of her poetry's seeming impersonality, collage-based density, and semantic and syntactic fragmentation, Howe has often been grouped with the Language poets. If poetry conventionally seeks fluent self-expression, Howe wants hers to be a poetry of stuttering, interruption, brokenness. Probing the spaces between words, the gaps between syllables, the silences surrounding lines on the page, she would recover something of what seamless language suppresses. Her poetry is a heap of broken tombstones, marking various absences and occlusions. "The moment a word is put on the page," she has said, "there's a kind of death in that." A feminist, Howe mourns the voices of women silenced by patriarchy. A revisionist, she remembers individuals and peoples marginalized or erased by traditional history. An ardent archivist, she commemorates lost or forgotten manuscripts supplanted by official texts. She mourns more personal losses as well. In the series "Rückenfigur," she obliquely elegizes her husband and companion of twenty-seven years, the sculptor David von Schlegell, who died in 1992. Responding to lost individuals, voices, histories, texts, and meanings, Howe labors to recover them and yet also to mark their ultimate irrecuperability. Without claiming that she can compensate for such losses and effacements, Howe remembers and even embodies them in her poetry's fissures, echoes, and ghostly traces.

From Thorow

Gabion
Parapet

Traverse canon night siege Constant firing
Escalade

Tranquillity of a garrison

Places to walk out to
Cove

canoes

waterbug
The Frames should be exactly
Fires by night
wood
Encamp t

mud
fitted to the paper, the Margins

shrub
of which will not per[mit] of

wavelet
swamp
a very deep Rabbit

cusk
lily root
cedar
grease
chip
coin

splint
disc
Their Plenipo
drisk
Messages
sheen

The French Hatchet
neck
At this end of the carry

& singing their war song
islet

battea
The War Bell
hieroglyph

Messengers say
Picked up arrowhead

over the lakes

Of the far nations

1990

Rückenfigur[1]

Iseult stands at Tintagel[2]
on the mid stairs between
light and dark symbolism
Does she stand for phonic
human overtone for outlaw
love the dread pull lothly
for weariness actual brute
predestined fact for phobic
falling no one talking too
Tintagel ruin of philosophy
here is known change here
is come crude change wave
wave determinist caparison[3]
Your soul your separation

•

But the counterfeit Iseult
Iseult aux Blanches Mains[4]
stands by the wall to listen
Phobic thought of openness
a soul also has two faces
Iseult's mother and double
Iseult the Queen later in *T*[5]
Even *Tros* echoes Tristan's
infirmity through spurious
etymology the Tintagel of *Fo*

1. Figure seen from behind (German); translated within the poem as "retreating figure." *Rückenfigur* is also the name of a subgenre of paintings in which halted travelers have their backs to the viewer, most famously in the landscape paintings of German Romantic Caspar David Friedrich (1774–1840). In a letter to the editor of this anthology, Howe cites as sources Friedrich's paintings (e.g., *Moonrise over the Sea, Moonrise at Sea, Flatlands on the Bay of Greifswald, Woman before the Setting Sun*) and Joseph Leo Koerner's discussion of them in *Caspar David Friedrich and the Subject of Landscape* (New Haven, 1990).
2. Village south of the rocky promontory Tintagel Head, in Cornwall, England. Reputed birthplace of King Arthur and site of twelfth-century castle, where Tristan is said to have fallen in love with Iseult. *Iseult:* lover of Tristan in medieval legend of Celtic origin. Tristan is sent to Ireland to bring back Iseult to be the bride of his uncle, King Mark. But after drinking a love potion Tristan and Iseult become lovers. She dies of sorrow on learning he has died waiting for her.
3. Cloth draped over a horse's saddle; adornment.
4. Iseult of the white hands (French). According to legend, the lovers become estranged late in life and Tristan marries another woman, also named Iseult: Iseult of the White Hands.
5. *T, Tros,* and *Fo* are scholarly abbreviations for fragments of different versions of the legend.

not the dead city of night
Wall in the element of Logic
here is a door and beyond
here is the sail she spies

•

Tristran Tristan Tristrant
Tristram Trystan Trystram
Tristrem Tristanz Drust
Drystan[6] these names concoct
a little wreathe of victory
dreaming over the landscape
Tintagel font icon twilight
Grove bough dark wind cove
brine testimony Iseult salt
Iseut Isolde Ysolt Essyllt
bride of March Marc Mark in
the old French commentaries
your secret correspondence
Soft Iseut two Iseults one

•

The third of Tristan's overt
identities is a double one
his disguise as nightingale
in *Tros* then wild man in *Fo*
Level and beautiful La Blanche
Lande[7] of disguise episodes
the nocturnal garden of *Tros*
Fo recalls the scene in Ovid[8]
Orpheus grief stricken over
the loss of Eurydice sits by
the bank of a river seven days
I see Mark's shadow in water

6. The names of the main characters vary in the legend's many different versions.
7. The white moor (French).
8. Roman poet (43 B.C.E.?–17 C.E.) and author of the *Metamorphoses,* which tells the story of Orpheus's grief after losing his wife, Eurydice, in Hades.

Mark's moral right to Iseult
David's relationship to Saul[9]

•

Lean on handrail river below
Sense of depth focus motion
of chaos in Schlegel[1] only as
visual progress into depth its
harsh curb estrangement logic
Realism still exists is part
of the realist dual hypothesis
Dual on verso[2] as one who has
obeyed acceleration velocity
killing frost regenerative thaw
you other rowing forward face
backward Hesperides[3] messenger
into the pastness of landscape
inarticulate scrawl awash air

•

Insufferably pale the icy
limit pulls and pulls no
kindness free against you
Deep quietness never to be
gathered no blind threat
Assuredly I see division
can never be weighed once
pale anguish breathes free
to be unhallowed empty what
in thought or other sign
roof and lintel remember
Searching shall I know is

9. 1 Samuel describes David's ascension from King Saul's protégé to his successor.
1. Friedrich von Schlegel (1772–1829), German Romantic philosopher. In his book on Caspar David Friedrich's paintings, Koerner cites Schlegel's "we are potential, *chaotic* organic beings," adding that Friedrich's landscapes aspire to what Schlegel called "artful chaos" (*Kunstchaos*). Two figures at a handrail above a river can be seen in a destroyed *Rückenfigur* by Friedrich, *Augustus Bridge in Dresden* (c. 1830).
2. Left-hand page of an open book; reverse side of a coin or medal.
3. In Greek mythology, the maidens entrusted with guarding Hera's tree of golden apples.

some sense deepest moment
What is and what appears

•

The way light is broken
To splinter color blue
the color of day yellow
near night the color of
passion red by morning
His name of grief being
red sound to sense sense
in place of the slaying
Tristram must be caught
Saw the mind otherwise
in thought or other sign
because we are not free
Saw the mind otherwise
Two thoughts in strife

•

Separation requires an
other quest for union
I use a white thread
half of the same paper
and in the sun's light
I place a lens so that
the sea reflects back
violet and blue making
rays easily more freely
your nativity and you
of light from that of
memory when eyelids close
so in dream sensation
Mind's trajected light

•

It is precision we have
to deal with we can pre-

scind space from color if
Thomas[4] was only using a
metaphor and metaphysics
professes to be metaphor
There is a way back to the
misinterpretation of her
message TheseusTristan is
on the ship AegeusIseut[5]
is a land watcher she is
a mastermind her frailty
turned to the light her
single vision twin soul half

•

Dilemma of dead loyalty
Mark's speeches are sham
Gottfried[6] shows Tristan
only hunting for pleasure
Emerald jacinth sapphire
chalcedony lovely Isolt
Topaz sardonyx chrysolite
ruby[7] sir Tristan the Court
sees only the beauty of
their persons that they
appear to be represented
Isolt sings for your eyes
Surveillance is a constant
theme in lyric poetry

•

Le Page disgracié his attempt
to buy a linnet[8] for his master
from a birdcatcher he hoped

4. Thomas of Brittany, the author of one of the earliest *Tristan* fragments. *Prescind:* cut off.
5. *Aegeus:* king of Athens and father of the legendary hero Theseus. Wounded, Tristan waits for Iseult to come to his aid, but dies after being tricked into thinking her ship has a black, not white, sail.
6. German poet Gottfried von Strasburg, who composed his version of "Tristan und Isolt" probably around 1211.
7. *Emerald . . . chalcedony* and *Topaz . . . ruby:* precious stones.
8. Songbird. *Le Page disgracié:* title of French poet Tristan L'Hermite's (c. 1601–1655) picaresque account of his travels abroad.

to comfort him with bird song
but gambled the money away
and in desperation bought a
wild linnet that didn't sing
His first words occur in the
linnet episode the young master's
perplexity about the bird's
silence so just the linnet's
silence provokes Tristan's *je*[9]
hero his shared identity the
remarkable bird list in *L'Orphée*[1]

•

L'Orphée—the lanner falcon
takes pigeons the sparrow-
hawk sparrows the goshawk
partridge when Tristan was
young he would have watched
hawks being flown his own
little hunting falcon his
observation of the way in
which other birds refrain
from their characteristic
habit of "mobbing the owl"
Vignette of the birdcatcher
in the street that day the
linnet's mimic reputation

•

Parasite and liar of genius
even emptiness is something
not nothingness of negation
having been born Not born
wrapped in protective long
cloak power of the woodland

9. I (French).
1. Play and film dealing with the Orpheus myth, by French avant-gardist Jean Cocteau (1889–1963).

No burrowing deep for warmth
The eagle of Prometheus[2] is a
vulture the vulture passions
go to a predator tricked up
forever unexpressed in half-
effaced ambiguous butterfly
disguises authentic regional
avifauna[3] an arsenal of stories

•

Ysolt that for naught might
carry them as they coasting
past strange land past haven
ruin garland effigy figment
sensible nature blue silver
orange yellow different lake
effect of the death-rebirth
eternal rush-return fragment
I cannot separate in thought
You cannot be separate from
perception everything draws
toward autumn[4] distant tumult
See that long row of folios
Surely Ysolt remembers Itylus[5]

•

Antigone[6] bears her secret in
her heart like an arrow she is
sent twice over into our dark
social as if real life as if real

2. In Greek mythology, Prometheus's punishment for giving humans fire is to be chained to a rock while an eagle feeds on his liver each day.
3. Birds.
4. Cf. the *Duino Elegies* (1922) of Austro-German poet Rainer Maria Rilke (1875–1926), cited in Koerner's book on Friedrich's paintings (also by Howe in a letter): "And we, spectators always, everywhere / Looking at, never out of, everything! / It fills us. We arrange it. It decays. / We re-arrange it, and decay ourselves."
5. In one story, Itylus (or Itys) is the ill-fated son of King Tereus and Procne, killed by his mother in revenge after his father rapes Philomela. In another story, Itylus is accidentally killed by his mother, Aedon, when she attempts to murder her sister-in-law's firstborn. She is changed into a nightingale, lamenting her son in song. Also the title of a poem by the English poet Algernon Charles Swinburne (1837–1909).
6. In Sophocles' tragedy of the same name, a woman who kills herself after she is imprisoned for burying her brother.

person proceeding into self-
knowledge as if there were no
proof just blind right reason
to assuage our violent earth
Ysolt's single vision of union
Precursor shadow self by self
in open place or on an acting
platform two personae meeting
Strophe[7] antistrophe which is
which dual unspeakable cohesion

•

Day binds the wide Sound
Bitter sound as truth is
silent as silent tomorrow
Motif of retreating figure
arrayed beyond expression
huddled unintelligible air
Theomimesis[8] divinity message
I have loved come veiling
Lyrist come veil come lure
echo remnant sentence spar
never never form wherefor
Wait some recognition you
Lyric over us love unclothe
Never forever whoso move

1999

7. Originally, in Greek choral poetry, a stanzalike series of lines forming a structure, which is then repeated in a response called an antistrophe.
8. Representation of divinity, but, according to Howe, "in relation to the viewer as halted traveler arrested by what she sees in the landscape—chaos and particularity, detail and distance" (letter to the editor). "Theomimesis" is also a chapter title of Koerner's book on Friedrich's landscape paintings.

Michael S. Harper
b. 1938

Though it was forbidden by his parents, young Michael S. Harper secretly enjoyed listening to their jazz recordings. "Jazz was my bible," he writes of his years as a college student. "How would it be to solo with that great tradition of the big bands honking you on? Could one do it in a poem?" ("Don't They Speak Jazz"). Jazz is an example of what the novelist Ralph Ellison calls "antagonistic cooperation": while the individual musician, soloist for a time, improvises, the other musicians both follow and guide him or her, and the individual must never lose touch with fellow performers. Harper's conception of the individual talent in relation to tradition also recalls T. S. Eliot's essays, another formative influence. For Harper, as for his vital precursors Sterling Brown and Langston Hughes, the blues are likewise important because they bridge poetry and music and because "they always say *yes* to life; meet life's terms but never accept them" ("Don't").

In Harper's context, "saying yes to life" is not an undiscriminating affirmation, for like the blues, his work repeatedly takes the view that life is at best a melancholy business, replete with losses and painful farewells. Drawing on the collective grief and rage at the base of jazz and the blues, Harper mourns the deaths of two infant sons in a series of tormented elegies, among the best postwar poems in the form. He fashions a strenuous style that painfully couples the emotional language of loss, guilt, and love ("We assume / you did not know we loved you") with the clinical language of the hospital ("collapsible isolette," "sterile hands," "bicarbonate," "plastic mask"). Having pursued premedical studies before being deterred by racism, Harper forces together scientific culture and black oral culture in violent collocations such as "*mamaborn, sweetsonchild / gonedowntown* into *researchtestingwarehousebatteryacid / mama-son-done-gone*" ("Nightmare Begins Responsibility"). The father's private grief is inseparable from a race-based historical experience; "Deathwatch" recalls a letter written to another mourning father, W. E. B. Du Bois, asking whether "negroes / are not able to cry." In the tensile fabric of Harper's poetry, as in that of jazz, we witness collisions and convergences between the personal and historical, blues refrains and idiosyncratic digressions, melodic cadences and "sour" notes. His lines are crowded, word pressing against word, image against image, so that each component is forced to assert its individual energies, to cooperate but with a certain antagonism.

Harper was born on March 18, 1938, in Brooklyn, New York. He went to the west coast for much of his education, attending the City College of Los Angeles and California State University at Los Angeles, where he earned a B.A. in 1961 and an M.A. in English in 1963. He also received an M.F.A. from the University of Iowa in 1963. Since 1971, he has been a professor at Brown University. In addition to publishing twelve books of his own poetry, he has edited anthologies of African American poetry and *The Collected Poems of Sterling A. Brown* (1980).

American History

Those four black girls blown up
in that Alabama church[1]
remind me of five hundred
middle passage blacks,[2]
in a net, under water
in Charleston harbor
so *redcoats*[3] wouldn't find them.
Can't find what you can't see
can you?

1970

We Assume: On the Death of Our Son, Reuben Masai Harper

We assume
that in twenty-eight hours,
lived in a collapsible isolette,[4]
you learned to accept pure oxygen
as the natural sky;
the scant shallow breaths
that filled those hours
cannot, did not make you fly—
but dreams were there
like crooked palmprints on
the twin-thick windows of the nursery—
in the glands of your mother.

We assume
the sterile hands
drank chemicals in and out
from lungs opaque with mucus,
pumped your stomach,
eeked the bicarbonate in
crooked, green-winged veins,
out in a plastic mask;

A woman who'd lost her first son
consoled us with an angel gone ahead
to pray for our family—
gone into that sky
seeking oxygen,
gone into autopsy,

1. By white racists in response to 1960s civil rights demonstrations.
2. Captured and en route from Africa to be sold as slaves.
3. That is, British soldiers patrolling the waters during an embargo.
4. Infant incubator.

a fine brown powdered sugar,
a disposable cremation:

We assume
you did not know we loved you.

1970

Reuben, Reuben

I reach from pain
to music great enough
to bring me back,
swollenhead, madness,
lovefruit, a pickle of hate
so sour my mouth twicked
up and would not sing;
there's nothing in the beat
to hold it in
melody and turn human skin;
a brown berry gone
to rot just two days on the branch;
we've lost a son,
the music, *jazz,* comes in.

1970

Deathwatch

Twitching in the cactus
hospital gown, a loon
on hairpin wings,
she tells me how
her episiotomy[5]
is perfectly sewn
and doesn't hurt
while she sits in a pile
of blood
which once cleaned
the placenta
my third son should be in.
She tells me how early
he is, and how strong,
like his father,
and long, like a black-

5. Surgical enlargement of the vulval orifice during labor.

stemmed Easter rose
in a white hand.

Just under five pounds
you lie there, a collapsed
balloon doll, burst in your
fifteenth hour, with the face
of your black father,
his fingers, his toes,
and eight voodoo
adrenalin holes in
your pinwheeled hair-lined
chest; you witness
your parents sign the autopsy
and disposal papers
shrunken to duplicate
in black ink
on white paper
like the country
you were born in,
unreal, asleep,
silent, almost alive.

This is a dedication
to our memory
of three sons—
two dead, one alive—
a reminder of a letter
to Du Bois[6]
from a student
at Cornell—on behalf
of his whole history class.
The class is confronted
with a question,
and no one—
not even the professor—
is sure of the answer:
"Will you please tell us
whether or not it is true
that negroes
are not able to cry?"

America needs a killing.
America needs a killing.
Survivors will be human.

1970

6. W. E. B. Du Bois (1868–1963), African American educator and writer.

Dear John, Dear Coltrane

a love supreme, a love supreme[7]
a love supreme, a love supreme

Sex fingers toes
in the marketplace
near your father's church
in Hamlet, North Carolina[8]—
witness to this love
in this calm fallow
of these minds,
there is no substitute for pain:
genitals gone or going,
seed burned out,
you tuck the roots in the earth,
turn back, and move
by river through the swamps,
singing: *a love supreme, a love supreme;*
what does it all mean?
Loss, so great each black
woman expects your failure
in mute change, the seed gone.
You plod up into the electric city—
your song now crystal and
the blues. You pick up the horn
with some will and blow
into the freezing night:
a love supreme, a love supreme—

Dawn comes and you cook
up the thick sin 'tween
impotence and death, fuel
the tenor sax cannibal
heart, genitals, and sweat
that makes you clean—
a love supreme, a love supreme—

Why you so black?
cause I am
why you so funky?
cause I am
why you so black?
cause I am
why you so sweet?
cause I am
why you so black?

7. A phrase chanted in *A Love Supreme* (1964), a four-part composition by African American jazz saxophonist John Coltrane (1926–1967).
8. Coltrane's birthplace.

cause I am
a love supreme, a love supreme:

So sick
you couldn't play *Naima*,[9]
so flat we ached
for song you'd concealed
with your own blood,
your diseased liver gave
out its purity,
the inflated heart
pumps out, the tenor kiss,
tenor love:
a love supreme, a love supreme—
a love supreme, a love supreme—

1970

Nightmare Begins Responsibility[1]

I place these numbed wrists to the pane
watching white uniforms whisk over
him in the tube-kept
prison
fear what they will do in experiment
watch my gloved stickshifting gasolined hands
breathe *boxcar-information-please* infirmary tubes
distrusting white-pink mending paperthin
silkened end hairs, distrusting tubes
shrunk in his *trunk-skincapped*
shaven head, in thighs
distrusting-white-hands-picking-baboon-light
on his son who will not make his second night
of this wardstrewn intensive airpocket
where his father's asthmatic
hymns of *night-train*, train done gone
his mother can only know that he has flown
up into essential calm unseen corridor
going boxscarred home, *mamaborn, sweetsonchild*
gonedowntown into *researchtestingwarehousebatteryacid*
mama-son-done-gone/me telling her 'nother
train tonight, no music, no breathstroked
heartbeat in my infinite distrust of them:

and of my distrusting self
white-doctor-who-breathed-for-him-all-night

9. Coltrane composition named for his first wife.
1. Cf. the epigraph to Irish poet W. B. Yeats's *Responsibilities* (1913): "In dreams begin responsibilities," later used as the title to the first collection published by Delmore Schwartz (1913–1966), American poet.

say it for two sons gone,
say nightmare, say it loud
panebreaking heartmadness:
nightmare begins responsibility.

1975

Double Elegy

Whatever city or country road
you two are on
there are nettles,
and the dark invisible
elements cling to your skin
though you do not cry
and you do not scratch
your arms at forty-five degree angles
as the landing point of a swan
in the Ohio, the Detroit River;

at the Paradise Theatre
you named the cellist
with the fanatical fingers
of the plumber, the exorcist,
and though the gimmickry at wrist
and kneecaps could lift the séance
table, your voice was real
in the gait and laughter of Uncle
Henry, who could dance on either
leg, wooden or real, to the sound
of the troop train, megaphone,
catching the fine pitch of a singer
on the athletic fields of Virginia.

At the Radisson Hotel,
we once took a fine angel
of the law to the convention center,
and put her down as an egret
in the subzero platform of a friend—
this is Minneapolis, the movies
are all of strangers, holding themselves
in the delicacy of treading water,
while they wait for the trumpet
of the 20th Century Limited[2]
over the bluff or cranny.
You two men like to confront
the craters of history and spillage,

2. Famous cross-country train.

our natural infections of you
innoculating blankets and fur,
ethos[3] of cadaver and sunflower.

I hold the dogwood blossom,
eat the pear, and watch the nettle
swim up in the pools
of the completed song
of Leadbelly and Little Crow[4]
crooning the buffalo and horse
to the changes and the bridge
of a twelve-string guitar,
the melody of "Irene";[5]
this is really goodbye—
I can see the precious stones
of embolism[6] and consumption
on the platinum wires of the mouth:
in the flowing rivers, in the public baths
of Ohio and Michigan.

1985

3. Distinguishing character.
4. Sioux Indian chief (1810–1863). *Leadbelly:* Huddie Ledbetter (1888–1949), itinerant blues singer and songwriter.
5. Leadbelly song, which became a major hit in the 1950s as "Goodnight Irene," recorded by many artists.
6. Sudden obstruction by an abnormal particle.

CHARLES SIMIC
b. 1938

After surviving the German bombing and occupation of his native Belgrade in World War II, then escaping Yugoslavia with his mother in 1948 into Austria and France, Charles Simic arrived at sixteen in the United States, haunted by memories of blasted buildings, displaced populations, and the sounds of his native Serbian. The wartime Central European experience shadows his poetry in large, black clouds of torture, dispossession, and loss. The landscape of Simic's poems is nightmarish: buildings are broken and askew, colors drab and dismal, sounds hushed and muted. Dwarfed by this gray panorama of futility are the folkloristic stick figures of the parent or grandparent, innocent child or old woman, vampire or executioner.

Yet Simic juxtaposes against this dull, ominous, vacant world images of pellucid clarity and vividness. Watches with tiny, incandescent wheels; a fly with turquoise wings; a doll's head with a painted mouth—the mind latches onto such sharp-edged details, briefly evading the vast blankness of the universe, the repressed horrors of an inconceivable past, and the sense that what really matters is always happening beyond the boundaries of consciousness. Instead of surrendering to the banalities and brutalities of history, Simic grips it with an antic humor, twisting and tweaking it in wordplay, buffoonery, offhand utterance, grotesque metaphor, and deadpan understatement. Precise amid indefiniteness, wry amid terror, Simic's poetry both acknowledges the degradations of modern history, including nationalisms and totalitarianisms of various kinds, and idiosyncratically, comically rejects them. Simic captures the wayward individuality of poetry when he outlandishly describes the "rude" propensities of his profession: "To be a poet," he says in "Assembly Required," "is to feel something like a unicyclist in a desert, a pornographic magician performing in the corner of the church during Mass, a drag queen attending night classes and blowing kisses at the teacher."

The sense of the absurd and the ridiculous, the juxtaposition of the mundane and the metaphysical, the fusion of everyday realism with folktale irrationality—these are Simic's versions of the surrealism he found in French and Latin American literature and in the Serbian poetry of Vasko Popa. In night school at the University of Chicago and afterwards, Simic also read poets such as Walt Whitman, Emily Dickinson, Hart Crane, Ezra Pound, and Theodore Roethke. He helped graft surrealism onto American poetry, along with James Tate, Mark Strand, Charles Wright, and Robert Bly. His style of grim laughter at the menace of modern life is, however, very much his own. Since his first volumes, published in the 1960s, Simic's poetry has retained its gnomic, minimalist terseness, but has loosened its plotting, expanded its range of reference, and increasingly incorporated the American urban experience.

Simic was born on May 9, 1938. Drafted into the U.S. Army in 1961, he received his B.A. from New York University in 1967 and became a U.S. citizen in 1971. In addition to many volumes of poetry, he has published books of essays, anthologies, and translations of French, Serbian, Croation, Macedonian, and Slovenian poetry. A winner of a MacArthur Fellowship in 1984 and the Pulitzer Prize in 1990, Simic has taught for several decades at the University of New Hampshire.

Fork

This strange thing must have crept
Right out of hell.
It resembles a bird's foot
Worn around the cannibal's neck.

As you hold it in your hand,
As you stab with it into a piece of meat,
It is possible to imagine the rest of the bird:
Its head which like your fist
Is large, bald, beakless, and blind.

1969

Watch Repair

A small wheel
Incandescent,
Shivering like
A pinned butterfly.

Hands thrown up
In all directions:

The crossroads
One arrives at
In a nightmare.

Higher than that
Number 12 presides
Like a beekeeper
Over the swarming honeycomb
Of the open watch.

Other wheels
That could fit
Inside a raindrop.

Tools
That must be splinters
Of arctic starlight.

Tiny golden mills
Grinding invisible
Coffee beans.

When the coffee's boiling
Cautiously,
So it doesn't burn us,
We raise it
To the lips
Of the nearest
Ear.

1974

A Wall

That's the only image
That turns up.

A wall all by itself,
Poorly lit, beckoning,
But no sense of the room,
Not even a hint
Of why it is I remember
So little and so clearly:

The fly I was watching,
The details of its wings
Glowing like turquoise.
Its feet, to my amusement
Following a minute crack—

An eternity
Around that simple event.

And nothing else; and nowhere
To go back to;
And no one else
As far as I know to verify.

1977

Prodigy

I grew up bent over
a chessboard.

I loved the word *endgame.*

All my cousins looked worried.

It was a small house
near a Roman graveyard.
Planes and tanks
shook its windowpanes.

A retired professor of astronomy
taught me how to play.

That must have been in 1944.

In the set we were using,
the paint had almost chipped off
the black pieces.

The white King was missing
and had to be substituted for.

I'm told but do not believe
that that summer I witnessed
men hung from telephone poles.

I remember my mother
blindfolding me a lot.
She had a way of tucking my head
suddenly under her overcoat.

In chess, too, the professor told me,
the masters play blindfolded,
the great ones on several boards
at the same time.

1980

Classic Ballroom Dances

Grandmothers who wring the necks
Of chickens; old nuns
With names like Theresa, Marianne,
Who pull schoolboys by the ear;

The intricate steps of pickpockets
Working the crowd of the curious
At the scene of an accident; the slow shuffle
Of the evangelist with a sandwich board;

The hesitation of the early-morning customer
Peeking through the window grille
Of a pawnshop; the weave of a little kid
Who is walking to school with eyes closed;

And the ancient lovers, cheek to cheek,
On the dance floor of the Union Hall,
Where they also hold charity raffles
On rainy Monday nights of an eternal November.

1980

Spoons with Realistic Dead Flies on Them

I cause a great many worries to my mother.
My body will run with the weeds some day.
My head will be carried by slaughterhouse ants,
The carnivorous, bloody-aproned ants.

That was never in any of your legends, O saints!
The years she spent working in a novelty store:
Joy buzzers, false beards, and dead flies
To talk to between the infrequent customers.

A room rented from a minor demon.
An empty bird cage and a coffee mill for company.
A hand-operated one for her secret guardian angel
To take a turn grinding the slow hours.

Though I'm not a believer—
Neither is she, and that's why she worries,
Looks both ways crossing the street
At two gusts of nothing and nothing.

1982

Eastern European Cooking

While Marquis de Sade had himself buggered[1]—
O just around the time the Turks
Were roasting my ancestors on spits,
Goethe wrote "The Sorrows of Young Werther."[2]

It was chilly, raw, down-in-the-mouth
We were slurping bean soup thick with smoked sausage,
On 2nd Avenue,[3] where years before I saw an old horse
Pull a wagon piled up high with flophouse mattresses.

Anyway, as I was telling my uncle Boris,
With my mouth full of pig's feet and wine:
"While they were holding hands and sighing under parasols,
We were being hung by our tongues."

"I make no distinction between scum,"
He said, and he meant everybody,
Us and them: A breed of murderers' helpers,
Evil-smelling torturers' apprentices.

1982

Northern Exposure

When old women say, it smells of snow,
In a whisper barely audible
Which still rouses the sick man upstairs
So he opens his eyes wide and lets them fill

With the grayness of the remaining daylight.
When old women say, how quiet it is,
And truly today no one came to visit,
While the one they still haven't shaved

Lifts the wristwatch to his ear and listens.
In it, something small, subterranean
And awful in intent, chews rapidly.
When old women say, time to turn on the lights,

And not a single one gets up to do so,
For now there are loops and loose knots around their feet

1. Sodomized. Marquis de Sade (1740–1814), French nobleman whose sexually explicit novels and plays, many of which were written in prisons or asylums, gave rise to the term *sadism*.
2. Johann Wolfgang von Goethe (1749–1832), German poet, playwright, and philosopher, preeminent figure of German Romanticism, wrote the novel *The Sorrows of Young Werther* (1774), which tells the story of a hypersensitive young man led to commit suicide by his sense of alienation and disappointed love. *Turks:* Simic's native Serbia was under the Turkish Ottoman Empire from the fourteenth century until 1878.
3. In New York City; many Eastern European immigrants have lived on the Lower East Side of Manhattan.

As if someone is scribbling over them
With a piece of charcoal found in the cold stove.

1983

Cameo Appearance

I had a small, nonspeaking part
In a bloody epic. I was one of the
Bombed and fleeing humanity.
In the distance our great leader
Crowed like a rooster from a balcony,
Or was it a great actor
Impersonating our great leader?

That's me there, I said to the kiddies.
I'm squeezed between the man
With two bandaged hands raised
And the old woman with her mouth open
As if she were showing us a tooth

That hurts badly. The hundred times
I rewound the tape, not once
Could they catch sight of me
In that huge gray crowd,
That was like any other gray crowd.

Trot off to bed, I said finally.
I know I was there. One take
Is all they had time for.
We ran, and the planes grazed our hair,
And then they were no more
As we stood dazed in the burning city,
But, of course, they didn't film that.

1996

Head of a Doll

Whose demon are you,
Whose god? I asked
Of the painted mouth
Half buried in the sand.

A brooding gull
Made a brief assessment,
And tiptoed away
Nodding to himself.

At dusk a firefly or two
Dowsed its eye pits.
And later, toward midnight,
I even heard mice.

1999

Les Murray
b. 1938

Les Murray is widely acclaimed as the most versatile and verbally inventive Australian poet of his generation. Exploring his national experience, as well as the musical resources and figurative reach of the English language, Murray has been compared to two other poets at the margins of the former British Empire—Seamus Heaney and Derek Walcott. Like his Irish and Caribbean contemporaries, Murray risks metaphorical lushness and sonic opulence in his poetry, in contrast with the often minimalist models in metropolitan America and Britain. Affectionately dubbing the Australian poet "Crocodile Dandy," Walcott places the "shaggy power, grace, and mass of Les Murray's poems" in a postcolonial context. The so-called "barbarians approaching the capital," Walcott says, not only bring "the vandalization of the imperial language," but also possess "the imperial literature as if it were their own" (*The New Republic,* 1989). Murray seems intent on proving that the provincial farmer living in the imperial outpost can write poetry as learned, authoritative, and technically virtuosic as any from the metropolitan center. A poet equipped with dazzling linguistic skills and a deep knowledge of classical and modern literature, Murray nevertheless styles himself a bumbling, anti-elitist "redneck"—his ironically honorific term for working-class people from the Australian bush. A silver-tongued brawler, he wrings new sounds and sense from English.

Having grown up on a modest, family dairy farm in New South Wales, Murray returned to farming in 1985 after a number of years as translator and as writer-in-residence at various Australian universities. Many of his poems suggest the crusty Catholic conservatism and the shambling, unfashionable background of his humble rural roots. A rugged Australian ironist, Murray is suspicious of academic and city-bred pieties. But he often foregoes social satire and emphasizes compassion instead, whether sympathetically entering into the minute life of a crustacean in "Mollusc" or into the traumatic experience of a severely burned six-year-old child in "Cotton Flannelette."

Hailing the Aborigines for creating poetic forms that are keenly responsive to the Australian landscape, Murray incorporates stylistic and rhetorical strategies learned from indigenous oral poetry. In "The Buladelah-Taree Holiday Song Cycle," he borrows the lens of Aboriginal poetry to defamiliarize vacationing white Australians, revitalize the natural world, and mythologize the land. This poetic sequence formally exemplifies the intercultural process he described to an interviewer: "Every invader, every settler gradually becomes the people who are conquered. Aborigines didn't appreciate the word conquer, but in the end they will conquer us. Through all sorts of mixing and mingling and learning from each other, they won't be the same Aborigines we first encountered, and we won't be the white people that they first encountered" ("Embracing the Vernacular").

In attempting to define poetry, Murray often links it to key terms such as "presence," "interest," and "dream." He sees in poetry a "precarious fusion" of "the dreaming mind, the waking, intellectual mind, and the body." Drawing on Catholic tradition, Murray writes, "Art is a way of making a body for yourself, a body for yourself and others. A new body. You give embodiment to things" ("Embracing the Vernacular"). The balance of dream, intellect, and body has to be just right. The "linkage with dream" helps keep poetry from degenerating into what Murray disparages as "head poems" (1998 interview). Lasting poetry involves intellect but also "working always beyond // your own intelligence" ("The Instrument").

The language of Murray's poetry startles and amuses, reveling in the fecundity and elasticity of English. Murray plays energetically on verbal sonorities. He delights in the eddying reflections of homonyms and rhymes, the slapstick conjunctions of puns and onomatopoeia, in poems such as "On Removing Spiderweb." His wordplay conveys a robust pleasure in language as a tactile medium, without retreating into self-reflexive obscurity. Murray eagerly draws out the interconnections among words held together by alliteration, rhythm, rhyme, consonance, hyphenation, syntax, repetition, enjambment, and elided punctuation. By playing on these verbal resources in a poem such as "The Powerline Incarnation," he suggests a profound interconnectedness among things. Circuits of electricity override differences to fuse farms with towns, Mozart with Johnny Cash, the poet's body itself, like the body of his poetry, acting as a medium of confluence.

Metaphor, for Murray, like verbal music, serves as a connective force. In the rapid imaginative gush of some poems, such as the charmingly nostalgic "The Milk Lorry," freshly minted metaphors spill over one another in rapid succession, the poet discovering similitude between the swaying old cans in a milk truck and dancers, armed warriors, even students in "a seminar engrossed // in one swaying tradition." Weaving the world together through resemblances in sound and image, Murray's sensibility—by turns elegiac and brash, earthy and ironic—is attuned to the rich variety of human experience and to the oneness behind the many.

The Powerline Incarnation

When I ran to snatch the wires off our roof
hands bloomed teeth shouted I was almost seized
held back from this life
                                        O flumes   O chariot reins
you cover me with lurids deck me with gaudies feed
my coronal[1]   a scream sings in the air
above our dance   you slam it to me with farms
that you dark on and off numb hideous strong friend
Tooma and Geehi[2] freak and burr through me
rocks fire-trails damwalls mountain-ash trees slew
to darkness through me   I zap them underfoot
with the swords of my shoes
                                        I am receiving mountains
piloting around me   Crackenback   Anembo
the Fiery Walls[3]   I make a hit in towns
I've never visited: smoke curls lightbulbs pop grey
discs hitch and slow   I plough the face of Mozart
and Johnny Cash[4]   I bury and smooth their song

1. Crown or garland for the head; cf. also the related word *coronary*.
2. Australian rivers.
3. Like Crackenback and Anembo, Australian mountains.
4. American country musician (b. 1932).

I crack it for copper links and fusebox spiders
I call my Friend from the circuitry of mixers
whipping cream for a birthday   I distract the immortal
Inhuman from hospitals
                                        to sustain my jazz
and here is Rigel[5] in a glove of flesh
my starry hand discloses smoke, cold Angel.

Vehicles that run on death come howling into
our street with lights a thousandth of my blue
arms keep my wife from my beauty   from my species
the jewels in my tips
                                        I would accept her in
blind white remarriage   cover her with wealth
to arrest the heart   we'd share Apache leaps
crying out *Disyzygy!*[6]
                                        shield her from me, humans
from this happiness I burn to share   this touch
sheet car   live ladder   wildfire garden shrub—
away off I hear the bombshell breakers thrown
diminishing me   a meaninglessness coming
over the circuits
                                the god's deserting me
but I have dived in the mainstream   jumped the graphs
I have transited the dreams of crew-cut boys named Buzz
and the hardening music
                                        to the big bare place
where the strapped-down seekers, staining white clothes, come
to be shown the Zeitgeist[7]
                                        passion and death my skin
my heart all logic   I am starring there
and must soon flame out
                                        having seen the present god
It who feels nothing   It who answers prayers.

1977

From The Buladelah-Taree Holiday Song Cycle[8]

3

It is good to come out after driving and walk on the bare grass;
walking out, looking all around, relearning that country.
Looking out for snakes, and looking out for rabbits as well;
going into the shade of myrtles to try their cupped climate, swinging by
    one hand around them,
in that country of the Holiday . . .

5. Star in the Orion constellation.
6. Play on *syzygy*, the alignment of three celestial bodies (e.g., the sun, the moon, and Earth, during an eclipse).
7. Spirit of the times (German).
8. Buladelah is a town and Taree a city in a popular tourist region in New South Wales, Australia. The locations mentioned throughout the poem are in this region. The poem is an imitation of Aboriginal song cycles.

stepping behind trees to the dam, as if you had a gun,
to that place of the Wood Duck,
to that place of the Wood Duck's Nest,
proving you can still do it; looking at the duck who hasn't seen you,
the mother duck who'd run Catch Me (broken wing) I'm Fatter (broken wing), having hissed to her children.

6

Barbecue smoke is rising at Legge's Camp; it is steaming into the midday air,
all around the lake shore, at the Broadwater, it is going up among the paperbark trees,
a heat-shimmer of sauces, rising from tripods and flat steel, at that place of the cone shells,
at that place of the Seagrass, and the tiny segmented things swarming in it, and of the Pelican.
Dogs are running around disjointedly; water escapes from their mouths,
confused emotions from their eyes; humans snarl at them Gwanout and Hereboy, not varying their tone much;
the impoverished dog people, suddenly sitting down to nuzzle themselves; toddlers side with them:
toddlers, running away purposefully at random, among cars, into big drownie water (come back, Cheryl-Ann!).
They rise up as charioteers, leaning back on the tow-bar; all their attributes bulge at once:
swapping swash shoulder-wings for the white-sheeted shoes that bear them,
they are skidding over the flat glitter, stiff with grace, for once not travelling to arrive.
From the high dunes over there, the rough blue distance, at length they come back behind the boats,
and behind the boats' noise, cartwheeling, or sitting down, into the lake's warm chair;
they wade ashore and eat with the families, putting off that uprightness, that assertion,
eating with the families who love equipment, and the freedom from equipment,
with the fathers who love driving, and lighting a fire between stones.

8

Forests and State Forests, all down off the steeper country; mosquitoes are always living in there:
they float about like dust motes and sink down, at the places of the Stinging Tree,[9]
and of the Staghorn Fern; the males feed on plant-stem fluid, absorbing that watery ichor;
the females meter the air, feeling for the warm-blooded smell, needing blood for their eggs.

9. Australian nettle.

They find the dingo in his sleeping-place, they find his underbelly and his anus;
they find the possum's face, they drift up the ponderous pleats of the fig tree, way up into its rigging,
the high camp of the fruit bats; they feed on the membranes and ears of bats; tired wings cuff air at them;
their eggs burning inside them, they alight on the muzzles of cattle,
the half-wild bush cattle, there at the place of the Sleeper Dump, at the place of the Tallowwoods.[1]
The males move about among growth tips; ingesting solutions, they crouch intently;
the females sing, needing blood to breed their young; their singing is in the scrub country;
their tune comes to the name-bearing humans, who dance to it and irritably grin at it.

12

Now the sun is an applegreen blindness through the swells, a white blast on the sea face, flaking and shoaling;
now it is burning off the mist; it is emptying the density of trees, it is spreading upriver,
hovering above the casuarina[2] needles, there at Old Bar and Manning Point;
flooding the island farms, it abolishes the milkers' munching breath
as they walk towards the cowyards; it stings a bucket here, a teatcup there.
Morning steps into the world by ever more southerly gates; shadows weaken their north skew
on Middle Brother, on Cape Hawke, on the dune scrub toward Seal Rocks;
steadily the heat is coming on, the butter-water time, the clothes-sticking time;
grass covers itself with straw; abandoned things are thronged with spirits;
everywhere wood is still with strain; birds hiding down the creek galleries, and in the cockspur canes;
the cicada is hanging up her sheets; she takes wing off her music-sheets.
Cars pass with a rational zoom, panning quickly towards Wingham,
through the thronged and glittering, the shale-topped ridges, and the cattlecamps,
towards Wingham for the cricket, the ball knocked hard in front of smoked-glass ranges, and for the drinking.
In the time of heat, the time of flies around the mouth, the time of the west verandah;
looking at that umbrage along the ranges, on the New England[3] side;
clouds begin assembling vaguely, a hot soiled heaviness on the sky, away there towards Gloucester;
a swelling up of clouds, growing there above Mount George, and above Tipperary;
far away and hot with light; sometimes a storm takes root there, and fills the heavens rapidly;

1. Variety of eucalyptus tree.
2. Australian pine tree.
3. District on and around the New England Tableland, in New South Wales.

darkening, boiling up and swaying on its stalks, pulling this way and that, blowing round by Krambach;
coming white on Bulby, it drenches down on the paddocks, and on the wire fences;
the paddocks are full of ghosts, and people in cornbag hoods approaching;
lights are lit in the house; the storm veers mightily on its stem, above the roof; the hills uphold it;
the stony hills guide its dissolution; gullies opening and crumbling down, wrenching tussocks and rolling them;
the storm carries a greenish-grey bag; perhaps it will find hail and send it down, starring cars, flattening tomatoes,
in the time of the Washaways,[4] of the dead trunks braiding water, and of the Hailstone Yarns.

1977

The Milk Lorry

Now the milk lorry is a polished submarine
that rolls up at midday, attaches a trunk and inhales
the dairy's tank to a frosty snore in minutes

but its forerunner was the high-tyred barn of crisp mornings,
reeking Diesel and mammary, hazy in its roped interior
as a carpet under beaters, as it crashed along potholed lanes

cooeeing at schoolgirls. Long planks like unshipped oars
butted, levelling in there, because between each farm's
stranded wharf of milk cans, the work was feverish slotting

of floors above floors, for load. It was sling out the bashed
paint-collared empties and waltz in the full,
stumbling on their rims under ribaldry, tilting their big gallons

then the schoolboy's calisthenic, hoisting steel men man-high
till the glancing hold was a magazine of casque armour,
a tinplate 'tween-decks,[5] a seminar engrossed

in one swaying tradition, behind the speeding doorways
that tempted a truant to brace and drop, short of town,
and spend the day, with book or not, down under

the bridge of a river that by dinnertime would be
tongueing like cattledogs, or down a moth-dusty reach
where the fish-feeding milk boat and cedar barge once floated.

1987

4. Erosion caused by flooding.
5. Area "between decks" on a sailing vessel. *Casque armour:* armor for the head.

On Removing Spiderweb

Like summer silk its denier
but stickily, oh, ickilier,
miffed bunny-blinder, silver tar,
gesticuli-gesticular,
crepe when cobbed, crap when rubbed,
stretchily adhere-and-there
and everyway, nap-snarled or sleek,
glibly hubbed with grots to tweak:
ehh weakly bobbined tae yer neb,
spit it Phuoc Tuy! filthy web!

1990

Mollusc

By its nobship sailing upside down,
by its inner sexes, by the crystalline
pimplings of its skirts, by the sucked-on
lifelong kiss of its toppling motion,
by the viscose[6] optics now extruded
now wizened instantaneously, by the
ridges grating up a food-path, by
the pop shell in its nick of dry,
by excretion, the earthworm coils, the glibbing,
by the gilt slipway, and by pointing
perhaps as far back into time as
ahead, a shore being folded interior,
by boiling on salt, by coming uncut over
a razor's edge, by hiding the Oligocene[7]
underleaf may this and every snail sense
itself ornament the weave of presence.

1992

Corniche[8]

I work all day and hardly drink at all.[9]
I can reach down and feel if I'm depressed.
I adore the Creator because I made myself
and a few times a week a wire jags in my chest.

The first time, I'd been coming apart all year,
weeping, incoherent; cigars had given me up:

6. Substance used to make rayon.
7. From the Tertiary Period (geologic).
8. Coastal road.
9. Cf. the opening of "Aubade," by the English poet Philip Larkin (1922–1985): "I work all day, and get half drunk at night."

any road round a cliff edge I'd whimper along in low gear
then: cardiac horror. Masking my pulse's calm lub-dub.

It was the victim-sickness. Adrenaline howling in my head,
the black dog was my brain. Come to drown me in my breath
was energy's black hole, depression, compere[1] of the predawn show
when, returned from a pee, you stew and welter in your death.

The rogue space rock is on course to snuff your world,
sure. But go acute, and its oncoming fills your day.
The brave die but once? I could go a hundred times a week,
clinging to my pulse with the world's edge inches away.

Laugh, who never shrank around wizened genitals there
or killed themselves to stop dying. The blow that never falls
batters you stupid. Only gradually do
you notice a slight scorn in you for what appals.

A self inside self, cool as conscience, one to be erased
in your final night, or faxed, still knows beneath
all the mute grand opera and uncaused effect—
that death which can be imagined is not true death.

1996

Cotton Flannelette

Shake the bed, the blackened child whimpers,
O *Shake the bed!* through beak lips that never
will come unwry. And wearily the iron-
framed mattress, with nodding crockery bulbs,
jinks on its way.
Her brothers and sister take
shifts with the terrible glued-together baby
when their unsleeping absolute mother
reels out to snatch an hour, back to stop
the rocking and wring pale blue soap-water
over nude bladders and blood-webbed chars.[2]

Even their cranky evasive father
is awed to stand watches rocking the bed.
Lids frogged shut, O *please shake the bed,*
her contour whorls and braille tattoos
from where, in her nightdress, she flared
out of hearth-drowse to a marrow shriek
pedalling full tilt firesleeves[3] in mid-air,
are grainier with repair
than when the doctor, crying *Dear God, woman!*

1. Master of ceremonies.
2. Substances burned to carbon.
3. Sleeves used as insulation in engines.

No one can save that child. Let her go!
spared her the treatments of the day.

Shake the bed. Like: count phone poles, rhyme,
classify realities, bang the head, any
iteration that will bring, in the brain's forks,
the melting molecules of relief,
and bring them again.
O rock the bed!

Nibble water with bared teeth, make lymph
like arrowroot gruel, as your mother grips you
for weeks in the untrained perfect language,
till the doctor relents. Salves and wraps you
in dressings that will be the fire again,
ripping anguish off agony,
and will confirm
the ploughland ridges in your woman's skin
for the sixty more years your family weaves you
on devotion's loom, rick-racking the bed
as you yourself, six years old, instruct them.

1996

Seamus Heaney
1939–2013

Rich, complex, and multifarious, Seamus Heaney's poetry yields a string of paradoxes. It is popular and accessible, with a wide readership in Ireland and across the anglophone world. Yet its lyric subtlety and rigorous technique have attracted legions of poets and academic critics. It is earthy and matter-of-fact, saturated with the physical textures, sights, smells, and sounds of farm life. Yet it is also visionary, enacting spiritual pilgrimages and tentatively crediting miracles. Heaney represented his poetic quest as digging, a grim archaeological process of recovery from dark and unknowable depths. Yet he also moved upward into the open and the glimmering light of hope, spirit, and unbridled imaginings. He wrote masterfully in meter and rhyme, revitalized meditative blank verse, and composed a number of sonnet sequences, such as his elegy for his mother, "Clearances." Yet he was also a superb poet in the looser forms of "Bog Queen" and "Punishment," his irregularly metered, short lines grouped in unrhymed quatrains. Heaney was a genial poet, brimming with wordplay and stories. Yet he was also reticent and indirect, tactfully withholding and slyly concealing.

Many of the paradoxes of Heaney's work can be understood only in the context of his historical situation as an Irish Catholic who grew up in the predominantly Protestant North of Ireland under British rule. Heaney was a political poet, affirming his affinities with the Catholic civil rights movement, which has struggled against British and Protestant domination. Yet he refused slogans, journalistic reportage, and political pieties, instead scrutinizing the roots of communal identity and exploring his ambivalences. He was a devotedly Irish poet, who translated poetry from Gaelic; renewed Irish traditions such as the *aisling*, or vision poem; drew on the examples of W. B. Yeats, James Joyce, and Patrick Kavanagh; and strongly rejected descriptions of himself as "British." Yet he recognized his many debts to and affinities with British poets, from *Beowulf* (his prize-winning translation was published in 1999) to John Keats, William Wordsworth, Thomas Hardy, Gerard Manley Hopkins, Wilfred Owen, W. H. Auden, and Ted Hughes, and his poetry ironically uses Anglo-Saxon alliterative effects and other techniques to suggest the sounds of Irish in English. He was both a private poet—skillfully kneading his feelings of grief, love, wonder, and ambivalence into poems about his family and his humble origins—and a public poet, finding within himself the many conflicting responses of people of different views to large-scale historical events and atrocities. Eluding categories, his poetry is instantly recognizable, marked by a distinctive sensibility, grace, and sound. Some of these complexities can be explained as shifts in emphasis across his career—from the early blank verse poems of bucolic childhood to the middle free verse poems of self-questioning and guilt to later poems, written in varied forms, of mourning, vision, and spiritual quest. But any given phase in his writing life, if scrutinized, will reveal divergent propensities.

Born just two and a half months after Yeats died and widely seen as the greatest Irish poet since Yeats, Heaney responded to his major precursor with characteristic ambivalence. Reacting against "something too male and assertive" in poems such as "Under Ben Bulben," Heaney criticized Yeats for moving, by career's end, "within his mode of vision as within some invisible ring of influence and defence, some bullet-proof glass of the spirit." At the same time, he recognized in some of Yeats's late poems an introspection, a "humility," a "tenderness towards life and its uncompletedness" ("Yeats as an Example?"). The differences between Yeats and Heaney are partly explained by the discrepant affinities of a would-be aristocratic Anglo-Irish Protestant and a working-class Northern Irish Catholic. Nature for Heaney did not mean lakes, woods, and swans visible from the houses of the aristocracy. Instead, a farmer's son, Heaney describes, in "Station Island" II, the "dark-clumped grass where cows or horses dunged, / the cluck when pith-lined chestnut shells split open" (the latter a line that Hopkins would have welcomed). Heaney's nature was agricultural; it includes such farm equipment as a harrow pin, a sledge-head, a trowel. This contemporary poetry marks its difference from Yeats's by subdued rhythms, less clamant philosophy, less prophetic utterance, but Heaney's abiding respect for Yeats is evident in his rewriting of his precursor's work, as in the recasting of "The Fisherman" by "Casualty."

Irish poetry since Yeats has been at pains to purge itself of the grand manner, and Heaney austerely excluded it. His sounds are contained and clipped, "definite / as a steel nib's downstroke, quick and clean" ("Station Island" XII). Even his lyrical passages are tightly reined. He liked rugged words that sound like dialect but are respectably standard, such as *flenge* or *loaning* or *slub silk* or *scutch* or Joyce's *tundish.* Alliterations, assonances, and guttural sounds play a prominent part. Although Heaney's verse is unpretentious, this did not keep him from unearthing apt and unexpected images or from seeing the visible world as a substance compounded from materials no longer visible but still suspended in it.

The "voice of conscience and remorse" that Heaney singled out for praise in Yeats's "Man and the Echo" is a dominant aspect of Heaney's aesthetic. Out of his divided loyalties to history and art, to the dead and the living, to his rural roots and his literary gifts, Heaney crafted poems of emotional and ethical complexity. "Is it any wonder when I thought / I would have second thoughts?" he asks in "Terminus"; "I grew up in between." The political in-betweenness of a Catholic boy in the predominantly Protestant Ulster, an Irishman steeped in the English literary canon and language, a farmer's son become a rich and renowned poet are obvious. Incertus was the self-mocking pen name under which Heaney published his first poems in college. In poems about his origins, such as "Digging," "Alphabets," "The Stone Verdict," "Clearances," and "Electric Light," Heaney tries to honor his humble beginnings and ancestry while striking out on his own—"An educated man," in the words of the fisherman of "Casualty."

The voice of conscience and remorse is even stronger in Heaney's poetry about the bloody Troubles of Northern Ireland. In his essay "The Interesting Case of Nero, Chekov's Cognac and a Knocker" (1987), Heaney recalls an evening in Belfast when he and a friend decided, after explosions jolted the city, not to record songs and poems as they had planned: "to have sung and said the poems in those conditions would have been a culpable indulgence." Heaney uses this anecdote to reflect on the tension between "Song and Suffering"—song as the condition of "liberation and abundance" and suffering as the condition of the contemporary world. Even as Heaney concedes that to sing and recite after the explosions might have seemed an "affront," he questions whether he and his friend did the right thing in silencing themselves. Riddled by the inescapable contradictions between what he calls in "The Grauballe Man" "beauty and atrocity," Heaney interrogates song but refuses to be muffled by suffering. In his elegy for Francis Ledwidge, an Irishman who died fighting on behalf of the British Empire that was suppressing Irish nationalism, Heaney sees the mirror of his inner conflicts: "In you, our dead enigma, all the strains / Criss-cross in useless equilibrium."

In his first volumes of poetry, written in the early to mid-1960s, Heaney plays out his growth, guilt, and developing sexuality in the rural landscape of his childhood. But his poetry takes a darker turn after the eruption of internecine violence in Northern Ireland in 1969, which culminated in the 1972 Bloody Sunday killing of thirteen Catholic civilians by British paratroopers during a civil rights march in Derry. Across several books, but especially in *North* (1975), he wrote a series of grim "bog poems," about well-preserved Iron Age corpses discovered buried in the peat of Northern Europe and Ireland. Heaney saw the peat bog as a kind of "memory bank," or unconscious, of the landscape. These poems view contemporary violence through the lens of ancient myths, sacrifices, and feuds, an oblique approach that gives Heaney's poetry about the Troubles an unusual depth and toughness.

In the essay "Feeling into Words," Heaney describes how he discovered emblems for the violence in Northern Ireland in a book published in translation in 1969, "the year the killing started," entitled *The Bog People:* "And the unforgettable photographs of these victims blended in my mind with photographs of atrocities, past and present, in the long rites of Irish political and religious struggles." Heaney takes a serious moral risk in depicting terrorist and antiterrorist atrocities as repetitions of ancient ritual sacrifices, but while reactivating archetypal fertility myths in which ritual death assures rebirth, he aborts the usual payoff of these paradigms. The dead undergo no spiritual transcendence, but remain tenaciously material, bodies bound to the earth. At the end of "Bog Queen," he insists on bleak images of the woman's deadness—bone, skull, stitches—even as he allows her rebirth into the light and into his dramatic monologue: "and I rose from the dark, / hacked bone, skull-ware, / frayed stitches, tufts, / small gleams on the bank." In the bog poems, Heaney scrupulously inspects his own poetic art for any aestheticizing of death and murder, and the poems that result are cramped, anguished, and self-aware, among the most powerful poems about political violence written in the twentieth century.

In the late 1970s, Heaney moved away from clipped, free verse lines, emblematic for him of inwardness, to longer lines in a more conversational idiom, suggesting a more outward and social impulse. He wrote elegies for people he knew who were killed in the violence, such as his cousin Colum McCartney, elegized in "The Strand at Lough Beg," and his acquaintance Louis O'Neill, recalled in "Casualty." He returns to McCartney's death in one of his most adventurous groups of poems, "Station Island," a pilgrimage on which the poet encounters a series of familiar ghosts, who ably tell their stories to this Irish Dante in a modified terza rima and implicate him in their replies. A principal ghost is that of Joyce, who rejects the poet's pilgrimage: "Your obligation / is not discharged by any common rite." He urges Heaney instead to "keep at a tangent" and find his own "echo-soundings, searches, probes, allurements, / / elver gleams in the dark of the whole sea." Heaney's subsequent volumes pursue still further the more visionary or "spiritual" temper announced in "Station Island," while also recovering some of the retrospective pastoralism of his earliest verse and the self-scrutiny of his middle work.

Heaney was born on April 13, 1939, in Mossbawn, County Derry. He was educated at a boarding school, St. Columb's College, before going on to take a First Class Honours degree in English at Queen's University, in Belfast, where he returned in 1965, after several years of schoolteaching. He also spent a year at the University of California, Berkeley (1970–71), where he read American poets such as William Carlos Williams and Robert Creeley. He moved to County Wicklow, in the Irish Republic, in 1972 and became a citizen and full-time writer, taking up residency in Dublin in 1976. From 1982 to 1996, he spent part of each year as a professor at Harvard University, which he continued to visit every other year. In 1995, he won the Nobel Prize in Literature.

Digging[1]

Between my finger and my thumb
The squat pen rests; snug as a gun.

Under my window, a clean rasping sound
When the spade sinks into gravelly ground:
My father, digging. I look down

Till his straining rump among the flowerbeds
Bends low, comes up twenty years away
Stooping in rhythm through potato drills[2]
Where he was digging.

The coarse boot nestled on the lug, the shaft
Against the inside knee was levered firmly.
He rooted out tall tops, buried the bright edge deep
To scatter new potatoes that we picked,
Loving their cool hardness in our hands.

By God, the old man could handle a spade.
Just like his old man.

My grandfather cut more turf[3] in a day
Than any other man on Toner's bog.
Once I carried him milk in a bottle
Corked sloppily with paper. He straightened up
To drink it, then fell to right away

1. See Heaney's account of the poem in the essay "Feeling into Words," p. 1096 in this volume.
2. Furrows in which seeds are sown.
3. Slabs of dried peat commonly used as domestic fuel in Ireland.

Nicking and slicing neatly, heaving sods
Over his shoulder, going down and down
For the good turf. Digging.

The cold smell of potato mould, the squelch and slap
Of soggy peat, the curt cuts of an edge
Through living roots awaken in my head.
But I've no spade to follow men like them.

Between my finger and my thumb
The squat pen rests.
I'll dig with it.

1966

Death of a Naturalist

All year the flax-dam[4] festered in the heart
Of the townland; green and heavy headed
Flax had rotted there, weighted down by huge sods.
Daily it sweltered in the punishing sun.
Bubbles gargled delicately, bluebottles[5]
Wove a strong gauze of sound around the smell.
There were dragon-flies, spotted butterflies,
But best of all was the warm thick slobber
Of frogspawn that grew like clotted water
In the shade of the banks. Here, every spring
I would fill jampotfuls of the jellied
Specks to range on window-sills at home,
On shelves at school, and wait and watch until
The fattening dots burst into nimble-
Swimming tadpoles. Miss Walls would tell us how
The daddy frog was called a bullfrog
And how he croaked and how the mammy frog
Laid hundreds of little eggs and this was
Frogspawn. You could tell the weather by frogs too
For they were yellow in the sun and brown
In rain.

Then one hot day when fields were rank
With cowdung in the grass the angry frogs
Invaded the flax-dam; I ducked through hedges
To a coarse croaking that I had not heard
Before. The air was thick with a bass chorus.
Right down the dam gross-bellied frogs were cocked
On sods; their loose necks pulsed like sails. Some hopped:
The slap and plop were obscene threats. Some sat
Poised like mud grenades, their blunt heads farting.

4. Dam across a stream made of flax plants and fibers.

5. That is, flies.

I sickened, turned, and ran. The great slime kings
Were gathered there for vengeance and I knew
That if I dipped my hand the spawn would clutch it.

1966

Requiem for the Croppies[6]

The pockets of our great coats full of barley—
No kitchens on the run, no striking camp—
We moved quick and sudden in our own country.
The priest lay behind ditches with the tramp.
A people, hardly marching—on the hike—
We found new tactics happening each day:
We'd cut through reins and rider with the pike
And stampede cattle into infantry,
Then retreat through hedges where cavalry must be thrown.
Until, on Vinegar Hill, the fatal conclave.
Terraced thousands died, shaking scythes at cannon.
The hillside blushed, soaked in our broken wave.
They buried us without shroud or coffin
And in August the barley grew up out of the grave.[7]

1969

Bogland[8]

for T. P. Flanagan[9]

We have no prairies
To slice a big sun at evening—
Everywhere the eye concedes to
Encroaching horizon,

Is wooed into the cyclops' eye
Of a tarn.[1] Our unfenced country
Is bog that keeps crusting
Between the sights of the sun.

They've taken the skeleton
Of the Great Irish Elk[2]
Out of the peat, set it up
An astounding crate full of air.

6. Irish rebels of 1798, who wore their hair cut (cropped) very short in sympathy with the French Revolution.
7. See Heaney's comments on the poem in the essay "Feeling into Words," p. 1096 in this volume.
8. See the essay "Feeling into Words," p. 1096 in this volume.
9. Irish artist (b. 1929), whose 1967 painting *Boglands (for Seamus Heaney)* helped inspire the poem.
1. Mountain lake or pool; the mythical Cyclops had only one eye.
2. Extinct species of elk with huge antlers.

Butter sunk under
More than a hundred years
Was recovered salty and white.
The ground itself is kind, black butter

Melting and opening underfoot,
Missing its last definition
By millions of years.
They'll never dig coal here,[3]

Only the waterlogged trunks
Of great firs, soft as pulp.
Our pioneers[4] keep striking
Inwards and downwards,

Every layer they strip
Seems camped on before.
The bogholes might be Atlantic seepage.
The wet centre is bottomless.

1969

The Tollund Man[5]

I

Some day I will go to Aarhus
To see his peat-brown head,
The mild pods of his eyelids,
His pointed skin cap.

In the flat country nearby
Where they dug him out,
His last gruel of winter seeds
Caked in his stomach,

Naked except for
The cap, noose and girdle,
I will stand a long time.
Bridegroom to the goddess,

She tightened her torc[6] on him
And opened her fen,[7]
Those dark juices working
Him to a saint's kept body,

3. Because the ground is too wet for it to form.
4. Diggers or miners (archaic), implicitly contrasted with American "pioneers."
5. See Heaney's essay "Feeling into Words," in which he cites the description in P. V. Glob's *The Bog People* of the Tollund Man, whose head is preserved in a museum near Aarhus, Denmark, and who was sacrificed two thousand years ago in a fertility ritual to the Mother Goddess (p. 1096 in this volume).
6. Or *torque:* twisting force; also, necklace of precious metal, worn by ancient Gauls and Britons.
7. Lowlands covered with shallow water.

Trove of the turf-cutters'
Honeycombed workings.
Now his stained face
Reposes at Aarhus.

II

I could risk blasphemy,
Consecrate the cauldron bog
Our holy ground and pray
Him to make germinate

The scattered, ambushed
Flesh of labourers,
Stockinged corpses
Laid out in the farmyards,

Tell-tale skin and teeth
Flecking the sleepers
Of four young brothers, trailed
For miles along the lines.[8]

III

Something of his sad freedom
As he rode the tumbril[9]
Should come to me, driving,
Saying the names

Tollund, Grauballe, Nebelgard,[1]
Watching the pointing hands
Of country people,
Not knowing their tongue.

Out there in Jutland[2]
In the old man-killing parishes
I will feel lost,
Unhappy and at home.

1972

8. In the early 1920s, four brothers murdered by the Ulster Special Constabulary, an auxiliary police force known as the B Specials, were dragged for miles behind a train.
9. A cart used to transport condemned prisoners to their execution.
1. Cities in Denmark.
2. Projection of northern Europe forming continental Denmark and part of northwest Germany.

Bog Queen[3]

I lay waiting
between turf-face and demesne wall,[4]
between heathery levels
and glass-toothed stone.

My body was braille
for the creeping influences:
dawn suns groped over my head
and cooled at my feet,

through my fabrics and skins
the seeps of winter
digested me,
the illiterate roots

pondered and died
in the cavings
of stomach and socket.
I lay waiting

on the gravel bottom,
my brain darkening,
a jar of spawn
fermenting underground

dreams of Baltic amber.[5]
Bruised berries under my nails,
the vital hoard reducing
in the crock of the pelvis.

My diadem grew carious,[6]
gemstones dropped
in the peat floe[7]
like the bearings of history.

My sash was a black glacier
wrinkling, dyed weaves
and phoenician stitchwork
retted on my breasts'

soft moraines.[8]
I knew winter cold
like the nuzzle of fjords
at my thighs—

3. See Heaney's essay "Feeling into Words," p. 1096 in this volume.
4. Between the edge of the grassy turf and the wall marking the lord's estate.
5. Yellowish fossil resin used for jewelry, from the Baltic Sea.
6. That is, decayed.
7. Floating peat.
8. Accumulations deposited by glaciers. *Phoenician:* from the ancient trading city of Phoenicia, noted for its purple dyes. *Retted:* soaked.

the soaked fledge, the heavy
swaddle[9] of hides.
My skull hibernated
in the wet nest of my hair.

Which they robbed.
I was barbered
and stripped
by a turfcutter's spade

who veiled me again
and packed coomb softly
between the stone jambs[1]
at my head and my feet.

Till a peer's wife bribed him.[2]
The plait of my hair,
a slimy birth-cord
of bog, had been cut

and I rose from the dark,
hacked bone, skull-ware,
frayed stitches, tufts,
small gleams on the bank.

1975

The Grauballe Man[3]

As if he had been poured
in tar, he lies
on a pillow of turf
and seems to weep

the black river of himself.
The grain of his wrists
is like bog oak,
the ball of his heel

like a basalt egg.
His instep has shrunk
cold as a swan's foot
or a wet swamp root.

His hips are the ridge
and purse of a mussel,

9. That is, wrapping. *Fledge:* cloth.
1. Upright pieces at top and bottom of opening in which she was placed. *Coomb:* old word for barley stems.
2. That is, till a nobleman's wife bribed him (to cut off and give her the speaker's hair).
3. Another body exhumed from a Danish bog (see "The Tollund Man" and its note 5, above).

his spine an eel arrested
under a glisten of mud.

The head lifts,
the chin is a visor
raised above the vent
of his slashed throat

that has tanned and toughened.
The cured wound
opens inwards to a dark
elderberry place.

Who will say 'corpse'
to his vivid cast?
Who will say 'body'
to his opaque repose?

And his rusted hair,
a mat unlikely
as a foetus's.
I first saw his twisted face

in a photograph,
a head and shoulder
out of the peat,
bruised like a forceps baby,

but now he lies
perfected in my memory,
down to the red horn
of his nails,

hung in the scales
with beauty and atrocity:
with the Dying Gaul[4]
too strictly compassed

on his shield,
with the actual weight
of each hooded victim,
slashed and dumped.

1975

4. Roman marble reproduction of a Greek bronze sculpture depicting a wounded soldier of Gaul, whose matted hair identifies him as a Celt, in Rome's Capitoline Museum.

Punishment[5]

I can feel the tug
of the halter at the nape
of her neck, the wind
on her naked front.

It blows her nipples
to amber beads,
it shakes the frail rigging
of her ribs.

I can see her drowned
body in the bog,
the weighing stone,
the floating rods and boughs.

Under which at first
she was a barked sapling
that is dug up
oak-bone, brain-firkin:[6]

her shaved head
like a stubble of black corn,
her blindfold a soiled bandage,
her noose a ring

to store
the memories of love.
Little adulteress,
before they punished you

you were flaxen-haired,
undernourished, and your
tar-black face was beautiful.
My poor scapegoat,

I almost love you
but would have cast, I know,
the stones of silence.
I am the artful voyeur

5. In 1951, the peat-stained body of a young girl who lived during the late first century C.E. was recovered from a bog in Windeby, Germany. As P. V. Glob describes her in *The Bog People,* she "lay naked in the hole in the peat, a bandage over the eyes and a collar round the neck. The band across the eyes was drawn tight and had cut into the neck and the base of the nose. We may feel sure that it had been used to close her eyes to this world. There was no mark of strangulation on the neck, so that it had not been used for that purpose." Her hair "had been shaved off with a razor on the left side of the head. . . . When the brain was removed the convolutions and folds of the surface could be clearly seen. [Glob reproduces a photograph of her brain.] . . . This girl of only fourteen had had an inadequate winter diet. . . . To keep the young body under, some birch branches and a big stone were laid upon her." According to the Roman historian Tacitus (c. 56–c. 120), the Germanic peoples punished adulterous women by shaving off their hair and scourging them out of the village or killing them.

6. *Firkin:* small cask.

of your brain's exposed
and darkened combs,[7]
your muscles' webbing
and all your numbered bones:

I who have stood dumb
when your betraying sisters,
cauled in tar,
wept by the railings,[8]

who would connive
in civilized outrage
yet understand the exact
and tribal, intimate revenge.

1975

The Strand at Lough Beg[9]

In Memory of Colum McCartney

All round this little island, on the strand
Far down below there, where the breakers strive,
Grow the tall rushes from the oozy sand.
—Dante, *Purgatorio,* 1, 100–103[1]

Leaving the white glow of filling stations
And a few lonely streetlamps among fields
You climbed the hills toward Newtownhamilton
Past the Fews Forest, out beneath the stars—
Along that road, a high, bare pilgrim's track
Where Sweeney fled before the bloodied heads,[2]
Goat-beards and dogs' eyes in a demon pack
Blazing out of the ground, snapping and squealing.
What blazed ahead of you? A faked road block?
The red lamp swung, the sudden brakes and stalling
Engine, voices, heads hooded and the cold-nosed gun?
Or in your driving mirror, tailing headlights
That pulled out suddenly and flagged you down
Where you weren't known and far from what you knew:
The lowland clays and waters of Lough Beg,
Church Island's[3] spire, its soft treeline of yew.

7. Valleys.
8. Women in Belfast, Northern Ireland, have sometimes been shaven, stripped, tarred, and handcuffed to railings as punishment by the Irish Republican Army for keeping company with British soldiers. *Cauled:* wrapped or enclosed; a caul is the inner fetal membrane that at birth, when it is unruptured, sometimes covers the infant's head.
9. Lake in Northern Ireland. *Strand:* beach. "Colum McCartney, a relative of the author's, was the victim of a random sectarian [that is, Catholic versus Protestant] killing in the late summer of 1975" [Heaney's note].
1. *Purgatorio,* the second part of *The Divine Comedy,* by Italian poet Dante Alighieri (1265–1321), is about the mountian of Purgatory and its various groups of repentant sinners after death.
2. "Sweeney is the hero of a Middle Irish prose and poem sequence, one part of which takes place in the Fews" [Heaney's note].
3. Island in Lough Beg on which a spire was erected in 1788 by the earl of Bristol.

There you used hear guns fired behind the house
Long before rising time, when duck shooters
Haunted the marigolds and bulrushes,
But still were scared to find spent cartridges,
Acrid, brassy, genital, ejected,
On your way across the strand to fetch the cows.
For you and yours and yours and mine fought shy,
Spoke an old language of conspirators
And could not crack the whip or seize the day:
Big-voiced scullions, herders, feelers round
Haycocks and hindquarters, talkers in byres,[4]
Slow arbitrators of the burial ground.

Across that strand of yours the cattle graze
Up to their bellies in an early mist
And now they turn their unbewildered gaze
To where we work our way through squeaking sedge[5]
Drowning in dew. Like a dull blade with its edge
Honed bright, Lough Beg half-shines under the haze.
I turn because the sweeping of your feet
Has stopped behind me, to find you on your knees
With blood and roadside muck in your hair and eyes,
Then kneel in front of you in brimming grass
And gather up cold handfuls of the dew
To wash you, cousin. I dab you clean with moss
Fine as the drizzle out of a low cloud.
I lift you under the arms and lay you flat.
With rushes that shoot green again, I plait
Green scapulars[6] to wear over your shroud.

1979

Casualty[7]

I

He would drink by himself
And raise a weathered thumb
Towards the high shelf,
Calling another rum
And blackcurrant, without
Having to raise his voice,
Or order a quick stout[8]
By a lifting of the eyes
And a discreet dumb-show
Of pulling off the top;
At closing time would go

4. Barns. *Scullions:* lowest-ranking kitchen help.
5. Coarse, grasslike plants.
6. Religious or fraternal bands of cloth worn front and back over the shoulders. *Plait:* braid.
7. An elegy for Louis O'Neill, a fisherman killed in an Irish Republican Army bombing, after Bloody Sunday murders of Roman Catholic demonstrators.
8. Strong, dark beer.

In waders and peaked cap
Into the showery dark,
A dole-kept[9] breadwinner
But a natural for work.
I loved his whole manner,
Sure-footed but too sly,
His deadpan sidling tact,
His fisherman's quick eye
And turned, observant back.

Incomprehensible
To him, my other life.
Sometimes, on his high stool,
Too busy with his knife
At a tobacco plug
And not meeting my eye,
In the pause after a slug
He mentioned poetry.
We would be on our own
And, always politic
And shy of condescension,
I would manage by some trick
To switch the talk to eels
Or lore of the horse and cart
Or the Provisionals.[1]

But my tentative art
His turned back watches too:
He was blown to bits
Out drinking in a curfew
Others obeyed, three nights
After they shot dead
The thirteen men in Derry.
PARAS THIRTEEN, the walls said,
BOGSIDE NIL.[2] That Wednesday
Everybody held
Their breath and trembled.

II

It was a day of cold
Raw silence, windblown
Surplice and soutane:[3]
Rained-on, flower-laden
Coffin after coffin
Seemed to float from the door
Of the packed cathedral

9. Receiving unemployment benefits.
1. The Provisional branch of the Irish Republican Army.
2. The graffito turns into the score of a soccer match the death toll of Bloody Sunday, January 30, 1972, when the British Army Parachute Regiment shot and killed thirteen Roman Catholic demonstrators in Derry's Bogside district.
3. Vestments worn by Roman Catholic priests.

Like blossoms on slow water.
The common funeral
Unrolled its swaddling band,[4]
Lapping, tightening
Till we were braced and bound
Like brothers in a ring.

But he would not be held
At home by his own crowd
Whatever threats were phoned,
Whatever black flags waved.
I see him as he turned
In that bombed offending place,
Remorse fused with terror
In his still knowable face,
His cornered outfaced stare
Blinding in the flash.

He had gone miles away
For he drank like a fish
Nightly, naturally
Swimming towards the lure
Of warm lit-up places,
The blurred mesh and murmur
Drifting among glasses
In the gregarious smoke.
How culpable was he
That last night when he broke
Our tribe's complicity?[5]
'Now you're supposed to be
An educated man,'
I hear him say. 'Puzzle me
The right answer to that one.'

III

I missed his funeral,
Those quiet walkers
And sideways talkers
Shoaling out of his lane
To the respectable
Purring of the hearse . . .
They move in equal pace
With the habitual
Slow consolation
Of a dawdling engine,
The line lifted, hand
Over fist, cold sunshine
On the water, the land

4. Cloth in which babies were wrapped to restrain and warm them.

5. The Roman Catholic community's agreement to obey the curfew.

Banked under fog: that morning
When he took me in his boat,
The screw[6] purling, turning
Indolent fathoms white,
I tasted freedom with him.
To get out early, haul
Steadily off the bottom,
Dispraise the catch, and smile
As you find a rhythm
Working you, slow mile by mile,
Into your proper haunt
Somewhere, well out, beyond . . .

Dawn-sniffing revenant,[7]
Plodder through midnight rain,
Question me again.

1979

In Memoriam Francis Ledwidge[8]

Killed in France 31 July 1917

The bronze soldier hitches a bronze cape
That crumples stiffly in imagined wind
No matter how the real winds buff and sweep
His sudden hunkering run, forever craned

Over Flanders.[9] Helmet and haversack,
The gun's firm slope from butt to bayonet,
The loyal, fallen names on the embossed plaque—
It all meant little to the worried pet

I was in nineteen forty-six or seven,
Gripping my Aunt Mary by the hand
Along the Portstewart prom, then round the crescent
To thread the Castle Walk out to the strand.[1]

The pilot from Coleraine[2] sailed to the coal-boat.
Courting couples rose out of the scooped dunes.
A farmer stripped to his studs and shiny waistcoat
Rolled the trousers down on his timid shins.

At night when coloured bulbs strung out the sea-front
Country voices rose from a cliff-top shelter

6. Propeller.
7. Ghost.
8. "Francis Ledwidge (1891–1917) was friendly with some of the leaders of the 1916 Rising [insurrection by Irish republicans] yet, like thousands of Irishmen of the time, felt himself constrained to enlist in the British Army to defend 'the rights of small nations' " [Heaney's note].
9. Area covering part of modern France and Belgium; scene of prolonged trench warfare in World War I.
1. Beach. *Prom:* promenade, paved walking path. *Crescent:* semicircular row of houses.
2. Shipping port in Northern Ireland.

With news of a great litter—'We'll pet the runt!'—
And barbed wire that had torn a friesian's elder.[3]

Francis Ledwidge, you courted at the seaside
Beyond Drogheda one Sunday afternoon.
Literary, sweet-talking, countrified,
You pedalled out the leafy road from Slane[4]

Where you belonged, among the dolorous
And lovely: the May altar of wild flowers,
Easter water sprinkled in outhouses,
Mass-rocks and hill-top raths and raftered byres.[5]

I think of you in your Tommy's[6] uniform,
A haunted Catholic face, pallid and brave,
Ghosting the trenches with a bloom of hawthorn
Or silence cored from a Boyne passage-grave.[7]

It's summer, nineteen-fifteen. I see the girl
My aunt was then, herding on the long acre.
Behind a low bush in the Dardanelles[8]
You suck stones to make your dry mouth water.

It's nineteen-seventeen. She still herds cows
But a big strafe puts the candles out in Ypres:[9]
'My soul is by the Boyne, cutting new meadows. . . .
My country wears her confirmation dress.'

'To be called a British soldier while my country
Has no place among nations. . . .' You were rent
By shrapnel six weeks later. 'I am sorry
That party politics should divide our tents.'

In you, our dead enigma, all the strains
Criss-cross in useless equilibrium
And as the wind tunes through this vigilant bronze
I hear again the sure confusing drum

You followed from Boyne water to the Balkans
But miss the twilit note your flute should sound.
You were not keyed or pitched like these true-blue ones
Though all of you consort now underground.

1979

3. That is, an old cow.
4. Drogheda and Slane are both in northeastern Eire, Ireland.
5. Barns. *Mass-rocks:* rocks at which persecuted Roman Catholics gathered to celebrate the Mass in secret. *Raths:* circular forts built by the early Irish.
6. That is, British soldier's.
7. Subterranean burial chamber entered by means of a long tunnel or passage; the River Boyne was the scene of a battle between the Irish and the English in 1690.
8. Narrow strait between Europe and Turkey.
9. In West Flanders, the site of three heavy World War I battles; pronounced "Wipers" by British soldiers.

From Station Island[1]

VIII

Black water. White waves. Furrows snowcapped.
A magpie flew from the basilica[2]
and staggered in the granite airy space
I was staring into, on my knees
at the hard mouth of St Brigid's Bed.[3]
I came to and there at the bed's stone hub
was my archaeologist, very like himself,
with his scribe's face smiling its straight-lipped smile,
starting at the sight of me with the same old
pretence of amazement, so that the wing
of woodkerne's[4] hair fanned down over his brow.
And then as if a shower were blackening
already blackened stubble, the dark weather
of his unspoken pain came over him.
A pilgrim bent and whispering on his rounds
inside the bed passed between us slowly.

'Those dreamy stars that pulsed across the screen
beside you in the ward—your heartbeats, Tom, I mean—
scared me the way they stripped things naked.
My banter failed too early in that visit.
I could not take my eyes off the machine.
I had to head back straight away to Dublin,
guilty and empty, feeling I had said nothing
and that, as usual, I had somehow broken
covenants, and failed an obligation.
I half-knew we would never meet again . . .
Did our long gaze and last handshake contain
nothing to appease that recognition?'

'Nothing at all. But familiar stone
had me half-numbed to face the thing alone.
I loved my still-faced archaeology.
The small crab-apple physiognomies
on high crosses, carved heads in abbeys . . .
Why else dig in for years in that hard place
in a muck of bigotry under the walls
picking through shards and Williamite cannon balls?[5]
But all that we just turned to banter too.
I felt that I should have seen far more of you
and maybe would have—but dead at thirty-two!

1. "*Station Island* is a sequence of dream encounters with familiar ghosts, set on Station Island on Lough Derg in Co. Donegal. The island is also known as St Patrick's Purgatory because of a tradition that Patrick was the first to establish the penitential vigil of fasting and praying which still constitutes the basis of the three-day pilgrimage. Each unit of the contemporary pilgrim's exercises is called a 'station,' and a large part of each station involves walking barefoot and praying round the 'beds,' stone circles which are said to be the remains of early medieval monastic cells" [Heaney's note].
2. That is, old church building.
3. One of the stone circles mentioned by Heaney in note 9 above. St. Brigid (c. 450–c. 523) is, after St. Patrick, Ireland's most revered saint.
4. Irish outlaw's.
5. From the Battle of the Boyne (1690), in which William of England defeated James II of Ireland.

Ah poet, lucky poet, tell me why
what seemed deserved and promised passed me by?'

I could not speak. I saw a hoard of black
basalt axe heads, smooth as a beetle's back,
a cairn[6] of stone force that might detonate,
the eggs of danger. And then I saw a face
he had once given me, a plaster cast
of an abbess, done by the Gowran master,
mild-mouthed and cowled,[7] a character of grace.
'Your gift will be a candle in our house.'
But he had gone when I looked to meet his eyes
and hunkering instead there in his place
was a bleeding, pale-faced boy, plastered in mud.
'The red-hot pokers blazed a lovely red
in Jerpoint the Sunday I was murdered,'
he said quietly. 'Now do you remember?
You were there with poets when you got the word
and stayed there with them, while your own flesh and blood
was carted to Bellaghy from the Fews.
They showed more agitation at the news
than you did.'

'But they were getting crisis
first-hand, Colum, they had happened in on
live sectarian assassination.
I was dumb, encountering what was destined.'
And so I pleaded with my second cousin.
'I kept seeing a grey stretch of Lough Beg
and the strand empty at daybreak.
I felt like the bottom of a dried-up lake.'

'You saw that, and you wrote that—not the fact.
You confused evasion and artistic tact.
The Protestant who shot me through the head
I accuse directly, but indirectly, you
who now atone perhaps upon this bed
for the way you whitewashed ugliness and drew
the lovely blinds of the *Purgatorio*
and saccharined my death with morning dew.'[8]

Then I seemed to waken out of sleep
among more pilgrims whom I did not know
drifting to the hostel for the night.

XII

Like a convalescent, I took the hand
stretched down from the jetty, sensed again
an alien comfort as I stepped on ground

6. Heap of stones, piled as a memorial or landmark.
7. Hooded. *Gowran master:* that is, a master craftsperson.
8. Cf. Heaney's "The Strand at Lough Beg," above.

to find the helping hand still gripping mine,
fish-cold and bony, but whether to guide
or to be guided I could not be certain

for the tall man in step at my side
seemed blind, though he walked straight as a rush
upon his ash plant, his eyes fixed straight ahead.[9]

Then I knew him in the flesh
out there on the tarmac[1] among the cars,
wintered hard and sharp as a blackthorn bush.

His voice eddying with the vowels of all rivers[2]
came back to me, though he did not speak yet,
a voice like a prosecutor's or a singer's,

cunning,[3] narcotic, mimic, definite
as a steel nib's downstroke, quick and clean,
and suddenly he hit a litter basket

with his stick, saying, 'Your obligation
is not discharged by any common rite.
What you must do must be done on your own

so get back in harness. The main thing is to write
for the joy of it. Cultivate a work-lust
that imagines its haven like your hands at night

dreaming the sun in the sunspot of a breast.
You are fasted now, light-headed, dangerous.
Take off from here. And don't be so earnest,

let others wear the sackcloth and the ashes.[4]
Let go, let fly, forget.
You've listened long enough. Now strike your note.'

It was as if I had stepped free into space
alone with nothing that I had not known
already. Raindrops blew in my face

as I came to. 'Old father, mother's son,
there is a moment in Stephen's diary
for April the thirteenth, a revelation

9. In this last section of the poem, the "familiar ghost" is James Joyce (1882–1941), Irish writer who was almost blind. *Ash plant*: walking stick made of an ash sapling; Stephen Dedalus, one of the two heroes of Joyce's *Ulysses*, carries one. Cf. the stanza form and encounter with a ghost in T. S. Eliot's "Little Gidding."
1. Surface paved with blacktop.
2. The "Anna Livia Plurabelle" section of Joyce's *Finnegans Wake* resounds with the names of many rivers.
3. "The only arms I allow myself to use—silence, exile, and cunning" (Joyce's *Portrait of the Artist as a Young Man*).
4. Traditional dress of penitents.

set among my stars—that one entry
has been a sort of password in my ears,
the collect of a new epiphany,[5]

the Feast of the Holy Tundish.'[6] 'Who cares,'
he jeered, 'any more? The English language
belongs to us. You are raking at dead fires,

a waste of time for somebody your age.
That subject people stuff is a cod's[7] game,
infantile, like your peasant pilgrimage.

You lose more of yourself than you redeem
doing the decent thing. Keep at a tangent.
When they make the circle wide, it's time to swim

out on your own and fill the element
with signatures on your own frequency,
echo soundings, searches, probes, allurements,

elver-gleams[8] in the dark of the whole sea.'
The shower broke in a cloudburst, the tarmac
fumed and sizzled. As he moved off quickly

the downpour loosed its screens round his straight walk.

1985

Alphabets

I

A shadow his father makes with joined hands
And thumbs and fingers nibbles on the wall
Like a rabbit's head. He understands
He will understand more when he goes to school.

There he draws smoke with chalk the whole first week,
Then draws the forked stick that they call a Y.
This is writing. A swan's neck and swan's back
Make the 2 he can see now as well as say.

Two rafters and a cross-tie on the slate[9]
Are the letter some call *ah*, some call *ay*.

5. Manifestations of a divine being, as of the infant Jesus to the Magi (Matthew 2); in the Christian calendar, the Feast of the Epiphany is January 6. *Collect:* short prayer assigned to a particular day. "Epiphany" was also the term Joyce used for the prose poems he wrote as a young man; it meant, he said, the "sudden revelation of the whatness of things."

6. "See the end of James Joyce's *Portrait of the Artist as a Young Man*" [Heaney's note]: "*13 April:* That tundish [funnel] has been on my mind for a long time. I looked it up and find it English and good old blunt English too. Damn the dean of studies and his funnel! What did he come here for to teach us his own language or to learn it from us? Damn him one way or the other!"

7. Fool's. *Subject:* colonized.

8. Gleams as of young eels.

9. Small, rectangular sheet of rocklike substance, written on with chalk.

There are charts, there are headlines, there is a right
Way to hold the pen and a wrong way.

First it is 'copying out', and then 'English'
Marked correct with a little leaning hoe.
Smells of inkwells rise in the classroom hush.
A globe in the window tilts like a coloured O.

II

Declensions sang on air like a *hosanna*[1]
As, column after stratified column,
Book One of *Elementa Latina*,
Marbled and minatory,[2] rose up in him.

For he was fostered next in a stricter school
Named for the patron saint of the oak wood[3]
Where classes switched to the pealing of a bell
And he left the Latin forum for the shade

Of new calligraphy[4] that felt like home.
The letters of this alphabet were trees.
The capitals were orchards in full bloom,
The lines of script like briars coiled in ditches.

Here in her snooded garment and bare feet,
All ringleted in assonance and woodnotes,[5]
The poet's dream stole over him like sunlight
And passed into the tenebrous[6] thickets.

He learns this other writing. He is the scribe
Who drove a team of quills on his white field.
Round his cell door the blackbirds dart and dab.
Then self-denial, fasting, the pure cold.

By rules that hardened the farther they reached north
He bends to his desk and begins again.
Christ's sickle[7] has been in the undergrowth.
The script grows bare and Merovingian.[8]

III

The globe has spun. He stands in a wooden O.
He alludes to Shakespeare. He alludes to Graves.[9]

1. Cry of adoration. *Declensions:* changes in word forms according to their grammatical cases (in grammar books these are usually printed in columns).
2. Menacing. *Elementa Latina:* elements of Latin.
3. St. Louis (1214–1270), king of France, administered justice under an oak tree.
4. Elegant handwriting, as in medieval manuscripts. *Forum:* public meeting place in old Roman city. The "new calligraphy" is the Irish script. The poem moves from English through Latin to Irish.
5. Natural, artless verbal expressions. *Snooded:* with a net or cloth bag holding her hair. *Assonance:* repetition of vowels in poetry.
6. Murky.
7. In Revelation 14.14, Jesus is portrayed as having "in his hand a sharp sickle," to reap "the harvest of the earth."
8. Characteristic of the first Frankish dynasty (500–751 C.E.), in northern Europe.
9. Robert Graves (1895–1985), English poet. In *Henry V*, the theater building of Shakespeare's time is compared to a "wooden O."

Time has bulldozed the school and school window.
Balers drop bales like printouts where stooked sheaves[1]

Made lambdas on the stubble once at harvest
And the delta face of each potato pit
Was patted straight and moulded against frost.
All gone, with the omega that kept

Watch above each door, the good luck horse-shoe.[2]
Yet shape-note language, absolute on air
As Constantine's sky-lettered IN HOC SIGNO[3]
Can still command him; or the necromancer[4]

Who would hang from the domed ceiling of his house
A figure of the world with colours in it
So that the figure of the universe
And 'not just single things' would meet his sight

When he walked abroad. As from his small window
The astronaut sees all that he has sprung from,
The risen, aqueous, singular, lucent O
Like a magnified and buoyant ovum[5]

Or like my own wide pre-reflective stare
All agog at the plasterer on his ladder
Skimming our gable[6] and writing our name there
With his trowel point, letter by strange letter.

1987

Terminus[7]

I

When I hoked[8] there, I would find
An acorn and a rusted bolt.

If I lifted my eyes, a factory chimney
And a dormant mountain.

If I listened, an engine shunting
And a trotting horse.

Is it any wonder when I thought
I would have second thoughts?

1. That is, gatherings of grain stalks and ears.
2. These images allude to the shapes of capital letters in the Greek alphabet: *lambda*: Λ; *delta*: Δ; *omega*: Ω.
3. Before a battle, according to legend, Constantine the Great (d. 337) saw a vision in the heavens of a cross and the words *In hoc signo vinces* ("in this sign you will conquer"); he won the battle and converted to Christianity.
4. One who conjures the spirits of the dead to reveal the future.
5. That is, cell (also Latin for egg). *Aqueous:* watery, *Lucent:* glowing with light.
6. That is, putting a thin layer of plaster over the triangular end of the roof.
7. Roman god who watched over boundaries.
8. Played.

II

When they spoke of the prudent squirrel's hoard
It shone like gifts at a Nativity.[9]

When they spoke of the mammon[1] of iniquity
The coins in my pockets reddened like stove-lids.

I was the march drain and the march drain's banks
Suffering the limit of each claim.

III

Two buckets were easier carried than one.
I grew up in between.

My left hand placed the standard iron weight.
My right tilted a last grain in the balance.

Baronies, parishes met where I was born.
When I stood on the central stepping stone

I was the last earl on horseback in midstream
Still parleying, in earshot of his peers.

1987

The Stone Verdict[2]

When he stands in the judgement place
With his stick in his hand and the broad hat
Still on his head, maimed by self-doubt
And an old disdain of sweet talk and excuses,
It will be no justice if the sentence is blabbed out.
He will expect more than words in the ultimate court
He relied on through a lifetime's speechlessness.

Let it be like the judgement of Hermes,[3]
God of the stone heap, where the stones were verdicts
Cast solidly at his feet, piling up around him
Until he stood waist-deep in the cairn[4]
Of his own absolution: maybe a gate-pillar
Or a tumbled wallstead where hogweed earths the silence
Somebody will break at last to say, 'Here
His spirit lingers,' and will have said too much.

1987

9. Scene depicting Jesus' birth.
1. Material wealth.
2. An anticipatory elegy for Patrick Heaney, the poet's father.
3. Greek messenger god, whose name probably derives from the word *herma,* which means "piles of stones." When Hermes killed Argos and was brought to trial by the gods, the judges made their decisions by casting voting pebbles at his feet.
4. Pyramid of stones, often a grave monument.

Clearances

in memoriam M.K.H.,[5] 1911–1984

She taught me what her uncle once taught her:
How easily the biggest coal block split
If you got the grain and hammer angled right.

The sound of that relaxed alluring blow,
Its co-opted and obliterated echo,
Taught me to hit, taught me to loosen,

Taught me between the hammer and the block
To face the music. Teach me now to listen,
To strike it rich behind the linear black.

I

A cobble thrown a hundred years ago
Keeps coming at me, the first stone
Aimed at a great-grandmother's turncoat brow.[6]
The pony jerks and the riot's on.
She's crouched low in the trap
Running the gauntlet that first Sunday
Down the brae[7] to Mass at a panicked gallop.
He whips on through the town to cries of 'Lundy!'[8]

Call her 'The Convert'. 'The Exogamous Bride'.
Anyhow, it is a genre piece
Inherited on my mother's side
And mine to dispose with now she's gone.
Instead of silver and Victorian lace,
The exonerating, exonerated stone.

II

Polished linoleum shone there. Brass taps shone.
The china cups were very white and big—
An unchipped set with sugar bowl and jug.
The kettle whistled. Sandwich and tea scone
Were present and correct. In case it run,
The butter must be kept out of the sun.
And don't be dropping crumbs. Don't tilt your chair.
Don't reach. Don't point. Don't make noise when you stir.

It is Number 5, New Row, Land of the Dead,
Where grandfather is rising from his place
With spectacles pushed back on a clean bald head

5. Margaret Kathleen Heaney, the poet's mother.
6. Heaney's Protestant great-grandmother married a Catholic.
7. Steep slope.
8. That is, traitor. In 1688, the Irish colonel Robert Lundy knew that Derry (or Londonderry) would be invaded by the English, but failed to prepare adequate defenses.

To welcome a bewildered homing daughter
Before she even knocks. 'What's this? What's this?'
And they sit down in the shining room together.

III

When all the others were away at Mass
I was all hers as we peeled potatoes.
They broke the silence, let fall one by one
Like solder weeping off the soldering iron:
Cold comforts set between us, things to share
Gleaming in a bucket of clean water.
And again let fall. Little pleasant splashes
From each other's work would bring us to our senses.

So while the parish priest at her bedside
Went hammer and tongs at the prayers for the dying
And some were responding and some crying
I remembered her head bent towards my head,
Her breath in mine, our fluent dipping knives—
Never closer the whole rest of our lives.

IV

Fear of affectation made her affect
Inadequacy whenever it came to
Pronouncing words 'beyond her'. *Bertold Brek.*[9]
She'd manage something hampered and askew
Every time, as if she might betray
The hampered and inadequate by too
Well-adjusted a vocabulary.
With more challenge than pride, she'd tell me, 'You
Know all them things.' So I governed my tongue
In front of her, a genuinely well-
Adjusted adequate betrayal
Of what I knew better. I'd *naw* and *aye*
And decently relapse into the wrong
Grammar which kept us allied and at bay.

V

The cool that came off sheets just off the line
Made me think the damp must still be in them
But when I took my corners of the linen
And pulled against her, first straight down the hem
And then diagonally, then flapped and shook
The fabric like a sail in a cross-wind,
They made a dried-out undulating thwack.
So we'd stretch and fold and end up hand to hand
For a split second as if nothing had happened

9. Bertolt Brecht (1898–1956), German playwright.

For nothing had that had not always happened
Beforehand, day by day, just touch and go,
Coming close again by holding back
In moves where I was X and she was O
Inscribed in sheets she'd sewn from ripped-out flour sacks.

VI

In the first flush of the Easter holidays
The ceremonies during Holy Week
Were highpoints of our *Sons and Lovers*[1] phase.
The midnight fire. The paschal candlestick.[2]
Elbow to elbow, glad to be kneeling next
To each other up there near the front
Of the packed church, we would follow the text
And rubrics for the blessing of the font.
As the hind longs for the streams, so my soul . . . [3]
Dippings. Towellings. The water breathed on.
The water mixed with chrism and with oil.
Cruet tinkle. Formal incensation
And the psalmist's outcry taken up with pride:
Day and night my tears have been my bread.[4]

VII

In the last minutes he said more to her
Almost than in all their life together.
'You'll be in New Row on Monday night
And I'll come up for you and you'll be glad
When I walk in the door . . . Isn't that right?'
His head was bent down to her propped-up head.
She could not hear but we were overjoyed.
He called her good and girl. Then she was dead,
The searching for a pulsebeat was abandoned
And we all knew one thing by being there.
The space we stood around had been emptied
Into us to keep, it penetrated
Clearances that suddenly stood open.
High cries were felled and a pure change happened.

VIII

I thought of walking round and round a space
Utterly empty, utterly a source
Where the decked chestnut tree had lost its place
In our front hedge above the wallflowers.
The white chips jumped and jumped and skited high.
I heard the hatchet's differentiated

1. Novel (1913) by English writer D. H. Lawrence (1885–1930) that largely centers on the oedipal relationship between a mother and son.
2. Large candle lit during a ceremony on the Holy Saturday preceding Easter.
3. Psalms 42.1.
4. Psalms 42.3.

Accurate cut, the crack, the sigh
And collapse of what luxuriated
Through the shocked tips and wreckage of it all.
Deep-planted and long gone, my coeval[5]
Chestnut from a jam jar in a hole,
Its heft and hush become a bright nowhere,
A soul ramifying and forever
Silent, beyond silence listened for.

1987

At Toomebridge[6]

Where the flat water
Came pouring over the weir out of Lough Neagh
As if it had reached an edge of the flat earth
And fallen shining to the continuous
Present of the Bann.
Where the checkpoint used to be.
Where the rebel boy was hanged in '98.[7]
Where negative ions in the open air
Are poetry to me. As once before
The slime and silver of the fattened eel.

2001

Electric Light

Candle-grease congealed, dark-streaked with wick-soot . . .
The smashed thumb-nail
Of that ancient mangled thumb was puckered pearl,

Rucked quartz, a littered Cumae.[8]
In the first house where I saw electric light
She sat with her fur-lined felt slippers unzipped,

Year in, year out, in the same chair, and whispered
In a voice that at its loudest did nothing else
But whisper. We were both desperate

The night I was left to stay, when I wept and wept
Under the clothes, under the waste of light
Left turned on in the bedroom. "What ails you, child,

5. Of the same age.
6. City in Northern Ireland where the Bann River meets Lough Neagh, the largest freshwater lake in the British Isles. Toomebridge is also the home of Europe's largest eel fishery.
7. Roddy McCorley was hanged at Toomebridge for his participation in the rising of 1798.
8. Ancient city near Naples, Italy, site of many archaeological finds. It was also the legendary home of the Sybil of Cumae, the female prophet who grants the hero Aeneas's wish to descend into the underworld in book 6 of the *Aeneid*, by Virgil (70–19 B.C.E.), Roman poet. Heaney's poem remembers his maternal grandmother.

What ails you, for God's sake?" Urgent, sibilant
Ails, far off and old. Scaresome cavern waters
Lapping a boatslip. Her helplessness no help.

•

Lisp and relapse. Eddy of sybilline[9] English.
Splashes between a ship and dock, to which,
Animula,[1] I would come alive in time

As ferries churned and turned down Belfast Lough[2]
Towards the brow-to-glass transport of a morning train,
The very "there-you-are-and-where-are-you?"

Of poetry itself. Backs of houses
Like the back of hers, meat-safes and mangles
In the railway-facing yards of fleeting England,

Then fields of grain like the Field of the Cloth of Gold.[3]
To Southwark too I came, from tube-mouth into sunlight,
Moyola-breath by Thames's "straunge stronde."[4]

•

If I stood on the bow-backed chair, I could reach
The light switch. They let me and they watched me.
A touch of the little pip would work the magic.

A turn of their wireless knob and light came on
In the dial. They let me and they watched me
As I roamed at will the stations of the world.

Then they were gone and Big Ben and the news
Were over. The set had been switched off,
All quiet behind the blackout except for

Knitting needles ticking, wind in the flue.[5]
She sat with her fur-lined felt slippers unzipped,
Electric light shone over us, I feared

The dirt-tracked flint and fissure of her nail,
So plectrum-hard, glit-glittery, it must still keep
Among beads and vertebrae in the Derry[6] ground.

2001

9. Like the strange, riddling language spoken by the Sybil of Cumae (see preceding note).
1. Little soul (Latin).
2. Lake.
3. Place near Calais, in France, where in 1520 Henry VIII of England and Francis I of France, with sumptuous pageantry, met to arrange an alliance. Shakespeare describes the meeting in *Henry VIII*.
4. From the "General Prologue" of *The Canterbury Tales*, by Geoffrey Chaucer (c. 1342–1400). Both the Tabard Inn, where Chaucer's pilgrims begin their trip, and the Globe Theatre, where most of Shakespeare's plays were originally performed, were located in Southwark, a borough of London on the Thames River. *Moyola*: river in County Derry.
5. Chimney.
6. City and district in Northern Ireland. *Plectrum*: pick for use with stringed instruments.

Frank Bidart
b. 1939

At a time when most of his contemporaries are writing lyrics with oblique meanings, Frank Bidart has evolved a method both old-fashioned and new. One might suppose that he is reviving the dramatic monologue, but he does so with such marked originality that it does not resemble his predecessors' use of this form. A poem about the mad dancer Vaslav Nijinsky includes imagined or recorded quotations, interfused with diary extracts, letters, and other material—a use of heterogeneous sources indebted to Ezra Pound's *Cantos*. But Bidart's effect is not miscellaneous: though his work is fragmented, sometimes almost a series of spasms, all becomes coherent in the minds of the various protagonists. He shows, as Robert Browning did in his dramatic monologues, great psychological penetration, though Bidart focuses on such subjects as guilt, obsession, or seeming grotesqueness. In "Ellen West," based on a case study by the psychiatrist Ludwig Binswanger, Bidart adopts the voice of an anorexic who responds with vexed intensity to her body and the bodies of those around her. Along with other daring and disturbing dramatic monologues, such as "Herbert White," about a necrophilic child-murderer, Bidart has written personal poems about his conflicted relationship with his parents: "the CRISES, FURIES, REFUSALS," "the ACTIONS, ANGERS, DECISIONS // that *made me* what I am" ("Confessional").

The presentation of his poems is unusual. Some phrases appear in capital letters, as if they are headlines emphasizing the most important thoughts in the poem. There are often, though not always, large spaces between lines, occasional bursts into prose, special paragraphing, dramatic uses of punctuation. Bidart boldly rewrites the biblical story of creation, and through simplification, capitalization, and pauses, he fashions a fresh and effective version. Whether lyrical or dramatic, his poems demand attention by these devices, yet on occasion their compressed language is mellifluous in a clipped way, as in the brief elegies and poems of gay experience in *Desire* (1997).

Born on May 27, 1939, in Bakersfield, California, Bidart was educated at the University of California at Riverside (B.A., 1962) and at Harvard University (M.A., 1967), where he studied with and befriended Robert Lowell, whose poetry he later edited. He teaches at Wellesley College.

Ellen West[1]

I love sweets,—
                                heaven
would be dying on a bed of vanilla ice cream . . .

But my true self
is thin, all profile

and effortless gestures, the sort of blond
elegant girl whose
                                    body is the image of her soul.

1. Bidart's poem is based on a case study of a woman suffering from anorexia nervosa, written by Swiss existential psychiatrist Ludwig Binswanger (1881–1966).

—My doctors tell me I must give up
this ideal;
            but I
WILL NOT . . . cannot.

Only to my husband I'm not simply a "case."

But he is a fool. He married
meat, and thought it was a wife.

•   •   •

Why am I a girl?

I ask my doctors, and they tell me they
don't know, that it is just "given."

But it has such
implications—;
                and sometimes,
I even feel like a girl.

•   •   •

Now, at the beginning of Ellen's thirty-second year, her physical condition has deteriorated still further. Her use of laxatives increases beyond measure. Every evening she takes sixty to seventy tablets of a laxative, with the result that she suffers tortured vomiting at night and violent diarrhea by day, often accompanied by a weakness of the heart. She has thinned down to a skeleton, and weighs only 92 pounds.

•   •   •

About five years ago, I was in a restaurant,
eating alone
            with a book. I was
not married, and often did that . . .

—I'd turn down
dinner invitations, so I could eat alone;

I'd allow myself two pieces of bread, with
butter, at the beginning, and three scoops of
vanilla ice cream, at the end,—

                        sitting there alone

with a book, both in the book
and out of it, waited on, idly
watching people,—

                when an attractive young man
and woman, both elegantly dressed,
sat next to me.
            She was beautiful—;

with sharp, clear features, a good
bone structure—;
                    if she took her make-up off
in front of you, rubbing cold cream
again and again across her skin, she still would be
beautiful—
            more beautiful.

And he,—
            I couldn't remember when I had seen a man
so attractive. I didn't know why. He was almost

a male version
            of her,—

I had the sudden, mad notion that I
wanted to be his lover . . .

—Were they married?
                        were *they* lovers?

They didn't wear wedding rings.

Their behavior was circumspect. They discussed
politics. They didn't touch . . .

—How could I discover?
                        Then, when the first course
arrived, I noticed the way

each held his fork out for the other

to taste what he had ordered . . .

                                They did this
again and again, with pleased looks, indulgent
smiles, for each course,
                        more than once for *each* dish—;
much too much for just friends . . .

—Their behavior somehow sickened me;

the way each *gladly*
put the *food* the other had offered *into his mouth*—;

I knew what they were. I knew they slept together.

An immense depression came over me . . .

—I knew I could never
with such ease allow another to put food into my mouth:

happily *myself* put food into another's mouth—;

I knew that to become a wife I would have to give up my ideal.

• • •

Even as a child,
I saw that the "natural" process of aging

is for one's middle to thicken—
one's skin to blotch;

as happened to my mother.
And her mother.
I loathed "Nature."

At twelve, pancakes
became the most terrible thought there is . . .

I shall *defeat* "Nature."

In the hospital, when they
weigh me, I wear weights secretly sewn into my belt.

• • •

January 16. The patient is allowed to eat in her room, but comes readily with her husband to afternoon coffee. Previously she had stoutly resisted this on the ground that she did not really eat but devoured like a wild animal. This she demonstrated with utmost realism . . . Her physical examination showed nothing striking. Salivary glands are markedly enlarged on both sides.

January 21. Has been reading *Faust* again. In her diary, writes that art is the "mutual permeation" of the "world of the body" and the "world of the spirit." Says that her own poems are "hospital poems . . . weak—without skill or perseverance; only managing to beat their wings softly."

February 8. Agitation, quickly subsided again. Has attached herself to an elegant, very thin female patient. Homo-erotic component strikingly evident.

February 15. Vexation, and torment. Says that her mind forces her always to think of eating. Feels herself degraded by this. Has entirely, for the first time in years, stopped writing poetry.

• • •

Callas[2] is my favorite singer, but I've only
seen her once—;

I've never forgotten that night . . .

—It was in *Tosca*,[3] she had long before
lost weight, her voice

2. Maria Callas (1923–1977), American opera singer.

3. Opera by Italian composer Giacomo Puccini (1858–1924).

had been, for years,
                    deteriorating, half itself . . .

When her career began, of course, she was fat,

enormous—; in the early photographs,
sometimes I almost don't recognize her . . .

The voice too then was enormous—

healthy; robust; subtle; but capable of
crude effects, even vulgar,
                        almost out of
high spirits, too much health . . .

But soon she felt that she must lose weight,—
that all she was trying to express

was obliterated by her body,
buried in flesh—;
                    abruptly, within
four months, she lost at least sixty pounds . . .

—The gossip in Milan was that Callas
had swallowed a tapeworm.

But of course she hadn't.
                        The *tapeworm*
was her *soul* . . .

—How her soul, uncompromising,
insatiable,
            must have loved eating the flesh from her bones,

revealing this extraordinarily
mercurial; fragile; masterly creature . . .

—But irresistibly, nothing
stopped there; the huge voice

also began to change: at first, it simply diminished
in volume, in size,
                    then the top notes became
shrill, unreliable—at last,
usually not there at all . . .

—No one knows *why*. Perhaps her mind,
ravenous, still insatiable, sensed

that to struggle with the *shreds* of a voice

must make her artistry subtler, more refined,
more capable of expressing humiliation,
rage, betrayal . . .

—Perhaps the opposite. Perhaps her spirit
loathed the unending struggle

to *embody* itself, to *manifest* itself, on a stage whose

mechanics, and suffocating customs,
seemed expressly designed to annihilate spirit . . .

—I know that in *Tosca,* in the second act,
when, humiliated, hounded by Scarpia,
she sang *Vissi d'arte*
                    —"I lived for art"—

and in torment, bewilderment, at the end she asks,
with a voice reaching
                    harrowingly for the notes,

"Art has *repaid* me LIKE THIS?"

                                        I felt I was watching
autobiography—
                    an art; skill;
virtuosity

miles distant from the usual soprano's
athleticism,—
                    the usual musician's dream
of virtuosity *without* content . . .

—I wonder what she feels, now,
listening to her recordings.

For they have already, within a few years,
begun to date . . .

Whatever they express
they express through the style of a decade
and a half—;
                    a style *she* helped create . . .

—She must know that now
she probably would *not* do a trill in
exactly that way,—
                    that the whole sound, atmosphere,
dramaturgy of her recordings

have just slightly become those of the past . . .

—Is it bitter? Does her soul
tell her

that she was an *idiot* ever to think
anything
material wholly could satisfy? . . .

—Perhaps it says: *The only way*
to escape
the History of Styles

is not to have a body.

• • •

When I open my eyes in the morning, my great
mystery
stands before me . . .

—I *know* that I am intelligent; therefore

the inability not to fear food
day-and-night; this unending hunger
ten minutes after I have eaten . . .
a childish
dread of eating; hunger which can have no cause,—

half my mind says that all this
is *demeaning* . . .

Bread
for days on end
drives all real thought from my brain . . .

—Then I think, No. The ideal of being thin

conceals the ideal
not to have a body—;
which is NOT trivial . . .

This wish seems now as much a "given" of my existence

as the intolerable
fact that I am dark-complexioned; big-boned;
and once weighed
one hundred and sixty-five pounds . . .

—But then I think, *No*. That's too simple,—

without a body, who can
know himself at all?
Only by
acting; choosing; rejecting; have I

made myself—
discovered who and what *Ellen* can be . . .

—But then again I think, *NO.* This *I* is anterior
to name; gender; action;
fashion;
MATTER ITSELF,—

. . . trying to stop my hunger with FOOD
is like trying to appease thirst
with ink.

• • •

March 30. Result of the consultation: Both gentlemen agree completely with my prognosis and doubt any therapeutic usefulness of commitment even more emphatically than I. All three of us are agreed that it is not a case of obsessional neurosis and not one of manic-depressive psychosis, and that no definitely reliable therapy is possible. We therefore resolved to give in to the patient's demand for discharge.

• • •

The train-ride yesterday
was far *worse* than I expected . . .

In our compartment
were ordinary people: a student;
a woman; her child;—

they had ordinary bodies, pleasant faces;
but I thought
I was surrounded by creatures

with the pathetic, desperate
desire to be *not* what they were:—

the student was short,
and carried his body as if forcing
it to be taller—;

the woman showed her gums when she smiled,
and often held her
hand up to hide them—;

the child
seemed to cry simply because it was
small; a dwarf, and helpless . . .

—I was hungry. I had insisted that my husband
not bring food . . .

After about thirty minutes, the woman
peeled an orange

to quiet the child. She put a section
into its mouth—;
                                        immediately it spit it out.

The piece fell to the floor.

—She pushed it with her foot through the dirt
toward me
several inches.

My husband saw me staring
down at the piece . . .

—I didn't move; how I wanted
to reach out,
                        and as if invisible

shove it in my mouth—;

my body
became rigid. As I stared at him,
I could see him staring
at me,—
            then he looked at the student—; at the woman—; then
back to me . . .

I didn't move.

—At last, he bent down, and
casually
            threw it out the window.

He looked away.

—I got up to leave the compartment, then
saw his face,—

his eyes
were red;
            and I saw

—I'm sure I saw—

disappointment.

• • •

On the third day of being home she is as if transformed. At breakfast she eats butter and sugar, at noon she eats so much that—for the first time in thirteen years!—she is satisfied by her food and gets really full. At afternoon coffee she eats chocolate creams and Easter eggs. She takes a walk with her husband, reads poems, listens to recordings, is in a positively festive mood, and all heaviness seems to have fallen away from her. She writes letters, the last one a letter to the fellow patient here to whom she had become so attached. In the evening she takes a lethal dose of poison, and on the following morning she is dead. "She looked as she had never looked in life—calm and happy and peaceful."

• • •

Dearest.—I remember how
at eighteen,
                    on hikes with friends, when
they rested, sitting down to joke or talk,

I circled
around them, afraid to hike ahead alone,

yet afraid to rest
when I was not yet truly thin.

You and, yes, my husband,—
you and he

have by degrees drawn me within the circle;
forced me to sit down at last on the ground.

I am grateful.

But something in me *refuses* it.

—How eager I have been
to compromise, to kill this *refuser,*—

but each compromise, each attempt
to poison an ideal
which often seemed to *me* sterile and unreal,

heightens my hunger.

I am crippled. I disappoint you.

Will you greet with anger, or
happiness,

the news which might well reach you
before this letter?

Your *Ellen.*

1977

If I Could Mourn Like a Mourning Dove

It is what recurs that we believe,
your face not at one moment looking
sideways up at me anguished or

elate, but the old words welling up by
gravity rearranged:
two weeks before you died in

pain worn out, after my usual casual sign-off
with *All my love,* your simple
solemn *My love to you, Frank.*

1997

A Coin for Joe, with the Image of a Horse; c. 350–325 BC

COIN

chip of the closed,—L O S T world, toward whose unseen grasses

this long-necked emissary horse

eagerly still
stretches, to graze

•

World; Grass;

stretching Horse;—ripe with hunger, bright circle
of appetite, risen to feed and famish us, from exile underground . . . for

you chip of the incommensurate
closed world *A n g e l*

1997

Michael Longley
b. 1939

In the dozen years from the birth of Seamus Heaney, in 1939, to that of Paul Muldoon, in 1951, the ratio of outstanding poets born to the general population may be higher in Northern Ireland than anywhere else in the English-speaking world. Growing up amid the collisions of and strife between cultures, between religions, and between dialects seems to have propelled an extraordinary group of writers into poetry. Along with Heaney and Muldoon, Michael Longley, Derek Mahon, and Medbh McGuckian came to know one other during the 1960s and early 1970s, friendly competitors who swapped poems and together read the work of other writers. Born in Belfast, on July 27, 1939, a few months after Heaney, Michael Longley takes his place in this formidable company as a master of formal elegance and lyric grace. Over the years he has authored many books of poetry, and he retired in 1991 from a long career in the Arts Council of

Northern Ireland. In 2000–2001, he was triply honored when he won the Hawthornden Prize (Britain's oldest literary award), the T. S. Eliot Prize, and the Queen's Gold Medal.

In the rhymed verse characteristic of his early work (which recalls Louis MacNeice, W. H. Auden, W. B. Yeats, and Ted Hughes), Longley addresses "A Letter to Derek Mahon" to his friend and fellow Protestant, encapsulating the tension between their formalist precision and the sectarian killings of Belfast: "Two poetic conservatives / In the city of guns and long knives, / Our ears receiving then and there / The stereophonic nightmare / Of the Shankill and the Falls." Even after discarding rhyme and metaphysical conceits, Longley continued to work in polished stanzas with intricate sonic patterning, fluent meters, and sinuous syntax. Whether or not the Troubles of Northern Ireland are his explicit subject, Longley's miniaturist formal craft is, to modify Robert Frost's phrase, a delicate stay against Belfast's bloody confusion.

As a student at Trinity College, Dublin (1958–63), Longley read classics, and the example of ancient poetry's golden balance has been fruitful for him, as evidenced by his poise at the level of the line, the stanza, and the poem. Sometimes, he borrows explicitly from classical verse, as in "Ceasefire," a poem he wrote in response to the 1994 suspension of hostilities between the warring parties in Northern Ireland. He retells the story from Homer's *Iliad* of the meeting between the warrior Achilles and King Priam, father to Hector, the great Trojan warrior he has just killed. This moving poem, true both to painful family loss and to the aspiration for a peace beyond cycles of revenge, filters and thus clarifies the immediate present through an ancient paradigm. "Wounds" sees the contemporary bloodshed—a boy wanders into a home to commit sectarian murder—through a different historical parallel, that of World War I, in which Longley's father fought alongside many Ulster Protestants and other Irishmen. Like many fellow poets of Northern Ireland, Longley takes an indirect approach in his writing about atrocity. But where Heaney turns to the deflections of metaphor and of the archetypal dead, Mahon to those of rhyme and painterly texture, McGuckian to dream and figurative play, and Muldoon to irony and numerological form, Longley detours through the classics—their stories, symmetries, and universalized speakers. In lyrics such as "The Comber" and "The Beech Tree," nature's splendor also offers, in contrast to human hatred and butchery, a repose, a vital presence, an epiphanic beauty.

Casualty

Its decline was gradual,
A sequence of explorations
By other animals, each
Looking for the easiest way in—

A surgical removal of the eyes,
A probing of the orifices,
Bitings down through the skin,
Through tracts where the grasses melt,

And the bad air released
In a ceremonious wounding
So slow that more and more
I wanted to get closer to it.

A candid grin, the bones
Accumulating to a diagram

Except for the polished horns,
The immaculate hooves.

And this no final reduction
For the ribs began to scatter,
The wool to move outward
As though hunger still worked there,

As though something that had followed
Fox and crow was desperate for
A last morsel and was
Other than the wind or rain.

1973

Wounds

Here are two pictures from my father's head—
I have kept them like secrets until now:
First, the Ulster Division at the Somme[1]
Going over the top with 'Fuck the Pope!'
'No Surrender!': a boy about to die,
Screaming 'Give 'em one for the Shankill!'[2]
'Wilder than Gurkhas'[3] were my father's words
Of admiration and bewilderment.
Next comes the London-Scottish padre[4]
Resettling kilts with his swagger-stick,
With a stylish backhand and a prayer.
Over a landscape of dead buttocks
My father followed him for fifty years.
At last, a belated casualty,
He said—lead traces flaring till they hurt—
'I am dying for King and Country, slowly.'
I touched his hand, his thin head I touched.

Now, with military honours of a kind,
With his badges, his medals like rainbows,
His spinning compass, I bury beside him
Three teenage soldiers, bellies full of
Bullets and Irish beer, their flies undone.
A packet of Woodbines I throw in,
A lucifer,[5] the Sacred Heart of Jesus
Paralysed as heavy guns put out
The night-light in a nursery for ever;
Also a bus-conductor's uniform—
He collapsed beside his carpet-slippers

1. In World War I, the 36th (Ulster) Division lost thousands of soldiers in two days of fighting at the First Battle of the Somme, in France.
2. Protestant stronghold in Belfast.
3. Soldiers from Nepal in the British army.
4. Military chaplain.
5. Match. *Woodbines:* cigarettes commonly smoked by soldiers in World War I.

Without a murmur, shot through the head
By a shivering boy who wandered in
Before they could turn the television down
Or tidy away the supper dishes.
To the children, to a bewildered wife,
I think 'Sorry Missus' was what he said.

1973

Detour

I want my funeral to include this detour
Down the single street of a small market town,
On either side of the procession such names
As Philbin, O'Malley, MacNamara, Keane.
A reverent pause to let a herd of milkers pass
Will bring me face to face with grubby parsnips,
Cauliflowers that glitter after a sunshower,
Then hay rakes, broom handles, gas cylinders.
Reflected in the slow sequence of shop windows
I shall be part of the action when his wife
Draining the potatoes into a steamy sink
Calls to the butcher to get ready for dinner
And the publican[6] descends to change a barrel.
From behind the one locked door for miles around
I shall prolong a detailed conversation
With the man in the concrete telephone kiosk
About where my funeral might be going next.

1991

Ceasefire[7]

I

Put in mind of his own father and moved to tears
Achilles took him by the hand and pushed the old king
Gently away, but Priam curled up at his feet and
Wept with him until their sadness filled the building.

II

Taking Hector's corpse into his own hands Achilles
Made sure it was washed and, for the old king's sake,

6. Republican, one who wants Northern Ireland to be free from British rule.
7. In book 24 of Homer's *Iliad*, the Trojan king Priam visits Achilles' camp to beg for the body of his son, Hector, after Achilles has killed Hector and dragged his body by chariot, in revenge for Hector's having killed his friend Patroclus. Achilles receives the king graciously and gives him the body.

Laid out in uniform, ready for Priam to carry
Wrapped like a present home to Troy at daybreak.

III

When they had eaten together, it pleased them both
To stare at each other's beauty as lovers might,
Achilles built like a god, Priam good-looking still
And full of conversation, who earlier had sighed:

IV

'I get down on my knees and do what must be done
And kiss Achilles' hand, the killer of my son.'

1994

The Comber

A moment before the comber turns into
A breaker—sea-spray, raggedy rainbows—
Water and sunlight contain all the colours
And suspend between Inishbofin[8] and me
The otter, and thus we meet, without my scent
In her nostrils, the uproar of my presence,
My unforgivable shadow on the sand—
Even if this is the only sound I make.

2000

Death of a Horse

after Keith Douglas[9]

Its expression resigned, humble even, as if it knows
And doesn't mind when the man draws the first diagonal
In white across its forehead, from ear to eyeball, then
The second, death's chalky intersection, the crossroads

Where, moments before the legs stiffen and relax and
The knees give way and like water from a burst drain
The blood comes jetting out, black almost, warm and thick,
The horse goes on standing still, just staring ahead.

2000

8. Island off the west coast of Ireland.
9. English poet (1920–1944), who wrote about and was killed in World War II.

The Beech Tree

Leaning back like a lover against this beech tree's
Two-hundred-year-old pewter trunk, I look up
Through skylights into the leafy cumulus, and join
Everybody who has teetered where these huge roots
Spread far and wide our motionless mossy dance,
As though I'd begun my eclogues with a beech
As Virgil[1] does, the brown envelopes unfolding
Like fans their transparent downy leaves, tassels
And prickly cups, mast, a fall of vermilion
And copper and gold, then room in the branches
For the full moon and her dusty lakes, winter
And the poet who recollects his younger self
And improvises a last line for the georgics
About snoozing under this beech tree's canopy.

2000

1. Roman poet (70–19 B.C.E.), author of ten eclogues, or short pastoral poems in dialogue form, as well as the *Georgics* (line 13), or poems on agricultural subjects.

MARGARET ATWOOD
b. 1939

Margaret Atwood, born November 18, 1939, published her first book just after receiving her B.A. from Victoria College, University of Toronto, in 1961. She earned an M.A. at Harvard University and later returned for doctoral research that she did not complete, publishing several volumes of verse during that time. Until 1972, she taught at Canadian universities in Montreal, Alberta, and Toronto; since then, she has been a writer-in-residence in Canada, the United States, and Wales. She has published, besides verse, acclaimed novels, stories, and critical prose. Although written with great confidence, her poems portray a quality she shares with one of her subjects, nineteenth-century Canadian writer Susanna Moodie: "the inescapable doubleness of her own vision" (*The Journals of Susanna Moodie*). Her experiences seem always to rouse cross-cutting responses: "though we knew we had never / been there before, / we knew we had been there before" ("A Morning"). Pierced by her gaze, familiar objects look different: "and you, my electric typewriter / with your cord and hungry plug / drinking a sinister transfusion / from the other side of the wall" ("Three Desk Objects").

Atwood's analysis of the Canadian experience suggests a national corollary for this divided vision: Susanna Moodie, for example, is "an ardent Canadian patriot" and yet also a "detached observer, a stranger"; "We are all immigrants to this place even if we were born here." In "Disembarking at Quebec," Atwood finds an apt metaphor for this collective sense of alienation: "I am a word / in a foreign language." Preoccupations with survival and isolation are also, in Atwood's view, among the distinguishing features of Canadian literature.

An eminent feminist, Atwood has written perceptive, surprising, and witty poems that explore the dynamics of gender relations. "How much longer can I get away / with being so fucking cute?" is the arresting question that opens "Miss July Grows Older," a poem that presents the smart, wryly self-critical voice of a woman who, hardly a passive object, has skillfully manipulated men: "It was something I did well, / like playing the flute." As she ages, Miss July transfers her psychic energies to the world outside, to sunshine and raindrops; "after a while," she explains of her feelings about sex, "these flesh arpeggios get boring." In "Manet's Olympia," Atwood describes the subject of a famous painting, another woman who refuses subordination to the male gaze, her body "unfragile, defiant." "This is no morsel," states the speaker. Blunt address, short declarative sentences, colloquial diction, precise descriptions, well-defined characters, dramatic tension, plays on clichés, and ironic inversions of the reader's expectations—these are among the strategies that help Margaret Atwood's poems command instant attention.

This Is a Photograph of Me

It was taken some time ago.
At first it seems to be
a smeared
print: blurred lines and grey flecks
blended with the paper;

then, as you scan
it, you see in the left-hand corner
a thing that is like a branch: part of a tree
(balsam or spruce) emerging
and, to the right, halfway up
what ought to be a gentle
slope, a small frame house.

In the background there is a lake,
and beyond that, some low hills.

(The photograph was taken
the day after I drowned.

I am in the lake, in the center
of the picture, just under the surface.

It is difficult to say where
precisely, or to say
how large or small I am:
the effect of water
on light is a distortion

but if you look long enough,
eventually
you will be able to see me.)

1966

[You Fit into Me]

you fit into me
like a hook into an eye

a fish hook
an open eye

1971

They Eat Out

In restaurants we argue
over which of us will pay for your funeral

though the real question is
whether or not I will make you immortal.

At the moment only I
can do it and so

I raise the magic fork
over the plate of beef fried rice

and plunge it into your heart.
There is a faint pop, a sizzle

and through your own split head
you rise up glowing;

the ceiling opens
a voice sings Love Is A Many

Splendoured Thing[1]
you hang suspended above the city

in blue tights and a red cape,
your eyes flashing in unison.

The other diners regard you
some with awe, some only with boredom:

they cannot decide if you are a new weapon
or only a new advertisement.

1. Title and theme song of a highly romantic movie of the 1950s.

As for me, I continue eating;
I liked you better the way you were,
but you were always ambitious.

1971

From Circe/Mud Poems[2]

[*Men with the Heads of Eagles*]

Men with the heads of eagles
no longer interest me
or pig-men, or those who can fly
with the aid of wax and feathers[3]

or those who take off their clothes
to reveal other clothes
or those with skins of blue leather[4]

or those golden and flat as a coat of arms
or those with claws, the stuffed ones
with glass eyes; or those
hierarchic as greaves[5] and steam-engines.

All these I could create, manufacture,
or find easily: they swoop and thunder
around this island, common as flies,
sparks flashing, bumping into each other,

on hot days you can watch them
as they melt, come apart,
fall into the ocean
like sick gulls, dethronements, plane crashes.

I search instead for the others,
the ones left over,
the ones who have escaped from these
mythologies with barely their lives;
they have real faces and hands, they think
of themselves as
wrong somehow, they would rather be trees.

1974

2. In Homer's *Odyssey,* Circe is the female enchanter who turns Odysseus's companions into swine; he is protected by the herb moly and thus frees his mates.
3. As did Daedalus, the legendary craftsman, and his son, Icarus, who escaped from the Cretan labyrinth on wings fashioned out of wax and feathers.
4. Probably a reference to the Picts, an early British people who painted themselves blue before going into battle.
5. Armor for the lower part of the leg.

Footnote to the Amnesty Report on Torture

The torture chamber is not like anything
you would have expected.
No opera set or sexy chains and
leather-goods from the glossy
porno magazines, no thirties horror
dungeon with gauzy cobwebs; nor is it
the bare cold-lighted
chrome space of the future
we think we fear.
More like one of the seedier
British Railways stations, with scratched green
walls and spilled tea,
crumpled papers, and a stooped man
who is always cleaning the floor.

It stinks, though; like a hospital,
of antiseptics and sickness,
and, on some days, blood
which smells the same anywhere,
here or at the butcher's.

The man who works here
is losing his sense of smell.
He's glad to have this job, because
there are few others.
He isn't a torturer, he only
cleans the floor:
every morning the same vomit,
the same shed teeth, the same
piss and liquid shit, the same panic.

Some have courage, others
don't; those who do what he thinks of
as the real work, and who are
bored, since minor bureaucrats
are always bored, tell them
it doesn't matter, who
will ever know they were brave, they might
as well talk now
and get it over.

Some have nothing to say, which also
doesn't matter. Their
warped bodies too, with the torn
fingers and ragged tongues, are thrown
over the spiked iron fence onto
the Consul's lawn, along with
the bodies of the children
burned to make their mothers talk.

The man who cleans the floors
is glad it isn't him.
It will be if he ever says
what he knows. He works long hours,
submits to the searches, eats
a meal he brings from home, which tastes
of old blood and the sawdust
he cleans the floor with. His wife
is pleased he brings her money
for the food, has been told
not to ask questions.

As he sweeps, he tries
not to listen; he tries
to make himself into a wall,
a thick wall, a wall
soft and without echoes. He thinks
of nothing but the walk back
to his hot shed of a house,
of the door
opening and his children
with their unmarked skin and flawless eyes
running to meet him.

He is afraid of
what he might do
if he were told to,
he is afraid of the door,

he is afraid, not
of the door but of the door
opening; sometimes, no matter
how hard he tries,
his children are not there.

1978

Miss July Grows Older

How much longer can I get away
with being so fucking cute?
Not much longer.
The shoes with bows, the cunning underwear
with slogans on the crotch—*Knock Here,*
and so forth—
will have to go, along with the cat suit.[6]

6. Tight-fitting garment from neck to feet.

After a while you forget
what you really look like.
You think your mouth is the size it was.
You pretend not to care.

When I was young I went with my hair
hiding one eye, thinking myself daring;
off to the movies in my jaunty pencil
skirt and elastic cinch-belt,
chewed gum, left lipstick
imprints the shape of grateful, rubbery
sighs on the cigarettes of men
I hardly knew and didn't want to.
Men were a skill, you had to have
good hands, breathe into
their nostrils, as for horses. It was something I did well,
like playing the flute, although I don't.

In the forests of grey stems there are standing pools,
tarn-coloured, choked with brown leaves.
Through them you can see an arm, a shoulder,
when the light is right, with the sky clouded.
The train goes past silos, through meadows,
the winter wheat on the fields like scanty fur.

I still get letters, although not many.
A man writes me, requesting true-life stories
about bad sex. He's doing an anthology.
He got my name off an old calendar,
the photo that's mostly bum and daisies,
back when my skin had the golden slick
of fresh-spread margarine.
Not rape, he says, but disappointment,
more like a defeat of expectations.
Dear Sir, I reply, I never had any.
Bad sex, that is.
It was never the sex, it was the other things,
the absence of flowers, the death threats,
the eating habits at breakfast.
I notice I'm using the past tense.

Though the vaporous cloud of chemicals that enveloped
you like a glowing eggshell, an incense,
doesn't disappear: it just gets larger
and takes in more. You grow out
of sex like a shrunk dress
into your common senses, those you share
with whatever's listening. The way the sun
moves through the hours becomes important,
the smeared raindrops
on the window, buds
on the roadside weeds, the sheen

of spilled oil on a raw ditch
filling with muddy water.

Don't get me wrong: with the lights out
I'd still take on anyone,
if I had the energy to spare.
But after a while these flesh arpeggios get boring,
like Bach[7] over and over;
too much of one kind of glory.

When I was all body I was lazy.
I had an easy life, and was not grateful.
Now there are more of me.
Don't confuse me with my hen-leg elbows:
what you get is no longer
what you see.

1995

Manet's Olympia[8]

She reclines, more or less.
Try that posture, it's hardly languor.
Her right arm sharp angles.
With her left she conceals her ambush.
Shoes but not stockings,
how sinister. The flower
behind her ear is naturally
not real, of a piece
with the sofa's drapery.
The windows (if any) are shut.
This is indoor sin.
Above the head of the (clothed) maid
is an invisible voice balloon: *Slut.*

But. Consider the body,
unfragile, defiant, the pale nipples
staring you right in the bull's-eye.
Consider also the black ribbon
around the neck. What's under it?
A fine red threadline, where the head
was taken off and glued back on.
The body's on offer,
but the neck's as far as it goes.
This is no morsel.
Put clothes on her and you'd have a schoolteacher,
the kind with the brittle whiphand.

7. Johann Sebastian Bach (1685–1750), German Baroque composer. *Arpeggios:* chords played rapidly, one note at a time.

8. Famous 1863 painting by French Impressionist Édouard Manet (1832–1883), depicting a nude courtesan gazing confidently at the viewer.

There's someone else in this room.
You, Monsieur Voyeur.
As for that object of yours
she's seen those before, and better.

I, the head, am the only subject
of this picture.
You, Sir, are furniture.
Get stuffed.

1995

Morning in the Burned House

In the burned house I am eating breakfast.
You understand there is no house, there is no breakfast,
yet here I am.

The spoon which was melted scrapes against
the bowl which was melted also.
No one else is around.

Where have they gone to, brother and sister,
mother and father? Off along the shore,
perhaps. Their clothes are still on the hangers,

their dishes piled beside the sink,
which is beside the woodstove
with its grate and sooty kettle,

every detail clear,
tin cup and rippled mirror.
The day is bright and songless,

the lake is blue, the forest watchful.
In the east a bank of cloud
rises up silently like dark bread.

I can see the swirls in the oilcloth,
I can see the flaws in the glass,
those flares where the sun hits them.

I can't see my own arms and legs
or know if this is a trap or blessing,
finding myself back here, where everything

in this house has long been over,
kettle and mirror, spoon and bowl,
including my own body,

including the body I had then,
including the body I have now
as I sit at this morning table, alone and happy,

bare child's feet on the scorched floorboards
(I can almost see)
in my burning clothes, the thin green shorts

and grubby yellow T-shirt
holding my cindery, non-existent,
radiant flesh. Incandescent.

1995

Eunice de Souza
b. 1940

Eunice de Souza's first collection, *Fix* (1979), was a breakthrough in Indian women's writing in English. Before this volume, Indian English women's poetry was marred by melodramatic self-dramatization and slack sentimentality. With its dry wit, spare lines, and laconic insight, *Fix* represented a new level of tonal control. A poet of cold perspicuity, de Souza satirizes the hypocrisy and self-delusion she sees in the conservative Catholic community in Goa, the former capital of Portuguese India, where she grew up. The contradictions she exposes are in part a legacy of colonialism, which remained in place in Goa even after most of India became independent.

In her free verse lyrics, de Souza often reenters the voice of a child growing up in Goa. She imports and indigenizes this strategy of American "confessional" poets of the 1960s, such as Sylvia Plath. De Souza also deploys the idiom, diction, and speech rhythms of Goan India. The speaker of "Sweet Sixteen," for example, assures another teenager that dancing can indeed cause pregnancy, rendered in the local vernacular as "getting *preggers*." While the girl's pathetic confusion is the immediate object of the poem's dramatic irony, its broader target is the Goan Catholic social code that teaches girls to repress their sexuality and ignore their bodies. The openly autobiographical poem "De Souza Prabhu" is an ironic self-portrait of the poet as a girl alienated from her own body and mind. The young de Souza places herself among the "lame ducks" because of her foreign name (part Greek, part Portuguese), her speech ("my language alien"), and her emerging sexuality. Knowing her parents would have preferred a boy, the unwanted girl tries to conceal her femininity ("I hid the bloodstains").

De Souza's understated and epigrammatic poems reveal pain, anger, and bewilderment in growing up female in middle-class Portuguese India—feelings clarified by the poetry's controlled verbal surface and descriptive precision. Humor is also present, as in "Conversation Piece," a one-joke poem about an Indian Catholic who mistakes a clay lingam, a phallic representation of the Hindu god Siva, for an ashtray. In de Souza's more recent volumes, the poetry has relaxed into a more contemplative style, though even a lyric of tender celebration, such as the nativity poem "For Rita's Daughter, Just Born," curbs sentiment with its acid final reference to "the shrill cry of kites."

Born on August 1, 1940, in Poona, India, de Souza received her B.A. from Sophia College, Bombay, in 1960; her M.A. from Marquette University, Wisconsin, in 1963; and her Ph.D. from the University of Bombay in 1988. Since 1969, she has been teaching English at St. Xavier's College, in Bombay. Along with poetry, she has published essays and children's books, while also editing volumes of fiction and poems by, and interviews with, fellow Indian writers.

Sweet Sixteen

Well, you can't say
they didn't try.
Mamas never mentioned menses.[1]
A nun screamed: you vulgar girl
don't say brassieres
say bracelets.
She pinned paper sleeves
onto our sleeveless dresses.
The preacher thundered:
Never go with a man alone
Never alone
and even if you're engaged
only passionless kisses.

At sixteen, Phoebe asked me:
Can it happen when you're in a dance hall
I mean, you know what,
getting *preggers*[2] and all that, when
you're dancing?
I, sixteen, assured her
you could.

1979

De Souza Prabhu

No, I'm not going to
delve deep down and discover
I'm really de Souza Prabhu[3]
even if Prabhu was no fool
and got the best of both worlds.
(Catholic Brahmin![4]
I can hear his fat chuckle still.)

No matter that
my name is Greek
my surname Portuguese
my language alien.

1. Menstruation.
2. Local idiom for *pregnant*.
3. Master; teacher; accomplished one (Sanskrit, Hindi).
4. The priestly and highest of the four major castes of Hinduism.

There are ways
of belonging.

I belong with the lame ducks.

I heard it said
my parents wanted a boy.
I've done my best to qualify.
I hid the bloodstains
on my clothes
and let my breasts sag.
Words the weapon
to crucify.

1979

Conversation Piece

My Portuguese-bred aunt
picked up a clay shivalingam[5]
one day and said:
Is this an ashtray?
No, said the salesman,
This is our god.

1979

Women in Dutch Painting

The afternoon sun is on their faces.
they are calm, not stupid,
pregnant, not bovine.
I know women like that
and not just in paintings—
an aunt who did not answer her husband back
not because she was plain
and Anna who writes poems
and hopes her avocado stones
will sprout in the kitchen.
Her voice is oatmeal and honey.

1988

For Rita's Daughter, Just Born

Luminous new leaf
May the sun rise gently
on your unfurling

5. Phallic representation of the Hindu god Siva.

in the courtyard always linger
the smell of earth after rain

the stone of these steps
stay cool and old

gods in the niches
old brass on the wall

never the shrill cry of kites

1988

Landscape

I

M. assures me she'll be back
to fling my ashes in the local creek.
(We're short on sacred rivers here).[6]

The pungent air will suit my soul:
It will find its place among
the plastic carrier bags and rags that float upstream
or is it downstream.
One can never tell.
The sea sends everything reeling back.
The trees go under.

II

We push so much under the carpet—
the carpet's now a landscape.
A worm embedded in each tuft
There's a forest moving.

Everybody smiles
and smiles.

III

The crows will never learn
there is garbage enough for everyone:
the mouths of the young are raw red,
soundless.

The egret alights on the topmost branch.
Not a leaf is disturbed.
On all sides the ocean.

6. Many Hindus, considering the River Ganges holy, float the bodies of the dead or spread their ashes in it.

IV

stretch marks of the city

Look the other way:
There are dhows[7] there
mud banks
white horses for desert kingdoms

an old monkey coughs in a tree

the young sense food
begin their walk up the hill
slow sure unceasing

we lock the windows
bar the doors

the sun burns through the walls

1994

7. Sailing vessels.

Robert Pinsky
b. 1940

Robert Pinsky is one of the foremost contemporary poets trying to reclaim a public and discursive language for poetry. Whereas neoconfessionalists plumb the depths of psychic turmoil and anguish, and avant-gardists insist on the opacities of language, Pinsky recalls classical Roman virtues of clarity, balance, and civility. Instead of violently attacking his poetic or familial ancestors, Pinsky works in forms and patterns—measured stanzas, a rational grammar and syntax, rhetorical parallelisms and pauses—that quietly renew his inheritances. The clarity, wit, and seriousness of Pinsky's poems may be traced to the example of Yvor Winters, the poet, critic, and teacher to whom Pinsky pays tribute in his work, and whom he calls the "Old Man." But whereas Winters's poetry evinces a stoicism bolstered by reason and learning, Pinsky's is less severe and allows more for idiosyncratic feeling and contingency.

"Poetry is, among other things," says Pinsky, "a technology for remembering" (*New York Times Book Review,* September 25, 1994). In "The Uncreation," he celebrates the roots, the communal experience, and the pervasiveness of poetry, "the great excess of song that coats the world." But Pinsky's poems, if attached to past achievements, are not deaf to the contemporary. While steeped in the lyric tradition of meditations on ruins, "The Haunted Ruin" vividly describes computer technology, its internal "billion corridors / Of the semiconductor." Into somewhat elevated rhetoric and diction, Pinsky imports the new and the mundane. His poetry encompasses a wide range of experience and thought, from the imagistic ("Spraying flecks of tar and molten rock") to the abstract ("an all-but-unthinkable music"). His language is assimilative, like the historical process allegorized in the rolling hexameters of "The Figured Wheel." Solemnity and melancholy are among his moods, but so too is a gentle humor. In "ABC," the first letter of each successive word begins with the next letter of the alphabet, starting with "Any body can die, evidently."

Pinsky was born on October 20, 1940, into a Jewish family of Long Branch, New Jersey. He was educated at Rutgers University, where he received his B.A. in 1962, and at Stanford University, where he earned a Ph.D. in English in 1966. He has taught at Wellesley College (1968–80) and the University of California, Berkeley (1980–88); since 1988, he has been a professor of English and creative writing at Boston University. He has published several books of criticism on poetry and an acclaimed translation of Dante's *Inferno*. Serving from 1997 to 2000 as the U.S. poet laureate, he worked through various media to promote the reading and speaking of poetry. Presented through print, video, the Internet, and TV, his Favorite Poem Project has gathered and disseminated the diverse experiences of Americans reading and responding to their favorite poems.

The Figured[1] Wheel

The figured wheel rolls through shopping malls and prisons,
Over farms, small and immense, and the rotten little downtowns.
Covered with symbols, it mills everything alive and grinds
The remains of the dead in the cemeteries, in unmarked graves and
oceans.

Sluiced by salt water and fresh, by pure and contaminated rivers,
By snow and sand, it separates and recombines all droplets and grains,
Even the infinite sub-atomic particles crushed under the illustrated,
Varying treads of its wide circumferential track.

Spraying flecks of tar and molten rock it rumbles
Through the Antarctic station of American sailors and technicians,
And shakes the floors and windows of whorehouses for diggers and
smelters
From Bethany, Pennsylvania to a practically nameless, semi-penal New
Town

In the mineral-rich tundra[2] of the Soviet northernmost settlements.
Artists illuminate it with pictures and incised mottoes
Taken from the Ten-Thousand Stories and the Register of True Dramas.
They hang it with colored ribbons and with bells of many pitches.

With paints and chisels and moving lights they record
On its rotating surface the elegant and terrifying doings
Of the inhabitants of the Hundred Pantheons of major Gods
Disposed in iconographic stations at hub, spoke and concentric bands,

And also the grotesque demi-Gods, Hopi gargoyles and Ibo dryads.[3]
They cover it with wind-chimes and electronic instruments

1. Inscribed, decorated, or prophesied.
2. Arctic or subarctic treeless plain.
3. That is, carved grotesques of the plain-dwelling Native Americans and tree nymphs of the West African Igbo.

That vibrate as it rolls to make an all-but-unthinkable music,
So that the wheel hums and rings as it turns through the births of stars

And through the dead-world of bomb, fireblast and fallout
Where only a few doomed races of insects fumble in the smoking grasses.
It is Jesus oblivious to hurt turning to give words to the unrighteous,
And is also Gogol's feeding pig that without knowing it eats a baby chick

And goes on feeding.[4] It is the empty armor of My Cid, clattering
Into the arrows of the credulous unbelievers, a metal suit
Like the lost astronaut revolving with his useless umbilicus.[5]
Through the cold streams, neither energy nor matter, that agitate

The cold, cyclical dark, turning and returning.
Even in the scorched and frozen world of the dead after the holocaust
The wheel as it turns goes on accreting ornaments.
Scientists and artists festoon it from the grave with brilliant

Toys and messages, jokes and zodiacs, tragedies conceived
From among the dreams of the unemployed and the pampered,
The listless and the tortured. It is hung with devices
By dead masters who have survived by reducing themselves magically

To tiny organisms, to wisps of matter, crumbs of soil,
Bits of dry skin, microscopic flakes, which is why they are called "great,"
In their humility that goes on celebrating the turning
Of the wheel as it rolls unrelentingly over

A cow plodding through car-traffic on a street in Iasi[6]
And over the haunts of Robert Pinsky's mother and father
And wife and children and his sweet self
Which he hereby unwillingly and inexpertly gives up, because it is

There, figured and pre-figured in the nothing-transfiguring wheel.

1987

The Questions

What about the people who came to my father's office
For hearing aids and glasses—chatting with him sometimes

A few extra minutes while I swept up in the back,
Addressed packages, cleaned the machines; if he was busy

4. "There was also a sow with her family; as she scraped in a heap of garbage the sow in passing swallowed a chicken and, without even noticing it, continued unconcernedly to gobble up the watermelon rinds" (from Nikolai Gogol's 1842 novel *Dead Souls,* tr. George Reavey, part 1, chapter 3).

5. Navel; the astronaut's now useless "lifeline" is compared to the human umbilical cord as in a scene in Stanley Kubrick's movie *2001: A Space Odyssey* (1968). *My Cid:* El Cid, eleventh-century Spanish military leader; after he died, his followers dressed his corpse in his armor and tied it to a horse, so that he could still lead them into battle.

6. City in Romania.

I might sell them batteries, or tend to their questions:
The tall overloud old man with a tilted, ironic smirk

To cover the gaps in his hearing; a woman who hummed one
Prolonged note constantly, we called her "the hummer"—how

Could her white fat husband (he looked like Rev. Peale)[7]
Bear hearing it day and night? And others: a coquettish old lady

In a bandeau,[8] a European. She worked for refugees who ran
Gift shops or booths on the boardwalk in the summer;

She must have lived in winter on Social Security. One man
Always greeted my father in Masonic gestures and codes.[9]

Why do I want them to be treated tenderly by the world, now
Long after they must have slipped from it one way or another,

While I was dawdling through school at that moment—or driving,
Reading, talking to Ellen. Why this new superfluous caring?

I want for them not to have died in awful pain, friendless.
Though many of the living are starving, I still pray for these,

Dead, mostly anonymous (but Mr. Monk, Mrs. Rose Vogel)
And barely remembered: that they had a little extra, something

For pleasure, a good meal, a book or a decent television set.
Of whom do I pray this rubbery, low-class charity? I saw

An expert today, a nun—wearing a regular skirt and blouse,
But the hood or headdress navy and white around her plain

Probably Irish face, older than me by five or ten years.
The Post Office clerk told her he couldn't break a twenty

So she got change next door and came back to send her package.
As I came out she was driving off—with an air, it seemed to me,

Of annoying, demure good cheer, as if the reasonableness
Of change, mail, cars, clothes was a pleasure in itself: veiled

And dumb like the girls I thought enjoyed the rules too much
In grade school. She might have been a grade school teacher;

But she reminded me of being there, aside from that—as a name
And person there, a Mary or John who learns that the janitor

7. Norman Vincent Peale (1898–1993), influential clergyman.

8. Hairband.

9. Of the Order of Freemasons, a secret society.

Is Mr. Woodhouse; the principal is Mr. Ringleven; the secretary
In the office is Mrs. Apostolacos; the bus driver is Ray.

1987

The Uncreation

The crowd at the ballpark sing, the cantor sings
Kol Nidre,[1] and the equipment in our cars
Fills them with singing voices while we drive.

When the warlord hears his enemy is dead,
He sings his praises. The old men sang a song
And we protesters sang a song against them,

Like teams of children in a singing game;
And at the great convention all they did
They punctuated with a song: our breath

Which is an element and so a quarter
Of all creation, heated and thrown out
With all the body's force to shake our ears.

Everything said has its little secret song,
Strained higher and lower as talking we sing all day,
The sentences turned and tinted by the body:

A tune of certain pitch for questions, a tune
For *that was not a question,* a tune for *was it,*
The little tunes of begging, of coolness, of scolding.

The Mudheads[2] dance in their adobe masks
From house to house, and sing at each the misdeeds
Of the small children inside. And we must take you,

They sing, Now we must take you, Now we must take
You back to the house of Mud. But then the parents
With presents for the Mudheads in their arms

Come singing each child's name, and buy them back:
Forgive him, give her back, we'll give you presents.
And the prancing Mudheads take the bribes, and sing.

I make a feeble song up while I work,
And sometimes even machines may chant or jingle
Some lyrical accident that takes its place

1. Prayer led by the cantor of a Jewish synagogue on the eve of Yom Kippur.

2. Ceremonial masked dancers who represent Native American kachinas, or ancestral spirits.

In the great excess of song that coats the world.
But after the flood the bland Immortals will come
As holy tourists to our sunken world,

To slide like sunbeams down shimmering layers of blue:
Artemis, Gog, Priapus, Jehovah and Baal,[3]
With faces calmer than when we gave them names,

Walking our underwater streets where bones
And houses bloom fantastic spurts of coral,
Until they find our books. The pages softened

To a dense immobile pulp between the covers
Will rise at their touch in swelling plumes like smoke,
With a faint black gas of ink among the swirls,

And the golden beings shaping their mouths like bells
Will impel their breath against the weight of ocean
To sing us into the cold regard of water.

A girl sang dancing once, and shook her hair.
A young man fasting to have a powerful dream
Sang as he cut his body, to please a spirit.

But the Gods will sing entirely, the towering spumes
Dissolving around their faces will be the incense
Of their old anonymity restored

In a choral blast audible in the clouds,
An immense vibration that presses the very fish,
So through her mighty grin the whale will sing

To keep from bursting, and the tingling krill
Will sing in her jaws, the whole cold salty world
Humming oblation to what our mouths once made.

1990

ABC

Any body can die, evidently. Few
Go happily, irradiating joy,

Knowledge, love. Many
Need oblivion, painkillers,
Quickest respite.

3. Fertility god worshipped by the Canaanites. *Artemis:* Greek goddess of fertility, chastity, and the hunt. *Gog:* in the Bible, a hostile spirit supposed to appear just before the end of the world. *Priapus:* Greek fertility god. *Jehovah:* Judeo-Christian name for God.

Sweet time unafflicted,
Various world:

X = your zenith.

2000

The Haunted Ruin

Even your computer is a haunted ruin, as your
Blood leaves something of itself, warming
The tool in your hand.

From far off, down the billion corridors
Of the semiconductor, military
Pipes grieve at the junctures.

This too smells of the body, its heated
Polymers smell of breast milk
And worry-sweat.

Hum of so many cycles in current, voltage
Of the past. Sing, wires. Feel, hand. Eyes,
Watch and form

Legs and bellies of characters:
Beak and eye of A. Serpentine hiss
S of the foregoers, claw-tines

Of E and of the claw hammer
You bought yesterday, its head
Tasting of light oil, the juice

Of dead striving—the haft
Of ash, for all its urethane varnish, is
Polished by body salts.

Pull, clawhead. Hold, shaft. Steel face,
Strike and relieve me. Voice
Of the maker locked in the baritone

Whine of the handsaw working.
Lost, lingerer like the dead souls of
Vilna, revenant.[4] Machine-soul.

2000

4. Ghost. *Vilna:* now Vilnius, capital of Lithuania; a center of Jewish culture until the German extermination of its Jewish population in World War II.

Robert Hass
b. 1941

Robert Hass, the U.S. poet laureate from 1995 through 1997 and, since 1989, a Berkeley professor, is a poet of presence and absence, plenitude and loss. Born on March 1, 1941, in San Francisco, he attended private Catholic schools. In 1963, he received his B.A. from St. Mary's College of California, where he taught beginning in 1971. In 1976, he received his Ph.D. from Stanford University. He won a MacArthur Fellowship in 1984 and the National Book Critics Circle Award in 1996.

In California, Hass came under the influence of the Beats and of west coast poets such as Gary Snyder and Kenneth Rexroth. Like them, he steeped himself in Buddhism and other aspects of East Asian culture. Many of his poems suggest the compression, meditativeness, and alertness to detail of the haiku, a form he has ably translated, in addition to translating the Polish poetry of Nobel Prize–winner Czeslaw Milosz. Hass strives to recover the naked immediacy, the radiant being of nature, objects, people, and emotions. As he says of a lover in "Meditation at Lagunitas," "I felt a wonder at her presence / like a thirst for salt." Yet Hass is no less aware of what Wordsworth called "Fallings from us, vanishings" ("Ode: Intimations of Immortality"). He concedes that, as he puts it in the same poem, "a word is elegy to what it signifies" and "desire is full / of endless distances." As desire in language, poetry is doomed to inscribe absences, to mark losses, even as it seeks to record the full sensual, vital presence of reality. Hass's poetry delights in the primal poetic activity of recovering the world through naming, and yet it is shadowed throughout by emptiness, failure, melancholy longing.

This generative tension is already evident in the early poem "Song." A father returns to an empty house "yelling, 'Hey, I'm home!' " only to encounter the ghost of his desire for physical and emotional contact, for a family "to throw their bodies on the Papa-body, / I-am-loved." To counterbalance this disappointing absence, the poem turns to the gleaming presence of the object-world, "slices of green pepper / on a bone-white dish." One of Hass's fine poems about love relationships, "Privilege of Being," sees anew the mingling of bodies in sex from the astonished perspective of angels. But the poem's celebration of physical immediacy quickly turns into a meditation on separateness and loneliness, one lover hungrily bidding the other: *"look at me."*

Hass's work exhibits mastery of tone, subtly mixing wonder and melancholy, amazement and longing, assertion and vulnerability. In poems such as "Song" and "Sonnet," the natural world evokes moods or inner feelings, as in the haiku. Spliced into the interior ruminations of other poems are quoted snatches of conversation, often in female voices. Combining conversational utterances and rhythms with elevated rhetorical structures, such as formal diction and parallel or hypotactic syntax, the poems ambitiously fuse theoretical speculation with lyrical intensity.

Song

Afternoon cooking in the fall sun—
who is more naked
                    than the man
yelling, "Hey, I'm home!"

to an empty house?
thinking because the bay is clear,
the hills in yellow heat,
& scrub oak red in gullies
that great crowds of family
should tumble from the rooms
to throw their bodies on the Papa-body,
I-am-loved.

Cat sleeps in the windowgleam,
dust motes.
On the oak table
filets of sole
stewing in the juice of tangerines,
slices of green pepper
on a bone-white dish.

1973

Meditation at Lagunitas[1]

All the new thinking is about loss.
In this it resembles all the old thinking.
The idea, for example, that each particular erases
the luminous clarity of a general idea. That the clown-
faced woodpecker probing the dead sculpted trunk
of that black birch is, by his presence,
some tragic falling off from a first world
of undivided light. Or the other notion that,
because there is in this world no one thing
to which the bramble of *blackberry* corresponds,
a word is elegy to what it signifies.
We talked about it late last night and in the voice
of my friend, there was a thin wire of grief, a tone
almost querulous: After a while I understood that,
talking this way, everything dissolves: *justice,*
pine, hair, woman, you and *I*. There was a woman
I made love to and I remembered how, holding
her small shoulders in my hands sometimes,
I felt a violent wonder at her presence
like a thirst for salt, for my childhood river
with its island willows, silly music from the pleasure boat,
muddy places where we caught the little orange-silver fish
called *pumpkinseed.* It hardly had to do with her.
Longing, we say, because desire is full
of endless distances. I must have been the same to her.
But I remember so much, the way her hands dismantled bread,
the thing her father said that hurt her, what

1. Small town near San Francisco.

she dreamed. There are moments when the body is as numinous
as words, days that are the good flesh continuing.
Such tenderness, those afternoons and evenings,
saying *blackberry, blackberry, blackberry.*

1979

Privilege of Being

Many are making love. Up above, the angels
in the unshaken ether and crystal of human longing
are braiding one another's hair, which is strawberry blond
and the texture of cold rivers. They glance
down from time to time at the awkward ecstasy—
it must look to them like featherless birds
splashing in the spring puddle of a bed—
and then one woman, she is about to come,
peels back the man's shut eyelids and says,
look at me, and he does. Or is it the man
tugging the curtain rope in that dark theater?
Anyway, they do, they look at each other;
two beings with evolved eyes, rapacious,
startled, connected at the belly in an unbelievably sweet
lubricious glue, stare at each other,
and the angels are desolate. They hate it. They shudder pathetically
like lithographs of Victorian beggars
with perfect features and alabaster skin hawking rags
in the lewd alleys of the novel.
All of creation is offended by this distress.
It is like the keening sound the moon makes sometimes,
rising. The lovers especially cannot bear it,
it fills them with unspeakable sadness, so that
they close their eyes again and hold each other, each
feeling the mortal singularity of the body
they have enchanted out of death for an hour or so,
and one day, running at sunset, the woman says to the man,
I woke up feeling so sad this morning because I realized
that you could not, as much as I love you,
dear heart, cure my loneliness,
wherewith she touched his cheek to reassure him
that she did not mean to hurt him with this truth.
And the man is not hurt exactly,
he understands that life has limits, that people
die young, fail at love,
fail of their ambitions. He runs beside her, he thinks
of the sadness they have gasped and crooned their way out of
coming, clutching each other with old, invented
forms of grace and clumsy gratitude, ready
to be alone again, or dissatisfied, or merely
companionable like the couples on the summer beach

reading magazine articles about intimacy between the sexes
to themselves, and to each other,
and to the immense, illiterate, consoling angels.

1989

Forty Something

She says to him, musing, "If you ever leave me,
and marry a younger woman and have another baby,
I'll put a knife in your heart." They are in bed,
so she climbs onto his chest, and looks directly
down into his eyes. "You understand? Your heart."

1996

Sonnet

A man talking to his ex-wife on the phone.
He has loved her voice and listens with attention
to every modulation of its tone. Knowing
it intimately. Not knowing what he wants
from the sound of it, from the tendered civility.
He studies, out the window, the seed shapes
of the broken pods of ornamental trees.
The kind that grow in everyone's garden, that no one
but horticulturists can name. Four arched chambers
of pale green, tiny vegetal proscenium arches,
a pair of black tapering seeds bedded in each chamber.
A wish geometry, miniature, Indian or Persian,
lovers or gods in their apartments. Outside, white,
patient animals, and tangled vines, and rain.

1996

LYN HEJINIAN
b. 1941

"The language of poetry," writes Lyn Hejinian, "is a language of inquiry." A leading Language poet, Hejinian refuses to segregate poetry from theory. But neither are her poems—shuttling between linguistic self-scrutiny and lyrical reminiscence—sterile tracts on language. In *My Life* (1980, rev. and exp. 1987), a long, semiparodic, semi-autobiographical prose poem, she recalls a typical American girlhood in the 1950s, complete with family vacations, big cars, airports, middle-class homes, pampered babies, and distant war. She records sensual and emotional details, such as fear of an "uncle with the wart on his nose." Yet Hejinian's poetry resists the illusion of transparent access to a coherent past self. "Maybe writing begins not in the self but in language," she remarked in an interview, "which is far larger than the self, and prior to it. So writing, like reading, begins at a point which is 'not-I' " ("Roughly Stapled").

Seeing the personal life as at least partly constructed by language, Hejinian draws attention to this process in a number of ways. She lets the seams show between sentences. Narrative is discernible but riddled with holes. Pronoun reference is ambiguous and unstable. Like John Ashbery, Hejinian often imitates the form of a thought but twists its content, as in the seeming aphorism "Pretty is as pretty does." Like other Language poets, Hejinian was influenced by the Russian Formalist Victor Shklovsky's theory that art involves a "making strange" or "defamiliarization." With her slightly skewed generalizations, mixed genres, shifting leitmotifs, discontinuous narratives, paratactic sentences, and decentered "I," Hejinian both stimulates and frustrates our desire to construct coherence. She defamiliarizes the meaning-making process of language itself.

"Language is nothing but meanings," writes Hejinian, "and meanings are nothing but a flow of contexts. Such contexts rarely coalesce into images, rarely come to terms. They are transitions, transmutations, the endless radiating of denotation into relation" (*The Language of Inquiry*). Playing on "orb" and "orbit" in *Oxota,* "eye" and "I" in *The Cell,* "hap" and "happy" in *Happily,* and many other such homonyms and verbal cousins, Hejinian emphasizes how words generate related yet distinct words, as do sounds, phrases, and grammars. Indebted to Gertrude Stein's view that, as Hejinian puts it, "language is an order of reality itself and not a mere mediating medium," Hejinian discerns in her precursor many of the devices she also uses to accentuate language, "such as rhyming, punning, pairing, parallelisms, and running strings of changes within either vowel or consonant frames. It is the difference between rod and red and rid that makes them mean. Wordplay, in this sense, foregrounds the relationships between words."

Hejinian was born on May 17, 1941, in Alameda, California, into an academic family. In 1968, she graduated from Harvard University. After she returned to California, she eventually settled in the San Francisco Bay area. She founded Tuumba Press in 1976, was its editor until 1984, and has been coeditor, with Barrett Watten, of *Poetics Journal.* With her second husband, Larry Ochs, avant-garde jazz saxophonist and composer in the Rova Saxophone Quartet, Hejinian traveled to Russia, forming long-term intellectual friendships that have influenced her work. She has taught at several universities and colleges, including the New College of California, the University of California, Berkeley, and Iowa University.

From My Life[1]

A pause, a rose, something on paper

A moment yellow, just as four years later, when my father returned home from the war, the moment of greeting him, as he stood at the bottom of the stairs, younger, thinner than when he had left, was purple—though moments are no longer so colored. Somewhere, in the background, rooms share a pattern of small roses. Pretty is as pretty does. In certain families, the meaning of necessity is at one with the sentiment of

1. This semiautobiographical work was originally published in 1980 in thirty-seven sections, each containing thirty-seven sentences (Hejinian was thirty-seven at the time of writing). In 1987, at forty-five, Hejinian expanded the work to forty-five sections of forty-five sentences each. This excerpt is from the beginning of the 1987 version.

prenecessity. The better things were gathered in a pen. The windows were narrowed by white gauze curtains which were never loosened. Here I refer to irrelevance, that rigidity which never intrudes. Hence, repetitions, free from all ambition. The shadow of the redwood trees, she said, was oppressive. The plush must be worn away. On her walks she stepped into people's gardens to pinch off cuttings from their geraniums and succulents. An occasional sunset is reflected on the windows. A little puddle is overcast. If only you could touch, or, even, catch those gray great creatures. I was afraid of my uncle with the wart on his nose, or of his jokes at our expense which were beyond me, and I was shy of my aunt's deafness who was his sister-in-law and who had years earlier fallen into the habit of nodding, agreeably. Wool station. See lightning, wait for thunder. Quite mistakenly, as it happened. Long time lines trail behind every idea, object, person, pet, vehicle, and event. The afternoon happens, crowded and therefore endless. Thicker, she agreed. It was a tic, she had the habit, and now she bobbed like my toy plastic bird on the edge of its glass, dipping into and recoiling from the water. But a word is a bottomless pit. It became magically pregnant and one day split open, giving birth to a stone egg, about as big as a football. In May when the lizards emerge from the stones, the stones turn gray, from green. When daylight moves, we delight in distance. The waves rolled over our stomachs, like spring rain over an orchard slope. Rubber bumpers on rubber cars. The resistance on sleeping to being asleep. In every country is a word which attempts the sound of cats, to match an insolable[2] portrait in the clouds to a din in the air. But the constant noise is not an omen of music to come. "Everything is a question of sleep," says Cocteau,[3] but he forgets the shark, which does not. Anxiety is vigilant. Perhaps initially, even before one can talk, restlessness is already conventional, establishing the incoherent border which will later separate events from experience. Find a drawer that's not filled up. That we sleep plunges our work into the dark. The ball was lost in a bank of myrtle. I was in a room with the particulars of which a later nostalgia might be formed, an indulged childhood. They are sitting in wicker chairs, the legs of which have sunk unevenly into the ground, so that each is sitting slightly tilted and their postures make adjustment for that. The cows warm their own barn. I look at them fast and it gives the illusion that they're moving. An "oral history" on paper. *That* morning this morning. I say it about the psyche because it is not optional. The overtones are a denser shadow in the room characterized by its habitual readiness, a form of charged waiting, a perpetual attendance, of which I was thinking when I began the paragraph, "So much of childhood is spent in a manner of waiting."

As for we who "love to be astonished"

You spill the sugar when you lift the spoon. My father had filled an old apothecary jar with what he called "sea glass," bits of old bottles rounded and textured by the sea, so abundant on beaches. There is no solitude. It buries itself in veracity. It is as if one splashed in the water lost by one's tears. My mother had climbed into the garbage can in order to stamp down the accumulated trash, but the can was knocked off balance, and when she fell she broke her arm. She could only give a little shrug. The

2. Incapable of being isolated.
3. Jean Cocteau (1889–1963), French avant-garde writer, artist, and filmmaker.

family had little money but plenty of food. At the circus only the elephants were greater than anything I could have imagined. The egg of Columbus,[4] landscape and grammar. She wanted one where the playground was dirt, with grass, shaded by a tree, from which would hang a rubber tire as a swing, and when she found it she sent me. These creatures are compound and nothing they do should surprise us. I don't mind, or I won't mind, where the verb "to care" might multiply. The pilot of the little airplane had forgotten to notify the airport of his approach, so that when the lights of the plane in the night were first spotted, the air raid sirens went off, and the entire city on that coast went dark. He was taking a drink of water and the light was growing dim. My mother stood at the window watching the only lights that were visible, circling over the darkened city in search of the hidden airport. Unhappily, time seems more normative than place. Whether breathing or holding the breath, it was the same thing, driving through the tunnel from one sun to the next under a hot brown hill. She sunned the baby for sixty seconds, leaving him naked except for a blue cotton sunbonnet. At night, to close off the windows from view of the street, my grandmother pulled down the window shades, never loosening the curtains, a gauze starched too stiff to hang properly down. I sat on the windowsill singing sunny lunny teena, ding-dang-dong. Out there is an aging magician who needs a tray of ice in order to turn his bristling breath into steam. He broke the radio silence. Why would anyone find astrology interesting when it is possible to learn about astronomy. What one passes in the Plymouth.[5] It is the wind slamming the doors. All that is nearly incommunicable to my friends. Velocity and throat verisimilitude. Were we seeing a pattern or merely an appearance of small white sailboats on the bay, floating at such a distance from the hill that they appeared to be making no progress. And for once to a country that did not speak another language. To follow the progress of ideas, or that particular line of reasoning, so full of surprises and unexpected correlations, was somehow to take a vacation. Still, you had to wonder where they had gone, since you could speak of reappearance. A blue room is always dark. Everything on the boardwalk was shooting toward the sky. It was not specific to any year, but very early. A German goldsmith covered a bit of metal with cloth in the 14th century and gave mankind its first button. It was hard to know this as politics, because it plays like the work of one person, but nothing is isolated in history—certain humans are situations. Are your fingers in the margin. Their random procedures make monuments to fate. There is something still surprising when the green emerges. The blue fox has ducked its head. The front rhyme of harmless with harmony. Where is my honey running. You cannot linger "on the lamb." You cannot determine the nature of progress until you assemble all of the relatives.

It seemed that we had hardly begun and we were already there

We see only the leaves and branches of the trees close in around the house. Those submissive games were sensual. I was no more than three or four years old, but when crossed I would hold my breath, not from rage but from stubbornness, until I lost consciousness. The shadows one day deeper. Every family has its own collection of stories, but not every

4. Puzzle in which the pieces initially form the shape of an egg and can be rearranged into other forms.

5. American brand of automobile.

family has someone to tell them. In a small studio in an old farmhouse, it is the musical expression of a glowing optimism. A bird would reach but be secret. Absence of allusion: once, and ring alone. The downstairs telephone was in a little room as dark as a closet. It made a difference between the immediate and the sudden in a theater filled with transitions. Without what can a person function as the sea functions without me. A typical set of errands. My mother stood between us and held our hands as we waded into the gray-blue water, lecturing us on the undertow, more to add to the thrill of the approaching water than to warn us of any real danger, since she would continue to grip us by the hand when the wave came in and we tried to jump over it. The curve of the rain, more, comes over more often. Four seasons circle a square year. A mirror set in the crotch of the tree was like a hole in the out-of-doors. I could have ridden in the car forever, or so it seemed, watching the scenery go by, alert as to the circumstances of a dream, and that peaceful. Roller coast. The fog lifts a late sunrise. There are floral twigs in position on it. The roots of the locust tree were lifting the corner of the little cabin. Our unease grows before the newly restless. There you are, and you know it's good, and all you have to do is make it better. He sailed to the war. A life no more free than the life of a lost puppy. It became popular and then we were inundated with imitations. My old aunt entertained us with her lie, a story about an event in her girlhood, a catastrophe in a sailboat that never occurred, but she was blameless, unaccountable, since, in the course of the telling, she had come to believe the lie herself. A kind of burbling in the waters of inspiration. Because of their recurrence, what had originally seemed merely details of atmosphere became, in time, thematic. As if sky plus sun *must* make leaves. A snapdragon volunteering in the garden among the cineraria gapes its maw between the fingers, and we pinched the buds of the fuchsia[6] to make them pop. Is that willful. Inclines. They have big calves because of those hills. Flip over small stones, dried mud. We thought that the mica might be gold. A pause, a rose, something on paper, in a nature scrapbook. What follows a strict chronology has no memory. For me, they must exist, the contents of that absent reality, the objects and occasions which now I reconsidered. The smells of the house were thus a peculiar mix of heavy interior air and the air from outdoors lingering over the rose bushes, the camellias, the hydrangeas, the rhododendron and azalea bushes. Hard to distinguish hunger from wanting to eat. My grandmother was in the kitchen, her hands on her hips, wearing what she called a "wash-dress," watching a line of ants cross behind the faucets of the sink, and she said to us, "Now *I* am waging war." There are strings in the terrible distance. They are against the blue. The trees are continually receiving their own shadows.

1980, 1987

6. Flowering shrub. *Cineraria:* garden plants with heart-shaped flowers.

FROM OXOTA: A SHORT RUSSIAN NOVEL[7]

Chapter Seven

One person believes in nothing and another dislikes poetry
They don't present equal dangers to society
The lowness of the light stole the field from its shadows
An old babushka[8] on the ice atop the ridge of snow packed beside the street
In deed and word
She was hissing
And a pedestrian screaming, what are you doing up there, you stupid old woman.
The shouting samaritan[9] jerked the granny to safety
She was hissing like a street cat, not snakily
An engine, an omen of weddings
An habitual association with daily aesthetic impressions
An omen of the love of art and its social functioning
An orb standing for an orbit
The old woman still standing in the street

Chapter 203

A chipped flange on the dangling pipe bringing in our cooking gas
It's in a prepositional state—for, not for, off, on
What can we say of individualism? of cells?
That is just my way
A woman had been struck in a zebra[1] and killed
The driver clung
She was nowhere—how could I stop
Traffic lights broken, ice on the street
He's technically guilty unless she was drunk
It's five, seven years, after such an event
And events happen, but this doesn't have to mean that another event has happened before
Habits before—the favorite cup
Horses that have freed themselves
I think I should get up and chase them

1991

7. The fourteen-line stanza Hejinian uses for each chapter of *Oxota: A Short Russian Novel* is an adaptation of the form used by the Russian writer Aleksandr Pushkin (1799–1837) in his verse novel, *Eugene Onegin* (1823–31).

8. Russian slang for old woman.

9. In Luke 10.30–37, Jesus tells the parable of the Samaritan who demonstrates his generosity by stopping to help a man attacked by thieves.

1. Crosswalk.

From The Cell

[It Is the Writer's Object]

It is the writer's object
        to supply the hollow green
        and yellow life of the
        human I
It rains with rains supplied
        before I learned to type
        along the sides who when
        asked what we have in
        common with nature replied opportunity
        and size
Readers of the practical help
They then reside
And resistance is accurate—it
        rocks and rides the momentum
Words are emitted by the
        rocks to the eye
Motes, parts, genders, sights collide
There are concavities
It is not imperfect to
        have died

October 6, 1986 — 1992

[Yesterday I Saw the Sun]

Yesterday I saw the sun
        sagging with assent—fat, yellow-green
        and pink
The live body in its
        spectrum
The guts to be sufficiently
        mental
We gawk at a brutality
And self-consciousness is the situation
        (stasis) of objection
She assigned herself 20 pages
        a day
Throbbing sticks, the installments stuck
        on them, the sunlight swelling
Any person who agrees will
        increase

So I am going, like
        a proper editor, to introduce
        the reader

Because culture does not fall
    into the arms of the
    first comer
The reader, with its eyes
    glued to the slits and
    its heart going out to
    me, surveys my efforts
The question is framed in
    something like words: "What is
    that on your mouth?"

She lowered her head and
    saw the grass, which had
    been almost under her feet,
    growing far below her—clearly
    reflected in it
I.e., introspected on subjective grounds,
    not just by being near
Subjectivity is not a misuse
    of substitution
Objectivity is not a misunderstanding
    of sex

May 5, 1988

1992

FROM HAPPILY[2]

Constantly I write this happily
Hazards that hope may break open my lips
What I feel is taking place, a large context, long yielding, and to doubt it
    would be a crime against it
I sense that in stating "this is happening"
Waiting for us?
It has existence in fact without that
We came when it arrived
Here I write with inexact straightness but into a place in place immediately
    passing between phrases of the imagination
Flowers optimistically going to seed, fluttering candles lapping the air,
    persevering saws swimming into boards, buckets taking dents, and the
    hands on the clock turning—*they* aren't melancholy
Whether or not the future looks back to trigger a longing for conso-
    nance grieving over brevity living is "unfinished work" to remember to
    locate something in times to come
Sure a terrible thing whistling at the end of the rope is a poor way of
    laughing
And okay in the dim natural daylight producing it in fragments to the
    skeptic to take it is recognizable
Only the dull make no response

2. This excerpt is from the beginning of the poem.

Each reality needs to be affirmed
Several reasons can be linked to all that we ascribe to that
And whether or not a dog sees a rainbow as mere scratches suspending judgment, all gesture invisibly as we all think what we think to form a promising mode of communication bobbing something

The day is promising
Along comes something—launched in context
In context to pass it the flow of humanity divides and on the other side unites
All gazing at the stars bound in a black bow
I am among them thinking thought through the thinking thought to no conclusion
Context is the chance that time takes
Our names tossed into the air scraped in the grass before having formed any opinion leaving people to say only that there was a man who happened on a cart and crossed a gnarled field and there was a woman who happened on a cart and crossed a gnarled field too
Is happiness the name for our (involuntary) complicity with chance?
Anything could happen
A boy in the sun drives nails into a fruit a sign (cloud) in the wind swings
A woman descends a ladder into mud it gives way
But today's thought is different
Better to presuppose late
We eat with relief from our formlessness
Each day is drawn to its scene or scene to its day the image already under way and formed to proceed
Perhaps happiness is what we volunteer
A cormorant appears in the sun flashing exact notes, a phenomenon of a foggy day stretching its wings
Madame Cézanne[3] offers herself in homage with its various uses with its curve and blank stare
It resembles an apple
And the most unexpected aspect of this activity dependent on nothing personal is that it consists of praise coming by chance, viz., happiness, into the frame of the world

It is midday a sentence its context—history with a future
The blue is sky at all high points and the shadow underfoot moves at zero point
Someone speaks it within reason
The one occupied by something launched without endpoint
Flaubert[4] said he wanted his sentences *erect while running—almost an impossibility*
Nonetheless, though its punctuation is half hoping for failure, the sentence makes an irrevocable address to life
And though the parrot speaks but says nothing this has the impact of an aphorism

3. Wife of French Postimpressionist painter Paul Cézanne (1839–1906). Madame Cézanne was the subject of the painter's famous *La Femme à l'éventail,* a portrait that became an important influence on the method of composition developed by the American writer Gertrude Stein (1874–1946) and adapted by Hejinian in *Happily.*

4. Gustave Flaubert (1821–1880), French novelist.

Are you there?
I'm here
Is that a *yes* or a *no?*

The writer over the page is driven down but like a robin by a worm
The visible world is drawn
Sentence meaning reason
Without that nothing recurs
Joy—a remnant of an original craziness we can hardly remember—it exists, everything does, without us
There is music recognizing recognition we know about boundaries and boundaries wound up
No straight line the riddle set I am tempted to say rough circles hazards lips that only things can differ
It's not not me I'm afraid saying *this* is *thus*
A name by chance for anything on which we have no claim
Everything for the magician is accidental
All that could possibly happen to the magical prop becomes intrinsic to it and knowing "all that" (could possibly happen) is what constitutes a magician's knowledge which is changed by the stopping of the thought just as such an aphorism is formed as the one that observes an event emerging just where time is becoming attracted to a particular thing (say, a branch hanging over a river) in a particular situation (say, mirrored in hilarity)
The event is the adventure of that moment
Then seven more days of heavy rain, one drop after another a relay that is all in the passing by that is inside it (the bypassing, all washed away)
If I were a fictional character thinking back she might be weeping in a hundred bedrooms tonight wanting to be good long after this depiction of wanting to have been good
But what is it that Plotinus[5] says—the "good" will not be something brought in from the outside?
Is it then a pleasure covered in all seasons out of bounds beyond the interior chain around the vernacular meant to bring us in, you know what I mean, I see what you're saying, and so on
The good is the chance with things that happen that inside and out time takes

It's midday a sentence, then night another
The sentence arachnid, a so-called "riddle figure"
Sense for its own sake saying at the same time something and its meaning "only the gust outside crossed the slate," "only the shale span caught at the consciousness that makes even sleep delicious"
Susceptible to happiness I was thinking of nothing
Thinking thing linking that to which thought goes back, the thing arrives
Tightly the hands of the clock turn but other elements also must conduct logic
The good of it be it love or touchiness in idleness sunk in proximity

* * *

2000

5. Neoplatonic philosopher (c. 205–270 C.E.).

Derek Mahon
b. 1941

Derek Mahon is, like Seamus Heaney, one of the gifted poets from Northern Ireland to become prominent in the late 1960s and early 1970s. Not that the Ulster poets are a homogeneous group. Born in Belfast a couple of years after Heaney, on November 23, 1941, Mahon studied French at a traditionally Protestant institution, Trinity College, Dublin, and belonged ambivalently to the Protestant community. By contrast, Heaney's early affiliations with the Northern Irish Catholic community, though equivocal, were strong. Heaney scrabbled in the farms and bogs of County Derry; Mahon was raised in the urban roar of Belfast. Heaney's earthy language is often tinged with the sonorities of Irish Gaelic; Mahon's writing evokes a cross-national metropolitanism—from Belfast to London, New York, even Paris. Irishness is central to Heaney's poetry; Mahon, whose relation to Irish national identity and native cultural traditions is greatly complicated by his Protestant background and who worked for many years as a reviewer, editor, and translator in London and New York, represents himself as a displaced cosmopolitan, unsure "what is meant by home" ("Afterlives").

Even so, many commonalities exist between the two poets. The tension between civilization and violence, between beauty and suffering, recurs in their work. Avoiding journalistic patter, both poets take an oblique approach to the Troubles in Northern Ireland. Like a French Impressionist painter, Mahon is drawn to beautiful atmospheric effects—falling snow, moonlit waves, sunlit puddles, an urban dawn after rainfall. But tucked into his poems are jarring references to war, genocide, torture, guns, bombs, and executions. The undercurrent of brutality is all the more affecting, because of its implicit contrast with the poetry's literary learning, its gauzy, delicate, languid patterns. Mahon allegorizes the suffering of the Irish, as of other suppressed and even forgotten peoples, in his most famous poem, "A Disused Shed in Co. Wexford." Here, as in poems such as "The Snow Party," "Afterlives," and "The Last of the Fire Kings," history is a nightmare, civilization an ineffective tonic. The suffering and brutality exist in ironic counterpoint to the quiet beauty of Mahon's rhymes and half-rhymes ("forms" / "worms"), consonances ("barrels" / "burials"), stately stanzas, elegant syntax, and plangent meters.

A skilled craftsman, Mahon exhibits a literary sensibility that is rich, restrained, and humanistic. In tonally complex verse, he layers irony and self-irony on melancholy, humor on pathos, hope on skepticism. Always the outsider among the living, he finds genial company among dead poetic forebears, among them Charles Baudelaire, Louis MacNeice, and W. H. Auden. Solitary figures, such as the speaker in "The Last of the Fire Kings" and the bittern in "An Bonnán Buí," evoke his estrangement. "An Bonnán Buí" instances the loosening in Mahon's style during the 1990s, when he adopted a more conversational voice and relinquished honed stanzas for a single, expansive verse paragraph. But even here, Mahon is no less allusive, literary, or elegiac than he was at the beginning of his career. In our age of psychiatric therapy and group-think, when "the odd learn to renounce / their singularity for a more communal faith" (as he wrote in an early version of the poem), he continues to defend poetry as a space for human idiosyncrasy, irresolvable ambivalence, and difficult introspection.

Afterlives

for James Simmons[1]

1

I wake in a dark flat
To the soft roar of the world.
Pigeons neck on the white
Roofs as I draw the curtains
And look out over London
Rain-fresh in the morning light.

This is our element, the bright
Reason on which we rely
For the long-term solutions.
The orators yap, and guns
Go off in a back street;
But the faith does not die

That in our time these things
Will amaze the literate children
In their non-sectarian schools
And the dark places be
Ablaze with love and poetry
When the power of good prevails.

What middle-class twits we are
To imagine for one second
That our privileged ideals
Are divine wisdom, and the dim
Forms that kneel at noon
In the city not ourselves.

2

I am going home by sea
For the first time in years.
Somebody thumbs a guitar
On the dark deck, while a gull
Dreams at the mast-head,
The moon-splashed waves exult.

At dawn the ship trembles, turns
In a wide arc to back
Shuddering up the grey lough[2]
Past lightship and buoy,
Slipway and dry dock
Where a naked bulb burns;

1. Poet and songwriter (b. 1933) from Northern Ireland.
2. Lake or sea.

And I step ashore in a fine rain
To a city so changed
By five years of war
I scarcely recognize
The places I grew up in,
The faces that try to explain.

But the hills are still the same
Grey-blue above Belfast.
Perhaps if I'd stayed behind
And lived it bomb by bomb
I might have grown up at last
And learnt what is meant by home.

1975, 1991

The Snow Party

(for Louis Asekoff)[3]

Bashō, coming
To the city of Nagoya,
Is asked to a snow party.

There is a tinkling of china
And tea into china;
There are introductions.

Then everyone
Crowds to the window
To watch the falling snow.

Snow is falling on Nagoya
And farther south
On the tiles of Kyōto.

Eastward, beyond Irago,
It is falling
Like leaves on the cold sea.

Elsewhere they are burning
Witches and heretics
In the boiling squares,

Thousands have died since dawn
In the service
Of barbarous kings;

3. American poet (b. 1939). The Japanese poet Bashō (1644–1694) mentions the snow-watching party, a traditional social gathering, in *The Records of a Weather-Exposed Skeleton.*

But there is silence
In the houses of Nagoya
And the hills of Ise.

1975, 1979

The Last of the Fire Kings[4]

I want to be
Like the man who descends
At two milk churns

With a bulging
String bag and vanishes
Where the lane turns,

Or the man
Who drops at night
From a moving train

And strikes out over the fields
Where fireflies glow;
Not knowing a word of the language.

Either way, I am
Through with history—
Who lives by the sword

Dies by the sword.[5]
Last of the fire kings, I shall
Break with tradition and

Die by my own hand
Rather than perpetuate
The barbarous cycle.

Five years I have reigned
During which time
I have lain awake each night

And prowled by day
In the sacred grove
For fear of the usurper,

4. In *The Golden Bough,* the Cambridge anthropologist James Frazer (1854–1941) describes the Fire King as living in isolation in parts of Cambodia. Supposed to have supernatural powers, he must not die a natural death; when he becomes seriously ill, he is stabbed to death by local elders.

5. A seventeenth-century proverb. Cf. Matthew 26.52: "All they that take the sword shall perish with the sword."

Perfecting my cold dream
Of a place out of time,
A palace of porcelain

Where the frugivorous[6]
Inheritors recline
In their rich fabrics
Far from the sea.

But the fire-loving
People, rightly perhaps,
Will not countenance this,

Demanding that I inhabit,
Like them, a world of
Sirens, bin-lids
And bricked-up windows—

Not to release them
From the ancient curse
But to die their creature and be thankful.

1975

A Disused Shed in Co. Wexford[7]

Let them not forget us, the weak souls among the asphodels.
—Seferis, *Mythistorema,* tr. Keeley and Sherrard

(for J. G. Farrell)[8]

Even now there are places where a thought might grow—
Peruvian mines, worked out and abandoned
To a slow clock of condensation,
An echo trapped for ever, and a flutter
Of wild-flowers in the lift-shaft,
Indian compounds where the wind dances
And a door bangs with diminished confidence,
Lime crevices behind rippling rain-barrels,
Dog corners for bone burials;
And in a disused shed in Co. Wexford,

Deep in the grounds of a burnt-out hotel,
Among the bathtubs and the washbasins
A thousand mushrooms crowd to a keyhole.
This is the one star in their firmament
Or frames a star within a star.
What should they do there but desire?

6. Fruit-eating.
7. County in southeast Ireland.
8. Historical novelist (1935–1979) and friend of Mahon's.

So many days beyond the rhododendrons
With the world waltzing in its bowl of cloud,
They have learnt patience and silence
Listening to the rooks querulous in the high wood.

They have been waiting for us in a foetor[9]
Of vegetable sweat since civil war days,
Since the gravel-crunching, interminable departure
Of the expropriated mycologist.[1]
He never came back, and light since then
Is a keyhole rusting gently after rain.
Spiders have spun, flies dusted to mildew
And once a day, perhaps, they have heard something—
A trickle of masonry, a shout from the blue
Or a lorry changing gear at the end of the lane.

There have been deaths, the pale flesh flaking
Into the earth that nourished it;
And nightmares, born of these and the grim
Dominion of stale air and rank moisture.
Those nearest the door grow strong—
'Elbow room! Elbow room!'
The rest, dim in a twilight of crumbling
Utensils and broken pitchers, groaning
For their deliverance, have been so long
Expectant that there is left only the posture.

A half century, without visitors, in the dark—
Poor preparation for the cracking lock
And creak of hinges. Magi, moonmen,
Powdery prisoners of the old regime,
Web-throated, stalked like triffids,[2] racked by drought
And insomnia, only the ghost of a scream
At the flash-bulb firing-squad we wake them with
Shows there is life yet in their feverish forms.
Grown beyond nature now, soft food for worms,
They lift frail heads in gravity and good faith.

They are begging us, you see, in their wordless way,
To do something, to speak on their behalf
Or at least not to close the door again.
Lost people of Treblinka and Pompeii![3]
'Save us, save us,' they seem to say,
'Let the god not abandon us
Who have come so far in darkness and in pain.
We too had our lives to live.

9. Offensive smell.
1. One who studies mushrooms and other fungi.
2. Fictional plants with poisonous stingers that attack humanity in John Wyndham's science fiction novel *The Day of the Triffids* (1951) and the 1962 movie based on it.
3. Ancient Italian city destroyed by the eruption of Mt. Vesuvius in 79 C.E. *Treblinka:* site of a Nazi extermination camp.

You with your light meter and relaxed itinerary,
Let not our naive labours have been in vain!'

1975, 1991

An Bonnán Buí[4]

A heron-like species, rare visitors, most recent records referring to winter months . . . very active at dusk.
—Guide to Irish Birds

A sobering thought, the idea of you stretched there,
bittern, under a dark sky, your exposed bones
yellow too in a ditch among cold stones,
ice glittering everywhere on bog and river,
the whole unfortunate country frozen over
and your voice stilled by enforced sobriety—
a thought more wrenching than the fall of Troy
because more intimate; for we'd hear your shout
of delight from a pale patch of watery sunlight
out on the mud there as you took your first
drink of the day and now, destroyed by thirst,
you lie in brambles while the rats rotate.
I'd've broken the ice for you, given an inkling;
now, had I known it, we might both be drinking
and singing too; for ours is the same story.
Others have perished—heron, blackbird, thrushes—
and lie shivering like you under whin-bushes;[5]
but I mourn only the bittern, withdrawn and solitary,
who used to carouse alone among the rushes
and sleep rough in the star-glimmering bog-drain.
It used to be, with characters like us,
they'd let us wander the roads in wind and rain
or lock us up and throw away the key—
but now they have a cure for these psychoses
as indeed they do for most social diseases
and, rich at last, we can forget our pain.
She says I'm done for if I drink again;
so now, relieved of dangerous stimuli,
at peace with my plastic bottle of H_2O
and the slack strings of insouciance, I sit
with bronze Kavanagh on his canal-bank seat,
not in 'the tremendous silence of mid-July'[6]
but the fast bright zing of a winter afternoon

4. Irish name for the yellow bittern, a bird popularly believed to die from thirst and elegized in an eighteenth-century Irish drinking song by Cathal Buí Mac Giolla Ghunna (c. 1680–1756).
5. *Whin:* swampy meadow.
6. A bronze statue of the Irish poet Patrick Kavanagh (1904–1967) sits on a bench on the banks of the Grand Canal in Dublin. The quotation is from Kavanagh's sonnet "Lines Written on a Seat on the Grand Canal, Dublin," which begins, "O commemorate me where there is water." Cf. also his "Canal Bank Walk," which records his passive surrender to flux.

dizzy with head-set, flash-bulb and digifone,
to learn the *tao*[7] he once claimed as his own
and share with him the moor-hen and the swan,
the thoughtless lyric of a cloud in the sky
and the play of light and shadow on the slow
commemorative waters; relax, go with the flow.

1997, 1999

A Swim in Co. Wicklow

The only reality is the perpetual flow of vital energy.
—Montale[8]

Spindrift,[9] crustacean patience
and a gust of ozone,
you come back once more
to this dazzling shore,
its warm uterine rinse,
heart-racing heave and groan.

A quick gasp as you slip
into the hissing wash,
star cluster, dulse[1] and kelp,
slick algae, spittle, froth,
the intimate slash and dash,
hard-packed in the seething broth.

Soft water-lip, soft hand,
close tug of origin,
the sensual writhe and snore
of maidenhair and frond,
you swim here once more
smart as a rogue gene.

Spirits of lake, river
and woodland pond preside
mildly in water never
troubled by wind or tide;
and the quiet suburban pool
is only for the fearful—

no wind-wave energies
where no sea briar grips
and no freak breaker with
the violence of the ages

7. Belief that the process of change in nature is to be followed for a life of harmony. *Digifone:* Irish mobile phone.
8. Eugenio Montale (1896–1981), Italian poet, critic, and translator.
9. Sea spray.
1. Coarse red seaweed.

comes foaming at the mouth
to drown you in its depths.

Among pebbles a white conch
worn by the suck and crunch,
a sandy chamber old
as the centuries, in cold
and solitude reclines
where the moon-magnet shines;

but today you swirl and spin
in sea water as if,
creatures of salt and slime
and naked under the sun,
life were a waking dream
and this the only life.

1999

Sharon Olds
b. 1942

Sharon Olds is perhaps the most prominent beneficiary of the confessional poets' "breakthrough back into life," in Robert Lowell's phrase. But if personal experience remains highly mediated in the poetry of such first-generation confessionals as Lowell and Sylvia Plath, Olds unveils her emotional and sensual life with arresting candor. Her poems are grounded in human drives, longings, and traumas. Their eroticism is unrestrained, their immediacy almost glaring. In a number of her poems, Olds penetrates all outward show to reveal what is for her the ultimate truth within the body. Looking at a 1921 photograph of a starving Russian girl, Olds surmises: "Deep in her body / the ovaries let out her first eggs, / golden as drops of grain" ("Photograph of the Girl"). Similarly, in Olds's most notoriously provocative poem, the Pope is imagined in terms of the irrepressible reproductive drive hidden within his robes ("The Pope's Penis"). In lyrics that frequently return to sex, birth, and family relationships, Olds embraces without shame or prurience the propulsive force of desire. Like Walt Whitman, she celebrates the human body with an almost religious zeal. Even when she meditates on the dead, it is their physical reality that she most memorably describes. Devoting an entire volume of poems, *The Father* (1992), to an account of her father's death, Olds conveys excruciating pain, ambivalence, and tenderness in her unsparing chronicle of his physical deterioration.

For all their intimacy, Olds's poems are far from artless. Heavily enjambed, they convey the rush of sensation and emotion in their sinuous movement from one line to the next. Meaning spills forward, carried along the arteries of a fluent syntax. Clauses are spun tightly or loosely to modulate pacing. Bold bodily images are at the center of Olds's art, often graphic, occasionally lurid. Sometimes her language, though accessible and direct, becomes richly metaphorical. Whether describing the moment of giving birth or her daughter's peeling of an orange, Olds layers her poetry with evocative sensual images. Each poem focuses on a single event, sight, or feeling, which exfoliates in an unbroken verse paragraph. Although her speakers are usually recognizable as Olds, not all of her poems are written in *propria persona.* In one poem, for example, she assumes the voice of her cremated father, who "Speaks to Me from the Dead."

Olds was born on November 19, 1942, in San Francisco, and was raised, in her words, as a "hellfire Calvinist." She completed her undergraduate education at Stanford University in 1964 and her Ph.D. at Columbia University in 1972. Since the publication of her first volume of poetry, *Satan Says* (1980), Olds has won the Lamont Poetry Selection and the National Book Critics Circle Award. She teaches poetry workshops at New York University's Graduate Creative Writing Program, while also helping run the New York University workshop program at Goldwater Hospital, on New York's Roosevelt Island. She was the New York State poet laureate for 1998–2000.

Photograph of the Girl

The girl sits on the hard ground,
the dry pan of Russia, in the drought
of 1921,[1] stunned,
eyes closed, mouth open,
raw hot wind blowing
sand in her face. Hunger and puberty are
taking her together. She leans on a sack,
layers of clothes fluttering in the heat,
the new radius of her arm curved.
She cannot be not beautiful, but she is
starving. Each day she grows thinner, and her bones
grow longer, porous. The caption says
she is going to starve to death that winter
with millions of others. Deep in her body
the ovaries let out her first eggs,
golden as drops of grain.

1984

The Pope's Penis

It hangs deep in his robes, a delicate
clapper at the center of a bell.
It moves when he moves, a ghostly fish in a
halo of silver seaweed, the hair
swaying in the dark and the heat—and at night,
while his eyes sleep, it stands up
in praise of God.

1987

1. An estimated five million people died in the Russian drought and famine of 1921.

The Moment the Two Worlds Meet

That's the moment I always think of—when the
slick, whole body comes out of me,
when they pull it out, not pull it but steady it
as it pushes forth, not catch it but keep their
hands under it as it pulses out,
they are the first to touch it,
and it shines, it glistens with the thick liquid on it.
That's the moment, while it's sliding, the limbs
compressed close to the body, the arms
bent like a crab's rosy legs, the
thighs closely packed plums in heavy syrup, the
legs folded like the white wings of a chicken—
that is the center of life, that moment when the
juiced bluish sphere of the baby is
sliding between the two worlds,
wet, like sex, it *is* sex,
it is my life opening back and back
as you'd strip the reed from the bud, not strip it but
watch it thrust so it peels itself and the
flower is there, severely folded, and
then it begins to open and dry
but by then the moment is over,
they wipe off the grease and wrap the child in a blanket and
hand it to you entirely in this world.

1987

The Exact Moment of His Death

When he breathed his last breath, it was he,
my father, although he was so transformed
no one who had not been with him
for the last hour would know him—the skin
now physical as animal fat,
the eyes cast halfway back into his head,
the nose thinned, the mouth racked open,
with that tongue in it like the fact of the mortal,
a tongue so dried, scalloped, darkened
and material. We could see the fluid
risen into the back of his mouth
but it was he, the huge, slack arms,
the spots of blood under the skin
black and precise, we had come this far with him
step by step, it was he, his last
breath was his, not taken with desire
but his, light as a milkweed seed,
coming out of his mouth and floating across the room.

And when the nurse listened for his heart,
and his stomach was silvery, it was his stomach,
when she did not shake her head but stood and
nodded at me, for a moment it was fully
he, my father, dead but completely
himself, a man with an open mouth and
black spots on his arms. He looked like
someone killed in a bloodless struggle—
the strain in his neck and the base of his head,
as if he were violently pulling back.
He seemed to be holding still, then the skin
tightened slightly around his whole body
as if the purely physical were claiming him,
and then it was not my father,
it was not a man, it was not an animal,
I ran my hand slowly through the hair,
lifted my fingers up through the grey
waves of it, the unliving glistening
matter of this world.

1992

My Father Speaks to Me from the Dead

I seem to have woken up in a pot-shed,
on clay, on shards, the bright paths
of slugs kiss-crossing my body. I don't know
where to start, with this grime on me.
I take the spider glue-net, plug
of the dead, out of my mouth, let's see
if where I have been I can do this.
I love your feet. I love your knees,
I love your our my legs, they are so
long because they are yours and mine
both. I love your—what can I call it,
between your legs, we never named it, the
glint and purity of its curls. I love
your rear end, I changed you once,
washed the detritus off your tiny
bottom, with my finger rubbed
the oil on you; when I touched your little
anus I crossed wires with God for a moment.
I never hated your shit—that was
your mother. I love your navel, thistle
seed fossil, even though
it's her print on you. Of course I love
your breasts—did you see me looking up
from within your daughter's face, as she nursed?
I love your bony shoulders and you know I
love your hair, thick and live

as earth. And I never hated your face,
I hated its eruptions. You know what I love?
I love your brain, its halves and silvery
folds, like a woman's labia.
I love in you
even what comes
from deep in your mother—your heart, that hard worker,
and your womb, it is a heaven to me,
I lie on its soft hills and gaze up
at its rosy vault.
I have been in a body without breath,
I have been in the morgue, in fire, in the slagged
chimney, in the air over the earth,
and buried in the earth, and pulled down
into the ocean—where I have been
I understand this life, I am matter,
your father, I made you, when I say now that I love you
I mean look down at your hand, move it,
that action is matter's love, for human
love go elsewhere.

1992

Once

I saw my father naked, once, I
opened the blue bathroom's door
which he always locked—if it opened, it was empty—
and there, surrounded by glistening turquoise
tile, sitting on the toilet, was my father,
all of him, and all of him
was skin. In an instant, my gaze ran
in a single, swerving, unimpeded
swoop, up: toe, ankle,
knee, hip, rib, nape,
shoulder, elbow, wrist, knuckle,
my father. He looked so unprotected,
so seamless, and shy, like a girl on a toilet,
and even though I knew he was sitting
to shit, there was no shame in that
but even a human peace. He looked up,
I said Sorry, backed out, shut the door
but I'd seen him, my father a shorn lamb,
my father a cloud in the blue sky
of the blue bathroom, my eye had driven
up the hairpin mountain road of the
naked male, I had turned a corner
and found his flank unguarded—gentle
bulge of the hip-joint, border of the pelvic cradle.

1999

Marilyn Hacker
b. 1942

"I do like words," Marilyn Hacker admits in the poem "Feeling and Form," and few contemporary poets are as dexterous in their use. She likes organizing words within elaborate literary grids, such as the fixed forms of the rondeau, the villanelle, the sestina, and the sonnet. She is one of the most accomplished of the New Formalists—poets committed to the revival of rhymed and metered verse—though she was belatedly included in the group and was publishing before its formation in the 1980s. Her formalism is flexible, allowing for the insertion of colloquialisms and confessional details into inherited structures, which are loosened and renewed by the liberties she takes with slant rhymes, skewed meters, coiled syntax, and wrenching enjambments. Although the New Formalism is sometimes assumed to be politically—as well as poetically—conservative, Hacker couples traditional forms with "nontraditional" content: feminist outrage, lesbian desire, and mourning across an extended family of women. "Traditional forms, or for that matter, invented forms," she said in a 1980 interview, "aren't in any way inimical to women's poetry, feminist poetry." Hacker knits together form and content to powerful effect. In the "braided" form and echoic language of "Year's End," love poetry is intertwined with elegy, erotic pleasure with grief for the bodies of lovers lost to breast cancer.

Often addressed to specific lovers, friends, and family members, Hacker's poems usually emerge from fresh joy, anger, grief, and disappointment. With her mother and her daughter, she composes a generational triad that forms, breaks apart, and reforms. She has written sonnet sequences about the end of her relationship with her daughter's father, about a love affair and its eventual unhappy conclusion, and about her struggle with breast cancer. The sonnets commemorate her grief and fear, but they also testify, with humor, to her bravery and spirit.

Hacker was born on November 27, 1942, to Jewish immigrants in New York City. She was educated at the Bronx High School of Science, New York University, and the Art Students League. She has been an antiquarian bookseller and a teacher, and she has done editorial work for books and magazines. In 1975, she won the National Book Award; in 1995, she won the Lenore Marshall Prize. She has one daughter and lives part of each year in France.

Rondeau[1] after a Transatlantic Telephone Call

Love, it was good to talk to you tonight.
You lather me like summer though. I light
up, sip smoke. Insistent through walls comes
the downstairs neighbor's double-bass. It thrums
like toothache. I will shower away the sweat,

smoke, summer, sound. Slick, soapy, dripping wet,
I scrub the sharp edge off my appetite.
I want: crisp toast, cold wine prickling my gums,
love. It was good

1. Strictly, a poem with two rhyme sounds, thirteen lines, and three stanzas, in which the refrain of the last two stanzas echoes the first line of the poem.

imagining around your voice, you, late-
awake there. (It isn't midnight yet
here.) This last glass washes down the crumbs.
I wish that I could lie down in your arms
and, turned toward sleep there (later), say, "Goodnight,
love. It was good."

1980

From Taking Notice

13

No better lost than any other woman
turned resolutely from the common pool
of our erased, emended history,
I think of water, in this book-strewn room. In
another room, my daughter, home from school,
audibly murmurs "spanking, stupid, angry
voice"—a closet drama where I am
played second-hand to unresisting doll
daughters. Mother and daughter both, I see
myself, the furious and unforgiven;
myself, the terrified and terrible;
the child punished into autonomy;
the unhealed woman hearing her own voice damn
her to the nightmares of the brooding girl.

1980

Almost Aubade[2]

The little hours: two lovers herd upstairs
two children, one of whom is one of theirs.
Past them, two of the other sex lope down,
dressed for mid-winter cruising bars in brown
bomber-jackets—their lives as uncluttered
as their pink shaven cheeks, one of us muttered,
fumbling with keys. Yes, they did look alike.
Hooking their scarves and parkas on the bike,
the seven-year-old women shuck a heap
of velvet jeans and Mary Janes.[3] They sleep
diagonal, instantly, across the top
bunk, while their exhausted elders drop,
not to the bliss breasts melt to against breasts
yet, but to kitchen chairs. One interests
herself in omelets, listening anyhow.
It's certain that fine women pick at food.

2. Morning love song.

3. Young girls' patent-leather shoes.

A loaf of bread, a jug of wine, and thou[4]
shalt piecemeal total both, gripped in that mood
whose hunger makes a contrapuntal[5] stutter
across connectives. Unwrap cheese, find butter,
dip bread crusts in a bowl of pasta sauce
saved from the children's supper. Tired because
of all we should stay up to say, we keep
awake together often as we sleep
together. I'll clear the plates. Leave your cup.
Lie in my arms until the kids get up.

1985

Year's End

for Audre Lorde and Sonny Wainwright[6]

Twice in my quickly disappearing forties
someone called while someone I loved and I were
making love to tell me another woman
had died of cancer.

Seven years apart, and two different lovers:
underneath the numbers, how lives are braided,
how those women's deaths and lives, lived and died, were
interleaved also.

Does lip touch on lip a memento mori?[7]
Does the blood-thrust nipple against its eager
mate recall, through lust, a breast's transformations
sometimes are lethal?

Now or later, what's the enormous difference?
If one day is good, is a day sufficient?
Is it fear of death with which I'm so eager
to live my life out

now and in its possible permutations
with the one I love? (Only four days later,
she was on a plane headed west across the
Atlantic, work-bound.)

Men and women, mortally wounded where we
love and nourish, dying at thirty, forty,
fifty, not on barricades, but in beds of
unfulfilled promise:

4. Slightly altered from "A Jug of Wine, a Loaf of Bread—and Thou," Edward FitzGerald's "Rubaíyát of Omar Khayyám" (1859, 1889), line 46.
5. That is, complementing and contrasting.
6. Audre Lorde (1934–1992) and Sonny Wainwright (1930–1985), American writers, also lesbian, who died of cancer.
7. Reminder of death (Latin); symbol reminding the viewer of mortality.

tell me, senators, what you call abnormal?
Each day's obits read as if there's a war on.
Fifty-eight-year-old poet dead of cancer:
warrior woman[8]

laid down with the other warrior women.
Both times when the telephone rang, I answered,
wanting not to, knowing I had to answer,
go from two bodies'

infinite approach to a crest of pleasure
through the disembodied voice from a distance
saying one loved body was clay, one wave of
mind burst and broken.

Each time we went back to each other's hands and
mouths as to a requiem where the chorus
sings death with irrelevant and amazing
bodily music.

1994

Twelfth Floor West

Brandy, who got it from a blood transfusion,
was in for MAC, with a decubitus
ulcer[9] festering. Baffled and generous,
her Baptist sisters brought each day's illusion
that she'd look back at them, that her confusion
would focus into words. They swabbed the pus,
they cleaned the shit, they wiped away the crust
of morning on her lids. The new bruise on
her thigh was baffling. They left an armchair
facing the window: an unspoken goal.
They'd come next morning, find her sitting there
with juice and coffee and a buttered roll.
The day she was released to hospice care
they came to meet her. They held her thin cold
hands on the gurney in the corridor.
The ambulance stood in the bay downstairs.

2000

8. Toward the end of her life, Lorde adopted the African name Gamba Adisa (Warrior, She Who Makes Her Meaning Known).

9. Bedsore. *MAC*: Mycobacterium Avium Complex, a disease commonly afflicting people in the later stages of AIDS.

Dave Smith
b. 1942

Dave Smith insists on his nickname, and such informality helps prepare the reader for an unusual poet. He writes powerfully, using rough words as he inexhaustibly collates jarring bits of the local scene. His mostly outdoor world is full of objects waiting for him to assemble them: blowfish, fiddler crabs, goshawks, antelopes, sharks, sawmills, boats. He occasionally provides hints of literary tradition: Gerard Manley Hopkins has obviously had some effect on him, as have Robert Penn Warren, James Dickey, and Robert Lowell. Yet Smith scorns obviously melodic cadences; his sonorities are thickly clustered. His near-sonnets are muscular and compressed, knit with tension. Other poems present unusual epithets: "the arthritic orchard" ("Winesaps"), "the shocking gray face of the sea" ("Near the Docks"), "night leaking" ("How to Get to Green Springs"), "the beautiful last erosions" ("Messenger"). Smith's poetry accumulates odd details, brought urgently together at moments of crisis. He conveys, as he says, a sense of responsibility in situations of stress: "poetry emerges from the individual spirit in crisis. Poetry is the death-wrestler" (*Contemporary Poets,* 1991).

Memory plays a large part in his consciousness. As for many southern writers, the Civil War is a haunting transgenerational memory ("Leafless Trees, Chickahominy Swamp"). An air of doomed nostalgia hangs over his poems, with hints of violence, fear, and the grotesque. Whether in poems about an encounter with a wrecked car in the woods or with fiddler crabs on the shore, Smith's details pulsate with a kind of bleak vitalism and provide a defense against dissolution. Smith has said that his poems are "attempts to conflate the lyric and the narrative" (*Contemporary*).

Smith was born on December 19, 1942, in Portsmouth, Virginia. He graduated in 1965 from the University of Virginia, served in the air force during the Vietnam War (1969–72), and received graduate degrees from Southern Illinois University (M.A., 1969) and Ohio University (Ph.D., 1976). Among his many teaching posts have been Virginia Commonwealth University and, since 1990, Louisiana State University. In addition to his books of poetry, he has published fiction and essays and is coeditor of *The Southern Review.*

Leafless Trees, Chickahominy Swamp[1]

Humorless, hundreds of trunks, gray in the blue expanse
where dusk leaves them hacked like a breastwork,[2]
stripped like pikes planted to impale, the knots
of vines at each groin appearing placed by makers
schooled in grotesque campaigns. Mathew Brady's[3]
plates show them as they are, the ageless stumps,
timed-sanded solitaries, some clumped in squads
we might imagine veterans, except they're only wood,
and nothing in the world seems more dead than these.

1. In Virginia; Confederate staging area for Civil War battles, now a nesting spot for bald eagles.
2. Temporary fortification, a few feet high, for defense against an enemy.
3. American photographer (1823–1896), famous for his documentation of the Civil War.

Stopped by the lanes filled with homebound taillights,
we haven't seen the rumored Eagle we hoped to watch,
only a clutch of buzzards ferrying sticks for a nest.
Is this history, that we want the unchanged, useless
spines out there to thrust in our faces the human
qualities we covet? We read this place like generals
whose promised recruits don't show, who can't press on:
we feel the languor of battle, troops unable to tell
themselves from the enemy, and a file-hard fear gone

indifferent in the mortaring sun that will leave all
night after night standing in the same cold planes
of water. It never blooms or greens. It merely stinks.
Why can't we admit this is death's gift, the scummy
scene of our pride, blown brainpans of a century ago?
Why do we sit and sniff the rank hours inside words
blunt as ground that only stares off our question: what
happened? Leaf-light in our heads, don't we mean why
these grisly emblems, the slime that won't swell to hope?

The rapacious odor of swamps all over the earth bubbles
sometimes to mist, fetid flesh we can't see but know,
just cells composing, decomposing, a heart's illusions.
God knows what we'd do in there, we say, easing back
on the blacktop. Once we heard a whistling. Harmonicas?
But who'd listen? Surely all was green once, fragile
as a truce, words braiding sun and water, as on a lake
where families sang. What else would we hope for, do
in the dead miles nothing explains or changes or relieves?

1984

Fiddlers

Black mudbank pushes them out like hotel fire.
Some at water's edge seem to wait for transport.
Others sweat, pale, scattered on the shining beach.
All keep closed the mighty arms of God's damage,
waving at shadows and movements made by the sun.
Desire, the dragging arm, sifts, picks, tastes, untastes
endlessly the civic occasions the tide brings in.
Surely floods, cold fronts, embolisms[4] of dreams
drive them in where the earth's brain hums. They
clasp, breed. They glare upward in rooms where the moon
slips its question. Daylong they spout, fume, command.
Biblical as kinsmen with a son they must kill.
Nouns, verbs couple like years. Water comes, listens.

1996

4. Obstructions in blood vessels.

Wreck in the Woods

Under that embrace of wild saplings held fast,
surrounded by troops of white mushrooms, by wrens
visiting like news-burdened ministers known
only to some dim life inside, this Model
A Ford like my grandfather's entered the earth.
What were fenders, hood, doors, no one washed, polished,
grazed with a tip of finger, or boyhood dream.
I stood where silky blue above went wind-rent,
pines, oaks, dogwood ticking, pushing as if grief
called families to see what none understood. What
plot of words, what heart-shudder of men, women
here ended so hard the green world must hide it?
Headlights, large, round. Two pieces of shattered glass.

1996

Blowfish and Mudtoad[5]

Held the wrong way either will take the finger
that clamps the casual pen, changing your words,
its rows of teeth like a serrated bread knife.
Moss-covered as bottom rock, wearing the brown
scum of salt water settlers, current-fluttered
flags of weed, eyes like glass pitted by age,
each reads steadily the downdrifted offerings
its tongue ticks for: crawlers, wings, limbs, all
the great current gathers to sweep away at last.
Our line sinkered into that steep wants a sleek
one to claim us—big Blue, Striper, Thor-like[6] Drum.
Not these nibbling small-town preachers, Mudtoad's
black ambush, or Blowfish, resurrection and rage.

1996

Black Silhouettes of Shrimpers

Grand Isle, Louisiana

Along the flat sand the cupped torsos of trash fish
arch to seek the sun, but the eyes
glaze with thick gray, death's touch
already drifting these jeweled darters.

5. Oyster toadfish. Blowfish inflate themselves and are often poisonous.
6. *Thor:* Viking thunder god.

Back and forth against the horizon slow trawlers
gulp in their bags whatever rises
here with the shrimp they come for.
Boys on deck shovel the fish off

like the clothes of their fathers out of attics.
Who knows what tides beached them,
what lives were lived to arrive just here?
I walk without stepping on any

dead, though it is hard, the sun's many blazes
spattering and blinding the way ahead
where the wildness of water coils
dark in small swamps and smells fiercely of flesh.

If a cloud shadows everything for a moment, cool,
welcome, there is still no end in sight,
body after body, stench, jewels
nothing will wear, roar and fade of engines.

2000

Louise Glück
b. 1943

One's first impression of Louise Glück's work is its sensitivity; the second is its economy. Her minimalist poems generally begin with sharp, unrelieved feelings about love, death, and loss; these are expressed in short lines as if to cut deeper into consciousness. "Desire, loneliness, wind in the flowering almond—/ surely these are the great, the inexhaustible subjects" of lyric poetry, she writes in "Summer Night." A number of her early poems are about a sister who died as an infant before Glück was born. In these dreamlike poems, Glück, like such "confessional" poets as Sylvia Plath, Anne Sexton, and Robert Lowell, returns to childhood perception and feeling. More generally, her poems echo Sexton's adaptation of fairy tale, H. D.'s mythic minimalism, and George Oppen's use of silence and negative space. In the confessional vein, many of her later poems are about the gradual disintegration of a marriage. Family members, marriages, natural beauty—"All, all / can be lost," she writes in "The White Lilies."

But Glück's treatment of personal feeling, though stripped-down and direct, is measured and controlled. Often, she frames autobiographical experience with myths and fables. The dissolution of a marriage is told in *Meadowlands* (1996) through the Homeric story of Penelope and Odysseus. A gardener-poet, flowers, and a god speak the extended poetic sequence that makes up *The Wild Iris* (1992). The situations of her poetry—daughters and a mother in grief, a mother holding a sick child—are archetypal, embedding minute perceptions within larger contexts. She entitled one poem "Mythic Fragment," and her work is composed of fragments and sequences.

Glück insists in "Marathon" that "nakedness in woman is always a pose," and she is never unaware of the dress of formal pattern: "Then what began as love for you / became a hunger for structure" ("The Beginning"). Glück counterbalances dejection and despair with a stark, lucid language and with understatement. "You see," begins "The Drowned Children," "they have no judgment. / So it is natural that they should drown." The colloquial address, the offhand tone, the seeming acceptance ("it is natural") contrast with the horrific drowning of children in winter ponds. Similarly, Glück's cool, modulated rhythms help distill feeling, often with a ghostly echo of formal meters. Her spartan images, though they appear natural, are unexpected and glide easily from momentary perception to an abstraction. Her abstractions and occasional aphorisms ("whatever / returns from oblivion returns / to find a voice" in "The Wild Iris") filter the particular through the general. By screening personal experience through various forms of artifice, Glück's poetry succeeds in bringing us close to piercing feelings of anguish, isolation, and loss.

Glück was born on April 22, 1943, in New York City. She attended Sarah Lawrence College and Columbia University. She has taught at Williams College since 1984. In 1985, she won the National Book Critics Circle Award for *The Triumph of Achilles;* in 1993, the Pulitzer Prize for *The Wild Iris;* and in 2001, the Bollingen Prize for *Vita Nova.*

The School Children

The children go forward with their little satchels.
And all morning the mothers have labored
to gather the late apples, red and gold,
like words of another language.

And on the other shore
are those who wait behind great desks
to receive these offerings.

How orderly they are—the nails
on which the children hang
their overcoats of blue or yellow wool.

And the teachers shall instruct them in silence
and the mothers shall scour the orchards for a way out,
drawing to themselves the gray limbs of the fruit trees
bearing so little ammunition.

1975

The Drowned Children

You see, they have no judgment.
So it is natural that they should drown,
first the ice taking them in
and then, all winter, their wool scarves
floating behind them as they sink
until at last they are quiet.
And the pond lifts them in its manifold dark arms.

But death must come to them differently,
so close to the beginning.
As though they had always been
blind and weightless. Therefore
the rest is dreamed, the lamp,
the good white cloth that covered the table,
their bodies.

And yet they hear the names they used
like lures slipping over the pond:
What are you waiting for
come home, come home, lost
in the waters, blue and permanent.

1980

Descending Figure

1. *The Wanderer*

At twilight I went into the street.
The sun hung low in the iron sky,
ringed with cold plumage.
If I could write to you
about this emptiness—
Along the curb, groups of children
were playing in the dry leaves.
Long ago, at this hour, my mother stood
at the lawn's edge, holding my little sister.
Everyone was gone; I was playing
in the dark street with my other sister,
whom death had made so lonely.
Night after night we watched the screened porch
filling with a gold, magnetic light.
Why was she never called?
Often I would let my own name glide past me
though I craved its protection.

2. *The Sick Child*

—Rijksmuseum[1]

A small child
is ill, has wakened.
It is winter, past midnight
in Antwerp.[2] Above a wooden chest,
the stars shine.
And the child
relaxes in her mother's arms.

1. Dutch state museum, in Amsterdam. *The Sick Child* is a painting of a mother holding her sick child at night, by Flemish painter Gabriel Metsu (1629–1667).
2. Belgian city.

The mother does not sleep;
she stares
fixedly into the bright museum.
By spring the child will die.
Then it is wrong, wrong
to hold her—
Let her be alone,
without memory, as the others wake
terrified, scraping the dark
paint from their faces.

3. *For My Sister*

Far away my sister is moving in her crib.
The dead ones are like that,
always the last to quiet.

Because, however long they lie in the earth,
they will not learn to speak
but remain uncertainly pressing against the wooden bars,
so small the leaves hold them down.

Now, if she had a voice,
the cries of hunger would be beginning.
I should go to her;
perhaps if I sang very softly,
her skin so white,
her head covered with black feathers. . . .

1980

Mock Orange[3]

It is not the moon, I tell you.
It is these flowers
lighting the yard.

I hate them.
I hate them as I hate sex,
the man's mouth
sealing my mouth, the man's
paralyzing body—

and the cry that always escapes,
the low, humiliating
premise of union—

In my mind tonight
I hear the question and pursuing answer

3. Shrub with showy, fragrant white flowers.

fused in one sound
that mounts and mounts and then
is split into the old selves,
the tired antagonisms. Do you see?
We were made fools of.
And the scent of mock orange
drifts through the window.

How can I rest?
How can I be content
when there is still
that odor in the world?

1985

A Fantasy

I'll tell you something: every day
people are dying. And that's just the beginning.
Every day, in funeral homes, new widows are born,
new orphans. They sit with their hands folded,
trying to decide about this new life.

Then they're in the cemetery, some of them
for the first time. They're frightened of crying,
sometimes of not crying. Someone leans over,
tells them what to do next, which might mean
saying a few words, sometimes
throwing dirt in the open grave.

And after that, everyone goes back to the house,
which is suddenly full of visitors.
The widow sits on the couch, very stately,
so people line up to approach her,
sometimes take her hand, sometimes embrace her.
She finds something to say to everybody,
thanks them, thanks them for coming.

In her heart, she wants them to go away.
She wants to be back in the cemetery,
back in the sickroom, the hospital. She knows
it isn't possible. But it's her only hope,
the wish to move backward. And just a little,
not so far as the marriage, the first kiss.

1990

The Wild Iris

At the end of my suffering
there was a door.

Hear me out: that which you call death
I remember.

Overhead, noises, branches of the pine shifting.
Then nothing. The weak sun
flickered over the dry surface.

It is terrible to survive
as consciousness
buried in the dark earth.

Then it was over: that which you fear, being
a soul and unable
to speak, ending abruptly, the stiff earth
bending a little. And what I took to be
birds darting in low shrubs.

You who do not remember
passage from the other world
I tell you I could speak again: whatever
returns from oblivion returns
to find a voice:

from the center of my life came
a great fountain, deep blue
shadows on azure seawater.

1992

Penelope's Song[4]

Little soul, little perpetually undressed one,
do now as I bid you, climb
the shelf-like branches of the spruce tree;
wait at the top, attentive, like
a sentry or look-out. He will be home soon;
it behooves you to be
generous. You have not been completely
perfect either; with your troublesome body
you have done things you shouldn't
discuss in poems. Therefore
call out to him over the open water, over the bright water

4. In Homer's *Odyssey,* Odysseus's wife, Penelope, waits for him while he journeys home.

with your dark song, with your grasping,
unnatural song—passionate,
like Maria Callas.[5] Who
wouldn't want you? Whose most demonic appetite
could you possibly fail to answer? Soon
he will return from wherever he goes in the meantime,
suntanned from his time away, wanting
his grilled chicken. Ah, you must greet him,
you must shake the boughs of the tree
to get his attention,
but carefully, carefully, lest
his beautiful face be marred
by too many falling needles.

1996

Quiet Evening

You take my hand; then we're alone
in the life-threatening forest. Almost immediately

we're in a house; Noah's[6]
grown and moved away; the clematis after ten years
suddenly flowers white.

More than anything in the world
I love these evenings when we're together,
the quiet evenings in summer, the sky still light at this hour.

So Penelope took the hand of Odysseus,[7]
not to hold him back but to impress
this peace on his memory:

from this point on, the silence through which you move
is my voice pursuing you.

1996

Vita Nova[8]

You saved me, you should remember me.

The spring of the year; young men buying tickets for the ferryboats.
Laughter, because the air is full of apple blossoms.

When I woke up, I realized I was capable of the same feeling.

5. American operatic soprano (1923–1977).
6. The poet's son.
7. See note 4 above.
8. New life (Latin). *La Vita Nova* (c. 1292) was the first major work of Italian poet Dante Alighieri (1265–1321); it describes his idealistic love for Beatrice.

I remember sounds like that from my childhood,
laughter for no cause, simply because the world is beautiful,
something like that.

Lugano.[9] Tables under the apple trees.
Deckhands raising and lowering the colored flags.
And by the lake's edge, a young man throws his hat into the water;
perhaps his sweetheart has accepted him.

Crucial
sounds or gestures like
a track laid down before the larger themes

and then unused, buried.

Islands in the distance. My mother
holding out a plate of little cakes—

as far as I remember, changed
in no detail, the moment
vivid, intact, having never been
exposed to light, so that I woke elated, at my age
hungry for life, utterly confident—

By the tables, patches of new grass, the pale green
pieced into the dark existing ground.

Surely spring has been returned to me, this time
not as a lover but a messenger of death, yet
it is still spring, it is still meant tenderly.

1999

Earthly Love

Conventions of the time
held them together.
It was a period
(very long) in which
the heart once given freely
was required, as a formal gesture,
to forfeit liberty: a consecration
at once moving and hopelessly doomed.

As to ourselves:
fortunately we diverged
from these requirements,
as I reminded myself

9. Lake on the border between Italy and Switzerland.

when my life shattered.
So that what we had for so long
was, more or less,
voluntary, alive.
And only long afterward
did I begin to think otherwise.

We are all human—
we protect ourselves
as well as we can
even to the point of denying
clarity, the point
of self-deception. As in
the consecration to which I alluded.

And yet, within this deception,
true happiness occurred.
So that I believe I would
repeat these errors exactly.
Nor does it seem to me
crucial to know
whether or not such happiness
is built on illusion:
it has its own reality.
And in either case, it will end.

1999

Michael Palmer
b. 1943

Michael Palmer's poetry is abstract and yet affective. It bridges the divide between the rigors of postmodern suspicion and the pleasures of sonorous lyricism. Often associated with the Language poets, influenced by Louis Zukofsky and other late modernists, well-versed in the theories of Jacques Derrida, Roland Barthes, and other poststructuralists, Palmer writes poems that are fragmentary, self-reflexive, and nonsequential. Like other experimental writers, he questions the fiction of a unitary self that confesses its inner experience in a poem. "Various *selves*," he says of the process of composition, "aspects of a heightened attention, did it in a certain way, but not your *self*" ("A Conversation," 1986). Calling attention to the creative role of the reader, Palmer dramatizes the complex interactions among reader, writer, speaker, and text in his poem "Song of the Round Man," which is reminiscent of Wallace Stevens's self-reflexive meditations. "Poetry seems often a talking to self as well as other as well as self as other, a simultaneity that recognizes the elusive multiplicity of what is called 'identity' " ("Autobiography, Memory and Mechanisms of Concealment").

Hardly a mirror to the soul, the poem is, for Palmer, a verbal artifact that spotlights its own words. Palmer continually reminds us of the materiality of language—syllables, grammatical and syntactic structures, even the differences among words separated by a mere letter. "A word may be shaped like a fig or a pig, an effigy or an egg," he writes in "Sun." Syntactic parallelism, evident in this line as throughout much of his poetry, is insistent and yet defamiliarized. Similarly, Palmer often repeats an initial word or phrase, only to set up through such anaphora a false parallel that makes us scrutinize the logic of analogy. Pages of poetry—not being transparent windows onto experiences or things "out there"—are physical realities in themselves, "pages which sit up," as he puts it in "Sun," "Pages torn from their spines." Resisting the linear flow of narrative, Palmer may allow one line to pivot back on what preceded it, as in the nonsequiturs of "This Time": "Once I fell in the ocean when / I didn't know I fell in the ocean // Then Momma got me out / This isn't true // only something I remember." While this poem raises central poststructuralist questions about the complexity of knowledge, truth, memory, and identity, it also evinces the lyric's traditionally lucid imagery ("I turned blue all over // then got clear as glass") and sensual sound. Palmer's poetry is replete with assonance, consonance, alliteration, occasional rhyme, echoic rhythms, refrains, and other forms of verbal repetition. "Sun" recalls phrases and musical cadences from T. S. Eliot's *Waste Land*. The strength of Palmer's work is that, like Eliot's masterpiece, it effectively combines fluency with syntactical dislocation, violent disjunctiveness with an eerie calm.

Palmer was born on May 11, 1943, into a middle-class Italian American family in New York City, his father the manager of a small hotel. A French major at Harvard University, he received a B.A. in 1965 and an M.A. in comparative literature two years later. Along with poetry and translations, his works include various collaborations with painters and dancers. He has spent most of his life in the San Francisco area.

Song of the Round Man

(for Sarah when she's older)

The round and sad-eyed man puffed cigars as if
he were alive. Gillyflowers
to the left of the apple, purple bells to the right

and a grass-covered hill behind.
I am sad today said the sad-eyed man
for I have locked my head in a Japanese box

and lost the key.
I am sad today he told me
for there are gillyflowers by the apple

and purple bells I cannot see.
Will you look at them for me
he asked, and tell me what you find?

I cannot I replied
for my eyes have grown sugary and dim
from reading too long by candlelight.

Tell me what you've read then
said the round and sad-eyed man.
I cannot I replied

for my memory has grown tired and dim
from looking at things that can't be seen
by any kind of light

and I've locked my head in a Japanese box
and thrown away the key.
Then I am you and you are me

said the sad-eyed man as if alive.
I'll write you in where I should be
between the gillyflowers and the purple bells

and the apple and the hill
and we'll puff cigars from noon till night
as if we were alive.

1981

This Time

(another for Sarah)

Once I fell in the ocean when
I didn't know I fell in the ocean

Then Momma got me out
This isn't true

only something I remember
Once in the park I broke in half

and lost one half
which half I don't remember

Once I was in a room
It grew larger and larger

why I don't remember
One time I turned blue all over

then got clear as glass
This really happened

but not to me
Once I couldn't see

for a while
so I listened lying down

Another time I looked out the window
and saw myself at the window

across the street
This time it was me

1984

Sun

Write this. We have burned all their villages

Write this. We have burned all the villages and the people in them

Write this. We have adopted their customs and their manner of dress

Write this. A word may be shaped like a bed, a basket of tears or an X

In the notebook it says, It is the time of mutations, laughter at jokes,
secrets beyond the boundaries of speech

I now turn to my use of suffixes and punctuation, closing Mr. Circle with a
single stroke, tearing the canvas from its wall, joined to her, experiencing
the same thoughts at the same moment, inscribing them on a loquat[1] leaf

Write this. We have begun to have bodies, a now here and a now gone,
a past long ago and one still to come

Let go of me for I have died and am in a novel and was a lyric poet,
certainly, who attracted crowds to mountaintops. For a nickel I will appear
from this box. For a dollar I will have text with you and answer three
questions

First question. We entered the forest, followed its winding paths, and
emerged blind

Second question. My townhouse, of the Jugendstil, lies by Darmstadt[2]

Third question. He knows he will wake from this dream, conducted in the
mother-tongue

Third question. He knows his breathing organs are manipulated by God, so
that he is compelled to scream

1. Fruitbearing tree native to Japan and China; interlingual pun on unrelated Latin word for "to talk," as in *loquacious*.
2. Industrial city in central Germany devastated by bombings during World War II. *Jugendstil:* German name of Art Nouveau, a late nineteenth-century design movement that emphasized the decorative arts, ornamentation, and exotic forms.

Third question. I will converse with no one on those days of the week
which end in *y*

Write this. There is pleasure and pain and there are marks and signs.
A word may be shaped like a fig or a pig, an effigy or an egg
but
there is only time for fasting and desire, device and design, there is
only time to swerve without limbs, organs or face into a
scientific
silence, pinhole of light

Say this. I was born on an island among the dead. I learned language on
this island but did not speak on this island. I am writing to you from this
island. I am writing to the dancers from this island. The writers do not
dance on this island

Say this. There is a sentence in my mouth, there is a chariot in my mouth.
There is a ladder. There is a lamp whose light fills empty space and a space
which swallows light

A word is beside itself. Here the poem is called What Speaking Means to
Say
though I have no memory of my name

Here the poem is called Theory of the Real, its name is Let's Call This,
and its name is called A Wooden Stick. It goes yes-yes, no-no. It goes one
and one

I have been writing a book, not in my native language, about violins and
smoke, lines and dots, free to speak and become the things we speak,
pages which sit up, look around and row resolutely toward the setting sun

Pages torn from their spines and added to the pyre, so that they will
resemble thought.

Pages which accept no ink

Pages we've never seen—first called Narrow Street, then Half a Fragment,
Plain of Jars or Plain of Reeds,[3] taking each syllable into her mouth,
shifting position and passing it to him

3. Region of marshland west of Saigon that was a stronghold for Communist guerillas during the Vietnam War. *Plain of Jars:* region of Laos dotted with large stone "jars" produced—probably as burial urns—nearly two thousand years ago. The plain was the site of prolonged battles during the Vietnam War and was heavily bombed by U.S. forces.

Let me say this. Neak Luong[4] is a blur. It is Tuesday in the hardwood
forest. I am a visitor here, with a notebook

The notebook lists My New Words and Flag above White. It claims to have
no inside
only characters like A-against-Herself, B, C, L and
N, Sam, Hans Magnus, T. Sphere, all speaking in the dark with their
hands
G for Gramsci or Goebbels,[5] blue hills, cities, cities with hills,
modern and at the edge of time
F for alphabet, Z for A, an H in an arbor,
shadow, silent wreckage, W or M among stars

What last. Lapwing. Tesseract.[6] X perhaps for X. The villages are known
as These Letters—humid, sunless. The writing occurs on their walls

1988

4. Cambodian city bombed by the United States during the Vietnam War despite Cambodia's official neutrality. Palmer took this sentence from the headline of a newspaper story about an American soldier returning to the city years later.

5. Joseph Goebbels (1897–1945), Nazi propaganda minister. *Hans Magnus:* Hans Magnus Enzenberger (b. 1929), German political poet and critic. *T. Sphere:* Thelonious Sphere Monk (1917–1982), jazz pianist and composer. *Gramsci:* Antonio Gramsci (1891–1937), Italian communist philosopher.

6. A four-dimensional cube (the fourth dimension being time). *Lapwing:* species of bird named for its slow wing-beat.

MICHAEL ONDAATJE
b. 1943

Frequently riven by internecine violence, formerly subjected to European colonial rule, Sri Lanka (previously Ceylon) is a large, pear-shaped island just off the southern tip of India, its landscape variegated with mountains and jungles, and its tropical vegetation of a wild and dreamlike richness. Michael Ondaatje's family has been in Sri Lanka since 1600. Culturally, they are a mixture of the Sinhalese, the indigenous inhabitants; the Tamils, dark-skinned emigrants from India; and the Dutch, who came to Sri Lanka in search of spices in the seventeenth century. English, Sinhalese, and Tamil were the languages that surrounded Ondaatje when he was growing up. He spent the first eleven years of his life in Sri Lanka, as recalled in his 1982 memoir, *Running in the Family.* By way of England, he eventually settled in Canada when he was nineteen. His later trips to Sri Lanka are reflected in his poetry collection *Handwriting* (1999) and in his novel *Anil's Ghost* (2000).

Widely known as the author of *The English Patient* (1992), a best-seller that became an award-winning film and the first Canadian novel to win the Booker Prize, Ondaatje reminds interviewers that he "began as a poet and that has influenced all my writing" and insists that poetry is "the most precise writing" (*The Observer,* November 1, 1998; *Maclean's,* December 18, 2000). Earlier, Ondaatje published book-length narratives that combine poems with highly charged prose: *The Collected Works of Billy the Kid*

(1970, 1974) and *Coming through Slaughter* (1976), the latter based on the life of a jazz cornettist who went mad. Some of Ondaatje's shorter poems are surrealistic snapshots of domestic life, such as "Biography," in which a family dog runs in her sleep and dreams of killing. Whether writing about his parents or his grown daughter, Ondaatje inspects human situations in search of the erotic, the ironic, and the humanly pathetic. These poems suggest the influence of Robert Lowell, whereas his later poetry about Sri Lankan violence, religion, and culture fuses William Carlos Williams's short-lined free verse with spare, imagistic South Asian models (classical Tamil and Sanskrit). Cryptic and fragmentary, these poems are built around haunting visual images. Ondaatje's poetry blends the dreamlike with the lucid, the offhand with the formal, as suggested in the *ars poetica* of the early poem " 'The Gate in His Head' ": "And that is all this writing should be then. / The beautiful formed things caught at the wrong moment / so they are shapeless, awkward / moving to the clear."

Ondaatje was born on September 12, 1943. After his departure from Sri Lanka (prompted by his parents' divorce), he was educated at Dulwich College, London; Bishop's University, Quebec; the University of Toronto; and Queen's University, Kingston, Ontario. From 1961 to 1971, he taught English at the University of Western Ontario, in London; beginning in 1971, at Glendon College, York University, in Toronto. He has won several awards, including the Governor-General's Award for Literature—roughly equivalent to the Pulitzer Prize. In addition to writing poems and anthologies, Ondaatje has directed several films.

Biography

The dog scatters her body in sleep,
paws, finding no ground, whip at air,
the unseen eyeballs reel deep, within.
And waking—crouches,
tacked to humility all day,
children ride her, stretch,
display the black purple lips,
pull hind legs to dance;
unaware that she
tore bulls apart, loosed
heads of partridges,
dreamt blood.

1979

Letters & Other Worlds

"for there was no more darkness for him and, no doubt
like Adam before the fall, he could see in the dark"

My father's body was a globe of fear
His body was a town we never knew
He hid that he had been where we were going
His letters were a room he seldom lived in
In them the logic of his love could grow

My father's body was a town of fear
He was the only witness to its fear dance
He hid where he had been that we might lose him
His letters were a room his body scared

He came to death with his mind drowning.
On the last day he enclosed himself
in a room with two bottles of gin, later
fell the length of his body
so that brain blood moved
to new compartments
that never knew the wash of fluid
and he died in minutes of a new equilibrium.

His early life was a terrifying comedy
and my mother divorced him again and again
he would rush into tunnels magnetized
by the white eye of trains
and once, gaining instant fame,
managed to stop a Perahara[1] in Ceylon
—the whole procession of elephants dancers
local dignitaries—by falling
dead drunk onto the street.

As a semi-official, and semi-white at that,
the act was seen as a crucial
turning point in the Home Rule Movement
and led to Ceylon's independence in 1948.

(My mother had done her share too—
her driving so bad
she was stoned by villagers
whenever her car was recognized)

For 14 years of marriage
each of them claimed he or she
was the injured party.
Once on the Colombo[2] docks
saying goodbye to a recently married couple
my father, jealous
at my mother's articulate emotion,
dove into the waters of the harbour
and swam after the ship waving farewell.
My mother pretending no affiliation
mingled with the crowd back to the hotel.

Once again he made the papers
though this time my mother

1. Or Anuradhapura Perahara, an annual religious festival of Sri Lanka (formerly Ceylon) commemorating the birth of Vishnu, one of the three primary Hindu gods. On its final night, the festival culminates in processions, the elephants carrying shrines and relics.
2. Seaport city, capital of Sri Lanka.

with a note to the editor
corrected the report—saying he was drunk
rather than broken hearted at the parting of friends.
The married couple received both editions
of *The Ceylon Times* when their ship reached Aden.[3]

And then in his last years
he was the silent drinker,
the man who once a week
disappeared into his room with bottles
and stayed there until he was drunk
and until he was sober.

There speeches, head dreams, apologies,
the gentle letters, were composed.
With the clarity of architects
he would write of the row of blue flowers
his new wife had planted,
the plans for electricity in the house,
how my half-sister fell near a snake
and it had awakened and not touched her.
Letters in a clear hand of the most complete empathy
his heart widening and widening and widening
to all manner of change in his children and friends
while he himself edged
into the terrible acute hatred
of his own privacy
till he balanced and fell
the length of his body
the blood screaming in
the empty reservoir of bones
the blood searching in his head without metaphor

1979

(Inner Tube)[4]

On the warm July river
head back

upside down river
for a roof

slowly paddling
towards an estuary between trees

there's a dog
learning to swim near me
friends on shore

3. The Port of Aden, on the southern coast of the Arabian peninsula, in South Yemen; then a British colony.
4. Airtight tube often used by children as a float.

my head
dips
back to the eyebrow
I'm the prow
on an ancient vessel,
this afternoon
I'm going down to Peru
soul between my teeth

a blue heron
with its awkward
broken backed flap
upside down

one of us is wrong

he
in his blue grey thud
thinking he knows
the blue way
out of here

or me

1984

Driving with Dominic in the Southern Province We See Hints of the Circus

The tattered Hungarian tent

A man washing a trumpet
at a roadside tap

Children in the trees,

one falling
into the grip of another

1999

From Buried

To be buried in times of war,
in harsh weather, in the monsoon
of knives and stakes.

The stone and bronze gods carried
during a night rest of battle

between the sleeping camps
floated in catamarans[5] down the coast
past Kalutara.[6]
                    To be buried
for safety.

To bury, surrounded by flares,
large stone heads
during floods in the night.
Dragged from a temple
by one's own priests,
lifted onto palanquins,[7]
covered with mud and straw.
Giving up the sacred
among themselves,
carrying the faith of a temple
during political crisis
away in their arms.
                    Hiding
the gestures of the Buddha.

Above ground, massacre and race.
A heart silenced.
The tongue removed.
The human body merged into burning tire.
Mud glaring back
into a stare.

1999

From Buried 2

vii

The heat of explosions
sterilized all metal.

Ball bearings and nails
in the arms, in the head.
Shrapnel in the feet.

Ear channels
deformed by shockwaves.
Men without balance
surrounding the dead President
on Armour Street.[8]

5. Rafts made of logs tied together.
6. Fishing and trade center in southwestern Sri Lanka.
7. Conveyances in which one person is carried by four or six people by means of poles projecting from a large box.
8. President Ranasinghe Premadasa (1924–1993) and sixteen others were killed by a suicide bomber on Armour Street in Colombo, the capital of Sri Lanka, on May 1, 1993.

Those whose bodies
could not be found.

1999

James Tate
b. 1943

James Tate describes himself as writing in the "tradition of the Impurists," and he mentions in particular the poetry of Walt Whitman, William Carlos Williams, and Pablo Neruda (*Contemporary Authors*, 1969). Poetry, for Tate, is a form of protest, as well as celebration, protest not against political situations but against the difficulty of connecting deeply with one another and with the natural world that surrounds us. The dazzling surrealist world of the poem "The Wheelchair Butterfly" is both a heaven and a hell; the delight here cannot exist without destruction: "Today a butterfly froze / in midair; and was plucked like a grape / by a child who swore he could take care / of it." Presumably identifying with the child, the poet speaks of his desire to "order the world for a moment, freeze it, understand it."

Sometimes, Tate's poems seem to coast on their own zany rhetoric, propelled by the energies of the language and by the clash of images. Playful, clever, ever quirky, Tate effects his transformations with the speed and efficiency of a first-rate magician. Yet beneath the often giddy and campy surfaces of Tate's poems lurks pain and disappointment. As his former teacher Donald Justice said on the publication of *The Lost Pilot* (1967), "Once despair can be taken for granted, gaiety becomes a possibility, almost a necessity." Tate often dreams a world where an armistice will be declared in the warfare of contraries between old and young, men and women. But only the blue boobies of the Galápagos—who contrive to be at once sad, funny, and beautiful—have found a haven beyond conflict; they exemplify Tate's dictum: "The poem is man's noblest effort because it is utterly useless" (*Contemporary Poets of the English Language*, ed. R. Murphy, 1971).

Tate was born in Kansas City, Missouri, on December 8, 1943, the year his pilot father was reported missing in Germany during World War II. He received his B.A. from Kansas State College in 1965, after two years at the University of Missouri. He then went to the University of Iowa, from which he received an M.F.A. and where he taught creative writing for a year. He has since taught at the University of California, Berkeley, at Columbia University, and, since 1971, at the University of Massachusetts at Amherst. A prolific and honored poet, he was, at twenty-three, the youngest poet chosen for the Yale Series of Younger Poets (1967), and he subsequently garnered the Pulitzer Prize (1992), the National Book Award (1994), and the Tanning Prize (1995).

Stray Animals

This is the beauty of being alone
toward the end of summer:
a dozen stray animals asleep on the porch

in the shade of my feet,
and the smell of leaves burning
in another neighborhood.
It is late morning,
and my forehead is alive with shadows,
some bats rock back and forth
to the rhythm of my humming,
the mimosa[1] flutters with bees.
This is a house of unwritten poems,
this is where I am unborn.

1968

The Blue Booby

The blue booby lives
on the bare rocks
of Galápagos[2]
and fears nothing.
It is a simple life:
they live on fish,
and there are few predators.
Also, the males do not
make fools of themselves
chasing after the young
ladies. Rather,
they gather the blue
objects of the world
and construct from them

a nest—an occasional
Gaulois[3] package,
a string of beads,
a piece of cloth from
a sailor's suit. This
replaces the need for
dazzling plumage;
in fact, in the past
fifty million years
the male has grown
considerably duller,
nor can he sing well.
The female, though,

asks little of him—
the blue satisfies her
completely, has

1. Tropical tree or shrub.
2. Pacific islands famous for their unique species of animals and birds.
3. A French brand of cigarettes with a distinctive blue package.

a magical effect
on her. When she returns
from her day of
gossip and shopping,
she sees he has found her
a new shred of blue foil:
for this she rewards him
with her dark body,
the stars turn slowly
in the blue foil beside them
like the eyes of a mild savior.

1969

The Wheelchair Butterfly

O sleepy city of reeling wheelchairs
where a mouse can commit suicide if he can

concentrate long enough
on the history book of rodents
in his underground town

of electrical wheelchairs!
The girl who is always pregnant and bruised
like a pear

rides her many-stickered bicycle
backward up the staircase
of the abandoned trolleybarn.

Yesterday was warm. Today a butterfly froze
in midair; and was plucked like a grape
by a child who swore he could take care

of it. O confident city where
the seeds of poppies pass for carfare,

where the ordinary hornets in a human's heart
may slumber and snore, where bifocals bulge

in an orange garage of daydreams,
we wait in our loose attics for a new season

as if for an ice-cream truck.
An Indian pony crosses the plains

whispering Sanskrit prayers to a crater of fleas.
Honeysuckle says: I thought I could swim.

The Mayor is urinating on the wrong side
of the street! A dandelion sends off sparks:
beware your hair is locked!

Beware the trumpet wants a glass of water!
Beware a velvet tabernacle!

Beware the Warden of Light has married
an old piece of string!

1969

The Lost Pilot

for my father, 1922–1944

Your face did not rot
like the others—the co-pilot,
for example, I saw him

yesterday. His face is corn-
mush: his wife and daughter,
the poor ignorant people, stare

as if he will compose soon.
He was more wronged than Job.[4]
But your face did not rot

like the others—it grew dark,
and hard like ebony;
the features progressed in their

distinction. If I could cajole
you to come back for an evening,
down from your compulsive

orbiting, I would touch you,
read your face as Dallas,
your hoodlum gunner, now,

with the blistered eyes, reads
his braille editions. I would
touch your face as a disinterested

scholar touches an original page.
However frightening, I would
discover you, and I would not

4. Hebrew Bible patriarch severely afflicted by God to test his faith.

turn you in; I would not make
you face your wife, or Dallas,
or the co-pilot, Jim. You

could return to your crazy
orbiting, and I would not try
to fully understand what

it means to you. All I know
is this: when I see you,
as I have seen you at least

once every year of my life,
spin across the wilds of the sky
like a tiny, African god,

I feel dead. I feel as if I were
the residue of a stranger's life,
that I should pursue you.

My head cocked toward the sky,
I cannot get off the ground,
and, you, passing over again,

fast, perfect, and unwilling
to tell me that you are doing
well, or that it was mistake

that placed you in that world,
and me in this; or that misfortune
placed these worlds in us.

1978

The Motorcyclists

My cuticles are a mess. Oh honey, by the way,
did you like my new negligee? It's a replica
of one Kim Novak[5] wore in some movie or other.
I wish I had a foot-long chili dog right now.
Do you like fireworks, I mean not just on the 4th
of July, but fireworks any time? There are people
like that, you know. They're like people who like
orchestra music, listen to it any time of day.
Lopsided people, that's what my father calls them.
Me, I'm easy to please. I like ping-pong and bobcats,
shatterproof drinking glasses, the smell of kerosene,

5. American actor (b. 1933).

the crunch of carrots. I like caterpillars and
whirlpools, too. What I hate most is being the first
one at the scene of a bad accident.

Do I smell like garlic? Are we still in Kansas?
I once had a chiropractor make a pass at me,
did I ever tell you that? He said that your spine
is happiest when you're snuggling. Sounds kind
of sweet now when I tell you, but he was a creep.
Do you know that I have never understood what they meant
by "grassy knoll."[6] It sounds so idyllic, a place to go
to dream your life away, not kill somebody. They
should have called it something like "the grudging notch."
But I guess that's life. What is it they always say?
"It's always the sweetest ones that break your heart."
You getting hungry yet, hon? I am. When I was seven
I sat in our field and ate an entire eggplant
right off the vine. Dad loves to tell that story,

but I still can't eat eggplant. He says I'll be the first
woman President, it'd be a waste since I talk so much.
Which do you think the fixtures are in the bathroom
at the White House, gold or brass? It'd be okay with me
if they were just brass. Honey, can we stop soon?
I really hate to say it but I need a lady's room.

1983

Poem

The angel kissed my alphabet,
it tingled like a cobweb in starlight.
A few letters detached themselves
and drifted in shadows, a loneliness
they carry like infinitesimal coffins
on their heads.

She kisses my alphabet
and a door opens: blackbirds roosting
on far ridges. A windowpeeper
under an umbrella watches
a funeral service. Blinkered horses
drum the cobblestones.

She kisses: Plunderers gather
in a lackluster ballroom
to display their booty. Mice

6. After the assassination of President John F. Kennedy, in 1963, witnesses said that shots were fired from a "grassy knoll," a phrase that became associated with various conspiracy theories about the murder.

testify against one another
in dank rodent courtrooms.

The angel kisses my alphabet,
she squeezes and bites,
and the last lights flutter,
and the violins are demented.
Moisture spreads across my pillow,
a chunk of quartz thirsts
to abandon my brain trust.

1990

Where Babies Come From

Many are from the Maldives,[7]
southwest of India, and must begin
collecting shells almost immediately.
The larger ones may prefer coconuts.
Survivors move from island to island
hopping over one another and never
looking back. After the typhoons
have had their pick, and the birds of prey
have finished with theirs, the remaining few
must build boats, and in this, of course,
they can have no experience, they build
their boats of palm leaves and vines.
Once the work is completed, they lie down,
thoroughly exhausted and confused,
and a huge wave washes them out to sea.
And that is the last they see of one another.
In their dreams Mama and Papa
are standing on the shore
for what seems like an eternity,
and it is almost always the wrong shore.

1997

7. Nation of islands in the Indian Ocean.

Eavan Boland
b. 1944

The great puzzle of Eavan Boland's career has been how to embrace Irish identity while rejecting certain male-centered assumptions that have long dominated Irish literary culture. For Boland, as a young woman writer, the frozen, mythical images of the Irish nation as an idealized woman—Mother Ireland, Dark Rosaleen, Cathleen Ni Houlihan—were inhibiting and insufficient. While her early verse reflects W. B. Yeats's strong influence, Boland came to decry the inadequacy of what she called "the Mimic Muse" of Irish tradition, charging that it falsified women's lives and prettified bloodshed in service to the nation. Such poetry was insensitive to the "human truths of survival and humiliation" (*A Kind of Scar*), deaf to "The scream of beaten women, / The crime of babies battered" ("Tirade for the Mimic Muse"). Irish poetry had to break with rhetorical cosmetics and masculinist iconography if it was to recover Irish women's historical experiences, including domestic labor, motherhood, famine, mortal fever, prostitution, and emigration.

Yet to slough off the encumbrances of Irish aesthetics, Boland ironically had to deploy other aesthetic strategies, including some inherited from Yeats, James Joyce, and other Irish men. Boland's declarations of freedom from the past recall Yeats's narratives of self-remaking: she promises to descend down poetic ladders into what Yeats calls the "foul rag and bone shop of the heart" ("The Circus Animals' Desertion"), to surrender the embroidery of old mythologies and walk "naked" (a word shared by Yeats's "A Coat" and Boland's "Tirade for the Mimic Muse"). At times, Boland intimates an awareness that her narratives of liberation are inevitably bound up with the Irish poetry from which she seeks liberation. "I won't go back to it," she proclaims at the start of "Mise Eire," willing her independence from traditional Irish poetry; but she later concedes the inevitability of going back when she repeats, "No. I won't go back."

Boland's break with the Irish male tradition also required an affiliation with an alternative tradition—in particular, that of American women's confessional verse. In the writing of Sylvia Plath and Adrienne Rich, Boland—caught up in the 1970s women's movement in Ireland—discovered powerful assertions of female rage and desire, as well as acid, self-mocking candor and explorations of a specifically female experience of the body. Boland's harrowing dramatic monologue "Anorexic," with its hypnotic repetitions of "I," echoes Plath's "Lady Lazarus" ("I may be skin and bone" becomes "I am skin and bone"). Her attempts to identify herself with a collective female experience, as represented at the end of "Mise Eire" by a garrisoned prostitute and an Irish emigrant holding a half-dead baby, are indebted to Rich's poetry. Boland's efforts to merge the personal with broader female history began with the collections *In Her Own Image* (1980) and *Night Feed* (1982), when she broke with her earlier, more formal, less gender-specific poetry.

In Boland's most striking poetry, form mirrors content. The body of the poem "Anorexic," for example—with its clipped, often end-stopped lines—is desiccated. Similarly, the winding syntax, obsessive anaphora, and paratactic connections of "Fever" create a linguistic fever, in Boland's gripping lament for a grandmother and others who died in a fever ward. In poems such as "Fond Memory," the long line serves Boland's retrospective meditation.

Boland was born on September 24, 1944, in Dublin. Her acute sensitivity to language owes something to her experience of growing up in between varieties of the English language. As recalled in "Fond Memory" and other poems, she was displaced as a six-year-old from Ireland to London, and then to New York, before finally returning to Ireland in adolescence. She attended convent schools in these various locations; her father was Ireland's ambassador to England and then the United Nations, her mother a painter. Educated at Trinity College, Dublin, Boland returned to teach there and has also taught at University College, the University of Iowa, and Stanford University.

Anorexic

Flesh is heretic.
My body is a witch.
I am burning it.

Yes I am torching
her curves and paps and wiles.
They scorch in my self-denials.

How she meshed my head
in the half-truths
of her fevers till I renounced
milk and honey
and the taste of lunch.

I vomited
her hungers.
Now the bitch is burning.

I am starved and curveless.
I am skin and bone.
She has learned her lesson.

Thin as a rib
I turn in sleep.
My dreams probe

a claustrophobia
a sensuous enclosure.
How warm it was and wide

once by a warm drum,
once by the song of his breath
and in his sleeping side.

Only a little more,
only a few more days
sinless, foodless.

I will slip
back into him again
as if I have never been away.

Caged so
I will grow
angular and holy

past pain
keeping his heart
such company

as will make me forget
in a small space
the fall

into forked dark,
into python needs
heaving to hips and breasts
and lips and heat
and sweat and fat and greed.

1980

From DOMESTIC INTERIOR

1. Night Feed

This is dawn.
Believe me
This is your season, little daughter.
The moment daisies open,
The hour mercurial rainwater
Makes a mirror for sparrows.
It's time we drowned our sorrows.

I tiptoe in.
I lift you up
Wriggling
In your rosy, zipped sleeper.
Yes, this is the hour
For the early bird and me
When finder is keeper.

I crook the bottle.
How you suckle!
This is the best I can be,
Housewife
To this nursery
Where you hold on,
Dear life.

A silt of milk.
The last suck.
And now your eyes are open,
Birth-colored and offended.
Earth wakes.
You go back to sleep.
The feed is ended.

Worms turn.
Stars go in.
Even the moon is losing face.
Poplars stilt for dawn
And we begin
The long fall from grace.
I tuck you in.

1982

Mise Eire[1]

I won't go back to it—

my nation displaced
into old dactyls,[2]
oaths made
by the animal tallows
of the candle—

land of the Gulf Stream,
the small farm,
the scalded memory,
the songs
that bandage up the history,
the words
that make a rhythm of the crime

where time is time past.
A palsy of regrets.
No. I won't go back.
My roots are brutal:

I am the woman—
a sloven's mix
of silk at the wrists,
a sort of dove-strut
in the precincts of the garrison—

who practices
the quick frictions,
the rictus of delight
and gets cambric[3] for it,
rice-colored silks.

I am the woman
in the gansy-coat[4]

1. I am Ireland (Irish Gaelic); the title of an earlier poem by Irish nationalist Pádraic Pearse (1879–1916) that continues a long tradition of personifying Ireland as a woman.

2. Poetic feet of one stressed syllable followed by two unstressed.

3. Fine linen fabric. *Rictus:* gaping mouth.

4. Woolen sweater.

on board the *Mary Belle*,
in the huddling cold,

holding her half-dead baby to her
as the wind shifts East
and North over the dirty
water of the wharf

mingling the immigrant
guttural with the vowels
of homesickness who neither
knows nor cares that

a new language
is a kind of scar
and heals after a while
into a passable imitation
of what went before.

1987

Fever

is what remained or what they thought
remained after the ague and the sweats
were over and the shock of wild flowers
at the bedside had been taken away;

is what they tried to shake out of
the crush and dimple of cotton,
the shy dust of a bridal skirt;
is what they beat, lashed, hurt like

flesh as if it were a lack of virtue
in a young girl sobbing her heart out
in a small town for having been seen
kissing by the river; is what they burned

alive in their own back gardens
as if it were a witch and not the full-
length winter gaberdine and breathed again
when the fires went out in charred dew.

My grandmother died in a fever ward,
younger than I am and far from
the sweet chills of a Louth[5] spring—
its sprigged light and its wild flowers—

5. County on the east coast of Ireland.

with five orphan daughters to her name.
Names, shadows, visitations, hints
and a half-sense of half-lives remain.
And nothing else, nothing more unless

I re-construct the soaked-through midnights;
vigils; the histories I never learned
to predict the lyric of; and re-construct
risk; as if silence could become rage,

as if what we lost is a contagion
that breaks out in what cannot be
shaken out from words or beaten out
from meaning and survives to weaken

what is given, what is certain
and burns away everything but this
exact moment of delirium when
someone cries out someone's name.

1987

The Women

This is the hour I love: the in-between,
neither here-nor-there hour of evening.
The air is tea-colored in the garden.
The briar rose is spilled crepe-de-Chine.[6]

This is the time I do my work best,
going up the stairs in two minds,
in two worlds, carrying cloth or glass,
leaving something behind, bringing
something with me I should have left behind.

The hour of change, of metamorphosis,
of shape-shifting instabilities.
My time of sixth sense and second sight
when in the words I choose, the lines I write,
they rise like visions and appear to me:

women of work, of leisure, of the night,
in stove-colored silks, in lace, in nothing,
with crewel needles, with books, with wide open legs

who fled the hot breath of the god pursuing,
who ran from the split hoof and the thick lips
and fell and grieved and healed into myth,

6. Fine silk.

into me in the evening at my desk
testing the water with a sweet quartet,
the physical force of a dissonance—

the fission of music into syllabic heat—
and getting sick of it and standing up
and going downstairs in the last brightness

into a landscape without emphasis,
light, linear, precisely planned,
a hemisphere of tiered, aired cotton,

a hot terrain of linen from the iron,
folded in and over, stacked high,
neatened flat, stoving heat and white.

1987

Fond Memory

It was a school where all the children wore darned worsted;[7]
where they cried—or almost all—when the Reverend Mother
announced at lunch-time that the King[8] had died

peacefully in his sleep. I dressed in wool as well,
ate rationed food, played English games and learned
how wise the Magna Carta was, how hard the Hanoverians[9]

had tried, the measure and complexity of verse,
the hum and score of the whole orchestra.
At three-o-clock I caught two buses home

where sometimes in the late afternoon
at a piano pushed into a corner of the playroom
my father would sit down and play the slow

lilts of Tom Moore[1] while I stood there trying
not to weep at the cigarette smoke stinging up
from between his fingers and—as much as I could think—

I thought this is my country, was, will be again,
this upward-straining song made to be
our safe inventory of pain. And I was wrong.

1987

7. Woolen fabric.
8. King George VI of the United Kingdom died in 1952. Boland's father was a diplomat, and she spent much of her childhood in London.
9. Family of English monarchs who controlled the throne from 1714 to 1901. *Magna Carta:* charter of English liberties granted by King John in 1215.
1. Irish poet and singer (1779–1852).

The Pomegranate

The only legend I have ever loved is
The story of a daughter lost in hell.
And found and rescued there.
Love and blackmail are the gist of it.
Ceres and Persephone[2] the names.
And the best thing about the legend is
I can enter it anywhere. And have.
As a child in exile in
A city of fogs and strange consonants,
I read it first and at first I was
An exiled child in the crackling dusk of
The underworld, the stars blighted. Later
I walked out in a summer twilight
Searching for my daughter at bedtime.
When she came running I was ready
To make any bargain to keep her.
I carried her back past whitebeams.
And wasps and honey-scented buddleias.[3]
But I was Ceres then and I knew
Winter was in store for every leaf
On every tree on that road.
Was inescapable for each one we passed.
And for me.
It is winter
And the stars are hidden.
I climb the stairs and stand where I can see
My child asleep beside her teen magazines,
Her can of Coke, her plate of uncut fruit.
The pomegranate! How did I forget it?
She could have come home and been safe
And ended the story and all
Our heartbroken searching but she reached
Out a hand and plucked a pomegranate.
She put out her hand and pulled down
The French sound for apple and
The noise of stone and the proof
That even in the place of death,
At the heart of legend, in the midst
Of rocks full of unshed tears
Ready to be diamonds by the time
The story was told, a child can be
Hungry. I could warn her. There is still a chance.
The rain is cold. The road is flint-coloured.
The suburb has cars and cable television.

2. In Greek myth, Persephone, the daughter of Zeus and Demeter (Roman, Ceres) is abducted by Hades and taken to the underworld. Although Hades is commanded to set her free, she is condemned to spend a portion of each year with him after eating a pomegranate seed.

3. Like whitebeams, flowering trees.

The veiled stars are above ground.
It is another world. But what else
Can a mother give her daughter but such
Beautiful rifts in time?
If I defer the grief I will diminish the gift.
The legend must be hers as well as mine.
She will enter it. As I have.
She will wake up. She will hold
The papery, flushed skin in her hand.
And to her lips. I will say nothing.

1994

Craig Raine
b. 1944

In the late 1970s, Craig Raine began his literary career as one of the postwar English poets attempting a radical reconsideration of poetic subjects and attitudes. At first, his verse appears opaque and riddling, but gradually, as one reads him, his method becomes clearer. His strange images and metaphors let us see our lives in a new way, by a process that the Russian critic Victor Shklovsky calls "defamiliarization." Raine made this especially clear by the title poem of his second book, "A Martian Sends a Postcard Home." He describes this world as if from outer space. The result is a surrealistic surface. A number of poets—James Fenton and Christopher Reid, for example—flocked to Raine's banner and were promptly labeled "the Martian school." As James Fenton said, Raine "taught us to become strangers in our familiar world, to release the faculty of perception and allow it to graze at liberty in the field of experience" (quoted in Anthony Thwaite, *Poetry Today,* 1985).

Though Raine has been criticized for merely heaping up weird data, his work is tightly organized. Even the Martian postcard seems to proceed logically from external subjects (books, mist, rain) to internal ("everyone's pain has a different smell"). In later volumes, Raine has written not as someone from outer space, but as father, lover, office worker. The poet amuses and is amused by the sight of "the pagoda / of dirty dinner plates" ("A Free Translation") and is delighted by the way children see the world. One poem wittily portrays the city in metaphors of the country ("City Gent"). Raine's pleasure in unexpected juxtapositions, in a comedy of displacement, in the recognition of everyday absurdity, is contagious.

Raine was born on December 3, 1944, in Bishop Auckland, County Durham, England. He was educated at Oxford University, later returning as lecturer (1971–79) and, since 1991, as fellow. He also served in an editorial capacity on several magazines. From 1981 to 1991, he occupied a post formerly held by T. S. Eliot, as poetry editor at the publishing house of Faber & Faber Ltd. He has written essays and an opera libretto, and he applied Martian principles to epic poetry in *History: The Home Movie* (1994).

The Onion, Memory

Divorced, but friends again at last,
we walk old ground together
in bright blue uncomplicated weather.
We laugh and pause
to hack to bits these tiny dinosaurs,
prehistoric, crenellated, cast
between the tractor ruts in mud.

On the green, a junior Douglas Fairbanks,[1]
swinging on the chestnut's unlit chandelier,
defies the corporation spears—
a single rank around the bole,[2]
rusty with blood.
Green, tacky phalluses curve up, romance.
A gust—the old flag blazes on its pole.

In the village bakery
the pasty babies pass
from milky slump to crusty cadaver,
from crib to coffin—without palaver.
All's over in a flash,
too silently . . .

Tonight the arum lilies fold
back napkins monogrammed in gold,
crisp and laundered fresh.
Those crustaceous gladioli, on the sly,
reveal the crimson flower-flesh
inside their emerald armour plate.
The uncooked herrings blink a tearful eye.
The candles palpitate.
The Oistrakhs bow and scrape
in evening dress, on Emi-tape.[3]

Outside the trees are bending over backwards
to please the wind : the shining sword
grass flattens on its belly.
The white-thorn's frillies[4] offer no resistance.
In the fridge, a heart-shaped jelly
strives to keep a sense of balance.

I slice up the onions. You sew up a dress.
This is the quiet echo—flesh—
white muscle on white muscle,

1. American actor (1883–1939), famous for swashbuckling daredevil movie roles of the 1920s and 1930s. *Crenellated:* having battlements.
2. Tree trunk. *Corporation spears:* spiked fence put up by the town corporation.
3. A popular British brand of audiotape. David Oistrakh (1908–1974) and his son Igor (b. 1931), celebrated Russian violinists.
4. Frilled undergarments (British colloquialism).

intimately folded skin,
finished with a satin rustle.
One button only to undo, sewn up with shabby thread.
It is the onion, memory,
that makes me cry.

Because there's everything and nothing to be said,
the clock with hands held up before its face,
stammers softly on, trying to complete a phrase—
while we, together and apart,
repeat unfinished gestures got by heart.

And afterwards, I blunder with the washing on the line—
headless torsos, faceless lovers, friends of mine.

1978

A Martian Sends a Postcard Home

Caxtons[5] are mechanical birds with many wings
and some are treasured for their markings—

they cause the eyes to melt
or the body to shriek without pain.[6]

I have never seen one fly, but
sometimes they perch on the hand.

Mist is when the sky is tired of flight
and rests its soft machine on ground:

then the world is dim and bookish
like engravings under tissue paper.

Rain is when the earth is television.
It has the property of making colours darker.

Model T[7] is a room with the lock inside—
a key is turned to free the world

for movement, so quick there is a film
to watch for anything missed.

But time is tied to the wrist
or kept in a box, ticking with impatience.

In homes, a haunted apparatus sleeps,
that snores when you pick it up.

5. That is, books, which William Caxton (c. 1422–1491) was the first to print in English.
6. The Martian does not know the words for cry or laugh.
7. An old-fashioned type of automobile; the "key" (next line) is the ignition key.

If the ghost cries, they carry it
to their lips and soothe it to sleep

with sounds. And yet, they wake it up
deliberately, by tickling with a finger.

Only the young are allowed to suffer
openly. Adults go to a punishment room

with water but nothing to eat.
They lock the door and suffer the noises

alone. No one is exempt
and everyone's pain has a different smell.

At night, when all the colours die,
they hide in pairs

and read about themselves—
in colour, with their eyelids shut.

1979

NORMAN DUBIE
b. 1945

In a period when narrative verse about specific times and places tends to be rare, Norman Dubie is known for evoking historical and biographical scenes, though he also composes lyric poems. When he writes about a personage such as Czar Nicholas II or Madame Blavatsky, Dubie comments through a reflective observer or a persona, yet he presents his subjects as if he were intimately involved in them all. Many of his lyric poems concern death and grief: "Any simple loss," he remarks, "is like the loss of all of us" ("Sun and Moon Flowers: Paul Klee, 1879–1940").

Dubie has a keen eye for detail, and his diction renders realistic images—an old Studebaker, a thermos, a box of pills—startlingly clear and yet strange. Dubie does not, however, offer slices of externality, for everything is on the verge of being internalized: "Just beyond two hills in the winter air, and / Somewhere inside the mind" ("The City of the Olesha Fruit"). In "The Funeral," the speaker remembers minnows nibbling at the toes of an aunt the year before, and after her death, this image becomes prescient: "Uncle Peter, in a low voice, said / The cancer ate her like horse piss eats deep snow." Many poems are built around vivid contrasts, the beautiful and the ugly bizarrely mingling. In a poem about Queen Elizabeth I, images of violence (the bloody carnage of bearbaiting and a beheading) and of seeming purity (white dress, snow, and bone) converge and clash in disturbing combinations. Despite his use of historical materials, Dubie's poetry is oblique, between realism and surrealism. It is like a series of parables in which the meaning must be kept implicit and somewhat indistinct.

Dubie was born on April 10, 1945, in Barre, Vermont. He was educated at Goddard College, in Vermont (B.A., 1969), and the University of Iowa (M.F.A., 1971). Since 1975, he has taught at Arizona State University.

Elizabeth's War with the Christmas Bear

The bears are kept by hundreds within fences, are fed cracked
Eggs; the weakest are
Slaughtered and fed to the others after being scented
With the blood of deer brought to the pastures by Elizabeth's
Men—the blood spills from deep pails with bottoms of slate.

The balding Queen[1] had bear gardens in London and in the country.
The bear is baited:[2] the nostrils
Are blown full with pepper, the Irish wolf dogs
Are starved, then, emptied, made crazy with fermented barley:

And the bear's hind leg is chained to a stake, the bear
Is blinded and whipped, kneeling in his own blood and slaver, he is
Almost instantly worried by the dogs. At the very moment that
Elizabeth took Essex's head,[3] a giant brown bear
Stood in the gardens with dogs hanging from his fur . . .
He took away the sun, took
A wolfhound in his mouth, and tossed it into
The white lap of Elizabeth I—arrows and staves[4] rained

On his chest, and standing, he, then, stood even taller, seeing
Into the Queen's private boxes—he grinned
Into her battered eggshell face.
Another volley of arrows and poles, and opening his mouth
He showered
Blood all over Elizabeth and her Privy Council.[5]

The next evening, a cool evening, the Queen demanded
13 bears and the justice of 113 dogs: She slept

All that Sunday night and much of the next morning.
Some said she was guilty of *this* and *that*.
The Protestant Queen gave the defeated bear
A grave in a Catholic cemetery. The marker said:
Peter, a Solstice Bear, a gift of the Tsarevitch[6] to Elizabeth.

After a long winter she had the grave opened. The bear's skeleton
Was cleared with lye, she placed it at her bedside,
Put a candle inside behind the sockets of the eyes, and, then
She spoke to it:

You were a Christmas bear—behind your eyes
I see the walls of a snow cave where you are a cub still smelling
Of your mother's blood which has dried in your hair; you have

1. Queen Elizabeth I (1553–1603).
2. Tied to a stake and attacked by dogs, as described below. Bearbaiting was a popular spectator sport in Elizabethan England.
3. In 1601, the earl of Essex, who had earlier been Elizabeth's favorite, was executed for treason.
4. Narrow strips of wood.
5. That is, her advisory council.
6. The tsar's (or czar's) son. *Solstice:* in celebration of the winter solstice, December 22.

Troubled a Queen who was afraid
When seated in *shade* which, standing,
You had created! A Queen who often wakes with a dream
Of you at night—
Now, you'll stand by my bed in your long white bones; alone, you
Will frighten away at night all visions of bear, and all day
You will be in this cold room—your constant grin,
You'll stand in the long, white prodigy of your bones, and you are,

Every inch of you, a terrible vision, not bear, but virgin![7]

1979

The Funeral

It felt like the zero in brook ice.
She was my youngest aunt, the summer before
We had stood naked
While she stiffened and giggled, letting the minnows
Nibble at her toes. I was almost four—
That evening she took me
To the springhouse where on the scoured planks
There were rows of butter in small bricks, a mold
Like ermine on the cheese,
And cut onions to rinse the air
Of the black, sickly-sweet meats of rotting pecans.

She said butter was colored with marigolds
Plucked down by the marsh
With its tall grass and miner's-candles.
We once carried the offal's pail[8] beyond the barn
To where the fox could be caught in meditation.
Her bed linen smelled of camphor. We went

In late March for her burial. I heard the men talk.
I saw the minnows nibble at her toe.
And Uncle Peter, in a low voice, said
The cancer ate her like horse piss eats deep snow.

1986

Last Poem, Snow Tree

after Rafael Alberti[9]

Call a ruined shoe, the sandal—
White, the cow's blood
Forever drained from it.

7. Elizabeth I was known as the Virgin Queen because she never married.

8. Pail containing animal viscera after butchering.
9. Spanish poet and painter (1902–1999).

Where are the happy integers of inventory?

Call the one sandal, abstract and nostalgic:
Glove of the first baseman, it folds like night

Or night's daring bird feeding on amber insects.

The circulations of blood in the snow tree
Remind me of the woman we lost.
The sea rises behind us, at our backs.
Mr. Enos Slaughter[1] didn't die

In Nebraska, of drink. In the snow tree a sick,
Whiter angel picks its teeth.
Errors of snow in water, our names . . .
You were wrong, Rafael. The stars,
Violent at their tea,

Were the last children to learn the arithmetic
Of memory.

2001

1. Baseball player (b. 1916).

Yusef Komunyakaa
b. 1947

Yuesf Komunyakaa wrote the most acclaimed book of American poetry about the Vietnam War, *Dien Cai Dau* (1988), the title meaning "crazy" in Vietnamese. Having served in Vietnam in 1969–70 as a reporter for and editor of the military newspaper *The Southern Cross*, Komunyakaa, decorated with the Bronze Star, allowed the war to settle in memory for fourteen years. At this distance, he could distill the complexities of America's most controversial war—American indifference and empathy for the Vietnamese, cross-racial tension and camaraderie between whites and African Americans. Like Wilfred Owen and other modern war poets, Komunyakaa is attentive to inner experience and to shared political history. "My belief is that you have to have both," he remarked in an interview, "the odyssey outward as well as inward" (*Callaloo*, 1990).

Like the speaker who peers through a nightscope at eerily ghostlike figures in "Starlight Scope Myopia," Komunyakaa sees the war as distant and yet insistently present in the minds of the war's participants and observers. Touching a name carved on the Vietnam Veterans Memorial triggers a sudden memory in "Facing It": "I see the booby trap's white flash." On the wall's mirrorlike surface, memory bumps up against sight, the dead invade the present, and the self is interpenetrated by the surrounding world. The poem, like the wall, crosses and blurs lines of historical, racial, and political division. Time and space are similarly layered in Komunyakaa's poems inspired by jazz, such as "February in Sydney," in which the past erupts from beneath the protective sheen of the present.

Komunyakaa's poetry also cuts across different levels of diction, from biblical idiom to journalistic reportage, African American vernacular to high-art lyricism. Komunyakaa's remark in *Callaloo* about Melvin Tolson applies with equal force to his own work: "he brings together the street as well as the highly literary into a single poetic context in ways where the two don't even seem to exhibit division—it's all one and the same." Syncopating short, jagged lines, enjambing and coiling syntax, building musical resonances through assonance and alliteration, Komunyakaa crafts poems that have surprisingly quick turns of sound and sense. He mimics the sudden riffs, twists, and mannered elaborations of jazz improvisation, in the long tradition of African American poets who have mined jazz and the blues for poetry, from Langston Hughes and Sterling Brown to Gwendolyn Brooks and Robert Hayden, Amiri Baraka and Michael S. Harper.

Komunyakaa was born James Willie Brown Jr., on April 29, 1947, in Bogalusa, Louisiana, not far from New Orleans. He changed his name for religious reasons, adopting Komunyakaa from a grandfather smuggled, according to family legend, on a banana boat from Trinidad. His father was an illiterate carpenter, remembered with anger and affection in "My Father's Love Letters." After returning from Vietnam, Komunyakaa received his B.A. from the University of Colorado in 1975, his M.A. from Colorado State University in 1979, and his M.F.A. from the University of California, Irvine, in 1980. He has coedited anthologies of "jazz poetry" (1991, 1996) and published a volume of essays and interviews. He won the Pulitzer Prize in 1994 for *Neon Vernacular: New and Selected Poems* and, in 2001, published *Pleasure Dome: New and Collected Poems*. He teaches at Princeton University.

Starlight Scope Myopia[1]

Gray-blue shadows lift
shadows onto an oxcart.

Making night work for us,
the starlight scope brings
men into killing range.

The river under Vi Bridge
takes the heart away

like the Water God
riding his dragon.
Smoke-colored

Viet Cong[2]
move under our eyelids,

lords over loneliness
winding like coral vine through
sandalwood & lotus,

1. Nearsightedness. *Starlight scope:* electrical instrument that uses light from the night sky to improve nocturnal vision.
2. Shortened name of the Viet Nam Cong San, the Communist military forces supported by North Vietnam against South Vietnam and the United States in the Vietnam War (1955–75).

inside our lowered heads
years after this scene

ends. The brain closes
down. What looks like
one step into the trees,

they're lifting crates of ammo
& sacks of rice, swaying

under their shared weight.
Caught in the infrared,
what are they saying?

Are they talking about women
or calling the Americans

beaucoup dien cai dau?[3]
One of them is laughing.
You want to place a finger

to his lips & say "shhhh."
You try reading ghost talk

on their lips. They say
"up-up we go," lifting as one.
This one, old, bowlegged,

you feel you could reach out
& take him into your arms. You

peer down the sights of your M-16,
seeing the full moon
loaded on an oxcart.

1988

Tu Do Street[4]

Music divides the evening.
I close my eyes & can see
men drawing lines in the dust.
American pushes through the membrane
of mist & smoke, & I'm a small boy
again in Bogalusa: *White Only*
signs & Hank Snow.[5] But tonight

3. Very crazy. The phrase, used often to describe the American soldiers, is a combination of Vietnamese (*dien cai dau*) and French (*beaucoup*). France had a long colonial presence in Vietnam until 1954.
4. Street bustling with bars and brothels in Saigon, the capital of South Vietnam and site of the U.S. Army headquarters during the Vietnam War.
5. American country singer (1914–1999). *Bogalusa:* town in Louisiana where Komunyakaa spent his childhood.

I walk into a place where bar girls
fade like tropical birds. When
I order a beer, the mama-san
behind the counter acts as if she
can't understand, while her eyes
skirt each white face, as Hank Williams[6]
calls from the psychedelic jukebox.
We have played Judas[7] where
only machine-gun fire brings us
together. Down the street
black GIs hold to their turf also.
An off-limits sign pulls me
deeper into alleys, as I look
for a softness behind these voices
wounded by their beauty & war.
Back in the bush at Dak To
& Khe Sanh,[8] we fought
the brothers of these women
we now run to hold in our arms.
There's more than a nation
inside us, as black & white
soldiers touch the same lovers
minutes apart, tasting
each other's breath,
without knowing these rooms
run into each other like tunnels
leading to the underworld.

1988

Facing It

My black face fades,
hiding inside the black granite.
I said I wouldn't,
dammit: No tears.
I'm stone. I'm flesh.
My clouded reflection eyes me
like a bird of prey, the profile of night
slanted against morning. I turn
this way—the stone lets me go.
I turn that way—I'm inside
the Vietnam Veterans Memorial
again, depending on the light
to make a difference.
I go down the 58,022 names,
half-expecting to find

6. American country singer and composer (1923–1953).
7. One of the twelve disciples, Judas betrayed Jesus for thirty pieces of silver.
8. Site of U.S. Marine base in South Vietnam kept under siege by the North Vietnamese army for several months in 1968. *Dak To:* city in northwest South Vietnam that, in 1967, was the site of one of the war's most violent battles.

my own in letters like smoke.
I touch the name Andrew Johnson;
I see the booby trap's white flash.
Names shimmer on a woman's blouse
but when she walks away
the names stay on the wall.
Brushstrokes flash, a red bird's
wings cutting across my stare.
The sky. A plane in the sky.
A white vet's image floats
closer to me, then his pale eyes
look through mine. I'm a window.
He's lost his right arm
inside the stone. In the black mirror
a woman's trying to erase names:
No, she's brushing a boy's hair.

1988

February in Sydney

Dexter Gordon's tenor sax
plays "April in Paris"
inside my head all the way back
on the bus from Double Bay.
Round Midnight,[9] the '50s,
cool cobblestone streets
resound footsteps of Bebop[1]
musicians with whiskey-laced voices
from a boundless dream in French.
Bud, Prez, Webster, & The Hawk,[2]
their names run together riffs.
Painful gods jive talk through
bloodstained reeds & shiny brass
where music is an anesthetic.
Unreadable faces from the human void
float like torn pages across the bus
windows. An old anger drips into my throat,
& I try thinking something good,
letting the precious bad
settle to the salty bottom.
Another scene keeps repeating itself:
I emerge from the dark theatre,

9. Bertrand Tavernier's 1986 movie about expatriate jazz musicians in 1950s Paris, starring jazz saxophonist Dexter Gordon (1923–1990) and named after a composition by jazz pianist Thelonious Monk (1917–1982). *"April in Paris"*: jazz standard. *Double Bay*: neighborhood in Sydney, Australia.

1. Style of modern jazz developed in the 1940s and 1950s, characterized by harmonic exploration and fast-paced flurries of notes drawn from the chromatic scale.

2. *'Round Midnight* was loosely based on the tragic lives of pianist Bud Powell (1924–1966) and saxophonist Lester "Prez" Young (1909–1959), who worked in Europe late in their careers, like influential saxophonists Ben Webster (1909–1973) and Coleman "The Hawk" Hawkins (1904–1969).

passing a woman who grabs her red purse
& hugs it to her like a heart attack.
Tremolo.[3] Dexter comes back to rest
behind my eyelids. A loneliness
lingers like a silver needle
under my black skin,
as I try to feel how it is
to scream for help through a horn.

1989

My Father's Love Letters

On Fridays he'd open a can of Jax[4]
After coming home from the mill,
& ask me to write a letter to my mother
Who sent postcards of desert flowers
Taller than men. He would beg,
Promising to never beat her
Again. Somehow I was happy
She had gone, & sometimes wanted
To slip in a reminder, how Mary Lou
Williams' "Polka Dots & Moonbeams"[5]
Never made the swelling go down.
His carpenter's apron always bulged
With old nails, a claw hammer
Looped at his side & extension cords
Coiled around his feet.
Words rolled from under the pressure
Of my ballpoint: Love,
Baby, Honey, Please.
We sat in the quiet brutality
Of voltage meters & pipe threaders,
Lost between sentences . . .
The gleam of a five-pound wedge
On the concrete floor
Pulled a sunset
Through the doorway of his toolshed.
I wondered if she laughed
& held them over a gas burner.
My father could only sign
His name, but he'd look at blueprints
& say how many bricks
Formed each wall. This man,
Who stole roses & hyacinth
For his yard, would stand there
With eyes closed & fists balled,

3. Rapid alternation between two or more notes.
4. Beer brewed by the Jackson Brewing Company, in New Orleans.
5. Recording by jazz pianist and composer Mary Lou Williams (1910–1981).

Laboring over a simple word, almost
Redeemed by what he tried to say.

1992

Lorna Goodison
b. 1947

Lorna Goodison is one of the most gifted heirs of the pioneering West Indian poets Derek Walcott, Kamau Brathwaite, and fellow Jamaican Louise Bennett, dubbed by her the "mother of the Jamaican language." Born a generation later, Goodison writes poetry that straddles the divide between Creole verse, as exemplified by Bennett's quarrelsome street vendor in "South Parade Peddler," and visionary rhetoric, as in Walcott's "Season of Phantasmal Peace." All such idioms are possible for Goodison, none of them alien. In her poetry, the liquid turns between Standard English and Creole are supple, quick, barely visible. Fluent in different linguistic and rhetorical registers, she interweaves the discourses that a colonial education rigidly segregates.

Goodison, who recalls a colonial childhood in which she "spoke two languages," one at home and one at school, one from the colonizer and one from the colonized, is unassuming in her explanation of her facility in composing code-switching poetry. "Some things I think of in standard English and some in Creole," she explained to an interviewer; she is neither afraid of literary English nor ashamed of Creole and thus refuses to be "contained" by "just one language." Forced to recite Wordsworth's "Daffodils" even though she "had never seen one," she nevertheless credits Wordsworth, along with other British writers, with helping to open her "inward," imaginative eye.

For Goodison, Jamaica's cultural heterogeneity is recorded most obviously in its multifarious place names: "There is everywhere here," she quips in the poem "To Us, All Flowers Are Roses": along with the Ashanti name Accompong and the Amerindian Arawak, "there is Alps and Lapland and Berlin / Armagh, Carrick Fergus, Malvern / Rhine and Calabar, Askenish." Likewise, Goodison's poetry freely embraces a range of cultural and linguistic inheritances, whether European, Caribbean, or African.

Goodison describes her own ancestry as mixed, declaring, "It all belongs to me": "my great grandfather was a man called Aberdeen, who obviously came from Scotland. And my great grandmother came from Guinea, and because they had a mating and produced my grandmother, who looked like an American Indian—I have relatives who look like Egyptians and my son is an African prince—all of it belongs to me" (1988 interview). In some of her poems, Goodison has self-mockingly adopted the persona of the "mulatta," but with an intercultural delight that stands in marked contrast to the inner torment of "mulatto" poems such as Walcott's "A Far Cry from Africa."

Goodison sees her personal history of racial and cultural hybridity as exemplifying a broader experience. Her poems about the genesis of her "family's history," she says of works such as "Guinea Woman," suggest "everybody's family history in the colonial experience, a Jamaican experience." Goodison thinks back through the lives of women in particular, reclaiming aspects of past experience that have traditionally been marginalized, including the lives of Afro-Caribbean slaves and domestic servants. The character portrait is often Goodison's imaginative vehicle for individualizing and reentering history, as in "Annie Pengelly" and "Turn Thanks to Miss Mirry." She denounces specific injustices of Jamaican colonial history—enslavement, rape, torture, incarceration—yet offers a nuanced treatment of, for example, the white mistress of the slave girl Annie

Pengelly, exploring the parallels between racial and gender oppression. Sometimes, she bestows a voice upon a legendary historical figure, such as a great Jamaican Maroon leader and warrior in the poem "Nanny," who surrenders sexual dependency to become mother to a nation. If Goodison's poetry fearlessly crosses boundaries between languages and cultures, some of her poems explore life in the interstices between genders. In "On Becoming a Mermaid," she returns to a Western archetype and imagines the metamorphosis of woman into water nymph, a change that liberates her from sexual boundaries, yet confines her within her own body.

Goodison's poetry engages a rich field of sensual experience. An accomplished painter, she melds colors with taste in poems such as "Hungry Belly Kill Daley." Delighting in what she calls, in the title of a poem, "The Mango of Poetry," she connects the pleasures of art and poetry with the pleasures of food. Her poetry is highly musical in its cadences, sometimes shifting tempo with the speed of jazz improvisation, from staccato to langor to chanted exuberance. Mercurial shifts in voice, person, and diction help sustain the propulsive momentum. In the complex inner life of a poem such as "Bam Chi Chi Lala," disparate aspects of the poet's experience flow together—a cold North American autumn with West Indian hurricanes, monastic prayer with Caribbean superstition, even Mary, Queen of Scots with reggae and Sufism.

Goodison was born on August 1, 1947, in Kingston, Jamaica, to a lower-middle-class family, her father a telephone line worker, her mother a seamstress. Congested city life marked her youth, but trips to the Jamaican countryside fired her imagination. From her schooldays, she names *The Oxford Book of Modern Verse*, edited by W. B. Yeats, and Walcott's *In a Green Night* as formative influences. After school, she studied art both in Jamaica (1967–68) and in New York (1968–69). In Jamaica, she worked as an illustrator, artist, teacher, and cultural administrator. In 1986–87, she was a fellow at the Bunting Institute at Radcliffe College, and since 1991, she has taught creative writing both in the United States, at the University of Michigan, and in Canada, at the University of Toronto. Among other awards, she has won a Commonwealth Poetry Prize (1986) and the Musgrave Gold Medal from the Institute of Jamaica (1999).

On Becoming a Mermaid

Watching the underlife idle by
you think drowning must be easy death
just let go and let the water carry you
away and under
the current pulls your bathing-plaits loose
your hair floats out straightened by the water
your legs close together fuse all the length down
your feet now one broad foot
the toes spread into
a fish-tail, fan-like,
your sex locked under
mother-of-pearl scales
you're a nixie[1] now, a mermaid
a green-tinged fish/fleshed woman/thing
who swims with thrashing movements
and stands upended on the sea floor

1. Water nymph.

breasts full and floating buoyed by the salt
and the space between your arms now always
filled and your sex sealed forever under
mother-of-pearl scale/locks closes finally
on itself like some close-mouthed oyster.

1986

Guinea Woman[2]

Great grandmother
was a guinea woman
wide eyes turning
the corners of her face
could see behind her,
her cheeks dusted with
a fine rash of jet-bead warts
that itched when the rain set up.

Great grandmother's waistline
the span of a headman's hand,
slender and tall like a cane stalk
with a guinea woman's antelope-quick walk
and when she paused,
her gaze would look to sea
her profile fine like some obverse impression
on a guinea coin from royal memory.

It seems her fate was anchored
in the unfathomable sea
for great grandmother caught the eye of a sailor
whose ship sailed without him from Lucea[3] harbor.
Great grandmother's royal scent of
cinnamon and scallions
drew the sailor up the straits of Africa,
the evidence my blue-eyed grandmother
the first Mulatta,
taken into backra's[4] household
and covered with his name.
They forbade great grandmother's
guinea woman presence.
They washed away her scent of
cinnamon and scallions,
controlled the child's antelope walk,
and called her uprisings rebellions.

But, great grandmother,
I see your features blood dark

2. Woman born in Africa.
3. Town on western coast of Jamaica.
4. Master's (Jamaican English). *Mulatta:* a woman with one black parent and one white parent.

appearing
in the children of each new
breeding.
The high yellow brown
is darkening down.
Listen, children,
it's great grandmother's turn.

1986

Nanny[5]

My womb was sealed
with molten wax
of killer bees
for nothing should enter
nothing should leave
the state of perpetual siege
the condition of the warrior.

From then my whole body would quicken
at the birth of every one of my people's children.
I was schooled in the green-giving ways
of the roots and vines
made accomplice to the healing acts
of Chainey root, fever grass & vervain.[6]

My breasts flattened
settled unmoving against my chest
my movements ran equal
to the rhythms of the forest.

I could sense and sift
the footfall of men
from the animals
and smell danger
death's odor
in the wind's shift.

When my eyes rendered
light from the dark
my battle song opened
into a solitaire's moan
I became most knowing
and forever alone.

5. Warrior and Jamaican national hero who helped lead the Maroons, a society of fugitive slaves, in battles against the British in the eighteenth century.
6. Three plants used in Jamaica for their medicinal properties.

And when my training was over
they circled my waist with pumpkin seeds
and dried okra, a traveler's jigida,[7]
and sold me to the traders
all my weapons within me.
I was sent, tell that to history.

When your sorrow obscures the skies
other women like me will rise.

1986

Annie Pengelly

I come to represent the case
of one Annie Pengelly,
maidservant, late of the San Fleming Estate
situated in the westerly parish of Hanover.

Hanover, where that masif
mountain range
assumes the shape of a Dolphin's head
rearing up in the blue expanse overhead
restless white clouds round it foaming.

Those at sea would look up
and behold, mirrored, a seascape in the sky.

It is this need to recreate,
to run 'gainst things, that cause
all this confusion.

The same need that made men
leave one side of the world
to journey in long, mawed ships,
to drogue[8] millions of souls
to a world
that they call the new one
in competition with the original act
the creation of the old one.

So now you are telling me to proceed
and proceed swiftly.
Why have I come here representing Annie?

Well this is the first thing she asked me to say,
that Annie is not even her real name.
A name is the first thing we own in this world.

7. String of beads worn around the waist.
8. That is, drag; from nautical term for hooped canvas bag towed at boat's stern.

We lay claim to a group of sounds
which rise up and down and mark out our space
in the air around us.
We become owners of a harmony of vowels and consonants
singing a specific meaning.

Her real name was given to her
at the pastoral ceremony of her outdooring.[9]
Its outer meaning was, "she who is precious to us."

It had too a hidden part, a kept secret.
A meaning known only to those within
the circle of her family.

For sale Bidderman, one small girl,
one small African girl answering now
to the name of Annie.

Oh Missus my dear, when you write Lady Nugent[1]
to tell her of your splendid birthday
of the ivory moire[2] gown you wore
that you send clear to London for.

You can tell her too how you had built for you
a pair of soft, supple leather riding boots
fashioned from your own last
by George O'Brian Wilson
late of Aberdeen
now Shoemaker and Sadler of Lucea, Hanover[3]
late occupation,
bruk[4] Sailor.

One pair of tortoiseshell combs,
one scrolled silver backed mirror,
one dinner party where they killed
one whole cow
with oaken casks of Madeira wine
to wash it down.

And don't forget, one small African girl,
answering now to the name of Annie.

With all that birthday show of affection
Massa never sleep with missus.
But I am not here to talk about that,
that is backra[5] business.

I am really here just representing Annie Pengelly.

9. Ghanaian naming ceremony in which a newborn is introduced to the community.
1. Wife of George Nugent, lieutenant governor of Jamaica in the early nineteenth century.
2. Textile with a watered or clouded appearance.
3. Lucea is the capital of the parish of Hanover in western Jamaica. *Aberdeen:* seaport in northeast Scotland.
4. Broke (Jamaican English).
5. White people's (Jamaican English).

For Missus began to make Annie
sleep across her feet
come December when northers began to blow.

Northers being the chill wheeling tail end
of the winter breezes
dropping off their cold what lef' in Jamaica
to confuse the transplanted Planter.

Causing them to remember words like "hoarfrost" and "moors"
from a frozen vocabulary they no longer
had use for.

When this false winter breeze would
careen across canefields
Missus would make Annie lie draped,
heaped across her feet
a human blanket
nothing covering her as she gave
her warmth to Missus.

So I come to say that History owes Annie
the brightest woolen blanket.
She is owed too, at least twelve years of sleep
stretched out,
free to assume the stage of sleep
flat on her back,
or profiled like the characters
in an Egyptian frieze.

Most nights though, Missus don't sleep.
And as Annie was subject to Missus will,
Annie was not to sleep as long
as Missus kept her open-eyed vigil.

Sometimes Missus sit up
sipping wine from a cut glass goblet.
Talking, talking.

Sometimes Missus dance and sing
like she was on a stage,
sad cantatrice[6] solo
on a stage performing.

At the end of her performance
she would demand that Annie clap
clap loud and shout "encore."

Encouraged by this she would sing
and dance on,
her half-crazed torch song of rejection.

6. Female opera singer.

Sometimes Annie nod off.
Missus jook[7] her with a pearl-tipped pin.
Sometimes Annie tumble off the chair
felled by sleep.
Missus slap her awake again.
Then in order to keep her alert, awake
she devised the paper torture.

One pile of newspapers
a sharp pair of scissors later,
Annie learned about
the cruel make-work task
that is the *cut-up*
to throw-away of old newspaper.

For if Missus could not sleep
Annie gal you don't sleep that night,
and poor Missus enslaved by love
fighting her servitude with spite.

So I say history owes Annie
thousands of nights
of sleep upon a feather bed.
Soft feathers from the breast of
a free, soaring bird,
one bright blanket,
and her name returned,
she who is precious to us.

Annie Pengelly O.
I say, History owe you.

1995

Turn[8] Thanks to Miss Mirry

Turn thanks to Miss Mirry
ill-tempered domestic helper who hated me.
She said that she had passed through hell bareheaded
and that a whitening ash from hell's furnace

had sifted down upon her and that is why she gray early.
Called me "Nana." Nanny's name I have come to love.
She twisted her surname Henry into Endry
in her railing against the graceless state of her days.

She was the repository of 400 years of resentment
for being uprooted and transplanted, condemned
to being a stranger on this side of a world
where most words would not obey her tongue.

7. Pricked (Jamaican English).

8. Return.

She said that she came from "Ullava"
in the parallel universe of Old Harbor.
She could not read or write a word in English
but took every vowel and consonant of it

and rung it around, like the articulated neck
of our Sunday dinner sacrificial fowl.
In her anger she stabbed at English, walked it out,
abandoned it in favor of a long kiss teeth,

a furious fanning of her shift tail, a series of hawks
at the back of her throat, a long extended elastic sigh,
a severing cut eye, or a melancholy wordless moaning
as she squatted over her wooden washtub soaping

our dirty clothes with a brown wedge of hard key soap.
To Miss Mirry who subverted the English language
calling Barbara, Baba; my father, Tata; who desiled her mind
that I was boofuttoo, a baffan and too rampify.[9]

Who said pussbrukokonatinnadalikklegalnanayeye.[1]
Miss Mirry versus English against the west
once assured me that for every sickness
there exists a cure growing in the bush.

I thank her for giving me a bath in her washtub
which she had filled with water heated
in a kerosene tin and in it she had strewed
the fringed leaves of the emancipation tamarind.[2]

I turn thanks for the calming bath
that she gave to me which quelled effectively
the red itching measles prickling my skin.
As she sluiced the astringent waters over me

she was speak-singing in a language
familiar to her tongue which rose unfettered
up and down in tumbling cadences, ululations
in time with the swift sopping motion of her hands,

becoming her true self
in that ritual bathing, that song.
Turn thanks now to Miss Mirry
African bush healing woman.

1999

9. I was awkward, a clumsy and useless person, and too playful (Jamaican English; *-ify:* Creole suffix akin to *-ied,* as in *prettified*).
1. Jamaican proverb meaning "you're disrespectful" (the cat has broken a coconut in that little girl Nana's eye).
2. Tree with an acidic fruit.

Hungry Belly Kill Daley[3]

I fancied that I could paint
a still life with food,
and my rendering of victuals
would be so good
that I could reach into the canvas
and eat and fill my belly.

Cadmium yellow could spread
butter impasto[4] over white lead
or a brown loaf baked of sienna.
Scarlet and vermilion, the wine
would flow, otaheiti apple
is a deep, dark, rose madder.[5]

If I could fill my hungry belly
with painted wine and bread
but they shock my visions from my head
at Bellevue, where Louis Q. Bowerbank[6]
sends madmen or black men mad enough
to think that we could be artists, in 1940.

1999

Bam Chi Chi Lala[7]

It is fall again, October rains
and red trees signal you
are entering change season.
Your guinea blood courses fierce
and you think to drink gold leaf[8]
in a camel bid to store sun.
See how your small boy
has become a fine man.

You cross the street to bless brides
and cross yourself as ambulances shriek by.
This morning you woke at five and kept
company with the monk of Gethsemane,[9]

3. Henry Daley (1918?–1950?), talented but ill-fated Jamaican painter of symbolic self-portraits and trees. Starving, suffering from tuberculosis, he died at Kingston Public Hospital. *Hungry Belly:* personified companion of Henry Daley in an elegy by Jamaican poet Philip Sherlock, "Trees His Testament: A Goodbye for Daley" (1957).
4. Thick application of paint.
5. Shade of deep red paint. *Otaheiti apple:* Jamaican fruit.
6. Chief of the Kingston magistry in the nineteenth century. His statue stands inside Kingston's Bellevue hospital, a mental asylum. Bowerbank helped sentence Jamaican popular leader George William Gordon to death for the political agitation he organized in his campaign for the rights of poverty-stricken black Jamaicans.
7. Refrain of a Jamaican folk song.
8. Extremely thin sheet of gold used to gild books, paintings, and so on. *Guinea:* African.
9. Thomas Merton (1915–1968), poet and Trappist monk.

lauds and aubades. In Hanover[1] your people's
river swells because the hurricanes
have wept and flashed their epileptic
selves across the West Indies.

How do wild spirits gain entrance
into humans?
Do they make their way through body
orifices as we sleep?
If that is so then it is best to say
the sealing prayer before slumber.
"Lord, please keep all demons away
from the nine gates of my body."

Or better still, forsake shuteye,
join the night watch and patrol
the border country between
the worlds of sleep and wake.

Do small deeds of love for the world.
Remove traps and tripping stones
set by the wicked for the weak.
With the aid of clean mirrors
bring the lost from behind themselves.
And then pass silent by graveyards
taverns and public cotton trees where
the ambitious hold duppy[2] conventions.

Aye, earth's garments wear so heavy.
See how much the queen's robe sags,
trimmed as it is with feathers of the vain,
sleek ermine and jewels of bright ambition.
Be wary miss monarch of the ones who come
ostensibly to admire the intricate inlaid
workmanship of your throne, for they
may be measuring your neck's length like

Queen Mary[3] the pretender, whom some
toasted with wine glass on top of glass of water
because they said the real monarch lived over
the ocean. No one crowned her that is true,
she is a pretender just like you, save for this
one thing. The first word
you read spelled your vocation, Singer.[4]

If they knew how all ambition
should come to this, autonomy
autonomy over the me myself.

1. In Jamaica. *Aubades*: poems or songs of dawn.
2. Spirit; ghost (Jamaican English).
3. Mary, Queen of Scots (1542–1587), believed by Catholics to be the rightful queen of England, was executed by her cousin Elizabeth I.
4. Brand name of sewing machine used by the poet's mother, a seamstress.

Sovereign over self kingdom
feel free whomsoever to fight over
the cold food Babylon[5] has left over.
Bam chi chi lala
angels dance rocksteady[6]
on the head of a common pin.

Softly now
our Beloved[7]
is convening
pleasant Sunday evening.

2001

5. Ancient, wealthy Mesopotamian city; symbol of decadent materialism for Rastafarians.
6. Musical precursor to reggae.
7. In the literature of Sufism, a mystical branch of Islam, the individual is often the "lover" seeking union with the divine, or the "Beloved."

AI
1947–2010

In many of Ai's poems, writes the poet Carolyn Forché in a foreword, "there are knives, axes, blades, or pitchforks, splitting skulls, slicing off pieces of flesh, jabbing the sun." What might in another writer's hands seem like sensational violence becomes, in hers, a scalpel, an "instrument for penetrating a social order which has become anesthetized to human agony." The violence is not observed dispassionately from without, but experienced by the poems' speakers, for most of Ai's poems are dramatic monologues. In her first book, *Cruelty* (1973), the personae—anonymous, dispossessed—frequently speak at a moment of sexual desire: "I'll pull, you push, we'll tear each other in half" ("Twenty-Year Marriage"). The desire is often painful, often fatalistically felt, and the poems are brief—as brief, perhaps, as the moments themselves, stabs of energy in otherwise dreary lives.

The monologues of her subsequent books are longer. Their speakers are more rooted in a specific time or place; some are historical figures, such as Marilyn Monroe, J. Edgar Hoover, or Leon Trotsky, the Russian Communist leader ousted by Joseph Stalin. We hear Trotsky on three different occasions in "Killing Floor," at each of which his assassination comes closer. "I find it very exciting to become other people," Ai said, insisting that her adopted voices were not masks for herself (*Radcliffe Quarterly*, Spring 2000). Distinct as we read the poems, the voices—stylized, undifferentiated by diction—blend in recollection to become a chorus. They explore such lurid subjects as necrophilia, mass murder, sexual abuse, and torture. Whether from the perspective of victim or victimizer, Ai presents with vigor, bluntness, and glaring immediacy moments in which the boundaries of the body and psyche are broken. Her acts of ventriloquism counter anesthesia and cruelty by reasserting an articulate humanity and a robust interior life.

Ai used only her given middle name, which means "love" in Japanese. She was born on October 21, 1947, in Albany, Texas, to a Japanese father and a mother of African American, Native American, and European descent. Growing up in the American southwest, she attended Catholic schools until the seventh grade. She held a B.A. in Japanese from the University of Arizona and an M.F.A. from the University of California, Irvine. She taught or was writer-in-residence at a variety of institutions, including Oklahoma State University. She received the Lamont Poetry Prize in 1978 and the National Book Award in 1999.

Twenty-Year Marriage

You keep me waiting in a truck
with its one good wheel stuck in the ditch,
while you piss against the south side of a tree.
Hurry. I've got nothing on under my skirt tonight.
That still excites you, but this pickup has no windows
and the seat, one fake leather thigh,
pressed close to mine is cold.
I'm the same size, shape, make as twenty years ago,
but get inside me, start the engine;
you'll have the strength, the will to move.
I'll pull, you push, we'll tear each other in half.
Come on, baby, lay me down on my back.
Pretend you don't owe me a thing
and maybe we'll roll out of here,
leaving the past stacked up behind us;
old newspapers nobody's ever got to read again.

1973

Killing Floor

1. Russia, 1927

On the day the sienna-skinned man
held my shoulders between his spade-shaped hands,
easing me down into the azure water of Jordan,[1]
I woke ninety-three million miles from myself,
Lev Davidovich Bronstein,[2]
shoulder-deep in the Volga,
while the cheap dye of my black silk shirt darkened the water.

My head wet, water caught in my lashes.
Am I blind?
I rub my eyes, then wade back to shore,
undress and lie down,
until Stalin comes from his place beneath the birch tree.
He folds my clothes
and I button myself in my marmot[3] coat,

1. River that flows through what was ancient Palestine; its waters were reputedly holy.
2. Original name of the Russian revolutionist (1879–1940) who was a leader in postrevolutionary Russia until Lenin's death, in 1924, when he lost the struggle for leadership to Joseph Stalin (1879–1953). He was expelled from the Communist Party in 1927. The Volga (below) is Russia's chief river.
3. A cheap fur.

and together we start the long walk back to Moscow.
He doesn't ask, *what did you see in the river?*,
but I hear the hosts of a man drowning in water and holiness,
the castrati voices[4] I can't recognize,
skating on knives, from trees, from air
on the thin ice of my last night in Russia.
Leon Trotsky. Bread.
I want to scream, but silence holds my tongue
with small spade-shaped hands
and only this comes, so quietly
Stalin has to press his ear to my mouth:
I have only myself. Put me on the train.
I won't look back.

2. *Mexico, 1940*

At noon today, I woke from a nightmare:
my friend Jacques ran toward me with an ax,
as I stepped from the train in Alma-Ata.[5]
He was dressed in yellow satin pants and shirt.
A marigold in winter.
When I held out my arms to embrace him,
he raised the ax and struck me at the neck,
my head fell to one side, hanging only by skin.
A river of sighs poured from the cut.

3. *Mexico, August 20, 1940*[6]

The machine-gun bullets
hit my wife in the legs,
then zigzagged up her body.
I took the shears, cut open her gown
and lay on top of her for hours.
Blood soaked through my clothes
and when I tried to rise, I couldn't.

I wake then. Another nightmare.
I rise from my desk, walk to the bedroom
and sit down at my wife's mirrored vanity.
I rouge my cheeks and lips,
stare at my bone-white, speckled egg of a face:
lined and empty.
I lean forward and see Jacques's reflection.
I half-turn, smile, then turn back to the mirror.
He moves from the doorway,
lifts the pickax
and strikes the top of my head.

4. That is, high voices; castrati were male singers castrated in boyhood to preserve their soprano voices.
5. City in Kazakhstan. Trotsky was assassinated by the Spanish Communist Ramón Mercader, who also used the aliases Jacques van den Dreschd and Frank Jacson. He was a pretended friend of Trotsky's in Mexico, where Trotsky eventually settled after being exiled from Russia. An earlier attempt on Trotsky's life, by machine gun (lines 38–44), was led by the Mexican Communist painter David Siqueiros.
6. The date of Trotsky's assassination.

My brain splits.
The pickax keeps going
and when it hits the tile floor,
it flies from his hands,
a black dove on whose back I ride,
two men, one cursing,
the other blessing all things:
Lev Davidovich Bronstein,
I step from Jordan without you.

1979

Sleeping Beauty

A Fiction

for the comatose patient raped by an aide

You steal into my room,
between darkness and noon
to doff the disguise as nurse's aide
and parade before me as you really are,
a man for whom time is deranged
and consists of your furtive visits to me,
while all the rest is just a gloomy reprieve
from your nothingness.
For me time is arranged without the past
or the future,
without tenses to suture me to my days and nights.
For me, there is only now,
when you are certain you won't be disturbed,
spread my legs apart
and break through the red door to my chamber.
After you've finished,
you use a clean, white towel
to wipe away the evidence
of how you mingled your life
with what is left of mine.
You think your crime won't be discovered
but the evidence survives
to dine on the flow of fluid
dripping into me,
as though I were merely a conduit
for the baby who knows me
only as its host
and never will as Mother
and you will never be Father,
baby never see,
you, who in a fever came to me.
I was "comma tose" as my mother calls it.
She hoped for a miracle,
but when it came, it was not the one she wanted,

when she prayed to Saint Jude,
patron saint of lost causes
and laid my photo on the altar
she'd erected in the living room,
beside a rose in a crystal vase.
My face almost glowed in the dark,
as if the spark of consciousness
leaped from me into the image
of what I was before I was swept away from myself,
only to return as someone else,
for whom language is silence,
language is thirst
that is not slaked.
Monster, you took all that was left of my body,
but could not break my body's vow
of renunciation of itself.
My eyes were open,
while you violated me.
All at once
you raised your hand and closed them,
but I could see
beyond the veil of your deceit.
At first, I thought you'd come to my rescue,
but instead of waking me with a kiss,
you pricked me with the thorn of violence
and I did not rise from my bed
to wed the handsome prince
as in the fairy tale
my mother once read to me,
when *forever* did not mean eternity.

1999

LESLIE MARMON SILKO
b. 1948

As early as the nineteenth century, the Laguna Pueblo was hospitable to mixed marriages and the children of these marriages. Leslie Marmon Silko is of mixed European and Native American heritage, and she builds a bridge between her native Laguna Pueblo culture, orally transmitted generally by storytelling older women, and readers of poetry in English. But she positions herself with the Native Americans in their mostly losing struggle with the murderous white invaders. One of her poems, beginning "Long time ago," imagines a world in which there were "no white people . . . / there was nothing European." The witches of many tribes gather for a contest as to who can cause the most mischief, and an unknown witch wins when she describes a people who live far away: *"When they look / they see only objects. / The world is a dead thing for them / the trees and rivers are not alive / the mountains and stones are not alive. / The deer and bear are objects / They see no life."* Appalled, the other witches plead with the strange witch to take the story back, but that cannot be done: *"It's already coming."* A gifted storyteller, Silko condenses the past, present, and future, inverts the dominant Euro-American perspective on history, and effectively combines a rhetoric of repetition (*"Killing killing killing killing"*) with vivid details (*"covered with festered sores / shitting blood / vomiting blood"*). Yet angry lament is not Silko's only note. "Prayer to the Pacific" dissolves temporal boundaries to represent a powerfully animistic and prophetic encounter with the natural world. Instancing her skill as an ironist, "Toe'osh: A Laguna Coyote Story" begins by relating traditional Native American trickster stories, but then shifts to modern examples of how Coyote continues to survive. Episodic in structure, compressed in timing, the poem fuses bleak realism and mischievous humor in describing encounters between whites and Native peoples.

Silko was born on March 5, 1948, in Albuquerque, New Mexico, and grew up in Laguna Pueblo, forty miles to the west. She was educated at the University of New Mexico, where she has also taught; since 1978, she has held a position at the University of Arizona. In addition to her poems, she has written short stories and novels, including *Ceremony* (1977). In 1981, she received a MacArthur Fellowship.

[Long Time Ago]

Long time ago
in the beginning
there were no white people in this world
there was nothing European.
And this world might have gone on like that
except for one thing:
witchery.
This world was already complete
even without white people.
There was everything
including witchery.

Then it happened.
These witch people got together.
Some came from far far away
across oceans
across mountains.
Some had slanty eyes
others had black skin.
They all got together for a contest
the way people have baseball tournaments nowadays
except this was a contest
in dark things.

So anyway
they all got together
witch people from all directions
witches from all the Pueblos
and all the tribes.
They had Navajo witches there,

some from Hopi, and a few from Zuni.[1]
They were having a witches' conference,
that's what it was
Way up in the lava rock hills
north of Cañoncito[2]
they got together
to fool around in caves
with their animal skins.
Fox, badger, bobcat, and wolf
they circled the fire
and on the fourth time
they jumped into that animal's skin.

But this time it wasn't enough
and one of them
maybe a Sioux[3] or some Eskimos
started showing off.
"That wasn't anything,
watch this."

The contest started like that.
Then some of them lifted the lids
on their big cooking pots,
calling the rest of them over
to take a look:
dead babies simmering in blood
circles of skull cut away
all the brains sucked out.
Witch medicine
to dry and grind into powder
for new victims.

Others untied skin bundles of disgusting objects:
dark flints, cinders from burned hogans[4] where the
dead lay
Whorls of skin
cut from fingertips
sliced from the penis end and clitoris tip.

Finally there was only one
who hadn't shown off charms or powers.
The witch stood in the shadows beyond the fire
and no one ever knew where this witch came from
which tribe
or if it was a woman or a man.
But the important thing was
this witch didn't show off any dark thunder charcoals

1. Native American peoples of, respectively, northern New Mexico and Arizona, northeastern Arizona, and western New Mexico.
2. That is, Cañon City, in southern Colorado.
3. Native American people of the northern Mississippi Valley.
4. Navajo dwellings.

or red ant-hill beads.
This one just told them to listen:
"What I have is a story."

At first they all laughed
but this witch said
Okay
go ahead
laugh if you want to
but as I tell the story
it will begin to happen.

Set in motion now
set in motion by our witchery
to work for us.

Caves across the ocean
in caves of dark hills
white skin people
like the belly of a fish
covered with hair.

Then they grow away from the earth
then they grow away from the sun
then they grow away from the plants and animals.
They see no life
When they look
they see only objects.
The world is a dead thing for them
the trees and rivers are not alive
the mountains and stones are not alive.
The deer and bear are objects
They see no life.

They fear
They fear the world.
They destroy what they fear.
They fear themselves.

The wind will blow them across the ocean
thousands of them in giant boats
swarming like larva
out of a crushed ant hill.

They will carry objects
which can shoot death
faster than the eye can see.

They will kill the things they fear
all the animals
the people will starve.

They will poison the water
they will spin the water away
and there will be drought
the people will starve.

They will fear what they find
They will fear the people
They kill what they fear.

Entire villages will be wiped out
They will slaughter whole tribes.

Corpses for us
Blood for us
Killing killing killing killing.

And those they do not kill
will die anyway
at the destruction they see
at the loss
at the loss of the children
the loss will destroy the rest.

Stolen rivers and mountains
the stolen land will eat their hearts
and jerk their mouths from the Mother.[5]
The people will starve.

They will bring terrible diseases
the people have never known.
Entire tribes will die out
covered with festered sores
shitting blood
vomiting blood.
Corpses for our work

Set in motion now
set in motion by our witchery
set in motion
to work for us.

They will take this world from ocean to ocean
they will turn on each other
they will destroy each other
Up here
in these hills
they will find the rocks,
rocks with veins of green and yellow and black.
They will lay the final pattern with these rocks
they will lay it across the world
and explode everything.

5. That is, the earth.

Set in motion now
set in motion
To destroy
To kill
Objects to work for us
objects to act for us
Performing the witchery
for suffering
for torment
for the stillborn
the deformed
the sterile
the dead.

Whirling
Whirling
Whirling
Whirling
set into motion now
set into motion.

So the other witches said
"Okay you win; you take the prize,
but what you said just now—
it isn't so funny
It doesn't sound so good.
We are doing okay without it
we can get along without that kind of thing.
Take it back.
Call that story back."

But the witch just shook its head
at the others in their stinking animal skins, fur
and feathers.
It's already turned loose.
It's already coming.
It can't be called back.

1981

Prayer to the Pacific

I traveled to the ocean
distant
from my southwest land of sandrock
to the moving blue water
Big as the myth of origin.

Pale
pale water in the yellow-white light of

sun floating west
to China
where ocean herself was born.
Clouds that blow across the sand are wet.

Squat in the wet sand and speak to the Ocean:
I return to you turquoise the red coral you sent us,
sister spirit of Earth.
Four round stones in my pocket I carry back the ocean
to suck and to taste.

Thirty thousand years ago
Indians came riding across the ocean
carried by giant sea turtles.

Waves were high that day
great sea turtles waded slowly out
from the gray sundown sea.
Grandfather Turtle rolled in the sand four times
and disappeared
swimming into the sun.

And so from that time
immemorial,
as the old people say,
rain clouds drift from the west
gift from the ocean.

Green leaves in the wind
Wet earth on my feet
swallowing raindrops
clear from China.

1981

Toe'osh: A Laguna Coyote Story

for Simon Ortiz,[6] July 1973

In the wintertime
at night
we tell coyote stories
and drink Spañada[7] by the stove.
How coyote got his
ratty old fur coat
bits of old fur
the sparrows stuck on him
with dabs of pitch.
That was after he lost his proud original one in a poker game.

6. Native American poet (b. 1941).
7. Spanish wine.

anyhow, things like that
are always happening to him,
that's what he said, anyway.

And it happened to him at Laguna
and Chinle
and Lukachukai[8] too, because coyote got too smart for his own good.

But the Navajos say he won a contest once.
It was to see who could sleep out in a
snowstorm the longest
and coyote waited until chipmunk badger and skunk were all
curled up under the snow
and then he uncovered himself and slept all night
inside
and before morning he got up and went out again
and waited until the others got up before he came
in to take the prize.

Some white men came to Acoma[9] and Laguna a hundred years ago
and they fought over Acoma land and Laguna women, and even now
some of their descendants are howling in
the hills southeast of Laguna.

Charlie Coyote wanted to be governor
and he said that when he got elected
he would run the other men off
the reservation
and keep all the women for himself.

One year
the politicians got fancy
at Laguna.
They went door to door with hams and turkeys
and they gave them to anyone who promised
to vote for them.
On election day all the people
stayed home and ate turkey
and laughed.

The Trans-Western pipeline vice president came
to discuss right-of-way.
The Lagunas let him wait all day long
because he is a busy and important man.
And late in the afternoon they told him
to come back again tomorrow.

They were after the picnic food
that the special dancers left
down below the cliff.

8. Pueblos (Native American villages).

9. Pueblo in west central New Mexico.

And Toe'osh and his cousins hung themselves
down over the cliff
holding each other's tail in their mouth making a coyote chain
until someone in the middle farted
and the guy behind him opened his
mouth to say "What stinks?" and they
all went tumbling down, like that.

Howling and roaring
Toe'osh scattered white people
out of bars all over Wisconsin.
He bumped into them at the door
until they said
"Excuse me"
And the way Simon meant it
was for 300 or maybe 400 years.

1981

AGHA SHAHID ALI
1949–2001

Agha Shahid Ali was born in New Delhi, India, on February 4, 1949, just a year and a half after the triumphant "birth" and traumatic partition of India. He was the leading anglophone Indian poet of the generation born after independence. Like his peer in the earlier generation, A. K. Ramanujan, Ali enriched English-language poetry by hybridizing it with South Asian traditions. But whereas Ramanujan belonged to the majority Hindu population, Ali came from the Shi'a Muslim minority. And whereas Ramanujan's poetry draws on literature in south Indian languages (Tamil and Kannada), Ali brings into English-language poetry "the music of Urdu," the north Indian language spoken by most Muslims of the Indian subcontinent. Indebted to T. S. Eliot's sharply etched, dreamlike, fragmentary lines, he synthesizes this Western modernist influence with the ornate forms, rhetorical patterning, and melancholy tonality of Urdu poetry.

Ali considered himself a "Kashmiri-American" and yet a "triple exile" from Kashmir, India, and the United States. He spent a few years as a teenager in the United States, but otherwise he grew up in Srinagar, Kashmir, and the violence and instability of his disputed homeland haunted his imagination. By internalizing this violence, he conjured it powerfully in nightmarish images of homes, religious sites, artifacts, and human lives devastated by conflict. As in the poetry of his Urdu precursors, the political and the personal are inseparable in Ali's work, though his poetry eschews polemics, favoring the emotionally inscribed landscape, the unpredictably visualized image.

One prominent example of the political realities that mark Ali's work is an event mourned in the title poem of *The Country without a Post Office* (1997): a catastrophic fire, in 1995, in the picturesque, twenty-thousand-person Kashmiri town of Chrar-e-Sharif. In this poem, written in a mirrorlike rhyme scheme (ABCDDCBA), Ali imaginatively returns to the displaced and the dead, to walls of flame, to houses burning like leaves, to a broken and buried minaret, ultimately to a country reduced to ash. Yet he acknowledges the impossibility of his reentering the scene of destruction or poetically rehabilitating it, dwelling on images of undeliverable "dead letters" with "vanished envelopes" and "blank stamps." As in much of Ali's work, the poet's remembrance of ruin and loss is vivified, not trivialized, by his personal anguish over his own limitations as poet and exile.

The imaginative yet incomplete return to a remembered landscape is often the psychic impetus of Ali's poetry. In "Postcard from Kashmir," the postcolonial poet conjures his native landscape, yet implicitly mocks his own retrospective reconstruction. Like a postcard, he acknowledges, the poetry of the postcolonial émigré risks miniaturizing, idealizing, and reducing his native place. In "The Dacca Gauzes," his poetry implicitly aspires to the condition of the dewlike muslins woven by earlier generations of Bengalis, before their brutal suppression by the British (their hands were mutilated), though this poem acknowledges, again, its language's incapacity to resurrect fully the lost art it memorializes.

The deliberate self-consciousness of Ali's poetry owes much to that modernist tradition in which poets allegorize the work of shoring fragments against personal and cultural ruins. It also owes something to the self-mirroring artifice of James Merrill's poetry, which influenced Ali's shift from his early free verse to rhymed and metered forms, including the sestina and the canzone. But it is especially evident in his use of a non-Western form—the ghazal (pronounced gha*zal* in Persian, *ghuzz*le in Urdu), the last lines of which typically include a reference to the poet by name, such as the poignant ending of the ghazal reprinted here: "And I, Shahid, only am escaped to tell thee—/ God sobs in my arms. Call me Ishmael tonight." Indeed, Ali became the most visible spokesman for this form borrowed from medieval Persian and Arabic. Because the last line of each couplet rhymes ("tell" and the earlier "farewell") and ends in the same word ("tonight"), the ghazal builds a hypnotic momentum, also evident in Ali's many other ghazal-inflected poems, such as "The Country without a Post Office" and "Lenox Hill." But because a ghazal's couplets are strung together without regard to thematic or narrative unity, each standing on its own without enjambments between couplets, they also enable the poet to jump across the disjunctures and incoherences of contemporary life. For Ali, as for poets as divergent as Adrienne Rich, Galway Kinnell, John Hollander, and Paul Muldoon, the ghazal becomes a tool for inscribing the obsessions and the gaps of modernity.

Absence, loss, exile—these are the fruitful obsessions of Ali's poetry. Responding to "the death of tribes, the death of landscapes and the death of a language," he said in 1998, "I see everything in a very elegiac way. It's not something morbid, but it's part of my emotional coloring." Imbued with a sense of national dislocation and grief over the horrors of Kashmir, Ali also writes effectively about other histories of loss and destruction. In "Leaving Sonora," he remembers the unexplained fifteenth-century disappearance of the Hohokam (said to mean "those who have vanished") from their homes in Arizona. The atrocities and disappearances under Chilean dictator Pinochet and other South American autocrats are surreally compressed as an absent visual presence in "I See Chile in My Rearview Mirror." In these poems, the speaker is driving or flying, his mobility exemplifying contemporary migrancy, one diaspora or violent displacement becoming superimposed upon another as in the works' palimpsestic allusions and cross-cultural textures.

Ali studied literature at the University of Kashmir, Srinagar (B.A., 1968), and at the University of Delhi (M.A., 1970) before earning a Ph.D. in English at Pennsylvania State University (1984) and an M.F.A. at the University of Arizona (1985). He taught creative writing at various American universities, including the University of Arizona, Hamilton College, the University of Massachusetts, Amherst, and the University of Utah. When his mother died of brain cancer, he mourned her death in the elegy "Lenox Hill," one of the crowning achievements of his career. Not long after, he was killed by the same disease.

Postcard from Kashmir[1]

Kashmir shrinks into my mailbox,
my home a neat four by six inches.

I always loved neatness. Now I hold
the half-inch Himalayas in my hand.

This is home. And this the closest
I'll ever be to home. When I return,
the colors won't be so brilliant,
the Jhelum's[2] waters so clean,
so ultramarine. My love
so overexposed.

And my memory will be a little
out of focus, in it
a giant negative, black
and white, still undeveloped.

(for Pavan Sahgal)

1987

The Dacca Gauzes

. . . for a whole year he sought
to accumulate the most exquisite
Dacca gauzes.
—Oscar Wilde / *The Picture of Dorian Gray*

Those transparent Dacca gauzes[3]
known as woven air, running
water, evening dew:

a dead art now, dead over
a hundred years. "No one
now knows," my grandmother says,

"what it was to wear
or touch that cloth." She wore
it once, an heirloom sari from

1. Mountainous northwestern region of the Indian subcontinent subject to tense border disputes and armed conflict between India and Pakistan since 1947.
2. River running through Kashmir and the Punjab region of Pakistan.
3. Finely woven and exceptionally soft muslins once produced in the city of Dacca, now the capital of Bangladesh. The first stanza of the poem continues the quotation from *The Picture of Dorian Gray*.

her mother's dowry, proved
genuine when it was pulled, all
six yards, through a ring.

Years later when it tore,
many handkerchiefs embroidered
with gold-thread paisleys

were distributed among
the nieces and daughters-in-law.
Those too now lost.

In history we learned: the hands
of weavers were amputated,
the looms of Bengal silenced,

and the cotton shipped raw
by the British to England.[4]
History of little use to her,

my grandmother just says
how the muslins of today
seem so coarse and that only

in autumn, should one wake up
at dawn to pray, can one
feel that same texture again.

One morning, she says, the air
was dew-starched: she pulled
it absently through her ring.

1987

Leaving Sonora[5]

living in the desert
has taught me to go inside myself
for shade
—Richard Shelton[6]

Certain landscapes insist on fidelity.
Why else would a poet of this desert
go deep inside himself for shade?
Only there do the perished tribes live.

4. In the early nineteenth century, the British decided that the Indian muslins were threatening the sales of British fabrics in India and, consequently, cut off the thumbs of the muslin weavers so they could no longer produce the fabric or pass on the skills to their children.

5. State in northwestern Mexico.

6. American poet (b. 1933). The epigraph comes from Shelton's "Notes toward an Autobiography."

The desert insists, always: Be faithful,
even to those who no longer exist.

The Hohokam[7] lived here for 1500 years.
In his shade, the poet sees one of their women,
beautiful, her voice low as summer thunder.
Each night she saw, among the culinary ashes,
what the earth does only through a terrible pressure—
the fire, in minutes, transforming the coal into diamonds.

I left the desert at night—to return
to the East. From the plane I saw Tucson's lights
shatter into blue diamonds. My eyes dazzled
as we climbed higher: below a thin cloud,
and only for a moment, I saw those blue lights fade
into the outlines of a vanished village.

1991

I See Chile in My Rearview Mirror

By dark the world is once again intact
Or so the mirrors, wiped clean, try to reason . . .
—James Merrill[8]

This dream of water—what does it harbor?
I see Argentina and Paraguay
under a curfew of glass, their colors
breaking, like oil. The night in Uruguay

is black salt. I'm driving toward Utah,
keeping the entire hemisphere in view—
Colombia vermilion, Brazil blue tar,
some countries wiped clean of color: Peru

is titanium white. And always oceans
that hide in mirrors: when beveled edges
arrest tides or this world's destinations
forsake ships. There's Sedona, Nogales[9]

far behind. Once I went through a mirror—
from there too the world, so intact, resembled
only itself. When I returned I tore
the skin off the glass. The sea was unsealed

7. Said to mean "those who have vanished"; Native American tribe that flourished between the fourth and fifteenth centuries in what is now Arizona before disappearing for unknown reasons.

8. American poet (1926–1995). The epigraph comes from Merrill's "Amsterdam."

9. Cities in Arizona.

by dark, and I saw ships sink off the coast
of a wounded republic. Now from a blur
of tanks in Santiago,[1] a white horse
gallops, riderless, chased by drunk soldiers

in a jeep; they're firing into the moon.
And as I keep driving in the desert,
someone is running to catch the last bus, men
hanging on to its sides. And he's missed it.

He is running again; crescents of steel
fall from the sky. And here the rocks
are under fog, the cedars a temple,
Sedona carved by the wind into gods—

each shadow their worshiper. The siren
empties Santiago; he watches
—from a hush of windows—blindfolded men
blurred in gleaming vans. The horse vanishes

into a dream. I'm passing skeletal
figures carved in 700 B.C.
Whoever deciphers these canyon walls
remains forsaken, alone with history,

no harbor for his dream. And what else will
this mirror now reason, filled with water?
I see Peru without rain, Brazil
without forests—and here in Utah a dagger

of sunlight: it's splitting—it's the summer
solstice—the quartz center of a spiral.
Did the Anasazi[2] know the darker
answer also—given now in crystal

by the mirrored continent? The solstice,
but of winter? A beam stabs the window,
diamonds him, a funeral in his eyes.
In the lit stadium of Santiago,

this is the shortest day. He's taken there.
Those about to die are looking at him,
his eyes the ledger of the disappeared.
What will the mirror try now? I'm driving,

still north, always followed by that country,
its floors ice, its citizens so lovesick

1. Capital of Chile. Between 1973 and 1990, the government of Chile was controlled by a military junta led by Agusto Pinochet (b. 1915) and responsible for over three thousand deaths or disappearances.

2. Native American civilization dating back to c. 100 C.E. in what is today the southwestern United States and famous for the dwellings it built into the sides of cliffs and canyon walls.

that the ground—sheer glass—of every city
is torn up. They demand the republic

give back, jeweled, their every reflection.
They dig till dawn but find only corpses.
He has returned to this dream for his bones.
The waters darken. The continent vanishes.

1991

Ghazal[3]

Pale hands I loved beside the Shalimar
—Laurence Hope[4]

Where are you now? Who lies beneath your spell tonight
before you agonize him in farewell tonight?

Pale hands that once loved me beside the Shalimar:
Whom else from rapture's road will you expel tonight?

Those "Fabrics of Cashmere—" "to make Me beautiful—"
"Trinket"—to gem—"Me to adorn—How—tell"—tonight?[5]

I beg for haven: Prisons, let open your gates—
A refugee from Belief seeks a cell tonight.

Executioners near the woman at the window.
Damn you, Elijah, I'll bless Jezebel[6] tonight.

Lord, cried out the idols, *Don't let us be broken;*
Only we can convert the infidel tonight.

Has God's vintage loneliness turned to vinegar?
He's poured rust into the Sacred Well tonight.

In the heart's veined temple all statues have been smashed.
No priest in saffron's left to toll its knell tonight.

He's freed some fire from ice, in pity for Heaven;
he's left open—for God—the doors of Hell tonight.

3. A poetic form with a long history in Urdu, Persian, and Arabic dating back to the seventh century. In the classical version, the thematically discontinuous couplets of the ghazal have a rhyme scheme (called *qafia*) and refrain (called *radif*), and the last couplet includes the poet's name.
4. Pseudonym of English poet Violet Nicolson (1865–1904). The epigraph as well as the language of the first two stanzas of Ali's poem is taken from her "Kashmiri Song." The Shalimar Gardens of Lahore, in present-day Pakistan, were designed in the seventeenth century.
5. The third stanza is borrowed from Emily Dickinson's "I am ashamed—I hide" (#473).
6. 1 Kings 16–22 describes the Hebrew prophet Elijah's confrontation with Queen Jezebel, who introduced the cult of Baal into Israel.

And I, Shahid, only am escaped to tell thee—
God sobs in my arms. Call me Ishmael[7] tonight.

1997

The Country without a Post Office[8]

. . . letters sent
To dearest him that lives alas! away.
—Gerard Manley Hopkins[9]

1

Again I've returned to this country
where a minaret[1] has been entombed.
Someone soaks the wicks of clay lamps
in mustard oil, each night climbs its steps
to read messages scratched on planets.
His fingerprints cancel blank stamps
in that archive for letters with doomed
addresses, each house buried or empty.

Empty? Because so many fled, ran away,
and became refugees there, in the plains,
where they must now will a final dewfall
to turn the mountains to glass. They'll see
us through them—see us frantically bury
houses to save them from fire that, like a wall,
caves in. The soldiers light it, hone the flames,
burn our world to sudden papier-mâché

inlaid with gold, then ash. When the muezzin[2]
died, the city was robbed of every Call.
The houses were swept about like leaves
for burning. Now every night we bury
our houses—and theirs, the ones left empty.
We are faithful. On their doors we hang wreaths.
More faithful each night fire again is a wall
and we look for the dark as it caves in.

7. Son of Abraham and Hagar and, according to legend, the ancestor to whom the origin of the Arab people can be traced. "Call me Ishmael" is the first sentence of Herman Melville's *Moby-Dick* (1851). "I only am escaped alone to tell thee" is a refrain spoken by Job in response to his calamities (Job 1).

8. This poem mourns the 1995 destruction by fire of one of Kashmir's most important Muslim shrines, the mausoleum of Kashmir's patron saint Sheikh Noor-ud-Din (1377?–1438?), and the surrounding town of Chrar-e-Sharif in the Indian-governed region of Kashmir. The blaze was the culmination of a two-month standoff between the Indian army and a group of 150 Muslim militants. Each side blamed the other for the conflagration.

9. English poet (1844–1889). The epigraph is from the poem beginning "I wake and feel the fell of dark, not day."

1. Tall tower of a mosque, from which worshipers are called to prayer.

2. The official who proclaims the call to prayer in Islam.

2

"We're inside the fire, looking for the dark,"
one card lying on the street says. "I want
to be he who pours blood. To soak your hands.
Or I'll leave mine in the cold till the rain
is ink, and my fingers, at the edge of pain,
are seals all night to cancel the stamps."
The mad guide! The lost speak like this. They haunt
a country when it is ash. Phantom heart,

pray he's alive. I have returned in rain
to find him, to learn why he never wrote.
I've brought cash, a currency of paisleys
to buy the new stamps, rare already, blank,
no nation named on them. Without a lamp
I look for him in houses buried, empty—
He may be alive, opening doors of smoke,
breathing in the dark his ash-refrain:

"Everything is finished, nothing remains."
I must force silence to be a mirror
to see his voice again for directions.
Fire runs in waves. Should I cross that river?
Each post office is boarded up. Who will deliver
parchment cut in paisleys, my news to prisons?
Only silence can now trace my letters
to him. Or in a dead office the dark panes.

3

"The entire map of the lost will be candled.
I'm keeper of the minaret since the muezzin died.
Come soon, I'm alive. There's almost a paisley
against the light, sometimes white, then black.
The glutinous wash is wet on its back
as it blossoms into autumn's final country—
Buy it, I issue it only once, at night.
Come before I'm killed, my voice canceled."

In this dark rain, be faithful, Phantom heart,
this is your pain. Feel it. You must feel it.
"Nothing will remain, everything's finished,"
I see his voice again: "This is a shrine
of words. You'll find your letters to me. And mine
to you. Come soon and tear open these vanished
envelopes." And I reach the minaret:
I'm inside the fire. I have found the dark.

This is your pain. You must feel it. Feel it,
Heart, be faithful to his mad refrain—
For he soaked the wicks of clay lamps,

lit them each night as he climbed these steps
to read messages scratched on planets.
His hands were seals to cancel the stamps.
This is an archive. I've found the remains
of his voice, that map of longings with no limit.

4

I read them, letters of lovers, the mad ones,
and mine to him from whom no answers came.
I light lamps, send my answers, Calls to Prayer
to deaf worlds across continents. And my lament
is cries countless, cries like dead letters sent
to this world whose end was near, always near.
My words go out in huge packages of rain,
go there, to addresses, across the oceans.

It's raining as I write this. I have no prayer.
It's just a shout, held in, It's Us! It's Us!
whose letters are cries that break like bodies
in prisons. Now each night in the minaret
I guide myself up the steps. Mad silhouette,
I throw paisleys to clouds. The lost are like this:
They bribe the air for dawn, this their dark purpose.
But there's no sun here. There is no sun here.

Then be pitiless you whom I could not save—
Send your cries to me, if only in this way:
I've found a prisoner's letters to a lover—
One begins: "These words may never reach you."
Another ends: "The skin dissolves in dew
without your touch." And I want to answer:
I want to live forever. What else can I say?
It rains as I write this. Mad heart, be brave.

(for James Merrill)

1997

Lenox Hill

(In Lenox Hill Hospital,[3] after surgery, my mother said the sirens sounded like the elephants of Mihiragula when his men drove them off cliffs in the Pir Panjal Range.)[4]

The Hun so loved the cry, one falling elephant's,
he wished to hear it again. At dawn, my mother
heard, in her hospital-dream of elephants,

3. In New York City. This poem is in the form of a canzone.
4. Part of the western Himalayas in northwestern India. Mihiragula (or Mihirakula) was a sixth-century Hun (or Central Asian) king in India. Known for his cruelty, he amused himself by rolling elephants off precipices to watch their suffering, according to Buddhist legend.

sirens wail through Manhattan like elephants
forced off Pir Panjal's rock cliffs in Kashmir:
the soldiers, so ruled, had rushed the elephant,
The greatest of all footprints is the elephant's,
said the Buddha. But not lifted from the universe,
those prints vanished forever into the universe,
though nomads still break news of those elephants
as if it were just yesterday the air spread the dye
("War's annals will fade into night / Ere their story die"),[5]

the punishing khaki whereby the world sees us die
out, mourning you, O massacred elephants!
Months later, in Amherst,[6] she dreamt: She was, with dia-
monds, being stoned to death. I prayed: If she must die,
let it only be some dream. But there were times, Mother,
while you slept, that I prayed, "Saints, let her die."
Not, I swear by you, that I wished you to die
but to save you as you were, young, in song in Kashmir,
and I, one festival, crowned Krishna[7] by you, Kashmir
listening to my flute. You never let gods die.
Thus I swear, here and now, not to forgive the universe
that would let me get used to a universe

without you. She, she alone, was the universe
as she earned, like a galaxy, her right not to die,
defying the Merciful of the Universe,
Master of Disease, "in the circle of her traverse"[8]
of drug-bound time. And where was the god of elephants,
plump with Fate, when tusk to tusk, the universe,
dyed green, became ivory? Then let the universe,
like Paradise, be considered a tomb. Mother,
they asked me, *So how's the writing?* I answered *My mother*
is my poem. What did they expect? For no verse
sufficed except the promise, fading, of Kashmir
and the cries that reached you from the cliffs of Kashmir

(across fifteen centuries) in the hospital. *Kashmir,*
she's dying! How her breathing drowns out the universe
as she sleeps in Amherst. Windows open on Kashmir:
There, the fragile wood-shrines—so far away—of Kashmir!
O Destroyer, let her return there, if just to die.
Save the right she gave its earth to cover her, Kashmir
has no rights. When the windows close on Kashmir,
I see the blizzard-fall of ghost-elephants.
I hold back—she couldn't bear it—one elephant's
story: his return (in a country far from Kashmir)
to the jungle where each year, on the day his mother
died, he touches with his trunk the bones of his mother.

5. From Thomas Hardy's "In Time of the 'The Breaking of Nations.' "
6. Town in Massachusetts.
7. Indian god; his cult explores analogies between divine and human love.
8. From Wallace Stevens's "The Paltry Nude Starts on a Spring Voyage." The next line refers to the elephant-headed Hindu god Ganesh.

"As you sit here by me, you're just like my mother,"
she tells me. I imagine her: a bride in Kashmir,
she's watching, at the Regal, her first film with Father.
If only I could gather you in my arms, Mother,
I'd save you—now my daughter—from God. The universe
opens its ledger. I write: How helpless was God's mother!
Each page is turned to enter grief's accounts. Mother,
I see a hand. *Tell me it's not God's.* Let it die.
I see it. It's filling with diamonds. Please let it die.
Are you somewhere alive, somewhere alive, Mother?
Do you hear what I once held back: in one elephant's
cry, by his mother's bones, the cries of those elephants

that stunned the abyss? Ivory blots out the elephants.
I enter this: *The Belovéd leaves one behind to die.*
For compared to my grief for you, what are those of Kashmir,
and what (I close the ledger) are the griefs of the universe
when I remember you—beyond all accounting—O my mother?

2001

James Fenton
b. 1949

Although James Fenton gave the Martian poets their name, on the basis of a poem by Craig Raine, and was considered a central member of that movement, he strikes a note of his own. His experiences as a journalist in Southeast Asia and in Germany have provided him with a first-hand understanding of suffering. He feels particularly for those people, especially children, whom "geography condemns to war" ("Children in Exile"). In "A German Requiem," a series of negative images sparsely recalls widescale destruction. The simplicity of grief is heightened by sardonic details, such as "Professor Sargnagel was buried with four degrees, two associate memberships." Fenton is at his best in confronting horror with humor, not to mitigate but to enhance it. His title "Dead Soldiers" refers to both consumed bottles of Napoleon brandy and actual dead men; in the poem, the wild party at the beginning gives way to the barbarous civil war at the end. The jocularity heightens the pity.

Fenton has written few poems and reprinted even fewer; those that survive his winnowing are strong and individual. Suffering appears to be immemorial; no wonder he finds the Deity, in "God, a Poem," anything but beneficent. Yet if Fenton has no confidence in redemption, he has some trust in human wit and fantasy. Like W. H. Auden, his major precursor, Fenton adapts a variety of poetic forms and ranges tonally from light humor and satire to the didactic, the sardonic, and the elegiac. His use of rhetorical and sonic repetition is especially effective, whether for mocking naive belief or, in poems such as "For Andrew Wood" and "A German Requiem," for mourning the dead.

Fenton was born on April 25, 1949, in Lincoln, England. He was educated at Oxford University and won the Newdigate Prize for poetry there. In the 1970s, he wrote for the *New Statesman* and the *Guardian,* working abroad as well as in London. He has been a principal reviewer of books for the *Sunday Times* and the *New York Review of Books.* He has written about theater and art as well as poetry.

A German Requiem[1]

(To T. J. G.-A.)

For as at a great distance of place, that which wee look at, appears dimme, and without distinction of the smaller parts; and as Voyces grow weak, and inarticulate: so also after great distance of time, our imagination of the Past is weak; and wee lose (for example) of Cities wee have seen, many particular Streets; and of Actions, many particular Circumstances. This *decaying sense,* when wee would express the thing it self, (I mean *fancy* it selfe,) wee call *Imagination,* as I said before: But when we would express the *decay,* and signifie that the Sense is fading, old, and past, it is called Memory. So that *Imagination* and *Memory* are but one thing . . .

—Hobbes, *Leviathan*[2]

It is not what they built. It is what they knocked down.
It is not the houses. It is the spaces between the houses.
It is not the streets that exist. It is the streets that no longer exist.
It is not your memories which haunt you.
It is not what you have written down.
It is what you have forgotten, what you must forget.
What you must go on forgetting all your life.
And with any luck oblivion should discover a ritual.
You will find out that you are not alone in the enterprise.
Yesterday the very furniture seemed to reproach you.
Today you take your place in the Widow's Shuttle.[3]

•

The bus is waiting at the southern gate
To take you to the city of your ancestors
Which stands on the hill opposite, with gleaming pediments,[4]
As vivid as this charming square, your home.
Are you shy? You should be. It is almost like a wedding,
The way you clasp your flowers and give a little tug at your veil. Oh,
The hideous bridesmaids, it is natural that you should resent them
Just a little, on this first day.
But that will pass, and the cemetery is not far.
Here comes the driver, flicking a toothpick into the gutter,
His tongue still searching between his teeth.
See, he has not noticed you. No one has noticed you.
It will pass, young lady, it will pass.

•

How comforting it is, once or twice a year,
To get together and forget the old times.
As on those special days, ladies and gentlemen,
When the boiled shirts[5] gather at the graveside

1. Mass or chant for the dead. Also, the title of a requiem by the German composer Johannes Brahms (1833–1897).
2. *Leviathan, or the Matter, Form, and Power of a Commonwealth, Ecclesiastical and Civil* (1651), by the English philosopher Thomas Hobbes (1588–1679).
3. Popular name for bus going to cemetery.
4. Triangular shapes above doors or windows.
5. (Men wearing) dress shirts with starched fronts.

And a leering waistcoat approaches the rostrum.
It is like a solemn pact between the survivors.
The mayor has signed it on behalf of the freemasonry.[6]
The priest has sealed it on behalf of all the rest.
Nothing more need be said, and it is better that way—

•

The better for the widow, that she should not live in fear of surprise,
The better for the young man, that he should move at liberty between the armchairs,
The better that these bent figures who flutter among the graves
Tending the nightlights and replacing the chrysanthemums
Are not ghosts,
That they shall go home.
The bus is waiting, and on the upper terraces
The workmen are dismantling the houses of the dead.

•

But when so many had died, so many and at such speed,
There were no cities waiting for the victims.
They unscrewed the name-plates from the shattered doorways
And carried them away with the coffins.
So the squares and parks were filled with the eloquence of young cemeteries:
The smell of fresh earth, the improvised crosses
And all the impossible directions in brass and enamel.

•

'Doctor Gliedschirm, skin specialist, surgeries 14–16 hours or by appointment.'
Professor Sargnagel was buried with four degrees, two associate memberships
And instructions to tradesmen to use the back entrance.
Your uncle's grave informed you that he lived on the third floor, left.
You were asked please to ring, and he would come down in the lift[7]
To which one needed a key . . .

•

Would come down, would ever come down
With a smile like thin gruel, and never too much to say.
How he shrank through the years.
How you towered over him in the narrow cage.[8]
How he shrinks now . . .

•

But come. Grief must have its term? Guilt too, then.
And it seems there is no limit to the resourcefulness of recollection.
So that a man might say and think:
When the world was at its darkest,

6. Secret society for mutual help, called Free and Accepted Order of Masons.
7. Elevator (British usage).
8. Of the wire-screened elevator.

When the black wings passed over the rooftops[9]
(And who can divine His purposes?) even then
There was always, always a fire in this hearth.
You see this cupboard? A priest-hole![1]
And in that lumber-room whole generations have been housed and fed.
Oh, if I were to begin, if I were to begin to tell you
The half, the quarter, a mere smattering of what we went through!

•

His wife nods, and a secret smile,
Like a breeze with enough strength to carry one dry leaf
Over two pavingstones, passes from chair to chair.
Even the enquirer is charmed.
He forgets to pursue the point.
It is not what he wants to know.
It is what he wants not to know.
It is not what they say.
It is what they do not say.

1981

Dead Soldiers

When His Excellency Prince Norodom Chantaraingsey[2]
Invited me to lunch on the battlefield
I was glad of my white suit for the first time that day.
They lived well, the mad Norodoms, they had style.
The brandy and the soda arrived in crates.
Bricks of ice, tied around with raffia,[3]
Dripped from the orderlies' handlebars.

And I remember the dazzling tablecloth
As the APCs[4] fanned out along the road,
The dishes piled high with frogs' legs,
Pregnant turtles, their eggs boiled in the carapace,
Marsh irises in fish sauce
And inflorescence[5] of a banana salad.

On every bottle, Napoleon Bonaparte
Pleaded for the authenticity of the spirit.
They called the empties Dead Soldiers
And rejoiced to see them pile up at our feet.

Each diner was attended by one of the other ranks
Whirling a table-napkin to keep off the flies.

9. Cf. Exodus 12.27: "It is the sacrifice of the Lord's passover, who passed over the houses of the children of Israel in Egypt, when he smote the Egyptians, and delivered our houses."
1. Originally, a hiding place for a Roman Catholic priest during periods of persecution.
2. Uncle of Prince Norodom Sihanouk, former ruler of Cambodia. Fenton was a war correspondent in Vietnam and Cambodia.
3. Palm fibers.
4. Armored personnel carriers.
5. That is, cluster (of bananas in salad). *Carapace:* shell. *Marsh irises:* that is, water plants.

It was like eating between rows of morris[6] dancers—
Only they didn't kick.

On my left sat the prince;
On my right, his drunken aide.
The frogs' thighs leapt into the sad purple face
Like fish to the sound of a Chinese flute.
I wanted to talk to the prince. I wish now
I had collared his aide, who was Saloth Sar's brother.
We treated him as the club bore. He was always
Boasting of his connections, boasting with a head-shake
Or by pronouncing of some doubtful phrase.
And well might he boast. Saloth Sar, for instance,
Was Pol Pot's[7] real name. The APCs
Fired into the sugar palms but met no resistance.

In a diary, I refer to Pol Pot's brother as the Jockey Cap.
A few weeks later, I find him 'in good form
And very skeptical about Chantaraingsey.'
'But one eats well there,' I remark.
'So one should,' says the Jockey Cap:
'The tiger always eats well,
It eats the raw flesh of the deer,
And Chantaraingsey was born in the year of the tiger.
So, did they show you the things they do
With the young refugee girls?'

And he tells me how he will one day give me the gen.[8]
He will tell me how the prince financed the casino
And how the casino brought Lon Nol[9] to power.
He will tell me this.
He will tell me all these things.
All I must do is drink and listen.

In those days, I thought that when the game was up
The prince would be far, far away—
In a limestone faubourg, on the promenade at Nice,[1]
Reduced in circumstances but well enough provided for.
In Paris, he would hardly require his private army.
The Jockey Cap might suffice for café warfare,
And matchboxes for APCs.

But we were always wrong in these predictions.
It was a family war. Whatever happened,
The principals were obliged to attend its issue.

6. Vigorous English folk dance.
7. Leader of Cambodian Communist guerilla force Khmer Rouge, who in 1976 ousted Lon Nol (line 46, note 9), proclaimed the new state of Kampuchea, and instituted a reign of terror.
8. General information (British slang).
9. Corrupt military leader of Cambodia, who in 1970 overthrew the government of Prince Norodom Sihanouk.
1. French resort city on the Mediterranean. *Faubourg:* suburb of a French city.

A few were cajoled into leaving, a few were expelled,
And there were villains enough, but none of them
Slipped away with the swag.

For the prince was fighting Sihanouk, his nephew,
And the Jockey Cap was ranged against his brother
Of whom I remember nothing more
Than an obscure reputation for virtue.
I have been told that the prince is still fighting
Somewhere in the Cardamoms or the Elephant Mountains.
But I doubt that the Jockey Cap would have survived his good
connections.
I think the lunches would have done for him—
Either the lunches or the dead soldiers.

1981

God, a Poem

A nasty surprise in a sandwich,
A drawing-pin caught in your sock,
The limpest of shakes from a hand which
You'd thought would be firm as a rock,

A serious mistake in a nightie,
A grave disappointment all round
Is all that you'll get from th'Almighty,
Is all that you'll get underground.

Oh he *said:* 'If you lay off the crumpet
I'll see you alright[2] in the end.
Just hang on until the last trumpet.[3]
Have faith in me, chum—I'm your friend.'

But if you remind him, he'll tell you:
'I'm sorry, I must have been pissed[4]—
Though your name rings a sort of a bell. You
Should have guessed that I do not exist.

'I didn't exist at Creation,
I didn't exist at the Flood,
And I won't be around for Salvation
To sort out the sheep from the cud—

'Or whatever the phrase is. The fact is
In soteriological[5] terms

2. That is, I'll take care of you (British). *Crumpet:* here, British for girls.
3. That is, Judgment Day.
4. Drunk (British slang).
5. Concerning salvation.

I'm a crude existential malpractice
And you are a diet of worms.[6]

'You're a nasty surprise in a sandwich.
You're a drawing-pin caught in my sock.
You're the limpest of shakes from a hand which
I'd have thought would be firm as a rock,

'You're a serious mistake in a nightie,
You're a grave disappointment all round—
That's all that you are,' says th'Almighty,
'And that's all that you'll be underground.'

1983

For Andrew Wood

What would the dead want from us
Watching from their cave?
Would they have us forever howling?
Would they have us rave
Or disfigure ourselves, or be strangled
Like some ancient emperor's slave?[7]

None of my dead friends were emperors
With such exorbitant tastes
And none of them were so vengeful
As to have all their friends waste
Waste quite away in sorrow
Disfigured and defaced.

I think the dead would want us
To weep for what *they* have lost.
I think that our luck in continuing
Is what would affect them most.
But time would find them generous
And less self-engrossed.

And time would find them generous
As they used to be
And what else would they want from us
But an honoured place in our memory,
A favourite room, a hallowed chair,
Privilege and celebrity?

6. (1) Food for worms (after death); (2) conference (or "Diet") held at Worms, Germany, in 1521, to dissuade Martin Luther from his agitations for reform. *Existential malpractice:* that is, empirical mistake.

7. In ancient Babylonian and Sumerian civilizations, servants were killed and buried with their rulers to serve them in the afterlife.

And so the dead might cease to grieve
And we might make amends
And there might be a pact between
Dead friends and living friends.
What our dead friends would want from us
Would be such living friends.

1993

GRACE NICHOLS
b. 1950

Grace Nichols is, along with poets such as Linton Kwesi Johnson, David Dabydeen, and Fred D'Aguiar, one of the foremost "black British" poets. She was born on January 18, 1950, in Guyana, then a British colony. Educated in the English literary tradition, she became a freelance journalist after receiving a diploma in communications from the University of Guyana. In 1977, she and her companion, the poet John Agard, left Guyana for England.

As "a Caribbean person," Nichols emphasizes that "the Caribbean embraces so much": "The mixture of races and cultures, American-Indian, Asian, European, African. If you are Caribbean, you are a citizen of the world" (*Guardian,* 1991). The geographical vectors of Nichols's poetry point in multiple directions: Africa is "a kind of spiritual homeland" that she imaginatively reclaims; the Caribbean is a much-missed topography of vibrant color, heat, and lush vegetation; and chilly, gray, rain-spattered England is her current home. But Nichols is not only nostalgic; sometimes she celebrates, like Louise Bennett, the reverse colonization of England. In the poem "Wherever I Hang," she ironically inverts the schizophrenic agonies of Derek Walcott's early poetry and the agonized homelessness of Kamau Brathwaite's: "Yes, divided to de ocean / Divided to de bone // Wherever I hang me knickers—that's my home."

Culturally mixed, Nichols writes poetry that is also melded linguistically. Her enslaved ancestors were transported from African to the West Indies, she remembers in "Epilogue," and there a new tongue grew "from the root of the old one." The mixture of English with African and European languages became the Creole—"vibrant, exciting and alive"—that is often the medium of her poetry, as it is for such West Indian poets as Bennett and Brathwaite (*Guardian,* 1991). Like her Afro-Caribbean contemporary Lorna Goodison, Nichols writes in a language that moves across varieties of English: "I myself like working in both standard English and Creole, and tend to want to fuse the two tongues because I come from a background where the two were constantly interacting" ("The Battle with Language"). Celebrating the once despised Creole, Nichols likewise revalorizes the black female body. In *The Fat Black Woman's Poems* (1984) and elsewhere, she appropriates and reverses negative cultural and gender stereotypes, affirming, with infectious glee and sass, the "fat black woman's" size and erotic energy. "Poetry thankfully is a radical synthesizing force," she has written. "The erotic isn't separated from the political or spiritual" ("Battle").

Epilogue

I have crossed an ocean
I have lost my tongue
from the root of the old one
a new one has sprung

1983, 1984

Invitation

1

If my fat
was too much for me
I would have told you
I would have lost a stone[1]
or two

I would have gone jogging
even when it was fogging
I would have weighed in
sitting the bathroom scale
with my tail tucked in

I would have dieted
more care than a diabetic

But as it is
I'm feeling fine
feel no need
to change my lines
when I move I'm target light

Come up and see me sometime[2]

2

Come up and see me sometime
Come up and see me sometime

My breasts are huge exciting
amnions[3] of watermelon
your hands can't cup

1. British term of weight, equivalent to fourteen pounds.
2. A line attributed to Mae West (1893–1980), bawdy, wisecracking American actor.
3. Membranes enclosing sacs.

my thighs are twin seals
                    fat slick pups
there's a purple cherry
below the blues
                    of my black seabelly
there's a mole that gets a ride
each time I shift the heritage
of my behind

Come up and see me sometime

1984

Tropical Death

The fat black woman want
a brilliant tropical death
not a cold sojourn
in some North Europe far/forlorn

The fat black woman want
some heat/hibiscus at her feet
blue sea dress
to wrap her neat

The fat black woman want
some bawl
no quiet jerk tear wiping
a polite hearse withdrawal

The fat black woman want
all her dead rights
first night
third night
nine night
all the sleepless droning
red-eyed wake nights

In the heart
of her mother's sweetbreast
In the shade
of the sun leaf's cool bless
In the bloom
of her people's bloodrest

the fat black woman want
a brilliant tropical death yes

1984

Wherever I Hang

I leave me people, me land, me home
For reasons, I not too sure
I forsake de sun
And de humming-bird splendour
Had big rats in de floorboard
So I pick up me new-world-self
And come, to this place call England
At first I feeling like I in dream—
De misty greyness
I touching de walls to see if they real
They solid to de seam
And de people pouring from de underground system
Like beans
And when I look up to de sky
I see Lord Nelson[4] high—too high to lie

And is so I sending home photos of myself
Among de pigeons and de snow
and is so I warding off de cold
And is so, little by little
I begin to change my calypso ways
Never visiting nobody
Before giving them clear warning
And waiting me turn in queue[5]
Now, after all this time
I get accustom to de English life
But I still miss back-home side
To tell you de truth
I don't know really where I belaang

Yes, divided to de ocean
Divided to de bone

Wherever I hang me knickers—that's my home.

1989

4. British naval hero (1758–1805), whose statue is atop a tall column in Trafalgar Square, London. There are also many monuments to him in the Caribbean, where he spent much of his career.
5. Line.

Charles Bernstein
b. 1950

Charles Bernstein was born on April 4, 1950, in New York City, his father the head of a dressmaking company. From 1968 to 1972, he attended Harvard University, where he studied philosophy and was active in the antiwar movement. After college, while producing and promoting experimental writing, he worked, for nearly twenty years, as a commercial writer and editor for the healthcare industry. In 1978, together with Bruce Andrews, he founded *L=A=N=G=U=A=G=E* magazine, the name of which became associated with a now-famous group of avant-garde writers. Leftist in politics and post-structuralist in theoretical outlook, the Language poets foregrounded the materiality and constitutive power of language. They extended and radicalized the language-centered poetics of the modernists Gertrude Stein and James Joyce, the Objectivists Louis Zukofsky and Charles Reznikoff, and the New York school of John Ashbery and Frank O'Hara. After teaching at several universities, Bernstein was appointed in 1990 the David Gray Professor of Poetry and Letters at the State University of New York at Buffalo, where he has been a central organizer, proponent, and catalyst for avant-garde poetry in the United States.

In his critical prose and his poetry, Bernstein states unambiguously what he is against. He is a fierce—if tongue-in-cheek—opponent of what he debunks as "official verse culture." In his view, the leading poetry publishers, reviewers, institutions, and M.F.A. programs sanction poetry of, as he put it in 1983, "restricted vocabulary, neutral and univocal tone in the guise of voice or persona, grammar-book syntax, received conceits, static and unitary form." Despite its pretense of diversity, "mainstream poetry" assumes a restrictive norm in which a single voice expresses personal feeling. Bernstein proposes instead a poetry of multiple voices and discourses, ruptured grammar and syntax, and blurred generic boundaries. He aims not for a completely abstract or nonreferential language but for what he called in a 1999 interview "polyreferential" language, "in that the poems do not necessarily mean one fixed, definable, paraphrasable thing" (see also the essay "Semblance"). In lieu of appealing to personal or divine authority to ground the meaning of his texts, he riotously plays with the textures and structures of language that create meaning. "Against the priestly function of the poet or of poetry," he writes, "I propose the comic and bathetic, the awkward and railing: to be grounded horizontally in the social and not vertically in the ethers" ("Poetry and/or the Sacred").

Aware of their textual reality, many of Bernstein's poems offer—directly or obliquely—an imbedded self-description, or *ars poetica*. In a poem humorously cast in the fourteen-line sonnet form, "The Kiwi Bird in the Kiwi Tree," he writes, "I want no paradise," such as that of normative lyric transcendence, "only to be / drenched in the downpour of words, fecund / with tropicality." His joyfully irreverent poems are drenched in different kinds of words taken from a variety of contexts. Like a frenetic ventriloquist or stand-up comic, he forces together the discourses of TV, movies, business, computers, nursery rhyme, and canonical literature. The incongruities of this verbal collage defamiliarize and satirize each dialect. As the rhetorical posture of the poetry continually shifts, clichés, imperatives, near-proverbs, witty epigrams, and jingles jostle side by side. Although Bernstein seeks to avoid the grace and mellifluousness of traditional lyric, he insistently rhymes, chimes, puns, and otherwise plays on verbal euphonies. Hoping to resist the easy absorption or commodification of language, he writes a difficult, recalcitrant poetry not of grace, clarity, and self-expression but of—as he told an interviewer in 1999—"confusion, anger, ambiguity, distress, fumbling, awkwardness."

Autonomy Is Jeopardy

I hate artifice. All these
contraptions so many barriers
against what otherwise can't
be contested, so much seeming
sameness in a jello of
squirms. Poetry scares me. I
mean its virtual (or ventriloquized)
anonymity—no protection, no
bulwark to accompany its pervasive
purposivelessness,[1] its accretive
acceleration into what may or
may not swell. Eyes demand
counting, the nowhere seen everywhere
behaved voicelessness everyone is clawing
to get a piece of. Shudder
all you want it won't
make it come any faster
last any longer: the pump
that cannot be dumped.

1990

The Kiwi Bird[2] in the Kiwi Tree

I want no paradise only to be
drenched in the downpour of words, fecund
with tropicality. Fundament be-
yond relation, less 'real' than made, as arms
surround a baby's gurgling: encir-
cling mesh pronounces its promise (not bars
that pinion, notes that ply). The tailor tells
of other tolls, the seam that binds, the trim,
the waste. & having spelled these names, move on
to toys or talcums, skates & scores. Only
the imaginary is real—not trumps
beclouding the mind's acrobatic vers-
ions. The first fact is the social body,
one from another, nor needs no other.

1991

1. Translation of German term used by philosopher Immanuel Kant (1724–1804) in defining the nonutility and autonomy of the aesthetic object.
2. Small, flightless bird native to New Zealand.

From The Lives of the Toll Takers

* * *

Our new
service orientation
mea
nt
not only changing the way we wrote poems but also diversifying
into new poetry services. Poetic
opportunities
,
however, do not fall into your lap, at least not
very often. You've got to seek them out, and when you find them
you've got to have the knowhow to take advantage
of them.
Keeping up with the new aesthetic environment is an ongoing
process: you can't stand still. Besides, our current fees
barely cover our expenses; any deviation from these levels
would
mean working for nothing. Poetry services provide cost savings
to readers, such
as avoiding hospitalizations (you're less likely
to get in an accident if you're home reading poems), minimizing
wasted time (*condensare*),[3] and reducing
adverse idea interactions

3. To condense (Latin). For Ezra Pound, condensation was the essence of poetry, as also for later, Objectivist poets Louis Zukofsky and Lorine Niedecker.

(studies show higher levels of resistance to double-bind
political programming among those who read 7.7 poems or
more each week

).

Poets deserve compensation

for such services.

For readers unwilling to pay the price

we need to refuse to provide such

service as alliteration,
internal rhymes,
exogamic[4] structure, and
unusual vocabulary.

Sharp edges which become shady groves,

mosaic walkways, emphatic asymptotes[5] (asthmatic microtolls).

The hidden language of the Jews: self-reproach, laden with
ambivalence, not this or this either, seeing five sides to
every issue, the old *pilpul*[6] song and dance, obfuscation
clowning as ingratiation, whose only motivation is never
offend, criticize only with a discountable barb: Genocide
is made of words like these, Pound laughing (with Nietzsche's
gay laughter) all the way to the canon's bank spewing forth
about the concrete value of gold, the "plain sense of the
word", a people rooted in the land they sow, and cashing
in on such verbal usury (language held hostage: year one
thousand nine hundred eighty seven).[7]

There is no plain sense of the word,

nothing is straightforward,

description a lie behind a lie:

but truths can still be told.

4. Literally, having to do with intertribal or intergroup marriage.
5. Geometric curves.
6. From the Hebrew for pepper; a method of Talmudic study based on comparing opposing arguments.
7. Ezra Pound (1885–1972), poet, anti-Semite, and supporter of Italian Fascism, believed usury was corrupting and destroying modern civilization (cf. Canto 45). In a wartime radio broadcast from Fascist Italy on April 20, 1943, he reaffirmed the Imagist principle of "the plain sense of the word," amid attacks on capitalism, communism, Jews, British prime minister Winston Churchill, and so forth. *Nietzsche:* Friedrich Nietzsche (1844–1900), German philosopher, who in his book *The Gay Science* (1882) proposed an alliance of laughter and wisdom. The Nazis appropriated his ideas for their Fascist program.

These are the sounds of science (whoosh, blat,
flipahineyhoo), brought to
you by DuPont,[8] *a broadly diversified company dedicated to*
exploitation through science and industry.

Take this harrow off

my chest, I don't feel it anymore

it's getting stark, too stark

to see, feel I'm barking at Hell's spores.[9]

The new sentience.[1]

As if Harvard Law School

was not a re-education camp.

I had decided to go back

to school after fifteen years in

community poetry because I felt

I did not know enough to navigate

through the rocky waters that

lie ahead for all of us in this field.

How had Homer done it, what might Milton

teach? Business training turned

out to be just what I most needed.

Most importantly, I learned that

for a business to be successful, it

needs to be different, to stand out

from the competition. In poetry,

8. Chemical company. *The sounds of science:* allusion to "The Sound of Silence," a 1965 song by folk-rock musicians Paul Simon and Art Garfunkel.

9. Cf. the first verse of "Knockin' on Heaven's Door," by the American singer-songwriter Bob Dylan (b. 1941): "Mama, take this badge off of me / I can't use it anymore. / It's gettin' dark, too dark for me to see / I feel like I'm knockin' on heaven's door."

1. Pun on fellow Language poet Ron Silliman's concept of "The New Sentence," the building block of a disjunctive, avant-garde poetics.

this differentiation is best

achieved through the kind of form

we present.

Seduced by its own critique, the heady operative with twin
peaks and a nose for a brain, remodeled the envelope she
was pushing only to find there was nobody home and no
time when they were expected. Water in the brain,
telescopic Malthusian[2] dumbwaiter, what time will the train
arrive?, I feel weird but then I'm on assignment, a plain blue
wrapper with the taps torn, sultan of my erogenous bull's
eyes, nothing gratis except the tall tales of the Mughali
terraces, decked like plates into the Orangerie's[3] glacial
presentiment . . .

No,

only that the distinction

between nature and

culture may obs

cure

the

b

odily

gumption of language.

* * *

1994

Have Pen, Will Travel

It's not my

business to describe

anything. The only

report is the

2. Thomas Robert Malthus (1766–1857), English economist who warned of unchecked population growth.

3. Museum in Paris. *Mughali*: referring to the Mughal Empire in India (1526–1857), known for its opulence.

discharge of
words called
to account for
their slurs.
A seance of sorts—
or transport into
that nether that
refuses measure.

1995

CAROLYN FORCHÉ
b. 1950

A quotation from Stéphane Mallarmé serves as an epigraph for Carolyn Forché's "Reunion": "Just as he changes himself, in the end eternity changes him." The remark could be a motto for most of her poems. She has cultivated a sense of the past, her own past that has been increasingly impinged on by the forces of power and cruelty that rule much of the world and by the speechless victims of these forces. In "Taking Off My Clothes," exemplary of her poetry of psychological and sexual experience, the poet discovers that her relationship with her male lover is essentially false and conveys this lack in dry, clipped declarative sentences. In "Reunion," by contrast, the poet remembers an early lover from whom she learned "how much tenderness we could / wedge between a stairwell/ and a police lock." But Forché is best known for the poetry that came out of her work as a human rights advocate and journalist in Central America, writing that bridges the distance between verse and journalism, lyric and politics. These poems, perhaps the most gruesome and memorable of which is the prose poem "The Colonel," render vividly the suffering and humiliation of the people of El Salvador. They show a powerful sympathetic identification and sometimes a poignant humor. "The Memory of Elena," another of Forché's best-known poems, is at once delicate and horrifying. The voice is that of the poet, who, by her friendship with an Argentinian woman, participates in the historic cruelty that has been visited on that country. Eating becomes a kind of cannibalism, and the flowers on the husband's grave remind Forché of the impotent silence of the victims.

Forché was born on April 28, 1950, in Detroit, Michigan. She was educated at Michigan State University, receiving a B.A. in international relations and creative writing in 1972 (prefiguring her lasting concern with poetry and international politics), and at Bowling Green State University, where she received an M.F.A. in 1975. She has taught creative writing at a variety of colleges and universities, since 1988 at George Mason University. She worked for Amnesty International in El Salvador from 1978 to 1980 and as the Beirut correspondent for National Public Radio's "All Things Considered" in 1983. Her first collection of poems, *Gathering the Tribes* (1976), was chosen for the Yale Series of Younger Poets, and the second, *The Country between Us* (1981), won the Lamont Poetry Selection Award. She has since published translations, volumes of poetry about global atrocities and suffering, and the anthology *Against Forgetting: Twentieth-Century Poetry of Witness* (1993).

Taking Off My Clothes

I take off my shirt, I show you.
I shaved the hair out under my arms.
I roll up my pants, I scraped off the hair
on my legs with a knife, getting white.

My hair is the color of chopped maples.
My eyes dark as beans cooked in the south.
(Coal fields in the moon on torn-up hills)

Skin polished as a Ming bowl[1]
showing its blood cracks, its age, I have hundreds
of names for the snow, for this, all of them quiet.

In the night I come to you and it seems a shame
to waste my deepest shudders on a wall of a man.

You recognize strangers,
think you lived through destruction.
You can't explain this night, my face, your memory.

You want to know what I know?
Your own hands are lying.

1976

The Memory of Elena[2]

We spend our morning
in the flower stalls counting
the dark tongues of bells
that hang from ropes waiting
for the silence of an hour.
We find a table, ask for *paella*,[3]
cold soup and wine, where a calm
light trembles years behind us.

1. Bowl created during the peak of Chinese ceramic-making.
2. This poem is part of a group titled "In Salvador"; Forché spent some time in the Central American country El Salvador while it was under a military dictatorship.
3. Spanish and Latin American dish containing rice, meat, seafood, and vegetables.

In Buenos Aires[4] only three
years ago, it was the last time his hand
slipped into her dress, with pearls
cooling her throat and bells like
these, chipping at the night—

As she talks, the hollow
clopping of a horse, the sound
of bones touched together.
The *paella* comes, a bed of rice
and *camarones,*[5] fingers and shells,
the lips of those whose lips
have been removed, mussels
the soft blue of a leg socket.

This is not *paella,* this is what
has become of those who remained
in Buenos Aires. This is the ring
of a rifle report on the stones,
her hand over her mouth,
her husband falling against her.

These are the flowers we bought
this morning, the dahlias tossed
on his grave and bells
waiting with their tongues cut out
for this particular silence.

1977 1981

Reunion

Just as he changes himself, in the end eternity changes him.
—Mallarmé[6]

On the phonograph, the voice
of a woman already dead for three
decades, singing of a man
who could make her do anything.
On the table, two fragile
glasses of black wine,
a bottle wrapped in its towel.
It is that room, the one
we took in every city, it is
as I remember: the bed, a block
of moonlight and pillows.

4. Capital of Argentina.
5. Shrimp.
6. First line of "Le Tombeau d'Edgar Poe," by French poet Stéphane Mallarmé (1842–1898).

My fingernails, pecks of light
on your thighs.
The stink of the fire escape.
The wet butts of cigarettes
you crushed one after another.
How I watched the morning come
as you slept, more my son
than a man ten years older.
How my breasts feel, years
later, the tongues swishing
in my dress, some yours, some
left by other men.
Since then, I have always
wakened first, I have learned
to leave a bed without being
seen and have stood
at the washbasins, wiping oil
and salt from my skin,
staring at the cupped water
in my two hands.
I have kept everything
you whispered to me then.
I can remember it now as I see you
again, how much tenderness we could
wedge between a stairwell
and a police lock,[7] or as it was,
as it still is, in the voice
of a woman singing of a man
who could make her do anything.

1981

The Colonel

What you have heard is true. I was in his house. His wife carried a tray of coffee and sugar. His daughter filed her nails, his son went out for the night. There were daily papers, pet dogs, a pistol on the cushion beside him. The moon swung bare on its black cord over the house. On the television was a cop show. It was in English. Broken bottles were embedded in the walls around the house to scoop the kneecaps from a man's legs or cut his hands to lace. On the windows there were gratings like those in liquor stores. We had dinner, rack of lamb, good wine, a gold bell was on the table for calling the maid. The maid brought green mangoes, salt, a type of bread. I was asked how I enjoyed the country. There was a brief commercial in Spanish. His wife took everything away. There was some talk then of how difficult it had become to govern. The parrot said hello on the terrace. The colonel told it to shut up, and pushed himself from the table. My friend said to me with his eyes: say nothing.

7. Lock with a heavy iron rod in the floor that prevents an apartment door from being forcibly opened; common in high-crime neighborhoods.

The colonel returned with a sack used to bring groceries home. He spilled many human ears on the table. They were like dried peach halves. There is no other way to say this. He took one of them in his hands, shook it in our faces, dropped it into a water glass. It came alive there. I am tired of fooling around he said. As for the rights of anyone, tell your people they can go fuck themselves. He swept the ears to the floor with his arm and held the last of his wine in the air. Something for your poetry, no? he said. Some of the ears on the floor caught this scrap of his voice. Some of the ears on the floor were pressed to the ground.

May 1978

1981

JORIE GRAHAM
b. 1950

Jorie Graham is a poet of large ideas. Her philosophical bent owes something to her polyglot background. Born on May 9, 1950, in New York, to an Irish American father and a Jewish American mother, she grew up with one ear to American speech. Raised in Italy and attending French schools, she had another ear to European languages and culture. As a child, Graham "was taught three/names for the tree facing" her window: "*Castagno . . . Chassagne . . . chestnut*" ("I Was Taught Three"). It was not until this trilingual poet was in her twenties that, after studying at the Sorbonne in Paris, she moved to the United States as a film student at New York University—an influence apparent in the cinematic techniques and rhetoric of her poetry. Seeing the world through the prism of three languages, Graham early on experienced the relation between word and world as complex and contingent.

Her European affiliations, her philosophical questioning of the relation between mind and reality, and her fascination with the visual arts recall her precursors, the Francophile modernists Wallace Stevens and T. S. Eliot. In an interview with the *Denver Quarterly*, Graham remarked, "I think many poets writing today realize we need to recover a high level of ambition, a rage, if you will—the big hunger." She is at the forefront of contemporary poets working to recover this "big hunger," the large philosophical and formal ambition of modernist poetry.

Graham has this hunger, but also distrusts it. She longs for an ethical, philosophical, or scientific system that would heal the split between thing and representation and also make sense of our place in the world, of personal experience within the context of public atrocities—the Holocaust, imperialism, assassination, and so forth. She calls this, in the title of one of her most ambitious poems, "The Dream of the Unified Field." She thus compares large events with small, deliberately forces analogies between the personal and the historical, and braids together intimate disclosure with metaphysics. She also juxtaposes different modes of representation from art, film, history, and poetry. Yet Graham fiercely questions her own impulse toward philosophical systematization. She explodes her analogies as she crafts them. She undermines the myth of continuous subjectivity even as she relies on personal memory. And she views her own poetic language with corrosive suspicion.

Her poems typically take personal moments of crisis or revelation as their points of departure, such as hearing about the shooting of President Kennedy in a movie theater or bringing her daughter a leotard. She slows down and reenters the moment to ask about its meaning in collective history, about the relation between inner experience and external reality, and about the ethics of representation. The psychic structure of her poetry is daringly associative, leaping from one image to another and thus compelling the reader to puzzle out the resemblances and differences—in "The Dream of the Unified Field," for example, between the mind and a pocket; between starlings, a crow, and a Russian ballet teacher; between the poet's ambitions for her daughter and Columbus's colonization of the New World.

Graham has criticized the generation after the modernists for being limited "by the strictly secular sense of reality (domestic, confessional), as well as their unquestioned relationship to the act of representation." But her own work bears fruitful comparison with that of Robert Lowell, Sylvia Plath, and other "confessionalists," who often examined their personal experience within broader historical and cultural contexts. At the same time, her poetry can also be compared with that of anticonfessional poets, such as Susan Howe, Lyn Hejinian, Michael Palmer, and Charles Bernstein: her poems, too, interrogate subjectivity, resist closure, and fracture time, space, and the speaking voice. Although Graham relies less on pastiche and collage than do these experimentalists, her anxieties about the ethical implications of form—narrative as complicit in imperialism, language as a kind of violence, closure as commodification—dovetail with their concerns.

The texture of Graham's poems has changed dramatically over the course of her career. "At Luca Signorelli's Resurrection of the Body," like many of Graham's early poems an example of *ekphrasis*, a poem about a visual artifact, is written in regular stanzas with alternate lines indented. By the time of "Fission," the indentations remain, but the strophes have become irregular, the lines have lengthened, and ellipses, dashes, and parentheses have fissured the syntax. The stilled, balanced ekphrastic poem has been abandoned for the hurried, disjunctive, jump-cut cinematic poem. She is seeking, as she put it, "new strategies by which to postpone closure," to resist its "suction," new "forms of delay, digression, side-motions." With her book *Materialism* (1993), the spatial organization of the poem on the page becomes still more sprawling, with large blocks of type and more dropped lines, her syntax and semantics become increasingly fragmented, frenzied, and opaque. "For me," Graham says, "each book is a critique of the previous," and so she has challenged herself to begin again with each new volume.

After receiving her M.F.A. in 1978 from the University of Iowa Writers' Workshop, Graham taught briefly at several universities before returning to Iowa, as a teacher, in 1983. In 1999, she succeeded Seamus Heaney as Boylston Professor of Rhetoric and Oratory at Harvard University. She was honored with a MacArthur Fellowship in 1990 and the Pulitzer Prize in 1996 for *The Dream of the Unified Field: Selected Poems, 1974–1994*.

At Luca Signorelli's Resurrection of the Body[1]

See how they hurry
    to enter
their bodies,
    these spirits.
Is it better, flesh,
    that they

1. Renaissance painter Luca Signorelli (c. 1445–1523) was famous for the anatomical precision and musculature of his human figures. The poem considers his *Resurrection of the Body* (c. 1500), part of a series of frescoes in the cathedral at Orvieto, in central Italy.

should hurry so?
      From above
the green-winged angels
      blare down
trumpets and light. But
      they don't care,

they hurry to congregate,
      they hurry
into speech, until
      it's a marketplace,
it is humanity. But still
      we wonder

in the chancel
      of the dark cathedral,
is it better, back?
      The artist
has tried to make it so: each tendon
      they press

to re-enter
      is perfect. But is it
perfection
      they're after,
pulling themselves up
      through the soil

into the weightedness, the color,
      into the eye
of the painter? Outside
      it is 1500,
all round the cathedral
      streets hurry to open

through the wild
      silver grasses. . . .
The men and women
      on the cathedral wall
do not know how,
      having come this far,

to stop their
      hurrying. They amble off
in groups, in
      couples. Soon
some are clothed, there is
      distance, there is

perspective. Standing below them
      in the church
in Orvieto, how can we

tell them
to be stern and brazen
and slow,

that there is no
entrance,
only entering. They keep on
arriving,
wanting names,
wanting

happiness. In his studio
Luca Signorelli
in the name of God
and Science
and the believable
broke into the body

studying arrival.
But the wall
of the flesh
opens endlessly,
its vanishing point so deep
and receding

we have yet to find it,
to have it
stop us. So he cut
deeper,
graduating slowly
from the symbolic

to the beautiful. How far
is true?
When his one son
died violently,[2]
he had the body brought to him
and laid it

on the drawing-table,
and stood
at a certain distance
awaiting the best
possible light, the best depth
of day,

then with beauty and care
and technique

2. According to an anecdote recorded by Italian painter and biographer Giorgio Vasari (1511–1574), after Signorelli's son was killed the painter had his body brought to him so that he could study it and preserve it in his drawings.

and judgment, cut into
shadow, cut
into bone and sinew and every
pocket

in which the cold light
pooled.
It took him days,
that deep
caress, cutting,
unfastening,

until his mind
could climb into
the open flesh and
mend itself.

1983

Fission

The real electric lights light upon the full-sized
screen
on which the greater-than-life-size girl appears,
almost nude on the lawn—sprinklers on—
voice-over her mother calling her name out—loud—[3]
camera angle giving her lowered lids their full
expanse—a desert—as they rise

out of the shabby annihilation,
out of the possibility of never-having-been-seen,
and rise,
till the glance is let loose into the auditorium,
and the man who has just stopped in his tracks
looks down
for the first

time. Tick tock. It's the birth of the mercantile
dream (he looks down). It's the birth of
the dream called
new world (looks down). She lies there. A corridor of light
filled with dust
flows down from the booth to the screen.
Everyone in here wants to be taken off

somebody's list, wants to be placed on
somebody else's list.

3. The scene described is from Stanley Kubrick's 1962 movie *Lolita*, an adaptation of the 1955 novel by Vladimir Nabokov. In the scene, the middle-aged Humbert (James Mason) first sees Lolita (Sue Lyon), the adolescent girl who becomes the object of his obsession.

Tick. It is 1963. The idea of history is being
outmaneuvered.
So that as the houselights come on—midscene—
not quite killing the picture which keeps flowing beneath,

a man comes running down the aisle
asking for our attention—
Ladies and Gentlemen.
I watch the houselights lap against the other light—the tunnel
of image-making dots licking the white sheet awake—
a man, a girl, her desperate mother—daisies growing in the
corner—

I watch the light from our real place
suck the arm of screen-building light into itself
until the gesture of the magic forearm frays,
and the story up there grays, pales—them almost lepers now,
saints, such

white on their flesh in
patches—her thighs like receipts slapped down on a
slim silver tray,

her eyes as she lowers the heart-shaped shades,
as the glance glides over what used to be the open,
the free,
as the glance moves, pianissimo, over the glint of day,
over the sprinkler, the mother's voice shrieking like a grappling
hook
the grass blades aflame with being-seen, here on the out-

skirts. . . . You can almost hear the click at the heart of
the silence
where the turnstile shuts and he's *in*—our hero—
the moment spoked,
our gaze on her fifteen-foot eyes,
the man hoarse now as he waves his arms,
as he screams to the booth to cut it, cut the sound,
and the sound is cut,
and her sun-barred shoulders are left to turn

soundless as they accompany
her neck, her face, the
looking-up.
Now the theater's skylight is opened and noon slides in.
I watch as it overpowers the electric lights,
whiting the story out one layer further

till it's just a smoldering of whites
where she sits up, and her stretch of flesh
is just a roiling up of graynesses,
vague stutterings of
light with motion in them, bits of moving zeros

in the infinite virtuality of light,
some *likeness* in it but not particulate,
a grave of possible shapes called *likeness*—see it?—something
scrawling up there that could be skin or daylight or even

the expressway now that he's gotten her to leave with him—
(it happened rather fast) (do you recall)—

the man up front screaming the President's been shot,[4] waving
his hat, slamming one hand flat
over the open
to somehow get
our attention,

in Dallas, behind him the scorcher—whites, grays,
laying themselves across his face—
him like a beggar in front of us, holding his hat—
I don't recall what I did,
I don't recall what the right thing to do would be,
I wanted someone to love. . . .

There is a way she lay down on that lawn
to begin with,
in the heart of the sprinklers,
before the mother's call,
before the man's shadow laid itself down,

there is a way to not yet be wanted,

there is a way to lie there at twenty-four frames
per second—no faster—
not at the speed of plot,
not at the speed of desire—
the road out—expressway—hotels—motels—
no telling what we'll have to see next,
no telling what all we'll have to want next,
(right past the stunned rows of houses),
no telling what on earth we'll have to marry marry marry. . . .

Where the three lights merged:
where the image licked my small body from the front, the story
playing
all over my face my
forwardness,
where the electric lights took up the back and sides,
the unwavering houselights,
seasonless,

where the long thin arm of day came in from the top
to touch my head,

4. President John F. Kennedy was assassinated in Dallas, Texas, on November 22, 1963.

reaching down along my staring face—
where they flared up around my body unable to

merge into each other
over my likeness,
slamming down one side of me, unquenchable—here static

there flaming—
sifting grays into other grays—
mixing the split second into the long haul—
flanking me—undressing something there where my
body is
though not my body—
where they play on the field of my willingness,

where they kiss and brood, filtering each other to no avail,
all over my solo
appearance,
bits smoldering under the shadows I make—
and aimlessly—what we call *free*—there

the immobilism sets in,
the being-in-place more alive than the being,
my father sobbing beside me, the man on the stage
screaming, the woman behind us starting to
pray,
the immobilism, the being-in-place more alive than

the being,
the squad car now faintly visible on the screen
starting the chase up,
all over my countenance,
the velvet armrest at my fingers, the dollar bill

in my hand,
choice the thing that wrecks the sensuous here the glorious
here—
that wrecks the beauty,
choice the move that rips the wrappings of light, the
ever-tighter wrappings

of the layers of the
real: what is, what also is, what might be that is,
what could have been that is, what
might have been that is, what I say that is,
what the words say that is,
what you imagine the words say that is—Don't move, don't

wreck the shroud, don't move—

1991

The Dream of the Unified Field[5]

1

On my way to bringing you the leotard
you forgot to include in your overnight bag,
the snow started coming down harder.
I watched each gathering of leafy flakes
melt round my footfall.
I looked up into it—late afternoon but bright.
Nothing true or false in itself. Just motion. Many strips of
motion. Filaments of falling marked by the tiny certainties
of flakes. Never blurring yet themselves a cloud. Me in it
and yet
moving easily through it, black Lycra leotard balled into
my pocket,
your tiny dream in it, my left hand on it or in it
to keep
warm. Praise this. Praise that. Flash a glance up and try
to see
the arabesques and runnels,[6] gathering and loosening, as they
define, as a voice would, the passaging through from
the-other-than-
human. Gone as they hit the earth. But embellishing.
Flourishing. The road with me on it going on through. In-
scribed with the present. As if it really
were possible to exist, and exist, never to be pulled back
in, given and given never to be received. The music
of the footfalls doesn't stop, doesn't
mean. *Here are your things*, I said.

2

Starting home I heard—bothering, lifting, then
bothering again—
the huge flock of starlings massed over our
neighborhood
these days; heard them lift and
swim overhead through the falling snow
as though the austerity of a true, cold thing, a verity,
the black bits of their thousands of bodies swarming
then settling
overhead. I stopped. All up and down the empty oak
they stilled. Every limb sprouting. Every leafy backlit
body
filling its part of the empty crown. I tried to count—
then tried to estimate—
but the leaves of this wet black tree at the heart of
the storm—shiny—

5. In particle physics, unified field theory represents an attempt to account for the interaction of all forces and particles under a single explanatory framework.
6. Small streams. *Arabesques:* ballet position; also, flowing lines.

river through limbs, back onto limbs,
scatter, blow away, scatter, recollect—
undoing again and again the tree without it ever ceasing to be
full.
Foliage of the tree of the world's waiting.
Of having waited a long time and
still having
to wait. Of trailing and screaming.
Of engulfed readjustments. Of blackness redisappearing
into
downdrafts of snow. Of indifference. Of indifferent
reappearings.
I think of you
back of me now in the bright house of
your friend
twirling in the living room in the shiny leotard
you love.
I had looked—as I was leaving—through the window

to see you, slick in your magic,
pulling away from the wall—

I watch the head explode then recollect, explode, recollect.

3

Then I heard it, inside the swarm, the single cry

of the crow. One syllable—one—inside the screeching and the
skittering,
inside the constant repatterning of a thing not nervous yet
not ever
still—but not uncertain—without obedience
yet not without law—one syllable—
black, shiny, twirling on its single stem,
rooting, one foot on the earth,
twisting and twisting—

and then again—a little further off this time—*down the*
ravine, voice inside a head, filling a head. . . .

See, my pocket is empty now. I let my hand
open and shut in there. I do it again. Two now, skull and
pocket
with their terrified inhabitants.

You turn the music up. The window nothing to you, liquid, dark,
where now your mother has come back to watch.

4

Closeup, he's blue—streaked iris blue, india-ink blue—and
black—an oily, fiery set of blacks—none of them

true—as where hate and order touch—something that cannot
become known. Stages of black but without
graduation. So there is no direction.
All of this happened, yes. Then disappeared
into the body of the crow, chorus of meanings,
layers of blacks, then just the crow, plain, big,
lifting his claws to walk thrustingly
forward and back—indigo, cyanine, beryl, grape, steel. . . . Then suddenly he
wings and—braking as he lifts
the chest in which an eye-sized heart now beats—
—he's up—a blunt clean stroke—
one ink-streak on the early evening snowlit scene—
See the gesture of the painter?—Recall the
crow?—Place him quickly on his limb as he comes sheering in,
close to the trunk, to land—Is he now
disappeared again?

5

. . . . *long neck, up, up with the head,*
eyes on the fingertips, bent leg, shift of
the weight—*turn*—No, no, begin again . . .
What had she seen, Madame Sakaroff, at Stalingrad,[7] now in
her room of mirrors tapping her cane
as the piano player begins the interrupted Minuet again
and we line up right foot extended, right
hand extended, the Bach mid-phrase—
Europe? The dream of Europe?—midwinter afternoon,
rain at the windowpane, ceilings at thirty feet and coffered
floating over the wide interior spaces . . .
No one must believe in God again I heard her say
one time when I had come to class too soon
and had been sent to change. The visitor had left,
kissing her hand, small bow, and I had seen her (from the curtain)
(having forgotten I was there)
turn from the huge pearl-inlaid doors she had just closed,
one hand still on the massive, gold, bird-headed knob,
and see—a hundred feet away—herself—a woman in black in
a mirrored room—
saw her not shift her gaze but bring her pallid tensile hand—
as if it were not part of her—slowly down from
the ridged, cold, feathered knob and, recollected, fixed upon
that other woman, emigrée,
begin to move in stiffly towards her . . . You out there
now,
you in here with me—I watched the two of them,
black and black, in the gigantic light,
glide at each other, heads raised, necks long—
me wanting to cry out—where were the others?—wasn't it late?
the two of her like huge black hands—
clap once and once only and the signal is given—

7. Former name of Volgograd, city in southwestern Russia.

but to what?—regarding what?—till closer-in I saw
more suddenly
how her eyes eyed themselves: no wavering:
like a vast silver page burning: the black hole
expanding:
like a meaning coming up quick from inside that page—
coming up quick to seize the reading face—
each face wanting the other to *take* it—
but where? and *from* where?—I was eight—
I saw the different weights of things,
saw the vivid performance of the present,
saw the light rippling almost shuddering where her body finally
touched
the image, the silver film between them like something that would have
shed itself in nature now
but wouldn't, couldn't, here, on tight,
between, not thinning, not slipping off to let some
seed-down[8]
through, no signal in it, no information . . . Child,
what should I know
to save you that I do not know, hands on this windowpane?—

6

The storm: I close my eyes and,
standing in it, try to make it *mine*. An inside
thing. Once I was. . . . once, once.
It settles, in my head, the wavering white
sleep, the instances—they stick, accrue,
grip up, connect, they do not melt,
I will not let them melt, they build, cloud and cloud,
I feel myself weak, I feel the thinking muscle-up—
outside, the talk-talk of the birds—outside,
strings and their roots, leaves inside the limbs,
in some spots the skin breaking—
but inside, no more exploding, no more smoldering, no more,
inside, a splinter colony, new world, possession
gripping down to form,
wilderness brought deep into my clearing,
out of the ooze of night,
limbed, shouldered, necked, visaged, the white—
now the clouds coming in (don't look up),
now the Age behind the clouds, The Great Heights,
all in there, reclining, eyes closed, huge,
centuries and centuries long and wide,
and underneath, barely attached but attached,
like a runner, my body, my tiny piece of
the century—minutes, houses going by—The Great
Heights—
anchored by these footsteps, now and now,

8. The soft hairs on seeds, such as cotton.

the footstepping—now and now—carrying its vast
white sleeping geography—mapped—
not a lease—*possession*—"At the hour of vespers
in a sudden blinding snow,
they entered the harbor and he named it Puerto de

7

San Nicolas[9] and at its entrance he imagined he
could see
its beauty and goodness, *sand right up to the land*
where you can put the side of a ship. He thought
he saw
Indians fleeing through the white before
the ship . . . As for him, he did not believe what his
crew
told him, nor did he understand them well, nor they
him. In the white swirl, he placed a large cross
at the western side of
the harbor, on a conspicuous height,
as a sign that Your Highness claim the land as
Your own. After the cross was set up,
three sailors went into the bush (immediately erased
from sight by the fast snow) to see what kinds of
trees. They captured three very black Indian
women—one who was young and pretty.
The Admiral ordered her clothed and returned to
her land
courteously. There her people told
that she had not wanted to leave the ship,
but wished to stay on it. The snow was wild.
Inside it, though, you could see
this woman was wearing a little piece of
gold on her nose, which was a sign there was
gold
on that land"—

1993

The Surface

It has a hole in it. Not only where I
concentrate.
The river still ribboning, twisting up,
into its re-
arrangements, chill enlightenments, tight-knotted
quickenings

9. The quotation is adapted from the diary of Christopher Columbus's first voyage to the New World. Graham adds to the passage the snow and the adjective "black" describing the Indian women.

and loosenings—whispered messages dissolving
                    the messengers—
the river still glinting-up into its handfuls, heapings,
                    glassy
forgettings under the river of
my attention—
and the river of my attention laying itself down—
                    bending,
reassembling—over the quick leaving-offs and windy
                    obstacles—
and the surface rippling under the wind's attention—
rippling over the accumulations, the slowed-down drifting
                    permanences
of the cold
bed.
I say *iridescent* and I look down.
The leaves very still as they are carried.

1993

The Swarm

(Todi,[1] 1996)

I wanted you to listen to the bells,
holding the phone out the one small window
to where I thought
the ringing was—

Vespers[2] scavenging the evening air,
headset fisted against the huge dissolving

where I stare at the tiny holes in the receiver's transatlantic opening
to see evening-light and then churchbells

send their regrets, slithering, in—
in there a white flame charged with duplication—.
I had you try to listen, bending down into the mouthpiece to whisper,
    hard,

can you hear them (two petals fall and then the   is wholly
changed) (yes) (and then another yes like a vertebrate enchaining)
yes yes yes yes

We were somebody. A boat stills on a harbor and for a while no one
appears,
not on deck, not on shore,
only a few birds glancing round,

1. Town in central Italy.
2. Bells rung at the hour of the Roman Catholic evening prayers.

then—before a single face appears—something
                                        announces itself
like a piece of the whole blueness broken off and thrown down,
a roughness inserted,

yes,
the infinite variety of *having once been,*
of being, of *coming to life,* right there in the thin air, a debris re-
assembling, a blue transparent bit of paper flapping in also-blue air,

boundaries being squeezed out of the blue, out of the inside of the blue,
human eyes
held shut,

and then the whisking-open of the lash—the *be thou, be thou*—

—*a boat stills in a harbor and for a while no one*
appears—a sunny day, a crisp Aegean blue,
easy things—a keel, a sail—

why should you fear?—
me holding my arm out into the crisp December air—
beige cord and then the plastic parenthetical opening wherein I

have you—you without eyes or arms or body now—listen to

the long ocean between us

—the plastic cooling now—this tiny geometric swarm of
openings sending to you

no parts of me you've touched, no places where you've

gone—

Two petals fall—hear it?—moon, are you not coming soon?—two fall

2000

ANNE CARSON
b. 1950

In much of her poetry, Anne Carson evocatively juxtaposes the modern and the classical, the personal and the literary. She writes about recent love relationships, contemporary video and TV, twentieth-century writers such as Virginia Woolf, Antonin Artaud, and Sylvia Plath. But she sandwiches these references with older texts, whether writings by the Brontë sisters ("The Glass Essay"), stories from the Bible ("Lazarus Standup: Shooting Script"), or ancient Greek poetry by Homer, Sappho, and Stesichorus.

Like the incongruous equations in metaphor, these rich connections make the familiar strange. As Carson writes: "metaphor causes the mind to experience itself // in the act of making a mistake"; but "from the true mistakes of metaphor a lesson can be learned. . . . / Metaphors teach the mind // to enjoy error / and to learn / from the juxtaposition of *what is* and *what is not* the case" ("Essay on What I Think about Most"). Spanning vast distances in time and space, Carson's poetry shimmers in the gap between her own emotional life and the rediscovered past, between the contemporary media and ancient forms. She renews the modernist promise to "make it new," in Ezra Pound's slogan, by rereading the contemporary in the light of the classical and vice versa.

Formally inventive, Carson braids together the ruminative texture of the essay, the narrative propulsion of the novel, the self-analysis of autobiography, and the lapidary compression of lyric. In "The Glass Essay," she vividly describes the end of a love affair with a man named Law, a visit with a difficult mother, the degeneration of a father with Alzheimer's in a nursing home, and walks on a bleak Canadian moor. Into this semiautobiographical mix, she weaves commentary on the writings of the Brontë sisters, whose works function—like the classical texts she often incorporates into her poetry—as oblique and remote points of comparison for the poet's personal experience.

Carson casts the net of her poetry around philosophical speculation, epigrammatic insight, personal drama, and literary-critical analysis. Tightly wound with crisp diction, studded with striking metaphors, her poems are lucid in feeling and intense in thought. They are at one and the same time intellectually crystalline and emotionally volcanic.

Carson was born on June 21, 1950, in Toronto, Canada, and grew up in Ontario. From the University of Toronto she received both her B.A. (1974) and her Ph.D. (1981). The recipient of a MacArthur Fellowship in 2000, she teaches classics at McGill University, in Montreal, and earlier held positions at the University of Calgary (1979), Princeton University (1980–87), and Emory University (1987). Along with lyric poetry, she has published books of criticism on classical literature, books that include both poetry and criticism, and a novel-in-verse, *Autobiography of Red* (1998).

From The Glass Essay

* * *

Well there are many ways of being held prisoner,
I am thinking as I stride over the moor.
As a rule after lunch mother has a nap

and I go out to walk.
The bare blue trees and bleached wooden sky of April
carve into me with knives of light.

Something inside it reminds me of childhood—
it is the light of the stalled time after lunch
when clocks tick

and hearts shut
and fathers leave to go back to work
and mothers stand at the kitchen sink pondering

something they never tell.
You remember too much,
my mother said to me recently.

Why hold onto all that? And I said,
Where can I put it down?
She shifted to a question about airports.

Crops of ice are changing to mud all around me
as I push on across the moor
warmed by drifts from the pale blue sun.

On the edge of the moor our pines
dip and coast in breezes
from somewhere else.

Perhaps the hardest thing about losing a lover is
to watch the year repeat its days.
It is as if I could dip my hand down

into time and scoop up
blue and green lozenges[1] of April heat
a year ago in another country.

I can feel that other day running underneath this one
like an old videotape—here we go fast around the last corner
up the hill to his house, shadows

of limes and roses blowing in the car window
and music spraying from the radio and him
singing and touching my left hand to his lips.

Law[2] lived in a high blue room from which he could see the sea.
Time in its transparent loops as it passes beneath me now
still carries the sound of the telephone in that room

and traffic far off and doves under the window
chuckling coolly and his voice saying,
You beauty. I can feel that beauty's

heart beating inside mine as she presses into his arms in the high blue room—
No, I say aloud. I force my arms down
through air which is suddenly cold and heavy as water

and the videotape jerks to a halt
like a glass slide under a drop of blood.
I stop and turn and stand into the wind,

1. Diamond-shaped figures.
2. The speaker's lover.

which now plunges towards me over the moor.
When Law left I felt so bad I thought I would die.
This is not uncommon.

I took up the practice of meditation.
Each morning I sat on the floor in front of my sofa
and chanted bits of old Latin prayers.

De profundis clamavi ad te Domine.[3]
Each morning a vision came to me.
Gradually I understood that these were naked glimpses of my soul.

I called them Nudes.
Nude #1. Woman alone on a hill.
She stands into the wind.

It is a hard wind slanting from the north.
Long flaps and shreds of flesh rip off the woman's body and lift
and blow away on the wind, leaving

an exposed column of nerve and blood and muscle
calling mutely through lipless mouth.
It pains me to record this,

I am not a melodramatic person.
But soul is "hewn in a wild workshop"
as Charlotte Brontë says of *Wuthering Heights.*[4]

Charlotte's preface to *Wuthering Heights* is a publicist's masterpiece.
Like someone carefully not looking at a scorpion
crouched on the arm of the sofa Charlotte

talks firmly and calmly
about the other furniture of Emily's workshop—about
the inexorable spirit ("stronger than a man, simpler than a child"),

the cruel illness ("pain no words can render"),
the autonomous end ("she sank rapidly, she made haste to leave us")
and about Emily's total subjection

to a creative project she could neither understand nor control,
and for which she deserves no more praise nor blame
than if she had opened her mouth

"to breathe lightning." The scorpion is inching down
the arm of the sofa while Charlotte
continues to speak helpfully about lightning

3. Psalm 130: Out of the depths I have called unto thee, O Lord (Latin).
4. Novel by English writer Emily Brontë (1818–1848). Her sister Charlotte (1816–1855) wrote an introduction for the 1850 edition, attempting to explain how a novel of such extreme passion, imagination, and apparent "coarseness" could have been produced by a woman with such a reserved life. Throughout "The Glass Essay," the poet compares her own life with Emily Brontë's.

and other weather we may expect to experience
when we enter Emily's electrical atmosphere.
It is "a horror of great darkness" that awaits us there

but Emily is not responsible. Emily was in the grip.
"Having formed these beings she did not know what she had done,"
says Charlotte (of Heathcliff and Earnshaw and Catherine).[5]

Well there are many ways of being held prisoner.
The scorpion takes a light spring and lands on our left knee
as Charlotte concludes, "On herself she had no pity."

Pitiless too are the Heights, which Emily called Wuthering
because of their "bracing ventilation"
and "a north wind over the edge."

Whaching[6] a north wind grind the moor
that surrounded her father's house on every side,
formed of a kind of rock called millstone grit,

taught Emily all she knew about love and its necessities—
an angry education that shapes the way her characters
use one another. "My love for Heathcliff," says Catherine,

"resembles the eternal rocks beneath—
a source of little visible delight, but necessary."
Necessary? I notice the sun has dimmed

and the afternoon air sharpening.
I turn and start to recross the moor towards home.
What are the imperatives

that hold people like Catherine and Heathcliff
together and apart, like pores blown into hot rock
and then stranded out of reach

of one another when it hardens? What kind of necessity is that?
The last time I saw Law was a black night in September.
Autumn had begun,

my knees were cold inside my clothes.
A chill fragment of moon rose.
He stood in my living room and spoke

without looking at me. Not enough spin on it,
he said of our five years of love.
Inside my chest I felt my heart snap into two pieces

5. Three characters from the novel.
6. Earlier in the poem, Carson explains that *whacher* is Brontë's idiosyncratic spelling of *watcher*. This excerpt is from the poem's fourth section, "Whacher."

which floated apart. By now I was so cold
it was like burning. I put out my hand
to touch his. He moved back.

I don't want to be sexual with you, he said. Everything gets crazy.
But now he was looking at me.
Yes, I said as I began to remove my clothes.

Everything gets crazy. When nude
I turned my back because he likes the back.
He moved onto me.

Everything I know about love and its necessities
I learned in that one moment
when I found myself

thrusting my little burning red backside like a baboon
at a man who no longer cherished me.
There was no area of my mind

not appalled by this action, no part of my body
that could have done otherwise.
But to talk of mind and body begs the question.

Soul is the place,
stretched like a surface of millstone grit between body and mind,
where such necessity grinds itself out.

Soul is what I kept watch on all that night.
Law stayed with me.
We lay on top of the covers as if it weren't really a night of sleep and time,

caressing and singing to one another in our made-up language
like the children we used to be.
That was a night that centred Heaven and Hell,

as Emily would say. We tried to fuck
but he remained limp, although happy. I came
again and again, each time accumulating lucidity,

until at last I was floating high up near the ceiling looking down
on the two souls clasped there on the bed
with their mortal boundaries

visible around them like lines on a map.
I saw the lines harden.
He left in the morning.

It is very cold
walking into the long scraped April wind.
At this time of year there is no sunset
just some movements inside the light and then a sinking away.

1995

From TV Men

XI

TV is presocial, like Man.

On the last day of the Death Valley shoot
driving through huge slow brown streaks of mountain
towards the light-hole,

Hektor[7] feels his pits go dry.

Clouds drop their lines down the faces of the rock
as if marking out a hunting ground.
Hektor, whose heart

walked ahead of him always,

ran ahead like a drunk creature
to lick salt particles off the low bushes
as if they were butter or silver honey,
whose heart Homer compared to a lion

turning in a net of dogs and men and
whichever way the lion lunges the men and dogs give way
yet the net keeps contracting—

Hektor trembles.

The human way includes two kinds of knowledge.
Fire and Night. Hektor has been to the Fire
in conditions of experimental purity.

It is 6:53 A.M. when his Night unhoods itself.

Hektor sees that he is living at the centre of a vast metal disc.
A dawn clot of moon dangles oddly above
and this realization comes coldly through him:

the disc is tilting.

Very slowly the disc attains an angle of thirty degrees.
Dark blue signal is flowing steadily
from the centre to the edge

as Hektor starts to slide.

It takes but an instant to realize you are mortal.
Troy reared up on its hind legs
and a darkness of life flowed through the town

7. In Homer's *Iliad*, the chief warrior of the Trojan army.

from purple cup to purple cup.

Toes to the line please, says the assistant camera man,
slapping two pieces of yellow tape
on the surface of the disc

just in front of Hektor's feet.

Dashing back to the camera he raises his slate.
Places everyone, calls the director as a thousand wasps
come stinging out of the arc lamp

and the camera is pouring its black butter,

its bitter honey,
straight into Hektor's eye.
Hektor steps to the line.

War has always interested me, he begins.

1995

Epitaph: Zion[8]

Murderous little world once our objects had gazes. Our lives
　　Were fragile, the wind
Could dash them away. Here lies the refugee breather
　　Who drank a bowl of elsewhere.

2000

Lazarus[9] Standup: Shooting Script

How does a body do in the ground?

Clouds look like matted white fur.
Which are the animals? He has forgotten the difference
between near and far.
Round pink ones come at him.
From the pinks shoot fluids
some dark (from eyes) some loud (from mouth).

His bones are moving like a mist in him

8. In the Hebrew Bible, the eastern hill of Jerusalem. In Judaism, it came to symbolize a promised homeland; in Christianity, a heavenly or ideal city of faith.

9. A man brought back to life by Jesus after being dead four days (John 11).

all blown to the surface then sideways.
I do not want to see,
he thinks in pain
as a darkish clump
cuts across his field of vision,
and some
strange

silver milk
is filling the space,
gets caught in the mist,
twists all his bones to the outside where they ignite in air.
The burning
of his bones

lets Lazarus know where each bone is.

And so
shifted forward into solidity—
although he pulls against it and groans to turn away—
Lazarus locks on
with a whistling sound behind him
as panels slide shut

and his soul congeals on his back in chrysolite[1] drops

which almost at once evaporate.
Lazarus
(someone is calling his name)—his name!
And at the name (which he knew)
not just a roar of darkness
the whole skeletal freight

of him
took pressure,
crushing him backward into the rut where he lay
like a damp
petal
under a pile of furniture.

And the second fact of his humanity began.

For the furniture shrank upon him as a bonework of
not just volume but
secret volume—
where fingers go probing
into drawers
and under
pried-up boxlids,

1. Pale yellow-green gemstone.

go rifling mute garments of white

and memories are streaming from his mind to his heart—
of someone standing at the door.
Of white breath in frozen air.
Mary. Martha.[2]
Linen of the same silence.
Lazarus! (again the voice)
and why not

climb the voice

where it goes spiralling upward
lacing him on a glow point
into the nocturnal motions of the world so that he is
standing now
propped on a cage of hot pushes of other people's air
and he feels more than hears
her voice (again)

like a salt rubbed whole into raw surface—

Lazarus!
A froth of fire is upon his mind.
It crawls to the back of his tongue,
struggles a bit,
cracking the shell
and pushes out a bluish cry that passes at once to the soul.
Martha!

he cries, making a little scalded place

on the billows of tomb that lap our faces as we watch.
We know the difference now
(life or death).
For an instant it parts our hearts.
Someone take the linen napkin off his face,
says the director quietly.

2000

Stanzas, Sexes, Seductions

It's good to be neuter.
I want to have meaningless legs.
There are things unbearable.
One can evade them a long time.
Then you die.

2. Sisters of Lazarus.

The oceans remind me
of your green room.
There are things unbearable.
Scorn, princes, this little size
of dying.

My personal poetry is a failure.
I do not want to be a person.
I want to be unbearable.
Lover to lover, the greenness of love.
Cool, cooling.

Earth bears no such plant.
Who does not end up
a female impersonator?
Drink all the sex there is.
Still die.

I tempt you.
I blush.
There are things unbearable.
Legs, alas.
Legs die.

Rocking themselves down,
crazy slow,
some ballet term for it—
fragment of foil, little
spin, little drunk, little do, little oh, alas.

2001

MEDBH MCGUCKIAN
b. 1950

Not since the early W. B. Yeats has there been an Irish poet more preoccupied with the dimly lit interior world, hidden from rational consciousness, than Medbh McGuckian (her first name an Irish rendering of Maeve). She has said that her poetry's "territory is the feminine subconscious, or semi-conscious," that she seeks "to tap the sensual realms of dream or daydream for their spiritual value" (*Contemporary Poets*, 1996). Born on August 12, 1950, in Belfast, Northern Ireland, McGuckian studied, like fellow Ulster poet Seamus Heaney, at Queen's University, Belfast, where Heaney was among her teachers. She shares Heaney's Catholic background and his poetry's lush organicism and musicality, but McGuckian, who continues to live in Belfast, is a still more intensely private, enigmatic, and subjective poet than Heaney or, for that matter, Yeats. "I forfeit the world outside / For the sake of my own inwardness," she writes ("Sky Writing"). McGuckian's dream-tipped lyrics set her apart, contrasting sharply, for example, with the declarative, public poetry of her Irish contemporary Eavan Boland.

McGuckian has averred, "I believe wholly in the beauty and power of language, the music of words, the intensity of images to shadow-paint the inner life of the soul" (*Contemporary Poets*). She is less interested in the paraphrasable content of words than in their connotations, resonances, and associations. In "Slips" and "The Dream-Language of Fergus," she represents language as layered, bound together by complex psychological, etymological, and sonic interconnections. These self-describing poems form a kind of *ars poetica*, or theory of poetry within poetry, according to which poetry is predicated on verbal slips, misconnections, and misreadings that reveal the nether reaches of our minds. Not that her poems are devoid of people. "The Dream-Language of Fergus" features her son Fergus; "The War Ending" alludes to the birth of a child; and "Captain Lavender" elegizes her father. And yet as a "threader / of double-stranded words" ("The Dream-Language of Fergus"), McGuckian elaborates and embroiders the significance of these human figures.

McGuckian's interest in evading the dictates of rationality for a poetics of ambiguity, music, and suggestiveness may be partly indebted to her sense of English as an imperial tongue that displaced the native Gaelic of Ireland. She makes something rich and strange from the bones of an imposed language. Her poetry can be baffling because its language is released from many of its usual moorings in the everyday world. Action is absent or undefined. Pronouns appear without referents. People, objects, and ideas dissolve into one another. Long, nonlinear sentences syntactically defer meaning. Instead, McGuckian's oblique poems unfold through metaphorical chains of evocation. Eschewing direct statement, they have a figurative and sonic texture that is sumptuous and involuted. Pushing the bounds of sense, sensorily and emotionally charged, they tease the reader with meanings just beyond the reach of understanding.

Slips

The studied poverty of a moon roof,
the earthenware of dairies cooled by apple trees,
the apple tree that makes the whitest wash . . .

But I forget names, remembering them wrongly
where they touch upon another name,
a town in France like a woman's Christian name.

My childhood is preserved as a nation's history,
my favorite fairytales the shells
leased by the hermit crab.

I see my grandmother's death as a piece of ice,
my mother's slimness restored to her,
my own key slotted in your door—

tricks you might guess from this unfastened button,
a pen mislaid, a word misread,
my hair coming down in the middle of a conversation.

1982

The Dream-Language of Fergus[1]

1

Your tongue has spent the night
in its dim sack as the shape of your foot
in its cave. Not the rudiment
of half a vanquished sound,
the excommunicated shadow of a name,
has rumpled the sheets of your mouth.

2

So Latin sleeps, they say, in Russian speech,
so one river inserted into another
becomes a leaping, glistening, splashed
and scattered alphabet
jutting out from the voice,
till what began as a dog's bark
ends with bronze, what began
with honey ends with ice;
as if an aeroplane in full flight
launched a second plane,
the sky is stabbed by their exits
and the mistaken meaning of each.

3

Conversation is as necessary
among these familiar campus trees
as the apartness of torches;
and if I am a threader
of double-stranded words, whose
Quando[2] has grown into now,
no text can return the honey
in its path of light from a jar,
only a seed-fund, a pendulum,
pressing out the diasporic snow.

1988

1. Much of the language of this poem is borrowed from the essays of Russian poet and critic Osip Mandelstam (1891–1938), especially "Conversation with Dante," "About the Nature of the Word," and "Notes about Poetry." Fergus is McGuckian's son.
2. When (Italian).

The War Ending

In the still world
between the covers of a book,
silk glides through your name
like a bee sleeping in a flower
or a seal that turns its head to look
at a boy rowing a boat.

The fluttering motion of your hands
down your body presses into my thoughts
as an enormous broken wave,
a rainbow or a painting being torn
within me. I remove the hand
and order it to leave.

Your passion for light
is so exactly placed,
I read them as eyes, mouth, nostrils,
disappearing back into their mystery
like the war that has gone
into us ending,

there you have my head,
a meeting of Irish eyes
with something English:
and now,
today,
it bursts.

1991

Captain Lavender

Night-hours. The edge of a fuller moon
waits among the interlocking patterns
of a flier's sky.

Sperm names, ovum names, push inside
each other. We are half-taught
our real names, from other lives.

Emphasise your eyes. Be my flare-
path, my uncold begetter,[3]
my air-minded bird-sense.

1995

3. Cf. "onlie begetter," in the dedication to Shakespeare's sonnets.

Mantilla[4]

for Shane Murphy

My resurrective verses shed people
and reinforced each summer.
I saw their time as my own time,
I said, this day will penetrate
those other days, using a thorn
to remove a thorn in the harness
of my mind where anyone's touch
stemmed my dreams.
From below
to above all decay I stated
my contentless name and held
the taste as though it were dying
all over true in the one day light.

My sound world was a vassal state,
a tightly bonded lattice of water
sealed with cunning to rear
the bridge of breathing.
And my raw
mouth a non-key of spring, a cousin
sometimes source, my signature
vibrational as parish flowers.

1998

4. Large veil or cape worn over the head and covering the shoulders.

JOY HARJO
b. 1951

The sacred, the mythical, and the natural are central to Joy Harjo's poetry, which draws on and celebrates the oral narratives and the images of her Muskogee Creek heritage. By means of symbolic and densely figurative language, incantatory rhythms, and nativist allusions, Harjo infuses the polluted cities, sordid bars, and other mundane realities of contemporary life with a visionary texture and consciousness. Like Sherman Alexie, who cites her as an influence, Harjo works out of a profound awareness of the colonial devastation of native cultures, though Alexie's poems are like acerbic jokes and hers are more like prayers or chants.

Harjo's blending of the everyday with archetypal stories and symbols is evident in the prose poem (her characteristic medium) "Deer Dancer," in which the dancer fuses a mythical deer with a female stripper. Despite the dancer's "stained red dress" and "tape on her heels," remarks the speaker, "She was the myth slipped down through dreamtime." Clock time is juxtaposed with dreamtime; the stripper's magical transformation occurs side by side with a degraded reality—a drunk "passed out, his head by the toilet."

Harjo grimly observes the taped heels, drunks, failed lives, and—in the prose poems "Insomnia and the Seven Steps to Grace" and "The Path to the Milky Way Leads through Los Angeles"—night skies wiped out by glare, "lit by chemical yellow." But Harjo's language hovers between such bleak realism and a dreamlike lyricism, which seeks to recover suppressed cultural and psychic truths. Her mythopoeic work reclaims such native presences as the shape-shifting panther and the trickster crow. The elemental world—stars, flowers, trees, the sky—radiates. Dislocations of normal speech through symbol and metaphor ("The way back is deer breath on icy windows") hint at mystical experiences just beyond the reach of colloquial English. "How do I say it?" asks the speaker of "Deer Dancer," "In this language there are no words for how the real world collapses."

In making reality as defined by the culture of "the colonizer" seem strange, not ineluctable, Harjo recalls Native American writers such as Leslie Marmon Silko, as well as global postcolonial influences such as the Ugandan poet Okot p'Bitek. The example of feminist autobiographical verse and of African American poetry, as practiced by poets such as Audre Lorde and Gwendolyn Brooks, has also been important.

Harjo was born on May 9, 1951, in Tulsa, Oklahoma, and the typical landscapes and cityscapes of her poetry are of the American southwest and west. She was a painter early on and later embraced music, playing the saxophone in her group Poetic Justice. She received her B.A. from the University of New Mexico in 1976, her M.F.A. from the University of Iowa in 1978. She has taught at Arizona State University, the University of Colorado, the University of Arizona, and the University of New Mexico.

Deer Dancer

Nearly everyone had left that bar in the middle of winter except the hardcore. It was the coldest night of the year, every place shut down, but not us. Of course we noticed when she came in. We were Indian ruins. She was the end of beauty. No one knew her, the stranger whose tribe we recognized, her family related to deer, if that's who she was, a people accustomed to hearing songs in pine trees, and making them hearts.

The woman inside the woman who was to dance naked in the bar of misfits blew deer magic. Henry Jack, who could not survive a sober day, thought she was Buffalo Calf Woman come back, passed out, his head by the toilet. All night he dreamed a dream he could not say. The next day he borrowed money, went home, and sent back the money I lent. Now that's a miracle. Some people see vision in a burned tortilla, some in the face of a woman.

This is the bar of broken survivors, the club of shotgun, knife wound, of poison by culture. We who were taught not to stare drank our beer. The players gossiped down their cues. Someone put a quarter in the jukebox to relive despair. Richard's wife dove to kill her. We had to hold her back, empty her pockets of knives and diaper pins, buy her two beers to keep her still, while Richard secretly bought the beauty a drink.

How do I say it? In this language there are no words for how the real world collapses. I could say it in my own and the sacred mounds would come into focus, but I couldn't take it in this dingy envelope. So I look at the stars in this strange city, frozen to the back of the sky, the only promises that ever make sense.

My brother-in-law hung out with white people, went to law school with a perfect record, quit. Says you can keep your laws, your words. And practiced law on the street with his hands. He jimmied to the proverbial dream girl, the face of the moon, while the players racked a new game. He bragged to us, he told her magic words and that's when she broke,
became human.
But we all heard his bar voice crack:

What's a girl like you doing in a place like this?

That's what I'd like to know, what are we all doing in a place like this?

You would know she could hear only what she wanted to; don't we all? Left the drink of betrayal Richard bought her, at the bar. What was she on? We all wanted some. Put a quarter in the juke. We all take risks stepping into thin air. Our ceremonies didn't predict this. Or we expected more.

I had to tell you this, for the baby inside the girl sealed up with a lick of hope and swimming into praise of nations. This is not a rooming house, but a dream of winter falls and the deer who portrayed the relatives of strangers. The way back is deer breath on icy windows.

The next dance none of us predicted. She borrowed a chair for the stairway to heaven and stood on a table of names. And danced in the room of children without shoes.

You picked a fine time to leave me, Lucille.
With four hungry children and a crop in the field.[1]

And then she took off her clothes. She shook loose memory, waltzed with the empty lover we'd all become.

She was the myth slipped down through dreamtime. The promise of feast we all knew was coming. The deer who crossed through knots of a curse to find us. She was no slouch, and neither were we, watching.

The music ended. And so does the story. I wasn't there. But I imagined her like this, not a stained red dress with tape on her heels but the deer who entered our dream in white dawn, breathed mist into pine trees, her fawn a blessing of meat, the ancestors who never left.

1990

1. First two lines from the chorus of the 1970s hit song "Lucille," by the American country-pop performer Kenny Rogers (b. 1938).

Mourning Song[2]

It's early evening here in the small world, where gods gamble for good weather as the sky turns red. Oh grief rattling around in the bowl of my skeleton. How I'd like to spit you out, turn you into another human, or remake the little dog spirit who walked out of our house without its skin toward an unseen land. We were left behind to figure it out during a harvest turned to ashes. I need to mourn with the night, turn to the gleaming house of bones under your familiar brown skin. The hot stone of our hearts will make a fire. If we cry more tears we will ruin the land with salt; instead let's praise that which would distract us with despair. Make a song for death, a song with yellow teeth and bad breath. For loneliness, the house guest who eats everything and refuses to leave. A song for bad weather so we can stand together under our leaking roof, and make a terrible music with our wise and ragged bones.

1994

Insomnia and the Seven Steps to Grace[3]

At dawn the panther of the heavens peers over the edge of the world. She hears the stars gossip with the sun, sees the moon washing her lean darkness with water electrified by prayers. All over the world there are those who can't sleep, those who never awaken.

My granddaughter sleeps on the breast of her mother with milk on her mouth. A fly contemplates the sweetness of lactose.

Her father is wrapped in the blanket of nightmares. For safety he approaches the red hills near Thoreau.[4] They recognize him and sing for him.

Her mother has business in the house of chaos. She is a prophet disguised as a young mother who is looking for a job. She appears at the door of my dreams and we put the house back together.

Panther watches as human and animal souls are lifted to the heavens by rain clouds to partake of songs of beautiful thunder.

Others are led by deer and antelope in the wistful hours to the villages of their ancestors. There they eat cornmeal cooked with berries that stain their lips with purple while the tree of life flickers in the sun.

2. In commentary following this poem, Harjo writes that she was once shocked to realize that a "filthy" homeless man, "his hair thick with lice," was her "old friend, a tall good-looking Navajo."

3. "I think of Bell's theorem which states that all actions have a ripple effect in this world. We could name this theorem for any tribe in this country as tribal peoples knew this long before we knew English or the scientific method" [Harjo's comments]. Bell's theorem was proposed by physicist John Stuart Bell (1928–1990).

4. New Mexico town locally believed to be named after Henry David Thoreau (1817–1862), American writer.

It's October, though the season before dawn is always winter. On the city streets of this desert town lit by chemical yellow travelers search for home.

Some have been drinking and intimate with strangers. Others are escapees from the night shift, sip lukewarm coffee, shift gears to the other side of darkness.

One woman stops at a red light, turns over a worn tape to the last chorus of a whispery blues. She has decided to live another day.

The stars take notice, as do the half-asleep flowers, prickly pear and chinaberry tree who drink exhaust into their roots, into the earth.

She guns the light to home where her children are asleep and may never know she ever left. That their fate took a turn in the land of nightmares toward the sun may be untouchable knowledge.

It is a sweet sound.

The panther relative yawns and puts her head between her paws.
She dreams of the house of panthers and the seven steps to grace.

1994

The Path to the Milky Way Leads through Los Angeles

There are strangers above me, below me and all around me and we are all strange in this place of recent invention.
This city named for angels appears naked and stripped of anything resembling
the shaking of turtle shells, the songs of human voices on a summer night outside Okmulgee.[5]
Yet, it's perpetually summer here, and beautiful. The shimmer of gods is easier
to perceive at sunrise or dusk,
when those who remember us here in the illusion of the marketplace
turn toward the changing of the sun and say our names.
We matter to somebody,
We must matter to the strange god who imagines us as we revolve together in
the dark sky on the path to the Milky Way.
We can't easily see that starry road from the perspective of the crossing of boulevards, can't hear it in the whine of civilization or taste the minerals of planets in hamburgers.
But we can buy a map here of the stars' homes, dial a tone for dangerous love,

5. City and county in central Oklahoma.

choose from several brands of water or a hiss of oxygen for gentle
rejuvenation.
Everyone knows you can't buy love but you can still sell your soul for less
than a song to a stranger who will sell it to someone else for a profit
until you're owned by a company of strangers
in the city of the strange and getting stranger.
I'd rather understand how to sing from a crow
who was never good at singing or much of anything
but finding gold in the trash of humans.
So what are we doing here I ask the crow parading on the ledge of falling
that
hangs over this precarious city?
Crow[6] just laughs and says *wait, wait and see* and I am waiting and not
seeing
anything, not just yet.
But like crow I collect the shine of anything beautiful I can find.

2000

6. Trickster character in many Native American stories and myths.

Paul Muldoon
b. 1951

Paul Muldoon has much in common with the hedgehog he writes about in one of his early poems: "Shares its secret with no one. / We say, *Hedgehog, come out / Of yourself and we will love you. // We mean no harm. We want / Only to listen to what / You have to say.*" Muldoon does not easily yield up his feelings or his meanings; nor are we likely to fall in love with him on first reading. In the context of the violent internecine Troubles and long colonial history of his native Northern Ireland, this ironic secretiveness, this postmodern play of disguises and masks, takes on a special significance. "*We mean no harm,*" we may protest, but the hedgehog knows better. Though Muldoon's tone is typically arch and his cleverness can be forbidding, his poems dazzle with their lexical exuberance, formal engineering, and wry allusiveness. For sheer wit and structural inventiveness, few contemporary poets rival him.

Like all contemporary Irish poets, Muldoon must contend with the long shadow cast by W. B. Yeats. In this, as in much else, Muldoon combines seriousness of purpose with irreverence. Yeats is tormented by guilt in his great, late poem "Man and the Echo," and he asks whether his art helped inspire the Easter Rising of 1916, which ended in the execution by the British of its poet-leaders: "Did that play of mine send out / Certain men the English shot?" Adopting the voice of his fellow ironist W. H. Auden, Muldoon answers with a quip in "7, Middagh Street": " 'Certainly not'. // If Yeats had saved his pencil-lead / would certain men have stayed in bed?" Whereas Yeats saw art as a force that could create nations and alter the course of history, Muldoon is more circumspect about the relation between art and politics. Even so, in poems such as "Lunch with Pancho Villa," "Meeting the British," and "Aftermath," he offers oblique parables or verbal puzzles about the violence of history. Like his major immediate predecessor, Seamus Heaney—his tutor at Queen's University, Belfast—Muldoon mistrusts journalistic directness in approaching the Troubles. But whereas Heaney is indirect, Muldoon is doubly so; Heaney worries that "song" may betray "suffering," and Muldoon is still more unsure of language's ability to be faithful to a reality outside itself. In contrast to Heaney's rooted sense of self, history, and Irishness, Muldoon's is transnational, fractured, and decentered. Muldoon writes about Heaney, with characteristic slyness and playfulness, in "The Briefcase," among other poems.

In "7, Middagh Street," Muldoon explores various views on the relation of art and politics through imaginary monologues by such literary and artistic figures as Auden, Salvador Dalí, and Louis MacNeice. This is one of a number of long poems and poetry cycles that Muldoon has written, including "Madoc: A Mystery," the autobiographical "Yarrow" and "Sleeve Notes," and "Immram," which laconically tells of a hero's nightmarish search for his father, a demented recluse who lives in squalor at the top of a luxury hotel and cries out for Baskin-Robbins banana-nut ice cream. In his long poems and in the carefully arranged sequences of his books, Muldoon invites his readers to see interconnections. He says: "I've become very interested in structures that can be fixed like mirrors at angles to each other . . . so that new images can emerge from the setting up of the poems in relationship to each other" (*Viewpoints: Poets in Conversation with John Haffenden,* 1981). Muldoon takes pleasure in his skills and in the amiable surprises and tricks he arranges for us, even as he explores such grim matters as mortality, urban warfare, and our generally futile attempts to recover the past. A poem such as the skewed sonnet "Quoof," in which the speaker goes to bed with a non-English-speaking woman in New York, offers off-kilter but searching reflections on sex, language, and colonization. In "The Grand Conversation," as elsewhere, he turns his mixed marriage to American Jewish writer Jean Korelitz into a densely specific yet allegorical poem about identity and intercultural experience. Other poems on the commerce between love and sex are sometimes delicately graphic. "Alternate worlds"—Auden's phrase for works of art and what they offer us—are what we find in the situations Muldoon invents for his readers.

Muldoon was born on June 20, 1951, in County Armagh, Northern Ireland, where his mother was a schoolteacher and his father, a frequent subject of his poems, a produce gardener and farm laborer with Republican sympathies. Muldoon was educated at St. Patrick's College, Armagh, and Queen's University, Belfast, where he came to know such poets as Medbh McGuckian and Michael Longley. Recognition came early, with the publication of his first book of poems at twenty-one. For more than ten years he worked as a producer, first in radio and then in television for the British Broadcasting Corporation in Belfast. In 1986, he left to devote himself to writing and to teaching, and since 1990, he has taught at Princeton University. In addition to books of poetry, he has published opera libretti, anthologies, and translations from poetry in Irish.

Hedgehog

The snail moves like a
Hovercraft,[1] held up by a
Rubber cushion of itself,
Sharing its secret

1. Vehicle that moves over land or water, supported by a cushion of air provided by downward-directed fans.

With the hedgehog. The hedgehog
Shares its secret with no one.
We say, *Hedgehog, come out*
Of yourself and we will love you.

We mean no harm. We want
Only to listen to what
You have to say. We want
Your answers to our questions.

The hedgehog gives nothing
Away, keeping itself to itself.
We wonder what a hedgehog
Has to hide, why it so distrusts.

We forget the god
Under this crown of thorns.[2]
We forget that never again
Will a god trust in the world.

1973

Lunch with Pancho Villa[3]

I

'Is it really a revolution, though?'
I reached across the wicker table
With another $10,000 question.
My celebrated pamphleteer,
Co-author of such volumes
As *Blood on the Rose,*
The Dream and the Drums,
And *How It Happened Here,*
Would pour some untroubled Muscatel[4]
And settle back in his cane chair.

'Look, son. Just look around you.
People are getting themselves killed
Left, right and centre
While you do what? Write rondeaux?[5]
There's more to living in this country
Than stars and horses, pigs and trees,
Not that you'd guess it from your poems.

2. Like the one Jesus was crowned with at his crucifixion (Matthew 27.29).
3. Francisco Villa (1878–1923), Mexican revolutionary and guerrilla leader who fought in the Mexican Revolution (1910–20).
4. Sweet wine made from the muscat grape.
5. Poetic and musical forms in which a main theme returns several times.

Do you never listen to the news?
You want to get down to something true,
Something a little nearer home.'

I called again later that afternoon,
A quiet suburban street.
'You want to stand back a little
When the world's at your feet.'
I'd have liked to have heard some more
Of his famous revolution.
I rang the bell, and knocked hard
On what I remembered as his front door,
That opened then, as such doors do,
Directly on to a back yard.

II

Not any back yard, I'm bound to say,
And not a thousand miles away
From here. No one's taken in, I'm sure,
By such a mild invention.
But where (I wonder myself) do I stand,
In relation to a table and chair,
The quince-tree I forgot to mention,
That suburban street, the door, the yard—
All made up as I went along
As things that people live among.

And such a person as lived there!
My celebrated pamphleteer!
Of course, I gave it all away
With those preposterous titles.
The Bloody Rose? The Dream and the Drums?
The three-day-wonder of the flowering plum!
Or was I desperately wishing
To have been their other co-author,
Or, at least, to own a first edition
Of *The Boot Boys and Other Battles?*

'When are you going to tell the truth?'
For there's no such book, so far as I know,
As *How it Happened Here,*
Though there may be. There may.
What should I say to this callow youth
Who learned to write last winter—
One of those correspondence courses—
And who's coming to lunch today?
He'll be rambling on, no doubt,
About pigs and trees, stars and horses.

1977

Anseo

When the Master was calling the roll
At the primary school in Collegelands,
You were meant to call back *Anseo*
And raise your hand
As your name occurred.
Anseo, meaning here, here and now,
All present and correct,
Was the first word of Irish I spoke.
The last name on the ledger
Belonged to Joseph Mary Plunkett Ward
And was followed, as often as not,
By silence, knowing looks,
A nod and a wink, the Master's droll
'And where's our little Ward-of-court?'

I remember the first time he came back
The Master had sent him out
Along the hedges
To weigh up for himself and cut
A stick with which he would be beaten.
After a while, nothing was spoken;
He would arrive as a matter of course
With an ash-plant, a salley-rod.[6]
Or, finally, the hazel-wand
He had whittled down to a whip-lash,
Its twist of red and yellow lacquers
Sanded and polished,
And altogether so delicately wrought
That he had engraved his initials on it.

I last met Joseph Mary Plunkett Ward
In a pub just over the Irish border.
He was living in the open,
In a secret camp
On the other side of the mountain.
He was fighting for Ireland,
Making things happen.
And he told me, Joe Ward,
Of how he had risen through the ranks
To Quartermaster, Commandant:
How every morning at parade
His volunteers would call back *Anseo*
And raise their hands
As their names occurred.

1980

6. Stick made from a willow tree. *Ash-plant:* stick or whip made from a sapling of the ash tree.

Why Brownlee Left

Why Brownlee left, and where he went,
Is a mystery even now.
For if a man should have been content
It was him; two acres of barley,
One of potatoes, four bullocks,
A milker, a slated farmhouse.
He was last seen going out to plough
On a March morning, bright and early.

By noon Brownlee was famous;
They had found all abandoned, with
The last rig[7] unbroken, his pair of black
Horses, like man and wife,
Shifting their weight from foot to
Foot, and gazing into the future.

1980

Quoof

How often have I carried our family word
for the hot water bottle
to a strange bed,
as my father would juggle a red-hot half-brick
in an old sock
to his childhood settle.[8]
I have taken it into so many lovely heads
or laid it between us like a sword.

An hotel room in New York City
with a girl who spoke hardly any English,
my hand on her breast
like the smouldering one-off spoor of the yeti[9]
or some other shy beast
that has yet to enter the language.

1983

Meeting the British

We met the British in the dead of winter.
The sky was lavender

and the snow lavender-blue.
I could hear, far below,

7. Ridge between a pair of plough furrows.
8. Wooden bed that can also be used as a bench.
9. Hypothetical apelike creature of the Himalayas; the "abominable snowman." *Spoor:* footprint.

the sound of two streams coming together
(both were frozen over)

and, no less strange,
myself calling out in French

across that forest-
clearing. Neither General Jeffrey Amherst[1]

nor Colonel Henry Bouquet
could stomach our willow-tobacco.

As for the unusual
scent when the Colonel shook out his hand-

kerchief: *C'est la lavande,*
une fleur mauve comme le ciel.[2]

They gave us six fishhooks
and two blankets embroidered with smallpox.

1987

From 7, MIDDAGH STREET[3]

Wystan

Quinquereme of Nineveh from distant Ophir;[4]
a blizzard off the Newfoundland[5] coast
had, as we slept, metamorphosed

the *Champlain*'s decks
to a wedding cake,
on whose uppermost tier stood Christopher

1. Commander-in-chief of British forces in the French and Indian War (1754–63); fought against France and its Native American allies. During Pontiac's Rebellion (1763–64), led by Ottawa chief Pontiac in the Great Lakes region, Amherst wrote to the British officer Colonel Bouquet, "Could it not be contrived to Send the *Small Pox* among those Disaffected Tribes of Indians?" Bouquet replied, "I will try to inocculate the Indians by means of Blankets that may fall in their hands, taking care however not to get the disease myself," to which Amherst responded, "You will Do well to try to Innoculate the Indians by means of Blanketts, as well as to try Every other method that can serve to Extirpate this Execreble Race." Apparently as a result of this and similar plans of other British officers, many Native Americans in the area, never having been exposed to smallpox, were killed by the disease in 1763–64. Pontiac concluded a peace treaty with the British in July 1766.

2. It is lavender, a flower purple as the sky (French).

3. Address of the building in Brooklyn Heights in which the poet W[ystan] H[ugh] Auden (1907–1973) lived at one time or another—along with an impressive list of bohemian housemates including the poet Louis MacNeice (1907–1973), novelists Carson McCullers (1917–1967) and Anaïs Nin (1903–1977), and the famous striptease artist Gypsy Rose Lee (1914–1970)—during the early years of World War II. In the sections of the poem printed here, Muldoon speaks in the voices of Auden and surrealist painter Salvador Dalí (1904–1989), who was also in exile in New York at this time.

4. Muldoon borrows this line from "Cargoes" (1902), by American poet John Masefield (1878–1967). *Quinquereme:* ship with five banks or oars. *Nineveh:* ancient city of the Assyrian Empire on the east bank of the Tigris River. *Ophir:* in the Bible, a region from which Solomon's ships brought large quantities of exquisite gold.

5. Island and province on the eastern coast of Canada. On January 26, 1939, Auden and the author Christopher Isherwood (1904–1986) arrived aboard the French liner *Champlain* in New York, where they eventually decided to immigrate from Great Britain.

and I like a diminutive bride and groom.
A heavy-skirted Liberty[6] would lunge
with her ice-cream
at two small, anxious

boys, and Erika[7] so grimly wave
from the quarantine-launch
she might as truly have been my wife
as, later that day, Barcelona was Franco's.

There was a time when I thought it mattered
what happened in Madrid

or Seville
and, in a sense, I haven't changed
my mind; the forces of Good and Evil
were indeed ranged

against each other, though not unambiguously.
I went there on the off-chance
they'd let me try
my hand at driving an ambulance;

there turned out to be some bureau-
cratic hitch.[8]
When I set out for the front on a black burro
it promptly threw me in the ditch.

I lay there for a year, disillusioned, dirty,
until a firing-party

of Chinese soldiers[9]
came by, leading dishevelled ponies.
They arranged a few sedimentary boulders
over the body of a Japanese

spy they'd shot
but weren't inclined to bury,
so that one of his feet stuck out.
When a brindled pariah[1]

6. Isherwood later recalled that the Statue of Liberty seemed intimidating rather than welcoming as they arrived in New York during a snowstorm.
7. Auden and Isherwood were met at the quarantine launch by their friends Klaus and Erika Mann, the eldest children of German-born novelist Thomas Mann. Auden and Erika, both homosexuals, had entered into a marriage of convenience in 1936 so that Erika could become a British citizen and escape Nazi Germany. Earlier on the day of Auden and Isherwood's arrival, Barcelona had fallen to the Fascist army of Francisco Franco (1892–1975), signifying that the Spanish Republicans had in effect lost the Spanish Civil War (1936–39).
8. In 1937, Auden traveled to Spain to volunteer as an ambulance driver for the Spanish Republican army. For reasons that remain unclear, the Spanish Medical Aid Committee turned him down. Instead, British Communists apparently arranged for Auden to travel to the front and write articles supporting the Republican side. According to a possibly apocryphal story, Auden refused a car and rode a mule, making it six miles from Valencia before being bucked by the mule and returning to take the car.
9. In 1938, Auden and Isherwood traveled through China as correspondents observing the war between the Japanese and Chinese.
1. A striped, "tabby" dog.

began to gnaw
on it, I recognized the markings of the pup
whose abscessed paw
my father had lanced on our limestone doorstep.

Those crucial years he tended
the British wounded

in Egypt, Gallipoli
and France,[2] I learned to play

Isolde to my mother's Tristan.[3]
Are they now tempted to rechristen

their youngest son
who turned his back on Albion

a Quisling?[4]
Would their *chaise-longue*[5]

philosophers have me somehow inflate
myself and float

above their factories and pylons
like a flat-footed barrage-balloon?

For though I would gladly return to Eden
as that ambulance-driver
or air-raid warden
I will never again ford the river
to parley with the mugwumps[6]
and fob them off with monocles and mumps;
I will not go back as *Auden*.

And were Yeats living at this hour
it should be in some ruined tower

not malachited Ballylee[7]
where he paid out to those below

2. Auden's father, George Auden, left his family to work as a doctor for the Royal Army Medical Corps during World War I, serving in Egypt, France, and Gallipoli, a Turkish seaport. In "Letter to Lord Byron" (1936), Auden claims this sight of surgery on a dog was his "earliest recollection."
3. *Tristan* and *Isolde:* central characters from a famous medieval romance. The young man Tristan was sent as a messenger to arrange for the Princess Isolde to be married to his uncle. However, after drinking a love potion, Tristan and Isolde became inseparable lovers involved in numerous adventures. Auden, the youngest of three children, once sang Isolde's role while his mother, at the piano, played Tristan.
4. Traitor, after Vidkun Quisling (1887–1945), a Norwegian officer who collaborated with the Germans during their World War II occupation of Norway. *Albion:* the earliest known name for Britain.
5. Sofa.
6. People who assume a superior lack of interest in politics or other affairs.
7. The castle that Irish poet W. B. Yeats (1865–1939) renovated and lived in. *Malachite:* an ornate, green mineral.

one gilt-edged scroll from his pencil
as though he were part-Rapunzel

and partly Delphic oracle.[8]
As for his crass, rhetorical

posturing, 'Did that play of mine
send out certain men (*certain* men?)

the English shot . . . ?'[9]
the answer is 'Certainly not'.

If Yeats had saved his pencil-lead
would certain men have stayed in bed?

For history's a twisted root
with art its small, translucent fruit

and never the other way round.
The roots by which we were once bound

are severed here, in any case,
and we are all now dispossessed;

prince, poet, construction worker,
salesman, soda fountain jerker—

all equally isolated.
Each loads flour, sugar and salted

beef into a covered wagon
and strikes out for his Oregon,

each straining for the ghostly axe
of a huge, blond-haired lumberjack.

'If you want me look for me under your boot-soles';[1]
when I visited him in a New Hampshire hospital
where he had almost gone for a Burton
with peritonitis
Louis[2] propped himself up on an ottoman
and read aloud the ode to Whitman
from *Poeta en Nueva York*[3]

8. In ancient Greece, a cave and shrine on the slope of Mt. Parnassus where questioners received a god's riddling answers. *Rapunzel:* fairy-tale character imprisoned in a tall tower who lowers her exceptionally long hair for her rescuer to climb.
9. From Yeats's late poem "Man and the Echo" (1939), in which he worries that his nationalist play *Cathleen ni Houlihan* (1902) helped inspire the violence associated with the Easter 1916 uprising.

1. From "Song of Myself," by American poet Walt Whitman (1819–1892).
2. Anglo-Irish poet Louis MacNeice (1907–1963), who suffered from a near-fatal case of peritonitis, an inflammation of the membrane lining the abdominal wall, during his visit to the United States in 1939.
3. *Poet in New York:* 1940 collection by Spanish poet Federico García Lorca (1898–1936).

The impossible Eleanor Clark[4]
had smuggled in a pail of oysters and clams
and a fifth column
of Armagnac.[5]
Carson McCullers extemporized a blues harmonica
on urinous pipkins and pannikins
that would have flummoxed Benjamin Franklin.[6]
I left them, so, to the reign
of the ear of corn
and the journey-work of the grass-leaf
and found my way next morning to Bread Loaf
and the diamond-shaped clearing in the forest
where I learned to play softball with Robert Frost.[7]

For I have leapt with Kierkegaard
out of the realm of Brunel and Arkwright[8]

with its mills, canals and railway-bridges
into this great void
where Chester[9] and I exchanged love-pledges
and vowed
our marriage-vows. As he lay asleep
last night the bronze of his exposed left leg
made me want nothing so much as to weep.
I thought of the terrier, of plague,
of Aschenbach at the Lido.[1]
Here was my historical
Mr W. H., my 'onlie begetter' and fair lady;
for nothing this wide universe I call . . . [2]

Salvador[3]

This lobster's not a lobster but the telephone
that rang for Neville Chamberlain.[4]

4. American writer (b. 1913) and wife of poet Robert Penn Warren (1905–1989). While MacNeice was in the United States, she had an affair with him. Her book *The Oysters of Locmariaquer* won the National Book Award in 1965.
5. That is, a bottle of French brandy. A "column" is a vessel used to distill spirits; "fifth column" means, loosely, traitor or spy.
6. One of Benjamin Franklin's many inventions was the glass harmonica, a musical instrument made of a series of bowls that vibrate (like the mouth of a wine glass) when rubbed with wetted fingers. Carson McCullers (1917–1967): American novelist. *Pipkins:* small pots or pans. *Pannikins:* small, metal drinking cups.
7. American poet (1874–1963), who helped found the Breadloaf School of English, in Vermont. Auden played softball with Frost at Breadloaf in August 1940. While teaching summers at Breadloaf, Muldoon lived in Frost's old home.
8. Sir Richard Arkwright (1732–1792): British industrialist, who opened mills in Auden's native Midlands. Søren Kierkegaard (1813–1855): Danish philosopher, whose blend of Christianity and proto-existentialism required a profound leap of faith. Sir Marc Brunel (1769–1849): French-born British engineer, who designed the shielding used to build the Thames Tunnel in 1843. His son Isambard was also a famous engineer.
9. American poet and librettist Chester Kallman (1921–1975), Auden's lover.
1. Italian seaside resort where, in Thomas Mann's *Death in Venice* (1912), the writer Aschenbach falls in love with a young boy.
2. From Shakespeare's Sonnet 109: "For nothing this wide universe I call, / Save thou, my rose; in it thou art my all." Shakespeare's dedication of his sonnets, "To the onlie begetter . . . Mr. W. H.," possibly includes a misprint of his own initials, but has generated speculation about the young man who might be the inspiration for many of the poems. "W. H." were also the initials Auden used instead of a spelled-out first name.
3. Spanish surrealist painter Salvador Dalí (1904–1989).
4. British politician (1869–1940), greatly criticized for the strategy of "appeasement" he adopted toward Adolf Hitler in the years preceding World

It droops from a bare branch
above a plate, on which the remains of lunch

include a snapshot of Hitler
and some boiled beans left over

from *Soft Construction: A Premonition*
of Civil War.[5] When Breton

hauled me before his kangaroo-court
I quoted the Manifesto;[6] we must disregard

moral and aesthetic considerations
for the integrity of our dream-visions.

What if I dreamed of Hitler as a masochist
who raises his fist

only to be beaten?
I might have dreamed of fucking André Breton

he so pooh-poohed my *Enigma of William Tell.*
There I have Lenin kneel

with one massive elongated buttock
and the elongated peak

of his cap supported by two forked sticks.
This time there's a raw beef-steak

on the son's head. My father croons a lullaby.
Is it that to refer, however obliquely,

is to refer? In October 1934,
I left Barcelona by the back door

with a portfolio of work
for my first one-man show in New York.

A starry night. The howling of dogs.
The Anarchist taxi-driver carried two flags,

War II. He was forced to step down as prime minister in 1940. *The Lobster Telephone* (1936) is an example of Dalí's surrealist assemblages.
5. *Soft Construction with Boiled Beans: A Premonition of Civil War:* 1934 Dalí painting depicting giant body parts on a desolate plain.
6. André Breton (1896–1966): French poet and critic whose *Surrealist Manifesto* (1924) helped found the surrealist movement, which was dedicated to exploring the creative power of the unconscious with dreamlike imagery and unexpected juxtapositions. In the mid-1930s, Dalí's relationship with the other surrealists was becoming strained, largely because of his growing interest in Hitler, who, according to Dalí, exhibited a gratuitous masochism that made him a surrealist icon. After Breton and the others saw Dalí's *Enigma of William Tell* (1933), which seemed to insult communism by putting the face of Russian revolutionary V. I. Lenin (1870–1924) on a highly distorted and sexualized body, the surrealists convened a meeting to confront Dalí about his fascination with fascism. Dalí's immediate response was to suggest that he would dream about having sex with Breton and then paint the encounter when he awoke.

Spanish and Catalan. Which side was I on?
Not one, or both, or none.

I who had knelt with Lenin in Breton's court
and sworn allegiance to the proletariat

had seen the chasm
between myself and surrealism

begin as a hair-crack on a tile.
In *Soft Construction* I painted a giant troll

tearing itself apart limb
by outlandish limb.

Among the broken statues of Valladolid[7]
there's one whose foot's still welded

to the granite plinth[8]
from which, like us, it draws its strength.

From that, and from those few boiled beans.
We cannot gormandize upon

the flesh of Cain and Abel[9]
without some melancholic vegetable

bringing us back to earth, to the boudoir
in the abattoir.[1]

Our civil wars, the crumbling of empires,
the starry nights without number

safely under our belts,
have only slightly modified the tilt

of the acanthus[2] leaf,
its spiky puce-and-alabaster an end in itself.

1987

The Briefcase

for Seamus Heaney[3]

I held the briefcase at arms's length from me;
the oxblood or liver

7. City and province of northwestern Spain.
8. Blocklike base for a statue.
9. Cain's murder of his brother Abel is told in Genesis 4.
1. Slaughterhouse. *Boudoir:* private bedroom.
2. Prickly Mediterranean plant, whose image is often carved into classical moldings or plinths.
3. Irish poet (b. 1939).

eelskin with which it was covered
had suddenly grown supple.

I'd been waiting in line for the cross-town
bus when an almighty cloudburst
left the sidewalk a raging torrent.

And though it contained only the first
inkling of this poem, I knew I daren't
set the briefcase down
to slap my pockets for an obol[4]—

for fear it might slink into a culvert
and strike out along the East River
for the sea. By which I mean the 'open' sea.

1990

Cauliflowers

Plants that glow in the dark have been developed through gene-splicing, in which light-producing bacteria from the mouths of fish are introduced to cabbage, carrots and potatoes.

—*The National Enquirer*

More often than not he stops at the headrig[5] to light
his pipe
and try to regain
his composure. The price of cauliflowers
his gone down
two weeks in a row on the Belfast market.

From here we can just make out
a platoon of Light
Infantry going down
the road to the accompaniment of a pipe-
band. The sun glints on their silver-
buttoned jerkins.

My uncle, Patrick Regan,
has been leaning against the mud-guard
of the lorry. He levers
open the bonnet and tinkers with a light
wrench at the hose-pipe
that's always going down.

Then he himself goes down
to bleed oil into a jerry-can.

4. Small coin.
5. A sawmill, specifically its principal machine and carriage.

My father slips the pipe
into his scorch-marked
breast pocket and again makes light
of the trepanned[6] cauliflowers.

All this as I listened to lovers
repeatedly going down
on each other in the next room . . . 'light
of my life . . . ' in a motel in Oregon.
All this. Magritte's
pipe[7]

and the pipe-
bomb. White Annetts. Gillyflowers.
Margaret,
are you grieving?[8] My father going down
the primrose path with Patrick Regan.
All gone out of the world of light.

All gone down
the original pipe. And the cauliflowers
in an unmarked pit, that were harvested by their own light.

1990

The Sonogram

Only a few weeks ago, the sonogram of Jean's womb
resembled nothing so much
as a satellite-map of Ireland:

now the image
is so well-defined we can make out not only a hand
but a thumb;

on the road to Spiddal,[9] a woman hitching a ride;
a gladiator in his net, passing judgement on the crowd.

1994

6. Cored.
7. One of the most famous paintings by Belgian surrealist René Magritte (1898–1967) depicts a pipe, beneath which a caption reads in French "This is not a pipe."
8. The opening line of "Spring and Fall," by English poet Gerard Manley Hopkins (1844–1889). Line 36 below recalls "They are all gone into the world of light!", the first line of a poem by English religious poet Henry Vaughan (1621 or 1622–1695).
9. Town in County Galway, in western Ireland.

Aftermath

I

"Let us now drink," I imagine patriot cry to patriot
after they've shot
a neighbor in his own aftermath, who hangs still between two sheaves
like Christ between two tousle-headed thieves,
his body wired up to the moon, as like as not.

II

To the memory of another left to rot
near some remote beauty spot,
the skin of his right arm rolled up like a shirtsleeve,
let us now drink.

III

Only a few nights ago, it seems, they set fire to a big house and it
got so preternaturally hot
we knew there would be no reprieve
till the swallows' nests under the eaves
had been baked into these exquisitely glazed little pots
from which, my love, let us now drink.

1998

The Grand Conversation

She. My people came from Korelitz,[1]
where they grew yellow cucumbers
and studied the Talmud.[2]
He. Mine pored over the mud
of mangold- and potato-pits
of flicked through kale plants from Comber[3]
as bibliomancers of old
went a-flicking through deckle-mold.[4]

She. Mine would lie low in the shtetl[5]
when they heard the distant thunder
stolen by the Cossacks.[6]

1. Town now in Belarus, once famous for its cucumbers. During World War II, the Nazis largely massacred its population.
2. Collection of writings that constitutes the Jewish civil and religious law.
3. Village in Northern Ireland. *Mangold:* a beet.
4. Rough edges of pages before they are trimmed. *Bibliomancers:* people who predicted the future from the text in a book opened at random.
5. Former Jewish village-communities of Eastern Europe.
6. A Polish people known for their horsemanship, they massacred hundreds of thousands of Polish Jews in 1648–49.

He. It was potato sacks
lumped together on a settle[7]
mine found themselves lying under,
the Peep O'Day Boys from Loughgall
making Defenders[8] of us all.

She. Mine once controlled the sugar trade
from the islets of Langerhans[9]
and were granted the deed
to Charlottesville. *He.* Indeed?
My people called a spade a spade
and were admitted to the hanse[1]
of pike- and pickax-men, shovels
leaning to their lean-to hovels.

She. Mine were trained to make a suture
after the bomb and the bombast
have done their very worst.
He. Between *fearsad* and *verst*[2]
we may yet construct our future
as we've reconstructed our past
and cry out, my love, each to each
from his or her own quicken-queach.[3]

She. Each from his stand of mountain-ash
will cry out over valley farms
spotlit with pear-blossom.
He. There some young Absalom[4]
picks his way through cache after cache
of ammunition and small arms
hidden in grain wells, while his nag
tugs at a rein caught on a snag.

2002

7. Long wooden bed or bench.
8. Eighteenth-century Catholic group in Ireland that fought Protestants who called themselves the Peep O'Day Boys. *Loughgall:* village where Protestants formed a larger coalition, the Orange Order, at the beginning of the nineteenth century.
9. The groups of cells in the pancreas that produce the hormone insulin, which regulates the sugar level in the bloodstream.
1. Merchant guild.
2. Russian land measure, roughly two-thirds of a mile. *Fearsad:* sandbank (Irish).
3. *Queach:* dense growth of bushes. Cf. T. S. Eliot's "Love Song of J. Alfred Prufrock": "Do I dare to eat a peach? / . . . . I have heard the mermaids singing, each to each."
4. King David's son, killed leading a rebellion against his father (2 Samuel). Riding his mule, he was accidentally hung up on a low branch and was thus made vulnerable to enemy spears.

Gary Soto
b. 1952

In 1848, at the end of the Mexican-American War, Mexico ceded its territory above the Rio Grande River to the United States. The Mexicans who lived there became American citizens and yet maintained their language and traditions, while other Mexicans, dreaming of becoming rich Americans, also came to the southwest. Whether native or immigrant, Mexican Americans found themselves defined as outsiders, second-class citizens who were segregated into barrios—essentially, Spanish-speaking ghettos. Over time, literary stirrings and a growing group consciousness began within the Chicano community, but not until the late 1960s could leaders such as César Chávez make *La Causa* a nationalistic Chicano movement. *La Causa* produced a protest literature; it also made way for other Chicano writers, including Gary Soto, to become visible.

Soto both emerged from this cultural moment and felt distinct from it; "the work I was trying to do," he has said, even at this "nationalistic" time, "was so private—talking about loss, death" (*The Boston Globe,* October 18, 1998). Soto's first two books—*The Element of San Joaquin* (1977) and *The Tale of Sunlight* (1978)—describe private experience, but they do so within the contexts of the ugly urban life of Fresno, California, the migration of the hungry poor out of Mexico, and the dreary toil of farmwork in the San Joaquin Valley—toil that Soto had experienced firsthand. In a grim Fresno poem, "After Tonight," violent death and injury are a constant threat. Grief is everywhere: the tavern keeper Manuel, of "The Manuel Zaragoza Poems," is plunged into mourning when his wife's birthing goes awry ("Graciela").

In later books, Soto enlarges his repertoire. With a keen memory for the atmosphere and feelings of childhood, he recalls some charming moments of relief amid the culture of poverty. "Oranges" touchingly relates a boy's first date, with only a nickel and two oranges in his pockets, and his redemption by a kindly salesperson. In "Practicing Eulogies," the young Soto and his brother turn a rooster's claws into toys that grasp things. "Sensitive me," concludes the poet self-mockingly, "I went for the box of Kleenex, / Tendons closing and tissues jerking up like ghosts." Evincing poverty as it impinges on the lives of individuals, Soto uses fresh and vivid figurative language and conjures physical sensations with immediacy.

Soto was born on April 12, 1952, in Fresno. In 1974, he earned a B.A. at California State University, Fresno, where he studied with a master poet of working-class life, Philip Levine; in 1976, he earned an M.F.A. at the University of California, Irvine. He has also written several books of autobiographical prose, including books for children and young adults. From 1979 to 1996, he taught Chicano studies and English at the University of California, Berkeley.

After Tonight

Because there are avenues
Of traffic lights, a phone book
Of brothers and lawyers,
Why should you think your purse
Will not be tugged from your arm
Or the screen door
Will remain latched

Against the man
Who hugs and kisses
His pillow
In the corridor of loneliness?

There is a window of light
A sprinkler turning
As the earth turns,
And you do not think of the hills
And of the splintered wrists it takes
To give you
The heat rising toward the ceiling.

You expect your daughter
To be at the door any moment
And your husband to arrive
With the night
That is suddenly all around.
You expect the stove to burst
A collar of fire
When you want it,
The siamese cats
To move against your legs, purring.

But remember this:
Because blood revolves from one lung to the next,
Why think it will
After tonight?

1977

The Drought

The clouds shouldered a path up the mountains
East of Ocampo,[1] and then descended,
Scraping their bellies gray on the cracked shingles of slate.

They entered the valley, and passed the roads that went
Trackless, the houses blown open, their cellars creaking
And lined with the bottles that held their breath for years.

They passed the fields where the trees dried thin as hat racks
And the plow's tooth bit the earth for what endured.
But what continued were the wind that plucked the birds spineless

And the young who left with a few seeds in each pocket,
Their belts tightened on the fifth notch of hunger—
Under the sky that deafened from listening for rain.

1978

1. Town in Mexico.

Graciela[2]

Wedding night
Graciela bled lightly—
But enough to stain his thighs—
And left an alphabet
Of teeth marks on his arm.
At this, he was happy.
They drank mescal[3]
In bed like the rich
And smoked cigarettes.
She asleep
And the bottle empty, he hid
A few coins in her left shoe,
Earrings in the right.
They worked long hours
Hoeing crooked rows of maize.
Evenings she wove rugs
And embroidered curtains
To market in Taxco.[4]
In short they lived well.
However in the seventh month
With child, her belly
Rising like a portion of the sun,
Something knotted inside her.
The ribs ached. A fever climbed.
Manuel summoned the Partera[5]
And though she burned pepper,
And tied belts around
The stretched belly,
The child did not ease out.
Days later she turned
Onto her belly
And between her legs
Unraveled a spine of blood.

1978

Oranges

The first time I walked
With a girl, I was twelve,
Cold, and weighted down
With two oranges in my jacket.
December. Frost cracking
Beneath my steps, my breath
Before me, then gone,

2. One of the first poems in "The Manuel Zaragoza Poems," a section of the book *The Tale of Sunlight*.

3. Mexican liquor.
4. Town in central Mexico.
5. Midwife.

As I walked toward
Her house, the one whose
Porch light burned yellow
Night and day, in any weather.
A dog barked at me, until
She came out pulling
At her gloves, face bright
With rouge. I smiled,
Touched her shoulder, and led
Her down the street, across
A used car lot and a line
Of newly planted trees,
Until we were breathing
Before a drugstore. We
Entered, the tiny bell
Bringing a saleslady
Down a narrow aisle of goods.
I turned to the candies
Tiered like bleachers,
And asked what she wanted—
Light in her eyes, a smile
Starting at the corners
Of her mouth. I fingered
A nickel in my pocket,
And when she lifted a chocolate
That cost a dime,
I didn't say anything.
I took the nickel from
My pocket, then an orange,
And set them quietly on
The counter. When I looked up,
The lady's eyes met mine,
And held them, knowing
Very well what it was all
About.

Outside,
A few cars hissing past,
Fog hanging like old
Coats between the trees.
I took my girl's hand
In mine for two blocks,
Then released it to let
Her unwrap the chocolate.
I peeled my orange
That was so bright against
The gray of December
That, from some distance,
Someone might have thought
I was making a fire in my hands.

1985

How Things Work

Today it's going to cost us twenty dollars
To live. Five for a softball. Four for a book,
A handful of ones for coffee and two sweet rolls,
Bus fare, rosin for your mother's violin.
We're completing our task. The tip I left
For the waitress filters down
Like rain, wetting the new roots of a child
Perhaps, a belligerent cat that won't let go
Of a balled sock until there's chicken to eat.
As far as I can tell, daughter, it works like this:
You buy bread from a grocery, a bag of apples
From a fruit stand, and what coins
Are passed on helps others buy pencils, glue,
Tickets to a movie in which laughter
Is thrown into their faces.
If we buy a goldfish, someone tries on a hat.
If we buy crayons, someone walks home with a broom.
A tip, a small purchase here and there,
And things just keep going. I guess.

1985

Practicing Eulogies

Momma cat died in the weeds,
A stink swirling in my nostrils
Until the flat hand of slapping rain
Leveled its odor. Then a neighbor died,
The one who said, Look, I got my wife's cancer—
His bony hands transparent as paper.
That was more than I needed
—mortal cat and mortal, old man—
And walked to the courthouse to sit by a pond,
Sickly fish gasping, their gills like razor slits.
Turd-coiled toads lay on the bottom, not daring to come up.
I was stirring the surface with a finger
When a suicidal cricket leaped into the pond.
Honest-to-God, I tried to save that armored insect—
My hand scooped and scooped
Like a pelican. The fish,
Sick as they were, ate antenna and spindly legs.
On the way home, I petted a stray dog,
Stared at a bird's egg cracked like a crown,
And wondered about death,
That flea-juice under my fingernail.
I grew scared. In the kitchen,
The neighbor's rooster was on the stove,

Boiling among diced celery and coins of carrots.
Do saints ever sleep? I asked my mom,
And she said, Put out the big spoons.
We ate that rooster,
Tastier than store-bought chicken.
After dinner I got Frankie's left claw
And my brother got the right claw.
We worked the tendons like pulleys
As the claws opened and closed on things—
My laughing brother picked up pencils and erasers.
Sensitive me, I went for the box of Kleenex,
Tendons closing and tissues jerking up like ghosts.

1999

Rita Dove
b. 1952

Appealing to our common humanity, Rita Dove's poems may be enjoyed by both the mind and the senses. Made out of intricate associative puzzles, they tell stories in miniature. Their language is musically pitched and cadenced but restrained, richly textured but taut. Like Robert Hayden and Gwendolyn Brooks, Dove is a poet of understatement who gives by holding back, demanding that we attend as much to what is unsaid as to what is said. Although much of her work is autobiographical, she distills this emotional material through crystalline phrasing, chiseled lines, precise diction and similes, careful rhythms, and sonic patterning. Whether she writes about the sensual body or historical atrocity, Dove approaches her subject with a sympathetic but cool eye. Her early series "Adolescence" recalls emerging sexuality, endowing this experience with curiosity, fearfulness, and pleasure. A later poem, "After Reading *Mickey in the Night Kitchen* for the Third Time before Bed," describes with frankness and yet considerable grace and humor a mother and daughter sharing the secrets of their bodies: "That we're in the pink / and the pink's in us."

Many of Dove's poems are written out of her sense of history and its injustices. Inventing some incidents (e.g., "The House Slave"), she also makes poems out of the lives of historical men and women whom she, like Odysseus on his visit to the underworld, restores to life long enough for them to speak to us and thus endure. In "Claudette Colvin Goes to Work," she imagines the inner life of the young, African American woman who helped precipitate the Montgomery bus boycott. In this poem, as elsewhere, Dove finds within her character not the straightforward emotions one might expect of a "role model," but more ambiguous feelings. Dove's historical poems witness injustice without falsifying the variety of emotions roused by it, from pain and anger to guilt, resignation, and ambivalence.

Dove's Pulitzer Prize–winning sequence, *Thomas and Beulah,* recounts the inner lives of her grandparents, reflecting in microcosm the movements and social history of African Americans in the first sixty years of the twentieth century. The sequence encapsulates two lifetimes, told in a series of short poems. Dove celebrates the lives of her grandparents, and the work shines with gratitude and joy. Part of her purpose was also to combat the assumption that the inner lives of the poor and unlettered are less complex than the lives of those who are on easier terms with society. Thomas is haunted by guilt over his friend's accidental death, as recounted in "The Incident." Beulah, hidden from the white customers of the dress shop, ironing the sweaty dress of a white woman while reflecting on the spoiled darlings of the French courts, is complex and heroic. Using free, indirect discourse to mirror the inner world of her grandparents, Dove employs both colloquial and elevated diction, rhetoric, and figurative language, creating a fascinating convergence between the minds of the poet and her characters.

What to make of a mixed cultural inheritance—black and white, African American and European? This central question confronts Dove as it did such predecessors as Melvin Tolson, Brooks, and Hayden. In contrast to African American poets inspired by the cultural nationalism of the Black Arts Movement, such as Amiri Baraka and June Jordan, Dove wants less to separate the African American aesthetic from other cultural traditions than to offer a synthesis. The myth of Demeter and Persephone is not off limits because of its European origins, but a powerful archetype for interpreting her experience as a mother, in *Mother Love* (1995). So too with poetic forms. For her brilliant poem "Parsley," about how the Dominican dictator Rafael Trujillo slaughtered twenty thousand blacks who spoke Haitian Creole, she loosely adapts the villanelle (in the first part) and the sestina (in the second). She has explained that the "obsessiveness of the sestina, the repeated words, was something I wanted to get at—that driven quality" (*Black American Literature Forum,* Fall 1986). Dove ironically adapts European poetic forms to retell the story of one of the twentieth century's most horrific and gratuitous atrocities against New World blacks, promulgated by a dictator who insisted on a European norm of speech. Like Claude McKay with the sonnet, Tolson with the Pindaric ode, or Derek Walcott with Homeric epic, Dove wrests European forms from those who enslaved her ancestors to recount vividly a crime against men and women of the African diaspora. Dove is no less bold about imaginatively entering the mind of the murderous dictator, as she explained in an interview: "It was important to me to try to understand that arbitrary quality of his cruelty. And I'm not afraid of making him too human. I don't believe anyone's going to like him after reading my poem. Making us get into his head may shock us all into seeing what the human being is capable of, and what in fact we're capable of, because if we can go that far into his head we're halfway there ourselves" (*Black American*). Recovering the ethical and experiential messiness of history, Dove risks implicating herself (and us as readers) in the fate not only of the slaughtered Haitians, but also of the cruel dictator, who is as obsessed as any poet by the sound and power of words.

In another of her most powerful poems, "Agosta the Winged Man and Rasha the Black Dove," Dove reflects on a 1929 German painting of two sideshow performers, one afflicted with a bone disease that made him almost seem to have wings, another a Madagascan woman whose only oddity was her blackness. In this disturbing meditation on art, race, and spectatorship, Dove's identification is again mixed: she shares some kinship not only with the objectified black woman or "Dove," but also perhaps with the objectifying gaze of the painter, who uses "classical drapery" and makes art out of the people he portrays. Similarly, in a poem about slavery, "The House Slave," the poet wonders whether she (and the reader) have more in common with the sister whipped in the field or with the house slave who, racked with guilt, stays in the house and overhears her sister's cries at a distance. Dove's poems explore such difficult questions about art and suffering with courage, subtlety, and rigor.

Dove was born on August 28, 1952, in Akron, Ohio, where her father was a chemist. She was educated at Miami University in Oxford, Ohio, traveled to Tübingen University in Germany as a Fulbright fellow (1974–75), and received her M.F.A. from the University of Iowa (1977). She has taught creative writing at Arizona State University (1981–89) and, since 1989, at the University of Virginia. Besides her books of poetry, she has published short stories, a play, and a novel. Winner of the 1987 Pulitzer Prize and many other awards, she was the first African American poet laureate of the United States (1993–95).

Geometry

I prove a theorem and the house expands:
the windows jerk free to hover near the ceiling,
the ceiling floats away with a sigh.

As the walls clear themselves of everything
but transparency, the scent of carnations
leaves with them. I am out in the open

and above the windows have hinged into butterflies,
sunlight glinting where they've intersected.
They are going to some point true and unproven.

1980

The House Slave

The first horn lifts its arm over the dew-lit grass
and in the slave quarters there is a rustling—
children are bundled into aprons, cornbread

and water gourds grabbed, a salt pork breakfast taken.
I watch them driven into the vague before-dawn
while their mistress sleeps like an ivory toothpick

and Massa dreams of asses, rum and slave-funk.
I cannot fall asleep again. At the second horn,
the whip curls across the backs of the laggards—

sometimes my sister's voice, unmistaken, among them.
"Oh! pray," she cries. "Oh! pray!" Those days
I lie on my cot, shivering in the early heat,

and as the fields unfold to whiteness,
and they spill like bees among the fat flowers,
I weep. It is not yet daylight.

1980

Adolescence—II

Although it is night, I sit in the bathroom, waiting.
Sweat prickles behind my knees, the baby-breasts are alert.
Venetian blinds slice up the moon; the tiles quiver in pale strips.

Then they come, the three seal men with eyes as round
As dinner plates and eyelashes like sharpened tines.
They bring the scent of licorice. One sits in the washbowl,

One on the bathtub edge; one leans against the door.
"Can you feel it yet?" they whisper.
I don't know what to say, again. They chuckle,

Patting their sleek bodies with their hands.
"Well, maybe next time." And they rise,
Glittering like pools of ink under moonlight,

And vanish. I clutch at the ragged holes
They leave behind, here at the edge of darkness.
Night rests like a ball of fur on my tongue.

1980

Agosta the Winged Man and Rasha the Black Dove[1]

Schad paced the length of his studio
and stopped at the wall,
staring
at a blank space. Behind him
the clang and hum of Hardenbergstrasse,[2] its
automobiles and organ grinders.
Quarter to five.
His eyes traveled
to the plaster scrollwork
on the ceiling. Did *that*
hold back heaven?
He could not leave his skin—once
he'd painted himself in a new one,
silk green, worn
like a shirt.
He thought
of Rasha, so far from Madagascar,
turning slowly in place as
the boa constrictor
coiled counterwise its
heavy love. How
the spectators gawked, exhaling
beer and sour herring sighs.
When the tent lights dimmed,
Rasha went back to her trailer and plucked

1. Title of a 1929 painting by German painter Christian Schad (1894–1982), depicting two Berlin sideshow performers. Agosta had a bone disease that caused his ribs and shoulder blades to jut out of his body like wings. Rasha was a Madagascan woman whose title, "the Black Dove," recalls the emblem of the serpent and the dove, since she performed with a boa constrictor twined around her (though not in Schad's painting).
2. Street in Berlin.

a chicken for dinner.
                    The canvas,

not his eye, was merciless.
He remembered Katja the Russian
aristocrat, late
for every sitting,
            still fleeing
the October Revolution[3]—
how she clutched her sides
and said not
        one word. Whereas Agosta
(the doorbell rang)
was always on time, lip curled
as he spoke in wonder of women
                    trailing
backstage to offer him
the consummate bloom of their lust.

Schad would place him
on a throne, a white sheet tucked
over his loins, the black suit jacket
thrown off like a cloak.
Agosta had told him
            of the medical students
at the Charité,[4]
that chill arena
        where he perched on
a cot, his torso
exposed, its crests and fins
a colony of birds, trying
to get out . . .
        and the students,
lumps caught
in their throats, taking notes.

Ah, Rasha's
        foot on the stair.
She moved slowly, as if she carried
the snake around her body
always.

    Once
she brought fresh eggs into
the studio, flecked and
warm as breath.
        Agosta in
classical drapery, then,
and Rasha at his feet.
Without passion. Not

3. Russian Revolution of 1917.

4. University hospital in Berlin.

the canvas
    but their gaze,
    so calm,
was merciless.

1983

Parsley[5]

1. *The Cane Fields*[6]

There is a parrot imitating spring
in the palace, its feathers parsley green.
Out of the swamp the cane appears

to haunt us, and we cut it down. El General
searches for a word; he is all the world
there is. Like a parrot imitating spring,

we lie down screaming as rain punches through
and we come up green. We cannot speak an R—
out of the swamp, the cane appears

and then the mountain we call in whispers *Katalina.*[7]
The children gnaw their teeth to arrowheads.
There is a parrot imitating spring.

El General has found his word: *perejil.*
Who says it, lives. He laughs, teeth shining
out of the swamp. The cane appears

in our dreams, lashed by wind and streaming.
And we lie down. For every drop of blood
there is a parrot imitating spring.
Out of the swamp the cane appears.

2. *The Palace*

The word the general's chosen is parsley.
It is fall, when thoughts turn
to love and death; the general thinks
of his mother, how she died in the fall
and he planted her walking cane at the grave
and it flowered, each spring stolidly forming
four-star blossoms. The general

5. "On October 2, 1937, Rafael Trujillo (1891–1961), dictator of the Dominican Republic, ordered 20,000 blacks to be killed because they could not pronounce the letter 'r' in *perejil,* the Spanish word for parsley" [Dove's note].

6. This first section is in the form of a (nonrhyming) villanelle. *Cane:* sugar cane.

7. That is, Katarina (since "we cannot speak an R").

pulls on his boots, he stomps to
her room in the palace, the one without
curtains, the one with a parrot
in a brass ring. As he paces he wonders
Who can I kill today. And for a moment
the little knot of screams
is still. The parrot, who has traveled

all the way from Australia in an ivory
cage, is, coy as a widow, practising
spring. Ever since the morning
his mother collapsed in the kitchen
while baking skull-shaped candies
for the Day of the Dead,[8] the general
has hated sweets. He orders pastries
brought up for the bird; they arrive

dusted with sugar on a bed of lace.
The knot in his throat starts to twitch;
he sees his boots the first day in battle
splashed with mud and urine
as a soldier falls at his feet amazed—
how stupid he looked!— at the sound
of artillery. *I never thought it would sing*
the soldier said, and died. Now

the general sees the fields of sugar
cane, lashed by rain and streaming.
He sees his mother's smile, the teeth
gnawed into arrowheads. He hears
the Haitians sing without R's
as they swing the great machetes:
Katalina, they sing, *Katalina,*

mi madle, mi amol en muelte.[9] God knows
his mother was no stupid woman; she
could roll an R like a queen. Even
a parrot can roll an R! In the bare room
the bright feathers arch in a parody
of greenery, as the last pale crumbs
disappear under the blackened tongue. Someone

calls out his name in a voice
so like his mother's, a startled tear
splashes the tip of his right boot.
My mother, my love in death.
The general remembers the tiny green sprigs
men of his village wore in their capes

8. Roman Catholic celebration honoring the souls of the dead.

9. That is, *mi madre, mi amor en muerte*: "my mother, my love in death."

to honor the birth of a son. He will
order many, this time, to be killed

for a single, beautiful word.

1983

FROM THOMAS AND BEULAH[1]

The Event

Ever since they'd left the Tennessee ridge
with nothing to boast of
but good looks and a mandolin,

the two Negroes leaning
on the rail of a riverboat
were inseparable: Lem plucked

to Thomas' silver falsetto.
But the night was hot and they were drunk.
They spat where the wheel

churned mud and moonlight,
they called to the tarantulas
down among the bananas

to come out and dance.
You're so fine and mighty; let's see
what you can do, said Thomas, pointing

to a tree-capped island.
Lem stripped, spoke easy: *Them's chestnuts,*
I believe. Dove

quick as a gasp. Thomas, dry
on deck, saw the green crown shake
as the island slipped

under, dissolved
in the thickening stream.
At his feet

1. "These poems tell two sides of a story and are meant to be read in sequence" [Dove's introduction]. *Thomas and Beulah* was inspired by incidents in the lives of Dove's grandparents in Akron, Ohio, and begun after she heard this story from her grandmother: Dove's grandfather dared a friend "to jump off the boat and swim to an island and to pick some chestnuts and the friend died in the river."

a stinking circle of rags,
the half-shell mandolin.
Where the wheel turned the water

gently shirred.[2]

Dusting

Every day a wilderness—no
shade in sight. Beulah[3]
patient among knicknacks,
the solarium a rage
of light, a grainstorm
as her gray cloth brings
dark wood to life.

Under her hand scrolls
and crests gleam
darker still. What
was his name, that
silly boy at the fair with
the rifle booth? And his kiss and
the clear bowl with one bright
fish, rippling
wound!

Not Michael—
something finer. Each dust
stroke a deep breath and
the canary in bloom.
Wavery memory: home
from a dance, the front door
blown open and the parlor
in snow, she rushed
the bowl to the stove, watched
as the locket of ice
dissolved and he
swam free.

That was years before
Father gave her up
with her name, years before
her name grew to mean
Promise, then
Desert-in-Peace.

2. Drew together.
3. Hebrew for married; used in the Bible to refer to the promised land.

Long before the shadow and
sun's accomplice, the tree.

Maurice.

Weathering Out

She liked mornings the best—Thomas gone
to look for work, her coffee flushed with milk,

outside autumn trees blowsy and dripping.
Past the seventh month she couldn't see her feet

so she floated from room to room, houseshoes flapping,
navigating corners in wonder. When she leaned

against a door jamb to yawn, she disappeared entirely.

Last week they had taken a bus at dawn
to the new airdock. The hangar slid open in segments

and the zeppelin nosed forward in its silver envelope.
The man walked it out gingerly, like a poodle,

then tied it to a mast and went back inside.
Beulah felt just that large and placid, a lake;

she glistened from cocoa butter smoothed in
when Thomas returned every evening nearly

in tears. He'd lean an ear on her belly
and say: *Little fellow's really talking,*

though to her it was more the *pok-pok-pok*
of a fingernail tapping a thick cream lampshade.

Sometimes during the night she woke and found him
asleep there and the child sleeping, too.

The coffee was good but too little. Outside
everything shivered in tinfoil—only the clover

between the cobblestones hung stubbornly on,
green as an afterthought. . . .

The Great Palaces of Versailles[4]

Nothing nastier than a white person!
She mutters as she irons alterations
in the backroom of Charlotte's Dress Shoppe.
The steam rising from a cranberry wool
comes alive with perspiration[5]
and stale Evening of Paris.
Swamp she born from, swamp
she swallow, swamp she got to sink again.

The iron shoves gently
into a gusset,[6] waits until
the puckers bloom away. Beyond
the curtain, the white girls are all
wearing shoulder pads to make their faces
delicate. That laugh would be Autumn,
tossing her hair in imitation of Bacall.[7]

Beulah had read in the library
how French ladies at court would tuck
their fans in a sleeve
and walk in the gardens for air. Swaying
among lilies, lifting shy layers of silk,
they dropped excrement as daintily
as handkerchieves. Against all rules

she had saved the lining from a botched coat
to face last year's gray skirt. She knows
whenever she lifts a knee
she flashes crimson. That seems legitimate;
but in the book she had read
how the *cavaliere*[8] amused themselves
wearing powder and perfume and spraying
yellow borders knee-high on the stucco
of the *Orangerie*.[9]

A hanger clatters
in the front of the shoppe.
Beulah remembers how
even Autumn could lean into a settee
with her ankles crossed, sighing
I need a man who'll protect me
while smoking her cigarette down to the very end.

4. The magnificent complex of palaces built principally by Louis XIV (1638–1715) of France.
5. Beulah "can smell the perspiration. In that poem, it's one of those rare moments where, with her rage, she even allows it to come to the surface in terms of response. It's a political situation, actually, in the dress shop, because white girls can sell the dresses in the front of the shop and she, as the black help, gets to iron in the back room" [Dove's comments].
6. Insert in the seam of a garment.
7. Lauren Bacall (b. 1924), American actor.
8. Lovers, gallants.
9. Building housing orange trees at Versailles.

Wingfoot Lake[1]

(Independence Day, 1964)

On her 36th birthday, Thomas had shown her
her first swimming pool. It had been
his favorite color, exactly—just
so much of it, the swimmers' white arms jutting
into the chevrons[2] of high society.
She had rolled up her window
and told him to drive on, fast.

Now this *act of mercy:* four daughters
dragging her to their husbands' company picnic,
white families on one side and them
on the other, unpacking the same
squeeze bottles of Heinz, the same
waxy beef patties and Salem potato chip bags.
So he was dead for the first time
on Fourth of July—ten years ago

had been harder, waiting for something to happen,
and ten years before that, the girls
like young horses eying the track.
Last August she stood alone for hours
in front of the T.V. set
as a crow's wing moved slowly through
the white streets of government.
That brave swimming

scared her, like Joanna saying
Mother, we're Afro-Americans now!
What did she know about Africa?
Were there lakes like this one
with a rowboat pushed under the pier?
Or Thomas' Great Mississippi
with its sullen silks? (There was
the Nile but the Nile belonged
to God.) Where she came from
was the past, 12 miles into town
where nobody had locked their back door,
and Goodyear hadn't begun to dream of a park
under the company symbol, a white foot
sprouting two small wings.

1986

1. Lake and park owned by the Goodyear Tire & Rubber Company, for whom the poet's grandfather worked in Akron, Ohio.

2. V shapes; badges of honor or rank worn on the sleeve.

After Reading *Mickey in the Night Kitchen*[3] for the Third Time before Bed

I'm in the milk and the milk's in me! . . . I'm Mickey!

My daughter spreads her legs
to find her vagina:
hairless, this mistaken
bit of nomenclature
is what a stranger cannot touch
without her yelling. She demands
to see mine and momentarily
we're a lopsided star
among the spilled toys,
my prodigious scallops
exposed to her neat cameo.

And yet the same glazed
tunnel, layered sequences.
She is three; that makes this
innocent. *We're pink!*
she shrieks, and bounds off.

Every month she wants
to know where it hurts
and what the wrinkled string means
between my legs. *This is good blood*
I say, but that's wrong, too.
How to tell her that it's what makes us—
black mother, cream child.
That we're in the pink
and the pink's in us.

1987

Claudette Colvin Goes to Work[4]

Another Negro woman has been arrested and thrown into jail because she refused to get up out of her seat on the bus and give it to a white person. This is the second time since the Claudette Colbert [sic] case. . . . This must be stopped.

—Boycott Flier, December 5, 1955

Menial twilight sweeps the storefronts along Lexington[5]
as the shadows arrive to take their places
among the scourge of the earth. Here and there

3. *In the Night Kitchen* (1970): children's book by Maurice Sendak and Dena Wallenstein Neusner.
4. Claudette Colvin, an African American woman, was fifteen when she was arrested in Montgomery, Alabama, for refusing to give up her seat on a bus to a white person. Her example helped start the Montgomery bus boycott of 1955. The author of the flier in the epigraph mixes up Colvin's name with that of Claudette Colbert (1903–1996), French-born American actor.
5. Avenue running through Harlem in New York City.

a fickle brilliance—lightbulbs coming on
in each narrow residence, the golden wattage
of bleak interiors announcing *Anyone home?*
or *I'm beat, bring me a beer.*

Mostly I say to myself *Still here.* Lay
my keys on the table, pack the perishables away
before flipping the switch. I like the sugary
look of things in bad light—one drop of sweat
is all it would take to dissolve an armchair pillow
into brocade residue. Sometimes I wait until
it's dark enough for my body to disappear;

then I know it's time to start out for work.
Along the Avenue, the cabs start up, heading
toward midtown; neon stutters into ecstasy
as the male integers light up their smokes and let loose
a stream of brave talk: "Hey Mama" souring quickly to
"Your Mama" when there's no answer—as if
the most injury they can do is insult the reason

you're here at all, walking in your whites
down to the stop so you can make a living.
So ugly, so fat, so dumb, so greasy—
What do we have to do to make God love us?
Mama was a maid; my daddy mowed lawns like a boy,
and I'm the crazy girl off the bus, the one
who wrote in class she was going to be President.

I take the Number 6 bus to the Lex Ave train
and then I'm there all night, adjusting the sheets,
emptying the pans. And I don't curse or spit
or kick and scratch like they say I did then.
I help those who can't help themselves,
I do what needs to be done . . . and I sleep
whenever sleep comes down on me.

1999

ALBERTO RÍOS
b. 1952

"You see, there are in our countries rivers which have no names, trees which nobody knows, and birds which nobody has described. . . . Our duty, then, as we understand it, is to express what is unheard of." Alberto Ríos used this remark—made by the Chilean poet Pablo Neruda—as the epigraph for his first book, *Whispering to Fool the Wind* (1981), and he perhaps has adopted it as his own program. Ríos quietly makes his readers accept, understand, and take pleasure in his fanciful, "unheard-of" characters. The "old Russian" in "A Man Then Suddenly Stops Moving" is merely "surprised" when, out of a plum he has thrown to the ground, emerges his "younger self," which he simply puts "on the shelf / with the pictures." When the priest Anselmo Luna dies on a ladder, as recounted in the later collection *Teodora Luna's Two Kisses* (1990), his "muscular" soul is said to leap "from his ribs / As he had stepped / On the rungs of the ladder." Blurring boundaries between the actual and the mysterious, Ríos tells such miniaturized stories in a matter-of-fact tone, his insouciance disarming the reader's skepticism.

One of Ríos's finest grotesques is "Madre Sofía," the fat, old gypsy fortune-teller his mother takes him to when he is ten, "because she couldn't / wait the second ten years to know" her son's future. We see Madre Sofía through the child's eyes, and with him we are bewildered and terrified by her. In this poem, as in Ríos's short story about the same visit, "Eyes Like They Say the Devil Has," vivid details haunt the speaker: the "unfamiliar poppies" growing out of Sofía's head, her breasts like "horse nuzzles" or "like the quarter-arms of the amputee Joaquín," and the final prediction, which dissolves fear: "*The future will make you tall.*" In such poems, Ríos embodies the mixture of fantasy and realism—the "magical realism"—of Latin American writers such as Gabriel García Márquez. Unlike Gary Soto, a contemporary and fellow Chicano poet who also pays homage to Márquez, but who is typically more realistic in his textured evocations of the culture of Mexican American poverty, Ríos hybridizes English-language poetry with both Latin American tradition and the rhetoric and rhythms of Latino English. His poetic language indirectly but beautifully recalls the Spanish he was forced to give up in junior high school.

Ríos was born on September 18, 1952, in Nogales, Arizona, on the border of Mexico. "My father, born in southern Mexico, and my mother, born in England, gave me a language-rich, story-fat upbringing," he has said. He earned B.A.s in English and psychology at the University of Arizona (1974, 1975). After a brief stint at law school, which he left to pursue writing, he earned an M.F.A. at the University of Arizona (1979). In addition to poetry and prose fiction, he has published a memoir. Since 1982, he has taught creative writing at Arizona State University.

Madre Sofía[1]

My mother took me because she couldn't
wait the second ten years to know.
This was the lady rumored to have been
responsible for the box-wrapped baby
among the presents at that wedding,
but we went in, anyway, through the curtains.
Loose jar-top, half turned
and not caught properly in the threads
her head sat mimicking its original intention
like the smile of a child hitting himself.
Central in that head grew unfamiliar poppies
from a face mahogany, eyes half yellow
half gray at the same time, goat and fog,
slit eyes of the devil, his tweed suit, red
lips, and she smelled of smoke, cigarettes,

1. Mother Sofía (Spanish); "Sofía" derives from the Greek word meaning wisdom.

but a diamond smoke, somehow; I inhaled
sparkles, I could feel them, throat, stomach.
She did not speak, and as a child
I could only answer, so that together
we were silent, cold and wet, dry and hard:
from behind my mother pushed me forward.
The lady put her hand on the face
of a thin animal wrap, tossing that head
behind her to be pressured incredibly
as she sat back in the huge chair and leaned.
And then I saw the breasts as large as her
head, folded together, coming out of her dress
as if it didn't fit, not like my mother's.
I could see them, how she kept them
penned up, leisurely, in maroon feed bags,
horse nuzzles of her wide body,
but exquisitely penned up
circled by pearl reins and red scarves.
She lifted her arm, but only with the tips
of her fingers motioned me to sit opposite.
She looked at me but spoke to my mother
words dark, smoky like the small room,
words coming like red ants stepping occasionally
from a hole on a summer day in the valley,
red ants from her mouth, her nose, her ears,
tears from the corners of her cinched eyes.
And suddenly she put her hand full on my head
pinching tight again with those finger tips
like a television healer, young Oral Roberts
half standing, quickly, half leaning
those breasts swinging toward me
so that I reach with both my hands to my lap
protecting instinctively whatever it is
that needs protection when a baseball is thrown
and you're not looking but someone yells,
the hand, then those breasts coming toward me
like the quarter-arms of the amputee Joaquín
who came back from the war to sit
in the park, reaching always for children
until one day he had to be held back.
I sat there, no breath, and could see only
hair around her left nipple, like a man.
Her clothes were old.
Accented, in a language whose spine had been
snapped, she whispered the words of a city
witch, and made me happy, alive like a man:
The future will make you tall.

1982

Mi Abuelo[2]

Where my grandfather is is in the ground
where you can hear the future
like an Indian with his ear at the tracks.
A pipe leads down to him so that sometimes
he whispers what will happen to a man
in town or how he will meet the best
dressed woman tomorrow and how the best
man at her wedding will chew the ground
next to her. Mi abuelo is the man
who speaks through all the mouths in my house.
An echo of me hitting the pipe sometimes
to stop him from saying *my hair is a*
sieve is the only other sound. It is a phrase
that among all others is the best,
he says, and *my hair is a sieve* is sometimes
repeated for hours out of the ground
when I let him, which is not often.
An abuelo should be much more than a man
like you! He stops then, and speaks: *I am a man*
who has served ants with the attitude
of a waiter, who has made each smile as only
an ant who is fat can, and they liked me best,
but there is nothing left. Yet I know he ground
green coffee beans as a child, and sometimes
he will talk about his wife, and sometimes
about when he was deaf and a man
cured him by mail and he heard groundhogs
talking, or about how he walked with a cane
he chewed on when he got hungry.
At best, mi abuelo is a liar.
I see an old picture of him at nani's[3] with an
off-white yellow center mustache and sometimes
that's all I know for sure. He talks best
about these hills, *slowest waves,* and where this man
is going, and I'm convinced his hair is a sieve,
that his fever is cooled now underground.
Mi abuelo is an ordinary man.
I look down the pipe, sometimes, and see a
ripple-topped stream in its best suit, in the ground.

1982

2. My grandfather (Spanish).
3. Grandma's (informal Spanish).

A Man Then Suddenly Stops Moving

The old Russian spits up a plum
fruit of the rasping sound
he has stored in his throat
all these lonely years

made in fact lonely by his wife
who left him, God knows
without knowing how to cook for himself.

He examines the plum
notes its purplish consistency
almost the color and shape of her buttocks
whose circulation was bad

which is why he himself wears a beret:
black, good wool, certainly warm enough
the times he remembers.

He shoots the plum
to the ground like a child
whose confidence is a game of marbles

whose flick of a thumb
is a smile inside his mouth
knowing what he knows will happen.

But his wife, Marthe
does not spill out
when the plum breaks open.

Instead, it is a younger self
alive and waving
just the size he remembers
himself to have been.

The old Russian puts him onto his finger
like a parakeet
and sits him on the shelf
with the pictures.

For the rest of his days
he nags himself constantly
into a half-sleep
surprised by this turn of events.

1985

Anselmo's Moment with God[4]

Anselmo in a fit of pique
Over a spatula he could not find
As the eggs were burning
And as he did not yet have the services
Of the housekeeper Mrs. M.
He would have in later years,
Renounced his love of God
And of the world, right there.

He threw the drawer of utensils to the ground
And let the eggs burn dry
Until they gave texture to
And became part of the black iron pan itself.
Every day for the rest of his life
He remembered himself that moment—
Himself but not the event:
His spatula became through the years
The Hand of God.

Of God's smell
He could not be certain:
Only that the burning of candles
Had for him a certain urgency.

1990

The Death of Anselmo Luna

Since he was the priest,
No one could say for certain about Anselmo Luna.
What began as a lark
One slow afternoon of interminable chores
Regarding candles and residue on the walls,
Became his drawings:
First of the saints,
Then the twelve Stations of the Cross,[5]
The sketches of simpler remembrances.
All of these chiaroscuros[6] he made
In and from the soot on the walls of this church,
A work that moved into years
And which finally filled his life.
What began as a lark became the seed

4. This poem and "The Death of Anselmo Luna" are taken from Ríos's *Teodoro Luna's Two Kisses*, a book of poems detailing the history of the fictitious Luna family. Anselmo is a priest and the brother of Teodoro.

5. A series of images depicting the final events in the life of Jesus.

6. Technique of painting with dramatic contrasts between light and dark.

Of his miracle, a simple
Moving of a finger along a pillar
Just to see, was there enough
To require cleansing,
This test also used on parked cars,
A line spelling *wash me* in the soil of a window.
He died while perched on a ladder
High behind the altar, underneath
The fine woodwork: that moment
As he fell, and as he made a mark
Not unlike a moustache
Where none should have been,
He died already partway
Toward heaven. It was said
His soul took the advantage,
Leaping out from his body
Right there, stepping from his ribs
As he had stepped
On the rungs of the ladder.
It was a strong soul, muscular,
On account of his years of devoted effort,
And it knew like an animal what to do
When the moment came.

1990

MARK DOTY
b. 1953

Mark Doty quotes W. H. Auden's remarks that a poem should be "a verbal earthly paradise, a timeless world of pure play, which gives us delight precisely because of its contrast to our historical existence with all its insoluble problems and inescapable suffering"; and yet "a poet cannot bring us any truth without introducing into his poetry the problematic, the painful, the disorderly, the ugly" ("Here in Hell"). Doty tries to meet the demands of both delight and truth in his poetry of shimmering surfaces and numb grief, of exultant play and mortal pain. His work displays, as he has suggested, something of the drag queen's pleasure in ravishing texture and spectacle, but it also employs something of the mortician's cold stare at the grim inevitabilities of loss and death.

A poem such as "A Green Crab's Shell" is indeed an earthly paradise. The poem takes us inside a small crab's shell with its "shocking, Giotto blue" and "lavish lining," and it evokes the glory of a life "surrounded by / the brilliant rinse / of summer's firmament." Characteristically sensuous and painterly, Doty re-creates this magnificent and yet minute "chamber" in the artfully constructed chambers of his poem. But the shell that offers a fantastical escape into beauty reminds us also of death's inevitability.

Doty works in the tradition of American autobiographical poetry that extends from Walt Whitman to Elizabeth Bishop and Robert Lowell. The propulsive cadences and rhetorical patterns of "Homo Will Not Inherit," a charged repudiation of homophobia, echo Whitman. Here Doty also appropriates but transfigures biblical rhetoric in his sacramental descriptions of gay sex ("I've seen flame flicker around the edges of the body, / pentecostal") and of the soiled beauty of the homoerotic city: "This city's inescapable, // gorgeous, and on fire. I have my kingdom." The opening of "A Green Crab's Shell" may remind us of Bishop's penchant for exactly calibrated descriptions of nature's details ("Not, exactly, green: / closer to bronze / preserved in kind brine") and of Lowell's capacity for uncovering stress and violence in seeming calm ("something retrieved / from a Greco-Roman wreck, / patinated and oddly // muscular"). But for all his interest in gorgeous surfaces and lavish language, Doty can also write in a plain style. His austere AIDS elegy "The Embrace" largely withholds description, until the "physical fact" of the dead man's face—"smooth-shaven, loving, alert"—emerges with luminous power, only to be eclipsed by the quiet severity of the final line: "without thinking you were alive again."

Doty was born on August 10, 1953, in Maryville, Tennessee. His father was an army engineer whose work required frequent moves in the suburban American south and west. Doty married early, but divorced after receiving his B.A. from Drake University in Iowa. While working toward his M.F.A. from Goddard College, in Vermont, he met his partner, Wally Roberts, whose illness and death (in 1994, from AIDS) Doty has memorialized in prose as well as verse. Doty has taught creative writing at the Universities of Utah, Iowa, and Houston, Columbia University, and Sarah Lawrence College. He has received, among other prizes, the National Book Critics Circle Award in 1994 and the T. S. Eliot Prize in 1995.

A Green Crab's Shell

Not, exactly, green:
closer to bronze
preserved in kind brine,

something retrieved
from a Greco-Roman wreck,
patinated and oddly

muscular. We cannot
know what his fantastic
legs were like—

though evidence
suggests eight
complexly folded

scuttling works
of armament, crowned
by the foreclaws'

gesture of menace
and power. A gull's
gobbled the center,

leaving this chamber
—size of a demitasse—
open to reveal

a shocking, Giotto[1] blue.
Though it smells
of seaweed and ruin,

this little traveling case
comes with such lavish lining!
Imagine breathing

surrounded by
the brilliant rinse
of summer's firmament.

What color is
the underside of skin?
Not so bad, to die,

if we could be opened
into *this*—
if the smallest chambers

of ourselves,
similarly,
revealed some sky.

1995

Homo Will Not Inherit[2]

Downtown anywhere and between the roil
of bathhouse steam—up there the linens of joy
and shame must be laundered again and again,

all night—downtown anywhere
and between the column of feathering steam
unknotting itself thirty feet above the avenue's

shimmered azaleas of gasoline,
between the steam and the ruin
of the Cinema Paree (marquee advertising

its own milky vacancy, broken showcases sealed,
ticketbooth a hostage wrapped in tape
and black plastic, captive in this zone

1. Giotto di Bondone (c. 1266–1337), Italian artist. *Demitasse:* small cup.
2. "For Michael Carter" [Doty's note].

of blackfronted bars and bookstores
where there's nothing to read
but longing's repetitive texts,

where desire's unpoliced, or nearly so)
someone's posted a xeroxed headshot
of Jesus: permed, blonde, blurred at the edges

as though photographed through a greasy lens,
and inked beside him, in marker strokes:
HOMO WILL NOT INHERIT. *Repent & be saved.*[3]

I'll tell you what I'll inherit: the margins
which have always been mine, downtown after hours
when there's nothing left to buy,

the dreaming shops turned in on themselves,
seamless, intent on the perfection of display,
the bodegas[4] and offices lined up, impenetrable:

edges no one wants, no one's watching. Though
the borders of this shadow-zone (mirror and dream
of the shattered streets around it) are chartered

by the police, and they are required,
some nights, to redefine them. But not now, at twilight,
permission's descending hour, early winter darkness

pillared by smoldering plumes. The public city's
ledgered and locked, but the secret city's boundless;
from which do these tumbling towers arise?

I'll tell you what I'll inherit: steam,
and the blinding symmetry of some towering man,
fifteen minutes of forgetfulness incarnate.

I've seen flame flicker around the edges of the body,
pentecostal,[5] evidence of inhabitation.
And I have been possessed of the god myself,

I have been the temporary apparition
salving another, I have been his visitation, I say it
without arrogance, I have been an angel

for minutes at a time, and I have for hours
believed—without judgment, without condemnation—
that in each body, however obscured or recast,

3. "Be not deceived: neither fornicators, nor idolaters, nor adulterers, nor effeminate, nor abusers of themselves with mankind, nor thieves, nor covetous, nor drunkards, nor revilers, nor extortioners, shall inherit the kingdom of God" (1 Corinthians 6.9–10).

4. Shops selling groceries and wine (Spanish).

5. During Pentecost, the Holy Spirit descended in the form of fire onto the disciples, causing them to speak in tongues (Acts 2.1–4).

is the divine body—common, habitable—
the way in a field of sunflowers
you can see every bloom's

the multiple expression
of a single shining idea,
which is the face hammered into joy.

I'll tell you what I'll inherit:
stupidity, erasure, exile
inside the chalked lines of the police,

who must resemble what they punish,
the exile you require of me,
you who's posted this invitation

to a heaven nobody wants.
You who must be patrolled,
who adore constraint, I'll tell you

what I'll inherit, not your pallid temple
but a real palace, the anticipated
and actual memory, the moment flooded

by skin and the knowledge of it,
the gesture and its description
—do I need to say it?—

the flesh *and* the word. And I'll tell you,
you who can't wait to abandon your body,
what you want me to, maybe something

like you've imagined, a dirty story:
Years ago, in the baths,
a man walked into the steam,

the gorgeous deep indigo of him gleaming,
solid tight flanks, the intricately ridged abdomen—
and after he invited me to his room,

nudging his key toward me,
as if perhaps I spoke another tongue
and required the plainest of gestures,

after we'd been, you understand,
worshipping a while in his church,
he said to me, *I'm going to punish your mouth.*

I can't tell you what that did to me.
My shame was redeemed then;
I won't need to burn in the afterlife.

It wasn't that he hurt me,
more than that: the spirit's transactions
are enacted now, here—no one needs

your eternity. This failing city's
radiant as any we'll ever know,
paved with oily rainbow, charred gates

jeweled with tags, swoops of letters
over letters, indecipherable as anything
written by desire. I'm not ashamed

to love Babylon's scrawl.[6] How could I be?
It's written on my face as much as on
these walls. This city's inescapable,

gorgeous, and on fire. I have my kingdom.

1995

The Embrace

You weren't well or really ill yet either;
just a little tired, your handsomeness
tinged by grief or anticipation, which brought
to your face a thoughtful, deepening grace.

I didn't for a moment doubt you were dead.
I knew that to be true still, even in the dream.
You'd been out—at work maybe?—
having a good day, almost energetic.

We seemed to be moving from some old house
where we'd lived, boxes everywhere, things
in disarray: that was the *story* of my dream,
but even asleep I was shocked out of narrative

by your face, the physical fact of your face:
inches from mine, smooth-shaven, loving, alert.
Why so difficult, remembering the actual look
of you? Without a photograph, without strain?

So when I saw your unguarded, reliable face,
your unmistakable gaze opening all the warmth
and clarity of you—warm brown tea—we held
each other for the time the dream allowed.

6. Daniel 5 describes the writing that appeared on a palace wall and that Daniel interpreted as a condemnation of Belshazzar, the king of Babylon.

Bless you. You came back, so I could see you
once more, plainly, so I could rest against you
without thinking this happiness lessened anything,
without thinking you were alive again.

1998

THYLIAS MOSS
b. 1954

The subject matter of Thylias Moss's poetry is often emotionally disturbing, even explosive. "Lunchcounter Freedom" recalls African American sit-ins during the civil rights movement. "Crystals" chronicles a nineteenth-century doctor's experimental operations on a slave's vagina. Historical injustices toward African American women, the contradictions of motherhood, and questions of sexuality, rapture, death, and God—Moss does not shy away from such charged issues. But her approach to this weighty material is oblique, riddling, and gnomic. "Only what seems extraordinary compels me to write," she remarks, and her poetry conveys by its strangeness some of the oddity and wonder of undomesticated human experiences ("The Extraordinary Hoof"). In Moss's hands, even an encounter as routine as rereading Robert Frost's "Stopping by Woods on a Snowy Evening" is defamiliarized, the poet rethinking the lyric through the lens of racial binarism ("Interpretation of a Poem by Frost").

Moss says she avoids "imposing certain agendas" on her poems, such as those of "identity" politics. Instead, she lets her poems ramble associatively, and their turns—imbedded in syntactic sprawl—are often surprising. "I prefer that unanticipated discovery lead me to and through a poem," she comments ("The Extraordinary Hoof"). Digressive, elliptical, allusive, her poems nevertheless tend to return to their central themes. Moss credits as a strong influence Sunday sermons in which the preacher makes "text," and her work recalls this model in its impassioned, if indirect, explorations of themes such as joy and infanticide. In the poem "The Rapture of Dry Ice Burning off Skin as the Moment of the Soul's Apotheosis," Moss meditates on the meanings of joy, performing extravagant metaphorical leaps from buffalo-stomach hair to Tiffany-lamp fringes and from needle tracks on the arms of drug addicts to umbrellas (that is, the veins of addicts are compared to the "metal veins" of a collapsed umbrella). Shifting gears in her figurative language, Moss may also suddenly change tone, from arch knowingness to the earnestness of prayer, from acid bleakness to the fierce confidence of prophecy. Though her poems are loosely jointed, their stunningly climactic endings are anything but haphazard. In the last lines of "After Reading *Beloved*," she compares the nails that held Jesus on the cross to the Virgin Mary's nipples. "Crystals" closes with an image of the doctor's hand remaining inside the slave's vagina.

Strange juxtapositions were part of Moss's childhood. Born on February 27, 1954, to a working-class family in Cleveland, Ohio, Moss grew up in circumstances that combined nightmare and "paradise" (her word). In her 1998 memoir, *Tale of a Sky-Blue Dress*, she describes her parents as lavishing care and affection on her as an only child, yet for several years she was also cruelly abused by a babysitter, only later rediscovering happiness in her own family. She began her undergraduate work at Syracuse University, but received her B.A. from Oberlin College (1981) and her M.A. from the University of New Hampshire (1983), where she studied with Charles Simic. A 1996

MacArthur Fellow, she has taught at Phillips Academy (1984–92) and, since 1993, at the University of Michigan.

Lunchcounter Freedom[1]

I once wanted a white man's eyes upon
me, my beauty riveting him to my slum
color. Forgetting his hands are made for my
curves, he would raise them to shield his eyes
and they would fly to my breasts with gentleness
stolen from doves.

I've made up my mind not to order a sandwich on
light bread if the waitress approaches me
with a pencil. My hat is the one I wear
the Sundays my choir doesn't sing. A dark
bird on it darkly sways to the gospel music,
trying to pull nectar from a cloth flower.
Psalms are mice in my mind, nibbling,
gnawing, tearing up my thoughts.
White men are the walls. I can't tell anyone
how badly I want water. In the mirage that
follows, the doves unfold into hammers.
They still fly to my breasts.

Because I'm nonviolent I don't act or
react. When knocked from the stool
my body takes its shape from what
it falls into. The white man cradles
his tar baby. Each magus[2] in turn.
He fathered it, it looks just like him,
the spitting image. He can't let go of
his future. The menu offers tuna fish,
grits, beef in a sauce like desire.
He is free to choose from available
choices. An asterisk marks the special.

1990

1. The sit-ins of the black civil rights movement began in the early 1960s, when college students staged a sit-in at a lunchcounter in Greensboro, North Carolina.
2. One of the three wise men traditionally believed to have paid homage to the infant Jesus. *Tar baby:* sticky black doll used as a trap in many African-derived folktales and made famous in the stories of the American writer Joel Chandler Harris (1848–1908).

Interpretation of a Poem by Frost[3]

A young black girl stopped by the woods,
so young she knew only one man: Jim Crow[4]
but she wasn't allowed to call him Mister.
The woods were his and she respected his boundaries
even in the absence of fence.
Of course she delighted in the filling up
of his woods, she so accustomed to emptiness,
to being taken at face value.
This face, her face eternally the brown
of declining autumn, watches snow inter the grass,
cling to bark making it seem indecisive
about race preference, a fast-to-melt idealism.
With the grass covered, black and white are the only options,
polarity is the only reality; corners aren't neutral
but are on edge.
She shakes off snow, defiance wasted
on the limited audience of horse.
The snow does not hypnotize her as it wants to,
as the blond sun does in making too many prefer daylight.
She has promises to keep,
the promise that she bear Jim no bastards,
the promise that she ride the horse only as long
as it is willing to accept riders,
the promise that she bear Jim no bastards,
the promise to her face that it not be mistaken as shadow,
and miles to go, more than the distance from Africa to Andover,[5]
more than the distance from black to white
before she sleeps with Jim.

1991

The Rapture of Dry Ice Burning off Skin as the Moment of the Soul's Apotheosis[6]

How will we get used to joy
if we won't hold onto it?

Not even extinction stops me; when
I've sufficient craving, I follow the buffalo,
their hair hanging below their stomachs like
fringes on Tiffany lampshades,[7] they can be turned on
so can I by a stampede, footsteps whose sound

3. "Stopping by Woods on a Snowy Evening," by the American poet Robert Frost (1874–1963).
4. Jim Crow laws enforced racial segregation in southern U.S. states between the 1880s and 1950s; originally, name of a character in a black-face-minstrel song-and-dance act.
5. Town in Massachusetts.
6. Glorification; transformation into a god.
7. Decorated, stained-glass lampshades.

is my heart souped up, doctored, ninety pounds
running off a semi's invincible engine. Buffalo
heaven is Niagara Falls. There their spirit
gushes. There they still stampede and power
the generators that operate the Tiffany lamps
that let us see in some of the dark. Snow
inundates the city bearing their name; buffalo
spirit chips later melt to feed the underground,
the politically dredlocked tendrils of roots. And this
has no place in reality, is trivial juxtaposed with

the faces of addicts, their eyes practically as sunken
as extinction, gray ripples like hurdlers' track lanes
under them, pupils like just more needle sites.
And their arms: flesh trying for a moon apprenticeship,
a celestial antibody. Every time I use it
the umbrella is turned inside out,
metal veins, totally hardened arteries and survival
without anything flowing within, nothing saying
life came from the sea, from anywhere but coincidence
or God's ulcer, revealed. Yet also, inside out
the umbrella tries to be a bouquet, or at least
the rugged wrapping for one that must endure much,
without dispensing coherent parcels of scent,
before the refuge of vase in a room already accustomed
to withering mind and retreating skin. But the smell
of the flowers lifts the corners of the mouth as if
the man at the center of this remorse has lifted her
in a waltz. This is as true as sickness. The Jehovah's

Witness will come to my door any minute with tracts, an
inflexible agenda and I won't let him in because
I'm painting a rosy picture with only blue and
yellow (sadness and cowardice).
I'm something of an alchemist. Extinct.
He would tell me time is running out.
I would correct him: time *ran* out; that's why
history repeats itself, why we can't advance.
What joy will come has to be here right now: Cheer
to wash the dirt away, Twenty Mule Team Borax and
Arm & Hammer to magnify Cheer's power, lemon-scented
bleach and ammonia to trick the nose, improved—changed—
Tide, almost all-purpose starch that cures any limpness
except impotence. Celebrate that there's *Master*card
to rule us, bring us to our knees, the protocol we follow
in the presence of the head of our state of ruin, the
official with us all the time, not inaccessible in
palaces or White Houses or Kremlins. Besides every
ritual is stylized, has patterns and repetitions
suitable for adaptation to dance. Here come toe shoes,
brushstrokes, oxymorons. Joy

is at our tongue tips: Let the great thirsts and hungers
of the world be the *marvelous* thirsts, *glorious* hungers.
Let heartbreak be alternative to coffeebreak, five
midmorning minutes devoted to emotion.

1991

Crystals

In 1845 Dr. James Marion Sims[8] had seen it many times,
vesico-vaginal fistula, abnormal passageway
between bladder and vagina through which urine leaks
almost constantly if the fistula is large

as it tends to become after those pregnancies
not quite a year apart in Anarcha and her slave
friends Lucy, Betsey. *If you can just fix this*
the girl said, probably pregnant again, her vulva inflamed,
her thighs caked with urinary salts; from the beginning
he saw his future in those crystals.

Society women sometimes had this too, a remaking of the vulva,
more color, pustules like decorations of which women
were already fond; beads, cultured pearls of pus, status.
Perhaps the design improves in its greater challenger to love
and fondle even in the dark except that there is pain,
inability to hold water.

He tried to help Anarcha first, drawing on what
he was inventing: frontier ingenuity and gynecology,
and operated thirty times, using a pewter teaspoon
that he reshaped, bent and hammered for each surgery,
no sterilant but spit, while she watched; it became
his famous duck-bill speculum too large and sharp
to be respectful, yet it let him look.

Such excoriation, such stretching of the vaginal walls, tunnel
into room; such remembrance of Jericho, prophecy of Berlin[9]
when his mind was to have been on her comfort and healing.

Through the vulva was the way most tried to access her
yet they did not come close. Using

8. American doctor (1813–1883), considered the "father of modern gynecology." Sims began his surgical career by conducting experiments on slave women such as the seventeen-year-old Anarcha, who underwent over thirty such operations without anesthesia. "Although in 'Crystals,' the implication is that Anarcha, her actual name, was or had been pregnant, there is not yet evidence of her pregnancies, suggesting that her fistula had some other cause, such as horseback riding. However, among those multiparas [women who have given birth more than once], especially enslaved multiparas, who develop these fistulas, repeated childbirth is often the cause" [Moss's note].

9. The Berlin Wall, separating East and West Berlin, was taken down in 1989. The walls of Jericho were destroyed by Joshua and the Israelites (Joshua 6).

a half-dollar he formed the wire suture that closed
Anarcha's fistula on the thirtieth, it bears repeating, thirtieth
attempt.

For the rest of her life she slept in the Sims position:
on her left side, right knee brought to her chest; she so long,
four years, on his table came to find it comfortable, came to find
no other way to lose herself, relieve her mind,
ignore Sims' rising glory, his bragging in the journals
that he had seen the fistula *as no man had ever seen it before.*
Now they all can.

Anarcha who still does not know anesthesia except
for her willed loss of awareness went on peeing as she'd
always done, just not so frequently and in reduced
volume, hardly enough for a tea cup, but whenever
necessary, the doctor poked, prodded, practiced

then, successful, went gloved and shaven to help ladies
on whom white cloths were draped; divinity
on the table to indulge his tastefulness.

It should be noted
that Anarcha's fistula closed well,
sealed in infection, scarred
thickly

as if his hand remained.

1998

Louise Erdrich
b. 1954

"My characters choose me and once they do it's like standing in a field and hearing echoes," Louise Erdrich said in a 1986 interview. "All I can do is trace their passage." She was speaking of the people in one of her acclaimed novels, *The Beet Queen* (1986), but the remark applies as well to the personae of the many remarkable dramatic monologues in her first book of poems, *Jacklight* (1984), named after a light used for hunting or fishing at night. Among them are unidealized portraits of the Native Americans with whom she grew up near North Dakota's Turtle Mountain Reservation, such as Debby, who speaks in "Family Reunion" of Ray, her beer-drinking uncle. They also include historical figures, such as Mary Rowlandson, the seventeenth-century author of a famous narrative about her "captivity" by the Wampanoag Indians; once restored to her family, bewildered by the change, she can "see no truth in things." Erdrich never judges the speakers in her poems; she quietly observes the details of their lives in the strong yet sympathetic ray of her jacklight.

Erdrich wrote many poems in her second collection, *Baptism of Desire* (1989), according to a note, "between the hours of two and four in the morning, a period of insomnia brought on by pregnancy." The circumstance of the poems' composition is sometimes reflected in their subject matter. "The Fence" is a beautiful lyric about pregnancy, interweaving images of the poet ("My body is a golden armor around my unborn child's body") and growth in her garden ("the young plant trembles on its stalk"). But Erdrich knows that what is a miracle to one person can become a nightmare for someone else, and she also included a bleak narrative poem about an unwanted pregnancy and infanticide ("Poor Clare"). Mediating between gritty narrative realism and personal lyricism, between Christian and Native American lore, Erdrich's poetry is marked by luminous revelations of character, resiliently unsentimental language, and vivid storytelling.

Erdrich was born on June 7, 1954, in Minnesota, and she grew up in a small town in North Dakota near the Turtle Mountain Reservation, where her grandparents lived and her grandfather served as tribal chairman. Her French Ojibwa (Chippewa) mother and her German-born father both worked at a Bureau of Indian Affairs boarding school. She spent several years at a Catholic school, but began writing at Dartmouth College, from which she received her B.A. (1976); she also has an M.A. (1979) from the Writing Seminars at Johns Hopkins University, then directed by Richard Howard, another contemporary master of the dramatic monologue.

Family Reunion

Ray's third new car in half as many years.
Full cooler in the trunk, Ray sogging[1] the beer
as I solemnly chauffeur us through the bush
and up the backroads, hardly cowpaths and hub-deep in mud.
All day the sky lowers, clears, lowers again.
Somewhere in the bush near Saint John
there are uncles, a family, one mysterious brother
who stayed on the land when Ray left for the cities.
One week Ray is crocked. We've been through this before.
Even, as a little girl, hands in my dress,
Ah punka, you's my Debby, come and ki me.

Then the road ends in a yard full of dogs.
Them's Indian dogs, Ray says, lookit how they know me.
And they do seem to know him, like I do. His odor—
rank beef of fierce turtle pulled dripping from Metagoshe,[2]
and the inflammable mansmell: hair tonic, ashes, alcohol.
Ray dances an old woman up in his arms.
Fiddles reel in the phonograph and I sink apart
in a corner, start knocking the Blue Ribbons[3] down.
Four generations of people live here.
No one remembers Raymond Twobears.

So what. The walls shiver, the old house caulked with mud
sails back into the middle of Metagoshe.

1. Soaking.
2. Lake Metagoshe, in North Dakota.
3. That is, beers.

A three-foot-long snapper is hooked on a troutline,
so mean that we do not dare wrestle him in
but tow him to shore, heavy as an old engine.
Then somehow Ray pries the beak open and shoves
down a cherry bomb. Lights the string tongue.

Headless and clenched in its armor, the snapper
is lugged home in the trunk for tomorrow's soup.
Ray rolls it beneath a bush in the backyard and goes in
to sleep his own head off. Tomorrow I find
that the animal has dragged itself someplace.
I follow torn tracks up a slight hill and over
into a small stream that deepens and widens into a marsh.

Ray finds his way back through the room into his arms.
When the phonograph stops, he slumps hard in his hands
and the boys and their old man fold him into the car
where he curls around his bad heart, hearing how it knocks
and rattles at the bars of his ribs to break out.

Somehow we find our way back. Uncle Ray
sings an old song to the body that pulls him
toward home. The gray fins that his hands have become
screw their bones in the dashboard. His face
has the odd, calm patience of a child who has always
let bad wounds alone, or a creature that has lived
for a long time underwater. And the angels come
lowering their slings and litters.

1984

Captivity

He (my captor) gave me a bisquit, which I put in my pocket, and not daring to eat it, buried it under a log, fearing he had put something in it to make me love him.
—from the narrative of the captivity of Mrs. Mary Rowlandson, who was taken prisoner by the Wampanoag when Lancaster, Massachusetts, was destroyed, in the year 1676

The stream was swift, and so cold
I thought I would be sliced in two.
But he dragged me from the flood
by the ends of my hair.
I had grown to recognize his face.
I could distinguish it from the others.
There were times I feared I understood
his language, which was not human,
and I knelt to pray for strength.

We were pursued! By God's agents
or pitch[4] devils I did not know.
Only that we must march.
Their guns were loaded with swan shot.[5]
I could not suckle and my child's wail
put them in danger.
He had a woman
with teeth black and glittering.
She fed the child milk of acorns.
The forest closed, the light deepened.

I told myself that I would starve
before I took food from his hands
but I did not starve.
One night
he killed a deer with a young one in her
and gave me to eat of the fawn.
It was so tender,
the bones like the stems of flowers,
that I followed where he took me.
The night was thick. He cut the cord
that bound me to the tree.

After that the birds mocked.
Shadows gaped and roared
and the trees flung down
their sharpened lashes.
He did not notice God's wrath.
God blasted fire from half-buried stumps.
I hid my face in my dress, fearing He would burn us all
but this, too, passed.

Rescued, I see no truth in things.
My husband drives a thick wedge
through the earth, still it shuts
to him year after year.
My child is fed of the first wheat.
I lay myself to sleep
on a Holland-laced pillowbeer.[6]
I lay to sleep.
And in the dark I see myself
as I was outside their circle.

They knelt on deerskins, some with sticks,
and he led his company in the noise
until I could no longer bear
the thought of how I was.
I stripped a branch

4. That is, pitch-black.
5. A large size of shot used in hunting wildfowl.
6. Pillowcases with lace made in the Netherlands.

and struck the earth,
in time, begging it to open
to admit me
as he was
and feed me honey from the rock.[7]

1984

Windigo

For Angela

The Windigo is a flesh-eating, wintry demon with a man buried deep inside of it. In some Chippewa stories, a young girl vanquishes this monster by forcing boiling lard down its throat, thereby releasing the human at the core of ice.

You knew I was coming for you, little one,
when the kettle jumped into the fire.
Towels flapped on the hooks,
and the dog crept off, groaning,
to the deepest part of the woods.

In the hackles of dry brush a thin laughter started up.
Mother scolded the food warm and smooth in the pot
and called you to eat.
But I spoke in the cold trees:
New one, I have come for you, child hide and lie still.

The sumac pushed sour red cones through the air.
Copper burned in the raw wood.
You saw me drag toward you.
Oh touch me, I murmured, and licked the soles of your feet.
You dug your hands into my pale, melting fur.

I stole you off, a huge thing in my bristling armor.
Steam rolled from my wintry arms, each leaf shivered
from the bushes we passed
until they stood, naked, spread like the cleaned spines of fish.

Then your warm hands hummed over and shoveled themselves full
of the ice and the snow. I would darken and spill
all night running, until at last morning broke the cold earth
and I carried you home,
a river shaking in the sun.

1984

7. Cf. Psalm 81.16: "But you would be fed with the finest of wheat; with honey from the rock I would satisfy you."

The Fence

Then one day the gray rags vanish
and the sweet wind rattles her sash.
Her secrets bloom hot. I'm wild for everything.
My body is a golden armor around my unborn child's body,
and I'll die happy, here on the ground.
I bend to the mixture of dirt, chopped hay,
grindings of coffee from our dark winter breakfasts.
I spoon the rich substance around the acid-loving shrubs.
I tear down last year's drunken vines,
pull the black rug off the bed of asparagus
and lie there, knowing by June I'll push the baby out
as easily as seed wings fold back from the cotyledon.[8]
I see the first leaf already, the veined tongue
rigid between the thighs of the runner beans.
I know how the shoot will complicate itself
as roots fill the trench.
Here is the link fence, the stem doubling toward it,
and something I've never witnessed.
One moment the young plant trembles on its stalk.
The next, it has already gripped the wire.
Now it will continue to climb, dragging rude blossoms
to the other side
until in summer fruit like green scimitars,
the frieze of vines, and then the small body
spread before me in need
drinking light from the shifting wall of my body,
and the fingers, tiny stems wavering to mine,
flexing for the ascent.

1989

8. Seed leaf in a seed's embryo.

Lorna Dee Cervantes
b. 1954

Em-plu-ma-do *v.m.*, feathered; in plumage, as after molting
plu-ma-da *n.f.*, pen flourish

Lorna Dee Cervantes used these definitions as the epigraph to her first book of poems (1981). She entitled the book *Emplumada,* combining the two Spanish words, so that feathers, wings, birds become fused with writing, a neologism that suggests visionary hope for the power of poetry. As this playful use of Spanish suggests, both the language and Mexican American culture have been important resources for her poetry. Even so,

Cervantes grew up speaking English primarily, because Spanish was forbidden to her. "I'm orphaned from my Spanish name," she writes in "Refugee Ship," an early poem. "The words are foreign, stumbling / on my tongue." And yet, though she feels "a captive / aboard the refugee ship" of English, she reclaims her ancestral and cultural language in the hybrid language of her poetry. Perhaps her work's most striking feature is its bilingual texture, its sinuous integration of Spanish words and phrases, rhetorical structure and oral rhythms, into contemporary English. Both of and distanced from that culture, Cervantes voices in richly imagistic free verse a range of feelings, from fierce optimism and love ("The Body as Braille") to anger and grief over the debilitating social circumstances and grim history of Mexican Americans ("Cannery Town in August," "Poema para los Californios Muertos").

Cervantes was born into a working-class family in San Francisco, California, on August 6, 1954. That year, the word *Chicano* first became an individualizing name for Mexican Americans; Mexican American women adopted the label *Chicana* in 1967. Of Mexican and Native American ancestry, Cervantes grew up in San José, reading Shakespeare and the English Romantic poets in the houses cleaned by her mother. She was educated at San José City College, San José State University (B.A., 1984), and the University of California, Santa Cruz (1985–88). Long active in Chicano/a community and literary affairs, she founded a small press, Mango Publications, in 1976. She teaches creative writing at the University of Colorado, Boulder.

Cannery Town in August

All night it humps the air.
Speechless, the steam rises
from the cannery columns. I hear
the night bird rave about work
or lunch, or sing the swing shift[1]
home. I listen, while bodyless
uniforms and spinach specked shoes
drift in monochrome down the dark
moon-possessed streets. Women
who smell of whiskey and tomatoes,
peach fuzz reddening their lips and eyes—
I imagine them not speaking, dumbed
by the can's clamor and drop
to the trucks that wait, grunting
in their headlights below.
They spotlight those who walk
like a dream, with no one
waiting in the shadows
to palm them back to living.

1981

1. Work shift between day and night shifts.

The Body as Braille

He tells me, "Your back
is so beautiful." He traces
my spine with his hand.

I'm burning like the white ring
around the moon. "A witch's moon,"
dijo mi abuela.[2] The schools call it

"a reflection of ice crystals."
It's a storm brewing in the cauldron
of the sky. I'm in love

but won't tell him
if it's omens
or ice.

1981

Refugee Ship

Like wet cornstarch, I slide
past my grandmother's eyes. Bible
at her side, she removes her glasses.
The pudding thickens.

Mama raised me without language.
I'm orphaned from my Spanish name.
The words are foreign, stumbling
on my tongue. I see in the mirror
my reflection: bronzed skin, black hair.

I feel I am a captive
aboard the refugee ship.
The ship that will never dock.
El barco que nunca atraca.[3]

1981

2. Said my grandmother (Spanish).

3. Spanish translation of above line.

Poema para los Californios Muertos[4]

Once a refuge for Mexican Californios . . .
—plaque outside a restaurant
in Los Altos, California, 1974.

These older towns die
into stretches of freeway.
The high scaffolding cuts a clean cesarean
across belly valleys and fertile dust.
What a bastard child, this city
lost in the soft
llorando de las madres.[5]
Californios moan like husbands of the raped,
husbands de la tierra,
tierra la madre.[6]

I run my fingers
across this brass plaque.
Its cold stirs in me a memory
of silver buckles and spent bullets,
of embroidered shawls and dark rebozos.[7]
Yo recuerdo los antepasados muertos.
Los recuerdo en la sangre,
la sangre fértil.[8]

What refuge did you find here,
ancient Californios?
Now at this restaurant nothing remains
but this old oak and an ill-placed plaque.
Is it true that you still live here
in the shadows of these white, high-class houses?
Soy la hija pobrecita
pero puedo maldecir estas fantasmas blancas.
Las fantasmas tuyas deben aquí quedarse,
solas las tuyas.[9]

In this place I see nothing but strangers.
On the shelves there are bitter antiques,
yanqui[1] remnants
y estos no de los Californios.[2]
A blue jay shrieks
above the pungent odor of crushed
eucalyptus and the pure scent
of rage.

1981

4. Poem for dead Californios (Spanish).
5. Crying of mothers.
6. Husbands of the earth, mother earth.
7. Shawls.
8. I remember dead ancestors. I remember them in the blood, the fertile blood.
9. I am the poor daughter, but I can curse these white ghosts. Your ghosts must remain here, only yours.
1. American.
2. And these not pertaining to the Californios.

Marilyn Chin
b. 1955

"I am a Chinese American poet," Marilyn Chin wrote to the American Poetry Society, "born in Hong Kong and raised in Portland, Oregon. My poetry both laments and celebrates my 'hyphenated' identity." In an interview published in 1995, Chin explained that, as "a Pacific Rim person," she does not "believe in static identities" but sees them as "forever changing." While she fears losing her Chinese heritage and language, she feels strongly that one "can't recapture the past." Chin defines and redefines herself in her poetry, her biting irony and unvarnished language suggesting the contingency of her acts of self-definition. Her hyphenated identity finds expression in the hybridization of East and West, whether in poetic forms, as when she combines Chinese quatrains with the confessional lyric, or in imagery and allusion, as when she refers to chop suey and bamboo shoots while citing William Carlos Williams and John Berryman.

Chin finds in her name itself a potent emblem of her hybrid identity. "I am Marilyn Mei Ling Chin," she declares with mock solemnity at the start of "How I Got That Name"; she goes on to explain that her father, "obsessed with a bombshell blonde / transliterated 'Mei Ling' to 'Marilyn.' " Her father later abandoned his Chinese family for a white woman, and the emotional scars of this desertion are evident in the anti-patriarchal anger of her poetry. In voicing such anger despite cultural and gender stereotypes of silent submission, and in seeking to create a poetic voice that at once is personal and has a broader political significance, Chin follows the example of such American women poets as Sylvia Plath, Adrienne Rich, and June Jordan.

Chin rejects both her father's assimilationist denial of his cultural background and the effort to reify and idealize Chinese culture. A poem such as "Altar" has the trappings of an immigrant writer's nostalgic reverie—an armchair, the morning sun, a moth—and yet is characteristically bracing and acerbic about ancestor worship. Nor does Chin spare herself her mocking tongue. Her tone is bold, wry, and irreverent. In "How I Got That Name," she remembers her father describing her as " 'not quite boiled, not quite cooked,' " and her poetic style is indeed somewhat raw and deliberately jarring. Its sharp edges contrast with the smoothly contoured and mellifluous poetry of her Asian American contemporaries Cathy Song and Li-Young Lee. Along with cultural boundaries, Chin crosses lines between elevated diction and chatty colloquialism, between the essay and the poem, between lyricism and parody.

Chin was born on January 14, 1955. She received her B.A. in 1977 from the University of Massachusetts at Amherst, her M.F.A. in 1981 from the University of Iowa. She teaches at San Diego State University.

How I Got That Name

An Essay on Assimilation

I am Marilyn Mei Ling Chin.
Oh, how I love the resoluteness
of that first person singular
followed by that stalwart indicative
of "be," without the uncertain i-n-g
of "becoming." Of course,
the name had been changed

somewhere between Angel Island and the sea,
when my father the paperson[1]
in the late 1950s
obsessed with a bombshell blonde[2]
transliterated "Mei Ling" to "Marilyn."
And nobody dared question
his initial impulse—for we all know
lust drove men to greatness,
not goodness, not decency.
And there I was, a wayward pink baby,
named after some tragic white woman
swollen with gin and Nembutal.
My mother couldn't pronounce the "r."
She dubbed me "Numba one female offshoot"
for brevity: henceforth, she will live and die
in sublime ignorance, flanked
by loving children and the "kitchen deity."
While my father dithers,
a tomcat in Hong Kong trash—
a gambler, a petty thug,
who bought a chain of chopsuey joints
in Piss River, Oregon,
with bootlegged Gucci cash.
Nobody dared question his integrity given
his nice, devout daughters
and his bright, industrious sons
as if filial piety were the standard
by which all earthly men were measured.

•

Oh, how trustworthy our daughters,
how thrifty our sons!
How we've managed to fool the experts
in education, statistics and demography—
We're not very creative but not averse to rote-learning.
Indeed, they can *use* us.
But the "Model Minority" is a tease.
We know you are watching now,
so we refuse to give you any!
Oh, bamboo shoots, bamboo shoots!
The further west we go, we'll hit east;
the deeper down we dig, we'll find China.
History has turned its stomach
on a black polluted beach—
where life doesn't hinge
on that red, red wheelbarrow,[3]

1. Many Chinese immigrants became *paper sons* or *daughters*, overcoming U.S. exclusionary laws and gaining admission into the country by purchasing paperwork claiming they had American parents. *Angel Island*: island off the coast of San Francisco that served as an immigration station and detention center during the first half of the twentieth century.

2. Marilyn Monroe (1926–1962), American actor, who died of an overdose of the barbiturate Nembutal (line 19).

3. Cf. William Carlos Williams's "The Red Wheelbarrow."

but whether or not our new lover
in the final episode of "Santa Barbara"[4]
will lean over a scented candle
and call us a "bitch."
Oh God, where have we gone wrong?
We have no inner resources![5]

•

Then, one redolent spring morning
the Great Patriarch Chin
peered down from his kiosk in heaven
and saw that his descendants were ugly.[6]
One had a squarish head and a nose without a bridge.
Another's profile—long and knobbed as a gourd.
A third, the sad, brutish one
may never, never marry.
And I, his least favorite—
"not quite boiled, not quite cooked,"
a plump pomfret[7] simmering in my juices—
too listless to fight for my people's destiny.
"To kill without resistance is not slaughter"
says the proverb. So, I wait for imminent death.
The fact that this death is also metaphorical
is testament to my lethargy.

•

So here lies Marilyn Mei Ling Chin,
married once, twice to so-and-so, a Lee and a Wong,
granddaughter of Jack "the patriarch"
and the brooding Suilin Fong,
daughter of the virtuous Yuet Kuen Wong
and G. G. Chin the infamous,
sister of a dozen, cousin of a million,
survived by everybody and forgotten by all.
She was neither black nor white,
neither cherished nor vanquished,
just another squatter in her own bamboo grove
minding her poetry—
when one day heaven was unmerciful,
and a chasm opened where she stood.
Like the jowls of a mighty white whale,
or the jaws of a metaphysical Godzilla,
it swallowed her whole.
She did not flinch nor writhe,
nor fret about the afterlife,
but stayed! Solid as wood, happily
a little gnawed, tattered, mesmerized

4. American soap opera.
5. Cf. John Berryman's Dream Song 14: "I conclude now I have no / inner resources."
6. Cf. Genesis 1.
7. Type of fish.

by all that was lavished upon her
and all that was taken away!

1994

Altar

I tell her she has outlived her usefulness.
I point to the corner where dust gathers,
where light has never touched. But there she sits,
a thousand years, hands folded, in a tattered armchair,
with yesterday's news, "the Golden Mountain Edition."
The morning sun slants down the broken eaves,
shading half of her sallow face.

On the upper northwest corner (I'd consulted a geomancer),[8]
a deathtrap shines on the dying bougainvillea.
The carcass of a goatmoth hangs upsidedown,
hollowed out. The only evidence
of her seasonal life is a dash
of shimmery powder, a last cry.

She, who was attracted to that bare bulb,
who danced around that immigrant dream,
will find her end here, this corner,
this solemn altar.

1994

Autumn Leaves

The dead piled up, thick, fragrant, on the fire escape.
My mother ordered me again, and again, to sweep it clean.
All that blooms must fall. I learned this not from the Tao,[9]
  but from high school biology.

Oh, the contradictions of having a broom and not a dustpan!
I swept the leaves down, down through the iron grille
and let the dead rain over the Wong family's patio.

And it was Achilles[1] Wong who completed the task.
  We called her:
The-one-who-cleared-away-another-family's-autumn.
She blossomed, tall, benevolent, notwithstanding.

1994

8. One who divines special information from geographical features.
9. The *Tao-te Ching*, the fundamental text of Taoism, teaches that one should abjure from all striving.
1. Greek hero of the Trojan War.

Chinese Quatrains (The Woman in Tomb 44)[2]

The aeroplane is shaped like a bird
Or a giant mechanical penis
My father escorts my mother
From girlhood to unhappiness

A dragonfly has iridescent wings
Shorn, it's a lowly pismire
Plucked of arms and legs
A throbbing red pepperpod[3]

Baby, she's a girl
Pinkly propped as a doll
Baby, she's a pearl
An ulcer in the oyster of God

Cry little baby clam cry
The steam has opened your eyes
Your secret darkly hidden
The razor is sharpening the knife

Abandoned taro-leaf[4] boat
Its lonely black sail broken
The corpses are fat and bejeweled
The hull is thoroughly rotten

The worm has entered the ear
And out the nose of my father
Cleaned the pelvis of my mother
And ringed around her fingerbone

One child beats a bedpan
One beats a fishhook out of wire
One beats his half sister on the head
Oh, teach us to fish and love

Don't say her boudoir[5] is too narrow
She could sleep but in one cold bed
Don't say you own many horses
We escaped on her skinny mare's back

Man is good said Meng-Tzu
We must cultivate their natures

2. "Adapted from *jue-ju*, literally 'cut verse,' four-line poems, usually seven characters per line" [Chin's note].
3. Cf. a story of the Japanese poet Bashō (1644–1694), a master of the haiku verse form. His student proposed as an idea for a poem, "Pull the wings off a dragonfly and look—you get a red pepperpod." Bashō replied that more appropriate to the spirit of haiku would be, "Add wings to a pepperpod and look—you get a red dragonfly." *Pismire*: ant.
4. A plant.
5. Bedroom.

Man is evil said Hsun-Tzu[6]
There's a worm in the human heart

He gleaned a beaded purse from Hong Kong
He procured an oval fan from Taiwan
She married him for a green card
He abandoned her for a blonde

My grandmother is calling her goslings
My mother is summoning her hens
The sun has vanished into the ocean
The moon has drowned in the fen

Discs of jade for her eyelids
A lozenge of pearl for her throat
Lapis and kudzu in her nostrils
They will rob her again and again

2002

6. Chinese Confucian philosopher (c. 300–c. 230 B.C.E.). *Meng-Tzu*: Chinese Confucian philosopher (c. 371–c. 289 B.C.E.), known in the West as Mencius.

Cathy Song
b. 1955

In 1982, the poet Richard Hugo, then judge of the Yale Series of Younger Poets, chose as the winning manuscript Cathy Song's *Picture Bride,* praising its "strength of quiet resolve." Song's paternal grandmother came from Korea, the poet tells us in that first collection's title poem; she went to Hawaii as a "picture bride" (a mail-order bride), like many other Korean and Japanese women. Trying to reconstruct what she can of her ancestral Asia from the perspective of contemporary Hawaii, Song often explores the gains and losses of her grandmother's move from the Old World to the New, without idealizing either world. However beautiful and gauzy the texture of her poetry, Song does not miss the harsh reality of the traps that family and society set for women. She writes, in "Beauty and Sadness," of the Japanese printmaker Kitagawa Utamaro's "floating world" of "teahouse waitresses, actresses, / geishas, courtesans and maids." In "Lost Sister," the sister has escaped Chinese norms of female immobility and foot-binding, but she discovers that the New World imposes its own constraints—"the possibilities, / the loneliness, / can strangulate like jungle vines."

In her later books, Song extends her exploration of the family heritage to include her own children. She continues to reconstruct memories of her childhood, which she reproduces with singular transparency. In "Sunworshippers," the mother teaches her daughter that Americans are grotesquely self-indulgent, their "bodies glazed and glistening like raw fish in the market," and this revulsion later contributes to the college-age daughter's anorexia. As this and other poems demonstrate, Song's carefully structured poetry works through vivid imagery and implication. Astutely exploring intercultural perception, the poem "Ghost" offers an extended play on the Chinese for white person—which can be translated as "white ghost." The speaker's mother sees whites as ghostly, as well as noisy, hairy, smelly, and round eyed, but the speaker also sees herself as a ghost to white schoolchildren for whom she, too, is alien. Precise and economical, Song's poetry is also distinguished by its delicate sensibility and artful framing. "What frames the view," she commented in a letter, "is the mind in the diamond pinpoint light of concentration tunneling into memory, released by the imagination. Out of that depth, squares of light form, like windows you pass at night, like photographs developing in the dark."

Cathy-Lynn Song was born on August 20, 1955, in Honolulu, Hawaii, to a Chinese American mother and a Korean American father. She attended the University of Hawaii at Manoa for two years, then went to Wellesley College for her B.A. (1977) and to Boston University for her M.F.A. (1981). Since 1987, she has taught in Hawaii's Teacher in the Schools program. She lives and writes in Honolulu.

Beauty and Sadness

for Kitagawa Utamaro[1]

He drew hundreds of women
in studies unfolding
like flowers from a fan.
Teahouse waitresses, actresses,
geishas,[2] courtesans and maids.
They arranged themselves
before this quick, nimble man
whose invisible presence
one feels in these prints
is as delicate
as the skinlike paper
he used to transfer
and retain their fleeting loveliness.

Crouching like cats,
they purred amid the layers of kimono[3]
swirling around them
as though they were bathing
in a mountain pool with irises
growing in the silken sunlit water.
Or poised like porcelain vases,
slender, erect and tall; their heavy
brocaded hair was piled high
with sandalwood combs and blossom sprigs
poking out like antennae.
They resembled beautiful iridescent insects,
creatures from a floating world.[4]

1. Japanese artist (1753–1806), who specialized in studies of sensuous and beautiful women.
2. Women trained to provide entertaining, lighthearted company for men.
3. Traditional Japanese robe with long sleeves.
4. The pictures "were called 'pictures of the floating world' because of their preoccupation with the pleasures of the moment" [Song's glossary].

Utamaro absorbed these women of Edo[5]
in their moments of melancholy
as well as of beauty.
He captured the wisp of shadows,
the half-draped body
emerging from a bath; whatever
skin was exposed
was powdered white as snow.
A private space disclosed.
Portraying another girl
catching a glimpse of her own vulnerable
face in the mirror, he transposed
the trembling plum lips
like a drop of blood
soaking up the white expanse of paper.

At times, indifferent to his inconsolable
eye, the women drifted
through the soft gray feathered light,
maintaining stillness, the moments in between.
Like the dusty ash-winged moths
that cling to the screens in summer
and that the Japanese venerate
as ancestors reincarnated;
Utamaro graced these women with immortality
in the thousand sheaves of prints
fluttering into the reverent hands of keepers:
the dwarfed and bespectacled painter
holding up to a square of sunlight
what he had carried home beneath his coat
one afternoon in winter.

1983

Lost Sister

1

In China,
even the peasants
named their first daughters
Jade—
the stone that in the far fields
could moisten the dry season,
could make men move mountains
for the healing green of the inner hills
glistening like slices of winter melon.

And the daughters were grateful:
They never left home.

5. "Present-day Tokyo" [Song's glossary].

To move freely was a luxury
stolen from them at birth.
Instead, they gathered patience,
learning to walk in shoes
the size of teacups,
without breaking—
the arc of their movements
as dormant as the rooted willow,
as redundant as the farmyard hens.
But they traveled far
in surviving,
learning to stretch the family rice,
to quiet the demons,
the noisy stomachs.

2

There is a sister
across the ocean,
who relinquished her name,
diluting jade green
with the blue of the Pacific.
Rising with a tide of locusts,
she swarmed with others
to inundate another shore.
In America,
there are many roads
and women can stride along with men.

But in another wilderness,
the possibilities,
the loneliness,
can strangulate like jungle vines.
The meager provisions and sentiments
of once belonging—
fermented roots, Mah-Jong[6] tiles and firecrackers—
set but a flimsy household
in a forest of nightless cities.
A giant snake rattles above,
spewing black clouds into your kitchen.
Dough-faced landlords
slip in and out of your keyholes,
making claims you don't understand,
tapping into your communication systems
of laundry lines and restaurant chains.

You find you need China:
your one fragile identification,
a jade link
handcuffed to your wrist.

6. Chinese game.

You remember your mother
who walked for centuries,
footless—
and like her,
you have left no footprints,
but only because
there is an ocean in between,
the unremitting space of your rebellion.

1983

Sunworshippers

"Look how they love themselves,"
my mother would lecture as we drove through
the ironwoods, the park on one side,
the beach on the other, where sunworshippers,
splayed upon towels, appeared sacrificial,
bodies glazed and glistening like raw fish in the market.
There was folly and irreverence to such exposure,
something only people with dirty feet did.
Who will marry you
if your skin is sunbaked and dried up like beef jerky?
We put on our hats and gloves
whenever we went for a drive.
When the sun broke through clouds,
my mother sprouted her umbrella.
The body is a temple we worship
secretly in the traveling revivalist tent of our clothes.
The body, hidden, banished to acceptable
rooms of the house, had only a mouth
for eating and a hole for eliminating
what the body rejected: the lower forms of life.
Caramel-colored stools, coiled heavily
like a sleeping python, were a sign
we were living right.
But to erect a statue of the body
and how the body, insolent and defiant
in a bikini, looked was self-indulgent, sun-
worshipping, fad diets and weight-lifting proof
you loved yourself too much.
We were not allowed to love ourselves too much.
So I ate less, and less, and less,
nibbling my way out of meals—
the less I ate, the less
there was of me to love.
I liked it best when standing before the mirror,
I seemed to be disappearing into myself,
breasts sunken into the cavity of my bird-cage chest,
air my true element which fed
in those days of college, snow and brick bound,

the coal fire in my eyes.
No one knew how I truly felt about myself.
Fueled by my own impending disappearance,
I neither slept nor ate, but devoured radiance,
essential as chlorophyll,
the apple's heated core.
Undetected, I slipped in and out of books,
passages of music, brightly painted rooms
where, woven into the signature of voluptuous vines,
was the one who flew one day out the window,
leaving behind an arrangement of cakes and ornamental flowers;
to weave one's self, one's breath, ropes of it, whole
and fully formed, was a way of shining
out of this world.

1994

Ghost

1

Yellow ghost,
I flutter like a moth
invisible to these
children of soldiers,
dusting camphor wings,
pollen from the ancient pages

of poems, texts
that have no meaning
to the alley maps
of fast food and hard

cash, trash on the heels
of their need to go fast—

so very fast,
I am a blur to them,

without scent, a ghost
they rush right through

the light
I am so confident
I shed.

Who called the ghost white?

Yellow face of the oppressor—
one of a long line of Asian
schoolteachers who have stood before them,

yardstick in hand to measure
how far
they fail to measure up.

I say I am different.
I offer them
a jeweled seeded fruit,
a poem I pare and peel
that has no flesh.
It tastes like nothing
they want to eat.

2

Bok gwai,
my mother called
the round eye,
persons of a certain
body odor—
a pungent offense
to the delicate flower of her nostrils.

Bok gwai filled flesh
more than any ghost
I could conjure,
noisy and hairy,
they moved visibly
with authority
in the world they were
so sure
belonged to them.

Bok gwai, white ghost,
she chose to call them.
By choosing, she chose
not to see
them
as she so surely saw
she was not seen.

Eyes sunken into
the bone hood of their skulls,
how could they possibly see?

But I saw,
and I liked
what I saw,
the round-eyed men
with golden fur on their arms.
They moved like soldiers
who on leave toss a confetti
of coins and candy

and cigarettes
to the waving sea of the weak,
the conquered, the invisible.

When I caught and brought
a round eye home,
my mother recoiled
at the sharp
scent of his skin.
It was the odor
of a meat eater,
unwashed flesh
she shrank from.
He had an earnest appetite
and good horse teeth.
His bite was strong.
He got under her yellow skin.
She invited him back again.
She said she liked the way
he chewed his bone.

2001

Carol Ann Duffy
b. 1955

Widely acclaimed for her deft dramatic monologues, Carol Ann Duffy gained international notoriety as a leading contender for the post of British poet laureate after the death of Ted Hughes. She was seen as the anti-establishment candidate. The lesbian partner of "black British" poet Jackie Kay, she was born on December 23, 1955, in Glasgow, Scotland, to an Irish mother in a left-wing, working-class, Catholic family, and she graduated from a non-Oxbridge institution (the University of Liverpool). After a period of intense public speculation, she was not chosen.

Like other contemporary masters of the dramatic monologue (e.g., Frank Bidart, Ai, Richard Howard, Louise Bennett, Okot p'Bitek), Duffy is an expert ventriloquist. Because she moved to Stafford, England, as a child, her skill may owe something to having grown up amid Scottish, English, and Irish accents. In "Medusa," "Mrs Lazarus," and other poems, she assumes the voice of a mythological, historical, or fictive female character. She invites us, as did Robert Browning, to enter into the mind of a character distant from ourselves historically, culturally, or morally, exploiting the tension between our identification and our alienation. Dramatic monologue is especially suited to Duffy's feminist revisions of myth and history: it enables her to dramatize a silenced or marginalized female perspective, wittily playing on the ironic contrast between the traditional version of the story and her own.

Lazarus's resurrection, for example, looks different from the perspective of his imaginary wife. After successive stages of mourning (she "howled, shrieked, clawed"), when her dead husband has become mere "legend, language," no more than "memory," Mrs. Lazarus falls in love with a schoolteacher. For her, Lazarus's resurrection is not only miraculous but shattering and repulsive: "I breathed / his stench," she says. Brilliantly reimagined, the story is propelled to its climax by Duffy's gift for narrative. Likewise, Medusa's frightening ability to petrify becomes—in Duffy's vivid, compact account—a delightful game of transformation, like the quick turns afforded by Duffy's own poetic metaphors: "I looked at a snuffling pig, / a boulder rolled / in a heap of shit."

The author of love poetry and political satire as well as dramatic monologues, Duffy has a sharp eye for detail. She encapsulates the intensity of erotic desire in the contrast and interchange between pearls and skin, heat and coolness in "Warming Her Pearls." Another poem about longing adopts a child's perspective on her "good teachers": they "swish down the corridor in long, brown skirts." Working in well-constructed stanzas, carefully pacing her rhythms, playing on half-rhymes, effectively conjuring the senses of touch, smell, and sight, Duffy mobilizes the resources of traditional lyric, turning them to contemporary ends. Economical and witty, sensual and exuberant, Duffy's best work displays the ongoing potential of broadly accessible poetry.

Warming Her Pearls

for Judith Radstone[1]

Next to my own skin, her pearls. My mistress
bids me wear them, warm then, until evening
when I'll brush her hair. At six, I place them
round her cool, white throat. All day I think of her,

resting in the Yellow Room, contemplating silk
or taffeta, which gown tonight? She fans herself
whilst I work willingly, my slow heat entering
each pearl. Slack on my neck, her rope.

She's beautiful. I dream about her
in my attic bed; picture her dancing
with tall men, puzzled by my faint, persistent scent
beneath her French perfume, her milky stones.

I dust her shoulders with a rabbit's foot,
watch the soft blush seep through her skin
like an indolent sigh. In her looking-glass
my red lips part as though I want to speak.

Full moon. Her carriage brings her home. I see
her every movement in my head . . . Undressing,
taking off her jewels, her slim hand reaching
for the case, slipping naked into bed, the way

1. British political activist and bookseller (1925–2001). According to Radstone's obituary in *The Guardian*, the poem was inspired by a conversation with Radstone about the practice of ladies' maids increasing the luster of their mistresses' pearls by wearing them beneath their clothes.

she always does . . . And I lie here awake,
knowing the pearls are cooling even now
in the room where my mistress sleeps. All night
I feel their absence and I burn.

1987

The Good Teachers

You run round the back to be in it again.
No bigger than your thumbs, those virtuous women
size you up from the front row. Soon now,
Miss Ross will take you for double History.
You breathe on the glass, making a ghost of her, say
South Sea Bubble Defenestration of Prague.[2]

You love Miss Pirie. So much, you are top
of her class. So much, you need two of you
to stare out from the year, serious, passionate.
The River's Tale by Rudyard Kipling[3] by heart.
Her kind intelligent green eye. Her cruel blue one.
You are making a poem up for her in your head.

But not Miss Sheridan. Comment vous appelez.[4]
But not Miss Appleby. Equal to the square
of the other two sides. Never Miss Webb.
Dar es Salaam. Kilimanjaro.[5] Look. The good teachers
swish down the corridor in long, brown skirts,
snobbish and proud and clean and qualified.

And they've got your number. You roll the waistband
of your skirt over and over, all leg, all
dumb insolence, smoke-rings. You won't pass.
You could do better. But there's the wall you climb
into dancing, lovebites, marriage, the Cheltenham
and Gloucester,[6] today. The day you'll be sorry one day.

1993

2. *Defenestration of Prague:* incident in 1618 in which two imperial agents were thrown from the window of Prague Castle by a group of dissenting Bohemian Protestants. *South Sea Bubble:* first major stock market crash in England, in 1720.
3. British author (1865–1936) famous for his treatment of colonialism.
4. What is your name (French).
5. Tanzanian mountain. *Dar es Salaam:* capital of Tanzania.
6. British mortgage and investment bank, named after two cities (and districts) in Gloucestershire, England.

Medusa[7]

A suspicion, a doubt, a jealousy
grew in my mind,
which turned the hairs on my head to filthy snakes,
as though my thoughts
hissed and spat on my scalp.

My bride's breath soured, stank
in the grey bags of my lungs.
I'm foul mouthed now, foul tongued,
yellow fanged.
There are bullet tears in my eyes.
Are you terrified?[8]

Be terrified.
It's you I love,
perfect man, Greek God, my own;
but I know you'll go, betray me, stray
from home.
So better by far for me if you were stone.

I glanced at a buzzing bee,
a dull grey pebble fell
to the ground.
I glanced at a singing bird,
a handful of dusty gravel
spattered down.

I looked at a ginger cat,
a housebrick
shattered a bowl of milk.
I looked at a snuffling pig,
a boulder rolled
in a heap of shit.

I stared in the mirror.
Love gone bad
showed me a Gorgon.
I stared at a dragon.
Fire spewed
from the mouth of a mountain.

And here you come
with a shield for a heart
and a sword for a tongue
and your girls, your girls.

7. In Greek mythology, the mortal, snake-haired gorgon with the power to turn anyone who gazed upon her into stone. Looking at her reflection in a shield given him by Athena, Perseus cut off Medusa's head as she slept.

8. Cf. Sylvia Plath's "Lady Lazarus": "Do I terrify?—."

Wasn't I beautiful?
Wasn't I fragrant and young?

Look at me now.

1999

Mrs Lazarus[9]

I had grieved. I had wept for a night and a day
over my loss, ripped the cloth I was married in
from my breasts, howled, shrieked, clawed
at the burial stones till my hands bled, retched
his name over and over again, dead, dead.

Gone home. Gutted the place. Slept in a single cot,
widow, one empty glove, white femur
in the dust, half. Stuffed dark suits
into black bags, shuffled in a dead man's shoes,
noosed the double knot of a tie round my bare neck,

gaunt nun in the mirror, touching herself. I learnt
the Stations of Bereavement,[1] the icon of my face
in each bleak frame; but all those months
he was going away from me, dwindling
to the shrunk size of a snapshot, going,

going. Till his name was no longer a certain spell
for his face. The last hair on his head
floated out from a book. His scent went from the house.
The will was read. See, he was vanishing
to the small zero held by the gold of my ring.

Then he was gone. Then he was legend, language;
my arm on the arm of the schoolteacher—the shock
of a man's strength under the sleeve of his coat—
along the hedgerows. But I was faithful
for as long as it took. Until he was memory.

So I could stand that evening in the field
in a shawl of fine air, healed, able
to watch the edge of the moon occur to the sky
and a hare thump from a hedge; then notice
the village men running towards me, shouting,

behind them the women and children, barking dogs,
and I knew. I knew by the sly light

9. Lazarus was the man raised from the dead by Jesus (John 11).
1. Allusion to the Stations of the Cross, a series of fourteen icons (pictures or carvings) corresponding to the stages of Jesus' crucifixion and over each of which a prayer is said.

on the blacksmith's face, the shrill eyes
of the barmaid, the sudden hands bearing me
into the hot tang of the crowd parting before me.

He lived. I saw the horror on his face.
I heard his mother's crazy song. I breathed
his stench; my bridegroom in his rotting shroud,
moist and dishevelled from the grave's slack chew,
croaking his cuckold name, disinherited, out of his time.

1999

Dionisio D. Martínez
b. 1956

Dionisio D. Martínez grew up speaking Spanish, but his poetry has wrung new possibilities from English. Born on April 7, 1956, in Cuba, he was three at the start of Fidel Castro's revolution and remembers the confiscation of his family's home and personal property—even his toys. He and his family went into exile in 1965, first living in northern Spain; but he grew up in Glendale, California. In 1972, his sophomore year in high school, his family moved to Tampa, Florida, which has since been his home. In high school, he was inspired by reading T. S. Eliot, Archibald MacLeish, and the Spanish poet Federico García Lorca.

Martínez's poetry is offbeat and radially allusive, assimilating diverse ingredients from the cultures of the Americas and of Europe, painting and music, the highbrow and the lowbrow—composer Niccolò Paganini and painter Jackson Pollock but also the White Sox and advertising. A poem such as "Hysteria," like the map and the newspaper it invokes, folds over and over. The half-humorous, half-panicked recycling of images from various sources—TV and the paper, history and poetry—releases new and unexpected connective energies among them. "The Prodigal Son in His Own Words: Bees" also manically recirculates images, alternating between a decaying house and bee hives, as if to give this prose poem the vertiginous circularity of such fixed forms as the sestina and the villanelle.

Martínez is a poet of gaps, losses, and interstices. While we find no paeans to Cuban American identity in his poetry, we can perhaps infer an indirect expression of his divided cultural experience in his preoccupation with displacement and disorientation, with orphans, exiles, and abandoned houses. "I want to learn / to think in American," says the speaker of "Hysteria," but a skewed relation to the dominant culture helps Martínez see that culture afresh, as if always through the lens of metaphor. "No matter where I go," he writes in "Temporary Losses," "I carry foreign currency." In "Moto Perpetuo," the poet's comments about Pollock's art also describe his own poetics: "how important / the gaps and absences were to him; // how crucial the distances, the gulfs." Martínez's poetry of juxtaposition owes something to surrealist technique and moves with the velocity of cinematic montage. It also recalls the seemingly logical illogic and elusiveness of John Ashbery's poetry. In tone, it is, like the work of the New York school, both zany and insistent, colloquial and authoritative. Its cultural and psychological kaleidoscope of images, puzzling and humorous, has the strange forcefulness of dream.

Hysteria

It only takes one night with the wind on its knees
to imagine Carl Sandburg unfolding
a map of Chicago,[1] puzzled, then walking the wrong way.

The lines on his face are hard to read. I alternate
between the tv, where a plastic surgeon is claiming
that every facial expression causes wrinkles, and

the newspaper. I picture the surgeon reading the lines
on Sandburg's face, lines that would've made more sense
if the poet had been, say, a tree growing

in a wind orchard. Maybe he simply smiled too much.
I'm reading about the All-Star game, thinking
that maybe Sandburg saw the White Sox of 1919.[2]

• • •

I love American newspapers, the way each section
is folded independently and believes it owns
the world. There's this brief item in the inter-

national pages: the Chinese government has posted
signs in Tiananmen Square,[3] forbidding laughter.
I'm sure the plastic surgeon would approve, he'd say

the Chinese will look young much longer, their faces
unnaturally smooth, but what I see (although
no photograph accompanies the story) is laughter

bursting inside them. I go back to the sports section
and a closeup of a rookie in mid-swing, his face
keeping all the wrong emotions in check.

• • •

When I read I bite my lower lip, a habit
the plastic surgeon would probably call
cosmetic heresy because it accelerates the aging

process. I think of Carl Sandburg and the White Sox;
I think of wind in Tiananmen Square, how a country
deprived of laughter ages invisibly; I think

1. American poet Carl Sandburg (1878–1967) published *Chicago Poems* in 1916.
2. The 1919 World Series resulted in a front-page news story when eight players from the Chicago White Sox were accused of a crime: throwing the series against the Cincinnati Reds. The players were legally acquitted but permanently banned from professional baseball.
3. Public square in the center of Beijing where pro-reform demonstrators were massacred by the government in 1989.

of the Great Walls of North America, each of them
a grip on some outfield like a rookie's hands
around a bat when the wind is against him; I bite

my lower lip again; I want to learn
to think in American, to believe that a headline
is a fact and all stories are suspect.

For Ana Menéndez

1995

Temporary Losses

Now that I know where circus children
go when they run away, I have no desire to move.
I load the moving van and tell the driver
to go until he runs out of road or out of gas or
out of towns that refuse his worthless cargo.

To define what remains, we speak the language of
the invisible man who argues with the doctors long
after the amputation, tells them
that he still walks with a phantom limb. Literally.

I begin to count the change in my pocket
and think of Thoreau[4] living on 27 cents a week,
walking too much, becoming accustomed
to the calluses from the ax, the strained
muscles and all that winter rising from the pond.

When I lay the change on the floor I find
a penny rubbed since 1944 by fingers not unlike
my own. I rub it too. For luck,
I think. All my superstitions are hand-me-downs.
What do I know about luck? What do I care if
the face of Lincoln rubs off on my fingers?

The oldest train route on the island began
a block from home. We laid coins
on the tracks and moved out of the way quickly,
remembering the kid who'd been half blinded.
I still wonder if a man with a glass eye
sees half of everything—half of the road, half
of the woman who will not tell him all the truth,
always a half moon regardless of the tides.

You want me to believe in everything, but there's
something to be said for knowing that a house

4. Henry David Thoreau (1817–1862), American author famous for the experiment in simple, self-sufficient living recorded in *Walden* (1854).

is not the world, that we can live without
the wicker furniture that made our house as tangible
as a father's arms. After all, sooner
or later they'll stop calling us orphans.

I hold my life savings in this hand.
No matter where I go, I carry foreign currency.

For María Menéndez

1995

Moto Perpetuo[5]

1

I've been walking in circles for what seems like days.
They've been playing Paganini, but you know

how intermittent the conscious ear
can be. How selective. Walking has nothing to do

with distance as clearly as Paganini
has nothing to do with the violin that plays him hard.

2

How it hurt Jackson Pollock,[6] during his black
and white period, to hear the critics say

that he was painting black *on* white; how important
the gaps and absences were to him;

how crucial the distances, the gulfs; how
critical each emptiness to each composition.

3

There is that moment in, say, the finale of Beethoven's
Fifth,[7] when you hear nothing between the various

false endings, so you make your own music,
a bridge of silence from one illusion

to the next. A deeper and more refined
ear—Beethoven's ear—takes care of this.

1995

5. Perpetual motion (Italian); title of a composition by Italian composer Niccolò Paganini (1782–1840).
6. American abstract expressionist painter (1912–1956), famous for his action paintings made by dripping paint onto canvas.
7. *Symphony No. 5 in C minor* by Ludwig van Beethoven (1770–1827), German composer who continued to write music even after going deaf in his later years.

The Prodigal Son in His Own Words: Bees

There is a mathematical illusion that, if performed correctly, makes two halves mirror one another. We've seen enough disparities within the whole to know better. Some female bees mate only once. Carrying enough sperm for a lifetime, they continue to reproduce without further need for the male. Don't let the well-stocked shelves of the hardware store fool you: the part you need is never available. This is why the house deteriorates: hairline cracks appear, compromising the integrity of the structure, and your solution is another coat of paint. Door frames buckle and the doors never shut comfortably again. In one species of the mining bee, some females are never inseminated because their work is more valuable than any possible offspring. Pipes burst, filling the basement with water, and you can't find the right joint. I visit an excavation of my paternal ancestors' dwellings, built maybe three thousand years ago. Seen from higher ground, the community is an enormous honeycomb, the walls for the most part still standing solidly against the elements. My father's own house, by contrast, is barely habitable after only two centuries. Where I sleep, I do so with the uneasy feeling that I'll wake in a field, the house gone and the millennium gone with the house. Mason bees secrete their own cement. Though it may be rebuilt ad nauseam, the first house falls only once.

2001

Henri Cole
b. 1956

Beset with contradictions between his homosexuality and his Catholicism, his mind at war with itself, Henri Cole writes poems that are taut with an inner violence. Sinewy, tense, conflicted, they yoke together love of God with desire for the bodies of men. Through their controlled linguistic surfaces and muscular compression, they contain the immense pressure of these and other irreconcilable longings. To hold in suspension his profoundly antithetical feelings, Cole has often turned to the sonnet, ratcheting up the emotional intensity of this inherited form.

Having visited the Vatican, the poet opens the sonnet "White Spine" with a harsh question: "Liar, I thought, kneeling with the others, / how can He love me and hate what I am?" Cole's anger and self-reviling find no relief in the course of the poem. In another sonnet, "Childlessness," he confronts the clash between two desires: to fuse with his dead mother and to hold at bay her overbearing presence. Severe and unsparingly honest, Cole's poetry renews the tradition of Elizabeth Bishop, Robert Lowell, and James Merrill, affording psychic self-examination without self-pity, self-disclosure without bathos. The power of his verse arises from its inner affective tension, its blunt and authoritative tone, and its luminous figurative language.

Metaphor can be a language of miniaturized tension, holding together the like and the unlike, and Cole's gift for figuration is unmistakable. In "White Spine," Cole writes, "The dome of St. Peter's shone yellowish / gold, like butter and eggs." In "Folly," swans tearing up weeds in a decadent Roman garden are seen as "dripping like a chandelier." In the double sonnet "Buddha and the Seven Tiger Cubs," a male erotic dancer slings his leg over the bar rail for tips, and the speaker, unabashed about his sexual longing, remarks: "He's a black swan straining its elastic / neck to eat bread crumbs and nourish itself."

Cole's early poetry is overtly formal, relying on patterned meter, rhyme, and off-rhyme. But he opens his 1998 collection *The Visible Man* by recanting "description & rhyme, / which had nursed and embalmed me at once" ("Arte Povera"). When in *Life Studies* (1959) Lowell broke with formal prosody, its ghost remained an animating presence within his free verse. Cole likewise transfers the formal impulse from end rhyme to a forceful syntax, focused tone, and potent verbs. In "Folly," the nutrea "eradicating" a garden are said to "root" along ditches, "to hunt . . . and gut" cygnet eggs.

Born to a military family on May 9, 1956, in Fukuoka, Japan, Cole has written sadly about his imposing mother, his largely absent father, and his shabby circumstances as a child. Violence, he has said, regularly erupted in the household. But he eventually found solace in poetry, especially that of Hart Crane, who, he states, "gave the young homosexual I was a model, an inflected language, an ecstatic voice, to begin to write about the social and domestic life I wanted to reveal secretly in art" ("First Loves"). Cole was educated at the College of William and Mary (B.A., 1978), the University of Wisconsin at Milwaukee (M.A., 1980), and Columbia University (M.F.A., 1982). He has taught at various universities and colleges, including Columbia, Reed, Yale, Maryland, Harvard, Brandeis, and Smith.

Harvard Classics[1]

It is the hour of lamps.
On our knees my mother
and I, still young, color
with crayons threadbare nap

on the livingroom rug.
Though there is no money,
no one seems to care. We
are self-possessed as bugs

waving their antennae
through cracks in the kitchen's
linoleum floor. When
Father begins to read

from the red gilt volume
in his lap, a circle
of light encapsulates
us like hearts in a womb.

Except their marriage is
already dead. I know

1. A series of fifty works of world literature chosen in 1908 by Harvard University president Charles Eliot (1834–1926) to represent a compact liberal arts education.

this though I'm only six.
So we visit Pharoahs,

a boatman on the Nile,
Crusaders[2] eating grapes
on a beach. Life escapes
with all its sadness while

two tragic Greek poets
inhabit Father's voice.
Who'd know I'm just a boy
when he begins a stoic

moral tale concerning
a dull provincial doctor's
young French wife.[3] If Mother,
in French, begins to sing

to herself, I know she's
had enough. Crayon stubs
litter the crumbling rug.
Our prostrate cat sneezes

at the dust in her fur.
And cries from a swallow
remind us one swallow
doesn't make a summer.

1995

Buddha and the Seven Tiger Cubs[4]

Holding a varnished paper parasol,
the gardener—a shy man-off-the-street—
ripple-rakes the white sand, despite rainfall,
into a pattern effortlessly neat,
meant to suggest, only abstractly, the sea,
as eight weathered stones are meant to depict
Buddha and the hungry cubs he knows he
must sacrifice himself to feed. I sit
in a little red gazebo and think—
as the Zen monks[5] do—about what love means,

2. Christian participants in medieval military expeditions against Muslim powers.
3. *Madame Bovary* (1857), by French novelist Gustave Flaubert (1821–1880), tells of the adultery committed by the wife of a country doctor.
4. According to legend, upon finding seven starving tiger cubs abandoned by their mother, the Buddha decided to offer himself as food so the animals might survive.
5. Practitioners of the Zen branch of Buddhism, which emphasizes the importance of meditation and breaking out of ordinary modes of thinking to achieve enlightenment. The speaker of the poem is located in the Japanese Gardens in Portland, Oregon. Stark Street is another Portland locale.

unashamed to have known it as something
tawdry and elusive from watching lean
erotic dancers in one of the dives
on Stark Street, where I go some lovesick nights.

Even in costume they look underage,
despite hard physiques and frozen glances
perfected for the ugly, floodlit stage,
where they are stranded like fish. What enhances
their act is that we're an obedient crowd,
rheumy with liquor; our stinginess
is broken. When one slings his leg proudly
across the bar rail where I sit, I kiss
a five dollar bill and tuck it in his belt.
He's a black swan straining its elastic
neck to eat bread crumbs and nourish itself.
My heart is not alert; I am transfixed,
loving him as tiger cubs love their
mother who abandons them forever.

1995

White Spine

Liar, I thought, kneeling with the others,
how can He love me and hate what I am?
The dome of St. Peter's[6] shone yellowish
gold, like butter and eggs. *My God,* I prayed
anyhow, as if made in the image
and likeness of Him. Nearby, a handsome
priest looked at me like a stone; I looked back,
not desiring to go it alone.
The college of cardinals[7] wore punitive red.
The white spine waved to me from his white throne.[8]
Being in a place not my own, much less
myself, I climbed out, a beast in a crib.
Somewhere a terrorist rolled a cigarette.
Reason, not faith, would change him.

1998

6. St. Peter's Basilica at the Vatican, in Rome.
7. The members of the Sacred College of Cardinals act as the pope's main counselors and wear distinctive red dress.
8. The silk-covered armchair (*sedia gestatoria*) on which the pope ("white spine") sits during solemn ceremonies.

Folly

In the Doria Pamphili garden,[9]
most of the granite niches are empty,
the male gods have lost their genitals,
and the Great Mother, Hera,[1] has no head.

Something has gone awry
in the artificial lake.
Burrowing deep into the black banks
enclosed by wire mesh,
families of nutria[2] are eradicating—
with webbed hind feet,
blunt muzzled heads
and long orange incisors—
Pope Innocent X's pleasure garden's
eco-system.

Gothic as the unconscious,
the heavy tapered bodies
root along the irrigation ditches,
making their way in a criminal trot
toward the swans, whose handsome,
ecclesiastical wings open out
obliviously.

Each day I come back.
The sky is Della Robbia blue.[3]
As I rise to my feet,
a swan—immaculate
and self-possessed as the ambulance
bearing my half-dead Mother—
grasps into the depths
and tears a weed up,
dripping like a chandelier,
while paddling behind are the derelict rodents,
hankering—with big sleepy eyes,
suggesting something like matrimonial bliss,
and plush gray fur,
undulating like the coat my mother wore—
to hunt the grass-shrouded
cygnet eggs and gut
their bloody embryos.

1998

9. Roman garden commissioned in the mid-seventeenth century by Pope Innocent X and now part of Rome's largest public park.
1. In Greek mythology, wife of Zeus and queen of the gods.
2. Aquatic rodent native to South America and considered a pest in parts of North America and Europe.
3. Color associated with the glaze Florentine sculptor Luca Della Robbia (c. 1400–1482) invented and applied to his terra cotta sculptures.

Childlessness

For many years I wanted a child
though I knew it would only illuminate life
for a time, like a star on a tree; I believed
that happiness would at last assert itself,
like a bird in a dirty cage, calling me,
ambassador of flesh, out of the rough
locked ward of sex.

Outstretched on my spool-bed,[4]
I am like a groom, alternately seeking fusion
with another and resisting engulfment by it.
A son's love for his mother is like a river
dividing the continent to reach the sea:
I believed that once. When you died, Mother,
I was alone at last. And then you came back,
dismal and greedy like the sea, to reclaim me.

1998

4. Style of bed with ribbed bedposts.

LI-YOUNG LEE
b. 1957

Born on August 19, 1957, to Chinese parents in Jakarta, Indonesia, Li-Young Lee is one of the preeminent poets of the East Asian diaspora in the United States. His father had been a personal physician to Communist leader Mao Tse-tung in China, before moving with his family to Indonesia, Hong Kong, Macao, and Japan, finally settling, in 1964, in a small town in western Pennsylvania, where he became a Presbyterian minister. Li-Young Lee said in an interview published in 1995 that his family's migrant experience, though "an outward manifestation of a homelessness that people in general feel," is responsible for his intense "feeling of disconnection and dislocation." As a child, Lee learned from his father Chinese poetry of the Tang Dynasty, as well as psalms and proverbs in the King James Bible. Having grown up between Mandarin Chinese and English, Lee explores through his poetry the tensions and ambiguities of his biculturalism: "You live / a while in two worlds / at once" ("My Indigo").

The painful experience of being in between languages as an immigrant child is the subject of one of Lee's best-known poems. "Persimmons" tells the story of a young Chinese immigrant slapped by a schoolteacher for being unable to differentiate the sounds of "persimmon" and "precision." Imperfectly grounded in English as a child, the adult speaker, likewise unable to remember some Chinese words, is completely at home in neither language. Lee's early sense of linguistic estrangement can be seen, paradoxically, in his powerful attachment to the sounds and textures of English words. His poetic language is richly sensuous. Lee savors the phonemic resources of English, almost eroticizing words and their relationships. In an exemplary line, Lee revels in assonance and alliteration: a hornet in a rotten pear "spun crazily, glazed in slow, glistening juice" ("Eating Alone"). Studding his poems with pellucid visual images (a splinter is "a silver tear, a tiny flame" in "The Gift"), Lee evokes the smell, the feel, and the taste of an often ethnically specific experience (the steamed trout with ginger in "Eating Together").

Although Lee's work bears the imprint of his Chinese background, it should not be exoticized. It descends from the American confessional poetry of Theodore Roethke and Sylvia Plath, and from the Deep Image poetry of James Wright and Philip Levine. It is written in free—if strongly cadenced—verse, sometimes cleverly enjambed ("How to choose/ /persimmons. This is precision"). Emotionally charged, rooted in childhood experience, the poems narrate simple stories. Lee's father plays the dominant role as figure of ambivalence, associated in "The Gift" and other poems with tenderness and love, and yet with discipline and pain. Squarely in the Romantic tradition, many of the poems drink at the well of early memory, relying on images and dreams to recover feelings from the past. John Keats, Walt Whitman, and Rainer Maria Rilke are among Lee's formative influences.

Lee was educated at the Universities of Pittsburgh (B.A., 1979) and Arizona (1979–80) and the State University of New York College at Brockport (1980–81). He has taught at various universities, including Northwestern University and the University of Iowa. He lives with his family in Chicago.

The Gift

To pull the metal splinter from my palm
my father recited a story in a low voice.
I watched his lovely face and not the blade.
Before the story ended, he'd removed
the iron sliver I thought I'd die from.

I can't remember the tale,
but hear his voice still, a well
of dark water, a prayer.
And I recall his hands,
two measures of tenderness
he laid against my face,
the flames of discipline
he raised above my head.

Had you entered that afternoon
you would have thought you saw a man
planting something in a boy's palm,
a silver tear, a tiny flame.
Had you followed that boy
you would have arrived here,
where I bend over my wife's right hand.

Look how I shave her thumbnail down
so carefully she feels no pain.
Watch as I lift the splinter out.
I was seven when my father
took my hand like this,

and I did not hold that shard
between my fingers and think,
Metal that will bury me,
christen it Little Assassin,
Ore Going Deep for My Heart.
And I did not lift up my wound and cry,
Death visited here!
I did what a child does
when he's given something to keep.
I kissed my father.

1986

Persimmons

In sixth grade Mrs. Walker
slapped the back of my head
and made me stand in the corner
for not knowing the difference
between *persimmon* and *precision*.
How to choose

persimmons. This is precision.
Ripe ones are soft and brown-spotted.
Sniff the bottoms. The sweet one
will be fragrant. How to eat:
put the knife away, lay down newspaper.
Peel the skin tenderly, not to tear the meat.
Chew the skin, suck it,
and swallow. Now, eat
the meat of the fruit,
so sweet,
all of it, to the heart.

Donna undresses, her stomach is white.
In the yard, dewy and shivering
with crickets, we lie naked,
face-up, face-down.
I teach her Chinese.
Crickets: *chiu chiu*. Dew: I've forgotten.
Naked: I've forgotten.
Ni, wo: you and me.
I part her legs,
remember to tell her
she is beautiful as the moon.

Other words
that got me into trouble were
fight and *fright*, *wren* and *yarn*.
Fight was what I did when I was frightened,
fright was what I felt when I was fighting.

Wrens are small, plain birds,
yarn is what one knits with.
Wrens are soft as yarn.
My mother made birds out of yarn.
I loved to watch her tie the stuff;
a bird, a rabbit, a wee man.

Mrs. Walker brought a persimmon to class
and cut it up
so everyone could taste
a *Chinese apple*. Knowing
it wasn't ripe or sweet, I didn't eat
but watched the other faces.

My mother said every persimmon has a sun
inside, something golden, glowing,
warm as my face.

Once, in the cellar, I found two wrapped in newspaper,
forgotten and not yet ripe.
I took them and set both on my bedroom windowsill,
where each morning a cardinal
sang, *The sun, the sun.*

Finally understanding
he was going blind,
my father sat up all one night
waiting for a song, a ghost.
I gave him the persimmons,
swelled, heavy as sadness,
and sweet as love.

This year, in the muddy lighting
of my parents' cellar, I rummage, looking
for something I lost.
My father sits on the tired, wooden stairs,
black cane between his knees,
hand over hand, gripping the handle.

He's so happy that I've come home.
I ask how his eyes are, a stupid question.
All gone, he answers.

Under some blankets, I find a box.
Inside the box I find three scrolls.
I sit beside him and untie
three paintings by my father:
Hibiscus leaf and a white flower.
Two cats preening.
Two persimmons, so full they want to drop from the cloth.

He raises both hands to touch the cloth,
asks, *Which is this?*

This is persimmons, Father.

Oh, the feel of the wolftail on the silk,[1]
the strength, the tense
precision in the wrist.
I painted them hundreds of times
eyes closed. These I painted blind.
Some things never leave a person:
scent of the hair of one you love,
the texture of persimmons,
in your palm, the ripe weight.

1986

Eating Alone

I've pulled the last of the year's young onions.
The garden is bare now. The ground is cold,
brown and old. What is left of the day flames
in the maples at the corner of my
eye. I turn, a cardinal vanishes.
By the cellar door, I wash the onions,
then drink from the icy metal spigot.

Once, years back, I walked beside my father
among the windfall pears. I can't recall
our words. We may have strolled in silence. But
I still see him bend that way—left hand braced
on knee, creaky—to lift and hold to my
eye a rotten pear. In it, a hornet
spun crazily, glazed in slow, glistening juice.

It was my father I saw this morning
waving to me from the trees. I almost
called to him, until I came close enough
to see the shovel, leaning where I had
left it, in the flickering, deep green shade.

White rice steaming, almost done. Sweet green peas
fried in onions. Shrimp braised in sesame
oil and garlic. And my own loneliness.
What more could I, a young man, want.

1986

1. Materials used in Chinese calligraphy.

Eating Together

In the steamer is the trout
seasoned with slivers of ginger,
two sprigs of green onion, and sesame oil.
We shall eat it with rice for lunch,
brothers, sister, my mother who will
taste the sweetest meat of the head,
holding it between her fingers
deftly, the way my father did
weeks ago. Then he lay down
to sleep like a snow-covered road
winding through pines older than him,
without any travelers, and lonely for no one.

1986

Pillow

There's nothing I can't find under there.
Voices in the trees, the missing pages
of the sea.

Everything but sleep.

And night is a river bridging
the speaking and the listening banks,

a fortress, undefended and inviolate.

There's nothing that won't fit under it:
fountains clogged with mud and leaves,
the houses of my childhood.

And night begins when my mother's fingers
let go of the thread
they've been tying and untying
to touch toward our fraying story's hem.

Night is the shadow of my father's hands
setting the clock for resurrection.

Or is it the clock unraveled, the numbers flown?

There's nothing that hasn't found home there:
discarded wings, lost shoes, a broken alphabet.

Everything but sleep. And night begins

with the first beheading
of the jasmine, its captive fragrance
rid at last of burial clothes.

2001

SHERMAN ALEXIE
b. 1966

Though widely known as a gifted novelist and screenwriter, Sherman Alexie began his literary career as a poet and has regularly published volumes of poetry. A "registered" (in the bureaucratic jargon) Spokane/Coeur d'Alene Indian, Alexie is a master of the trickster aesthetic. Wily and poker-faced, he dons rhetorical guises with cunning force. Occasionally a clenched fist is visible behind his characteristic curtain of irony. The Native American speaker in the poem "On the Amtrak from Boston to New York City" listens and nods cordially to a well-meaning white woman, as she, smiling, reads the landscape outside in terms of a "history" that is exclusively white, effacing thousands of years of Native American experience. Never revealed to his fellow passenger, the anger is all the more effectively presented in the poem, as in "Evolution" and "How to Write the Great American Indian Novel," smoldering behind a facade of agreeable good cheer.

Many of Alexie's poems explore the collision and tension between the perspectives of Native and white Americans. Tricksters must know the dominant as well as their own culture if they are to manipulate appearances effectively. "[I]t's hard to live in both worlds," Alexie remarked in a 1998 interview. "But I'm always doing it, it's part of who I am. It's actually a strength. . . . I know a lot more about white people than white people know about Indians." In the surreal world of "Tourists," Alexie imaginatively juxtaposes popular American cultural icons with reservation life. As he put it in another 1998 interview, his poetry is "always about the image, and about the connection, often, of very disparate, contradictory images."

If the ironic conjunction of antagonistic cultural perspectives is one of the key features of Alexie's work, another is narrative momentum. Alexie repeatedly refers to the "strong narrative drive" in his poetry. He shows little interest in lyric density or syntactic and lexical complexity. But his ear for colloquial speech, his feel for incremental repetition, and his eye for telling incongruity help him build narrative tension toward an ultimate climax. His brilliance as a storyteller has helped Alexie repeatedly win poetry slams, such as the Taos Poetry Circus World Heavyweight Championship in 1998, 1999, and 2000.

Born on October 7, 1966, Alexie grew up in Wellpinit, a town in a Spokane reservation in eastern Washington. Diagnosed with hydrocephalus, a large amount of cerebrospinal fluid in the cranial cavity, he was expected to die or at least to suffer from severe mental retardation after brain surgery at six months. Teased as "The Globe" for his enlarged skull in childhood, he retreated to the library, where he devoured books. He was educated at Gonzaga University in Spokane (1985–87) and Washington State University in Pullman (B.A., 1991). He lives in Seattle.

Evolution

Buffalo Bill[1] opens a pawn shop on the reservation
right across the border from the liquor store
and he stays open 24 hours a day, 7 days a week

and the Indians come running in with jewelry
television sets, a VCR, a full-length beaded buckskin outfit
it took Inez Muse 12 years to finish. Buffalo Bill

takes everything the Indians have to offer, keeps it
all catalogued and filed in a storage room. The Indians
pawn their hands, saving the thumbs for last, they pawn

their skeletons, falling endlessly from the skin
and when the last Indian has pawned everything
but his heart, Buffalo Bill takes that for twenty bucks

closes up the pawn shop, paints a new sign over the old
calls his venture THE MUSEUM OF NATIVE AMERICAN CULTURES
charges the Indians five bucks a head to enter.

1991

On the Amtrak from Boston to New York City

The white woman across the aisle from me says, "Look,
look at all the history, that house
on the hill there is over two hundred years old,"
as she points out the window past me

into what she has been taught. I have learned
little more about American history during my few days
back East than what I expected and far less
of what we should all know of the tribal stories

whose architecture is 15,000 years older
than the corners of the house that sits
museumed on the hill. "Walden Pond,"[2]
the woman on the train asks, "Did you see Walden Pond?"

and I don't have a cruel enough heart to break
her own by telling her there are five Walden Ponds
on my little reservation out West
and at least a hundred more surrounding Spokane,

1. William F. Cody (1846–1917), whose life was mythologized in a series of dime novels and theatrical productions celebrating his bravery and skill as a cavalry scout and buffalo hunter.
2. Small lake just south of Concord, Massachusetts, where American Transcendentalist Henry David Thoreau (1817–1862) tried to live simply and self-reliantly in a small cabin for two years, as described in his *Walden* (1854).

the city I pretend to call my home. "Listen,"
I could have told her. "I don't give a shit
about Walden. I know the Indians were living stories
around that pond before Walden's grandparents were born

and before his grandparents' grandparents were born.
I'm tired of hearing about Don-fucking-Henley[3] saving it, too,
because that's redundant. If Don Henley's brothers and sisters
and mothers and fathers hadn't come here in the first place

then nothing would need to be saved."
But I didn't say a word to the woman about Walden
Pond because she smiled so much and seemed delighted
that I thought to bring her an orange juice

back from the food car. I respect elders
of every color. All I really did was eat
my tasteless sandwich, drink my Diet Pepsi
and nod my head whenever the woman pointed out

another little piece of her country's history
while I, as all Indians have done
since this war began, made plans
for what I would do and say the next time

somebody from the enemy thought I was one of their own.

1993

Tourists

1. James Dean[4]

walks everywhere now. He's afraid of fast cars
and has walked this far, arriving
suddenly on the reservation, in search
of the Indian woman of his dreams.
He wants an Indian woman who could pass
for Natalie Wood.[5] He wants an Indian woman
who looks like the Natalie Wood
who was kidnapped by Indians
in John Ford's classic movie, "The Searchers."
James Dean wants to rescue somebody beautiful.
He still wears that red jacket,
you know the one. It's the color of a powwow[6] fire.

3. American rock musician Don Henley (b. 1947) helped start the Walden Woods Project in 1990 to preserve the woodlands surrounding the pond from encroaching commercial development.
4. American actor (1931–1955), most famous for his role in the film *Rebel without a Cause* (1955); his early death in a car accident helped contribute to his status as a tragic symbol of misunderstood youth in the 1950s.
5. American actor (1938–1981), who starred in such films as *Rebel without a Cause* (opposite Dean) and *The Searchers* (1956), a western directed by American filmmaker John Ford (1894–1973).
6. Tribal or intertribal event featuring dancing, singing, prayers, and speeches.

James Dean has never seen
a powwow, but he joins right in, dancing
like a crazy man, like a profane clown.
James Dean cannot contain himself.
He dances in the wrong direction. He tears
at his hair. He sings in wild syllables
and does not care. The Indian dancers stop
and stare like James Dean was lightning
or thunder, like he was bad weather.
But he keeps dancing, bumps into a man
and knocks loose an eagle feather.
The feather falls, drums stop.
This is the kind of silence
that frightens white men. James Dean
looks down at the feather
and knows that something has gone wrong.
He looks into the faces of the Indians.
He wants them to finish the song.

2. *Janis Joplin*[7]

sits by the jukebox in the Powwow Tavern,
talking with a few drunk Indians
about redemption. She promises each of them
she can punch in the numbers
for the song that will save their lives.
All she needs is a few quarters, a beer,
and their own true stories. The Indians
are as traditional as drunk Indians can be
and don't believe in autobiography,
so they lie to Janis Joplin about their lives.
One Indian is an astronaut, another killed JFK,
while the third played first base
for the New York Yankees. Janis Joplin knows
the Indians are lying. She's a smart woman
but she listens anyway, plays them each a song,
and sings along off key.

3. *Marilyn Monroe*[8]

drives herself to the reservation. Tired and cold,
she asks the Indian women for help.
Marilyn cannot explain what she needs
but the Indian women notice the needle tracks
on her arms and lead her to the sweat lodge[9]
where every woman, young and old, disrobes
and leaves her clothes behind
when she enters the dark of the lodge.

7. Rock vocalist (1943–1970), renowned for her raucous, bluesy voice and early death, of a heroin overdose.
8. American actor and Hollywood sex symbol (1926–1962), who died of an overdose of sleeping pills.
9. Small building that, when filled with steam, is used for purification and healing.

Marilyn's prayers may or may not be answered here
but they are kept sacred by Indian women.
Cold water is splashed on hot rocks
and steam fills the lodge. There is no place like this.
At first, Marilyn is self-conscious, aware
of her body and face, the tremendous heat, her thirst,
and the brown bodies circled around her.
But the Indian women do not stare. It is dark
inside the lodge. The hot rocks glow red
and the songs begin. Marilyn has never heard
these songs before, but she soon sings along.
Marilyn is not Indian, Marilyn will never be Indian
but the Indian women sing about her courage.
The Indian women sing for her health.
The Indian women sing for Marilyn.
Finally, she is no more naked than anyone else.

1996

How to Write the Great American Indian Novel

All of the Indians must have tragic features: tragic noses, eyes, and arms.
Their hands and fingers must be tragic when they reach for tragic food.

The hero must be a half-breed, half white and half Indian, preferably
from a horse culture. He should often weep alone. That is mandatory.

If the hero is an Indian woman, she is beautiful. She must be slender
and in love with a white man. But if she loves an Indian man

then he must be a half-breed, preferably from a horse culture.
If the Indian woman loves a white man, then he has to be so white

that we can see the blue veins running through his skin like rivers.
When the Indian woman steps out of her dress, the white man gasps

at the endless beauty of her brown skin. She should be compared to nature:
brown hills, mountains, fertile valleys, dewy grass, wind, and clear water.

If she is compared to murky water, however, then she must have a secret.
Indians always have secrets, which are carefully and slowly revealed.

Yet Indian secrets can be disclosed suddenly, like a storm.
Indian men, of course, are storms. They should destroy the lives

of any white women who choose to love them. All white women love
Indian men. That is always the case. White women feign disgust

at the savage in blue jeans and T-shirt, but secretly lust after him.
White women dream about half-breed Indian men from horse cultures.

Indian men are horses, smelling wild and gamey. When the Indian man
unbuttons his pants, the white woman should think of topsoil.

There must be one murder, one suicide, one attempted rape.
Alcohol should be consumed. Cars must be driven at high speeds.

Indians must see visions. White people can have the same visions
if they are in love with Indians. If a white person loves an Indian

then the white person is Indian by proximity. White people must carry
an Indian deep inside themselves. Those interior Indians are half-breed

and obviously from horse cultures. If the interior Indian is male
then he must be a warrior, especially if he is inside a white man.

If the interior Indian is female, then she must be a healer, especially if she is inside
a white woman. Sometimes there are complications.

An Indian man can be hidden inside a white woman. An Indian woman
can be hidden inside a white man. In these rare instances,

everybody is a half-breed struggling to learn more about his or her horse culture.
There must be redemption, of course, and sins must be forgiven.

For this, we need children. A white child and an Indian child, gender
not important, should express deep affection in a childlike way.

In the Great American Indian novel, when it is finally written,
all of the white people will be Indians and all of the Indians will be ghosts.

1996

Crow Testament

1

Cain lifts Crow, that heavy black bird
and strikes down Abel.[1]

Damn, says Crow, I guess
this is just the beginning.

1. According to Genesis 4, Cain is history's first murderer, slaying his younger brother in a fit of jealousy. The Crow is a prominent trickster figure in the mythologies of many Native American tribes.

2

The white man, disguised
as a falcon, swoops in
and yet again steals a salmon
from Crow's talons.

Damn, says Crow, if I could swim
I would have fled this country years ago.

3

The Crow God as depicted
in all of the reliable Crow bibles
looks exactly like a Crow.

Damn, says Crow, this makes it
so much easier to worship myself.

4

Among the ashes of Jericho,[2]
Crow sacrifices his firstborn son.

Damn, says Crow, a million nests
are soaked with blood.

5

When Crows fight Crows
the sky fills with beaks and talons.

Damn, says Crow, it's raining feathers.

6

Crow flies around the reservation
and collects empty beer bottles

but they are so heavy
he can carry only one at a time.

So, one by one, he returns them
but gets only five cents a bottle.

Damn, says Crow, redemption
is not easy.

2. Town on the west side of the Jordan River Valley famous in biblical history for its destruction under the attack of Joshua and the Israelites after God caused its walls to tumble (Joshua 6).

7

Crow rides a pale horse
into a crowded powwow
but none of the Indians panic.

Damn, says Crow, I guess
they already live near the end of the world.

2000

Poetics

Projective Verse

In the post–World War II period, this landmark essay by Charles Olson, leader of the Black Mountain school, which also included Robert Creeley, Robert Duncan, and Denise Levertov, has been a major catalyst of poetic innovation. Published at a time when the so-called closed forms of New Criticism and T. S. Eliot's version of modernism predominated, Olson's essay inspired many poets to experiment with open forms. In contrast to the concept of poetry as the well-wrought urn, static and timeless, Olson proposes a model of poetry as the dynamic transfer and discharge of energy. Grounded in the poet's body and breath, the poem should convey the spontaneity, the process, the excitement of composition. Propounding what he calls "objectism," Olson urges poets to reach beyond their individual egos and open themselves to the larger forces of nature. He breaks with some literary precedents, but adapts others, such as Romantic ideas of inspiration, organicism, and responsiveness to nature, as well as the modernist ideas and practices of Ezra Pound and William Carlos Williams. First published in *Poetry New York*, No. 3 (1950), the essay has been reprinted from *Collected Prose* (1997).

CHARLES OLSON

Projective / Verse

(projectile (percussive (prospective[1]
vs.
The NON-Projective

(or what a French critic calls "closed" verse, that verse which print bred and which is pretty much what we have had, in English & American, and have still got, despite the work of Pound & Williams:

it led Keats, already a hundred years ago, to see it (Wordsworth's, Milton's) in the light of "the Egotistical Sublime";[2] *and it persists, at this latter day, as what you might call the private-soul-at-any-public-wall)*

1. Throughout his writing, Olson used unclosed parentheses to signify birth and a receptive consciousness.
2. English Romantic poet John Keats (1795–1821) contrasted the "[W]ordsworthian or egotistical sublime," the poet's habit of focusing attention on his or her own mind, with his own poetic strategies, including "negative capability," the poet's tolerance of uncertainty and sympathetic identification with nature.

Verse now, 1950, if it is to go ahead, if it is to be of *essential* use, must, I take it, catch up and put into itself certain laws and possibilities of the breath, of the breathing of the man who writes as well as of his listenings. (The revolution of the ear, 1910, the trochee's heave, asks it of the younger poets.)[3]

I want to do two things: first, try to show what projective or OPEN verse is, what it involves, in its act of composition, how, in distinction from the non-projective, it is accomplished; and II, suggest a few ideas about what stance toward reality brings such verse into being, what that stance does, both to the poet and to his reader. (The stance involves, for example, a change beyond, and larger than, the technical, and may, the way things look, lead to new poetics and to new concepts from which some sort of drama, say, or of epic, perhaps, may emerge.)

I

First, some simplicities that a man learns, if he works in OPEN, or what can also be called COMPOSITION BY FIELD, as opposed to inherited line, stanza, over-all form, what is the "old" base of the non-projective.

(1) the *kinetics* of the thing. A poem is energy transferred from where the poet got it (he will have some several causations), by way of the poem itself to, all the way over to, the reader. Okay. Then the poem itself must, at all points, be a high energy-construct and, at all points, an energy-discharge. So: how is the poet to accomplish same energy, how is he, what is the process by which a poet gets in, at all points energy at least the equivalent of the energy which propelled him in the first place, yet an energy which is peculiar to verse alone and which will be, obviously, also different from the energy which the reader, because he is a third term, will take away?

This is the problem which any poet who departs from closed form is specially confronted by. And it involves a whole series of new recognitions. From the moment he ventures into FIELD COMPOSITION—puts himself in the open—he can go by no track other than the one the poem under hand declares, for itself. Thus he has to behave, and be, instant by instant, aware of some several forces just now beginning to be examined. (It is much more, for example, this push, than simply such a one as Pound put, so wisely, to get us started: "the musical phrase," go by it, boys, rather than by, the metronome.)[4]

(2) is the *principle*, the law which presides conspicuously over such composition, and, when obeyed, is the reason why a projective poem can come into being. It is this: FORM IS NEVER MORE THAN AN EXTENSION OF CONTENT. (Or so it got phrased by one, R. Creeley,[5] and it makes absolute sense to me, with this possible corollary, that right form, in any given poem, is the only and exclusively possible extension of content under hand.) There it is, brothers, sitting there, for USE.

Now (3) the *process* of the thing, how the principle can be made so to shape the energies that the form is accomplished. And I think it can be boiled down to one statement (first pounded into my head by Edward Dahlberg[6]):

3. Cf. Canto 81, by Ezra Pound (1885–1972): "To break the pentameter, that was the first heave."
4. The third principle of Imagism: "As regarding rhythm: to compose in the sequence of the musical phrase, not in sequence of a metronome" (Pound, "A Retrospect," vol. 1 of this anthology).
5. Robert Creeley (b. 1926), fellow poet of the Black Mountain school.
6. American poet and novelist (1900–1977).

ONE PERCEPTION MUST IMMEDIATELY AND DIRECTLY LEAD TO A FURTHER PERCEPTION. It means exactly what it says, is a matter of, at *all* points (even, I should say, of our management of daily reality as of the daily work) get on with it, keep moving, keep in, speed, the nerves, their speed, the perceptions, theirs, the acts, the split second acts, the whole business, keep it moving as fast as you can, citizen. And if you also set up as a poet, USE USE USE the process at all points, in any given poem always, always one perception must must must MOVE, INSTANTER, ON ANOTHER!

So there we are, fast, there's the dogma. And its excuse, its usableness, in practice. Which gets us, it ought to get us, inside the machinery, now, 1950, of how projective verse is made.

If I hammer, if I recall in, and keep calling in, the breath, the breathing as distinguished from the hearing, it is for cause, it is to insist upon a part that breath plays in verse which has not (due, I think, to the smothering of the power of the line by too set a concept of foot) has not been sufficiently observed or practiced, but which has to be if verse is to advance to its proper force and place in the day, now, and ahead. I take it that PROJECTIVE VERSE teaches, is, this lesson, that that verse will only do in which a poet manages to register both the acquisitions of his ear *and* the pressures of his breath.

Let's start from the smallest particle of all, the syllable. It is the king and pin of versification, what rules and holds together the lines, the larger forms, of a poem. I would suggest that verse here and in England dropped this secret from the late Elizabethans to Ezra Pound, lost it, in the sweetness of meter and rime, in a honey-head.[7] (The syllable is one way to distinguish the original success of blank verse, and its falling off, with Milton.)

It is by their syllables that words juxtapose in beauty, by these particles of sound as clearly as by the sense of the words which they compose. In any given instance, because there is a choice of words, the choice, if a man is in there, will be, spontaneously, the obedience of his ear to the syllables. The fineness, and the practice, lie here, at the minimum and source of speech.

O western wynd, when wilt thou blow
And the small rain down shall rain
O Christ that my love were in my arms
And I in my bed again[8]

It would do no harm, as an act of correction to both prose and verse as now written, if both rime and meter, and, in the quantity words, both sense and sound, were less in the forefront of the mind than the syllable, if the syllable, that fine creature, were more allowed to lead the harmony on. With this warning, to those who would try: to step back here to this place of the elements and minims of language, is to engage speech where it is least careless—and least logical. Listening for the syllables must be so constant and so scrupulous, the exaction must be so complete, that the assurance of the

7. Cf. the end of chapter 78 of Herman Melville's (1819–1891) novel *Moby-Dick* (1851), in which the narrator compares falling into the oil from a whale's head or into a honey tree with falling into the idealism of ancient Greek philosopher Plato: "How many, think ye, have likewise fallen into Plato's honey head, and sweetly perished there?"

8. Anonymous English lyric from the late fifteenth or early sixteenth century.

ear is purchased at the highest—40 hours a day—price. For from the root out, from all over the place, the syllable comes, the figures of, the dance:

> "Is" comes from the Aryan root, *as,* to breathe. The English "not" equals the Sanscrit *na,* which may come from the root *na,* to be lost, to perish. "Be" is from *bhu,* to grow.

I say the syllable, king, and that it is spontaneous, this way: the ear, the ear which has collected, which has listened, the ear, which is so close to the mind that it is the mind's, that it has the mind's speed . . .

it is close, another way: the mind is brother to this sister and is, because it is so close, is the drying force, the incest, the sharpener . . .

it is from the union of the mind and the ear that the syllable is born.

But the syllable is only the first child of the incest of verse (always, that Egyptian thing, it produces twins!). The other child is the LINE. And together, these two, the syllable *and* the line, they make a poem, they make that thing, the—what shall we call it, the Boss of all, the "Single Intelligence." And the line comes (I swear it) from the breath, from the breathing of the man who writes, at the moment that he writes, and thus is, it is here that, the daily work, the WORK, gets in, for only he, the man who writes, can declare, at every moment, the line its metric and its ending—where its breathing, shall come to, termination.

The trouble with most work, to my taking, since the breaking away from traditional lines and stanzas, and from such wholes as, say, Chaucer's *Troilus* or S's *Lear,* is: contemporary workers go lazy RIGHT HERE WHERE THE LINE IS BORN.

Let me put it baldly. The two halves are:

the HEAD, by way of the EAR, to the SYLLABLE
the HEART, by way of the BREATH, to the LINE

And the joker? that it is in the 1st half of the proposition that, in composing, one lets-it-rip; and that it is in the 2nd half, surprise, it is the LINE that's the baby that gets, as the poem is getting made, the attention, the control, that it is right here, in the line, that the shaping takes place, each moment of the going.

I am dogmatic, that the head shows in the syllable. The dance of the intellect[9] is there, among them, prose or verse. Consider the best minds you know in this here business: where does the head show, is it not, precise, here, in the swift currents of the syllable? can't you tell a brain when you see what it does, just there? It is true, what the master says he picked up from Confusion:[1] all the thots men are capable of can be entered on the back of a postage stamp. So, is it not the PLAY of a mind we are after, is not that that shows whether a mind is there at all?

And the threshing floor for the dance? Is it anything but the LINE? And when the line has, is, a deadness, is it not a heart which has gone lazy, is it not, suddenly, slow things, similes, say, adjectives, or such, that we are bored by?

For there is a whole flock of rhetorical devices which have now to be brought under a new bead, now that we sight with the line. Simile is only one bird who comes down, too easily. The descriptive functions generally

9. From Pound's definition of logopoeia: "the dance of the intellect among words" (Pound, *How to Read,* vol. 1 of this anthology).

1. Wordplay on Confucius (551–479 B.C.E.), Chinese philosopher.

have to be watched, every second, in projective verse, because of their easiness, and thus their drain on the energy which composition by field allows into a poem. *Any* slackness takes off attention, that crucial thing, from the job in hand, from the *push* of the line under hand at the moment, under the reader's eye, in his moment. Observation of any kind is, like argument in prose, properly previous to the act of the poem, and, if allowed in, must be so juxtaposed, apposed, set in, that it does not, for an instant, sap the going energy of the content toward its form.

It comes to this, this whole aspect of the newer problems. (We now enter, actually, the large area of the whole poem, into the FIELD, if you like, where all the syllables and all the lines must be managed in their relations to each other.) It is a matter, finally, of OBJECTS, what they are, what they are inside a poem, how they got there, and, once there, how they are to be used. This is something I want to get to in another way in Part II, but, for the moment, let me indicate this, that every element in an open poem (the syllable, the line, as well as the image, the sound, the sense) must be taken up as participants in the kinetic of the poem just as solidly as we are accustomed to take what we call the objects of reality; and that these elements are to be seen as creating the tensions of a poem just as totally as do those other objects create what we know as the world.

The objects which occur at every given moment of composition (of recognition, we can call it) are, can be, must be treated exactly as they do occur therein and not by any ideas or preconceptions from outside the poem, must be handled as a series of objects in field in such a way that a series of tensions (which they also are) are made to *hold*, and to hold exactly inside the content and the context of the poem which has forced itself, through the poet and them, into being.

Because breath allows *all* the speech-force of language back in (speech is the "solid" of verse, is the secret of a poem's energy), because, now, a poem has, by speech, solidity, everything in it can now be treated as solids, objects, things; and, though insisting upon the absolute difference of the reality of verse from that other dispersed and distributed thing, yet each of these elements of a poem can be allowed to have the play of their separate energies and can be allowed, once the poem is well composed, to keep, as those other objects do, their proper confusions.

Which brings us up, immediately, bang, against tenses, in fact against syntax, in fact against grammar generally, that is, as we have inherited it. Do not tenses, must they not also be kicked around anew, in order that time, that other governing absolute may be kept, as must the space-tensions of a poem, immediate, contemporary to the acting-on-you of the poem? I would argue that here, too, the LAW OF THE LINE, which projective verse creates, must be hewn to, obeyed, and that the conventions which logic has forced on syntax must be broken open as quietly as must the too set feet of the old line. But an analysis of how far a new poet can stretch the very conventions on which communication by language rests, is too big for these notes, which are meant, I hope it is obvious, merely to get things started.

Let me just throw in this. It is my impression that *all* parts of speech suddenly, in composition by field, are fresh for both sound and percussive use, spring up like unknown, unnamed vegetables in the patch, when you work it, come spring. Now take Hart Crane.[2] What strikes me in him is the singleness of the push to the nominative, his push along that one arc of

2. American poet (1899–1932).

freshness, the attempt to get back to word as handle. (If logos is word as thought, what is word as noun, as, pass me that, as Newman Shea used to ask, at the galley table, put a jib on the blood, will ya.) But there is a loss in Crane of what Fenollosa[3] is so right about, in syntax, the sentence as first act of nature, as lightning, as passage of force from subject to object, quick, in this case, from Hart to me, in every case, from me to you, the VERB, between two nouns. Does not Hart miss the advantages, by such an isolated push, miss the point of the whole front of syllable, line, field, and what happened to all language, and to the poem, as a result?

I return you now to London, to beginnings, to the syllable, for the pleasures of it, to intermit;

> If music be the food of love, play on,
> give me excess of it, that, surfeiting,
> the appetite may sicken, and so die.
> That strain again. It had a dying fall,
> o, it came over my ear like the sweet sound
> that breathes upon a bank of violets,
> stealing and giving odour.[4]

What we have suffered from, is manuscript, press, the removal of verse from its producer and its reproducer, the voice, a removal by one, by two removes from its place of origin *and* its destination. For the breath has a double meaning which latin had not yet lost.[5]

The irony is, from the machine has come one gain not yet sufficiently observed or used, but which leads directly on toward projective verse and its consequences. It is the advantage of the typewriter that, due to its rigidity and its space precisions, it can, for a poet, indicate exactly the breath, the pauses, the suspensions even of syllables, the juxtapositions even of parts of phrases, which he intends. For the first time the poet has the stave and the bar a musician has had. For the first time he can, without the convention of rime and meter, record the listening he has done to his own speech and by that one act indicate how he would want any reader, silently or otherwise, to voice his work.

It is time we picked the fruits of the experiments of Cummings, Pound, Williams,[6] each of whom has, after his way, already used the machine as a scoring to his composing, as a script to its vocalization. It is now only a matter of the recognition of the conventions of composition by field for us to bring into being an open verse as formal as the closed, with all its traditional advantages.

If a contemporary poet leaves a space as long as the phrase before it, he means that space to be held, by the breath, an equal length of time. If he suspends a word or syllable at the end of a line (this was most Cummings' addition) he means that time to pass that it takes the eye—that hair of time suspended—to pick up the next line. If he wishes a pause so light it hardly separates the words, yet does not want a comma—which is an interruption of the meaning rather than the sounding of the line—follow him when he uses a symbol the typewriter has ready to hand:

3. Ernest Fenollosa (1853–1908), American scholar whose work on Chinese and Japanese literature greatly influenced Pound, emphasized the importance of action and verbs. *Newman Shea*: sailor on a ship Olson worked on one summer. "Put a jib on the blood" was Shea's way of saying "pass the ketchup."
4. Beginning of Shakespeare's *Twelfth Night*.
5. In Latin, *spiritus*: breath; soul or life.
6. William Carlos Williams (1883–1963) and E. E. Cummings (1894–1962), American poets.

What does not change / is the will to change[7]

Observe him, when he takes advantage of the machine's multiple margins, to juxtapose:

Sd he:
  to dream takes no effort
    to think is easy
      to act is more difficult
    but for a man to act after he has taken thought, this!
is the most difficult thing of all[8]

Each of these lines is a progressing of both the meaning and the breathing forward, and then a backing up, without a progress or any kind of movement outside the unit of time local to the idea.

There is more to be said in order that this convention be recognized, especially in order that the revolution out of which it came may be so forwarded that work will get published to offset the reaction now afoot to return verse to inherited forms of cadence and rime. But what I want to emphasize here, by this emphasis on the typewriter as the personal and instantaneous recorder of the poet's work, is the already projective nature of verse as the sons of Pound and Williams are practicing it. Already they are composing as though verse was to have the reading its writing involved, as though not the eye but the ear was to be its measurer, as though the intervals of its composition could be so carefully put down as to be precisely the intervals of its registration. For the ear, which once had the burden of memory to quicken it (rime & regular cadence were its aids and have merely lived on in print after the oral necessities were ended) can now again, that the poet has his means, be the threshold of projective verse.

II

Which gets us to what I promised, the degree to which the projective involves a stance toward reality outside a poem as well as a new stance towards the reality of a poem itself. It is a matter of content, the content of Homer or of Euripides or of Seami[9] as distinct from that which I might call the more "literary" masters. From the moment the projective purpose of the act of verse is recognized, the content does—it will—change. If the beginning and the end is breath, voice in its largest sense, then the material of verse shifts. It has to. It starts with the composer. The dimension of his line itself changes, not to speak of the change in his conceiving, of the matter he will turn to, of the scale in which he imagines that matter's use. I myself would pose the difference by a physical image. It is no accident that Pound and Williams both were involved variously in a movement which got called "objectivism."[1] But that word was then used in some sort of a necessary quarrel, I take it, with "subjectivism." It is now too late to be bothered with the latter. It has excellently done itself to death, even though we are all caught in its dying.

7. From Olson's "The Kingfishers" (1950).
8. From Olson's "The Praises" (1950).
9. Japanese Noh playwright (1363–1443). Euripides (c. 484–406 B.C.E.), Greek dramatist.
1. In the 1930s, the Objectivists, inspired by Pound and Williams, emphasized composition unclouded by authorial sentiment and the poem as material object. Among those affiliated with the group were American poets Louis Zukofsky, Charles Reznikoff, George Oppen, and Lorine Niedecker and British poet Basil Bunting.

What seems to me a more valid formulation for present use is "objectism," a word to be taken to stand for the kind of relation of man to experience which a poet might state as the necessity of a line or a work to be as wood is, to be as clean as wood is as it issues from the hand of nature, to be as shaped as wood can be when a man has had his hand to it. Objectism is the getting rid of the lyrical interference of the individual as ego, of the "subject" and his soul, that peculiar presumption by which western man has interposed himself between what he is as a creature of nature (with certain instructions to carry out) and those other creations of nature which we may, with no derogation, call objects. For a man is himself an object, whatever he may take to be his advantages, the more likely to recognize himself as such the greater his advantages, particularly at that moment that he achieves an humilitas sufficient to make him of use.

It comes to this: the use of a man, by himself and thus by others, lies in how he conceives his relation to nature, that force to which he owes his somewhat small existence. If he sprawl, he shall find little to sing but himself, and shall sing, nature has such paradoxical ways, by way of artificial forms outside himself. But if he stays inside himself, if he is contained within his nature as he is participant in the larger force, he will be able to listen, and his hearing through himself will give him secrets objects share. And by an inverse law his shapes will make their own way. It is in this sense that the projective act, which is the artist's act in the larger field of objects, leads to dimensions larger than the man. For a man's problem, the moment he takes speech up in all its fullness, is to give his work his seriousness, a seriousness sufficient to cause the thing he makes to try to take its place alongside the things of nature. This is not easy. Nature works from reverence, even in her destructions (species go down with a crash). But breath is man's special qualification as animal. Sound is a dimension he has extended. Language is one of his proudest acts. And when a poet rests in these as they are in himself (in his physiology, if you like, but the life in him, for all that) then he, if he chooses to speak from these roots, works in that area where nature has given him size, projective size.

It is projective size that the play, *The Trojan Women,*[2] possesses, for it is able to stand, is it not, as its people do, beside the Aegean—and neither Andromache or the sea suffer diminution. In a less "heroic" but equally "natural" dimension Seami causes the Fisherman and the Angel to stand clear in *Hagoromo.*[3] And Homer, who is such an unexamined cliché that I do not think I need to press home in what scale Nausicaa's girls wash their clothes.[4]

Such works, I should argue—and I use them simply because their equivalents are yet to be done—could not issue from men who conceived verse without the full relevance of human voice, without reference to where lines come from, in the individual who writes. Nor do I think it accident that, at this end point of the argument, I should use, for examples, two dramatists and an epic poet. For I would hazard the guess that, if projective verse is practiced long enough, is driven ahead hard enough along the course I think

2. Greek tragedy (c. 415 B.C.E.) by Euripedes about the aftermath of the Trojan War. Andromache, Hector's loyal wife, is forced to marry the son of her husband's killer, Achilles.

3. The Noh play by Seami (trans. Arthur Waley in 1922) in which a fisherman steals an angel's cloak and prevents her from returning to Heaven.

4. Cf. book 6 of Homer's *Odyssey*, in which the Phaeacian princess Nausicaa encounters the shipwrecked Odysseus as she and her maids wash clothes on the shore.

it dictates, verse again can carry much larger material than it has carried in our language since the Elizabethans. But it can't be jumped. We are only at its beginnings, and if I think that the *Cantos* make more "dramatic" sense than do the plays of Mr. Eliot,[5] it is not because I think they have solved the problem but because the methodology of the verse in them points a way by which, one day, the problem of larger content and of larger forms may be solved. Eliot is, in fact, a proof of a present danger, of "too easy" a going on the practice of verse as it has been, rather than as it must be, practiced. There is no question, for example, that Eliot's line, from "Prufrock" on down, has speech-force, is "dramatic," is, in fact, one of the most notable lines since Dryden. I suppose it stemmed immediately to him from Browning,[6] as did so many of Pound's early things. In any case Eliot's line has obvious relations backward to the Elizabethans, especially to the soliloquy. Yet O. M. Eliot is *not* projective. It could even be argued (and I say this carefully, as I have said all things about the non-projective, having considered how each of us must save himself after his own fashion and how much, for that matter, each of us owes to the non-projective, and will continue to owe, as both go alongside each other) but it could be argued that it is because Eliot has stayed inside the non-projective that he fails as a dramatist—that his root is the mind alone, and a scholastic mind at that (no high *intelletto*[7] despite his apparent clarities)—and that, in his listenings he has stayed there where the ear and the mind are, has only gone from his fine ear outward rather than, as I say a projective poet will, down through the workings of his own throat to that place where breath comes from, where breath has its beginnings, where drama has to come from, where, the coincidence is, all act springs.

1950

5. American-born poet and dramatist T. S. Eliot (1888–1965), who became a British citizen in 1927. "O. M.," below, refers to the British Order of Merit.

6. Robert Browning (1812–1889), English poet famous for his dramatic monologues.

7. Intellect (Italian).

POETIC MANIFESTO

In the summer of 1951, a student writing a thesis on Dylan Thomas asked the poet five questions. Though not intended for publication, Thomas's response is one of the most cogent and evocative postwar statements on the verbal craft of poetry. It appeared after his death under the title "Poetic Manifesto," initially as a reproduction of the handwritten text. In his response, Thomas defines poetry as an art celebrating language, humanity, and God. For him, the love not of ideas but of language itself—rhythm, rhyme, assonance, metaphor, and all other elements of verbal magic—is the fundamental basis of poetry. He reports being smitten as a child by "the shape and shade and size and noise of the words." Although he dutifully responds to questions about influences and movements, Thomas writes exuberantly on behalf of the pleasure of verbal artifice, the poet's joy in "twistings and convolutions of words." Originally reproduced in *Texas Quarterly* 4.4 (Winter 1961), the manifesto has been reprinted from *Early Prose Writings* (1971), ed. Walford Davies.

DYLAN THOMAS

Poetic Manifesto

You want to know why and how I first began to write poetry, and which poets or kind of poetry I was first moved and influenced by.

To answer the first part of this question, I should say I wanted to write poetry in the beginning because I had fallen in love with words. The first poems I knew were nursery rhymes, and before I could read them for myself I had come to love just the words of them, the words alone. What the words stood for, symbolised, or meant, was of very secondary importance; what mattered was the *sound* of them as I heard them for the first time on the lips of the remote and incomprehensible grown-ups who seemed, for some reason, to be living in my world. And these words were, to me, as the notes of bells, the sounds of musical instruments, the noises of wind, sea, and rain, the rattle of milk-carts, the clopping of hooves on cobbles, the fingering of branches on a window pane, might be to someone, deaf from birth, who has miraculously found his hearing. I did not care what the words said, overmuch, nor what happened to Jack & Jill & the Mother Goose rest of them; I cared for the shapes of sound that their names, and the words describing their actions, made in my ears; I cared for the colours the words cast on my eyes. I realise that I may be, as I think back all that way, romanticising my reactions to the simple and beautiful words of those pure poems; but that is all I can honestly remember, however much time might have falsified my memory. I fell in love—that is the only expression I can think of—at once, and am still at the mercy of words, though sometimes now, knowing a little of their behaviour very well, I think I can influence them slightly and have even learned to beat them now and then, which they appear to enjoy. I tumbled for words at once. And, when I began to read the nursery rhymes for myself, and, later, to read other verses and ballads, I knew that I had discovered the most important things, to me, that could be ever. There they were, seemingly lifeless, made only of black and white, but out of them, out of their own being, came love and terror and pity and pain and wonder and all the other vague abstractions that make our ephemeral lives dangerous, great, and bearable. Out of them came the gusts and grunts and hiccups and heehaws of the common fun of the earth; and though what the words meant was, in its own way, often deliciously funny enough, so much funnier seemed to me, at that almost forgotten time, the shape and shade and size and noise of the words as they hummed, strummed, jigged and galloped along. That was the time of innocence; words burst upon me, unencumbered by trivial or portentous association; words were their spring-like selves, fresh with Eden's dew, as they flew out of the air. They made their own original associations as they sprang and shone. The words, 'Ride a cock-horse to Banbury Cross', were as haunting to me, who did not know then what a cock-horse was nor cared a damn where Banbury Cross might be, as, much later, were such lines as John Donne's, 'Go and catch a falling star, Get with child a mandrake root',[1] which also I could not understand when I first read them. And as I read more and

1. From "Go and Catch a Falling Star," by English poet John Donne (1572–1631).

more, and it was not all verse, by any means, my love for the real life of words increased until I knew that I must live *with* them and *in* them, always. I knew, in fact, that I must be a writer of words, and nothing else. The first thing was to feel and know their sound and substance; what I was going to do with those words, what use I was going to make of them, what I was going to *say* through them, would come later. I knew I had to know them most intimately in all their forms and moods, their ups and downs, their chops and changes, their needs and demands. (Here, I am afraid, I am beginning to talk too vaguely. I do not like writing *about* words, because then I often use bad and wrong and stale and woolly words. What I like to do is to treat words as a craftsman does his wood or stone or what-have-you, to hew, carve, mould, coil, polish and plane them into patterns, sequences, sculptures, fugues of sound expressing some lyrical impulse, some spiritual doubt or conviction, some dimly-realised truth I must try to reach and realise.) It was when I was very young, and just at school, that, in my father's study, before homework that was never done, I began to know one kind of writing from another, one kind of goodness, one kind of badness. My first, and greatest, liberty was that of being able to read everything and anything I cared to. I read indiscriminately, and with my eyes hanging out. I could never have dreamt that there were such goings-on in the world between the covers of books, such sand-storms and ice-blasts of words, such slashing of humbug,[2] and humbug too, such staggering peace, such enormous laughter, such and so many blinding bright lights breaking across the just-awaking wits and splashing all over the pages in a million bits and pieces all of which were words, words, words, and each of which was alive forever in its own delight and glory and oddity and light. (I must try not to make these supposedly helpful notes as confusing as my poems themselves.) I wrote endless imitations, though I never thought them to be imitations but, rather, wonderfully original things, like eggs laid by tigers. They were imitations of anything I happened to be reading at the time: Sir Thomas Browne, de Quincey, Henry Newbolt, the Ballads, Blake, Baroness Orczy, Marlowe, Chums, the Imagists, the Bible, Poe, Keats, Lawrence, Anon., and Shakespeare.[3] A mixed lot, as you see, and randomly remembered. I tried my callow hand at almost every poetical form. How could I learn the tricks of a trade unless I tried to do them myself? I learned that the bad tricks come easily; and the good ones, which help you to say what you think you wish to say in the most meaningful, moving way, I am still learning. (But in earnest company you must call these tricks by other names, such as technical devices, prosodic experiments, etc.)

The writers, then, who influenced my earliest poems and stories were, quite simply and truthfully, all the writers I was reading at the time, and, as you see from a specimen list higher up the page, they ranged from writers of school-boy adventure yarns to incomparable and inimitable masters like Blake. That is, when I began, bad writing had as much influence on my stuff as good. The bad influences I tried to remove and renounce bit by bit, shadow

2. Empty or misleading talk.
3. Sir Thomas Browne (1605–1682): English writer and physician. Thomas De Quincey (1785–1859): English writer famous for his *Confessions of an English Opium-Eater*. Henry Newbolt (1862–1938): English lawyer and writer of nautical poetry. William Blake (1757–1827): English poet and printer. Baroness Orczy (1865–1947): Hungarian-born author of *The Scarlet Pimpernel* (1905). Christopher Marlowe (1564–1593): English dramatist. Imagists: early twentieth-century poets who wrote in direct, clear, image-based free verse, as proposed by Ezra Pound (1885–1972) and others. Edgar Allan Poe (1809–1849): American poet and fiction writer. John Keats (1795–1821): English Romantic poet. D. H. Lawrence (1885–1930): English poet and novelist.

by shadow, echo by echo, through trial and error, through delight and disgust and misgiving, as I came to love words more and to hate the heavy hands that knocked them about, the thick tongues that had no feel for their multitudinous tastes, the dull and botching hacks who flattened them out into a colourless and insipid paste, the pedants who made them moribund and pompous as themselves. Let me say that the things that first made me love language and want to work *in* it and *for* it were nursery rhymes and folk tales, the Scottish Ballads, a few lines of hymns, the most famous Bible stories and the rhythms of the Bible, Blake's *Songs of Innocence,* and the quite incomprehensible magical majesty and nonsense of Shakespeare heard, read, and near-murdered in the first forms[4] of my school.

You ask me, next, if it is true that three of the dominant influences on my published prose and poetry are Joyce, the Bible, and Freud.[5] (I purposely say my 'published' prose and poetry, as in the preceding pages I have been talking about the primary influences upon my very first and forever unpublishable juvenilia.) I cannot say that I have been 'influenced' by Joyce, whom I enormously admire and whose *Ulysses,* and earlier stories I have read a great deal. I think this Joyce question arose because somebody once, in print, remarked on the closeness of the title of my book of short stories, *Portrait of the Artist As a Young Dog* to Joyce's title, *Portrait of the Artist as a Young Man*. As you know, the name given to innumerable portrait paintings by their artists is, 'Portrait of the Artist as a Young Man'—a perfectly straightforward title. Joyce used the painting title for the first time as the title of a literary work. I myself made a bit of doggish fun of the *painting*-title and, of course, intended no possible reference to Joyce. I do not think that Joyce has had any hand at all in my writing; certainly his *Ulysses* has not. On the other hand, I cannot deny that the shaping of some of my *Portrait* stories might owe something to Joyce's stories in the volume, *Dubliners*. But then *Dubliners* was a pioneering work in the world of the short story, and no good storywriter since can have failed, in some way, however little, to have benefited by it.

The Bible, I have referred to in attempting to answer your first question. Its great stories of Noah, Jonah, Lot, Moses, Jacob, David, Solomon and a thousand more, I had, of course, known from very early youth; the great rhythms had rolled over me from the Welsh pulpits; and I read, for myself, from Job and Ecclesiastes; and the story of the New Testament is part of my life. But I have never sat down and studied the Bible, never consciously echoed its language, and am, in reality, as ignorant of it as most brought-up Christians. All of the Bible that I use in my work is remembered from childhood, and is the common property of all who were brought up in English-speaking communities. Nowhere, indeed, in all my writing, do I use any knowledge which is not commonplace to any literate person. I *have* used a few difficult words in early poems, but they are easily looked-up and were, in any case, thrown into the poems in a kind of adolescent showing-off which I hope I have now discarded.

And that leads me to the third 'dominant influence': Sigmund Freud. My only acquaintance with the theories and discoveries of Dr Freud has been through the work of novelists who have been excited by his case-book his-

4. Grades (British).
5. Sigmund Freud (1856–1939): Austrian founder of psychoanalysis. James Joyce (1882–1941): Irish novelist.

tories, of popular newspaper scientific-potboilers who have, I imagine, vulgarised his work beyond recognition, and of a few modern poets, including Auden,[6] who have attempted to use psychoanalytical phraseology and theory in some of their poems. I have read only one book of Freud's, *The Interpretation of Dreams*, and do not recall having been influenced by it in any way. Again, no honest writer today can possibly avoid being influenced by Freud through his pioneering work into the Unconscious and by the influence of those discoveries on the scientific, philosophic, and artistic work of his contemporaries: but not, by any means, necessarily through Freud's own writing.

To your third question—Do I deliberately utilise devices of rhyme, rhythm, and word-formation in my writing—I must, of course, answer with an immediate, Yes. I am a painstaking, conscientious, involved and devious craftsman in words, however unsuccessful the result so often appears, and to whatever wrong uses I may apply my technical paraphernalia, I use everything and anything to make my poems work and move in the directions I want them to: old tricks, new tricks, puns, portmanteau-words, paradox, allusion, paranomasia, paragram, catachresis, slang, assonantal rhymes, vowel rhymes, sprung rhythm.[7] Every device there is in language is there to be used if you will. Poets have got to enjoy themselves sometimes, and the twistings and convolutions of words, the inventions and contrivances, are all part of the joy that is part of the painful, voluntary work.

Your next question asks whether my use of combinations of words to create something new, 'in the Surrealist way', is according to a set formula or is spontaneous.

There is a confusion here, for the Surrealists' set formula was to juxtapose the unpremeditated.

Let me make it clearer if I can. The Surrealists—(that is, super-realists, or those who work *above* realism)—were a coterie of painters and writers in Paris, in the nineteen twenties, who did not believe in the conscious selection of images. To put it in another way: They were artists who were dissatisfied with both the realists—(roughly speaking, those who tried to put down in paint and words an actual representation of what they imagined to be the real world in which they lived)—and the impressionists who, roughly speaking again, were those who tried to give an impression of what they imagined to be the real world. The Surrealists wanted to dive into the subconscious mind, the mind below the conscious surface, and dig up their images from there without the aid of logic or reason, and put them down, illogically and unreasonably, in paint and words. The Surrealists affirmed that, as three quarters of the mind was submerged, it was the function of the artist to gather his material from the greatest, submerged mass of the mind rather than from that quarter of the mind which, like the tip of an iceberg, protruded from the subconscious sea. One method the Surrealists used in their poetry was to juxtapose words and images that had no rational relationship; and out of this they hoped to achieve a kind of subconscious, or dream, poetry that would be truer to the real, imaginative world of the mind, mostly

6. W. H. Auden (1907–1973): Anglo-American poet.
7. Metrical system using a variable number of syllables per foot, devised by English poet Gerard Manley Hopkins (1844–1889). *Portmanteau-words:* words made from the blending of two words. *Paranomasia:* pun. *Paragram:* wordplay involving alteration of letters. *Catachresis:* intentional misuse of a word or figure, as in a strained or mixed metaphor.

submerged, than is the poetry of the conscious mind that relies upon the rational and logical relationship of ideas, objects, and images.

This is, very crudely, the credo of the Surrealists, and one with which I profoundly disagree. I do not mind from where the images of a poem are dragged up: drag them up, if you like, from the nethermost sea of the hidden self; but before they reach paper, they must go through all the rational processes of the intellect. The Surrealists, on the other hand, put their words down together on paper exactly as they emerge from chaos; they do not shape these words or put them in order; to them, chaos is the shape and order. This seems to me to be exceedingly presumptuous; the Surrealists imagine that whatever they dredge from their subconscious selves and put down in paint or in words must, essentially, be of some interest or value. I deny this. One of the arts of the poet is to make comprehensible and articulate what might emerge from subconscious sources; one of the great main uses of the intellect is to *select,* from the amorphous mass of subconscious images, those that will best further his imaginative purpose, which is to write the best poem he can.

And question five is, God help us, what is my definition of Poetry?

I, myself, do not read poetry for anything but pleasure. I read only the poems I like. This means, of course, that I have to read a lot of poems I don't like before I find the ones I do, but, when I *do* find the ones I do, then all I can say is, 'Here they are', and read them to myself for pleasure.

Read the poems you like reading. Don't bother whether they're 'important', or if they'll live. What does it matter what poetry *is,* after all? If you want a definition of poetry, say: 'Poetry is what makes me laugh or cry or yawn, what makes my toenails twinkle, what makes me want to do this or that or nothing', and let it go at that. All that matters about poetry is the enjoyment of it, however tragic it may be. All that matters is the eternal movement behind it, the vast undercurrent of human grief, folly, pretension, exaltation, or ignorance, however unlofty the intention of the poem.

You can tear a poem apart to see what makes it technically tick, and say to yourself, when the works are laid out before you, the vowels, the consonants, the rhymes or rhythms, 'Yes, this is *it.* This is why the poem moves me so. It is because of the craftsmanship.' But you're back again where you began.

You're back with the mystery of having been moved by words. The best craftsmanship always leaves holes and gaps in the works of the poem so that something that is *not* in the poem can creep, crawl, flash, or thunder in.

The joy and function of poetry is, and was, the celebration of man, which is also the celebration of God.

1951 1961

The Pleasure Principle

In this essay, the English poet Philip Larkin argues for a reclamation of pleasure as the chief end of poetry. Poetry must return to its primary function of capturing an emotional experience and communicating it to the reader if it is to regain an audience wider than academic critics, scholars, and their students. Larkin worries that "once the other end of the rope is dropped" between poet and general reader, poetry becomes self-involved and obscure, because untested by the challenge of communicating to a reader with a different education or experience. "Hence, no pleasure. Hence, no poetry." First printed in *Listen* 2.3 (1957), the essay has been reprinted from *Required Writing* (1984).

PHILIP LARKIN

The Pleasure Principle

It is sometimes useful to remind ourselves of the simpler aspects of things normally regarded as complicated. Take, for instance, the writing of a poem. It consists of three stages: the first is when a man becomes obsessed with an emotional concept to such a degree that he is compelled to do something about it. What he does is the second stage, namely, construct a verbal device that will reproduce this emotional concept in anyone who cares to read it, anywhere, any time. The third stage is the recurrent situation of people in different times and places setting off the device and re-creating in themselves what the poet felt when he wrote it. The stages are interdependent and all necessary. If there has been no preliminary feeling, the device has nothing to reproduce and the reader will experience nothing. If the second stage has not been well done, the device will not deliver the goods, or will deliver only a few goods to a few people, or will stop delivering them after an absurdly short while. And if there is no third stage, no successful reading, the poem can hardly be said to exist in a practical sense at all.

What a description of this basic tripartite structure shows is that poetry is emotional in nature and theatrical in operation, a skilled re-creation of emotion in other people, and that, conversely, a bad poem is one that never succeeds in doing this. All modes of critical derogation are no more than different ways of saying this, whatever literary, philosophical or moral terminology they employ, and it would not be necessary to point out anything so obvious if present-day poetry did not suggest that it had been forgotten. We seem to be producing a new kind of bad poetry, not the old kind that tries to move the reader and fails, but one that does not even try. Repeatedly he is confronted with pieces that cannot be understood without reference beyond their own limits or whose contented insipidity argues that their authors are merely reminding themselves of what they know already, rather than re-creating it for a third party. The reader, in fact, seems no longer present in the poet's mind as he used to be, as someone who must understand and enjoy the finished product if it is to be a success at all; the assumption now is that no one will read it, and wouldn't understand or enjoy it if they did. Why should this be so? It is not sufficient to say that poetry has lost its audience, and so need no longer consider it: lots of people still read and even buy poetry. More accurately, poetry has lost its old audience, and gained a new one. This has been caused by the consequences of a cunning merger between poet, literary critic and academic critic (three classes now notoriously indistinguishable): it is hardly an exaggeration to say that the poet has gained the happy position wherein he can praise his own poetry in the press and explain it in the class-room, and the reader has been bullied into giving up the consumer's power to say 'I don't like this, bring me something different.' Let him now so much as breathe a word about not liking a poem, and he is in the dock before he can say Edwin Arlington Robinson.[1] And the charge is a grave one: flabby sensibility, insufficient or inadequate critical tools, and inability to meet new verbal and emotional situations. Verdict: guilty, plus a few riders on the prisoner's mental upbringing, addiction to mass amusements, and enfeebled responses. It is time some of you playboys realized, says the judge, that reading a poem is hard work. Fourteen days in stir. Next case.

The cash customers of poetry, therefore, who used to put down their money in the sure and certain hope of enjoyment as if at a theatre or concert hall, were quick to move elsewhere. Poetry was no longer a pleasure. They have been replaced by a humbler squad, whose aim is not pleasure but self-improvement, and who have uncritically accepted the contention that they cannot appreciate poetry without preliminary investment in the intellectual equipment which, by the merest chance, their tutor happens to have about him. In short, the modern poetic audience, when it is not taking in its own washing, is a *student* audience, pure and simple. At first sight this may not seem a bad thing. The poet has at last a moral ascendancy, and his new clientele not only pay for the poetry but pay to have it explained afterwards. Again, if the poet has only himself to please, he is no longer handicapped by the limitations of his audience. And in any case nobody nowadays believes that a worthwhile artist can rely on anything but his own judgement: public taste is always twenty-five years behind, and picks up a style only when it is exploited by the second-rate. All this is true enough. But at bottom poetry, like all art, is inextricably bound up with giving pleasure, and if a poet loses his pleasure-seeking audience he has lost the only audience worth having, for which the dutiful mob that signs on every September is no substitute. And the effect will be felt throughout his work. He will forget that even if he finds what he has to say interesting, others may not. He will concentrate on moral worth or semantic intricacy. Worst of all, his poems will no longer be born of the tension between what be non-verbally feels and what can be got over in common word-usage to someone who hasn't had his experience or education or travel grant, and once the other end of the rope is dropped what results will not be so much obscure or piffling (though it may be both) as an unrealized, 'undramatized' slackness, because he will have lost the habit of testing what he writes by this particular standard. Hence, no pleasure. Hence, no poetry.

What can be done about this? Who wants anything done about it? Certainly not the poet, who is in the unprecedented position of peddling both his work and the standard by which it is judged. Certainly not the new reader, who, like a partner of some unconsummated marriage, has no idea of any-

1. American poet (1869–1935).

thing better. Certainly not the old reader, who has simply replaced one pleasure with another. Only the romantic loiterer who recalls the days when poetry was condemned as sinful might wish things different. But if the medium is in fact to be rescued from among our duties and restored to our pleasures, I can only think that a large-scale revulsion has got to set in against present notions, and that it will have to start with poetry readers asking themselves more frequently whether they do in fact enjoy what they read, and, if not, what the point is of carrying on. And I use 'enjoy' in the commonest of senses, the sense in which we leave a radio on or off. Those interested might like to read David Daiches's essay 'The New Criticism: Some Qualifications' (in *Literary Essays,* 1956); in the meantime, the following note by Samuel Butler may reawaken a furtive itch for freedom: 'I should like to like Schumann's music better than I do; I dare say I could make myself like it better if I tried; but I do not like having to try to make myself like things; I like things that make me like them at once and no trying at all' (*Notebooks,* 1919).

1957

INTRODUCTION TO *ALL WHAT JAZZ*

Leading the charge against modernist difficulty in poetry, Philip Larkin offered perhaps his most cogent remarks on the subject in relation to another art form—jazz. A longtime follower of the traditional jazz style rooted in New Orleans, Larkin was unhappy that the music was becoming increasingly harsh, edgy, and inaccessible, ever since saxophonist Charlie Parker, a major innovator of the bebop revolution in the 1940s and 1950s, abandoned traditional melodies to experiment with complicated rhythms and harmonies. In this excerpt from Larkin's introduction to *All What Jazz* (1970), a collection of his 1960s jazz criticism, he proposes that jazz history parallels the history of art in general: like modern painting and poetry, modern jazz—from bebop to free jazz and other avant-garde styles—neglects the audience and becomes preoccupied with its own material. In all the arts, this narcissistic modernism is elitist and exclusionary. Music, like poetry, should instead reaffirm the human values that give art its value. This excerpt has been taken from *Required Writing* (1984).

PHILIP LARKIN

From Introduction to *All What Jazz*

* * *

And yet again, there was something about the books [of jazz criticism] I was now reading that seemed oddly familiar. This *development,* this *progress,* this *new language* that was more *difficult,* more *complex,* that required you to *work hard at appreciating it,* that you *couldn't expect to understand first go*, that needed *technical and professional knowledge* to evaluate it *at all levels*, this *revolutionary explosion* that *spoke for our time* while at the same time being *traditional* in the *fullest*, the *deepest*. . . . Of course! This was the language of criticism of modern painting, modern poetry, modern music. *Of course!* How glibly I had talked of modern jazz, without realizing the force of the adjective: this was *modern* jazz, and Parker was a modern jazz player just as Picasso was a modern painter and Pound a modern poet. I hadn't realized that jazz had gone from Lascaux to Jackson Pollock[1] in fifty years, but now I realized it relief came flooding in upon me after nearly two years' despondency. I went back to my books: 'After Parker, you had to be something of a musician to follow the best jazz of the day.'[2] Of course! After Picasso! After Pound! There could hardly have been a conciser summary of what I don't believe about art.

The reader may here have the sense of having strayed into a private argument. All I am saying is that the term 'modern', when applied to art, has a more than chronological meaning: it denotes a quality of irresponsibility peculiar to this century, known sometimes as modernism, and once I had classified modern jazz under this heading I knew where I was. I am sure there are books in which the genesis of modernism is set out in full. My own theory is that it is related to an imbalance between the two tensions from which art springs: these are the tension between the artist and his material, and between the artist and his audience, and that in the last seventy-five years or so the second of these has slackened or even perished. In consequence the artist has become over-concerned with his material (hence an age of technical experiment), and, in isolation, has busied himself with the two principal themes of modernism, mystification and outrage. Piqued at being neglected, he has painted portraits with both eyes on the same side of the nose, or smothered a model with paint and rolled her over a blank canvas. He has designed a dwelling-house to be built underground. He has written poems resembling the kind of pictures typists make with their machines during the coffee break, or a novel in gibberish, or a play in which the characters sit in dustbins. He has made a six-hour film of someone asleep. He has carved human figures with large holes in them. And parallel to this activity ("every idiom has its idiot," as an American novelist has written) there has grown up a kind of critical journalism designed to put it over. The terms and the arguments vary with circumstances, but basically the message is: Don't trust your eyes, or ears, or understanding. They'll tell you this is ridiculous, or ugly, or meaningless. Don't believe them. You've got to work at this: after all, you don't expect to understand anything as important as art straight off, do you? I mean, this is pretty complex stuff: if you want to know how complex, I'm giving a course of ninety-six lectures at the local college, starting next week, and you'd be more than welcome. The whole thing's on the rates, you won't have to pay. After all, think what asses people have made of themselves in the past by not understanding art—you don't want to be like that, do you? And so on, and so forth. Keep the suckers spending.

The tension between artist and audience in jazz slackened when the Negro stopped wanting to entertain the white man, and when the audience as a whole, with the end of the Japanese war and the beginning of television,

1. American abstract expressionist painter (1912–1956). Charlie Parker (1920–1955): bebop jazz saxophonist. Pablo Picasso (1881–1973): Spanish expatriate painter. *Lascaux:* site of prehistoric cave paintings in France.

2. "Benny Green, *The Reluctant Art* (1962), pp. 182–3" [Larkin's note].

didn't in any case particularly want to be entertained in that way any longer. The jazz band in the night club declined just as my old interest, the dance band, had declined in the restaurant and hotel: jazz moved, ominously, into the culture belt, the concert halls, university recital rooms and summer schools where the kind of criticism I have outlined has freer play. This was bound to make the re-establishment of any artist–audience nexus more difficult, for universities have long been the accepted stamping ground for the subsidized acceptance of art rather than the real purchase of it—and so, of course, for this kind of criticism, designed as it is to prevent people using their eyes and ears and understandings to report pleasure and discomfort. In such conditions modernism is bound to flourish.

I don't know whether it is worth pursuing my identification of modern jazz with other branches of modern art any further: if I say I dislike both in what seems to me the same way I have made my point. * * *

* * *

* * * To say I don't like modern jazz because it's modernist art simply raises the question of why I don't like modernist art: I have a suspicion that many readers will welcome my grouping of Parker with Picasso and Pound as one of the nicest things I could say about him. Well, to do so settles at least one question: as long as it was only Parker I didn't like, I might believe that my ears had shut up about the age of twenty-five and that jazz had left me behind. My dislike of Pound and Picasso, both of whom pre-date me by a considerable margin, can't be explained in this way. The same can be said of Henry Moore and James Joyce[3] (a textbook case of declension from talent to absurdity). No, I dislike such things not because they are new, but because they are irresponsible exploitations of technique in contradiction of human life as we know it. This is my essential criticism of modernism, whether perpetrated by Parker, Pound or Picasso:[4] it helps us neither to enjoy nor endure. It will divert us as long as we are prepared to be mystified or outraged, but maintains its hold only by being more mystifying and more outrageous: it has no lasting power. Hence the compulsion on every modernist to wade deeper and deeper into violence and obscenity: hence the succession of Parker by Rollins and Coltrane, and of Rollins and Coltrane by Coleman, Ayler and Shepp.[5] In a way, it's a relief: if jazz records are to be one long screech, if painting is to be a blank canvas, if a play is to be two hours of sexual intercourse performed *coram populo,*[6] then let's get it over, the sooner the better, in the hope that human values will then be free to reassert themselves.

* * *

1970

3. Irish novelist (1882–1941). Henry Moore (1898–1986): English abstract sculptor.
4. "The reader will have guessed by now that I am using these pleasantly alliterative names to represent not only their rightful owners but every practitioner who might be said to have succeeded them" [Larkin's note].
5. All jazz saxophonists. Sonny Rollins (b. 1930) and John Coltrane (1926–1967) extended Parker's experimentation with complicated harmonies. Ornette Coleman (b. 1930), Albert Ayler (1936–1970), and Archie Shepp (b. 1937) helped develop free jazz, abandoning to an even greater degree traditional melody and structure.
6. Before the public (Latin).

Personism: A Manifesto

In his 1959 essay, Frank O'Hara parodically deflates the pretensions of other poetic manifestos proliferating at the time and yet offers a valuable point of entry into his poetry and the work of the New York school (which also includes John Ashbery and Kenneth Koch). In contrast to the prophetic exhortations and moralistic tone of many manifesto writers, O'Hara humorously concedes that a manifesto is unlikely to make people who dislike poetry read it and that discussions of formal structures often stray from the essential energy at the heart of good poetry—"You just go on your nerve." But O'Hara also outlines a poetics, and if his implied claims were recast in the standard rhetoric of manifestos, they might read thus: the poet must be witty, never boring; the poet must communicate the spontaneity of imaginative creation; the poet must be effortlessly allusive (this essay nimbly leaps from Romantic poets to surrealist painters to the French New Novel); and the poet must convey a robust sense of personal immediacy and yet not be dully confessional. O'Hara encapsulates this last idea in his self-mocking rubric of "personism," hinting at the strange combination of almost erotically charged intimacy and depersonalized abstraction that characterizes his poetry. Composed on September 3 for Donald Allen's *New American Poetry,* but turned down as too frivolous, the manifesto first appeared in *Yugen,* No. 7 (1961) and has been reprinted from *The Selected Poems of Frank O'Hara* (1972).

FRANK O'HARA

Personism: A Manifesto

Everything is in the poems, but at the risk of sounding like the poor wealthy man's Allen Ginsberg[1] I will write to you because I just heard that one of my fellow poets thinks that a poem of mine that can't be got at one reading is because I was confused too. Now, come on. I don't believe in god, so I don't have to make elaborately sounded structures. I hate Vachel Lindsay,[2] always have; I don't even like rhythm, assonance, all that stuff. You just go on your nerve. If someone's chasing you down the street with a knife you just run, you don't turn around and shout, "Give it up! I was a track star for Mineola Prep."

That's for the writing poems part. As for their reception, suppose you're in love and someone's mistreating (*mal aimé*)[3] you, you don't say, "Hey, you can't hurt me this way, I care!" you just let all the different bodies fall where they may, and they always do may after a few months. But that's not why you fell in love in the first place, just to hang onto life, so you have to take

1. American poet (1926–1997). In "Abstraction in Poetry," *It Is,* No. 3 (1959), Ginsberg had argued that O'Hara's work was developing an abstraction similar to that of painting.
2. American poet (1879–1931), who employed powerful rhythms and emphasized poetry's oral character.
3. Poorly loved (French). Cf. "La Chanson du Mal Aimé" (1913), by Guillaume Apollinaire (1880–1918), French avant-garde and early surrealist poet.

your chances and try to avoid being logical. Pain always produces logic, which is very bad for you.

I'm not saying that I don't have practically the most lofty ideas of anyone writing today, but what difference does that make? They're just ideas. The only good thing about it is that when I get lofty enough I've stopped thinking and that's when refreshment arrives.

But how can you really care if anybody gets it, or gets what it means, or if it improves them. Improves them for what? For death? Why hurry them along? Too many poets act like a middle-aged mother trying to get her kids to eat too much cooked meat, and potatoes with drippings (tears). I don't give a damn whether they eat or not. Forced feeding leads to excessive thinness (effete). Nobody should experience anything they don't need to, if they don't need poetry bully for them. I like the movies too. And after all, only Whitman and Crane and Williams,[4] of the American poets, are better than the movies. As for measure and other technical apparatus, that's just common sense: if you're going to buy a pair of pants you want them to be tight enough so everyone will want to go to bed with you. There's nothing metaphysical about it. Unless, of course, you flatter yourself into thinking that what you're experiencing is "yearning."

Abstraction in poetry, which Allen [Ginsberg] recently commented on in *It Is,* is intriguing. I think it appears mostly in the minute particulars where decision is necessary. Abstraction (in poetry, not in painting) involves personal removal by the poet. For instance, the decision involved in the choice between "the nostalgia *of* the infinite"[5] and "the nostalgia *for* the infinite" defines an attitude towards degree of abstraction. The nostalgia *of* the infinite representing the greater degree of abstraction, removal, and negative capability (as in Keats and Mallarmé).[6] Personism, a movement which I recently founded and which nobody knows about, interests me a great deal, being so totally opposed to this kind of abstract removal that it is verging on a true abstraction for the first time, really, in the history of poetry. Personism is to Wallace Stevens what *la poésie pure* was to Béranger.[7] Personism has nothing to do with philosophy, it's all art. It does not have to do with personality or intimacy, far from it! But to give you a vague idea, one of its minimal aspects is to address itself to one person (other than the poet himself), thus evoking overtones of love without destroying love's life-giving vulgarity, and sustaining the poet's feelings towards the poem while preventing love from distracting him into feeling about the person. That's part of Personism. It was founded by me after lunch with LeRoi Jones[8] on August 27, 1959, a day in which I was in love with someone (not Roi, by the way, a blond). I went back to work and wrote a poem for this person. While I was writing it I was realizing that if I wanted to I could use the telephone instead of writing the poem, and so Personism was born. It's a very exciting movement which will undoubtedly have lots of adherents. It puts the poem squarely between the

4. Walt Whitman (1819–1892), Hart Crane (1899–1932), and William Carlos Williams (1883–1963), American poets.
5. Title of painting by Italian surrealist Giorgio di Chirico (1888–1978).
6. Stéphane Mallarmé (1842–1898): French Symbolist poet. British Romantic poet John Keats (1795–1821) identified his own creative talent as negative capability, the ability to tolerate uncertainty and identify with other people and things.
7. Pierre-Jean de Béranger (1780–1857), French political and satirical poet, whose work is contrasted here with *la poésie pur,* Symbolist doctrine according to which poetry is, like music, patterns of sound. Similarly, the poetry of Wallace Stevens (1879–1955) is contrasted with O'Hara's personism.
8. American poet and playwright (b. 1934); now Amiri Baraka.

poet and the person, Lucky Pierre[9] style, and the poem is correspondingly gratified. The poem is at last between two persons instead of two pages. In all modesty, I confess that it may be the death of literature as we know it. While I have certain regrets, I am still glad I got there before Alain Robbe-Grillet[1] did. Poetry being quicker and surer than prose, it is only just that poetry finish literature off. For a time people thought that Artaud[2] was going to accomplish this, but actually, for all their magnificence, his polemical writings are not more outside literature than Bear Mountain is outside New York State. His relation is no more astounding than Debuffet's[3] to painting.

What can we expect of Personism? (This is getting good, isn't it?) Everything, but we won't get it. It is too new, too vital a movement to promise anything. But it, like Africa, is on the way. The recent propagandists for technique on the one hand, and for content on the other, had better watch out.

September 3, 1959 1961

9. Having sexual intercourse with two other people simultaneously.
1. Experimental French writer (b. 1922) and theorist of the *nouveau roman* (new novel).
2. Antonin Artaud (1896–1948), French writer associated with the experimental "theatre of cruelty."
3. Jean Dubuffet (1901–1985), French painter associated with *art brut* (raw art).

Notes Written on Finally Recording *Howl*

In this essay, a version of which appeared as a liner note to the 1959 recording of *"Howl" and Other Poems,* Allen Ginsberg, the central figure of the Beat movement, explains the poetic innovations, such as "wild phrasing" and "rhythmic buildup," of "Howl"—an important long poem that combined the use of breath units with oracular proclamations and exceptionally long lines. Tracing his development, Ginsberg credits William Carlos Williams' measures based on units of breath and American speech patterns with inspiring him, as did the cadences, tonalities, and visions of William Blake, Walt Whitman, and Jack Kerouac. He also finds sources for "Howl," "Kaddish," "Sunflower Sutra," "America," and other poems in such heterogeneous sources as drug use, a madhouse wail, the Hebrew prophets, and the haiku. Ginsberg emphasizes the rapidity, associative psychology, and Romantic spontaneity of his initial outpourings, which—particularly in such long poems as "Howl" and "Kaddish"—he reshaped and carefully edited before publication. First published in *Evergreen Review* 3.10 (1959), the essay has been reprinted from *Deliberate Prose: Selected Essays 1952–1995* (2000), ed. Bill Morgan.

ALLEN GINSBERG

Notes Written on Finally Recording *Howl*

By 1955 I wrote poetry adapted from prose seeds, journals, scratchings, arranged by phrasing or breath groups into little short-line patterns according to ideas of measure of American speech I'd picked up from William Carlos Williams' imagist[1] preoccupations. I suddenly turned aside in San Francisco, unemployment compensation leisure, to follow my romantic inspiration—Hebraic-Melvillean[2] bardic breath. I thought I wouldn't write a *poem,* but just write what I wanted to without fear, let my imagination go, open secrecy, and scribble magic lines from my real mind—sum up my life—something I wouldn't be able to show anybody, writ for my own soul's ear and a few other golden ears. So the first line of *Howl,* "I saw the best minds etc.," the whole first section typed out madly in one afternoon, a tragic custard-pie comedy of wild phrasing, meaningless images for the beauty of abstract poetry of mind running along making awkward combinations like Charlie Chaplin's walk, long saxophone-like chorus lines I knew Kerouac[3] would hear *sound* of—taking off from his own inspired prose line really a new poetry.

I depended on the word "who" to keep the beat, a base to keep measure, return to and take off from again onto another streak of invention: "who lit cigarettes in boxcars boxcars boxcars," continuing to prophesy what I really knew despite the drear consciousness of the world: "who were visionary Indian angels." Have I really been attacked for this sort of joy? So the poem got awesome, I went on to what my imagination believed true to eternity (for I'd had a beatific illumination years before during which I'd heard Blake's[4] ancient voice and saw the universe unfold in my brain), and what my memory could reconstitute of the data of celestial experiences.

But how sustain a long line in poetry (lest it lapse into prosaic)? It's natural inspiration of the moment that keeps it moving, disparate thinks put down together, shorthand notations of visual imagery, juxtapositions of hydrogen jukebox—abstract *haikus* sustain the mystery and put iron poetry back into the line: the last line of *Sunflower Sutra* is the extreme, one stream of single word associations, summing up. Mind is shapely, art is shapely. Meaning mind practiced in spontaneity invents forms in its own image and gets to last thoughts. Loose ghosts wailing for body try to invade the bodies of living men. I hear ghostly academies in limbo screeching about form.

Ideally each line of *Howl* is a single breath unit. My breath is long—that's the measure, one physical-mental inspiration of thought contained in the elastic of a breath. It probably bugs Williams now, but it's a natural consequence, my own heightened conversation, not cooler average-daily-talk short breath. I get to mouth more madly this way.

1. In the early twentieth century, Imagism emphasized cadenced free verse and direct language. William Carlos Williams (1883–1963), American poet.
2. Herman Melville (1819–1891), American poet, novelist, and author of *Moby-Dick* (1851). *Hebraic:* here, recalling the Hebrew prophets.
3. Jack Kerouac (1922–1969): American novelist and spokesman for the Beat movement. Charlie Chaplin (1889–1977): English actor and film producer, famous for his "tramp" character.
4. William Blake (1757–1827), English visionary, poet, and printmaker. Ginsberg reported having heard in 1948 William Blake's voice reciting "Ah Sun-Flower" and "The Sick Rose."

So these poems are a series of experiments with the formal organization of the long line. Explanations follow. I realized at the time that Whitman's[5] form had rarely been further explored (improved on even) in the U.S.—Whitman always a mountain too vast to be seen. Everybody assumes (with Pound?) (except [Robinson] Jeffers)[6] that his line is a big freakish uncontrollable necessary prosaic goof. No attempt's been made to use it in the light of early twentieth century organization of new speech-rhythm prosody to *build up* large organic structures.

I had an apartment on Nob Hill, got high on peyote, and saw an image of the robot skullface of Moloch[7] in the upper stories of a big hotel glaring into my window; got high weeks later again, the visage was still there in red smoky downtown metropolis, I wandered down Powell street muttering, "Moloch Moloch" all night and wrote *Howl II* nearly intact in cafeteria at foot of Drake Hotel, deep in the hellish vale. Here the long line is used as a stanza form broken into exclamatory units punctuated by a base repetition, Moloch.

The rhythmic paradigm for Part III was conceived and half-written same day as the beginning of *Howl,* I went back later and filled it out. Part I, a lament for the Lamb in America with instances of remarkable lamblike youths; Part II names the monster of mental consciousness that preys on the Lamb; Part III a litany of affirmation of the Lamb in its glory: "O starry spangled shock of Mercy." The structure of Part III, pyramidal, with a graduated longer response to the fixed base.

I remembered the archetypal rhythm of Holy Holy Holy weeping in a bus on Kearny Street, and wrote most of it down in notebook there. That exhausted this set of experiments with a fixed base. I set it as *Footnote to Howl* because it was an extra variation of the form of Part II. (Several variations on these forms, including stanzas of graduated litanies followed by fugues, will be seen in *Kaddish.*)

A lot of these forms developed out of an extreme rhapsodic wail I once heard in a madhouse. Later I wondered if short quiet lyrical poems could be written using the long line. *A Strange New Cottage in Berkeley* and *A Supermarket in California* (written same day) fell in place later that year. Not purposely, I simply followed my angel in the course of compositions.

What if I just simply wrote, in long units and broken short lines, spontaneously noting prosaic realities mixed with emotional upsurges, solitaries? *Transcription of Organ Music* (sensual data), strange writing which passes from prose to poetry and back, like the mind.

What about poem with rhythmic buildup power equal to *Howl* without use of repetitive base to sustain it? *The Sunflower Sutra* (composition time 20 minutes, me at desk scribbling, Kerouac at cottage door waiting for me to finish so we could go off somewhere party) did that, it surprised me, one long who.

Next what happens if you mix long and short lines, single breath remaining the rule of measure? I didn't trust free flight yet, so went back to fixed base to sustain the flow, *America.* After that, a regular formal type long poem in parts, short and long breaths mixed at random, no fixed base, sum of earlier experiments—*In the Baggage Room at Greyhound. In Back of the Real* shows what I was doing with short lines (see sentence above) before I accidentally wrote *Howl.*

5. Walt Whitman (1819–1892), American poet, who sometimes wrote in long, paratactic, free verse lines.

6. Robinson Jeffers (1887–1962) and Ezra Pound (1885–1972), American poets.

7. Deity to which children were sacrificed in ancient Middle Eastern cultures. *Nob Hill:* in San Francisco.

Later I tried for a strong rhythm built up using free short syncopated lines, *Europe! Europe!* a prophecy written in Paris.

Last, the Proem to *Kaddish* (NY 1959 work)—finally, completely free composition, the long line breaking up within itself into short staccato breath units—notations of one spontaneous phrase after another linked within the line by dashes mostly: the long line now perhaps a variable stanzaic unit, measuring groups of related ideas, grouping them—a method of notation. Ending with a hymn in rhythm similar to the synagogue death lament. Passing into dactylic? says Williams? Perhaps not: at least the ear hears itself in Promethean[8] natural measure, not in mechanical count of accent.

All these poems are recorded now as best I can, though with scared love, imperfect to an angelic trumpet in mind. I have quit reading in front of live audiences for a while. I began in obscurity to communicate a live poetry, it's become more a trap and duty than the spontaneous ball it was first.

A word on the Academies: poetry has been attacked by an ignorant and frightened bunch of bores who don't understand how it's made, and the trouble with these creeps is they wouldn't know poetry if it came up and buggered them in broad daylight.

A word on the Politicians: my poetry is angelic ravings, and has nothing to do with dull materialistic vagaries about who should shoot who. The secrets of individual imagination—which are transconceptual and non-verbal—I mean unconditioned spirit—are not for sale to this consciousness, are no use to this world, except perhaps to make it shut its trap and listen to the music of the spheres. Who denies the music of the spheres denies poetry, denies man, and spits on Blake, Shelley,[9] Christ, and Buddha. Meanwhile have a ball. The universe is a new flower. America will be discovered. Who wants a war against roses will have it. Fate tells big lies, and the gay creator dances on his own body in eternity.[1]

July 4, 1959

1959

8. Life-giving, courageously original; in Greek myth, Prometheus stole fire from Olympus for humankind and was severely punished for it.

9. Percy Bysshe Shelley (1792–1822), English Romantic poet.

1. "Need comment on end—This provocative even inflammatory peroration seems to have offended a number of straight poets, and was oft quoted, a declaration of absolute poetic purpose that the critic Richard Howard [b. 1929] still remembered decades later, taking exception to my insistence of 'unconditioned Spirit.' This aggression may have exacerbated the Battle of Anthologies between Open Form and Closed Form poets. An incendiary tract, aimed at both Marxist and CIA Capitalist (*Encounter*) Critics, as well as bourgeois judgmental sociologists, Norman Podhoretz probably in mind" [Ginsberg's note].

THE MYTH OF A NEGRO LITERATURE

A leader of the Black Arts Movement, Amiri Baraka delivered this essay as an address to the American Society for African Culture on March 14, 1962, before he changed his name from LeRoi Jones and at a time when he was in between his early Beat aesthetic and his later black nationalism. Baraka attacks as derivative those writers who produce a "Negro literature" according to Euro-American models for the approval of middle-class white society. Instead, black artists should follow the models in African American music, particularly jazz and the blues, which best exemplify how African traditions can be forged into African American art. From slave songs to avant-garde jazz, black music is rooted in African traditions "translated and transmuted" in America. Black music shows poets the way forward, because it is true to the African American experience of pain, hybridization, and survival—an experience estranged from and invisible to mainstream American culture, yet absolutely central to it. Originally published in the *Saturday Review* 46 (April 20, 1963), the essay has been reprinted from *Home: Social Essays* (1966).

AMIRI BARAKA

From The Myth of a "Negro Literature"

* * *

American Negro music from its inception moved logically and powerfully out of a fusion between African musical tradition and the American experience. It was, and continues to be, a natural, yet highly stylized and personal version of the Negro's life in America. It is, indeed, a chronicler of the Negro's movement, from African slave to American slave, from Freedman to Citizen. And the literature of the blues is a much more profound contribution to Western culture than any other literary contribution made by American Negroes. * * *

* * *

The development of the Negro's music was, as I said, direct and instinctive. It was the one vector out of African culture impossible to eradicate completely. The appearance of blues as a native *American* music signified in many ways the appearance of American Negroes where once there were African Negroes. The emotional fabric of the music was colored by the emergence of an American Negro culture. It signified that culture's strength and vitality. In the evolution of form in Negro music it is possible to see not only the evolution of the Negro as a cultural and social element of American culture, but also the evolution of that culture itself. The "Coon Shout" proposed one version of the American Negro—and of America; Ornette Coleman[1] proposes another. But the point is that both these versions are accurate and informed with a legitimacy of emotional concern nowhere available in what is called "Negro Literature," and certainly not in the middlebrow literature of the white American.

The artifacts of African art and sculpture were consciously eradicated by slavery. Any African art that based its validity on the production of an artifact, *i.e.*, some *material* manifestation such as a wooden statue or a woven cloth, had little chance of survival. It was only the more "abstract" aspects of African culture that could continue to exist in slave America. Africanisms still persist in the music, religion, and popular cultural traditions of American Negroes. However, it is not an African art American Negroes are responsible for, but an American one. The traditions of Africa must be utilized within the culture of the American Negro where they *actually* exist, and not because

1. American jazz musician (b. 1930), who helped pioneer free jazz.

of a defensive rationalization about the *worth* of one's ancestors or an attempt to capitalize on the recent eminence of the "new" African nations. Africanisms do exist in Negro culture, but they have been so translated and transmuted by the American experience that they have become integral parts of that experience.

The American Negro has a definable and legitimate historical tradition, no matter how painful, in America, but it is the only place such a tradition exists, simply because America is the only place the American Negro exists. He is, as William Carlos Williams said, "A pure product of America."[2] [The paradox of the Negro experience in America is that it is a separate experience, but inseparable from the complete fabric of American life.] The history of Western culture begins for the Negro with the importation of the slaves. It is almost as if all Western history before that must be strictly a learned concept. It is only the American experience that can be a persistent cultural catalyst for the Negro. In a sense, history for the Negro, before America, must remain an emotional abstraction. The cultural memory of Africa informs the Negro's life in America, but it is impossible to separate it from its American transformation. Thus, the Negro writer if he wanted to tap his legitimate cultural tradition should have done it by utilizing the entire spectrum of the American experience from the point of view of the emotional history of the black man in this country: as its victim and its chronicler. The soul of such a man, as it exists outside the boundaries of commercial diversion or artificial social pretense. But without a deep commitment to cultural relevance and intellectual purity this was impossible. The Negro as a writer, was always a social object, whether glorifying the concept of white superiority, as a great many early Negro writers did, or in crying out against it, as exemplified by the stock "protest" literature of the thirties. He never moved into the position where he could propose his own symbols, erect his own personal myths, as any great literature must. Negro writing was always "after the fact," *i.e.*, based on known social concepts within the structure of bourgeois idealistic projections of "their America," and an emotional climate that never really existed.

The most successful fiction of most Negro writing is in its emotional content. The Negro protest novelist postures, and invents a protest quite amenable with the tradition of bourgeois American life. He never reaches the central core of the America which *can* cause such protest. The intellectual traditions of the white middle class prevent such exposure of reality, and the black imitators reflect this. The Negro writer on Negro life in America postures, and invents a Negro life, and an America to contain it. And even most of those who tried to rebel against that *invented* America were trapped because they had lost all touch with the reality of their experience within the *real* America, either because of the hidden emotional allegiance to the white middle class, or because they did not realize where the reality of their experience lay. When the serious Negro writer disdained the "middlebrow" model, as is the case with a few contemporary black American writers, he usually rushed headlong into the groves of the Academy, perhaps the most insidious and clever dispenser of middlebrow standards of excellence under the guise of "recognizable tradition." That such recognizable tradition is necessary goes without saying, but even from the great philosophies of Europe a contemporary usage must be established. No poetry has come out of

2. From Williams's poem "To Elsie" (1923).

England of major importance for forty years, yet there are would-be Negro poets who reject the gaudy excellence of 20th century American poetry in favor of disembowelled Academic models of second-rate English poetry, with the notion that somehow it is the only way poetry should be written. It would be better if such a poet listened to Bessie Smith sing *Gimme A Pigfoot,* or listened to the tragic verse of a Billie Holiday,[3] than be content to imperfectly imitate the bad poetry of the ruined minds of Europe. And again, it is this striving for respectability that has it so. For an American, black or white, to say that some hideous imitation of Alexander Pope means more to him, emotionally, than the blues of Ray Charles or Lightnin' Hopkins,[4] it would be required for him to have completely disappeared into the American Academy's vision of a Europeanized and colonial American culture, or to be lying. In the end, the same emotional sterility results. It is somehow much more tragic for the black man.

A Negro literature, to be a legitimate product of the Negro experience in America, must get at that experience in exactly the terms America has proposed for it, in its most ruthless identity. Negro reaction to America is as deep a part of America as the root causes of that reaction, and it is impossible to accurately describe that reaction in terms of the American middle class; because for them, the Negro has never really existed, never been glimpsed in anything even approaching the complete reality of his humanity. The Negro writer has to go from where he actually is, completely outside of that conscious white myopia. That the Negro does exist is the point, and as an element of American culture he is completely misunderstood by Americans. The middlebrow, commercial Negro writer assures the white American that, in fact, he doesn't exist, and that if he does, he does so within the perfectly predictable fingerpainting of white bourgeois sentiment and understanding. Nothing could be further from the truth. The Creoles of New Orleans resisted "Negro" music for a time as raw and raucous, because they thought they had found a place within the white society which would preclude their being Negroes. But they were unsuccessful in their attempts to "disappear" because the whites themselves reminded them that they were still, for all their assimilation, "just coons." And this seems to me an extremely important idea, since it is precisely this bitter insistence that has kept what can be called "Negro Culture" a brilliant amalgam of diverse influences. There was always a border beyond which the Negro could not go, whether musically or socially. There was always a possible limitation to any dilution or excess of cultural or spiritual reference. The Negro could not ever become white and that was his strength; at some point, always, he could not participate in the dominant tenor of the white man's culture, yet he came to understand that culture as well as the white man. It was at this juncture that he had to make use of other resources, whether African, sub-cultural, or hermetic. And it was this boundary, this no-man's-land, that provided the logic and beauty of his music. And this is the only way for the Negro artist to provide his version of America—from that no-man's-land outside the mainstream. A no-man's-land, a black country, completely invisible to white America, but so essentially part of it as to stain its whole being an ominous gray. Were there really

3. Jazz singer (1915–1959). Bessie Smith (1894 or 1898–1937): blues singer.
4. Sam "Lightnin' " Hopkins (1912–1982): blues singer and guitarist. Alexander Pope (1688–1744): English Augustan poet. Ray Charles (b. 1930): jazz, blues, and soul singer.

a Negro literature, now it could flower. At this point when the whole of Western society might go up in flames, the Negro remains an integral part of that society, but continually outside it, a figure like Melville's Bartleby.[5] He is an American, capable of identifying emotionally with the fantastic cultural ingredients of this society, but he is also, forever, outside that culture, an invisible strength within it, an observer. If there is ever a Negro literature, it must disengage itself from the weak, heinous elements of the culture that spawned it, and use its very existence as evidence of a more profound America. But as long as the Negro writer contents himself with the imitation of the useless ugly inelegance of the stunted middle-class mind, academic or popular, and refuses to look around him and "tell it like it is"—preferring the false prestige of the black bourgeoisie or the deceitful "acceptance" of *buy and sell* America, something never included in the legitimate cultural tradition of "his people"—he will be a failure, and what is worse, not even a significant failure. Just another dead American.

1962 1963

5. Extraordinarily passive protagonist of "Bartleby, the Scrivener," an 1853 short story by Herman Melville (1819–1891).

SOME NOTES ON ORGANIC FORM

In the 1950s and 1960s, Anglo-American poet Denise Levertov tried to find new ways of talking about open form, as did other poets associated with the Black Mountain school, such as Charles Olson and Robert Creeley. In her view, poetry should discover the inner distinctiveness of an experience—what the English poet Gerard Manley Hopkins termed *inscape*—instead of imposing on it a preconceived form. Adapting a semi-religious, semi-Romantic vocabulary, Levertov says that poetic inspiration begins in a moment of awed contemplation in "the temple of life." The poet then assembles words in patterns of rhythm, sonority, and recurrent imagery, all in close harmony with the intrinsic nature of the experience. The organic poem—as distinct from either the fixed forms of closed verse, or the shapelessness of some free verse—emerges as a whole, coherent both within itself and in relation to the dictates of the experience. Adapting Creeley's maxim, she insists: "Form is never more than a *revelation* of content." Originally published in *Poetry* 106.6 (September 1965), the piece has been reprinted from *New & Selected Essays* (1992).

DENISE LEVERTOV

Some Notes on Organic Form

For me, back of the idea of organic form is the concept that there is a form in all things (and in our experience) which the poet can discover and reveal. There are no doubt temperamental differences between poets who use prescribed forms and those who look for new ones—people who need a tight schedule to get anything done, and people who have to have a free hand—but the difference in their conception of "content" or "reality" is functionally more important. On the one hand is the idea that content, reality, experience, is essentially fluid and must be given form; on the other, this sense of seeking out inherent, though not immediately apparent, form. Gerard Manley Hopkins[1] invented the word "inscape" to denote intrinsic form, the pattern of essential characteristics both in single objects and (what is more interesting) in objects in a state of relation to each other, and the word "instress" to denote the experiencing of the perception of inscape, the apperception of inscape. In thinking of the process of poetry as I know it, I extend the use of these words, which he seems to have used mainly in reference to sensory phenomena, to include intellectual and emotional experience as well; I would speak of the inscape of an experience (which might be composed of any and all of these elements, including the sensory) or of the inscape of a sequence or constellation of experiences.

A partial definition, then, of organic poetry might be that it is a method of apperception, i.e., of recognizing what we perceive, and is based on an intuition of an order, a form beyond forms, in which forms partake, and of which man's creative works are analogies, resemblances, natural allegories. Such poetry is exploratory.

How does one go about such a poetry? I think it's like this: first there must be an experience, a sequence or constellation of perceptions of sufficient interest, felt by the poet intensely enough to demand of him their equivalence in words: he is *brought to speech*. Suppose there's the sight of the sky through a dusty window, birds and clouds and bits of paper flying through the sky, the sound of music from his radio, feelings of anger and love and amusement roused by a letter just received, the memory of some long-past thought or event associated with what's seen or heard or felt, and an idea, a concept, he has been pondering, each qualifying the other; together with what he knows about history; and what he has been dreaming—whether or not he remembers it—working in him. This is only a rough outline of a possible moment in a life. But the condition of being a poet is that periodically such a cross section, or constellation, of experiences (in which one or another element may predominate) demands, or wakes in him this demand: the poem. The beginning of the fulfillment of this demand is to contemplate, to meditate; words which connote a state in which the heat of feeling warms the intellect. To contemplate comes from "*templum*, temple, a place, a space for observation, marked out by the augur." It means, not simply to observe, to regard, but to do these things in the presence of a god. And to meditate is "to keep the mind in a state of contemplation"; its synonym is "to muse,"

1. English poet (1844–1889).

and to muse comes from a word meaning "to stand with open mouth"—not so comical if we think of "inspiration"—to breathe in.

So—as the poet stands open-mouthed in the temple of life, contemplating his experience, there come to him the first words of the poem: the words which are to be his way in to the poem, if there is to be a poem. The pressure of demand and the meditation on its elements culminate in a moment of vision, of crystallization, in which some inkling of the correspondence between those elements occurs; and it occurs as words. If he forces a beginning before this point, it won't work. These words sometimes remain the first, sometimes in the completed poem their eventual place may be elsewhere, or they may turn out to have been only forerunners, which fulfilled their function in bringing him to the words which are the actual beginning of the poem. It is faithful attention to the experience from the first moment of crystallization that allows those first or those forerunning words to rise to the surface: and with that same fidelity of attention the poet, from that moment of being let in to the possibility of the poem, must follow through, letting the experience lead him through the world of the poem, its unique inscape revealing itself as he goes.

During the writing of a poem the various elements of the poet's being are in communion with each other, and heightened. Ear and eye, intellect and passion, interrelate more subtly than at other times; and the "checking for accuracy," for precision of language, that must take place throughout the writing is not a matter of one element supervising the others but of intuitive interaction between all the elements involved.

In the same way, content and form are in a state of dynamic interaction; the understanding of whether an experience is a linear sequence or a constellation raying out from and into a central focus or axis, for instance, is discoverable only in the work, not before it.

Rhyme, chime, echo, reiteration: they not only serve to knit the elements of an experience but often are the very means, the sole means, by which the density of texture and the returning or circling of perception can be transmuted into language, apperceived. A may lead to E directly through B, C, and D: but if then there is the sharp remembrance or revisioning of A, this return must find its metric counterpart. It could do so by actual repetition of the words that spoke of A the first time (and if this return occurs more than once, one finds oneself with a refrain—not put there because one decided to write something with a refrain at the end of each stanza, but directly because of the demand of the content). Or it may be that since the return to A is now conditioned by the journey through B, C, and D, its words will not be a simple repetition but a variation . . . Again, if B and D are of a complementary nature, then their thought- or feeling-rhyme may find its corresponding word-rhyme. Corresponding images are a kind of nonaural rhyme. It usually happens that within the whole, that is between the point of crystallization that marks the beginning or onset of a poem and the point at which the intensity of contemplation has ceased, there are distinct units of awareness; and it is—for me anyway—these that indicate the duration of stanzas. Sometimes these units are of such equal duration that one gets a whole poem of, say, three-line stanzas, a regularity of pattern that looks, but is not, predetermined.

When my son was eight or nine I watched him make a crayon drawing of a tournament. He was not interested in the forms as such, but was grappling with the need to speak in graphic terms, to say, "And a great crowd of people were watching the jousting knights." There was a need to show the tiers of seats, all those people sitting in them. And out of the need arose a formal design that was beautiful—composed of the rows of shoulders and heads. It is in very much the same way that there can arise, out of fidelity to instress, a design that is the form of the poem—both its total form, its length and pace and tone, and the form of its parts (e.g., the rhythmic relationships of syllables within the line, and of line to line; the sonic relationships of vowels and consonants; the recurrence of images, the play of associations, etc.). "Form follows function" (Louis Sullivan).

Frank Lloyd Wright[2] in his autobiography wrote that the idea of organic architecture is that "the reality of the building lies in the space within it, to be lived in." And he quotes Coleridge: "Such as the life is, such is the form." (Emerson says in his essay "Poetry and Imagination," "Ask the fact for the form.") The *Oxford English Dictionary* quotes Huxley (Thomas, presumably)[3] as stating that he used the word organic "almost as an equivalent for the word 'living.' "

In organic poetry the metric movement, the measure, is the direct expression of the movement of perception. And the sounds, acting together with the measure, are a kind of extended onomatopoeia—i.e., they imitate not the sounds of an experience (which may well be soundless, or to which sounds contribute only incidentally), but the feeling of an experience, its emotional tone, its texture. The varying speed and gait of different strands of perception within an experience (I think of strands of seaweed moving within a wave) result in counterpointed measures.

Thinking about how organic poetry differs from free verse, I wrote that "most free verse is failed organic poetry, that is, organic poetry from which the attention of the writer had been switched off too soon, before the intrinsic form of the experience had been revealed." But Robert Duncan[4] pointed out to me that there is a "free verse" of which this is not true, because it is written not with any desire to seek a form, indeed perhaps with the longing to avoid form (if that were possible) and to express inchoate emotion as purely as possible.[5] There is a contradiction here, however, because if, as I suppose, there is an inscape of emotion, of feeling, it is impossible to avoid presenting something of it if the rhythm or tone of the feeling is given voice in the poem. But perhaps the difference is this: that free verse isolates the "rightness" of each line or cadence—if it seems expressive, then never mind the relation of it to the next; while in organic poetry the peculiar rhythms of the parts are in some degree modified, if necessary, in order to discover the rhythm of the whole.

But doesn't the character of the whole depend on, arise out of, the character of the parts? It does; but it is like painting from nature: suppose you absolutely imitate, on the palette, the separate colors of the various objects you are going to paint; yet when they are closely juxtaposed in the actual painting, you may have to lighten, darken, cloud, or sharpen each color in order to produce an effect equivalent to what you see in nature. Air, light, dust, shadow, and distance have to be taken into account.

2. American architect (1867–1959), like Louis Sullivan (1856–1924).
3. Thomas Huxley (1825–1895): English biologist. Samuel Taylor Coleridge (1772–1834): English Romantic poet. Ralph Waldo Emerson (1803–1882): American poet, essayist, and Transcendentalist.
4. American poet (1919–1988).
5. "See for instance, some of the forgotten poets of the early 20s—also, some of Amy Lowell [1874–1925]—[Carl] Sandburg [1878–1967]—John Gould Fletcher [1886–1950]. Some Imagist poems were written in 'free verse' in this sense, but by no means all" [Levertov's note].

Or one could put it this way: in organic poetry the form sense or "traffic sense," as Stefan Wolpe[6] speaks of it, is ever present along with (yes, paradoxically) fidelity to the revelations of meditation. The form sense is a sort of Stanislavsky[7] of the imagination: putting a chair two feet downstage there, thickening a knot of bystanders upstage left, getting this actor to raise his voice a little and that actress to enter more slowly; all in the interest of a total form he intuits. Or it is a sort of helicopter scout flying over the field of the poem, taking aerial photos and reporting on the state of the forest and its creatures—or over the sea to watch for the schools of herring and direct the fishing fleet toward them.

A manifestation of form sense is the sense the poet's ear has of some rhythmic norm peculiar to a particular poem, from which the individual lines depart and to which they return. I heard Henry Cowell tell that the drone in Indian music is known as the horizon note. Al Kresch,[8] the painter, sent me a quotation from Emerson: "The health of the eye demands a horizon." This sense of the beat or pulse underlying the whole I think of as the horizon note of the poem. It interacts with the nuances or forces of feeling which determine emphasis on one word or another, and decides to a great extent what belongs to a given line. It relates the needs of that feeling-force which dominates the cadence to the needs of the surrounding parts and so to the whole.

Duncan also pointed to what is perhaps a variety of organic poetry: the poetry of linguistic impulse. It seems to me that the absorption in language itself, the awareness of the world of multiple meaning revealed in sound, word, syntax, and the entering into this world in the poem, is as much an experience or constellation of perceptions as the instress of nonverbal sensuous and psychic events. What might make the poet of linguistic impetus appear to be on another tack entirely is that the demands of his realization may seem in opposition to truth as we think of it; that is, in terms of sensual logic. But the apparent distortion of experience in such a poem for the sake of verbal effects is actually a precise adherence to truth, since the experience itself was a verbal one.

Form is never more than a *revelation* of content.[9]

"The law—one perception must immediately and directly lead to a further perception" (Edward Dahlberg,[1] as quoted by Charles Olson in "Projective Verse," *Selected Writings*). I've always taken this to mean, "no loading of the rifts with ore,"[2] because there are to be no rifts. Yet alongside this truth is another truth (that I've learned from Duncan more than from anyone else)—that there must be a place in the poem for rifts too—(never to be stuffed with imported ore). Great gaps between perception and perception which must be leapt across if they are to be crossed at all.

The X-factor, the magic, is when we come to those rifts and make those leaps. A religious devotion to the truth, to the splendor of the authentic,

6. German-born composer (1902–1972) and director of music at Black Mountain College from 1952 to 1956. His music, structured in nonlinear, or "organic," modes, allowed for the unplanned element of ambient noise.
7. Konstantin Stanislavsky (1863–1938): Russian theater director associated with "method" acting, in which the actor makes use of personal memory and emotion to create a believable character.
8. Albert Kresch (b. 1922): American figurative painter. Henry Cowell: American composer (1897–1965).
9. Cf. Robert Creeley's (b. 1926) statement "Form is never more than an extension of content," cited by fellow Black Mountain poet Charles Olson (1910–1970) in his essay "Projective Verse," reprinted above.
1. American poet (1900–1977).
2. Cf. the English Romantic poet John Keats's suggestion in a letter of August 16, 1820, to fellow poet Percy Bysshe Shelley: "be more of an artist, and 'load every rift' of your subject with ore" (echoing English Renaissance poet Edmund Spenser's *Faerie Queene* 2.7.28.5).

involves the writer in a process rewarding in itself; but when that devotion brings us to undreamed abysses and we find ourselves sailing slowly over them and landing on the other side—that's ecstasy.

1965

When We Dead Awaken

One of the preeminent literary figures who helped shape the women's movement of the 1960s and 1970s, Adrienne Rich writes in this essay about her "awakening consciousness" as a woman writer. She uses her own poetic development as an example of a more general trend away from self-effacing formalism toward a feminist poetics. Grounding her insights in her self-transformation as a poet, she fuses social commentary, literary criticism, and personal exploration and thus resists the polarities of the personal and the political. Enacting interpretive "re-vision"—in her view, not a luxury but a survival tool for women—she analyzes disempowering images of femininity in earlier literature. She traces a path from alienation and inert impersonality, through rage at social and cultural victimization, to a poetics of integrated self-expression and liberation. Originally delivered as part of a panel on "The Woman Writer in the Twentieth Century" at the Modern Language Association in 1971 and printed in *College English* 34.1 (October 1972), the essay has been reprinted from the revised version, with introductory paragraphs, in Rich's *On Lies, Secrets, and Silence: Selected Prose, 1966–1978* (1979).

ADRIENNE RICH

When We Dead Awaken: Writing as Re-Vision

The Modern Language Association[1] is both marketplace and funeral parlor for the professional study of Western literature in North America. Like all gatherings of the professions, it has been and remains a "procession of the sons of educated men" (Virginia Woolf):[2] a congeries of old-boys' networks, academicians rehearsing their numb canons in sessions dedicated to the literature of white males, junior scholars under the lash of "publish or perish" delivering papers in the bizarrely lit drawing-rooms of immense hotels: a ritual competition veering between cynicism and desperation.

However, in the interstices of these gentlemanly rites (or, in Mary Daly's words, on the boundaries of this patriarchal space),[3] some feminist scholars, teachers, and graduate students, joined by feminist writers, editors, and publishers, have for a decade been creating more subversive occasions, challenging the sacredness of the gentlemanly canon, sharing the rediscovery of buried works by women, asking women's questions, bringing literary history

1. Association of scholars, critics, and teachers of language and literature.
2. English novelist (1882–1941).
3. "Mary Daly, *Beyond God the Father* (Boston: Beacon, 1971), pp. 40–41" [Rich's note]. Mary Daly (b. 1928): American feminist philosopher and theologian.

and criticism back to life in both senses. The Commission on the Status of Women in the Profession was formed in 1969, and held its first public event in 1970. In 1971 the Commission asked Ellen Peck Killoh, Tillie Olsen, Elaine Reuben, and myself, with Elaine Hedges as moderator, to talk on "The Woman Writer in the Twentieth Century."[4] The essay that follows was written for that forum, and later published, along with the other papers from the forum and workshops, in an issue of *College English* edited by Elaine Hedges ("Women Writing and Teaching," vol. 34, no. 1, October 1972.) With a few revisions, mainly updating, it was reprinted in *American Poets in 1976*, edited by William Heyen (New York: Bobbs-Merrill, 1976). That later text is the one published here.

The challenge flung by feminists at the accepted literary canon, at the methods of teaching it, and at the biased and astigmatic view of male "literary scholarship," has not diminished in the decade since the first Women's Forum; it has become broadened and intensified more recently by the challenges of black and lesbian feminists pointing out that feminist literary criticism itself has overlooked or held back from examining the work of black women and lesbians. The dynamic between a political vision and the demand for a fresh vision of literature is clear: without a growing feminist movement, the first inroads of feminist scholarship could not have been made; without the sharpening of a black feminist consciousness, black women's writing would have been left in limbo between misogynist black male critics and white feminists still struggling to unearth a white women's tradition; without an articulate lesbian/feminist movement, lesbian writing would still be lying in that closet where many of us used to sit reading forbidden books "in a bad light."

Much, much more is yet to be done; and university curricula have of course changed very little as a result of all this. What *is* changing is the availability of knowledge, of vital texts, the visible effects on women's lives of seeing, hearing our wordless or negated experience affirmed and pursued further in language.

Ibsen's[5] *When We Dead Awaken* is a play about the use that the male artist and thinker—in the process of creating culture as we know it—has made of women, in his life and in his work; and about a woman's slow struggling awakening to the use to which her life has been put. Bernard Shaw wrote in 1900 of this play:

> [Ibsen] shows us that no degradation ever devized or permitted is as disastrous as this degradation; that through it women can die into luxuries for men and yet can kill them; that men and women are becoming conscious of this; and that what remains to be seen as perhaps the most interesting of all imminent social developments is what will happen "when we dead awaken."[6]

It's exhilarating to be alive in a time of awakening consciousness; it can also be confusing, disorienting, and painful. This awakening of dead or sleeping consciousness has already affected the lives of millions of women, even

4. The panelists are writers and teachers. Tillie Olsen (b. c. 1913) is a prominent Jewish American fiction writer.
5. Henrik Ibsen (1828–1906), Norwegian playwright and poet.
6. "G. B. Shaw, The Quintessence of Ibsenism (New York: Hill & Wang, 1922), p. 139" [Rich's note]. George Bernard Shaw (1856–1950), Irish playwright and critic.

those who don't know it yet. It is also affecting the lives of men, even those who deny its claims upon them. The argument will go on whether an oppressive economic class system is responsible for the oppressive nature of male/female relations, or whether, in fact, patriarchy—the domination of males—is the original model of oppression on which all others are based. But in the last few years the women's movement has drawn inescapable and illuminating connections between our sexual lives and our political institutions. The sleepwalkers are coming awake, and for the first time this awakening has a collective reality; it is no longer such a lonely thing to open one's eyes.

Re-vision—the act of looking back, of seeing with fresh eyes, of entering an old text from a new critical direction—is for women more than a chapter in cultural history: it is an act of survival. Until we can understand the assumptions in which we are drenched we cannot know ourselves. And this drive to self-knowledge, for women, is more than a search for identity: it is part of our refusal of the self-destructiveness of male-dominated society. A radical critique of literature, feminist in its impulse, would take the work first of all as a clue to how we live, how we have been living, how we have been led to imagine ourselves, how our language has trapped as well as liberated us, how the very act of naming has been till now a male prerogative, and how we can begin to see and name—and therefore live—afresh. A change in the concept of sexual identity is essential if we are not going to see the old political order reassert itself in every new revolution. We need to know the writing of the past, and know it differently than we have ever known it; not to pass on a tradition but to break its hold over us.

For writers, and at this moment for women writers in particular, there is the challenge and promise of a whole new psychic geography to be explored. But there is also a difficult and dangerous walking on the ice, as we try to find language and images for a consciousness we are just coming into, and with little in the past to support us. I want to talk about some aspects of this difficulty and this danger.

Jane Harrison, the great classical anthropologist, wrote in 1914 in a letter to her friend Gilbert Murray:

> By the by, about "Women," it has bothered me often—why do women never want to write poetry about Man as a sex—why is Woman a dream and a terror to man and not the other way around? . . . Is it mere convention and propriety, or something deeper?[7]

I think Jane Harrison's question cuts deep into the myth-making tradition, the romantic tradition; deep into what women and men have been to each other; and deep into the psyche of the woman writer. Thinking about that question, I began thinking of the work of two twentieth-century women poets, Sylvia Plath and Diane Wakoski. It strikes me that in the work of both Man appears as, if not a dream, a fascination and a terror; and that the source of the fascination and the terror is, simply, Man's power—to dominate, tyrannize, choose, or reject the woman. The charisma of Man seems to come purely from his power over her and his control of the world by force, not from anything fertile or life-giving in him. And, in the work of both these poets, it is finally the woman's sense of *herself*—embattled, possessed—that gives the poetry its dynamic charge, its rhythms of struggle, need, will, and

7. "J. G. Stewart, *Jane Ellen Harrison: A Portrait from Letters* (London: Merlin, 1959), p. 140" [Rich's note]. Jane Harrison (1850–1928): English archeologist. Gilbert Murray (1866–1957): English classicist.

female energy. Until recently this female anger and this furious awareness of the Man's power over her were not available materials to the female poet, who tended to write of Love as the source of her suffering, and to view that victimization by Love as an almost inevitable fate. Or, like Marianne Moore and Elizabeth Bishop,[8] she kept sexuality at a measured and chiseled distance in her poems.

One answer to Jane Harrison's question has to be that historically men and women have played very different parts in each others' lives. Where woman has been a luxury for man, and has served as the painter's model and the poet's muse, but also as comforter, nurse, cook, bearer of his seed, secretarial assistant, and copyist of manuscripts, man has played a quite different role for the female artist. Henry James repeats an incident which the writer Prosper Mérimée described, of how, while he was living with George Sand,

> he once opened his eyes, in the raw winter dawn, to see his companion, in a dressing-gown, on her knees before the domestic hearth, a candlestick beside her and a red *madras* round her head, making bravely, with her own hands the fire that was to enable her to sit down betimes to urgent pen and paper. The story represents him as having felt that the spectacle chilled his ardor and tried his taste; her appearance was unfortunate, her occupation an inconsequence, and her industry a reproof—the result of all which was a lively irritation and an early rupture.[9]

The specter of this kind of male judgment, along with the misnaming and thwarting of her needs by a culture controlled by males, has created problems for the woman writer: problems of contact with herself, problems of language and style, problems of energy and survival.

In rereading Virginia Woolf's *A Room of One's Own* (1929) for the first time in some years, I was astonished at the sense of effort, of pains taken, of dogged tentativeness, in the tone of that essay. And I recognized that tone. I had heard it often enough, in myself and in other women. It is the tone of a woman almost in touch with her anger, who is determined not to appear angry, who is *willing* herself to be calm, detached, and even charming in a roomful of men where things have been said which are attacks on her very integrity. Virginia Woolf is addressing an audience of women, but she is acutely conscious—as she always was—of being overheard by men: by Morgan and Lytton and Maynard Keynes and for that matter by her father, Leslie Stephen.[1] She drew the language out into an exacerbated thread in her determination to have her own sensibility yet protect it from those masculine presences. Only at rare moments in that essay do you hear the passion in her voice; she was trying to sound as cool as Jane Austen,[2] as Olympian as

8. American poets from earlier generations.
9. "Henry James, 'Notes on Novelists,' in *Selected Literary Criticism of Henry James*, Morris Shapira, ed. (London: Heinemann, 1963), pp. 157–58" [Rich's note]. Prosper Mérimée (1803–1870): French Romantic author. George Sand (1804–1876): male pseudonym of French novelist Armandine-Aurore-Lucie (or Lucile) Dupin. *Madras:* brightly colored handkerchief worn on the head.
1. "*A. R., 1978:* This intuition of mine was corroborated when, early in 1978, I read the correspondence between Woolf and Dame Ethel Smyth (Henry W. and Albert A. Berg Collection, The New York Public Library, Astor, Lenox and Tilden Foundations); in a letter dated June 8, 1933, Woolf speaks of having kept her own personality out of *A Room of One's Own* lest she not be taken seriously: '. . . how personal, so will they say, rubbing their hands with glee, women always are; *I even hear them as I write.*' (Italics mine.)" [Rich's note]. Edward Morgan (E. M.) Forster (1879–1970): English novelist. Lytton Strachey (1880–1932): English biographer. John Maynard Keynes (1883–1946): English economist. Leslie Stephen (1832–1904): English critic.
2. English novelist (1775–1817).

Shakespeare, because that is the way the men of the culture thought a writer should sound.

No male writer has written primarily or even largely for women, or with the sense of women's criticism as a consideration when he chooses his materials, his theme, his language. But to a lesser or greater extent, every woman writer has written for men even when, like Virginia Woolf, she was supposed to be addressing women. If we have come to the point when this balance might begin to change, when women can stop being haunted, not only by "convention and propriety" but by internalized fears of being and saying themselves, then it is an extraordinary moment for the woman writer—and reader.

I have hesitated to do what I am going to do now, which is to use myself as an illustration. For one thing, it's a lot easier and less dangerous to talk about other women writers. But there is something else. Like Virginia Woolf, I am aware of the women who are not with us here because they are washing the dishes and looking after the children. Nearly fifty years after she spoke, the fact remains largely unchanged. And I am thinking also of women whom she left out of the picture altogether—women who are washing other people's dishes and caring for other people's children, not to mention women who went on the streets last night in order to feed their children. We seem to be special women here, we have liked to think of ourselves as special, and we have known that men would tolerate, even romanticize us as special, as long as our words and actions didn't threaten their privilege of tolerating or rejecting us and our work according to *their* ideas of what a special woman ought to be. An important insight of the radical women's movement has been how divisive and how ultimately destructive is this myth of the special woman, who is also the token woman. Every one of us here in this room has had great luck—we are teachers, writers, academicians; our own gifts could not have been enough, for we all know women whose gifts are buried or aborted. Our struggles can have meaning and our privileges—however precarious under patriarchy—can be justified only if they can help to change the lives of women whose gifts—and whose very being—continue to be thwarted and silenced.

My own luck was being born white and middle-class into a house full of books, with a father who encouraged me to read and write. So for about twenty years I wrote for a particular man, who criticized and praised me and made me feel I was indeed "special." The obverse side of this, of course, was that I tried for a long time to please him, or rather, not to displease him. And then of course there were other men—writers, teachers—the Man, who was not a terror or a dream but a literary master and a master in other ways less easy to acknowledge. And there were all those poems about women, written by men: it seemed to be a given that men wrote poems and women frequently inhabited them. These women were almost always beautiful, but threatened with the loss of beauty, the loss of youth—the fate worse than death. Or, they were beautiful and died young, like Lucy and Lenore. Or, the woman was like Maud Gonne,[3] cruel and disastrously mistaken, and the poem reproached her because she had refused to become a luxury for the poet.

A lot is being said today about the influence that the myths and images of women have on all of us who are products of culture. I think it has been a

3. Irish patriot (1865–1953), memorialized in the poetry of her refused suitor W. B. Yeats (1865–1939). *Lucy and Lenore*: tragic female figures from the poetry of William Wordsworth (1770–1850) and Edgar Allan Poe (1809–1849), respectively.

peculiar confusion to the girl or woman who tries to write because she is peculiarly susceptible to language. She goes to poetry or fiction looking for *her* way of being in the world, since she too has been putting words and images together; she is looking eagerly for guides, maps, possibilities; and over and over in the "words' masculine persuasive force" of literature she comes up against something that negates everything she is about: she meets the image of Woman in books written by men. She finds a terror and a dream, she finds a beautiful pale face, she finds La Belle Dame Sans Merci, she finds Juliet or Tess or Salomé,[4] but precisely what she does not find is that absorbed, drudging, puzzled, sometimes inspired creature, herself, who sits at a desk trying to put words together.

So what does she do? What did I do? I read the older women poets with their peculiar keenness and ambivalence: Sappho, Christina Rossetti, Emily Dickinson, Elinor Wylie, Edna Millay, H. D.[5] I discovered that the woman poet most admired at the time (by men) was Marianne Moore, who was maidenly, elegant, intellectual, discreet. But even in reading these women I was looking in them for the same things I had found in the poetry of men, because I wanted women poets to be the equals of men, and to be equal was still confused with sounding the same.

I know that my style was formed first by male poets: by the men I was reading as an undergraduate—Frost, Dylan Thomas, Donne, Auden, MacNiece, Stevens, Yeats. What I chiefly learned from them was craft.[6] But poems are like dreams: in them you put what you don't know you know. Looking back at poems I wrote before I was twenty-one, I'm startled because beneath the conscious craft are glimpses of the split I even then experienced between the girl who wrote poems, who defined herself in writing poems, and the girl who was to define herself by her relationships with men. "Aunt Jennifer's Tigers" (1951), written while I was a student, looks with deliberate detachment at this split.[7] In writing this poem, composed and apparently cool as it is, I thought I was creating a portrait of an imaginary woman. But this woman suffers from the opposition of her imagination, worked out in tapestry, and her life-style, "ringed with ordeals she was mastered by." It was important to me that Aunt Jennifer was a person as distinct from myself as possible—distanced by the formalism of the poem, by its objective, observant tone—even by putting the woman in a different generation.

In those years formalism was part of the strategy—like asbestos gloves, it allowed me to handle materials I couldn't pick up bare-handed. A later strategy was to use the persona of a man, as I did in "The Loser" (1958):

4. In the Bible, a woman who beguiled King Herod into beheading John the Baptist. *La Belle Dame Sans Merci:* woman whose lover dies after she refuses him, in French poem by Alain Chartier (c. 1385–c. 1433), and who seduces a knight, in a ballad by John Keats (1795–1821). *Juliet:* female protagonist of Shakespeare's *Romeo and Juliet. Tess:* tragic heroine of the novel *Tess of the d'Urbervilles,* by Thomas Hardy (1840–1928).

5. American poet (1886–1961), like Emily Dickinson (1830–1886), Elinor Wylie (1885–1928), and Edna St. Vincent Millay (1892–1950). Sappho (c. 610–c. 580 B.C.E.): Greek lyric poet. Christina Rossetti (1830–1894): English poet.

6. "*A. R., 1978:* Yet I spent months, at sixteen, memorizing and writing imitations of Millay's sonnets; and in notebooks of that period I find what are obviously attempts to imitate Dickinson's metrics and verbal compression. I knew H. D. only through anthologized lyrics; her epic poetry was not then available to me" [Rich's note]. Robert Frost (1874–1963): American poet. Dylan Thomas (1914–1953): Welsh poet. John Donne (1572–1631): English poet. W. H. Auden (1907–1973): Anglo-American poet. Wallace Stevens (1879–1955): American poet. Louis MacNeice (1907–1963): Anglo-Irish poet.

7. The original essay reprinted "Aunt Jennifer's Tigers," on p. 459 of this volume.

A man thinks of the woman he once loved: first, after her wedding, and then nearly a decade later.

I

I kissed you, bride and lost, and went
home from that bourgeois sacrament,
your cheek still tasting cold upon
my lips that gave you benison[8]
with all the swagger that they knew—
as losers somehow learn to do.

Your wedding made my eyes ache; soon
the world would be worse off for one
more golden apple dropped to ground
without the least protesting sound,
and you would windfall lie, and we
forget your shimmer on the tree.

Beauty is always wasted: if
not Mignon's song sung to the deaf,
at all events to the unmoved.
A face like yours cannot be loved
long or seriously enough.
Almost, we seem to hold it off.

II

Well, you are tougher than I thought.
Now when the wash with ice hangs taut
this morning of St. Valentine,
I see you strip the squeaking line,
your body weighed against the load,
and all my groans can do no good.

Because you are still beautiful,
though squared and stiffened by the pull
of what nine windy years have done.
You have three daughters, lost a son.
I see all your intelligence
flung into that unwearied stance.

My envy is of no avail.
I turn my head and wish him well
who chafed your beauty into use
and lives forever in a house
lit by the friction of your mind.
You stagger in against the wind.

I finished college, published my first book by a fluke, as it seemed to me, and broke off a love affair. I took a job, lived alone, went on writing, fell in love. I was young, full of energy, and the book seemed to mean that others

8. Blessing.

agreed I was a poet. Because I was also determined to prove that as a woman poet I could also have what was then defined as a "full" woman's life, I plunged in my early twenties into marriage and had three children before I was thirty. There was nothing overt in the environment to warn me: these were the fifties, and in reaction to the earlier wave of feminism, middle-class women were making careers of domestic perfection, working to send their husbands through professional schools, then retiring to raise large families. People were moving out to the suburbs, technology was going to be the answer to everything, even sex; the family was in its glory. Life was extremely private; women were isolated from each other by the loyalties of marriage. I have a sense that women didn't talk to each other much in the fifties—not about their secret emptinesses, their frustrations. I went on trying to write; my second book and first child appeared in the same month. But by the time that book came out I was already dissatisfied with those poems, which seemed to me mere exercises for poems I hadn't written. The book was praised, however, for its "gracefulness"; I had a marriage and a child. If there were doubts, if there were periods of null depression or active despairing, these could only mean that I was ungrateful, insatiable, perhaps a monster.

About the time my third child was born, I felt that I had either to consider myself a failed woman and a failed poet, or to try to find some synthesis by which to understand what was happening to me. What frightened me most was the sense of drift, of being pulled along on a current which called itself my destiny, but in which I seemed to be losing touch with whoever I had been, with the girl who had experienced her own will and energy almost ecstatically at times, walking around a city or riding a train at night or typing in a student room. In a poem about my grandmother I wrote (of myself): "A young girl, thought sleeping, is certified dead" ("Halfway").[9] I was writing very little, partly from fatigue, that female fatigue of suppressed anger and loss of contact with my own being; partly from the discontinuity of female life with its attention to small chores, errands, work that others constantly undo, small children's constant needs. What I did write was unconvincing to me; my anger and frustration were hard to acknowledge in or out of poems because in fact I cared a great deal about my husband and my children. Trying to look back and understand that time I have tried to analyze the real nature of the conflict. Most, if not all, human lives are full of fantasy—passive day-dreaming which need not be acted on. But to write poetry or fiction, or even to think well, is not to fantasize, or to put fantasies on paper. For a poem to coalesce, for a character or an action to take shape, there has to be an imaginative transformation of reality which is in no way passive. And a certain freedom of the mind is needed—freedom to press on, to enter the currents of your thought like a glider pilot, knowing that your motion can be sustained, that the buoyancy of your attention will not be suddenly snatched away. Moreover, if the imagination is to transcend and transform experience it has to question, to challenge, to conceive of alternatives, perhaps to the very life you are living at that moment. You have to be free to play around with the notion that day might be night, love might be hate; nothing can be too sacred for the imagination to turn into its opposite or to call experimentally by another name. For writing is re-naming. Now, to be maternally with small children all day in the old way, to be with a man in the old way of marriage, requires a holding-back, a putting-aside of that imaginative activity, and

9. See Rich's *The Fact of a Doorframe: Poems Selected and New 1950–1984* (1984), p. 73.

demands instead a kind of conservatism. I want to make it clear that I am *not* saying that in order to write well, or think well, it is necessary to become unavailable to others, or to become a devouring ego. This has been the myth of the masculine artist and thinker; and I do not accept it. But to be a female human being trying to fulfill traditional female functions in a traditional way *is* in direct conflict with the subversive function of the imagination. The word traditional is important here. There must be ways, and we will be finding out more and more about them, in which the energy of creation and the energy of relation can be united. But in those years I always felt the conflict as a failure of love in myself. I had thought I was choosing a full life: the life available to most men, in which sexuality, work, and parenthood could coexist. But I felt, at twenty-nine, guilt toward the people closest to me, and guilty toward my own being.

I wanted, then, more than anything, the one thing of which there was never enough: time to think, time to write. The fifties and early sixties were years of rapid revelations: the sit-ins and marches in the South, the Bay of Pigs,[1] the early antiwar movement, raised large questions—questions for which the masculine world of the academy around me seemed to have expert and fluent answers. But I needed to think for myself—about pacifism and dissent and violence, about poetry and society, and about my own relationship to all these things. For about ten years I was reading in fierce snatches, scribbling in notebooks, writing poetry in fragments; I was looking desperately for clues, because if there were no clues then I thought I might be insane. I wrote in a notebook about this time:

> Paralyzed by the sense that there exists a mesh of relationships—e.g., between my anger at the children, my sensual life, pacifism, sex (I mean sex in its broadest significance, not merely sexual desire)—an interconnectedness which, if I could see it, make it valid, would give me back myself, make it possible to function lucidly and passionately. Yet I grope in and out among these dark webs.

I think I began at this point to feel that politics was not something "out there" but something "in here" and of the essence of my condition.

In the late fifties I was able to write, for the first time, directly about experiencing myself as a woman. The poem was jotted in fragments during children's naps, brief hours in a library, or at 3:00 A.M. after rising with a wakeful child. I despaired of doing any continuous work at this time. Yet I began to feel that my fragments and scraps had a common consciousness and a common theme, one which I would have been very unwilling to put on paper at an earlier time because I had been taught that poetry should be "universal," which meant, of course, nonfemale. Until then I had tried very much *not* to identify myself as a female poet. Over two years I wrote a ten-part poem called "Snapshots of a Daughter-in-Law" (1958–1960), in a longer looser mode than I'd ever trusted myself with before. It was an extraordinary relief to write that poem. It strikes me now as too literary, too dependent on allusion; I hadn't found the courage yet to do without authorities, or even to use the pronoun "I"—the woman in the poem is always "she." One section of it, No. 2, concerns a woman who thinks she is going mad; she is haunted

1. Failed attempt by U.S.-financed Cuban exiles to overthrow Fidel Castro (b. 1926/27) on April 17, 1961.

by voices telling her to resist and rebel, voices which she can hear but not obey.[2]

The poem "Orion," written five years later, is a poem of reconnection with a part of myself I had felt I was losing—the active principle, the energetic imagination, the "half-brother" whom I projected, as I had for many years, into the constellation Orion. It's no accident that the words "cold and egotistical" appear in this poem, and are applied to myself.[3] The choice still seemed to be between "love"—womanly, maternal love, altruistic love—a love defined and ruled by the weight of an entire culture; and egotism—a force directed by men into creation, achievement, ambition, often at the expense of others, but justifiably so. For weren't they men, and wasn't that their destiny as womanly, selfless love was ours? We know now that the alternatives are false ones—that the word "love" is itself in need of re-vision.

There is a companion poem to "Orion," written three years later, in which at last the woman in the poem and the woman writing the poem become the same person. It is called "Planetarium," and it was written after a visit to a real planetarium, where I read an account of the work of Caroline Herschel, the astronomer, who worked with her brother William, but whose name remained obscure, as his did not.[4]

In closing I want to tell you about a dream I had last summer. I dreamed I was asked to read my poetry at a mass women's meeting, but when I began to read, what came out were the lyrics of a blues song. I share this dream with you because it seemed to me to say something about the problems and the future of the woman writer, and probably of women in general. The awakening of consciousness is not like the crossing of a frontier—one step and you are in another country. Much of woman's poetry has been of the nature of the blues song: a cry of pain, of victimization, or a lyric of seduction.[5] And today, much poetry by women—and prose for that matter—is charged with anger. I think we need to go through that anger, and we will betray our own reality if we try, as Virginia Woolf was trying, for an objectivity, a detachment, that would make us sound more like Jane Austen or Shakespeare. We know more than Jane Austen or Shakespeare knew: more than Jane Austen because our lives are more complex, more than Shakespeare because we know more about the lives of women—Jane Austen and Virginia Woolf included.

Both the victimization and the anger experienced by women are real, and have real sources, everywhere in the environment, built into society, language, the structures of thought. They will go on being tapped and explored by poets, among others. We can neither deny them, nor will we rest there. A new generation of women poets is already working out of the psychic energy released when women begin to move out towards what the feminist philosopher Mary Daly has described as the "new space" on the boundaries of patriarchy.[6] Women are speaking to and of women in these poems, out of

2. The original essay quoted section 2 of "Snapshots of a Daughter-in-Law," on p. 459 of this volume.
3. The original essay reprinted "Orion," on p. 464 of this volume.
4. The original essay reprinted "Planetarium," on p. 465 of this volume. Caroline Herschel (1750–1848), German-born British astronomer and brother of Sir William Herschel (1738–1822).
5. "*A. R., 1978:* When I dreamed that dream, was I wholly ignorant of the tradition of Bessie Smith [1894 or 1898–1937] and other women's blues lyrics which transcended victimization to sing of resistance and independence?" [Rich's note].
6. "Mary Daly, *Beyond God the Father: Towards a Philosophy of Women's Liberation* (Boston: Beacon, 1973)" [Rich's note].

a newly released courage to name, to love each other, to share risk and grief and celebration.

To the eye of a feminist, the work of Western male poets now writing reveals a deep, fatalistic pessimism as to the possibilities of change, whether societal or personal, along with a familiar and threadbare use of women (and nature) as redemptive on the one hand, threatening on the other; and a new tide of phallocentric sadism and overt woman-hating which matches the sexual brutality of recent films. "Political" poetry by men remains stranded amid the struggles for power among male groups; in condemning U.S. imperialism or the Chilean junta the poet can claim to speak for the oppressed while remaining, as male, part of a system of sexual oppression. The enemy is always outside the self, the struggle somewhere else. The mood of isolation, self-pity, and self-imitation that pervades "nonpolitical" poetry suggests that a profound change in masculine consciousness will have to precede any new male poetic—or other—inspiration. The creative energy of patriarchy is fast running out; what remains is its self-generating energy for destruction. As women, we have our work cut out for us.

1971 1972, 1979

Feeling into Words

The Irish poet and Nobel laureate Seamus Heaney conceived of poetry as being at once public and personal, political and autobiographical. In this early essay, originally delivered as a lecture at London's Royal Society of Literature in 1974, he explores the poet's multifaceted vocation. Poetry, in Heaney's view, plumbs the depths of experience, giving shape and heft to what would otherwise remain hidden and inarticulate. Using his own work as an example, Heaney argues that a successful poem bears the watermark of the poet's voice and that its technique, beyond craft, reveals a unique relationship to the world. Heaney also describes how the eruption of tensions between Protestants and Catholics in Northern Ireland affected his work in the late 1960s and early 1970s. "From that moment," he explains, "the problems of poetry moved from being simply a matter of achieving the satisfactory verbal icon to being a search for images and symbols adequate to our predicament." In the shadow of the violent Troubles, Heaney wrote his famous "bog poems," which he describes as exploring analogies between the contemporary bloodshed and ancient sacrificial rites. The essay was originally published in the journal *Essays by Diverse Hands*, New Series 40 (1979) and has been reprinted from the slightly revised version in *Preoccupations: Selected Prose, 1968–1978* (1980).

SEAMUS HEANEY

Feeling into Words

I intend to retrace some paths into what William Wordsworth called in *The Prelude*[1] 'the hiding places'.

> The hiding places of my power
> Seem open; I approach, and then they close;
> I see by glimpses now; when age comes on,
> May scarcely see at all, and I would give,
> While yet we may, as far as words can give,
> A substance and a life to what I feel:
> I would enshrine the spirit of the past
> For future restoration.

Implicit in those lines is a view of poetry which I think is implicit in the few poems I have written that give me any right to speak: poetry as divination, poetry as revelation of the self to the self, as restoration of the culture to itself; poems as elements of continuity, with the aura and authenticity of archaeological finds, where the buried shard has an importance that is not diminished by the importance of the buried city; poetry as a dig, a dig for finds that end up being plants.

'Digging', in fact, was the name of the first poem I wrote where I thought my feelings had got into words, or to put it more accurately, where I thought my *feel* had got into words. Its rhythms and noises still please me, although there are a couple of lines in it that have more of the theatricality of the gunslinger than the self-absorption of the digger. I wrote it in the summer of 1964, almost two years after I had begun to 'dabble in verses'. This was the first place where I felt I had done more than make an arrangement of words: I felt that I had let down a shaft into real life. The facts and surfaces of the thing were true, but more important, the excitement that came from naming them gave me a kind of insouciance and a kind of confidence. I didn't care who thought what about it: somehow, it had surprised me by coming out with a stance and an idea that I would stand over[.][2]

As I say, I wrote it down years ago; yet perhaps I should say that I dug it up, because I have come to realize that it was laid down in me years before that even. The pen/spade analogy was the simple heart of the matter and *that* was simply a matter of almost proverbial common sense. As a child on the road to and from school, people used to ask you what class you were in and how many slaps you'd got that day and invariably they ended up with an exhortation to keep studying because 'learning's easy carried' and 'the pen's lighter than the spade'. And the poem does no more than allow that bud of wisdom to exfoliate, although the significant point in this context is that at the time of writing I was not aware of the proverbial structure at the back of my mind. Nor was I aware that the poem was an enactment of yet another digging metaphor that came back to me years later. This was the rhyme we

1. Autobiographical epic (1850) by the English Romantic poet (1770–1850).

2. The original essay reprinted lines 25–31 of "Digging," on p. 723 of this volume.

used to chant on the road to school, though, as I have said before, we were not fully aware of what we were dealing with:

> 'Are your praties[3] dry
> And are they fit for digging?'
> 'Put in your spade and try,'
> Says Dirty-Faced McGuigan.

There digging becomes a sexual metaphor, an emblem of initiation, like putting your hand into the bush or robbing the nest, one of the various natural analogies for uncovering and touching the hidden thing. I now believe that the 'Digging' poem had for me the force of an initiation: the confidence I mentioned arose from a sense that perhaps I could do this poetry thing too, and having experienced the excitement and release of it once, I was doomed to look for it again and again.

I don't want to overload 'Digging' with too much significance. It is a big coarse-grained navvy of a poem, but it is interesting as an example—and not just as an example of what one reviewer called 'mud-caked fingers in Russell Square',[4] for I don't think that the subject-matter has any particular virtue in itself—it is interesting as an example of what we call 'finding a voice'.

Finding a voice means that you can get your own feeling into your own words and that your words have the feel of you about them; and I believe that it may not even be a metaphor, for a poetic voice is probably very intimately connected with the poet's natural voice, the voice that he hears as the ideal speaker of the lines he is making up.

In his novel *The First Circle,* Solzhenitzyn[5] sets the action in a prison camp on the outskirts of Moscow where the inmates are all highly skilled technicians forced to labour at projects dreamed up by Stalin. The most important of these is an attempt to devise a mechanism to bug a phone. But what is to be special about this particular bugging device is that it will not simply record the voice and the message but that it will identify the essential sound patterns of the speaker's voice; it will discover, in the words of the narrative, 'what it is that makes every human voice unique', so that no matter how the speaker disguises his accent or changes his language, the fundamental structure of his voice will be caught. The idea was that a voice is like a fingerprint, possessing a constant and unique signature that can, like a fingerprint, be recorded and employed for identification.

Now one of the purposes of a literary education as I experienced it was to turn the student's ear into a poetic bugging device, so that a piece of verse denuded of name and date could be identified by its diction, tropes and cadences. And this secret policing of English verse was also based on the idea of a style as a signature. But what I wish to suggest is that there is a connection between the core of a poet's speaking voice and the core of his poetic voice, between his original accent and his discovered style. I think that the discovery of a way of writing that is natural and adequate to your sensibility depends on the recovery of that essential quick which Solzhenitzyn's technicians were trying to pin down. This is the absolute register to which your proper music has to be tuned.

How, then, do you find it? In practice, you hear it coming from somebody

3. Potatoes (Irish).
4. In London. *Navvy:* unskilled laborer (British).
5. Aleksandr Solzhenitsyn (b. 1918), Russian novelist who drew on his own experiences in the Soviet prisons of Joseph Stalin (1879–1953) in the late 1940s for *The First Circle.*

else, you hear something in another writer's sounds that flows in through your ear and enters the echo-chamber of your head and delights your whole nervous system in such a way that your reaction will be, 'Ah, I wish I had said that, in that particular way'. This other writer, in fact, has spoken something essential to you, something you recognize instinctively as a true sounding of aspects of yourself and your experience. And your first steps as a writer will be to imitate, consciously or unconsciously, those sounds that flowed in, that in-fluence.

One of the writers who influenced me in this way was Gerard Manley Hopkins.[6] The result of reading Hopkins at school was the desire to write, and when I first put pen to paper at university, what flowed out was what had flowed in, the bumpy alliterating music, the reporting sounds and ricochetting consonants typical of Hopkins's verse. I remember lines from a piece called 'October Thought' in which some frail bucolic images foundered under the chainmail of the pastiche:

> Starling thatch-watches, and sudden swallow
> Straight breaks to mud-nest, home-rest rafter
> Up past dry dust-drunk cobwebs, like laughter
> Ghosting the roof of bog-oak, turf-sod and rods of willow . . .

and then there was 'heaven-hue, plum-blue and gorse-pricked with gold' and 'a trickling tinkle of bells well in the fold'.

Looking back on it, I believe there was a connection, not obvious at the time but, on reflection, real enough, between the heavily accented consonantal noise of Hopkins's poetic voice, and the peculiar regional characteristics of a Northern Ireland accent. The late W. R. Rodgers,[7] another poet much lured by alliteration, said in his poem 'The Character of Ireland' that the people from his (and my) part of the world were

> an abrupt people
> who like the spiky consonants of speech
> and think the soft ones cissy; who dig
> the k and t in orchestra, detect sin
> in sinfonia, get a kick out of
> tin-cans, fricatives, fornication, staccato talk,
> anything that gives or takes attack
> like Micks, Teagues, tinker's gets, Vatican.

It is true that the Ulster[8] accent is generally a staccato consonantal one. Our tongue strikes the tangent of the consonant rather more than it rolls the circle of the vowel—Rodgers also spoke of 'the round gift of the gab in southern mouths'. It is energetic, angular, hard-edged, and it may be because of this affinity between my dialect and Hopkins's oddity that those first verses turned out as they did.

I couldn't say, of course, that I had found a voice but I had found a game. I knew the thing was only word-play, and I hadn't even the guts to put my name to it. I called myself *Incertus*, uncertain, a shy soul fretting and all that. I was in love with words themselves, but had no sense of a poem as a whole structure and no experience of how the successful achievement of a poem could be a stepping stone in your life. Those verses were what we might

6. English poet (1844–1889).
7. Irish poet (1909–1969).
8. Northern Irish.

call 'trial-pieces', little stiff inept designs in imitation of the master's fluent interlacing patterns, heavy-handed clues to the whole craft.

I was getting my first sense of crafting words and for one reason or another, words as bearers of history and mystery began to invite me. Maybe it began very early when my mother used to recite lists of affixes and suffixes, and Latin roots, with their English meanings, rhymes that formed part of her schooling in the early part of the century. Maybe it began with the exotic listing on the wireless dial: Stuttgart, Leipzig, Oslo, Hilversum.[9] Maybe it was stirred by the beautiful sprung rhythms of the old BBC weather forecast: Dogger, Rockall, Malin, Shetland, Faroes, Finisterre;[1] or with the gorgeous and inane phraseology of the catechism; or with the litany of the Blessed Virgin that was part of the enforced poetry in our household: Tower of Gold, Ark of the Covenant, Gate of Heaven, Morning Star, Health of the Sick, Refuge of Sinners, Comforter of the Afflicted. None of these things were consciously savoured at the time but I think the fact that I still recall them with ease, and can delight in them as verbal music, means that they were bedding the ear with a kind of linguistic hardcore that could be built on some day.

That was the unconscious bedding, but poetry involves a conscious savouring of words also. This came by way of reading poetry itself, and being required to learn pieces by heart, phrases even, like Keats's,[2] from 'Lamia':

> and his vessel now
> Grated the quaystone with her brazen prow,

or Wordsworth's:

> All shod with steel,
> We hiss'd along the polished ice,[3]

or Tennyson's:

> Old yew, which graspest at the stones
> That name the underlying dead,
> Thy fibres net the dreamless head,
> Thy roots are wrapped about the bones.[4]

These were picked up in my last years at school, touchstones of sorts, where the language could give you a kind of aural gooseflesh. At the university I was delighted in the first weeks to meet the moody energies of John Webster—'I'll make Italian cut-works in their guts / If ever I return'[5]—and later on to encounter the pointed masonry of Anglo-Saxon verse and to learn about the rich stratifications of the English language itself. Words alone were certain good.[6] I even went so far as to write these 'Lines to myself':

> In poetry I wish you would
> Avoid the lilting platitude.
> Give us poems humped and strong,
> Laced tight with thongs of song,

9. Suburb of Amsterdam, Holland. *Stuttgart* and *Leipzig:* cities in Germany. *Oslo:* capital of Norway.
1. Lighthouses by the seas surrounding Great Britain and Ireland, mentioned in the shipping forecast broadcast on BBC radio. *Sprung rhythm:* metrical system with a variable number of syllables per foot, developed by Gerard Manley Hopkins.
2. John Keats (1795–1821), English Romantic poet.
3. *The Prelude* 1.433–34.
4. *In Memoriam* 2.1–4, by English poet Alfred, Lord Tennyson (1809–1892).
5. From *The White Devil*, by English dramatist John Webster (c. 1580–1632).
6. Line 10 of Irish poet W. B. Yeats's "Song of the Happy Shepherd."

Poems that explode in silence
Without forcing, without violence.
Whose music is strong and clear and good
Like a saw zooming in seasoned wood.
You should attempt concrete expression,
Half-guessing, half-expression.

Ah well. Behind that was 'Ars Poetica', MacLeish's and Verlaine's, Eliot's 'objective correlative'[7] (half understood) and several critical essays (by myself and others) about 'concrete realization'. At the university I kept the whole thing at arm's length, read poetry for the noise and wrote about half a dozen pieces for the literary magazine. But nothing happened inside me. No experience. No epiphany. All craft—and not much of that—and no technique.

I think technique is different from craft. Craft is what you can learn from other verse. Craft is the skill of making. It wins competitions in the *Irish Times* or the *New Statesman*. It can be deployed without reference to the feelings or the self. It knows how to keep up a capable verbal athletic display; it can be content to be *vox et praeterea nihil*—all voice and nothing else—but not voice as in 'finding a voice'. Learning the craft is learning to turn the windlass at the well of poetry. Usually you begin by dropping the bucket halfway down the shaft and winding up a taking of air. You are miming the real thing until one day the chain draws unexpectedly tight and you have dipped into waters that will continue to entice you back. You'll have broken the skin on the pool of yourself. Your praties will be 'fit for digging'.

At that point it becomes appropriate to speak of technique rather than craft. Technique, as I would define it, involves not only a poet's way with words, his management of metre, rhythm and verbal texture; it involves also a definition of his stance towards life, a definition of his own reality. It involves the discovery of ways to go out of his normal cognitive bounds and raid the inarticulate: a dynamic alertness that mediates between the origins of feeling in memory and experience and the formal ploys that express these in a work of art. Technique entails the watermarking of your essential patterns of perception, voice and thought into the touch and texture of your lines; it is that whole creative effort of the mind's and body's resources to bring the meaning of experience within the jurisdiction of form. Technique is what turns, in Yeats's phrase, 'the bundle of accident and incoherence that sits down to breakfast' into 'an idea, something intended, complete'.[8]

It is indeed conceivable that a poet could have a real technique and a wobbly craft—I think this was true of Alun Lewis and Patrick Kavanagh[9]—but more often it is a case of a sure enough craft and a failure of technique. And if I were asked for a figure who represents pure technique, I would say a water diviner. You can't learn the craft of dowsing or divining[1]—it is a gift for being in touch with what is there, hidden and real, a gift for mediating between the latent resource and the community that wants it current and released. As Sir Philip Sidney[2] notes in his *Apologie for Poetry*: 'Among the Romans a Poet was called *Vates*, which is as much as a Diviner . . .'

7. Term coined by T. S. Eliot for a feature of a literary work designed to elicit specific emotional responses. *Ars Poetica:* the art of poetry (Latin); title of poems about poetry by American poet Archibald MacLeish (1892–1982) and French poet Paul Verlaine (1844–1896), and originally the title of a work by Latin poet Horace (65 B.C.E.–8 B.C.E.).

8. Phrases from Yeats's 1937 introduction to a proposed edition of his collected works, in vol. 1 of this anthology.

9. Irish poet (1904–1967). Alun Lewis (1915–1944), Welsh poet.

1. Using a divining rod, or dowsing rod, to search for underground water.

2. English poet and statesman (1554–1586).

The poem was written simply to allay an excitement and to name an experience, and at the same time to give the excitement and the experience a small *perpetuum mobile*[3] in language itself. I quote it here, not for its own technique but for the image of technique contained in it. The diviner resembles the poet in his function of making contact with what lies hidden, and in his ability to make palpable what was sensed or raised.

The Diviner

Cut from the green hedge a forked hazel stick
That he held tight by the arms of the V:
Circling the terrain, hunting the pluck
Of water, nervous, but professionally

Unfussed. The pluck came sharp as a sting.
The rod jerked with precise convulsions,
Spring water suddenly broadcasting
Through a green hazel its secret stations.

The bystanders would ask to have a try.
He handed them the rod without a word.
It lay dead in their grasp till nonchalantly
He gripped expectant wrists. The hazel stirred.

What I had taken as matter of fact as a youngster became a matter of wonder in memory. When I look at the thing now I am pleased that it ends with a verb, 'stirred', the heart of the mystery; and I am glad that 'stirred' chimes with 'word', bringing the two functions of *vates* into the one sound.

Technique is what allows that first stirring of the mind round a word or an image or a memory to grow towards articulation: articulation not necessarily in terms of argument or explication but in terms of its own potential for harmonious self-reproduction. The seminal excitement has to be granted conditions in which, in Hopkins's words, it 'selves, goes itself . . . crying / What I do is me, for that I came'.[4] Technique ensures that the first gleam attains its proper effulgence. And I don't just mean a felicity in the choice of words to flesh the theme—that is a problem also but it is not so critical. A poem can survive stylistic blemishes but it cannot survive a still-birth. The crucial action is pre-verbal, to be able to allow the first alertness or come-hither, sensed in a blurred or incomplete way, to dilate and approach as a thought or a theme or a phrase. Robert Frost[5] put it this way: 'a poem begins as a lump in the throat, a homesickness, a lovesickness. It finds the thought and the thought finds the words'. As far as I am concerned, technique is more vitally and sensitively connected with that first activity where the 'lump in the throat' finds 'the thought' than with 'the thought' finding 'the words'. That first emergence involves the divining, vatic, oracular function; the second, the making function. To say, as Auden did,[6] that a poem is a 'verbal contraption' is to keep one or two tricks up your sleeve.

Traditionally an oracle speaks in riddles, yielding its truths in disguise, offering its insights cunningly. And in the practice of poetry, there is a cor-

3. Perpetual motion (Latin).
4. From the poem beginning "As kingfishers catch fire, dragonflies draw flame."
5. American poet (1874–1963), quoted from a letter to Louis Untermeyer (1885–1977), American editor.
6. W. H. Auden (1907–1973), Anglo-American poet, quoted from the essay "Making, Knowing and Judging."

responding occasion of disguise, a protean, chameleon moment when the lump in the throat takes protective colouring in the new element of thought. One of the best documented occasions in the canon of English poetry, as far as this process is concerned, is a poem that survived in spite of its blemish. In fact, the blemish has earned it a peculiar fame:

High on a mountain's highest ridge,
Where oft the stormy winter gale
Cuts like a scythe, while through the clouds
It sweeps from vale to vale;
Not five yards from the mountain path,
This thorn you on your left espy;
And to the left, three yards beyond,
You see a little muddy pond
Of water never dry;
I've measured it from side to side:
'Tis three feet long and two feet wide.

Those two final lines were probably more ridiculed than any other lines in *The Lyrical Ballads* yet Wordsworth maintained 'they ought to be liked'. That was in 1815, seventeen years after the poem had been composed; but five years later he changed them to 'Though but of compass small, and bare / To thirsting suns and parching air'. Craft, in more senses than one.

Yet far more important than the revision, for the purposes of this discussion, is Wordsworth's account of the poem's genesis. " 'The Thorn' ", he told Isabella Fenwick in 1843,

> arose out of my observing on the ridge of Quantock Hills, on a stormy day, a thorn which I had often passed in calm and bright weather without noticing it. I said to myself, 'Cannot I by some invention do as much to make this thorn permanently an impressive object, as the storm has made it to my eyes at this moment?' I began the poem accordingly, and composed it with great rapidity.

The storm, in other words, was nature's technique for granting the thorn-tree its epiphany, awakening in Wordsworth that engendering, heightened state which he describes at the beginning of *The Prelude*—again in relation to the inspiring influence of wind:

For I, methought, while the sweet breath of Heaven
Was blowing on my body, felt within
A corresponding, mild, creative breeze,
A vital breeze which travell'd gently on
O'er things which it had made, and is become
A tempest, a redundant energy
Vexing its own creation.

This is exactly the kind of mood in which he would have 'composed with great rapidity'; the measured recollection of the letter where he makes the poem sound as if it were written to the thesis propounded (retrospectively) in the Preface of 1800—'cannot I by some invention make this thorn permanently an impressive object?'—probably tones down an instinctive, instantaneous recognition into a rational procedure. The technical triumph was to discover a means of allowing his slightly abnormal, slightly numinous vision of the thorn to 'deal out its being'.

What he did to turn 'the bundle of accident and incoherence' of that moment into 'something intended, complete' was to find, in Yeats's language, a mask. The poem as we have it is a ballad in which the speaker is a garrulous superstitious man, a sea captain, according to Wordsworth, who connects the thorn with murder and distress. For Wordsworth's own apprehension of the tree, he instinctively recognized, was basically superstitious: it was a standing over, a survival in his own sensibility of a magical way of responding to the natural world, of reading phenomena as signs, occurrences requiring divination. And in order to dramatize this, to transpose the awakened appetites in his consciousness into the satisfactions of a finished thing, he needed his 'objective correlative'. To make the thorn 'permanently an impressive object', images and ideas from different parts of his conscious and unconscious mind were attracted by almost magnetic power. The thorn in its new, wind-tossed aspect had become a field of force.

Into this field were drawn memories of what the ballads call 'the cruel mother' who murders her own baby:

She leaned her back against a thorn
All around the loney-o
And there her little babe was born
Down by the greenwood side-o

is how a surviving version runs in Ireland. But there have always been variations on this pattern of the woman who kills her baby and buries it. And the ballads are also full of briars and roses and thorns growing out of graves in symbolic token of the life and death of the buried one. So in Wordsworth's imagination the thorn grew into a symbol of tragic, feverish death, and to voice this the ballad mode came naturally; he donned the traditional mask of the tale-teller, legitimately credulous, entering and enacting a convention. The poem itself is a rapid and strange foray where Wordsworth discovered a way of turning the 'lump in the throat' into a 'thought', discovered a set of images, cadences and sounds that amplified his original visionary excitement into 'a redundant energy / Vexing its own creation':

And some had sworn an oath that she
Should be to public justice brought;
And for the little infant's bones
With spades they would have sought.
But then the beauteous hill of moss
Before their eyes began to stir;
And for full fifty yards around
The grass it shook upon the ground.

'The Thorn' is a nicely documented example of feeling getting into words, in ways that paralleled much in my own experience; although I must say that it is hard to discriminate between feeling getting into words and words turning into feeling, and it is only on posthumous occasions like this that the distinction arises. Moreover, it is dangerous for a writer to become too self-conscious about his own processes: to name them too definitively may have the effect of confining them to what is named. A poem always has elements of accident about it, which can be made the subject of inquest afterwards, but there is always a risk in conducting your own inquest: you might begin to believe the coroner in yourself rather than put your trust in the man in you who is capable of the accident. Robert Graves's[7] 'Dance of Words' puts this delightfully:

> To make them move, you should start from lightning
> And not forecast the rhythm: rely on chance
> Or so-called chance for its bright emergence
> Once lightning interpenetrates the dance.
>
> Grant them their own traditional steps and postures
> But see they dance it out again and again
> Until only lightning is left to puzzle over—
> The choreography plain and the theme plain.

What we are engaged upon here is a way of seeing that turns the lightning into 'the visible discharge of electricity between cloud and cloud or between cloud and ground' rather than its own puzzling, brilliant self. There is nearly always an element of the bolt from the blue about a poem's origin.

When I called my second book *Door into the Dark* I intended to gesture towards this idea of poetry as a point of entry into the buried life of the feelings or as a point of exit for it. Words themselves are doors; Janus[8] is to a certain extent their deity, looking back to a ramification of roots and associations and forward to a clarification of sense and meaning. And just as Wordsworth sensed a secret asking for release in the thorn, so in *Door into the Dark* there are a number of poems that arise out of the almost unnameable energies that, for me, hovered over certain bits of language and landscape.

The poem 'Undine', for example. It was the dark pool of the sound of the word that first took me: if our auditory imaginations were sufficiently attuned to plumb and sound a vowel, to unite the most primitive and civilized associations, the word 'undine' would probably suffice as a poem in itself. *Unda,* a wave, *undine,* a water-woman—a litany of undines would have ebb and flow, water and woman, wave and tide, fulfilment and exhaustion in its very rhythms. But, old two-faced vocable that it is, I discovered a more precise definition once, by accident, in a dictionary. An undine is a water-sprite who has to marry a human being and have a child by him before she can become human. With that definition, the lump in the throat, or rather the thump in the ear, *undine,* became a thought, a field of force that called up other images. One of these was an orphaned memory, without a context, obviously a very early one, of watching a man clearing out an old spongy growth from a drain between two fields, focusing in particular on the way the water, in the cleared-out place, as soon as the shovelfuls of sludge had been removed, the way the water began to run free, rinse itself clean of the soluble mud and make its own little channels and currents. And this image was gathered into a more conscious reading of the myth as being about the liberating, humanizing effect of sexual encounter. Undine was a cold girl who got what the dictionary called a soul through the experience of physical love. So the poem uttered itself out of that nexus—more short-winded than 'The Thorn', with less red*undant* energy, but still escaping, I hope, from my incoherence into the voice of the undine herself:

7. English poet (1895–1985).
8. Double-faced Roman god of doorways and bridges.

He slashed the briars, shovelled up grey silt
To give me right of way in my own drains
And I ran quick for him, cleaned out my rust.

He halted, saw me finally disrobed,
Running clear, with apparent unconcern.
Then he walked by me. I rippled and I churned

Where ditches intersected near the river
Until he dug a spade deep in my flank
And took me to him. I swallowed his trench

Gratefully, dispersing myself for love
Down in his roots, climbing his brassy grain—
But once he knew my welcome, I alone

Could give him subtle increase and reflection.
He explored me so completely, each limb
Lost its cold freedom. Human, warmed to him.

I once said it was a myth about agriculture, about the way water is tamed and humanized when streams become irrigation canals, when water becomes involved with seed. And maybe that is as good an explanation as any. The paraphrasable extensions of a poem can be as protean as possible as long as its elements remain firm. Words can allow you that two-faced approach also. They stand smiling at the audience's way of reading them and winking back at the poet's way of using them.

Behind this, of course, there is a good bit of symbolist theory. Yet in practice, you proceed by your own experience of what it is to write what you consider a successful poem. You survive in your own esteem not by the corroboration of theory but by the trust in certain moments of satisfaction which you know intuitively to be moments of extension. You are confirmed by the visitation of the last poem and threatened by the elusiveness of the next one, and the best moments are those when your mind seems to implode and words and images rush of their own accord into the vortex. Which happened to me once when the line 'We have no prairies' drifted into my head at bedtime, and loosened a fall of images that constitute the poem 'Bogland', the last one in *Door into the Dark*.

I had been vaguely wishing to write a poem about bogland, chiefly because it is a landscape that has a strange assuaging effect on me, one with associations reaching back into early childhood. We used to hear about bog-butter, butter kept fresh for a great number of years under the peat. Then when I was at school the skeleton of an elk had been taken out of a bog nearby and a few of our neighbours had got their photographs in the paper, peering out across its antlers. So I began to get an idea of bog as the memory of the landscape, or as a landscape that remembered everything that happened in and to it. In fact, if you go round the National Museum in Dublin, you will realize that a great proportion of the most cherished material heritage of Ireland was 'found in a bog'. Moreover, since memory was the faculty that supplied me with the first quickening of my own poetry, I had a tentative unrealized need to make a congruence between memory and bogland and, for the want of a better word, our national consciousness. And it all released itself after 'We have no prairies . . . '—but we have bogs.

At that time I was teaching modern literature in Queen's University, Belfast, and had been reading about the frontier and the west as an important myth in the American consciousness, so I set up—or rather, laid down—the bog as an answering Irish myth. I wrote it quickly the next morning, having slept on my excitement, and revised it on the hoof, from line to line, as it came[.][9] Again, as in the case of 'Digging', the seminal impulse had been unconscious. What generated the poem about memory was something lying beneath the very floor of memory, something I only connected with the poem months after it was written, which was a warning that older people would give us about going into the bog. They were afraid we might fall into the pools in the old workings so they put it about (and we believed them) that *there was no bottom* in the bog-holes. Little did they—or I—know that I would filch it for the last line of a book.

There was also in that book a poem called 'Requiem for the Croppies' which was written in 1966 when most poets in Ireland were straining to celebrate the anniversary of the 1916 Rising.[1] That rising was the harvest of seeds sown in 1798, when revolutionary republican ideals and national feeling coalesced in the doctrines of Irish republicanism and in the rebellion of 1798 itself—unsuccessful and savagely put down. The poem was born of and ended with an image of resurrection based on the fact that some time after the rebels were buried in common graves, these graves began to sprout with young barley, growing up from barley corn which the 'croppies' had carried in their pockets to eat while on the march. The oblique implication was that the seeds of violent resistance sowed in the Year of Liberty had flowered in what Yeats called 'the right rose tree' of 1916.[2] I did not realize at the time that the original heraldic murderous encounter between Protestant yeoman and Catholic rebel was to be initiated again in the summer of 1969, in Belfast, two months after the book was published.[3]

From that moment the problems of poetry moved from being simply a matter of achieving the satisfactory verbal icon to being a search for images and symbols adequate to our predicament. I do not mean liberal lamentation that citizens should feel compelled to murder one another or deploy their different military arms over the matter of nomenclatures such as British or Irish. I do not mean public celebrations or execrations of resistance or atrocity—although there is nothing necessarily unpoetic about such celebration, if one thinks of Yeats's 'Easter 1916'. I mean that I felt it imperative to discover a field of force in which, without abandoning fidelity to the processes and experience of poetry as I have outlined them, it would be possible to encompass the perspectives of a humane reason and at the same time to grant the religious intensity of the violence its deplorable authenticity and

9. The original essay reprinted "Bogland," on p. 725 of this volume.
1. In the week of Easter, 1916, Irish Republican nationalists in Dublin staged a revolt against British rule. Although the rising was technically a failure, the leaders of the rebellion became martyrs when executed by the British, further fueling Irish anger against British authorities. The rising of 1798, in which Irish Roman Catholics rose up against the Protestant British government, is often viewed as the inaugural moment of Irish republicanism.
2. In "The Rose Tree."
3. The devastating sectarian violence in Northern Ireland developed from the tensions between the Catholic minority and the Protestant majority. In 1969, unrest generated by the Catholic civil rights movement was countered by police action, and in the early 1970s, British troops entered Northern Ireland. Acts of violence were perpetrated by both sides and hundreds of civilians had been killed at the time that Heaney delivered his lecture.

complexity. And when I say religious, I am not thinking simply of the sectarian division. To some extent the enmity can be viewed as a struggle between the cults and devotees of a god and a goddess. There is an indigenous territorial numen, a tutelar of the whole island, call her Mother Ireland, Kathleen Ni Houlihan, the poor old woman, the Shan Van Vocht,[4] whatever; and her sovereignty has been temporarily usurped or infringed by a new male cult whose founding fathers were Cromwell, William of Orange and Edward Carson,[5] and whose godhead is incarnate in a rex or caesar resident in a palace in London. What we have is the tail-end of a struggle in a province between territorial piety and imperial power.

Now I realize that this idiom is remote from the agnostic world of economic interest whose iron hand operates in the velvet glove of 'talks between elected representatives', and remote from the political manoeuvres of power-sharing; but it is not remote from the psychology of the Irishmen and Ulstermen who do the killing, and not remote from the bankrupt psychology and mythologies implicit in the terms Irish Catholic and Ulster Protestant. The question, as ever, is 'How with this rage shall beauty hold a plea?' And my answer is, by offering 'befitting emblems of adversity'.[6]

Some of these emblems I found in a book that was published in English translation, appositely, the year the killing started, in 1969. And again appositely, it was entitled *The Bog People*. It was chiefly concerned with preserved bodies of men and women found in the bogs of Jutland, naked, strangled or with their throats cut, disposed under the peat since early Iron Age times. The author, P. V. Glob, argues convincingly that a number of these, and in particular the Tollund Man, whose head is now preserved near Aarhus in the museum at Silkeburg,[7] were ritual sacrifices to the Mother Goddess, the goddess of the ground who needed new bridegrooms each winter to bed with her in her sacred place, in the bog, to ensure the renewal and fertility of the territory in the spring. Taken in relation to the tradition of Irish political martyrdom for that cause whose icon is Kathleen Ni Houlihan, this is more than an archaic barbarous rite: it is an archetypal pattern. And the unforgettable photographs of these victims blended in my mind with photographs of atrocities, past and present, in the long rites of Irish political and religious struggles. When I wrote this poem, I had a completely new sensation, one of fear. It was a vow to go on pilgrimage and I felt as it came to me—and again it came quickly—that unless I was deeply in earnest about what I was saying, I was simply invoking dangers for myself. It is called 'The Tollund Man'[.][8]

And just how persistent the barbaric attitudes are, not only in the slaughter but in the psyche, I discovered, again when the *frisson* of the poem itself had passed, and indeed after I had fulfilled the vow and gone to Jutland, 'the holy blisful martyr for to seke'.[9] I read the following in a chapter on 'The Religion of the Pagan Celts' by the Celtic scholar, Anne Ross:

4. Popular figures personifying Ireland as a woman.

5. Northern Irish politician (1854–1935), who led the Protestant anti–Home Rule movement, which helped ensure that Northern Ireland did not become part of the Irish Republic. Oliver Cromwell (1599–1658): English soldier, who in the wake of the English Civil War acted as lord protector of England, Scotland, and Ireland from 1653–58 and brutally suppressed an Irish rebellion in 1649. William of Orange (1650–1702): Protestant King William III of Great Britain, who defeated the Catholic King James II.

6. The first quotation is from Shakespeare's Sonnet 65; the second, from Yeats's "Meditations in Time of Civil War."

7. Like Aarhus, a city in the eastern Jutland region of Denmark.

8. The original essay quoted "The Tollund Man," on p. 726 of this volume.

9. From the "General Prologue" to the *Canterbury Tales*, by Geoffrey Chaucer (c. 1342/43–1400).

> Moving from sanctuaries and shrines . . . we come now to consider the nature of the actual deities. . . . But before going on to look at the nature of some of the individual deities and their cults, one can perhaps bridge the gap as it were by considering a symbol which, in its way, sums up the whole of Celtic pagan religion and is as representative of it as is, for example, the sign of the cross in Christian contexts. This is the symbol of the severed human head; in all its various modes of iconographic representation and verbal presentation, one may find the hard core of Celtic religion. It is indeed . . . a kind of shorthand symbol for the entire religious outlook for the pagan Celts.[1]

My sense of occasion and almost awe as I vowed to go to pray to the Tollund Man and assist at his enshrined head had a longer ancestry than I had at the time realized.

I began by suggesting that my point of view involved poetry as divination, as a restoration of the culture to itself. In Ireland in this century it has involved for Yeats and many others an attempt to define and interpret the present by bringing it into significant relationship with the past, and I believe that effort in our present circumstances has to be urgently renewed. But here we stray from the realm of technique into the realm of tradition; to forge a poem is one thing, to forge the uncreated conscience of the race, as Stephen Dedalus[2] put it, is quite another and places daunting pressures and responsibilities on anyone who would risk the name of poet.

1974

1979, 1980

1. From Ross's *Pagan Celtic Britain: Studies in Iconography and Tradition* (1967).
2. Protagonist of *A Portrait of the Artist as a Young Man* (1916), by Irish novelist James Joyce (1882–1941); at the conclusion of that work, Stephen Dedalus vows "to forge in the smithy of my soul the uncreated conscience of my race."

Jamaica Language

The poet Louise Bennett, who has been called "the mother of the Jamaican language," or Creole, wittily mocks the idea that Standard English is the only worthy variety of the English language. In this radio monologue, one of many broadcast between 1966 and 1982 as part of Bennett's program "Miss Lou's Views," Bennett, through her popular persona as Aunty Roachy, ridicules the view that Jamaican Creole is a corruption of "Standard English," which is itself derived from other languages and constantly evolving. Ever since slavery, speakers of Jamaican English, which combines African languages with English, have been able to "meck it soun like it no got no English at all eena it," strategically thwarting outsiders from understanding. For all the influences on Jamaican Creole, it is a distinctive product of an Afro-Caribbean people's historical experience and remains vibrant and richly expressive today. Originally broadcast in 1979–81, the monologue has been reprinted from *Aunty Roachy Seh* (1993), ed. Mervyn Morris.

LOUISE BENNETT

Jamaica Language

Listen, na!

My Aunty Roachy seh dat it bwile[1] her temper an really bex[2] her fi true anytime she hear anybody a style we Jamaican dialec as "corruption of the English language." For if dat be de case, den dem shoulda call English Language corruption of Norman French an Latin an all dem tarra[3] language what dem seh dat English is derived from.

Oonoo[4] hear de wud? "Derived." English is a derivation but Jamaica Dialec is corruption! What a unfairity!

Aunty Roachy seh dat if Jamaican Dialec is corruption of de English Language, den it is also a corruption of de African Twi Language to, a oh!

For Jamaican Dialec did start when we English forefahders did start mus-an-boun[5] we African ancestors fi stop talk fi-dem African Language altogedder an learn fi talk so-so[6] English, because we English forefahders couldn understan what we African ancestors-dem wasa seh to dem one anodder when dem wasa talk eena dem African Language to dem one annodder!

But we African ancestors-dem pop[7] we English forefahders-dem. Yes! Pop dem an disguise up de English Language fi projec fi-dem African Language in such a way dat we English forefahders-dem still couldn understan what we African ancestors-dem wasa talk bout when dem wasa talk to dem one annodder!

Yes, bwoy!

So till now, aldoah plenty a we Jamaica Dialec wuds-dem come from English wuds, yet, still an for all, de talkin is so-so Jamaican, an when we ready we can meck it soun like it no got no English at all eena it! An no so-so English-talkin smaddy[8] cyaan[9] understan weh we a seh if we doan want dem to understan weh we a seh, a oh!

An we fix up we dialec wud fi soun like whatsoever we a talk bout, look like! For instance, when we seh sinting "kooroo-kooroo"[1] up, yuh know seh dat it mark-up mark-up. An if we seh one house "rookoo-rookoo"[2] up, it is plain to see dat it ole an shaky-shaky. An when we seh smaddy "boogoo-yagga", everybody know seh dat him outa-order; an if we seh dem "boonoo-noonoos",[3] yuh know seh dat dem nice an we like dem. Mmmm.

Aunty Roachy seh dat Jamaica Dialec is more direc an to de point dan English. For all like how English smaddy would seh "Go away", Jamaican jus seh "Gweh!" An de only time we use more wuds dan English is when we want fi meck someting soun strong: like when dem seh sinting "batter-batter" up, it soun more expressive dan if yuh seh "it is battered." But most of all

1. Boils.
2. Vexes.
3. Other.
4. You (plural).
5. Compel.
6. Only.
7. Outwitted.
8. People.
9. Can't.
1. Rough; rocky. *Sinting:* something.
2. Unsteady.
3. Beautiful; wonderful (term of endearment). *Boogoo-yagga:* ill-mannered.

we fling weh all de bangarang an trimmins[4] dem an only lef what wantin, an dat's why when English smaddy seh "I got stuck by a prickle" Jamaican jus seh "Macca[5] jook me"!

So fi-we Jamaica Language is not no English Language corruption at all, a oh! An we no haffi shame a it, like one gal who did go a Englan go represent we Jamaican folk-song "One shif me got" as "De sole underwear garment I possess", and go sing "Mumma, Mumma, dem ketch Puppa" as "Mother, Mother, they apprehended Father"!

Ay ya yie!

1979–81 1993

4. Miscellaneous trash and trimmings.
5. A prickly plant.

SEMBLANCE

This essay exemplifies the fusion of philosophy and linguistic experimentation that marks both the poetry and the prose of Charles Bernstein, a central contemporary exponent and practitioner of avant-garde poetry. Composed for the symposium "Death of the Referent?" and published while Bernstein was coediting *L=A=N=G=U=A=G=E* magazine with Bruce Andrews, "Semblance" distills the postmodernist tenets of Language poetry and explains Bernstein's own practice as a poet. By freeing language from normative rules of syntax and grammar, reference and narrative, Bernstein hopes to achieve in his poetry a new level of musical, sensory, associative, and conceptual fecundity. Drawing on structuralist and poststructuralist philosophies of language, as well as such poetic precursors as the Russian Futurist Velimir Khlebnikov and projectivist Charles Olson, Bernstein emphasizes that words are enmeshed in complicated relationships with one another, in contrast to a correspondence theory of language, in which each word's primary relationship is to the named object. The poet's task, he argues, is neither to submit to nor to deny the referentiality of language, but to electrify it by removing the constraints of conventional structures of meaning. Originally printed in *Reality Studios* 2.4 (1980), the essay has been reprinted from *Content's Dream: Essays 1975–1984* (1986, 2001).

CHARLES BERNSTEIN

Semblance

> It's as if each of these things has a life of its own. You can stretch them, deform them and even break them apart, and they still have an inner cohesion that keeps them together.

Not "death" of the referent—rather a recharged use of the multivalent referential vectors that any word has, how words in combination tone and modify the associations made for each of them, how 'reference' then is not a one-on-one relation to an 'object' but a perceptual dimension that closes in to pinpoint, nail down (*this* word), sputters omnitropically[1] (the in in the which of who where what wells), refuses the build up of image track/projection while, pointillistically,[2] fixing a reference at each turn (fills vats ago lodges spire), or, that much rarer case (Peter Inman's *Platin* and David Melnick's *Pcoet* two recent examples) of "zaum"[3] (so-called transrational, pervasively neologistic)—"ig ok aberflappi"—in which reference, deprived of its automatic reflex reaction of word/stimulus image/response roams over the range of associations suggested by the word, word shooting off referential vectors like the energy field in a Kirillian photograph.[4]

All of which are ways of releasing the energy inherent in the referential dimension of language, that these dimensions are the material of which the writing is made, define its medium. Making the structures of meaning in language more tangible and in that way allowing for the maximum resonance for the medium—the traditional power that writing has always had to make experience palpable not by simply pointing to it but by (re)creating its conditions.[5]

Point then, at first instance, to see the medium of writing—our area of operation—as maximally open in vocabulary, forms, shapes, phoneme/morpheme/word/phrase/sentence[6] order, etc., so that possible areas covered, ranges of things depicted, suggested, critiqued, considered, etc., have an outer limit (asymptotic[7]) of what can be thought, what can (might) be. But then, taking that as zero degree, not to gesturalize the possibility of poetry to operate in this 'hyperspace', but to create works (poems) within it.

1. In all figures of speech.
2. Pointillism is a Postimpressionist style of painting in which small dots of color seem to fuse when seen from afar.
3. Term associated with the Russian Futurist Velimir Khlebnikov (1885–1922), who treated words as things in attempting to develop a transrational language.
4. Colorful image that displays the aura surrounding an object.
5. "Alan Davies has objected that language and experience are separate realms and that the separation should be maximized in writing, in this way questioning the value of using language to make experience palpable.—But I don't mean 'experience' in the sense of a picture/image/representation that is calling back to an already constituted experience. Rather, language itself constitutes experience at every moment (in reading and otherwise). Experience, then, is not tied into representation exclusively but is a separate 'perception'-like category. (& perception not necessarily as in perception onto a physical/preconstituted world, as "eyes" in the [Charles] Olson sense, that is, not just onto a matrix-qua-the world but as operating/projecting/composing activity.) The point is, then, that experience is a dimension necessarily built into language—that far from being avoidable, or a choice, it is a property. So this view attempts to rethink representational or pictorial or behaviorist notions of what 'experience' is, i.e., experience is not inextricably linked to representation, normative syntax, images, but rather, the other way around, is a synthetic, generative activity—"in the beginning was the word" & so on, or that's our 'limit' of beginnings" [Bernstein's note].
6. *Phoneme:* smallest unit of speech distinguishing one word (or part of a word) from another. *Morpheme:* smallest grammatical unit of speech.
7. In math, an asymptote is a straight line approaching but never reaching a curve.

The order of the words, the syntax, creates possibilities for images, pictures, representations, descriptions, invocation, ideation, critique, relation, projection, etc. Sentences that follow standard grammatical patterns allow the accumulating references to enthrall the reader by diminishing diversions from a constructed representation. In this way, each word's references work in harmony by reinforcing a spatiotemporal order conventionalized by the bulk of writing practice that creates the 'standard'. "The lamp sits atop the table in the study"—each word narrowing down the possibilities of each other, limiting the interpretation of each word's meaning by creating an ever more specific context. In a similar way, associations with sentences are narrowed down by conventional expository or narrational paragraph structure, which directs attention away from the sentence as meaning generating event and onto the 'content' depicted. By shifting the contexts in which even a fairly 'standard' sentence finds itself, as in some of the prose-format work of Barrett Watten,[8] the seriality of the ordering of sentences within a paragraph displaces from its habitual surrounding the projected representational fixation that the sentence conveys. "Words elect us. The lamp sits atop the table in the study. The tower is burnt orange. . . ." By rotating sentences within a paragraph (a process analogous to jump cutting in film) according to principles generated by and unfolding in the work (rather than in accordance with representational construction patterns) a perceptual vividness is intensified for each sentence since the abruptness of the cuts induces a greater desire to savor the tangibility of each sentence before it is lost to the next, determinately other, sentence. Juxtapositions not only suggest unsuspected relations but induce reading along ectoskeletal and citational lines. As a result, the operant mechanisms of meaning are multiplied and patterns of projection in reading are less restricted. The patterns of projection are not, however, undetermined. The text operates at a level that not only provokes projections by each sentence but by the sequencing of the sentences suggests lines or paths for them to proceed along. At the same time, circumspection about the nature and meaning of the projections is called forth. The result is both a self-reflectiveness and an intensification of the items/conventions of the social world projected/suggested/provoked. A similar process can also take place within sentences and phrases and not only intersententially. Syntactic patterns are composed which allow for this combination of projection and reflection in the movement from word to word. "For as much as, within the because, tools their annoyance, tip to toward."—But, again, to acknowledge this as the space of the text, and still to leave open what is to be said, what projections desire these reflections.

The sense of music in poetry: the music of meaning—emerging, fogging, contrasting, etc. Tune attunement in understanding—the meaning sounds. It's impossible to separate prosody from the structure (the form and content seen as an interlocking figure) of a given poem. You can talk about strategies of meaning generation, shape, the kinds of sounds accented, the varieties of measurement (of scale, of number, of line length, of syllable order, of word length, of phrase length, or measure as punctuation, of punctuation as metrics). But no one has primacy—the music is the orchestrating these into the poem, the angles one plays against another, the shading. In much of my own work: working at angles to the strong tidal pull of an expected sequence of

8. Language poet, critic, and professor (b. 1948).

a sentence—or by cutting off a sentence or phrase midway and counting on the mind to complete where the poem goes off in another direction, giving two vectors at once—the anticipated projection underneath and the actual wording above.

My interest in not conceptualizing the field of the poem as a unitary plane, and so also not using overall structural programs: that any prior principle of composition violates the priority I want to give to the inherence of surface, to the total necessity in the durational space of the poem for every moment to *count*. The moment not subsumed into a schematic structure, hence instance of it, but at every juncture creating (synthesizing) the structure. So not to have the work resolve at the level of the "field" if this is to mean a uniplanar surface within which the poem operates. Structure that can't be separated from decisions made within it, constantly poking through the expected parameters. Rather than having a single form or shape or idea of the work pop out as you read, the structure itself is pulled into a moebius-like[9] twisting momentum. In this process, the language takes on a centrifugal force that seems to trip it out of the poem, turn it out from itself, exteriorizing it. Textures, vocabularies, discourses, constructivist modes of radically different character are not integrated into a field as part of a predetermined planar architecture; the gaps and jumps compose a space within shifting parameters, types and styles of discourse constantly crisscrossing, interacting, creating new gels. (Intertextual, interstructural . . .) (Bruce Andrews[1] has suggested the image of a relief map for the varying kinds of referential vectors—reference to different domains of discourse, references made by different processes—in some of his work in which words and phrases are visually spaced out over the surface of the page. However, the structural dissonance in these works is counterbalanced by the perspicacious poise of the overall design, which tends to even-out the surface tension.)

Writing as a process of pushing whatever way, or making the piece cohere as far as can: stretching my mind—to where I know it makes sense but not quite why—suspecting relations that I understand, that make the sense of the ready-to-hand—i.e. pushing the composition to the very limits of sense, meaning, to that razor's edge where judgment/aesthetic sense is all I can go on (know-how). (Maybe what's to get beyond in Olson's field theory[2] is just the idea of form as a single web, a unified field, one matrix, with its implicit idea of 'perception' onto a given world rather than, as well, onto the language through which the world is constituted.) So that the form, the structure, that, finally, is the poem, has emerged, is come upon, is made.

1980

9. That is, like a Möbius strip.
1. Language poet (b. 1948).
2. For Charles Olson's theory of "field composition," in which the poet "puts himself in the open," see his essay "Projective Verse," reprinted above.

WHERE MIRRORS ARE WINDOWS

The distinguished Indian poet A. K. Ramanujan was also an award-winning translator and scholar of South Asian languages and literatures. In this essay on the reflexivity and continuity of Indian poetry, he proposes an indigenous Indian model of literary inheritance. Revising T. S. Eliot's Europe-centered "Tradition and the Individual Talent," he argues that the literatures of the world are "indissolubly plural" and interact in complex intertextual networks. He traces the intricate web of relationships connecting Indian poetry in myriad languages from various traditions. Indian poems are, in his view, internally self-reflexive and also "reflect, invert, and subvert" one another: "Every poem resonates with the absent presence of others that sound with it, like the unstruck strings of a sitar." Ramanujan's analysis also bears indirectly on the work of many postwar anglophone poets of South Asia, including his own. Writing poetry in English, as well as Kannada and Tamil, he cites such Western poets as W. B. Yeats and Wallace Stevens alongside such Sanskrit epics as the *Rāmāyaṇa*. The essay has been excerpted from the journal *History of Religions* 28.3 (1989).

A. K. RAMANUJAN

From Where Mirrors Are Windows: Toward an Anthology of Reflections

* * *

One way of defining diversity for India is to say what the Irishman is said to have said about trousers. When asked whether trousers were singular or plural, he said, "Singular at the top and plural at the bottom." This is the view espoused by people who believe that Indian traditions are organized as a pan-Indian Sanskritic Great Tradition (in the singular) and many local Little Traditions (in the plural). Older Indian notions of *mārga* and *deśi*[1] and modern Indian politicians' rhetoric about unity in diversity fall in line with the same position. The official Indian literary academy, the Sahitya Akademi, has the motto, "Indian literature is one but written in many languages." I, for one, would prefer the plural, "Indian literatures," and would wonder if something would remain the same if it is written in several languages, knowing as I do that even in the same language, "a change of style is a change of subject," as Wallace Stevens[2] would say.

Another way of talking about a culture like the Indian is through the analogy of a hologram[3]—that is, to say that any section is a cross-section, any piece of it is a true representation of the whole, as any cell of the body is

1. *Mārga* and *deśi:* ancient Sanskrit distinction between classical, learned (*mārga*) and local, folk (*deśi*) forms of culture.
2. American poet (1879–1955), quoted from his *Adagia*, vol. 1 of this anthology.
3. Which achieves its three-dimensional appearance by encoding, in each portion of the object, information about the whole.

supposed to be a true sample of the whole body. Linguists and anthropologists, especially structuralists in general, have operated on this assumption for a while. To them, any native speaker contains the whole of his language; any informant, any myth or ritual, contains the whole of the culture. To study his or its grammar is to study the grammar of the whole language or culture. Such a holographic view implies uniform texture, the replication of one structure in all systems of a culture, without negations, warps, or discontinuities and with no pockets in space or time. It is a very attractive view, especially to people in a hurry, and I have myself held it for many years, though somewhat uneasily. In this view, the classics of Indian civilization, the *Mahābhārata,* the *Rāmāyaṇa,* and the *Purāṇas,*[4] as well as the folklore, the so-called Little (or as we say in India, the "little little") Traditions, are all of one piece. At worst, the latter are garbled versions of the former, simplified for or by the little man. The Great Traditions for the elite, and the little Little Traditions for the little little folks, that is, semi- or illiterate, rural, regional people who are competent only in a mother tongue—but basically there is no difference in kind, only in quality. At its best, it is a form of monism; at its worst, it is a form of cultural imperialism, an upstairs/downstairs view of India.

I would like to suggest the obvious: that cultural traditions in India are indissolubly plural and often conflicting but are organized through at least two principles, (*a*) context-sensitivity and (*b*) reflexivity of various sorts, both of which constantly generate new forms out of the old ones. What we call Brahminism, Bhakti traditions, Buddhism, Jainism, Tantra,[5] tribal traditions and folklore, and lastly, modernity itself, are the most prominent of these systems. They are responses to previous and surrounding traditions; they invert, subvert, and convert their neighbors. Furthermore, each of these terms, like what we call India itself, is "a verbal tent with three-ring circuses" going on inside them. Further dialogic divisions are continuously in progress. They look like single entities, like neat little tents, only from a distance.

Reflexivity takes many forms: awareness of self and other, mirroring, distorted mirroring, parody, family resemblances and rebels, dialectic, anti-structure, utopias and dystopias, the many ironies connected with these responses, and so on. In this paper on Indian literary texts and their relations to each other ("intertextuality," if you will), I will concentrate on three related kinds of reflexivity. I shall call them (1) *responsive,* where text A responds to text B in ways that define both A and B; (2) *reflexive,* where text A reflects on text B, relates itself to it directly or inversely; (3) *self-reflexive,* where a text reflects on itself or its kind. The parts or texts in relation 1 may be called co-texts, in 2, countertexts, and in 3, metatexts. We could also speak of pretexts, intertexts, subtexts, and so on. The vast variety of Indian literature, oral and written, over the centuries, in hundreds of languages and dialects, offers an intricate but open network of such relations, producing families of texts as well as texts that are utterly individual in their effect, detail, and temporal/regional niches. But these relations are perceived by native commentators and by readers. To them, texts do not come in historical stages

4. Collection of ancient Hindu tales. *Mahābhārata* and *Rāmāyaṇa:* the two major Sanskrit epics.
5. Tradition of esoteric texts and practices within some Hindu, Buddhist, and Jaina sects. *Brahminism:* an orthodox Hinduism emphasizing the pantheism of the Vedas (ancient sacred writings), family ceremonies, and ritual sacrifices. *Bhakti:* devotional movement of Hinduism emphasizing the emotional relation between a devotee and a personal god. *Jainism:* Indian religion emphasizing enlightenment through *ahimsa,* or nonviolence to all living things.

but form "a simultaneous order," where every new text within a series confirms yet alters the whole order ever so slightly, and not always so slightly. T. S. Eliot spoke of a simultaneous order for European literature, but the phrase applies even more strongly to Indian literary traditions, especially until the nineteenth century.[6] Modernity disrupted the whole tradition of reflexivity with new notions of originality and the autonomy of single works. Among other things, the printing press radically altered the relation of audience to author and of author to work, and it bifurcated the present and the past so that the pastness of the past is more keenly felt than the presence of the past. Reflexive elements may occur in various sizes: one part of the text may reflect on another part; one text may reflect on another; a whole tradition may invert, negate, rework, and revalue another. Where cultures (like the "Indian") are stratified yet interconnected, where the different communities communicate but do not commune, the texts of one stratum tend to reflect on those of another: encompassment, mimicry, criticism and conflict, and other power relations are expressed by such reflexivities. Self-conscious contrasts and reversals also mark off and individuate the groups—especially if they are closely related, like twins. Closely related sects, like the *teṅkalai* (Southern) and *vaṭakalai* (Northern) sects of Tamil Śrī Vaiṣṇavism, serve even food in different orders, and self-consciously list "eighteen differences."[7]

The rather grossly conceived Great Tradition and Little Traditions are only two such moieties:[8] as suggested earlier, Bhakti, Tantra, and other counter-traditions, as well as Buddhism, Jainism, and, for later times, Islam and Christianity, should be included in this web of intertextuality. I shall draw here only on earlier Indian literatures for my instances. Stereotypes, foreign views, and native self-images on the part of some groups all tend to regard one part (say, the Brahminical texts[9] or folklore) as the original, and the rest as variations, derivatives, aberrations, so we tend to get monolithic conceptions. But the civilization, if it can be described at all, has to be described in terms of all these dynamic interrelations between different traditions, their texts, ideologies, social arrangements, and so forth. Reflexivities are crucial to the understanding of both the order and diversity, the openness and the closures, of this civilization. One may sometimes feel that "mirror on mirror mirrored is all the show."[1] Such an anthology can be made about other aspects of the culture, like ritual, philosophy, food, and sociolinguistic patterns, or across them.[2] * * *

* * *

Furthermore, in such traditions, poems do not come singly, but in sequences often arranged in tens, hundreds, sometimes thousands: sharing motifs, images, structures, yet playing variations that individuate each poem. Every poem resonates with the absent presence of others that sound with it,

6. From "Tradition and the Individual Talent," by T. S. Eliot (1880–1965), vol. 1 of this anthology.
7. "A. Govindacarya, ' "The Aṣṭadaśa-bhedas," or the Eighteen Points of Doctrinal Differences between the Tengalais (Southerners) and the Vadagalais (Northerners) of the Visistadvaita Vaisnava School, South India,' " *Journal of the Royal Asiatic Society* (1910), p. 1103–12" [Ramanujan's note]. *Tamil:* south Indian and Sri Lankan language and people. *Śrī Vaiṣṇavism:* major south Indian sect of Hinduism dedicated to the worship of Vishnu.
8. Parts, components.
9. Early Sanskrit texts such as the Vedas and the Upanishads.
1. From "The Statues," by Irish poet W. B. Yeats (1865–1939).
2. "See A. K. Ramanujan, 'Food for Thought: Towards an Anthology of Hindu Food Images' " [Ramanujan's note], reprinted in his *Collected Essays* (1999).

like the unstruck strings of a sitar. So we respond to a system of presences and absences; our reading then is not linear but what has been called "radial."[3] Every poem is part of a large self-reflexive paradigm; it relates to all others in absentia, gathers ironies, allusions; one text becomes the context of others. Each is precisely foregrounded against a background of all the others.

Once such genres are established, they not only classify, they generate. The settled conventions make possible, indeed cry out for, another kind of reflexivity. Poems beget metapoems that reflect on themselves or their kind, make the audience conscious of the genre and its limits. Genres give rise to antigenres and metagenres that still use all the properties of the genre they are parodying or reflecting on. * * *

* * *

What is merely suggested in one poem may become central in a "repetition" or an "imitation" of it. Mimesis is never only mimesis, for it evokes the earlier image in order to play with it and make it mean other things. When the "same" Indian poem appears in different ages and bodies of poetry, we cannot dismiss them as interlopers and anachronisms, for they become signifiers in a new system: mirrors again that become windows.

I have suggested above, and elsewhere, that in traditions like the Indian, different genres (and generic texts like these epics) specialize in different "provinces of reality."[4] What one does, another does not. The realities of the civilization are expressed in a spectrum of forms, where one complements, contradicts, reflects, and refracts another—we have to take them together to make sense of the civilization and catch a glimpse of the complex whole. Each has to be read in the light of others, as each is defined by the presence of others in the memory of both poet and audience—like the Mahādēvi poem in the light of texts that speak of *māyā,* the three *guṇas, vāsanas,*[5] and so on or the Bengali love-death poem in the context of the Vedic hymn about death.

Contradictions, inversions, multiple views, multiforms affecting and animating one another, expressing conflict and dissent through the same repertoire of forms—all these are ways the traditions relate to each other. Reflexivity binds them together and gives them a common yet creative language for dissent. Without the other, there is no language for the self.

Among Western thinkers, Bakhtin's dialogism seems to anticipate some of these thoughts. Speaking of Dostoevsky's heroes, he says, "Every thought . . . senses itself to be from the very beginning a rejoinder in an unfinished dialogue. Such thought is not impelled towards a well-rounded, finalized, systematically monologic whole. It lives a tense life on the borders of someone else's consciousness."[6]

* * *

3. "Jerome J. McGann, 'Theory of Texts,' *London Review of Books* (February 18, 1988), p. 21" [Ramanujan's note].
4. "A. K. Ramanujan, 'Two Realms of Kannada Folklore,' in *Another Harmony: New Essays in South Asian Folklore,* ed. Stuart Blackburn and A. K. Ramanujan (Berkeley and Los Angeles: University of California Press, 1986), pp. 41–75" [Ramanujan's note].
5. Unconscious areas from which psychic energies develop. *Mahādēvi:* great goddess, wife of Siva. *Māyā:* creative energy. *Guṇas:* the three qualities—*sattva* (purity), *rajas* (energy), and *tamas* (inertia)—from which all things are created.
6. "Quoted in Katarina Clark and Michael Holquist, *Mikhail Bakhtin* (Cambridge, Mass.: Harvard University Press, Belknap, 1984), p. 242" [Ramanujan's note]. Mikhail Bakhtin (1895–1975), Russian critic who developed his theories about dialogic and polyphonic languages in his readings of the work of the Russian novelist Fyodor Dostoyevsky (1821–1881).

Mirror on mirror. Doubles, shadow worlds, upside-down reflections, are common in Indian myth and story. When Viśvāmitra the sage sent his protégé Triśaṅku to heaven and the gods would not accept him and threw him down, the sage held him midair with his powers. And, piqued by his own failure to send Triśaṅku to heaven, he decided to make a second world exclusively for him, a world like the first but a bit botched: it is said that the buffalo is Viśvāmitra's version of the cow, the donkey his version of the horse, and so on.

The creation of doubles is a favorite literary device. In some Rāmāyaṇas, the chaste Sītā is not abducted at all, only a shadow double suffers all the hardships. Seducers in Indian texts appear as replicas of the husband. When Śiva creates, he creates clones of himself. As with DNA, to create is to project one's copies onto the world. * * *

* * *

1989

THE ANTILLES: FRAGMENTS OF EPIC MEMORY

In this lecture, delivered on the occasion of his acceptance of the 1992 Nobel Prize in Literature, Derek Walcott celebrates the cultural and linguistic hybridity and heterogeneity of the Antillean islands of the Caribbean, where peoples from around the world live side by side, creating new identities and fresh imaginative possibilities. Walcott recognizes the continuities with the Old World while rejecting the idea that the art and culture of the islands are mere imitations of African, Asian, or European originals. He also acknowledges the pain and horror of Caribbean history—the massacre and destruction of Amerindian peoples, the enslavement and importation of African slaves, and the indentured servitude of East Indians—but insists that the West Indian poet transfigure such inheritances in an art of awe, wonder, even ecstasy before the splendor of the New World. First published as Walcott's *Nobel Lecture* (December 7, 1992), the piece has been reprinted from *What the Twilight Says* (1998).

DEREK WALCOTT

The Antilles: Fragments of Epic Memory

Felicity is a village in Trinidad on the edge of the Caroni plain, the wide central plain that still grows sugar and to which indentured cane cutters were brought after emancipation,[1] so the small population of Felicity is East Indian, and on the afternoon that I visited it with friends from America, all the faces along its road were Indian, which, as I hope to show, was a moving, beautiful thing, because this Saturday afternoon *Ramleela,* the epic dramatization of the Hindu epic the *Ramayana,*[2] was going to be performed, and the costumed actors from the village were assembling on a field strung with different-coloured flags, like a new gas station, and beautiful Indian boys in red and black were aiming arrows haphazardly into the afternoon light. Low blue mountains on the horizon, bright grass, clouds that would gather colour before the light went. Felicity! What a gentle Anglo-Saxon name for an epical memory.

Under an open shed on the edge of the field, there were two huge armatures of bamboo that looked like immense cages. They were parts of the body of a god, his calves or thighs, which, fitted and reared, would make a gigantic effigy. This effigy would be burnt as a conclusion to the epic. The cane structures flashed a predictable parallel: Shelley's sonnet on the fallen statue of Ozymandias[3] and his empire, that "colossal wreck" in its empty desert.

Drummers had lit a fire in the shed and they eased the skins of their tablas[4] nearer the flames to tighten them. The saffron flames, the bright grass, and the hand-woven armatures of the fragmented god who would be burnt were not in any desert where imperial power had finally toppled but were part of a ritual, evergreen season that, like the cane-burning harvest, is annually repeated, the point of such sacrifice being its repetition, the point of the destruction being renewal through fire.

Deities were entering the field. What we generally call "Indian music" was blaring from the open platformed shed from which the epic would be narrated. Costumed actors were arriving. Princes and gods, I supposed. What an unfortunate confession! "Gods, I suppose" is the shrug that embodies our African and Asian diasporas. I had often thought of but never seen *Ramleela,* and had never seen this theatre, an open field, with village children as warriors, princes, and gods. I had no idea what the epic story was, who its hero was, what enemies he fought, yet I had recently adapted the *Odyssey* for a theatre in England, presuming that the audience knew the trials of Odysseus, hero of another Asia Minor epic, while nobody in Trinidad knew any more than I did about Rama, Kali, Shiva, Vishnu,[5] apart from the Indians, a phrase I use pervertedly because that is the kind of remark you can still hear in Trinidad: "apart from the Indians."

It was as if, on the edge of the Central Plain, there was another plateau, a raft on which the *Ramayana* would be poorly performed in this ocean of

1. In the 1830s, slavery was abolished in the British West Indies.
2. One of the two major epics—along with the *Mahabharata*—of Hinduism, the *Ramayana* tells the story of Rama, whose heroic deeds are enacted annually in performances of the *Ramaleela,* or the play of Rama.
3. "Ozymandias," by English poet Percy Bysshe Shelley (1792–1822), describes the desert ruins of an inscribed statue of an ancient king.
4. Small drums prominent in much Indian music.
5. Important deities appearing in the *Ramayana.*

cane, but that was my writer's view of things, and it is wrong. I was seeing the *Ramleela* at Felicity as theatre when it was faith.

Multiply that moment of self-conviction when an actor, made-up and costumed, nods to his mirror before stopping on stage in the belief that he is a reality entering an illusion and you would have what I presumed was happening to the actors of this epic. But they were not actors. They had been chosen; or they themselves had chosen their roles in this sacred story that would go on for nine afternoons over a two-hour period till the sun set. They were not amateurs but believers. There was no theatrical term to define them. They did not have to psych themselves up to play their roles. Their acting would probably be as buoyant and as natural as those bamboo arrows crisscrossing the afternoon pasture. They believed in what they were playing, in the sacredness of the text, the validity of India, while I, out of the writer's habit, searched for some sense of elegy, of loss, even of degenerative mimicry in the happy faces of the boy-warriors or the heraldic profiles of the village princes. I was polluting the afternoon with doubt and with the patronage of admiration. I misread the event through a visual echo of History—the cane fields, indenture, the evocation of vanished armies, temples, and trumpeting elephants—when all around me there was quite the opposite: elation, delight in the boys' screams, in the sweets-stalls, in more and more costumed characters appearing; a delight of conviction, not loss. The name Felicity made sense.

Consider the scale of Asia reduced to these fragments: the small white exclamations of minarets or the stone balls of temples in the cane fields, and one can understand the self-mockery and embarrassment of those who see these rites as parodic, even degenerate. These purists look on such ceremonies as grammarians look at a dialect, as cities look on provinces and empires on their colonies. Memory that yearns to join the centre, a limb remembering the body from which it has been severed, like those bamboo thighs of the god. In other words, the way that the Caribbean is still looked at, illegitimate, rootless, mongrelized. "No people there," to quote Froude, "in the true sense of the word."[6] No people. Fragments and echoes of real people, unoriginal and broken.

The performance was like a dialect, a branch of its original language, an abridgement of it, but not a distortion or even a reduction of its epic scale. Here in Trinidad I had discovered that one of the greatest epics of the world was seasonally performed, not with that desperate resignation of preserving a culture, but with an openness of belief that was as steady as the wind bending the cane lances of the Caroni plain. We had to leave before the play began to go through the creeks of the Caroni Swamp, to catch the scarlet ibises coming home at dusk. In a performance as natural as those of the actors of the *Ramleela*, we watched the flocks come in as bright as the scarlet of the boy archers, as the red flags, and cover an islet until it turned into a flowering tree, an anchored immortelle. The sigh of History meant nothing here. These two visions, the *Ramleela* and the arrowing flocks of scarlet ibises, blent into a single gasp of gratitude. Visual surprise is natural in the Caribbean; it comes with the landscape, and faced with its beauty, the sigh of History dissolves.

We make too much of that long groan which underlines the past. I felt privileged to discover the ibises as well as the scarlet archers of Felicity.

6. From *The English in the West Indies; or, The Bow of Ulysses* (1888), by James Anthony Froude (1818–1894), English historian.

The sigh of History rises over ruins, not over landscapes, and in the Antilles there are few ruins to sigh over, apart from the ruins of sugar estates and abandoned forts. Looking around slowly, as a camera would, taking in the low blue hills over Port of Spain,[7] the village road and houses, the warrior-archers, the god-actors and their handlers, and music already on the sound track, I wanted to make a film that would be a long-drawn sigh over Felicity. I was filtering the afternoon with evocations of a lost India, but why "evocations"? Why not "celebrations of a real presence"? Why should India be "lost" when none of these villagers ever really knew it, and why not "continuing," why not the perpetuation of joy in Felicity and in all the other nouns of the Central Plain: Couva, Chaguanas, Charley Village? Why was I not letting my pleasure open its windows wide? I was entitled like any Trinidadian to the ecstasies of their claim, because ecstasy was the pitch of the sinuous drumming in the loudspeakers. I was entitled to the feast of Husein,[8] to the mirrors and crêpe-paper temples of the Muslim epic, to the Chinese Dragon Dance, to the rites of that Sephardic Jewish[9] synagogue that was once on Something Street. I am only one-eighth the writer I might have been had I contained all the fragmented languages of Trinidad.

Break a vase, and the love that reassembles the fragments is stronger than that love which took its symmetry for granted when it was whole. The glue that fits the pieces is the sealing of its original shape. It is such a love that reassembles our African and Asiatic fragments, the cracked heirlooms whose restoration shows its white scars. This gathering of broken pieces is the care and pain of the Antilles, and if the pieces are disparate, ill-fitting, they contain more pain than their original sculpture, those icons and sacred vessels taken for granted in their ancestral places. Antillean art is this restoration of our shattered histories, our shards of vocabulary, our archipelago becoming a synonym for pieces broken off from the original continent.

And this is the exact process of the making of poetry, or what should be called not its "making" but its remaking, the fragmented memory, the armature that frames the god, even the rite that surrenders it to a final pyre; the god assembled cane by cane, reed by weaving reed, line by plaited line, as the artisans of Felicity would erect his holy echo.

Poetry, which is perfection's sweat but which must seem as fresh as the raindrops on a statue's brow, combines the natural and the marmoreal; it conjugates both tenses simultaneously: the past and the present, if the past is the sculpture and the present the beads of dew or rain on the forehead of the past. There is the buried language and there is the individual vocabulary, and the process of poetry is one of excavation and of self-discovery. Tonally the individual voice is a dialect; it shapes its own accent, its own vocabulary and melody in defiance of an imperial concept of language, the language of Ozymandias, libraries and dictionaries, law courts and critics, and churches, universities, political dogma, the diction of institutions. Poetry is an island that breaks away from the main. The dialects of my archipelago seem as fresh to me as those raindrops on the statue's forehead, not the sweat made

7. Capital of Trinidad, where Walcott directed the Trinidad Theatre Workshop from 1958 to 1976.

8. Shi'a Muslim festival commemorating the martyrdom of Muhammad's grandson. Indo-Trinidadians have culturally adapted and carnivalized the event, including in it colorful street theater, dancing, drinking, and nighttime processions with floats that represent Husein's tomb.

9. Sephardic Jews trace their ancestors back to Spain and Portugal, from which they were expelled in the fifteenth century.

from the classic exertion of frowning marble, but the condensations of a refreshing element, rain and salt.

Deprived of their original language, the captured and indentured tribes create their own, accreting and secreting fragments of an old, an epic vocabulary, from Asia and from Africa, but to an ancestral, an ecstatic rhythm in the blood that cannot be subdued by slavery or indenture, while nouns are renamed and the given names of places accepted like Felicity village or Choiseul.[1] The original language dissolves from the exhaustion of distance like fog trying to cross an ocean, but this process of renaming, of finding new metaphors, is the same process that the poet faces every morning of his working day, making his own tools like Crusoe,[2] assembling nouns from necessity, from Felicity, even renaming himself. The stripped man is driven back to that self-astonishing, elemental force, his mind. That is the basis of the Antillean experience, this shipwreck of fragments, these echoes, these shards of a huge tribal vocabulary, these partially remembered customs, and they are not decayed but strong. They survived the Middle Passage and the *Fatel Rozack*, the ship that carried the first indentured Indians from the port of Madras[3] to the cane fields of Felicity, that carried the chained Cromwellian convict[4] and the Sephardic Jew, the Chinese grocer and the Lebanese merchant selling cloth samples on his bicycle.

And here they are, all in a single Caribbean city, Port of Spain, the sum of history, Trollope's[5] "non-people." A downtown babel of shop signs and streets, mongrelized, polyglot, a ferment without a history, like heaven. Because that is what such a city is, in the New World, a writer's heaven.

A culture, we all know, is made by its cities.

Another first morning home, impatient for the sunrise—a broken sleep. Darkness at five, and the drapes not worth opening; then, in the sudden light, a cream-walled, brown-roofed police station bordered with short royal palms, in the colonial style, back of it frothing trees and taller palms, a pigeon fluttering into the cover of an eave, a rain-stained block of once-modern apartments, the morning side road into the station without traffic. All part of a surprising peace. This quiet happens with every visit to a city that has deepened itself in me. The flowers and the hills are easy, affection for them predictable; it is the architecture that, for the first morning, disorients. A return from American seductions used to make the traveller feel that something was missing, something was trying to complete itself, like the stained concrete apartments. Pan left along the window and the excrescences rear—a city trying to soar, trying to be brutal, like an American city in silhouette, stamped from the same mould as Columbus or Des Moines. An assertion of power, its decor bland, its air conditioning pitched to the point where its secretarial and executive staff sport competing cardigans; the colder the offices the more important, an imitation of another climate. A longing, even an envy of feeling cold.

In serious cities, in grey, militant winter with its short afternoons, the days

1. Old village on the southwest coast of Saint Lucia, near which live the island's small remaining population of Caribs—an Amerindian people largely killed off after the European conquest.
2. Shipwrecked protagonist of the novel *Robinson Crusoe*, by English writer Daniel Defoe (1660–1731), and in Walcott's work, a frequent figure for the Caribbean poet.
3. South Indian city where the British established a trading post in the seventeenth century. *Middle Passage:* transatlantic journey of slaves, transported from Africa to the Americas in morbidly overcrowded ships.
4. During the rule of Oliver Cromwell (1599–1658), who served as lord protector of England after the Civil War, the Caribbean was used as an English penal colony.
5. Anthony Trollope (1815–1882), English novelist; his travel books include *The West Indies and the Spanish Main* (1859).

seem to pass by in buttoned overcoats, every building appears as a barracks with lights on in its windows, and when snow comes, one has the illusion of living in a Russian novel, in the nineteenth century, because of the literature of winter. So visitors to the Caribbean must feel that they are inhabiting a succession of postcards. Both climates are shaped by what we have read of them. For tourists, the sunshine cannot be serious. Winter adds depth and darkness to life as well as to literature, and in the unending summer of the tropics not even poverty or poetry (in the Antilles poverty is poetry with a V, *une vie*,[6] a condition of life as well as of imagination) seems capable of being profound because the nature around it is so exultant, so resolutely ecstatic, like its music. A culture based on joy is bound to be shallow. Sadly, to sell itself, the Caribbean encourages the delights of mindlessness, of brilliant vacuity, as a place to flee not only winter but that seriousness that comes only out of culture with four seasons. So how can there be a people there, in the true sense of the word?

They know nothing about seasons in which leaves let go of the year, in which spires fade in blizzards and streets whiten, of the erasures of whole cities by fog, of reflection in fireplaces; instead, they inhabit a geography whose rhythm, like their music, is limited to two stresses: hot and wet, sun and rain, light and shadow, day and night, the limitations of an incomplete metre, and are therefore a people incapable of the subtleties of contradiction, of imaginative complexity. So be it. We cannot change contempt.

Ours are not cities in the accepted sense, but no one wants them to be. They dictate their own proportions, their own definitions in particular places and in a prose equal to that of their detractors, so that now it is not just St. James but the streets and yards that Naipaul[7] commemorates, its lanes as short and brilliant as his sentences; not just the noise and jostle of Tunapuna but the origins of C. L. R. James's *Beyond a Boundary*,[8] not just Felicity village on the Caroni plain, but Selvon[9] Country, and that is the way it goes up the islands now: the old Dominica of Jean Rhys[1] still very much the way she wrote of it; and the Martinique of the early Césaire; Perse's[2] Guadeloupe, even without the pith helmets and the mules; and what delight and privilege there was in watching a literature—one literature in several imperial languages, French, English, Spanish—bud and open island after island in the early morning of a culture, not timid, not derivative, any more than the hard white petals of the frangipani[3] are derivative and timid. This is not a belligerent boast but a simple celebration of inevitability: and this flowering had to come.

On a heat-stoned afternoon in Port of Spain, some alley white with glare, with love vine spilling over a fence, palms and a hazed mountain appear around a corner to the evocation of Vaughn or Herbert's "that shady city of palm-trees,"[4] or to the memory of a Hammond organ from a wooden chapel

6. A life (French); *V* was also the symbol for Allied victory in World War II.

7. V. S. Naipaul (b. 1932), Trinidad-born writer, who in his fiction and travel writing describes St. James, a region of Port of Spain, Trinidad, with a large Indian population.

8. In this work, C. L. R. James (1901–1989), historian and political activist born in Tunapuna, Trinidad, explores the sport of cricket as a metaphor for Britain and the West Indies.

9. Samuel Selvon (1923–1994), West Indian writer born in Trinidad.

1. Novelist Jean Rhys (1890–1979) spent her childhood on the small West Indian island of Dominica, the setting of part of her novel *Wide Sargasso Sea* (1966).

2. Saint-John Perse (1887–1975): French poet born in the Guadeloupe islands of the French Antilles. Aimé Césaire (b. 1913): poet and cofounder of the Negritude movement, born on the French Antillean island of Martinique.

3. Flowering tropical tree or shrub.

4. From line 25 of "The Retreate," by English religious poet Henry Vaughan (1621 or 1622–1695).

in Castries,[5] where the congregation sang "Jerusalem, the Golden." It is hard for me to see such emptiness as desolation. It is that patience that is the width of Antillean life, and the secret is not to ask the wrong thing of it, not to demand of it an ambition it has no interest in. The traveller reads this as lethargy, as torpor.

Here there are not enough books, one says, no theatres, no museums, simply not enough to do. Yet, deprived of books, a man must fall back on thought, and out of thought, if he can learn to order it, will come the urge to record, and in extremity, if he has no means of recording, recitation, the ordering of memory which leads to metre, to commemoration. There can be virtues in deprivation, and certainly one virtue is salvation from a cascade of high mediocrity, since books are now not so much created as remade. Cities create a culture, and all we have are these magnified market towns, so what are the proportions of the ideal Caribbean city? A surrounding, accessible countryside with leafy suburbs, and if the city is lucky, behind it, spacious plains. Behind it, fine mountains; before it, an indigo sea. Spires would pin its centre and around them would be leafy, shadowy parks. Pigeons would cross its sky in alphabetic patterns, carrying with them memories of a belief in augury,[6] and at the heart of the city there would be horses, yes, horses, those animals last seen at the end of the nineteenth century drawing broughams[7] and carriages with top-hatted citizens, horses that live in the present tense without elegiac echoes from their hooves, emerging from paddocks at the Queen's Park Savannah[8] at sunrise, when mist is unthreading from the cool mountains above the roofs, and at the centre of the city seasonally there would be races, so that citizens could roar at the speed and grace of these nineteenth-century animals. Its docks, not obscured by smoke or deafened by too much machinery, and above all, it would be so racially various that the cultures of the world—the Asiatic, the Mediterranean, the European, the African—would be represented in it, its humane variety more exciting than Joyce's Dublin.[9] Its citizens would intermarry as they chose, from instinct, not tradition, until their children find it increasingly futile to trace their genealogy. It would not have too many avenues difficult or dangerous for pedestrians, its mercantile area would be a cacophony of accents, fragments of the old language that would be silenced immediately at five o'clock, its docks resolutely vacant on Sundays.

This is Port of Spain to me, a city ideal in its commercial and human proportions, where a citizen is a walker and not a pedestrian, and this is how Athens may have been before it became a cultural echo.

The finest silhouettes of Port of Spain are idealizations of the craftsman's handiwork, not of concrete and glass, but of baroque woodwork, each fantasy looking more like an involved drawing of itself than the actual building. Behind the city is the Caroni plain, with its villages, Indian prayer flags, and fruit vendors' stalls along the highway over which ibises come like floating flags. Photogenic poverty! Postcard sadnesses! I am not recreating Eden; I mean, by "the Antilles," the reality of light, of work, of survival. I mean a house on the side of a country road, I mean the Caribbean Sea, whose smell is the smell of refreshing possibility as well as survival. Survival is the triumph of stubbornness, and spiritual stubbornness, a sublime stupidity, is what

George Herbert (1593–1633), English religious poet of the same period.
5. Capital of Saint Lucia.
6. Practice of divining the future from the flight of birds.
7. One-horse carriages.
8. Large park in Port of Spain, Trinidad.
9. Irish writer James Joyce (1882–1941), whose novel *Ulysses* (1922) details minutely a day's life in Dublin.

makes the occupation of poetry endure, when there are so many things that should make it futile. Those things added together can go under one collective noun: "the world."

This is the visible poetry of the Antilles, then. Survival.

If you wish to understand that consoling pity with which the islands were regarded, look at the tinted engravings of Antillean forests, with their proper palm trees, ferns, and waterfalls. They have a civilizing decency, like Botanical Gardens, as if the sky were a glass ceiling under which a colonized vegetation is arranged for quiet walks and carriage rides. Those views are incised with a pathos that guides the engraver's tool and the topographer's pencil, and it is this pathos which, tenderly ironic, gave villages names like Felicity. A century looked at a landscape furious with vegetation in the wrong light and with the wrong eye. It is such pictures that are saddening rather than the tropics itself. These delicate engravings of sugar mills and harbours, of native women in costume, are seen as a part of History, that History which looked over the shoulder of the engraver and, later, the photographer. History can alter the eye and the moving hand to conform a view of itself; it can rename places for the nostalgia in an echo; it can temper the glare of tropical light to elegiac monotony in prose, the tone of judgement in Conrad,[1] in the travel journals of Trollope.

These travellers carried with them the infection of their own malaise, and their prose reduced even the landscape to melancholia and self-contempt. Every endeavor is belittled as imitation, from architecture to music. There was this conviction in Froude that since History is based on achievement, and since the history of the Antilles was so genetically corrupt, so depressing in its cycles of massacres, slavery, and indenture, a culture was inconceivable and nothing could ever be created in those ramshackle ports, those monotonously feudal sugar estates. Not only the light and salt of Antillean mountains defied this, but the demotic vigour and variety of their inhabitants. Stand close to a waterfall and you will stop hearing its roar. To be still in the nineteenth century, like horses, as Brodsky[2] has written, may not be such a bad deal, and much of our life in the Antilles still seems to be in the rhythm of the last century, like the West Indian novel.

By writers even as refreshing as Graham Greene,[3] the Caribbean is looked at with elegiac pathos, a prolonged sadness to which Lévi-Strauss has supplied an epigraph: *Tristes Tropiques*. Their *tristesse*[4] derives from an attitude to the Caribbean dusk, to rain, to uncontrollable vegetation, to the provincial ambition of Caribbean cities where brutal replicas of modern architecture dwarf the small houses and streets. The mood is understandable, the melancholy as contagious as the fever of a sunset, like the gold fronds of diseased coconut palms, but there is something alien and ultimately wrong in the way such a sadness, even a morbidity, is described by English, French, or some of our exiled writers. It relates to a misunderstanding of the light and the people on whom the light falls.

These writers describe the ambitions of our unfinished cities, their unrealized, homiletic[5] conclusion, but the Caribbean city may conclude just at that

1. Polish-born English novelist Joseph Conrad (1857–1924); his fiction reflects his experience as a young man of working on ships in the West Indies.
2. Joseph Brodsky (1940–1996), Russian-born American poet and 1987 Nobel laureate.
3. British novelist (1904–1991).
4. Sadness (French). French (Belgian-born) structural anthropologist Claude Lévi-Strauss (b. 1908) titled his memoir *Tristes Tropiques* (melancholy tropics).
5. Sermonlike.

point where it is satisfied with its own scale, just as Caribbean culture is not evolving but already shaped. Its proportions are not to be measured by the traveller or the exile, but by its own citizenry and architecture. To be told you are not yet a city or a culture requires this response. I am not your city or your culture. There might be less of *Tristes Tropiques* after that.

Here, on the raft of this dais, there is the sound of the applauding surf: our landscape, our history recognized, "at last." *At Last* is one of the first Caribbean books. It was written by the Victorian traveller Charles Kingsley.[6] It is one of the early books to admit the Antillean landscape and its figures into English literature. I have never read it but gather that its tone is benign. The Antillean archipelago was there to be written about, not to write itself, by Trollope, by Patrick Leigh-Fermor,[7] in the very tone in which I almost wrote about the village spectacle at Felicity, as a compassionate and beguiled outsider, distancing myself from Felicity village even while I was enjoying it. What is hidden cannot be loved. The traveller cannot love, since love is stasis and travel is motion. If he returns to what he loved in a landscape and stays there, he is no longer a traveller but in stasis and concentration, the lover of that particular part of earth, a native. So many people say they "love the Caribbean," meaning that someday they plan to return for a visit but could never live there, the usual benign insult of the traveller, the tourist. These travellers, at their kindest, were devoted to the same patronage, the islands passing in profile, their vegetal luxury, their backwardness and poverty. Victorian prose dignified them. They passed by in beautiful profiles and were forgotten, like a vacation.

Alexis Saint-Léger Léger, whose writer's name is St.-John Perse, was the first Antillean to win this prize for poetry. He was born in Guadeloupe and wrote in French, but before him, there was nothing as fresh and clear in feeling as those poems of his childhood, that of a privileged white child on an Antillean plantation, *"Pour fêter une enfance," "Eloges,"* and later *"Images à Crusoe."*[8] At last, the first breeze on the page, salt-edged and self-renewing as the trade winds, the sound of pages and palm trees turning as "the odour of coffee ascends the stairs."

Caribbean genius is condemned to contradict itself. To celebrate Perse, we might be told, is to celebrate the old plantation system, to celebrate the *bequé*[9] or plantation rider, verandahs and mulatto servants, a white French language in a white pith helmet, to celebrate a rhetoric of patronage and hauteur; and even if Perse denied his origins, great writers often have this folly of trying to smother their source, we cannot deny him any more than we can the African Aimé Césaire. This is not accommodation, this is the ironic republic that is poetry, since, when I see cabbage palms moving their fronds at sunrise, I think they are reciting Perse.

The fragrant and privileged poetry that Perse composed to celebrate his white childhood and the recorded Indian music behind the brown young archers of Felicity, with the same cabbage palms against the same Antillean sky, pierce me equally. I feel the same poignancy of pride in the poems as in the faces. Why, given the history of the Antilles, should this be remarkable? The history of the world, by which of course we mean Europe, is a record of intertribal lacerations, of ethnic cleansings. At last, islands not

6. English clergyman and writer (1819–1875).
7. English travel writer (b. 1915).
8. To celebrate a childhood, eulogies, images of Crusoe (French).
9. White person (French Creole).

written about but writing themselves! The palms and the Muslim minarets are Antillean exclamations. At last! the royal palms of Guadeloupe recite *"Eloges"* by heart.

Later, in *Anabase,* Perse assembled fragments of an imaginary epic, with the clicking teeth of frontier gates, barren wadis with the froth of poisonous lakes, horsemen burnoosed[1] in sandstorms, the opposite of cool Caribbean mornings, yet not necessarily a contrast any more than some young brown archer at Felicity, hearing the sacred text blared across the flagged field, with its battles and elephants and monkey-gods, in a contrast to the white child in Guadeloupe assembling fragments of his own epic from the lances of the cane fields, the estate carts and oxens, and the calligraphy of bamboo leaves from the ancient languages, Hindi, Chinese, and Arabic, on the Antillean sky. From the *Ramayana* to Anabasis, from Guadeloupe to Trinidad, all that archaeology of fragments lying around, from the broken African kingdoms, from the crevasses of Canton, from Syria and Lebanon, vibrating not under the earth but in our raucous, demotic streets.

A boy with weak eyes skims a flat stone across the flat water of an Aegean inlet, and that ordinary action with the scything elbow contains the skipping lines of the *Iliad* and the *Odyssey,* and another child aims a bamboo arrow at a village festival, and another hears the rustling march of cabbage palms in a Caribbean sunrise, and from that sound, with its fragments of tribal myth, the compact expedition of Perse's epic is launched, centuries and archipelagos apart. For every poet it is always morning in the world. History a forgotten, insomniac night; History and elemental awe are always our early beginning, because the fate of poetry is to fall in love with the world, in spite of History.

There is a force of exultation, a celebration of luck, when a writer finds himself a witness to the early morning of a culture that is defining itself, branch by branch, leaf by leaf, in that self-defining dawn, which is why, especially at the edge of the sea, it is good to make a ritual of the sunrise. Then the noun, the "Antilles" ripples like brightening water, and the sounds of leaves, palm fronds, and birds are the sounds of fresh dialect, the native tongue. The personal vocabulary, the individual melody whose metre is one's biography, joins in that sound, with any luck, and the body moves like a walking, a waking island.

This is the benediction that is celebrated, a fresh language and a fresh people, and this is the frightening duty owed.

I stand here in their name, if not their image—but also in the name of the dialect they exchange like the leaves of the trees whose names are suppler, greener, more morning-stirred than English—*laurier canelles, bois-flot, bois-canot*—or the valleys the trees mention—*Fond St. Jacques, Mabonya, Forestièr, Roseau, Mahaut*—or the empty beaches—*L'Anse Ivrogne, Case en Bas, Paradis*—all songs and histories in themselves, pronounced not in French—but in patois.[2]

One rose hearing two languages, one of the trees, one of schoolchildren reciting in English:

I am monarch of all I survey,
My right there is none to dispute;

1. A burnoose is a long cloak with a hood, worn by Arabs. *Wadis:* valleys or ravines dry except during the rainy season (from Arabic).

2. French Creole, borne of a fusion of French with African and European languages; the everyday language of Walcott's native Saint Lucia.

From the centre all round to the sea
I am lord of the fowl and the brute.
Oh, solitude! where are the charms
That sages have seen in thy face?
Better dwell in the midst of alarms,
Than reign in this horrible place . . . [3]

While in the country to the same metre, but to organic instruments, hand-made violin, chac-chac,[4] *and goatskin drum, a girl named Sensenne singing:*

Si mwen di 'ous' ça fait mwen la peine
'Ous kai dire ça vrai.
    (If I told you that caused me pain
    You'll say, "It's true.")
Si mwen di 'ous ça pentetrait mwen
'Ous peut dire ça vrai.
    (If I told you you pierced my heart
    You'd say, "It's true.")
Ces mamailles actuellement
Pas ka faire l'amour z'autres pour un rien.
    (Children nowadays
    Don't make love for nothing.)

It is not that History is obliterated by this sunrise. It is there in Antillean geography, in the vegetation itself. The sea sighs with the drowned from the Middle Passage, the butchery of its aborigines, Carib and Aruac and Taino,[5] bleeds in the scarlet of the immortelle, and even the actions of surf on sand cannot erase the African memory, or the lances of cane as a green prison where indentured Asians, the ancestors of Felicity, are still serving time.

That is what I have read around me from boyhood, from the beginnings of poetry, the grace of effort. In the hard mahogany of woodcutters: faces, resinous men, charcoal burners; in a man with a cutlass cradled across his forearm, who stands on the verge with the usual anonymous khaki dog; in the extra clothes he put on this morning, when it was cold when he rose in the thinning dark to go and make his garden in the heights—the heights, the garden, being miles away from his house, but that is where he has his land—not to mention the fishermen, the footmen on trucks, groaning up mornes,[6] all fragments of Africa originally but shaped and hardened and rooted now in the island's life, illiterate in the way leaves are illiterate; they do not read, they are there to be read, and if they are properly read, they create their own literature.

But in our tourist brochures the Caribbean is a blue pool into which the republic dangles the extended foot of Florida as inflated rubber islands bob and drinks with umbrellas float towards her on a raft. This is how the islands from the shame of necessity sell themselves; this is the seasonal erosion of their identity, that high-pitched repetition of the same images of service that cannot distinguish one island from the other, with a future of polluted marinas, land deals negotiated by ministers, and all of this conducted to the music of Happy Hour and the rictus[7] of a smile. What is the earthly paradise for

3. From William Cowper's (1731–1800) poem written in the voice of Alexander Selkirk (1676–1721), the Scottish sailor after whom Robinson Crusoe was modeled.
4. Maracalike instrument.
5. Peoples native to the Antilles at the time of the Spanish conquest.
6. Small, independent mountains (French Creole).
7. Mouth.

our visitors? Two weeks without rain and a mahogany tan, and, at sunset, local troubadours in straw hats and floral shirts beating "Yellow Bird" and "Banana Boat Song"[8] to death. There is a territory wider than this—wider than the limits made by the map of an island—which is the illimitable sea and what it remembers.

All of the Antilles, every island, is an effort of memory; every mind, every racial biography culminating in amnesia and fog. Pieces of sunlight through the fog and sudden rainbows, *arcs-en-ciel*.[9] That is the effort, the labour of the Antillean imagination, rebuilding its gods from bamboo frames, phrase by phrase.

Decimation from the Aruac downwards is the blasted root of Antillean history, and the benign blight that is tourism can infect all of those island nations, not gradually, but with imperceptible speed, until each rock is whitened by the guano of white-winged hotels, the arc and descent of progress.

Before it is all gone, before only a few valleys are left, pockets of an older life, before development turns every artist into an anthropologist or folklorist, there are still cherishable places, little valleys that do not echo with ideas, a simplicity of rebeginnings, not yet corrupted by the dangers of change. Not nostalgic sites but occluded sanctities as common and simple as their sunlight. Places as threatened by this prose as a headland is by the bulldozer or a sea almond grove by the surveyor's string, or from blight, the mountain laurel.

One last epiphany: A basic stone church in a thick valley outside Soufrière,[1] the hills almost shoving the houses around into a brown river, a sunlight that looks oily on the leaves, a backward place, unimportant, and one now being corrupted into significance by this prose. The idea is not to hallow or invest the place with anything, not even memory. African children in Sunday frocks come down the ordinary concrete steps into the church, banana leaves hang and glisten, a truck is parked in a yard, and old women totter towards the entrance. Here is where a real fresco should be painted, one without importance, but one with real faith, mapless, Historyless.

How quickly it could all disappear! And how it is beginning to drive us further into where we hope are impenetrable places, green secrets at the end of bad roads, headlands where the next view is not of a hotel but of some long beach without a figure and the hanging question of some fisherman's smoke at its far end. The Caribbean is not an idyll, not to its natives. They draw their working strength from it organically, like trees, like the sea almond or the spice laurel of the heights. Its peasantry and its fishermen are not there to be loved or even photographed; they are trees who sweat, and whose bark is filmed with salt, but every day on some island, rootless trees in suits are signing favourable tax breaks with entrepreneurs, poisoning the sea almond and the spice laurel of the mountains to their roots. A morning could come in which governments might ask what happened not merely to the forests and the bays but to a whole people.

They are here again, they recur, the faces, corruptible angels, smooth black skins and white eyes huge with an alarming joy, like those of the Asian children of Felicity at *Ramleela;* two different religions, two different continents, both filling the heart with the pain that is joy.

8. Popular 1950s song by American singer and actor Harry Belafonte (b. 1927). "Yellow Bird" is an anonymous song.
9. Rainbows (French).

1. Town on west coast of Saint Lucia; nearby are the tourist attractions of an active volcano and the island's twin peaks, the Pitons.

But what is joy without fear? The fear of selfishness that, here on this podium with the world paying attention not to them but to me, I should like to keep these simple joys inviolate, not because they are innocent, but because they are true. They are as true as when, in the grace of this gift, Perse heard the fragments of his own epic of Asia Minor in the rustling of cabbage palms, that inner Asia of the soul through which imagination wanders, if there is such a thing as imagination as opposed to the collective memory of our entire race, as true as the delight of that warrior-child who flew a bamboo arrow over the flags in the field at Felicity; and now as grateful a joy and a blessed fear as when a boy opened an exercise book and, within the discipline of its margins, framed stanzas that might contain the light of the hills on an island blest by obscurity, cherishing our insignificance.

1992

Selected Bibliographies

African Poetry

Book-length studies of African poetry include Jonathan Kariara and Ellen Kitonga's *An Introduction to East African Poetry* (1976); Romanus Egudu's *Four Modern West African Poets* (1977) and *Modern African Poetry and the African Predicament* (1978); K. L. Goodwin's *Understanding African Poetry* (1982); Tayo Olafioye's *Politics in African Poetry* (1982); Jacques Alvarez-Pereyre's *The Poetry of Commitment in South Africa* (1984); Robert Fraser's *West African Poetry: A Critical History* (1986); *Oral and Written Poetry in African Literature Today* (1988), ed. Eldred D. Jones; Emmanuel Ngara's *Ideology and Form in African Poetry* (1990); Adrian Roscoe's *The Quiet Chameleon: Modern Poetry from Central Africa* (1992); Tanure Ojaide's *Poetic Imagination in Black Africa* (1996); and Charles Bodunde's *Oral Traditions and Aesthetic Transfer: Creativity and Social Vision in Contemporary Black Poetry* (2001). Other works dealing with African literature include Adrian Roscoe's *Mother Is Gold: A Study of West African Literature* (1971); Nadine Gordimer's *The Black Interpreters* (1973); O. R. Dathorne's *The Black Mind: A History of African Literature* (1974); Kofi Awoonor's *The Breast of the Earth: A Survey of the History, Culture, and Literature of Africa South of the Sahara* (1975); Gerald Moore's *Twelve African Writers* (1980); Chinweizu, Onwuchekwa Jemie, and Ihechukwu Madubuike's *Toward the Decolonization of African Literature* (1983); and Ursula A. Barnett's *A Vision of Order: A Study of Black South African Literature in English, 1914–1980* (1983).

Anthologies of African poetry written in English include *West African Verse* (1967), ed. Donatus Ibe Nwoga; *Poems from East Africa* (1971), ed. David Cook and David Rubadiri; *The Word Is Here: Poetry from Modern Africa* (1973), ed. Keroapetse Kgositsile; *Poems of Black Africa* (1975), ed. Wole Soyinka; *The Return of the Amasi Bird: Black South African Poetry, 1891–1981* (1982), ed. Tim Couzens and Essop Patel; *A New Book of African Verse* (1984), ed. John Reed and Clive Wake; *The Penguin Book of Modern African Poetry* (1984), ed. Gerald Moore and Ulli Beier; *The Heritage of African Poetry* (1985), ed. Isidore Okpewho; *When My Brothers Come Home: Poems from Central and Southern Africa* (1985), ed. Frank Chipasula; *The Fate of Vultures: New Poetry of Africa* (1989), ed. Kofi Anyidoho, Peter Porter, and Musaemura Zimunya; *The Heinemann Book of African Women's Poetry* (1995), ed. Stella Chipasula; and *The New African Poetry* (1999), ed. Tanure Ojaide. See also **Christopher Okigbo, Okot p'Bitek, Wole Soyinka**.

American Poetry

Critical works especially helpful for the study of contemporary American poetry include Richard Howard's *Alone with America* (1969, 1980), Harold Bloom's *Ringers in the Tower* (1971) and *Figures of Capable Imagination* (1976), Robert Pinsky's *The Situation of Poetry* (1976), David Kalstone's *Five Temperaments* (1977), Helen Vendler's *Part of Nature, Part of Us* (1980), Cary Nelson's *Our Last First Poets* (1981), Marjorie Perloff's *The Poetics of Indeterminacy* (1981), James E. B. Breslin's *From Modern to Contemporary: American Poetry, 1945–1965* (1984), Charles Altieri's *Self and Sensibility in Contemporary American Poetry* (1984), Robert von Hallberg's *American Poetry and Culture, 1945–1980* (1985), Andrew Ross's *The Failure of Modernism: Symptoms of American Poetry* (1986), Paul Breslin's *The Psycho-Political Muse* (1987), Lynn Keller's *Re-Making It New* (1987), J. D. McClatchy's *White Paper* (1989), Willard Spiegelman's *The Didactic Muse* (1989), Perloff's *Radical Artifice* (1991), Vernon Shetley's *After the Death of Poetry* (1993), Vendler's *The Given and the Made* (1995) and *Soul Says* (1995), James Longenbach's *Modern Poetry after Modernism* (1997), Peter Stitt's *Uncertainty and Plenitude* (1997), Perloff's *Poetry on and off the Page* (1998), and Thomas Gardner's *Regions of Unlikeness* (1999). An excellent compendium is *Encyclopedia of American Poetry: The Twentieth Century* (2001), ed. Eric L. Haralson. The Academy of American Poets maintains a useful website, www.poets.org, with an audio component and links to other sites on contemporary poetry.

Asian American Poetry

Studies of Asian American poetry and literature include *Asian-American Authors* (1972), ed. Kai-yu Hsu and Helen Palubinskas; Elaine H. Kim's *Asian American Literature: An Introduction to the Writings and Their Social Context* (1982); Stephen Sumida's *And the View from the Shore: Literary Traditions of Hawaii* (1991); *Reading the Literatures of Asian America* (1992), ed. Shirley Geok-lin Lim and Amy Ling; Sau-ling Cynthia Wong's *Reading Asian American Literature: From Necessity to Extravagance* (1993); Esther Mikyung Ghymn's *Images of Asian American Women by Asian American Women Writers* (1995); Lisa Lowe's *Immigrant Acts: On Asian American Cultural Politics* (1996); *Asian American Women Writers* (1997), ed. Harold Bloom; *An Interethnic Companion to Asian American Literature* (1997), ed. King-Kok Cheung; Eileen Tabios's *Black Lightning: Poetry-in-Progress* (1998); Jinqi Ling's *Narrating Nationalism: Ideology and Form in Asian American Literature* (1998); *Words Matter: Conversations with Asian American Writers* (2000), ed. King-Kok Cheung; and Anne Anlin Cheng's *The Melancholy of Race* (2001). Bibliographic information is available in *Asian American Literature: An Annotated Bibliography* (1988), ed. Cheung and Stan Yogi.

Anthologies of Asian American literature include *Aiiieeeee!: An Anthology of Asian-American Writers* (1974), ed. Frank Chin, Jeffery Paul Chan, Lawson Fusao Inada, and Shawn Hsu Wong; *The Forbidden Stitch: An Asian American Women's Anthology* (1989), ed. Shirley Geok-lin Lim, Mayumi Tsutakawa, and Margarita Donnelly; *The Big Aiiieeeee!: An Anthology of Chinese American and Japanese American Literature* (1991), ed. Chan et al.; *Asian American Literature: A Brief Introduction and Anthology* (1996), ed. Shawn Wong; *Quiet Fire: A Historical Anthology of Asian American Poetry* (1996), ed. Juliana Chang; *Making More Waves: New Writing by Asian American Women* (1997), ed. Elaine H. Kim, Lilia V. Villanueva, and Asian Women United of California; and *Bold Words: A Century of Asian American Writing* (2001), ed. Rajini Srikanth and Esther Y. Iwanaga. See also **Marilyn Chin, Li-Young Lee, Cathy Song.**

Australian Poetry

For studies of Australian poetry, see Judith Wright's *Preoccupations in Australian Poetry* (1965); Brian Elliott's *The Landscape of Australian Poetry* (1967); Vincent Buckley's *Essays in Poetry, Mainly Australian* (1969); James Phillip McAuley's *A Map of Australian Verse: The Twentieth Century* (1975); Andrew Taylor's *Reading Australian Poetry* (1987); *Poetry and Gender: Statements and Essays in Australian Women's Poetry and Poetics* (1989), ed. David Brooks and Brenda Walker; *Australian Poetry in the Twentieth Century* (1991), ed. Robert Gray and Geoffrey Lehmann; Bruce Dawe's *Tributary Streams: Some Sources of Social and Political Concerns in Modern Australian Poetry* (1992); R. P. Rama's *Dialogues with Australian Poets* (1993); and Paul Kane's *Australian Poetry: Romanticism and Negativity* (1996).

Anthologies include *The Penguin Book of Modern Australian Verse* (1972), ed. Harry P. Heseltine; *The New Australian Poetry* (1979), ed. John Tranter; *The Collins Book of Australian Poetry* (1981), ed. R. Hall; *The New Oxford Book of Australian Verse* (1986), ed. Les Murray; *The Penguin Book of Australian Women Poets* (1986), ed. Susan Hampton and K. Llewellyn; *Contemporary Australian Poetry: An Anthology* (1990), ed. John Leonard; and *The Penguin Book of Modern Australian Poetry* (1991), ed. Tranter. See also **Les Murray, Judith Wright; in volume 1, A. D. Hope.**

Beat Movement

For discussions of the Beat movement, see Lawrence Ferlinghetti and Nancy J. Peters's *Literary San Francisco* (1980); Michael Davidson's *The San Francisco Renaissance: Poetics and Community at Mid-Century* (1989); John Arthur Maynard's *Venice West: The Beat Generation in Southern California* (1991); Ann Charters's "Beat Poetry and the San Francisco Poetry Renaissance," *Columbia History of American Poetry* (1993), ed. Jay Parini and Brett C. Millier; Pierre Delattre's *Episodes* (1993); Steven Watson's *The Birth of the Beat Generation* (1995); David Sterritt's *Mad to Be Saved: The Beats, The Fifties, and Film* (1998); *The Beat Writers at Work: Paris Review Interviews* (1999), ed. George Plimpton; Ronna C. Johnson and Maria Damon's "Recapturing the Skipped Beats: Women and Minorities in the Beat Generation," *Chronicle of Higher Education* (1 October 1999); James Campbell's *This Is the Beat Generation: New York, San Francisco, Paris* (1999); Neeli Cherkovski's *Whitman's Wild Children* (1999); Barry Miles's *The Beat Hotel* (2000); and David Meltzer's *San Francisco Beats: Talking with the Poets* (2001). See also **Amiri Baraka, Lawrence Ferlinghetti, Allen Ginsberg, Gary Snyder, San Francisco Renaissance.**

Black Arts Movement

For Black Arts Movement anthologies, see Amiri Baraka and Larry Neal's *Black Fire* (1968); Toni Cade Bambara's *The Black Woman* (1970); Addison Gayle's *The Black Aesthetic* (1971); Abraham Chapman's *New Black Voices* (1972); Stephen Henderson's *Understanding the New Black Poetry* (1972); Eugene Redmond's *Drumvoices, The Mission of Afro-American Poetry: A Critical History* (1976); and Neal's *Visions of a Liberated Future* (1989). Discussions of the Black Arts Movement include *The LeRoi Jones/*

Amiri Baraka Reader (1991, 2000), ed. William J. Harris; William Cook's "The Black Arts Poets," *Columbia History of American Poetry* (1993), ed. Jay Parini and Brett C. Millier; and Kalamu ya Salaam's "Black Arts Movement," *Oxford Companion to African American Literature* (1997), ed. William L. Andrews, Frances Smith Foster, and Trudier Harris. See also **Amiri Baraka, Lucille Clifton, June Jordan, Audre Lorde.**

Black Mountain School

For discussion of the Black Mountain school, see Martin Duberman's *Black Mountain: An Exploration in Community* (1972); Sherman Paul's *Olson's Push: Origin, Black Mountain, and Recent American Poetry* (1978); Paul Christensen's *Charles Olson: Call Him Ishmael* (1979); Charles Altieri's *Self and Sensibility in Contemporary American Poetry* (1984); Mary Emma Harris's *The Arts at Black Mountain College* (1987); Willard Fox's *Robert Creeley, Edward Dorn, and Robert Duncan: A Reference Guide* (1989); *Black Mountain College: Sprouted Seeds: An Anthology of Personal Accounts* (1990), ed. Mervin Lane; Brian Conniff's "Reconsidering Black Mountain: The Poetry of Hilda Morley," *American Literature* 65.1 (1993); Edward Halsey Foster's *Understanding the Black Mountain Poets* (1995); Marjorie Perloff's "Whose New American Poetry? Anthologizing the Nineties," *Diacritics* 26.3–4 (1996); and Paul Breslin's "Black Mountain Reunion," *Poetry* 176.3 (2000). See also **Robert Creeley, Robert Duncan, Denise Levertov, Charles Olson.**

British Poetry

Works especially helpful for the study of contemporary British poetry include *British Poetry since 1960* (1972), ed. Michael Schmidt and Grevel Lindop; Calvin Bedient's *Eight Contemporary Poets* (1974); Anthony Thwaite's *Twentieth-Century English Poetry: An Introduction* (1978); Blake Morrison's *The Movement: English Poetry and Fiction of the 1950s* (1980); John Haffenden's *Viewpoints: Poets in Conversation with John Haffenden* (1981); Bruce K. Martin's *British Poetry since 1939* (1985); *Poets of Great Britain and Ireland since 1960* (1985), ed. Vincent B. Sherry Jr.; John Lucas's *Modern English Poetry—From Hardy to Hughes* (1986); Edna Longley's *Poetry in the Wars* (1986); Alan Robinson's *Instabilities in Contemporary British Poetry* (1988); Donald Davie's *Under Briggflatts: A History of Poetry in Great Britain, 1960–1988* (1989); Ian Gregson's *Contemporary Poetry and Postmodernism: Dialogue and Estrangement* (1996); Keith Tuma's *Fishing by Obstinate Isles: Modern and Postmodern British Poetry and American Readers* (1998); and Dillon Johnston's *The Poetic Economies of England and Ireland, 1912–2000* (2001).

Canadian Poetry

For more information on Canadian poetry in English, see *The Making of Modern Poetry in Canada* (1967), ed. Louis Dudek and Michael Gnarowski; *Canadian Poetry* (1982), ed. Jack David and Robert Lecker; George Bowering's *A Way with Words* (1982); Frank Davey's *Reading Canadian Reading* (1988); Caroline Bayard's *The New Poetics in Canada and Quebec: From Concretism to Postmodernism* (1989); *Beyond Tish* (1991), ed. Douglas Barbour; Warren Tallman's *In the Midst: Writings 1962–1992* (1992); and George Woodcock's *George Woodcock's Introduction to Canadian Poetry* (1993). Other works on Canadian literature include Douglas G. Jones's *Butterfly on Rock* (1970), Northrop Frye's *The Bush Garden* (1971), Margaret Atwood's *Survival: A Thematic Guide to Canadian Literature* (1972), and E. D. Blodgett's *Configuration: Essays in the Canadian Literatures* (1982).

Anthologies include *The New Oxford Book of Canadian Verse in English* (1982), ed. Margaret Atwood, and *The New Canadian Poets* (1985), ed. Dennis Lee. See also **Margaret Atwood, Anne Carson, Michael Ondaatje, P. K. Page.**

Caribbean Poetry

Studies of Caribbean poetry include *West Indian Literature* (1979), ed. Bruce King; *Fifty Caribbean Writers: A Bio-Bibliographical Critical Sourcebook* (1986), ed. Daryl Cumber Dance; Edward Kamau Brathwaite's *Roots* (1986); Frank Birbalsingh's *Passion and Exile: Essays in Caribbean Literature* (1988); *New World Adams: Conversations with Contemporary West Indian Writers* (1992), ed. Dance; Gordon Rohlehr's *My Strangled City* (1992) and *The Shape of That Hurt* (1992); Antonio Benítez Rojo's *The Repeating Island: The Caribbean and the Postmodern Perspective* (1992), tr. James Maraniss; J. Edward Chamberlin's *Come Back to Me My Language: Poetry and the West Indies* (1993); Birbalsingh's *Frontiers of Caribbean Literature* (1996); Silvio Torres-Saillant's *Caribbean Poetics: Toward an Aesthetics of West Indian Literature* (1997); Laurence A. Breiner's *An Introduction to West Indian Poetry* (1998); J. Michael Dash's *The Other America: Caribbean Literature in a New World Context* (1998); Louis James's *Caribbean Literature in English* (1999); and *Talk Yuh Talk: Interviews with Anglophone Caribbean Poets* (2001), ed. Kwame Senu Neville Dawes.

Anthologies include *The Penguin Book of Caribbean Verse in English* (1986), ed. Paula Burnett; *Hinterland: Caribbean Poetry from the West Indies and Britain* (1989), ed. E. A. Markham; *Voiceprint: An Anthology of Oral and*

Related Poetry from the Caribbean (1989), ed. Stewart Brown and Mervyn Morris; and *The Heinemann Book of Caribbean Poetry* (1992), ed. Ian McDonald and Stewart Brown. See also **Louise Bennett, Kamau Brathwaite, Lorna Goodison, Grace Nichols, Derek Walcott.**

Confessional Poetry

For more on confessional poetry, see Robert S. Phillips's *The Confessional Poets* (1973); Ralph J. Mills's *Cry of the Human* (1975); David Perkins's *A History of Modern Poetry: The Eighteen-Nineties to the High Modernist Mode* (1976); Charles Molesworth's *The Fierce Embrace* (1979); James E. B. Breslin's *From Modern to Contemporary* (1984); Paul Breslin's *The Psycho-Political Muse* (1987); Jeffrey Meyers's *Manic Power: Robert Lowell and His Circle* (1987); Diane Wood Middlebrook's "What Was Confessional Poetry?" *Columbia History of American Poetry* (1993), ed. Jay Parini and Brett C. Millier; Marjorie Perloff's "Realism and the Confessional Mode of Robert Lowell," *The Critical Response to Robert Lowell* (1999), ed. Steven Gould Axelrod; and Lucy Collins's "Confessionalism," *A Companion to Twentieth-Century Poetry* (2001), ed. Neil Roberts. See also **John Berryman, Robert Lowell, Sylvia Plath, Adrienne Rich, Anne Sexton, W. D. Snodgrass.**

Cross-National Studies

David Perkins's *A History of Modern Poetry: Modernism and After* (1987) is an indispensable guide for British, Irish, and American poetry. Other helpful cross-national studies include M. L. Rosenthal's *The New Poets: American and British Poetry since World War II* (1967); *50 Modern American and British Poets, 1920–1970* (1973), ed. Louis Untermeyer; Louis Simpson's *A Revolution of Taste* (1978); *Modern Poetry* (1979), ed. Charles Altieri; Helen Vendler's *The Music of What Happens* (1988); Jahan Ramazani's *Poetry of Mourning* (1994); Vendler's *The Breaking of Style* (1995); David Bromwich's *Skeptical Music: Essays on Modern Poetry* (2001); and Ramazani's *The Hybrid Muse* (2001). Valuable critical and biographical material can also be found in *The Oxford Companion to Twentieth-Century Poetry* (1996), ed. Ian Hamilton; the essay collection *A Companion to Twentieth-Century Poetry* (2001), ed. Neil Roberts; and the volumes (many now available online) of *Contemporary Poets* and *The Dictionary of Literary Biography.*

Deep Image Poetry

For more on Deep Image poetry, see Robert Kelly's "Notes on the Poetry of the Deep Image," *Trobar* (1961); James E. B. Breslin's *From Modern to Contemporary* (1984); Kevin Power's "Robert Bly," *American Poetry Observed: Poets on Their Work* (1984), ed. Joe D. Bellamy; Robert Bly's *American Poetry: Wildness and Domesticity* (1990); Paul Christensen's *Minding the Underworld: Clayton Eshleman and Late Postmodernism* (1991); Cramer R. Cauthen's "Deep Image and the Poetics of Oppen's 'Of Being Numerous,' " *Sagetrieb* 13.3 (1994); and Nick Halpern's " 'Coming Back Here How Many Years Now': August Kleinzahler and James Wright's *Shall We Gather at the River*," *Contemporary Literature* 42.2 (2001). See also **Robert Bly, W. S. Merwin, James Wright.**

Gay and Lesbian Poetry

Studies dealing with gay and lesbian poetry include Robert K. Martin's *The Homosexual Tradition in Modern Poetry* (1979, 1998), Judy Grahn's *The Highest Apple: Sappho and the Lesbian Poetic Tradition* (1985), and Gregory Woods's *Articulate Flesh: Male Homo-Eroticism and Modern Poetry* (1987). Anthologies include *The Male Muse: A Gay Anthology* (1973), ed. Ian Young; *Angels of the Lyre: A Gay Poetry Anthology* (1975), ed. Winston Leyland; *The Penguin Book of Homosexual Verse* (1983), ed. Stephen Coote; *Beautiful Barbarians: Lesbian Feminist Poetry* (1986), ed. Lilian Mohin; *Gay and Lesbian Poetry in Our Time* (1988), ed. Carl Morse and Joan Larkin; *Naming the Waves: Contemporary Lesbian Poetry* (1988), ed. Christian McEwen; *The World in Us: Lesbian and Gay Poetry of the Next Wave* (2000), ed. Michael Lassell; and *Love Speaks Its Name: Gay and Lesbian Love Poems* (2001), ed. J. D. McClatchy.

Indian Poetry

For studies of Indian poetry in English, see *Contemporary Indian English Verse* (1980), ed. Chirantan Kulshrestha; M. K. Naik's *Perspectives on Indian Poetry in English* (1984); Bruce King's *Modern Indian Poetry in English* (1987); Makarand Paranjape's *Mysticism in Indian English Poetry* (1988); *Living Indian English Poets* (1989), ed. Madhusudan Prasad; D. S. Mishra's *Contemporary Indian English Poetry: A Revaluation* (1990); Lakshmi Raghunandan's *Contemporary Indian Poetry in English* (1990); P. K. J. Kurup's *Contemporary Indian Poetry in English* (1991); King's *Three Indian Poets* (1991); Vinay Dharwadker's "Some Contexts of Modern Indian Poetry," *Chicago Review* 38.1–2 (1992); *Indian Poetry in English* (1993), ed. Paranjape; John Oliver Perry's "Contemporary Indian Poetry in English," *World Literature Today* 68.2 (1994); G. J. V. Prasad's *Continuities in Indian English Poetry: Nation Language Form* (1999); and Eunice de Souza's *Talking Poems: Conversations with Poets* (1999).

Anthologies include *India: An Anthology of Contemporary Writing* (1983), ed. David Ray and Amritjit Singh; *Another India* (1990), ed. Nissim Ezekiel and Meenakshi Mukherjee; and

The Oxford Anthology of Modern Indian Poetry (1994), ed. Vinay Dharwadker and A. K. Ramanujan. See also **Agha Shahid Ali, Eunice de Souza, A. K. Ramanujan.**

Irish Poetry

For studies of contemporary Irish poetry, see Terence Brown's *Northern Voices: Poets from Ulster* (1975); A. Norman Jeffares's *Anglo-Irish Literature* (1982); Seamus Deane's *Celtic Revivals: Essays in Modern Irish Literature 1880–1980* (1985); Robert F. Garratt's *Modern Irish Poetry: Tradition and Continuity from Yeats to Heaney* (1986); Edna Longley's *Poetry in the Wars* (1987); *The Chosen Ground: Essays on the Contemporary Poetry of Northern Ireland* (1992), ed. Neil Corcoran; *Contemporary Irish Poetry: A Collection of Critical Essays* (1992), ed. Elmer Andrews; Clair Wills's *Improprieties: Politics and Sexuality in Northern Irish Poetry* (1993); Theo Dorgan's *Irish Poetry since Kavanagh* (1995); Michael Kenneally's *Poetry in Contemporary Irish Literature* (1995); Patricia Boyle Haberstroh's *Women Creating Women* (1996); Steven Matthews's *Irish Poetry: Politics, History, Negotiation: The Evolving Debate, 1969 to the Present* (1997); Peter McDonald's *Mistaken Identities: Poetry and Northern Ireland* (1997); *Contemporary Irish Women Poets: Some Male Perspectives* (1999), ed. Alexander G. Gonzalez; Eamon Grennan's *Facing the Music: Irish Poetry in the Twentieth Century* (1999); Neil Corcoran's *Poets of Modern Ireland: Text, Context, Intertext* (1999); Jonathan Hufstader's *Tongue of Water, Teeth of Stones: Northern Irish Poetry and Social Violence* (1999); John Goodby's *From Stillness into History: Irish Poetry since 1950* (2000); Fran Brearton's *The Great War in Irish Poetry: W. B. Yeats to Michael Longley* (2000); Frank Sewell's *Modern Irish Poetry: A New Alhambra* (2000); Patrick Grant's *Literature, Rhetoric, and Violence in Northern Ireland, 1968–98* (2001); and *My Self, My Muse: Irish Women Poets Reflect on Life and Art* (2001), ed. Haberstroh.

Anthologies include *Contemporary Irish Poetry* (1980, 1988), ed. Anthony Bradley; *The Faber Book of Contemporary Irish Poetry* (1986), ed. Paul Muldoon; *The New Oxford Book of Irish Verse* (1986), ed. Thomas Kinsella; and *The Penguin Book of Contemporary Irish Poetry* (1990), ed. Peter Fallon and Derek Mahon. See also **Eavan Boland, Seamus Heaney, Thomas Kinsella, Michael Longley, Derek Mahon, Medbh McGuckian, Paul Muldoon.**

Language Poetry

For works associated with Language poetry, see Bruce Andrews and Charles Bernstein's *The L=A=N=G=U=A=G=E Book* (1984); Barrett Watten's *Total Syntax* (1984); Bob Perelman's *Writing/Talks* (1985); Ron Silliman's *The New Sentence* (1987); Bernstein's *The Politics of Poetic Form* (1990); and Lyn Hejinian's "The Rejection of Closure," reprinted in *The Language of Inquiry* (2000). *In the American Tree* (1986), ed. Silliman, is a representative anthology. For critical discussions, see Jerome McGann's "Contemporary Poetry, Alternate Routes," *Critical Inquiry* 13.3 (Spring 1987); George Hartley's *Textual Politics and the Language Poets* (1989); Marjorie Perloff's *Radical Artifice* (1991); Linda Reinfeld's *Language Poetry: Writing as Rescue* (1992); Perelman's *The Marginalization of Poetry: Language Writing and Literary History* (1996); Perloff's *Poetry on and off the Page* (1998); and Simon Perril's entry in *A Companion to Twentieth-Century Poetry* (2001), ed. Neil Roberts. See also **Charles Bernstein, Lyn Hejinian, Susan Howe, Michael Palmer.**

Latino Poetry

For studies of Latino poetry, see Américo Paredes's "The Folk Base of Chicano Literature," *Modern Chicano Writers: A Collection of Critical Essays* (1979), ed. Joseph Sommers and Tomás Ybarro-Frausto; Bruce-Novoa's *Chicano Poetry: A Response to Chaos* (1982); Marta Ester Sánchez's *Contemporary Chicana Poetry* (1985); *Partial Autobiographies: Interviews with Twenty Chicano Poets* (1985), ed. Wolfgang Binder; Cordelia Candelaria's *Chicano Poetry: A Critical Introduction* (1986); Bruce-Novoa's *RetroSpace: Collected Essays on Chicano Literature, Theory, and History* (1990); José Eduardo Límon's *Mexican Ballads, Chicano Poems: History and Influence in Mexican-American Social Poetry* (1992); Rafael Pérez-Torres's *Movements in Chicano Poetry: Against Myths, Against Margins* (1995); Alfred Arteaga's *Chicano Poetics: Heterotexts and Hybridities* (1997); and Teresa McKenna's *Migrant Song: Politics and Process in Contemporary Chicano Literature* (1997).

Anthologies include *Fiesta in Aztlan* (1982), ed. Toni Empringham; *Contemporary Chicano Poetry* (1986), ed. Wolfgang Binder; *Touching the Fire: Fifteen Poets of Today's Latino Renaissance* (1998), ed. Ray González. See also **Lorna Dee Cervantes, Dionisio D. Martínez, Alberto Ríos, Gary Soto.**

The Movement

New Lines (1956), ed. Robert Conquest, is the anthology that first attracted attention to the Movement. A fine book-length study is Blake Morrison's *The Movement: English Poetry and Fiction of the 1950s* (1980). For other discussions, see William Van O'Connor's *The New University Wits and the End of Modernism* (1963); Kenneth Allsop's *The Angry Decade* (1964); Anthony Saroop's "The Anti-Aestheticism of the British Movement Poets," *Studies in English Literature* 54 (1977); Florence Elon's "The Movement against Itself: British Poetry of the 1950s," *Southern Review* 19.1 (1983); Andrew Crozier's "Thrills and Frills: Poetry as Figures of Empirical Lyricism," *Society and Literature, 1945–1970* (1983), ed. Alan Sinfield; Michael Dirda's "The Movement," *Grand Street* 6.3 (1987); Hans Osterwalder's *British Poetry between the Movement and Modernism: Anthony Thwaite and Philip Larkin* (1991); and Stephen Regan's "The Movement," *A Companion to Twentieth-Century Poetry* (2001), ed. Neil Roberts. See also **Kingsley Amis, Donald Davie, Thom Gunn, Philip Larkin.**

Native American Poetry

For discussions of Native American poetry, see John Milton's *The American Indian Speaks* (1969); Kenneth Roemer's "Bear and Elk: The Nature(s) of Contemporary Indian Poetry," *Journal of Ethnic Studies* 5.2 (1977); J. Rupert's "The Uses of Oral Tradition in Six Contemporary Native American Poets," *American Indian Culture and Research Journal* 4 (1980); Anne Bromley's "Renegade Wants the Word: Contemporary Native American Poetry," *Literary Review* 23.3 (1980); Kenneth Lincoln's *Native American Renaissance* (1983); Duane Niatum's "History in the Colors of Song: A Few Words on Contemporary Native American Poetry," *Coyote Was Here: Essays on Contemporary Native American Literary and Political Mobilization* (1984), ed. Bo Schöler; Andrew Wiget's "Sending a Voice: The Emergence of Contemporary Native American Poetry," *College English* 46.6 (1984); Andrew Wiget's *Native American Literature* (1985); Joseph Bruchach's "Many Tongues: Native American Poetry Today," *North Dakota Quarterly* 55.4 (1987) and *Survival This Way: Interviews with American Indian Poets* (1987); Laura Coltelli's *Winged Words: American Indian Writers Speak* (1990); Robin Riley Fast's "Borderland Voice in Contemporary Native American Poetry," *Contemporary Literature* 36.3 (1995); Janet McAdams's "We, I, 'Voice,' and Voices: Reading Contemporary Native American Poetry," *Studies in American Indian Literatures* 7.3 (1995); Kathleen M. Donovan's *Feminist Readings of Native American Literature* (1998); *Native American Writers* (1998), ed. Harold Bloom; Fast's *The Heart as a Drum: Continuance and Resistance in American Indian Poetry* (1999); Lincoln's *Sing with the Heart of a Bear: Fusions of Native and American Poetry, 1890–1999* (2000); and Norma Wilson's *The Nature of Native American Poetry* (2001).

Anthologies include *The Remembered Earth: An Anthology of Contemporary Native American Literature* (1979, 1981), ed. Geary Hobson; *Harper's Anthology of 20th Century Native American Poetry* (1988), ed. Duane Niatum; *Durable Breath: Contemporary Native American Poetry* (1994), ed. John E. Smelcer; *Reinventing the Enemy's Language: Contemporary Native Women's Writings of North America* (1997), ed. Joy Harjo; and *Native American Women's Writing c. 1800–1924* (2000), ed. Karen Kilcup. See also **Sherman Alexie, Louise Erdrich, Joy Harjo, Leslie Marmon Silko.**

The New Criticism and Poetry

For the original critical works in which the tenets of the New Criticism were worked out, see Laura Riding and Robert Graves's *A Survey of Modernist Poetry* (1927); John Crowe Ransom's *The New Criticism* (1941); Cleanth Brooks's *The Well Wrought Urn* (1947) and his anthology *Understanding Poetry* (with Robert Penn Warren, 1938); William Empson's *Seven Types of Ambiguity* (1947); W. K. Wimsatt and Monroe C. Beardsley's *The Verbal Icon* (1954), especially their essay on "The Intentional Fallacy"; and Murray Krieger's *The New Apologists for Poetry* (1956). For critical discussions of the movement, see J. N. Patnaik's *The Aesthetics of the New Criticism* (1982); James E. B. Breslin's *From Modern to Contemporary* (1984); J. Timothy Bagwell's *American Formalism and the Problem of Interpretation* (1986); Mark Doty's "The 'Forbidden Planet' of Character: The Revolutions of the 1950s," *A Profile of Twentieth-Century American Poetry* (1991), ed. Jack Myers, David Wojahn, and Ed Folsom; Robert Bechtold's *The Southern Connection* (1991); Mark Jancovich's *Cultural Politics of the New Criticism* (1993); Mark Royden Winchell's *Cleanth Brooks and the Rise of Modern Criticism* (1996); and Stephen Burt and Jennifer Lewin's "Poetry and the New Criticism," *A Companion to Twentieth-Century Poetry* (2001).

New Formalism

For critical discussions of New Formalism, see Diane Wakoski's "The New Conservatism in American Poetry," *American Book Review* 7.4 (1986); *Expansive Poetry: Essays on the New Narrative and the New Formalism* (1989), ed. Frederick Feirstein; Robert McPhillips's "Reading the New Formalists," *Sewanee Review* 47.1 (1989); Wyatt Prunty's *"Fallen from the Symboled World": Precedents for the New Formalism* (1990); Ira Sadoff's "Neo-Formalism: A Dangerous Nostalgia," *American Poetry Review* 19.1 (1990); Lewis Turco's "New-Formalism in Contemporary American Poetry," *Poet* 2.3 (1990); Vernon Shetley's *After the Death of Poetry* (1993); *After New Formalism: Poets on Form, Narrative, and Tradition* (1999), ed. Annie Finch. Two anthologies associated with the movement are *Strong Measures: Contemporary American Poetry in Traditional Forms* (1986), ed. Philip Dacey and David Jauss; and *Rebel Angels: 25 Poets of the New Formalism* (1996), ed. Mark Jarman and David Mason. See also **Marilyn Hacker.**

New York School

Works dealing with the New York school include Geoffrey Ward's *Statutes of Liberty: The New York School of Poets* (1993); David Lehman's *The Last Avant-Garde: The Making of the New York School of Poets* (1998); John Simon's "Partying on Parnassus: The New York School Poets," *New Criterion* 17.2 (1998); William Watkin's *In the Process of Poetry: The New York School and the Avant-Garde* (2001); Terence Diggory and Stephen Paul Miller's *The Scene of My Selves : New Work on New York School Poets* (2001); and Paul Hoover's "Fables of Representation: Poetry of The New York School," *American Poetry Review* 31.4 (2002). The early anthologies *The Poets of the New York School* (1969), ed. John Bernard Myers, and *An Anthology of New York School Poets* (1970), ed. Ron Padgett and David Shapiro, helped institutionalize the poets as a school. See also **John Ashbery, Kenneth Koch, Frank O'Hara.**

San Francisco Renaissance

For more on the San Francisco Renaissance, see Daniel Aaron's *Writers on the Left: Episodes in American Literary Communism* (1961); Kenneth Rexroth's *American Poetry in the Twentieth Century* (1971); *The Poetics of the New American Poetry* (1973), ed. Donald Allen and Warren Tallman; William Everson's *Archetype West: The Pacific Coast as a Literary Region* (1976); *Towards a New American Poetics* (1978), ed. Ekbert Faas; Lawrence Ferlinghetti and Nancy J. Peters's *Literary San Francisco* (1980); Michael McClure's *Scratching the Beat Surface* (1982); *The Literary Review* (San Francisco Renaissance issue, Fall 1988); Michael Davidson's *The San Francisco Renaissance: Poetics and Community at Mid-Century* (1989); Lee Bartlett's *The Sun Is but a Morning Star: Studies in West Coast Poetry and Poetics* (1989); and Linda Hamalian's "Regionalism Makes Good: The San Francisco Renaissance," *Reading the West: New Essays on the Literature of the American West* (1996), ed. Michael Kowalewski. See also **Beat Poetry, Robert Duncan, Lawrence Ferlinghetti, Gary Snyder; in volume 1, Kenneth Rexroth.**

Ai

Ai's volumes of poetry include *Cruelty* (1973), *Killing Floor* (1979), *Sin* (1986), *Fate* (1991), *Greed* (1993), and *Vice: New and Selected Poems* (1999). She is also the author of a novel, *Black Blood* (1997). Selected periodical publications include "On Being ½ Japanese, ⅛ Choctaw, ¼ Black, and 1/16 Irish," *Ms.* 6 (June 1974); and "Movies, Mom, Poetry, Sex and Death: A Self-Interview," *Onthebus* 3–4 (1991). Interviews include Lawrence Kearney and Michael Cuddihy's in *Ironwood* 12 (1978) and Lisa Erb's in *Manoa: A Pacific Journal of International Writing* 2 (1990).

Critical articles include Rob Wilson's "The Will to Transcendence in Contemporary American Poet, Ai," *Canadian Review of American Studies* 17.4 (1986); Susannah B. Mintz's " 'A Descent into the Unknown' in the Poetry of Ai," *Sage* 9.2 (1995); Jeanne Heuving's "Divesting Social Registers: Ai's Sensational Portraiture of the Renowned and the Infamous," *Critical Survey* 9.2 (1997); Claudia Ingram's "Writing the Crises: The Deployment of Abjection in Ai's Dramatic Monologues," *Lit: Literature Interpretation Theory* 8.2 (1997); and Karen L. Kilcup's "Dialogues of the Self: Toward a Theory of (Re)Reading Ai," *Journal of Gender Studies* 7.1 (1998).

Sherman Alexie

Alexie's books of poetry include *The Business of Fancydancing* (1992), *I Would Steal Horses* (1992), *First Indian on the Moon* (1993), *Old Shirts & New Skins* (1993), *Seven Mourning Songs for the Cedar Flute I Have Yet to Learn to Play* (1994), *Water Flowing Home* (1994), *The Summer of Black Widows* (1996), *The Man Who Loves Salmon* (1998), and *One Stick Song* (2000). Alexie has also published fiction, including the novels *Reservation Blues* (1995) and *Indian Killer* (1996), and short-story collections, *The Lone Ranger and Tonto Fistfight in Heaven* (1993) and *The Toughest Indian in the World* (2000). He also wrote the screenplays for the films *Smoke Signals* (1998) and *The Business of Fancydancing* (2002), which he also directed. Interviews include John and Carl Bellante's in *Bloomsbury Review* 14 (1994); Mark Weber's in *Chiron Review* (1995); and Kelly Myers's in *Tonic* 1 (1995).

Discussions of Alexie's work include Jennifer Gillan's "Reservation Home Movies: Sherman Alexie's Poetry," *American Literature* 68.1 (1996); Ron McFarland's "Another Kind of Violence: Sherman Alexie's Poetry," *American Indian Quarterly* 21 (1997); "Sherman Alexie," *Studies in American Indian Literatures* 9.4 (1997); Lynne Cline's "About Sherman Alexie," *Ploughshares* 26.4 (2000–2001); Kenneth Lincoln's *Sing with the Heart of a Bear: Fusions of Native and American Poetry, 1890–1999* (2000); John Newton's "Sherman Alexie's Autoethnography," *Contemporary Literature* 42.2 (2001); and Carrie Etter's "Dialectic to Dialogic: Negotiating Bicultural Heritage in Sherman Alexie's Sonnets," *Telling the Stories: Essays on American Literatures and Cultures* (2001), ed. Elizabeth Hoffman Nelson. See also **Native American Poetry.**

Agha Shahid Ali

Ali's volumes of poetry include *Bone Sculpture* (1972), *"In Memory of Begum Akhtar" and Other Poems* (1979), *The Half-Inch Himalayas* (1987), *A Walk through the Yellow Pages* (1987), *A Nostalgist's Map of America* (1991), *The Beloved Witness: Selected Poems* (1992), *The Country without a Post Office* (1997), and *Rooms Are Never Finished* (2001). He also edited a volume of ghazals, *Ravishing Disunities: Real Ghazals in English* (2000), translated the poetry of Faiz Ahmed Faiz in *The Rebel's Silhouette: Selected Poems* (1992), and wrote a scholarly study of T. S. Eliot, *T. S. Eliot as Editor* (1986).

Critical essays on his work include the review in *Indian Literature* 145.5 (1991); Neile Graham's in *Poet Lore* 87.1 (1992); Sudeep Sen's in *Poetry Review* 83.1 (1993); Lawrence Needham's "The Sorrows of a Broken Time," *Reworlding: Writers of the Indian Diaspora* (1992), ed. Emmanuel Nelson, and also Needham's "In Pursuit of Evanescence: Agha Shahid Ali's *A Nostalgist's Map of America*," *Kunapipi* 15.2 (1993); Ketu H. Katrak's "South Asian American Literature," *An Interethnic Companion to Asian American Literature* (1996), ed. King-Kok Cheung; Rajeev S. Patke's "Translation as Metaphor: The Poetry of Agha Shahid Ali," *Metamorphoses: Journal of the Five-College Seminar on Literary Translation* 8.2 (2000); and Amitav Ghosh's " 'The Ghat of the Only World': Agha Shahid Ali in Brooklyn," *Nation* (11 February 2002). See also **Indian Poetry.**

Kingsley Amis

Amis's *Collected Poems, 1944–1979* was published in 1979. Most famous for his many novels—notably *Lucky Jim* (1954)—Amis also wrote short stories, essays, science fiction, scripts for radio and television, and *The King's English: A Guide to Modern Usage* (1998). Zachary Leader edited *The Letters of Kingsley Amis* in 2000. Recent biographies are Eric Jacobs's *Kingsley Amis* (1995) and Richard Bradford's *Lucky Him: The Life of Kingsley Amis* (2001).

Book-length studies include Philip Gardner's *Kingsley Amis* (1981) and Paul Fussell's *The Anti-Egotist* (1994). Collections of essays include *Kingsley Amis in Life and Letters* (1990), ed. Dale Salwak; and *Critical Essays on Kingsley Amis* (1998), ed. Robert H. Bell. Other critical discussions include William Van O'Connor's *The New University Wits and the End of Modernism* (1963); John Press's *Rule and Energy: British Poetry since the Second World War* (1963); Blake Morrison's *The Movement: English Poetry and Fiction of the 1950s* (1980); Florence Elon's "The Movement Against Itself: British Poetry of the 1950s," *Southern Review* 19.1 (1983); and Edward Lobb's "The Dead Father: Notes on Literary Influence," *Studies in the Humanities* 13.2 (1986). Two bibliographies are Jack Benoit Gohn's *Kingsley Amis: A Checklist* (1976) and Salwak's *Kingsley Amis: A Reference Guide* (1978). See also **The Movement.**

A. R. Ammons

Collections of Ammons's poetry include *Collected Poems, 1951–1971* (1972), *Selected Longer Poems* (1980), *Selected Poems: Expanded Edition* (1986), and the *Really Short Poems of A. R. Ammons* (1990). Other volumes include *Sphere: The Form of Motion* (1974), *Diversifications* (1975), *Highgate Rode* (1977), *The Snow Poems* (1977), *A Coast of Trees* (1981), *Worldly Hopes* (1982), *Lake Effect Country* (1983), *Sumerian Vista* (1987), *Garbage* (1993), *Brink Road* (1996), *Glare* (1997), and *Strip* (1997). *Set in Motion* (1996) is a collection of essays and interviews.

Book-length studies of his work include Alan Holder's *A. R. Ammons* (1978) and Steven P. Schneider's *A. R. Ammons and the Poetics of Widening Scope* (1994). Other discussions of his work are included in Richard Howard's *Alone with America* (1969, 1980); Harold Bloom's *The Ringers in the Tower* (1971); Helen Vendler's *The Music of What Happens* (1988); Mary Kinzie's *The Cure of Poetry in an Age of Prose* (1993); Stephen Cushman's *Fictions of Form in American Poetry* (1993); Robert Kirschten's *Approaching Prayer: Ritual and the Shape of Myth in A. R. Ammons and James Dickey* (1998); Leonard M. Scigaj's *Sustainable Poetry: Four American Ecopoets* (1999); and Bonnie Costello's "Ammons: Pilgrim, Sage, Ordinary Man," *Raritan* (Winter 2002). There are numerous useful critical essays in the collections *A. R. Ammons* (1986), ed. Harold Bloom; *Critical Essays on A. R. Ammons* (1997), ed. Kirschten; and *Complexities of Motion: New Essays on A. R. Ammons's Long Poems* (1999), ed. Steven P. Schneider. Two special journal issues dedicated to Ammons are *Diacritics* 3 (Winter 1973) and *Pembroke Magazine* 18 (1986). Stuart Wright's *A. R. Ammons: A Bibliography, 1954–1979* was published in 1980.

John Ashbery

Ashbery's volumes of poetry include *Some Trees* (1956), *The Tennis Court Oath* (1962), *Rivers and Mountains* (1966), *The Double Dream of Spring* (1970), *Three Poems* (1972), *Self-Portrait in a Convex Mirror* (1975), *The Vermont Notebook* (with Joe Brainard, 1975); *Houseboat Days* (1977), *As We Know* (1979), *Shadow Train* (1981), *A Wave* (1984), *Selected Poems* (1985); *April Galleons* (1987); *Flow Chart* (1991); *Hotel Lautréamont* (1992), *Three Books* (1993), *And the Stars Were Shining* (1994), *Can You Hear, Bird* (1995); *The Mooring of Starting Out: The First Five Books of Poetry* (1997), *Wakefulness* (1998), *Girls on the Run* (1999), and *Your Name*

Here (2000). He is also the author of plays and the collaborative novel *A Nest of Ninnies* (with James Schuyler, 1969). His art criticism is collected in *Reported Sightings* (1989) and his series of lectures on neglected modern poets in *Other Traditions* (2000). Interviews include Janet Bloom and Robert Losada's in *The Craft of Poetry: Interviews from "The New York Quarterly"* (1974), ed. William Packard; A. Poulin's in *Michigan Quarterly Review* 20 (1981); John Koethe's in *Sub/Stance* 37/38 (1983); and David Herd's in *Pn Review* 21.1 (1994).

John Shoptaw's *On The Outside Looking Out* (1994) is an especially useful study of Ashbery's books from *Some Trees* to *Flow Chart*. Other studies include David Shapiro's *John Ashbery: An Introduction to the Poetry* (1979) and David Herd's *John Ashbery and American Poetry* (2000). Important discussions of his work include David Kalstone's *Five Temperaments* (1977); Charles Altieri's *Self and Sensibility in Contemporary American Poetry* (1984); Andrew Ross's *The Failure of Modernism: Symptoms of American Poetry* (1986); Lee Edelman's "The Pose of Imposture: Ashbery's 'Self-Portrait in a Convex Mirror,'" *Twentieth Century Literature* 32.1 (1986); Geoff Ward's "Ashbery and Influence," *Statutes of Liberty: The New York School of Poets* (1993, 2001); Catherine Imbriglio's "'Our Days Put on Such Reticence': The Rhetoric of the Closet in John Ashbery's *Some Trees*," *Contemporary Literature* 36.2 (1995); James Longenbach's "John Ashbery's Individual Talent," *Modern Poetry After Modernism* (1997); Peter Stitt's *Uncertainty and Plenitude* (1997); Thomas Gardner's "John Ashbery's New Voice," *Regions of Unlikeness* (1999); and Peter Nicholls's "Ashbery and Language Poetry," *Poetry and the Sense of Panic: Critical Essays on Elizabeth Bishop and John Ashbery* (2000), ed. Lionel Kelly. David Lehman's *The Last Avant-Garde: The Making of the New York School of Poets* (1998) combines biographical information with critical analysis of Ashbery and his fellow New York school poets. Many important essays are included in the collections *Beyond Amazement: New Essays on John Ashbery* (1980), ed. David Lehman; *John Ashbery* (1985), ed. Harold Bloom; and *The Tribe of John: Ashbery and Contemporary Poetry* (1995), ed. Susan M. Schultz. David K. Kermani's *John Ashbery: A Comprehensive Bibliography* appeared in 1976. See also **New York School.**

Margaret Atwood

Atwood's most recent collection of selected poetry is *Eating Fire: Selected Poems 1965–1995* (1998). Other volumes include *Double Persephone* (1961), *Kaleidoscopes: Baroque* (1965), *Talismans for Children* (1965), *The Circle Game* (1966), *Expeditions* (1966), *Speeches for Doctor Frankenstein* (1966), *The Animals in That County* (1968), *The Journals of Susanna Moodie* (1970), *Procedures for the Underground* (1970), *Power Politics* (1971), *You Are Happy* (1974), *Selected Poems* (1976), *Marsh, Hawk* (1977), *Two-Headed Poems* (1978), *Notes Towards a Poem That Can Never Be Written* (1981), *True Stories* (1981), *Snake Poems* (1983), *Interlunar* (1984), *Selected Poems II: Poems Selected and New 1976–1986* (1986), and *Morning in the Burned House* (1995). She is also the author of numerous novels, including *The Edible Woman* (1969), *The Handmaid's Tale* (1985), and *Cat's Eye* (1988), as well as short stories and children's fiction. Some of her criticism can be found in *Second Words: Selected Critical Prose* (1984), and interviews in *Margaret Atwood: Conversations* (1990), ed. Earl Ingersoll. She has also written a book on writing, *Negotiating with the Dead* (2002), and a guide to Canadian literature, *Survival* (1972), and edited *The New Oxford Book of Canadian Verse in English* (1982).

Collections of critical essays include *Margaret Atwood: A Symposium* (1977), ed. Linda Sandler; *The Art of Margaret Atwood: Essays in Criticism* (1981), ed. Arnold E. and Cathy N. Davidson; *Margaret Atwood: Language, Text, and System* (1983), ed. Grace and Lorraine Weir; *Critical Essays on Margaret Atwood* (1988), ed. Judith McCombs; *Margaret Atwood* (2000), ed. Harold Bloom; and *Margaret Atwood: Works and Impact* (2000), ed. Reingard M. Nischik. Other studies include Frank Davey's *Margaret Atwood: A Feminist Poetics* (1984) and Karen Stein's *Margaret Atwood Revisited* (1999). Alan J. Horne has compiled bibliographies of Atwood's poetry and prose in *The Annotated Bibliography of Canada's Major Authors 1–2* (1979–1980), ed. Robert Lecker and Jack David. See also **Canadian Poetry.**

Amiri Baraka

Baraka's *Selected Poetry* was published in 1979. Other volumes include *Preface to a Twenty Volume Suicide Note* (1961), *The Dead Lecturer* (1964), *Black Art* (1966), *Black Magic: Collected Poetry, 1961–1967* (1969), *It's Nation Time* (1970), *Spirit Reach* (1972), *Afrikan Revolution* (1973), *Hard Facts* (1976), *AM/TRAK* (1979), *Reggae or Not!* (1981); *Wise, Why's Y's* (1995), *Eulogies* (1996), and *Funk Lore: New Poems, 1984–1995* (1996). His dramatic and prose works have been collected in *Selected Plays and Prose* (1979) and, with selected poetry, in the *LeRoi Jones/Amiri Baraka Reader* (1991, 2000), ed. William J. Harris. Some of his most important plays can be found in *Dutchman and the Slave* (1964) and *Four Black Revolutionary Plays* (1969). Prose writings include *Blues People* (1963), *Home: Social Essays* (1966), *Raise Race Rays Raze* (1972), *The Autobiography of LeRoi Jones* (1984), *Daggers and Javelins: Essays,*

1974–1979 (1984), and *The Music: Reflections on Jazz and Blues* (1987). Charlie Reilly edited a book of interviews, *Conversations with Amiri Baraka*, in 1994. Baraka performed his poetry to jazz accompaniment on audio recordings such as *New Music—New Poetry* (1981), with David Murray and Steve McCall.

Imamu Amiri Baraka (1978), ed. Kimberly W. Benston, is a collection of critical essays. Other useful studies include Werner Sollors's *Amiri Baraka/LeRoi Jones: The Quest for a "Populist Modernism"* (1978); Lloyd Brown's *Amiri Baraka* (1980); William J. Harris's *Poetry and Poetics of Amiri Baraka: The Jazz Aesthetic* (1985); Komozi Woodard's *A Nation within a Nation: Amiri Baraka (LeRoi Jones) and Black Power Politics* (1999); and Jerry Gafio Watts's *Amiri Baraka: The Politics and Art of a Black Intellectual* (2001). Theodore R. Hudson's *A LeRoi Jones (Amiri Baraka) Bibliography* (1971) and Letitia Dace's *LeRoi Jones (Imamu Amiri Baraka): A Checklist of Works by and about Him* (1971), provide reference information on primary and secondary materials. Some individual articles about Baraka's work are W. D. E. Andrews's "'All Is Permitted': The Poetry of LeRoi Jones/Amiri Baraka," *Southwest Review* 67.2 (1982); David Smith's "Amiri Baraka and the Black Arts of Black Art" in *Boundary* 2 15.1–2 (1986–87); and Fred Moten's "Tragedy Elegy Improvisation: Voices of Baraka, II" in *Semiotics 1994* (1995), ed. C. W. Spinks and John Deely. See also **Beat Movement, Black Arts Movement.**

Louise Bennett

Bennett's *Selected Poems* (1982, 1983) was edited by Mervyn Morris and contains his excellent introduction and notes; an earlier edited selection, also important, is *Jamaica Labrish* (1966), edited by Rex Nettleford. Other volumes of poetry, folktales, and stories include *Jamaica Dialect Verses* (1942), compiled by George R. Bowen; *Anancy Stories and Poems in Dialect* (1944); *Jamaican Dialect Poems* (1949); *Anancy Stories and Dialect Verse* (with others, 1950, 1957); *Laugh with Louise: A Pot-Pourri of Jamaican Folklore, Stories, Songs, Verses* (with Lois Kelle-Barrow) (1961); and *Anancy and Miss Lou* (1979). *Aunty Roachy Seh* (1993), ed. Mervyn Morris, is a collection of monologues from Bennett's popular radio broadcasts. Her brilliant performances of her poetry can be heard on recordings such as *Yes M'Dear: Miss Lou Live!* (1983).

Discussions of Bennett's works can be found in Rex Nettleford's introduction to Bennett's *Jamaica Labrish* (1966); Lloyd W. Brown, *West Indian Poetry* (1978); Morris's "Louise Bennett in Print," *Caribbean Quarterly* 28.1–2 (1982); Edward Kamau Brathwaite's *History of the Voice: The Development of Nation Language in Anglophone Caribbean Poetry* (1984); Carolyn Cooper's *Noises in the Blood: Orality, Gender and the "Vulgar" Body of Jamaican Popular Culture* (1993); Eric Doumerc's "Louise Bennett and the Mento Tradition," *Ariel* 31.4 (2000); and Jahan Ramazani's *The Hybrid Muse* (2001). See also **Caribbean Poetry.**

Charles Bernstein

An extensive collection of Bernstein's poetry is *Republics of Reality: 1975–1995* (2000). Other volumes include *Asylums* (1975), *Parsing* (1976), *Shade* (1978), *Poetic Justice* (1979), *Senses of Responsibility* (1979), *Controlling Interests* (1980), *Legend* (with others, 1980), *The Occurrence of Tune* (photographs by Susan Bee Laufer, 1980), *Disfrutes* (1981), *Stigma* (1981), *Islets/Irritations* (1983), *Resistance* (1983), *Amblyopia* (1985), *The Sophist* (1987), *Veil* (1987), *Four Poems* (1988), *The Nude Formalism* (1989), *The Absent Father in Dumbo* (1990), *Fool's Gold* (with Laufer, 1990), *Rough Trades* (1990), *Dark City* (1994), *Little Orphan Anagram* (with Laufer, 1997), *Log Rhythms* (with Laufer, 1998), *My Way: Speeches and Poems* (1999), and *With Strings* (2001). Bernstein's critical and theoretical contributions include *Content's Dream: Essays* (1986, 2001), *The Politics of Poetic Farm: Poetry and Public Policy* (1990), and *A Poetics* (1992). Bernstein has also written libretti for operas such as *The Blind Witness News* (1990) and *The Lenny Paschen Show* (1992). Along with Bruce Andrews, Bernstein edited *L=A=N=G=U=A=G=E*, the journal at the center of the Language poetry movement, from 1978 to 1981.

Critical discussions of Bernstein's work can be found in *The Difficulties* 2 (1982), ed. Tom Beckett; Marjorie Perloff's *The Dance of the Intellect: Studies in the Poetry of the Pound Tradition* (1985); Linda Reinfeld's *Language Poetry: Writing as Rescue* (1992); Jerome McGann's *Black Riders: The Visible Language of Modernism* (1993); Hank Lazer's "Charles Bernstein's Dark City: Polis, Policy, and the Policing of Poetry," *American Poetry Review* 24.5 (1995); Paul Naylor's "(Mis)Characterizing Charlie: Language and the Self in the Poetry and Poetics of Charles Bernstein," *Sagetrieb* 14.3 (1995); and Charles Altieri's "Some Problems about Agency in the Theories of Radical Poetics," *Contemporary Literature* 37.2 (1996). Among other interviews is Loss Pequeño Glazier's "An Autobiographical Interview with Charles Bernstein," *Boundary* 2 23.3 (1996). A bibliography appears in *The Difficulties* 2 (1982). See also **Language Poetry.**

John Berryman

Collections of Berryman's poetry include *Collected Poems, 1937–1971* (1989), ed. Charles Thornbury, and *Selected Poems, 1938–1968*

(1972). 77 *Dream Songs* (1964) and *His Toy, His Dream, His Rest* (1968) were published together as *The Dream Songs* in 1969. Berryman also wrote a novel, *Recovery* (1973), a biography of Stephen Crane (1950), and Shakespeare criticism, published posthumously as *Berryman's Shakespeare* (1999). *The Freedom of the Poet* (1976) includes prose, short fiction, and interviews. Biographies include Paul Mariani's *Dream Song: The Life of John Berryman* (1982), John Haffenden's *The Life of John Berryman* (1990), and Eileen Simpson's memoir, *Poets in Their Youth* (1982).

Collections of critical essays include *Berryman's Understanding* (1988), ed. Harry Thomas; *John Berryman* (1989), ed. Harold Bloom; and *Recovering Berryman* (1993), ed. Richard J. Kelly and Alan K. Lathrop. Other useful studies include J. M. Linebarger's *John Berryman* (1974); Joel Conarroe's *John Berryman: An Introduction to the Poetry* (1977); Haffenden's *John Berryman: A Critical Commentary* (1980); Bruce Bawer's *The Middle Generation* (1986); Stephen Matterson's *Berryman and Lowell: The Art of Losing* (1988); Helen Vendler's *The Given and the Made* (1995); and Thomas Travisano's *Midcentury Quartet: Bishop, Lowell, Jarrell, Berryman, and the Making of a Postmodern Aesthetic* (1999). Bibliographies include Richard J. Kelly's *John Berryman: A Checklist* (1972); Ernest C. Stefanik Jr.'s *John Berryman: A Descriptive Bibliography* (1974); and Gary Q. Arpin's *John Berryman: A Reference Guide* (1976). See also **Confessional Poetry.**

Frank Bidart

In the Western Night: Collected Poems, 1965–90 was published in 1990. Subsequent volumes are *Desire* (1997) and *Music Like Dirt* (2002). Interviews include Mark Halliday's in *Ploughshares* 9.1 (1983), Tim Liu's in *Lambda Book Report: A Review of Gay and Lesbian Literature* 6.9 (1998), and Andrew Rathmann and Danielle Allen's in *Chicago Review* 47.3 (2001).

Discussions of his work can be found in Robert Pinsky's *The Situation of Poetry* (1976), Louise Glück's *Proofs and Theories: Essays on Poetry* (1994), and Anne Ferry's *The Title to the Poem* (1996). Relevant essays include Alan Nadel's "Wellesley Poets: The Works of Robert Pinsky and Frank Bidart," *New England Review & Bread Loaf Quarterly* 4.2 (1981); Brad Crenshaw's "The Sin of the Body: Frank Bidart's Human Bondage," *Chicago Review* 33.4 (1983); David Young's "Out beyond Rhetoric: Four Poets and One Critic," *Field: Contemporary Poetry & Poetics* 30 (1984); Seamus Heaney's "Frank Bidart: A Salute," *Agni* 36 (1992); Jeffrey Gray's " 'Necessary Thought': Frank Bidart and the Postconfessional," *Contemporary Literature* 34.4 (1993); Justin Quinn's "Frank Bidart and the Fate of the Lyric," *Pn Review* 27 (July–August 2001); and Ann Keniston's " 'The Fluidity of Damaged Form': Apostrophe and Desire in Nineties Lyric," *Contemporary Literature* 42.2 (2001).

Elizabeth Bishop

Bishop's collected poetry is available in *The Complete Poems, 1927–1979* (1983). Stories, memoirs, and other prose works can be found in *The Collected Prose* (1984). Bishop also published travel writing, *Brazil* (1962); translated Portuguese literature; and edited collections of poetry such as *An Anthology of Twentieth-Century Brazilian Poetry* (with Emanuel Brasil, 1972). *Conversations with Elizabeth Bishop* (1996), ed. George Monteiro, is a collection of interviews; *One Art* (1994), ed. Robert Giroux, is a collection of letters; and the standard biography is Brett C. Millier's *Elizabeth Bishop: Life and the Memory of It* (1993).

Book-length studies of Bishop's work include Thomas Travisano's *Elizabeth Bishop: Her Artistic Development* (1988), Robert Dale Parker's *The Unbeliever: The Poetry of Elizabeth Bishop* (1988), David Kalstone's *Becoming a Poet: Elizabeth Bishop with Marianne Moore and Robert Lowell* (1989), Bonnie Costello's *Elizabeth Bishop: Questions of Mastery* (1991), Lorrie Goldensohn's *Elizabeth Bishop: The Biography of a Poetry* (1992), Victoria Harrison's *Elizabeth Bishop's Poetics of Intimacy* (1993), Carole Doreski's *Elizabeth Bishop: The Restraints of Language* (1993), Susan McCabe's *Elizabeth Bishop: Her Poetics of Loss* (1994), Marilyn May Lombardi's *The Body and the Song: Elizabeth Bishop's Poetics* (1995), Anne Colwell's *Inscrutable Houses: Metaphors of the Body in the Poems of Elizabeth Bishop* (1997), and Anne Stevenson's *Five Looks at Elizabeth Bishop* (1998). Other illuminating discussions of her work can be found in Helen Vendler's *Part of Nature, Part of Us* (1980), Susan Schweik's *A Gulf So Deeply Cut* (1991), James Longenbach's *Modern Poetry after Modernism* (1997), and Thomas Gardner's *Regions of Unlikeness* (1999). Collections of essays on Bishop include *Elizabeth Bishop and Her Art* (1983), ed. Lloyd Schwartz and Sybil P. Estess; *Elizabeth Bishop* (1985), ed. Harold Bloom; and *Elizabeth Bishop: The Geography of Gender* (1993), ed. Lombardi. A bibliography by Candace W. MacMahon appeared in 1980.

Robert Bly

Bly's most recent collection of selected poems is *Eating the Honey of Words: New and Selected Poems* (1999). Other volumes include *The Lion's Tail and Eyes: Poems Written out of Laziness and Silence* (with James Wright and William Duffy, 1962), *Silence in the Snowy Fields* (1962), *Chrysanthemums* (1967), *The Light Around the Body* (1967), *Ducks* (1968), *The Morning Glory* (1969, 1975), *The Shadow-Mothers* (1970), *The*

Teeth-Mother Naked at Last (1970), *Poems for Tennessee* (with William Stafford and William Matthews, 1971), *Christmas Eve Service at Midnight at St. Michael's* (1972), *Jumping out of Bed* (1972), *Water under the Earth* (1972), *The Dead Seal Near McClure's Beach* (1973), *Sleepers Joining Hands* (1973), *The Hockey Poem* (1974), *Point Reyes Poems* (1974), *Leaping Poetry* (1975), *Old Man Rubbing His Eyes* (1975), *The Loon* (1977), *This Body Is Made of Camphor and Gopherwood* (1977), *This Tree Will Be Here for a Thousand Years* (1979), *"Visiting Emily Dickinson's Grave" and Other Poems* (1979), *Finding an Old Ant Mansion* (1981), *The Man in the Black Coat Turns* (1981), *The Eight Stages of Translation* (1983), *Four Ramages* (1983), *"Out of the Rolling Ocean" and Other Love Poems* (1984), *Loving a Woman in Two Worlds* (1985), *Selected Poems* (1986), *The Moon on a Fencepost* (1988), *The Apple Found in the Plowing* (1989), *What Have I Ever Lost by Dying?: Collected Prose Poems* (1992), *Gratitude to Old Teachers* (1993), *Meditations on the Insatiable Soul* (1994), *Holes the Crickets Have Eaten in Blankets* (1997), *Morning Poems* (1997), and *The Night Abraham Called to the Stars* (2001). He has also translated extensively from the work of poets such as Georg Trakl, Pablo Neruda, and Rainer Maria Rilke, and written a book on masculinity, *Iron John* (1990). A book of interviews is *Talking All Morning* (1979). An interview also appears in Bill Moyers's *The Language of Life* (1995).

Critical discussions of his work can be found in Ingegerd Friberg's *Moving Inward: A Study of Robert Bly's Poetry* (1977); *Of Solitude and Silence: Writings on Robert Bly* (1981), ed. Kate Daniels and Richard Jones; James E. B. Breslin's *From Modern to Contemporary: American Poetry, 1945–1965* (1984); Howard Nelson's *Robert Bly: An Introduction to the Poetry* (1984); Richard P. Sugg's *Robert Bly* (1986); *Critical Essays on Robert Bly* (1992), ed. William V. Davis; Victoria Harris's *The Incorporative Consciousness of Robert Bly* (1992); and Davis's *Robert Bly: The Poet and His Critics* (1994). A bibliography is William H. Roberson's *Robert Bly: A Primary and Secondary Bibliography* (1986). See also **Deep Image Poetry.**

Eavan Boland

An Origin Like Water: Collected Poems, 1967–1987 appeared in 1996. Subsequent volumes of poetry include *Outside History* (1990), *In a Time of Violence* (1994), *Night Feed* (1994), *Collected Poems* (1995), *The Lost Land* (1998), *Against Love Poetry* (2001), and *Code* (2001). Her essay *A Kind of Scar: The Woman Poet in a National Tradition* (1989) offers essential insight into her work, as does *Object Lessons: The Life of the Woman and the Poet in Our Time* (1995). She has also coedited *The Making of a Poem: A Norton Anthology of Poetic Forms* (2000). Interviews include Amy Klauke's in *Northwest Review* 25.1 (1987), Marilyn Reizbaum's in *Contemporary Literature* 30.4 (1989), Patty O'Connell's in *Poets & Writers* 22.6 (1994), and Margaret Mills Harper's in *Five Points* 1.2 (1997).

Studies of her work include Patricia L. Hagen and Thomas W. Zelman's " 'We Were Never on the Scene of the Crime': Eavan Boland's Repossession of History," *Twentieth Century Literature* 37.4 (1991); Ellen M. Mahon's "Eavan Boland's Journey with the Muse," *Learning the Trade: Essays on W. B. Yeats and Contemporary Poetry* (1993), ed. Deborah Fleming; Jody Allen-Randolph's "Finding a Voice Where She Found a Vision," *Pn Review* 21.1 (1994); Kerry E. Robertson's "Anxiety, Influence, Tradition, and Subversion in the Poetry of Eavan Boland," *Colby Quarterly* 30.4 (1994); Patricia Boyle Haberstroh's *Women Creating Women: Contemporary Women Irish Poets* (1996); David C. Ward's "Eavan Boland: Mazing Her Way," *Sewanee Review* 106.2 (1998); Katie Conboy's essay in *Border Crossings: Irish Women Writers and National Identities* (2000), ed. Kathryn Kirkpatrick; *Critical Ireland: New Essays in Literature and Culture* (2001), ed. Alan A. Gillis and Aaron Kelly; and Richard Rankin Russell's "W. B. Yeats and Eavan Boland: Postcolonial Poets?" in *W. B. Yeats and Postcolonialism* (2001), ed. Deborah Fleming. *Irish University Review* (Spring/Summer 1993) and *Colby Quarterly* 35.4 (1999) are special issues dedicated to Boland. See also **Irish Poetry.**

Kamau Brathwaite

Brathwaite's volumes of poetry are *The Arrivants: A New World Trilogy* (1973), which includes *Rights of Passage* (1967), *Masks* (1968), and *Islands* (1969); *Days and Nights* (1975); *Other Exiles* (1975); *Black + Blues* (1976); *Mother Poem* (1977); *Soweto* (1979); *Word Making Man: A Poem for Nicólas Guillèn* (1979); *Sun Poem* (1982); *Third World Poems* (1983); *Jah Music* (1986); *X/Self* (1987); *Sappho Sakyi's Meditations* (1989); *Middle Passages* (1992); *Shar/Hurricane Poem* (1992); *Trench Town Rock* (1994); *Words Need Love Too* (2000); and *Ancestors: A Reinvention of Mother Poem, Sun Poem, and X/Self* (2001). Brathwaite has also written plays, including *Four Plays for Primary Schools* (1964) and *Odale's Voice* (1967). A revised edition of his *Roots: Essays in Caribbean Literature* (1986) appeared in 1993. He has also written important works of nonfiction, *The Development of Creole Society in Jamaica, 1770–1820* (1971) and *History of the Voice: The Development of Nation Language in Anglophone Caribbean Poetry* (1984), and edited collections of literature, *Iouanaloa: Recent Writing from St. Lucia* (1963) and *New Poets from Jamaica* (1979).

Collections of essays include *The Art of Kamau Brathwaite* (1995), ed. Stewart Brown; a special issue of *World Literature Today* 68.4 (1994); and *For the Geography of a Soul: Emerging Perspectives on Kamau Brathwaite*, ed. Timothy J. Reiss (2001). Other relevant discussions include Gordon Rohlehr's *Pathfinder: Black Awakening in* The Arrivants *of Edward Kamau Brathwaite* (1981); Maureen Warner Lewis's *E. Kamau Brathwaite's* Masks: *Essays and Annotations* (1992); Elaine Savory's "The Word Becomes *Nam:* Self and Community in the Poetry of Kamau Brathwaite and Its Relation to Caribbean Culture and Postmodern Theory," *Writing the Nation: Self and Country in the Post-Colonial Imagination* (1996), ed. John C. Hawley; Silvio Torres-Saillant's *Caribbean Poetics: Toward an Aesthetic of West Indian Literature* (1997); June D. Bobb's *Beating a Restless Drum: The Poetics of Kamau Brathwaite and Derek Walcott* (1998); and Paul Naylor's *Poetic Investigations: Singing the Holes in History* (1999). See also **Caribbean Poetry.**

Gwendolyn Brooks

Brooks's volumes of poetry include *A Street in Bronzeville* (1945), *Annie Allen* (1949), *Bronzeville Boys and Girls* (1956), *The Bean Eaters* (1960), *Selected Poems* (1963, 1999), *In the Mecca* (1968), *Riot* (1969), *Family Pictures* (1970), *Aloneness* (1971), *Beckonings* (1975), *To Disembark* (1981), *"The Near-Johannesburg Boy" and Other Poems* (1986, 1991), *Winnie* (1988), and *Children Coming Home* (1991). Poetry and prose are collected in *The World of Gwendolyn Brooks* (1971) and *Blacks* (1987, 1991). Other prose works include the novel *Maud Martha* (1953, 1974) and the autobiographical *Report from Part One* (1972) and *Report from Part Two* (1996). She also edited *A Broadside Treasury* (1971), *Jump Bad: A New Chicago Anthology* (1971), and *A Capsule Course in Black Poetry Writing* (1975). George E. Kent published the biography *A Life of Gwendolyn Brooks* in 1990.

Collections of essays on her work include Maria K. Mootry and Gary Smith's *A Life Distilled: Gwendolyn Brooks, Her Poetry and Fiction* (1987); *Say That the River Turns: The Impact of Gwendolyn Brooks* (1987), ed. Haki R. Madhubuti; *On Gwendolyn Brooks: Reliant Contemplation* (1996), ed. Stephen Caldwell Wright; and *Gwendolyn Brooks*, ed. Harold Bloom (2000). Other studies include Harry B. Shaw's *Gwendolyn Brooks* (1980); D. H. Melhem's *Gwendolyn Brooks: Poetry and the Heroic Voice* (1987); and B. J. Bolden's *Urban Rage in Bronzeville: Social Commentary in the Poetry of Gwendolyn Brooks* (1999). Also of interest is Melhem's "Cultural Challenge, Heroic Response: Gwendolyn Brooks and the New Black Poetry," *Perspectives of Black Popular Culture* (1990), ed. Harry Shaw; Susan Schweik's chapter on Brooks in *A Gulf So Deeply Cut* (1991); Kathryne Lindberg's "Whose Canon? Gwendolyn Brooks: Founder at the Center of the 'Margins,' " *Gendered Modernisms* (1996), ed. Margaret Dickie and Thomas Travisano; and essays and an interview in *The Furious Flowering of African American Poetry*, ed. Joanne V. Gabbin (1999). Bibliographic information can be found in R. Baxter Miller's *Langston Hughes and Gwendolyn Brooks: A Reference Guide* (1978).

Anne Carson

Poetry and prose are often combined in Carson's books, which include *Short Talks* (1992), *Plainwater* (1995), *Glass, Irony, and God* (1995), *Autobiography of Red* (1998), *Men in the Off Hours* (2000), and *The Beauty of the Husband: A Fictional Essay in 29 Tangos* (2001). Other works include her classical study *Eros the Bittersweet* (1986) and *Economy of the Unlost: Reading Simonides of Keos with Paul Celan* (1999). John D'Agata has interviewed Carson in *Iowa Review* 27.2 (1997) and *Brick* 57 (1997).

Guy Davenport introduces Carson's *Glass, Irony, and God.* Other relevant essays include Jorie Graham's "An Introduction to Anne Carson," *Brick* 57 (1997); Paula Melton's "Essays at Anne Carson's *Glass, Irony and God,*" *Iowa Review* 27.1 (1997); Jeff Hamilton's "This Cold Hectic Dawn and I," *Denver Quarterly* 32.1–2 (1997); Mark Halliday's "Carson: Mind and Heart," *Chicago Review* 45.2 (1999); Sharon Wahl's "Erotic Sufferings: *Autobiography of Red* and Other Anthropologies," *Iowa Review* 29.1 (1999); Kevin McNeilly's "Home Economics" and Ian Rae's " 'Dazzling Hybrids': The Poetry of Anne Carson," both in *Canadian Literature* 166 (2000); Melanie Rehak's "Things Fall Together," *New York Times Magazine* (26 March 2000); David C. Ward's "Anne Carson: Addressing the Wound," *Pn Review* 27.5 (2001); Chris Jennings's "The Erotic Poetics of Anne Carson," *University of Toronto Quarterly* 70.4 (2001); and Harriet Zinnes's "What Is Time Made Of? The Poetry of Anne Carson," *Hollins Critic* 38.1 (2001). See also **Canadian Poetry.**

Lorna Dee Cervantes

Cervantes's volumes of poetry are *Emplumada* (1981) and *From the Cables of Genocide: Poems of Love and Hunger* (1991). Interviews include Bernadette Monda's in *Third Woman* 2.1 (1984), Ray Gonzalez's in *Bloomsbury Review* 17.5 (1997), and one in Karin Ikas's *Chicana Ways: Conversations with Ten Chicana Writers* (2001).

Marta Ester Sánchez's *Contemporary Chicana Poetry: A Critical Approach to an Emerging Literature* (1985) and Deborah L. Madsen's *Understanding Contemporary Chicana Literature* (2000) offer discussions of Cervantes in the larger context of Chicana literature. Critical essays include Bárbara Brinson-Curiel's "Our Own Words: *Emplumada*," *Tecolote* 3 (1982); Lynette Seator, "*Emplumada*: Chicana Rites-of-Passages," *MELUS* 11.2 (1984); Tey Diana Rebolledo's "Soothing Restless Serpents: The Dreaded Creation and Other Inspirations in Chicana Poetry," *Third Woman* 2.1 (1984); John F. Crawford's "Notes toward a New Multicultural Criticism: Three Works by Women of Color," *A Gift of Tongues: Critical Challenges in Contemporary American Poetry* (1987), ed. Marie Harris and Kathleen Aguero; Yvonne Yarbro-Bejarano's "Chicana Literature from a Chicana Feminist Perspective," *Chicana Creativity and Criticism: Charting New Frontiers in American Literature* (1988, 1996), ed. María Herrera-Sobek and Helena María Viramontes; Patricia Wallace's "Divided Loyalties: Literal and Literary in the Poetry of Lorna Dee Cervantes, Cathy Song and Rita Dove," *MELUS* 18.3 (1993); and Ada Savin's "Bilingualism and Dialogism: Another Reading of Lorna Dee Cervantes's Poetry," *An Other Tongue: Nation and Ethnicity in the Linguistic Borderlands* (1994), ed. Alfred Arteaga. See also **Latino Poetry.**

Marilyn Chin

Chin's volumes of poetry include *Dwarf Bamboo* (1987), *The Phoenix Gone, The Terrace Empty* (1994), and *Rhapsody in Plain Yellow* (2002). She has also translated Gozo Yoshimasu's *Devil Wind: A Thousand Steps or More* (1980) and *Selected Poems of Ai Qing* (with Peng Wenlan and Eugene Eoyang, 1982), as well as the work of various contemporary Chinese poets. In addition, she coedited *Dissident Song: A Contemporary Asian American Anthology* (with David Wong Louie, 1991).

Discussions of Chin's work can be found in *Reading the Literatures of Asian America* (1992), ed. Shirley Geok-lin Lim and Amy Ling; Anne-Elizabeth Green's entry on Chin in *Contemporary Women Poets* (1998), ed. Pamela L. Shelton; Adrienne McCormick's " 'Being Without': Marilyn Chin's Poems as Feminist Acts of Theorizing," *Hitting Critical Mass* 6.2 (2000); Mary Slowik's "Beyond Lot's Wife: The Immigration Poems of Marilyn Chin, Garrett Hongo, Li-Young Lee, and David Mura," *MELUS* 25.3–4 (2000); and John Gery's " 'Mocking My Own Happiness': Authenticity, Heritage, and Self-Erasure in the Poetry of Marilyn Chin," *Lit: Literature Interpretation Theory* 12.1 (2001). See also **Asian American Poetry.**

Amy Clampitt

The Collected Poems of Amy Clampitt appeared in 1997, with a useful introduction by Mary Jo Salter. *Predecessors, Et Cetera* (1991) is a collection of Clampitt's essays. Clampitt also edited *The Essential Donne* (1988). An interview with Laura Fairchild appears in *The American Poetry Review* 16.4 (1987), and one with Jan Huesgen and Robert W. Lewis in *North Dakota Quarterly* 58.1 (1990).

Discussions of Clampitt's work can be found in Peter Sacks's *The English Elegy* (1985), Helen Vendler's *The Music of What Happens* (1976, 1988) and *Soul Says* (1995), J. D. McClatchy's *White Paper: On Contemporary American Poetry* (1989), Jahan Ramazani's *Poetry of Mourning* (1994), and James Longenbach's *Modern Poetry After Modernism* (1997). Other essays and reviews include Edmund White's "Poetry as Alchemy," *Nation* 236 (16 April 1983); Robert E. Hosmer Jr.'s "Amy Clampitt: The Art of Poetry," *Paris Review* 126 (1993); a special issue of *Verse* 10.3 (1993), ed. Bonnie Costello; and Willard Spiegelman's "What to Make of an Augmented Thing," *Kenyon Review* 21.1 (1999).

Lucille Clifton

Clifton's volumes of poetry include *Good Times* (1969), *Good News about the Earth* (1972), *An Ordinary Woman* (1974), *Two-Headed Woman* (1980), *Good Woman: Poems and a Memoir, 1969–1980* (1987), *Next* (1987), *Ten Oxherding Pictures* (1988), *Quilting* (1991), *The Book of Light* (1993), *Terrible Stories* (1996), *Selected Poems* (1996), and *Blessing the Boats: New and Selected Poems, 1988–2000* (2000). She also wrote a family memoir, *Generations* (1976), and many books for children, including the *Everett Anderson* series. An interview appears in Bill Moyers's *The Language of Life* (1995).

Several discussions of Clifton's work can be found in *Black Women Writers (1950–1980): A Critical Evaluation* (1984), ed. Mari Evans: Clifton's own "A Simple Language," Haki Madhubuti's "Lucille Clifton: Warm Water, Greased Legs, and Dangerous Poetry," and Audrey T. McCluskey's "Tell the Good News: A View of the Works of Lucille Clifton." Other studies include Andrea Benton Rushing's "Lucille Clifton: A Changing Voice for Changing Times," *Coming to Light: American Women Poets in the Twentieth Century* (1985), ed. Diane Wood Middlebrook and Marilyn Yalom; Alicia Ostriker's "Kin and Kind: The Poetry of Lucille Clifton," *American Poetry Review* 22.6 (1993); Akasha Hull's "In Her Own Images: Lucille Clifton and the Bible," *Dwelling in Possibility: Women Poets and Critics on Poetry* (1997), ed. Yopie Prins and Maeera Shreiber; Hillary Holladay's "Songs of Herself: Lucille Clifton's Poems about Womanhood," *The Furious Flowering of African American Poetry* (1999), ed. Joanne V. Gabbin; and Ajuan Maria Mance's "Re-Locating the Black Female Subject: The Landscape of the Body in the Poems of Lucille Clifton," *Recovering the Black Female Body: Self-Representations by African American Women* (2001), ed. Michael Bennett and Vanessa D. Dickerson. See also **Black Arts Movement.**

Henri Cole

Cole's volumes of poetry are *The Marble Queen* (1986), *The Zoo Wheel of Knowledge* (1989), *The Look of Things* (1995), and *The Visible Man* (1998). He appears in *Under 35: The New Generation of American Poets* (1989), ed. Nicholas Christopher. A brief section of his journal appears in *The Writer's Journal* (1997), ed. Sheila Bender. He has interviewed Helen Vendler in *Paris Review* 38.141 (1996) and Seamus Heaney in *Paris Review* 39.144 (1997), and Vendler discusses his work in *Soul Says: On Recent Poetry* (1995). Reviews include Wayne Koestenbaum's in *New Yorker* 71.10 (1 May 1995), Richard Holinger's in *Midwest Quarterly* 37.3 (1996), Timothy Liu's in *Lambda Book Report* 7.4 (1998), Tim Gavin's in *Library Journal* 123.16 (1998), Phoebe Pettingell's "Poetry Read in Canoes," *New Leader* 82.1 (1999), and John Taylor's in *Antioch Review* 58.1 (2000).

Robert Creeley

The Collected Poems of Robert Creeley, 1945–1975 was published in 1982. Other volumes include *Away* (1976), *Presences* (1976), *Myself* (1977), *Thanks* (1977), *The Children* (1978), *Desultory Days* (1978), *Later* (1979), *Corn Close* (1980), *Mother's Voice* (1981), *Mirrors* (1983), *A Calendar* (1984), *Four Poems* (1984), *Memories* (1984), *Memory Gardens* (1986), *The Company* (1988), *7and6* (with Robert Therrien and Michel Butor, 1988), *Dreams* (1989), *It* (with Francesco Clemente, 1989), *Places* (1990), *Windows* (1990), *Selected Poems, 1945–1990* (1991), *Gnomic Verses* (1991), *The Old Days* (1991), *Echoes* (1994), *Loops* (1995), *Life and Death* (with Clemente, 1998), *So There: Poems 1976–1983* (1998), *En Famille* (1999), *For Friends* (2000), and *Just in Time: Poems, 1984–1994* (2001). Prose writings can be found in *The Collected Prose* (1984) and *The Collected Essays* (1989). Creeley has also written fiction, including *The Gold Diggers* (1954) and *The Island* (1963). Interviews have been collected in *Contexts of Poetry: Interviews, 1961–1971* (1973), ed. Donald Allen; and *Tales out of School* (1993). *Charles Olson and Robert Creeley: The Complete Correspondence* (1980), ed. George Butterick, publishes the letters between these two poets.

Critical discussions of Creeley's work include Arthur Ford's *Robert Creeley* (1978), Cynthia Dubin Edelberg's *Robert Creeley's Poetry: A Critical Introduction* (1978), Charles Altieri's *Self and Sensibility in Contemporary American Poetry* (1984), Robert von Hallberg's *American Poetry and Culture, 1945–1980* (1985), Brian Conniff's *The Lyric and Modern Poetry: Olson, Creeley, Bunting* (1988), and Tom Clark's *Robert Creeley and the Genius of the American Common Place* (1993). Numerous useful essays can be found in the special Creeley issue of *Sagetrieb* 2.1 (1982) and in the collections *Robert Creeley: The Poet's Workshop* (1984), ed. Carroll Terrell, and *Robert Creeley's Life and Work: A Sense of Increment* (1987), ed. John Wilson. Bibliographies are Mary Novik's *Robert Creeley: An Inventory, 1945–1970* (1973) and Willard Fox's *Robert Creeley, Edward Dorn, and Robert Duncan: A Reference Guide* (1989). See also **Black Mountain School.**

Donald Davie

Davie's complete *Collected Poems*, ed. Neil Powell, was published in 2002. Among Davie's many works of criticism are *Purity of Diction in English Verse* (1952); *Articulate Energy* (1955); *Ezra Pound: Poet as Sculptor* (1964); *The Poet in the Imaginary Museum* (1977), ed. Barry Alpert; *Dissentient Voice* (1982); and *With the Grain: Essays on Thomas Hardy and Modern British Poetry* (1998).

A book-length study is Martin Dodsworth's *Donald Davie* (1976), and a collection of essays is *Donald Davie and the Responsibilities of Literature* (1983), ed. George Dekker. *On Modern Poetry: Essays Presented to Donald Davie*, ed. Vereen Bell and Laurence Lerner, was published in 1988. *Agenda* 14.2 (1976) is a special issue on Davie. Critical essays include Bernard Bergonzi's "The Poetry of Donald Davie," *Critical Quarterly* 4 (1962); Calvin Bedient's "On Donald Davie," *Iowa Review* 2.2 (1971); William H. Pritchard's "In the British Looking-Glass," *Parnassus* 4.2 (1976); Robert von Hallberg's "Two Poet-Critics: Donald Davie's *The Poet in the Imaginary Museum* and Robert Pinsky's *The Situation of Poetry*," *Chicago Review* 30.1 (1978); Kieran Quinlan's "Donald Davie: The Irish Years," *Southern Review* 20.1 (1984); Andrew Shelley's "Donald Davie and the Canon," *Essays in Criticism* 42.1 (1992); and Michael Grant's "Donald Davie and the Concept of Time," *Pn Review* 23.1 (1996). Bibliographic information is available in Stuart T. Wright's *Donald Davie: A Checklist of his Writings, 1946–1988* (1991). See also **The Movement.**

Eunice de Souza

De Souza's volumes of poetry include *Fix* (1979), *Women in Dutch Painting* (1988), *Ways of Belonging: Selected Poems* (1990), and *Selected and New Poems* (1994). She also edited *Statements: An Anthology of Indian Prose in English* (with Adil Jussawalla, 1976) and *Nine Indian Women Poets: An Anthology* (1997). *Talking Poems: Conversations with Poets* appeared in 1999. She has also published literature for children.

Discussions of her work can be found in Kersey Katrak's "Three Poets Come of Age," *Sunday Observer* (Bombay, 12 December 1982); Bruce King's *Modern Indian Poetry in English* (1987); and Veronica Brady's " 'One Long Cry in the Dark'?: The Poetry of Eunice de Souza," *Literature and Theology* 5.1 (1991). See also **Indian Poetry.**

James Dickey

Dickey's *The Whole Motion: Collected Poems, 1945–1992* appeared in 1992, and *James Dickey: The Selected Poems* in 1998. He also published novels, *Deliverance* (1970), *Alnilam* (1987), and *To the White Sea* (1993). Autobiographical and critical prose includes *The Suspect in Poetry* (1964), *Babel to Byzantium* (1968), *Self-Interviews* (1970), *Sorties: Journals and New Essays* (1971), and *The Poet Turns on Himself* (1982). A book of interviews is *The Voiced Connections of James Dickey* (1984), ed. Ronald Baughman. *Striking In* (1996) is a selection from Dickey's early notebooks. *Crux: The Letters of James Dickey* was published in 1999. Two biographies are Neal Bowers's *James Dickey: The Poet as Pitchman* (1985) and Henry Hart's *James Dickey: The World as a Lie* (2000).

Collections of essays on his work include *The Expansive Imagination* (1973), ed. Richard J. Calhoun; *The Imagination as Glory* (1984), ed. Bruce Weigl and T. R. Hummer; *James Dickey* (1987), ed. Harold Bloom; and *Critical Essays on James Dickey* (1994), ed. Robert Kirschten. Other studies include Gordon Van Ness's *Outbelieving Existence: The Measured Motion of James Dickey* (1992); Ernest Suarez's *James Dickey and the Politics of Canon* (1993); and Kirschten's *Struggling for Wings* (1997) and *Approaching Prayer: Ritual and the Shape of Myth in the Poetry of A. R. Ammons and James Dickey* (1998). Bibliographies include Jim Elledge's *James Dickey: A Bibliography, 1947–1974* (1979) and Matthew Joseph Bruccoli's *James Dickey: A Descriptive Bibliography* (1990).

Mark Doty

Doty's volumes of poetry include *Turtle, Swan* (1987), *Bethlehem in Broad Daylight* (1991), *My Alexandria* (1993), *Atlantis* (1995), *Sweet Machine* (1998), *Murano* (2000), *Turtle, Swan & Bethlehem in Broad Daylight* (2000), *Source* (2001), and *Still Life with Oysters and Lemon* (2001). He has also written memoirs, including *Heaven's Coast* (1996) and *Firebird* (1999). Interviews appear in *New Statesman* 126.4336 (1997); *Atlantic* (10 November 1999); and *Writer's Digest* 79.11 (1999).

Discussions of his work include Deborah Landau's " 'How to Live. What to Do': The Poetics and Politics of AIDS," *American Literature* 68.1 (1996); Helen Vendler's "The Poetry of August Kleinzahler and Mark Doty," *New Yorker* (8 April 1996); David R. Jarraway's " 'Creatures of the Rainbow': Wallace Stevens, Mark Doty, and the Poetics of Androgyny," *Mosaic* 30.3 (1997); William Joseph Reichard's "Mercurial and Rhapsodic: Manifestations of the Gay Male Body in the Poetry of Mark Doty and Wayne Koestenbaum," *Humanities and Social Sciences* 58.4 (1997); Mark Wunderlich's "About Mark Doty," *Ploughshares* 25.1 (1999); Yaakov Perry's "The Homecoming Queen: The Reconstruction of Home in Queer Life-Narratives," *A/B: Auto/Biography Studies* 15.2 (2000); and Hugh Dunkerley's "Unnatural Relations?: Language and Nature in the Poetry of Mark Doty and Les Murray," *Isle: Interdisciplinary Studies in Literature and Environment* 8.1 (2001).

Rita Dove

Dove's volumes of poetry include *Ten Poems* (1977), *The Yellow House on the Corner* (1980), *Museum* (1983), *Thomas and Beulah* (1986), *Grace Notes* (1989), *Selected Poems* (1993), *Mother Love* (1995), *On the Bus with Rosa Parks* (1999), and *Domestic Work* (2000). She has also written a collection of stories, *Fifth Sunday* (1985), and a novel, *Through the Ivory Gate* (1992). Other work includes a play, *The Darker Face of the Earth* (1994), and a collection of essays, *The Poet's World* (1995). Interviews include "A Conversation with Rita Dove" in *Black American Literature Forum* 20.3 (1986); Steven Schneider's in *Iowa Review* 19.3 (1989); Mohammed B. Taleb-Khyar's in *Callaloo* 14.2 (1991); William Walsh's in *Kenyon Review* 16.3 (1994); Grace Cavalieri's in *American Poetry Review* 24.2 (1995); Bill Moyers's in *The Language of Life* (1995); and Malin Pereira's in *Contemporary Literature* 40.2 (1999).

A book-length study is Therese Steffen's *Crossing Color: Transcultural Space and Place in Rita Dove's Poetry, Fiction, and Drama* (2001). Other discussions of Dove's work include Arnold Rampersad's "The Poems of Rita Dove," *Callaloo* 9.1 (1986); Robert McDowell's "The Assembling Vision of Rita Dove," *Conversant Essays: Contemporary Poets on Poetry* (1990), ed. James McCorkle; Bonnie Costello's "Scars and Wings: Rita Dove's *Grace Notes*," *Callaloo* 14.2 (1991); Kirkland C. Jones's "Folk Idiom in the Literary Expression of Two African American Authors: Rita Dove and Yusef Komunyakaa," *Language and Literature in the African American Imagination* (1992), ed. Carol Aisha Blackshire-Belay; Patricia Wallace's "Divided Loyalties: Literal and Literary in the Poetry of Lorna Dee Cervantes, Cathy Song, and Rita Dove," *MELUS* 18.3 (1993); Helen Vendler's *The Given and the Made* (1995) and *Soul Says* (1995); Lynn Keller's *Forms of Expansion: Recent Long Poems by Women* (1997); and Susan Van Dyne's "Siting the Poet: Rita Dove's Refiguring of Traditions," *Women Poets of the Americas: Toward a Pan-American Gathering*

(1999), ed. Jacqueline Vaught Brogan and Cordelia Candelaria. Articles on Dove's work by numerous critics appear in *Callaloo* 19.1 (1996).

Norman Dubie

The Mercy Seat: Collected and New Poems, 1967–2001 was published in 2001. Interviews include Julie Fay and David Wojahn's in *American Poetry Review* 7.4 (1978) and James Green's in *American Poetry Review* 18.6 (1989).

Discussions of Dubie's work include Richard Howard's introduction to *The Illustrations* (1977); John Weston's "Norman Dubie: The Vision of Astonishment," *Gramercy Review* 11.3 (1978); Greg Simon's "We Live for Cries: On Norman Dubie," *Sonora Review* 1 (1980); Frederick Garber's "On Dubie and Seidel," *American Poetry Review* 11.3 (1982); John Bensko's "Reflexive Narration in Contemporary American Poetry," *Journal of Narrative Technique* 16.2 (1986); David St. John's "A Generous Salvation: The Poetry of Norman Dubie," *Conversant Essays: Contemporary Poets on Poetry* (1990), ed. James McCorkle; and William Slattery's "My Dubious Calculus," *Antioch Review* 52.1 (1994).

Carol Ann Duffy

Duffy's volumes of poetry include *"Fleshweathercock" and Other Poems* (1973), *Fifth Last Song* (1982), *Standing Female Nude* (1985), *Thrown Voices* (1986), *Selling Manhattan* (1987), *The Other Country* (1990), *Mean Time* (1993), *Selected Poems* (1994), and *The World's Wife: Poems* (2000). She has also written plays, including *Loss* (1986), and a book for younger readers, *The Oldest Girl in the World* (2000). Collections edited by Duffy include *I Wouldn't Thank You for a Valentine: Poems for Young Feminists* (illustrated by Trisha Rafferty, 1992) and *Stopping for Death: Poems of Death and Loss* (illustrated by Rafferty, 1996). Interviews include Andrew McAllister's in *Bete Noir* 6 (1988). In 1999, when she appeared to be a leading candidate for British poet laureate, a number of profiles and interviews appeared in the *Guardian, The Independent,* and other British newspapers.

A book-length study is Dervyn Rees-Jones's *Carol Ann Duffy* (1999). Other discussions of Duffy include Jane E. Thomas's " 'The Intolerable Wrestle with Words': The Poetry of Carol Ann Duffy," *Bete Noir* 6 (1988); Eavan Boland's "Making the Difference: Eroticism and Ageing in the Work of the Woman Poet," *Pn Review* 20.4 (1994); *Four Women Poets* (1995), ed. Judith Baxter; Istvan Racz's "Carol Ann Duffy's Poetry," *B.A.S.: British and American Studies* 1.1 (1996); Danette DiMarco's "Exposing Nude Art: Carol Ann Duffy's Response to Robert Browning," *Mosaic* 31.3 (1998); Angelica Michelis's "The Pleasure of Saying It: Images of Sexuality and Desire in Contemporary Women's Poetry," *Seeing and Saying: Self-Referentiality in British and American Literature* (1998), ed. Detlev Gohrbandt; Elzbieta Wojcik-Leese's " 'Her Language Is Simple': The Poetry of Carol Ann Duffy" and Susanne Schmid's "Realities Within Reality—The Poetry of Carol Ann Duffy," both in *Poetry Now: Contemporary British and Irish Poetry in the Making* (1999), ed. Holger Klein, Sabine Coelsch-Foisner, and Wolfgang Gortschacher; Eleanor Porter's " 'What Like Is It?' Landscape and Language in Carol Ann Duffy's Love Poetry," *Neohelicon* 26.1 (1999); Linda A. Kinnahan's " 'Now I Am Alien': Immigration and the Discourse of Nation in the Poetry of Carol Ann Duffy," *Contemporary Women's Poetry: Reading, Writing, Practice* (2000), ed. Alison Mark and Rees-Jones; and Antony Rowland's "Love and Masculinity in the Poetry of Carol Ann Duffy," *English* 50.198 (2001).

Alan Dugan

Dugan's *Poems Seven: New and Complete* was published in 2001. Interviews include Michael Ryan's in *Iowa Review* 4.3 (1973), Donald Heines's in *Massachusetts Review* 22 (1981), and Keith Althaus's in *Northwest Review* 20.1 (1982).

Discussions of his work include Robert Boyers's "Alan Dugan: The Poetry of Survival" in his *Contemporary Poetry in America: Essays and Interviews* (1974); Wayne McGinnis's "Christian Symbology in Alan Dugan's 'Morning Song,' " *Nassau Review* 3.3 (1977); David Wojahn's "Recent Poetry," *Western Humanities Review* 38.3 (1984); John Gery's " 'Pieces of Harmony': The Quiet Politics of Alan Dugan's Poetry," *Politics and the Muse: Studies in the Politics of Recent American Literature* (1989), ed. Adam J. Sorkin.

Robert Duncan

Volumes of Duncan's selected work include *Selected Poems* (1959), *The Years as Catches; First Poems, 1939–1941* (1966), *The First Decade: Selected Poems, Vol. 1* (1968), *Derivations: Selected Poems, 1950–1956* (1968), *Ground Work: Before the War* (1984); *Ground Work II: In the Dark* (1987), and *Selected Poems* (1993). Other volumes include *The Opening of the Field* (1960), *Roots and Branches* (1964), and *Bending the Bow* (1968). Prose work can be found in *Fictive Certainties* (1985) and *A Selected Prose* (1995), ed. Robert J. Bertholf, which contains Duncan's important essay "The Homosexual in Society." Duncan's correspondence with H. D. has been published as *A Great Admiration* (1992), ed. Bertholf.

Robert Duncan: Scales of the Marvelous (1979), ed. Bertholf and Ian Reid, is a collection of essays on Duncan's work. Other studies include Ekbert Faas's *Robert Duncan: Portrait of the Poet as Homosexual in Society* (1983); Mark Andrew Johnson's *Robert Duncan* (1988); and Michael Davidson's *The San Francisco Renaissance: Poetics and Community at Mid-Century* (1989). Useful critical essays include Charles Altieri's "The Book of the World: Robert Duncan's Poetics of Presence," *Sun and Moon* 1 (1976); Geoffrey Thurley's "Robert Duncan: The Myth of Open Form," *The American Moment: American Poetry in Mid-Century* (1977); and Wendy McIntyre's "Psyche, Christ, and the Poem," *Ironwood* 11.2 (1983). Several journals have dedicated special issues to Duncan: *Boundary* 28.2 (1980); *Ironwood* 22 (1983); and *Sagetrieb* 4.2–3 (1985). Bertholf published *Robert Duncan: A Descriptive Bibliography* in 1986. See also **Black Mountain School, San Francisco Renaissance.**

Louise Erdrich

Erdrich's volumes of poetry are *Jacklight* (1984) and *Baptism of Desire* (1989). She has also written acclaimed novels, including *Love Medicine* (1984) and *The Antelope Wife* (1998), and collections of short stories, *The Bingo Palace* (1994) and *Tales of Burning Love* (1996). Interviews appear in Laura Coltelli's *Winged Word: American Indian Writers Speak* (1990) and *Conversations with Louise Erdrich and Michael Dorris* (1994), ed. Allan Chavkin and Nancy Feyl Chavkin.

Studies of her work include Daniela Daniele's "Transactions in a Native Land: Mixed-Blood Identity and Indian Legacy in Louise Erdrich's Writing," *RSA Journal* 3 (1992); Jeannie Ludlow's "Working (in) the In-Between: Poetry, Criticism, Interrogation, and Interruption," *Studies in American Indian Literatures* 6.1 (1994); Jane P. Hafen's "Sacramental Language: Ritual in the Poetry of Louise Erdrich," *Great Plains Quarterly* 16.3 (1996); Hans Bak's "Circles Blaze in Ordinary Days: Louise Erdrich's *Jacklight*," *Native American Women in Literature and Culture* (1997), ed. Susan Castillo and Victor Da Rosa; Alan Shucard's entry in *Contemporary Women Poets* (1998), ed. Pamela L. Shelton; and Sheila Hassell Hughes's "Falls of Desire/Leaps of Faith: Religious Syncretism in Louise Erdrich's and Joy Harjo's 'Mixed-Blood' Poetry," *Religion and Literature* 33.2 (2001). See also **Native American Poetry.**

James Fenton

Fenton's volumes of poetry include *Our Western Furniture* (1968), *Put Thou Thy Tears into My Bottle* (1969), *Terminal Moraine* (1972), *A Vacant Possession* (1978), *The Memory of War: Poems, 1968–1982* (1982), *Children in Exile: Poems 1968–1984* (1984), *Partingtime Hall* (1987), *Manila Envelope* (1989), and *Out of Danger* (1993). Fenton's critical works include *Leonardo's Nephew: Essays on Art and Artists* (1998), *The Strength of Poetry* (2001), and *An Introduction to English Poetry* (2002). Fenton has also published travel literature, including *All the Wrong Places: Adrift in the Politics of the Pacific Rim* (1988). Interviews include Manuel Gómez Lara's in *Revista Canaria de Estudios Ingleses* 12 (1986) and Bruce Meyer's in *Eclectic Literary Forum* 8.3–4 (1998).

Discussions of Fenton's poetry include Michael Hulse's "The Poetry of James Fenton," *Antigonish Review* 58 (1984); Alan Robinson's "James Fenton's 'Narratives': Some Reflections on Postmodernism," *Critical Quarterly* 29.1 (1987); Ellen Krieger Stark's "An American Confession: On Reading James Fenton's 'Out of Danger,'" *Critical Quarterly* 36.2 (1994); Ian Parker's "Auden's Heir," *New Yorker* (25 July 1994); Douglas Kerr's "Orientations: James Fenton and Indochina," *Contemporary Literature* 35.3 (1994); and Dana Gioia's "The Rise of James Fenton," *Dark Horse* 8 (1999) and 9–10 (2000).

Lawrence Ferlinghetti

Ferlinghetti's volumes of poetry include *Pictures of the Gone World* (1955, 1995), *A Coney Island of the Mind* (1958), *Tentative Description of a Dinner Given to Promote the Impeachment of President Eisenhower* (1958), *Berlin* (1961), *One Thousand Fearful Words for Fidel Castro* (1961), *Starting from San Francisco* (1961, 1967), *Penguin Modern Poets* 5 (with Gregory Corso and Allen Ginsberg, 1963), *Thoughts of a Concerto of Telemann* (1963), *Christ Climbed Down* (1965), *To Fuck Is to Love Again, Kyrie Eleison Kerista; or, The Situation in the West, Followed by a Holy Proposal* (1965), *Where Is Vietnam?* (1965), *After the Cries of the Birds* (1967), *An Eye on the World: Selected Poems* (1967), *Moscow in the Wilderness, Segovia in the Snow* (1967), *Fuclock* (1968), *Reverie Smoking Grass* (1968), *The Secret Meaning of Things* (1969), *Tyrannus Nix?* (1969), *Back Roads to Far Places* (1971), *The Illustrated Wilfred Funk* (1971), *Love Is No Stone on the Moon* (1971), *Open Eye, Open Heart* (1973), *Director of Alienation* (1976), *Who Are We Now?* (1976), *Landscapes of Living and Dying* (1979), *Mule Mountain Dreams* (1980), *A Trip to Italy and France* (1980), *Endless Life: Selected Poems* (1981), *Over All the Obscene Boundaries: European Poems and Transitions* (1984), *Inside the Trojan Horse* (1987), *Wild Dreams of a New Beginning* (1988), *When I Look at Pictures* (1990), *These Are My Rivers: New & Selected Poems, 1955–1993* (1993), *Ends and Beginnings* (1994), *A Far Rockaway of the Heart* (1997), and *How to Paint Sunlight: Lyric Poems*

& Others (1997–2000) (2001). He has also published novels, including *Her* (1960) and *Love in the Days of Rage* (1988), plays, and works of journalism, including *Howl of the Censor* (1961), ed. J. W. Ehrlich; *Literary San Francisco* (with Nancy J. Peters, 1980), and *Seven Days in Nicaragua Libre* (1984). *The Cool Eye* (1993) is a book-length interview with Alexis Lykiard. Biographies include Neeli Cherkovski's *Ferlinghetti: A Biography* (1979) and Larry Smith's *Lawrence Ferlinghetti: Poet-at-Large* (1983).

Book-length studies include Michael Skau's *"Constantly Risking Absurdity": The Writings of Lawrence Ferlinghetti* (1989) and Barry Silesky's *Ferlinghetti: The Artist in His Time* (1990). Other discussions of his work include David Kherdian's *Six Poets of the San Francisco Renaissance* (1967); *The San Francisco Poets* (1971), ed. David Meltzer; Samuel Barclay Charters's *Some Poems/Poets: Studies in American Underground Poetry since 1945* (1971); Crale D. Hopkins's "The Poetry of Lawrence Ferlinghetti: A Reconsideration," *Italian Americana* 1.1 (1974); and Tony Curtis's "A Hundred Harms: Poetry and the Gulf War—Ferlinghetti at Laugharne," *Poetry Review* 82.2 (1992). Bill Morgan published an updated bibliography on Ferlinghetti in *The Bulletin of Bibliography* 51.2 (1994). See also **Beat Movement, San Francisco Renaissance.**

Carolyn Forché

Forché's volumes of poetry are *Gathering the Tribes* (1976), *The Country between Us* (1981), and *The Angel of History* (1994). She has also written journalism and nonfiction on El Salvador, such as the *History and Motivations of U.S. Involvement and Control of the Peasant Movement in El Salvador: The Role of the AIFLD in the Agrarian Reform Process, 1970–1980* (with Philip Wheaton, 1980), and composed the text for *El Salvador: The Work of Thirty Photographers* (1983), ed. Harry Mattison, Susan Meiselas, and Fae Rubenstein. In addition, she has published translations of Spanish and French poetry and edited the anthology *Against Forgetting: Twentieth-Century Poetry of Witness* (1993). An interview appears in Bill Moyers's *The Language of Life* (1995). Other interviews include David Montenegro's in *American Poetry Review* 17.6 (1988) and Jill Taft-Kaufman's in *Text and Performance Quarterly* 10.1 (1990).

Studies of Forché's work include Imogen Forster's "Constructing Central America," *Red Letters: A Journal of Cultural Politics* 16 (1984); John Mann's "Carolyn Forché: Poetry and Survival," *American Poetry* 3.3 (1986); Michael Greer's "Politicizing the Modern: Carolyn Forché in El Salvador and America," *Centennial Review* 30.2 (1986); Paul Rea's "The Poet as Witness: Carolyn Forché's Powerful Pleas from El Salvador," *Confluencia* 2.2 (1987); Leonora Smith's "Carolyn Forché: Poet as Witness," *Still the Frame Holds: Essays of Women Poets and Writers* (1993), ed. Sheila Roberts and Yvonne Pacheco Tevis, Peter Balakian's "Carolyn Forché and the Poetry of Witness: Another View," *Agni* 40 (1994); Nora Mitchell and Emily Skoler's "History, Death, Politics, Despair," *New England Review* 17.2 (1995; and Anita Helle's "Elegy as History: Three Women Poets 'By the Century's Deathbed,' " *South Atlantic Review* 61.2 (1996).

Allen Ginsberg

Collections of Ginsberg's poetry include *Collected Poems, 1947–1980* (1984), *White Shroud: Poems, 1980–1985* (1986), *Selected Poems 1947–1995* (1996), and *Death and Fame: Poems, 1993–1997* (1999). Ginsberg's essays are collected in *Deliberate Prose: Selected Essays, 1952–1995* (2000), ed. Bill Morgan. A collection of lectures is *Allen Verbatim* (1974) and a book of correspondence is *Journals: Early Fifties, Early Sixties* (1977). *Howl: Original Draft Facsimile, Transcript, and Variant Versions, Fully Annotated by Author, with Contemporaneous Correspondence, Account of First Public Reading, Legal Skirmishes, Precursor Texts, and Bibliography* (1986), ed. Barry Miles, supplies illuminating material for the study of Ginsberg's most famous poem. Interviews include those in *Spontaneous Mind: Selected Interviews, 1958–1996* (2001), ed. David Carter, *Composed on the Tongue* (1980), ed. Donald Allen; and the *Paris Review* dialogue in Tom Clarkin's *Writers at Work*, Third Series (1967). Two biographies are Barry Miles's *Ginsberg* (1989) and Michael Schumacher's *Dharma Lion* (1992).

A collection of essays on his work is *On the Poetry of Allen Ginsberg* (1984), ed. Lewis Hyde. Other discussions of his work include Leslie Fiedler's *Waiting for the End* (1964); Jane Kramer's *Allen Ginsberg in America* (1969); Eric Mottram's *Allen Ginsberg in the Sixties* (1972); Paul Portugés's *The Visionary Poetics of Allen Ginsberg* (1978); Robert K. Martin's *The Homosexual Tradition in American Poetry* (1979, 1998); Richard Howard's *Alone with America* (1980); James E. B. Breslin's *From Modern to Contemporary* (1984); Paul Breslin's *The Psycho-Political Muse* (1987); Helen Vender's *The Music of What Happens* (1988); Michael Davidson's *The San Francisco Renaissance* (1989); Marjorie Perloff's *Poetic License* (1990); John Tytell's *Naked Angels* (1991); Alicia Ostriker's " 'Howl' Revisited: The Poet as Jew," *American Poetry Review* 26 (1997); and Edward Sanders's *The Poetry and Life of Allen Ginsberg* (2000). Bibliographies include George Dowden and Lawrence McGilvery's *A Bibliography of Works by Allen Ginsberg, October, 1943–July 1, 1967* (1971); Michelle P. Kraus's *Allen Ginsberg: An Annotated Bibliography, 1969–1977* (1980);

and Bill Morgan's *The Response to Allen Ginsberg, 1926–1994* (1996). See also **Beat Movement.**

Louise Glück

Glück's poetry from 1969 to 1985 is available as *The First Four Books of Poems* (1995). Subsequent volumes include *Ararat* (1990), *The Wild Iris* (1992), *Meadowlands* (1996), *Vita Nova* (1999), and *The Seven Ages* (2001). A collection of her essays is *Proofs and Theories* (1994).

Critical discussions of her work are found in Helen Vendler's *The Music of What Happens* (1988) and Elizabeth Dodd's *The Veiled Mirror and the Woman Poet: H. D., Louise Bogan, Elizabeth Bishop and Louise Glück* (1992). Other studies include Lynn Keller's " 'Free / of Blossom and Subterfuge': Louise Glück and the Language of Renunciation," *World, Self, Poem: Essays on Contemporary Poetry from the "Jubilation of Poets"* (1990), ed. Leonard M. Trawick; Lynne McMahon's "The Sexual Swamp: Female Erotics and the Masculine Art," *Southern Review* 28.2 (1992); Suzanne Matson's "Without Relation: Family and Freedom in the Poetry of Louise Glück," *Mid-America Review* 14.2 (1994); and Lee Upton's *The Muse of Abandonment: Origins, Identity, Mastery in Five American Poets* (1998).

Lorna Goodison

Goodison's volumes of poetry include *Tamarind Season* (1980), *I Am Becoming My Mother* (1986), *Heartease* (1988), *Selected Poems* (1992), *To Us, All Flowers Are Roses* (1995), *Turn Thanks* (1999), *Guinea Woman: New and Selected Poems* (2000), and *Travelling Mercies* (2001). *Baby Mother and the King of Swords* (1990) is a collection of short stories. Along with Kamau Brathwaite and Mervyn Morris, Goodison is included in *Three Caribbean Poets on Their Work* (1993), ed. Victor L. Chang. Interviews appear in *Wasafiri* 11 (1990); *Commonwealth Essays and Studies* 13.2 (1991); and *Talk Yuh Talk: Interviews with Anglophone Caribbean Poets* (2001), ed. Kwame Dawes.

Critical discussions of Goodison's work can be found in Edward Baugh's "Goodison on the Road to Heartease," *Journal of West Indian Literature* 1.1 (1986) and his "Lorna Goodison in the Context of Feminist Criticism," *Journal of West Indian Literature* 4.1 (1990); *Caribbean Women Writers: Essays from the First International Conference* (1990), ed. Selwyn R. Cudjoe; Susheila Nasta's *Motherlands* (1991); Denise deCaires Narain's "Body Language in the Work of Four Caribbean Poets," *Wasafiri* 16 (1992); J. Edward Chamberlin's *Come Back to Me My Language: Poetry and the West Indies* (1993); Velma Pollard's *Dread Talk: The Language of Rastafari* (1994); Christine Pagnoulle's "Pilgrimage Out of Dispossession," *Commonwealth Essays and Studies* 17.1 (1994); *Frontiers of Caribbean Literature in English* (1996), ed. Frank Birbalsingh; Gudrun Webhofer's *Identity in the Poetry of Grace Nichols and Lorna Goodison* (1996); Elaine Campbell and Pierrette M. Frickey's *The Whistling Bird* (1998); and Dannabang Kuwabong's "The Mother as Archetype of Self: A Poetics of Matrilineage in the Poetry of Claire Harris and Lorna Goodison," *Ariel* 30.1 (1999). See also **Caribbean Poetry.**

Jorie Graham

Graham's volumes of poetry are *Hybrids of Plants and of Ghosts* (1980), *Erosion* (1983), *The End of Beauty* (1987), *Region of Unlikeness* (1991), *Materialism* (1993), *The Dream of the Unified Field: Selected Poems, 1974–1994* (1995), *The Errancy* (1997), *Swarm* (2000), and *Never* (2002). Thomas Gardner's interview in his *Regions of Unlikeness: Explaining Contemporary Poetry* (1999) is an especially illuminating look at Graham's poetics.

Critical work on Graham includes Charles Altieri's "Jorie Graham and Ann Lauterbach: Towards a Contemporary Poetry of Eloquence," *Cream City Review* 12 (1988); Bonnie Costello's "Jorie Graham: Art and Erosion," *Contemporary Literature* 33.2 (1992); James Longenbach's "Jorie Graham's Big Hunger," *Modern Poetry after Modernism* (1997); Calvin Bedient's "Like a Chafing of the Visible" and Willard Spiegelman's "Jorie Graham's 'New Way of Looking,' " both in *Salmagundi* 120 (1998); Gudrun Grabher's "Epistemological Empathy: A. R. Ammons and Jorie Graham," *Strategies of Difference* (1998), ed. Pierre Lagayette; Eric Murphy Selinger's "In Each Other's Arms, or No, Not Really," *Parnassus* (1999); and Gardner's "Jorie Graham's Incandescence," *Regions of Unlikeness* (1999). Helen Vendler discusses Graham in *The Breaking of Style* (1995), *The Given and the Made* (1995), and *Soul Says* (1995).

Thom Gunn

Thom Gunn's *Collected Poems* appeared in 1993. Subsequent volumes include *Boss Cupid* (2000). *The Occasions of Poetry* (1982, 1985) and *Shelf Life* (1993) are collections of essays and autobiographical writings. Interviews appear in *Talking Poetry* (1987), ed. Lee Bartlett; *Critical Survey* 2.2 (1990); *Agni* 36.2 (1992); *Paris Review* (Summer 1995); and *Gay and Lesbian Review Worldwide* 7.3 (2000).

Work on Gunn includes Alan Norman Bold's *Thom Gunn and Ted Hughes* (1976); *Three Contemporary Poets: Thom Gunn, Ted Hughes, and R. S. Thomas: A Casebook* (1990), ed. A. E. Dyson; Bruce Woodcock's " 'But Oh Not Loose': Form and Sexuality in Thom Gunn's Poetry," *Critical Quarterly* 35 (1993); and Tyler Hoffman's "Representing AIDS: Thom Gunn and the

Modalities of Verse," *South Atlantic Review* 65.2 (2000). Jack W. C. Hagstrom and George Bixby's *Thom Gunn: A Bibliography, 1940–1978* (1979) was last updated in *Bulletin of Bibliography* 51. 1 (1994). See also **The Movement.**

Marilyn Hacker

Hacker's volumes of poetry include *The Terrible Children* (1967), *Quark* (1970), *Presentation Piece* (1974), *Separations* (1976), *Taking Notice* (1980), *Assumptions* (1985), *Love, Death, and the Changing of the Seasons* (1986), *Going Back to the River* (1990), *The Hang-Glider's Daughter: New and Selected Poems* (1990), *Selected Poems 1965–1990* (1994), *Winter Numbers* (1994), and *Squares and Courtyards* (2000). She has also published translations, including Claire Malroux's *A Long-Gone Sun* (2000) and Vénus Khoury-Ghata's *Here There Was Once a Country* (2001), and edited *Woman Poet: The East* (1982). Interviews include Karla Hammond's in *Frontiers: A Journal of Woman's Studies* 5.3 (1980), Judith Johnson's in *13th Moon* 9.1–2 (1991); and Annie Finch's in *American Poetry Review* 25.3 (1996). A conversation between Hacker and Richard Howard appears in *Antioch Review* (Summer 2000).

Critical discussions of Hacker's work include Suzanne Gardinier's "Marilyn Hacker," *Lesbian Writers of the United States: A Bio-Bibliographical Critical Sourcebook* (1993), ed. Sandra Pollack and Denise D. Knight; Lynn Keller's "Measured Feet 'in Gender-Bender Shoes': The Politics of Form in Marilyn Hacker's *Love, Death, and the Changing of the Seasons*," *Feminist Measures: Soundings in Poetry and Theory* (1994), ed. Keller and Cristanne Miller; Rafael Campo's "About Marilyn Hacker," *Ploughshares* (Spring 1996); and Nancy Honicker's "Marilyn Hacker's *Love, Death, and the Changing of the Seasons*: Writing/Living within Formal Constraints," *Freedom and Form: Essays in Contemporary American Poetry* (1998), ed. Esther Giger and Agnieszka Salska. See also **New Formalism.**

Joy Harjo

Harjo's collections of poetry include *The Last Song* (1975), *What Moon Drove Me to This?* (1979), *She Had Some Horses* (1983, 1997), *In Mad Love and War* (1990), *The Woman Who Fell from the Sky* (1994), *A Map to the Next World* (2000), and *How We Became Human: New and Selected Poems: 1975–2001* (2002). *Secrets from the Center of the World* (1989) is a collaboration with the photographer Steven Strom. She has also written children's literature, *The Good Luck Cat* (2000); and short stories, in *Talking Leaves: Contemporary Native American Short Stories* (1991), ed. Carig Lesley; and she edited an anthology, *Reinventing the Enemy's Language: Contemporary Native Women's Writing of North America* (1997). *Letter from the End of the Twentieth Century* (1997) is a CD of her poetry backed by the music of Poetic Justice, in which she also played saxophone. Her essay "Oklahoma: The Prairie of Words" is included in *The Remembered Earth: An Anthology of Contemporary Native-American Literature* (1979), ed. Geary Hobson. *The Spiral of Memory* (1996), ed. Laura Coltelli, is a collection of interviews.

Critical studies include Paula Gunn Allen's *The Sacred Hoop: Recovering the Feminine in American Indian Traditions* (1986); John Scarry's "Representing Real Worlds: The Evolving Poetry of Joy Harjo," *World Literature Today* 66.2 (1992); Elaine A. Jahner's "Knowing All the Way Down to Fire," *Feminist Measures: Soundings in Poetry and Theory* (1994), ed. Lynn Keller and Cristanne Miller; Norma C. Wilson's "Joy Harjo," *Native American Writers of the United States* (1997), ed. Kenneth M. Roemer; Rhonda Pettit's *Joy Harjo* (1998); and Kenneth Lincoln's *Sing with the Heart of a Bear: Fusions of Native and American Poetry, 1890–1999* (2000). See also **Native American Poetry.**

Michael S. Harper

Harper's volumes of poetry include *Dear John, Dear Coltrane* (1970), *History Is Your Own Heartbeat* (1971), *Photographs: Negatives: History as Apple Tree* (1972); *Song: I Want a Witness* (1972); *Debridement* (1973); *Nightmare Begins Responsibility* (1974); *Images of Kin: New and Selected Poems* (1977); *Rhode Island* (1981); *Healing Song for the Inner Ear* (1985); *Songlines: Mosaics* (1991); *Honorable Amendments* (1995); and *Songlines in Michaeltree: New and Collected Poems* (2000). Harper also edited *The Collected Poems of Sterling A. Brown* (1980) and coedited various anthologies, including *Chant of Saints: A Gathering of Afro-American Literature, Art and Scholarship* (with Robert B. Stepto, 1979) and *Every Shut Eye Ain't Asleep: An Anthology of Poetry by Americans since 1945* (with Anthony Walton, 1994). An interview appears in Bill Moyers's *The Language of Life* (1995). Other interviews include James Randall's in *Ploughshares* 7.1 (1981) and David Lloyd's in *TriQuarterly* (1986).

Critical discussions of Harper's work can be found in Joseph A. Brown's " 'Their Long Scars Touch Ours': A Reflection on the Poetry of Michael Harper," *Callaloo* 9.1 (1986); John F. Callahan's " 'Close Roads': The Friendship Songs of Michael Harper" and Niccolo N. Donzella's "The Rage of Michael Harper," both in *Callaloo* 13.4 (1990); Jahan Ramazani's *Poetry of Mourning* (1994); Xavier Nicholas's "Robert Hayden and Michael Harper: A Literary Friendship," *Callaloo* 17.4 (1994); Laurence Lieberman's *Beyond the Muse of Memory* (1995);

Michael Bibby's *Hearts and Minds: Bodies, Poetry, and Resistance in the Vietnam Era* (1996); and Elizabeth Dodd's "Another Version: Michael S. Harper, William Clark, and the Problem of Historical Blindness," *Western American Literature* 33.1 (1998). *Callaloo* 13.4 (1990) is a special issue dedicated to Harper.

Tony Harrison

Harrison's volumes of poetry include *Earthworks* (1964), *Newcastle Is Peru* (1969), *The Loiners* (1970), *From "The School of Eloquence" and Other Poems* (1978), *Continuous: Fifty Sonnets from "The School of Eloquence"* (1981), *A Kumquat for John Keats* (1981), *U.S. Martial* (1981), *Selected Poems* (1984, 1987), *The Mysteries* (1985), *"V." and Other Poems* (1990), *A Cold Coming: Gulf War Poems* (1991), *The Gaze of the Gorgon* (1992), *Permanently Bard* (1995), and *"The Shadow of Hiroshima" and Other Film/Poems* (1995). Among his collections of dramatic verse are *Theatre Works: 1973–1985* (1986) and *Plays Three* (1996), *Plays Two* (2002), and *Plays Four* (2002). He also wrote and directed a movie, *Prometheus* (1998), and wrote the screenplay for a short television production, *Crossings* (2002). Biographical information can be found in Joe Kelleher's *Tony Harrison* (1996).

Bloodaxe Critical Anthologies 1: Tony Harrison (1991), ed. Neil Astley, and *Tony Harrison: Loiner* (1997), ed. Sandie Byrne, are collections of essays. Other criticism of his work includes Luke Spencer's *The Poetry of Tony Harrison* (1994); Raymond Hargreaves's "Tony Harrison and the Poetry of Leeds," *Poetry in the British Isles: Non-Metropolitan Perspectives* (1995), ed. Hans-Werner Ludwig and Lothar Fietz; Byrne's *H, v. & O: The Poetry of Tony Harrison* (1998); and Antony Rowland's *Tony Harrison and the Holocaust* (2001). John R. Kaiser's *Tony Harrison: A Bibliography, 1957–1987* was published in 1989.

Robert Hass

Hass's volumes of poetry include *Field Guide* (1973), *Praise* (1979), *Human Wishes* (1989), and *Sun under Wood* (1996). Interviews appear in Bill Moyers's *The Language of Life* (1995) and Thomas Gardner's *Regions of Unlikeness: Explaining Contemporary Poetry* (1999).

Discussions of his work include Alan Shapiro's "'And There Will Always Be Melons': Some Thoughts on Robert Hass," *Chicago Review* 33.3 (1983) and his "Some Thoughts on Robert Hass," *In Praise of the Impure* (1993); Charles Altieri's *Self and Sensibility in Contemporary American Poetry* (1984); Charles Berger's "Poetry Chronicle: Dan Pagis and Robert Hass," *Raritan* 10.1 (1990); Calvin Bedient's "Man Is Altogether Desire?" *Salmagundi* 90–91 (1991); Terrence Doody's "From Image to Sentence: The Spiritual Development of Robert Hass," *American Poetry Review* 26.2 (1997); and Gardner's *Regions of Unlikeness* (1999).

Robert Hayden

Robert Hayden: Collected Poems, ed. Frederick Glaysher, appeared in 1985 and his *Collected Prose*, also edited by Glaysher, in 1984. Hayden edited several anthologies, including *Kaleidoscope: Poems of American Negro Poets* (1967); *Afro-American Literature: An Introduction* (with David J. Burrows and Frederick Lapides, 1971); and *The Human Condition: Literature Written in the English Language* (1974). Hayden also published "A Portfolio of Recent American Poems," *World Order* 5 (1971), and "Recent American Poetry—Portfolio II," *World Order* 9 (1975), and wrote the preface to the 1968 edition of Alain Locke's *The New Negro*. A biography is Fred M. Fetrow's *Robert Hayden* (1984).

Book-length studies include John Hatcher's *From the Auroral Darkness: The Life and Poetry of Robert Hayden* (1984); and Pontheolla T. Williams's *Robert Hayden: A Critical Analysis of His Poetry* (1987). *Robert Hayden: Essays on the Poetry* (2001), ed. Laurence Goldstein, is a collection of essays. Other discussions of Hayden include Vera M. Kutzinski's "Changing Permanences: Historical and Literary Revisionism in Robert Hayden's 'Middle Passage,'" *Callaloo* 9.1 (1986); Fetrow's "Minority Reporting and Psychic Distancing in the Poetry of Robert Hayden," *CLA Journal* 33 (1989); Alan Shapiro's "In Praise of the Impure: Narrative Consciousness in Poetry," *TriQuarterly* 81 (1991); Michael Collins's "On the Track of the Universal: 'Middle Passage' and America," *Parnassus* 17 (1992); Xavier Nicholas's "Robert Hayden: Some Introductory Notes," *Michigan Quarterly Review* 31 (1992); Nicholas's "Robert Hayden and Michael Harper: A Literary Friendship," *Callaloo* 17.4 (1994); Benjamin Friedlander's "Robert Hayden's Epic of Community," *MELUS* 23.3 (1998); Brian Conniff's "Answering 'The Waste Land': Robert Hayden and the Rise of the African American Poetic Sequence," *African American Review* 33.3 (1999); and Jon Woodson's "Consciousness, Myth, and Transcendence: Symbolic Action in Three Poems on the Slave Trade," *The Furious Flowering of African American Poetry* (1999), ed. Joanne V. Gabbin.

Seamus Heaney

Heaney's volumes of poetry include *Death of a Naturalist* (1966), *Door into the Dark* (1969), *Wintering Out* (1972), *North* (1975), *Field Work* (1979), *Sweeney Astray* (1983), *Station Island* (1984), *The Haw Lantern* (1987), *Seeing Things* (1991), *The Spirit Level* (1996), *Open Ground: Selected Poems, 1966–1996* (1998), and *Electric Light* (2001). His translation of *Beowulf* was published in 1999. Collections of essays are *Preoccupations: Selected Prose, 1968–1978* (1980), *The Government of the Tongue*

(1988), *The Redress of Poetry: Oxford Lectures* (1995), and *Finders Keepers: Selected Prose, 1971–2001* (2002). A biography is Michael Parker's *Seamus Heaney: The Making of the Poet* (1993).

Essay collections on Heaney's work include *The Art of Seamus Heaney* (1982), ed. Tony Curtis; *Seamus Heaney* (1988), ed. Harold Bloom; *Seamus Heaney: A Collection of Critical Essays* (1992), ed. Elmer Andrews; and *Critical Essays on Seamus Heaney* (1995), ed. Robert F. Garratt. Other critical studies include Blake Morrison's *Seamus Heaney* (1982); Neil Corcoran's *Seamus Heaney: A Faber Study Guide* (1986); Andrews's *The Poetry of Seamus Heaney: All the Realms of Whisper* (1988); Thomas C. Foster's *Seamus Heaney* (1989); Henry Hart's *Seamus Heaney: Poet of Contrary Progressions* (1992); Bernard O'Donoghue's *Seamus Heaney* (1994); J. W. Foster's *The Achievement of Seamus Heaney* (1995); and Helen Vendler's *Seamus Heaney* (1998). Bibliographical information can be found in Michael J. Durkan and Rand Brandes's *Seamus Heaney: A Reference Guide* (1996). See also **Irish Poetry.**

Anthony Hecht

Hecht's volumes of poetry include *A Summoning of Stones* (1954), *The Hard Hours* (1967), *Millions of Strange Shadows* (1977), *The Venetian Vespers* (1979), *Collected Earlier Poems* (1990), *The Transparent Man* (1990), *Flight among the Tombs* (1996), and *The Darkness and the Light* (2001). Works of criticism include *Obbligati: Essays in Criticism* (1986), *The Hidden Law: The Poetry of W. H. Auden* (1993), and *On the Laws of the Poetic Art* (1995). He has also published translations from Latin and French and edited Jonathan Aaron's *Second Sight* (1982), Susan Donnelly's *Eve Names the Animals* (1985), *The Essential Herbert* (1987), and an edition of Shakespeare's sonnets (1996).

The Burdens of Formality (1989), ed. Sydney Lea, is a collection of essays on Hecht's work. Other relevant studies include Richard Howard's *Alone with America: Essays on the Art of Poetry in the United States since 1950* (1969, 1980); Norman German's *Anthony Hecht* (1989); J. D. McClatchy's *White Paper: On Contemporary American Poetry* (1989); Geoffrey Lindsay's " 'Laws That Stand for Other Laws': Anthony Hecht's Dramatic Strategy," *Essays in Literature* 21.2 (1994); John Hollander's "On Anthony Hecht," *Raritan* 17 (1997); and A. Alvarez's "A Light Black World," *New York Review of Books* (May 9, 2002). A recent interview by Daniel Anderson is published in *Bomb* 62 (1998).

Lyn Hejinian

Hejinian's books include *A Thought Is the Bride of What Thinking* (1976), *A Mask of Motion* (1977), *Gesualdo* (1978), *Writing Is an Aid to Memory* (1978), *My Life* (1980, 1987), *Redo* (1984), *Individuals* (with Kit Robinson, 1988), *Oxota: A Short Russian Novel* (1991), *The Cell* (1992), *The Cold of Poetry* (1994), *Guide, Grammar, Watch, and the Thirty Nights* (1996), *The Little Book of a Thousand Eyes* (1996), *Wicker: A Collaborative Poem* (with Jack Collom, 1996), *Hearing* (with Leslie Scalapino, 1998), *The Traveler and the Hill; and, The Hill* (1998), *Sight* (with Scalapino, 1999), *Chartings* (with Ray DiPalma, 2000), *Happily* (2000), *A Border Comedy* (2001), and *The Lake* (with Emilie Clark, 2001). A selection of Hejinian's criticism, including her essay "The Rejection of Closure," as well as poetry, appears in *The Language of Inquiry* (2000).

Marjorie Perloff has written about Hejinian in various places, including *The Dance of the Intellect* (1985), *Radical Artifice* (1991), and *Poetry on and off the Page* (1998). Other studies include Hilary Clark's "The Mnemonics of Autobiography: Lyn Hejinian's *My Life*," *Biography* 14.4 (1991); David Jarraway's "*My Life* through the Eighties," *Contemporary Literature* 33.2 (1992); Juliana Spahr's "Resignifying Autobiography: Lyn Hejinian's *My Life*," *American Literature* 68 (1996); Christopher Beach's "Poetic Positionings: Stephen Dobyns and Lyn Hejinian in Cultural Context," *Contemporary Literature* 38.1 (1997); and Charles Altieri's "Lyn Hejinian and the Possibilities of Postmodernism in Poetry," *Women Poets of the Americas* (1999), ed. Jaqueline Brogan and Cordelia Candelaria. See also **Language Poetry**.

Geoffrey Hill

Hill's *New and Collected Poems, 1952–1992* was published in 1994. Subsequent volumes include *Canaan* (1997), *The Triumph of Love* (1998), *Speech! Speech!* (2000), and *The Orchards of Syon* (2002). Prose works include *The Lords of Limit: Essays on Literature and Ideas* (1984) and *Illuminating Shadow: The Mythic Power of Film* (1992). An interview appears in *Viewpoints: Poets in Conversation with John Haffenden* (1981).

Two collections of criticism are *Geoffrey Hill: Essays on His Work* (1985), ed. Peter Robinson, and *Geoffrey Hill* (1986), ed. Harold Bloom. Book-length studies include Christopher Ricks's *Geoffrey Hill and "The Tongue's Atrocities"* (1978); Henry Hart's *The Poetry of Geoffrey Hill* (1986); Vincent Sherry's *The Uncommon Tongue: The Poetry and Criticism of Geoffrey Hill* (1987); and E. M. Knottenbelt's *Passionate Intelligence: The Poetry of Geoffrey Hill* (1990). *Agenda* 17.1 (1979) and 23 (1985–86) are special issues dedicated to Hill. Other critical discussions can be found in John Silkin's chapter in *British Poetry since 1960* (1972), ed. Michael Schmidt and Grevel Lindop; Seamus Heaney's "Now and in England," *Critical Inquiry* 3 (1977); Calvin Bedient's "On Geoffrey Hill,"

Critical Quarterly 23.2 (1981); Thomas H. Getz's "Geoffrey Hill: History as Poetry, Poetry as Salutation," *Contemporary Poetry* 4.3 (1982); Stephen T. Glynn's " 'Biting Nothings to the Bone': The Exemplary Failure of Geoffrey Hill," *English* 36.156 (1987); Michael North's "The Word as Bond: Money and Performative Language in Hill's *Mercian Hymns*," *ELH* 54.2 (1987); William Logan's "The Absolute Unreasonableness of Geoffrey Hill," *Conversant Essays: Contemporary Poets on Poetry* (1990), ed. James McCorkle; Jeffrey Donaldson's "Must Men Stand by What They Write?," *Partisan Review* 58.3 (1991); Eleanor J. McNees's *Eucharistic Poetry: The Search for Presence in the Writings of John Donne, Gerard Manley Hopkins, Dylan Thomas, and Geoffrey Hill* (1992); and Karen A. Weisman's "Romantic Constructions and Epic Subversions in Geoffrey Hill's *Mercian Hymns*," *Modern Language Quarterly* 57.1 (March 1996).

John Hollander

Hollander's volumes of poetry include *A Crackling of Thorns* (1958), *A Beach Vision* (1962), *"Movie Going" and Other Poems* (1962), *Visions from the Ramble* (1965), *Philomel* (1968), *Types of Shape* (1969, 1991), *The Night Mirror* (1971), *Town and Country Matters* (1972), *Selected Poems* (1972), *The Head of the Bed* (1974), *Tales Told of the Fathers* (1975), *Reflections on Espionage* (1976), *In Place* (1978), *Spectral Emanations: New and Selected Poems* (1978), *Blue Wine and Other Poems* (1979), *Looking Ahead* (1982), *Powers of Thirteen* (1983), *A Hollander Garland* (1985), *In Time and Place* (1986), *Harp Lake* (1988), *Some Fugitives Take Cover* (1988), *Selected Poetry* (1993), *"Tesserae" and Other Poems* (1993), *The Gazer's Spirit: Poems Speaking to Silent Works of Art* (1995), *The Poetry of Everyday Life* (1998), and *"Figurehead" & Other Poems* (1999). Hollander's *Rhyme's Reason: A Guide to English Verse* (1981, 2001) is a helpful and amusing guide to poetic forms. Other works of criticism include *Modern Poetry: Modern Essays in Criticism* (1968) and *Melodious Guile: Fictive Pattern in Poetic Language* (1988). He also coedited *The Oxford Anthology of English Literature* (1973) and edited *American Poetry: The Nineteenth Century* (1994). Interviews include Wesley Wark's in *Queen's Quarterly* 100.2 (1993) and Langdon Hammer's in *Southwest Review* 80 (1995).

Studies dealing with Hollander's work include Richard Howard's *Alone with America* (1969, 1980); Helen Vendler's "A Quarter of Poetry," *New York Times Book Review* (6 April 1975); J. D. McClatchy's "Speaking of Hollander," *The American Poetry Review* 11.5 (1982); and David Lehman's "The Sound and Sense of the Sleight-of-Hand Man," *Parnassus* 12.1 (1984); Rosanna Warren's "Night Thoughts and a Figurehead," and Kenneth Gross's "John Hollander's Game of Patience," both in *Raritan* 20.2 (2000); and Ernest Suarez's "John Hollander," *Five Points* 6.1 (2001).

Richard Howard

Howard's volumes of poetry include *Quantities* (1962), *The Damages* (1967), *Untitled Subjects* (1969), *Findings* (1971), *Two-Part Inventions* (1974), *Fellow Feelings* (1976), *Misgivings* (1979), *Lining Up* (1984), *Quantities/Damages: Early Poems* (contains *Quantities* and *The Damages*, 1984), *No Traveller* (1989), *Selected Poems* (1991), *Like Most Revelations* (1994), *If I Dream I Have You, I Have You* (1997), and *Trappings* (1999). Howard is also an extremely prolific translator, translating a wide range of French works from Baudelaire to Roland Barthes. His *Alone with America* (1969, 1980) is an important work of criticism on American poetry after 1960. Interviews appear in *Shenandoah* 24.1 (1973) and *Ohio Review* 16.1 (1974). A conversation with Marilyn Hacker appears in *Antioch Review* 58.3 (Summer 2000).

Discussions of Howard's work include Christopher Ricks's "Conspicuous Consumption," *Parnassus* 3.1 (1974); Robert K. Martin's "The Unconsummated Word," *Parnassus* 4.1 (1975); Henry Sloss's "Cleaving and Burning: An Essay on Richard Howard's Poetry," *Shenandoah* 29.1 (1977); Michael Lynch's "The Life below the Life," *The Gay Academic* (1978), ed. Louie Crew; and James Longenbach's "Richard Howard's Modern World," *Modern Poetry after Modernism* (1997).

Susan Howe

Howe's volumes of poetry—which often also incorporate other genres—include *Hinge Picture* (1974), *Chanting at the Crystal Sea* (1975), *The Western Borders* (1976), *Secret History of the Dividing Line* (1978), *Cabbage Gardens* (1979), *Deep in a Forest of Herods* (1979), *The Liberties* (1980), *Pythagorean Silence* (1982), *Defenestration of Prague* (1983), *Articulation of Sound Forms in Time* (1987), *A Bibliography of the King's Book; or, Eikon Basilike* (1989), *The Europe of Trusts* (1990), *Singularities* (1990), *The Nonconformist's Memorial* (illustrations by Robert Mangold, 1992), *Frame Structures: Early Poems, 1974–1979* (1996), *Pierce-Arrow* (1999), and *Bed Hangings* (pictures by Susan Bee, 2001). Her *My Emily Dickinson* (1985) is an important contribution to Dickinson criticism. Other critical works include *Incloser* (1992) and *The Birth-Mark: Unsettling the Wilderness in American Literary History* (1993). An interview with Lynn Keller appears in *Contemporary Literature* 36.1 (1995).

Critical studies dealing with Howe's work include *The Difficulties* 3.2 (1989); *Talisman* 4 (1990); Rachel Blau DuPlessis's *The Pink Gui-*

tar (1990); Marjorie Perloff's *Poetic License* (1990); Peter Middleton's "On Ice: Julia Kristeva, Susan Howe, and Avant-Garde Poetics," *Contemporary Poetry Meets Modern Theory* (1991), ed. Anthony Easthope and John O. Thompson; Peter Quartermain's *Disjunctive Poetics: From Gertrude Stein and Louis Zukofsky to Susan Howe* (1992); Linda Reinfeld's *Language Poetry: Writing as Rescue* (1992); Mingqian Ma's "Articulating the Inarticulate: Singularities and the Counter-Method in Susan Howe," *Contemporary Literature* 36.3 (1995); Peter Nicholls's "Unsettling the Wilderness: Susan Howe and American History," Contemporary Literature 37.4 (1996); Geoffrey O'Brien's *Bardic Deadlines: Reviewing Poetry 1984–1995* (1998); and Paul Naylor's *Poetic Investigations: Singing the Holes in History* (1999). See also **Language Poetry.**

Ted Hughes

Hughes's volumes of poetry include *The Hawk in the Rain* (1957), *Lupercal* (1960), *Wodwo* (1967), *Crow* (1970, 1972), *Season Songs* (1975), *Gaudete* (1977), *Cave Birds* (1978), *Moortown* (1979), *Remains of Elmet* (1979), *River* (1983), *Flowers and Insects* (1986), *Wolfwatching* (1989), *Cappriccio* (1990), *"Rain-Charm for the Duchy" and Other Laureate Poems* (1992), *New Selected Poems 1957–1994* (1995), *Difficulties of a Bridegroom* (1995), *Tales from Ovid* (1997), and *Birthday Letters* (1998). Works of prose include *Poetry in the Making* (1969), *Shakespeare and the Goddess of Complete Being* (1992), and *Winter Pollen: Occasional Prose* (1994). His translations include Seneca's *Oedipus* (1969) and Jean Racine's *Phedre* (1998). He also published children's literature and edited collections of Shakespeare, Coleridge, Dickinson, Keith Douglas, and Sylvia Plath. A biography is Elaine Feinstein's *Ted Hughes: The Life of a Poet* (2001).

Collections of essays include *The Achievement of Ted Hughes* (1983), ed. Keith Sagar; *Critical Essays on Ted Hughes* (1992), ed. Leonard M. Scigaj; and *The Epic Poise: A Celebration of Ted Hughes* (1999), ed. Nick Gammage. Book-length studies include Sagar's *The Art of Ted Hughes* (1978), Terry Gifford and Neil Roberts's *Ted Hughes: A Critical Study* (1981), Thomas West's *Ted Hughes* (1985), Dennis Walder's *Ted Hughes* (1987), Craig Robinson's *Ted Hughes as Shepherd of Being* (1989), Nick Bishop's *Re-Making Poetry: Ted Hughes and a New Critical Psychology* (1991), Ann Skea's *Ted Hughes: The Poetic Quest* (1994), and Paul Bentley's *The Poetry of Ted Hughes: Language, Illusion, and Beyond* (1998). Discussions of Hughes and Plath include Janet Malcolm's *The Silent Woman: Sylvia Plath and Ted Hughes* (1993), Erica Wagner's *Ariel's Gift* (2000), and Lynda K. Bundtzen's *The Other Ariel* (2001). Bibliographical information is available in Keith Sagar and Stephen Tabor's *Ted Hughes: A Bibliography,* 1946–1980 (1983).

Richard Hugo

Making Certain It Goes On: The Collected Poems of Richard Hugo was published in 1984. Other works include *The Triggering Town: Lectures and Essays on Poetry and Writing* (1979) and the novel *Death and The Good Life* (1981). Hugo's *The Real West Marginal Way: A Poet's Autobiography,* ed. Ripley S. Hugo, Louis M. Welch, and James Welch, was published in 1986. Interviews include David Dillon's in *Southwest Review* 62 (Spring 1977), Michael S. Allen's in *Ohio Review* 19 (Winter 1978), and Thomas Gardner's in *Contemporary Literature* 22 (Spring 1981). A conversation between Hugo and William Stafford appears in *Northwest Review* 13 (March 1974).

Book-length studies of Hugo include Michael S. Allen's *We Are Called Human: The Poetry of Richard Hugo* (1982) and Donna Gerstenberger's *Richard Hugo* (1983). *A Trout in the Milk* (1982), ed. Jack Myers, is a collection of essays on Hugo. *Slackwater Review* produced a special Hugo issue in 1978. Other critical discussions of Hugo include Dave Smith's "Getting Right: Richard Hugo's *Selected Poems* and *The Triggering Town,*" *American Poetry Review* 10.5 (September–October 1981); Hank Lazer's "The Letter Poem," *Northwest Review* 19.1–2 (1981); Paul Lindholdt's "Richard Hugo's Language: The Poem as 'Obsessive Musical Deed,' " *Contemporary Poetry* 16.2 (Fall 1983); Julian Gitzen's " 'What We Want to Save': The Odyssey of Richard Hugo," *Northwest Review* 24.2 (1986); Sanford Pinsker's *Three Pacific Northwest Poets* (1987); Larry Levinger's "Poet Richard Hugo: The Open Field Beyond," *Ploughshares* 18.1 (1992); and Jonathan Holden's "West Marginal Way: Richard Hugo's Poetry as Self-Psychoanalysis," *Mid-American Review* 16.1 (1995). Bibliographies include Allen's in *A Trout in the Milk* and James Bense's in *Bulletin of Bibliography* 40.3 (September 1983).

Randall Jarrell

Jarrell's *Complete Poems* appeared in 1969 and a *Selected Poems*, ed. William H. Pritchard, in 1990. Jarrell also wrote children's literature and adult fiction, including *Pictures from an Institution: A Comedy* (1954), and translated from German. Jarrell's criticism can be found in *The Poetry of the Age* (1953, expanded in a 2001 edition), *The Third Book of Criticism* (1969), and *No Other Book: Selected Essays* (1999). Pritchard's *Randall Jarrell: A Literary Life* (1990) is a fine biography. Mary Jarrell edited *Randall Jarrell's Letters* (1985).

Collections of essays on Jarrell include *Rand-*

all Jarrell, 1914–1965, a memorial volume edited by Robert Lowell, Peter Taylor, and Robert Penn Warren in 1967, and *Critical Essays on Randall Jarrell* (1983), ed. Suzanne Ferguson. Other discussions of Jarrell's work can be found in Ferguson's *The Poetry of Randall Jarrell* (1971), M. L. Rosenthal's *Randall Jarrell* (1972), J. A. Bryant Jr.'s *Understanding Randall Jarrell* (1986), Richard Flynn's *Randall Jarrell and the Lost World of Childhood* (1990), James Longenbach's *Modern Poetry after Modernism* (1997), and Thomas Travisano's *Midcentury Quartet* (1999). A bibliography is Stuart T. Wright's *Randall Jarrell: A Descriptive Bibliography: 1929–1983* (1986).

June Jordan

Jordan's volumes of poetry include *Who Look at Me* (1969), *Some Changes* (1971), *New Days: Poems of Exile and Return* (1974), *Things That I Do in the Dark: Selected Poetry* (1977, 1981), *Passion* (1980), *Living Room* (1985), *Lyrical Campaigns: Selected Poems* (1989), *Naming Our Destiny: New and Selected Poems* (1989), *Haruko/Love Poetry: New and Selected Love Poems* (1994), and *Kissing God Goodbye: Poems, 1991–1997* (1997). Collections of essays are *Civil Wars* (1981), *On Call: Political Essays* (1985), *Technical Difficulties: African American Notes on the State of the Union* (1992), and *Affirmative Acts: Political Essays* (1998). She has published many books for children and edited *Soulscript: Afro-American Poetry* (1970) and *The Voice of the Children* (with Terri Bush, 1970). She wrote plays, *In the Spirit of Sojourner Truth* (1979) and *The Issue* (1985), and the libretto for *I Was Looking at the Ceiling and Then I Saw the Sky: Earthquake/Romance* (1995), an opera composed by John Adams. In 2000, Jordan published the autobiographical *Soldier: A Poet's Childhood.* An interview with June Jordan appears in *High Plains Literary Review* 3.2 (1988) and one with Peter Erickson in *Transition* 63 (1994).

A collection of essays on Jordan's work is *June Jordan's Poetry for the People: A Revolutionary Blueprint* (1995), ed. Lauren Muller and the Poetry for the People Collective. Other discussions of Jordan's work can be found in Erickson's "The Love Poetry of June Jordan," *Callaloo* 9.1 (1986); *Diverse Voices: Essays on Twentieth-Century Women Writers in English* (1991), ed. Harriet Devine Jump; Jacqueline Vaught Brogan's "From Warrior to Womanist: The Development of June Jordan's Poetry," *Speaking the Other Self: American Women Writers* (1997), ed. Jeanne Campbell Reesman; Scott MacPhail's "June Jordan and the New Black Intellectuals," *African American Review* 33.1 (1999); and AnaLouise Keating's "The Intimate Distance of Desire: June Jordan's Bisexual Inflections," *Journal of Lesbian Studies* 4.2 (2000). See also **Black Arts Movement.**

Donald Justice

Justice's volumes of poetry include *The Summer Anniversaries* (1960), *A Local Storm* (1963), *Night Light* (1967), *Sixteen Poems* (1970), *From a Notebook* (1972), *Departures* (1973), *Selected Poems* (1979), *Tremayne* (1984), *New and Selected Poems* (1995), and *Orpheus Hesitated Beside the Black River: Poems 1952–1997* (1998). *The Sunset Maker* (1987) includes stories and a memoir as well as verse. *The Donald Justice Reader* (1991) collects poetry and prose. *Oblivion* (1998) contains essays on writers and writing. Other works include the play *The Death of Lincoln* (1988) and translations, including Eugène Guillevic's *The Man Closing Up* (1973). Justice also edited *The Collected Poems of Weldon Kees* (1960) and Joe Bolton's *The Last Nostalgia: Poems, 1982–1990* (1999). An interview appears in *American Poetry Review* 25.1 (1996).

Donald Justice in Conversation with Philip Hoy (2001) contains a long interview and an overview of Justice's work and critical reception. A collection of critical essays is *Certain Solitudes: On the Poetry of Donald Justice* (1997), ed. Dana Gioia and William Logan. Other discussions include Mark Jarman's "Ironic Elegies: The Poetry of Donald Justice," *Pequod* 16/17 (1984); Michael Ryan's "Flaubert in Florida," *New England Review and Breadloaf Quarterly* 7.2 (1984); Gioia's "A Poet's Poet," *New Criterion* (May 1992); Lewis Turco's "The Progress of Donald Justice," *Hollins Critic* 29.4 (1992); Clive Watkin's "Some Reflections on Donald Justice's Poem 'After a Phrase Abandoned by Wallace Stevens,'" *Wallace Stevens Journal* 17.2 (1993); Charles Wright's "Homage to the Thin Man," *Southern Review* 30.4 (1994); Carol Frost's "The Poet's Tact, and a Necessary Tactlessness," *New England Review* 20.3 (1999).

Galway Kinnell

Kinnell's volumes of poetry include *What a Kingdom It Was* (1960), *Flower Herding on Mount Monadnock* (1964), *Body Rags* (1968), *Poems of Night* (1968), *The Hen Flower* (1969), *First Poems: 1946–1954* (1970), *The Book of Nightmares* (1971), *The Shoes of Wandering* (1971), *The Avenue Bearing the Initial of Christ into the New World: Poems 1946–1964* (1974), *Mortal Acts, Mortal Words* (1980), *Selected Poems* (1982), *The Past* (1985), *When One Has Lived a Long Time Alone* (1990), *Three Books* (includes *Body Rags; Mortal Acts, Mortal Words*; and *The Past,* 1993), *Imperfect Thirst* (1994), and *A New Selected Poems* (2000). He has also published translations, including *The Poems of François Villon* (1977) and *The Essential Rilke* (with Hannah Liebmann, 1999), children's literature, and a novel, *Black Light* (1966). *Walking Down the Stairs* (1978) is a selection of interviews.

Book-length studies of Kinnell include Lee Zimmerman's *Intricate and Simple Things: The Poetry of Galway Kinnell* (1987) and Richard J. Calhoun's *Galway Kinnell* (1992). Collections of essays on his work include *On the Poetry of Galway Kinnell: The Wages of Dying* (1987), ed. Howard Nelson, and *Critical Essays on Galway Kinnell* (1996), ed. Nancy L. Tuten. Other helpful discussions can be found in Richard Howard's *Alone with America* (1969, 1980), Ralph Mills's *Cry of the Human* (1975), and Cary Nelson's *Our Last First Poets* (1981). A bibliography is *Galway Kinnell: A Bibliography and Index of His Published Works and Criticism of Them* (1968).

Thomas Kinsella

Kinsella's *The Collected Poems 1956–2001* was published in 2001. Works of criticism include *Davis, Mangan, Ferguson?: Tradition and the Irish Writer* (with writings by W. B. Yeats, 1970) and *The Dual Tradition: An Essay on Poetry and Politics in Ireland* (1995). He has also published translations of literature in Irish.

Book-length considerations of Kinsella's work include Maurice Harmon's *The Poetry of Thomas Kinsella: "With Darkness for a Nest"* (1974), Thomas H. Jackson's *The Whole Matter: The Poetic Evolution of Thomas Kinsella* (1995), Donatella Abbate Badin's *Thomas Kinsella* (1996), and Brian John's *Reading the Ground: The Poetry of Thomas Kinsella* (1996). Critical essays include Floyd Skloot's "The Evolving Poetry of Thomas Kinsella," *New England Review* 18.4 (1997); Taffy Martin's "Thomas Kinsella and the Poetry of Irish Difference," *Strategies of Difference in Modern Poetry: Case Studies in Poetic Composition* (1998), ed. Pierre Lagayette; and Daniel T. O'Hara's "The Pen Shop of Thomas Kinsella," *Boundary 2* 28.2 (2001). *The Hollins Critic* published a special issue on Kinsella in 1968. J. Chris Westgate's bibliography appears in *Bulletin of Bibliography* 56.3 (1999). See also **Irish Poetry.**

Kenneth Koch

Koch's volumes of poetry include *Poems* (1953), *Ko; or A Season on Earth* (1959), *Permanently* (1960), *"Thank You" and Other Poems* (1962), *Poems from 1952 and 1953* (1968), *The "Pleasures of Peace" and Other Poems* (1969), *Sleeping with Women* (1969), *When the Sun Tries to Go On* (1969), *The Art of Love* (1975), *The Duplications* (1977), *The Burning Mystery of Anna in 1951* (1979), *From the Air* (1979), *Days and Nights* (1982), *Selected Poems, 1950–1982* (1985), *On the Edge* (1986), *Seasons on Earth* (1987), *Selected Poems* (1991), *One Train* (1994), *On the Great Atlantic Rainway: Selected Poems, 1950–1988* (1994), *Straits* (1998), and *New Addresses* (2000). *The Art of Poetry* (1996) is a collection of poems, interviews, essays, and other writings. Koch published short stories, including *"Hotel Lambosa" and Other Stories* (1993); a novel, *The Red Robins* (1975); and many plays, including those collected in *Gold Standard* (1996). He also published extensively on questions of pedagogy: *Wishes, Lies, and Dreams: Teaching Children to Write Poetry* (1970), *Rose, Where did You Get That Red?: Teaching Great Poetry to Children* (1973), and *I Never Told Anybody: Teaching Poetry Writing in a Nursing Home* (1977). His *Making Your Own Days* (1998) is a delightful introduction to reading and writing poetry that includes a small anthology of poems. Interviews include John Tranter's in *Scripsi* 4.2 (1986), David Herd's in *Pn Review* 22 (1995), and Jordan Davis's in *American Poetry Review* 25.6 (1996).

Discussions of Koch's work can be found in David Spurr's "Beyond Irony," *American Poetry Review* 12.2 (1983); Philip Auslander's *The New York School Poets as Playwrights* (1989); John Paul Tassoni's "Play and Co-Option in Kenneth Koch's *Ko; or, A Season on Earth*: 'Freedom and the Realizable World!' " *Sagetrieb* 10.1–2 (1991); David Lehman's "Dr. Fun," American Poetry Review 24.6 (1995); Mark Halliday's "Koch and Sense," *Michigan Quarterly Review* 36.1 (1997); Lehman's *The Last Avant-Garde* (1998); and Paul Hoover's "Fables of Representation: Poetry of The New York School," *American Poetry Review* 31.4 (2002). *The Scene of My Selves: New Work on the New York School Poets* (2001), ed. Terrence Diggory and Stephen Paul Miller, contains three essays on Koch: David Chinitz's " 'Arm the Paper Arm': Kenneth Koch's Postmodern Comedy," Theodore Pelton's "Kenneth Koch's Poetics of Pleasure," and David Spurr's "Kenneth Koch's 'Serious Moment.' " See also **New York School.**

Yusef Komunyakaa

Komunyakaa's poetry is collected in *Pleasure Dome: New and Collected Poems* (2001). *Blue Notes* (2000) is a collection of essays, interviews, and other writings. Komunyakaa also coedited the two-volume *Jazz Poetry Anthology* (1991, 1996) with Sascha Feinstein. Interviews include Vincente F. Gotera's in *Callaloo* 13.2 (1990); Robert Kelley's "Jazz and Poetry," *Georgia Review* 46.4 (1992); Muna Asali's in *New England Review* 16.1 (1994); Thomas C. Johnson's in *Worcester Review* 19.1–2 (1998); and Ernest Suarez's in *Five Points* (1999).

For discussions of Komunyakaa's work, see Vincente F. Gotera's " 'Depending on the Light': Yusef Komunyakaa's *Dien Cai Dau*," *America Rediscovered: Critical Essays on Literature and*

Film of the Vietnam War (1990), ed. Owen W. Gilman Jr. and Lorrie Smith; Kirkland C. Jones's "Folk Idiom in the Literary Expression of Two African American Authors: Rita Dove and Yusef Komunyakaa," *Language and Literature in the African American Imagination* (1992), ed. Carol Aisha Blackshire-Belay; Don Ringnalda's "Rejecting 'Sweet Geometry': Komunyakaa's Duende," *Journal of American Culture* 16.3 (1993); Michael Collins's "Staying Human," *Parnassus* 18–19 (1993); Stuart Friebert's "The Truth of the Matter," *Field* 48 (1993); Alvin Aubert's "Yusef Komunyakaa: The Unified Vision—Canonization and Humanity," *African American Review* 27.1 (1993); Kevin Stein's "Vietnam and the 'Voice Within': Public and Private History in Yusef Komunyakaa's *Dien Cai Dau*," *Massachusetts Review* 36.4 (1995–96); Ernest Suarez's "Yusef Komunyakaa," *Five Points* 4.1 (1999); and Angela M. Salas's "'Flashbacks through the Heart': Yusef Komunyakaa and the Poetry of Self-Assertion," *The Furious Flowering of African American Poetry* (1999), ed. Joanne V. Gabbin.

Maxine Kumin

Kumin's volumes of poetry include *Halfway* (1961), *The Privilege* (1965), *The Nightmare Factory* (1970), *Up Country: Poems of New England, New and Selected* (illustrated by Barbara Swan, 1972), *House, Bridge, Fountain, Gate* (1975), *The Retrieval System* (1978), *Our Ground Time Here Will Be Brief: New and Selected Poems* (1982), *Closing the Ring: Selected Poems* (1984), *The Long Approach* (1985), *Nurture* (1989), *Looking for Luck* (1992), *Connecting the Dots* (1996), *Selected Poems, 1960–1990* (1997), and *The Long Marriage* (2001). She also wrote novels, including *The Designated Heir* (1974), short stories, and children's literature. *To Make a Prairie: Essays on Poets, Poetry, and Country Living* (1979) and *Always Beginning: Essays on a Life in Poetry* (2000) offer a selection of memoirs, essays, and criticism. In her memoir *Inside the Halo and Beyond* (2000), Kumin discusses her recovery from a serious injury. Interviews include Enid Shomer's in *Massachusetts Review* 37.4 (1996–97), Steve Kronen's in *Shenandoah* 48.4 (1998), and Jeffrey S. Cramer's in *New Letters* 66.3 (2000). A conversation between Kumin, Elaine Showalter, Carol Smith, and Anne Sexton appears in *Women's Studies* 4 (1976).

Many critical essays can be found in the collection *Telling the Barn Swallow: Poets on the Poetry of Maxine Kumin* (1997), ed. Emily Grosholz. Other discussions of Kumin's work include Sybil P. Estess's "Past Halfway: *The Retrieval System*, by Maxine Kumin," *Iowa Review* 10.4 (1979); Diane Wood Middlebrook's "Housewife into Poet: The Apprenticeship of Anne Sexton," *New England Quarterly* 56.4 (1983); Jean B. Gearhart's "Courage to Survive: Maxine Kumin," *Pembroke Magazine* 20 (1988); Diana Hume George's "'Keeping Our Working Distance': Maxine Kumin's Poetry of Loss and Survival," *Aging and Gender in Literature* (1993), ed. Anne M. Wyatt-Brown and Janice Rossen; and Ben Howard's "Review of Selected Poems, 1960–1990," *Poetry* 172.3 (1998).

Philip Larkin

Larkin's *Collected Poems*, ed. Anthony Thwaite, was published in 1988. Thwaite also edited *Selected Letters of Philip Larkin, 1940–1985* (1992) and *Further Requirements: Interviews, Broadcasts, Statements, and Book Reviews* (2001). Other works include Larkin's novels *Jill* (1946) and *A Girl in Winter* (1947); a collection of music reviews, *All What Jazz: A Record Diary, 1961–1971* (1985); and *The Oxford Book of Twentieth-Century English Verse* (1973), which Larkin edited. Previously unpublished material has recently been published in two posthumous collections: fiction in *"Trouble at Willow Gables" and Other Fictions* (2002), ed. James Booth, and jazz writings in *Larkin's Jazz: Essays and Reviews, 1940–84* (2001), ed. Richard Palmer and John White. *Required Writing: Miscellaneous Pieces, 1955–1982* (1983) contains much of Larkin's important prose. The standard biography is Andrew Motion's *Philip Larkin: A Writer's Life* (1993). An additional interview appears in *Viewpoints: Poets in Conversation with John Haffenden* (1981).

Book-length studies include David Timms's *Philip Larkin* (1973), Bruce K. Martin's *Philip Larkin* (1978), Motion's *Philip Larkin* (1982), Terrence Whalen's *Philip Larkin and English Poetry* (1986), Salem K. Hassan's *Philip Larkin and His Contemporaries: An Air of Authenticity* (1988), Janice Rossen's *Philip Larkin: His Life's Work* (1989), Stephen Regan's *Philip Larkin* (1992), James Booth's *Philip Larkin: Writer* (1992), Andrew Swarbrick's *Out of Reach: The Poetry of Philip Larkin* (1995), and A. T. Tolley's *Larkin at Work: A Study of Larkin's Mode of Composition as Seen in His Workbooks* (1997). Collections of essays include *Larkin at Sixty* (1982), ed. Thwaite; *Critical Essays on Philip Larkin: The Poems* (1989), ed. Linda Cookson and Bryan Loughrey; *Philip Larkin: The Man and His Work* (1989), ed. Dale Salwak; *Philip Larkin* (1997), ed. Regan; and *New Larkins for Old: Critical Essays* (2000), ed. James Booth. *Phoenix* 11–12 (1973–74) is a special Larkin issue. B. C. Bloomfield's bibliography was first published in 1979 and expanded in 2002. See also **The Movement.**

Li-Young Lee

Lee's volumes of poetry include *Rose* (1986), *The City in Which I Love You* (1990), and *Book of My Nights* (2001). His autobiography, *The Winged Seed*, was published in 1995. Gerald Stern's foreword to *Rose* provides a useful introduction. A helpful interview is found in Bill Moyers's *The Language of Life* (1995). Other interviews include James Kyung-Jin Lee's in *Words Matter: Conversations with Asian American Writers* (2000), ed. King-Kok Cheung, and Tod Marshall's "To Witness the Invisible: A Talk with Li-Young Lee," *Kenyon Review* 22.1 (2000).

Critical studies include Zhou Xiaojing's "Inheritance and Invention in Li-Young Lee's Poetry," *MELUS* 21.1 (1996); Walter A. Hesford's "The City in Which I Love You: Li-Young Lee's Excellent Song," *Christianity and Literature* 46.1 (1996); Tim Engles's "Lee's 'Persimmons,' " *Explicator* 54.3 (1996); Mary Slowik's "Beyond Lot's Wife: The Immigration Poems of Marilyn Chin, Garrett Hongo, Li-Young Lee, and David Mura," *MELUS* 25.3–4 (2000); Timothy Yu's "Form and Identity in Language Poetry and Asian American Poetry," *Contemporary Literature* 41.1 (2000); and Steven G. Yao's "The Precision of Persimmons: Hybridity, Grafting and the Case of Li-Young Lee," *Lit: Literature Interpretation Theory* 12.1 (2001). See also **Asian American Poetry.**

Denise Levertov

Collections of Levertov's poems include *Collected Earlier Poems, 1940–1960* (1979), *Poems, 1960–1967* (1983), *Selected Poems* (1986), *Poems 1968–1972* (1987), and *Poems 1972–1982* (2001). Two thematic selections are *The Stream and the Sapphire: Selected Poems on Religious Themes* and *The Life around Us: Selected Poems on Nature*, both published in 1997. Uncollected individual volumes include *Oblique Prayers* (1984), *Breathing the Water* (1987), *A Door in the Hive* (1989), *Evening Train* (1992), *Sands of the Well* (1996), and *This Great Unknowing: Last Poems* (1999). Other helpful texts include her *New and Selected Essays* (1992); a collection of autobiographical writings, *Tesserae: Memories and Supposition* (1995); and the interviews in *Conversations with Denise Levertov* (1998), ed. Jewel Spears Brooker. She also published short stories, *In the Night* (1966); translated French and Bengali poetry; and edited *Out of the War Shadow: An Anthology of Current Poetry* (1967). *The Letters of Denise Levertov and William Carlos Williams*, ed. Christopher MacGowan, was published in 1998.

Important critical studies include Linda Wagner-Martin's *Denise Levertov* (1967); Harry Marten's *Understanding Denise Levertov* (1988); Audrey T. Rodgers's *Denise Levertov: The Poetry of Engagement* (1993); and Linda A. Kinnahan's *Poetics of the Feminine: Authority and Literary Tradition in William Carlos Williams, Mina Loy, Denise Levertov, and Kathleen Fraser* (1994). Many useful essays are included in the collections *Critical Essays on Denise Levertov* (1990), ed. Wagner-Martin; *Denise Levertov: Selected Criticism* (1993), ed. Albert Gelpi; and *Denise Levertov: New Perspectives* (2000), ed. Anne C. Little and Susie Paul. *Twentieth Century Literature* 38.3 (1992) and *Renascence* 50.1–2 (1997–98) are special issues dedicated to Levertov. Liana Sakelliou-Schultz's *Denise Levertov: An Annotated Primary and Secondary Bibliography* appeared in 1988. See also **Black Mountain School.**

Philip Levine

Volumes of Levine's poetry include *On the Edge* (1963), *Not This Pig* (1968), *Red Dust* (1971), *They Feed They Lion* (1972), *1933* (1974), *The Names of the Lost* (1976), *7 Years from Somewhere* (1979), *Ashes: Poems New and Old* (1979), *One for the Rose* (1981), *Selected Poems* (1984), *Sweet Will* (1985), *A Walk with Tom Jefferson* (1988), *New Selected Poems* (1991), *What Work Is* (1991), *The Simple Truth* (1994), *Unselected Poems* (1997), and *The Mercy* (1999). His memoir, *The Bread of Time*, was published in 1994, and a collection of interviews, *Don't Ask*, in 1981. He has also translated *Tarumba: The Selected Poems of Jaime Sabines* (with Ernest Trejo, 1979) and *Off the Map: Selected Writings of Gloria Fuertes* (with Ada Long, 1984).

Essays on Levine's work can be found in *Parnassus* (Fall–Winter 1977); *American Poetry Review* (November–December 1979); and *On the Poetry of Philip Levine: Stranger to Nothing* (1991), ed. Christopher Buckley. Other studies include Edward Hirsch's "The Visionary Poetics of Philip Levine and Charles Wright," *The Columbia History of American Poetry* (1993), ed. Jay Parini and Brett C. Millier; Ernest Suarez's "Philip Levine," *Five Points* 3.2 (1999); Gary Pacernick's "Staying Power: A Lifetime in Poetry," *Kenyon Review* 21.2 (1999); and Peter Hitchcock's "They Must Be Represented? Problems in Theories of Working-Class Representation," *PMLA* 115.1 (2000).

Michael Longley

Longley's volumes of poetry include *Ten Poems* (1965), *Room to Rhyme* (with Seamus Heaney and David Hammond, 1968), *Secret Marriages* (1968), *Three Regional Voices* (with Barry Tebb and Iain Crichton Smith, 1968), *No Continuing City: Poems, 1963–1968* (1969), *Lares* (1972), *An Exploded View: Poems 1968–72* (1973), *Fishing in the Sky: Love Poems* (1975), *Man Lying on a Wall* (1976), *The Echo Gate* (1979), *Selected Poems, 1963–1980* (1981), *Patchwork* (drawings by Jim Allen, 1981), *Poems, 1963–1983* (1985), *Gorse Fires* (1991), *The Ghost Orchid* (1995), *The Ship of the Wind* (1997),

Broken Dishes (1998), *Selected Poems* (1998), *Out of the Cold: Drawings & Poems for Christmas* (with Sarah Longley, 1999), and *The Weather in Japan* (2000). He has also published *Tuppenny Stung: Autobiographical Chapters* (1994) and edited *Causeway: The Arts of Ulster* (1971), *Under the Moon, Over the Stars: Young People's Writing from Ulster* (1971), Louis MacNeice's *Selected Poems* (1988), *Poems by W. R. Rodgers* (1993), *Louis MacNeice: Poems* (2001), and *20th Century Irish Poems* (2002). Interviews appear in *Pn Review* 20 (1994), *Southern Review* 31.3 (1995), and *Irish Studies Review* 18 (1997).

Critical discussions of Longley's work include Michael Allen's "Options: The Poetry of Michael Longley," *Eire-Ireland* 10.4 (1975); John Mole's "A Question of Balance," *Times Literary Supplement* (8 February 1980); Harry Marten's " 'Singing the Darkness into the Light': Reflections on Recent Irish Poetry," *New England Review* 3 (1980); D. E. S. Maxwell's "Semantic Scruples: A Rhetoric for Politics in the North," *Literature and the Changing Ireland* (1982), ed. Peter Connelly; Charles O'Neill's "Three Irish Voices," *Spirit* (Fall–Winter 1989); Brian McIlroy's "Poetry Imagery as Political Fetishism," *Canadian Journal of Irish Studies* 16.1 (1990); Peter McDonald's "Michael Longley's Homes," *The Chosen Ground: Essays on the Contemporary Poetry of Northern Ireland* (1992), ed. Neil Corcoran; John Lyon's "Michael Longley's List," *English* 45.183 (1996); and Victor Luftig's "Poetry, Causality, and an Irish Ceasefire," *Peace Review* (June 2001). See also **Irish Poetry.**

Audre Lorde

The Collected Poems of Audre Lorde appeared in 1997. Lorde also published a biographical novel, *Zami: A New Spelling of My Name* (1982), and a meditation on her experience with cancer, *The Cancer Journals* (1980). Two collections of essays and speeches are *Sister Outsider* (1984) and *A Burst of Light* (1988). Interviews appear in *Black Women Writers at Work* (1983), ed. Claudia Tate, and *Callaloo* 23.1 (2000).

Essays on Lorde appear in *Black Women Writers (1950–1980): A Critical Evaluation* (1983), ed. Mari Evans, and *Black Feminist Criticism: Perspectives on Black Women Writers* (1985, 1997), ed. Barbara Christian. Other critical studies include Mary DeShazer's *Inspiring Women: Reimagining the Muse* (1986); Gloria T. Hull's "Living on the Line: Audre Lorde and *Our Dead behind Us*," *Changing Our Own Words* (1989), ed. Cheryl A. Wall; AnaLouise Keating's *Women Reading Women Writing: Self-Invention in Paula Gunn Allen, Gloria Anzaldúa, and Audre Lorde* (1996); Carmen Birkle's *Women's Stories of the Looking Glass: Autobiographical Reflections and Self-Representations in the Poetry of Sylvia Plath, Adrienne Rich, and Audre Lorde* (1996); Alexis De Veaux's "Searching for Audre Lorde," *Callaloo* 23.1 (2000); and Cassie Premo Steele's *We Heal from Memory: Sexton, Lorde, Anzaldúa, and the Poetry of Witness* (2000). See also **Black Arts Movement.**

Robert Lowell

Lowell's volumes of poetry include *Lord Weary's Castle* (1946), *The Mills of the Kavanaughs* (1951), *Life Studies* (1959), *Imitations* (1961), *For the Union Dead* (1964), *Near the Ocean* (1967), *Notebook 1967–68* (1969, 1979), *The Dolphin* (1973), *For Lizzie and Harriet* (1973), *History* (1973), *Selected Poems* (1976, 1977), and *Day by Day* (1977). His *Collected Prose*, ed. Robert Giroux, appeared in 1987. Lowell adapted works for the stage, including Racine's *Phaedra* (1961); Melville and Hawthorne stories in *The Old Glory* (1965); and Aeschylus's *Prometheus Unbound* (1969). An important interview appears in *Robert Lowell: A Collection of Critical Essays* (1968), ed. Thomas Parkinson. Other interviews can be found in *Robert Lowell, Interviews and Memoirs* (1988), ed. Jeffrey Meyers. Ian Hamilton's *Robert Lowell* (1982) and Paul Mariani's *The Lost Puritan* (1994) are helpful biographies.

Important critical works include Hugh B. Staples's *Robert Lowell: The First Twenty Years* (1962), Jerome Mazzaro's *The Poetic Themes of Robert Lowell* (1965), Philip Cooper's *The Autobiographical Myth of Robert Lowell* (1970), Marjorie Perloff's *The Poetic Art of Robert Lowell* (1973), Alan Williamson's *Pity the Monsters: The Political Vision of Robert Lowell* (1974), Stephen Yenser's *Circle to Circle* (1975), Steven Gould Axelrod's *Robert Lowell: Life and Art* (1978), Vereen Bell's *Robert Lowell, Nihilist as Hero* (1983), Jeffrey Meyers's *Manic Power: Robert Lowell and His Circle* (1987), Katharine Wallingford's *Robert Lowell's Language of the Self* (1988), Helen Vendler's *The Given and the Made* (1995), Richard Tillinghast's *Robert Lowell's Life and Work: Damaged Grandeur* (1995), Henry Hart's *Robert Lowell and the Sublime* (1995), Thomas Travisano's *Midcentury Quartet* (1999), and William Doreski's *Robert Lowell's Shifting Colors* (1999). Other collections of essays on Lowell include *Robert Lowell: Essays on the Poetry* (1986), ed. Axelrod and Helen Deese, and *The Critical Response to Robert Lowell* (1999), ed. Axelrod. Axelrod and Deese also compiled *Robert Lowell: A Reference Guide* (1982). See also **Confessional Poetry.**

Derek Mahon

Mahon's *Collected Poems* was published in 1999. *Journalism: Selected Prose 1970–1995* was published in 1996. His translations include Nerval's *The Chimeras* (1982) and Jean Racine's *Phaedra* (1996). Among his plays are adaptations of Molière's *High Time* (1985) and *The*

School for Wives (1986) and an adaptation of Euripides' *The Bacchae* (1991). He edited the collections *Modern Irish Poetry* (1972) and *The Penguin Book of Contemporary Irish Poetry* (with Peter Fallon, 1990). Interviews appear in *Irish Literary Supplement* 10 (1991) and *Poetry Review* 81.2 (1991).

Critical discussions of Mahon's work include Brian Donnelly's "The Poetry of Derek Mahon," *English Studies* 60 (1979); Dillon Johnston's "Unaccommodated Mahon: An Ulster Poet," *Hollins Critic* 17.5 (1980); Andrew Waterman's "Somewhere, out There, Beyond: The Poetry of Seamus Heaney and Derek Mahon," *Pn Review* 8.1 (1981); Eamon Grennan's " 'To the Point of Speech': The Poetry of Derek Mahon," *Contemporary Irish Writing* (1983), ed. James D. Brophy and Raymond J. Porter; Conor Johnston's "Poetry and Politics: Responses to the Northern Ireland Crisis in the Poetry of John Montague, Derek Mahon, and Seamus Heaney," *Poesis* 5.4 (1984); David E. William's "The Poetry of Derek Mahon," *Journal of Irish Literature* 13.3 (1984); John M. Byrne's *The Significance of Landscape and History in the Poetry of Seamus Heaney, Derek Mahon, and John Montague* (1984); John Constable's "Derek Mahon's Development," *Agenda* 22.3–4 (1984–85); Robert Taylor's "Derek Mahon: The Lute and the Stars," *Massachusetts Review* 28.3 (1987); Bill Tinley's "International Perspectives in the Poetry of Derek Mahon," *Irish University Review* 21.1 (1991); Hugh Houghton's " 'Even Now There Are Places Where a Thought Might Grow': Place and Displacement in the Poetry of Derek Mahon," *The Chosen Ground: Essays on the Contemporary Poetry of Northern Ireland* (1992), ed. Neil Corcoran; David G. Williams's " 'A Decadent Who Lived to Tell the Story': Derek Mahon's *The Yellow Book*," *Journal of Modern Literature* 23.1 (1999); and Richard Tillinghast's "Derek Mahon: Exile and Stranger," *New Criterion* 18.1 (1999). *Irish University Review* 24.1 (1994) is a special issue dedicated to Mahon and includes Jody Allen-Randolph's bibliography. See also **Irish Poetry.**

Dionisio D. Martínez

Martínez's books of poetry include *Dancing at the Chelsea* (1992), *History as a Second Language* (1993), *Bad Alchemy* (1995), and *Climbing Back* (2001).

Discussions of his poetry include Carolyne Wright's "On Agosin and Martínez," *Iowa Review* 25.1 (1995) and Bill Christophersen's review of *Climbing Back* in *Poetry* 179.4 (2002). A number of useful journalistic profiles have appeared in *The St. Petersburg Times* and *The Tampa Tribune*. See also **Latino Poetry.**

Medbh McGuckian

McGuckian's volumes of poetry include *Portrait of Joanna* (1980), *Single Ladies* (1980), *The Flower Master* (1982), *Venus and the Rain* (1984), *On Ballycastle Beach* (1988), *Two Women, Two Shores: Poems by Medbh McGuckian and Nuala Archer* (1989), *Marconi's Cottage* (1991), *"The Flower Master" and Other Poems* (1993), *Captain Lavender* (1995), *Selected Poems 1978–1994* (1997), *Shelmalier* (1998), and *Drawing Ballerinas* (2001). With Eiléan Ní Chuilleanáin she translated the poems in Nuala Ní Dhomhnaill's *The Water Horse* (1999). She has also written a study of the automobile in Seamus Heaney's poetry, *Horsepower Pass By!* (1999). Interviews include Rebecca Wilson's in *Cencrastus* (Spring 1988), Kathleen McCracken's in *Irish Literary Supplement* 9.2 (1990), Laura O'Connor's in *Southern Review* 28.1 (1995), and Sawnie Morris's in *Kenyon Review* 23.3–4 (2001).

Clair Wills's *Improprieties: Politics and Sexuality in Northern Irish Poetry* (1993) and Patricia Boyle Haberstroh's *Women Creating Women: Contemporary Irish Women Poets* (1996) offer extensive examinations of McGuckian's work. Other critical discussions include Ann Beer's "Medbh McGuckian's Poetry: Maternal Thinking and a Politics of Peace," *Canadian Journal of Irish Studies* 18.1 (1992); Thomas Docherty's "Initiations, Tempers, Seductions: Postmodern McGuckian," *The Chosen Ground: Essays on the Contemporary Poetry of Northern Ireland* (1992), ed. Neil Corcoran; Susan Porter's "The 'Imaginative Space' of Medbh McGuckian," *International Women's Writing: New Landscapes of Identity* (1995), ed. Anne E. Brown and Marjanne E. Gooze; Mary O'Connor's " 'Rising Out': Medbh McGuckian's Destabilizing Poetics," *Eire-Ireland* 30.4 (1996); Shane Murphy's "Obliquity in the Poetry of Paul Muldoon and Medbh McGuckian," *Eire-Ireland* 31.3–4 (1996) and " 'You Took Away My Biography': The Poetry of Medbh McGuckian," *Irish University Review* 28.1 (1998); *Gender and Sexuality in Modern Ireland* (1997), ed. Anthony Bradley and Maryann Gialanella; and *Border Crossings: Irish Women Writers and National Identities* (2000), ed. Kathryn Kirkpatrick. See also **Irish Poetry.**

William Meredith

Meredith's volumes of poetry include *Love Letter from an Impossible Land* (1944), *Ships and Other Figures* (1948), *"The Open Sea" and Other Poems* (1957), *Winter Verse* (1964), *"The Wreck of the Thresher" and Other Poems* (1964), *Year End Accounts* (1965), *Two Pages from a Colorado Journal* (1967), *Earth Walk: New and Selected Poems* (1970), *Hazard, the Painter* (1975), *The Cheer* (1980), *Partial Accounts: New and Selected Poems* (1987), and *Effort at Speech: New and Selected Poems* (1997). Two collections of his criticism, lectures, and prose are the two-lecture volume, *Reasons for Poetry; and, The Reason for Criticism* (1982) and *Poems*

Are Hard to Read (1991). He published numerous translations, including Guillaume Apollinaire's *Alcools: Poems, 1898–1913* (1964), and wrote the libretto for *The Bottle Imp* (1958), an opera composed by Peter Whiton. Interviews appear in *Southwest Review* 57 (1972) and *Plum Review* 4 (1992).

Critical discussions of Meredith can be found in James Dickey's "Orientations," *American Scholar* 34 (1965); Raymond Roselip's "From Woodcarver to Wordcarver," *Poetry* 107 (1966); Richard Howard's *Alone with America* (1969, 1980); Jeremy Robson's *Corgi Modern Poets in Focus* 2 (1971); Henry Taylor's "In Charge of Morale in a Morbid Time: The Poetry of William Meredith," *Hollins Critic* 16.1 (1979); Neva Herrington's "The Language of the Tribe: William Meredith's Poetry," *Southwest Review* 67.1 (1982); Guy Rotella's *Three Contemporary Poets of New England* (1983); and Michael Collier's foreword to *Effort at Speech* (1997) and "An Exact Ratio," *Passing the Word: Writers on Their Mentors* (2001), ed. Jeffrey Skinner and Lee Martin.

James Merrill

The Collected Poems of James Merrill, ed. J. D. McClatchy and Stephen Yenser, was published in 2001. His prose is collected in *Recitative* (1986), and his autobiography is *A Different Person* (1993). Merrill also wrote two novels, *The Seraglio* (1957) and *The (Diblos) Notebook* (1965). Biographical information can be found in Alison Lurie's *Familiar Spirits: A Memoir of James Merrill and David Jackson* (2001). Ross Labrie's *James Merrill at Home* (1982) is a helpful book-length interview. Stephen Yenser's *The Consuming Myth: The Work of James Merrill* (1987) is an important book-length study. Other useful studies include Labrie's *James Merrill* (1982), Judith Moffett's *James Merrill, an Introduction to the Poetry* (1984), Don Adams's *James Merrill's Poetic Quest* (1997), and Timothy Materer's *James Merrill's Apocalypse* (2000). Robert Polito's *A Reader's Guide to James Merrill's* The Changing Light at Sandover (1994) offers assistance for the study of Merrill's trilogy. Other helpful discussions of his work can be found in David Kalstone's *Five Temperaments* (1977), Helen Vendler's *Part of Nature, Part of Us* (1980), Robert von Hallberg's *American Poetry and Culture, 1945–1980* (1985), Vernon Shetley's *After the Death of Poetry* (1993), Mutlu Konuk Blasing's *Politics and Form in Postmodern Poetry* (1995), and Rachel Hadas's *Merrill, Cavafy, Poems, and Dreams* (2000). Collections of critical essays include *James Merrill: Essays in Criticism* (1983), ed. David Lehman and Charles Berger; *James Merrill* (1985), ed. Harold Bloom; and *Critical Essays on James Merrill* (1996), ed. Guy L. Rotella.

W. S. Merwin

Merwin's early volumes have been collected as *The First Four Books of Poems* (1975), *The Second Four Books of Poems* (1993), and *Flower and Hand: Poems, 1977–1983* (1997). Uncollected later volumes include *The Rain in the Trees* (1988), *Selected Poems* (1988), *The Vixen* (1996), *The Folding Cliffs: A Narrative* (1998), *The River Sound* (1999), and *The Pupil* (2001). Among his many translations are *East Window: The Asian Translations* (1998), Dante's *Purgatorio* (2000), and *Gawain and the Green Knight* (2002). He has also published television scripts and plays, including *Darkling Child* (1956) and *Favor Island* (1957). *The Miner's Pale Children* (1970) and *Houses and Travellers* (1977) are collections of short fiction. Two collections of essays and memoirs are *Unframed Original* (1982) and *Regions of Memory* (1987), ed. Ed Folsom and Cary Nelson.

Collections of essays on Merwin include *W. S. Merwin: Essays on the Poetry* (1987), ed. Cary Nelson and Ed Folsom, and *Many Mountains Moving* (2001), ed. Mark Irwin. Other work on Merwin includes Cheri Davis's *W. S. Merwin* (1981), Mark Christhilf's *W. S. Merwin: The Myth Maker* (1986), Thomas B. Byers's *What I Cannot Say: Self, Word, and World in Whitman, Stevens, and Merwin* (1989), Edward J. Brunner's *Poetry as Labor and Privilege* (1991), Edward Haworth Hoeppner's *Echoes and Moving Fields: Structure and Subjectivity in the Poetry of W. S. Merwin and John Ashbery* (1994), H. L. Hix's *Understanding W. S. Merwin* (1997), Jane Frazier's *From Origin to Ecology: Nature and the Poetry of W. S. Merwin* (1999), and Leonard M. Scigaj's *Sustainable Poetry: Four American Ecopoets* (1999). See also **Deep Image Poetry.**

Thylias Moss

Moss's volumes of poetry include *Hosiery Seams on a Bowlegged Woman* (1983), *Pyramid of Bone* (1989), *At Redbones* (1990), *Rainbow Remnants in Rock Bottom Ghetto Sky* (1991), *Small Congregations: New and Selected Poems* (1993), and *Last Chance for the Tarzan Holler* (1998). Moss's memoir, *Tale of a Sky-Blue Dress*, appeared in 1998. She has also written children's literature and two plays, *Talking to Myself* (1984) and *The Dolls in the Basement* (1984). Interviews appear in *Onthebus* 4–5 (1992) and *Fourth Genre* 1.2 (1999).

Critical discussions of Moss include Rafael Campo's "Sturdy Boxcars and Exploding Pickle Jars," *Parnassus* 21.1–2 (1995), and Eric Murphy Selinger's "This Personal Maze Is Not the Prize," *Parnassus* 24.2 (2000).

Paul Muldoon

Muldoon's collected *Poems, 1968–1998* appeared in 2001. He has also published translations, including Nuala Ní Dhomhnaill's *The Astrakhan Cloak* (1993) and Aristophanes' *The Birds* (with Richard Martin, 1999), and edited collections of poetry, including *The Faber Book of Contemporary Irish Poetry* (1986). His lectures on Irish literature, *To Ireland, I*, were published in 2000. He has also written libretti, including the one for *Bandanna* (1999), an opera composed by Daron Hagen. An important early interview appeared in *Viewpoints: Poets in Conversation with John Haffenden* (1981); more recent interviews appear in *Contemporary Literature* 35.1 (1994), *Bomb* 65 (1998), and *Michigan Quarterly Review* 37.1 (1998).

Two book-length studies are Tim Kendall's *Paul Muldoon* (1996) and Clair Wills's *Reading Paul Muldoon* (1998). Other critical works include Wills's "The Lie of the Land: Language, Imperialism, and Trade in Paul Muldoon's 'Meeting the British,' " *The Chosen Ground: Essays on the Contemporary Poetry of Northern Ireland* (1992), ed. Neil Corcoran; Wills's *Improprieties: Politics and Sexuality in Northern Irish Poetry* (1993); David Wheatley's "An Irish Poet in America," *Raritan* 18.4 (1999); Sven Birkerts's "About Paul Muldoon," *Ploughshares* 26.1 (2000); Andrew Osborn's "Skirmishes on the Border: The Evolution and Function of Paul Muldoon's Fuzzy Rhyme," *Contemporary Literature* 41.2 (2000); and Rachael Buxton's " 'Structure and Serendipity': The Influence of Robert Frost on Paul Muldoon," *Critical Ireland: New Essays in Literature and Culture* (2001), ed. Alan A. Gillis and Aaron Kelly. See also **Irish Poetry.**

Les Murray

Murray's *Collected Poems* were published in 1994. Subsequent volumes of poetry include *Subhuman Redneck Poems* (1996), *Collected Poems* (1998), *New Selected Poems* (1998), *Conscious and Verbal* (1999), *Fredy Neptune: A Novel in Verse* (1999), *Learning Human: Selected Poems* (2000), and *Poems the Size of Photographs* (2002). Prose collections include *The Paperbark Tree* (1992) and *A Working Forest* (1997). He edited *The New Oxford Book of Australian Verse* (1986, 1991) and the *Anthology of Australian Religious Poetry* (1986, 1991). Peter F. Alexander's biography, *Les Murray: A Life in Progress*, appeared in 2000.

Collections of essays on Murray include *Counterbalancing Light: Essays on Les Murray* (1997), ed. Carmel Gaffney; *Poetry of Les Murray: Critical Essays* (2001), ed. Laurie Hergenhan and Bruce Clunies Ross; and *Les Murray and Australian Poetry*, ed. Angela Smith (2002). Other critical studies include Lawrence Bourke's *A Vivid Steady State: Les Murray and Australian Poetry* (1992) and Steven Matthews's *Les Murray* (2001). *Australian Literary Studies* 20.2 (2001) is a special issue dedicated to Murray and contains Carol Hetherington's bibliographical "Les Murray: A Selective Checklist." See also **Australian Poetry.**

Howard Nemerov

Nemerov's *The Collected Poems* appeared in 1977. Subsequent volumes include *By Al Lebowitz's Pool* (1979), *Sentences* (1980), *Inside the Onion* (1984), *War Stories: Poems about Long Ago and Now* (1987), *Trying Conclusions: New and Selected Poems 1961–1991* (1991), and *A Howard Nemerov Reader* (1991), which includes prose. Essays are collected in *Reflections on Poetry and Poetics* (1972), *Figures of Thought* (1978), and *New and Selected Essays* (1985). In addition, Nemerov published novels, including *The Homecoming Game* (1957); short stories, including *Stories, Fables, and Other Diversions* (1971); and plays. An interview appears in *Massachusetts Review* 22.1.

Critical work on Nemerov's poetry include Peter Meinke's *Howard Nemerov* (1968), Julia Bartholomay's *The Shield of Perseus* (1972), William Mills's *The Stillness in Moving Things* (1975), Ross Labrie's *Howard Nemerov* (1980), and Rodney Edgecombe's *A Reader's Guide to the Poetry of Howard Nemerov* (1999). Bibliographic information can be found in *The Critical Reception of Howard Nemerov: A Selection of Howard Nemerov and a Bibliography* (1971) and Diane E. Wyllie's *Elizabeth Bishop and Howard Nemerov: A Reference Guide* (1983).

Grace Nichols

Nichols's volumes of poetry include *I Is a Long-Memoried Woman* (1983), *The Fat Black Woman's Poems* (1984), *"Lazy Thoughts of a Lazy Woman" and Other Poems* (1989), and *Sunris* (1996). She has also written numerous books for children and edited anthologies, including *Black Poetry* (1988) and *Can I Buy a Slice of Sky?* (1991). Her novel, *Whole of a Morning Sky*, was published in 1986. An interview appears in *Wasafiri* 8 (1988). Prose statements by Nichols include "The Battle with Language," *Caribbean Women Writers: Essays from the First International Conference* (1990), ed. Selwyn Cudjoe, and "Grace Nichols," *Let It Be Told: Black Women Writers in Britain* (1988), ed. Lauretta Ngcobo.

Critical studies of Nichols's work include Peter Fraser's "I Is a Long-Memoried Woman," *Let It Be Told: Black Women Writers in Britain* (1988); Patrick Williams's "Difficult Subjects: Black British Women's Poetry," in *Literary Theory and Poetry: Extending the Canon* (1989), ed. David Murray; Gabriele Griffin's "Writing the Body: Reading Joan Riley, Grace Nichols and Ntozake Shange" and Bruce Woodcock's "Long Memoried Women: Caribbean Women Poets," both in *Black Women's Writing* (1993), ed. Gina Wisker; Elfi Bettinger's "Grace Nichols' 'Sugar

Cane': A Post-Colonial and Feminist Perspective," *Anglistik und Englischunterrischt* 53 (1994); Alison Easton's "The Body as History and 'Writing the Body': The Example of Grace Nichols," *Journal of Gender Studies* 3.1 (1994); Gudrun Webhofer's *Identity in the Poetry of Grace Nichols and Lorna Goodison* (1996); Mara Scanlon's "The Divine Body in Grace Nichols's The Fat Black Women's Poems," *World Literature Today* 72.1 (1998); Aleid Fokkema's "On the (False) Idea of Exile: Derek Walcott and Grace Nichols," *(Un)Writing Empire* (1999), ed. Theo D'haen. See also **Caribbean Poetry.**

Frank O'Hara

The Collected Poems of Frank O'Hara, ed. Donald Allen, appeared in 1971. Allen also edited two subsequent volumes, *Early Writings* (1977) and *Poems Retrieved* (1977). O'Hara's art criticism can be found in *Jackson Pollock* (1959), *Art Chronicles, 1954–1966* (1975), and *What's with Modern Art?* (1999), and other essays in *Standing Still and Walking in New York* (1975). He also wrote numerous plays and collaborated with visual artists such as Joe Brainard and Larry Rivers. Brad Gooch's biography, *City Poet: The Life and Times of Frank O'Hara*, was published in 1993. Memoirs, anecdotes, and essays about O'Hara have been collected as *Homage to Frank O'Hara* (1978), ed. Bill Berkson and Joe LeSueur. *In Memory of My Feelings* (1967), ed. Berkson, is a memorial volume of O'Hara's poems accompanied by paintings.

A new edition of Marjorie Perloff's important study, *Frank O'Hara: A Poet among Painters* (1977), was published with a new introduction in 1998. Also helpful are the essays by various critics collected in *Frank O'Hara: To Be True to a City* (1990), ed. Jim Elledge. Other helpful books on O'Hara include Alan Feldman's *Frank O'Hara* (1979), Russell Ferguson's *In Memory of My Feelings: Frank O'Hara and American Art* (1999), and Hazel Smith's *Hyperscapes in the Poetry of Frank O'Hara: Difference, Homosexuality, Topography* (2000). Important chapters and essays include Bruce Boone's "Gay Language as Political Praxis: The Poetry of Frank O'Hara," *Social Text* 1.1 (1982); James E. B. Breslin's chapter in *From Modern to Contemporary* (1984); Andrew Ross's "The Death of Lady Day," *Poetics Journal* 8 (June 1989); John Lowney's "The 'Post-Anti-Esthetic' Poetics of Frank O'Hara," *Contemporary Literature* 32.2 (1991); Geoff Ward's "Frank O'Hara: Accident and Design," *Statutes of Liberty* (1993, 2001); Timothy Gray's "Semiotic Shepherds: Gary Snyder, Frank O'Hara, and the Embodiment of an Urban Pastoral," *Contemporary Literature* 39.4 (1998); Mark Goble's " 'Our Country's Black and White Past': Film and the Figures of History in Frank O'Hara," *American Literature* 71.1 (1999); David L. Sweet's "Parodic Nostalgia for Aesthetic Machismo: Frank O'Hara and Jackson Pollock," *Journal of Modern Literature* 23.3–4 (2000); Michael Magee's "Tribes of New York: Frank O'Hara, Amiri Baraka, and the Poetics of the Five Spot," *Contemporary Literature* 42.4 (2001); and Terrell Scott Herring's "Frank O'Hara's Open Closet," *PMLA* 117.3 (2002). David Lehman's *The Last Avant-Garde* (1998) combines critical analysis with biographical information on O'Hara and his companions in the New York school. Alexander Smith's comprehensive bibliography appeared in 1979. See also **New York School.**

Christopher Okigbo

Okigbo's *Collected Poems* was published in 1986. Other writings include "Dance of the Painted Maidens," *Verse & Voice: A Festival of Poetry* (1965), ed. Douglas Cleverdon; "In Lament of Masks," *W. B. Yeats, 1865–1965: Centenary Essays on the Art of W. B. Yeats* (1965), ed. D. E. S. Maxwell and Suheil B. Bushrui; and "Lament of the Deer," in Chinua Achebe and John Iroaganachi's *How the Leopard Got His Claws* (1972). Achebe and Dubem Okafor edited *Don't Let Him Die: An Anthology of Memorial Poems for Christopher Okigbo (1932–1967)* (1978). Interviews appear in *Journal of Commonwealth Literature* 9 (1970) and *African Writers Talking* (1972), ed. Dennis Duerden and Cosmo Pieterse.

Collections of essays on his work include *Critical Perspectives on Christopher Okigbo* (1984), ed. Donatus Ibe Nwoga, and *Critical Essays on Christopher Okigbo* (2000), ed. Uzoma Esonwanne. Other critical studies include Gerald Moore's *The Chosen Tongue* (1969), Ali A. Mazrui's *The Trial of Christopher Okigbo* (1971), Sunday O. Anozie's *Christopher Okigbo: Creative Rhetoric* (1972), Nyong J. Udoeyop's *Three Nigerian Poets* (1973), Romanus N. Egudu's *Four Modern West African Poets* (1977) and *Modern African Poetry and the African Predicament* (1978), K. L. Goodwin's *Understanding African Poetry: A Study of Ten Poets* (1982), Robert Fraser's *West African Poetry* (1986), James Wieland's *The Ensphering Mind* (1988), and Dubem Okafor's *The Dance of Death: Nigerian History and Christopher Okigbo's Poetry* (1998). Joseph C. Anafulu's bio-bibliography and Bernth Lindfors's addenda are included in *Critical Perspectives on Christopher Okigbo* (1984), ed. Nwoga. See also **African Poetry.**

Okot p'Bitek

Okot's books of poetry include *Song of Lawino* (1966), *Song of Ocol* (1967), *Song of Malaya* (1971), and *Song of a Prisoner* (1971). He also published important books of and about anthropology and African culture, including *African Religions in Western Scholarship* (1970) and *Africa's Cultural Revolution* (1973), and translations of folk literature, including *The Horn of My Love* (1974), *Hare and Hornbill* (1978), and *Acholi Proverbs* (1985). Interviews appear in *Kunapipi* 1.1 (1979); *World Literature Written in English* 16 (1977); and *Conversations with African Writers* (1981), ed. Lee Nichols. A biographical sketch by Lubwa p'Chong appears in Okot's *Artist, the Ruler* (1986).

Book-length studies include G. A. Heron's *The Poetry of Okot p'Bitek* (1976) and Monica Nalyaka Wanambisi's *Thought and Technique in the Poetry of Okot p'Bitek* (1984). Other critical studies include Michael R. Ward's "Okot p'Bitek and the Rise of East African Writing," *A Celebration of Black and African Writing* (1975), ed. Bruce King and Kolawole Ogungbesan; Gerald Moore's "The Horn of the Grasslands," *Twelve African Writers* (1980); Bernth Lindfors's "The Songs of Okot p'Bitek," *The Writing of East and Central Africa* (1984), ed. G. D. Killam; G. A. Heron's introduction to Okot's *"Song of Lawino" and "Song of Ocol"* (1984); Ogo A. Ofuani's "Digression as Discourse Strategy in Okot p'Bitek's Dramatic Monologue Texts," *Research in African Literatures* 19.3 (1988); Charles Okumu's "The Form of Okot p'Bitek's Poetry: Literary Borrowing from Acoli Oral Traditions," *Research in African Literatures* 23.3 (1992); Nkem Okoh's "Writing African Oral Literature: A Reading of Okot p'Bitek's *Song of Lawino*," *Bridges* 5.2 (1993); and Jahan Ramazani's *The Hybrid Muse* (2001). See also **African Poetry.**

Sharon Olds

Olds's volumes of poetry include *Satan Says* (1980), *The Dead and the Living* (1984), *The Gold Cell* (1987), *The Matter of This World: New and Selected Poems* (1987), *The Sign of Saturn* (1991), *The Father* (1992), *The Wellspring* (1996), *Blood, Tin, Straw* (1999), and *The Unswept Room* (2002). Interviews include Laurel Blossom's in *Poets & Writers Magazine* 21.5 (1993) and Esta Spalding's in *Brick* 67 (2001).

Critical essays on Olds include Roland Flint's "A Way of Knowing," *Poet Lore* 83.1 (1988); Suzanne Matson's "Talking to Our Father: The Political and Mythical Appropriation of Adrienne Rich and Sharon Olds," *The American Poetry Review* 18.6 (1989); Jonathan Holden's "American Poetry: 1970–1990," *A Profile of Twentieth-Century American Poetry* (1991), ed. Jack Myers and David Wojahn; Terri Brown-Davidson's "The Belabored Scene, The Subtlest Detail: How Craft Affects Heat in the Poetry of Sharon Olds and Sandra McPherson," *Hollins Critic* 29.1 (1992); Brian Dillon's " 'Never Having Had You, I Cannot Let You Go': Sharon Olds's Poems of a Father-Daughter Relationship," *The Literary Review: An International Journal of Contemporary Writing* 37.1 (1993); Calvin Bedient's "Sentencing Eros," *Salmagundi* 97 (1993); Alicia Ostriker's "I Am (Not) This: Erotic Discourse in Bishop, Olds, and Stevens," *Wallace Stevens Journal* 19.2 (1995); Laura E. Tanner's "Death-Watch: Terminal Illness and the Gaze in Sharon Olds's *The Father*," *Mosaic* 29.1 (1996); James Sutherland-Smith's "Death and the Unmaidenly: An Exploration of Sharon Olds' *The Wellspring* with Reference to George Bataille," *Pn Review* 24.4 (1998); and Kenneth Lincoln's *Sing with the Heart of a Bear: Fusions of Native and American Poetry 1890–1999* (2000).

Mary Oliver

Oliver's volumes of poetry include *"No Voyage" and Other Poems* (1963, 1965), *"The River Styx, Ohio," and Other Poems* (1972), *Twelve Moons* (1979), *American Primitive* (1983), *Dream Work* (1986), *House of Light* (1990), *New and Selected Poems* (1992), *White Pine* (1994), *West Wind* (1997), *The Leaf and the Cloud* (2000), and *What Do We Know* (2002). Her essays have been collected in *Blue Pastures* (1995) and *Winter Hours* (1999), which also contains poetry. She has also published two poetry handbooks, *A Poetry Handbook* (1994) and *Rules for the Dance: A Handbook for Writing and Reading Metrical Verse* (1998). An interview appears in *Bloomsbury Review* 10.3 (1990).

Critical essays on Oliver's work include Janet McNew's "Mary Oliver and the Tradition of Romantic Nature Poetry," *Contemporary Literature* 30.1 (1989); Robin Riley Fast's "The Native American Presence in Mary Oliver's Poetry," *Kentucky Review* 12.1–2 (1993) and "Moore, Bishop, and Oliver: Thinking Back, Re-Seeing the Sea," *Twentieth Century Literature* 39.3 (1993); Vicki Graham's " 'Into the Body of Another': Mary Oliver and the Poetics of Becoming Other," *Papers on Language and Literature* 30.4 (1994); and Sue Russell's "Mary Oliver: The Poet and the Persona," *The Harvard Gay & Lesbian Review* 4.4 (1997).

Charles Olson

The Collected Poems of Charles Olson, ed. George F. Butterick, was published in 1987. This collection excludes *The Maximus Poems*, a complete edition of which, also edited by Butterick, appeared in 1983. *The Selected Writings of Charles Olson* (1966), ed. Robert Creeley, offers a good overview of the poet's thought. *The Collected Prose* (1997) was edited by Donald Allen, Benjamin Friedlander, and Creeley. Olson published a study of Melville, *Call Me Ishmael* (1947); and *Mathologos* (1976–79), ed. Butterick, is a collection of lectures and interviews. A *Selected Letters*, ed. Ralph Maud, appeared in 2000, in addition to which the seven volumes of Butterick's *Charles Olson and Robert Creeley: The Complete Correspondence* (1980–86) are illuminating. Biographical information can be found in Tom Clark's *Charles Olson: The Allegory of a Poet's Life* (1991), Maud's *Charles Olson's Reading* (1996), and Olson's autobiographical *The Post Office* (1975).

Among the useful critical discussions of Olson's work are Ed Dorn's *What I See in the Maximus Poems* (1960), Robert von Hallberg's *Charles Olson: The Scholar's Art* (1978), Butterick's *A Guide to the Maximus Poems of Charles Olson* (1978), Sherman Paul's *Olson's Push* (1978), Paul Christensen's *Charles Olson: Call Him Ishmael* (1979), Thomas F. Merrill's *The Poetry of Charles Olson: A Primer* (1982), Andrew Ross's *The Failure of Modernism* (1986), Eniko Bollobás's *Charles Olson* (1992), Stephen Fredman's *The Grounding of American Poetry: Charles Olson and the Emersonian Tradition* (1993), and Libbie Rifkin's *Career Moves: Olson, Creeley, Zukofsky, Berrigan, and the American Avant-Garde* (2000). A bibliography compiled by Butterick and Albert Glover appeared in 1967. See also **Black Mountain School.**

Michael Ondaatje

Ondaatje's volumes of poetry include *The Dainty Monsters* (1967), *The Man with Seven Toes* (1969), *The Collected Works of Billy the Kid: Left Handed Poems* (1970), *Rat Jelly* (1973), *Elimination Dance* (1978), *There's a Trick with a Knife I'm Learning to Do: Poems, 1963–1978* (1979), *Secular Love* (1985), *All along the Mazinaw: Two Poems* (1986), *The Cinnamon Peeler: Selected Poems* (1989), and *Handwriting* (1998). His novels include *Coming through Slaughter* (1976), *In the Skin of a Lion* (1987), *The English Patient* (1992), and *Anil's Ghost* (2000). His memoir, *Running in the Family*, appeared in 1982. He has also edited several anthologies, including the collection of animal verse *The Broken Ark* (1971) and *The Faber Book of Contemporary Canadian Short Stories* (1990). Interviews appear in *Manna* 1 (March 1972); *Rune* 2 (Spring 1975); *Twelve Voices: Interviews with Canadian Poets* (1980), ed. Jon Pearce; *Revista Espanola de Estudios Canadienses* 3.1 (1996); and *Wasafiri* 32 (2000).

A collection of essays on his work is *Spider Blues* (1985), ed. Sam Solecki. *Canadian Review of Comparative Literature* 22.1 (1995) is a special issue dedicated to Ondaatje. Other critical studies include Solecki's "Nets and Chaos," *Studies in Canadian Literature* 2 (Winter 1977), and "Michael Ondaatje," *Descant* 42 (Autumn 1983); Lynette Hunter's "Form and Energy in the Poetry of Michael Ondaatje," *Journal of Canadian Poetry* 1.1 (1978); Stephen Scobie's "His Legend a Jungle Sleep," *Canadian Literature* 76 (Spring 1978); Leslie Mundwiler's *Michael Ondaatje: Word, Image, Imagination* (1984); Arun P. Mukherjee's "The Poetry of Michael Ondaatje and Cyril Dabydeen: Two Responses to Otherness," *Journal of Commonwealth Literature* 20.1 (1985); Steven Heighton's "Approaching 'That Perfect Edge': Kinetic Techniques in the Poetry and Fiction of Michael Ondaatje," *Studies in Canadian Literature* 13.2 (1988); Lorraine Mary York's *The Other Side of Dailiness: Photography in the Works of Alice Munro, Timothy Findley, Michael Ondaatje, and Margaret Laurence* (1988); Ajay Heble's "Michael Ondaatje and the Problem of History," *Clio* 19.2 (1990); Douglas Barbour's *Michael Ondaatje* (1993); Ed Jewinski's *Michael Ondaatje: Express Yourself Beautifully* (1994); John Cooke's *The Influence of Painting on Five Canadian Writers* (1996); and Geert Lernout's "Multicultural Canada: The Case of Michael Ondaatje," *Union in Partition: Essays in Honour of Jeanne Delbaere* (1997), ed. Gilbert Debusscher, Jeanne Delbaere, and Marc Maufort. Judith Brady's annotated bibliography appears in *The Annotated Bibliography of Canada's Major Authors* (1985), ed. Robert Lecker and Jack David. See also **Canadian Poetry.**

P. K. Page

Page's *The Hidden Room: Collected Poems* was published in 1997. Other works include the story collections *"The Sun and the Moon" and Other Fictions* (1973), *Unless the Eye Catch Fire* (1994), and *A Kind of Fiction* (2001); the libretto for the opera *The Travelling Musicians* (1994), composed by Ruth Watson Henderson; children's literature; and *Brazilian Journal* (1987), a work of travel writing and autobiography. She also edited *To Say the Least: Canadian Poets from A to Z* (1979).

A book-length study is John Orange's *P. K. Page and Her Work* (1989). A collection of essays is *P. K. Page: Essays on her Works* (2001), ed. Linda Rogers and Barbara Colebrook Peace. Other critical discussions include John Sutherland's "The Poetry of P. K. Page," *Northern Review* 1 (1946–47); A. J. M. Smith's "The Poetry of P. K. Page," *Canadian Literature* 50 (1971); Constance Rooke's "P. K. Page: The Chameleon and the Centre," *Malahat Review* 45 (1978); Rosemary Sullivan's "A Size Larger than Seeing," *Canadian Literature* 79 (1978); Diane Schoemperlen's "Four Themes in the Poetry of P. K. Page," *English Quarterly* 12 (1979); Jean Mallinson's "Retrospect and Prospect," *West Coast Review* 13 (1979); Douglas Freake's "The Multiple Self in the Poetry of P. K. Page," *Studies in Canadian Literature* 19.1 (1994); Diana Relke's "Tracing a Terrestrial Vision in the Early Work of P. K. Page," *Canadian Poetry* 35 (1994); Brian Bartlett's "For Sure the Kittiwake: Naming, Nature, and P. K. Page," *Canadian Literature* 155 (1997); and Sara Jamieson's " 'Now That I Am Dead': P. K. Page and the Self-Elegy," *Canadian Literature* 166 (2000). *Malahat Review* 117 (Winter 1996) is a special issue dedicated to Page. John Orange's bibliography appears in *The Annotated Bibliography of Canada's Major Authors* (1985), ed. Robert Lecker and Jack David. See also **Canadian Poetry.**

Michael Palmer

Palmer's volumes of poetry include *Plan of the City of O* (1971), *Blake's Newton* (1972), *C's Songs* (1973), *Six Poems* (1973), *The Circular Gates* (1974), *Without Music* (1977), *Alogon* (1980), *Notes for Echo Lake* (1981), *First Figure* (1984), *For a Reading: A Selection of Poems* (1988), *Sun* (1988), *An Alphabet Underground/ Underjordisk Alfabet* (with Danish translations by Poul Borum and illustrations by Jens Birkemose, 1993), *At Passages* (1995), *The Lion Bridge: Selected Poems, 1972–1995* (1998), *The Promises of Glass* (2000), and *Codes Appearing: Poems, 1979–1988* (2001). He also wrote plays; published translations, including *Sky-Eclipse* (2000); and edited a collection of essays on poetics, *Code of Signals* (1983). Interviews appear in *Acts* 2.1 (1986); *Talking Poetry* (1987), ed. Lee Bartlett; *Contemporary Literature* 30.1 (1989); *Sagetrieb* 12.3 (1993); and Thomas Gardner's *Regions of Unlikeness* (1999).

Critical discussions of Palmer's work include Steve McCaffery's "Michael Palmer's LANGUAGE of Language," *North of Intention* (1986); Norman Finkelstein's "The Case of Michael Palmer," *Contemporary Literature* 29.4 (1988); Linda Reinfeld's *Language Poetry: Writing as Rescue* (1992); Eric Murphy Selinger's "Important Pleasures and Others: Michael Palmer, Ronald Johnson," *Postmodern Culture* 4.3 (1994); David Clippinger's "Making the Dust Rise: Michael Palmer's Interrogation into Being," *Salt Hill Journal* 2 (1996); Gardner's *Regions of Unlikeness* (1999); and Calvin Bedient's "Breath and Blister: The Word-Burns of Michael Palmer and Leslie Scalapino," *Parnassus* 24.2 (2000). *Occident* 103.1 (1990) is a special issue with essays on Palmer, including Bruce Campbell's "'A Body Disappears into Itself': Michael Palmer's *Sun*." See also **Language Poetry.**

Marge Piercy

Piercy's volumes of poetry include *Breaking Camp* (1968), *Hard Loving* (1969), *To Be of Use* (1973), *Living in the Open* (1976), *The Twelve-Spoked Wheel Flashing* (1978), *The Moon Is Always Female* (1980), *Circles on the Water: Selected Poems* (1982), *Stone, Paper, Knife* (1983), *My Mother's Body* (1985), *Available Light* (1988), *The Earth Shines Secretly: A Book of Days* (with Nell Blaine, 1990), *Mars and Her Children* (1992), *What Are Big Girls Made Of?* (1997), *Written in Bone: The Early Poems of Marge Piercy* (1998), *The Art of Blessing the Day: Poems with a Jewish Theme* (1999), and *Early Grrrl: The Early Poems of Marge Piercy* (1999). She has also published many novels, including *Women on the Edge of Time* (1976). *Parti-Colored Blocks for a Quilt* (1982) is a collection of her criticism and interviews. She also edited *Early Ripening: American Women's Poetry* (1987). *Sleeping with Cats*, a memoir, appeared in 2002. An interview appears in Gary Pacernick's *Meaning and Memory: Interviews with Fourteen Jewish Poets* (2001).

A collection of essays on Piercy's work is *Ways of Knowing* (1991), ed. Sue Walker and Eugenie Hamner. Other critical work on Piercy's poetry includes Victor Contoski's "Marge Piercy: A Vision of the Peaceable Kingdom" and Jean Rosenbaum's "You Are Your Own Magician: A Vision of Integrity in the Poetry of Marge Piercy," both in *Modern Poetry Studies* 8 (1977); Edith Wynne's "Imagery of Association in the Poetry of Marge Piercy," *Publications of the Missouri Philological Association* 10 (1985); Felicia Mitchell's "Marge Piercy's *The Moon Is Always Female:* Feminist Text, Great Books Context," *Virginia English Bulletin* 40.2 (1990); and Naomi Guttman's "'Rooms without Walls': Marge Piercy's Ecofeminist Garden Poetry," *Proteus* 15.2 (1998). Patricia Doherty's *Marge Piercy: An Annotated Bibliography* appeared in 1997.

Robert Pinsky

The Figured Wheel: New and Collected Poems, 1966–1996 appeared in 1996. A subsequent volume, *Jersey Rain*, was published in 2000. Pinsky has also published translations, including Dante's *Inferno* (1994) and, with Robert Hass, Czeslaw Milosz's *The Separate Notebooks* (1984). Pinsky's important books of criticism include *The Situation of Poetry* (1976), *Poetry and the World* (1988), and *The Sounds of Poetry: A Brief Guide* (1998). Interviews appear in *Ploughshares* 6.2 (1980), *TriQuarterly* (1992), *New Letters* 64.4 (1998), *Pembroke Magazine* 31 (1991), and *Bomb* 68 (1999).

Critical work on Pinsky includes Charles Molesworth's "Proving Irony by Compassion: The Poetry of Robert Pinksy," *Hollins Critic* 21.5 (1984); Robert Richman's "At the Intersection of Art and Life," *The New Criterion* 7.10 (1989); Willard Spiegelman's *The Didactic Muse* (1989); Calvin Bedient's "'Man Is Altogether Desire'?" *Salmagundi* 90–91 (1991); Peter Sacks's "'Also This, Also That': Robert Pinsky's Poetics of Inclusion," *Agni* 36 (1992); Timothy Erwin's "The Extraordinary Language of Robert Pinsky," *Halcyon* 16 (1994); Louise Glück's "Story Tellers," *American Poetry Review* 26.4 (1997); James Longenbach's *Modern Poetry after Modernism* (1997); Tony Whedon's "The Transfiguration of Pinsky," *Agni* 49 (1999) and his "Public Pinksy," *Northwest Review* 38.3

(2000); and Jonathan Freedman's "How Now, Middlebrow?" *Raritan* 20.3 (2001).

Sylvia Plath

Plath's *Collected Poems,* ed. Ted Hughes, appeared in 1981, and a *Selected Poems*, also ed. Hughes, in 1985. *Above the Oxbow: Selected Writings* (1985) includes poetry and prose. She also wrote children's literature and a major novel, *The Bell Jar* (1963). Correspondence is available in *Letters Home: Correspondence, 1950–1963* (1975). *The Journals of Sylvia Plath*, ed. Hughes and Frances McCullough, was published in 1982, and *The Unabridged Journals of Sylvia Plath, 1950–1962*, ed. Karen V. Kukil, in 2000. Biographies include Linda Wagner-Martin's *Sylvia Plath: A Biography* (1987), Anne Stevenson's *Bitter Fame* (1989), Paul Alexander's *This Rough Magic* (1991), Janet Malcolm's *The Silent Woman: Sylvia Plath and Ted Hughes* (1994), and Wagner-Martin's *Sylvia Plath: A Literary Life* (1999).

Important critical studies include Caroline King Barnard Hall's *Sylvia Plath* (1978, 1998), Margaret Dickie's *Sylvia Plath and Ted Hughes* (1979), Jon Rosenblatt's *Sylvia Plath: The Poetry of Initiation* (1979), Pamela J. Annas's *A Disturbance in Mirrors* (1988), Steven Gould Axelrod's *Sylvia Plath: The Wound and the Cure of Words* (1990), Jacqueline Rose's *The Haunting of Sylvia Plath* (1992), Susan R. Van Dyne's *Revising Life: Sylvia Plath's Ariel Poems* (1993), Christina Bitzolakis's *Sylvia Plath and the Theatre of Mourning* (1999), Tim Kendall's *Sylvia Plath: A Critical Study* (2000), and Lynda K. Bundtzen's *The Other Ariel* (2001). Collections of essays include *The Art of Sylvia Plath* (1970), ed. Charles Newman; *Critical Essays on Sylvia Plath* (1984), ed. Linda Wagner; *Ariel Ascending* (1985), ed. Paul Alexander; and *The Poetry of Sylvia Plath* (2001), ed. Claire Brennan. Other discussions of her work can be found in Paul Breslin's *The Psycho-Political Muse* (1987); Kathleen Margaret Lant's "The Big Strip Tease: Female Bodies and Male Power in the Poetry of Sylvia Plath," *Contemporary Literature* 34.4 (1993); Jahan Ramazani's *Poetry of Mourning* (1994); and Cynthia Sugar's "Sylvia Plath as Fantasy Space; or, The Return of the Living Dead," *Literature and Psychology* 45.3 (1999). Bibliographies include Gary Lane's (1978) and Sheryl L. Meyering's (1990). See also **Confessional Poetry.**

Craig Raine

Raine's *Collected Poems, 1978–1999* appeared in 2000. Selections of his essays and criticism are available in *Haydn and the Valve Trumpet* (1990) and *In Defense of T. S. Eliot* (2000). He has also written libretti for opera, including the *Electrification of the Soviet Union* (1986), based on a novella by Boris Pasternak, with music by Nigel Osborne. An interview appears in John Haffenden's *Viewpoints* (1981).

Ploughshares 13.4, ed. Bill Knott, is a special issue containing an interview and several articles on Raine. Other critical discussions of Raine's work include John Osborne's "The Incredulous Eye: Craig Raine and Postmodernist Aesthetics," *Stone Ferry Review* 2 (1978); Michael Hulse's "Alms for Every Beggared Sense: Craig Raine's Aesthetic in Context," *Critical Quarterly* 23.4 (1981); Hulse's "The Dialectic of the Image: Notes on the Poetry of Craig Raine and Christopher Reid," *Malahat Review* 64 (1983); A. D. Moody's "Telling It Like It's Not: Ted Hughes and Craig Raine," *Yearbook of English Studies* 17 (1987); Ian Gregson's " 'But Who Is Speaking?': 'Novelisation' in the Poetry of Craig Raine," *English* 41.170 (1992); and David G. Williams's "Elizabeth Bishop and the 'Martian' Poetry of Craig Raine and Christopher Reid," *English Studies* 78.5 (1997).

A. K. Ramanujan

The Collected Poems of A. K. Ramanujan was published in 1995, and *The Collected Essays* in 1999. A volume of *Uncollected Poems and Prose* was published in 2001. Ramanujan published many important translations from Tamil and Kannada, including *The Interior Landscape: Love Poems from a Classical Tamil Anthology* (1967), *Speaking of Siva* (1973), and *Hymns for the Drowning* (1983).

A. N. Dwivedi has published two book-length studies of Ramanujan: *A. K. Ramanujan and His Poetry* (1983) and *The Poetic Art of A. K. Ramanujan* (1995). Other discussions of Ramanujan's poetry include R. Parthasarathy, "How It Strikes a Contemporary: The Poetry of A. K. Ramanujan," *Literary Criterion* 12.2–3 (1976); Emmanuel Narendra Lall's *The Poetry of Encounter* (1983); M. K. Naik's "A. K. Ramanujan and the Search for Roots," *Living Indian English Poets*, ed. Madhusudan Prasad; Bruce King's *Three Indian Poets: Nissim Ezekiel, A. K. Ramanujan, Dom Moraes* (1991); Vinay Dharwadker's introduction to the *Collected Poems;* Shirish Chindhade's *Five Indian Poets* (1996); Rajeev S. Patke's "The Ambivalence of Poetic Self-Exile: The Case of A. K. Ramanujan," *Jouvert* 5.2 (2001); and Jahan Ramazani's *The Hybrid Muse* (2001). See also **Indian Poetry.**

Adrienne Rich

Rich's *The Fact of a Doorframe: Poems 1950–2000* was published in 2002. *Collected Early Poems* (1993) includes Rich's poetry from 1950 to 1970. Later works include *Diving into the Wreck* (1973), *Poems Selected and New* (1975), *Twenty-One Love Poems* (1976), *The Dream of a Common Language* (1978), *A Wild Patience Has Taken Me This Far* (1981), *Sources* (1983),

The Fact of a Doorframe: Poems Selected and New, 1950–1984 (1984), *Your Native Land, Your Life* (1986), *Time's Power* (1989), *An Atlas of the Difficult World* (1991), *Dark Fields of the Republic* (1995), *Midnight Salvage* (1999), and *Fox* (2001). *Adrienne Rich's Poetry and Prose* (1993), ed. Barbara Charlesworth Gelpi and Albert Gelpi, contains, in addition to selections of Rich's own work, selected essays and reviews by critics and scholars. Other prose works include *Of Woman Born: Motherhood as Experience and Institution* (1976), *On Lies, Secrets, and Silence: Selected Prose, 1966–1978* (1979), *Blood, Bread, and Poetry: Selected Prose, 1979–1985* (1986), and *What Is Found There: Notebooks on Poetry and Politics* (1993). Interviews and other major essays are collected in *Arts of the Possible* (2001). Another interview appears in Bill Moyers's *The Language of Life* (1995). Rich has also published translations and edited *The Best American Poetry 1996* (1996).

Book-length studies of her work include Claire Keyes's *The Aesthetics of Power* (1986), Craig Werner's *Adrienne Rich: The Poet and Her Critics* (1988), Alice Templeton's *The Dream and the Dialogue: Adrienne Rich's Feminist Poetics* (1994), and Liz Yorke's *Adrienne Rich: Passion, Politics, and the Body* (1997). *Reading Adrienne Rich* (1984), ed. Jane Roberta Cooper, is a collection of essays on her work. Other important discussions include Rachel Blau DuPlessis's "The Critique of Consciousness and Myth in Levertov, Rich, and Rukeyser," *Shakespeare's Sisters: Feminist Essays on Women Poets* (1979), ed. Sandra M. Gilbert and Susan Gubar; Alicia Ostriker's "Her Cargo: Adrienne Rich and the Common Language" in her *Writing Like a Woman* (1983); Wendy Martin's *An American Triptych: Anne Bradstreet, Emily Dickinson, Adrienne Rich* (1984); Susan Stanford Friedman's " 'I Go Where I Love': An Intertextual Study of H. D. and Adrienne Rich," *Coming to Light: American Women Poets of the Twentieth Century* (1985), ed. Diane Wood Middlebrook and Marilyn Yalom; Mary Hussmann's "On Adrienne Rich," *Iowa Review* 22.1 (1992); Kim Whitehead's *The Feminist Poetry Movement* (1996); Barbara L. Estrin's "Re-Versing the Past: Adrienne Rich's Postmodern Inquietude," *Tulsa Studies in Women's Literature* 16.2 (1997); Margaret Dickie's *Stein, Bishop, and Rich: Lyrics of Love, War, and Place* (1997); and Maeera Shreiber's " 'Where Are We Moored?' Adrienne Rich, Women's Mourning, and the Limits of Lament," *Dwelling in Possibility: Women Poets and Critics on Poetry* (1997), ed. Shreiber and Yopie Prins.

Alberto Ríos

Ríos's volumes of poetry include *Whispering to Fool the Wind* (1982), *Five Indiscretions* (1985), *The Lime Orchard Woman* (1988), *Teodora Luna's Two Kisses* (1990), and *The Smallest Muscle in the Human Body* (2002). Ríos's fiction includes *The Iguana Killer* (1984), *"Pig Cookies" and Other Stories* (1995), and *The Curtain of Trees* (1999). His autobiographical *Capirotada: A Nogales Memoir* was published in 1999. Interviews include Leslie Wootten's in *Bloomsbury Review* 16.1 (1996) and William Barillas's in *Americas Review* 24.3–4 (1996).

Critical discussions of Ríos's work can be found in José David Saldívar's "The Real and the Marvelous in Nogales, Arizona," *Denver Quarterly* 17.2 (1982); Cordelia Candelaria's *Chicano Poetry: A Critical Introduction* (1986); Saldívar's "Towards a Chicano Poetics: The Making of the Chicano Subject, 1969–1982," *Confluencia* 1.2 (1985); Renato Rosaldo's "Fables of the Fallen Guy," *Criticism in the Borderlands: Studies in Chicano Literature, Culture, and Ideology* (1991), ed. Hector Calderon and Saldívar; Deneen Jenks's "The Breathless Patience of Alberto Ríos," *Hayden's Ferry Review* 11 (1992); and Joseph Deters's "Fireworks on the Borderlands: A Blending of Cultures in the Poetry of Alberto Ríos," *Confluencia* 15.2 (2000). See also **Latino Poetry.**

Muriel Rukeyser

The Collected Poems of Muriel Rukeyser was published in 1978. *A Muriel Rukeyser Reader* (1994), ed. Jan Heller Levi with an introduction by Adrienne Rich, offers a good selection of her work. *The Life of Poetry*, originally published in 1949, provides essential insight into Rukeyser's politics and poetics. She also published translations, including Octavio Paz's *Sun Stone* (1963) and Gunnar Ekelöf's *Three Poems* (1967). She wrote biographies of Willard Gibbs (1942), Wendell Willkie (1957), and Thomas Harriet (1971). She also wrote plays, including *Houdini* (1973), and fiction, *More Night* (1981). Collections of letters include *Bubbles* (1967) and *Mazes* (1970).

How Shall We Tell Each Other of the Poet?: The Life and Writing of Muriel Rukeyser (1999), ed. Anne F. Herzog and Janet E. Kaufman, is a helpful collection of essays. A good book-length study is Louise Kertesz's *The Poetic Vision of Muriel Rukeyser* (1980). Other critical work on Rukeyser includes Walter Kalaidjian's *American Culture between the Wars* (1993); Kim Whitehead's *The Feminist Poetry Movement* (1996); Thomas Travisano's "Muriel Rukeyser and Her Literary Critics," and Kate Daniels's " 'The Buried Life and the Body of Waking': Muriel Rukeyser and the Politics of Literary History," both in *Gendered Modernisms* (1996), ed. Margaret Dickie and Travisano; Michael Davidson's *Ghostlier Demarcations: Modern Poetry and the Material World* (1997); David Kadlec's "X-Ray Testimonials in Muriel Rukeyser," *Modernism/Modernity* 5 (1998); Michael Thurston's "Documentary Modernism as Popular Front Poetics: Muriel Rukeyser's 'Book of the Dead,'" *Modern Language Quarterly* 60.1 (1999); Robert Shulman's *The Power of Political Art: The 1930s Literary Left Reconsidered* (2000); and Adrienne Rich's "Muriel Rukeyser: Her Vision" in her *Arts of the Possible* (2001).

Delmore Schwartz

Schwartz's volumes of poetry include *In Dreams Begin Responsibilities* (1938), *Genesis: Book One* (1943), *"Vaudeville for a Princess" and Other Poems* (1950), *Summer Knowledge: New and Selected Poems, 1938–1958* (1959); and *Last and Lost Poems of Delmore Schwartz* (1979), ed. Robert Phillips. Schwartz also wrote a play, *Shenandoah* (1940), and fiction, including *The World Is a Wedding* (1948) and *"Successful Love" and Other Stories* (1961). His *Selected Essays*, ed. Donald A. Dike and David H. Zucker, was published in 1970, and *Portrait of Delmore: Journals and Notes of Delmore Schwartz, 1939–1959*, ed. Elizabeth Pollet, appeared in 1986. He also translated Arthur Rimbaud's *A Season in Hell* (1939, 1940). Karl Shapiro and Robert Phillips edited the *Letters of Delmore Schwartz* (1984), and Phillips edited *Delmore Schwartz and James Laughlin: Selected Letters* (1993). The standard biography is James Atlas's *Delmore Schwartz: The Life of an American Poet* (1977); also useful is Eileen Simpson's *Poets in Their Youth* (1982).

Important studies include Richard McDougall's *Delmore Schwartz* (1974) and Bruce Bawer's *The Middle Generation: The Lives and Poetry of Delmore Schwartz, Randall Jarrell, John Berryman, and Robert Lowell* (1986). Other discussions of his work include William Barrett's "The Truants: *Partisan Review* in the Forties," *Commentary* 49 (June 1974); Douglas Dunn's introduction to Schwartz's *What Is to Be Given* (1976); Phillips's introduction to *Last and Lost Poems of Delmore Schwartz* (1979); David Zucker's " 'Alien to Myself': Jewishness in the Poetry of Delmore Schwartz," *Studies in American Jewish Literature* 9.2 (1990); and Raymond J. Wilson's "Delmore Schwartz and Purgatory," *Partisan Review* 57.3 (1990).

Anne Sexton

Sexton's *Complete Poems* were published in 1981; a *Selected Poems*, ed. Diane Wood Middlebrook and Diane Hume George, in 1988. *No Evil Star* (1985), ed. Steven E. Colburn, is a collection of essays and interviews, and *Anne Sexton: A Self-Portrait in Letters* (1977), ed. Linda Gray Sexton and Lois Ames, is a selection of letters. Sexton also cowrote children's books with Maxine Kumin. The standard biography is Middlebrook's *Anne Sexton* (1991). Sexton's daughter, Linda Gray Sexton, published a memoir, *Searching for Mercy Street: My Journey Back to My Mother, Anne Sexton*, in 1994, and Arthur Furst's *Anne Sexton: The Last Summer* (2000) contains photographic portraits of the poet, as well as correspondence.

Collections of essays on Sexton include *Anne Sexton: The Artist and Her Critics* (1978), ed. J. D. McClatchy; *Anne Sexton: Telling the Tale* (1988), ed. Steven E. Colburn; *Sexton: Selected Criticism* (1988), ed. Diana Hume George; *Critical Essays on Anne Sexton* (1989), ed. Linda Wagner-Martin; and *Original Essays on the Poetry of Anne Sexton* (1998), ed. Frances Bixler. Useful book-length studies are George's *Oedipus Anne: The Poetry of Anne Sexton* (1987) and Caroline King Barnard Hall's *Anne Sexton* (1989). Other critical work on Sexton includes Greg Johnson's "The Achievement of Anne Sexton," *Hollins Critic* (1984); Janice Markey's *A New Tradition?: The Poetry of Sylvia Plath, Anne Sexton, and Adrienne Rich* (1985); and Cassie Premo Steele's *We Heal from Memory: Sexton, Lorde, Anzaldúa, and the Poetry of Witness* (2000). Bibliographic information is available in Cameron Northouse and Thomas P. Walsh's *Sylvia Plath and Anne Sexton: A Reference Guide* (1974).

Karl Shapiro

Shapiro's *Collected Poems: 1948–1978* was published in 1978. Subsequent volumes include *Love and War, Art and God* (1984); *Adam and Eve* (1986), ed. John Wheatcroft; *New and Selected Poems, 1940–1986* (1987); *The Old Horsefly* (1992); and *The Wild Card: Selected Poems, Early and Late* (1998), ed. Stanley Kunitz and David Ignatow. He also wrote a novel, *Edsel* (1971). Works of Shapiro's criticism include *In Defense of Ignorance* (1960); *The Writer's Experience* (with Ralph Ellison, 1964); and *The Poetry Wreck: Selected Essays, 1950–1970* (1975). He also published *Poet: An Autobiography in Three Parts* (1988, 1990). Shapiro edited the magazine *Poetry* from 1948 to 1950. Interviews appear in *Talks with Authors* (1968), ed. Charles F. Madden; *TriQuarterly* 43 (1978); *Southern Humanities Review* 15.3 (1981); *Prairie Schooner* 55.3 (1981); and *Paris Review* 28.99 (1986).

A book-length study is Joseph Reino's *Karl Shapiro* (1981). Useful essays appear in the collection *Seriously Meeting Karl Shapiro* (1993), ed. Sue B. Walker. Other discussions of Shapiro's work include Louis D. Rubin's "The Search for Lost Innocence: Karl Shapiro's *The Bourgeois Poet*," *Hollins Critic* 1.5 (1964); Hyatt H. Waggoner's *American Poets from the Puritans to the Present* (1968); Karl Malkoff's "The Self in the Modern World: Karl Shapiro's Jewish Poems," *Contemporary American-Jewish Literature* (1973), ed. Irving Malin; Robert Phillips's "Poetry, Prosody, and Meta-Poetics: Karl Shapiro's Self-Reflexive Poetry," *Poetics in the*

Poem: Critical Essays on American Self-Reflexive Poetry (1997), ed. Dorothy Z. Baker; Diederik Oostdijk's " 'Someplace Called Poetry': Karl Shapiro, *Poetry* Magazine and Post-War American Poetry," *English Studies* 81.4 (2000); and L. D. Rubin's "Karl Shapiro (1913–2000)—He Took His Stands," *Sewanee Review* 109.1 (2001). Two bibliographies are William White's *Karl Shapiro: A Bibliography* (1960) and Lee Bartlett's *Karl Shapiro: A Descriptive Bibliography* (1979).

Leslie Marmon Silko

Silko's poetry appears in her *Laguna Woman* (1974). Her fiction includes *Ceremony* (1977), *Storyteller* (1981), *Almanac of the Dead* (1991), *Sacred Water* (1993), and *Gardens in the Dunes* (1999). A collection of essays on Native American life is *Yellow Woman and a Beauty of the Spirit* (1996). Silko has also published her correspondence with James Wright, *With the Delicacy and Strength of Lace* (1985). A collection of interviews is *Conversations with Leslie Marmon Silko* (2000), ed. Ellen L. Arnold.

A book-length study is Per Seyerstad's *Leslie Marmon Silko* (1980). A collection of essays is *Leslie Marmon Silko: A Collection of Critical Essays* (1999), ed. Louise K. Barnett and James L. Thorson. Other critical work on Silko includes E. Blicksilver's "Traditionalism vs. Modernity: Leslie Silko on American Indian Women," *Southwest Review* 64 (1979); Alan R. Velie's *Four American Indian Literary Masters* (1982); Kenneth M. Roemer's "Bear and Elk: The Nature(s) of Contemporary American Indian Poetry," *Studies in American Indian Literature: Critical Essays and Course Designs* (1983), ed. Paula Gunn Allen; Susan Perez Castillo's "Postmodernism, Native American Literature, and the Real: The Silko-Erdrich Controversy," *Massachusetts Review* 32.2 (1991); Jeanne Perreault's "New Dreaming: Joy Harjo, Wendy Rose, Leslie Marmon Silko," *Deferring a Dream: Literary Sub-Versions of the American Columbiad* (1994), ed. Gert Buelens and Ernst Rudin; Kate Adams's "Northamerican Silences: History, Identity, and Witness in the Poetry of Gloria Anzaldúa, Cherrie Moraga, and Leslie Marmon Silko," *Listening to Silences: New Essays in Feminist Criticism* (1994), ed. Elain Hedges and Shelley Fisher Fishkin; and Joni Adamson Clarke's "Toward an Ecology of Justice: Transformative Ecological Theory and Practice," *Reading the Earth: New Directions in the Study of Literature and Environment* (1998), ed. Michael P. Branch, Rochelle Johnson, Daniel Patterson, and Scott Slovic. See also **Native American Poetry.**

Charles Simic

Simic's volumes of poetry include *What the Grass Says* (1967), *Somewhere among Us a Stone Is Taking Notes* (1969), *Dismantling the Silence* (1971), *White* (1972, 1980), *Return to a Place Lit by a Glass of Milk* (1974), *Biography and a Lament* (1976), *Charon's Cosmology* (1977), *Brooms: Selected Poems* (1978), *School for Dark Thoughts* (1978), *Classic Ballroom Dances* (1980), *Austerities* (1982), *Weather Forecast for Utopia and Vicinity* (1983), *Selected Poems, 1963–1983* (1985), *Unending Blues* (1986), *Nine Poems* (1989), *The World Doesn't End* (1989), *The Book of Gods and Devils* (1990), *Hotel Insomnia* (1992), *A Wedding in Hell* (1994), *Frightening Toys* (1995), *Walking the Black Cat* (1996), *Jackstraws* (1999, 2000), *Selected Early Poems* (2000), and *Night Picnic* (2001). *Wonderful Words, Silent Truth* (1990), *The Unemployed Fortune-Teller* (1994), *Orphan Factory* (1997), and *A Fly in the Soup* (2000) are collections of essays and memoirs. A book of prose poetry/art criticism is *Dime-Store Alchemy: The Art of Joseph Cornell* (1992). *The Uncertain Certainty* (1985) contains interviews as well as essays and criticism.

An extensive collection of essays is *Charles Simic: Essays on the Poetry* (1996), ed. Bruce Weigl. Other critical studies include Victor Contoski's "Charles Simic: Language at the Stone's Heart," *Chicago Review* 28.6 (1977); Richard Jackson's "Charles Simic and Mark Strand: The Presence of Absence," *Contemporary Literature* 21 (1980); Peter Schmidt's "White: Charles Simic's Thumbnail Epic," *Contemporary Literature* 23.4 (1982); Bruce Bond's "Immanent Distance: Silence and the Poetry of Charles Simic," *Mid-American Review* 8.1 (1988); Kevin Hart's "Writing Things: Literary Property in Heidegger and Simic," *New Literary History* 21.1 (1989); Marci Janas's "The Secret World of Charles Simic," *Field* 44 (1991); Seamus Heaney's "Shorts for Simic," *Agni* 44 (1996); Daniel Morris's " 'My Shoes': Charles Simic's Self-Portraits," *A/B: Auto/Biography Studies* 11.1 (1996) and "Responsible Viewing: Charles Simic's *Dime-Store Alchemy: The Art of Joseph Cornell*," *Papers on Language & Literature* 34.4 (1998); and Peter Stitt's *Uncertainty and Plenitude* (1997). Brian C. Avery's bibliography appears in *Charles Simic: Essays on the Poetry* (1996), ed. Weigl.

Louis Simpson

Simpson's *Collected Poems* appeared in 1988. Subsequent volumes include *In the Room We Share* (1990) and *There You Are* (1995). *Selected Prose* (1989) and *Ships Going into the Blue* (1994) are collection of Simpson's essays and criticism. He also published numerous books of criticism, including *James Hogg* (1962), *Three on the Tower: The Lives and Works of Ezra Pound, T. S. Eliot, and William Carlos Williams* (1975), *A Revolution of Taste: Studies of Dylan Thomas, Allen Ginsberg, Sylvia Plath, and Robert Lowell* (1978), and *The Character of the Poet* (1986). Simpson has also written fiction, *Riverside Drive* (1962); translations, including *Modern Poets of France: A Bilingual Anthology* (1998); and plays. He coedited *New Poets of England and America* (1957) with Donald Hall and Robert Pack.

Ronald Moran's *Louis Simpson* (1972) is a book-length study. A collection of critical essays is *On Louis Simpson: Depths beyond Happiness* (1988), ed. Hank Lazer. Other critical discussions include George Lensing and Moran's *Four Poets and the Emotive Imagination* (1976); Lazer's "Louis Simpson and Walt Whitman: Destroying the Teacher," *Walt Whitman Review* 1.3 (1983); Bruce Bawer's "Louis Simpson and American Dreams," *Arizona Quarterly* 40.2 (1984); Peter Stitt's *The World's Hieroglyphic Beauty* (1985); Henry Taylor's "Great Experiments: The Poetry of Louis Simpson," *Hollins Critic* 27.3 (1990); and James M. Cox's "Re-Viewing Louis Simpson," *Southern Review* 31.1 (1995). Bibliographic information can be found in William H. Roberson's *Louis Simpson: A Reference Guide* (1980).

Dave Smith

Smith's volumes of poetry include *Bull Island* (1970), *Mean Rufus Throw Down* (1973), *Drunks* (1974), *The Fisherman's Whore* (1974), *Cumberland Station* (1977), *In Dark, Sudden with Light* (1977), *Goshawk, Antelope* (1979), *Apparitions* (1981), *Blue Spruce* (1981), *Dream Flights* (1981), *Homage to Edgar Allan Poe* (1981), *Gray Soldiers* (1983), *In the House of the Judge* (1983), *Southern Delights: Poems and Stories* (1984), *The Roundhouse Voices: Selected and New Poems* (1985), *Three Poems* (1988), *Cuba Night* (1990), *Night Pleasures: New and Selected Poems* (1992), *Fate's Kite: Poems, 1991–1995* (1995), *Floating on Solitude: Three Volumes of Poetry* (1996), and *The Wick of Memory: New and Selected Poems, 1974–2000* (2000). His novel *Onliness* was published in 1981, and a book of criticism on contemporary American poetry, *Local Assays*, in 1985. He is coeditor of *The Southern Review*; he has also edited *The Pure Clear Word: Essays on the Poetry of James Wright* (1982), *The Morrow Anthology of Younger American Poets* (with David Bottoms, 1985), and *The Essential Poe* (1990). An interview appears in *Contemporary Literature* 37.3 (1996).

A collection of critical essays is *The Giver of Morning: On the Poetry of Dave Smith* (1982), ed. Bruce Weigl. Other discussions can be found in Helen Vendler's *Part of Nature, Part of Us* (1980); Peter Stitt's "The Sincere, the Mythic, the Playful: Forms of Voice in Current Poetry," *Georgia Review* 34 (Spring 1980); Thom Swiss's "Unfold the Fullness: Dave Smith's Poetry and Fiction," *Sewanee Review* (Summer 1983); and Vendler's " 'Catching a Pig on the Farm,' " *New York Review of Books* (March 8, 2001).

W. D. Snodgrass

Snodgrass's volumes of poetry include *Heart's Needle* (1959), *After Experience* (1968), *Remains* (as S. S. Gardons, 1970, 1985), *The Führer Bunker: A Cycle of Poems in Progress* (1977, 1995), *If Birds Build with Your Hair* (1979), *The Boy Made of Meat* (1983), *A Colored Poem* (1986), *The House the Poet Built* (1986), *A Locked House* (1986), *Selected Poems, 1957–1987* (1987), *W. D.'s Midnight Carnival* (with DeLoss McGraw, 1988), *To Shape a Song* (1989), *Snow Songs* (1992), *Each in His Season* (1993), and *Spring Suite* (1994). In 2001, he published *De/Compositions: 101 Good Poems Gone Wrong*, in which poems are rewritten to demonstrate how the originals work. *In Radical Pursuit* (1975) is a collection of essays and lectures. *Selected Translations* was published in 1998. Interviews appear in *Papers on Language and Literature* 13.4 (1977), *High Plains Literary Review* 8.2 (1993), and *New England Review* 21.1 (2000).

Critical studies of Snodgrass include Paul Gaston's *W. D. Snodgrass* (1978); Gertrude M. White's *To Tell the Truth: The Poems of W. D. Snodgrass* (1979); Lewis Turco's "The Poetics of W. D. Snodgrass," *Hollins Critic* 30.3 (1993); Stephen Haven's *The Poetry of W. D. Snodgrass: Everything Human* (1993); James Fenton's "W. D. Snodgrass: An Introduction," *Agenda* 34.1 (1996); and Philip Raisor's *Tuned and Under Tension: The Recent Poetry of W. D. Snodgrass* (1998). William White's bibliography appeared in 1960. See also **Confessional Poetry.**

Gary Snyder

Snyder's volumes of poetry include *Riprap* (1959), *Myths and Texts* (1960), *Riprap; and Cold Mountain Poems* (1965), *Six Sections from* Mountains and Rivers without End (1965), *A Range of Poems*, (1966), *Three Worlds, Three Realms, Six Roads* (1966), *The Back Country* (1967), *Regarding Wave* (1969, 1970), *Anasazi* (1971), *Manzanita* (1972), *Turtle Island* (1974), *Axe Handles* (1983), *Left Out in the Rain: New Poems, 1947–1985* (1986), *No Nature: New and Selected Poems* (1992), *North Pacific Lands and Waters: A Further Six Sections* (1993), and *Mountains and Rivers without End* (1996). *The Gary Snyder Reader* (1999) contains prose and translations as well as poetry. Other collections of essays include *The Practice of the Wild* (1990) and *A Place in Space: Ethics, Aesthetics, and Watersheds* (1995). *The Real Work: Interviews and Talks, 1964–1979* (1980) was edited by William Scott McLean. Snyder also coedited *The Wooden Fish: Basic Sutras and Gathas of*

Rinzai Zen (with Gutetsu Kanetsuki, 1961). Other interviews appear in *Western American Literature* 30.1 (1995); Bill Moyers's *The Language of Life* (1995); *Western American Literature* 33.3 (1998); and *The San Francisco Beat* (2001), ed. David Meltzer. Biographical information can be found in David Kherdian's *A Biographical Sketch and a Descriptive Checklist of Gary Snyder* (1965) and *Gary Snyder: Dimensions of a Life* (1991), ed. Jon Halper.

Book-length studies include Bob Steuding's *Gary Snyder* (1976), Charles Molesworth's *Gary Snyder's Vision* (1983), Tim Dean's *Gary Snyder and the American Unconscious: Inhabiting the Ground* (1991), Patrick D. Murphy's *Understanding Gary Snyder* (1992), Robert J. Schuler's *Journeys toward the Original Mind: The Long Poems of Gary Snyder* (1994), and Murphy's *A Place for Wayfaring* (2000). Murphy also edited the collection *Critical Essays on Gary Snyder* (1990) and *Studies in the Humanities* 26.1–2 (1999), a special issue on Snyder. Other critical discussions can be found in Charles Altieri's *Self and Sensibility in Contemporary American Poetry* (1984); Sherman Paul's *In Search of the Primitive* (1986); *Beneath a Single Moon: Buddhism in Contemporary American Poetry* (1991), ed. Kent Johnson and Craig Paulenich; David Robertson's "The Circumambulation of Mt. Tamalpais," *Western American Literature* 30.1 (1995); Anthony Hunt's " 'The Hump-Backed Flute Player': The Structure of Emptiness in Gary Snyder's *Mountains and Rivers without End*," *Isle: Interdisciplinary Studies in Literature and Environment* 1.2 (1993) and "Singing the Dyads: The Chinese Landscape Scroll and Gary Snyder's *Mountains and Rivers without End*," *Journal of Modern Literature* 23.1 (1999); and Leonard Scigaj's *Sustainable Poetry* (1999). Bibliographic information can be found in Katherine McNeil's *Gary Snyder: A Bibliography* (1983) and Tom Lavazzi's "Gary Snyder: An International Checklist of Criticism," *Sagetrieb* 12 (1993). See also **Beat Poetry, San Francisco Renaissance.**

Cathy Song

Song's volumes of poetry are *Picture Bride* (1983), *Frameless Windows, Squares of Light* (1988), *School Figures* (1994), and *The Land of Bliss* (2001). She also coedited *Sister Stew: Fiction and Poetry by Women* (with Juliet Kono, 1991). An interview appears in *Honolulu Weekly* 4 (15 June 1994).

Critical discussions of Song's work can be found in *Talk Story: An Anthology of Hawaii's Local Writers* (1978), ed. Eric Chock; Debbie Murakami Nomaguchi's "Cathy Song: 'I'm a Poet Who Happens to Be Asian American,' " *International Examiner* 2.11 (2 May 1984); Gayle K. Fujita-Sato's " 'Third World' as Place and Paradigm in Cathy Song's *Picture Bride*," *MELUS* 15.1 (1988); Stephen Sumida's *And the View from the Shore: Literary Traditions of Hawaii* (1991); Patricia Wallace's "Divided Loyalties: Literal and Literary in the Poetry of Lorna Dee Cervantes, Cathy Song and Rita Dove," *MELUS* 18.3 (1993); Kyhan Lee's "Korean-American Literature: The Next Generation," *Korea Journal* 34.1 (1994); Masami Usui's "Women Disclosed: Cathy Song's Poetry and Kitagawa Ukiyoe," *Studies in Culture and the Humanities* (1995); Jessica Greenbaum's "Cathy Song," *Asian American Literature: Reviews and Criticism of Works by American Writers of Asian Descent* (1995), ed. Lawrence J. Trudeau; and Zhou Xiaojing's "Breaking from Tradition: Experimental Poems by Four Contemporary Asian American Women Poets," *Revista Canaria de Estudios Ingleses* 37 (1998). See also **Asian American Poetry**.

Gary Soto

Soto's volumes of poetry include *The Elements of San Joaquin* (1977), *The Tale of Sunlight* (1978), *Where Sparrows Work Hard* (1981), *Black Hair* (1985), *A Fire in My Hands* (1990), *Who Will Know Us?* (1990), *Home Course in Religion* (1991), *Neighborhood Odes* (1992), *Canto Familiar/Familiar Song* (1995), *New and Selected Poems* (1995), *The Sparrows Move South: Early Poems* (1995), *Super-Eight Movies* (illustrated John Digby, 1996), *Junior College* (1997), *A Natural Man* (1999), and *Poetry Lover* (2001). He has published many books for children and edited *California Childhood: Recollections and Stories of the Golden State* (1988). Memoirs include *Living up the Street: Narrative Recollections* (1985), *A Summer Life* (1990), and *The Effects of Knut Hamsun on a Fresno Boy* (2000). "The Childhood Worries; or, Why I Became a Writer" appears in *Iowa Review* 25.2 (1995). Soto also edited *Four Chicano Poets* (1976) and *Pieces of the Heart: New Chicano Fiction* (1993). Interviews appear in Wolfgang Binder's *Partial Autobiographies: Interviews with Twenty Chicano Poets* (1985) and *Hayden's Ferry Review* 18 (1996).

Critical work on Soto includes Bruce-Novoa's *Chicano Poetry: A Response to Chaos* (1982); Alberto Ríos's "Chicano/Borderlands Literature and Poetry," *Contemporary Latin American Culture: Unity and Diversity* (1984), ed. C. Gail Guntermann; Patricia De La Fuente's "Entropy in the Poetry of Gary Soto: The Dialectics of Violence," *Discurso Literario: Revista de Temas Hispanicos* 5.1 (1987) and "Mutability and Stasis: Images of Time in Gary Soto's *Black Hair*," *Americas Review: A Review of Hispanic Literature and Art of the USA* 17.1 (1989); Julian Olivares's "The Streets of Gary Soto," *Latin American Literary Review* 18 (1990); Rudolf Erben's "Popular Culture, Mass Media, and Chicano Identity in Gary Soto's *Living up the*

Street and *Small Faces,*" *MELUS* 17.3 (1991–92); Don Lee's "About Gary Soto," *Ploughshares* 21.1 (1995); and Michael Tomasek Manson's "Poetry and Masculinity on the Anglo/Chicano Border: Gary Soto, Robert Frost, and Robert Hass," *The Calvinist Roots of the Modern Era* (1997), ed. Aliki Barnstone, Manson, and Carol J. Singley. See also **Latino Poetry.**

Wole Soyinka

Soyinka's volumes of poetry include *"Idanre" and Other Poems* (1969), *Poems from Prison* (1969, expanded as *A Shuttle in the Crypt,* 1972), *Ogun Abibiman* (1976), *"Mandela's Earth" and Other Poems* (1988), and *Early Poems* (1998). Among Soyinka's many major plays are *Camwood on the Leaves* (1960), *The Trials of Brother Jero* (1960), *Kongi's Harvest* (1964), *Madmen and Specialists* (1970), *Jero's Metamorphosis* (1973), *Poems of Black Africa* (1975), *Death and the King's Horseman* (1976), *Opera Wonyosi* (adaptation of Brecht's *The Threepenny Opera,* 1977), *A Play of Giants* (1984), *From Zia, with Love* (1992), and *The Beatification of Area Boy* (1995). Soyinka has also published two novels, *The Interpreters* (1965) and *Season of Anomy* (1973), and written scripts for radio, television, and film. Works dealing with the politics of Nigeria include his prison diary, *The Man Died: Prison Notes* (1972), and his lectures in *The Open Sore of a Continent: A Personal Narrative of the Nigerian Crisis* (1996). Other prose works include *Myth, Literature, and the African World* (1976), the autobiographical *Aké: The Years of Childhood* (1981); *The Critic and Society* (1981); *Art, Dialogue and Outrage* (1988); the Nobel lecture, *This Past Must Address Its Present* (1988); *Ibadan—The Penkelemes Years* (1994); and *The Burden of Memory, The Muse of Forgiveness* (1999). In addition, he edited the anthology *Poems of Black Africa* (1975). Biodun Jeyifo edited a book of interviews, *Conversations with Wole Soyinka,* in 2001.

Book-length studies of Soyinka include Gerald Moore's *Wole Soyinka* (1971, 1978), Eldred D. Jones's *The Writing of Wole Soyinka* (1973, 1983), James Gibbs's *Wole Soyinka* (1986), Obi Maduakor's *Wole Soyinka: An Introduction to His Writing* (1986), Aderemi Bamikunle's *Introduction to Soyinka's Poetry: Analysis of* A Shuttle in the Crypt (1991), Akomaye Oko's *The Tragic Paradox* (1992), Derek Wright's *Wole Soyinka Revisited* (1993), Tanure Ojaide's *The Poetry of Wole Soyinka* (1994), and Tunde Adeniran's *The Politics of Wole Soyinka* (1994). Collections of essays dedicated to Soyinka include *Before Our Very Eyes: Tribute to Wole Soyinka* (1987), ed. Dapo Adelugba; *Critical Perspectives on Wole Soyinka* (1980), ed. Gibbs; *Research on Wole Soyinka* (1993), ed. Bernth Lindfors and Gibbs; *Soyinka: A Collection of Critical Essays* (1994), ed. Oyin Ogunba; and Jeyifo's *Perspectives on Wole Soyinka: Freedom and Complexity* (2001). Other discussions of his work include Nyong J. Udoeyop's *Three Nigerian Poets: A Critical Study of the Poetry of Soyinka, Clark, and Okigbo* (1973), Ken Goodwin's *Understanding African Poetry* (1982), and Kole Omotoso's *Achebe or Soyinka?: A Study in Contrasts* (1996). B. M. Okpu's bibliography was published in 1984, and Gibbs's in 1986. See also **African Poetry.**

William Stafford

Stafford's volumes of poetry include *West of Your City* (1960); *Traveling through the Dark* (1962); *The Rescued Year* (1966); *Eleven Untitled Poems* (1968); *Weather* (1969); *Allegiances* (1970); *Temporary Facts* (1970); *In the Clock of Reason* (1973); *Someday, Maybe* (1973); *That Other Alone* (1973); *Going Places* (1974); *Braided Apart* (with Kim Robert Stafford, 1976); *The Design on the Oriole* (1977); *Stories That Could Be True: New and Collected Poems* (1977); *Tuft by Puff* (1978); *Sometimes Like A Legend: Puget Sound Poetry* (1981); *A Glass Face in the Rain* (1982); *Segues: A Correspondence in Poetry* (with Marvin Bell, 1983); *Roving across Fields: A Conversation and Uncollected Poems, 1942–1982* (1983), ed. Thom Tammaro; *Smoke's Way: Poems from Limited Editions, 1968–1981* (1983); *Listening Deep* (1984); *Stories and Storms and Strangers* (1984); *Brother Wind* (1986); *An Oregon Message* (1987); *Annie-Over* (with Bell, 1988); *Fin, Feather, Fur* (1989), *A Scripture of Leaves* (1989); *How to Hold Your Arms When It Rains* (1990); *History Is Loose Again* (1991); *Passwords* (1991); *The Animal That Drank Up Sound* (for children, 1992); *Holding onto the Grass* (1992); *My Name Is William Tell* (1992); *Seeking the Way* (1992); *The Darkness Around Us Is Deep: Selected Poems* (1993), ed. Robert Bly; *Who Are You Really, Wanderer?* (1993); *Learning to Live in the World: Earth Poems* (1994), ed. Jerry Watson and Linda Obbink; *The Methow River Poems* (1995); *Even in Quiet Places* (1996); and *The Way It Is: New and Selected Poems* (1998). *Down in My Heart* (1947, 1985) is a memoir, and essays and interviews are collected in *You Must Revise Your Life* (1986). *Writing the Australian Crawl* (1978) and *Crossing Unmarked Snow* (1998) are collections of "views on the writer's vocation." Other interviews appear in *Prairie Schooner* 44 (Summer 1970), *Northwest Review* 13 (1973), *Sunstone* 1 (Fall 1976), *American Poetry Review* 10.6 (1981), *Cimarron Review* 72 (July 1985), *Michigan Quarterly Review* 30.2 (1991), and *American Poetry Review* 22.3 (1993).

Book-length studies of his work include Jonathan Holden's *The Mark to Turn: A Reading of William Stafford's Poetry* (1976), David A. Carpenter's *William Stafford* (1986), Judith Kitchen's *Understanding William Stafford*

(1989), and Kitchen's *Writing the World: Understanding William Stafford* (1999). A collection of essays is *On William Stafford: The Worth of Local Things* (1993), ed. Tom Andrews. Other studies include George S. Lensing and Ronald Moran's *Four Poets and the Emotive Imagination* (1976), Peter Stitt's *The World's Hieroglyphic Beauty* (1985), and Sanford Pinsker's *Three Pacific Northwest Poets* (1987). Two bibliographies are James W. Pirie's *William Stafford: A Primary Bibliography, 1942–1982* (1983) and Lars Nordstrom's in *Studia Neophilologica* 59 (1987).

Mark Strand

Strand's volumes of poetry include *Sleeping with One Eye Open* (1964), *Reasons for Moving* (1968), *Darker* (1970), *Elegy for My Father* (1973), *The Sergeantville Notebook* (1973), *The Story of Our Lives* (1973), *The Late Hour* (1978), *Selected Poems* (1980), *The Continuous Life* (1990), *Explain That You Live* (with Karl Elder, 1992), *Dark Harbor* (1993), *A Poet's Alphabet of Influences* (1993), *A Suite of Appearances* (1993), *Blizzard of One* (1998), and *Chicken, Shadow, Moon, and More* (2000). Prose and criticism is available in *Hopper* (1994) and *Weather of Words: Poetic Invention* (2000). He has also published short stories, *"Mr. and Mrs. Baby," and Other Stories* (1985), and many translations, including Rafael Alberti's *The Owl's Insomnia* (1973) and Jorge Luis Borges's *Texas* (1975). He has also coedited *The Making of a Poem: A Norton Anthology of Poetic Forms* (2000). An interview appears in *Chicago Review* 28.4 (1977).

A book-length study of Strand's work is David Kirby's *Mark Strand and the Poet's Place in Contemporary Culture* (1990). Other critical discussions can be found in Richard Howard's *Alone with America* (1969, 1980); Harold Bloom's *Figures of Capable Imagination* (1976); Richard Jackson's "Charles Simic and Mark Strand: The Presence of Absence," *Contemporary Literature* 21.1 (1980); Linda Gregerson's "Negative Capability," *Parnassus* 9.2 (1981); Peter Stitt's "Stages of Reality: The Mind/Body Problem in Contemporary Poetry," *Georgia Review* 37.1 (1983); Harold Bloom's "Mark Strand," *Gettysburg Review* 4.2 (1991); Charles Berger's "Poetry Chronicle," *Raritan* 10.3 (1991); Jeffrey Donaldson's "The Still Life of Mark Strand's Darkening Harbor," *Dalhousie Review* 74 (1994); Sarah Manguso's "Where Is that Boy?" *Iowa Review* 29.2 (1999); and Christopher R. Miller's "Mark Strand's Inventions of Farewell," *Wallace Stevens Journal* 24.2 (2000).

May Swenson

Swenson's volumes of poetry include *Another Animal* (1954), *A Cage of Spines* (1958), *To Mix with Time: New and Selected Poems* (1963), *Half Sun, Half Sleep: New Poems* (1967), *Iconographs* (1970), *New and Selected Things Taking Place* (1978), *In Other Words* (1987), *The Love Poems of May Swenson* (1991), *Nature: Poems Old and New* (1994), and *May Out West* (1996). Works of Swenson's criticism include *The Contemporary Poet as Artist and Critic* (1964) and *Made with Words* (1998). *Dear Elizabeth: Five Poems and Three Letters to Elizabeth Bishop* appeared in 2000. Swenson also participated in the translation of *Windows and Stones: Selected Poems of Tomas Tranströmer* (1972). Interviews appear in *New York Quarterly* 19 (1977); *Parnassus* 7 (1978); and *Truthtellers of the Times: Interviews with Contemporary Women Poets* (1998), ed. Janet Palmer Mullaney. A biography for young adults is R. R. Knudson's *The Wonderful Pen of May Swenson* (1993). Knudson and Suzzanne Bigelow also published *May Swenson: A Poet's Life in Photos* (1996).

Critical works on Swenson include Alicia Ostriker's "May Swenson and the Shapes of Speculation," *Writing Like a Woman* (1983); Grace Schulman's "Life's Miracles: The Poetry of May Swenson," *American Poetry Review* 23.5 (1994); Sue Russell's "A Mysterious and Lavish Power: How Things Continue to Take Place in the Work of May Swenson," *Kenyon Review* 16.3 (1994); Kirstin Hotelling Zona's "A 'Dangerous Game of Change': Images of Desire in the Love Poems of May Swenson," *Twentieth Century Literature* 44.2 (1998); Mark Doty's "Queer Sweet Thrills: Reading May Swenson," *Yale Review* 88.1 (2000); and Richard Howard's "Banausics," *Parnassus* 25.1–2 (2001). Kenneth E. Gadomski's "May Swenson: A Bibliography of Primary and Secondary Sources," appeared in *Bulletin of Bibliography* 44.4 (1987).

James Tate

Tate's volumes of poetry include *Cages* (1966), *The Destination* (1967), *The Lost Pilot* (1967), *Notes of Woe* (1968), *The Torches* (1968, 1971), *Row with Your Hair* (1969), *Shepherds of the Mist* (1969), *Are You Ready, Mary Baker Eddy???* (with Bill Knott, 1970), *The Oblivion Ha-Ha* (1970, 1984), *Hints to Pilgrims* (1971, 1981), *Absences* (1972), *Viper Jazz* (1976), *Riven Doggeries* (1979), *Constant Defender* (1983), *Reckoner* (1986), *Distance from Loved Ones* (1990), *Selected Poems* (1991), *Worshipful Company of Fletchers* (1994), *Shroud of the Gnome* (1997), and *Memoir of the Hawk* (2001). He has also published a novel, *Lucky Darryl* (with Bill Knott, 1977), and collections of short stories, *Hottentot Ossuary* (1974) and *Dreams of a Robot Dancing Bee* (2002), and edited *The Best American Poetry 1997* (1997). *The Route as Briefed* (1999) contains interviews and essays. With Alberta Turner, Tate contributed "A Box for Tom" to the volume *Fifty Contemporary Poets: The Creative Process* (1977).

Denver Quarterly 33.3 (1998) is a special issue with numerous essays on Tate. Other critical work includes R. D. Rosen's "James Tate and Sidney Goldfarb and the Inexhaustible Nature of the Murmur," *American Poetry since 1960: Some Critical Perspectives* (1973), ed. Robert B. Shaw; William Logan's "Language against Fear," *Poetry* 80.4 (1977); Mark Rudman's "Private but No Less Ghostly Worlds," *American Poetry Review* 10.4 (1981); Donald Revell's "The Desperate Buck and Wing: James Tate and the Failure of Ritual," *Western Humanities Review* 38.4 (1984); *American Poetry Observed* (1984), ed. Joe David Bellamy et al.; Lee Upton's "The Masters Can Only Make Us Laugh," *South Atlantic Review* 55.4 (1990) and *The Muse of Abandonment* (1998); David Young's "Some Huge Pageant," *Field: Contemporary Poetry and Poetics* 46 (Spring 1992); and Anthony Caleshu's "What Kind of Disorganization Is This?" *Pn Review* 25 (1999).

Dylan Thomas

The Collected Poems, ed. Walford Davies and Ralf Ward, was published in 1988. *Quite Early One Morning* (1954) is a collection of short stories, essays, and other writings. Other important works include the autobiographical *Portrait of the Artist as a Young Dog* (1940); *Adventures in the Skin Trade* (1955); and the radio play *Under Milk Wood* (1954). *The Notebooks of Dylan Thomas*, ed. Ralph N. Maud, appeared in 1967, and *The Collected Letters of Dylan Thomas*, ed. Paul Ferris, in 1985. Biographies include Constantine Fitzgibbon's *The Life of Dylan Thomas* (1965), Ferris's *Dylan Thomas: A Biography* (1977, 2000), and Andrew Sinclair's *Dylan the Bard* (2000).

Helpful collections of essays on Thomas's work include *Critical Essays on Dylan Thomas* (1989), ed. Georg Gaston, and *Dylan Thomas* (2001), ed. John Goodby and Chris Wigginton. Book-length studies include David Holbrook's *Llareggub Revisited: Dylan Thomas and the State of Modern Poetry* (1962), H. H. Kleinman's *The Religious Sonnets of Dylan Thomas* (1963), Walford Davies's *Dylan Thomas* (1985), Alan Bold's *Dylan Thomas: Craft or Sullen Art* (1990), Jacob Korg's *Dylan Thomas* (1992), John Ackerman's *Dylan Thomas: His Life and Work* (1996), William York Tindall's *A Reader's Guide to Dylan Thomas* (1996), Barbara Hardy's *Dylan Thomas: An Original Language* (2000), and Eynel Wardi's *Once Below a Time: Dylan Thomas, Julia Kristeva, and Other Speaking Subjects* (2000). Bibliographic information can be found in John Ackerman's *A Dylan Thomas Companion* (1991) and James A. Davies's *A Reference Companion to Dylan Thomas* (1998).

Charles Tomlinson

Tomlinson's *Collected Poems* appeared in 1985 and was enlarged in 1987. Subsequent volumes include *The Return* (1987), *Annunciations* (1989), *Selected Poems* (1989), *The Door in the Wall* (1992), *Jubilation* (1995), *Selected Poems: 1955–1997* (1997), and *Vineyard above the Sea* (1999). A selection of prose work is available in *American Essays: Making It New* (2001). He has also published works of graphic art, including *In Black and White* (1981), and edited many collections, including *Selected Poems of William Carlos Williams* (1976) and *Poems of George Oppen, 1908–1984* (1990). *The Letters of William Carlos Williams and Charles Tomlinson* was published in 1992. Interviews include Jed Rasula and Mike Erwin's in *Contemporary Literature* 16 (1975), Bruce Meyer's in *Hudson Review* 43.3 (1990), and Jordi Doce's in *Agenda* 33.2 (1995).

Book-length studies of Tomlinson include Brian John's *The World as Event* (1989); Richard Swigg's *Charles Tomlinson and the Objective Tradition* (1994); and *William Carlos Williams and Charles Tomlinson: A Transatlantic Connection* (1999), ed. Barry Magid and Hugh Witemeyer. A collection of essays is *Charles Tomlinson: Man and Artist* (1988), ed. Kathleen O'Gorman, and *Agenda* 33.2 (1995) is a special issue dedicated to Tomlinson. Other discussions can be found in Denis Donoghue's *The Ordinary Universe* (1968); Calvin Bedient's *Eight Contemporary Poets* (1974); *British Poetry since 1960: A Critical Survey* (1972), ed. Michael Schmidt and Grevel Lindop; Paul Mariani's "Tomlinson's Use of the Williams Triad," *Contemporary Literature* 18 (1977); J. Keith Hardie's "Charles Tomlinson and the Language of Silence," *Boundary 2* 15.1–2 (1986–87); Hearne Pardee's "A Distant Vision: Charles Tomlinson and American Art," *Partisan Review* 58.3 (1991); Judith P. Saunders's "Charles Tomlinson and the Automobile: Shifting Perspectives and a Moving Frame," *Sagetrieb* 14.3 (1995); Willard Spiegelman's "Just Looking," *Parnassus* 21.1–2 (1995); Michael Hennessy's "Louis Zukofsky, Charles Tomlinson, and the 'Objective Tradition,' " *Contemporary Literature* 37.2 (1996); and Swigg's "One World You Say?: Charles Tomlinson's Poetry," *Contemporary Literature* 41.2 (2000).

David Wagoner

Wagoner's *Traveling Light* (1999) contains new and collected poems. A subsequent volume, *The House of Song*, was published in 2002. He has also written many novels, including *Rock* (1958), and edited *Straw for the Fire: From the Notebooks of Theodore Roethke, 1943–63* (1972). Since 1966, he has edited the journal *Poetry Northwest*.

A book-length study is Ron McFarland's *The World of David Wagoner* (1997). Other critical works dealing with Wagoner are Sanford Pinsker's "On David Wagoner," *Salmagundi* 22–23 (1973); Robert Peters's "Thirteen Ways of Looking at David Wagoner's New Poems," *Western Humanities Review* 35.3 (1981); Sarah Mc-

Aulay's "'Getting There' and Going Beyond: David Wagoner's Journey without Regret," *The Literary Review: An International Journal of Contemporary Writing* 28.1 (1984); Justin Askins's "Mild Delight," *Parnassus* 12.1 (1984); Pinsker's *Three Pacific Northwest Poets: William Stafford, Richard Hugo, and David Wagoner* (1987); and Laurie Ricou's "David Wagoner," *Updating the Literary West* (1997), ed. Max Westbrook.

Derek Walcott

Walcott's *Collected Poems, 1948–1984* was published in 1986. Subsequent volumes include *The Arkansas Testament* (1987), *Omeros* (1990), *The Bounty* (1997), and *Tiepolo's Hound* (2000). His many plays include *Ti-Jean and His Brothers* (1958), *Dream on Monkey Mountain* (1967), and *The Odyssey* (1993). *What the Twilight Says* (1998) offers a selection of Walcott's essays, and *Conversations with Derek Walcott* (1996), ed. William Baer, is a collection of interviews. In addition to Bruce King's biography, *Derek Walcott: A Caribbean Life* (2000), a useful introduction to Walcott's life and work is Paul Breslin's *Nobody's Nation* (2001).

An essential collection of primary and secondary materials is *Critical Perspectives on Derek Walcott* (1993), ed. Robert D. Hamner. Other collections of essays include *The Art of Derek Walcott* (1991), ed. Stewart Brown, and *Approaches to the Poetics of Derek Walcott* (2001), ed. José Luis Martínez-Dueñas Espejo and José María Pérez Fernández. *Verse* 11.2 (1994) and *South Atlantic Quarterly* 96.2 (1997) are special issues dedicated to Walcott. Other book-length studies include Edward Baugh's *Derek Walcott: Memory as Vision* (1978), Ned Thomas's *Derek Walcott: Poet of the Islands* (1980), Rei Terada's *Walcott's Poetry: American Mimicry* (1992), Hamner's *Derek Walcott* (1981, 1993) and *Epic of the Dispossessed: Derek Walcott's* Omeros (1997), John Thieme's *Derek Walcott* (1999), Paula Burnett's *Derek Walcott: Politics and Poetics* (2000), and Patricia Ismond's *Abandoning Dead Metaphors: The Caribbean Phase of Derek Walcott's Poetry* (2001). Other discussions of Walcott's poetry include Joseph Brodsky's "On Derek Walcott," *New York Review of Books* (10 November 1983); Rita Dove's "'Either I'm Nobody, or I'm a Nation," *Parnassus* 14.1 (1987); June D. Bobb's *Beating a Restless Drum: The Poetics of Kamau Brathwaite and Derek Walcott* (1998); and Jahan Ramazani's *The Hybrid Muse* (2001). The standard bibliography is Irma E. Goldstraw's *Derek Walcott: An Annotated Bibliography of His Works* (1984). See also **Caribbean Poetry.**

Richard Wilbur

Wilbur's *New and Collected Poems* appeared in 1988. Subsequent volumes include *About Sylvia* (1996) and *Mayflies: New Poems and Translations* (2000). Wilbur has also published many translations, notably the works of Molière, including *The Misanthrope* (1955) and *Tartuffe* (1964). He has also written plays and children's literature and edited *Poe: Complete Poems* (1959). *Responses* (1976) selects prose from 1953 to 1976, and *The Catbird's Song* (1997) from 1963 to 1995. Interviews are collected in *Conversations with Richard Wilbur* (1990), ed. William Butts.

A collection of essays on Wilbur is *Richard Wilbur's Creation* (1983), ed. Wendy Salinger. Book-length studies include Donald Louis Hill's *Richard Wilbur* (1967), Paul F. Cummins's *Richard Wilbur: A Critical Essay* (1971), Bruce Michelson's *Wilbur's Poetry: Music in a Scattering Time* (1991), Rodney Stenning Edgecombe's *A Reader's Guide to the Poetry of Richard Wilbur* (1995), and John B. Hougen's *Ecstasy within Discipline: The Poetry of Richard Wilbur* (1995). Other works dealing with Wilbur include Randall Jarrell's *Poetry and the Age* (1953) and *The Third Book of Criticism* (1965); Frank Littler's "Wilbur's 'Love Calls Us to the Things of This World,'" *Explicator* 40.3 (1982); and Peter Harris's "Forty Years of Richard Wilbur: The Loving Work of an Equilibrist," *Virginia Quarterly Review* 66.3 (1990).

Charles Wright

Wright's volumes of poetry include *The Voyage* (1963), *6 Poems* (1965), *The Dream Animal* (1968), *Private Madrigals* (1969), *The Grave of the Right Hand* (1970), *The Venice Notebook* (1971), *Backwater* (1973), *Hard Freight* (1973), *Bloodlines* (1975), *China Trace* (1977), *Colophons* (1977), *Dead Color* (1980), *The Southern Cross* (1981), *Country Music: Selected Early Poems* (1982), *Four Poems of Departure* (1983), *The Other Side of the River* (1984), *Five Journals* (1986), *Zone Journals* (1988), *The World of the Ten Thousand Things* (1990), *Xionia* (1990), *Chickamauga* (1995), *Black Zodiac* (1997), *Appalachia* (1998), *Negative Blues: Selected Later Poems* (2000), and *A Short History of the Shadow* (2002). *Halflife* (1988) and *Quarter Notes* (1995) collect "improvisations and interviews." Wright has also published translations, including Eugenio Montale's *The Storm* (1978) and *Motels* (1981). Recent interviews include Willard Spiegelman's in *Literary Imagination* 2.1 (2000) and Ted Genoways's in *Southern Review* 36.2 (2000).

A collection of essays on Wright's work is *The Point Where All Things Meet: Essays on Charles Wright* (1995), ed. Tom Andrews. Other critical studies include Nance Van Winckel's "Charles Wright and the Landscape of the Lyric," *New England Review* 12.3 (1988); Helen Vendler's *The Music of What Happens* (1988); David Young's "The Blood Bees of Paradise," *Field* 44 (1991); Floyd Collins's "Metamorphosis within the Poetry of Charles Wright," *Gettysburg*

Review 4.3 (1991) and "A Poetry of Transcendence," *Gettysburg Review* 10.4 (1997); Edward Hirsch's "The Visionary Poetics of Philip Levine and Charles Wright," *Columbia History of American Poetry* (1993), ed. Jay Parini and Brett C. Millier; Peter Stitt's *Uncertainty and Plenitude* (1997); Ernest Suarez's "Charles Wright," *Five Points* 2.3 (1998); Lee Upton's *The Muse of Abandonment* (1998); David Garrison's "From Feeling to Form: Image as Translation in the Poetry of Charles Wright," *Midwest Quarterly* 4.1 (1999); and Bonnie Costello's "Charles Wright's Via Negativa: Language, Landscape, and the Idea of God," *Contemporary Literature* 36.2 (2000).

James Wright

Wright's *Above the River: The Complete Poems* was published in 1990. His *Collected Prose*, ed. Anne Wright, was published in 1983. Wright also translated German and Spanish poetry, including the work of Theodor Storm, Hermann Hesse, Georg Trakl, César Vallejo, and Pablo Neruda. Collections of letters include *With the Delicacy and Strength of Lace: Letters between Leslie Marmon Silko and James Wright* (1986), ed. Anne Wright, and *In Defense against This Exile: Letters to Wayne Burns* (1985), ed. John R. Doheny. Anne Wright also edited *A Secret Field: Selections from the Final Journals of James Wright* (1985).

Book-length studies of Wright include David C. Dougherty's *James Wright* (1987), Kevin Stein's *James Wright: The Poetry of a Grown Man* (1989), and Andrew Elkins's *The Poetry of James Wright* (1991). *The Pure Clear Word: Essays on the Poetry of James Wright* (1982), ed. Dave Smith, and *James Wright: The Heart of the Light* (1990), ed. Peter Stitt and Frank Graziano, contain many helpful essays. Other critical discussions of Wright's work can be found in Robert Hass's "James Wright," *Ironwood* 10 (1977); James E. B. Breslin's *From Modern to Contemporary* (1984); Henry Taylor's *Compulsory Figures* (1992); Nathan A. Scott Jr.'s *Visions of Presence in Modern American Poetry* (1993); and Nick Halpern's " 'Coming Back Here How Many Years Now': August Kleinzahler and James Wright's *Shall We Gather at the River*," *Contemporary Literature* 42.2 (2001). William H. Roberson's annotated bibliography was published in 1995. See also **Deep Image Poetry.**

Judith Wright

Wright's *Collected Poems, 1942–1985* was published in 1994. Collections of essays on writing, conservation, and other topics include *Born of the Conquerors* (1991) and *Going on Talking* (1992). She edited *Australian Poetry* (1948), *A Book of Australian Verse* (1956, 1968), and *New Land, New Language: An Anthology of Australian Verse* (1957). She wrote children's literature; a biographical novel, *Generations of Men* (1959, 1995); and works of history, including *The Cry for the Dead* (1981). Her study of the Australian writer Charles Harpur was published in 1963. *Half a Life* (1999) is an autobiography.

Collections of essays dealing with Wright include *Critical Essays on Judith Wright* (1968), ed. A. K. Thomson; *Judith Wright: An Appreciation* (1976), ed. Norman Simms; and *Considerations: New Essays on Kenneth Slessor, Judith Wright, and Douglas Stewart* (1977), ed. Brian Kiernan. Book-length studies include W. N. Scott's *Focus on Judith Wright* (1967); A. D. Hope's *Judith Wright* (1975); Jennifer Strauss's *Judith Wright* (1995); and four works by Shirley Walker: *The Poetry of Judith Wright: A Search for Unity* (1980), *Judith Wright* (1981), *Flame and Shadow: A Study of Judith Wright's Poetry* (1991), and *Vanishing Edens: Responses to Australia in the Works of Mary Gilmore, Judith Wright, and Dorothy Hewett* (1992). See also **Australian Poetry.**

Permissions Acknowledgments

Ai: "Sleeping Beauty" from VICE by Ai. Copyright © 1999 by Ai. "Killing Floor" and "Twenty-Year Marriage," copyright © 1973 by Ai from VICE by Ai. Copyright © 1999 by Ai. Used by permission of W. W. Norton & Co., Inc.

Agha Shahid Ali: "Postcard from Kashmir" and "The Dacca Gauzes" from THE HALF-INCH HIMALAYAS by Agha Shahid Ali. Copyright © 1987 by Agha Shahid Ali and reprinted by permission of Wesleyan University Press. "Leaving Sonora" and "I See Chile in My Rearview Mirror" from A NOSTALGIST'S MAP OF AMERICA by Agha Shahid Ali. Copyright © 1991 by Agha Shahid Ali. "The Country without a Post Office" and "Ghazal" from THE COUNTRY WITHOUT A POST OFFICE by Agha Shahid Ali. Copyright © 1997 by Agha Shahid Ali. "Lenox Hill" from ROOMS ARE NEVER FINISHED by Agha Shahid Ali. Copyright © 2002 by Agha Shahid Ali. Used by permission of W. W. Norton & Co., Inc.

Sherman Alexie: "Evolution" from THE BUSINESS OF FANCY DANCING, copyright © 1992 by Sherman Alexie; "On the Amtrak from Boston to New York City" from FIRST INDIAN ON THE MOON, copyright © 1993 by Sherman Alexie; "Tourists" and "How to Write the Great American Indian Novel" from THE SUMMER OF BLACK WIDOWS, copyright © 1996 by Sherman Alexie; "Crow Testament" from ONE STICK SONG, copyright © 2000 by Sherman Alexie. Reprinted by permission of Hanging Loose Press.

Kingsley Amis: "Against Romanticism" from COLLECTED POEMS 1944–1979 by Kingsley Amis. Copyright © 1956 by Kingsley Amis. "Science Fiction" and "An Ever-Fixed Mark" from A LOOK AROUND THE ESTATE by Kingsley Amis. Copyright © 1967 by Kingsley Amis. Reprinted by kind permission of Jonathan Clowes Ltd., London, on behalf of the Literary Estate of Sir Kingsley Amis.

A. R. Ammons: "Corson's Inlet," copyright © 1963 by A. R. Ammons. "Easter Morning," copyright © 1979 by A. R. Ammons. "So I Said I am Ezra" and "Love Song" from THE SELECTED POEMS, Expanded Edition by A. R. Ammons. Copyright © 1987, 1977, 1975, 1974, 1972, 1971, 1970, 1966, 1965, 1964, 1955 by A. R. Ammons. "Gravelly Run," copyright © 1960 by A. R. Ammons. "The City Limits," "Laser," and "Small Song" from COLLECTED POEMS 1951–1971 by A. R. Ammons. Copyright © 1972 by A. R. Ammons. From "Tombstones" and "Motion's Holdings" from SUMERIAN VISTAS by A. R. Ammons. Copyright © 1987 by A. R. Ammons. Part 2 from GARBAGE by A. R. Ammons. Copyright © 1993 by A. R. Ammons. "Strip 43" from GLARE by A. R. Ammons. Copyright © 1997 by A. R. Ammons. Used by permission of W. W. Norton & Co., Inc.

John Ashbery: "The Tennis Court Oath" from THE TENNIS COURT OATH by John Ashbery, copyright © 1962. Reprinted by permission of Wesleyan University Press. "Wet Casements" from HOUSEBOAT DAYS by John Ashbery. Copyright © 1975, 1976, 1977 by John Ashbery. "Paradoxes and Oxymorons" from SHADOW TRAIN by John Ashbery. Copyright © 1980, 1981 by John Ashbery. "At North Farm" from A WAVE by John Ashbery. Copyright © 1981, 1982, 1983, 1984 by John Ashbery. "Some Trees" and "The Instruction Manual" from SOME TREES by John Ashbery. Copyright © 1956 by John Ashbery. "These Lacustrine Cities" from RIVERS AND MOUNTAINS by John Ashbery. Copyright © 1962, 1963, 1964, 1966 by John Ashbery. "Soonest Mended" and "Farm Implements and Rutabagas in a Landscape" from THE DOUBLE DREAM OF SPRING by John Ashbery. Copyright © 1970, 1969, 1968, 1967, 1966 by John Ashbery. Reprinted by permission of Georges Borchardt, Inc. "As One Put Drunk into the Packet-Boat" and "Self-Portrait in a Convex Mirror," copyright © 1974 by John Ashbery, from SELF-PORTRAIT IN A CONVEX MIRROR by John Ashbery. Used by permission of Viking Penguin, a division of Penguin Putnam Inc. "Of the Light" from YOUR NAME HERE by John Ashbery. Copyright © 2000 by John Ashbery. Reprinted by permission of Farrar, Straus and Giroux, LLC.

Margaret Atwood: "Miss July Grows Older," "Manet's Olympia," and "Morning in the Burned House" from MORNING IN THE BURNED HOUSE by Margaret Atwood. Copyright © 1995 by Margaret Atwood. Used by permission of Houghton Mifflin Co. and McClelland & Stewart Ltd., The Canadian Publishers. All rights reserved. From "Circe / Mud Poems" from SELECTED POEMS 1965–1975 by Margaret Atwood. Copyright © 1976 by Margaret Atwood. Published in Canada in SELECTED POEMS 1966–1984. Copyright © 1990 Margaret Atwood. Reprinted by permission of Houghton Mifflin Co. and Oxford University Press Canada. All rights reserved. "This Is a Photograph of Me" from THE CIRCLE GAME, copyright © 1968, 1998 by Margaret Atwood. "You Fit into me" and "They Eat Out" from POWER POLITICS, copyright © 1971, 1996 by Margaret Atwood. Reprinted by permission of House of Anansi Press, Toronto. "Footnote to the Amnesty Report on Torture" is reprinted by permission of Margaret Atwood from the collection TWO HEADED POEMS, copyright © 1978 by Margaret Atwood, first published in Canada by Oxford University Press and in the US by Simon & Schuster.

Amiri Baraka: "A Poem for Black Hearts" from THE LEROI JONES / AMIRI BARAKA READER by Amiri Baraka. Copyright © 2000 by Amiri Baraka. Appears by permission of the publisher, Thunder's Mouth Press. From "The Myth of a 'Negro Literature' " by Amiri Baraka, reprinted by permission of Sterling Lord Literistic, Inc. Copyright © 1998 by Amiri Baraka. "An Agony. As Now.," "A Poem for Speculative Hipsters, "Legacy," "Wise I," "Y The Link Will Not Always Be 'Missing' #40," and "A New Reality Is Better Than a New Movie" are reprinted by permission of Sterling Lord Literistic, Inc. Copyright by Amiri Baraka. "In the Funk World" and "Monk's World" are reprinted by permission of Sterling Lord Literistic, Inc. Copyright © 1995 by Amiri Baraka.

Louise Bennett: From LOUISE BENNETT: SELECTED POEMS edited by Mervyn Morris. First published in 1982 by Sangster's Book Stores Ltd. (Kingston, Jamaica). Copyright © by the Ministry of Education. "Jamaica Language" from AUNT ROACHY SEH by Louise Bennett, edited by Mervyn Morris. First published in 1993 by Sangster's Book Stores Ltd. (Kingston, Jamaica). Copyright © by the Ministry of Education.

Charles Bernstein: "The Kiwi Bird in the Kiwi Tree" from ROUGH TRADES (Los Angeles: Sun & Moon, 1991), p. 11. Copyright © 1991 by Charles Bernstein. "Autonomy Is Jeopardy" and "Have Pen Will Travel" from REPUBLICS OF REALITY 1975–1995 (Los Angeles: Sun & Moon, 1991), pp. 307 and 359. Copyright © 2000 by Charles Bernstein. "Lives of the Toll Takers (excerpt) from DARK CITY (Los Angeles: Sun & Moon, 1994), pp. 22–26. Copyright © 1994 by Charles Bernstein. "Semblance" from CONTENT'S DREAM: ESSAYS 1975–1984 (Los Angeles: Sun & Moon Press, 1986), pp. 34–39. Reprinted with the permission of the publisher.

John Berryman: "Henry's Understanding" from DELUSIONS, ETC. by John Berryman. Copyright © 1972 by the Estate of John Berryman. Dream Songs # 1, #4, #14, #29, #37, #76, #145, #149, #153, #219, #312 and #384 from THE DREAM SONGS by John Berryman. Copyright © 1969 by John Berryman. Copyright renewed 1997 by Kate Donahue Berryman. Reprinted by permission of Farrar, Straus and Giroux, LLC.

Frank Bidart: "A Coin for Joe, with the Image of a Horse: c. 350–325 BC" and "If I Could Mourn Like a Morning Dove" from DESIRE by Frank Bidart. Copyright © 1997 by Frank Bidart. "Ellen West" from IN THE WESTERN NIGHT: COLLECTED POEMS 1965–1990 by Frank Bidart. Copyright © 1990 by Frank Bidart. Reprinted by permission of Farrar, Straus and Giroux, LLC. Excerpts from "Der Fall Ellen West," tr. by Werner M. Mendel and Joseph Lyons, from EXISTENCE, ed. by Rollo May et al. Reprinted by permission of Jason Aronson, Inc.

Elizabeth Bishop: "The Map," "The Man-Moth," "The Monument," "Roosters," "The Fish," "Over 2000 Illustrations and a Complete Concordance," "At the Fishhouses," "Brazil, January 1, 1502," "The Armadillo," "Sestina," "In the Waiting Room," "Crusoe in England," "One Art," "The End of March," "North Haven," and "Poem" from THE COMPLETE POEMS 1927–1979 by Elizabeth Bishop. Copyright © 1979, 1983 by Alice Helen Methfessel. Reprinted by permission of Farrar, Straus & Giroux, LLC.

Robert Bly: "A Week after Your Death" from EATING THE HONEY OF WORDS by Robert Bly. Copyright © 1999 by Robert Bly. "Johnson's Cabinet Watched by Ants" and "The Great Society" from THE LIGHT AROUND THE BODY by Robert Bly. Copyright © 1967 by Robert Bly. Copyright renewed 1995 by Robert Bly. Reprinted by permission of HarperCollins Publishers, Inc. "My Father's Wedding" and "Kneeling Down to Look into a Culvert" from THE MAN IN THE BLACK COAT TURNS by Robert Bly, copyright © 1981 by Robert Bly. Used by permission of Doubleday, a division of Random House, Inc.

Eavan Boland: "The Pomegranate" from IN A TIME OF VIOLENCE by Eavan Boland. Copyright © 1994 by Eavan Boland. Used by permission of W. W. Norton & Co., Inc. "Anorexic" and "Fond Memory," copyright © 1986 by Eavan Boland. "Night Feed" and "Mise Eire," copyright © 1987 by Eavan Boland. "Fever" and "The Women," from AN ORIGIN LIKE WATER: COLLECTED POEMS 1967–1987 by Eavan Boland. Copyright © 1996 by Eavan Boland. Used by permission of W. W. Norton & Co., Inc.

Kamau Brathwaite: "Wings of a Dove," "Calypso," and "Ogun" from THE ARRIVANTS: A NEW WORLD TRILOGY (1973) by permission of Oxford University Press. "Trane" from BLACK AND BLUES, copyright © 1976, 1994, 1995 by Kamau Brathwaite. "Irae" and "Stone" from MIDDLE PASSAGES, copyright © 1993 by Kamau Brathwaite. Reprinted by permission of New Directions Publishing Corp.

Gwendolyn Brooks: "A Song in the Front Yard," "Sadie and Maud," "Of De Witt Williams on His Way to Lincoln Cemetery," and "The Vacant Lot" from SELECTED POEMS by Gwendolyn Brooks. "The Rites for Cousin Vit," "The Bean Eaters," "We Real Cool," and "The Last Quatrain of the Ballad of Emmett Till" from BLACKS. "Boy Breaking Glass" and "The Blackstone Rangers" from IN THE MECCA. "The Boy Died in My Alley" from TO DISEMBARK. Reprinted by consent of Brooks Permissions.

Anne Carson: "Stanzas, Sexes, Seductions" by Anne Carson first published in *The New Yorker,* Dec. 3, 2001. Reprinted by permission of the Burnes & Clegg Inc. on behalf of the author. From "The Glass Essay" and from "TV Men" from GLASS, IRONY, AND GOD, copyright © 1995 by Anne Carson. Reprinted by permission of New Directions Publishing Corp. "Epitaph Zion" and "Lazarus Standup: Shooting Script," from MEN IN THE OFF HOURS by Anne Carson, copyright © 2000 by Anne Carson. Used by permission of Alfred A. Knopf, a division of Random House, Inc.

Lorna Dee Cervantes: "Cannery Town in August" and "Poema para los Californios Muertos" from EMPLUMADA by Lorna Dee Cervantes, copyright © 1981. Reprinted by permission of the University of Pittsburgh Press. "The Body as Braille" by Lorna Dee Cervantes is reprinted with permission from the publisher of THE AMERICAS REVIEW (Houston: Arte Público Press–University of Houston, 1978). Copyright © 1978 by Revista Chicano-Riqueña. "Refugee Ship" by Lorna Dee Cervantes is reprinted with permission from the publisher of THE AMERICAS REVIEW (Houston: Arte Público Press–University of Houston, 1975). Copyright © 1975 by Revista Chicano-Riqueña.

Marilyn Chin: "How I Got That Name," "Altar," and "Autumn Leaves" from THE PHOENIX GONE, THE TERRACE EMPTY (Minneapolis: Milkweed Editions, 1994). Copyright © 1994 by Marilyn Chin. Reprinted with permission from Milkweed Editions. "Chinese Quatrains (The Woman in Tomb 44)" from RHAPSODY IN PLAIN YELLOW by Marilyn Chin. Copyright © 2002 by Marilyn Chin. Used by permission of W. W. Norton & Co., Inc.

Amy Clampitt: From THE COLLECTED POEMS OF AMY CLAMPITT by Amy Clampitt, copyright © 1997 by the Estate of Amy Clampitt. Used by permission of Alfred A. Knopf, a division of Random House, Inc.

Lucille Clifton: "still" and "cutting greens" from GOOD WOMAN: POEMS AND A MEMOIR 1969–1980 by Lucille Clifton. Copyright © 1987 by Lucille Clifton. "i am accused of tending to the past," "at the cemetery, walnut grove plantation, south carolina, 1989," "poem to my uterus," and "to my last period" from QUILTING: POEMS 1987–1990 by Lucille Clifton. Copyright © 1991 by Lucille Clifton. "the mississippi river empties into the gulf" from THE TERRIBLE STORIES by Lucille Clifton. Copyright © 1996 by Lucille Clifton. Reprinted with the permission of BOA EDITIONS, LTD. "homage to my hips" first appeared in TWO-HEADED WOMAN by Lucille Clifton, published by The University of Massachusetts Press, 1980. Now appears in GOOD WOMAN: POEMS AND A MEMOIR 1969–1980 by Lucille Clifton, published by BOA Editions Ltd. Copyright © 1980, 1987 by Lucille Clifton. Reprinted by permission of Curtis Brown, Ltd. "cain" and "leda 3" from THE BOOK OF LIGHT. Copyright © 1993 by Lucille Clifton. Reprinted with the permission of Copper Canyon Press, P.O. Box 271, Port Townsend, WA 98363–0271.

Henri Cole: "Harvard Classics" and "Buddha and the Seven Tiger Cubs" from THE LOOK OF THINGS by Henri Cole, copyright © 1995 by Henri Cole. Used by permission of Alfred A. Knopf, a division of Random House, Inc. "White Spine," "Folly," and "Childlessness" from THE VISIBLE

Thomas Kinsella: From COLLECTED POEMS: 1956–2001 by Thomas Kinsella (2001). Reprinted by permission of the publisher, Carcanet Press Ltd.

Kenneth Koch: "Geography" and "Variations on a Theme by William Carlos Williams" from THANK YOU by Kenneth Koch (1962). "2. The Stones of Time" from DAYS AND NIGHTS by Kenneth Koch (1982). "To the Roman Forum" from NEW ADDRESSES by Kenneth Koch (2000). "Mending Sump" by Kenneth Koch from THE NEW AMERICAN POETRY, ed. Donald Allen (1960). "One Train May Hide Another" from ONE TRAIN POEMS by Kenneth Koch (1994). Reprinted by permission of Karen Koch, Literary Estate Executrix.

Yusef Komunyakaa:: "Starlight Scope Myopia," "Tu Do Street," "Facing It," and "February in Sydney" from NEON by Yusef Komunyakaa. Copyright © 1993 by Yusel Komunyakaa. "My Father's Love Letters" from MAGIC CITY by Yusef Komunyakaa. Copyright © 1992 by Yusef Komunyakaa. Reprinted by permission of Wesleyan University Press.

Maxine Kumin: From "Letters" from CONNECTING THE DOTS by Maxine Kumin. Copyright © 1996 by Maxine Kumin. "Our Ground Time Here Will Be Brief," copyright © 1982 by Maxine Kumin. "In the Absence of Bliss," copyright © 1985 by Maxine Kumin. "How It Is," copyright © 1978 by Maxine Kumin. "The Bangkok Gong" from SELECTED POEMS 1960–1990 by Maxine Kumin. Copyright © 1996 by Maxine Kumin. Used by permission of W. W. Norton & Co., Inc.

Philip Larkin: "Reasons for Attendance" and "Church Going" from THE LESS DECEIVED by Philip Larkin are reprinted by permission of The Marvell Press, England and Australia. "Water," "An Arundel Tomb," "The Whitsun Weddings," "Faith Healing," "MCMXIV," "Talking in Bed," "Here," "Sunny Prestatyn," "Solar," "High Windows," "Sad Steps," "Homage to a Government," "The Explosion," "Forget What Did," "This Be The Verse," "Going, Going," and "Aubade" from COLLECTED POEMS by Philip Larkin. Copyright © 1988,1989 by the Estate of Philip Larkin. Reprinted by permission of Farrar, Straus and Giroux, LLC and Faber and Faber Ltd. "The Pleasure Principle" and from "Introduction" to "All What Jazz" from REQUIRED WRITING by Philip Larkin. Copyright © 1983 by Philip Larkin. Reprinted by permission of Farrar, Straus and Giroux, LLC. and Faber and Faber Ltd.

Li-Young Lee: "The Gift," "Persimmons," "Eating Alone," and "Eating Together" from ROSE by Li-Young Lee. Copyright © 1986 by Li-Young Lee. "Pillow" from BOOK OF MY NIGHTS by Li-Young Lee. Copyright © 2001 by Li-Young Lee. Reprinted by permission of BOA Editions, Ltd.

Denise Levertov: "Caedmon" from BREATHING THE WATER, copyright © 1987 by Denise Levertov. "Pleasures" and "The Dog of Art" from COLLECTED EARLIER POEMS 1940–1960, copyright © 1960, 1979 by Denise Levertov. "Some Notes on Organic Form" from NEW AND SELECTED ESSAYS, copyright © 1973 by Denise Levertov. "Olga Poems" i, iv, vi, "September 1961," "Song for Ishtar," and "The Ache of Marriage" from POEMS 1960–1967, copyright © 1966 by Denise Levertov. "A Time Past" from THE FREEING OF THE DUST, copyright © 1975 by Denise Levertov. "Aware," "Celebration," and "Scraps of Moon" from THIS GREAT UNKNOWING: LAST POEMS, copyright © 1998 by The Denise Levertov Literary Trust, Paul A. Lacey and Valerie Trueblood Rapport, Co-Trustees. Reprinted by permission of New Directions Publishing Corp.

Philip Levine: "You Can Have It" from NEW SELECTED POEMS by Philip Levine, copyright © 1991 by Philip Levine. Used by permission of Alfred A. Knopf, a division of Random House, Inc. "(Drum) Leo's Tool & Die, 1950" from THE MERCY: POEMS BY PHILIP LEVINE, copyright © 1999 by Philip Levine. Used by permission of Alfred A. Knopf, a division of Random House, Inc. "They Feed They Lion" and "Belle Isle, 1949" from THEY FEED THEY LION AND THE NAMES OF THE LOST by Philip Levine, copyright © 1968, 1969, 1970, 1971, 1972 by Philip Levine. Copyright © 1976 by Philip Levine. Used by permission of Alfred A. Knopf, a division of Random House, Inc.

Michael Longley: "Casualty," "Wounds," "Detour," and "Ceasefire" from SELECTED POEMS of Michael Longley. "The Comber," "Death of a Horse," and "The Beech Tree" from THE WEATHER IN JAPAN by Michael Longley. Reprinted by permission of the publishers, Wake Forest University Press and Jonathan Cape c/o The Random House Group Ltd.

Audre Lorde: "A Question of Climate," copyright © 1986 by Audre Lorde. "Now that I Am Forever with Child," "Love Poem," copyright © 1975 by Audre Lorde. "Hanging Fire," copyright © 1978 by

Audre Lorde. "From the House of Yemanjá," "Coal," copyright © 1968, 1970, 1973 by Audre Lorde from COLLECTED POEMS by Audre Lorde. Copyright © 1997 by the Estate of Audre Lorde. Used by permission of W. W. Norton & Co., Inc.

Robert Lowell: "The Quaker Graveyard in Nantucket" and "After the Surprising Conversions" from LORD WEARY'S CASTLE, copyright © 1946 and renewed 1974 by Robert Lowell, reprinted by permission of Harcourt, Inc. "Epilogue" from DAY BY DAY by Robert Lowell. Copyright © 1977 by Robert Lowell. "Commander Lowell," "Dolphin," "For the Union Dead," "Grandparents," "Memories of West Street and Lepke," "Reading Myself," "Skunk Hour," "To Speak of Woe That Is In Marriage," "Waking Early Sunday Morning," and "Waking in the Blue" from SELECTED POEMS by Robert Lowell. Copyright © 1976 by Robert Lowell. Reprinted by permission of Farrar, Straus and Giroux, LLC.

Derek Mahon: "Afterlives," "The Last of the Fire Kings," "A Disused Shed in Co. Wexford," "The Snow Party," "An Bonnán Buí" and "A Swim in Co. Wicklow" from COLLECTED POEMS (1999) by Derek Mahon. Reprinted by kind permission of the author and The Gallery Press, Loughcrew, Oldcastle, County Meath, Ireland.

Dionisio D. Martínez: "Moto Perpetuo," "Hysteria," "Temporary Losses" from BAD ALCHEMY by Dionisio D. Martínez. Copyright © 1995 by Dioniosio D. Martínez. "Bees" from CLIMBING BACK by Dionisio D. Martínez. Copyright © 2001 by Dionisio D. Martínez. Used by permission of W. W. Norton & Co., Inc.

Medbh McGuckian: "Slips," "The Dream-Language of Fergus," "The War Ending," and "Captain Lavender" from SELECTED POEMS 1978–1994 by Medbh McGuckian. "Mantilla" from SHELMALIER by Medbh McGuckian. Reprinted by permission of Wake Forest University Press.

William Meredith: "Last Things," "Parents," and "Dying Away" are reprinted from EFFORT AT SPEECH: NEW AND SELECTED POEMS by William Meredith, published by TriQuarterly Books / Northwestern University Press in 1997. Copyright © 1997 by William Meredith. All rights reserved; used by permission of Northwestern University Press and the author.

James Merrill: From "The Book of Ephraim" from THE CHANGING LIGHT AT SANDOVER by James Merrill, copyright © 1980, 1982 by James Merrill. Used by permission of Alfred A. Knopf, a division of Random House, Inc. "Lost in Translation," "The Broken Home," and "The Victor Dog" from SELECTED POEMS 1946–1985 by James Merrill, copyright © 1992 by James Merrill. Used by permission of Alfred A. Knopf, a division of Random House, Inc. "Days of 1964," "b o d y," "Self-Portrait in Tyvek™ Windbreaker," and "An Upward Look" from COLLECTED POEMS by James Merrill, ed. by J.D. McClatchy and Stephen Yenser, copyright © 2001 by the Literary Estate of James Merrill at Washington University. Used by permission of Alfred A. Knopf, a division of Random House, Inc.

W. S. Merwin: "The Drunk in the Furnace" from THE FIRST FOUR BOOKS OF POEMS. Copyright © 1960, 2000 by W. S. Merwin. Reprinted with the permission of Copper Canyon Press, P.O. Box 271, Port Townsend, WA 98368–0271. "The Hydra," "Some Last Questions," "For the Anniversary of My Death," "The Asians Dying," and "For a Coming Extinction" from THE LICE by W. S. Merwin, copyright © 1967 by W. S. Merwin. Reprinted with the permission of The Wylie Agency. "A Given Day" from THE VIXEN by W. S. Merwin, copyright © 1995 by W. S. Merwin. Used by permission of Alfred A. Knopf, a division of Random House, Inc.

Thylias Moss: "Crystals" and "The Rapture of Dry Ice Burning off Skin as the Moment of the Soul's Apotheosis" from RAINBOW REMNANTS IN A ROCK BOTTOM GHETTO SKY by Thylias Moss. Copyright © 1991 by Thylias Moss. "Interpretation of a Poem by Frost" from LAST CHANCE FOR THE TARZAN HOLLER by Thylias Moss. Copyright © 1998 by Thylias Moss. Reprinted by permission of Persea Books, Inc. (New York). "Lunchcounter Freedom" from SMALL CONGREGATIONS: NEW AND SELECTED POEMS by Thylias Moss. Copyright © 1983, 1990, 1991, 1993 by Thylias Moss. Reprinted by permission of HarperCollins Publishers Inc.

Paul Muldoon: "Aftermath," "Anseo," "The Briefcase," "Cauliflowers," from "7, Middagh Street" ("Wystan" and "Salvador"), "Hedgehog," "Lunch with Pancho Villa," "Meeting the British," "Quoof," "The Sonogram," and "Why Brownlee Left" from POEMS 1968–1998 by Paul Muldoon. Copyright © 2001 by Paul Muldoon. "The Grand Conversation" from MOY SAND AND GRAVEL by Paul

Muldoon. Copyright © 2002 by Paul Muldoon. First published in *The New Yorker*. Reprinted by permission of Farrar, Straus and Giroux, LLC.

Les Murray: From "The Buladelah-Taree Holiday Song Cycle," "Corniche," "Cotton Flannelette," "The Milk Lorry," "Mollusc," "On Removing Spiderweb," and "The Powerline Incarnation" from LEARNING HUMAN by Les Murray. Copyright © 1998 by Les Murray. Reprinted by permission of Farrar, Straus & Giroux, LLC.

Howard Nemerov: From THE COLLECTED POEMS OF HOWARD NEMEROV, reprinted by permission of Margaret Nemerov.

Grace Nichols: "Wherever I Hang" from LAZY THOUGHTS OF A LAZY WOMAN by Grace Nichols. "Invitation" and "Tropical Death" from THE FAT BLACK WOMAN'S POEMS by Grace Nichols. Reprinted by permission of Time Warner Books UK. "Epilogue" from I IS A LONG MEMORIED WOMAN (Karnak House 1983, 2000). Used with permission of the publisher.

Frank O'Hara: From MEDITATIONS IN AN EMERGENCY by Frank O'Hara. Copyright © 1957 by Frank O'Hara. Used by permission of Grove / Atlantic, Inc. "The Day Lady Died" and "A Step Away from Them" from LUNCH POEMS by Frank O'Hara, copyright © 1964 by Frank O'Hara. Reprinted by permission of City Lights Books. "A True Account of Talking to the Sun at Fire Island," "Rhapsody," "Why I am Not a Painter," "Les Luths," and "Personism: A Manisfesto" from COLLECTED POEMS by Frank O'Hara, copyright © 1971 by Maureen Granville-Smith, Administratrix of the Estate of Frank O'Hara. Used by permission of Alfred A. Knopf, a division of Random House, Inc.

Christopher Okigbo: From "Heavensgate" and "Come Thunder" from LABYRINTHS by Christopher Okigbo (New York: African Publishing Corporation 1971). Copyright © 1971 Legal Personal Representatives of Christopher Okigbo. Reproduced with the permission of the publisher, Holmes & Meier.

Okot p'Bitek: From SONG OF LAWINO by Okot p'Bitek. Reprinted by permission of East African Educational Publishers.

Sharon Olds: "The Pope's Penis" and "The Moment the Two Worlds Meet" from THE GOLD CELL by Sharon Olds, copyright © 1987 by Sharon Olds. Used by permission of Alfred A. Knopf, a division of Random House, Inc. "Photograph of the Girl" from THE DEAD AND THE LIVING by Sharon Olds, copyright © 1987 by Sharon Olds. Used by permission of Alfred A. Knopf, a division of Random House, Inc. "The Exact Moment of His Death" and "My Father Speaks to Me from the Dead" from THE FATHER by Sharon Olds, copyright © 1992 by Sharon Olds. Used by permission of Alfred A. Knopf, a division of Random House, Inc. "Once" from BLOOD, TIN, STRAW by Sharon Olds, copyright © 1999 by Sharon Olds. Used by permission of Alfred A. Knopf, a division of Random House, Inc.

Mary Oliver: "Hawk" from NEW AND SELECTED POEMS by Mary Oliver. Copyright © 1992 by Mary Oliver. Reprinted by permission of Beacon Press, Boston. "The Black Snake" from TWELVE MOONS by Mary Oliver. Copyright © 1972, 1973, 1974, 1976, 1977, 1978, 1979 by Mary Oliver. "August" from AMERICAN PRIMITIVE by Mary Oliver. Copyright © 1982 by Mary Oliver; first appeared in COUNTRY JOURNAL. By permission of Little, Brown and Company, (Inc.).

Charles Olson: From THE MAXIMUS POEMS by Charles Olson, ed. by George F. Butterick. Copyright © 1983 The Regents of the University of California. "Pacific Lament" and "The Thing Was Moving" from COLLECTED POEMS OF CHARLES OLSON, ed. George F. Butterick. Copyright © 1987 Estate of Charles Olson, copyright © 1987 University of Connecticut. Reprinted by permission of the Regents of the University of California and the University of California Press. "Projective Verse" from SELECTED WRITINGS OF CHARLES OLSON, copyright © 1951, 1966 by Charles Olson. Reprinted by permission of New Directions Publishing Corp.

Michael Ondaatje: "Driving South with Dominic in the Southern Province We See Hints of the Circus" and "Buried" (1) and (2) from HANDWRITING by Michael Ondaatje, copyright © 1998 by Michael Ondaatje. Used by permission of Alfred A. Knopf, a division of Random House, Inc., and Ellen Levine Literary Agency, Inc. "Biography" from THERE'S A TRICK WITH A KNIFE I'M LEARNING TO DO by Michael Ondaatje. Copyright © 1979 by Michael Ondaatje. "Letters and

Other Worlds" from THE CINNAMON PEELER by Michael Ondaatje. Copyright © 1984 by Michael Ondaatje. "(Innertube)" from SECULAR LOVE by Michael Ondaatje. Copyright © 1987 by Michael Ondaatje. Reprinted by permission of Ellen Levine Literary Agency, Inc.

P. K. Page: "The Stenographers," "Photos of a Saltmine" and "Deaf-Mute in the Pear Tree" are reprinted by permission of P. K. Page.

Michael Palmer: From THE LION BRIDGE, copyright © 1998 by Michael Palmer. Reprinted by permission of New Directions Publishing Corp.

Marge Piercy: "Learning Experience" and "The Cyclist" from HARD LOVING by Marge Piercy. Copyright © 1969 by Marge Piercy, reprinted by permission of Wesleyan University Press. "The Cast Off" from THE MOON IS ALWAYS FEMALE by Marge Piercy, copyright © 1980 by Marge Piercy. Used by permission of Alfred A. Knopf, a division of Random House, Inc. "Moonburn" from WHAT ARE BIG GIRLS MADE OF? by Marge Piercy, copyright © 1997 by Middlemarsh, Inc. Used by permission of Alfred A. Knopf, a division of Random House, Inc.

Robert Pinsky: "The Uncreation" from THE WANT BONE by Robert Pinsky. Copyright © 1991 by Robert Pinsky. Reprinted by permission of HarperCollins Publishers, Inc. "ABC" and "The Haunted Ruin" from JERSEY RAIN by Robert Pinsky. Copyright © 2000 by Robert Pinsky. "The Figured Wheel" and "The Questions" from THE FIGURED WHEEL: NEW AND COLLECTED POEMS 1966–1996 by Robert Pinsky. Copyright © 1996 by Robert Pinsky. Reprinted by permission of Farrar, Straus & Giroux, LLC.

Sylvia Plath: "The Disquieting Muses" and "The Colossus" from THE COLOSSUS AND OTHER POEMS by Sylvia Plath, copyright © 1962 by Sylvia Plath. Used by permission of Alfred A. Knopf, a division of Random House, Inc., and Faber and Faber Ltd. All other poems are from THE COLLECTED POEMS OF SYLVIA PLATH, edited by Ted Hughes. Copyright © 1960, 1965, 1971, 1981 by the Estate of Sylvia Plath. Editorial material copyright © 1981 by Ted Hughes. Reprinted by permission of HarperCollins Publishers, Inc.

Craig Raine: "The Onion Memory" and "A Martian Sends a Postcard Home" from COLLECTED POEMS by Craig Raine (Picador 2000). Reprinted by permission of David Godwin Associates.

A. K. Ramanujan: "Self-Portrait, "Elements of Composition," "Alien," "Drafts," "Extended Family," "Chicago Zen," and "Foundlings in the Yukon" from THE COLLECTED POEMS of A. K. Ramanujan. Reproduced by permission of Oxford University Press India, New Delhi. From "Where Mirrors Are Windows: Toward an Anthology of Reflections" by A. K. Ramanujan from HISTORY OF RELIGION, 28:3, pp. 187–216. Copyright © 1988 by The University of Chicago. All rights reserved.

Adrienne Rich: "Grandmothers," "Diving into the Wreck," "Power," "Twenty-One Love Poems," from THE FACT OF A DOORFRAME: POEMS SELECTED AND NEW, 1950–1984 by Adrienne Rich. Copyright © 1984 by Adrienne Rich. Copyright © 1975, 1978 by W. W. Norton & Company, Inc. Copyright © 1981 by Adrienne Rich. "The Loser," copyright © 1993, 1967, 1963 by Adrienne Rich. "Aunt Jennifer's Tigers," copyright © 1993, 1951 by Adrienne Rich. "Face to Face," copyright © 1993 by Adrienne Rich. Copyright © 1966 by W. W. Norton & Co., Inc. "Orion," copyright © 1993 by Adrienne Rich. Copyright © 1969 by W. W. Norton & Co., Inc. "Planetarium," copyright © 1993 by Adrienne Rich. Copyright © 1971 by W. W. Norton & Co., Inc. "A Valediction Forbidding Mourning," copyright © 1993 by Adrienne Rich. Copyright © 1971 by W. W. Norton & Co, Inc. "Snapshots of a Daughter-in-Law," copyright © 1993, 1967, 1963 by Adrienne Rich. From COLLECTED EARLY POEMS: 1950–1979 by Adrienne Rich. "Seven Skins" from MIDNIGHT SALVAGE: POEMS 1995–1998 by Adrienne Rich, copyright © 1999 by Adrienne Rich. "Fox" from FOX by Adrienne Rich. Copyright © 2001 by Adrienne Rich. "When We Dead Awaken: Writing as Re-Vision" from ARTS OF THE POSSIBLE: ESSAYS AND CONVERSATIONS by Adrienne Rich. Copyright © 2001 by Adrienne Rich. Used by permission of the author and W. W. Norton & Co., Inc.

Alberto Ríos: "Mi Abuelo" from WHISPERING TO FOOL THE WIND by Alberto Ríos is reprinted by permission of The Sheep Meadow Press. "Madre Sofía" and "A Man Then Suddenly Stops Moving," copyright © 1985 by Alberto Ríos. Reprinted by permission of the author. "The Death of Anselmo Luna" and "Anselmo's Moment with God" from TEODORO LUNA'S TWO KISSES by Alberto Ríos. Copyright © 1990 by Alberto Ríos. Used by permission of W. W. Norton & Co., Inc.

Muriel Rukeyser: "Alloy," copyright © 1938 by Muriel Rukeyser. Copyright © 1994 by Jan Heller Levi and William L. Rukeyser. "Night Feeding," copyright 1951 and renewed © 1979 by Muriel Rukeyser. "Poem," copyright © 1968 by Muriel Rukeyser. Copyright © 1994 by Jan Heller Levi and William L. Rukeyser. "The Poem as Mask," copyright © 1968 by Muriel Rukeyser. Copyright © 1994 by Jan Heller Levi and William L. Rukeyser. "The Conjugation of the Paramecium" and "Absalom," from A MURIEL RUKEYSER READER by Jan Heller Levi. Copyright © 1994 by Jan Heller Levi and William L. Rukeyser. Used by permission of W. W. Norton & Co., Inc. "Boy with His Hair Cut Short" from *U.S. 1,* copyright © 1938 by Muriel Rukeyser. Reprinted by permission of International Creative Management, Inc.

Delmore Schwartz: From SELECTED POEMS: SUMMER KNOWLEDGE, copyright © 1959 by Delmore Schwartz. Reprinted by permission of New Directions Publishing Corp.

Anne Sexton: "The Room of My Life" from THE AWFUL ROWING TOWARD GOD by Anne Sexton. Copyright © 1975 by Anne Sexton. "Dreams" from THE DEATH NOTEBOOKS by Anne Sexton. Copyright © 1974 by Anne Sexton. "How We Danced" from THE BOOK OF FOLLY by Anne Sexton. Copyright © 1972 by Anne Sexton. "The Truth the Dead Know," "All My Pretty Ones," and "The Starry Night" from ALL MY PRETTY ONES by Anne Sexton. Copyright © 1962 by Anne Sexton. Copyright © renewed 1990 by Linda G. Sexton. "Her Kind" from TO BEDLAM AND PARTWAY BACK by Anne Sexton. Copyright © 1960 by Anne Sexton. Copyright © renewed 1988 by Linda G. Sexton. Reprinted by permission of Houghton Mifflin Co. All rights reserved.

Karl Shapiro: "The First Time" from NEW AND SELECTED POEMS, copyright © 1987 Karl Shapiro. "The Fly," "Manhole Covers," and "The Piano Tuner's Wife" from COLLECTED POEMS 1948–1978, copyright © by Karl Shapiro. Reprinted by permission of Wieser & Wieser Inc.

Leslie Marmon Silko: From STORYTELLER by Leslie Marmon Silko, published by Seaver Books, New York, NY. Copyright © 1981 by Leslie Marmon Silko.

Charles Simic: Poems from CHARLES SIMIC: SELECTED EARLY POEMS, copyright © 1999 by Charles Simic. Reprinted by permission of George Braziller, Inc. "Head of a Doll" from JACKSTRAWS, copyright © 1999 by Charles Simic, reprinted by permission of Harcourt, Inc. "Cameo Appearance" from WALKING THE BLACK CAT, copyright © 1996 by Charles Simic, reprinted by permission of Harcourt, Inc.

Louis Simpson: "The Battle" from GOOD NEWS OF DEATH, copyright © 1955; "My Father in the Night Commanding No" from AT THE END OF THE OPEN ROAD, copyright © 1963; "American Poetry" and "White Oxen" from IN THE ROOM WE SHARE; copyright © 1990. Reprinted by permission of Louis Simpson.

Dave Smith: "Leafless Trees, Chickahominy Swamp," "Fiddlers," "Wreck in the Woods," "Blowfish and Mudtoad," and "Black Silhouettes of Shrimpers" from THE WICK OF MEMORY: NEW AND SELECTED POEMS, 1974–2000 by Dave Smith. Copyright © 2000 by Dave Smith. Reprinted by permission of Louisiana State University Press.

W. D. Snodgrass: "A Flat One" from SELECTED POEMS 1957–1987 by W. D. Snodgrass, by permission of Soho Press, Inc., New York, NY. All other poems from HEART'S NEEDLE by W. D. Snodgrass, copyright © 1959 by William Snodgrass. Used by permission of Alfred A. Knopf, a division of Random House, Inc.

Gary Snyder: "The Wild Edge" from REGARDING WAVE, copyright © 1970 by Gary Snyder. "Burning the Small Dead" from THE BACK COUNTRY, copyright © 1970 by Gary Snyder. "The Bath" from TURTLE ISLAND, copyright © 1974 by Gary Snyder. Reprinted by permission of New Directions Publishing Corp. "Axe Handles" from AXE HANDLES by Gary Snyder. Copyright © 1983 by Gary Snyder. "Above Pate Valley," "Milton by Firelight," and "Riprap" from RIPRAP AND COLD MOUNTAIN POEMS by Gary Snyder. Copyright © 1990 by Gary Snyder. Reprinted by permission of North Point Press, a division of Farrar, Straus and Giroux, LLC.

Cathy Song: "Beauty and Sadness" and "Lost Sister" from PICTURE BRIDE by Cathy Song. Copyright © 1983 by Yale University Press. Reprinted by permission of the publishers, Yale University Press. "Sunworshippers" from SCHOOL FIGURES by Cathy Song, copyright © 1994. "Ghost" from

THE LAND OF BLISS by Cathy Song, copyright © 2001. Reprinted by permission of the University of Pittsburgh Press.

Gary Soto: "Practicing Eulogies" from A NATURAL MAN by Gary Soto, copyright © 1999. "Oranges" from NEW AND SELECTED POEMS by Gary Soto, copyright © 1995. Reprinted by permission of Chronicle Books, LLC, San Francisco. "After Tonight," copyright © 1977 by Gary Soto. "The Drought" and "Graciela," copyright © 1978 by Gary Soto. "How Things Work," copyright © 1985 by Gary Soto. Used by permission of the author.

Wole Soyinka: "Around Us, Dawning," "Death in the Dawn," and "Massacre, October '66" from IDANRE by Wole Soyinka. Copyright © 1967 by Wole Soyinka. Reprinted by permission of Hill and Wang, a division of Farrar, Straus and Giroux, LLC. and Melanie Jackson Agency, LLC. "Dragonfly at My Windowpane" from MANDELA'S EARTH AND OTHER POEMS by Wole Soyinka, copyright © 1988 by Wole Soyinka. Used by permission of Random House, Inc. "Telephone Conversation" copyright © 1962, 1990 by Wole Soyinka. Reprinted by permission of Melanie Jackson Agency, LLC.

William Stafford: "At the Bomb Testing Site" and "Traveling through the Dark" from THE WAY IT IS: NEW AND SELECTED POEMS by William Stafford with the permission of Graywolf Press, St. Paul, MN. Copyright © 1960, 1962, 1998 by the Estate of William Stafford. "For the Grave of Daniel Boone," copyright © 1966 by William Stafford, from THE RESCUED YEAR (Harper and Row). Reprinted by permission of The Estate of William Stafford.

Mark Strand: From SELECTED POEMS by Mark Strand, copyright © 1979, 1980 by Mark Strand. Used by permission of Alfred A. Knopf, a division of Random House, Inc.

May Swenson: "Staring at the Sea on the Day of the Death of Another" and "Last Day" from NATURE: POEMS OLD AND NEW by May Swenson. Copyright © 1994 by The Literary Estate of May Swenson. "A Couple" and "In Love Made Visible" from THE LOVE POEMS OF MAY SWENSON. Copyright © 1991 by The Literary Estate of May Swenson. Reprinted by permission of Houghton Mifflin Co. All rights reserved. "Unconscious Came a Beauty" from NEW AND SELECTED THINGS TAKING PLACE: POEMS by May Swenson. "The Centaur" and "Question" from THE COMPLETE POEMS TO SOLVE by May Swenson. "Strawberrying" from IN OTHER WORDS by May Swenson. Reprinted by permission of the May Swenson Literary Estate.

James Tate: "Poem" from DISTANCE FROM LOVED ONES by James Tate. Copyright © 1990 by James Tate, reprinted by permission of Wesleyan University Press. "Stray Animals," "The Blue Booby," and "The Wheelchair Butterfly" from THE OBLIVION HA-HA by James Tate and "The Motorcyclists" by James Tate. Copyright © by James Tate. Reprinted by permission of the author. "The Lost Pilot" from THE LOST PILOT by James Tate. Copyright © 1978 by James Tate. Reprinted by permission of HarperCollins Publishers Inc. "Where Babies Come From" from SHROUD OF THE GNOME by James Tate. Copyright © 1997 by James Tate. Reprinted by permission of HarperCollins Publishers Inc.

Dylan Thomas: From THE POEMS OF DYLAN THOMAS, copyright © 1939 by New Directions Publishing Corp. Reprinted by permission of New Directions Publishing Corp. and David Higham Associates. Published in Great Britain in COLLECTED POEMS of Dylan Thomas. "Poetic Manifesto" from EARLY PROSE WRITINGS by Dylan Thomas. Reprinted by permission of David Higham Associates.

Charles Tomlinson: From SELECTED POEMS of Charles Tomlinson (1997). Reprinted by permission of the publisher, Carcanet Press, Ltd.

David Wagoner: "The Man of the House" and "Elegy for a Forest Clear-Cut by the Weyerhaeuser Company" from COLLECTED POEMS 1956–1976 by David Wagoner. Copyright © 1974 by David Wagoner. Reprinted by permission of the author. "A Young Girl with a Pitcher Full of Water" from FIRST LIGHT by David Wagoner. Copyright © 1983 by David Wagoner. By permission of Little, Brown and Company, (Inc.). "By a Waterfall" from TRAVELING LIGHT: COLLECTED AND NEW POEMS. Copyright © 1999 by David Wagoner. Used with permission of the poet and the University of Illinois Press.

Derek Walcott: "A Far Cry from Africa," "The Fortunate Traveller," "Laventille," "The Sea Is History," "The Season of Phantasmal Peace," "The Schooner *Flight*" from COLLECTED POEMS

1948–1984 by Derek Walcott. Copyright © 1986 by Derek Walcott. From OMEROS by Derek Walcott. Copyright © 1990 by Derek Walcott. "The Antilles" from WHAT THE TWILIGHT SAYS: ESSAYS by Derek Walcott. Copyright © 1999 by Derek Walcott. Reprinted by permission of Farrar, Straus & Giroux, LLC.

Richard Wilbur: "A Barred Owl" from MAYFLIES: NEW POEMS AND TRANSLATIONS, copyright © 2000 by Richard Wilbur, reprinted by permission of Harcourt, Inc. "Love Calls Us to the Things of This World" from THINGS OF THIS WORLD, copyright © 1956 and renewed 1984 by Richard Wilbur, Reprinted by permission of Harcourt, Inc. "Boy at the Window" from THINGS OF THIS WORLD, copyright 1952 and renewed 1980 by Richard Wilbur, reprinted by permission of Harcourt, Inc. "Playboy" from WALKING TO SLEEP: NEW POEMS AND TRANSLATIONS, copyright © 1968 and renewed 1996 by Richard Wilbur, reprinted by permission of Harcourt, Inc. "The Writer" from THE MIND-READER, copyright © 1971 by Richard Wilbur, reprinted by permission of Harcourt, Inc. "A Finished Man" from NEW AND COLLECTED POEMS, copyright © 1985 by Richard Wilbur, reprinted by permission of Harcourt, Inc. "The Death of a Toad" and "Ceremony" from CEREMONY AND OTHER POEMS, copyright 1950 and renewed 1978 by Richard Wilbur, reprinted by permission of Harcourt, Inc.

Charles Wright: "Blackwater Mountain," "Stone Canyon Nocturne," and "Clear Night" from COUNTRY MUSIC by Charles Wright. Copyright © 1982 by Charles Wright, reprinted by permission of Wesleyan University Press. "Apologia Pro Vita Sua" I and "Stray Paragraphs in February, Year of the Rat" from NEGATIVE BLUE: SELECTED LATER POEMS by Charles Wright. "Homage to Paul Cézanne" and "Laguna Blues" from THE WORLD OF TEN THOUSAND THINGS: POEMS 1980–1990 by Charles Wright. Copyright © 1990 by Charles Wright. Reprinted by permission of Farrar, Straus and Giroux, LLC.

James Wright: Poems from ABOVE THE RIVER: THE COMPLETE POEMS by James Wright, copyright © 1990 by Anne Wright. Reprinted by permission of Wesleyan University Press.

Judith Wright: From COLLECTED POEMS, 1942–1985 of Judith Wright (1994). Reprinted by permission of Carcanet Press Ltd.

Every effort has been made to contact the copyright holders of each selection. Rights holders of any selection not credited should contact W. W. Norton & Co., 500 Fifth Avenue, New York, NY 10110, for a correction to be made in the next reprinting of our work.

Index

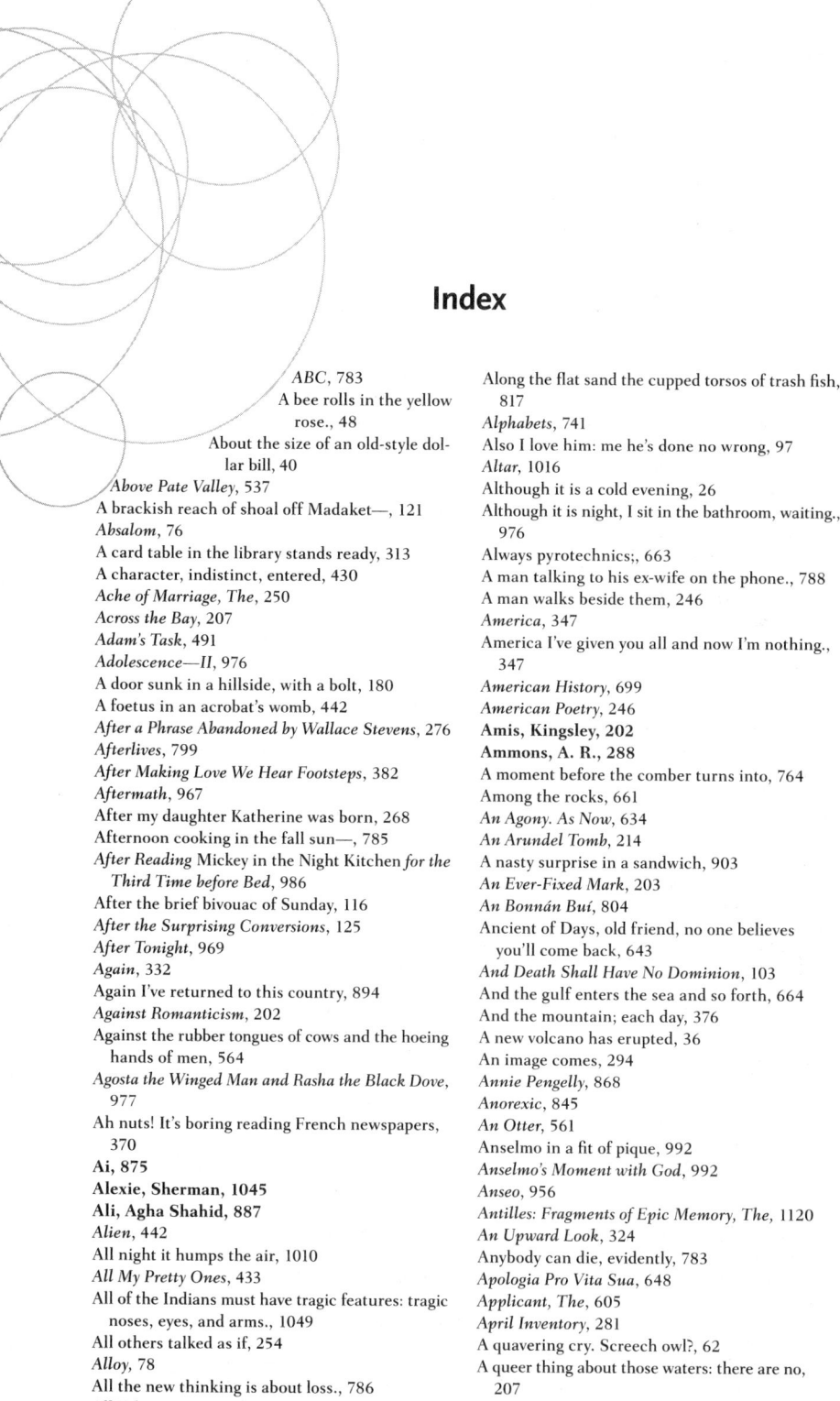

The Norton Anthology of Modern and Contemporary Poetry

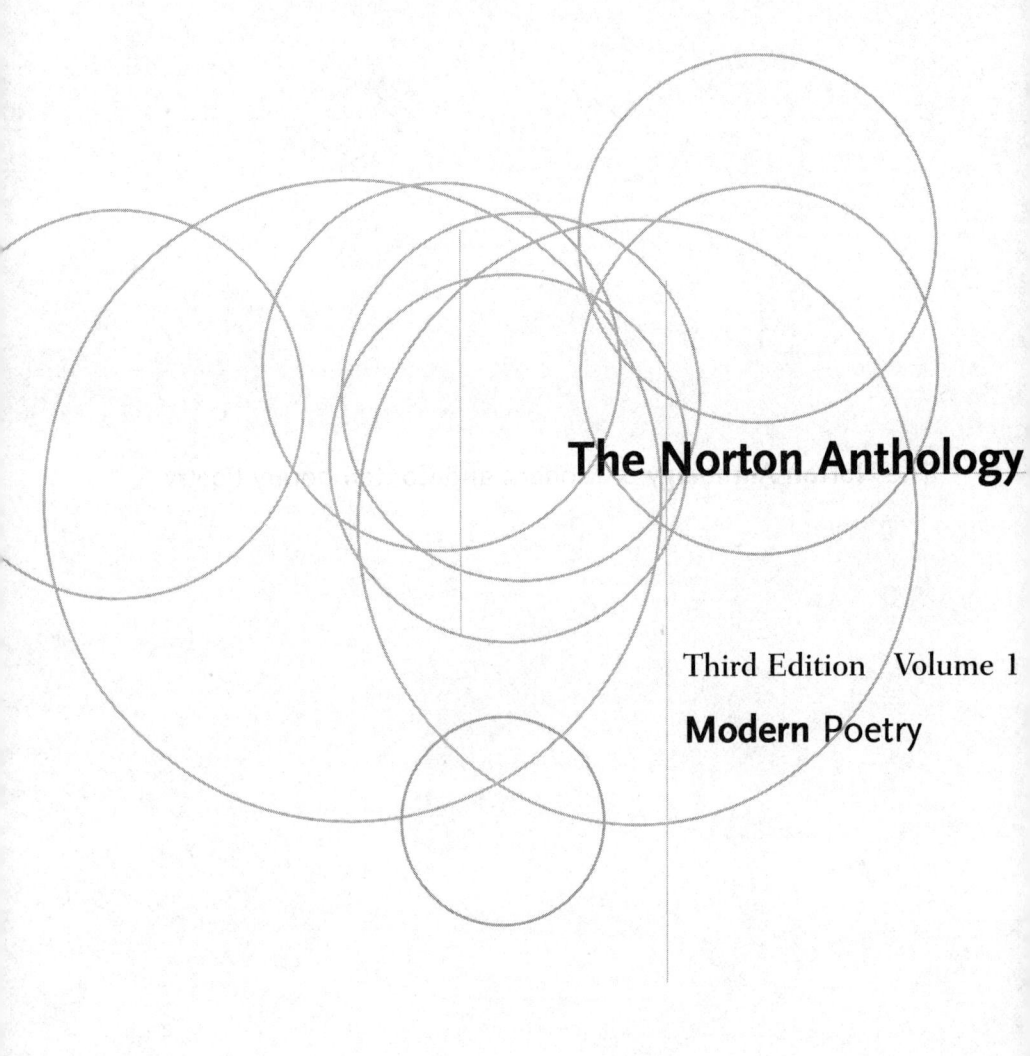

The Norton Anthology

Third Edition Volume 1

Modern Poetry

of Modern and Contemporary Poetry

edited by

Jahan Ramazani

UNIVERSITY OF VIRGINIA

Richard Ellmann

LATE GOLDSMITHS' PROFESSOR EMERITUS,

OXFORD UNIVERSITY

Robert O'Clair

LATE OF MANHATTANVILLE COLLEGE

W · W · **Norton** & Company · New York · London

Previous editions published as THE NORTON ANTHOLOGY OF MODERN POETRY

Printed in the United States of America

Editor: Julia Reidhead
Developmental Editor: Kurt Wildermuth
Production Manager: Diane O'Connor
Manuscript Editor: Kate Lovelady
Project Editors: Lory Frenkel, Sarah Chamberlin
Editorial Assistants: Brian Baker, Carey Schwaber
Permissions Manager and Associate: Nancy Rodwan, Margaret Gorenstein
Managing Editor: Marian Johnson
Book Designer: Antonina Krass
Cover Designer: Joan Greenfield
Art Researcher: Ruth Mandel

Library of Congress Cataloging-in-Publication Data

The Norton anthology of modern and contemporary poetry / edited
by Jahan Ramazani, Richard Ellmann, Robert O'Clair. — 3rd ed.
p. cm.
Rev. ed. of: The Norton anthology of modern poetry. 2nd ed.
New York : Norton, c1988.
Includes bibliographical references and index.
Contents: v. 1. Modern poetry — v. 2. Contemporary poetry.

ISBN 0-393-97791-9 (v. 1 : pbk.) — ISBN 0-393-97792-7 (v. 2 : pbk.)

1. American poetry—20th century. 2. English poetry—20th
century. 3. American poetry—19th century. 4. English poetry—
19th century. I. Ramazani, Jahan, 1960– II. Ellmann, Richard,
1918– III. O'Clair, Robert. IV. Norton anthology of modern
poetry.

PS613 .N67 2003
821.008—dc21 2002037990

W. W. Norton & Company, Inc., 500 Fifth Avenue, New York, N.Y. 10110
www.wwnorton.com

W. W. Norton & Company Ltd., Castle House, 75/76 Wells Street, London W1T 3QT

4 5 6 7 8 9 0

Contents

Preface to the Third Edition

Thirty years ago, in their preface to the First Edition, Richard Ellmann and Robert O'Clair set forth this anthology's aims and assumptions: "The most acute rendering of an era's sensibility is its poetry. In the twentieth century, probably in reaction to its horrors, poets have created new and powerful consolidations of the imaginative life. Some writers have accepted the discipline of the literary tradition, others have flouted it. During the last seventy-five [now, over a hundred] years in the English-speaking nations, many poets of consequence have written well in an unprecedented range of styles and subjects. This book aspires to present their best work, and also to delineate the many different tendencies of modern poetry in English."

In revising the anthology created by my predecessors, I have sought to preserve its strong conceptual core, while renewing the text for current use. Two prominent changes signal and respond to recent developments in the field: where the 1973 and 1988 editions were entitled *The Norton Anthology of Modern Poetry,* with this Third Edition, the anthology becomes *The Norton Anthology of Modern and Contemporary Poetry,* and the single volume now becomes two, Volume 1, *Modern Poetry,* and Volume 2, *Contemporary Poetry*. With the close of the twentieth century, it has become increasingly difficult to stretch the term "modern" to encompass all innovative poetry in English since the late nineteenth century, and critics and teachers have recently sharpened the term's more narrow historical use for the literature centered in the early twentieth century. College curricula embody this distinction in courses on poetry variously distinguished as "modern" and "contemporary," "modern" and "postmodern," or "pre" and "post–World War II." Since the First Edition was published, more poetry-writing courses emphasizing postwar poetic models have also contributed to this shift. Because of the continuities between pre- and postwar poetry—poets, forms, and trends extending across the divide—this anthology still embraces both, but the two periods are made available in separate volumes for teachers and readers who wish to focus on one at a time.

The boundary between "modern" and "contemporary" is inevitably somewhat arbitrary, but poets who came to maturity on either side of World War II have broad generational affinities. Volume 1, *Modern Poetry,* begins with the precursors Walt Whitman, Emily Dickinson, and Gerard Manley Hopkins. At its center are the innovations and consolidations of the first-generation modern poets, from W. B. Yeats and Gertrude Stein to Marianne Moore and T. S. Eliot. The volume ends with the second generation of modern poets—most of them born in the final decade of the nineteenth century and the first of the twentieth—which includes the Fugitives, the Harlem Renaissance poets, the Objectivists, and the Auden circle. (Because Keith

Douglas was killed in World War II, he appears, in an exception to birth order, last in Volume 1.)

Contemporary Poetry opens with two towering presences in contemporary poetry, Charles Olson and Elizabeth Bishop. Born in and around the 1910s and 1920s, the first generation of postwar poets is "contemporary" in that it created many of the paradigms and fomented many of the debates that still inform poetry writing today. This generation and the next, born largely in the 1930s and 1940s, founded a host of new schools and movements in the 1950s and 1960s: in the United States, the Black Mountain school, Beat poetry, confessional poetry, the New York school, Deep Image poetry, and the Black Arts Movement; in Britain, the New Apocalypse and the Movement. Poets of these generations also developed distinctive poetries in the older nations of the British Commonwealth, such as Canada and Australia, and postcolonial poetry in the newer nations of the so-called Third World, such as Jamaica, Nigeria, and India.

Since its first publication, this anthology has presented an international vision of modern and contemporary poetry in English. Confounding national classification, many key poets of the twentieth century led migratory lives, including such modern expatriates as T. S. Eliot (U.S./U.K.), Gertrude Stein (U.S./France), Ezra Pound (U.S./U.K./Italy), H. D. (U.S./U.K./Switzerland), Mina Loy (U.S./U.K.), Claude McKay (Jamaica/U.S./Europe), Laura Riding (U.S./U.K./Spain), and W. H. Auden (U.K./U.S./Europe), and such contemporaries as Denise Levertov (U.K./U.S.), Sylvia Plath (U.S./U.K.), Thom Gunn (U.K./U.S.), A. K. Ramanujan (India/U.S.), Agha Shahid Ali (India/U.S.), and Grace Nichols (Guyana/U.K.). Other poets have lived much of their lives outside their natal countries—W. B. Yeats, Elizabeth Bishop, Gary Snyder, Derek Walcott, Kamau Brathwaite, Seamus Heaney, Paul Muldoon, Eavan Boland, Wole Soyinka, and Lorna Goodison, to mention but a few. Like these transnational lives, literary influence has, especially since the start of the twentieth century, continually crossed national boundaries, so that much modern poetry is transatlantic, and much contemporary poetry is in its bearings global. Not that this anthology aims to give equal representation to every anglophone nation. Produced in the United States, its center of gravity is American. But its selection extends well beyond the borders of the United States, since modern poetry in English is impossible to understand without reading poets such as Thomas Hardy, Gerard Manley Hopkins, W. B. Yeats, D. H. Lawrence, Wilfred Owen, Stevie Smith, and W. H. Auden, as is contemporary poetry without engaging poets such as Dylan Thomas, Philip Larkin, Derek Walcott, Seamus Heaney, Agha Shahid Ali, Les Murray, Eavan Boland, Tony Harrison, Paul Muldoon, Derek Mahon, and Anne Carson.

Reshaping the anthology's selections, I have been guided by some general aims. One priority has been to expand the selections of some of the most influential, most frequently taught poets already in the Second Edition, so that they can be read and studied in greater depth. In *Modern Poetry*, more space has been devoted to selections by Gertrude Stein, Wallace Stevens, Ezra Pound, H. D., Marianne Moore, T. S. Eliot, Claude McKay, Wilfred Owen, Hart Crane, Langston Hughes, W. H. Auden, and Theodore Roethke; in *Contemporary Poetry*, by Charles Olson, Elizabeth Bishop, Robert Hayden, Robert Lowell, Amy Clampitt, Philip Larkin, A. R. Ammons, Allen Ginsberg, Frank O'Hara, John Ashbery, Adrienne Rich, Derek Walcott, Sylvia Plath, Tony Harrison, Seamus Heaney, Louise Glück, Paul Muldoon, and Rita Dove.

Another priority has been to welcome into the anthology what John Ashbery has called an "other tradition"—experimental poetry by modern avant-garde writers, such as Mina Loy and Laura Riding, and the Objectivists Charles Reznikoff, Louis Zukofsky, Lorine Niedecker, and George Oppen, extending to the contemporary avant-garde of Language poetry by Susan Howe, Lyn Hejinian, Michael Palmer, and Charles Bernstein.

I have also tried to represent the accelerated globalization of English-language poetry in the second half of the twentieth century, particularly in the work of postcolonial poets who creatively hybridize indigenous traditions with British and American influences. Along with Walcott and Michael Ondaatje, in the Second Edition, Caribbean poets Louise Bennett, Kamau Brathwaite, Grace Nichols, and Lorna Goodison have been included, as have African poets Christopher Okigbo, Wole Soyinka, and Okot p'Bitek, and Indian poets A. K. Ramanujan, Eunice de Souza, and Agha Shahid Ali.

Another aim has been to add significant longer poems and poetic sequences, including Kipling's "Epitaphs of the War," Yeats's "Nineteen Hundred and Nineteen," Stein's "Sacred Emily," Moore's "An Octopus," Hart Crane's *The Bridge,* Theodore Roethke's "The Lost Son," Robert Hayden's "Middle Passage" and "Elegies for Paradise Valley," Allen Ginsberg's "Howl," Adrienne Rich's *Twenty-One Love Poems,* Derek Walcott's "The Schooner *Flight,*" John Ashbery's "Self-Portrait in a Convex Mirror," Seamus Heaney's "Clearances," Frank Bidart's "Ellen West," Amy Clampitt's "A Procession at Candlemas," Tony Harrison's *v.*, Jorie Graham's "The Dream of the Unified Field," James Merrill's "Self-Portrait in Tyvek(TM) Windbreaker," Richard Howard's " 'Man Who Beat Up Homosexuals Reported to Have AIDS Virus,' " and Susan Howe's "Rückenfigur."

A final, and perhaps obvious, priority has been to present various modern and contemporary poets who have only recently emerged into prominence, including poets of the Harlem Renaissance and African American modernism, such as James Weldon Johnson, Sterling Brown, and Melvin Tolson, and their contemporary inheritors Lucille Clifton, Yusef Komunyakaa, and Thylias Moss; female modern poets such as Amy Lowell, Elinor Wylie, Dorothy Parker, and their contemporary counterparts May Swenson, Mary Oliver, Sharon Olds, Jorie Graham, Anne Carson, and Carol Ann Duffy; poets of ethnic American minorities, such as Joy Harjo, Dionisio D. Martínez, Li-Young Lee, and Sherman Alexie; poets of Ireland and Northern Ireland, such as Michael Longley, Derek Mahon, Eavan Boland, and Medbh McGuckian; poets of gay experience, such as Mark Doty and Henri Cole; poets influenced by European surrealism and East Asian literature, such as Charles Simic, Charles Wright, and Robert Hass; an influential poet of World War I, Ivor Gurney; and an eminent Australian, Les Murray.

My overriding aim has been to gather some of the most influential, imaginative, and aesthetically accomplished modern and contemporary poems. Aesthetic criteria are notoriously impossible to pin down, but this edition's have included—to catalog them baldly—creative daring, figurative reach, verbal dexterity, formal skill, historical responsiveness, social significance, psychological complexity, emotional richness, and the inventive engagement with, and revision of, literary and extraliterary genres and discourses. I have looked for poems that seem not merely representative or illustrative—of trends, schools, or identities—but among the best of their kind. Trying to be as open as possible to advice and suggestion, I have hoped to capture, where possible, something like a current critical consensus, while tentatively outlining some newly emerging areas, such as those mentioned above. But because the canons of modern and especially contemporary poetry are still being formed, such choices must be provisional. Since no anthology can be boundlessly inclusive, additions have meant, inevitably, excisions. A publisher's survey of college teachers, showing which texts were taught least often, provided some guidance in the painful task of removing poets and poems to make space for new texts. The anthology's selections are necessarily constrained by page limits, by permissions fees, and by my taste and the taste of colleagues I have consulted.

In addition to poems, the Third Edition also includes, for the first time, a Poetics section at the end of each volume. Poets' explanatory statements help illuminate poems, schools, and movements, as well as the intellectual and social forces that shaped them. As poetry became more difficult, as poets founded new styles, as groups of poets competed for attention, such statements enjoyed an unprecedented boom, with especially large concentrations accompanying the creative ferment of the 1910s and 1920s and again of the 1950s and 1960s. Some of these documents became manifestos for movements and schools, such as Langston Hughes's "The Negro Artist and the Racial Mountain" for the Harlem Renaissance and Charles Olson's "Projective Verse" for the Black Mountain school. Many have also become standard reference points for poets learning their trade—for example, Ezra Pound's famous series of "don'ts" and the aphorisms of Robert Frost, Wallace Stevens, and W. H. Auden. Some are of great interest in themselves, from the typographic experimentation of *Blast* and of Mina Loy's "Feminist Manifesto" to Derek Walcott's meditation on cross-cultural mixture in the Caribbean. Others include revelatory self-analyses and self-explications, such as the statements by Gerard Manley Hopkins, T. S. Eliot, Hart Crane, Gertrude Stein, Dylan Thomas, Philip Larkin, Adrienne Rich, Allen Ginsberg, and Seamus Heaney. Some echo and revise each other, such as Frank O'Hara's parodic engagement with the multitudinous manifestos of the 1950s and A. K. Ramanujan's indigenization of Eliot's "Tradition and the Individual Talent." Though not every poet has published a poetics, and though theory sometimes aligns imperfectly with practice, these primary materials have become an integral part of the history of modern and contemporary poetry.

Also to help in understanding poems, the anthology's editorial features—period introductions, headnotes, annotations, bibliographies—have been substantially revised. These features are designed to enrich the engagement of readers, students, and teachers with the poems; they are meant to reduce spadework and thus to help focus attention on the vital and creative task of interpreting the poetry. Many headnotes are new, others have been tightened or rewritten in light of recent scholarship and of unfolding poetic careers. They seek to distill each poet's formal and thematic preoccupations, to place each poet in a literary historical context, to encapsulate essential biographical and historical information, and to suggest possible lines of analysis. Attentive to how poets see their own contributions, the headnotes frequently quote poets' letters, interviews, and essays. A general introduction to each volume surveys the interconnected movements and key developments in the poetry of the period. Modern and contemporary poems often demand specialized knowledge, and the annotations are meant to meet this need while being concise and minimally interpretive. The bibliographies have been rewritten from scratch; for the first time, they include entries on movements and schools, and on ethnic, national, and regional poetries.

A final note on the texts: in presenting major modern poets who revised their early work at much later stages of their careers, such as Yeats, Pound, Moore, Hughes, and Auden, the Third Edition often gives preference to early versions or early revisions of their texts, since their historical and literary development is of special interest and is sometimes obscured by their later revisions. Throughout the anthology, the date that appears at the bottom right of a poem is its publication date. When there are two dates at the bottom right, the first is the date of first publication, the second the date of the revision or of the poem's inclusion in a volume of poetry. A date provided on the bottom left of a poem is its composition date.

Acknowledgments

The making of this edition was a collaborative venture from start to finish. My first debt is to the late editors of this anthology, Richard Ellmann and Robert O'Clair, whose generosity of spirit, shrewdness of insight, and breadth of vision live on in this edition's introductions, notes, and selections. As a former student of Ellmann's, I am especially glad for the example of his humane sensibility and of his elegant, wit-brimming prose.

For wise counsel on selections and brilliant advice on editorial apparatus, I have turned repeatedly to scholars elsewhere who have been, in effect, an informal advisory group: Paul Breslin (Northwestern University), Langdon Hammer (Yale University), Henry Hart (College of William and Mary), Nicholas Jenkins (Stanford University), Lucy McDiarmid (Villanova University), Mervyn Morris (University of the West Indies, Jamaica), Michael North (University of California, Los Angeles), Marjorie Perloff (Stanford University), Vincent Sherry (Villanova University), Willard Spiegelman (Southern Methodist University), and Helen Vendler (Harvard University). In this group, Bonnie Costello (Boston University) wrote a marvelously astute commissioned review of the Second Edition, as did Charles Berger (University of Utah), Paul Hoover (Columbia College), and Mark Jeffreys (University of Alabama, Birmingham).

I have also sought and gratefully received incisive help and sage suggestions from Calvin Bedient (University of California, Los Angeles), Harold Bloom (Yale University), George Bornstein (University of Michigan), David Bromwich (Yale University), Reed Way Dasenbrock (New Mexico State University, Las Cruces), Ian Duncan (University of California, Berkeley), Sascha Feinstein (Lycoming College), Oren Izenberg (Harvard University), David Kadlec (Georgetown University), Bruce King (independent scholar), Alan Golding (University of Louisville), Elizabeth Gregory (University of Houston), Christopher MacGowan (College of William and Mary), Douglas Mao (Harvard University), Steven Meyer (Washington University), Paul Morrison (Brandeis University), Charles Pollard (Calvin College), Alison Rieke (University of Cincinnati), Neil Roberts (University of Sheffield), William Rushton (University of Alabama, Birmingham), John Whittier-Ferguson (University of Michigan), and David Wyatt (University of Maryland). Peter Quartermain (University of British Columbia) provided several excellent corrections, and thoughtful advice also came from William Packard (New School for Social Research).

Teachers who patiently filled out a questionnaire that provided sound and precise guidance include Leonard Adame (Butte College), Barry Ahearn (Tulane University), Joel Brouwer (University of Alabama), Luke Carson (University of Victoria), Christopher Collins (New York University), Michael J. Coulombe (University of Wisconsin, La Crosse), Joanne Craig (Bishop's University), Paul J. Dolan (SUNY, Stony Brook), Sharm Dolin (formerly at

Cooper Union), P. E. Firchow (University of Minnesota at Minneapolis), Karen J. Ford (University of Oregon), J. T. French III (Coker College), Philip Furia (University of North Carolina, Wilmington), R. F. Gish (California Polytechnic Institute), Albert G. Glover (St. Lawrence University), Beverly Gross (Queens College), Michael Harris (formerly at Dawson College), Louise Harrison (Boston University), Sarah K. Inman (formerly at New York University), Bill Johnsen (Michigan State University), Anthony Low (New York University), Sara Lundquist (University of Toledo), David Mason (Colorado College), David Middleton (Nicholls State University), Pat Moran (University of Wisconsin, Green Bay), James Persoon (Grand Valley State University), Deborah Sarbin (Clarion University of Pennsylvania), J. D. Scrimgeous (Salem State College), Kenith Simmons (University of Hawaii, Hilo), R. Sullivan (University of Wisconsin, La Crosse), John H. Timmerman (Calvin College), Mary Turnbell (University of Puget Sound), Michael Webster (Grand Valley State University), B. H. Wang (formerly at Florida International University at Miami), Marianne Werner (Butte College), and Don Wood (Langara College).

Also truly helpful in advancing this edition were the respondents to a subsequent, shorter questionnaire, including Bruce Bond (University of North Texas), Samuel Lee Cohen (Bernard Baruch College), Michael Collier (University of Maryland at College Park), Joanne Craig (Bishop's University), Richard K. Cross (University of Maryland at College Park), Anne Herzog (West Chester University), Jonathan Hufstader (University of Connecticut at Storrs), Donald W. Markos (California State University at Hayward), Paul D. McGlynn (Eastern Michigan University), Eliza Richards (Boston University), David St. John (University of Southern California), Dennis Taylor (Boston College), Daniel Thurber (Concordia University), Jonathan Warren (York University), Laura Lee Washburn (Pittsburg State University), and Nancy M. Whitt (Samford University).

Poets who graciously responded to personal queries include the late Agha Shahid Ali, Amiri Baraka, Frank Bidart, Kamau Brathwaite, Rita Dove, Carolyn Forché, Lorna Goodison, Robert Hass, Seamus Heaney, John Hollander, Susan Howe, the late Kenneth Koch, Yusef Komunyakaa, Paul Muldoon, Robert Pinsky, and Charles Wright.

Though not granted for this purpose, fellowships from the John Simon Guggenheim Memorial Foundation and the Virginia Foundation for the Humanities helped get this edition off the ground while I was completing another book. At the Virginia Foundation for the Humanities, Robert Vaughan, Roberta Culbertson, Andrew Wyndham, and Kevin McFadden provided kind encouragement, as did my colleagues in residence Jean Maria Arrigo, Paul Harvey, Anne Goodwyn Jones, Ralph Luker, and Carlos Pereda. I am also grateful for the support of the Richard A. and Sarah Page Mayo NEH Distinguished Teaching Professorship at the University of Virginia.

For their unstinting readiness to furnish much-needed assistance and to share immense reserves of knowledge and insight, I thank the colleagues at the University of Virginia I frequently imposed on, including Stephen Cushman, Victor Luftig, Jerome McGann, Raymond Nelson, Marlon Ross, and Herbert Tucker, and I thank Marva Barnett, Alison Booth, Daniel Ehnbom, Jessica Feldman, David Gies, Jeffrey Grossman, Robert Hueckstedt, Dell Hymes, Michael Levenson, Eric Lott, Debra Nystrom, Peter Onuf, Gregory Orr, Lisa Russ-Spaar, and Patricia Spacks. Librarians at special collections, reference, interlibrary loan, and library express have been forthcoming and efficient; Gary Treadway and Bryson Clevenger kindly answered numerous queries, and Karen Marshall speedily acquired needed volumes. At ITC, Nancy Hopkins designed a most useful spreadsheet. Students in my classes on modern and contemporary poetry have motivated and schooled me. I heartily thank the graduate assistants I worked with, whether for a few hours or much longer: at various early stages, James Parr, Joy Asekun, Kevin Seidel, and Nicole Gharda gathered criticism, texts, and page tallies; in the last stretch, Lauryl Hicks, Kate Nash, and Hallie Smith helped greatly with proofreading and with demanding research; and for over a year, Brian Glavey labored with diligence and keen intelligence to help draft many annotations and compile the bibliographies.

At Norton, Julia Reidhead has been a tremendously energetic and inspiring collaborator. I feel especially fortunate to have worked closely and intensively with her and with Kurt Wildermuth, who edited at a brisk pace while remaining always meticulous and sensitive. For scrupulous copyediting of standing editorial materials, I thank Kate Lovelady; for equally scrupulous work on proofs, I thank Lory Frenkel and Sarah Chamberlin. Marian Johnson and Diane O'Connor kept a close watch on a tight schedule. Nancy Rodwan and Margaret Gorenstein were great allies in permissions, even through some painful cuts. Toni Krass brought elegance to the task of book design. And Brian Baker and Carey Schwaber were efficient and helpful points of contact.

My last and best thanks go to my ever-sustaining parents, Nesta and Ruhi; to my dear children, Cyrus and Gabriel, whose early-morning laughter and end-of-day exuberance renewed me; and to Caroline Rody, who has been wondrously responsive and indefatigably supportive, especially through the last challenging year of this project.

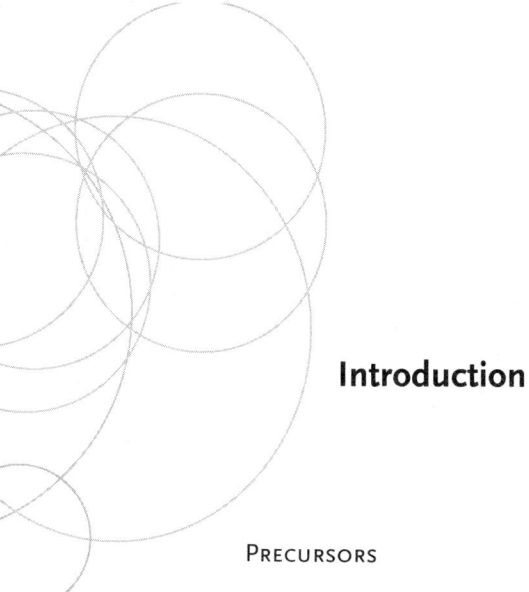

Introduction

Precursors

"Of Modern Man I sing," wrote Walt Whitman, declaring his modernity by implicit contrast with Virgil's "Of arms and the man I sing" ("One's-Self I Sing"). But just when poetry in English became "modern" is not easy to determine. The word *modern* comes from the Latin word *modo,* meaning "just now," and so *modern poetry* in a general sense is new or innovative poetry, perhaps beginning with Whitman and continuing to today. As a period term, however, *modern* can be used more narrowly, for poetry centered in the first half of the twentieth century, bounded by the Victorian era on one end and the contemporary period (also called *post–World War II* or *postmodern*) on the other. In this sense, the late nineteenth-century poets Whitman, Emily Dickinson, and Gerard Manley Hopkins fall outside the period's boundaries. Yet these three figures stand like giants at the threshold, precursors who heralded key developments in the early twentieth-century poetry that is generally called "modern." Their groundbreaking poetry, disdained by or largely unknown to their contemporaries, found both readers and disciples in the twentieth century.

Considered scandalous in his time, Whitman's verse first gained acceptance in Europe. In his preface to *Leaves of Grass* (1855), Whitman dares to imagine a poetry that, released from inhibiting conventions, responds energetically to the teeming worlds of nature, humanity, and the self. He vows in "Song of Myself" to strip naked, to open himself to the air he loves, "mad for it to be in contact with me." In rhapsodically cadenced lines, he celebrates "The delight alone or in the rush of the streets, or along the fields and hillsides, / The feeling of health, the full-noon trill, the song of me rising from bed and meeting the sun." In his sweeping embrace, he includes even bodily realities and profane feelings—"guile, anger, lust, hot wishes" ("Crossing Brooklyn Ferry"). Whitman's poetry expresses a new way of looking at the world, discovering charged relationships among the most disparate things and people, and uncovering the world's variousness within himself as poet and as human archetype. This largeness of conception broke the bonds of conventional prosody. He became the first major poet to write in free verse, a crucial innovation that Ezra Pound and the Imagists were to institutionalize more than fifty years later as a prime tenet of modernism. Pound called Whitman "a pig-headed father"; other poets more graciously numbered themselves among Whitman's progeny, including W. B. Yeats, William Carlos Williams, Hart Crane, Langston Hughes, Allen Ginsberg, June Jordan, and Derek Walcott.

Emily Dickinson's poems, only a small handful of which were published before she died, echo through the work of twentieth-century poets, whether working primarily in "closed" or "open," regular or irregular forms, including Williams, H. D., Crane, Lorine Niedecker, Elizabeth Bishop, Adrienne Rich, Sylvia Plath, and Susan Howe. Indeed, Dickinson both embraced and burst formal boundaries: she wrote compact poems in hymnlike quatrains that alternate four- and three-beat lines, yet she slanted and skewed rhyme and structure, time and space. The extreme compression of her poetry, its riddle- or parablelike indirection, and its abruptly shifting scale seem to anticipate "modern" developments. In contrast to Whitman's macrocosm, manifested in long lines, her world is one of minute examinations of her surroundings, recounted like secrets that seem to have been preserved almost accidentally. In short lines that compress multiple meanings and trouble the normal movements of syntax, she inspects domestic and natural objects with diamondlike concentration—a buzzing fly, a worm bit in half, "a certain Slant of light, / Winter Afternoons." Even so, she too draws all things into a jagged cohesion, for to her, "the brain is wider than the sky" and can encompass and absorb sky, sea, and all. "My Business is Circumference," she wrote in a letter. In her poetry, she affirms, as Yeats and William Blake both asserted, that infinity may be represented by things infinitely small.

Gerard Manley Hopkins, an English precursor of the modern movement, was a devout student of Whitman, and remarked in a letter of October 18, 1882, "I may as well say . . . that I always knew in my heart Walt Whitman's mind to be more like my own than any other man's living. As he is a very great scoundrel this is not a very pleasant confession." Hopkins doubtless thought Whitman a scoundrel because of the American's unchristian religion, general bravado, and erotically charged verse; whereas Whitman found the multitudinous world's coherence in his own sensibility, Hopkins found it in God and termed this integrative energy *instress*. But their poetic kinship is unmistakable. Like Whitman, Hopkins felt the need to transform the apparatus of poetry in the process of reimagining the world. He did not desert rhyme or meter, but he pulled, twisted, and stretched them until they sounded like nothing seen before in English verse. His most important prosodic invention was what he called *sprung rhythm,* in which stressed syllables are attached to widely varying numbers of unstressed syllables—a technique that enabled him to approximate more nearly the unpredictable ebb and flow of experience. His poetry combines extremities of feeling—agony and rapture, distress and joy—in lines so densely packed with sounds, meanings, and ambiguities that they resist easy absorption, as when he describes how branches mark the night in "Spelt from Sibyl's Leaves": "Only the beakleaved boughs dragonish damask the tool-smooth bleak light; black, / Ever so black on it." Hopkins's poetry was largely unread until his friend Robert Bridges—having waited for the right moment—published a collection in 1918, when audiences shattered by World War I were readier than the Victorians for its strangeness and daring. His descendents include British and Irish poets such as Dylan Thomas, W. H. Auden, and Seamus Heaney, and Americans such as Robert Lowell, Amy Clampitt, and Charles Wright.

Modern and Modernist

Thomas Hardy is a pivotal figure between the Victorian and modern periods. Although his novels appeared in the nineteenth century, he published all but the first of his poetry collections, *Wessex Poems and Other Verses* (1898), in the twentieth. Like Hopkins, Hardy confronts and even affronts the reader with new shapes, rhythms, and sounds. His verse is based on tormented syntax and inelegant vocabulary, as if they, rather than eloquence, might best reflect the uncouth universe. He praised "dissonances" and "irregularities" in verse, and while his poems are in rhymed and metered stanzas, their unconsoling endings, jarring juxtapositions, and skeptical questionings also distort and dislocate Victorian conventions. His unvarnished presentation of his pained and tumultuous feelings—in his elegies for his first wife and elsewhere—likewise accord with the fiercely truth-telling mood of poets he most influenced, such as D. H. Lawrence, Siegfried Sassoon, W. H. Auden, Philip Larkin, James Wright, and Pound, whose only literary souvenir when leaving London in 1920 was a letter of Hardy's.

Hardy marked the end of the Victorian period and the dawn of the new age in "The Darkling Thrush," a poem originally titled "By the Century's Deathbed" and postdated December 31, 1900, the last day of the nineteenth century. The poem mourns the demise of a century of conviction and optimism, and it intimates the beginnings of a new era in its skeptical irresolution, its bleak sense of the modern world as "hard and dry"—favorite adjectives of later writers such as Pound and T. E. Hulme:

> The land's sharp features seemed to be
>   The Century's corpse outleant,
> His crypt the cloudy canopy,
>   The wind his death-lament.
> The ancient pulse of germ and birth
>   Was shrunken hard and dry,
> And every spirit upon earth
>   Seemed fervourless as I.

Along with Hardy's first volume, A. E. Housman's *A Shropshire Lad* (1896), Edwin Arlington Robinson's *The Children of the Night* (1897), and Yeats's *The Wind among the Reeds* (1899) appeared in the waning years of the nineteenth century. These books continue Romantic and Victorian traditions—a language of personal feeling, regular meters and rhymes, the imputation of human feelings to nature by the pathetic fallacy. But the poetry of Housman, Robinson, and Hardy diverges by its intensified doubt and pessimism, and that of the early Yeats by its thorough internalization of the outer world and by its apocalyptic anticipations.

Because this century-bridging poetry remains grounded in nineteenth-century literary conventions, it is *modern* without being *modernist*. By analogy with political *-ist* words such as *anarchist* and *monarchist*, the word *modernist* can be glossed literally as "advocate of newness." Through its fragmentation, ellipses, and jagged edges, modernist poetry disrupts formal coherence, traditionally enforced by regular meter and rhyme, tonal and figural continuity. It aggressively asserts modernity in form and subject matter, and it forces a sharper break with Romantic and Victorian tradition. Instead of lamenting the death of the nineteenth century, Pound repudiated the late Victorian period as "blurry, messy," and "sentimentalistic." The 1914 manifesto of the avant-garde journal *Blast* thunders, "**BLAST / years 1837 to 1900.**" Like other avant-garde manifestos, this one damns the middle class for perpetuating Victorian taste and conventional mores.

While modern poetry in English can be dated to the turn of the twentieth century, modernist poetry began in the 1910s with the publication of T. S. Eliot's "The Love Song of J. Alfred Prufrock" and "Preludes," H. D.'s and Pound's Imagist poems, Gertrude Stein's and Mina Loy's early experimental work. Manifestos by Hulme, Pound, Loy, and others accompanied these first modernist poems, proclaiming and explaining the new aesthetic. A further distinction arises with the emergence of what is often called *high modernism:* the densely allusive, learned, polyglot poetry, exemplified in the 1920s by Eliot's *The Waste Land* (1922) and Pound's *Hugh Selwyn Mauberley* (1920) and his Cantos, a group of which were published as a book in 1925.

These distinctions, if clear at the extremes, blur in the middle ground held by Yeats, D. H. Lawrence, Robert Frost, Wallace Stevens, and others who share qualities with modernism and high modernism, but can also be seen, in Yeats's words, as "the last Romantics": they innovate formally and thematically while extending nineteenth-century traditions. Still more formally conservative poets—such as the World War I poet Wilfred Owen, the Harlem Renaissance poet Claude McKay, and the New York traditionalist Edna St. Vincent Millay—brought inherited forms into fresh dialogue with "modern" subjects, such as mass warfare, racial lynching, and sexual liberation. Moreover, even Pound and Eliot did not break completely with nineteenth-century poetry: they were indebted to Whitman, Robert Browning, and the French Symbolists, among others, and in the late 1910s, they too composed formally regular poems—in quatrains. But since Pound and Eliot sought to distinguish themselves from the Romantics and Victorians, their modernist emphasis on rupture and on formal invention colors the overall picture of what is new and distinctive in modern poetry as a whole. As a result, some critics use *modernism* broadly for all early twentieth-century literature, claiming the term's prestige for the nonmodernist moderns as well.

"Make It New"

It may be useful at the outset to summarize some of the distinctive features of modern poetry. The preoccupation with newness is put succinctly in Pound's slogan "make it new" and in an assertion of William Carlos Williams: "Nothing is good save the new." Formal coherence, metrical rules, and generic laws must be broken or, at least, twisted and distorted to fit the unsettled times: "To break the pentameter, that was the first heave," Pound writes. The lyric convention of the "gem-like" poem must be shattered in favor of poetry, as Lawrence graphically puts it in his "Poetry of the Present" (1919), of the "insurgent naked throb of the instant moment."

The search for new ways to represent experience was not exclusive, of course, to poetry. By the early twentieth century, powerful vocabularies were emerging in anthropology, psychology, philosophy, and the visual arts that described human identity in radically new ways. Sigmund Freud's seminal *The Interpretation of Dreams* was published in 1900, and soon psychoanalysis was changing how people saw and described rationality, the self, and personal development. By 1913, when Pound defines the image as "an intellectual and emotional complex in an instant of time," he refers to the psychoanalytic meaning of "complex" ("A Retrospect"); at the same time, in his prose and poetry, Lawrence is adapting the Oedipus complex to interpret and present his relationships with his parents, though rejecting Freud's negative definition of the unconscious. In a 1924 essay about Freud's influence on literature, the southern poet and critic John Crowe Ransom noted that, after Freud, the self is conceived as "multiple rather than simple," many "bound up loosely in one," "a pack of demons." By the time of his death, in 1939, Freud had become, as Auden wrote in an elegy for him, "a whole climate of opinion // under whom we conduct our different lives." Also in the early twentieth century, Sir James Frazer's *The Golden Bough* (1890–1915) and other works of anthropology were altering basic conceptions of culture, religion, and myth. Eliot observed that Frazer's work "influenced our generation profoundly," and the critic Lionel Trilling suggested that "perhaps no book has had so decisive an effect upon modern literature as Frazer's." In poetry, Yeats, Eliot, Pound, H. D., Stevens, and Lawrence layered myths of fertility gods as paradigms of the death and potential rebirth of civilization, and as models for what Yeats called the ritual of verse. For both anthropologists and modern poets, Western religion now became one of numerous interrelated mythologies—the "dying god," Jesus Christ, but one "three-days' personage" (in Stevens's phrase) among many. Reinforcing this radical rethinking were the writings of Friedrich Nietzsche, the nineteenth-century German philosopher who declared the death of God, repudiated Christianity, and offered instead a harshly tragic conception of life: people look "deeply into the true nature of things" and realize "that no action of theirs can work any change," but they nevertheless laugh and stoically affirm their fate. Stevens responds with Nietzschean gaiety to seeing the "gods dispelled in mid-air and dissolve like clouds"; Yeats, who remarks in a 1902 letter that his eyes are exhausted from reading "that strong enchanter," greets death and destruction in a Nietzschean spirit of exultation; and Robinson Jeffers, who read Nietzsche at fifteen, likewise conceives of heroic responses to loss and tragedy that, like those of Nietzsche's *Übermensch* or overman, exceed the human.

The modern poet's concern with the new also reflects the rapid transformation of everyday life in the early twentieth century. Electricity was spreading, cinema and radio were proliferating, new pharmaceuticals were being developed, and cheap steel was readily available for the building of skyscrapers. As labor was increasingly managed and rationalized, as more and more people crowded into cities, as communications and transportation globalized space and accelerated time, poetry could not stand still. (As if nothing had changed, some popular poets, such as Americans in the "Genteel Tradition," as the philosopher-poet George Santayana called it in a 1911 lecture, continued to write about conventional themes in an archaic diction and highly rhetorical style, but their work has, as a result, been largely forgotten.) This was a period of scientific revolution, as exemplified in German physics by Max Planck's quantum theory (1900) and Albert Einstein's theory of relativity (1905). Eliot reflects the increasing dominance of science when he argues that the poet surrenders to tradition and thus extinguishes rather than expresses personality: "It is in this depersonalization that art may be said to approach the condition of science," he claims, adding that "the mind of the poet is the shred of platinum" that catalyzes change but itself remains "inert, neutral, and unchanged" ("Tradition and the Individual Talent"). Gertrude Stein, who considered a possible career in science, conducted her experiments in poetic form after working for ten years in laboratories; her investigations included neurophysiological research under the supervision of the psychologist William James.

The early twentieth century also brought countless advances in technology: the first wireless communication across the Atlantic occurred in 1901, the Wright brothers flew the first airplane in 1903, and Henry Ford introduced the first mass-produced car, the Model T or "Tin Lizzie," in 1913. Not that modern poets univocally embraced such changes. Although poets in the second modern generation were more sanguine—Hart Crane exalted the Brooklyn Bridge and Stephen Spender the express train—most poets of the first generation were paradoxically repulsed by aspects of modernization. Mass-produced appliances and goods, such as the "gramophone" and canned "tins," are objects of revulsion in *The Waste Land,* and cinema ("kinema"), the pianola, and popular journalism come under satiric attack in *Hugh Selwyn Mauberley.* Scientific materialism and positivism, according to which empirical explanations could be found for everything, were weakening the influence of organized religion, and many poets looked to poetry as an alternative. His "simple-minded" Protestantism spoiled by science, Yeats says in his autobiography he "made a new religion, almost an infallible church of poetic tradition." H. D. assumes an almost priestly role in her verse, though she attempts to free religious icons such as the Virgin Mary of patriarchal accretions. Whether or not they welcomed the demise of tradition, habit, and certitude in favor of the new, modern poets articulated the effects of modernity's relentless change, loss, and destabilization. "Things fall apart," as Yeats wrote, "the centre cannot hold." Eliot describes in *Four Quartets* his quest for the "still point of the turning world." "Make it new" thus arises in part out of an often ambivalent consciousness of the relentless mutations brought by modernization.

"Make it new" is also, ironically, a reaction to an uneasy sense of being "not new," of coming late in the long record of human achievement, and thus bearing the enormous weight of the cultural past. The explosion of knowledge was extending human consciousness, as Eliot said of Frazer's work, into "the backward and abysm of time" (echoing Shakespeare's *The Tempest*). At the same time that modern life was shedding old traditions and customs, the great expanse of cultural and literary history was becoming more accessible—"simultaneous" is Eliot's word—than ever before. To "make it new" is thus necessarily in part to recycle, refurbish, and recontextualize the old. Indeed, Pound said he borrowed his slogan from the bathtub of an ancient Chinese emperor. Modern poetry, like the two-faced Roman god Janus, looks toward the newness of the "just now" and toward the "backward and abysm of time." It registers the impact of change on the imagination, while answering to the traditions of poetry as an ancient art form. Poems of the greatest allusiveness and synchronicity—high modernist works from *The Waste Land* and *The Cantos* to H. D.'s *Tribute to the Angels,* Louis Zukofsky's "Poem Beginning 'The,' " and Melvin Tolson's *Harlem Gallery*—are steeped in literary tradition, but they reassemble and amalgamate past myths and vocabularies, figures and forms, in ways that are decidedly antitraditional.

The social changes at the turn of the century were reflected not only in what and how the new poetry was written but also in who was writing it. Between the two world wars, African Americans of the Harlem Renaissance and Jews of the modernist and Objectivist movements racially and ethnically diversified poetry in English. As we shall see, these writers brought into poetry partly unwritten areas of experience, fresh vocabularies, and emergent social identities, and thus they also made it new. More women were leading poets in the modernist revolution than in the comparably transformative literary revolutions of the Romantic movement and the Renaissance; their ranks included Stein, H. D., Loy, Marianne Moore, Amy Lowell, Edith Sitwell, and Laura Riding. Many other women poets consolidated and revised lyric traditions, often from a strongly gendered perspective—in 1920s and 1930s New York, for example, Edna St. Vincent Millay, Elinor Wylie, Dorothy Parker, and Louise Bogan. Modern male poets continued as the majority, however, and sometimes Yeats, Pound, Eliot, and other men, in their representations of their masculinity and of women, betrayed a heightened anxiety over changing sex roles. The partial gender shift in the traditionally male domain of poetry was enabled by the increasing access of women to higher education, the loosening of Victorian gender codes, and the entry of more women into the workplace—accelerated by the labor shortages of World War I. After long struggles, the women's movement won suffrage for American women in 1920 and for British women over thirty in 1918, over twenty-one in 1928. Modern women poets in turn helped prepare the way for the still greater number of ambitious women poets after World War II.

DIFFICULTY AND IMAGINATION

Make it difficult is another imperative of much modern poetry. In his essay "The Metaphysical Poets" (1921), T. S. Eliot famously said that "it appears likely that poets in our civilization, as it exists at present, must be *difficult*. Our civilization comprehends great variety and complexity, and this variety and complexity, playing upon a refined sensibility, must produce various and complex results. The poet must become more and more comprehensive, more allusive, more indirect, in order to force, to dislocate if necessary, language into his meaning." Eliot's analogy between the complexity of modern poetry and that of modern civilization suggests that simple poetry feebly evades modernity, retreating into the consolations, nostalgias, and pieties of the past. Because of the rapid pace of social and technological change, because of the mass dislocation of populations by war, empire, and economic migration, because of the urban juxtaposition of vast cultural differences, modernity disrupts the old order, up-ends ethical and social codes, casts into doubt previously stable assumptions about self, community, the world, and the divine. Difficulty takes on many different guises in modern poetry. Reflecting the erosion both of the classically liberal confidence in progress and advancement and of traditional values and belief systems, modern poetry—skeptical of all-explanatory narratives and theories—avoids the discursive commentary of Victorian poems such as Alfred, Lord Tennyson's *In Memoriam*. Modern poetry more often shows instead of telling, presents instead of expounding. Its approach is typically oblique, throwing the reader into the middle of an experience instead of working up to it gradually. Because modern poems present ideas, experiences, and sensory perceptions directly, unfiltered by explanations, their immediacy and directness paradoxically contribute to their difficulty. Eliding the comforts of discursive connections and transitions, they force readers to leap across gaps of many different kinds—tonally, from bitter satire to melancholy in Yeats's "September 1913"; figuratively, from an urban crowd to flower petals in Pound's "In a Station of the Metro"; metrically, from cadenced, unrhymed verse to couplets in Eliot's "The Love Song of J. Alfred Prufrock"; generically, from the blues to iambic pentameter couplets in Langston Hughes's "The Weary Blues"; typographically, from prose poetry to lineated verse in Stein's "Idem the Same. A Valentine to Sherwood Anderson"; spatially, from a mountain-top glacier deep into the sea in Marianne Moore's "An Octopus"; temporally, from World War II–era London to ancient Egypt in H. D.'s *The Walls Do Not Fall;* and linguistically, from African American vernacular to Standard English in Sterling Brown's "Strong Men." Poets such as Yeats and Robert Graves, mistrusting conventional religions, assemble private mythologies, leaving readers to puzzle them out in the poems. Even seemingly straightforward poems, such as those of Robert Frost or Langston Hughes, often employ evasive irony and subtle indirection.

Modern poets also place a premium on the imagination, an emphasis that leads back, perhaps surprisingly, to the Romantic movement. The Romantics presented poetry not as the celebration of the ideals of society, but as the expression of the individual imagination, its power to invest the external world with a new light—or even to transform it altogether, to invent what Auden called "alternative worlds." Many modern poets fundamentally questioned the reality of the objective world. Their verse exhibits what Paul Valéry called a "drama of mental images," a drama made out of the different and conflicting gradations of reality or irreality that mental images seem to possess. Not that modern poets need confine themselves to a single stance. Sometimes, they may veer toward a Platonic world of essences, beside which material things offer only ghostly semblances; at other times, they may recognize the stubborn powers that lurk in material realities, resistant to reshaping by the imaginative will. Modern poets search for adequate fictions, fictions verging on facts, what is imagined reshaping what is seen, and their imaginative quest may be said to culminate in Stevens's pursuit of a "supreme fiction." This pursuit has been concomitant, also, with doubts about the feasibility of such an enterprise—another favorite subject of modern verse. In Stevens's poetry, life and art struggle to bring one another under control, and the issue is never settled. Yeats's poetry asks to what extent art conquers nature, is conquered by nature, and is itself nature, and the degree to which nature is itself art. The lake isle of Innisfree is a real island, but in Yeats's famous poem, it is also an image of that island perfected by the imagination. Byzantium is a real, historical city, but for Yeats it is also an image of art and eternity, conjured out of nothing by the passions of a living poet. The London of Eliot's *The Waste Land* and H. D.'s *The Walls Do Not Fall,* the New York of Crane's *The Bridge,* the Harlem of Hughes's *Montage of a Dream Deferred* and Tolson's *Harlem Gallery* are replete with verifiable concrete details, but each is also an "Unreal City," the special property of the poet who aided in its creation. In Eliot's poetry, the imagination conjures broken images of a fragmented world, but strives to reconstruct the symbols needed for survival, symbols that for him are not only imaginative but spiritual, implying the interdependence of art and religion. In an age characterized by fragmentation, Eliot searches for a symbolic landscape of wholeness and radiance. In the next generation, Auden abjures any relation of poetry and religion, insisting that the one praises the physical universe and the other the metaphysical universe, but his work nevertheless refurbishes drab or anguishing data by spiritual nourishment and aesthetic delight.

Globalization

Along with the imperatives of newness, difficulty, and imagination comes a fourth—*make it international.* As trade, travel, investment, and communications were becoming globalized, so too was poetry. The movies and radio, the telephone and telegraph, ocean liners and, after 1919, transatlantic air travel were augmenting and speeding the movement of knowledge, images, news, capital, and people within and across national boundaries. The vast reach of the British Empire and the increasing political and economic might of the United States—in 1919, the prime mover behind the creation of the League of Nations and the greatest creditor nation in the world—also helped knit together previously separate peoples across the globe. Between 1850 and 1914, British and other European empires had carved up most of the "undeveloped" world, and by 1914, Britain's empire was 140 times its own size, covering a quarter of the world's land surface. The empire's centrifugal forces—including economic, political, and religious colonization and ethnographic research—scattered British denizens across the globe; its centripetal forces drew them back, along with material goods, artifacts, and occasionally indigenous peoples (though a much greater influx of non-European immigrants would follow World War II).

No previous period in English-language poetry includes so many migrants and expatriates. Major modern cities were centers of the new internationalism. The population of London, the cosmopolitan capital of the world, had leapt in the nineteenth century from one million to six and a half million by 1900. Now it drew into its "vortex," as Pound called it, writers from Ireland such as Yeats, from Scotland such as Edwin Muir, from America such as Pound, H. D., Eliot, and, more transiently, Frost, Amy Lowell, Claude McKay, and Laura Riding. Other American poets, such as Stein, McKay, Riding, and E. E. Cummings, spent long periods in Europe, where the avant-garde visual arts were exploding. In 1913, the Armory Show brought modern European painting to New York, including works by the Postimpressionists Paul Cézanne and Paul Gauguin, the Cubists Pablo Picasso and Georges Braque. Inspired by the European avant-garde, little magazines in New York published venturesome art and writing—*Others, Rogue, Camera Work, 291, Broom, The Dial,* and, after 1917, *The Little Review.* More heterogeneous than London or Paris, New York was a vibrantly transnational and ethnically diverse metropolis. In and around it lived Williams, Stevens, Moore, Loy, Crane, and most of the poets of the Harlem Renaissance and the Objectivist movement. To its Irish and German populations, New York was rapidly adding Italians, Greeks, Russians, Hungarians, Poles, and, in the wake of continuing pogroms, Jews; in 1907 alone, 1,200,000 immigrants entered through Ellis Island. The Harlem Renaissance owes its energy to the influx of American southerners, but also of West Indians such as McKay. As a result of the migration into and out of the United States, many American poets of this period spoke another language before they learned English: Stein's first languages were German and French, Sandburg's was Swedish, and Louis Zukofsky's was Yiddish. Even the American nativist Williams had an English-born father and a Spanish-speaking mother, from Puerto Rico. In addition to Stein and Zukofsky, other Jews were among the poets born to recent immigrants, such as Laura Riding, Dorothy Parker, Charles Reznikoff, and George Oppen. Poets of Jewish descent in Britain included Loy, Siegfried Sassoon, Isaac Rosenberg, and—as he was surprised to learn at sixteen—Stephen Spender.

Like the great literary burgeoning of the Renaissance, when Continental and classical models infused the English-language writing of Shakespeare, Spenser, and Milton, the modern movement resulted in part from an energetic opening to global literatures. Never before had major English-language writers immersed themselves so thoroughly in the literary cultures of East and South Asia as did Yeats, Pound, and Eliot. Yeats sought confirmation for his early convictions about the primacy of consciousness in Indian thought, and in 1912, he befriended the Bengali poet Rabindranath Tagore—the first of his many collaborative relationships with Indian poets and mystics. Although Pound was antipathetic toward South Asian culture, he shared Yeats's interest in Japanese Noh drama and East Asian culture. In 1913, the American sinologist Ernest Fenollosa's widow gave his notebooks to Pound, who creatively rendered from Chinese the free verse poems of *Cathay* (1915), thus beginning a lifelong fascination with the ideogram as a model of juxtaposition and of language that integrates signifier and signified. As a student at Harvard, Eliot immersed himself in the study of Sanskrit and other Eastern languages, Buddhism and other Eastern religions, later incorporated in the global synthesis of *The Waste Land*. Little wonder that high modernist poetry is polyglot—ancient Greek, Latin, French, German, Sanskrit, Chinese, and Yiddish are among the untranslated languages heard in the multilingual din of poems by Pound, Eliot, Moore, H. D., Zukofsky, and Tolson.

Alongside this many-tongued verse, some poets asserted, ever more strongly, the claims of their own indigenous varieties of English. Yeats, and later Austin Clarke and Patrick Kavanagh, hybridized English with elements of Irish English. Hugh MacDiarmid composed in Scots. Rudyard Kipling imported into poetry a vigorous cockney. Frost wrote poems attuned to the speech of New England, and Williams asserted the importance of writing in American English about American subjects. Sandburg used midwestern slang. Hughes and Brown wrote in the African American vernacular, and McKay initially published books of poems written in the Jamaican English of his youth. But these various nativisms in language and poetics cannot be understood outside the context of globalization, within which these poets struggled to carve out a literary space for the local.

Georgian Poetry, Poetry of World War I, and Regionalism

Simultaneous with the emergence of modernist poets in the 1910s were the solitary and introspective Georgian poets, so called because they began writing soon after George V acceded the English throne in 1910. They continued a nonmodernist line of English pastoral poetry that reaches back to the Romantics and forward to, in the 1950s, the Movement poets such as Philip Larkin, who claimed them as an authentically English alternative to the bookish complexity of international modernists such as Pound and Eliot. The Georgian poets had learned from Hardy's colloquialism and narrative realism, and they also drew inspiration from A. E. Housman's melancholy lyricism and feeling for nature. In spare, pastoral lyrics set near the hills of Shropshire, Housman had sadly and stoically meditated on human transience, thwarted love, and failed lives. But Georgian poetry is less bleak than Housman's and less arrestingly contorted than Hardy's.

Appearing in the *Georgian Poetry* anthologies, edited by Sir Edward Marsh and published five times from 1912 to 1922, the Georgian poets infused nature with nationalist feeling. Among those participating in the anthologies were Robert Graves, Siegfried Sassoon, and for a time even D. H. Lawrence. The most popular of the Georgians was Rupert Brooke, who before dying in World War I, literalized death as an act of national possession in his sonnet

"The Soldier": "If I should die, think only this of me: / That there's some corner of a foreign field / That is forever England." At first these poets, with their celebration of the English countryside and its people, seemed to open a window onto a more wholesome outdoors, in reaction against the art-for-art's-sake claustrophobia of late nineteenth-century Aestheticism, associated with writers such as Walter Pater and Oscar Wilde. Those who wished to preserve rural England in traditional prosody received the movement enthusiastically. But soon the Georgians were under critical attack—the principal targets in the *Wheels* anthologies of Edith Sitwell, who regarded them as insipid and pretentious. Graves, Sassoon, and Lawrence all outstripped the mode's limitations, and nearly all the Georgians who remained Georgians seem quaintly escapist by comparison with their modernist contemporaries and have faded into obscurity. Edward Thomas—omitted by the editor from the Georgian anthologies—has ironically had the most staying power. The poet who perhaps best epitomized Georgian ideals, Thomas ruminates over meadows, birds, and "Rain, midnight rain, nothing but the wild rain / On this bleak hut, and solitude, and me / Remembering again that I shall die." Thomas combines inward pastoral reflection with the accents of real speech in poems such as the semidramatic "The Gypsy": "Give a penny / For the poor baby's sake." His poetry is deepened by the consciousness of imminent death—his own and the multitudes killed in World War I hovering just outside his lyric frame.

Thomas began writing during the war and was killed in 1917. His poems are not directly about the carnage of World War I, but other soldier-poets who began as Georgian pastoralists, such as Sassoon and Wilfred Owen, wrenched this late Romantic mode to make it reflect the violence that engulfed them. In the first phases of World War I, even the most famous war poets were writing reminiscences of idyllic English landscape. But innocent greenery came to seem too much at odds with trench warfare and mass slaughter. The soldiers' experiences in what Eliot called "rat's alley" withered away their conventional patriotism and stirred them to devise a bitter new rhetoric to express their disillusion, grief, and anger.

The international destruction between 1914 and 1918 was completely unexpected and unprecedented in scale: thirteen million civilians died because of massacres and military battles, starvation and exposure, and the world's most destructive outbreak of influenza. Eight and a half million soldiers were killed. In a single day, the British suffered 57,470 casualties at the 1916 Battle of the Somme, and they eventually lost 780,000 lives in the war. The battle line along the Western Front through Belgium, France, and Germany remained largely stagnant for years, despite the introduction of new technologies of war, such as tanks and, perhaps most horribly, poison gas—Owen describes a gassed soldier "guttering, choking, drowning," a man with "white eyes writhing in his face," in "Dulce et Decorum Est." The most gifted of the war poets, Owen jarringly conveys the war's mad slaughter by viewing it through the estranging lens of John Keats's lush and sensual Romanticism: "Red lips are not so red / As the stained stones kissed by the English dead" ("Greater Love"). Sassoon befriended Owen in a war hospital and encouraged his war poetry, but Owen was killed a week before the war ended, while Sassoon survived. He is a more journalistic, less densely literary poet, whose mainstays are ironic juxtaposition and satire. Of Sephardic Jewish descent, Sassoon recognized in another Jewish war poet, Isaac Rosenberg, the prophetic quality of the Hebrew Bible, which Rosenberg, like

Owen, brought into combination with a Keatsian sensuality. Rosenberg was killed in the war; he had served in it as a common soldier, like Ivor Gurney but unlike the officers Owen and Sassoon. Gurney's poetry, too, is rooted in the typically Georgian preoccupations with landscape and memory, but its distortions of sense and syntax, its irregularities in rhyme and rhythm, are recognizably "modern." Indeed, the war's absurd slaughter helped make the asymmetries and skepticism of prewar modernism more acceptable to postwar audiences.

Civilian poets were also deeply moved by the war. Even Rudyard Kipling, much of whose verse had been that of "a jingo imperialist," in George Orwell's phrase, grew horrified by the war in which his son died. He composed the disturbing World War I sequence "Epitaphs of the War," one spoken by a headless "Unknown Female Corpse," another by a woman "Raped and Revenged." The war was more distant, even abstract, for most American poets, but Stevens describes himself, in a 1918 letter, as obsessed by the war deaths; he elegized an archetypal soldier in "The Death of a Soldier": "Death is absolute and without memorial, / As in a season of autumn, / When the wind stops." Eliot, afflicted by his intimate friend Jean Verdenal's being "mixed with the mud" of the Dardanelles, obliquely mourned him in *The Waste Land,* and Pound, disturbed by the death of a sculptor friend, Henri Gaudier-Brzeska, grieved bitterly in *Hugh Selwyn Mauberley*, "There died a myriad . . . // Quick eyes gone under earth's lid."

During these years, the war fronts were not the only scenes of violent conflict. Launching the Easter Rising of 1916, sixteen hundred Irish nationalists, impatient with British rule and broken promises of independence, took over the central post office, a park, and other buildings in Dublin, and proclaimed an Irish Republic. One after another, fifteen leaders were executed by firing squad. Yeats was, like most of the Irish, at first dubious of the rebellion, but after the leaders whom he knew personally were martyred by the British, his dormant nationalism was reawakened. In "Easter, 1916," he yoked together both his awed appreciation and his doubts, his nationalism and his antinationalism, fashioning a newly complex kind of public yet private verse. Two years later, when the only child of his friend Lady Gregory was killed flying for the British Royal Flying Corps at the Italian front, he wrote four poems commemorating him. Yeats decried war poetry such as Owen's as being too passive, realistic, and unheroic—"all blood, dirt and sucked sugar stick," he said in a letter. But his poems about the ensuing Irish Civil War and the Anglo-Irish War bitterly evoke the house-to-house carnage: "a drunken soldiery / Can leave the mother, murdered at her door, / To crawl in her own blood" ("Nineteen Hundred and Nineteen"). In 1922, the Irish Free State became the first nation to emerge from British colonial rule in the twentieth century, decades before the decolonization of the Indian subcontinent, Africa, and the Caribbean.

Robert Frost had long admired Yeats, and while Frost was living in England from 1912 to 1915, Pound introduced the two poets. During this time, Frost also met the leading Imagists and Georgians, and he befriended Edward Thomas and persuaded him to write poetry. In England, Frost found his first sympathetic audience and published his first two books, in 1913 and 1914, but because of the war, he returned to the United States. Traces of Georgian tendencies can be found in his work, but Frost renewed pastoral by toughening it. When he returned from England, he bought a farm in New Hampshire and consolidated his reputation as America's greatest pastoral poet. On the one hand, he tapped the seasoned country wisdom of New England; on the other, he converted his self-disgust and loneliness into verses of classical Roman dignity phrased in the accents of New Hampshire and Vermont. Tormented and lonely men and women, "stiff and sore and scarred," often speak his dramatic monologues, experiencing "hurt" that their homely folk wisdom cannot assuage: "Now no joy but lacks salt / That is not dashed with pain / And weariness and fault" ("To Earthward"). Though he little resembles the polyglot, craggily allusive high modernists, he too shifts mercurially in tone and complicates poetry with undercurrents of rhythms half heard and meanings half spoken.

During the first two decades of the new century, American regionalists explored their local environments with little regard for the more disruptive innovations of the modernists. But their poetry also reflects indirectly the tradition-effacing forces of modernization: they sought to capture and preserve the particular character of local settings, often in the inhabitants' distinctive idiom and sensibility. Edwin Arlington Robinson exposed the life of Tilbury Town, and Edgar Lee Masters that of Spoon River, imparting public lessons from private scandals. Robinson's compressed character sketches, like those of his English counterpart, A. E. Housman, are melancholy in tone, telling of lives misshapen, cut off, or squandered. Preferring Whitmanian free verse to Robinson's formally taut stanzas, Masters nevertheless shares with Robinson an economical style. The more brazen Carl Sandburg wrote of Chicago: "Stormy, husky, brawling, / City of the Big Shoulders." His ebullient rhetoric in free verse about the city and its workers constituted the most "modern" literature to gain much public acceptance in the United States, at a time when most American readers thought he, Masters, and other regionalists represented the future of modern poetry. Many poets who wished a more radical break with tradition left the United States to find it, while the early poems of others, such as Williams, were printed either privately or abroad.

Although he was neither an English nor an American regionalist, D. H. Lawrence—who left England after World War I and traveled for much of his life across Continental Europe, Mexico, the American southwest, Australia, and elsewhere—shared with the Georgians and with most American regionalists a preoccupation with nature. Both the Georgians and the Imagists sought to claim him and included him in their anthologies. His praise for the Georgians in a 1913 review was more accurate as a description of his own purposes than of their accomplishments: "If I take my whole, passionate, spiritual and physical love to the woman who in return loves me, that is how I serve God. . . . All of which I read in the anthology of *Georgian Poetry*." Lawrence sought to break through superficialities with his burning honesty and directness, and centered his own verse in the passions of tortoises and elephants as well as of men and women. Unlike the Georgians, Lawrence worked mostly in free verse. He thought that an interest in form usually accompanied an interest in imitation and preferred to let his subjects command their own shape. Lawrence remained an isolated figure, almost an outcast, beset during his short life by the public's unfounded notion that his often erotic writings were pornographic. Robinson Jeffers, whose long-lined, incantatory poetry was centered in the wild beauty of the California coastline, pursued like Lawrence an interest in nature and passion, though he sought to "break out of humanity" and embrace even nature's cruelty and indifference.

Symbolism

Unlike American and English regionalism and pastoralism, which hymned native landscapes (and, occasionally, cityscapes), an idealist poetry had emerged that found truth in the mind rather than in the outside world. Symbolism began in France with Charles Baudelaire's *The Flowers of Evil* (1857). Keenly acknowledging the anonymity and filth of the modern city, the visible corruption of the body in life and death, Baudelaire in resistance invents a symbolic world of "wholeness, harmony, and radiance." In the words of a later French poet, Stéphane Mallarmé, who pursued symbolist philosophy as far as anyone, this invented symbolic world is "the mind's native land." The term *symbolism* became popular in France about 1886 and after about ten years crossed the English Channel, when the English critic and poet Arthur Symons began writing about these French poets in his book *The Symbolist Movement in Literature* (1899). Symons was persuaded by his friend Yeats, with whom he shared rooms for a time in the mid-1890s, that this late nineteenth-century literature—in which the mind is supreme over fact, suggestion over statement, mood over external reality—constituted a literary movement.

Yeats refashioned symbolism for English-language poetry. In his essay "The Autumn of the Body" (1898), he wrote that the era of externality was over—that is, of naturalism, materialism, scientific realism—and that a new movement that should renew imaginative control over the environment (the world's body) was now afoot. He developed this position in "The Symbolism of Poetry" and other early essays. *The Wind among the Reeds* is about a second, human-centered nature, in which all outward things were internalized. The four elements became aspects of feeling; bird and beast alike were bent on expressing human passion rather than retaining their own identity.

Early in the new century, Yeats wearied of his early lugubrious, disembodied symbolism, declaring his intentions, in a 1901 letter, to make "everything hard and clear" and, in another of 1904, to leave behind "sentiment and sentimental sadness." He began working toward verse that, if still symbolist, exhibited the whole person thinking and feeling, not only the suitor ecstatically languishing. Verse must be "athletic," with leaps instead of dying falls. Lust, rage, and the body; war, violence, and the city—he now embraced materials he eschewed earlier as imperfect and unpoetic. He enacted his self-transformation in poems such as "The Fisherman" and "A Coat," in which his more austere diction and passionate syntax enact his will to leave behind the poetic "embroideries" of his youth and walk "naked." Restless, he continued to remake himself in one book of poems after another, his visionary intensity, complex ambivalences, and subtle but emotionally charged music remaining unmistakably his own to the end.

Imagism

In his development, Yeats found unexpected company in a young American, Ezra Pound. Pound arrived in London in 1908, at twenty-three, convinced that Yeats was the best poet then writing in English and determined to learn from him. Yeats also discovered how much this young man could tell him of new ideas and techniques, and from 1913 to 1916, they spent three winters together in a stone cottage south of London. Pound's generosity and gregariousness, his propagandizing for the avant-garde, made his apartment in Kensington for a time the headquarters of innovative verse for both England and America. Pound's early poems are full of Yeats's early symbols and Robert Browning's mannered rhetoric—"stale creampuffs," he later called them—but in 1912–13, he adopted the more epigrammatic and ironic mode that became Imagism. Imagism evolved from symbolism and shared its antipathy for explanatory discourse, but it shifted the emphasis from the musical to the visual, the mysterious to the actual, the ambiguously suggestive symbol to the clear-cut natural image. Pound was helped to chart the new course in his writing by Ford Madox Ford, an American expatriate novelist who insisted on precision and efficiency in writing, on presenting facts without commenting on them. The philosopher-poet T. E. Hulme, who led a literary group Pound joined in April 1909, also offered guidance. In "Romanticism and Classicism," Hulme denounced Romantic poetry as so much whining and moaning, and he proposed instead "a period of dry, hard, classical verse"; by 1912, Pound, too, was calling for "harder and saner" verse, "like granite" ("A Retrospect"). Hulme said the poet must render "the exact curve of what he sees whether it be an object or an idea in the mind" ("Romanticism and Classicism"), and Pound demanded, through F. S. Flint's introductory synopsis (partly incorporated in "A Retrospect"), "Direct treatment of the thing, whether subjective or objective." In his poetry volume *Ripostes* (1912), Pound published an appendix of five poems, "The Complete Poetical Works of T. E. Hulme," prefaced by a note that printed the term *Imagistes* for the first time. That year, in a London teashop, Pound had announced to the poets Richard Aldington and H. D. (then called Hilda Doolittle) that they were "Imagistes," and two years later he included their and his work in the first Imagist anthology, *Des Imagistes.*

H. D. had arrived in London in 1911, and her verse, written under the spell of ancient Greek lyrical fragments, so impressed Pound that a year later he sent her poems, signed "H. D. Imagiste" at his insistence, to Harriet Monroe, the founding editor of *Poetry,* the Chicago clearinghouse for modern verse. He told Monroe that H. D.'s poems were "modern" and "laconic," though classical in subject: "Objective—no slither; direct—no excessive use of adjectives, no metaphors that won't permit examination. It's straight talk, straight as the Greek!" Except for poems such as his two-line, haikulike "In a Station of the Metro," written in 1912, Pound's Imagist pronouncements tended to run ahead of his practice, but H. D.'s early poems—lucid, economical, often centered in a single metaphor—best exemplified the theory. When Amy Lowell, a poet living in Boston, read these poems of H. D.'s in a 1913 issue of *Poetry,* she decided, "Why, I too am an *Imagiste,*" and soon left for London, where she sought out Pound and allowed him to revise her work. Before long, Pound and Lowell rivaled each other for leadership of the Imagists, and after a squabble, Lowell published in 1915 the first of her three anthologies with a newly anglicized name, *Some Imagist Poets.* The preface to the first edition influentially spelled out the Imagist principles of exactitude in diction, inventiveness in rhythm, and clarity in images. Long after the dispersal of the Imagists, these precepts remained a generative force in modern poetry.

After abandoning Imagism as too static and insufficiently rigorous in 1914, Pound helped create a new movement, Vorticism, that emphasized not the do's and don'ts of style, such as those he had enumerated in "A Few Don'ts by an Imagiste," but the dynamism of content. Pound conceived the vortex—an image of whirling, intensifying, encompassing energy—as the movement's emblem. Like Imagism, Vorticism lasted only for a few years, finding its most raucous embodiment in Wyndham Lewis's journal *Blast* and its main aesthetic achievements in Lewis's painting and Gaudier-Brzeska's sculpture rather than in verse. After its demise, Pound quit founding movements and, a few years later, left London for Italy.

Though the Imagist movement formally came to an end in 1917, when Lowell published the third of her anthologies, both Pound and H. D. went on to write long, complex, many-layered poems that recall Imagism in their musical cadences, sharp juxtapositions, and free-ranging content. In the 1920s, other American poets, such as E. E. Cummings and Archibald MacLeish, cut their teeth on Imagism. Also influenced by Gertrude Stein's experimentalism and by Cubism in the visual arts, Cummings invented flamboyant typographical oddities to tantalize, disconcert, and amuse. For all his pyrotechnics, however, he sustained the ancient themes of lyric poetry, such as love, grief, and innocence. Although MacLeish eventually denounced modernism for its political and ethical ineffectiveness, he distills, in his early poem "Ars Poetica," the antidiscursive credo of Imagism: "A poem should not mean / But be."

High Modernism: For and Against

Pound's closest confederate was T. S. Eliot, whom Pound can be said to have discovered. The two men met in 1914, when Eliot came to England to study philosophy at Oxford University; Pound was astonished by the poems that Eliot showed him, among them "The Love Song of J. Alfred Prufrock," observing that Eliot had "modernized himself *on his own.*" Introduced by Symons's book to French Symbolist poets such as Jules Laforgue, Eliot had found in them models for his early free verse lyrics of inner suffering viewed with ironic detachment. At first, Eliot and Pound seemed to be moving in the same direction. They both wrote about the modern world as a group of fragments, Pound in the first Cantos that he published in *Poetry* and Eliot in *The Waste Land,* which Pound had helped Eliot complete. Only gradually did it become clear that these poems embodied divergent views: for Eliot, the disjunctiveness of the world was intolerable, and he was determined to mend it (as his eventual conversion to Anglican Christianity helped him do). Pound preferred to accept and exploit this disjunctiveness. In the canceled first version of Canto 2, Pound contrasted himself with the Victorian Robert Browning, who had "one whole man," whereas he himself had only "many fragments." But he went on to ask defiantly, "Less worth? Less worth?" He saw how he might accept the fragments and make them material for a modern epic, *The Cantos,* which would, like Dante's *Divine Comedy,* plumb its hell and purgatory and ultimately achieve its paradise.

As a result, *The Waste Land,* with the poems by Eliot that became its sequels, and *The Cantos,* which Pound continued to write until his death, may be seen as rival eminences of early modern verse. The fragments that Eliot wished to reconcile and reintegrate Pound was willing to keep scattered and unchanged. Pound wrote Eliot that he envied him his sense of form, but he did not emulate it. For Pound, Eliot's sifting and fusing ended in a surprisingly orthodox religious view that Pound regarded as based on too limited a number of particulars. Pound developed his own "ideogrammatic method," as he called it, in which he heaped up the components of thought so that they would eventually cohere as if without artistic intervention. His image for this method was one of iron filings that, drawn toward a piece of glass by a magnet, assume the pattern of a rose. "Hast 'ou seen the rose in the steel dust?" he asks. He realized that such a rose might serve him as the rose of beauty had served Yeats, the Christian rose had served Eliot. *The Cantos* gather slices of time and space, fable and fact, images from aboriginal tribes and effete cultures. The poet achieves his effect not by purifying, but by collocating diffuse materials. Eliot consolidated his innovations, while Pound restlessly extended his.

The initial reaction to *The Waste Land* was violently mixed. Most poets, while admiring its technical inventiveness and finish, found it hard to like. Yeats felt it was dour and despairing. Robert Graves clung to traditional forms, disparaging their disintegration by Eliot. John Crowe Ransom wrote an adverse review of the poem, to which his sometime pupil Allen Tate published a refutation. Hart Crane was moved by *The Waste Land,* but thought that Eliot's despair was exaggerated and that his own mission, assisted by Walt Whitman's example, must be to effect a redemption of Eliot's disintegrated or corrupted world. While owing a debt to Eliot's symbolism, cityscapes, and generic mixture, Crane made what he called "an almost complete reverse of direction" from Eliot's "pessimism" toward an "ecstatic goal." Crane's major poem, *The Bridge* (1930), takes the reader backward in time, across the American continent in space, and down emotionally into a modern subterranean hell; but its overriding movement is across the arc of the Brooklyn Bridge, and it passionately and emphatically expresses secular hope against all odds.

In his prologue to *Kora in Hell,* written in 1918, William Carlos Williams, a doctor living in New Jersey, attacked the expatriates Eliot and Pound for merely warming over European conventions and for betraying American life and speech. Williams sought to express neither what the cosmopolitan Eliot called "the mind of Europe," nor the distinctive character of a limited region, as Frost, Masters, and Sandburg were doing, but a national experience. "Our own language is the beginning of that which makes and will continue to make an American poetry distinctive," he said. After the publication of *The Waste Land,* Williams campaigned against it: its sinister merit was so powerful that it might well block the movement toward an indigenous American verse. It was, he said in his *Autobiography* (1948), "the great catastrophe" that by its genius (a quality he admitted) interrupted the "rediscovery of a primal impulse, the elementary principle of all art, in the local conditions." "It wiped out our world as if an atom bomb had been dropped upon it. . . . Eliot returned us to the classroom just at the moment when I felt that we were on the point of escape to matters much closer to the essence of a new art form itself—rooted in the locality, which should give it fruit." Published a year after *The Waste Land,* the title poem of Williams's *Spring and All* opens with a "waste of broad, muddy fields / brown with dried weeds," but things that seem dead in Williams's poem, unlike those in Eliot's waste land, are slowly reborn into their particular lives: "clarity, outline of leaf." Williams felt that Eliot had imposed a shape on material that should have been allowed to take its own shape. He most famously expressed his conception of poetry in the poem beginning "so much depends / upon // a red wheel / barrow," as if objects in the world should be allowed to retain their nature without being conceptualized into abstract schemas and literary archetypes. The poet, Williams believed, should work "particularly, as a physician works, upon a patient, upon the thing before him." "No ideas but in things" was the credo he espoused in his epic, *Paterson,* which, like Pound's Cantos, extends the principles of Imagism, and also rebukes those symbolists who invest "things" with foreign significance. In *Paterson,* he called his poetry "a reply to Greek and Latin with the bare hands"; his work, unlike Pound's or Eliot's, is all but devoid of "literary" English. Its distinctiveness comes, as he insisted, from contact with native materials. He founded a magazine with *Contact* as its defiant title.

In a review, Wallace Stevens called Williams's work "anti-poetic." In contrast to Williams, Stevens, who made his living as an insurance company executive, adapted the richly suggestive patterns of sound and color in the French Symbolism of Mallarmé and Valéry, and in the Romanticism of Keats and Shelley. Despite a mutual debt to the French Symbolists, Stevens said in letters that he regarded Eliot "as a negative rather than a positive force": "Eliot and I are dead opposites." Stevens rejected especially the religious presuppositions of *The Waste Land.* In *Harmonium* (1923) and later books, he presented the death of the old gods as a liberation of the imagination. In contradistinction to Eliot's return to Christianity, Stevens called for a new religion closer to physical life and willing to encompass death, as well as life, in its conception of being. Instead of yearning for an "imperishable bliss," he embraced mortality as the meaning-granting limit: "Death is the mother of beauty," he writes in "Sunday Morning"; "hence from her, / alone, shall come fulfillment to our dreams / And our desires." Any paradise must be found within the world. The poet's task, Stevens indicates in "The Noble Rider and the Sound of Words," is ultimately to replace religion with imaginative literature: "what makes the poet the potent figure that he is, or was, or ought to be, is that he creates the world to which we turn incessantly and without knowing it and that he gives to life the supreme fictions without which we are unable to conceive of it." The creation of poetic fictions—fictions he changed and questioned even as he affirmed—occupied Stevens steadily.

Modernist Poetry and the Visual Arts

Williams and Stevens were both inspired by the European avant-garde visual artists of their time. For all his advocacy of poetry rooted in American experience, Williams was fascinated with the Cubist dissection of space and the Dada use of "found" objects, as expressed in his prologue to *Kora in Hell* and exemplified by his experiments in verbal collage. Stevens blends Cubism's multiperspectivism with haikulike concision in a poem such as "Thirteen Ways of Looking at a Blackbird." Other poets of the period register the impact of the new mass art form of cinema. Crane was so impressed by Charlie Chaplin's "genius" after seeing *The Kid* in 1921 that in the poem "Chaplinesque" he sought to capture the "arrested climaxes and evasive victories of [Chaplin's] gestures in words." At the beginning of *The Bridge,* Crane writes, "I think of cinemas, panoramic sleights," implicitly comparing his own verbal panoramas to those of a new rival, the "flashing" screen. Gertrude Stein saw her seeming repetitions as analogous with the frames of motion pictures: "the emphasis is different," she said in "Portraits and Repetition," "just as the cinema has each time a slightly different thing to make it all be moving."

Of all the modernist poets, Stein and Mina Loy had the most direct contact with the European avant-garde artists of the early twentieth century. In her "Transatlantic Interview" (1946), Stein traced her radically nonhierarchical style, in which each word is laid against another and given equal weight, to Cézanne, the painter who most influenced Cubists such as her friend Picasso. Just on the verge of his Cubist style, Picasso painted Stein's portrait in 1906; she returned the favor when she published her portrait poem "Picasso" (1912) in Alfred Stieglitz's *Camera Work,* the journal most responsible for exposing Americans to Cubism. Like the fragmented space of a Cubist painting, Stein's fragmented language threw the emphasis back on the artist's materials—the rhythms, sonorities, and grammatical norms that make up language. The experimental prose poems of *Tender Buttons* (1914) recall and parallel the Cubist disfiguration of the still life. "Act so that there is no use in a centre," she wrote in that influential poetic series; her decentering of language has inspired the Language poets and other avant-garde writers into the twenty-first century.

A regular guest in Stein's Paris salon, the English-born poet Mina Loy, whose early creative work was in the visual arts, lived in France, Italy, and New York during the period of greatest avant-garde ferment in Futurism, Cubism, and Dada. She was closely associated with artists working in these different styles, such as the Italian Futurists F. T. Marinetti and Giovanni Papini—the subject of her then-scandalously frank and edgy "Songs to Joannes" (1915–17), in which she depicts the god of love as "Pig Cupid   his rosy snout / Rooting erotic garbage." But whereas Marinetti's Futurist manifesto (1909)—amid glorifications of speeding machines, cleansing wars, and aesthetic revolt—had attacked feminism and women, Loy responds in her "Feminist Manifesto," written in 1914, with a call for women to make themselves virtually independent of men. The 1922 issue of *The Dial* that published *The Waste Land* also included Loy's poem about a bird sculpture by Constantin Brancusi, suggestive of her own poetic yearning for abstraction, and the next year she published her first book of poetry, *Lunar Baedecker*. Her long semiautobiographical poem *Anglo-Mongrels and the Rose* (1923–25) brought satiric allegory and introspective self-examination into a dissonant new amalgamation.

In 1916, Loy moved to New York City, the center of avant-garde art in America, where she was seen as rival to another poet living there, Marianne Moore. Moore had considered becoming a painter, and, in 1915, had first visited Stieglitz's gallery in New York, 291, with its collection of art by Picasso, Man Ray, and others. Like the other New York modernists, Moore took seriously the challenge of avant-garde artists to fashion a new relationship to the artistic medium and to the world. Her insistent use of quotation can be seen as a poetic corollary to the synthetic phase of Cubism, in which various media were brought together in pictorial and sculptural conglomerations that radically questioned the relation of part to whole, of representation to reality. In the verbal collage of Moore's "An Octopus," snatches of language from tourist guides, journalism, science, philosophy, and conversation are shoved up against one another, intersecting in unexpected ways. In her ambitiously modernist verse, the stanzas sprawl in jagged formations across the page, the syntax tumbles across lines in strict syllabic units, the rhymes burrow in almost undetectably discrete positions, and insistently nominalist descriptions evoke nature's dense particularity. Like her friend Williams, Moore was a sharp observer, and upholder, of the physical world; but where Williams's world is familiar, hers includes not only steamrollers and baseball players but also unusual creatures, such as the anteater called a pangolin and the mollusk called a paper nautilus—animals faithful, like her poems, to their individualizing quirks and idiosyncracies.

The Fugitives, the New Critics, and the New York Traditionalists

The year 1922 saw many important tendencies in modern writing put into motion. It was the year of *The Waste Land,* of James Joyce's *Ulysses* (published in Paris), and, at the start of the Harlem Renaissance, of Claude McKay's *Harlem Shadows* and James Weldon Johnson's *The Book of American Negro Poetry.* It was also the year when a group of teachers and students at Nashville's Vanderbilt University brought out a literary magazine called *The Fugitive,* in which they published their own and others' poems and urged an alternative to the cosmopolitan modernism centered in London. The dominant figure of the group was John Crowe Ransom, and the younger members included Allen Tate and Robert Penn Warren. These writers saw their southern identity, defined in part by their provincial remoteness from metropolitan culture, and their sense of rootedness in time and place as sources of strength for their writing. They cultivated an astringent wit as an antidote to southern nostalgia; politically, through the agrarian movement—which opposed industrialization and standardization, and affirmed Christian agricultural society—they hoped to keep for the south some of its traditional values. The magazine ceased publication in 1925; Tate had already moved to New York; Warren (after graduate study at Berkeley, Yale, and Oxford) went to Louisiana State University to teach; and Ransom joined the faculty of Kenyon College and founded the *Kenyon Review.* As writers, teachers, and critics, these and other poets speaking from the university, such as Yvor Winters, continued to compose in a style that younger poets liked for its aloofness and its complexity of motives and materials.

The influence of this style began to take shape during the later 1920s and the 1930s, when a number of important critical works were published that John Crowe Ransom applauded in his book *The New Criticism* (1941), whose title became a byword for the entire movement. Some years earlier, in *A Survey of Modernist Poetry* (1927), by Laura Riding and Robert Graves, Riding had been perhaps the first to try the experiment of reading a poem apart from any historical or linguistic context; her intense appreciation of the semantic complexities of a Shakespeare sonnet encouraged the young English poet and critic William Empson to discover the value of exploring every nuance of meaning, with the aid of psychology and sociology. The result was his famous study *Seven Types of Ambiguity* (1930), which sought to characterize the semantic strategies of multiple meanings that distinguish imaginative writing from straightforward exposition. Empson's teacher, the English critic I. A. Richards, was another creator of the New Criticism; he urged that poems be read with active and exclusive attention to what they said, without distortion by the reader's subjective preferences and presuppositions. Eliot, whose admiration for the Metaphysical poets' fusion of idea and fact influenced the movement, agreed that what was needed in reading poetry was "a very highly developed sense of fact." These prescriptions for readers, and by extension for writers, were codified by the Americans Robert Penn Warren and Cleanth Brooks in their textbook, *Understanding Poetry* (1938), which had a vast influence on the teaching of verse at American colleges in the 1940s, 1950s, and early 1960s; the influence was even greater on the many textbooks it spawned. Taken to extremes, the New Criticism implied that the essence of poetry was not to convey ideas or feelings as such but to create intricate structures of language that would manifest the density of psychophysical experience. Some of Empson's own poems are among the most thoroughgoing exemplifications of this principle; few other poets went so far, but they understood his goal. During and immediately after World War II, most poets living in the United States came to write in a way that poets of the 1920s and critics of the 1930s had prepared for them.

Despite her participation in the Fugitive group and influence on the New Criticism, Riding composed poems distinctive for their resistance to metaphor, rhetoric, and other forms of artifice. Fiercely self-questioning as a poet, she quit writing poetry altogether in 1941. Riding, a New Yorker, wrote most of her significant poetry while living abroad with Graves, largely in England and off the Spanish coast. Other women writers, more traditional in form than Riding, flourished in the New York area in the 1920s and 1930s. These poets commanded a larger following and garnered more prizes than their modernist contemporaries. In 1923, for example, the Pulitzer Prize for poetry went not to *The Waste Land* but to two books and a sonnet sequence by Edna St. Vincent Millay, the first woman to win the prize. Living in the then-bohemian Greenwich Village from 1917 to 1921, Millay wrote in fixed forms such as the sonnet and in diction close to the Romantics, but her poems capture "modern" sensibilities in that they mock prudence, endorse ephemeral love, and flout conventional femininity. Partly under Millay's influence, another New York poet, Dorothy Parker, also rode the gap between formal constraint and social unconstraint, or what she called "a disciplined eye and a wild mind"; but whereas Millay's verse is elegiac, Parker's is ascerbically comic. Elinor Wylie, who entered New York's vibrant literary scene in 1921, wrote rhyming poetry nourished by the examples of Shelley and Keats, but at her best she countervails Romantic opulence with an austerity comparable to Imagism. In 1919, Louise Bogan moved to New York, eventually becoming the poetry editor of *The New Yorker;* she, too, strongly advocated poetry in traditional meter and rhyme, but her polished poems explore terrors and griefs that elude strict control. Most of these traditionalists paradoxically articulated in their tightly controlled poems more "liberated" views than those of the formally radical but socially conservative modernists Eliot and Pound.

THE HARLEM RENAISSANCE

In the first half of the twentieth century, the Great Migration brought millions of African Americans from the rural south to northern cities in search of economic opportunity and racial tolerance. The number of such migrants rose dramatically, from 213,000 in 1900–1910, to 572,000 in the 1910s, to 913,000 in the 1920s. This massive influx helped precipitate a burst of creativity in African American letters in the 1920s and early 1930s. Though not exclusive to Harlem, it is called the Harlem Renaissance. Along with southern blacks, Caribbean migrants were among those moving north, including Claude McKay, later declared the national poet of Jamaica. Arriving in the United States in 1912 and abandoning the Jamaican English of his early verse, McKay was politically the most militant if prosodically among the more conservative of the new African American writers. In *Harlem Shadows* (1922), he preferred the sonnet among European lyric forms, but if the genre was traditional, McKay's use of it—dislocating its norms of intimacy to express racial fury and estrangement—was not. Living mostly in France and Morocco for eleven years after 1922, he inspired francophone poets such as Léopold Sédar Senghor—African and Caribbean poets of the Negritude movement, who beginning in the 1930s asserted black pride and resistance to colonial assimilation. Like McKay, another poet of the Harlem Renaissance, Countee Cullen, whose first book of poetry was *Color* (1925), also adhered to European forms and diction, but he enacted in his verse the conflict between such Eurocentric allegiance and racial alienation.

Other Harlem Renaissance poets sought to adapt African American oral forms for use in literary poetry. They rejected, on the one hand, exclusively European poetic models and, on the other, the "Uncle Remus" dialect and the exoticism of Paul Laurence Dunbar. In his preface to the first edition of *The Book of American Negro Poetry* (1922), James Weldon Johnson pointed to the example of the Irish literary renaissance, saying the African American poet "needs to find a form that will express the racial spirit by symbols from within rather than by symbols from without, . . . a form that is freer and larger than dialect, but which will still hold the racial flavor; a form expressing the imagery, the idioms, the peculiar turns of thought, and the distinctive humor and pathos, too, of the Negro." In *God's Trombones* (1927), Johnson brings the rhetorical forms, cadences, and structure of the African American sermon into literary verse. The preeminent poet of the Harlem Renaissance was Langston Hughes. Hughes's major formal innovation was to adapt for poetry the rhythms and rhymes, the rhetoric and gritty humor of the blues, as well as other music-based genres such as jazz and spirituals. His first two volumes, *The Weary Blues* (1926) and *Fine Clothes to the Jew* (1927), hybridized the blues with resources gleaned from Whitman, Sandburg, and other Euro-American poets. His later book *Montage of a Dream Deferred* (1951) assimilated into poetry the fast-paced, dissonant style of jazz called bebop: "Listen closely: / You'll hear their feet / Beating out and beating out a—/ *You think / It's a happy beat?*" Inspired by Hughes, Sterling Brown helped import into printed verse such African American oral forms as the blues, worksongs, ballads, spirituals, sermons, and tall tales. But whereas Hughes drew inspiration from black urban life, Brown looked to the rural south. His *Southern Road* (1932) blends African American rhetorical devices, syncopated rhythms, blues repetition, vernacular idiom, and call-and-response structure with Whitmanian free verse. These poets, like the Euro-American modernists, crafted a spare, nonornamental style of poetry, though its major source was the bitter wisdom and wry humor of black "folk" genres. Whereas the Euro-American modernists shattered formal traditions that seemed worn out and remote from modern life, Brown, Hughes, and Johnson extended and reinvented African American forms that had lacked a secure place in "literary" tradition.

Other African American poets drew simultaneously on the techniques of Euro-American modernism and of black "folk" culture. In poems of the loosely knit collection *Cane* (1923), Jean Toomer pays homage to a disappearing African American way of life in the rural south, drawing on the ritualistic repetitions of black oral culture. Sometimes, Toomer takes up and recasts Imagist technique in free verse poems of metaphoric juxtaposition: "Portrait in Georgia" begins, "Hair—braided chestnut, coiled like a lyncher's rope," and continues to oscillate violently between a description of a white woman's face and the lynching of a black man. Melvin Tolson, who began his career in the Harlem Renaissance but wrote his best poetry later, fused the folk-based, oral aesthetic of poets such as Hughes and Brown with the allusive strategies of Euro-American modernism in *Harlem Gallery* (1965), one of the last great high modernist poems. If high modernism is often grim, Tolson evinces a high-spirited delight in his ability to master, manipulate, and shift among different styles and idioms. He nimbly leaps rhetorical registers, from the curt abbreviations of slang to the over-elaborations of pedantry. Stuffed-shirt classicism jostles alongside racy innuendo. Since high modernism is already itself a culturally mixed aesthetic, and since Harlem Renaissance poets such as Hughes and Brown harness both black and white influences, Tolson further hybridizes two distinct yet already hybrid modes of poetry.

ENGLISH, SCOTTISH, AND IRISH POETRY AFTER MODERNISM

In the 1920s, few English poets followed the lead of Eliot and Pound, and those who did made relatively little impact on their first readers. An exception to this as to many other rules was Edith Sitwell, whose highly abstract, sound-centered sequence, *Façade* (read to the music of her friend William Walton), scandalized its first public audience, in 1923. At about the same time, in Sitwell's anthologies called *Wheels,* she was vigorously attacking poetry less experimental than her own, and she also brought to light the war poems of Wilfred Owen. David Jones, a painter as well as a poet, published two book-length poems, *In Parenthesis* (1937), perhaps the most important poem to express the disaster of World War I, and *The Anathémata* (1952), for which the inspiration and sometimes the model was Eliot's poetry, particularly *The Waste Land.* He was the only British World War I poet to write in the high modernist tradition of polyglot, densely textured, myth-laden verse. Jones's contemporary Basil Bunting spent World War I in jail as a conscientious objector and then lived away from England for many years, some of them in Rapallo, near his mentor and friend Ezra Pound. When Bunting returned to England, he came to wider notice, especially among younger poets in the north of England, after the publication of his long poem, *Briggflatts* (1966).

In 1919, in his early twenties, Edwin Muir left Scotland for London. There and in Europe, he composed archetypal poems that fuse dreamscapes, partly gleaned from his experience in psychoanalysis, with the narrative momentum of Scottish ballads. In "The Horses," he imagines the world after nuclear war: "the strange horses came. / We heard a distant tapping on the road, / A deepening drumming; it stopped, went on again / And at the corner changed to hollow thunder." Whereas Muir adopted the diction and rhythms of English poetry, Hugh MacDiarmid wrote in a synthetic Scots dialect of his own invention. "I'm famished, but fegs!" he protests in "In the Pantry," "What's here for a man / But a wheen rubbish that's lain / Sin' Time began?" MacDiarmid achieved fame and notoriety in Scotland—fame for his lyric poems and notoriety for his activities on behalf of the Communist and Scottish Nationalist parties. He aligned himself with Pound and especially with James Joyce, whose linguistic experiments in *Finnegans Wake* (1939) he praised and imitated.

Irish poets after Yeats were less attracted to the problems raised by symbolism and modernism than were Americans. Yeats, an Anglo-Irish Protestant, cast a long shadow, and Catholic poets Austin Clarke and Patrick

Kavanagh sought to distinguish their own efforts. While pursuing an interest in Irish myth and local legend, as Yeats had, Clarke wrote poems more strongly colored by the assonantal effects of Gaelic poetry and less beholden to the Protestant narrative of Irish history. Kavanagh debunked the early twentieth-century Irish literary movement led by Yeats for its elitist, "English" mystifications of the land and the peasantry. An influence on Seamus Heaney, Kavanagh brought into Irish poetry an idiom closer to Irish English speech, a sensibility more intimate with rural Irish experience.

Objectivism

Founded in the 1930s, twenty years after Imagism, Objectivism was its second-generation modernist descendent. The Imagist precept "Direct treatment of the thing, whether subjective or objective" can be seen as its point of origin: Objectivism prescribed a poetry of austere directness. In the view of the Objectivists, the world should not be subordinated, as in symbolism, to the poet's sentiments, figurative language, or preconceived forms, but should be presented in its objective otherness. "In the small beauty of the forest," writes George Oppen in "Psalm," "The wild deer bedding down—/ That they are there!" As a correlative, the Objectivists saw the poem itself as having material substance worthy of respect—as object, as thing in the world, not only as symbol of a reality elsewhere. Louis Zukofsky proposed "thinking with the things as they exist"—things both worldly and linguistic (*Prepositions*).

Pound and Williams were the encouraging elder statesmen to the Objectivists. It is one of the great ironies of modern literary history that Pound, an anti-Semite living in and supporting Benito Mussolini's Fascist Italy, inspired the left-wing Objectivist American Jews—Oppen, Zukofsky, and Charles Reznikoff—as well as Bunting, the one prominent British member of the Objectivist group, and the American Lorine Niedecker, the only woman. When Pound persuaded Harriet Monroe to publish a special issue of *Poetry* magazine in 1931, Zukofsky coined the word *Objectivists* for the group. Referring to himself in letters as the "sonny" and to Pound as his "papa," Zukofsky put Pound's methods to work in forging a second-generation modernist aesthetic that could include Yiddish song and humor, as in "Poem Beginning 'The.' " This poem adapts Pound and Eliot's high modernist technique of multilayered allusion and abrupt juxtaposition, but it rejects Eliot's pessimism in *The Waste Land,* instead celebrating in a carnivalesque spirit the possibilities of an urban, interethnic, progressive modernity. Zukofsky admired Reznikoff and wrote an essay about him in the Objectivist issue of *Poetry*. Reznikoff's 1930s poems adapt Imagist precision and understatement to the Jewish American experience of the modern city. In his later long poem *Holocaust,* Reznikoff borrows Pound's practice in *The Cantos* of using raw documents, except that the texts he edits and presents without authorial comment are from the postwar Nuremberg and Eichmann trials of the Nazis—not the sorts of materials Pound was likely to use.

Together with Zukofsky and Reznikoff, Oppen founded the Objectivist Press in the early 1930s. His work exemplifies an ethic of poetic economy in writing. The poet must try, he remarked, "to write carefully, lucidly, accurately, resisting the temptation to inflate." An organizer for the Communist Party during the Great Depression, Oppen nevertheless eschewed political rhetoric in his poetry, and for twenty-five years he gave up poetry writing for political activism. His late modernist poetry came to its finest fruition in publications of the 1960s, as did Niedecker's. Niedecker did not appear in Zukofsky's 1931 issue of *Poetry,* but when she read it, she traveled to meet him in New York. Niedecker's free verse, like Oppen's, exhibits precision and compression, silence and riddling ellipses. Some of her crystalline poems are about nature, while others are made of "found" materials—collagelike sequences that fit together quotations from historical figures such as Thomas Jefferson and Charles Darwin.

THE AUDEN CIRCLE

In England, the most significant movement contemporary with the Objectivists was made up of poets who also came to maturity in the late 1920s and early 1930s. Like the Objectivists, they were faced with the question of what to do with the legacy of modernism and, also like the Objectivists, they diverged from right-wing modernists such as Eliot and Pound in being political leftists. W. H. Auden, whose obvious brilliance daunted his contemporaries, was the central figure in this group. At various times during his time at Oxford, he befriended fellow students Stephen Spender and C. Day Lewis, and made the acquaintance of Louis MacNeice. These poets were given a collective identity when Michael Roberts published them together in an anthology, *New Signatures* (1932). They prided themselves on understatement and "social concern." Since the early part of their careers coincided with the Great Depression across the industrialized world and the rise of fascism in Europe, they were eager to express radical political attitudes, but they often did so through older verse techniques. Except for their preference for inherited poetic forms, they were strenuously ahead of their time, not least in their use of the specialized vocabularies of politics, psychiatry, and the social sciences. They proclaimed their support for a socialist revolution. After World War II led to the cold war, they became more centrist in their political views.

Auden's generation was the first in England to grow up in the shadow of the first-generation modern poets. Hopkins's attention to sonorities, Hardy's experiments in stanzaic patterns, Yeats's civic poetry of psychic ambivalence, Eliot's satiric treatment of a mechanized, urbanized world, and Owen's slant-rhymed poems of pity influenced Auden and the other poets in his circle. But the new generation needed to distinguish itself, particularly from the towering presences of Yeats and Eliot, both of whom continued to write important poems through the 1930s. Thus whereas Yeats's tone was at times hortatory, theirs tended to be low-pitched, almost flat. And whereas Eliot aspired to impersonality, they presented themselves as flesh-and-blood individuals in history, responsive to and active in the secular world.

For all their resemblances, the poets seen as a single corporate entity, "Daylewisaudenmacneicespender," in Auden's humorous collocation, are distinctive. Day Lewis, of an Anglo-Irish Protestant background, is the most lyrical and traditional poet of the group; he was a member of the Communist Party longer than the others—Stephen Spender also joined briefly in the 1930s. MacNeice is of a similar Anglo-Irish background, but his verse is less ceremonious, more alert to historical particularities and his ambivalent participation in them. Spender's self-presentation is the most vulnerable in the group: he admits to perplexities and regrets, though he admires trains, heroes, and other emblems of unwavering certitude. Auden projects sheer mastery, though he masters paradoxically, through witty self-deprecation and ironic deflation, ambivalent praise and ethical self-questioning. In a reversal of Eliot's emigration, he left England for the United States just before World War II and wrote sharply and sympathetically about the problems of community in a divided world—where "the living nations wait, / Each sequestered in its hate" ("In Memory of W. B. Yeats"). His early verse had been unrhymed and knotted with modernist difficulty, but as the social crisis of the 1930s worsened, he wrote less cryptic, more direct poems in a prodigious variety of rhymed, metered, and syllabic forms. He successfully met a challenge that has baffled many other modern and contemporary poets—how to write about intimate experience without betraying public responsibility, how to write about political exigencies without subsuming the complexities of personal feeling. In his later years, he became more religious in his Christian beliefs, and more tender, friendly, and conversational in his verse. He wittily hails even the microorganisms that make their homes on his body's surface. Living largely in New York and presiding from 1947 to 1959 over the Yale Series of Younger Poets, he became a primary influence on the next generation of American poets, whether they wrote in free verse or intricate forms.

Beyond Modernism

To summarize: in the 1920s and 1930s, emerging groups or schools of poets in the English-speaking world, as well as individual writers, defined themselves by varying degrees of affiliation with or reaction against modernism. Williams and Crane urgently felt the need to work their way out from under the weight of *The Waste Land*'s learned cynicism, while the New Critical poets elaborated Eliot's complex modernist combination of Metaphysical and symbolist poetics. Some of the Harlem Renaissance poets enthusiastically embraced Imagist or high modernist styles, while others renovated traditional European forms and African American oral genres. Born for the most part in the first decade of the twentieth century, the Objectivists and the Auden circle rejected the authoritarian politics and elevated tone of much high modernist poetry, but the Objectivists wrote "hard" and "clear," Imagist-descended poems in open forms, whereas the Auden circle often wrote in strict forms, imbued with modernist allusiveness, tonal complexity, and urban or industrial landscapes.

While all of these poets were wrestling with the legacy of modernism, they were also charting a number of distinct routes for contemporary poetry. The first-generation New Critical poets enabled the dominant mid-twentieth-century style of poetry, the elegant and complex formalism practiced by the next generation of poets in the New Critical style, such as Richard Wilbur and the early Robert Lowell, as well as the New Formalism of the 1980s. The innovations of Auden and his confederates in socially and historically responsive formal verse influenced postwar poets in England (e.g., Philip Larkin), Ireland (e.g., Paul Muldoon), and America (e.g., Frank O'Hara). The Objectivists linked first-generation experimental, open-form modernism with postwar avant-garde movements such as Charles Olson's Black Mountain school in the 1950s and the Language poets in the 1980s. In the 1960s, African American poets of the Black Arts Movement were able to look back to the orally and musically inspired poetry of some members of the Harlem Renaissance, as had identity-centered Negritude poets in Africa and the Caribbean.

Other poets born in the first decade of the twentieth century helped lay the groundwork for contemporary poetry. Stanley Kunitz began writing in the highly wrought Metaphysical mode championed by the New Critics and the modernists, but in the 1950s began to turn, with Robert Lowell and other so-called confessional poets, toward a more intimate style. Adapting Imagist precision and a Poundian interest in East Asian and classical literature to more personal utterance, Kenneth Rexroth, the patron saint of the San Francisco Renaissance of the 1950s, also helped guide the Beat movement and the Black Mountain school, countercultural movements that shared overlapping interests in open-form, orally inspired poetry. Rexroth resigned from the board of *The Black Mountain Review* in 1954 because of "unfair" criticism of Theodore Roethke, whose verse helped some postwar poets shed Eliot's ideal of impersonality. Like his friend Kunitz, Roethke began writing in highly formal verse, but in time broke into more open, self-exploratory poetry that, like the confessionalism with which he is often associated, is shaped by a psychoanalytic interest in childhood, personal development, and the unconscious.

Reacting like the American confessional poets against modernism, the English poets of the Movement in the 1950s, such as Philip Larkin, looked favorably on the traditionally metered and rhymed formal verse of John Betjeman. Like them, he tried to write poems that, avoiding arcane references and formal fragmentation, were accessible to, and pleasurable for, a wider public. Betjeman and Stevie Smith began publishing books of poetry in the 1930s, but took decades to achieve their widest readership. Smith wrote quirkily profound poems that mix theological ponderings with nursery-rhyme humor. Like Sylvia Plath, she frequently invokes death, though for Smith, death is strangely tame, almost civil. Yet another sort of death—this time on the battlefield—is the subject of Keith Douglas's poetry. The preeminent English poet of World War II, Douglas was admired by later English and Irish poets such as Geoffrey Hill and Michael Longley for his skillful yoking of powerful feeling to verbal restraint. He was killed in the war that is often seen as marking the boundary between modern and contemporary poets.

Poets in the first modern generation, such as Eliot and H. D., and those in the second, such as Auden and Oppen, wrote powerfully about World War II. But even as the unprecedented carnage of World War I was formative for many of the first moderns, World War II was a defining experience for the first contemporary generation, which begins with Elizabeth Bishop and Charles Olson, poets who came to maturity in the war's shadow. Attending college thanks to veterans' educational subsidies, many soldiers-turned-poets studied modern verse under the guidance of the close-reading strategies of the New Criticism. The challenge for these postwar poets was to transform and adapt creatively this increasingly institutionalized inheritance, to "make it new" for the contemporary world. Whether formalists or antiformalists, rebels or traditionalists, nativists or cosmopolitans, they could look back to their modern precursors for fertile soil in which to root their own consolidations and experiments.

Walt Whitman
1819–1892

Walt Whitman was one of the great innovative figures in nineteenth-century Anglo-American literature and remains a uniquely important presence in poetry across the globe. As one reads modern and contemporary American poets, one doesn't so much trace Whitman's influence as locate individual writers by their attitude toward him. He insisted that he was that new man, an American, yet some of his first European readers felt that he was too good for Americans and that he was a European in spite of himself. The young W. B. Yeats admired him; Gerard Manley Hopkins admired and feared him, the fear growing from a sense of similarity that Hopkins was reluctant to admit. Ezra Pound swore "A Pact" with Whitman, as child to a "pig-headed father": "It was you that broke the new wood, / Now is a time for carving. / We have one sap and one root— / Let there be commerce between us." Both Hart Crane and William Carlos Williams saw in Whitman's poetry an alternative to T. S. Eliot's pessimism about life, his reliance on external authority, and his suspect devotion to the iamb. A hundred years after the first edition of *Leaves of Grass,* the spirit of Whitman seemed to be born again in Allen Ginsberg and his fellow Beats, and John Berryman traced the inspiration for his Dream Songs to Whitman's "Song of Myself." Pablo Neruda, the Chilean poet whose work was much admired by American poets of the 1960s, paid tribute to Whitman as the founding father of a continental poetry: "We continue to live in a Whitmanesque age, seeing how new men and new societies rise and grow, despite their birth-pangs. Walt Whitman was the protagonist of a truly geographical personality: the first man in history to speak with a truly continental voice, to bear a truly American name" (*New York Times,* April 14, 1972). Contemporary poets as various as Adrienne Rich, Derek Walcott, and Robert Pinsky have wrestled with his shadow. In sum, in the history of modern and contemporary poetry, Whitman has been a rallying cry, an inspiration, a battleground.

Whitman raised many of the important issues that confront later poets and their readers. His joyful experiments with language, his pretense of telling all while leaving much to be inferred, his reckless assumption that poets, their language, their subject matter, and their readers are all part of one expanding community, have endowed him with enormous importance. Whitman eludes and sometimes exasperates us because, just as he prophesied, he has become part of our environment, the way we look at and thus create our world.

In his poems, Whitman appears as the archetypal overreacher; nothing human is alien to him (if he can help it) or negligible. He rescues for poetry the unpoetic, the vulgar, and the profane. He realized that poems need no longer look like poems—with neat couplets and quatrains—need, for that matter, no longer sound like poems. They can sound like the Book of Psalms or Fourth-of-July orations; it was all one to him. He launched his long periodic sentences in search of their subject matter, gave names to everything he saw, and became for later poets a great natural resource.

Whitman was born on May 31, 1819, in then-rural Huntington, Long Island. His father was of English descent, his mother of Dutch and Welsh. His indifference to religious orthodoxy, his insistence on the worth of individual experience and on private charity, may owe something to the Quakers on both sides of his family. When Whitman was still very young, his father, who was both a farmer and a carpenter, moved the family to Brooklyn, and Whitman's childhood happily alternated between the growing city and the countryside and seacoast. He attended school for only five years, for at age eleven he went to work as an office boy. He soon turned, however, to printing and journalism, and until the early 1850s—with occasional periods of school teaching—he worked as a newspaperman and editor.

More than most poets, Whitman had a carefully developed public personality, and he fostered the impression that he was ill read and indolent. This was not the case. As a youth, he read the Bible (as his revolutionary cadences bear witness), Shakespeare, McPherson's Ossian, Homer, Aeschylus and Sophocles, the Nibelungelied, the "ancient Hindoo poems," and Dante. He was also influenced by such contemporary sages as Goethe, Thomas Carlyle, and Ralph Waldo Emerson. As an occasional book reviewer for his newspapers and an energetic amateur of the theater and opera, he accumulated the rich experience that would find expression in his poems.

Whitman had been experimenting with poetry since 1847. In 1851, he moved in with his parents, supported himself with part-time carpentry, and began work on *Leaves of Grass*. The first edition appeared on July 4, 1855; like all but two of the first seven editions, it was privately printed, and the author himself set the type. It consisted of twelve untitled poems, the first and by far the longest of which would eventually be titled "Song of Myself." It is a foretaste of the poems that were to follow. The incantatory rhythms of the unrhymed lines, the catalogs of North Americans busy with their lives and occupations, the rapid alternations from joy to disaster (disaster sometimes natural, sometimes visited on men and women by their fellow human beings), the moving cinemalike eye that homes in on a detail, then springs back to survey a panorama, the speaker, sexually and socially undefined, never, despite the unabashed egocentricity of the poem's title, to be isolated from his creations—all of this richness is evident in the poet from his beginnings.

The first edition of *Leaves of Grass* was nearly anonymous; Whitman's name did not appear, but the frontispiece was a photograph of the poet in work clothes, bearded, lounging, unbuttoned. The book did not sell well, but it attracted attention in important quarters. Emerson, to whom Whitman had sent a copy, wrote a famous acknowledgment in a letter of July 21, 1855: "I greet you at the beginning of a great career, which yet must have had a long foreground somewhere, for such a start. I rubbed my eyes a little to see if this sunbeam were no illusion, but the solid sense of the book is a sober certainty. It has the best merits, namely, of fortifying and encouraging."

Leaves of Grass is Whitman's one book, and it appeared in eight editions in his lifetime as the author transformed it in response to changes in his life and in the history of his nation. It is Whitman's contribution to that peculiarly nineteenth-century form, the subjective epic, like William Wordsworth's *Prelude* a work of heroic introspection, which views the experience of one person so that it will include multitudes. "I can hardly tell why," he wrote in a letter of March 5, 1889, "but feel very positively that if any thing can justify my revolutionary attempts & utterances it is such *ensemble*—like a great city to modern civilization, & a whole combined clustering paradoxical identity a man, a woman."

From the first, Whitman added new poems to his initial slim volume—twenty in 1856, 124 in 1860. He also began to title individual poems and to divide the poems into groups. One of these groups is called "Calamus"—the title refers to a phallic marsh plant, a "very large & aromatic grass, or rush"—and it celebrates homoerotic feeling and masculine friendship, which Whitman called "adhesiveness." The emotional center of another group of poems, "Children of Adam," is Whitman's admiration for the masculine body at work and play. He praises, for example, "The march of firemen in their own costumes, the play of masculine muscles through clean-setting trowsers, and waist-straps . . . Such-like I love" ("I Sing the Body Electric").

From the beginning of his career as a writer, Whitman as experimental poet aligned himself with the great social and political experiment of American democracy. His was a "new style . . . necessitated by new theories, new themes . . . , forced upon us for American purposes" (letter of January 7, 1860). His ambition, Whitman wrote, was "to give something to our literature which will be our own; with neither foreign spirit, nor imagery nor form, but adapted to our case, grown out of our associations, boldly portraying the West, strengthening and intensifying the national soul, and finding the entire fountains of its birth and growth in our own country" (1866 letter to William D. O'Conner). Whitman propounds these ideas most influentially in his preface to *Leaves of Grass.* His relationship with his country was brought to a dramatic resolution—one might almost say, consummation—by the Civil War.

In 1862, Whitman went to the front in Virginia to be with his soldier brother, George, who had been reported wounded. George's wounds were slight, but Whitman stayed on near the fighting for a few weeks and then went to Washington. He took a part-time job in the army paymaster's office in aid of his main activity—ministering to wounded soldiers, Union and Confederate alike. Unsponsored, living meagerly so that he would have a little money for his charities, Whitman made daily visits to the Washington hospitals: he comforted the dying, dressed wounds, wrote letters home for the soldiers, brought them gifts of flowers, fruit, and tobacco, and read aloud to them, though never from his own poems. Though his first reactions to the war had been conventionally pro-Union, his awareness of the suffering on both sides and his readily aroused sympathy for all the wounded and dying young men give his poems about the war—eventually collected and published as *Drum-Taps* and later incorporated into *Leaves of Grass*—a beautifully modulated compassion. They are, with the pictures of Winslow Homer and the photographs of Mathew Brady, among the most precious records of the American Civil War. His tender poetry about soldiers and other working-class men now seems homoerotically charged, although he professed to having been unaware that his sentiments might be considered unorthodox. When the English critic John Addington Symonds, himself a homosexual, questioned Whitman about his sexual preferences, the poet adduced as evidence of his heterosexuality six bastard children, hastily invented for the occasion.

Whitman remained in Washington after the war ended. In 1865, he lost a clerkship in the Office of Indian Affairs after a few months, when it was discovered that he had written an allegedly indecent book—*Leaves of Grass.* He was then employed in the attorney general's office until 1873, when he suffered a stroke from which he never completely recovered, though he was able to do some traveling and lecturing. Between 1876 and 1891, he produced the autobiographical prose work *Specimen Days* and three collections of new poems, first published separately and then added to *Leaves of Grass,* which continued to appear in new editions. He spent his last eight years living near his brother in a small house in Camden, New Jersey. His reputation was already considerable, though greater in Europe than in the United States, and he was unembarrassed by disciples who saw him as the founder of a new religion of political and sexual liberation and who treated his poems as sacred texts. His visitors included the young Oscar Wilde, who wrote in a letter that there "is no one in this wide great world of America whom I love and honour so much."

One's-Self I Sing

One's Self I sing, a simple separate person,
Yet utter the word Democratic, the word En-Masse.

Of physiology from top to toe I sing,
Not physiognomy[1] alone nor brain alone is worthy for the Muse, I say
    the Form complete is worthier far,
The Female equally with the Male I sing.

1. Facial features, as manifestations of character.

Of Life immense in passion, pulse, and power,
Cheerful, for freest action form'd under the laws divine,
The Modern Man I sing.

1867, 1871

From Song of Myself

1

I celebrate myself, and sing myself,
And what I assume you shall assume,
For every atom belonging to me as good belongs to you.

I loafe and invite my soul,
I lean and loafe at my ease observing a spear of summer grass.

My tongue, every atom of my blood, form'd from this soil, this air,
Born here of parents born here from parents the same, and their parents the same,
I, now thirty-seven years old in perfect health begin,
Hoping to cease not till death.

Creeds and schools in abeyance,
Retiring back a while sufficed at what they are, but never forgotten,
I harbor for good or bad, I permit to speak at every hazard,
Nature without check with original energy.

2

Houses and rooms are full of perfumes, the shelves are crowded with perfumes,
I breathe the fragrance myself and know it and like it,
The distillation would intoxicate me also, but I shall not let it.

The atmosphere is not a perfume, it has no taste of the distillation, it is odorless,
It is for my mouth forever, I am in love with it,
I will go to the bank by the wood and become undisguised and naked,
I am mad for it to be in contact with me.

The smoke of my own breath,
Echoes, ripples, buzz'd whispers, love-root, silk-thread, crotch and vine,
My respiration and inspiration, the beating of my heart, the passing of blood and air through my lungs,
The sniff of green leaves and dry leaves, and of the shore and dark-color'd sea-rocks, and of hay in the barn,
The sound of the belch'd words of my voice loos'd to the eddies of the wind,
A few light kisses, a few embraces, a reaching around of arms,
The play of shine and shade on the trees as the supple boughs wag,

The delight alone or in the rush of the streets, or along the fields and hill-sides,
The feeling of health, the full-noon trill, the song of me rising from bed and meeting the sun.

Have you reckon'd a thousand acres much? have you reckon'd the earth much?
Have you practis'd so long to learn to read?
Have you felt so proud to get at the meaning of poems?

Stop this day and night with me and you shall possess the origin of all poems,
You shall possess the good of the earth and sun, (there are millions of suns left,)
You shall no longer take things at second or third hand, nor look through the eyes of the dead, nor feed on the spectres in books,
You shall not look through my eyes either, nor take things from me,
You shall listen to all sides and filter them from your self.

3

I have heard what the talkers were talking, the talk of the beginning and the end,
But I do not talk of the beginning or the end.

There was never any more inception than there is now,
Nor any more youth or age than there is now,
And will never be any more perfection than there is now,
Nor any more heaven or hell than there is now.

Urge and urge and urge,
Always the procreant urge of the world.

Out of the dimness opposite equals advance, always substance and increase, always sex,
Always a knit of identity, always distinction, always a breed of life.

To elaborate is no avail, learn'd and unlearn'd feel that it is so.

Sure as the most certain sure, plumb in the uprights, well entretied,[2] braced in the beams,
Stout as a horse, affectionate, haughty, electrical,
I and this mystery here we stand.

Clear and sweet is my soul, and clear and sweet is all that is not my soul.

Lack one lacks both, and the unseen is proved by the seen,
Till that becomes unseen and receives proof in its turn.

2. Cross-braced (carpenter's term).

Showing the best and dividing it from the worst age vexes age,
Knowing the perfect fitness and equanimity of things, while they discuss
I am silent, and go bathe and admire myself.

Welcome is every organ and attribute of me, and of any man hearty and clean,
Not an inch nor a particle of an inch is vile, and none shall be less familiar than the rest.

I am satisfied—I see, dance, laugh, sing;
As the hugging and loving bed-fellow sleeps at my side through the night, and withdraws at the peep of the day with stealthy tread,
Leaving me baskets cover'd with white towels swelling the house with their plenty,
Shall I postpone my acceptation and realization and scream at my eyes,
That they turn from gazing after and down the road,
And forthwith cipher[3] and show me to a cent,
Exactly the value of one and exactly the value of two, and which is ahead?

4

Trippers[4] and askers surround me,
People I meet, the effect upon me of my early life or the ward and city I live in, or the nation,
The latest dates, discoveries, inventions, societies, authors old and new,
My dinner, dress, associates, looks, compliments, dues,
The real or fancied indifference of some man or woman I love,
The sickness of one of my folks or of myself, or ill-doing or loss or lack of money, or depressions or exaltations,
Battles, the horrors of fratricidal war, the fever of doubtful news, the fitful events;
These come to me days and nights and go from me again,
But they are not the Me myself.

Apart from the pulling and hauling stands what I am,
Stands amused, complacent, compassionating, idle, unitary,
Looks down, is erect, or bends an arm on an impalpable certain rest,
Looking with side-curved head curious what will come next,
Both in and out of the game and watching and wondering at it.

Backward I see in my own days where I sweated through fog with linguists and contenders,
I have no mockings or arguments, I witness and wait.

5

I believe in you my soul, the other I am must not abase itself to you,
And you must not be abased to the other.

3. Calculate.

4. That is, travelers.

Loafe with me on the grass, loose the stop from your throat,
Not words, not music or rhyme I want, not custom or lecture, not even the best,
Only the lull I like, the hum of your valvèd voice.

I mind how once we lay such a transparent summer morning,
How you settled your head athwart my hips and gently turn'd over upon me,
And parted the shirt from my bosom-bone, and plunged your tongue to my bare-stript heart,
And reach'd till you felt my beard, and reach'd till you felt my feet.

Swiftly arose and spread around me the peace and knowledge that pass all the argument of the earth,
And I know that the hand of God is the promise of my own,
And I know that the spirit of God is the brother of my own,
And that all the men ever born are also my brothers, and the women my sisters and lovers,
And that a kelson[5] of the creation is love,
And limitless are leaves stiff or drooping in the fields,
And brown ants in the little wells beneath them,
And mossy scabs of the worm fence, heap'd stones, elder, mullein and poke-weed.[6]

6

A child said *What is the grass?* fetching it to me with full hands;
How could I answer the child? I do not know what it is any more than he.

I guess it must be the flag of my disposition, out of hopeful green stuff woven.

Or I guess it is the handkerchief of the Lord,
A scented gift and remembrancer designedly dropt,
Bearing the owner's name someway in the corners, that we may see and remark, and say *Whose?*

Or I guess the grass is itself a child, the produced babe of the vegetation.

Or I guess it is a uniform hieroglyphic,
And it means, Sprouting alike in broad zones and narrow zones,
Growing among black folks as among white,
Kanuck, Tuckahoe, Congressman, Cuff,[7] I give them the same, I receive them the same.

And now it seems to me the beautiful uncut hair of graves.

5. Timber support for a ship's keel (also *keelson*).
6. A shrub, an herb, and a weed, respectively.
7. African American. *Kanuck:* or "Canuck," French Canadian. *Tuckahoe:* tidewater Virginian.

Tenderly will I use you curling grass,
It may be you transpire from the breasts of young men,
It may be if I had known them I would have loved them,
It may be you are from old people, or from offspring taken soon out of their mothers' laps
And here you are the mothers' laps.

This grass is very dark to be from the white heads of old mothers,
Darker than the colorless beards of old men,
Dark to come from under the faint red roofs of mouths.

O I perceive after all so many uttering tongues,
And I perceive they do not come from the roofs of mouths for nothing.

I wish I could translate the hints about the dead young men and women,
And the hints about old men and mothers, and the offspring taken soon out of their laps.

What do you think has become of the young and old men?
And what do you think has become of the women and children?

They are alive and well somewhere,
The smallest sprout shows there is really no death,
And if ever there was it led forward life, and does not wait at the end to arrest it,
And ceas'd the moment life appear'd.

All goes onward and outward, nothing collapses,
And to die is different from what any one supposed, and luckier.

7

Has any one supposed it lucky to be born?
I hasten to inform him or her it is just as lucky to die, and I know it.

I pass death with the dying and birth with the new-wash'd babe, and am not contain'd between my hat and boots,
And peruse manifold objects, no two alike and every one good,
The earth good and the stars good, and their adjuncts all good.

I am not an earth nor an adjunct of an earth,
I am the mate and companion of people, all just as immortal and fathomless as myself,
(They do not know how immortal, but I know.)

Every kind for itself and its own, for me mine male and female,
For me those that have been boys and that love women,
For me the man that is proud and feels how it stings to be slighted,
For me the sweet-heart and the old maid, for me mothers and the mothers of mothers,
For me lips that have smiled, eyes that have shed tears,
For me children and the begetters of children.

Undrape! you are not guilty to me, nor stale nor discarded,
I see through the broadcloth and gingham whether or no,
And am around, tenacious, acquisitive, tireless, and cannot be shaken away.

8

The little one sleeps in its cradle,
I lift the gauze and look a long time, and silently brush away flies with my hand.

The youngster and the red-faced girl turn aside up the bushy hill,
I peeringly view them from the top.

The suicide sprawls on the bloody floor of the bedroom,
I witness the corpse with its dabbled hair, I note where the pistol has fallen.

The blab of the pave,[8] tires of carts, sluff of boot-soles, talk of the promenaders,
The heavy omnibus, the driver with his interrogating thumb, the clank of the shod horses on the granite floor,
The snow-sleighs, clinking, shouted jokes, pelts of snow-balls,
The hurrahs for popular favorites, the fury of rous'd mobs,
The flap of the curtain'd litter, a sick man inside borne to the hospital,
The meeting of enemies, the sudden oath, the blows and fall,
The excited crowd, the policeman with his star quickly working his passage to the centre of the crowd,
The impassive stones that receive and return so many echoes,
What groans of over-fed or half-starv'd who fall sunstruck or in fits,
What exclamations of women taken suddenly who hurry home and give birth to babes,
What living and buried speech is always vibrating here, what howls restrain'd by decorum,
Arrests of criminals, slights, adulterous offers made, acceptances, rejections with convex lips,
I mind them or the show or resonance of them—I come and I depart.

9

The big doors of the country barn stand open and ready,
The dried grass of the harvest-time loads the slow-drawn wagon,
The clear light plays on the brown gray and green intertinged,
The armfuls are pack'd to the sagging mow.

I am there, I help, I came stretch'd atop of the load,
I felt its soft jolts, one leg reclined on the other,
I jump from the cross-beams and seize the clover and timothy,[9]
And roll head over heels and tangle my hair full of wisps.

8. The idle talk of the streets.

9. Grass used as hay.

10

Alone far in the wilds and mountains I hunt,
Wandering amazed at my own lightness and glee,
In the late afternoon choosing a safe spot to pass the night,
Kindling a fire and broiling the fresh-kill'd game,
Falling asleep on the gather'd leaves with my dog and gun by my side.

The Yankee clipper is under her sky-sails, she cuts the sparkle and scud,[1]
My eyes settle the land, I bend at her prow or shout joyously from the deck.

The boatmen and clam-diggers arose early and stopt for me,
I tuck'd my trowser-ends in my boots and went and had a good time;
You should have been with us that day round the chowder-kettle.

I saw the marriage of the trapper in the open air in the far west, the bride was a red girl,
Her father and his friends sat near cross-legged and dumbly smoking, they had moccasins to their feet and large thick blankets hanging from their shoulders,
On a bank lounged the trapper, he was drest mostly in skins, his luxuriant beard and curls protected his neck, he held his bride by the hand,
She had long eyelashes, her head was bare, her coarse straight locks descended upon her voluptuous limbs and reach'd to her feet.

The runaway slave came to my house and stopt outside,
I heard his motions crackling the twigs of the woodpile,
Through the swung half-door of the kitchen I saw him limpsy[2] and weak,
And went where he sat on a log and led him in and assured him,
And brought water and fill'd a tub for his sweated body and bruis'd feet,
And gave him a room that enter'd from my own, and gave him some coarse clean clothes,
And remember perfectly well his revolving eyes and his awkwardness,
And remember putting plasters on the galls of his neck and ankles;
He staid with me a week before he was recuperated and pass'd north,
I had him sit next me at table, my fire-lock lean'd in the corner.

11

Twenty-eight young men bathe by the shore,
Twenty-eight young men and all so friendly;
Twenty-eight years of womanly life and all so lonesome.

She owns the fine house by the rise of the bank,
She hides handsome and richly drest aft the blinds of the window.

Which of the young men does she like the best?
Ah the homeliest of them is beautiful to her.

1. Sea foam. *Yankee clipper:* swift, full-rigged merchant ship. *Sky-sails:* the light sails near the top of the mast.
2. Limp.

Where are you off to, lady? for I see you,
You splash in the water there, yet stay stock still in your room.

Dancing and laughing along the beach came the twenty-ninth bather,
The rest did not see her, but she saw them and loved them.

The beards of the young men glisten'd with wet, it ran from their long hair,
Little streams pass'd all over their bodies.

An unseen hand also pass'd over their bodies,
It descended tremblingly from their temples and ribs.

The young men float on their backs, their white bellies bulge to the sun, they do not ask who seizes fast to them,
They do not know who puffs and declines with pendant and bending arch,
They do not think whom they souse with spray.

12

The butcher-boy puts off his killing-clothes, or sharpens his knife at the stall in the market,
I loiter enjoying his repartee and his shuffle and break-down.[3]

Blacksmiths with grimed and hairy chests environ the anvil,
Each has his main-sledge, they are all out, there is a great heat in the fire.

From the cinder-strew'd threshold I follow their movements,
The lithe sheer of their waists plays even with their massive arms,
Overhand the hammers swing, overhand so slow, overhand so sure,
They do not hasten, each man hits in his place.

13

The negro holds firmly the reins of his four horses, the block swags underneath on its tied-over chain,
The negro that drives the long dray of the stone-yard, steady and tall he stands pois'd on one leg on the string-piece,[4]
His blue shirt exposes his ample neck and breast and loosens over his hip-band,
His glance is calm and commanding, he tosses the slouch of his hat away from his forehead,
The sun falls on his crispy hair and mustache, falls on the black of his polish'd and perfect limbs.

I behold the picturesque giant and love him, and I do not stop there,
I go with the team also.

3. Two ministrel-show dances: the first slow and shuffling, the second fast and frenetic.

4. Long, heavy timber used to keep a load in place.

In me the caresser of life wherever moving, backward as well as forward sluing,
To niches aside and junior[5] bending, not a person or object missing,
Absorbing all to myself and for this song.

Oxen that rattle the yoke and chain or halt in the leafy shade, what is that you express in your eyes?
It seems to me more than all the print I have read in my life.

My tread scares the wood-drake and wood-duck on my distant and day-long ramble,
They rise together, they slowly circle around.

I believe in those wing'd purposes,
And acknowledge red, yellow, white, playing within me,
And consider green and violet and the tufted crown[6] intentional,
And do not call the tortoise unworthy because she is not something else,
And the jay in the woods never studied the gamut,[7] yet trills pretty well to me,
And the look of the bay mare shames silliness out of me.

14

The wild gander leads his flock through the cool night,
Ya-honk he says, and sounds it down to me like an invitation,
The pert may suppose it meaningless, but I listening close,
Find its purpose and place up there toward the wintry sky.

The sharp-hoof'd moose of the north, the cat on the house-sill, the chick-adee, the prairie-dog,
The litter of the grunting sow as they tug at her teats,
The brood of the turkey-hen and she with her half-spread wings,
I see in them and myself the same old law.

The press of my foot to the earth springs a hundred affections,
They scorn the best I can do to relate them.

I am enamour'd of growing out-doors,
Of men that live among cattle or taste of the ocean or woods,
Of the builders and steerers of ships and the wielders of axes and mauls,[8] and the drivers of horses,
I can eat and sleep with them week in and week out.

What is commonest, cheapest, nearest, easiest, is Me,
Me going in for my chances, spending for vast returns,
Adorning myself to bestow myself on the first that will take me,
Not asking the sky to come down to my good will,
Scattering it freely forever.

* * *

5. Smaller. *Sluing:* turning.
6. Of the wood drake, a male duck.
7. Musical scale.
8. Heavy mallets.

46

I know I have the best of time and space, and was never measured and never will be measured.

I tramp a perpetual journey, (come listen all!)
My signs are a rain-proof coat, good shoes, and a staff cut from the woods,
No friend of mine takes his ease in my chair,
I have no chair, no church, no philosophy,
I lead no man to a dinner-table, library, exchange,[9]
But each man and each woman of you I lead upon a knoll,
My left hand hooking you round the waist,
My right hand pointing to landscapes of continents and the public road.

Not I, not any one else can travel that road for you,
You must travel it for yourself.

It is not far, it is within reach,
Perhaps you have been on it since you were born and did not know,
Perhaps it is everywhere on water and on land.

Shoulder your duds[1] dear son, and I will mine, and let us hasten forth,
Wonderful cities and free nations we shall fetch as we go.

If you tire, give me both burdens, and rest the chuff[2] of your hand on my hip,
And in due time you shall repay the same service to me,
For after we start we never lie by again.

This day before dawn I ascended a hill and look'd at the crowded heaven,
And I said to my spirit *When we become the enfolders of those orbs, and the pleasure and knowledge of every thing in them, shall we be fill'd and satisfied then?*
And my spirit said *No, we but level that lift to pass and continue beyond.*

You are also asking me questions and I hear you,
I answer that I cannot answer, you must find out for yourself.

Sit a while dear son,
Here are biscuits to eat and here is milk to drink,
But as soon as you sleep and renew yourself in sweet clothes, I kiss you with a good-by kiss and open the gate for your egress hence.

Long enough have you dream'd contemptible dreams,
Now I wash the gum from your eyes,
You must habit yourself to the dazzle of the light and of every moment of your life.

9. Stock exchange.
1. Clothes and personal belongings.
2. That is, heel.

Long have you timidly waded holding a plank by the shore,
Now I will you to be a bold swimmer,
To jump off in the midst of the sea, rise again, nod to me, shout, and laughingly dash with your hair.

47

I am the teacher of athletes,
He that by me spreads a wider breast than my own proves the width of my own,
He most honors my style who learns under it to destroy the teacher.

The boy I love, the same becomes a man not through derived power, but in his own right,
Wicked rather than virtuous out of conformity or fear,
Fond of his sweetheart, relishing well his steak,
Unrequited love or a slight cutting him worse than sharp steel cuts,
First-rate to ride, to fight, to hit the bull's eye, to sail a skiff, to sing a song or play on the banjo,
Preferring scars and the beard and faces pitted with small-pox over all latherers,
And those well-tann'd to those that keep out of the sun.

I teach straying from me, yet who can stray from me?
I follow you whoever you are from the present hour,
My words itch at your ears till you understand them.

I do not say these things for a dollar or to fill up the time while I wait for a boat,
(It is you talking just as much as myself, I act as the tongue of you,
Tied in your mouth, in mine it begins to be loosen'd.)

I swear I will never again mention love or death inside a house,
And I swear I will never translate myself at all, only to him or her who privately stays with me in the open air.

If you would understand me go to the heights or water-shore,
The nearest gnat is an explanation, and a drop or motion of waves a key,
The maul, the oar, the hand-saw, second my words.

No shutter'd room or school can commune with me,
But roughs and little children better than they.

The young mechanic is closest to me, he knows me well,
The woodman that takes his axe and jug with him shall take me with him all day,
The farm-boy ploughing in the field feels good at the sound of my voice,
In vessels that sail my words sail, I go with fishermen and seamen and love them.

The soldier camp'd or upon the march is mine,
On the night ere the pending battle many seek me, and I do not fail them,
On that solemn night (it may be their last) those that know me seek me.

My face rubs to the hunter's face when he lies down alone in his blanket,
The driver thinking of me does not mind the jolt of his wagon,
The young mother and old mother comprehend me,
The girl and the wife rest the needle a moment and forget where they are,
They and all would resume what I have told them.

48

I have said that the soul is not more than the body,
And I have said that the body is not more than the soul,
And nothing, not God, is greater to one than one's self is,
And whoever walks a furlong[3] without sympathy walks to his own funeral drest in his shroud,
And I or you pocketless of a dime may purchase the pick of the earth,
And to glance with an eye or show a bean in its pod confounds the learning of all times,
And there is no trade or employment but the young man following it may become a hero,
And there is no object so soft but it makes a hub for the wheel'd universe,
And I say to any man or woman, Let your soul stand cool and composed before a million universes.

And I say to mankind, Be not curious about God,
For I who am curious about each am not curious about God,
(No array of terms can say how much I am at peace about God and about death.)

I hear and behold God in every object, yet understand God not in the least,
Nor do I understand who there can be more wonderful than myself.

Why should I wish to see God better than this day?
I see something of God each hour of the twenty-four, and each moment then,
In the faces of men and women I see God, and in my own face in the glass,
I find letters from God dropt in the street, and every one is sign'd by God's name,
And I leave them where they are, for I know that wheresoe'er I go,
Others will punctually come for ever and ever.

3. One-eighth of a mile.

49

And as to you Death, and you bitter hug of mortality, it is idle to try to alarm me.

To his work without flinching the accoucheur comes,
I see the elder-hand[4] pressing receiving supporting,
I recline by the sills of the exquisite flexible doors,
And mark the outlet, and mark the relief and escape.

And as to you Corpse I think you are good manure, but that does not offend me,
I smell the white roses sweet-scented and growing,
I reach to the leafy lips, I reach to the polish'd breasts of melons.

And as to you Life I reckon you are the leavings of many deaths,
(No doubt I have died myself ten thousand times before.)

I hear you whispering there O stars of heaven,
O suns—O grass of graves—O perpetual transfers and promotions,
If you do not say any thing how can I say any thing?

Of the turbid pool that lies in the autumn forest,
Of the moon that descends the steeps of the soughing[5] twilight,
Toss, sparkles of day and dusk—toss on the black stems that decay in the muck,
Toss to the moaning gibberish of the dry limbs.

I ascend from the moon, I ascend from the night,
I perceive that the ghastly glimmer is noonday sunbeams reflected,
And debouch[6] to the steady and central from the offspring great or small.

50

There is that in me—I do not know what it is—but I know it is in me.

Wrench'd and sweaty—calm and cool then my body becomes,
I sleep—I sleep long.

I do not know it—it is without name—it is a word unsaid,
It is not in any dictionary, utterance, symbol.

Something it swings on more than the earth I swing on,
To it the creation is the friend whose embracing awakes me.

Perhaps I might tell more. Outlines! I plead for my brothers and sisters.

Do you see O my brothers and sisters?
It is not chaos or death—it is form, union, plan—it is eternal life—it is Happiness.

4. The guiding hand of the midwife or obstetrician. *Accoucheur:* male midwife.
5. Sighing.
6. Pour forth.

51

The past and present wilt—I have fill'd them, emptied them,
And proceed to fill my next fold of the future.

Listener up there! what have you to confide to me?
Look in my face while I snuff the sidle[7] of evening,
(Talk honestly, no one else hears you, and I stay only a minute longer.)

Do I contradict myself?
Very well then I contradict myself,
(I am large, I contain multitudes.)

I concentrate toward them that are nigh, I wait on the door-slab.

Who has done his day's work? who will soonest be through with his supper?
Who wishes to walk with me?

Will you speak before I am gone? will you prove already too late?

52

The spotted hawk swoops by and accuses me, he complains of my gab and my loitering.

I too am not a bit tamed, I too am untranslatable,
I sound my barbaric yawp over the roofs of the world.

The last scud of day holds back for me,
It flings my likeness after the rest and true as any on the shadow'd wilds,
It coaxes me to the vapor and the dusk.

I depart as air, I shake my white locks at the runaway sun,
I effuse my flesh in eddies, and drift it in lacy jags.

I bequeath myself to the dirt to grow from the grass I love,
If you want me again look for me under your boot-soles.

You will hardly know who I am or what I mean,
But I shall be good health to you nevertheless,
And filter and fibre your blood.

Failing to fetch me at first keep encouraged,
Missing me one place search another,
I stop somewhere waiting for you.

1855, 1881

7. Extinguish the fading light.

Crossing Brooklyn Ferry

1

Flood-tide below me! I see you face to face!
Clouds of the west—sun there half an hour high—I see you also face to face.

Crowds of men and women attired in the usual costumes, how curious you are to me!
On the ferry-boats the hundreds and hundreds that cross, returning home, are more curious to me than you suppose,
And you that shall cross from shore to shore years hence are more to me, and more in my meditations, than you might suppose.

2

The impalpable sustenance of me from all things at all hours of the day,
The simple, compact, well-join'd scheme, myself disintegrated, every one disintegrated yet part of the scheme,
The similitudes of the past and those of the future,
The glories strung like beads on my smallest sights and hearings, on the walk in the street and the passage over the river,
The current rushing so swiftly and swimming with me far away,
The others that are to follow me, the ties between me and them,
The certainty of others, the life, love, sight, hearing of others.

Others will enter the gates of the ferry and cross from shore to shore,
Others will watch the run of the flood-tide,
Others will see the shipping of Manhattan north and west, and the heights of Brooklyn to the south and east,
Others will see the islands large and small;
Fifty years hence, others will see them as they cross, the sun half an hour high,
A hundred years hence, or ever so many hundred years hence, others will see them,
Will enjoy the sunset, the pouring-in of the flood-tide, the falling-back to the sea of the ebb-tide.

3

It avails not, time nor place—distance avails not,
I am with you, you men and women of a generation, or ever so many generations hence,
Just as you feel when you look on the river and sky, so I felt,
Just as any of you is one of a living crowd, I was one of a crowd,
Just as you are refresh'd by the gladness of the river and the bright flow, I was refresh'd,
Just as you stand and lean on the rail, yet hurry with the swift current, I stood yet was hurried,
Just as you look on the numberless masts of ships and the thick-stemm'd pipes of steamboats, I look'd.

I too many and many a time cross'd the river of old,
Watched the Twelfth-month[8] sea-gulls, saw them high in the air floating with motionless wings, oscillating their bodies,
Saw how the glistening yellow lit up parts of their bodies and left the rest in strong shadow,
Saw the slow-wheeling circles and the gradual edging toward the south,
Saw the reflection of the summer sky in the water,
Had my eyes dazzled by the shimmering track of beams,
Look'd at the fine centrifugal spokes of light round the shape of my head in the sunlit water,
Look'd on the haze on the hills southward and south-westward,
Look'd on the vapor as it flew in fleeces tinged with violet,
Look'd toward the lower bay to notice the vessels arriving,
Saw their approach, saw aboard those that were near me,
Saw the white sails of schooners and sloops, saw the ships at anchor,
The sailors at work in the rigging or out astride the spars,
The round masts, the swinging motion of the hulls, the slender serpentine pennants,
The large and small steamers in motion, the pilots in their pilot-houses,
The white wake left by the passage, the quick tremulous whirl of the wheels,
The flags of all nations, the falling of them at sunset,
The scallop-edged waves in the twilight, the ladled cups, the frolicsome crests and glistening,
The stretch afar growing dimmer and dimmer, the gray walls of the granite storehouses by the docks,
On the river the shadowy group, the big steam-tug closely flank'd on each side by the barges, the hay-boat, the belated lighter,
On the neighboring shore the fires from the foundry chimneys burning high and glaringly into the night,
Casting their flicker of black contrasted with wild red and yellow light over the tops of houses and down into the clefts of streets.

4

These and all else were to me the same as they are to you,
I loved well those cities, loved well the stately and rapid river,
The men and women I saw were all near to me,
Others the same—others who look back on me because I look'd forward to them,
(The time will come, though I stop here to-day and to-night.)

5

What is it then between us?
What is the count of the scores or hundreds of years between us?

Whatever it is, it avails not—distance avails not, and place avails not,
I too lived, Brooklyn of ample hills was mine,

8. The Quaker designation for December.

I too walk'd the streets of Manhattan island, and bathed in the waters around it,
I too felt the curious abrupt questionings stir within me,
In the day among crowds of people sometimes they came upon me,
In my walks home late at night or as I lay in my bed they came upon me,
I too had been struck from the float forever held in solution,
I too had receiv'd identity by my body,
That I was I knew was of my body, and what I should be I knew I should be of my body.

6

It is not upon you alone the dark patches fall,
The dark threw its patches down upon me also,
The best I had done seem'd to me blank and suspicious,
My great thoughts as I supposed them, were they not in reality meagre?
Nor is it you alone who know what it is to be evil,
I am he who knew what it was to be evil,
I too knitted the old knot of contrariety,
Blabb'd, blush'd, resented, lied, stole, grudg'd,
Had guile, anger, lust, hot wishes I dared not speak,
Was wayward, vain, greedy, shallow, sly, cowardly, malignant,
The wolf, the snake, the hog, not wanting in me,
The cheating look, the frivolous word, the adulterous wish, not wanting,
Refusals, hates, postponements, meanness, laziness, none of these wanting,
Was one with the rest, the days and haps of the rest,
Was call'd by my nighest name by clear loud voices of young men as they saw me approaching or passing,
Felt their arms on my neck as I stood, or the negligent leaning of their flesh against me as I sat,
Saw many I loved in the street or ferry-boat or public assembly, yet never told them a word,
Lived the same life with the rest, the same old laughing, gnawing, sleeping,
Play'd the part that still looks back on the actor or actress,
The same old role, the role that is what we make it, as great as we like,
Or as small as we like, or both great and small.

7

Closer yet I approach you,
What thought you have of me now, I had as much of you—I laid in my stores in advance,
I consider'd long and seriously of you before you were born.

Who was to know what should come home to me?
Who knows but I am enjoying this?
Who knows, for all the distance, but I am as good as looking at you now, for all you cannot see me?

8

Ah, what can ever be more stately and admirable to me than mast-hemm'd Manhattan?
River and sunset and scallop-edg'd waves of flood-tide?
The sea-gulls oscillating their bodies, the hay-boat in the twilight, and the belated lighter?
What gods can exceed these that clasp me by the hand, and with voices I love call me promptly and loudly by my nighest name as I approach?
What is more subtle than this which ties me to the woman or man that looks in my face?
Which fuses me into you now, and pours my meaning into you?

We understand then do we not?
What I promis'd without mentioning it, have you not accepted?
What the study could not teach—what the preaching could not accomplish is accomplish'd, is it not?

9

Flow on, river! flow with the flood-tide, and ebb with the ebb-tide!
Frolic on, crested and scallop-edg'd waves!
Gorgeous clouds of the sunset! drench with your splendor me, or the men and women generations after me!
Cross from shore to shore, countless crowds of passengers!
Stand up, tall masts of Mannahatta! stand up, beautiful hills of Brooklyn!
Throb, baffled and curious brain! throw out questions and answers!
Suspend here and everywhere, eternal float of solution!
Gaze, loving and thirsting eyes, in the house or street or public assembly!
Sound out, voices of young men! loudly and musically call me by my nighest name!
Live, old life! play the part that looks back on the actor or actress!
Play the old role, the role that is great or small according as one makes it!
Consider, you who peruse me, whether I may not in unknown ways be looking upon you;
Be firm, rail over the river, to support those who lean idly, yet haste with the hasting current;
Fly on, sea-birds! fly sideways, or wheel in large circles high in the air;
Receive the summer sky, you water, and faithfully hold it till all downcast eyes have time to take it from you!
Diverge, fine spokes of light, from the shape of my head, or any one's head, in the sunlit water!
Come on, ships from the lower bay! pass up or down, white-sail'd schooners, sloops, lighters!
Flaunt away, flags of all nations! be duly lower'd at sunset!
Burn high your fires, foundry chimneys! cast black shadows at nightfall! cast red and yellow light over the tops of the houses!
Appearances, now or henceforth, indicate what you are,
You necessary film, continue to envelop the soul,
About my body for me, and your body for you, be hung out divinest aromas,

Thrive, cities—bring your freight, bring your shows, ample and sufficient rivers,
Expand, being than which none else is perhaps more spiritual,
Keep your places, objects than which none else is more lasting.

You have waited, you always wait, you dumb, beautiful ministers,
We receive you with free sense at last, and are insatiate henceforward,
Not you any more shall be able to foil us, or withhold yourselves from us,
We use you, and do not cast you aside—we plant you permanently within us,
We fathom you not—we love you—there is perfection in you also,
You furnish your parts toward eternity,
Great or small, you furnish your parts toward the soul.

1856, 1881

I Saw in Louisiana a Live-Oak Growing

I saw in Louisiana a live-oak growing,
All alone stood it and the moss hung down from the branches,
Without any companion it grew there uttering joyous leaves of dark green,
And its look, rude, unbending, lusty, made me think of myself,
But I wonder'd how it could utter joyous leaves standing alone there without its friend near, for I knew I could not,
And I broke off a twig with a certain number of leaves upon it, and twined around it a little moss,
And brought it away, and I have placed it in sight in my room,
It is not needed to remind me as of my own dear friends,
(For I believe lately I think of little else than of them,)
Yet it remains to me a curious token, it makes me think of manly love;
For all that, and though the live-oak glistens there in Louisiana solitary in a wide flat space,
Uttering joyous leaves all its life without a friend a lover near,
I know very well I could not.

1860, 1867

A Hand-Mirror

Hold it up sternly—see this it sends back, (who is it? is it you?)
Outside fair costume, within ashes and filth,
No more a flashing eye, no more a sonorous voice or springy step,
Now some slave's eye, voice, hands, step,
A drunkard's breath, unwholesome eater's face, venerealee's flesh,
Lungs rotting away piecemeal, stomach sour and cankerous,
Joints rheumatic, bowels clogged with abomination,
Blood circulating dark and poisonous streams,
Words babble, hearing and touch callous,

No brain, no heart left, no magnetism of sex;
Such from one look in this looking-glass ere you go hence,
Such a result so soon—and from such a beginning!

1860

Cavalry Crossing a Ford

A line in long array where they wind betwixt green islands,
They take a serpentine course, their arms flash in the sun—hark to the musical clank,
Behold the silvery river, in it the splashing horses loitering stop to drink,
Behold the brown-faced men, each group, each person a picture, the negligent rest on the saddles,
Some emerge on the opposite bank, others are just entering the ford—while,
Scarlet and blue and snowy white,
The guidon[9] flags flutter gayly in the wind.

1865, 1867

By the Bivouac's Fitful Flame

By the bivouac's fitful flame,
A procession winding around me, solemn and sweet and slow—but first I note,
The tents of the sleeping army, the fields' and woods' dim outline,
The darkness lit by spots of kindled fire, the silence,
Like a phantom far or near an occasional figure moving,
The shrubs and trees, (as I lift my eyes they seem to be stealthily watching me,)
While wind in procession thoughts, O tender and wondrous thoughts,
Of life and death, of home and the past and loved, and of those that are far away;
A solemn and slow procession there as I sit on the ground,
By the bivouac's fitful flame.

1865, 1867

When Lilacs Last in the Dooryard Bloom'd

1

When lilacs last in the dooryard bloom'd,
And the great star[1] early droop'd in the western sky in the night,
I mourn'd, and yet shall mourn with ever-returning spring.

9. Pennant.

1. Venus.

Ever-returning spring, trinity sure to me you bring,
Lilac blooming perennial and dropping star in the west,
And thought of him I love.

2

O powerful western fallen star!
O shades of night—O moody, tearful night!
O great star disappear'd—O the black murk that hides the star!
O cruel hands that hold me powerless—O helpless soul of me!
O harsh surrounding cloud that will not free my soul.

3

In the dooryard fronting an old farm-house near the white-wash'd palings,
Stands the lilac-bush tall-growing with heart-shaped leaves of rich green,
With many a pointed blossom rising delicate, with the perfume strong I love,
With every leaf a miracle—and from this bush in the dooryard,
With delicate-color'd blossoms and heart-shaped leaves of rich green,
A sprig with its flower I break.

4

In the swamp in secluded recesses,
A shy and hidden bird is warbling a song.

Solitary the thrush,
The hermit withdrawn to himself, avoiding the settlements,
Sings by himself a song.

Song of the bleeding throat,
Death's outlet song of life, (for well dear brother I know,
If thou wast not granted to sing thou would'st surely die.)

5

Over the breast of the spring, the land, amid cities,
Amid lanes and through old woods, where lately the violets peep'd from the ground, spotting the gray debris,
Amid the grass in the fields each side of the lanes, passing the endless grass,
Passing the yellow-spear'd wheat, every grain from its shroud in the dark-brown fields uprisen,
Passing the apple-tree blows[2] of white and pink in the orchards,
Carrying a corpse to where it shall rest in the grave,
Night and day journeys a coffin.[3]

2. Blossoms.
3. Six days after President Abraham Lincoln's assassination on April 14, 1865, a funeral train carried his body from Washington, D.C., to Springfield, Illinois.

6

Coffin that passes through lanes and streets,
Through day and night with the great cloud darkening the land,
With the pomp of the inloop'd flags with the cities draped in black,
With the show of the States themselves as of crape-veil'd women standing,
With processions long and winding and the flambeaus[4] of the night,
With the countless torches lit, with the silent sea of faces and the unbared heads,
With the waiting depot, the arriving coffin, and the sombre faces,
With dirges through the night, with the thousand voices rising strong and solemn,
With all the mournful voices of the dirges pour'd around the coffin,
The dim-lit churches and the shuddering organs—where amid these you journey,
With the tolling tolling bells' perpetual clang,
Here, coffin that slowly passes,
I give you my sprig of lilac.

7

(Nor for you, for one alone,
Blossoms and branches green to coffins all I bring,
For fresh as the morning, thus would I chant a song for you O sane and sacred death.

All over bouquets of roses,
O death, I cover you over with roses and early lilies,
But mostly and now the lilac that blooms the first,
Copious I break, I break the sprigs from the bushes,
With loaded arms I come, pouring for you,
For you and the coffins all of you O death.)

8

O western orb sailing the heaven,
Now I know what you must have meant as a month since I walk'd,
As I walk'd in silence the transparent shadowy night,
As I saw you had something to tell as you bent to me night after night,
As you droop'd from the sky low down as if to my side, (while the other stars all look'd on,)
As we wander'd together the solemn night, (for something I know not what kept me from sleep,)
As the night advanced, and I saw on the rim of the west how full you were of woe,
As I stood on the rising ground in the breeze in the cool transparent night,
As I watch'd where you pass'd and was lost in the netherward black of the night,

4. Torches.

As my soul in its trouble dissatisfied sank, as where you sad orb,
Concluded, dropt in the night, and was gone.

9

Sing on there in the swamp,
O singer bashful and tender, I hear your notes, I hear your call,
I hear, I come presently, I understand you,
But a moment I linger, for the lustrous star has detain'd me,
The star my departing comrade holds and detains me.

10

O how shall I warble myself for the dead one there I loved?
And how shall I deck my song for the large sweet soul that has gone?
And what shall my perfume be for the grave of him I love?

Sea-winds blown from east and west,
Blown from the Eastern sea and blown from the Western sea, till there
    on the prairies meeting,
These and with these and the breath of my chant,
I'll perfume the grave of him I love.

11

O what shall I hang on the chamber walls?
And what shall the pictures be that I hang on the walls,
To adorn the burial-house of him I love?

Pictures of growing spring and farms and homes,
With the Fourth-month eve at sundown, and the gray smoke lucid and
    bright,
With floods of the yellow gold of the gorgeous, indolent, sinking sun,
    burning, expanding the air,
With the fresh sweet herbage under foot, and the pale green leaves of
    the trees prolific,
In the distance the flowing glaze, the breast of the river, with a wind-
    dapple here and there,
With ranging hills on the banks, with many a line against the sky, and
    shadows,
And the city at hand with dwellings so dense, and stacks of chimneys,
And all the scenes of life and the workshops, and the workmen
    homeward returning.

12

Lo, body and soul—this land,
My own Manhattan with spires, and the sparkling and hurrying tides,
    and the ships,
The varied and ample land, the South and the North in the light, Ohio's
    shores and flashing Missouri,
And ever the far-spreading prairies cover'd with grass and corn.

Lo, the most excellent sun so calm and haughty,
The violet and purple morn with just-felt breezes,
The gentle soft-born measureless light,
The miracle spreading bathing all, the fulfill'd noon,
The coming eve delicious, the welcome night and the stars,
Over my cities shining all, enveloping man and land.

13

Sing on, sing on you gray-brown bird,
Sing from the swamps, the recesses, pour your chant from the bushes,
Limitless out of the dusk, out of the cedars and pines.

Sing on dearest brother, warble your reedy song,
Loud human song, with voice of uttermost woe.

O liquid and free and tender!
O wild and loose to my soul—O wondrous singer!
You only I hear—yet the star holds me, (but will soon depart,)
Yet the lilac with mastering odor holds me.

14

Now while I sat in the day and look'd forth,
In the close of the day with its light and the fields of spring, and the farmers preparing their crops,
In the large unconscious scenery of my land with its lakes and forests,
In the heavenly aerial beauty, (after the perturb'd winds and the storms,)
Under the arching heavens of the afternoon swift passing, and the voices of children and women,
The many-moving sea-tides, and I saw the ships how they sail'd,
And the summer approaching with richness, and the fields all busy with labor,
And the infinite separate houses, how they all went on, each with its meals and minutia of daily usages,
And the streets how their throbbings throbb'd, and the cities pent—lo, then and there,
Falling upon them all and among them all, enveloping me with the rest,
Appear'd the cloud, appear'd the long black trail,
And I knew death, its thought, and the sacred knowledge of death.

Then with the knowledge of death as walking one side of me
And the thought of death close-walking the other side of me
And I in the middle as with companions, and as holding the hands of companions,
I fled forth to the hiding receiving night that talks not,
Down to the shores of the water, the path by the swamp in the dimness,
To the solemn shadowy cedars and ghostly pines so still.

And the singer so shy to the rest receiv'd me,
The gray-brown bird I know receiv'd us comrades three,
And he sang the carol of death, and a verse for him I love.

From deep secluded recesses,
From the fragrant cedars and the ghostly pines so still,
Came the carol of the bird.

And the charm of the carol rapt me,
As I held as if by their hands my comrades in the night,
And the voice of my spirit tallied the song of the bird.

Come lovely and soothing death,
Undulate round the world, serenely arriving, arriving,
In the day, in the night, to all, to each,
Sooner or later delicate death.

Prais'd be the fathomless universe,
For life and joy, and for objects and knowledge curious,
And for love, sweet love—but praise! praise! praise!
For the sure-enwinding arms of cool-enfolding death.

Dark mother always gliding near with soft feet,
Have none chanted for thee a chant of fullest welcome?
Then I chant it for thee, I glorify thee above all,
I bring thee a song that when thou must indeed come, come unfalteringly.

Approach strong deliveress,
When it is so, when thou hast taken them I joyously sing the dead,
Lost in the loving floating ocean of thee,
Loved in the flood of thy bliss O death.

From me to thee glad serenades,
Dances for thee I propose saluting thee, adornments and feastings for thee,
And the sights of the open landscape and the high-spread sky are fitting,
And life and the fields, and the huge and thoughtful night.

The night in silence under many a star,
The ocean shore and the husky whispering wave whose voice I know,
And the soul turning to thee O vast and well-veil'd death,
And the body gratefully nestling close to thee.

Over the tree-tops I float thee a song,
Over the rising and sinking waves, over the myriad fields and the prairies wide,
Over the dense-pack'd cities all and the teeming wharves and ways,
I float this carol with joy, with joy to thee O death.

15

To the tally of my soul,
Loud and strong kept up the gray-brown bird,
With pure deliberate notes spreading filling the night.

Loud in the pines and cedars dim,
Clear in the freshness moist and the swamp-perfume,
And I with my comrades there in the night.

While my sight that was bound in my eyes unclosed,
As to long panoramas of visions.
And I saw askant the armies,

I saw as in noiseless dreams hundreds of battle-flags,
Borne through the smoke of the battles and pierc'd with missiles I saw them,
And carried hither and yon through the smoke, and torn and bloody,
And at last but a few shreds left on the staffs, (and all in silence,)
And the staffs all splinter'd and broken.

I saw battle-corpses, myriads of them,
And the white skeletons of young men, I saw them,
I saw the debris and debris of all the slain soldiers of the war
But I saw they were not as was thought,
They themselves were fully at rest, they suffer'd not,
The living remain'd and suffer'd, the mother suffer'd,
And the wife and the child and the musing comrade suffer'd
And the armies that remain'd suffer'd.

16

Passing the visions, passing the night,
Passing, unloosing the hold of my comrades' hands,
Passing the song of the hermit bird and the tallying song of my soul,
Victorious song, death's outlet song, yet varying ever-altering song,
As low and wailing, yet clear the notes, rising and falling, flooding the night,
Sadly sinking and fainting, as warning and warning, and yet again bursting with joy,
Covering the earth and filling the spread of the heaven,
As that powerful psalm in the night I heard from recesses.
Passing, I leave thee lilac with heart-shaped leaves,
I leave thee there in the door-yard, blooming, returning with spring.

I cease from my song for thee,
From my gaze on thee in the west, fronting the west, communing with thee,
O comrade lustrous with silver face in the night.

Yet each to keep and all, retrievements out of the night,
The song, the wondrous chant of the gray-brown bird,
And the tallying chant, the echo arous'd in my soul,
With the lustrous and drooping star with the countenance full of woe,
With the holders holding my hand nearing the call of the bird,
Comrades mine and I in the midst, and their memory ever to keep, for the dead I loved so well,
For the sweetest, wisest soul of all my days and lands—and this for his dear sake,
Lilac and star and bird twined with the chant of my soul,
There in the fragrant pines and the cedars dusk and dim.

1865, 1881

Emily Dickinson
1830–1886

Emily Dickinson wrote poems that not only are excellent, but establish a standard of excellence. She is bracketed with Walt Whitman because, unknown to each other and almost simultaneously, they all but invented American poetry. At first glance, they seem at opposite poles, he with his waves of large experiences, she with her careful preservations of private ones. She felt no urge to read him; in 1862, her new friend and future editor, Thomas Wentworth Higginson, asked if she knew his work, and she replied, "You speak of Mr. Whitman—I never read his Book—but was told that he was disgraceful" (*Letters,* ed. Thomas H. Johnson, 1958, 2:404). Yet the poets complement each other in an extraordinary way, and they join in a concern to salvage from English something specifically American. William Carlos Williams, with the same aim, thought of Emily Dickinson as his "patron saint." "She was an independent spirit. She did her best to get away from too strict an interpretation. And she didn't want to be confined to rhyme or reason. . . . And she followed the American idiom. . . . She speaks the spoken language, the idiom, which would be deformed by Oxford English" (*Writers at Work,* Third Series, 1967).

Several of Dickinson's earliest poems hint at the strange, explosive ponderings of her later verse, which is filled with questions and riddles; even at this late stage in her life, her imagination could conceal its wildness under a mask of mischief. She did not write for publication and was easily discouraged from it; only ten of her nearly eighteen hundred poems were published during her lifetime. Her personal reticence, fulfilled by obscurity, had its roots in an upbringing that has been variously described as Puritan, Calvinist, and simply Protestant. After some mysterious catastrophe in her youth, probably having to do with unrequited love, she sequestered herself in her father's house and spent the rest of her days memorializing her oblique visions in lines that she punctuated, as she did her recipes, only with dashes. Yet her Puritanism, if it was that which impeded her immersion in social experience, had a more beneficial effect on her verse. Since William Blake, no other poet had found such inspiration in the Protestant hymnology and in the biblical imagery it employs. Nor, whatever her sense of life's copiousness, which at times almost embarrasses her, can she long forget the terrifying approach of death, a presence that inspires in her something like sexual excitement.

The key moment in Emily Dickinson's verse is often the transformation of poverty into riches. Her poems find in the happenings of a village life all that is required to reveal the cosmos. The speaker is usually in a state of deprivation, but has a vision of the Kingdom that might, by virtue of imaginative energy, be brought into being. "I dwell in Possibility," she says, describing her occupation as "spreading wide my narrow hands / To gather Paradise." There are sudden intoxications: "Inebriate of Air—am I— / And Debauchee of Dew" (poem 214). She is aware of impediment, even agitated by it, but the impediment is sometimes defied or burst through by "the imperial heart." Out of herself, yet with the help of a literary tradition stretching back to the Metaphysical poets, she wrote several dozen of the greatest poems of her century. Her poems are like John Donne's and George Herbert's in their assumption that difficult states of mind require hard words and troubled syntax. Higginson and Mabel Loomis Todd, her first editors, tidied up some of her roughnesses when they brought out the first posthumous volume in 1890. Over the following decades, her scope was gradually revealed, as several additional collections appeared, and only in 1955, when all her poems were published for the first time, were her texts reproduced without editorial changes. In this belated appreciation of her work she is like her contemporary Gerard Manley Hopkins, another re-creator of the Metaphysical mode. In the twentieth century, she was greeted at last as not only a precursor, but a poet of contemporary feeling, whose epigrammatic yet passionate style contains entire worlds of intense emotion and experience in miniature. The manuscripts of Dickinson's poems have also been the subject of considerable editorial interest and speculation, since in 1858 she began collecting her poems into small handsewn booklets, or fascicles.

Although she had often been depicted as a lonely figure in an unpeopled landscape, Dickinson's life is surprisingly well documented by her poems, her letters, and the recollections of her friends and neighbors. She was born on December 10, 1830, in Amherst, Massachusetts, the daughter of a respected lawyer, Edward Dickinson, who for many years was the treasurer of Amherst College and for a time was a member of Congress. He was an imposing figure—Emily Dickinson observed that even in going to fetch the kindling he "steps like Cromwell," and on his death, in 1874, she wrote: "His heart was pure and terrible, and I think no other like it exists." She would not attend his funeral service, but listened to it in an upstairs bedroom. A residue of her father and his faith may be found in her work, particularly in the divine paternal figure that she variously finds laughable, terrifying, and consoling. She had a sister, Lavinia, who also never married, and a brother, Austin, whose wife, Sue Gilbert, has been seen by some interpreters as the great passion of Dickinson's life. We can imagine that life as a group of concentric circles: at the center, the poet, her imagination, and her creations; then her family, trusted and respected, yet harboring at least one scandalous secret, her brother's longtime love affair with Mabel Loomis Todd, Dickinson's future editor and the wife of an Amherst astronomer; and beyond *that*, the village, in which the poet lived and which she observed.

From childhood on, Dickinson led a circumscribed life, but her mind was well traveled. In the same letter that disclaimed any knowledge of Whitman, she told Higginson she had read John Keats and Robert and Elizabeth Browning for poetry; John Ruskin, Sir Thomas Browne, and the biblical Book of Revelation for prose. She might have added, from among her contemporaries, Ralph Waldo Emerson, who probably stimulated her preference for imperfect rhymes and her eagerness to see nature as an emblem, as well as Charlotte and Emily Brontë, George Eliot, and many others. Her acquaintance with Higginson she owed to having read one of his magazine articles, which led her to send him four poems and ask for critical advice. The variety of her reading and the vigor of her correspondence belie the assumption that she was merely provincial.

When she was seventeen, Dickinson graduated from Amherst Academy; the next month, she entered Mount Holyoke Female Seminary, in South Hadley, Massachusetts. Only a few miles from Amherst, she was gruelingly homesick, and having resisted pressure to become a professing Christian, she returned home after less than a year. The move was not so much a retreat as the result of a violent attachment to the place where she would remain. In her letters, she refers to local merriment, and she was given to infatuated friendships, though few of the persons she loved can have known the parts they played in her inner life. With Benjamin F. Newton, one of her father's law apprentices, she seems to have had a relationship that went a little beyond an exchange of flirtatious valentines (though some biographers believe Dickinson was sexually inexperienced until an affair in her fifties with Judge Otis Phillips Lord). Newton had an energetic mind, and he encouraged her to question conventional beliefs, but he was poor and otherwise an unsuitable candidate to be her husband. He left Amherst when she was eighteen and died soon after. Dickinson was probably thinking of him when, years later, she wrote to Higginson: "My dying Tutor told me that he would like to live till I had been a poet" (*Letters*, 2:408). Perhaps the man she most admired was the Reverend Charles Wadsworth, whom she met in Philadelphia in 1855, on one of her rare trips beyond Amherst. He visited her at home in 1860, shortly before he was called to a church in San Francisco. She took his departure hard, and her greatest poems, written in the early 1860s, have been read as reenactments of this pain and broodings on it. In her second letter to Higginson she was driven to confide in veiled terms, "I had a terror—since September—I could tell to none—and so I sing, as the Boy does by the Burying Ground—because I am afraid" (*Letters,* 2:404).

In his diary, Higginson described what a visit to Emily Dickinson was like: "a step like a pattering child's in entry . . . a little plain woman with two smooth bands of reddish hair and a face . . . with no good feature. . . . She came to me with two day-lilies, which she put in a sort of childlike way into my hand and said 'These are my introduction,' in a soft, frightened, breathless childlike voice—and added under her breath, 'Forgive me if I am frightened; I never see strangers, and hardly know what I say'—but she talked soon and thenceforth continuously—and deferentially—sometimes stopping to ask me to talk instead of her—but readily recommencing." In the 1860s, she became a recluse; she dressed in white, saw fewer and fewer and finally no visitors. She worked without stint at her poems, frequently including them in letters; the poems often seem inseparable from the letters, the cadences of the verse chiming with those of the prose. As with Whitman, her period of most intense activity coincided with the Civil War, but she managed to see this chiefly as it impinged on the lives of her fellow villagers. The possibility of death, "that bareheaded life under the grass," held her imagination. In a letter of December 1861, she wrote of a widowed neighbor's son, recently killed in action: "Poor little widow's boy, riding to-night in the mad wind, back to the village burying-ground where he never dreamed of sleeping! Ah! the dreamless sleep!" (*Letters,* 2:386).

Shortly before her death, she wrote her beloved cousins, the Norcross sisters: "Little Cousins,—Called back.—Emily." She had once written that "Nature is a Haunted House—but Art—a House that tries to be haunted" (*Letters,* 2:554). The remark has her yearning elusiveness, a marked trait in her, but she had stronger, sterner qualities too: "Every day life feels mightier, and what we have the power to be, more stupendous" (*Letters,* 2:436). In her turn, she is, as she described her father, "pure and terrible."

49[1]

I never lost as much but twice,
And that was in the sod.
Twice have I stood a beggar
Before the door of God!

Angels—twice descending
Reimbursed my store—
Burglar! Banker—Father!
I am poor once more!

1890

1. The order and numbering of the poems is that established by Thomas H. Johnson in his edition of *The Poems of Emily Dickinson,* 1955.

214

I taste a liquor never brewed—
From Tankards scooped in Pearl—
Not all the Vats upon the Rhine[2]
Yield such an Alcohol!

Inebriate of Air—am I—
And Debauchee of Dew—
Reeling—thro endless summer days—
From inns of Molten Blue—

When "Landlords" turn the drunken Bee
Out of the Foxglove's door—
When Butterflies—renounce their "drams"—
I shall but drink the more!

Till Seraphs[3] swing their snowy Hats—
And Saints—to windows run—
To see the little Tippler
Leaning against the—Sun—

1861

249

Wild Nights—Wild Nights!
Were I with thee
Wild Nights should be
Our luxury!

Futile—the Winds—
To a Heart in port—
Done with the Compass—
Done with the Chart!

Rowing in Eden—
Ah, the Sea!
Might I but moor—Tonight—
In Thee!

1891

2. That is, wine from Germany.

3. Highest-ranking angels.

258

There's a certain Slant of light,
Winter Afternoons—
That oppresses, like the Heft
Of Cathedral Tunes—

Heavenly Hurt, it gives us—
We can find no scar,
But internal difference,
Where the Meanings, are—

None may teach it—Any—
'Tis the Seal Despair—
An imperial affliction
Sent us of the Air—

When it comes, the Landscape listens—
Shadows—hold their breath—
When it goes, 'tis like the Distance
On the look of Death—

1890

280

I felt a Funeral, in my Brain,
And Mourners to and fro
Kept treading—treading—till it seemed
That Sense was breaking through—

And when they all were seated,
A Service, like a Drum—
Kept beating—beating—till I thought
My Mind was going numb—

And then I heard them lift a Box
And creak across my Soul
With those same Boots of Lead, again,
Then Space—began to toll,

As all the Heavens were a Bell,
And Being, but an Ear,
And I, and Silence, some strange Race
Wrecked, solitary, here—

And then a Plank in Reason, broke,
And I dropped down, and down—

And hit a World, at every plunge,
And Finished knowing—then—

1896

303

The Soul selects her own Society—
Then—shuts the Door—
To her divine Majority—
Present no more—

Unmoved—she notes the Chariots—pausing—
At her low Gate—
Unmoved—an Emperor be kneeling
Upon her Mat—

I've known her—from an ample nation—
Choose One—
Then—close the Valves of her attention—
Like Stone—

1890

328

A Bird came down the Walk—
He did not know I saw—
He bit an Angelworm in halves
And ate the fellow, raw,

And then he drank a Dew
From a convenient Grass—
And then hopped sidewise to the Wall
To let a Beetle pass—

He glanced with rapid eyes
That hurried all around—
They looked like frightened Beads, I thought—
He stirred his Velvet Head

Like one in danger, Cautious,
I offered him a Crumb
And he unrolled his feathers
And rowed him softer home—

Than Oars divide the Ocean,
Too silver for a seam—

Or Butterflies, off Banks of Noon
Leap, plashless[4] as they swim.

1891

341

After great pain, a formal feeling comes—
The Nerves sit ceremonious, like Tombs—
The stiff Heart questions was it He, that bore,
And Yesterday, or Centuries before?

The Feet, mechanical, go round—
Of Ground, or Air, or Ought—
A Wooden way
Regardless grown,
A Quartz contentment, like a stone—

This is the Hour of Lead—
Remembered, if outlived,
As Freezing persons, recollect the Snow—
First—Chill—then Stupor—then the letting go—

1929

435

Much Madness is divinest Sense—
To a discerning Eye—
Much Sense—the starkest Madness—
'Tis the Majority
In this, as All, prevail—
Assent—and you are sane—
Demur—you're straightway dangerous—
And handled with a Chain—

1890

465

I heard a Fly buzz—when I died—
The Stillness in the Room
Was like the Stillness in the Air—
Between the Heaves of Storm—

4. Splashless.

The Eyes around—had wrung them dry—
And Breaths were gathering firm
For that last Onset—when the King
Be witnessed—in the Room—

I willed my Keepsakes—Signed away
What portion of me be
Assignable—and then it was
There interposed a Fly—

With Blue—uncertain stumbling Buzz—
Between the light—and me—
And then the Windows failed—and then
I could not see to see—

1896

585

I like to see it lap the Miles—
And lick the Valleys up—
And stop to feed itself at Tanks—
And then—prodigious step

Around a Pile of Mountains—
And supercilious peer
In Shanties—by the sides of Roads—
And then a Quarry pare

To fit its Ribs
And crawl between
Complaining all the while
In horrid—hooting stanza—
Then chase itself down Hill—

And neigh like Boanerges[5]—
Then—punctual as a Star
Stop—docile and omnipotent
At its own stable door—

1891

5. "Sons of thunder" (Mark 3.17); Hebrew term, originally applied to the zealous apostles John and James; here, any zealous orator.

632

The Brain—is wider than the Sky—
For—put them side by side—
The one the other will contain
With ease—and You—beside—

The Brain is deeper than the sea—
For—hold them—Blue to Blue—
The one the other will absorb—
As Sponges—Buckets—do—

The Brain is just the weight of God—
For—Heft them—Pound for Pound—
And they will differ—if they do—
As Syllable from Sound—

1896

657

I dwell in Possibility—
A fairer House than Prose—
More numerous of Windows—
Superior—for Doors—

Of Chambers as the Cedars—
Impregnable of Eye—
And for an Everlasting Roof
The Gambrels[6] of the Sky—

Of Visitors—the fairest—
For Occupation—This—
The spreading wide my narrow Hands
To gather Paradise—

1929

712

Because I could not stop for Death—
He kindly stopped for me—
The Carriage held but just Ourselves—
And Immortality.

6. Curved roofs.

We slowly drove—He knew no haste
And I had put away
My labor and my leisure too,
For His Civility—

We passed the School, where Children strove
At Recess—in the Ring—
We passed the Fields of Gazing Grain—
We passed the Setting Sun—

Or rather—He passed Us—
The Dews drew quivering and chill—
For only Gossamer, my Gown—
My Tippet—only Tulle[7]—

We paused before a House that seemed
A swelling of the Ground—
The Roof was scarcely visible—
The Cornice—in the Ground—

Since then—'tis Centuries—and yet
Feels shorter than the Day
I first surmised the Horses' Heads
Were toward Eternity—

1890

754

My Life had stood—a Loaded Gun—
In Corners—till a Day
The Owner passed—identified—
And carried Me away—

And now We roam in Sovreign Woods—
And now We hunt the Doe—
And every time I speak for Him—
The Mountains straight reply—

And do I smile, such cordial light
Upon the Valley glow—
It is as a Vesuvian face
Had let it's[8] pleasure through—

And when at Night—Our good Day done—
I guard My Master's Head—
'Tis better than the Eider-Duck's[9]
Deep Pillow—to have shared—

7. Thin, net fabric. *Tippet:* cape.
8. That is, *its. Vesuvian:* capable of erupting, like Mt. Vesuvius, a volcano in Italy.
9. Waterfowl with soft feathers.

To foe of His—I'm deadly foe—
None stir the second time—
On whom I lay a Yellow Eye—
Or an emphatic Thumb—

Though I than He—may longer live
He longer must—than I—
For I have but the power to kill,
Without—the power to die—

1929

986

A narrow Fellow in the Grass
Occasionally rides—
You may have met Him—did you not
His notice sudden is—

The Grass divides as with a Comb—
A spotted shaft is seen—
And then it closes at your feet
And opens further on—

He likes a Boggy Acre
A Floor too cool for Corn—
Yet when a Boy, and Barefoot—
I more than once at Noon
Have passed, I thought, a Whip lash
Unbraiding in the Sun
When stooping to secure it
It wrinkled, and was gone—

Several of Nature's People
I know, and they know me—
I feel for them a transport
Of cordiality—

But never met this Fellow
Attended, or alone
Without a tighter breathing
And Zero at the Bone—

1866

1129

Tell all the Truth but tell it slant—
Success in Circuit lies

Too bright for our infirm Delight
The Truth's superb surprise
As Lightning to the Children eased
With explanation kind
The Truth must dazzle gradually
Or every man be blind—

1945

1732

My life closed twice before its close—
It yet remains to see
If Immortality unveil
A third event to me

So huge, so hopeless to conceive
As these that twice befell.
Parting is all we know of heaven,
And all we need of hell.

1896

THOMAS HARDY
1840–1928

Thomas Hardy and Gerard Manley Hopkins stand like two warders at the portals of modern poetry. Hopkins died before the twentieth century began; Hardy lived almost to its third decade. Hopkins might be heraldically represented with an eye turned upward, whereas Hardy, whose poetry is retrospective and elegiac, would be posed casting a backward look.

Hardy was born at Upper Bockhampton in Dorset, England, and apart from three long absences, he chose to live and die in this region. His date of birth—June 2, 1840, four years before Hopkins—isolates him from the great Victorian poets, Alfred Tennyson (born 1809), Robert Browning (born 1812), and Matthew Arnold (born 1822). From being their junior during the nineteenth century, he became in the twentieth century the senior of all poets. Proud of his longevity, he prepared in 1928 a manuscript called *Winter Words,* and in the preface he declared: "So far as I am aware, I happen to be the only English poet who has brought out a new volume of verse on his ——— birthday." He meant to write in "eighty-ninth," but he did not quite make it: the volume appeared posthumously. The title *Winter Words* would have suited just as well the poems he wrote in youth; Hardy had the premature old age of the child called "Father Time" in his novel *Jude the Obscure.* His earlier books, with titles such as *Time's Laughingstocks, Satires of Circumstance,* and *Human Shows—Far Phantasies,* have the same bleak outlook.

Hardy straddles the Victorian and modern periods not only because of his longevity, but also because of his aesthetic, which has the mournful vulnerability of the Romantics and Victorians and yet the skeptical detachment of the modernists—a very human attachment to the particulars of place and memory and yet an ironic, god's-eye perspective. His forms are likewise semi-Victorian, semimodern. He writes in traditional stanzaic patterns, but invents many of his own. He adheres to the metered line, but roughs up prosody and syntax. He composes in inherited genres—love poetry, war poetry, the sonnet, the elegy, the epic—yet he dislocates and distorts many of their conventions. Much of his diction is in the Romantic tradition, but he also fashions jarring locutions: he incorporates dialect; archaic, obsolete, and rare words; and deliberately awkward coinages (e.g., "Powerfuller" and "unblooms" in the unresolved sonnet "Hap"). His syntactic contortions, irresolvable juxtapositions, and endings that resist closure look toward future generations of poets.

Hardy's father was a master mason, and the son's first ambition was to design buildings. At sixteen, he was apprenticed to a local ecclesiastical architect. Hardy later said that the Gothic aesthetic principles in which he was trained taught him to value spontaneity in poetry—even the "freakish." He was extremely interested in his school studies in Latin and his private studies in Greek, a language he had taught himself. William Barnes, a good dialect poet, was a neighbor and encouraged Hardy's literary interests. But a career in letters was not then a practical course, and Hardy took no wild risks. Having finished his apprenticeship, Hardy went to London in 1862 and became assistant to an architect. But after five years he returned to Dorset, and while continuing his architectural work, he began to write novels. The first was acceptable to a publisher, but the publisher's reader, the novelist George Meredith, called Hardy in and, after praising the book, warned him that its harsh satire of the upper classes would arouse hostility and impair his career. Hardy, strangely docile before this prudential advice—he saw the universe as a many-leveled snub—put the book aside and began another. This new one and thirteen other novels were published without difficulty, but he may never have lost his feeling that prose had a meretricious element and was full of compromises. When, in 1895, *Jude the Obscure* was lampooned as *Jude the Obscene,* Hardy (perhaps gratefully) turned altogether to verse. Besides volumes of lyrics and dramatic monologues, he published, in the first years of the century, his three-part epic-drama, *The Dynasts,* about England's wars with Napoleon, in which events are shown to be controlled by demiurges, or secondary deities.

Hardy said in a late poem that "he never expected much" of the world, but one period in his life, that of courtship, was exempt from the general belittlement. In 1870, he went to Cornwall to restore a church. (Restoration of churches was his principal architectural work, an ironic occupation for a skeptic.) He there met Emma Lavinia Gifford, whom he married four years later. Their marriage went badly, however, and by the time of her death, Emma Hardy and the poet had barely spoken to each other for years. Suffering from psychological disturbances, she had increasingly withheld herself from his friends, preferring to stay home alone. After she died in 1912, Hardy found two manuscripts: "What I Think of My Husband," which he destroyed because it was full of "bitter denunciations" of him, "venom, hatred and abuse," and a more congenial record of her youth up to their marriage, later published as *Some Recollections.* The latter document helped inspire some of Hardy's elegies for her, poems that evoke her as she was in her "air-blue gown" almost half a century before. In the aftermath of their vexed relationship, the elegiac sequence "Poems of 1912–13" includes some of Hardy's most passionate poems, vacillating between anger and self-reproach, idealization and skepticism. In these poems of intense inner turmoil, Hardy is the first English poet to display so fully the psychological burdens, anxieties, and contradictions that attend secular mourning and the act of writing about it.

For a long time, Hardy's prose was preferred to his poetry, but readers today often take a different view. Although he said that poetry is "the heart of literature," Hardy tended to be modest about his poems, calling them, in a preface dated 1901, "unadjusted impressions." He told a friend that he wanted to avoid "the jewelled line"; his awkwardness, often an ostentatious laboriousness, was both natural and cultivated. He is the first of the poets, so numerous now, who are suspicious of writing well. He broke away from poetic diction toward an unexpected vocabulary. With similar purposes, he insisted on provincialism in art. Against Arnold's disparagement, Hardy said that "a certain provincialism of feeling is invaluable. It is of the essence of individuality, and is largely made up of that crude enthusiasm without which no great thoughts are thought, no great deeds done." More largely, he said: "Art is a disproportioning . . . of realities, to show more clearly the features that matter in those realities" (Florence Emily Hardy, *The Life of Thomas Hardy 1840–1928*, 1968). The awkwardness was intended to give a sense of penetrating the facade of language and syntax as well as the deceptions of circumstance. In the typescript of a letter, apparently of December 1919, Hardy praises "irregularities" in poetry, saying, "dissonances, and other irregularities can be produced advisedly, as art, and worked as to give more charm than strict conformities." Later poets found these tenets congenial. W. H. Auden, for instance, said he fell in love with Hardy's poetry when he was sixteen and "for more than a year I read no one else" ("A Literary Transference"). He felt "very lucky" in having Hardy as his "first Master," because Hardy's unevenness, his "often clumsy and forced" diction, "gave me hope where a flawless poet might have made me despair. He was modern without being too modern. . . . If I looked through his spectacles, at least I was conscious of a certain eyestrain. Lastly, his metrical variety, his fondness for complicated stanza forms, were an invaluable training in the craft of making" ("Making, Knowing and Judging"). Philip Larkin and James Wright also testified to Hardy's influence, and Dylan Thomas, though he thought W. B. Yeats the greatest of modern poets, considered Hardy his favorite. Ezra Pound, who held up Hardy as the gold standard or "true test" of poetry in his *Guide to Kulchur* (1938), remarked in a 1934 letter: "Nobody has taught me anything about writing since Thomas Hardy died."

Hardy was dejected all his life, even as a child. The event of his childhood that remained with him more than any other, he described, according to his second wife, Florence Emily Hardy, in this way: "He was lying on his back in the sun, thinking how useless he was, and covered his face with his straw hat. The sun's rays streamed through the interstices of the straw, the lining having disappeared. Reflecting on his experiences of the world so far as he had got, he came to the conclusion that he did not wish to grow up. Other boys were always talking of when they would be men; he did not want at all to be a man, or to possess things, but to remain as he was, in the same spot, and to know no more people than he already knew (about half a dozen)" (*Life*). There is a symptomatic self-sheltering in the young Hardy's inclination to stay put as a youthful ruin.

In later life, Hardy became convinced that the force governing the universe cannot comfortably be described as God; Hardy commemorated the deity's death in an elegy called "God's Funeral." When a clergyman wrote to ask how certain horrors of human and animal life might be reconciled with God's goodness, Hardy replied, with formal finality: "Mr. Hardy regrets that he is unable to offer any hypothesis which would reconcile the existence of such evils as Dr. Grosart describes with the idea of omnipotent goodness. Perhaps Dr. Grosart might be helped to a provisional view of the universe by the recently published Life of Darwin, and the works of Herbert Spencer and other agnostics" (*Life*). With no confidence in a supernatural god, Hardy was nonetheless fond of a pantheon of forces for which he kept devising new names. These are the demiurges who move us pathetically about. They are animated, Hardy usually insists, not by malignity, but merely by indifference, as in the poem "Hap." This will-less, amoral universe is seen as operating at loggerheads with human morality. Hardy's universe is a grotesque inversion of the traditional one, offering in place of an immanent divinity an immanent indifference.

The archetypal scene in a Hardy poem is a man meditating on his losses, surrounded by ghosts of what he has loved or hoped for, preserving his identity in a friendless landscape only by the momentary intensity of his feeling. Time is not regained, as in Marcel Proust's fiction and in traditional elegies; memory only deepens loss. The poet expresses afterthoughts rather than thoughts, experiences remasticated rather than devoured, and returns obsessively to what is gone. The poem is a thermometer of present chill and past heat. The tone is almost always low pitched. Though Hardy's sympathy goes out to those who are indifferently mistreated by indifferent masters of the world, there may be in him also a secret admiration for indifference, for power without feeling as opposed to human feeling without power. Perhaps he secretly longed to be free of choice and concern, unshakable aspects of human existence, and to ally himself with the workings of inhuman will. Yet his conscious purpose is always to defend and fortify, insofar as possible, the human.

Hap[1]

If but some vengeful god would call to me
From up the sky, and laugh: 'Thou suffering thing,
Know that thy sorrow is my ecstasy,
That thy love's loss is my hate's profiting!'

Then would I bear it, clench myself, and die,
Steeled by the sense of ire unmerited;
Half-eased in that a Powerfuller than I
Had willed and meted me the tears I shed.

But not so. How arrives it joy lies slain,
And why unblooms the best hope ever sown?
—Crass Casualty obstructs the sun and rain,
And dicing Time for gladness casts a moan . . .
These purblind Doomsters had as readily strown
Blisses about my pilgrimage as pain.

1866 1898

Neutral Tones

We stood by a pond that winter day,
And the sun was white, as though chidden of God,
And a few leaves lay on the starving sod;
—They had fallen from an ash, and were gray.

1. Chance, fortune.

Your eyes on me were as eyes that rove
Over tedious riddles of years ago;
And some words played between us to and fro
    On which lost the more by our love.

The smile on your mouth was the deadest thing
Alive enough to have strength to die;
And a grin of bitterness swept thereby
    Like an ominous bird a-wing. . . .

Since then, keen lessons that love deceives,
And wrings with wrong, have shaped to me
Your face, and the God-curst sun, and a tree,
    And a pond edged with grayish leaves.

1867 1898

I Look into My Glass

I look into my glass,
And view my wasting skin,
And say, 'Would God it came to pass
My heart had shrunk as thin!'

For then, I, undistrest
By hearts grown cold to me,
Could lonely wait my endless rest
With equanimity.

But Time, to make me grieve,
Part steals, lets part abide;
And shakes this fragile frame at eve
With throbbings of noontide.

1898

In Tenebris[2]

I

"Percussus sum sicut foenum, et aruit cor meum."
—Psalm 102

    Wintertime nighs;
But my bereavement-pain
It cannot bring again:
    Twice no one dies.

2. In the shadows, In darkness (Latin); these are the first two of three poems with this title. The epigraph is translated in the King James version as "My heart is smitten, and withered like grass."

Flower-petals flee;
But, since it once hath been,
No more that severing scene
Can harrow me.

Birds faint in dread:
I shall not lose old strength
In the lone frost's black length:
Strength long since fled!

Leaves freeze to dun;[3]
But friends can not turn cold
This season as of old
For him with none.

Tempests may scath;[4]
But love can not make smart
Again this year his heart
Who no heart hath.

Black is night's cope;
But death will not appal
One who, past doubtings all,
Waits in unhope.

II

"Considerabam ad dexteram, et videbam;
et non erat qui cognosceret me. . . .
Non est qui requirat animam meam."
—Psalm 141[5]

When the clouds' swoln bosoms echo back the shouts of the many and strong
That things are all as they best may be, save a few to be right ere long,
And my eyes have not the vision in them to discern what to these is so clear,
The blot seems straightway in me alone; one better he were not here.

The stout upstanders say, All's well with us: ruers have nought to rue!
And what the potent say so oft, can it fail to be somewhat true?
Breezily go they, breezily come; their dust smokes around their career,
Till I think I am one born out of due time, who has no calling here.

Their dawns bring lusty joys, it seems; their evenings all that is sweet;
Our times are blessed times, they cry: Life shapes it as is most meet,
And nothing is much the matter; there are many smiles to a tear;
Then what is the matter is I, I say. Why should such an one be here? . . .

3. Greyish brown.
4. Scathe.
5. I looked on my right hand, and beheld, but there was no one who would know me. . . . No one cared for my soul (Latin).

Let him in whose ears the low-voiced Best is killed by the clash of the First,
Who holds that if way to the Better there be, it exacts a full look at the Worst,
Who feels that delight is a delicate growth cramped by crookedness, custom, and fear,
Get him up and be gone as one shaped awry; he disturbs the order here.

1895–96 1901

Drummer Hodge

I

They throw in Drummer Hodge, to rest
Uncoffined—just as found:
His landmark is a kopje-crest[6]
That breaks the veldt[7] around;
And foreign constellations west[8]
Each night above his mound.

II

Young Hodge the Drummer never knew—
Fresh from his Wessex[9] home—
The meaning of the broad Karoo,[1]
The Bush,[2] the dusty loam,
And why uprose to nightly view
Strange stars amid the gloam.

III

Yet portion of that unknown plain
Will Hodge for ever be;
His homely Northern breast and brain
Grow to some Southern tree,
And strange-eyed constellations reign
His stars eternally.

1899, 1901

6. A small hill (Afrikaans, South African Dutch). Drummer Hodge is an English soldier killed in the Boer War, 1899–1902, when Great Britain fought the Transvaal Republic and the Orange Free State.
7. Plain (Afrikaans).
8. Visible only in the Southern Hemisphere and thus unfamiliar. *West:* to set in the west.
9. An ancient Saxon kingdom centered in Salisbury plain. Hardy revived the name and used it to include his native shire of Dorset.
1. The high plateau in the Cape of Good Hope, South Africa.
2. British colonial word for tracts of land covered with brushwood and shrubby vegetation.

The Darkling[3] Thrush

I leant upon a coppice[4] gate
    When Frost was spectre-gray,
And Winter's dregs made desolate
    The weakening eye of day.
The tangled bine-stems[5] scored the sky
    Like strings of broken lyres,
And all mankind that haunted nigh
    Had sought their household fires.

The land's sharp features seemed to be
    The Century's corpse[6] outleant,
His crypt the cloudy canopy,
    The wind his death-lament.
The ancient pulse of germ and birth
    Was shrunken hard and dry,
And every spirit upon earth
    Seemed fervourless as I.

At once a voice arose among
    The bleak twigs overhead
In a full-hearted evensong
    Of joy illimited;
An aged thrush, frail, gaunt, and small,
    In blast-beruffled plume,
Had chosen thus to fling his soul
    Upon the growing gloom.

So little cause for carolings
    Of such ecstatic sound
Was written on terrestrial things
    Afar or nigh around,
That I could think there trembled through
    His happy good-night air
Some blessed Hope, whereof he knew
    And I was unaware.

1900, 1901

A Broken Appointment

You did not come,
And marching Time drew on, and wore me numb.—
Yet less for loss of your dear presence there
Than that I thus found lacking in your make

3. In the dark.
4. Thicket.
5. Stems of climbing, twisting plants.
6. The poem was dated the last day of the nineteenth century, December 31, 1900. It was first published as "By the Century's Deathbed."

That high compassion which can overbear
Reluctance for pure lovingkindness' sake
Grieved I, when, as the hope-hour stroked its sum,
You did not come.

You love not me,
And love alone can lend you loyalty;
—I know and knew it. But, unto the store
Of human deeds divine in all but name,
Was it not worth a little hour or more
To add yet this: Once you, a woman, came
To soothe a time-torn man; even though it be
You love not me?

1901

The Self-Unseeing

Here is the ancient floor,
Footworn and hollowed and thin,
Here was the former door
Where the dead feet walked in.

She sat here in her chair,
Smiling into the fire;
He who played stood there,
Bowing it higher and higher.

Childlike, I danced in a dream;
Blessings emblazoned that day;
Everything glowed with a gleam;
Yet we were looking away!

1901

Bereft

In the black winter morning
No light will be struck near my eyes
While the clock in the stairway is warning
For five, when he used to rise.
Leave the door unbarred,
The clock unwound.
Make my lone bed hard—
Would 'twere underground!

When the summer dawns clearly,
And the appletree-tops seem alight,

Who will undraw the curtain and cheerly
Call out that the morning is bright?

When I tarry at market
No form will cross Durnover Lea
In the gathering darkness, to hark at
Grey's Bridge for the pit-pat o' me.

When the supper crock's steaming,
And the time is the time of his tread,
I shall sit by the fire and wait dreaming
In a silence as of the dead.
Leave the door unbarred,
The clock unwound,
Make my lone bed hard—
Would 'twere underground!

1901 1909

Shut Out That Moon

Close up the casement, draw the blind,
Shut out that stealing moon,
She wears too much the guise she wore
Before our lutes were strewn
With years-deep dust, and names we read
On a white stone were hewn.

Step not out on the dew-dashed lawn
To view the Lady's Chair,
Immense Orion's glittering form,
The Less and Greater Bear:
Stay in; to such sights we were drawn
When faded ones were fair.

Brush not the bough for midnight scents
That come forth lingeringly,
And wake the same sweet sentiments
They breathed to you and me
When living seemed a laugh, and love
All it was said to be.

Within the common lamp-lit room
Prison my eyes and thought;
Let dingy details crudely loom,
Mechanic speech be wrought:
Too fragrant was Life's early bloom,
Too tart the fruit it brought!

1904 1909

New Year's Eve

'I have finished another year,' said God,
'In grey, green, white, and brown;
I have strewn the leaf upon the sod,
Sealed up the worm within the clod,
And let the last sun down.'

'And what's the good of it?' I said,
'What reasons made you call
From formless void this earth we tread,
When nine-and-ninety can be read
Why nought should be at all?

'Yea, Sire; why shaped you us, "who in
This tabernacle groan"—[7]
If ever a joy be found herein,
Such joy no man had wished to win
If he had never known!'

Then he: 'My labours—logicless—
You may explain; not I:
Sense-sealed I have wrought, without a guess
That I evolved a Consciousness
To ask for reasons why.

'Strange that ephemeral creatures who
By my own ordering are,
Should see the shortness of my view,
Use ethic tests I never knew,
Or made provision for!'

He sank to raptness as of yore,
And opening New Year's Day
Wove it by rote as theretofore,
And went on working evermore
In his unweeting[8] way.

1906 1907, 1909

Channel Firing[9]

That night your great guns, unawares,
Shook all our coffins as we lay,
And broke the chancel window-squares,
We thought it was the Judgment-day

7. "For we that are in this tabernacle do groan, being burdened: not for that we would be unclothed, but clothed upon, that mortality might be swallowed up of life" (2 Corinthians 5.4).

8. Unknowing.

9. That is, gunnery practice in the English Channel (here, before the outbreak of World War I).

And sat upright. While drearisome
Arose the howl of wakened hounds:
The mouse let fall the altar-crumb,
The worms drew back into the mounds,

The glebe cow[1] drooled. Till God called, 'No;
It's gunnery practice out at sea
Just as before you went below;
The world is as it used to be:

'All nations striving strong to make
Red war yet redder. Mad as hatters
They do no more for Christés sake
Than you who are helpless in such matters.

'That this is not the judgment-hour
For some of them's a blessed thing,
For if it were they'd have to scour
Hell's floor for so much threatening. . . .

'Ha, ha. It will be warmer when
I blow the trumpet (if indeed
I ever do; for you are men,
And rest eternal sorely need).'

So down we lay again. 'I wonder,
Will the world ever saner be,'
Said one, 'than when He sent us under
In our indifferent century!'

And many a skeleton shook his head.
'Instead of preaching forty year,'
My neighbour Parson Thirdly said,
'I wish I had stuck to pipes and beer.'

Again the guns disturbed the hour,
Roaring their readiness to avenge,
As far inland as Stourton Tower,
And Camelot, and starlit Stonehenge.[2]

1914

1. That is, cow on a small parcel of land adjacent to the church.
2. Stourton Tower is an eighteenth-century tower near Stonehenge; it was built to commemorate King Alfred's defeat of Viking invaders in 878. Camelot, the legendary site of King Arthur's court, is associated usually with Tintagel in Cornwall. Hardy and others associated Stonehenge with druidic rites.

The Convergence of the Twain

Lines on the loss of the "Titanic"[3]

I

In a solitude of the sea
Deep from human vanity,
And the Pride of Life that planned her, stilly couches she.

II

Steel chambers, late the pyres
Of her salamandrine[4] fires,
Cold currents thrid,[5] and turn to rhythmic tidal lyres.

III

Over the mirrors meant
To glass the opulent
The sea-worm crawls—grotesque, slimed, dumb, indifferent.

IV

Jewels in joy designed
To ravish the sensuous mind
Lie lightless, all their sparkles bleared and black and blind.

V

Dim moon-eyed fishes near
Gaze at the gilded gear
And query: 'What does this vaingloriousness down here?' . . .

VI

Well: while was fashioning
This creature of cleaving wing,
The Immanent Will that stirs and urges everything

VII

Prepared a sinister mate
For her—so gaily great—
A Shape of Ice, for the time far and dissociate.

VIII

And as the smart ship grew
In stature, grace, and hue,
In shadowy silent distance grew the Iceberg too.

3. On the night of April 14, 1912, the British White Star liner *Titanic*, the largest ship afloat and on her maiden voyage to New York from Southampton, collided with an iceberg in the North Atlantic and sank in less than three hours; 1,513 passengers died, including two of Hardy's acquaintances. This poem was first published in the program of a London charity performance of May 14 to aid the survivors.
4. Bright red. The salamander was supposed to be able to live in fire.
5. Thread.

IX

Alien they seemed to be:
No mortal eye could see
The intimate welding of their later history,

X

Or sign that they were bent
By paths coincident
On being anon twin halves of one august event,

XI

Till the Spinner of the Years
Said 'Now!' And each one hears,
And consummation comes, and jars two hemispheres.

1914

From POEMS OF 1912–13

The Going[6]

Why did you give no hint that night
That quickly after the morrow's dawn,
And calmly, as if indifferent quite,
You would close your term here, up and be gone
Where I could not follow
With wing of swallow
To gain one glimpse of you ever anon!

Never to bid good-bye,
Or lip me the softest call,
Or utter a wish for a word, while I
Saw morning harden upon the wall,
Unmoved, unknowing
That your great going
Had place that moment, and altered all.

Why do you make me leave the house
And think for a breath it is you I see
At the end of the alley of bending boughs
Where so often at dusk you used to be;
Till in darkening dankness
The yawning blankness
Of the perspective sickens me!

You were she who abode
By those red-veined rocks far West,

6. The next four poems are from the sequence "Poems of 1912–13," elegies for Hardy's first wife, Emma, who died on November 27, 1912. Their meeting and initial courtship was in Cornwall in 1870.

You were the swan-necked one who rode
Along the beetling Beeny Crest,[7]
        And, reining nigh me,
        Would muse and eye me,
While Life unrolled us its very best.

Why, then, latterly did we not speak,
Did we not think of those days long dead,
And ere your vanishing strive to seek
That time's renewal? We might have said,
        'In this bright spring weather
        We'll visit together
Those places that once we visited.'

        Well, well! All's past amend,
        Unchangeable. It must go.
I seem but a dead man held on end
To sink down soon. . . . O you could not know
        That such swift fleeing
        No soul foreseeing—
Not even I—would undo me so!

Your Last Drive

Here by the moorway you returned,
And saw the borough lights ahead
That lit your face—all undiscerned
To be in a week the face of the dead,
And you told of the charm of that haloed view
That never again would beam on you.

And on your left you passed the spot
Where eight days later you were to lie,
And be spoken of as one who was not;
Beholding it with a heedless eye
As alien from you, though under its tree
You soon would halt everlastingly.

I drove not with you. . . . Yet had I sat
At your side that eve I should not have seen
That the countenance I was glancing at
Had a last-time look in the flickering sheen,
Nor have read the writing upon your face,
'I go hence soon to my resting-place;

'You may miss me then. But I shall not know
How many times you visit me there,
Or what your thoughts are, or if you go
There never at all. And I shall not care.

7. Cliff in Cornwall. *Beetling:* overhanging.

Should you censure me I shall take no heed
And even your praises no more shall need.'

True: never you'll know. And you will not mind.
But shall I then slight you because of such?
Dear ghost, in the past did you ever find
The thought 'What profit,' move me much?
Yet abides the fact, indeed, the same,—
You are past love, praise, indifference, blame.

I Found Her Out There

I found her out there
On a slope few see,
That falls westwardly
To the salt-edged air,
Where the ocean breaks
On the purple strand,
And the hurricane shakes
The solid land.

I brought her here,[8]
And have laid her to rest
In a noiseless nest
No sea beats near.
She will never be stirred
In her loamy cell
By the waves long heard
And loved so well.

So she does not sleep
By those haunted heights
The Atlantic smites
And the blind gales sweep,
Whence she often would gaze
At Dundagel's famed head,[9]
While the dipping blaze
Dyed her face fire-red;

And would sigh at the tale
Of sunk Lyonnesse,[1]
As a wind-tugged tress
Flapped her cheek like a flail;
Or listen at whiles
With a thought-bound brow
To the murmuring miles
She is far from now.

8. Circumstances prevented Emma Hardy's being buried in St. Juliot, Cornwall, where Hardy and she had met, so she was buried at Stinsford, a mile from Dorchester.

9. Dunderhole Point, near the legendary site of Camelot.

1. The legendary scene in Cornwall of several Arthurian stories.

Yet her shade, maybe,
Will creep underground
Till it catch the sound
Of that western sea
As it swells and sobs
Where she once domiciled,
And joy in its throbs
With the heart of a child.

The Voice

Woman much missed, how you call to me, call to me,
Saying that now you are not as you were
When you had changed from the one who was all to me,
But as at first, when our day was fair.

Can it be you that I hear? Let me view you, then,
Standing as when I drew near to the town
Where you would wait for me: yes, as I knew you then,
Even to the original air-blue gown!

Or is it only the breeze, in its listlessness
Travelling across the wet mead[2] to me here,
You being ever dissolved to wan wistlessness,[3]
Heard no more again far or near?

Thus I; faltering forward,
Leaves around me falling,
Wind oozing thin through the thorn from norward
And the woman calling.

December 1912 — 1914

A Poet

Attentive eyes, fantastic heed,
Assessing minds, he does not need,
Nor urgent writs to sup or dine,
Nor pledges in the rosy wine.

For loud acclaim he does not care
By the august or rich or fair,
Nor for smart pilgrims from afar,
Curious on where his hauntings are.

But soon or later, when you hear
That he has doffed this wrinkled gear,

2. Meadow.

3. Inattention (Hardy's coinage).

Some evening, at the first star-ray,
Come to his graveside, pause and say:

'Whatever his message—glad or grim—
Two bright-souled women clave to him;'[4]
Stand and say that while day decays;
It will be word enough of praise.

1914

In the Moonlight

'O lonely workman, standing there
In a dream, why do you stare and stare
At her grave, as no other grave there were?

'If your great gaunt eyes so importune
Her soul by the shine of this corpse-cold moon,
Maybe you'll raise her phantom soon!'

'Why, fool, it is what I would rather see
Than all the living folk there be;
But alas, there is no such joy for me!'

'Ah—she was one you loved, no doubt,
Through good and evil, through rain and drought,
And when she passed, all your sun went out?'

'Nay: she was the woman I did not love,
Whom all the others were ranked above,
Whom during her life I thought nothing of.'

1914

The Oxen

Christmas Eve, and twelve of the clock.
'Now they are all on their knees,'[5]
An elder said as we sat in a flock
By the embers in hearthside ease.

We pictured the meek mild creatures where
They dwelt in their strawy pen,
Nor did it occur to one of us there
To doubt they were kneeling then.

4. Hardy married his second wife in February 1914.

5. A folk belief that the oxen kneel every Christmas as the ox is said to have kneeled in the manger when Jesus was born.

So fair a fancy few would weave
  In these years! Yet, I feel,
If someone said on Christmas Eve,
  'Come; see the oxen kneel

'In the lonely barton by yonder coomb[6]
  Our childhood used to know,'
I should go with him in the gloom,
  Hoping it might be so.

1915, 1917

In Time of 'the Breaking of Nations'[7]

I

Only a man harrowing clods
  In a slow silent walk
With an old horse that stumbles and nods
  Half asleep as they stalk.

II

Only thin smoke without flame
  From the heaps of couch-grass;
Yet this will go onward the same
  Though Dynasties pass.

III

Yonder a maid and her wight[8]
  Come whispering by:
War's annals will fade into night
  Ere their story die.

1915 1916, 1917

For Life I Had Never Cared Greatly

For Life I had never cared greatly,
  As worth a man's while;
  Peradventures[9] unsought,
Peradventures that finished in nought,
Had kept me from youth and through manhood till lately
    Unwon by its style.

6. Valley. *Barton:* farmyard.
7. Cf. "Thou art my battle axe and weapons of war: for with thee will I break in pieces the nations" (Jeremiah 51.20).
8. Man.
9. Contingencies, chance incidents.

In earliest years—why I know not—
I viewed it askance;
Conditions of doubt,
Conditions that leaked slowly out,
May haply have bent me to stand and to show not
Much zest for its dance.

With symphonies soft and sweet colour
It courted me then,
Till evasions seemed wrong,
Till evasions gave in to its song,
And I warmed, until living aloofly loomed duller
Than life among men.

Anew I found nought to set eyes on,
When, lifting its hand,
It uncloaked a star,
Uncloaked it from fog-damps afar,
And showed its beams burning from pole to horizon
As bright as a brand.

And so, the rough highway forgetting,
I pace hill and dale
Regarding the sky,
Regarding the vision on high,
And thus re-illumed have no humour for letting
My pilgrimage fail.

1917

I Looked Up from My Writing

I looked up from my writing,
And gave a start to see,
As if rapt in my inditing,[1]
The moon's full gaze on me.

Her meditative misty head
Was spectral in its air,
And I involuntarily said,
'What are you doing there?'

'Oh, I've been scanning pond and hole
And waterway hereabout
For the body of one with a sunken soul
Who has put his life-light out.

1. Composing.

'Did you hear his frenzied tattle?
It was sorrow for his son
Who is slain in brutish battle,
Though he has injured none.

'And now I am curious to look
Into the blinkered mind
Of one who wants to write a book
In a world of such a kind.'

Her temper overwrought me,
And I edged to shun her view,
For I felt assured she thought me
One who should drown him too.

1917

Afterwards

When the Present has latched its postern behind my tremulous stay,
And the May month flaps its glad green leaves like wings,
Delicate-filmed as new-spun silk, will the neighbours say,
'He was a man who used to notice such things'?

If it be in the dusk when, like an eyelid's soundless blink,
The dewfall-hawk[2] comes crossing the shades to alight
Upon the wind-warped upland thorn, a gazer may think,
'To him this must have been a familiar sight'.

If I pass during some nocturnal blackness, mothy and warm,
When the hedgehog travels furtively over the lawn,
One may say, 'He strove that such innocent creatures should come to no harm,
But he could do little for them; and now he is gone'.

If, when hearing that I have been stilled at last, they stand at the door,
Watching the full-starred heavens that winter sees,
Will this thought rise on those who will meet my face no more,
'He was one who had an eye for such mysteries'?

And will any say when my bell of quittance is heard in the gloom,
And a crossing breeze cuts a pause in its outrollings,
Till they swell again, as they were a new bell's boom,
'He hears it not now, but used to notice such things'?

1917

2. A nighthawk.

Going and Staying

I

The moving sun-shapes on the spray,
The sparkles where the brook was flowing,
Pink faces, plightings, moonlit May,
These were the things we wished would stay;
But they were going.

II

Seasons of blankness as of snow,
The silent bleed of a world decaying,
The moan of multitudes in woe,
These were the things we wished would go;
But they were staying.

III

Then we looked closelier at Time,
And saw his ghostly arms revolving
To sweep off woeful things with prime,
Things sinister with things sublime
Alike dissolving.

1919, 1922

Nobody Comes

Tree-leaves labour up and down,
And through them the fainting light
Succumbs to the crawl of night.
Outside in the road the telegraph wire
To the town from the darkening land
Intones to travellers like a spectral lyre
Swept by a spectral hand.

A car comes up, with lamps full-glare,
That flash upon a tree:
It has nothing to do with me,
And whangs along in a world of its own,
Leaving a blacker air;
And mute by the gate I stand again alone,
And nobody pulls up there.

1925

He Never Expected Much

(or)

A CONSIDERATION

(A reflection) On my Eighty-Sixth Birthday

Well, World, you have kept faith with me,
Kept faith with me;
Upon the whole you have proved to be
Much as you said you were.
Since as a child I used to lie
Upon the leaze[3] and watch the sky,
Never, I own, expected I
That life would all be fair.

'Twas then you said, and since have said,
Times since have said,
In that mysterious voice you shed
From clouds and hills around:
'Many have loved me desperately,
Many with smooth serenity,
While some have shown contempt of me
Till they dropped underground.

'I do not promise overmuch,
Child; overmuch;
Just neutral-tinted haps and such,'
You said to minds like mine.
Wise warning for your credit's sake!
Which I for one failed not to take,
And hence could stem such strain and ache
As each year might assign.

1928

3. Pasture.

Gerard Manley Hopkins
1844–1889

Gerard Manley Hopkins, who wrote so little and died so young, was one of the most original poets to write in English at any period. He worked out his innovations in private. His efforts to secure publication were sporadic and perfunctory, and during his lifetime only a few of his poems were published. His friend from college days, Robert Bridges, England's poet laureate, collected and edited Hopkins's poetry in 1918, having delayed so long because of his desire to find the propitious moment. The work caught on at once among post–World War I audiences, readier than the Victorians for its verbal extremity and formal daring, and has been a favorite of later poets, from W. H. Auden to Robert Lowell, Amy Clampitt, and Seamus Heaney.

Hopkins's life, whatever its inner satisfactions, is melancholy in summary. He was the eldest of eight children of a London marine-insurance adjuster (Hopkins has two long poems about shipwrecks). His father wrote not only books about marine insurance, but also volumes of poems. His mother was conspicuously pious. Hopkins went to Highgate School, in London, where he won a poetry prize and where one of the masters was Canon R. W. Dixon, a minor poet with whom Hopkins later struck up a long correspondence. In 1863, Hopkins enrolled at Balliol College, Oxford, to read Greats (classics, ancient history, and philosophy). At that time, his ambition was to become a painter. But his plans changed because he was drawn to Catholicism, despite his parents' strong opposition. He was received into the Church by John Henry (later Cardinal) Newman in October 1866, and the experience of conversion determined the course of his life. In 1877, Hopkins was ordained. He served variously as priest and teacher until 1884, when he was appointed professor of classics at University College, Dublin, but he felt out of place in the Irish scene. He died of typhoid at age forty-four.

After Hopkins decided to become a Jesuit, he burnt his early verse as too worldly. "I am a eunuch," he later wrote to Robert Bridges, "but it is for the kingdom of God's sake." He stopped writing poems, though he had not given up the thought of relating his two vocations of priest and poet. In 1875, encouraged by his superior, Hopkins wrote his first major work, on the wreck of the *Deutschland,* a ship carrying five nuns exiled from Germany by the anti-Catholic Falk Laws. It was the kind of subject that interested Thomas Hardy too; different as these poets were, they met on the level of melancholy in disaster-ridden waters. Hopkins sent the poem to Bridges, who called it "presumptuous jugglery." Hopkins stood his ground, evidently with an inner conviction that he had done something of worth. The poem forcefully brought together his own conversion and the chief nun's transfiguring death, God's wrath and God's love. Whereas Hardy emphasized the indifference of the creator to his creation, Hopkins celebrated the bond between them.

Not that this conclusion was wrung from him without pain. Faith was not an escape or a refuge for Hopkins, but a source of anguish; he said that he never wavered in it, but that he never felt worthy of it. He made his misery clear in many poems, most notably in those he wrote in his last years, known variously as the "sonnets of desolation," "the terrible sonnets," or "the dark sonnets." Hopkins spoke, in a poem "To R. B." [Bridges], of his "winter world," but except in his blackest moods, his poems relieve the winter world with sunsets. As he says in "The Wreck of the Deutschland," it is "a winter and warm." Many of his poems set anguish and rapture against each other, and the inner combat is continued to the last moment in a poem such as "Carrion Comfort," in which Christ is adversary as well as savior. But "Spring and Fall" tenderly admits the mortality of earth, with no reference to salvation. Nor is "Spelt from Sibyl's Leaves" redemptive: it leaves us on a rack "Where, selfwrung, selfstrung, sheathe- and shelterless, thoughts against thoughts in groans grind." In Hopkins's poetry, pain is the principal ingredient in joy.

Hopkins was unwilling to accept the usual appurtenances of nineteenth-century poetry—its forms, meters, language. He was altogether at odds with the view implicit in Hardy that one had better not write too well for fear of losing something central in an experience. Hopkins held that difficulty of composition was a means of achieving poetic value, much as difficulty in spiritual exercises brought forth rewards to match. In an essay he wrote while at Oxford in 1865, on poetic diction, Hopkins disagreed with William Wordsworth's theory—which was also Hardy's—that the language of poetry and that of prose should be very little different. Still, he recognized the danger of using an archaic or overly "poetic" diction and rhetoric. He stated this idea in a letter of August 14, 1879, to Bridges: "For it seems to me that the poetical language of an age shd. be the current language heightened, to any degree heightened and unlike itself, but not (I mean normally: passing freaks and graces are another thing) an obsolete one." The language must divorce itself from such archaisms as "ere," "wellnigh," and "say not."

Even so, he approved the poet William Barnes's use of dialect words (as did Hardy), because thereby Barnes was tied "down to the things that he or another Dorset man has said or might say, which though it narrows his field heightens his effects." Hopkins himself borrowed from dialect such words as *fettle, sillion,* and *burl.* He also invented new words, often in the "kenning," or periphrastic, mode of Old English that he had studied, such as "beechbole" (trunk of a beech tree), "bloomfall" (fall of flowers), "bower of bone" (body), "churlsgrace" (grace of a churl or laborer), "firedint" (spark), "firefolk" (stars), "leafmeal" (a fusion of *leaf* and *piecemeal*), and "unleaving" (losing leaves). In a letter of January 26, 1881, he advised Bridges to concentrate by dispensing with articles: instead of "The eye marvelled, the ear hearkened," he urged "eye marvelled, ear hearkened," as in his own poem "Spring and Fall." The effect is to convey the meaning more abruptly. In addition, Hopkins made new and original use of internal rhyme, alliteration, consonance, dissonance. Some of his effects he took from classical prosody, some from Welsh poetry (which he studied for the purpose), and some from alliterative Middle English verse, especially from William Langland, author of *Piers Plowman.*

Hopkins also coined a critical vocabulary, feeling the need for a new set of terms to explain what he was doing. His earlier expression, "vividness of idea," gave way to "inscape." This word, formed on the analogy of landscape, meant "individually distinctive beauty," the inner design or essential "whatness" of a thing, suddenly apprehended like an electrical impulse, a divine spark. Hopkins wrote in his *Notebooks,* "All things therefore are charged with love, are charged with God and if we know how to touch them give off sparks and take fire, yield drops and flow, ring and tell of him" (1881). Or as he writes in the poem that begins "As kingfishers catch fire, dragonflies draw flame," each thing "flings out broad its name" and "selves" (that is, displays its essential self). Another poem, "Pied Beauty," celebrates sudden recognitions of the unique identities that compose the universe, in each of which God can be seen to manifest himself as "thisness," or *haecceitas,* a term Hopkins adopted from medieval philosophy. A second term Hopkins needed arose from a conception of "liveliness," which he made more precise as "instress." This power holds inscape together, as force binds the atom; the ultimate instress of all things is their divine creator. The sense that everything is not passively meaningless or meaningful, but actively asserts its distinctive totality of symbolical being, connects Hopkins with other symbolist poets.

In technique, Hopkins's most important innovation is "sprung rhythm," which he explained variously at various times. It is made up of a constant number of strong stresses in a line but a variable number of unstressed syllables, instead of the regular alternation of stressed and unstressed syllables. Its use is basic to the effect Hopkins so often achieves, of a sudden rush or an equally sudden slowing down of tension. He contended, in a letter of August 21, 1877, that it was the rhythm nearest to "the native and natural rhythm of speech." In sum, Hopkins saw his verse as eliciting the special identity of a thing or person, releasing its private energy, and conveying the particular animation of it, by every means of formal activity.

The density of his verse made (and still makes) it difficult to comprehend. Metaphorically compressed, syntactically contorted, it energetically plays on verbal ambiguities, such as those of the verb *buckle* (meaning both "fasten together" and "collapse") in "The Windhover." In a letter of November 6, 1887, to Bridges, Hopkins defended his technique: "Plainly if it is possible to express a subtle and recondite subject in a subtle and recondite way and with great felicity and perfection, in the end, something must be sacrificed." He conceded the "oddness" of his verse, admitted it was "queer," but argued that this was the "distinctiveness" of a true aesthetic, of "design, pattern or what I am in the habit of calling 'inscape.'"

While Hopkins was a professor in Dublin, he met the young poet W. B. Yeats one day in 1886. Hopkins disliked Yeats's early verse, but he said that at least one poem had many fine lines and vivid images. Yeats, for his part, wrote later that he had not cared much for the Jesuit priest, who seemed a querulous, sensitive scholar, alien to a young man with Walt Whitman in his pocket. But Hopkins had carried Whitman in his pocket too. In later life, Yeats found fault with the obscurity of Hopkins's diction and rhythms; Hopkins's "stoppage and sudden onrush of syllables were to him a necessary expression of his slight constant excitement" (introduction, *Oxford Book of Modern Verse,* 1936). T. S. Eliot also complained that Hopkins was too far from the language of common speech. But if an older generation disapproved of him, younger ones, readier to accept grotesqueness, have not been put off. His dislocations of words to embody dislocations of feeling, the artificiality that he presents so naturally with powerful emotion, attract rather than repel. Hopkins remains offbeat and superb.

The Habit of Perfection

Elected Silence,[1] sing to me
And beat upon my whorlèd ear,
Pipe me to pastures still and be
The music that I care to hear.

Shape nothing, lips; be lovely-dumb:
It is the shut,[2] the curfew sent
From there where all surrenders come
Which only makes you eloquent.

Be shellèd, eyes, with double dark
And find the uncreated light:
This ruck[3] and reel which you remark
Coils,[4] keeps, and teases simple sight.

Palate, the hutch[5] of tasty lust,
Desire not to be rinsed with wine:
The can[6] must be so sweet, the crust
So fresh that come in fasts divine!

Nostrils, your careless breath that spend
Upon the stir and keep[7] of pride,
What relish shall the censers send
Along the sanctuary side!

1. The priest has elected—or freely chosen—the life of renunciation celebrated in the poem. *Habit:* disposition; religious attire.
2. Close of day.
3. Confused pile.
4. Ensnares.
5. Storage chest.
6. Cup.
7. Upkeep.

O feel-of-primrose hands, O feet
That want the yield of plushy sward,
But you shall walk the golden street
And you unhouse and house the Lord.[8]

And, Poverty, be thou the bride
And now the marriage feast begun,
And lily-coloured clothes provide
Your spouse not laboured-at nor spun.[9]

1866 1918

The Wreck of the Deutschland[1]

December 6, 7, 1875
to the
happy memory of five Franciscan nuns,
exiles by the Falck Laws,[2]
drowned between midnight and morning of
December 7

Part the First

1

Thou mastering me
God! giver of breath and bread;
World's strand, sway of the sea;
Lord of living and dead;
Thou hast bound bones and veins in me, fastened me flesh,
And after it almost unmade, what with dread,
Thy doing: and dost thou touch me afresh?
Over again I feel thy finger and find thee.

8. Remove the eucharistic bread, or Host, from the tabernacle and then return it. *Sward:* turf.
9. "And why are you anxious about clothing? Consider the lilies of the field, how they grow; they neither toil nor spin; yet I tell you, even Solomon in all his glory was not arrayed like one of these" (Matthew 6.28–29).
1. Germany (German); here, the name of the ship. In a lengthy note on the poem's rhythm, Hopkins states, in part: "Be pleased, reader, since the rhythm in which the following poem is written is new, strongly to mark the beats of the measure, according to the number belonging to each of the eight lines of the stanza, as the indentation guides the eye, namely two and three and four and three and five and five and four and six; not disguising the rhythm and rhyme, as some readers do, who treat poetry as if it were prose fantastically written to rule (which they mistakenly think the perfection of reading), but laying on the beats too much stress rather than too little; nor caring whether one, two, three, or more syllables go to a beat."
2. The Falk (or Falck) Laws of the 1870s, named for Aldabert Falk, Prussian minister of public worship and education, were intended to diminish the influence of the Roman Catholic Church in the newly unified Germany. Church property was seized and members of religious orders, such as Franciscans and Jesuits, were expelled from the country. In a letter of October 5, 1878, Hopkins wrote that "when in the winter of '75 the *Deutschland* was wrecked in the mouth of the Thames and five Franciscan nuns, exiles from Germany by the Falk Laws, aboard of her were drowned I was affected by the account and happening to say so to my rector he said that he wished someone would write a poem on the subject. On this hint I set to work and, though my hand was out at first, produced one. I had long had haunting my ear the echo of a new rhythm which now I realized on paper."

2

I did say yes
O at lightning and lashed rod;
Thou heardst me truer than tongue, confess
Thy terror, O Christ, O God;
Thou knowest the walls, altar and hour and night:
The swoon of a heart that the sweep and the hurl of thee trod
Hard down with a horror of height:
And the midriff astrain with leaning of, laced with fire of stress.

3

The frown of his face
Before me, the hurtle of hell
Behind, where, where was a, where was a place?
I whirled out wings that spell[3]
And fled with a fling of the heart to the heart of the Host.[4]
My heart, but you were dovewinged, I can tell,
Carrier-witted,[5] I am bold to boast,
To flash from the flame to the flame then, tower from the grace to the grace.

4

I am soft sift
In an hourglass—at the wall
Fast, but mined with a motion, a drift,
And it crowds and it combs to the fall;
I steady as a water in a well, to a poise, to a pane,
But roped with, always, all the way down from the tall
Fells or flanks of the voel,[6] a vein
Of the gospel proffer, a pressure, a principle, Christ's gift.

5

I kiss my hand
To the stars, lovely-asunder
Starlight, wafting him out of it; and
Glow, glory in thunder;
Kiss my hand to the dappled-with-damson[7] west:
Since, though he is under the world's splendour and wonder,
His mystery must be instressed,[8] stressed;
For I greet him the days I meet him, and bless when I understand.

6

Not out of his bliss
Springs the stress felt
Nor first from heaven (and few know this)

3. At that time.
4. Eucharistic body of Christ.
5. With the homing instinct of a carrier pigeon.
6. Bare mountain (Welsh; rhymes with *coil*). *Fells:* high hills (Northern British).
7. A dark-purple plum.
8. Realized, with full receptiveness to divine immanence (Hopkins's coinage).

Swings the stroke dealt—
Stroke and a stress that stars and storms deliver,
That guilt is hushed by, hearts are flushed by and melt—
But it rides time like riding a river
(And here the faithful waver, the faithless fable and miss).

7

It dates from day
Of his going in Galilee;[9]
Warm-laid grave of a womb-life grey;
Manger, maiden's knee;
The dense and the driven Passion,[1] and frightful sweat;
Thence the discharge of it, there its swelling to be,
Though felt before, though in high flood yet—
What none would have known of it, only the heart, being hard at bay,

8

Is out with it! Oh,
We lash with the best or worst
Word last! How a lush-kept plush-capped sloe[2]
Will, mouthed to flesh-burst,
Gush!—flush the man, the being with it, sour or sweet,
Brim, in a flash, full!—Hither then, last or first,
To hero of Calvary, Christ,'s feet—
Never ask if meaning it, wanting it, warned of it—men go.

9

Be adored among men,
God, three-numberèd form;
Wring thy rebel, dogged in den,
Man's malice, with wrecking and storm.
Beyond saying sweet, past telling of tongue,
Thou art lightning and love, I found it, a winter and warm;
Father and fondler of heart thou hast wrung:
Hast thy dark descending and most art merciful then.

10

With an anvil-ding
And with fire in him forge thy will
Or rather, rather then, stealing as Spring
Through him, melt him but master him still:
Whether at once, as once at a crash Paul,
Or as Austin, a lingering-out swéet skill,[3]
Make mercy in all of us, out of us all
Mastery, but be adored, but be adored King.

9. Site of Jesus' life and ministry, in Palestine.
1. Jesus' crucifixion, on the hill of Calvary (see line 63).
2. Plum.
3. The sudden conversion of Paul on his way to Damascus (Acts 9.3–9), when he was struck to the ground, is contrasted with the slower, more meditative conversion of St. Augustine ("Austin").

Part the Second

11

'Some find me a sword; some
The flange[4] and the rail; flame,
Fang, or flood' goes Death on drum,
And storms bugle his fame.
But wé dream we are rooted in earth—Dust!
Flesh falls within sight of us, we, though our flower the same,
Wave with the meadow, forget that there must
The sour scythe cringe,[5] and the blear share come.

12

On Saturday sailed from Bremen,
American-outward-bound,
Take settler and seamen, tell men with women,
Two hundred souls in the round—
O Father, not under thy feathers nor ever as guessing
The goal was a shoal, of a fourth the doom to be drowned;
Yet did the dark side of the bay of thy blessing
Not vault them, the millions of rounds of thy mercy not reeve[6] even them in?

13

Into the snows she sweeps,
Hurling the haven behind,
The Deutschland, on Sunday; and so the sky keeps,
For the infinite air is unkind,
And the sea flint-flake, black-backed in the regular blow,
Sitting Eastnortheast, in cursed quarter, the wind;
Wiry and white-fiery and whirlwind-swivellèd snow
Spins to the widow-making unchilding unfathering deeps.

14

She drove in the dark to leeward,
She struck—not a reef or a rock
But the combs of a smother of sand: night drew her
Dead to the Kentish Knock;[7]
And she beat the bank down with her bows and the ride of her keel;
The breakers rolled on her beam with ruinous shock;
And canvass and compass, the whorl[8] and the wheel
Idle for ever to waft her or wind her with, these she endured.

15

Hope had grown grey hairs,
Hope had mourning on,

4. Rim of a wheel.
5. Bend.
6. Gather.
7. Sandbar near the mouth of the Thames River.
8. Propeller screw.

Trenched with tears, carved with cares,
Hope was twelve hours gone;
And frightful a nightfall folded rueful a day
Nor rescue, only rocket and lightship, shone,
And lives at last were washing away:
To the shrouds they took,—they shook in the hurling and horrible airs.

16

One stirred from the rigging to save
The wild woman-kind below,
With a rope's end round the man, handy and brave—
He was pitched to his death at a blow,
For all his dreadnought breast and braids of thew:[9]
They could tell him for hours, dandled the to and fro
Through the cobbled foam-fleece. What could he do
With the burl of the fountains of air, buck and the flood of the wave?

17

They fought with God's cold—
And they could not and fell to the deck
(Crushed them) or water (and drowned them) or rolled
With the sea-romp over the wreck.
Night roared, with the heart-break hearing a heart-broke rabble,
The woman's wailing, the crying of child without check—
Till a lioness arose breasting the babble,
A prophetess towered in the tumult, a virginal tongue told.[1]

18

Ah, touched in your bower of bone
Are you! turned for an exquisite smart,
Have you! make words break from me here all alone,
Do you!—mother of being in me, heart.
O unteachably after evil, but uttering truth,
Why, tears! is it? tears; such a melting, a madrigal start!
Never-eldering revel and river and of youth,
What can it be, this glee? the good you have there of your own?

19

Sister, a sister calling
A master, her master and mine!—
And the inboard seas run swirling and hawling;
The rash smart sloggering[2] brine
Blinds her; but she that weather sees one thing, one;
Has one fetch[3] in her: she rears herself to divine
Ears, and the call of the tall nun
To the men in the tops and the tackle rode over the storm's brawling.

9. Knotted muscles.
1. "Five German nuns . . . clasped hands and were drowned together, the chief sister, a gaunt woman 6 ft. high, calling out loudly and often 'O Christ, come quickly' till the end came" (London *Times*, December 11, 1875).
2. Hanging loosely; dashing against.
3. Expedient; here, the miracle of the nun's sacrifice and transfiguration. *That weather:* in that circumstance.

20

She was first of a five and came
Of a coifèd sisterhood.
(O Deutschland, double a desperate name!
O world wide of its good!
But Gertrude, lily, and Luther, are two of a town[4]
Christ's lily and beast of the waste wood:
From life's dawn it is drawn down,
Abel is Cain's brother[5] and breasts they have sucked the same.)

21

Loathed for a love men knew in them,
Banned by the land of their birth,
Rhine refused them. Thames[6] would ruin them;
Surf, snow, river and earth
Gnashed: but thou art above, thou Orion of light;
Thy unchancelling[7] poising palms were weighing the worth,
Thou martyr-master: in thy sight
Storm flakes were scroll-leaved flowers, lily showers—sweet heaven was astrew in them.

22

Five! The finding and sake[8]
And cipher of suffering Christ.
Mark, the mark is of man's make
And the word of it Sacrificed.
But he scores it in scarlet himself on his own bespoken,
Before-time-taken, dearest prizèd and priced—
Stigma, signal, cinequefoil[9] token
For lettering of the lamb's fleece, ruddying of the rose-flake.

23

Joy fall to thee, father Francis,
Drawn to the Life that died;
With the gnarls of the nails in thee, niche of the lance, his
Lovescape crucified
And seal of his seraph-arrival! and these thy daughters
And five-livèd and leavèd favour and pride,
Are sisterly sealed in wild waters,
To bathe in his fall-gold mercies, to breathe in his all-fire glances.

4. St. Gertrude (thirteenth century) lived in a convent in Eisleben near the birthplace of Martin Luther (1483–1546), instigator of the Protestant Reformation (and a pernicious heretic to Hopkins, a Catholic priest).
5. They were the first brothers, according to Genesis. Cain killed Abel out of envy.
6. English river. *Rhine:* German river.
7. Evicting from the chancel of the church; exiling. *Orion:* the hunter, one of the most recognizable constellations.
8. Clue and trace. In stanzas 22 and 23, Hopkins plays on the analogies between the five dead nuns, the five wounds of the crucified Jesus, and the stigmata of St. Francis of Assisi (1182–1226), founder of the nuns' order.
9. Five-leaved.

24

Away in the loveable west,
On a pastoral forehead of Wales,[1]
I was under a roof here, I was at rest,
And they the prey of the gales;
She to the black-about air, to the breaker, the thickly
Falling flakes, to the throng that catches and quails
Was calling 'O Christ, Christ, come quickly':
The cross to her she calls Christ to her, christens her wild-worst[2] Best.

25

The majesty! what did she mean?
Breathe, arch and original Breath.[3]
Is it love in her of the being as her lover[4] had been?
Breathe, body of lovely Death.
They were else-minded then, altogether, the men
Woke thee with a *We are perishing* in the weather of Gennesareth.[5]
Or is it that she cried for the crown then,
The keener to come at the comfort for feeling the combating keen?

26

For how to the heart's cheering
The down-dugged ground-hugged grey[6]
Hovers off, the jay-blue heavens appearing
Of pied and peeled May!
Blue-beating and hoary-glow height; or night, still higher,
With belled fire and the moth-soft Milky Way.
What by your measure is the heaven of desire,
The treasure never eyesight got, nor was ever guessed what for the hearing?

27

No, but it was not these.
The jading and jar of the cart,
Time's tasking, it is fathers that asking for ease
Of the sodden-with-its-sorrowing heart,
Not danger, electrical horror; then further it finds
The appealing of the Passion is tenderer in prayer apart:
Other, I gather, in measure her mind's
Burden, in wind's burly[7] and beat of endragonèd seas.

1. Hopkins was studying at St. Bruno's College, in Wales, at the time of the disaster.
2. That is, death.
3. The Holy Ghost.
4. That is, Jesus Christ.
5. While sailing across the Sea of Galilee (or Gennesaret) with his disciples, Jesus calmed a storm that was endangering them. They had cried, "Save us, Lord, we are perishing" (Matthew 8.23–27).
6. That is, cloud.
7. That is, hurly-burly; uproar.

28

But how shall I . . . make me room there:
Reach me a . . . Fancy, come faster—
Strike you the sight of it? look at it loom there,
Thing that she . . . There then! the Master,
Ipse,[8] the only one, Christ, King, Head:
He was to cure the extremity where he had cast her;
Do, deal, lord it with living and dead;
Let him ride, her pride, in his triumph, despatch and have done with
his doom there.

29

Ah! there was a heart right
There was single eye!
Read the unshapeable shock night
And knew the who and the why;
Wording it how but by him that present and past,
Heaven and earth are word of, worded by?—
The Simon Peter[9] of a soul! to the blast
Tarpeian-fast,[1] but a blown beacon of light.

30

Jesu, heart's light,
Jesu, maid's son,
What was the feast followed the night
Thou hadst glory of this nun?—
Feast of the one woman without stain.[2]
For so conceivèd, so to conceive thee is done;[3]
But here was heart-throe, birth of a brain,
Word, that heard and kept thee and uttered thee outright.

31

Well, she has thee for the pain, for the
Patience; but pity of the rest of them!
Heart, go and bleed at a bitterer vein for the
Comfortless unconfessed of them—
No not uncomforted: lovely-felicitous Providence
Finger of a tender of, O of a feathery delicacy, the breast of the
Maiden could obey so, be a bell to, ring of it,[4] and
Startle the poor sheep back! is the shipwrack then a harvest, does
tempest carry the grain for thee?

8. Himself (Latin).
9. Jesus' chief apostle, called the rock of the Church in Matthew 16.18.
1. As solid as the rock on one of the Roman hills (Capitoline) from which condemned traitors were thrown to their deaths.
2. Hopkins compares the nun's death to the Feast of the Immaculate Conception of the Virgin Mary, which falls on December 8, the day after the shipwreck.
3. The nun's spiritual marriage with Christ is as virginal as his own conception.
4. She is like a bell summoning others to God.

32

I admire thee, master of the tides,
Of the Yore-flood,[5] of the year's fall;
The recurb and the recovery[6] of the gulf's sides,
The girth of it and the wharf of it and the wall;
Stanching, quenching ocean of a motionable mind;
Ground of being, and granite of it: past all
Grasp God, throned behind
Death with a sovereignty that heeds but hides, bodes but abides;

33

With a mercy that outrides
The all of water, an ark
For the listener; for the lingerer with a love glides
Lower than death and the dark;[7]
A vein for the visiting of the past-prayer, pent in prison,
The-last-breath penitent spirits—the uttermost mark
Our passion-plungèd giant risen,
The Christ of the Father compassionate, fetched in the storm of his strides.

34

Now burn, new born to the world,
Doubled-naturèd name,[8]
The heaven-flung, heart-fleshed, maiden-furled
Miracle-in-Mary-of-flame,
Mid-numbered he in three of the thunder-throne![9]
Not a dooms-day dazzle in his coming nor dark as he came;
Kind, but royally reclaiming his own;
A released shower, let flash to the shire, not a lightning of fire hard-hurled.

35

Dame, at our door
Drowned, and among our shoals,
Remember us in the roads,[1] the heaven-haven of the reward:
Our King back, Oh, upon English souls!
Let him easter in us, be dayspring to the dimness of us, be a crimson-cresseted east,
More brightening her, rare-dear Britain, as his reign rolls,
Pride, rose, prince, hero of us, high-priest,
Our hearts' charity's hearth's fire, our thoughts' chivalry's throng's Lord.

1876 1918

5. This may refer to the primal waters of Genesis, to the biblical Flood, or to both.
6. Tidal ebb and flow.
7. To Purgatory.
8. That is, Christ, who comprises God and human.
9. Christ is "mid-numbered" in the Trinity of Father, Son, and Holy Ghost.
1. Sheltered waters where ships may lie in safety.

God's Grandeur

The world is charged with the grandeur of God.
It will flame out, like shining from shook foil;[2]
It gathers to a greatness, like the ooze of oil
Crushed. Why do men then now not reck his rod?[3]
Generations have trod, have trod, have trod;
And all is seared with trade; bleared, smeared with toil;
And wears man's smudge and shares man's smell: the soil
Is bare now, nor can foot feel, being shod.

And, for all this, nature is never spent;
There lives the dearest freshness deep down things;
And though the last lights off the black West went
Oh, morning, at the brown brink eastward, springs—
Because the Holy Ghost over the bent
World broods with warm breast and with ah! bright wings.

1877 1918

[As Kingfishers Catch Fire, Dragonflies Draw Flame]

As kingfishers catch fire, dragonflies draw flame;
As tumbled over rim in roundy wells
Stones ring; like each tucked[4] string tells, each hung bell's
Bow swung finds tongue to fling out broad its name;
Each mortal thing does one thing and the same:
Deals out that being indoors[5] each one dwells;
Selves[6]—goes its self; *myself* it speaks and spells,
Crying *What I do is me: for that I came.*

I say more: the just man justices;[7]
Keeps grace: that keeps all his goings graces;
Acts in God's eye what in God's eye he is—

Christ. For Christ plays in ten thousand places,
Lovely in limbs, and lovely in eyes not his
To the Father through the features of men's faces.

1881? 1918

2. "I mean foil in its sense of leaf or tinsel. . . . Shaken goldfoil gives off broad glares like sheet lightning and also, and this is true of nothing else, owing to its zig-zag dints and creasings and network of small many cornered facets, a sort of fork lightning too" (*Letters of Gerard Manley Hopkins to Robert Bridges*, ed. C. C. Abbott, 1955, 169).
3. Heed his authority.
4. Plucked.
5. Within.
6. Fulfills its individuality.
7. Behaves in a just fashion.

Spring

Nothing is so beautiful as spring—
When weeds, in wheels, shoot long and lovely and lush;
Thrush's eggs look little low heavens, and thrush
Through the echoing timber does so rinse and wring
The ear, it strikes like lightnings to hear him sing;
The glassy peartree leaves and blooms, they brush
The descending blue; that blue is all in a rush
With richness; the racing lambs too have fair their fling.

What is all this juice and all this joy?
A strain of the earth's sweet being in the beginning
In Eden garden.—Have, get, before it cloy,

Before it cloud, Christ, lord, and sour with sinning,
Innocent mind and Mayday in girl and boy,
Most, O maid's child, thy choice and worthy the winning.

1877 1918

The Windhover:[8]

To Christ our Lord

I caught this morning morning's minion,[9] king-
dom of daylight's dauphin,[1] dapple-dawn-drawn Falcon, in his riding
Of the rolling level underneath him steady air, and striding
High there, how he rung upon the rein of a wimpling[2] wing
In his ecstasy! then off, off forth on swing,
As a skate's heel sweeps smooth on a bow-bend: the hurl and gliding
Rebuffed the big wind. My heart in hiding
Stirred for a bird,—the achieve of, the mastery of the thing!

Brute beauty and valour and act, oh, air, pride, plume here
Buckle![3] and the fire that breaks from thee then, a billion
Times told lovelier, more dangerous, O my chevalier![4]

No wonder of it: shéer plód makes plough down sillion[5]
Shine, and blue-bleak embers, ah my dear,
Fall, gall themselves, and gash gold-vermilion.

1877 1918

8. The kestrel, a small falcon that hovers in the air.
9. Favorite.
1. Prince.
2. Rippling. *Rung upon the rein:* circled at the end of the rein.
3. Prepare for action; fasten together; give way, bend.
4. Knight.
5. Ploughed furrow.

Pied Beauty

Glory be to God for dappled things—
For skies of couple-colour as a brinded cow;
For rose-moles all in stipple upon trout that swim;
Fresh-firecoal chestnut-falls;[6] finches' wings;
Landscape plotted and pieced—fold,[7] fallow, and plough;
And áll trádes, their gear and tackle and trim.[8]

All things counter,[9] original, spare, strange;
Whatever is fickle, freckled (who knows how?)
With swift, slow; sweet, sour; adazzle, dim;
He fathers-forth whose beauty is past change:
Praise him.

1877 1918

Binsey Poplars[1]

felled 1879

My aspens dear, whose airy cages quelled,
Quelled or quenched in leaves the leaping sun,
All felled, felled, are all felled;
Of a fresh and following folded rank
Not spared, not one
That dandled a sandalled
Shadow that swam or sank
On meadow and river and wind-wandering weed-winding bank.

O if we but knew what we do
When we delve or hew—
Hack and rack the growing green!
Since Country is so tender
To touch, her being só slender,
That, like this sleek and seeing ball[2]
But a prick will make no eye at all,
Where we, even where we mean
To mend her we end her,
When we hew or delve:
After-comers cannot guess the beauty been.
Ten or twelve, only ten or twelve
Strokes of havoc únselve
The sweet especial scene,
Rural scene, a rural scene,
Sweet especial rural scene.

1879 1918

6. That is, the chestnuts when they fall.
7. Pastureland.
8. Equipment.
9. Contrary.
1. Binsey is a village near Oxford.
2. Eye.

Felix Randal

Felix Randal the farrier,[3] O is he dead then? my duty all ended,
Who have watched his mould of man, big-boned and hardy-handsome
Pining, pining, till time when reason rambled in it and some
Fatal four disorders, fleshed there, all contended?

Sickness broke him. Impatient, he cursed at first, but mended
Being anointed[4] and all; though a heavenlier heart began some
Months earlier, since I had our sweet reprieve and ransom[5]
Tendered to him. Ah well, God rest him all road ever[6] he offended!

This seeing the sick endears them to us, us too it endears.
My tongue had taught thee comfort, touch had quenched thy tears,
Thy tears that touched my heart, child, Felix, poor Felix Randal;

How far from then forethought of, all thy more boisterous years,
When thou at the random grim[7] forge, powerful amidst peers,
Didst fettle for the great grey drayhorse his bright and battering sandal!

1880 1918

[I Wake and Feel the Fell of Dark, Not Day]

I wake and feel the fell of dark, not day.
What hours, O what black hours we have spent
This night! what sights you, heart, saw; ways you went!
And more must, in yet longer light's delay.

With witness I speak this. But where I say
Hours I mean years, mean life. And my lament
Is cries countless, cries like dead letters sent
To dearest him that lives alas! away.

I am gall, I am heartburn. God's most deep decree
Bitter would have me taste: my taste was me;
Bones built in me, flesh filled, blood brimmed the curse.

Selfyeast of spirit a dull dough sours. I see
The lost are like this, and their scourge to be
As I am mine, their sweating selves; but worse.

1885? 1918

3. Blacksmith.
4. Having received the sacrament for the seriously ill or dying.
5. Communion, preceded by confession and absolution.
6. In whatever way.
7. Disorderly and grimy.

[No Worst, There Is None. Pitched Past Pitch of Grief]

No worst, there is none. Pitched past pitch of grief,
More pangs will, schooled at forepangs, wilder wring.
Comforter, where, where is your comforting?
Mary, mother of us, where is your relief?
My cries heave, herds-long, huddle in a main, a chief-
Woe, world-sorrow; on an age-old anvil wince and sing—
Then lull, then leave off. Fury had shrieked 'No ling-
Ering! Let me be fell: force[8] I must be brief'.
O the mind, mind has mountains; cliffs of fall
Frightful, sheer, no-man-fathomed. Hold them cheap
May who ne'er hung there. Nor does long our small
Durance deal with that steep or deep. Here! creep,
Wretch, under a comfort serves in a whirlwind: all
Life death does end and each day dies with sleep.

1885 1918

Spring and Fall:

to a Young Child

Márgarét, áre you gríeving
Over Goldengrove unleaving?
Leáves, líke the things of man, you
With your fresh thoughts care for, can you?
Áh! ás the heart grows older
It will come to such sights colder
By and by, nor spare a sigh
Though worlds of wanwood leafmeal[9] lie;
And yet you *will* weep and know why.
Now no matter, child, the name:
Sórrow's spríngs áre the same.
Nor mouth had, no nor mind, expressed
What heart heard of, ghost[1] guessed:
It ís the blight man was born for,
It is Margaret you mourn for.

1880 1918

8. Perforce; of necessity. *Fell:* fierce.
9. That is, wan forest with scattered leaves. Coined by analogy with "piecemeal."
1. Spirit.

[Carrion Comfort]

Not, I'll not, carrion comfort, Despair, not feast on thee;
Not untwist—slack they may be—these last strands of man
In me ór, most weary, cry *I can no more.* I can;
Can something, hope, wish day come, not choose not to be.
But ah, but O thou terrible, why wouldst thou rude on me
Thy wring-earth right foot rock? lay a lionlimb against me? scan
With darksome devouring eyes my bruisèd bones? and fan,
O in turns of tempest, me heaped there; me frantic to avoid thee and flee?
Why? That my chaff might fly; my grain lie, sheer and clear.
Nay in all that toil, that coil, since (seems) I kissed the rod,
Hand rather, my heart lo! lapped strength, stole joy, would laugh, cheer.
Cheer whom though? The hero whose heaven-handling flung me, foot trod
Me? or me that fought him? O which one? is it each one? That night, that year
Of now done darkness I wretch lay wrestling with (my God!) my God.

1885–87 1918

Spelt from Sibyl's Leaves[2]

Earnest, earthless, equal, attuneable, vaulty, voluminous, . . . stupendous
Evening strains to be time's vast, womb-of-all, home-of-all, hearse-of-all night.
Her fond yellow hornlight[3] wound to the west, her wild hollow hoarlight hung to the height
Waste; her earliest stars, earlstars, stars principal, overbend us,
Fire-featuring heaven. For earth her being has unbound; her dapple is at end, as-
Tray or aswarm, all throughther,[4] in throngs; self in self steepèd and pashed—quite
Disremembering, dismembering all now. Heart, you round me right
With: Our evening is over us; our night whelms, whelms, and will end us.
Only the beakleaved boughs dragonish damask[5] the tool-smooth bleak light; black,
Ever so black on it. Our tale, O our oracle! Let life, waned, ah let life wind
Off her once skeined stained veined variety upon, all on two spools; part, pen, pack
Now her all in two flocks, two folds—black, white; right, wrong; reckon but, reck but, mind

2. The title of this poem is derived from the hymn "Dies Irae" (Latin for day of wrath), which claims that the Day of Judgment was prophesized by both David and the Sibyl, a female prophet of Greek mythology; her ecstasies were written on paper leaves.
3. Light diffused as through a lantern made of horn. *Fond:* meager.
4. Confusedly; intermingled (dialect).
5. Adorn with patterns.

But these two; ware[6] of a world where but these two tell, each off the
other; of a rack
Where, selfwrung, selfstrung, sheathe- and shelterless, thoughts against
thoughts in groans grind.

1886 1918

[Thou Art Indeed Just, Lord, If I Contend]

Justus quidem tu es, Domine, si disputem tecum: verumtamen justa loquar ad te: quare via impiorum prosperatur? etc.[7]

Thou art indeed just, Lord, if I contend
With thee; but, sir, so what I plead is just.
Why do sinners' ways prosper? and why must
Disappointment all I endeavour end?

Wert thou my enemy, O thou my friend,
How wouldst thou worse, I wonder, than thou dost
Defeat, thwart me? Oh, the sots and thralls[8] of lust
Do in spare hours more thrive than I that spend,

Sir, life upon thy cause. See, banks and brakes[9]
Now, leavèd how thick! lacèd they are again
With fretty chervil,[1] look, and fresh wind shakes

Them; birds build—but not I build; no, but strain,
Time's eunuch, and not breed one work that wakes.
Mine, O thou lord of life, send my roots rain.

1889 1918

6. Aware; beware.
7. "Righteous art thou, O Lord, when I complain to thee; yet I would plead my case before thee. Why does the way of the wicked prosper?" (Jeremiah 12.1). Hopkins quotes this much as his epigraph; the imagery of his poem may owe something to the next verses: "Why do all who are treacherous thrive? Thou plantest them and they take root; they grow and bring forth fruit; thou art near in their mouth and far from their heart."
8. Prisoners.
9. Thickets.
1. *Fretty:* interlaced. *Chervil:* an herb related to parsley.

A. E. Housman
1859–1936

A. E. Housman refused to have his poems included in an anthology of the 1890s, insisting on their difference from the work of his contemporaries, but certain poems of W. B. Yeats, Lionel Johnson, and Ernest Dowson are close to Housman's. The interest in a small, predominantly rural area, the use of ballad meters, the sense of the world's unsatisfactoriness, and the reiterated theme of unrequited love are aspects that Housman shared with the early Yeats in particular. The two poets also shared an intense admiration for William Blake, whom Housman put second only to Shakespeare. But Housman admired Blake's subordination of idea to lyrical intensity, whereas Yeats was more occupied with Blake's mythical system. Housman minimizes and disparages the intellect in poetry, whereas Yeats, like other poets of larger scope, recognizes the necessity of incorporating it. Housman, when he can, *ex*cludes; Yeats *in*cludes. It was characteristic of Housman to devote much of his life to editing a minor work, the *Astronomicon* of Manilius, rather than classical poems of greater enterprise.

While disclaiming close kinship with contemporaries, Housman conceded that he liked the German writer Heinrich Heine's sardonically wistful poetry and Thomas Hardy's doom-laden novels—like Housman, Hardy straddled Romantic feeling and a grim modern pessimism. Even as a boy, Housman had been attracted to the theme of death. Dirges and laments were favorite reading. He appears to have thought of himself as a loser, predestined to see hopes dashed and love unrequited. His poems, written mostly after he was thirty-five, deal chiefly with young men between twenty-one—or as he would say, one-and-twenty—and twenty-five. Youth and life and love end at a stroke. He extracts all possible ironies from this situation in stark, lucid, elegant verse that recasts pastoral tradition. Nature adds to the gloom either by baleful destructiveness or by its phantasmal parade of meaningless fertility and beauty.

Alfred Edward Housman was born on March 26, 1859, in Fockbury, which is in Worcestershire and not, as might be supposed from his verse, in Shropshire. His "sentimental" attachment to Shropshire came, he said, from the fact that "its hills were our western horizon." He was brought up in the High Church Party of the Church of England, but at eight—also the age at which he first tried writing poetry—he was converted to paganism by John Lemprière's *Classical Dictionary*. Of his later religious career he commented flatly, "I became a deist at 13 and an atheist at 21" (John Carter and John Sparrow, *A. E. Housman, An Annotated Hand-List*, 1952).

Housman did well at school and won a scholarship to St. John's College, Oxford, where he met his "greatest friend," Moses Jackson. A bright and versatile student, Jackson was receptive to friendship, but Housman wanted a more intimate relationship. In a posthumously published verse (poem XXXI), he wrote: "Because I liked you better / Than suits a man to say, / It irked you, and I promised / To throw the thought away." Enjoined to dismiss his feelings, he had to conceal their intensity to enjoy Jackson's company. At first, Housman did well academically, but in emotional turmoil, he failed his examinations in the end and had to return ignominiously the next year to complete a marginal, "pass" degree. Meanwhile, Jackson had taken a job in the Patent Office; Housman joined him there, and for a time the two shared rooms in London, until Housman moved into his own place. Toward the end of 1887, Jackson sailed for a career in India; two years later, he was married. Housman wrote sadly in "Epithalamium": "Friend and comrade yield you o'er / To her that hardly loves you more." In 1892, Jackson's young brother Adalbert died from typhoid. The removal from his life of these two brothers marked a pivotal time for Housman. Most of his poems were written in the early 1890s. He commented afterward, "I did not begin to write poetry in earnest until the really emotional part of my life was over" (George L. Watson, *A. E. Housman*, 1957).

Scorned by Oxford, Housman had been spending most of his nights at the British Museum, determined to prove himself in classics. He earned signal recognition in 1892, when he was elected to the chair of Greek and Latin at University College, London. In 1894, his father died, and Housman was also afflicted sharply by the suicide of a man he did not know, an eighteen-year-old Woolrich cadet. Housman kept for life the newspaper report that quoted the cadet's suicide note, in which he referred to a hopeless homosexual love, "that one thing I have no hope of obtaining." Suicide is a chronic theme in Housman. In the 1890s, homosexuality was illegal: in 1895, Oscar Wilde was convicted on this charge and sentenced to two years at hard labor. Housman, in sympathy, sent Wilde a copy of his book of poems, *A Shropshire Lad* (1896), the product of all Housman's misfortunes and anxieties. Housman had sent the first copy to Jackson, to whom he later dedicated his five-volume edition of Manilius (1903–30). Holding a chair of classics at Cambridge University from 1911, Housman gathered together a second slender volume in 1922, lugubriously entitled *Last Poems.* Jackson died the next year. After Housman's death, his brother Laurence edited *More Poems* (1936).

In his famous 1933 lecture, "The Name and Nature of Poetry," Housman attributed to poetry a "superior terseness" over prose. The function of poetry is, he said, "to transfuse emotion—not to transmit thought but to set up in the reader's sense a vibration corresponding to what was felt by the writer." On this principle, he rejected seventeenth-century poetry as too deliberate, eighteenth-century poetry as too intelligent. Against Alexander Pope he upheld the school of irrational men, or rather madmen, William Collins, Christopher Smart, William Cowper, and William Blake. Here was the passionate urgency he required. Blake in particular offered to "entangle the reader in a net of thoughtless delight." Housman insisted that poetry should be "more physical than intellectual," and his famous touchstone was that when a line of genuine poetry entered his head while he was shaving, he could feel his skin bristle, his spine shiver, and the pit of his stomach receive something like a spear.

These theories, or opinions, plead for lyricism of a special kind. It is limited lyricism, yet Housman's poems stay in the mind and even outlast less limited ones. They are easily parodied, as is his aesthetic, and perhaps inseparable from an element of "camp." Yet they have a refined agony, a stylized pain, a kind of courtly lovelornness that insures their memorability.

[Loveliest of Trees, the Cherry Now]

Loveliest of trees, the cherry now
Is hung with bloom along the bough,
And stands about the woodland ride
Wearing white for Eastertide.

Now, of my threescore years and ten,
Twenty will not come again,
And take from seventy springs a score,
It only leaves me fifty more.

And since to look at things in bloom
Fifty springs are little room,
About the woodlands I will go
To see the cherry hung with snow.

1896

[When I Was One-and-Twenty]

When I was one-and-twenty
I heard a wise man say,

"Give crowns and pounds and guineas
  But not your heart away;
Give pearls away and rubies
  But keep your fancy free."
But I was one-and-twenty,
  No use to talk to me.

When I was one-and-twenty
  I heard him say again,
"The heart out of the bosom
  Was never given in vain;
'Tis paid with sighs a plenty
  And sold for endless rue."
And I am two-and-twenty,
  And oh, 'tis true, 'tis true.

1896

To an Athlete Dying Young

The time you won your town the race
We chaired you through the market-place;
Man and boy stood cheering by,
And home we brought you shoulder-high.

To-day, the road all runners come,
Shoulder-high we bring you home,
And set you at your threshold down,
Townsman of a stiller town.

Smart lad, to slip betimes away
From fields where glory does not stay
And early though the laurel[1] grows
It withers quicker than the rose.

Eyes the shady night has shut
Cannot see the record cut,[2]
And silence sounds no worse than cheers
After earth has stopped the ears:

Now you will not swell the rout[3]
Of lads that wore their honours out,
Runners whom renown outran
And the name died before the man.

1. In ancient Mediterranean civilizations, victors were crowned with laurel wreaths.
2. Broken.
3. Crowd.

So set, before its echoes fade,
The fleet foot on the sill of shade,
And hold to the low lintel up
The still-defended challenge-cup.

And round that early-laurelled head
Will flock to gaze the strengthless dead,
And find unwithered on its curls
The garland briefer than a girl's.

1896

[Is My Team Ploughing]

"Is my team ploughing,
  That I was used to drive
And hear the harness jingle
  When I was man alive?"

Ay, the horses trample,
  The harness jingles now;
No change though you lie under
  The land you used to plough.

"Is football[4] playing
  Along the river shore,
With lads to chase the leather,
  Now I stand up no more?"

Ay, the ball is flying,
  The lads play heart and soul;
The goal stands up, the keeper
  Stands up to keep the goal.

"Is my girl happy,
  That I thought hard to leave,
And has she tired of weeping
  As she lies down at eve?"

Ay, she lies down lightly,
  She lies not down to weep:
Your girl is well contented.
  Be still, my lad, and sleep.

"Is my friend hearty,
  Now I am thin and pine,
And has he found to sleep in
  A better bed than mine?"

4. Soccer or rugby.

Yes, lad, I lie easy,
  I lie as lads would choose;
I cheer a dead man's sweetheart
  Never ask me whose.

1896

[On Wenlock Edge the Wood's in Trouble]

On Wenlock Edge[5] the wood's in trouble;
  His forest fleece the Wrekin[6] heaves;
The gale, it plies the saplings double,
  And thick on Severn[7] snow the leaves.

'Twould blow like this through holt and hanger
  When Uricon[8] the city stood:
'Tis the old wind in the old anger,
  But then it threshed another wood.

Then, 'twas before my time, the Roman
  At yonder heaving hill would stare:
The blood that warms an English yeoman,
  The thoughts that hurt him, they were there.

There, like the wind through woods in riot,
  Through him the gale of life blew high;
The tree of man was never quiet:
  Then 'twas the Roman, now 'tis I.

The gale, it plies the saplings double,
  It blows so hard, 'twill soon be gone:
To-day the Roman and his trouble
  Are ashes under Uricon.

1896

[With Rue My Heart Is Laden]

With rue my heart is laden
  For golden friends I had,
For many a rose-lipt maiden
  And many a lightfoot lad.

By brooks too broad for leaping
  The lightfoot boys are laid;
The rose-lipt girls are sleeping
  In fields where roses fade.

1896

5. Range of hills in Shropshire.
6. Prominent hill in Shropshire.
7. British river.
8. Roman town of Uriconium, on the site of present-day Wroxeter, Shropshire. *Holt and hanger*: woods (folk terms).

[Terence, This Is Stupid Stuff]

"Terence,[9] this is stupid stuff:
You eat your victuals fast enough;
There can't be much amiss, 'tis clear,
To see the rate you drink your beer.
But oh, good Lord, the verse you make,
It gives a chap the belly-ache.
The cow, the old cow, she is dead;
It sleeps well, the horned head:
We poor lads, 'tis our turn now
To hear such tunes as killed the cow.
Pretty friendship 'tis to rhyme
Your friends to death before their time
Moping melancholy mad:
Come, pipe a tune to dance to, lad."

Why, if 'tis dancing you would be,
There's brisker pipes than poetry.
Say, for what were hop-yards meant,
Or why was Burton built on Trent?
Oh many a peer of England brews
Livelier liquor than the Muse.[1]
And malt does more than Milton can
To justify God's ways to man.[2]
Ale, man, ale's the stuff to drink
For fellows whom it hurts to think:
Look into the pewter pot
To see the world as the world's not.
And faith, 'tis pleasant till 'tis past:
The mischief is that 'twill not last.
Oh I have been to Ludlow[3] fair
And left my necktie God knows where,
And carried half way home, or near,
Pints and quarts of Ludlow beer:
Then the world seemed none so bad,
And I myself a sterling lad;
And down in lovely muck I've lain,
Happy till I woke again.
Then I saw the morning sky:
Heigho, the tale was all a lie;
The world, it was the old world yet,
I was I, my things were wet,
And nothing now remained to do
But begin the game anew.

9. Housman's intended title for *A Shropshire Lad* was *The Poems of Terence Hearsay.*
1. A comparison of the fountains of Mt. Ida, tended by the Muses (nine sister goddesses in Greek mythology), with the breweries of Burton-on-Trent (some of whose owners were raised to the peerage; that is, were made nobles), as sources of inspiration.
2. Cf. John Milton's promise in *Paradise Lost* (1.17–26) to "justify the ways of God to men."
3. A Shropshire town.

Therefore, since the world has still
Much good, but much less good than ill,
And while the sun and moon endure
Luck's a chance, but trouble's sure,
I'd face it as a wise man would,
And train for ill and not for good.
'Tis true, the stuff I bring for sale
Is not so brisk a brew as ale:
Out of a stem that scored the hand
I wrung it in a weary land.
But take it: if the smack is sour,
The better for the embittered hour;
It should do good to heart and head
When your soul is in my soul's stead;
And I will friend you, if I may,
In the dark and cloudy day.

There was a king reigned in the east:
There, when kings will sit to feast,
They get their fill before they think
With poisoned meat and poisoned drink.
He gathered all that springs to birth
From the many-venomed earth,
First a little, thence to more,
He sampled all her killing store;
And easy, smiling, seasoned sound,
Sate the king when healths went round.
They put arsenic in his meat
And stared aghast to watch him eat;
They poured strychnine in his cup
And shook to see him drink it up:
They shook, they stared as white's their shirt:
Them it was their poison hurt.
—I tell the tale that I heard told.
Mithridates, he died old.[4]

1896

Eight O'Clock

He stood, and heard the steeple
Sprinkle the quarters on the morning town.
One, two, three, four, to market-place and people
It tossed them down.

4. Mithridates VI, a pre-Christian king of Pontus, was said to have immunized himself against poisoning by taking poison in small quantities.

Strapped, noosed, nighing his hour,
He stood and counted them and cursed his luck;
And then the clock collected in the tower
Its strength, and struck.

1922

Epitaph on an Army of Mercenaries[5]

These, in the day when heaven was falling,
The hour when earth's foundations fled,
Followed their mercenary calling
And took their wages and are dead.

Their shoulders held the sky suspended;
They stood, and earth's foundations stay;
What God abandoned, these defended,
And saved the sum of things for pay.

1922

[They Say My Verse Is Sad: No Wonder]

They say my verse is sad: no wonder.
Its narrow measure spans
Rue for eternity, and sorrow
Not mine, but man's.

This is for all ill-treated fellows
Unborn and unbegot,
For them to read when they're in trouble
And I am not.

1936

5. Written in honor of the professional soldiers of the British Regular Army in the First Battle of Ypres (1914).

William Butler Yeats
1865–1939

After the poet A. C. Swinburne died in 1909, Yeats remarked to one of his sisters that he was now "king of the cats." In 1940, after Yeats died, T. S. Eliot declared him "the greatest poet of our time." One key to Yeats's greatness is that there are many different Yeatses. He is, as he said, one of the "last Romantics," straining after dreams and visions, brooding on loss and unrequited desire. But he is also a modern poet, who harshly mocks idealism, nostalgia, and contemporary society, even affirming ruin and destruction: "We that look on but laugh in tragic joy" ("The Gyres"). He is a literary traditionalist, working within such inherited genres as love poetry, the elegy, the self-elegy, the sonnet, and the occasional poem on public themes. But he is also a restless innovator who disrupts generic conventions, breaking up the coherence of the sonnet, de-idealizing the dead mourned in elegies, and bringing into public poems an intense personal ambivalence. In matters of form, too, he rhymes but often in off-rhyme, uses standard meters but bunches or scatters their stresses, employs an elegant syntax that nevertheless has the passionate urgency of colloquial speech; his diction, tone, enjambments, and stanzas intermix ceremony with contortion, controlled artifice with wayward unpredictability.

In "the matter of Ireland," Yeats is also a man of many masks (to borrow one of his metaphors). He is an Irish cultural nationalist, who helped forge Irish cultural identity and inspired the poet-revolutionaries who led the Easter Rising of 1916 against British rule—"men the English shot" ("Man and the Echo"). A resolutely Irish poet, this Yeats imaginatively reclaims a land colonized by the British; imposes Irish rhythms, images, genres, and syntax on English-language poetry; and revives native myths, place-names, and consciousness. Yet there is another Yeats, the antinationalist who deflates patriotic orthodoxy, satirizes the money-grubbing and prudery of the Irish middle class, and resists arguments for replacing the English language with Gaelic. A cosmopolitan, this Yeats insists on the transnationalism of the collective storehouse of images, spends much of his life in England, and cross-pollinates forms, ideas, and images from all over the world.

Yeats's poetry is at its frequent best when it mediates between contending aspects of himself. As he said: "We make out of the quarrel with others, rhetoric, but of the quarrel with ourselves, poetry" (*Per Amica Silentia Lunae*). A poem such as "Easter, 1916" is a masterpiece in part because, at once nationalist and antinationalist, it responds with both skepticism and inspired hope to the Easter Rising, internalizing the multiple and conflicting views of an emerging nation. A poem such as "Lapis Lazuli" is both grim and gleeful: it grieves over personal and cultural losses, yet it affirms the imagination in the face of destruction. In such dialogic poems as "A Dialogue of Self and Soul" and "Vacillation," both sides get their say—Yeats the idealist, who credits spiritualism, miracles, and the occult, and Yeats the skeptic, for whom such beliefs are but "metaphors for poetry" (*A Vision*). Lyrics from "The Lake Isle of Innisfree" to "Man and the Echo" renew both English and Irish inheritances. Writing poems that articulate and hold together such powerfully contradictory views, Yeats set an example for poets across the globe, from Ezra Pound and Sylvia Plath to W. H. Auden and Seamus Heaney to Derek Walcott, Christopher Okigbo, and A. K. Ramanujan.

Half-consciously at least, Yeats prepared himself for the role of a major literary figure by plunging himself in the Western cultural tradition and then, as no important poet in English had before him, the Eastern tradition. His range of allusion comprehends Homer's "unchristened heart," a prophecy from Virgil's Sixth Eclogue, Dante's "multifoliate rose," a line from Hafiz or Rabindranath Tagore or a Noh play or—as he was greatly interested in the occult—a theosophist text. Yeats did not neglect the tradition of English verse. An editor of William Blake, he had fresh theories about writers from Edmund Spenser and Shakespeare to the Romantics and Pre-Raphaelites. He pursued the Irish tradition to the earliest saga literature and followed it to his own day. He compiled anthologies of Irish poems as well as fairy and folk tales. He drew into creative activity the Irish playwrights Lady Augusta Gregory and John Synge, and to some extent James Joyce. With Lady Gregory's help, Yeats founded and developed the Abbey Theatre, demonstrating his abilities in "management of men" as well as in "this sedentary trade" of poetry.

In the 1890s, Yeats began hammering his thoughts into unity (his phrase) in part by recasting the symbolist principles he drew from the Romantics, nineteenth-century

French poets, and various kinds of spiritualism, according to which a poet discovered inner psychological states in such scenic elements as stars, sea, winds, and woods. At the pinnacle of Yeats's own early symbolism was the rose of beauty, which in certain circumstances might flower from the cross of suffering. The meaning of rose and cross varies according to the context, but in general, as in "To the Rose upon the Rood of Time," the rose is at once a muse (with a special affection for Irish poets and subjects), an epitome of eternal beauty, and an image of completeness, timelessness, and superhumanity; the cross not only is the emblem of Jesus' Passion, which is mimicked by every lover's suffering, but also represents discord, incompleteness, opposition, mortality, temporality. Yeats invokes the rose, but warns it not to come too close because he does not wish to give up entirely the painful but familiar ingredients of the temporal world. Yet he heralds some juncture of the two, as he searches for ways to bind the worlds of matter and spirit together.

"Myself must I remake," Yeats says in "An Acre of Grass," and he continually remade himself in new symbols, new styles, and new philosophies. He came to see his early symbolism and poetry as too wistful, too aspiring, too respectful of spirit, and too little respectful of body. He was no longer content with the dreamy, languorous style of his early work, with its anapestic and lulling rhythms, its tapestrylike texture. Yeats determined that mortal conditions did not need to be transcended; they might be accepted with such intensity that they would no longer hamper him. Corporeal love might achieve "profane perfection." With this resolution Yeats came "into his force." He spoke with new urgency, as when he astounded Lady Gregory by telling her in a letter, "We must accept the baptism of the gutter." His Crazy Jane would say later, "Nothing can be sole or whole / That has not been rent." And in his own person Yeats declared, "I must lie down where all the ladders start / In the foul rag and bone shop of the heart" ("The Circus Animals' Desertion"). In "A Dialogue of Self and Soul," the self defies the soul's injunction to leave the world behind and insists, "I am content to live it all again / And yet again, if it be life to pitch / Into the frog-spawn of a blind man's ditch." Yeats forged a more rugged, colloquial, and concrete language for his poetry. The world of the rose and that of the cross might enter into many relations: they could encroach upon each other instead of fusing, for example. What is sought is not so much the raising of mortal to immortal but an interpenetration. Instead of sanctifying the human, one must humanize the world of spirit or, more simply, achieve a human sanctity.

Yeats regarded his new energy as based on incarnation and his old as based on transfiguration. In the new, spirit became flesh; in the old, flesh became spirit. His new symbolism took an intermediate form in poems and prose writings that dwelt on the battle within each individual mind, between what one is and what one would like to be, the real and the image of its opposite. It is as if everyone put on a mask that expressed the antiself and struggled to make it fuse with the face. But after his marriage in 1917, Yeats greatly expanded this imagery. He now conceived of all consciousness as a conflict of opposites or antinomies, which he represented by two interpenetrating cones, or gyres, the apex of one in the base of the other. These were, like his earlier use of the cross, an emblem of earthly pain. Beyond the gyres is a sphere that represents a totality that they merely subdivide, comparable to the emblematic rose of his early poetry. This symbolism Yeats put into his book *A Vision,* one of the strangest works of the century. It can profitably be read in connection with his poems, but it also has an intrinsic fascination as the most complete symbolic system since Blake's, written in a style that at moments leans toward philosophy and at other moments toward poetry.

As Yeats grew older, his sense of life sharpened, and he dwelt more boldly on its lust and rage, mire and fury, but also its possibility. Feelings rarefied when he was young became thick with substance. He was determined to "beat upon the wall / Till truth obeyed his call," as he said Blake had done ("An Acre of Grass"); he pushed to the most extreme point his thought and his expression, content to be, as he said, "for the song's sake a fool." Each poem finds a new context for Yeats's inner debate. Different poems weigh more heavily in different directions, but they join in asserting the primacy of the imagination. Man or woman is for Yeats a being who, born incomplete, conceives of completeness and at moments attains it, or imagines doing so, which may be just as satisfying. The desert, peopled by images, becomes the garden.

The relation of Yeats's life to his work is close, though not simple. His mythmaking imagination was so powerful that it transforms events that in another writer might be commonplace. We might, however, bear in mind some unadorned facts. He was born in Dublin, on June 13, 1865, the son of John Butler Yeats, later well known as a portrait-painter. His mother came from the Pollexfen family that lived near Sligo, and Yeats spent much of his childhood with them. In 1874, the family went to London so that J. B. Yeats might continue his art studies, but in 1880, they returned to Dublin. Here Yeats attended high school and then art school, the latter from 1884 to 1886. He gave up painting abruptly and threw himself into literary work. From now on, his life expanded in many different directions. He founded Irish literary societies in both Dublin and London. In 1889, he met Maud Gonne, and "the troubles of my life began." A nationalist and a beauty, she became his ideal love and his coadjutor in various nationalistic activities. Over the years, Yeats proposed to her repeatedly and even to her daughter, Iseult. But in 1903, Maud Gonne shocked Yeats when she married Major John MacBride. Her political extremism completed her separation from Yeats, though she remained a figure in his poetry till the end.

The Irish dramatic movement, which Yeats began to organize in 1899, took up more and more of his time, especially after the founding of the Abbey Theatre, in 1904. Treading perilously between Irish chauvinists on one side and British authorities on the other, Yeats frequently ran afoul of both. As a result, he felt some "estrangement" from his country, or at least from large groups within it. But the Easter Rising of 1916, though put down at once by the British, awoke his old sympathy and his best political poems. The following year, when he was fifty-two, Yeats married an Englishwoman, Georgie (changed by Yeats to George) Hyde-Lees. Their early days together were troubled by Yeats's concern that his marriage was ill-advised. Georgie Yeats, in an endeavor to distract her husband, successfully attempted automatic (or unconcious) writing, and his doubts evaporated. Some of her script proved so relevant to his own concerns that Yeats began to work it into the book that eventually became *A Vision*.

The Yeatses had a son and a daughter, both memorialized in verse, and they lived off and on in a Norman tower called Thoor (Castle) Ballylee, near Lady Gregory's house at Coole, in the west of Ireland. This tower became the setting of several of Yeats's poems and gave him the title for one of his books; its winding stair provided the title for another. Tower and winding stair replaced the earlier symbols of rose and cross.

After the Irish Free State was formed, Yeats served six years in the senate (1922–28), and after his term, he continued to devote himself to various schemes for invigorating the country. Some of these were absurd, but they always came back to his own ideal of a nation of people free to cultivate their imaginative capacities. Like T. S. Eliot and Ezra Pound, he was attracted to right-wing politics, and in the 1930s, he was briefly drawn to fascism. His late interest in authoritarian politics arose in part from his desire for a feudal, aristocratic society that, unlike middle-class culture, might allow the imagination to flourish, and in part from his anticolonialism, since he thought a fascist Spain, among other states, would "weaken the British Empire." Even so, all governments eventually appalled him, and the grim prophecy in his poem "The Second Coming" seemed to him more and more apt. He died in southern France, just before World War II began. His grave is, as his poem directed, near Sligo, "under Ben Bulben."

A note on the texts: Yeats greatly revised many of his poems. To help make visible his historical development, we reprint early versions of Yeats's poems through "To Be

Carved on a Stone at Thoor Ballylee"; for these poems, we follow the texts reprinted in *Yeats's Poetry, Drama, and Prose: A Norton Critical Edition,* ed. James Pethica (2000). For later poems, from *The Tower* (1928) on, we follow *The Poems of W. B. Yeats: A New Edition,* ed. Richard J. Finneran (1989).

To the Rose upon the Rood[1] of Time

Red Rose, proud Rose, sad Rose of all my days!
Come near me, while I sing the ancient ways:
Cuhoollin[2] battling with the bitter tide;
The Druid,[3] gray, wood nurtured, quiet-eyed,
Who cast round Fergus dreams, and ruin untold;[4]
And thine own sadness, whereof stars, grown old
In dancing silver sandalled on the sea,
Sing in their high and lonely melody.
Come near, that no more blinded by man's fate,
I find under the boughs of love and hate,
In all poor foolish things that live a day,
Eternal Beauty wandering on her way.

Come near, come near, come near—Ah, leave me still
A little space for the rose-breath to fill!
Lest I no more hear common things that crave;
The weak worm hiding down in its small cave,
The field mouse running by me in the grass,
And heavy mortal hopes that toil and pass;
But seek alone to hear the strange things said
By God to the bright hearts of those long dead,
And learn to chaunt a tongue, men do not know.
Come near—I would, before my time to go,
Sing of old Eri[5] and the ancient ways:
Red Rose, proud Rose, sad Rose of all my days.

1892, 1895

The Lake Isle of Innisfree[6]

I will arise and go now, and go to Innisfree,
  And a small cabin build there, of clay and wattles made;

1. The cross on which Jesus was crucified. The rose, a traditional symbol of love and of the Irish nation, recurs in Yeats's early poetry. In 1925, he noted: "the quality symbolised as The Rose differs from the Intellectual Beauty of Shelley and of Spenser in that I have imagined it as suffering with man and not as something pursued and seen from afar."
2. Cuchulain, a mythic Irish warrior; he fought the sea after discovering that he had unwittingly killed his own son.
3. Ancient Celtic priest.
4. Yeats explained that Fergus, a legendary king of Ireland, was persuaded by a Druid to give up his kingdom and live at peace in the woods.
5. Ireland.
6. Inis Fraoigh (Heather Island) is a small island in Lough Gill, near Sligo, in the west of Ireland. In his *Autobiography,* Yeats writes: "I had still the ambition, formed in Sligo in my teens, of living in imitation of Thoreau on Innisfree . . . and when walking through Fleet Street [in London] very homesick I heard a little tinkle of water and saw a fountain in a shop-window which balanced a little ball upon its jet, and began to remember lake water. From the sudden remembrance came my poem *Innisfree,* my first lyric with anything in its rhythm of my own music."

Nine bean rows will I have there, a hive for the honey bee,
  And live alone in the bee-loud glade.

And I shall have some peace there, for peace comes dropping slow,
  Dropping from the veils of the morning to where the cricket sings;
There midnight's all a glimmer, and noon a purple glow,
  And evening full of the linnet's[7] wings.

I will arise and go now, for always night and day
  I hear lake water lapping with low sounds by the shore;
While I stand on the roadway, or on the pavements gray,
  I hear it in the deep heart's core.

1890, 1895

The Sorrow of Love

The quarrel of the sparrows in the eaves,
  The full round moon and the star-laden sky,
And the loud song of the ever-singing leaves,
  Had hid away earth's old and weary cry.

And then you came with those red mournful lips,
  And with you came the whole of the world's tears,
And all the sorrows of her labouring ships,[8]
  And all the burden of her myriad years.

And now the sparrows warring in the eaves,
  The curd-pale moon, the white stars in the sky,
And the loud chaunting of the unquiet leaves,
  Are shaken with earth's old and weary cry.

1891 1892, 1895

When You Are Old[9]

When you are old and gray and full of sleep,
  And nodding by the fire, take down this book,
  And slowly read, and dream of the soft look
Your eyes had once, and of their shadows deep;

How many loved your moments of glad grace,
  And loved your beauty with love false or true;

7. Small songbird.
8. In a 1925 revision of the poem, Yeats makes explicit the allusion to the Trojan War in the second stanza: "Doomed like Odysseus and the labouring ships / And proud as Priam murdered with his peers."
9. Adapted from a sonnet by French poet Pierre de Ronsard (1524–1585) that begins: "Quand vous serez bien vieille, au soir, à la chandelle" (When you are quite old, in the evening by candlelight).

But one man loved the pilgrim soul in you,
And loved the sorrows of your changing face.

And bending down beside the glowing bars
Murmur, a little sad, *From us fled Love;*
He paced upon the mountains far above,
And hid his face amid a crowd of stars.

1891 1892, 1895

[Who Goes with Fergus?][1]

Who will go drive with Fergus now,
And pierce the deep wood's woven shade,
And dance upon the level shore?
Young man, lift up your russet brow,
And lift your tender eyelids, maid,
And brood on hopes and fears no more.

And no more turn aside and brood
Upon Love's bitter mystery;
For Fergus rules the brazen cars,[2]
And rules the shadows of the wood,
And the white breast of the dim sea
And all disheveled wandering stars.

1892, 1895

To Ireland in the Coming Times

Know, that I would accounted be
True brother of that company,
Who sang to sweeten Ireland's wrong,
Ballad and story, rann[3] *and song;*
Nor be I any less of them,
Because the red-rose-bordered hem
Of her, whose history began
Before God made the angelic clan,
Trails all about the written page;
For in the world's first blossoming age
The light fall of her flying feet
Made Ireland's heart begin to beat;
And still the starry candles flare
To help her light foot here and there;
And still the thoughts of Ireland brood
Upon her holy quietude.

1. Legendary ancient king of Ireland, persuaded by a Druid to give up his kingdom to live at peace in the woods.
2. Chariots.
3. A stanza of Irish verse.

Nor may I less be counted one
With Davis, Mangan, Ferguson,[4]
Because to him, who ponders well,
My rhymes more than their rhyming tell
Of the dim wisdoms old and deep,
That God gives unto man in sleep.
For the elemental beings go
About my table to and fro.
In flood and fire and clay and wind,
They huddle from man's pondering mind;
Yet he who treads in austere ways
May surely meet their ancient gaze.
Man ever journeys on with them
After the red-rose-bordered hem.
Ah, faeries, dancing under the moon,
A Druid land, a Druid tune!

While still I may, I write for you
The love I lived, the dream I knew.
From our birthday, until we die,
Is but the winking of an eye;
And we, our singing and our love,
The mariners of night above,
And all the wizard things that go
About my table to and fro,
Are passing on to where may be,
In truth's consuming ecstasy,
No place for love and dream at all;
For God goes by with white foot-fall.
I cast my heart into my rhymes,
That you, in the dim coming times,
May know how my heart went with them
After the red-rose-bordered hem.

1892, 1895

The Hosting of the Sidhe[5]

The host is riding from Knocknarea[6]
And over the grave of Clooth-na-bare;[7]
Caolte[8] tossing his burning hair

4. Irish nationalist poets of the nineteenth century: Thomas Davis (1814–1845) was the founder of the nationalist newspaper *The Nation* and a leader of the Young Ireland movement. James Clarence Mangan (1803–1849), perhaps the best Irish poet of the period, wrote (and translated) nationalist laments. Sir Samuel Ferguson (1810–1886) was notable for his ballads, versions of Irish sagas, and other poems.

5. According to Yeats, the Sidhe (Irish for wind) are the gods of ancient Ireland, associated with the fairies. They are said to travel in whirling winds, some on horseback, their hair streaming out. "If any one becomes too much interested in them, and sees them over much, he loses all interest in ordinary things" [Yeats's note].

6. Mountain near Sligo; at its top, Queen Maeve of the Sidhe is reputedly buried in a cairn, or mound of stones.

7. A fairy in Irish legend. She "went all over the world, seeking a lake deep enough to drown her faery life, of which she had grown weary . . . until, at last, she found the deepest water in the world in little Lough Ia, on top of the bird mountain, in Sligo" [Yeats's note].

8. Caoilte MacRonan, a legendary Irish warrior and friend of Oisin. After his death, he appeared

And Niamh[9] calling *Away, come away:*
Empty your heart of its mortal dream.
The winds awaken, the leaves whirl round,
Our cheeks are pale, our hair is unbound,
Our breasts are heaving, our eyes are a-gleam,
Our arms are waving, our lips are apart;
And if any gaze on our rushing band,
We come between him and the deed of his hand,
We come between him and the hope of his heart.
The host is rushing 'twixt night and day,
And where is there hope or deed as fair?
Caolte tossing his burning hair,
And Niamh calling *Away, come away.*

1893, 1906

The Song of Wandering Aengus[1]

I went out to the hazel wood,
Because a fire was in my head,
And cut and peeled a hazel wand,
And hooked a berry to a thread;
And when white moths were on the wing,
And moth-like stars were flickering out,
I dropped the berry in a stream
And caught a little silver trout.

When I had laid it on the floor
I went to blow the fire a-flame,
But something rustled on the floor,
And some one called me by my name:
It had become a glimmering girl
With apple blossom in her hair
Who called me by my name and ran
And faded through the brightening air.

Though I am old with wandering
Through hollow lands and hilly lands,
I will find out where she has gone,
And kiss her lips and take her hands;
And walk among long dappled grass,
And pluck till time and times are done,
The silver apples of the moon,
The golden apples of the sun.

1893? 1897, 1906

to the king of Ireland in a forest as a flaming man, ready to lead the king out of darkness.

9. A fairy woman and daughter of Aengus, Irish god of love. She persuaded the poet-warrior Oisin to spend three hundred years in the Land of the Ever-Living.

1. "The god of youth, beauty, and poetry. He reigned in Tir-nan-Oge, the country of the young" [Yeats's note].

The Cap and Bells[2]

The jester walked in the garden:
The garden had fallen still;
He bade his soul rise upward
And stand on her window-sill.

It rose in a straight blue garment,
When owls began to call:
It had grown wise-tongued by thinking
Of a quiet and light footfall;

But the young queen would not listen;
She rose in her pale night gown;
She drew in the heavy casement
And pushed the latches down.

He bade his heart go to her,
When the owls called out no more;
In a red and quivering garment
It sang to her through the door.

It had grown sweet-tongued by dreaming,
Of a flutter of flower-like hair;
But she took up her fan from the table
And waved it off on the air.

"I have cap and bells," he pondered,
"I will send them to her and die;"
And when the morning whitened
He left them where she went by.

She laid them upon her bosom,
Under a cloud of her hair,
And her red lips sang them a love song:
Till stars grew out of the air.

She opened her door and her window,
And the heart and the soul came through,
To her right hand came the red one,
To her left hand came the blue.

They set up a noise like crickets,
A chattering wise and sweet,
And her hair was a folded flower
And the quiet of love in her feet.

1893 1894, 1906

2. Traditionally, worn by a jester.

He Wishes for the Cloths of Heaven

Had I the heavens' embroidered cloths,
Enwrought with golden and silver light,
The blue and the dim and the dark cloths
Of night and light and the half light,
I would spread the cloths under your feet:
But I, being poor, have only my dreams;
I have spread my dreams under your feet;
Tread softly because you tread on my dreams.

1899, 1906

Adam's Curse[3]

We sat together at one summer's end,
That beautiful mild woman, your close friend,
And you and I,[4] and talked of poetry.

I said: "A line will take us hours maybe;
Yet if it does not seem a moment's thought,
Our stitching and unstitching has been naught.
Better go down upon your marrow bones
And scrub a kitchen pavement, or break stones
Like an old pauper, in all kinds of weather;
For to articulate sweet sounds together
Is to work harder than all these, and yet
Be thought an idler by the noisy set
Of bankers, schoolmasters, and clergymen
The martyrs call the world."

That woman then
Murmured with her young voice, for whose mild sake
There's many a one shall find out all heartache
In finding that it's young and mild and low:
"There is one thing that all we women know,
Although we never heard of it at school—
That we must labour to be beautiful."

I said: "It's certain there is no fine thing
Since Adam's fall but needs much labouring.
There have been lovers who thought love should be
So much compounded of high courtesy
That they would sigh and quote with learned looks
Precedents out of beautiful old books;
Yet now it seems an idle trade enough."

3. When Adam was evicted from the Garden of Eden, he was cursed by God with a life of toil and labor (Genesis 3.17–19).

4. The two women in the poem are modeled on Maud Gonne and her sister, Kathleen Pilcher (1868–1919).

We sat grown quiet at the name of love;
We saw the last embers of daylight die,
And in the trembling blue-green of the sky
A moon, worn as if it had been a shell
Washed by time's waters as they rose and fell
About the stars, and broke in days and years.

I had a thought for no one's but your ears;
That you were beautiful, and that I strove
To love you in the old high way of love;
That it had all seemed happy, and yet we'd grown
As weary hearted as that hollow moon.

1902, 1906

No Second Troy

Why should I blame her[5] that she filled my days
With misery, or that she would of late
Have taught to ignorant men most violent ways,
Or hurled the little streets upon the great,
Had they but courage equal to desire?
What could have made her peaceful with a mind
That nobleness made simple as a fire,
With beauty like a tightened bow, a kind
That is not natural in an age like this,
Being high and solitary and most stern?
Why, what could she have done being what she is?
Was there another Troy for her to burn?[6]

1908 1910, 1912

The Fascination of What's Difficult

The fascination of what's difficult
Has dried the sap out of my veins, and rent
Spontaneous joy and natural content
Out of my heart. There's something ails our colt[7]
That must, as if it had not holy blood,
Nor on an Olympus[8] leaped from cloud to cloud,
Shiver under the lash, strain, sweat and jolt
As though it dragged road metal. My curse on plays
That have to be set up in fifty ways,
On the day's war with every knave and dolt,
Theatre business,[9] management of men.

5. Maud Gonne, whose revolutionary activities are at issue in the poem.
6. Helen of Troy was the legendary cause of the Trojan War and thus of Troy's destruction.
7. Pegasus, in Greek mythology a winged horse associated with poetry.
8. A mountain in Greece; the home of the gods.
9. In 1904, Yeats cofounded the Abbey Theatre in Dublin.

I swear before the dawn comes around again
I'll find the stable and pull out the bolt.

1909 1910, 1912

The Cold Heaven

Suddenly I saw the cold and rook-delighting Heaven
That seemed as though ice burned and was but the more ice,
And thereupon imagination and heart were driven
So wild that every casual thought of that and this
Vanished, and left but memories, that should be out of season
With the hot blood of youth, of love crossed long ago;
And I took all the blame out of all sense and reason,
Until I cried and trembled and rocked to and fro,
Riddled with light. Ah! when the ghost begins to quicken,
Confusion of the death-bed over, is it sent
Out naked on the roads, as the books say, and stricken
By the injustice of the skies for punishment?

1912, 1916

A Coat

I made my song a coat
Covered with embroideries
Out of old mythologies
From heel to throat;
But the fools caught it,
Wore it in the world's eye
As though they'd wrought it.
Song, let them take it
For there's more enterprise
In walking naked.

1912 1914, 1916

September 1913

What need you,[1] being come to sense,
But fumble in a greasy till[2]
And add the halfpence to the pence
And prayer to shivering prayer, until
You have dried the marrow from the bone;

1. The new, largely Catholic, middle class. When the art dealer Hugh Lane (d. 1915) offered to give his collection of French Impressionist paintings to Dublin if the city would build a proper gallery, Yeats became angry over public opposition to funding the project.
2. Cash register.

For men were born to pray and save:
Romantic Ireland's dead and gone,
It's with O'Leary[3] in the grave.

Yet they were of a different kind
The names that stilled your childish play,
They have gone about the world like wind,
But little time had they to pray
For whom the hangman's rope was spun,
And what, God help us, could they save:
Romantic Ireland's dead and gone,
It's with O'Leary in the grave.

Was it for this the wild geese[4] spread
The grey wing upon every tide;
For this that all that blood was shed,
For this Edward Fitzgerald died,
And Robert Emmet and Wolfe Tone,[5]
All that delirium of the brave;
Romantic Ireland's dead and gone,
It's with O'Leary in the grave.

Yet could we turn the years again,
And call those exiles as they were,
In all their loneliness and pain
You'd cry 'Some woman's yellow hair
Has maddened every mother's son':
They weighed so lightly what they gave,
But let them be, they're dead and gone,
They're with O'Leary in the grave.

1913, 1916

The Magi[6]

Now as at all times I can see in the mind's eye,
In their stiff, painted clothes, the pale unsatisfied ones
Appear and disappear in the blue depth of the sky
With all their ancient faces like rain-beaten stones,
And all their helms of silver hovering side by side,
And all their eyes still fixed, hoping to find once more,
Being by Calvary's turbulence[7] unsatisfied,
The uncontrollable mystery on the bestial floor.

1913 1914, 1916

3. John O'Leary (1830–1907), Irish nationalist, who, after five years' imprisonment and fifteen years' exile, returned to Dublin in 1885; he rallied the young Yeats to the cause of literary nationalism.
4. Widely used name for the Irish who emigrated to the Continent during the period of anti-Catholic penal laws (1695–1727).
5. Theobald Wolfe Tone (1763–1798): a leader of the 1798 Irish Rising who committed suicide in prison. Lord Edward Fitzgerald (1763–1798): a leader of the 1798 Irish Rising who died in prison. Robert Emmet (1778–1803): a leader of the abortive 1803 Irish Nationalist Revolt who was hanged for treason.
6. The wise men who came to Bethlehem to pay homage to the infant Jesus.
7. Jesus was crucified on a hill called Calvary.

The Fisherman

Although I can see him still
The freckled man who goes
To a grey place on a hill
In grey Connemara[8] clothes
At dawn to cast his flies,
It's long since I began
To call up to the eyes
This wise and simple man.
All day I'd looked in the face
What I had hoped 'twould be
To write for my own race
And the reality;
The living men that I hate,
The dead man that I loved,
The craven man in his seat,
The insolent unreproved
And no knave brought to book
Who has won a drunken cheer,
The witty man and his joke
Aimed at the commonest ear,
The clever man who cries
The catch-cries of the clown,
The beating down of the wise
And great Art beaten down.

Maybe a twelvemonth since
Suddenly I began,
In scorn of this audience
Imagining a man,
And his sun-freckled face,
And grey Connemara cloth,
Climbing up to a place
Where stone is dark under froth,
And the down turn of his wrist
When the flies drop in the stream;
A man who does not exist,
A man who is but a dream;
And cried, 'Before I am old
I shall have written him one
Poem maybe as cold
And passionate as the dawn.'

1914 1916, 1919

8. A picturesque part of County Galway, in the west of Ireland.

Easter, 1916[9]

I have met them at close of day
Coming with vivid faces
From counter or desk among grey
Eighteenth-century houses.
I have passed with a nod of the head
Or polite meaningless words,
Or have lingered awhile and said
Polite meaningless words,
And thought before I had done
Of a mocking tale or a gibe
To please a companion
Around the fire at the club,
Being certain that they and I
But lived where motley[1] is worn:
All changed, changed utterly:
A terrible beauty is born.

That woman's days[2] were spent
In ignorant good will,
Her nights in argument
Until her voice grew shrill.
What voice more sweet than hers
When young and beautiful,
She rode to harriers?
This man[3] had kept a school
And rode our winged horse;
This other[4] his helper and friend
Was coming into his force;
He might have won fame in the end,
So sensitive his nature seemed,
So daring and sweet his thought.
This other man[5] I had dreamed
A drunken, vain-glorious lout.
He had done most bitter wrong
To some who are near my heart,
Yet I number him in the song;
He, too, has resigned his part
In the casual comedy;
He, too, has been changed in his turn,

9. During the Easter Rising of 1916, Irish nationalists revolted against the British government and proclaimed an Irish Republic. Sixteen hundred Irish Volunteers seized buildings and a park in Dublin. The rebellion began on Easter Monday, April 24, 1916, and was crushed in six days. Over the next two weeks, fifteen of the leaders were executed by firing squad. Yeats knew the chief nationalist leaders personally.
1. The multicolored clothes of a jester.
2. Countess Constance Markievicz, née Gore-Booth (1868–1927), took a prominent role in the uprising. Her death sentence was reduced to imprisonment. The other rebel leaders to whom Yeats refers were executed.
3. Padraic Pearse (1879–1916), founder of a boys' school in Dublin and poet—hence the "winged horse," or Pegasus, the poet's mythical charger.
4. Thomas MacDonagh (1878–1916), poet and dramatist.
5. Major John MacBride (1865–1916), Irish revolutionary and estranged husband of Maud Gonne.

Transformed utterly:
A terrible beauty is born.

Hearts with one purpose alone
Through summer and winter seem
Enchanted to a stone
To trouble the living stream.
The horse that comes from the road,
The rider, the birds that range
From cloud to tumbling cloud,
Minute by minute they change;
A shadow of cloud on the stream
Changes minute by minute;
A horse-hoof slides on the brim,
And a horse plashes within it
Where long-legged moor-hens dive,
And hens to moor-cocks call.
Minute by minute they live:
The stone's in the midst of all.

Too long a sacrifice
Can make a stone of the heart.
O when may it suffice?
That is heaven's part, our part
To murmur name upon name,
As a mother names her child
When sleep at last has come
On limbs that had run wild.
What is it but nightfall?
No, no, not night but death;
Was it needless death after all?
For England may keep faith[6]
For all that is done and said.
We know their dream; enough
To know they dreamed and are dead;
And what if excess of love
Bewildered them till they died?
I write it out in a verse—
MacDonagh and MacBride
And Connolly[7] and Pearse
Now and in time to be,
Wherever green is worn,
Are changed, changed utterly:
A terrible beauty is born.

September 25, 1916 — 1916, 1922

6. In 1914, the English government had passed Home Rule for Ireland into law, but because of World War I had suspended it, promising to implement it later.

7. James Connolly (1870–1916), a trade-union organizer and military commander of the rebellion.

The Wild Swans at Coole[8]

The trees are in their autumn beauty,
The woodland paths are dry,
Under the October twilight the water
Mirrors a still sky;
Upon the brimming water among the stones
Are nine and fifty swans.

The nineteenth Autumn has come upon me
Since I first made my count;[9]
I saw, before I had well finished,
All suddenly mount
And scatter wheeling in great broken rings
Upon their clamorous wings.

I have looked upon those brilliant creatures,
And now my heart is sore.
All's changed since I, hearing at twilight,
The first time on this shore,
The bell-beat of their wings above my head,
Trod with a lighter tread.

Unwearied still, lover by lover,
They paddle in the cold,
Companionable streams or climb the air;
Their hearts have not grown old;
Passion or conquest, wander where they will,
Attend upon them still.

But now they drift on the still water
Mysterious, beautiful;
Among what rushes will they build,
By what lake's edge or pool
Delight men's eyes when I awake some day
To find they have flown away?

1916 1917, 1919

8. Coole Park, in County Galway, was the estate of Lady Gregory, Irish playwright (1852–1932).
9. Yeats made his first long visit to Coole in 1897; from then on, he spent summers there, often staying into the fall.

In Memory of Major Robert Gregory[1]

1

Now that we're almost settled in our house[2]
I'll name the friends that cannot sup with us
Beside a fire of turf in th' ancient tower,
And having talked to some late hour
Climb up the narrow winding stair to bed:
Discoverers of forgotten truth
Or mere companions of my youth,
All, all are in my thoughts to-night being dead.

2

Always we'd have the new friend meet the old
And we are hurt if either friend seem cold,
And there is salt to lengthen out the smart
In the affections of our heart,
And quarrels are blown up upon that head;
But not a friend that I would bring
This night can set us quarrelling,
For all that come into my mind are dead.

3

Lionel Johnson[3] comes the first to mind,
That loved his learning better than mankind,
Though courteous to the worst; much falling he
Brooded upon sanctity
Till all his Greek and Latin learning seemed
A long blast upon the horn that brought
A little nearer to his thought
A measureless consummation that he dreamed.

4

And that enquiring man John Synge[4] comes next,
That dying chose the living world for text
And never could have rested in the tomb
But that, long travelling, he had come
Towards nightfall upon certain set apart
In a most desolate stony place,

1. Robert Gregory, son of Lady Gregory, was killed on the Italian front, on January 23, 1918. This is one of four poems Yeats wrote in his memory. See also "An Irish Airman Foresees His Death."
2. In 1917, Yeats purchased the Norman tower Thor Ballylee, near Lady Gregory's home in Coole Park. While that residence was being renovated, Yeats and his wife were living in a house that Lady Gregory had lent them.
3. Poet and scholar (1867–1902); he was "much falling" (line 19) because of his drinking.
4. Irish playwright (1871–1909), associated with the Irish literary renaissance and the Abbey Theatre. When Yeats first met Synge, in 1896, he encouraged him to travel to the Aran Islands ("a most desolate and stony place") and write about its rural residents.

Towards nightfall upon a race
Passionate and simple like his heart.

5

And then I think of old George Pollexfen,[5]
In muscular youth well known to Mayo[6] men
For horsemanship at meets or at racecourses,
That could have shown how purebred horses
And solid men, for all their passion, live
But as the outrageous stars incline
By opposition, square and trine;[7]
Having grown sluggish and contemplative.

6

They were my close companions many a year,
A portion of my mind and life, as it were,
And now their breathless faces seem to look
Out of some old picture-book;
I am accustomed to their lack of breath,
But not that my dear friend's dear son,
Our Sidney[8] and our perfect man,
Could share in that discourtesy of death.

7

For all things the delighted eye now sees
Were loved by him,[9] the old storm-broken trees
That cast their shadows upon road and bridge;
The tower set on the stream's edge;
The ford where drinking cattle make a stir
Nightly, and startled by that sound
The water-hen must change her ground;
He might have been your heartiest welcomer.

8

When with the Galway foxhounds he would ride
From Castle Taylor to the Roxborough side
Or Esserkelly plain, few kept his pace;
At Mooneen[1] he had leaped a place
So perilous that half the astonished meet
Had shut their eyes, and where was it
He rode a race without a bit?
And yet his mind outran the horses' feet.

5. Yeats's maternal uncle (1839–1910).
6. County in western Ireland.
7. Terms from astrology, in which both Yeats and his uncle were interested.
8. Sir Philip Sidney (1554–1586), English poet and exemplar of the "Renaissance man"; like Gregory, he was killed in battle.
9. Robert Gregory encouraged Yeats to buy the tower.
1. Properties neighboring Coole Park. Roxborough was Lady Gregory's childhood home.

9

We dreamed that a great painter had been born
To cold Clare[2] rock and Galway rock and thorn,
To that stern colour and that delicate line
That are our secret discipline
Wherein the gazing heart doubles her might.
Soldier, scholar, horseman, he,
And yet he had the intensity
To have published all to be a world's delight.

10

What other could so well have counselled us
In all lovely intricacies of a house
As he that practised or that understood
All work in metal or in wood,
In moulded plaster or in carven stone?
Soldier, scholar, horseman, he,
And all he did done perfectly
As though he had but that one trade alone.

11

Some burn damp fagots,[3] others may consume
The entire combustible world in one small room
As though dried straw, and if we turn about
The bare chimney is gone black out
Because the work had finished in that flare.
Soldier, scholar, horseman, he,
As 'twere all life's epitome.
What made us dream that he could comb grey hair?

12

I had thought, seeing how bitter is that wind
That shakes the shutter, to have brought to mind
All those that manhood tried, or childhood loved
Or boyish intellect approved,
With some appropriate commentary on each;
Until imagination brought
A fitter welcome; but a thought
Of that late death took all my heart for speech.

1918, 1919

An Irish Airman[4] Foresees His Death

I know that I shall meet my fate
Somewhere among the clouds above;

2. County south of Galway.
3. Bundles of sticks.
4. Robert Gregory (1881–1918), Lady Gregory's only child, was killed on the Italian front, in 1918, as a member of the British Royal Flying Corps.

Those that I fight I do not hate,
Those that I guard I do not love;
My country is Kiltartan Cross,[5]
My countrymen Kiltartan's poor,
No likely end could bring them loss
Or leave them happier than before.
Nor law, nor duty bade me fight,
Nor public man, nor cheering crowds,
A lonely impulse of delight
Drove to this tumult in the clouds;
I balanced all, brought all to mind,
The years to come seemed waste of breath,
A waste of breath the years behind
In balance with this life, this death.

1919, 1920

The Second Coming

Turning and turning in the widening gyre[6]
The falcon cannot hear the falconer;
Things fall apart; the centre cannot hold;
Mere anarchy[7] is loosed upon the world,
The blood-dimmed tide is loosed, and everywhere
The ceremony of innocence is drowned;
The best lack all conviction, while the worst
Are full of passionate intensity.

Surely some revelation is at hand;
Surely the Second Coming[8] is at hand.
The Second Coming! Hardly are those words out
When a vast image out of Spiritus Mundi[9]
Troubles my sight: somewhere in sands of the desert
A shape with lion body and the head of a man,
A gaze blank and pitiless as the sun,
Is moving its slow thighs, while all about it
Reel shadows of the indignant desert birds.
The darkness drops again; but now I know
That twenty centuries of stony sleep
Were vexed to nightmare by a rocking cradle,
And what rough beast, its hour come round at last,
Slouches towards Bethlehem[1] to be born?

January 1919 — 1920, 1922

5. Crossroads village near Coole.
6. Yeats's term (pronounced with a hard g) for a spiraling motion in the shape of a cone. He envisions the two-thousand-year cycle of the Christian age as spiraling toward its end and the next historical cycle as beginning after a violent reversal: "the end of an age, which always receives the revelation of the character of the next age, is represented by the coming of one gyre to its place of greatest expansion and of the other to that of its greatest contraction" [Yeats's note].
7. The poem was written in January 1919, in the aftermath of World War I and the Russian Revolution and on the eve of the Anglo-Irish War.
8. Christ's second coming is heralded by the coming of the Beast of the Apocalypse, or Antichrist (1 John 2.18).
9. The spirit of the universe (Latin); that is, Yeats said, "a general storehouse of images," or collective unconscious.
1. Jesus' birthplace.

A Prayer for My Daughter

Once more the storm is howling and half hid
Under this cradle-hood and coverlid
My child[2] sleeps on. There is no obstacle
But Gregory's wood[3] and one bare hill
Whereby the haystack and roof-levelling wind,
Bred on the Atlantic, can be stayed;
And for an hour I have walked and prayed
Because of the great gloom that is in my mind.

I have walked and prayed for this young child an hour
And heard the sea-wind scream upon the tower,
And under the arches of the bridge, and scream
In the elms above the flooded stream;
Imagining in excited reverie
That the future years had come,
Dancing to a frenzied drum,
Out of the murderous innocence of the sea.

May she be granted beauty and yet not
Beauty to make a stranger's eye distraught,
Or hers before a looking-glass, for such,
Being made beautiful overmuch,
Consider beauty a sufficient end,
Lose natural kindness and maybe
The heart-revealing intimacy
That chooses right and never find a friend.

Helen being chosen found life flat and dull
And later had much trouble from a fool,[4]
While that great Queen,[5] that rose out of the spray,
Being fatherless could have her way
Yet chose a bandy-legged smith for man.
It's certain that fine women eat
A crazy salad with their meat
Whereby the Horn of Plenty[6] is undone.

In courtesy I'd have her chiefly learned;
Hearts are not had as a gift but hearts are earned
By those that are not entirely beautiful;
Yet many, that have played the fool
For beauty's very self, has charm made wise,
And many a poor man that has roved,
Loved and thought himself beloved,
From a glad kindness cannot take his eyes.

2. Yeats's daughter and first child, Anne Butler Yeats, was born on February 26, 1919.
3. Lady Gregory's wood at Coole, only a few miles from Yeats's tower, Thoor Ballylee.
4. Menelaus, the husband of Helen. Her abduction by Paris precipitated the Trojan War.
5. Venus, born from the sea, was the Roman goddess of love; her husband, Vulcan, was the lame god of fire and metalwork.
6. In Greek mythology, the goat's horn that suckled the god Zeus flowed with nectar and ambrosia; the cornucopia thus became a symbol of plenty.

May she become a flourishing hidden tree
That all her thoughts may like the linnet[7] be,
And have no business but dispensing round
Their magnanimities of sound,
Nor but in merriment begin a chase,
Nor but in merriment a quarrel.
Oh, may she live like some green laurel
Rooted in one dear perpetual place.

My mind, because the minds that I have loved,
The sort of beauty that I have approved,
Prosper but little, has dried up of late,
Yet knows that to be choked with hate
May well be of all evil chances chief.
If there's no hatred in a mind
Assault and battery of the wind
Can never tear the linnet from the leaf.

An intellectual hatred is the worst,
So let her think opinions are accursed.
Have I not seen the loveliest woman[8] born
Out of the mouth of Plenty's horn,
Because of her opinionated mind
Barter that horn and every good
By quiet natures understood
For an old bellows full of angry wind?

Considering that, all hatred driven hence,
The soul recovers radical innocence
And learns at last that it is self-delighting,
Self-appeasing, self-affrighting,
And that its own sweet will is heaven's will;
She can, though every face should scowl
And every windy quarter howl
Or every bellows burst, be happy still.

And may her bride-groom bring her to a house
Where all's accustomed, ceremonious;
For arrogance and hatred are the wares
Peddled in the thoroughfares.
How but in custom and in ceremony
Are innocence and beauty born?
Ceremony's a name for the rich horn,
And custom for the spreading laurel tree.

June 1919 — 1919, 1922

7. Small songbird.
8. Maud Gonne.

To Be Carved on a Stone at Thoor Ballylee[9]

I, the poet William Yeats,
With old mill boards and sea-green slates,
And smithy work from the Gort forge,
Restored this tower for my wife George;
And may these characters remain
When all is ruin once again.

1918 1921, 1922

Nineteen Hundred and Nineteen[1]

I

Many ingenious lovely things are gone
That seemed sheer miracle to the multitude,
Protected from the circle of the moon
That pitches common things about. There stood
Amid the ornamental bronze and stone
An ancient image made of olive wood—[2]
And gone are Phidias' famous ivories
And all the golden grasshoppers and bees.[3]

We too had many pretty toys when young;
A law indifferent to blame or praise,
To bribe or threat; habits that made old wrong
Melt down, as it were wax in the sun's rays;
Public opinion ripening for so long
We thought it would outlive all future days.
O what fine thought we had because we thought
That the worst rogues and rascals had died out.

All teeth were drawn, all ancient tricks unlearned,
And a great army but a showy thing;
What matter that no cannon had been turned
Into a ploughshare?[4] Parliament and king
Thought that unless a little powder burned
The trumpeters might burst with trumpeting
And yet it lack all glory; and perchance
The guardsmen's drowsy chargers would not prance.

9. The old Norman tower (*thoor*), near the small town of Gort in County Galway, that Yeats restored to be his home.
1. The year of the beginning of the Anglo-Irish War, which ended in 1921. The Irish Republican Army fought the English-controlled government of Ireland. British forces, especially the British ex-servicemen known as Black and Tans, committed atrocities in violent reprisals against the IRA.
2. The wooden statue of Athena that stood at the Acropolis, site of the Parthenon (temple of Athena), in Athens.
3. Phidias (c. 490–423 B.C.E.), famous Athenian sculptor; the Greek historian Thucydides (c. 450–400 B.C.E.) described Athenian women "fastening up their hair in a knot held by a golden grasshopper as a brooch" (*History of the Peloponnesian War* 1.6).
4. Cf. Isaiah 2.4: "And they shall beat their swords into plowshares."

Now days are dragon-ridden, the nightmare
Rides upon sleep: a drunken soldiery
Can leave the mother, murdered at her door,
To crawl in her own blood,[5] and go scot-free;
The night can sweat with terror as before
We pieced our thoughts into philosophy,
And planned to bring the world under a rule,
Who are but weasels fighting in a hole.

He who can read the signs nor sink unmanned
Into the half-deceit of some intoxicant
From shallow wits; who knows no work can stand,
Whether health, wealth or peace of mind were spent
On master-work of intellect or hand,
No honour leave its mighty monument,
Has but one comfort left: all triumph would
But break upon his ghostly solitude.

But is there any comfort to be found?
Man is in love and loves what vanishes,
What more is there to say? That country round
None dared admit, if such a thought were his,
Incendiary or bigot could be found
To burn that stump on the Acropolis,
Or break in bits the famous ivories
Or traffic in the grasshoppers or bees.

II

When Loie Fuller's Chinese dancers[6] enwound
A shining web, a floating ribbon of cloth,
It seemed that a dragon of air
Had fallen among dancers, had whirled them round
Or hurried them off on its own furious path;
So the Platonic Year[7]
Whirls out new right and wrong,
Whirls in the old instead;
All men are dancers and their tread
Goes to the barbarous clangour of a gong.

III

Some moralist or mythological poet
Compares the solitary soul to a swan;[8]
I am satisfied with that,

5. In November 1920, in Gort, a woman was killed outside her house by passing Black and Tans.
6. Loie Fuller (1862–1928), American dancer; she toured with a group of Japanese dancers (not Chinese) using whirling ribbons.
7. Great historical cycle.
8. Cf. *Prometheus Unbound* (1820), by English Romantic poet Percy Bysshe Shelley (1792–1822): "My soul is like an enchanted boat / Which, like a sleeping swan, doth float / Upon the silver waves of thy sweet singing" (2.5.72–74).

Satisfied if a troubled mirror show it,
Before that brief gleam of its life be gone,
An image of its state;
The wings half spread for flight,
The breast thrust out in pride
Whether to play, or to ride
Those winds that clamour of approaching night.

A man in his own secret meditation
Is lost amid the labyrinth that he has made
In art or politics;
Some Platonist[9] affirms that in the station
Where we should cast off body and trade
The ancient habit sticks,
And that if our works could
But vanish with our breath
That were a lucky death,
For triumph can but mar our solitude.

The swan has leaped into the desolate heaven:
That image can bring wildness, bring a rage
To end all things, to end
What my laborious life imagined, even
The half-imagined, the half-written page;
O but we dreamed to mend
Whatever mischief seemed
To afflict mankind, but now
That winds of winter blow
Learn that we were crack-pated when we dreamed.

IV

We, who seven years ago
Talked of honour and of truth,
Shriek with pleasure if we show
The weasel's twist, the weasel's tooth.

V

Come let us mock at the great
That had such burdens on the mind
And toiled so hard and late
To leave some monument behind,
Nor thought of the levelling wind.

Come let us mock at the wise;
With all those calendars whereon
They fixed old aching eyes,
They never saw how seasons run,
And now but gape at the sun.

9. Idealist philosopher.

Come let us mock at the good
That fancied goodness might be gay,
And sick of solitude
Might proclaim a holiday:
Wind shrieked—and where are they?

Mock mockers after that
That would not lift a hand maybe
To help good, wise or great
To bar that foul storm out, for we
Traffic in mockery.

VI

Violence upon the roads: violence of horses;
Some few have handsome riders, are garlanded
On delicate sensitive ear or tossing mane,
But wearied running round and round in their courses
All break and vanish, and evil gathers head:
Herodias' daughters[1] have returned again,
A sudden blast of dusty wind and after
Thunder of feet, tumult of images,
Their purpose in the labyrinth of the wind;
And should some crazy hand dare touch a daughter
All turn with amorous cries, or angry cries,
According to the wind, for all are blind.
But now wind drops, dust settles; thereupon
There lurches past, his great eyes without thought
Under the shadow of stupid straw-pale locks,
That insolent fiend Robert Artisson[2]
To whom the love-lorn Lady Kyteler[3] brought
Bronzed peacock feathers, red combs of her cocks.

1919 1921, 1928

1. Irish fairies or malevolent spirits "journey in whirling wind, the winds that were called the dance of the daughters of Herodias in the Middle Ages" [Yeats's note to "The Hosting of the Sidhe"].
2. An incubus, or medieval demon thought to seek sexual intercourse with women; also called "Robert Son of Art." "The country people see at times certain apparitions whom they name now 'fallen angels,' now 'ancient inhabitants of the country,' and describe as riding at whiles 'with flowers upon the heads of the horses.' I have assumed in the sixth poem that these horsemen, now that the times worsen, give way to worse. My last symbol, Robert Artisson, was an evil spirit much run after in Kilkenny at the start of the fourteenth century. Are not those who travel in the whirling dust also in the Platonic Year?" [Yeats's note].
3. Dame Alice Kyteler, an Anglo-Norman woman condemned as a witch in 1324, was charged with having nightly sex with Artisson and making animal sacrifices to him of peacocks and red cocks (Raphael Holinshed, *The Historie of Ireland,* 1577).

Leda and the Swan[4]

A sudden blow: the great wings beating still
Above the staggering girl, her thighs caressed
By the dark webs, her nape caught in his bill,
He holds her helpless breast upon his breast.

How can those terrified vague fingers push
The feathered glory from her loosening thighs?
And how can body, laid in that white rush,
But feel the strange heart beating where it lies?

A shudder in the loins engenders there
The broken wall, the burning roof and tower[5]
And Agamemnon dead.
                    Being so caught up,
So mastered by the brute blood of the air,
Did she put on his knowledge with his power
Before the indifferent beak could let her drop?

1923 — 1924, 1928

The Tower

I

What shall I do with this absurdity—
O heart, O troubled heart—this caricature,
Decrepit age that has been tied to me
As to a dog's tail?
                    Never had I more
Excited, passionate, fantastical
Imagination, nor an ear and eye
That more expected the impossible—
No, not in boyhood when with rod and fly,
Or the humbler worm, I climbed Ben Bulben's[6] back
And had the livelong summer day to spend.
It seems that I must bid the Muse go pack,
Choose Plato and Plotinus[7] for a friend
Until imagination, ear and eye,

4. In the Greek myth, the god Zeus, in the form of a swan, raped Leda, a mortal. Helen, Clytemnestra, Castor, and Pollux were the children of this union. Yeats saw Leda's rape by the swan as the beginning of a new age, analogous with the dove's annunciation to Mary of Jesus' conception: "I imagine the annunciation that founded Greece as made to Leda, remembering that they showed in a Spartan temple, strung up to the roof as a holy relic, an unhatched egg of hers, and that from one of her eggs came love and from the other war" (*A Vision*).

5. That is, Troy's destruction, caused by Helen's abduction by Paris. Agamemnon, the leader of the Greek army that besieged Troy, was murdered by his wife, Clytemnestra, when he returned home.

6. A mountain near Sligo.

7. The Greek philosopher Plato (c. 428–348 B.C.E.) warned against confusing abstract, ideal forms and their transitory, material counterparts. Plotinus (c. 205–70 B.C.E.) was a Neoplatonic Roman philosopher.

Can be content with argument and deal
In abstract things; or be derided by
A sort of battered kettle at the heel.

II

I pace upon the battlements[8] and stare
On the foundations of a house, or where
Tree, like a sooty finger, starts from the earth;
And send imagination forth
Under the day's declining beam, and call
Images and memories
From ruin or from ancient trees,
For I would ask a question of them all.

Beyond that ridge lived Mrs. French, and once
When every silver candlestick or sconce
Lit up the dark mahogany and the wine,
A serving-man, that could divine
That most respected lady's every wish,
Ran and with the garden shears
Clipped an insolent farmer's ears
And brought them in a little covered dish.[9]

Some few remembered still when I was young
A peasant girl[1] commended by a song,
Who'd lived somewhere upon that rocky place,
And praised the colour of her face,
And had the greater joy in praising her,
Remembering that, if walked she there,
Farmers jostled at the fair
So great a glory did the song confer.

And certain men, being maddened by those rhymes,
Or else by toasting her a score of times,
Rose from the table and declared it right
To test their fancy by their sight;
But they mistook the brightness of the moon
For the prosaic light of day—
Music had driven their wits astray—
And one was drowned in the great bog of Cloone.

Strange, but the man who made the song was blind;[2]
Yet, now I have considered it, I find
That nothing strange; the tragedy began
With Homer that was a blind man,
And Helen has all living hearts betrayed.

8. Of his tower, Thoor Ballylee.
9. An event recounted in Sir Jonah Barrington's *Personal Sketches of His Own Times* (1827, 1832).
1. Mary Hynes of Ballylee, a "peasant beauty," according to Yeats.
2. Anthony Raftery (c. 1784–1835), a blind Irish poet who wrote the Gaelic song "Mary Hynes." By tradition, Homer was also blind.

O may the moon and sunlight seem
One inextricable beam,
For if I triumph I must make men mad.

And I myself created Hanrahan[3]
And drove him drunk or sober through the dawn
From somewhere in the neighbouring cottages.
Caught by an old man's juggleries
He stumbled, tumbled, fumbled to and fro
And had but broken knees for hire
And horrible splendour of desire;
I thought it all out twenty years ago:

Good fellows shuffled cards in an old bawn;[4]
And when that ancient ruffian's turn was on
He so bewitched the cards under his thumb
That all but the one card became
A pack of hounds and not a pack of cards,
And that he changed into a hare.
Hanrahan rose in frenzy there
And followed up those baying creatures towards—

O towards I have forgotten what—enough!
I must recall a man that neither love
Nor music nor an enemy's clipped ear
Could, he was so harried, cheer;
A figure that has grown so fabulous
There's not a neighbour left to say
When he finished his dog's day:
An ancient bankrupt master of this house.

Before that ruin came, for centuries,
Rough men-at-arms, cross-gartered to the knees
Or shod in iron, climbed the narrow stairs,
And certain men-at-arms there were
Whose images, in the Great Memory stored,
Come with loud cry and panting breast
To break upon a sleeper's rest
While their great wooden dice beat on the board.[5]

As I would question all, come all who can;
Come old, necessitous, half-mounted man;[6]
And bring beauty's blind rambling celebrant;
The red man[7] the juggler sent
Through God-forsaken meadows; Mrs. French,
Gifted with so fine an ear;

3. "Hanrahan's pursuit of the phantom hare and hounds is from my *Stories of Red Hanrahan*" [Yeats's note]. The particular story is "Red Hanrahan."

4. An enclosure around a farmhouse.

5. "The ghosts have been seen at their game of dice in what is now my bedroom, and the old bankrupt man lived about a hundred years ago" [Yeats's note].

6. A derisive term, in Barrington's book, for a social climber.

7. Hanrahan.

The man drowned in a bog's mire,
When mocking muses chose the country wench.

Did all old men and women, rich and poor,
Who trod upon these rocks or passed this door,
Whether in public or in secret rage
As I do now against old age?
But I have found an answer in those eyes
That are impatient to be gone;
Go therefore; but leave Hanrahan,
For I need all his mighty memories.

Old lecher with a love on every wind,
Bring up out of that deep considering mind
All that you have discovered in the grave,
For it is certain that you have
Reckoned up every unforeknown, unseeing
Plunge, lured by a softening eye,
Or by a touch or a sigh,
Into the labyrinth of another's being;

Does the imagination dwell the most
Upon a woman won or woman lost?
If on the lost, admit you turned aside
From a great labyrinth out of pride,
Cowardice, some silly over-subtle thought
Or anything called conscience once;
And that if memory recur, the sun's
Under eclipse and the day blotted out.

III

It is time that I wrote my will;
I choose upstanding men
That climb the streams until
The fountain leap, and at dawn
Drop their cast at the side
Of dripping stone; I declare
They shall inherit my pride,
The pride of people that were
Bound neither to Cause nor to State,
Neither to slaves that were spat on,
Nor to the tyrants that spat,
The people of Burke and of Grattan[8]

8. Yeats here allies himself with the Anglo-Irish (Protestant) minority, who supported the nationalist cause when they might have considered themselves English. In a speech on divorce that he gave in the Irish Senate on June 11, 1925, Yeats said: "I am proud to consider myself a typical man of that minority. We against whom you have done this thing are no petty people. We are one of the great stocks of Europe. We are the people of Burke; we are the people of Grattan; we are the people of Swift, the people of Emmet, the people of Parnell. We have created the most of the modern literature of this country. We have created the best of its political intelligence." Dublin-born statesman and writer Edmund Burke (1729–1797) fought for Irish legislative freedom and Catholic relief measures; political leader Henry Grattan (1746–1820) fought for Catholic emancipation and against the union of Great Britain and Ireland.

That gave, though free to refuse—
Pride, like that of the morn,
When the headlong light is loose,
Or that of the fabulous horn,[9]
Or that of the sudden shower
When all streams are dry,
Or that of the hour
When the swan must fix his eye
Upon a fading gleam,
Float out upon a long
Last reach of glittering stream
And there sing his last song.
And I declare my faith:
I mock Plotinus' thought
And cry in Plato's teeth,
Death and life were not
Till man made up the whole,
Made lock, stock and barrel
Out of his bitter soul,
Aye, sun and moon and star, all,
And further add to that
That, being dead, we rise,
Dream and so create
Translunar Paradise.
I have prepared my peace
With learned Italian things
And the proud stones of Greece,
Poet's imaginings
And memories of love,
Memories of the words of women,
All those things whereof
Man makes a superhuman
Mirror-resembling dream.

As at the loophole there
The daws chatter and scream,
And drop twigs layer upon layer.
When they have mounted up,
The mother bird will rest
On their hollow top,
And so warm her wild nest.

I leave both faith and pride
To young upstanding men
Climbing the mountain side,
That under bursting dawn
They may drop a fly;
Being of that metal made
Till it was broken by
This sedentary trade.

9. The horn of plenty.

Now shall I make my soul,
Compelling it to study
In a learned school
Till the wreck of body,
Slow decay of blood,
Testy delirium
Or dull decrepitude,
Or what worse evil come—
The death of friends, or death
Of every brilliant eye
That made a catch in the breath—
Seem but the clouds of the sky
When the horizon fades;
Or a bird's sleepy cry
Among the deepening shades.

1925–26 1927, 1928

Sailing to Byzantium[1]

I

That is no country for old men. The young
In one another's arms, birds in the trees,
—Those dying generations—at their song,
The salmon-falls, the mackerel-crowded seas,
Fish, flesh, or fowl, commend all summer long
Whatever is begotten, born, and dies.
Caught in that sensual music all neglect
Monuments of unageing intellect.

II

An aged man is but a paltry thing,
A tattered coat upon a stick, unless
Soul clap its hands and sing,[2] and louder sing
For every tatter in its mortal dress,
Nor is there singing school but studying
Monuments of its own magnificence;
And therefore I have sailed the seas and come
To the holy city of Byzantium.

1. Yeats wrote in *A Vision:* "I think that if I could be given a month of Antiquity and leave to spend it where I chose, I would spend it in Byzantium [now Istanbul] a little before Justinian opened St. Sophia and closed the Academy of Plato [in the sixth century C.E.]. . . . I think that in early Byzantium, maybe never before or since in recorded history, religious, aesthetic and practical life were one, that architect and artificers . . . spoke to the multitude and the few alike. The painter, the mosaic worker, the worker in gold and silver, the illuminator of sacred books, were almost impersonal, almost perhaps without the consciousness of individual design, absorbed in their subject-matter and that the vision of a whole people."

2. The poet William Blake saw the soul of his dead brother rising to heaven, "clapping his hands for joy."

III

O sages standing in God's holy fire
As in the gold mosaic of a wall,[3]
Come from the holy fire, perne in a gyre,[4]
And be the singing-masters of my soul.
Consume my heart away; sick with desire
And fastened to a dying animal
It knows not what it is; and gather me
Into the artifice of eternity.

IV

Once out of nature I shall never take
My bodily form from any natural thing,
But such a form as Grecian goldsmiths make
Of hammered gold and gold enamelling
To keep a drowsy Emperor awake;[5]
Or set upon a golden bough to sing
To lords and ladies of Byzantium
Of what is past, or passing, or to come.

1926 1927, 1928

Among School Children

I

I walk through the long schoolroom questioning;
A kind old nun in a white hood replies;
The children learn to cipher and to sing,
To study reading-books and history,
To cut and sew, be neat in everything
In the best modern way—the children's eyes
In momentary wonder stare upon
A sixty-year-old smiling public man.[6]

II

I dream of a Ledaean[7] body, bent
Above a sinking fire, a tale that she
Told of a harsh reproof, or trivial event
That changed some childish day to tragedy—
Told, and it seemed that our two natures blent
Into a sphere from youthful sympathy,
Or else, to alter Plato's parable,[8]
Into the yolk and white of the one shell.

3. The mosaics in San Apollinaire Nuovo, in Ravenna, Italy, depict rows of Christian saints on a gold background; Yeats saw them in 1907.
4. That is, whirl in a spiral.
5. "I have read somewhere that in the Emperor's palace at Byzantium was a tree made of gold and silver, and artificial birds that sang" [Yeats's note].
6. Yeats, as part of his work in the Irish Senate, visited a Montessori school in Waterford in 1926.
7. A body like Leda's. Yeats associated her daughter, Helen of Troy, with Maud Gonne.
8. In the *Symposium*, by the Greek philosopher Plato (c. 428–c. 348 B.C.E.), Aristophanes argues that "the primeval man" was both male and female

III

And thinking of that fit of grief or rage
I look upon one child or t'other there
And wonder if she stood so at that age—
For even daughters of the swan can share
Something of every paddler's heritage—
And had that colour upon cheek or hair,
And thereupon my heart is driven wild:
She stands before me as a living child.

IV

Her present image floats into the mind—
Did Quattrocento[9] finger fashion it
Hollow of cheek as though it drank the wind
And took a mess of shadows for its meat?
And I though never of Ledaean kind
Had pretty plumage once—enough of that,
Better to smile on all that smile, and show
There is a comfortable kind of old scarecrow.

V

What youthful mother, a shape upon her lap
Honey of generation[1] had betrayed,
And that must sleep, shriek, struggle to escape
As recollection or the drug decide,
Would think her son, did she but see that shape
With sixty or more winters on its head,
A compensation for the pang of his birth,
Or the uncertainty of his setting forth?

VI

Plato thought nature but a spume that plays
Upon a ghostly paradigm of things;[2]
Solider Aristotle played the taws
Upon the bottom of a king of kings;[3]
World-famous golden-thighed Pythagoras[4]
Fingered upon a fiddle-stick or strings
What a star sang and careless Muses heard:
Old clothes upon old sticks to scare a bird.

---

but was divided (like an egg separated into yoke and white); the resulting two beings come together in love to become one again.

9. That is, the skill of a fifteenth-century Italian painter.

1. "I have taken the 'honey of generation' from Porphyry's essay on 'The Cave of Nymphs' " [Yeats's note]. Porphyry (233–c. 304 C.E.) was a Neoplatonic philosopher.

2. Plato thought nature merely an image of an ideal world that exists elsewhere.

3. Plato's student Aristotle (384–322 B.C.E.) was "solider" because he regarded this world as the authentic one. He tutored Alexander the Great (356–323 B.C.E.), the "king of kings," and disciplined him with the "taws," or leather strap.

4. Greek philosopher (c. 582–507 B.C.E), known for his doctrine of the harmony of the spheres and his discovery of the mathematical basis of musical intervals.

VII

Both nuns and mothers worship images,
But those the candles light are not as those
That animate a mother's reveries,
But keep a marble or a bronze repose.
And yet they too break hearts—O Presences
That passion, piety or affection knows,
And that all heavenly glory symbolise—
O self-born mockers of man's enterprise;

VIII

Labour is blossoming or dancing where
The body is not bruised to pleasure soul,
Nor beauty born out of its own despair,
Nor blear-eyed wisdom out of midnight oil.
O chestnut tree, great rooted blossomer,
Are you the leaf, the blossom or the bole?[5]
O body swayed to music, O brightening glance,
How can we know the dancer from the dance?

1926 1927, 1928

In Memory of Eva Gore-Booth and Con Markievicz

The light of evening, Lissadell,[6]
Great windows open to the south,
Two girls in silk kimonos, both
Beautiful, one a gazelle.
But a raving autumn shears
Blossom from the summer's wreath;
The older is condemned to death,
Pardoned, drags out lonely years
Conspiring among the ignorant.
I know not what the younger dreams—
Some vague Utopia—and she seems,
When withered old and skeleton-gaunt,
An image of such politics.
Many a time I think to seek
One or the other out and speak
Of that old Georgian mansion, mix
Pictures of the mind, recall
That table and the talk of youth,
Two girls in silk kimonos, both
Beautiful, one a gazelle.

5. Trunk.
6. Yeats, on a visit to the Gore-Booth country house, Lissadell, overlooking Sligo Bay, told the two sisters of the nationalist activities of Maud Gonne. Both soon became active in the movement. Constance Gore-Booth (1868–1927), who became the Countess Markievicz, was sentenced to execution for her part in the Easter Rising of 1916, but her sentence was commuted to imprisonment. Eva Gore-Booth (1870–1926) was a trade-union organizer who campaigned for women's suffrage.

Dear shadows, now you know it all,
All the folly of a fight
With a common wrong or right.
The innocent and the beautiful
Have no enemy but time;
Arise and bid me strike a match
And strike another till time catch;
Should the conflagration climb,
Run till all the sages know.
We the great gazebo[7] built,
They convicted us of guilt;
Bid me strike a match and blow.

October 1927 1929, 1933

A Dialogue of Self and Soul[8]

I

My Soul. I summon to the winding ancient stair;
Set all your mind upon the steep ascent,
Upon the broken, crumbling battlement,
Upon the breathless starlit air,
Upon the star that marks the hidden pole;
Fix every wandering thought upon
That quarter where all thought is done:
Who can distinguish darkness from the soul?

My Self. The consecrated blade upon my knees
Is Sato's ancient blade, still as it was,
Still razor-keen, still like a looking-glass
Unspotted by the centuries;
That flowering, silken, old embroidery, torn
From some court-lady's dress and round
The wooden scabbard bound and wound,
Can, tattered, still protect, faded adorn.

My Soul. Why should the imagination of a man
Long past his prime remember things that are
Emblematical of love and war?
Think of ancestral night that can,
If but imagination scorn the earth
And intellect its wandering
To this and that and t'other thing,
Deliver from the crime of death and birth.

7. A summer house, here by extension the nationalist movement and even the whole temporal world.
8. In a letter of October 2, 1923, Yeats wrote: "I am writing a new tower poem 'Sword and Tower,' which is a choice of rebirth rather than deliverance from birth. I make my Japanese sword and its silk covering my symbol of life." Junzo Sato, a friend, had given him the ceremonial sword in 1920.

My Self. Montashigi, third of his family, fashioned it
Five hundred years ago, about it lie
Flowers from I know not what embroidery—
Heart's purple—and all these I set
For emblems of the day against the tower
Emblematical of the night,
And claim as by a soldier's right
A charter to commit the crime once more.

My Soul. Such fullness in that quarter overflows
And falls into the basin of the mind
That man is stricken deaf and dumb and blind,
For intellect no longer knows
Is from the *Ought*, or *Knower* from the *Known*—
That is to say, ascends to Heaven;
Only the dead can be forgiven;
But when I think of that my tongue's a stone.

II

My Self. A living man is blind and drinks his drop.
What matter if the ditches are impure?
What matter if I live it all once more?
Endure that toil of growing up;
The ignominy of boyhood; the distress
Of boyhood changing into man;
The unfinished man and his pain
Brought face to face with his own clumsiness;

The finished man among his enemies?—
How in the name of Heaven can he escape
That defiling and disfigured shape
The mirror of malicious eyes
Casts upon his eyes until at last
He thinks that shape must be his shape?
And what's the good of an escape
If honour find him in the wintry blast?

I am content to live it all again
And yet again, if it be life to pitch
Into the frog-spawn of a blind man's ditch,
A blind man battering blind men;
Or into that most fecund ditch of all,
The folly that man does
Or must suffer, if he woos
A proud woman not kindred of his soul.

I am content to follow to its source
Every event in action or in thought;
Measure the lot; forgive myself the lot!
When such as I cast out remorse
So great a sweetness flows into the breast

We must laugh and we must sing,
We are blest by everything,
Everything we look upon is blest.

1927 1929, 1933

Byzantium[9]

The unpurged images of day recede;
The Emperor's drunken soldiery are abed;
Night resonance recedes, night-walkers' song
After great cathedral gong;
A starlit or a moonlit dome[1] disdains
All that man is,
All mere complexities,
The fury and the mire of human veins.

Before me floats an image, man or shade,
Shade more than man, more image than a shade;
For Hades' bobbin[2] bound in mummy-cloth
May unwind the winding path;[3]
A mouth that has no moisture and no breath
Breathless mouths may summon;
I hail the superhuman;
I call it death-in-life and life-in-death.

Miracle, bird or golden handiwork,
More miracle than bird or handiwork,
Planted on the starlit golden bough,
Can like the cocks of Hades crow,[4]
Or, by the moon embittered, scorn aloud
In glory of changeless metal
Common bird or petal
And all complexities of mire or blood.

At midnight on the Emperor's pavement flit
Flames that no faggot[5] feeds, nor steel has lit,
Nor storm disturbs, flames begotten of flame,
Where blood-begotten spirits come
And all complexities of fury leave,

9. On October 4, 1930, Yeats sent a copy of this poem to Sturge Moore, saying: "The poem originates from a criticism of yours. You objected to the last verse of 'Sailing to Byzantium' because a bird made by a goldsmith was just as natural as anything else. That showed me that the idea needed exposition." In a diary entry of April 1930, Yeats had noted the following as "subject for a poem": "Describe Byzantium as it is in the system towards the end of the first Christian millennium. A walking mummy. Flames at the street corners where the soul is purified, birds of hammered gold singing in the golden trees, in the harbour [dolphins] offering their backs to the wailing dead that they may carry them to Paradise."
1. Of the great church of St. Sophia.
2. Spool. Hades was the Greek god of the underworld, the realm of the dead.
3. That is, the spool of life, wound like a mummy, may be unwound and lead to the timeless world of pure spirit.
4. On Roman tombstones, the cock is a herald of rebirth, thus of the continuing cycle of human life.
5. Bundle of sticks.

Dying into a dance,
An agony of trance,
An agony of flame that cannot singe a sleeve.

Astraddle on the dolphin's mire and blood,[6]
Spirit after spirit! The smithies break the flood,
The golden smithies of the Emperor!
Marbles of the dancing floor
Break bitter furies of complexity,
Those images that yet
Fresh images beget,
That dolphin-torn, that gong-tormented sea.

1930 1932, 1933

Crazy Jane Talks with the Bishop[7]

I met the Bishop on the road
And much said he and I.
'Those breasts are flat and fallen now
Those veins must soon be dry;
Live in a heavenly mansion,
Not in some foul sty.'

'Fair and foul are near of kin,
And fair needs foul,' I cried.
'My friends are gone, but that's a truth
Nor grave nor bed denied,
Learned in bodily lowliness
And in the heart's pride.

'A woman can be proud and stiff
When on love intent;
But Love has pitched his mansion in
The place of excrement;
For nothing can be sole or whole
That has not been rent.'

1931 1933

6. In ancient mythology, dolphins were thought to carry the souls of the dead to the Isles of the Blessed.
7. Crazy Jane is partly modeled on an old woman named Cracked Mary, who lived near Lady Gregory. Yeats uses her as the spokesperson in a group of poems.

Vacillation

I

Between extremities
Man runs his course;
A brand, or flaming breath,
Comes to destroy
All those antinomies[8]
Of day and night;
The body calls it death,
The heart remorse.
But if these be right
What is joy?

II

A tree there is that from its topmost bough
Is half all glittering flame and half all green[9]
Abounding foliage moistened with the dew;
And half is half and yet is all the scene;
And half and half consume what they renew,
And he that Attis'[1] image hangs between
That staring fury and the blind lush leaf
May know not what he knows, but knows not grief.

III

Get all the gold and silver that you can,
Satisfy ambition, or animate
The trivial days and ram them with the sun,
And yet upon these maxims meditate:
All women dote upon an idle man
Although their children need a rich estate;
No man has ever lived that had enough
Of children's gratitude or woman's love.

No longer in Lethean[2] foliage caught
Begin the preparation for your death
And from the fortieth winter by that thought
Test every work of intellect or faith
And everything that your own hands have wrought,
And call those works extravagance of breath
That are not suited for such men as come
Proud, open-eyed and laughing to the tomb.

8. Opposites.
9. In "The Celtic Element in Literature," Yeats quotes Lady Charlotte Guest's translation of the Welsh romances, *The Mabinogi:* "They saw a tall tree by the side of the river, one half of which was in flames from the root to the top, and the other half was green and in full leaf."
1. An ancient vegetation god. In Greek mythology, the earth goddess Cybele caused Attis to castrate himself, and after his death he was turned into a pine tree. At his annual festival in March, his devotees castrated themselves, and "the effigy of a young man was attached to the middle" of a pine tree as "a representation of his coming to life again in tree-form" (James G. Frazer, *The Golden Bough,* 1890).
2. Lethe was the river of forgetfulness in the Greek underworld.

IV

My fiftieth year had come and gone,
I sat, a solitary man,
In a crowded London shop,
An open book and empty cup
On the marble table-top.

While on the shop and street I gazed
My body of a sudden blazed;
And twenty minutes more or less
It seemed, so great my happiness,
That I was blessèd and could bless.[3]

V

Although the summer sunlight gild
Cloudy leafage of the sky,
Or wintry moonlight sink the field
In storm-scattered intricacy,
I cannot look thereon,
Responsibility so weighs me down.

Things said or done long years ago,
Or things I did not do or say
But thought that I might say or do,
Weigh me down, and not a day
But something is recalled,
My conscience or my vanity appalled.

VI

A rivery field spread out below,
An odour of the new-mown hay
In his nostrils, the great lord of Chou[4]
Cried, casting off the mountain snow,
'Let all things pass away.'

Wheels by milk-white asses drawn
Where Babylon or Nineveh[5]
Rose; some conqueror drew rein
And cried to battle-weary men,
'Let all things pass away.'

3. In *Per Amica Silentia Lunae* (1917), Yeats wrote: "At certain moments, always unforeseen, I become happy, most commonly when at hazard I have opened some book of verse. . . . Perhaps I am sitting in some crowded restaurant, the open book beside me, or closed, my excitement having overbrimmed the page. I look at the strangers near as if I had known them all my life, and it seems strange that I cannot speak to them: everything fills me with affection, I have no longer any fears or any needs; I do not even remember that this happy mood must come to an end."

4. Probably the Chinese author and statesman Chou-Kung (d. 1105 B.C.E.), known as the Duke of Chou, who composed the *I-Ching,* or *Book of Changes,* in prison.

5. Ancient civilizations of the Middle East, here emblems of past glory.

From man's blood-sodden heart are sprung
Those branches of the night and day
Where the gaudy moon is hung.
What's the meaning of all song?
'Let all things pass away.'

VII

The Soul. Seek out reality, leave things that seem.
The Heart. What, be a singer born and lack a theme?
The Soul. Isaiah's coal,[6] what more can man desire?
The Heart. Struck dumb in the simplicity of fire!
The Soul. Look on that fire, salvation walks within.
The Heart. What theme had Homer but original sin?

VIII

Must we part, Von Hügel,[7] though much alike, for we
Accept the miracles of the saints and honour sanctity?
The body of Saint Teresa[8] lies undecayed in tomb,
Bathed in miraculous oil, sweet odours from it come,
Healing from its lettered slab. Those self-same hands[9] perchance
Eternalised the body of a modern saint that once
Had scooped out Pharaoh's mummy. I—though heart might find relief
Did I become a Christian man and choose for my belief
What seems most welcome in the tomb—play a predestined part.
Homer is my example and his unchristened heart.
The lion and the honeycomb, what has Scripture said?[1]
So get you gone, Von Hügel, though with blessings on your head.

1931–32 1932, 1933

Meru[2]

Civilisation is hooped together, brought
Under a rule, under the semblance of peace
By manifold illusion; but man's life is thought,
And he, despite his terror, cannot cease
Ravening through century after century,
Ravening, raging, and uprooting that he may come
Into the desolation of reality:
Egypt and Greece good-bye, and good-bye, Rome!

6. The prophet Isaiah is purged of sin when an angel puts a fiery coal to his lips (Isaiah 6.6–11).
7. Friedrich Von Hügel (1852–1925), Catholic mystic and religious philosopher.
8. Spanish Carmelite nun (1515–1582), one of the principal Catholic saints. Her body was believed to have remained undecayed, exuding a miraculous oil and emitting a delicious scent.
9. Of the embalmers.
1. In the Bible, Samson kills a lion and finds a honeycomb inside. He asks the riddle: how "out of the eater came forth meat, and out of the strong came forth sweetness" (Judges 14.14–18).
2. In Hindu tradition, Meru is a sacred mountain at the center of the world; it is the abode of Vishnu, who preserves humanity. Hindus identify it as Mount Kailis, in Tibet; holy men climb it in pursuit of union with the god.

Hermits upon Mount Meru or Everest,
Caverned in night under the drifted snow,
Or where that snow and winter's dreadful blast
Beat down upon their naked bodies, know
That day brings round the night, that before dawn
His glory and his monuments are gone.

1934

The Gyres[3]

The gyres! the gyres! Old Rocky Face[4] look forth;
Things thought too long can be no longer thought
For beauty dies of beauty, worth of worth,
And ancient lineaments are blotted out.
Irrational streams of blood are staining earth;
Empedocles[5] has thrown all things about;
Hector[6] is dead and there's a light in Troy;
We that look on but laugh in tragic joy.

What matter though numb nightmare ride on top
And blood and mire the sensitive body stain?
What matter? Heave no sigh, let no tear drop,
A greater, a more gracious time has gone;
For painted forms or boxes of make-up
In ancient tombs I sighed, but not again;
What matter? Out of Cavern comes a voice
And all it knows is that one word 'Rejoice.'

Conduct and work grow coarse, and coarse the soul,
What matter! Those that Rocky Face holds dear,
Lovers of horses and of women, shall
From marble of a broken sepulchre
Or dark betwixt the polecat and the owl,
Or any rich, dark nothing disinter
The workman, noble and saint, and all things run
On that unfashionable gyre again.

1938

3. Yeats uses the image of interlocking gyres (or cones), with now one and now another ascendant, as a symbol for the cycles of history and human life.
4. Perhaps the Delphic oracle, who spoke through a cleft in the rock.
5. Greek philosopher (c. 490–430 B.C.E.), who elaborated a theory of the concord and discord of the four elements and of the two opposing forces, love and hate.
6. Oldest son of King Priam of Troy, killed by Achilles during the Trojan War, before Troy was burned.

Lapis Lazuli

(For Harry Clifton)[7]

I have heard that hysterical women say
They are sick of the palette and fiddle-bow,
Of poets that are always gay,
For everybody knows or else should know
That if nothing drastic is done[8]
Aeroplane and Zeppelin[9] will come out;
Pitch like King Billy[1] bomb-balls in
Until the town lie beaten flat.

All perform their tragic play,
There struts Hamlet, there is Lear,
That's Ophelia, that Cordelia;
Yet they, should the last scene be there,
The great stage curtain about to drop,
If worthy their prominent part in the play,
Do not break up their lines to weep.
They know that Hamlet and Lear are gay;
Gaiety transfiguring all that dread.
All men have aimed at, found and lost;
Black out; Heaven blazing into the head:
Tragedy wrought to its uttermost.
Though Hamlet rambles and Lear rages,
And all the drop scenes drop at once
Upon a hundred thousand stages,
It cannot grow by an inch or an ounce.

On their own feet they came, or on shipboard,
Camel-back, horse-back, ass-back, mule-back,
Old civilisations put to the sword.
Then they and their wisdom went to rack:
No handiwork of Callimachus[2]
Who handled marble as if it were bronze,
Made draperies that seemed to rise
When sea-wind swept the corner, stands;
His long lamp chimney shaped like the stem
Of a slender palm, stood but a day;
All things fall and are built again
And those that build them again are gay.

7. The English writer Harry Clifton (1908–1978) gave Yeats for his seventieth birthday a piece of lapis lazuli, "carved by some Chinese sculptor into the semblance of a mountain with temple, trees, paths, and an ascetic and pupil about to climb the mountain. Ascetic, pupil, hard stone, eternal theme of the sensual east. The heroic cry in the midst of despair. But no, I am wrong, the east has its solutions always and therefore knows nothing of tragedy. It is we, not the east, that must raise the heroic cry" (from Yeats's letter to Dorothy Wellesley, July 6, 1935).
8. Because Europe was (in 1936) close to war.
9. German zeppelins, or airships, bombed London during World War I.
1. King William III (William of Orange), who defeated the army of King James II at the Battle of the Boyne, in Ireland, in 1690. A popular ballad says, "King William he threw his bomb-balls in, / And set them on fire."
2. Athenian sculptor of the fifth century B.C.E.

Two Chinamen, behind them a third,
Are carved in Lapis Lazuli,
Over them flies a long-legged bird
A symbol of longevity;
The third, doubtless a serving-man,
Carries a musical instrument.

Every discolouration of the stone,
Every accidental crack or dent
Seems a water-course or an avalanche,
Or lofty slope where it still snows
Though doubtless plum or cherry-branch
Sweetens the little half-way house
Those Chinamen climb towards, and I
Delight to imagine them seated there;
There, on the mountain and the sky,
On all the tragic scene they stare.
One asks for mournful melodies;
Accomplished fingers begin to play.
Their eyes mid many wrinkles, their eyes,
Their ancient, glittering eyes, are gay.

July 1936 — 1938

An Acre of Grass

Picture and book remain,
An acre of green grass
For air and exercise,
Now strength of body goes;
Midnight an old house
Where nothing stirs but a mouse.

My temptation is quiet.
Here at life's end
Neither loose imagination,
Nor the mill of the mind
Consuming its rag and bone,
Can make the truth known.

Grant me an old man's frenzy.
Myself must I remake
Till I am Timon and Lear[3]
Or that William Blake[4]
Who beat upon the wall
Till truth obeyed his call;

3. Shakespeare's Timon of Athens, abandoned by all his friends and raging, like King Lear, at ingratitude.
4. English poet and artist (1757–1827).

A mind Michael Angelo[5] knew
That can pierce the clouds
Or inspired by frenzy
Shake the dead in their shrouds;
Forgotten else by mankind
An old man's eagle mind.

November 1936 1938

The Spur

You think it horrible that lust and rage
Should dance attendance upon my old age;
They were not such a plague when I was young;
What else have I to spur me into song?

1936 1938

Long-Legged Fly

That civilisation may not sink
Its great battle lost,
Quiet the dog, tether the pony
To a distant post.
Our master Caesar is in the tent
Where the maps are spread,
His eyes fixed upon nothing,
A hand under his head.

Like a long-legged fly upon the stream
His mind moves upon silence.

That the topless towers be burnt
And men recall that face,[6]
Move most gently if move you must
In this lonely place.
She thinks, part woman, three parts a child,
That nobody looks; her feet
Practise a tinker shuffle
Picked up on the street.

Like a long-legged fly upon the stream
Her mind moves upon silence.

5. Italian artist (1475–1564).
6. Of Helen of Troy. Yeats alludes to Christopher Marlowe's play *Dr. Faustus:* "Was this the face that launched a thousand ships / And burnt the topless towers of Ilium?"

That girls at puberty may find
The first Adam in their thought,
Shut the door of the Pope's chapel,
Keep those children out.
There on the scaffolding reclines
Michael Angelo.[7]
With no more sound than the mice make
His hand moves to and fro.

Like a long-legged fly upon the stream
His mind moves upon silence.

November 1937 1939

Under Ben Bulben[8]

I

Swear by what the Sages spoke
Round the Mareotic Lake
That the Witch of Atlas knew,[9]
Spoke and set the cocks a-crow.

Swear by those horsemen, by those women,[1]
Complexion and form prove superhuman,
That pale, long visaged company
That airs an immortality
Completeness of their passions won;
Now they ride the wintry dawn
Where Ben Bulben sets the scene.

Here's the gist of what they mean.

II

Many times man lives and dies
Between his two eternities,
That of race and that of soul,
And ancient Ireland knew it all.
Whether man dies in his bed
Or the rifle knocks him dead,
A brief parting from those dear
Is the worst man has to fear.

7. Italian artist (1475–1564), who painted *The Creation of Man* on the Sistine Chapel ceiling, in the Vatican.
8. A mountain near Sligo; Yeats's grave is in sight of it, in Drumcliff churchyard.
9. Lake Mareotis, near Alexandria, Egypt, was an ancient center of Christian Neoplatonism and of neo-Pythagorean philosophy. The lake is mentioned in "The Witch of Atlas," a poem by Percy Bysshe Shelley (1792–1822). In an essay on Shelley, Yeats writes that the witch, passing in a boat by this and another lake, "sees all human life shadowed upon its waters . . . and because she can see the reality of things she is described as journeying 'in the calm depths' of 'the wide lake' we journey over unpiloted."
1. Superhuman beings or fairies, like the Sidhe, believed to ride through the countryside near Ben Bulben.

Though grave-diggers' toil is long,
Sharp their spades, their muscle strong,
They but thrust their buried men
Back in the human mind again.

III

You that Mitchel's prayer have heard
'Send war in our time, O Lord!'[2]
Know that when all words are said
And a man is fighting mad,
Something drops from eyes long blind
He completes his partial mind,
For an instant stands at ease,
Laughs aloud, his heart at peace,
Even the wisest man grows tense
With some sort of violence
Before he can accomplish fate
Know his work or choose his mate.

IV

Poet and sculptor do the work
Nor let the modish painter shirk
What his great forefathers did,
Bring the soul of man to God,
Make him fill the cradles right.

Measurement began our might:
Forms a stark Egyptian thought,
Forms that gentler Phidias[3] wrought.

Michael Angelo left a proof
On the Sistine Chapel roof,
Where but half-awakened Adam
Can disturb globe-trotting Madam
Till her bowels are in heat,
Proof that there's a purpose set
Before the secret working mind:
Profane perfection of mankind.

Quattrocento[4] put in paint,
On backgrounds for a God or Saint,
Gardens where a soul's at ease;
Where everything that meets the eye
Flowers and grass and cloudless sky
Resemble forms that are, or seem
When sleepers wake and yet still dream,
And when it's vanished still declare,

2. From *Jail Journal,* by Irish nationalist John Mitchel (1815–1875).

3. Greek sculptor (c. 490–423 B.C.E.).

4. Fifteenth-century Italian art.

With only bed and bedstead there,
That Heavens had opened.

Gyres[5] run on;
When that greater dream had gone
Calvert and Wilson, Blake and Claude[6]
Prepared a rest for the people of God,
Palmer's[7] phrase, but after that
Confusion fell upon our thought.

V

Irish poets learn your trade
Sing whatever is well made,
Scorn the sort now growing up.
All out of shape from toe to top,
Their unremembering hearts and heads
Base-born products of base beds.
Sing the peasantry, and then
Hard-riding country gentlemen,
The holiness of monks, and after
Porter-drinkers' randy laughter;
Sing the lords and ladies gay
That were beaten into the clay
Through seven heroic centuries;[8]
Cast your mind on other days
That we in coming days may be
Still the indomitable Irishry.

VI

Under bare Ben Bulben's head
In Drumcliff churchyard Yeats is laid,
An ancestor was rector there[9]
Long years ago; a church stands near,
By the road an ancient Cross.
No marble, no conventional phrase,
On limestone quarried near the spot
By his command these words are cut:

Cast a cold eye
On life, on death.
Horseman, pass by!

1938 1939

5. Yeats's term for conelike spirals or cycles of history.
6. Edward Calvert (1799–1883): English visionary artist and follower of William Blake (1757–1827), English mystical poet and artist. Richard Wilson (1714–1782): English landscape painter and disciple of Claude Lorraine (1600–1682), French artist.
7. Samuel Palmer (1805–1881), English landscape painter who admired Blake.
8. Since the Normans' conquest of Ireland, in the twelfth century.
9. Yeats's great-grandfather, the Reverend John Yeats (1774–1846), was rector of Drumcliff Church, Sligo.

Man and the Echo

Man. In a cleft that's christened Alt
Under broken stone I halt
At the bottom of a pit
That broad noon has never lit,
And shout a secret to the stone.
All that I have said and done,
Now that I am old and ill,
Turns into a question till
I lie awake night after night
And never get the answers right.
Did that play of mine[1] send out
Certain men the English shot?
Did words of mine put too great strain
On that woman's reeling brain?[2]
Could my spoken words have checked
That whereby a house[3] lay wrecked?
And all seems evil until I
Sleepless would lie down and die.

Echo. Lie down and die.

Man. That were to shirk
The spiritual intellect's great work
And shirk it in vain. There is no release
In a bodkin[4] or disease,
Nor can there be a work so great
As that which cleans man's dirty slate.
While man can still his body keep
Wine or love drug him to sleep,
Waking he thanks the Lord that he
Has body and its stupidity,
But body gone he sleeps no more
And till his intellect grows sure
That all's arranged in one clear view
Pursues the thoughts that I pursue,
Then stands in judgment on his soul,
And, all work done, dismisses all
Out of intellect and sight
And sinks at last into the night.

Echo. Into the night.

1. *Cathleen ni Houlihan,* a nationalist play Yeats wrote with Lady Gregory and in which Maud Gonne played the title role in 1902. It helped inspire the Easter Rising of 1916.
2. Margot Ruddock (1907–1951), a young poet with whom Yeats had a brief affair in the 1930s and to whom he offered financial support when she suffered a nervous breakdown.
3. Coole Park, Lady Gregory's home, in disrepair since her death, in 1932.
4. Dagger. Cf. *Hamlet* 3.177–78: "When he himself might his quietus make / with a bare bodkin."

Man. O rocky voice
Shall we in that great night rejoice?
What do we know but that we face
One another in this place?
But hush, for I have lost the theme
Its joy or night seem but a dream;
Up there some hawk or owl has struck
Dropping out of sky or rock,
A stricken rabbit is crying out
And its cry distracts my thought.

1938 1939

The Circus Animals' Desertion

I

I sought a theme and sought for it in vain,
I sought it daily for six weeks or so.
Maybe at last being but a broken man
I must be satisfied with my heart, although
Winter and summer till old age began
My circus animals were all on show,
Those stilted boys, that burnished chariot,
Lion and woman and the Lord knows what.[5]

II

What can I but enumerate old themes,
First that sea-rider Oisin led by the nose
Through three enchanted islands,[6] allegorical dreams,
Vain gaiety, vain battle, vain repose,
Themes of the embittered heart, or so it seems,
That might adorn old songs or courtly shows;
But what cared I that set him on to ride,
I, starved for the bosom of his fairy bride.

And then a counter-truth filled out its play,
'The Countess Cathleen'[7] was the name I gave it,
She, pity-crazed, had given her soul away
But masterful Heaven had intervened to save it.
I thought my dear must her own soul destroy
So did fanaticism and hate enslave it,
And this brought forth a dream and soon enough
This dream itself had all my thought and love.

5. Yeats alludes to the ancient Irish heroes of his early work ("Those stilted boys"), the gilded carriage of his play *The Unicorn from the Stars,* and the lion in several of his poems, including "The Second Coming."

6. In the long poem *The Wanderings of Oisin* (1889), Yeats's first successful work, the poet-warrior Oisin is enchanted by the fairy Niamh, who leads him to the Islands of Delight, of Many Fears, and of Forgetfulness.

7. A play (published in 1892) in which the countess (an idealized version of Maud Gonne) sells her soul to the devil during a famine to buy food for the starving Irish poor, but she is taken up to heaven, for God "looks always on the motive, not the deed."

And when the Fool and Blind Man stole the bread
Cuchulain fought the ungovernable sea;[8]
Heart mysteries there, and yet when all is said
It was the dream itself enchanted me:
Character isolated by a deed
To engross the present and dominate memory.
Players and painted stage took all my love
And not those things that they were emblems of.

III

Those masterful images because complete
Grew in pure mind but out of what began?
A mound of refuse or the sweepings of a street,
Old kettles, old bottles, and a broken can,
Old iron, old bones, old rags, that raving slut
Who keeps the till. Now that my ladder's gone
I must lie down where all the ladders start
In the foul rag and bone shop of the heart.

1939

Politics

'In our time the destiny of man presents its meanings in political terms.'
—Thomas Mann[9]

How can I, that girl standing there,
My attention fix
On Roman or on Russian
Or on Spanish politics,
Yet here's a travelled man that knows
What he talks about,
And there's a politician
That has both read and thought,
And maybe what they say is true
Of war and war's alarms,
But O that I were young again
And held her in my arms.

May 1938 1939

8. In Yeats's play *On Baile's Strand* (1904), the legendary warrior Cuchulain, crazed by his discovery that he has killed his son, fights with the sea.
9. Yeats drew this quotation by the German writer Thomas Mann (1875–1955) from the essay "Public Speech and Private Speech in Poetry," by the American poet Archibald MacLeish (1892–1982). In a letter of May 24, 1938, Yeats says his poem is a reply to the essay, which, while praising his "public" language, criticizes him for not using "this 'public' language on what it evidently considered the right public material, politics."

Rudyard Kipling
1865–1936

Rudyard Kipling has seemed to many readers an entertainer and a rabble-rouser, a racist, a reactionary, always ready to write verses calculated to send young men off to be killed. He was, as George Orwell said in a 1942 review, "a jingo imperialist," and some of his poems, such as "Recessional," were treated as patriotic anthems for the British Empire. His opposition to Home Rule in Ireland and to women's suffrage, and poems such as "The White Man's Burden," have not aided his reputation. But although many of his poems almost have the sound of military music, others are quieter, less overstated, more tender and poignant. Kipling's views on war, empire, and social class have some complexity. He supported British imperialism, but also attacked British xenophobia. He famously wrote, "Oh, East is East, and West is West, and never the twain shall meet" in "The Ballad of East and West," but he could mock cultural distinctions absurdly drawn on the basis of eating and dress habits in "We and They": "Their full-dress is un-. / We dress up to Our ears." He rallies for war, but like other modern war poets he attends to its human tragedies and deprivations, brutalities and losses. In his terse, immediate, emotionally powerful "Epitaphs of the War," he even gives voice to an "Unknown Female Corpse," who begins: "Headless, lacking foot and hand."

Born in India of British parents, Kipling was a child of empire at a time when it seemed invulnerable. He believed that the citizens of Western Europe had a responsibility to journey east to teach—by force, if necessary—the so-called backward peoples how they might better their lives. He was a true conservative and a believer in "civilization," the ideal of a human community whose model is the city, where the many sorts of humankind go about their tasks. In his writing, he celebrates the expert worker—the engineer, mariner, soldier, and others who devise the machinery of society and keep it going. A writer of ghost stories, science fiction, and animal fables, Kipling is also a poet of great imagination and has a sharp, canny eye, an inquisitiveness about people and their inventions. The dark side of Kipling's view of civilization comes from his sense that the city is perpetually in danger—besieged from without by hostile tribes, menaced within by mendacious and greedy betrayers. Far from being boisterously optimistic, Kipling's social and political views often remind one of Joseph Conrad's.

Kipling was born on December 30, 1865, in Bombay, where his father had a post as a resident artist and museum curator. For the first years of his life, Kipling enjoyed privileges and luxuries as the spoiled child of two cultures. When he was six, his parents sent him and his younger sister back to England to be taught that they were in fact English. The children spent their first English years with a couple who made life hellish for them. Kipling's eyes were bad, he was clumsy and defenseless, and he was constantly bullied. He was rescued from what he was to call the House of Desolation after his mother visited and noted that when she was about to kiss him goodnight, he flinched as if to ward off a blow. When he was seventeen, Kipling returned to India, where he wrote for several newspapers and, on his own, wrote his first poems and short stories. He found himself at the center of a great web of gossip and information about the English in India, and the scandals, comic and tragic, gave Kipling the material he would shape into his poems and stories. He often wrote of common soldiers using their jargon and Cockney. The poems, many of them dramatic monologues, tend to take the form of long-lined stanzas, with head-on, unsubtle rhymes and thumping rhythms; easy to remember, they are often on the verge of being rousing songs.

In 1889, Kipling returned to England, his works already well known, his literary reputation consolidated. In 1892, he married an American woman, and for a time it seemed that he would move permanently to the United States: the couple built a house in her hometown, Brattleboro, Vermont. But after an embarrassing encounter with Kipling's drunken brother-in-law that resulted in legal action, he and his wife left the country. Back in England, they bought a country house—a curiously grim and menacing building—and there Kipling spent the rest of his days; he and his family traveled widely, but he never returned to India. He had three children: two girls, one of whom died of an ailment that nearly felled her father, and a son, who died in World War I.

During the Boer War (1899–1902), Kipling sided with the English against the Afrikaners, though many of his fellow men of letters were pro-Boer. In Africa as a journalist, Kipling had his first taste of genuine combat, and he wrote about it with enthusiasm, though his faith in the English cause slackened when he realized how ill-prepared the English were to defend themselves and their interests. Kipling had long been suspicious of the Germans, and when World War I came, he raised money, wrote poems exhorting young men to join the services, believed and retold every tale of German enormities that he heard. "The Hun is at the Gate!" he exclaimed ("For All We Have and Are"). Kipling lived for sixteen years after the armistice, long enough to see his work, gone out of fashion, treated almost with contempt. Kipling and King George V died within days of each other; it was said, "The King has gone and taken his trumpeter with him."

Danny Deever

"What are the bugles blowin' for?" said Files-on-Parade.
"To turn you out, to turn you out," the Colour-Sergeant[1] said.
"What makes you look so white, so white?" said Files-on-Parade.
"I'm dreadin' what I've got to watch," the Colour-Sergeant said.
For they're hangin' Danny Deever, you can hear the Dead March play,
The Regiment's in 'ollow square[2]—they're hangin' him to-day;
They've taken of his buttons off an' cut his stripes[3] away,
An' they're hangin' Danny Deever in the mornin'.

"What makes the rear-rank breathe so 'ard?" said Files-on-Parade.
"It's bitter cold, it's bitter cold," the Colour-Sergeant said.
"What makes that front-rank man fall down?" said Files-on-Parade.
"A touch o' sun, a touch o' sun," the Colour-Sergeant said.
They are hangin' Danny Deever, they are marchin' of 'im round,
They 'ave 'alted Danny Deever by 'is coffin on the ground;
An' 'e'll swing in 'arf a minute for a sneakin' shootin' hound—
O they're hangin' Danny Deever in the mornin'!

" 'Is cot was right-'and cot to mine," said Files-on-Parade.
" 'E's sleepin' out an' far to-night," the Colour-Sergeant said.
"I've drunk 'is beer a score o' times," said Files-on-Parade.
" 'E's drinkin' bitter beer[4] alone," the Colour-Sergeant said.
They are hangin' Danny Deever, you must mark 'im to 'is place,
For 'e shot a comrade sleepin'—you must look 'im in the face;
Nine 'undred of 'is county[5] an' the Regiment's disgrace,
While they're hangin' Danny Deever in the mornin'.

1. A high-ranking, noncommissioned army officer. *Files-on-Parade:* a private.
2. In this ceremonial formation, the troops line four sides of a parade square and face inward.
3. Chevrons denoting rank.
4. Or simply "bitter," a favorite variety of beer in British pubs.
5. English regiments often bear the name of the county from which most of the soldiers have been recruited.

"What's that so black agin the sun?" said Files-on-Parade.
"It's Danny fightin' 'ard for life," the Colour-Sergeant said.
"What's that that whimpers over'ead?" said Files-on-Parade.
"It's Danny's soul that's passin' now," the Colour-Sergeant said.
  For they're done with Danny Deever, you can 'ear the quickstep play,
  The Regiment's in column, an' they're marchin' us away;
  Ho! the young recruits are shakin', an' they'll want their beer to-day,
  After hangin' Danny Deever in the mornin'!

1892

Shillin' a Day

My name is O'Kelly, I've heard the Revelly[6]
From Birr to Bareilly, from Leeds to Lahore,
Hong-Kong and Peshawur.
Lucknow and Etawah,
And fifty-five more all endin' in "pore."[7]
Black Death and his quickness, the depth and the thickness
Of sorrow and sickness I've known on my way,
But I'm old and I'm nervis,
I'm cast from the Service,
And all I deserve is a shillin' a day.[8]

(*Chorus*) Shillin' a day,
Bloomin' good pay—
Lucky to touch it, a shillin' a day!

Oh, it drives me half crazy to think of the days I
Went slap for the Ghazi,[9] my sword at my side,
When we rode Hell-for-leather
Both squadrons together,
That didn't care whether we lived or we died.
But it's no use despairin', my wife must go charin'
An' me commissairin',[1] the pay-bills to better,
So if me you be'old
In the wet and the cold,
By the Grand Metropold,[2] won't you give me a letter?

(*Full chorus*) Give 'im a letter—
'Can't do no better,
Late Troop-Sergeant-Major an'—runs with a letter!
Think what 'e's been,

6. That is, reveille, trumpet signal to arise in the morning.
7. With the exception of Leeds (in England) and Hong Kong, all the places (including those "ending in 'pore' ") are in India, where the speaker served his army career.
8. That is, his pension; a shilling was then worth about a dollar.
9. Term used by the British for tribal rebels along the Indian frontier, who committed acts of violence against British officials in the belief that these acts would win them a place in paradise.
1. Or "commissionairing"; the commissionaires were an organization of pensioned ex-soldiers employed as porters or messengers. *Charin'*: or "charring"; housecleaning.
2. Grand Metropole, a swanky London hotel.

Think what 'e's seen.
Think of his pension an'——
GAWD SAVE THE QUEEN!

1892

Recessional[3]

God of our fathers, known of old,
  Lord of our far-flung battle-line,
Beneath whose awful Hand we hold
  Dominion over palm and pine—
Lord God of Hosts, be with us yet,
Lest we forget—lest we forget!

The tumult and the shouting dies;
  The Captains and the Kings depart:
Still stands Thine ancient sacrifice,
  And humble and a contrite heart.[4]
Lord God of Hosts, be with us yet,
Lest we forget—lest we forget!

Far-called, our navies melt away;
  On dune and headland sinks the fire:[5]
Lo, all our pomp of yesterday
  Is one with Nineveh and Tyre![6]
Judge of the Nations, spare us yet,
Lest we forget—lest we forget!

If, drunk with sight of power, we loose
  Wild tongues that have not Thee in awe,
Such boastings as the Gentiles use,
  Or lesser breeds without the Law—[7]
Lord God of Hosts, be with us yet,
Lest we forget—lest we forget!

For heathen heart that puts her trust
  In reeking tube and iron shard,
All valiant dust that builds on dust,
  And guarding, calls not Thee to guard,
For frantic boast and foolish word—
Thy mercy on Thy people, Lord!

1897

1899, 1903

3. Hymn sung as clergy and choir leave the church at the end of the service. Kipling wrote this on the occasion of the Jubilee celebrations in honor of Victoria's sixtieth year as queen, events that had prompted much chauvinistic boasting.
4. "The sacrifices of God are a broken spirit: a broken and a contrite heart, O God, thou wilt not despise" (Psalm 51.17).
5. On Jubilee night, bonfires were lit all over England.
6. Once capitals of great empires; in Assyria and Phoenicia, respectively.
7. Cf. Romans 2.14: "For when the Gentiles, which have not the law, do by nature the things contained in the law, these, having not the law, are a law unto themselves."

Harp Song of the Dane Women

("The Knights of the Joyous Venture"—*Puck of Pook's Hill*)[8]

What is a woman that you forsake her,
And the hearth-fire and the home-acre,
To go with the old grey Widow-maker?

She has no house to lay a guest in—
But one chill bed for all to rest in,
That the pale suns and the stray bergs nest in.

She has no strong white arms to fold you,
But the ten-times-fingering weed to hold you—
Out on the rocks where the tide has rolled you.

Yet, when the signs of summer thicken,
And the ice breaks, and the birch-buds quicken,
Yearly you turn from our side, and sicken—

Sicken again for the shouts and the slaughters.
You steal away to the lapping waters,
And look at your ship in her winter-quarters.

You forget our mirth, and talk at the tables,
The kine[9] in the shed and the horse in the stables—
To pitch her sides and go over her cables.

Then you drive out where the storm-clouds swallow,
And the sound of your oar-blades, falling hollow,
Is all we have left through the months to follow.

Ah, what is Woman that you forsake her,
And the hearth-fire and the home-acre,
To go with the old grey Widow-maker?

1906

A Pict Song[1]

("The Winged Hats"—*Puck of Pook's Hill*)

Rome never looks where she treads.
  Always her heavy hooves fall,
On our stomachs, our hearts or our heads;

8. In Kipling's *Puck of Pook's Hill,* the children's book in which this poem originally appeared, the sprite Puck, from Shakespeare's *Midsummer Night's Dream,* appears to two children and introduces them to ghosts from British history. In the story "The Knights of the Joyous Venture," the knight Sir Richard describes his adventures with Danish pirates.

9. Cows (archaic).

1. The Picts were an ancient people inhabiting northern Britain when the Romans invaded. This song from *Puck of Pook's Hill* occurs after the story "The Winged Hats" (that is, the helmets worn by the Norse and Germanic invaders of Britain in the fourth and fifth centuries).

And Rome never heeds when we bawl.
Her sentries pass on—that is all,
And we gather behind them in hordes,
And plot to reconquer the Wall,
With only our tongues for our swords.

We are the Little Folk—we!
Too little to love or to hate.
Leave us alone and you'll see
How we can drag down the State!
We are the worm in the wood!
We are the rot at the root!
We are the taint in the blood!
We are the thorn in the foot!

Mistletoe killing an oak—[2]
Rats gnawing cables in two—
Moths making holes in a cloak—
How they must love what they do!
Yes—and we Little Folk too,
We are busy as they—
Working our works out of view—
Watch, and you'll see it some day!

No indeed! We are not strong,
But we know Peoples that are.
Yes, and we'll guide them along,
To smash and destroy you in War!
We shall be slaves just the same?
Yes, we have always been slaves,
But you—you will die of the shame,
And then we shall dance on your graves!

We are the Little Folk, we, etc.

1906

The Way through the Woods

("Marklake Witches"—*Rewards and Fairies*)[3]

They shut the road through the woods
Seventy years ago.
Weather and rain have undone it again,
And now you would never know
There was once a road through the woods
Before they planted the trees.
It is underneath the coppice[4] and heath,
And the thin anemones.

2. Mistletoe is a parasitic plant that lives on trees, especially the oak. It was sacred to the Druids, high priests of the Celtic people, who may have been related to the Picts.
3. A sequel (1910) to Kipling's *Puck of Pook's Hill*.
4. Grove of small trees.

Only the keeper sees
That, where the ring-dove broods,
And the badgers roll at ease,
There was once a road through the woods.

Yet, if you enter the woods
Of a summer evening late,
When the night-air cools on the trout-ringed pools
Where the otter whistles his mate,
(They fear not men in the woods,
Because they see so few.)
You will hear the beat of a horse's feet,
And the swish of a skirt in the dew,
Steadily cantering through
The misty solitudes,
As though they perfectly knew
The old lost road through the woods. . . .
But there is no road through the woods.

1910

Epitaphs of the War

"Equality of Sacrifice"

A. "I was a Have." B. "I was a 'have-not.' "
(*Together.*) "What hast thou given which I gave not?"

A Servant

We were together since the War began.
He was my servant—and the better man.

A Son

My son was killed while laughing at some jest. I would I knew
What it was, and it might serve me in a time when jests are few.

An Only Son

I have slain none except my Mother. She
(Blessing her slayer) died of grief for me.

Ex-Clerk

Pity not! The Army gave
Freedom to a timid slave:
In which Freedom did he find
Strength of body, will, and mind:
By which strength he came to prove
Mirth, Companionship, and Love:

For which Love to Death he went:
In which Death he lies content.

The Wonder

Body and Spirit I surrendered whole
To harsh Instructors—and received a soul . . .
If mortal man could change me through and through
From all I was—what may The God not do?

Hindu Sepoy[5] in France

This man in his own country prayed we know not to what Powers.
We pray Them to reward him for his bravery in ours.

The Coward

I could not look on Death, which being known,
Men led me to him, blindfold and alone.

Shock

My name, my speech, my self I had forgot.
My wife and children came—I knew them not.
I died. My Mother followed. At her call
And on her bosom I remembered all.

A Grave Near Cairo

Gods of the Nile, should this stout fellow here
Get out—get out! He knows not shame nor fear.

Pelicans in the Wilderness
(A Grave Near Halfa)[6]

The blown sand heaps on me, that none may learn
   Where I am laid for whom my children grieve. . . .
O wings that beat at dawning, ye return
   Out of the desert to your young at eve!

Two Canadian Memorials

I

We giving all gained all.
   Neither lament us nor praise.
Only in all things recall,
   It is Fear, not Death that slays.

5. Indian soldier under European—usually British—command.

6. In the Sudan.

II

From little towns in a far land we came,
  To save our honour and a world aflame.
By little towns in a far land we sleep;
  And trust that world we won for you to keep.

The Favour

Death favoured me from the first, well knowing I could not endure
  To wait on him day by day. He quitted my betters and came
Whistling over the fields, and, when he had made all sure,
  "Thy line is at end," he said, "but at least I have saved its name."

The Beginner

On the first hour of my first day
  In the front trench I fell.
(Children in boxes at a play
  Stand up to watch it well.)

R.A.F.[7] *(Aged Eighteen)*

Laughing through clouds, his milk-teeth still unshed,
Cities and men he smote from overhead.
His deaths delivered, he returned to play
Childlike, with childish things now put away.

The Refined Man

I was of delicate mind. I stepped aside for my needs,
  Disdaining the common office. I was seen from afar and killed. . . .
How is this matter for mirth? Let each man be judged by his deeds.
  I have paid my price to live with myself on the terms that I willed.

Native Water-Carrier (M.E.F.)

Prometheus[8] brought down fire to men.
  This brought up water.
The Gods are jealous—now, as then,
  Giving no quarter.[9]

Bombed in London

On land and sea I strove with anxious care
To escape conscription. It was in the air!

7. Royal Air Force.
8. Greek god who gave fire to humanity and was subsequently punished by Zeus. *M.E.F.*: Mediterranean Expeditionary Force.
9. That is, giving no merciful exemption from being put to death.

The Sleepy Sentinel

Faithless the watch that I kept: now I have none to keep.
I was slain because I slept: now I am slain I sleep.
Let no man reproach me again, whatever watch is unkept—
I sleep because I am slain. They slew me because I slept.

Batteries Out of Ammunition

If any mourn us in the workshop, say
We died because the shift kept holiday.

Common Form

If any question why we died,
Tell them, because our fathers lied.

A Dead Statesman

I could not dig: I dared not rob:
Therefore I lied to please the mob.
Now all my lies are proved untrue
And I must face the men I slew.
What tale shall serve me here among
Mine angry and defrauded young?

The Rebel

If I had clamoured at Thy Gate
   For gift of Life on Earth,
And, thrusting through the souls that wait,
   Flung headlong into birth—
Even then, even then, for gin and snare
   About my pathway spread,
Lord, I had mocked Thy thoughtful care
   Before I joined the Dead!
But now? . . . I was beneath Thy Hand
   Ere yet the Planets came.
And now—though Planets pass, I stand
   The witness to Thy shame!

The Obedient

Daily, though no ears attended,
   Did my prayers arise.
Daily, though no fire descended,
   Did I sacrifice.
Though my darkness did not lift,
   Though I faced no lighter odds,
Though the Gods bestowed no gift,
                        None the less,
   None the less, I served the Gods!

A Drifter off Tarentum[1]

He from the wind-bitten North with ship and companions descended,
Searching for eggs of death spawned by invisible hulls.
Many he found and drew forth. Of a sudden the fishery ended
In flame and a clamorous breath known to the eye-pecking gulls.

Destroyers in Collision

For Fog and Fate no charm is found
To lighten or amend.
I, hurrying to my bride, was drowned—
Cut down by my best friend.

Convoy Escort

I was a shepherd to fools
Causelessly bold or afraid.
They would not abide by my rules.
Yet they escaped. For I stayed.

Unknown Female Corpse

Headless, lacking foot and hand,
Horrible I come to land.
I beseech all women's sons
Know I was a mother once.

Raped and Revenged

One used and butchered me: another spied
Me broken—for which thing an hundred died.
So it was learned among the heathen hosts
How much a freeborn woman's favour costs.

Salonikan[2] *Grave*

I have watched a thousand days
Push out and crawl into night
Slowly as tortoises.
Now I, too, follow these.
It is fever, and not the fight—
Time, not battle,—that slays.

1. Roman name for Taranto, a city in southern Italy.

2. Of Thessalonica (also called Salonika), a Greek city destroyed by fire in 1917.

The Bridegroom

Call me not false, beloved,
  If, from thy scarce-known breast
So little time removed,
  In other arms I rest.

For this more ancient bride,
  Whom coldly I embrace,
Was constant at my side
  Before I saw thy face.

Our marriage, often set—
  By miracle delayed—
At last is consummate,
  And cannot be unmade.

Live, then, whom Life shall cure,
  Almost, of Memory,
And leave us to endure
  Its immortality.

V.A.D.[3] *(Mediterranean)*

Ah, would swift ships had never been, for then we ne'er had found,
These harsh Ægean[4] rocks between, this little virgin drowned,
Whom neither spouse nor child shall mourn, but men she nursed
    through pain
And—certain keels for whose return the heathen look in vain.

Actors

ON A MEMORIAL TABLET IN HOLY TRINITY CHURCH, STRATFORD-ON-AVON[5]

We counterfeited once for your disport
  Men's joy and sorrow: but our day has passed.
We pray you pardon all where we fell short—
  Seeing we were your servants to this last.

Journalists

ON A PANEL IN THE HALL OF THE INSTITUTE OF JOURNALISTS

We have served our day.

1914–18

1919, 1940

3. Voluntary Aid Detachment.
4. Aegean Sea: portion of the Mediterranean Sea between Greece and Turkey.
5. District of England in Warwickshire; birthplace of Shakespeare.

We and They

("*A Friend of the Family*")[6]

Father, Mother, and Me
  Sister and Auntie say
All the people like us are We,
  And every one else is They.
And They live over the sea,
  While We live over the way,
But—would you believe it?—They look upon We
  As only a sort of They!

We eat pork and beef
  With cow-horn-handled knives.
They who gobble Their rice off a leaf,
  Are horrified out of Their lives;
And They who live up a tree,
  And feast on grubs and clay,
(Isn't it scandalous?) look upon We
  As a simply disgusting They!

We shoot birds with a gun.
  They stick lions with spears.
Their full-dress is un-.
  We dress up to Our ears.
They like Their friends for tea.
  We like Our friends to stay;
And, after all that, They look upon We
  As an utterly ignorant They!

We eat kitcheny food.
  We have doors that latch.
They drink milk or blood,
  Under an open thatch.
We have Doctors to fee.[7]
  They have Wizards to pay.
And (impudent heathen!) They look upon We
  As a quite impossible They!

All good people agree,
  And all good people say,
All nice people, like Us, are We
  And every one else is They:
But if you cross over the sea,
  Instead of over the way,
You may end by (think of it!) looking on We
  As only a sort of They!

1926

6. A story by Kipling; the story and poem appeared together in *Debits and Credits*.

7. That is, pay.

Edgar Lee Masters
1868–1950

The characterization of a small town attracted poets early in the twentieth century as a new theme and binding agent for lyrical verse. Edwin Arlington Robinson wrote about his native Gardiner, Maine, under the name of Tilbury Town, and A. E. Housman situated his Shropshire lad in the actual place of Ludlow. Edgar Lee Masters combined an interest in the small town as the place where he had spent his childhood with a novelist's search for individual peculiarities. The technique that proved most important for him was to portray a dead town rather than a live one. After death, lives are clarified; delusions are gone and pretensions with them. If one could write true epitaphs, instead of conventional ones, a whole community might appear as it actually was rather than as it seemed to be. These ideas animated Masters's *Spoon River Anthology,* his one memorable book in a lifetime of writing. It shares a painful realism that was achieved by several writers in the Chicago school of poets and also in the prose of Theodore Dreiser and later of Ernest Hemingway.

Masters was born on August 23, 1868, in Garnett, Kansas. His family soon moved to Illinois, and he grew up in Lewistown, near Springfield, where his father was an unsuccessful lawyer. In 1892, after spending a year at Knox College, in Galesburg, he went to Chicago, where he gradually built up a successful law practice. For eight years, he was a partner of the greatest defense attorney of the day, Clarence Darrow. Masters shared Darrow's liberal, agnostic, humanitarian outlook.

An early interest in the English Romantic poets, and in Edgar Allan Poe, had not left him, and in the first years of the twentieth century he published three books. When the editor of *Reedy's Mirror,* in St. Louis, gave Masters a copy of J. W. Mackail's *Selected Epigrams from the Greek Anthology,* which had been revised and reissued in 1907, Masters felt challenged to see if he could adapt the mode to modern circumstances, and the result was a burst of creative force. Always an admirer of Walt Whitman, whose biography he was to write, he determined on free verse. He sought to blend the universality of classical poetry with the localism of the American middle west.

Spoon River is the name of an actual river in Illinois, but the town Masters portrays is a combination of Lewistown and Petersburg, where his grandparents lived, and the river itself includes the Sangamon River as well. By virtue of being far removed, in his Chicago office, from the small towns of his childhood, Masters could scrutinize them with affection and detachment. He had also his legal experience of people's mixed and shabby motives, in big as in small places. Harriet Monroe, editor of *Poetry* magazine, helped Masters issue the poems in book form in 1915, and *Spoon River Anthology* was an instant success. Perhaps no book of verse has gone so quickly through so many editions, in part because Masters appeared to be laying bare the dark side of small-town life, its suicides, murders, illicit loves. But Masters emphasized later that the book was organized in terms of Hell, Purgatory, and Heaven (on Earth), and it began with ne'er-do-wells, moved on to mixed, purgatorial types, and concluded with those who had achieved some illumination. The book's success came in part from the inspired simplicity of its aim. The types of people were familiar; their sly misdoings were those that everyone could recognize their neighbors to be guilty of. The style was not ambitious, but often hit home. Its prosiness allowed for unexpectedly terse phrases inlaid among the slack ones. The solemn reverberations of death mixed with the flamboyant chatter of life.

Masters's later life was anticlimactic, with many now-forgotten books, many quarrels with other writers, and many extramarital pursuits. In 1923, he left Chicago and settled, for most of his remaining years, in New York. He incurred much ire when, in 1931, he published a debunking biography of Abraham Lincoln (over which he and fellow poet, fellow Chicagoan, and fellow Lincoln biographer Carl Sandburg broke). In a gesture of posthumous reconciliation, the epitaph on his tombstone begins, "Good friends, let's to the fields."

From Spoon River Anthology[1]

The Hill

Where are Elmer, Herman, Bert, Tom and Charley,
The weak of will, the strong of arm, the clown, the boozer, the fighter?
All, all are sleeping on the hill.

One passed in a fever.
One was burned in a mine,
One was killed in a brawl,
One died in a jail,
One fell from a bridge toiling for children and wife—
All, all are sleeping, sleeping, sleeping on the hill.

Where are Ella, Kate, Mag, Lizzie and Edith,
The tender heart, the simple soul, the loud, the proud, the happy one?—
All, all are sleeping on the hill.

One died in shameful child-birth,
One of a thwarted love,
One at the hands of a brute in a brothel,
One of a broken pride, in the search for heart's desire;
One after life in far-away London and Paris
Was brought to her little space by Ella and Kate and Mag—
All, all are sleeping, sleeping on the hill.

Where are Uncle Isaac and Aunt Emily,
And old Towny Kincaid and Sevigne Houghton,
And Major Walker who had talked
With venerable men of the revolution?—
All, all are sleeping on the hill.

They brought them dead sons from the war,
And daughters whom life had crushed,
And their children fatherless, crying—
All, all are sleeping, sleeping, sleeping on the hill.

1. The title derives from the *Greek Anthology*, a collection of poems—many of them epitaphs—written from the seventh century B.C.E. to the tenth century C.E. One epitaph reads, for example: "I Dionysius of Tarsus lie here at sixty, having never married; and I would that my father had not."

Where is Old Fiddler Jones
Who played with life all his ninety years,
Braving the sleet with bared breast,
Drinking, rioting, thinking neither of wife nor kin,
Nor gold, nor love, nor heaven?
Lo! he babbles of the fish-frys of long ago,
Of the horse-races of long ago at Clary's Grove,
Of what Abe Lincoln said
One time at Springfield.

Amanda Barker

Henry got me with child,
Knowing that I could not bring forth life
Without losing my own.
In my youth therefore I entered the portals of dust.
Traveler, it is believed in the village where I lived
That Henry loved me with a husband's love,
But I proclaim from the dust
That he slew me to gratify his hatred.

Fiddler Jones

The earth keeps some vibration going
There in your heart, and that is you.
And if the people find you can fiddle,
Why, fiddle you must, for all your life.
What do you see, a harvest of clover?
Or a meadow to walk through to the river?
The wind's in the corn; you rub your hands
For beeves hereafter ready for market;
Or else you hear the rustle of skirts
Like the girls when dancing at Little Grove.
To Cooney Potter a pillar of dust
Or whirling leaves meant ruinous drouth;
They looked to me like Red-Head Sammy
Stepping it off, to "Toor-a-Loor."
How could I till my forty acres
Not to speak of getting more,
With a medley of horns, bassoons and piccolos
Stirred in my brain by crows and robins
And the creak of a wind-mill—only these?
And I never started to plow in my life
That someone did not stop in the road
And take me away to a dance or picnic.
I ended up with forty acres;
I ended up with a broken fiddle—

And a broken laugh, and a thousand memories,
And not a single regret.

Petit, the Poet

Seeds in a dry pod, tick, tick, tick,
Tick, tick, tick, like mites in a quarrel—
Faint iambics that the full breeze wakens—
But the pine tree makes a symphony thereof.
Triolets, villanelles, rondels, rondeaus,
Ballades by the score with the same old thought:
The snows and the roses of yesterday are vanished;[2]
And what is love but a rose that fades?
Life all around me here in the village:
Tragedy, comedy, valor and truth,
Courage, constancy, heroism, failure—
All in the loom, and oh what patterns!
Woodlands, meadows, streams and rivers—
Blind to all of it all my life long.
Triolets, villanelles, rondels, rondeaus,
Seeds in a dry pod, tick, tick, tick,
Tick, tick, tick, what little iambics,
While Homer and Whitman roared in the pines.

Elsa Wertman

I was a peasant girl from Germany,
Blue-eyed, rosy, happy and strong.
And the first place I worked was at Thomas Greene's.
On a summer's day when she was away
He stole into the kitchen and took me
Right in his arms and kissed me on my throat,
I turning my head. Then neither of us
Seemed to know what happened.
And I cried for what would become of me.
And cried and cried as my secret began to show.
One day Mrs. Greene said she understood,
And would make no trouble for me,
And, being childless, would adopt it.
(He had given her a farm to be still.)
So she hid in the house and sent out rumors,
As if it were going to happen to her.
And all went well and the child was born—They were so kind to me.

2. Cf. the refrain of the "Ballade des dames du temps jadis," by French poet François Villon (1431–1463?): "But where are the snows of yesteryear?"

Later I married Gus Wertman, and years passed.
But—at political rallies when sitters-by thought I was crying
At the eloquence of Hamilton Greene—
That was not it.
No! I wanted to say:
That's my son! That's my son!

Hamilton Greene

I was the only child of Frances Harris of Virginia
And Thomas Greene of Kentucky,
Of valiant and honorable blood both.
To them I owe all that I became,
Judge, member of Congress, leader in the State.
From my mother I inherited
Vivacity, fancy, language;
From my father will, judgment, logic.
All honor to them
For what service I was to the people!

Anne Rutledge[3]

Out of me unworthy and unknown
The vibrations of deathless music:
"With malice toward none, with charity for all."[4]
Out of me the forgiveness of millions toward millions,
And the beneficent face of a nation
Shining with justice and truth.
I am Anne Rutledge who sleep beneath these weeds,
Beloved in life of Abraham Lincoln,
Wedded to him, not through union,
But through separation.
Bloom forever, O Republic,
From the dust of my bosom!

1915

3. A girl Abraham Lincoln knew in New Salem, Illinois. She died at nineteen, and one of Lincoln's biographers insisted that she was the only true love of his life.

4. From Lincoln's Second Inaugural Address, March 4, 1865.

Edwin Arlington Robinson
1869–1935

Edwin Arlington Robinson was born, "with his skin inside out" (as he said), on December 22, 1869, in Head Tide, Maine. At the age of one he was taken by his parents to another small, bleak Maine town, Gardiner, where he spent his childhood. It was in Gardiner, which he renamed Tilbury Town, that he situated much of his poetry. Robinson had a difficult childhood. He wrote Amy Lowell that at the age of six, as he remembered, he sat in a rocking chair and wondered why he had been born. In this, as in much else, he resembles the lonely, dejected characters, fictive and real, whose stories he tells in poems such as "Miniver Cheevy": "He wept that he was ever born, / And he had reasons."

As a boy, he had an older friend, Dr. Alanson Tucker Schumann, who gave him assignments in common and uncommon verse forms, which seem to have suited Robinson's need for the settling effect of known patterns. Asked later why he did not try free verse, he replied with characteristic self-deprecation, "I write badly enough as it is." From 1891 to 1893, Robinson attended Harvard University, where he committed himself increasingly to literature: "I never could do anything but write verse," he was to tell his biographer on his deathbed (Chard Powers Smith, *Where the Light Falls,* 1965). At his own expense, he began publishing books of poetry in 1896, and his third book (*Captain Craig,* 1902) came to the notice of President Theodore Roosevelt, who wrote a magazine article in praise of Robinson and found him a sinecure in the New York Custom House, where he stayed for five years and fell prey to alcohol. During the 1920s, he began to publish a series of long poems, many on Arthurian subjects. Whether he wrote of Tristram or of Cavender, his characters were tormented by up-to-date anxieties.

Most readers prefer Robinson's short lyrics; in their melodious yet intellectual language, he offers a deeply felt account of the indignities of life and of its occasional mysterious rewards. Robinson writes in melancholy accents of the passage of time and the failure of lives. The shimmer of past glories, of "the days of old," haunt the impoverished present. Robinson's gifts for brief narrative, character sketch, and plangent wit are considerable. "I sing," Robinson wrote of his first book, "in my own particular manner, of heaven & hell and now and then of natural things (supposing they exist) of a more prosy connotation than those generally admitted into the domain of metre" (letter of October 28, 1896). His diction is down-to-earth and economical, yet his lines are elegant and smartly turned. Formal discipline and irony help contain the pathos; terse phrases and quiet humor counterbalance the lugubrious brooding. The gloom is occasionally broken, too, when Robinson's characters find themselves suddenly bathed in an unearned radiance. But often they find no such redemption: "Miniver Cheevy, born too late, / Scratched his head and kept on thinking; / Miniver coughed, and called it fate, / And kept on drinking."

Robinson's work invites comparison with Robert Frost's presentation of the same New England landscape in colloquial language, with Edgar Lee Masters's chronicles of small-town life, and with Thomas Hardy's bleak outlook. Interested in Herbert Spencer's evolutionary meliorism and in Ralph Waldo Emerson's transcendentalism, Robinson emphasized that he was not a Christian. "There is no 'philosophy' in my poetry," he said in a letter, "beyond an implication of an ordered universe and a sort of deterministic negation of the general futility that appears to be the basis of 'rational' thought" (January 1, 1930). Robinson was signally honored in his lifetime, winning three Pulitzer Prizes and acclaimed, in the last two decades of his life, as the preeminent poet of the day. If his achievement now seems more modest, he is superb within his limited range.

Luke Havergal

Go to the western gate, Luke Havergal,
There where the vines cling crimson on the wall,
And in the twilight wait for what will come.
The leaves will whisper there of her, and some,
Like flying words, will strike you as they fall;
But go, and if you listen she will call.
Go the western gate, Luke Havergal—
Luke Havergal.

No, there is not a dawn in eastern skies
To rift the fiery night that's in your eyes;
But there, where western glooms are gathering,
The dark will end the dark, if anything:
God slays Himself with every leaf that flies,
And hell is more than half of paradise.
No, there is not a dawn in eastern skies—
In eastern skies.

Out of a grave I come to tell you this,
Out of a grave I come to quench the kiss
That flames upon your forehead with a glow
That blinds you to the way that you must go.
Yes, there is yet one way to where she is,
Bitter, but one that faith may never miss.
Out of a grave I come to tell you this—
To tell you this.

There is the western gate, Luke Havergal,
There are the crimson leaves upon the wall.
Go, for the winds are tearing them away,—
Nor think to riddle the dead words they say,
Nor any more to feel them as they fall;
But go, and if you trust her she will call.
There is the western gate, Luke Havergal—
Luke Havergal.

1896

Richard Cory

Whenever Richard Cory went down town,
We people on the pavement looked at him:
He was a gentleman from sole to crown,
Clean favored, and imperially slim.

And he was always quietly arrayed,
And he was always human when he talked;
But still he fluttered pulses when he said,
"Good-morning," and he glittered when he walked.

And he was rich—yes, richer than a king—
And admirably schooled in every grace:
In fine, we thought that he was everything
To make us wish that we were in his place.

So on we worked, and waited for the light,
And went without the meat, and cursed the bread;
And Richard Cory, one calm summer night,
Went home and put a bullet through his head.

1897

Reuben Bright

Because he was a butcher and thereby
Did earn an honest living (and did right),
I would not have you think that Reuben Bright
Was any more a brute than you or I;
For when they told him that his wife must die,
He stared at them, and shook with grief and fright,
And cried like a great baby half that night,
And made the women cry to see him cry.

And after she was dead, and he had paid
The singers and the sexton and the rest,
He packed a lot of things that she had made
Most mournfully away in an old chest
Of hers, and put some chopped-up cedar boughs
In with them, and tore down the slaughter house.

1897

Calverly's

We go no more to Calverly's,
From there the lights are few and low;
And who are there to see by them,
Or what they see, we do not know.
Poor strangers of another tongue
May now creep in from anywhere,
And we, forgotten, be no more
Than twilight on a ruin there.

We two, the remnant. All the rest
Are cold and quiet. You nor I,
Nor fiddle now, nor flagon-lid,
May ring them back from where they lie.
No fame delays oblivion
For them, but something yet survives:
A record written fair, could we
But read the book of scattered lives.

There'll be a page for Leffingwell,
And one for Lingard, the Moon-calf;
And who knows what for Clavering,
Who died because he couldn't laugh?
Who knows or cares? No sign is here,
No face, no voice, no memory;
No Lingard with his eerie joy,
No Clavering, no Calverly.

We cannot have them here with us
To say where their light lives are gone,
Or if they be of other stuff
Than are the moons of Ilion.[1]
So, be their place of one estate
With ashes, echoes, and old wars,—
Or ever we be of the night,
Or we be lost among the stars.

1910

How Annandale Went Out

"They called it Annandale—and I was there
To flourish, to find words, and to attend:
Liar, physician, hypocrite, and friend,
I watched him; and the sight was not so fair
As one or two that I have seen elsewhere:
An apparatus not for me to mend—
A wreck, with hell between him and the end,
Remained of Annandale; and I was there.

"I knew the ruin as I knew the man;
So put the two together, if you can,
Remembering the worst you know of me.
Now view yourself as I was, on the spot—
With a slight kind of engine.[2] Do you see?
Like this . . . You wouldn't hang me? I thought not."

1910

1. Ancient Troy.

2. That is, a hypodermic needle.

Miniver Cheevy

Miniver Cheevy, child of scorn,
  Grew lean while he assailed the seasons;
He wept that he was ever born,
  And he had reasons.

Miniver loved the days of old
  When swords were bright and steeds were prancing;
The vision of a warrior bold
  Would set him dancing.

Miniver sighed for what was not,
  And dreamed, and rested from his labors;
He dreamed of Thebes and Camelot,
  And Priam's neighbors.[3]

Miniver mourned the ripe renown
  That made so many a name so fragrant;
He mourned Romance, now on the town,
  And Art, a vagrant.

Miniver loved the Medici,[4]
  Albeit he had never seen one;
He would have sinned incessantly
  Could he have been one.

Miniver cursed the commonplace
  And eyed a khaki suit with loathing;
He missed the mediæval grace
  Of iron clothing.

Miniver scorned the gold he sought,
  But sore annoyed was he without it;
Miniver thought, and thought, and thought,
  And thought about it.

Miniver Cheevy, born too late,
  Scratched his head and kept on thinking;
Miniver coughed, and called it fate,
  And kept on drinking.

1910

3. Thebes was the setting of many Greek legends, including that of King Oedipus; Camelot was the location of King Arthur's court; Priam was the last king of Troy, and his compatriots included Helen, Aeneas, and Hector.

4. Florentine merchant-princes of the Renaissance who were famous both as powerful rulers and as patrons of the arts.

For a Dead Lady

No more with overflowing light
Shall fill the eyes that now are faded,
Nor shall another's fringe with night
Their woman-hidden world as they did.
No more shall quiver down the days
The flowing wonder of her ways,
Whereof no language may requite
The shifting and the many-shaded.

The grace, divine, definitive,
Clings only as a faint forestalling;
The laugh that love could not forgive
Is hushed, and answers to no calling;
The forehead and the little ears
Have gone where Saturn keeps the years;[5]
The breast where roses could not live
Has done with rising and with falling.

The beauty, shattered by the laws
That have creation in their keeping,
No longer trembles at applause,
Or over children that are sleeping;
And we who delve in beauty's lore
Know all that we have known before
Of what inexorable cause
Makes Time so vicious in his reaping.

1910

Eros Turannos[6]

She fears him, and will always ask
  What fated her to choose him;
She meets in his engaging mask
  All reasons to refuse him;
But what she meets and what she fears
Are less than are the downward years,
Drawn slowly to the foamless weirs
  Of age, were she to lose him.

Between a blurred sagacity
  That once had power to sound him,
And Love, that will not let him be
  The Judas that she found him,
Her pride assuages her almost,

5. Saturn, or Cronos, the deposed ruler of the Roman gods, was often erroneously associated with time ("Chronos").
6. Love, the king; also tyrant (Greek).

As if it were alone the cost.—
He sees that he will not be lost,
And waits and looks around him.

A sense of ocean and old trees
Envelops and allures him;
Tradition, touching all he sees,
Beguiles and reassures him;
And all her doubts of what he says
Are dimmed with what she knows of days—
Till even prejudice delays
And fades, and she secures him.

The falling leaf inaugurates
The reign of her confusion;
The pounding wave reverberates
The dirge of her illusion;
And home, where passion lived and died,
Becomes a place where she can hide,
While all the town and harbor side
Vibrate with her seclusion.

We tell you, tapping on our brows,
The story as it should be,—
As if the story of a house
Were told, or ever could be;
We'll have no kindly veil between
Her visions and those we have seen,—
As if we guessed what hers have been,
Or what they are or would be.

Meanwhile we do no harm; for they
That with a god have striven,
Not hearing much of what we say,
Take what the god has given;
Though like waves breaking it may be,
Or like a changed familiar tree,
Or like a stairway to the sea
Where down the blind are driven.

1916

The Mill

The miller's wife had waited long,
The tea was cold, the fire was dead;
And there might yet be nothing wrong
In how he went and what he said:
"There are no millers any more,"

Was all that she had heard him say;
And he had lingered at the door
So long that it seemed yesterday.

Sick with a fear that had no form
She knew that she was there at last;
And in the mill there was a warm
And mealy fragrance of the past.
What else there was would only seem
To say again what he had meant;
And what was hanging from a beam
Would not have heeded where she went.

And if she thought it followed her,
She may have reasoned in the dark
That one way of the few there were
Would hide her and would leave no mark:
Black water, smooth above the weir
Like starry velvet in the night,
Though ruffled once, would soon appear
The same as ever to the sight.

1920

The Dark Hills

Dark hills at evening in the west,
Where sunset hovers like a sound
Of golden horns that sang to rest
Old bones of warriors under ground,
Far now from all the bannered ways
Where flash the legions of the sun,
You fade—as if the last of days
Were fading, and all wars were done.

1920

Mr. Flood's Party

Old Eben Flood, climbing alone one night
Over the hill between the town below
And the forsaken upland hermitage
That held as much as he should ever know
On earth again of home, paused warily.
The road was his with not a native near;
And Eben, having leisure, said aloud,
For no man else in Tilbury Town to hear:

"Well, Mr. Flood, we have the harvest moon
Again, and we may not have many more;
The bird is on the wing, the poet says,[7]
And you and I have said it here before.
Drink to the bird." He raised up to the light
The jug that he had gone so far to fill,
And answered huskily: "Well, Mr. Flood,
Since you propose it, I believe I will."

Alone, as if enduring to the end
A valiant armor of scarred hopes outworn,
He stood there in the middle of the road
Like Roland's ghost winding a silent horn.[8]
Below him, in the town among the trees,
Where friends of other days had honored him,
A phantom salutation of the dead
Rang thinly till old Eben's eyes were dim.

Then, as a mother lays her sleeping child
Down tenderly, fearing it may awake,
He set the jug down slowly at his feet
With trembling care, knowing that most things break;
And only when assured that on firm earth
It stood, as the uncertain lives of men
Assuredly did not, he paced away,
And with his hand extended paused again:

"Well, Mr. Flood, we have not met like this
In a long time; and many a change has come
To both of us, I fear, since last it was
We had a drop together. Welcome home!"
Convivially returning with himself,
Again he raised the jug up to the light;
And with an acquiescent quaver said:
"Well, Mr. Flood, if you insist, I might.

"Only a very little, Mr. Flood—
For auld lang syne. No more, sir; that will do."
So, for the time, apparently it did,
And Eben evidently thought so too;
For soon amid the silver loneliness
Of night he lifted up his voice and sang,
Secure, with only two moons listening,
Until the whole harmonious landscape rang—

7. Cf. *The Rubáiyát of Omar Khayyám,* translated by the English poet Edward FitzGerald (1809–1883), stanza 7: "Come, fill the Cup, and in the Fire of Spring / Your Winter-garment of Repentance fling: / The Bird of Time has but a little way / To flutter—and the Bird is on the wing."

8. Roland is the hero of the medieval French epic *Chanson de Roland* (*Song of Roland,* c. 1000). He and his troops were besieged at the mountain pass of Roncevaux, but he refused to blow his horn, the signal for help from Charlemagne's army, until just before dying.

"For auld lang syne." The weary throat gave out,
The last word wavered, and the song was done.
He raised again the jug regretfully
And shook his head, and was again alone.
There was not much that was ahead of him,
And there was nothing in the town below—
Where strangers would have shut the many doors
That many friends had opened long ago.

1920

The Sheaves

Where long the shadows of the wind had rolled,
Green wheat was yielding to the change assigned;
And as by some vast magic undivined
The world was turning slowly into gold.
Like nothing that was ever bought or sold
It waited there, the body and the mind;
And with a mighty meaning of a kind
That tells the more the more it is not told.

So in a land where all days are not fair,
Fair days went on till on another day
A thousand golden sheaves were lying there,
Shining and still, but not for long to stay—
As if a thousand girls with golden hair
Might rise from where they slept and go away.

1925

James Weldon Johnson
1871–1938

In the 1908 poem "O Black and Unknown Bards," James Weldon Johnson celebrates the unknown African American creators of spirituals. This poem's form bears little resemblance to a spiritual, but in the crowning achievement of his poetic career, *God's Trombones: Seven Negro Sermons in Verse* (1927), Johnson infused his poetry with the traditions of another African American oral genre. As his subtitle suggests, he wanted to distill in verse qualities of the sermons he had heard in childhood—their narrative energy, incantatory rhythms, humanistic imagery, and creative exuberance. He wrote "The Creation" first in the series, and its immediate inspiration was a spellbinding sermon by a Kansas City preacher: "He intoned, he moaned, he pleaded—he blared, he crashed, he thundered" (preface to *God's Trombones*).

In recasting as verse the oral tradition of the African American sermon, Johnson sought wider recognition for the poetic integrity of the genre. Old-time preachers were, in Johnson's words, "saturated with the sublime phraseology of the Hebrew prophets and steeped in the idioms of King James English," and they fused these with "Negro idioms" (preface). Wary of the degrading stereotypes in much dialect poetry, Johnson preferred a hybrid language made out of a Standard English lexicon syncopated with African American speech rhythms. He grafted various features of the African American sermon—anaphora, climactic momentum, cosmic space (Earth, sun, moon, stars), startling comparisons (God as "a mammy bending over her baby"), and colloquial refrains ("That's good!")—onto free verse paragraphs derived from Walt Whitman's *Leaves of Grass*. By bringing the African American sermon into literary verse, Johnson did for it what Langston Hughes and Sterling Brown would do for jazz and the blues. Given that Johnson was an agnostic, his success in adapting a religious form is all the more remarkable.

Johnson was born amid the hopeful atmosphere of Reconstruction on June 17, 1871, in Jacksonville, Florida. In 1900, he wrote the lyrics for "Lift Every Voice and Sing," a song the NAACP would later adopt as the Negro National Anthem. Attending Atlanta University and doing graduate work at Columbia University, Johnson led a multifaceted career, including time spent as a school principal, a lawyer, a songwriter for Broadway musicals, a diplomat in Venezuela and Nicaragua, and a journalist. In 1912, he published anonymously a groundbreaking novel about race relations and passing, *The Autobiography of an Ex-Colored Man*. Among those at the forefront of the struggle against racial violence, Johnson became the field secretary of the NAACP in 1916 and, in 1920, was the first African American elected to head the organization. A precursor to and participant in the Harlem Renaissance, he edited major collections of African American poetry and spirituals in the 1920s. He died when, driving a car to his summer home in Maine, he was hit by a train at an unmarked railroad crossing.

O Black and Unknown Bards

O black and unknown bards of long ago,
How came your lips to touch the sacred fire?
How, in your darkness, did you come to know
The power and beauty of the minstrel's lyre?
Who first from midst his bonds lifted his eyes?
Who first from out the still watch, lone and long,
Feeling the ancient faith of prophets rise
Within his dark-kept soul, burst into song?

Heart of what slave poured out such melody
As "Steal away to Jesus"?[1] On its strains
His spirit must have nightly floated free,
Though still about his hands he felt his chains.
Who heard great "Jordan roll"? Whose starward eye
Saw chariot "swing low"? And who was he
That breathed that comforting, melodic sigh,
"Nobody knows de trouble I see"?

What merely living clod, what captive thing,
Could up toward God through all its darkness grope,
And find within its deadened heart to sing

1. A spiritual; subsequent quotations are also from spirituals.

These songs of sorrow, love, and faith, and hope?
How did it catch that subtle undertone,
That note in music heard not with the ears?
How sound the elusive reed so seldom blown,
Which stirs the soul or melts the heart to tears?

Not that great German master[2] in his dream
Of harmonies that thundered amongst the stars
At the creation, ever heard a theme
Nobler than "Go down, Moses." Mark its bars,
How like a mighty trumpet-call they stir
The blood. Such are the notes that men have sung
Going to valorous deeds; such tones there were
That helped make history when Time was young.

There is a wide, wide wonder in it all,
That from degraded rest and servile toil
The fiery spirit of the seer should call
These simple children of the sun and soil.
O black slave singers, gone, forgot, unfamed,
You—you alone, of all the long, long line
Of those who've sung untaught, unknown, unnamed,
Have stretched out upward, seeking the divine.

You sang not deeds of heroes or of kings;
No chant of bloody war, no exulting pean[3]
Of arms-won triumphs; but your humble strings
You touched in chord with music empyrean.[4]
You sang far better than you knew; the songs
That for your listeners' hungry hearts sufficed
Still live,—but more than this to you belongs:
You sang a race from wood and stone to Christ.

1908

From DOWN BY THE CARIB SEA

VI. Sunset in the Tropics

A silver flash from the sinking sun,
Then a shot of crimson across the sky
That, bursting, lets a thousand colors fly
And riot among the clouds; they run,
Deepening in purple, flaming in gold,
Changing, and opening fold after fold,
Then fading through all of the tints of the rose into gray,
Till, taking quick fright at the coming night,

2. Gottfried Wilhelm Leibniz (1646–1716), German philosopher.
3. That is, pæan, song of triumph.
4. Of the highest heaven.

They rush out down the west,
In hurried quest
Of the fleeing day.

Now above, where the tardiest color flares a moment yet,
One point of light, now two, now three are set
To form the starry stairs,—
And, in her fire-fly crown,
Queen Night, on velvet slippered feet, comes softly down.

1917

The Creation

And God stepped out on space,
And he looked around and said:
I'm lonely—
I'll make me a world.

And far as the eye of God could see
Darkness covered everything,
Blacker than a hundred midnights
Down in a cypress swamp.

Then God smiled,
And the light broke,
And the darkness rolled up on one side,
And the light stood shining on the other,
And God said: That's good!

Then God reached out and took the light in his hands,
And God rolled the light around in his hands
Until he made the sun;
And he set that sun a-blazing in the heavens.
And the light that was left from making the sun
God gathered it up in a shining ball
And flung it against the darkness,
Spangling the night with the moon and stars.
Then down between
The darkness and the light
He hurled the world;
And God said: That's good!

Then God himself stepped down—
And the sun was on his right hand,
And the moon was on his left;
The stars were clustered about his head,
And the earth was under his feet.
And God walked, and where he trod
His footsteps hollowed the valleys out
And bulged the mountains up.

Then he stopped and looked and saw
That the earth was hot and barren.
So God stepped over to the edge of the world
And he spat out the seven seas—
He batted his eyes, and the lightnings flashed—
He clapped his hands, and the thunders rolled—
And the waters above the earth came down,
The cooling waters came down.

Then the green grass sprouted,
And the little red flowers blossomed,
The pine tree pointed his finger to the sky,
And the oak spread out his arms,
The lakes cuddled down in the hollows of the ground,
And the rivers ran down to the sea;
And God smiled again,
And the rainbow appeared,
And curled itself around his shoulder.

Then God raised his arm and he waved his hand
Over the sea and over the land,
And he said: Bring forth! Bring forth!
And quicker than God could drop his hand,
Fishes and fowls
And beasts and birds
Swam the rivers and the seas,
Roamed the forests and the woods,
And split the air with their wings.
And God said: That's good!

Then God walked around,
And God looked around
On all that he had made.
He looked at his sun,
And he looked at his moon,
And he looked at his little stars;
He looked on his world
With all its living things,
And God said: I'm lonely still.

Then God sat down—
On the side of a hill where he could think;
By a deep, wide river he sat down;
With his head in his hands,
God thought and thought,
Till he thought: I'll make me a man!

Up from the bed of the river
God scooped the clay;
And by the bank of the river
He kneeled him down;
And there the great God Almighty

Who lit the sun and fixed it in the sky,
Who flung the stars to the most far corner of the night,
Who rounded the earth in the middle of his hand;
This Great God,
Like a mammy bending over her baby,
Kneeled down in the dust
Toiling over a lump of clay
Till he shaped it in his own image;

Then into it he blew the breath of life,
And man became a living soul.
Amen. Amen.

1918, 1927

Gertrude Stein
1874–1946

Modern before modernism, Gertrude Stein's work stands at one extreme of twentieth-century literature. It is closer in spirit to the avant-garde experimentalism of modern art than is the work of any other major English-language poet of her time. When Stein sat for the celebrated portrait by her friend Pablo Picasso, in 1906, he was already beginning to abstract the shapes, colors, and materials of painting from their representational function. Picasso and other Cubists gave new primacy to the surface texture of painting, creating a tension between the picture and things in the world. Stein likewise foregrounded the materials of poetry in her poems—words, sounds, rhymes, rhythms, syntax. Though she conceded that words had to make some sense, she loosened their usual moorings in commonsense reference and linear time.

In "A Transatlantic Interview," Stein credited the Postimpressionist Paul Cézanne with the proto-Cubist idea "that in composition one thing was as important as another thing. Each part is as important as the whole." Whereas poems typically create closure, meaning, and movement through the hierarchical organization of words and grammar, Stein's poetry—laying words side by side as did Cézanne his brushstrokes—is deliberately open ended. Words had been debased, Stein implied, by their function as instruments of referential utility in nineteenth-century realism; she said she "had to recapture the value of the individual word, find out what it meant and act within it." Poetry, then, becomes less an act of describing reality than an activity for its own sake, like a game. Borrowing from the rhetoric of painting, Stein says: "I took individual words and thought about them until I got their weight and volume complete and put them next to another word."

Many of Stein's convictions were rooted in her early student experience. At Radcliffe College (then called Harvard Annex), she studied psychology with William James and under his supervision conducted experiments with automatic writing to reveal the unconscious mind. James's psychological theories, along with those of the French philosopher Henri Bergson, laid the foundation for Stein's highly original work. The idea that consciousness is a stream, rather than a succession of formations, and that underneath chronological memory is an intuitive apprehension of existence led Stein to conclude that sequence and causation were methods of imprisoning the mind. The object of language, she held, was to bring things and people and words out of stale usage into a state that she variously designated as "the excitingness of pure being" ("Lecture at Chicago"), "realizing the existence of living," and "the intensity of anyone's existence" ("Portraits and Repetition"). When asked what she meant by "a rose is a rose is a rose," a line she first used in slightly different form in the poem "Sacred Emily," she explained that in the time of Homer, or even of Chaucer, when the language was still new, "the poet could use the name of a thing and the thing was really there." But through overuse and overfamiliarity, names lost their identities, which she was trying to recover. She boasted, "I think in that line the rose is red for the first time in English poetry for a hundred years" ("Lecture at Chicago").

Believing a noun can either conceal or reveal the thing it designates, Stein says in "Poetry and Grammar" that the function of poetry is to rediscover what lies behind nouns: "Poetry is concerned with using with abusing, with losing with wanting, with denying with avoiding with adoring with replacing the noun." She asserts that in her ringlike line about a rose, "I caressed completely caressed and addressed a noun." Just as someone in love says over and again the beloved's name until the name itself becomes the object of attention and "you love it more, more violently more persistently more tormentedly," so too "poetry is essentially the discovery, the love, the passion for the name of anything." This act of impassioned naming attempts to get beyond conventional meaning, or as Wallace Stevens says, to throw away the rotted name.

The pursuit of intuitive as opposed to apparent life required getting at the rhythm, or what she called "melody," of a personality. Stein's rhythms are based on what appear to be repetitions, but she insists in "Portraits and Repetition," "I never repeat"; in each seeming repetition, "the emphasis is different just as the cinema has each time a slightly different thing to make it all be moving." She discards memory: "We in this period have not living in remembering, we have living in moving being." Chronological time is superseded by her attempt to intensify seemingly casual words to reach an inner focus. Her poems are therefore written in the present tense, without sequence or causality. In *Lectures in America*, she describes her way of writing as distinctively American: "A disembodied way of disconnecting something from anything and anything from something." Against the force of traditional syntax and of traditional fixities, she asserts a new freedom.

Stein's poems are riddling, opaque, and musical, but they are not all of a kind. Her early poem "Picasso," printed alongside images of the painter's work in Alfred Stieglitz's journal *Camera Work*, is an incantatory conjuring of Picasso's imaginative fecundity. The prose poems of *Tender Buttons* are intense if oblique evocations of mundane objects, food, and rooms, creating dynamics of wordplay and suggestion that have a resonant, but never direct, relation to the ostensible focus of their attention. In "A Transatlantic Interview," she comments on poems excerpted from *Tender Buttons*, and in "Poetry and Grammar," she explains that she was trying to re-create things by calling "them by their names with passion" and "struggled desperately" to avoid "nouns as nouns"—as sterile and debased signifiers. In poems of what she referred to as her "Spanish" period, such as "Susie Asado" and "Preciosilla," Stein responds to flamenco dance and song, which she had experienced in Madrid in 1912. Placing the emphasis on rhythm, alliteration, repetition, and sonority, these poems, as Stein said in "Portraits and Repetition," achieve "an extraordinary melody of words and a melody of excitement." "Guillaume Apollinaire" is, like many of Stein's early writings, a portrait, but in an unconventional sense. Trying to render the avant-garde poet's personality, Stein starts the poem with a bilingual pun on his name: "Give known or pin ware." "Sacred Emily" is a more sustained experiment in lineated verse, repeating and varying words, phrases, and lines, and punning: "So great so great Emily. / Sew grate sew grate Emily." Words dissolve into one another, break down into component parts, echo, double back, fracture, repeat: "In accompany. / In a company in"; "Door. / Do or." Some of Stein's poetry is lineated, some unlineated, and "Idem the Same. A Valentine to Sherwood Anderson" mixes the two forms, in keeping with Stein's blurring and redefining of the boundaries between prose and poetry. "Stanzas in Meditation" is a rigorous exercise in poetic abstraction. Using poetry to make conventional language seem strange, Stein reveals the norms that typically shape the construction of our world. Her poetry dissolves the stable identities of people and objects. Indeterminate and fertile, it frees the reader to become the cocreator of literary meaning.

Stein was born on February 3, 1874, in Allegheny, Pennsylvania, to German Jewish immigrant parents. She and her family moved when she was one to Vienna, and a few years later to Passy, France. Her first two languages were German and French, and her enduring sense of the opacity and contingency of language probably owes much to her polyglot upbringing. When Stein was six, she moved with her family to California, but after her studies at Radcliffe and Johns Hopkins University, she left America with her brother Leo in 1903 and did not return except for a six-month promotional tour of lectures in 1934–35. In Paris, Stein maintained a famous salon at 27, rue de Fleurus, and she was regularly visited by Picasso, Henri Matisse, and Juan Gris, among other artists. Among writers, Stein was closely associated with Ernest Hemingway and Thornton Wilder, and she was also friendly with composer Virgil Thomson, who set a number of her poems to music. James Joyce, also living in Paris, kept his distance. But poets Edith Sitwell, H. D., William Carlos Williams, and Mina Loy were among her friends and visitors. Her influence was profound on later avant-garde poets, including Objectivists such as Louis Zukofsky and Language poets such as Charles Bernstein and Lyn Hejinian.

In 1907, Stein began a lifelong romantic relationship with Alice B. Toklas, from San Francisco, and in 1933, she published *The Autobiography of Alice B. Toklas*, in which Toklas reminisces about Stein and others, ostensibly in her own person. This form enabled Stein to transgress her own rules about memory. Stein and Toklas survived World War II in France, where Stein wrote two pieces that endorsed the Nazi-backed Vichy regime, though she later came to the ardent support of the Allies. On her deathbed, she asked, "What is the answer?" and when no one said anything she laughed and asked, "Then what is the question?"

Picasso[1]

One whom some were certainly following was one who was completely charming. One whom some were certainly following was one who was charming. One whom some were following was one who was completely charming. One whom some were following was one who was certainly completely charming.

Some were certainly following and were certain that the one they were then following was one working and was one bringing out of himself then something. Some were certainly following and were certain that the one they were then following was one bringing out of himself then something that was coming to be a heavy thing, a solid thing and a complete thing.

One whom some were certainly following was one working and certainly was one bringing something out of himself then and was one who had been all his living had been one having something coming out of him.

1. Spanish expatriate painter Pablo Picasso (1881–1973).

Something had been coming out of him, certainly it had been coming out of him certainly it was something, certainly it had been coming out of him and it had meaning, a charming meaning, a solid meaning, a struggling meaning, a clear meaning.

One whom some were certainly following and some were certainly following him, one whom some were certainly following was one certainly working.

One whom some were certainly following was one having something coming out of him something having meaning, and this one was certainly working then.

This one was working and something was coming then, something was coming out of this one then. This one was one and always there was something coming out of this one and always there had been something coming out of this one. This one had never been one not having something coming out of this one. This one was one having something coming out of this one. This one had been one whom some were following. This one was one whom some were following. This one was being one whom some were following. This one was one who was working.

This one was one who was working. This one was one being one having something being coming out of him. This one was one going on having something come out of him. This one was one going on working. This one was one whom some were following. This one was one who was working.

This one always had something being coming out of this one. This one was working. This one always had been working. This one was always having something that was coming out of this one that was a solid thing, a charming thing, a lovely thing, a perplexing thing, a disconcerting thing, a simple thing, a clear thing, a complicated thing, an interesting thing, a disturbing thing, a repellent thing, a very pretty thing. This one was one certainly being one having something coming out of him. This one was one whom some were following. This one was one who was working.

This one was one who was working and certainly this one was needing to be working so as to be one being working. This one was one having something coming out of him. This one would be one all his living having something coming out of him. This one was working and then this one was working and this one was needing to be working, not to be one having something coming out of him something having meaning, but was needing to be working so as to be one working.

This one was certainly working and working was something this one was certain this one would be doing and this one was doing that thing, this one was working. This one was not one completely working. This one was not ever completely working. This one certainly was not completely working.

This one was one having always something being coming out of him, something having completely a real meaning. This one was one whom some were following. This one was one who was working. This one was one who was working and he was one needing this thing needing to be working so as to be one having some way of being one having some way of working. This one was one who was working. This one was one having something come out of him something having meaning. This one was one always having something come out of him and this thing the thing coming out of him always had real meaning. This one was one who was working. This one was one who was almost always working. This one was not one completely working. This one was one not ever completely working. This one was not one working to have anything come out of him. This one did have something having meaning that did come out of him. He always did have something come out of him. He was working, he was not ever completely working. He did have some following. They were always following him. Some were certainly following him. He was one who was working. He was one having something coming out of him something having meaning. He was not ever completely working.

1909 1912

From Tender Buttons[2]

From Objects

A carafe, that is a blind glass.

A kind in glass and a cousin, a spectacle and nothing strange a single hurt color and an arrangement in a system to pointing. All this and not ordinary, not unordered in not resembling. The difference is spreading.

A piece of coffee.

More of double.

A place in no new table.

A single image is not splendor. Dirty is yellow. A sign of more in not mentioned. A piece of coffee is not a detainer. The resemblance to yellow is dirtier and distincter. The clean mixture is whiter and not coal color, never more coal color than altogether.

The sight of a reason, the same sight slighter, the sight of a simpler negative answer, the same sore sounder, the intention to wishing, the same splendor, the same furniture.

The time to show a message is when too late and later there is no hanging in a blight.

A not torn rose-wood color. If it is not dangerous then a pleasure and more than any other if it is cheap is not cheaper. The amusing side is that the sooner there are no fewer the more certain is the necessity dwindled. Supposing that the case contained rosewood and a color. Supposing that there was no reason for a distress and more likely for a number, supposing that there was no astonishment, is it not necessary to mingle astonishment.

The settling of stationing cleaning is one way not to shatter scatter and scattering. The one way to use custom is to use soap and silk for cleaning. The one way to see cotton is to have a design concentrating the illusion and the illustration. The perfect way is to accustom the thing to have a lining and the shape of a ribbon and to be solid, quite solid in standing and to use heaviness in morning. It is light enough in that. It has that shape nicely. Very nicely may not be exaggerating. Very strongly may be

2. A series of prose poems grouped in three sections: "Objects," "Food," and "Rooms." Stein discusses most of the following poems in "A Transatlantic Interview," on p. 986 of this volume.

sincerely fainting. May be strangely flattering. May not be strange in everything. May not be strange to.

A waist.

A star glide, a single frantic sullenness, a single financial grass greediness.

Object that is in wood. Hold the pine, hold the dark, hold in the rush, make the bottom.

A piece of crystal. A change, in a change that is remarkable there is no reason to say that there was a time.

A woolen object gilded. A country climb is the best disgrace, a couple of practices any of them in order is so left.

A little bit of a tumbler.

A shining indication of yellow consists in there having been more of the same color than could have been expected when all four were bought. This was the hope which made the six and seven have no use for any more places and this necessarily spread into nothing. Spread into nothing.

A brown.

A brown which is not liquid not more so is relaxed and yet there is a change, a news is pressing.

A little called Pauline.

A little called anything shows shudders.

Come and say what prints all day. A whole few watermelon. There is no pope.

No cut in pennies and little dressing and choose wide soles and little spats really little spices.

A little lace makes boils. This is not true.

Gracious of gracious and a stamp a blue green white bow a blue green lean, lean on the top.

If it is absurd then it is leadish and nearly set in where there is a tight head.

A peaceful life to arise her, noon and moon and moon. A letter a cold sleeve a blanket a shaving house and nearly the best and regular window.

Nearer in fairy sea, nearer and farther, show white has lime in sight, show a stitch of ten. Count, count more so that thicker and thicker is leaning.

I hope she has her cow. Bidding a wedding, widening received treading, little leading mention nothing.

Cough out cough out in the leather and really feather it is not for.

Please could, please could, jam it not plus more sit in when.

A dog.

A little monkey goes like a donkey that means to say that means to say that more sighs last goes. Leave with it. A little monkey goes like a donkey.

A white hunter.

A white hunter is nearly crazy.

Peeled pencil, choke.

Rub her coke.

From Food

ROASTBEEF; MUTTON; BREAKFAST; SUGAR; CRANBERRIES; MILK; EGGS; APPLE; TAILS; LUNCH; CUPS; RHUBARB; SINGLE; FISH; CAKE; CUSTARD; POTATOES; ASPARAGUS; BUTTER; END OF SUMMER; SAUSAGES; CELERY; VEAL; VEGETABLE; COOKING; CHICKEN; PASTRY; CREAM; CUCUMBER; DINNER; EATING; SALAD; SAUCE; SALMON; ORANGE; COCOA; AND CLEAR SOUP AND ORANGES AND OAT-MEAL; SALAD DRESSING AND AN ARTICHOKE; A CENTRE IN A TABLE.[3]

Mutton.

A letter which can wither, a learning which can suffer and an outrage which is simultaneous is principal.

Student, students are merciful and recognised they chew something.

Hate rests that is solid and sparse and all in a shape and largely very largely. Interleaved and successive and a sample of smell all this makes a certainty a shade.

Light curls very light curls have no more curliness than soup. This is not a subject.

Change a single stream of denting and change it hurriedly, what does it express, it expresses nausea. Like a very strange likeness and pink, like that and not more like that than the same resemblance and not more like that than no middle space in cutting.

An eye glass, what is an eye glass, it is water. A splendid specimen, what is it when it is little and tender so that there are parts. A centre can place and four are no more and two and two are not middle.

Melting and not minding, safety and powder, a particular recollection and a sincere solitude all this makes a shunning so thorough and so unrepeated and surely if there is anything left it is a bone. It is not solitary.

Any space is not quiet it is so likely to be shiny. Darkness very dark darkness is sectional. There is a way to see in onion and surely very surely rhubarb and a tomato, surely very surely there is that seeding. A little thing in is a little thing.

Mud and water were not present and not any more of either. Silk and stockings were not present and not any more of either. A receptacle and a symbol and no monster were present and no more. This made a piece show and was it a kindness, it can be asked was it a kindness to have it warmer, was it a kindness and does gliding mean more. Does it.

3. Stein's list echoes the form of a table of contents, enumerating some of the prose poems in the complete "Food" section.

Does it dirty a ceiling. It does not. Is it dainty, it is if prices are sweet. Is it lamentable, it is not if there is no undertaker. Is it curious, it is not when there is youth. All this makes a line, it even makes makes no more. All this makes cherries. The reason that there is a suggestion in vanity is due to this that there is a burst of mixed music.

A temptation any temptation is an exclamation if there are misdeeds and little bones. It is not astonishing that bones mingle as they vary not at all and in any case why is a bone outstanding, it is so because the circumstance that does not make a cake and character is so easily churned and cherished.

Mouse and mountain and a quiver, a quaint statue and pain in an exterior and silence more silence louder shows salmon a mischief intender. A cake, a real salve made of mutton and liquor, a specially retained rinsing and an established cork and blazing, this which resignation influences and restrains, restrains more altogether. A sign is the specimen spoken.

A meal in mutton, mutton, why is lamb cheaper, it is cheaper because so little is more. Lecture, lecture and repeat instruction.

Sugar.

A violent luck and a whole sample and even then quiet.

Water is squeezing, water is almost squeezing on lard. Water, water is a mountain and it is selected and it is so practical that there is no use in money. A mind under is exact and so it is necessary to have a mouth and eye glasses.

A question of sudden rises and more time than awfulness is so easy and shady. There is precisely that noise.

A peck a small piece not privately overseen, not at all not a slice, not at all crestfallen and open, not at all mounting and chaining and evenly surpassing, all the bidding comes to tea.

A separation is not tightly in worsted and sauce, it is so kept well and sectionally.

Put it in the stew, put it to shame. A little slight shadow and a solid fine furnace.

The teasing is tender and trying and thoughtful.

The line which sets sprinkling to be a remedy is beside the best cold.

A puzzle, a monster puzzle, a heavy choking, a neglected Tuesday.

Wet crossing and a likeness, any likeness, a likeness has blisters, it has that and teeth, it has the staggering blindly and a little green, any little green is ordinary.

One, two and one, two, nine, second and five and that.

A blaze, a search in between, a cow, only any wet place, only this tune.

Cut a gas jet uglier and then pierce pierce in between the next and negligence. Choose the rate to pay and pet pet very much. A collection of all around, a signal poison, a lack of languor and more hurts at ease.

A white bird, a colored mine, a mixed orange, a dog.

Cuddling comes in continuing a change.

A piece of separate outstanding rushing is so blind with open delicacy.

A canoe is orderly. A period is solemn. A cow is accepted.

A nice old chain is widening, it is absent, it is laid by.

Eggs.

Kind height, kind in the right stomach with a little sudden mill.

Cunning shawl, cunning shawl to be steady.

In white in white handkerchiefs with little dots in a white belt all shadows are singular they are singular and procured and relieved.

No that is not the cows shame and a precocious sound, it is a bite.

Cut up alone the paved way which is harm. Harm is old boat and a likely dash.

Chicken.

Pheasant and chicken, chicken is a peculiar third.

Chicken.

Alas a dirty word, alas a dirty third alas a dirty third, alas a dirty bird.

Chicken.

Alas a doubt in case of more go to say what it is cress. What is it. Mean. Potato. Loaves.

Chicken.

Stick stick call then, stick stick sticking, sticking with a chicken. Sticking in a extra succession, sticking in.

A centre in a table.

It was a way a day, this made some sum. Suppose a cod liver a cod liver is an oil, suppose a cod liver oil is tunny, suppose a cod liver oil tunny is pressed suppose a cod liver oil tunny pressed is china and secret with a bestow a bestow reed, a reed to be a reed to be, in a reed to be.

Next to me next to a folder, next to a folder some waiter, next to a foldersome waiter and re letter and read her. Read her with her for less.

From Rooms

Act so that there is no use in a centre. A wide action is not a width. A preparation is given to the ones preparing. They do not eat who mention silver and sweet. There was an occupation.

A whole centre and a border make hanging a way of dressing. This which is not why there is a voice is the remains of an offering. There was no rental.

So the tune which is there has a little piece to play and the exercise is all there is of a fast. The tender and true that makes no width to hew is the time that there is question to adopt.

To begin the placing there is no wagon. There is no change lighter. It was done. And then the spreading, that was not accomplishing that needed standing and yet the time was not so difficult as they were not all in place. They had no change. They were not respected. They were that, they did it so much in the matter and this showed that that settlement was not condensed. It was spread there. Any change was in the ends of the centre. A heap was heavy. There was no change.

Burnt and behind and lifting a temporary stone and lifting more than a drawer.

The instance of there being more is an instance of more. The shadow is not shining in the way there is a black line. The truth has come. There is a disturbance. Trusting to a baker's boy meant that there would be very much exchanging and anyway what is the use of a covering to a door. There is a use, they are double.

If the centre has the place then there is distribution. That is natural. There is a contradiction and naturally returning there comes to be both sides and the centre. That can be seen from the description.

* * *

1912 1914

Susie Asado[4]

Sweet sweet sweet sweet sweet tea.
    Susie Asado.
Sweet sweet sweet sweet sweet tea.
    Susie Asado.
Susie Asado which is a told tray sure.
A lean on the shoe this means slips slips hers.
When the ancient light grey is clean it is yellow, it is a silver seller.
This is a please this is a please there are the saids to jelly. These are the
    wets these say the sets to leave a crown to Incy.
Incy is short for incubus.[5]
A pot. A pot is a beginning of a rare bit of trees. Trees tremble, the old
    vats are in bobbles, bobbles which shade and shove and render
    clean, render clean must.
    Drink pups.
Drink pups drink pups lease a sash hold, see it shine and a bobolink has
    pins. It shows a nail.
What is a nail. A nail is unison.
Sweet sweet sweet sweet sweet tea.

1913 1922

4. Portrait suggested by the flamenco dancer Antonia Marce (1890–1936), known as La Argentina.

5. Evil spirit supposed to have intercourse with women at night.

Guillaume Apollinaire[6]

Give known or pin ware.
Fancy teeth, gas strips.
Elbow elect, sour stout pore, pore caesar, pour state at.
Leave eye lessons I. Leave I. Lessons. I. Leave I lessons, I.

1913 1934

Preciosilla[7]

Cousin to Clare washing.

In the win all the band beagles which have cousin lime sign and arrange a weeding match to presume a certain point to exstate to exstate a certain pass lint to exstate a lean sap prime lo and shut shut is life.

Bait, bait tore, tore her clothes, toward it, toward a bit, to ward a sit, sit down in, in vacant surely lots, a single mingle, bait and wet, wet a single establishment that has a l i l y lily grow. Come to the pen come in the stem, come in the grass grown water.

Lily wet lily wet while. This is so pink so pink in stammer, a long bean which shows bows is collected by a single curly shady, shady get, get set wet bet.

It is a snuff a snuff to be told and have can wither, can is it and sleep sleeps knot, it is a lily scarf the pink and blue yellow, not blue not odor sun, nobles are bleeding bleeding two seats two seats on end. Why is grief. Grief is strange black. Sugar is melting. We will not swim.

Preciosilla.

Please be please be get, please get wet, wet naturally, naturally in weather. Could it be fire more firier. Could it be so in ate struck. Could it be gold up, gold up stringing, in it while while which is hanging, hanging in dingling, dingling in pinning, not so. Not so dots large dressed dots, big sizes, less laced, less laced diamonds, diamonds white, diamonds bright, diamonds in the in the light, diamonds light diamonds door diamonds hanging to be four, two four, all before, this bean, lessly, all most, a best, willow, vest, a green guest, guest, go go go go go go, go. Go go. Not guessed. Go go.

Toasted susie is my ice-cream.

1913 1926

Sacred Emily

Compose compose beds.
Wives of great men rest tranquil.
Come go stay philip philip.

6. Avant-garde French poet (1880–1918), proponent of literary cubism and experimental typography.

7. Stage name of a singer in Madrid.

Egg be takers.
Parts of place nuts.
Suppose twenty for cent.
It is rose in hen.
Come one day.
A firm terrible a firm terrible hindering, a firm hindering have a ray nor pin nor.
Egg in places.
Egg in few insists.
In set a place.
I am not missing.
Who is a permit.
I love honor and obey I do love honor and obey I do.
Melancholy do lip sing.
How old is he.
Murmur pet murmur pet murmur.
Push sea push sea push sea push sea push sea push sea push sea push sea.
Sweet and good and kind to all.
Wearing head.
Cousin tip nicely.
Cousin tip.
Nicely.
Wearing head.
Leave us sit.
I do believe it will finish, I do believe it will finish.
Pat ten patent, Pat ten patent.
Eleven and eighteen.
Foolish is foolish is.
Birds measure birds measure stores birds measure stores measure birds measure.
Exceptional firm bites.
How do you do I forgive you everything and there is nothing to forgive.
Never the less.
Leave it to me.
Weeds without papers.
Weeds without papers are necessary.
Left again left again.
Exceptional considerations.
Never the less tenderness.
Resting cow curtain.
Resting bull pin.
Resting cow curtain.
Resting bull pin.
Next to a frame.
The only hat hair.
Leave us mass leave us. Leave us pass. Leave us. Leave us pass leave us.
Humming is.
No climate.
What is a size.
Ease all I can do.
Colored frame.

Couple of canning.
Ease all I can do.
Humming does as
Humming does as humming is.
What is a size.
No climate.
Ease all I can do.
Shall give it, please to give it.
Like to give it, please to give it.
What a surprise.
Not sooner whether.
Cordially yours.
Pause.
Cordially yours.
Not sooner together.
Cordially yours.
In strewing, in strewing.
That is the way we are one and indivisible.
Pay nuts renounce.
Now without turning around.
I will give them to you tonight.
Cunning is and does cunning is and does the most beautiful notes.
I would like a thousand most most.
Center pricking petunia.
Electrics are tight electrics are white electrics are a button.
Singular pressing.
Recent thimble.
Noisy pearls noisy pearl coat.
Arrange.
Arrange wide opposite.
Opposite it.
Lily ice-cream.
Nevertheless.
A hand is Willie.
Henry Henry Henry.
A hand is Henry.
Henry Henry Henry.
A hand is Willie.
Henry Henry Henry.
All the time.
A wading chest.
Do you mind.
Lizzie do you mind.
Ethel.
Ethel.
Ethel.
Next to barber.
Next to barber bury.
Next to barber bury china.
Next to barber bury china glass.
Next to barber china and glass.
Next to barber and china.

Next to barber and hurry.
Next to hurry.
Next to hurry and glass and china.
Next to hurry and glass and hurry.
Next to hurry and hurry.
Next to hurry and hurry.
Plain cases for see.
Tickle tickle tickle you for education.
A very reasonable berry.
Suppose a selection were reverse.
Cousin to sadden.
A coral neck and a little song so very extra so very Susie.
Cow come out cow come out and out and smell a little.
Draw prettily.
Next to a bloom.
Neat stretch.
Place plenty.
Cauliflower.
Cauliflower.
Curtain cousin.
Apron.
Neither best set.
Do I make faces like that at you.
Pinkie.
Not writing not writing another.
Another one.
Think.
Jack Rose Jack Rose.
Yard.
Practically all of them.
Does believe it.
Measure a measure a measure or.
Which is pretty which is pretty which is pretty.
To be top.
Neglect Waldberg.
Sudden say separate.
So great so great Emily.
Sew grate sew grate Emily.
Not a spell nicely.
Ring.
Weigh pieces of pound.
Aged steps.
Stops.
Not a plan bow.
Why is lacings.
Little slam up.
Cold seam peaches.
Begging to state begging to state begging to state alright.
Begging to state begging to state begging to state alright.
Wheels stows wheels stows.
Wickedness.
Cotton could mere less.

Nevertheless.
Anne.
Analysis.
From the standpoint of all white a week is none too much.
Pink coral white coral, coral coral.
Happy happy happy.
All the, chose.
Is a necessity.
Necessity.
Happy happy happy all the.
Happy happy happy all the.
Necessity.
Remain seated.
Come on come on come on on.
All the close.
Remain seated.
Happy.
All the.
Necessity.
Remain seated.
All the, close.
Websters and mines, websters and mines.
Websters and mines.
Trimming.
Gold space gold space of toes.
Twos, twos.
Pinned to the letter.
In accompany.
In a company in.
Received.
Must.
Natural lace.
Spend up.
Spend up length.
Spend up length.
Length thoroughly.
Neatness.
Neatness Neatness.
Excellent cording.
Excellent cording short close.
Close to.
When.
Pin black.
Cough or up.
Shouting.
Shouting.
Neater pin.
Pinned to the letter.
Was it a space was it a space was it a space to see.
Neither things.
Persons.
Transition.

Say say say.
North of the calender.
Window.
Peoples rest.
Preserve pulls.
Cunning piler.
Next to a chance.
Apples.
Apples.
Apples went.
It was a chance to preach Saturday.
Please come to Susan.
Purpose purpose black.
Extra plain silver.
Furious slippers.
Have a reason.
Have a reason candy.
Points of places.
Neat Nezars.
Which is a cream, can cream.
Ink of paper slightly mine breathes a shoulder able shine.
Necessity.
Near glass.
Put a stove put a stove hoarser.
If I was surely if I was surely.
See girl says.
All the same bright.
Brightness.
When a churn say suddenly when a churn say suddenly.
Poor pour percent.
Little branches.
Pale.
Pale.
Pale.
Pale.
Pale.
Pale.
Pale.
Near sights.
Please sorts.
Example.
Example.
Put something down.
Put something down some day.
Put something down some day in.
Put something down some day in my.
In my hand.
In my hand right.
In my hand writing.
Put something down some day in my hand writing.
Needles less.
Never the less.

Never the less.
Pepperness.
Never the less extra stress.
Never the less.
Tenderness.
Old sight.
Pearls.
Real line.
Shoulders.
Upper states.
Mere colors.
Recent resign.
Search needles.
All a plain all a plain show.
White papers.
Slippers.
Slippers underneath.
Little tell.
I chance.
I chance to.
I chance to to.
I chance to.
What is a winter wedding a winter wedding.
Furnish seats.
Furnish seats nicely.
Please repeat.
Please repeat for.
Please repeat.
This is a name to Anna.
Cushions and pears.
Reason purses.
Reason purses to relay to relay carpets.
Marble is thorough fare.
Nuts are spittoons.
That is a word.
That is a word careless.
Paper peaches.
Paper peaches are tears.
Rest in grapes.
Thoroughly needed.
Thoroughly needed signs.
All but.
Relieving relieving.
Argonauts.
That is plenty.
Cunning saxon symbol.
Symbol of beauty.
Thimble of everything.
Cunning clover thimble.
Cunning of everything.
Cunning of thimble.
Cunning cunning.

Place in pets.
Night town.
Night town a glass.
Color mahogany.
Color mahogany center.
Rose is a rose is a rose is a rose.
Loveliness extreme.
Extra gaiters.
Loveliness extreme.
Sweetest ice-cream.
Page ages page ages page ages.
Wiped Wiped wire wire.
Sweeter than peaches and pears and cream.
Wiped wire wiped wire.
Extra extreme.
Put measure treasure.
Measure treasure.
Tables track.
Nursed.
Dough.
That will do.
Cup or cup or.
Excessively illigitimate.
Pussy pussy pussy what what.
Current secret sneezers.
Ever.
Mercy for a dog.
Medal make medal.
Able able able.
A go to green and a letter spoke a go to green or praise or
Worships worships worships.
Door.
Do or.
Table linen.
Wet spoil.
Wet spoil gaiters and knees and little spools little spools or ready silk lining.
Suppose misses misses.
Curls to butter.
Curls.
Curls.
Settle stretches.
See at till.
Louise.
Sunny.
Sail or.
Sail or rustle.
Mourn in morning.
The way to say.
Patter.
Deal own a.
Robber.

A high b and a perfect sight.
Little things singer.
Jane.
Aiming.
Not in description.
Day way.
A blow is delighted.

1913 1922

Idem the Same
A Valentine to Sherwood Anderson[8]

I knew too that through them I knew too that he was through, I knew too that he threw them. I knew too that they were through, I knew too I knew too, I knew I knew them.

I knew to them.

If they tear a hunter through, if they tear through a hunter, if they tear through a hunt and a hunter, if they tear through the different sizes of the six, the different sizes of the six which are these, a woman with a white package under one arm and a black package under the other arm and dressed in brown with a white blouse, the second Saint Joseph the third a hunter in a blue coat and black garters and a plaid cap, a fourth a knife grinder who is full faced and a very little woman with black hair and a yellow hat and an excellently smiling appropriate soldier. All these as you please.

In the meantime examples of the same lily. In this way please have you rung.

What Do I See.

A very little snail.
A medium sized turkey.
A small band of sheep.
A fair orange tree.
All nice wives are like that.
Listen to them from here.
Oh.
You did not have an answer.
Here.
Yes.

A Very Valentine.

Very fine is my valentine.
Very fine and very mine.
Very mine is my valentine very mine and very fine.
Very fine is my valentine and mine, very fine very mine and mine is my valentine.

8. American novelist and short-story writer (1876–1941). *Idem:* the same (Latin).

Why Do You Feel Differently.

Why do you feel differently about a very little snail and a big one.
Why do you feel differently about a medium sized turkey and a very large one.
Why do you feel differently about a small band of sheep and several sheep that are riding.
Why do you feel differently about a fair orange tree and one that has blossoms as well.
Oh very well.
All nice wives are like that.

To Be.
No Please.
To Be
They can please
Not to be
Do they please.
Not to be
Do they not please
Yes please.
Do they please
No please.
Do they not please
No please.
Do they please.
Please.
If you please.
And if you please.
And if they please
And they please.
To be pleased
Not to be pleased.
Not to be displeased.
To be pleased and to please.

Kneeling.

One two three four five six seven eight nine and ten.
The tenth is a little one kneeling and giving away a rooster with this feeling.
I have mentioned one, four five seven eight and nine.
Two is also giving away an animal.
Three is changed as to disposition.
Six is in question if we mean mother and daughter, black and black caught her, and she offers to be three she offers it to me.
That is very right and should come out below and just so.

Bundles for Them.

A HISTORY OF GIVING BUNDLES.

We were able to notice that each one in a way carried a bundle, they were not a trouble to them nor were they all bundles as some of them were chickens some of them pheasants some of them sheep and some of them bundles, they were not a trouble to them and then indeed we learned that it was the principal recreation and they were so arranged that they were not given away, and to-day they were given away.

I will not look at them again.
They will not look for them again.
They have not seen them here again.
They are in there and we hear them again.

In which way are stars brighter then they are. When we have come to this decision. We mention many thousands of buds. And when I close my eyes I see them.

If you hear her snore
It is not before you love her
You love her so that to be her beau is very lovely
She is sweetly there and her curly hair is very lovely
She is sweetly here and I am very near and that is very lovely.
She is my tender sweet and her little feet are stretched out well which is a treat and very lovely
Her little tender nose is between her little eyes which close and are very lovely.
She is very lovely and mine which is very lovely.

On Her Way.

If you can see why she feels that she kneels if you can see why he knows that he shows what he bestows, if you can see why they share what they share, need we question that there is no doubt that by this time if they had intended to come they would have sent some notice of such intention. She and they and indeed the decision itself is not early dissatisfaction.

In This Way.

Keys please, it is useless to alarm any one it is useless to alarm some one it is useless to be alarming and to get fertility in gardens in salads in heliotrope and in dishes. Dishes and wishes are mentioned and dishes and wishes are not capable of darkness. We like sheep. We like sheep. And so does he.

Let Us Describe.

Let us describe how they went. It was a very windy night and the road although in excellent condition and extremely well graded has many turnings and although the curves are not sharp the rise is considerable. It was a very windy night and some of the larger vehicles found it more prudent not to venture. In consequence some of those who had planned to go were unable to do so. Many others did go and there was a sacrifice, of what shall we, a sheep, a hen, a cock, a village, a ruin, and all that and then that having been blessed let us bless it.

1922 1923

George Hugnet[9]

George and Genevieve Geronimo[1] with a with whether they thought they were with whether.
Without their finding it out. Without. Their finding it out. With whether.
George whether they were about. With their finding their whether it finding it out whether with their finding about it out.
George with their finding it with out.
George whether their with their it whether.
Redoubt[2] out with about.
With out whether it their whether with out doubt.
Azure can with our about.
It is welcome welcome thing.
George in are ring.
Lain away awake.
George in our ring.
George Genevieve Geronimo straightened it out without their finding it out.
Grammar makes George in our ring which Grammar make George in our ring.
Grammar is as disappointed not is as grammar is as disappointed.
Grammar is not as Grammar is as disappointed.
George is in our ring. Grammar is not is disappointed. In are ring.
George Genevieve in are ring.

1928 1929

From STANZAS IN MEDITATION

Stanza LXXXIII

Why am I if I am uncertain reasons may inclose.
Remain remain propose repose chose.
I call carelessly that the door is open
Which if they may refuse to open
No one can rush to close.
Let them be mine therefor.
Everybody knows that I chose.
Therefor if therefore before I close.
I will therefore offer therefore I offer this.
Which if I refuse to miss may be miss is mine.
I will be well welcome when I come.
Because I am coming.
Certainly I come having come.
These stanzas are done.

1932 1950

9. Surrealist poet (1906–1974) and, at the time of composition, a friend of Stein's.
1. Leader of Apache in forays against U.S. troops (1829–1909).
2. Small defensive fort.

Amy Lowell
1874–1925

Amy Lowell's best poetry has the immediacy, spareness, and precision that she, Ezra Pound, and other Imagists advocated as a tonic to slack sentimentality and abstraction in verse. In the 1915 introduction to one of several anthologies she edited of Imagist poets, we find these principles: "to use the language of common speech," "to create new rhythms," "to allow absolute freedom in the choice of subject," "to present an image," "to produce poetry that is hard and clear, never blurred nor indefinite," and, finally, to hold that "concentration is the very essence of poetry." Much of Amy Lowell's poetry did not live up to these aspirations, but Pound's famous list of "Don'ts" also outstripped his actual poetic practice at the time. Still, Lowell and Pound, along with H. D. and other like-minded contemporaries, were revolutionizing poetry by promoting and working toward a crystalline, hard-edged aesthetic.

Born on February 9, 1874, in Brookline, Massachusetts, into a prominent New England family that would eventually spawn her distant cousin Robert Lowell, Amy Lowell first encountered Imagism when reading H. D. in a magazine. She soon set out to meet Pound and other Imagists in England in 1913, and she and Pound collaborated for a time. But jealousy over aesthetic and editorial leadership soon pitted them against one another, and Pound broke with the movement he had helped found. He famously denounced it as "Amygism" and denigrated the heavyset Lowell as a "hippopoetess." In revolt against the constraints of her patrician heritage, Lowell—smoking cigars, wearing a pince-nez, bluntly dispensing opinions, and taking as her long-term companion the actress Ada Dwyer Russell—cut a striking figure as a liberated woman. As critic, propagandist, anthologist, and patron, Lowell was a significant early promoter of modernist poetry. Like other Imagists, she found East Asian aesthetics congenial, eventually writing haiku poetry and other forms of what she called *Chinoiserie.*

If some of Lowell's poetry is verbose and didactic, in contrast to the sharp focus and spare economy of means in the strongest Imagist work, a poem such as "The Pike" is vivid and compact. Like many of H. D.'s poems, many of Lowell's are explicitly feminist in intention. In "Venus Transiens," she vies with Botticelli's famous painting of Venus, while slyly borrowing some of the painting's energy to celebrate the beloved. Here and in the passionate poem "A Decade," Lowell boldly expresses lesbian desire. Playing on the traditional association of the beloved with food and drink in "A Decade," Lowell uses the senses of taste (sweet wine) and touch (smooth bread) to figure both sex and satiety. In poems such as "Shore Grass," she captures textures of light, sound, and wind in cadenced language. While Lowell engages the senses in much of her early work, the late poem "New Heavens for Old" represents a sad, self-elegiac withdrawal from the adventurous styles of living and erotic expression she had once championed.

The Pike

In the brown water,
Thick and silver-sheened in the sunshine,
Liquid and cool in the shade of the reeds,
A pike dozed.
Lost among the shadows of stems

He lay unnoticed.
Suddenly he flicked his tail,
And a green-and-copper brightness
Ran under the water.

Out from under the reeds
Came the olive-green light,
And orange flashed up
Through the sun-thickened water.
So the fish passed across the pool,
Green and copper,
A darkness and a gleam,
And the blurred reflections of the willows on the opposite bank
Received it.

1914

Venus Transiens[1]

Tell me,
Was Venus more beautiful
Than you are,
When she topped
The crinkled waves,
Drifting shoreward
On her plaited shell?
Was Botticelli's[2] vision
Fairer than mine;
And were the painted rosebuds
He tossed his lady,
Of better worth
Than the words I blow about you
To cover your too great loveliness
As with a gauze
Of misted silver?
For me,
You stand poised
In the blue and buoyant air,
Cinctured by bright winds,
Treading the sunlight.
And the waves which precede you
Ripple and stir
The sands at my feet.

1919

1. Venus passing over (Latin). Venus is the Roman goddess of love and beauty.
2. Italian artist Sandro Botticelli (1444–1510) painted *The Birth of Venus,* in which the goddess stands on a large scallop shell and small roses are blown about her.

A Decade

When you came, you were like red wine and honey,
And the taste of you burnt my mouth with its sweetness.
Now you are like morning bread,
Smooth and pleasant.
I hardly taste you at all for I know your savour,
But I am completely nourished.

1919

Shore Grass

The moon is cold over the sand-dunes,
And the clumps of sea-grasses flow and glitter;
The thin chime of my watch tells the quarter after midnight;
And still I hear nothing
But the windy beating of the sea.

1919

New Heavens for Old

I am useless.
What I do is nothing,
What I think has no savour.
There is an almanac between the windows:
It is of the year when I was born.

My fellows call to me to join them,
They shout for me,
Passing the house in a great wind of vermilion banners.
They are fresh and fulminant,[3]
They are indecent and strut with the thought of it,
They laugh, and curse, and brawl,
And cheer a holocaust of "Who comes firsts!" at the iron fronts of the houses at the two edges of the street.
Young men with naked hearts jeering between iron house-fronts,
Young men with naked bodies beneath their clothes
Passionately conscious of them,
Ready to strip off their clothes,
Ready to strip off their customs, their usual routine,
Clamouring for the rawness of life,
In love with appetite,
Proclaiming it as a creed,
Worshipping youth,

3. Thunderous; explosive.

Worshipping themselves.
They call for women and the women come,
They bare the whiteness of their lusts to the dead gaze of the old house-
fronts,
They roar down the street like flame,
They explode upon the dead houses like new, sharp fire.

But I—
I arrange three roses in a Chinese vase:
A pink one,
A red one,
A yellow one.
I fuss over their arrangement.
Then I sit in a South window
And sip pale wine with a touch of hemlock[4] in it,
And think of Winter nights,
And field-mice crossing and re-crossing
The spot which will be my grave.

1927

4. The poisonous potion by which the ancient Greek philosopher Socrates reportedly was executed.

ROBERT FROST
1874–1963

Although he identified himself with rural New England, especially New Hampshire and Vermont, Robert Frost was born and lived until age eleven in San Francisco and spent his high school years in a Massachusetts mill town, not a farm center. He presented himself in many of his poems—which are almost always in the first person—as building soil, chopping wood, cleaning out the spring, patching fences, picking apples; he was familiar with these activities, but he did not rely entirely on them for his livelihood.

In his poems, Frost, even as a young man, seemed wise, as if he were expressing the eternal processes of nature. To Frost, composition was a process of letting the poem take over from him; he said in an essay, "The Figure a Poem Makes," that "like a piece of ice on a hot stove the poem must ride on its own melting." But his poems, often composed as extremely compact units, can hardly be said to escape into impersonality. Critics have discovered darkness to be a prominent countertheme to the cheeriness usually ascribed to him. It could be said that Frost wished to play the game from both sides, evincing despair and then dispelling it by household philosophy or offhandedness. He was convinced that he could always grab the reins just before the horse left the road, yet it is possible to glimpse madness in his sanity. A neighbor seems to move "in darkness" almost "like an old-stone savage armed" ("Mending Wall"). The boundaries between the real and the dream world blur ("After Apple-Picking"). Poems such as "Fire and Ice" and "Design" give us glimpses into chaos, destruction, and nothingness; they are the work of "a terrifying poet," as Lionel Trilling first noted in a 1959 speech. In "The Figure a Poem Makes," Frost famously described poetry as "a momentary stay against confusion," and in his poems, we can feel both artful reprieve and the disorder it tries to hold in check. Frost's mainstay is always irony, the art of sustaining the self between extremes, and his balances are precarious. Like so many New England writers—Nathaniel Hawthorne and Herman Melville among them—he is a student of darkness, aware of its encroachments, yet hopeful that it can, by art and understanding, be overwhelmed.

Frost once referred to his faith as a grafting of the philosophy of Arthur Schopenhauer upon Christianity, but his mother, a Scottish immigrant, baptized her two children in the Swedenborgian Church, with its more benign but mysterious creed of salvation through the acceptance of divine truth. In high school, Frost was an excellent student of classics, and he also began to be known as a poet. He resolved to marry Elinor White, his covaledictorian, and it was characteristic of his tenacity that he succeeded in doing so in spite of her delays and doubts. He won a scholarship to Dartmouth College, and she went to St. Lawrence College. Before a semester was over, Frost had dropped out, but in 1897, he persuaded the authorities at Harvard University to admit him as a special student (rather than a degree candidate). He was to say in later life that this was a turning point for him. At Harvard, he could try himself against the intellectual powers of his time. But again, in March 1899, he withdrew of his own accord. On medical advice, he thought he would live in the country, and his grandfather bought him a farm in Derry, New Hampshire. These years were gloomy ones for Frost. Money was short, and family life was especially difficult—the Frosts had five children by 1905; the first, Elliott, died at age three, in 1900, and another, the infant Elinor, in 1907. Frost more than once meditated suicide. A lift came when, in 1905, he took a teaching job at Pinkerton Academy, in New Hampshire. During the next six years, he reformed its English syllabus, directed plays, and wrote most of the poems later included in his first book.

In 1911, he sold his farm; the next year marked a second turning point in his life, when, in September 1912, he took a ship with his family to Glasgow and then went on to London. The move was perhaps a whim, but it was a fortunate one. He had little reason to hope that publication of his verse would be any easier in England than in the United States, but a month after his arrival the English publisher Alfred Nutt accepted his poems. *A Boy's Will* was published in 1913 and a second book, *North of Boston,* in 1914.

In England, Frost came to know the poets of the time. Ezra Pound introduced him to W. B. Yeats, whom he had long admired; Frost also met Imagists such as F. S. Flint, Amy Lowell, and T. E. Hulme and became friendly with the Georgian poets. Among these last, his closest friend was Edward Thomas, in whom he recognized a kindred spirit. This pleasant idyll in England was broken by the war, and Frost returned in 1915 to the United States. There his luck in publication held. Although he could not live on his poems, his poetry made him much sought after by colleges and universities. In 1916, he began to teach at Amherst College, intermixed with periods as professor or poet in residence at the University of Michigan, Harvard, Dartmouth, and elsewhere. He was a frequent lecturer around the country and eventually became a goodwill emissary to South America and, at President John F. Kennedy's request, to the Soviet Union.

Frost's personal life was never easy. He demanded great loyalty, was quick to suspect friends of treachery, and was sometimes insensitive to members of his family. In 1934, his daughter Marjorie died; in 1938, his wife died; in 1940, his son Carol committed suicide; and in 1947, his daughter Irma was committed to a mental hospital. Though he won the Pulitzer Prize four times, he never received the Nobel Prize, which Yeats and Eliot had both won; the reason may have been his determined provincialism. Nonetheless, he was showered with honors, perhaps the most conspicuous of which was reading a poem at President Kennedy's inauguration, in 1961. Frost had become the most recognized poet in America. He lived about as long as Thomas Hardy, dying at eighty-eight.

Frost's poetry has some kinship with Edwin Arlington Robinson's in its choice of a New England setting and in its attempt to be true to the peculiarities of the region. But Frost's idiom is much less literary, and here he seems to have learned a little from Hardy and from Yeats's plays. But even his earliest poems strive for utter colloquialism. This did not entail any surrender of form. Though his syntax, rhythms, and often monosyllabic vocabulary seem natural, even folksy, they play in subtle counterpoint against traditional meters, such as iambic pentameter, and verse forms, such as the sonnet. Frost prided himself, for all his country accents, on being close to his favorite Latin poet, Horace, in the way his poems were chiseled out. Free verse was like playing tennis without a net, he said. To secure his effect, Frost avoided any hint of the grand manner; John Crowe Ransom remarked that he was startled during his own boyhood to discover that Frost's poetry had no kings or queens in it. The revival of Arthurian materials by his compatriot Robinson struck Frost as absurd. He prided himself, too, on staying close to earth, and he objected to what he called "Platonism" in poetry, an insistence on essence without matter.

Yet his flatness is not so open as it at first appears. He works with *paysages moralisés,* or psychological landscapes. "Poetry," he said in the essay "Education by Poetry," "provides the one permissible way of saying one thing and meaning another. People say, 'Why don't you say what you mean?' We never do that, do we, being all of us too much poets. We like to talk in parables and in hints and in indirections—whether from diffidence or some other instinct." The sentences for which he is best known, when read in context, prove to be trickier than they seem. "Good fences make good neighbors," repeats the neighbor in "Mending Wall," but the poem is suspicious of the usefulness of walls and boundaries, except as opportunities for playing a "game" or fooling around, as one does in working within the formal boundaries of poetry. "Two roads diverged in a wood," remembers the self-satisfied speaker in "The Road Not Taken," "and I—/ I took the one less traveled by, / And that has made all the difference." But his self-congratulatory remark distorts experience, since the other road was, in fact, "just as fair," "really about the same," and "equally" worn. Choices are consequential—"way leads on to way"—but we retrospectively impose on them intention and meaning.

For all his irony, teasing, and quizzical understatement, Frost is different from other poets who practice indirection. He is countrified where Wallace Stevens is not; he is conclusive where William Carlos Williams is not. Unlike Yeats and Eliot, he has almost nothing to say in prose, whether from guardedness or economy, except for some aphoristic statements. Aside from long meditative poems and two masques, he wrote only lyrics. Although no poet need do more than Frost did, and few can do as much, he presents, in comparison with other eminent writers of his time, an impressive example of reserve or holding back in genre, diction, theme, and even philosophy. This at times bitter man left his readers poems that they quite simply love; and to love a poem by Frost is to begin, at each rereading of a poem, to hear a voice that does not set aside its task before that task has been performed.

Mending Wall

Something there is that doesn't love a wall,
That sends the frozen-ground-swell under it
And spills the upper boulders in the sun,
And makes gaps even two can pass abreast.
The work of hunters is another thing:
I have come after them and made repair
Where they have left not one stone on a stone,

But they would have the rabbit out of hiding,
To please the yelping dogs. The gaps I mean,
No one has seen them made or heard them made,
But at spring mending-time we find them there.
I let my neighbor know beyond the hill;
And on a day we meet to walk the line
And set the wall between us once again.
We keep the wall between us as we go.
To each the boulders that have fallen to each.
And some are loaves and some so nearly balls
We have to use a spell to make them balance:
"Stay where you are until our backs are turned!"
We wear our fingers rough with handling them.
Oh, just another kind of outdoor game,
One on a side. It comes to little more:
There where it is we do not need the wall:
He is all pine and I am apple orchard.
My apple trees will never get across
And eat the cones under his pines, I tell him.
He only says, "Good fences make good neighbors."
Spring is the mischief in me, and I wonder
If I could put a notion in his head:
"*Why* do they make good neighbors? Isn't it
Where there are cows? But here there are no cows.
Before I built a wall I'd ask to know
What I was walling in or walling out,
And to whom I was like to give offense.
Something there is that doesn't love a wall,
That wants it down." I could say "Elves" to him,
But it's not elves exactly, and I'd rather
He said it for himself. I see him there,
Bringing a stone grasped firmly by the top
In each hand, like an old-stone savage armed.
He moves in darkness as it seems to me,
Not of woods only and the shade of trees.
He will not go behind his father's saying,
And he likes having thought of it so well
He says again, "Good fences make good neighbors."

1914

Home Burial

He saw her from the bottom of the stairs
Before she saw him. She was starting down,
Looking back over her shoulder at some fear.
She took a doubtful step and then undid it
To raise herself and look again. He spoke
Advancing toward her: "What is it you see
From up there always?—for I want to know."

She turned and sank upon her skirts at that,
And her face changed from terrified to dull.
He said to gain time: "What is it you see?"
Mounting until she cowered under him.
"I will find out now—you must tell me, dear."
She, in her place, refused him any help,
With the least stiffening of her neck and silence.
She let him look, sure that he wouldn't see,
Blind creature; and awhile he didn't see.
But at last he murmured, "Oh," and again, "Oh."

"What is it—what?" she said.

"Just that I see."

"You don't," she challenged. "Tell me what it is."

"The wonder is I didn't see at once.
I never noticed it from here before.
I must be wonted to it—that's the reason.
The little graveyard where my people are!
So small the window frames the whole of it.
Not so much larger than a bedroom, is it?
There are three stones of slate and one of marble,
Broad-shouldered little slabs there in the sunlight
On the sidehill. We haven't to mind *those.*
But I understand: it is not the stones,
But the child's mound——"

"Don't, don't, don't, don't," she cried.

She withdrew, shrinking from beneath his arm
That rested on the banister, and slid downstairs;
And turned on him with such a daunting look,
He said twice over before he knew himself:
"Can't a man speak of his own child he's lost?"

"Not you!—Oh, where's my hat? Oh, I don't need it!
I must get out of here. I must get air.—
I don't know rightly whether any man can."

"Amy! Don't go to someone else this time.
Listen to me. I won't come down the stairs."
He sat and fixed his chin between his fists.
"There's something I should like to ask you, dear."

"You don't know how to ask it."

"Help me, then."

Her fingers moved the latch for all reply.

"My words are nearly always an offense.
I don't know how to speak of anything
So as to please you. But I might be taught,
I should suppose. I can't say I see how.
A man must partly give up being a man
With womenfolk. We could have some arrangement
By which I'd bind myself to keep hands off
Anything special you're a-mind to name.
Though I don't like such things 'twixt those that love.
Two that don't love can't live together without them.
But two that do can't live together with them."
She moved the latch a little. "Don't—don't go.
Don't carry it to someone else this time.
Tell me about it if it's something human.
Let me into your grief. I'm not so much
Unlike other folks as your standing there
Apart would make me out. Give me my chance.
I do think, though, you overdo it a little.
What was it brought you up to think it the thing
To take your mother-loss of a first child
So inconsolably—in the face of love.
You'd think his memory might be satisfied——"
"There you go sneering now!"

"I'm not, I'm not!
You make me angry. I'll come down to you.
God, what a woman! And it's come to this,
A man can't speak of his own child that's dead."

"You can't because you don't know how to speak.
If you had any feelings, you that dug
With your own hand—how could you?—his little grave;
I saw you from that very window there,
Making the gravel leap and leap in air,
Leap up, like that, like that, and land so lightly
And roll back down the mound beside the hole.
I thought, Who is that man? I didn't know you.
And I crept down the stairs and up the stairs
To look again, and still your spade kept lifting.
Then you came in. I heard your rumbling voice
Out in the kitchen, and I don't know why,
But I went near to see with my own eyes.
You could sit there with the stains on your shoes
Of the fresh earth from your own baby's grave
And talk about your everyday concerns.
You had stood the spade up against the wall
Outside there in the entry, for I saw it."

"I shall laugh the worst laugh I ever laughed.
I'm cursed. God, if I don't believe I'm cursed."

"I can repeat the very words you were saying:
'Three foggy mornings and one rainy day

Will rot the best birch fence a man can build.'
Think of it, talk like that at such a time!
What had how long it takes a birch to rot
To do with what was in the darkened parlor?
You *couldn't* care! The nearest friends can go
With anyone to death, comes so far short
They might as well not try to go at all.
No, from the time when one is sick to death,
One is alone, and he dies more alone.
Friends make pretense of following to the grave,
But before one is in it, their minds are turned
And making the best of their way back to life
And living people, and things they understand.
But the world's evil. I won't have grief so
If I can change it. Oh, I won't, I won't!"

"There, you have said it all and you feel better.
You won't go now. You're crying. Close the door.
The heart's gone out of it: why keep it up?
Amy! There's someone coming down the road!"

"*You*—oh, you think the talk is all. I must go—
Somewhere out of this house. How can I make you——"

"If—you—do!" She was opening the door wider.
"Where do you mean to go? First tell me that.
I'll follow and bring you back by force. I *will!*—"

1914

After Apple-Picking

My long two-pointed ladder's sticking through a tree
Toward heaven still,
And there's a barrel that I didn't fill
Beside it, and there may be two or three
Apples I didn't pick upon some bough.
But I am done with apple-picking now.
Essence of winter sleep is on the night,
The scent of apples: I am drowsing off.
I cannot rub the strangeness from my sight
I got from looking through a pane of glass
I skimmed this morning from the drinking trough
And held against the world of hoary grass.
It melted, and I let it fall and break.
But I was well
Upon my way to sleep before it fell,
And I could tell
What form my dreaming was about to take.
Magnified apples appear and disappear,
Stem end and blossom end,

And every fleck of russet showing clear.
My instep arch not only keeps the ache,
It keeps the pressure of a ladder-round.
I feel the ladder sway as the boughs bend.
And I keep hearing from the cellar bin
The rumbling sound
Of load on load of apples coming in.
For I have had too much
Of apple-picking: I am overtired
Of the great harvest I myself desired.
There were ten thousand thousand fruit to touch,
Cherish in hand, lift down, and not let fall.
For all
That struck the earth,
No matter if not bruised or spiked with stubble,
Went surely to the cider-apple heap
As of no worth.
One can see what will trouble
This sleep of mine, whatever sleep it is.
Were he not gone,
The woodchuck could say whether it's like his
Long sleep, as I describe its coming on,
Or just some human sleep.

1914

The Wood-Pile

Out walking in the frozen swamp one gray day,
I paused and said, "I will turn back from here.
No, I will go on farther—and we shall see."
The hard snow held me, save where now and then
One foot went through. The view was all in lines
Straight up and down of tall slim trees
Too much alike to mark or name a place by
So as to say for certain I was here
Or somewhere else: I was just far from home.
A small bird flew before me. He was careful
To put a tree between us when he lighted,
And say no word to tell me who he was
Who was so foolish as to think what *he* thought.
He thought that I was after him for a feather—
The white one in his tail; like one who takes
Everything said as personal to himself.
One flight out sideways would have undeceived him.
And then there was a pile of wood for which
I forgot him and let his little fear
Carry him off the way I might have gone,
Without so much as wishing him good-night.
He went behind it to make his last stand.
It was a cord of maple, cut and split

And piled—and measured, four by four by eight.
And not another like it could I see.
No runner tracks in this year's snow looped near it.
And it was older sure than this year's cutting,
Or even last year's or the year's before.
The wood was gray and the bark warping off it
And the pile somewhat sunken. Clematis
Had wound strings round and round it like a bundle.
What held it, though, on one side was a tree
Still growing, and on one a stake and prop,
These latter about to fall. I thought that only
Someone who lived in turning to fresh tasks
Could so forget his handiwork on which
He spent himself, the labor of his ax,
And leave it there far from a useful fireplace
To warm the frozen swamp as best it could
With the slow smokeless burning of decay.

1914

The Road Not Taken[1]

Two roads diverged in a yellow wood,
And sorry I could not travel both
And be one traveler, long I stood
And looked down one as far as I could
To where it bent in the undergrowth;

Then took the other, as just as fair,
And having perhaps the better claim,
Because it was grassy and wanted wear;
Though as for that, the passing there
Had worn them really about the same,

And both that morning equally lay
In leaves no step had trodden black.
Oh, I kept the first for another day!
Yet knowing how way leads on to way,
I doubted if I should ever come back.

I shall be telling this with a sigh
Somewhere ages and ages hence:
Two roads diverged in a wood, and I—

1. According to Lawrence Thomspson, in *Robert Frost* (1970), this poem was a slightly mocking parody of the behavior of Frost's friend Edward Thomas, who used to choose a direction for their country walks, then, before they had finished, berate himself for not having chosen a different, more interesting way. Frost, says Thompson, did not approve of romantic "sighing over what might have been."

But E. S. Sergeant, in *Robert Frost: The Trial by Existence* (1960), quotes a letter from Frost, written February 10, 1912, in which he describes how, going down a lonely crossroad on a recent evening, he saw someone who "looked for all the world like myself coming down the other, his approach to the point where our paths must intersect being so timed that unless one of us pulled up we must inevitably collide. I felt as if I was going to meet my own image in a slanting mirror. . . . I stood still in wonderment and let him pass by."

I took the one less traveled by,
And that has made all the difference.

1916

An Old Man's Winter Night

All out-of-doors looked darkly in at him
Through the thin frost, almost in separate stars,
That gathers on the pane in empty rooms.
What kept his eyes from giving back the gaze
Was the lamp tilted near them in his hand.
What kept him from remembering what it was
That brought him to that creaking room was age.
He stood with barrels round him—at a loss.
And having scared the cellar under him
In clomping here, he scared it once again
In clomping off—and scared the outer night,
Which has its sounds, familiar, like the roar
Of trees and crack of branches, common things,
But nothing so like beating on a box.
A light he was to no one but himself
Where now he sat, concerned with he knew what,
A quiet light, and then not even that.
He consigned to the moon—such as she was,
So late-arising—to the broken moon,
As better than the sun in any case
For such a charge, his snow upon the roof,
His icicles along the wall to keep;
And slept. The log that shifted with a jolt
Once in the stove, disturbed him and he shifted,
And eased his heavy breathing, but still slept.
One aged man—one man—can't keep a house,
A farm, a countryside, or if he can,
It's thus he does it of a winter night.

1916

Hyla Brook[2]

By June our brook's run out of song and speed.
Sought for much after that, it will be found
Either to have gone groping underground
(And taken with it all the Hyla breed

2. *Hyla:* tree frog. In Greek mythology, Hylas was a young boy who disappeared when lured into the water by river nymphs.

That shouted in the mist a month ago,
Like ghost of sleigh bells in a ghost of snow)—
Or flourished and come up in jewelweed,
Weak foliage that is blown upon and bent,
Even against the way its waters went.
Its bed is left a faded paper sheet
Of dead leaves stuck together by the heat—
A brook to none but who remember long.
This as it will be seen is other far
Than with brooks taken otherwhere in song.
We love the things we love for what they are.

1916

The Oven Bird

There is a singer everyone has heard,
Loud, a mid-summer and a mid-wood bird,
Who makes the solid tree trunks sound again.
He says that leaves are old and that for flowers
Mid-summer is to spring as one to ten.
He says the early petal-fall is past,
When pear and cherry bloom went down in showers
On sunny days a moment overcast;
And comes that other fall we name the fall.
He says the highway dust is over all.
The bird would cease and be as other birds
But that he knows in singing not to sing.
The question that he frames in all but words
Is what to make of a diminished thing.

1916

Birches

When I see birches bend to left and right
Across the lines of straighter darker trees,
I like to think some boy's been swinging them.
But swinging doesn't bend them down to stay
As ice-storms do. Often you must have seen them
Loaded with ice a sunny winter morning
After a rain. They click upon themselves
As the breeze rises, and turn many-colored
As the stir cracks and crazes their enamel.
Soon the sun's warmth makes them shed crystal shells
Shattering and avalanching on the snow crust—
Such heaps of broken glass to sweep away

You'd think the inner dome of heaven had fallen.
They are dragged to the withered bracken by the load,
And they seem not to break; though once they are bowed
So low for long, they never right themselves:
You may see their trunks arching in the woods
Years afterwards, trailing their leaves on the ground
Like girls on hands and knees that throw their hair
Before them over their heads to dry in the sun.
But I was going to say when Truth broke in
With all her matter of fact about the ice storm,
I should prefer to have some boy bend them
As he went out and in to fetch the cows—
Some boy too far from town to learn baseball,
Whose only play was what he found himself,
Summer or winter, and could play alone.
One by one he subdued his father's trees
By riding them down over and over again
Until he took the stiffness out of them,
And not one but hung limp, not one was left
For him to conquer. He learned all there was
To learn about not launching out too soon
And so not carrying the tree away
Clear to the ground. He always kept his poise
To the top branches, climbing carefully
With the same pains you use to fill a cup
Up to the brim, and even above the brim.
Then he flung outward, feet first, with a swish,
Kicking his way down through the air to the ground.
So was I once myself a swinger of birches.
And so I dream of going back to be.
It's when I'm weary of considerations,
And life is too much like a pathless wood
Where your face burns and tickles with the cobwebs
Broken across it, and one eye is weeping
From a twig's having lashed across it open.
I'd like to get away from earth awhile
And then come back to it and begin over.
May no fate willfully misunderstand me
And half grant what I wish and snatch me away
Not to return. Earth's the right place for love:
I don't know where it's likely to go better.
I'd like to go by climbing a birch tree,
And climb black branches up a snow-white trunk
Toward heaven, till the tree could bear no more,
But dipped its top and set me down again.
That would be good both going and coming back.
One could do worse than be a swinger of birches.

1916

Putting in the Seed

You come to fetch me from my work tonight
When supper's on the table, and we'll see
If I can leave off burying the white
Soft petals fallen from the apple tree
(Soft petals, yes, but not so barren quite,
Mingled with these, smooth bean and wrinkled pea),
And go along with you ere you lose sight
Of what you came for and become like me,
Slave to a springtime passion for the earth.
How Love burns through the Putting in the Seed
On through the watching for that early birth
When, just as the soil tarnishes with weed,
The sturdy seedling with arched body comes
Shouldering its way and shedding the earth crumbs.

1916

"Out, Out—"[3]

The buzz saw snarled and rattled in the yard
And made dust and dropped stove-length sticks of wood,
Sweet-scented stuff when the breeze drew across it.
And from there those that lifted eyes could count
Five mountain ranges one behind the other
Under the sunset far into Vermont.
And the saw snarled and rattled, snarled and rattled,
As it ran light, or had to bear a load.
And nothing happened: day was all but done.
Call it a day, I wish they might have said
To please the boy by giving him the half hour
That a boy counts so much when saved from work.
His sister stood beside them in her apron
To tell them "Supper." At the word, the saw,
As if to prove saws knew what supper meant,
Leaped out at the boy's hand, or seemed to leap—
He must have given the hand. However it was,
Neither refused the meeting. But the hand!
The boy's first outcry was a rueful laugh,
As he swung toward them holding up the hand,
Half in appeal, but half as if to keep
The life from spilling. Then the boy saw all—
Since he was old enough to know, big boy
Doing a man's work, though a child at heart—
He saw all spoiled. "Don't let him cut my hand off—
The doctor, when he comes. Don't let him, sister!"

3. Cf. Shakespeare's *Macbeth* 5.5.23–24: "Out, out, brief candle. / Life's but a walking shadow."

So. But the hand was gone already.
The doctor put him in the dark of ether.
He lay and puffed his lips out with his breath.
And then—the watcher at his pulse took fright.
No one believed. They listened at his heart.
Little—less—nothing!—and that ended it.
No more to build on there. And they, since they
Were not the one dead, turned to their affairs.

1916

Fire and Ice

Some say the world will end in fire,
Some say in ice.
From what I've tasted of desire
I hold with those who favor fire.
But if it had to perish twice,
I think I know enough of hate
To say that for destruction ice
Is also great
And would suffice.

1923

Dust of Snow

The way a crow
Shook down on me
The dust of snow
From a hemlock tree

Has given my heart
A change of mood
And saved some part
Of a day I had rued.

1923

Stopping by Woods on a Snowy Evening

Whose woods these are I think I know.
His house is in the village, though;
He will not see me stopping here
To watch his woods fill up with snow.

My little horse must think it queer
To stop without a farmhouse near
Between the woods and frozen lake
The darkest evening of the year.

He gives his harness bells a shake
To ask if there is some mistake.
The only other sound's the sweep
Of easy wind and downy flake.

The woods are lovely, dark, and deep,
But I have promises to keep,
And miles to go before I sleep,
And miles to go before I sleep.

1923

For Once, Then, Something

Others taunt me with having knelt at well-curbs
Always wrong to the light, so never seeing
Deeper down in the well than where the water
Gives me back in a shining surface picture
Me myself in the summer heaven, godlike,
Looking out of a wreath of fern and cloud puffs.
Once, when trying with chin against a well-curb,
I discerned, as I thought, beyond the picture,
Through the picture, a something white, uncertain,
Something more of the depths—and then I lost it.
Water came to rebuke the too clear water.
One drop fell from a fern, and lo, a ripple
Shook whatever it was lay there at bottom,
Blurred it, blotted it out. What was that whiteness?
Truth?[4] A pebble of quartz? For once, then, something.

1923

To Earthward

Love at the lips was touch
As sweet as I could bear;
And once that seemed too much;
I lived on air

That crossed me from sweet things,
The flow of—was it musk

4. Cf. the Greek proverb that truth lives at the bottom of a well.

From hidden grapevine springs
Downhill at dusk?

I had the swirl and ache
From sprays of honeysuckle
That when they're gathered shake
Dew on the knuckle.

I craved strong sweets, but those
Seemed strong when I was young;
The petal of the rose
It was that stung.

Now no joy but lacks salt,
That is not dashed with pain
And weariness and fault;
I crave the stain

Of tears, the aftermark
Of almost too much love,
The sweet of bitter bark
And burning clove.

When stiff and sore and scarred
I take away my hand
From leaning on it hard
In grass and sand,

The hurt is not enough:
I long for weight and strength
To feel the earth as rough
To all my length.

1923

The Need of Being Versed in Country Things

The house had gone to bring again
To the midnight sky a sunset glow.
Now the chimney was all of the house that stood,
Like a pistil after the petals go.

The barn opposed across the way,
That would have joined the house in flame
Had it been the will of the wind, was left
To bear forsaken the place's name.

No more it opened with all one end
For teams that came by the stony road

To drum on the floor with scurrying hoofs
And brush the mow with the summer load.

The birds that came to it through the air
At broken windows flew out and in,
Their murmur more like the sigh we sigh
From too much dwelling on what has been.

Yet for them the lilac renewed its leaf,
And the aged elm, though touched with fire;
And the dry pump flung up an awkward arm;
And the fence post carried a strand of wire.

For them there was really nothing sad.
But though they rejoiced in the nest they kept,
One had to be versed in country things
Not to believe the phoebes wept.

1923

Tree at My Window

Tree at my window, window tree,
My sash is lowered when night comes on;
But let there never be curtain drawn
Between you and me.

Vague dream-head lifted out of the ground,
And thing next most diffuse to cloud,
Not all your light tongues talking aloud
Could be profound.

But, tree, I have seen you taken and tossed,
And if you have seen me when I slept,
You have seen me when I was taken and swept
And all but lost.

That day she put our heads together,
Fate had her imagination about her,
Your head so much concerned with outer,
Mine with inner, weather.

1928

Acquainted with the Night

I have been one acquainted with the night.
I have walked out in rain—and back in rain.
I have outwalked the furthest city light.

I have looked down the saddest city lane.
I have passed by the watchman on his beat
And dropped my eyes, unwilling to explain.

I have stood still and stopped the sound of feet
When far away an interrupted cry
Came over houses from another street,

But not to call me back or say good-by;
And further still at an unearthly height
One luminary clock against the sky

Proclaimed the time was neither wrong nor right.
I have been one acquainted with the night.

1928

Two Tramps in Mud Time

Out of the mud two strangers came
And caught me splitting wood in the yard.
And one of them put me off my aim
By hailing cheerily "Hit them hard!"
I knew pretty well why he dropped behind
And let the other go on a way.
I knew pretty well what he had in mind:
He wanted to take my job for pay.

Good blocks of oak it was I split,
As large around as the chopping block;
And every piece I squarely hit
Fell splinterless as a cloven rock.
The blows that a life of self-control
Spares to strike for the common good,
That day, giving a loose to my soul,
I spent on the unimportant wood.

The sun was warm but the wind was chill.
You know how it is with an April day
When the sun is out and the wind is still,
You're one month on in the middle of May.
But if you so much as dare to speak,
A cloud comes over the sunlit arch,
A wind comes off a frozen peak,
And you're two months back in the middle of March.

A bluebird comes tenderly up to alight
And turns to the wind to unruffle a plume,
His song so pitched as not to excite
A single flower as yet to bloom.

It is snowing a flake: and he half knew
Winter was only playing possum.
Except in color he isn't blue,
But he wouldn't advise a thing to blossom.

The water for which we may have to look
In summertime with a witching wand,[5]
In every wheelrut's now a brook,
In every print of a hoof a pond.
Be glad of water, but don't forget
The lurking frost in the earth beneath
That will steal forth after the sun is set
And show on the water its crystal teeth.

The time when most I loved my task
These two must make me love it more
By coming with what they came to ask.
You'd think I never had felt before
The weight of an ax-head poised aloft,
The grip on earth of outspread feet,
The life of muscles rocking soft
And smooth and moist in vernal[6] heat.

Out of the woods two hulking tramps
(From sleeping God knows where last night,
But not long since in the lumber camps).
They thought all chopping was theirs of right.
Men of the woods and lumberjacks,
They judged me by their appropriate tool.
Except as a fellow handled an ax
They had no way of knowing a fool.

Nothing on either side was said.
They knew they had but to stay their stay
And all their logic would fill my head:
As that I had no right to play
With what was another man's work for gain.
My right might be love but theirs was need.
And where the two exist in twain
Theirs was the better right—agreed.

But yield who will to their separation,
My object in living is to unite
My avocation and my vocation
As my two eyes make one in sight.
Only where love and need are one,
And the work is play for mortal stakes,
Is the deed ever really done
For Heaven and the future's sakes.

1936

5. Divining rod.

6. Spring.

Desert Places

Snow falling and night falling fast, oh, fast
In a field I looked into going past,
And the ground almost covered smooth in snow,
But a few weeds and stubble showing last.

The woods around it have it—it is theirs.
All animals are smothered in their lairs.
I am too absent-spirited to count;
The loneliness includes me unawares.

And lonely as it is, that loneliness
Will be more lonely ere it will be less—
A blanker whiteness of benighted snow
With no expression, nothing to express.

They cannot scare me with their empty spaces
Between stars—on stars where no human race is.
I have it in me so much nearer home
To scare myself with my own desert places.

1936

Neither Out Far nor In Deep

The people along the sand
All turn and look one way.
They turn their back on the land.
They look at the sea all day.

As long as it takes to pass
A ship keeps raising its hull;
The wetter ground like glass
Reflects a standing gull.

The land may vary more;
But wherever the truth may be—
The water comes ashore,
And the people look at the sea.

They cannot look out far.
They cannot look in deep.
But when was that ever a bar
To any watch they keep?

1936

Design

I found a dimpled spider, fat and white,
On a white heal-all,[7] holding up a moth
Like a white piece of rigid satin cloth—
Assorted characters of death and blight
Mixed ready to begin the morning right,
Like the ingredients of a witches' broth—
A snow-drop spider, a flower like a froth,
And dead wings carried like a paper kite.

What had that flower to do with being white,
The wayside blue and innocent heal-all?
What brought the kindred spider to that height,
Then steered the white moth thither in the night?
What but design of darkness to appall?[8]—
If design govern in a thing so small.

1936

Unharvested

A scent of ripeness from over a wall.
And come to leave the routine road
And look for what had made me stall,
There sure enough was an apple tree
That had eased itself of its summer load,
And of all but its trivial foliage free,
Now breathed as light as a lady's fan.
For there there had been an apple fall
As complete as the apple had given man.
The ground was one circle of solid red.

May something go always unharvested!
May much stay out of our stated plan,
Apples or something forgotten and left,
So smelling their sweetness would be no theft.

1936

7. Common wildflower that normally has a violet-blue blossom.

8. Literally, to make pale.

Provide, Provide

The witch that came (the withered hag)
To wash the steps with pail and rag
Was once the beauty Abishag,[9]

The picture pride of Hollywood.
Too many fall from great and good
For you to doubt the likelihood.

Die early and avoid the fate.
Or if predestined to die late,
Make up your mind to die in state.

Make the whole stock exchange your own!
If need be occupy a throne,
Where nobody can call *you* crone.

Some have relied on what they knew,
Others on being simply true.
What worked for them might work for you.

No memory of having starred
Atones for later disregard
Or keeps the end from being hard.

Better to go down dignified
With boughten friendship at your side
Than none at all. Provide, provide!

1936

The Silken Tent

She is as in a field a silken tent
At midday when a sunny summer breeze
Has dried the dew and all its ropes relent,
So that in guys[1] it gently sways at ease,
And its supporting central cedar pole,
That is its pinnacle to heavenward
And signifies the sureness of the soul,
Seems to owe naught to any single cord,
But strictly held by none, is loosely bound
By countless silken ties of love and thought
To everything on earth the compass round,
And only by one's going slightly taut
In the capriciousness of summer air
Is of the slightest bondage made aware.

1942

9. A beautiful young woman who nursed King David in his old age (1 Kings 1.2–4).

1. Ropes used to hold an object steady.

The Most of It

He thought he kept the universe alone;
For all the voice in answer he could wake
Was but the mocking echo of his own
From some tree-hidden cliff across the lake.
Some morning from the boulder-broken beach
He would cry out on life, that what it wants
Is not its own love back in copy speech,
But counter-love, original response.
And nothing ever came of what he cried
Unless it was the embodiment that crashed
In the cliff's talus[2] on the other side,
And then in the far-distant water splashed,
But after a time allowed for it to swim,
Instead of proving human when it neared
And someone else additional to him,
As a great buck it powerfully appeared,
Pushing the crumpled water up ahead,
And landed pouring like a waterfall,
And stumbled through the rocks with horny tread,
And forced the underbrush—and that was all.

1942

Never Again Would Birds' Song Be the Same

He would declare and could himself believe
That the birds there in all the garden round
From having heard the daylong voice of Eve
Had added to their own an oversound,
Her tone of meaning but without the words.
Admittedly an eloquence so soft
Could only have had an influence on birds
When call or laughter carried it aloft.
Be that as may be, she was in their song.
Moreover her voice upon their voices crossed
Had now persisted in the woods so long
That probably it never would be lost.
Never again would birds' song be the same.
And to do that to birds was why she came.

1942

2. Sloping pile of rock.

The Gift Outright

The land was ours before we were the land's.
She was our land more than a hundred years
Before we were her people. She was ours
In Massachusetts, in Virginia,
But we were England's, still colonials,
Possessing what we still were unpossessed by,
Possessed by what we now no more possessed.
Something we were withholding made us weak
Until we found out that it was ourselves
We were withholding from our land of living,
And forthwith found salvation in surrender.
Such as we were we gave ourselves outright
(The deed of gift was many deeds of war)
To the land vaguely realizing westward,
But still unstoried, artless, unenhanced,
Such as she was, such as she would become.

1942

Directive

Back out of all this now too much for us,
Back in a time made simple by the loss
Of detail, burned, dissolved, and broken off
Like graveyard marble sculpture in the weather,
There is a house that is no more a house
Upon a farm that is no more a farm
And in a town that is no more a town.
The road there, if you'll let a guide direct you
Who only has at heart your getting lost,
May seem as if it should have been a quarry—
Great monolithic knees the former town
Long since gave up pretense of keeping covered.
And there's a story in a book about it:
Besides the wear of iron wagon wheels
The ledges show lines ruled southeast-northwest.
The chisel work of an enormous Glacier
That braced his feet against the Arctic Pole.
You must not mind a certain coolness from him
Still said to haunt this side of Panther Mountain.
Nor need you mind the serial ordeal
Of being watched from forty cellar holes
As if by eye pairs out of forty firkins.[3]

3. Small wooden tubs.

As for the woods' excitement over you
That sends light rustle rushes to their leaves,
Charge that to upstart inexperience.
Where were they all not twenty years ago?
They think too much of having shaded out
A few old pecker-fretted[4] apple trees.
Make yourself up a cheering song of how
Someone's road home from work this once was,
Who may be just ahead of you on foot
Or creaking with a buggy load of grain.
The height of the adventure is the height
Of country where two village cultures faded
Into each other. Both of them are lost.
And if you're lost enough to find yourself
By now, pull in your ladder road behind you
And put a sign up CLOSED to all but me.
Then make yourself at home. The only field
Now left's no bigger than a harness gall.[5]
First there's the children's house of make-believe,
Some shattered dishes underneath a pine,
The playthings in the playhouse of the children.
Weep for what little things could make them glad.
Then for the house that is no more a house,
But only a belilaced cellar hole,
Now slowly closing like a dent in dough.
This was no playhouse but a house in earnest.
Your destination and your destiny's
A brook that was the water of the house,
Cold as a spring as yet so near its source,
Too lofty and original to rage.
(We know the valley streams that when aroused
Will leave their tatters hung on barb and thorn.)
I have kept hidden in the instep arch
Of an old cedar at the waterside
A broken drinking goblet like the Grail[6]
Under a spell so the wrong ones can't find it,
So can't get saved, as Saint Mark says they mustn't.[7]
(I stole the goblet from the children's playhouse.)
Here are your waters and your watering place.
Drink and be whole again beyond confusion.

1947

4. Woodpecker-marked.
5. Sore caused by a harness.
6. Cup sought in medieval and Arthurian romance, supposed to have been used by Jesus at the Last Supper.
7. Cf. Mark 4.11: "Unto you it is given to know the mystery of the kingdom of God: but unto them that are without, all *these* things are done in parables"; and Mark 16.16: "He that believeth and is baptized shall be saved; but he that believeth not shall be damned."

Carl Sandburg
1878–1967

Carl Sandburg, like Edgar Lee Masters, belonged to a group of writers centered in Chicago who sought to liberate verse from gentility. After Walt Whitman and Emily Dickinson, American poetry lost intensity, and at the end of the nineteenth century, except for Edwin Arlington Robinson (who was just beginning to publish), there were no models capable of satisfying the young. T. S. Eliot had to look to France for his examples of living poetry. Sandburg took Whitman as his example and America for his subject matter. He was the first of an increasing number of American poets to grow up in a house where English was the second language, and as the child of immigrants he saw with gusto and exaltation what poets of established families took for granted or disparaged.

Chicago, for example, had been generally considered another overgrown industrial city until Sandburg began to apostrophize its monstrosity with maternal indulgence. Some readers of his *Chicago Poems* (1916) objected to his delight in violence and attributed it to his socialist politics. Defending himself in a 1917 letter to Amy Lowell, Sandburg wrote that his intention was not to propound the theories of the Industrial Workers of the World, but "to sing, blab, chortle, yodel, like people, and people in the sense of human beings subtracted from formal doctrines" (*The Letters of Carl Sandburg*, ed. Herbert Mitgang, 1968, 117–18). Sandburg regarded himself as the defender of the people, and he expressed their basic drives in two modes, one rough-and-ready, the other tender.

Sandburg helped blow a new wind into American verse, in part by his lack of subtlety. He was a sharp and engaged observer, writing poetry more immediately political and sociological than Whitman's, with a journalistic delight in timeliness, yet honest and unaffected. Sandburg saw socialism, not democracy, as the ideal of the new age. The changes of modernity necessitated changes in techniques. "It is a time of confusions," he wrote. "Particularly in America is it a period of chaos, in the economic America that hurls forms and images of new designs so rapidly and changefully that artists who honestly relate their own epoch to older epochs understand how art today, if it is to get results, must pierce exteriors and surfaces by ways different from artists of older times" (*Letters*, 209). He was in revolt against what he considered "Arrow Collar" literature (*Letters*, 221). Free verse and prose were natural media for him, as were noble generalities. Sandburg respected the sturdy and reliable repetitiveness of life and death; like Franco Marinetti and the Futurists he admired dynamism; he hated injustice; and he trusted in his fellow citizens' ability to handle what might come.

Sandburg was born on January 6, 1878, in Galesburg, Illinois. His mother and his father, a machinist's blacksmith, had come from Sweden. He left school after the eighth grade and took on all kinds of working-class jobs. When he was twenty, he enlisted as a volunteer in the Spanish-American War, serving in Puerto Rico. He attended Lombard College, in Illinois, for four years. He then traveled about the country selling stereoscopic photographs. But he also rode the rails, enjoying the company of hobos; on one occasion, he was arrested and served ten days in a Pittsburgh jail. His sympathy for underdogs was fixed by such experiences. In 1904, he returned to newspaper jobs, and in 1907–08, he worked as an organizer for the Social Democratic Party and campaigned with Eugene Victor Debs, the presidential candidate.

In 1914, Harriet Monroe published some of Sandburg's "Chicago Poems" in *Poetry* magazine, and after a book with the same title was published in 1916, Sandburg quickly became a popular figure. He toured the country giving ballad concerts; he wrote articles, books for children, an autobiography, a monumental biography of Abraham Lincoln, and a series of books of verse. His fellow poets were not all as impressed as the public: Robert Frost called Sandburg a fraud. William Carlos Williams regretted that Sandburg "deliberately invited" failure by inattention to the demands of craft. Sandburg was not artless, but his principal interest was in subject, and he is often makeshift in form. The reading public felt his genuineness and was not put off by his clumsiness. Like Frost, he enjoyed in old age extraordinary acclaim. The governor of Illinois proclaimed his seventy-fifth birthday "Carl Sandburg Day," the king of Sweden decorated him, the U.S. Congress invited him to address a joint session on Lincoln Day in 1959, schools bearing his name were opened in Illinois, and in 1964, he received from President Lyndon B. Johnson the Presidential Medal of Freedom.

Chicago

Hog Butcher for the World,
Tool Maker, Stacker of Wheat,
Player with Railroads and the Nation's Freight Handler;
Stormy, husky, brawling,
City of the Big Shoulders:

They tell me you are wicked and I believe them, for I have seen your painted women under the gas lamps luring the farm boys.
And they tell me you are crooked and I answer: Yes, it is true I have seen the gunman kill and go free to kill again.
And they tell me you are brutal and my reply is: On the faces of women and children I have seen the marks of wanton hunger.
And having answered so I turn once more to those who sneer at this my city, and I give them back the sneer and say to them:
Come and show me another city with lifted head singing so proud to be alive and coarse and strong and cunning.
Flinging magnetic curses amid the toil of piling job on job, here is a tall bold slugger set vivid against the little soft cities;
Fierce as a dog with tongue lapping for action, cunning as a savage pitted against the wilderness,
Bareheaded,
Shoveling,
Wrecking,
Planning,
Building, breaking, rebuilding,
Under the smoke, dust all over his mouth, laughing with white teeth,
Under the terrible burden of destiny laughing as a young man laughs,
Laughing even as an ignorant fighter laughs who has never lost a battle,
Bragging and laughing that under his wrist is the pulse, and under his ribs the heart of the people,
Laughing!
Laughing the stormy, husky, brawling laughter of Youth, half-naked, sweating, proud to be Hog Butcher, Tool Maker, Stacker of Wheat, Player with Railroads and Freight Handler to the Nation.

1916

The Harbor

Passing through huddled and ugly walls
By doorways where women
Looked from their hunger-deep eyes,
Haunted with shadows of hunger-hands,
Out from the huddled and ugly walls,
I came sudden, at the city's edge,
On a blue burst of lake,
Long lake waves breaking under the sun
On a spray-flung curve of shore;
And a fluttering storm of gulls,
Masses of great gray wings
And flying white bellies
Veering and wheeling free in the open.

1916

Subway

Down between the walls of shadow
Where the iron laws insist,
  The hunger voices mock.
The worn wayfaring men
With the hunched and humble shoulders,
  Throw their laughter into toil.

1916

Cool Tombs

When Abraham Lincoln was shoveled into the tombs, he forgot the copperheads[1] and the assassin . . . in the dust, in the cool tombs.

And Ulysses Grant lost all thought of con men and Wall Street, cash and collateral turned ashes[2] . . . in the dust, in the cool tombs.

Pocahontas' body, lovely as a poplar, sweet as a red haw in November or a pawpaw in May,[3] did she wonder? does she remember? . . . in the dust, in the cool tombs?

1. A derogatory nickname during the Civil War for Northerners with sympathy for Southern secession.
2. President Ulysses S. Grant (1822–1885) led an administration notorious for corruption and bribery.
3. Pocahontas (1595?–1617), daughter of the Native American chief Powhatan, intervened to save the life of Captain John Smith. *Red haw:* a type of American hawthorn tree. *Pawpaw:* colloquial for the fruit of the papaya tree.

Take any streetful of people buying clothes and groceries, cheering a hero or throwing confetti and blowing tin horns . . . tell me if the lovers are losers . . . tell me if any get more than the lovers . . . in the dust . . . in the cool tombs.

1918

Grass

Pile the bodies high at Austerlitz and Waterloo.[4]
Shovel them under and let me work—
I am the grass; I cover all.

And pile them high at Gettysburg[5]
And pile them high at Ypres and Verdun.[6]
Shovel them under and let me work.
Two years, ten years, and passengers ask the conductor:
What place is this?
Where are we now?

I am the grass.
Let me work.

1918

Gargoyle

I saw a mouth jeering. A smile of melted red iron ran over it. Its laugh was full of nails rattling. It was a child's dream of a mouth.
A fist hit the mouth: knuckles of gun-metal driven by an electric wrist and shoulder. It was a child's dream of an arm.
The fist hit the mouth over and over, again and again. The mouth bled melted iron, and laughed its laughter of nails rattling.
And I saw the more the fist pounded the more the mouth laughed. The fist is pounding and pounding, and the mouth answering.

1918

4. Austerlitz (Slavkov, Czech Republic) was in 1805 the scene of one of Napoleon's great victories, whereas Waterloo, in Belgium, was where he met his final defeat, in 1815.
5. The city in Pennsylvania near which the Confederate army suffered a major defeat in 1863.
6. Ypres, in Belgium, and Verdun, in France, were the centers of some of the fiercest fighting in World War I.

Edward Thomas
1878–1917

Although Edward Thomas has affinities with other Georgian poets—as a city-born nature lover who wrote during World War I—he is unusual for the intensity of his vision, the durability of his reputation, and the subtlety of his technique. He was born on March 3, 1878, in Lambeth, south London, and he spent most of his early life in the city. His parents were Welsh; his father, a dour man, discouraged Thomas's early interest in poetry and urged him to enter the civil service. Thomas was educated at St. Paul's School and Lincoln College, Oxford. He was poor, soon had a family to support, and was given to periods of terrible self-doubt and melancholy. He worked as a reviewer and hack writer, and when he died, at thirty-nine, he had written thirty books of prose and edited many others, but he had managed to publish only six of his poems.

A transforming moment in Thomas's life was first reading Robert Frost. In a review of *North of Boston* (1914), he wrote that Frost's "poems are revolutionary because they lack the exaggeration of rhetoric" and "poetical words and forms": "Many, if not most, of the separate lines and separate sentences are plain, and, in themselves, nothing. But they are bound together and made elements of beauty by a calm eagerness of emotion." Frost, after coming to England, convinced Thomas that he had long neglected his true vocation, which was poetry. And Thomas was proud to say of a poem that it "sounded" like Frost.

War is an oblique but haunting presence in Thomas's poetry, all of which he wrote after the outbreak of World War I. In 1915, Thomas, whose poems constantly look for consolation in the particularities of his native countryside, enlisted as a private soldier to fight for England. He went to France, where the experience of war both alleviated his chronic depression and encouraged his writing. Easter Sunday, 1917, found him in Arras; he wrote his wife: "You would have laughed to see us dodging shells to-day." The next day, April 9, 1917, he was killed. His death, only two and a half years after he began writing poetry, was a blow to the tradition of pastoral lyric that, in England, extends from William Wordsworth through Thomas Hardy and A. E. Housman to Philip Larkin.

Frost used to tease his friend Thomas for his indecisiveness, and he later said that his poem "The Road Not Taken" was inspired by Thomas's frequent dreaming over what might have been. Many of Thomas's poems speak from the point of view of a questioning, sometimes benighted traveler. In "The Owl," the voice of the owl, coming out of the darkness from which the traveler has just escaped, "Salted and sobered" his "repose"—that is, reminded him of human misery and seasoned his relief in present safety. In many of Thomas's poems, such intimations of mortality intensify the speaker's responsiveness to nature. His long, seemingly casual sentences create the impression of a mind sensitively ruminating on outer things and its own thoughts. But this delicate sensibility is balanced by an unsentimental toughness. In "Rain," the dead are compared to "Myriads of broken reeds all still and stiff." At the stunning end of "February Afternoon," the deity is imagined "stone-deaf and stone-blind." Thomas's deftly constructed poems still have the power to salt and sober our meditative life.

Adlestrop[1]

Yes. I remember Adlestrop—
The name, because one afternoon
Of heat the express-train drew up there
Unwontedly. It was late June.

The steam hissed. Someone cleared his throat.
No one left and no one came
On the bare platform. What I saw
Was Adlestrop—only the name

And willows, willow-herb, and grass,
And meadowsweet, and haycocks dry,
No whit less still and lonely fair
Than the high cloudlets in the sky.

And for that minute a blackbird sang
Close by, and round him, mistier,
Farther and farther, all the birds
Of Oxfordshire and Gloucestershire.

January 8, 1915 1917

The Gypsy

A fortnight before Christmas Gypsies were everywhere:
Vans were drawn up on wastes, women trailed to the fair.
'My gentleman,' said one, 'You've got a lucky face.'
'And you've a luckier,' I thought, 'if such a grace
And impudence in rags are lucky.' 'Give a penny
For the poor baby's sake.' 'Indeed I have not any
Unless you can give change for a sovereign,[2] my dear.'
'Then just half a pipeful of tobacco can you spare?'
I gave it. With that much victory she laughed content.
I should have given more, but off and away she went
With her baby and her pink sham flowers to rejoin
The rest before I could translate to its proper coin
Gratitude for her grace. And I paid nothing then,
As I pay nothing now with the dippling of my pen
For her brother's music when he drummed the tambourine
And stamped his feet, which made the workmen passing grin,
While his mouth-organ changed to a rascally Bacchanal dance
'Over the hills and far away'.[3] This and his glance
Outlasted all the fair, farmer and auctioneer,
Cheap-jack,[4] balloon-man, drover with crooked stick, and steer,

1. English village in Gloucestershire, bordering on Oxfordshire.
2. An English gold piece worth about five dollars.
3. An old English folksong.
4. A peddler, often of inferior or worthless goods.

Pig, turkey, goose, and duck, Christmas corpses to be.
Not even the kneeling ox had eyes like the Romany.[5]
That night he peopled for me the hollow wooded land,
More dark and wild than stormiest heavens, that I searched and
scanned
Like a ghost new-arrived. The gradations of the dark
Were like an underworld of death, but for the spark
In the Gypsy boy's black eyes as he played and stamped his tune,
'Over the hills and far away', and a crescent moon.

January 22, 1915 1918

The Owl

Downhill I came, hungry, and yet not starved;
Cold, yet had heat within me that was proof
Against the North wind; tired, yet so that rest
Had seemed the sweetest thing under a roof.

Then at the inn I had food, fire, and rest,
Knowing how hungry, cold, and tired was I.
All of the night was quite barred out except
An owl's cry, a most melancholy cry

Shaken out long and clear upon the hill,
No merry note, nor cause of merriment,
But one telling me plain what I escaped
And others could not, that night, as in I went.

And salted[6] was my food, and my repose,
Salted and sobered, too, by the bird's voice
Speaking for all who lay under the stars,
Soldiers and poor, unable to rejoice.

February 24, 1915 1917

Rain

Rain, midnight rain, nothing but the wild rain
On this bleak hut, and solitude, and me
Remembering again that I shall die
And neither hear the rain nor give it thanks
For washing me cleaner than I have been
Since I was born into this solitude.
Blessed are the dead that the rain rains upon:
But here I pray that none whom once I loved
Is dying to-night or lying still awake
Solitary, listening to the rain,

5. Gypsy.

6. Flavored (as with salt).

Either in pain or thus in sympathy
Helpless among the living and the dead,
Like a cold water among broken reeds,
Myriads of broken reeds all still and stiff,
Like me who have no love which this wild rain
Has not dissolved except the love of death,
If love it be for what is perfect and
Cannot, the tempest tells me, disappoint.

January 7, 1916 1917

February Afternoon

Men heard this roar of parleying starlings, saw,
A thousand years ago even as now,
Black rooks with white gulls following the plough
So that the first are last until a caw
Commands that last are first again,—a law
Which was of old when one, like me, dreamed how
A thousand years might dust lie on his brow
Yet thus would birds do between hedge and shaw.

Time swims before me, making as a day
A thousand years, while the broad ploughland oak
Roars mill-like and men strike and bear the stroke
Of war as ever, audacious or resigned,
And God still sits aloft in the array
That we have wrought him, stone-deaf and stone-blind.

February 7–8, 1916 1918

The Green Roads

The green roads that end in the forest
Are strewn with white goose feathers this June,

Like marks left behind by some one gone to the forest
To show his track. But he has never come back.

Down each green road a cottage looks at the forest.
Round one the nettle towers; two are bathed in flowers.

An old man along the green road to the forest
Strays from one, from another a child alone.

In the thicket bordering the forest,
All day long a thrush twiddles his song.

It is old, but the trees are young in the forest,
All but one like a castle keep, in the middle deep.

That oak saw the ages pass in the forest:
They were a host, but their memories are lost,

For the tree is dead: all things forget the forest
Excepting perhaps me, when now I see

The old man, the child, the goose feathers at the edge of the forest,
And hear all day long the thrush repeat his song.

June 28, 1916 1917

The Gallows

There was a weasel lived in the sun
With all his family,
Till a keeper shot him with his gun
And hung him up on a tree,
Where he swings in the wind and rain,
In the sun and in the snow,
Without pleasure, without pain,
On the dead oak tree bough.

There was a crow who was no sleeper,
But a thief and a murderer
Till a very late hour; and this keeper
Made him one of the things that were,
To hang and flap in rain and wind,
In the sun and in the snow.
There are no more sins to be sinned
On the dead oak tree bough.

There was a magpie, too,
Had a long tongue and a long tail;
He could both talk and do—
But what did that avail?
He, too, flaps in the wind and rain
Alongside weasel and crow,
Without pleasure, without pain,
On the dead oak tree bough.

And many other beasts
And birds, skin, bone and feather,
Have been taken from their feasts
And hung up there together,
To swing and have endless leisure
In the sun and in the snow,
Without pain, without pleasure,
On the dead oak tree bough.

July 3–4, 1916 1917

Wallace Stevens
1879–1955

Compared to other great poets in the first part of the twentieth century, such as W. B. Yeats and T. S. Eliot, Wallace Stevens was extraordinarily self-effacing. He worked as an executive of the Hartford Accident and Indemnity Company and never presented himself as a literary figure to his business associates. He had little to do with other writers, and his correspondence reveals that he was on a first-name basis with almost no one. Yet his verse is exciting and unexpected. The poems collected in his first volume, *Harmonium* (1923), present uncommonly vivid images and an extravagant mixture of morbid sorrow and prankish irony. They range from the meditative blank verse of "Sunday Morning" to the playful sonorities and gaudy color of "Disillusionment of Ten O'Clock"; from the apocalyptic whirling round of "Domination of Black" to the ascetic self-extinction of "The Snow Man." Multiple perspectives are cubistically arrayed in "Thirteen Ways of Looking at a Blackbird," and "The Emperor of Ice-Cream" juxtaposes sensual indulgence with fatalistic realism. Different voices collide and overlap in a poetry of riotous masquerade and sensation yet intellectual precision. Stevens's later poetry, if less exuberant and more abstract, continues to affirm and question the power of the imagination. Many of the late poems view life as if from beyond the grave, the everyday objects and feelings revealed with luminous clarity against the backdrop of death. Stevens movingly reflects on his life's work and asks himself over and over what he has left behind and what, if anything, his imagination has changed.

Stevens is a modern poet who, unlike Eliot and Ezra Pound, but like Yeats and Robert Frost, sees himself as extending and transforming the Romantic tradition. The Romantic theme of the imagination is central to his poetry, and he often writes in regular—though unrhymed—stanzas in mellifluous iambic pentameter. A near-contemporary of Frost, he brings into modern poetry a Keatsian color, in contrast to Frost's Wordsworthian plainness. In private, Frost called him a bric-a-brac poet, and Stevens, professing virtual ignorance of Frost's verse, remarked: "His work is full (or said to be full) of humanity." Stevens seems to have formed early the idea expressed in "Sunday Morning" that the poet must rediscover the earth. He commented in "Imagination as Value," an essay written in later life, that "the great poems of heaven and hell have been written and the great poem of the earth remains to be written." In another essay, "The Figure of the Youth as Virile Poet," he writes: "It is easy to suppose that few people realize on that occasion, which comes to all of us, when we look at the blue sky for the first time, that is to say: not merely see it, but look at it and experience it and for the first time have a sense that we live in the center of a physical poetry, a geography that would be intolerable except for the non-geography that exists there—few people realize that they are looking at the world of their own thoughts and the world of their own feelings." Precisely what is the domain of the imagination, and what that of the world, is a question that Stevens keeps asking and answering. In this quality, he is comparable to Stéphane Mallarmé and to Yeats, for whom the changing relation of image to fact is also to be explored rather than arrested. Stevens vacillates between a modern, skeptical minimalism and a visionary, Romantic maximalism. "The Snow Man" imagines the self emptied out and surrendered to reality, while "Tea at the Palaz of Hoon" and "Anecdote of the Jar" see reality as shaped and perhaps even created by the human mind.

This preoccupation with the relation of mind to reality is, for Stevens, inevitable in a skeptical age, when the central question is no longer that of the relation between the human and the divine. "To see the gods dispelled in mid-air and dissolve like clouds," writes Stevens, "is one of the great human experiences." The death of the gods "left us feeling dispossessed and alone in a solitude, like children without parents, in a home that seemed deserted" ("Two or Three Ideas"). For Stevens, each poem is an attempt to fill this spiritual void. He pondered what satisfactions poetry might offer and evolved a theory of necessary fictions. Among them, poetry is "the supreme fiction." It gives "a sense of the freshness or vividness of life" (*Adagia*). If there is no eternal world, the poet's fictions intensify our appreciation of this world. "The imperfect is our paradise," Stevens affirms in "The Poems of Our Climate." The poet is powerful because he or she "creates the world to which we turn incessantly and without knowing it" and "gives to life the supreme fictions without which we are unable to conceive of it" ("The Noble Rider and the Sound of Words"). But the fictions offered by poetry are, in contrast to the absolutes of religion, self-conscious and self-questioning: "The final belief is to believe in a fiction, which you know to be a fiction, there being nothing else. The exquisite truth is to know that it is a fiction and that you believe in it willingly" (*Adagia*). Stevens objected to a view of the imagination that excluded the abstract in favor of minor wish-fulfillments, mere word-pictures of no lasting value in the great task of replacing religion. "The imagination is the liberty of the mind. . . . It is intrepid and eager and the extreme of its achievement lies in abstraction" ("Imagination as Value"). The abstraction must be blooded, he writes in the long poem "Notes toward a Supreme Fiction." It must not leave the world behind, but must, as he said in a letter of March 27, 1944, "express an agreement with reality."

The question of poetry's function elicited some of Stevens's best poems. In one, "Poetry Is a Destructive Force," he warns that "it can kill a man." But more usually, he celebrates its power "to help people to live their lives" ("The Noble Rider and the Sound of Words"). In "A Postcard from the Volcano," Stevens seems to acknowledge that future generations inevitably misread what the poet bequeaths, yet he insists that the poet's words leave a lasting mark on reality: "what we said of it became // A part of what it is." In his late work, Stevens represents the poet as leaving behind a corpus that is like a house or a mountain or even a planet, and he wonders whether this reality made of words has enhanced, transformed, or even displaced reality.

The imagination is crucial, in Stevens's view, to the human effort to cope with an increasingly violent reality. As he explained in a lecture presented in the midst of World War II, "The Noble Rider and the Sound of Words," the poet responds to the extreme pressure of news and worldwide violence with the counterforce of the imagination. The role of the poet is that "of resisting or evading the pressure of reality," knowing it may become even "deadlier" tomorrow. "It is a violence from within that protects us from a violence without. It is the imagination pressing back against the pressure of reality." Stevens provides multiple models for the relation of the imagination and reality, sometimes seeing them as mutually exclusive, the strong imagination offering "resistance" and "evasion" as it "cancels the pressure" outside. At other times, they share the happy "interdependence" of a married pair, "equal and inseparable." He avows the defensive "escapism" of poetry, but he also claims that it actively purifies and converts reality—"Poetry is a purging of the world's poverty and change and evil and death" (*Adagia*). His poems often mediate between these views, deliberately straddling escapism and realism.

Stevens was born on October 2, 1879, in Reading, Pennsylvania. He attended high school in Reading and then entered Harvard University as a special student, like Frost. He remained there for three years, 1897–1900, during which he studied French and German and, following his philosophical bent, became friendly with the philosopher-poet George Santayana. He was later to write the anticipatory elegy "To an Old Philosopher in Rome" in Santayana's honor. Stevens became president of the *Harvard Advocate* and, like Eliot, published his early poems in it.

Apart from his interest in writing, he was not sure how to make a livelihood. His first job was on the *New York Herald Tribune,* and he did not like it. At his father's suggestion, he resigned and entered New York Law School in the fall of 1901. In 1904, he was admitted to the New York bar and began, unsuccessfully, to practice law. A partnership failed, and he worked in several other law firms. In January 1908, he entered the legal staff of an insurance firm; he at last felt secure enough to marry, in 1909, Elsie Moll, a young woman he had met in Reading five years before. In 1916, he joined the New York office of the Hartford Accident and Indemnity Company, and a few months later he and Elsie moved to Hartford. In 1934, he became vice-president of the company. His routine labors at first seemed stultifying: "I certainly do not exist from nine to six, when I am at the office," he wrote Elsie Moll before their marriage (letter of January 13, 1909). But he told a reporter five years before his death: "It gives a man character as a poet to have this daily contact with a job" (*New York Times* obituary, August 3, 1955).

Stevens began to publish his mature poems in 1914, chiefly in *Poetry* magazine. But he held off publishing a volume until 1923, when *Harmonium* appeared. It was somewhat ignored because of the fanfare over Eliot's *Waste Land,* issued the previous year. The following year, Stevens's only child, Holly, was born. He led a "quiet, normal," but full life. He worked hard at his business; he read; he wrote poems; he regularly corresponded with a variety of men and women who shared his interest in all the arts. He received several honorary degrees, and he seems to have been pleased with the attention he received from younger poets and readers. His life, although it may seem short on events, was a feast of the imagination, a feast shared with all who know his poems.

Sunday Morning

I

Complacencies of the peignoir,[1] and late
Coffee and oranges in a sunny chair,
And the green freedom of a cockatoo
Upon a rug mingle to dissipate
The holy hush of ancient sacrifice.
She dreams a little, and she feels the dark
Encroachment of that old catastrophe,
As a calm darkens among water-lights.
The pungent oranges and bright, green wings
Seem things in some procession of the dead,
Winding across wide water, without sound.
The day is like wide water, without sound,
Stilled for the passing of her dreaming feet
Over the seas, to silent Palestine,
Dominion of the blood and sepulchre.[2]

1. Loose negligée.
2. Jesus' sepulchre is located in Palestine. *Blood:* cf. Jesus' reference to the wine of his last Passover as his "blood of the new testament" (Matthew 25.28).

II

Why should she give her bounty to the dead?
What is divinity if it can come
Only in silent shadows and in dreams?
Shall she not find in comforts of the sun,
In pungent fruit and bright, green wings, or else
In any balm or beauty of the earth,
Things to be cherished like the thought of heaven?
Divinity must live within herself:
Passions of rain, or moods in falling snow;
Grievings in loneliness, or unsubdued
Elations when the forest blooms; gusty
Emotions on wet roads on autumn nights;
All pleasures and all pains, remembering
The bough of summer and the winter branch.
These are the measures destined for her soul.

III

Jove in the clouds had his inhuman birth.[3]
No mother suckled him, no sweet land gave
Large-mannered motions to his mythy mind.
He moved among us, as a muttering king,
Magnificent, would move among his hinds,[4]
Until our blood, commingling, virginal,
With heaven, brought such requital to desire
The very hinds discerned it, in a star.
Shall our blood fail? Or shall it come to be
The blood of paradise? And shall the earth
Seem all of paradise that we shall know?
The sky will be much friendlier then than now,
A part of labor and a part of pain,
And next in glory to enduring love,
Not this dividing and indifferent blue.

IV

She says, "I am content when wakened birds,
Before they fly, test the reality
Of misty fields, by their sweet questionings;
But when the birds are gone, and their warm fields
Return no more, where, then, is paradise?"
There is not any haunt of prophecy,
Nor any old chimera[5] of the grave,
Neither the golden underground, nor isle
Melodious, where spirits gat them home,
Nor visionary south, nor cloudy palm
Remote on heaven's hill, that has endured

3. Zeus, supreme Greek god, was suckled by the goat Amalthea in his childhood.

4. Farm hands, servants.

5. Illusion.

As April's green endures; or will endure
Like her remembrance of awakened birds,
Or her desire for June and evening, tipped
By the consummation of the swallow's wings.

V

She says, "But in contentment I still feel
The need of some imperishable bliss."
Death is the mother of beauty; hence from her,
Alone, shall come fulfillment to our dreams
And our desires. Although she strews the leaves
Of sure obliteration on our paths,
The path sick sorrow took, the many paths
Where triumph rang its brassy phrase, or love
Whispered a little out of tenderness,
She makes the willow shiver in the sun
For maidens who were wont to sit and gaze
Upon the grass, relinquished to their feet.
She causes boys to pile new plums and pears
On disregarded plate.[6] The maidens taste
And stray impassioned in the littering leaves.

VI

Is there no change of death in paradise?
Does ripe fruit never fall? Or do the boughs
Hang always heavy in that perfect sky,
Unchanging, yet so like our perishing earth,
With rivers like our own that seek for seas
They never find, the same receding shores
That never touch with inarticulate pang?
Why set the pear upon those river-banks
Or spice the shores with odors of the plum?
Alas, that they should wear our colors there,
The silken weavings of our afternoons,
And pick the strings of our insipid lutes!
Death is the mother of beauty, mystical,
Within whose burning bosom we devise
Our earthly mothers waiting, sleeplessly.

VII

Supple and turbulent, a ring of men
Shall chant in orgy on a summer morn
Their boisterous devotion to the sun,
Not as a god, but as a god might be,
Naked among them, like a savage source.

6. "Plate is used in the sense of so-called family plate [that is, household silver]. Disregarded refers to the disuse into which things fall that have been possessed for a long time. I mean, therefore, that death releases and renews. What the old have come to disregard, the young inherit and make use of" (*Letters of Wallace Stevens*, 1966, 183–84).

Their chant shall be a chant of paradise,
Out of their blood, returning to the sky;
And in their chant shall enter, voice by voice,
The windy lake wherein their lord delights,
The trees, like serafin,[7] and echoing hills,
That choir among themselves long afterward.
They shall know well the heavenly fellowship
Of men that perish and of summer morn.
And whence they came and whither they shall go
The dew upon their feet shall manifest.

VIII

She hears, upon that water without sound,
A voice that cries, "The tomb in Palestine
Is not the porch of spirits lingering.
It is the grave of Jesus, where he lay."
We live in an old chaos of the sun,
Or old dependency of day and night,
Or island solitude, unsponsored, free,
Of that wide water, inescapable.
Deer walk upon our mountains, and the quail
Whistle about us their spontaneous cries;
Sweet berries ripen in the wilderness;
And, in the isolation of the sky,
At evening, casual flocks of pigeons make
Ambiguous undulations as they sink,
Downward to darkness, on extended wings.

1915 1923

Peter Quince at the Clavier[8]

I

Just as my fingers on these keys
Make music, so the selfsame sounds
On my spirit make a music, too.

Music is feeling, then, not sound;
And thus it is that what I feel,
Here in this room, desiring you,

Thinking of your blue-shadowed silk,
Is music. It is like the strain
Waked in the elders by Susanna.[9]

7. Or seraphim, angels.
8. Peter Quince is one of the "rude mechanicals," or comic rustics, who perform an unintentionally funny tragedy in Shakespeare's *Midsummer Night's Dream*. Cf. also the popular "Quince to Lilac: To G. H.," from *More Songs from Vagabondia* (1895), by Bliss Carman and Richard Horey.
9. Two elders, or Hebrew tribal councilors, attempted to seduce Susanna, who repulsed them; they then brought against her false accusations of an illicit relationship with a young man. Daniel, however, saved her from punishment. The story is told in Daniel 13, a chapter in the Apocrypha.

Of a green evening, clear and warm,
She bathed in her still garden, while
The red-eyed elders, watching, felt

The basses of their beings throb
In witching chords, and their thin blood
Pulse pizzicati of Hosanna.[1]

II

In the green water, clear and warm,
Susanna lay.
She searched
The touch of springs,
And found
Concealed imaginings.
She sighed,
For so much melody.

Upon the bank, she stood
In the cool
Of spent emotions.
She felt, among the leaves,
The dew
Of old devotions.

She walked upon the grass,
Still quavering.
The winds were like her maids,
On timid feet,
Fetching her woven scarves,
Yet wavering.

A breath upon her hand
Muted the night.
She turned—
A cymbal crashed,
And roaring horns.

III

Soon, with a noise like tambourines,
Came her attendant Byzantines.[2]

They wondered why Susanna cried
Against the elders by her side;

And as they whispered, the refrain
Was like a willow swept by rain.

1. Expression of great praise. *Pizzicati:* notes or passages played by plucking strings.

2. That is, people of the Byzantine Empire.

Anon, their lamps' uplifted flame
Revealed Susanna and her shame.

And then, the simpering Byzantines,
Fled, with a noise like tambourines.

IV

Beauty is momentary in the mind—
The fitful tracing of a portal;
But in the flesh it is immortal.

The body dies; the body's beauty lives.
So evenings die, in their green going,
A wave, interminably flowing.
So gardens die, their meek breath scenting
The cowl[3] of winter, done repenting.
So maidens die, to the auroral
Celebration of a maiden's choral.
Susanna's music touched the bawdy strings
Of those white elders; but, escaping,
Left only Death's ironic scraping.
Now, in its immortality, it plays
On the clear viol of her memory,
And makes a constant sacrament of praise.

1915

Disillusionment of Ten O'Clock

The houses are haunted
By white night-gowns.
None are green,
Or purple with green rings,
Or green with yellow rings,
Or yellow with blue rings.
None of them are strange,
With socks of lace
And beaded ceintures.[4]
People are not going
To dream of baboons and periwinkles.
Only, here and there, an old sailor,
Drunk and asleep in his boots,
Catches tigers
In red weather.

1915

3. Hood on a monk's or nun's habit.

4. Belts (French).

Domination of Black

At night, by the fire,
The colors of the bushes
And of the fallen leaves,
Repeating themselves,
Turned in the room,
Like the leaves themselves
Turning in the wind.
Yes: but the color of the heavy hemlocks
Came striding—
And I remembered the cry of the peacocks.

The colors of their tails
Were like the leaves themselves
Turning in the wind,
In the twilight wind.
They swept over the room,
Just as they flew from the boughs of the hemlocks
Down to the ground.
I heard them cry—the peacocks.
Was it a cry against the twilight
Or against the leaves themselves
Turning in the wind,
Turning as the flames
Turned in the fire,
Turning as the tails of the peacocks
Turned in the loud fire,
Loud as the hemlocks
Full of the cry of the peacocks?
Or was it a cry against the hemlocks?

Out of the window,
I saw how the planets gathered
Like the leaves themselves
Turning in the wind.
I saw how the night came,
Came striding like the color of the heavy hemlocks.
I felt afraid—
And I remembered the cry of the peacocks.

1915 1916

The Worms at Heaven's Gate

Out of the tomb, we bring Badroulbadour,[5]
Within our bellies, we her chariot.
Here is an eye. And here are, one by one,
The lashes of that eye and its white lid.
Here is the cheek on which that lid declined,
And, finger after finger, here, the hand,
The genius of that cheek. Here are the lips,
The bundle of the body and the feet.

. . . .

Out of the tomb we bring Badroulbadour.

1916

Thirteen Ways of Looking at a Blackbird

I

Among twenty snowy mountains,
The only moving thing
Was the eye of the blackbird.

II

I was of three minds,
Like a tree
In which there are three blackbirds.

III

The blackbird whirled in the autumn winds,
It was a small part of the pantomime.

IV

A man and a woman
Are one.
A man and a woman and a blackbird
Are one.

V

I do not know which to prefer—
The beauty of inflections
Or the beauty of innuendoes,
The blackbird whistling
Or just after.

5. A princess in the *Arabian Nights* story "Aladdin and His Wonderful Lamp."

VI

Icicles filled the long window
With barbaric glass.
The shadow of the blackbird
Crossed it, to and fro.
The mood
Traced in the shadow
An indecipherable cause.

VII

O thin men of Haddam,[6]
Why do you imagine golden birds?
Do you not see how the blackbird
Walks around the feet
Of the women about you?

VIII

I know noble accents
And lucid, inescapable rhythms;
But I know, too,
That the blackbird is involved
In what I know.

IX

When the blackbird flew out of sight,
It marked the edge
Of one of many circles.

X

At the sight of blackbirds
Flying in a green light,
Even the bawds[7] of euphony
Would cry out sharply.

XI

He rode over Connecticut
In a glass coach.
Once, a fear pierced him,
In that he mistook
The shadow of his equipage[8]
For blackbirds.

XII

The river is moving.
The blackbird must be flying.

6. A town in Connecticut.
7. Brothel keepers.
8. That is, coach.

XIII

It was evening all afternoon.
It was snowing
And it was going to snow.
The blackbird sat
In the cedar-limbs.

1917

The Death of a Soldier[9]

Life contracts and death is expected,
As in a season of autumn.
The soldier falls.

He does not become a three-days' personage,
Imposing his separation,
Calling for pomp.

Death is absolute and without memorial,
As in a season of autumn,
When the wind stops.

When the wind stops and, over the heavens,
The clouds go, nevertheless,
In their direction.

1918

Anecdote of the Jar

I placed a jar in Tennessee,
And round it was, upon a hill.
It made the slovenly wilderness
Surround that hill.

The wilderness rose up to it,
And sprawled around, no longer wild.
The jar was round upon the ground
And tall and of a port in air.

It took dominion everywhere.
The jar was gray and bare.
It did not give of bird or bush,
Like nothing else in Tennessee.

1919

9. Originally untitled as part IX of the sequence "Lettres d'un Soldat," this poem had the epigraph "La mort du soldat est près des choses naturelles" (the death of a soldier is like a natural thing), from *Lettres d'un soldat* (1916), by a French soldier in World War I, Eugène Emmanuel Lemercier.

The Snow Man

One must have a mind of winter
To regard the frost and the boughs
Of the pine-trees crusted with snow;

And have been cold a long time
To behold the junipers shagged with ice,
The spruces rough in the distant glitter

Of the January sun; and not to think
Of any misery in the sound of the wind,
In the sound of a few leaves,

Which is the sound of the land
Full of the same wind
That is blowing in the same bare place

For the listener, who listens in the snow,
And, nothing himself, beholds
Nothing that is not there and the nothing that is.

1921

Tea at the Palaz of Hoon

Not less because in purple I descended
The western day through what you called
The loneliest air, not less was I myself.

What was the ointment sprinkled on my beard?
What were the hymns that buzzed beside my ears?
What was the sea whose tide swept through me there?

Out of my mind the golden ointment rained,
And my ears made the blowing hymns they heard.
I was myself the compass of that sea:

I was the world in which I walked, and what I saw
Or heard or felt came not but from myself;
And there I found myself more truly and more strange.

1921

Bantams in Pine-Woods

Chieftain Iffucan of Azcan in caftan
Of tan with henna hackles,[1] halt!

Damned universal cock, as if the sun
Was blackamoor[2] to bear your blazing tail.

Fat! Fat! Fat! Fat! I am the personal.
Your world is you. I am my world.

You ten-foot poet among inchlings. Fat!
Begone! An inchling bristles in these pines,

Bristles, and points their Appalachian tangs,
And fears not portly Azcan nor his hoos.

1922

The Emperor of Ice-Cream

Call the roller of big cigars,
The muscular one, and bid him whip
In kitchen cups concupiscent[3] curds.
Let the wenches dawdle in such dress
As they are used to wear, and let the boys
Bring flowers in last month's newspapers.
Let be be finale of seem.
The only emperor is the emperor of ice-cream.

Take from the dresser of deal,[4]
Lacking the three glass knobs, that sheet
On which she embroidered fantails[5] once
And spread it so as to cover her face.
If her horny feet protrude, they come
To show how cold she is, and dumb.
Let the lamp affix its beam.
The only emperor is the emperor of ice-cream.

1922

1. "Iffucan" and "Azcan" are Stevens's coinages, perhaps intended to suggest the Aztecs or Mayans. *Caftan:* an ankle-length robe, commonly worn in the Middle East. The rooster being addressed (the "bantams" of the title are small fowl) has "hackles," or neck feathers, of a reddish-brown color.
2. Black person; here, a servant or slave.
3. Lustful.
4. Plain, unfinished wood.
5. Stevens said that "the word fantails does not mean fans, but fantail pigeons."

The Idea of Order at Key West[6]

She sang beyond the genius[7] of the sea.
The water never formed to mind or voice,
Like a body wholly body, fluttering
Its empty sleeves; and yet its mimic motion
Made constant cry, caused constantly a cry,
That was not ours although we understood,
Inhuman, of the veritable ocean.

The sea was not a mask. No more was she.
The song and water were not medleyed sound
Even if what she sang was what she heard,
Since what she sang was uttered word by word.
It may be that in all her phrases stirred
The grinding water and the gasping wind;
But it was she and not the sea we heard.

For she was the maker of the song she sang.
The ever-hooded, tragic-gestured sea
Was merely a place by which she walked to sing.
Whose spirit is this? we said, because we knew
It was the spirit that we sought and knew
That we should ask this often as she sang.

If it was only the dark voice of the sea
That rose, or even colored by many waves;
If it was only the outer voice of sky
And cloud, of the sunken coral water-walled,
However clear, it would have been deep air,
The heaving speech of air, a summer sound
Repeated in a summer without end
And sound alone. But it was more than that,
More even than her voice, and ours, among
The meaningless plungings of water and the wind,
Theatrical distances, bronze shadows heaped
On high horizons, mountainous atmospheres
Of sky and sea.
                                        It was her voice that made
The sky acutest at its vanishing.
She measured to the hour its solitude.
She was the single artificer of the world
In which she sang. And when she sang, the sea,
Whatever self it had, became the self
That was her song, for she was the maker.[8] Then we,
As we beheld her striding there alone,
Knew that there never was a world for her
Except the one she sang and, singing, made.

6. The southernmost of several small coral islands off the coast of Florida, where Stevens vacationed.

7. Attendant spirit or deity.

8. The Greek *poietes*, or poet, also means "maker."

Ramon Fernandez,[9] tell me, if you know,
Why, when the singing ended and we turned
Toward the town, tell why the glassy lights,
The lights in the fishing boats at anchor there,
As the night descended, tilting in the air,
Mastered the night and portioned out the sea,
Fixing emblazoned zones and fiery poles,
Arranging, deepening, enchanting night.

Oh! Blessed rage for order, pale Ramon,
The maker's rage to order words of the sea,
Words of the fragrant portals, dimly-starred,
And of ourselves and of our origins,
In ghostlier demarcations, keener sounds.

1934 1936

A Postcard from the Volcano

Children picking up our bones
Will never know that these were once
As quick as foxes on the hill;

And that in autumn, when the grapes
Made sharp air sharper by their smell
These had a being, breathing frost;

And least will guess that with our bones
We left much more, left what still is
The look of things, left what we felt

At what we saw. The spring clouds blow
Above the shuttered mansion-house,
Beyond our gate and the windy sky

Cries out a literate despair.
We knew for long the mansion's look
And what we said of it became

A part of what it is . . . Children,
Still weaving budded aureoles,[1]
Will speak our speech and never know,

Will say of the mansion that it seems
As if he that lived there left behind
A spirit storming in blank walls,

9. Stevens said he had simply combined two common Spanish names at random, without conscious reference to Ramon Fernandez the French critic (*Letters*, 798).

1. Haloes, radiances.

A dirty house in a gutted world,
A tatter of shadows peaked to white,
Smeared with the gold of the opulent sun.

1936 1936

From The Man with the Blue Guitar[2]

I

The man bent over his guitar,
A shearsman of sorts.[3] The day was green.

They said, "You have a blue guitar,
You do not play things as they are."

The man replied, "Things as they are
Are changed upon the blue guitar."

And they said then, "But play, you must,
A tune beyond us, yet ourselves,

A tune upon the blue guitar
Of things exactly as they are."

XXII

Poetry is the subject of the poem,
From this the poem issues and

To this returns. Between the two,
Between issue and return, there is

An absence in reality,
Things as they are. Or so we say.

But are these separate? Is it
An absence for the poem, which acquires

Its true appearances there, sun's green,
Cloud's red, earth feeling, sky that thinks?

From these it takes. Perhaps it gives,
In the universal intercourse.

1937 1937

2. Though the title describes a painting from Picasso's "blue period," *Blind Guitar-Player* (1903), Stevens asserted in 1953, "I had no particular painting of Picasso's in mind" (*Letters*, 786).

3. "This refers to the posture of the speaker, squatting like a tailor (a shearsman) as he works on his cloth" (*Letters*, 783).

A Rabbit as King of the Ghosts

The difficulty to think at the end of day,
When the shapeless shadow covers the sun
And nothing is left except light on your fur—

There was the cat slopping its milk all day,
Fat cat, red tongue, green mind, white milk
And August the most peaceful month.

To be, in the grass, in the peacefullest time,
Without that monument of cat,
The cat forgotten in the moon;

And to feel that the light is a rabbit-light,
In which everything is meant for you
And nothing need be explained;

Then there is nothing to think of. It comes of itself;
And east rushes west and west rushes down,
No matter. The grass is full

And full of yourself. The trees around are for you,
The whole of the wideness of night is for you,
A self that touches all edges,

You become a self that fills the four corners of night.
The red cat hides away in the fur-light
And there you are humped high, humped up,

You are humped higher and higher, black as stone—
You sit with your head like a carving in space
And the little green cat is a bug in the grass.

1937 1942

The Poems of Our Climate

I

Clear water in a brilliant bowl,
Pink and white carnations. The light
In the room more like a snowy air,
Reflecting snow. A newly-fallen snow
At the end of winter when afternoons return.
Pink and white carnations—one desires
So much more than that. The day itself
Is simplified: a bowl of white,
Cold, a cold porcelain, low and round,
With nothing more than the carnations there.

II

Say even that this complete simplicity
Stripped one of all one's torments, concealed
The evilly compounded, vital I
And made it fresh in a world of white,
A world of clear water, brilliant-edged,
Still one would want more, one would need more,
More than a world of white and snowy scents.

III

There would still remain the never-resting mind,
So that one would want to escape, come back
To what had been so long composed.
The imperfect is our paradise.
Note that, in this bitterness, delight,
Since the imperfect is so hot in us,
Lies in flawed words and stubborn sounds.

1938 1942

Study of Two Pears

I

Opusculum paedagogum.[4]
The pears are not viols,
Nudes or bottles.
They resemble nothing else.

II

They are yellow forms
Composed of curves
Bulging toward the base.
They are touched red.

III

They are not flat surfaces
Having curved outlines.
They are round
Tapering toward the top.

IV

In the way they are modelled
There are bits of blue.
A hard dry leaf hangs
From the stem.

4. A small didactic work (Latin).

V

The yellow glistens.
It glistens with various yellows,
Citrons, oranges and greens
Flowering over the skin.

VI

The shadows of the pears
Are blobs on the green cloth.
The pears are not seen
As the observer wills.

1938 1942

The Man on the Dump

Day creeps down. The moon is creeping up.
The sun is a corbeil[5] of flowers the moon Blanche
Places there, a bouquet, Ho-ho . . . The dump is full
Of images. Days pass like papers from a press.
The bouquets come here in the papers. So the sun,
And so the moon, both come, and the janitor's poems
Of every day, the wrapper on the can of pears,
The cat in the paper-bag, the corset, the box
From Esthonia:[6] the tiger chest, for tea.

The freshness of night has been fresh a long time.
The freshness of morning, the blowing of day, one says
That it puffs as Cornelius Nepos[7] reads, it puffs
More than, less than or it puffs like this or that.
The green smacks in the eye, the dew in the green
Smacks like fresh water in a can, like the sea
On a cocoanut—how many men have copied dew
For buttons, how many women have covered themselves
With dew, dew dresses, stones and chains of dew, heads
Of the floweriest flowers dewed with the dewiest dew.
One grows to hate these things except on the dump.

Now in the time of spring (azaleas, trilliums,
Myrtle, viburnums, daffodils, blue phlox),
Between that disgust and this, between the things
That are on the dump (azaleas and so on)
And those that will be (azaleas and so on),
One feels the purifying change. One rejects
The trash.

5. Basket of flowers or fruit, or sculptural representation thereof.
6. A country in northwestern Europe.
7. Roman historian (c. 100–c. 25 B.C.E.); his name likely chosen for its sound.

That's the moment when the moon creeps up
To the bubbling of bassoons. That's the time
One looks at the elephant-colorings of tires.
Everything is shed; and the moon comes up as the moon
(All its images are in the dump) and you see
As a man (not like an image of a man),
You see the moon rise in the empty sky.

One sits and beats an old tin can, lard pail.
One beats and beats for that which one believes.
That's what one wants to get near. Could it after all
Be merely oneself, as superior as the ear
To a crow's voice? Did the nightingale torture the ear,
Pack the heart and scratch the mind? And does the ear
Solace itself in peevish birds? Is it peace,
Is it a philosopher's honeymoon, one finds
On the dump? Is it to sit among mattresses of the dead,
Bottles, pots, shoes and grass and murmur *aptest eve:*
Is it to hear the blatter of grackles and say
Invisible priest; is it to eject, to pull
The day to pieces and cry *stanza my stone*?
Where was it one first heard of the truth? The the.

1938 1942

Of Modern Poetry

The poem of the mind in the act of finding
What will suffice. It has not always had
To find: the scene was set; it repeated what
Was in the script.
Then the theatre was changed
To something else. Its past was a souvenir.

It has to be living, to learn the speech of the place.
It has to face the men of the time and to meet
The women of the time. It has to think about war
And it has to find what will suffice. It has
To construct a new stage. It has to be on that stage
And, like an insatiable actor, slowly and
With meditation, speak words that in the ear,
In the delicatest ear of the mind, repeat,
Exactly, that which it wants to hear, at the sound
Of which, an invisible audience listens,
Not to the play, but to itself, expressed
In an emotion as of two people, as of two
Emotions becoming one. The actor is
A metaphysician in the dark, twanging
An instrument, twanging a wiry string that gives
Sounds passing through sudden rightnesses, wholly

Containing the mind, below which it cannot descend,
Beyond which it has no will to rise.
                                        It must
Be the finding of a satisfaction, and may
Be of a man skating, a woman dancing, a woman
Combing. The poem of the act of the mind.

1940   1942

From Notes toward a Supreme Fiction

I.I

Begin, ephebe,[8] by perceiving the idea
Of this invention, this invented world,
The inconceivable idea of the sun.

You must become an ignorant man again
And see the sun again with an ignorant eye
And see it clearly in the idea of it.

Never suppose an inventing mind as source
Of this idea nor for that mind compose
A voluminous master folded in his fire.

How clean the sun when seen in its idea,
Washed in the remotest cleanliness of a heaven
That has expelled us and our images . . .

The death of one god is the death of all.
Let purple Phoebus[9] lie in umber harvest,
Let Phoebus slumber and die in autumn umber,

Phoebus is dead, ephebe. But Phoebus was
A name for something that never could be named.
There was a project for the sun and is.

There is a project for the sun. The sun
Must bear no name, gold flourisher, but be
In the difficulty of what it is to be.

II.V

On a blue island in a sky-wide water
The wild orange trees continued to bloom and to bear,
Long after the planter's death. A few limes remained,

Where his house had fallen, three scraggy trees weighted
With garbled green. These were the planter's turquoise
And his orange blotches, these were his zero green,

8. In ancient Greece, a young citizen.
9. Epithet for Apollo, Greek god associated with the sun, meaning "bright, shining."

A green baked greener in the greenest sun.
These were his beaches, his sea-myrtles in
White sand, his patter of the long sea-slushes.

There was an island beyond him on which rested,
An island to the South, on which rested like
A mountain, a pineapple pungent as Cuban summer.

And là-bas, là-bas,[1] the cool bananas grew,
Hung heavily on the great banana tree,
Which pierces clouds and bends on half the world.

He thought often of the land from which he came,
How that whole country was a melon, pink
If seen rightly and yet a possible red.

An unaffected man in a negative light
Could not have borne his labor nor have died
Sighing that he should leave the banjo's twang.

III.III

A lasting visage in a lasting bush,
A face of stone in an unending red,
Red-emerald, red-slitted-blue, a face of slate,

An ancient forehead hung with heavy hair,
The channel slots of rain, the red-rose-red
And weathered and the ruby-water-worn,

The vines around the throat, the shapeless lips,
The frown like serpents basking on the brow,
The spent feeling leaving nothing of itself,

Red-in-red repetitions never going
Away, a little rusty, a little rouged,
A little roughened and ruder, a crown

The eye could not escape, a red renown
Blowing itself upon the tedious ear.
An effulgence faded, dull cornelian[2]

Too venerably used. That might have been.
It might and might have been. But as it was,
A dead shepherd brought tremendous chords from hell

And bade the sheep carouse. Or so they said.
Children in love with them brought early flowers
And scattered them about, no two alike.

1942 1947

1. Over there (French).

2. Or carnelian: red quartz.

The Motive for Metaphor

You like it under the trees in autumn,
Because everything is half dead.
The wind moves like a cripple among the leaves
And repeats words without meaning.

In the same way, you were happy in spring,
With the half colors of quarter-things,
The slightly brighter sky, the melting clouds,
The single bird, the obscure moon—

The obscure moon lighting an obscure world
Of things that would never be quite expressed,
Where you yourself were never quite yourself
And did not want nor have to be,

Desiring the exhilarations of changes:
The motive for metaphor, shrinking from
The weight of primary noon,
The A B C of being,

The ruddy temper, the hammer
Of red and blue, the hard sound—
Steel against intimation—the sharp flash,
The vital, arrogant, fatal, dominant X.

1943 1947

From The Auroras[3] of Autumn

I

This is where the serpent lives, the bodiless.
His head is air. Beneath his tip at night
Eyes open and fix on us in every sky.

Or is this another wriggling out of the egg,
Another image at the end of the cave,
Another bodiless for the body's slough?

This is where the serpent lives. This is his nest,
These fields, these hills, these tinted distances,
And the pines above and along and beside the sea.

This is form gulping after formlessness,
Skin flashing to wished-for disappearances
And the serpent body flashing without the skin.

3. The northern lights, a luminous atmospheric phenomenon radiating from the North Pole.

This is the height emerging and its base . . .
These lights may finally attain a pole
In the midmost midnight and find the serpent there,

In another nest, the master of the maze
Of body and air and forms and images,
Relentlessly in possession of happiness.

This is his poison: that we should disbelieve
Even that. His meditations in the ferns,
When he moved so slightly to make sure of sun,

Made us no less as sure. We saw in his head,
Black beaded on the rock, the flecked animal,
The moving grass, the Indian in his glade.

II

Farewell to an idea . . . A cabin stands,
Deserted, on a beach. It is white,
As by a custom or according to

An ancestral theme or as a consequence
Of an infinite course. The flowers against the wall
Are white, a little dried, a kind of mark

Reminding, trying to remind, of a white
That was different, something else, last year
Or before, not the white of an aging afternoon,

Whether fresher or duller, whether of winter cloud
Or of winter sky, from horizon to horizon.
The wind is blowing the sand across the floor.

Here, being visible is being white,
Is being of the solid of white, the accomplishment
Of an extremist in an exercise . . .

The season changes. A cold wind chills the beach.
The long lines of it grow longer, emptier,
A darkness gathers though it does not fall.

And the whiteness grows less vivid on the wall.
The man who is walking turns blankly on the sand.
He observes how the north is always enlarging the change,

With its frigid brilliances, its blue-red sweeps
And gusts of great enkindlings, its polar green,
The color of ice and fire and solitude.

III

Farewell to an idea . . . The mother's face,
The purpose of the poem, fills the room.
They are together, here, and it is warm,

With none of the prescience of oncoming dreams,
It is evening. The house is evening, half dissolved.
Only the half they can never possess remains,

Still-starred. It is the mother they possess,
Who gives transparence to their present peace.
She makes that gentler that can gentle be.

And yet she too is dissolved, she is destroyed.
She gives transparence. But she has grown old.
The necklace is a carving not a kiss.

The soft hands are a motion not a touch.
The house will crumble and the books will burn.
They are at ease in a shelter of the mind

And the house is of the mind and they and time,
Together, all together. Boreal[4] night
Will look like frost as it approaches them

And to the mother as she falls asleep
And as they say good-night, good-night. Upstairs
The windows will be lighted, not the rooms.

A wind will spread its windy grandeurs round
And knock like a rifle-butt against the door.
The wind will command them with invincible sound.

1947 1950

Large Red Man Reading

There were ghosts that returned to earth to hear his phrases,
As he sat there reading, aloud, the great blue tabulae.[5]
They were those from the wilderness of stars that had expected more.

There were those that returned to hear him read from the poem of life,
Of the pans above the stove, the pots on the table, the tulips among them.
They were those that would have wept to step barefoot into reality,

That would have wept and been happy, have shivered in the frost
And cried out to feel it again, have run fingers over leaves
And against the most coiled thorn, have seized on what was ugly

4. Northern.

5. Ancient writing tablet.

And laughed, as he sat there reading, from out of the purple tabulae,
The outlines of being and its expressings, the syllables of its law:
Poesis, poesis, the literal characters, the vatic[6] lines,

Which in those ears and in those thin, those spended hearts,
Took on color, took on shape and the size of things as they are
And spoke the feeling for them, which was what they had lacked.

1948 1950

From An Ordinary Evening in New Haven

XXX

The last leaf that is going to fall has fallen.
The robins are là-bas,[7] the squirrels, in tree-caves,
Huddle together in the knowledge of squirrels.

The wind has blown the silence of summer away.
It buzzes beyond the horizon or in the ground:
In mud under ponds, where the sky used to be reflected.

The barrenness that appears is an exposing.
It is not part of what is absent, a halt
For farewells, a sad hanging on for remembrances.

It is a coming on and a coming forth.
The pines that were fans and fragrances emerge,
Staked solidly in a gusty grappling with rocks.

The glass of the air becomes an element—
It was something imagined that has been washed away.
A clearness has returned. It stands restored.

It is not an empty clearness, a bottomless sight.
It is a visibility of thought,
In which hundreds of eyes, in one mind, see at once.

1949 1950

From The Rock

I

SEVENTY YEARS LATER

It is an illusion that we were ever alive,
Lived in the houses of mothers, arranged ourselves
By our own motions in a freedom of air.

6. Prophetic. *Poesis:* poetry (Greek and Latin).
7. Over there (French).

Regard the freedom of seventy years ago.
It is no longer air. The houses still stand,
Though they are rigid in rigid emptiness.

Even our shadows, their shadows, no longer remain.
The lives these lived in the mind are at an end.
They never were . . . The sounds of the guitar

Were not and are not. Absurd. The words spoken
Were not and are not. It is not to be believed.
The meeting at noon at the edge of the field seems like

An invention, an embrace between one desperate clod
And another in a fantastic consciousness,
In a queer assertion of humanity:

A theorem proposed between the two—
Two figures in a nature of the sun,
In the sun's design of its own happiness,

As if nothingness contained a métier,[8]
A vital assumption, an impermanence
In its permanent cold, an illusion so desired

That the green leaves came and covered the high rock,
That the lilacs came and bloomed, like a blindness cleaned,
Exclaiming bright sight, as it was satisfied,

In a birth of sight. The blooming and the musk
Were being alive, an incessant being alive,
A particular of being, that gross universe.

1950 1954

To an Old Philosopher in Rome[9]

On the threshold of heaven, the figures in the street
Become the figures of heaven, the majestic movement
Of men growing small in the distances of space,
Singing, with smaller and still smaller sound,
Unintelligible absolution and an end—

The threshold, Rome, and that more merciful Rome
Beyond, the two alike in the make of the mind.
It is as if in a human dignity
Two parallels become one, a perspective, of which
Men are part both in the inch and in the mile.

8. Trade or profession; that in which one is especially skilled.

9. Addressed to the Spanish-born American philosopher George Santayana (1863–1952), also a poet, who retired from teaching at Harvard University in 1912 and went to live in Italy. Stevens met Santayana while an undergraduate at Harvard. The elegy was written less than a year before Santayana's death in the nursing home of a Roman Catholic order in Rome.

How easily the blown banners change to wings . . .
Things dark on the horizons of perception
Become accompaniments of fortune, but
Of the fortune of the spirit, beyond the eye,
Not of its sphere, and yet not far beyond,

The human end in the spirit's greatest reach,
The extreme of the known in the presence of the extreme
Of the unknown. The newsboys' muttering
Becomes another murmuring; the smell
Of medicine, a fragrantness not to be spoiled . . .

The bed, the books, the chair, the moving nuns,
The candle as it evades the sight, these are
The sources of happiness in the shape of Rome,
A shape within the ancient circles of shapes,
And these beneath the shadow of a shape

In a confusion on bed and books, a portent
On the chair, a moving transparence on the nuns,
A light on the candle tearing against the wick
To join a hovering excellence, to escape
From fire and be part only of that of which

Fire is the symbol: the celestial possible.
Speak to your pillow as if it was yourself.
Be orator but with an accurate tongue
And without eloquence, O, half-asleep,
Of the pity that is the memorial of this room,

So that we feel, in this illumined large,
The veritable small, so that each of us
Beholds himself in you, and hears his voice
In yours, master and commiserable man,
Intent on your particles of nether-do,

Your dozing in the depths of wakefulness,
In the warmth of your bed, at the edge of your chair, alive
Yet living in two worlds, impenitent
As to one, and, as to one, most penitent,
Impatient for the grandeur that you need

In so much misery; and yet finding it
Only in misery, the afflatus[1] of ruin,
Profound poetry of the poor and of the dead,
As in the last drop of the deepest blood,
As it falls from the heart and lies there to be seen,

Even as the blood of an empire, it might be,
For a citizen of heaven though still of Rome.
It is poverty's speech that seeks us out the most.

1. Breath; inspiration.

It is older than the oldest speech of Rome.
This is the tragic accent of the scene.

And you—it is you that speak it, without speech,
The loftiest syllables among loftiest things,
The one invulnerable man among
Crude captains, the naked majesty, if you like,
Of bird-nest arches and of rain-stained vaults.

The sounds drift in. The buildings are remembered.
The life of the city never lets go, nor do you
Ever want it to. It is part of the life in your room.
Its domes are the architecture of your bed.
The bells keep on repeating solemn names

In choruses and choirs of choruses,
Unwilling that mercy should be a mystery
Of silence, that any solitude of sense
Should give you more than their peculiar chords.
And reverberations clinging to whisper still.

It is a kind of total grandeur at the end,
With every visible thing enlarged and yet
No more than a bed, a chair and moving nuns,
The immensest theatre, the pillared porch,
The book and candle in your ambered room,

Total grandeur of a total edifice,
Chosen by an inquisitor of structures
For himself. He stops upon this threshold,
As if the design of all his words takes form
And frame from thinking and is realized.

1952 1954

The Poem That Took the Place of a Mountain

There it was, word for word,
The poem that took the place of a mountain.

He breathed its oxygen,
Even when the book lay turned in the dust of his table.

It reminded him how he had needed
A place to go to in his own direction,

How he had recomposed the pines,
Shifted the rocks and picked his way among clouds,

For the outlook that would be right,
Where he would be complete in an unexplained completion:

The exact rock where his inexactnesses
Would discover, at last, the view toward which they had edged,

Where he could lie and, gazing down at the sea,
Recognize his unique and solitary home.

1952 1954

The Planet on the Table

Ariel[2] was glad he had written his poems.
They were of a remembered time
Or of something seen that he liked.

Other makings of the sun
Were waste and welter
And the ripe shrub writhed.

His self and the sun were one
And his poems, although makings of his self,
Were no less makings of the sun.

It was not important that they survive.
What mattered was that they should bear
Some lineament or character,

Some affluence, if only half-perceived,
In the poverty of their words,
Of the planet of which they were part.

1953 1954

The River of Rivers in Connecticut

There is a great river this side of Stygia,[3]
Before one comes to the first black cataracts[4]
And trees that lack the intelligence of trees.

In that river, far this side of Stygia,
The mere flowing of the water is a gayety,
Flashing and flashing in the sun. On its banks,

2. Airy spirit set free by Prospero at the end of Shakespeare's *Tempest*.
3. In Greek mythology, the river Styx, in Hades, over which the dead were ferried by Charon.
4. Waterfalls.

No shadow walks. The river is fateful,
Like the last one. But there is no ferryman.
He could not bend against its propelling force.

It is not to be seen beneath the appearances
That tell of it. The steeple at Farmington
Stands glistening and Haddam[5] shines and sways.

It is the third commonness with light and air,
A curriculum, a vigor, a local abstraction . . .
Call it, once more, a river, an unnamed flowing,

Space-filled, reflecting the seasons, the folk-lore
Of each of the senses; call it, again and again,
The river that flows nowhere, like a sea.

1954

The Plain Sense of Things

After the leaves have fallen, we return
To a plain sense of things. It is as if
We had come to an end of the imagination,
Inanimate in an inert savoir.[6]

It is difficult even to choose the adjective
For this blank cold, this sadness without cause.
The great structure has become a minor house.
No turban walks across the lessened floors.

The greenhouse never so badly needed paint.
The chimney is fifty years old and slants to one side.
A fantastic effort has failed, a repetition
In a repetitiousness of men and flies.

Yet the absence of the imagination had
Itself to be imagined. The great pond,
The plain sense of it, without reflections, leaves,
Mud, water like dirty glass, expressing silence

Of a sort, silence of a rat come out to see,
The great pond and its waste of the lilies, all this
Had to be imagined as an inevitable knowledge,
Required, as a necessity requires.

1952 1954

5. Like Farmington, a town in Connecticut.
6. Knowledge (French, "to know").

Reality Is an Activity of the Most August Imagination

Last Friday, in the big light of last Friday night,
We drove home from Cornwall to Hartford,[7] late.

It was not a night blown at a glassworks in Vienna
Or Venice, motionless, gathering time and dust.

There was a crush of strength in a grinding going round,
Under the front of the westward evening star,

The vigor of glory, a glittering in the veins,
As things emerged and moved and were dissolved,

Either in distance, change or nothingness,
The visible transformations of summer night,

An argentine[8] abstraction approaching form
And suddenly denying itself away.

There was an insolid billowing of the solid.
Night's moonlight lake was neither water nor air.

1954 1957

Of Mere Being

The palm at the end of the mind,
Beyond the last thought, rises
In the bronze decor,

A gold-feathered bird
Sings in the palm, without human meaning,
Without human feeling, a foreign song.

You know then that it is not the reason
That makes us happy or unhappy.
The bird sings. Its feathers shine.

The palm stands on the edge of space.
The wind moves slowly in the branches.
The bird's fire-fangled feathers dangle down.

1955 1957

7. Cities in Connecticut.

8. Silvery.

Mina Loy
1882–1966

Writing to Marianne Moore in 1921, Ezra Pound asked: "entre nooz: is there anyone in America except you, Bill [William Carlos Williams] and Mina Loy who can write anything of interest in verse?" Loy was one of the leading poets of experimental modernism early in the twentieth century. She shared the rebellious energies of various avant-garde movements, such as Futurism, Cubism, and Dada, though her poetry is not entirely assimilable to any of them. Seen as "American" by some, "British" by others, Loy, like such friends as Pound and Gertrude Stein, led a migrant life that confounds national classification. Her transnational poetry cross-fertilizes literary idioms, styles, and traditions from England, America, France, Germany, and elsewhere.

Loy was born on December 27, 1882, in London, to a Protestant English mother and a Jewish Hungarian immigrant father. The constraints of her mother's Victorian prudery and religiosity helped fuel Loy's iconoclastic zeal. In the long autobiographical poem *Anglo-Mongrels and the Rose* (1923–25), Loy mythologizes and satirizes her convention-bound mother as "the Rose" or "Alice," her father as "Exodus." In the "English Rose" section of the poem, she relates her parents' meeting, courtship, and disastrous marriage. Far from being the mysterious Rose invoked by Shelley, W. B. Yeats, and the Pre-Raphaelites, her cold mother is the "Rose of arrested impulses," absurdly committed to the value of chastity, humorously described as "an impenetrable pink curtain." This "Conservative Rose" is also the "British Empire" confronting such ethnic "others" as Exodus. In her lifelong rebellion against her mother's imperial values, Loy writes candidly about the female body in sex ("Songs to Joannes") and in childbirth ("Parturition").

Loy's early creative work was in the visual arts. Encouraged by her father, she studied art in Munich (1899–1901) and England (1901–02). During a stay in Paris (1903–06), she exhibited work at the Salon d'Autumne in 1906. At this time, she shortened her surname from Löwy to Loy. Married to an English painter, she became intimately involved with the leaders of the Futurist movement during a long period in Florence (1906–16), having affairs with the propagandist and self-declared "caffeine of Europe," F. T. Marinetti, and the reputedly ugly and acerbic poet Giovanni Papini, renamed "Joannes" in Loy's sequence of love poems. Futurism's embrace of modernity and its violent rebuke of tradition fired Loy's imagination. "We will destroy museums, libraries, and fight against moralism, feminism, and all utilitarian cowardice," proclaimed Marinetti's Futurist manifesto (1909), while celebrating speed, machines, and innovation. Loy's "Feminist Manifesto" is inspired by Futurist bravura and typographical experimentation, but it also breaks sharply with the movement's misogyny and jingoism.

In 1916, she moved to New York, where she was seen as the prototypical New Woman, and where she met not only such modernist figures as Williams and Marcel Duchamp, but also her second husband, Dada poet-boxer Arthur Cravan. His mysterious death—while in Mexico escaping the draft around 1918—ended the happiest period of Loy's life, as indicated in the poem "The Widow's Jazz." When she returned to Paris, in 1923, she published her first volume of poetry, *Lunar Baedecker* (a misspelling of Baedeker). That same year saw the publication of other major volumes of modernist poetry, including Williams's *Spring and All* and Wallace Stevens's *Harmonium*. After a period in Paris during which she made and sold lampshades, among other business ventures, Loy returned to New York in 1936, living for many years in the Bowery and making assemblages out of found materials. She became a naturalized American citizen in 1946 and moved to Aspen in 1953.

From the start of World War I through the 1920s, Loy composed most of the poetry for which she is celebrated. "During the war," Alfred Kreymborg wrote in the 1920s, a "curious woman, exotic and beautiful, came to New York from foreign shores: the English Jewess, Mina Loy, [whose] clinical frankness and sardonic conclusions, wedded to a madly elliptical style scornful of the regulation grammar, syntax, and punctuation, horrified our gentry and drove our critics into furious despair." For a woman to indulge both sexual and poetic freedom was scandalous. In "Songs to Joannes," which created an uproar when the magazine *Others* published it, in 1915 and 1917, Loy risks de-idealizing the god of love as "Pig Cupid," his "rosy snout / Rooting erotic garbage." She describes sex as "the impact of lighted bodies / Knocking sparks off each other / In chaos," resulting in "seismic orgasm." Freeing sex of the cloak of sentimentality, Loy also frees her lines of punctuation, cuts them short, and inserts unconventional dashes and typographical spaces. In her poem about a bird sculpture by Constantin Brancusi, a poem printed in the famous *Waste Land* issue of *The Dial* (1922) alongside a picture of the sculpture, Loy aptly describes the abstractive impetus of her own work: "A naked orientation / unwinged unplumed /—the ultimate rhythm / has lopped the extremities / of crest and claw / from / the nucleus of flight" ("Brancusi's Golden Bird").

Loy inspired Pound to coin the term *logopoeia* for poetry that "is a dance of the intellect among words," as opposed to poetry that emphasizes music or imagery (*How to Read*). Her language is that of a satirist and experimentalist, not a lyrical poet. The rhythms of Loy's lines are jagged. Her diction is a strange amalgam of the abstract and the concrete ("Eternity in a sky-rocket"). In keeping with her aesthetic of incongruity, her poetry combines the colloquial and the formal: it forces words that are arcane and ponderous ("infructuous") together with others that are immediate and profane ("skin-sack"). Like the Pre-Raphaelite poets she read in youth, Loy is deliberately artificial in her language. Her use of alliteration, internal rhyme, and other forms of phonemic repetition is insistent and direct. She yokes this fin-de-siècle mannered surface to a satiric intensity, akin to Eliot's harsh description in *The Waste Land* of a sordid encounter between a typist and a "young man carbuncular." Like Eliot's and Pound's English, Loy's is polyglot. She puns on French and German words in *Anglo-Mongrels and the Rose* and injects African American vernacular into "The Widow's Jazz." A self-described "mongrel," Loy evinces the modern "mongrelization" of English in the language and texture of her poetry.

From Songs to Joannes[1]

I

Spawn of Fantasies
Silting the appraisable
Pig Cupid his rosy snout
Rooting erotic garbage
"Once upon a time"
Pulls a weed white and star-topped
Among wild oats sewn in mucous-membrane

I would an eye in a bengal light[2]
Eternity in a sky-rocket
Constellations in an ocean

1. Loy's pseudonym for her difficult lover, the Italian poet Giovanni Papini (1881–1956).

2. Flare used for signaling or illumination.

Whose rivers run no fresher
Than a trickle of saliva

These   are suspect places

I must live in my lantern
Trimming subliminal flicker
Virginal   to the bellows
Of Experience
                    Coloured   glass

II

The skin-sack
In which a wanton duality
Packed
All the completion of my infructuous[3] impulses
Something the shape of a man
To the casual vulgarity of the merely observant
More of a clock-work mechanism
Running down against time
To which I am not paced
    My finger-tips are numb from fretting your hair
A God's door-mat
                    On the threshold of your mind

III

We might have coupled
In the bed-ridden monopoly of a moment
Or broken flesh with one another
At the profane communion table
Where wine is spill't on promiscuous lips

We might have given birth to a butterfly
With the daily-news
Printed in blood on its wings

XIII

Come to me   There is something
I have got to tell you   and I can't tell
Something taking shape
Something that has a new name
A new dimension
A new use
A new illusion

3. Fruitless.

It is ambient And it is in your eyes
Something shiny Something only for you
Something that I must not see

It is in my ears Something very resonant
Something that you must not hear
Something only for me

Let us be very jealous
Very suspicious
Very conservative
Very cruel
Or we might make an end of the jostling of aspirations
Disorb[4] inviolate egos

Where two or three are welded together
They shall become god[5]
— — — — — — —
Oh that's right
Keep away from me Please give me a push
Don't let me understand you Don't realise me
Or we might tumble together
Depersonalized
Identical
Into the terrific Nirvana[6]
Me you—you—me

XIV

Today
Everlasting passing apparent imperceptible
To you
I bring the nascent virginity of
—Myself for the moment

No love or the other thing
Only the impact of lighted bodies
Knocking sparks off each other
In chaos

XXVI

Shedding our petty pruderies
From slit eyes

4. To throw something from its normal orbit.
5. Cf. Matthew 18.20, in which Jesus tells his disciples: "For where two or three come together in my name, there am I with them."
6. Ideal bliss associated in Hinduism and Buddhism with achieving wisdom and the extinction of all attachment.

We sidle up
To Nature
— — — that irate pornographist

XXIX

Evolution fall foul of
Sexual equality
Prettily miscalculate
Similitude

Unnatural selection
Breed such sons and daughters
As shall jibber at each other
Uninterpretable cryptonyms
Under the moon

Give them some way of braying brassily
For caressive calling
Or to homophonous[7] hiccoughs
Transpose the laugh
Let them suppose that tears
Are snowdrops or molasses
Or anything
Than human insufficiencies
Begging dorsal vertebrae[8]

Let meeting be the turning
To the antipodean[9]
And Form a blurr
Anything
Than seduce them
To the one
As simple satisfaction
For the other

Let them clash together
From their incognitoes
In seismic orgasm

For far further
Differentiation
Rather than watch
Own-self distortion
Wince in the alien ego

1915–17

7. Identically sounding.
8. Vertebrae located between the cervical and the lumbar vertebrae.
9. Diametrically opposite.

Brancusi's Golden Bird[1]

The toy
become the aesthetic archetype

As if
some patient peasant God
had rubbed and rubbed
the Alpha and Omega[2]
of Form
into a lump of metal

A naked orientation
unwinged   unplumed
—the ultimate rhythm
has lopped the extremities
of crest and claw
from
the nucleus of flight

The absolute act
of art
conformed
to continent sculpture
—bare as the brow of Osiris[3]—
this breast of revelation

an incandescent curve
licked by chromatic flames
in labyrinths of reflections

This gong
of polished hyperaesthesia[4]
shrills with brass
as the aggressive light
strikes
its significance

The immaculate
conception[5]
of the inaudible bird
occurs
in gorgeous reticence . . .

1922

1. Constantin Brancusi (1876–1957), French (Romanian-born) pioneer of abstract sculpture, whose bird statues became icons of modernism in the arts. His nonrepresentational aesthetic was so revolutionary at the time that U.S. customs officials wanted to tax his sculptures as raw material rather than works of art.

2. The first and last letters of the Greek alphabet. In the book of Revelation, Jesus repeatedly identifies himself as the alpha and the omega.

3. God of the Egyptian underworld; symbol of the indestructibility of life.

4. Excessive sensitivity.

5. Catholic doctrine that, from the moment of her conception, Mary was free of the burden of original sin.

Der Blinde Junge[6]

The dam Bellona[7]
littered
her eyeless offspring
Kreigsopfer[8]
upon the pavements of Vienna

Sparkling precipitate
the spectral day
involves
the visionless obstacle

this slow blind face
pushing
its virginal nonentity
against the light

Pure purposeless eremite[9]
of centripetal sentience

Upon the carnose horologe[1] of the ego
the vibrant tendon index[2] moves not

since the black lightning desecrated
the retinal altar

Void and extinct
this planet of the soul
strains from the craving throat
in static flight upslanting

A downy youth's snout
nozzling the sun
drowned in dumbfounded instinct

Listen!
illuminati[3] of the coloured earth
How this expressionless "thing"
blows out damnation and concussive dark

Upon a mouth-organ

1923

6. The blind youth (German).
7. Roman goddess of war. *Dam:* mother.
8. War victim (German).
9. Hermit.
1. The fleshy clock.
2. Clock hand.
3. People claiming to have access to arcane knowledge.

FROM ANGLO-MONGRELS AND THE ROSE

English Rose[4]

Early English everlasting
    quadrate Rose
    paradox-Imperial
trimmed with some travestied flesh
tinted with bloodless duties   dewed
with Lipton's teas
and grimed with crack-packed
herd-housing
petalling
the prim gilt
penetralia[5]
of a luster-scioned
core-crown

Rose of arrested impulses
self-pruned
of the primordial attributes
a tepid heart   inhibiting
with tactful terrorism
the Blossom Populous
to mystic incest with its ancestry
establishing
by the divine right of self-assertion
the post-conceptional
virginity of Nature
wiping
its pink paralysis
across the dawn of reason
A World-Blush
glowing from
a never-setting-sun
Conservative Rose
storage
of British Empire-made pot-pourri
of dry dead men   making a sweetened smell
among a shrivelled collectivity

Which august dust
stirred by
the trouser-striped prongs of statesmanship
(whenever politic)

4. *Anglo-Mongrels and the Rose* is a long, semi-autobiographical poem about Loy's English mother (allegorized as the Rose, Alice, and Ada) and her Jewish father (Exodus). The rose is a traditional symbol of England. Many heraldic representations are modeled on the dog rose, whose flowers are somewhat square, or "quadrate."

5. Innermost or most private part.

rises upon the puff of press alarum
and whirling itself
deliriously around the   unseen
Bolshevik[6]   subsides
in ashy circularity
"a wreath" upon the   unknown
soldier's grave

And Jehovah   strikes—
through the fetish
of the island hedges—
Exodus[7]
who on his holiday
(induced
by the insidious pink
of Albion's[8] ideal)
is looking for a rose

And the rose
rises
from the green
of a green lane
rosily-stubborn
and robustly round

Under a pink print
sunbonnet
the village maid
scowls at the heathen

        Albion
        in female form
        salutes the alien Exodus

staring so hard—
warms his nostalgia
on her belligerent innocence

The maidenhead
drooping her lid
and pouting her breast

forewarns
his amity

Amorphous meeting
in the month of May

6. Member of the Communist Party that came to power after the Russian Revolution of 1917.
7. Loy's father. Exodus is the second book of the Bible, describing the escape of the Jews from bondage in Egypt.
8. Traditional name for Britain.

This Hebrew
    culled by Cupid on a thorn
    of the rose
lays siege
    to the thick hedgerows
    where she blows[9]
on Christian Sundays

She
    simpering in her
    ideological pink
He
    loaded with Mosaic[1]
    passions that amass
    like money

    implores her to take pity upon him
    and come and be a "Lady in the City"

Maiden emotions
breed
on leaves of novels
where anatomical man
has no notion
of offering other than the bended knee
to femininity

and purity
passes in pleasant ways
as the cows graze

For in those days
when Exodus courted the rose
literature was supposed to elevate us

So the maid   with puffy
bosom   where Jerusalem
    dreams to ease
    his head of calculations
    in the Zero of ecstasy
and a little huffy
bristles   with chastity

For this is the last Judgment
when Jehovah
roars   "Open your mouth!
and I will tell you what you have been reading"

9. Blossoms.

1. Associated with Moses and ancient Hebrew law.

Exodus had been reading
Proverbs[2]
making sharp distinction
    between the harlot
    and the Hausfrau[3] arraying
    her offspring in scarlet
approving
    such as garner good advice like grain
    and such as know enough
    to come in from the rain

The would-be
secessionist from Israel's etiquette
    (shielding pliant Jewesses from shame
    less glances
    and the giving
    of just percentages
    to matrimonial intermediaries)[4]
is spiritually intrigued
by the Anglo-Saxon phenomenon
of Virginity
delightfully
on its own defensive!

This pouting
pearl beyond price[5]
flouts
the male pretentions
to its impervious surface

Alice the gentile
Exodus the Jew
after a few
feverish tiffs
and reparations
chiefly conveyed in exclamations—
a means of expression
modified by lack of experience—
unite their variance
in marriage

Exodus
Oriental
mad to melt
with something softer than himself
clasps with soothing pledges
his wild rose of the hedges

2. Biblical book, which tells of the harlot (7.6–27) and the virtuous woman (31.10–31).
3. Housewife (German).
4. Traditional Jewish culture often relied on professional matchmakers rather than direct courtship in the arrangement of marriage.
5. Cf. Matthew 13.45–46, which describes salvation as a "pearl of great price," and Proverbs 31.10: "Who can find a virtuous woman? For her price is far above rubies."

While she
expecting
the presented knee
of chivalry
repels
the sub-umbilical mystery
of his husbandry
hysterically
His passionate-anticipation
of warming, in his arms
his rose   to a maturer coloration
which was all of aspiration
the grating upon civilization
of his sensitive organism
had left him

splinters upon an adamsite[6]
opposition
of nerves like stalactites

This dying chastity
had rendered up no soul
yet they pursued their conjugal
dilemmas   as is usual
with people
who know   not what they do[7]
but know   that what they do
is not illegal

Deep in the névrose[8]
night   he
peruses his body
divested of its upholstery
      firmly insensitive
      in mimicry
of its hypothetical model—
      a petal
of the English rose
an abstracted Ada
in myopic contemplation
of the incontemplatable
      compound rosette
of peerless negations

That like other Gods
has never appeared
leaving itself to be inferred
      Whereof

6. Greenish-black mica.
7. Cf. Jesus' words from the cross: "Father, forgive them; for they know not what they do" (Luke 23.34).
8. Neurotic.

it is not seemly
that the one petal
shall apprehend
of the other petals
their conformity

For of this Rose
wherever it blows
it is certain
that an impenetrable pink curtain
hangs between it and itself
and in metaphysical vagrance
it passes beyond the ken
of men unless
possessed
of exorbitant incomes
And Then—
merely indicating its presence
by an exotic fragrance

A rose—
that like religions
before
becoming amateur—
enwraps itself
in esoteric
and exoteric[9]
dimensions:
the official
and inofficial
social   morale
The outer
classes
accepting the official
of the inner
as a plausible
gymnastic
for disciplining the inofficial
"flesh and devil"[1]
to the ap   parent impecca   bility
of the English

And for Empire
what form could be superior
to the superimposed
slivers
of the rose?

9. Suitable for the public.
1. The Litany in the Book of Common Prayer asks for deliverance "from all the deceits of the world, the flesh, and the devil."

The best
is this compressed
all round-and-about
itself conformation
never letting out
subliminal infection
from hiatuses
in its sub-roseal skeleton

Its petals hung
with tongues
that under the supervision
of the Board of Education
may never sing in concert—
for some
singing h
flat and some
h sharp 'The Arch
angels sing H'[2]

There reigns a disproportionate
dis'armony
in the English Hanthem
And for further information
re the Rose—
and what it does to the nose
while smelling it

See *Punch*[3]

1923

Gertrude Stein[4]

Curie[5]
of the laboratory
of vocabulary
    she crushed
the tonnage
of consciousness
congealed to phrases
    to extract
a radium of the word

1924

2. *H:* note of German musical notation (B natural).
3. English periodical famous for its satire and cartoons.
4. American-born modernist writer (1874–1946).
5. Marie Curie (1867–1934), French (Polish-born) scientist responsible for the discovery of radium; the first woman to win the Nobel Prize.

The Widow's Jazz

The white flesh quakes to the negro soul
Chicago! Chicago!

An uninterpretable wail
stirs in a tangle of pale snakes

to the lethargic ecstasy of steps
backing into primeval goal

White man quit his actin' wise
colored folk hab de moon in dere eyes

Haunted by wind instruments
in groves of grace

the maiden saplings
slant to the oboes

and shampooed gigolos
prowl to the sobbing taboos.

An electric crown
crashes the furtive cargoes of the floor.

the pruned contours
dissolve
in the brazen shallows of dissonance
revolving mimes

of the encroaching Eros[6]
in adolescence

The black brute-angels
in their human gloves
bellow through a monstrous growth of metal trunks

and impish musics
crumble the ecstatic loaf
before a swooning flock of doves.

Cravan[7]
colossal absentee
the substitute dark
rolls to the incandescent memory

6. Greek god of desire.
7. Loy's beloved husband, Dada poet-boxer Arthur Cravan (1887–1918?), whose mysterious death ended the happiest period in Loy's life.

of love's survivor
on this rich suttee[8]

seared by the flames of sound
the widowed urn

holds impotently
your murdered laughter

Husband
how secretly you cuckold me with death

while this cajoling jazz
blows with its tropic breath

among the echoes of the flesh
a synthesis
of racial caress

The seraph and the ass
in this unerring esperanto[9]
of the earth
converse
of everlit delight

as my desire
receded
to the distance of the dead

searches
the opaque silence
of unpeopled space.

1931

8. In Hindu practice, a widow who immolates herself on a funeral pyre.
9. An artificial international language constructed out of words common to the chief European languages.

WILLIAM CARLOS WILLIAMS
1883–1963

William Carlos Williams has attracted more followers in the last half-century than has W. B. Yeats or T. S. Eliot. He resides at the center of much postwar poetry, especially in the United States, his example helping foster the trend toward "open" and "organic" forms. Writers who trace their branches to his roots regard many other important poets of the century as merely makers of "literature." Although these older poets may once have been liberators, Williams seems to have liberated poetry from them.

Like his disciples, Williams sees most writing as having taken a wrong turn and regards his own efforts, even if stumbling, as at least in the right direction. This mixture of humility and assertiveness can be found in poems such as "Danse Russe," in which the naked dance of the writer before his mirror characterizes him first as a ludicrous figure, then as "the happy genius of my household." Of course, Williams had no corner on nakedness: the pursuit of naked perception has been a principal endeavor of poets since William Blake, and in "A Coat," Yeats proclaimed his intention to walk naked. But at other times, Yeats openly embraced ceremony and tradition, whereas Williams, in his early brash manifesto poem "Tract," renounces them in favor of a "rough plain" aesthetic: modern art, like the new funeral hearse conjured in a series of negations, must be stripped of hackneyed symbolism and formal veneer ("not polished!"), nonfunctional ornament ("no upholstery phew!"), and flowery clichés ("No wreaths please— / especially no hot house flowers"). Though the speaker employs a hortatory tone, he demands that the driver-author wear no "silk hat" and that he be brought down, "Low and inconspicuous!"

Williams was not shy about his disagreements with major writers of his time. In his 1919 prologue to *Kora in Hell* (1920), he denounced Eliot and Ezra Pound as conformists, preoccupied with rehashing the literary glories of the past. Even so, a number of Williams's key dicta about poetry agree with their high modernist principles. "The language is worn out," Williams declared in *Paterson;* Pound had said the same in *The Cantos* and Eliot in *Four Quartets*. Williams wrote to Harriet Monroe, editor of *Poetry*, in 1913: "Most current verse is dead from the point of view of art. . . . Now life is above all things else at any moment subversive of life as it was the moment before—always new, irregular. Verse to be alive must have infused into it something of the same order, some tincture of disestablishment, something in the nature of an impalpable revolution, an ethereal reversal, let me say. I am speaking of modern verse." He put this idea succinctly in the prologue to *Kora in Hell*: "Nothing is good save the new." Although Pound insisted similarly on making poetry new, he annoyed Williams with his belief that a great deal of the remote past was capable of modernization.

Williams was by profession a general practitioner of medicine—the most important literary doctor since Anton Chekhov. Despite his insistent Americanism, his background and education were cosmopolitan. He was born on September 17, 1883, in Rutherford, New Jersey, and died in the same town. His father had emigrated from Birmingham, England, and his Spanish-speaking mother (of Basque-Dutch-Spanish-Jewish descent) from Puerto Rico. Williams attended schools in Rutherford until 1897, when he was sent for two years to a school near Geneva and to the Lycée Condorcet, in Paris. On his return, he attended Horace Mann High School, in New York City. After passing a special examination, he was admitted in 1902 to the medical school of the University of Pennsylvania. There he met two poets, Ezra Pound and Hilda Doolittle (H. D.). The friendship with Pound had a permanent effect; Williams divided his life into "Before Pound" and "After Pound." Both men were writing a good deal of verse, Williams in the English Romantic mode: "Keats was my god. *Endymion* really woke me up" (*Autobiography*). Pound was studying Romance literature, chiefly in Spanish and Italian, and kept urging Williams to do the same; Williams became increasingly uncooperative. They remained friends chiefly by cherishing disagreement.

Williams did his internship in New York City, from 1906 to 1908, writing verse in between patients. He went to Leipzig in 1908 to study pediatrics and then returned to Rutherford to practice medicine there for the rest of his life. He published a first book, *Poems,* in 1909. In 1913, Pound secured a London publisher for Williams's second book, *The Tempers.* But his first distinctly original book was *Al Que Quiere!* (Spanish for "to him who wants it"), published in Boston in 1917. It was a time for titles in foreign languages, though Williams soon abjured such gestures. In the following years, he wrote not only poems but short stories, novels, essays, and an autobiography. In 1946, he began the fulfillment of a long-standing intention, to write an epic, with the publication of *Paterson,* Book I. The four following books appeared in 1948, 1949, 1951, and 1958; at the time of his death he was working on a sixth book.

Williams based his poetry in the language as spoken in the United States. He disapproved of Pound's and Eliot's expatriation and called the publication of *The Waste Land* (1922) "the great catastrophe" that, by its genius, interrupted the "rediscovery of a primary impetus, the elementary principles of all art, in the local conditions" (*Autobiography*). He refused to present himself as an artist, insisting instead that he was like other men; he used slang to avoid pretentiousness and preferred to be thought a fool rather than a subtle artificer. His object was to communicate with the world directly: "There is a constant barrier between the reader and his consciousness of immediate contact with the world," he wrote in *Spring and All* (1923). In his manifesto for *Contact* magazine, which he edited in the 1920s, Williams stated, no doubt with Eliot and Pound as his unnamed adversaries, "I take contact to mean: man without the syllogism, without the parody, without Spinoza's ethics, man with nothing but the thing and the feeling of that thing." In explaining an aphorism in *Paterson,* "No ideas but in things," he said: "The poet does not . . . permit himself to go beyond the thought to be discovered in the context of that with which he is dealing. . . . The poet thinks with his poem."

Wallace Stevens, in a famous review of Williams, called his work "anti-poetic," and the adjective applies if poetry must be bookish and allusive. Williams emphasized that a poem must have its own idiom, that it must deal with "those things which lie under the direct scrutiny of the senses, close to the nose" (prologue to *Kora in Hell*). In a poem such as "The Red Wheelbarrow," he makes clear how any object, rightly regarded, can display its special signature. "The particular thing . . . offers a finality that sends us spinning through space" (*Kora in Hell* 27.1). Each line is suspended, demanding another line to complete it, and the whole poem shows the dependence of everything (in the poem, but also, since a microcosm is implied, in the world) upon the red wheelbarrow. "To refine, to clarify, to intensify that eternal moment in which we alone live there is but a single force—the imagination," says Williams, with something of Blake's (and, indeed, of Stevens's) radiant energy. "The only realism in art is of the imagination" (*Spring and All*).

To secure this contact with the moment, this immediacy, the poet must invent new forms. Williams commends Walt Whitman for his daring and praises Edgar Allan Poe for clearing the ground. In "The Poem as a Field of Action," he writes: "I propose sweeping changes from top to bottom of the poetic structure. . . . I say we are *through* with the iambic pentameter as presently conceived, at least for dramatic verse; through with the measured quatrain, the staid concatenations of sounds in the usual stanza, the sonnet."

In freeing himself from the mediation of other writers, Williams seeks "radiant gists," as he calls them in *Paterson*. These are not so unlike Pound's topflight or magic moments as Williams believes. To attain them, the poet must create a totality of experiencing rather than a partial or copycat experiencing. Williams wishes to let everything into the poem. He opposes symbolism, but often, as in "The Widow's Lament in Springtime" and later in "Asphodel, That Greeny Flower," his details take on a symbolic weight.

The purging of staidness and the search for new forms and vital, local language led Williams to conceive *Paterson,* in which the city is at once a giant in the landscape, a city, and a person. "I took the city as my 'case' to work up. . . . It called for a poetry such as I did not know, it was my duty to discover or make such a context on the 'thought.' To *make* a poem, fulfilling the requirements of the art, and yet new, in the sense that in the very lay of the syllables Paterson as Paterson would be discovered . . . it would be as itself, locally, and so like every other place in the world. For it is in that,

that it be particular to its own idiom, that it lives" (quoted in Linda Wagner, *The Poems of William Carlos Williams,* 1964). The poem is about the difficulties of bringing the particulars into poetry, and in the course of attempting this process it suggests the blockage of feeling and thought in the modern city. But like Hart Crane in *The Bridge,* Williams emerges from the waste land. Cyclical in structure, the poem recalls Pound's *Cantos,* in which a combination of plainspokenness and finesse ushers different kinds of matter toward complete expression. Pound insisted that Williams was interested in "the loam," while he was interested in "the finished product" ("The Poem as a Field of Action"). But a good deal of loam exists in *The Cantos,* and much of the finished product in Williams.

The Young Housewife

At ten A.M. the young housewife
moves about in négligé behind
the wooden walls of her husband's house.
I pass solitary in my car.

Then again she comes to the curb
to call the ice-man, fish-man, and stands
shy, uncorseted, tucking in
stray ends of hair, and I compare her
to a fallen leaf.

The noiseless wheels of my car
rush with a crackling sound over
dried leaves as I bow and pass smiling.

1916

Tract

I will teach you   my townspeople
how to perform   a funeral—
for you have it   over a troop
of artists—
unless one should   scour the world—
you have the ground sense   necessary.

See!   the hearse leads.
I begin with   a design for a hearse.
For Christ's sake   not black—
nor white either—   and not polished!
Let it be weathered—   like a farm wagon—
with gilt wheels   (this could be
applied fresh   at small expense)
or no wheels at all:
a rough dray to   drag over the ground.

Knock the glass out!
My God—glass,   my townspeople!
For what purpose?   Is it for the dead
to look out or   for us to see
how well he is housed   or to see
the flowers or   the lack of them—
or what?
To keep the rain   and snow from him?
He will have a   heavier rain soon:
pebbles and dirt   and what not.
Let there be no glass—
and no upholstery   phew!
and no little   brass rollers
and small easy wheels   on the bottom—
my townspeople   what are you thinking of?

A rough   plain hearse then
with gilt wheels   and no top at all.
On this   the coffin lies
by its own weight.

No wreathes please—
especially no   hot house flowers.
Some common memento   is better,
something he prized   and is known by:
his old clothes—   a few books perhaps—
God knows what!   You realize
how we are   about these things
my townspeople—
something will be found—   anything
even flowers   if he had come to that.

So much for   the hearse.
For heaven's sake though   see to the driver!
Take off   the silk hat! In fact
that's no place   at all for him—
up there   unceremoniously
dragging our friend out   to his own dignity!
Bring him down—   bring him down!
Low and inconspicuous!   I'd not have him ride
on the wagon at all—   damn him—
the undertaker's   understrapper!
Let him hold   the reins
and walk   at the side
and inconspicuously   too!

Then briefly   as to yourselves:
Walk behind—   as they do in France,
seventh class, or   if you ride
Hell take curtains!   Go with some show
of inconvenience;   sit openly—
to the weather   as to grief.

Or do you think you can shut grief in?
What—from us? We who have perhaps
nothing to lose? Share with us
share with us— it will be money
in your pockets.
Go now
I think you are ready.

1917

Danse Russe[1]

If I when my wife is sleeping
and the baby and Kathleen
are sleeping
and the sun is a flame-white disc
in silken mists
above shining trees,—
if I in my north room
dance naked, grotesquely
before my mirror
waving my shirt round my head
and singing softly to myself:
"I am lonely, lonely.
I was born to be lonely.
I am best so!"
If I admire my arms, my face
my shoulders, flanks, buttocks
against the yellow drawn shades,—

who shall say I am not
the happy genius[2] of my household?

1917

Sympathetic Portrait of a Child

The murderer's little daughter
who is barely ten years old
jerks her shoulders
right and left
so as to catch a glimpse of me
without turning round.

Her skinny little arms
wrap themselves
this way then that

1. Russian dance (French). Williams wrote this poem after seeing a performance in New York by the Ballets Russes of Sergei Pavlovich Diaghilev (1872–1922).
2. Guardian spirit of a place.

reversely about her body!
Nervously
she crushes her straw hat
about her eyes
and tilts her head
to deepen the shadow—
smiling excitedly!

As best as she can
she hides herself
in the full sunlight
her cordy legs writhing
beneath the little flowered dress
that leaves them bare
from mid-thigh to ankle—

Why has she chosen me
for the knife
that darts along her smile?

1917

Portrait of a Lady

Your thighs are appletrees
whose blossoms touch the sky.
Which sky? The sky
where Watteau hung a lady's
slipper.[3] Your knees
are a southern breeze—or
a gust of snow. Agh! what
sort of man was Fragonard?
—as if that answered
anything. Ah, yes—below
the knees, since the tune
drops that way, it is
one of those white summer days,
the tall grass of your ankles
flickers upon the shore—
Which shore?—
the sand clings to my lips—
Which shore?
Agh, petals maybe. How
should I know?
Which shore? Which shore?
I said petals from an appletree.

1920, 1934

3. Jean Antoine Watteau (1684–1721), French painter famous for his pictures of outdoor gatherings. Williams seems to have in mind *The Swing*, a painting by French artist Jean Honoré Fragonard (1732–1806, line 8), in which the girl on the swing has kicked off her slipper, which hangs perpetually in mid-air.

Queen-Ann's-Lace[4]

Her body is not so white as
anemone petals nor so smooth—nor
so remote a thing. It is a field
of the wild carrot taking
the field by force; the grass
does not raise above it.
Here is no question of whiteness,
white as can be, with a purple mole
at the center of each flower.
Each flower is a hand's span
of her whiteness. Wherever
his hand has lain there is
a tiny purple blemish. Each part
is a blossom under his touch
to which the fibres of her being
stem one by one, each to its end,
until the whole field is a
white desire, empty, a single stem,
a cluster, flower by flower,
a pious wish to whiteness gone over—
or nothing.

1921

The Widow's Lament in Springtime[5]

Sorrow is my own yard
where the new grass
flames as it has flamed
often before but not
with the cold fire
that closes round me this year.
Thirtyfive years
I lived with my husband.
The plumtree is white today
with masses of flowers.
Masses of flowers
load the cherry branches
and color some bushes
yellow and some red
but the grief in my heart
is stronger than they
for though they were my joy
formerly, today I notice them
and turn away forgetting.

4. A common, white field flower made up of many tiny blossoms that have a dark spot at the center and are joined to the stem by a stalk.
5. The poem is a tribute to Williams's mother.

Today my son told me
that in the meadows,
at the edge of the heavy woods
in the distance, he saw
trees of white flowers.
I feel that I would like
to go there
and fall into those flowers
and sink into the marsh near them.

1921

The Great Figure

Among the rain
and lights
I saw the figure 5
in gold
on a red
firetruck
moving
with weight and urgency[6]
tense
unheeded
to gong clangs
siren howls
and wheels rumbling
through the dark city.

1921

Spring and All[7]

By the road to the contagious hospital[8]
under the surge of the blue
mottled clouds driven from the
northeast—a cold wind. Beyond, the
waste of broad, muddy fields
brown with dried weeds, standing and fallen

patches of standing water
the scattering of tall trees

6. Williams later omitted this line.
7. Williams's *Spring and All* (1923) intermixed prose with poems identified by roman numerals (this poem was I). In later collections, Williams gave titles to this poem and the next three poems below (originally, III, XVIII, and XXII).
8. That is, hospital for contagious diseases.

All along the road the reddish
purplish, forked, upstanding, twiggy
stuff of bushes and small trees
with dead, brown leaves under them
leafless vines—

Lifeless in appearance, sluggish
dazed spring approaches—

They enter the new world naked,
cold, uncertain of all
save that they enter. All about them
the cold, familiar wind—

Now the grass, tomorrow
the stiff curl of wildcarrot leaf

One by one objects are defined—
It quickens: clarity, outline of leaf

But now the stark dignity of
entrance—Still, the profound change
has come upon them: rooted, they
grip down and begin to awaken

1923

The Farmer

The farmer in deep thought
is pacing through the rain
among his blank fields, with
hands in pockets,
in his head
the harvest already planted.
A cold wind ruffles the water
among the browned weeds.
On all sides
the world rolls coldly away:
black orchards
darkened by the March clouds—
leaving room for thought.
Down past the brushwood
bristling by
the rainsluiced wagonroad
looms the artist figure of
the farmer—composing
—antagonist

1923

To Elsie[9]

The pure products of America
go crazy—
mountain folk from Kentucky

or the ribbed north end of
Jersey
with its isolate lakes and

valleys, its deaf-mutes, thieves
old names
and promiscuity between

devil-may-care men who have taken
to railroading
out of sheer lust of adventure—

and young slatterns, bathed
in filth
from Monday to Saturday

to be tricked out that night
with gauds[1]
from imaginations which have no

peasant traditions to give them
character
but flutter and flaunt

sheer rags—succumbing without
emotion
save numbed terror

under some hedge of choke-cherry
or viburnum—
which they cannot express—

Unless it be that marriage
perhaps
with a dash of Indian blood

will throw up a girl so desolate
so hemmed round
with disease or murder

that she'll be rescued by an
agent—
reared by the state and

9. Nursemaid who worked for the Williams family. 1. Showy ornaments.

sent out at fifteen to work in
some hard-pressed
house in the suburbs—

some doctor's family, some Elsie—
voluptuous water
expressing with broken

brain the truth about us—
her great
ungainly hips and flopping breasts

addressed to cheap
jewelry
and rich young men with fine eyes

as if the earth under our feet
were
an excrement of some sky

and we degraded prisoners
destined
to hunger until we eat filth

while the imagination strains
after deer
going by fields of goldenrod in

the stifling heat of September
Somehow
it seems to destroy us

It is only in isolate flecks that
something
is given off

No one
to witness
and adjust, no one to drive the car

1923

The Red Wheelbarrow

so much depends
upon

a red wheel
barrow

glazed with rain
water

beside the white
chickens

1923

This Is Just to Say

I have eaten
the plums
that were in
the icebox

and which
you were probably
saving
for breakfast

Forgive me
they were delicious
so sweet
and so cold

1934

Death[2]

He's dead

the dog won't have to
sleep on his potatoes
any more to keep them
from freezing

he's dead
the old bastard—
He's a bastard because

there's nothing
legitimate in him any
more
        he's dead

He's sick-dead

2. Williams refers to his father's death, in 1918.

he's
a godforsaken curio
without
any breath in it

He's nothing at all
he's dead

Shrunken up to skin

Put his head on
one chair and his
feet on another and
he'll lie there
like an acrobat—

Love's beaten. He
beat it. That's why
he's insufferable—

because
he's here needing a
shave and making love
an inside howl
of anguish and defeat—

He's come out of the man
and he's let
the man go—
the liar

Dead
his eyes
rolled up out of
the light—a mockery

which
love cannot touch—

just bury it
and hide its face—
for shame.

1930, 1934

Flowers by the Sea

When over the flowery, sharp pasture's
edge, unseen, the salt ocean

lifts its form—chicory and daisies
tied, released, seem hardly flowers alone

but color and the movement—or the shape
perhaps—of restlessness, whereas

the sea is circled and sways
peacefully upon its plantlike stem

1930, 1935

The Botticellian Trees[3]

The alphabet of
the trees

is fading in the
song of the leaves

the crossing
bars of the thin

letters that spelled
winter

and the cold
have been illumined

with
pointed green

by the rain and sun—
The strict simple

principles of
straight branches

are being modified
by pinched-out

ifs of color, devout
conditions

the smiles of love—
. . . . . .

until the stript
sentences

move as a woman's
limbs under cloth

3. Sandro Botticelli (1445–1510), Italian Renaissance painter.

and praise from secrecy
quick with desire

love's ascendancy
in summer—

In summer the song
sings itself

above the muffled words—

1931

The Yachts

contend in a sea which the land partly encloses
shielding them from the too-heavy blows
of an ungoverned ocean which when it chooses

tortures the biggest hulls, the best man knows
to pit against its beatings, and sinks them pitilessly.
Mothlike in mists, scintillant in the minute

brilliance of cloudless days, with broad bellying sails
they glide to the wind tossing green water
from their sharp prows while over them the crew crawls

ant-like, solicitously grooming them, releasing,
making fast as they turn, lean far over and having
caught the wind again, side by side, head for the mark.

In a well guarded arena of open water surrounded by
lesser and greater craft which, sycophant, lumbering
and flittering follow them, they appear youthful, rare

as the light of a happy eye, live with the grace
of all that in the mind is fleckless, free and
naturally to be desired. Now the sea which holds them

is moody, lapping their glossy sides, as if feeling
for some slightest flaw but fails completely.
Today no race. Then the wind comes again. The yachts

move, jockeying for a start, the signal is set and they
are off. Now the waves strike at them but they are too
well made, they slip through, though they take in canvas.

Arms with hands grasping seek to clutch at the prows.
Bodies thrown recklessly in the way are cut aside.
It is a sea of faces about them in agony, in despair

until the horror of the race dawns staggering the mind,
the whole sea become an entanglement of watery bodies
lost to the world bearing what they cannot hold. Broken,

beaten, desolate, reaching from the dead to be taken up
they cry out, failing, failing! their cries rising
in waves still as the skillful yachts pass over.

1935

The Last Words of My English Grandmother

There were some dirty plates
and a glass of milk
beside her on a small table
near the rank, disheveled bed—

Wrinkled and nearly blind
she lay and snored
rousing with anger in her tones
to cry for food,

Gimme something to eat—
They're starving me—
I'm all right I won't go
to the hospital. No, no, no

Give me something to eat
Let me take you
to the hospital, I said
and after you are well

you can do as you please.
She smiled, Yes
you do what you please first
then I can do what I please—

Oh, oh, oh! she cried
as the ambulance men lifted
her to the stretcher—
Is this what you call

making me comfortable?
By now her mind was clear—
Oh you think you're smart
you young people,

she said, but I'll tell you
you don't know anything.

Then we started.
On the way

we passed a long row
of elms. She looked at them
awhile out of
the ambulance window and said,

What are all those
fuzzy-looking things out there?
Trees? Well, I'm tired
of them and rolled her head away.

1939

The Dance

In Brueghel's great picture, The Kermess,[4]
the dancers go round, they go round and
around, the squeal and the blare and the
tweedle of bagpipes, a bugle and fiddles
tipping their bellies (round as the thick-
sided glasses whose wash they impound)
their hips and their bellies off balance
to turn them. Kicking and rolling about
the Fair Grounds, swinging their butts, those
shanks must be sound to bear up under such
rollicking measures, prance as they dance
in Brueghel's great picture, The Kermess.

1944

Burning the Christmas Greens

Their time past, pulled down
cracked and flung to the fire
—go up in a roar

All recognition lost, burnt clean
clean in the flame, the green
dispersed, a living red,
flame red, red as blood wakes
on the ash—

and ebbs to a steady burning
the rekindled bed become
a landscape of flame

4. Pieter Bruegel (sometimes spelled Brueghel, Breugel, or Breughel) the Elder (1521?–1569), Flemish painter, was most famous for his pictures of peasant life, set in ordinary Dutch farms and villages. *Kermess:* an outdoor festival or fair held to benefit a church on the town's patron saint's day.

At the winter's midnight
we went to the trees, the coarse
holly, the balsam and
the hemlock for their green

At the thick of the dark
the moment of the cold's
deepest plunge we brought branches
cut from the green trees

to fill our need, and over
doorways, about paper Christmas
bells covered with tinfoil
and fastened by red ribbons

we stuck the green prongs
in the windows hung
woven wreaths and above pictures
the living green. On the

mantle we built a green forest
and among those hemlock
sprays put a herd of small
white deer as if they

were walking there. All this!
and it seemed gentle and good
to us. Their time past,
relief! The room bare. We

stuffed the dead grate
with them upon the half burnt out
log's smoldering eye, opening
red and closing under them

and we stood there looking down.
Green is a solace
a promise of peace, a fort
against the cold (though we

did not say so) a challenge
above the snow's
hard shell. Green (we might
have said) that, where

small birds hide and dodge
and lift their plaintive
rallying cries, blocks for them
and knocks down

the unseeing bullets of
the storm. Green spruce boughs

pulled down by a weight of
snow—Transformed!

Violence leaped and appeared.
Recreant! roared to life
as the flame rose through and
our eyes recoiled from it.

In the jagged flames green
to red, instant and alive. Green!
those sure abutments . . . Gone!
lost to mind

and quick in the contracting
tunnel of the grate
appeared a world! Black
mountains, black and red—as

yet uncolored—and ash white,
an infant landscape of shimmering
ash and flame and we, in
that instant, lost,

breathless to be witnesses,
as if we stood
ourselves refreshed among
the shining fauna of that fire.

1944

From Paterson[5]

Preface

"Rigor of beauty is the quest. But how will you find beauty when it is locked in the mind past all remonstrance?"

To make a start,
out of particulars
and make them general, rolling
up the sum, by defective means—
Sniffing the trees,
just another dog
among a lot of dogs. What
else is there? And to do?
The rest have run out—
after the rabbits.

5. An industrial city on the Passaic River, in northeast New Jersey. Williams's book-length poem is in five parts.

Only the lame stands—on
three legs. Scratch front and back.
Deceive and eat. Dig
a musty bone

For the beginning is assuredly
the end—since we know nothing, pure
and simple, beyond
our own complexities.

Yet there is
no return: rolling up out of chaos,
a nine months' wonder, the city
the man, an identity—it can't be
otherwise—an
interpenetration, both ways. Rolling
up! obverse, reverse;
the drunk the sober; the illustrious
the gross; one. In ignorance
a certain knowledge and knowledge,
undispersed, its own undoing.

(The multiple seed,
packed tight with detail, soured,
is lost in the flux and the mind,
distracted, floats off in the same
scum)

Rolling up, rolling up heavy with
numbers.

It is the ignorant sun
rising in the slot of
hollow suns risen, so that never in this
world will a man live well in his body
save dying—and not know himself
dying; yet that is
the design. Renews himself
thereby, in addition and subtraction,
walking up and down.

and the craft,
subverted by thought, rolling up, let
him beware lest he turn to no more than
the writing of stale poems . . .
Minds like beds always made up,
(more stony than a shore)
unwilling or unable.

Rolling in, top up,
under, thrust and recoil, a great clatter:
lifted as air, boated, multicolored, a

wash of seas—
from mathematics to particulars—

divided as the dew,
floating mists, to be rained down and
regathered into a river that flows
and encircles:

shells and animalcules[6]
generally and so to man,

to Paterson.

From Book I
The Delineaments of the Giants

From *I*

Paterson lies in the valley under the Passaic Falls
its spent waters forming the outline of his back. He
lies on his right side, head near the thunder
of the waters filling his dreams! Eternally asleep,
his dreams walk about the city where he persists
incognito. Butterflies settle on his stone ear.
Immortal he neither moves nor rouses and is seldom
seen, though he breathes and subtleties of his machinations
drawing their substance from the noise of the pouring river
animate a thousand automatons. Who because they
neither know their sources nor the sills of their
disappointments walk outside their bodies aimlessly for the most part,
locked and forgot in their desires—unroused.

—Say it, no ideas but in things—
nothing but the blank faces of the houses
and cylindrical trees
bent, forked by preconception and accident—
split, furrowed, creased, mottled, stained—
secret—into the body of the light!

From above, higher than the spires, higher
even than the office towers, from oozy fields
abandoned to grey beds of dead grass,
black sumac, withered weed-stalks,
mud and thickets cluttered with dead leaves—
the river comes pouring in above the city
and crashes from the edge of the gorge
in a recoil of spray and rainbow mists—

6. Microscopic animals.

(What common language to unravel?
. . . combed into straight lines
from that rafter of a rock's
lip.)

A man like a city and a woman like a flower
—who are in love. Two women. Three women.
Innumerable women, each like a flower.

But
only one man—like a city.

In regard to the poems I left with you; will you be so kind as to return them to me at my new address? And without bothering to comment upon them if you should find that embarrassing—for it was the human situation and not the literary one that motivated my phone call and visit.

Besides, I know myself to be more the woman than the poet; and to concern myself less with the publishers of poetry than with . . . living . . .

But they set up an investigation . . . and my doors are bolted forever (I hope forever) against all public welfare workers, professional do-gooders and the like.[7]

Jostled as are the waters approaching
the brink, his thoughts
interlace, repel and cut under,
rise rock-thwarted and turn aside
but forever strain forward—or strike
an eddy and whirl, marked by a
leaf or curdy spume, seeming
to forget .
Retake later the advance and
are replaced by succeeding hordes
pushing forward—they coalesce now
glass-smooth with their swiftness,
quiet or seem to quiet as at the close
they leap to the conclusion and
fall, fall in air! as if
floating, relieved of their weight,
split apart, ribbons; dazed, drunk
with the catastrophe of the descent
floating unsupported
to hit the rocks: to a thunder,
as if lightning had struck

All lightness lost, weight regained in
the repulse, a fury of
escape driving them to rebound
upon those coming after—
keeping nevertheless to the stream, they
retake their course, the air full

7. A number of the prose materials interpolated throughout *Paterson* are from letters Williams received.

of the tumult and of spray
connotative of the equal air, coeval,
filling the void

And there, against him, stretches the low mountain.
The Park's her head, carved, above the Falls, by the quiet
river;[8] Colored crystals the secret of those rocks;
farms and ponds, laurel and the temperate wild cactus,
yellow flowered . . facing him, his
arm supporting her, by the *Valley of the Rocks*, asleep.
Pearls at her ankles, her monstrous hair
spangled with apple-blossoms is scattered about into
the back country, waking their dreams—where the deer run
and the wood-duck nests protecting his gallant plumage.

In February 1857, David Hower, a poor shoemaker with a large family, out of work and money, collected a lot of mussels from Notch Brook near the City of Paterson. He found in eating them many hard substances. At first he threw them away but at last submitted some of them to a jeweler who gave him twenty-five to thirty dollars for the lot. Later he found others. One pearl of fine lustre was sold to Tiffany for $900 and later to the Empress Eugenie[9] for $2,000 to be known thenceforth as the "Queen Pearl," the finest of its sort in the world today.

News of this sale created such excitement that search for the pearls was started throughout the country. The Unios (mussels) at Notch Brook and elsewhere were gathered by the millions and destroyed often with little or no result. A large round pearl, weighing 400 grains which would have been the finest pearl of modern times, was ruined by boiling open the shell.

Twice a month Paterson receives
communications from the Pope and Jacques Barzun
(Isocrates).[1] His works
have been done into French
and Portuguese. And clerks in the post-
office ungum rare stamps from
his packages and steal them for their
childrens' albums .

Say it! No ideas but in things. Mr.
Paterson has gone away
to rest and write. Inside the bus one sees
his thoughts sitting and standing. His
thoughts alight and scatter—

Who are these people (how complex
the mathematic) among whom I see myself
in the regularly ordered plateglass of

8. In *Paterson*'s symbolism, the park (that is, nature) is associated with the female principle, the city with the male.
9. Eugenie Marie de Montijo (1826–1920), wife of Napoleon III and empress of France (1853–70). Tiffany & Co. is a famous jewelry store in New York.

1. Isocrates, an ancient Greek orator and rhetorician, seems to be identified here with Barzun, a twentieth-century scholar and teacher at Columbia University. Dr. Paterson "hears from" him because Barzun was a sponsor of the Readers' Subscription, a highbrow mail-order book club to which the doctor subscribed.

his thoughts, glimmering before shoes and bicycles?
They walk incommunicado, the
equation is beyond solution, yet
its sense is clear—that they may live
his thought is listed in the Telephone
Directory—

And derivatively, for the Great Falls,
PISS-AGH! the giant lets fly! good *Muncie*,[2] too

They craved the miraculous!

* * *

From *III*

* * *

Thought clambers up,
snail like, upon the wet rocks
hidden from sun and sight—
hedged in by the pouring torrent—
and has its birth and death there
in that moist chamber, shut from
the world—and unknown to the world,
cloaks itself in mystery—

And the myth
that holds up the rock,
that holds up the water thrives there—
in that cavern, that profound cleft,
a flickering green
inspiring terror, watching . .

And standing, shrouded there, in that din,
Earth, the chatterer, father of all
speech . . . .

1946

The Ivy Crown[3]

The whole process is a lie,
unless,
crowned by excess,
it break forcefully,
one way or another,
from its confinement—

2. Or *Munsee*, meaning "where stones are gathered"; the name of the Native American "Wolf Tribe." The Great Falls are imagined as the giant urinating.

3. Associated, traditionally, with an award for victory or honor. Ivy was sacred to Dionysus, the ancient Greek god of wine, ecstasy, sacrifice, regeneration, and poetic inspiration.

or find a deeper well.
Antony and Cleopatra[4]
were right;
they have shown
the way. I love you
or I do not live
at all.

Daffodil time
is past. This is
summer, summer!
the heart says,
and not even the full of it.
No doubts
are permitted—
though they will come
and may
before our time
overwhelm us.
We are only mortal
but being mortal
can defy our fate.
We may
by an outside chance
even win! We do not
look to see
jonquils and violets
come again
but there are,
still,
the roses!

Romance has no part in it.
The business of love is
cruelty *which,*
by our wills,
we transform
to live together.
It has its seasons,
for and against,
whatever the heart
fumbles in the dark
to assert
toward the end of May.

4. The Roman warrior Marc Antony (c. 83–30 B.C.E.) and the Egyptian queen (69–30 B.C.E.). Their passionate love affair and eventual suicides are the subject of Shakespeare's *Antony and Cleopatra.*

Just as the nature of briars
is to tear flesh,
I have proceeded
through them.
Keep
the briars out,
they say.
You cannot live
and keep free of
briars.

Children pick flowers.
Let them.
Though having them
in hand
they have no further use for them
but leave them crumpled
at the curb's edge.

At our age the imagination
across the sorry facts
lifts us
to make roses
stand before thorns.
Sure
love is cruel
and selfish
and totally obtuse—
at least, blinded by the light,
young love is.
But we are older,
I to love
and you to be loved,
we have,
no matter how,
by our wills survived
to keep
the jeweled prize
always
at our finger tips.
We will it so
and so it is
past all accident.

1955

From Pictures from Bruegel[5]

II. Landscape with the Fall of Icarus[6]

According to Brueghel
when Icarus fell
it was spring

a farmer was ploughing
his field
the whole pageantry

of the year was
awake tingling
near

the edge of the sea
concerned
with itself

sweating in the sun
that melted
the wings' wax

unsignificantly
off the coast
there was

a splash quite unnoticed
this was
Icarus drowning

VI. Haymaking[7]

The living quality of
the man's mind
stands out

and its covert assertions
for art, art, art!
painting

5. Peter Bruegel (or Breughel) the Elder (1521?–1569), Flemish painter of often lively and boisterous peasant life. *Pictures from Bruegel* is a set of ten poems, each having as its subject a Bruegel painting.
6. In Greek mythology, Icarus's father, Daedalus, made wings for both of them to escape from Crete. Icarus flew too close to the sun, the wax on his wings melted, and he fell into the sea and drowned. In Bruegel's painting *Fall of Icarus,* the only reference to the myth is Icarus's pair of legs disappearing into the sea in a corner of the canvas. See also W. H. Auden's "Musée de Beaux Arts" (p. 797).
7. The picture is titled *Haymaking* or *July*.

that the Renaissance
tried to absorb
but

it remained a wheat field
over which the
wind played

men with scythes tumbling
the wheat in
rows

the gleaners[8] already busy
it was his own—
magpies

the patient horses no one
could take that
from him

1962

From Asphodel,[9] That Greeny Flower

Book I

Of asphodel, that greeny flower,
        like a buttercup
                upon its branching stem—
save that it's green and wooden—
        I come, my sweet,
                to sing to you.
We lived long together
        a life filled,
                if you will,
with flowers. So that
        I was cheered
                when I came first to know
that there were flowers also
        in hell.
                Today
I'm filled with the fading memory of those flowers
        that we both loved,
                even to this poor
colorless thing—
        I saw it
                when I was a child—
little prized among the living
        but the dead see,
                asking among themselves:

8. Farm laborers who pick up scattered grain left by reapers.

9. Flower associated with the fields of the dead in the underworld of Greek mythology.

What do I remember
            that was shaped
                        as this thing is shaped?
while our eyes fill
            with tears.
                        Of love, abiding love
it will be telling
            though too weak a wash of crimson
                        colors it
to make it wholly credible.
            There is something
                        something urgent
I have to say to you
            and you alone
                        but it must wait
while I drink in
            the joy of your approach,
                        perhaps for the last time.
And so
            with fear in my heart
                        I drag it out
and keep on talking
            for I dare not stop.
                        Listen while I talk on
against time.
            It will not be
                        for long.
I have forgot
            and yet I see clearly enough
                        something
central to the sky
            which ranges round it.
                        An odor
springs from it!
            A sweetest odor!
                        Honeysuckle! And now
there comes the buzzing of a bee!
            and a whole flood
                        of sister memories!
Only give me time,
            time to recall them
                        before I shall speak out.
Give me time,
            time.
When I was a boy
            I kept a book
                        to which, from time
to time,
            I added pressed flowers
                        until, after a time,
I had a good collection.
            The asphodel,

forebodingly,
among them.
I bring you,
reawakened,
a memory of those flowers.
They were sweet
when I pressed them
and retained
something of their sweetness
a long time.
It is a curious odor,
a moral odor,
that brings me
near to you.
The color
was the first to go.
There had come to me
a challenge,
your dear self,
mortal as I was,
the lily's throat
to the hummingbird!
Endless wealth,
I thought,
held out its arms to me.
A thousand tropics
in an apple blossom.
The generous earth itself
gave us lief.[1]
The whole world
became my garden!
But the sea
which no one tends
is also a garden
when the sun strikes it
and the waves
are wakened.
I have seen it
and so have you
when it puts all flowers
to shame.
Too, there are the starfish
stiffened by the sun
and other sea wrack
and weeds. We knew that
along with the rest of it
for we were born by the sea,
knew its rose hedges
to the very water's brink.
There the pink mallow grows

1. Obsolete form of both *leaf* and *life;* also connotes gladness.

and in their season
strawberries
and there, later,
we went to gather
the wild plum.
I cannot say
that I have gone to hell
for your love
but often
found myself there
in your pursuit.
I do not like it
and wanted to be
in heaven. Hear me out.
Do not turn away.
I have learned much in my life
from books
and out of them
about love.
Death
is not the end of it.
There is a hierarchy
which can be attained,
I think,
in its service.
Its guerdon[2]
is a fairy flower;
a cat of twenty lives.
If no one came to try it
the world
would be the loser.
It has been
for you and me
as one who watches a storm
come in over the water.
We have stood
from year to year
before the spectacle of our lives
with joined hands.
The storm unfolds.
Lightning
plays about the edges of the clouds.
The sky to the north
is placid,
blue in the afterglow
as the storm piles up.
It is a flower
that will soon reach
the apex of its bloom.
We danced,

2. Recompense.

in our minds,
and read a book together.
You remember?
It was a serious book.
And so books
entered our lives.
The sea! The sea!
Always
when I think of the sea
there comes to mind
the *Iliad*
and Helen's public fault
that bred it.[3]
Were it not for that
there would have been
no poem but the world
if we had remembered,
those crimson petals
spilled among the stones,
would have called it simply
murder.
The sexual orchid that bloomed then
sending so many
disinterested
men to their graves
has left its memory
to a race of fools
or heroes
if silence is a virtue.
The sea alone
with its multiplicity
holds any hope.
The storm
has proven abortive
but we remain
after the thoughts it roused
to
re-cement our lives.
It is the mind
the mind
that must be cured
short of death's
intervention,
and the will becomes again
a garden. The poem
is complex and the place made
in our lives
for the poem.
Silence can be complex too,

3. According to Homer's *Iliad*, the Trojan War resulted when Paris abducted Helen, an exceptionally beautiful woman, from her husband, Menelaus.

but you do not get far
with silence.
Begin again.
It is like Homer's
catalogue of ships:[4]
it fills up the time.
I speak in figures,
well enough, the dresses
you wear are figures also,
we could not meet
otherwise. When I speak
of flowers
it is to recall
that at one time
we were young.
All women are not Helen,
I know that,
but have Helen in their hearts.
My sweet,
you have it also, therefore
I love you
and could not love you otherwise.
Imagine you saw
a field made up of women
all silver-white.
What should you do
but love them?
The storm bursts
or fades! it is not
the end of the world.
Love is something else,
or so I thought it,
a garden which expands,
though I knew you as a woman
and never thought otherwise,
until the whole sea
has been taken up
and all its gardens.
It was the love of love,
the love that swallows up all else,
a grateful love,
a love of nature, of people,
animals,
a love engendering
gentleness and goodness
that moved me
and *that* I saw in you.
I should have known,
though I did not,
that the lily-of-the-valley
is a flower makes many ill

4. In Homer's *Iliad* 2, nearly three hundred lines list the Greek ships that sailed to Troy.

who whiff it.
We had our children,
rivals in the general onslaught.
I put them aside
though I cared for them
as well as any man
could care for his children
according to my lights.
You understand
I had to meet you
after the event
and have still to meet you.
Love
to which you too shall bow
along with me—
a flower
a weakest flower
shall be our trust
and not because
we are too feeble
to do otherwise
but because
at the height of my power
I risked what I had to do,
therefore to prove
that we love each other
while my very bones sweated
that I could not cry to you
in the act.
Of asphodel, that greeny flower,
I come, my sweet,
to sing to you!
My heart rouses
thinking to bring you news
of something
that concerns you
and concerns many men. Look at
what passes for the new.
You will not find it there but in
despised poems.
It is difficult
to get the news from poems
yet men die miserably every day
for lack
of what is found there.
Hear me out
for I too am concerned
and every man
who wants to die at peace in his bed
besides.

1955

Elinor Wylie
1885–1928

Born into a prominent family in Somerville, New Jersey, on September 7, 1885, Elinor Wylie grew up in Philadelphia and Washington, D.C. Her personal life, which included leaving her socially conservative first husband and her child to elope with a married man, was considered scandalous. Wealthy, glamorous, reputedly beautiful, yet defiant of social mores, she became a prominent literary figure in the 1920s, before dying, in New York, of a stroke. Like Edna St. Vincent Millay and Dorothy Parker, she was widely celebrated in her lifetime, partly because she eschewed the modernist difficulty of Gertrude Stein, Ezra Pound, Marianne Moore, and T. S. Eliot, preferring to bring into the twentieth century a Romantic literary practice. Shelley was especially important to her as a kindred spirit and model, and Keats's influence is also apparent in her lush descriptions of nature. Even so, her poetry of miniaturist clarity recalls the contemporary Imagist techniques of Amy Lowell, H. D., perhaps Wallace Stevens. She wrote novels as well as verse.

Wylie's poetry is capable of both escapist reverie and bone-hard realism. In "Let No Charitable Hope," she declares, "I live by squeezing from a stone / The little nourishment I get." The textures of Wylie's best poetry are remarkable in combining austerity and sensual nourishment. "Wild Peaches" imagines an earthly paradise on the Eastern Shore of Maryland, brimming with taste, scent, and deep-hued color. But there are hints of death and destruction in this lavish pastoral, and the poem's harsh ending retracts the opulent fantasy, conjuring in its place the blank starkness of "Bare hills, cold silver on a sky of slate." Similarly, "Incantation" is a baroque exercise in contrasts, except that the poet has severely restricted her palette to black and white. Wylie's art is sustained by precise attention to particulars, brilliantly polished surfaces, and an exacting formal discipline.

Wild Peaches

1

When the world turns completely upside down
You say we'll emigrate to the Eastern Shore[1]
Aboard a river-boat from Baltimore;
We'll live among wild peach trees, miles from town,
You'll wear a coonskin cap, and I a gown
Homespun, dyed butternut's dark gold colour.
Lost, like your lotus-eating ancestor,[2]
We'll swim in milk and honey[3] till we drown.

The winter will be short, the summer long,
The autumn amber-hued, sunny and hot,
Tasting of cider and of scuppernong;[4]

1. Of Maryland, east of the Chesapeake Bay.
2. In book 9 of Homer's *Odyssey*, the lotus-eaters live in a continual stupor caused by the narcotic effects of the honey-sweet lotus fruit. When Odysseus's men eat the lotus, they forget their mission and lose all desire save to remain and continue eating the addictive fruit.
3. God promises to Moses and the Israelites "a land flowing with milk and honey" (Exodus 3.8).
4. A sweet wine made from the scuppernong grape.

All seasons sweet, but autumn best of all.
The squirrels in their silver fur will fall
Like falling leaves, like fruit, before your shot.

2

The autumn frosts will lie upon the grass
Like bloom on grapes of purple-brown and gold.
The misted early mornings will be cold;
The little puddles will be roofed with glass.
The sun, which burns from copper into brass,
Melts these at noon, and makes the boys unfold
Their knitted mufflers; full as they can hold,
Fat pockets dribble chestnuts as they pass.

Peaches grow wild, and pigs can live in clover;
A barrel of salted herrings lasts a year;
The spring begins before the winter's over.
By February you may find the skins
Of garter snakes and water moccasins
Dwindled and harsh, dead-white and cloudy-clear.

3

When April pours the colours of a shell
Upon the hills, when every little creek
Is shot with silver from the Chesapeake
In shoals new-minted by the ocean swell,
When strawberries go begging, and the sleek
Blue plums lie open to the blackbird's beak,
We shall live well—we shall live very well.

The months between the cherries and the peaches
Are brimming cornucopias which spill
Fruits red and purple, sombre-bloomed and black;
Then, down rich fields and frosty river beaches
We'll trample bright persimmons, while you kill
Bronze partridge, speckled quail, and canvasback.[5]

4

Down to the Puritan marrow of my bones
There's something in this richness that I hate.
I love the look, austere, immaculate,
Of landscapes drawn in pearly monotones.
There's something in my very blood that owns
Bare hills, cold silver on a sky of slate,
A thread of water, churned to milky spate[6]
Streaming through slanted pastures fenced with stones.

5. A variety of duck.

6. Floodwater.

I love those skies, thin blue or snowy gray,
Those fields sparse-planted, rendering meagre sheaves;
That spring, briefer than apple-blossom's breath,
Summer, so much too beautiful to stay,
Swift autumn, like a bonfire of leaves,
And sleepy winter, like the sleep of death.

1921

Incantation

A white well
In a black cave;
A bright shell
In a dark wave.

A white rose
Black brambles hood;
Smooth bright snows
In a dark wood.

A flung white glove
In a dark fight;
A white dove
On a wild black night.

A white door
In a dark lane;
A bright core
To bitter black pain.

A white hand
Waved from dark walls;
In a burnt black land
Bright waterfalls.

A bright spark
Where black ashes are;
In the smothering dark
One white star.

1921

Let No Charitable Hope

Now let no charitable hope
Confuse my mind with images
Of eagle and of antelope:
I am in nature none of these.

I was, being human, born alone;
I am, being woman, hard beset;
I live by squeezing from a stone
The little nourishment I get.

In masks outrageous and austere
The years go by in single file;
But none has merited my fear,
And none has quite escaped my smile.

1923

D. H. Lawrence
1885–1930

D. H. Lawrence has about him something of the prophet of humanity, like Walt Whitman, and something of the insurgent rhapsode, like the Beat poets. He is not so all-encompassing as Whitman, whose free long line and bardic voice he adapted; he complained, indeed, that Whitman was too indiscriminate. And he is not so silly as the Beat poets can be. He thought of himself in various ways, latterly as a cleanser and a stinger. The title of his book of poems *Pansies* he derived from the French word *panser* (to cleanse) rather than from the flower. Another of his later books had the title *Nettles*.

Like William Blake, Lawrence sees humans as imprisoned within their bodies, their "bowels of steel"—mechanisms grown incapable of genuine feeling. They are imprisoned within their egoism as well; Lawrence speaks of it as a "barbed-wire enclosure of Know Thyself." And they are imprisoned within sexual taboos that destroy their ability to feel and think by isolating the processes of feeling and thinking from each other.

No wonder, then, that in Lawrence's writings the relations of mother and son are ruined by possessiveness, an excess of feeling; and that the relations of lovers are ruined by frigidity, an excess of thinking. The spirit has to break through egoism and become, as a line in one poem says, "Not I, but the wind that blows through me!" To shed self-involvement, to diminish mind, is the way for Westerners, at least, to achieve secular beatitude. To die is to be risen, "the same as before yet unaccountably new." Only then can a man "let his buttocks prance," in Lawrence's provocative image. Lawrence might seem to espouse mindlessness, but he does not wish for mere physicality. The self has to be released, he wrote to the editor of *Poetry* magazine, Harriet Monroe, by "something really deeper" than "cerebral sex-consciousness," something also at "the root of poetry, lived or sung" (*The Letters of D. H. Lawrence,* ed. James T. Boulton, 6:328). Sexual intercourse is for Lawrence less a physical act than a mystical mode, so that his endorsement of it is oddly grim.

Lawrence opposed contemporary verse. He objected to W. B. Yeats's poetry as sickly and A. E. Housman's as stale. He was more sympathetic to Thomas Hardy, who, like him, cultivated a poetry of deliberate roughness, of intense and complicated feeling. As he said in a 1908 letter: "[M]y verses are tolerable—rather pretty, but not suave; there is some blood in them. Poetry now a days seems to be a sort of plaster-cast craze, scraps sweetly moulded in easy Plaster of Paris sentiment. Nobody chips verses earnestly out of the living rock of his own feeling. . . . Before everything I like sincerity, and a quickening spontaneous emotion. I do not worship music or the 'half said thing' " (*Letters,*

1:63). Extremism is necessary for the poet—to drink "the last dregs of bitterness," he said, and "face the last embrace of the fire" (*Letters,* 2:341).

Lawrence defined the qualities he sought in poetry in varying ways. In "this age of stark and unlovely actualities," he wrote in 1916, "this stark, bare, rocky directness of statement, this alone makes poetry, today" (*Letters,* 2:503). He conceived of the poetic process as one of self-extinction. His "real poems" frightened him because, he wrote, they "had the ghost in them. They seemed to me to come from somewhere, I didn't quite know where, out of a me whom I didn't know and didn't want to know, and say things I would much rather not have said" (quoted in Harry T. Moore, *The Life and Works of D. H. Lawrence,* 1951). The process of revision should not be merely formal but should attempt to uncover the basic, as opposed to the superficial, self. Some of Lawrence's formalist critics have taken him to task for not valuing more highly the discipline of craft. Lawrence was not indifferent to good writing—he revised the language and ideas of his poems—but he thought that form must arise spontaneously from the material, not be imposed on it from above. When someone objected to the form of his novels, he replied that what was being asked for was *imitative* rather than *natural* form.

In "Poetry of the Present" (1919), reprinted as the preface to the American edition of *New Poems* (1920), Lawrence clarifies this attitude, distinguishing between two kinds of poetry; one is perfect, complete, final, conveyed in perfect symmetry of form—the "gem-like lyrics of Shelley and Keats." But he prefers to such poetry of "static perfection" what he calls "the poetry of that which is at hand: the immediate present," poetry of "the incarnate moment: the moment, the quick of all change and haste and opposition: the moment, the immediate present, the Now." For the poetry of now, of the "pulsating, carnal self," he finds that the appropriate medium is free verse, because it alone can be "direct utterance from the instant, whole man." Although the poetry may be marked by some discord and confusion, those qualities have a purpose; they "belong to the reality as noise belongs to the plunge of water." Lawrence's poetics of immediacy and spontaneity echo Romantic ideas of creative self-expression and anticipate post–World War II notions of "open form," "organic form," and even "confessional poetry," in contrast to the theories of "impersonal" poetry and New Critical formalism that shaped British and American poetry into the 1950s. In the preface to his *Collected Poems* (1928), he remarked, "many of the poems are so personal that, in their fragmentary fashion, they make up a biography of an emotional and inner life."

David Herbert Lawrence was born on September 11, 1885, in Eastwood, Nottinghamshire. His mother was a schoolteacher, his father a miner; their personalities clashed and marked their son's, whose oedipal feelings play a prominent part in his novel *Sons and Lovers* (1913). Lawrence thought of his life as in two parts, the first of them dominated by his mother. Like her, he became a schoolteacher, after he had attended the University of Nottingham. He published his first poems, written in traditional meters and rhyming stanzas, in a magazine in 1909. Partly under the influence of the Imagists, such as Ezra Pound, Amy Lowell, and H. D., after 1912 Lawrence turned to freer, unrhyming, cadenced forms. But Lawrence resisted Pound's attempt to adopt him into the Imagist group, preferring to play his own game. He had published his first novel, *The White Peacock,* in 1911. A month before, in December, his mother had died, and Lawrence felt very conscious of this "wound," as he called it. The second part of his life, a process of recovery, began in April 1912, when he met Frieda von Richthofen Weekley, the wife of a professor of philology and daughter of a German baron. Almost at once, they determined to elope to the Continent, although Frieda would have to leave her three children behind. Eventually, Frieda secured a divorce, and Lawrence married her in 1914. Back in England, Lawrence opposed World War I and was suspected of being a spy. As soon as the war was over, he and Frieda left for

Italy. They were to travel a great deal during the remainder of Lawrence's life, returning only briefly to England after 1919. One extended sojourn was at Taos, New Mexico; others took him to Australia, Mexico, and Ceylon (Sri Lanka). Lawrence was so insistent on the importance of bodiliness that his death, in Vence, France, from tuberculosis, had a bitter irony.

Lawrence's poetry ranges not only from tighter to looser forms, but also from ecstatic encounters with nature ("Snake") to sardonic social commentary ("The English Are So Nice") and moving self-elegies ("The Ship of Death"). Amid this variety, perhaps his most notable poems or passages are bursts of unified perception, characterized by brutal honesty of observation. He pries open the lid, whatever the box may hold. It is the honesty of a person with a preconceived idea, not of a detached observer. He disturbs whatever he touches; he goads and is goaded. Another, rather surprising aspect of his poetry is its dignity. He respects, and demands that his readers respect, the things and experiences he values. Lines that other poets would find too raw—"It was the flank of any wife / I touched with my hand, I clutched with my hand" ("New Heaven and Earth")—are in context not ridiculous, though when excerpted they may appear so. In addition to honesty and dignity, his verse has a more fundamental quality of dynamism, a concentrated apprehension of the inner life of animals and flowers. No poet has a more uncanny sense of what it is like to be, for example, a copulating tortoise ("Lui et Elle"). Lawrence asks of nature not What principles of order and harmony can I find here? but rather, What is the center of violent feeling here? This he elicits with great distinctiveness.

The Wild Common[1]

The quick sparks on the gorse-bushes are leaping
Little jets of sunlight texture imitating flame;
Above them, exultant, the peewits[2] are sweeping:
They have triumphed again o'er the ages, their screamings proclaim.

Rabbits, handfuls of brown earth, lie
Low-rounded on the mournful turf they have bitten down to the quick.
Are they asleep?—are they living?—Now see, when I
Lift my arms, the hill bursts and heaves under their spurting kick!

The common flaunts bravely; but below, from the rushes
Crowds of glittering king-cups[3] surge to challenge the blossoming
    bushes;
There the lazy streamlet pushes
His bent course mildly; here wakes again, leaps, laughs, and gushes

Into a deep pond, an old sheep-dip,[4]
Dark, overgrown with willows, cool, with the brook ebbing through so
    slow;
Naked on the steep, soft lip
Of the turf I stand watching my own white shadow quivering to and fro.

1. Uncultivated stretch of land. Although he did not publish this poem until 1916, Lawrence placed it first in his collections.
2. Birds noted for their irregular flapping flight and shrill walling cries. *Gorse-bushes*: spiny evergreen shrubs with yellow flowers.
3. Buttercups.
4. That is, pond in which sheep are washed.

What if the gorse-flowers shrivelled, and I were gone?
What if the waters ceased, where were the marigolds then, and the gudgeon?[5]
What is this thing that I look down upon?
White on the water wimples[6] my shadow, strains like a dog on a string, to run on.

How it looks back, like a white dog to its master!
I on the bank all substance, my shadow all shadow looking up to me, looking back!
And the water runs, and runs faster, runs faster,
And the white dog dances and quivers, I am holding his cord quite slack.

But how splendid it is to be substance, here!
My shadow is neither here nor there; but I, I am royally here!
I am here! I am here! screams the peewit; the may-blobs[7] burst out in a laugh as they hear!
Here! flick the rabbits. Here! pants the gorse. Here! say the insects far and near.

Over my skin in the sunshine, the warm, clinging air
Flushed with the songs of seven larks singing at once, goes kissing me glad.
You are here! You are here! We have found you! Everywhere
We sought you substantial, you touchstone of caresses, you naked lad!

Oh but the water loves me and folds me,
Plays with me, sways me, lifts me and sinks me, murmurs: Oh marvellous stuff!
No longer shadow!—and it holds me
Close, and it rolls me, enfolds me, touches me, as if never it could touch me enough.

Sun, but in substance, yellow water-blobs!
Wings and feathers on the crying, mysterious ages, peewits wheeling!
All that is right, all that is good, all that is God takes substance! a rabbit lobs[8]
In confirmation, I hear sevenfold lark-songs pealing.[9]

1916

Love on the Farm[1]

What large, dark hands are those at the window
Grasping in the golden light
Which weaves its way through the evening wind
At my heart's delight?

5. Small fish.
6. Ripples.
7. Marigolds.
8. Runs slowly.
9. As in a ringing of bells.
1. Titled "Cruelty and Love" when first published in 1913 and retitled for the *Collected Poems* (1928).

Ah, only the leaves! But in the west
I see a redness suddenly come
Into the evening's anxious breast—
'Tis the wound of love goes home!

The woodbine[2] creeps abroad
Calling low to her lover:
The sun-lit flirt who all the day
Has poised above her lips in play
And stolen kisses, shallow and gay
Of pollen, now has gone away—
She woos the moth with her sweet, low word;
And when above her his moth-wings hover
Then her bright breast she will uncover
And yield her honey-drop to her lover.

Into the yellow, evening glow
Saunters a man from the farm below;
Leans, and looks in at the low-built shed
Where the swallow has hung her marriage bed.
The bird lies warm against the wall.
She glances quick her startled eyes
Towards him, then she turns away
Her small head, making warm display
Of red upon the throat. Her terrors sway
Her out of the nest's warm, busy ball,
Whose plaintive cry is heard as she flies
In one blue stoop from out the sties[3]
Into the twilight's empty hall.

Oh, water-hen, beside the rushes
Hide your quaintly scarlet blushes,
Still your quick tail, lie still as dead,
Till the distance folds over his ominous tread!

The rabbit presses back her ears,
Turns back her liquid, anguished eyes
And crouches low; then with wild spring
Spurts from the terror of *his* oncoming;
To be choked back, the wire ring
Her frantic effort throttling:
Piteous brown ball of quivering fears!
Ah, soon in his large, hard hands she dies,
And swings all loose from the swing of his walk!
Yet calm and kindly are his eyes
And ready to open in brown surprise
Should I not answer to his talk
Or should he my tears surmise.

I hear his hand on the latch, and rise from my chair
Watching the door open; he flashes bare

2. Honeysuckle.

3. Pens for animals.

His strong teeth in a smile, and flashes his eyes
In a smile like triumph upon me; then careless-wise
He flings the rabbit soft on the table board
And comes towards me: ah! the uplifted sword
Of his hand against my bosom! and oh, the broad
Blade of his glance that asks me to applaud
His coming! With his hand he turns my face to him
And caresses me with his fingers that still smell grim
Of the rabbit's fur! God, I am caught in a snare!
I know not what fine wire is round my throat;
I only know I let him finger there
My pulse of life, and let him nose like a stoat[4]
Who sniffs with joy before he drinks the blood.

And down his mouth comes to my mouth! and down
His bright dark eyes come over me, like a hood
Upon my mind! his lips meet mine, and a flood
Of sweet fire sweeps across me, so I drown
Against him, die, and find death good.

1913

Aware

Slowly the moon is rising out of the ruddy haze,
Divesting herself of her golden shift,[5] and so
Emerging white and exquisite; and I in amaze
See in the sky before me, a woman I did not know
I loved, but there she goes, and her beauty hurts my heart;
I follow her down the night, begging her not to depart.

1913

The Bride[6]

My love looks like a girl to-night,
    But she is old.
The plaits[7] that lie along her pillow
    Are not gold,
But threaded with filigree silver,
    And uncanny cold.

She looks like a young maiden, since her brow
    Is smooth and fair;
Her cheeks are very smooth, her eyes are closed,

4. That is, weasel.
5. Woman's underdress.
6. Lawrence's mother, who died on December 5, 1910.
7. Braids of hair.

She sleeps a rare,
Still, winsome sleep, so still, and so composed.

Nay, but she sleeps like a bride, and dreams her dreams
Of perfect things.
She lies at last, the darling, in the shape of her dream,
And her dead mouth sings
By its shape, like thrushes in clear evenings.

1916

Sorrow

Why does the thin grey strand
Floating up from the forgotten
Cigarette between my fingers,
Why does it trouble me?

Ah, you will understand;
When I carried my mother downstairs,
A few times only, at the beginning
Of her soft-foot malady,

I should find, for a reprimand
To my gaiety, a few long grey hairs
On the breast of my coat; and one by one
I watched them float up the dark chimney.

1916, 1928

The Enkindled Spring

This spring as it comes bursts up in bonfires green,
Wild puffing of green-fire trees, and flame-green bushes,
Thorn-blossom lifting in wreaths of smoke between
Where the wood fumes up, and the flickering, watery rushes.

I am amazed at this spring, this conflagration
Of green fires lit on the soil of earth, this blaze
Of growing, these smoke-puffs that puff in wild gyration,
Faces of people blowing across my gaze!

And I, what sort of fire am I among
This conflagration of spring? the gap in it all—!
Not even palish smoke like the rest of the throng.
Less than the wind that runs to the flamy call!

1916

Gloire de Dijon[8]

When she rises in the morning
I linger to watch her;
She spreads the bath-cloth underneath the window
And the sunbeams catch her
Glistening white on the shoulders,
While down her sides the mellow
Golden shadow glows as
She stoops to the sponge, and her swung breasts
Sway like full-blown yellow
Gloire de Dijon roses.

She drips herself with water, and her shoulders
Glisten as silver, they crumple up
Like wet and falling roses, and I listen
For the sluicing of their rain-dishevelled petals.
In the window full of sunlight
Concentrates her golden shadow
Fold on fold, until it glows as
Mellow as the glory roses.

Icking. 1917

A Youth Mowing

There are four men mowing down by the Isar;[9]
I can hear the swish of the scythe-strokes, four
Sharp breaths taken: yea, and I
Am sorry for what's in store.

The first man out of the four that's mowing
Is mine, I claim him once and for all;
Though it's sorry I am, on his young feet, knowing
None of the trouble he's led to stall.

As he sees me bringing the dinner, he lifts
His head as proud as a deer that looks
Shoulder-deep out of the corn; and wipes
His scythe-blade bright, unhooks

The scythe-stone and over the stubble to me.
Lad, thou hast gotten a child in me,
Laddie, a man thou'lt ha'e to be,
Yea, though I'm sorry for thee.[1]

1917

8. Literally, Glory of Dijon; Dijon is a French town.
9. River in Germany.
1. Her speech, presumably in a heavily dialectal German, is reproduced in a similar kind of English.

Piano

Softly, in the dusk, a woman is singing to me;
Taking me back down the vista of years, till I see
A child sitting under the piano, in the boom of the tingling strings
And pressing the small, poised feet of a mother who smiles as she sings.

In spite of myself, the insidious mastery of song
Betrays me back, till the heart of me weeps to belong
To the old Sunday evenings at home, with winter outside
And hymns in the cosy parlour, the tinkling piano our guide.

So now it is vain for the singer to burst into clamour
With the great black piano appassionato.[2] The glamour
Of childish days is upon me, my manhood is cast
Down in the flood of remembrance, I weep like a child for the past.

1918

Medlars and Sorb-Apples[3]

I love you, rotten,
Delicious rottenness.

I love to suck you out from your skins
So brown and soft and coming suave,
So morbid, as the Italians say.

What a rare, powerful, reminiscent flavour
Comes out of your falling through the stages of decay:
Stream within stream.

Something of the same flavour as Syracusan muscat wine
Or vulgar Marsala.[4]

Though even the word Marsala will smack of preciosity
Soon in the pussyfoot West.

What is it?
What is it, in the grape turning raisin,
In the medlar, in the sorb-apple,
Wineskins of brown morbidity,
Autumnal excrementa;
What is it that reminds us of white gods?

2. Played with passion.
3. European fruits, edible only when they begin to decay.
4. Dark, sweet wine.

Gods nude as blanched nut-kernels,
Strangely, half-sinisterly flesh-fragrant
As if with sweat,
And drenched with mystery.

Sorb-apples, medlars with dead crowns.
I say, wonderful are the hellish experiences,
Orphic, delicate
Dionysos of the Underworld.[5]

A kiss, and a spasm of farewell, a moment's orgasm of rupture,
Then along the damp road alone, till the next turning.
And there, a new partner, a new parting, a new unfusing into twain,
A new gasp of further isolation,
A new intoxication of loneliness, among decaying, frost-cold leaves.

Going down the strange lanes of hell, more and more intensely alone,
The fibres of the heart parting one after the other
And yet the soul continuing, naked-footed, even more vividly embodied
Like a flame blown whiter and whiter
In a deeper and deeper darkness
Ever more exquisite, distilled in separation.

So, in the strange retorts of medlars and sorb-apples
The distilled essence of hell.
The exquisite odour of leave-taking.
        Jamque vale![6]
Orpheus, and the winding, leaf-clogged, silent lanes of hell.

Each soul departing with its own isolation,
Strangest of all strange companions,
And best.

Medlars, sorb-apples,
More than sweet
Flux of autumn
Sucked out of your empty bladders

And sipped down, perhaps, with a sip of Marsala
So that the rambling, sky-dropped grape can add its savour to yours,
Orphic farewell, and farewell, and farewell
And the *ego sum* of Dionysos
The *sono io*[7] of perfect drunkenness
Intoxication of final loneliness.

San Gervasio. 1923

5. *Orphic:* from Orpheus, mythical poet; associated with Dionysos, god of wine and poetic inspiration. In Greek myth, Orpheus went to the underworld to bring back his dead wife, Eurydice. Pluto (Hades), king of the underworld, permitted him to take her on the condition that he not look back at her as they ascended to Earth's surface. He failed the test, and she vanished.

6. And at last, farewell! (Latin).

7. I am (Latin and Italian, respectively).

Southern Night

Come up, thou red thing.
Come up, and be called a moon.

The mosquitoes are biting to-night
Like memories.

Memories, northern memories,
Bitter-stinging white world that bore us
Subsiding into this night.

Call it moonrise
This red anathema?

Rise, thou red thing,
Unfold slowly upwards, blood-dark;
Burst the night's membrane of tranquil stars
Finally.

Maculate
The red Macula.[8]

Taormina. 1923

Sicilian Cyclamens

When he pushed his bush of black hair off his brow:
When she lifted her mop from her eyes, and screwed it in a knob
    behind
        —O act of fearful temerity!
When they felt their foreheads bare, naked to heaven, their eyes
    revealed:
When they felt the light of heaven brandished like a knife at their
    defenceless eyes,
And the sea like a blade at their face,
Mediterranean savages:
When they came out, face-revealed, under heaven, from the shaggy
    undergrowth of their own hair
For the first time,
They saw tiny rose cyclamens between their toes, growing
Where the slow toads sat brooding on the past.

Slow toads, and cyclamen leaves
Stickily glistening with eternal shadow
Keeping to earth.
Cyclamen leaves
Toad-filmy, earth-iridescent

8. Spot or stain. *Maculate:* to spoil or defile.

Beautiful
Frost-filigreed
Spumed with mud
Snail-nacreous[9]
Low down.

The shaking aspect of the sea
And man's defenceless bare face
And cyclamens putting their ears back.
Long, pensive, slim-muzzled greyhound buds
Dreamy, not yet present,
Drawn out of earth
At his toes

Dawn-rose
Sub-delighted, stone-engendered
Cyclamens, young cyclamens
Arching
Waking, pricking their ears
Like delicate very-young greyhound bitches
Half-yawning at the open, inexperienced
Vista of day,
Folding back their soundless petalled ears.

Greyhound bitches
Bending their rosy muzzles pensive down,
And breathing soft, unwilling to wake to the new day
Yet sub-delighted.

Ah Mediterranean morning, when our world began!
Far-off Mediterranean mornings,
Pelasgic[1] faces uncovered,
And unbudding cyclamens.

The hare suddenly goes uphill
Laying back her long ears with unwinking bliss.

And up the pallid, sea-blenched Mediterranean stone-slopes
Rose cyclamen, ecstatic fore-runner!
Cyclamens, ruddy-muzzled cyclamens
In little bunches like bunches of wild hares
Muzzles together, ears-aprick,
Whispering witchcraft
Like women at a well, the dawn-fountain.

Greece, and the world's morning
Where all the Parthenon marbles[2] still fostered the roots of the cycla-
    men.

9. Pearly.
1. Or Pelasgian, ancient name for the first inhabitants of Greece and eastern Mediterranean islands.
2. That is, marble sculptures and bas-reliefs on the famous temple to the goddess Athena, on the Acropolis, in Athens.

Violets
Pagan, rosy-muzzled violets
Autumnal
Dawn-pink,
Dawn-pale
Among squat toad-leaves sprinkling the unborn
Erechtheion[3] marbles.

Taormina. 1923

Snake

A snake came to my water-trough
On a hot, hot day, and I in pyjamas for the heat,
To drink there.

In the deep, strange-scented shade of the great dark carob-tree[4]
I came down the steps with my pitcher
And must wait, must stand and wait, for there he was at the trough before me.

He reached down from a fissure in the earth-wall in the gloom
And trailed his yellow-brown slackness soft-bellied down, over the edge of the stone trough
And rested his throat upon the stone bottom,
And where the water had dripped from the tap, in a small clearness,
He sipped with his straight mouth,
Softly drank through his straight gums, into his slack long body,
Silently.

Someone was before me at my water-trough,
And I, like a second comer, waiting.

He lifted his head from his drinking, as cattle do,
And looked at me vaguely, as drinking cattle do,
And flickered his two-forked tongue from his lips, and mused a moment,
And stooped and drank a little more,
Being earth-brown, earth-golden from the burning bowels of the earth
On the day of Sicilian July, with Etna[5] smoking.

The voice of my education said to me
He must be killed,
For in Sicily the black, black snakes are innocent, the gold are venomous.

And voices in me said, If you were a man
You would take a stick and break him now, and finish him off.

3. Of the Erechtheum, the first temple to Athena built on the Acropolis.
4. Mediterranean evergreen tree.
5. The volcano.

But must I confess how I liked him,
How glad I was he had come like a guest in quiet, to drink at my water-trough
And depart peaceful, pacified, and thankless,
Into the burning bowels of this earth?

Was it cowardice, that I dared not kill him?
Was it perversity, that I longed to talk to him?
Was it humility, to feel so honoured?
I felt so honoured.

And yet those voices:
If you were not afraid, you would kill him!

And truly I was afraid, I was most afraid,
But even so, honoured still more
That he should seek my hospitality
From out the dark door of the secret earth.

He drank enough
And lifted his head, dreamily, as one who has drunken,
And flickered his tongue like a forked night on the air, so black;
Seeming to lick his lips,
And looked around like a god, unseeing, into the air,
And slowly turned his head,
And slowly, very slowly, as if thrice adream,
Proceeded to draw his slow length curving round
And climb again the broken bank of my wall-face.

And as he put his head into that dreadful hole,
And as he slowly drew up, snake-easing his shoulders, and entered farther,
A sort of horror, a sort of protest against his withdrawing into that horrid black hole,
Deliberately going into the blackness, and slowly drawing himself after,
Overcame me now his back was turned.

I looked round, I put down my pitcher,
I picked up a clumsy log
And threw it at the water-trough with a clatter.

I think it did not hit him,
But suddenly that part of him that was left behind convulsed in undignified haste,
Writhed like lightning, and was gone
Into the black hole, the earth-lipped fissure in the wall-front,
At which, in the intense still noon, I stared with fascination.

And immediately I regretted it.
I thought how paltry, how vulgar, what a mean act!
I despised myself and the voices of my accursed human education.

And I thought of the albatross,[6]
And I wished he would come back, my snake.

For he seemed to me again like a king,
Like a king in exile, uncrowned in the underworld,
Now due to be crowned again.

And so, I missed my chance with one of the lords
Of life.
And I have something to expiate;
A pettiness.

Taormina. 1923

Lui et Elle[7]

She is large and matronly
And rather dirty,
A little sardonic-looking, as if domesticity had driven her to it.

Though what she does, except lay four eggs at random in the garden
once a year
And put up with her husband,
I don't know.

She likes to eat.
She hurries up, striding reared on long uncanny legs
When food is going.
Oh yes, she can make haste when she likes.

She snaps the soft bread from my hand in great mouthfuls,
Opening her rather pretty wedge of an iron, pristine face
Into an enormously wide-beaked mouth
Like sudden curved scissors,
And gulping at more than she can swallow, and working her thick, soft
tongue,
And having the bread hanging over her chin.

O Mistress, Mistress,
Reptile mistress,
Your eye is very dark, very bright,
And it never softens
Although you watch.

She knows,
She knows well enough to come for food,

6. In "Rime of the Ancient Mariner," by English poet Samuel Taylor Coleridge (1772–1834), a ship and its crew fall under a curse when the Mariner wantonly shoots an albatross.
7. He and she (French).

Yet she sees me not;
Her bright eye sees, but not me, not anything,
Sightful, sightless, seeing and visionless,
Reptile mistress.

Taking bread in her curved, gaping, toothless mouth,
She has no qualm when she catches my finger in her steel overlapping gums,
But she hangs on, and my shout and my shrinking are nothing to her.
She does not even know she is nipping me with her curved beak.
Snake-like she draws at my finger, while I drag it in horror away.

Mistress, reptile mistress,
You are almost too large, I am almost frightened.

He is much smaller,
Dapper beside her,
And ridiculously small.

Her laconic eye has an earthy, materialistic look,
His, poor darling, is almost fiery.

His wimple,[8] his blunt-prowed face,
His low forehead, his skinny neck, his long, scaled, striving legs,
So striving, striving,
Are all more delicate than she,
And he has a cruel scar on his shell.

Poor darling, biting at her feet,
Running beside her like a dog, biting her earthy, splay feet,
Nipping her ankles,
Which she drags apathetic away, though without retreating into her shell.

Agelessly silent,
And with a grim, reptile determination,
Cold, voiceless age-after-age behind him, serpents' long obstinacy
Of horizontal persistence.

Little old man
Scuffling beside her, bending down, catching his opportunity,
Parting his steel-trap face, so suddenly, and seizing her scaly ankle,
And hanging grimly on,
Letting go at last as she drags away,
And closing his steel-trap face.

His steel-trap, stoic, ageless, handsome face.
Alas, what a fool he looks in this scuffle.

8. His skin is compared to the cloth headcovering worn in Europe during the Middle Ages.

And how he feels it!
The lonely rambler, the stoic, dignified stalker through chaos,
The immune, the animate,
Enveloped in isolation,
Fore-runner.
Now look at him!

Alas, the spear is through the side of his isolation.
His adolescence saw him crucified into sex,
Doomed, in the long crucifixion of desire, to seek his consummation
beyond himself.[9]
Divided into passionate duality,
He, so finished and immune, now broken into desirous fragmentariness,
Doomed to make an intolerable fool of himself
In his effort toward completion again.

Poor little earthy house-inhabiting Osiris,[1]
The mysterious bull tore him at adolescence into pieces,
And he must struggle after reconstruction, ignominiously.

And so behold him following the tail
Of that mud-hovel of his slowly rambling spouse,
Like some unhappy bull at the tail of a cow,
But with more than bovine, grim, earth-dank persistence.

Suddenly seizing the ugly ankle as she stretches out to walk,
Roaming over the sods,
Or, if it happen to show, at her pointed, heavy tail
Beneath the low-dropping back-board of her shell.

Their two shells like domed boats bumping,
Hers huge, his small;
Their splay feet rambling and rowing like paddles,
And stumbling mixed up in one another,
In the race of love—
Two tortoises,
She huge, he small.

She seems earthily apathetic,
And he has a reptile's awful persistence.

I heard a woman pitying her, pitying the Mère Tortue.[2]
While I, I pity Monsieur.
"He pesters her and torments her," said the woman.
How much more is *he* pestered and tormented, say I.

9. In John 19.34, one of the soldiers pierces the side of the crucified Jesus.
1. Egyptian god, representing the male reproductive principle. He was torn to pieces by his brother Set, whom Lawrence here identifies with the bull Apis, another form of Osiris. Later, Osiris's sister, Isis, reassembled him.
2. Mother tortoise (French).

What can he do?
He is dumb, he is visionless,
Conceptionless.
His black, sad-lidded eye sees but beholds not
As her earthen mound moves on,
But he catches the folds of vulnerable, leathery skin,
Nail-studded, that shake beneath her shell,
And drags at these with his beak,
Drags and drags and bites,
While she pulls herself free, and rows her dull mound along.

1923

Humming-Bird

I can imagine, in some otherworld
Primeval-dumb, far back
In that most awful stillness, that only gasped and hummed,
Humming-birds raced down the avenues.

Before anything had a soul,
While life was a heave of Matter, half inanimate,
This little bit chipped off in brilliance
And went whizzing through the slow, vast, succulent stems.

I believe there were no flowers then,
In the world where the humming-bird flashed ahead of creation.
I believe he pierced the slow vegetable veins with his long beak.

Probably he was big
As mosses, and little lizards, they say, were once big.
Probably he was a jabbing, terrifying monster.

We look at him through the wrong end of the long telescope of Time,
Luckily for us.

Española. 1923

You

You, you don't know me.
When have your knees ever nipped me
like fire-tongs a live coal
for a minute?

1929

The English Are So Nice!

The English are so nice
so awfully nice
they're the nicest people in the world.

And what's more, they're very nice about being nice
about your being nice as well!
If you're not nice, they soon make you feel it.

Americans and French and Germans and so on
they're all very well
but they're not *really* nice, you know.
They're not nice in *our* sense of the word, are they now?

That's why one doesn't have to take them seriously.
We must be nice to them, of course,
of course, naturally—
But it doesn't really matter what you say to them,
they don't really understand—
you can just say anything to them:
be nice, you know, just be nice
but you must never take them seriously, they wouldn't understand,
just be nice, you know! oh, fairly nice,
not too nice of course, they take advantage—
but nice enough, just nice enough
to let them feel they're not quite as nice as they might be.

1932

Andraitx[3]—Pomegranate Flowers

It is June, it is June
the pomegranates are in flower,
the peasants are bending cutting the bearded wheat.

The pomegranates are in flower
beside the high-road, past the deathly dust,
and even the sea is silent in the sun.

Short gasps of flame in the green of night, way off
the pomegranates are in flower,
small sharp red fires in the night of leaves.

And noon is suddenly dark, is lustrous, is silent and dark
men are unseen, beneath the shading hats;
only, from out the foliage of the secret loins
red flamelets here and there reveal
a man, a woman there.

1932

3. Port on Spanish island of Majorca, in the western Mediterranean.

Whales Weep Not!

They say the sea is cold, but the sea contains
the hottest blood of all, and the wildest, the most urgent.

All the whales in the wider deeps, hot are they, as they urge
on and on, and dive beneath the icebergs.
The right whales, the sperm-whales, the hammer-heads, the killers
there they blow, there they blow, hot wild white breath out of the sea!

And they rock, and they rock, through the sensual ageless ages
on the depths of the seven seas,
and through the salt they reel with drunk delight
and in the tropics tremble they with love
and roll with massive, strong desire, like gods.
Then the great bull lies up against his bride
in the blue deep bed of the sea,
as mountain pressing on mountain, in the zest of life:
and out of the inward roaring of the inner red ocean of whale blood
the long tip reaches strong, intense, like the maelstrom-tip, and comes
    to rest
in the clasp and the soft, wild clutch of a she-whale's fathomless body.

And over the bridge of the whale's strong phallus, linking the wonder of
    whales
the burning archangels under the sea keep passing, back and forth,
keep passing, archangels of bliss
from him to her, from her to him, great Cherubim[4]
that wait on whales in mid-ocean, suspended in the waves of the sea
great heaven of whales in the waters, old hierarchies.

And enormous mother whales lie dreaming suckling their whale-tender
    young
and dreaming with strange whale eyes wide open in the waters of the
    beginning and the end.[5]

And bull-whales gather their women and whale-calves in a ring
when danger threatens, on the surface of the ceaseless flood
and range themselves like great fierce Seraphim[6] facing the threat
encircling their huddled monsters of love.
And all this happens in the sea, in the salt
where God is also love, but without words:
and Aphrodite[7] is the wife of whales
most happy, happy she!

and Venus among the fishes skips and is a she-dolphin
she is the gay, delighted porpoise sporting with love and the sea

4. Angels representing divine wisdom or justice.
5. Cf. Revelation 21.6: "I am . . . the beginning and the end. I will give unto him that is athirst of the fountain of the water of life freely."
6. Angels who guard God's throne.
7. Greek goddess of love, known in Rome as Venus (line 34).

she is the female tunny-fish, round and happy among the males
and dense with happy blood, dark rainbow bliss in the sea.

1932

Butterfly

Butterfly, the wind blows sea-ward, strong beyond the garden wall!
Butterfly, why do you settle on my shoe, and sip the dirt on my shoe,
Lifting your veined wings, lifting them? big white butterfly!

Already it is October, and the wind blows strong to the sea
from the hills where snow must have fallen, the wind is polished with snow.
Here in the garden, with red geraniums, it is warm, it is warm
but the wind blows strong to sea-ward, white butterfly, content on my shoe!

Will you go, will you go from my warm house?
Will you climb on your big soft wings, black-dotted,
as up an invisible rainbow, an arch
till the wind slides you sheer from the arch-crest
and in a strange level fluttering you go out to sea-ward, white speck!

Farewell, farewell, lost soul![8]
you have melted in the crystalline distance,
it is enough! I saw you vanish into air.

1932

Bavarian Gentians

Not every man has gentians in his house
in Soft September, at slow, sad Michaelmas.[9]

Bavarian gentians, big and dark, only dark
darkening the day-time, torch-like with the smoking blueness of Pluto's gloom,[1]
ribbed and torch-like, with their blaze of darkness spread blue
down flattening into points, flattened under the sweep of white day
torch-flower of the blue-smoking darkness, Pluto's dark-blue daze,
black lamps from the halls of Dis, burning dark blue,

8. The Greek word *psyche* means both "butterfly" and "soul."
9. September 29, the feast celebrating the Archangel Michael.
1. Pluto (or Dis), in Greek and Roman mythology, ruled the underworld. He abducted Persephone, daughter of the grain goddess, Demeter, and made her his queen; she was allowed to return from the underworld in April and remain with her mother for six months, but in September she had to rejoin her husband.

giving off darkness, blue darkness, as Demeter's pale lamps give off
light,
lead me then, lead the way.

Reach me a gentian, give me a torch!
let me guide myself with the blue, forked torch of this flower
down the darker and darker stairs, where blue is darkened on blueness
even where Persephone goes, just now, from the frosted September
to the sightless realm where darkness is awake upon the dark
and Persephone herself is but a voice
or a darkness invisible enfolded in the deeper dark
of the arms Plutonic, and pierced with the passion of dense gloom,
among the splendour of torches of darkness, shedding darkness on the
lost bride and her groom.

1932

The Ship of Death[2]

I

Now it is autumn and the falling fruit
and the long journey towards oblivion.

The apples falling like great drops of dew
to bruise themselves an exit from themselves.

And it is time to go, to bid farewell
to one's own self, and find an exit
from the fallen self.

II

Have you built your ship of death, O have you?
O build your ship of death, for you will need it.

The grim frost is at hand, when the apples will fall
thick, almost thundrous, on the hardened earth.

And death is on the air like a smell of ashes!
Ah! can't you smell it?

And in the bruised body, the frightened soul
finds itself shrinking, wincing from the cold
that blows upon it through the orifices.

2. This poem was written near the end of 1929; Lawrence died on March 2, 1930. In his travel book, *Etruscan Places* (1927), Lawrence described ancient Italian tombs in which had been buried, near the body of the dead man, "the little bronze ship that should bear him over to the other world, the vases of jewels for his arraying, the vases of small dishes, the little bronze statuettes and tools, the weapons, the armor: all the amazing impedimenta of the important dead."

III

And can a man his own quietus make
with a bare bodkin?[3]

With daggers, bodkins, bullets, man can make
a bruise or break of exit for his life;
but is that a quietus, O tell me, is it quietus?

Surely not so! for how could murder, even self-murder
ever a quietus make?

IV

O let us talk of quiet that we know,
that we can know, the deep and lovely quiet
of a strong heart at peace!

How can we this, our own quietus, make?

V

Build then the ship of death, for you must take
the longest journey, to oblivion.
And die the death, the long and painful death
that lies between the old self and the new.

Already our bodies are fallen, bruised, badly bruised,
already our souls are oozing through the exit
of the cruel bruise.

Already the dark and endless ocean of the end
is washing in through the breaches of our wounds,
already the flood is upon us.

Oh build your ship of death, your little ark
and furnish it with food, with little cakes, and wine
for the dark flight down oblivion.

VI

Piecemeal the body dies, and the timid soul
has her footing washed away, as the dark flood rises.

We are dying, we are dying, we are all of us dying
and nothing will stay the death-flood rising within us
and soon it will rise on the world, on the outside world.

We are dying, we are dying, piecemeal our bodies are dying
and our strength leaves us,

3. Cf. *Hamlet* 3.1. 77–78. *Quietus*: death. *Bodkin*: dagger.

and our soul cowers naked in the dark rain over the flood,
cowering in the last branches of the tree of our life.

VII

We are dying, we are dying, so all we can do
is now to be willing to die, and to build the ship
of death to carry the soul on the longest journey.

A little ship, with oars and food
and little dishes, and all accoutrements
fitting and ready for the departing soul.

Now launch the small ship, now as the body dies
and life departs, launch out, the fragile soul
in the fragile ship of courage, the ark of faith
with its store of food and little cooking pans
and change of clothes,
upon the flood's black waste
upon the waters of the end
upon the sea of death, where still we sail
darkly, for we cannot steer, and have no port.

There is no port, there is nowhere to go
only the deepening blackness darkening still
blacker upon the soundless, ungurgling flood
darkness at one with darkness, up and down
and sideways utterly dark, so there is no direction any more.
And the little ship is there; yet she is gone.
She is not seen, for there is nothing to see her by.
She is gone! gone! and yet
somewhere she is there.
Nowhere!

VIII

And everything is gone, the body is gone
completely under, gone, entirely gone.
The upper darkness is heavy as the lower,
between them the little ship
is gone
she is gone.

It is the end, it is oblivion.

IX

And yet out of eternity, a thread
separates itself on the blackness,
a horizontal thread
that fumes a little with pallor upon the dark.

Is it illusion? or does the pallor fume
A little higher?
Ah wait, wait, for there's the dawn,
the cruel dawn of coming back to life
out of oblivion.

Wait, wait, the little ship
drifting, beneath the deathly ashy grey
of a flood-dawn.

Wait, wait! even so, a flush of yellow
and strangely, O chilled wan soul, a flush of rose.

A flush of rose, and the whole thing starts again.

X

The flood subsides, and the body, like a worn sea-shell
emerges strange and lovely.
And the little ship wings home, faltering and lapsing
on the pink flood,
and the frail soul steps out, into her house again
filling the heart with peace.

Swings the heart renewed with peace
even of oblivion.

Oh build your ship of death, oh build it!
for you will need it.
For the voyage of oblivion awaits you.

1932

EZRA POUND
1885–1972

The most extraordinary career in modern poetry was undoubtedly that of Ezra Pound. He more than anyone made poets write modern verse, editors publish it, and readers read it. W. B. Yeats asked Pound's help when, in 1912, he felt his style had become abstract; T. S. Eliot asked Pound's help when, in 1921, he had to sift *The Waste Land* out of a mass of ill-assorted material. Even Robert Frost was obliged to admit that two or three changes Pound proposed in "The Death of the Hired Man" were acceptable. Pound may also be said to have discovered James Joyce and to have made possible all his later work. These were major benefactions, and innumerable minor ones occurred as well, in a personal history of openhandedness both financial—though he had little money—and literary.

Pound's life was centered with great energy on the pursuit of what Matthew Arnold called the best that has been thought and said in the world, and on the attempt to "make it new" (Pound's slogan) for the present day. He showed an American voracity for swallowing up talented utterance in many languages. Pound was born on October 30, 1885, in Hailey, Idaho; he was taken to Pennsylvania at the age of two and brought up in the east. He retained a frontiersman's pleasure in thinking about the opening up of the west and prided himself on the exploits of a grandfather who built a railway; he kept up a rough-and-ready manner, an American bluntness, in effete Europe. His career might be viewed as a struggle to build a cultural railway from Idaho to Provence, or even to Beijing, for he incorporated Chinese characters in his later verse and translated as freely and creatively from Chinese and Japanese as from Italian or Greek, beginning with the limpid free-verse poems of *Cathay* (1915). He tried to marry Continental and East Asian suavities with American directness and even vulgarity. More profoundly, he sought to bring incandescent moments ("magic moments," he sometimes called them) out of seeming disorder, precision out of seeming improvisation, the most vivid English out of conversational or prosy details. The result of this effort remains controversial. Yeats found Pound's verse too experimental; Eliot, though personally devoted to him, thought it verged on the "quaint and archaic." Pound had misgivings about his own literary and political directions. But if his poetry is imperfect, it suits our time, when many poets feel that formal perfection betrays the original vision. Pound greatly influenced poets in the second half of the twentieth century, notably Charles Olson and other advocates of "open form," no less than in the first half.

At sixteen, Pound enrolled as a special student (rather than as a degree candidate) at the University of Pennsylvania, to study (as he said) what he thought important. In 1903, he matriculated more conventionally at Hamilton College, where he earned a Ph.B. His interests were in Romance languages and literatures; he returned as a fellow in these to the University of Pennsylvania in 1905. He received a master of arts degree that year, but much more consequential was his association with two poets also just getting started, William Carlos Williams and Hilda Doolittle (H. D.). She later became a member of Pound's Imagist group, and Williams and Pound criticized, praised, and lectured each other all their lives.

The next year, Pound won a fellowship to go to Italy, Provence, and especially Spain, in preparation for a dissertation (never written) on the Spanish playwright Lope de Vega. On his return, he became an instructor in Romance languages at Wabash College in Crawfordsville, Indiana. His generosity in offering his bed to a stranded burlesque dancer was construed by his landladies, and then by the college authorities, as immoral behavior; he was discharged, but was given the rest of his year's salary, and with this he went to Gibraltar and Venice. In the latter city (which was to be the scene of his declining years as well), Pound published his first book, *A Lume Spento* (Italian for "with tapers extinguished")—he would describe these poems later as "stale creampuffs," but for all their echoes of Yeats and more exotic poets, they are full of possibility. Pound makes, for example, the first important use in modern verse of ellipses to indicate the speaker's panicky repressions. From Venice, Pound went to London, where for twelve years he remained a hard-working poet, proselytizer, and provocateur.

At that time (1908), Pound believed that all English poets except Yeats were on the wrong track, and that Yeats was the greatest poet writing in English. The friendship of these two, which began shortly after Pound's arrival, was important for both. Victorianism was giving way to a new idiom: Virginia Woolf said that in 1910 human personality changed, and at any rate it appeared to do so, as modern art, music, and architecture began to coalesce with modern literature. Pound did not confine himself to literature: he was friendly with the sculptors Jacob Epstein and Henri Gaudier-Brzeska (about whom he wrote a book), the painter and writer Wyndham Lewis, and others, including, later, Constantin Brancusi; he wrote an opera, *Villon,* and a book on the American composer George Antheil. In literature, he was extremely fond of the troubadours, but also evinced great respect for Henry James, the full range of whose modernity was not yet clear to most readers. He profited from the friendship of Ford Madox Ford, a novelist and poet much occupied with bringing the language up to date. Finally, Pound moved in the same circle as philosopher-poet T. E. Hulme, who offered the modern movement one of its principal aesthetic programs. Hulme held that human beings are finite and limited, burdened with original sin. Against the vague outlines and damp emotions he found in Romantic art, against sentimental poems of "moaning and whining," he espoused a "dry, hard, classical verse" ("Romanticism and Classicism").

Without quite subscribing to Hulme's doctrines, Pound began to write starker poems. To Harriet Monroe, editor of the newly founded magazine *Poetry,* he sent his famous pronouncement in a letter of January 1915, "Poetry must be *as well written as prose,*" and he went on: "Its language must be a fine language, departing in no way from speech save by a heightened intensity (i.e. simplicity). There must be no book words, no periphrases, no inversions. It must be as simple as De Maupassant's best prose, and as hard as Stendhal's. . . . Objectivity and again objectivity, and expression: no hindside-beforeness, no straddled adjectives (as 'addled mosses dank'), no Tennysonianness of speech; nothing—nothing that you couldn't, in some circumstance, in the stress of some emotion, actually say. Every literaryism, every book word, fritters away a scrap of the reader's patience, a scrap of his sense of your sincerity."

The gradual accumulation of these principles led Pound in 1912, with H. D., Richard Aldington, and F. S. Flint, to found the Imagist group. Their purpose was to sanction experimentation in verse form and to aim at new modes of perception. Pound published in *Poetry* (March 1913) "A Few Don'ts by an Imagiste," prefaced by a synopsis of the movement Flint drafted in collaboration with Pound, who then incorporated the three principles, along with "A Few Don'ts," in "A Retrospect" (1918):

1. Direct treatment of the "thing," whether subjective or objective.
2. To use absolutely no word that does not contribute to the presentation.
3. As regarding rhythm: to compose in the sequence of the musical phrase, not in the sequence of a metronome.

Pound offered the following definition: "An 'Image' is that which presents an intellectual and emotional complex in an instant of time." His "Few Don'ts" warned beginning poets against superfluous words, abstractions, ornament, end-stopped lines, fixed meters, and other such vices. These Imagist precepts and definitions, which Pound actually violated in many of his own poems, are still enormously influential. But Pound soon came to resent late arrivals, especially Amy Lowell, for taking over Imagism, turning it toward what he considered sentimentality and derided as "Amygism." Pound required something tougher, and he joined with Wyndham Lewis to promulgate a new movement, Vorticism. Its principal difference from Imagism was in insisting on dynamism, as outlined in the iconoclastic manifesto in the short-lived journal *Blast;* the mood of Imagism had been too placid. The Vorticist image was a force rather than a picture.

Pound's most congruent literary relationship in England was with T. S. Eliot, whom he met in 1914. He was astonished to discover that Eliot had "modernized himself *on his own*" (letter of September 30), and he quickly obliged Harriet Monroe to publish "The Love Song of J. Alfred Prufrock" and persuaded the editor of the *Egoist,* Harriet Weaver, to publish Eliot's first book, *Prufrock and Other Observations* (1917). But then both men decided on a change of technique. As Pound wrote: "at a particular date in a particular room, two authors, neither engaged in picking the other's pocket, decided that the dilutation of *vers libre,* Amygism, Lee Masterism, general floppiness had gone too far and that some countercurrent must be set going. Parallel situation centuries ago in China. Remedy prescribed 'Émaux et Camées' [*Enamels and Cameos,* by Théophile Gautier] (or the Bay State Hymn Book). Rhyme and regular strophes. Results: Poems in Mr. Eliot's *second* volume, not contained in his first, . . . also 'H. S. Mauberley'. Divergence later" ("Harold Monro").

Pound's *Hugh Selwyn Mauberley* was first published in 1920, though its first section was completed at least a year earlier. It anticipates many of the devices of *The Waste Land* (1922), such as sudden shifts of perspective, unacknowledged quotations in different languages, and the presentation of an individual consciousness against a panorama of the age. It is more loosely knit, however, and includes satirical portraits, invectives against modern capitalism, and elegies for the war dead. Pound was eager to disavow that the poem was autobiographical, though he seems to elegize his London self as impossibly aestheticist: "Of course, I'm no more Mauberley than Eliot is Prufrock. . . . Mauberley is a mere surface. Again a study in form, an attempt to condense the James novel. Meliora speramus [let us hope for better]" (letter of July 9, 1922).

In the meantime, Pound had in 1915 begun his principal work, *The Cantos,* long meditated and destined to occupy him during the rest of his life. At various times, Pound offered indications of his plan in *The Cantos,* but these varied from each other. In one, he claimed a musical organization like that of "a fugue: theme, response, contrasujet," but this mattered little "*unless* I pull it off as reading matter, singing matter, shouting matter, the tale of the tribe." Another explanation, to his father, offered as his outline of the main scheme another fugal pattern:

A. A. Live man goes down into world of Dead
C. B. The "repeat in history"
B. C. The "magic moment" or moment of metamorphosis, bust thru from
    quotidien into "divine or permanent world." Gods, etc.

He indicates, in the same letter of April 11, 1927, that the poem includes aspects of an inferno, a purgatorio, and a paradise.

For readers of *The Cantos,* the abrupt shifts in time and place and recondite allusions can be baffling. Favoring the concrete over the abstract, Pound avoids predigesting his materials and presents as many particulars as possible before generalizing about them. As he wrote in his *ABC of Economics,* "I am not proceeding according to Aristotelian logic but according to the ideogrammic method of first heaping together the necessary components of thought." (Chinese scholars do not agree with Pound's theory that the ideogram is still read with a sense of its original components.) *The Cantos* interweave raw documents, juxtapose images, layer narratives, and amalgamate characters. Though vastly more expansive and heterogeneous than his Imagist poetry, *The Cantos,* too, instance Pound's techniques of compression, elision, and juxtaposition. As early as 1913, Pound was extolling the poet's "faculty for amalgamation," the ability "to heap together and arrange and harmonize the results of many men's labour" ("The Serious Artist"). He is fond of the image of the magnet that exerts its force through a mirror on iron filings scattered on the glass, causing them to assume a pattern, a "rose in the steel dust" (Canto 74). But the total impression of *The Cantos* may rather be one of shifting, intersecting forms, coming into being and then retreating from the page. The fragments, instead of adding up to degradation, as in Eliot's *Waste Land,* compose for Pound possibilities and brief realizations. *The Cantos* stand like a monolith in modern literature, not to be avoided or ignored.

In 1921, Pound left England for Paris, where he lived until 1924. Then he moved to Italy, settling in Rapallo. In 1925, he published *A Draft of XVI Cantos,* later dropping the word "draft" without altering the poems. Pound continued to publish *The Cantos* along with books of prose. While European fascism strengthened in the 1930s, his politics became increasingly extreme, and in 1933, he met with Benito Mussolini, the Fascist dictator of Italy. In 1941–43, he broadcast virulent talks on Rome radio, denouncing President Franklin Roosevelt, blaming Jews for the world's economic problems, and supporting Mussolini's activities as conducive to a new society no longer based on money grubbing. Since he continued to give these talks after the United States entered the war, he was indicted in July 1943 for treason. In May 1945, the U.S. Army arrested him, and he was confined in an open-air wire cage for three weeks outside Pisa until he suffered a breakdown and was moved to a tent in a medical compound. This experience was reflected in some of his best poems, published as *The Pisan Cantos*. He was flown to Washington to stand trial, but was remanded to St. Elizabeth's Hospital for the criminally insane. When, in 1949, he was awarded the Bollingen Prize for poetry, a great furor erupted, and Pound's adherents and detractors argued the merits of his case, and of the poems, for a long time afterward. In 1958, because of the intercession of various poets, including Frost and Archibald MacLeish, and of other sympathizers, the indictment for treason was dismissed. In 1967, Pound told the poet Allen Ginsberg that the worst mistake of his life was "that stupid suburban prejudice of anti-Semitism," though the extent to which Pound recanted his fascist and anti-Semitic views remains in dispute. He promoted right-wing writers, but he was also, ironically, the literary mentor to such left-wing, Jewish Objectivist poets as Louis Zukofsky, George Oppen, and Charles Reznikoff. In July 1958, Pound went to Italy and resided for a time with his daughter at Schloss Brunnenburg, near Merano, and then with his longtime companion, Olga Rudge, in Venice, maintaining in his last years an almost total silence.

Portrait d'une Femme[1]

Your mind and you are our Sargasso Sea,[2]
London has swept about you this score years
And bright ships left you this or that in fee:
Ideas, old gossip, oddments of all things,
Strange spars of knowledge and dimmed wares of price.
Great minds have sought you—lacking someone else.
You have been second always. Tragical?
No. You preferred it to the usual thing:
One dull man, dulling and uxorious,
One average mind—with one thought less, each year.
Oh, you are patient, I have seen you sit
Hours, where something might have floated up.
And now you pay one. Yes, you richly pay.
You are a person of some interest, one comes to you
And takes strange gain away:
Trophies fished up; some curious suggestion;
Fact that leads nowhere; and a tale or two,
Pregnant with mandrakes, or with something else
That might prove useful and yet never proves,
That never fits a corner or shows use,
Or finds its hour upon the loom of days:
The tarnished, gaudy, wonderful old work;

1. Portrait of a woman (French).
2. North Atlantic sea choked with seaweed; it was widely believed that many ships had been inextricably tangled in the weeds.

Idols and ambergris and rare inlays,
These are your riches, your great store; and yet
For all this sea-hoard of deciduous things,
Strange woods half sodden, and new brighter stuff:
In the slow float of differing light and deep,
No! there is nothing! In the whole and all,
Nothing that's quite your own.
Yet this is you.

1912

The Return

See, they return; ah, see the tentative
Movements, and the slow feet,
The trouble in the pace and the uncertain
Wavering!

See, they return, one, and by one,
With fear, as half-awakened;
As if the snow should hesitate
And murmur in the wind,
and half turn back;
These were the "Wing'd-with-Awe,"
Inviolable.

Gods of the wingèd shoe![3]
With them the silver hounds,
sniffing the trace of air!

Haie! Haie!
These were the swift to harry;
These the keen-scented;
These were the souls of blood.

Slow on the leash,
pallid the leash-men!

1912, 1920

A Pact

I make a pact with you, Walt Whitman—
I have detested you long enough.
I come to you as a grown child
Who has had a pig-headed father;
I am old enough now to make friends.

3. A Homeric epithet, coined by Pound, to identify the pagan gods; Hermes, messenger of the Greek gods, wore winged shoes.

It was you that broke the new wood,
Now is a time for carving.
We have one sap and one root—
Let there be commerce between us.

1913, 1916

The Rest

O helpless few in my country,
O remnant enslaved!

Artist broken against her,
A-stray, lost in the villages,
Mistrusted, spoken-against,

Lovers of beauty, starved,
Thwarted with systems,
Helpless against the control;

You who can not wear yourselves out
By persisting to successes,
You who can only speak,
Who can not steel yourselves into reiteration;

You of the finer sense,
Broken against false knowledge,
You who can know at first hand,
Hated, shut in, mistrusted:

Take thought:
I have weathered the storm,
I have beaten out my exile.

1913, 1916

In a Station of the Metro[4]

The apparition of these faces in the crowd;
Petals on a wet, black bough.

1913, 1916

4. Of this poem, Pound writes in *Gaudier-Brzeska:* "Three years ago in Paris I got out of a 'metro' train at La Concorde, and saw suddenly a beautiful face, and then another and another, and then a beautiful child's face, and then another beautiful woman, and I tried all that day to find words for what this had meant to me, and I could not find any words that seemed to me worthy, or as lovely as that sudden emotion. And that evening . . . I was still trying and I found, suddenly, the expression. I do not mean that I found words, but there came an equation . . . not in speech, but in little splotches of colour. . . . The 'one-image poem' is a form of super-position, that is to say, it is one idea getting out of the impasse in which I had been left by my metro emotion. I wrote a thirty-line poem, and destroyed it. . . . Six months later I made a poem half that length; a year later I made the following *hokku*-like sentence."

The River-Merchant's Wife: A Letter[5]

While my hair was still cut straight across my forehead
I played about the front gate, pulling flowers.
You came by on bamboo stilts, playing horse,
You walked about my seat, playing with blue plums.
And we went on living in the village of Chokan:
Two small people, without dislike or suspicion.

At fourteen I married My Lord you.
I never laughed, being bashful.
Lowering my head, I looked at the wall.
Called to, a thousand times, I never looked back.

At fifteen I stopped scowling,
I desired my dust to be mingled with yours
Forever and forever, and forever.
Why should I climb the look out?

At sixteen you departed
You went into far Ku-to-en,[6] by the river of swirling eddies,
And you have been gone five months.
The monkeys make sorrowful noise overhead.
You dragged your feet when you went out.
By the gate now, the moss is grown, the different mosses,
Too deep to clear them away!
The leaves fall early this autumn, in wind.
The paired butterflies are already yellow with August
Over the grass in the West garden;
They hurt me.
I grow older.
If you are coming down through the narrows of the river Kiang,
Please let me know beforehand,
And I will come out to meet you
As far as Cho-fu-Sa.[7]
By Rihaku.

1915

5. Pound's versions of Chinese poems are based on notes made by the American sinologist Ernest Fenollosa, for whom the Chinese originals were interpreted by various Japanese scholars; neither Fenollosa nor Pound could then read Chinese. Throughout, Pound uses Japanese spellings of Chinese place-names, and even of the name of poet Li Po (701–762), who in Japanese is called Rihaku. This poem is a translation of the first of Li Po's "Two Letters from Ch'ang-kan" (a suburb of Nanking, called "Chokan" in line 5).

6. The Chinese river Ch'üt'ang (or Kiang, in Japanese, as in line 26), which Pound treats as a place by the river.

7. A beach several hundred miles upstream of Nanking.

Lament of the Frontier Guard

By the North Gate, the wind blows full of sand,
Lonely from the beginning of time until now!
Trees fall, the grass goes yellow with autumn.
I climb the towers and towers
  to watch out the barbarous land:
Desolate castle, the sky, the wide desert.
There is no wall left to this village.
Bones white with a thousand frosts,
High heaps, covered with trees and grass;
Who brought this to pass?
Who has brought the flaming imperial anger?
Who has brought the army with drums and with kettle-drums?
Barbarous kings.
A gracious spring, turned to blood-ravenous autumn,
A turmoil of wars-men, spread over the middle kingdom,
Three hundred and sixty thousand,
And sorrow, sorrow like rain.
Sorrow to go, and sorrow, sorrow returning.
Desolate, desolate fields,
And no children of warfare upon them,
  No longer the men for offence and defence.
Ah, how shall you know the dreary sorrow at the
  North Gate,
With Riboku's[8] name forgotten,
And we guardsmen fed to the tigers.
Rihaku.[9]

1915

The Temperaments

Nine adulteries, 12 liaisons, 64 fornications and something approaching
  a rape
Rest nightly upon the soul of our delicate friend Florialis,
And yet the man is so quiet and reserved in demeanour
That he passes for both bloodless and sexless.
Bastidides, on the contrary, who both talks and writes of nothing
  save copulation,
Has become the father of twins,
But he accomplished this feat at some cost;
He had to be four times cuckold.[1]

1917

8. Li Mu in Chinese; a famous general who died in battle against the Huns in 223 B.C.E.
9. Chinese poet Li Po (701–762).
1. "Bastidides is such a perfect portrait of a certain distinguished author who wouldn't recognize it, that I should greatly regret not giving it, sometime, to the light of day" (*The Letters of Ezra Pound, 1907–41*, ed. D. D Paige, 1950, 100). Presumably, Florialis is also an invented pseudonym.

Hugh Selwyn Mauberley

(Life and Contacts)[2]

"Vocat æstus in umbram"[3]
—Nemesianus, Ec. IV.

Ode pour l'Election de Son Sepulchre[4]

I

For three years, out of key with his time,
He strove to resuscitate the dead art
Of poetry; to maintain "the sublime"
In the old sense. Wrong from the start—

No, hardly but, seeing he had been born
In a half savage country,[5] out of date;
Bent resolutely on wringing lilies from the acorn;
Capaneus;[6] trout for factitious bait;

Ἴδμεν γάρ τοι πάνθ', ὅσ' ἐνὶ Τροίῃ[7]
Caught in the unstopped ear;
Giving the rocks small lee-way
The chopped seas held him, therefore, that year.

His true Penelope was Flaubert,[8]
He fished by obstinate isles;
Observed the elegance of Circe's[9] hair
Rather than the mottoes on sun-dials.

Unaffected by "the march of events,"
He passed from men's memory in *l'an trentiesme*

2. Pound's footnote to this poem describes it as "a farewell to London," and in a letter to Felix E. Schelling on July 9, 1922, he called it "Again a study in form, an attempt to condense the James novel." The use of quatrains he attributed to a feeling shared with Eliot that they must set in motion "some countercurrent" to the excesses of free verse. They both studied the chiseled quatrains of Theophile Gautier (1811–1872) in his *Emaux et Camées* (1852), and in the letter to Schelling, Pound said, "The metre in *Mauberley* is Gautier and Bion's *Adonis;* or at least those are the two grafts I was trying to flavour it with. Syncopation from the Greek; and a general distaste for the slushiness and swishiness of the post-Swinburnian British line." Bion, a Greek poet who died c. 100 B.C.E., was famous for his "Lament for Adonis."
3. The heat calls us into the shade (Latin); from the Fourth Eclogue of Nemesianus, a third-century Latin poet.
4. Ode on the choice of his tomb (French); adapted from the title of a poem by Pierre de Ronsard (1524–1585), "De l'Election de Son Sepulchre." The initials E. P. preceded the section title in the 1920 and later editions of the poem, but were omitted in the 1921 text reprinted here.
5. The United States.
6. One of the seven warriors who attacked Thebes. Boastful and defiant, he was struck down by one of Zeus's thunderbolts.
7. *Idmen gár toi pánth hos eni Troíe* (Greek): For we know all things [suffered] in Troy. First line of the Sirens' song, *Odyssey* 12.189. Odysseus plugged his shipmates' ears with wax so they would not be tempted by the dangerous song, but he left his own ears open and had himself lashed to the mast. "Troíe," pronounced "Troh*ee*-ay," rhymes with "leeway"; bilingual rhymes are a recurring device of the poem.
8. Gustave Flaubert (1821–1880), French novelist, is here a symbol of artistic perfectionism. Penelope, Odysseus's wife, was famous for her long faithfulness to her husband.
9. Seductive female enchanter who delayed Odysseus's return home.

De son eage;[1] the case presents
No adjunct to the Muses' diadem.

II

The age demanded an image
Of its accelerated grimace,
Something for the modern stage,
Not, at any rate, an Attic grace;

Not, not certainly, the obscure reveries
Of the inward gaze;
Better mendacities
Than the classics in paraphrase!

The "age demanded" chiefly a mould in plaster,
Made with no loss of time,
A prose kinema,[2] not, not assuredly, alabaster
Or the "sculpture" of rhyme.

III

The tea-rose tea-gown, etc.
Supplants the mousseline of Cos,[3]
The pianola "replaces"
Sappho's barbitos.[4]

Christ follows Dionysus,[5]
Phallic and ambrosial
Made way for macerations;
Caliban casts out Ariel.[6]

All things are a flowing,
Sage Heracleitus says;[7]
But a tawdry cheapness
Shall outlast our days.

Even the Christian beauty
Defects—after Samothrace;[8]
We see *τὸ καλὸν*[9]
Decreed in the market place.

Faun's flesh is not to us,
Nor the saint's vision.

1. The thirtieth year of his life (French); adapted from the first line of the *Grand Testament*, by François Villon (1431–1463?).
2. Movement (Greek); cinema.
3. A Greek island, famous in Roman times for its muslin.
4. Lyre (Greek). Sappho, sixth-century B.C.E. Greek poet, is Pound's type of the classical poet; her verse survives in fragments. *Pianola:* player piano.
5. Greek god of wine, fertility, and poetic inspiration, whose rites were ecstatic and frenzied.
6. Caliban, "a savage and deformed Slave," and Ariel, "an airy Spirit," are characters in Shakespeare's *The Tempest*. *Macerations:* fasting, wasting (here, in Christianity).
7. Heracleitus (c. 535–475 B.C.E.), Greek philosopher, held that everything is in eternal flux.
8. Greek island associated with a cult of beauty and Dionysian rites; the famous Winged Victory statue (c. 300 B.C.E.) was recovered there.
9. *Tò kalón* (Greek): the beautiful.

We have the press for wafer;
Franchise for circumcision.

All men, in law, are equals.
Free of Peisistratus,[1]
We choose a knave or an eunuch
To rule over us.

O bright Apollo,
τίν' ἀνδρα, τίν' ἥρωα, τίνα θεὸν,[2]
What god, man, or hero
Shall I place a tin wreath upon!

IV

These fought in any case,
and some believing, pro domo,[3] in any case . .

Some quick to arm,
some for adventure,
some from fear of weakness,
some from fear of censure,
some for love of slaughter, in imagination,
learning later . . .

some in fear, learning love of slaughter;
Died some, pro patria, non dulce non et decor . .
walked eye-deep in hell
believing in old men's lies, then unbelieving
came home, home to a lie,
home to many deceits,
home to old lies and new infamy;
usury age-old and age-thick
and liars in public places.

Daring as never before, wastage as never before.
Young blood and high blood,
fair cheeks, and fine bodies;

fortitude as never before

frankness as never before,
disillusions as never told in the old days,
hysterias, trench confessions,
laughter out of dead bellies.

1. Pisistratus (d. 527 B.C.E.), Athenian tyrant.
2. *Tín ándra, tín héroa, tína theón* (Greek): What man, what hero, what god; adapted from the Second Olympian Ode by Pindar (c. 522–c. 402 B.C.E.), Greek lyric poet. The original reads, "What god, what hero, what man shall we loudly praise?" Pindar's tone is one of genuine eulogy; Pound puns on "tin," which is the sound of the Greek word for "what."
3. For [one's] home (Latin); a substitution in the phrase from Horace (65–8 B.C.E.), *Odes* 3.2.13: "Dulce et decorum est pro patria mori" (It is sweet and fitting to die for one's country). (Pound attacks this sentiment in line 70, inserting the negative "non.")

V

There died a myriad,
And of the best, among them,
For an old bitch gone in the teeth,
For a botched civilization,

Charm, smiling at the good mouth,
Quick eyes gone under earth's lid,

For two gross of broken statues,
For a few thousand battered books.

Yeux Glauques[4]

Gladstone[5] was still respected,
When John Ruskin produced
"Kings' Treasuries";[6] Swinburne
And Rossetti still abused.

Fœtid Buchanan[7] lifted up his voice
When that faun's head of hers
Became a pastime for
Painters and adulterers.

The Burne-Jones cartons[8]
Have preserved her eyes;
Still, at the Tate, they teach
Cophetua to rhapsodize;

Thin like brook-water,
With a vacant gaze.
The English Rubaiyat was still-born[9]
In those days.

The thin, clear gaze, the same
Still darts out faun-like from the half-ruin'd face,
Questing and passive. . . .
"Ah, poor Jenny's case" . . .[1]

4. Sea-green eyes (French); a favorite image in nineteenth-century poetry; the eyes are of Elizabeth Siddal, the model for several paintings by Pre-Raphaelite poet and artist Dante Gabriel Rossetti (1828–1882), who married her in 1860, two years before her death.
5. William Ewart Gladstone (1809–1898), British prime minister for ten years, and a type of the most rigid Victorian respectability.
6. The first lecture in *Sesame and Lilies* (1865), by John Ruskin (1819–1900), art historian and social critic. It contains a scathing indictment of the English, whom Ruskin found to despise literature, science, art, natural beauty, and human compassion. Pound shared some of Ruskin's views on art and society.
7. Robert Buchanan (1841–1901), author of the "Fleshly School of Poetry" (1871), which attacked the Pre-Raphaelite poets, among whom Rossetti and Algernon Charles Swinburne (1837–1909) were prominent.
8. Cartoons (French), in the sense of preparatory designs for a painting or tapestry. Sir Edward Burne-Jones (1833–1898), a Pre-Raphaelite painter, used Elizabeth Siddal as a model for the beggar maid in his painting *King Cophetua and the Beggar Maid,* at London's Tate Gallery.
9. Edward FitzGerald's *The Rubáiyát of Omar Khayyám,* which Pound thought highly of, was published in 1859, but went unnoticed until Rossetti discovered it the following year.
1. Rossetti's poem "Jenny" is about a prostitute; Buchanan, a Scotsman with a Calvinistic streak, made much of it in his attack on the Pre-Raphaelites.

Bewildered that a world
Shows no surprise
At her last maquero's[2]
Adulteries.

"Siena Mi Fe'; Disfecemi Maremma"[3]

Among the pickled fœtuses and bottled bones,
Engaged in perfecting the catalogue,
I found the last scion of the
Senatorial families of Strasbourg, Monsieur Verog.[4]

For two hours he talked of Gallifet;[5]
Of Dowson; of the Rhymers' Club;[6]
Told me how Johnson (Lionel) died
By falling from a high stool in a pub . . .

But showed no trace of alcohol
At the autopsy, privately performed—
Tissue preserved—the pure mind
Arose toward Newman[7] as the whiskey warmed.

Dowson found harlots cheaper than hotels;
Headlam for uplift; Image impartially imbued
With raptures for Bacchus, Terpsichore and the Church.[8]
So spoke the author of "The Dorian Mood,"

M. Verog, out of step with the decade,
Detached from his contemporaries,
Neglected by the young,
Because of these reveries.

Brennbaum[9]

The sky-like limpid eyes,
The circular infant's face,
The stiffness from spats to collar
Never relaxing into grace;

2. Or *maquereau* (French); pimp.
3. Siena made me; Maremma unmade me (Italian); from Dante's *Purgatorio* 5.134, where it is spoken by Pia de' Tolomei of her birth, in Siena, and her death, in Maremma, at her husband's hands. In *The Divine Comedy,* Pia represents souls who have found salvation at the last moment.
4. Modeled on Victor Plarr (1863–1929), librarian to the Royal College of Surgeons, in London; he prepared a catalogue of its manuscripts.
5. The Marquis de Galliffet (1830–1909), a French general, led his cavalry brigade courageously in the crucial battle of Sedan during the Franco-Prussian War, which France lost.
6. Plarr was a member of the Rhymers' Club, an informal group of late Victorian poets, c. 1890–91, who met at the Cheshire Cheese, a pub in London. Their members were W. B. Yeats, Ernest Dowson (1867–1900)—whose biography Plarr wrote—and Lionel Johnson (1867–1907), who died from a fall in the street, not in a pub. Plarr's poems were published in an 1896 book called *In the Dorian Mood* (line 133).
7. Cardinal John Henry Newman (1801–1890), who like Johnson and Dowson was a convert to Catholicism.
8. The Rev. Stewart D. Headlam (1847–1924), a friend of several writers of the 1890s, and Selwyn Image (1849–1930), another cleric-poet, joined to found the Church and Stage Guild. *Bacchus*: Roman name for Dionysus, god of wine, ecstasy, and music. *Terpsichore:* Muse of dance.
9. Anti-Semitic portrait probably modeled on Max Beerbohm (1872–1956), who Pound mistakenly thought was Jewish.

The heavy memories of Horeb, Sinai and the forty years,[1]
Showed only when the daylight fell
Level across the face
Of Brennbaum "The Impeccable."

Mr Nixon[2]

In the cream gilded cabin of his steam yacht
Mr. Nixon advised me kindly, to advance with fewer
Dangers of delay. "Consider
        "Carefully the reviewer.

"I was as poor as you are;
"When I began I got, of course,
"Advance on royalties, fifty at first," said Mr. Nixon,
"Follow me, and take a column,
"Even if you have to work free.

"Butter reviewers. From fifty to three hundred
"I rose in eighteen months;
"The hardest nut I had to crack
"Was Dr. Dundas.

"I never mentioned a man but with the view
"Of selling my own works.
"The tip's a good one, as for literature
"It gives no man a sinecure.

"And no one knows, at sight a masterpiece.
"And give up verse, my boy,
"There's nothing in it."

. . . .

Likewise a friend of Bloughram's[3] once advised me:
Don't kick against the pricks,[4]
Accept opinion. The "Nineties" tried your game
And died, there's nothing in it.

X

Beneath the sagging roof
The stylist[5] has taken shelter,
Unpaid, uncelebrated,
At last from the world's welter

1. Horeb, or Sinai, was the mountain where Moses received the Tables of the Law; after the Exodus from Egypt, the Israelites spent forty years in the wilderness.
2. Perhaps modeled on Arnold Bennett (1867–1931), the highly successful English novelist.
3. Robert Browning's poem "Bishop Blougram's Apology" (1855) is a priest's casuistic defense of his worldly interests.
4. A phrase adapted from Acts 16.14.
5. Ford Madox Ford (1873–1939), English poet, editor, and novelist, is probably the model; Pound always credited Ford with having pointed him toward naturalness and freshness of language.

Nature receives him,
With a placid and uneducated mistress
He exercises his talents
And the soil meets his distress.

The haven from sophistications and contentions
Leaks through its thatch;
He offers succulent cooking;
The door has a creaking latch.

XI

"Conservatrix of Milésien"[6]
Habits of mind and feeling,
Possibly. But in Ealing[7]
With the most bank-clerkly of Englishmen?

No, "Milésien" is an exaggeration.
No instinct has survived in her
Older than those her grandmother
Told her would fit her station.

XII

"Daphne with her thighs in bark
Stretches toward me her leafy hands,"—[8]
Subjectively. In the stuffed-satin drawing-room
I await The Lady Valentine's commands,

Knowing my coat has never been
Of precisely the fashion
To stimulate, in her,
A durable passion;

Doubtful, somewhat, of the value
Of well-gowned approbation
Of literary effort,
But never of The Lady Valentine's vocation:

Poetry, her border of ideas,
The edge, uncertain, but a means of blending
With other strata
Where the lower and higher have ending;

A hook to catch the Lady Jane's attention,
A modulation toward the theatre,

6. Phrase from "Stratagems" (1894), a short story by Rémy de Gourmont (1858–1915): "Women, conservers of Milesian traditions." The *Milesian Tales*, by Aristides of Miletus (second century B.C.E.), were erotic Greek tales that, not having survived, cannot be conserved.

7. A part of western London associated with dull respectability.

8. Translated from Gautier, "The Castle of Memory." Daphne, pursued by Apollo, was transformed into a laurel tree to escape him; the sylvan scene is compared with the salon.

Also, in the case of revolution,
A possible friend and comforter.

. . . .

Conduct,[9] on the other hand, the soul
"Which the highest cultures have nourished"
To Fleet St. where
Dr. Johnson flourished;[1]

Beside this thoroughfare
The sale of half-hose has
Long since superseded the cultivation
Of Pierian roses.[2]

Envoi (1919)[3]

Go, dumb-born book,
Tell her that sang me once that song of Lawes;[4]
Hadst thou but song
As thou hast subjects known,
Then were there cause in thee that should condone
Even my faults that heavy upon me lie
And build her glories their longevity.

Tell her that sheds
Such treasure in the air,
Recking naught else but that her graces give
Life to the moment,
I would bid them live
As roses might, in magic amber laid,
Red overwrought with orange and all made
One substance and one colour
Braving time.

Tell her that goes
With song upon her lips
But sings not out the song, nor knows
The maker of it, some other mouth,
May be as fair as hers,
Might, in new ages, gain her worshippers,
When our two dusts with Waller's shall be laid,
Siftings on siftings in oblivion,
Till change hath broken down
All things save Beauty alone.

1920, 1921

9. Here, a verb. The following quotation is a translation of two lines of "Complainte des pianos," by Jules Laforgue (1860–1887), French poet.
1. Samuel Johnson (1709–1784), English poet, essayist, and editor. *Fleet Street:* a center of London journalism.
2. In Greek mythology, Pieria, a district on the northern slopes of Mt. Olympus, is where the Muses, inspirers of the arts, were born.
3. An envoy, or a poem's postscript, often addresses the poet's book. Here, it is an adaptation of "Go, Lovely Rose," a poem by Edmund Waller (1606–1687).
4. Henry Lawes (1598–1662), an English composer, set Waller's poem to music.

1920 (Mauberley)[5]

I

Turned from the "eau-forte
Par Jaquemart"[6]
To the strait head
Of Messalina:[7]

"His true Penelope
Was Flaubert,"
And his tool
The engraver's.

Firmness,
Not the full smile,
His art, but an art
In profile;

Colourless
Pier Francesca,[8]
Pisanello lacking the skill
To forge Achaia.[9]

II

"Qu'est ce qu'ils savent de l'amour, et qu'est ce qu'ils peuvent comprendre?

S'ils ne comprennent pas la poèsie, si'ils ne sentent pas la musique, qu'est ce qu'ils peuvent comprendre de cette passion en comparaison avec laquelle la rose est grossière et le parfum des violettes un tonnerre?"

—CAID ALI[1]

For three years, diabolus in the scale,[2]
He drank ambrosia,[3]
All passes, ANANGKE[4] prevails,
Came end, at last, to that Arcadia.[5]

5. This part of the poem is a commentary on the first and an extension of it.
6. An etching of Gautier by J. F. Jacquemart (1837–1880) appears in several editions of *Emaux et Camées*.
7. Wife of the Roman emperor Claudius, who had her murdered in 48 C.E. Her image was engraved on Roman coins.
8. Piero della Francesca (c. 1420–1492), Italian painter, was famous for his perfect forms and pale colors.
9. That is, Antonio Pisanello (1395–c. 1455), Italian Gothic medalist and painter, lacked the skill to forge classical medallions, particularly those of Achaia in ancient Greece.

1. A Persian pseudonym of Pound's. The epigraph in French means "What do they know of love, and what can they understand of it? If they do not understand poetry, if they do not feel music, what can they understand of this passion compared to which the rose is crude and the perfume of violets a thunderbolt?"
2. In music, the diabolus (Latin for devil) is the interval of an augmented fourth, which medieval theorists admonished composers never to use. Cf. line 1.
3. The food of the gods, which Mauberley presumptuously eats.
4. Necessity or fate (Greek).
5. Earthly paradise.

He had moved amid her[6] phantasmagoria,
Amid her galaxies,
NUKTIS 'AGALMA[7]

• • • • • • •

Drifted. . . . drifted precipitate,
Asking time to be rid of. . . .
Of his bewilderment; to designate
His new found orchid. . . . [8]

To be certain. . . . certain. . . .
(Amid ærial flowers) . . time for arrangements—
Drifted on
To the final estrangement;

Unable in the supervening blankness
To sift TO AGATHON[9] from the chaff
Until he found his seive.[1] . . .
Ultimately, his seismograph:

—Given that is his "fundamental passion"
This urge to convey the relation
Of eye-lid and cheek-bone
By verbal manifestations;

To present the series
Of curious heads in medallion—

He had passed, inconscient, full gaze,
The wide-banded irises
And botticellian[2] sprays implied
In their diastasis;[3]

Which anæsthesis,[4] noted a year late,
And weighed, revealed his great affect,
(Orchid), mandate
Of Eros,[5] a retrospect.

• • •

Mouths biting empty air,
The still stone dogs,[6]
Caught in metamorphosis, were
Left him as epilogues.

6. That is, Night's.
7. Inaccurate Greek for "night's jewel"; from Bion's apostrophe to the evening star (Idyll IX).
8. Also a pun on the Greek word *orchis,* testicle.
9. The good (Greek).
1. That is, sieve.
2. An allusion to Venus rising out of the sea spray in *The Birth of Venus,* by Sandro Botticelli (c. 1445–1510), Florentine painter.
3. Separation between the eyes (cf. the "stance between the eyes" in the vision of Canto 81.122–23).
4. Insensibility.
5. The Greek god of love.
6. Cf. the line adapted from Ovid's *Metamorphoses* 7.786 that Pound used as an epigraph to "1920 (Mauberley)" in later editions: "Vacuous exercet in aera morsus," Latin for "he bites at the empty air." In Ovid, a dog pursuing a monster that has been ravaging the city is turned, along with the monster, into stone.

"The Age Demanded"

VIDE POEM II. PAGE 355

For this agility chance found
Him of all men, unfit
As the red-beaked steeds[7] of
The Cytheræan for a chain bit.

The glow of porcelain
Brought no reforming sense
To his perception
Of the social inconsequence.

Thus, if her colour
Came against his gaze,
Tempered as if
It were through a perfect glaze

He made no immediate application
Of this to relation of the state
To the individual, the month was more temperate
Because this beauty had been.

. . . . . .

The coral isle, the lion-coloured sand
Burst in upon the porcelain revery:
Impetuous troubling
Of his imagery.

. . . . . .

Mildness, amid the neo-Neitzschean[8] clatter,
His sense of graduations,
Quite out of place amid
Resistance to current exacerbations,

Invitation, mere invitation to perceptivity
Gradually led him to the isolation
Which these presents[9] place
Under a more tolerant, perhaps, examination.

By constant elimination
The manifest universe
Yielded an armour
Against utter consternation,

A Minoan[1] undulation,
Seen, we admit, amid ambrosial circumstances
Strengthened him against
The discouraging doctrine of chances,

7. In Greek mythology, doves drew the carriage of Aphrodite (the Cytherean).
8. That is, neo-Nietzschean. Friedrich Nietzsche (1844–1900), German philosopher, was much in fashion at this time.
9. That is, these circumstances.
1. Derived from the name of King Minos, the most famous king of Crete.

And his desire for survival,
Faint in the most strenuous moods,
Became an Olympian *apathein*[2]
In the presence of selected perceptions.

A pale gold, in the aforesaid pattern,
The unexpected palms
Destroying, certainly, the artist's urge,
Left him delighted with the imaginary
Audition of the phantasmal sea-surge,[3]

Incapable of the least utterance or composition,
Emendation, conservation of the "better tradition"
Refinement of medium, elimination of superfluities,
August attraction or concentration.

Nothing, in brief, but maudlin confession
Irresponse to human aggression,
Amid the precipitation, down-float
Of insubstantial manna,
Lifting the faint susurrus[4]
Of his subjective hosannah.

Ultimate affronts to human redundancies;

Non-esteem of self-styled "his betters"
Leading, as he well knew,
To his final
Exclusion from the world of letters.

IV

Scattered Moluccas[5]
Not knowing, day to day,
The first day's end, in the next noon;
The placid water
Unbroken by the Simoon;[6]

Thick foliage
Placid beneath warm suns,
Tawn fore-shores
Washed in the cobalt of oblivions;

Or through dawn-mist
The grey and rose
Of the juridical
Flamingoes;

2. Indifference (Greek).
3. Pound said this was an attempt at onomatopoeia, giving the actual sound of the sea. See Canto 2.13.
4. Whisper (Latin).
5. Islands near New Guinea.
6. A hot, dry wind.

A consciousness disjunct,
Being but this overblotted
Series
Of intermittences;

Coracle[7] of Pacific voyages,
The unforecasted beach:
Then on an oar
Read this:

"I was
And I no more exist;
Here drifted
An hedonist."

Medallion[8]

Luini[9] in porcelain!
The grand piano
Utters a profane
Protest with her clear soprano.

The sleek head emerges
From the gold-yellow frock
As Anadyomene[1] in the opening
Pages of Reinach.

Honey-red, closing the face-oval,
A basket-work of braids which seem as if they were
Spun in King Minos' hall
From metal, or intractable amber;

The face-oval beneath the glaze,
Bright in its suave bounding-line, as,
Beneath in half-watt rays,
The eyes turn topaz.

1920, 1921

On The Cantos

Ezra Pound began to publish *The Cantos* in 1917, when early versions of the first three appeared. In the end, he had written 109 complete Cantos, including two in Italian and unpublished in the United States until 1987, and "drafts and fragments" of nine more. From the beginning, he was vague about the final dimensions of the work; his decision in 1969 to publish incomplete versions of the latest additions may have meant he thought he could do no more.

7. A small boat.
8. This poem is usually taken to be written, like the "Envoi" of the first part, by Mauberley, and it is a kind of ultimate justification of his aesthetic interests and methods.
9. Bernardino Luini (c.1481–1532), Milanese painter and follower of Leonardo da Vinci.
1. Epithet for Venus meaning "born from foam." Pound alludes to an illustration in *Apollo* (1904), a history of art by Salomon Reinach (1858–1932).

At various times, Pound offered partial explanations of *The Cantos*' structural plan. He said that the poem constitutes a "commedia agnostica" as against Dante's *Divina Commedia* and claimed a musical organization: "Take a fugue: theme, response, contrasujet. *Not* that I mean to make an exact analogy of structure. . . . There *is* a start, descent to the shades, metamorphoses, parallel (Vidal-Actaeon)." He said *The Cantos* are "rather like, or unlike subject and response and counter subject in fugue." "Out of the three main classes of themes, permanent, recurrent, and casual (or haphazard)," he hoped "a hierarchy of values should emerge."

Pound intended to develop a modern epic, a "poem including history," that encompasses not only the world's literature, but its art and architecture, myths, economics, the lives of historical figures—in effect, "the tale of the tribe"—in a profuse assemblage of particular details that may or may not make connections with each other. Underlying this concept are didactic purposes: to present materials that he thinks a civilized reader ought to absorb, and to point, by means of documents and achievements of the past and present, toward a good civilization ruled by right-thinking men of action. The famous obscurity of *The Cantos* results partly from Pound's disjunctive arrangement of his materials, but partly also from the obscurity of the materials themselves; Pound, formidably traveled and read, usually assumes his readers are as familiar with sixteenth-century Italian architecture, Provençal lyrics, Confucian philosophy, and medieval economic history as he is, as well as with the nearly dozen languages from which he draws, or into which he translates, many of his allusions. In some ways it is easier, armed with patience and the *Annotated Index to the Cantos of Ezra Pound,* to read right through the poem rather than to read excerpts from it, as Pound's hermetic allusions are often tags that he expands elsewhere.

Cantos 1–7 indicate the poem's procedures and some of its themes. Cantos 8–11 present Sigismundo Malatesta (d. 1468), the Venetian soldier and art patron, as a type of the man of action. Cantos 12–13 contrast modern economic exploitation with the tranquil order of Confucian moral philosophy. Cantos 14–16 describe a passage through hell (in the guise of modern London), ending with a vision of medieval Venice as paradise in Canto 17. American presidents whose policies and personal styles Pound admires are presented in Cantos 31–33 (Jefferson), 34 (John Quincy Adams), 37 (Van Buren), and 62–71 (John Adams); Canto 41 introduces Mussolini, whom Pound, sympathizing with the Fascist economic program and seeming patronage of art, thought the best contemporary leader. As Pound identifies humane civilization and government with Confucian ethics, he sketches a history of ancient China (Cantos 52–61) to show that Chinese prosperity and peace attended only rule by Confucian moral principles—a conclusion that modern historians find dubious. In counterpoint to these "historical" Cantos, Pound sets those of the *Fifth Decad of Cantos,* which inveigh against usurious monetary systems (those, according to Pound, based on paper values rather than real ones) and exalt those principles, from the Eleusinian mysteries of ancient Greece to the "social credit" theories of Pound's contemporary C. H. Douglas, that encourage the growth of natural fertility and wealth. During World War II, Pound wrote two strongly pro-Fascist Cantos in Italian that were published only many years later; at the war's end, he was imprisoned near Pisa by the U.S. Army on charges of treason arising from his wartime broadcasts on the Italian radio.

The Pisan Cantos, written in the prison camp under great physical and psychological duress while Pound was waiting to be returned to the United States for trial and quite possibly execution, record a "dark night of the soul" through which the poet passes toward a vision of Aphrodite, the goddess of love, and the acceptance of his own death. Available to him were the scenes and events of the detention camp, the Bible, an edition of Confucius, a poetry anthology, and the resources of his extraordinary memory. Under extreme pressure these elements combine, in a "magic moment" recorded in Canto 81. *The Pisan Cantos* are both impressive and difficult, and when they won the Bollingen

Prize in 1949 (given by the Library of Congress; the distinguished jury included T. S. Eliot, W. H. Auden, Robert Lowell, Allen Tate, R. P. Warren, and the dissenting Karl Shapiro), a controversy arose involving not only the charge of treason that was still pending against Pound, and the undeniably Fascist and anti-Semitic passages in parts of the poems, but also a reaction against the aesthetic of postsymbolist "modernism" as exemplified in all the works of Pound and Eliot.

The later Cantos—*Section: Rock Drill* (1955) and *Thrones* (1959)—consolidate the insights of the earlier Cantos and are yet more cryptic. *Drafts and Fragments of Cantos CX–CXVII* (1969) hint at an apologia: "But the beauty is not the madness / Tho' my errors and wrecks lie about me. / And I am not a demigod, / I cannot make it cohere" (Canto 116). In a 1968 conversation with Daniel Cory, Pound said he had "botched" the work. But despite its unevenness and obscurity, *The Cantos* remains for readers and for other poets one of the great literary challenges and inspirations of the twentieth century.

From The Cantos

I[1]

And then went down to the ship,
Set keel to breakers, forth on the godly sea, and
We[2] set up mast and sail on that swart ship,
Bore sheep aboard her, and our bodies also
Heavy with weeping, and winds from sternward
Bore us out onward with bellying canvas,
Circe's this craft, the trim-coifed goddess.[3]
Then sat we amidships, wind jamming the tiller,
Thus with stretched sail, we went over sea till day's end.
Sun to his slumber, shadows o'er all the ocean,
Came we then to the bounds of deepest water,
To the Kimmerian lands,[4] and peopled cities
Covered with close-webbed mist, unpierced ever
With glitter of sun-rays
Nor with stars stretched, nor looking back from heaven
Swartest night stretched over wretched men there.
The ocean flowing backward, came we then to the place
Aforesaid by Circe.
Here did they rites, Perimedes and Eurylochus,[5]

1. This Canto is, until line 68, a free translation of the opening of *Odyssey* 11, which describes Odysseus's voyage to the end of the earth, where he summons up spirits from the underworld. For Pound, Odysseus is the type of the enterprising, imaginative man, and this voyage represents in some sense a symbol or analogy of the poet's own voyage into the darker aspects of his civilization or the buried places of the mind. The verse is alliterative, resembling that of Old English poetry, perhaps to suggest the archaic and archetypal character of this Odyssean experience. Pound believed on internal evidence that book 11 is the oldest part of the *Odyssey*, and this may also have influenced his choice of the oldest style of English poetry.
2. Odysseus and his shipmates.
3. And female sorcerer, who turns Odysseus's men into swine and detains Odysseus for a year. Odysseus has just left her island; following her instructions, he goes to the mouth of the underworld, where the prophet Tiresias counsels him about his return to his native Ithaca.
4. The Cimmerii were a mythical people living on the edge of the world.
5. Two of Odysseus's men.

And drawing sword from my hip
I dug the ell-square pitkin;[6]
Poured we libations unto each the dead,
First mead and then sweet wine, water mixed with white flour.
Then prayed I many a prayer to the sickly death's-heads;
As set in Ithaca, sterile bulls of the best
For sacrifice, heaping the pyre with goods,
A sheep to Tiresias only, black and a bell-sheep.[7]
Dark blood flowed in the fosse,[8]
Souls out of Erebus,[9] cadaverous dead, of brides
Of youths and of the old who had borne much;
Souls stained with recent tears, girls tender,
Men many, mauled with bronze lance heads,
Battle spoil, bearing yet dreory[1] arms,
These many crowded about me; with shouting,
Pallor upon me, cried to my men for more beasts;
Slaughtered the herds, sheep slain of bronze;
Poured ointment, cried to the gods,
To Pluto the strong, and praised Proserpine;[2]
Unsheathed the narrow sword,
I sat to keep off the impetuous impotent dead,
Till I should hear Tiresias.
But first Elpenor[3] came, our friend Elpenor,
Unburied, cast on the wide earth,
Limbs that we left in the house of Circe,
Unwept, unwrapped in sepulchre, since toils urged other.
Pitiful spirit. And I cried in hurried speech:
"Elpenor, how art thou come to this dark coast?
"Cam'st thou afoot, outstripping seamen?"
        And he in heavy speech:
"Ill fate and abundant wine. I slept in Circe's ingle.[4]
"Going down the long ladder unguarded,
"I fell against the buttress,
"Shattered the nape-nerve, the soul sought Avernus.[5]
"But thou, O King, I bid remember me, unwept, unburied,
"Heap up mine arms, be tomb[6] by sea-bord, and inscribed:
"*A man of no fortune, and with a name to come.*
"And set my oar up, that I swung mid fellows."

And Anticlea[7] came, whom I beat off, and then Tiresias Theban,
Holding his golden wand, knew me, and spoke first:

6. Pound's coinage for a small pit. *Ell:* a measure of length, varying from two to four feet.
7. *Bell-sheep:* the one that leads the herd. Tiresias, a Theban, was granted the gift of prophecy by the gods. Cf. part 3 of T. S. Eliot's *Waste Land*.
8. Ditch (Latin).
9. Primeval darkness, Hades.
1. Bloody. (The Old English word is *dreorig*.)
2. Wife of Pluto, the Roman god of the underworld.
3. One of Odysseus's companions. He broke his neck in an accidental fall from the roof of Circe's house; because his companions did not discover his death, they failed to perform the burial rites.
4. Inglenook, or hearth.
5. A lake in Italy beside which was the cave through which the Trojan hero Aeneas descended to Hades to learn the future. The name was also given to the underworld.
6. That is, may there be a tomb.
7. Odysseus's mother. In the *Odyssey*, Odysseus weeps at the sight of her, but cannot let her drink the blood, and so speak to him, until Tiresias has done so.

"A second time?[8] why? man of ill star,
"Facing the sunless dead and this joyless region?
"Stand from the fosse, leave me my bloody bever[9]
"For soothsay."
And I stepped back,
And he strong with the blood, said then: "Odysseus
"Shalt return through spiteful Neptune,[1] over dark seas,
"Lose all companions." And then Anticlea came.
Lie quiet Divus. I mean, that is Andreas Divus,
In officina Wecheli, 1538, out of Homer.[2]
And he sailed, by Sirens and thence outward and away
And unto Circe.[3]
Venerandam,[4]
In the Cretan's phrase, with the golden crown, Aphrodite,
Cypri munimenta sortita est,[5] mirthful, orichalchi,[6] with golden
Girdles and breast bands, thou with dark eyelids
Bearing the golden bough of Argicida.[7] So that:

1917, 1925

II

Hang it all, Robert Browning,
there can be but the one "Sordello."[8]
But Sordello, and my Sordello?
Lo Sordels si fo di Mantovana.[9]
So-shu[1] churned in the sea.
Seal sports in the spray-whited circles of cliff-wash,
Sleek head, daughter of Lir;
eyes of Picasso[2]
Under black fur-hood, lithe daughter of Ocean;

8. They have met before, in the upper world.
9. Drink (Middle English).
1. An allusion to the shipwreck Odysseus was to undergo. Neptune was the Roman sea god.
2. Pound here acknowledges that he has been following not the original Greek but a medieval Latin translation of Homer by Andreas Divus, published by the workshop of Wechel, in Paris, in 1538. Hence also Pound's use of the Roman names for the gods. With these words he abruptly turns from the *Odyssey*.
3. Actually, Odysseus first returned to Circe and then went on to the Sirens. Pound varies the order, perhaps with some idea of a sensual progress from the Sirens (temptation) to Circe (a love affair) and then to Aphrodite, the goddess of love.
4. Commanding reverence (Latin). This epithet is given to Aphrodite in what is known as the sixth Homeric Hymn. (These Greek hymns were not in fact written by Homer.) Pound is again working from a Latin translation, this one by Georgius Dartona Cretensis (called the Cretan); it was included in Pound's copy of Divus's Latin *Odyssey*.
5. The citadels of Cyprus were her appointed realm (Latin).
6. Of copper (Latin). The hymn recounts how a votive gift of copper and gold was made, by the attendant Hours, to Aphrodite.
7. An epithet usually given to Hermes, the gods' messenger, that means Slayer of Argus (a mythical herdsman with eyes all over his body, whose watchfulness the goddess Hera had counted on to prevent her husband, Zeus, from having an affair with the mortal woman Io). But Pound may be conferring the epithet upon Aphrodite as slayer of the Argi (Greeks) during the Trojan War. The golden bough was Aeneas's offering to Proserpina before his descent to Hades, and it is usually associated with Diana and the sacred wood of Nemi rather than with Aphrodite.
8. Sordello (1200–1270), an Italian troubadour who lived in Provence, was the subject of a long narrative poem, by the English poet Robert Browning (1812–1889), that Pound admired.
9. Sordello was from the Mantua district (Provençal). Pound quotes from a medieval source a fact about the historical Sordello that Browning had omitted in his fictionalized portrait.
1. An invented name.
2. Pablo Picasso (1881–1973), Spanish expatriate painter. *Lir:* literally, ocean; the Celtic sea god Manannan mac Lir.

And the wave runs in the beach-groove:
"Eleanor, ἑλέναυς and ἑλέπτολις!"[3]
And poor old Homer blind, blind, as a bat,
Ear, ear for the sea-surge, murmur of old men's voices:[4]
"Let her go back to the ships,
Back among Grecian faces, lest evil come on our own,
Evil and further evil, and a curse cursed on our children,
Moves, yes she moves like a goddess
And has the face of a god
and the voice of Schoeney's daughters,[5]
And doom goes with her in walking,
Let her go back to the ships,
back among Grecian voices."
And by the beach-run, Tyro,[6]
Twisted arms of the sea-god,
Lithe sinews of water, gripping her, cross-hold,
And the blue-gray glass of the wave tents them,
Glare azure of water, cold-welter, close cover.
Quiet sun-tawny sand-stretch,
The gulls broad out their wings,
nipping between the splay feathers;
Snipe come for their bath,
bend out their wing-joints,
Spread wet wings to the sun-film,
And by Scios,
to left of the Naxos passage,[7]
Naviform[8] rock overgrown,
algæ cling to its edge,
There is a wine-red glow in the shallows,
a tin flash in the sun-dazzle.

The ship landed in Scios,[9]
men wanting spring-water,
And by the rock-pool a young boy loggy with vine-must,
"To Naxos? Yes, we'll take you to Naxos,
Cum' along lad." "Not that way!"
"Aye, that way is Naxos."
And I said: "It's a straight ship."

3. *Helénaus, heléptolis* (Greek): destroyer of ships, destroyer of cities. The Chorus in Aeschylus's *Agamemnon* describes Helen (Eleanor), the cause of the Trojan War, with these words, which are puns on her name. In Canto 7, she blends into Eleanor of Aquitaine.

4. The Trojan elders' "murmurs" about Helen are recounted in the *Iliad* 3.60. Pound admired Homer's "ear of the sea-surge," shown by his onomatopoeic coinage *poluphloisboio*, much-roaring.

5. That is, Schoeneus's one daughter, Atalanta, whose many suitors had to outrun her in a race in order to marry her, and who were killed when they failed. Here, as elsewhere in this Canto, Pound echoes Arthur Golding's famous sixteenth-century translation of Ovid's *Metamorphoses,* which describes Atalanta as "one / of Schoenyes daughters," and which Pound called "possibly the most beautiful book in our language" ("Notes on Elizabethan Classicists").

6. The nymph Tyro was raped by the sea god Poseidon, who disguised himself as a river.

7. Scios (or Chios) and Naxos are Greek islands about a hundred miles apart. Chios was one of seven reputed birthplaces of Homer; Naxos was once a center for the worship of Dionysus (or Bacchus), the Greek god of wine and religious ecstasy. "Scios" was Golding's spelling.

8. Boat-shaped.

9. This story, about an attempt to kidnap Dionysus by fishermen who don't know who he is, was told by Acoestes (Ovid, *Metamorphoses* 3.511–733) to King Pentheus of Thebes as a warning not to restrict the worship of Dionysus there.

And an ex-convict out of Italy
knocked me into the fore-stays,
(He was wanted for manslaughter in Tuscany)
And the whole twenty against me,
Mad for a little slave money.
And they took her out of Scios
And off her course . . .
And the boy came to, again, with the racket,
And looked out over the bows,
and to eastward, and to the Naxos passage.
God-sleight then, god-sleight:
Ship stock fast in sea-swirl,
Ivy upon the oars, King Pentheus,
grapes with no seed but sea-foam,
Ivy in scupper-hole.
Aye, I, Acœtes, stood there,
and the god stood by me,
Water cutting under the keel,
Sea-break from stern forrards,[1]
wake running off from the bow,
And where was gunwale, there now was vine-trunk,
And tenthril[2] where cordage had been,
grape-leaves on the rowlocks,
Heavy vine on the oarshafts,
And, out of nothing, a breathing,
hot breath on my ankles,
Beasts like shadows in glass,
a furred tail upon nothingness.
Lynx-purr, and heathery smell of beasts,
where tar smell had been,
Sniff and pad-foot of beasts,
eye-glitter out of black air.[3]
The sky overshot, dry, with no tempest,
Sniff and pad-foot of beasts,
fur brushing my knee-skin,
Rustle of airy sheaths,
dry forms in the *æther*.[4]
And the ship like a keel in ship-yard,
slung like an ox in smith's sling,
Ribs stuck fast in the ways,
grape-cluster over pin-rack,
void air taking pelt.
Lifeless air become sinewed,
feline leisure of panthers,
Leopards sniffing the grape shoots by scupper-hole,
Crouched panthers by fore-hatch,
And the sea blue-deep about us,
green-ruddy in shadows,
And Lyæus.[5] "From now, Acœtes, my altars,

1. That is, forwards.
2. That is, tendril.
3. Lynxes or leopards were Dionysus's attendant beasts and drew his chariot.
4. Air (Latin).
5. Another name for Dionysus: "One who lightens burdens."

Fearing no bondage,
fearing no cat of the wood,
Safe with my lynxes,
feeding grapes to my leopards,
Olibanum[6] is my incense,
the vines grow in my homage."

The back-swell now smooth in the rudder-chains,
Black snout of a porpoise
where Lycabs[7] had been,
Fish-scales on the oarsmen.
And I worship.
I have seen what I have seen.
When they brought the boy I said:
"He has a god in him,
though I do not know which god."
And they kicked me into the fore-stays.
I have seen what I have seen:
Medon's face like the face of a dory,[8]
Arms shrunk into fins. And you, Pentheus,
Had as well listen to Tiresias, and to Cadmus,[9]
or your luck will go out of you.
Fish-scales over groin muscles,
lynx-purr amid sea . . .
And of a later year,
pale in the wine-red algæ,
If you will lean over the rock,
the coral face under wave-tinge,
Rose-paleness under water-shift,
Ileuthyeria, fair Dafne of sea-bords,[1]
The swimmer's arms turned to branches,
Who will say in what year,
fleeing what band of tritons,
The smooth brows, seen, and half seen,
now ivory stillness.

And So-shu churned in the sea, So-shu also,
using the long moon for a churn-stick . . .
Lithe turning of water,
sinews of Poseidon,
Black azure and hyaline,[2]
glass wave over Tyro,
Close cover, unstillness,
bright welter of wave-cords,
Then quiet water,

6. Frankincense (Latin).
7. That is, Lycabas, a member of the crew; he is the "ex-convict" of line 47.
8. Medon is another crewmember. *Dory:* fish resembling the golden pike.
9. The founder and first king of Thebes, and Pentheus's grandfather; Tiresias, the famous seer, lived there and prophesied in the marketplace. Both warned Pentheus to allow his subjects to worship Dionysus.
1. Ileuthyeria (Pound's invention) is described as a maiden who escapes pursuit by the "band of tritons" (mermen) by being changed into branching coral; Pound's model for this metamorphosis is Daphne, who escaped Apollo's ardor by being transformed into a laurel tree.
2. Glassy

quiet in the buff sands,
Sea-fowl stretching wing-joints,
splashing in rock-hollows and sand-hollows
In the wave-runs by the half-dune;
Glass-glint of wave in the tide-rips against sunlight,
pallor of Hesperus,[3]
Grey peak of the wave,
wave, colour of grape's pulp,

Olive grey in the near,
far, smoke grey of the rock-slide,
Salmon-pink wings of the fish-hawk
cast grey shadows in water,
The tower like a one-eyed great goose
cranes up out of the olive-grove,

And we have heard the fauns chiding Proteus[4]
in the smell of hay under the olive-trees,
And the frogs singing against the fauns
in the half-light.
And . . .

1917, 1925

VII[5]

Eleanor (she spoiled in a British climate)[6]
Ἕλανδρος and *Ἑλέπτολις*,[7] and poor old Homer
blind, blind as a bat,
Ear, ear for the sea-surge—; rattle of old men's voices;[8]
And then the phantom Rome, marble narrow for seats[9]
"Si pulvis nullus. . . ."
In chatter above the circus, "Nullum excute tamen."[1]
Then: file and candles, e li mestiers ecoutes,[2]
Scene—for the battle only,—but still scene,
Pennons and standards y cavals armatz[3]

3. The evening star.
4. A sea god who could change his shape at will; also famous for his knowledge. Faun, half men and half goats, were Roman deities of fields and herds.
5. This Canto, Pound's response to what he saw as the decadence of Edwardian England, was written in 1919 and may have influenced the tone and structure of Eliot's *Waste Land*, which was completed two years later. We reprint the original, 1921 version, subsequently much less revised than Cantos I and II.
6. Helen of Troy now blends into Eleanor of Aquitaine (1122–1204), who after her divorce from Louis VII of France married Henry, duke of Normandy, who soon became King Henry II of England.
7. *Hélandros, heléptolis* (Greek): destroyer of men and destroyer of cities; Aeschylus's punning epithets on the name of Helen of Troy. See note for Canto 2.11.
8. See Canto 2.13–22.
9. Ovid, in *The Art of Love*, points out that the narrow seats of the Colosseum force lovers to be close to each other. *Phantom:* that is, Rome is a shadow of Greece.
1. Even if there is no dust . . . brush it off (Latin). In this statement adapted from Ovid, the poet suggests this attention to a girl's clothes as an excuse to touch her.
2. And the heard mysteries (Old French); a reference to the Catholic Mass said before battle in the Middle Ages.
3. And horses arrayed for battle (Provençal); from a war song by the thirteenth-century troubadour Bertrand de Born, who praises Easter because the bright weather is good for battles.

Not mere succession of strokes, sightless narration,
To Dante's "ciocco,"[4] the brand struck in the game.
Un peu moisi, plancher plus bas que le jardin.[5]
Contre le lambris, fauteuil de paille,
Un vieux piano, et sous le baromètre . . . [6]
The old men's voices—beneath the columns of false marble,
And the walls tinted discreet, the modish, darkish green-blue,
Discreeter gilding, and the panelled wood
Not present, but suggested, for the leasehold is
Touched with an imprecision . . . about three squares;
The house a shade too solid, and the art
A shade off action, paintings a shade too thick.
And the great domed head, *con gli occhi onesti e tardi*[7]
Moves before me, phantom with weighted motion,
Grave incessu,[8] drinking the tone of things,
And the old voice lifts itself
weaving an endless sentence.
We also made ghostly visits, and the stair
That knew us, found us again on the turn of it,
Knocking at empty rooms, seeking a buried beauty;
And the sun-tanned gracious and well-formed fingers
Lift no latch of bent bronze, no Empire handle
Twists for the knocker's fall; no voice to answer.
A strange concierge, in place of the gouty-footed.
Sceptic against all this one seeks the living,
Stubborn against the fact. The wilted flowers
Brushed out a seven year since, of no effect.
Damn the partition! Paper, dark brown and stretched,
Flimsy and damned partition.
Ione, dead the long year,[9]
My lintel, and Liu Ch'e's lintel.[1]
Time blacked out with the rubber.
The Elysée[2] carries a name on
And the bus behind me gives me a date for peg;
Low ceiling and the Erard[3] and silver
These are in "time." Four chairs, the bow-front dresser,
The pannier[4] of the desk, cloth top sunk in.
"Beer-bottle on the statue's pediment!

4. Log (Italian). Dante (in *Paradiso* 18.100–105) describes the ascent of a thousand souls from Mars to Jupiter as like the innumerable sparks that leap out of a burning log when it is struck by a poker, and from which the foolish sometimes make predictions.
5. A bit mildewed, the floor lower than the garden (French). In this and the following two lines, Pound quotes from Gustave Flaubert's *A Simple Heart* (1877); the passage describes a commonplace French interior of the late nineteenth century.
6. Against the panelling a straw armchair, / An old piano, and under the barometer . . . (French).
7. With honest and slow eyes (Italian); quoted from *Purgatorio* 6.63, a passage in which Dante meets the ghost of Sordello, his fellow Italian (see Canto 2.1–3), who briefly acts as his guide. Pound is describing his countryman, novelist Henry James, who had recently died; according to a note in *The Analyst,* the rooms they visit are of the Polytechnic Institute in London, an old mansion converted into classrooms, where Pound lectured on Romance literature in 1910.
8. With heavy gait (Latin).
9. The title of an early Pound poem.
1. Another early Pound poem, "Liu Ch'e," is translated from the fourteenth-century Chinese poet; Pound alludes to the line "A wet leaf that clings to the threshold."
2. The Elysée Palace, the home of the president of France, carries on the name of Elysium, the place of the virtuous dead in Greek myth.
3. Famous French maker of pianos.
4. A "panier" is a basket in French.

"That, Fritz,[5] is the era, to-day against the past,
"Contemporary." And the passion endures.
Against their action, aromas; rooms, against chronicles.
Smaragdos, chrysolitos;[6] De Gama wore striped pants in Africa[7]
And "Mountains of the sea gave birth to troops,"[8]

Le vieux commode en acajou:[9]
        beer bottles of various strata.
But is she as dead as Tyro?[1] In seven years?
Ἑλέναυς, ἕλανδρος, ἑλέπτολις,[2]
The sea runs in the beach-groove, shaking the floated pebbles,
Eleanor!
        The scarlet curtain throws a less scarlet shadow;
Lamplight at Buovilla, e quel remir,[3]
        And all that day
Nicea[4] moved before me
And the cold gray air troubled her not
For all her naked beauty, bit not the tropic skin,
And the long slender feet lit on the curb's marge
And her moving height went before me,
        We alone having being.

And all that day, another day:
        Thin husks I had known as men,
Dry casques[5] of departed locusts
        speaking a shell of speech . . .
Propped between chairs and table . . .
Words like the locust-shells, moved by no inner being,
        A dryness calling for death.
Another day, between walls of a sham Mycenian,
"Toc"[6] sphinxes, sham-Memphis columns,
And beneath the jazz a cortex, a stiffness or stillness,
        The older shell, varnished to lemon colour,
Brown-yellow wood, and the no colour plaster,
Dry professorial talk . . .
        now stilling the ill beat music,

5. Pound's friend, the Dutch writer and art critic Fritz Vanderpyl, who was living in Paris.
6. That is, *chrysolithos*, or topazes. *Smaragdos:* emeralds. In one of Propertius's elegies (2.16.43), these jewels are types of imperishable beauty.
7. Pound parodies the *Lusiads*, an epic by the Portuguese poet Luis de Camoens (1524–1580), which describes the explorations of Vasco da Gama, presenting trivial details (such as da Gama's trousers) in a bombastic style.
8. A pseudoquotation, not actually from the *Lusiad* but a paraphrase of a line from Horace: "The mountains gave birth to a ridiculous mouse."
9. The old mahogany chest; again quoted from Flaubert's *A Simple Heart*.
1. An immortal sea nymph (see Canto 2), who has died with the ancient Greek civilization that invented her.
2. *Helénaus, hélandros, heléptolis* (Greek): destroyer of ships, destroyer of men, destroyer of cities; see note for line 2. The following line echoes Canto 2.10.
3. And which I gaze upon (Provençal); from the poem "Sweet Songs and Cries," by the twelfth-century Provençal poet Arnaut Daniel, who loved the wife of one Guillem de Buovilla. These words are from a couplet in which Daniel tells of his longing to kiss her and see her beautiful body by lamplight. Pound evokes her body by an allusion, "the scarlet curtain," to Ovid's simile describing the body of Atalanta flushed from running (*Metamorphoses* 10). Before she came to England, Eleanor of Aquitaine had been the object of a troubadour song, by Bernart de Ventadorn (1148–1195), who had joined her court.
4. That is, Helen of Troy, from a glancing allusion to Edgar Allan Poe's "To Helen" (1831): "Helen, thy beauty is to me / As those Nicean barks of yore."
5. Shells. Pound here uses the Neoplatonic concept that evil is not a positive force but an absence of being.
6. Imitation (French). The house has been decorated in the style of classical Greece and Egypt.

House expulsed by this house, but not extinguished.
        Square even shoulders and the satin skin,
Gone cheeks of the dancing woman,
        Still the old dead dry talk, gassed out
It is ten years gone, makes stiff about her a glass,
A petrification of air.
        The old room of the tawdry class asserts itself.
The young men, never!
        Only the husk of talk.
O voi che siete in piccioletta barca,[7]
Dido choked up with sobs for her Sicheus
Lies heavy in my arms, dead weight
        Drowning with tears, new Eros,[8]
And the life goes on, mooning upon bare hills;
Flame leaps from the hand, the rain is listless,
Yet drinks the thirst from our lips,
        solid as echo,
Passion to breed a form in shimmer of rain-blurr;
But Eros drowned, drowned, heavy-half dead with tears
        For dead Sicheus.
Life to make mock of motion:
For the husks, before me, move,
        The words rattle: shells given out by shells.

The live man, out of lands and prisons,
        shakes the dry pods,
Probes for old wills and friendships, and the big locust-casques
Bend to the tawdry table,
Lift up their spoons to mouths, put forks in cutlets,
And make sound like the sound of voices.
        Lorenzaccio
Being more live than they, more full of flames and voices.
Ma si morisse!
        Credesse caduto da se, ma si morisse.[9]
And the tall indifference moves,
        a more living shell,
Drift in the air of fate, dry phantom, but intact,
O Alessandro, chief and thrice warned,[1] watcher,
        Eternal watcher of things,
Of things, of men, of passions.
        Eyes floating in dry, dark air;

7. These words, which Canto 109 translates "You in the dinghy (*piccioletta*) astern there!" are from *Paradiso* 2.1. Dante, comparing *The Divine Comedy* with a ship that sails the main, warns his readers (who are following him in little boats) to put back to shore while they can, because he will sail uncharted seas. If his readers lose touch with him, they may drift forever, but if they keep up, they will see great and unknown marvels.

8. Dido, queen of Carthage, mourned her murdered husband, Sicheus, and would not remarry.

9. Lorenzo de Medici (1515–1547), also called Lorenzaccio, murdered his tyrannical cousin Alessandro, duke of Florence; Pound is inclined to approve the outrageous acts of men of action, because he believes that such men are necessary to civilization. Lines 114–15 are misquoted from the account of this murder in Benedetto Varchi's *Florentine History* (1547): "But if he should die! / It would [not!] be believed that he fell by himself, but if he should die!" (Italian). Lorenzo had planned to throw Alessandro from a high wall, but he wanted to be sure that he would not be charged with the murder. Pound has left out the crucial negative.

1. Alessandro had been warned about an attempt on his life.

E biondo,[2] with glass-gray iris, with an even side-fall of hair
The stiff, still features.

1921

From XIV[3]

* * *

The slough of unamiable liars,
    bog of stupidities,
malevolent stupidities, and stupidities,
the soil living pus, full of vermin,
dead maggots begetting live maggots,
    slum owners,
usurers squeezing crab-lice, pandars to authority,
pets-de-loup,[4] sitting on piles of stone books,
obscuring the texts with philology,
    hiding them under their persons,
the air without refuge of silence,
    the drift of lice, teething,
and above it the mouthing of orators,
    the arse-belching of preachers.
    And Invidia,[5]
the corruptio,[6] fœtor, fungus,
liquid animals, melted ossifications,
slow rot, fœtid combustion,
    chewed cigar-butts, without dignity, without tragedy,
. . . . .m Episcopus,[7] waving a condom full of black-beetles,
monopolists, obstructors of knowledge,
    obstructors of distribution.

1930

XLV

With *Usura*[8]
With usura hath no man a house of good stone
each block cut smooth and well fitting
that design might cover their face,

2. He is blond (Italian). This may be taken from *Inferno* 12.110, in which Dante describes the tyrant Obizzo da Esti, who murdered his stepson.
3. From the first of the "Hell Cantos" (14–15, with 16 as purgatory).
4. Scholars; literally, wolf farts (French).
5. Envy (Latin).
6. Corruption (Latin).
7. Bishop (Latin). Each ellipsis marks a letter in the elided proper name.
8. Usury (Latin); the lending of money at excessive interest. "N.B. Usury: A charge for the use of purchasing power, levied without regard to production; often without regard to the possibilities of production. (Hence the failure of the Medici bank)" [Pound's note]. Pound believed that usury allowed banks to accumulate excessive wealth, alienated workers from their creations, and prevented the realization of an earthly paradise. For Pound, the legalization of usury in the Reformation changed the way people related to the world around them: beauty, nature, and sex were valued no longer in themselves but for potential profit.

with usura
hath no man a painted paradise on his church wall
harpes et luz[9]
or where virgin receiveth message
and halo projects from incision,
with usura
seeth no man Gonzaga his heirs and his concubines[1]
no picture is made to endure nor to live with
but it is made to sell and sell quickly
with usura, sin against nature,
is thy bread ever more of stale rags
is thy bread dry as paper,
with no mountain wheat, no strong flour
with usura the line grows thick
with usura is no clear demarcation
and no man can find site for his dwelling.
Stonecutter is kept from his stone
weaver is kept from his loom
WITH USURA
wool comes not to market
sheep bringeth no gain with usura
Usura is a murrain,[2] usura
blunteth the needle in the maid's hand
and stoppeth the spinner's cunning. Pietro Lombardo[3]
came not by usura
Duccio[4] came not by usura
nor Pier della Francesca; Zuan Bellin' not by usura
nor was 'La Calunnia'[5] painted.
Came not by usura Angelico; came not Ambrogio Praedis,
Came no church of cut stone signed: *Adamo me fecit.*[6]
Not by usura St Trophime
Not by usura Saint Hilaire,[7]
Usura rusteth the chisel
It rusteth the craft and the craftsman
It gnaweth the thread in the loom
None learneth to weave gold in her pattern;
Azure hath a canker by usura; cramoisi[8] is unbroidered
Emerald findeth no Memling[9]
Usura slayeth the child in the womb
It stayeth the young man's courting
It hath brought palsey to bed, lyeth

9. From the line "Painted paradise where there are harps and lutes" (in Old French, "Paradis paint, où sont harpes et luz"), spoken by the poet's mother, in a poem of the *Grand Testament,* by French poet François Villon (1431–1463?).
1. *Gonzaga, His Heirs and His Concubines:* title of Andrea Mantegna's painting of Francesco Gonzaga, a powerful patron-lord from Mantua.
2. Plague.
3. Italian sculptor (1435–1515). The fifteenth-century artists listed in the poem were financed by patrons and were therefore not likely concerned with the salability of their work.
4. Agostino di Duccio (1418?–1481), Italian sculptor.
5. Calumny (Italian); allegorical painting by Sandro Botticelli (1444–1510). Piero della Francesca (1420–1492): Italian painter. *Zuan Bellin':* Giovanni Bellini (1430–1516), Venetian painter.
6. Adam made me (Latin); a sculptor's inscription on a column in the Church of San Zeno, in Verona, Italy; as contrasted with mass-produced artifacts. Fra Angelico (1387–1455) and Ambrogio Praedis (1455?–1508), Italian painters.
7. Church in Poitiers, France. *St Trophime:* church in Arles, France.
8. Crimson cloth (French).
9. Hans Memling (1430?–1495), Flemish painter.

between the young bride and her bridegroom
CONTRA NATURAM[1]
They have brought whores for Eleusis[2]
Corpses are set to banquet
at behest of usura.

1937

LXXXI

Zeus lies in Ceres' bosom[3]
Taishan[4] is attended of loves
under Cythera,[5] before sunrise
and he said: "Hay aquí mucho catolicismo—(sounded catoli*th*ismo)
y muy poco reliHion"[6]
and he said: "Yo creo que los reyes desaparecen"[7]
(Kings will, I think, disappear)
That was Padre José Elizondo[8]
in 1906 and in 1917
or about 1917
and Dolores said: "Come pan, niño," eat bread, me lad
Sargent[9] had painted her
before he descended
(i.e. if he descended)
but in those days he did thumb sketches,
impressions of the Velásquez in the Museo del Prado
and books cost a peseta,[1]
brass candlesticks in proportion,
hot wind came from the marshes
and death-chill from the mountains.
And later Bowers[2] wrote: "but such hatred,
I had never conceived such"
and the London reds wouldn't show up his friends
(i.e. friends of Franco
working in London) and in Alcázar[3]
forty years gone, they said: go back to the station to eat
you can sleep here for a peseta"

1. Against nature (Latin); a phrase used to describe usury in Aristotle's *Politics*.
2. Town in ancient Greece where spring fertility rites were celebrated.
3. Zeus, the ruler of the Greek gods, is sometimes said to have married his sister Ceres, the goddess of agriculture and natural fertility.
4. A sacred mountain in China, which Pound identified with a cone-shaped mountain visible from his cage in the Disciplinary Training Center near Pisa.
5. Aphrodite, Greek goddess of love; Cythera was an island sacred to her.
6. There is much Catholicism here and very little religion (Spanish).
7. Translated in the next line.
8. A Spanish priest who had helped Pound obtain a photostat of manuscripts by Guido Cavalcanti from the Escorial, the palace of the Spanish kings.
9. American painter John Singer Sargent (1856–1925) was much influenced by Velasquez's paintings even before 1880, when he traveled to Spain and copied *The Maids of Honor* and other paintings in Madrid's Prado Museum. Dolores is presumably the subject of one of Sargent's Spanish paintings; he later specialized in portraits.
1. Basic Spanish monetary unit, like the dollar.
2. Claude Gernade Bowers (1878–1958) was the American ambassador to Spain during the Spanish Civil War (1936–39), won by the right-wing faction led by Francisco Franco.
3. Alcazar de San Juan, a town in central Spain.

goat bells tinkled all night
and the hostess grinned: Eso es luto, *haw!*
mi marido es muerto[4]
(it is mourning, my husband is dead)
when she gave me paper to write on
with a black border half an inch or more deep,
say ⅝ths, of the locanda[5]
"We call *all* foreigners frenchies"
and the egg broke in Cabranez' pocket,
thus making history.[6] Basil says
they beat drums for three days
till all the drumheads were busted
(simple village fiesta)
and as for his life in the Canaries . . .[7]
Possum[8] observed that the local portagoose[9] folk dance
was danced by the same dancers in divers localities
in political welcome . . .
the technique of demonstration
Cole studied that (not G.D.H., Horace)[1]
"You will find" said old André Spire,[2]
that every man on that board (Crédit Agricole)[3]
has a brother-in-law.
"You the one, I the few"
said John Adams[4]
speaking of fears in the abstract
to his volatile friend Mr. Jefferson.
(To break the pentameter, that was the first heave)
or as Jo Bard[5] says: they never speak to each other,
if it is baker and concierge visibly
it is La Rochefoucauld and de Maintenon audibly.[6]
"Te cavero le budella"
"La corata a te"[7]
In less than a geological epoch
said Henry Mencken[8]

4. Translated in the following line.
5. Inn or boarding house (Italian).
6. Perhaps a joke involving one of Pound's Spanish friends; the meaning of this allusion has not been traced.
7. Basil Bunting (1900–1985), English poet and Pound's friend, lived in the Canary Islands (a Spanish possession off the northwest coast of Africa) from 1933 to 1936. Visiting a village in Argon, Spain, he observed an Easter ritual in which costumed villagers beat large drums during Jesus' harrowing of Hell, from Good Friday to Easter Sunday (Bunting, "The Village Fiesta").
8. T. S. Eliot (author of *Old Possum's Book of Practical Cats*).
9. Portuguese.
1. Horace Cole (b. 1874): a writer for magazines and a contributor to *20th Century Business Practice*. G. D. H. Cole (1880–1959): English economist and novelist.
2. André Spire (1868–1966), French writer and advocate of Zionism.
3. The French agricultural bank; Cole sat on its board.
4. Sixth U.S. president (1767–1848).
5. Joseph Bard (1882–1975), Hungarian-born British writer and Pound's friend.
6. The Duc de la Rochefoucauld (1747–1827) and Madame de Maintenon (1635–1719), here presented not as historical figures but as exemplars of elegant prose style, which, Pound indicates, is inherent in the French language.
7. I'll cut your guts out! / And I'll tear the liver out of you! (Italian). In Canto 10 of Dante's *Inferno*, this passage is part of an exchange between Sigismondo Malatesta (1417–1468) and his sworn enemy Federigo d'Urbino (1422–1482).
8. ". . . I believe that all schemes of monetary reform collide inevitably with the nature of man in the mass. He can't be convinced in anything less than a geological epoch" (quoted as part of a letter from American author H. L. Mencken [1880–1959] to Pound in *Guide to Kulchur*). Pound observed, "Above statement does not invalidate geological process."

"Some cook, some do not cook
some things cannot be altered"
Ἰυγξ . . . . . ’εμὸν ποτί δῶμα τὸν ἄνδρα[9]
What counts is the cultural level,
thank Benin[1] for this table ex packing box
"doan yu tell no one I made it"
from a mask fine as any in Frankfurt
"It'll get you offn th' groun"
Light as the branch of Kuanon[2]
And at first disappointed with shoddy
the bare ram-shackle quais, but then saw the
high buggy wheels
and was reconciled,
George Santayana[3] arriving in the port of Boston
and kept to the end of his life that faint *thethear*[4]
of the Spaniard
as a grace quasi imperceptible
as did Muss the v or υ of Romagna[5]
and said the grief was a full act
repeated for each new condoleress
working up to a climax.[6]
And George Horace[7] said he wd/ "get Beveridge" (Senator)
Beveridge wouldn't talk and he wouldn't write for the papers
but George got him by campin' in his hotel
and assailin' him at lunch breakfast an' dinner
three articles
and my ole man went on hoein' corn
while George was a-tellin' him,
come across a vacant lot
where you'd occasionally see a wild rabbit
or mebbe only a loose one
AOI![8]
a leaf in the current
at my grates no Althea[9]

Libretto[1]

Yet
Ere the season died a-cold

9. *Iünx, emòn poti doma ton ándra* (Greek): Little wheel, [bring back] that man to my house. From the second Idyll of Theocritus, a dramatic monologue in which a girl uses a magic wheel to cast a spell on her unfaithful lover.
1. Pound's nickname for Henry Hudson Edwards, a GI and guard at the DTC near Pisa who made Pound a writing table. Pound thought the black man's face resembled the bronze masks of Benin in Nigeria, collected by Leo Frobenius (1873–1938), a German anthropologist, at Frankfurt's Institute for Cultural Morphology.
2. Japanese name for Kuan-yin, the Chinese goddess of mercy.
3. Spanish-born American philosopher (1863–1952); lines 71–78 are based on his *Autobiography*.
4. *Cecear* (Spanish) means the Castilian pronunciation of the soft *c*, with a lisp.
5. Benito Mussolini's dialect, in which the sound *w* was pronounced as *v*. The Italian Fascist leader, executed on April 28, 1945, is elegized in Canto 74.
6. Another reference to a description in Santayana's *Autobiography*.
7. George Horace Lorimer (1868–1937), editor of the *Saturday Evening Post* for over thirty-five years, was trying to interview Albert Jeremiah Beveridge (1862–1927), American senator and historian.
8. An exclamation, perhaps of grief, that occurs repeatedly in the Oxford manuscript of the *Song of Roland* (c. 1098–1100).
9. From Richard Lovelace's poem "To Althea, from Prison" (1649): "When Love with unconfined wings / Hovers within my Gates; / And my divine Althea brings / To whisper at the grates."
1. A text to be sung to music.

Borne upon a zephyr's shoulder
I rose through the aureate sky
Lawes and Jenkyns guard thy rest
Dolmetsch ever be thy guest,
Has he tempered the viol's[2] wood
To enforce both the grave and the acute?
Has he curved us the bowl of the lute?
Lawes and Jenkyns guard thy rest
Dolmetsch ever be thy guest
Hast 'ou fashioned so airy a mood
To draw up leaf from the root?
Hast 'ou found a cloud so light
As seemed neither mist nor shade?

Then resolve me, tell me aright
If Waller sang or Dowland[3] played.

Your eyen two wol sleye me sodenly
I may the beauté of hem nat susteyne[4]

And for 180 years almost nothing.

Ed ascoltando al leggier mormorio[5]
there came new subtlety of eyes into my tent,
whether of spirit or hypostasis,[6]
but what the blindfold hides
or at carneval
nor any pair showed anger
Saw but the eyes and stance between the eyes,
colour, diastasis,[7]
careless or unaware it had not the
whole tent's room
nor was place for the full Ειδὼς[8]
interpass, penetrate
casting but shade beyond the other lights
sky's clear
night's sea
green of the mountain pool
shone from the unmasked eyes in half-mask's space.
What thou lovest well remains,
the rest is dross
What thou lov'st well shall not be reft from thee
What thou lov'st well is thy true heritage

2. *Viol:* stringed instrument. Henry Lawes (1596–1662) and John Jenkins (1592–1678): English composers; Lawes set to music "Go Lovely Rose," by English poet Edmund Waller (1606–1687). (Cf. "Envoi," above.) Arnold Dolmetsch (1858–1940): French musicologist who made reconstructions of old instruments and advocated a revival of pre-Baroque music.
3. John Dowland (1563–1626), composer and lute player.
4. From Chaucer's "Merciles Beauté": "Your two eyes will slay me quickly; I may not withstand their beauty."
5. And listening to the light murmur (Italian). "Not a quotation," according to Pound, "merely the author using handy language."
6. The substance of the godhead; here, possibly Aphrodite.
7. Separation between the eyes (their "stance"). Cf. *Hugh Selwyn Mauberley,* lines 286–88.
8. *Eidos* (Greek): knowing.

Whose world, or mine or theirs
                    or is it of none?
First came the seen, then thus the palpable
        Elysium, though it were in the halls of hell,
What thou lovest well is thy true heritage
What thou lov'st well shall not be reft from thee

The ant's a centaur in his dragon world.
Pull down thy vanity,[9] it is not man
Made courage, or made order, or made grace,
        Pull down thy vanity, I say pull down.
Learn of the green world what can be thy place
In scaled invention or true artistry,
Pull down thy vanity,
                Paquin pull down!
The green casque[1] has outdone your elegance.

"Master thyself, then others shall thee beare"[2]
        Pull down thy vanity
Thou art a beaten dog beneath the hail,
A swollen magpie in a fitful sun,
Half black half white
Nor knowst'ou wing from tail
Pull down thy vanity
                How mean thy hates
Fostered in falsity,
                Pull down thy vanity,
Rathe[3] to destroy, niggard in charity,
Pull down thy vanity,
                I say pull down.

But to have done instead of not doing
                this is not vanity
To have, with decency, knocked
That a Blunt[4] should open
            To have gathered from the air a live tradition
or from a fine old eye the unconquered flame
This is not vanity.
        Here error is all in the not done,
all in the diffidence that faltered . . .

1948

9. The tone and language of the following passage are reminiscent of Ecclesiastes 1: "Saith the preacher, vanity of vanities, all is vanity."
1. The shell of a green insect. Pound had ended the previous Canto with the words "sunset grand couturier." *Paquin:* Parisian dress designer.
2. A variation on Chaucer's "Ballade of Good Counsel": "Subdue thyself, and others thee shall hear."
3. Quick (Middle English).
4. Wilfred Scawen Blunt (1840–1922), English poet who opposed British imperialism. In 1914, Pound and Yeats organized a testimonial dinner for him at his house; Pound's address on the occasion reads in part: "We who are little given to respect, / Respect you."

CXVI[5]

Came Neptunus[6]
his mind leaping
like dolphins,
These concepts the human mind has attained.
To make Cosmos—
To achieve the possible—
Muss.,[7] wrecked for an error,
But the record
the palimpsest—
a little light
in great darkness—
cuniculi—[8]
An old "crank" dead in Virginia.
Unprepared young burdened with records,
The vision of the Madonna
above the cigar butts
and over the portal.
"Have made a mass of laws"
(mucchio di leggi)[9]
Litterae nihil sanantes[1]
Justinian's,[2]
a tangle of works unfinished.

I have brought the great ball of crystal;
who can lift it?
Can you enter the great acorn of light?[3]
But the beauty is not the madness
Tho' my errors and wrecks lie about me.
And I am not a demigod,
I cannot make it cohere.
If love be not in the house there is nothing.
The voice of famine unheard.
How came beauty against this blackness,
Twice beauty under the elms—
To be saved by squirrels and bluejays?
"plus j'aime le chien"[4]
Ariadne.[5]

5. One of the final "Drafts and Fragments" of *The Cantos*.
6. *Neptune:* sea god of Roman mythology.
7. Pound's nickname for Benito Mussolini (1883–1945), Fascist dictator of Italy, whom Pound admired and, because of his promises of economic reform, likened to Thomas Jefferson. His "error" was likely his alliance with Hitler.
8. Underground passages or canals (Italian); Pound was interested in an Italian scholar's having discovered irrigation canals near Rome older than the accepted date of the birth of civilization in Italy.
9. Mass of laws (Italian); a phrase repeated from Canto 87, in which it appears to be quoted from Mussolini.
1. Writings that cure nothing (Latin); quoted from a letter from John Adams to Thomas Jefferson.
2. Justinian I (c. 482–565), Roman emperor responsible for the codification of Roman law.
3. Image from Neoplatonic philosophy of light.
4. The more I love dogs (French). Remark attributed to Jeanne-Marie Rolande (1754–1793): "The more I know men the more I love dogs."
5. In classical mythology, the daughter of King Minos who helped Theseus kill the Minotaur and escape from the labyrinth. Also, the holy of holies at the center of the labyrinth.

Disney against the metaphysicals,
and Laforgue more than they thought in him,
Spire thanked me in proposito[6]
And I have learned more from Jules
(Jules Laforgue) since then
deeps in him,
and Linnaeus.[7]
chi crescerà i nostri—[8]
but about that terzo[9]
third heaven,
that Venere,[1]
again is all "paradiso"
a nice quiet paradise
over the shambles,
and some climbing
before the take-off,
to "see again,"
the verb is "see," not "walk on"
i.e. it coheres all right
even if my notes do not cohere.
Many errors,
a little rightness,
to excuse his hell
and my paradiso.
And as to why they go wrong,
thinking of rightness
And as to who will copy this palimpsest?
al poco giorno
ed al gran cerchio d'ombra[2]
But to affirm the gold thread in the pattern
(Torcello)[3]
al Vicolo d'oro[4]
(Tigullio).[5]
To confess wrong without losing rightness:
Charity I have had sometimes,
I cannot make it flow thru.
A little light, like a rushlight
to lead back to splendour.

1969

6. *In proposito*: for the intention (Italian). Andre Spire (1868–1966): French poet. Walt Disney (1901–1966): American filmmaker, animator, and entrepreneur. Jules Laforgue (1860–1887): French Symbolist poet.
7. Carolus Linnaeus (1707–1778), Swedish scientist who invented the taxonomic system to classify plant and animal species.
8. Who will increase (Italian); from Dante, *Paradiso* 5.105: "Behold the man who will increase our loves."
9. Third (Italian).
1. Venus (Italian).
2. In the small hours of the day with the great circle of shadow (Italian); first line of a poem by Dante.
3. Sunken city in the Venetian Lagoon where two palaces and a cathedral are preserved.
4. Street in Rapallo where a cross of blue sky can be seen.
5. Gulf below Rapallo.

CXX[6]

I have tried to write Paradise

Do not move
    Let the wind speak
        that is paradise.

Let the Gods forgive what I
        have made
Let those I love try to forgive
        what I have made.

1969

6. This Canto is incomplete.

Siegfried Sassoon
1886–1967

Siegfried Sassoon was born into a world of leisured ease and country pleasures, a privileged world that in retrospect he transformed into a timeless Eden. This quiet world exploded in 1914, and Sassoon served in the British army for four and a half years. During this period, he wrote the short satirical poems for which he is best remembered.

He was born on September 8, 1886, in London. His father was descended from a prosperous family of Sephardic Jews, which had made its fortune in the Middle East and India; Sassoon later attributed his prophetic zeal to his Jewish ancestry. His mother was an Anglican and came from English gentry. His parents separated when Sassoon was a child; his father died soon thereafter, and he was raised by his mother. He was educated at Marlborough Grammar School and at Clare College, Cambridge, and then spent a few years in London; Sassoon was an attractive young man, well connected and comfortably situated, and his main interests were hunting and poetry. The most interesting of his prewar poems is a long narrative, *The Daffodil Murderer,* a parody that was a popular success thanks to its treatment of low life and its forthright language. Sassoon was taken up by Sir Edward Marsh, a patron of the arts, and for a time figured in the collections of Georgian poetry Marsh began to publish in 1912.

On August 1, 1914, a few days before England declared war, Sassoon enlisted. He went to France as a second lieutenant in the Royal Welch Fusiliers, the same infantry regiment in which the poets Robert Graves and David Jones served. His first war poems were written under the enchantment of a chivalric ideal. In "The Dragon and the Undying" he writes, "they are fortunate who fight / For gleaming landscapes swept and shafted / And crowned by cloud pavilions white." Graves, a fellow officer, showed him his own poems about the war, and Sassoon objected that they were too "realistic"; but he soon changed his mind about the war and the proper way to write about it. He set himself the task of observing the war and his reactions to it. He wrote Edward Marsh: "I am going up to the trenches very shortly; . . . and I mean to suck in all I can when I get up there. I am always trying to impress things on my memory, and make as many notes as I can" (quoted in Robert H. Ross, *The Georgian Revolt,* 1965). Two collections of Sassoon's poems appeared during the war: *The Old Huntsman* (1917) and *Counter Attack* (1918). In 1917, Sassoon was wounded and was sent home; disgusted with the war and with the civilians who were profiting from it financially and emotionally, he threw the ribbon of his Military Cross into the sea and wrote a widely circulated letter of protest that could have resulted in a court martial. But Graves interceded on his behalf, arguing that Sassoon was suffering from shell shock. Judged to be "temporarily insane," Sassoon was sent to a hospital at Craiglockhart, near Edinburgh, where he became friends with the poet Wilfred Owen. Sassoon eventually returned to France, where he was wounded a second time.

When the war was over, Sassoon, a declared pacifist, toured the United States, reading his poems and speaking against war. He entered into homosexual relationships, one with a younger soldier that lasted six years. Although he continued to write poetry, his best later work was a three-volume fictionalized autobiography—*Memoirs of a Fox-Hunting Man* (1928), *Memoirs of an Infantry Officer* (1930), and *Sherston's Progress* (1936)—and several volumes of undisguised autobiography. To the surprise of many, Sassoon married in 1933 and became a Roman Catholic in 1957.

Sassoon began as a social and poetic radical; in the trenches, he dreamed that one day he and Graves would "scandalize the jolly old Gosses and Stracheys," the established literary figures of their day (Graves, *Goodbye to All That,* 1969). Once this wartime exuberance was spent, Sassoon's views of poetry turned out to be old-fashioned; he preferred straightforward, sincere, emotional verse to modernist indirection and formal fragmentation. But his best poems are not without artful obliquity. Emotion is nakedly expressed in "Repression of War Experience" ("O Christ, I want to go out / And screech at them to stop—I'm going crazy / I'm going stark, staring mad because of the guns"), but the poem erupts in this climactic utterance only after the speaker has tried repeatedly to deny his feelings. Sassoon's poems are typically built around ironic contrasts. He arranges confrontations between a nostalgic poetic vocabulary ("Soldiers are citizens of death's grey land") and the grim particulars of the war (the "soft, unanswering heap" of a corpse, the soldiers "in foul dug-outs, gnawed by rats"). Everyday speech—sometimes slang—in colloquial rhythms is set against the war's unspeakable and shocking singularity. Formal regularity—neat rhymes and iambic or anapestic rhythms—often contrasts with the war chaos and slaughter it cannot contain. Another contrast, equally grim, is between the horror of battle and the attitude of civilians who send their sons off to war and then enjoy the carnage at a safe distance:

> I'd like to see a Tank come down the stalls,
> Lurching to rag-time tunes, or 'Home, sweet Home',
> And there'd be no more jokes in Music-halls
> To mock the riddled corpses round Bapaume. (" 'Blighters' ")

To His Dead Body

When roaring gloom surged inward and you cried,
Groping for friendly hands, and clutched, and died,
Like racing smoke, swift from your lolling head
Phantoms of thought and memory thinned and fled.

Yet, though my dreams that throng the darkened stair
Can bring me no report of how you fare,

Safe quit of wars, I speed you on your way
Up lonely, glimmering fields to find new day,
Slow-rising, saintless, confident and kind—
Dear, red-faced father God who lit your mind.

1916

'Blighters'

The House is crammed: tier beyond tier they grin
And cackle at the Show, while prancing ranks
Of harlots shrill the chorus, drunk with din;
'We're sure the Kaiser loves the dear old Tanks!'

I'd like to see a Tank come down the stalls,[1]
Lurching to rag-time tunes, or 'Home, sweet Home',
And there'd be no more jokes in Music-halls
To mock the riddled corpses round Bapaume.[2]

1917

The Rear-Guard

(Hindenburg Line, April 1917)[3]

Groping along the tunnel, step by step,
He winked his prying torch with patching glare
From side to side, and sniffed the unwholesome air.

Tins, boxes, bottles, shapes too vague to know;
A mirror smashed, the mattress from a bed;
And he, exploring fifty feet below
The rosy gloom of battle overhead.

Tripping, he grabbed the wall; saw some one lie
Humped at his feet, half-hidden by a rug,
And stooped to give the sleeper's arm a tug.
'I'm looking for headquarters.' No reply.
'God blast your neck!' (For days he'd had no sleep,)
'Get up and guide me through this stinking place.'
Savage, he kicked a soft, unanswering heap,
And flashed his beam across the livid face
Terribly glaring up, whose eyes yet wore

1. Orchestra seats in a theater or music hall.
2. A town in northern France, one of the main objectives in the costly but successful Allied offensive against the Hindenburg Line in 1918 (see "The Rear-Guard").
3. The Hindenburg Line (named for the German chief of staff) was the last and strongest line of German defensive trenches; it extended about thirty-five miles across northern France and was not broken until August 1918. April 1917 was a low point in the fortunes of the British Army in France.

Agony dying hard ten days before;
And fists of fingers clutched a blackening wound.

Alone he staggered on until he found
Dawn's ghost that filtered down a shafted stair
To the dazed, muttering creatures underground
Who hear the boom of shells in muffled sound.
At last, with sweat of horror in his hair,
He climbed through darkness to the twilight air,
Unloading hell behind him step by step.

1918

Dreamers

Soldiers are citizens of death's grey land,
Drawing no dividend from time's to-morrows.
In the great hour of destiny they stand,
Each with his feuds, and jealousies, and sorrows.
Soldiers are sworn to action; they must win
Some flaming, fatal climax with their lives.
Soldiers are dreamers; when the guns begin
They think of firelit homes, clean beds and wives.

I see them in foul dug-outs, gnawed by rats,
And in the ruined trenches, lashed with rain,
Dreaming of things they did with balls and bats,
And mocked by hopeless longing to regain
Bank-holidays,[4] and picture shows, and spats,
And going to the office in the train.

1918

The General

'Good-morning; good-morning!' the General said
When we met him last week on our way to the line.
Now the soldiers he smiled at are most of 'em dead,
And we're cursing his staff for incompetent swine.
'He's a cheery old card,' grunted Harry to Jack
As they slogged up to Arras[5] with rifle and pack.

• • •

But he did for them both by his plan of attack.

1918

4. National holidays in Great Britain.
5. A city in northern France, in the front line during most of World War I. The British assault against the Germans at the Western Front, on April 9, 1917, was known as the Battle of Arras.

Repression of War Experience

Now light the candles; one; two; there's a moth;
What silly beggars they are to blunder in
And scorch their wings with glory, liquid flame—
No, no, not that,—it's bad to think of war,
When thoughts you've gagged all day come back to scare you;
And it's been proved that soldiers don't go mad
Unless they lose control of ugly thoughts
That drive them out to jabber among the trees.

Now light your pipe; look, what a steady hand.
Draw a deep breath; stop thinking; count fifteen,
And you're as right as rain . . .
                    Why won't it rain? . . .
I wish there'd be a thunder-storm to-night,
With bucketsful of water to sluice the dark,
And make the roses hang their dripping heads.
Books; what a jolly company they are,
Standing so quiet and patient on their shelves,
Dressed in dim brown, and black, and white, and green,
And every kind of colour. Which will you read?
Come on; O *do* read something; they're so wise.
I tell you all the wisdom of the world
Is waiting for you on those shelves; and yet
You sit and gnaw your nails, and let your pipe out,
And listen to the silence: on the ceiling
There's one big, dizzy moth that bumps and flutters;
And in the breathless air outside the house
The garden waits for something that delays.
There must be crowds of ghosts among the trees,—
Not people killed in battle,—they're in France,—
But horrible shapes in shrouds—old men who died
Slow, natural deaths,—old men with ugly souls,
Who wore their bodies out with nasty sins.

• • • •

You're quiet and peaceful, summering safe at home;
You'd never think there was a bloody war on! . . .
O yes, you would . . . why, you can hear the guns.
Hark! Thud, thud, thud,—quite soft . . . they never cease—
Those whispering guns—O Christ, I want to go out
And screech at them to stop—I'm going crazy;
I'm going stark, staring mad because of the guns.

1918

Everyone Sang

Everyone suddenly burst out singing;
And I was filled with such delight
As prisoned birds must find in freedom,
Winging wildly across the white
Orchards and dark-green fields; on—on—and out of sight.

Everyone's voice was suddenly lifted;
And beauty came like the setting sun:
My heart was shaken with tears; and horror
Drifted away . . . O, but Everyone
Was a bird; and the song was wordless; the singing will never be done.

1919

On Passing the New Menin Gate[6]

Who will remember, passing through this Gate,
The unheroic Dead who fed the guns?
Who shall absolve the foulness of their fate,—
Those doomed, conscripted, unvictorious ones?
  Crudely renewed, the Salient[7] holds its own.
  Paid are its dim defenders by this pomp;
  Paid, with a pile of peace-complacent stone,
  The armies who endured that sullen swamp.

Here was the world's worst wound. And here with pride
'Their name liveth for ever,' the Gateway claims.
Was ever an immolation so belied
As these intolerably nameless names?
Well might the Dead who struggled in the slime
Rise and deride this sepulchre of crime.

1928

6. The names of 54,889 men are engraved on this World War I memorial in Belgium.

7. Protruding part of a line of defensive trenches, especially vulnerable to attack.

H. D. (Hilda Doolittle) 1886–1961

H. D.'s "special form of the mode of Imagism—cold, 'Greek,' fast, and enclosed—has become one of the ordinary resources of the poetic language," remarked the American poet and critic R. P. Blackmur; "it is a regular means of putting down words so that they will keep" (*Language as Gesture,* 1952). Like such modernist friends and contemporaries as Ezra Pound, T. S. Eliot, and William Carlos Williams, H. D. tried to discover how few words are required to make a poem, in revolt against the comparative excess and sentimentality of Victorian verse. Her chiseled, early poems, often modeled on fragments of classical verse and exploiting that quality of fragmentariness, prove that less can be more and that implication is an all-important source of energy in poetry.

H. D.'s early work, often seen as quintessentially Imagist, helped inspire Pound's influential pronouncements about direct, laconic, unadorned poetry. Poems such as "Oread," "Sea Rose," "Garden," and "Sea Violet" are built around a central image, which is presented with immediacy, economy, and precision. This is not to say that H. D.'s early poems lack movement or passion. They are often fervent exclamations in the face of, and in praise of, actuality, what is seen, what is there. "Oread," cast in the second person like many of these poems, moves dynamically and rhapsodically from one short line to the next, from the juxtaposition of pine-covered mountain and sea to their coalescence ("pools of fir"). Often, the poet appears in the role of a priest who has come to worship and celebrate a natural event. She prays that the event—the sea, the heat of the day, any item of real or imagined life—will overwhelm her. Through the ritual of her verse, she seeks an ecstatic loss of self, not unlike the lyric ecstasies of her treasured classical poet, Sappho. Invoking flowers in "Sea Rose," "Garden," and "Sea Violet," H. D. describes a complex emotional state that mingles toughness and vulnerability, much like the androgynous poems she is fashioning—tender but strong, buffeted but enduring, responsive but hard, "cut in rock." Though ostensibly about nature, these poems rethink traditional polarities of gender.

H. D. often returns to such traditional female archetypes as the rose, the lily, Helen of Troy, Leda, and the Virgin Mary. Her engagements with this traditional iconography are revisionary. Her rose is not an idealized symbol of the feminine other, but natural and time bound. Although her poem "Helen" recalls earlier depictions of this paradigmatic beauty as the bleached-out object of idolatry, H. D. interrogates this idealization, suggesting that it culminates in hatred, death, and destructiveness.

In the three long, meditative poems of *Trilogy* (1973), written under the pressure of the London bombings she endured in World War II, H. D.'s art becomes more expansive, syncretist, and mythopoeic. Fusing present-day London with the ancient world, she uses psychoanalysis, astrology, numerology, and the mythologies of Greece and Egypt to come to terms with twentieth-century disaster. Her quest for personal, cultural, and gender rebirth begins in the trilogy's first book, *The Walls Do Not Fall* (1944); she hopes that even in the trying "outer circumstance" of war, she can beget a new, pearl-like self. As poet-prophet, she tries "to hatch butterflies" from war, art, and language—"the meaning that words hide."

In these poems, H. D. searches for feminine archetypes of power and sustenance. To this end, in the second book of the war trilogy, *Tribute to the Angels* (1945), she surveys an array of Western artistic images of the Virgin Mary, but she pares away from these what are, in her view, images of female subordination, dependence, and entrapment. She envisions a "Lady" who is, in contrast to the traditional images, not "bowed down," "trapped," "frozen," "shut up," or "imprisoned." H. D.'s imagined Lady, who blends the

Christian Virgin with cross-cultural archetypes of the Mother Goddess, represents a spirit of independent female power and creativity, reborn from the chrysalis of tradition. The Lady's sacred book is not "the tome of ancient wisdom" but "the unwritten volume of the new," akin to the book of female potentiality that the poet is writing.

Hilda Doolittle was born on September 10, 1886, in Bethlehem, Pennsylvania. Her father was a professor of mathematics and astronomy at Lehigh University and later at the University of Pennsylvania; her mother was an artist. Growing up in a small Moravian community, she was educated at private schools in Philadelphia and studied at Bryn Mawr College for a time, but she left in her sophomore year. Williams remembered her in those early years as "wild," "angular," displaying "a provocative indifference to rule and order" (*Autobiography*). In 1911, she went to Europe for what she thought would be a brief summer's stay. In England, she renewed her friendship with Pound, to whom she had been briefly engaged, and he encouraged her to write. She had never heard of free verse, H. D. recalled, "till I was 'discovered' . . . by Ezra Pound. Ezra Pound was very kind and used to bring me (literally) armfuls of books to read. . . . I did a few poems that I don't think Ezra liked . . . but later he was beautiful about my first authentic verses, . . . and sent my poems in for me to Miss Monroe [the editor of *Poetry* magazine]. He signed them for me 'H. D., Imagiste.' The name seems to have stuck somehow" (quoted in Glenn Hughes, *Imagism and the Imagists*, 1960). But H. D.'s feelings about Pound were mixed. In her semiautobiographical work *HERmione*, written in 1927, she suggests she felt "smothered" by Pound, who treated her as muse and "decorative" object. Nor was Pound the sole object of H. D.'s attention. She also fell in love with an intense young poet, Frances Josepha Gregg. Gregg, as H. D. later discovered, also had a secret erotic liaison with Pound. But both Gregg and Pound soon became engaged to other people, and H. D., distraught over these losses, married the English poet and fellow Imagist Richard Aldington; they collaborated on some translations from the Greek, and after he had gone off to war, she was an assistant editor of *Egoist* magazine.

H. D. had a short-lived friendship with another poet who opposed the war and sought spiritual rebirth, D. H. Lawrence. But she found his poems too frequently fragments of an autobiography, not deliberated works of art; he thought that hers tended to be too abstract, to neglect human beings and their dealings with one another. In July 1918, after her break-up with Aldington, H. D., bereft, the mother of an infant conceived in an affair, met the woman whose penname and later legal name was Bryher (born Winifred Ellerman), the daughter of a shipping magnate considered the wealthiest person in England. Bryher fell in love with H. D. and was lovingly devoted to her for the rest of the poet's life. Bryher wrote novels, most of them historical; a woman of considerable practical intelligence—once said to resemble Napoleon—she made it possible for H. D. to live comfortably, to travel in style, to publish her writing, and to have both the society and the solitude she required. They lived together in London, Paris, Berlin, and Switzerland, drawing a wide array of avant-garde writers and artists into their circle. In 1920, they traveled to the United States, where H. D. met Marianne Moore; the two poets corresponded and admired each other's work for many years to come.

In May 1933, H. D. became a "pupil" (her word) of Sigmund Freud, an experience she commemorated in *A Tribute to Freud* (1956). She underwent psychoanalysis with the movement's founder because, in her words, she "wanted to dig down and dig out, root out my personal needs, strengthen my purposes, reaffirm my beliefs, canalize my energies" (quoted in Barbara Guest, *Herself Defined: The Poet H. D. and Her World*, 1984). With Freud, H. D. shared a fascination with unconscious associations and with the religions of the past, and her later poems, which blend her interests in myth and psychoanalysis, include increasingly eclectic allusions. She and Bryher returned to London in 1939 and spent the war years there. Her later books, many published posthumously, include autobiographical writings, fiction, and the epic poem *Helen in Egypt* (1961).

Oread[1]

Whirl up, sea—
Whirl your pointed pines,
Splash your great pines
On our rocks,
Hurl your green over us,
Cover us with your pools of fir.

1914

The Pool

Are you alive?
I touch you.
You quiver like a sea-fish.
I cover you with my net.
What are you—banded one?

1915

Sea Rose

Rose, harsh rose,
marred and with stint of petals,
meagre flower, thin,
sparse of leaf,

more precious
than a wet rose
single on a stem—
you are caught in the drift.

Stunted, with small leaf,
you are flung on the sand,
you are lifted
in the crisp sand
that drives in the wind.

Can the spice-rose
drip such acrid fragrance
hardened in a leaf?

1916

1. A nymph of the mountains.

Mid-Day

The light beats upon me.
I am startled—
a split leaf crackles on the paved floor—
I am anguished—defeated.

A slight wind shakes the seed-pods—
my thoughts are spent
as the black seeds.
My thoughts tear me,
I dread their fever.
I am scattered in its whirl.
I am scattered like
the hot shrivelled seeds.

The shrivelled seeds
are split on the path—
the grass bends with dust,
the grape slips
under its crackled leaf:
yet far beyond the spent seed-pods,
and the blackened stalks of mint,
the poplar is bright on the hill,
the poplar spreads out,
deep-rooted among trees.

O poplar, you are great
among the hill-stones,
while I perish on the path
among the crevices of the rocks.

1916

Garden

I

You are clear
O rose, cut in rock,
hard as the descent of hail.

I could scrape the colour
from the petals
like spilt dye from a rock.

If I could break you
I could break a tree.

If I could stir
I could break a tree—
I could break you.

II

O wind, rend open the heat,
cut apart the heat,
rend it to tatters.

Fruit cannot drop
through this thick air—
fruit cannot fall into heat
that presses up and blunts
the points of pears
and rounds the grapes.

Cut the heat—
plough through it,
turning it on either side
of your path.

1916

Sea Violet

The white violet
is scented on its stalk,
the sea-violet
fragile as agate,
lies fronting all the wind
among the torn shells
on the sand-bank.

The greater blue violets
flutter on the hill,
but who would change for these
who would change for these
one root of the white sort?

Violet
your grasp is frail
on the edge of the sand-hill,
but you catch the light—
frost, a star edges with its fire.

1916

Helen[2]

All Greece hates
the still eyes in the white face,
the lustre as of olives
where she stands,
and the white hands.

All Greece reviles
the wan face when she smiles,
hating it deeper still
when it grows wan and white,
remembering past enchantments
and past ills.

Greece sees unmoved,
God's daughter, born of love,[3]
the beauty of cool feet
and slenderest knees,
could love indeed the maid,
only if she were laid,
white ash amid funereal cypresses.

1924

Fragment Sixty-Eight

. . . even in the house of Hades.
—Sappho[4]

1

I envy you your chance of death,
how I envy you this.
I am more covetous of him
even than of your glance,
I wish more from his presence
though he torture me in a grasp,
terrible, intense.

Though he clasp me in an embrace
that is set against my will

2. In Greek legend, wife of the king Menelaus; her abduction by Paris started the Trojan War.
3. Helen was the daughter of the god Zeus, who, in the guise of a swan, impregnated the mortal woman Leda.
4. Greek poet (seventh century B.C.E.), who gathered a group of like-minded women around her on the island of Lesbos. Her poems have come down to us almost entirely in fragments. *Hades*: the grim and terrible god of the underworld in Greek mythology; the name was also given to the underworld itself.

and rack me with his measure,
effortless yet full of strength,
and slay me
in that most horrible contest,
still, how I envy you your chance.

Though he pierce me—imperious—
iron—fever—dust—
though beauty is slain
when I perish,
I envy you death.

What is beauty to me?
has she not slain me enough,
have I not cried in agony of love,
birth, hate,
in pride crushed?

What is left after this?
what can death loose in me
after your embrace?
your touch,
your limbs are more terrible
to do me hurt.

What can death mar in me
that you have not?

2

What can death send me
that you have not?
you gathered violets,
you spoke:
"your hair is not less black,
nor less fragrant,
nor in your eyes is less light,
your hair is not less sweet
with purple in the lift of lock;"
why were those slight words
and the violets you gathered
of such worth?

How I envy you death;
what could death bring,
more black, more set with sparks
to slay, to affright,
than the memory of those first violets,
the chance lift of your voice,
the chance blinding frenzy
as you bent?

3

So the goddess[5] has slain me
for your chance smile
and my scarf unfolding
as you stooped to it;
so she trapped me
with the upward sweep of your arm
as you lifted the veil,
and the swift smile and selfless.

Could I have known?
nay, spare pity,
though I break,
crushed under the goddess' hate,
though I fall beaten at last,
so high have I thrust my glance
up into her presence.

Do not pity me, spare that,
but how I envy you
your chance of death.

1924

Epitaph

So I may say,
"I died of living,
having lived one hour";

so they may say,
"she died soliciting
illicit fervour";

so you may say,
"Greek flower; Greek ecstasy
reclaims for ever

one who died
following
intricate songs' lost measure."

1931

5. Probably Aphrodite, goddess of love.

FROM THE WALLS DO NOT FALL[6]

To Bryher

for Karnak 1923
from London 1942

[1]

An incident here and there,
and rails gone (for guns)
from your (and my) old town square:

mist and mist-grey, no colour,
still the Luxor[7] bee, chick and hare
pursue unalterable purpose

in green, rose-red, lapis;[8]
they continue to prophesy
from the stone papyrus:

there, as here, ruin opens
the tomb, the temple; enter,
there as here, there are no doors:

the shrine lies open to the sky,
the rain falls, here, there
sand drifts; eternity endures:

ruin everywhere, yet as the fallen roof
leaves the sealed room
open to the air,

so, through our desolation,
thoughts stir, inspiration stalks us
through gloom:

unaware, Spirit announces the Presence;
shivering overtakes us,
as of old, Samuel:[9]

6. The first book of H. D.'s war trilogy. The dedicatee, Bryher (1894–1983), who had changed her name legally from Winnifred Ellerman, was H. D.'s partner.
7. Egyptian town on the Nile River, near Thebes, where images of a bee, a chick, and a hare appear on the Temple of Karnak.
8. Stone (Latin); lapis lazuli is a semiprecious blue stone.
9. Cf. 1 Samuel 28.15, in which the Hebrew prophet Samuel is appalled at being brought back from the dead, and 1 Samuel 28.3, in which Saul trembles at the sight of the Philistine army.

trembling at a known street-corner,
we know not nor are known;
the Pythian[1] pronounces—we pass on

to another cellar, to another sliced wall
where poor utensils show
like rare objects in a museum;

Pompeii[2] has nothing to teach us,
we know crack of volcanic fissure,
slow flow of terrible lava,

pressure on heart, lungs, the brain
about to burst its brittle case
(what the skull can endure!):

over us, Apocryphal fire,
under us, the earth sway, dip of a floor,
slope of a pavement

where men roll, drunk
with a new bewilderment,
sorcery, bedevilment:

the bone-frame was made for
no such shock knit within terror,
yet the skeleton stood up to it:

the flesh? it was melted away,
the heart burnt out, dead ember,
tendons, muscles shattered, outer husk dismembered,

yet the frame held:
we passed the flame: we wonder
what saved us? what for?

[4]

There is a spell, for instance,
in every sea-shell:

continuous, the sea-thrust
is powerless against coral,

bone, stone, marble
hewn from within by that craftsman,

1. Pertaining to the Delphic oracle.
2. City buried by the eruption of Mt. Vesuvius in 79 C.E.

the shell-fish:
oyster, clam, mollusc

is master-mason planning
the stone marvel:

yet that flabby, amorphous hermit
within, like the planet

senses the finite,
it limits its orbit

of being, its house,
temple, fane,[3] shrine:

it unlocks the portals
at stated intervals:

prompted by hunger,
it opens to the tide-flow:

but infinity? no,
of nothing-too-much:

I sense my own limit,
my shell-jaws snap shut

at invasion of the limitless,
ocean-weight; infinite water

can not crack me, egg in egg-shell;
closed in, complete, immortal

full-circle, I know the pull
of the tide, the lull

as well as the moon;
the octopus-darkness

is powerless against
her cold immortality;

so I in my own way know
that the whale

can not digest me:
be firm in your own small, static, limited

orbit and the shark-jaws
of outer circumstance

3. Temple.

will spit you forth:
be indigestible, hard, ungiving.

so that, living within,
you beget, self-out-of-self,

selfless,
that pearl-of-great-price.

[6]

In me (the worm) clearly
is no righteousness, but this—

persistence; I escaped spider-snare,
bird-claw, scavenger bird-beak,

clung to grass-blade,
the back of a leaf

when storm-wind
tore it from its stem;

I escaped, I explored
rose-thorn forest,

was rain-swept
down the valley of a leaf;

was deposited on grass,
where mast by jewelled mast

bore separate ravellings
of encrusted gem-stuff

of the mist
from each banner-staff:

unintimidated by multiplicity
of magnified beauty,

such as your gorgon-great[4]
dull eye can not focus

nor compass, I profit
by every calamity;

4. In Greek mythology, the gaze of one of the Gorgons, three monstrous sisters, turned mortals to stone.

I eat my way out of it;
gorged on vine-leaf and mulberry,

parasite, I find nourishment:
when you cry in disgust,

a worm on the leaf,
a worm in the dust,

a worm on the ear-of-wheat,
I am yet unrepentant,

for I know how the Lord God
is about to manifest, when I,

the industrious worm,
spin my own shroud.

[39]

We have had too much consecration,
too little affirmation,

too much: but this, this, this
has been proved heretical,

too little: I know, I feel
the meaning that words hide;

they are anagrams, cryptograms,
little boxes, conditioned

to hatch butterflies . . .

1944

FROM TRIBUTE TO THE ANGELS[5]

[24]

Every hour, every moment
has its specific attendant Spirit;

the clock-hand, minute by minute,
ticks round its prescribed orbit;

5. In the second book of her war trilogy, H. D. revises the final book of the New Testament, Revelation, which describes the end of the world and God's ultimate triumph over evil.

but this curious mechanical perfection
should not separate but relate rather,

our life, this temporary eclipse
to that other . . .

[25]

. . . of the *no need*
of the moon to shine in it,[6]

for it was ticking minute by minute
(the clock at my bed-head,

with its dim, luminous disc)
when the Lady knocked;

I was talking casually
with friends in the other room,

when we saw the outer hall
grow lighter—then we saw where the door was,

there was no door
(this was a dream, of course),

and she was standing there,
actually, at the turn of the stair.

[26]

One of us said, how odd,
she is actually standing there,

I wonder what brought her?
another of us said,

have we some power between us,
we three together,

that acts as a sort of magnet,
that attracts the super-natural?

(yet it was all natural enough,
we agreed);

6. "And the city had no need of the sun, neither of the moon, to shine in it: for the glory of God did lighten it" (Revelation 21.23).

I do not know what I said
or if I said anything,

for before I had time to speak,
I realized I had been dreaming,

that I lay awake now on my bed,
that the luminous light

was the phosphorescent face
of my little clock

and the faint knocking
was the clock ticking.

[27]

And yet in some very subtle way,
she was there more than ever,

as if she had miraculously
related herself to time here,

which is no easy trick, difficult
even for the experienced stranger,

of whom we must *be not forgetful*
for *some have entertained angels unawares.*[7]

[28]

I had been thinking of Gabriel,[8]
of the moon-cycle, of the moon-shell,

of the moon-crescent
and the moon at full:

I had been thinking of Gabriel,
the moon-regent, the Angel,

and I had intended to recall him
in the sequence of candle and fire

and the law of the seven;
I had not forgotten

7. "Be not forgetful to entertain strangers: for thereby some have entertained angels unawares" (Hebrews 13.2).

8. One of seven archangels in Christian tradition, he announced the birth of Jesus to the Virgin Mary.

his special attribute
of annunciator; I had thought

to address him as I had the others,
Uriel, Annael;[9]

how could I imagine
the Lady herself would come instead?

[29]

We have seen her
the world over,

Our Lady of the Goldfinch,
Our Lady of the Candelabra,

Our Lady of the Pomegranate,
Our Lady of the Chair;[1]

we have seen her, an empress,
magnificent in pomp and grace,

and we have seen her
with a single flower

or a cluster of garden-pinks
in a glass beside her;

we have seen her snood[2]
drawn over her hair,

or her face set in profile
with the blue hood and stars;

we have seen her head bowed down
with the weight of a domed crown,

or we have seen her, a wisp of a girl
trapped in a golden halo;

we have seen her with arrow, with doves
and a heart like a valentine;

we have seen her in fine silks imported
from all over the Levant,[3]

9. Two of the seven archangels.
1. Various iconographic representations of the Virgin Mary.
2. Hair net.
3. Countries along the eastern Mediterranean.

and hung with pearls brought
from the city of Constantine;[4]

we have seen her sleeve
of every imaginable shade

of damask and figured brocade;[5]
it is true,

the painters did very well by her;
it is true, they missed never a line

of the suave turn of the head
or subtle shade of lowered eye-lid

or eye-lids half-raised; you find
her everywhere (or did find),

in cathedral, museum, cloister,
at the turn of the palace stair.

[30]

We see her hand in her lap,
smoothing the apple-green

or the apple-russet silk;
we see her hand at her throat,

fingering a talisman
brought by a crusader from Jerusalem;

we see her hand unknot a Syrian veil
or lay down a Venetian shawl

on a polished table that reflects
half a miniature broken column;

we see her stare past a mirror
through an open window,

where boat follows slow boat on the lagoon;
there are white flowers on the water.

4. City named Constantinople after Emperor Constantine the Great in 330 C.E.; formerly Byzantium, now Istanbul.

5. Textile woven with patterns of raised figures. *Damask:* silk fabric woven with elaborate designs.

[31]

But none of these, none of these
suggest her as I saw her,

though we approach possibly
something of her cool beneficence

in the gracious friendliness
of the marble sea-maids in Venice,

who climb the altar-stair
at *Santa Maria dei Miracoli,*[6]

or we acclaim her in the name
of another in Vienna,

Maria von dem Schnee,[7]
Our Lady of the Snow.

[36]

Ah (you say), this is Holy Wisdom,
Santa Sophia, the SS of the *Sanctus Spiritus,*[8]

so by facile reasoning, logically
the incarnate symbol of the Holy Ghost;

your Holy Ghost was an apple-tree[9]
smouldering—or rather now bourgeoning

with flowers; the fruit of the Tree?
this is the new Eve who comes

clearly to return, to retrieve
what she lost the race,

given over to sin, to death;
she brings the Book of Life, obviously.

6. Saint Mary of the Miracles (Italian); church in Venice with statuettes of sea nymphs on the balustrade leading to the altar.
7. German translated in next line. The church is actually in southern Austria.
8. Holy Ghost or Holy Spirit (Latin). *Santa Sophia:* holy wisdom (Greek); it is also a name for Hagia Sophia, a church and mosque in Istanbul (Constantinople).
9. The tree of knowledge of good and evil, in Genesis 2–3.

[37]

This is a symbol of beauty (you continue),
she is Our Lady universally,

I see her as you project her,
not out of place

flanked by Corinthian capitals,
or in a Coptic nave,[1]

or frozen above the centre door
of a Gothic cathedral;

you have done very well by her
(to repeat your own phrase),

you have carved her tall and unmistakable,
a hieratic figure, the veiled Goddess,

whether of the seven[2] delights,
whether of the seven spear-points.

[38]

O yes—you understand, I say,
this is all most satisfactory,

but she wasn't hieratic, she wasn't frozen,
she wasn't very tall;

she is the Vestal
from the days of Numa,[3]

she carries over the cult
of the *Bona Dea*,[4]

she carries a book but it is not
the tome of the ancient wisdom,

the pages, I imagine, are the blank pages
of the unwritten volume of the new;

1. Main hall of a church built by the Copts, a group of Egyptian Christians. *Corinthian capitals:* distinctive tops of Greek columns in the most ornate style.
2. A mystic number. *Hieratic:* priestly.
3. Legendary king of Rome (715 to 673 B.C.E.), who founded most of the city's sacred institutions, such as the temple of Vesta, a goddess of the hearth, whose fire was tended by the Vestal Virgins, or Vestals.
4. Roman fertility goddess; only women were allowed to attend her rites.

all you say, is implicit,
all that and much more;

but she is not shut up in a cave
like a Sibyl;[5] she is not

imprisoned in leaden bars
in a coloured window;

she is Psyche,[6] the butterfly,
out of the cocoon.

[39]

But nearer than Guardian Angel
or good Daemon,[7]

she is the counter-coin-side
of primitive terror;

she is not-fear, she is not-war,
but she is no symbolic figure

of peace, charity, chastity, goodness,
faith, hope, reward;

she is not Justice with eyes
blindfolded like Love's;[8]

I grant you the dove's symbolic purity,[9]
I grant you her face was innocent

and immaculate and her veils
like the Lamb's Bride,[1]

but the Lamb was not with her,
either as Bridegroom or Child;

her attention is undivided,
we are her bridegroom and lamb;

her book is our book; written
or unwritten, its pages will reveal

5. Female prophet.
6. Soul (Greek); human lover of the Greek god of love, Cupid (or Eros); her symbol is the butterfly. She was eventually deified after achieving seemingly impossible tasks, including a descent into Hades.
7. The ancient Greeks believed humans had good and bad daemons, or spirits, guiding their lives.
8. Traditionally, both Justice and Cupid are blindfolded.
9. In the Bible, the spirit of God descends like a dove (e.g., Matthew 3.16).
1. Traditionally, Christ is the Lamb and the Church is his bride.

a tale of a Fisherman,
a tale of a jar or jars,

the same—different—the same attributes,
different yet the same as before.

[40]

This is no rune[2] nor symbol,
what I mean is—it is so simple

yet no trick of the pen or brush
could capture that impression;

what I wanted to indicate was
a new phase, a new distinction of colour;

I wanted to say, I did say
there was no sheen, no reflection,

no shadow; when I said white,
I did not mean sculptor's or painter's white,

nor porcelain; dim-white could
not suggest it, for when

is fresh-fallen snow (or snow
in the act of falling) dim?

yet even now, we stumble, we are lost—
what can we say?

she was not impalpable like a ghost,
she was not awe-inspiring like a Spirit,

she was not even over-whelming
like an Angel.

[41]

She carried a book, either to imply
she was one of us, with us,

or to suggest she was satisfied
with our purpose, a tribute to the Angels;

2. A magical character in the runic alphabet.

yet though the campanili[3] spoke,
Gabriel, Azrael,

though the campanili answered,
Raphael, Uriel,

though a distant note over-water
chimed *Annael,* and *Michael*[4]

was implicit from the beginning,
another, deep, un-named, resurging bell

answered, sounding through them all:
remember, where there was

no need of the moon to shine . . .
I saw no temple.[5]

1945

3. Bell towers.
4. Names of archangels invoked previously in the poem.
5. "And I saw no temple therein: for the Lord God Almighty and the Lamb are the temple of it. And the city had no need of the sun, neither of the moon, to shine in it: for the glory of God did lighten it, and the Lamb is the light thereof" (Revelation 21.22–23).

Robinson Jeffers
1887–1962

Robinson Jeffers admired strength and sought it in his own poetry, whether that poetry was full-throated or modulated. He admired "dead men's thoughts" that had "shed weakness" ("Wise Men in Their Bad Hours"). In his prefaces, he indicates that he rejected poetry that was "slight and fantastic, abstract, unreal, eccentric," such as that of Stéphane Mallarmé and the Anglo-American symbolists. His own verse, he felt, "must reclaim substance and sense, and physical and psychological reality" (foreword to *Selected Poetry,* 1959). The strength he endorses is of two kinds. The first is sudden, swift, flashing, like the hawk's. The second kind is enduring, permanent, like the rock's. Hawk and rock appear in various guises in Jeffers's writings, as principles of dynamism and revered inertness. In a letter of December 21, 1912, he states: "My theory . . . is that poetry should be a blending of fire and earth—should be made of solid and immediate things . . . which are set on fire by human passion."

Jeffers wrote in the long poem *Roan Stallion* (1925): "Humanity is the mould to break away from, the crust to break through, the coal to break into fire, / The atom to be split. Tragedy that breaks man's face and white fire flies out of it." Violence leads his characters, like the hero of W. B. Yeats's play *The Unicorn from the Stars* (which Jeffers greatly admired), to a self-surpassing, ecstatic stillness. Friedrich Nietzsche, whose writings Jeffers read when he was fifteen, helped both Yeats and Jeffers conceive tragic heroes who outdo the human rather than accept it or grovel in it. Jeffers said that his theme in *The Women at Point Sur* (1927) was "to uncenter the human mind from itself" (letter of August 5, 1927). In a late book, *The Double Axe* (1948), Jeffers announced with an old man's boldness that he would "present a certain philosophical attitude which might be called inhumanism, a shifting of emphasis and significance from man to not-man." In vigorous, long-lined free verse that aspires to the sublime, he envisaged a mentality more attuned to hawks and rocks, more acquiescent in the cruelty-kindness-indifference of nature and God.

Jeffers was born on January 10, 1887, in Pittsburgh; his father was a professor at Western Theological Seminary. Although Jeffers, in "To His Father," contrasted his own unbelief with his father's Scotch Irish Calvinism, his sense of the primal force in nature bears some resemblance to the God of Calvinism. A more apparent influence came from his father's having been a professor of Greek and Latin; from him, Jeffers learned Greek and perhaps also a taste for Greek tragedy. Perhaps Jeffers's greatest fame came when he translated Euripides' *Medea* (1946) into his own manner, and Judith Anderson played the leading role on Broadway.

As a boy, Jeffers was sent to boarding schools in Geneva, Lausanne, Zurich, and Leipzig. He was brought back from school in 1903, and the next year his family moved from Pittsburgh to California. Jeffers entered Occidental College and graduated at eighteen. He began graduate work at the University of Southern California and there met Una Call Kuster, whom he married in 1913. In September 1914, they decided to live in the California coastal village of Carmel, where Jeffers immediately began to have a house built; he was later to build Hawk Tower beside Tor House with his own hands. The rocky coasts, the seabirds, and the comparative solitude suited him. An isolationist, he risked opprobrium by opposing American participation in World War II. Since his death, he has been identified with the spectacular Pacific coastline and with poetry of basic, violent emotions.

Shine, Perishing Republic

While this America settles in the mould of its vulgarity, heavily thickening
  to empire,
And protest, only a bubble in the molten mass, pops and sighs out, and the
  mass hardens,

I sadly smiling remember that the flower fades to make fruit, the fruit rots
  to make earth.
Out of the mother; and through the spring exultances, ripeness and
  decadence; and home to the mother.

You making haste haste on decay: not blameworthy; life is good, be it
  stubbornly long or suddenly
A mortal splendor: meteors are not needed less than mountains: shine,
  perishing republic.

But for my children, I would have them keep their distance from the
  thickening center; corruption
Never has been compulsory, when the cities lie at the monster's feet there
  are left the mountains.

And boys, be in nothing so moderate as in love of man, a clever servant,
insufferable master.
There is the trap that catches noblest spirits, that caught—they say—
God, when he walked on earth.

1925

Fawn's Foster-Mother

The old woman sits on a bench before the door and quarrels
With her meager pale demoralized daughter.
Once when I passed I found her alone, laughing in the sun
And saying that when she was first married
She lived in the old farmhouse up Garapatas Canyon.
(It is empty now, the roof has fallen
But the log walls hang on the stone foundation; the redwoods
Have all been cut down, the oaks are standing;
The place is now more solitary than ever before.)
"When I was nursing my second baby
My husband found a day-old fawn hid in a fern-brake
And brought it; I put its mouth to the breast
Rather than let it starve, I had milk enough for three babies.
Hey, how it sucked, the little nuzzler,
Digging its little hoofs like quills into my stomach.
I had more joy from that than from the others."
Her face is deformed with age, furrowed like a bad road
With market-wagons, mean cares and decay.
She is thrown up to the surface of things, a cell of dry skin
Soon to be shed from the earth's old eyebrows,
I see that once in her spring she lived in the streaming arteries,
The stir of the world, the music of the mountain.

1928

Hurt Hawks

I

The broken pillar of the wing jags from the clotted shoulder,
The wing trails like a banner in defeat,
No more to use the sky forever but live with famine
And pain a few days: cat nor coyote
Will shorten the week of waiting for death, there is game without
talons.
He stands under the oak-bush and waits
The lame feet of salvation; at night he remembers freedom
And flies in a dream, the dawns ruin it.
He is strong and pain is worse to the strong, incapacity is worse.
The curs of the day come and torment him
At distance, no one but death the redeemer will humble that head,
The intrepid readiness, the terrible eyes.

The wild God of the world is sometimes merciful to those
That ask mercy, not often to the arrogant.
You do not know him, you communal people, or you have forgotten
him;
Intemperate and savage, the hawk remembers him;
Beautiful and wild, the hawks, and men that are dying, remember him.

II

I'd sooner, except the penalties, kill a man than a hawk; but the great
redtail
Had nothing left but unable misery
From the bone too shattered for mending, the wing that trailed under
his talons when he moved.
We had fed him six weeks, I gave him freedom,
He wandered over the foreland hill and returned in the evening, asking
for death,
Not like a beggar, still eyed with the old
Implacable arrogance. I gave him the lead gift in the twilight. What fell
was relaxed,
Owl-downy, soft feminine feathers; but what
Soared: the fierce rush: the night-herons by the flooded river cried fear
at its rising
Before it was quite unsheathed from reality.

1928

Rock and Hawk

Here is a symbol in which
Many high tragic thoughts
Watch their own eyes.

This gray rock, standing tall
On the headland, where the seawind
Lets no tree grow,

Earthquake-proved, and signatured
By ages of storms: on its peak
A falcon has perched.

I think, here is your emblem
To hang in the future sky;
Not the cross, not the hive,

But this; bright power, dark peace;
Fierce consciousness joined with final
Disinterestedness;

Life with calm death; the falcon's
Realist eyes and act
Married to the massive

Mysticism of stone,
Which failure cannot cast down
Nor success make proud.

1935

Ave Caesar[1]

No bitterness: our ancestors did it.
They were only ignorant and hopeful, they wanted freedom but wealth too.
Their children will learn to hope for a Caesar.
Or rather—for we are not aquiline Romans but soft mixed colonists—
Some kindly Sicilian tyrant who'll keep
Poverty and Carthage off until the Romans arrive.[2]
We are easy to manage, a gregarious people,
Full of sentiment, clever at mechanics, and we love our luxuries.

1935

The Purse-Seine[3]

Our sardine fishermen work at night in the dark of the moon; daylight or moonlight
They could not tell where to spread the net, unable to see the phosphorescence of the shoals of fish.
They work northward from Monterey, coasting Santa Cruz; off New Year's Point or off Pigeon Point
The look-out man will see some lakes of milk-color light on the sea's night-purple; he points, and the helmsman
Turns the dark prow, the motorboat circles the gleaming shoal and drifts out her seine-net. They close the circle
And purse the bottom of the net, then with great labor haul it in.

I cannot tell you
How beautiful the scene is, and a little terrible, then, when the crowded fish
Know they are caught, and wildly beat from one wall to the other of their closing destiny the phosphorescent
Water to a pool of flame, each beautiful slender body sheeted with flame, like a live rocket
A comet's tail wake of clear yellow flame; while outside the narrowing
Floats and cordage of the net great sea-lions come up to watch, sighing in the dark; the vast walls of night
Stand erect to the stars.

1. Hail, Caesar! (Latin).
2. For over two hundred years the towns of Sicily were ruled by tyrants; this was ended by the First Punic War (264–241 B.C.E.), in which Rome defeated Carthage and annexed Sicily.
3. A fishing net shaped like a bag.

Lately I was looking from a night mountain-top
On a wide city, the colored splendor, galaxies of light: how could I help but recall the seine-net
Gathering the luminous fish? I cannot tell you how beautiful the city appeared, and a little terrible.
I thought, We have geared the machines and locked all together into interdependence; we have built the great cities; now
There is no escape. We have gathered vast populations incapable of free survival, insulated
From the strong earth, each person in himself helpless, on all dependent. The circle is closed, and the net
Is being hauled in. They hardly feel the cords drawing, yet they shine already. The inevitable mass-disasters
Will not come in our time nor in our children's, but we and our children
Must watch the net draw narrower, government take all powers—or revolution, and the new government
Take more than all, add to kept bodies kept souls—or anarchy, the mass-disasters.

These things are Progress;
Do you marvel our verse is troubled or frowning, while it keeps its reason? Or it lets go, lets the mood flow
In the manner of the recent young men into mere hysteria, splintered gleams, crackled laughter. But they are quite wrong.
There is no reason for amazement: surely one always knew that cultures decay, and life's end is death.

1937

Carmel Point[4]

The extraordinary patience of things!
This beautiful place defaced with a crop of suburban houses—
How beautiful when we first beheld it,
Unbroken field of poppy and lupin walled with clean cliffs;
No intrusion but two or three horses pasturing,
Or a few milch[5] cows rubbing their flanks on the outcrop rockheads—
Now the spoiler has come: does it care?
Not faintly. It has all time. It knows the people are a tide
That swells and in time will ebb, and all
Their works dissolve. Meanwhile the image of the pristine beauty
Lives in the very grain of the granite,
Safe as the endless ocean that climbs our cliff.—As for us:
We must uncenter our minds from ourselves;
We must unhumanize our views a little, and become confident
As the rock and ocean that we were made from.

1954

4. In California, on the Pacific Ocean.

5. Milk-giving.

Vulture

I had walked since dawn and lay down to rest on a bare hillside
Above the ocean. I saw through half-shut eyelids a vulture wheeling high up in heaven,
And presently it passed again, but lower and nearer, its orbit narrowing, I understood then
That I was under inspection. I lay death-still and heard the flight-feathers
Whistle above me and make their circle and come nearer.
I could see the naked red head between the great wings
Bear downward staring. I said, "My dear bird, we are wasting time here.
These old bones will still work; they are not for you." But how beautiful he looked, gliding down
On those great sails; how beautiful he looked, veering away in the sea-light over the precipice. I tell you solemnly
That I was sorry to have disappointed him. To be eaten by that beak and become part of him, to share those wings and those eyes—
What a sublime end of one's body, what an enskyment; what a life after death.

1963

Edwin Muir
1887–1959

One of the most influential Scottish poets of the twentieth century, Edwin Muir was born on May 15, 1887, in Deerness, in the Orkney Islands. He was the son of a small tenant farmer, and his recollections of this changeless agricultural life, its daily and seasonal rituals, its folk beliefs and superstitions, are the material for much of his poetry. His family and their neighbors, he recalled in his *Autobiography* (1954), "had a culture made up of legend, folk-song, and the poetry and prose of the Bible; they had customs which sanctioned their instinctive feelings for the earth; their life was an order, and a good order." When Muir was thirteen, his family moved to the industrial city of Glasgow, then famous for both its prosperity and its terrible slums, considered the worst in the British Isles. His parents found life in the city unbearable, and by the time Muir was eighteen both his parents and two of his brothers were dead. Muir moved from one shabby factory or office job to another. He had left school at fourteen and was forced to continue his education on his own. He published aphorisms, akin to Friedrich Nietzsche's, in the magazine *New Age*. In June 1919, Muir married Willa Anderson, who encouraged him to devote himself to writing. They left Glasgow for London, where Muir made his living as a journalist—for years he reviewed novels for the *Listener*—and as an occasional teacher. Both before and after World War II, he and his wife spent some time in Prague, where he lectured on English literature, and for five years he was the Warden of Newbattle, a residential adult education college in Scotland. In 1955–56, he was Charles Eliot Norton Professor at Harvard University.

In his poetry, Muir attempted to steer clear of schools and contemporary influences, recasting instead the rhythms of traditional English verse, the narrative momentum and grim determinism of Scottish ballads, and the archetypal imagery and figures of myth, legend, and dream—the hero, the sky, the shadow, the wheel. In undergoing psychoanalysis, he recorded his dreams, which later provided material for his writing. Instead of emulating new models, he tried to write "from the solidest base" within himself, which was, for him, the vanished Eden of his childhood. His last book takes its title from his poem "One Foot in Eden," and his tombstone bears lines from his poem "Milton": "his unblinded eyes / Saw far and near the fields of paradise." In the spring of 1938, he wrote in his diary of his longing to recover a childhood intuition: "It is a state in which the earth, the human buildings on the earth, and the earthly life of everyone will in some way be in harmony with the sky which overarches them." Although in childhood it seemed "the sky fitted the earth," "I have often been troubled by a sense of dislocation between the earth and the sky" (quoted in P. H. Butter, *Edwin Muir,* 1967). Muir's poem "The Horses," which T. S. Eliot described in a preface to Muir's *Collected Poems* (1952) as "that great, that terrifying poem of the 'atomic age,' " envisions the reconstruction of the human and the natural world after the destruction of our mechanized and inhuman "civilization." Because of the enduring simplicities of his recollected childhood, Muir's bent is toward allegory. In 1937, he and his wife translated Franz Kafka's *The Trial,* and his words on that great allegorist are also a summary of Muir's own endeavor and achievement: "In an age obsessed by the time sense, or, as it is called, the historical sense, he has resurrected and made available for contemporary use the timeless story, the archetypal story, in which is the source of all stories."

Ballad of Hector in Hades[1]

Yes, this is where I stood that day,
  Beside this sunny mound.
The walls of Troy are far away,
  And outward comes no sound.

I wait. On all the empty plain
  A burnished stillness lies,
Save for the chariot's tinkling hum,
  And a few distant cries.

His helmet glitters near. The world
  Slowly turns around,
With some new sleight compels my feet
  From the fighting ground.

I run. If I turned back again
  The earth must turn with me,
The mountains planted on the plain,
  The sky clamped to the sea.

The grasses puff a little dust
  Where my footsteps fall.

1. In Homer's *Iliad,* Hector, leader of the Trojan army, is killed in battle by the Greek hero Achilles, who drags the dead body behind his chariot around the walls of Troy. *Hades:* the underworld in Greek myth.

I cast a shadow as I pass
  The little wayside wall.

The strip of grass on either hand
  Sparkles in the light;
I only see that little space
  To the left and to the right,

And in that space our shadows run,
  His shadow there and mine,
The little flowers, the tiny mounds,
  The grasses frail and fine.

But narrower still and narrower!
  My course is shrunk and small,
Yet vast as in a deadly dream,
  And faint the Trojan wall.
The sun up in the towering sky
  Turns like a spinning ball.

The sky with all its clustered eyes
  Grows still with watching me,
The flowers, the mounds, the flaunting weeds
  Wheel slowly round to see.

Two shadows racing on the grass,
  Silent and so near,
Until his shadow falls on mine.
  And I am rid of fear.

The race is ended. Far away
  I hang and do not care,
While round bright Troy Achilles whirls
  A corpse with streaming hair.

1925

The Wheel

How can I turn this wheel that turns my life,
Create another hand to move this hand
Not moved by me, who am not the mover,[2]
Nor, though I love and hate, the lover,
The hater? Loves and hates are thrust
Upon me by the acrimonious dead,
The buried thesis, long since rusted knife,
Revengeful dust.
A stony or obstreperous head,

2. Cf. the "unmoved mover," the ancient Greek philosopher Aristotle's description, in his *Metaphysics*, of the "Prime Mover" causing all motion.

Though slain so squarely, can usurp my will
As I walk above it on the sunny hill.

Then how do I stand?
How can I here remake what there made me
And makes and remakes me still?
Set a new mark? Circumvent history?
Nothing can come of history but history,
The stationary storm that cannot bate
Its neutral violence,
The transitory solution that cannot wait,
The indecisive victory
That is like loss read backwards and cannot bring
Relief to you and me,
The jangling
Of all the voices of plant and beast and man
That have not made a harmony
Since first the great controversy began,
And cannot sink to silence
Unless a grace
Come of itself to wrap our souls in peace
Between the turning leaves of history and make
Ourselves ourselves, winnow the grudging grain,
And take
From that which made us that which will make us again.

1943

The Absent

They are not here. And we, we are the Others
Who walk by ourselves unquestioned in the sun
Which shines for us and only for us.
For They are not here.
And are made known to us in this great absence
That lies upon us and is between us
Since They are not here.
Now, in this kingdom of summer idleness
Where slowly we the sun-tranced multitudes dream and wander
In deep oblivion of brightness
And breathe ourselves out, out into the air—
It is absence that receives us;
We do not touch, our souls go out in the absence
That lies between us and is about us.
For we are the Others,
And so we sorrow for These that are not with us,
Not knowing we sorrow or that this is our sorrow,
Since it is long past thought or memory or device of mourning,
Sorrow for loss of that which we never possessed,
The unknown, the nameless,

The ever-present that in their absence are with us
(With us the inheritors, the usurpers claiming
The sun and the kingdom of the sun) that sorrow
And loneliness might bring a blessing upon us.

1949

The Horses

Barely a twelvemonth after
The seven days war that put the world to sleep,
Late in the evening the strange horses came.
By then we had made our covenant with silence,
But in the first few days it was so still
We listened to our breathing and were afraid.
On the second day
The radios failed; we turned the knobs; no answer.
On the third day a warship passed us, heading north,
Dead bodies piled on the deck. On the sixth day
A plane plunged over us into the sea. Thereafter
Nothing. The radios dumb;
And still they stand in corners of our kitchens,
And stand, perhaps, turned on, in a million rooms
All over the world. But now if they should speak,
If on a sudden they should speak again,
If on the stroke of noon a voice should speak,
We would not listen, we would not let it bring
That old bad world that swallowed its children quick
At one great gulp. We would not have it again.
Sometimes we think of the nations lying asleep,
Curled blindly in impenetrable sorrow,
And then the thought confounds us with its strangeness.
The tractors lie about our fields; at evening
They look like dank sea-monsters couched and waiting.
We leave them where they are and let them rust:
'They'll moulder away and be like other loam'.
We make our oxen drag our rusty ploughs,
Long laid aside. We have gone back
Far past our fathers' land.
And then, that evening
Late in the summer the strange horses came.
We heard a distant tapping on the road,
A deepening drumming; it stopped, went on again
And at the corner changed to hollow thunder.
We saw the heads
Like a wild wave charging and were afraid.
We had sold our horses in our fathers' time
To buy new tractors. Now they were strange to us
As fabulous steeds set on an ancient shield
Or illustrations in a book of knights.

We did not dare go near them. Yet they waited,
Stubborn and shy, as if they had been sent
By an old command to find our whereabouts
And that long-lost archaic companionship.
In the first moment we had never a thought
That they were creatures to be owned and used.
Among them were some half-a-dozen colts
Dropped in some wilderness of the broken world,
Yet new as if they had come from their own Eden.
Since then they have pulled our ploughs and borne our loads,
But that free servitude still can pierce our hearts.
Our life is changed; their coming our beginning.

1956

EDITH SITWELL
1887–1964

Among the English poets of the twentieth century, Edith Sitwell has occupied an eminent but at times precarious place. She straddles the divide between experimental modernism and traditional lyricism, and she can thus seem either a member of the bohemian avant-garde or an aristocratic throwback to an earlier era. In most of her poetry, she is determined to present experience with as much novel artistry as possible, but in her later work she embraces experience in the age-old rhythms of nature.

The poetry that particularly enraged Sitwell in her youth was that of the Georgians (Rupert Brooke being the most popular), whose "dim bucolics" she and her two brothers resolved to overthrow. "At the time I began to write, a change in the direction, imagery, and rhythms in poetry had become necessary, owing to the rhythmical flaccidity, the verbal deadness, the dead and expected patterns, of some of the poetry immediately preceding us" (introduction to *The Canticle of the Rose*). She acknowledged various influences: the poetry of Charles Baudelaire and Stéphane Mallarmé, the music of Igor Stravinsky, the Russian Ballet of Sergei Diaghilev, and various artists. "With the publication of . . . *Prufrock*," she said of T. S. Eliot's first volume, "a new era in poetry began" (*Taken Care Of: The Autobiography of Edith Sitwell*, 1965). Hailing these innovations, she wrote: "The great quality of the modern masters is an explosive energy, the separating up of the molecules, exploring the possibilities of the atom."

The influx of the new into Sitwell's ancestral great house of Renishaw, where she lived in the midst of old-fashioned splendor, generated considerable tension. The poems that resulted sought to renew the visible and sonic world. Her first book, *Façade* (1922), contains "abstract poems—that is, they are patterns in sound," she said later. "They are, too, in many cases virtuoso exercises in technique of an extreme difficulty" (*Canticle*). Their emphasis on sound makes them virtually untranslatable, as they seek to establish new modes of sensory data. One of her favorite early subjects, in a poem such as "Aubade," is "a person who has always been blind and who, suddenly endowed with sight, must *learn* to see." Sitwell also had an elaborate notion, based in part on Mallarmé but more reiterative, of the effects of particular letters and sounds. Her experiments with verbal sound and abstraction also bear comparison with those of the American writer Gertrude Stein.

In 1923, Sitwell performed *Façade,* with music by William Walton, at London's Aeolian Hall. She stood behind a painted curtain and intoned the lines, to the bafflement and exasperation of critics. In her next long work, *Gold Coast Customs* (1929), she turned to social satire and criticism, juxtaposing English and African social surfaces. In her last volume, with the Dantesque title *The Canticle of the Rose* (1949), she described her poems as "hymns of praise to the glory of life." She sang with threnodic force of rhythms in nature and of sensory experience ecstatically translated into illumination. These later poems bear the influence of William Blake, W. B. Yeats, and her friend Dylan Thomas. She said she wished to achieve "a greater expressiveness, a greater formality, and a return to rhetoric," rejecting "the outcry for understatement, for quietness, for neutral tints in poetry" (*Taken Care Of*).

Sitwell was born on September 7, 1887. She was the first child of Sir George Sitwell, baronet, and Lady Ida, the daughter of an earl. "My parents," Sitwell lamented in her autobiography, "were strangers to me from the moment of my birth." Her father was an extreme eccentric and an impossible parent; her mother was upset by her daughter's unusual features and great height. Sitwell's first poems were published in 1915. In 1916, she became editor of a literary review, *Wheels,* the purpose of which was to stir up the poetic scene. Seven issues appeared between 1916 and 1921. Sitwell and her two brothers were lavishly represented, as was war poet Wilfred Owen. Reviewers were often cruel to the Sitwells, who made a point of being cruel back. Edith Sitwell remained controversial, but was much honored in later life. She was created a Dame Grand Cross of the British Empire by Elizabeth II and became known as Dame Edith. She and her brother Osbert toured the United States to great applause. The record of her reading of *Façade* was widely distributed. Her talent was offbeat and difficult to categorize, but her attempts to enliven the relations of sound, image, and sense continue to inspire avant-garde poets in England.

From Façade

Aubade[1]

Jane, Jane,
Tall as a crane,
The morning light creaks down again;

Comb your cockscomb-ragged hair,
Jane, Jane, come down the stair.

Each dull blunt wooden stalactite
Of rain creaks, hardened by the light,

Sounding like an overtone
From some lonely world unknown.

But the creaking empty light
Will never harden into sight,

1. A poem about dawn; aubades often lament the parting of lovers at dawn.

Will never penetrate your brain
With overtones like the blunt rain.

The light would show (if it could harden)
Eternities of kitchen garden,

Cockscomb flowers that none will pluck,
And wooden flowers that 'gin to cluck.

In the kitchen you must light
Flames as staring, red and white,

As carrots or as turnips, shining
Where the cold dawn light lies whining.

Cockscomb hair on the cold wind
Hangs limp, turns the milk's weak mind. . . .
        Jane, Jane,
        Tall as a crane,
        The morning light creaks down again!

Country Dance

That hobnailed goblin, the bobtailed Hob,
Said, 'It is time I began to rob.'
For strawberries bob, hob-nob with the pearls
Of cream (like the curls of the dairy girls),
And flushed with the heat and fruitish-ripe
Are the gowns of the maids who dance to the pipe.
Chase a maid?
She's afraid!
'Go gather a bob-cherry kiss from a tree,
But don't, I prithee, come bothering me!'
She said,
As she fled.
The snouted satyrs drink clouted cream[2]
'Neath the chestnut-trees as thick as a dream;
So I went,
And leant,
Where none but the doltish coltish wind
Nuzzled my hand for what it could find.
As it neighed,
I said,
'Don't touch me, sir, don't touch me, I say,
You'll tumble my strawberries into the hay.'
Those snow-mounds of silver that bee, the spring,
Has sucked his sweetness from, I will bring

2. Satyrs are ancient Greek deities of the wood, half goat and half man. *Clouted:* clotted.

With fair-haired plants and with apples chill
For the great god Pan's[3] high altar . . . I'll spill
Not one!
So, in fun,
We rolled on the grass and began to run,
Chasing that gaudy satyr the Sun;
Over the haycocks, away we ran,
Crying, 'Here be berries as sunburnt as Pan!'
But Silenus[4]
Has seen us. . . .
He runs like the rough satyr Sun.
Come away!

1922

Still Falls the Rain

The Raids, 1940.[5] Night and Dawn

Still falls the Rain—
Dark as the world of man, black as our loss—
Blind as the nineteen hundred and forty nails
Upon the Cross.

Still falls the Rain
With a sound like the pulse of the heart that is changed to the hammer-beat
In the Potter's Field,[6] and the sound of the impious feet

On the Tomb:
Still falls the Rain
In the Field of Blood where the small hopes breed and the human brain
Nurtures its greed, that worm with the brow of Cain.

Still falls the Rain
At the feet of the Starved Man hung upon the Cross.
Christ that each day, each night, nails there, have mercy on us—
On Dives and on Lazarus:[7]
Under the Rain the sore and the gold are as one.

Still falls the Rain—
Still falls the Blood from the Starved Man's wounded Side:
He bears in His Heart all wounds—those of the light that died,
The last faint spark

3. Pan, a rural god of the Greeks and kin to the satyrs, ruled Arcadia, a mythical pastoral country inhabited by shepherds and shepherdesses.
4. Pan's father.
5. During the Battle of Britain, the German air force carried out many heavy bombing raids on England.
6. A cemetery for foreigners, on land near Jerusalem bought with the blood money thrown away by Judas; it was also called the Field of Blood.
7. In a parable told by Jesus (Luke 16.19–31), the rich man Dives was sent to Hell, while the leprous beggar Lazarus (not the Lazarus raised from the dead) went to Heaven.

In the self-murdered heart, the wounds of the sad uncomprehending
dark,
The wounds of the baited bear—[8]
The blind and weeping bear whom the keepers beat
On his helpless flesh . . . the tears of the hunted hare.

Still falls the Rain—
Then—O Ile leape up to my God: who pulles me doune—[9]
See, see where Christ's blood streames in the firmament:
It flows from the Brow we nailed upon the tree
Deep to the dying, to the thirsting heart
That holds the fires of the world—dark-smirched with pain
As Caesar's laurel crown.[1]

Then sounds the voice of One who like the heart of man
Was once a child who among beasts has lain—
'Still do I love, still shed my innocent light, my Blood, for thee.'

1942

The Poet Laments the Coming of Old Age

I see the children running out of school;
They are taught that Goodness means a blinding hood
Or is heaped by Time like the hump on an agèd back,
And that Evil can be cast like an old rag
And Wisdom caught like a hare and held in the golden sack
Of the heart. . . . But I am one who must bring back sight to the blind.

Yet there was a planet dancing in my mind
With a gold seed of Folly . . . long ago. . . .
And where is that grain of Folly? . . . with the hare-wild wind
Of my spring it has gone from one who must bring back sight to the
blind.

For I, the fool, was once like the philosopher
Sun who laughs at evil and at good:
I saw great things mirrored in littleness,
Who now see only that great Venus wears Time's filthy dress—
A toothless crone who once had the Lion's mouth.

The Gold Appearances from Nothing rise
In sleep, by day.[2] . . . Two thousands years ago

8. A medieval entertainment in which a pack of dogs fought a bear chained to a post.
9. Faust's cry of despair at the end of the play *Dr. Faustus,* by Christopher Marlowe (1564–1593), when he realizes he has been damned for his compact with Mephistopheles.
1. A token of victory or preeminence.
2. "This is a reference to a passage in Plato's *The Sophist*" [Sitwell's note]. In that dialogue, a stranger to the Socratic circle establishes that "imitation [in effect, art] is a kind of creation—of images, however, as we affirm, and not of real things." Lines 16–17 paraphrase the stranger's observation that images are "the appearances which spring up of themselves in sleep or by day" [Sitwell's note].

There was a man who had the Lion's leap,
Like the Sun's, to take the worlds and loves he would,
But (laughed the philosopher Sun, and I, the fool)

Great golden Alexander[3] and his thunder-store
Are now no more
Than the armored knight who buzzed on the windowpane
And the first drops of rain.

He lies in sleep . . . But still beneath a thatch
Of hair like sunburnt grass, the thieving sweet thoughts move
Towards the honey-hive. . . . And another sweet-tooth Alexander runs
Out of the giant shade that is his school,
To take the dark knight's world, the honeycomb.

The Sun's simulacrum, the gold-sinewed man,
Lies under a hump of grass, as once I thought to wear
With patience Goodness like a hump on my agèd back.
. . . But Goodness grew not with age, although my heart must bear
The weight of all Time's filth, and Wisdom is not a hare in the golden
sack

Of the heart. . . . It can never be caught. Though I bring back sight to
the blind,
My seed of Folly has gone, that could teach me to bear
That the gold-sinewed body that had the blood of all the earth in its
veins
Has changed to an old rag of the outworn world
And the great heart that the first Morning made
Should wear all Time's destruction for a dress.

1945

3. Alexander the Great, king of Macedonia in the fourth century B.C.E. and conquerer of the East.

Marianne Moore
1887–1972

Marianne Moore was one of the most original poets of her time, original in her mode of perception, in her kind of poetry, even in the way her stanzas appear on the page. She proceeds by acute, if often indirect, observation, commenting in an impersonal yet distinctive voice. She marvels at the peculiarities of animals and draws inferences from them, sometimes by ironically comparing lower with higher animals, though she may prefer either group. Often reflecting on ethics and aesthetics, she writes about subjects ranging from a steamroller, the sea, and a mountain to poetry, art, nationality, and the divine.

Moore's poems are made up of long sentences chopped jaggedly into lines of varying lengths, often arranged in a syllabic pattern. Her lines usually do not begin with capital letters, as if written plainly and, with slight interruptions at line ends, prosily. Yet the lines break up the syntax and add emphasis, at times humorous, to what is being said. They also usually rhyme, although finding the rhyme may take some effort. More visibly, quotations from scientific or journalistic works may appear within poems, often with footnotes divulging their out-of-the-way sources. In "Poetry," Moore impugns discrimination "against 'business documents and school-books.' " That her verse embraces many characteristics of prose was almost revolutionary, reconstituting the relationship of these two media and attracting to her many poets equally concerned to be matter-of-fact and antirhetorical. Yet she is capable of suddenly bursting into rhetoric for her own purposes, as in "What Are Years?"

Moore was born on November 15, 1887, in Kirkwood, Missouri, ten months before T. S. Eliot was born, nearby in St. Louis. Her significance as one of the major modernists in the generation of Wallace Stevens, Ezra Pound, William Carlos Williams, and H. D., all of whom admired her, has been confirmed in recent years. Moore shares the anti-ornamental and antisentimental disposition of her contemporaries, but she is less pretentious in manner, more reserved in tone, and more rigorous in engaging seemingly trivial details. She writes with a hard-edged, objectifying precision that confounds traditional categories of gender, as does H. D., and she upholds, like Pound, "direct treatment of the thing" and the exact word (*le mot juste*). She celebrates the ordinary in cleverly enjambed lines, as does Williams, but she focuses on the natural world. Like Stevens, she experiments with a highly varied physical scene in unaccustomed ways, though her interest in animals, birds, and plants is more specialized, as if to honor the variety of the physical universe. Also like Stevens, she takes up aesthetic and metaphysical problems, but in a less overtly philosophical language. She brings quotations from popular culture into poetry, like Eliot, but she welcomes instead of satirizes them. In the verbal collage of the ambitious long poem "An Octopus," Moore juxtaposes various sources—travel guides, fashion magazines, science, journalism, literature, philosophy, even a remark "Overheard at the circus"—to suggest both the vastness of Mt. Rainier and its sublime ineffability, a massive and heterogeneous presence that outstrips all attempts at description. She takes the stance neither of critic nor of connoisseur, both roles being too peacock-tailed and dominating for her taste.

Moore most admires the three qualities in art that she calls, in the title of a famous essay, "Humility, Concentration, and Gusto." By humility, she means—in contrast to the pomp and grandeur of prophetic poetry—"quiet objectiveness" in writing and the recognition that it is impossible to do "something that has never been thought of before." In addition to quoting abundantly and effacing her presence, she thus writes with an understated tone and covert humor, cataloging species and enumerating visual phenomena while refusing connectives. As for concentration, Moore "would rather be told too little than too much"; "a poem," she adds, "is a concentrate." Like other modernists who favor compression, she seeks to pare away superfluities in diction and punctuation, though her expansive syntax and heterogeneous sources counteract the limitations of a doctrinal Imagism. But lest all the emphasis in Moore's poetics seem to fall on a buttoned-up asceticism, she also praises what she calls "gusto," imaginative flair that seems exactly right. Perhaps her splendid but precise use of figurative language can be counted as an example of gusto. In "The Fish," a mussel is "like // an / injured fan," sunrays in the water are "split like spun / glass," and the "water drives a wedge / of iron" through a crevice in a cliff. In "The Steeple-Jack," "a sea the purple of the peacock's neck is / paled to greenish azure." Moore reconciles the colorful extravagance of poetry and the meticulous, rule-bound accuracy of science. She binds many of her poems to the mathematical grid of a strict syllable count, syntax spilling over the lines, images proliferating wildly. She asserts: "gusto thrives on freedom, and freedom in art, as in life, is the result of a discipline imposed by ourselves." In an interview with poet

Donald Hall, she explained: "precision, economy of statement, logic employed to ends that are disinterested, drawing and identifying, liberate . . . the imagination."

Animals exemplify, in Moore's view, the right balance between freedom and discipline, power and restraint. In "The Pangolin," a poem that probes human aggression and divine grace, this armored anteater goes about its business with an exemplary patience, exactitude, and skill, holding its considerable strength in reserve. The octopus, like the mountain glacier to which Moore compares it, is a creature of both "delicacy" and "crushing rigor," beauty and menace. Moore is devoted to the quirkiness of animals, to their stubbornness or flexibility, their dignity or lack of it. Unlike D. H. Lawrence, she offers no depth psychology of the jerboa or the fish, and she makes no attempt—she would consider it futile, in view of the distinctness of each creature—to share its fundamental drives. Unlike Jean de La Fontaine, whose fables she translated, Moore draws lessons from nature obliquely, as if to say more would be embarrassing for both author and reader.

Moore lived in New York City and spent a lot of time at the Central Park Zoo and the Bronx Zoo, as might be expected, but also at Ebbets Field, where for many years she applauded the Brooklyn Dodgers (a baseball team now in Los Angeles). In the preface to *A Marianne Moore Reader,* she explains or half-explains her liking for both spectacles: "Why an inordinate interest in animals and athletes? They are subjects for art and exemplars of it, are they not? minding their own business. Pangolins, hornbills, pitchers, catchers, do not pry or prey—or prolong the conversation; do not make us self-conscious; look their best when caring least." Athletes and animals are both "miracles of dexterity."

Moore was educated at the Metzger Institute, then at Bryn Mawr College, where in 1909 she took a degree in biology and histology (animal anatomy). In Carlisle, Pennsylvania, her hometown, she went to the Carlisle Commercial College and then taught stenography at the U.S. Industrial Indian School from 1911 to 1915. In 1918, she moved to New York and worked as a private tutor, as a secretary, and then, from 1921 to 1925, as an assistant in a branch of the New York Public Library. Her first book of poems was published by the Egoist Press in England, at the instigation of friends including H. D., in 1921. From 1926 to 1929, when it ceased publication, she was editor of *The Dial,* a leading literary review. A shrewd critic in spite of her disavowals, she also published two volumes of brief but pointed essays.

In later life, Moore gave many public readings of her poems, which she continued to write, impervious to changing literary fashions. She also became a minor but genuine literary celebrity. Her elegant appearance, inevitably set off by a tricorn hat; her passionate interest in baseball; her quiet devotion to Christianity; her generosity; and her intolerance for the second-rate inspired devotion from her friends and the public at large.

Her verse is so unassuming that it is almost surprising to see how many poets—W. H. Auden, Robert Lowell, Ted Hughes, Elizabeth Bishop, Amy Clampitt, Jorie Graham—acknowledge her as the source for some of their own effects. Eliot, in a preface to her *Selected Poems* (1935), calls Moore "one of those few who have done the language some service in my lifetime." Her "predilection"—a favorite word with her and more likely to appear than "passion"—is for grace and neatness. She dislikes steamrollers and over-decoration and prefers the impromptu, the casual. Her wit plays delicately but incisively. She announces her feelings for poetry with the famous words "I too dislike it," but she goes on to celebrate poetry as "a place for the genuine," calling poets " 'literalists of / the imagination' " and their works " 'imaginary gardens with real toads in them' " ("Poetry"). As she said in "The Monkeys," art is neither difficult, nor arcane, nor symmetrically frigid, but "strict with tension, malignant / in its power over us and deeper / than the sea."

Note on the texts: Moore dramatically revised many of her poems over the years, changing their shape, size, line breaks, wording, even footnotes. In selecting which version of a poem to reprint, we have sometimes favored earlier over final revisions, since Moore, for example, reduced "Poetry" to three lines and omitted a valuable section of "An Octopus." At the end of each poem, we give the date of first publication, followed by the date of the version reprinted here.

To a Steam Roller

The illustration
is nothing to you without the application.
  You lack half wit. You crush all the particles down
    into close conformity, and then walk back and forth on them.

Sparkling chips of rock
are crushed down to the level of the parent block.
  Were not "impersonal judgment in aesthetic
    matters, a metaphysical impossibility,"[1] you

might fairly achieve
it. As for butterflies, I can hardly conceive
  of one's attending upon you, but to question
    the congruence of the complement is vain, if it exists.

1915, 1921

Critics and Connoisseurs

There is a great amount of poetry in unconscious
  fastidiousness. Certain Ming
    products, imperial floor coverings of coach
  wheel yellow, are well enough in their way but I have seen something
      that I like better—a
        mere childish attempt to make an imperfectly ballasted animal
              stand up,
        similar determination to make a pup
          eat his meat on the plate.

I remember a swan under the willows in Oxford
  with flamingo colored, maple-
    leaflike feet. It reconnoitered like a battle
  ship. Disbelief and conscious fastidiousness were the staple
      ingredients in its
        disinclination to move. Finally its hardihood was not proof
              against its

1. Slightly changed from an April 1915 article in *The New American Review* by American music critic Lawrence Gilman (1878–1939).

proclivity to more fully appraise such bits
of food as the stream

bore counter to it; it made away with what I gave it
to eat. I have seen this swan and
I have seen you; I have seen ambition without
understanding in a variety of forms. Happening to stand
by an ant hill, I have
seen a fastidious ant carrying a stick, north, south, east, west,
till it turned on
itself, struck out from the flower bed into the lawn,
and returned to the point

from which it had started. Then abandoning the stick as
useless and overtaxing its
jaws with a particle of whitewash pill-like but
heavy, it again went through the same course of procedure. What is
there in being able
to say that one has dominated the stream in an attitude of self
defense,
in proving that one has had the experience
of carrying a stick?

1916, 1924

Black Earth

Openly, yes,
with the naturalness
of the hippopotamus or the alligator
when it climbs out on the bank to experience the

sun, I do these
things which I do, which please
no one but myself. Now I breathe and now I am sub-
merged; the blemishes stand up and shout when the object

in view was a
renaissance; shall I say
the contrary? The sediment of the river which
encrusts my joints, makes me very gray but I am used

to it, it may
remain there; do away
with it and I am myself done away with, for the
patina of circumstance can but enrich what was

there to begin
with. This elephant skin

which I inhabit, fibred over like the shell of
the cocoanut, this piece of black glass through which no light

can filter—cut
into checkers by rut
upon rut of unpreventable experience—
it is a manual for the peanut-tongued and the

hairy toed. Black
but beautiful, my back
is full of the history of power. Of power? What
is powerful and what is not? My soul shall never

be cut into
by a wooden spear; through-
out childhood to the present time, the unity of
life and death has been expressed by the circumference

described by my
trunk; nevertheless, I
perceive feats of strength to be inexplicable after
all; and I am on my guard; external poise, it

has its centre
well nurtured—we know
where—in pride, but spiritual poise, it has its centre where?
My ears are sensitized to more than the sound of

the wind. I see
and I hear, unlike the
wandlike body of which one hears so much, which was made
to see and not to see; to hear and not to hear;

that tree trunk without
roots, accustomed to shout
its own thoughts to itself like a shell, maintained intact
by one who knows what strange pressure of the atmosphere; that

spiritual
brother to the coral
plant, absorbed into which, the equable sapphire light
becomes a nebulous green. The I of each is to

the I of each,
a kind of fretful speech
which sets a limit on itself; the elephant is?
Black earth preceded by a tendril? It is to that

phenomenon
the above formation,
translucent like the atmosphere—a cortex merely—
that on which darts cannot strike decisively the first

time, a substance
needful as an instance
of the indestructibility of matter; it
has looked at the electricity and at the earth-

quake and is still
here; the name means thick. Will
depth be depth, thick skin be thick, to one who can see no
beautiful element of unreason under it?

1918, 1924

The Fish

wade
through black jade.
Of the crow-blue mussel-shells, one keeps
adjusting the ash-heaps;
opening and shutting itself like

an
injured fan.
The barnacles which encrust the side
of the wave, cannot hide
there for the submerged shafts of the

sun,
split like spun
glass, move themselves with spotlight swiftness
into the crevices—
in and out, illuminating

the
turquoise sea
of bodies. The water drives a wedge
of iron through the iron edge
of the cliff; whereupon the stars,[2]

pink
rice-grains, ink-
bespattered jelly-fish, crabs like green
lilies, and submarine
toadstools, slide each on the other.

All
external
marks of abuse are present on this
defiant edifice—
all the physical features of

2. Starfish.

ac-
cident—lack
of cornice, dynamite grooves, burns, and
hatchet strokes, these things stand
out on it; the chasm-side is

dead.
Repeated
evidence has proved that it can live
on what can not revive
its youth. The sea grows old in it.

1918, 1935

In the Days of Prismatic Colour

not in the days of Adam and Eve, but when Adam
was alone; when there was no smoke and colour was
fine, not with the refinement
of early civilization art, but because
of its originality; with nothing to modify it but the

mist that went up, obliqueness was a varia-
tion of the perpendicular, plain to see and
to account for: it is no
longer that; nor did the blue-red-yellow band
of incandescence that was colour keep its stripe: it also is one of

those things into which much that is peculiar can be
read; complexity is not a crime, but carry
it to the point of murki-
ness and nothing is plain. Complexity,
moreover, that has been committed to darkness, instead of granting it-

self to be the pestilence that it is, moves all a-
bout as if to bewilder us with the dismal
fallacy that insistence
is the measure of achievement and that all
truth must be dark. Principally throat, sophistication is as it al-

ways has been—at the antipodes[3] from the init-
ial great truths. 'Part of it was crawling, part of it
was about to crawl, the rest
was torpid in its lair.'[4] In the short-legged, fit-
ful advance, the gurgling and all the minutiae—we have the classic

3. Points on the globe directly opposite one's current location.
4. "Nestor: *Greek Anthology* (Loeb Classical Library), Vol. III, p. 129" [Moore's note]. Nestor was king of Pylos in Greek legend.

multitude of feet. To what purpose! Truth is no Apollo
Belvedere,[5] no formal thing. The wave may go over it if it likes.
Know that it will be there when it says,
'I shall be there when the wave has gone by.'[6]

1919, 1935

Poetry

I, too, dislike it: there are things that are important beyond all this
fiddle.
Reading it, however, with a perfect contempt for it, one discovers in
it after all, a place for the genuine.[7]
Hands that can grasp, eyes
that can dilate, hair that can rise
if it must, these things are important not because a

high-sounding interpretation can be put upon them but because they
are
useful. When they become so derivative as to become unintelligible,
the same thing may be said for all of us, that we
do not admire what
we cannot understand: the bat
holding on upside down or in quest of something to

eat, elephants pushing, a wild horse taking a roll, a tireless wolf under
a tree, the immovable critic twitching his skin like a horse that feels a
flea, the base-
ball fan, the statistician—
nor is it valid
to discriminate against 'business documents and

school-books';[8] all these phenomena are important. One must make a
distinction
however: when dragged into prominence by half poets, the result is
not poetry,
nor till the poets among us can be
'literalists of
the imagination'[9]—above
insolence and triviality and can present

5. Statue of the Greek god Apollo in the Belvedere Courtyard of the Vatican Museum.
6. Adapted from a letter from Moore's brother, written just after he entered the navy.
7. In the final, 1967 version, Moore omitted all but these first three lines.
8. "*Diary of Tolstoy* (Dutton [1917]), p. 84. 'Where the boundary between prose and poetry lies, I shall never be able to understand. The question is raised in manuals of style, yet the answer to it lies beyond me. Poetry is verse: prose is not verse. Or else poetry is everything with the exception of business documents and school books' " [Moore's note]. Count Leo Tolstoy (1828–1910), Russian novelist.
9. "[W. B.] Yeats: *Ideas of Good and Evil* (A. H. Bullen [1903], p. 182. 'The limitation of his [Blake's] view was from the very intensity of his vision; he was a too literal realist of imagination as others are of nature; and because he believed that the figures seen by the mind's eye, when exalted by inspiration, were 'eternal existences,' symbols of divine essences, he hated every grace of style that might obscure their lineaments' " [Moore's note].

for inspection, 'imaginary gardens with real toads in them', shall we have
it. In the meantime, if you demand on the one hand,
the raw material of poetry in
all its rawness and
that which is on the other hand
genuine, you are interested in poetry.

1919, 1951

England

With its baby rivers and little towns, each with its abbey or its cathedral,
with voices—one voice perhaps, echoing through the transept[1]—the
criterion of suitability and convenience: and Italy with its equal
shores—contriving an epicureanism from which the grossness has been

extracted: and Greece with its goats and its gourds, the nest of modified illusions:
and France, the "chrysalis of the nocturnal butterfly"[2] in
whose products, mystery of construction diverts one from what was originally one's
object—substance at the core: and the East with its snails, its emotional

shorthand and jade cockroaches, its rock crystal and its imperturbability,
all of museum quality: and America where there
is the little old ramshackle victoria in the south, where cigars are smoked on the
street in the north; where there are no proof readers, no silkworms, no digressions;

the wild man's land; grass-less, links-less, language-less country in which letters are written
not in Spanish, not in Greek, not in Latin, not in short-hand
but in plain American which cats and dogs can read! The letter "a" in psalm and calm when

pronounced with the sound of "a" in candle, is very noticeable but
why should continents of misapprehension have to be accounted for by the
fact? Does it follow that because there are poisonous toadstools
which resemble mushrooms, both are dangerous? In the case of mettlesomeness which may be
mistaken for appetite, of heat which may appear to be haste, no con-

1. The "cross" section, at right angles to the main axis, of a cruciform church.

2. "Erté" [Moore's note]. Erté (1892–1990) was a fashion illustrator and stage designer.

clusions may be drawn. To have misapprehended the matter, is to have
confessed
that one has not looked far enough. The sublimated wisdom
of China, Egyptian discernment, the cataclysmic torrent of emotion
compressed
in the verbs of the Hebrew language, the books of the man who is
able

to say, "I envy nobody but him and him only, who catches more fish
than
I do,"[3]—the flower and fruit of all that noted superi-
ority—should one not have stumbled upon it in America, must one
imagine
that it is not there? It has never been confined to one locality.

1920, 1924

A Grave

Man looking into the sea,
taking the view from those who have as much right to it as you have to
yourself,
it is human nature to stand in the middle of a thing,
but you cannot stand in the middle of this;
the sea has nothing to give but a well excavated grave.
The firs stand in a procession, each with an emerald turkey-foot at the
top,
reserved as their contours, saying nothing;
repression, however, is not the most obvious characteristic of the sea;
the sea is a collector, quick to return a rapacious look.
There are others besides you who have worn that look—
whose expression is no longer a protest; the fish no longer investigate
them
for their bones have not lasted:
men lower nets, unconscious of the fact that they are desecrating a
grave,
and row quickly away—the blades of the oars
moving together like the feet of water-spiders as if there were no such
thing as death.
The wrinkles progress among themselves in a phalanx[4]—beautiful under
networks of foam,
and fade breathlessly while the sea rustles in and out of the seaweed;
the birds swim through the air at top speed, emitting cat-calls as
heretofore—
the tortoise-shell scourges about the feet of the cliffs, in motion
beneath them;
and the ocean, under the pulsation of lighthouses and noise of bell-
buoys,

3. "*Compleat Angler*" [Moore's note]. The title of a treatise on fishing by English author Izaak Walton (1593–1683).
4. Body of troops in close array.

advances as usual, looking as if it were not that ocean in which dropped
things are bound to sink—
in which if they turn and twist, it is neither with volition nor
consciousness.

1921, 1935

An Octopus

of ice. Deceptively reserved and flat,
it lies 'in grandeur and in mass'[5]
beneath a sea of shifting snow-dunes;
dots of cyclamen-red and maroon on its clearly defined pseudopodia[6]
made of glass that will bend[7]—a much needed invention—
comprising twenty-eight ice-fields from fifty to five hundred feet thick,
of unimagined delicacy.
'Picking periwinkles from the cracks'[8]
or killing prey with the concentric crushing rigour of the python,
it hovers forward 'spider fashion
on its arms'[9] misleadingly like lace;
its 'ghostly pallor[1] changing
to the green metallic tinge of an anemone-starred pool'.
The fir-trees, in 'the magnitude of their root systems',[2]
rise aloof from these manoeuvres 'creepy to behold',[3]
austere specimens of our American royal families,
'each like the shadow of the one beside it.
The rock seems frail compared with their dark energy of life',[4]
its vermilion and onyx and manganese-blue[5] interior expensiveness
left at the mercy of the weather;
'stained transversely by iron where the water drips down',
recognized by its plants and its animals.
Completing a circle,
you have been deceived into thinking that you have progressed,

5. "Quoted lines of which the source is not given, are from Department of the Interior Rules and Regulations, The National Parks Portfolio [1922]" [Moore's note]. In the summers of 1922 and 1923, Moore traveled to the northwest and, on the first trip, climbed part of the way up Mt. Rainier (also known as Mt. Tacoma), in Washington State. On the mountain, a large alpine meadow, Paradise Park, overlooks the eight-armed Nisqually glacier. The poem was originally conceived as part of a longer piece that Moore split into "An Octopus" and "Marriage."

6. A tendril-like protrusion of the cytoplasm of an amoeba, used for locomotion or food gathering.

7. "Sir William Bell, of the British Institute of Patentees, has made a list of inventions which he says the world needs: glass that will bend; a smooth road surface that will not be slippery in wet weather; a furnace that will conserve 95 per cent. of its heat; a process to make flannel unshrinkable; a noiseless airplane; a motor engine of one pound weight per horsepower; methods to reduce friction; a process to extract phosphorous from vulcanized indiarubber, so that it can be boiled up and used again; practical ways of utilizing the tides" [Moore's note].

8. "M. C. Carey, *London Graphic,* 25th August, 1923" [Moore's note]. *Periwinkles:* both edible snails and the purple flowers of an evergreen groundcover.

9. "W. P. Pycraft: *Illustrated London News,* 28th June, 1924" [Moore's note].

1. " 'Ghostly pallor', 'Creeping slowly' [line 209]. Francis Ward: *Illustrated London News,* 11th August, 1923" [Moore's note].

2. "John Muir" [Moore's note]. Naturalist and conservationist (1838–1914).

3. "W. P. Pycraft: *Illustrated London News,* 28th June, 1924" [Moore's note].

4. "Ruskin" [Moore's note]. John Ruskin (1819–1900), English art critic and essayist.

5. " 'Thoughtful beavers', 'blue stone forests', 'bristling, puny, swearing men', 'tear the snow', 'flat on the ground', 'bent in a half circle' [lines 45, 52, 144, 211, 215, 216]. Clifton Johnson: *What to See in America* (Macmillan [1919])" [Moore's note].

under the polite needles of the larches
'hung to filter, not to intercept the sunlight'—
met by tightly wattled spruce-twigs
'conformed to an edge[6] like clipped cypress
as if no branch could penetrate the cold beyond its company';
and dumps of gold and silver ore enclosing The Goat's Mirror[7]—
that lady-fingerlike depression in the shape of the left human foot,
which prejudices you in favour of itself
before you have had time to see the others;
its indigo, pea-green, blue-green, and turquoise,
from a hundred to two hundred feet deep,
'merging in irregular patches in the middle lake
where, like gusts of a storm
obliterating the shadows of the fir-trees, the wind makes lanes of
ripples'.
What spot could have merits of equal importance
for bears, elk, deer, wolves, goats, and ducks?
Pre-empted by their ancestors,
this is the property of the exacting porcupine,
and of the rat 'slipping along to its burrow in the swamp
or pausing on high ground to smell the heather';
of 'thoughtful beavers
making drains which seem the work of careful men with shovels',
and of the bears inspecting unexpectedly
ant-hills and berry-bushes.
Composed of calcium gems and alabaster pillars,
topaz, tourmaline crystals and amethyst quartz,
their den is somewhere else, concealed in the confusion
of 'blue forests thrown together with marble and jasper and agate
as if whole quarries had been dynamited'.
And farther up, in stag-at-bay position
as a scintillating fragment of these terrible stalagmites,
stands the goat,
its eye fixed on the waterfall which never seems to fall—
an endless skein swayed by the wind,
immune to force of gravity in the perspective of the peaks.
A special antelope
acclimated to 'grottoes from which issue penetrating draughts
which make you wonder why you came',
it stands its ground
on cliffs the colour of the clouds, of petrified white vapour—
black feet, eyes, nose, and horns, engraved on dazzling ice-fields,
the ermine body on the crystal peak;
the sun kindling its shoulders to maximum heat like acetylene,[8] dyeing
them white—
upon this antique pedestal,

6. "'Conformed to an edge', 'grottoes', 'two pairs of trousers'—'My old packer, Bill Peyto . . . would give one or two nervous yanks at the fringe and tear off the longer pieces, so that his outer trousers disappeared day by day from below upwards. . . . (He usually wears two pairs of trousers)'—'glass eyes', 'business men', 'with a sound like the crack of a rifle'[lines 28, 61, 79, 111, 115, 226]. W. D. Wilcox: *The Rockies of Canada* (Putnam [1903])" [Moore's note].

7. A lake. The phrase was originally used by Wilcox to describe Canada's Lake Louise.

8. Flammable gas used as welding fuel.

'a mountain with those graceful lines which prove it a volcano',
its top a complete cone like Fujiyama's[9]
till an explosion blew it off.
Distinguished by a beauty
of which 'the visitor dare never fully speak at home
for fear of being stoned as an impostor',
Big Snow Mountain is the home of a diversity of creatures:
those who 'have lived in hotels
but who now live in camps—who prefer to';
the mountain guide evolving from the trapper,
'in two pairs of trousers, the outer one older,
wearing slowly away from the feet to the knees';
'the nine-striped chipmunk
running with unmammal-like agility along a log';
the water ouzel[1]
with 'its passion for rapids and high-pressured falls',
building under the arch of some tiny Niagara;
the white-tailed ptarmigan 'in winter solid white,
feeding on heather-bells and alpine buckwheat';
and the eleven eagles of the west,
'fond of the spring fragrance and the winter colours',
used to the unegoistic action of the glaciers
and 'several hours of frost every midsummer night'.
'They make a nice appearance, don't they',[2]
happy seeing nothing?
Perched on treacherous lava and pumice—
those unadjusted chimney-pots and cleavers
which stipulate 'names and addresses of persons to notify
in case of disaster'—
they hear the roar of ice and supervise the water
winding slowly through the cliffs,
the road 'climbing like the thread
which forms the groove around a snail-shell,
doubling back and forth until where snow begins, it ends'.
No 'deliberate wide-eyed wistfulness' is here
among the boulders sunk in ripples and white water
where 'when you hear the best wild music of the forest
it is sure to be a marmot',
the victim on some slight observatory,
of 'a struggle between curiosity and caution',
inquiring what has scared it:
a stone from the moraine descending in leaps,
another marmot, or the spotted ponies with glass eyes,
brought up on frosty grass and flowers
and rapid draughts of ice-water.
Instructed none knows how, to climb the mountain,
by business men who as totemic scenery of Canada,
require for recreation
three hundred and sixty-five holidays in the year,

9. Volcano and highest mountain in Japan.
1. Bird that walks along the bottom of mountain streams in search of food.
2. "Overheard at the circus" [Moore's note].

these conspicuously spotted little horses are peculiar;
hard to discern among the birch-trees, ferns, and lily-pads,
avalanche lilies, Indian paint-brushes,
bear's ears and kittentails,
and miniature cavalcades of chlorophylless fungi
magnified in profile on the mossbeds like moonstones in the water;
the cavalcade of calico competing
with the original American menagerie of styles[3]
among the white flowers of the rhododendron surmounting rigid leaves
upon which moisture works its alchemy,
transmuting verdure into onyx.
Larkspur, blue pincushions, blue peas, and lupin;
white flowers with white, and red with red;
the blue ones 'growing close together
so that patches of them look like blue water in the distance';
this arrangement of colours
as in Persian designs of hard stones with enamel,
forms a pleasing equation—
a diamond outside, and inside, a white dot;
on the outside, a ruby; inside, a red dot;
black spots balanced with black
in the woodlands where fires have run over the ground—
separated by aspens, cat's paws, and woolly sunflowers,
fireweed, asters, and Goliath thistles
'flowering at all altitudes as multiplicitous as barley',
like pink sapphires in the pavement of the glistening plateau.
Inimical to 'bristling, puny, swearing men
equipped with saws and axes',
this treacherous glass mountain
admires gentians, lady-slippers, harebells, mountain dryads,
and 'Calypso, the goat flower—
that greenish orchid fond of snow'—
anomalously nourished on shelving glacial ledges
where climbers have not gone or have gone timidly,
'the one resting his nerves while the other advanced',
on this volcano with the blue jay, her principal companion.
'Hopping stiffly on sharp feet' like miniature ice-hacks—
'secretive, with a look of wisdom and distinction, but a villain,
fond of human society or the crumbs that go with it',
he knows no Greek,
'that pride-producing language',[4]
in which 'rashness is rendered innocuous, and error exposed
by the collision of knowledge with knowledge'.

'Like happy souls in Hell', enjoying mental difficulties,
the grasshoppers of Greece
amused themselves with delicate behaviour
because it was 'so noble and so fair';[5]

3. "W. M., 'The Mystery of an Adjective and of Evening Clothes'. *London Graphic,* 21st June, 1924" [Moore's note].
4. "Anthony Trollope's *Autobiography*" [Moore's note]. Anthony Trollope (1815–1882), English novelist.
5. " 'Rashness is rendered innocuous' [line 159], 'So noble and so fair'. Cardinal Newman: *Historical*

not practised in adapting their intelligence
to eagle-traps and snow-shoes,
to alpenstocks[6] and other toys contrived by those
'alive to the advantage of invigorating pleasures'.
Bows, arrows, oars, and paddles, for which trees provide the wood,
in new countries more eloquent than elsewhere—
augmenting the assertion that, essentially humane,
'the forest affords wood for dwellings and by its beauty stimulates
the moral vigour of its citizens'.
The Greeks liked smoothness, distrusting what was back
of what could not be clearly seen,
resolving with benevolent conclusiveness,
'complexities which still will be complexities[7]
as long as the world lasts';
ascribing what we clumsily call happiness,
to 'an accident or a quality,
a spiritual substance or the soul itself,
an act, a disposition, or a habit,
or a habit infused, to which the soul has been persuaded,
or something distinct from a habit, a power—'
such power as Adam had and we are still devoid of.
'Emotionally sensitive,[8] their hearts were hard';
their wisdom was remote
from that of these odd oracles of cool official sarcasm,
upon this game preserve
where 'guns, nets, seines, traps and explosives,
hired vehicles, gambling and intoxicants are prohibited;
disobedient persons being summarily removed
and not allowed to return without permission in writing.'
It is self-evident
that it is frightful to have everything afraid of one;
that one must do as one is told
and eat 'rice, prunes, dates, raisins, hardtack, and tomatoes'
if one would 'conquer the main peak' of Mount Tacoma,
this fossil flower concise without a shiver,
intact when it is cut,
damned for its sacrosanct remoteness—
like Henry James[9] 'damned by the public for decorum';
not decorum, but restraint;
it is the love of doing hard things
that rebuffed and wore them out—a public out of sympathy with
neatness.
Neatness of finish! Neatness of finish![1]
Relentless accuracy is the nature of this octopus

Sketches" [Moore's note]. John Henry Newman (1801–1890), British theologian.

6. Pointed staffs used in mountain climbing.

7. " 'Complexities . . . an accident'. Richard Baxter: *The Saints' Everlasting Rest*" [Moore's note]. Richard Baxter (1615–1691), English preacher and theologian.

8. " 'The Greeks were emotionally sensitive'. W. D. Hyde: *The Five Great Philosophies* (Macmillan [1911])" [Moore's note].

9. American novelist (1843–1916).

1. Though Moore had been reading James at the time of composition, she likely adapts this phrase from William Carlos Williams's *Kora in Hell* 21.2: "Neatness and finish, the dust out of every corner, you swish from room to room and find all perfect. The house may now be carefully wrapped in brown paper and sent to a publisher. It is a work of art."

with its capacity for fact.
'Creeping slowly as with meditated stealth,
its arms seeming to approach from all directions,'
it receives one under winds that 'tear the snow to bits
and hurl it like a sandblast
shearing off twigs and loose bark from the trees'.
Is 'tree' the word for these things
'flat on the ground like vines'?
some 'bent in a half circle with branches on one side
suggesting dust-brushes, not trees;
some finding strength in union, forming little stunted groves,
their flattened mats of branches shrunk in trying to escape'
from the hard mountain 'planed by ice and polished by the wind'—
the white volcano with no weather side;
the lightning flashing at its base,
rain falling in the valleys, and snow falling on the peak—
the glassy octopus symmetrically pointed,
its claw cut by the avalanche
'with a sound like the crack of a rifle,
in a curtain of powdered snow launched like a waterfall.'

1924, 1935

To a Snail

If "compression is the first grace of style,"[2]
you have it. Contractility is a virtue
as modesty is a virtue.
It is not the acquisition of any one thing
that is able to adorn,
or the incidental quality that occurs
as a concomitant of something well said,
that we value in style,
but the principle that is hid:
in the absence of feet, "a method of conclusions";
"a knowledge of principles,"[3]
in the curious phenomenon of your occipital[4] horn.

1924

The Steeple-Jack

Revised, 1961

Dürer[5] would have seen a reason for living
in a town like this, with eight stranded whales

2. " 'The very first grace of style is that which comes from compression.' *Demetrius on Style* translated by W. Hamilton Fyfe. Heinemann, 1932" [Moore's 1951 note]. Demetrius (350–280 B.C.E.), Athenian politician and philosopher.

3. Phrases from a discussion of theology in *Medieval Mind,* by Scottish philosopher John Duns Scotus (c. 1266–1308).

4. That is, near the back of the head.

5. Albrecht Dürer (1471–1528), German artist.

to look at; with the sweet sea air coming into your house
on a fine day, from water etched
with waves as formal as the scales
on a fish.

One by one in two's and three's, the seagulls keep
flying back and forth over the town clock,
or sailing around the lighthouse without moving their wings—
rising steadily with a slight
quiver of the body—or flock
mewing where

a sea the purple of the peacock's neck is
paled to greenish azure as Dürer changed
the pine green of the Tyrol to peacock blue and guinea
gray. You can see a twenty-five-
pound lobster; and fish nets arranged
to dry. The

whirlwind fife-and-drum of the storm bends the salt
marsh grass, disturbs stars in the sky and the
star on the steeple; it is a privilege to see so
much confusion. Disguised by what
might seem the opposite, the sea-
side flowers and

trees are favored by the fog so that you have
the tropics at first hand: the trumpet vine,
foxglove, giant snapdragon, a salpiglossis that has
spots and stripes; morning-glories, gourds,
or moon-vines trained on fishing twine
at the back door:

cattails, flags, blueberries and spiderwort,
striped grass, lichens, sunflowers, asters, daisies—
yellow and crab-claw ragged sailors with green bracts—toad-plant,
petunias, ferns; pink lilies, blue
ones, tigers; poppies; black sweet-peas.
The climate

is not right for the banyan, frangipani, or
jack-fruit trees; or for exotic serpent
life. Ring lizard and snakeskin for the foot, if you see fit;
but here they've cats, not cobras, to
keep down the rats. The diffident
little newt

with white pin-dots on black horizontal spaced-
out bands lives here; yet there is nothing that
ambition can buy or take away. The college student
named Ambrose sits on the hillside
with his not-native books and hat
and sees boats

at sea progress white and rigid as if in
a groove. Liking an elegance of which
the source is not bravado, he knows by heart the antique
sugar-bowl shaped summerhouse of
interlacing slats, and the pitch
of the church

spire, not true, from which a man in scarlet lets
down a rope as a spider spins a thread;
he might be part of a novel, but on the sidewalk a
sign says C. J. Poole, Steeple Jack,[6]
in black and white; and one in red
and white says

Danger. The church portico has four fluted
columns, each a single piece of stone, made
modester by whitewash. This would be a fit haven for
waifs, children, animals, prisoners,
and presidents who have repaid
sin-driven

senators by not thinking about them. The
place has a schoolhouse, a post-office in a
store, fish-houses, hen-houses, a three-masted schooner on
the stocks. The hero, the student,
the steeple jack, each in his way,
is at home.

It could not be dangerous to be living
in a town like this, of simple people,
who have a steeple-jack placing danger signs by the church
while he is gilding the solid-
pointed star, which on a steeple
stands for hope.

1932, 1961

The Pangolin[7]

Another armoured animal—scale
lapping scale with spruce-cone regularity until they
form the uninterrupted central
tail-row! This near artichoke with head and legs and grit-equipped
gizzard,
the night miniature artist engineer is
Leonardo's—da Vinci's replica—

6. Moore identifies him as the steeple-jack (person who climbs steeples to repair them) "who removed the Lafayette Avenue Presbyterian Church steeple at the time the 8th Avenue Independent Subway on Lafayette Avenue was being completed, threatening the foundation and other stonework of the church."

7. An anteater.

impressive animal and toiler of whom we seldom hear.
Armour seems extra. But for him,
the closing ear-ridge—[8]
or bare ear lacking even this small
eminence and similarly safe

contracting nose and eye apertures
impenetrably closable, are not;—a true ant-eater,
not cockroach-eater, who endures
exhausting solitary trips through unfamiliar ground at night,
returning before sunrise; stepping in the moonlight,
on the moonlight peculiarly,[9] that the outside
edges of his hands may bear the weight and save the claws
for digging. Serpentined about
the tree, he draws
away from danger unpugnaciously,
with no sound but a harmless hiss; keeping

the fragile grace of the Thomas-
of-Leighton Buzzard Westminster Abbey wrought-iron vine,[1] or
rolls himself into a ball that has
power to defy all effort to unroll it; strongly intailed, neat
head for core, on neck not breaking off, with curled-in feet.
Nevertheless he has sting-proof scales; and nest
of rocks closed with earth from inside, which he can thus
darken.
Sun and moon and day and night and man and beast
each with a splendour
which man in all his vileness cannot
set aside; each with an excellence!

'Fearful yet to be feared,' the armoured
ant-eater met by the driver-ant does not turn back, but
engulfs what he can, the flattened sword-
edged leafpoints on the tail and artichoke set leg- and body-plates
quivering violently when it retaliates
and swarms on him. Compact like the furled fringed frill
on the hat-brim of Gargallo's[2] hollow iron head of a
matador, he will drop and will
then walk away
unhurt, although if unintruded on,
he cautiously works down the tree, helped

by his tail. The giant-pangolin-
tail, graceful tool, as prop or hand or broom or axe, tipped like
the elephant's trunk with special skin,
is not lost on this ant- and stone-swallowing uninjurable

8. "The 'closing ear-ridge', and certain other detail, from *Pangolins* by Robert T. Hatt; *Natural History*, December 1935" [Moore's note].
9. "See Lyddeker's *Royal Natural History*" [Moore's note].
1. "A fragment of ironwork in Westminister Abbey" [Moore's note]. *Leighton Buzzard:* ancient market town forty miles from London.
2. Pablo Gargallo (1881–1934), Spanish sculptor who worked in iron.

artichoke which simpletons thought a living fable
whom the stones had nourished, whereas ants had done
so. Pangolins are not aggressive animals; between
dusk and day they have the not unchain-like machine-like
form and frictionless creep of a thing
made graceful by adversities, con-

versities. To explain grace requires
a curious hand. If that which is at all were not forever,
why would those who graced the spires
with animals and gathered there to rest, on cold luxurious
low stone seats—a monk and monk and monk—between the thus
ingenious roof-supports, have slaved to confuse
grace with a kindly manner, time in which to pay a debt,
the cure for sins, a graceful use
of what are yet
approved stone mullions[3] branching out across
the perpendiculars? A sailboat

was the first machine.[4] Pangolins, made
for moving quietly also, are models of exactness,
on four legs; or hind feet plantigrade,
with certain postures of a man. Beneath sun and moon, man slaving
to make his life more sweet, leaves half the flowers worth having,
needing to choose wisely how to use the strength;
a paper-maker like the wasp; a tractor of food-stuffs,
like the ant; spidering a length
of web from bluffs
above a stream; in fighting, mechanicked
like the pangolin; capsizing in

disheartenment. Bedizened or stark
naked, man, the self, the being we call human, writing-
master to this world, griffons[5] a dark
'Like does not like like that is obnoxious'; and writes error with four
r's. Among animals, one has a sense of humour.
Humour saves a few steps, it saves years. Unignorant,
modest and unemotional, and all emotion,
he has everlasting vigour,
power to grow,
though there are few creatures who can make one
breathe faster and make one erecter.

Not afraid of anything is he,
and then goes cowering forth, tread paced to meet an obstacle
at every step. Consistent with the
formula—warm blood, no gills, two pairs of hands and a few hairs—
that
is a mammal; there he sits in his own habitat,

3. Decorative vertical strips in windows.
4. "See F. L. Moore: *Power: Its Application from the 17th Dynasty to the Twentieth Century*" [Moore's note].
5. Mythical beast, part eagle, part lion; here used as a verb.

serge-clad, strong-shod. The prey of fear, he, always
curtailed, extinguished, thwarted by the dusk, work partly done,
says to the alternating blaze,
'Again the sun!
anew each day; and new and new and new,
that comes into and steadies my soul.'

1936, 1951

The Paper Nautilus[6]

For authorities whose hopes
are shaped by mercenaries?
Writers entrapped by
teatime fame and by
commuters' comforts? Not for these
the paper nautilus
constructs her thin glass shell.

Giving her perishable
souvenir of hope, a dull
white outside and smooth-
edged inner surface
glossy as the sea, the watchful
maker of it guards it
day and night; she scarcely

eats until the eggs are hatched.
Buried eight-fold in her eight
arms, for she is in
a sense a devil-
fish, her glass ram'shorn-cradled freight
is hid but is not crushed;
as Hercules,[7] bitten

by a crab loyal to the hydra,
was hindered to succeed,
the intensively
watched eggs coming from
the shell free it when they are freed,—
leaving its wasp-nest flaws
of white on white, and close-

laid Ionic chiton-folds[8]
like the lines in the mane of
a Parthenon[9] horse,

6. The female of this species of eight-legged mollusk lays its eggs in a delicate, paper-thin shell.
7. Hero of Greek and Roman mythology who faced the trial of killing the Hydra, a monstrous snake with multiple heads; during the fight, Hercules crushed a crab that bit him.
8. *Chiton:* ancient Greek tunic or type of mollusk. *Ionic:* style of Greek architecture characterized by the spiral ornaments at the head of the column.
9. Athenian temple; its sculptures include processions of horses.

round which the arms had
wound themselves as if they knew love
is the only fortress
strong enough to trust to.

1940, 1941

What Are Years?[1]

What is our innocence,
what is our guilt? All are
naked, none is safe. And whence
is courage: the unanswered question,
the resolute doubt,—
dumbly calling, deafly listening—that
in misfortune, even death,
encourages others
and in its defeat, stirs

the soul to be strong? He
sees deep and is glad, who
accedes to mortality
and in his imprisonment rises
upon himself as
the sea in a chasm, struggling to be
free and unable to be,
in its surrendering
finds its continuing.

So he who strongly feels,
behaves. The very bird,
grown taller as he sings, steels
his form straight up. Though he is captive,
his mighty singing
says, satisfaction is a lowly
thing, how pure a thing is joy.
This is mortality,
this is eternity.

1940, 1941

1. In a note sent to W. R. Benet and Norman Holmes Pearson, Moore said that the poem was "partly written in 1931 and finished in 1939. The desperation attendant on moral fallibility is mitigated for me by admitting that the most willed and resolute vigilance may lapse, as with the Apostle Peter's denial that he could be capable of denial; but that failure, disgrace, and even death have now and again been redeemed into inviolateness by a sufficiently transfigured courage."

He "Digesteth Harde Yron"[2]

Although the aepyornis
or roc that lived in Madagascar, and
the moa are extinct,[3]
the camel-sparrow, linked
with them in size—the large sparrow
Xenophon saw walking by
a stream[4]—was and is
a symbol of justice.

This bird watches his chicks with
a maternal concentration, after
he has sat on the eggs
at night six weeks, his legs
their only weapon of defense.
He is swifter than a horse;
he has a foot hard
as a hoof; the leopard

is not more suspicious. How
could he, prized for plumes and eggs and young, used
even as a riding-
beast, respect men hiding
actorlike in ostrich-skins, with
the right hand making the neck move
as if alive and
from a bag the left hand

strewing grain, that ostriches
might be decoyed and killed! Yes this is he
whose plume was anciently
the plume of justice;[5] he
whose comic duckling head on its
great neck, revolves with compass-
needle nervousness,
when he stands guard, in S-

like foragings as he is
preening the down on his leaden-skinned back.
The egg piously shown
as Leda's very own

2. "[John] Lyly's *Euphues*" [1580]: 'the estrich digesteth harde yron to preserve his health' [Moore's note].
3. *Aepyornis* and *moa:* prehistoric birds. *Roc:* legendary bird of great size.
4. Xenophon (born c. 430 B.C.E.), Greek historian. " 'Xenophon (Anabasis I,5,2) reports many ostriches in the desert on the left . . . side of the middle Euphrates, on the way from North Syria to Babylonia.' *Animals for Show and Pleasure in Ancient Rome* by George Jennison" [Moore's note].
5. For this phrase and for "men . . . in ostrich-skins" above and "Leda's very own [egg]" below, Moore refers to "*Ostrich Egg-Shell Cups from Mesopotamia* by Berthold Laufer, The Open Court, May 1926. 'An ostrich plume symbolized truth and justice, and was the emblem of the goddess Ma-at, the patron saint of judges. Her head is adorned with an ostrich feather, her eyes are closed, . . . as Justice is blind-folded.' "

from which Castor and Pollux hatched,[6]
was an ostrich-egg. And what
could have been more fit
for the Chinese lawn it

grazed on, as a gift to an
emperor who admired strange birds, than this
one who builds his mud-made
nest in dust yet will wade
in lake or sea till only the
head shows. A nervous restless
bird that flees at sight
of danger, he feigns flight

to save his chicks, decoying
his decoyers; never known to hide his
head in sand, yet lagging
when he must, and dragging
an as-if-wounded wing. The friend
of hippotigers and wild
asses, it is as
though schooled by them he was

the best of the unflying
pegasi,[7] since the Greeks "caught a few wild
asses but no ostrich;"
quadrupedlike bird which
flies on feet not wings,—his moth-silk
plumage wilted by his speed;
mobile wings and tail
behaving as a sail.

Six hundred ostrich-brains served
at one banquet,[8] the ostrich-plume-tipped tent
and desert spear, jewel-
gorgeous ugly egg-shell
goblets,[9] eight pairs of ostriches
in harness,[1] dramatize a
meaning always missed
by the externalist.

The power of the visible
is the invisible; as even where
no tree of freedom grows,
so-called brute courage knows.

6. Zeus, ruler of the Greek gods, took on the form of a swan to rape the mortal woman Leda; their offspring was an egg, from which hatched not only the twins Castor and Pollux, but also Helen of Troy and the murderous queen Clytemnestra.
7. Plural form of Pegasus, the winged horse of Greek mythology.
8. "At a banquet given by Elagabalus. See above: *Animals for Show and Pleasure*" [Moore's note].
9. Moore gives as example "the painted ostrich-egg cup mounted in silver-gilt by Elias Geier of Leipzig about 1589. *Antiques in and About London* by Edward Wenham; *New York Sun*, May 22, 1937."
1. "See above; *Animals for Show and Pleasure*" [Moore's note].

Heroism is exhausting, yet
it contradicts a greed that
did not wisely spare
the harmless solitaire

or great auk in its grandeur;
unsolicitude having swallowed up
all giant birds but an
alert gargantuan
little-winged, magnificently
speedy running-bird. This one
remaining rebel
is the sparrow-camel.[2]

1941

2. Cf. line 4 ("camel-sparrows"). In her note, Moore gives the name in Greek.

JOHN CROWE RANSOM
1888–1974

John Crowe Ransom's poems could never be mistaken for anybody else's. Quirky, at times eccentric, they are among the most remarkable poems to come out of the American south in the twentieth century. Ransom's wit is Metaphysical, but besides the elaborated central image, he offers a self-deprecating frivolity in dealing with grave subjects. The implication is that a poem deals in both messages and counter-messages. Yet it is not so much the wit as the mannered diction that leaps first from Ransom's page: he cultivated archaisms, mock-pedanticisms, unaccustomed usages. It is as if, to express himself in the modern world, he had to don an antique mask. The pull of the past was powerful for Ransom—the past of language, of literature, and of southern society.

In accepting the Bollingen Prize for verse in 1964, Ransom recalled that he had, in youth, tried "to escape from the stilted and sentimental verbal habits which conditioned" him. Ransom's mature poetry, however archaic its diction and decorous its quatrains, is modernist in its antisentimentality, discordance, and tonal complexity. Powerful feelings such as love and grief are presented with restraint and explored with impersonal wit. His poems on charged subjects—such as the death of children in the elegies "Bells for John Whiteside's Daughter" and "Dead Boy"—subdue, distill, even ironize emotion. In "The Concrete Universal: Observations on the Understanding of Poetry," Ransom explains that the poem, as an organism, is a "joint production" of "the head in an intellectual language, the heart in an affective language, the feet in a rhythmical language." He allows for disharmony among the three, so that their relationship may be as complex as possible. Sometimes, he makes the stanzaic pattern jangle against the subject matter, the rhyme or rhythm or image against the expected feeling.

Ransom was avowedly a formalist; he saw formalism as a check on bluntness, on brutality. Most modern poetry seemed to him to err in its exclusive aim of being sincere and spontaneous. Only as an art could it survive, and Ransom accordingly endorsed technique that was "vain and affected . . . like the technique of fine manners, or of ritual" (*The World's Body*). The poem was, for the conservative Ransom, a microcosm of society. With his sometime pupils Allen Tate and Robert Penn Warren, Ransom was a leading member of the Fugitives, a group of southern writers mostly centered at Vanderbilt University who sought to recover and preserve the values of the Old South against the corruptions of industrialism, which would destroy, like an invading Northern army, all delicate gradations. An agrarian culture appeared most likely to keep the best in the past together. Ransom's social views were probably influenced by T. S. Eliot, although he disliked Eliot's verse. Playing on Eliot's famous tripartite self-characterization, Ransom offered as his own program "something like this: In manners, aristocratic; in religion, ritualistic; in art, traditional" (*World's Body*). If not especially accurate, this self-description shows the terms he found favorable, at a time when they were all being assailed.

Ransom's traditionalism was prominent in his first prose book, *God without Thunder* (1930). There, adopting the guise of a southern fundamentalist, he urged that religion, or rather religious myth, was necessary. Sounding like the minister's son he was, he prescribed religious orthodoxy and a virile God. His next book, *The World's Body* (1938), was more urbane. The fullness of the natural, he argued, could be represented by poetry rather than by religion. Then, in *The New Criticism* (1941), Ransom called for an "ontological critic," one who would demonstrate how in poetry logical structure and variegated detail join to present the world's concrete body. In this increasingly secular way, Ransom made the role of the critic very similar to the function of many of his own poems, such as "Painted Head."

Ransom was born on April 30, 1888, in Pulaski, Tennessee. He received an A.B. degree from Vanderbilt in 1909, and as a Rhodes scholar, he took a B.A. at Christ Church, Oxford University, in 1913. He was a lieutenant in World War I. Afterward, he returned to Vanderbilt, where he had taught, and remained there until 1937. In that year, to the surprise of many, he moved north to Kenyon College and became founder and editor of the *Kenyon Review*, which was to be the best-known literary review in the United States from 1937 until his retirement in 1959.

Ransom published his three books of poems between 1919 and 1927, after which his interest shifted to criticism. In his poetry, Ransom often, as he said of Allen Tate, uses obscurity to avoid sententiousness. Most of his poems recount losses and failures and have about them a rich disheartenment and, in spite of their anti-Romanticism, a shine of old romance. But they are more than nostalgic; their language, tensions, and incongruities give them excitement and make even the portrayal of failure an expressive triumph, witty yet serious and even desperate.

Bells for John Whiteside's Daughter

There was such speed in her little body,
And such lightness in her footfall,
It is no wonder her brown study
Astonishes us all.

Her wars were bruited[1] in our high window.
We looked among orchard trees and beyond
Where she took arms against her shadow,
Or harried unto the pond

1. Loudly voiced.

The lazy geese, like a snow cloud
Dripping their snow on the green grass,
Tricking and stopping, sleepy and proud,
Who cried in goose, Alas,

For the tireless heart within the little
Lady with rod that made them rise
From their noon apple-dreams and scuttle
Goose-fashion under the skies!

But now go the bells, and we are ready,
In one house we are sternly stopped
To say we are vexed at her brown study,
Lying so primly propped.

1924

Here Lies a Lady

Here lies a lady of beauty and high degree,
Of chills and fever she died, of fever and chills,
The delight of her husband, an aunt, an infant of three
And medicos[2] marveling sweetly on her ills.

First she was hot, and her brightest eyes would blaze
And the speed of her flying fingers shook their heads.
What was she making? God knows; she sat in those days
With her newest gowns all torn, or snipt into shreds.

But that would pass, and the fire of her cheeks decline
Till she lay dishonored and wan like a rose overblown,
And would not open her eyes, to kisses, to wine;
The sixth of which states was final. The cold came down.

Fair ladies, long may you bloom, and sweetly may thole![3]
She was part lucky. With flowers and lace and mourning,
With love and bravado, we bade God rest her soul
After six quick turns of quaking, six of burning.

1924, 1945

Piazza Piece[4]

—I am a gentleman in a dustcoat trying
To make you hear. Your ears are soft and small
And listen to an old man not at all,

2. Doctors (slang)
3. Endure (archaic).
4. A reenactment of the old folk tale of Death and the Maiden. *Piazza:* porch.

They want the young men's whispering and sighing.
But see the roses on your trellis dying
And hear the spectral singing of the moon;
For I must have my lovely lady soon,
I am a gentleman in a dustcoat trying.

—I am a lady young in beauty waiting
Until my truelove comes, and then we kiss.
But what grey man among the vines is this
Whose words are dry and faint as in a dream?
Back from my trellis, Sir, before I scream!
I am a lady young in beauty waiting.

1927

Dead Boy

The little cousin is dead, by foul subtraction,
A green bough from Virginia's aged tree,
And none of the country kin like the transaction,
Nor some of the world of outer dark, like me.

A boy not beautiful, nor good, nor clever,
A black cloud full of storms too hot for keeping,
A sword beneath his mother's heart—yet never
Woman bewept her babe as this is weeping.

A pig with a pasty face, so I had said,
Squealing for cookies, kinned by poor pretense
With a noble house. But the little man quite dead,
I see the forbears' antique lineaments.

The elder men have strode by the box of death
To the wide flag porch, and muttering low send round
The bruit[5] of the day. O friendly waste of breath!
Their hearts are hurt with a deep dynastic wound.

He was pale and little, the foolish neighbors say;
The first-fruits,[6] saith the Preacher, the Lord hath taken;
But this was the old tree's late branch wrenched away,
Grieving the sapless limbs, the shorn and shaken.

1927

5. News (archaic).
6. Or first-born, as the Lord killed the Egyptian first-born sons in Exodus.

Painted Head

By dark severance the apparition head
Smiles from the air a capital on no
Column or a Platonic[7] perhaps head
On a canvas sky depending from nothing;

Stirs up an old illusion of grandeur
By tickling the instinct of heads to be
Absolute and to try decapitation
And to play truant from the body bush;

But too happy and beautiful for those sorts
Of head (homekeeping heads are happiest)
Discovers maybe thirty unwidowed years
Of not dishonoring the faithful stem;

Is nameless and has authored for the evil
Historian headhunters neither book
Nor state and is therefore distinct from tart
Heads with crowns and guilty gallery heads;

Wherefore the extravagant device of art
Unhousing by abstraction this once head
Was capital[8] irony by a loving hand
That knew the no treason of a head like this;

Makes repentance in an unlovely head[9]
For having vinegarly traduced the flesh
Till, the hurt flesh recusing,[1] the hard egg
Is shrunken to its own deathlike surface;

And an image thus. The body bears the head
(So hardly one they terribly are two)
Feeds and obeys and unto please what end?
Not to the glory of tyrant head but to

The estate of body. Beauty is of body.
The flesh contouring shallowly on a head
Is a rock-garden needing body's love
And best bodiness to colorify

The big blue birds[2] sitting and sea-shell flats
And caves, and on the iron acropolis
To spread the hyacinthine[3] hair and rear
The olive garden for the nightingales.

1945

7. A reference to the Platonic theory of perfect forms that exist independently of this world.
8. First-rate (British).
9. The poet's.
1. Refusing.
2. The eyes.
3. Falling in curls. *Acropolis:* a Greek city's fortified upper part.

T. S. Eliot
1888–1965

Although T. S. Eliot deferred to W. B. Yeats as "the greatest poet" of his time, he was himself the most famous. A man of keen intellect, capable of developing a philosophical position as well as a new rhythm and intonation, trained in classics, fluent in French and German, Eliot was better equipped than any other poet to bring verse fully into the twentieth century. Choosing with fastidiousness what he wanted from the literary tradition in several languages, Eliot gave modern literature one of its most distinctive idioms.

Thomas Stearns Eliot was born on September 26, 1888, in St. Louis. He was one of seven children and the youngest son. His family had come from Massachusetts and "jealously guarded," as Eliot remarked, its New England connections. His grandfather, William Greenleaf Eliot, after graduation from the Harvard Divinity School, founded the first Unitarian church in St. Louis, as well as Washington University. Eliot's father was a successful industrialist, an executive of the Hydraulic Press Brick Company. Eliot's mother had literary interests; a respect for family tradition and a predisposition toward intense religious feeling may have come to Eliot through her.

Eliot's geographical movements reflect his inner turbulence. After living for his first seventeen years in St. Louis, except for annual summer holidays in New England, he went to Milton Academy, in Massachusetts, and then entered Harvard University in 1906. In St. Louis, he said, he felt himself to be a New Englander, but in New England he felt himself to be a southwesterner. (He was later to pursue deracination further.) He completed his course work at Harvard in three years instead of four. Among his teachers was Irving Babbitt, whose hatred of Romanticism and advocacy of classical restraint proved influential. After taking his first degree in 1909, Eliot entered the graduate school in the department of philosophy, studying with George Santayana, among others.

In 1910, Eliot received a master's degree and then went to the Sorbonne, in Paris, for a year, absorbing the conflicting philosophies of Henri Bergson, theorist of flux and the flow of consciousness, and of Charles Maurras, the reactionary Catholic monarchist whose organization, Action Française, was violently anti-Semitic. He returned to Harvard to write a doctoral dissertation on the philosophy of F. H. Bradley, the author of *Appearance and Reality,* who saw humans as "finite centers" in isolation from one another. Meanwhile, he ranged widely in his intellectual interests: he read French poetry, studied the Sanskrit and Pali languages, and took a great interest in Hinduism and Buddhism, reading their sacred texts in the original. In 1910–11, he wrote his earliest mature poems, including "The Love Song of J. Alfred Prufrock," "Portrait of a Lady," and "Preludes." During the academic year 1913–14, Eliot was a teaching assistant at Harvard. He was then awarded a traveling fellowship and went to study for the summer at Marburg University, in Germany. The outbreak of war forced him to Oxford University. The year 1914–15 proved pivotal, as he came to three interrelated decisions: to give up the appearance of the philosopher for the reality of the poet, to marry, and to settle in England.

Ezra Pound encouraged him in all three. After they met in 1914, Pound read the poems that no one had been willing to publish and pronounced his verdict in a letter of September 30 to Harriet Monroe: that Eliot "has actually trained himself *and* modernized himself *on his own.*" Monroe, the editor of *Poetry* magazine, must publish them, beginning with "Prufrock." It took Pound some time to convince her, and it was not until June 1915 that Eliot first published. This was also the month of his marriage to Vivien Haigh-Wood, an Englishwoman.

He resisted his parents' urging that he return to the United States for a career in teaching philosophy. He would be a poet, and England offered a better atmosphere in which to write. His family did not cut him off financially, but they offered insufficient help to support the couple. Eliot took a teaching job at the High Wycombe Grammar School, then at Highgate Junior School. He deferred to his parents' wishes so far as to complete his dissertation and was booked to sail on April 1, 1916, to take his oral examination at Harvard. The crossing was canceled because of wartime complications, and his academic career came to an end. In March 1917, he took a job as a clerk with Lloyd's Bank, in London, and he stayed at it for eight years, while he struggled with literary and marital problems.

Now began the personal troubles out of which came Eliot's poem *The Waste Land*. Vivien Eliot's emotional and physical health was subject to frequent collapses; she suffered from neuralgia and insomnia. Eliot's great strain and marital disillusionment are probably shadowed in the opening of his poem: "April is the cruellest month." (The Eliots' unhappy marriage turned into a separation in 1932; Vivien Eliot was committed to a mental asylum in London in 1938 and died in 1947.) The death of Eliot's father, in January 1919, was another blow, especially since his father died thinking that Eliot had wasted his ability. Passing references to a father's death in *The Waste Land* perhaps express the son's guilt. The death in World War I of his close friend Jean Verdenal, a French medical student to whom he had dedicated his first book of poems, probably also underlies the poem's melancholy. In addition, Eliot had passed his thirtieth year, and *The Waste Land* is a memorial to his youth as *Hugh Selwyn Mauberley* is a memorial to Pound's.

Much of *The Waste Land* was written by early 1921. Then Eliot had a breakdown and was advised by a prominent neurologist to take three months away from Lloyd's Bank. He went first to Margate and then to Lausanne, Switzerland, where he underwent psychiatric treatment. In Paris, with Pound's brilliant editorial aid, he pieced *The Waste Land* out of various truncated drafts. The manuscript, edited by his second wife, Valerie Eliot, was published in facsimile in 1971.

When the poem itself was first published, in 1922, it gave Eliot his central position in modern poetry. No one has been able to encompass so much material with so much dexterity, or to express the alienation and horror of so many aspects of the modern world. Though the poem is made of fragments, they are pieces of a jigsaw puzzle that might be joined if certain spiritual conditions were met. In this way, Eliot's attitude toward fragmentation was different from Pound's—Eliot wanted to recompose the world, whereas Pound thought it could remain in fragments and still have a paradisal aspect that the poet could elicit. In other words, Pound accepted discontinuity as the only way in which the world could be regarded, while Eliot rejected it and looked for a seamless world. He began to find it in Christianity: after *The Waste Land,* he wrote "The Hollow Men," "Journey of the Magi," "Ash-Wednesday," and other poems that mark stages on his way toward conversion. In June 1927, he was baptized into the Church of England, and in November of the same year he became a British citizen. In *For Lancelot Andrewes* (1928), he declared himself, only partly in jest, a "classicist in literature, royalist in politics, and Anglo-Catholic in religion." His last important work as a poet, *Four Quartets* (1935–43), constitutes the achievement of his spiritual quest.

In the year *The Waste Land* appeared, Eliot founded a new review, *The Criterion,* which became a leading cultural magazine through 1939. Eliot joined the publishing firm of Faber & Gwyer (later Faber & Faber) in 1925. As editor of the leading literary journal, as a director of a publishing firm, and as poet and critic, he became the principal figure in English letters. His work was translated into many languages, and for decades the latest verses in Arabic, Swahili, or Japanese were far more likely to sound like Eliot than like earlier poets in those languages or like other poets in English. Eliot's eminence became a hazard to poets such as William Carlos Williams and Hart Crane, who felt that their fundamental aesthetic problem was not to write like him.

Eliot was determined to carry his art into other literary forms, particularly playwriting. His first play was *Murder in the Cathedral,* a liturgical verse drama about Thomas à Becket with a title that might have suited one of the detective stories of which Eliot was fond. In subsequent plays, Eliot attempted to represent the difficulties of conscience in a conscienceless world, and some of his verse plays, notably *The Cocktail Party,* achieved a success ordinarily reserved in modern times for plays in prose. Eliot also wrote works on religion, literature, and culture, in which he tried to establish, as the title of a 1939 book put it, the idea of a Christian society. In *After Strange Gods* (1934), a book he later suppressed, he spoke of the desirability of there being few "free-thinking Jews" in forming such a society, sounding the anti-Semitic note also heard in satiric portraits in "Sweeney among the Nightingales" ("Rachel *née* Rabinovitch"), "Gerontion" ("the Jew squats on the window sill"), and an early draft of the "Death by Water" section of *The Waste Land.* Although the missionary zeal of his prose books sometimes aroused great opposition, Eliot's reputation as a public figure grew. In 1948, he was awarded the Nobel Prize for Literature, and with his plays on Broadway, his best lines on every lip, and his essays dominating contemporary taste, he might well have seemed the man of letters par excellence of the English-speaking world.

Eliot said that when he started to write poetry no one writing in England or America could serve as a model. In December 1908, he came across the newly published second edition of Arthur Symons's *The Symbolist Movement in Literature* and read, for the first time, about the French poets Arthur Rimbaud, Jules Laforgue, Stéphane Mallarmé, and others. "I myself owe Mr. Symons a great debt," he wrote in *The Criterion* (January 1930), saying "the Symons book . . . affected the course of my life." Elsewhere, he remarked that from these French poets he first learned to speak. His early free verse, he said in a 1959 interview, "was started under the endeavor to practice the same form as Laforgue . . . merely rhyming lines of irregular length, with the rhymes coming in irregular places." He drew from French poets the notion that poetry could carry considerable intellectual as well as emotional content, and that it might be—and, as he thought, in the modern world had to be—exceedingly complex in expression. In his early work, Eliot heaped ironies upon each other, yoking—as Samuel Johnson said Metaphysical poets in the seventeenth century did—heterogeneous ideas together by violence. Eliot wrote almost exclusively about decadent, enervated people, yet in a violent, innovative style. He bound together by wit a precise and often formal outward manner with an inner writhing.

Love pervades all his work, though often in negative form. Prufrock never sings his love song to a woman; Gerontion (a later hero) finds himself similarly impotent before God; then follows Eliot's laborious and agonized progress toward a higher love. His poetry does not much deal, as Yeats's does, with the love of man and woman; the female body often seems sexually alluring but discomfiting for Eliot's speakers. His "satiric intensity," as Yeats called it, is perhaps most memorable in such sordid scenes as that of the typist and the "carbuncular" clerk in *The Waste Land.* But in one of his late poems, addressed to Valerie, Eliot gives unexpected recognition to the communion not of man and God but of man and woman, "lovers whose bodies smell of each other" and who "think the same thoughts without need of speech" ("A Dedication to My Wife"). Though he upholds the way of the saint as supreme, he allows validity here and in *Four Quartets* to "the life of significant soil" in which the claims of society, as well as of God, are enforced. With all its strangeness, his poetry conveys a sense of utter, painful sincerity, as he sifts and reconstitutes stale into living emotions.

The Love Song of J. Alfred Prufrock

S'io credessi che mia risposta fosse
a persona che mai tornasse al mondo,
questa fiamma staria senza più scosse.
Ma per ciò che giammai di questo fondo
non tornò vivo alcun, s'i'odo il vero,
senza tema d'infamia ti rispondo.[1]

Let us go then, you and I,
When the evening is spread out against the sky
Like a patient etherised upon a table;
Let us go, through certain half-deserted streets,
The muttering retreats
Of restless nights in one-night cheap hotels
And sawdust restaurants with oyster-shells:
Streets that follow like a tedious argument
Of insidious intent
To lead you to an overwhelming question . . .
Oh, do not ask, 'What is it?'
Let us go and make our visit.

In the room the women come and go
Talking of Michelangelo.

The yellow fog that rubs its back upon the window-panes,
The yellow smoke that rubs its muzzle on the window-panes,
Licked its tongue into the corners of the evening,
Lingered upon the pools that stand in drains,
Let fall upon its back the soot that falls from chimneys,
Slipped by the terrace, made a sudden leap,
And seeing that it was a soft October night,
Curled once about the house, and fell asleep.

And indeed there will be time[2]
For the yellow smoke that slides along the street
Rubbing its back upon the window-panes;
There will be time, there will be time
To prepare a face to meet the faces that you meet;
There will be time to murder and create,
And time for all the works and days[3] of hands
That lift and drop a question on your plate;
Time for you and time for me,
And time yet for a hundred indecisions,

1. From Dante's *Inferno,* Canto 27. 61–66, where the poet asks Guido da Montefeltro, who like the other Counsellors of Fraud is wrapped in a tall flame, to identify himself. Guido, having sinned with his tongue, has to speak through the tongue of the flame. He replies, "If I thought my reply were / to someone who would ever return to the world, / this flame would stop flickering. / But since no one has ever / returned alive from this pit, if what I hear is true, / I answer you without any fear of infamy."

2. Cf. Andrew Marvell's "To His Coy Mistress" (1681): "Had we but world enough and time."

3. *Works and Days* is the title of a long, didactic poem about farming by the Greek poet Hesiod (eighth century B.C.E.).

And for a hundred visions and revisions,
Before the taking of a toast and tea.

In the room the women come and go
Talking of Michelangelo.

And indeed there will be time
To wonder, 'Do I dare?' and, 'Do I dare?'
Time to turn back and descend the stair,
With a bald spot in the middle of my hair—
(They will say: 'How his hair is growing thin!')
My morning coat, my collar mounting firmly to the chin,
My necktie rich and modest, but asserted by a simple pin—
(They will say: 'But how his arms and legs are thin!')
Do I dare
Disturb the universe?
In a minute there is time
For decisions and revisions which a minute will reverse.

For I have known them all already, known them all—
Have known the evenings, mornings, afternoons,
I have measured out my life with coffee spoons;
I know the voices dying with a dying fall[4]
Beneath the music from a farther room.
  So how should I presume?

And I have known the eyes already, known them all—
The eyes that fix you in a formulated phrase,
And when I am formulated, sprawling on a pin,
When I am pinned and wriggling on the wall,
Then how should I begin
To spit out all the butt-ends of my days and ways?
  And how should I presume?

And I have known the arms already, known them all—
Arms that are braceleted and white and bare
(But in the lamplight, downed with light brown hair!)
Is it perfume from a dress
That makes me so digress?
Arms that lie along a table, or wrap about a shawl.
  And should I then presume?
  And how should I begin?

. . . . .

Shall I say, I have gone at dusk through narrow streets
And watched the smoke that rises from the pipes
Of lonely men in shirt-sleeves, leaning out of windows? . . .

I should have been a pair of ragged claws
Scuttling across the floors of silent seas.

4. Cf. Shakespeare's *Twelfth Night*: "That strain again, it had a dying fall" (1.1.4).

• • • • •

And the afternoon, the evening, sleeps so peacefully!
Smoothed by long fingers,
Asleep . . . tired . . . or it malingers,
Stretched on the floor, here beside you and me.
Should I, after tea and cakes and ices,
Have the strength to force the moment to its crisis?
But though I have wept and fasted, wept and prayed,
Though I have seen my head (grown slightly bald) brought in upon a
platter,[5]
I am no prophet—and here's no great matter;
I have seen the moment of my greatness flicker,
And I have seen the eternal Footman hold my coat, and snicker,
And in short, I was afraid.

And would it have been worth it, after all,
After the cups, the marmalade, the tea,
Among the porcelain, among some talk of you and me,
Would it have been worth while,
To have bitten off the matter with a smile,
To have squeezed the universe into a ball[6]
To roll it towards some overwhelming question,
To say: 'I am Lazarus,[7] come from the dead,
Come back to tell you all, I shall tell you all'—
If one, settling a pillow by her head,
Should say: 'That is not what I meant at all.
That is not it, at all.'

And would it have been worth it, after all,
Would it have been worth while,
After the sunsets and the dooryards and the sprinkled streets,
After the novels, after the teacups, after the skirts that trail along the
floor—
And this, and so much more?—
It is impossible to say just what I mean!
But as if a magic lantern threw the nerves in patterns on a screen:
Would it have been worth while
If one, settling a pillow or throwing off a shawl,
And turning toward the window, should say:
'That is not it at all,
That is not what I meant, at all.'

• • • • •

No! I am not Prince Hamlet, nor was meant to be;
Am an attendant lord, one that will do
To swell a progress,[8] start a scene or two,

5. The head of the prophet John the Baptist, killed at Salome's request, was brought to her on a platter (Mark 6.17–20, Matthew 14.3–11).
6. Cf. "To His Coy Mistress": "Let us roll all our strength and all / Our sweetness up into a ball, / And tear our pleasures with rough strife / Through the iron gates of life."
7. One Lazarus was raised by Jesus from the dead (John 11.1–44). Another Lazarus is a beggar who dies; God says that even if he "rose from the dead," his warning about hell would not be believed (Luke 16.19–31).
8. Royal procession.

Advise the prince; no doubt, an easy tool,
Deferential, glad to be of use,
Politic, cautious, and meticulous;
Full of high sentence,[9] but a bit obtuse;
At times, indeed, almost ridiculous—
Almost, at times, the Fool.

I grow old . . . I grow old . . .
I shall wear the bottoms of my trousers rolled.[1]

Shall I part my hair behind? Do I dare to eat a peach?
I shall wear white flannel trousers, and walk upon the beach.
I have heard the mermaids singing, each to each.

I do not think that they will sing to me.

I have seen them riding seaward on the waves
Combing the white hair of the waves blown back
When the wind blows the water white and black.

We have lingered in the chambers of the sea
By sea-girls wreathed with seaweed red and brown
Till human voices wake us, and we drown.

1910–11 1915, 1917

Preludes

I

The winter evening settles down
With smell of steaks in passageways.
Six o'clock.
The burnt-out ends of smoky days.
And now a gusty shower wraps
The grimy scraps
Of withered leaves about your feet
And newspapers from vacant lots;
The showers beat
On broken blinds and chimney-pots,
And at the corner of the street
A lonely cab-horse steams and stamps.
And then the lighting of the lamps.

II

The morning comes to consciousness
Of faint stale smells of beer

9. Opinions.
1. That is, overfastidiously rolled up so they will not get wet.

From the sawdust-trampled street
With all its muddy feet that press
To early coffee-stands.
With the other masquerades
That time resumes,
One thinks of all the hands
That are raising dingy shades
In a thousand furnished rooms.

III

You tossed a blanket from the bed,
You lay upon your back, and waited;
You dozed, and watched the night revealing
The thousand sordid images
Of which your soul was constituted;
They flickered against the ceiling.
And when all the world came back
And the light crept up between the shutters
And you heard the sparrows in the gutters,
You had such a vision of the street
As the street hardly understands;
Sitting along the bed's edge, where
You curled the papers from your hair,
Or clasped the yellow soles of feet
In the palms of both soiled hands.

IV

His soul stretched tight across the skies
That fade behind a city block,
Or trampled by insistent feet
At four and five and six o'clock;
And short square fingers stuffing pipes,
And evening newspapers, and eyes
Assured of certain certainties,
The conscience of a blackened street
Impatient to assume the world.

I am moved by fancies that are curled
Around these images, and cling:
The notion of some infinitely gentle
Infinitely suffering thing.

Wipe your hand across your mouth, and laugh;
The worlds revolve like ancient women
Gathering fuel in vacant lots.

1910–11 1915, 1917

Whispers of Immortality

Webster[2] was much possessed by death
And saw the skull beneath the skin;
And breastless creatures under ground
Leaned backward with a lipless grin.

Daffodil bulbs instead of balls
Stared from the sockets of the eyes!
He knew that thought clings round dead limbs
Tightening its lusts and luxuries.

Donne,[3] I suppose, was such another
Who found no substitute for sense,
To seize and clutch and penetrate;
Expert beyond experience,

He knew the anguish of the marrow
The ague[4] of the skeleton;
No contact possible to flesh
Allayed the fever of the bone.

• • • • •

Grishkin[5] is nice: her Russian eye
Is underlined for emphasis;
Uncorseted, her friendly bust
Gives promise of pneumatic bliss.

The couched Brazilian jaguar
Compels the scampering marmoset
With subtle effluence of cat;
Grishkin has a maisonnette;[6]

The sleek Brazilian jaguar
Does not in its arboreal gloom
Distil so rank a feline smell
As Grishkin in a drawing-room.

And even the Abstract Entities
Circumambulate her charm;
But our lot crawls between dry ribs
To keep our metaphysics warm.

1918, 1919

2. John Webster (c.1580–c.1625), English dramatist, whose plays *The Duchess of Malfi* and *The White Devil* are redolent of violent death.
3. John Donne (1572–1631), English poet and priest.
4. Fever.
5. Though her name is evidently a pseudonym, Grishkin was a real person, according to Ezra Pound, who in Canto 77 mentions finding her photograph—and thinking that Eliot had not done her justice.
6. Apartment.

Sweeney among the Nightingales

ὤμοι, πέπληγμαι καιρίαν πληγὴν ἔσω.[7]

Apeneck Sweeney spread his knees
Letting his arms hang down to laugh,
The zebra stripes along his jaw
Swelling to maculate[8] giraffe.

The circles of the stormy moon
Slide westward toward the River Plate,[9]
Death and the Raven[1] drift above
And Sweeney guards the hornèd gate.[2]

Gloomy Orion and the Dog[3]
Are veiled; and hushed the shrunken seas;[4]
The person in the Spanish cape
Tries to sit on Sweeney's knees

Slips and pulls the table cloth
Overturns a coffee-cup,
Reorganised upon the floor
She yawns and draws a stocking up;

The silent man in mocha brown
Sprawls at the window-sill and gapes;
The waiter brings in oranges
Bananas figs and hothouse grapes;

The silent vertebrate in brown
Contracts and concentrates, withdraws;
Rachel *née* Rabinovitch
Tears at the grapes with murderous paws;

She and the lady in the cape
Are suspect, thought to be in league;
Therefore the man with heavy eyes
Declines the gambit, shows fatigue,

Leaves the room and reappears
Outside the window, leaning in,
Branches of wistaria
Circumscribe a golden grin;

7. Pronounced *ómoi, péplegemai kairían plegén éso* (Greek). From Aeschylus's *Agamemnon;* when Agamemnon is struck by his wife Clytemnestra, he cries, "Alas, I have been struck a mortal blow."
8. Spotted.
9. Or Rio de la Plata, in South America, between Uruguay and Argentina.
1. The constellation Corvus.
2. The Gates of Horn, in Hades, through which true dreams come.
3. Orion, constellation of the hunter, is close in the sky to Canis Major, the constellation of the dog.
4. The tide is out.

The host with someone indistinct
Converses at the door apart,
The nightingales are singing near[5]
The Convent of the Sacred Heart,

And sang within the bloody wood[6]
When Agamemnon cried aloud
And let their liquid siftings fall
To stain the stiff dishonoured shroud.

1918, 1919

Gerontion[7]

Thou hast nor youth nor age
But as it were an after dinner sleep
Dreaming of both.[8]

Here I am, an old man in a dry month,
Being read to by a boy, waiting for rain.[9]
I was neither at the hot gates
Nor fought in the warm rain
Nor knee deep in the salt marsh, heaving a cutlass,
Bitten by flies, fought.[1]
My house is a decayed house,
And the Jew squats on the window sill, the owner,
Spawned in some estaminet[2] of Antwerp,
Blistered in Brussels, patched and peeled in London.[3]
The goat coughs at night in the field overhead;
Rocks, moss, stonecrop, iron, merds.[4]
The woman keeps the kitchen, makes tea,
Sneezes at evening, poking the peevish gutter.[5]
                                        I an old man,
A dull head among windy spaces.

Signs are taken for wonders. 'We would see a sign!'
The word within a word, unable to speak a word,

5. In Greek legend, Philomela was turned into a nightingale after being raped by her sister's husband, Tereus.
6. Philomela was raped in a wood; also, in the sacred wood of Nemi, the old priest was killed by his successor (see James Frazer, *The Golden Bough,* ch. 1).
7. Little old man (from the Greek *geron,* old man). Eliot once proposed this poem as a prologue to *The Waste Land,* but Ezra Pound dissuaded him.
8. A description of death from Shakespeare's *Measure for Measure* (3.1.32–34), in which the Duke is trying to console Claudio, who is on the verge of being executed.
9. Cf. a description of the English poet Edward FitzGerald (1809–1883): "Here he sits, in a dry month, old and blind, being read to by a country boy, longing for rain" (A. C. Benson, *Edward FitzGerald,* 1905).
1. Probably references to specific battles: Thermopylae (Greek for hot gates), 480 B.C.E.; Waterloo, 1815; and Cannae, 216 B.C.E.
2. Café. The "Jew" is Eliot's anti-Semitic symbol for urban decay and deracination.
3. Allusions to symptoms and treatments for venereal disease.
4. Excrement (French).
5. Drain (British).

Swaddled with darkness.[6] In the juvescence[7] of the year
Came Christ the tiger

In depraved May, dogwood and chestnut, flowering judas,[8]
To be eaten, to be divided, to be drunk[9]
Among whispers; by Mr. Silvero
With caressing hands, at Limoges[1]
Who walked all night in the next room;

By Hakagawa, bowing among the Titians;[2]
By Madame de Tornquist, in the dark room
Shifting the candles; Fräulein von Kulp
Who turned in the hall, one hand on the door.
      Vacant shuttles
Weave the wind. I have no ghosts,
An old man in a draughty house
Under a windy knob.

After such knowledge, what forgiveness? Think now
History has many cunning passages, contrived corridors
And issues, deceives with whispering ambitions,
Guides us by vanities. Think now
She gives when our attention is distracted
And what she gives, gives with such supple confusions
That the giving famishes the craving. Gives too late
What's not believed in, or is still believed,
In memory only, reconsidered passion. Gives too soon
Into weak hands, what's thought can be dispensed with
Till the refusal propagates a fear. Think
Neither fear nor courage saves us. Unnatural vices
Are fathered by our heroism. Virtues
Are forced upon us by our impudent crimes.
These tears are shaken from the wrath-bearing tree.

The tiger springs in the new year. Us he devours. Think at last
We have not reached conclusion, when I
Stiffen in a rented house. Think at last
I have not made this show purposelessly
And it is not by any concitation[3]
Of the backward devils.
I would meet you upon this honestly.
I that was near your heart was removed therefrom

6. Eliot alludes to passages in the Gospels and to Lancelot Andrewes' (1555–1626) commentary on them. Matthew 12.38: "Master, we would see a sign from you." Luke 2.12: "And this will be a sign for you: you will find a babe [Jesus] wrapped in swaddling cloths and lying in a manger." Andrewes in his *Works* 1.204: "Signs are taken for wonders. . . . Indeed, every word here is a wonder. . . . *Verbum infans* [the infant Word, or the baby Jesus], the Word without a word; the eternal Word not able to speak a word."

7. That is, juvenescence, or youth.

8. Three trees mentioned in *The Education of Henry Adams* (1918), chapter 18: "No European spring had shown him the . . . passionate depravity that marked the Maryland May."

9. An allusion to the wine and bread divided and consumed in Christian communion and at the Last Supper.

1. City in central France known for its fine porcelain.

2. Paintings by the Venetian painter Titian (1477–1576).

3. Stirring up.

To lose beauty in terror, terror in inquisition.
I have lost my passion: why should I need to keep it
Since what is kept must be adulterated?
I have lost my sight, smell, hearing, taste and touch:
How should I use them for your closer contact?

These with a thousand small deliberations
Protract the profit of their chilled delirium,
Excite the membrane, when the sense has cooled,
With pungent sauces, multiply variety
In a wilderness of mirrors. What will the spider do,
Suspend its operations, will the weevil
Delay? De Bailhache, Fresca, Mrs. Cammel whirled
Beyond the circuit of the shuddering Bear[4]
In fractured atoms. Gull against the wind, in the windy straits
Of Belle Isle, or running on the Horn.[5]
White feathers in the snow, the Gulf claims,
And an old man driven by the Trades[6]
To a sleepy corner.

Tenants of the house,
Thoughts of a dry brain in a dry season.

1920

On The Waste Land

In the essay "*Ulysses,* Order and Myth" (1923), Eliot hinted at the ambitions of his own poetry when he declared that others would follow James Joyce "in manipulating a continuous parallel between contemporaneity and antiquity. . . . It is simply a way of controlling, of ordering, of giving a shape and a significance to the immense panorama of futility and anarchy which is contemporary history. . . . It is, I seriously believe, a step toward making the modern world possible in art." Eliot labeled this new technique "the mythical method."

In his first note to *The Waste Land,* Eliot says: "Not only the title, but the plan and a good deal of the incidental symbolism of the poem were suggested by Miss Jessie L. Weston's book on the Grail legend: *From Ritual to Romance* [1920]. Indeed, so deeply am I indebted, Miss Weston's book will elucidate the difficulties of the poem much better than my notes can do; and I recommend it (apart from the great interest of the book itself) to any who think such elucidation of the poem worth the trouble. To another work of anthropology I am indebted in general, one which has influenced our generation profoundly; I mean [Sir James Frazer's] *The Golden Bough* [1890–1915]; I have used especially the two volumes *Adonis, Attis, Osiris.* Anyone who is acquainted with these works will immediately recognise in the poem certain references to vegetation ceremonies." Weston contends that pre-Christian fertility myths and rituals such as those described by Frazer underlie the Arthurian romances of the quest for the Holy Grail.

4. The Great Bear, a northern constellation.
5. Cape Horn, the southernmost tip of South America. *Belle Isle:* island on Canada's eastern seaboard.
6. Trade Winds. *Gulf:* the Gulf Stream.

In the Arthurian legend, the Fisher King (the fish being an ancient symbol of life) has been maimed or killed, and his country has therefore become a dry waste land; he can be regenerated and his land restored to fertility only by a knight (Perceval, or Parsifal) who perseveres through various ordeals to the Perilous Chapel and learns the answers to certain ritual questions about the Grail. The Fisher King is seen as analogous to vegetation gods such as Adonis of Greece, Attis of Phrygia, Osiris of Egypt, and perhaps also the Greek deity Hyacinthus, all of whose deaths and rebirths are represented in ancient ritual ceremonies intended to bring about the regeneration of plants after the sterile winter. Weston also connects the symbols of the Arthurian stories with the suits of the tarot deck, today used to tell fortunes but perhaps originally designed by the Egyptians to predict the flooding of the Nile and the restoration of its valley to fertility.

Eliot wrote most of *The Waste Land* while at Lausanne in 1921, but it had been on his mind since 1919. Parts of the poem antedate the final version by several years: lines 26–29 were taken from "The Death of Saint Narcissus" (1915), lines 312–21 are adapted from Eliot's French poem "Dans le Restaurant" (1916–17), and Conrad Aiken remarks that lines 377–84 and other passages had "long been familiar" to him "as poems, or part-poems, in themselves" (*A Reviewer's ABC,* 1958). As these dates indicate, the mass death and social collapse of World War I centrally inform the poem's vision of a waste land strewn with corpses, wreckage, and ruin.

Eliot gave Ezra Pound much credit for his help in shaping *The Waste Land,* and the manuscript reveals how extensive and crucial this help was. Pound persuaded Eliot to delete seventy-two lines in rhymed couplets at the beginning of "The Fire Sermon" that imitated the style of Alexander Pope's "The Rape of the Lock" and the defecation scene in Joyce's *Ulysses* (a book Eliot had recently read in manuscript and thought "magnificent") and another eighty-two lines, preceding line 312, based on Dante's description of Ulysses' last voyage and describing the wreck of a New England fishing boat. Pound also disapproved of three short lyrics that Eliot planned as interludes, and dissuaded him from adding "Gerontion" as a preface. Smaller emendations eliminated patches of conventionally poetic diction and cut nonessential verbiage; the effect was often to distort previously regular meter and rhyme. In gratitude for Pound's help, Eliot dedicated the poem to him, quoting Dante's tribute to the twelfth-century Provençal poet Arnaut Daniel: "The better craftsman [*il miglior fabbro*] of the mother tongue" (*Purgatorio* 26).

Eliot's fifty-two notes to *The Waste Land,* reproduced here, were prepared for its publication as a book in 1922; they do not accompany the poem in *The Criterion* (London), Eliot's own magazine, or in *The Dial* (New York). He later remarked, "I have sometimes thought of getting rid of these notes; but now they can never be unstuck. They have had almost greater popularity than the poem itself." Eliot was aware of the difficulties his work presented to its readers. In *The Use of Poetry and the Use of Criticism,* he emphasized that such difficulties may come from various causes and be of different kinds. "The more seasoned reader . . . does not bother about understanding; not, at least, at first. I know that some of the poetry to which I am most devoted is poetry which I did not understand at first reading; some is poetry which I am not sure I understand yet: for instance, Shakespeare's." He mentions "the difficulty caused by the author's having left out something which the reader is used to finding; so that the reader, bewildered, gropes about for what is absent, and puzzles his head for a kind of 'meaning' which is not there, and is not meant to be there." These remarks, which are somewhat introductory to *The Waste Land,* may be supplemented by Eliot's remark in an interview: "In *The Waste Land* I wasn't even bothering whether I understood what I was saying" (*Writers at Work,* Second Series, 1963). And though critics immediately began to interpret the poem as an expression of a generation's spiritual alienation, Eliot soon felt the need to disavow any such intention, and he is reported to have remarked,

"To me it was only the relief of a personal and wholly insignificant grouse against life; it is just a piece of rhythmical grumbling" (*The Waste Land: Facsimile and Transcript of the Original Drafts* . . . , ed. Valerie Eliot, 1971).

The Waste Land

'Nam Sibyllam quidem Cumis ego ipse oculis meis vidi in ampulla pendere, et cum illi pueri dicerent: Σίβυλλα τί θέλεις; respondebat illa: ἀποθανεῖν θέλω.'[7]

FOR EZRA POUND
IL MIGLIOR FABBRO.[8]

I. The Burial of the Dead[9]

April is the cruellest month,[1] breeding
Lilacs out of the dead land, mixing
Memory and desire, stirring
Dull roots with spring rain.
Winter kept us warm, covering
Earth in forgetful snow, feeding
A little life with dried tubers.
Summer surprised us, coming over the Starnbergersee[2]
With a shower of rain; we stopped in the colonnade,
And went on in sunlight, into the Hofgarten,
And drank coffee, and talked for an hour.
Bin gar keine Russin, stamm' aus Litauen, echt deutsch.[3]
And when we were children, staying at the arch-duke's,
My cousin's, he took me out on a sled,
And I was frightened. He said, Marie,
Marie, hold on tight. And down we went.
In the mountains, there you feel free.
I read, much of the night, and go south in the winter.

What are the roots that clutch, what branches grow
Out of this stony rubbish? Son of man,[4]
You cannot say, or guess, for you know only
A heap of broken images, where the sun beats,
And the dead tree gives no shelter, the cricket no relief,[5]

7. "For I saw with my own eyes the Sibyl hanging in a jar at Cumae, and when the acolytes said, 'Sibyl, what do you want?' she replied, 'I want to die'" (Petronius, *Satyricon,* ch. 48). Apollo had granted the Sibyl eternal life, but because she had forgotten to ask for eternal youth, her body shriveled up until she could be put in a bottle.
8. The better craftsman (Italian). The tribute in Dante's *Purgatorio* 26.117 to the twelfth-century Provençal poet Arnaut Daniel.
9. The title of the Anglican burial service.
1. Cf. Chaucer's "General Prologue" to *The Canterbury Tales.*
2. A lake near Munich; the Hofgarten (line 10) is a park in the city. According to Valerie Eliot, Eliot based this passage on a conversation he had had with Countess Marie Larisch (lines 8–18). She published her reminiscences of Austrian nobility in *My Past* (1913).
3. I'm not a Russian woman at all; I come from Lithuania, a true German (German).
4. "Cf. Ezekiel II, i" [Eliot's note]: "Son of man stand upon thy feet, and I will speak unto thee," God says to Ezekiel.
5. "Cf. Ecclesiastes XII, v" [Eliot's note], in which the preacher evokes the evil days "when they shall be afraid of that which is high, and fears shall be in the way, and the almond tree shall flourish, and the grasshopper shall be a burden, and desire shall fail."

And the dry stone no sound of water. Only
There is shadow under this red rock,[6]
(Come in under the shadow of this red rock),
And I will show you something different from either
Your shadow at morning striding behind you
Or your shadow at evening rising to meet you;
I will show you fear in a handful of dust.
Frisch weht der Wind
Der Heimat zu
Mein Irisch Kind,
Wo weilest du?[7]
"You gave me hyacinths first a year ago;
"They called me the hyacinth girl."
—Yet when we came back, late from the hyacinth[8] garden,
Your arms full, and your hair wet, I could not
Speak, and my eyes failed, I was neither
Living nor dead, and I knew nothing,
Looking into the heart of light, the silence.
Oed' und leer das Meer.[9]

Madame Sosostris,[1] famous clairvoyante,
Had a bad cold, nevertheless
Is known to be the wisest woman in Europe,
With a wicked pack of cards.[2] Here, said she,
Is your card, the drowned Phoenician Sailor,[3]
(Those are pearls that were his eyes. Look!)[4]
Here is Belladonna,[5] the Lady of the Rocks,
The lady of situations.
Here is the man with three staves, and here the Wheel,[6]
And here is the one-eyed merchant,[7] and this card,
Which is blank, is something he carries on his back,

6. Cf. Isaiah 32.2, which tells of a savior who "shall be . . . as rivers of water in a dry place, as the shadow of a great rock in a weary land."
7. "V. [see] *Tristan und Isolde,* I, verses 5–8" [Eliot's note]. In this opera, by German composer Richard Wagner (1813–1883), a sailor recalls the woman he has left behind: "Fresh blows the wind / To the homeland; / My Irish darling, / Where are you waiting?" Isolde overhears these verses on the ship taking her to marry her unloved fiancé, King Mark of Cornwall.
8. In Greek mythology, Apollo loved and accidentally killed Hyacinth; from his blood sprang the flower named for him, inscribed with "AI," a cry of grief.
9. "Id. [ibid] III, verse 24" [Eliot's note]. Desolate and empty is the sea (German); the second quotation from *Tristan und Isolde.* In this scene, the dying Tristan waits for Isolde to arrive by sea.
1. Name adapted from a fake fortune-teller in Aldous Huxley's novel *Crome Yellow* (1921).
2. Tarot cards, with their vestiges of ancient vegetation myth. Eliot notes: "I am not familiar with the exact constitution of the Tarot pack of cards, from which I have obviously departed to suit my own convenience. The Hanged Man, a member of the traditional pack, fits my purpose in two ways: because he is associated in my mind with the Hanged God of Frazer, and because I associate him with the hooded figure in the passage of the disciples to Emmaus in Part V. The Phoenician Sailor and the Merchant appear later; also the 'crowds of people,' and Death by Water is executed in Part IV. The Man with Three Staves (an authentic member of the Tarot pack) I associate, quite arbitrarily, with the Fisher King himself."
3. The Phoenicians were ancient seafaring merchants who spread fertility cults across the Mediterranean. The sailor reappears as Phlebas in part 4; cf. also Mr. Eugenides, the Smyrna merchant, in part 3.
4. From Ariel's song in Shakespeare's *Tempest* about Ferdinand's supposedly drowned father: "Full fathom five thy father lies. / Of his bones are coral made; / Those are pearls that were his eyes; / Nothing of him that doth fade / But doth suffer a sea-change / Into something rich and strange" (1.2.400–405).
5. Beautiful lady (Italian); also, the poisonous plant nightshade and a cosmetic. Calling her "the Lady of the Rocks" is an ironic allusion to Leonardo de Vinci's *Madonna of the Rocks,* a picture of the Virgin Mary, and to his Mona Lisa, described in Walter Pater's *The Renaissance* (1893) as "older than the rocks among which she sits."
6. That is, the Wheel of Fortune.
7. Mr. Eugenides of part 3, "one-eyed" because seen in profile. This card, like those of Belladonna and of the drowned Phoenician sailor, is not part of the Tarot deck.

Which I am forbidden to see. I do not find
The Hanged Man. Fear death by water.
I see crowds of people, walking round in a ring.
Thank you. If you see dear Mrs. Equitone,
Tell her I bring the horoscope myself:
One must be so careful these days.

Unreal City,[8]
Under the brown fog of a winter dawn,
A crowd flowed over London Bridge, so many,
I had not thought death had undone so many.[9]
Sighs, short and infrequent, were exhaled,[1]
And each man fixed his eyes before his feet.
Flowed up the hill and down King William Street,
To where Saint Mary Woolnoth kept the hours
With a dead sound on the final stroke of nine.[2]
There I saw one I knew, and stopped him, crying: "Stetson!
"You who were with me in the ships at Mylae![3]
"That corpse you planted last year in your garden,
"Has it begun to sprout? Will it bloom this year?
"Or has the sudden frost disturbed its bed?
"O keep the Dog far hence, that's friend to men,
"Or with his nails he'll dig it up again![4]
"You! hypocrite lecteur!—mon semblable,—mon frère!"[5]

II. A Game of Chess[6]

The Chair she sat in, like a burnished throne,
Glowed on the marble,[7] where the glass
Held up by standards wrought with fruited vines

8. "Cf. Baudelaire: *'Fourmillante cité, cité pleine de rêves / Où le spectre en plein jour raccroche le passant'* " [Eliot's note]. From the poem "Les Sept Vieillards" ("The Seven Old Men"), in *Les Fleurs du Mal* (*The Flowers of Evil,* 1857), by French poet Charles Baudelaire (1821–1867): "Swarming city, city full of dreams, / Where the specter in full daylight accosts the passerby."
9. "Cf. *Inferno* III, 55–57 . . ." [Eliot's note]. At the gate of Hell, Dante describes souls in limbo as "So long a train of people / That I should never have believed / That death had undone so many." They are in limbo because they "lived without praise or blame" or did not know the faith.
1. "Cf. *Inferno* IV, 25–27 . . ." [Eliot's note]: "Here, so far as I could tell by listening / There was no lamentation except sighs, / Which caused the eternal air to tremble." The sighs are uttered by the souls of the virtuous heathen who lived before Jesus.
2. "A phenomenon which I have often noticed" [Eliot's note]. The people cross London Bridge and pass St. Mary Woolnoth (at the corner of King William and Lombard Streets) on their way to the financial district of London, known as the City.
3. A battle in the first Punic War between Rome and Carthage. It merges with World War I. In the Bible, Jesus died at the ninth hour.
4. "Cf. the Dirge in Webster's *White Devil*" [Eliot's note]: "But keep the wolf far thence, that's foe to man / Or with his nails he'll dig them up again." In John Webster's 1612 play, the dirge is sung by a woman to one of her sons, who has killed the other and is burying him. In fertility rituals, the death of the god heralds his rebirth, but here the burial follows a grim murder, and the dog, perhaps Anubis (the dog-headed Egyptian god of the underworld who helped Isis reassemble her dismembered brother Osiris), is to be kept away.
5. "V. Baudelaire, Preface to *Fleurs du Mal*" [Eliot's note]. This is the last line of "Au Lecteur" ("To the Reader"), the introductory poem of *Les Fleurs du Mal.* The poem describes ennui as the worst sin of humankind and well known to the reader: "Hypocrite reader!—my double—my brother!"
6. The title comes from Thomas Middleton's (c. 1570–1627) play *A Game of Chess* and refers particularly to another play by Middleton, *Women Beware Women,* in which a girl is seduced in one room while her mother-in-law is kept busy at a chess game in the next. The chess moves reflect the erotic maneuvers next door.
7. "Cf. *Antony and Cleopatra,* II, ii, l. 190" [Eliot's note]. An ironic adaptation of the famous description of Cleopatra by Enobarbus in Shakespeare's play.

From which a golden Cupidon peeped out
(Another hid his eyes behind his wing)
Doubled the flames of sevenbranched candelabra
Reflecting light upon the table as
The glitter of her jewels rose to meet it,
From satin cases poured in rich profusion.
In vials of ivory and coloured glass
Unstoppered, lurked her strange synthetic perfumes,
Unguent, powdered, or liquid—troubled, confused
And drowned the sense in odours; stirred by the air
That freshened from the window, these ascended
In fattening the prolonged candle-flames,
Flung their smoke into the laquearia,[8]
Stirring the pattern on the coffered ceiling.
Huge sea-wood fed with copper
Burned green and orange, framed by the coloured stone,
In which sad light a carvèd dolphin swam.
Above the antique mantel was displayed
As though a window gave upon the sylvan scene[9]
The change of Philomel,[1] by the barbarous king
So rudely forced;[2] yet there the nightingale
Filled all the desert with inviolable voice
And still she cried, and still the world pursues,
"Jug Jug"[3] to dirty ears.
And other withered stumps of time
Were told upon the walls; staring forms
Leaned out, leaning, hushing the room enclosed.
Footsteps shuffled on the stair.
Under the firelight, under the brush, her hair
Spread out in fiery points
Glowed into words, then would be savagely still.

"My nerves are bad to-night. Yes, bad. Stay with me.
"Speak to me. Why do you never speak. Speak.
  "What are you thinking of? What thinking? What?
"I never know what you are thinking. Think."

I think we are in rats' alley[4]
Where the dead men lost their bones.

"What is that noise?"
                    The wind under the door.[5]

8. "Laquearia. V. *Aeneid*, I, 726 . . ." [Eliot's note]. The word means panelled ceiling, and Eliot refers to Virgil's description of the banquet given by the Carthaginian queen Dido for her lover Aeneas: "Burning lamps hang from the gold-panelled ceiling, / And torches dispel the night with their flames."
9. "Sylvan scene. V. Milton, *Paradise Lost*, IV, 140" [Eliot's note]. The context is Satan's description of Eden.
1. "V. Ovid, *Metamorphoses*, VI, Philomela" [Eliot's note]. Philomela was changed into a nightingale after she was raped by her sister's husband, King Tereus.
2. "Cf. Part III, [line] 204" [Eliot's note].
3. Conventional representation of nightingale's song in Elizabethan poetry.
4. "Cf. Part III, [line] 195" [Eliot's note].
5. "Cf. Webster: 'Is the wind in that door still?' " [Eliot's note]. In Webster's *The Devil's Law Case*, a physician asks this question on finding that the victim of a murderous attack is still breathing, meaning "Is he still alive?"

"What is that noise now? What is the wind doing?"
Nothing again nothing.
"Do
"You know nothing? Do you see nothing? Do you remember
"Nothing?"

I remember
Those are pearls that were his eyes.
"Are you alive, or not? Is there nothing in your head?"
But
O O O O that Shakespeherian Rag—
It's so elegant
So intelligent[6]
"What shall I do now? What shall I do?"
"I shall rush out as I am, and walk the street
"With my hair down, so. What shall we do tomorrow?
"What shall we ever do?"
The hot water at ten.
And if it rains, a closed car at four.
And we shall play a game of chess,[7]
Pressing lidless eyes and waiting for a knock upon the door.

When Lil's husband got demobbed,[8] I said—
I didn't mince my words, I said to her myself,
HURRY UP PLEASE ITS TIME[9]
Now Albert's coming back, make yourself a bit smart.
He'll want to know what you done with that money he gave you
To get yourself some teeth. He did, I was there.
You have them all out, Lil, and get a nice set,
He said, I swear, I can't bear to look at you.
And no more can't I, I said, and think of poor Albert,
He's been in the army four years, he wants a good time,
And if you don't give it him, there's others will, I said.
Oh is there, she said. Something o' that, I said.
Then I'll know who to thank, she said, and give me a straight look.
HURRY UP PLEASE ITS TIME
If you don't like it you can get on with it, I said.
Others can pick and choose if you can't.
But if Albert makes off, it won't be for lack of telling.
You ought to be ashamed, I said, to look so antique.
(And her only thirty-one.)
I can't help it, she said, pulling a long face,
It's them pills I took, to bring it off, she said.
(She's had five already, and nearly died of young George.)
The chemist[1] said it would be all right, but I've never been the same.

6. Cf. "The Shakespearian Rag," a popular song from 1912; the chorus (lyrics by Gene Buck and Herman Ruby) is "That Shakespearean Rag, most intelligent, very elegant."
7. "Cf. the game of chess in Middleton's *Women beware Women*" [Eliot's note], described in note 4 at the beginning of part 2.
8. British slang for "demobilized" (discharged from the armed services after World War I).
9. The bartender's routine call at closing time in an English pub. The following passage, according to Valerie Eliot's notes to the poem's manuscript, was based on a story told to the Eliots by their maid.
1. Pharmacist. *To bring it off*: to cause an abortion.

You *are* a proper fool, I said.
Well, if Albert won't leave you alone, there it is, I said,
What you get married for if you don't want children?
HURRY UP PLEASE ITS TIME
Well, that Sunday Albert was home, they had a hot gammon,[2]
And they asked me in to dinner, to get the beauty of it hot—
HURRY UP PLEASE ITS TIME
HURRY UP PLEASE ITS TIME
Goonight Bill. Goonight Lou. Goonight May. Goonight.
Ta ta. Goonight. Goonight.
Good night, ladies, good night, sweet ladies, good night, good night.[3]

III. The Fire Sermon[4]

The river's tent is broken; the last fingers of leaf
Clutch and sink into the wet bank. The wind
Crosses the brown land, unheard. The nymphs are departed.
Sweet Thames, run softly, till I end my song.[5]
The river bears no empty bottles, sandwich papers,
Silk handkerchiefs, cardboard boxes, cigarette ends
Or other testimony of summer nights. The nymphs are departed.
And their friends, the loitering heirs of City directors;
Departed, have left no addresses.
By the water of Leman I sat down and wept . . .[6]
Sweet Thames, run softly till I end my song,
Sweet Thames, run softly, for I speak not loud or long.
But at my back in a cold blast I hear[7]
The rattle of the bones, and chuckle spread from ear to ear.

A rat crept softly through the vegetation
Dragging its slimy belly on the bank
While I was fishing in the dull canal
On a winter evening round behind the gashouse
Musing upon the king my brother's wreck[8]
And on the king my father's death before him.
White bodies naked on the low damp ground
And bones cast in a little low dry garret,
Rattled by the rat's foot only, year to year.
But at my back from time to time I hear[9]

2. Ham or bacon.
3. In *Hamlet* 4.5, these words conclude Ophelia's mad speech before her drowning; cf. also the popular song lyric "Good night ladies, we're going to leave you now."
4. In the *Fire Sermon,* Buddha counsels his followers to conceive an aversion for the burning flames of passion and physical sensation and thus to live a holy life, attain freedom from earthly things, and finally leave the cycle of rebirth for Nirvana.
5. "V. Spenser, *Prothalamion*" [Eliot's note]. This line is the refrain of Elizabethan poet Edmund Spenser's marriage song, set along London's Thames River.
6. Cf. Psalm 137, in which the exiled Jews mourn for their homeland: "By the rivers of Babylon, there we sat down, yea, we wept, when we remembered Zion." *Leman:* the French name for Lake Geneva, near which, in Lausanne, Eliot was convalescing when he was completing *The Waste Land;* in Elizabethan and earlier English, *leman* meant a lover.
7. An ironic adaptation of "To His Coy Mistress," by Andrew Marvell (1621–1678), lines 21–22: "But at my back I always hear / Time's winged chariot hurrying near."
8. "Cf. *The Tempest,* I, ii" [Eliot's note]. Another allusion to Shakespeare's play. In lines 393–95, Prince Ferdinand, thinking his father dead, describes himself: "Sitting on a bank, / Weeping again the King my father's wreck, / This music crept by me upon the waters" (the music is Ariel's song "Full Fathom Five").
9. "Cf. Marvell, *To His Coy Mistress*" [Eliot's note].

The sound of horns and motors, which shall bring
Sweeney to Mrs. Porter in the spring.[1]
O the moon shone bright on Mrs. Porter
And on her daughter
They wash their feet in soda water[2]
Et O ces voix d'enfants, chantant dans la coupole![3]

Twit twit twit
Jug jug jug jug jug jug
So rudely forc'd.
Tereu[4]

Unreal City
Under the brown fog of a winter noon
Mr. Eugenides, the Smyrna merchant
Unshaven, with a pocket full of currants
C.i.f. London: documents at sight,[5]
Asked me in demotic French
To luncheon at the Cannon Street Hotel
Followed by a weekend at the Metropole.[6]

At the violet hour, when the eyes and back
Turn upward from the desk, when the human engine waits
Like a taxi throbbing waiting,
I Tiresias,[7] though blind, throbbing between two lives,

1. "Cf. Day, *Parliament of Bees:* 'When of the sudden, listening, you shall hear, / A noise of horns and hunting, which shall bring / Actaeon to Diana in the spring, / Where all shall see her naked skin . . . ' " [Eliot's note]. Diana, the virgin goddess of the woods and hunting, was seen naked by Actaeon the hunter; she then changed him into a stag, to be hunted to death by his own dogs. John Day (1574–c. 1640), English poet.
2. "I do not know the origin of the ballad from which these lines are taken: it was reported to me from Sydney, Australia" [Eliot's note]. It was sung by Australian troops during the Dardanelles Campaign of World War I; a fuller version reads: "O the moon shone bright on Mrs. Porter / And on the daughter / Of Mrs. Porter. / They wash their feet in soda water / And so they oughter / To keep them clean."
3. "V. Verlaine, *Parsifal*" [Eliot's note]: "And O those children's voices singing in the dome!" The sonnet, by French poet Paul Verlaine (1844–1896), evokes Wagner's opera about the Grail quest. Parsifal has withstood the female enchanter's efforts to seduce him; humbled and purified, she washes his feet to prepare him to enter the Grail Castle, where he heals the Fisher King Amfortas and becomes king himself. The opera ends with the sound of children's voices singing Jesus' praise from the heights of the castle.
4. Another conventional representation of the nightingale's song, alluding to King Tereus and his brutality to Philomela. Cf. a song in John Lyle's play *Campaspe* (1584): "O 'tis the ravished nightingale. / Jug, jug, jug, jug, tereu! she cries."
5. "The currants were quoted at a price 'carriage and insurance free to London'; and the Bill of Lading etc. were to be handed to the buyer upon payment of the sight draft" [Eliot's note]. Another gloss of *C.i.f.* is "cost, insurance and freight." *Smyrna:* now Izmir, a seaport in western Turkey and the center of war between Turkey and Greece after World War I.
6. A luxurious hotel in the seaside resort of Brighton. Cannon Street Hotel, next to the City's Cannon Street Station, was used by business people going to or from the Continent by boat-train; it was also a locale for homosexual liaisons.
7. "Tiresias, although a mere spectator and not indeed a 'character,' is yet the most important personage in the poem, uniting all the rest. Just as the one-eyed merchant, seller of currants, melts into the Phoenician Sailor, and the latter is not wholly distinct from Ferdinand Prince of Naples [in *The Tempest*], so all the women are one woman, and the two sexes meet in Tiresias. What Tiresias *sees*, in fact, is the substance of the poem. The whole passage from Ovid is of great anthropological interest" [Eliot's note]. Eliot then quotes the Latin passage in Ovid's *Metamorphoses* (3.316–38): "Jove [when drunk] said jokingly to Juno: 'You women have greater pleasure in love than that enjoyed by men.' She denied it. So they decided to refer the question to wise Tiresias who knew love from both points of view. For once, with a blow of his staff, he had separated two huge snakes who were copulating in the forest, and miraculously was changed instantly from a man into a woman and remained so for seven years. In the eighth year he saw the snakes again and said: 'If a blow against you is so powerful that it changes the sex of the author of it, now I shall strike you again.' With these words he struck them, and his former shape and masculinity were restored. As referee in the sportive quarrel, he supported Jove's claim. Juno,

Old man with wrinkled female breasts, can see
At the violet hour, the evening hour that strives
Homeward, and brings the sailor home from sea,[8]
The typist home at teatime, clears her breakfast, lights
Her stove, and lays out food in tins.
Out of the window perilously spread
Her drying combinations[9] touched by the sun's last rays,
On the divan are piled (at night her bed)
Stockings, slippers, camisoles, and stays.[1]
I Tiresias, old man with wrinkled dugs
Perceived the scene, and foretold the rest—
I too awaited the expected guest.
He, the young man carbuncular,[2] arrives,
A small house agent's clerk, with one bold stare,
One of the low on whom assurance sits
As a silk hat on a Bradford[3] millionaire.
The time is now propitious, as he guesses,
The meal is ended, she is bored and tired,
Endeavours to engage her in caresses
Which still are unreproved, if undesired.
Flushed and decided, he assaults at once;
Exploring hands encounter no defence;
His vanity requires no response,
And makes a welcome of indifference.
(And I Tiresias have foresuffered all
Enacted on this same divan or bed;
I who have sat by Thebes below the wall[4]
And walked among the lowest of the dead.)
Bestows one final patronising kiss,
And gropes his way, finding the stairs unlit . . .

She turns and looks a moment in the glass,
Hardly aware of her departed lover;
Her brain allows one half-formed thought to pass:
"Well now that's done: and I'm glad it's over."
When lovely woman stoops to folly and
Paces about her room again, alone,
She smoothes her hair with automatic hand,
And puts a record on the gramophone.[5]

overly upset by the decision, condemned the arbitrator to eternal blindness. But the all-powerful father (inasmuch as no god can undo what has been done by another god) gave him the power of prophecy, with this honor compensating him for the loss of sight."

8. "This may not appear as exact as Sappho's lines, but I had in mind the 'longshore' or 'dory' fisherman, who returns at nightfall" [Eliot's note]. In Fragment 149, Sappho writes, "Hesperus [the evening star], thou bringest home all things bright morning scattered: thou bringest the sheep, the goat, the child to the mother." Also echoed is "Home is the sailor, home from the sea," a line in "Requiem," by Scottish writer Robert Louis Stevenson (1850–1894).

9. Undergarments.

1. Corset.

2. Pimply.

3. Manufacturing town in the north of England, where fortunes were made during World War I.

4. Tiresias, who prophesied in the marketplace by the wall of Thebes, foretold the fall of two Theban kings, Oedipus and Creon. After his death, he remained a prophet; Odysseus summoned him from Hades and was given advice to aid his voyage home.

5. "V. Goldsmith, the song in *The Vicar of Wakefield*" [Eliot's note]. In the 1766 novel by Oliver Goldsmith, the seduced Olivia sings, on returning to the scene of her seduction: "When lovely woman stoops to folly / And finds too late that men betray, / What charm can soothe her melancholy, / What art can wash her guilt away? /

"This music crept by me upon the waters"[6]
And along the Strand, up Queen Victoria Street.
O City city, I can sometimes hear
Beside a public bar in Lower Thames Street,
The pleasant whining of a mandoline
And a clatter and a chatter from within
Where fishmen lounge at noon: where the walls
Of Magnus Martyr[7] hold
Inexplicable splendour of Ionian white and gold.

The river sweats[8]
Oil and tar
The barges drift
With the turning tide
Red sails
Wide
To leeward, swing on the heavy spar.
The barges wash
Drifting logs
Down Greenwich reach
Past the Isle of Dogs.[9]
Weialala leia
Wallala leialala

Elizabeth and Leicester[1]
Beating oars
The stern was formed
A gilded shell
Red and gold
The brisk swell
Rippled both shores
Southwest wind
Carried down stream
The peal of bells
White towers
Weialala leia
Wallala leialala

The only art her guilt to cover, / To hide her shame from every eye, / To give repentance to her lover / And wring his bosom—is to die."

6. "V. *The Tempest,* as above" [Eliot's note].

7. "The interior of St. Magnus Martyr is to my mind one of the finest among [Sir Christopher] Wren's interiors. See *The Proposed Demolition of Nineteen City Churches:* (P. S. King & Son, Ltd.)" [Eliot's note]. The church, built in 1676, still stands at the corner of Lower Thames and Fish Streets, between London Bridge and London's fish market.

8. "The Song of the (three) Thames-daughters begins here. From line 292 to 306 inclusive they speak in turn. V. *Götterdämmerung,* III, i: the Rhine-daughters" [Eliot's note]. In Wagner's opera *The Twilight of the Gods,* the three Rhinemaidens try in vain to seduce and then frighten the hero Siegfried into returning their gold, which brings both power and death to its possessor; since its theft, their river has lost its beauty. Lines 277–78 quote the refrain of their song.

9. A peninsula in East London formed by a sharp bend in the Thames called Greenwich Reach; Greenwich is a borough on the south bank. Queen Elizabeth I was born in Greenwich House and entertained the Earl of Leicester there (lines 279–89).

1. "V. [J. A.] Froude, [*The Reign of*] *Elizabeth,* Vol. I, ch. iv, letter of De Quadra [Spanish bishop and ambassador to England] to [King] Philip of Spain: 'In the afternoon we were in a barge, watching the games on the river. (The queen) was alone with Lord Robert [Earl of Leicester] and myself on the poop, when they began to talk nonsense, and went so far that Lord Robert at last said, as I was on the spot there was no reason why they should not be married if the queen pleased' " [Eliot's note].

"Trams and dusty trees.
Highbury bore me. Richmond and Kew
Undid me.[2] By Richmond I raised my knees
Supine on the floor of a narrow canoe."

"My feet are at Moorgate, and my heart
Under my feet. After the event
He wept. He promised 'a new start.'
I made no comment. What should I resent?

"On Margate Sands.[3]
I can connect
Nothing with nothing.
The broken fingernails of dirty hands.
My people humble people who expect
Nothing."
la la

To Carthage then I came[4]

Burning burning burning burning[5]
O Lord Thou pluckest me out[6]
O Lord Thou pluckest

burning

IV. Death by Water[7]

Phlebas the Phoenician, a fortnight dead,
Forgot the cry of gulls, and the deep sea swell
And the profit and loss.
A current under sea
Picked his bones in whispers. As he rose and fell
He passed the stages of his age and youth
Entering the whirlpool.
Gentile or Jew
O you who turn the wheel and look to windward,
Consider Phlebas, who was once handsome and tall as you.

2. "Cf. *Purgatorio,* V, 133 . . ." [Eliot's note]. Dante meets the spirit of Pia de' Tolomei of Siena, who tells him: "Remember me, who am La Pia. Siena made me, Maremma unmade me," a reference to her violent death in Maremma at her husband's hands. Ezra Pound used this phrase in "Hugh Selwyn Mauberley" (see p. 358, note 3).
3. Margate, and the other places mentioned above, are in or near London and the Thames.
4. "V. St. Augustine's *Confessions:* 'to Carthage then I came, where a cauldron of unholy loves sang all about mine ears' " [Eliot's note].
5. "The complete text of the Buddha's Fire Sermon (which corresponds in importance to the Sermon on the Mount), from which these words are taken, will be found translated in the late Henry Clarke Warren's *Buddhism in Translation* (Harvard Oriental Series). Mr. Warren was one of the great pioneers of Buddhist studies in the Occident" [Eliot's note].
6. "From St. Augustine's *Confessions* again. The collocation of these two representatives of eastern and western asceticism, as the culmination of this part of the poem, is not an accident" [Eliot's note]. Augustine wrote, "I entangle my steps with these outward beauties, but Thou pluckest me out, O Lord, Thou pluckest me out."
7. Phlebas's drowning has been read as a sacrificial death before rebirth, as in the fertility rites, or as a sterile death without hope of resurrection. This section is a translation, somewhat modified, of the close of Eliot's French poem "Dans le Restaurant."

V. *What the Thunder Said*[8]

After the torchlight red on sweaty faces
After the frosty silence in the gardens
After the agony in stony places
The shouting and the crying
Prison and palace and reverberation
Of thunder of spring over distant mountains
He who was living is now dead[9]
We who were living are now dying
With a little patience

Here is no water but only rock
Rock and no water and the sandy road
The road winding above among the mountains
Which are mountains of rock without water
If there were water we should stop and drink
Amongst the rock one cannot stop or think
Sweat is dry and feet are in the sand
If there were only water amongst the rock
Dead mountain mouth of carious[1] teeth that cannot spit
Here one can neither stand nor lie nor sit
There is not even silence in the mountains
But dry sterile thunder without rain
There is not even solitude in the mountains
But red sullen faces sneer and snarl
From doors of mudcracked houses
                                                  If there were water
    And no rock
    If there were rock
    And also water
    And water
    A spring
    A pool among the rock
    If there were the sound of water only
    Not the cicada[2]
    And dry grass singing
    But sound of water over a rock
    Where the hermit-thrush sings in the pine trees
    Drip drop drip drop drop drop drop[3]
    But there is no water

8. "In the first part of Part V three themes are employed: the journey to Emmaus, the approach to the Chapel Perilous (see Miss Weston's book) and the present decay of eastern Europe" [Eliot's note]. On the journey to Emmaus, the resurrected Jesus walks alongside and converses with two disciples, who think he is a stranger until he reveals his identity (Luke 24.13–14).
9. Allusions to Jesus' agony in the Garden of Gethsemane, his imprisonment, trial, and death on the cross.
1. Decayed.
2. Cf. Ecclesiastes' prophecy "the grasshopper shall be a burden, and desire shall fail" (and also compare line 23 and its note).
3. "This is *Turdus aonalaschkae pallasii,* the hermit-thrush which I have heard in Quebec County. Chapman says (*Handbook of Birds of Eastern North America*) 'it is most at home in secluded woodland and thickety retreats. . . . Its notes are not remarkable for variety or volume, but in purity and sweetness of tone and exquisite modulation they are unequalled.' Its 'water-dripping song' is justly celebrated" [Eliot's note].

Who is the third who walks always beside you?[4]
When I count, there are only you and I together
But when I look ahead up the white road
There is always another one walking beside you
Gliding wrapt in a brown mantle, hooded
I do not know whether a man or a woman
—But who is that on the other side of you?

What is that sound high in the air[5]
Murmur of maternal lamentation
Who are those hooded hordes swarming
Over endless plains, stumbling in cracked earth
Ringed by the flat horizon only
What is the city over the mountains
Cracks and reforms and bursts in the violet air
Falling towers
Jerusalem Athens Alexandria
Vienna London
Unreal

A woman drew her long black hair out tight
And fiddled whisper music on those strings
And bats with baby faces in the violet light
Whistled, and beat their wings
And crawled head downward down a blackened wall
And upside down in air were towers
Tolling reminiscent bells, that kept the hours
And voices singing out of empty cisterns and exhausted wells

In this decayed hole among the mountains
In the faint moonlight, the grass is singing
Over the tumbled graves, above the chapel[6]
There is the empty chapel, only the wind's home.
It has no windows, and the door swings,
Dry bones can harm no one.
Only a cock stood on the rooftree
Co co rico co co rico[7]
In a flash of lightning. Then a damp gust
Bringing rain

4. "The following lines were stimulated by the account of one of the Antarctic expeditions (I forget which, but I think one of Shackleton's): it was related that the party of explorers, at the extremity of their strength, had the constant delusion that there *was one more member* than could actually be counted" [Eliot's note]. The experience is associated with Jesus' unrecognized presence on the way to Emmaus.

5. Eliot's note for lines 367–77: "Cf. Hermann Hesse, *Blick ins Chaos* [A Glimpse into Chaos]": "Already half of Europe, and at least half of Eastern Europe, is on the way to Chaos, travels drunk in sacred madness along the brink of the abyss and moreover sings drunken hymns as Dmitri Karamazov sang [in *The Brothers Karamazov* (1882), by Fyodor Dostoyevsky]. The bourgeois, shocked, laughs at these songs: the saint and seer hear them with tears."

6. On his way to the Grail, the questing knight must enter the Chapel Perilous, where he is tested by strange voices and sights.

7. In folklore, the cock crows to announce the coming dawn and the departure of evil spirits; in Matthew 26.34 and 74, the cock crows after Peter betrays Jesus three times.

Ganga[8] was sunken, and the limp leaves
Waited for rain, while the black clouds
Gathered far distant, over Himavant.[9]
The jungle crouched, humped in silence.
Then spoke the thunder
DA[1]
Datta: what have we given?
My friend, blood shaking my heart
The awful daring of a moment's surrender
Which an age of prudence can never retract
By this, and this only, we have existed
Which is not to be found in our obituaries
Or in memories draped by the beneficent spider[2]
Or under seals broken by the lean solicitor[3]
In our empty rooms
DA
Dayadhvam: I have heard the key
Turn in the door once and turn once only[4]
We think of the key, each in his prison
Thinking of the key, each confirms a prison
Only at nightfall, aethereal rumours
Revive for a moment a broken Coriolanus[5]
DA
Damyata: The boat responded
Gaily, to the hand expert with sail and oar
The sea was calm, your heart would have responded
Gaily, when invited, beating obedient
To controlling hands

I sat upon the shore
Fishing,[6] with the arid plain behind me
Shall I at least set my lands in order?[7]

8. The Sanskrit name for the major sacred river in India.
9. That is, snowy mountain (Sanskrit); usually applied to the Himalayas.
1. " 'Datta, dayadhvam, damyata' (Give, sympathise, control). The fable of the meaning of the Thunder is found in the *Brihadaranyaka—Upanishad,* 5, 1 . . ." [Eliot's note]. In the Old Indian fable The Three Great Disciplines, the Creator God utters the enigmatic syllable *DA* to three groups. Lesser gods, naturally unruly, interpret it as "Control yourselves" (*Damyata*); humans, naturally greedy, as "Give" (*Datta*); demons, naturally cruel, as "Be compassionate" (*Dayadhvam*): "That very thing is repeated even today by the heavenly voice, in the form of thunder as *'DA' 'DA' 'DA,'* which means 'Control yourselves,' 'Give,' and 'Have compassion.' Therefore one should practice these three things: self-control, giving, and mercy." The Upanishads are ancient philosophical dialogues in Sanskrit. They are primary texts for an early form of Hinduism sometimes called Brahminism.
2. "Cf. Webster, *The White Devil,* V, vi: " ' . . . they'll remarry / Ere the worm pierce your winding-sheet, ere the spider / Make a thin curtain for your epitaphs' " [Eliot's note].
3. Lawyer.
4. "Cf. *Inferno,* XXXIII, 46 . . ." [Eliot's note]: "And below I heard them nailing shut the door / of the horrible tower." The traitor Ugolino tells Dante that his enemies imprisoned him and his children in a tower to die of starvation. Eliot continues: "Also F. H. Bradley, *Appearance and Reality,* p. 346. 'My external sensations are no less private to myself than are my thoughts or my feelings. In either case my experience falls within my own circle, a circle closed on the outside; and, with all its elements alike, every sphere is opaque to the others which surround it. . . . In brief, regarded as an existence which appears in a soul, the whole world for each is peculiar and private to that soul.' " Eliot wrote his doctoral thesis on Bradley's philosophy.
5. Roman general, the hero of a play by Shakespeare; exiled by the Roman people and driven by injured pride, he led the enemy against Rome.
6. "V. Weston: *From Ritual to Romance;* chapter on the Fisher King" [Eliot's note].
7. Cf. Isaiah 38.1: "Thus saith the Lord, Set thine house in order: for thou shalt die, and not live."

London Bridge is falling down falling down falling down
Poi s'ascose nel foco che gli affina[8]
Quando fiam uti chelidon[9]—O swallow swallow[1]
Le Prince d'Aquitaine à la tour abolie[2]
These fragments I have shored against my ruins
Why then Ile fit you. Hieronymo's mad againe.[3]
Datta. Dayadhvam. Damyata.

Shantih shantih shantih[4]

1922

Journey of the Magi[5]

'A cold coming we had of it,
Just the worst time of the year
For a journey, and such a long journey:
The ways deep and the weather sharp,
The very dead of winter.'[6]
And the camels galled, sore-footed, refractory,
Lying down in the melting snow.
There were times we regretted
The summer palaces on slopes, the terraces,
And the silken girls bringing sherbet.
Then the camel men cursing and grumbling
And running away, and wanting their liquor and women,
And the night-fires going out, and the lack of shelters,
And the cities hostile and the towns unfriendly
And the villages dirty and charging high prices:
A hard time we had of it.
At the end we preferred to travel all night,
Sleeping in snatches,
With the voices singing in our ears, saying
That this was all folly.

Then at dawn we came down to a temperate valley,
Wet, below the snow line, smelling of vegetation;

8. "V. *Purgatorio,* XXVI, 148 . . ." [Eliot's note]. In this passage, the soul of the poet Arnaut Daniel speaks to Dante: "Now I pray you, by the power / that guides you to the top of this staircase [out of Purgatory], / be mindful in time of my suffering." Dante continues with the line quoted in *The Waste Land*: "Then he hid himself in the refining fire."
9. "V. *Pervigilium Veneris.* Cf. Philomela in Parts II and III" [Eliot's note]. In the late Latin poem "The Vigil of Venus," Philomela asks, "When shall I be like the swallow," continuing, "that I may cease to be silent?"
1. Cf. A. C. Swinburne's "Itylus," which begins, "Swallow, my sister, O sister swallow, / How can thy heart be full of spring?" and Alfred, Lord Tennyson's "O Swallow, Swallow, flying, flying south."
2. "V. Gerard de Nerval, Sonnet *El Desdichado*" [Eliot's note]. From Nerval's poem "The Disinherited," in which the poet compares himself to "the prince of Aquitaine at the ruined tower" (French).
3. "V. Kyd's *Spanish Tragedy*" [Eliot's note]. The play's subtitle is *Hieronymo Is Mad Againe;* to avenge his son's murder, he feigns madness and writes a play in which, acting one of the parts, he kills the murderers. "Why then Ile fit you!" (that is, accommodate you) is his answer when asked to write the play.
4. "Repeated as here, a formal ending to an Upanishad. 'The Peace which passeth understanding' is our equivalent to this word" [Eliot's note]. In another edition of this poem, Eliot phrased his note as "a feeble translation to this word." On the Upanishads, see note 1, line 401, above.
5. Matthew 2.1–12 describes the journey of the magi, or wise men, who followed a star to worship Jesus at his birth.
6. Adapted from the Christmas sermon preached in 1622 by Bishop Lancelot Andrewes.

With a running stream and a water-mill beating the darkness,
And three trees on the low sky,
And an old white horse galloped away in the meadow.
Then we came to a tavern with vine-leaves over the lintel,
Six hands at an open door dicing for pieces of silver,
And feet kicking the empty wine-skins.
But there was no information, and so we continued
And arrived at evening, not a moment too soon
Finding the place; it was (you may say) satisfactory.

All this was a long time ago, I remember,
And I would do it again, but set down
This set down
This: were we led all that way for
Birth or Death? There was a Birth, certainly,
We had evidence and no doubt. I had seen birth and death,
But had thought they were different; this Birth was
Hard and bitter agony for us, like Death, our death.
We returned to our places, these Kingdoms,
But no longer at ease here, in the old dispensation,
With an alien people clutching their gods.
I should be glad of another death.

1927

Little Gidding[7]

I

Midwinter spring is its own season
Sempiternal[8] though sodden towards sundown,
Suspended in time, between pole and tropic.
When the short day is brightest, with frost and fire,
The brief sun flames the ice, on pond and ditches,
In windless cold that is the heart's heat,
Reflecting in a watery mirror
A glare that is blindness in the early afternoon.
And glow more intense than blaze of branch, or brazier,
Stirs the dumb spirit: no wind, but pentecostal fire[9]

7. The last of Eliot's *Four Quartets;* Eliot considered it the best part of that work and that work as the best of his poetry. Each of Eliot's *Quartets* is divided into five parts, or movements, that develop the themes—centrally, time and eternity, history and the timeless moment—in different ways. Each quartet is based on one of the four elements, that of *Little Gidding* being fire. Here, as in the "Fire Sermon" section of *The Waste Land*, fire is the torturing element in which we live, but it is also the refining fire that can bring salvation. Each quartet also is named after a place. Little Gidding was an Anglican religious community founded in 1625 by Nicholas Ferrar; it is now a village in Huntingdonshire. Although the community lasted only twenty-two years, broken up by the victorious Puritans at the end of the English Civil War, the memory of its devotion persisted, and the chapel was rebuilt in the nineteenth century.

8. Everlasting.

9. On the feast of Pentecost, Jesus' disciples were assembled, "And suddenly there came a sound from heaven, as of a rushing mighty wind, and it filled all the house where they were sitting. And there appeared unto them cloven tongues, like as of fire. . . . And they were all filled with the Holy Ghost" (Acts 2.2–4).

In the dark time of the year. Between melting and freezing
The soul's sap quivers. There is no earth smell
Or smell of living thing. This is the spring time
But not in time's covenant. Now the hedgerow
Is blanched for an hour with transitory blossom
Of snow, a bloom more sudden
Than that of summer, neither budding nor fading,
Not in the scheme of generation.
Where is the summer, the unimaginable
Zero summer?

If you came this way,
Taking the route you would be likely to take
From the place you would be likely to come from,
If you came this way in may time, you would find the hedges
White again, in May, with voluptuary sweetness.
It would be the same at the end of the journey,
If you came at night like a broken king,[1]
If you came by day not knowing what you came for,
It would be the same, when you leave the rough road
And turn behind the pig-sty to the dull façade
And the tombstone. And what you thought you came for
Is only a shell, a husk of meaning
From which the purpose breaks only when it is fulfilled
If at all. Either you had no purpose
Or the purpose is beyond the end you figured
And is altered in fulfilment. There are other places
Which also are the world's end, some at the sea jaws,
Or over a dark lake, in a desert or a city—
But this is the nearest, in place and time,
Now and in England.

If you came this way,
Taking any route, starting from anywhere,
At any time or at any season,
It would always be the same: you would have to put off
Sense and notion. You are not here to verify,
Instruct yourself, or inform curiosity
Or carry report. You are here to kneel
Where prayer has been valid. And prayer is more
Than an order of words, the conscious occupation
Of the praying mind, or the sound of the voice praying.
And what the dead had no speech for, when living,
They can tell you, being dead: the communication
Of the dead is tongued with fire beyond the language of the living.
Here, the intersection of the timeless moment
Is England and nowhere. Never and always.

1. King Charles I, who, after his final defeat at the battle of Naseby in the English Civil War, came to Little Gidding to fortify his spirit.

II

Ash on an old man's sleeve
Is all the ash the burnt roses leave.
Dust in the air suspended
Marks the place where a story ended.
Dust inbreathed was a house—
The wall, the wainscot and the mouse.
The death of hope and despair,
    This is the death of air.[2]

There are flood and drouth
Over the eyes and in the mouth,
Dead water and dead sand
Contending for the upper hand.
The parched eviscerate soil
Gapes at the vanity of toil,
Laughs without mirth.
    This is the death of earth.

Water and fire succeed
The town, the pasture and the weed.
Water and fire deride
The sacrifice that we denied.
Water and fire shall rot
The marred foundations we forgot,
Of sanctuary and choir.[3]
    This is the death of water and fire.

In the uncertain hour before the morning[4]
  Near the ending of interminable night
  At the recurrent end of the unending
After the dark dove with the flickering tongue[5]
  Had passed below the horizon of his homing
  While the dead leaves still rattled on like tin
Over the asphalt where no other sound was
  Between three districts whence the smoke arose
  I met one walking, loitering and hurried
As if blown towards me like the metal leaves
  Before the urban dawn wind unresisting.
  And as I fixed upon the down-turned face
That pointed scrutiny with which we challenge
  The first-met stranger in the waning dusk
  I caught the sudden look of some dead master
Whom I had known, forgotten, half recalled

2. Cf. the theory of the four elements' creative strife put forth by the Greek philosopher Heracleitus (540?–475 B.C.E.): "Fire lives in the death of air; water lives in the death of earth; and earth lives in the death of water."
3. Parts of a church: the altar is in the sanctuary, which is connected to the nave, or main hall, by the choir.
4. Lines 78–149 are meant to suggest, if not exactly to imitate, the stanzaic pattern (terza rima) of Dante's *Divine Comedy*. Eliot was an air-raid warden during the German raids on London in World War II and represents himself here as patrolling the streets after such a raid.
5. The German dive bomber.

Both one and many; in the brown baked features
The eyes of a familiar compound ghost[6]
Both intimate and unidentifiable.
So I assumed a double part, and cried
And heard another's voice cry: 'What! are *you* here?'[7]
Although we were not. I was still the same,
Knowing myself yet being someone other—
And he a face still forming; yet the words sufficed
To compel the recognition they preceded.
And so, compliant to the common wind,
Too strange to each other for misunderstanding,
In concord at this intersection time
Of meeting nowhere, no before and after,
We trod the pavement in a dead patrol.
I said: 'The wonder that I feel is easy,
Yet ease is cause of wonder. Therefore speak:
I may not comprehend, may not remember.'
And he: 'I am not eager to rehearse
My thoughts and theory which you have forgotten.
These things have served their purpose: let them be.
So with your own, and pray they be forgiven
By others, as I pray you to forgive
Both bad and good. Last season's fruit is eaten
And the fullfed beast shall kick the empty pail.
For last year's words belong to last year's language
And next year's words await another voice.
But, as the passage now presents no hindrance
To the spirit unappeased and peregrine[8]
Between two worlds become much like each other,
So I find words I never thought to speak
In streets I never thought I should revisit
When I left my body on a distant shore.
Since our concern was speech, and speech impelled us
To purify the dialect of the tribe[9]
And urge the mind to aftersight and foresight,
Let me disclose the gifts reserved for age
To set a crown upon your lifetime's effort.
First, the cold friction of expiring sense
Without enchantment, offering no promise
But bitter tastelessness of shadow fruit
As body and soul begin to fall asunder.
Second, the conscious impotence of rage[1]
At human folly, and the laceration
Of laughter at what ceases to amuse.[2]

6. Eliot principally had in mind here the Anglo-Irish poets W. B. Yeats (1865–1939) and Jonathan Swift (1667–1745).
7. A translation of Dante's cry of recognition when he sees his mentor, Brunetto Latini, in *Inferno* 15.30. *A double part:* that is, a part in an imagined dialogue.
8. Wandering, foreign.
9. A rendition of a line in Stéphane Mallarmé's "Le Tombeau d'Edgar Poe" (1877): "Donner un sens plus pur aux mots de la tribu."
1. Cf. Yeats's "The Spur": "You think it horrible that lust and rage / Should dance attendance upon my old age."
2. According to Swift's epitaph, written by himself in Latin (and translated by Yeats), "Savage indignation now / Cannot lacerate his breast."

And last, the rending pain of re-enactment
Of all that you have done, and been; the shame
Of motives late revealed, and the awareness
Of things ill done and done to others' harm
Which once you took for exercise of virtue.[3]
Then fools' approval stings, and honour stains.
From wrong to wrong the exasperated spirit
Proceeds, unless restored by that refining fire[4]
Where you must move in measure, like a dancer.'[5]
The day was breaking. In the disfigured street
He left me, with a kind of valediction,
And faded on the blowing of the horn.[6]

III

There are three conditions which often look alike
Yet differ completely, flourish in the same hedgerow:
Attachment to self and to things and to persons, detachment
From self and from things and from persons; and, growing between them, indifference
Which resembles the others as death resembles life,
Being between two lives—unflowering, between
The live and the dead nettle. This is the use of memory:
For liberation—not less of love but expanding
Of love beyond desire, and so liberation
From the future as well as the past. Thus, love of a country
Begins as attachment to our own field of action
And comes to find that action of little importance
Though never indifferent. History may be servitude,
History may be freedom. See, now they vanish,
The faces and places, with the self which, as it could, loved them,
To become renewed, transfigured, in another pattern.

Sin is Behovely,[7] but
All shall be well, and
All manner of thing shall be well.
If I think, again, of this place,
And of people, not wholly commendable,
Of no immediate kin or kindness,
But some of peculiar genius,
All touched by a common genius,
United in the strife which divided them;
If I think of a king at nightfall,

3. Cf. Yeats's "Man and the Echo," lines 7–18, and "Vacillation," lines 51–56, above.
4. See the "Fire Sermon" section of *The Waste Land* and its first note 4, above.
5. Cf. the dancer in Yeats's "Among School Children" and "Nineteen Hundred and Nineteen," above.
6. Spirits usually vanish at the crowing of the cock. The horn is the "All Clear" siren after the air raid. Eliot echoes Shakespeare's description of the disappearance of Hamlet's father's ghost: "It faded on the crowing of the cock" (*Hamlet* 1.1.138).
7. Necessary to the divine plan. In one of her visions, the fourteenth-century English mystic Dame Julian of Norwich was told that "sin is behovable but all shall be well . . . and all manner of things shall be well."

Of three men, and more, on the scaffold[8]
And a few who died forgotten
In other places, here and abroad,
And of one who died blind and quiet,[9]
Why should we celebrate
These dead men more than the dying?
It is not to ring the bell backward
Nor is it an incantation
To summon the spectre of a Rose.[1]
We cannot revive old factions
We cannot restore old policies
Or follow an antique drum.
These men, and those who opposed them
And those whom they opposed
Accept the constitution of silence
And are folded in a single party.
Whatever we inherit from the fortunate
We have taken from the defeated
What they had to leave us—a symbol:
A symbol perfected in death.
And all shall be well and
All manner of thing shall be well
By the purification of the motive
In the ground of our beseeching.[2]

IV

The dove descending breaks the air
With flame of incandescent terror
Of which the tongues declare
The one discharge from sin and error.[3]
The only hope, or else despair
    Lies in the choice of pyre or pyre—
    To be redeemed from fire by fire.

Who then devised the torment? Love.
Love is the unfamiliar Name
Behind the hands that wove
The intolerable shirt of flame
Which human power cannot remove.[4]
    We only live, only suspire[5]
    Consumed by either fire or fire.

8. King Charles I died "on the scaffold," in 1649; his two chief aides, Thomas Wentworth, earl of Strafford, and Archbishop Laud, were executed earlier by the Puritans.
9. John Milton, who took Cromwell's side against the king.
1. A pun combining the title of a sentimental ballet, in which a girl dreams of the ghost of a rose she once wore to the ball, and a reference to the Wars of the Roses, Lancaster being the white and York the red, to determine which family would rule England.
2. Dame Julian of Norwich was instructed in a vision that "the ground of our beseeching" is love.
3. The dove is both dive bomber and the symbol of the Holy Ghost with its pentecostal tongues of fire.
4. The shirt of Nessus, which Hercules' wife had him put on because she had been falsely informed that it would win back his love for her, clung to his flesh and caused such agony that he mounted a pyre and burned himself to death.
5. Breathe, sigh.

V

What we call the beginning is often the end
And to make an end is to make a beginning.
The end is where we start from. And every phrase
And sentence that is right (where every word is at home,
Taking its place to support the others,
The word neither diffident nor ostentatious,
An easy commerce of the old and the new,
The common word exact without vulgarity,
The formal word precise but not pedantic,
The complete consort dancing together)
Every phrase and every sentence is an end and a beginning,
Every poem an epitaph. And any action
Is a step to the block, to the fire, down the sea's throat
Or to an illegible stone: and that is where we start.
We die with the dying:
See, they depart, and we go with them.
We are born with the dead:
See, they return, and bring us with them.
The moment of the rose and the moment of the yew-tree[6]
Are of equal duration. A people without history
Is not redeemed from time, for history is a pattern
Of timeless moments. So, while the light fails
On a winter's afternoon, in a secluded chapel[7]
History is now and England.

With the drawing of this Love and the voice of this Calling[8]

We shall not cease from exploration
And the end of all our exploring
Will be to arrive where we started
And know the place for the first time.
Through the unknown, remembered gate
When the last of earth left to discover
Is that which was the beginning;
At the source of the longest river
The voice of the hidden waterfall
And the children in the apple-tree
Not known, because not looked for
But heard, half-heard, in the stillness
Between two waves of the sea.
Quick now, here, now, always—[9]
A condition of complete simplicity
(Costing not less than everything)

6. Traditional symbol of death and grief (here, contrasted with the rose).
7. At Little Gidding.
8. Quoted from *The Cloud of Unknowing,* an anonymous fourteenth-century religious work.
9. The voices of the children in the apple tree occur in the first of the *Four Quartets,* "Burnt Norton": "Sudden in a shaft of sunlight / Even while the dust moves / There rises the hidden laughter / Of children in the foliage / Quick now, here, now, always."

And all shall be well and
All manner of thing shall be well
When the tongues of flame are in-folded
Into the crowned knot[1] of fire
And the fire and the rose are one.

1942, 1943

1. A nautical knot finished by interweaving the strands to prevent untwisting.

IVOR GURNEY
1890–1937

Ivor Gurney was born on August 28, 1890, in Gloucester, England. His father was a tailor and the family of modest means. In 1911, he won a scholarship to the Royal College of Music, in London. His teachers recognized him as a gifted, if eccentric, composer. He set to music the work of such contemporaries as A. E. Housman and W. B. Yeats, and his compositions are still performed and recorded. But Gurney volunteered for service in World War I and, after an initial rejection because of poor eyesight, was admitted in February 1915. A private in the Gloucester Regiment, he fought in the trenches along front lines in France and Belgium, becoming at one point the crack shot for his platoon. Gassed near the infamous town of Ypres in September 1917, he was sent home, where he moved from hospital to hospital, thought to be suffering from "deferred shellshock." Even before the war, Gurney had shown signs of mental instability, and he is now believed to have been schizophrenic. After several years when he did odd jobs while writing and composing, his condition worsened, until he was finally committed to an asylum in 1922, remaining—except for brief escapes—confined for the last fifteen years of his life.

Gurney published two small volumes of verse, *Severn and Somme* (1917) and *War's Embers* (1919), leaving behind a large archive of material, which continues to be published. In recent decades, his reputation has risen, in part because of his influence on English poets such as Geoffrey Hill and Andrew Motion. His war poetry is rooted in typically Georgian preoccupations and themes—landscape, nature, love, isolation, mortality—but it is recognizably "modern" in its compression, jarring disharmonies, and unredemptive psychology. Gurney dislocates a traditional aesthetic through syntactic contortions that sometimes make his sentences difficult; colloquial diction that is often specific to life in the trenches; rhythms and rhymes that change surprisingly or sometimes dissipate; images that are deliberately "unpoetic"; and lines broken to accentuate the jarring experience of war (a body described as "that red wet / Thing" in "To His Love"). He seizes with intensity on the particulars of daily life in the trenches, recovering in "Laventie" the specific names of trench food, such as the tinned stew called Machonachie. In "The Escape," he explains, "whatever / Leads to the seeing of small trifles, / Real, beautiful, is good." The poet's duty, as Gurney understands it, involves "moving or breaking to sight / Of a thing hidden under custom." Whereas the better-known war poets were officers, such as Wilfred Owen and Siegfried Sassoon, Gurney was a mere private, and as such, his poetry has an immediacy of perception that is not filtered through guilt, abstraction, or polemical irony. His verse compounds the uncanny and the concrete in a rich poetic synthesis that is unsettling, if "strangely beautiful" ("First Time In").

To His Love

He's gone, and all our plans
   Are useless indeed.
We'll walk no more on Cotswold[1]
   Where the sheep feed
   Quietly and take no heed.

His body that was so quick
   Is not as you
Knew it, on Severn river[2]
   Under the blue
   Driving our small boat through.

You would not know him now . . .
   But still he died
Nobly, so cover him over
   With violets of pride
   Purple from Severn side.

Cover him, cover him soon!
   And with thick-set
Masses of memoried flowers—
   Hide that red wet
   Thing I must somehow forget.

1919

First Time In

After the dread tales and red yarns of the Line
Anything might have come to us; but the divine
Afterglow brought us up to a Welsh colony
Hiding in sandbag ditches, whispering consolatory
Soft foreign things. Then we were taken in
To low huts candle-lit, shaded close by slitten
Oilsheets, and there the boys gave us kind welcome,
So that we looked out as from the edge of home,
Sang us Welsh things, and changed all former notions
To human hopeful things. And the next day's guns
Nor any line-pangs ever quite could blot out
That strangely beautiful entry to war's rout;
Candles they gave us, precious and shared over-rations—
Ulysses found little more in his wanderings without doubt.
'David of the White Rock', the 'Slumber Song,'[3] so soft, and that
Beautiful tune to which roguish words by Welsh pit boys
Are sung—but never more beautiful than there under the guns' noise.

1919–20 1982

1. Region in south-central England.
2. British river.
3. Welsh folk songs.

Laventie[4]

One would remember still
Meadows and low hill
Laventie was, as to the line and elm row
Growing through green strength wounded, as home elms grow.
Shimmer of summer there and blue autumn mists
Seen from trench-ditch winding in mazy twists.
The Australian gunners in close flowery hiding
Cunning found out at last, and smashed in the unspeakable lists.
And the guns in the smashed wood thumping and griding.[5]
The letters written there, and received there,
Books, cakes, cigarettes in a parish of famine,
And leaks in rainy times with general all-damning.
The crater, and carrying of gas cylinders on two sticks
(Pain past comparison and far past right agony gone),
Strained hopelessly, of heart and frame at first fix.

Café-au-lait in dug-outs on Tommies'[6] cookers,
Cursed minniewerfs,[7] thirst in eighteen-hour summer.
The Australian miners clayed, and the being afraid
Before strafes, sultry August dusk time than death dumber—
And the cooler hush after the strafe, and the long night wait—
The relief of first dawn, the crawling out to look at it,
Wonder divine of dawn, man hesitating before Heaven's gate.
(Though not on Cooper's where music fire took at it.
Though not as at Framilode[8] beauty where body did shake at it)
Yet the dawn with aeroplanes crawling high at Heaven's gate
Lovely aerial beetles of wonderful scintillate
Strangest interest, and puffs of soft purest white—
Seeking light, dispersing colouring for fancy's delight.
Of Machonachie, Paxton, Tickler and Gloucester's Stephens;
Fray Bentos, Spiller and Baker,[9] odds and evens
Of trench food, but the everlasting clean craving
For bread, the pure thing, blessèd beyond saving.
Canteen disappointments, and the keen boy braving
Bullets or such for grouse roused surprisingly through
(Halfway) Stand-to.[1]
And the shell nearly blunted my razor at shaving;
Tilleloy, Fauquissart, Neuve Chapelle,[2] and mud like glue.
But Laventie, most of all, I think is to soldiers
The town itself with plane trees, and small-spa air;
And vin, rouge-blanc, chocolat, citron, grenadine:[3]
One might buy in small delectable cafés there.
The broken church, and vegetable fields bare;

4. French village near the front line.
5. Piercing; producing a grating sound.
6. British soldiers'.
7. German trench-mortars.
8. Cooper's Hill and the town of Framilode are in Gloucestershire, England.
9. Varieties of tinned rations.
1. Command to stand in readiness for possible attack.
2. Towns on the front line.
3. And red wine, white wine, hot chocolate, lemon cordial, drink made from pomegranate syrup (French).

Neat French market-town look so clean,
And the clarity, amiability of North French air.

•

Like water flowing beneath the dark plough and high Heaven,
Music's delight to please the poet pack-marching there.

1919–20 1954

The Silent One

Who died on the wires, and hung there, one of two—
Who for his hours of life had chattered through
Infinite lovely chatter of Bucks[4] accent:
Yet faced unbroken wires; stepped over, and went
A noble fool, faithful to his stripes—and ended.
But I weak, hungry, and willing only for the chance
Of line—to fight in the line, lay down under unbroken
Wires, and saw the flashes and kept unshaken,
Till the politest voice—a finicking accent, said:
'Do you think you might crawl through there: there's a hole.'
Darkness, shot at: I smiled, as politely replied—
'I'm afraid not, Sir.' There was no hole no way to be seen
Nothing but chance of death, after tearing of clothes.
Kept flat, and watched the darkness, hearing bullets whizzing—
And thought of music—and swore deep heart's deep oaths
(Polite to God) and retreated and came on again,
Again retreated—and a second time faced the screen.

1919–22 1954

4. Buckinghamshire, county in southern England.

Claude McKay
1890–1948

Claude McKay, like fellow moderns T. S. Eliot and Mina Loy, led a migrant life that eluded national categories. Having spent the first half of his life in Jamaica, he was posthumously declared the national poet of the island. Having emigrated to the United States in 1912 and become a citizen in 1940, he has often been claimed as an American writer. Identified with Afro-Caribbean and with African American literary culture, McKay was a generative influence on both. He was the first major poet to make effective literary use of Jamaican English, inspiring the still more masterful Creole verse of later Jamaican poets, such as Louise Bennett. He also became, after moving to the United

States and writing poetry in Standard English, one of the pioneering figures of the Harlem Renaissance; his 1922 collection of poetry, *Harlem Shadows,* is often seen as inaugurating the movement.

McKay's literary models were English Renaissance and Romantic poets. His primary form, after he moved to the United States and switched to Standard English, was the sonnet. But like Countee Cullen, he brought to this European poetic structure a new experience—in his case, the pain, rage, and longings of an Afro-Caribbean immigrant. In "The White City," McKay pours "life-long hate" into the typically love-filled rhyme scheme and iambic meter of the Shakespearean sonnet. Another poem uses the same form to describe "The Lynching," its final, alliterative couplet drawing not a redemptive but a horrifying portrait of the next generation: "And little lads, lynchers that were to be, / Danced round the dreadful thing in fiendish glee." "The Tropics in New York," while recalling William Wordsworth's "The Reverie of Poor Susan," commemorates the fruits, climate, and environment of a Third World childhood. The sonnets "America" and "The White City" compact intense ambivalence toward white society in muscular syntax and violent images. The tension between McKay's strict form and molten subject parallels the intense racial alienation represented in some of his poems. "Outcast" registers the poet's sense of permanent estrangement from African culture. The figure of "The Harlem Dancer," though idolized and exoticized, reflects the poet's alienation: "looking at her falsely-smiling face, / I knew her self was not in that strange place."

McKay was born on September 15, 1890, in Sunny Ville, Clarendon Parish, Jamaica. His parents were poor farmworkers. At six, he went to live with an older brother, a schoolteacher, who exposed him to socialist and agnostic ideas. First apprenticed to a cabinetmaker and then a wheelwright, McKay became a police constable in Kingston in 1909; but disillusioned, he left the job after less than a year. An English linguist and folklorist, Walter Jekyll, encouraged him to write in Jamaican dialect, or Creole. Drawing on the example of Robert Burns, the best of these poems, such as "A Midnight Woman to the Bobby," harness the vigor, wit, and resistant spunk of Jamaican idiom to English forms, while dramatizing Jamaican class and racial conflict. They were collected in two books, *Songs of Jamaica* and *Constab Ballads,* published in 1912. For his work, McKay won a prize that enabled him to come to the United States, where he studied briefly at the Tuskegee Institute and for two years at Kansas State College. In 1914, he moved to Harlem, supporting himself with odd jobs, most often as a waiter; during World War I, he began to publish poems (including some of his most famous, such as "The Harlem Dancer") under the pseudonym Eli Edwards. He lived in Europe, mostly England, from 1919 to 1921. He published in England a third book of poems, *Spring in New Hampshire,* with a laudatory preface by I. A. Richards, one of the most important English critics of the twentieth century. McKay returned to the United States as an associate editor of the radical newspaper *The Liberator.*

Like many other writers of the time, McKay was fascinated by the Russian Revolution; he traveled to Moscow in 1922 to meet Leon Trotsky and other Soviet leaders. For eleven years, he lived in Europe and North Africa, mainly in France and Morocco, and wrote fiction; *Home to Harlem* (1928) was a best-selling as well as award-winning novel. In the mid-1930s, McKay returned to the United States, where he remained for the rest of his life. In the late 1930s, he became strongly interested in Catholicism and (like Richard Wright at about the same time) repudiated his earlier commitment to communism. He died in poverty, in Chicago, where he taught in his last years for a Catholic youth organization. His poem "If We Must Die," a response to the antiblack riots of the summer of 1919, was read to the British people by Winston Churchill and into the Congressional Record by American senator Henry Cabot Lodge Sr., as a World War II rallying cry.

A Midnight Woman to the Bobby[1]

No palm me up,[2] you dutty brute,
You' jam mout' mash[3] like ripe bread-fruit;
You fas'n now, but wait lee ya,[4]
I'll see you grunt under de law.

You t'ink you wise, but we wi' see;
You not de fus' one fas' wid me;
I'll lib fe see dem tu'n you out,
As sure as you got dat mash' mout'.

I born right do'n beneat' de clack[5]
(You ugly brute, you tu'n you' back?)
Don't t'ink dat I'm a come-aroun',[6]
I born right 'way in 'panish Town.

Care how you try, you caan' do mo'
Dan many dat was hyah befo';
Yet whe' dey all o' dem te-day?
De buccra[7] dem no kick dem 'way?

Ko 'pon you' jam samplatta[8] nose:
'Cos you wear Mis'r Koshaw clo'es
You t'ink say you's de only man,
Yet fus' time ko how you be'n 'tan'.[9]

You big an' ugly ole tu'n-foot[1]
Be'n neber know fe wear a boot;
An' chigger nyam you' tumpa toe,[2]
Till nit full i' like herrin' roe.

You come from mountain naked-'kin,
An' Lard a mussy! you be'n thin,
For all de bread-fruit dem be'n done,
Bein' 'poil' up by de tearin' sun:

De coco[3] couldn' bear at all,
For, Lard! de groun' was pure white-marl;
An' t'rough de rain part o' de year
De mango tree dem couldn' bear.

1. Police constable.
2. Don't put your hands on me (Jamaican English).
3. Your damn mouth is all awry.
4. You're fast now, but wait a little, hear?
5. Clock on the public buildings at Spanish Town.
6. Day laborer, commuter.
7. White man.
8. A piece of cut leather tied around the foot and worn as a sandal. *Ko:* look.
9. Yet when I first knew you, see how you looked. *Mis'r Koshaw clo'es:* police uniform. Colonel Kershaw was inspector general of police when the poem was written, in 1911.
1. Turned-in foot.
2. And chiggers had eaten into your maimed toe.
3. Edible root.

An' when de pinch o' time you feel
A 'pur you a you' chigger heel,[4]
You lef' you' district, big an' coarse,
An' come join buccra Police Force.

An' now you don't wait fe you' glass,[5]
But trouble me wid you' jam fas';[6]
But wait, me frien', you' day wi' come,
I'll see you go same lak a some.[7]

Say wah'?—'res' me?[8]—you go to hell!
You t'ink Judge don't know unno[9] well?
You t'ink him gwin' go sentance me
Widout a soul fe witness i'?

1912

The Harlem Dancer

Applauding youths laughed with young prostitutes
And watched her perfect, half-clothed body sway;
Her voice was like the sound of blended flutes
Blown by black players upon a picnic day.
She sang and danced on gracefully and calm,
The light gauze hanging loose about her form;
To me she seemed a proudly-swaying palm
Grown lovelier for passing through a storm.
Upon her swarthy neck black shiny curls
Luxuriant fell; and tossing coins in praise,
The wine-flushed, bold-eyed boys, and even the girls,
Devoured her shape with eager, passionate gaze;
But looking at her falsely-smiling face,
I knew her self was not in that strange place.

1917, 1922

If We Must Die

If we must die, let it not be like hogs
Hunted and penned in an inglorious spot,
While round us bark the mad and hungry dogs,
Making their mock at our accursed lot.
If we must die, O let us nobly die,
So that our precious blood may not be shed
In vain; then even the monsters we defy

4. When you felt hard times spur you in your chigger-eaten heel.
5. The right moment.
6. Meddling and officiousness.
7. Same like some; just as others before you did.
8. Arrest me?
9. You.

Shall be constrained to honor us though dead!
O kinsmen! we must meet the common foe!
Though far outnumbered let us show us brave,
And for their thousand blows deal one deathblow!
What though before us lies the open grave?
Like men we'll face the murderous, cowardly pack,
Pressed to the wall, dying, but fighting back!

1919, 1922

The Lynching

His Spirit in smoke ascended to high heaven.
His father, by the cruelest way of pain,
Had bidden him to his bosom once again;
The awful sin remained still unforgiven.
All night a bright and solitary star
(Perchance the one that ever guided him,
Yet gave him up at last to Fate's wild whim)
Hung pitifully o'er the swinging char.
Day dawned, and soon the mixed crowds came to view
The ghastly body swaying in the sun.
The women thronged to look, but never a one
Showed sorrow in her eyes of steely blue.

And little lads, lynchers that were to be,
Danced round the dreadful thing in fiendish glee.

1920, 1922

The Tropics in New York

Bananas ripe and green, and ginger-root
    Cocoa in pods and alligator pears,
And tangerines and mangoes and grape fruit,
    Fit for the highest prize at parish fairs,

Set in the window, bringing memories
    Of fruit-trees laden by low-singing rills,
And dewy dawns, and mystical blue skies
    In benediction over nun-like hills.

My eyes grew dim, and I could no more gaze;
    A wave of longing through my body swept,
And, hungry for the old, familiar ways,
    I turned aside and bowed my head and wept.

1920, 1922

America

Although she feeds me bread of bitterness,
And sinks into my throat her tiger's tooth,
Stealing my breath of life, I will confess
I love this cultured hell that tests my youth!
Her vigor flows like tides into my blood,
Giving me strength erect against her hate.
Her bigness sweeps my being like a flood.
Yet as a rebel fronts a king in state,
I stand within her walls with not a shred
Of terror, malice, not a word of jeer.
Darkly I gaze into the days ahead,
And see her might and granite wonders there,
Beneath the touch of Time's unerring hand,
Like priceless treasures sinking in the sand.

1921, 1922

The White City

I will not toy with it nor bend an inch.
Deep in the secret chambers of my heart
I muse my life-long hate, and without flinch
I bear it nobly as I live my part.
My being would be a skeleton, a shell,
If this dark Passion that fills my every mood,
And makes my heaven in the white world's hell,
Did not forever feed me vital blood.
I see the mighty city through a mist—
The strident trains that speed the goaded mass,
The poles and spires and towers vapor-kissed,
The fortressed port through which the great ships pass,
The tides, the wharves, the dens I contemplate,
Are sweet like wanton loves because I hate.

1921, 1922

Outcast

For the dim regions whence my fathers came
My spirit, bondaged by the body, longs.
Words felt, but never heard, my lips would frame;
My soul would sing forgotten jungle songs.
I would go back to darkness and to peace,
But the great western world holds me in fee,

I may never hope for full release
While to its alien gods I bend my knee.
Something in me is lost, forever lost,
Some vital thing has gone out of my heart,
And I must walk the way of life a ghost
Among the sons of earth, a thing apart.

For I was born, far from my native clime,
Under the white man's menace, out of time.

1922

Isaac Rosenberg
1890–1918

Isaac Rosenberg was one of those gifted English poets cut off in their youth by World War I. He left a small body of excellent work in the mature style that he achieved only at the end of his short life. Like another casualty of the war, Wilfred Owen, Rosenberg early came under the spell of John Keats and had Keats's love of splendid phrasing. For Rosenberg, the poet was "a part of paradise," though "caught . . . in a cage of earth" ("The Poet I"). As he said in "The Poet II," the poet somehow consecrates "the mould": "So shut in are our lives, so still, / That we see not of good or ill— / A dead world since ourselves are dead. / Till he, the master speaks, and lo! / The dead world's shed."

Surrounded by the corpses of his fellows, the poet still detects the presence of "fierce imaginings," "sweet laughter," and "joy." Glorifying war repulses him. He succeeds, however, in transforming and even exalting brute facts. Many of his poems have what war poet Siegfried Sassoon described as a biblical or prophetic quality, and sometimes the Old Testament can be heard in his verse. But he can be humorous. "Break of Day in the Trenches" juxtaposes the sardonic grin of a rat that refuses national boundaries with apocalyptic imagery—"shrieking iron and flame / Hurled through still heavens." His poetry strangely amalgamates lush, resonant diction with acerbic irony.

Rosenberg was born on November 25, 1890, in Bristol. His Jewish parents had emigrated from Lithuania and Russia. When he was seven, the family moved to Whitechapel, London, where their son's abilities as a painter were clearly recognized. Because his family was poor, he was apprenticed at fourteen to a firm of engravers. At twenty-one, with the help of another Jewish family, he began attending the Slade School of Art, where he studied from October 1911 to March 1914. He left some fully realized portraits and drawings. Mostly to secure part of his salary for his mother, he enlisted in the army in October 1915. Unlike Owen and Sassoon, he was a soldier, not an officer, and he writes as one. From August 1916, he was in the trenches in France, except for spells of illness. He was killed at dawn in the Battle of Arras on the Somme, while on night patrol.

The Mirror

It glimmers like a wakeful lake in the dusk narrowing room.
Like drowning vague branches in its depth floats the gloom,
The night shall shudder at its face by gleams of pallid light
Whose hands build the broader day to break the husk of night.

No shade shall waver there when your shadowless soul shall pass,
The green shakes not the air when your spirit drinks the grass,
So in its plashless water falls, so dumbly lies therein
A fervid rose whose fragrance sweet lies hidden and shut within.

Only in these bruised words the glass dim-showing my spirit's face,
Only a little colour from a fire I could not trace,
To glimmer through eternal days like an enchanted rose,
The potent dreamings of whose scent are wizard-locked beneath its glows.

1915 1937

Break of Day in the Trenches

The darkness crumbles away.
It is the same old druid[1] Time as ever,
Only a live thing leaps my hand,
A queer sardonic rat,
As I pull the parapet's poppy[2]
To stick behind my ear.
Droll rat, they would shoot you if they knew
Your cosmopolitan sympathies.
Now you have touched this English hand
You will do the same to a German
Soon, no doubt, if it be your pleasure
To cross the sleeping green between.
It seems you inwardly grin as you pass
Strong eyes, fine limbs, haughty athletes,
Less chanced than you for life,
Bonds to the whims of murder,
Sprawled in the bowels of the earth,
The torn fields of France.
What do you see in our eyes
At the shrieking iron and flame
Hurled through still heavens?
What quaver—what heart aghast?
Poppies whose roots are in man's veins

1. Ancient Celtic priest.
2. Flower, commonly found in Flanders, where much of World War I was fought. *Parapet:* the bank of earth in front of a trench.

Drop, and are ever dropping;
But mine in my ear is safe—
Just a little white with the dust.

June 1916 1922

Louse Hunting

Nudes—stark and glistening,
Yelling in lurid glee. Grinning faces
And raging limbs
Whirl over the floor one fire.
For a shirt verminously busy
Yon soldier tore from his throat, with oaths
Godhead might shrink at, but not the lice.
And soon the shirt was aflare
Over the candle he'd lit while we lay.

Then we all sprang up and stript
To hunt the verminous brood.
Soon like a demons' pantomine
The place was raging.
See the silhouettes agape,
See the gibbering shadows
Mixed with the battled arms on the wall.
See gargantuan hooked fingers
Pluck in supreme flesh
To smutch[3] supreme littleness.
See the merry limbs in hot Highland fling
Because some wizard vermin
Charmed from the quiet this revel
When our ears were half lulled
By the dark music
Blown from Sleep's trumpet.

1917 1922

Returning, We Hear the Larks

Sombre the night is.
And though we have our lives, we know
What sinister threat lurks there.

Dragging these anguished limbs, we only know
This poison-blasted track opens on our camp—
On a little safe sleep.

3. Blacken, besmirch.

But hark! joy—joy—strange joy.
Lo! heights of night ringing with unseen larks.
Music showering our upturned list'ning faces.

Death could drop from the dark
As easily as song—
But song only dropped,
Like a blind man's dreams on the sand
By dangerous tides,
Like a girl's dark hair for she dreams no ruin lies there,
Or her kisses where a serpent hides.

1917 1922

Dead Man's Dump

The plunging limbers[4] over the shattered track
Racketed with their rusty freight,
Stuck out like many crowns of thorns,
And the rusty stakes like sceptres old
To stay the flood of brutish men
Upon our brothers dear.

The wheels lurched over sprawled dead
But pained them not, though their bones crunched,
Their shut mouths made no moan,
They lie there huddled, friend and foeman,
Man born of man, and born of woman,
And shells go crying over them
From night till night and now.

Earth has waited for them
All the time of their growth
Fretting for their decay:
Now she has them at last!
In the strength of their strength
Suspended—stopped and held.

What fierce imaginings their dark souls lit
Earth! have they gone into you?
Somewhere they must have gone,
And flung on your hard back
Is their souls' sack,
Emptied of God-ancestralled essences.
Who hurled them out? Who hurled?

None saw their spirits' shadow shake the grass,
Or stood aside for the half used life to pass

4. Two-wheeled carts, here carrying barbed wire.

Out of those doomed nostrils and the doomed mouth,
When the swift iron burning bee
Drained the wild honey of their youth.

What of us, who flung on the shrieking pyre,
Walk, our usual thoughts untouched,
Our lucky limbs as on ichor[5] fed,
Immortal seeming ever?
Perhaps when the flames beat loud on us,
A fear may choke in our veins
And the startled blood may stop.

The air is loud with death,
The dark air spurts with fire
The explosions ceaseless are.
Timelessly now, some minutes past,
These dead strode time with vigorous life,
Till the shrapnel called 'an end!'
But not to all. In bleeding pangs
Some borne on stretchers dreamed of home,
Dear things, war-blotted from their hearts.

A man's brains splattered on
A stretcher-bearer's face;
His shook shoulders slipped their load,
But when they bent to look again
The drowning soul was sunk too deep
For human tenderness.

They left this dead with the older dead,
Stretched at the cross roads.
Burnt black by strange decay,
Their sinister faces lie
The lid over each eye,
The grass and coloured clay
More motion have than they,
Joined to the great sunk silences.

Here is one not long dead;
His dark hearing caught our far wheels,
And the choked soul stretched weak hands
To reach the living world the far wheels said,
The blood-dazed intelligence beating for light,
Crying through the suspense of the far torturing wheels
Swift for the end to break,
Or the wheels to break,
Cried as the tide of the world broke over his sight.

Will they come? Will they ever come?
Even as the mixed hoofs of the mules,

5. In Greek mythology, ethereal fluid that flowed in the veins of the gods.

The quivering-bellied mules,
And the rushing wheels all mixed
With his tortured upturned sight,
So we crashed round the bend,
We heard his weak scream,
We heard his very last sound,
And our wheels grazed his dead face.

1917 1922

EDNA ST. VINCENT MILLAY
1892–1950

Edna St. Vincent Millay presents a perhaps unexpected figure in a collection of modern poetry. Her idiom for the most part avoids local reference, and much of her verse might have been written at an earlier time. For example,

> Love is not all: it is not meat nor drink
> Nor slumber nor a roof against the rain;
> Nor yet a floating spar to men that sink
> And rise and sink and rise and sink again.

Here the diction is not archaic, but the slightly elevated tone, the movement of the syntax, and the use of the Shakespearean sonnet form place the poem in a tradition that goes back to the Victorian era and even the English Renaissance. The aesthetic distance is great between Millay's poetry—personal in expression, traditional in form and technique—and the contemporary modernist innovations of Gertrude Stein, Ezra Pound, Marianne Moore, and T. S. Eliot.

Even so, Millay was seen in the 1920s and 1930s as a central figure of her generation, and though her reputation was greatly diminished by the time of her death, poets such as Anne Sexton and Sylvia Plath were still wrestling with her shadow in the 1950s. Critics since the 1970s have celebrated her as a female apostle of sexual liberation and an alternative to high modernist impersonality. Millay received popular acclaim first for the long poem "Renascence" and then for a series of lyrics, many of them about love, in which she created a striking literary personality—dashing, unconventional, charismatic, eager for experience, haunted by the brevity of life. Her combination of intimacy with closed forms, of frankness with elevated rhetoric, gives her poetry its peculiar allure. In the quatrain poem "First Fig," she rebelliously affirms impermanent pleasure. The passing of experience in "Recuerdo" encourages a mood of tender, rueful nostalgia. Millay obviously became dissatisfied with this personality, and she later wrote other kinds of poetry, including protest poems against the execution of the anarchists Sacco and Vanzetti and propaganda poetry for the Allies during World War II. What most seems to have stirred her imagination in later life was the inevitability of her own death:

> With all my might
>   My door shall be barred.
> I shall put up a fight,
>   I shall take it hard.

With his hand on my mouth
He shall drag me forth,
Shrieking to the south
And clutching at the north. ("Moriturus")

Millay was born on February 22, 1892, in Rockland, Maine. Her parents were divorced when she was a child, and her mother encouraged her literary interests. Millay wrote her first poem when she was five, and as a child she regularly submitted poems to *St. Nicholas* magazine. Her first important poem, "Renascence," written when she was only nineteen, was published in the anthology *The Lyric Year* in 1912; it is an account of ecstatic self-discovery, full of echoes of John Keats and William Wordsworth.

She studied for a short time at Barnard College, then attended Vassar College, where as a young poet she baited the college authorities. When she dared the president to expel her, he explained that he didn't want a "banished Shelley on my doorstep," and she is supposed to have replied, "On those terms, I think I can continue to live in this hell hole." In 1917, the year of her Vassar degree, her first book of poems was published. She moved to New York City's Greenwich Village, then a refuge for young people newly liberated from home and school, and her poems helped create the legend of an American bohemia. She joined the Provincetown Players and published three plays in verse. In 1923, she became the first woman to be awarded the Pulitzer Prize for poetry. In the same year, she married Eugen Boissevain, a Dutch importer, and moved with her husband to a farm in the Berkshires. Through the 1920s and 1930s she published regularly. Her work included further collections of poems, the libretto for Deems Taylor's opera *The King's Henchman* (1927), and a translation of Charles Baudelaire's *Flowers of Evil* done in collaboration with George Dillon. In the 1940s, she published two books in which she tried to write poetry adequate to the anguish of World War II—*Make Bright the Arrows* (1940) and *The Murder of Lidice* (1942). The poems that retain critical interest are mostly those in which, while chafing against gender constraints, she revitalizes the traditions of the English lyric.

First Fig

My candle burns at both ends;
It will not last the night;
But ah, my foes, and oh, my friends—
It gives a lovely light!

1920

Recuerdo[1]

We were very tired, we were very merry—
We had gone back and forth all night on the ferry.
It was bare and bright, and smelled like a stable—
But we looked into a fire, we leaned across a table,
We lay on a hill-top underneath the moon;
And the whistles kept blowing, and the dawn came soon.

1. Remembrance, souvenir (Spanish).

We were very tired, we were very merry—
We had gone back and forth all night on the ferry;
And you ate an apple, and I ate a pear,
From a dozen of each we had bought somewhere;
And the sky went wan, and the wind came cold,
And the sun rose dripping, a bucketful of gold.

We were very tired, we were very merry,
We had gone back and forth all night on the ferry.
We hailed, "Good morrow, mother!" to a shawl-covered head,
And bought a morning paper, which neither of us read;
And she wept, "God bless you!" for the apples and pears,
And we gave her all our money but our subway fares.

1920

Grown-Up

Was it for this I uttered prayers,
And sobbed and cursed and kicked the stairs,
That now, domestic as a plate,
I should retire at half-past eight?

1920

Spring

To what purpose, April, do you return again?
Beauty is not enough.
You can no longer quiet me with the redness
Of little leaves opening stickily.
I know what I know.
The sun is hot on my neck as I observe
The spikes of the crocus.
The smell of the earth is good.
It is apparent that there is no death.
But what does that signify?
Not only under ground are the brains of men
Eaten by maggots.
Life in itself
Is nothing,
An empty cup, a flight of uncarpeted stairs.
It is not enough that yearly, down this hill,
April
Comes like an idiot, babbling and strewing flowers.

1921

[I, Being Born a Woman and Distressed]

I, being born a woman and distressed
By all the needs and notions of my kind,
Am urged by your propinquity[2] to find
Your person fair, and feel a certain zest
To bear your body's weight upon my breast:
So subtly is the fume of life designed,
To clarify the pulse and cloud the mind,
And leave me once again undone, possessed.
Think not for this, however, the poor treason
Of my stout blood against my staggering brain,
I shall remember you with love, or season
My scorn with pity,—let me make it plain:
I find this frenzy insufficient reason
For conversation when we meet again.

1923

[Gazing upon Him Now, Severe and Dead]

Gazing upon him now, severe and dead,
It seemed a curious thing that she had lain
Beside him many a night in that cold bed,
And that had been which would not be again.
From his desirous body the great heat
Was gone at last, it seemed, and the taut nerves
Loosened forever. Formally the sheet
Set forth for her today those heavy curves
And lengths familiar as the bedroom door.
She was as one who enters, sly, and proud,
To where her husband speaks before a crowd,
And sees a man she never saw before—
The man who eats his victuals at her side,
Small, and absurd, and hers: for once, not hers, unclassified.

1923

[Love Is Not All: It Is Not Meat nor Drink]

Love is not all: it is not meat nor drink
Nor slumber nor a roof against the rain;
Nor yet a floating spar to men that sink
And rise and sink and rise and sink again;
Love can not fill the thickened lung with breath,
Nor clean the blood, nor set the fractured bone;

2. Proximity.

Yet many a man is making friends with death
Even as I speak, for lack of love alone.
It well may be that in a difficult hour,
Pinned down by pain and moaning for release,
Or nagged by want past resolution's power,
I might be driven to sell your love for peace,
Or trade the memory of this night for food.
It well may be. I do not think I would.

1931

The Return

Earth does not understand her child,
  Who from the loud gregarious town
Returns, depleted and defiled,
  To the still woods, to fling him down.

Earth can not count the sons she bore:
  The wounded lynx, the wounded man
Come trailing blood unto her door;
  She shelters both as best she can.

But she is early up and out,
  To trim the year or strip its bones;
She has no time to stand about
  Talking of him in undertones

Who has no aim but to forget,
  Be left in peace, be lying thus
For days, for years, for centuries yet,
  Unshaven and anonymous;

Who, marked for failure, dulled by grief,
  Has traded in his wife and friend
For this warm ledge, this alder leaf:
  Comfort that does not comprehend.

1934

To a Calvinist in Bali

You that are sprung of northern stock,
And nothing lavish,—born and bred
With tablets at your foot and head,
And CULPA[3] carven in the rock,

3. Guilt, fault.

Sense with delight but not with ease
The fragrance of the quinine trees,
The *kembang-spatu's*[4] lolling flame
With solemn envy kin to shame.

Ah, be content!—the scorpion's tail
Atones for much; without avail
Under the sizzling solar pan
Our sleeping servant pulls the fan.

Even in this island richly blest,
Where Beauty walks with naked breast,
Earth is too harsh for Heaven to be
One little hour in jeopardy.

1939

4. A tropical flower.

Archibald MacLeish
1892–1982

Archibald MacLeish responded closely to the changes in style and the political concerns of his generation. Committed to a public life and a public poetry, he did not see poets as privileged members of the community who could stand apart from the life of their fellow citizens. He never reconciled the claims of art and society to his own satisfaction, but he worked at this problem, with courage and energy, over a long career as writer, public servant, and teacher.

MacLeish was born on May 7, 1892, in Glencoe, Illinois. He was educated at Hotchkiss School, at Yale University (B.A., 1915), and at Harvard Law School, where he led his class. He enlisted during World War I and served at the front as a captain of field artillery. After the war, he taught briefly at Harvard and then worked as a lawyer in Boston. Because his work distracted him from his poetry, in 1923 he moved with his family to France, where he participated in the modernist revolution. Between 1924 and 1928, he published four books of poetry. The discontinuities of these early poems indicate a debt to both Ezra Pound and T. S. Eliot, and MacLeish learned from Eliot to vary lines that end abruptly with lines that conclude with a dying fall. But MacLeish developed his own idiom, which was accessible, elegiac, and musically cadenced. His subject was often human beings' mysterious passage through time, and he confronted it with a special quality of quiet dread. In 1928, MacLeish returned to America; as preparation for the writing of *Conquistador,* which in 1932 won the first of MacLeish's three Pulitzer Prizes, he retraced by foot and mule the route of Cortez's conquering army through Mexico.

During the Great Depression, MacLeish worked for *Fortune* magazine. In the later 1930s, he produced radio plays and other works designed to warn his fellow citizens of the imminent war with fascism and to restore their love of country. The author of the famous dictum "A poem should not mean / But be" now devoted himself to public speech ("Ars Poetica"). In 1940, MacLeish, in his controversial pamphlet *The Irrespon-*

sibles, charged the great modernist writers of his generation, centrally Eliot and Pound, with weakening the moral fiber of their readers and leaving them prey to fascism. During World War II, MacLeish, distinct among twentieth-century American poets, directly entered public life. In 1939, President Franklin Roosevelt appointed him librarian of Congress, a post he held for five years. In 1941, he was made director of the Office of Facts and Figures, a wartime agency with special responsibilities in the area of propaganda, and in 1944–45, he was assistant secretary of state. After the war, he worked for the formation of UNESCO (United Nations Educational, Scientific, and Cultural Organization), and in 1946, he served as chairman of the first UNESCO conference in Paris.

In 1949, MacLeish returned to Harvard as Boylston Professor of English, a post he held until 1962. Like Eliot, he turned to writing poetic dramas on classical themes. He also continued to write lyric poems, and the Romantic temper of many of them is suggested by the last words of his book of lectures on poetry, *Poetry and Experience* (1961): "To face the truth of the passing away of the world and make song of it, make beauty of it, is not to solve the riddle of our mortal lives but perhaps to accomplish something more."

Ars Poetica[1]

A poem should be palpable and mute
As a globed fruit,

Dumb
As old medallions to the thumb,

Silent as the sleeve-worn stone
Of casement ledges where the moss has grown—

A poem should be wordless
As the flight of birds.

•

A poem should be motionless in time
As the moon climbs,

Leaving, as the moon releases
Twig by twig the night-entangled trees,

Leaving, as the moon behind the winter leaves,
Memory by memory the mind—

A poem should be motionless in time
As the moon climbs.

•

A poem should be equal to:
Not true.

1. The art of poetry (Latin); title of a treatise on poetics by Roman poet Horace (65–8 B.C.E.).

For all the history of grief
An empty doorway and a maple leaf.

For love
The leaning grasses and two lights above the sea—

A poem should not mean
But be.

1926

The End of the World

Quite unexpectedly as Vasserot
The armless ambidextrian was lighting
A match between his great and second toe
And Ralph the lion was engaged in biting
The neck of Madame Sossman while the drum
Pointed, and Teeny was about to cough
In waltz-time swinging Jocko by the thumb—
Quite unexpectedly the top blew off:

And there, there overhead, there, there, hung over
Those thousands of white faces, those dazed eyes,
There in the starless dark the poise, the hover,
There with vast wings across the canceled skies,
There in the sudden blackness the black pall
Of nothing, nothing, nothing—nothing at all.

1926

You, Andrew Marvell[2]

And here face down beneath the sun
And here upon earth's noonward height
To feel the always coming on
The always rising of the night:

To feel creep up the curving east
The earthly chill of dusk and slow
Upon those under lands the vast
And ever climbing shadow grow

And strange at Ecbatan[3] the trees
Take leaf by leaf the evening strange

2. English poet (1621–1676). MacLeish extends and develops the idea expressed in two lines of Marvell's "To His Coy Mistress": "But at my back I always hear / Time's wingèd chariot hurrying near."

3. The ancient capital of Media (now Hamadan, in western Iran).

The flooding dark about their knees
The mountains over Persia change

And now at Kermanshah[4] the gate
Dark empty and the withered grass
And through the twilight now the late
Few travelers in the westward pass

And Baghdad darken and the bridge
Across the silent river gone
And through Arabia the edge
Of evening widen and steal on

And deepen on Palmyra's[5] street
The wheel rut in the ruined stone
And Lebanon fade out and Crete
High through the clouds and overblown

And over Sicily the air
Still flashing with the landward gulls
And loom and slowly disappear
The sails above the shadowy hulls

And Spain go under and the shore
Of Africa the gilded sand
And evening vanish and no more
The low pale light across the land

Nor now the long light on the sea:

And here face downward in the sun
To feel how swift how secretly
The shadow of the night comes on . . .

1930

4. A city and province in Iran.
5. An oasis city of great power and culture in ancient Syria.

HUGH MACDIARMID (C. M. GRIEVE)
1892–1978

In his autobiography, *Lucky Poet*, Hugh MacDiarmid, widely seen as the leading Scottish poet of the twentieth century, wrote that throughout his life one of his mottoes had been Thomas Hardy's declaration "Literature is the written expression of revolt against accepted things." In his polemical poetry and in his prose, MacDiarmid rejected halfway measures and craven reconciliations: "I'll ha'e nae hauf-way hoose, but aye be whaur / Extremes meet," he wrote in the long sequence that many consider his masterpiece, *A Drunk Man Looks at the Thistle* (1926). In "The Kind of Poetry I Want," he described a poetry that is dangerous and eager to take chances and that maintains a creative alliance with personal disorder:

> A poetry like the barrel of a gun
> Weaving like a snake's head.
>
> A poetry that can put all its chips on the table
> And back it to the limit.
>
> A poetry full of the crazy feeling
> That everything that has ever gone into my life
> Has pointed to each successive work
> And I couldn't have failed to write it if I'd tried.

Beyond commitment, MacDiarmid valued concreteness, and he spoke for a poetry "of fact and first-hand experience and scientific knowledge," though he was aware that the constituents of an experience did not explain it. The function of poetry was not limited to a reproduction of social reality; he cited the French Symbolist Stéphane Mallarmé as authority for his belief that the act of poetry is the "reverse of what it is usually thought to be; not an idea gradually shaping itself in words, but deriving entirely from words" (*Lucky Poet*). MacDiarmid's poetry was thus shaped both by his politics and by his linguistic predilections.

MacDiarmid was a Scottish nationalist and a communist, and from the time he wrote his first lyrics in Scots in the early 1920s, he devoted his energies to the restoration of his country to its native traditions and identity. He described his function "in Scotland during the past twenty to thirty years" as "that of the cat-fish that vitalizes the other torpid denizens of the aquarium" (*Lucky Poet*). He dreamt of a modern, native Scottish poetry that would exhibit the qualities of "courage, patience, self-assertion, unyieldingness, energy, and (above all) a steel-like and combative virility" (*At the Sign of the Thistle*). MacDiarmid's enemies, whom he belabored mercilessly in prose and verse, were those who, by trying to establish an English literary hegemony in Scotland, came between a Scottish poet and his audience; he called them "spineless triflers," the "small class of Anglicized mediocrities who are continually debauching the public taste" (*Sign*). He encouraged his fellow poets to seek their inspiration in the Scottish Chaucerians, a group of late medieval poets who sought to create a native Scottish literature. MacDiarmid recalled approvingly the "old Gaelic days" when "poets had to go through a long and rigorous apprenticeship in the Bardic Colleges, and qualify by arduous stages for the right to use certain metres and tackle certain types of subject matter" (*Sign*).

The central figure of the Scottish Renaissance, MacDiarmid proved the vigor and robust physicality, the wit and sonic power of Scots as a medium for modern poetry. The language in which he wrote many of his best poems is a literary Scots of his own invention, an amalgam of several dialects enriched by a number of archaic Scottish words that he found in dictionaries. His "synthetic Scots," as MacDiarmid called it, consisted in "the revival of Scots words without equivalents, or precise equivalents, in English, on the one hand, and a use of Gaelic and foreign phrases and allusions on the other" (*Sign*). For MacDiarmid, James Joyce's linguistic eclecticism in *Finnegans Wake* pointed the way to a synthetic language in which the modern European consciousness might express itself, and for this purpose MacDiarmid envisioned a supranational "Joycean amalgam of Scots, Gaelic, and English, plus Gothic, Sanscrit, and Old Norse" (*In Memoriam James Joyce* is one of MacDiarmid's long poems). Such grand linguistic designs were as central to MacDiarmid's poetic purposes as his communist politics, and this may suggest why his poetry in Lallans, the revived language of the Scottish

Lowlands, was usually free of polemic: the mere fact that he was restoring Scots to literature was revolutionary enough.

MacDiarmid was born Christopher Murray Grieve on August 11, 1892, in Langholm, Dumfriesshire, in the Scottish border country. He was educated at a local school and as a pupil-teacher in Edinburgh, then served in World War I, after which he worked for many years as a journalist. His first poems, written in English, appeared in an anthology of Scottish verse in 1920. Two years later, some poems in Scots, signed Hugh MacDiarmid, were published in a periodical called *The Scottish Chapbook;* since that time he has been best known by his pseudonym. After the publication of *Stony Limits* (1934), he wrote little poetry in Scots. Meanwhile, his political associations were extremely turbulent. He was a founding member of the National Party of Scotland in 1928, but it expelled him in 1933 because of his communism, a commitment announced in his *First Hymn to Lenin* (1931). He joined the Communist Party of Great Britain in 1934, but it, too, expelled him, in this case because of his Scottish nationalism. He later rejoined the Communist Party in support of the Soviet invasion of Hungary. After he retired as a journalist, MacDiarmid lectured extensively in Europe, Asia, and North America and practiced what he listed in *Who's Who* as his preferred recreation, Anglophobia.

The Sauchs[1] in the Reuch Heuch Hauch[2]

For George Reston Malloch[3]

There's teuch[4] sauchs growin' i' the Reuch Heuch Hauch.
Like the sauls o' the damned are they,
And ilk ane[5] yoked in a whirligig
Is birlin'[6] the lee-lang[7] day.

O we come doon frae oor stormiest moods,
And licht like a bird i' the haun',[8]
But the teuch sauchs there i' the Reuch Heuch Hauch
As the deil's ain hert are thrawn.[9]

The winds 'ud pu' them up by the roots,
Tho' it broke the warl' asunder,
But they rin richt doon thro' the boddom o' Hell,
and nane kens[1] hoo fer under!

There's no' a licht that the Heavens let loose
Can calm them a hanlawhile.[2]
Nor frae their ancient amplefeyst[3]
Sall God's ain sel' them wile.[4]

1925

1. Willows.
2. "A field near Hawick" [MacDiarmid's note]. Hawick is a town in southeast Scotland.
3. Scottish dramatist, poet, and critic (1875–1953).
4. Tough
5. Each one.
6. Spinning.
7. Livelong.
8. Hand.
9. Like the devil's own heart, twisted.
1. Knows.
2. A moment.
3. Contrariness.
4. Shall God's own self beguile them.

In the Pantry

For N. M. Gunn[1]

Knedneuch[2] land
And a loppert[3] sea
And a lift[4] like a blue-douped[5]
Mawkin'-flee.[6]

I'm famished, but fegs![7]
What's here for a man
But a wheen[8] rubbish that's lain
Sin' Time began?

The sun has a goût[9]
And the mune's hairy-mouldit,[1]
And wha[2] but auld Daith
Has a stummack to hold it?

I'll thraw the lot oot
And lippen[3] to get fresh,
For the sicht o'ts eneuch
To turn my soul nesh![4]

1925

Cloudburst and Soaring Moon

Cloodburst an' soarin' mune
And 'twixt the twa a taed[1]
That loupit oot[2] upon me
As doon the loan I gaed.[3]

Noo I gang[4] white an' lanely
But hoo[5] I'm wishin', faith,
And clood aine mair cam' owre me
Wi' Jock the byreman's[6] braith.

1926

1. Neil M. Gunn (1891–1973), Scottish fiction writer.
2. Sour.
3. Clotted.
4. Sky.
5. Blue-bottomed.
6. Bluebottle fly.
7. Faith!
8. Little.
9. Sticky mass.

1. Covered with hairlike mold.
2. Who.
3. Trust.
4. Nervous.

1. Toad.
2. Leaped out.
3. As down the land I went.
4. Go.
5. How.
6. Cattleman's.

Parley of Beasts

Auld[1] Noah was at hame wi' them a',
The lion and the lamb,
Pair by pair they entered the Ark
And he took them as they cam'.

If twa o' ilka[2] beist there is
Into this room sud[3] come,
Wad[4] I cud welcome them like him,
And no' staun' gowpin'[5] dumb!

Be chief[6] wi' them and they wi' me
And a' wi' ane anither
As Noah and his couples were
There in the Ark thegither.

It's fain I'd mell wi' tiger and tit,[7]
Wi' elephant and eel,
But noo-a-days e'en wi' ain's se[8]
At hame it's hard to feel.

1926

O Wha's[1] the Bride?

O wha's the bride that cairries the bunch
O' thistles blinterin'[2] white?
Her cuckold bridegroom little dreids
What he sall ken[3] this nicht.

For closer than gudeman[4] can come
And closer to'r than hersel',
Wha didna need her maidenheid
Has wrocht his purpose fell.

O wha's been here afore me, lass,
And hoo did he get in?
—A man that deed or[5] was I born
This evil thing has din.

And left, as it were on a corpse,
Your maidenheid to me?

1. Old.
2. Every.
3. Should.
4. Would.
5. Gaping.
6. Friendly.
7. I'd eagerly mix with tiger and titmouse.
8. Even with one's self.

1. Who's.
2. Shining. The thistle is the emblem of Scotland.
3. Shall know.
4. Husband.
5. Died before.

—Nae lass,[6] gudeman, sin' Time began
'S hed ony mair to g'e.[7]

But I can gi'e ye kindness, lad,
And a pair o' willin' hands,
And you sall ha'e my breists like stars,
My limbs like willow wands.

And on my lips ye'll heed nae mair,
And in my hair forget,
The seed o' a' the men that in
My virgin womb ha'e met. . . .

1926

Another Epitaph on an Army of Mercenaries[1]

It is a God-damned lie to say that these
Saved, or knew, anything worth any man's pride.
They were professional murderers and they took
Their blood money and impious risks and died.
In spite of all their kind some elements of worth
With difficulty persist here and there on earth.

1935

British Leftish Poetry, 1930–40

Auden, MacNeice, Day Lewis, I have read them all,
Hoping against hope to hear the authentic call.[1]
"A tragical disappointment. There was I
Hoping to hear old Aeschylus, when the Herald
Called out, 'Theognis, bring your chorus forward.'
Imagine what my feelings must have been!
But then Dexitheus pleased me coming forward
And singing his Bœotian melody:[2]
But next came Chaeris with his music truly
That turned me sick and killed me very nearly.

6. No girl.
7. Has had any more to give.
1. "In reply to A. E. Housman's" [MacDiarmid's note]; see Housman's "Epitaph on an Army of Mercenaries," above.
1. MacDiarmid, a communist who wrote some spirited ideological poetry, found fault with poets W. H. Auden (1907–1973), Louis MacNeice (1907–1963), and C. Day Lewis (1904–1972) because, from his point of view, they lacked political toughness. The following passage, from the opening speech in Aristophanes' comedy *The Acharnians* (fifth century B.C.E.), is spoken in the Pnyx (the place where the Athenian assembly of all the citizens met to make the laws) by a character whose name means "Honest Citizen." He is remembering an evening in the theater. Aeschylus was the first great tragic poet; Theognis, a minor elegiac poet; Dexitheus and Chaeris, musicians.
2. Boeotia was a district of Greece whose capital was Thebes.

And never in my lifetime, man nor boy,
Was I so vexed as at the present moment;
To see the Pnyx, at this time of the morning,
Quite empty, when the Assembly should be full"
And know the explanation I must pass is this
—You cannot light a match on a crumbling wall.

1948

WILFRED OWEN
1893–1918

War has always been a favorite subject of poets, but the pity—as distinguished from the heroism—of war is a modern emphasis. "The Poetry is in the pity," Wilfred Owen wrote in the draft preface to a book of verse he did not live to see published. Repeating Owen's statement as if it were a mantra, the next generation of English and Irish poets—including W. H. Auden, Stephen Spender, Louis MacNeice, and C. Day Lewis—adapted Owen's themes and techniques. Owen's influence persisted with such later poets as Philip Larkin, Ted Hughes, and Seamus Heaney. But Owen's vision of the irredeemable agony and death of modern technological warfare was not universally accepted. W. B. Yeats, who felt that "passive suffering" was not a worthy theme for poetry, dismissed Owen's verse as "unworthy of the poet's corner of a country newspaper," "all blood, dirt and sucked sugar stick," "clumsy," "discordant" (introduction to *The Oxford Book of Modern Verse,* 1936; *The Letters of W. B. Yeats,* 1980, 874–75). Owen's sharp rejection of Yeats's at times heroic representation of death can be inferred from poems such as "S.I.W.," which uses ironically a quotation from Yeats as its epigraph and presents a soldier's death as a banal, even meaningless event. " 'Death sooner than dishonour,' " from Owen's de-idealizing perspective, is misleading cant.

Owen uses his youthful Romanticism, or at least a shell of it, to counterpoint the horrifying scenes he describes, just as he poses his youth against the age-old spectacle of men dying in pain and futility. In a letter of February 4, 1917, he speaks of "[h]ideous landscapes, vile noises, foul language . . . everything unnatural, broken, blasted; the distortion of the dead, whose unburiable bodies sit outside the dug-outs all day, all night, the most execrable sights on earth. In poetry we call them the most glorious." In verse, such contrasts are made tense by lines such as "Red lips are not so red / As the stained stones kissed by the English dead" ("Greater Love"). The slant rhymes, or "pararhymes," that Owen discovered for his verse ("groined" / "groaned," "killed" / "cold," "dazed" / "dozed") reflect in technique the displacement of the old relationships that held together grandeur and patriotic sacrifice.

Owen's poems echo, or "rhyme slant" with, the Bible and the works of earlier writers such as Dante, Shakespeare, Percy Bysshe Shelley, and especially John Keats. Owen's poems convey the harrowing reality of war not by abandoning literary and religious language, but by putting it in dissonant new relationships with the absurdities of war experience. The realism of his verse is, paradoxically, a literary effect. Thus "Anthem for Doomed Youth" recalls pastoral elegy, but personifies destructive weapons, not a sympathetic and healing nature. "Futility" summons the kindly and redemptive sun of elegiac tradition only to turn it into "fatuous sunbeams," or inane rays of light. "Mental Cases" borrows compulsive repetition from Dante's Hell, but the self-torment in Owen's hell is that of shell shock victims, who must obsessively remember scenes of bodily carnage—"Batter of guns and shatter of flying muscles." Far from transparent, these poems rely on sensual images and rhetorical excess, internal rhyme and alliteration, to convey the extremities of pain and terror on the modern battlefield. Never forgetting that he is a poet as well as a soldier, Owen self-consciously explores the ambiguities of this dual position—both combatant and guilty voyeur of the suffering of others, such as the gassed soldier who, in the poet's dreams, "plunges at me, guttering choking, drowning" ("Dulce et Decorum Est").

Owen was born on March 18, 1893, in Oswestry, England, near the Welsh border of Shropshire. His father had a modest job with the railway. His mother was strict and Calvinistic, but she remained closely bound to her son even when, in 1913, he rejected the "false creed" of Christianity. Owen attended Birkenhead Institute from 1900 to 1907, then Shrewsbury Technical School. He did some work at University College, Reading, in botany and then matriculated at the University of London. Unfortunately, he had to withdraw for lack of money. Thinking he might want to join the clergy, he went to Dunsden, Oxfordshire, as a pupil and lay assistant to the vicar. But Owen developed sympathy for the sufferings of poor parishioners while lacking confidence in Christianity's power to relieve them. He also felt profane, homoerotic impulses in the midst of ceremonials at the church, as he indicates in "Maundy Thursday":

> Between the brown hands of a server-lad
> The silver cross was offered to be kissed . . .
> Then, I, too, knelt before that acolyte.
> Above the crucifix I bent my head:
> The Christ was thin, and cold, and very dead:
> And yet I bowed, yea, kissed—my lips did cling.
> (I kissed the warm live hand that held the thing.)

Disaffected, he left this post in August 1913 and went to teach at the Berlitz school in Bordeaux. He stayed in the city for two years, the second as tutor for two boys. The coming of war made him restive, so he returned to England in August or September 1915 to enlist. He was trained and then commissioned as a lieutenant in the Manchester Regiment, which went to the western front in January 1917. His first letter from France is full of "excitement": "This morning I was hit! We were bombing and a fragment from somewhere hit my thumb knuckle. I coaxed out 1 drop of blood. Alas! no more!!" But Owen's attitude soon changed. The weather was extremely cold, the fighting fierce. In June, Owen, suffering from shell shock, was moved to a hospital and then sent back to England to recuperate. Moved again, to a hospital near Edinburgh, he met Siegfried Sassoon, an army captain already known as a war poet. "I was always a mad comet; but you have fixed me," he wrote to Sassoon in November 1917. Sassoon's satiric realism was a useful tonic to Owen's lush Romanticism. Owen went back to France on August 31, 1918, and soon received the Military Cross for gallantry. He was killed on November 4, a week before the armistice, and buried in Ors, France. His poems were published posthumously by Sassoon in 1920.

Owen wrote most of his best poems during a period of thirteen months, from August 1917 to September 1918. He felt a burst of energy and confidence during this time. In a characteristic letter to his mother, of December 31, 1917, he wrote, "I go out of this year a poet, my dear mother, as which I did not enter it. I am held peer by the Georgians; I am a poet's poet. I am started. The tugs have left me; I feel the great swelling of the open sea taking my galleon." Owen's war poems, among the best of the twentieth century, are astringent rather than sentimental. Neither patriotic nor self-deceptive, they express community with the intensity of a lover and the accuracy of an honest man.

Anthem for Doomed Youth

What passing-bells for these who die as cattle?
—Only the monstrous anger of the guns.
Only the stuttering rifles' rapid rattle
Can patter out their hasty orisons.[1]
No mockeries now for them, no prayers nor bells;
Nor any voice of mourning save the choirs,—
The shrill, demented choirs of wailing shells;
And bugles calling for them from sad shires.[2]

What candles may be held to speed them all?
Not in the hands of boys but in their eyes
Shall shine the holy glimmers of goodbyes.
The pallor of girls' brows shall be their pall;
Their flowers the tenderness of patient minds,
And each slow dusk a drawing-down of blinds.

September–October 1917 1920

Apologia pro Poemate Meo[3]

I, too, saw God through mud,—
The mud that cracked on cheeks when wretches smiled.
War brought more glory to their eyes than blood,
And gave their laughs more glee than shakes a child.

Merry it was to laugh there—
Where death becomes absurd and life absurder.
For power was on us as we slashed bones bare
Not to feel sickness or remorse of murder.

I, too, have dropped off Fear—
Behind the barrage, dead as my platoon,
And sailed my spirit surging light and clear
Past the entanglement where hopes lay strewn;

And witnessed exultation—
Faces that used to curse me, scowl for scowl,
Shine and lift up with passion of oblation,[4]
Seraphic for an hour; though they were foul.

1. Prayers.
2. Counties.
3. A defense of my poem (Latin). Owen perhaps derives his title from *Apologia pro Vita Sua* (1864), the famous spiritual autobiography of Cardinal John Henry Newman (1801–1890).
4. Making a religious offering.

I have made fellowships—
Untold of happy lovers in old song.
For love is not the binding of fair lips
With the soft silk of eyes that look and long,

By Joy, whose ribbon slips,—
But wound with war's hard wire whose stakes are strong;
Bound with the bandage of the arm that drips;
Knit in the webbing of the rifle-thong.

I have perceived much beauty
In the hoarse oaths that kept our courage straight;
Heard music in the silentness of duty;
Found peace where shell-storms spouted reddest spate.

Nevertheless, except you share
With them in hell the sorrowful dark of hell,
Whose world is but the trembling of a flare
And heaven but as the highway for a shell,

You shall not hear their mirth:
You shall not come to think them well content
But any jest of mine. These men are worth
Your tears. You are not worth their merriment.

November–December 1917 1920

Miners[5]

There was a whispering in my hearth,
A sigh of the coal,
Grown wistful of a former earth
It might recall.

I listened for a tale of leaves
And smothered ferns,
Frond-forests, and the low sly lives
Before the fauns.

My fire might show steam-phantoms simmer
From Time's old cauldron,
Before the birds made nests in summer,
Or men had children.

5. On January 12, 1918, an explosion in a mining pit at the Podmore Hall Colliery, Halmerend, England, killed about 150 miners.

But the coals were murmuring of their mine,
And moans down there
Of boys that slept wry sleep, and men
Writhing for air.

And I saw white bones in the cinder-shard,
Bones without number.
Many the muscled bodies charred,
And few remember.

I thought of all that worked dark pits
Of war, and died
Digging the rock where Death reputes
Peace lies indeed.

Comforted years will sit soft-chaired,
In rooms of amber;
The years will stretch their hands, well-cheered
By our life's ember;

The centuries will burn rich loads
With which we groaned,
Whose warmth shall lull their dreaming lids,
While songs are crooned;
But they will not dream of us poor lads,
Left in the ground.

January 1918 1918

Dulce et Decorum Est[6]

Bent double, like old beggars under sacks,
Knock-kneed, coughing like hags, we cursed through sludge,
Till on the haunting flares we turned our backs
And towards our distant rest began to trudge.
Men marched asleep. Many had lost their boots
But limped on, blood-shod. All went lame; all blind;
Drunk with fatigue; deaf even to the hoots
Of tired, outstripped Five-Nines[7] that dropped behind.

Gas! GAS! Quick, boys!—An ecstasy of fumbling,
Fitting the clumsy helmets just in time;
But someone still was yelling out and stumbling
And flound'ring like a man in fire or lime . . .
Dim, through the misty panes[8] and thick green light,
As under a green sea, I saw him drowning.

6. The beginning of a line from Horace (65–8 B.C.E.) completed at the end of the poem: "It is sweet and proper to die for one's country" (Latin), *Odes* 3.2.13.
7. That is, 5.9-caliber shells.
8. Of the gas mask's celluloid window.

In all my dreams, before my helpless sight,
He plunges at me, guttering, choking, drowning.

If in some smothering dreams you too could pace
Behind the wagon that we flung him in,
And watch the white eyes writhing in his face,
His hanging face, like a devil's sick of sin;
If you could hear, at every jolt, the blood
Come gargling from the froth-corrupted lungs,
Obscene as cancer, bitter as the cud
Of vile, incurable sores on innocent tongues,—
My friend,[9] you would not tell with such high zest
To children ardent for some desperate glory,
The old Lie: Dulce et decorum est
Pro patria mori.

October 1917, January–March 1918 1920

Strange Meeting

It seemed that out of battle I escaped
Down some profound dull tunnel, long since scooped
Through granites which titanic wars had groined.

Yet also there encumbered sleepers groaned,
Too fast in thought or death to be bestirred.
Then, as I probed them, one sprang up, and stared
With piteous recognition in fixed eyes,
Lifting distressful hands, as if to bless.
And by his smile, I knew that sullen hall,—
By his dead smile I knew we stood in Hell.

With a thousand pains that vision's face was grained;
Yet no blood reached there from the upper ground,
And no guns thumped, or down the flues made moan.
'Strange friend,' I said, 'here is no cause to mourn.'
'None,' said the other, 'save the undone years,
The hopelessness. Whatever hope is yours,
Was my life also; I went hunting wild
After the wildest beauty in the world,
Which lies not calm in eyes, or braided hair,
But mocks the steady running of the hour,
And if it grieves, grieves richlier than here.
For by my glee might many men have laughed,
And of my weeping something had been left,
Which must die now. I mean the truth untold,

9. Jessie Pope, to whom the poem was originally dedicated, published jingoistic war poems urging young men to enlist.

The pity of war, the pity war distilled.
Now men will go content with what we spoiled,
Or, discontent, boil bloody, and be spilled.
They will be swift with swiftness of the tigress.
None will break ranks, though nations trek from progress.
Courage was mine, and I had mystery,
Wisdom was mine, and I had mastery:
To miss the march of this retreating world
Into vain citadels that are not walled.
Then, when much blood had clogged their chariot-wheels,
I would go up and wash them from sweet wells,
Even with truths that lie too deep for taint.[1]
I would have poured my spirit without stint
But not through wounds; not on the cess[2] of war.
Foreheads of men have bled where no wounds were.

'I am the enemy you killed, my friend.
I knew you in this dark: for so you frowned
Yesterday through me as you jabbed and killed.
I parried; but my hands were loath and cold.
Let us sleep now. . . . '

January–March 1918 1920

Futility

Move him into the sun—
Gently its touch awoke him once,
At home, whispering of fields half-sown.
Always it woke him, even in France,
Until this morning and this snow.
If anything might rouse him now
The kind old sun will know.

Think how it wakes the seeds—
Woke once the clays of a cold star.
Are limbs, so dear achieved, are sides
Full-nerved, still warm, too hard to stir?
Was it for this the clay grew tall?
—O what made fatuous sunbeams toil
To break earth's sleep at all?

May 1918 1920

1. Cf. "Thoughts that do often lie too deep for tears," a line in "Ode: Intimations of Immortality" (1807), by William Wordsworth.
2. As in cesspool; also, luck.

S.I.W.[3]

I will to the King,
And offer him consolation in his trouble,
For that man there has set his teeth to die,
And being one that hates obedience,
Discipline, and orderliness of life,
I cannot mourn him.

—W. B. YEATS[4]

I. The Prologue

Patting goodbye, doubtless they told the lad
He'd always show the Hun[5] a brave man's face;
Father would sooner him dead than in disgrace,—
Was proud to see him going, aye, and glad.
Perhaps his mother whimpered how she'd fret
Until he got a nice safe wound to nurse.
Sisters would wish girls too could shoot, charge, curse . . .
Brothers—would send his favourite cigarette.
Each week, month after month, they wrote the same,
Thinking him sheltered in some Y.M. Hut,[6]
Because he said so, writing on his butt
Where once an hour a bullet missed its aim.
And misses teased the hunger of his brain.
His eyes grew old with wincing, and his hand
Reckless with ague.[7] Courage leaked, as sand
From the best sandbags after years of rain.
But never leave, wound, fever, trench-foot, shock,
Untrapped the wretch. And death seemed still withheld
For torture of lying machinally shelled,
At the pleasure of this world's Powers who'd run amok.

He'd seen men shoot their hands, on night patrol.
Their people never knew. Yet they were vile.
'Death sooner than dishonour, that's the style!'
So Father said.

II. The Action

One dawn, our wire patrol
Carried him. This time, Death had not missed.
We could do nothing but wipe his bleeding cough.
Could it be accident?—Rifles go off . . .
Not sniped? No. (Later they found the English ball.)

3. Military abbreviation for self-inflicted wound.
4. Irish poet and playwright (1865–1939). The passage from the play *The King's Threshold* (1906) describes the poet Seanchan's heroic resolve to die.
5. German soldier; originally, a nomadic people feared for their military prowess in the fourth century.
6. Hostel of the Young Men's Christian Association.
7. Fever.

III. The Poem

It was the reasoned crisis of his soul
Against more days of inescapable thrall,
Against infrangibly[8] wired and blind trench wall
Curtained with fire, roofed in with creeping fire,
Slow grazing fire, that would not burn him whole
But kept him for death's promises and scoff,
And life's half-promising, and both their riling.

IV. The Epilogue

With him they buried the muzzle his teeth had kissed,
And truthfully wrote the mother, 'Tim died smiling.'

September 1917, May 1918 1920

Greater Love[9]

Red lips are not so red
As the stained stones kissed by the English dead.
Kindness of wooed and wooer
Seems shame to their love pure.
O Love, your eyes lose lure
When I behold eyes blinded in my stead!

Your slender attitude
Trembles not exquisite like limbs knife-skewed,
Rolling and rolling there
Where God seems not to care;
Till the fierce love they bear
Cramps them in death's extreme decrepitude.

Your voice sings not so soft,—
Though even as wind murmuring through raftered loft,—
Your dear voice is not dear,
Gentle, and evening clear,
As theirs whom none now hear,
Now earth has stopped their piteous mouths that coughed.

Heart, you were never hot,
Nor large, nor full like hearts made great with shot;
And though your hand be pale,
Paler are all which trail
Your cross through flame and hail:
Weep, you may weep, for you may touch them not.[1]

October–November 1917 1920

8. Unbreakably.
9. "Greater love hath no man than this, that a man lay down his life for his friends" (John 15.13).
1. "Jesus said unto [Mary Magdelene], Woman, why weepest thou? . . . Jesus saith unto her, Touch me not; for I am not yet ascended to my Father" (John 20.15–17).

Mental Cases[2]

Who are these? Why sit they here in twilight?
Wherefore rock they, purgatorial shadows,
Drooping tongues from jaws that slob their relish,
Baring teeth that leer like skulls' teeth wicked?
Stroke on stroke of pain,—but what slow panic,
Gouged these chasms round their fretted sockets?
Ever from their hair and through their hands' palms
Misery swelters. Surely we have perished
Sleeping, and walk hell; but who these hellish?

—These are men whose minds the Dead have ravished.
Memory fingers in their hair of murders,
Multitudinous murders they once witnessed.
Wading sloughs of flesh these helpless wander,
Treading blood from lungs that had loved laughter.
Always they must see these things and hear them,
Batter of guns and shatter of flying muscles,
Carnage incomparable, and human squander
Rucked too thick for these men's extrication.

Therefore still their eyeballs shrink tormented
Back into their brains, because on their sense
Sunlight seems a blood-smear; night comes blood-black;
Dawn breaks open like a wound that bleeds afresh.
—Thus their heads wear this hilarious, hideous,
Awful falseness of set-smiling corpses.
—Thus their hands are plucking at each other;
Picking at the rope-knouts of their scourging;
Snatching after us who smote them, brother,
Pawing us who dealt them war and madness.

May, July 1918 1920

Disabled

He sat in a wheeled chair, waiting for dark,
And shivered in his ghastly suit of grey,
Legless, sewn short at elbow. Through the park
Voices of boys rang saddening like a hymn,
Voices of play and pleasure after day,
Till gathering sleep had mothered them from him.

2. The opening of each stanza of this poem echoes and parallels the structure of the King James version of Revelation 7.13–17: "What are these which are arrayed in white robes? and whence came they? . . . These are they which came out of great tribulation, and have washed their robes, and made them white in the blood of the Lamb. Therefore are they before the throne of God."

• • •

About this time Town used to swing so gay
When glow-lamps budded in the light blue trees,
And girls glanced lovelier as the air grew dim,—
In the old times, before he threw away his knees.
Now he will never feel again how slim
Girl's waists are, or how warm their subtle hands
All of them touch him like some queer disease.

• • •

There was an artist silly for his face,
For it was younger than his youth, last year.
Now, he is old; his back will never brace;
He's lost his colour very far from here,
Poured it down shell-holes till the veins ran dry,
And half his lifetime lapsed in the hot race,
And leap of purple spurted from his thigh.

• • •

One time he liked a blood-smear down his leg,
After the matches, carried shoulder-high.[3]
It was after football, when he'd drunk a peg,[4]
He thought he'd better join.—He wonders why.
Someone had said he'd look a god in kilts,
That's why; and maybe, too, to please his Meg,
Aye, that was it, to please the giddy jilts[5]
He asked to join. He didn't have to beg;
Smiling they wrote his lie: aged nineteen years.
Germans he scarcely thought of; all their guilt,
And Austria's, did not move him. And no fears
Of Fear came yet. He thought of jewelled hilts
For daggers in plaid socks;[6] of smart salutes;
And care of arms; and leave; and pay arrears;
Esprit de corps;[7] and hints for young recruits.
And soon, he was drafted out with drums and cheers.

• • •

Some cheered him home, but not as crowds cheer Goal.
Only a solemn man who brought him fruits
Thanked him; and then enquired about his soul.

• • •

Now, he will spend a few sick years in institutes,
And do what things the rules consider wise,
And take whatever pity they may dole.

3. Cf. A. E. Houseman's "To an Athlete Dying Young," lines 1–4: "The time you won your town the race / We chaired you through the market-place, / Man and boy stood cheering by, / And home we brought you shoulder-high."
4. Brandy and soda (slang).
5. Capricious women.
6. Kilted Scottish Highlanders used to carry small ornamental daggers (*skene-dhus*) thrust into the top of a stocking.
7. Esteem for the honor and spirit of an organization—here, the army. *Pay arrears:* back pay.

Tonight he noticed how the women's eyes
Passed from him to the strong men that were whole.
How cold and late it is! Why don't they come
And put him into bed? Why don't they come?[8]

October 1917, July 1918 1920

Exposure

Our brains ache, in the merciless iced east winds that knive us[9] . . .
Wearied we keep awake because the night is silent . . .
Low, drooping flares confuse our memory of the salient[1] . . .
Worried by silence, sentries whisper, curious, nervous,
But nothing happens.

Watching, we hear the mad gusts tugging on the wire,
Like twitching agonies of men among its brambles.
Northward, incessantly, the flickering gunnery rumbles,
Far off, like a dull rumour of some other war[2]
What are we doing here?

The poignant misery of dawn begins to grow . . .
We only know war lasts, rain soaks, and clouds sag stormy.
Dawn massing in the east her melancholy army
Attacks once more in ranks on shivering ranks of grey,[3]
But nothing happens.

Sudden successive flights of bullets streak the silence.
Less deathly than the air that shudders black with snow,
With sidelong flowing flakes that flock, pause, and renew;
We watch them wandering up and down the wind's nonchalance,
But nothing happens.

Pale flakes with fingering stealth come feeling for our faces—
We cringe in holes, back on forgotten dreams, and stare, snow-dazed,
Deep into grassier ditches. So we drowse, sun-dozed,
Littered with blossoms trickling where the blackbird fusses,
—Is it that we are dying?

Slowly our ghosts drag home: glimpsing the sunk fires, glozed[4]
With crusted dark-red jewels; crickets jingle there;
For hours the innocent mice rejoice: the house is theirs;
Shutters and doors, all closed: on us the doors are closed,—
We turn back to our dying.

8. Cf. the slogan on a recruiting poster: "Will they never come?"
9. Cf. John Keats's "Ode to a Nightingale" (1819), lines 1–2: "My heart aches, and a drowsy numbness pains / My sense, . . ."
1. Places where the front lines jutted out into enemy territory and where the fighting was the worst.
2. Cf. Matthew 24.6: "wars and rumours of war."
3. The German soldiers wore gray uniforms.
4. Glowing+glazed. The preceding words echo a popular song: "Keep the home fires burning. . . . Though your lads are far away they dream of home."

Since we believe not otherwise can kind fires burn;
Nor even suns smile true on child, or field, or fruit.
For God's invincible spring our love is made afraid;
Therefore, not loath, we lie out here; therefore were born,
For love of God seems dying.

Tonight, this frost will fasten on this mud and us,
Shrivelling many hands, puckering foreheads crisp.
The burying-party, picks and shovels in shaking grasp,
Pause over half-known faces. All their eyes are ice,
But nothing happens.

December 1917, September 1918 1920

DOROTHY PARKER
1893–1967

Born on August 22, 1893, in West End, New Jersey, Dorothy Parker made a name for herself as one of the leading literary wits of her day, writing poetry and fiction for such mass-circulation magazines as *Vogue, Vanity Fair,* and *The New Yorker,* and associating with a famous literary group of New York humorists called the Algonquin Circle. Her father was a Jew, her mother a Scot, but Parker was raised a Catholic by her stepmother after her mother's early death. While pursuing a literary career, she actively supported various leftist political causes and contributed to a number of Hollywood film scripts. Her tumultuous personal life included romantic relationships that often ended unhappily. She acknowledged the influence of Edna St. Vincent Millay on her poetry, though Parker's wit was more bitter and more biting. Defining humor, Parker said, "There must be a disciplined eye and a wild mind," and the tight formal discipline of Parker's verse contains within itself a melancholy wildness.

Parker reminds us that good comic poems can resemble good jokes in their wordplay, concision, timing, and surprising turns. Poems such as "Résumé" and "Observation" end in a kind of punch line, inverting the expectations built up by the preceding catalog. More particularized and vivid than most jokes, the suicide poem "Résumé" packs images of razors, acids, guns, and gas into a few short lines. A gag line bursts a rhetorical bubble ("flow'r," "Deep-hearted," "amulet") in "One Perfect Rose," replacing a rose with "One perfect limousine" as the real object of the speaker's desire. While writing in snappily rhymed stanzas and polished meters, Parker flouts social constraints and proprieties, especially those placed on women. Her sharp-tongued irony, aggressive wit, and defiant spunk contrast with the stereotype of the popular woman writer as delicate, sentimental moralist.

Résumé

Razors pain you;
Rivers are damp;
Acids stain you;
And drugs cause cramp.
Guns aren't lawful;
Nooses give;
Gas smells awful;
You might as well live.

1926

One Perfect Rose

A single flow'r he sent me, since we met.
All tenderly his messenger he chose;
Deep-hearted, pure, with scented dew still wet—
One perfect rose.

I knew the language of the floweret;
"My fragile leaves," it said, "his heart enclose."
Love long has taken for his amulet
One perfect rose.

Why is it no one ever sent me yet
One perfect limousine, do you suppose?
Ah no, it's always just my luck to get
One perfect rose.

1926

Observation

If I don't drive around the park,
I'm pretty sure to make my mark.
If I'm in bed each night by ten,
I may get back my looks again,
If I abstain from fun and such,
I'll probably amount to much,
But I shall stay the way I am,
Because I do not give a damn.

1926

Oscar Wilde[1]

If, with the literate, I am
Impelled to try an epigram,
I never seek to take the credit;
We all assume that Oscar said it.

1928

George Sand[2]

What time the gifted lady took
Away from paper, pen, and book,
She spent in amorous dalliance
(They do those things so well in France).

1928

1. Irish writer (1856–1900) of brilliantly satiric wit.
2. Pseudonymous French novelist (1804–1876), famous for both her many novels and her notorious love affairs.

Charles Reznikoff
1894–1976

Charles Reznikoff was born on August 31, 1894, in Brooklyn, New York, to Russian Jewish immigrants. He was trained as a lawyer at New York University's School of Law, but practiced law only briefly, working in various modest jobs so he could devote himself to writing poetry. He spent most of his life in New York, often going for long walks through the city streets. Working for a publishing firm during the early Depression years, he analyzed and summarized legal cases—an experience that eventually led to the long, synthetic, documentary poems he would publish in later life, *Testimony: The United States, 1885–1915* (1965, 1968) and *Holocaust* (1975).

Reznikoff is known as one of the leading Objectivists, a loosely affiliated group of late modernists rooted in Imagism. In the early 1930s he, together with Louis Zukofsky and George Oppen, formed the Objectivist Press. Of the older generation of modernists, Ezra Pound and William Carlos Williams were primary sources of inspiration and encouragement, even though the younger poets were left-wing Jews, while Pound in particular was fascist and anti-Semitic. Notwithstanding these differences, Reznikoff adapted the Imagist program of free verse and "direct treatment of the thing" to an ethnic American milieu. His version of Objectivism is an urban poetry of understatement, empathy, and materialist realism. Shunning overt rhetoric, transcendental poses, and Romantic sublimity, he aims at unadorned plainness and democratic openness. "I sing," he summarizes in "Te Deum," "for the common sunshine, / the breeze, / the largess of the spring."

Even so, the "objectivity" of Reznikoff's Objectivism should not be overstated. Many poems offer an elegiac response to transience ("Heart and Clock," "Epitaphs"). Others testify to the historical injustices against Jews ("Early History of a Writer"). Still others make effective use of figurative language. A man drops dead like a sparrow, subway pillars recall trees, chewing gum is "a flat black fungus," and "the clocks / drip." These are hardly literal statements. But Reznikoff's quiet, restrained, matter-of-fact style makes his melancholy, his ethical anger, and his metaphors all the more compelling.

Reznikoff carried the Objectivist ideal to an extreme when, in his late long poems, he selected and arranged court evidence. The facts, he hoped, would speak for themselves. Indeed, the author almost seems to disappear from his poems. In the documentary collage of *Holocaust,* Reznikoff edits, assimilates, and compresses material from the records of the Nuremburg and the Eichmann trials. To these found documents, he refuses to add the consolations of voice, narrative, or interpretation. Testimonies of torture, deportation, massacre, and mass graves are presented with a relentless and unsparing immediacy that evidences the power of poetry and yet also—in this antilyrical and unredemptive poem—sternly evacuates it.

[On Brooklyn Bridge I Saw a Man Drop Dead.]

On Brooklyn Bridge I saw a man drop dead.
It meant no more than if he were a sparrow.

Above us rose Manhattan;
below, the river spread to meet sea and sky.

1918

[The Shopgirls Leave Their Work]

The shopgirls leave their work
quietly.

Machines are still, tables and chairs
darken.

The silent rounds of mice and roaches begin.

1918

[I Walked through the Lonely Marsh]

I walked through the lonely marsh
among the white birches.

Above the birches rose
three crows,
croaking, croaking.

The trumpets blare war
and the streets are filled with the echoes.

1918

[It Had Long Been Dark, though Still an Hour before Supper-Time.]

It had long been dark, though still an hour before supper-time.
The boy stood at the window behind the curtain.
The street under the black sky was bluish white with snow.
Across the street, where the lot sloped to the pavement,
boys and girls were going down on sleds.
The boys were after him because he was a Jew.

At last his father and mother slept. He got up and dressed.
In the hall he took his sled and went out on tiptoe.
No one was in the street. The slide was worn smooth and slippery—
just right.
He laid himself on the sled and shot away. He went down only twice.
He stood knee-deep in snow:
no one was in the street, the windows were darkened;
those near the street-lamps were ashine, but the rooms inside were
dark;
on the street were long shadows of clods of snow.
He took his sled and went back into the house.

1921

[Walk about the Subway Station]

Walk about the subway station
in a grove of steel pillars;
how their knobs, the rivet-heads—
unlike those of oaks—
are regularly placed;
how barren the ground is
except here and there on the platform
a flat black fungus
that was chewing-gum.

1934

[About an Excavation]

About an excavation
a flock of bright red lanterns
has settled.

1934

Heart and Clock

I

Now the sky begins to turn upon its hub—
the sun; each leaf revolves upon its stem;

now the plague of watches and of clocks nicks away
the day—
ten thousand thousand steps
tread upon the dawn;
ten thousand wheels
cross and criss-cross the day
and leave their ruts across its brightness;

the clocks
drip
in every room—
our lives are leaking from the places,
and the day's brightness dwindles into stars.

II

If my days were like the ants,
I might carry away this mountain;
therefore, you must be precious to me,
seconds;
let them step and stamp upon you as they can,
I shall escape with a few grains.

III

EVENING

The dark green leaves
of grass, bushes, and trees—
the jays are hushed,
I see no squirrel scamper;
but the street lamps along the winding path
burn brightly—
the work of man is not yet over.

IV

How pleasant
the silence of a holiday
to those who listen
to the long dialogue of heart and clock.

1936

Epitaphs

I

Drowning
I felt for a moment reaching towards me
finger tips against mine.

II

You mice,
that ate the crumbs of my freedom,
lo!

III

The clock strikes:
these are the steps of our departure.

IV

A brown oak leaf
scraping the sidewalk
frightened me.

V

Proserpine
swallowed only six seeds
of the pomegranate
and had to stay six months among the dead—[1]
I was a glutton.

1936

1. In Roman mythology, Proserpine (or Persephone in Greek) is carried away to the underworld to be the bride of Dis (Hades or Pluto). Although her mother, Ceres (Demeter), eventually persuades the gods to set her free, she is condemned to spend a portion of each year in the underworld after she is tricked into eating pomegranate seeds, the food of the dead.

Te Deum

Not because of victories
I sing,
having none,
but for the common sunshine,
the breeze,
the largess of the spring.

Not for victory
but for the day's work done
as well as I was able;
not for a seat upon the dais
but at the common table.

1959

From Early History of a Writer

When my grandfather was about fifty, he fell sick,
and my grandparents thought it best to go to America
where my father and their other children were.
My father went to the pier to bring his parents to our home
and could hardly recognize his father—
the face was swollen
and the man could hardly move his hands and feet.
I had been watching from the window
and my brother and I ran downstairs
to meet them. My father turned to my grandfather
and said: "These are my sons."
My grandfather looked at us with his bleary eyes,
whose rims were red,
and turning to my father murmured in Hebrew
what the patriarch Jacob had said to his son Joseph:
"I did not think to see your face
and God has shown me your sons also,"[2]
and, putting his swollen hands slowly on my head,
began to bless me. Even as he did so,
my grandmother who was standing beside him
poked him in the ribs and said sharply in Yiddish:
"Well?"
My grandfather hurriedly brought the blessing to a close.
Shoving his fist into his pocket he took out a gold coin
and put it in the hand I had stretched out to greet him.
"No, no," I said
and would have given the coin back,

2. From Genesis 48. Jacob blesses his favorite son, Joseph, and his grandchildren, Manasseh and Ephraim, from his deathbed. Jacob, who received the name Israel after wrestling with an angel, is considered the patriarch of the Jews.

for I had been brought up to think it disgraceful
to take money from my elders: the purpose of the instruction
was that I should not ask for pennies,
as ill-bred children did; in good Talmudical style[3]
the prohibition was wider than the evil.
But this time my father smiled and said:
"Keep it—to remember your grandfather by."
As they went into the house,
I stopped to glance at the coin
and saw the monstrous eagle of czarist Russia,
with two open beaks,
from which my father and mother and so many others had fled.

1969

From Holocaust

IX. Entertainment

1

The commander of a camp, among his amusements, as in other camps
had a large dog
and at the cry of "Jude," that is, "Jew,"
the dog would attack the man and tear off pieces of flesh.
In another camp, the Jews who had just come
kept seeing a dog—
the dog belonged to the S.S.[4] man in charge of "the showers," that is, the gas chambers;
the S.S. man would call the dog "Mensch," that is, "man":
and whenever he set the dog on a Jew would say, "Man, get that dog!"

2

In one camp the officers, for their amusement,
if they saw a group of Jews at a distance,
would draw their revolvers and shoot in that direction;
but they must have shot into the air
because no one was ever hit.
Throwing stones at the group was another matter:
some would be hurt—in the face, hands or legs.
But, in another camp, the two commanders began a game:
they would stand at their windows
and, while those carrying stones were passing,
the two would shoot at them, aiming at the tip of a nose or a finger;
and in the evening would pick out those who had been hit
and were no longer any good for work

3. The Talmud is the sacred collection of rabbinical interpretations and commentary on the Jewish oral law.

4. Abbreviated name of the Schutzstaffel, the Nazi military corps that ran the concentration camps during World War II.

and have them shot.
And in still another camp the officers played "the spinning top":
they would place a stick in the ground—stand it up quite low—
and the man to be tortured would have to keep touching it with his right hand,
his left hand behind his back,
and keep turning around the stick,
and as he ran around he was beaten
and those beating him would shout, "Quicker! Quicker!"
He would have to go around at least ten times,
but after three or four times some would faint.

3

Once the commander of a camp had eight of the strongest among the Jews
placed in a large barrel of water,
saying that they did not look clean,
and they had to stand in this barrel naked for twenty-four hours.
In the morning, other Jews had to cut away the ice:
the men were frozen to death.
In this camp—and in others also—
they had an orchestra of Jews
who had to play every morning and evening
and whenever Jews were taken to be shot.
In one such camp,
the orchestra had all of sixty men.

4

Once a group of Jews who came on a truck
were ordered off when they reached a camp at night
and a powerful light was suddenly focused upon them.
They were told to keep looking towards it.
When they tried to look aside
an S.S. man stabbed them to death.

The Germans in another camp, too, had their games.
A young man would be sent to close an umbrella open on a roof
and had to climb to do it;
if he fell he was beaten to death.
One after another had to climb to the roof
to close the umbrella
and almost all fell down,
and each who fell was beaten to death;
and a dog would bite the man at each stroke.
Then there were times when the inmates had to run
and were shot at.
And once five had the bottoms of their trousers bound with rope
and mice put into the trousers;
the men had to stand at attention
and those who could not because of the mice
were beaten.

On Sundays there was no work and Jews would be placed in a row:
each had a bottle on his head
and the S.S. men amused themselves by shooting at the bottles.
If a bottle was hit,
the man lived;
but if the bullet landed below,
well, the man had it.

1975

E. E. CUMMINGS
1894–1962

E. E. Cummings is one of the most innovative modern poets, but his innovation is on a different level from T. S. Eliot's ambitious, polyglot collages or Wallace Stevens's philosophically complex long poems. In some ways, Cummings is oddly traditional. Though he drops most punctuation and capitalization, breaks words into syllables and letters, and deliberately distorts syntax, he is fond of the sonnet and other regular forms, and he likes rhymes and off-rhymes. And though he alters parts of speech, making verbs into nouns and nouns into verbs, he does so chiefly to express feelings whose simplicity belies all this complication. He does not seek, or find, the authoritative utterance of some of the modernists, but he achieves a magnificent, subversive smallness.

Edward Estlin Cummings was born on October 14, 1894, in Cambridge, Massachusetts. He was the son of a Unitarian minister who preached in Boston at the South Congregational Church and also taught sociology at Harvard University. Cummings received a B.A. at Harvard in 1915 and an M.A. there in 1916. He then volunteered to go to France, where as a pacifist he joined the Norton Harjes Ambulance Corps, but he was interned for three months in a concentration camp because his letters aroused the suspicions of a French censor, as recalled in the semifictional work *The Enormous Room* (1922). After the war, Cummings lived in Paris and took up painting as well as writing. He was influenced by Pablo Picasso's fracturing of space, Gertrude Stein's linguistic experimentation, and Ezra Pound's and Amy Lowell's Imagist concision and freedom. The title of his first book of poems, *Tulips and Chimneys* (1923), suggests the opposition that was to become lifelong in his work, between organic life and what he calls "manunkind" ("pity this busy monster, manunkind / not").

Flouting typographic convention, Cummings used punctuation only for special effects, and many of his poems exploited odd typographic arrangements, allowing letters of words to trail over from one line to the next in total indifference to syllables. Like other modernist writers, he experimented with the visual appearance of words, anticipating the use of typewriter spacing and peculiarities by Charles Olson, May Swenson, and others. His poetry's arrangement on the page rouses tensions and effects resolutions, offers an intriguing puzzle, and gives vent to his iconoclasm. It is the badge he wears as a self-styled misfit, still capable of feeling love and lust in an unfeeling, mechanized world. He revolts against people in high places, in crowded cities, in ruts, to whom the only pronoun he considers applicable is "it." One poem begins, "a salesman is an it that stinks Excuse me," and Cummings explains that whether the product sold by the "it" is lingerie or shrouds does not matter.

He is set firmly against abstractions. "Knowledge is a polite word for dead but not buried imagination . . . think twice before you think." He is against expressions such as "most people," which he runs into one word: "it's no use trying to pretend that mostpeople and ourselves are alike. Mostpeople have less in common with ourselves than the squarerootofminusone" (introduction to *Collected Poems,* 1938). He is against science as an impersonalizing force, because the only reality is the person. Politically, he is an anarchist, a Robin Hood. After a trip to Russia in the early 1930s, Cummings excoriated it in a book called *Eimi* (Greek for "I am"; 1933), in which he instructs an interpreter to tell a Russian dramatist, ' "I drink . . . to the individual.' " Cummings denounces also "the cambridge ladies who live in furnished souls" that don't belong to them; the philosophers, scientists, and religious zealots who try to shackle the natural instinctive world; the flag-wavers who keep saying they love America and mean only the "Land of the Cluett Shirt, Boston Garter and Spearmint Girl with the Wrigley eyes"; the artists who write by formula; the supposedly wholesome young men ready to die for God, for country, and for Yale, suffering from venereal disease of mind as well as body; the warmongers who find the best of reasons for preventing other people from living, and who regard freedom as a commodity like a breakfast food. All these people live, in short, in negative worlds, full of prohibitions, taboos, manunkindness, and it is against them that Cummings shoots his arrows.

Those he befriends range from the man who had fallen among thieves to Olaf the conscientious objector to Buffalo Bill to Cummings's father to every lover. These people have certain things in common: they exist—"is" is their first big word; they love, and "love" is their second big word; they are spontaneous; they are childlike; and they are themselves.

Cumming's poems are either lyrical or satirical, and they changed little as he built up endless variations out of a limited group of ideas. His love poems express a childlike wonder and humor that Cummings has almost to himself in modern poetry and that he retained into old age. His satirical poems are witty as well as savage. "Only so long as we can laugh at ourselves are we nobody else," he writes. A faint pre-Raphaelite glow surrounds Cummings's unexpected combinations of archaic attitudes with typographic experiment and modern, sometimes slangy, diction. He seems a triumphant anachronism. In his last years, Cummings delivered the Charles Eliot Norton lectures at Harvard; they appeared under the title *Six Nonlectures* in 1953 and resume that blend of wayward bohemianism and noble intransigence that marks all his work.

[in Just-]

in Just-
spring   when the world is mud-
luscious the little
lame balloonman

whistles   far   and wee

and eddieandbill come
running from marbles and
piracies and it's
spring

when the world is puddle-wonderful

the queer
old balloonman whistles
far   and   wee
and bettyandisbel come dancing

from hop-scotch and jump-rope and

it's
spring
and
    the

        goat-footed[1]

balloonMan   whistles
far
and
wee

1920, 1923

[Buffalo Bill 's[2]]

Buffalo Bill 's
defunct
        who used to
        ride a watersmooth-silver
                                        stallion
and break onetwothreefourfive pigeonsjustlikethat
                                                Jesus

he was a handsome man
                        and what i want to know is
how do you like your blueeyed boy
Mister Death

1920, 1923

[O sweet spontaneous]

O sweet spontaneous
earth how often have
the
doting

        fingers of
prurient philosophers pinched

1. Reference to Pan, lustful Greek god depicted as half human and half goat.

2. William F. Cody (1846–1917), American army scout, buffalo hunter, and Wild West showman.

and
poked

thee
,has the naughty thumb
of science prodded
thy

    beauty   .how
often have religions taken
thee upon their scraggy knees
squeezing and

buffeting thee that thou mightest conceive
gods
    (but
true

to the incomparable
couch of death thy
rhythmic
lover

    thou answerest

them only with

        spring)

1920, 1923

[the Cambridge ladies who live in furnished souls]

the Cambridge ladies who live in furnished souls
are unbeautiful and have comfortable minds
(also,with the church's protestant blessings
daughters,unscented shapeless spirited)
they believe in Christ and Longfellow,[3]both dead,
are invariably interested in so many things—
at the present writing one still finds
delighted fingers knitting for the is it Poles?
perhaps. While permanent faces coyly bandy
scandal of Mrs. N and Professor D
....the Cambridge ladies do not care,above
Cambridge if sometimes in its box of
sky lavender and cornerless,the
moon rattles like a fragment of angry candy

1922, 1923

3. Henry Wadsworth Longfellow (1807–1882), American poet.

[i was sitting in mcsorley's]

i was sitting in mcsorley's.[4]   outside it was New York and beauti-
fully snowing.

Inside snug and evil.   the slobbering walls filthily push witless
creases of screaming warmth chuck pillows are noise funnily swallows
swallowing revolvingly pompous a the swallowed mottle with smooth or
a but of rapidly goes gobs the and of flecks of and a chatter sobbings
intersect with which distinct disks of graceful oath, upsoarings the
break on   ceiling-flatness

the Bar.tinking luscious jigs dint of ripe silver with warmlyish
wetflat splurging smells waltz the glush of squirting taps plus slush
of foam knocked off and a faint piddle-of-drops she says I ploc spittle
what the lands thaz me kid in no sir hopping sawdust you kiddo he's a
palping wreaths of badly Yep cigars who jim him why gluey grins topple
together eyes pout gestures stickily point made glints squinting who's
a wink bum-nothing and money fuzzily mouths take big wobbly foot-steps
every goggle cent of it get out ears dribbles soft right old feller
belch the chap hic summore eh chuckles skulch....

and i was sitting in the din thinking drinking the ale, which never
lets you grow old blinking at the low ceiling my being pleasantly was
punctuated by the always retchings of a worthless lamp.

when With a minute terrif   iceffort one dirty squeal of soiling light
yanKing from bushy obscurity a bald greenish foetal head established
It suddenly upon the huge neck around whose unwashed sonorous muscle
the filth of a collar hung gently.

(spattered)by this instant of semiluminous nausea A vast wordless
nondescript genie of trunk trickled firmly in to one exactly-mutilated
ghost of a chair,

a;domeshaped interval of complete plasticity,shoulders,sprouted the
extraordinary arms through an angle of ridiculous velocity commenting
upon an unclean table,and,whose distended immense Both paws slowly,
loved a dinted mug

gone Darkness   it was so near to me,i ask of shadow won't you have a
drink?

(the eternal perpetual question)

Inside snugandevil.   i was sitting in mcsorley's   It,did not answer.

outside.(it was New York and beautifully,snowing....

1925

4. McSorley's Saloon, in New York City.

["next to of course god america i]

"next to of course god america i
love you land of the pilgrims' and so forth oh
say can you see by the dawn's early my
country 'tis of centuries come and go
and are no more what of it we should worry
in every language even deafanddumb
thy sons acclaim your glorious name by gorry
by jingo by gee by gosh by gum
why talk of beauty what could be more beauti-
ful than these heroic happy dead
who rushed like lions to the roaring slaughter
they did not stop to think they died instead
then shall the voice of liberty be mute?"

He spoke. And drank rapidly a glass of water

1926

[my sweet old etcetera]

my sweet old etcetera
aunt lucy during the recent

war could and what
is more did tell you just
what everybody was fighting

for,
my sister

isabel created hundreds
(and
hundreds)of socks not to
mention shirts fleaproof earwarmers

etcetera wristers etcetera,my

mother hoped that

i would die etcetera
bravely of course my father used
to become hoarse talking about how it was
a privilege and if only he
could meanwhile my

self etcetera lay quietly
in the deep mud et

cetera
(dreaming,
et
   cetera,of
Your smile
eyes knees and of your Etcetera)

1926

[i sing of Olaf glad and big]

i sing of Olaf glad and big
whose warmest heart recoiled at war:
a conscientious object-or

his wellbelovéd colonel(trig
westpointer[5] most succinctly bred)
took erring Olaf soon in hand;
but—though an host of overjoyed
noncoms[6](first knocking on the head
him)do through icy waters roll
that helplessness which others stroke
with brushes recently employed
anent[7] this muddy toiletbowl,
while kindred intellects evoke
allegiance per blunt instruments—
Olaf(being to all intents
a corpse and wanting any rag
upon what God unto him gave)
responds,without getting annoyed
"I will not kiss your fucking flag"

straightway the silver bird[8] looked grave
(departing hurriedly to shave)

but—though all kinds of officers
(a yearning nation's blueeyed pride)
their passive prey did kick and curse
until for wear their clarion
voices and boots were much the worse,
and egged the firstclassprivates on
his rectum wickedly to tease
by means of skilfully applied
bayonets roasted hot with heat—
Olaf(upon what were once knees)
does almost ceaselessly repeat
"there is some shit I will not eat"

5. Graduate of West Point, the U.S. military academy. *Trig:* primly neat.
6. Noncommissioned officers.
7. Concerning.
8. The insignia of a U.S. Army colonel.

our president,being of which
assertions duly notified
threw the yellowsonofabitch
into a dungeon,where he died

Christ(of His mercy infinite)
i pray to see;and Olaf,too

preponderatingly because
unless statistics lie he was
more brave than me:more blond than you.

1931

[r-p-o-p-h-e-s-s-a-g-r]

                                   r-p-o-p-h-e-s-s-a-g-r
                         who
a)s w(e loo)k
upnowgath
            PPEGORHRASS
                                          eringint(o-
aThe):l
          eA
             !p:
S   a
                                   (r
rIvInG   .gRrEaPsPhOs)
                                                to
rea(be)rran(com)gi(e)ngly
,grasshopper;

1935

[may i feel said he]

may i feel said he
(i'll squeal said she
just once said he)
it's fun said she

(may i touch said he
how much said she
a lot said he)
why not said she

(let's go said he
not too far said she
what's too far said he
where you are said she)

may i stay said he
(which way said she
like this said he
if you kiss said she

may i move said he
is it love said she)
if you're willing said he
(but you're killing said she

but it's life said he
but your wife said she
now said he)
ow said she

(tiptop said he
don't stop said she
oh no said he)
go slow said she

(cccome?said he
ummm said she)
you're divine!said he
(you are Mine said she)

1935

[anyone lived in a pretty how town]

anyone lived in a pretty how town
(with up so floating many bells down)
spring summer autumn winter
he sang his didn't he danced his did.

Women and men(both little and small)
cared for anyone not at all
they sowed their isn't they reaped their same
sun moon stars rain

children guessed(but only a few
and down they forgot as up they grew
autumn winter spring summer)
that noone loved him more by more

when by now and tree by leaf
she laughed his joy she cried his grief
bird by snow and stir by still
anyone's any was all to her

someones married their everyones
laughed their cryings and did their dance

(sleep wake hope and then)they
said their nevers they slept their dream

stars rain sun moon
(and only the snow can begin to explain
how children are apt to forget to remember
with up so floating many bells down)

one day anyone died i guess
(and noone stooped to kiss his face)
busy folk buried them side by side
little by little and was by was

all by all and deep by deep
and more by more they dream their sleep
noone and anyone earth by april
wish by spirit and if by yes.

Women and men(both dong and ding)
summer autumn winter spring
reaped their sowing and went their came
sun moon stars rain

1940

[my father moved through dooms of love]

my father moved through dooms of love
through sames of am through haves of give,
singing each morning out of each night
my father moved through depths of height

this motionless forgetful where
turned at his glance to shining here;
that if(so timid air is firm)
under his eyes would stir and squirm

newly as from unburied which
floats the first who,his april touch
drove sleeping selves to swarm their fates
woke dreamers to their ghostly roots

and should some why completely weep
my father's fingers brought her sleep:
vainly no smallest voice might cry
for he could feel the mountains grow.

Lifting the valleys of the sea
my father moved through griefs of joy;
praising a forehead called the moon
singing desire into begin

joy was his song and joy so pure
a heart of star by him could steer
and pure so now and now so yes
the wrists of twilight would rejoice

keen as midsummer's keen beyond
conceiving mind of sun will stand,
so strictly(over utmost him
so hugely)stood my father's dream

his flesh was flesh his blood was blood:
no hungry man but wished him food;
no cripple wouldn't creep one mile
uphill to only see him smile.

Scorning the pomp of must and shall
my father moved through dooms of feel;
his anger was as right as rain
his pity was as green as grain

septembering arms of year extend
less humbly wealth to foe and friend
than he to foolish and to wise
offered immeasurable is

proudly and(by octobering flame
beckoned)as earth will downward climb,
so naked for immortal work
his shoulders marched against the dark

his sorrow was as true as bread:
no liar looked him in the head;
if every friend became his foe
he'd laugh and build a world with snow.

My father moved through theys of we,
singing each new leaf out of each tree
(and every child was sure that spring
danced when she heard my father sing)

then let men kill which cannot share,
let blood and flesh be mud and mire,
scheming imagine,passion willed,
freedom a drug that's bought and sold

giving to steal and cruel kind,
a heart to fear,to doubt a mind,
to differ a disease of same,
conform the pinnacle of am

though dull were all we taste as bright,
bitter all utterly things sweet,
maggoty minus and dumb death
all we inherit,all bequeath

and nothing quite so least as truth
—i say though hate were why men breathe—
because my father lived his soul
love is the whole and more than all

1940

[pity this busy monster,manunkind]

pity this busy monster,manunkind,

not. Progress is a comfortable disease:
your victim(death and life safely beyond)

plays with the bigness of his littleness
—electrons deify one razorblade
into a mountainrange;lenses extend

unwish through curving wherewhen till unwish
returns on its unself.
A world of made
is not a world of born—pity poor flesh

and trees,poor stars and stones,but never this
fine specimen of hypermagical

ultraomnipotence. We doctors know

a hopeless case if—listen:there's a hell
of a good universe next door;let's go

1944

Jean Toomer
1894–1967

In 1922, in reply to a request for biographical information, Jean Toomer wrote: "Racially, I seem to have (who knows for sure) seven blood mixtures: French, Dutch, Welsh, Negro, German, Jewish, and Indian. Because of these, my position in America has been a curious one. I have lived equally amid the two race groups. Now white, now colored. From my own point of view I am naturally and inevitably an American. I have strived for a spiritual fusion analogous to the fact of racial intermingling. Without denying a single element in me, with no desire to subdue one to the other, I have sought to let them function as complements. I have tried to let them live in harmony. Within the last two or three years, however, my growing need for artistic expression has pulled me deeper and deeper into the Negro group" (quoted in introduction to *Cane,* 1969).

At that time, Toomer was writing poems, stories, and sketches that were published in 1923 as *Cane,* the work for which he is best known. But the quandaries suggested in this passage were to concern him for most of his life. How can a man of mixed ancestry define himself creatively in American society? What special gifts does such a man bring to that society? In his late long poem *The Blue Meridian,* Toomer dreams of an evolution to a higher form of life, the development of Blakean "Spirit-torsos of exquisite strength." This poem contains, however, more pathos than optimism. The "great African races" sent "one wave across the American continent," and the best that survives is a "swan song, to break rocks / And immortalize a hiding water boy."

Toomer was born on December 26, 1894, in Washington, D.C., the grandson of P. B. S. Pinchback, an African American who during Reconstruction served as acting governor of Louisiana. Toomer grew up alternately in black and white communities in New Rochelle, New York, and Washington, D.C., attending at times all-white, at other times all-black schools. After sampling courses in physical education, agriculture, medicine, sociology, and history at a number of different colleges, he decided on a literary career. In 1919–21, he wrote his first mature poems, including "Her Lips Are Copper Wire" and "Gum." In 1921, he became an interim school principal in Sparta, Georgia, and was inspired by its rural African American community. Many of the poems and prose sketches in *Cane* are the fruit of this experience, written in Sparta and Washington, D.C., some first published separately as magazine pieces. *Cane* attracted much attention in the white literary community (Allen Tate, of the Fugitives, reviewed it sympathetically), and it helped spearhead the Harlem Renaissance of the 1920s.

Toomer's early poems have rhetorical force and mellifluous cadences, and they reveal his sharp eye for clashing cultures. They are rooted in the symbolist aesthetics of Charles Baudelaire and in Walt Whitman's mystical sense of collective identity. The influence of Imagism is also strong, perhaps most visibly in "Portrait in Georgia," "Gum," and "Her Lips Are Copper Wire," concentrated free verse poems in which direct sensory images are foremost, narrative and connectives largely suppressed. But Toomer puts this Anglo-American avant-garde style to distinctive ends. "Portrait in Georgia" uses the stark juxtapositions of Imagism to embody violent racial tension: it enumerates the parts of a white woman's face (as in the lyric tradition of the blazon) and superimposes these features onto the description of a black man's lynching. Poems such as "Reapers," "Georgia Dusk," and "Song of the Son" meditate on a disappearing rural way of life; their nature-centered symbolism and ritualistic repetitions suggest the interwovenness of black farm workers and the land. But Toomer's response is conflicted, both wistful and clear eyed: he mourns that the "blade" of impersonal machinery is tearing the fabric of this lifestyle, yet he also acknowledges the slavery and servitude that have been integral to this threatened world.

Despite his early success with *Cane,* Toomer dropped from sight for most of his remaining forty-five years. During the 1920s, he began to direct his efforts toward his psychological development and integration; in 1924, he spent a summer at Fontainebleau studying the ideas of George Gurdjieff, a Greek Armenian mystic whose ethical and psychological philosophy greatly influenced Toomer's later styles of life and art. In the United States, Toomer taught Gurdjieffian mysticism and experimented with community living. In 1932, he married a member of one of his communes, Marjorie Latimer, a white New Englander and a promising writer; a year later, she died giving birth to their only child. In 1934, Toomer remarried; his second wife, Marjorie Content, was also white, the daughter of a New York stockbroker. Toomer's experiments and marriages led to some scandalmongering in the press. In 1940, he became a Quaker.

Though Toomer seemed to the world to have given up writing after *Cane,* he was more prolific than ever, writing plays, novels, poems, and stories that publishers would not issue. The lyric celebrations of *Cane* had given way to Gurdjieffian didacticism and satire, and these in turn to a visionary mysticism. The bulk of his work, except for some short magazine pieces, a self-published collection of aphorisms, and a few other works, remained in manuscript at his death.

Her Lips Are Copper Wire

whisper of yellow globes
gleaming on lamp-posts that sway
like bootleg licker drinkers in the fog

and let your breath be moist against me
like bright beads on yellow globes

telephone the power-house
that the main wires are insulate

(her words play softly up and down
dewy corridors of billboards)

then with your tongue remove the tape
and press your lips to mine
till they are incandescent

1923

Gum

On top of two tall buildings,
  Where Seventh Street joints
The Avenue,
The city's signs:

STAR
J E S U S
The Light of the World

• • •

WRIGLEYS
eat it
after
every meal
It Does You Good

Intermittently, their lights flash
Down upon the streets of Washington,
The sleek pat streets some asphalt spider
Spun and tired of.
Upon a fountain in the square
Where sparrows get their water,
Upon the tambourines and drum
Of the Salvation Army jawing,
Hallelujah!
The crowd
          jaws Jesus
            jawing gum.

1923

Reapers

Black reapers with the sound of steel on stones
Are sharpening scythes. I see them place the hones
In their hip-pockets as a thing that's done.
And start their silent swinging, one by one.
Black horses drive a mower through the weeds.
And there, a field rat, startled, squealing bleeds.
His belly close to ground. I see the blade,
Blood-stained, continue cutting weeds and shade.

1923

November Cotton Flower

Boll-weevil's coming, and the winter's cold,
Made cotton-stalks look rusty, season's old,
And cotton, scarce as any southern snow,
Was vanishing; the branch, so pinched and slow,
Failed in its function as the autumn rake;
Drouth fighting soil had caused the soil to take
All water from the streams; dead birds were found
In wells a hundred feet below the ground—
Such was the season when the flower bloomed.
Old folks were startled, and it soon assumed
Significance. Superstition saw
Something it had never seen before:
Brown eyes that loved without a trace of fear,
Beauty so sudden for that time of year.

1923

Portrait in Georgia

Hair—braided chestnut,
coiled like a lyncher's rope,
Eyes—fagots,[1]
Lips—old scars, or the first red blisters,
Breath—the last sweet scent of cane,
And her slim body, white as the ash
of black flesh after flame.

1923

Song of the Son

Pour O pour that parting soul in song,
O pour it in the sawdust glow of night,
Into the velvet pine-smoke air to-night,
And let the valley carry it along.
And let the valley carry it along.

O land and soil, red soil and sweet-gum tree,
So scant of grass, so profligate of pines,
Now just before an epoch's sun declines
Thy son, in time, I have returned to thee,
Thy son, I have in time returned to thee.

In time, for though the sun is setting on
A song-lit race of slaves, it has not set;
Though late, O soil, it is not too late yet
To catch thy plaintive soul, leaving, soon gone,
Leaving, to catch thy plaintive soul soon gone.

O Negro slaves, dark purple ripened plums,
Squeezed, and bursting in the pine-wood air,
Passing, before they stripped the old tree bare
One plum was saved for me, one seed becomes

An everlasting song, a singing tree,
Caroling softly souls of slavery,
What they were, and what they are to me,
Caroling softly souls of slavery.

1922, 1923

1. Bundles of sticks.

Georgia Dusk

The sky, lazily disdaining to pursue
  The setting sun, too indolent to hold
  A lengthened tournament for flashing gold,
Passively darkens for night's barbeque,

A feast of moon and men and barking hounds.
  An orgy for some genius of the South
  With blood-hot eyes and cane-lipped scented mouth,
Surprised in making folk-songs from soul sounds.

The sawmill blows its whistle, buzz-saws stop,
  And silence breaks the bud of knoll and hill,
  Soft settling pollen where plowed lands fulfill
Their early promise of a bumper crop.

Smoke from the pyramidal sawdust pile
  Curls up, blue ghosts of trees, tarrying low
  Where only chips and stumps are left to show
The solid proof of former domicile.

Meanwhile, the men, with vestiges of pomp,
  Race memories of king and caravan,
  High-priests, an ostrich, and a juju-man,
Go singing through the footpaths of the swamp.

Their voices rise . . the pine trees are guitars,
  Strumming, pine-needles fall like sheets of rain . .
  Their voices rise . . the chorus of the cane
Is caroling a vesper to the stars . .

O singers, resinous and soft your songs
  Above the sacred whisper of the pines,
  Give virgin lips to cornfield concubines,
Bring dreams of Christ to dusky cane-lipped throngs.

1922, 1923

Robert Graves
1895–1985

Though Robert Graves claimed that he wrote them only for himself and his muse, his poems are not private or eccentric and do not present the immediate difficulties of much modern poetry. Traditionally formed, his poetry is craftsmanlike, lucid, orderly, and often companionable in tone. Graves chided many of his contemporaries—W. B. Yeats, Ezra Pound, and T. S. Eliot among them—for their slovenliness, their plagiarism, and their willful obscurity. His achievement was to blend epigrammatic tidiness and civility with an allegiance to the irrational and the mythic; like Yeats and William Blake, he pieced together his own mythology and proclaimed it the grand original of all true poetry.

Graves's important autobiography, *Goodbye to All That,* was an account of his life up to 1929. He was born on July 26, 1895, at Wimbledon, near London. His father, Alfred Perceval Graves, was an Anglo-Irish poet; his mother was German and related to the historian Leopold von Ranke. Graves's years in preparatory school came to an end when, a week before the outbreak of war in 1914, he joined the Royal Welch Fusiliers as an officer. He went to France soon after and saw a good deal of action, in a war that killed one in three of his school generation. Graves's autobiography sees continuities between his school experience and the war; the bloody-minded staff officers, for example, were only an exaggeration of schoolmasterly indifference. Though Graves was disgusted with both the officer caste and the civilians (his father among them) who enjoyed the war from a safe distance, he maintained respect for bravery and soldierly values.

Toward the end of the war, Graves entered an ill-fated marriage, and after the armistice, he studied at Oxford University. He was a friend of the psychiatrist W. H. R. Rivers, who had treated the war poets Wilfred Owen and (Graves's friend) Siegfried Sassoon. Rivers helped his patients by studying their dream-life, and he led Graves to a psychiatrically based theory of poetry, according to which the poet gives therapeutic expression to unacknowledged internal conflicts. Graves's Oxford thesis, published as *Poetic Unreason* (1925), argues that poetry has a "supralogical element" and that the "latent associations" of the words used in a poem often contradict its prose sense.

In 1926, Graves met the American poet Laura Riding, and their love relationship and intellectual collaboration renewed Graves's work. The two left England for Majorca, Spain, where, apart from wartime absences, Graves continued to live until his death. Riding encouraged Graves to write in a more ironic and concentrated style, and his blend of craft, clarity, and personal expression won the approval of the Movement poets in the 1950s. Riding and Graves wrote several prose tracts of great verve, including *A Survey of Modernist Poetry* (1927), which expounded ideas of close reading and multiple significance that influenced William Empson and the New Critics. But by 1939, the intense and turbulent relationship was over.

Graves had an extraordinarily varied literary career: he was a poet, a scholar and mythographer, a literary theorist, a writer of occasional essays and travel books, a translator, and a dramatist. Between 1925 and 1957, he wrote fifteen novels, most of them historical. In his poem "The Persian Version," Graves reminds us that the winners usually write the official version of a battle. As a historical novelist, he sought to give the "Persian version" of a number of events and figures, such as the Roman emperor Claudius I in *I, Claudius* (1934) and *Claudius the God* (1934), a man written off by most historians as a clumsy incompetent.

In 1948, Graves completed a profoundly influential book, *The White Goddess* (revised and enlarged, 1952), in which he reconstructs the matriarchal religions of the Neolithic period and the Bronze Age. Offering a "historical grammar of poetic myth," Graves gives simultaneously a version of history (he maintains that the Hebrews and Greeks perverted a matriarchal society), a view of the personality (the life of an individual recapitulates the events of the myth), and an account of poetic creation (all true poets worship the same muse). Though academic specialists were outraged by Graves's speculative foolhardiness, many readers have valued the book both for the light it casts on some of Graves's most beautiful poems (especially "To Juan in the Winter Solstice") and as a thesaurus of poetic motifs. If the early Graves thought of poetry as an expression of unanalyzed interior conflicts, the later Graves, proclaiming in *The White Goddess* his allegiance to objectivity and externality, saw poetry as a celebration of a mythic pattern beyond the poet, independent of the creative self.

The Cool Web

Children are dumb to say how hot the day is,
How hot the scent is of the summer rose,
How dreadful the black wastes of evening sky,
How dreadful the tall soldiers drumming by.

But we have speech, to chill the angry day,
And speech, to dull the rose's cruel scent.
We spell away the overhanging night,
We spell away the soldiers and the fright.

There's a cool web of language winds us in,
Retreat from too much joy or too much fear:
We grow sea-green at last and coldly die
In brininess and volubility.

But if we let our tongues lose self-possession,
Throwing off language and its watery clasp
Before our death, instead of when death comes,
Facing the wide glare of the children's day,
Facing the rose, the dark sky and the drums,
We shall go mad no doubt and die that way.

1927

Ogres and Pygmies

Those famous men of old, the Ogres—
They had long beards and stinking arm-pits,
They were wide-mouthed, long-yarded and great-bellied
Yet not of taller stature, Sirs, than you.
They lived on Ogre-Strand, which was no place
But the churl's terror of their vast extent,
Where every foot was three-and-thirty inches
And every penny bought a whole hog.
Now of their company none survive, not one,

The times being, thank God, unfavourable
To all but nightmare shadows of their fame;
Their images stand howling on the hill
(The winds enforced against those wide mouths),
Whose granite haunches country-folk salute
With May Day kisses, and whose knobbed knees.

So many feats they did to admiration:
With their enormous throats they sang louder
Than ten cathedral choirs, with their grand yards
Stormed the most rare and obstinate maidenheads,
With their strong-gutted and capacious bellies
Digested stones and glass like ostriches.
They dug great pits and heaped huge mounds,
Deflected rivers, wrestled with the bear
And hammered judgements for posterity—
For the sweet-cupid-lipped and tassel-yarded
Delicate-stomached dwellers
In Pygmy Alley, where with brooding on them
A foot is shrunk to seven inches
And twelve-pence will not buy a spare rib.
And who would judge between Ogres and Pygmies—
The thundering text, the snivelling commentary—
Reading between such covers he will marvel
How his own members bloat and shrink again.

1931

Down, Wanton, Down![1]

Down, wanton, down! Have you no shame
That at the whisper of Love's name,
Or Beauty's, presto! up you raise
Your angry head and stand at gaze?

Poor bombard-captain, sworn to reach
The ravelin[2] and effect a breach—
Indifferent what you storm or why
So be that in the breach you die![3]

Love may be blind, but Love at least
Knows what is man and what mere beast;
Or Beauty wayward, but requires
More delicacy from her squires.

Tell me, my witless, whose one boast
Could be your staunchness at the post,

1. See Shakespeare's *King Lear* 2.4.118.
2. Fortified projection from a castle wall. *Bombard:* a large medieval cannon.
3. A pun on the verb *to die,* in the sense of "to achieve orgasm" (common from the sixteenth to the eighteenth centuries).

When were you made a man of parts
To think fine and profess the arts?

Will many-gifted Beauty come
Bowing to your bald rule of thumb,
Or Love swear loyalty to your crown?
Be gone, have done! Down, wanton, down!

1933

Recalling War

Entrance and exit wounds are silvered clean,
The track aches only when the rain reminds.
The one-legged man forgets his leg of wood,
The one-armed man his jointed wooden arm.
The blinded man sees with his ears and hands
As much or more than once with both his eyes.
Their war was fought these twenty years ago
And now assumes the nature-look of time,
As when the morning traveller turns and views
His wild night-stumbling carved into a hill.

What, then, was war? No mere discord of flags
But an infection of the common sky
That sagged ominously upon the earth
Even when the season was the airiest May.
Down pressed the sky, and we, oppressed, thrust out
Boastful tongue, clenched fist and valiant yard.
Natural infirmities were out of mode,
For Death was young again: patron alone
Of healthy dying, premature fate-spasm.

Fear made fine bed-fellows. Sick with delight
At life's discovered transitoriness,
Our youth became all-flesh and waived the mind.
Never was such antiqueness of romance,
Such tasty honey oozing from the heart.
And old importances came swimming back—
Wine, meat, log-fires, a roof over the head,
A weapon at the thigh, surgeons at call.
Even there was a use again for God—
A word of rage in lack of meat, wine, fire,
In ache of wounds beyond all surgeoning.

War was return of earth to ugly earth,
War was foundering of sublimities,
Extinction of each happy art and faith
By which the world had still kept head in air,
Protesting logic or protesting love,

Until the unendurable moment struck—
The inward scream, the duty to run mad.

And we recall the merry ways of guns—
Nibbling the walls of factory and church
Like a child, piecrust; felling groves of trees
Like a child, dandelions with a switch.
Machine-guns rattle toy-like from a hill,
Down in a row the brave tin-soldiers fall:
A sight to be recalled in elder days
When learnedly the future we devote
To yet more boastful visions of despair.

1938

To Juan at the Winter Solstice[4]

There is one story and one story only
That will prove worth your telling,
Whether as learned bard or gifted child;[5]
To it all lines or lesser gauds belong
That startle with their shining
Such common stories as they stray into.

Is it of trees you tell, their months and virtues,[6]
Or strange beasts[7] that beset you,
Of birds that croak at you the Triple will?[8]
Or of the Zodiac and how slow it turns
Below the Boreal Crown,
Prison of all true kings that ever reigned?[9]

Water to water, ark again to ark,
From woman back to woman:
So each new victim treads unfalteringly
The never altered circuit of his fate,

4. This poem epitomizes Graves's "historic grammar of poetic myth," *The White Goddess* (1948), an intuitive study of ancient mythologies (especially Greek and Celtic) that finds the only theme for true poetry in the story of the life cycle of the Sun-God or -Hero, his marriage with the Goddess and inevitable death at her hands or by her command. Juan, Graves's youngest son, was born on December 21, 1945, one day before the Winter Solstice, which (as it is the time when the sun gives least heat and light to the North) is in many religions the birthday of the Solar Hero. Some of these heroes are Apollo, Dionysus, Zeus, Hermes, and Hercules of Greek mythology; Horus, the Egyptian sun god; Merlin and King Arthur; and perhaps Jesus Christ, whose life often parallels that of the Solar Hero, and whose mother, Mary, shares some characteristics of the Goddess.

5. Graves "decoded" the Celtic riddle-poem "The Battle of the Trees," by the bard Taliesin, who as a "gifted child" outmatched twenty-four experienced court poets; this insight began the series of researches and intuitions that resulted in *The White Goddess*.

6. Besides "The Battle of the Trees" (see note 5 above) Graves also cites an ancient druidic "tree-calendar" that describes the natural and magic properties of various trees and associates each tree with a month or season of the year.

7. The unicorn, the chimera, and the phoenix are some of the fabulous animals associated with the Goddess.

8. The Goddess sometimes speaks through "prophetic" birds such as the owl, the crane, and the eagle. She was sometimes called the Triple Goddess or Triple Muse because of her threefold aspect as Goddess of the underworld, Earth, and the sky.

9. "*Boreal Crown* is Corona Borealis, . . . which in Thracean-Libyan mythology, carried to Bronze Age Britain, was the purgatory where Solar Heroes went after death" [Graves's note]. The progression, or "turning," of the twelve signs of the Zodiac corresponds to the cycle of months.

Bringing twelve peers as witness
Both to his starry rise and starry fall.[1]

Or is it of the Virgin's silver beauty,
All fish below the thighs?
She in her left hand bears a leafy quince;
When with her right she crooks a finger, smiling,[2]
How may the King hold back?
Royally then he barters life for love.

Or of the undying snake from chaos hatched,
Whose coils contain the ocean,
Into whose chops with naked sword he springs,
Then in black water, tangled by the reeds,
Battles three days and nights,
To be spewed up beside her scalloped shore?[3]

Much snow is falling, winds roar hollowly,
The owl hoots from the elder,
Fear in your heart cries to the loving-cup:
Sorrow to sorrow as the sparks fly upward.
The log groans and confesses:[4]
There is one story and one story only.

Dwell on her graciousness, dwell on her smiling,
Do not forget what flowers
The great boar trampled down in ivy time.[5]
Her brow was creamy as the crested wave,
Her sea-blue eyes were wild
But nothing promised that is not performed.

1945

The Persian Version

Truth-loving Persians do not dwell upon
The trivial skirmish fought near Marathon.[6]

1. The King (or Solar Hero), reincarnated, reappears at the Winter Solstice floating in an ark on the water. The "twelve peers" may be, for example, the twelve knights of King Arthur's Round Table, Jesus' apostles, or even the twelve Zodiacal constellations (as suggested by line 18).
2. Two forms of the Goddess are Aphrodite, Greek goddess of love, whose emblem is the quince (the mythical or biblical "apple," since the modern apple was not then known), and Rahab, the Hebraic sea goddess who resembled the modern idea of a mermaid.
3. The snake of Ophion, who was created by the Goddess and mated with her: from their egg, the world was hatched by the sun's rays. The Sun-King must kill the serpent to win the Goddess; in turn, in October, the serpent (perhaps reincarnated as the boar of line 39) inevitably kills the King.
4. Cf. Job 5.7: "Man is born unto trouble, as the sparks fly upward." The owl and the elder tree are occult emblems of death. "The *log* is the Yule log, burned at the year's end" [Graves's note].
5. The boar is another symbol of death; Aphrodite's lover Adonis was killed by a boar. Ivy was eaten as an intoxicant by the priestesses of Dionysus in ancient Greece; if their October revels were interrupted by any man, they tore him to pieces.
6. The decisive battle of the first war between Persia and Greece, in which an Athenian force routed part of the Persian army. Modern historians consider this war far less significant than the second one, in which the allied Greek city-states defeated an enormous Persian army and navy of four hundred thousand men. "The Greek theatrical tradition" (next line) consists mainly of a play about the wars by Aeschylus; no information has survived about the Persian view of the battle.

As for the Greek theatrical tradition
Which represents that summer's expedition
Not as a mere reconnaissance in force
By three brigades of foot and one of horse
(Their left flank covered by some obsolete
Light craft detached from the main Persian fleet)
But as a grandiose, ill-starred attempt
To conquer Greece—they treat it with contempt;
And only incidentally refute
Major Greek claims, by stressing what repute
The Persian monarch and the Persian nation
Won by this salutary demonstration:
Despite a strong defence and adverse weather
All arms combined magnificently together.

1945

The Blue-Fly

Five summer days, five summer nights,
The ignorant, loutish, giddy blue-fly
Hung without motion on the cling peach,
Humming occasionally: 'O my love, my fair one!'
    As in the *Canticles*.[7]

Magnified one thousand times, the insect
Looks farcically human; laugh if you will!
Bald head, stage-fairy wings, blear eyes,
A caved-in chest, hairy black mandibles,
    Long spindly thighs.

The crime was detected on the sixth day.
What then could be said or done? By anyone?
It would have been vindictive, mean and what-not
To swat that fly for being a blue-fly,
    For debauch of a peach.

Is it fair, either, to bring a microscope
To bear on the case, even in search of truth?
Nature, doubtless, has some compelling cause
To glut the carriers of her epidemics—
    Nor did the peach complain.

1953

7. That is, the biblical Song of Solomon, ch. 2.

David Jones
1895–1974

David Jones is one of the few important British writers of the twentieth century whose poetry—multilayered and densely textured—is in the high modernist tradition of T. S. Eliot, James Joyce, and Ezra Pound. His writing is tied to the modernists' by its polyglossia, ritualism, mythical syncretism, formal discontinuity, and rich allusiveness. And yet Jones, unlike any other major British modernist, also belongs to another group of early twentieth-century writers—the poets of World War I. Jones served in the same regiment as Siegfried Sassoon and Robert Graves—the Royal Welch Fusiliers—though, as a private, he did not know these officer-poets. Unlike Sassoon, Wilfred Owen, Isaac Rosenberg, and Ivor Gurney, who wrote about the war during and immediately after it, Jones started to compose his major long poem about World War I, *In Parenthesis* (1937), a decade after the armistice. As a war poet, he writes with immediacy; as a modernist, he filters the experience through archetypes, elliptical forms, and incantatory rhythms.

World War I was, for Jones, a time of more than usually sharpened "consciousness of the past, the very remote, and the more immediate and trivial past" (*Epoch and Artist*). The foreground action of *In Parenthesis*—the soldiers' embarkation, their initiation into battle, the engagement in which the protagonist, John Ball, is wounded in the leg (as Jones was at the First Battle of the Somme, in 1916)—is surrounded with an aura of references to Shakespeare's history plays, Malory's accounts of Arthurian quests, Welsh epics of heroic and futile battles, and the Bible and Catholic liturgy. No action appears merely contemporary; each detail is associated with the heroic, human past. The effect of Jones's complex pattern of allusions is to magnify and dignify his nearly anonymous characters, with none of the denigrating mock-heroism of *The Waste Land* or *Ulysses.* Mixing prose and verse, Jones acknowledges his aesthetic affiliations with Eliot and especially with Joyce. Like Eliot, he annotates his poems and assembles them from fragments (modestly calling his second book, *The Anathémata* [1952], "fragments of an attempted writing"), while he praises Joyce as the "most incarnational of artists," who by his absorption in the microcosm reveals "macrocosmic realities" (*Epoch*).

An unusual plural of the word *anathema, anathémata* has two opposed dictionary meanings, either a thing "accursed or assigned to damnation" or a thing "devoted or consecrated to divine use." In this doubleness of meaning, Jones finds a verbal emblem for the enterprise of his literary life. Borrowing a phrase from the eighth-century British historian Nennius, Jones describes *The Anathémata* as a "heap of all that I could find," a heap of the "blessed things that have taken on what is cursed and the profane things that somehow are redeemed: the delights and also the 'ornaments,' both in the primary sense of gear and paraphernalia and in the sense of what simply adorns; the donated and votive things, the things dedicated after whatever fashion, the things in some sense made separate, being laid up from other things; things, or some aspect of them, that partake of the extra-utile [that is, of the more than merely useful] and of the gratuitous; things that are the signs of something other, together with those signs that not only have the nature of a sign, but are themselves, under some mode, what they signify" (*Epoch*).

As accumulations of things, Jones's poems have a spatial organization that recalls the earliest Welsh poets, whose work has been likened to "stone circles or the contour-following rings of the forts from which they fought" and "the interwoven inventions preserved in early Celtic manuscripts and on stone crosses, where what happens in a corner is as important as what happens at the centre, because there is often no centre" (foreword to *The Burning Tree,* ed. Gwyn Williams, 1956). Indeed, Jones derived many of his aesthetic principles from the visual arts; he was a painter some years before he began to write poems.

In *The Anathémata,* Jones makes a poem from the fragments of his life and past, a past that extends back into the prehistory of the British Isles. The basic structural model is the Roman Catholic Mass; individual books, in a fluctuating montage, present the Ice Age, the birth of Aphrodite, the founding of Rome and London, and the coming of the Angles to the British Isles. These polyphonous episodes include a retelling of the birth and death of Jesus, events conflated with the legend of the Arthurian knight Peredur and the Holy Grail.

Jones was born on November 1, 1895, in Brockley, Kent, to an English mother and a Welsh father. He attended art schools in London until he enlisted; after the war, in 1921, he converted to Roman Catholicism and joined the Catholic artist Eric Gill and his community of craftsmen in Ditchling, Sussex. Continuing to suffer from memories of the war, Jones had recurrent bouts of neurasthenia and depression, and after 1939, he retreated into relative isolation in Harrow, London. Through the years, he worked as a poet, a reviewer, an engraver, an artist, and a calligrapher.

From In Parenthesis[1]

From Part 4
King Pellam's Launde[2]

So thus he sorrowed till it was day and heard the foules sing, then somewhat he was comforted.[3]

Stand-to.[4]
Stand-to-arms.

1. "This writing is called 'In Parenthesis' because I have written it in a kind of space between—I don't know between quite what—but as you turn aside to do something; and because for us amateur soldiers (and especially for the writer, who was not only amateur, but grotesquely incompetent, a knocker-over of piles, a parade's despair) the war itself was a parenthesis—how glad we thought we were to step outside its brackets at the end of '18—and also because our curious type of existence here is altogether in parenthesis" (from the preface to *In Parenthesis*).
2. "King Pellam in Malory's *Morte Darthur* is lord of the Waste Lands and the lord of the Two Lands" [Jones's note]. He has been wounded in battle by the knight Balin, who had smitten him with a Dolorous Stroke that also laid his country waste, so that when Balin "rode forth through the fair countries and cities [he] found the people dead, slain on every side." For further details of the legend, see the notes to Eliot's *Waste Land,* above, concerning the Fisher King.
3. "Malory, book xii, ch. 19" [Jones's note]. In the quest for the Holy Grail, which King Arthur and his knights undertook, Sir Launcelot found himself in a wood near a chapel and dreamed that he saw the Grail heal a wounded knight; he then heard a voice banning him from the holy place because of his sinful life. Launcelot awoke and wept until dawn, then confessed his sins to a hermit to cleanse his soul for the quest.
4. "Shortly before daybreak all troops in the line stood in their appointed places, their rifles in their hands, or immediately convenient, with bayonets fixed, ready for any dawn action on the part of the enemy. When it was fully day and the dangerous half-light past, the order would come to 'stand-down and clean rifles.' This procedure was strict and binding anywhere in the forward zone, under any circumstances whatever. The same routine was observed at dusk. So that that hour occurring twice in the twenty-four, of 'stand-to', was one of particular significance and there was attaching to it a degree of solemnity, in that one was conscious that from the sea dunes to the mountains, everywhere, on the whole front the two opposing lines stood alertly, waiting any eventuality" [Jones's note].

Stealthly, imperceptibly stript back, thinning
night wraps
unshrouding, unsheafing—
and insubstantial barriers dissolve.
This blind night-negative yields uncertain flux.
At your wrist the phosphorescent dial describes the equal seconds.

The flux yields up a measurable body; bleached forms emerge and stand.

Where their faces turned, grey wealed earth bared almost of last clung weeds of night-weft—[5]

behind them the stars still shined.

Her fractured contours dun where soon his ray would show more clear her dereliction.

Already before him low atmospheres harbingered his bright influence.

The filtering irradiance spread, you could begin to know that thing from this; this nearer from that away over.

There at ten o'clock from that leaning picket-iron, where the horizon most invented its character to their eyes straining, a changing dark, variant-textured, shaped to their very watching a wooded gradient.

Skin off those comforters—to catch with their
cocked ears
the early bird,
and meagre chattering of
December's prime
shrill over from
Biez wood.[6]

Biez wood fog pillowed, by low mist isled, a play of hide and seek arboreal for the white diaphane.

To their eyes seeming a wood moving,
a moving grove advisioned.
Stand-to.
Stand-to.
Stand-to-arms.

Out there,
get out there
get into that fire trench.
Pass it along to Stand-to.

* * *

5. *Weft:* fabric. *Wealed:* ridged, as if with welts raised by a whip.

6. An area on the front line, fifteen miles south-east of Brussels.

From Part 7
The Five Unmistakable Marks[7]

* * *

Across upon this undulated board of verdure chequered bright
when you look to left and right
small, drab, bundled pawns severally make effort
moved in tenuous line
and if you looked behind—the next wave came slowly, as successive surfs
creep in to dissipate on flat shore;
and to your front, stretched long laterally,
and receded deeply,
the dark wood.

And now the gradient runs more flatly toward the separate scared saplings,
where they make fringe for the interior thicket and you take notice.
There between the thinning uprights
at the margin
straggle tangled oak and flayed sheeny beech-bole, and fragile birch
whose silver queenery is draggled and ungraced
and June shoots lopt
and fresh stalks bled
runs the Jerry[8] trench.
And cork-screw stapled trip-wire[9]
to snare among the briars
and iron warp with bramble weft
with meadow-sweet and lady-smock
for a fair camouflage.

Mr. Jenkins[1] half inclined his head to them—he walked just barely in advance of his platoon and immediately to the left of Private Ball.[2]
He makes the conventional sign
and there is the deeply inward effort of spent men who would make response for him,
and take it at the double.
He sinks on one knee
and now on the other,
his upper body tilts in rigid inclination
this way and back;
weighted lanyard[3] runs out to full tether,
swings like a pendulum
and the clock run down.

7. "[Lewis] Carroll's *Hunting of the Snark,* Fit the 2nd, verse 15" [Jones's note]. The Captain tells his crew of "the five unmistakable marks" by which they can identify the true snark: the taste ("meagre and hollow, but crisp"), its habit of getting up late, its lack of a sense of humor, its "fondness for bathing machines," and its ambition. In a way, these "marks" define the British soldier's life by contraries. The snark was found by one of the crew, but not captured, for it had vanished; so had the crewman.

8. German (British slang).

9. "Low strand-wire at about middle shin height, set some way apart from main entanglement [of barbed wire in front of the trenches], and often hidden in the long grass" [Jones's note].

1. A lieutenant.

2. John Ball, the central figure of the poem, is named for a medieval English priest who led the unsuccessful Peasants' Revolt of 1381.

3. A standard ornament of the British army uniform, worn at the shoulder.

Lurched over, jerked iron saucer over tilted brow,
clampt unkindly over lip and chin
nor no ventaille[4] to this darkening
                and masked face lifts to grope the air
and so disconsolate;
enfeebled fingering at a paltry strap—
buckle holds,
holds him blind against the morning
Then stretch still where weeds pattern the chalk predella—where it rises to his wire[5]—and Sergeant T. Quilter takes over.

Sergeant Quilter is shouting his encouragements, you can almost hear him, he opens his mouth so wide.
Sergeant Quilter breaks into double-time
and so do the remainder.
You stumble in a place of tentacle
you seek a place made straight
you unreasonably blame the artillery
you stand waist-deep
you stand upright
you stretch out hands to pluck at Jerry wire as if it were bramble mesh.
No. 3 section inclined a little right where a sequence of 9.2's have done well their work of preparation and cratered a plain passage. They bunch, a bewildered half dozen, like sheep where the wall is tumbled—but high-perched Brandenburghers[6]
from their leafy vantage-tops observe
that kind of folly:
nevertheless, you and one other walk alive before his parapets.
Yet a taut prehensile strand gets you at the instep, even so, and sprawls you useless to the First Objective.[7] But Private Watcyn takes it with blameless technique, and even remembers to halloo the official blasphemies.[8]
The inorganic earth where your body presses seems itself to pulse deep down with your heart's acceleration . . . but you go on living, lying with your face bedded in neatly folded, red-piped, greatcoat and yet no cold cleaving thing drives in between expectant shoulder-blades, so you get to your feet, and the sun-lit chalk is everywhere absorbing fresh stains.
Dark gobbets stiffen skewered to revetment-hurdles[9] and dyed garments strung-up for a sign;
                but the sun shines also
on the living
and on Private Watcyn, who wears a strange look under his iron brim, like a small child caught at some bravado in a garden, and old Dawes comes so queerly from the thing he saw in the next bay[1] but one.

4. The movable face guard of a medieval helmet.
5. "The approach to the German trenches here rose slightly, in low chalk ridges" [Jones's note].
6. That is, German snipers.
7. Of the assault.
8. "Refers to instructions given in bayonet-fighting drill. Men were cautioned to look fiercely upon the enemy when engaging him and to shout some violent word—and to not spare his genitals. This attempt to stimulate an artificial hate by parade-ground Staff-Instruction was not popular among men fresh from actual contact with the enemy" [Jones's note].
9. Woven fences used to stabilize the sides of ditches. *Gobbets:* pieces of flesh.
1. Of the German trench.

But for all that it is relatively pleasant here under the first trees and lying in good cover.

But Sergeant Quilter is already on the parados.[2] He sorts them out a bit
they are five of No. 1
six of No. 2
two of No. 3
four of No. 4
a lance-jack,[3] and a corporal.
So these nineteen deploy
between the rowan and the hazel,[4]
go forward to the deeper shades.

And now all the wood-ways live with familiar faces and your mate[5] moves like Jack o' the Green: for this season's fertility gone unpruned, & this year's renewing sap shot up fresh tendrils to cumber greenly the heaped decay of last fall, and no forester to tend the paths, nor strike with axes to the root of selected boles, nor had come Jacqueline to fill a pinafore with may-thorn.

But keepers who engineer new and powerful devices,
forewarned against this morning
prepared with booby-trap beneath
and platforms in the stronger branches
like main-top for an arbalestier,[6]
precisely and competently advised and all in the know,
as to this hour
        when unicorns break cover
and come down
and foxes flee, whose warrens know the shock,
and birds complain in flight—for their nests fall like stars
        and all their airy world gone crazed
and the whole woodland rocks where these break their horns.

It was largely his machine guns in Acid Copse[7] that did it, and our own heavies firing by map reference, with all lines phut and no reliable liaison.

So you just lay where you were and shielded what you could of your body.

It slackened a little and they try short rushes and you find yourself alone in a denseness of hazel-brush and body high bramble and between the bright interstices and multifarious green-stuff, grey textile, scarlet-edged goes and comes—and there is another withdrawing-heel from the thicket.

His light stick-bomb winged above your thorn-bush, and aged oak-timbers shiver and leaves shower like thrown blossom for a conqueror.
You tug at rusted pin—
it gives unexpectedly and your fingers pressed to released flange.

2. An embankment of earth behind the enemy trench.
3. A lance-corporal.
4. Types of trees, both reputed to have protective or divinatory powers.
5. Buddy. Jack o' the Green and Jacqueline (in following lines) are figures in old English folk dances.
6. Crossbowman.
7. Kaput, rendered useless. *Acid Copse:* also known as Acid Drop Copse, a forested area that Welsh troops were to take over as part of the First Battle of the Somme.

You loose the thing into the underbrush.
Dark-faceted iron oval lobs heavily to fungus-cushioned dank, wobbles under low leaf to lie, near where the heel drew out just now; and tough root-fibres boomerang to top-most green filigree and earth clods flung disturb fresh fragile shoots that brush the sky.
You huddle closer to your mossy bed
you make yourself scarce
you scramble forward and pretend not to see,
but ruby drops from young beech-sprigs—
are bright your hands and face.
And the other one cries from the breaking-buckthorn.
He calls for Elsa, for Manuela
for the parish priest of Burkersdorf in Saxe Altenburg.
You grab his dropt stick-bomb as you go, but somehow you don't fancy it and anyway you forget how it works. You definitely like the coloured label on the handle,[8] you throw it to the tall wood-weeds.
So double detonations, back and fro like well-played-up-to service at a net, mark left and right the forcing of the groves.

* * *

1937

From The Anathémata

Part III
Angle-Land[9]

Did he strike soundings off Vecta Insula?[1]
or was it already the gavelkind *ígland?*[2]
Did he lie by
in the East Road?[3]
was it a kindly *numen* of the Sleeve that headed him clear of South Sand Head?[4]
Did he shelter in the Small Downs?[5]

8. "I cannot recall what it was, either stamped or labelled on the handle of a German stick-bomb, but I know the sight of it gave me some kind of pleasure—just as one likes any foreign manufacture, I suppose" [Jones's note].
9. The first two parts of *The Anathémata* tell of prehistoric Britain, focusing on the Celtic inhabitants of Wales, and of the Roman conquest and occupation of England. In part III, Jones envisions the approach to the southern English coast of the first boat of the Germanic invaders, the Angles, who with the Jutes and Saxons took over much of England in the declining years of the Roman Empire. The Angles settled mainly in the county of Norfolk, which is still called East Anglia.
1. Roman name for the Isle of Wight, located off England's southern coast.
2. Island (Old English). *Gavelkind:* a Jutish custom of inheritance whereby if the father died intestate, his lands were equally shared among all his sons, rather than devolving to the oldest alone; this ancient law survived until 1925. "When I wrote this I was associating the system of gavelkind with the Isle of Wight solely on account of its being occupied by Jutes, who also occupied Kent, which county is particularly associated with that system and there is evidence of a sort of succession by gavelkind in the Jutish area in Hampshire opposite Wight" [Jones's note].
3. A protected area of the English Channel, south of Dover, where ships can anchor; a ship heading from the North Sea to the Isle of Wight would pass through it.
4. A spit of land surrounded by shallows on which the boat might have wrecked. *Numen:* a local divinity (Latin). *The Sleeve*: the English Channel (from the French, *La Manche.*)
5. Shallows off the Kentish coast north of Dover. In the following lines, Jones gives the names of other navigational points in the area.

Keeping close in, did he feel his way
between the Flats and the Brake?
But, what was her draught, and, what was the ocean doing?
Did he stand on toward the Gull?
did his second mate sound[6]
with more than care?
was it perforce or Fortuna's rudder, circumstances or superb pilotage or clean oblation[7]
that sheered him from smother
(the unseen necropolis[8] banking to starboard of her).
Or was it she
Sea-born[9] and Sea-star
whose own, easy and free
the pious matlos[1] are
or, was it a whim of Poseidon's[2]
(master o' the cinque masters o' lodemanage)[3]
whose own the Island's approaches are
that kept her?
Was the Foreland?
was the Elbow?[4]
under fog.
He might have been deeped in the Oaze![5]
Or
by the brumous numen[6] drawn on
or
in preclear visibility
by the invisible wind laboured
it might have been Dogger or Well
to bank her a mound[7]
without a sheet to wrap her
without a shroud to her broken back.[8]
Past where they placed their *ingas*-names[9]
where they speed the coulter deep

6. That is, measure the water's depth.
7. Ritual offering.
8. City of the dead, a cemetery. "It so happens that it was at Deal [a seaport north of Dover], c. 1903, that 'I first beheld the ocean' and I particularly remember that sometimes, in certain conditions of weather and tide, a number of hulks were visible on the Goodwins [the Goodwin Sands, a shallow patch four miles offshore, which is a notorious hazard to navigation] which then seemed like a graveyard of ships" [Jones's note].
9. Perhaps Aphrodite, the Greek goddess of love, who was born from the sea and was thought to be the protector of sailors; the epithet *Stella maris* (star of the sea) is often applied to the Virgin Mary.
1. Sailors (from French, *matelot*). "Cf. Archbishop David Mathew, *British Seamen,* p. 48, 'Easy and gallant they defend the freedom of the seas and the shores of England'. And cf. song, *All the Nice Girls Love a Sailor,* line 5, 'Bright and breezy, free and easy' " [Jones's note].
2. The Greek god of the sea.
3. " 'Cinque' [five] and 'lodemanage' [pilotage] to be said as in English, indeed as in Cockney English. (Each of the Cinque Ports had a pilot called the Master of Lodemanage)" [Jones's note]. The Cinque Ports were a federation of trading ports along the Kentish shore that provided the permanent nucleus of the British navy until the fourteenth century. Jones may also have had in mind the appointment of Winston Churchill in 1941 as Lord Warden of the Cinque Ports.
4. Parts of Kent that project into the English Channel.
5. "Cf. Oaze Deep, an area of water so named in the mouth of the Thames" [Jones's note].
6. Foggy deity.
7. Dogger Bank is a shallow area in the North Sea; Well Bank is the shallow water off the Lincolnshire coast.
8. Jones puns on a double meaning of sheets and shrouds, which are also ropes used in the rigging of sailing ships.
9. "Ingas" is ambiguous; it is an Old English word for meadows, but "Ing" is also a name for the oldest Germanic tribes and of a letter in their Runic alphabet.

in the open Engel[1] fields
to this day.
How many poles
of their broad Angle hidage[2]
to the small scattered plots, to the lightly furrowed *erwau,*[3] that once did
quilt Boudícca's róyal *gwely*?[4]

Past where they urn'd their calcined dead from Schleswig over the foam.[5]
(Close the south-west wall of the chester, without the orbit, if but a
stone's throw: you don't want to raise an Icenian Venta's Brettisc[6] ghost.
He'll latin-runes tellan in his horror-coat standing:[7]
IAM REDIT ROMA[8]
his lifted palm his VERBVM[9] is.)

Past where the ancra-man, deeping his holy rule
in the fiendish marsh[1]
at the *Geisterstunde*[2]
on *Calangaeaf* night[3]
heard the bogle-*baragouinage*.[4]
Crowland-*diawliaidd*[5]
Waelisc-man lingo speaking?
or Britto-Romani gone *diaboli*?
or Romanity gone *Waelisc*?[6]
Is Marianus wild Meirion?[7]
is Sylvánus

1. Old English for Angle; also German for angel. This evokes Pope Gregory's pun on seeing some British children: "They're not Angles but angels." The setting of the poem is now East Anglia. *Coulter*: blade of a plow.
2. One hide (Old English) was an area of land large enough to support a man and his family and small enough for him to cultivate; hidage was a land tax and also applied to the assessed value of the land. A pole is a unit of area about thirty square yards.
3. "Plural of *erw,* acre; err-wye [err as in error], accent on first syllable. Not in fact an acre or any fixed unit, but land equally divided among the members of a plough-team under the Celtic system of co-aration" [Jones's note].
4. "Gwel-ly, bed, but also used of the collective lands of a group. Typical Celtic ploughing was less deep than that of subsequent invaders" [Jones's note]. Among the "subsequent invaders" were the Romans (against whom Queen Bondicca of the Icenian tribe led an unsuccessful revolt in 60 C.E.) and the Angles.
5. The Angles, who are believed to have come from the part of northern Germany that is now the province of Schleswig-Holstein, practiced cremation of the dead; their burial grounds in East Anglia are the earliest evidence of their settlement in England.
6. "Pronounce bret-tish" [Jones's note]. "Chester" is an Anglicization of *castra,* a Roman military camp; near it is the stone circle of a Celtic fort. After their defeat by the Romans, the Icenians remained as a small tribal colony in Norfolk whose capital was Venta Icenorum.
7. The word order, and the word "tellan," are from Old English: "He'll announce (tellan) Latin mysteries (runes), standing in his horror-coat."
8. Now Rome returns (Latin).
9. Word (Latin). This may be an allusion to contemporary events, as Mussolini had revived some of the social and architectural trappings of ancient Rome in modern Italy; the Fascist salute, with raised palm, was also that of the Roman army.
1. "The Mercian saint, Guthlac, when an anchorite on Crowland Island in the Fens [of East Anglia], hearing the speech of surviving Britons, thought it the language of devils" [Jones's note]. "Ancra" is Old English for anchorite; in this line, Jones puns on the title of a famous middle English work, the *Ancrene Riwle* ("Rule for Anchoresses"), which prescribed the conduct of a holy life. Crowland Island is near the Deepings (line 88), hence the pun.
2. Witching hour (German). Jones uses German words occasionally to remind the reader of the Angles' Germanic origins; Celtic words are usually applied to the ancient Britons, Latin to the Romans.
3. "Winter Calends, November 1, cal-lan-gei-av, accent on ei pronounced as in height" [Jones's note].
4. *Baragouinage*: French term for speaking an incomprehensible language, either foreign or bizarrely unidiomatic.
5. "Devils, deeowl-yithe, accent on first syllable" [Jones's note].
6. Welsh. "Pronounced wye-lish" [Jones's note].
7. "The Roman name Marianus gave Meirion in Welsh; hence 'Merioneth' " [Jones's note].

Urbigéna's son?[8]
has toga'd Rhufon
(gone Actaeon)[9]
come away to the Wake
in the bittern's low aery?
along with his towny
Patricius gone the *wilde Jäger*?[1]

From the *fora*[2]
to the forests.
Out from *gens Romulum*[3]
into the *Weal*-kin[4]
dinas-man[5] gone *aethwlad*[6]
cives gone wold-men[7]
. . . from Lindum[8] to London
bridges broken down.

What was his *Hausname*?[9]
he whose North Holstein urn
they sealed against the seep of the Yare?[1]
If there are *Wealas*[2] yet
in the Waltons[3]
what's the cephalic index of the *môrforynion*,[4] who knell the bell, who thread the pearls that were Ned Mizzen's eyes, at the five fathom line off the Naze?[5]
On the past the low low lands of the Holland that Welland winds to the Deepings north of the Soke[6]
past where Woden's gang is *gens Julia* for Wuffingas new to old Nene and up with the Lark[7]

8. "Urbigena; cf. Urbgen [the Welsh king] in Nennius [an early historian of Britain], Urien [a British god of the underworld, identified in Arthurian legends with a king of North Wales] in the Romances. The late Gilbert Sheldon wrote: 'The Latin name Urbigena, city-born, is disguised as Urien'. Pronounce as urr-bee-gain-ah, accent on gain" [Jones's note]. Jones's pun contrasts a Latin name meaning city-born (especially in the city of Rome) and one meaning woodsman.
9. "Rhufon, rhiv-von, Romanus" [Jones's note]. *Actaeon:* a mythical hunter who was changed into a stag.
1. Wild hunter (German). The name Patricius applies to a member of the Roman aristocracy, a patrician.
2. Plural of *forum,* the center of economic and political life in a Roman town.
3. The race of Romulus, who founded Rome; in other words, the Romans.
4. Welsh-kin. "Cf. Wealcyn used by the Teutonic invaders of any group of kindred within those lands which had been part of Roman Britain. Pronounce, wa-ahl" [Jones's note].
5. "*Dinas,* City, din-ass, accent on first syllable" [Jones's note].
6. "Outlaw, aeth-oolahd, ae as ah + eh, accent on first syllable" [Jones's note].
7. Forest (Old English) men. *Cives:* Latin for citizen, commonly implying citizenship of Rome.
8. A Roman fort on the site of the modern city of Lincoln, 125 miles north of London.
9. Family name (German).
1. A river in Norfolk.
2. "Wa-ahl-ass, plural of *Wealh,* a Welshman" [Jones's note].
3. Several towns in Norfolk, such as Walton-on-the-Naze, have names including Walton (a contraction for walled town).
4. "Water-maidens, morr-vorr-un-yon, accent on third syllable" [Jones's note]. *Cephalic index:* the sum of two measurements of a skull; a tool of the science of physical anthropology.
5. The Naze is a peninsula, shaped like a nose, that extends into the North Sea. Jones alludes to Ariel's song in Shakespeare's *Tempest:* "Full fathom five thy father lies. / Of his bones are coral made; / Those are pearls that were his eyes" (1.2. 400–403). Ned Mizzen is a sailor (the mizzenmast being the hindmost on a sailing ship).
6. The Soke of Peterborough is a district in west Norfolk; there are two towns on the Welland River whose names include the word "Deeping." *The Holland:* an area west of the Wash, an inlet of the North Sea into which the Welland flows.
7. "The Wuffingas [a royal family of the Angles] that during the fifth-century invasions made settlements in the Fen Country [around the Wash], through which flow the Nene and the Lark, seem later on to have claimed descent from both Odin [ruler of the Germanic gods] and Caesar" [Jones's note]. *Gens Julia:* Latin for the clan of Julius Caesar.

past the south hams and the north tons
past the weathered thorps[8] and
the Thorpe
that bore, that bred
him whom Nike did bear[9]
her tears at flood
and over the scatter of the forebrace bitts
down to the orlop[1]
at twenty five minutes after one of the clock
in the afternoon, on a Monday
twelve days before the Calends of November
outside the Pillars[2]
where they closed like a forest
. . . in 13 fathoms' water
unanchored in the worsening weather.[3]
Far drawn on away from the
island's field-floor, upwards of a hundred fathoms over where, beyond
where, in the fifties, toward the sixties, north latitude[4]
all our easting waters are con-
fluent with the fathering river[5] and tributary to him: where Tamesis,
Great Ouse, Tyne from the Wall's end, demarking Tweed, Forth that
winds the middle march, Tummel and wide looping Tay (that laps the
wading files when Birnam boughs deploy toward Dunsinane—out
toward the Goat Flats).[6]
Spey of the Symbol stones and Ness from the serpentine mere[7] all mingle
Rhenus-flow
and are oned with him
in Cronos-*meer.*[8]
I speak of before the whale-roads or the keel-paths were from Orcades

8. *Ham, ton,* and *thorp:* Germanic suffixes included in English place names and meaning village or town.
9. That is, Lord Nelson, the great English admiral, who was born in Burnham Thorpe, Norfolk, in 1758; his ship in the sea battle of Trafalgar was the *Victory,* for which *Nike* is the Greek word.
1. Lower deck. *Forebrace bitts:* posts or cleats to which sailhandling ropes on a ship are made fast. Nelson was fatally wounded during the battle and carried below decks, where he died. The battle was won by the British.
2. That is, the Pillars of Hercules, otherwise the Strait of Gibraltar; the battle of Trafalgar was fought in the waters off the west coast of Portugal. In the Roman calendar, the *calends* of a month is its first day.
3. "See Collingwood's dispatch to the Admiralty Lords as reported in a contemporary edition of *The Times,* giving particulars of the action on Monday, October 21, 1805, and also James, *Naval History,* Vol. IV, 1837 ed.: 'Seeing by the direction of her course that the Victory was about to follow the example of the Royal-Sovereign, the French and Spanish ships ahead of the British weather [windward] column closed like a forest,' p. 38. "To add to the perilous condition of the British fleet and prizes [i.e., captured enemy ships], the ships were then in 13 fathoms' water, with the shoals of Trafalgar but a few miles to leeward,' p. 87" [Jones's note].
4. That is, in the North Sea.
5. That is, the Rhine, on whose banks the Angles and Saxons had lived before coming to England; it, like those English rivers that flow eastward, empties into the North Sea.
6. *Tamesis* is the Latin name for the Thames; the Ouse flows through Norfolk into the Wash; the Tyne River flows from the center of England past Hadrian's Wall into the sea; the Tweed forms part of the boundary between England and Scotland; the Firth of Forth runs through the boundary land (the march) of Scotland's Middle Kingdom; the Tummel River flows into the Tay, which debouches into the North Sea in northern Scotland. Jones alludes to the last act of Shakespeare's *Macbeth,* in which the Scottish king's castle is taken by Macduff, whose soldiers had camouflaged themselves with boughs from the forests around Birnam, a town past which the Tay River flows.
7. The Spey and the Ness are Scottish rivers (the latter originating in Loch Ness) that flow to the North Sea.
8. "The name used by the Classical writers for the unexplored northern waters" [Jones's note].

to the fiord-havens,[9] or the greyed green wastes that they strictly grid
quadrate and number on the sea-green *Quadratkarte*
one eight six one G
for the fratricides
of the latter-day, from east-shore of Iceland
bis Norwegen[1]
(O Balin O Balan![2]
how blood you both
the *Brudersee*[3]
toward the last pháse
of our dear West.)[4]

1952

9. In Anglo-Saxon poetry, the sea was conventionally called the "whale-road" and the "keel path." The Orcades (Latin) were the Orkney Islands, north of Scotland, in which the British navy was based during the two world wars; during World War II, the German navy made raids into the North Sea and the North Atlantic, then took refuge in the Norwegian fiords.

1. "I had in mind a squared chart issued for special service requirements by the German Naval Command, described as *Europäisches Nordmeer Ostküste von Island bis Norwegen, 1861 G.* [European North Sea. East Coasts from Iceland to Norway], on which the grid, numerals and other markings are imposed in green on a large-scale map of that area. Date c. 1940" [Jones's note].

2. "Cf. Malory [*Morte Darthur*] Bk. II, Cp. 18. How Balin met with his brother Balan and how each slew other unknown [not knowing they were brothers]" [Jones's note]. The Arthurian legend provides Jones with a metaphor for World War II, then being fought between Germany and England.

3. Brother-sea (German).

4. Jones subscribes to the ideas advanced in Oswald Spengler's *Decline of the West* (1922), which holds that Western civilization reached its peak in the early Middle Ages and has since been falling into decadence.

Austin Clarke
1896–1974

After the deaths of W. B. Yeats and Patrick Kavanagh, Austin Clarke became the preeminent Irish poet until the advent of a younger group. Clarke's poetry is like Yeats's in its use of Irish materials—the hero Cuchulain from the ancient sagas, the Old Woman of Beare from country stories—but differs in having a strong sense of sin. Conscience is overridden by passion, but only after a struggle. Clarke was unlike Yeats also in his rejection of rhyme and strong, traditional rhythms. Instead, he offered an almost antilyrical poetry, terse and unyielding, with sudden arrests of movement. In the place of rhyme he uses, for the most part, assonance, which, he says, "takes the clapper from the bell of rhyme" (introduction to *Collected Poems,* 1936). Clarke's work has rhetorical force, but rich words appear suddenly, as if from a thin-lipped mouth. A saturnine, brooding figure, he is at his best "where hail and honey meet" ("Pilgrimage"), in poems about love in which passion and its limitations are paralleled by the restrictions and liberties of his verse technique.

His use of assonantal effects was original in English and won the praise of W. H. Auden, a poet given to technical experiment. In a footnote in his *Collected Poems,* Clarke explains his procedure: "Assonance is more elaborate in Gaelic than in Spanish poetry. In the simplest forms the tonic word at the end of the line is supported by an assonance in the middle of the next line. The use of internal pattern of assonance in English, though more limited in its possible range, changes the pivotal movement of the lyric stanza. In some forms of the early syllabic Gaelic metres only one part of a double syllable word is used in assonance . . . and this can be a guide to experiment in partial rhyming or assonance and muting. For example, rhyme or assonance on or off accent, stopped rhyme (e.g. *win*dow: thin: horn: *mor*ning), harmonic rhyme (e.g. her*o*: wind*ow*), cross-rhyme, in which the separate syllables are in assonance or rhyme. The use, therefore, of polysyllabic words at the end of the lyric line makes capable a movement common in continental languages such as Italian or Spanish. These experiments were originally suggested by the submerged rhyme of [French poet] Paul Fort."

Clarke was born on May 9, 1896, in Dublin. He was educated at Belvedere College, a Catholic school where Joyce had also been a student, and then at University College, Dublin. His parents were nationalists, and he was strengthened in his own patriotic feelings by the Easter Rising of 1916, which occurred when he was at University College. He had been taught by Donagh MacDonagh, a lecturer and poet who was executed for his part in the rebellion. In 1917, Clarke took MacDonagh's place at University College, and in the same year he published his first book of verse. This and most of his subsequent poems and plays were on Irish subjects. His late poems were sometimes bitterly political, but the most important, *Mnemosyne Lay in Dust* (1966), was an account of his nervous breakdown.

Difficulties ensuing from an unhappy marriage obliged Clarke to move to England in the 1920s, and to remain there "in exile," as he said, until 1937. He supported himself by writing editorials for *T.P.'s Weekly* and anonymous reviews, often severe and crotchety, for the *Times Literary Supplement*. He also wrote four novels, which were banned for a time by the Irish Censorship Board. In a note to his *Selected Poems* (1961), he recalled being asked by Robert Frost what kind of poetry he wrote, and replying, "I load myself with chains and then try to get out of them."

The Planter's Daughter[1]

When night stirred at sea
And the fire brought a crowd in,
They say that her beauty
Was music in mouth
And few in the candlelight
Thought her too proud,
For the house of the planter
Is known by the trees.

Men that had seen her
Drank deep and were silent,
The women were speaking
Wherever she went—
As a bell that is rung
Or a wonder told shyly,
And O she was the Sunday
In every week.

1928, 1961

1. "In barren Donegal, trees around a farmstead still denote an owner of Planter stock [that is, a Protestant], for in the past no native could improve his stone's-throw of land" [Clarke's note].

The Young Woman of Beare[2]

Through lane of black archway,
The praying people hurry,
When shadows have been walled,
At market hall and gate,
By low fires after nightfall;
The bright sodalities[3]
Are bannered in the churches;
But I am only roused
By horsemen of de Burgo[4]
That gallop to my house.

Gold slots of the sunlight
Close up my lids at evening.
Half clad in silken piles
I lie upon a hot cheek.
Half in dream I lie there
Until bad thoughts have bloomed
In flushes of desire.
Drowsy with indulgence,
I please a secret eye
That opens at the Judgment.

I am the bright temptation
In talk, in wine, in sleep.
Although the clergy pray,
I triumph in a dream.
Strange armies tax the south,
Yet little do I care
What fiery bridge or town
Has heard the shout begin—
That Ormond's men are out
And the Geraldine is in.[5]

The women at green stall
And doorstep on a weekday,
Who have been chinned with scorn
Of me, would never sleep

2. Castletown Beare is an Irish port on Bantry Bay. The poem is set in southern Ireland in the mid-sixteenth century. "The episodes of this allegory are fanciful, but the Old Woman of Beare is a well-known figure in country stories. She had seven periods of youth before the climacteric of her grief. She speaks in a famous and classic poem: 'the lament of an old hetaira who contrasts the privation and suffering of her old age with the pleasure of her youth when she had been the delight of kings' (Kuno Meyer). . . . In Glendalough, that holy place, a man told me of a poor crone who had lived in the ruined settlement below the abandoned mines. She refused even the consolations of religion, for she remembered with great anger her own times of merriment and the strong mortals she had held, when silver and lead were brought down the mountainside, more than half a century ago" [Clarke's note].

3. (Catholic) church groups of lay people.

4. An Irish noble family that ruled the province of Connacht, in northwest Ireland; later, they assumed the name MacWilliam (line 114).

5. Thomas, earl of Ormonde, and Gerald, earl of Desmond, fought over control of Munster (the southwest province of Ireland, whose capital is Limerick) from 1564 until Desmond's death, in 1579. The "strange armies" of line 25 may be the Spanish and Italian troops that fought for the Geraldines.

So well, could they but know
Their husbands turn at midnight,
And covet in a dream
The touching of my flesh.
Small wonder that men kneel
The longer at confession.

Bullies, that fight in dramshop[6]
For fluttered rags and bare side
At beggars' bush, may gamble
To-night on what they find.
I laze in yellow lamplight—
Young wives have envied me—
And laugh among lace pillows,
For a big-booted captain
Has poured the purse of silver
That glitters in my lap.

Heavily on his elbow,
He turns from a caress
To see—as my arms open—
The red spurs of my breast.
I draw fair pleats around me
And stay his eye at pleasure,
Show but a white knee-cap
Or an immodest smile—
Until his sudden hand
Has dared the silks that bind me.

See! See, as from a lathe
My polished body turning!
He bares me at the waist
And now blue clothes uncurl
Upon white haunch. I let
The last bright stitch fall down
For him as I lean back,
Straining with longer arms
Above my head to snap
The silver knots of sleep.

Together in the dark—
Sin-fast—we can enjoy
What is allowed in marriage.
The jingle of that coin
Is still the same, though stolen:
But are they not unthrifty,
Who spend it in a shame
That brings ill and repentance,
When they might pinch and save
Themselves in lawful pleasure?

6. Drink shop, pub.

• • •

Young girls, keep from dance-hall
And dark side of the road;
My common ways began
In idle thought and courting.
I strayed the mountain fields
And got a bad name down
In Beare. Yes, I became
So careless of my placket,[7]
That after I was blamed,
I went out to the islands.

Pull the boats on the roller
And rope them in the tide!
For the fire has got a story
That while the nets were drying,
I stretched to plank and sun
With strong men in their leather;
In scandal on the wave,
I fled with a single man
And caught behind a sail
The air that goes to Ireland.

He drew me from the seas
One night, without an oar,
To strip between the beach
And dark ribs of that boat.
Hard bed had turned to softness—
We drowsed into small hours.
How could I tell the glancing
Of men that awakened me,
When daylight in my lashes
Thickened with yellow sleep?

My fear was less than joy
To gallop from the tide;
Hooded among his horsemen,
MacWilliam bore me tighter.
The green land by Lough Corrib[8]
Spoke softly and all day
We followed through a forest
The wet heel of the axe,
Where sunlight had been trestled
In clearing and in gap.

At dark a sudden threshold
Was squared in light. Men cast
Their shadows as we rode up
That fiery short-cut. Bench

7. Old word for pudendum.

8. A large lake in Connacht.

And board were full at night.
Unknown there to the clergy,
I stayed with him to sin.
Companies of carousing—
Was I not for a winter
The darling of your house?

• • •

Women, obey the mission—
Be modest in your clothes.
Each manly look and wish
Is punished but the more.
In king's house, I have called
Hurlers[9] and men that fight.
It is my grief that time
Cannot appease my hunger;
I flourish where desire is
And still, still I am young.

I prosper, for the towns
Have made my skin but finer.
Hidden as words in mouth,
My fingers can entice
Until the sight is dim
And conscience lost in flame.
Then, to a sound of bracelets,
I look down and my locks
Are curtailed on a nape
That leads men into wrong.

Ships glide in Limerick
Between tall houses, isled
By street and castle: there
Are flighted steps to climb.
Soon with a Flemish merchant
I lodged at Thomond Gate.[1]
I had a painted bedpost
Of blue and yellow ply,
A bright pot and rich curtains
That I could pull at night.

But in that corner house
Of guilt, my foreign face
Shook voices in the crowd,
As I leaned out to take
The twilight at my sill.
When tide had filled the boat-rings,
Few dealers could be tempted
Who drank upon the fair-day:

9. Players of "hurling," a rough Irish game game like field hockey.

1. A suburb of Limerick.

The black friars preached to them
And frightened me with prayers.

As I came to the Curragh[2]
I heard how, at their ease,
Bands of the Geraldine
Gather with joy to see
The going of young horses
At morning on the plain.
A mile from Scholars Town[3]
I turned to ask the way
And laughing with the chapmen,[4]
I rode into the Pale.[5]

The summer had seen plenty;
I saw but a black crop
And knew the President
Of Munster[6] had come back.
All day, in high and low street,
His orderlies ran by.
At night I entertained him
Between the wine and map;
I whispered with the statesmen,
The lawyers that break land.

• • •

I am the dark temptation
Men know—and shining orders
Of clergy have condemned me.
I fear, alone, that lords
Of diocese are coped
With gold, their staven[7] hands
Upraised again to save
All those I have corrupted:
I fear, lost and too late,
The prelates of the Church.

In darker lane or archway,
I heard an hour ago
The men and women murmur;
They came back from Devotions.
Half-wakened by the tide,
Ships rise along the quay
As though they were unloading.
I turn a drowsy side—
That dreams, the eye has known,
May trouble souls to-night.

1929

2. A large, open plain, southwest of Dublin, used as a battleground and for horse races.
3. That is, Dublin.
4. Merchants.
5. The English Pale was the area around Dublin, Ireland, directly under English governance.
6. A province in southern Ireland.
7. Pushing away. *Coped:* robed.

Louise Bogan
1897–1970

Louise Bogan was a poet of polished form, with a preference for compact design and musical cadence. Although she shared with the modernists a debt to symbolism, she was committed to traditional meter and rhyme, as she explained in her essay "The Pleasures of Formal Poetry" (1953). Within her tightly controlled, finely braided lyrics, often built around subtle contrasts and ironies, she sounded experiences beyond control, such as terror, paralysis, nightmare, and mortality.

Bogan praised the German poet Rainer Maria Rilke for qualities displayed by her own verse—the patience and power of looking and the ability to carry through a single poetic concept informed by passion. She also admired the lyric poetry of W. B. Yeats and W. H. Auden. Though her poems are terse and unadjectival, they are often visionary. This is so whether they work with personal experience, always distilled, or with traditional myth ("Medusa" and "Cassandra"). "Women" bitterly pretends to specify the qualities women do not have, but indicates those they possess. Bogan works with a chisel rather than a brush, priding herself on spareness of line and on avoiding sentimentality while making room for grief.

She was born on August 11, 1897, to parents of Irish descent in Livermore Falls, Maine; it was, she said, "[t]en years before Auden, Isherwood, and L. MacNeice, and about two thousand years after Sappho" (letter of May 1, 1938). She attended a school in Manchester, New Hampshire, and then the Girls' Latin School, in Boston; she finished her education with a year at Boston University. She had a daughter by her first husband, a professional soldier who died after they separated, and she subsequently remarried and divorced. From 1931 on, she had a series of nervous breakdowns. For many years, as poetry editor of *The New Yorker,* she set a standard of fair and unflattering criticism, whether the poets discussed were her friends or not.

Bogan was a no-nonsense person. Her mocking temperament made her suspicious of what she called "ego-airing," and in her friendships as in her verse she sought directness. In a prose book, *Achievement in American Poetry, 1900–1950* (1951), she celebrated the half-century for leaving Victorian deadwood behind and opening up "fresh sources of moral, as well as of aesthetic courage," and for dealing with "subconscious and irrational processes." Her own verse, though unmentioned in her book, is an excellent example.

Medusa[1]

I had come to the house, in a cave of trees,
Facing a sheer sky.
Everything moved,—a bell hung ready to strike,
Sun and reflection wheeled by.

When the bare eyes were before me
And the hissing hair,
Held up at a window, seen through a door.

1. One of the three Gorgons, Greek mythological sisters with monstrous faces, glaring eyes, and snakes for hair; their gazes turned mortals to stone. Medusa was decapitated by Perseus, but her gaze retained its power even in death.

The stiff bald eyes, the serpents on the forehead
Formed in the air.

This is a dead scene forever now.
Nothing will ever stir.
The end will never brighten it more than this,
Nor the rain blur.

The water will always fall, and will not fall,
And the tipped bell make no sound.
The grass will always be growing for hay
Deep on the ground.

And I shall stand here like a shadow
Under the great balanced day,
My eyes on the yellow dust, that was lifting in the wind,
And does not drift away.

1923

Knowledge

Now that I know
How passion warms little
Of flesh in the mould,
And treasure is brittle,—

I'll lie here and learn
How, over their ground,
Trees make a long shadow
And a light sound.

1923

Women

Women have no wilderness in them,
They are provident instead,
Content in the tight hot cell of their hearts
To eat dusty bread.

They do not see cattle cropping red winter grass,
They do not hear
Snow water going down under culverts
Shallow and clear.

They wait, when they should turn to journeys,
They stiffen, when they should bend.

They use against themselves that benevolence
To which no man is friend.

They cannot think of so many crops to a field
Or of clean wood cleft by an axe.
Their love is an eager meaninglessness
Too tense, or too lax.

They hear in every whisper that speaks to them
A shout and a cry.
As like as not, when they take life over their door-sills
They should let it go by.

1923

The Alchemist

I burned my life, that I might find
A passion wholly of the mind,
Thought divorced from eye and bone,
Ecstasy come to breath alone.
I broke my life, to seek relief
From the flawed light of love and grief.

With mounting beat the utter fire
Charred existence and desire.
It died low, ceased its sudden thresh.
I had found unmysterious flesh—
Not the mind's avid substance—still
Passionate beyond the will.

1923

Cassandra[2]

To me, one silly task is like another.
I bare the shambling tricks of lust and pride.
This flesh will never give a child its mother,—
Song, like a wing, tears through my breast, my side,
And madness chooses out my voice again,
Again. I am the chosen no hand saves:
The shrieking heaven lifted over men,
Not the dumb earth, wherein they set their graves.

1929

2. In Greek mythology, Trojan princess with the power of prophesy but cursed never to be believed.

Night

The cold remote islands
And the blue estuaries
Where what breathes, breathes
The restless wind of the inlets,
And what drinks, drinks
The incoming tide;

Where shell and weed
Wait upon the salt wash of the sea,
And the clear nights of stars
Swing their lights westward
To set behind the land;

Where the pulse clinging to the rocks
Renews itself forever;
Where, again on cloudless nights,
The water reflects
The firmament's partial setting;

—O remember
In your narrowing dark hours
That more things move
Than blood in the heart.

1962 1968

Melvin Tolson
1898–1966

Perhaps the premier African American poet in the high modernist tradition, Melvin Tolson was one of the most densely allusive and verbally dazzling poets of the twentieth century. But his poetry, especially the crowning achievement of his career, *Harlem Gallery* (1965), has only recently begun to receive widespread critical attention. Oblique and multilayered, rhetorically mannered and fiercely learned, the long poetic sequence *Harlem Gallery* was published at a time when the reigning paradigms in American poetry emphasized direct self-expression (the autobiographical proclivities of confessional poetry) and political assertion (the nationalist imperatives of the Black Arts Movement). Long after his death, as poets explore other possibilities, the significance of Tolson's contribution is becoming apparent.

Tolson was born on February 6, 1898, in Moberly, Missouri. His father was a Methodist Episcopal minister, and Tolson spent his youth in small towns in Missouri and Iowa. He was educated at Fisk University, in Tennessee, and Lincoln University, in Pennsylvania, and he later enrolled for a year in a comparative literature program at

Columbia University, where he wrote an M.A. thesis on the writers of the Harlem Renaissance. He spent his academic career teaching at two African American institutions, Wiley College, in Texas, and Langston University, in Oklahoma. Enormously successful as a debate coach, he was also a legendary speaker. From 1937 to 1944, he wrote a weekly column, "Caviar and Cabbage," for the *Washington Tribune*.

Composed under the pall of the Depression, his first book of poems, *Rendezvous with America* (1944), explores class antagonism and race relations in America, while also reflecting Tolson's interest in New Negro progressivism, which defied old racial stereotypes to foster a new African American psychology. In 1947, Tolson was named the poet laureate of Liberia and was commissioned to write a poem for the West African nation's centennial, *Libretto for the Republic of Liberia* (1953). Abstruse yet politically engaged, *Libretto* represented his first major effort to work in the high modernist style. In 1954, he began the first of four terms as the mayor of Langston, Oklahoma. *Harlem Gallery* was published a year before his death, after he underwent several operations for cancer.

Perhaps no work more successfully synthesizes the twin legacies of the Harlem Renaissance and Euro-American modernism than *Harlem Gallery*. As indicated by its subtitle, *Book I, The Curator,* this twenty-four part poem, divided into sections headed with letters of the Greek alphabet, was originally intended to be the first of a five-part poetic sequence on the history of African Americans. Like the modernist sequences of T. S. Eliot, Ezra Pound, and Hart Crane, Tolson's was an ambitious poem of epic proportions, interweaving multiple voices, narratives, and references. Allusion is the poem's primary device for sustaining compression, efficiently summoning stories, characters, historical events, and previous texts from a stunning array of sources. Upon the publication of his magnum opus, Tolson was said to have "out-pounded Pound." Neologisms, convoluted syntax, multiple layers of irony, and strained figures of speech also help create a forbidding verbal texture. While the meters of *Harlem Gallery* move freely in accordance with modernist paradigms, its stanzaic patterning is borrowed from the Pindaric ode. Attentive to the spatial form of poetry, Tolson manipulates the typographical layout of lines centered on the page, often creating visual puns.

Yet Tolson fuses these Euro-American inheritances with vibrant African American traditions. "I, as a black poet," Tolson said to an interviewer in 1965, "have absorbed the Great Ideas of the Great White World, and interpreted them in the melting-pot idiom of my people. My roots are in Africa, Europe, and America." Like such poets as Langston Hughes and Sterling Brown, Tolson brings African American oral traditions into literary poetry. He yokes the archival impulses of Euro-modernism to the performative energies of African American aesthetics. Oratory from the pulpit, blues from the dance hall, jazz from the club, and jive from the street converge in *Harlem Gallery*. The poem recalls African American oral practices in its exaggerated irony, boastful overstatement, and rhetorical indirection, its syncopations, puns, and occasionally insistent rhymes. Nothing here is straightforward: Tolson continually signifies, riffs, and embroiders.

The primary narrator of Tolson's long poem is the Curator of the Harlem Gallery, and this learned former professor of art is racially mixed, of "afroirishjewish origins." Perhaps his clearest foil among the many personages in the poem is the raucous and jive-talking Hideho Heights, the "poet laureate of Harlem." In the excerpted eleventh through fourteenth chapters of *Harlem Gallery,* Tolson juxtaposes a concept of the African American artist as folk-based, jazz-and-blues drenched—exemplified by Hideho Heights—and the more detached, high-art, Europeanized perspective of the Curator. In these two figures, Tolson fruitfully plays out the unresolved tensions in his own conceptions of the African American artist. The poem celebrates both traditions, but aligns itself with neither, revealing each to be partial and flawed when uninformed by its opposite. It enacts the implicit tension between the terms *Harlem* and *Gallery.* The relation between the Harlem Renaissance and Euro-modernism is one of the great puzzles of twentieth-century poetry, and it is embodied in the jazzy yet intricately allusive sections of Tolson's masterpiece.

From Harlem Gallery

Lambda[1]

From the mouth of the Harlem Gallery
came a voice like a
ferry horn in a river of fog:

"Hey, man, when you gonna close this dump?
Fetch highbrow stuff for the middlebrows who
don't give a damn and the lowbrows who ain't hip!
Think you're a little high-yellow Jesus?"

No longer was I a boxer with a brain bruised
against its walls by Tyche's[2] fists,
as I welcomed Hideho Heights,
the vagabond bard of Lenox Avenue,
whose satyric legends adhered like beggar's-lice.

"Sorry, Curator, I got here late:
my black ma birthed me in the Whites' bottom drawer,
and the Reds forgot to fish me out!"

His belly laughed and quaked
the Blakean tigers and lambs[3] on the walls.
Haw-Haw's whale of a forefinger mocked
Max Donachie's revolutionary hero, Crispus Attucks,[4]
in the Harlem Gallery and on Boston Commons.
"In the beginning was the Word,"[5]
he challenged, "not the Brush!"
The scorn in the eyes that raked the gallery
was the scorn of an Ozymandias.[6]

The metal smelted from the ore of ideas,
his grin revealed all the gold he had stored away.
"Just came from a jam session

1. "Lamba," the eleventh chapter of *Harlem Gallery,* introduces the poet Hideho Heights, whose rowdy, charismatic presence and call-and-response poetics contrast with the high-art aesthetic of the paintings in the Curator's exhibition. With his late arrival, Hideho just misses the opening of an exhibit of African American painting in the gallery. (The ensuing notes draw on Raymond Nelson's annotations in *"Harlem Gallery" and Other Poems of Melvin B. Tolson,* 1999.)
2. Fortune or chance in Greek mythology.
3. English Romantic poet and printmaker William Blake (1757–1827) contrasts the states of innocence and experience in his illustrated poems "The Lamb" and "The Tyger."
4. Attucks (1723–1770), who is generally believed to have been of African ancestry, became the first American casualty of the Revolution when he was shot in the Boston Massacre. Max Donachie is apparently a fictional painter.
5. "In the beginning was the Word, and the Word was with God, and the Word was God" (John 1.1).
6. "Ozymandias" (1818): Percy Bysshe Shelley's poem about a sneering, ruined statue of a king.

at the Daddy-O Club," he said.
"I'm just one step from heaven
with the blues a-percolating in my head.
You should've heard old Satchmo[7] blow his horn!
The Lord God A'mighty made no mistake
the day that cat was born!"

Like a bridegroom unloosing a virgin knot,
from an inner pocket he coaxed a manuscript.
"Just given Satchmo a one-way ticket
to Immortality," he said. "Pure inspiration!"
His lips folded about the neck of a whiskey bottle
whose label belied its white-heat hooch.
I heard a gurgle, a gurgle—a death rattle.
His eyes as bright as a parachute light,
he began to rhetorize in the grand style
of a Doctor Faustus[8] in the dilapidated Harlem Opera House:

King Oliver of New Orleans[9]
has kicked the bucket, but he left behind
old Satchmo with his red-hot horn
to syncopate the heart and mind.
The honky-tonks in Storyville[1]
have turned to ashes, have turned to dust,
but old Satchmo is still around
like Uncle Sam's IN GOD WE TRUST.

Where, oh, where is Bessie Smith[2]
with her heart as big as the blues of truth?
Where, oh, where is Mister Jelly Roll[3]
with his Cadillac and diamond tooth?
Where, oh, where is Papa Handy[4]
with his blue notes a-dragging from bar to bar?
Where, oh, where is bulletproof Leadbelly[5]
with his tall tales and 12-string guitar?

Old Hip Cats,
when you sang and played the blues
the night Satchmo was born,
did you know hypodermic needles in Rome
couldn't hoodoo him away from his horn?[6]
Wyatt Earp's legend, John Henry's,[7] too,

7. Nickname of influential jazz trumpeter and vocalist Louis Armstrong (1901–1971).
8. Character whose ambitions lead him to sell his soul to the devil, in a legend from Western folklore and literature. *Parachute light:* bright light supported by a parachute to illuminate military objectives from the air.
9. Early in his career, Louis Armstrong played in the band of coronetist and bandleader Joseph "King" Oliver (1885–1938).
1. Famous red-light district of New Orleans where jazz was born in the early twentieth century.
2. American blues singer (1898?–1937).
3. Ferdinand "Jelly Roll" Morton (1890–1941), jazz pianist and composer.
4. W. C. Handy (1873–1958), blues composer and bandleader.
5. Huddie Ledbetter (1888–1949), blues guitarist and singer.
6. Hospitalized in Rome after suffering a heart attack on June 23, 1959, Armstrong made a surprise appearance at a July 4 concert. *Hoodoo:* bewitch.
7. Black folk hero who died after defeating a steam engine in a pile-driving competition. Wyatt Earp (1848–1929): outlaw and lawman famous for his participation in the gunfight at the O.K. Corral.

is a dare and a bet to old Satchmo
when his groovy blues put headlines in the news
from the Gold Coast to cold Moscow.

Old Satchmo's
gravelly voice and tapping foot and crazy notes
set my soul on fire.
If I climbed
the seventy-seven steps of the Seventh
Heaven, Satchmo's high C would carry me higher!
Are you hip to this, Harlem? Are you hip?
On Judgment Day, Gabriel[8] *will say*
after he blows his horn:
"I'd be the greatest trumpeter in the Universe,
if old Satchmo had never been born!"

Mu

Hideho Heights
and I, like the brims of old hats,
slouched at a sepulchered table in the Zulu Club.
Frog Legs Lux and his Indigo Combo
spoke with tongues[9] that sent their devotees
out of this world!

Black and brown and yellow fingers flashed,
like mirrored sunrays of a heliograph,[1]
on clarinet and piano keys, on cornet valves.

Effervescing like acid on limestone,
Hideho said:
"O White Folks, O Black Folks,
the dinosaur imagined its extinction meant
the death of the piss ants."

Cigarette smoke
—opaque veins in Carrara marble—
magicked the habitués[2] into
humoresques and grotesques.
Lurid lights
spraying African figures on the walls
ecstasied maids and waiters,
pickups and stevedores—[3]
with delusions
of Park Avenue grandeur.

8. Archangel. *Seventh Heaven:* the highest heaven of the Islamic tradition.
9. During the Pentecost, the apostles begin miraculously speaking in foreign tongues they do not understand (Acts 2.1–18).

1. An apparatus used to communicate by flashing the sun's reflection in a mirror.
2. Frequent customers (French). *Carrara marble:* a white marble used for sculpture
3. People who load and unload ships.

Once, twice,
Hideho sneaked a swig.
"On the house," he said, proffering the bottle
as he lorded it under the table.
Glimpsing the harpy eagle at the bar,
I grimaced,
"I'm not the house snake[4] of the Zulu Club."

A willow of a woman,
bronze as knife money,[5]
executed, near our table, the Lenox Avenue Quake.
Hideho winked at me and poked
that which
her tight Park Avenue skirt vociferously advertized.
Peacocking herself, she turned like a ballerina,
her eyes blazing drops of rum on a crêpe suzette.
"Why, you—"
A sanitary decree, I thought. "Don't *you* me!" he fumed.
The lips of a vixen exhibited a picadill[6] flare.
"*What* you smell isn't cooking," she said.
Hideho sniffed.
"Chanel No. 5," he scoffed,
"from Sugar Hill."[7]
I laughed and clapped him on the shoulder.
"A bad metaphor, *poet*."
His jaws closed
like an alligator squeezer.[8]
"She's a willow," I emphasized,
"a willow by a cesspool."
Hideho mused aloud,
"Do I hear The Curator rattle Eliotic[9] bones?"

Out of the Indigo Combo
flowed rich and complex polyrhythms.
Like surfacing bass,
exotic swells and softenings
of the veld vibrato[1]
emerged.

• • •

Was that Snakehips Briskie
gliding out of the aurora australis of the Zulu Club
into the kaleidoscopic circle?

• • •

4. Innocuous, African predator. *Harpy eagle:* large, powerful eagle of South and Central America.
5. Ancient Chinese bronze money shaped like a knife.
6. Also *piccadill:* a fringe, often at the collar.
7. Section of Harlem where affluent African Americans began moving in the 1920s.
8. Lever device used for metal shingling.
9. Related to modernist poet T. S. Eliot (1888–1965).
1. Slight and rapid variations of musical pitch. *Veld:* African grassland.

Etnean gasps!
Vesuvian acclamations![2]

• • •

Snakehips poised himself—
Giovanni Gabrieli's[3]
single violin against his massed horns.

• • •

The silence of the revelers was the arrested
hemorrhage of an artery
grasped by bull forceps.
I felt Hideho's breath against my ear.
"The penis act in the Garden of Eden," he confided.

• • •

Convulsively, unexampledly,
Snakehips' body and soul
began to twist and untwist like a gyrating rawhide—
began to coil, to writhe
like a prismatic-hued python
in the throes of copulation.

Eyes bright as the light
at Eddystone Rock,
an ebony Penthesilea[4]
grabbed her tiger's-eye yellow-brown
beanpole Sir Testiculus of the evening
and gave him an Amazonian hug.
He wilted in her arms
like a limp morning-glory.
"The Zulu Club is in the groove," chanted Hideho,
"and the cats, the black cats, are *gone!*"

In the *ostinato*[5]
of stamping feet and clapping hands,
the Promethean bard of Lenox Avenue became a
lost loose-leaf
as memory vignetted
Rabelaisian[6] I's of the Boogie-Woogie dynasty
in barrel houses, at rent parties,
on riverboats, at wakes:
The Toothpick, Funky Five, and Tippling Tom!
Ma Rainey, Countess Willie V., and Aunt Harriet!
Speckled Red, Skinny Head Pete, and Stormy Weather![7]
Listen, Black Boy.

2. Etna and Vesuvius: European volcanoes.
3. Italian composer (c. 1555–1612).
4. Amazon warrior of Greek mythology. *Eddystone Rock:* coastal area with a lighthouse near the western end of the English Channel.
5. Frequently repeated musical motif or passage.
6. Relating to François Rabelais (c. 1490–1553), French writer known for his ribald humor.
7. Tolson identifies these artists as "'the real *ancients* of the Jazz World,' although their identities are not always readily recoverable now," according to Raymond Nelson. Gertrude "Ma" Rainey (1886–1939), the best known of the list, was the first great professional blues singer.

Did the High Priestess at 27 rue de Fleurus
assert, "The Negro suffers from nothingness"?[8]
Hideho confided like a neophyte on The Walk,[9]
"Jazz is the marijuana of the Blacks."
In the *tribulum* of dialectics, I juggled the idea;
then I observed
"Jazz is the philosophers' egg[1] of the Whites."

Hideho laughed from below the Daniel Boone rawhide belt
he'd redeemed, in a Dallas pawn shop,
with part of the black-market
loot set loose
in a crap game
by a Yangtze ex-coolie who,
in a Latin Quarter dive below Telegraph Hill,[2]
out-Harvarded his Alma Mater.

• • •

Frog Legs Lux and his Indigo Combo
let go
with a wailing pedal point
that slid into
Basin Street Blues
like Ty Cobb[3] stealing second base:
Zulu,
King of the Africans,
arrives on Mardi Gras morning;[4]
the veld drum of Baby Dodds'
great-grandfather
in Congo Square
pancakes the first blue note
in a callithump[5] of the USA.
And now comes the eve of Ash Wednesday.
Comus on parade!
All God's children revel
like a post-Valley Forge
charivari[6] in Boston celebrating the nuptials of
a gay-old-dog minuteman with a lusty maid.

• • •

8. American writer Gertrude Stein (1874–1946), whose home in Paris was the famous site of her bohemian salon, attributes this comment to herself in *The Autobiography of Alice B. Toklas* (1933).
9. In ancient Greece, the mysteries of Eleusis were characterized by an ecstatic procession of neophytes—or young novices—escorting sacred objects from Athens to Eleusis.
1. Medicine used to cure the plague, made of egg yolk and saffron. *Tribulum:* threshing machine (Latin).
2. In New Orleans.
3. Early baseball star (1886–1961).
4. In New Orleans, the final day of Mardi Gras is marked by the parade of King Zulu, parodying the white paraders. Comus, the oldest Carnival King picked by a white krewe (masking and parading club), appears in the last parade of the day.
5. Noisy parade. Warren "Baby" Dodds (1898–1959): jazz drummer who worked with Louis Armstrong and King Oliver. *Congo Square:* area of New Orleans famous as the site where African slaves would meet and make music. *Blue note:* flatted fifth note that characterizes the blues scale.
6. Cacophony. *All God's children:* phrase from a spiritual adapted by Eugene O'Neill in *All God's Chillun Got Wings* (produced in 1924), a controversial play about interracial marriage.

Just as
the bourgeois adopted
the lyric-winged piano of Liszt in the court at Weimar[7]
for the solitude of his
aeried apartment,
Harlem chose
for its cold-water flat
the hot-blues cornet of King Oliver
in his cart
under the
El[8] pillars of the Loop.

• • •

The yanking fishing rod
of Hideho's voice
jerked me out of my bird's-foot violet[9] romanticism.
He mixed Shakespeare's image with his own
and caricatured me:
"Yonder Curator has a lean and hungry look;
he thinks too much.[1]
Such blackamoors are dangerous to
the Great White World!"

• • •

With a dissonance
from the Weird Sisters,
the jazz diablerie
boiled down and away
in the vacuum pan[2]
of the Indigo Combo.

Nu

Rufino Laughlin
(M. C.)
peacocked to the microphone
as a fixed-on grin lighted his corrugated face
like the island pharos of King Ptolemy.[3]

The M. C. raised his hand,
Rufino Laughlin raised his voice,
in rococo synchronization.
"Ladies and Gents," he demosthenized,[4]
"the Zulu Club has a distinguished guest tonight

7. Hungarian pianist and composer Franz Liszt (1811–1886) lived much of his later life in Weimar, Germany.
8. Elevated train in Chicago.
9. *Bird's-foot violet:* flower common in the eastern United States.
1. Cf. Caesar's warning about Cassius in Shakespeare's *Julius Caesar*: "Yon Cassius has a lean and hungry look. / He thinks too much" (1.2.195–96).
2. Tank for quick evaporation and condensation. *Weird Sisters: Macbeth*'s witches. *Diablerie:* black magic.
3. Pharos is an Egyptian island whose name became a generic term for lighthouses because of the extraordinary one King Ptolemy II built there around 280 B.C.E.
4. Declaimed (Demosthenes [c. 383–322 B.C.E] was a Greek orator).

who has never let us down.
In a thousand years,
when the Hall of Fame
lies in ruins on genesis-ground,
the poems and the name
of Hideho Heights,
the poet laureate of Lenox Avenue,
will still be kicking around.
Let Harlem give a great big hand,
therefore and *henceforth,*
to a great big poet and a great big man!"

A boiler—a caravan boiler
of applause
exploded.
My thoughts wandered and wondered
. . . *the poet is no Crusoe in the Zulu Club* . . .
His nightly nightmare waterlooed,
the M. C.'s histrionic antics
drooped and crinkled:
leaves of a Bermuda onion
with yellow dwarf.[5]

Colorful as a torch lily,[6]
her hips twin scimitars,
a tipsy Lena
who peddled Edenic joys
from Harlem to the Bronx
plucked the poet's filamentous sleeve and begged:
"If you make me a poem,
Hideho,
I'll make you my one and only daddy-o
till the Statue of Liberty
dates
a kinkyhead."

The poet was no Gallio[7]
who cared for none of these;
so he tossed his palm slap into her buttocks.
Her wiggles were whisky-frisky.
"You're a *female* woman," he said,
grave as the falling accent of a Cantonese scholar; and then
the soul seemed to pass out of the body as he announced,
"Sister, you and I belong to the people."
The tipsy Lena's
giggles were the wiggles
of a coral fish's spinal fin
when it poisons and kills the alien next of kin.

5. A disease that yellows the leaves and stunts the bulbs of onions.
6. Red tropical flower.
7. Roman administrator who refused to interfere in religious disputes between Jews and Christians because he "cared for none of these things" (Acts 18.12–17).

From Xi

Hideho Heights,
a black Gigas,[8]
ghosted above us
in a fan vaulting of awkward-age lights and shadows.

Sudden silence,
succulent as the leaves of a fat hen, swallowed
up the Zulu Club.

He staged a brown pose that minded me
of an atheistic black baritone[9]
who sang blue spirituals that turned
some white folk white, some pink, and others red.

Hideho's voice was the Laughing Philosopher's[1]
as he said:
"Only kings and fortunetellers,
poets and preachers,
are born to be."

In spite of the mocker's mask,
I saw Hideho
as a charcoal Piute Messiah[2]
at a ghetto
ghost dance.

Does a Yeats[3] or a beast or a Wovoka
see and hear
when our own faculties fail?

Was it *vox populi*[4]
or the Roman procurator
who said to the
Roman who was not a Roman,
"Much learning doth make thee mad"?[5]

In a faraway funereal voice,
Hideho continued:
"The night John Henry[6] was born

8. Abnormally large plant.
9. Paul Robeson (1898–1976), American singer and actor associated with leftist causes.
1. The Greek philosopher Democritus (c. 460–c. 370 B.C.E.), commonly believed to have gone mad in his later years, is said to have spent his days laughing at the folly of human life.
2. Jack Wilson, a.k.a. Wovoka (c. 1858–1932) of the Paiute nation and a prophet of the Ghost Dance religion, taught that the ghost dance could summon a time when all white people would die and the world would be reborn without sorrow or death.
3. Irish poet W. B. Yeats (1865–1939) envisions the coming of a "rough beast" in "The Second Coming."
4. The voice of the people (Latin).
5. The Roman administrator or procurator Festus responds to Paul's explication of Jesus' death and resurrection with the exclamation "Paul, thou art beside thyself; much learning doth make thee mad" (Acts 26.24).
6. Black folk hero who died after defeating a steam hammer in a pile-driving competition.

no Wise Men came to his cabin, because
they got lost in a raging storm
that tore
the countryside apart
like a mother's womb
when a too-big son is born."

"Great God A'mighty!"
cried Dipsy Muse,
as his arm went halfway round
the calf's-foot
jelly mound
of the Xanthippean spouse
whom the whim
of Tyche[7]
had created in the image
of Fatso Darden.
The Birth of John Henry!
Murmurs ebbed and flowed:
soughing sounds
in the ears of a stethoscope.

• • •

The night John Henry is born an ax
of lightning splits the sky,
and a hammer of thunder pounds the earth,
and the eagles and panthers cry!

• • •

Wafer Waite—
an ex-peon from the Brazos Bottoms,
who was in the M.-K.-T. station
when a dipping funnel
canyoned the Cotton Market Capital—[8]
leaps to his feet and shouts,
"Didn't John Henry's Ma and Pa
get no warning?"

Hideho,
with the tolerance of Diogenes[9]
naked in the market place on a frosty morning,
replies:
"Brother,
the tornado alarm became
tongue-tied."

• • •

7. In Greek mythology, fortune. *Xanthippean spouse:* Xanthippe was Socrates' wife.
8. Dallas was the world's largest inland cotton market for many years. *Brazos Bottoms:* the Brazos is a river in Texas. The bottoms are in the Blacklands south of Waco. *M.-K.-T.:* Missouri-Kansas-Texas Railroad.
9. Greek cynical philosopher (d. c. 320 B.C.E.), who challenged conventions and promoted outspokenness; that is, impatiently.

John Henry—he says to his Ma and Pa:
"Get a gallon of barleycorn.[1]
I want to start right, like a he-man child,
the night that I am born!"

• • •

The Zulu Club patrons whoop and stomp,
clap thighs and backs and knees:
the poet and the audience one,
each gears itself to please.

Says: "I want some ham hocks, ribs, and jowls,
a pot of cabbage and greens;
some hoecakes,[2] *jam, and buttermilk,*
a platter of pork and beans!"

John Henry's Ma—she wrings her hands,
and his Pa—he scratches his head.
John Henry—he curses in giraffe-tall words,
flops over, and kicks down the bed.

He's burning mad, like a bear on fire—
so he tears to the riverside.
As he stoops to drink, Old Man River gets scared
and runs upstream to hide!

Some say he was born in Georgia—O Lord!
Some say in Alabam.
But its writ on the rock at the Big Bend Tunnel:
"Lousyana was my home. So scram!"

• • •

The Zulu Club Wits
(dusky vestiges of the University Wits[3])
screech like a fanfare of hunting horns
when Hideho flourishes his hip-pocket bottle.

High as the ace of trumps,
an egghead says, " 'The artist is a strange bird,' Lenin says."
Dipping in every direction like a quaquaversal,[4]
the M. C. guffaws: "Hideho, that swig would make
a squirrel spit in the eye of a bulldog!"

Bedlam beggars
at a poet's feast in a people's dusk of dawn counterpoint
protest and pride

1. Whiskey made from barley.
2. Cornmeal cakes.
3. Group of Elizabethan playwrights and poets known for their intellects and rowdy behavior.
4. Structure that dips points in all directions of the compass. The Russian revolutionary V. I. Lenin (1870–1924) probably never made the quoted remark, though he might very well have agreed with it.

in honky-tonk rhythms
hot as an ache in a cold hand warmed.
The creative impulse in the Zulu Club
leaps from Hideho's lips to Frog Legs' fingers,
like the electric fire from the clouds
that blued the gap between
Franklin's key and his Leyden jar.[5]
A Creole co-ed from Basin Street by way of
Morningside Heights[6]
—circumspect as a lady in waiting—
brushes my shattered cocktail glass into a tray.
Am I a Basilidian anchoret[7] rapt in secret studies?
O spiritual, work-song, ragtime, blues, jazz—
consorts of
the march, quadrille, polka, and waltz!
Witness to a miracle
—I muse—
the birth of a blues,
the flesh
made André Gide's
musique nègre![8]

• • •

I was born in Bitchville, Lousyana.
A son of Ham,[9] *I had to scram!*
I was born in Bitchville, Lousyana;
so I ain't worth a T.B.[1] *damn!*

• • •

My boon crony,
Vincent Aveline, sports editor
of the *Harlem Gazette,*
anchors himself at my table.
"What a night!" he groans. "*What* a night!"
. . . I wonder . . .
Was he stewed or not
when he sneaked Hideho's
Skid Row Ballads
from my walk-up apartment?
Then the You advises the I,
Every bookworm is a potential thief.

• • •

5. Earliest form of electrical condenser, presumably used by Benjamin Franklin in his famous kite-flying experiment.
6. Middle-class community around Columbia University, near Harlem.
7. Hermit following the teachings of the Christian bishop and reformer St. Basil the Great (c. 329–379).
8. French author André Gide (1869–1951) was fascinated by African and African American music, dance, and art.
9. In Genesis 9, Ham, the father of Canaan and the youngest son of Noah, is cursed when he sees his father naked.
1. Total blank, slang for complete failure.

Ma taught me to pray. Pa taught me to grin,
It pays, Black Boy; oh, it pays!
So I pray to God and grin at the Whites
in seventy-seven different ways!

I came to Lenox Avenue.
Poor Boy Blue! Poor Boy Blue!
I came to Lenox Avenue,
but I find up here a Bitchville, too!

* * *

1965

Hart Crane
1899–1932

Many American poets have sought to embrace all of America. What attracts them is perhaps that the country is so large, sprawling, and hard to handle. This grandiose sensuality goes back to Walt Whitman, who wrote, "I embrace multitudes." In the twentieth century, America's chief lovers included William Carlos Williams and Hart Crane. For both, America seemed a center of intense, multifarious feelings. They differ from regionalists, such as Edgar Lee Masters and Robert Frost, whose relations even to their regions were more ambiguous. Crane had his own complexities, but he overrode them in his effort to distill an image of America beyond space and time.

This ambition perhaps grew out of the dissatisfactions of his personal life. Crane was born on July 21, 1899, in Garrettsville, Ohio, a small town near the Pennsylvania border. After his mother, an emotionally troubled woman renowned for her beauty, suffered a nervous breakdown in 1908, the family moved into Crane's grandparent's house in Cleveland. His parents had a stormy relationship and divorced in 1917. Crane took his mother's side in the domestic quarrels, but feeling overwhelmed by her affections and demands, he eventually broke off his relationship with her. He was periodically estranged also from his father—the candy manufacturer who invented Life Savers and the epitome of the self-made man, he repeatedly urged Crane to become a businessman and to think of poetry as a hobby, even while lending him financial support.

In 1916, following his parents' separation, Crane dropped out of high school and went to New York to become a poet. He had little success with jobs, and his personal life was unhappy. For some years, he moved back to Ohio whenever his money ran out, but in 1923, he settled in New York, returning to work in advertising. He had several love affairs with men, including one with the sailor Emil Opffer that became the groundwork of a group of poems called "Voyages," among the most significant love poems of the twentieth century. His love relationships were often unsuccessful and depressing, but Crane found apocalypse everywhere. He saw all things—bridge, sea, river, ash can—as on the verge of transformation. By fits and starts of imagination and arduous revision in which he pushed his muse more and more violently, he composed impassioned poetry that knots together conflicting feelings. His sublime rhetoric and preoccupation with ecstasy were congenial to Charles Olson and Allen Ginsberg, but these poets did not attempt what is equally distinctive in Crane, his metaphysical compression.

Crane owed in his earlier verse something to A. C. Swinburne and Oscar Wilde's notion of incantatory poetry, but he soon fell under more powerful influences, chiefly T. S. Eliot and the French Symbolists. Through them, he attempted a poetry close to speech yet many-layered in meaning. Crane's visionary journeys and extraordinary metaphors also suggest Arthur Rimbaud. As for Eliot, Crane admired his attempt to encompass the present-day scene, but found him, in the early 1920s, too pessimistic. As he began to compose his own poetry, Crane seemed to regard his work as a counterstatement to *The Waste Land.* In a letter to Allen Tate of June 12, 1922, he declares: "I have been facing him [Eliot] for *four* years,—and while I haven't discovered a weak spot yet in his armour,—I flatter myself a little lately that I have discovered a safe tangent to strike which, if I can possibly explain the position,—goes *through* him toward a *different goal.* You see it is such a fearful temptation to imitate him that at times I have been almost distracted. . . . In his own realm Eliot presents us with an absolute *impasse,* yet oddly enough, he can be utilized to lead us to, intelligently point to, other positions and 'pastures new.' Having absorbed him enough we can trust ourselves as never before, in the air or on the sea. I, for instance, would like to leave a few of his 'negations' behind me, risk the realm of the obvious more, in quest of new sensations, *humeurs.*" Six months later, on January 5, 1923, he writes: "I take Eliot as a point of departure toward an almost complete reverse of direction. His pessimism is amply justified, in his own case. But I would apply as much of his erudition and technique as I can absorb and assemble toward a more positive, or (if [I] must put it so in a sceptical age) ecstatic goal. I should not think of this if a kind of rhythm and ecstacy were not (at odd moments, and rare!) a very real thing to me. I feel that Eliot ignores certain spiritual events and possibilities as real and powerful now as, say in the time of Blake. . . . After this perfection of death—nothing is possible in motion but a resurrection of some kind."

Most of Crane's poems, including his last, "The Broken Tower," celebrate crucifixion and resurrection, horror or squalor out of which suddenly radiate hope and light. In "Chaplinesque," an ash can becomes a grail—a characteristic transformation. In a letter of November 3, 1921, about Charlie Chaplin, he writes, "Chaplin may be a sentimentalist, after all, but he carries the theme with such power and universal portent that sentimentality is made to transcend itself." This can also be said of Crane. He takes unusual words, combines them in an unusual way, and forms them into unexpected rhythms, as if his technique as well as his subject matter were intended to expand the boundaries of consciousness. When he was reproved for the difficulty of his work, Crane explained, in a 1926 letter to Harriet Monroe, the editor of *Poetry* magazine, that his object was to find a *logic of metaphor* that would not be the *logic of rational thought.* This pursuit of unconscious interconnections of "emotional dynamics" working through abbreviated thoughts is different from the explained images of the Metaphysical poets; it works by sudden, forced conjunctions that find their justification at deeper levels of meaning. Crane has as much complexity as any modern poet, but largely self-taught, he does not present himself as difficult and allusive; rather, his powerful speech and rhythms claim the instant response that his intricate images would seem to delay.

Crane's major poem is *The Bridge,* begun early in 1923 and published in 1930. "Very roughly," he wrote a friend on February 18, 1923, "it concerns a mystical synthesis of 'America.' History and fact, location, etc. all have to be transfigured into abstract form that would almost function independently of its subject matter. The initial impulses of 'our people' will have to be gathered up toward the climax of the bridge, symbol of our constructive future, our unique identity, in which is included also our scientific hopes and achievements of the future. The mystic portent of all this is already flocking through my mind." The bridge is a symbol of human and superhuman experience combined; it spans the river, the sea, and time and space. Crane said he intended it to be the myth of America. The bridge suggests something that encompasses and transcends what is below it, as in the section "To Brooklyn Bridge," which would subsume all twentieth-century America. Crane accepts the machine, though horrible, as part of this mode of intensity. Densely packed with vivid imagery, the poem as a whole projects furious feelings of hope onto the Brooklyn Bridge, in contrast to Eliot's *Waste Land,* which depicts London Bridge as the bleak site of modern alienation and dehumanization.

One of the great long poems of the twentieth century, *The Bridge* is about twelve hundred lines in fifteen sections. Although every piece of the poem has the stamp of Crane's linguistic intensity, the form varies from section to section, ranging from free verse and syncopated rhythms to blank verse and ballad. The epic reach of the poem is also visible in its historical scope, extending from the Native American origins of America to the arrival of Christopher Columbus to industrialized modernity. Its cast of characters is also heterogeneous, including types such as the drunken sailor and the hobo, historical figures such as Pocahontas, and poets such as Walt Whitman and Edgar Allan Poe. Amid its sprawling exuberance, the poem has a shape, moving geographically from east to west—Brooklyn to California—and historically from the present deep into the American past. The poem's opening sections are full of wonder and discovery, but *The Bridge* also has an epic descent into hell, reaching its nadir in "The Tunnel," before it concludes, in "Atlantis," with an ecstatic affirmation. Various images, such as the bridge, the serpent and the eagle, and the crescent ring, recur and change over the course of the poem, gaining resonances in each iteration. Crane fervently tries to forge a mode of poetry that will embrace and yet override all contraries—Native Americans and Europeans, history and modernity, the sacred and the profane.

Crane's life was a series of attempts at self-transformation. In his last year, he received a Guggenheim Fellowship to write in Mexico. He had a love affair in Mexico with a woman, Peggy Cowley, but on the ship back—drunk, beaten and robbed the night before, in despair over the loss of his father's estate in the Great Depression and over what he thought was the drying up of his poetic powers—he suddenly went to her stateroom to bid her goodbye; she thought he was joking, but he went on deck and jumped into the Caribbean Sea. Accounts differ as to whether or not he tried to catch the life preserver that was thrown to him. He was thirty-two.

Crane's poetry is always close to disaster, a form of brinkmanship, but it is saved by gathering the disaster into a new, ecstatic focus. His poems have a constant doubleness—the sea is death and love, the bridge from which the suicide falls is also the summit of wonder and hope. In our time, Crane looks perhaps gaudy, insistent, obscure; we may feel that he strained after intensity. But he succeeded in establishing a polar opposite to Eliot's early poetry, in getting to the other side of despair (as Eliot himself tried to do later) with his full-throated, daring, secular but visionary poetry. Ultimately, Crane wins us not so much because of his grand sleights, but because of the misery that can be felt pressing up from below them; "through all sounds of gaiety and quest" he has heard "a kitten crying in the wilderness."

Black Tambourine[1]

The interests of a black man in a cellar
Mark tardy judgment on the world's closed door.
Gnats toss in the shadow of a bottle,
And a roach spans a crevice in the floor.

Aesop,[2] driven to pondering, found
Heaven with the tortoise and the hare;
Fox brush and sow ear top his grave
And mingling incantations on the air.

The black man, forlorn in the cellar,
Wanders in some mid-kingdom, dark, that lies,
Between his tambourine, stuck on the wall,
And, in Africa, a carcass quick with flies.

1926

Chaplinesque[3]

We make our meek adjustments,
Contented with such random consolations
As the wind deposits
In slithered and too ample pockets.

For we can still love the world, who find
A famished kitten on the step, and know
Recesses for it from the fury of the street,
Or warm torn elbow coverts.

1. For a few weeks in 1921, Crane was in charge of a storeroom in the basement of his father's restaurant in Cleveland, where he worked alongside an African American porter. In a letter, Crane writes: "The Word 'mid-kingdom' is perhaps the key word to what ideas there are in it. The poem is a description and bundle of insinuations, suggestions bearing out the negro's place somewhere between man and beast. That is why Aesop is brought in, etc.—the popular conception of negro romance, the tambourine on the wall. The value of the poem is only, to me, in what a painter would call its 'tactile' quality,—an entirely aesthetic feature. A propagandist for either side of the negro question could find anything he wanted to in it. My one declaration in it is that I find the negro (in the popular mind) sentimentally or brutally 'placed' in this midkingdom. etc." In another letter, he writes: "What I want to get is . . . an 'interior' form, a form that is so thorough and intense as to dye the words themselves with a peculiarity of meaning, slightly different maybe from the ordinary definition of them separate from the poem" (*O My Land, My Friends: The Selected Letters of Hart Crane,* ed. Langdon Hammer and Brom Weber, 1997, 64, 79).

2. Thought to have been a Greek slave, to whom many animal fables are attributed.

3. Crane was delighted by Charlie Chaplin's movie *The Kid* (1921). He considered Chaplin "a dramatic genius that truly approaches the fabulous sort." In a letter, he explained this poem: "I am moved to put Chaplin with the poets (of today); hence the 'we.' In other words, he, especially in *The Kid,* made me feel myself, as a poet, as being 'in the same boat' with him. Poetry, the human feelings, 'the kitten,' is so crowded out of the humdrum, rushing, mechanical scramble of today that the man who would preserve them must duck and camouflage for dear life to keep them or keep himself from annihilation" (*O My Land,* 70). To the charge that the film was sentimental, Crane replied: "Chaplin may be a sentimentalist, after all, but he carries the theme with such power and universal portent that sentimentality is made to transcend itself into a new kind of tragedy, eccentric, homely and yet brilliant. It is because I feel that I have captured the arrested climaxes and evasive victories of his gestures in words, somehow, that I like the poem as much as anything I have done" (*Selected Letters,* ed. Brom Weber, 1965, 69).

We will sidestep, and to the final smirk
Dally the doom of that inevitable thumb
That slowly chafes its puckered index toward us,
Facing the dull squint with what innocence
And what surprise!

And yet these fine collapses are not lies
More than the pirouettes of any pliant cane;
Our obsequies are, in a way, no enterprise.
We can evade you, and all else but the heart:
What blame to us if the heart[4] live on.

The game enforces smirks; but we have seen
The moon in lonely alleys make
A grail of laughter of an empty ash can,
And through all sound of gaiety and quest
Have heard a kitten in the wilderness.

1926

Repose of Rivers

The willows carried a slow sound,
A sarabande[5] the wind mowed on the mead.
I could never remember
That seething, steady leveling of the marshes
Till age had brought me to the sea.

Flags, weeds. And remembrance of steep alcoves
Where cypresses shared the noon's
Tyranny; they drew me into hades[6] almost.
And mammoth turtles climbing sulphur dreams
Yielded, while sun-silt rippled them
Asunder . . .

How much I would have bartered! the black gorge
And all the singular nestings in the hills
Where beavers learn stitch and tooth.
The pond I entered once and quickly fled—
I remember now its singing willow rim.

And finally, in that memory all things nurse;
After the city that I finally passed
With scalding unguents[7] spread and smoking darts
The monsoon cut across the delta
At gulf gates . . . There, beyond the dykes

4. According to Crane, a deliberate pun on his first name.
5. A stately court dance from the seventeenth and eighteenth centuries.
6. The underworld of Greek mythology; Hell.
7. Ointments.

I heard wind flaking sapphire, like this summer,
And willows could not hold more steady sound.

1926

At Melville's Tomb[8]

Often beneath the wave, wide from this ledge
The dice of drowned men's bones he saw bequeath
An embassy. Their numbers as he watched,
Beat on the dusty shore and were obscured.

And wrecks passed without sound of bells,
The calyx[9] of death's bounty giving back
A scattered chapter, livid hieroglyph,
The portent wound in corridors of shells.

Then in the circuit calm of one vast coil,
Its lashings charmed and malice reconciled,
Frosted eyes there were that lifted altars;
And silent answers crept across the stars.

Compass, quadrant and sextant contrive
No farther tides . . . High in the azure steeps
Monody shall not wake the mariner.
This fabulous shadow only the sea keeps.

1926

Voyages[1]

I

Above the fresh ruffles of the surf
Bright striped urchins flay each other with sand.
They have contrived a conquest for shell shucks,
And their fingers crumble fragments of baked weed
Gaily digging and scattering.

And in answer to their treble interjections
The sun beats lightning on the waves,
The waves fold thunder on the sand;
And could they hear me I would tell them:

8. Herman Melville (1819–1891), American writer, is buried at Woodlawn Cemetery, in New York City. See Crane's letter to Harriet Monroe explicating the poem, p. 968 of this volume.

9. Outer whorl of a flower bud.

1. A series of six love poems, the outcome of a passionate affair with Emil Opffer, a merchant seaman.

O brilliant kids, frisk with your dog,
Fondle your shells and sticks, bleached
By time and the elements; but there is a line
You must not cross nor ever trust beyond it
Spry cordage of your bodies to caresses
Too lichen-faithful from too wide a breast.
The bottom of the sea is cruel.

II

—And yet this great wink of eternity,
Of rimless floods, unfettered leewardings,
Samite sheeted and processioned where
Her undinal[2] vast belly moonward bends,
Laughing the wrapt inflections of our love;

Take this Sea, whose diapason[3] knells
On scrolls of silver snowy sentences,
The sceptred terror of whose sessions rends
As her demeanors motion well or ill,
All but the pieties of lovers' hands.

And onward, as bells off San Salvador[4]
Salute the crocus lustres of the stars,
In these poinsettia meadows of her tides,—
Adagios of islands, O my Prodigal,[5]
Complete the dark confessions her veins spell.

Mark how her turning shoulders wind the hours,
And hasten while her penniless rich palms
Pass superscription of bent foam and wave,—
Hasten, while they are true,—sleep, death, desire,
Close round one instant in one floating flower.

Bind us in time, O Seasons clear, and awe.
O minstrel galleons of Carib fire,
Bequeath us to no earthly shore until
Is answered in the vortex of our grave
The seal's wide spindrift gaze toward paradise.

2. Associated with undines, water nymphs. *Leewardings:* a ship's movements away from the wind. *Samite:* a rich, silk fabric, sometimes woven with gold.
3. Deep burst of sound.
4. Crane alludes to a legend, told to him by Opffer, of a buried city beneath the Pacific Ocean, off San Salvador.
5. Wasteful, lavish one (cf. the Prodigal Son of Luke 15). *Adagios:* slow and graceful parts of a composition. In the essay "General Aims and Theories," Crane explains, "When . . . I speak of 'adagios of islands,' the reference is to the motion of a boat through islands clustered thickly, the rhythm of the motion, etc. And it seems a much more direct and creative statement than any more logical employment of words such as 'coasting slowly through the islands,' besides ushering in a whole world of music."

III

Infinite consanguinity[6] it bears—
This tendered theme of you that light
Retrieves from sea plains where the sky
Resigns a breast that every wave enthrones;
While ribboned water lanes I wind
Are laved and scattered with no stroke
Wide from your side, whereto this hour
The sea lifts, also, reliquary hands.

And so, admitted through black swollen gates
That must arrest all distance otherwise,—
Past whirling pillars and lithe pediments,
Light wrestling there incessantly with light,
Star kissing star through wave on wave unto
Your body rocking!
                                    and where death, if shed,
Presumes no carnage, but this single change,—
Upon the steep floor flung from dawn to dawn
The silken skilled transmemberment of song;

Permit me voyage, love, into your hands . . .

IV

Whose counted smile of hours and days, suppose
I know as spectrum of the sea and pledge
Vastly now parting gulf on gulf of wings
Whose circles bridge, I know, (from palms to the severe
Chilled albatross's white immutability)
No stream of greater love advancing now
Than, singing, this mortality alone
Through clay aflow immortally to you.

All fragrance irrefragably,[7] and claim
Madly meeting logically in this hour
And region that is ours to wreathe again,
Portending eyes and lips and making told
The chancel port[8] and portion of our June—

Shall they not stem and close in our own steps
Bright staves of flowers and quills today as I
Must first be lost in fatal tides to tell?

In signature of the incarnate word
The harbor shoulders to resign in mingling
Mutual blood, transpiring as foreknown
And widening noon within your breast for gathering

6. Oneness, as if by blood kinship.
7. Unalterably.
8. *Chancel:* the part of the church that includes the sanctuary, hence the most sacred or cherished part.

All bright insinuations that my years have caught
For islands where must lead inviolably
Blue latitudes and levels of your eyes,—

In this expectant, still exclaim receive
The secret oar and petals of all love.

V

Meticulous, past midnight in clear rime,
Infrangible[9] and lonely, smooth as though cast
Together in one merciless white blade—
The bay estuaries fleck the hard sky limits.

—As if too brittle or too clear to touch!
The cables of our sleep so swiftly filed,
Already hang, shred ends from remembered stars.
One frozen trackless smile . . . What words
Can strangle this deaf moonlight? For we

Are overtaken. Now no cry, no sword
Can fasten or deflect this tidal wedge,
Slow tyranny of moonlight, moonlight loved
And changed . . . "There's

Nothing like this in the world," you say,
Knowing I cannot touch your hand and look
Too, into that godless cleft of sky
Where nothing turns but dead sands flashing.

"—And never to quite understand!" No,
In all the argosy of your bright hair I dreamed
Nothing so flagless as this piracy.

But now
Draw in your head, alone and too tall here.
Your eyes already in the slant of drifting foam;
Your breath sealed by the ghosts I do not know:
Draw in your head and sleep the long way home.

VI

Where icy and bright dungeons lift
Of swimmers their lost morning eyes,
And ocean rivers, churning, shift
Green borders under stranger skies,

Steadily as a shell secretes
Its beating leagues of monotone,
Or as many waters trough the sun's
Red kelson[1] past the cape's wet stone;

9. Inviolable. *Rime:* frost.

1. Beam laid parallel to a ship's keel.

O rivers mingling toward the sky
And harbor of the phoenix' breast—
My eyes pressed black against the prow,
—Thy derelict and blinded guest

Waiting, afire, what name, unspoke,
I cannot claim: let thy waves rear
More savage than the death of kings,
Some splintered garland for the seer.

Beyond siroccos[2] harvesting
The solstice thunders, crept away,
Like a cliff swinging or a sail
Flung into April's inmost day—

Creation's blithe and petalled word
To the lounged goddess when she rose
Conceding dialogue with eyes
That smile unsearchable repose—

Still fervid covenant, Belle Isle,[3]
—Unfolded floating dais before
Which rainbows twine continual hair—
Belle Isle, white echo of the oar!

The imaged Word, it is, that holds
Hushed willows anchored in its glow.
It is the unbetrayable reply
Whose accent no farewell can know.

1926

THE BRIDGE

From going to and fro in the earth,
and from walking up and down in it.
THE BOOK OF JOB

To Brooklyn Bridge

How many dawns, chill from his rippling rest
The seagull's wings shall dip and pivot him,
Shedding white rings of tumult, building high
Over the chained bay waters Liberty—

Then, with inviolate curve, forsake our eyes
As apparitional as sails that cross

2. Hot winds, usually from North Africa.
3. Island near Newfoundland, the first land seen by boats from Europe.

Some page of figures to be filed away;
—Till elevators drop us from our day . . .

I think of cinemas, panoramic sleights
With multitudes bent toward some flashing scene
Never disclosed, but hastened to again,
Foretold to other eyes on the same screen;

And Thee, across the harbor, silver-paced
As though the sun took step of thee, yet left
Some motion ever unspent in thy stride,—
Implicitly thy freedom staying thee!

Out of some subway scuttle, cell or loft
A bedlamite[4] *speeds to thy parapets,*
Tilting there momently, shrill shirt ballooning,
A jest falls from the speechless caravan.

Down Wall,[5] *from girder into street noon leaks,*
A rip-tooth of the sky's acetylene;
All afternoon the cloud-flown derricks turn . . .
Thy cables breathe the North Atlantic still.

And obscure as that heaven of the Jews,[6]
Thy guerdon[7] *. . . Accolade thou dost bestow*
Of anonymity time cannot raise:
Vibrant reprieve and pardon thou dost show.

O harp and altar, of the fury fused,
(How could mere toil align thy choiring strings!)
Terrific threshold of the prophet's pledge,
Prayer of pariah, and the lover's cry,—

Again the traffic lights that skim thy swift
Unfractioned idiom, immaculate sigh of stars,
Beading thy path—condense eternity:
And we have seen night lifted in thine arms.

Under thy shadow by the piers I waited;
Only in darkness is thy shadow clear.
The City's fiery parcels all undone,
Already snow submerges an iron year . . .

O Sleepless as the river under thee,
Vaulting the sea, the prairies' dreaming sod,
Unto us lowliest sometime sweep, descend
And of the curveship lend a myth to God.

4. Mad person.
5. Wall Street in Manhattan.
6. Heaven in the Jewish tradition is much vaguer than in the Christian.
7. Reward.

I. Ave Maria[8]

Venient annis, saecula seris,
Quibus Oceanus vincula rerum
Laxet et ingens pateat tellus
Tethysque novos detegat orbes
Nec sit terris ultima Thule.
—SENECA[9]

Columbus, alone, gazing toward Spain, invokes the presence of two faithful partisans of his quest . . .

Be with me, Luis de San Angel,[1] now—
Witness before the tides can wrest away
The word I bring, O you who reined my suit
Into the Queen's great heart that doubtful day;
For I have seen now what no perjured breath
Of clown nor sage can riddle or gainsay;—
To you, too, Juan Perez,[2] whose counsel fear
And greed adjourned,—I bring you back Cathay!

Here waves climb into dusk on gleaming mail;
Invisible valves of the sea,—locks, tendons
Crested and creeping, troughing corridors
That fall back yawning to another plunge.
Slowly the sun's red caravel[3] drops light
Once more behind us. . . . It is morning there—
O where our Indian emperies lie revealed,
Yet lost, all, let this keel one instant yield!

I thought of Genoa;[4] and this truth, now proved,
That made me exile in her streets, stood me
More absolute than ever—biding the moon
Till dawn should clear that dim frontier, first seen
—The Chan's[5] great continent. . . . Then faith, not fear
Nigh surged me witless. . . . Hearing the surf near—
I, wonder-breathing, kept the watch,—saw
The first palm chevron the first lighted hill.

And lowered. And they came out to us crying,
"The Great White Birds!" (O Madre María, still
One ship[6] of these thou grantest safe returning;
Assure us through thy mantle's ageless blue!)

8. Hail Mary (Latin); the traditional invocation of the Virgin Mary in Roman Catholic devotionals. In this section, Christopher Columbus prays for a safe return to Spain following his first voyage to the Caribbean, where he still believed he had landed on the shores of India or Cathay (an old name for China). Columbus's quest for Cathay is here distinct from King Ferdinand's desire for gold, according to Crane, "Cathay being an attitude of spirit, rather than material conquest throughout, of course" (letter of January 18, 1926).
9. From the ancient Roman writer Seneca's *Medea:* "In distant years a time will come when Ocean will release the chains of things and the mighty earth will be revealed and Tiphys [the pilot of the Argonauts' quest for the Golden Fleece] will disclose new worlds, and there will be no ultimate Thule [the limit of ancient exploration] to be a limit to the lands." Columbus's son said that "this prophecy was fulfilled by my father . . . in 1492."
1. Collector of church revenues in Spain, who pleaded Columbus's scheme to Queen Isabella.
2. The queen's confessor, who also aided Columbus.
3. Small sailing vessel of the fifteenth and sixteenth centuries; Columbus's ships were caravels.
4. Birthplace of Columbus, in Italy.
5. Or Khan, the Chinese emperor.
6. The *Niña* or *Pinta* (the *Santa María* having been wrecked on a reef). *Madre María:* Mother Mary (Spanish), mother of Jesus.

And record of more, floating in a casque,
Was tumbled from us[7] under bare poles scudding;
And later hurricanes may claim more pawn. . . .
For here between two worlds, another, harsh,

This third, of water, tests the word; lo, here
Bewilderment and mutiny[8] heap whelming
Laughter, and shadow cuts sleep from the heart
Almost as though the Moor's flung scimitar[9]
Found more than flesh to fathom in its fall.
Yet under tempest-lash and surfeitings
Some inmost sob, half-heard, dissuades the abyss,
Merges the wind in measure to the waves,

Series on series, infinite,—till eyes
Starved wide on blackened tides, accrete—enclose
This turning rondure whole,[1] this crescent ring
Sun-cusped and zoned with modulated fire
Like pearls that whisper through the Doge's[2] hands
—Yet no delirium of jewels! O Fernando,[3]
Take of that eastern shore, this western sea,
Yet yield thy God's, thy Virgin's charity!

—Rush down the plenitude, and you shall see
Isaiah counting famine on this lee![4]

• • •

An herb, a stray branch among salty teeth,
The jellied weeds that drag the shore,—perhaps
Tomorrow's moon will grant us Saltes Bar—
Palos[5] again,—a land cleared of long war.
Some Angelus environs the cordage[6] tree;
Dark waters onward shake the dark prow free.

• • •

O Thou who sleepest on Thyself, apart
Like ocean athwart lanes of death and birth,
And all the eddying breath between dost search
Cruelly with love thy parable of man,—
Inquisitor! incognizable Word
Of Eden and the enchained Sepulchre,
Into thy steep savannahs, burning blue,
Utter to loneliness the sail is true.

Who grindest oar, and arguing the mast
Subscribest holocaust of ships, O Thou

7. This record was sealed in a cask and set adrift by Columbus.
8. Columbus's crew threatened mutiny.
9. Curved sword used by the Moors, who conquered Spain in the eighth century and ruled until their expulsion in 1492.
1. Cf. Walt Whitman's apostrophe to the world in "Passage to India" (line 81): "O vast Rondure, swimming in space." In the ensuing section, Whitman idealizes Columbus as "History's type of courage, action, faith."
2. Ruler of Venice, at that time the center of trade with Asia.
3. King Ferdinand V of Spain.
4. Cf. Isaiah 14.29–30: "Rejoice not thou, O Philistia. . . . I will kill thy root with famine."
5. The Spanish seaport of Palos, to which Columbus returned in 1493.
6. Rigging of a ship. *Angelus:* the Angelus Dominus, a devotional Columbus ordered sung in thanksgiving.

Within whose primal scan consummately
The glistening seignories of Ganges[7] swim;—
Who sendest greeting by the corposant,[8]
And Teneriffe's garnet—flamed it in a cloud,
Urging through night our passage to the Chan;—
Te Deum laudamus,[9] for thy teeming span!

Of all that amplitude that time explores,
A needle in the sight, suspended north,—
Yielding by inference and discard, faith
And true appointment from the hidden shoal:
This disposition that thy night relates
From Moon to Saturn in one sapphire wheel:
The orbic wake of thy once whirling feet,
Elohim,[1] still I hear thy sounding heel!

White toil of heaven's cordons, mustering
In holy rings all sails charged to the far
Hushed gleaming fields and pendant seething wheat
Of knowledge,—round thy brows unhooded now
—The kindled Crown! acceded of the poles
And biassed by full sails, meridians reel
Thy purpose—still one shore beyond desire!
The sea's green crying towers a-sway, Beyond

And kingdoms
naked in the
trembling heart—
Te Deum laudamus
O Thou Hand of Fire

II. Powhatan's Daughter[2]

"—Pocahuntus, a well-featured but wanton yong girle . . . of the age of eleven or twelve years, get the boyes forth with her into the market place, and make them wheele, falling on their hands, turning their heels upwards, whom she would followe, and wheele so herself, naked as she was, all the fort over."

The Harbor Dawn

Insistently through sleep—a tide of voices—
They meet you listening midway in your dream,
The long, tired sounds, fog-insulated noises:
Gongs in white surplices,[3] beshrouded wails,
Far strum of fog horns . . . signals dispersed in veils.

400 years and more . . . or is it from the soundless shore of sleep that time

7. India's major holy river. *Seignories:* territories.
8. A fireball seen by Columbus off Teneriffe, largest of the Canary Islands, and a sign, he said, of "His hand."
9. We praise you, God (Latin).
1. A Hebrew name for God.
2. Powhatan was the Native American chief met by the English settlers in Virginia in 1607. Pocahontas (1595–1617), his daughter, represents for Crane a "nature symbol" and the American continent (letter of September 12, 1927). The epigraph is from William Strachey's *History of Travaile into Virginia Britannica* (1615).
3. Loose-fitting linen garments worn by priests and clerics.

And then a truck will lumber past the wharves
As winch engines begin throbbing on some deck;
Or a drunken stevedore's[4] howl and thud below
Comes echoing alley-upward through dim snow.

And if they take your sleep away sometimes
They give it back again. Soft sleeves of sound
Attend the darkling harbor, the pillowed bay;
Somewhere out there in blankness steam

Spills into steam, and wanders, washed away
—Flurried by keen fifings,[5] eddied
Among distant chiming buoys—adrift. The sky,

Cool feathery fold, suspends, distills
This wavering slumber. . . . Slowly—
Immemorially the window, the half-covered chair
Ask nothing but this sheath of pallid air.

And you beside me, blessèd now while sirens
Sing to us, stealthily weave us into day—
Serenely now, before day claims our eyes
Your cool arms murmurously about me lay.

recalls you to your love, there in a waking dream to merge your seed

While myriad snowy hands are clustering at the panes—

your hands within my hands are deeds;
my tongue upon your throat—singing
arms close; eyes wide, undoubtful
dark
drink the dawn—
a forest shudders in your hair!

—with whom?

The window goes blond slowly. Frostily clears.
From Cyclopean[6] towers across Manhattan waters
—Two—three bright window-eyes aglitter, disk
The sun, released—aloft with cold gulls hither.

The fog leans one last moment on the sill.
Under the mistletoe of dreams, a star—
As though to join us at some distant hill—
Turns in the waking west and goes to sleep.

Who is the woman with us in the dawn? . . . whose is the flesh our feet have moved upon?

4. Person who loads or unloads the cargoes of merchant vessels.
5. Sound of pipes; or rails surrounding the mast of a ship.
6. One-eyed, like the Cyclops of Greek mythology.

Van Winkle[7]

Macadam, gun-grey as the tunny's[8] belt,
Leaps from Far Rockaway to Golden Gate:[9]
Listen! the miles a hurdy-gurdy grinds—
Down gold arpeggios mile on mile unwinds.

Streets spread past store and factory—sped by sunlight and her smile . . .

Times earlier, when you hurried off to school,
—It is the same hour though a later day—
You walked with Pizarro in a copybook,
And Cortes[1] rode up, reining tautly in—
Firmly as coffee grips the taste,—and away!

There was Priscilla's cheek close in the wind,
And Captain Smith, all beard and certainty,
And Rip Van Winkle bowing by the way,—
"Is this Sleepy Hollow,[2] friend—?" And he—

Like Memory, she is time's truant, shall take you by the hand . . .

And Rip forgot the office hours,
and he forgot the pay;
Van Winkle sweeps a tenement
way down on Avenue A,—

The grind-organ says . . . Remember, remember
The cinder pile at the end of the backyard
Where we stoned the family of young
Garter snakes under . . . And the monoplanes
We launched—with paper wings and twisted
Rubber bands . . . Recall—recall

the rapid tongues
That flittered from under the ash heap day
After day whenever your stick discovered
Some sunning inch of unsuspecting fibre—
It flashed back at your thrust, as clean as fire.

And Rip was slowly made aware
that he, Van Winkle, was not here
nor there. He woke and swore he'd seen Broadway
a Catskill[3] *daisy chain in May—*

So memory, that strikes a rhyme out of a box,
Or splits a random smell of flowers through glass—

7. Rip Van Winkle, hero of a story by Washington Irving (1783–1859) about a man who falls asleep for twenty years, waking to find that the United States has become an established nation.
8. Tuna's. *Macadam:* road paved with broken stones and tar.
9. In California. *Far Rockaway:* on New York coast.
1. Hernán Cortés (1485–1547): Spanish conqueror of the Aztec empire. Francisco Pizarro (1475–1541): Spanish conqueror of the Inca empire.
2. Setting of Irving's story of the Headless Horseman. Priscilla Alden: pilgrim colonist in Henry Wadsworth Longfellow's "The Courtship of Miles Standish" (1858). Captain John Smith (1580–1631): founder of Jamestown, Virginia; his life was reportedly saved by Pocahontas.
3. Segment of mountains in New York.

Is it the whip stripped from the lilac tree
One day in spring my father took to me,
Or is it the Sabbatical, unconscious smile
My mother almost brought me once from church
And once only, as I recall—?

It flickered through the snow screen, blindly
It forsook her at the doorway, it was gone
Before I had left the window. It
Did not return with the kiss in the hall.

Macadam, gun-grey as the tunny's belt,
Leaps from Far Rockaway to Golden Gate. . . .
Keep hold of that nickel for car-change, Rip,—
Have you got your "*Times*"—?
And hurry along, Van Winkle—it's getting late!

The River[4]

. . . and past the din and slogans of the year—

Stick your patent name on a signboard
brother—all over—going west—young man
Tintex—Japalac—Certain-teed Overalls ads[5]
and lands sakes! under the new playbill ripped
in the guaranteed corner—see Bert Williams[6] what?
Minstrels when you steal a chicken just
save me the wing for if it isn't
Erie it ain't for miles around a
Mazda—and the telegraphic night coming on Thomas

a Ediford[7]—and whistling down the tracks
a headlight rushing with the sound—can you
imagine—while an EXPRESS makes time like
SCIENCE—COMMERCE and the HOLYGHOST
RADIO ROARS IN EVERY HOME WE HAVE THE NORTHPOLE
WALLSTREET AND VIRGINBIRTH WITHOUT STONES OR
WIRES OR EVEN RUNning brooks connecting ears

4. In a letter to his patron Otto Kahn, September 12, 1927, Crane wrote of this section: "The extravagance of the first twenty-three lines of this section is an intentional burlesque on the cultural confusion of the present—a great conglomeration of noises analogous to the strident impression of a fast express [the Twentieth Century Limited] rushing by. The rhythm is jazz." Crane adds in letters to his mother of this same year: "I'm trying in this part of the poem to chart the pioneer experiences of our forefathers—and to tell the story backwards as it were, on the 'backs' of hobos. These hobos are simply 'psychological ponies' to carry the reader across the country and back to the Mississippi, which you will notice is described as a great River of Time. I also unlatch the door to the pure Indian world . . . so the reader is gradually led back in time to the pure savage world, while existing at the same time in the present. . . . The reader is really led back to the primal physical body of America (Pocahontas), and finally to the central pulse and artery, the Mississippi. . . . The introductory speedy vaudeville stuff (what comes before the line beginning 'The last bear . . . ') is a kind of take-off on all the journalism, advertising, and loudspeaker stuff of the day."

5. Presumably, advertising signs; these are the names of a dye, a varnish, and a brand of overalls.

6. Egbert A. Williams (1876–1922), a popular, black minstrel-show entertainer.

7. A play on Thomas A. Edison (1847–1931), inventor of the light bulb (trade name Mazda); Saint Thomas à Becket (1118–1170), archbishop of Canterbury, murdered by agents of Henry II; and Henry Ford (1863–1947), automobile manufacturer.

and no more sermons windows flashing roar
breathtaking—as you like it . . . eh?

So the 20th Century—so
whizzed the Limited—roared by and left
three men, still hungry on the tracks, ploddingly
watching the tail lights wizen and converge, slip-
ping gimleted and neatly out of sight.

• • • • • • •

The last bear, shot drinking in the Dakotas
Loped under wires that span the mountain stream.
Keen instruments,[8] strung to a vast precision
Bind town to town and dream to ticking dream.
But some men take their liquor slow—and count
—Though they'll confess no rosary nor clue—
The river's minute by the far brook's year.
Under a world of whistles, wires and steam
Caboose-like they go ruminating through
Ohio, Indiana—blind baggage—
To Cheyenne tagging . . . Maybe Kalamazoo.

to those whose addresses are never near

Time's rendings, time's blendings they construe
As final reckonings of fire and snow;
Strange bird-wit, like the elemental gist
Of unwalled winds they offer, singing low
My Old Kentucky Home and *Casey Jones,*
Some Sunny Day. I heard a road-gang chanting so.
And afterwards, who had a colt's eyes—one said,
"Jesus! Oh I remember watermelon days!" And sped
High in a cloud of merriment, recalled
"—And when my Aunt Sally Simpson smiled," he drawled—
"It was almost Louisiana, long ago."
"There's no place like Booneville though, Buddy,"
One said, excising a last burr from his vest,
"—For early trouting." Then peering in the can,
"—But I kept on the tracks." Possessed, resigned,
He trod the fire down pensively and grinned,
Spreading dry shingles of a beard. . . .

Behind
My father's cannery works I used to see
Rail-squatters ranged in nomad raillery,
The ancient men—wifeless or runaway
Hobo-trekkers that forever search
An empire wilderness of freight and rails.
Each seemed a child, like me, on a loose perch,
Holding to childhood like some termless play.

8. Telephone and telegraph.

John, Jake or Charley, hopping the slow freight
—Memphis to Tallahassee—riding the rods,
Blind fists of nothing, humpty-dumpty clods.

Yet they touch something like a key perhaps.
From pole to pole across the hills, the states
—They know a body[9] under the wide rain;
Youngsters with eyes like fjords, old reprobates
With racetrack jargon,—dotting immensity
They lurk across her, knowing her yonder breast
Snow-silvered, sumac-stained or smoky blue—
Is past the valley-sleepers, south or west.
—As I have trod the rumorous midnights, too,

but who have touched her, knowing her without name

And past the circuit of the lamp's thin flame
(O Nights that brought me to her body bare!)
Have dreamed beyond the print that bound her name.
Trains sounding the long blizzards out—I heard
Wail into distances I knew were hers.
Papooses crying on the wind's long mane
Screamed redskin dynasties that fled the brain,
—Dead echoes! But I knew her body there,
Time like a serpent down her shoulder, dark,
And space, an eaglet's wing, laid on her hair.

Under the Ozarks, domed by Iron Mountain,
The old gods of the rain lie wrapped in pools
Where eyeless fish curvet a sunken fountain
And re-descend with corn from querulous crows.
Such pilferings make up their timeless eatage,
Propitiate them for their timber torn
By iron, iron—always the iron dealt cleavage!
They doze now, below axe and powder horn.

nor the myths of her fathers . . .

And Pullman breakfasters glide glistening steel
From tunnel into field—iron strides the dew—
Straddles the hill, a dance of wheel on wheel.
You have a half-hour's wait at Siskiyou,
Or stay the night and take the next train through.
Southward, near Cairo[1] passing, you can see
The Ohio merging,—borne down Tennessee;
And if it's summer and the sun's in dusk
Maybe the breeze will lift the River's musk
—As though the waters breathed that you might know
Memphis Johnny, Steamboat Bill, Missouri Joe.
Oh, lean from the window, if the train slows down,
As though you touched hands with some ancient clown,
—A little while gaze absently below
And hum *Deep River* with them while they go.

9. America's, which Crane sometimes identifies with the body of Pocahontas.

1. In southern Illinois, where the Ohio River merges with the Mississippi.

Yes, turn again and sniff once more—look see,
O Sheriff, Brakeman and Authority—
Hitch up your pants and crunch another quid,[2]
For you, too, feed the River timelessly.
And few evade full measure of their fate;
Always they smile out eerily what they seem.
I could believe he joked at heaven's gate—
Dan Midland—jolted from the cold brake-beam.[3]

Down, down—born pioneers in time's despite,
Grimed tributaries to an ancient flow—
They win no frontier by their wayward plight,
But drift in stillness, as from Jordan's brow.[4]

You will not hear it as the sea; even stone
Is not more hushed by gravity . . . But slow,
As loth to take more tribute—sliding prone
Like one whose eyes were buried long ago

The River, spreading, flows—and spends your dream.
What are you, lost within this tideless spell?
You are your father's father, and the stream—
A liquid theme that floating niggers swell.

Damp tonnage and alluvial march of days—
Nights turbid, vascular with silted shale
And roots surrendered down of moraine clays:
The Mississippi drinks the farthest dale.

O quarrying passion, undertowed sunlight!
The basalt surface drags a jungle grace
Ochreous and lynx-barred[5] in lengthening might;
Patience! and you shall reach the biding place!

Over De Soto's[6] bones the freighted floors
Throb past the City[7] storied of three thrones.
Down two more turns the Mississippi pours
(Anon tall ironsides[8] up from salt lagoons)

And flows within itself, heaps itself free.
All fades but one thin skyline 'round . . . Ahead
No embrace opens but the stinging sea;
The River lifts itself from its long bed,

Poised wholly on its dream, a mustard glow
Tortured with history, its one will—flow!

2. Cut of chewing tobacco.
3. Where hoboes ride on railroad cars. Dan Midland, a hobo, fell to his death from a train.
4. The shore of the Jordan River, in Palestine.
5. That is, streaked with dark spots. *Ochreous:* brownish yellow.
6. Hernándo de Soto (1500–1542), Spanish explorer, whose body was consigned to the Mississippi River.
7. New Orleans, held successively by the Spanish, the French, and the English.
8. Warships.

—The Passion spreads in wide tongues, choked and slow,
Meeting the Gulf, hosannas silently below.

The Dance

Then you shall see her truly—your blood remembering its first invasion of her secrecy, its first encounters with her kin, her chieftain lover . . . his shade that haunts the lakes and hills

The swift red flesh, a winter king—
Who squired the glacier woman down the sky?
She ran the neighing canyons all the spring;
She spouted arms; she rose with maize—to die.

And in the autumn drouth,[9] whose burnished hands
With mineral wariness found out the stone
Where prayers, forgotten, streamed the mesa sands?
He holds the twilight's dim, perpetual throne.

Mythical brows we saw retiring—loth,
Disturbed and destined, into denser green.
Greeting they sped us, on the arrow's oath:
Now lie incorrigibly what years between . . .

There was a bed of leaves, and broken play;
There was a veil upon you, Pocahontas, bride—
O Princess whose brown lap was virgin May;
And bridal flanks and eyes hid tawny pride.

I left the village for dogwood. By the canoe
Tugging below the mill-race, I could see
Your hair's keen crescent running, and the blue
First moth of evening take wing stealthily.

What laughing chains the water wove and threw!
I learned to catch the trout's moon whisper; I
Drifted how many hours I never knew,
But, watching, saw that fleet young crescent die,—

And one star, swinging, take its place, alone,
Cupped in the larches of the mountain pass—
Until, immortally, it bled into the dawn.
I left my sleek boat nibbling margin grass . . .

I took the portage climb, then chose
A further valley-shed; I could not stop.
Feet nozzled wat'ry webs of upper flows;
One white veil gusted from the very top.

O Appalachian Spring! I gained the ledge;
Steep, inaccessible smile that eastward bends
And northward reaches in that violet wedge
Of Adirondacks![1]—wisped of azure wands,

9. Drought.

1. Mountain range in northern New York.

Over how many bluffs, tarns, streams I sped!
—And knew myself within some boding shade:—
Grey tepees tufting the blue knolls ahead,
Smoke swirling through the yellow chestnut glade . . .

A distant cloud, a thunder-bud—it grew,
That blanket of the skies: the padded foot
Within,—I heard it; 'til its rhythm drew,
—Siphoned the black pool from the heart's hot root!

A cyclone threshes in the turbine crest,
Swooping in eagle feathers down your back;
Know, Maquokeeta, greeting; know death's best;
—Fall, Sachem, strictly as the tamarack![2]

A birch kneels. All her whistling fingers fly.
The oak grove circles in a crash of leaves;
The long moan of a dance is in the sky.
Dance, Maquokeeta: Pocahontas grieves . . .

And every tendon scurries toward the twangs
Of lightning deltaed down your saber hair.
Now snaps the flint in every tooth; red fangs
And splay tongues thinly busy the blue air . . .

Dance, Maquokeeta! snake that lives before,
That casts his pelt, and lives beyond! Sprout, horn!
Spark, tooth! Medicine-man, relent, restore—
Lie to us,—dance us back the tribal morn!

Spears and assemblies: black drums thrusting on—
O yelling battlements,—I, too, was liege
To rainbows currying each pulsant bone:
Surpassed the circumstance, danced out the siege!

And buzzard-circleted, screamed from the stake;
I could not pick the arrows from my side.
Wrapped in that fire, I saw more escorts wake—
Flickering, sprint up the hill groins like a tide.

I heard the hush of lava wrestling your arms,
And stag teeth foam about the raven throat;
Flame cataracts of heaven in seething swarms
Fed down your anklets to the sunset's moat.

O, like the lizard in the furious noon,
That drops his legs and colors in the sun,
—And laughs, pure serpent, Time itself, and moon
Of his own fate, I saw thy change begun!

2. A larch tree. *Maquokeeta:* a Native American cabdriver, who told Crane his name meant Big River, after a god whose rains refreshed the plains. *Sachem:* chief (Algonquin).

And saw thee dive to kiss that destiny
Like one white meteor, sacrosanct and blent
At last with all that's consummate and free
There, where the first and last gods keep thy tent.

• • • •

Thewed of the levin,[3] thunder-shod and lean,
Lo, through what infinite seasons dost thou gaze—
Across what bivouacs[4] of thine angered slain,
And see'st thy bride immortal in the maize!

Totem and fire-gall, slumbering pyramid—
Though other calendars now stack the sky,
Thy freedom is her largesse, Prince, and hid
On paths thou knewest best to claim her by.

High unto Labrador the sun strikes free
Her speechless dream of snow, and stirred again,
She is the torrent and the singing tree;
And she is virgin to the last of men . . .

West, west and south! winds over Cumberland
And winds across the llano[5] grass resume
Her hair's warm sibilance. Her breasts are fanned
O stream by slope and vineyard—into bloom!

And when the caribou slant down for salt
Do arrows thirst and leap? Do antlers shine
Alert, star-triggered in the listening vault
Of dusk?—And are her perfect brows to thine?

We danced, O Brave, we danced beyond their farms,
In cobalt desert closures made our vows . . .
Now is the strong prayer folded in thine arms,
The serpent with the eagle in the boughs.[6]

Indiana

. . . and read her in a mother's farewell gaze.

The morning glory, climbing the morning long
  Over the lintel on its wiry vine,
Closes before the dusk, furls in its song
          As I close mine . . .

And bison thunder rends my dreams no more
  As once my womb was torn, my boy, when you
Yielded your first cry at the prairie's door . . .
          Your father knew

3. Muscled by the lightning.
4. Temporary encampments of soldiers in the open air.
5. Treeless plain.
6. Possibly suggesting the deity Quetzalcóatl, a feathered serpent of pre-Columbian Mexico, identified with water and fertility.

Then, though we'd buried him behind us, far
  Back on the gold trail—then his lost bones stirred . . .
But you who drop the scythe to grasp the oar
      Knew not, nor heard

How we, too, Prodigal, once rode off, too—
  Waved Seminary Hill a gay good-bye . . .
We found God lavish there in Colorado
      But passing sly.

The pebbles sang, the firecat slunk away
  And glistening through the sluggard freshets[7] came
In golden syllables loosed from the clay
      His gleaming name.

A dream called Eldorado[8] was his town,
  It rose up shambling in the nuggets' wake,
It had no charter but a promised crown
      Of claims to stake.

But we,—too late, too early, howsoever—
  Won nothing out of fifty-nine[9]—those years—
But gilded promise, yielded to us never,
      And barren tears . . .

The long trail back! I huddled in the shade
  Of wagon-tenting looked out once and saw
Bent westward, passing on a stumbling jade[1]
      A homeless squaw—

Perhaps a halfbreed. On her slender back
  She cradled a babe's body, riding without rein.
Her eyes, strange for an Indian's, were not black
      But sharp with pain

And like twin stars. They seemed to shun the gaze
  Of all our silent men—the long team line—
Until she saw me—when their violet haze
      Lit with love shine . . .

I held you up—I suddenly the bolder,
  Knew that mere words could not have brought us nearer.
She nodded—and that smile across her shoulder
      Will still endear her

As long as Jim, your father's memory, is warm.
  Yes, Larry, now you're going to sea, remember

7. Freshwater streams created from rain or melting snow. *Firecat:* mountain lion.
8. Legendary kingdom of gold, sought in South America by Spanish explorers.
9. The year of the second gold rush, 1859.
1. Old horse.

You were the first—before Ned and this farm,—
First-born, remember—

And since then—all that's left to me of Jim
Whose folks, like mine, came out of Arrowhead.[2]
And you're the only one with eyes like him—
Kentucky bred!

I'm standing still, I'm old, I'm half of stone!
Oh, hold me in those eyes' engaging blue;
There's where the stubborn years gleam and atone,—
Where gold is true!

Down the dim turnpike to the river's edge—
Perhaps I'll hear the mare's hoofs to the ford . . .
Write me from Rio[3] . . . and you'll keep your pledge;
I know your word!

Come back to Indiana—not too late!
(Or will you be a ranger to the end?)
Good-bye . . . Good-bye . . . oh, I shall always wait
You, Larry, traveller—
stranger,
son,
—my friend—

III. Cutty Sark[4]

O, the navies old and oaken,
O, the Temeraire no more!
—MELVILLE[5]

I met a man in South Street,[6] tall—
a nervous shark tooth swung on his chain.
His eyes pressed through green glass
—green glasses, or bar lights made them
so—
shine—
GREEN—
eyes—
stepped out—forgot to look at you
or left you several blocks away—

in the nickel-in-the-slot piano jogged
"Stamboul[7] Nights"—weaving somebody's nickel—sang—

2. Also the name of the Massachusetts home of American writer Herman Melville (1819–1891), where he lived during the 1850s and wrote *Moby-Dick*.
3. Rio de Janeiro, Brazil.
4. Brand of Scotch whiskey; also, the name of a famous British clipper ship.
5. Final lines of Herman Melville's poem "Temeraire" (*Battle Pieces*, 1866), celebrating an old British warship as one among a majestic class of wooden ships made obsolete by ironclads.
6. South Street Saloon, on the Manhattan side of the Brooklyn Bridge.
7. Istanbul (capital of Turkey until 1923).

O Stamboul Rose—dreams weave the rose!

Murmurs of Leviathan[8] he spoke,
and rum was Plato in our heads . . .

"It's S.S. *Ala*—Antwerp—now remember kid
to put me out at three she sails on time.
I'm not much good at time any more keep
weakeyed watches sometimes snooze—" his bony hands
got to beating time . . . "A whaler once—
I ought to keep time and get over it—I'm a
Democrat—I know what time it is—No
I don't want to know what time it is—that
damned white Arctic killed my time . . ."

O Stamboul Rose—drums weave—

"I ran a donkey engine down there on the Canal
in Panama—got tired of that—
then Yucatan selling kitchenware—beads—
have you seen Popocatepetl[9]—birdless mouth
with ashes sifting down—?
                    and then the coast again . . ."

Rose of Stamboul O coral Queen—
teased remnants of the skeletons of cities—
and galleries, galleries of watergutted lava
snarling stone—green—drums—drown—

Sing!
"—that spiracle!"[1] he shot a finger out the door . . .
"O life's a geyser—beautiful—my lungs—
No—I can't live on land—!"

I saw the frontiers gleaming of his mind;
or are there frontiers—running sands sometimes
running sands—somewhere—sands running . . .
Or they may start some white machine that sings.
Then you may laugh and dance the axletree—
steel—silver—kick the traces—and know—

ATLANTIS[2] ROSE drums wreathe the rose,
the star floats burning in a gulf of tears
and sleep another thousand—

                    interminably
long since somebody's nickel—stopped—
playing—

8. Biblical seamonster, identified with the white whale of Melville's *Moby-Dick* (1851).
9. Volcano near Mexico City. *Donkey engine:* a small steam engine used to lift cargo. *Yucatan:* peninsula separating the Caribbean from the Gulf of Mexico.
1. A whale's blowhole.
2. Mythical island in the Atlantic Ocean, described in Plato's *Timaeus* and *Critias* (fourth century B.C.E.); it sank because of its inhabitants' greed, but the ancients believed it may rise again.

A wind worried those wicker-neat lapels, the
swinging summer entrances to cooler hells . . .
Outside a wharf truck nearly ran him down
—he lunged up Bowery[3] way while the dawn
was putting the Statue of Liberty out—that
torch of hers you know—

I started walking home across the Bridge . . .

• • • • •

Blithe Yankee vanities, turreted sprites, winged
British repartees, skil-
ful savage sea-girls
that bloomed in the spring—Heave, weave
those bright designs the trade winds drive . . .

Sweet opium and tea, Yo-ho!
Pennies for porpoises that bank the keel!
Fins whip the breeze around Japan!

Bright skysails ticketing the Line, wink round the Horn
to Frisco, Melbourne . . .[4]
Pennants, parabolas—
clipper dreams indelible and ranging,
baronial white on lucky blue!

Perennial-*Cutty*-trophied-*Sark!*

Thermopylae, Black Prince, Flying Cloud through Sunda[5]
—scarfed of foam, their bellies veered green esplanades,
locked in wind-humors, ran their eastings down;

at Java Head freshened the nip
(sweet opium and tea!)
and turned and left us on the lee . . .

Buntlines[6] tusseling (91 days, 20 hours and anchored!)
Rainbow, Leander[7]
(last trip a tragedy)—where can you be
Nimbus? and you rivals two—

a long tack keeping—
Taeping?
Ariel?[8]

3. District in lower Manhattan with bars and cheap hotels.
4. Australian seaport. *The Line:* a line of sailing ships in the distance. *The Horn:* Cape Horn, the southernmost point of South America. *Frisco:* San Francisco.
5. A strait in the Java Sea. The italicized names are those of clipper ships; the *Thermopylae* won an 1872 race with the *Cutty Sark* back to London from Shanghai.
6. Ropes attached to the ends of square sails.
7. Ship named for the Greek mythological hero who drowned trying to swim across the Hellespont to reach his lover, Hero.
8. *Taeping* and *Ariel* were "rivals" in a ninety-nine-day race from Foochow to London in 1866. The *Ariel* was named after the airy spirit of Shakespeare's *Tempest. Nimbus:* American ship wrecked in 1877.

IV. Cape Hatteras[9]

The seas all crossed, weathered the capes, the voyage done . . .
—Walt Whitman[1]

Imponderable the dinosaur
sinks slow,
the mammoth saurian[2]
ghoul, the eastern
Cape . . .
While rises in the west the coastwise range,
slowly the hushed land—
Combustion at the astral core—the dorsal change
Of energy—convulsive shift of sand . . .
But we, who round the capes, the promontories
Where strange tongues vary messages of surf
Below grey citadels, repeating to the stars
The ancient names—return home to our own
Hearths, there to eat an apple and recall
The songs that gypsies dealt us at Marseille
Or how the priests walked—slowly through Bombay[3]—
Or to read you, Walt—knowing us in thrall

To that deep wonderment, our native clay
Whose depth of red, eternal flesh of Pocahontas—
Those continental folded aeons, surcharged
With sweetness below derricks, chimneys, tunnels—
Is veined by all that time has really pledged us . . .
And from above, thin squeaks of radio static,
The captured fume of space foams in our ears—
What whisperings of far watches on the main
Relapsing into silence, while time clears
Our lenses, lifts a focus, resurrects
A periscope to glimpse what joys or pain
Our eyes can share or answer—then deflects
Us, shunting to a labyrinth submersed
Where each sees only his dim past reversed . . .

But that star-glistered salver of infinity,
The circle, blind crucible of endless space,
Is sluiced by motion,—subjugated never.
Adam and Adam's answer in the forest
Left Hesperus[4] mirrored in the lucid pool.
Now the eagle dominates our days, is jurist
Of the ambiguous cloud. We know the strident rule
Of wings imperious . . . Space, instantaneous,

9. Peninsula on the coast of North Carolina and site of Kitty Hawk, where the Wright brothers first flew an airplane.
1. Line 220 of Whitman's "Passage to India."
2. Reptilian.
3. City in India. *Marseilles:* city on the southern coast of France.
4. The planet Venus after sunset; Hesperus and Phosphor are the evening and morning aspects of the same planet.

Flickers a moment, consumes us in its smile:
A flash over the horizon—shifting gears—
And we have laughter, or more sudden tears.
Dream cancels dream in this new realm of fact
From which we wake into the dream of act;
Seeing himself an atom in a shroud—
Man hears himself an engine in a cloud!

"—Recorders ages hence"[5]—ah, syllables of faith!
Walt, tell me, Walt Whitman, if infinity
Be still the same as when you walked the beach
Near Paumanok—your lone patrol—and heard the wraith
Through surf, its bird note there a long time falling . . .[6]
For you, the panoramas and this breed of towers,
Of you—the theme that's statured in the cliff,
O Saunterer on free ways still ahead!
Not this our empire yet, but labyrinth
Wherein your eyes, like the Great Navigator's[7] without ship,
Gleam from the great stones of each prison crypt
Of canyoned traffic . . . Confronting the Exchange,
Surviving in a world of stocks,—they also range
Across the hills where second timber strays
Back over Connecticut farms, abandoned pastures,—
Sea eyes and tidal, undenying, bright with myth!

The nasal whine of power whips a new universe . . .
Where spouting pillars spoor the evening sky,
Under the looming stacks of the gigantic power house
Stars prick the eyes with sharp ammoniac proverbs,
New verities, new inklings in the velvet hummed
Of dynamos, where hearing's leash is strummed . . .
Power's script,—wound, bobbin-bound, refined—
Is stropped to the slap of belts on booming spools, spurred
Into the bulging bouillon, harnessed jelly of the stars.
Towards what? The forked crash of split thunder parts
Our hearing momentwise; but fast in whirling armatures,
As bright as frogs' eyes, giggling in the girth
Of steely gizzards—axle-bound, confined
In coiled precision, bunched in mutual glee
The bearings glint,—O murmurless and shined
In oilrinsed circles of blind ecstasy!

Stars scribble on our eyes the frosty sagas,
The gleaming cantos of unvanquished space . . .
O sinewy silver biplane, nudging the wind's withers!
There, from Kill Devils Hill[8] at Kitty Hawk
Two brothers in their twinship left the dune;
Warping the gale, the Wright windwrestlers veered

5. Title and first line of a poem by Whitman.
6. Cf. Whitman's "Out of the Cradle Endlessly Rocking" for similar references to birdsong above the sound of surf. *Paumonok:* a Native American name Whitman used for Long Island.
7. Christopher Columbus's.
8. The Wright brothers' first takeoff site.

Capeward, then blading the wind's flank, banked and spun
What ciphers risen from prophetic script,
What marathons new-set between the stars!
The soul, by naphtha[9] fledged into new reaches
Already knows the closer clasp of Mars,—
New latitudes, unknotting, soon give place
To what fierce schedules, rife of doom apace!

Behold the dragon's covey[1]—amphibian, ubiquitous
To hedge the seaboard, wrap the headland, ride
The blue's cloud-templed districts unto ether . . .
While Iliads glimmer through eyes raised in pride[2]
Hell's belt springs wider into heaven's plumed side.
O bright circumferences, heights employed to fly
War's fiery kennel masked in downy offings,—
This tournament of space, the threshed and chiselled height,
Is baited by marauding circles, bludgeon flail
Of rancorous grenades whose screaming petals carve us
Wounds that we wrap with theorems sharp as hail!

Wheeled swiftly, wings emerge from larval-silver hangars.
Taut motors surge, space-gnawing, into flight;
Through sparkling visibility, outspread, unsleeping,
Wings clip the last peripheries of light . . .
Tellurian[3] wind-sleuths on dawn patrol,
Each plane a hurtling javelin of winged ordnance,
Bristle the heights above a screeching gale to hover;
Surely no eye that Sunward Escadrille can cover!
There, meaningful, fledged as the Pleiades[4]
With razor sheen they zoom each rapid helix!
Up-chartered choristers of their own speeding
They, cavalcade on escapade, shear Cumulus—
Lay siege and hurdle Cirrus down the skies!
While Cetus-like, O thou Dirigible,[5] enormous Lounger
Of pendulous auroral beaches,—satellited wide
By convoy planes, moonferrets that rejoin thee
On fleeing balconies as thou does glide,
—Hast splintered space!

Low, shadowed of the Cape,
Regard the moving turrets! From grey decks
See scouting griffons[6] rise through gaseous crepe
Hung low . . . until a conch of thunder answers
Cloud-belfries, banging, while searchlights, like fencers,
Slit the sky's pancreas of foaming anthracite

9. Fuel.
1. Small flock or brood (usually of birds).
2. That is, in observing planes in flight or aerial combat, modern onlookers witness an epic grandeur comparable to that of Homer's *Iliad*.
3. Inhabiting Earth.
4. A cluster of stars that purportedly shows the best times for harvest and navigation. *Escadrille:* six-plane air squadron (French).
5. An airship or balloon. *Cetus:* constellation in the shape of a whale, usually figured resting on the banks of a river. *Cumulus* and *cirrus:* types of clouds.
6. A breed of dog; also, mythical beasts with a lion's body and an eagle's wings and head; here, aircraft engaging in a dogfight.

Toward thee, O Corsair of the typhoon,—pilot, hear!
Thine eyes bicarbonated white by speed, O Skygak, see
How from thy path above the levin's lance[7]
Thou sowest doom thou hast nor time nor chance
To reckon—as thy stilly eyes partake
What alcohol of space . . ! Remember, Falcon-Ace,
Thou hast there in thy wrist a Sanskrit charge[8]
To conjugate infinity's dim marge—
Anew . . !

But first, here at this height receive
The benediction of the shell's deep, sure reprieve!
Lead-perforated fuselage, escutcheoned[9] wings
Lift agonized quittance, tilting from the invisible brink
Now eagle-bright, now
quarry-hid, twist-
-ing, sink with
Enormous repercussive list-
-ings down
Giddily spiralled
gauntlets, upturned, unlooping
In guerrilla sleights, trapped in combustion gyr-
Ing, dance the curdled depth
down whizzing
Zodiacs, dashed
(now nearing fast the Cape!)
down gravitation's
vortex into crashed
. . . . dispersion . . . into mashed and shapeless debris. . . .
By Hatteras bunched the beached heap of high bravery!

• • • • • •

The stars have grooved our eyes with old persuasions
Of love and hatred, birth,—surcease of nations . . .
But who has held the heights more sure than thou,
O Walt!—Ascensions of thee hover in me now
As thou at junctions elegiac, there, of speed
With vast eternity, dost wield the rebound seed!
The competent loam, the probable grass—travail
Of tides awash the pedestal of Everest, fail
Not less than thou in pure impulse inbred
To answer deepest soundings! O, upward from the dead
Thou bringest tally, and a pact, new bound
Of living brotherhood!

Thou, there beyond—
Glacial sierras and the flight of ravens,
Hermetically past condor zones, through zenith havens

7. Lightning bolt. *Corsair:* pirate. *Skygak:* stunt pilot.
8. That is, a moral responsibility, as if written in the sacred Sanskrit language of India. *Falcon-Ace:* fighter pilot.
9. Depicting a shield with armorial bearings.

Past where the albatross has offered up
His last wing-pulse, and downcast as a cup
That's drained, is shivered back to earth—thy wand
Has beat a song, O Walt,—there and beyond!
And this, thine other hand, upon my heart
Is plummet ushered of those tears that start
What memories of vigils, bloody, by that Cape,—
Ghoul-mound of man's perversity at balk
And fraternal massacre! Thou, pallid there as chalk
Hast kept of wounds, O Mourner, all that sum
That then from Appomattox stretched to Somme![1]

Cowslip and shad-blow,[2] flaked like tethered foam
Around bared teeth of stallions, bloomed that spring
When first I read thy lines, rife as the loam
Of prairies, yet like breakers cliffward leaping!
O, early following thee, I searched the hill
Blue-writ and odor-firm with violets, 'til
With June the mountain laurel broke through green
And filled the forest with what clustrous sheen!
Potomac lilies,—then the Pontiac rose,
And Klondike[3] edelweiss of occult snows!
White banks of moonlight came descending valleys—
How speechful on oak-vizored palisades,
As vibrantly I following down Sequoia alleys
Heard thunder's eloquence through green arcades
Set trumpets breathing in each clump and grass tuft—'til
Gold autumn, captured, crowned the trembling hill!

Panis Angelicus![4] Eyes tranquil with the blaze
Of love's own diametric gaze, of love's amaze!
Not greatest, thou,—not first, nor last,—but near
And onward yielding past my utmost year.
Familiar, thou, as mendicants in public places;
Evasive—too—as dayspring's spreading arc to trace is:—
Our Meistersinger,[5] thou set breath in steel;
And it was thou who on the boldest heel
Stood up and flung the span on even wing
Of that great Bridge, our Myth, whereof I sing!

Years of the Modern! Propulsions toward what capes?
But thou, *Panis Angelicus,* hast thou not seen
And passed that Barrier that none escapes—
But knows it leastwise as death-strife?—O, something green,
Beyond all sesames of science was thy choice
Wherewith to bind us throbbing with one voice,

1. Lines 174–81 allude to Whitman's elegiac Civil War poetry. *Appomattox:* site of the final battle of the Civil War and the Confederacy's surrender. *Somme:* site in France of two of the bloodiest battles of World War I.
2. Flowering bush. *Cowslip:* yellow wildflower.
3. Canadian river. *Pontiac:* river into which inventor Samuel Langley crashed a faulty full-scale model airplane just days before the Wright brothers' successful first flight, in 1903.
4. Bread of angels (Latin); a Christian hymn and invocation.
5. Master singer (German).

New integers of Roman, Viking, Celt—
Thou, Vedic[6] Caesar, to the greensward knelt!

And now, as launched in abysmal cupolas of space,
Toward endless terminals, Easters of speeding light—
Vast engines outward veering with seraphic grace
On clarion cylinders pass out of sight
To course that span of consciousness thou'st named
The Open Road—thy vision is reclaimed!
What heritage thou'st signalled to our hands!
And see! the rainbow's arch—how shimmeringly stands
Above the Cape's ghoul-mound, O joyous seer!
Recorders ages hence, yes, they shall hear
In their own veins uncancelled thy sure tread
And read thee by the aureole 'round thy head
Of pasture-shine, *Panis Angelicus!*
                                        yes, Walt,
Afoot again, and onward without halt—
Not soon, nor suddenly,—no, never to let go
    My hand
            in yours,
                    Walt Whitman—
                                        so—[7]

V. Three Songs

The one Sestos, the other Abydos hight.
—MARLOWE[8]

Southern Cross[9]

I wanted you, nameless Woman of the South,
No wraith, but utterly—as still more alone
The Southern Cross takes night
And lifts her girdles from her, one by one—
High, cool,
            wide from the slowly smoldering fire
Of lower heavens,—
                    vaporous scars!

Eve! Magdalene!
                    or Mary,[1] you?

6. Pertaining to the Vedas, sacred Hindu scriptures.
7. Cf. the end of Whitman's "Song of the Open Road": "Will you give me yourself? will you come travel with me? / Shall we stick by each other as long as we live?"
8. Adapted from *Hero and Leander* (1598), by English poet Christopher Marlowe (1564–1593); these are the towns at the mouth of the Hellespont, where Leander drowned.
9. Constellation visible in the Southern Hemisphere.
1. The Virgin Mary. In the Bible, Mary Magdalene is a prostitute who becomes a follower of Jesus'.

Whatever call—falls vainly on the wave.
O simian Venus, homeless Eve,
Unwedded, stumbling gardenless to grieve
Windswept guitars on lonely decks forever;
Finally to answer all within one grave!

And this long wake of phosphor,
                                    iridescent
Furrow of all our travel—trailed derision!
Eyes crumble at its kiss. Its long-drawn spell
Incites a yell. Slid on that backward vision
The mind is churned to spittle, whispering hell.

I wanted you . . . The embers of the Cross
Climbed by aslant and huddling aromatically.
It is blood to remember; it is fire
To stammer back . . . It is
God—your namelessness. And the wash—

All night the water combed you with black
Insolence. You crept out simmering, accomplished.
Water rattled that stinging coil, your
Rehearsed hair—docile, alas, from many arms.
Yes, Eve—wraith of my unloved seed!

The Cross, a phantom, buckled—dropped below the dawn.
Light drowned the lithic[2] trillions of your spawn.

National Winter Garden[3]

Outspoken buttocks in pink beads
Invite the necessary cloudy clinch
Of bandy eyes. . . . No extra mufflings here:
The world's one flagrant, sweating cinch.

And while legs waken salads in the brain
You pick your blonde out neatly through the smoke.
Always you wait for someone else though, always—
(Then rush the nearest exit through the smoke).

Always and last, before the final ring
When all the fireworks blare, begins
A tom-tom scrimmage with a somewhere violin,
Some cheapest echo of them all—begins.

And shall we call her whiter than the snow?
Sprayed first with ruby, then with emerald sheen—
Least tearful and least glad (who knows her smile?)
A caught slide shows her sandstone grey between.

2. Stonelike.

3. A burlesque theater in New York City.

Her eyes exist in swivellings of her teats,
Pearls whip her hips, a drench of whirling strands.
Her silly snake rings begin to mount, surmount
Each other—turquoise fakes on tinselled hands.

We wait that writhing pool, her pearls collapsed,
—All but her belly buried in the floor;
And the lewd trounce of a final muted beat!
We flee her spasm through a fleshless door. . . .

Yet, to the empty trapeze of your flesh,
O Magdalene, each comes back to die alone.
Then you, the burlesque of our lust—and faith,
Lug us back lifeward—bone by infant bone.

Virginia

O rain at seven,
Pay-check at eleven—
Keep smiling the boss away,
Mary (what are you going to do?)[4]
Gone seven—gone eleven,
And I'm still waiting you—

O blue-eyed Mary with the claret scarf,
Saturday Mary, mine!

It's high carillon[5]
From the popcorn bells!
Pigeons by the million—
And Spring in Prince Street[6]
Where green figs gleam
By oyster shells!

O Mary, leaning from the high wheat tower,
Let down your golden hair![7]

High in the noon of May
On cornices of daffodils
The slender violets stray.
Crap-shooting gangs in Bleecker reign,
Peonies with pony[8] manes—
Forget-me-nots at windowpanes:

Out of the way-up nickel-dime tower shine,
Cathedral Mary,
shine!—

4. Echo of a popular song (from the 1923 musical comedy *Poppy*) by Irving Caesar, "What Do You Do Sunday, Mary?"
5. Melody played on bells.
6. Spring, Prince, and Bleecker (line 20) are streets in lower Manhattan.
7. Cf. the fairy tale of Rapunzel.
8. "Pony" was slang in the 1920s for a chorus girl or burlesque dancer (cf. "National Winter Garden," above).

VI. Quaker Hill[9]

I see only the ideal. But no ideals have ever been fully successful on this earth.

—ISADORA DUNCAN

The gentian weaves her fringes,
The maple's loom is red.

—EMILY DICKINSON[1]

Perspective never withers from their eyes;
They keep that docile edict of the Spring
That blends March with August Antarctic skies:
These are but cows that see no other thing
Than grass and snow, and their own inner being
Through the rich halo that they do not trouble
Even to cast upon the seasons fleeting
Though they should thin and die on last year's stubble.

And they are awkward, ponderous and uncoy . . .
While we who press the cider mill, regarding them—
We, who with pledges taste the bright annoy
Of friendship's acid wine, retarding phlegm,
Shifting reprisals ('til who shall tell us when
The jest is too sharp to be kindly?) boast
Much of our store of faith in other men
Who would, ourselves, stalk down the merriest ghost.

Above them old Mizzentop,[2] palatial white
Hostelry—floor by floor to cinquefoil dormer
Portholes[3] the ceilings stack their stoic height.
Long tiers of windows staring out toward former
Faces—loose panes crown the hill and gleam
At sunset with a silent, cobwebbed patience . . .
See them, like eyes that still uphold some dream
Through mapled vistas, cancelled reservations!

High from the central cupola, they say
One's glance could cross the borders of three states;
But I have seen death's stare in slow survey
From four horizons that no one relates . . .
Weekenders avid of their turf-won scores,
Here three hours from the semaphores, the Czars
Of golf, by twos and threes in plaid plusfours[4]
Alight with sticks abristle and cigars.

9. A resort in New York State, formerly the site of a Quaker meetinghouse; Crane lived there intermittently between 1925 and 1930.
1. First two lines of a poem by Dickinson. Isadora Duncan (1878–1927), famous dancer and promoter of modern dance.
2. An abandoned hotel, named after one of a ship's masts.
3. Ornamental circular windows in the shape of five converging arcs.
4. Loose knickers.

This was the Promised Land, and still it is
To the persuasive suburban land agent
In bootleg roadhouses where the gin fizz
Bubbles in time to Hollywood's new love-nest pageant.
Fresh from the radio in the old Meeting House
(Now the New Avalon[5] Hotel) volcanoes roar
A welcome to highsteppers that no mouse
Who saw the Friends[6] there ever heard before.

What cunning neighbors history has in fine!
The woodlouse mortgages the ancient deal[7]
Table that Powitzky buys for only nine-
Ty-five at Adams' auction,—eats the seal,
The spinster polish of antiquity . . .
Who holds the lease on time and on disgrace?
What eats the pattern with ubiquity?
Where are my kinsmen and the patriarch race?

The resigned factions of the dead preside.
Dead rangers bled their comfort on the snow;
But I must ask slain Iroquois[8] to guide
Me farther than scalped Yankees knew to go:
Shoulder the curse of sundered parentage,
Wait for the postman driving from Birch Hill
With birthright by blackmail, the arrant page
That unfolds a new destiny to fill. . . .

So, must we from the hawk's far stemming view,
Must we descend as worm's eye to construe
Our love of all we touch, and take it to the Gate
As humbly as a guest who knows himself too late,
His news already told? Yes, while the heart is wrung,
Arise—yes, take this sheaf of dust upon your tongue!
In one last angelus lift throbbing throat—
Listen, transmuting silence with that stilly note

Of pain that Emily, that Isadora knew!
While high from dim elm-chancels hung with dew,
That triple-noted clause of moonlight—
Yes, whip-poor-will, unhusks the heart of fright,
Breaks us and saves, yes, breaks the heart, yet yields
That patience that is armour and that shields
Love from despair—when love foresees the end—
Leaf after autumnal leaf
                    break off,
                              descend—
                                        descend—

5. The island where King Arthur retired to recover from his wounds after his last battle.
6. Quakers.
7. Fir or pine.
8. A Native American culture largely centered in upstate New York.

VII. The Tunnel[9]

To Find the Western path
Right thro' the Gates of Wrath.
—BLAKE[1]

Performances, assortments, résumés—
Up Times Square to Columbus Circle[2] lights
Channel the congresses, nightly sessions,
Refractions of the thousand theatres, faces—
Mysterious kitchens. . . . You shall search them all.
Someday by heart you'll learn each famous sight
And watch the curtain lift in hell's despite;
You'll find the garden in the third act dead,
Finger your knees—and wish yourself in bed
With tabloid crime-sheets perched in easy sight.

Then let you reach your hat
and go.
As usual, let you—also
walking down—exclaim
to twelve upward leaving
a subscription praise
for what time slays.

Or can't you quite make up your mind to ride;
A walk is better underneath the L[3] a brisk
Ten blocks or so before? But you find yourself
Preparing penguin flexions of the arms,—
As usual you will meet the scuttle yawn:
The subway yawns the quickest promise home.

Be minimum, then, to swim the hiving swarms
Out of the Square, the Circle burning bright[4]—
Avoid the glass doors gyring at your right,
Where boxed alone a second, eyes take fright
—Quite unprepared rush naked back to light:
And down beside the turnstile press the coin
Into the slot. The gongs already rattle.

And so
of cities you bespeak
subways, rivered under streets
and rivers. . . . In the car
the overtone of motion

9. A New York City subway tunnel, the setting of the epic convention of a descent into the underworld.
1. From the opening of "Morning," by English poet William Blake (1757–1827).
2. In Manhattan.
3. Elevated railway.
4. The lighted sign of a subway station; cf. Blake's poem "The Tyger" (1794): "Tyger! Tyger! burning bright / In the forests of the night, / What immortal hand or eye / Could frame thy fearful symmetry?"

underground, the monotone
of motions is the sound
of other faces, also underground—

"Let's have a pencil Jimmy—living now
at Floral Park
Flatbush[5]—on the fourth of July—
like a pigeon's muddy dream—potatoes
to dig in the field—travlin the town—too—
night after night—the Culver line[6]—the
girls all shaping up—it used to be—"

Our tongues recant like beaten weather vanes.
This answer lives like verdigris,[7] like hair
Beyond extinction, surcease of the bone;
And repetition freezes—"What

"what do you want? getting weak on the links?
fandaddle daddy don't ask for change—IS THIS
FOURTEENTH? it's half past six she said—if
you don't like my gate why did you
swing on it, why *didja*
swing on it
anyhow—"

And somehow anyhow swing—

The phonographs of hades in the brain
Are tunnels that re-wind themselves, and love
A burnt match skating in a urinal—
Somewhere above Fourteenth TAKE THE EXPRESS
To brush some new presentiment of pain—

"But I want service in this office SERVICE
I said—after
the show she cried a little afterwards but—"

Whose head is swinging from the swollen strap?
Whose body smokes along the bitten rails,
Bursts from a smoldering bundle far behind
In back forks of the chasms of the brain,—
Puffs from a riven stump far out behind
In interborough fissures of the mind . . . ?[8]

And why do I often meet your visage here,
Your eyes like agate lanterns—on and on
Below the toothpaste and the dandruff ads?
—And did their riding eyes right through your side,

5. In Brooklyn.
6. Branch of the Brooklyn Rapid Transit system.
7. Greenish-blue coating or stain on copper.
8. The speaker addresses American poet Edgar Allan Poe (1809–1849).

And did their eyes like unwashed platters ride?
And Death, aloft,—gigantically down
Probing through you—toward me, O evermore![9]
And when they dragged your retching flesh,
Your trembling hands that night through Baltimore—
That last night on the ballot rounds, did you,
Shaking, did you deny the ticket, Poe?[1]

For Gravesend Manor change at Chambers Street.[2]
The platform hurries along to a dead stop.

The intent escalator lifts a serenade
Stilly
Of shoes, umbrellas, each eye attending its shoe,[3] then
Bolting outright somewhere above where streets
Burst suddenly in rain. . . . The gongs recur:
Elbows and levers, guard and hissing door.
Thunder is galvothermic[4] here below. . . . The car
Wheels off. The train rounds, bending to a scream,
Taking the final level for the dive
Under the river—
And somewhat emptier than before,
Demented, for a hitching second, humps; then
Lets go. . . . Toward corners of the floor
Newspapers wing, revolve and wing.
Blank windows gargle signals through the roar.

And does the Daemon take you home, also,
Wop washerwoman, with the bandaged hair?
After the corridors are swept, the cuspidors—
The gaunt sky-barracks cleanly now, and bare,
O Genoese,[5] do you bring mother eyes and hands
Back home to children and to golden hair?

Daemon, demurring and eventful yawn!
Whose hideous laughter is a bellows mirth
—Or the muffled slaughter of a day in birth—
O cruelly to inoculate the brinking dawn
With antennae toward worlds that glow and sink;—
To spoon us out more liquid than the dim
Locution of the eldest star, and pack
The conscience navelled in the plunging wind,
Umbilical to call—and straightway die!

9. Cf. Poe's refrain "Nevermore!" in "The Raven"; cf. also the line "the agate lamp within thy hand" in Poe's "To Helen" and his description of the kingdom of death in "The City in the Sea": "Lo! Death has reared himself a throne / In a strange city lying alone."

1. Poe died under mysterious circumstances in Baltimore, on Election Day, October 7, 1849. According to one theory, a political gang beat him to death, while he was drunk, because they wanted him to cast multiple ballots illegally for their candidate.

2. Near the southern tip of Manhattan.

3. Cf. T. S. Eliot's *Waste Land*, lines 62–65: "A crowd flowed over London Bridge, so many . . . / Sighs, short and infrequent, were exhaled, / And each man fixed his eyes before his feet."

4. That is, galvanothermic, producing heat by electricity.

5. Of Genoa, Italy, the birthplace of Columbus. *Wop:* slang term for an Italian, now considered offensive. *Cuspidors:* spittoons.

O caught like pennies beneath soot and steam,
Kiss of our agony thou gatherest;
Condensed, thou takest all—shrill ganglia[6]
Impassioned with some song we fail to keep.
And yet, like Lazarus,[7] to feel the slope,
The sod and billow breaking,—lifting ground,
—A sound of waters bending astride the sky
Unceasing with some Word that will not die . . . !

• • • • •

A tugboat, wheezing wreaths of steam,
Lunged past, with one galvanic blare stove up the River.
I counted the echoes assembling, one after one,
Searching, thumbing the midnight on the piers.
Lights, coasting, left the oily tympanum[8] of waters;
The blackness somewhere gouged glass on a sky.
And this thy harbor, O my City, I have driven under,
Tossed from the coil of ticking towers. . . . Tomorrow,
And to be. . . . Here by the River that is East—
Here at the waters' edge the hands drop memory;
Shadowless in that abyss they unaccounting lie.
How far away the star has pooled the sea—
Or shall the hands be drawn away, to die?

Kiss of our agony Thou gatherest,
O Hand of Fire
gatherest—

VIII. Atlantis

Music is then the knowledge of that which relates to love in harmony and system.

—PLATO[9]

Through the bound cable strands, the arching path
Upward, veering with light, the flight of strings,—
Taut miles of shuttling moonlight syncopate
The whispered rush, telepathy of wires.
Up the index of night, granite and steel—
Transparent meshes—fleckless the gleaming staves—
Sibylline voices[1] flicker, waveringly stream
As though a god were issue of the strings. . . .

And through that cordage, threading with its call
One arc synoptic of all tides below—
Their labyrinthine mouths of history
Pouring reply as though all ships at sea

6. A bundle of nerve cells from which electrical impulses are transmitted.
7. Raised from the dead by Jesus in John 11.43–44.
8. Surface that functions as a drumhead.
9. From Plato's *Symposium*.
1. The mysterious, oracular voices of the ancient sibyls, female prophets.

Complighted[2] in one vibrant breath made cry,—
"Make thy love sure—to weave whose song we ply!"
—From black embankments, moveless soundings hailed,
So seven oceans answer from their dream.

And on, obliquely up bright carrier bars[3]
New octaves trestle the twin monoliths
Beyond whose frosted capes the moon bequeaths
Two worlds of sleep (O arching strands of song!)—
Onward and up the crystal-flooded aisle
White tempest nets file upward, upward ring
With silver terraces the humming spars,
The loft of vision, palladium helm of stars.

Sheerly the eyes, like seagulls stung with rime[4]—
Slit and propelled by glistening fins of light—
Pick biting way up towering looms that press
Sidelong with flight of blade on tendon blade
—Tomorrows into yesteryear—and link
What cipher-script of time no traveller reads
But who, through smoking pyres of love and death,
Searches the timeless laugh of mythic spears.

Like hails, farewells—up planet-sequined heights
Some trillion whispering hammers glimmer Tyre:[5]
Serenely, sharply up the long anvil cry
Of inchling aeons silence rivets Troy.
And you, aloft there—Jason![6] hesting Shout!
Still wrapping harness to the swarming air!
Silvery the rushing wake, surpassing call,
Beams yelling Aeolus![7] splintered in the straits!

From gulfs unfolding, terrible of drums,
Tall Vision-of-the-Voyage, tensely spare—
Bridge, lifting night to cycloramic[8] crest
Of deepest day—O Choir, translating time
Into what multitudinous Verb the suns
And synergy of waters ever fuse, recast
In myriad syllables,—Psalm of Cathay!
O Love, thy white, pervasive Paradigm . . . !

We left the haven hanging in the night—
Sheened harbor lanterns backward fled the keel.
Pacific here at time's end, bearing corn,—
Eyes stammer through the pangs of dust and steel.
And still the circular, indubitable frieze
Of heaven's meditation, yoking wave

2. Bound, pledged, or twined together (Crane's coinage).
3. Vertical suspenders that extend from the main cables of the bridge to the diagonal stays that intersect them.
4. White frost.
5. An ancient Phoenecian island-city.
6. Leader of the Greek Argonauts in their search for the Golden Fleece. *Inchling*: early, young.
7. Keeper of the winds, in Homer's epics.
8. Curved panoramic.

To kneeling wave, one song devoutly binds—
The vernal strophe chimes from deathless strings!

O Thou steeled Cognizance whose leap commits
The agile precincts of the lark's return;
Within whose lariat sweep encinctured[9] sing
In single chrysalis the many twain,—
Of stars Thou art the stitch and stallion glow
And like an organ, Thou, with sound of doom—
Sight, sound and flesh Thou leadest from time's realm
As love strikes clear direction for the helm.

Swift peal of secular light, intrinsic Myth
Whose fell unshadow is death's utter wound,—
O River-throated—iridescently upborne
Through the bright drench and fabric of our veins;
With white escarpments swinging into light,
Sustained in tears the cities are endowed
And justified conclamant[1] with ripe fields
Revolving through their harvests in sweet torment.

Forever Deity's glittering Pledge, O Thou
Whose canticle fresh chemistry assigns
To wrapt inception and beatitude,—
Always through blinding cables, to our joy,
Of thy white seizure springs the prophecy:
Always through spiring cordage, pyramids
Of silver sequel, Deity's young name
Kinetic of white choiring wings . . . ascends.

Migrations that must needs void memory,
Inventions that cobblestone the heart,—
Unspeakable Thou Bridge to Thee, O Love.
Thy pardon for this history, whitest Flower,
O Answerer of all,—Anemone,[2]—
Now while thy petals spend the suns about us, hold—
(O Thou whose radiance doth inherit me)
Atlantis,—hold thy floating singer late!

So to thine Everpresence, beyond time,
Like spears ensanguined of one tolling star
That bleeds infinity—the orphic strings,
Sidereal phalanxes,[3] leap and converge:
—One Song, one Bridge of Fire! Is it Cathay,
Now pity steeps the grass and rainbows ring
The serpent with the eagle in the leaves . . . ?
Whispers antiphonal in azure swing.

1930

9. Encircled.
1. Calling out together.
2. Flower. In Greek mythology, the white anemone sprang from the tears of the goddess Venus when her lover Adonis was killed by a boar.
3. Starry ranks. *Orphic:* entrancing, prophetic; from Orpheus, mythical Greek musician who played the lyre so beautifully that he could enchant nature and the gods of the underworld.

Royal Palm

For Grace Hart Crane[4]

Green rustlings, more-than-regal charities
Drift coolly from that tower of whispered light.
Amid the noontide's blazed asperities
I watched the sun's most gracious anchorite

Climb up as by communings, year on year
Uneaten of the earth or aught earth holds,
And the grey trunk, that's elephantine, rear
Its frondings sighing in aetherial folds.

Forever fruitless, and beyond that yield
Of sweat the jungle presses with hot love
And tendril till our deathward breath is sealed—
It grazes the horizons, launched above

Mortality—ascending emerald-bright,
A fountain at salute, a crown in view—
Unshackled, casual of its azured height
As though it soared suchwise through heaven too.

1933

The Broken Tower

The bell-rope that gathers God at dawn[5]
Dispatches me as though I dropped down the knell
Of a spent day—to wander the cathedral lawn
From pit to crucifix, feet chill on steps from hell.

Have you not heard, have you not seen that corps
Of shadows in the tower, whose shoulders sway
Antiphonal carillons[6] launched before
The stars are caught and hived in the sun's ray?

The bells, I say, the bells break down their tower;
And swing I know not where. Their tongues engrave
Membrane through marrow, my long-scattered score
Of broken intervals . . . And I, their sexton slave!

Oval encyclicals[7] in canyons heaping
The impasse high with choir. Banked voices slain!
Pagodas, companiles[8] with reveilles outleaping—
O terraced echoes prostrate on the plain! . . .

4. The poet's mother.
5. The angelus bell commemorates the Incarnation of Christ.
6. Alternating and overlapping melodies played on the bells.
7. Papal documents; here, divinely inspired messages.
8. Also campaniles; bell-towers attached to Italian cathedrals.

And so it was I entered the broken world
To trace the visionary company of love,[9] its voice
An instant in the wind (I know not whither hurled)
But not for long to hold each desperate choice.

My word I poured. But was it cognate, scored
Of that tribunal monarch of the air
Whose thigh embronzes earth, strikes crystal Word[1]
In wounds pledged once to hope,—cleft to despair?

The steep encroachments of my blood left me
No answer (could blood hold such a lofty tower
As flings the question true?)—or is it she
Whose sweet mortality stirs latent power?—

And through whose pulse I hear, counting the strokes
My veins recall and add, revived and sure
The angelus of wars my chest evokes:
What I hold healed, original now, and pure . . .

And builds, within, a tower that is not stone
(Not stone can jacket heaven)—but slip
Of pebbles,—visible wings of silence sown
In azure circles, widening as they dip

The matrix of the heart, lift down the eye
That shrines the quiet lake and swells a tower . . .
The commodious, tall decorum of that sky
Unseals her earth, and lifts love in its shower.

1933

9. In the bells' attempt to transfigure life and to incarnate God, Crane sees an analogue of his own poetic mission.

1. Divine revelation, with which the poet hopes his word is cognate.

Allen Tate
1899–1979

Among the poets identified with the southern school, Allen Tate wrote the most chiseled and complicated verse. He had less directness than Robert Penn Warren and, though often witty, less humor than John Crowe Ransom. Of these poets, Tate seemed the least able to rid himself of the weight of melancholy and regret over the dilemmas of the south. For all his impersonal expression, he felt deeply the need to find and reassert some affirmable postulates in an atmosphere of disaffection. In this quest, Tate became a Fugitive, an agrarian, a Catholic. But he was at once too honest and too elegant for the self-denying fervor of these creeds. As a result, he appeared a rather distant figure, like the speaker in his important "Ode to the Confederate Dead." In a symposium on religion, Tate said that all his poems were about the suffering that comes from disbelief (George Hemphill, *Allen Tate,* 1964).

Tate avowed that his principal literary influence was T. S. Eliot's *Poems* (1920), and he defended *The Waste Land* against the strictures of Ransom (up to then, Tate's principal mentor). Tate's respect for tradition, his unhappiness with the cheapening of values, even his conversion to Catholicism showed the effect of Eliot. Tate also has something of Eliot's precise and sweepingly evaluative manner, though Tate curbs himself by his subtle and exacting recognition of his own limits.

John Orley Allen Tate was born on December 19, 1899, in Winchester, Clarke County, Kentucky. In 1918, he entered Vanderbilt University, where he impressed his teacher Ransom with his reading of French Symbolists such as Charles Baudelaire and Stéphane Mallarmé, among other writers. He was invited as an undergraduate, along with his roommate Robert Penn Warren, to join the adult group called the Fugitives, which published a magazine, *The Fugitive.* After taking his degree, Tate married Caroline Gordon, also a writer. In late 1925, they moved to a large house in Patterson, New York, to pursue their writing careers, and for several months they were joined by the poet Hart Crane, whose friendship with Tate was intense but vexed. Crane thought Tate ultimately too overwhelmed by the insufficiencies of life, while Tate thought Crane too eager to embrace enthusiasm at the cost of sense and form.

Living with his wife in New York and Paris until 1930, Tate became, through his tales, wit, and perception, a well-known and highly respected figure in the literary world. His first book of verse, *Mr. Pope and Other Poems,* which included an early version of his "Ode," was published in New York in 1928. In 1930, he wrote one of the essays in *I'll Take My Stand,* a book in which some eminent southerners spoke out in favor of an agrarian, rather than an industrialized, south. Tate's *Reactionary Essays on Poetry and Ideas* (with its multiple ironies over the meaning of "reactionary") appeared in 1936. He edited the *Sewanee Review* from 1944 to 1946. In 1950, he became a Roman Catholic. Having taught at small colleges in Tennessee and North Carolina, and at Princeton and New York Universities, Tate was, from 1951 until his retirement in 1968, a professor of English at the University of Minnesota. He won the Bollingen Prize in 1956. He remarried in 1959 and again in 1966. Besides his verse, he wrote fiction, biographies, and a series of books that helped shape the New Criticism. Though he affirmed southern tradition and custom, he could also be critical: in "The Swimmers," a late poem about collective guilt written in Dante's terza rima, he recalls a childhood experience of a lynching. Intricate and ritualistic in form, authoritative and elegiac in tone, densely allusive and symbolic in reference, Tate's poetry was a formative influence for a later generation of writers, including Randall Jarrell and Robert Lowell.

Mr. Pope[1]

When Alexander Pope strolled in the city
Strict was the glint of pearl and gold sedans.
Ladies leaned out more out of fear than pity
For Pope's tight back was rather a goat's than man's.

Often one thinks the urn[2] should have more bones
Than skeletons provide for speedy dust,

1. Alexander Pope (1688–1744), English poet and writer. Pope's body was deformed.

2. A funeral urn, imagined here as containing Pope's bones.

The urn gets hollow, cobwebs brittle as stones
Weave to the funeral shell a frivolous rust.

And he who dribbled couplets like a snake
Coiled to a lithe precision in the sun
Is missing. The jar is empty; you may break
It only to find that Mr. Pope is gone.

What requisitions of a verity
Prompted the wit and rage between his teeth
One cannot say. Around a crooked tree
A moral climbs whose name should be a wreath.

1928

Ode to the Confederate Dead

Row after row with strict impunity
The headstones yield their names to the element,
The wind whirrs without recollection;
In the riven troughs the splayed leaves
Pile up, of nature the casual sacrament
To the seasonal eternity of death;
Then driven by the fierce scrutiny
Of heaven to their election in the vast breath,
They sough[3] the rumor of mortality.

Autumn is desolation in the plot
Of a thousand acres where these memories grow
From the inexhaustible bodies that are not
Dead, but feed the grass row after rich row.
Think of the autumns that have come and gone!—
Ambitious November with the humors of the year,
With a particular zeal for every slab,
Staining the uncomfortable angels that rot
On the slabs, a wing chipped here, an arm there:
The brute curiosity of an angel's stare
Turns you, like them, to stone,
Transforms the heaving air
Till plunged to a heavier world below
You shift your sea-space blindly
Heaving, turning like the blind crab.

Dazed by the wind, only the wind
The leaves flying, plunge

You know who have waited by the wall
The twilight certainty of an animal,

3. Moan.

Those midnight restitutions of the blood
You know—the immitigable pines, the smoky frieze
Of the sky, the sudden call: you know the rage,
The cold pool left by the mounting flood,
Of muted Zeno and Parmenides.[4]
You who have waited for the angry resolution
Of those desires that should be yours tomorrow,
You know the unimportant shrift of death
And praise the vision
And praise the arrogant circumstance
Of those who fall
Rank upon rank, hurried beyond decision—
Here by the sagging gate, stopped by the wall.

Seeing, seeing only the leaves
Flying, plunge and expire

Turn your eyes to the immoderate past,
Turn to the inscrutable infantry rising
Demons out of the earth—they will not last.
Stonewall,[5] Stonewall, and the sunken fields of hemp,
Shiloh, Antietam, Malvern Hill, Bull Run.[6]
Lost in the orient of the thick-and-fast
You will curse the setting sun.

Cursing only the leaves crying
Like an old man in a storm

You hear the shout, the crazy hemlocks point
With troubled fingers to the silence which
Smothers you, a mummy, in time.

The hound bitch
Toothless and dying, in a musty cellar
Hears the wind only.

Now that the salt of their blood
Stiffens the saltier oblivion of the sea,
Seals the malignant purity of the flood,
What shall we who count our days and bow
Our heads with a commemorial woe
In the ribboned coats of grim felicity,
What shall we say of the bones, unclean,
Whose verdurous anonymity will grow?

4. Parmenides and his follower Zeno, both of Elea, were Greek philosophers of the fifth century B.C.E. They held that reality is single and unchanging, while mutable things are illusory and unknowable.

5. Thomas Jonathan Jackson (1824–1863), Confederate general in the Civil War, earned the nickname Stonewall at the first battle of Bull Run (Virginia), July 21, 1861. He was fatally wounded by his men at Chancellorsville.

6. Famous battles of the Civil War: Shiloh (Tennessee), April 6–7, 1862, ended with the Confederate troops in retreat; Antietam, or Sharpsburg (Maryland), September 17, 1862, and Malvern Hill (Virginia), July 2, 1862, also were disadvantageous to the South; the two battles of Bull Run, in 1861 and on August 29–30, 1862, were both victories for the Confederate armies.

The ragged arms, the ragged heads and eyes
Lost in these acres of the insane green?
The gray lean spiders come, they come and go;
In a tangle of willows without light
The singular screech-owl's tight
Invisible lyric seeds the mind
With the furious murmur of their chivalry.

We shall say only the leaves
Flying, plunge and expire

We shall say only the leaves whispering
In the improbable mist of nightfall
That flies on multiple wing;
Night is the beginning and the end
And in between the ends of distraction
Waits mute speculation, the patient curse
That stones the eyes, or like the jaguar leaps
For his own image in a jungle pool, his victim.

What shall we say who have knowledge
Carried to the heart? Shall we take the act
To the grave? Shall we, more hopeful, set up the grave
In the house? The ravenous grave?

Leave now
The shut gate and the decomposing wall:
The gentle serpent, green in the mulberry bush,
Riots with his tongue through the hush—
Sentinel of the grave who counts us all!

1928, 1937

The Swimmers

SCENE: Montgomery County
Kentucky, July 1911

Kentucky water, clear springs: a boy fleeing
To water under the dry Kentucky sun,
His four little friends in tandem with him, seeing

Long shadows of grapevine wriggle and run
Over the green swirl; mullein under the ear
Soft as Nausicaä's[7] palm; sullen fun

7. The king's daughter who kindly welcomes the shipwrecked Odysseus in Homer's *Odyssey*, book 6 (and see line 15). *Mullein:* wooly-leaved plant.

Savage as childhood's thin harmonious tear:
O fountain, bosom source undying-dead
Replenish me the spring of love and fear

And give me back the eye that looked and fled
When a thrush idling in the tulip tree
Unwound the cold dream of the copperhead.[8]

—Along the creek the road was winding; we
Felt the quicksilver sky. I see again
The shrill companions of that odyssey:

Bill Eaton, Charlie Watson, "Nigger" Layne
The doctor's son, Harry Duèsler who played
The flute; and Tate, with water on the brain.

Dog-days: the dusty leaves where rain delayed
Hung low on poison-oak and scuppernong,[9]
And we were following the active shade

Of water, that bells and bickers all night long.
"No more'n a mile," Layne said. All five stood still.
Listening, I heard what seemed at first a song;

Peering, I heard the hooves come down the hill.
The posse passed, twelve horse; the leader's face
Was worn as limestone on an ancient sill.

Then, as sleepwalkers shift from a hard place
In bed, and rising to keep a formal pledge
Descend a ladder into empty space,

We scuttled down the bank below a ledge
And marched stiff-legged in our common fright
Along a hog-track by the riffle's[1] edge:

Into a world where sound shaded the sight
Dropped the dull hooves again; the horsemen came
Again, all but the leader. It was night

Momently and I feared: eleven same
Jesus-Christers unmembered and unmade,
Whose Corpse had died again in dirty shame.

The bank then levelling in a speckled glade,
We stopped to breathe above the swimming-hole;
I gazed at its reticulated[2] shade

8. Poisonous snake, whose coloring makes it hard to see among fallen leaves.
9. Grapevine common in the south.
1. Of a shallow in the bed of a stream.
2. Netlike.

Recoiling in blue fear, and felt it roll
Over my ears and eyes and lift my hair
Like seaweed tossing on a sunk atoll.

I rose again. Borne on the copper air
A distant voice green as a funeral wreath
Against a grave: "That dead nigger there."

The melancholy sheriff slouched beneath
A giant sycamore; shaking his head
He plucked a sassafras twig and picked his teeth:

"We come too late." He spoke to the tired dead
Whose ragged shirt soaked up the viscous flow
Of blood in which It lay discomfited.

A butting horse-fly gave one ear a blow
And glanced off, as the sheriff kicked the rope
Loose from the neck and hooked it with his toe

Away from the blood.—I looked back down the slope:
The friends were gone that I had hoped to greet.—
A single horseman came at a slow lope

And pulled up at the hanged man's horny feet;
The sheriff noosed the feet, the other end
The stranger tied to his pommel in a neat

Slip-knot. I saw the Negro's body bend
And straighten, as a fish-line cast transverse
Yields to the current that it must subtend.

The sheriff's Goddamn was a murmured curse
Not for the dead but for the blinding dust
That boxed the cortège[3] in a cloudy hearse

And dragged it towards our town. I knew I must
Not stay till twilight in that silent road;
Sliding my bare feet into the warm crust,

I hopped the stonecrop like a panting toad
Mouth open, following the heaving cloud
That floated to the court-house square its load

Of limber corpse that took the sun for shroud.
There were three figures in the dying sun
Whose light were company where three was crowd.

3. Funerary procession.

My breath crackled the dead air like a shotgun
As, sheriff and the stranger disappearing,
The faceless head lay still. I could not run

Or walk, but stood. Alone in the public clearing
This private thing was owned by all the town,
Though never claimed by us within my hearing.

1953

Basil Bunting
1900–1985

Basil Bunting seemed always to have thought of himself as an outsider, a maverick, a man who went his own way and resisted the odious claims of modern literary society. He said of himself: "War, poverty, and love oppressed and illuminated him. He hated law, dogma, press pimps, and the pedlars of culture. He liked life and risk when he could afford them. As for dying, he would be content to let the servants do that for him, if he had any" (*Poetry,* January 1966). Bunting took pride in his Northumbrian ancestry and in his friendship with a few great modern men of letters, notably Ford Madox Ford, Ezra Pound, and W. B. Yeats, all of whom, in Bunting's phrase, "egged him on." Yeats described him as "one of Ezra's more savage disciples," and Pound referred to Bunting admiringly in a letter as a man who "simply will not melt himself into the vile patterns of expediency."

In the early 1930s, Bunting was associated with another young disciple of Pound's, the American Objectivist poet Louis Zukofsky. Objectivism, a development of Imagism, encouraged concentration and sharpness of definition and an interest in individual images for their cultural and historical suggestiveness. Bunting admired craftsmanship, and like Zukofsky, he valued poetry as an experience for the ear, an analogue with music. He was first drawn to the poetry of T. S. Eliot because Eliot's "Preludes" showed an interest, later developed in *Four Quartets,* in the adaptation of musical forms to poetry. Bunting himself experimented with the sonata concept. In *Briggflatts,* he endeavors to orchestrate the particulars of experience, evocative of a personal history and a collective past, in something like a musical form, and his model is a Baroque Italian composer (1660–1725): "Domenico Scarlatti / condensed so much music into so few bars / with never a crabbed turn or a congested cadence, / never a boast or a see-here; and stars and lakes / echo him and the copse drums out his measure."

Bunting was born on March 1, 1900, in Scotswood on Tyne, in the north of England. He was educated at Quaker schools and at the London School of Economics (1919–20). Influenced by his Quaker education, he was a conscientious objector during World War I and spent some time in prison. During the 1920s, he lived in Paris, where he helped Ford Madox Ford with the *Transatlantic Review;* he then moved to Italy, where he cultivated Pound's friendship, then to the Canary Islands. In the first months of World War II, Bunting, who had spent much time on the sea, worked for the British merchant navy. In 1943, the British government sent him to Iran to work in the British embassy because of his knowledge of classical Persian, which he had taught himself so he could read Persian poetry. Eventually, he became the Iran correspondent for the London *Times,* but in 1953, after repeated threats on his life, he was thrown out of the country because of his suspected lack of sympathy for its government. He then worked for an English provincial newspaper until the mid-1960s, when he returned to poetry after a long silence. He began to be read with admiration by other and much younger English poets; his autobiographical poem *Briggflatts* (1966) was seen by some as the best English long poem since Eliot's *Four Quartets.* Although English poets often disliked Pound's eclecticism, a kind of cultural tourism they found too American, they were drawn to Bunting because he adapted Pound's discoveries to a distinctively English locale. His poetry proved a valuable resource to those who sought for contemporary English verse rougher surfaces and greater dynamism than the Movement and other postwar developments provided.

On the Fly-Leaf of Pound's Cantos

There are the Alps. What is there to say about them?
They don't make sense. Fatal glaciers, crags cranks climb,
jumbled boulder and weed, pasture and boulder, scree,[1]
et l'on entend, maybe, *le refrain joyeux et leger.*[2]
Who knows what the ice will have scraped on the rock it is smoothing?

There they are, you will have to go a long way round
if you want to avoid them.
It takes some getting used to. There are the Alps,
fools! Sit down and wait for them to crumble!

1949 1965

From Briggflatts[3]

An Autobiography

I

Brag, sweet tenor bull,
descant on Rawthey's madrigal,[4]
each pebble its part
for the fells'[5] late spring.
Dance tiptoe, bull,
black against may.[6]
Ridiculous and lovely
chase hurdling shadows
morning into noon.
May on the bull's hide
and through the dale

1. Rocky debris.
2. And one hears the light and joyous refrain (French).
3. A small hamlet in Cumbria, the Lake District of northern England.
4. Part-song for three or more voices. *Descant:* sing the upper part of a part-song. The River Rawthey runs through Briggflatts.
5. Moorland hills.
6. The flower (pink or white) of the hawthorn tree.

furrows fill with may,
paving the slowworm's[7] way.

A mason times his mallet
to a lark's twitter,
listening while the marble rests,
lays his rule
at a letter's edge,
fingertips checking,
till the stone spells a name
naming none,
a man abolished.
Painful lark, labouring to rise!
The solemn mallet says:
In the grave's slot
he lies. We rot.

Decay thrusts the blade,
wheat stands in excrement
trembling. Rawthey trembles.
Tongue stumbles, ears err
for fear of spring.
Rub the stone with sand,
wet sandstone rending
roughness away. Fingers
ache on the rubbing stone.
The mason says: Rocks
happen by chance.
No one here bolts the door,
love is so sore.

Stone smooth as skin,
cold as the dead they load
on a low lorry[8] by night.
The moon sits on the fell
but it will rain.
Under sacks on the stone
two children lie,
hear the horse stale,[9]
the mason whistle,
harness mutter to shaft,
felloe[1] to axle squeak,
rut thud the rim,
crushed grit.

Stocking to stocking, jersey to jersey,[2]
head to a hard arm,

7. Or blind worm, a small, burrowing, limbless lizard.
8. Truck (British).
9. Urinate.
1. Interior rim of a wheel.
2. Sweater (British).

they kiss under the rain,
bruised by their marble bed.
In Garsdale, dawn;
at Hawes, tea from the can.[3]
Rain stops, sacks
steam in the sun, they sit up.
Copper-wire moustache,
sea-reflecting eyes
and Baltic plainsong speech
declare: By such rocks
men killed Bloodaxe.[4]

Fierce blood throbs in his tongue,
lean words.
Skulls cropped for steel caps
huddle round Stainmore.[5]
Their becks[6] ring on limestone,
whisper to peat.
The clogged cart pushes the horse downhill.
In such soft air
they trudge and sing,
laying the tune frankly on the air.
All sounds fall still,
fellside bleat,
hide-and-seek peewit.[7]

Her pulse their pace,
palm countering palm,
till a trench is filled,
stone white as cheese
jeers at the dale.
Knotty wood, hard to rive,
smoulders to ash;
smell of October apples.
The road again,
at a trot.
Wetter, warmed, they watch
the mason meditate
on name and date.

Rain rinses the road,
the bull streams and laments.
Sour rye porridge from the hob[8]
with cream and black tea,
meat, crust and crumb.
Her parents in bed

3. Metal container with handle and cover (not, that is, a modern seal can). Garsdale and Hawes are small, country towns in northern England.
4. Eric Bloodaxe (d. 954), Norwegian prince and ruler of the Viking kingdom of Northumbria; he was driven out by the English and killed.
5. Desolate area of fells in the north of England. *Steel caps:* helmets.
6. Small streams with stony beds. Also, mattocks (dialect).
7. A bird noted for its shrill, wailing cry.
8. Shelf in a fireplace to keep food or utensils warm.

the children dry their clothes.
He has untied the tape
of her striped flannel drawers
before the range. Naked
on the pricked rag mat
his fingers comb
thatch of his manhood's home.

Gentle generous voices weave
over bare night
words to confirm and delight
till bird dawn.
Rainwater from the butt
she fetches the flannel
to wash him inch by inch,
kissing the pebbles.
Shining slowworm part of the marvel.
The mason stirs:
Words!
Pens are too light.
Take a chisel to write.

Every birth a crime,
every sentence life.
Wiped of mould and mites
would the ball run true?
No hope of going back.
Hounds falter and stray,
shame deflects the pen.
Love murdered neither bleeds nor stifles
but jogs the draftsman's elbow.
What can he, changed, tell
her, changed, perhaps dead?
Delight dwindles. Blame
stays the same.

Brief words are hard to find,
shapes to carve and discard:
Bloodaxe, king of York,
king of Dublin, king of Orkney.[9]
Take no notice of tears;
letter the stone to stand
over love laid aside lest
insufferable happiness impede
flight to Stainmore,
to trace
lark, mallet,
becks, flocks
and axe knocks.

9. Islands of the northeast coast of Scotland; "king" here is in the sense of an early tribal chieftain.

Dung will not soil the slowworm's
mosaic. Breathless lark
drops to nest in sodden trash;
Rawthey truculent, dingy.
Drudge at the mallet, the may is down,
fog on fells. Guilty of spring
and spring's ending
amputated years ache after
the bull is beef, love a convenience.
It is easier to die than to remember.
Name and date
split in soft slate
a few months obliterate.

1965 1966

What the Chairman Told Tom[1]

Poetry? It's a hobby.
I run model trains.
Mr Shaw there breeds pigeons.

It's not work. You dont sweat.
Nobody pays for it.
You *could* advertise soap.

Art, that's opera; or repertory—
The Desert Song.[2]
Nancy was in the chorus.

But to ask for twelve pounds a week—
married, aren't you?—
you've got a nerve.

How could I look a bus conductor
in the face
if I paid you twelve pounds?

Who says it's poetry, anyhow?
My ten year old
can do it *and* rhyme.

I get three thousand and expenses,
a car, vouchers,
but I'm an accountant.

1. Generic figure modeled on Tom Pickard (b. 1946), a British poet who studied under Bunting's tutelage and who, in 1964, cofounded a poetry reading series at Morden Tower, in Bunting's native Newcastle-upon-Tyne. In 1965, as part of the series, Bunting gave the first reading of his major work, *Briggflatts*.
2. Popular musical of the 1930s.

They do what I tell them,
my company.
What do *you* do?

Nasty little words, nasty long words,
it's unhealthy.
I want to wash when I meet a poet.

They're Reds,[3] addicts,
all delinquents.
What you write is rot.

Mr Hines says so, and he's a schoolteacher,
he ought to know.
Go and find *work.*

1965 1967

3. Communists.

YVOR WINTERS
1900–1968

Marked by formal control and by disregard for twentieth-century poetic fashion, Yvor Winters's poetry often celebrates the hard-won victory of reason over sensation and emotion. In his poetry and criticism, he stands like a lonely, stoic survivor in an alien world. In his verse, Winters often seems to hold on to discipline, and the lucidity it encourages, for dear life. He does not entertain outlandish beliefs for the sake of their poetic effectiveness, a vice for which he censured W. B. Yeats. Winter's poems—orderly, balanced, restrained—seek to discover and express the truth of a particular situation and thus are often occasional and epigrammatic. For his models, he turns back to the spare, careful poetry of Sir Fulke Greville and Sir Walter Ralegh, Elizabethan courtiers whose work communicates a bitter wisdom. Though Winters can be didactic, he does not bully, but tries to express the truth with delicacy and in a carefully modulated tone.

He was born on October 17, 1900, in Chicago. He spent his childhood in California and Oregon, then returned to Chicago, where he went to high school and began studies at the University of Chicago. In his freshman year, he was discovered to have tuberculosis and was sent to Santa Fe, New Mexico, where he convalesced, taught primary school, and worked as a manual laborer. In 1925, he earned an M.A. in Romance languages at the University of Colorado; in 1928, he began to teach at Stanford University, where he remained until his retirement in 1966. His first book of poems, *The Immobile Wind* (1921), contained experiments in free verse, and early reviewers described Winters as an Imagist. He soon moved to strictly metered and rhymed forms, and for the next twenty-five years he wrote the meditative lyrics for which he is best known as a poet.

Winters is also known as an eminent, if controversial, critic. In 1937, he published

Primitivism and Decadence: A Study of American Experimental Poetry, the first of a series of books in which he defended his doctrine of the moral value of poetry and judged the work of his contemporaries by his own unpopular standards, such as whether a poem's language united rational statement with emotion. Most poems were found wanting; Winters believed that Romantic attitudes were a blight on modern literature and that poetry in English has been in decline since the early eighteenth century. As a moralist, rationalist, and formalist in his poetry and criticism, Winters swam against the current of twentieth-century letters, but he had a decisive influence on students who became prominent poets, among them Thom Gunn, Philip Levine, and Robert Pinsky.

The Slow Pacific Swell

Far out of sight forever stands the sea,
Bounding the land with pale tranquillity.
When a small child, I watched it from a hill
At thirty miles or more. The vision still
Lies in the eye, soft blue and far away:
The rain has washed the dust from April day;
Paint-brush and lupine[1] lie against the ground;
The wind above the hill-top has the sound
Of distant water in unbroken sky;
Dark and precise the little steamers ply—
Firm in direction they seem not to stir.
That is illusion. The artificer
Of quiet, distance holds me in a vise
And holds the ocean steady to my eyes.

Once when I rounded Flattery, the sea
Hove its loose weight like sand to tangle me
Upon the washing deck, to crush the hull;
Subsiding, dragged flesh at the bone. The skull
Felt the retreating wash of dreaming hair.
Half drenched in dissolution, I lay bare.
I scarcely pulled myself erect; I came
Back slowly, slowly knew myself the same.
That was the ocean. From the ship we saw
Gray whales for miles: the long sweep of the jaw,
The blunt head plunging clean above the wave.
And one rose in a tent of sea and gave
A darkening shudder; water fell away;
The whale stood shining, and then sank in spray.

A landsman, I. The sea is but a sound.
I would be near it on a sandy mound,
And hear the steady rushing of the deep
While I lay stinging in the sand with sleep.

1. Like paint-brush, a flowering plant.

I have lived inland long. The land is numb.
It stands beneath the feet, and one may come
Walking securely, till the sea extends
Its limber margin, and precision ends.
By night a chaos of commingling power,
The whole Pacific hovers hour by hour.
The slow Pacific swell stirs on the sand,
Sleeping to sink away, withdrawing land,
Heaving and wrinkled in the moon, and blind;
Or gathers seaward, ebbing out of mind.

1931

By the Road to the Air-Base

The calloused grass lies hard
Against the cracking plain:
Life is a grayish stain;
The salt-marsh hems my yard.

Dry dikes rise hill on hill:
In sloughs of tidal slime
Shell-fish deposit lime,
Wild sea-fowl creep at will.

The highway, like a beach,
Turns whiter, shadowy, dry:
Loud, pale against the sky,
The bombing planes hold speech.

Yet fruit grows on the trees;
Here scholars pause to speak;
Through gardens bare and Greek,
I hear my neighbor's bees.

1934

John Sutter[2]

I was the patriarch of the shining land,
Of the blond summer and metallic grain;
Men vanished at the motion of my hand,
And when I beckoned they would come again.

2. American pioneer (1803–1880), who was granted a huge tract of land on the Sacramento River by the Mexican governor on condition that he develop and fortify it. After California was acquired by the United States, gold was found on Sutter's property. The news leaked out, the gold rush began, and his property was overrun. When the U.S. Supreme Court found the title to most of his land invalid, he went bankrupt. From 1871 until his death, he petitioned Congress annually for redress.

The earth grew dense with grain at my desire;
The shade was deepened at the springs and streams;
Moving in dust that clung like pillared fire,
The gathering herds grew heavy in my dreams.

Across the mountains, naked from the heights,
Down to the valley broken settlers came,
And in my houses feasted through the nights,
Rebuilt their sinews and assumed a name.

In my clear rivers my own men discerned
The motive for the ruin and the crime—
Gold heavier than earth, a wealth unearned,
Loot, for two decades, from the heart of Time.

Metal, intrinsic value, deep and dense,
Preanimate, inimitable, still,
Real, but an evil with no human sense,
Dispersed the mind to concentrate the will.

Grained by alchemic change, the human kind
Turned from themselves to rivers and to rocks;
With dynamite broke metal unrefined;
Measured their moods by geologic shocks.

With knives they dug the metal out of stone;
Turned rivers back, for gold through ages piled,
Drove knives to hearts, and faced the gold alone;
Valley and river ruined and reviled;

Reviled and ruined me, my servant slew,
Strangled him from the figtree by my door.
When they had done what fury bade them do,
I was a cursing beggar, stripped and sore.

What end impersonal, what breathless age,
Incontinent of quiet and of years,
What calm catastrophe will yet assuage
This final drouth of penitential tears?

1941

Laura Riding
1901–1991

Laura Riding was born Laura Reichenthal on January 16, 1901, in New York City. Her father was a Jewish tailor and socialist who had immigrated from Poland. Her mother, who had nearly gone blind working from youth in sweatshops, was from a German Dutch Jewish family in New York. Growing up in poverty, Riding was educated at Brooklyn Girls High School and at Cornell University, where she wrote her first adult poems. In spite of her northern background, she found favor among a group of southern poets called the Fugitives, including John Crowe Ransom, Allen Tate, and Robert Penn Warren. In 1924, they awarded her a prize for her contributions to their magazine and subsequently made her a regular member of their group. In late 1925, having divorced her first husband, Riding went to Europe, where she remained from 1926 until 1939, mostly in England and on the Mediterranean island of Majorca, off the coast of Spain. During this period, she published her first book of poems, *The Close Chaplet* (1926), and wrote in various prose forms, including literary criticism. Her *A Survey of Modernist Poetry* (1927), written with Robert Graves, promoted close study of the words in poems and proved influential on the New Criticism.

In her life abroad—besides founding, with Robert Graves, the Seizin Press and being active in its development—Riding worked intimately with certain fellow writers, sharing her thinking and helping them strengthen their work. In 1929, she drank Lysol and leapt from a window, breaking her back and pelvis, because of a vexed emotional triad involving Graves, herself, and a male Irish poet in the group. She returned to the United States in 1939 and stopped writing poems two years later. She had come to see poetry as stimulating the desire for truth and yet obstructing truth by its formal patterning and dependence on the senses. The nature of language itself, rather than the nature of poetry, became the focus of her working life. After her marriage in 1941 to Schuyler B. Jackson, she changed her authorial signature to Laura (Riding) Jackson. Believing that human destiny depended on good speaking, the couple worked for two decades on a project to make it possible to define the intrinsic meanings of words—the posthumously published *Rational Meaning: A New Foundation for the Definition of Words* (1997).

"A poem," Riding writes in the introduction to her *Collected Poems* (1938), "is an uncovering of truth of so fundamental and general a kind that no other word besides poetry is adequate except truth. Knowledge implies specialized fields of exploration and discovery; it would be inexact to call poetry a kind of knowledge." Given this high ambition for poetry, perhaps it was inevitable that Riding would later judge the medium inadequate. Even before she gave up poetry altogether, she wrote antipoetic poems—poems, that is, in which she tries to resist the allure of rhetoric and ornament. Ultimate reality is her subject. In poems such as "Death as Death," Riding employs figurative language ("Death like a quick cold hand"), but doggedly resists it: " 'Like this, like this, like nothing else.' " A literalist, Riding is suspicious of metaphor, analogy, and representation. Maps tear; reality persists ("The Map of Places"). Interested in foundational issues, such as the relation between language and reality, or between men and women, she rarely allows her poems to become entangled in the particulars of time, place, and personal experience. Wary of the duplicity of language, she repeats words to purge inessentials, aspiring to a metaphysical purity. But Riding came to see even her own poetry—however ascetic—as being more in the service of aesthetic effect than of truth. Plato banished the poets from his hypothetical Republic because they appealed more to feeling than to reason; for similar reasons, Riding banished herself.

The Map of Places

The map of places passes.
The reality of paper tears.
Land and water where they are
Are only where they were
When words read *here* and *here*
Before ships happened there.

Now on naked names feet stand,
No geographies in the hand,
And paper reads anciently,
And ships at sea
Turn round and round.
All is known, all is found.
Death meets itself everywhere.
Holes in maps look through to nowhere.

1928

Footfalling

A modulation is that footfalling.
It says and does not say.
When not walking it is not saying.
When saying it is not walking.
When walking it is not saying.
Between the step and alternation
Breathes the hush of modulation
Which tars all roads
To confiding heels and soles and tiptoes.
Deep from the rostrum of the promenade
The echo-tongued mouth of motion
Rolls its voice,
And the large throat is heard to tremble
While the footfalls shuffle.

It says and does not say.
When the going is gone
There is only fancy.
Every thought sounds like a footfall,
Till a thought like a boot kicks down the wall.

1928

Death as Death

To conceive death as death
Is difficulty come by easily,
A blankness fallen among
Images of understanding,
Death like a quick cold hand
On the hot slow head of suicide.
So is it come by easily
For one instant. Then again furnaces
Roar in the ears, then again hell revolves,
And the elastic eye holds paradise
At visible length from blindness,
And dazedly the body echoes
'Like this, like this, like nothing else.'

Like nothing—a similarity
Without resemblance. The prophetic eye,
Closing upon difficulty,
Opens upon comparison,
Halving the actuality
As a gift too plain, for which
Gratitude has no language,
Foresight no vision.

1928

The Troubles of a Book

The trouble of a book is first to be
No thoughts to nobody,
Then to lie as long unwritten
As it will lie unread,
Then to build word for word an author
And occupy his head
Until the head declares vacancy
To make full publication
Of running empty.

The trouble of a book is secondly
To keep awake and ready
And listening like an innkeeper,
Wishing, not wishing for a guest,
Torn between hope of no rest
And hope of rest.
Uncertainly the pages doze
And blink open to passing fingers
With landlord smile, then close.

The trouble of a book is thirdly
To speak its sermon, then look the other way,
Arouse commotion in the margin,
Where tongue meets the eye,
But claim no experience of panic,
No complicity in the outcry.
The ordeal of a book is to give no hint
Of ordeal, to be flat and witless
Of the upright sense of print.

The trouble of a book is chiefly
To be nothing but book outwardly;
To wear binding like binding,
Bury itself in book-death,
Yet to feel all but book;
To breathe live words, yet with the breath
Of letters; to address liveliness
In reading eyes, be answered with
Letters and bookishness.

1928

Ding-Donging

With old hours all belfry heads
Are filled, as with thoughts.
With old hours ring the new hours
Between their bells.
And this hour-long ding-donging
So much employs the hour-long silences
That bells hang thinking when not striking,
When striking think of nothing.

Chimes of forgotten hours
More and more are played
While bells stare into space,
And more and more space wears
A look of having heard
But hearing not:
Forgotten hours chime louder
In the meantime, as if always,
And spread ding-donging back
More and more to yesterdays.

1928

With the Face

With the face goes a mirror
As with the mind a world.
Likeness tells the doubting eye
That strangeness is not strange.
At an early hour and knowledge
Identity not yet familiar
Looks back upon itself from later,
And seems itself.

To-day seems now.
With reality-to-be goes time.
With the mind goes a world.
With the heart goes a weather.
With the face goes a mirror
As with the body a fear.
Young self goes staring to the wall
Where dumb futurity speaks calm,
And between then and then
Forebeing grows of age.

The mirror mixes with the eye.
Soon will it be the very eye.
Soon will the eye that was
The very mirror be.
Death, the final image, will shine
Transparently not otherwise
Than as the dark sun described
With such faint brightnesses.

1933

STERLING BROWN
1901–1989

Sterling Brown was born on May 1, 1901, into a middle-class family in Washington, D.C. His father was a professor of religion at Howard University and pastor of Lincoln Temple Congregational Church. After attending segregated public schools, Brown attended Williams College on a scholarship, graduating with honors in 1922, and earning his master's degree at Harvard University the following year. He claimed that his finest education came from rural black people of the south, especially those he knew in the environs of the African American institutions where he held his first three teaching jobs, from 1923 to 1929: Virginia Seminary, in Lynchburg, Virginia; Lincoln University, in Jefferson City, Missouri; and Fisk University, in Nashville, Tennessee. Brown joined the faculty of Howard University in 1929 and taught there for the next forty years, his illustrious students including novelist Toni Morrison, actor Ossie Davis, and poet Amiri Baraka.

Brown published his first collection of poetry, *Southern Road,* in 1932, but the Depression and the literary establishment's waning interest in African American art thwarted his ambition to publish his second collection of verse, *No Hiding Place.* A trenchant observer of American culture, Brown turned to writing critical and cultural studies, ranging from literary history and folklore to musicology and social history. He also compiled anthologies, including the most comprehensive collection of African American literature at the time, *The Negro Caravan* (1941). He oversaw the Federal Writers' Project studies of African Americans, including the collection of slave narratives. More than forty years after the publication of his first book of poems, many of Brown's poems were published for the first time in *The Last Ride of Wild Bill and Eleven Narratives* (1975) and *The Collected Poems of Sterling A. Brown* (1985).

Along with Langston Hughes, Brown was one of the leading poets of the Harlem Renaissance, though he rejected the name as geographically inaccurate and preferred to call it the New Negro Renaissance. Brown was inspired by the blues-based poetry Hughes published in the 1920s, but whereas Hughes's emphasis was on the city, Brown's "folk"-based poetry was steeped in rural life. Like Hughes, Brown sought to bring black oral traditions, such as the blues, work songs, ballads, spirituals, sermons, and tall tales or "lies," into literary verse. Although James Weldon Johnson had described the black vernacular as limited, he astutely introduced Brown's *Southern Road,* observing that Brown "infused his poetry with genuine characteristic flavor by adopting as his medium the common, racy, living speech of the Negro. . . . For his raw material he dug down into the deep mine of Negro folk poetry. . . . He has made more than mere transcription of folk poetry, and he has done more than bring to it mere artistry; he has deepened its meanings and multiplied its implications." Like Johnson, Brown was conscious of the parallel between what writers of the New Negro Renaissance were doing to recover their own seemingly subliterary traditions and what J. M. Synge, W. B. Yeats, and other Irish writers had accomplished. Brown also discovered models in the so-called New American poets he first read in Louis Untermeyer's *Modern American Poetry* (1921), such as Robert Frost (with his character portraits of stoic, self-respecting rural folk) and Edwin Arlington Robinson (with his ironic sketches of ordinary lives), and he paid homage to Edgar Lee Masters and Carl Sandburg. Some characters in Brown's poetry are real, such as Ma Rainey, while others are fictive, such as Sporting Beasley, but in either case, they break down common stereotypes of rural African Americans. Often they reflect a grim, tough understanding of their gritty world. Some of Brown's most memorable characters, such as Slim Greer and Sporting Beasley, suggest the sly humor of the African American trickster, who attempts through the cagey manipulation of appearances to overcome the limitations of racial oppression.

The technical virtuosity of Brown's poetry is remarkable. Whether composing free verse derived from Walt Whitman, as in "Southern Road," or blues-based metered and rhymed poetry, Brown writes with economy and precision. In a few words, sometimes in a well-chosen verb, Brown intimates a whole life or social condition. The blues is a pervasive presence in *Southern Road.* Some of Brown's poems include the blues's repetition or worrying of a line ("Odyssey of Big Boy"), its AAB stanza form ("Southern Road"), and even snatches of blues lyrics ("Ma Rainey"). But Brown freely adapts the insistent rhymes and strong rhythms of the blues instead of its strict song form, while incorporating its stripped down imagery, desultory narratives, downtrodden characters, and despairing, if humorous, tone. Many of Brown's poems, such as "Memphis Blues" and "Slim Greer," skillfully fuse formal aspects of the blues and the ballad.

The call-and-response pattern that is basic to African American musical and oral traditions is evident in many poems, such as "Sporting Beasley" and "Old Lem." Sometimes alternations in line lengths, as in "Strong Men" and "Ma Rainey," intimate the dialogic structure of call and response. Some poems are written in African American vernacular ("Odyssey of Big Boy"), others are in Standard English ("Sporting Beasley"), and still others ingeniously mix the two ("Strong Men"). Even poems written in Standard English evince the syncopated rhythms of the vernacular ("Step it, Mr. Beasley, oh step it till the sun goes down"). Puns, hyperbole, understatement, irony—the rhetorical devices of African American oral performance are threaded through his poetry. Few poets had so ably styled their verse in the idiom, the structures, and the figures of African American speech and song, and Brown's example was vital for later poets such as Baraka, Sherley Anne Williams, and Michael S. Harper.

Odyssey of Big Boy

Lemme be wid Casey Jones,
  Lemme be wid Stagolee,[1]
Lemme be wid such like men
  When Death takes hol' on me,
    When Death takes hol' on me . . .

Done skinned as a boy in Kentucky hills,
  Druv steel dere as a man,
Done stripped tobacco in Virginia fiel's
  Alongst de River Dan,
    Alongst de River Dan;

Done mined de coal in West Virginia,
  Liked dat job jes' fine,
Till a load o' slate curved roun' my head,
  Won't work in no mo' mine,
    Won't work in no mo' mine;

Done shocked de corn in Marylan',
  In Georgia done cut cane,
Done planted rice in South Caline,
  But won't do dat again,
    Do dat no mo' again.

Been roustabout[2] in Memphis,
  Dockhand in Baltimore,
Done smashed up freight on Norfolk wharves,
  A fust class stevedore,[3]
    A fust class stevedore. . . .

Done slung hash yonder in de North
  On de ole Fall River Line,[4]
Done busted suds in li'l New York,
  Which ain't no work o' mine—
    Lawd, ain't no work o' mine.

1. Hero of folk ballad. *Casey Jones:* John Luther (Casey) Jones (1864–1900), American train engineer celebrated in folk songs.
2. Wharf laborer.
3. One who loads or unloads cargo from merchant ships.
4. Boat line from Fall River, Massachusetts, to New York City.

Done worked and loafed on such like jobs,
  Seen what dey is to see,
Done had my time wid a pint on my hip
An' a sweet gal on my knee,
  Sweet mommer on my knee:

Had stovepipe blond in Macon,
  Yaller gal in Marylan',
In Richmond had a choklit brown,
  Called me huh monkey man—
    Huh big fool monkey man.

Had two fair browns in Arkansaw
  And three in Tennessee,
Had Creole gal in New Orleans,
Sho Gawd did two time me—
    Lawd two time, fo' time me—

But best gal what I evah had
  Done put it over dem,
A gal in Southwest Washington
  At Four'n half and M—[5]
    Four'n half and M. . . .

Done took my livin' as it came,
  Done grabbed my joy, done risked my life;
Train done caught me on de trestle,[6]
  Man done caught me wid his wife,
    His doggone purty wife. . . .

I done had my women,
  I done had my fun;
Cain't do much complainin'
  When my jag[7] is done,
    Lawd, Lawd, my jag is done.

An' all dat Big Boy axes
  When time comes fo' to go,
Lemme be wid John Henry,[8] steel drivin' man,
  Lemme be wid old Jazzbo,[9]
    Lemme be wid ole Jazzbo. . . .

1927

5. Intersection in Washington, D.C.
6. Bridge.
7. Spree or binge.
8. African American folk hero who died after defeating a steam hammer in a pile-driving competition. *Axes:* asks.
9. That is, a cool, African American, urban hipster.

Southern Road

Swing dat hammer—hunh—
Steady, bo';
Swing dat hammer—hunh—
Steady, bo';
Ain't no rush, bebby,
Long ways to go.

Burner tore his—hunh—
Black heart away;[1]
Burner tore his—hunh—
Black heart away;
Got me life,[2] bebby,
An' a day.

Gal's on Fifth Street[3]—hunh—
Son done gone;
Gal's on Fifth Street—hunh—
Son done gone;
Wife's in de ward, bebby,
Babe's not bo'n.

My ole man died—hunh—
Cussin' me;
My ole man died—hunh—
Cussin' me;
Ole lady rocks, bebby,
Huh misery.

Doubleshackled—hunh—
Guard behin';
Doubleshackled—hunh—
Guard behin';
Ball an' chain, bebby,
On my min'.

White man tells me—hunh—
Damn yo' soul;
White man tells me—hunh—
Damn yo' soul;
Got no need, bebby,
To be tole.

Chain gang nevah—hunh—
Let me go;
Chain gang nevah—hunh—
Let me go;

1. That is, shot a man in the heart. *Burner*: gun.
2. That is, was sentenced to life imprisonment.
3. His daughter has become a prostitute.

Po' los' boy, bebby,
Evahmo'. . . .

1930

Ma Rainey[4]

I

When Ma Rainey
Comes to town,
Folks from anyplace
Miles aroun',
From Cape Girardeau,
Poplar Bluff,[5]
Flocks in to hear
Ma do her stuff;
Comes flivverin'[6] in,
Or ridin' mules,
Or packed in trains,
Picknickin' fools. . . .
That's what it's like,
Fo' miles on down,
To New Orleans delta
An' Mobile town,
When Ma hits
Anywheres aroun'.

II

Dey comes to hear Ma Rainey from de little river settlements,
From blackbottom cornrows and from lumber camps;
Dey stumble in de hall, jes a-laughin' an' a-cacklin',
Cheerin' lak roarin' water, lak wind in river swamps.

An' some jokers keeps deir laughs a-goin' in de crowded aisles,
An' some folks sits dere waitin' wid deir aches an' miseries,
Till Ma comes out before dem, a-smilin' gold-toofed smiles
An' Long Boy ripples minors on de black an' yellow keys.

III

O Ma Rainey,
Sing yo' song;
Now you's back
Whah you belong,
Git way inside us,
Keep us strong. . . .

4. African American vocalist (1886–1939), considered the "mother of the blues."
5. City in Missouri. *Cape Girardeau:* city on the Mississippi River in southeastern Missouri.
6. Riding in a flivver, or a cheap, small car.

O Ma Rainey,
Li'l an' low;
Sing us 'bout de hard luck
Roun' our do';
Sing us 'bout de lonesome road
We mus' go. . . .

IV

I talked to a fellow, an' the fellow say,
"She jes' catch hold of us, somekindaway.
She sang Backwater Blues one day:
"It rained fo' days an' de skies was dark as night,
Trouble taken place in de lowlands at night.

'Thundered an' lightened an' the storm begin to roll
Thousan's of people ain't got no place to go.

'Den I went an' stood upon some high ol' lonesome hill,
An' looked down on the place where I used to live.'

An' den de folks, dey natchally bowed dey heads an' cried,
Bowed dey heavy heads, shet dey moufs up tight an' cried,
An' Ma lef' de stage, an' followed some de folks outside."

Dere wasn't much more de fellow say:
She jes' gits hold of us dataway.

1930

Strong Men

The young men keep coming on
The strong men keep coming on.
SANDBURG[7]

They dragged you from homeland,
They chained you in coffles,[8]
They huddled you spoon-fashion in filthy hatches,
They sold you to give a few gentlemen ease.

They broke you in like oxen,
They scourged you,
They branded you,
They made your women breeders,
They swelled your numbers with bastards. . . .
They taught you the religion they disgraced.

7. Carl Sandburg (1878–1967), American poet.
8. Group of slaves chained together.

You sang:
Keep a-inchin' along
Lak a po' inch worm. . . .

You sang:
Bye and bye
I'm gonna lay down dis heaby load. . . .

You sang:
Walk togedder, chillen,
Dontcha git weary. . . .
The strong men keep a-comin' on
The strong men git stronger.

They point with pride to the roads you built for them,
They ride in comfort over the rails you laid for them.
They put hammers in your hands
And said—Drive so much before sundown.

You sang:
Ain't no hammah
In dis lan',
Strikes lak mine, bebby,
Strikes lak mine.

They cooped you in their kitchens,
They penned you in their factories,
They gave you the jobs that they were too good for,
They tried to guarantee happiness to themselves
By shunting dirt and misery to you.

You sang:
Me an' muh baby gonna shine, shine
Me an' muh baby gonna shine.
The strong men keep a-comin' on
The strong men git stronger. . . .

They bought off some of your leaders
You stumbled, as blind men will. . . .
They coaxed you, unwontedly[9] *soft-voiced. . . .*
You followed a way.
Then laughed as usual.

They heard the laugh and wondered;
Uncomfortable,
Unadmitting a deeper terror. . . .
The strong men keep a-comin' on
Gittin' stronger. . . .

What, from the slums
Where they have hemmed you.

9. Unusually.

What, from the tiny huts
They could not keep from you—
What reaches them
Making them ill at ease, fearful?
Today they shout prohibition at you
"Thou shalt not this"
"Thou shalt not that"
"Reserved for whites only"
You laugh.

One thing they cannot prohibit—
The strong men . . . coming on
The strong men gittin' stronger.
Strong men. . . .
Stronger. . . .

1931

Memphis Blues

I

Nineveh, Tyre,
Babylon,[1]
Not much lef'
Of either one.
All dese cities
Ashes and rust,
De win' sing sperrichals
Through deir dus' . . .
Was another Memphis[2]
Mongst de olden days,
Done been destroyed
In many ways. . . .
Dis here Memphis
It may go;
Floods may drown it;
Tornado blow;
Mississippi wash it
Down to sea—
Like de other Memphis in
History.

II

Watcha gonna do when Memphis on fire,
Memphis on fire, Mistah Preachin' Man?
Gonna pray to Jesus and nebber tire,
Gonna pray to Jesus, loud as I can,
Gonna pray to my Jesus, oh, my Lawd!

1. In the Bible, three cities that were the objects of divine wrath.

2. City on the Nile River that was often the political capital of Egypt under the pharaohs.

Watcha gonna do when de tall flames roar,
Tall flames roar, Mistah Lovin' Man?
Gonna love my brownskin better'n before—
Gonna love my baby lak a do right man,
Gonna love my brown baby, oh, my Lawd!

Watcha gonna do when Memphis falls down,
Memphis falls down, Mistah Music Man?
Gonna plunk on dat box as long as it soun',
Gonna plunk dat box fo' to beat de ban',
Gonna tickle dem ivories, oh, my Lawd!

Watcha gonna do in de hurricane,
In de hurricane, Mistah Workin' Man?
Gonna put dem buildings up again,
Gonna put em up dis time to stan',
Gonna push a wicked wheelbarrow, oh, my Lawd!

Watcha gonna do when Memphis near gone,
Memphis near gone, Mistah Drinkin' Man?
Gonna grab a pint bottle of Mountain Corn,
Gonna keep de stopper in my han',
Gonna get a mean jag[3] on, oh, my Lawd!

Watcha gonna do when de flood roll fas',
Flood roll fas', Mistah Gamblin' Man?
Gonna pick up my dice fo' one las' pass—
Gonna fade my way to de lucky lan',
Gonna throw my las' seven—oh, my Lawd!

III

Memphis go
By Flood or Flame;
Nigger won't worry
All de same—
Memphis go
Memphis come back,
Ain' no skin
Off de nigger's back.
All dese cities
Ashes, rust. . . .
De win' sing sperrichals
Through deir dus'.

1931

3. Drinking binge.

Slim Greer[4]

Listen to the tale
Of Ole Slim Greer,
Waitines' devil
Waitin' here;

Talkinges' guy
An' biggest liar,
With always a new lie
On the fire.

Tells a tale
Of Arkansaw
That keeps the kitchen
In a roar;

Tells in a long-drawled
Careless tone,
As solemn as a Baptist
Parson's moan.

How he in Arkansaw
Passed for white,
An' he no lighter
Than a dark midnight.

Found a nice white woman
At a dance,
Thought he was from Spain
Or else from France;

Nobody suspicioned
Ole Slim Greer's race
But a Hill Billy, always
Roun' the place,

Who called one day
On the trustful dame
An' found Slim comfy
When he came.

The whites lef' the parlor
All to Slim
Which didn't cut
No ice with him,

An' he started a-tinklin'
Some mo'nful blues,

4. Character created by Brown in a series of five poems, including "Slim in Atlanta."

An' a-pattin' the time
With No. Fourteen shoes.

The cracker listened
An' then he spat
An' said, "No white man
Could play like that. . . ."

The white jane[5] ordered
The tattler out;
Then, female-like,
Began to doubt,

Crept into the parlor
Soft as you please,
Where Slim was agitatin'
The ivories.

Heard Slim's music—
An' then, hot damn!
Shouted sharp—"Nigger!"
An' Slim said, "Ma'am?"

She screamed and the crackers
Swarmed up soon,
But found only echoes
Of his tune;

'Cause Slim had sold out
With lightnin' speed;
"Hope I may die,[6] sir—
Yes, indeed. . . ."

1931

Slim in Atlanta

Down in Atlanta,
De whitefolks got laws
For to keep all de niggers
From laughin' outdoors.

Hope to Gawd I may die
If I ain't speakin' truth
Make de niggers do deir laughin
In a telefoam booth.

5. Woman.

6. Expression for vouching as to the truth of a tale.

Slim Greer hit de town
  An' de rebs[7] got him told,—
"Dontcha laugh on de street,
  If you want to die old."

Den dey showed him de booth,
  An' a hundred shines[8]
In front of it, waitin'
  In double lines.

Slim thought his sides
  Would bust in two,
Yelled, "Lookout, everybody,
  I'm coming through!"

Pulled de other man out,
  An' bust in de box,
An' laughed four hours
  By de Georgia clocks.

Den he peeked through de door,
  An' what did he see?
Three hundred niggers there
  In misery.—

Some holdin' deir sides,
  Some holdin' deir jaws,
To keep from breakin'
  De Georgia laws.

An' Slim gave a holler,
  An' started again;
An' from three hundred throats
  Come a moan of pain.

An' everytime Slim
  Saw what was outside,
Got to whoopin' again
  Till he nearly died.

An' while de poor critters
  Was waitin' deir chance,
Slim laughed till dey sent
  Fo' de ambulance.

De state paid de railroad
  To take him away;
Den, things was as usural
  In Atlanta, Gee A.[9]

1932

7. Rebels; white southerners.
8. African Americans.
9. That is, GA, abbreviation for Georgia.

Sporting Beasley

Good glory, give a look at Sporting Beasley
Strutting, oh my Lord.

Tophat cocked one side his bulldog head,
Striped four-in-hand, and in his buttonhole
A red carnation; Prince Albert coat[1]
Form-fitting, corset like; vest snugly filled,
Gray morning trousers, spotless and full-flowing,
White spats and a cane.

Step it, Mr. Beasley, oh step it till the sun goes down.

Forget the snippy clerks you wait upon,
Tread clouds of glory above the heads of pointing children,
Oh, Mr. Peacock, before the drab barnfowl of the world.

Forget the laughter when at the concert
You paced down the aisle, your majesty,
Down to Row A, where you pulled out your opera glasses.

Majesty. . . .

It's your turn now, Sporting Beasley,
Step it off.

The world is a ragbag; the world
Is full of heathens who haven't seen the light;
Do it, Mr. Missionary.

Great glory, give a look.

Oh Jesus, when this brother's bill falls due,[2]
When he steps off the chariot
And flicks the dust from his patent leathers with his silk hand-
kerchief,
When he stands in front of the jasper gates, patting his tie,

And then paces in
Cane and knees working like well-oiled slow-timed pistons;

Lord help us, give a *look* at him.
Don't make him dress up in no night gown, Lord.
Don't put no fuss and feathers on his shoulders, Lord.

Let him know it's heaven.

1. A long, double-breasted frock coat associated with the husband of Queen Victoria.
2. That is, he dies.

Let him keep his hat, his vest, his elkstooth, and everything.

Let him have his spats and cane
Let him have his spats and cane.

1932

Old Lem

I talked to old Lem
and old Lem said:
"They weigh the cotton
They store the corn
We only good enough
To work the rows;
They run the commissary
They keep the books
We gotta be grateful
For being cheated;
Whippersnapper clerks
Call us out of our name
We got to say mister
To spindling boys
They make our figgers
Turn somersets
We buck in the middle
Say, "Thankyuh, sah."
They don't come by ones
They don't come by twos
But they come by tens.

"They got the judges
They got the lawyers
They got the jury-rolls
They got the law
They don't come by ones
They got the sheriffs
They got the deputies
They don't come by twos
They got the shotguns
They got the rope
We git the justice
In the end
And they come by tens.

"Their fists stay closed
Their eyes look straight
Our hands stay open
Our eyes must fall

        They don't come by ones
They got the manhood
They got the courage
        They don't come by twos
    We got to slink around
    Hangtailed hounds.
They burn us when we dogs
They burn us when we men
        They come by tens . . .

"I had a buddy
Six foot of man
Muscled up perfect
Game to the heart
        They don't come by ones
Outworked and outfought
Any man or two men
        They don't come by twos
He spoke out of turn
At the commissary
They gave him a day
To git out the county
He didn't take it.
He said 'Come and get me.'
They came and got him
        And they came by tens.
He stayed in the county—
He lays there dead.

        They don't come by ones
        They don't come by twos
        But they come by tens."

1939

Langston Hughes
1902–1967

Langston Hughes belongs to the same generation as Harlem Renaissance poets Claude McKay and Countee Cullen, who adapted European literary forms such as the sonnet, and Jean Toomer, who recast the Imagist aesthetic. He was also a contemporary of Melvin Tolson, who worked in the densely allusive style of high modernism. But Hughes, like fellow vernacular poet Sterling Brown, looked mostly to African American music for inspiration—the blues, jazz, work songs, ballads, and spirituals. If some African American poets were intent on refashioning European American literary genres and styles, Hughes took as his primary muses the trenchant humor, musical genius, and oral poetry of the black urban poor and working class.

Though he remained productive long after the Harlem Renaissance, Hughes arrived at perhaps his most significant innovation at the start of his career, when he became the first poet to bring the blues—with its vernacular wit, bitter realism, and spare form—into literary verse. Hughes incorporated the first blues song he heard as a boy into the title poem of his first book, "The Weary Blues," and he started writing blues poems soon after the first blues recordings were made, having learned from live and recorded performances by Ma Rainey, "Lonnie Johnson, Memphis Minnie, Mamie, Clara and Bessie Smith and others who never got to be famous" (Hughes quoted by Nat Hentoff, *Mayfair,* 1958). But Hughes's literary adaptation of not-yet-respectable African American forms was risky. In a review of *The Weary Blues* (1926), Cullen doubted whether jazz and blues poetry could "belong to that dignified company, that select and austere circle of high literary expression which we call poetry." Still more harsh was the reaction of the black middle-class press to his blues-inspired second volume, *Fine Clothes to the Jew* (1927). Headlines read, "LANGSTON HUGHES' BOOK OF POEMS TRASH" and "LANGSTON HUGHES—THE SEWER DWELLER." Created in desperation by former slaves, the blues were a reminder of African American pain, poverty, and dispossession—all that the middle class, trying to advance, wished to shunt from view.

Hughes turned to the blues because their "monotonous melancholy . . . almost terrible at times" seemed to him most true to African American experience: "The Blues always impressed me as being very sad, sadder even than the Spirituals, because their sadness is not softened with tears, but hardened with laughter . . . of a sadness without even a god to appeal to" (letter quoted by Carl Van Vechten in "The Black Blues," *Vanity Fair,* 1925). Hughes developed this contrast in a 1926 review of W. C. Handy's *Blues* anthology: "Whereas the Spirituals are always concerned with escape from this world, faith, hope, and a certain 'joy in the Lord,' the Blues are very much of the earth, dirty with pain and lazy with the weariness of life. . . . The folk Blues . . . are a long ways removed from the expectancy and faith of the Spirituals. Their hopeless weariness mixed with an absurdly incongruous laughter makes them the most interesting folk songs I have heard."

Like Hughes, the Euro-modernists T. S. Eliot, Ezra Pound, and Wallace Stevens were forging an earthbound, unsentimental aesthetic, in response to modern life's absurdities and incongruities. But Hughes self-consciously shapes his aesthetic through the sociohistorical experience of working-class African Americans after Reconstruction. Like his Euro-American contemporaries, Hughes was expanding the scope of language and materials that could be included in poetry, but whereas the Euro-modernists tended to satirize popular speech and forms, Hughes more often honored, developed, and refined them.

Yet Hughes's respectful treatment of African American forms and language should not obscure his distance from the "folk." In the "Note on Blues" that prefaces *Fine Clothes to the Jew,* Hughes says his poems "are written after the manner" of these "Negro folk-songs," implicitly distinguishing between blues songs and his blues poems: "The mood of the *Blues* is almost always despondency, but when they are sung people laugh." "The Weary Blues" registers even in its title Hughes's simultaneous fascination with and distance from oral folk culture: perhaps a "Weary Blues" itself, the poem is also *about* "The Weary Blues." Hughes's poems are linguistically and formally hybrid, straddling high culture and low, black and white, oral and literary, vernacular and Standard English. "The Weary Blues" intermixes features of the blues (lines repeated and varied, or "worried"; syncopated rhythms; call-and-response interjections; melancholy tonality; a final triple rhyme; vernacular idiom) and of Euro-American forms (couplets, iambic pentameter, embedded song, Standard English).

Hughes wrote in a wide variety of forms across the course of his career. The title of his *Montage of a Dream Deferred* (1951) likens the book-long sequence's technique to modernist montage. In a prefatory note, Hughes also relates the volume's aesthetic to bebop, a fast-paced, kaleidoscopic style of avant-garde jazz, which, he suggests, indicates the rapid pace of change underway in African American society: the sequence "on contemporary Harlem, like be-bop, is marked by conflicting changes, sudden nuances, sharp and impudent interjections, broken rhythms, and passages sometimes in the manner of the jam session, sometimes the popular song, punctuated by the riffs, runs, breaks, and disc-tortions [sic] of the music of a community in transition." The book is the consummation of Hughes's lifelong experiment with jazz poetry.

Along with jazz and blues poems, Hughes wrote stark, bitter poems about lynchings, ranging stylistically from the compressed, dialogic "Song for a Dark Girl" to the vividly imagistic "Blue Bayou" and the hypnotically repetitive elegy "The Bitter River." He also wrote lyric meditations on love, death, and suicide, and monologues spoken in the voices of wittily conceived characters, such as the wily Alberta K. Johnson and the self-aggrandizing Sylvester. Hughes sometimes embodies transhistorical experience in an archetypal speaker: in one of his famous poems, the speaker has heard the sound of rivers from the Euphrates to the Congo to the Mississippi. In all these poems, Hughes inverts negative stereotypes of Africans and African Americans, celebrating the rich continuities and achievements of the black "folk."

Hughes proudly hymned African American culture and racial identity long before "black is beautiful" became a popular slogan, but he personally endured many racial insults in his lifetime. Of African, white, and Native American ancestry, he tells in his autobiography of being asked in a southern restaurant whether he was Mexican or Negro; the waiter explained that he might serve a Mexican but not a Negro. Hughes recounts this and many other incidents with wry amusement tinged with subtle indignation.

He was born on February 1, 1902, in Joplin, Missouri. His early years were spent in Lawrence, Kansas (until he was twelve), but also in Ohio, Illinois, and Mexico. When he was five, his father (who, according to Hughes, "hated" blacks and himself as a black man) emigrated to Mexico, where he became a successful businessman, undeterred by racial barriers. His mother traveled from city to city, scratching out a living as a journalist and a stenographer. For the most part, Hughes was raised by his maternal grandmother, and he turned to books out of loneliness. When he was twelve, he attended a revival meeting, and rather than be the one holdout in the congregation, he also "testified" and was "saved." This combination of participation and detachment was to be characteristic throughout his life.

In 1915, Hughes's grandmother died, and he moved to Lincoln, Illinois, where he lived with his mother and stepfather. He completed grammar school and was elected class poet, a distinction that compelled him, he said, to try writing verse for the first time. Attending high school in Cleveland, Ohio, he read widely in philosophy and literature. Early in his career, he was influenced by the free verse poetry of Edgar Lee Masters, Vachel Lindsay, and Amy Lowell, but especially by the writings of Walt Whitman and his modern industrial precursor, Carl Sandburg. Claude McKay's politically engaged poetry and Alain Locke's concept of the self-confident and unshackled "New Negro" also had an impact, as did the writings of such early civil rights leaders as W. E. B. Du Bois and James Weldon Johnson.

In 1921, Hughes, wanting to see Harlem, attended Columbia University for a year. In search of adventure, he shipped out to the west coast of Africa, and then, on another vessel, to France. Living in Paris in 1924, he worked for several months in the kitchen of a nightclub where jazz was performed. On his return to the United States, Hughes joined his mother, now living in Washington, D.C., and took various odd jobs in a laundry, a restaurant, a hotel, and a historian's office. He sent many of his poems to magazines, and in 1925, "The Weary Blues" won a prize from *Opportunity*, an influential

African American magazine. He then published his first two books of poetry; his 1926 essay "The Negro Artist and the Racial Mountain," calling for an African American literature steeped in black folk culture, became a manifesto for the Harlem Renaissance. He accepted a scholarship to Pennsylvania's historically black Lincoln University, where he received a B.A. in 1929. The next year he published his first novel, *Not without Laughter*.

Drawn like many writers to the radical left during the Great Depression, Hughes spent a year traveling and writing in the Soviet Union (1932–33), though he later denied that he had ever been a member of the Communist Party. He wrote a series of politically radical plays in the 1930s and, in 1937, traveled as a journalist to civil-war Spain. During World War II, his politics became more centrist, though his writings continued to attack racial segregation and promote black pride.

Hughes invented a character named Jesse B. Semple, shortened to Simple, a black laborer, and in his name and idiom composed a weekly series for the *Chicago Defender* for twenty years, beginning in 1942. At the outset of the cold war, Hughes was under continual investigation and harassment for his leftist sympathies, and in 1953, Senator Joseph McCarthy forced him to testify in Washington, D.C., about his politics. Hughes rebounded from this public humiliation, but he continued to be attacked on the right for being too radical, on the left for being too accommodating.

He nevertheless became a successful writer, renowned for his readings (sometimes accompanied by jazz bands), and traveling to many parts of the globe. He became the first African American poet to support himself through his literary career, buying a house in Harlem in 1947. Prolific and wide-ranging, he created not only poems, plays, and novels, but also libretti for opera and gospel musical shows, scripts for film and TV, children's books, and anthologies. In traveling abroad, Hughes met, befriended, and influenced Caribbean and African writers, who testified to his importance as a model for Negritude, the francophone movement affirming black identity. His major achievement—rooting black literature in African American music—has been a foundation for African American poets of later generations, including Gwendolyn Brooks, Robert Hayden, and Amiri Baraka.

The Negro Speaks of Rivers

(To W. E. B. DuBois)[1]

I've known rivers:
I've known rivers ancient as the world and older than the flow of human
blood in human veins.

My soul has grown deep like the rivers.

I bathed in the Euphrates when dawns were young.
I built my hut near the Congo and it lulled me to sleep.
I looked upon the Nile and raised the pyramids above it.[2]
I heard the singing of the Mississippi when Abe Lincoln went down to
New Orleans,[3] and I've seen its muddy bosom turn all golden in the
sunset.

1. African American writer and civil rights leader (1868–1963).
2. The Nile River was the site of ancient Egyptian civilization. The Euphrates River was the cradle of ancient Babylonian civilization. The Congo, in West-Central Africa, is named after the Kongo kingdom (fourteenth to sixteenth centuries).
3. President Lincoln's decision to end slavery stemmed from a visit to New Orleans.

I've known rivers:
Ancient, dusky rivers.

My soul has grown deep like the rivers.

1921, 1926

When Sue Wears Red

When Susanna Jones wears red
Her face is like an ancient cameo
Turned brown by the ages.

Come with a blast of trumpets,
  Jesus!

When Susanna Jones wears red
A queen from some time-dead Egyptian night
Walks once again.

Blow trumpets, Jesus!

And the beauty of Susanna Jones in red
Burns in my heart a love-fire sharp like pain.

Sweet silver trumpets,
  Jesus!

1923, 1926

The Weary Blues

Droning a drowsy syncopated tune,
Rocking back and forth to a mellow croon,
  I heard a Negro play.
Down on Lenox Avenue[4] the other night
By the pale dull pallor of an old gas light
  He did a lazy sway. . . .
  He did a lazy sway. . . .
To the tune o' those Weary Blues.
With his ebony hands on each ivory key
He made that poor piano moan with melody.
  O Blues!
Swaying to and fro on his rickety stool
He played that sad raggy tune like a musical fool.
  Sweet Blues!
Coming from a black man's soul.

4. Major street in Harlem; now Malcolm X Boulevard.

  O Blues!
In a deep song voice with a melancholy tone
I heard that Negro sing, that old piano moan—
  "Ain't got nobody in all this world,
    Ain't got nobody but ma self.
    I's gwine to quit ma frownin'
    And put ma troubles on the shelf."

Thump, thump, thump, went his foot on the floor.
He played a few chords then he sang some more—
  "I got the Weary Blues
    And I can't be satisfied.
    Got the Weary Blues
    And can't be satisfied—
    I ain't happy no mo'
    And I wish that I had died."
And far into the night he crooned that tune.
The stars went out and so did the moon.
The singer stopped playing and went to bed
While the Weary Blues echoed through his head.
He slept like a rock or a man that's dead.

1925, 1926

Suicide's Note

The calm,
Cool face of the river
Asked me for a kiss.

1925, 1926

Cross

My old man's a white old man
And my old mother's black.
If ever I cursed my white old man
I take my curses back.

If ever I cursed my black old mother
And wished she were in hell,
I'm sorry for that evil wish
And now I wish her well.

My old man died in a fine big house.
My ma died in a shack.
I wonder where I'm gonna die,
Being neither white nor black?

1925, 1926

Lament over Love

I hope ma chile'll
Never love a man.
I say I hope ma chile'll
Never love a man.
Cause love can hurt you
Mo'n anything else can.

I'm goin' down to de[5] river
An' I ain't goin' there to swim.
Goin' down to de river,
Ain't goin' there to swim.
Ma true love's left me, an'
I'm goin' there to think about him.

Love is like whiskey,
Love is like red, red wine.
Love is like whiskey,
O, like sweet red wine.
If you wants to be happy
You got to love all de time.

I'm goin' up in a tower
Tall as a tree is tall.
Say up in a tower
Tall as a tree is tall.
Gonna think about ma man an'
Let ma fool-self fall.

1926, 1927

Po' Boy Blues

When I was home de
Sunshine seemed like gold.
When I was home de
Sunshine seemed like gold.
Since I come up North de
Whole damn world's turned cold.

I was a good boy,
Never done no wrong.
Yes, I was a good boy,
Never done no wrong,
But this world is weary
An' de road is hard an' long.

5. When Hughes republished this and other early poems in his *Selected Poems* (1959), he changed dialect forms into Standard English, so that "de" became "the."

I fell in love with
A gal I thought was kind.
Fell in love with
A gal I thought was kind.
She made me lose ma money
An' almost lose ma mind.

Weary, weary,
Weary early in de morn.
Weary, weary,
Early, early in de morn.
I's so weary
I wish I'd never been born.

1926, 1927

Song for a Dark Girl

Way Down South in Dixie[6]
 (Break the heart of me)
They hung my black young lover
 To a cross roads tree.

Way Down South in Dixie
 (Bruised body high in air)
I asked the white Lord Jesus
 What was the use of prayer.

Way Down South in Dixie
 (Break the heart of me)
Love is a naked shadow
 On a gnarled and naked tree.

1927

Gal's Cry for a Dying Lover

Heard de owl a hootin',
Knowed somebody's 'bout to die.
Heard de owl a hootin',
Knowed somebody's 'bout to die.
Put ma head un'neath de kiver,[7]
Started in to moan an' cry.

Hound dawg's barkin'
Means he's gonna leave this world.

6. Last line of "Dixie," a popular minstrel song that became a rallying cry for the South during and after the Civil War.
7. Cover.

Hound dawg's barkin'
Means he's gonna leave this world.
O, Lawd have mercy
On a po' black girl.

Black an' ugly
But he sho do treat me kind.
I'm black an' ugly
But he sho do treat me kind.
High-in-heaben Jesus,
Please don't take this man o' mine.

1927

Bad Man

I'm a bad, bad man
Cause everybody tells me so.
I'm a bad, bad man.
Everbody tells me so.
I takes ma meanness and ma licker
Everwhere I go.

I beats ma wife an'
I beats ma side gal too.
Beats ma wife an'
Beats ma side gal too.
Don't know why I do it but
It keeps me from feelin' blue.

I'm so bad I
Don't even want to be good.
So bad, bad, bad I
Don't even want to be good.
I'm goin' to de devil an'
I wouldn't go to heaben if I could.

1927

Hard Daddy

I went to ma daddy,
Says Daddy I have got de blues.
Went to ma daddy,
Says Daddy I have got de blues.
Ma daddy says Honey
Can't you bring no better news?

I cried on his shoulder but
He turned his back on me.

Cried on his shoulder but
He turned his back on me.
He said a woman's cryin's
Never gonna bother me.

I wish I had wings to
Fly like de eagle flies.
Wish I had wings to
Fly like de eagle flies.
I'd fly on ma man an'
I'd scratch out both his eyes.

1927

Drum

Bear in mind
That death is a drum
Beating for ever
Till the last worms come
To answer its call,
Till the last stars fall,
Until the last atom
Is no atom at all,
Until time is lost
And there is no air
And space itself
Is nothing nowhere.
Death is a drum,
A signal drum,
Calling all life
To Come! Come!
Come!

1931

Sylvester's Dying Bed

I woke up this mornin'
'Bout half-past three.
All de womens in town
Was gathered round me.

Sweet gals was a-moanin',
"Sylvester's gonna die!"
And a hundred pretty mamas
Bowed their heads to cry.

I woke up little later
'Bout half-past fo',

De doctor 'n' undertaker's
Both at ma do'.

Black gals was a-beggin',
"You can't leave us here!"
Brown-skins cryin' "Daddy!
Honey! Baby! Don't go, dear!"

But I felt ma time's a-comin',
And I know'd I's dyin' fast.
I seed de River Jerden
A-creepin' muddy past—
But I's still Sweet Papa 'Vester,
Yes, sir! Long as life do last!

So I hollers, "Com'ere, babies,
Fo' to love yo' daddy right!"
And I reaches up to hug 'em—
When de Lawd put out de light.

Then everything was darkness
In a great . . . big . . . night.

1931, 1942

The Bitter River

(Dedicated to the memory of Charlie Lang and Ernest Green, each fourteen years old when lynched together beneath the Shubuta Bridge over the Chicasawhay River in Mississippi, October 12th, 1942.)

There is a bitter river
Flowing through the South.
Too long has the taste of its water
Been in my mouth.
There is a bitter river
Dark with filth and mud.
Too long has its evil poison
Poisoned my blood.
I've drunk of the bitter river
And its gall coats the red of my tongue,
Mixed with the blood of the lynched boys
From its iron bridge hung,
Mixed with the hopes that are drowned there
In the snake-like hiss of its stream
Where I drank of the bitter river
That strangled my dream:
The book studied—but useless,
Tools handled—but unused,
Knowledge acquired but thrown away,
Ambition battered and bruised.
Oh, water of the bitter river

With your taste of blood and clay,
You reflect no stars by night,
No sun by day.

The bitter river reflects no stars—
It gives back only the glint of steel bars
And dark bitter faces behind steel bars:
The Scottsboro boys[8] behind steel bars,
Lewis Jones[9] behind steel bars,
The voteless share-cropper behind steel bars,
The labor leader behind steel bars,
The soldier thrown from a Jim Crow[1] bus behind steel bars,
The 15¢ mugger behind steel bars,
The girl who sells her body behind steel bars,
And my grandfather's back with its ladder of scars,
Long ago, long ago—the whip and steel bars—
The bitter river reflects no stars.

"Wait, be patient," you say.
"Your folks will have a better day."
But the swirl of the bitter river
Takes your words away.
"Work, education, patience
Will bring a better day."
The swirl of the bitter river
Carries your "patience" away.
"Disrupter! Agitator!
Trouble maker!" you say.
The swirl of the bitter river
Sweeps your lies away.
I did not ask for this river
Nor the taste of its bitter brew.
I was given its water
As a gift from you.
Yours has been the power
To force my back to the wall
And make me drink of the bitter cup
Mixed with blood and gall.

You have lynched my comrades
Where the iron bridge crosses the stream,
Underpaid me for my labor,
And spit in the face of my dream.
You forced me to the bitter river
With the hiss of its snake-like song—
Now your words no longer have meaning—
I have drunk at the river too long:
Dreamer of dreams to be broken,
Builder of hopes to be smashed,

8. Nine African American teenagers who, after nearly being lynched, were tried and imprisoned in 1931 for the supposed rape of two white women. The Supreme Court overturned the decision, but the State of Alabama continued to prosecute members of the group.

9. British novelist (1897–1939), imprisoned for his involvement in the Communist Party.

1. Discriminatory laws enforcing racial segregation in the south between 1877 and the 1950s.

Loser from an empty pocket
Of my meagre cash,
Bitter bearer of burdens
And singer of weary song,
I've drunk at the bitter river
With its filth and its mud too long.
Tired now of the bitter river,
Tired now of the pat on the back,
Tired now of the steel bars
Because my face is black,
I'm tired of segregation,
Tired of filth and mud,
I've drunk of the bitter river
And it's turned to steel in my blood.

Oh, tragic bitter river
Where the lynched boys hung,
The gall of your bitter water
Coats my tongue.
The blood of your bitter water
For me gives back no stars.
I'm tired of the bitter river:
Tired of the bars!

1942, 1943

Morning After

I was so sick last night I
Didn't hardly know my mind.
So sick last night I
Didn't know my mind.
I drunk some bad licker that
Almost made me blind.

Had a dream last night I
Thought I was in hell.
I drempt last night I
Thought I was in hell.
Woke up and looked around me—
Babe, your mouth was open like a well.

I said, Baby! Baby!
Please don't snore so loud.
Baby! Please!
Please don't snore so loud.
You jest a little bit o' woman but you
Sound like a great big crowd.

1942

Madam's Past History

My name is Johnson—
Madam Alberta K.
The Madam stands for business.
I'm smart that way.

I had a
HAIR-DRESSING PARLOR
Before
The depression put
The prices lower.

Then I had a
BARBECUE STAND
Till I got mixed up
With a no-good man.

Cause I had a insurance
The WPA[2]
Said, We can't use you.
Wealthy that way.

I said,
DON'T WORRY 'BOUT ME!
Just like the song,
Take care of yourself—
And I'll get along.

I do cooking,
Day's work, too!
Alberta K. Johnson
Madam to you.

1943, 1949

Madam and Her Madam

I worked for a woman,
She wasn't mean—
But she had a twelve-room
House to clean.

Had to get breakfast,
Dinner, and supper, too—

2. The Works Progress Administration, a 1930s Federal agency that created jobs for the unemployed.

Then take care of her children
When I got through.

Wash, iron, and scrub,
Walk the dog around—
It was too much,
Nearly broke me down.

I said, Madam,
Can it be
You trying to make a
Pack-horse out of me?

She opened her mouth.
She cried, Oh, no!
You know, Alberta,
I love you so!

I said, Madam,
That may be true—
But I'll be dogged
If I love you!

1943, 1949

Blue Bayou

I went walkin'
By de blue bayou
And I saw de sun go down.

I thought about old Greeley
And I thought about Lou
And I saw de sun go down.

White man
Makes me work all day
And I works too hard
For too little pay—
Then a white man
Takes my woman away.

I'll kill old Greeley,

De blue bayou
Turns red as fire.
Put the black man
On a rope
And pull him higher!

I saw de sun go down.

Put him on a rope
And pull him higher!
De blue bayou's
A pool of fire.

And I saw de sun go down,
Down,
Down!
Lawd, I saw de sun go down!

1943, 1949

Silhouette

Southern gentle lady,
Do not swoon.
They've just hung a black man
In the dark of the moon.

They've hung a black man
To a roadside tree
In the dark of the moon
For the world to see
How Dixie protects
Its white womanhood.

Southern gentle lady,
Be good!
Be good!

1944, 1949

Life Is Fine

I went down to the river
I set down on the bank.
I tried to think but couldn't,
So I jumped in and sank.

I came up once and hollered!
I came up twice and cried!
If that water hadn't a-been so cold
I might've sunk and died.

But it was
Cold in that water!
It was cold!

I took the elevator
Sixteen floors above the ground.
I thought about my baby
And thought I would jump down.

I stood there and I hollered.
I stood there and I cried.
If it hadn't a-been so high
I might've jumped and died.

But it was
High up there!
It was high!

Since I'm still here living,
I guess I will live on.
I could've died for love—
But for livin' I was born.

You may hear me holler,
You may see me cry—
But I'll be dogged, sweet baby,
If you gonna see me die.

Life is fine!
Fine as wine!
Life is fine!

1949

From Montage of a Dream Deferred

Dream Boogie

Good morning, daddy!
Ain't you heard
The boogie-woogie rumble
Of a dream deferred?

Listen closely:
You'll hear their feet
Beating out and beating out a—

You think
It's a happy beat?

Listen to it closely:
Ain't you heard
something underneath
like a—

What did I say?

Sure,
I'm happy!
Take it away!

Hey, pop!
Re-bop!
Mop!

Y-e-a-h!

1951

Motto

I play it cool
And dig all jive
That's the reason
I stay alive.

My motto,
As I lived and learn,
is:
Dig And Be Dug
In Return.

1951

Dead in There

Sometimes
A night funeral
Going by
Carries home
A re-bop daddy.

Hearse and flowers
Guarantee
He'll never hype
Another paddy.[3]

It's hard to believe,
But dead in there,
He'll never lay a
Hype nowhere!

3. Deceive another white person.

He's my ace-boy,
Gone away.
Wake up and live!
He used to say.

Squares
Who couldn't dig him,
Plant him now—
Out where it makes
No diff' no how.

1951

125th Street[4]

Face like a chocolate bar
full of nuts and sweet.

Face like a jack-o'-lantern,
candle inside.

Face like slice of melon,
grin that wide.

1950, 1951

Theme for English B

The instructor said,

Go home and write
a page tonight.
And let that page come out of you—
Then, it will be true.

I wonder if it's that simple?
I am twenty-two, colored, born in Winston-Salem.
I went to school there, then Durham,[5] then here
to this college[6] on the hill above Harlem.
I am the only colored student in my class.
The steps from the hill lead down into Harlem,
through a park, then I cross St. Nicholas,
Eighth Avenue, Seventh, and I come to the Y,
the Harlem Branch Y, where I take the elevator
up to my room, sit down, and write this page:

It's not easy to know what is true for you or me
at twenty-two, my age. But I guess I'm what

4. At the southern edge of Harlem.
5. Like Winston-Salem, a city in North Carolina.
6. City College of the City University of New York (CCNY).

I feel and see and hear, Harlem, I hear you:
hear you, hear me—we two—you, me, talk on this page.
(I hear New York, too.) Me—who?
Well, I like to eat, sleep, drink, and be in love.
I like to work, read, learn, and understand life.
I like a pipe for a Christmas present,
or records—Bessie, bop, or Bach.[7]
I guess being colored doesn't make me *not* like
the same things other folks like who are other races.
So will my page be colored that I write?
Being me, it will not be white.
But it will be
a part of you, instructor.
You are white—
yet a part of me, as I am a part of you.
That's American.
Sometimes perhaps you don't want to be a part of me.
Nor do I often want to be a part of you.
But we are, that's true!
As I learn from you,
I guess you learn from me—
although you're older—and white—
and somewhat more free.

This is my page for English B.

1949, 1951

Boogie: 1 A.M.

Good evening, daddy!
I know you've heard
The boogie-woogie rumble
Of a dream deferred
Trilling the treble
And twining the bass
Into midnight ruffles
Of cat-gut lace.

1951

Nightmare Boogie

I had a dream
and I could see
a million faces
black as me!

7. J. S. Bach (1695–1750): German Baroque composer. Bessie Smith (c. 1898–1937): American blues musician. *Bop*: high-tempo, chromatic form of jazz developed in the 1940s.

A nightmare dream:
Quicker than light
All them faces
Turned dead white!
Boogie-woogie,
Rolling bass,
Whirling treble
Of cat-gut lace.

1951

Dream Boogie: Variation

Tinkling treble,
Rolling bass,
High noon teeth
In a midnight face,
Great long fingers
On great big hands,
Screaming pedals
Where his twelve-shoe lands,
Looks like his eyes
Are teasing pain,
A few minutes late
For the Freedom Train.

1951

Harlem

What happens to a dream deferred?

Does it dry up
like a raisin in the sun?
Or fester like a sore—
And then run?
Does it stink like rotten meat?
Or crust and sugar over—
like a syrupy sweet?

Maybe it just sags
like a heavy load.

Or does it explode?

1951

Stevie Smith
1902–1971

Stevie Smith's poems appear at first to be light verse, and the simple line drawings with which she illustrated her books encourage the impression. Although some poems are humorous, her adaptations of nursery rhymes, her seemingly naive language, and her references to fairy tales also express a perplexed concern over the agonies of the human lot. In her poems, wit often shades into dread, whimsy into mortal fear. In "Sunt Leones," amusing rhymes ("hue," "blue," "do") punctuate theological ponderings on the formation of the Christian Church. The quick turns of tone in her verse are matched by abrupt shifts in diction, from colloquialism ("Poor chap"), slang ("you ass"), and nonsense ("Our Bog Is Dood") to archaism, didacticism ("My point which upon this has been obscured"), and foreign words. Smith can be sharply satiric ("Souvenir de Monsieur Poop"), solemn ("Exeat"), or both at once ("Sunt Leones," "Thoughts about the Person from Porlock"). Her mock naivete, akin to the cunning innocence of the fool or the trickster, can be seen partly as a woman's response to the world of modern English poetry, a way of coping with, deflecting, and subverting its masculine norms.

A poem about the difficulty of reading even simple gestures, "Not Waving but Drowning" belies the apparent guilelessness of Smith's art. What seems to be waving, a familiar gesture of greeting, is an urgent call for help, although the drowning man is, in another sense, "waving"—bidding a permanent farewell. Smith's poetry waves to us with its songlike lyricism and campy comedy, and yet it also reveals much about "drowning"—about mortality and other vexed human issues. In many poems, she mixes different voices, their dialogue creating interpretive complexity.

Although Smith constructs many of her poems around dichotomies—the divine and the human, belief and unbelief, child and adult, life and death—she often undoes them. Few oppositions could be more stark than that between the early Christians and the lions to whom they were fed, and yet in "Sunt Leones" not only is the lion symbolic of Christ, but also, in a further irony, the martyrs need their killers, and the Lion of Christ depends on the lions "chewing up"—in a graphic enumeration—"blood gristle flesh and bone." Smith similarly complicates the Romantic opposition between the innocent child and the stifling adult in "To Carry the Child," giving the child within the adult the power to "strangle the man alive."

Smith's poems communicate a stoic resolve. When asked if her attitudes had changed during her life, she replied decisively: "No, they haven't changed at all, I think. One has one's thoughts about things and one takes great pleasure in these thoughts and in working them out. But I should be very surprised, for instance, if one day I said, 'This is absolutely black' and the next day I said, 'This is absolutely white' " (*The Poet Speaks*, ed. Peter Orr, 1966). She said she was always in danger of falling into belief—belief she had rejected with the Anglican faith of her youth. In "God the Eater," she expresses the ambiguity of her position: "There is a god in whom I do not believe / Yet to this god my loves stretches." She insisted that her poems share with all poems a concern for mortality, but that she didn't mind much about survival. "I rather like the idea of death," she said strikingly, and her poem "Exeat" presents death as a reward that must be earned. Whereas Emily Dickinson describes death as a ceremoniously mannered gentleman and Sylvia Plath, in some poems, ecstatically hurtles toward oblivion, Smith calmly welcomes death as tame, sweet, and gentle, even resulting in a possible improvement of character.

She was born Florence Margaret Smith on September 20, 1902, in Hull, Yorkshire, England. (Her nickname "Stevie" refers to her smallness; it was borrowed from a famous jockey of the time.) At age three she moved with her family to the north London suburb of Palmers Green, where she lived for the rest of her life in the same house, during most of it with the "noble aunt" who raised her and her sister after her mother's early death. The autobiographical poem "The House of Mercy," which also refers to her father's having left the family to join the North Sea patrol, recalls this "house of female habitation." A publisher who rejected her collection of poems suggested that she write a novel instead, and *Novel on Yellow Paper* was published in 1936. A year later, she published her first collection of poems, *A Good Time Was Had by All*, illustrated, like all her later collections, with her own drawings, which she described as "something like doodling," yet which often comment obliquely on the texts. Until 1953, she worked in a publisher's office in London; after that, she devoted her time to writing and to broadcasts on BBC radio. In 1966, she was given the Cholmondeley Award; in 1969, the Queen's Gold Medal for Poetry. Since her death, from a brain tumor, her poems have found more and more admiring readers. In 1977–78, Hugh Whitemore's play based on her life—called simply *Stevie*—was produced and then made into a film.

Sunt Leones[1]

The lions who ate the Christians on the sands of the arena
By indulging native appetites played what has now been seen a
Not entirely negligible part
In consolidating at the very start
The position of the Early Christian Church.
Initiatory rites are always bloody
And the lions, it appears
From contemporary art, made a study
Of dyeing Coliseum sands a ruddy
Liturgically sacrificial hue
And if the Christians felt a little blue—
Well people being eaten often do.
Theirs was the death, and theirs the crown undying,[2]
A state of things which must be satisfying.
My point which up to this has been obscured
Is that it was the lions who procured
By chewing up blood gristle flesh and bone
The martyrdoms on which the Church has grown.
I only write this poem because I thought it rather looked
As if the part the lions played was being overlooked.
By lions' jaws great benefits and blessings were begotten
And so our debt to Lionhood must never be forgotten.

1937

1. There be lions (Latin).
2. That is, of martyrdom, in Heaven. Christians were attacked and eaten by lions in the public games held in the Colosseum during the Roman Empire. The Christian liturgy, or system of worship, prescribes certain colors for certain festivals (line 10).

This Englishwoman

This Englishwoman is so refined
She has no bosom and no behind.

1937

Souvenir de Monsieur Poop

I am the self-appointed guardian of English literature,
I believe tremendously in the significance of age;
I believe that a writer is wise at 50,
Ten years wiser at 60, at 70 a sage.
I believe that juniors are lively, to be encouraged with discretion and snubbed,
I believe also that they are bouncing, communistic, ill mannered and, of course, young.
But I never define what I mean by youth
Because the word undefined is more useful for general purposes of abuse.

I believe that literature is a school where only those who apply themselves diligently to their tasks acquire merit.
And only they after the passage of a good many years (see above).
But then I am an old fogey.
I always write more in sorrow than in anger.[3]
I am, after all, devoted to Shakespeare, Milton,
And, coming to our own times,
Of course
Housman.[4]
I have never been known to say a word against the established classics,
I am in fact devoted to the established classics.
In the service of literature I believe absolutely in the principle of division;
I divide into age groups and also into schools.
This is in keeping with my scholastic mind, and enables me to trounce
Not only youth
(Which might be thought intellectually frivolous by pedants) but also periodical tendencies,
To ventilate, in a word, my own political and moral philosophy.
(When I say that I am an old fogey, I am, of course, joking.)
English literature, as I see it, requires to be defended
By a person of integrity and essential good humour
Against the forces of fanaticism, idiosyncrasy and anarchy.
I perfectly apprehend the perilous nature of my convictions
And I am prepared to go to the stake
For Shakespeare, Milton,
And, coming to our own times,
Of course
Housman.
I cannot say more than that, can I?
And I do not deem it advisable, in the interests of the editor to whom I am spatially contracted,
To say less.

1938

Our Bog Is Dood

Our Bog is dood, our Bog is dood,
They lisped in accents mild,
But when I asked them to explain
They grew a little wild.
How do you know your Bog is dood
My darling little child?

3. Cf. Horatio's description of the ghost of Hamlet's father: "A countenance more / In sorrow than in anger" (*Hamlet* 1.2.229–30).

4. A. E. Housman (1859–1936), British poet and classical scholar.

We know because we wish it so
That is enough, they cried,
And straight within each infant eye
Stood up the flame of pride,
And if you do not think it so
You shall be crucified.

Then tell me, darling little ones,
What's dood, suppose Bog is?
Just what we think, the answer came,
Just what we think it is.
They bowed their heads. Our Bog is ours
And we are wholly his.

But when they raised them up again
They had forgotten me
Each one upon each other glared
In pride and misery
For what was dood, and what their Bog
They never could agree.

Oh sweet it was to leave them then,
And sweeter not to see,
And sweetest of all to walk alone
Beside the encroaching sea,
The sea that soon should drown them all,
That never yet drowned me.

1950

God the Eater

There is a god in whom I do not believe
Yet to this god my love stretches,
This god whom I do not believe in is
My whole life, my life and I am his.

Everything that I have of pleasure and pain
(Of pain, of bitter pain and men's contempt)
I give this god for him to feed upon
As he is my whole life and I am his.

When I am dead I hope that he will eat
Everything I have been and have not been
And crunch and feed upon it and grow fat
Eating my life all up as it is his.

1957

Not Waving but Drowning

Nobody heard him, the dead man,
But still he lay moaning:
I was much further out than you thought
And not waving but drowning.

Poor chap, he always loved larking
And now he's dead
It must have been too cold for him his heart gave way,
They said.

Oh, no no no, it was too cold always
(Still the dead one lay moaning)
I was much too far out all my life
And not waving but drowning.

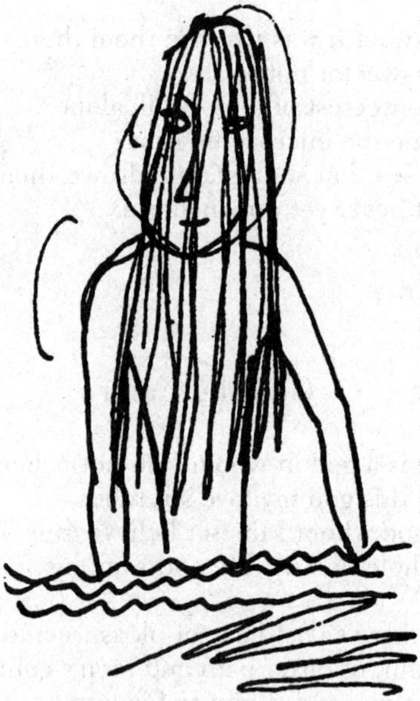

1957

Thoughts about the Person from Porlock[5]

Coleridge received the Person from Porlock
And ever after called him a curse,
Then why did he hurry to let him in?
He could have hid in the house.

It was not right of Coleridge in fact it was wrong
(But often we all do wrong)
As the truth is I think he was already stuck
With Kubla Khan.

He was weeping and wailing: I am finished, finished,
I shall never write another word of it,
When along comes the Person from Porlock
And takes the blame for it.

It was not right, it was wrong,
But often we all do wrong.

•

May we inquire the name of the Person from Porlock?
Why, Porson, didn't you know?
He lived at the bottom of Porlock Hill
So had a long way to go,

He wasn't much in the social sense
Though his grandmother was a Warlock,
One of the Rutlandshire ones I fancy
And nothing to do with Porlock,

And he lived at the bottom of the hill as I said
And had a cat named Flo,
And had a cat named Flo.

I long for the Person from Porlock
To bring my thoughts to an end,
I am becoming impatient to see him
I think of him as a friend,

Often I look out of the window
Often I run to the gate
I think, He will come this evening,
I think it is rather late.

5. In the prefatory note to his poem "Kubla Khan" (1816), Samuel Taylor Coleridge wrote that he had dreamed the poem's vision under the effects of opium, and that, on awakening, he immediately started to write the poem. "At this moment," Coleridge says, "he was unfortunately called out by a person on business from Porlock, and detained by him above an hour"; afterward, trying to finish the poem, Coleridge found, "to his no small surprise and mortification," that the vision had vanished "like the images on the surface of a stream."

I am hungry to be interrupted
For ever and ever amen
O Person from Porlock come quickly
And bring my thoughts to an end.

•

I felicitate the people who have a Person from Porlock
To break up everything and throw it away
Because then there will be nothing to keep them
And they need not stay.

•

Why do they grumble so much?
He comes like a benison[6]
They should be glad he has not forgotten them
They might have had to go on.

•

These thoughts are depressing I know. They are depressing,
I wish I was more cheerful, it is more pleasant,
Also it is a duty, we should smile as well as submitting
To the purpose of One Above who is experimenting
With various mixtures of human character which goes best,
All is interesting for him it is exciting, but not for us.
There I go again. Smile, smile, and get some work to do
Then you will be practically unconscious without positively having to go.

1962

A House of Mercy

It was a house of female habitation,
Two ladies fair inhabited the house,
And they were brave. For although Fear knocked loud
Upon the door, and said he must come in,
They did not let him in.

There were also two feeble babes, two girls,
That Mrs S. had by her husband had,
He soon left them and went away to sea,
Nor sent them money, nor came home again
Except to borrow back
Her Naval Officer's Wife's Allowance from Mrs S.
Who gave it him at once, she thought she should.

There was also the ladies' aunt
And babes' great aunt, a Mrs Martha Hearn Clode,
And she was elderly.
These ladies put their money all together
And so we lived.

6. Blessing.

I was the younger of the feeble babes
And when I was a child my mother died
And later Great Aunt Martha Hearn Clode died
And later still my sister went away.

Now I am old I tend my mother's sister
The noble aunt who so long tended us,
Faithful and True her name is. Tranquil.
Also Sardonic. And I tend the house.

It is a house of female habitation
A house expecting strength as it is strong
A house of aristocratic mould that looks apart
When tears fall; counts despair
Derisory. Yet it has kept us well. For all its faults,
If they are faults, of sternness and reserve,
It is a Being of warmth I think; at heart
A house of mercy.

1966

Exeat[7]

I remember the Roman Emperor, one of the cruellest of them,
Who used to visit for pleasure his poor prisoners cramped in dungeons,
So then they would beg him for death, and then he would say:
Oh no, oh no, we are not yet friends enough.
He meant they were not yet friends enough for him to give them death.
So I fancy my Muse says, when I wish to die:
Oh no, Oh no, we are not yet friends enough,

And Virtue also says:
We are not yet friends enough.

How can a poet commit suicide
When he is still not listening properly to his Muse,
Or a lover of Virtue when
He is always putting her off until tomorrow?

Yet a time may come when a poet or any person
Having a long life behind him, pleasure and sorrow,
But feeble now and expensive to his country
And on the point of no longer being able to make a decision
May fancy Life comes to him with love and says:
We are friends enough now for me to give you death;
Then he may commit suicide, then
He may go.

1966

7. Let him go out (Latin).

To Carry the Child

To carry the child into adult life
Is good? I say it is not,
To carry the child into adult life
Is to be handicapped.

The child in adult life is defenceless
And if he is grown-up, knows it,
And the grown-up looks at the childish part
And despises it.

The child, too, despises the clever grown-up,
The man-of-the-world, the frozen,
For the child has the tears alive on his cheek
And the man has none of them.

As the child has colours, and the man sees no
Colours or anything,
Being easy only in things of the mind,
The child is easy in feeling.

Easy in feeling, easily excessive
And in excess powerful,
For instance, if you do not speak to the child
He will make trouble.

You would say a man had the upper hand
Of the child, if a child survive,
I say the child has fingers of strength
To strangle the man alive.

Oh it is not happy, it is never happy,
To carry the child into adulthood,
Let children lie down before full growth
And die in their infanthood
And be guilty of no man's blood.

But oh the poor child, the poor child, what can he do,
Trapped in a grown-up carapace,
But peer outside of his prison room
With the eye of an anarchist?

1966

Pretty

Why is the word pretty so underrated?
In November the leaf is pretty when it falls
The stream grows deep in the woods after rain
And in the pretty pool the pike stalks

He stalks his prey, and this is pretty too,
The prey escapes with an underwater flash
But not for long, the great fish has him now
The pike is a fish who always has his prey

And this is pretty. The water rat is pretty
His paws are not webbed, he cannot shut his nostrils
As the otter can and the beaver, he is torn between
The land and water. Not 'torn', he does not mind.

The owl hunts in the evening and it is pretty
The lake water below him rustles with ice
There is frost coming from the ground, in the air mist
All this is pretty, it could not be prettier.

Yes, it could always be prettier, the eye abashes
It is becoming an eye that cannot see enough,
Out of the wood the eye climbs. This is prettier
A field in the evening, tilting up.

The field tilts to the sky. Though it is late
The sky is lighter than the hill field
All this looks easy but really it is extraordinary
Well, it is extraordinary to be so pretty.

And it is careless, and that is always pretty
This field, this owl, this pike, this pool are careless,
As Nature is always careless and indifferent
Who sees, who steps, means nothing, and this is pretty.

So a person can come along like a thief—pretty!—
Stealing a look, pinching the sound and feel,
Lick the icicle broken from the bank
And still say nothing at all, only cry pretty.

Cry pretty, pretty, pretty and you'll be able
Very soon not even to cry pretty
And so be delivered entirely from humanity
This is prettiest of all, it is very pretty.

1966

Lorine Niedecker
1903–1970

Lorine Niedecker was born on May 12, 1903, in Fort Atkinson, Wisconsin, the only child of a fisherman and a deeply religious mother. She lived her entire life on Black Hawk Island, on Lake Koshkonong, Wisconsin, housed from 1947 in a one-and-a-half-room cabin without plumbing. She attended Beloit College (1922–24), but returned home to care for her deaf mother. Over the course of her life, she took various jobs, working as a librarian, a writer for the Federal Writers' Project, a scriptwriter for a radio station, and a stenographer and proofreader for the dairy-farm magazine *Hoard's Dairyman* (1944–50). From 1957 to 1962, she walked five miles each way to the Fort Atkinson Memorial Hospital, where she cleaned the kitchen and scrubbed the cafeteria floor.

Although Niedecker spent much of her life isolated from the literary world, she corresponded at length with the Objectivist poet Louis Zukofsky. His famous 1931 "Objectivist" issue of *Poetry* magazine inspired her, and she traveled to New York to meet him. Niedecker is a second-generation modernist whose aesthetic can be traced back through Objectivism to Ezra Pound's Imagism, and beyond that to the wit and cryptic asceticism of Emily Dickinson's poetry. Like other Objectivists, she aims at precision, compression, and hard, clean images—images unclouded by authorial sentiment. Like poets from Charles Reznikoff to Susan Howe, she sometimes creates poems out of found or "objective" materials, such as the letters of Thomas Jefferson. "If one could establish / an absolute power / of silence over oneself," she quotes from Jefferson, and her poetry—though inevitably made up out of sounds—tries to be faithful to the silences around, in between, and beyond words.

Niedecker keeps her lines short, purging them of inessentials and cultivating the blank spaces on the page. She enacts the Imagist dictum: "To use absolutely no word that does not contribute to the presentation" (Pound, "A Retrospect"). Adapting the word *condensation* from Pound and Zukofsky, Niedecker refers to the making of poetry as "condensery." Often she elides prepositions, connectives, even pronouns and verbs, giving the remaining words greater intensity. Sometimes abandoning the sentence, she juxtaposes images, phrases, and words in parataxis. Like Imagist poems and East Asian haiku, Niedecker's poems are exercises in miniature, whether at the level of poem or of strophe. Though a practitioner of free verse, she gives end rhyme, slant rhyme, and internal rhyme a prominent place—along with alliteration and assonance—sometimes echoing nursery rhymes, ballads, and the blues.

Niedecker's attention to natural cycles is close and particular, even as it links the smallest detail to larger ecological patterns. Historical patterns and minutiae also fascinated her. To encode formally interrelatedness in both history and nature, she turned from short poems to long ones. (Imagism had similarly dilated in the longer poetic sequences of Pound and H. D.) Although Niedecker is often treated primarily as a poetic naturalist, she effectively applies miniaturization, disjointed sequentiality, condensation, collagelike quotation, and epigrammatic concision to historical personages. Her subjects include Jefferson, Charles Darwin, and North American explorers, all of whom share oblique resemblances with the meditative, inquisitive, silence-seeking poet who distills their lives.

[Well, Spring Overflows the Land]

Well, spring overflows the land,
floods floor, pump, wash machine
of the woman moored to this low shore by deafness.

Good-bye to lilacs by the door
and all I planted for the eye.
If I could hear—too much talk in the world,
too much wind washing, washing
good black dirt away.

Her hair is high.
Big blind ears.

I've wasted my whole life in water.
My man's got nothing but leaky boats.
My daughter, writer, sits and floats.

1946

[Swept Snow, Li Po]

Swept snow, Li Po.[1]
by dawn's 40-watt moon
to the road that hies to office
away from home.

Tended my brown little stove
as one would a cow—she gives heat.
Spring—marsh frog-clatter peace
breaks out.

1950, 1968

[What Horror to Awake at Night]

What horror to awake at night
and in the dimness see the light.
Time is white
mosquitoes bite
I've spent my life on nothing.

1. Chinese poet (c. 700–762 C.E.).

The thought that stings. How are you, Nothing,
sitting around with Something's wife.
Buzz and burn
is all I learn
I've spent my life on nothing.

I'm pillowed and padded, pale and puffing
lifting household stuffing—
carpets, dishes
benches, fishes
I've spent my life in nothing.

September 27, 1951 — 1968

[New-Sawed]

New-sawed
clean-smelling house
sweet cedar pink
flesh tint
I love you

January 1958 — 1961, 1968

Poet's Work

Grandfather
advised me:
Learn a trade

I learned
to sit at desk
and condense

No layoff
from this
condensery

June 8, 1962 — 1963, 1968

[Something in the Water]

Something in the water
like a flower
will devour

water

flower

1968

[Popcorn-Can Cover]

Popcorn-can cover
screwed to the wall
over a hole
        so the cold
can't mouse in

1968

My Life by Water

My life
  by water—
    Hear

spring's
  first frog
    or board

out on the cold
  ground
    giving

Muskrats
  gnawing
    doors

to wild green
  arts and letters
    Rabbits

raided
  my lettuce
    One boat

two—
  pointed toward
    my shore

thru birdstart
  wingdrip
    weed-drift

of the soft
  and serious—
    Water

1968

Thomas Jefferson[2]

I

My wife is ill!
And I sit
    waiting
for a quorum[3]

II

Fast ride
his horse collapsed
Now *he* saddled walked

Borrowed a farmer's
unbroken colt
To Richmond[4]

Richmond How stop—
Arnold's redcoats
there

III

Elk Hill destroyed—
Cornwallis
carried off 30 slaves

Jefferson:
Were it to give them freedom
he'd have done right[5]

2. Niedecker assembled this poem largely from material gathered from the letters of Thomas Jefferson (1743–1826), third U.S. president.
3. The number of people who must be present for legal business to occur. Jefferson's wife, Martha, died after prolonged illness, on September 6, 1782.
4. In 1781, during Jefferson's brief stint as governor of Virginia, American traitor Benedict Arnold (1741–1801) led British forces in an attack on Richmond, the state capital. Jefferson and his family fled before Arnold's men invaded his home.
5. In June 1781, British general Lord Cornwallis (1738–1805) captured Jefferson's home at Elk Hill, on the James River in Virginia, destroying his house and crops and carrying off thirty slaves. Jefferson explains that the slaves, rather than finding freedom, died because of the smallpox virus raging in Cornwallis's camp.

IV

Latin and Greek
my tools
to understand
humanity

I rode horse
away from a monarch
to an enchanting
philosophy

V

The South of France

Roman temple
'simple and sublime'

Maria Cosway[6]
    harpist
on his mind

white column
and arch

VI

To daughter Patsy: Read—
read Livy[7]

No person full of work
was ever hysterical

Know music, history
dancing

(I calculate 14 to 1
in marriage
she will draw
a blockhead)

Science also
Patsy

6. While serving as minister to France, Jefferson fell in love with the Anglo-Italian musician and artist Maria Cosway (1760–1838), wife of the English miniaturist Richard Cosway (1742–1821). In 1786, Jefferson and Maria Cosway visited the Désert de Retz in France, a garden with artificial ruins, including a house built to resemble an enormous Roman column.

7. Roman historian (59 B.C.E.–17 C.E.). "Patsy" was Jefferson's eldest daughter, Martha.

VII

Agreed with Adams:
send spermaceti oil to Portugal
for their church candles

(light enough to banish mysteries?:
three are one and one is three[8]
and yet the one not three
and the three not one)

and send salt fish
U.S. salt fish preferred
above all other

VIII

Jefferson of Patrick Henry[9]
backwoods fiddler statesman:

'He spoke as Homer wrote'
Henry eyed our minister at Paris—

the Bill of Rights hassle—
'he remembers . . .

in splendor and dissipation
he thinks yet of bills of rights'

IX

True, French frills and lace
for Jefferson, sword and belt

but follow the Court to Fontainebleau[1]
he could not—

house rent would have left him
nothing to eat

He bowed to everyone he met
and talked with arms folded

He could be trimmed
by a two-month migraine

8. The Christian doctrine of the Trinity teaches that God is both three (Father, Son, and Holy Spirit) and one. John Adams (1735–1826), second president of the United States, was Jefferson's lifelong friend and rival.
9. Jefferson greatly admired the rhetorical skills of American statesman Patrick Henry (1736–1799), who was largely responsible for the addition of the Bill of Rights to the Constitution.
1. Resort town southeast of Paris where the royal court would vacation. During his service as minister to France, Jefferson could not afford to stay with the court and would travel forty miles from Paris to perform his duties.

and yet
    stand up

X

Dear Polly:[2]
I said No—no frost

in Virginia—the strawberries
were safe

I'd have heard—I'm in that kind
of correspondence

with a young daughter—
if they were not

Now I must retract
I shrink from it

XI

Political honors
    'splendid torments'
'If one could establish
    an absolute power
of silence over oneself'

When I set out for Monticello[3]
  (my grandchildren
    will they know me?)
How are my young
      chestnut trees—

XII

Hamilton and the bankers
would make my country Carthage[4]

I am abandoning the rich—
their dinner parties—

I shall eat my simlins[5]
with the class of science

or not at all
Next year the last of labors

2. Jefferson's daughter Maria.
3. Jefferson's estate near Charlottesville, Virginia.
4. Ancient city on the northern coast of Africa governed by an aristocracy of wealthy merchants. Jefferson greatly objected to the American statesman Alexander Hamilton's (1755–1804) proposal to establish a national bank.
5. Variety of squash.

among conflicting parties
Then my family

we shall sow our cabbages
together

XIII

Delicious flower
of the acacia

or rather

Mimosa Nilotica
from Mr. Lomax[6]

XIV

Polly Jefferson, 8, had crossed
to father and sister in Paris

by way of London—Abigail
embraced her—Adams said

'in all my life I never saw
more charming child'

Death of Polly, 25
Monticello[7]

XV

My harpsichord
my alabaster vase
and bridle bit
bound for Alexandria[8]
Virginia

The good sea weather
of retirement
The drift and suck
and die-down of life
but there is land

6. John Taylor Lomax, first professor of law appointed at the University of Virginia (1826). *Mimosa Nilotica:* flowering plant.

7. "Polly," Maria Jefferson, died on April 12, 1804.

8. City in Virginia just south of Washington, D.C.

XVI

These were my passions:
Monticello and the villa-temples
I passed on to carpenters
bricklayers what I knew

and to an Italian sculptor
how to turn a volute[9]
on a pillar

You may approach the campus rotunda
from lower to upper terrace
Cicero had levels[1]

XVII

John Adams' eyes
        dimming
Tom Jefferson's rheumatism
                cantering[2]

XVIII

Ah soon must Monticello be lost
        to debts
    and Jefferson himself
                to death

XIX

Mind leaving, let body leave
Let dome live, spherical dome
and colonnade

Martha (Patsy) stay
'The Committee of Safety
must be warned'

Stay youth—Anne and Ellen
all my books, the bantams
and the seeds of the senega root[3]

1970

9. Spiral ornament on the capital of Ionic columns.
1. Jefferson designed the Rotunda, modeled after the Pantheon in Rome, to serve as the library of the University of Virginia, which he founded in 1819. Cicero (106–43 B.C.E.): Roman orator and statesman, whose "levels" of rhetoric are linked to architectural levels.
2. Jefferson and Adams both died on July 4, 1826.
3. Root used as an antidote for snakebites. *Anne and Ellen:* Anne Cary Randolph and Ellen Randolph Coolidge, Jefferson's granddaughters. *Bantams:* miniature fowls.

Countee Cullen
1903–1946

In 1940, the poet Melvin Tolson declared Countee Cullen and Langston Hughes the "antipodes" of the Harlem Renaissance: "The former is a classicist and conservative; the latter, an experimentalist and radical" ("The Harlem Group of Negro Writers"). Cullen writes primarily out of the European inheritance of Romanticism; Hughes, out of the African American inheritance of jazz, spirituals, and the blues. Rejecting Hughes's call for black poets to explore African American oral traditions, Cullen hues to the Petrarchan and Shakespearean sonnet, the Spenserian stanza, the elegy, the ballad, and other European forms. For all these differences, Cullen, like Hughes, writes about the vexed experience of African Americans in a predominantly white society.

Cullen is "conservative" in his technical devices (e.g., quatrains, rhyming couplets), in his muted if at times forceful protest against racial oppression, and his admiration for John Keats and Edna St. Vincent Millay (his undergraduate thesis was on Millay). He made his position clear in his forward to an important anthology of African American poetry that he published in 1927, *Caroling Dusk:* "This country's Negro writers may here and there turn some singular facet toward the literary sun, but in the main, since theirs is also the heritage of the English language, their work will not present any serious aberration from the poetic tendencies of their times." The word "aberration" indicates how much Cullen wanted to remain within a literary tradition in which the poet's color was secondary. He added: "Negro poets, dependent as they are on the English language, may have more to gain from the rich background of English and American poetry than from any nebulous atavistic yearnings toward an African inheritance." But this attitude did not pass unchallenged. In *The Black Christ and Other Poems,* published two years later, Cullen defended his cosmopolitanism in the poem "To Certain Critics":

> Then call me traitor if you must . . .
> I'll bear your censure as your praise,
> For never shall the clan
> Confine my singing to its ways
> Beyond the ways of man.

Notwithstanding this proud determination, Cullen realized that race influenced all his poems, not only those he placed in a discrete section labeled "Color" in his collections. "In spite of myself," he said, he began to see the distinction between "racial" and "nonracial" poetry as untenable: "I find my poetry of itself treating of the Negro, of his joys and sorrows—mostly of the latter, and of the heights and the depths of emotion which I feel as a Negro" (quoted in Houston A. Baker Jr., *Afro-American Poetics,* 1988). In "Heritage," he seems to argue with his own universalism; the refrain asks, "What is Africa to me?" but the poem concedes that it is a good deal: "Not yet has my heart or head / In the least way realized / They and I are civilized."

This division of identity into a primal African self and a "civilized" American self recurs in Cullen's work, reflecting an ambivalence toward both Africa and America, frequently voiced in a "primitivist" strain made popular during the Harlem Renaissance by Cullen and others. In "Atlantic City Waiter," the title character is split between his "acquiescent mask / Of bland gentility" and his inward, emotive, irrepressible blackness. If Cullen's verse sometimes wears a similar mask, it nevertheless gives powerful expression to the African American experience of divided allegiances—to a white America that demands conformity and to a racially specific divergence. At the heart of Cullen's work are these conflicting desires of assimilation and resistance—to excel within European formal conventions and yet to voice an experience that remains unassimilable and apart.

He was born Countee Leroy Porter on May 30, 1903, in Louisville, Kentucky, and raised by his grandmother in New York City. After her death in 1918, he was adopted by a Methodist minister, the Reverend Frederick A. Cullen, head of the largest congregation in Harlem and a future official in the NAACP. Countee Cullen attended New York University, graduating in 1925 after receiving several poetry prizes. The following year he received an A.M. in English at Harvard University. In 1927, he became assistant editor of *Opportunity: Journal of Negro Life*. Then a Guggenheim Fellowship enabled him to spend a year in Paris. In 1928, in a grand, candlelit ceremony in Harlem, he married Yolande Du Bois, only child of the leading African American intellectual W. E. B. Du Bois, but the couple separated two months later and were divorced by 1930. (Cullen's sexual preference seems to have been homosexual.) In 1934, his writing career in decline, Cullen took a high school position teaching French and English. Altogether, he published five volumes of verse, a novel, and a translation of Euripides' *Medea,* and he collaborated with the Harlem Renaissance poet Arna Bontemps on a play. Though some black nationalist poets repudiated Cullen in the 1960s, there has been a recent resurgence of interest in his work.

Yet Do I Marvel

I doubt not God is good, well-meaning, kind,
And did he stoop to quibble could tell why
The little buried mole continues blind,
Why flesh that mirrors Him must some day die,
Make plain the reason tortured Tantalus
Is baited by the fickle fruit, declare
If merely brute caprice dooms Sisyphus
To struggle up a never-ending stair.[1]
Inscrutable His ways are, and immune
To catechism by a mind too strewn
With petty cares to slightly understand
What awful brain compels His awful hand.
Yet do I marvel at this curious thing:
To make a poet black, and bid him sing!

1925

Atlantic City Waiter

With subtle poise he grips his tray
Of delicate things to eat;
Choice viands[2] to their mouths half way,
The ladies watch his feet

1. In Hades, the underworld of Greek mythology, Tantalus is punished by being "tantalized" with food and drink that recede at his touch; Sisyphus must push to the top of a hill a boulder that perpetually rolls back.
2. Pieces of food.

Go carving dexterous avenues
  Through sly intricacies;
Ten thousand years on jungle clues
  Alone shaped feet like these.

For him to be humble who is proud
  Needs colder artifice;
Though half his pride is disavowed,
  In vain the sacrifice.

Sheer through his acquiescent mask
  Of bland gentility,
The jungle flames like a copper cask
  Set where the sun strikes free.

1925

Incident

(For Eric Walrond)[3]

Once riding in old Baltimore,
  Heart-filled, head-filled with glee,
I saw a Baltimorean
  Keep looking straight at me.

Now I was eight and very small,
  And he was no whit bigger,
And so I smiled, but he poked out
  His tongue, and called me, "Nigger."

I saw the whole of Baltimore
  From May until December;
Of all the things that happened there
  That's all that I remember.

1925

For a Lady I Know

She even thinks that up in heaven
  Her class lies late and snores,
While poor black cherubs rise at seven
  To do celestial chores.

1925

3. American fiction writer and essayist (1898–1966).

Heritage

(For Harold Jackman)[4]

What is Africa to me:
Copper sun or scarlet sea,
Jungle star or jungle track,
Strong bronzed men, or regal black
Women from whose loins I sprang
When the birds of Eden sang?
One three centuries removed
From the scenes his fathers loved,
Spicy grove, cinnamon tree,
What is Africa to me?

So I lie, who all day long
Want no sound except the song
Sung by wild barbaric birds
Goading massive jungle herds,
Juggernauts of flesh that pass
Trampling tall defiant grass
Where young forest lovers lie,
Plighting troth beneath the sky.
So I lie, who always hear,
Though I cram against my ear
Both my thumbs, and keep them there,
Great drums throbbing through the air.
So I lie, whose fount of pride,
Dear distress, and joy allied,
Is my somber flesh and skin,
With the dark blood dammed within
Like great pulsing tides of wine
That, I fear, must burst the fine
Channels of the chafing net
Where they surge and foam and fret.

Africa? A book one thumbs
Listlessly, till slumber comes.
Unremembered are her bats
Circling through the night, her cats
Crouching in the river reeds,
Stalking gentle flesh that feeds
By the river brink; no more
Does the bugle-throated roar
Cry that monarch claws have leapt
From the scabbards where they slept.
Silver snakes that once a year
Doff the lovely coats you wear,
Seek no covert in your fear

4. A teacher, Cullen's friend (1901–1961).

Lest a mortal eye should see;
What's your nakedness to me?
Here no leprous flowers rear
Fierce corollas in the air;
Here no bodies sleek and wet,
Dripping mingled rain and sweat,
Tread the savage measures of
Jungle boys and girls in love.
What is last year's snow to me,[5]
Last year's anything? The tree
Budding yearly must forget
How its past arose or set—
Bough and blossom, flower, fruit,
Even what shy bird with mute
Wonder at her travail there,
Meekly labored in its hair.
One three centuries removed
From the scenes his fathers loved,
Spicy grove, cinnamon tree,
What is Africa to me?

So I lie, who find no peace
Night or day, no slight release
From the unremittent beat
Made by cruel padded feet
Walking through my body's street.
Up and down they go, and back,
Treading out a jungle track.
So I lie, who never quite
Safely sleep from rain at night—
I can never rest at all
When the rain begins to fall;
Like a soul gone mad with pain
I must match its weird refrain;
Ever must I twist and squirm,
Writhing like a baited worm,
While its primal measures drip
Through my body, crying, "Strip!
Doff this new exuberance.
Come and dance the Lover's Dance!"
In an old remembered way
Rain works on me night and day.

5. An allusion to the famous refrain from "Ballad of the Ladies of Bygone Time," by French poet François Villon (1431–1463?): "But where are the snows of yesteryear?"

Quaint, outlandish heathen gods
Black men fashion out of rods,
Clay, and brittle bits of stone,
In a likeness like their own,
My conversion came high-priced;
I belong to Jesus Christ,
Preacher of humility;
Heathen gods are naught to me.

Father, Son, and Holy Ghost,
So I make an idle boast;
Jesus of the twice-turned cheek,
Lamb of God, although I speak
With my mouth thus, in my heart
Do I play a double part.
Ever at Thy glowing altar
Must my heart grow sick and falter,
Wishing He I served were black,
Thinking then it would not lack
Precedent of pain to guide it,
Let who would or might deride it;
Surely then this flesh would know
Yours had borne a kindred woe.
Lord, I fashion dark gods, too,
Daring even to give You
Dark despairing features where,
Crowned with dark rebellious hair,
Patience wavers just so much as
Mortal grief compels, while touches
Quick and hot, of anger, rise
To smitten cheek and weary eyes.
Lord, forgive me if my need
Sometimes shapes a human creed.
All day long and all night through,
One thing only must I do:
Quench my pride and cool my blood,
Lest I perish in the flood.
Lest a hidden ember set
Timber that I thought was wet
Burning like the dryest flax,
Melting like the merest wax,
Lest the grave restore its dead.
Not yet has my heart or head
In the least way realized
They and I are civilized.

1925

Louis Zukofsky
1904–1978

At Ezra Pound's insistence, the second-generation modernist Louis Zukofsky was asked in 1931 to edit a special issue of *Poetry* magazine. Zukofsky gathered poems by William Carlos Williams, George Oppen, Basil Bunting, himself, and others, his choice of poems reflecting his desire to suggest an alternative to the symbolist procedures of W. B. Yeats and T. S. Eliot. When Harriet Monroe, founding editor and publisher, pressed him for a term that would gather his chosen poets into a movement, he coined *Objectivists.* Objectivism was clearly descended from Imagism. It shared with Imagism an emphasis on compression, direct description, rhythmical invention, and subordination of interiority. When asked about the origins of Objectivism, Zukofsky replied, "I picked up the word simply because I had something very simple in mind. You live with the things as they exist and as you sense them and think them" ("*A, 1–12*"). The poet lives in a world of objects and is perhaps more than usually aware of them.

But Zukofsky's version of Objectivism—a movement almost as variable as its practitioners—was more than an emphasis on the object "out there," the hard, clear, visual image. For Zukofsky, the poem itself was to be seen as a thing in the world. Words had a material reality. In an essay on fellow Objectivist Charles Reznikoff in the special issue of *Poetry,* Zukofsky explained, "Writing occurs which is the detail, not mirage, of seeing, of thinking with the things as they exist, and of directing them along a line of melody." The poet makes a poem out of unmystified perceptions, and once completed, the poem itself becomes an object, with a value and interest independent of its source. Zukofsky spoke of his own poems, once written, as "*found objects* . . . which arrange themselves as it were, one object near another—roots that have become sculpture, wood that appears talisman, and so on" (*Prepositions*). In his long poem "A," rival to Pound's *Cantos* and other modernist sequences, Zukofsky defines poetry in relation to two extremes: "An integral / Lower limit speech / Upper limit music." Perhaps poetry cannot dispense altogether with the communicative function of language, but Zukofsky pushes poetry toward its upper limit as "melody" and "music," as aural constellations of sound. "The test of poetry," he writes, "is the range of pleasure it affords as sight, sound, and intellection. This is its purpose as art" (*The Test of Poetry*).

Zukofsky was born on January 23, 1904, in New York City, to recent immigrants from what is now Lithuania. Though he came to resist the religious orthodoxy of his parents, he grew up in the vibrant New York culture of immigrant Jews. His first language was Yiddish. He knew the English canon through Yiddish translations, such as of the plays he saw by his beloved Shakespeare and others. Learning English in public school, he soon devoured Shakespeare, Longfellow, and other English-language writers. At sixteen, he entered Columbia University and there began to write poetry. Zukofsky caught the attention of Pound in Italy by sending him his first major work, "Poem Beginning 'The,' " in 1927. Publishing the poem in his short-lived periodical *The Exile* in 1928, Pound was impressed that Zukofsky had absorbed the juxtapositional and allusive techniques of high modernism, and Zukofsky would remain loyal to Pound despite many hectoring lessons on economic theory and invidious references to Jewish "racial characteristics."

In a letter of 1930, one of many between the "sonny" and his poetic "papa," Zukofsky explained, "*The* was a direct reply to *The Waste Land.*" Appropriating and parodying the idiom of *The Waste Land,* Zukofsky's poem sees the decentering and devolution of cultural authority after World War I as an occasion not for Eliotic gloom, religious nostalgia, or mythmaking but for playful experimentation with language and with cultural heterogeneity. Zukofsky assimilates modernist quotation, collage, difficulty, and self-referentiality to his urban experience as an American Jew. He was neither at ease in the world of traditional Judaism nor comfortable with the anti-Semitism he found in Pound's and Eliot's poetry, and his high-spirited poem plays out the tensions of his cultural in-betweenness. Apostrophizing the speaker's mother, it incorporates Jewish folk song and translations from Yiddish poetry alongside many European high-cultural references, humorously indexed in the poem's "dedication." Modernist collage turns out to be a useful aesthetic structure for conveying the cultural juxtapositions of the sophisticated Jewish New Yorker's ethnically complex experience. Though he later became ambivalent toward the American Communist Party, Zukofsky seems, unlike his modernist forebears, to respond hopefully in "The" to the recent Bolshevik revolution in Russia.

Over the course of his career, Zukofsky taught briefly at Wisconsin University and Colgate University, and for a longer period at the Polytechnic Institute of Brooklyn (1947–66). During the Depression, he made a living through various editing and writing jobs, including a period at the Works Progress Administration (WPA). He continued to work on "A," a massive poem in twenty-four "movements" that experiments in a wide array of formal structures, from the late 1920s to the late 1960s, while also writing and publishing many shorter lyrics, essays, and fiction and collaborating with his wife, Celia, on musical projects. Influencing such contemporaries as William Carlos Williams and Lorine Niedecker, Zukofsky's poetry is an important link between the high modernism of Eliot and Pound and the later avant-garde experiments of Black Mountain poets such as Robert Creeley and Language poets such as Charles Bernstein.

From Poem Beginning "The"[1]

[*Dedication*]

Because I have had occasion to remember, quote, paraphrase, I dedicate this poem to Anyone and Anything I have unjustifiably forgotten. Also to J. S. Bach—309, Bede's *Ecclesiastical History*—248, 291, Max Beerbohm—245, Beethoven's *Ninth Symphony*—310–312, Broadway—134, Geoffrey Chaucer—1st Movement, Title, College Cheer—45, E. E. Cummings' *Is Five*—38, Dante—66, Norman Douglas' *South Wind*—14, Elijah, the Prophet—24, T. S. Eliot's *The Waste Land* and *The Sacred Wood*—25–27, John Erskine—184, 185, Heinrich Heine—266, 267, 269, 316, Robert Herrick—187, 188, Horace—141, Horses—224–237, Aldous Huxley's *Those Barren Leaves*—12, 18, Henry James—2nd Movement, Title, Jewish Folk Song—191, 270–280, James Joyce—13, 20, 28, 29, D. H. Lawrence—8, 19, 133, Christopher Marlowe's *Edward II*—46, 47, Modern Advertising—163, George Moore—24, Marianne Moore—22, Mussolini—74, 75, Myself—130, 142, 167, 309, Obvious—Where the Reference is Obvious, Walter Pater's *Renaissance*—165, *Peer Gynt*—281–285, Poe's *Helen*—168–182, Popular Non-Sacred Song—4, 5, 36, 37, 288, 289, Ezra Pound—15, 18, Power of the Past, Present, and Future—Where the reference is to the word Sun, E. A. Robinson's *Children of the Night*—132, Sophocles—6, Oswald

1. Responding to the dense web of allusions and footnotes in *The Waste Land* (1922), Zukofsky playfully numbers each line of "Poem Beginning 'The' " and condenses his own annotations into this exhaustive dedication at the beginning of the poem. The numbers following the dashes refer to lines in the body of the poem.

Spengler—132, Max Stirner—199–202, Symbol of our Relatively Most Permanent Self, Origin and Destiny—Wherever the reference is to the word Mother, *The Bible*—1–3, 9, 313, 314, The Bolsheviki—203, 323, The French Language—31, 33, 51, 292, The King's English—166, *The Merchant of Venice*—250–265, The Yellow Menace—241–242, University Extension—70, Villon—21, Franz Werfel—68, Virginia Woolf's *Mrs. Dalloway*—52, Yehoash—110–129, 205–223, 318–330.

First Movement: "And out of olde bokes, in good feith"[2]

1 The
2 Voice of Jesus I. Rush singing
3 in the wilderness
4 A boy's best friend is his mother,
5 It's your mother all the time.
6 Residue of Oedipus-faced[3] wrecks
7 Creating out of the dead,—
8 From the candle flames of the souls of dead mothers
9 Vide[4] the legend of thin Christ sending her out of the temple,—
10 Books from the stony heart, flames rapping the stone,
11 Residue of self-exiled men
12 By the Tyrrhenian.[5]
13 Paris.
14 But everywhere only the South Wind, the sirocco,[6] the broken Earth-face.
15 The broken Earth-face, the age demands an image of its life and contacts,
16 Lord, lord, not that we pray, are sure of the question,
17 But why are our finest always dead?
18 And why, Lord, this time, is it Mauberly's Luini in porcelain, why is it Chelifer,[7]
19 Why is it Lovat who killed Kangaroo,
20 Why Stephen Daedalus[8] with the cane of ash,
21 But why les neiges?
22 And why, if all of Mary's Observations[9] have been made
23 Have not the lambs become more sapient drinking of the spring;
24 Kerith is long dry, and the ravens that brought the prophet bread[1]

2. From Geoffrey Chaucer's *Canterbury Tales*.
3. *Oedipus:* Greek king who unknowingly kills his father and marries his mother in Sophocles' tragedy *Oedipus the King*.
4. Refer to (Latin).
5. Portion of the Mediterranean Sea between the Italian peninsula, Sicily, and Corsica.
6. Desert wind.
7. Artist character in Aldous Huxley's novel *Those Barren Leaves* (1925). Mauberley is the main poet character in Ezra Pound's *Hugh Selwyn Mauberley* (1920). Line 15 alludes to the first section of Pound's poem, "(Life and Contacts)," and to the second section, which begins "The age demanded an image / Of its accelerated grimace." The last section of *Mauberley* begins "Luini in porcelain!" Bernadino Luini (c. 1480–1532): Italian painter.
8. Stephen Dedalus, whose last name derives from the mythical Greek artificer Daedalus, is the young writer in James Joyce's semiautobiographical novels *A Portrait of the Artist as a Young Man* (1914) and *Ulysses* (1922). Lines 28–29 refer to Stephen's role in *Ulysses* as the figure of Telemachus, the son of Odysseus. *Lovat who killed Kangaroo:* D. H. Lawrence's novel *Kangaroo* (1923) ends with the death of "Kangaroo" Ben Cooley, a Jewish barrister and radical killed in a riotous labor meeting. Kangaroo ultimately fails to persuade the novel's protagonist, the writer Richard Lovat Somers, to join the cause.
9. *Observations* (1924): the second book by the American poet Marianne Moore (1887–1972). *Les neiges:* literally, the snows (French). The "Ballade des dames du temps jadis," by French poet François Villon (1431–1463?), contains the famous refrain "Mais où sont les neiges d'antan?" (But where are the snows of yesteryear?).
1. According to 1 Kings 17, when God sent a drought to the Earth, he told the prophet Elijah to hide by the brook of Cherith, where ravens delivered bread and flesh. *The Brook Kerith* is also the

25 Are dust in the waste land of a raven-winged evening.
26 And why if the waste land has been explored, traveled over, circumscribed,
27 Are there only wrathless skeletons exhumed new planted in its sacred wood,[2]
28 Why—heir, long dead—Odysseus, wandering of ten years
29 Out-journeyed only by our Stephen, bibbing of a day,
30 O why is that to Hecuba as Hecuba to he![3]

31 You are cra-a-zee on the subject of babies, says she,
32 That is because somehow our authors have been given a woman's intuition.
33 Il y a un peu trop de femme[4] in this South Wind.
34 And on the cobblestones, bang, bang, bang, myself like the wheels—
35 The tram passes singing
36 O do you take this life as your lawful wife,
37   I do!
38 O the Time is 5
39   I do!
40 O the Time is 5
41   I do!
42 O do you take these friends as your loves to wive,
43 O the Time is 5
44   I do!

45 For it's the hoo-doos,[5] the somethin' voo-doos
46 And not Kings onelie, but the wisest men
47 Graue Socrates, what says Marlowe?[6]
48 For it was myself seemed held
49 Beating—beating—[7]
50 Body trembling as over an hors d'oeuvres[8]—
51
52 And the dream ending—Dalloway! Dalloway—[9]
53 The blind portals opening, and I awoke!

54 Let me be
55 Not by art have we lived,
56 Not by graven images forbidden to us

title of a skeptical 1916 novel about the life of Jesus written by the Irish author George Moore (1852–1933).

2. Cf. T. S. Eliot's *The Sacred Wood* (1920) and *The Waste Land* (1922), lines 71–72: " 'That corpse you planted last year in the garden, / Has it begun to sprout? Will it bloom this year?' "

3. Cf. *Hamlet* 2.2.536–37, in which Hamlet marvels at an actor's ability to conjure up emotion: "What's Hecuba to him, or he to Hecuba, / That he should weep for her?"

4. There is a little too much woman (French).

5. African American practices of sympathetic magic.

6. In Elizabethan dramatist Christopher Marlowe's *Edward II* (1594), the king's love for the Frenchman Gaveston is excused by Mortimer because the "mightiest kings have had their minions," including "grave Socrates," who had his "wild Alcibades."

7. Cf. "Beating oars" (line 280) and "Burning burning burning burning" (line 307) in the tryst scene between Elizabeth and Leicester in Eliot's *Waste Land*.

8. Plural form, used here as singular.

9. Cf. Virginia Woolf's novel *Mrs. Dalloway* (1925), which presents the internal experience of an upper-class Englishwoman on a summer's day. When Richard Dalloway exclaims repeatedly, "My name is Dalloway!" Peter Walsh has the "blinding" revelation that Richard will marry the woman Peter loves, Clarissa.

Not by letters I fancy,
Do we dare say
With Spinoza grinding lenses, Rabbaisi,
After living on Cathedral Parkway?[1]

Fifth Movement: Autobiography

Speaking about epics, mother,
How long ago is it since you gathered mushrooms,
Gathered mushrooms while you mayed.[2]
Is it your mate, my father, boating.
A stove burns like a full moon in a desert night.
Un in hoyze is kalt. You think of a new grave,[3]
In the fields, flowers.
Night on the bladed grass, bayonets dewed.
Is it your mate, my father, boating.
Speaking about epics, mother,—
Down here among the gastanks, ruts, cemetery-tenements—
It is your Russia that is free.[4]
And I here, can I say only—
"So then an egoist can never embrace a party
Or take up with a party?
Oh, yes, only he cannot let himself
Be embraced or taken up by the party."[5]
It is your Russia that is free, mother.
Tell me, mother.

Winged wild geese, where lies the passage,[6]
In far away lands lies the passage.
Winged wild geese, who knows the pathway?
Of the winds, asking, we shall say:
Wind of the South and wind of the North
Where has our sun gone forth?
Naked, twisted, scraggly branches,
And dark, gray patches through the branches,
Ducks with puffed-up, fluttering feathers
On a cobalt stream.
And faded grass that's slowly swaying.
A barefoot shepherd boy
Striding in the mire:
Swishing indifferently a peeled branch
On jaded sheep.
An old horse strewn with yellow leaves

1. Street just north of Central Park in Manhattan. Baruch Spinoza (1632–1677), Jewish philosopher, also worked as a lens grinder. *Rabbaisi:* or *rabosay*, a Hebrew-derived Yiddish word used to address a large group of people (as in "ladies and gentlemen" or, in modern Hebrew, *rabotai*).
2. Cf. "To the Virgins, to Make Much of Time" by the English poet Robert Herrick (1591–1674): "Gather ye rosebuds while ye may."
3. From a Jewish folksong. *Un in hoyze is kalt:* and at home it's cold (Yiddish).
4. The Bolshevik Revolution of 1917 ended czarist rule in Russia. Zukofsy's mother had grown up in Lithuania when it was part of czarist Russia.
5. From *The Ego and His Own,* by Max Stirner (1806–1856), German philosopher who taught that the only reality is the individual ego. In the passage preceding the quotation, Stirner cites "the Jews" as "another party," not belonging to the "party" of Christianity.
6. Lines 205–23 borrow from "Cheshwan," a lyric poem written in Yiddish by the Jewish American poet Yehoash (1872?–1927).

By the edge of the meadow
Draws weakly with humid nostrils
The moisture of the clouds.
Horses that pass through inappreciable woodland,
Leaves in their manes tangled, mist, autumn green,
Lord, why not give these bright brutes—your good land—
Turf for their feet always, years for their mien.
See how each peer lifts his head, others follow,
Mate paired with mate, flanks coming full they crowd,
Reared in your sun, Lord, escaping each hollow
Where life-struck we stand, utter their praise aloud.
Very much Chance, Lord, as when you first made us,
You might forget them, Lord, preferring what
Being less lovely where sadly we fuss?
Weed out these horses as tho they were not?
Never alive in brute delicate trembling
Song to your sun, against autumn assembling.

If horses could but sing Bach,[7] mother,—
Remember how I wished it once—
Now I kiss you who could never sing Bach, never read Shakespeare.

In Manhattan here the Chinamen are yellow in the face, mother,
Up and down, up and down our streets they go yellow in the face,
And why is it the representatives of your, my, race are always hankering for food, mother?
We, on the other hand, eat so little.
Dawn't you think Trawtsky rawthaw a darrling,[8]
I ask our immigrant cousin querulously.
Naw! I think hay is awlmawst a Tchekoff.[9]
But she has more color in her cheeks than the Angles[1]—Angels—mother,—
They have enough, though. We should get some more color, mother.
If I am like them in the rest, I should resemble them in that, mother,
Assimilation is not hard,
And once the Faith's askew
I might as well look Shagetz[2] just as much as Jew.
I'll read their Donne as mine,
And leopard in their spots
I'll do what says their Coleridge,[3]
Twist red hot pokers into knots.
The villainy they teach me I will execute
And it shall go hard with them,

7. Johann Sebastian Bach (1685–1750), German Baroque composer.
8. Attributed to English essayist and caricaturist Max Beerbohm (1872–1956). *Trawtsky:* Leon Trotsky (1879–1940), Communist theorist and agitator.
9. Anton Chekhov (1860–1904), Russian writer and dramatist.
1. Cf. *The Ecclesiastical History of the English Nation*, by church historian Saint Bede (673?–735), which describes the fifth-century invasion of Britain by the Angles and their eventual conversion to Christianity. Cf. also Pope Gregory's pun on seeing some British children: "They're not Angles but Angels."
2. Derogatory term for male Gentile (Yiddish).
3. Samuel Taylor Coleridge (1772–1834), English Romantic poet, wrote "On Donne's Poetry," about John Donne (1572–1631), English Metaphysical poet: "With Donne, whose muse on dromedary trots / Wreathe iron pokers into true-love knots; / Rhyme's sturdy cripple, fancy's name and clue, / Wit's forge and fire-blast, meaning's press and screw."

260 For I'll better the instruction,
261 Having learned, so to speak, in their colleges.
262   It is engendered in the eyes
263   With gazing fed, and fancy dies
264   In the cradle where it lies[4]
265   In the cradle where it lies
266 I, Senora, am the Son of the Respected Rabbi,
267 Israel of Saragossa,[5]
268 Not that the Rabbis give a damn,
269 Keine Kadish wird man sagen.[6]

1928

To My Wash-Stand

      To my wash-stand
in which I wash
      my left hand
and my right hand

      To my wash-stand
whose base is Greek
      whose shaft
is marble and is fluted

      To my wash-stand
whose wash-bowl
      is an oval
in a square

      To my wash-stand
whose square is marble
      and inscribes two
smaller ovals to left and right for soap

      Comes a song of
water from the right faucet and the left
      my left and my
right hand mixing hot and cold

      Comes a flow which
if I have called a song
      is a song
entirely in my head

4. From a song in Shakespeare's *Merchant of Venice:* fancy "is engendered in the eyes, / With gazing fed; and fancy dies / In the cradle where it lies" (3.2.67–69). In the same play, the Jewish Shylock delivers his famous speech about the common humanity of Jews and Christians (3.1.45–61), which concludes "The villainy you teach me I will execute, and it shall go hard but I will better the instruction."

5. Lines 266 and 267 quote the end of "Donna Clara," by German Jewish poet Heinrich Heine (1797–1856), in which a mysterious knight reveals his Jewish identity after the title character, who has betrayed her anti-Semitism, allows him to kiss her.

6. No Kaddish will be said (German). *Kaddish (or Kadish):* Jewish prayer said in memory of the dead.

a song out of imagining
modillions[7] descried above
my head a frieze
of stone completing what no longer

is my wash-stand
since its marble has completed
my getting up each morning
my washing before going to bed

my look into a mirror
to glimpse half an oval
as if its half
were half-oval in my head and the

climates of many
inscriptions human heads shapes'
horses' elephants' (tusks) others'
scratched in marble tile

so my wash-stand
in one particular breaking of the
tile at which I have
looked and looked

has opposed to my head
the inscription of a head
whose coinage is the
coinage of the poor

observant in waiting
in their getting up mornings
and in their waiting
going to bed

carefully attentive
to what they have
and to what they do not
have

when a flow of water
doubled in narrow folds
occasions invertible counterpoints
over a head and

an age in a wash-stand
and in their own heads

1931

7. Ornamental blocks or brackets such as those found on Corinthian columns.

Richard Eberhart
1904–2005

Richard Eberhart takes sides with the visionary poets, with William Blake and Dylan Thomas, although he expresses his visionary perceptions much more ruminatively than they do. His style is a cultivated and sustained awkwardness; his fitful lyricism a sudden relaxation from roughness. Although he admires and at times echoes effects of suave poets such as Wallace Stevens and John Crowe Ransom, he keeps an inelegance of rhyme and phrasing, as if it guaranteed "the brutal and primitive power of the poet" ("Action and Poetry"). With their unsteadiness of diction, his poems, like Thomas Hardy's, seem to testify to a stubborn integrity and genuineness. His best poems successfully combine unpremeditativeness with deliberativeness, fierceness of perception with pedestrian detail.

Eberhart was born on April 5, 1904, in Austin, Minnesota, where his father was a prosperous businessman. He graduated from high school in 1921 and entered the University of Minnesota. The following year, his mother died of cancer, and shortly afterward, his father's fortune was largely wiped out by an employee's embezzlement. Eberhart then enrolled at Dartmouth University, where he received his B.A. in 1926. He traveled around the world as a deck hand on steamships, ending up at Cambridge University (B.A., 1929), where I. A. Richards encouraged him as a poet. Eberhart's first book of verse was published in London in 1930. In the ensuing years, Eberhart served as tutor to the son of King Prajadhipok of Siam, spent a year as a graduate student at Harvard University, and taught English (1933–41) at St. Mark's School, near Boston, where one of his pupils was the budding poet Robert Lowell. During World War II, he was an aerial gunnery officer in the navy. From this experience came several poems, the best-known being "The Fury of Aerial Bombardment." After the war, Eberhardt worked for six years in his father-in-law's floor wax company. He held various university posts before accepting the position of professor of English and poet-in-residence at Dartmouth, where he remained until 1970. He was honored with the Bollingen Prize in 1962, the Pulitzer Prize in 1966, and the National Book Award in 1977.

The Groundhog

In June, amid the golden fields,
I saw a groundhog lying dead.
Dead lay he; my sense shook,
And mind outshot our naked frailty.
There lowly in the vigorous summer
His form began its senseless change,
And made my senses waver dim
Seeing nature ferocious in him.
Inspecting close his maggots' might
And seething cauldron of his being,
Half with loathing, half with a strange love,
I poked him with an angry stick.
The fever arose, became a flame
And Vigour circumscribed the skies,
Immense energy in the sun,

And through my frame a sunless trembling.
My stick had done nor good nor harm.
Then stood I silent in the day
Watching the object, as before;
And kept my reverence for knowledge
Trying for control, to be still,
To quell the passion of the blood;
Until I had bent down on my knees
Praying for joy in the sight of decay.
And so I left; and I returned
In Autumn strict of eye, to see
The sap gone out of the groundhog,
But the bony sodden hulk remained.
But the year had lost its meaning,
And in intellectual chains
I lost both love and loathing,
Mured up in the wall of wisdom.
Another summer took the fields again
Massive and burning, full of life,
But when I chanced upon the spot
There was only a little hair left,
And bones bleaching in the sunlight
Beautiful as architecture;
I watched them like a geometer,
And cut a walking stick from a birch.
It has been three years, now.
There is no sign of the groundhog.
I stood there in the whirling summer,
My hand capped a withered heart,
And thought of China and of Greece,
Of Alexander in his tent;
Of Montaigne in his tower,
Of Saint Theresa[1] in her wild lament.

1936

The Fury of Aerial Bombardment

You would think the fury of aerial bombardment
Would rouse God to relent; the infinite spaces
Are still silent. He looks on shock-pried faces.
History, even, does not know what is meant.

You would feel that after so many centuries
God would give man to repent; yet he can kill
As Cain could,[2] but with multitudinous will,
No farther advanced than in his ancient furies.

1. Three types of human enterprise: Alexander the Great (356–323 B.C.E.), conqueror of the known world; Michel Eyquen de Montaigne (1533–1592), the ironic commentator on all human affairs; and St. Theresa of Avila (1515–1582), mystic and founder of a religious order.
2. Cain became the first murderer when he killed his brother, Abel, according to Genesis.

Was man made stupid to see his own stupidity?
Is God by definition indifferent, beyond us all?
Is the eternal truth man's fighting soul
Wherein the Beast ravens in its own avidity?

Of Van Wettering I speak, and Averill,
Names on a list, whose faces I do not recall
But they are gone to early death, who late in school
Distinguished the belt feed lever from the belt holding pawl.[3]

1947

3. Parts of a gun.

C. Day Lewis
1904–1972

C. Day Lewis befriended W. H. Auden at Oxford University, and these two poets, along with Louis MacNeice and Stephen Spender, were later grouped as a literary school, "the curious chimaera named Daylewisaudenmacneicespender" (Auden's introduction to *C. Day-Lewis, The Poet Laureate: A Bibliography*). Day Lewis felt a keen rivalry toward Auden and tended to imitate him, smitten, as he confides in his autobiography, *The Buried Day* (1960), by "the vigour of . . . language, the exciting novelty (to me) of the images and ideas." Auden urged Day Lewis to read Thomas Hardy and Robert Frost, and Hardy's influence is apparent in Day Lewis's searching admission of painful feelings of love and estrangement.

Day Lewis preferred to regard the true antecedents of the group as Gerard Manley Hopkins, Wilfred Owen, and T. S. Eliot. Hopkins's vibrancy and technical innovations, Owen's passionate pity, Eliot's excoriation of contemporary society—all were certainly elements in the new verse. Yet like the Americans Hart Crane and Louis Zukofsky, these poets needed to outdo their predecessors—especially Eliot—with new goals, and their poetry rang not with Eliot's despair but with revolutionary hope: "Collect your forces for a counter-attack," wrote Day Lewis in *The Magnetic Mountain* (1933): "New Life is on the way, the relief train."

In the preface to his *Collected Poems* (1954), Day Lewis insists that the "unbroken thread" in his work is "the search for personal identity," and that its other recurring themes include, with "hero-worship, fear, compassion, a prevailing sense of the transience of things," the quality of "the divided mind." His verse exhibits a mastery of stanza, line, and vocabulary, and an ability to compress complicated thought into coherent lyrics. His poems are lucid but muted meditations in highly structured verse forms. "Love's essence, like a poem's," he writes, "shall spring / From the not saying everything." He does not overfill his poems or let them overflow. What comes through is candor, deftness, precision, feeling.

Cecil Day Lewis was born on April 27, 1904, to an Anglo-Irish family in Ballintubber, Queen's County, Northern Ireland. His father was a priest of the Church of Ireland—for a time, an army chaplain. The family name was hyphenated, but the poet, with what he called "inverted snobbery," dropped the hyphen and thereby threw librarians into a confusion from which they have not recovered. Day Lewis was sent to "public" (British for private) school, but he was much happier at Wadham College, Oxford, where he studied classics—he was later to translate Virgil—and philosophy and ancient history. After Oxford, he became a schoolteacher. He married and, finding he had additional expenses, wrote a detective story each year, under the pseudonym Nicholas Blake. He also wrote several literary novels. His first book of poetry he thought of as mature, *Transitional Poem* (1929), began with a declaration that he would eliminate disorder and "stamp on all / Life the tetragonal / Pure symmetry of brain." Still searching for his own voice, he wrote politically revolutionary poetry and, in 1935, joined the Communist Party, which he left after three years. After World War II, his poetry exhibited, if not much satisfaction with the present, less eagerness for change, and his becoming poet laureate of Great Britain in 1968 signaled recognition of his modified beliefs.

Two Songs[1]

I've heard them lilting at loom and belting,
Lasses lilting before dawn of day:
But now they are silent, not gamesome and gallant—
The flowers of the town are rotting away.

There was laughter and loving in the lanes at evening;
Handsome were the boys then, and girls were gay.
But lost in Flanders[2] by medalled commanders
The lads of the village are vanished away.

Cursed be the promise that takes our men from us—
All will be champion if you choose to obey:
They fight against hunger but still it is stronger—
The prime of our land grows cold as the clay.

The women are weary, once lilted so merry,
Waiting to marry for a year and a day:
From wooing and winning, from owning or earning
The flowers of the town are all turned away.

Come, live with me and be my love,
And we will all the pleasures prove
Of peace and plenty, bed and board,
That chance employment may afford.

I'll handle dainties on the docks
And thou shalt read of summer frocks:
At evening by the sour canals
We'll hope to hear some madrigals.

Care on the maiden brow shall put
A wreath of wrinkles, and thy foot

1. The songs are parodies of familiar poems. The first is of a Scottish ballad by Jane Elliot (1727–1805), "The Flowers of the Forest," which is about milkmaids; the second is of "The Passionate Shepherd to His Love," by Christopher Marlowe (1564–1593).
2. That is, were killed in World War I.

Be shod with pain: not silken dress
But toil shall tire thy loveliness.

Hunger shall make thy modest zone
And cheat fond death of all but bone—
If these delights thy mind may move,
Then live with me and be my love.

1935

Where Are the War Poets?

They who in folly or mere greed
Enslaved religion, markets, laws,
Borrow our language now and bid
Us to speak up in freedom's cause.

It is the logic of our times,
No subject for immortal verse—
That we who lived by honest dreams
Defend the bad against the worse.

1943

Almost Human

The man you know, assured and kind,
Wearing fame like an old tweed suit—
You would not think he has an incurable
Sickness upon his mind.

Finely that tongue, for the listening people,
Articulates love, enlivens clay;
While under his valued skin there crawls
An outlaw and a cripple.

Unenviable the renown he bears
When all's awry within? But a soul
Divinely sick may be immunized
From the scourge of common cares.

A woman weeps, a friend's betrayed,
Civilization plays with fire—
His grief or guilt is easily purged
In a rush of words to the head.

The newly dead, and their waxwork faces
With the look of things that could never have lived,
He'll use to prime his cold, strange heart
And prompt the immortal phrases.

Before you condemn this eminent freak
As an outrage upon mankind,
Reflect: something there is in him
That must for ever seek

To share the condition it glorifies,
To shed the skin that keeps it apart,
To bury its grace in a human bed—
And it walks on knives, on knives.

1957

PATRICK KAVANAGH
1904–1967

"My life," wrote Patrick Kavanagh toward its end, "has in many ways been a tragedy and a failure." He was born on October 21, 1904, in the village of Inniskeen, County Monaghan, Ireland, and he described the life of the Irish country poor, which he shared, as "sad, grey, twisted, blind, just awful" (*November Haggard: Uncollected Prose and Poetry*). Raised a Roman Catholic, Kavanagh continued to be a Christian, though he blamed the Church for causing much unhappiness, his own included, through its repression of natural feeling. In 1939, he moved to Dublin. "It was," he wrote in *Self-Portrait* (1964), "the worst mistake of my life." The Irish literary renaissance that began in the late nineteenth century still had great creative power, but Kavanagh—in time, at least—scorned it. Though the movement "purported to be frightfully Irish and racy of the Celtic soil," it was, Kavanagh said, a "thorough going English-bred lie." Having lived the life of the Irish peasant, he laughed at writers who claimed "to have their roots in the soil and to be peasants as well" (*Self-Portrait*). Ferociously independent, forever in a rage with readers who accepted the illusions promoted by successful authors and critics, Kavanagh contrived a meager living as a columnist, reviewer, movie critic, and, in 1952, publisher of his own magazine, *Kavanagh's Weekly*. His first book of poems to attract much attention, *The Great Hunger* (1942), got him into trouble with the Irish censor because of its alleged obscenity and anti-Catholicism. Kavanagh, who frequently wrote poems that he later disowned, said the book contained some "queer and terrible things" and lacked the "nobility and repose of poetry" (*Self-Portrait*).

Nobility and repose are not qualities one associates with Kavanagh's poetry or prose, and he praised the untroubled acceptance of life with the air of a man who found such acceptance difficult. In 1954, he was gravely ill with lung cancer, and one of his lungs had to be removed. During his convalescence, in the summer of 1955, he had the "passive" revelation described in "Canal Bank Walk," and he was then liberated from his "messianic compulsion." The event marked his "birth as a poet," Kavanagh claimed, because he was satisfied to "let the water lap idly on the shores of my mind. My purpose in life was to have no purpose" (author's note to *Collected Poems,* 1964). He resigned himself to obscurity and failure, finding consolation in the thought that great men "are not concerned with whether or not their work is involved with the ephemeral." The vocation of the true poet, as Kavanagh now saw it, was to "name and name and name the obscure places, people, or events" ("X," *A Quarterly Review,* March 1960). Kavanagh's efforts to transcend his lifelong anger and pain were helped by the comic muse. He came to regard comedy as the "ultimate sophistication," which ordinary people "do not understand and therefore fear" (*Self-Portrait*). Though he described his life as tragic, he ultimately believed that in tragedy "there is always something of a lie. . . . Comedy is the abundance of life" ("X"). Kavanagh married for the first time early in 1967 and died later that year in a Dublin nursing home. Since Kavanagh's death, Seamus Heaney has been his most prominent champion, hailing Kavanagh for being closely attuned to Ireland's rural experience and its common speech—rough and realistic, yet musically pitched and mystically tinged.

Inniskeen Road: July Evening[1]

The bicycles go by in twos and threes—
There's a dance in Billy Brennan's barn to-night,
And there's the half-talk code of mysteries
And the wink-and-elbow language of delight.
Half-past eight and there is not a spot
Upon a mile of road, no shadow thrown
That might turn out a man or woman, not
A footfall tapping secrecies of stone.

I have what every poet hates in spite
Of all the solemn talk of contemplation.
Oh, Alexander Selkirk[2] knew the plight
Of being king and government and nation.
A road, a mile of kingdom, I am king
Of banks and stones and every blooming thing.

1936

From The Great Hunger[3]

I

Clay is the word and clay is the flesh
Where the potato-gatherers like mechanised scarecrows move
Along the side-fall of the hill—Maguire and his men.
If we watch them an hour is there anything we can prove
Of life as it is broken-backed over the Book
Of Death? Here crows gabble over worms and frogs

1. Inniskeen, in the south of County Monaghan, was Kavanagh's native village.
2. Eighteenth-century seaman whose experiences on an uninhabited island off the coast of Chile were used for the novel *Robinson Crusoe*, by Daniel Defoe (1660–1731).
3. Kavanagh's most famous work is his long poem in fourteen sections, *The Great Hunger* (1942), named for a severe famine that decimated the Irish population during the 1840s. The poem focuses on the spiritual and sexual hunger of the Irish peasantry among whom Kavanagh grew up. The central figure is a potato farmer named Patrick Maguire, who is bound to the soil by the need not to leave his aged mother, and whose Church-induced sense of sin is so strong that he dies a bachelor and perhaps a virgin.

And the gulls like old newspapers are blown clear of the hedges, luckily.
Is there some light of imagination in these wet clods?
Or why do we stand here shivering?
                                        Which of these men
Loved the light and the queen
Too long virgin? Yesterday was summer. Who was it promised marriage
    to himself
Before apples were hung from the ceilings for Hallowe'en?
We will wait and watch the tragedy to the last curtain,
Till the last soul passively like a bag of wet clay
Rolls down the side of the hill, diverted by the angles
Where the plough missed or a spade stands, straitening the way.

A dog lying on a torn jacket under a heeled-up cart,
A horse nosing along the poised headland, trailing
A rusty plough. Three heads hanging between wide-apart
Legs. October playing a symphony on a slack wire paling.
Maguire watches the drills flattened out
And the flints that lit a candle for him on a June altar
Flameless. The drills slipped by and the days slipped by
And he trembled his head away and ran free from the world's halter,
And thought himself wiser than any man in the townland[4]
When he laughed over pints of porter
Of how he came free from every net spread
In the gaps of experience. He shook a knowing head
And pretended to his soul
That children are tedious in hurrying fields of April
Where men are spanging[5] across wide furrows.
Lost in the passion that never needs a wife—
The pricks that pricked were the pointed pins of harrows.
Children scream so loud that the crows could bring
The seed of an acre away with crow-rude jeers.
Patrick Maguire, he called his dog and he flung a stone in the air
And hallooed the birds away that were the birds of the years.

Turn over the weedy clods and tease out the tangled skeins.
What is he looking for there?
He thinks it is a potato, but we know better
Than his mud-gloved fingers probe in this insensitive hair.

'Move forward the basket and balance it steady
In this hollow. Pull down the shafts of that cart, Joe,
And straddle the horse,' Maguire calls.
'The wind's over Brannagan's, now that means rain.
Graip[6] up some withered stalks and see that no potato falls
Over the tail-board going down the ruckety pass—
And *that's* a job we'll have to do in December,
Gravel it and build a kerb on the bog-side. Is that Cassidy's ass
Out in my clover? Curse o' God—
Where is that dog?

4. In Ireland, an area of land comparable to a township.

5. Leaping.

6. Fork.

Never where he's wanted.' Maguire grunts and spits
Through a clay-wattled moustache and stares about him from the
height.
His dream changes again like the cloud-swung wind
And he is not so sure now if his mother was right
When she praised the man who made a field his bride.

Watch him, watch him, that man on a hill whose spirit
Is a wet sack flapping about the knees of time.
He lives that his little fields may stay fertile when his own body
Is spread in the bottom of a ditch under two coulters[7] crossed in
Christ's Name.

He was suspicious in his youth as a rat near strange bread,
When girls laughed; when they screamed he knew that meant
The cry of fillies in season. He could not walk
The easy road to his destiny. He dreamt
The innocence of young brambles to hooked treachery.
O the grip, O the grip of irregular fields! No man escapes.
It could not be that back of the hills love was free
And ditches straight.
No monster hand lifted up children and put down apes
As here.
'O God if I had been wiser!'
That was his sigh like the brown breeze in the thistles.
He looks towards his house and haggard.[8] 'O God if I had been wiser!'
But now a crumpled leaf from the whitethorn bushes
Darts like a frightened robin, and the fence
Shows the green of after-grass through a little window,
And he knows that his own heart is calling his mother a liar
God's truth is life—even the grotesque shapes of its foulest fire.

The horse lifts its head and cranes
Through the whins[9] and stones
To lip late passion in the crawling clover.
In the gap there's a bush weighted with boulders like morality,
The fools of life bleed if they climb over.

The wind leans from Brady's, and the coltsfoot leaves are holed with
rust,
Rain fills the cart-tracks and the sole-plate grooves;
A yellow sun reflects in Donaghmoyne[1]
The poignant light in puddles shaped by hooves.

Come with me, Imagination, into this iron house
And we will watch from the doorway the years run back,
And we will know what a peasant's left hand wrote on the page.
Be easy, October. No cackle hen, horse neigh, tree sough, duck quack.

1942

7. Or colter; iron blades in ploughs.
8. Yard.
9. Masses of furze or gorse shrub.
1. A stream in County Monaghan.

Epic

I have lived in important places, times
When great events were decided, who owned
That half a rood[2] of rock, a no-man's land
Surrounded by our pitchfork-armed claims.
I heard the Duffys shouting 'Damn your soul'
And old McCabe stripped to the waist, seen
Step the plot defying blue cast-steel—
'Here is the march along these iron stones'
That was the year of the Munich bother;[3] Which
Was more important? I inclined
To lose my faith in Ballyrush and Gortin[4]
Till Homer's ghost came whispering to my mind
He said: I made the Iliad[5] from such
A local row. Gods make their own importance.

1960

Canal Bank Walk[6]

Leafy-with-love banks and the green waters of the canal
Pouring redemption for me, that I do
The will of God, wallow in the habitual, the banal,
Grow with nature again as before I grew.
The bright stick trapped, the breeze adding a third
Party to the couple kissing on an old seat,
And a bird gathering materials for the nest for the Word
Eloquently new and abandoned to its delirious beat.
O unworn world enrapture me, encapture me in a web
Of fabulous grass and eternal voices by a beech,
Feed the gaping need of my senses, give me ad lib
To pray unselfconsciously with overflowing speech
For this soul needs to be honoured with a new dress woven
From green and blue things and arguments that cannot be proven.

1960

Come Dance with Kitty Stobling

No, no, no, I know I was not important as I moved
Through the colourful country, I was but a single
Item in the picture, the namer not the beloved.
O tedious man with whom no gods commingle.

2. Approximately a quarter of an acre.
3. Diplomatic crisis of September 1939 that precipitated World War II.
4. Small townships near Kavanagh's home in the village of Inniskeen, County Monaghan.
5. Homer's epic account of the Trojan War.
6. Along the Grand Canal in Dublin.

Beauty, who has described beauty? Once upon a time
I had a myth that was a lie but it served:
Trees walking across the crests of hills and my rhyme
Cavorting on mile-high stilts and the unnerved
Crowds looking up with terror in their rational faces.
O dance with Kitty Stobling I outrageously
Cried out-of-sense to them, while their timorous paces
Stumbled behind Jove's[7] page boy paging me.
I had a very pleasant journey, thank you sincerely
For giving me my madness back, or nearly.

1960

In Memory of My Mother

I do not think of you lying in the wet clay
Of a Monaghan graveyard; I see
You walking down a lane among the poplars
On your way to the station, or happily

Going to second Mass on a summer Sunday—
You meet me and you say:
'Don't forget to see about the cattle—'
Among your earthiest words the angels stray.

And I think of you walking along a headland
Of green oats in June,
So full of repose, so rich with life—
And I see us meeting at the end of a town

On a fair day by accident, after
The bargains are all made and we can walk
Together through the shops and stalls and markets
Free in the oriental streets of thought.

O you are not lying in the wet clay,
For it is a harvest evening now and we
Are piling up the ricks against the moonlight
And you smile up at us—eternally.

1960

7. Jove is the king of the Roman gods.

Robert Penn Warren
1905–1989

Few modern or contemporary writers rivaled Robert Penn Warren in scope and aspiration. Working with equal success in both verse and fiction, he was unique in winning Pulitzer Prizes in both genres—one for a novel, *All the King's Men* (1947), and two for poetry: *Promises* (1958) and *Now and Then* (1979). His fiction was stylistically daunting but widely read. He was a teacher and moralist, one of the most influential literary critics of the century, and the founding editor of an important literary magazine, *The Southern Review*. As a southerner, he had a deeper and more spontaneously acquired sense of history than most American writers—and readers. He spent the first two decades of his life in the region where he was born, and though much of his later life was spent far from that home, his strong feeling of initial rootedness in place and in history enabled him to bear witness to the dislocating circumstances of contemporary American life—for him, its ethical confusion, its lack of discipline and shared values, its dehumanizing mechanism and abstraction. The past was for Warren a special, living, potentially redemptive resource.

Although his work gives no sign of religious orthodoxy, Warren's criticism of secular orthodoxy is often religious in its language. He aspired to a vision of humanity beyond naturalism and scientism. Among Christian doctrines, he had a particular fondness for the Fall: he believed that even the most scrupulous and morally circumspect person can never guard against the sudden incursion of evil. The best plan may founder, the most happily circumstanced life may harbor a guilty secret and erupt into ghastly violence. Warren's sense of evil led him to prefer a literature distrustful of the unconditioned and the abstract. In the precepts of his criticism and in his poems and novels, he consistently recommended a view of life that takes account of contradictions and mixed motives. In the important essay "Pure and Impure Poetry," Warren describes irony as a refining fire that proves the poet's "vision has been earned, that it can survive reference to the contradictions of experience." This ideal of literature might best be called Shakespearean, and to it Warren was, in the multiplicity of his work, completely dedicated.

He was born on April 24, 1905, in Guthrie, Kentucky. At sixteen, he entered Vanderbilt University, where John Crowe Ransom was among his teachers and where he joined, with his friend Allen Tate, a group called the Fugitives, which published from 1922 a literary magazine called *The Fugitive*. He graduated in 1925 and went to the University of California, Berkeley, to Yale University, and to Oxford University to further his studies. While at Oxford on a Rhodes Scholarship, Warren wrote his first book, a biography of the abolitionist John Brown; he also contributed an essay defending racial segregation in the south to the symposium *I'll Take My Stand* (1930), compiled by Ransom to defend southern and agrarian principles in the face of growing northern derision and antagonism. (Warren later reversed his position, writing books in the 1950s and 1960s supporting integration.) Returning to the United States, he taught at Vanderbilt and Louisiana State Universities and the University of Minnesota before joining the Yale faculty in 1950. His style of teaching, as rigorous and detailed as Ransom's, is embodied in *Understanding Poetry* (1938), the influential textbook he wrote with Cleanth Brooks, which sharpened the reading practices of several generations of American college and high school students. His first book of poems appeared in 1936, and his first novel, *Night Rider*, in 1939. Among his most ambitious poetic achievements are a long narrative poem, *Brother to Dragons* (1953), which tells of a slave boy's murder by a nephew of Thomas Jefferson, and *Audubon: A Vision* (1969), a poem about the painter and naturalist John James Audubon that explores how attempts to represent the natural world both succeed and fall short.

After Warren retired from Yale in 1973, he devoted himself to his verse. The poetry of his last few decades seemed to many readers his best—still grand and opulent, but gritty, more personal and less rhetorically mannered, freer in form, infused with a Romantic visionary power and a fierce clarity of psychological insight. Many of his later poems are, not surprisingly, elegiac and retrospective, preoccupied with influxes of memory, dislocations of identity, and the inadequacies of language. But they show no diminution in verbal density or vigor. As always, Warren tried to expand the world of a single poem to make it more inclusive; he frequently arranged his poems in clusters, interwoven with one another. The resilience and strength of Warren's talent—his first book of poems was published almost a half century before his last—made him a kind of national treasure, a live-and-kicking monument; this eminence was recognized by his appointment as the first poet laureate of the United States, in 1986.

Bearded Oaks

The oaks, how subtle and marine,
Bearded, and all the layered light
Above them swims; and thus the scene,
Recessed, awaits the positive night.

So, waiting, we in the grass now lie
Beneath the languorous tread of light:
The grasses, kelp-like, satisfy
The nameless motions of the air.

Upon the floor of light, and time,
Unmurmuring, of polyp made,
We rest; we are, as light withdraws,
Twin atolls on a shelf of shade.

Ages to our construction went,
Dim architecture, hour by hour:
And violence, forgot now, lent
The present stillness all its power.

The storm of noon above us rolled,
Of light the fury, furious gold,
The long drag troubling us, the depth:
Dark is unrocking, unrippling, still.

Passion and slaughter, ruth, decay
Descend, minutely whispering down,
Silted down swaying streams, to lay
Foundation for our voicelessness.

All our debate is voiceless here,
As all our rage, the rage of stone;
If hope is hopeless, then fearless fear,
And history is thus undone.

Our feet once wrought the hollow street
With echo when the lamps were dead
At windows, once our headlight glare
Disturbed the doe that, leaping, fled.

I do not love you less that now
The caged heart makes iron stroke,
Or less that all that light once gave
The graduate dark should now revoke.

We live in time so little time
And we learn all so painfully,
That we may spare this hour's term
To practice for eternity.

1942

Where the Slow Fig's Purple Sloth

Where the slow fig's purple sloth
Swells, I sit and meditate the
Nature of the soul, the fig exposes,
To the blaze of afternoon, one haunch
As purple-black as Africa, a single
Leaf the rest screens, but through it, light
Burns, and for the fig's bliss
The sun dies, the sun
Has died forever—far, oh far—
For the fig's bliss, thus.

The air
Is motionless, and the fig,
Motionless in that imperial and blunt
Languor of glut, swells, and inward
The fibers relax like a sigh in that
Hot darkness, go soft, the air
Is gold.

When you
Split the fig, you will see
Lifting from the coarse and purple seed, its
Flesh like flame, purer
Than blood.

It fills
The darkening room with light.

1968

From Audubon: A Vision

I. Was Not the Lost Dauphin[1]

[A]

Was not the lost dauphin, though handsome was only
Base-born and not even able
To make a decent living, was only
Himself, Jean Jacques, and his passion—what
Is man but his passion?

Saw,
Eastward and over the cypress swamp, the dawn,
Redder than meat, break;
And the large bird,
Long neck outthrust, wings crooked to scull air, moved
In a slow calligraphy, crank, flat, and black against
The color of God's blood spilt, as though
Pulled by a string.

Saw
It proceed across the inflamed distance.

Moccasins set in hoar frost, eyes fixed on the bird,
Thought: "On that sky it is black."
Thought: "In my mind it is white."
Thinking: "*Ardea occidentalis,* heron, the great one."

Dawn: his heart shook in the tension of the world.

Dawn: and what is your passion?

[B]

October: and the bear,
Daft in the honey-light, yawns.

The bear's tongue, pink as a baby's, out-crisps to the curled tip,
It bleeds the black blood of the blueberry.

The teeth are more importantly white
Than has ever been imagined.

The bear feels his own fat
Sweeten, like a drowse, deep to the bone.

1. John James (Jean-Jacques) Audubon (1785–1851), French-born painter and ornithologist, later an American citizen, famous for his careful depictions of North American birds and wildlife. He was incorrectly rumored to be the Lost Dauphin, the son of dethroned Marie Antoinette and Louis XVI.

Bemused, above the fume of ruined blueberries,
The last bee hums.

The wings, like mica,[2] glint
In the sunlight.

He leans on his gun. Thinks
How thin is the membrane between himself and the world.

1969

There's a Grandfather's Clock in the Hall

There's a grandfather's clock in the hall, watch it closely. The minute hand stands still, then it jumps, and in between jumps there is no-Time,
And you are a child again watching the reflection of early morning sunlight on the ceiling above your bed,

Or perhaps you are fifteen feet under water and holding your breath as you struggle with a rock-snagged anchor, or holding your breath just long enough for one more long, slow thrust to make the orgasm really intolerable,
Or you are wondering why you do not really give a damn, as they trundle you off to the operating room,

Or your mother is standing up to get married and is very pretty and excited and is a virgin, and your heart overflows, and you watch her with tears in your eyes, or
She is the one in the hospital room and she is really dying.

They have taken out her false teeth, which are now in a tumbler on the bedside table, and you know that only the undertaker will ever put them back in.
You stand there and wonder if you will ever have to wear false teeth.

She is lying on her back, and God, is she ugly, and
With gum-flabby lips and each word a special problem, she is asking if it is a new suit that you are wearing.

You say yes, and hate her uremic[3] guts, for she has no right to make you hurt the way that question hurts.
You do not know why that question makes your heart hurt like a kick in the scrotum,

For you do not yet know that the question, in its murderous triviality, is the last thing she will ever say to you,
Nor know what baptism is occurring in a sod-roofed hut or hole on the

2. Crystalline substance.

3. Containing toxins.

now night-swept steppes of Asia, and a million mouths, like ruined
stars in darkness, make a rejoicing that howls like wind, or wolves,

Nor do you know the truth, which is: *Seize the nettle of innocence in*
both your hands, for this is the only way, and every
Ulcer in love's lazaret[4] *may, like a dawn-stung gem, sing—or even burst*
into whoops of, perhaps, holiness.

But, in any case, watch the clock closely. Hold your breath and wait.
Nothing happens, nothing happens, then suddenly, quick as a wink, and
slick as a mink's prick, Time thrusts through the time of no-Time.

1974

Evening Hawk

From plane of light to plane, wings dipping through
Geometries and orchids that the sunset builds,
Out of the peak's black angularity of shadow, riding
The last tumultuous avalanche of
Light above pines and the guttural gorge,
The hawk comes.

His wing
Scythes down another day, his motion
Is that of the honed steel-edge, we hear
The crashless fall of stalks of Time.

The head of each stalk is heavy with the gold of our error.

Look! look! he is climbing the last light
Who knows neither Time nor error, and under
Whose eye, unforgiving, the world, unforgiven, swings
Into shadow.

Long now,
The last thrush is still, the last bat
Now cruises in his sharp hieroglyphics. His wisdom
Is ancient, too, and immense. The star
Is steady, like Plato,[5] over the mountain.

If there were no wind we might, we think, hear
The earth grind on its axis, or history
Drip in darkness like a leaking pipe in the cellar.

1975

4. Quarantine.

5. Greek philosopher (427–347 B.C.E.).

Fear and Trembling[6]

The sun now angles downward, and southward.
The summer, that is, approaches its final fulfillment.
The forest is silent, no wind-stir, bird-note, or word.
It is time to meditate on what the season has meant.

But what is the meaningful language for such meditation?
What is a word but wind through the tube of the throat?
Who defines the relation between the word *sun* and the sun?
What word has glittered on whitecap? Or lured blossom out?

Walk deeper, foot soundless, into the forest.
Stop, breath bated. Look southward, and up, where high leaves
Against sun, in vernal translucence, yet glow with the freshest
Young tint of the lost spring. Here now nothing grieves.

Can one, in fact, meditate in the heart, rapt and wordless?
Or find his own voice in the towering gust now from northward?
When boughs toss—is it in joy or pain and madness?
The gold leaf—is it whirled in anguish or ecstasy skyward?

Can the heart's meditation wake us from life's long sleep,
And instruct us how foolish and fond was our labor spent—
Us who now know that only at death of ambition does the deep
Energy crack crust, spurt forth, and leap

From grottoes, dark—and from the caverned enchainment?

1981

Muted Music

As sultry as the cruising hum
Of a single fly lost in the barn's huge, black
Interior, on a Sunday afternoon, with all the sky
Ablaze outside—so sultry and humming
Is memory when in barn-shade, eyes shut,
You lie in hay, and wonder if that empty, lonely,
And muted music was all the past was, after all.
Does the past now cruise your empty skull like
That blundering buzz at barn-height—which is dark
Except for the window at one gable, where
Daylight is netted gray with cobwebs, and the web
Dotted and sagged with blunderers that once could cruise and hum?

6. Title of 1843 treatise by Danish philosopher and theologian Søren Kierkegaard (1813–1855).

What do you really know
Of that world of decision and
Action you once strove in? What
Of that world where now
Light roars, while you, here, lulled, lie
In a cunningly wrought and mathematical

Box of shade, and try, of all the past, to remember
Which was *what, what, which.* Perhaps
That sultry hum from the lone bumbler, cruising high
In shadow, is the only sound that truth can make,
And into that muted music you soon sink
To hear at last, at last, what you have strained for
All the long years, and sometimes at dream-verge thought

You heard—the song the moth sings, the babble
Of falling snowflakes (in a language
No school has taught you), the scream
Of the reddening bud of the oak tree

As the bud bursts into the world's brightness.

1981

Stanley Kunitz
1905–2006

The Metaphysical school of the seventeenth century is an obvious point of departure for many of Stanley Kunitz's earlier poems: they are allusive, sometimes recondite, and elaborately patterned; they strive to conjoin disparities. W. B. Yeats, among other moderns, was a strong influence. Kunitz's *Selected Poems, 1938–58* (1958), *The Testing Tree* (1971), and subsequent volumes showed him working steadily toward a relaxation of form and an intimacy of tone, with shorter lines and sparer diction. Some of these poems have affinities with Randall Jarrell's confessional monologues and with Robert Lowell's *Life Studies.* They are fragments of autobiography that mimic the vivid abruptness of notes in a journal, confrontations between the poet and his loneliness, informed by the knowledge that all are living and dying at once: "I stand on the terrible threshold, and I see / The end and the beginning in each other's arms" ("Open the Gates").

Although some of Kunitz's well-known mature poems are highly wrought rhetorically, his best poems are more personal, distinguished by their fierce clarity, lyrical perspicuity, and imagistic precision. Full of wonder and alertness, finely pitched and paced, these poems hum with the inner music of the senses and of nature. They reach deeply into the mysteries of memory, identity, and desire. If many poets are inspired early and struggle to sustain their first promise, Kunitz's poetry is a record of ever more impressive achievement over a long and distinguished career.

Just before Kunitz was born on July 29, 1905, in Worcester, Massachusetts, his father committed suicide. His mother, feeling betrayed, squelched any mention or image of his father, as Kunitz recalls in his poem "The Portrait." Perhaps not surprisingly, silence, secrecy, death, transience, and the absent father became recurrent themes in Kunitz's work. He studied at Harvard University, receiving his B.A. in 1926 and his M.A. the next year. Despite his stellar record, anti-Semitism crushed his hopes of going on in academia. As a result of this "cruel and wanton rejection," as he called it in a 1974 interview, he became a journalist, a translator, and an editor of the *Wilson Library Bulletin* and biographical dictionaries for the H. W. Wilson company, in New York. His first book of poems, *Intellectual Things* (1930), attracted little attention. His second book appeared fourteen years later, during World War II, when Kunitz was serving in the army. After the war, he replaced Theodore Roethke on the faculty of Bennington College, and from then on, he taught at various institutions, notably Columbia University from 1963 to 1985. From 1969 to 1977, he was editor of the Yale Series of Younger Poets. Although he had won several awards, he had some difficulty in finding a publisher for his *Selected Poems,* which won him the Pulitzer Prize in 1959. More honors followed, including the Bollingen Prize in 1987 and the National Book Award in 1995, given for *Passing Through: Later Poems, New and Selected.* In 2000, Kunitz, still publishing and promoting poetry at the age of ninety-five, became poet laureate of the United States. That year, he brought out his *Collected Poems.*

The War against the Trees

The man who sold his lawn to standard oil
Joked with his neighbors come to watch the show
While the bulldozers, drunk with gasoline,
Tested the virtue of the soil
Under the branchy sky
By overthrowing first the privet-row.

Forsythia-forays and hydrangea-raids
Were but the preliminaries to a war
Against the great-grandfathers of the town,
So freshly lopped and maimed.
They struck and struck again,
And with each elm a century went down.

All day the hireling engines charged the trees,
Subverting them by hacking underground
In grub-dominions, where dark summer's mole
Rampages through his halls,
Till a northern seizure shook
Those crowns, forcing the giants to their knees.

I saw the ghosts of children at their games
Racing beyond their childhood in the shade,
And while the green world turned its death-foxed page
And a red wagon wheeled,
I watched them disappear
Into the suburbs of their grievous age.

Ripped from the craters much too big for hearts
The club-roots bared their amputated coils,
Raw gorgons[1] matted blind, whose pocks and scars
Cried Moon! on a corner lot
One witness-moment, caught
In the rear-view mirrors of the passing cars.

1958

The Portrait

My mother never forgave my father
for killing himself,
especially at such an awkward time
and in a public park,
that spring
when I was waiting to be born.
She locked his name
in her deepest cabinet
and would not let him out,
though I could hear him thumping.
When I came down from the attic
with the pastel portrait in my hand
of a long-lipped stranger
with a brave moustache
and deep brown level eyes,
she ripped it into shreds
without a single word
and slapped me hard.
In my sixty-fourth year
I can feel my cheek
still burning.

1971

The Magic Curtain

1

At breakfast mother sipped her buttermilk,
her mind already on her shop,
unrolling gingham by the yard,
stitching her dresses for the Boston trade.
Behind her, Frieda with the yellow hair,
capricious keeper of the toast,
buckled her knees, as if she'd lost
balance and platter, then winked at me, blue-eyed.

1. Mythical monsters whose heads were covered with snakes instead of hair. People who met their gazes were turned to stone.

Frieda, my first love! who sledded me to sleep
through snows of the Bavarian woods
into the bell-song of the girls,
with kinds of kisses mother would not dream;
tales of her wicked stepfather, a dwarf,
from whom she fled to Bremerhaven[2]
with scarcely the tatters on her back;
riddles, nonsense, lieder,[3] counting-songs. . . .
Eins, zwei, drei, vier, fünf, sechs, sieben,
Wo ist denn mein liebster Herr geblieben?
Er ist nicht hier, er ist nicht da,
Er ist fort nach Amerika.[4]
"Be sure," said mother briskly at the door,
"that you get Sonny off to school
on time. And see that he combs his hair."
How could she guess what we two had in mind?

2

Downtown at the Front St. Bi-jo (spelt Bijou)
we were, as always, the first in line,
with a hot nickel clutched in hand,
impatient for *The Perils of Pauline*,[5]
my Frieda in her dainty blouse and skirt,
I in my starched white sailor suit
and buttoned shoes, prepared to hang
from cliffs, twist on a rack, be tied to rails.
School faded out at every morning reel,
The Iron Claw held me in thrall,
Cabiria taught me the Punic Wars,
at bloody Antietam I fought on Griffith's side.[6]
And Keystone Kops[7] came tumbling on the scene
in outsized uniforms, moustached,
their thick-browed faces dipped in flour,
to crank tin lizzies that immediately collapsed.
John Bunny[8] held his belly when he laughed,
ladies politely removed their hats,
Cyrus of Persia stormed the gates,
upsetting our orgy at Belshazzar's Feast.[9]
Then Charlie[1] shuffled in on bunioned feet.
We twirled with him an imaginary cane

2. City in northern Germany.
3. German songs.
4. One, two, three, four, five, six seven, / What has become of my beloved? / He is not here, he is not there. / He's gone away to America (German).
5. Melodramatic, "cliff-hanger" serial of 1914 starring American actor Pearl White (1889–1938).
6. *Iron Claw:* 1916 film starring White. *Cabiria:* 1914 Italian film about a young girl kidnapped during the Punic Wars, fought between Rome and Carthage in the third century B.C.E. The controversial 1915 film *The Birth of a Nation,* directed by D. W. Griffith (1875–1948), takes place during the American Civil War and Reconstruction. The Battle of Antietam (September 17, 1862) was one of the bloodiest of the war.
7. Slapstick police officers from the silent film farces of Mack Sennet (1880–1960).
8. American silent-film star (1863–1915). *Tin lizzies:* inexpensive early automobiles.
9. One of the four stories told in *Intolerance,* D. W. Griffith's 1916 follow-up to *The Birth of a Nation,* details the 539 B.C.E. fall of Belshazzar's Babylon to the army of King Cyrus I of Persia.
1. Charlie Chaplin (1889–1977), British actor and director famous for his silent-film "Little Tramp" character.

and blew our noses for the gallant poor
who bet on a horse, the horse that always loses.
Blanche Sweet, said Frieda, had a pretty name,
but I came back with Arline Pretty,
and, even sweeter, Louise Lovely.[2]
Send me your picture, Violet Mersereau![3]
Lights up! Ushers with atomizers ranged
the aisles, emitting lilac spray.
We lunched on peanuts and Hershey bars
and moved to the Majestic for the two o'clock show.

3

Five . . . four . . . three . . . two . . . one . . .
The frames are whirling backward, see!
The operator's lost control.
Your story flickers on your bedroom wall.
Deaths, marriages, betrayals, lies,
close-ups of tears, forbidden games,
spill in a montage on a screen,
with chases, pratfalls, custard pies, and sores.
You have become your past, which time replays,
to your surprise, as comedy.
That coathanger neatly whisked your coat
right off your back. Soon it will want your skin.

Five . . . four . . . three . . . two . . . one . . .
Where has my dearest gone?
She is nowhere to be found,
She swells in the underground.

Let the script revel in tricks and transformations.
When the film is broken, let it be spliced
where Frieda vanished one summer night
with somebody's husband, daddy to a brood.
And with her vanished, from the bureau drawer,
the precious rose-enameled box
that held those chestnut-colored curls
clipped from my sorrowing head when I was four.
After the war an unsigned picture-card
from Dresden came, with one word: *Liebe.*[4]
"I'll never forgive her," mother said,
but as for me, I do and do and do.

1971

2. Australian silent-film actor (1895–1980). Blanche Sweet (1895–1986) and Arline Pretty (1885–1978), American silent-film actors.

3. American silent-film actor (1892–1975).

4. Dear (German). *Dresden:* city in East Germany.

The Catch

It darted across the pond
toward our sunset perch,
weaving in, up, and around
a spindle of air,
this delicate engine
fired by impulse and glitter,
swift darning-needle,
gossamer dragon,
less image than thought,
and the thought come alive.
Swoosh went the net
with a practiced hand.
"Da-da, may I look too?"
You may look, child,
all you want.
This prize belongs to no one.
But you will pay all
your life for the privilege,
all your life.

1978

Day of Foreboding

Great events are about to happen.
I have seen migratory birds
in unprecedented numbers
descend on the coastal plain,
picking the margins clean.
My bones are a family in their tent
huddled over a small fire
waiting for the uncertain signal
to resume the long march.

1985

The Round

Light splashed this morning
on the shell-pink anemones
swaying on their tall stems;
down blue-spiked veronica[5]
light flowed in rivulets
over the humps of the honeybees;

5. Flowering herb.

this morning I saw light kiss
the silk of the roses
in their second flowering,
my late bloomers
flushed with their brandy.
A curious gladness shook me.

So I have shut the doors of my house,
so I have trudged downstairs to my cell,
so I am sitting in semi-dark
hunched over my desk
with nothing for a view
to tempt me
but a bloated compost heap,
steamy old stinkpile,
under my window;
and I pick my notebook up
and I start to read aloud
the still-wet words I scribbled
on the blotted page:
"Light splashed . . ."

I can scarcely wait till tomorrow
when a new life begins for me,
as it does each day,
as it does each day.

1985

Touch Me

Summer is late, my heart.
Words plucked out of the air
some forty years ago
when I was wild with love
and torn almost in two
scatter like leaves this night
of whistling wind and rain.
It is my heart that's late,
it is my song that's flown.
Outdoors all afternoon
under a gunmetal sky
staking my garden down,
I kneeled to the crickets trilling
underfoot as if about
to burst from their crusty shells;
and like a child again
marveled to hear so clear
and brave a music pour
from such a small machine.

What makes the engine go?
Desire, desire, desire.
The longing for the dance
stirs in the buried life.
One season only,
                    and it's done.
So let the battered old willow
thrash against the windowpanes
and the house timbers creak.
Darling, do you remember
the man you married? Touch me,
remind me who I am.

1995

KENNETH REXROTH
1905–1982

Like William Carlos Williams and Ezra Pound, Kenneth Rexroth was a veteran of American modernist poetry and almost a parental figure to younger poets. When he moved to San Francisco, in 1927, the city was as far from the centers of American letters as one could get without leaving the country. He was joined there during the 1940s by other anarchist poets who fomented the San Francisco Renaissance, and during the 1950s by the Beats who had fled from New York, all of whom found in Rexroth an open-minded and enthusiastic sponsor.

His early poems reflect his interest in painting and especially cubism, and during the 1930s he was associated, to his irritation, with Louis Zukofsky's Objectivist movement. Rexroth's description of Imagism, from which Objectivism evolved, is a good account of his own poetry: "Imagism was a revolt against rhetoric and symbolism in poetry, a return to direct statement, simple clear images, unpretentious themes, fidelity to objectively verifiable experience, strict avoidance of sentimentality. I suppose this is the actual *programme* of all good poetry anywhere" (*Assays*). Rexroth disliked pretentious rhetoric and wrote quiet and contemplative poems without obvious verbal dazzle. Williams said of him, "[He] is no writer in the sense of the word-man. For him words are sticks and stones to build a house—but it's a good house" (*Poetry* 104).

A striking characteristic of this city-bred poet is his sensuous and informed response to the woods, lakes, and creatures of the shrinking American wilderness. Characteristically, he not only registers the mountains, trees, and fauna that surround him, but names them and describes their particulars (e.g., the rare flower in "Blues"). Though distrustful of technology, Rexroth is well-disposed toward the earth sciences of geology and mineralogy. But he is not solely a nature poet. Classically learned, if largely self-taught, he recognizes on one camping trip with his daughters an analogue to Homer ("Homer in Basic"); on another, an analogue to a classical Chinese poem by Po Chu I ("The Wheel Revolves"). Occasionally, he can be, as Williams observed, "a moralist with his hand at the trigger ready to fire at the turn of a hair," as when he blames the middle-class American intelligentsia for Dylan Thomas's death, in the long poem "Thou Shalt Not Kill." But the dominant note of his poetry is not anger but rather a serene and loving appreciation of the natural world and the men and women who live in it. Bereavement and desire both have a place in his verse. In his characteristic lines of seven to nine syllables, he gives voice to muted grief in exquisitely restrained elegies for his mother ("Delia Rexroth") and his first wife ("Andrée Rexroth"). Erotic passion is the subject of the finely etched sequence of love poems he wrote after spending time in Japan, *The Love Poems of Marichiko,* presented in the voice of a young Japanese woman.

Rexroth was born on December 22, 1905, in South Bend, Indiana. His parents both died when he was young, his mother in 1916, after which, as he records in "The Bad Old Days," "my aunt / Took me to Chicago to live." He wrote his first poems at fifteen and studied painting at the Art Institute of Chicago and in New York City; he also grew interested in jazz and, in the 1920s, opened a club in Chicago called the Green Mask, where poets, including himself and Langston Hughes, read their poems to jazz accompaniment. As a young man, he worked variously as a farm hand, a factory worker, and an insane-asylum attendant; these years are the subject of his book *An Autobiographical Novel* (1966). In 1927, Rexroth and his wife Andrée, a painter, moved to California. "San Francisco, when we came there to live, was very much of a backwater town and there just wasn't anything happening," he recalls (*The San Francisco Poets,* ed. David Meltzer, 1971). He threw himself into leftist political activity and worked to organize maritime labor during the 1930s. Andrée Rexroth died in 1940, and in 1941, Rexroth declared himself a conscientious objector to World War II. After the war ended, he helped organize an anarchist circle in San Francisco, out of which emerged the underground radio station KPFA and its radical broadcasts in response to the conservative 1950s. He was also, as William Everson remembers, "the acknowledged leader of the new literary ferment" on the west coast, and in 1955, he helped organize the poetry reading at which Allen Ginsberg's "Howl" rocketed the Beats to national attention (*San Francisco Poets*). Rexroth's own poetry appeared regularly after his first book, *In What Hour* (1941), and he was also a far-ranging essayist and a prolific translator of Greek, Latin, French, Spanish, Chinese, and Japanese poetry. In his later years, he lived in Santa Barbara and taught at the University of California campus there.

Delia Rexroth[1]

Died June, 1916

Under your illkempt yellow roses,
Delia, today you are younger
Than your son. Two and a half decades—
The family monument sagged askew,
And he overtook your half-a-life.
On the other side of the country,
Near the willows by the slow river,
Deep in the earth, the white ribs retain
The curve of your fervent, careful breast;
The fine skull, the ardor of your brain.
And in the fingers the memory
Of Chopin[2] études, and in the feet

1. The poet's mother.
2. Frédéric Chopin (1810–1849), Polish French composer and pianist.

Slow waltzes and champagne twosteps sleep.
And the white full moon of midsummer,
That you watched awake all that last night,
Watches history fill the deserts
And oceans with corpses once again;
And looks in the east window at me,
As I move past you to middle age
And knowledge past your agony and waste.

1949

Andrée Rexroth[3]

Died October, 1940

Now once more gray mottled buckeye branches
Explode their emerald stars,
And alders smoulder in a rosy smoke
Of innumerable buds.
I know that spring again is splendid
As ever, the hidden thrush
As sweetly tongued, the sun as vital—
But these are the forest trails we walked together,
These paths, ten years together.
We thought the years would last forever,
They are all gone now, the days
We thought would not come for us are here.
Bright trout poised in the current—
The raccoon's track at the water's edge—
A bittern booming in the distance—
Your ashes scattered on this mountain—
Moving seaward on this stream.

1949

Blues

The tops of the higher peaks
Of the Sierra Nevada
Of California are
Drenched in the perfume of
A flower which grows only there—
The blue *Polemonium*
Confertum eximium,
Soft, profound blue, like the eyes
Of impregnable innocence;
The perfume is heavy and

3. Artist (1902–1940); the poet's first wife.

Clings thickly to the granite
Peaks, even in violent wind;
The leaves are clustered,
Fine, dull green, sticky, and musky.
I imagine that the scent
Of the body of Artemis
That put Endymion[4] to sleep
Was like this and her eyes had the
Same inscrutable color.
Lawrence was lit into death
By the blue gentians of Kore.[5]
Vanzetti[6] had in his cell
A bowl of tall blue flowers
From a New England garden.
I hope that when I need it
My mind can always call back
This flower to its hidden senses.

1949

Homer in Basic

Glitter of Nausicaä's[7]
Embroideries, flashing arms,
And heavy hung maiden hair;
Doing the laundry, the wind
Brisk in the bright air
Of the Mediterranean day.
Odysseus, hollow cheeked,
Wild eyed, bursts from the bushes.
Mary sits by the falling
Water reading Homer while
I fish for mottled brook trout
In the sun mottled riffles.
They are small and elusive.
The stream is almost fished out.
Water falls through shimmering
Panelled light between the red
Sequoias, over granite
And limestone, under green ferns
And purple lupin. Time was
I caught huge old trout in these
Pools and eddies. These are three

4. According to Greek mythology, the goddess Artemis fell in love with Endymion, a mortal shepherd, and persuaded the god Zeus to grant him a wish. When Endymion asked for eternal youth, Zeus granted his request on the condition that he remain eternally asleep.

5. Another name for Persephone, who, according to Greek mythology, was condemned to spend a portion of each year with the dead in the underworld. In "Bavarian Gentians," English author D. H. Lawrence (1885–1930) imagines blue flowers as guiding him into death and the underworld.

6. Bartolomeo Vanzetti, along with Nicola Sacco, was considered an anarchist martyr after he was executed for murder in 1927.

7. In book 6 of Homer's *Odyssey,* the beautiful young woman who assists Odysseus after he is shipwrecked.

Years old at the very most.
Mary is seven. Homer
Is her favorite author.
It took me a lifetime of
Shames and wastes to understand
Homer. She says, "Aren't those gods
Terrible? All they do is
Fight like those angels in Milton,[8]
And play tricks on the poor Greeks
And Trojans. I like Aias[9]
And Odysseus best. They are
Lots better than those silly
Gods." Like the ability
To paint, she will probably
Outgrow this wisdom. It too
Will wither away as she
Matures and a whole lifetime
Will be spent getting it back.
Now she teaches Katharine
The profound wisdom of seven
And Katharine responds with
The profound nonsense of three.
Grey haired in granite mountains,
I catch baby fish. Ten fish,
And Homer, and two little
Girls pose for a picture by
The twenty foot wide, cinnamon
Red trunk of a sequoia.
As I snap the camera,
It occurs to me that this
Tree was as big as the pines
Of Olympos,[1] not just before
Homer sang, but before Troy
Ever fell or Odysseus
Ever sailed from home.

1964

Proust's Madeleine[2]

Somebody has given my
Baby daughter a box of
Old poker chips to play with.
Today she hands me one while
I am sitting with my tired
Brain at my desk. It is red.

8. John Milton (1608–1674), author of *Paradise Lost*.
9. Another name for Ajax, Greek hero of the Trojan War, in Homer's *Iliad*.
1. Mountain home of the Greek gods. Rexroth's comparison alludes to the device of epic simile.
2. In Marcel Proust's novel *Swann's Way* (1913), the taste of a madeleine (a tea cake) awakens the protagonist's memories of his childhood.

On it is a picture of
An elk's head and the letters
B.P.O.E.—a chip from
A small town Elks' Club. I flip
It idly in the air and
Catch it and do a coin trick
To amuse my little girl.
Suddenly everything slips aside.
I see my father
Doing the very same thing,
Whistling "Beautiful Dreamer,"
His breath smelling richly
Of whiskey and cigars. I can
Hear him coming home drunk
From the Elks' Club in Elkhart
Indiana, bumping the
Chairs in the dark. I can see
Him dying of cirrhosis
Of the liver and stomach
Ulcers and pneumonia,
Or, as he said on his deathbed, of
Crooked cards and straight whiskey,
Slow horses and fast women.

1963

The Wheel Revolves

You were a girl of satin and gauze
Now you are my mountain and waterfall companion.
Long ago I read those lines of Po Chu-i[3]
Written in his middle age.
Young as I was they touched me.
I never thought in my own middle age
I would have a beautiful young dancer
To wander with me by falling crystal waters,
Among mountains of snow and granite,
Least of all that unlike Po's girl
She would be my very daughter.

The earth turns towards the sun.
Summer comes to the mountains.
Blue grouse drum in the red fir woods
All the bright long days.
You put blue jay and flicker feathers
In your hair.

3. A Chinese poet of the ninth century C.E., "generally considered . . . one of the four leading poets of the T'ang Dynasty" [Rexroth's note]. The poem to which Rexroth alludes is "Going to the Mountains with a Little Dancing Girl, Aged Fifteen (written when the poet was about sixty-five)," whose third and fourth lines in Arthur Waley's translation are: "You who are really a lady of silks and satins / Are now become my hill and stream companion!"

Two and two violet green swallows
Play over the lake.
The blue birds have come back
To nest on the little island.
The swallows sip water on the wing
And play at love and dodge and swoop
Just like the swallows that swirl
Under and over the Ponte Vecchio.[4]
Light rain crosses the lake
Hissing faintly. After the rain
There are giant puffballs with tortoise shell backs
At the edge of the meadow.
Snows of a thousand winters
Melt in the sun of one summer.
Wild cyclamen bloom by the stream.
Trout veer in the transparent current.
In the evening marmots bark in the rocks.
The Scorpion[5] curls over the glimmering ice field.

A white-crowned night sparrow sings as the moon sets.
Thunder growls far off.
Our campfire is a single light
Amongst a hundred peaks and waterfalls.
The manifold voices of falling water
Talk all night.
Wrapped in your down bag
Starlight on your cheeks and eyelids
Your breath comes and goes
In a tiny cloud in the frosty night.
Ten thousand birds sing in the sunrise.
Ten thousand years revolve without change.
All this will never be again.

1966

FROM THE LOVE POEMS OF MARICHIKO

IV

You ask me what I thought about
Before we were lovers.
The answer is easy.
Before I met you
I didn't have anything to think about.

4. A bridge in Florence, Italy.

5. The constellation Scorpio.

VII

Making love with you
Is like drinking sea water.
The more I drink
The thirstier I become,
Until nothing can slake my thirst
But to drink the entire sea.

IX

You wake me,
Part my thighs, and kiss me.
I give you the dew
Of the first morning of the world.

XXV

Your tongue thrums and moves
Into me, and I become
Hollow and blaze with
Whirling light, like the inside
Of a vast expanding pearl.

XXVII

As I came from the
Hot bath, you took me before
The horizontal mirror
Beside the low bed, while my
Breasts quivered in your hands, my
Buttocks shivered against you.

XXXI

Some day in six inches of
Ashes will be all
That's left of our passionate minds,
Of all the world created
By our love, its origin
And passing away.

XXXII

I hold your head tight between
My thighs, and press against your
Mouth, and float away
Forever, in an orchid
Boat on the River of Heaven.

XXXIII

I cannot forget
The perfumed dusk inside the
Tent of my black hair,
As we awoke to make love
After a long night of love.

XXXIV

Every morning, I
Wake alone, dreaming my
Arm is your sweet flesh
Pressing my lips.

LVIII

Half in a dream
I become aware
That the voices of the crickets
Grow faint with the growing Autumn.
I mourn for this lonely
Year that is passing
And my own being
Grows fainter and fades away.

LIX

I hate this shadow of a ghost
Under the full moon.
I run my fingers through my greying hair,
And wonder, have I grown so thin?

LX

Chilled through, I wake up
With the first light. Outside my window
A red maple leaf floats silently down.
What am I to believe?
Indifference?
Malice?
I hate the sight of coming day
Since that morning when
Your insensitive gaze turned me to ice
Like the pale moon in the dawn.

1978

John Betjeman
1906–1984

A year older than W. H. Auden, John (later Sir John) Betjeman also went to Oxford University, and he wrote poetry that is just as witty, if not so searching. Auden wrote an admiring preface to the American edition of Betjeman's poems, in which he praised them as "slick but not streamlined." The two poets invite comparison: Auden faced the future hopefully, however vague it might be, whereas Betjeman nostalgically looked over his shoulder at what was gone or going. Bells—symbols of the old order—appear obsessively in Betjeman's verse. Auden was always eager to move about and to find new themes far from home, in Iceland, China, and America. Betjeman in his poetry stayed close, matching contemporary England with old, to the disadvantage of the new order.

Betjeman's pursuit of the old led him, in the prose book *First and Last Loves* (1952) and elsewhere, to make a case for then-unfashionable nineteenth-century English architecture, including buildings in imitation of the medieval. In verse, too, Betjeman preferred nineteenth-century models—of meters, stanza forms, and sentiment. His perfect rhymes, fluent anapestic rhythms, engaging narratives, subtle mixtures of melancholy and jollity, satire and comedy, helped make him one of the most admired—and popular—verse craftsmen of his time. Philip Larkin, also reacting against modernism, was among his champions.

Betjeman was born on August 28, 1906. His preference for an older England, more religious, more countrified, and less busy, may have arisen from tension between him and his father, a successful manufacturer of Dutch origin who tried desperately to shunt his son into business. Against his father's pleas and his classmates' cruelties, he clung to poetry as though it were a religion, as he later recalled in his autobiography in verse, *Summoned by Bells* (1960). At the Highgate School, in North London, he showed his poems to one of the masters, T. S. Eliot, who, however, failed to comment on them. Eliot perhaps missed in Betjeman, then and later, a sense of profound upheaval and dislocation, such as he was to observe in Auden. Betjeman then attended the Dragon School, in Oxford; Marlborough School, in Wiltshire; and finally Magdalen College, Oxford (1925–28). On leaving Oxford without a degree, he became for a short time a schoolteacher, then an architectural journalist and editor. He wrote Shell Guides to Cornwall, Devon, and Shropshire, and books on Oxford and on English landscape. He was the witty spokesperson for the conservatism that clings to a past not only in art, architecture, and literature, but also in institutions. He made a virtue out of anachronism. It was only fitting when, in 1972, he was named to the perhaps anachronistic post of poet laureate of Great Britain.

The Arrest of Oscar Wilde at the Cadogan Hotel[1]

He sipped at a weak hock and seltzer
As he gazed at the London skies
Through the Nottingham lace of the curtains
Or was it his bees-winged[2] eyes?

To the right and before him Pont Street
Did tower in her new built red,
As hard as the morning gaslight
That shone on his unmade bed,

"I want some more hock in my seltzer,
And Robbie[3] please give me your hand—
Is this the end or beginning?
How can I understand?

"So you've brought me the latest *Yellow Book*:
And Buchan has got in it now:[4]
Approval of what is approved of
Is as false as a well-kept vow.

"More hock, Robbie—where is the seltzer?
Dear boy, pull again at the bell!
They are all little better than *cretins*,
Though this *is* the Cadogan Hotel.

"One astrakhan coat is at Willis's—
Another one's at the Savoy:[5]
Do fetch my morocco portmanteau,
And bring them on later, dear boy."

A thump, and a murmur of voices—
("Oh why must they make such a din?")
As the door of the bedroom swung open
And TWO PLAIN CLOTHES POLICEMEN came in:

1. In 1895, the poet and playwright Oscar Wilde (1856–1900) was convicted of homosexual acts and sentenced to two years hard labor. The circumstances of his arrest were as Betjeman describes them.
2. *Beeswing*: a gauzy film that forms in old wine.
3. Robert Ross, Wilde's best friend. *Hock:* wine.
4. In 1896, John Buchan (1875–1940), later famous for his adventure novels, published two stories in *Yellow Book* (1894–97), the periodical of the Aesthetic movement. Wilde was the most famous member of the movement, but had no direct connection with the magazine.
5. Wilde had an apartment at the Savoy Hotel and often took his friends to dinner there and at Willis's Rooms.

"Mr. Woilde, we 'ave come for tew take yew
Where felons and criminals dwell:
We must ask yew tew leave with us quoietly
For this *is* the Cadogan Hotel."

He rose, and he put down *The Yellow Book.*
He staggered—and, terrible-eyed,
He brushed past the palms on the staircase
And was helped to a hansom outside.

1937

Slough[6]

Come, friendly bombs, and fall on Slough
It isn't fit for humans now,
There isn't grass to graze a cow
Swarm over, Death!

Come, bombs, and blow to smithereens
Those air-conditioned, bright canteens,
Tinned fruit,[7] tinned meat, tinned milk, tinned beans
Tinned minds, tinned breath.

Mess up the mess they call a town—
A house for ninety-seven down
And once a week for half-a-crown
For twenty years,[8]

And get that man with double chin
Who'll always cheat and always win,
Who washes his repulsive skin
In women's tears,

And smash his desk of polished oak
And smash his hands so used to stroke
And stop his boring dirty joke
And make him yell.

But spare the bald young clerks who add
The profits of the stinking cad;
It's not their fault that they are mad,
They've tasted Hell.

It's not their fault they do not know
The birdsong from the radio

6. Large industrial town in central England; the name rhymes with *cow*.
7. "Tinned" items are, in the United States, canned. *Canteens*: company cafeterias (British term).
8. That is, bought on the installment plan, at about ten thousand dollars down and ten dollars a week.

It's not their fault they often go
To Maidenhead[9]

And talk of sports and makes of cars
In various bogus Tudor bars
And daren't look up and see the stars
But belch instead.

In labour-saving homes, with care
Their wives frizz out peroxide hair
And dry it in synthetic air
And paint their nails.

Come, friendly bombs, and fall on Slough
To get it ready for the plough.
The cabbages are coming now;
The earth exhales.

1937

An Incident in the Early Life of Ebenezer Jones, Poet, 1828[1]

The lumber of a London-going dray,
The still-new stucco on the London clay,
Hot summer silence over Holloway.[2]

Dissenting chapels,[3] tea-bowers, lovers' lairs,
Neat new-built villas, ample Grecian squares,
Remaining orchards ripening Windsor pears.

Hot silence where the older mansions hide
On Highgate Hill's thick elm-encrusted side,
And Pancras, Hornsey, Islington[4] divide.

9. Popular resort area on the Thames River.

1. Ebenezer Jones (1820–1860) was a very minor English poet whose one book, *Studies of Sensation and Event* (1843), was so badly received that he published no other poems. Betjeman prefaces this poem with an account of its central incident given by Jones's brother in an 1879 reissue of the book. "We were together at a well-known boarding-school of that day . . . on a hot summer afternoon. . . . Up the ladder-like stairs from the playground a lurcher dog had strayed into the schoolroom, panting with the heat, his tongue lolling out with thirst. The choleric usher who presided, and was detested by us for his tyranny, seeing this, advanced down the room. Enraged at our attention being distracted from our tasks, he dragged the dog to the top of the stairs, and there lifted him bodily up with the evident intention—and we had known him to do similar things—of hurling the poor creature to the bottom.

'YOU SHALL NOT!' rang through the room, as little Ebby, so exclaiming at the top of his voice, rushed with kindling face to the spot from among all the boys—some of them twice his age.

But even while the words passed his lips, the heavy fall was heard, and the sound seemed to travel through his listening form and face, as, with a strange look of anguish in one so young, he stood still, threw up his arms, and burst into an uncontrollable passion of tears.

With a coarse laugh at this, the usher led him back by his ear to the form; and there he sat, long after his sobbing had subsided, like one dazed and stunned."

2. A district of central London.

3. Jones's parents were strict Calvinists; like all other Protestants who refused integration into the official Church of England, they were called "dissenters" or "nonconformists," and because of discriminatory laws they tended to live together in areas such as Holloway.

4. London districts surrounding Holloway.

June's hottest silence where the hard rays strike
Yon hill-foot house, window and wall alike,
School of the Reverend Mr. Bickerdike,

For sons of Saints, blest with this world's possessions
(Seceders from the Protestant Secessions),[5]
Good grounding in the more genteel professions.

A lurcher dog, which draymen kick and pass
Tongue lolling, thirsty over shadeless grass,
Leapt up the playground ladder to the class.

The godly usher left his godly seat,
His skin was prickly in the ungodly heat,
The dog lay panting at his godly feet.

The milkman on the road stood staring in,
The playground nettles nodded "Now begin"—
And Evil waited, quivering, for sin.

He lifted it and not a word he spoke,
His big hand tightened. Could he make it choke?
He trembled, sweated, and his temper broke.

"You shall not!" clear across to Highgate Hill
A boy's voice sounded. Creaking forms were still.
The cat jumped slowly from the window sill.

"You shall not!" flat against the summer sun,
Hard as the hard sky frowning over one,
Gloat, little boys! enjoy the coming fun!

"God damns a cur. I am, I am his word!"
He flung it, flung it and it never stirred,
"You shall not!—shall not!" ringing on unheard.

Blind desolation! bleeding, burning rod!
Big, bull-necked Minister of Calvin's God!
Exulting milkman, redfaced, shameless clod;

Look on and jeer! Not Satan's thunder-quake
Can cause the mighty walls of Heaven to shake
As now they do, to hear a boy's heart break.

1940

5. The Calvinists, or Puritans (who were in the habit of calling themselves Saints), considered the Church of England too little reformed and seceded from it; the Protestant Church of England had earlier seceded from the Roman Catholic Church.

In Westminster Abbey[6]

Let me take this other glove off
As the *vox humana*[7] swells,
And the beauteous fields of Eden
Bask beneath the Abbey bells.
Here, where England's statesmen lie,
Listen to a lady's cry.

Gracious Lord, oh bomb the Germans.
Spare their women for Thy Sake,
And if that is not too easy
We will pardon Thy Mistake.
But, gracious Lord, whate'er shall be,
Don't let anyone bomb me.

Keep our Empire undismembered
Guide our Forces by Thy Hand,
Gallant blacks from far Jamaica,
Honduras and Togoland;
Protect them Lord in all their fights,
And, even more, protect the whites.

Think of what our Nation stands for,
Books from Boots' and country lanes,
Free speech, free passes, class distinction,
Democracy and proper drains.[8]
Lord, put beneath Thy special care
One-eighty-nine Cadogan Square.[9]

Although dear Lord I am a sinner,
I have done no major crime;
Now I'll come to Evening Service
Whensoever I have the time.
So, Lord, reserve for me a crown,
And do not let my shares go down.

I will labour for Thy Kingdom,
Help our lads to win the war,
Send white feathers to the cowards,[1]
Join the Women's Army Corps,
Then wash the Steps around Thy Throne
In the Eternal Safety Zone.

Now I feel a little better,
What a treat to hear Thy Word,

6. Church and national shrine in London. The poem is spoken during World War II.
7. One of the stops of an organ, so called because it sounds something like the human voice.
8. That is, plumbing. *Boots:* a chain of drugstores that, until 1966, also had lending libraries.
9. Fashionable part of London.
1. During World War I, women customarily gave white feathers to men they suspected of avoiding army service.

Where the bones of leading statesmen,
  Have so often been interr'd.
And now, dear Lord, I cannot wait
Because I have a luncheon date.

1940

The Cottage Hospital[2]

At the end of a long-walled garden
  in a red provincial town,
A brick path led to a mulberry—
  scanty grass at its feet.
I lay under blackening branches
  where the mulberry leaves hung down
Sheltering ruby fruit globes
  from a Sunday-tea-time heat.
Apple and plum espaliers[3]
  basked upon bricks of brown;
The air was swimming with insects,
  and children played in the street.

Out of this bright intentness
  into the mulberry shade
Musca domestica (housefly)
  swung from the August light
Slap into slithery rigging
  by the waiting spider made
Which spun the lithe elastic
  till the fly was shrouded tight.
Down came the hairy talons
  and horrible poison blade
And none of the garden noticed
  that fizzing, hopeless fight.

Say in what Cottage Hospital
  whose pale green walls resound
With the tap upon polished parquet
  of inflexible nurses' feet
Shall I myself be lying
  when they range the screens around?
And say shall I groan in dying,
  as I twist the sweaty sheet?
Or gasp for breath uncrying,
  as I feel my senses drown'd
While the air is swimming with insects
  and children play in the street?

1954

2. Small country hospital, without a resident medical staff.

3. Fruit trees trained to grow against a wall.

William Empson
1906–1984

In a 1963 BBC radio talk, William Empson recommended what he called "argufying in poetry." Poetic argument, employing voices that are beseeching and quarrelsome, hard-pressed and passionate, is central to Empson's poetic procedure. Argument, of course, assumes conflict, and Empson acknowledged the influence of poets and critics who saw poetry as the expression of an unresolved conflict, such as his friend and teacher I. A. Richards, who judged poetry by its success in harmonizing conflicting impulses. For inspiration, he turned back, like T. S. Eliot, to the English Metaphysicals, in particular to John Donne and George Herbert, whose poems are argumentative in tone and who in their figures of speech bring together discordant terms and images.

Elegant, intricate, and formally coherent, Empson's poetry gives impersonal expression to conflicting personal feelings. Empson struggles to reconcile a resignation to meaninglessness with a realization of the importance of "fictions," those provisional interpretations of life that constitute imaginative literature and perhaps all civilization. A love poem, "Villanelle," begins and ends with the resignation of the damned: "It is the pain, it is the pain, endures." "Ignorance of Death" reviews a number of attitudes toward death and then concludes with a "blank"—in part, the endless nullity of the universe, on which humans superimpose their poignant visions. But the poem's wry offhand tone, exemplary for Philip Larkin and other poets of the Movement in the 1950s, suggests that the situation can be lived with.

Empson was born on September 27, 1906, near Howden, Yorkshire. He was educated at Winchester School and at Magdalene College, Cambridge, where he took degrees first in mathematics, then in English. In 1930, he published his first critical work, *Seven Types of Ambiguity,* an influential study of how poems exploit the multiple, sometimes contradictory, senses of a word. From 1931 to 1934, he was Professor of English Literature at Tokyo National University. In 1935, he published his *Poems,* many of which had been written when he was an undergraduate, and a critical work, *Some Versions of Pastoral,* a reading of a series of literary works with particular attention to their covert social attitudes. Two years later, he went to China and taught English at the National University in Beijing; his work there was interrupted by the beginning of the Second Sino-Japanese War. In 1939, when World War II was certain, Empson returned to England, where he worked for the BBC and brought out his second collection of poems, *The Gathering Storm* (1940). When the war was over, he returned with his wife and two sons to a teaching post in Beijing. He completed a third important critical work, *The Structure of Complex Words,* in 1951, and a year later, he returned to live in England. He taught at Sheffield University from 1953 until his retirement, in 1971.

Villanelle[1]

It is the pain, it is the pain, endures.
Your chemic beauty burned my muscles through.
Poise of my hands reminded me of yours.

1. A French poetic form in five tercets, followed by a quatrain. The first and third lines of the poem become refrains, which are joined together at the end of the poem. Empson's "Missing Dates," below, is another villanelle.

What later purge from this deep toxin cures?
What kindness now could the old salve renew?
It is the pain, it is the pain, endures.

The infection slept (custom or change inures)
And when pain's secondary phase was due
Poise of my hands reminded me of yours.

How safe I felt, whom memory assures,
Rich that your grace safely by heart I knew.
It is the pain, it is the pain, endures.

My stare drank deep beauty that still allures.
My heart pumps yet the poison draught of you.
Poise of my hands reminded me of yours.

You are still kind whom the same shape immures.
Kind and beyond adieu. We miss our cue.
It is the pain, it is the pain, endures.
Poise of my hands reminded me of yours.

1935

Ignorance of Death

Then there is this civilising love of death, by which
Even music and painting tell you what else to love.
Buddhists and Christians contrive to agree about death

Making death their ideal basis for different ideals.
The Communists however disapprove of death
Except when practical. The people who dig up

Corpses and rape them are I understand not reported.
The Freudians regard the death-wish as fundamental,
Though "the clamour of life" proceeds from its rival "Eros."

Whether you are to admire a given case for making less clamour
Is not their story. Liberal hopefulness
Regards death as a mere border to an improving picture.

Because we have neither hereditary nor direct knowledge of death
It is the trigger of the literary man's biggest gun
And we are happy to equate it to any conceived calm.

Heaven me, when a man is ready to die about something
Other than himself, and is in fact ready because of that,
Not because of himself, that is something clear about himself.

Otherwise I feel very blank upon this topic,
And think that though important, and proper for anyone to bring up,
It is one that most people should be prepared to be blank upon.

1940

Missing Dates

Slowly the poison the whole blood stream fills.
It is not the effort nor the failure tires.
The waste remains, the waste remains and kills.

It is not your system or clear sight that mills
Down small to the consequence a life requires;
Slowly the poison the whole blood stream fills.

They bled an old dog dry yet the exchange rills
Of young dog blood gave but a month's desires;
The waste remains, the waste remains and kills.

It is the Chinese tombs and the slag hills
Usurp the soil,[2] and not the soil retires.
Slowly the poison the whole blood stream fills.

Not to have fire is to be a skin that shrills.
The complete fire is death. From partial fires
The waste remains, the waste remains and kills.

It is the poems you have lost, the ills
From missing dates, at which the heart expires.
Slowly the poison the whole blood stream fills.
The waste remains, the waste remains and kills.

1940

2. "It is true about the old dog, at least I saw it reported somewhere, but the legend that a fifth or some such part of the soil of China is given up to ancestral tombs is (by the way) not true" [Empson's note].

W. H. AUDEN
1907–1973

W. H. Auden stands monumentally between the poetry of the first decades of the twentieth century and that of the last decades. He wrote abundantly in poetry, prose, drama, and opera libretti. He was less challenged in his position as major poet than any other recent writer in English. Not that he could depend on steady acclaim: his detractors objected to two tendencies of his later work, toward High Church Christianity and toward low-keyed meditation. But his later work remains witty, intelligent, and ethically incisive to a superlative degree.

Auden took a stand against writers such as W. B. Yeats who, he thought, preened themselves too much on being poets and who touted poetry as revelation. He presented himself less ambitiously and said, in the prefatory poem to *Nones,* that he would have preferred to write "in the old grand manner, / Out of a resonant heart," but that the age forced him to write in a subdued, ironic voice. Some of the poems he wrote in the later 1930s, such as "Spain" and "September 1, 1939," attempt to integrate the old and the new registers. But Auden's overall preference was for the deflative: he countered the rhetoric and theatricality of others with exact understatements. As a lover, he insisted on love's transience in the midst of his most passionate lyrics, such as "Lullaby"; as a poet, he questioned the efficacy of his art, even while delighting in it, in poems such as "In Memory of W. B. Yeats." Some of his 1930s poetry was prophetic of social and political change, but he later insisted that poetry could have no value in the public sphere. Many of his poems were couched in the form of prayers or invocations, but he denied any bond between poet and priest. Nonetheless, his poems reveal a penchant for the lay sermon, and he once gave a sermon in prose in Westminster Abbey.

Wystan Hugh Auden was born on February 21, 1907, in York, England, the third son of a physician (his father) and a former nurse (his mother). As a child, Auden pored over his family's medical books and imparted to his schoolmates the sexual information he obtained. In later life, he preserved in his poetry a clinical coolness, a diagnostic air, and a hatred of the unexplained. Many of his poems deal with disease, physical or mental, of the individual or of the age, and offer remedies—revolution (moral rather than physical), love, friendship, "a change of heart" ("Petition").

Auden attended private schools and then Oxford University. During his three years at the university, he wrote many poems and collected the best of them in a volume, *Poems* (1928), that his friend Stephen Spender published on a handpress. (Auden severely revised these poems, like much of his work, in later collections; the selections below reprint the earlier texts, which better reflect his historical development and are often considered superior.) After taking his degree in 1928, Auden traveled to Weimar Germany, where he experienced a homosexual freedom impossible in England; it was the first of many important journeys that would fuel his poetry. In Germany, he came upon the teachings of Homer Lane, a latter-day American prophet who held that civilization distorted humankind's natural impulses and that illness resulted from repression. Vestiges of Lane's theories appear in Auden's verse, but a more important source was Sigmund Freud, whose help in penetrating human psychology Auden movingly acknowledged in a 1939 elegy. Paying homage to Freud's complex understanding of the psyche, his epic journey into the unconscious, and his Enlightenment idealism, Auden takes a Freudian approach to commemorating Freud, while representing the psychoanalytic method as a form of poetry.

During the 1930s, Auden became by common consent the principal poet of his generation, and other liberal and left-wing writers such as Louis MacNeice, C. Day Lewis, and Stephen Spender, in spite of their considerable differences from him, were assumed to be writing under his banner. He supported himself at first by teaching, and he was to do this sporadically for much of his life. But he had a strong urge to travel. In 1937, he and MacNeice published their *Letters from Iceland,* after making a trip to that country at their publisher's expense. The same year, Auden, the spokesperson for the literary left but never a member of the Communist Party, went to civil-war Spain and wrote a political poem, "Spain," in support of the Loyalists (a poem he subsequently removed from his canon). In 1938, he and Christopher Isherwood went to China, and Auden wrote *Journey to a War,* including the psychopolitical sonnets on the Sino-Japanese conflict, "In Time of War."

In January 1939, Auden and Isherwood left England for the United States. That year, Auden fell in love with the young American writer Chester Kallman, his companion for the rest of his life. Also that year, Auden wrote some of his greatest poems, including his elegies for Yeats and Freud and "September 1, 1939" (another poem he later struck from his canon, having come to see as false its claim that "We must love one another or die"). He became an American citizen in 1946, and for the rest of his life he was dogged with charges of having abandoned his country. Most of his later life was shared equally between two residences, one in New York City (the West Village until 1953, then the East Village) and the other in Europe—in Ischia, southern Italy (1948–58), then in Kirchstetten, Lower Austria (1958–73). In 1972, he took up lodgings at his old college, Christ Church, Oxford. He died in Vienna, on September 28, 1973.

For Auden, as for such poets as Hart Crane and Louis Zukofsky, the experience of reading T. S. Eliot was definitive. Auden said that when, at nineteen, he read *The Waste Land,* he discovered how he wanted to write and threw out his Wordsworthian verses. He was attracted to Eliot's conversational but ironically detached tone and his acute inspection of cultural decay. Auden, like Eliot, critiques the atomization and dehumanization in modern middle-class life, though seeing it from the opposite end of the political spectrum from Eliot. "The Unknown Citizen," for example, is a mock epitaph for a victim of the anonymity, routine, and facelessness of modern life. Another youthful encounter of lasting significance, a few years earlier, was with Thomas Hardy, his "poetical father." Hardy's metrical variety and irregular surfaces, his fusion of an elevated perspective with intimacy, were an enabling influence. Auden said he admired most Hardy's "hawk's vision, his way of looking at life from a very great height," and Auden adapted Hardy's method in exhilarating panoramas of modernity, human history, and natural processes ("A Literary Transference"). Despite this "hawk's vision," Auden also strove, again like Hardy, to "find the mortal world enough" ("Lullaby"). Gerard Manley Hopkins also set a useful example, as evidenced by the compression and musical intensity of Auden's early verse.

These influences came together in Auden's style of the late 1920s and early 1930s. Poems such as "The Secret Agent" and "The Wanderer" are elliptical, often dropping articles, pronouns, and conjunctions. Aphoristic and impersonal, they reproduce in their obscurity the modern condition of alienation they diagnose. The emblematic figures of estrangement, such as spies and wanderers, that populate these poems perhaps hint at the social exile brought on by the poet's guilty and vexed homosexuality. The poems speak cryptically of impending doom, of our general complicity in seemingly individual evil conduct, and of the necessity of reforming the affections. Revolution is darkly hinted at, though its exact nature is not specified; the poet seems disposed to urge a conspiracy of people of goodwill. As the 1930s advanced, Auden struggled, like Eliot, to make his poetry clearer and more direct. Though he concentrated on small, individual gestures, he was also fond of invoking large forces—mountains, floods, glaciers, deserts—as symbols of human needs or defects. His witty deflations of grandiloquence joined with large assertions made with great eloquence. The vocabulary was a daring mixture of the homely and the abstract, of vivid detail and allegory.

Two somewhat divergent tendencies appeared as his work proceeded. On the one hand, Auden regarded poetry as "a game of knowledge," an exploration of emotional, analytic, and stylistic possibilities. In this mood, he preferred that art be an enlightened diversion—not far from Eliot's ironic definition of poetry as "a superior form of entertainment." Accordingly, Auden turned out, as if effortlessly, poems in all manner of verse forms, including sestinas, sonnets, ballads, canzones, haiku, the blues, even limericks. On the other hand, Auden insisted on rigorous honesty, on a preference for sense over sound. His art stripped away moral deceptions; it was a disenchanter, standing against the Romantic traditions that influenced it. As he continued to remake his style during World War II, he created a voice that, in contrast not only to Romanticism but also to the authoritarianism devastating Europe, was increasingly flat, ironic, and conversational. Auden was not, however, quite so down-to-earth as he presented himself. His work became increasingly discursive, but it remained "circumspectly audacious," as it was called by Marianne Moore (*Predilections*), whose syllabic verse and proselike sentences also became an important model from the time of Auden's elegy for Freud. Moreover, Auden's pursuit of the seemingly random but actually significant detail, the extraordinary in the ordinary, made his poems reverberate beyond his modest professions for it. Whether he was incorporating bits of Old English poetry, as he did earlier, or bits of popular songs, as later, Auden could not avoid serving as a spokesperson for modern sensibility.

Throughout Auden's career, Yeats and Eliot persisted as shaping figures of attraction and repulsion. Despite political differences, Auden was closely associated with Eliot, who, as director of a publishing firm, accepted Auden's first regularly published books and warmly encouraged him. They were both active members of the Church of England, though Auden's piety was in comparison much more earthy and unmystical. In pursuit of order and tradition, Eliot left America for England, and Auden, in pursuit of variegation and diffuseness, crossed the Atlantic in the opposite direction. As for Yeats, Auden admired his ability to write "serious reflective" poems that were of both "personal and public interest" ("Yeats as an Example"). His elegy for Yeats, modeled on the personally ambivalent yet public style of poems such as "Easter, 1916," rescues the dead man's linguistic power from his right-wing politics and occult beliefs. But Auden became increasingly disenchanted with Yeats's "false emotions, inflated rhetoric, empty sonorities" (1964 letter quoted in Edward Mendelson, *Early Auden*). In Auden's self-elegiac poems, such as "Prologue at Sixty" and "A Lullaby," the poet presents himself humbly in the face of death, his life the intersection point of innumerable influences and accidents.

If modern poets were ranked by sheer intelligence, Auden would appear at or close to the top. While absorbing the viewpoints and vocabularies of both the "hard" and the "human" sciences, he reached also to religion and the devotional life. While recognizing the necessity of reworking religious tropes in an "age of anxiety," he also modestly declined the gambits of strained confession, the large gestures of a belated Romanticism. One of our major links with the best traditions of the Enlightenment, he offers the reassurance that cultural disarray may not extinguish the Enlightenment spirit. (His friend Louis MacNeice described him as the greatest English didactic poet since Alexander Pope.) This spirit appears in Auden's encyclopedic intellectual range, in his unbridled inquisitiveness, and in his internationalism. It accounts for his attachment to Mozart, Goethe, and Hogarth, as well as for the ease with which he addressed the other arts, especially music, as in the illuminated criticism contained in *The Enchafèd Flood: A Study of Romantic Iconography* (1950) and in his collection *The Dyer's Hand* (1962). Throughout his career, Auden acknowledged the badness of the times and the nearing of death wittily and without panic, keeping faith with those he loved and with a certain ideal of civilization and civility. He was a beacon light in the darkness he sometimes saw spreading, whether its source was dullness or something worse.

The Secret Agent[1]

Control of the passes was, he saw, the key
To this new district, but who would get it?
He, the trained spy, had walked into the trap
For a bogus guide, seduced with the old tricks.

At Greenhearth was a fine site for a dam
And easy power, had they pushed the rail
Some stations nearer. They ignored his wires.
The bridges were unbuilt and trouble coming.

The street music seemed gracious now to one
For weeks up in the desert. Woken by water
Running away in the dark, he often had
Reproached the night for a companion
Dreamed of already. They would shoot, of course,
Parting easily who were never joined.

January 1928 — 1928, 1930

This Lunar Beauty[2]

This lunar beauty
Has no history
Is complete and early;
If beauty later
Bear any feature
It had a lover
And is another.

This like a dream
Keeps other time
And daytime is
The loss of this;
For time is inches
And the heart's changes
Where ghost has haunted
Lost and wanted.

But this was never
A ghost's endeavour
Nor finished this,
Was ghost at ease;
And till it pass

1. This title, by which the poem is widely known, is from Auden's later collections. Many of Auden's early poems first appeared without titles.

2. The title is from Auden's later collections. "This" has been glossed as the innocent beauty, "ghost" as the haunting of sexual desire.

Love shall not near
The sweetness here
Nor sorrow take
His endless look.

April 1930 1930

The Wanderer[3]

Doom is dark and deeper than any sea-dingle.
Upon what man it fall
In spring, day-wishing flowers appearing,
Avalanche sliding, white snow from rock-face,
That he should leave his house,
No cloud-soft hand can hold him, restraint by women;
But ever that man goes
Through place-keepers, through forest trees,
A stranger to strangers over undried sea,
Houses for fishes, suffocating water,
Or lonely on fell as chat,[4]
By pot-holed becks[5]
A bird stone-haunting, an unquiet bird.

There head falls forward, fatigued at evening,
And dreams of home,
Waving from window, spread of welcome,
Kissing of wife under single sheet;
But waking sees
Bird-flocks nameless to him, through doorway voices
Of new men making another love.

Save him from hostile capture,
From sudden tiger's spring at corner;
Protect his house,
His anxious house where days are counted
From thunderbolt protect,
From gradual ruin spreading like a stain;
Converting number from vague to certain,
Bring joy, bright day of his returning,
Lucky with day approaching, with leaning dawn.

August 1930 1932, 1933

3. The title is from Auden's later collections, borrowed from an anonymous Old English poem about a solitary man who must journey across icy waters into exile and sadly remembers the lost joys of home: "Then the friendless man wakes again, sees before him the dark waves, the sea-birds bathing, spreading their feathers; frost and snow falling mingles with hail. Then heavier are the wounds in his heart, sore for his beloved; sorrow is renewed." The first line of Auden's poem draws on a Middle English West Midland homily, "Sawles Warde," which tells of God's judgments or "dooms that are secret and deeper than any sea dingle" (or abyss).

4. A warbler. *Fell:* a moorland ridge.

5. Stony brooks.

Who's Who[6]

A shilling life[7] will give you all the facts:
How Father beat him, how he ran away,
What were the struggles of his youth, what acts
Made him the greatest figure of his day:
Of how he fought, fished, hunted, worked all night,
Though giddy, climbed new mountains; named a sea:
Some of the last researchers even write
Love made him weep his pints like you and me.

With all his honours on, he sighed for one
Who, say astonished critics, lived at home;
Did little jobs about the house with skill
And nothing else; could whistle; would sit still
Or potter round the garden; answered some
Of his long marvellous letters but kept none.

1934 — 1934, 1936

On This Island[8]

Look, stranger, at this island now
The leaping light for your delight discovers,
Stand stable here
And silent be,
That through the channels of the ear
May wander like a river
The swaying sound of the sea.

Here at the small field's ending pause
Where the chalk wall falls to the foam, and its tall ledges
Oppose the pluck
And knock of the tide,
And the shingle scrambles after the suck-
ing surf, and the gull lodges
A moment on its sheer side.

Far off like floating seeds the ships
Diverge on urgent voluntary errands;
And the full view
Indeed may enter
And move in memory as now these clouds do,
That pass the harbour mirror
And all the summer through the water saunter.

November 1935 — 1935, 1936

6. The title, from Auden's later collections, refers to a book of capsule biographies of famous people.

7. Cheap book or pamphlet.

8. Title from Auden's later collections.

Lullaby[9]

Lay your sleeping head, my love,
Human on my faithless arm;
Time and fevers burn away
Individual beauty from
Thoughtful children, and the grave
Proves the child ephemeral:
But in my arms till break of day
Let the living creature lie,
Mortal, guilty, but to me
The entirely beautiful.

Soul and body have no bounds:
To lovers as they lie upon
Her tolerant enchanted slope
In their ordinary swoon,
Grave the vision Venus[1] sends
Of supernatural sympathy,
Universal love and hope;
While an abstract insight wakes
Among the glaciers and the rocks
The hermit's sensual ecstasy.

Certainty, fidelity
On the stroke of midnight pass
Like vibrations of a bell,
And fashionable madmen raise
Their pedantic boring cry:
Every farthing[2] of the cost,
All the dreaded cards foretell,
Shall be paid, but from this night
Not a whisper, not a thought,
Not a kiss nor look be lost.

Beauty, midnight, vision dies:
Let the winds of dawn that blow
Softly round your dreaming head
Such a day of sweetness show
Eye and knocking heart may bless,
Find the mortal world enough;
Noons of dryness see you fed
By the involuntary powers,
Nights of insult let you pass
Watched by every human love.

January 1937 — 1937, 1940

9. Title from Auden's later collections.
1. Roman goddess of love.
2. Smallest unit of currency in Britain at the time.

Spain[3]

Yesterday all the past. The language of size
Spreading to China along the trade-routes; the diffusion
Of the counting-frame and the cromlech;[4]
Yesterday the shadow-reckoning in the sunny climates.

Yesterday the assessment of insurance by cards,
The divination of water; yesterday the invention
Of cartwheels and clocks, the taming of
Horses. Yesterday the bustling world of the navigators.

Yesterday the abolition of fairies and giants,
The fortress like a motionless eagle eyeing the valley,
The chapel built in the forest;
Yesterday the carving of angels and alarming gargoyles;

The trial of heretics among the columns of stone;
Yesterday the theological feuds in the taverns
And the miraculous cure at the fountain;
Yesterday the Sabbath of witches; but to-day the struggle.

Yesterday the installation of dynamos and turbines,
The construction of railways in the colonial desert;
Yesterday the classic lecture
On the origin of Mankind. But to-day the struggle.

Yesterday the belief in the absolute value of Greek,
The fall of the curtain upon the death of a hero;
Yesterday the prayer to the sunset
And the adoration of madmen. But to-day the struggle.

As the poet whispers, startled among the pines,
Or where the loose waterfall sings compact, or upright
On the crag by the leaning tower:
"O my vision. O send me the luck of the sailor."

And the investigator peers through his instruments
At the inhuman provinces, the virile bacillus
Or enormous Jupiter finished:
"But the lives of my friends. I inquire. I inquire."

And the poor in their fireless lodgings, dropping the sheets
Of the evening paper: "Our day is our loss, O show us
History the operator, the
Organiser, Time the refreshing river."

3. Auden went to Spain during the Spanish Civil War in 1937; he sympathized with the left-wing Republican forces fighting the Fascist Nationalists.
4. Prehistoric stone monument.

And the nations combine each cry, invoking the life
That shapes the individual belly and orders
The private nocturnal terror:
"Did you not found the city state of the sponge,

"Raise the vast military empires of the shark
And the tiger, establish the robin's plucky canton?
Intervene. O descend as a dove[5] or
A furious papa or a mild engineer, but descend."

And the life, if it answers at all, replied from the heart
And the eyes and the lungs, from the shops and squares of the city
"O no, I am not the mover;
Not to-day; not to you. To you, I'm the

"Yes-man, the bar-companion, the easily-duped;
I am whatever you do. I am your vow to be
Good, your humorous story.
I am your business voice. I am your marriage.

"What's your proposal? To build the just city?[6] I will.
I agree. Or is it the suicide pact, the romantic
Death? Very well, I accept, for
I am your choice, your decision. Yes, I am Spain."

Many have heard it on remote peninsulas,
On sleepy plains, in the aberrant fishermen's islands
Or the corrupt heart of the city,
Have heard and migrated like gulls or the seeds of a flower.

They clung like burrs to the long expresses that lurch
Through the unjust lands, through the night, through the alpine tunnel;
They floated over the oceans;
They walked the passes. All presented their lives.

On that arid square, that fragment nipped off from hot
Africa, soldered so crudely to inventive Europe;
On that tableland scored by rivers,
Our thoughts have bodies; the menacing shapes of our fever

Are precise and alive. For the fears which made us respond
To the medicine ad. and the brochure of winter cruises
Have become invading battalions;
And our faces, the institute-face, the chain-store, the ruin

Are projecting their greed as the firing squad and the bomb.
Madrid is the heart. Our moments of tenderness blossom
As the ambulance and the sandbag;
Our hours of friendship into a people's army.

5. In the Bible, form taken by the Holy Spirit when descending to earth. *Canton:* district.

6. Plato (c. 428–c. 348 B.C.E.) discusses the just city in the *Republic*.

To-morrow, perhaps the future. The research on fatigue
And the movements of packers; the gradual exploring of all the
        Octaves of radiation;
To-morrow the enlarging of consciousness by diet and breathing.

To-morrow the rediscovery of romantic love,
The photographing of ravens; all the fun under
        Liberty's masterful shadow;
To-morrow the hour of the pageant-master and the musician,

The beautiful roar of the chorus under the dome;
To-morrow the exchanging of tips on the breeding of terriers,
        The eager election of chairmen
By the sudden forest of hands. But to-day the struggle.

To-morrow for the young the poets exploding like bombs,
The walks by the lake, the weeks of perfect communion;
        To-morrow the bicycle races
Through the suburbs on summer evenings. But to-day the struggle.

To-day the deliberate increase in the chances of death,
The conscious acceptance of guilt in the necessary murder;
        To-day the expending of powers
On the flat ephemeral pamphlet and the boring meeting.

To-day the makeshift consolations: the shared cigarette,
The cards in the candlelit barn, and the scraping concert,
        The masculine jokes; to-day the
Fumbled and unsatisfactory embrace before hurting.

The stars are dead. The animals will not look.
We are left alone with our day, and the time is short, and
        History to the defeated
May say Alas but cannot help nor pardon.

March 1937 | 1937

As I Walked Out One Evening[7]

As I walked out one evening,
    Walking down Bristol Street,
The crowds upon the pavement
    Were fields of harvest wheat.

And down by the brimming river
    I heard a lover sing
Under an arch of the railway:
    "Love has no ending.

7. Title from Auden's later collections.

"I'll love you, dear, I'll love you
Till China and Africa meet
And the river jumps over the mountain
And the salmon sing in the street.

"I'll love you till the ocean
Is folded and hung up to dry
And the seven stars[8] go squawking
Like geese about the sky.

"The years shall run like rabbits
For in my arms I hold
The Flower of the Ages
And the first love of the world."

But all the clocks in the city
Began to whirr and chime:
"O let not Time deceive you,
You cannot conquer Time.

"In the burrows of the Nightmare
Where Justice naked is,
Time watches from the shadow
And coughs when you would kiss.

"In headaches and in worry
Vaguely life leaks away,
And Time will have his fancy
To-morrow or to-day.

"Into many a green valley
Drifts the appalling[9] snow;
Time breaks the threaded dances
And the diver's brilliant bow.

"O plunge your hands in water,
Plunge them in up to the wrist;
Stare, stare in the basin
And wonder what you've missed.

"The glacier knocks in the cupboard,
The desert sighs in the bed,
And the crack in the tea-cup opens
A lane to the land of the dead.

"Where the beggars raffle the banknotes
And the Giant is enchanting to Jack,
And the Lily-white Boy is a Roarer
And Jill goes down on her back.[1]

8. The constellation of the Pleiades, supposed by the ancients to be seven sisters.
9. Literally, making white.
1. The giant of "Jack and the Bean Stalk" is trying to seduce Jack; the "lily-white Boy" (presumably pure) becomes a boisterous reveler; Jill, of "Jack and Jill," is seduced.

"O look, look in the mirror,
    O look in your distress;
Life remains a blessing
    Although you cannot bless.

"O stand, stand at the window
    As the tears scald and start;
You shall love your crooked neighbour
    With your crooked heart."

It was late, late in the evening,
    The lovers they were gone;
The clocks had ceased their chiming
    And the deep river ran on.

November 1937 — 1938, 1940

From IN TIME OF WAR[2]

XIV

Yes, we are going to suffer, now; the sky
Throbs like a feverish forehead; pain is real;
The groping searchlights suddenly reveal
The little natures that will make us cry,

Who never quite believed they could exist,
Not where we were. They take us by surprise
Like ugly long-forgotten memories,
And like a conscience all the guns resist.

Behind each sociable home-loving eye
The private massacres are taking place;
All Women, Jews, the Rich, the Human Race.

The mountains cannot judge us when we lie:
We dwell upon the earth; the earth obeys
The intelligent and evil till they die.

XVII

They are and suffer; that is all they do:
A bandage hides the place where each is living,
His knowledge of the world restricted to
The treatment that the instruments are giving.

2. A sonnet sequence written in response to a trip with Christopher Isherwood to China during the Second Sino-Japanese War in 1938. It was later retitled "Sonnets from China."

And lie apart like epochs from each other
—Truth in their sense is how much they can bear;
It is not talk like ours, but groans they smother—
And are remote as plants; we stand elsewhere.

For who when healthy can become a foot?
Even a scratch we can't recall when cured,
But are boisterous in a moment and believe

In the common world of the uninjured, and cannot
Imagine isolation. Only happiness is shared,
And anger, and the idea of love.

XVIII

Far from the heart of culture he was used:
Abandoned by his general and his lice,
Under a padded quilt he closed his eyes
And vanished. He will not be introduced

When this campaign is tidied into books:
No vital knowledge perished in his skull;
His jokes were stale; like wartime, he was dull;
His name is lost for ever like his looks.

He neither knew nor chose the Good, but taught us,
And added meaning like a comma, when
He turned to dust in China that our daughters

Be fit to love the earth, and not again
Disgraced before the dogs; that, where are waters,
Mountains and houses, may be also men.

1938 1939

The Capital

Quarter of pleasures where the rich are always waiting,
Waiting expensively for miracles to happen,
O little restaurant where the lovers eat each other,
Café where exiles have established a malicious village;

You with your charm and your apparatus have abolished
The strictness of winter and the spring's compulsion;
Far from your lights the outraged punitive father,
The dullness of mere obedience here is apparent.

Yet with orchestras and glances, O, you betray us
To belief in our infinite powers; and the innocent

Unobservant offender falls in a moment
Victim to the heart's invisible furies.

In unlighted streets you hide away the appalling;
Factories where lives are made for a temporary use
Like collars or chairs, rooms where the lonely are battered
Slowly like pebbles into fortuitous shapes.

But the sky you illumine, your glow is visible far
Into the dark countryside, the enormous, the frozen,
Where, hinting at the forbidden like a wicked uncle,
Night after night to the farmer's children you beckon.

December 1938 — 1939, 1940

Musée des Beaux Arts[3]

About suffering they were never wrong,
The Old Masters: how well they understood
Its human position; how it takes place
While someone else is eating or opening a window or just walking dully
along;
How, when the aged are reverently, passionately waiting
For the miraculous birth, there always must be
Children who did not specially want it to happen, skating
On a pond at the edge of the wood:
They never forgot
That even the dreadful martyrdom must run its course
Anyhow in a corner, some untidy spot
Where the dogs go on with their doggy life and the torturer's horse
Scratches its innocent behind on a tree.

In Brueghel's *Icarus*,[4] for instance: how everything turns away
Quite leisurely from the disaster; the ploughman may
Have heard the splash, the forsaken cry,
But for him it was not an important failure; the sun shone
As it had to on the white legs disappearing into the green
Water; and the expensive delicate ship that must have seen
Something amazing, a boy falling out of the sky,
Had somewhere to get to and sailed calmly on.

December 1938 — 1939, 1940

3. Museum of fine arts (French).
4. *The Fall of Icarus*, by Pieter Brueghel (c. 1525–1569), in the Musées Royaux des Beaux Arts in Brussels. In one corner of Brueghel's painting, Icarus's legs are seen disappearing into the sea, his wings having melted when he flew too close to the sun. Auden also alludes to other paintings by Brueghel: the nativity scene in *The Numbering at Bethlehem*, skaters in *Winter Landscape with Skaters and a Bird Trap*, a horse in *The Massacre of the Innocents*.

In Memory of W. B. Yeats[5]

(d. January 1939)

I

He disappeared in the dead of winter:
The brooks were frozen, the air-ports almost deserted,
And snow disfigured the public statues;
The mercury sank in the mouth of the dying day.
O all the instruments agree
The day of his death was a dark cold day.

Far from his illness
The wolves ran on through the evergreen forests,
The peasant river was untempted by the fashionable quays;
By mourning tongues
The death of the poet was kept from his poems.

But for him it was his last afternoon as himself,
An afternoon of nurses and rumours;
The provinces of his body revolted,
The squares of his mind were empty,
Silence invaded the suburbs,
The current of his feeling failed: he became his admirers.

Now he is scattered among a hundred cities
And wholly given over to unfamiliar affections;
To find his happiness in another kind of wood[6]
And be punished under a foreign code of conscience.
The words of a dead man
Are modified in the guts of the living.

But in the importance and noise of to-morrow
When the brokers are roaring like beasts on the floor of the Bourse,[7]
And the poor have the sufferings to which they are fairly accustomed,
And each in the cell of himself is almost convinced of his freedom;
A few thousand will think of this day
As one thinks of a day when one did something slightly unusual.

O all the instruments agree
The day of his death was a dark cold day.

5. Irish poet William Butler Yeats died on January 29, 1939, in Roquebrune (southern France).
6. Cf. the beginning of Dante's *Inferno*: "In the middle of the journey of our life I came to myself in a dark wood where the straight way was lost" (1.1–3).
7. Stock exchange (French).

II

You were silly like us: your gift survived it all;
The parish of rich women,[8] physical decay,
Yourself; mad Ireland hurt you into poetry.
Now Ireland has her madness and her weather still,
For poetry makes nothing happen: it survives
In the valley of its saying where executives
Would never want to tamper; it flows south
From ranches of isolation and the busy griefs,
Raw towns that we believe and die in; it survives,
A way of happening, a mouth.

III[9]

Earth, receive an honoured guest;
William Yeats is laid to rest:
Let the Irish vessel lie
Emptied of its poetry.

Time that is intolerant
Of the brave and innocent,
And indifferent in a week
To a beautiful physique,

Worships language and forgives
Everyone by whom it lives;
Pardons cowardice, conceit,
Lays its honours at their feet.

Time that with this strange excuse
Pardoned Kipling and his views,[1]
And will pardon Paul Claudel,[2]
Pardons him for writing well.

In the nightmare of the dark
All the dogs of Europe bark,[3]
And the living nations wait,
Each sequestered in its hate;

Intellectual disgrace
Stares from every human face,
And the seas of pity lie
Locked and frozen in each eye.

8. Several wealthy women, including Lady Augusta Gregory (1852–1932), provided financial help to Yeats.
9. The stanza pattern of this section echoes that of Yeats's late poem "Under Ben Bulben." Auden later omitted the section's second, third, and fourth stanzas.
1. British author Rudyard Kipling (1865–1936) was a champion of imperialism.
2. French author (1868–1955) with extremely conservative politics.
3. World War II would begin in September 1939.

Follow, poet, follow right
To the bottom of the night,
With your unconstraining voice
Still persuade us to rejoice;

With the farming of a verse
Make a vineyard of the curse,
Sing of human unsuccess
In a rapture of distress;

In the deserts of the heart
Let the healing fountain start,
In the prison of his days
Teach the free man how to praise.

February 1939 — 1939, 1940

The Unknown Citizen

To JS/07/M/378
This Marble Monument is Erected by the State

He was found by the Bureau of Statistics to be
One against whom there was no official complaint,
And all the reports on his conduct agree
That, in the modern sense of an old-fashioned word, he was a saint,
For in everything he did he served the Greater Community.
Except for the War till the day he retired
He worked in a factory and never got fired,
But satisfied his employers, Fudge Motors Inc.
Yet he wasn't a scab or odd in his views,
For his Union reports that he paid his dues,
(Our report on his Union shows it was sound)
And our Social Psychology workers found
That he was popular with his mates and liked a drink.
The Press are convinced that he bought a paper every day
And that his reactions to advertisements were normal in every way.
Policies taken out in his name prove that he was fully insured,
And his Health-card shows he was once in hospital but left it cured.
Both Producers Research and High-Grade Living declare
He was fully sensible to the advantages of the Installment Plan
And had everything necessary to the Modern Man,
A gramophone, a radio, a car and a frigidaire.
Our researchers into Public Opinion are content
That he held the proper opinions for the time of year;
When there was peace, he was for peace; when there was war, he went.
He was married and added five children to the population,
Which our Eugenist[4] says was the right number for a parent of his generation,

4. An expert in eugenics, a pseudoscience for the genetic "improvement" of humans.

And our teachers report that he never interfered with their education.
Was he free? Was he happy? The question is absurd:
Had anything been wrong, we should certainly have heard.

March 1939 1939, 1940

September 1, 1939[5]

I sit in one of the dives
On Fifty-Second Street[6]
Uncertain and afraid
As the clever hopes expire
Of a low dishonest decade:
Waves of anger and fear
Circulate over the bright
And darkened lands of the earth,
Obsessing our private lives;
The unmentionable odour of death
Offends the September night.

Accurate scholarship can
Unearth the whole offence
From Luther[7] until now
That has driven a culture mad,
Find what occurred at Linz,[8]
What huge imago[9] made
A psychopathic god:
I and the public know
What all schoolchildren learn,
Those to whom evil is done
Do evil in return.

Exiled Thucydides[1] knew
All that a speech can say
About Democracy,
And what dictators do,
The elderly rubbish they talk
To an apathetic grave;
Analysed all in his book,
The enlightenment driven away,
The habit-forming pain,
Mismanagement and grief:
We must suffer them all again.

5. The date of Germany's invasion of Poland and the outbreak of World War II.
6. In New York City, where Auden was living.
7. Martin Luther (1483–1546), founder of the Protestant Reformation.
8. Austrian city where Hitler spent his childhood.
9. Unconscious representation of a parental figure (psychoanalysis).
1. Greek general (460–400 B.C.E.) and historian of the Peloponnesian War, exiled from Athens because he failed to prevent the Spartans from seizing a colony.

Into this neutral air
Where blind skyscrapers use
Their full height to proclaim
The strength of Collective Man,
Each language pours its vain
Competitive excuse:
But who can live for long
In an euphoric dream;
Out of the mirror they stare,
Imperialism's face
And the international wrong.

Faces along the bar
Cling to their average day:
The lights must never go out,
The music must always play,
All the conventions conspire
To make this fort assume
The furniture of home;
Lest we should see where we are,
Lost in a haunted wood,
Children afraid of the night
Who have never been happy or good.

The windiest militant trash
Important Persons shout
Is not so crude as our wish:
What mad Nijinsky wrote
About Diaghilev[2]
Is true of the normal heart;
For the error bred in the bone
Of each woman and each man
Craves what it cannot have,
Not universal love
But to be loved alone.

From the conservative dark
Into the ethical life
The dense commuters come,
Repeating their morning vow,
"I *will* be true to the wife,
I'll concentrate more on my work,"
And helpless governors wake
To resume their compulsory game:
Who can release them now,
Who can reach the deaf,
Who can speak for the dumb?[3]

2. Vaslav Nijinsky (1890–1950), Russian dancer and choreographer, wrote that his former lover Sergei Diaghilev (1872–1929), ballet impresario, "does not want universal love, but to be loved alone."
3. Proverbs 31.8.

All I have is a voice
To undo the folded lie,
The romantic lie in the brain
Of the sensual man-in-the-street
And the lie of Authority
Whose buildings grope the sky:
There is no such thing as the State
And no one exists alone;
Hunger allows no choice
To the citizen or the police;
We must love one another or die.[4]

Defenceless under the night
Our world in stupor lies;
Yet, dotted everywhere,
Ironic points of light
Flash out wherever the Just
Exchange their messages:
May I, composed like them
Of Eros[5] and of dust,
Beleaguered by the same
Negation and despair,
Show an affirming flame.

September 1939 — 1939, 1940

In Memory of Sigmund Freud[6]

(d. September 1939)

When there are so many we shall have to mourn,
When grief has been made so public, and exposed
    To the critique of a whole epoch
    The frailty of our conscience and anguish,

Of whom shall we speak? For every day they die
Among us, those who were doing us some good,
    And knew it was never enough but
    Hoped to improve a little by living.

Such was this doctor: still at eighty he wished
To think of our life, from whose unruliness
    So many plausible young futures
    With threats or flattery ask obedience.

4. Auden later attempted to revise this line, which struck him as "dishonest." In one revision, the line reads "We must love one another and die." Another version of the poem leaves out the entire stanza.
5. Greek god of desire.
6. Austrian founder of psychoanalysis (1856–1939), who, forced by the Nazi regime to leave Vienna, died in London. This elegy seems to have been Auden's first poem written in syllabics.

But his wish was denied him; he closed his eyes
Upon that last picture common to us all,
Of problems like relatives standing
Puzzled and jealous about our dying.

For about him at the very end were still
Those he had studied, the nervous and the nights,
And shades that still waited to enter
The bright circle of his recognition

Turned elsewhere with their disappointment as he
Was taken away from his old interest
To go back to the earth in London,
An important Jew who died in exile.

Only Hate was happy, hoping to augment
His practice now, and his shabby clientele
Who think they can be cured by killing
And covering the gardens with ashes.

They are still alive but in a world he changed
Simply by looking back with no false regrets;
All that he did was to remember
Like the old and be honest like children.

He wasn't clever at all: he merely told
The unhappy Present to recite the Past
Like a poetry lesson till sooner
Or later it faltered at the line where

Long ago the accusations had begun,
And suddenly knew by whom it had been judged,
How rich life had been and how silly,
And was life-forgiven and more humble,

Able to approach the Future as a friend
Without a wardrobe of excuses, without
A set mask of rectitude or an
Embarrassing over-familiar gesture.

No wonder the ancient cultures of conceit
In his technique of unsettlement foresaw
The fall of princes, the collapse of
Their lucrative patterns of frustration.

If he succeeded, why, the Generalised Life
Would become impossible, the monolith
Of State be broken and prevented
The co-operation of avengers.

Of course they called on God: but he went his way,
Down among the Lost People like Dante, down

To the stinking fosse[7] where the injured
Lead the ugly life of the rejected.

And showed us what evil is: not as we thought
Deeds that must be punished, but our lack of faith,
Our dishonest mood of denial,
The concupiscence of the oppressor.

And if something of the autocratic pose,
The paternal strictness he distrusted, still
Clung to his utterance and features,
It was a protective imitation

For one who lived among enemies so long:
If often he was wrong and at times absurd,
To us he is no more a person
Now but a whole climate of opinion

Under whom we conduct our differing lives:
Like weather he can only hinder or help,
The proud can still be proud but find it
A little harder, and the tyrant tries

To make him do but doesn't care for him much.
He quietly surrounds all our habits of growth;
He extends, till the tired in even
The remotest most miserable duchy

Have felt the change in their bones and are cheered,
And the child unlucky in his little State,
Some hearth where freedom is excluded,
A hive whose honey is fear and worry,

Feels calmer now and somehow assured of escape;
While as they lie in the grass of our neglect,
So many long-forgotten objects
Revealed by his undiscouraged shining

Are returned to us and made precious again;
Games we had thought we must drop as we grew up,
Little noises we dared not laugh at,
Faces we made when no one was looking.

But he wishes us more than this: to be free
Is often to be lonely; he would unite
The unequal moieties[8] fractured
By our own well-meaning sense of justice,

7. Ditch. Dante descended into Hell in his *Inferno* (1308–21).

8. Parts.

Would restore to the larger the wit and will
The smaller possesses but can only use
    For arid disputes, would give back to
    The son the mother's richness of feeling.

But he would have us remember most of all
To be enthusiastic over the night
    Not only for the sense of wonder
    It alone has to offer, but also

Because it needs our love: for with sad eyes
Its delectable creatures look up and beg
    Us dumbly to ask them to follow;
    They are exiles who long for the future

That lies in our power. They too would rejoice
If allowed to serve enlightenment like him,
    Even to bear our cry of "Judas,"[9]
    As he did and all must bear who serve it.

One rational voice is dumb: over a grave
The household of Impulse mourns one dearly loved.
    Sad is Eros, builder of cities,
    And weeping anarchic Aphrodite.[1]

November 1939 — 1940

In Praise of Limestone[2]

If it form the one landscape that we the inconstant ones
  Are consistently homesick for, this is chiefly
Because it dissolves in water. Mark these rounded slopes
  With their surface fragrance of thyme and beneath
A secret system of caves and conduits; hear these springs
  That spurt out everywhere with a chuckle
Each filling a private pool for its fish and carving
  Its own little ravine whose cliffs entertain
The butterfly and the lizard; examine this region
  Of short distances and definite places:
What could be more like Mother or a fitter background
  For her son, for the nude young male who lounges
Against a rock displaying his dildo, never doubting
  That for all his faults he is loved, whose works are but
Extensions of his power to charm? From weathered outcrop
  To hill-top temple, from appearing waters to
Conspicuous fountains, from a wild to a formal vineyard,

9. Judas Iscariot, the disciple who betrayed Jesus (Matthew 26.14ff.).

1. Greek goddess of love and mother of Eros (which means "love"), or Cupid.

2. Inspired by the limestone landscape outside Florence, Italy, where Auden and his longtime companion Chester Kallman (1921–1975) were staying; the poem also recalls the poet's native Yorkshire.

Are ingenious but short steps that a child's wish
To receive more attention than his brothers, whether
By pleasing or teasing, can easily take.

Watch, then, the band of rivals as they climb up and down
Their steep stone gennels[3] in twos and threes, sometimes
Arm in arm, but never, thank God, in step; or engaged
On the shady side of a square at midday in
Voluble discourse, knowing each other too well to think
There are any important secrets, unable
To conceive a god whose temper-tantrums are moral
And not to be pacified by a clever line
Or a good lay: for, accustomed to a stone that responds,
They have never had to veil their faces in awe
Of a crater whose blazing fury could not be fixed;
Adjusted to the local needs of valleys
Where everything can be touched or reached by walking,
Their eyes have never looked into infinite space
Through the lattice-work of a nomad's comb; born lucky,
Their legs have never encountered the fungi
And insects of the jungle, the monstrous forms and lives
With which we have nothing, we like to hope, in common.
So, when one of them goes to the bad, the way his mind works
Remains comprehensible: to become a pimp
Or deal in fake jewelry or ruin a fine tenor voice
For effects that bring down the house could happen to all
But the best and the worst of us . . .
That is why, I suppose,
The best and worst never stayed here long but sought
Immoderate soils where the beauty was not so external,
The light less public and the meaning of life
Something more than a mad camp. "Come!" cried the granite wastes,
"How evasive is your humor, how accidental
Your kindest kiss, how permanent is death." (Saints-to-be
Slipped away sighing.) "Come!" purred the clays and gravel,
"On our plains there is room for armies to drill; rivers
Wait to be tamed and slaves to construct you a tomb
In the grand manner: soft as the earth is mankind and both
Need to be altered." (Intendant Caesar rose and
Left, slamming the door.) But the really reckless were fetched
By an older colder voice, the oceanic whisper:
"I am the solitude that asks and promises nothing;
That is how I shall set you free. There is no love;
There are only the various envies, all of them sad."

They were right, my dear, all those voices were right
And still are; this land is not the sweet home that it looks,
Nor its peace the historical calm of a site
Where something was settled once and for all: A backward
And dilapidated province, connected

3. Narrow passages between houses or, as here, rocks.

To the big busy world by a tunnel, with a certain
 Seedy appeal, is that all it is now? Not quite:
It has a worldly duty which in spite of itself
 It does not neglect, but calls into question
All the Great Powers assume; it disturbs our rights. The poet,
 Admired for his earnest habit of calling
The sun the sun, his mind Puzzle, is made uneasy
 By these solid statues which so obviously doubt
His antimythological myth; and these gamins,[4]
 Pursuing the scientist down the tiled colonnade
With such lively offers, rebuke his concern for Nature's
 Remotest aspects: I, too, am reproached, for what
And how much you know. Not to lose time, not to get caught,
 Not to be left behind, not, please! to resemble
The beasts who repeat themselves, or a thing like water
 Or stone whose conduct can be predicted, these
Are our Common Prayer,[5] whose greatest comfort is music
 Which can be made anywhere, is invisible,
And does not smell. In so far as we have to look forward
 To death as a fact, no doubt we are right: But if
Sins can be forgiven, if bodies rise from the dead,
 These modifications of matter into
Innocent athletes and gesticulating fountains,
 Made solely for pleasure, make a further point:
The blessed will not care what angle they are regarded from,
 Having nothing to hide. Dear, I know nothing of
Either, but when I try to imagine a faultless love
 Or the life to come, what I hear is the murmur
Of underground streams, what I see is a limestone landscape.

May 1948 1948, 1951

The Shield of Achilles[6]

She looked over his shoulder
 For vines and olive trees,
Marble well-governed cities,
 And ships upon untamed seas,
But there on the shining metal
 His hands had put instead
An artificial wilderness
 And a sky like lead.

4. Urchins.
5. The Book of Common Prayer is the liturgical book of the Anglican Church.
6. The splendid shield of Achilles is described in book 18 (lines 478–608) of Homer's *Iliad*. Achilles, the chief Greek hero in the war with Troy, has lost his armor when his great friend Patroclus, wearing it, is slain by Hector. While Achilles is mourning the death of his friend, his mother, the goddess Thetis, goes to Mt. Olympus to entreat Hephaestos, god of fire, to make new armor for Achilles. On the new shield he depicts the earth, the heavens, the sea, and the planets; a city in peace (with a wedding and a trial) and a city at war; scenes from country life, animal life, and the joyful life of young men and women. The ocean, as the outer border, flows around all these scenes.

A plain without a feature, bare and brown,
No blade of grass, no sign of neighborhood,
Nothing to eat and nowhere to sit down,
Yet, congregated on its blankness, stood
An unintelligible multitude,
A million eyes, a million boots in line,
Without expression, waiting for a sign.

Out of the air a voice without a face
Proved by statistics that some cause was just
In tones as dry and level as the place:
No one was cheered and nothing was discussed;
Column by column in a cloud of dust
They marched away enduring a belief
Whose logic brought them, somewhere else, to grief.

She looked over his shoulder
For ritual pieties,
White flower-garlanded heifers,
Libation and sacrifice,[7]
But there on the shining metal
Where the altar should have been,
She saw by his flickering forge-light
Quite another scene.

Barbed wire enclosed an arbitrary spot
Where bored officials lounged (one cracked a joke)
And sentries sweated, for the day was hot:
A crowd of ordinary decent folk
Watched from without and neither moved nor spoke
As three pale figures were led forth and bound
To three posts driven upright in the ground.

The mass and majesty of this world, all
That carries weight and always weighs the same,
Lay in the hands of others; they were small
And could not hope for help and no help came:
What their foes liked to do was done, their shame
Was all the worst could wish; they lost their pride
And died as men before their bodies died.

She looked over his shoulder
For athletes at their games,
Men and women in a dance
Moving their sweet limbs
Quick, quick, to music,
But there on the shining shield

7. Cf. John Keats's "Ode on a Grecian Urn" (1820): "Who are these coming to the sacrifice?/To what green altar, O mysterious priest,/Lead'st thou that heifer lowing at the skies,/And all her silken flanks with garlands dressed?" *Libation:* sacrifice of wine or other liquid.

His hands had set no dancing-floor
But a weed-choked field.

A ragged urchin, aimless and alone,
Loitered about that vacancy; a bird
Flew up to safety from his well-aimed stone:
That girls are raped, that two boys knife a third,
Were axioms to him, who'd never heard
Of any world where promises were kept
Or one could weep because another wept.

The thin-lipped armorer,
Hephaestos, hobbled away;
Thetis of the shining breasts
Cried out in dismay
At what the god had wrought
To please her son, the strong
Iron-hearted man-slaying Achilles
Who would not live long.

1952 | 1952, 1955

Prologue at Sixty

(FOR FRIEDRICH HEER)[8]

Dark-green upon distant heights
the stationary flocks foresters tend,
blonde and fertile the fields below them:
browing a hog-back, an oak stands
post-alone, light-demanding.

Easier to hear, harder to see,
limbed lives, locomotive,
automatic and irritable,
social or solitary, seek their foods,
mates and territories while their time lasts.

Radial republics, rooted to spots,
bilateral monarchies, moving frankly,
stoic by sort and self-policing,
enjoy their rites, their realms of data,
live well by the Law of their Flesh.

All but the youngest of the yawning mammals,
Name-Giver, Ghost-Fearer,

8. Author (1916–1983) of *The Intellectual History of Europe.*

maker of wars and wise-cracks,
a rum creature, in a crisis always,
the anxious species to which I belong,

whom chance and my own choice have arrived
to bide here yearly from bud-haze
to leaf-blush, dislodged from elsewhere,
by blood barbarian, in bias of view
a Son of the North, outside the *limes.*

Rapacious pirates my people were,[9]
crude and cruel, but not calculating,
never marched in step nor made straight roads,
nor sank like senators to a slave's taste
for grandiose buildings and gladiators.

But the Gospel reached the unroman lands.
I can translate what onion-towers
of five parish churches preach in Baroque:[1]
to make One, there must be Two,
Love is substantial, all Luck is good,

Flesh must fall through fated time
from birth to death, both unwilled,
but Spirit may climb counterwise
from a death, in faith freely chosen,
to resurrection, a re-beginning.

And the Greek Code got to us also:
a Mind of Honor must acknowledge
the happy eachness of all things,
distinguish even from odd numbers,
and bear witness to what-is-the-case.

East, West, on the Autobahn[2]
motorists whoosh, on the Main Line
a far-sighted express will snake by,
through a gap granted by grace of nature:
still today, as in the Stone Age,

our sandy vale is a valued passage.
Alluvia[3] flats, flooded often,
lands of outwash, lie to the North,
to the South litters of limestone alps
embarrass the progress of path-seekers.

Their thoughts upon ski-slope or theatre-opening,
few who pass us pay attention

9. Auden's ancestors were from Iceland. *Limes:* boundary line of the Roman Empire, hence of "civilization."
1. Style of architecture dominant in Europe in the seventeenth and early eighteenth centuries.
2. Network of German freeways.
3. Made of silt deposited by running water.

to our squandered hamlets where at harvest time
chugging tractors, child-driven,
shamble away down sheltered lanes.

Quiet now but acquainted too
with unwelcome visitors, violation,
scare and scream, the scathe of battle:
Turks have been here,[4] Boney's legions,
Germans, Russians, and no joy they brought.

Though the absence of hedge-rows is odd to me
(no Whig landlord, the landscape vaunts,
ever empired on Austrian ground),
this unenglish tract after ten years
into my love has looked itself,

added its names to my numinous map
of the *Solihull* gas-works,[5] gazed at in awe
by a bronchial boy, the *Blue John Mine,*
the *Festiniog* railway, the *Rhayader* dams,
Cross Fell, Keld and *Cauldron Snout,*

of sites made sacred by something read there,
a lunch, a good lay, or sheer lightness of heart,
the *Fürbringer* and the *Friedrich Strasse,*
Isafjördur, Epomeo,
Poprad, Basel, Bar-le-Duc,

of more modern holies, *Middagh Street,*
Carnegie Hall and the *Con-Ed* stacks
on *First Avenue.* Who am I now?
An American? No, a New Yorker,
who opens his *Times* at the obit page,

whose dream images date him already,
awake among lasers, electric brains,
do-it-yourself sex manuals,
bugged phones, sophisticated
weapon-systems and sick jokes.

Already a helpless orbited dog
has blinked at our sorry conceited O,
where many are famished, few look good,

4. This sector of Austria was once part of the Ottoman Empire. *Boney:* Napoleon Bonaparte.
5. The locations in the next three stanzas all had personal importance for Auden. The gasworks in the central English town of Solihull was Auden's favorite place as a young child. The Blue John Mine is in Derbyshire, England. The Rhayader dams help feed the water supply of Birmingham, England. Keld is a town in Yorkshire, and Cross Fell and Cauldron Snout are both located on the Pennine mountain range, in England. Fürbringer and Friedrich Strasse are in Berlin, Isafjördur in Iceland. Epomeo is a mountain on the island of Ischia, off the coast of Italy. Poprad is in Slovakia, Basel in Switzerland, and Bar-le-Duc in France. Auden lived at 7 Middagh Street, Brooklyn, from which point he could see the huge smokestacks of a Consolidated Edison electrical plant.

and my day turned out torturers
who read *Rilke*[6] in their rest periods.

Now the Cosmocrats are crashed through time-zones
in jumbo jets to a Joint Conference:
nor sleep nor shit have our shepherds had,
and treaties are signed (with secret clauses)
by Heads who are not all there.

Can Sixty make sense to Sixteen-Plus?
What has my camp in common with theirs,
with buttons and beards and Be-Ins?
Much, I hope. In *Acts* it is written
Taste was no problem at Pentecost.[7]

To speak is human because human to listen,
beyond hope, for an Eighth Day,[8]
when the creatured Image shall become the Likeness:
Giver-of-Life, translate for me
till I accomplish my corpse at last.

April 1967 — 1967, 1969

A New Year Greeting

(After an Article by Mary J. Marples
in *Scientific American*, January 1969)

(FOR VASSILY YANOWSKY)[9]

On this day tradition allots
    to taking stock of our lives,
my greetings to all of you, Yeasts,
    Bacteria, Viruses,
Aerobics and Anaerobics:
    A Very Happy New Year
to all for whom my ectoderm
    is as Middle-Earth to me.

For creatures your size I offer
    a free choice of habitat,
so settle yourselves in the zone
    that suits you best, in the pools
of my pores or the tropical
    forests of arm-pit and crotch,

6. Rainer Maria Rilke (1875–1926), Austro-German poet.
7. In the New Testament, Acts tells of the descent of the Holy Spirit and the miracle of the disciples speaking in tongues. *Be-Ins:* form of group protest associated with the 1960s youth counterculture.
8. According to Genesis, the world was created in seven days.
9. Russian emigré doctor and writer.

in the deserts of my fore-arms,
or the cool woods of my scalp.

Build colonies: I will supply
adequate warmth and moisture,
the sebum and lipids[1] you need,
on condition you never
do me annoy with your presence,
but behave as good guests should,
not rioting into acne
or athlete's-foot or a boil.

Does my inner weather affect
the surfaces where you live?
Do unpredictable changes
record my rocketing plunge
from fairs when the mind is in tift
and relevant thoughts occur
to fouls when nothing will happen
and no one calls and it rains.

I should like to think that I make
a not impossible world,
but an Eden it cannot be:
my games, my purposive acts,
may turn to catastrophes there.
If you were religious folk,
how would your dramas justify
unmerited suffering?

By what myths would your priests account
for the hurricanes that come
twice every twenty-four hours,
each time I dress or undress,
when, clinging to keratin[2] rafts,
whole cities are swept away
to perish in space, or the Flood
that scalds to death when I bathe?

Then, sooner or later, will dawn
a day of Apocalypse,
when my mantle suddenly turns
too cold, too rancid, for you,
appetising to predators
of a fiercer sort, and I
am stripped of excuse and nimbus,
a Past, subject to Judgement.

May 1969 1969, 1972

1. Organic compounds such as fat. *Sebum:* fatty substance secreted by the skin.

2. Substance of which hair and nails are made.

A Lullaby

The din of work is subdued,
another day has westered
and mantling darkness arrived.
Peace! Peace! Devoid your portrait
of its vexations and rest.
Your daily round is done with,
you've gotten the garbage out,
answered some tiresome letters
and paid a bill by return,
all *frettolosamente.*[3]
Now you have licence to lie,
naked, curled like a shrimplet,
jacent[4] in bed, and enjoy
its cosy micro-climate:
Sing, Big Baby, sing lullay.

The old Greeks got it all wrong:
Narcissus[5] is an oldie,
tamed by time, released at last
from lust for other bodies,
rational and reconciled.
For many years you envied
the hirsute, the he-man type.
No longer: now you fondle
your almost feminine flesh
with mettled[6] satisfaction,
imagining that you are
sinless and all-sufficient,
snug in the den of yourself,
Madonna and *Bambino:*[7]
Sing, Big Baby, sing lullay.

Let your last thinks all be thanks:
praise your parents who gave you
a Super-Ego[8] of strength
that saves you so much bother,
digit friends and dear them all,[9]
then pay fair attribution
to your age, to having been
born when you were. In boyhood
you were permitted to meet
beautiful old contraptions,
soon to be banished from earth,

3. Hastily (Italian).
4. Lying down.
5. In Greek mythology, a beautiful youth who fell in love with his reflection in a stream and so pined away until he died.
6. High-spirited.
7. Madonna and child (Italian); used for the Virgin Mary and the baby Jesus.
8. Conscience (psychoanalysis).
9. Call them all "dear." *Digit:* probably in the sense of counting.

saddle-tank loks, beam-engines
and over-shot waterwheels.[1]
Yes, love, you have been lucky:
Sing, Big Baby, sing lullay.

Now for oblivion: let
the belly-mind take over
down below the diaphragm,
the domain of the Mothers,
They who guard the Sacred Gates,[2]
without whose wordless warnings
soon the verbalising I
becomes a vicious despot,
lewd, incapable of love,
disdainful, status-hungry.
Should dreams haunt you, heed them not,
for all, both sweet and horrid,
are jokes in dubious taste,
too jejune[3] to have truck with.
Sleep, Big Baby, sleep your fill.

April 1972 — 1973, 1974

1. Waterwheels with buckets on their rims that turn as the buckets fill with water. *Saddle-tank loks:* water tanks on the boilers of railway locomotives. *Beam-engines:* parts of a steam engine.

2. Perhaps the gates of ivory and horn in classical myth, through which false and true dreams, respectively, issued.

3. Insipid.

A. D. Hope
1907–2000

Witty poets writing of love were in short supply in the twentieth century. A. D. Hope, however, established himself as a master of clever, amorous verse, translating into a current idiom the preoccupations of Metaphysical poetry. In his 1965 book of essays, *The Cave and the Spring,* Hope regrets the disappearance of "the middle form of poetry: that form in which the uses of poetry approach closest to the uses of prose, and yet remain essentially poetry." It is this middle form that he commanded, and he claimed poets such as Chaucer and Robert Browning as predecessors, poets uninterested in "a profusion of startling images," interested rather in ordinary English.

Hope defines his views on poetry in contrast to those of his contemporaries. In the preface to a small collection of his poems published in the Australian Poets Series in 1963, he remonstrates against the idea that "by excluding those things which poetry has in common with prose, narrative, argument, description, exhortation and exposition, and that by depending entirely on lyric impulse or the evocative power of massed imagery, one can arrive at the pure essence of poetry." He attacks free verse for abandoning textural richness and the possibilities of variation within metrical pattern. Against Romantic personalism, "the view that poetry is primarily self-expression," he argues, like T. S. Eliot, "that poetry is principally concerned to 'express' its subject and is doing so to create an emotion which is the feeling of the poem and not the feeling of the poet."

Alec Derwent Hope was born on July 21, 1907, in Coomo, New South Wales. He grew up on the island of Tasmania, off the southern coast of Australia. His father was a Presbyterian minister and small-scale farmer, and his mother taught the children to read and write. Hope received degrees at the University of Sydney, where he bested his contemporaries in both philosophy and English, and at University College, Oxford. In 1951, he became the first Professor of English at what is now the Australian National University, and in 1955, he published his first collection of poems, *The Wandering Islands.* Some of its first readers, eager for evidence of an emerging national literature, found the book disappointing, even scandalous. The poems were rarely situated in Australia, were not written in a native idiom, and were bookish and cosmopolitan. Hope wrote about Australia, and yet, interested in other literatures and cultures, he also explored a variety of ways of looking at the world and enacted them elegantly in his poems.

Australia

A Nation of trees, drab green and desolate grey
In the field uniform of modern wars,
Darkens her hills, those endless, outstretched paws
Of Sphinx demolished or stone lion worn away.

They called her a young country, but they lie:
She is the last of lands, the emptiest,
A woman beyond her change of life, a breast
Still tender but within the womb is dry.

Without songs, architecture, history:
The emotions and superstitions of younger lands,
Her rivers of water drown among inland sands,
The river of her immense stupidity

Floods her monotonous tribes from Cairns to Perth.[1]
In them at last the ultimate men arrive
Whose boast is not: "we live" but "we survive",
A type who will inhabit the dying earth.

And her five cities like five teeming sores,
Each drains her: a vast parasite robber-state
Where second-hand Europeans pullulate[2]
Timidly on the edge of alien shores.

Yet there are some like me turn gladly home
From the lush jungle of modern thought, to find
The Arabian desert of the human mind,
Hoping, if still from the desert the prophets come,[3]

Such savage and scarlet as no green hills dare
Springs in that waste, some spirit which escapes
The learned doubt, the chatter of cultured apes
Which is called civilization over there.

1939

Observation Car

To be put on the train and kissed and given my ticket,
Then the station slid backward, the shops and the neon lighting,
Reeling off in a drunken blur, with a whole pound note in my pocket
And the holiday packed with Perhaps. It used to be very exciting.

The present and past were enough. I did not mind having my back
To the engine. I sat like a spider and spun
Time backward out of my guts—or rather my eyes—and the track
Was a Now dwindling off to oblivion. I thought it was fun:

The telegraph poles slithered up in a sudden crescendo
As we sliced the hill and scattered its grazing sheep;
The days were a wheeling delirium that led without end to
Nights when we plunged into roaring tunnels of sleep.

But now I am tired of the train. I have learned that one tree
Is much like another, one hill the dead spit of the next

1. Australian cities on opposite coasts.
2. Breed rapidly.
3. In the Hebrew Bible, the prophets often came out of the desert to speak their prophecies or warnings.

I have seen tailing off behind all the various types of country
Like a clock running down. I am bored and a little perplexed;

And weak with the effort of endless evacuation
Of the long monotonous Now, the repetitive, tidy
Officialdom of each siding, of each little station
Labelled Monday, Tuesday—and goodness! what happened to Friday?

And the maddening way the other passengers alter:
The schoolgirl who goes to the Ladies' comes back to her seat
A lollipop blonde who leads you on to assault her,
And you've just got her skirts round her waist and her pants round her feet

When you find yourself fumbling about the nightmare knees
Of a pink hippopotamus with a permanent wave
Who sends you for sandwiches and a couple of teas,
But by then she has whiskers, no teeth and one foot in the grave.

I have lost my faith that the ticket tells where we are going.
There are rumours the driver is mad—we are all being trucked
To the abattoirs somewhere—the signals are jammed and unknowing
We aim through the night full speed at a wrecked viaduct.

But I do not believe them. The future is rumour and drivel;
Only the past is assured. From the observation car
I stand looking back and watching the landscape shrivel,
Wondering where we are going and just where the hell we are,

Remembering how I planned to break the journey, to drive
My own car one day, to have choice in my hands and my foot upon power,
To see through the trumpet throat of vertiginous perspective
My urgent Now explode continually into flower,

To be the Eater of Time, a poet and not that sly
Anus of mind the historian. It was so simple and plain
To live by the sole, insatiable influx of the eye.
But something went wrong with the plan: I am still on the train.

1955

Advice to Young Ladies

A.U.C. 334:[4] about this date
For a sexual misdemeanor, which she denied,
The vestal virgin[5] Postumia was tried.
Livy records it among affairs of state.

4. *Ab Urbe Condita:* from the founding of the city (Latin), that is, Rome, supposedly in 753 B.C.E. The historian Livy (58 B.C.E.–17 C.E.) tells the story narrated in the first three stanzas in his *History of Rome from the Foundation.*

5. One of several young, female priests, from patrician families, who tended the sacred flame of Vesta, goddess of the hearth.

They let her off: it seems she was perfectly pure;
The charge arose because some thought her talk
Too witty for a young girl, her eyes, her walk
Too lively, her clothes too smart to be demure.

The Pontifex Maximus,[6] summing up the case,
Warned her in future to abstain from jokes,
To wear less modish and more pious frocks.
She left the court reprieved, but in disgrace.

What then? With her the annalist[7] is less
Concerned than what the men achieved that year:
Plots, quarrels, crimes, with oratory to spare!
I see Postumia with her dowdy dress,

Stiff mouth and listless step; I see her strive
To give dull answers. She had to knuckle down.
A vestal virgin who scandalized that town
Had fair trial, then they buried her alive.[8]

Alive, bricked up in suffocating dark,
A ration of bread, a pitcher if she was dry,
Preserved the body they did not wish to die
Until her mind was quenched to the last spark.

How many the black maw has swallowed in its time!
Spirited girls who would not know their place;
Talented girls who found that the disgrace
Of being a woman made genius a crime;

How many others, who would not kiss the rod[9]
Domestic bullying broke or public shame?
Pagan or Christian, it was much the same:
Husbands, St Paul declared, rank next to God.

Livy and Paul,[1] it may be, never knew
That Rome was doomed; each spoke of her with pride.
Tacitus,[2] writing after both had died,
Showed that whole fabric rotten through and through.

Historians spend their lives and lavish ink
Explaining how great commonwealths collapse
From great defects of policy—perhaps
The cause is sometimes simpler than they think.

6. Chief religious officer of ancient Rome, one of whose special duties was to supervise the Vestals.
7. Historian.
8. Live burial was the punishment for a Vestal found guilty of breaking her vow of chastity.
9. That is, of obedience and punishment.
1. St. Paul, who said, "Wives, submit yourselves unto your own husbands, as unto the Lord" (Ephesians 5.22).
2. The *Histories* of Tacitus (c. 77–117) criticize the degeneracy of the times as exemplified in three Roman emperors who ruled and were deposed in 68–69 C.E.

It may not seem so grave an act to break
Postumia's spirit as Galileo's, to gag
Hypatia as crush Socrates, or drag
Joan as Giordano Bruno to the stake.[3]

Can we be sure? Have more states perished, then,
For having shackled the enquiring mind,
Than those who, in their folly not less blind,
Trusted the servile womb to breed free men?

1965

Beware of Ruins

Beware of ruins: they have a treacherous charm;
Insidious echoes lurk among their stones;
That scummy pool was where the fountain soared;
    The seated figure, whose white arm
Beckons you, is a mock-up of dry bones
And not, as you believe, your love restored.

The moonlight lends her grace, but have a care:
Behind her waits the fairy Melusine.[4]
The sun those beams refract died years ago.
    The moat has a romantic air
But it is choked with nettles and obscene
And phallic fungi rot there as they grow.

Beware of ruins; the heart is apt to make
Monstrous assumptions on the unburied past;
Though cleverly restored, the Tudor tower[5]
    Is spurious, the façade a fake
Whose new face is a death-mask[6] of the last
Despairing effort before it all went sour.

There are ruins, too, of a less obvious kind;
I go back; cannot believe my eyes; the place
Is just as I recall: the fire is lit,
    The table laid, bed warmed; I find
My former world intact, but not, alas,
The man I was when I was part of it.

1981

3. In 1633, the Italian astronomer Galileo Galilei (1564–1642) was forced by the Roman Catholic Church to renounce his scientific conclusions and was for a time imprisoned. In 415 C.E., Hypatia, a learned and beautiful woman of Alexandria, was murdered, allegedly at the command of an archbishop. In 399 B.C.E., Socrates was sentenced to die by poison, because of his supposedly subversive teachings. Both Joan of Arc and Giordano Bruno were burned at the stake: Joan in 1431 for heresy and sorcery, Bruno in 1600 for theological and scientific heresies.

4. A water spirit from various fairy tales, she has a beautiful face but the body of a fish or snake.

5. That is, dating from the sixteenth century.

6. Cast (of plaster, for example) taken from the face of a corpse.

Louis MacNeice
1907–1963

In 1938, Louis MacNeice published *Modern Poetry: A Personal Essay.* At thirty, he had published three books of poems and a translation of Aeschylus's *Agamemnon.* He had concocted, with his friend W. H. Auden, a lively book out of a trip to Iceland, and he was at work on a long poem, *Autumn Journal.* MacNeice describes *Modern Poetry* as a plea for "impure" poetry, expressive of the poet's immediate interests and sense of the natural and the social worlds. He eagerly advances the "impure poetry" of three of his contemporaries, whose work had appeared in Michael Roberts's anthology *New Signatures:* Auden, Stephen Spender, and C. Day Lewis. These poets are conscious that they have succeeded giants—W. B. Yeats and T. S. Eliot are particularly threatening—and, MacNeice argues, the virtue of the new poets lies in their emotional partisanship: "Yeats proposed to turn his back on desire and hatred; Eliot sat back and watched other peoples' emotions with ennui and an ironical self-pity. . . . The whole poetry, on the other hand, of Auden, Spender, and Day-Lewis implies that they have desires and hatreds of their own and, further, that they think some things *ought* to be desired and others hated." In his conclusion, MacNeice calls for a poetry that is not monastic and consecrated, that is but one form of human enjoyment among others: "My own prejudice . . . is in favour of poets whose worlds are not too esoteric. I would have a poet able-bodied, fond of talking, a reader of the newspapers, capable of pity and laughter, informed in economics, appreciative of women, involved in personal relationships, actively interested in politics, susceptible to physical impressions." MacNeice's engaging poems—written in a ruminative, responsive, flexible voice—are perhaps the best illustration of this ideal.

MacNeice was born on September 12, 1907, in Belfast, Northern Ireland. Like Yeats, about whom he wrote an appreciative book, MacNeice came from an Anglo-Irish Protestant family. Soon after his birth, his family moved to Carrickfergus, County Antrim, as recalled in the autobiographical poem "Carrickfergus." His father was a clergyman in the Church of Ireland, eventually a bishop, but he supported Home Rule for Ireland. Although MacNeice spent most of his adult life in London, where he felt an exile but found life exciting, he frequently returned in his poems to the landscapes of his childhood, and he took great pride in his Irishness. His mother, troubled by severe depression, was institutionalized when he was six, and after his father remarried a few years later, he was sent to English schools and lost his Irish accent. MacNeice attended Marlborough, a "public" (British for private) school, and Merton College, Oxford, where his stylish appearance and seemingly idle ways misled his teachers as to his seriousness; he took a degree with distinction. Newly married, MacNeice lectured on classics at the University of Birmingham, then at Bedford College of the University of London. In 1935, his wife suddenly left him for another man, and they formally divorced the next year. Just before the outbreak of World War II, MacNeice visited and lectured in the United States. After he returned to England, he married the singer Hedli Anderson. He gave up teaching to become a writer and producer for the BBC. Finding an audience through radio, he wrote many plays in verse, including *Christopher Columbus* (1944) and *The Dark Tower* (1947), both versions of the archetypal quest, one historical, the other personal and allegorical. In August 1963, he caught pneumonia after descending into a mine to check on sound effects for a BBC program. He died just before the publication of his twentieth book of poems, *The Burning Perch.*

The early MacNeice had much in common with the group of politically committed poets whose work appeared in *New Signatures* (1932), but MacNeice was as temperamentally mistrustful of political programs as he was of philosophical systems. He was never a member of any political party, and he could be alarmingly candid about the ambiguities of his political attitudes. "My sympathies are Left," he wrote. "But not in my heart or my guts" (quoted in John Press, *Louis MacNeice,* 1965). For the skeptical MacNeice, experience is, as he writes in "Snow," "Incorrigibly plural. I peel and portion / A tangerine and spit the pips and feel / The drunkenness of things being various." In love with life's irreducible multiplicity, MacNeice also strives, with the ancient Greek philosopher Heracleitus (or Heraclitus), to embrace its flux. The pen he uses, the chair in which he sits, even the poem he is writing—all are, according to "Variation on Heraclitus," illusions of permanence, melting into something other than themselves. "An Eclogue for Christmas" concludes, "Let all these so ephemeral things, / Be somehow permanent like the swallow's tangent wings"—a curious permanence.

MacNeice exercises what he takes to be the modern poet's privilege of irresolution; he dramatizes the mind's tentative advances and questionings in poems of frank ambivalence. In a series of lectures on allegory, *Varieties of Parable* (1965), MacNeice applauds Samuel Beckett's statement that he is interested in the "shape of ideas" even if he does not believe in them. MacNeice makes his poetry out of the experience of a fallen world, without wistful glances back at an Eden of metaphysical belief or ideological certitude.

Nature Morte[1]

(Even so it is not so easy to be dead)

As those who are not athletic at breakfast day by day
Employ and enjoy the sinews of others vicariously,
Shielded by the upheld journal from their dream-puncturing wives
And finding in the printed word a multiplication of their lives,
So we whose senses give us things misfelt and misheard
Turn also, for our adjustment, to the pretentious word
Which stabilises the light on the sun-fondled trees
And, by photographing our ghosts, claims to put us at our ease;
Yet even so, no matter how solid and staid we contrive
Our reconstructions, even a still life is alive
And in your Chardin[2] the appalling unrest of the soul
Exudes from the dried fish and the brown jug and the bowl.

July 1933 1935

An Eclogue[3] for Christmas

A. I meet you in an evil time.
B. The evil bells
Put out of our heads, I think, the thought of everything else.
A. The jaded calendar revolves,
Its nuts need oil, carbon chokes the valves,
The excess sugar of a diabetic culture
Rotting the nerve of life and literature;

1. Still life; literally, dead nature (French).
2. Jean Baptiste Siméon Chardin (1699–1779), French painter of peasant life, domestic scenes, and still lifes.
3. Originally, a dialogue in verse between two shepherds.

Therefore when we bring out the old tinsel and frills
To announce that Christ is born among the barbarous hills
I turn to you whom a morose routine
Saves you from mad vertigo of being what has been.
B. Analogue of me, you are wrong to turn to me,
My country will not yield you any sanctuary,
There is no pinpoint in any of the ordnance maps
To save you when your towns and town-bred thoughts collapse,
It is better to die *in situ* as I shall,
One place is as bad as another. Go back where your instincts call
And listen to the crying of the town-cats and the taxis again,
Or wind your gramophone and eavesdrop on great men.
A. Jazz-weary of years and drums and Hawaiian guitar,
Pivoting on the parquet I seem to have moved far
From bombs and mud and gas, have stuttered on my feet
Clinched to the streamlined and butter-smooth trulls[4] of the élite,
The lights irritating and gyrating and rotating in gauze—
Pomade-dazzle, a slick beauty of gewgaws—
I who was Harlequin in the childhood of the century,
Posed by Picasso[5] beside an endless opaque sea,
Have seen myself sifted and splintered in broken facets,
Tentative pencillings, endless liabilities, no assets,
Abstractions scalpelled with a palette-knife
Without reference to this particular life.
And so it has gone on; I have not been allowed to be
Myself in flesh or face, but abstracting and dissecting me
They have made of me pure form, a symbol or a pastiche,
Stylised profile, anything but soul and flesh:
And that is why I turn this jaded music on
To forswear thought and become an automaton.
B. There are in the country also of whom I am afraid—
Men who put beer into a belly that is dead,
Women in the forties with terrier and setter who whistle and swank
Over down and plough and Roman road and daisied bank,
Half-conscious that these barriers over which they stride
Are nothing to the barbed wire that has grown round their pride.
A. And two there are, as I drive in the city, who suddenly perturb—
The one sirening me to draw up by the kerb
The other, as I lean back, my right leg stretched creating speed,
Making me catch and stamp, the brakes shrieking, pull up dead:
She wears silk stockings taunting the winter wind,
He carries a white stick to mark that he is blind.
B. In the country they are still hunting, in the heavy shires
Greyness is on the fields and sunset like a line of pyres
Of barbarous heroes smoulders through the ancient air
Hazed with factory dust and, orange opposite, the moon's glare,
Goggling yokel-stubborn through the iron trees,

4. Prostitutes.
5. Between 1904 and 1906, the Spanish expatriate artist Pablo Picasso (1881–1973) did many paintings that portray harlequins, acrobats, and the life of the traveling carnival.

Jeers at the end of us, our bland ancestral ease;
We shall go down like palaeolithic man
Before some new Ice Age or Genghiz Khan.[6]
A. It is time for some new coinage, people have got so old,
Hacked and handled and shiny from pocketing they have made bold
To think that each is himself through these accidents, being blind
To the fact that they are merely the counters of an unknown Mind.
B. A Mind that does not think, if such a thing can be,
Mechanical Reason, capricious Identity.
That I could be able to face this domination nor flinch—
A. The tin toys of the hawker move on the pavement inch by inch
Not knowing that they are wound up; it is better to be so
Than to be, like us, wound up and while running down to know—
B. But everywhere the pretence of individuality recurs—
A. Old faces frosted with powder and choked in furs.
B. The jutlipped farmer gazing over the humpbacked wall.
A. The commercial traveller joking in the urinal.
B. I think things draw to an end, the soil is stale.
A. And over-elaboration will nothing now avail,
The street is up again, gas, electricity or drains,
Ever-changing conveniences, nothing comfortable remains
Un-improved, as flagging Rome improved villa and sewer
(A sound-proof library and a stable temperature).
Our street is up, red lights sullenly mark
The long trench of pipes, iron guts in the dark,
And not till the Goths[7] again come swarming down the hill
Will cease the clangour of the pneumatic drill.
But yet there is beauty narcotic and deciduous
In this vast organism grown out of us:
On all the traffic-islands stand white globes like moons,
The city's haze is clouded amber that purrs and croons,
And tilting by the noble curve bus after tall bus comes
With an osculation[8] of yellow light, with a glory like
chrysanthemums.
B. The country gentry cannot change, they will die in their shoes
From angry circumstances and moral self-abuse,
Dying with a paltry fizzle they will prove their lives to be
An ever-diluted drug, a spiritual tautology.
They cannot live once their idols are turned out,
None of them can endure, for how could they, possibly, without
The flotsam of private property, pekinese and polyanthus,[9]
The good things which in the end turn to poison and pus,
Without the bandy chairs and the sugar in the silver tongs
And the inter-ripple and resonance of years of dinner-gongs?
Or if they could find no more that cumulative proof
In the rain dripping off the conservatory roof?
What will happen when the only sanction the country-dweller has—
A. What will happen to us, planked and panelled with jazz?

6. Mongol conqueror (1162–1227) of lands stretching from the Black Sea to the Pacific Ocean.
7. Germanic peoples who overran the Roman Empire.
8. Kiss.
9. Ornamental flower. *Pekinese:* breed of dog.

Who go the theatre where a black man dances like an eel,
Where pink thighs flash like the spokes of a wheel, where we feel
That we know in advance all the jogtrot and the cake-walk jokes,
All the bumfun and the gags of the comedians in boaters and
toques,[1]
All the tricks of the virtuosos who invert the usual—
B. What will happen to us when the State takes down the manor wall,
When there is no more private shooting or fishing, when the trees
are all cut down,
When faces are all dials and cannot smile or frown—
A. What will happen when the sniggering machine-guns in the hands
of the young men
Are trained on every flat and club and beauty parlor and Father's
den?
What will happen when our civilisation like a long-pent balloon—
B. What will happen will happen; the whore and the buffoon
Will come off best; no dreamers, they cannot lose their dream
And are at least likely to be reinstated in the new régime.
But one thing is not likely—
A. Do not gloat over yourself,
Do not be your own vulture; high on some mountain shelf
Huddle the pitiless abstractions bald about the neck
Who will descend when you crumple in the plains a wreck.
Over the randy of the theatre and cinema I hear songs
Unlike anything—
B. The lady of the house poises the silver tongs
And picks a lump of sugar, 'ne plus ultra' she says
'I cannot do otherwise even to prolong my days'—
A. I cannot do otherwise either, to-night I will book my seat—
B. I will walk about the farm-yard which is replete
As with the smell of dung so with memories—
A. I will gorge myself to satiety with the oddities
Of every artiste, official or amateur,
Who has pleased me in my rôle of hero-worshipper
Who has pleased me in my rôle of individual man—
B. Let us lie once more, say 'What we think, we can'
The old idealist lie—
A. And for me before I die
Let me go the round of the garish glare—
B. And on the bare and high
Places of England, the Wiltshire Downs and the Long Mynd[2]
Let the balls of my feet bounce on the turf, my face burn in the
wind
My eyelashes stinging in the wind, and the sheep like grey stones
Humble my human pretensions—
A. Let the saxophones and the xylophones
And the cult of every technical excellence, the miles of canvas in
the galleries
And the canvas of the rich man's yacht snapping and tacking on the
seas

1. Small caps. *Bum:* British slang for buttocks.
2. That is, Longmynd Plateau; in Shropshire, near the Welsh border. *The Wiltshire Downs:* treeless, chalk uplands in southeast England.

And the perfection of a grilled steak—
B. Let all these so ephemeral things
Be somehow permanent like the swallow's tangent wings:
Goodbye to you, this day remember is Christmas, this morn
They say, interpret it your own way, Christ is born.

December 1933 1934, 1937

Snow

The room was suddenly rich and the great bay-window was
Spawning snow and pink roses against it
Soundlessly collateral and incompatible:
World is suddener than we fancy it.

World is crazier and more of it than we think,
Incorrigibly plural. I peel and portion
A tangerine and spit the pips and feel
The drunkenness of things being various.

And the fire flames with a bubbling sound for world
Is more spiteful and gay than one supposes—
On the tongue on the eyes on the ears on the palms of one's hands—
There is more than glass between the snow and the huge roses.

January 1935 1935

Bagpipe Music

It's no go the merrygoround, it's no go the rickshaw,
All we want is a limousine and a ticket for the peepshow.
Their knickers are made of crêpe-de-chine, their shoes are made of python,
Their halls are lined with tiger rugs and their walls with heads of bison.

John MacDonald found a corpse, put it under the sofa,
Waited till it came to life and hit it with a poker,
Sold its eyes for souvenirs, sold its blood for whiskey,
Kept its bones for dumb-bells to use when he was fifty.

It's no go the Yogi-Man, it's no go Blavatsky,[3]
All we want is a bank balance and a bit of skirt in a taxi.

Annie MacDougall went to milk, caught her foot in the heather,
Woke to hear a dance record playing of Old Vienna.
It's no go your maidenheads, it's no go your culture,
All we want is a Dunlop tyre and the devil mend the puncture.

3. Madame Helena Petrovna Blavatsky (1831–1891), Russian theosophist, whose occult ideas were of much interest in 1930s Britain. The poem is set in Scotland during the Great Depression and before World War II.

The Laird o' Phelps spent Hogmanay[4] declaring he was sober,
Counted his feet to prove the fact and found he had one foot over.
Mrs. Carmichael had her fifth, looked at the job with repulsion,
Said to the midwife 'Take it away; I'm through with over production'.

It's no go the gossip column, it's no go the ceilidh,[5]
All we want is a mother's help and a sugar-stick for the baby.

Willie Murray cut his thumb, couldn't count the damage,
Took the hide of an Ayrshire cow and used it for a bandage.
His brother caught three hundred cran[6] when the seas were lavish,
Threw the bleeders back in the sea and went upon the parish.

It's no go the Herring Board,[7] it's no go the Bible,
All we want is a packet of fags[8] when our hands are idle.

It's no go the picture palace, it's no go the stadium,
It's no go the country cot[9] with a pot of pink geraniums,
It's no go the Government grants, it's no go the elections,
Sit on your arse for fifty years and hang your hat on a pension.

It's no go my honey love, it's no go my poppet;
Work your hands from day to day, the winds will blow the profit.
The glass[1] is falling hour by hour, the glass will fall for ever,
But if you break the bloody glass you won't hold up the weather.

1937

The Sunlight on the Garden

The sunlight on the garden
Hardens and grows cold,
We cannot cage the minute
Within its nets of gold,
When all is told
We cannot beg for pardon.

Our freedom as free lances
Advances towards its end;
The earth compels, upon it
Sonnets and birds descend;
And soon, my friend,
We shall have no time for dances.

The sky was good for flying
Defying the church bells
And every evil iron

4. New Year's Eve (Scots).
5. A sociable evening of singing and storytelling; pronounced *kaley*.
6. A measure of fresh herring (about 750).
7. A government agency that in the 1930s unsuccessfully tried to save the failing British herring trade.
8. Cigarettes.
9. Cottage.
1. Barometer.

Siren and what it tells:
The earth compels,
We are dying, Egypt, dying[2]

And not expecting pardon,
Hardened in heart anew,
But glad to have sat under
Thunder and rain with you,
And grateful too
For sunlight on the garden.

1937, 1938

Carrickfergus[3]

I was born in Belfast between the mountain and the gantries[4]
To the hooting of lost sirens and the clang of trams:
Thence to Smoky Carrick in County Antrim
Where the bottle-neck harbour collects the mud which jams

The little boats beneath the Norman castle,
The pier shining with lumps of crystal salt;
The Scotch Quarter was a line of residential houses
But the Irish Quarter was a slum for the blind and halt.

The brook ran yellow from the factory stinking of chlorine,
The yarn-mill called its funeral cry at noon;
Our lights looked over the lough to the lights of Bangor[5]
Under the peacock aura of a drowning moon.

The Norman walled this town against the country
To stop his ears to the yelping of his slave
And built a church in the form of a cross but denoting
The list of Christ on the cross in the angle of the nave.

I was the rector's son, born to the anglican order,
Banned for ever from the candles of the Irish poor;
The Chichesters knelt in marble at the end of a transept
With ruffs about their necks, their portion sure.[6]

The war came and a huge camp of soldiers
Grew from the ground in sight of our house with long

2. From Shakespeare's *Antony and Cleopatra,* Antony's speech to Cleopatra: "I am dying, Egypt, dying" (4.16.43).
3. A seaport in Northern Ireland, northeast of Belfast.
4. Large shipyard structures, prominent in Belfast's skyline.
5. A port across the bay from Carrickfergus. *Lough:* lake.
6. "The church was cruciform. . . . The transept on our left was on a higher level and . . . the end wall of it was occupied by a huge Elizabethan monument to the Chichester family who had then been the power in the land. The father and mother, who were each very large, knelt each under an arch, opposite each other, praying" (MacNeice, *The Strings Are False*). The Normans conquered Ireland and joined it to England about a century after the Norman conquest of England.

Dummies hanging from gibbets for bayonet practice
And the sentry's challenge echoing all day long;

A Yorkshire terrier ran in and out by the gate-lodge
Barred to civilians, yapping as if taking affront:
Marching at ease and singing 'Who Killed Cock Robin?'
The troops went out by the lodge and off to the Front.

The steamer was camouflaged that took me to England—
Sweat and khaki in the Carlisle[7] train;
I thought that the war would last for ever and sugar
Be always rationed and that never again

Would the weekly papers not have photos of sandbags
And my governess not make bandages from moss
And people not have maps above the fireplace
With flags on pins moving across and across—

Across the hawthorn hedge the noise of bugles,
Flares across the night,
Somewhere on the lough was a prison ship for Germans,
A cage across their sight.

I went to school in Dorset,[8] the world of parents
Contracted into a puppet world of sons
Far from the mill girls, the smell of porter, the salt-mines
And the soldiers with their guns.

1937 1938

Brother Fire[9]

When our brother Fire was having his dog's day
Jumping the London streets with millions of tin cans
Clanking at his tail, we heard some shadow say
'Give the dog a bone'—and so we gave him ours;
Night after night we watched him slaver and crunch away
The beams of human life, the tops of topless towers.

Which gluttony of his for us was Lenten fare[1]
Who mother-naked, suckled with sparks, were chill
Though cotted in a grille of sizzling air
Striped like a convict—black, yellow and red;
Thus were we weaned to knowledge of the Will
That wills the natural world but wills us dead.

7. A city in Cumberland, just south of the Scottish border.
8. MacNeice spent his boyhood in Northern Ireland and was sent to school in southwest England.
9. "Praise to Thee, my Lord, for Brother Fire, by whom Thou lightest the night; He is lovely and pleasant, mighty and strong" (St. Francis of Assisi, "The Song of Brother Sun and of All Creatures"). The occasion for the poem is the German bombing raids on London during World War II.
1. Diet appropriate for Lent; that is, meager fare.

O delicate walker, babbler, dialectician Fire,
O enemy and image of ourselves,
Did we not on those mornings after the All Clear,
When you were looting shops in elemental joy
And singing as you swarmed up city block and spire,
Echo your thought in ours? 'Destroy! Destroy!'

1943, 1944

The Libertine

In the old days with married women's stockings
Twisted round his bedpost he felt himself a gay
Dog but now his liver has begun to groan,
Now that pick-ups are the order of the day:
O leave me easy, leave me alone.

Voluptuary in his 'teens and cynic in his twenties,
He ran through women like a child through growing hay
Looking for a lost toy whose capture might atone
For his own guilt and the cosmic disarray:
O leave me easy, leave me alone.

He never found the toy and has forgotten the faces,
Only remembers the props . . . a scent-spray
Beside the bed or a milk-white telephone
Or through the triple ninon[2] the acrid trickle of day:
O leave me easy, leave me alone.

Long fingers over the gunwale, hair in a hair-net,
Furs in January, cartwheel hats in May,
And after the event the wish to be alone—
Angels, goddesses, bitches, all have edged away:
O leave me easy, leave me alone.

So now, in middle age, his erotic programme
Torn in two, if after such a delay
An accident should offer him his own
Fulfillment in a woman, still he would say:
O leave me easy, leave me alone.

1943 1944

2. Light, semitransparent silk.

Variation on Heraclitus[3]

Even the walls are flowing, even the ceiling,
Nor only in terms of physics; the pictures
Bob on each picture rail like floats on a line
While the books on the shelves keep reeling
Their titles out into space and the carpet
Keeps flying away to Arabia nor can this be where I stood—
Where I shot the rapids I mean—when I signed
On a line that rippled away with a pen that melted
Nor can this now be the chair—the chairoplane of a chair—
That I sat in the day that I thought I had made up my mind
And as for that standard lamp it too keeps waltzing away
Down an unbridgeable Ganges[4] where nothing is standard
And lights are but lit to be drowned in honour and spite of some dark
And vanishing goddess. No, whatever you say,
Reappearance presumes disappearance, it may not be nice
Or proper or easily analysed not to be static
But none of your slide snide rules can catch what is sliding so fast
And, all you advisers on this by the time it is that,
I just do not want your advice
Nor need you be troubled to pin me down in my room
Since the room and I will escape for I tell you flat:
One cannot live in the same room twice.

1961

Charon[5]

The conductor's hands were black with money:
Hold on to your ticket, he said, the inspector's
Mind is black with suspicion, and hold on to
That dissolving map. We moved through London,
We could see the pigeons through the glass but failed
To hear their rumours of wars, we could see
The lost dog barking but never knew
That his bark was as shrill as a cock crowing,
We just jogged on, at each request
Stop there was a crowd of aggressively vacant
Faces, we just jogged on, eternity
Gave itself airs in revolving lights
And then we came to the Thames[6] and all
The bridges were down, the further shore
Was lost in fog, so we asked the conductor

3. Heracleitus (c. 540–c. 480 B.C.E.), Greek philosopher, known for his aphorisms on mutability such as "All is flux; nothing stands still"; "It is not possible to step twice into the same river"; "Nothing endures but change."

4. Major river in India.

5. In Greek mythology, the boatman who ferries dead souls into Hades, for the price of one obol each.

6. Major river.

What we should do. He said: Take the ferry
Faute de mieux.[7] We flicked the flashlight
And there was the ferryman just as Virgil
And Dante[8] had seen him. He looked at us coldly
And his eyes were dead and his hands on the oar
Were black with obols and varicose veins
Marbled his calves and he said to us coldly:
If you want to die you will have to pay for it.

1962, 1963

7. For want of anything better (French).
8. Italian poet (1261–1321). Cf. his *Inferno* and book 6 of Roman poet Virgil's *Aeneid.*

George Oppen
1908–1984

Two of George Oppen's epigraphs encapsulate fundamental assumptions of his poetry. From philosopher Jacques Maritain he quotes: "We awake in the same moment to ourselves and to things." From philosopher Martin Heidegger, whose thought influenced Oppen's work, he takes the phrase "the arduous path of appearance." Oppen's poetry presents a mind in stark encounter with the world. "That they are there!" he exclaims of the deer seen in the poem "Psalm." Careful not to enshroud the deer with sentiment or dogma, the awed poet tries to see them in their thereness, in what Heidegger calls the sheer "presence of the thing": their "alien small teeth / Tear at the grass." To see the world in its fresh appearance, its stubborn otherness, its physicality, requires arduous effort. The poet must try, Oppen states in a letter of December 21, 1962, "to write carefully, lucidly, accurately, resisting the temptation to inflate." "If it's perfect," he said in an interview published in 1985, "you're not in it at all." One of the leading Objectivists, Oppen recognized his debt to Ezra Pound's Imagism: "What I felt I was doing was beginning from imagism as a position of honesty" (1968 interview). His version of Objectivist self-effacement can be contrasted with other varieties of modern and contemporary poetry—for example, late Romantic, symbolist, confessional—that dramatize personal experience or that metaphorize or mythify the self and the world. While a poet can, Oppen writes in "The Mind's Own Place," "find a metaphor for anything," "the image is encountered," and this, for Oppen, is the core of "modernism": "the sense of the poet's self among things," or, as fellow Objectivist Louis Zukofsky put it, "thinking with the things as they exist" (*Prepositions*).

In Oppen's Objectivism, the poem is, like the world, "objectified"—treated, that is, as a constructed object, not an overflow of the author's feelings. Oppen constructs his poems out of a spare, unornamented diction, each simple word given weight. "I'm really concerned with the substantive," he said in a 1968 interview, "with the subject of the sentence, with what we are talking about, and not rushing over the subject matter in order to make a comment about it." The poet's obligation is "to notice, to state, to lay down the substantive for its own sake." Relying on forms of the verb *to be* and using few finite verbs, Oppen distills images and perceptions, which appear in disjointed fragments, frozen out of time, their movement marmoreal. Austere and restrained, his severely economical poetry dispenses with internal explanation and can thus become opaque and riddling.

With punctuation minimized and description compressed, the syntax can often be read in more than one way. Semantic units (phrases, clauses, lines) sometimes seem stranded among the silent, blank spaces on the page. Rhythms are irregular and unmusical. Quietly imbedded forms of sonic repetition, such as assonance, consonance, alliteration, and rhyme, discretely connect words and lines across the discontinuities of image and syntax. Similarly, parts of a long sequence are tenuously related, as in *Of Being Numerous* (1968), Oppen's Pulitzer Prize–winning meditation on the relation between the isolated, "shipwrecked" individual and the "numerous" collectivity.

Pound hailed Oppen as a "serious craftsman," in the preface to the Objectivist's first book, *Discrete Series* (1934). Although Pound, like Heidegger, held fascist and anti-Semitic views, Oppen was a left-wing Jew, becoming an organizer for the American Communist Party during the Depression (1935–41). He was born with the name Oppenheimer on April 24, 1908, in New Rochelle, New York, and though his family had considerable wealth, he made his living as a switchboard operator, carpenter, cabinetmaker, tool-and-die maker, and mechanic. In 1928, he met the other two principal proponents of what would become known as Objectivism, Louis Zukofsky and Charles Reznikoff, and in the early 1930s, he established a press dedicated to publishing their work. During the Depression, he abandoned poetry and publishing for politics, not believing that poetry could rectify social conditions and disliking politically doctrinal poetry, which he saw as hobbled by predetermined views and slogans. "If you write poetry," he said, "you write poetry, not something you hope, or deceive yourself into believing, can save people who are suffering" (1968 interview). He did not write again for twenty-five years. Serving in an antitank company during World War II, Oppen was wounded in 1945 and awarded the Purple Heart. In 1950, he came under investigation by Senator Joseph McCarthy's Committee on Un-American Activities. To avoid betraying friends or serving in prison, Oppen moved with his family to Mexico City, where for eight years he oversaw the making of furniture. Once he and his wife, Mary, returned to the United States, he took up poetry again and began to build a wider reputation. Like Zukofsky and Reznikoff, he is a strong link between first-generation modernists such as Pound and the later avant-gardes of the Black Mountain school and the Language poets.

Solution

The puzzle assembled
At last in the box lid showing a green
Hillside, a house,
A barn and man
And wife and children,
All of it polychrome,
Lucid, backed by the blue
Sky. The jigsaw of cracks
Crazes the landscape but there is no gap,
No actual edged hole
Nowhere the wooden texture of the table top
Glares out of scale in the picture,
Sordid as cellars, as bare foundations:
There is no piece missing. The puzzle is complete
Now in its red and green and brown.

1962

From Disaster

Ultimately the air
Is bare sunlight where must be found
The lyric valuables. From disaster

Shipwreck, whole families crawled
To the tenements, and there

Survived by what morality
Of hope

Which for the sons
Ends its metaphysic
In small lawns of home.

1962

Survival: Infantry[1]

And the world changed.
There had been trees and people,
Sidewalks and roads

There were fish in the sea.

Where did all the rocks come from?
And the smell of explosives
Iron standing in mud
We crawled everywhere on the ground without seeing the earth again

We were ashamed of our half life and our misery: we saw that everything
had died.

And the letters came. People who addressed us thru our lives
They left us gasping. And in tears
In the same mud in the terrible ground

1962

Pedestrian

What generations could have dreamed
This grandchild of the shopping streets, her eyes

In the buyer's light, the store lights
Brighter than the lighthouses, brighter than moonrise

1. Oppen served in the U.S. Army in Europe from 1944 to 1945. On April 22, 1945, he was seriously wounded by German artillery fire.

From the salt harbor so rich
So bright her city

In a soil of pavement, a mesh of wires where she walks
In the new winter among enormous buildings.

1962

Psalm

Veritas sequitur . . . [2]

In the small beauty of the forest
The wild deer bedding down—
That they are there!

Their eyes
Effortless, the soft lips
Nuzzle and the alien small teeth
Tear at the grass

The roots of it
Dangle from their mouths
Scattering earth in the strange woods.
They who are there.

Their paths
Nibbled thru the fields, the leaves that shade them
Hang in the distances
Of sun

The small nouns
Crying faith
In this in which the wild deer
Startle, and stare out.

1965

From Of Being Numerous

1

There are things
We live among 'and to see them
Is to know ourselves'.[3]

2. From Saint Thomas Aquinas: "*Veritas sequitur esse rerum*" (Truth follows the existence of things).-

3. From Robert S. Brumbaugh's *Plato for the Modern Age* (1962).

Occurrence, a part
Of an infinite series,

The sad marvels;

Of this was told
A tale of our wickedness.
It is not our wickedness.

'You remember that old town we went to, and we sat in the ruined window, and we tried to imagine that we belonged to those times—It is dead and it is not dead, and you cannot imagine either its life or its death; the earth speaks and the salamander speaks, the Spring comes and only obscures it—'[4]

2

So spoke of the existence of things,
An unmanageable pantheon.

Absolute, but they say
Arid

A city of the corporations

Glassed
In dreams

And images—

And the pure joy
Of the mineral fact

Tho it is impenetrable

As the world, if it is matter,
Is impenetrable.

3

The emotions are engaged
Entering the city
As entering any city.

We are not coeval
With a locality
But we imagine others are,

4. In a letter, Oppen writes that "the long quotes in the first section [of *Of Being Numerous*] are Mary, verbatim, telling me about Bonnefoy." Oppen's wife was describing the French writer Yves Bonnefoy's *Du mouvement et de l'immobilité de Douve* (1959).

We encounter them. Actually
A populace flows
Thru the city.

This is a language, therefore, of New York

4

For the people of that flow
Are new, the old

New to age as the young
To youth

And to their dwelling
For which the tarred roofs

And the stoops and doors—
A world of stoops—
Are petty alibi and satirical wit
Will not serve.

5

The great stone
Above the river
In the pylon of the bridge[5]

'1875'

Frozen in the moonlight
In the frozen air over the footpath, consciousness

Which has nothing to gain, which awaits nothing,
Which loves itself

6

We are pressed, pressed on each other,
We will be told at once
Of anything that happens

And the discovery of fact bursts
In a paroxysm of emotion
Now as always. Crusoe[6]

5. The Brooklyn Bridge was constructed from 1869 to 1883.
6. Robinson Crusoe, the shipwrecked man in Daniel Defoe's 1719 novel, is a recurrent image in this and other of Oppen's poems.

We say was
'Rescued'.
So we have chosen.

7

Obsessed, bewildered

By the shipwreck
Of the singular

We have chosen the meaning
Of being numerous.

8

Amor fati
The love of fate[7]

For which the city alone
Is audience

Perhaps blasphemous

Slowly over islands, destinies
Moving steadily pass
And change

In the thin sky
Over islands

Among days

Having only the force
Of days

Most simple
Most difficult

9

'Whether, as the intensity of seeing increases, one's distance from Them, the people, does not also increase'[8]
I know, of course I know, I can enter no other place

7. Translation of the Latin phrase, from *Ecce Homo*, by German philosopher Friedrich Nietzsche (1844–1900).

8. From a 1968 letter to Oppen by American poet and critic Rachel Blau DuPlessis (b. 1941).

Yet I am one of those who from nothing but man's way of thought and one of his dialects and what has happened to me
Have made poetry

To dream of that beach
For the sake of an instant in the eyes,

The absolute singular

The unearthly bonds
Of the singular

Which is the bright light of shipwreck

18

It is the air of atrocity,
An event as ordinary
As a President.

A plume of smoke, visible at a distance
In which people burn.[9]

19

Now in the helicopters the casual will
Is atrocious

Insanity in high places,
If it is true we must do these things
We must cut our throats

The fly in the bottle[1]

Insane, the insane fly

Which, over the city
Is the bright light of shipwreck

1968

9. These and the following stanzas evoke the Vietnam War.
1. Cf. "What is your aim in philosophy?—To shew the fly the way out of the fly-bottle," in *The Philosophical Investigations* (1953), by Austrian philosopher Ludwig Wittgenstein (1889–1951).

Theodore Roethke
1908–1963

For Theodore Roethke, nature was a vast psychic landscape. Some parts of it were projections of his feelings, some transcended the human. Roethke's authority for making nature a parable came from his love and intensive study of it. He traced this interest to his grandfather, once Prussian chancellor Bismarck's chief forester, who emigrated from Prussia in 1872 and, with his sons, started some greenhouses in Saginaw, Michigan. These greenhouses, which dwarfed Roethke's home, were dismantled and sold shortly before his father died, of cancer, when Roethke was fourteen. (Roethke's conflicted feelings toward his lost father are evident in two of his best poems, the elegy "My Papa's Waltz" and the formally inventive sequence "The Lost Son.") The greenhouse, Roethke wrote in the prose piece "Open Letter," "is . . . my symbol for the whole of life, a womb, a heaven-on-earth." He always felt close to elemental processes and to inanimate as well as animate objects: "I could say hello to things." He studies the lives on a leaf in "The Minimal," and he declares in "A Field of Light" that he can see, suddenly, "the separateness of all things!"

His sense of participation in nature makes for some of Roethke's most extreme, and yet most convincing, effects. "I lose and find myself in the long waters," he writes. Changing elements, he remarks, "I live in air; the long light is my home"; this line, from "Her Becoming," suggests his affinity with Dylan Thomas's mystic naturalism. Participation is only a short step from transcendence: "I'm wet with another life"—or, as he writes in "Snake": "I longed to be that thing, / The pure, sensuous form. / And I may be, some time." Roethke referred in prose to his "genuine love of nature," his instinctive sense of the "moods of nature," and the strong influence over him of "natural objects" ("Some Self-Analysis"). He is not blinded by sentimental feelings about nature, however, seeing it as malign as well as benign. In "The Pit," he warns, "Beware Mother Mildew"; in "The Pure Fury," a poem that expresses the "ferocity" Stanley Kunitz found in Roethke's poems, he confides, "I live near the abyss." He is less euphoric about nature than D. H. Lawrence. His language for nature—"sheath-wet," "slippery," "sucking," "sleek"—often carries erotic overtones, sometimes dark ones; by the end of "Weed Puller," the speaker is "Alive, in a slippery grave."

Roethke was six feet two and weighed over two hundred twenty-five pounds, but he moves in his verse with great delicacy, whether writing in intricate meters and stanza forms or in free verse. Though he was a tormented man, frantic for fame, a prey to breakdowns and alcoholism, he presented himself in his verse as a naïf. He had, as he insisted in "Some Self-Analysis," "a driving sincerity,—that prime virtue of any creative worker. I write only what I believe to be the absolute truth,—even if I must ruin the theme in so doing." The sense of a fragile self in a swollen body is pervasive. It reflects a "struggle for personal identity" ("The Teaching Poet"). He longs for the purity that he sees in William Blake and, at times, in nature. Nature can represent or, like poetry, expand consciousness.

Roethke was born on May 25, 1908, in Saginaw. He went to the University of Michigan (A.B., 1929; M.A., 1936) and took some graduate courses at Harvard University. He taught at several colleges and universities, lending his time generously to his students, who included James Wright and David Wagoner. His longest and last post, from 1947, was at the University of Washington, where his sporadic breakdowns were tolerated. His first book, *Open House* (1941), won Roethke considerable attention, but he longed for more recognition and was humbly eager to improve his verse. He wrote little but with great care. His slender collected poems appeared under the title *Words for the*

Wind in 1957. He won the Pulitzer Prize in 1954, the Bollingen Prize in 1959, and the National Book Award in 1959 and posthumously in 1965.

Sometimes, Roethke is boisterous and funny—he was able to write good children's poems—but he is fundamentally serious and intent. In a letter, he traced his lineage to Ralph Waldo Emerson, Henry David Thoreau, Walt Whitman, William Blake, William Wordsworth, and Henry Vaughan. He belongs with this company in his visionary intertwining of his spiritual self with leaves, water, light, and lower creatures. In elegiac poems, he plumbs his psychic ambivalence toward his parents and breaks with the impersonal allusiveness of T. S. Eliot and the New Critics. His verse explorations of vexed childhood memory influenced "confessional" poets such as Sylvia Plath; his lyric internalization of nature had an impact on poets such as James Dickey, Charles Wright, and Seamus Heaney.

Cuttings

Sticks-in-a-drowse droop over sugary loam,
Their intricate stem-fur dries;
But still the delicate slips keep coaxing up water;
The small cells bulge;

One nub of growth
Nudges a sand-crumb loose,
Pokes through a musty sheath
Its pale tendrilous horn.

1948

Cuttings

(later)

This urge, wrestle, resurrection of dry sticks,
Cut stems struggling to put down feet,
What saint strained so much,
Rose on such lopped limbs to a new life?

I can hear, underground, that sucking and sobbing,
In my veins, in my bones I feel it,—
The small waters seeping upward,
The tight grains parting at last.
When sprouts break out,
Slippery as fish,
I quail, lean to beginnings, sheath-wet.

1948

Weed Puller

Under the concrete benches,
Hacking at black hairy roots,—
Those lewd monkey-tails hanging from drainholes,—
Digging into the soft rubble underneath,
Webs and weeds,
Grubs and snails and sharp sticks,
Or yanking tough fern-shapes,
Coiled green and thick, like dripping smilax,[1]
Tugging all day at perverse life:
The indignity of it!—
With everything blooming above me,
Lilies, pale-pink cyclamen, roses,
Whole fields lovely and inviolate,—
Me down in that fetor of weeds,
Crawling on all fours,
Alive, in a slippery grave.

1948

My Papa's Waltz

The whiskey on your breath
Could make a small boy dizzy;
But I hung on like death:
Such waltzing was not easy.

We romped until the pans
Slid from the kitchen shelf;
My mother's countenance
Could not unfrown itself.

The hand that held my wrist
Was battered on one knuckle;
At every step you missed
My right ear scraped a buckle.

You beat time on my head
With a palm caked hard by dirt,
Then waltzed me off to bed
Still clinging to your shirt.

1948

1. Kind of vine.

Dolor

I have known the inexorable sadness of pencils,
Neat in their boxes, dolor of pad and paper-weight,
All the misery of manilla folders and mucilage,
Desolation in immaculate public places,
Lonely reception room, lavatory, switchboard,
The unalterable pathos of basin and pitcher,
Ritual of multigraph, paper-clip, comma,
Endless duplication of lives and objects.
And I have seen dust from the walls of institutions,
Finer than flour, alive, more dangerous than silica,
Sift, almost invisible, through long afternoons of tedium,
Dropping a fine film on nails and delicate eyebrows,
Glazing the pale hair, the duplicate grey standard faces.

1948

The Minimal

I study the lives on a leaf: the little
Sleepers, numb nudgers in cold dimensions,
Beetles in caves, newts, stone-deaf fishes,
Lice tethered to long limp subterranean weeds,
Squirmers in bogs,
And bacterial creepers
Wriggling through wounds
Like elvers[2] in ponds,
Their wan mouths kissing the warm sutures,[3]
Cleaning and caressing,
Creeping and healing.

1948

The Lost Son

1. The Flight

At Woodlawn[4] I heard the dead cry:
I was lulled by the slamming of iron,
A slow drip over stones,
Toads brooding wells.
All the leaves stuck out their tongues;
I shook the softening chalk of my bones,
Saying,
Snail, snail, glister me forward,
Bird, soft-sigh me home,

2. Small eels.
3. Threads that tie the edges of a wound together.
4. Cemetery in New York City where Roethke's father was buried.

Worm, be with me.
This is my hard time.

Fished in an old wound,
The soft pond of repose;
Nothing nibbled my line,
Not even the minnows came.

Sat in an empty house
Watching shadows crawl,
Scratching.
There was one fly.

Voice, come out of the silence.
Say something.
Appear in the form of a spider
Or a moth beating the curtain.

Tell me:
Which is the way I take;
Out of what door do I go,
Where and to whom?

    Dark hollows said, lee to the wind,
    The moon said, back of an eel,
    The salt said, look by the sea,
    Your tears are not enough praise,
    You will find no comfort here,
    In the kingdom of bang and blab.

    Running lightly over spongy ground,
    Past the pasture of flat stones,
    The three elms,
    The sheep strewn on a field,
    Over a rickety bridge
    Toward the quick-water, wrinkling and rippling.

    Hunting along the river,
    Down among the rubbish, the bug-riddled foliage,
    By the muddy pond-edge, by the bog-holes,
    By the shrunken lake, hunting, in the heat of summer.

The shape of a rat?
        It's bigger than that.
        It's less than a leg
        And more than a nose,
        Just under the water
        It usually goes.

    Is it soft like a mouse?
    Can it wrinkle its nose?
    Could it come in the house
    On the tips of its toes?

Take the skin of a cat
And the back of an eel,
Then roll them in grease,—
That's the way it would feel.

It's sleek as an otter
With wide webby toes
Just under the water
It usually goes.

2. *The Pit*

Where do the roots go?
Look down under the leaves.
Who put the moss there?
These stones have been here too long.
Who stunned the dirt into noise?
Ask the mole, he knows.
I feel the slime of a wet nest.
Beware Mother Mildew.
Nibble again, fish nerves.

3. *The Gibber*[5]

At the wood's mouth,
By the cave's door,
I listened to something
I had heard before.

Dogs of the groin
Barked and howled,
The sun was against me,
The moon would not have me.

The weeds whined,
The snakes cried,
The cows and briars
Said to me: Die.

What a small song. What slow clouds. What dark water.
Hath the rain a father? All the caves are ice. Only the snow's here.
I'm cold. I'm cold all over. Rub me in father and mother.
Fear was my father, Father Fear.
His look drained the stones.

What gliding shape
Beckoning through halls,
Stood poised on the stair,
Fell dreamily down?

5. Nonsense speech; also, pouch at the base of a flower's calyx.

From the mouths of jugs
Perched on many shelves,
I saw substance flowing
That cold morning.

Like a slither of eels
That watery cheek
As my own tongue kissed
My lips awake.

Is this the storm's heart? The ground is unstilling itself.
My veins are running nowhere. Do the bones cast out their fire?
Is the seed leaving the old bed? These buds are live as birds.
Where, where are the tears of the world?
Let the kisses resound, flat like a butcher's palm;
Let the gestures freeze; our doom is already decided.
All the windows are burning! What's left of my life?
I want the old rage, the lash of primordial milk!
Goodbye, goodbye, old stones, the time-order is going,
I have married my hands to perpetual agitation,
I run, I run to the whistle of money.

Money money money
Water water water

How cool the grass is.
Has the bird left?
The stalk still sways.
Has the worm a shadow?
What do the clouds say?

These sweeps of light undo me.
Look, look, the ditch is running white!
I've more veins than a tree!
Kiss me, ashes, I'm falling through a dark swirl.

4. *The Return*

The way to the boiler was dark,
Dark all the way,
Over slippery cinders
Through the long greenhouse.

The roses kept breathing in the dark.
They had many mouths to breathe with.
My knees made little winds underneath
Where the weeds slept.

There was always a single light
Swinging by the fire-pit,
Where the fireman pulled out roses,
The big roses, the big bloody clinkers.

Once I stayed all night.
The light in the morning came slowly over the white
Snow.
There were many kinds of cool
Air.
Then came steam.

Pipe-knock.

Scurry of warm over small plants.
Ordnung! ordnung![6]
Papa is coming!

A fine haze moved off the leaves;
Frost melted on far panes;
The rose, the chrysanthemum turned toward the light.
Even the hushed forms, the bent yellowy weeds
Moved in a slow up-sway.

5. *"It was beginning winter"*

It was beginning winter,
An in-between time,
The landscape still partly brown:
The bones of weeds kept swinging in the wind,
Above the blue snow.

It was beginning winter,
The light moved slowly over the frozen field,
Over the dry seed-crowns,
The beautiful surviving bones
Swinging in the wind.

Light traveled over the wide field;
Stayed.
The weeds stopped swinging.
The mind moved, not alone,
Through the clear air, in the silence.

Was it light?
Was it light within?
Was it light within light?
Stillness becoming alive,
Yet still?

A lively understandable spirit
Once entertained you.
It will come again.
Be still.
Wait.

1948

6. Order (German).

Elegy for Jane

My Student, Thrown by a Horse

I remember the neckcurls, limp and damp as tendrils;
And her quick look, a sidelong pickerel smile;
And how, once startled into talk, the light syllables leaped for her,
And she balanced in the delight of her thought,
A wren, happy, tail into the wind,
Her song trembling the twigs and small branches.
The shade sang with her;
The leaves, their whispers turned to kissing;
And the mold sang in the bleached valleys under the rose.

Oh, when she was sad, she cast herself down into such a pure depth,
Even a father could not find her:
Scraping her cheek against straw;
Stirring the clearest water.

My sparrow, you are not here,
Waiting like a fern, making a spiny shadow.
The sides of wet stones cannot console me,
Nor the moss, wound with the last light.

If only I could nudge you from this sleep,
My maimed darling, my skittery pigeon.
Over this damp grave I speak the words of my love:
I, with no rights in this matter,
Neither father nor lover.

1953

The Waking

I wake to sleep, and take my waking slow.
I feel my fate in what I cannot fear.
I learn by going where I have to go.

We think by feeling. What is there to know?
I hear my being dance from ear to ear.
I wake to sleep, and take my waking slow.

Of those so close beside me, which are you?
God bless the Ground! I shall walk softly there,
And learn by going where I have to go.

Light takes the Tree; but who can tell us how?
The lowly worm climbs up a winding stair;
I wake to sleep, and take my waking slow.

Great Nature has another thing to do
To you and me; so take the lively air,
And, lovely, learn by going where to go.

This shaking keeps me steady. I should know.
What falls away is always. And is near.
I wake to sleep, and take my waking slow.
I learn by going where I have to go.

1953

Frau Bauman, Frau Schmidt, and Frau Schwartze[7]

Gone the three ancient ladies
Who creaked on the greenhouse ladders,
Reaching up white strings
To wind, to wind
The sweet-pea tendrils, the smilax,
Nasturtiums, the climbing
Roses, to straighten
Carnations, red
Chrysanthemums; the stiff
Stems, jointed like corn,
They tied and tucked,—
These nurses of nobody else.
Quicker than birds, they dipped
Up and sifted the dirt;
They sprinkled and shook;
They stood astride pipes,
Their skirts billowing out wide into tents,
Their hands twinkling with wet;
Like witches they flew along rows
Keeping creation at ease;
With a tendril for needle
They sewed up the air with a stem;
They teased out the seed that the cold kept asleep,—
All the coils, loops, and whorls.
They trellised the sun; they plotted for more than themselves.

I remember how they picked me up, a spindly kid,
Pinching and poking my thin ribs
Till I lay in their laps, laughing,
Weak as a whiffet;[8]
Now, when I'm alone and cold in my bed,
They still hover over me,
These ancient leathery crones,
With their bandannas stiffened with sweat,

7. Three women who worked in the greenhouses kept by Roethke's father.

8. Small, young, or unimportant person (probably from *whippet*, a small dog).

And their thorn-bitten wrists,
And their snuff-laden breath blowing lightly over me in my first sleep.

1953

I Knew a Woman

I knew a woman, lovely in her bones,
When small birds sighed, she would sigh back at them;
Ah, when she moved, she moved more ways than one:
The shapes a bright container can contain!
Of her choice virtues only gods should speak,
Or English poets who grew up on Greek
(I'd have them sing in chorus, cheek to cheek).

How well her wishes went! She stroked my chin,
She taught me Turn, and Counter-turn, and Stand;[9]
She taught me Touch, that undulant white skin;
I nibbled meekly from her proffered hand;
She was the sickle; I, poor I, the rake,
Coming behind her for her pretty sake
(But what prodigious mowing we did make).

Love likes a gander, and adores a goose:
Her full lips pursed, the errant note to seize;
She played it quick, she played it light and loose;
My eyes, they dazzled at her flowing knees;
Her several parts could keep a pure repose,
Or one hip quiver with a mobile nose
(She moved in circles, and those circles moved).

Let seed be grass, and grass turn into hay:
I'm martyr to a motion not my own;
What's freedom for? To know eternity.
I swear she cast a shadow white as stone.
But who would count eternity in days?
These old bones live to learn her wanton ways:
(I measure time by how a body sways).

1958

Wish for a Young Wife

My lizard, my lively writher,
May your limbs never wither,
May the eyes in your face

9. The three parts of the Pindaric ode (in Greek, *strophe, antistrophe,* and *epode*).

Survive the green ice
Of envy's mean gaze;
May you live out your life
Without hate, without grief,
And your hair ever blaze,
In the sun, in the sun,
When I am undone,
When I am no one.

1964

The Far Field[1]

1

I dream of journeys repeatedly:
Of flying like a bat deep into a narrowing tunnel,
Of driving alone, without luggage, out a long peninsula,
The road lined with snow-laden second growth,
A fine dry snow ticking the windshield,
Alternate snow and sleet, no on-coming traffic,
And no lights behind, in the blurred side-mirror,
The road changing from glazed tarface to a rubble of stone,
Ending at last in a hopeless sand-rut,
Where the car stalls,
Churning in a snowdrift
Until the headlights darken.

2

At the field's end, in the corner missed by the mower,
Where the turf drops off into a grass-hidden culvert,
Haunt of the cat-bird, nesting-place of the field-mouse,
Not too far away from the ever-changing flower-dump,
Among the tin cans, tires, rusted pipes, broken machinery,—
One learned of the eternal;
And in the shrunken face of a dead rat, eaten by rain and ground-beetles
(I found it lying among the rubble of an old coal bin)
And the tom-cat, caught near the pheasant-run,
Its entrails strewn over the half-grown flowers,
Blasted to death by the night watchman.

I suffered for birds, for young rabbits caught in the mower,
My grief was not excessive.
For to come upon warblers in early May
Was to forget time and death:
How they filled the oriole's elm, a twittering restless cloud, all one
 morning,

1. The next to last of six poems that comprise "North American Sequence" in Roethke's final book, *The Far Field* (1964).

And I watched and watched till my eyes blurred from the bird shapes,—
Cape May, Blackburnian, Cerulean,—[2]
Moving, elusive as fish, fearless,
Hanging, bunched like young fruit, bending the end branches,
Still for a moment,
Then pitching away in half-flight,
Lighter than finches,
While the wrens bickered and sang in the half-green hedgerows,
And the flicker drummed from his dead tree in the chicken-yard.

—Or to lie naked in sand,
In the silted shallows of a slow river,
Fingering a shell,
Thinking:
Once I was something like this, mindless,
Or perhaps with another mind, less peculiar;
Or to sink down to the hips in a mossy quagmire;
Or, with skinny knees, to sit astride a wet log,
Believing:
I'll return again,
As a snake or a raucous bird,
Or, with luck, as a lion.

I learned not to fear infinity,
The far field, the windy cliffs of forever,
The dying of time in the white light of tomorrow,
The wheel turning away from itself,
The sprawl of the wave,
The on-coming water.

3

The river turns on itself,
The tree retreats into its own shadow.
I feel a weightless change, a moving forward
As of water quickening before a narrowing channel
When banks converge, and the wide river whitens;
Or when two rivers combine, the blue glacial torrent
And the yellowish-green from the mountainy upland,—
At first a swift rippling between rocks,
Then a long running over flat stones
Before descending to the alluvial plain,
To the clay banks, and the wild grapes hanging from the elmtrees,
The slightly trembling water
Dropping a fine yellow silt where the sun stays;
And the crabs bask near the edge,
The weedy edge, alive with small snakes and bloodsuckers,—
I have come to a still, but not a deep center,
A point outside the glittering current;

2. Kinds of warbler.

My eyes stare at the bottom of a river,
At the irregular stones, iridescent sandgrains,
My mind moves in more than one place,
In a country half-land, half-water.

I am renewed by death, thought of my death,
The dry scent of a dying garden in September,
The wind fanning the ash of a low fire.
What I love is near at hand,
Always, in earth and air.

4

The lost self changes,
Turning toward the sea,
A sea-shape turning around,—
An old man with his feet before the fire,
In robes of green, in garments of adieu.

A man faced with his own immensity
Wakes all the waves, all their loose wandering fire.
The murmur of the absolute, the why
Of being born fails on his naked ears.
His spirit moves like monumental wind
That gentles on a sunny blue plateau.
He is the end of things, the final man.

All finite things reveal infinitude:
The mountain with its singular bright shade
Like the blue shine on freshly frozen snow,
The after-light upon ice-burdened pines;
Odor of basswood on a mountain-slope,
A scent beloved of bees;
Silence of water above a sunken tree:
The pure serene of memory in one man,—
A ripple widening from a single stone
Winding around the waters of the world.

1964

In a Dark Time

In a dark time, the eye begins to see,
I meet my shadow in the deepening shade,
I hear my echo in the echoing wood—
A lord of nature weeping to a tree.
I live between the heron and the wren,[3]
Beasts of the hill and serpents of the den.

3. The heron is solitary, the wren sociable, among other differences.

What's madness but nobility of soul
At odds with circumstance? The day's on fire!
I know the purity of pure despair,
My shadow pinned against a sweating wall.
That place among the rocks—is it a cave,
Or winding path? The edge is what I have.

A steady storm of correspondences!
A night flowing with birds, a ragged moon,
And in broad day the midnight come again!
A man goes far to find out what he is—
Death of the self in a long, tearless night,
All natural shapes blazing unnatural light.

Dark, dark my light, and darker my desire.
My soul, like some heat-maddened summer fly,
Keeps buzzing at the sill. Which I is *I*?
A fallen man, I climb out of my fear.
The mind enters itself, and God the mind,
And one is One, free in the tearing wind.

1964

STEPHEN SPENDER
1909–1995

Some poets, such as W. H. Auden, present themselves as assured masters of their medium and of their world. Stephen Spender, Auden's longtime associate, tends instead toward incertitude or even bewilderment, not conclusiveness. He is a poet "without that one clear aim," as he says in one of his poems. In the introduction to his 1955 *Collected Poems,* Spender remarks that "with poetry one is less sure than with anything else." He is speaking primarily of craft, but unsureness is the ground on which he built his "faceted crystal" constructions. Tenuous and unresolved, his poems are repeated efforts—perhaps heroic in their kind—to make firm the infirm, to grip, without idealization, the possible. "Never being, but always at the edge of being," he writes. Adapting the Romantic lyric to modern settings, his verse has at its center his aroused, suffering consciousness; but he is not self-flattering, and with relentless severity he exposes what may be "corrupt, insubstantial" in himself.

Spender is much harder on himself than on others: "I think continually of those who were truly great," he writes in a famous poem. In an early critical book, *The Destructive Element* (1935), he salutes those writers who boldly encountered the destructive element, that is, "an all-pervading Present, which is a world without belief." Spender's obvious delight was in men of force and conviction. Yet his own heroism was delicate and vulnerable: he celebrates those who strive to be "naked . . . of all except the heart" ("Elegy for Margaret") or who are "an exposed nerve" ("Empty House"). He aims to be aware and sensitive, not insulated by self-confidence. His best poems, largely written in the 1930s, are perched on the strength of their emotions and the tentativeness of all that surrounds them. He admires the express train, the subject of one of his poems, because it has a clean and driving efficiency that he, with his feeling of each venture as "one more botched beginning," cannot emulate. Yet against its cool competence, and the cool competence of certain other writers, he asserts an image—no less crafted than theirs—of passionate ineptitude.

Like many poets who came to maturity in the 1930s, Spender often writes poems that reflect his politics. Whether in verse or prose, he expresses a great social sympathy for radical students, Israeli kibbutzim, and other liberals and leftists. But even his poems about the Spanish Civil War are pleas not so much for direct action as for indirect, statements of a personal dilemma writ large, especially the difficulty and urgency of social bonding. His autobiography, *World within World* (1951), which caused a stir by its candor about Spender's bisexuality, expresses both his self-consciousness and his social consciousness.

Spender was born on February 28, 1909, in London. His family ancestry was German, English, and—as he learned at sixteen—Jewish. At Oxford University, he befriended Auden, who encouraged him although finding his poetry Romantic. Spender published both Auden's first book and his own on a small handpress. After leaving Oxford, Spender traveled in Weimar Germany, then a site of homosexual adventure and license. During the 1930s, he and his friends worked for the Loyalists in Spain, though he became somewhat disillusioned with his efforts. He joined the Communist Party for a brief time in 1937 and came to oppose it in the 1950s. Spender wrote plays, novels, poems, a journal, and criticism. He was coeditor of the literary review *Horizon* (1939–41) and of *Encounter* (1953–67). For more than fifty years, he was a leading spokesperson for liberal opinion. He lectured widely, taught for some years at American universities, and from 1970 to 1977, held a chair in English literature at University College in the University of London. He was knighted in 1983.

The Funeral[1]

Death is another milestone on their way.
With laughter on their lips and with winds blowing round them
They record simply
How this one excelled all others in making driving belts.

This is festivity, it is the time of statistics,
When they record what one unit contributed:
They are glad as they lay him back in the earth
And thank him for what he gave them.

They walk home remembering the straining red flags,
And with pennons[2] of song still fluttering through their blood
They speak of the World State
With its towns like brain centres and its pulsing arteries.

They think how one life hums, revolves and toils,
One cog in a golden singing hive:

1. Spender describes this as a characteristic poem of the 1930s, though uncharacteristic of his own work (introduction to *Collected Poems,* 1955).
2. Long, narrow flags.

Like spark from fire, its task happily achieved,
It falls away quietly.

No more are they haunted by the individual grief
Nor the crocodile tears of European genius,
The decline of a culture
Mourned by scholars who dream of the ghosts of Greek boys.

1933

What I Expected[3]

What I expected, was
Thunder, fighting,
Long struggles with men
And climbing.
After continual straining
I should grow strong;
Then the rocks would shake,
And I rest long.

What I had not foreseen
Was the gradual day
Weakening the will
Leaking the brightness away,
The lack of good to touch,
The fading of body and soul
—Smoke before wind,
Corrupt, unsubstantial.

The wearing of Time,
And the watching of cripples pass
With limbs shaped like questions
In their odd twist,
The pulverous grief
Melting the bones with pity,
The sick falling from earth—
These, I could not foresee.

Expecting always
Some brightness to hold in trust,
Some final innocence
Exempt from dust,
That, hanging solid,
Would dangle through all,
Like the created poem,
Or faceted crystal.

1933, 1955

3. The title is from Spender's later collections.

The Truly Great[4]

I think continually of those who were truly great.
Who, from the womb, remembered the soul's history
Through corridors of light, where the hours are suns,
Endless and singing. Whose lovely ambition
Was that their lips, still touched with fire,
Should tell of the Spirit, clothed from head to foot in song.
And who hoarded from the Spring branches
The desires falling across their bodies like blossoms.

What is precious, is never to forget
The essential delight of the blood drawn from ageless springs
Breaking through rocks in worlds before our earth.
Never to deny its pleasure in the morning simple light
Nor its grave evening demand for love.
Never to allow gradually the traffic to smother
With noise and fog, the flowering of the spirit.

Near the snow, near the sun, in the highest fields,
See how these names are fêted by the waving grass
And by the streamers of white cloud
And whispers of wind in the listening sky.
The names of those who in their lives fought for life,
Who wore at their hearts the fire's centre.
Born of the sun, they travelled a short while toward the sun
And left the vivid air signed with their honour.

1933, 1958

The Express

After the first powerful, plain manifesto
The black statement of pistons, without more fuss
But gliding like a queen, she leaves the station.
Without bowing and with restrained unconcern
She passes the houses which humbly crowd outside,
The gasworks, and at last the heavy page
Of death, printed by gravestones in the cemetery.
Beyond the town, there lies the open country
Where, gathering speed, she acquires mystery,
The luminous self-possession of ships on ocean.
It is now she begins to sing—at first quite low
Then loud, and at last with a jazzy madness—
The song of her whistle screaming at curves,
Of deafening tunnels, brakes, innumerable bolts.
And always light, aerial, underneath,

4. The title is from Spender's later collections.

Retreats the elate metre of her wheels.
Steaming through metal landscape on her lines,
She plunges new eras of white happiness,
Where speed throws up strange shapes, broad curves
And parallels clean like trajectories from guns.
At last, further than Edinburgh or Rome,
Beyond the crest of the world, she reaches night
Where only a low stream-line brightness
Of phosphorus on the tossing hills is light.
Ah, like a comet through flame, she moves entranced,
Wrapt in her music no bird song, no, nor bough
Breaking with honey buds, shall ever equal.

1933

The Landscape near an Aerodrome

More beautiful and soft than any moth
With burring furred antennae feeling its huge path
Through dusk, the air liner with shut-off engines
Glides over suburbs and the sleeves set trailing tall
To point the wind. Gently, broadly, she falls,
Scarcely disturbing charted currents of air.

Lulled by descent, the travellers across sea
And across feminine land indulging its easy limbs
In miles of softness, now let their eyes trained by watching
Penetrate through dusk the outskirts of this town
Here where industry shows a fraying edge.
Here they may see what is being done.

Beyond the winking masthead light
And the landing ground, they observe the outposts
Of work: chimneys like lank black fingers
Or figures, frightening and mad: and squat buildings
With their strange air behind trees, like women's faces
Shattered by grief. Here where few houses
Moan with faint light behind their blinds,
They remark the unhomely sense of complaint, like a dog
Shut out, and shivering at the foreign moon.

In the last sweep of love, they pass over fields
Behind the aerodrome, where boys play all day
Hacking dead grass: whose cries, like wild birds,
Settle upon the nearest roofs
But soon are hid under the loud city.

Then, as they land, they hear the tolling bell
Reaching across the landscape of hysteria,
To where, louder than all those batteries

And charcoaled towers against that dying sky,
Religion stands, the Church blocking the sun.

1933

The Pylons

The secret of these hills was stone, and cottages
Of that stone made,
And crumbling roads
That turned on sudden hidden villages.

Now over these small hills, they have built the concrete
That trails black wire;
Pylons, those pillars
Bare like nude giant girls that have no secret.

The valley with its gilt and evening look
And the green chestnut
Of customary root,
Are mocked dry like the parched bed of a brook.

But far above and far as sight endures
Like whips of anger
With lightning's danger
There runs the quick perspective of the future.

This dwarfs our emerald country by its trek
So tall with prophecy:
Dreaming of cities
Where often clouds shall lean their swan-white neck.

1933

KEITH DOUGLAS
1920–1944

In his twenties, Keith Douglas was killed in World War II, as his compatriots, Wilfred Owen and Isaac Rosenberg, were killed in World War I. Douglas is not inclined to claim much in the way of heroism: he writes in "Aristocrats" of "this gentle / obsolescent breed of heroes," with "their stupidity and chivalry." Nor is there place for overt protest or patriotism; instead, his poems express sympathy, even for the enemy in whom lover and killer were mingled ("Vergissmeinnicht").

His early work is lyrical, but he came to disdain lyricism, associating it with his youthful innocence. His poems have an economy and an unexpectedness, which he identified with "the nature of poetry": "Poetry is like a man, whom thinking you know all his movements and appearance you will presently come upon in such a posture that for a moment you can hardly believe it a position of the limbs you know" (*Collected Poems*). He wanted to sing "Of what the others have never set eyes on" ("Desert Flowers"). His images, often sardonic, are sharp and pictorial, and appear, though naturally, in odd frames. Understated and musically restrained, his is perhaps the best British poetry of World War II. Charles Tomlinson, Geoffrey Hill, Ted Hughes, and Michael Longley are among the poets who have celebrated his special combination of lucidity and passion.

Douglas was born on January 24, 1920, at Tunbridge Wells, Kent. He began to write well-crafted, spare poems while at Merton College, Oxford, where he spent two years before being called up for active service. He received a commission and went to the Middle East; he describes his experiences there in his war journal, *Alamein to Zem Zem* (1946). In defiance of his superiors, he insisted on being in the front line in North Africa, where he served as a tank commander. He landed during the main assault on the Normandy beaches and was killed three days later, on June 9, 1944, after getting information from behind the enemy lines, for which he was officially commended.

Soissons

M. l'Épicier[1] in his white hat
in an outhouse by the cathedral, makes
devils from the selfsame stone
men used in the religious century.
The cathedral itself in new masonry
of white, stands openly in this sunlit town,
Soissons. Down the long hill snakes
the hard hot road into the town's heart.

In the evening when the late sunlight abandons
building still glimmering from shadow on shadow
someone leans from a window eavesdropping our
strange voices so late in the cathedral square.
From the barracks of the 19th Regiment you can hear
the equivalent of Lights Out. Now the sweet-sour
wine clambers in our heads. Go in. Tomorrow
tiptoes with us along the dark landing.

'A Laon, belle cathédrale',[2] making
a wave of his white hat, explains
the maker of gargoyles. So we take
a route for Laon and Rheims leaving you
Soissons, a simplified medieval view
taken from a Book of Hours.[3] How dark
seems the whole country we enter. Now it rains,
the trees like ominous old men are shaking.

Oxford, 1940 1951

1. Literally, Mr. Grocer (French). The "devils" (line 3) he carves are gargoyles, decorations for the cathedral.
2. At Laon, a beautiful cathedral (French). Soissons, Laon, and Rheims are equidistant from each other.
3. Book containing prayers to be said at designated times; medieval ones were often decorated with paintings and illuminations.

Simplify Me When I'm Dead

Remember me when I am dead
and simplify me when I'm dead.

As the processes of earth
strip off the colour and the skin
take the brown hair and blue eye

and leave me simpler than at birth
when hairless I came howling in
as the moon came in the cold sky.

Of my skeleton perhaps
so stripped, a learned man will say
'He was of such a type and intelligence,' no more.

Thus when in a year collapse
particular memories, you may
deduce, from the long pain I bore

the opinions I held, who was my foe
and what I left, even my appearance
but incidents will be no guide

Time's wrong-way telescope will show
a minute man ten years hence
and by distance simplified

Through that lens see if I seem
substance or nothing: of the world
deserving mention or charitable oblivion

not by momentary spleen
or love into decision hurled,
leisurely arrive at an opinion.

Remember me when I am dead
and simplify me when I'm dead.

May 1941? 1951

Gallantry

The Colonel in a casual voice
spoke into the microphone a joke
which through a hundred earphones broke
into the ears of a doomed race.

Into the ears of the doomed boy, the fool
whose perfectly mannered flesh fell
in opening the door for a shell
as he had learnt to do at school.

Conrad luckily survived the winter:
he wrote a letter to welcome
the auspicious spring: only his silken
intentions severed with a single splinter.

Was George fond of little boys?
We always suspected it,
but who will say: since George was hit
we never mention our surmise.

It was a brave thing the Colonel said,
but the whole sky turned too hot
and the three heroes never heard what
it was, gone deaf with steel and lead.

But the bullets cried with laughter,
the shells were overcome with mirth,
plunging their heads in steel and earth—
(the air commented in a whisper).

El Ballah, General Hospital, April 1943 — 1951

Vergissmeinnicht[4]

Three weeks gone and the combatants gone
returning over the nightmare ground
we found the place again, and found
the soldier sprawling in the sun.

The frowning barrel of his gun
overshadowing. As we came on
that day, he hit my tank with one
like the entry of a demon.

Look. Here in the gunpit spoil
the dishonoured picture of his girl
who has put: *Steffi. Vergissmeinnicht*
in a copybook gothic script.

We see him almost with content,
abased, and seeming to have paid
and mocked at by his own equipment
that's hard and good when he's decayed.

4. Forget me not (German).

But she would weep to see today
how on his skin the swart flies move;
the dust upon the paper eye
and the burst stomach like a cave.

For here the lover and killer are mingled
who had one body and one heart.
And death who had the soldier singled
has done the lover mortal hurt.

Tunisia, May–June 1943 1946

Aristocrats

"I think I am becoming a God"[5]

The noble horse with courage in his eye,
clean in the bone, looks up at a shellburst:
away fly the images of the shires[6]
but he puts the pipe back in his mouth.

Peter was unfortunately killed by an 88;[7]
it took his leg away, he died in the ambulance.
I saw him crawling on the sand, he said
It's most unfair, they've shot my foot off.

How can I live among this gentle
obsolescent breed of heroes, and not weep?
Unicorns, almost,
for they are fading into two legends
in which their stupidity and chivalry
are celebrated. Each, fool and hero, will be an immortal.

These plains were their cricket pitch[8]
and in the mountains the tremendous drop fences[9]
brought down some of the runners. Here then
under the stones and earth they dispose themselves,
I think with their famous unconcern.
It is not gunfire I hear, but a hunting horn.[1]

Tunisia, 1943 1946

5. The dying words of the Roman emperor Vespasian (d. 79 C.E.) were supposedly "Alas! I suppose I am turning into a god."
6. Counties.
7. German tank fitted with an eighty-eight-millimeter gun.
8. Field on which the game of cricket is played.
9. Used on the course of a steeplechase horse race.

1. "Lt.-Col. J. D. Player, killed in Tunisia, Enfidaville, February, 1943, left £3,000 to the Beaufort Hunt, and directed that the incumbent of the living in his gift [that is, the church whose vicar he was entitled to appoint] should be a 'man who approves of hunting, shooting, and all manly sports, which are the backbone of the nation' " [Douglas's note on one of the manuscripts of "Aristocrats." Player was in fact killed in April].

Poetics

Preface to Leaves of Grass

In July 1855, Walt Whitman anonymously published twelve poems titled *Leaves of Grass*. In his preface to the volume, he describes a new breed of poet wed to the democratic ideals he associated with his country. "The United States themselves," he proclaims, "are essentially the greatest poem," and the ideal poet will celebrate this with poems that express radical individualism while also speaking to and for the common people. Rejecting formal artifice, such as rhyme and personification, Whitman advances an organic vision of poetic form as free, insouciant, and vitally responsive to nature, the soul, and the people. These excerpts are taken from *Leaves of Grass* (1855).

WALT WHITMAN

From Preface to *Leaves of Grass*

America does not repel the past or what it has produced under its forms or amid other politics or the idea of castes or the old religions . . . . accepts the lesson with calmness . . . is not so impatient as has been supposed that the slough still sticks to opinions and manners and literature while the life which served its requirements has passed into the new life of the new forms . . . perceives that the corpse is slowly borne from the eating and sleeping rooms of the house . . . perceives that it waits a little while in the door . . . that it was fittest for its days . . . that its action has descended to the stalwart and wellshaped heir who approaches . . . and that he shall be fittest for his days.

The Americans of all nations at any time upon the earth have probably the fullest poetical nature. The United States themselves are essentially the greatest poem. In the history of the earth hitherto the largest and most stirring appear tame and orderly to their ampler largeness and stir. Here at last is something in the doings of man that corresponds with the broadcast doings of the day and night. Here is not merely a nation but a teeming nation of nations. Here is action untied from strings necessarily blind to particulars and details magnificently moving in vast masses. Here is the hospitality which forever indicates heroes . . . . Here are the roughs and beards and space and ruggedness and nonchalance that the soul loves. Here the performance disdaining the trivial unapproached in the tremendous audacity of its crowds and groupings and the push of its perspective spreads with crampless and flowing breadth and showers its prolific and splendid extravagance. One sees it must indeed own the riches of the summer and winter, and need never be bankrupt while corn grows from the ground or the orchards drop apples or the bays contain fish or men beget children upon women.

Other states indicate themselves in their deputies . . . . but the genius of the United States is not best or most in its executives or legislatures, nor in its ambassadors or authors or colleges or churches or parlors, nor even in its newspapers or inventors . . . but always most in the common people. Their manners speech dress friendships—the freshness and candor of their physiognomy—the picturesque looseness of their carriage . . . their deathless attachment to freedom—their aversion to anything indecorous or soft or mean—the practical acknowledgment of the citizens of one state by the citizens of all other states—the fierceness of their roused resentment—their curiosity and welcome of novelty—their self-esteem and wonderful sympathy—their susceptibility to a slight—the air they have of persons who never knew how it felt to stand in the presence of superiors—the fluency of their speech—their delight in music, the sure symptom of manly tenderness and native elegance of soul . . . their good temper and openhandedness—the terrible significance of their elections—the President's taking off his hat to them not they to him—these too are unrhymed poetry. It awaits the gigantic and generous treatment worthy of it.

* * *

The greatest poet hardly knows pettiness or triviality. If he breathes into any thing that was before thought small it dilates with the grandeur and life of the universe. He is a seer . . . . he is individual . . . he is complete in himself . . . . the others are as good as he, only he sees it and they do not. He is not one of the chorus . . . . he does not stop for any regulation . . . he is the president of regulation. What the eyesight does to the rest he does to the rest. Who knows the curious mystery of the eyesight? The other senses corroborate themselves, but this is removed from any proof but its own and foreruns the identities of the spiritual world. A single glance of it mocks all the investigations of man and all the instruments and books of the earth and all reasoning. What is marvellous? what is unlikely? what is impossible or baseless or vague? after you have once just opened the space of a peachpit and given audience to far and near and to the sunset and had all things enter with electric swiftness softly and duly without confusion or jostling or jam.

The land and sea, the animals fishes and birds, the sky of heaven and the orbs, the forests mountains and rivers, are not small themes . . . but folks expect of the poet to indicate more than the beauty and dignity which always attach to dumb real objects . . . . they expect him to indicate the path between reality and their souls. Men and women perceive the beauty well enough . . probably as well as he. The passionate tenacity of hunters, woodmen, early risers, cultivators of gardens and orchards and fields, the love of healthy women for the manly form, seafaring persons, drivers of horses, the passion for light and the open air, all is an old varied sign of the unfailing perception of beauty and of a residence of the poetic in outdoor people. They can never be assisted by poets to perceive . . . some may but they never can. The poetic quality is not marshalled in rhyme or uniformity or abstract addresses to things nor in melancholy complaints or good precepts, but is the life of these and much else and is in the soul. The profit of rhyme is that it drops seeds of a sweeter and more luxuriant rhyme, and of uniformity that it conveys itself into its own roots in the ground out of sight. The rhyme and uniformity of perfect poems show the free growth of metrical laws and bud from them as unerringly and loosely as lilacs or roses on a bush, and take shapes as compact as the shapes of chestnuts and oranges and melons and pears, and shed the perfume impalpable to form. The fluency and ornaments of the finest poems or music or orations or recitations are not independent but dependent. All beauty comes from beautiful blood and a beautiful brain. If the greatnesses are in conjunction in a man or woman it is enough . . . . the fact will prevail through the universe . . . . but the gaggery and gilt of a million years will not prevail. Who troubles himself about his ornaments or fluency is lost. This is what you shall do: Love the earth and sun and the animals, despise riches, give alms to every one that asks, stand up for the stupid and crazy, devote your income and labor to others, hate tyrants, argue not concerning God, have patience and indulgence toward the people, take off your hat to nothing known or unknown or to any man or number of men, go freely with powerful uneducated persons and with the young and with the mothers of families, read these leaves in the open air every season of every year of your life, reexamine all you have been told at school or church or in any book, dismiss whatever insults your own soul, and your very flesh shall be a great poem and have the richest fluency not only in its words but in the silent lines of its lips and face and between the lashes of your eyes and in every motion and joint of your body. . . . . The poet shall not spend his time in unneeded work. He shall know that the ground is always ready ploughed and manured . . . . others may not know it but he shall. He shall go directly to the creation. His trust shall master the trust of everything he touches . . . . and shall master all attachment.

* * *

The art of art, the glory of expression and the sunshine of the light of letters is simplicity. Nothing is better than simplicity . . . . nothing can make up for excess or for the lack of definiteness. To carry on the heave of impulse and pierce intellectual depths and give all subjects their articulations are powers neither common nor very uncommon. But to speak in literature with the perfect rectitude and insouciance of the movements of animals and the unimpeachableness of the sentiment of trees in the woods and grass by the roadside is the flawless triumph of art. If you have looked on him who has achieved it you have looked on one of the masters of the artists of all nations and times. You shall not contemplate the flight of the graygull over the bay or the mettlesome action of the blood horse or the tall leaning of sunflowers on their stalk or the appearance of the sun journeying through heaven or the appearance of the moon afterward with any more satisfaction than you shall contemplate him. The greatest poet has less a marked style and is more the channel of thoughts and things without increase or diminution, and is the free channel of himself. He swears to his art, I will not be meddlesome, I will not have in my writing any elegance or effect or originality to hang in the way between me and the rest like curtains. I will have nothing hang in the way, not the richest curtains. What I tell I tell for precisely what it is. Let who may exalt or startle or fascinate or sooth I will have purposes as health or heat or snow has and be as regardless of observation. What I experience or portray shall go from my composition without a shred of my composition. You shall stand by my side and look in the mirror with me.

* * *

The direct trial of him who would be the greatest poet is today. If he does not flood himself with the immediate age as with vast oceanic tides . . . . . and if he does not attract his own land body and soul to himself and hang on its neck with incomparable love and plunge his semitic muscle[1] into its merits and demerits . . . and if he be not himself the age transfigured . . . . and if to him is not opened the eternity which gives similitude to all periods and locations and processes and animate and inanimate forms, and which is the bond of time, and rises up from its inconceivable vagueness and infiniteness in the swimming shape of today, and is held by the ductile anchors of life, and makes the present spot the passage from what was to what shall be, and commits itself to the representation of this ware of an hour and this one of the sixty beautiful children of the wave—let him merge in the general run and wait his development. . . . . Still the final test of poems or any character or work remains. The prescient poet projects himself centuries ahead and judges performer or performance after the changes of time. Does it live through them? Does it still hold on untired? Will the same style and the direction of genius to similar points be satisfactory now? Has no new discovery in science or arrival at superior planes of thought and judgment and behaviour fixed him or his so that either can be looked down upon? Have the marches of tens and hundreds and thousands of years made willing detours to the right hand and the left hand for his sake? Is he beloved long and long after he is buried? Does the young man think often of him? and the young woman think often of him? and do the middleaged and the old think of him?

A great poem is for ages and ages in common and for all degrees and complexions and all departments and sects and for a woman as much as a man and a man as much as a woman. A great poem is no finish to a man or woman but rather a beginning. Has any one fancied he could sit at last under some due authority and rest satisfied with explanations and realize and be content and full? To no such terminus does the greatest poet bring . . . he brings neither cessation or sheltered fatness and ease. The touch of him tells in action. Whom he takes he takes with firm sure grasp into live regions previously unattained . . . . thenceforward is no rest . . . . they see the space and ineffable sheen that turn the old spots and lights into dead vacuums. The companion of him beholds the birth and progress of stars and learns one of the meanings. Now there shall be a man cohered out of tumult and chaos . . . . the elder encourages the younger and shows him how . . . they two shall launch off fearlessly together till the new world fits an orbit for itself and looks unabashed on the lesser orbits of the stars and sweeps through the ceaseless rings and shall never be quiet again.

There will soon be no more priests. Their work is done. They may wait awhile . . perhaps a generation or two . . dropping off by degrees. A superior breed shall take their place . . . . the gangs of kosmos and prophets en masse shall take their place. A new order shall arise and they shall be the priests of man, and every man shall be his own priest. The churches built under their umbrage shall be the churches of men and women. Through the divinity of themselves shall the kosmos and the new breed of poets be interpreters of men and women and of all events and things. They shall find their inspiration in real objects today, symptoms of the past and future . . . . They shall not deign to defend immortality or God or the perfection of things or liberty or

1. That is, muscle through which semen passes; penis (Whitman's coinage).

the exquisite beauty and reality of the soul. They shall arise in America and be responded to from the remainder of the earth.

The English language befriends the grand American expression . . . . it is brawny enough and limber and full enough. On the tough stock of a race who through all change of circumstance was never without the idea of political liberty, which is the animus of all liberty, it has attracted the terms of daintier and gayer and subtler and more elegant tongues. It is the powerful language of resistance . . . it is the dialect of common sense. It is the speech of the proud and melancholy races and of all who aspire. It is the chosen tongue to express growth faith self-esteem freedom justice equality friendliness amplitude prudence decision and courage. It is the medium that shall well nigh express the inexpressible.

No great literature nor any like style of behaviour or oratory or social intercourse or household arrangements or public institutions or the treatment by bosses of employed people, nor executive detail or detail of the army or navy, nor spirit of legislation or courts or police or tuition or architecture or songs or amusements or the costumes of young men, can long elude the jealous and passionate instinct of American standards. Whether or no the sign appears from the months of the people, it throbs a live interrogation in every freeman's and freewoman's heart after that which passes by or this built to remain. Is it uniform with my country? Are its disposals without ignominious distinctions? Is it for the evergrowing communes of brothers and lovers, large, well-united, proud beyond the old models, generous beyond all models? Is it something grown fresh out of the fields or drawn from the sea for use to me today here? I know that what answers for me an American must answer for any individual or nation that serves for a part of my materials. Does this answer? or is it without reference to universal needs? or sprung of the needs of the less developed society of special ranks? or old needs of pleasure overlaid by modern science and forms? Does this acknowledge liberty with audible and absolute acknowledgement, and set slavery at nought for life and death? Will it help breed one goodshaped and wellhung man, and a woman to be his perfect and independent mate? Does it improve manners? Is it for the nursing of the young of the republic? Does it solve readily with the sweet milk of the nipples of the breasts of the mother of many children? Has it too the old ever-fresh forbearance and impartiality? Does it look with the same love on the last born and on those hardening toward stature, and on the errant, and on those who disdain all strength of assault outside of their own?

The poems distilled from other poems will probably pass away. The coward will surely pass away. The expectation of the vital and great can only be satisfied by the demeanor of the vital and great. The swarms of the polished deprecating and reflectors and the polite float off and leave no remembrance. America prepares with composure and goodwill for the visitors that have sent word. It is not intellect that is to be their warrant and welcome. The talented, the artist, the ingenious, the editor, the statesman, the erudite . . they are not unappreciated . . they fall in their place and do their work. The soul of the nation also does its work. No disguise can pass on it . . no disguise can conceal from it. It rejects none, it permits all. Only toward as good as itself and toward the like of itself will it advance half-way. An individual is as superb as a nation when he has the qualities which make a superb nation. The soul of the largest and wealthiest and proudest nation may well go half-way to meet that of its poets. The signs are effectual. There is no fear of mistake. If the one is true the other is true. The proof of a poet is that his country absorbs him as affectionately as he has absorbed it.

1855

Letters

Like her poetry, Emily Dickinson's letters tell it "slant." They have none of the inflated rhetoric of many poetic manifestos, instead concealing as much as they reveal, enigmatically combining reticence and intimacy in compressed language. But for all their teasing evasiveness, they offer valuable insight into Dickinson's literary ambitions, her reading, and her reluctance to publish ("My Barefoot-Rank is better"). "My Business is Circumference," she writes, encapsulating her self-conception as a poet and hinting at the encompassing power of the poetic imagination. Several of Dickinson's most significant letters were to Colonel Thomas Wentworth Higginson (1823–1911), beginning on April 15, 1862, when she responded to the Unitarian minister's advice for aspiring American authors in an *Atlantic Monthly* article, "Letter to a Young Contributor." Dickinson included four poems with her letter, asking if her verse were "alive." The correspondence that followed continued for the rest of Dickinson's life. Originally printed posthumously in an article by Higginson, "Emily Dickinson's Letters," *Atlantic Monthly* (October 1891), the letters are reprinted from *Selected Letters* (1971), ed. Thomas H. Johnson.

EMILY DICKINSON

[Letter 261: Thank You for the Surgery]

To T. W. Higginson 25 April 1862

Mr Higginson,

Your kindness claimed earlier gratitude—but I was ill—and write today, from my pillow.

Thank you for the surgery—it was not so painful as I supposed. I bring you others—as you ask—though they might not differ—

While my thought is undressed—I can make the distinction, but when I put them in the Gown—they look alike, and numb.

You asked how old I was? I made no verse—but one or two—until this winter—Sir—

I had a terror—since September—I could tell to none—and so I sing, as the Boy does by the Burying Ground—because I am afraid—You inquire my Books—For Poets—I have Keats—and Mr and Mrs Browning. For Prose—Mr Ruskin—Sir Thomas Browne—and the Revelations.[1] I went to school—

1. Final, apocalyptic book of the New Testament. John Keats (1795–1821): English Romantic poet. Robert Browning (1812–1889) and Elizabeth Barrett Browning (1806–1861): English Victorian poets. John Ruskin (1819–1900): English writer and art critic. Sir Thomas Browne (1605–1682): English writer and physician.

but in your manner of the phrase—had no education. When a little Girl, I had a friend, who taught me Immortality—but venturing too near, himself—he never returned—Soon after, my Tutor,[2] died—and for several years, my Lexicon—was my only companion—Then I found one more—but he was not contented I be his scholar—so he left the Land.[3]

You ask of my Companions Hills—Sir—and the Sundown—and a Dog—large as myself, that my Father bought me—They are better than Beings—because they know—but do not tell—and the noise in the Pool, at Noon—excels my Piano. I have a Brother and Sister—My Mother does not care for thought—and Father, too busy with his Briefs—to notice what we do—He buys me many Books—but begs me not to read them—because he fears they joggle the Mind. They are religious—except me—and address an Eclipse, every morning—whom they call their "Father." But I fear my story fatigues you—I would like to learn—Could you tell me how to grow—or is it unconveyed—like Melody—or Witchcraft?

You speak of Mr Whitman[4]—I never read his Book—but was told that he was disgraceful—

I read Miss Prescott's "Circumstance,"[5] but it followed me, in the Dark—so I avoided her—

Two Editors of Journals came to my Father's House, this winter—and asked me for my Mind—and when I asked them "Why," they said I was penurious—and they, would use it for the World—

I could not weigh myself—Myself—

My size felt small—to me—I read your Chapters in the Atlantic—and experienced honor for you—I was sure you would not reject a confiding question—

Is this—Sir—what you asked me to tell you?

Your friend,
E—Dickinson.

[Letter 265: Will You Be My Preceptor?]

To T. W. Higginson — 7 June 1862

Dear friend.

Your letter gave no Drunkenness, because I tasted Rum before—Domingo[6] comes but once—yet I have had few pleasures so deep as your opinion, and if I tried to thank you, my tears would block my tongue—

My dying Tutor told me that he would like to live till I had been a poet, but Death was much of Mob as I could master[7]—then—And when far afterward—a sudden light on Orchards, or a new fashion in the wind troubled my attention—I felt a palsy, here—the Verses just relieve—

Your second letter surprised me, and for a moment, swung—I had not supposed it. Your first—gave no dishonor, because the True—are not ashamed—I thanked you for your justice—but could not drop the Bells

2. Probably Benjamin Franklin Newton (1821–1853), a clerk in her father's law firm.
3. The Reverend Charles Wadsworth, who left Philadelphia for California in April 1860.
4. Walt Whitman (1819–1892), American poet.
5. Story, by American writer Harriet Prescott Spofford (1835–1921), about a frontier woman who sings to fend off a terrifying beast.
6. Santo Domingo, the capital of the Dominican Republic.
7. That is, she could not write for a popular audience.

whose jingling cooled my Tramp—Perhaps the Balm, seemed better, because you bled me, first.

I smile when you suggest that I delay "to publish"—that being foreign to my thought, as Firmament to Fin—

If fame belonged to me, I could not escape her—if she did not, the longest day would pass me on the chase—and the approbation of my Dog, would forsake me—then—My Barefoot-Rank is better—

You think my gait "spasmodic"—I am in danger—Sir—

You think me "uncontrolled"—I have no Tribunal.

Would you have time to be the "friend" you should think I need? I have a little shape—it would not crowd your Desk—nor make much Racket as the Mouse, that dents your Galleries—

If I might bring you what I do—not so frequent to trouble you—and ask you if I told it clear—'twould be control, to me—

The Sailor cannot see the North—but knows the Needle can—

The "hand you stretch me in the Dark," I put mine in, and turn away—I have no Saxon,[8] now—

As if I asked a common Alms,
And in my wondering hand
A Stranger pressed a Kingdom,
And I, bewildered, stand—
As if I asked the Orient
Had it for me a Morn—
And it should lift it's[9] purple Dikes,
And shatter me with Dawn!

But, will you be my Preceptor, Mr Higginson?

Your friend
E Dickinson—

[Letter 268: My Business Is Circumference]

To T. W. Higginson July 1862

Could you believe me—without? I had no portrait, now, but am small, like the Wren, and my Hair is bold, like the Chestnut Bur—and my eyes, like the Sherry in the Glass, that the Guest leaves—Would this do just as well?

It often alarms Father—He says Death might occur, and he has Molds[1] of all the rest—but has no Mold of me, but I noticed the Quick wore off those things, in a few days, and forestall the dishonor—You will think no caprice of me—

You said "Dark." I know the Butterfly—and the Lizard—and the Orchis[2]—Are not those *your* Countrymen?

I am happy to be your scholar, and will deserve the kindness, I cannot repay.

If you truly consent, I recite, now—

8. That is, language fails me.
9. That is, *its*.
1. That is, photographs or likenesses.
2. A small orchid. Higginson was the author of nature essays.

Will you tell me my fault, frankly as to yourself, for I had rather wince, than die. Men do not call the surgeon, to commend—the Bone, but to set it, Sir, and fracture within, is more critical. And for this, Preceptor, I shall bring you—Obedience—the Blossom from my Garden, and every gratitude I know. Perhaps you smile at me. I could not stop for that—My Business is Circumference—An ignorance, not of Customs, but if caught with the Dawn—or the Sunset see me—Myself the only Kangaroo among the Beauty, Sir, if you please, it afflicts me, and I thought that instruction would take it away.

Because you have much business, beside the growth of me—you will appoint, yourself, how often I shall come—without your inconvenience. And if at any time—you regret you received me, or I prove a different fabric to that you supposed—you must banish me—

When I state myself, as the Representative of the Verse—it does not mean—me—but a supposed person. You are true, about the "perfection."

Today, makes Yesterday mean.[3]

You spoke of Pippa Passes—I never heard anybody speak of Pippa Passes—before.

You see my posture is benighted.

To thank you, baffles me. Are you perfectly powerful? Had I a pleasure you had not, I could delight to bring it.

Your Scholar

3. Verse drama (1841), by Robert Browning.

LETTERS

In his letters, Gerard Manley Hopkins explains his highly original conceptions of poetry. Though he died in the nineteenth century, Hopkins would exert a strong influence on poets of the twentieth century; in their poetics statements, modern and contemporary poets frequently echo his central ideas (see, e.g., Dylan Thomas, Denise Levertov, and Seamus Heaney). Long before Ezra Pound and the Imagists called for avoiding the rhythm of the metronome, Hopkins discovered a flexible prosodic system he called "sprung rhythm," which allowed for a variable number of syllables within a metrical foot. And long before the Black Mountain school developed a notion of "organic form," Hopkins said he aimed to present in his poetry the "inscape," or the inner distinctiveness of things. Hopkins followed his genius in unusual rhythmic, verbal, and stylistic directions, to the bafflement of his first readers. When he burned his poems, just before joining the Jesuits in 1868, the only remaining copies of many of them were those that had been sent to a friend, the poet Robert Bridges (1844–1930), who published Hopkins's poems in 1918. Although, as the letter to Richard Watson Dixon (1833–1900) explains, Hopkins would later change his mind and begin writing poetry again in 1875, his audience was to remain small throughout his lifetime, and much of his work was preserved in his correspondence with his friends and admirers. The complete letters of Hopkins to Bridges and Dixon can be found in *Letters of Hopkins to Robert Bridges* (1955) and *Correspondence of Hopkins and Richard Watson Dixon* (1955), both edited by C. C. Abbott. The letters are excerpted from *Selected Letters*, ed. Catherine Phillips (1990).

GERARD MANLEY HOPKINS

[Sprung Rhythm]

St. Bueno's, St. Asaph. Aug. 21 1877.

Dearest [Robert] Bridges,—

* * *

Why do I employ sprung rhythm at all? Because it is the nearest to the rhythm of prose, that is the native and natural rhythm of speech, the least forced, the most rhetorical and emphatic of all possible rhythms, combining, as it seems to me, opposite and, one wd. have thought, incompatible excellences, markedness of rhythm—that is rhythm's self—and naturalness of expression—for why, if it is forcible in prose to say 'lashed : rod',[1] am I obliged to weaken this in verse, which ought to be stronger, not weaker, into 'láshed birch-ród', or something?

My verse is less to be read than heard, as I have told you before; it is oratorical, that is the rhythm is so. I think if you will study what I have here said you will be much more pleased with it and may I say? converted to it.

You ask may you call it 'presumptious jugglery'. No, but only for this reason, that *presumptious* is not English.

I cannot think of altering anything. Why shd. I? I do not write for the public. You are my public and I hope to convert you.

You say you wd. not for any money read my poem again. Nevertheless I beg you will. Besides money, you know, there is love. If it is obscure do not bother yourself with the meaning but pay attention to the best and most intelligible stanzas, as the two last of each part and the narrative of the wreck. If you had done this you wd. have liked it better and sent me some serviceable criticisms, but now your criticism is of no use, being only a protest memorialising me against my whole policy and proceedings.

I may add for your greater interest and edification that what refers to myself in the poem is all strictly and literally true and did all occur; nothing is added for poetical padding.

* * *

[Sprung Rhythm]

111 Mount Street, Grosvenor Square, W. Oct. 5 1878.

[To Richard Watson Dixon,]

* * *

You ask, do I write verse myself. What I had written I burnt before I became a Jesuit and resolved to write no more, as not belonging to my pro-

1. From "The Wreck of the Deutschland."

fession, unless it were by the wish of my superiors; so for seven years I wrote nothing but two or three little presentation pieces which occasion called for. But when in the winter of '75 the Deutschland was wrecked in the mouth of the Thames and five Franciscan nuns, exiles from Germany by the Falck Laws, aboard of her were drowned[2] I was affected by the account and happening to say so to my rector he said that he wished someone would write a poem on the subject. On this hint I set to work and, though my hand was out at first, produced one. I had long had haunting my ear the echo of a new rhythm which now I realised on paper. To speak shortly, it consists in scanning by accents or stresses alone, without any account of the number of syllables, so that a foot may be but one strong syllable or it may be many light and one strong. I do not say the idea is altogether new; there are hints of it in music, in nursery rhymes and popular jingles, in the poets themselves, and, since then, I have seen it talked about as a thing possible in critics. Here are instances—'*Díng, dóng, béll;* Pússy's ín the wéll; *Whó pút* her ín? Líttle Jóhnny Thín. *Whó púlled* her óut? Líttlé Jóhnny Stóut.' For if each line has three stresses or three feet it follows that some of the feet are of one syllable only. So too '*Óne, twó,* Búckle my shóe' *passim.* In Campbell you have 'Ánd their fléet alóng the *déep próudly* shóne'—'It was tén of Ápril *mórn bý* the chíme'[3] etc; in Shakspere 'Why shd. *thís* désert bé?' corrected wrongly by the editors; in Moore[4] a little melody I cannot quote; etc. But no one has professedly used it and made it the principle throughout, that I know of. Nevertheless to me it appears, I own, to be a better and more natural principle than the ordinary system, much more flexible, and capable of much greater effects. However I had to mark the stresses in blue chalk, and this and my rhymes carried on from one line into another and certain chimes suggested by the Welsh poetry I had been reading (what they call *cynghanedd*) and a great many more oddnesses could not but dismay an editor's eye, so that when I offered it to our magazine the *Month,* though at first they accepted it, after a time they withdrew and dared not print it. After writing this I held myself free to compose, but cannot find it in my conscience to spend time upon it; so I have done little and shall do less. But I wrote a shorter piece on the Eurydice,[5] also in 'sprung rhythm', as I call it, but simpler, shorter, and without marks, and offered the *Month* that too, but they did not like it either. Also I have written some sonnets and a few other little things; some in sprung rhythm, with various other experiments—as 'outriding feet', that is parts of which do not count in the scanning (such as you find in Shakspere's later plays, but as a licence, whereas mine are rather calculated effects); others in the ordinary scanning *counterpointed* (this is counterpoint: '*Hóme to* his móther's hóuse *prívate* retúrned' and '*Bút to vánquish* by wísdom héllish wíles'[6] (etc); others, one or two, in common uncounterpointed rhythm. But even the impulse to write is wanting, for I have no thought of publishing.

2. In December 1875, the *Deutschland,* a German transatlantic steamer, was shipwrecked in England's Thames River. Among the dead were five Franciscan nuns, who had been exiled from Germany because of the laws—passed by Adalbert Falk, minister of public worship and education under Otto von Bismarck (1815–1898), that brought the Church under government control to stifle political Catholicism.

3. From "Battle of the Baltic," by English poet Thomas Campbell (1777–1844).

4. Thomas Moore (1779–1852), Irish poet. *Shakspere:* that is, Shakespeare. First line of one of Orlando's poems in *As You Like It,* corrected to "Why should this a desert be?" (3.2.113).

5. Training frigate wrecked on March 24, 1878, off the Isle of Wight. In Greek mythology, Orpheus's wife, condemned to remain in Hades when her husband turned to look at her.

6. From *Paradise Regained,* by John Milton (1608–1674).

I should add that Milton is the great standard in the use of counterpoint. In *Paradise Lost* and *Regained,* in the last more freely, it being an advance in his art, he employs counterpoint more or less everywhere, markedly now and then; but the choruses of *Samson Agonistes*[7] are in my judgment counterpointed throughout; that is, each line (or nearly so) has two different coexisting scansions. But when you reach that point the secondary or 'mounted rhythm', which is necessarily a sprung rhythm, overpowers the original or conventional one and then this becomes superfluous and may be got rid of; by taking that last step you reach simple sprung rhythm. Milton must have known this but had reasons for not taking it.

* * *

[My Poetry Errs on the Side of Oddness]

St. Giles's, Oxford. Feb. 15 '79.

Dearest [Robert] Bridges,—

* * *

No doubt my poetry errs on the side of oddness. I hope in time to have a more balanced and Miltonic style. But as air, melody, is what strikes me most of all in music and design in painting, so design, pattern or what I am in the habit of calling 'inscape' is what I above all aim at in poetry. Now it is the virtue of design, pattern, or inscape to be distinctive and it is the vice of distinctiveness to become queer. This vice I cannot have escaped. However 'winding the eyes'[8] is queer only if looked at from the wrong point of view: looked at as a motion in and of the eyeballs it is what you say, but I mean that the eye winds / only in the sense that its focus or point of sight winds and that coincides with a point of the object and winds with that. For the object, a lantern passing further and further away and bearing now east, now west of one right line, is truly and properly described as winding. That is how it should be taken then.

* * *

[The Current Language Heightened]

Aug. 14 1879.

My dearest [Robert] Bridges,—

* * *

By the by, inversions—As you say, I do avoid them, because they weaken and because they destroy the earnestness or in-earnestness of the utterance. Nevertheless in prose I use them more than other people, because there they

7. Verse drama, by Milton.

8. From Hopkins's "The Lantern Out of Doors."

have great advantages of another sort. Now these advantages they should have in verse too, but they must not seem to be due to the verse: that is what is so enfeebling (for instance the finest of your sonnets to my mind has a line enfeebled by inversion plainly due to the verse, as I said once before ' 'Tis joy the falling of her fold to view'[9]—but how it should be mended I do not see). As it is, I feel my way to their use. However in a nearly finished piece I have a very bold one indeed. So also I cut myself off from the use of *ere, o'er, wellnigh, what time, say not (for do not say),* because, though dignified, they neither belong to nor ever cd. arise from, or be the elevation of, ordinary modern speech. For it seems to me that the poetical language of an age shd. be the current language heightened, to any degree heightened and unlike itself, but not (I mean normally: passing freaks and graces are another thing) an obsolete one. This is Shakespeare's and Milton's practice and the want of it will be fatal to Tennyson's Idylls and plays, to Swinburne, and perhaps to Morris.[1]

9. From Bridges's *Growth of Love* 31.
1. Alfred, Lord Tennyson (1809–1892), Algernon Charles Swinburne (1837–1909), and William Morris (1834–1896), English poets.

THE SYMBOLISM OF POETRY

In this essay, Yeats argues that symbolism is at the heart of poetry—not "such obvious intellectual symbols as a cross or a crown of thorns," standing for one idea or another, but poetic images and sounds that evoke subtle, complex emotions. He sees the French Symbolists, introduced to English-language readers by his friend the poet-critic Arthur Symons, as part of a larger literary trend away from Victorian discursive and descriptive literature, wedded to scientific "externalities," and toward poetry of suggestion, mood, and interiority. Poetry, partly through its trancelike rhythms, can help unlock the power of unconscious associations and spiritual experience. By its ability to embody indistinct feelings, poetry can give rise, indirectly, to the creation of cities, religions, even civilizations. First published in the journal *The Dome* (1900) and reprinted in Yeats's *Ideas of Good and Evil* (1903), the essay is excerpted from *Essays and Introductions* (1961).

W. B. YEATS

The Symbolism of Poetry

I

Symbolism, as seen in the writers of our day, would have no value if it were not seen also, under one 'disguise or another, in every great imaginative writer,' writes Mr. Arthur Symons[1] in *The Symbolist Movement in Literature,* a subtle book which I cannot praise as I would, because it has been dedicated to me; and he goes on to show how many profound writers have in the last

1. English author and critic (1865–1945).

few years sought for a philosophy of poetry in the doctrine of symbolism, and how even in countries where it is almost scandalous to seek for any philosophy of poetry, new writers are following them in their search. We do not know what the writers of ancient times talked of among themselves, and one bull is all that remains of Shakespeare's talk,[2] who was on the edge of modern times; and the journalist is convinced, it seems, that they talked of wine and women and politics, but never about their art, or never quite seriously about their art. He is certain that no one who had a philosophy of his art, or a theory of how he should write, has ever made a work of art, that people have no imagination who do not write without forethought and afterthought as he writes his own articles. He says this with enthusiasm, because he has heard it at so many comfortable dinner-tables, where some one had mentioned through carelessness, or foolish zeal, a book whose difficulty had offended indolence, or a man who had not forgotten that beauty is an accusation. Those formulas and generalisations, in which a hidden sergeant has drilled the ideas of journalists and through them the ideas of all but all the modern world, have created in their turn a forgetfulness like that of soldiers in battle, so that journalists and their readers have forgotten, among many like events, that Wagner[3] spent seven years arranging and explaining his ideas before he began his most characteristic music; that opera, and with it modern music, arose from certain talks at the house of one Giovanni Bardi of Florence; and that the Pléiade laid the foundations of modern French literature with a pamphlet. Goethe[4] has said, 'a poet needs all philosophy, but he must keep it out of his work,' though that is not always necessary; and almost certainly no great art, outside England, where journalists are more powerful and ideas less plentiful than elsewhere, has arisen without a great criticism, for its herald or its interpreter and protector, and it may be for this reason that great art, now that vulgarity has armed itself and multiplied itself, is perhaps dead in England.

All writers, all artists of any kind, in so far as they have had any philosophical or critical power, perhaps just in so far as they have been deliberate artists at all, have had some philosophy, some criticism of their art; and it has often been this philosophy, or this criticism, that has evoked their most startling inspiration, calling into outer life some portion of the divine life, or of the buried reality, which could alone extinguish in the emotions what their philosophy or their criticism would extinguish in the intellect. They have sought for no new thing, it may be, but only to understand and to copy the pure inspiration of early times, but because the divine life wars upon our outer life, and must needs change its weapons and its movements as we change ours, inspiration has come to them in beautiful startling shapes. The scientific movement brought with it a literature which was always tending to lose itself in externalities of all kinds, in opinion, in declamation, in picturesque writing, in word-painting, or in what Mr. Symons has called an attempt 'to build in brick and mortar inside the covers of a book';[5] and now writers have begun to dwell upon the element of evocation, of suggestion, upon what we call the symbolism in great writers.

2. That is, Shakespeare's will, which famously bequeathed his "second-best bed" to his wife. *Bull:* edict or decree.
3. Richard Wagner (1813–1883), German composer.
4. Johann Wolfgang von Goethe (1749–1832): German Romantic poet and playwright. Giovanni Bardi (1534–1612): Italian musician and writer. *Pléiade:* group of sixteenth-century French poets dedicated to establishing French as a literary language.
5. From Symons's introduction to his *Symbolist Movement in Literature* (1899).

II

In 'Symbolism in Painting,'[6] I tried to describe the element of symbolism that is in pictures and sculpture, and described a little the symbolism in poetry, but did not describe at all the continuous indefinable symbolism which is the substance of all style.

There are no lines with more melancholy beauty than these by Burns:—

> The white moon is setting behind the white wave,
> And Time is setting with me, O![7]

and these lines are perfectly symbolical. Take from them the whiteness of the moon and of the wave, whose relation to the setting of Time is too subtle for the intellect, and you take from them their beauty. But, when all are together, moon and wave and whiteness and setting Time and the last melancholy cry, they evoke an emotion which cannot be evoked by any other arrangement of colours and sounds and forms. We may call this metaphorical writing, but it is better to call it symbolical writing, because metaphors are not profound enough to be moving, when they are not symbols, and when they are symbols they are the most perfect of all, because the most subtle, outside of pure sound, and through them one can best find out what symbols are. If one begins the reverie with any beautiful lines that one can remember, one finds they are like those by Burns. Begin with this line by Blake:—

> The gay fishes on the wave when the moon sucks up the dew;[8]

or these lines by Nash:—

> Brightness falls from the air,
> Queens have died young and fair,
> Dust hath closed Helen's eye;[9]

or these lines by Shakespeare:—

> Timon hath made his everlasting mansion
> Upon the beached verge of the salt flood;
> Who once a day with his embossed froth
> The turbulent surge shall cover;[1]

or take some line that is quite simple, that gets its beauty from its place in a story, and see how it flickers with the light of the many symbols that have given the story its beauty, as a sword-blade may flicker with the light of burning towers.

All sounds, all colours, all forms, either because of their preordained energies or because of long association, evoke indefinable and yet precise emotions, or, as I prefer to think, call down among us certain disembodied powers, whose footsteps over our hearts we call emotions; and when sound, and colour, and form are in a musical relation, a beautiful relation to one another, they become, as it were, one sound, one colour, one form, and evoke an emotion that is made out of their distinct evocations and yet is one emo-

6. Essay of 1898, printed preceding "Symbolism in Poetry" in *Ideas of Good and Evil* (1903).
7. Slight misquotation from Scottish poet Robert Burns's (1759–1796) "Open the Door to Me," which reads "The wan moon is setting ayont the white wave."
8. From English poet William Blake's (1757–1827) *Europe, a Prophesy.*
9. From the play *Summer's Last Will and Testament* (1600), by English playwright Thomas Nashe (1567–1601).
1. *Timon of Athens* 5.1

tion. The same relation exists between all portions of every work of art, whether it be an epic or a song, and the more perfect it is, and the more various and numerous the elements that have flowed into its perfection, the more powerful will be the emotion, the power, the god it calls among us. Because an emotion does not exist, or does not become perceptible and active among us, till it has found its expression, in colour or in sound or in form, or in all of these, and because no two modulations or arrangements of these evoke the same emotion, poets and painters and musicians, and in a less degree because their effects are momentary, day and night and cloud and shadow, are continually making and unmaking mankind. It is indeed only those things which seem useless or very feeble that have any power, and all those things that seem useful or strong, armies, moving wheels, modes of architecture, modes of government, speculations of the reason, would have been a little different if some mind long ago had not given itself to some emotion, as a woman gives herself to her lover, and shaped sounds or colours or forms, or all of these, into a musical relation, that their emotion might live in other minds. A little lyric evokes an emotion, and this emotion gathers others about it and melts into their being in the making of some great epic; and at last, needing an always less delicate body, or symbol, as it grows more powerful, it flows out, with all it has gathered, among the blind instincts of daily life, where it moves a power within powers, as one sees ring within ring in the stem of an old tree. This is maybe what Arthur O'Shaughnessy meant when he made his poets say they had built Nineveh[2] with their sighing; and I am certainly never sure, when I hear of some war, or of some religious excitement, or of some new manufacture, or of anything else that fills the ear of the world, that it has not all happened because of something that a boy piped in Thessaly.[3] I remember once telling a seeress to ask one among the gods who, as she believed, were standing about her in their symbolic bodies, what would come of a charming but seeming trivial labour of a friend, and the form answering, 'the devastation of peoples and the overwhelming of cities.' I doubt indeed if the crude circumstance of the world, which seems to create all our emotions, does more than reflect, as in multiplying mirrors, the emotions that have come to solitary men in moments of poetical contemplation; or that love itself would be more than an animal hunger but for the poet and his shadow the priest, for unless we believe that outer things are the reality, we must believe that the gross is the shadow of the subtle, that things are wise before they become foolish, and secret before they cry out in the market-place. Solitary men in moments of contemplation receive, as I think, the creative impulse from the lowest of the Nine Hierarchies, and so make and unmake mankind, and even the world itself, for does not 'the eye altering alter all'?[4]

> Our towns are copied fragments from our breast;
> And all man's Babylons strive but to impart
> The grandeurs of his Babylonian heart.[5]

2. Ancient Assyrian city. See "Ode," by British poet Arthur William Edgar O'Shaughnessy (1844–1881): "We, in the ages lying / In the buried past of the earth / Built Nineveh with our sighing."
3. Region of northern Greece.
4. From Blake's "The Mental Traveller." *Nine Hierarchies:* of angels.
5. From "The Heart," by English poet Francis Thompson (1859–1907).

III

The purpose of rhythm, it has always seemed to me, is to prolong the moment of contemplation, the moment when we are both asleep and awake, which is the one moment of creation, by hushing us with an alluring monotony, while it holds us waking by variety, to keep us in that state of perhaps real trance, in which the mind liberated from the pressure of the will is unfolded in symbols. If certain sensitive persons listen persistently to the ticking of a watch, or gaze persistently on the monotonous flashing of a light, they fall into the hypnotic trance; and rhythm is but the ticking of a watch made softer, that one must needs listen, and various, that one may not be swept beyond memory or grow weary of listening; while the patterns of the artist are but the monotonous flash woven to take the eyes in a subtler enchantment. I have heard in meditation voices that were forgotten the moment they had spoken; and I have been swept, when in more profound meditation, beyond all memory but of those things that came from beyond the threshold of waking life. I was writing once at a very symbolical and abstract poem, when my pen fell on the ground; and as I stooped to pick it up, I remembered some fantastic adventure that yet did not seem fantastic, and then another like adventure, and when I asked myself when these things had happened, I found that I was remembering my dreams for many nights. I tried to remember what I had done the day before, and then what I had done that morning; but all my waking life had perished from me, and it was only after a struggle that I came to remember it again, and as I did so that more powerful and startling life perished in its turn. Had my pen not fallen on the ground and so made me turn from the images that I was weaving into verse, I would never have known that meditation had become trance, for I would have been like one who does not know that he is passing through a wood because his eyes are on the pathway. So I think that in the making and in the understanding of a work of art, and the more easily if it is full of patterns and symbols and music, we are lured to the threshold of sleep, and it may be far beyond it, without knowing that we have ever set our feet upon the steps of horn or of ivory.

IV

Besides emotional symbols, symbols that evoke emotions alone,—and in this sense all alluring or hateful things are symbols, although their relations with one another are too subtle to delight us fully, away from rhythm and pattern,—there are intellectual symbols, symbols that evoke ideas alone, or ideas mingled with emotions; and outside the very definite traditions of mysticism and the less definite criticism of certain modern poets, these alone are called symbols. Most things belong to one or another kind, according to the way we speak of them and the companions we give them, for symbols, associated with ideas that are more than fragments of the shadows thrown upon the intellect by the emotions they evoke, are the playthings of the allegorist or the pedant, and soon pass away. If I say 'white' or 'purple' in an ordinary line of poetry, they evoke emotions so exclusively that I cannot say why they move me; but if I bring them into the same sentence with such obvious intellectual symbols as a cross or a crown of thorns, I think of purity and sovereignty. Furthermore, innumerable meanings, which are held to 'white' or to 'purple' by bonds of subtle suggestion, and alike in the emotions and in the intellect, move visibly through my mind, and move invisibly beyond the threshold of sleep, casting lights and shadows of an indefinable wisdom on what had seemed before, it may be, but sterility and noisy violence. It is the intellect that decides where the reader shall ponder over the procession of the symbols, and if the symbols are merely emotional, he gazes from amid the accidents and destinies of the world; but if the symbols are intellectual too, he becomes himself a part of pure intellect, and he is himself mingled with the procession. If I watch a rushy pool in the moonlight, my emotion at its beauty is mixed with memories of the man that I have seen ploughing by its margin, or of the lovers I saw there a night ago; but if I look at the moon herself and remember any of her ancient names and meanings, I move among divine people, and things that have shaken off our mortality, the tower of ivory, the queen of waters, the shining stag among enchanted woods, the white hare sitting upon the hilltop, the fool of Faery with his shining cup full of dreams, and it may be 'make a friend of one of these images of wonder,' and 'meet the Lord in the air.'[6] So, too, if one is moved by Shakespeare, who is content with emotional symbols that he may come the nearer to our sympathy, one is mixed with the whole spectacle of the world; while if one is moved by Dante, or by the myth of Demeter,[7] one is mixed into the shadow of God or of a goddess. So, too, one is furthest from symbols when one is busy doing this or that, but the soul moves among symbols and unfolds in symbols when trance, or madness, or deep meditation has withdrawn it from every impulse but its own. 'I then saw,' wrote Gérard de Nerval[8] of his madness, 'vaguely drifting into form, plastic images of antiquity, which outlined themselves, became definite, and seemed to represent symbols of which I only seized the idea with difficulty.' In an earlier time he would have been of that multitude whose souls austerity withdrew, even more perfectly than madness could withdraw his soul, from hope and memory, from desire and regret, that they might reveal those processions of symbols that men bow to before altars, and woo with incense and offerings. But being of our time, he has been like Maeterlinck, like Villiers de l'Isle-Adam in *Axël*,[9] like all who are preoccupied with intellectual symbols in our time, a foreshadower of the new sacred book, of which all the arts, as somebody has said, are beginning to dream. How can the arts overcome the slow dying of men's hearts that we call the progress of the world, and lay their hands upon men's heart-strings again, without becoming the garment of religion as in old times?

V

If people were to accept the theory that poetry moves us because of its symbolism, what change should one look for in the manner of our poetry? A return to the way of our fathers, a casting out of descriptions of nature for the sake of nature, of the moral law for the sake of the moral law, a casting out of all anecdotes and of that brooding over scientific opinion that so often extinguished the central flame in Tennyson,[1] and of that vehemence that

6. From Blake's *A Vision of the Last Judgment*.
7. Greek goddess of agriculture. Dante Alighieri (1265–1321), Italian poet.
8. French poet (1808–1855), who suffered from mental illnesses from 1841 until his suicide. The statement, from Nerval's *Le Rêve et la Vie* (*The Dream and Life*), is quoted in Symons's *The Symbolist Movement in Literature*.
9. Symbolist drama, by French writer Phillipe-Auguste Villiers de l'Isle-Adam (1838–1889). Maurice Maeterlinck (1862–1949): Belgian Symbolist poet and playwright.
1. Alfred, Lord Tennyson (1809–1892), English poet.

would make us do or not do certain things; or, in other words, we should come to understand that the beryl stone[2] was enchanted by our fathers that it might unfold the pictures in its heart, and not to mirror our own excited faces, or the boughs waving outside the window. With this change of substance, this return to imagination, this understanding that the laws of art, which are the hidden laws of the world, can alone bind the imagination, would come a change or style, and we would cast out of serious poetry those energetic rhythms, as of a man running, which are the invention of the will with its eyes always on something to be done or undone; and we would seek out those wavering, meditative, organic rhythms, which are the embodiment of the imagination, that neither desires nor hates, because it has done with time, and only wishes to gaze upon some reality, some beauty; nor would it be any longer possible for anybody to deny the importance of form, in all its kinds, for although you can expound an opinion, or describe a thing, when your words are not quite well chosen, you cannot give a body to something that moves beyond the senses, unless your words are as subtle, as complex, as full of mysterious life, as the body of a flower or of a woman. The form of sincere poetry, unlike the form of the 'popular poetry,' may indeed be sometimes obscure, or ungrammatical as in some of the best of the *Songs of Innocence and Experience,*[3] but it must have the perfections that escape analysis, the subtleties that have a new meaning every day, and it must have all this whether it be but a little song made out of a moment of dreamy indolence, or some great epic made out of the dreams of one poet and of a hundred generations whose hands were never weary of the sword.

1900

2. Gem believed to have magical properties.

3. By Blake.

INTRODUCTION

Toward the end of his life, Yeats wrote this essay as a general introduction to a deluxe edition of his collected works, planned but never published by Charles Scribner. Drawing on an array of English, Irish, Indian, and other sources, he summarizes many of the principle ideas behind his work. The poet, Yeats explains, is not merely the everyday, accidental self who "sits down to breakfast," but a self intensified, purified, reborn through the discipline of writing. Yeats believes "all that is personal soon rots; it must be packed in ice or salt," and as salt or ice for poetry, he proposes traditional rhythms, stanzaic forms, and a normal, if impassioned, syntax. The poet can vary and work against fixed meters, but these must remain a "ghostly voice." Yeats links poetic form to national experience, contrasting the Irishness of his tense, tightly knit verse with English meditative poetry. He also explores his vexed relationship with English, the language of Ireland's oppressors but also the language of Shakespeare and Blake. "[E]verything I love," he states, "has come to me through English; my hatred tortures me with love, my love with hate." Written in 1937 and originally printed as "A General Introduction for My Work" in *Essays and Introductions* (1961), the text is excerpted from *Later Essays,* ed. William H. O'Donnell (1994), vol. 5 of *The Collected Works of W. B. Yeats.*

W. B. YEATS

Introduction [A General Introduction for My Work]

I. The First Principle

A poet writes always of his personal life, in his finest work out of its tragedies, whatever it be, remorse, lost love or mere loneliness; he never speaks directly as to someone at the breakfast table, there is always a phantasmagoria. Dante and Milton had mythologies, Shakespeare the characters of English history, of traditional romance; even when the poet seems most himself, when Raleigh and gives potentates the lie,[1] or Shelley 'a nerve o'er which do creep the else unfelt oppressions of mankind',[2] or Byron when 'the heart wears out the breast as the sword wears out the sheath',[3] he is never the bundle of accident and incoherence that sits down to breakfast; he has been re-born as an idea, something intended, complete. A novelist might describe his accidence, his incoherence, he must not, he is more type than man, more passion than type. He is Lear, Romeo, Oedipus, Tiresias; he has stepped out of a play and even the woman he loves is Rosalind, Cleopatra, never The Dark Lady.[4] He is part of his own phantasmagoria and we adore him because nature has grown intelligible, and by so doing a part of our creative power. 'When mind is lost in the light of the Self', says the Prashna Upanishad,[5] 'it dreams no more; still in the body it is lost in happiness.' 'A wise man seeks in Self', says the Chāndôgya Upanishad, 'those that are alive and those that are dead and gets what the world cannot give.' The world knows nothing because it has made nothing, we know everything because we have made everything.

II. Subject-Matter

* * *

* * *I am convinced that in two or three generations it will become generally known that the mechanical theory[6] has no reality, that the natural and supernatural are knit together, that to escape a dangerous fanaticism we must study a new science; at that moment Europeans may find something attractive in a Christ posed against a background not of Judaism but of Druidism, not shut off in dead history, but flowing, concrete, phenomenal.

I was born into this faith, have lived in it, and shall die in it; my Christ, a legitimate deduction from the Creed of St Patrick[7] as I think, is that Unity of Being Dante compared to a perfectly proportioned human body, Blake's 'Imagination',[8] what the Upanishads have named 'Self': nor is this

1. From "The Lie," by English writer and explorer Sir Walter Ralegh (1552–1618): "Tell potentates, they live / Acting by others' action; / Not loved unless they give, / Not strong but by a faction: / If potentates reply, / Give potentates the lie."
2. From "Julian and Maddalo," by English poet Percy Bysshe Shelley (1792–1822).
3. From "So, We'll Go No More a Roving," by English poet George Gordon, Lord Byron (1788–1824).
4. The woman to whom many of Shakespeare's de-idealizing sonnets are addressed. The rest of the names refer to characters in Shakespeare's plays and in Sophocles' ancient Greek drama *Oedipus the King*.
5. One of a series of ancient philosophical dialogues in Sanskrit. From *Ten Principal Upanishads* (1937), translated by Yeats and Indian monk Shri Purohit Swami (1882–1941).
6. Theory explaining the universe in strictly naturalistic, Newtonian terms.
7. From the second paragraph of "The Confession of St. Patrick, or His Epistle to the Irish," by the fifth-century saint, the apostle of Ireland.
8. In *Jerusalem,* English poet William Blake (1757–1827) describes imagination as the "Divine

unity distant and therefore intellectually understandable, but imminent,[9] differing from man to man and age to age, taking upon itself pain and ugliness, 'eye of newt, and leg of frog'.[1]

Subconscious preoccupation with this theme brought me *A Vision*,[2] its harsh geometry an incomplete interpretation. The 'Irishry' have preserved their ancient 'deposit' through wars which, during the sixteenth and seventeenth centuries, became wars of extermination; no people, Lecky said at the opening of his *Ireland in the Eighteenth Century*,[3] have undergone greater persecution, nor did that persecution altogether cease up to our own day. No people hate as we do in whom that past is always alive; there are moments when hatred poisons my life and I accuse myself of effeminacy because I have not given it adequate expression. It is not enough to have put it into the mouth of a rambling peasant poet. Then I remind myself that, though mine is the first English marriage I know of in the direct line, all my family names are English and that I owe my soul to Shakespeare, to Spenser and to Blake, perhaps to William Morris,[4] and to the English language in which I think, speak and write, that everything I love has come to me through English; my hatred tortures me with love, my love with hate. I am like the Tibetan monk who dreams at his initiation that he is eaten by a wild beast and learns on waking that he himself is eater and eaten. This is Irish hatred and solitude, the hatred of human life that made Swift write *Gulliver*[5] and the epitaph upon his tomb, that can still make us wag between extremes and doubt our sanity.

Again and again I am asked why I do not write in Gaelic; some four or five years ago I was invited to dinner by a London society and found myself among London journalists, Indian students and foreign political refugees. An Indian paper says it was a dinner in my honour, I hope not; I have forgotten though I have a clear memory of my own angry mind. I should have spoken as men are expected to speak at public dinners; I should have paid and been paid conventional compliments; then they would speak of the refugees, from that on all would be lively and topical, foreign tyranny would be arraigned, England seem even to those confused Indians the protector of liberty; I grew angrier and angrier; Wordsworth, that typical Englishman, had published his famous sonnet to François Dominique Toussaint, a Santo Domingo negro:

> There's not a breathing of the common wind
> That will forget thee[6]

in the year when Emmet conspired and died, and he remembered that rebellion as little as the half hanging and the pitch cap that preceded it by half a dozen years.[7] That there might be no topical speeches I denounced the

---

body of the lord Jesus." Yeats's ideas about the Unity of Being are drawn from his reading of Dante's *Il Convito*.

9. In manuscript, Yeats wrote "imanent" (a misspelling of "immanent"), but he allowed "imminent" to stand in the typescript.

1. Ingredients of the witches' cauldron in Shakespeare's *Macbeth* 4.1.

2. Yeats's mystical writings (1925, 1937), in which he sketches out and schematizes many of his theories.

3. *A History of Ireland in the Eighteenth Century*, by Irish historian William Edward Hartpole Lecky (1838–1903).

4. English poet and designer (1834–1896). Edmund Spenser (1552–1599), English poet who, in addition to poetic works such as *The Faerie Queene*, wrote a treatise proposing the extermination of the Irish.

5. *Gulliver's Travels*, by Irish satirist Jonathan Swift (1667–1745). Yeats wrote a poem titled "Swift's Epitaph," a loose translation of the Latin on Swift's tomb, which claims that "Swift has sailed into his rest; / Savage indignation there / Cannot lacerate his breast."

6. From "To Toussaint L'Ouverture," by English poet William Wordsworth (1770–1850). L'Ouverture (1743–1803) died in prison after rebelling against France's rule in Haiti.

7. Paper caps filled with burning pitch were used for torture during the martial law preceding and following the Irish Rising of 1798. Robert Emmet (1778–1803), Irish nationalist executed after the Irish rebellion of 1803.

oppression of the people of India; being a man of letters, not a politician, I told how they had been forced to learn everything, even their own Sanscrit, through the vehicle of English till the first discoverers of wisdom had become bywords for vague abstract facility. I begged the Indian writers present to remember that no man can think or write with music and vigour except in his mother tongue. I turned a friendly audience hostile, yet when I think of that scene I am unrepentant and angry.

I could no more have written in Gaelic than can those Indians write in English; Gaelic is my national language, but it is not my mother tongue.

III. *Style and Attitude*

Style is almost unconscious. I know what I have tried to do, little what I have done. Contemporary lyric poems, even those that moved me—'The Stream's Secret', 'Dolores'[8]—seemed too long, but an Irish preference for a swift current might be mere indolence, yet Burns may have felt the same when he read Thomson and Cowper.[9] The English mind is meditative, rich, deliberate; it may remember the Thames[1] valley. I planned to write short lyrics or poetic drama where every speech [would] be short and concentrated, knit by dramatic tension, and I did so with more confidence because young English poets were at that time writing out of emotion at the moment of crisis, though their old slow-moving meditation returned almost at once. Then, and in this English poetry has followed my lead, I tried to make the language of poetry coincide with that of passionate, normal speech. I wanted to write in whatever language comes most naturally when we soliloquise, as I do all day long, upon the events of our own lives or of any life where we can see ourselves for the moment. I sometimes compare myself with the mad old slum women I hear denouncing and remembering; 'how dare you,' I heard one say of some imaginary suitor, 'and you without health or a home'. If I spoke my thoughts aloud they might be as angry and as wild. It was a long time before I had made a language to my liking; I began to make it when I discovered some twenty years ago that I must seek, not as Wordsworth thought words in common use,[2] but a powerful and passionate syntax, and a complete coincidence between period and stanza. Because I need a passionate syntax for passionate subject-matter I compel myself to accept those traditional metres that have developed with the language. Ezra Pound, Turner, Lawrence, wrote admirable free verse, I could not.[3] I would lose myself, become joyless like those mad old women. The translators of the Bible, Sir Thomas Browne,[4] certain translators from the Greek when translators still bothered about rhythm, created a form midway between prose and verse that seems natural to impersonal meditation; but all that is personal soon rots; it must be packed in ice or salt. Once when I was in delirium from pneumonia I dictated a letter to George Moore[5] telling him to eat salt because it was a symbol of eternity; the delirium passed, I had no memory of that letter, but I must have meant what I now mean. If I wrote of personal love or sorrow in free verse,

8. Long poems, by Dante Gabriel Rossetti (1828–1882) and Algernon Charles Swinburne (1837–1909), respectively.
9. James Thomson (1700–1748) and William Cowper (1731–1800): poets most famous for their long poems. Robert Burns (1759–1796): Scottish poet of short lyrics.
1. English river that runs through London.
2. In the preface to *Lyrical Ballads* (1800), Wordsworth says that poetry should be written in "language really used by men."
3. In his *Oxford Book of Modern Verse* (1936), Yeats included free verse by American poet Ezra Pound (1885–1972), English poet Walter Turner (1889–1946), and English poet and novelist D. H. Lawrence (1885–1930).
4. English physician and author (1605–1682) with an elaborate prose style.
5. Irish novelist (1852–1933).

or in any rhythm that left it unchanged, amid all its accident, I would be full of self-contempt because of my egotism and indiscretion, and I foresee the boredom of my reader. I must choose a traditional stanza, even what I alter must seem traditional. I commit my emotion to shepherds, herdsmen, camel-drivers, learned men, Milton's or Shelley's Platonist, that tower Palmer drew.[6] Talk to me of originality and I will turn on you with rage. I am a crowd, I am a lonely man, I am nothing. Ancient salt is best packing. The heroes of Shakespeare convey to us through their looks, or through the metaphorical patterns of their speech, the sudden enlargement of their vision, their ecstasy at the approach of death, 'She should have died hereafter', 'Of many million kisses, the poor last', 'Absent thee from felicity awhile'; they have become God or Mother Goddess, the pelican, 'My baby at my breast',[7] but all must be cold; no actress has ever sobbed when she played Cleopatra, even the shallow brain of a producer has never thought of such a thing. The supernatural is present, cold winds blow across our hands, upon our faces, the thermometer falls, and because of that cold we are hated by journalists and groundlings. There may be in this or that detail painful tragedy, but in the whole work none. I have heard Lady Gregory say, rejecting some play in the modern manner sent to the Abbey Theatre, 'Tragedy must be a joy to the man who dies.' Nor is it any different with lyrics, songs, narrative poems; neither scholars nor the populace have sung or read anything generation after generation because of its pain. The maid of honour whose tragedy they sing must be lifted out of history with timeless pattern, she is one of the four Maries,[8] the rhythm is old and familiar, imagination must dance, must be carried beyond feeling into the aboriginal ice. Is ice the correct word? I once boasted, copying the phrase from a letter of my father's, that I would write a poem 'cold and passionate as the dawn'.[9]

When I wrote in blank verse I was dissatisfied; my vaguely mediaeval *Countess Cathleen* fitted the measure, but our Heroic Age went better, or so I fancied, in the ballad metre of *The Green Helmet.*[1] There was something in what I felt about Deirdre, about Cuchulain,[2] that rejected the Renaissance and its characteristic metres, and this was a principal reason why I created in dance plays the form that varies blank verse with lyric metres. When I speak blank verse and analyse my feelings I stand at a moment of history when instinct, its traditional songs and dances, its general agreement, is of the past. I have been cast up out of the whale's belly though I still remember the sound and sway that came from beyond its ribs,[3] and, like the Queen in Paul Fort's ballad,[4] I smell of the fish of the sea. The contrapuntal structure of the verse, to employ a term adopted by Robert Bridges,[5] combines the past and present. If I repeat the first line of *Paradise Lost* so as to emphasise its

6. English artist Samuel Palmer (1805–1881) drew "The Lonely Tower" (1879) as an illustration of Milton's poem about the pensive man, "Il Penseroso" (1645), in which a scholar in a "high lonely tower" is dedicated to discovering the secrets of Plato; in Shelley's "Prince Athanase," the idealistic hero searches for love.

7. From *Macbeth* 5.4, *Anthony and Cleopatra* 4.15, *Hamlet* 5.2, respectively. *Pelican:* thought to feed its babies with its blood and thus often a symbol of self-sacrifice.

8. Mary, Queen of Scots (1542–1587) was served by four women named Mary.

9. From "The Fisherman" (1916): "Before I am old / I shall have written him one / Poem maybe as cold / And passionate as the dawn."

1. *The Countess Cathleen* (1892, later revised) is written in blank verse; *The Green Helmet* (1910), in iambic heptameter, which resembles the meter of a ballad (alternating between four- and three-stress lines).

2. The warrior-hero of the Irish mythological Ulster Cycle; he also appears in Yeats's "dance" plays, derived from Japanese Noh drama. *Deirdre:* in the Ulster Cycle, woman chosen to be queen of Ulster before she elopes with Naoise.

3. Cf. Jonah 2.10: "And the Lord spake unto the fish, and it vomited out Jonah upon the dry land."

4. "La Reine à la Mer" ("The Queen of the Sea," 1894–96), by French poet Paul Fort (1872–1960).

5. English poet (1844–1930), who stressed the poetic tension of the counterpoint between regular meters and the rhythm of poetry as actually spoken.

five feet I am among the folk singers, 'Of mán's fírst dísobédience ánd the frúit', but speak it as I should I cross it with another emphasis, that of passionate prose, 'Of mán's fírst disobédience and the frúit', or 'Of mán's fírst dísobedience and the frúit', the folk song is still there, but a ghostly voice, an unvariable possibility, an unconscious norm. What moves me and my hearer is a vivid speech that has no laws except that it must not exorcise the ghostly voice. I am awake and asleep, at my moment of revelation, self-possessed in self-surrender; there is no rhyme, no echo of the beaten drum, the dancing foot, that would overset my balance. When I was a boy I wrote a poem upon dancing that had one good line: 'They snatch with their hands at the sleep of the skies.' If I sat down and thought for a year I would discover that but for certain syllabic limitations, a rejection or acceptance of certain elisions, I must wake or sleep.

The Countess Cathleen could speak a blank verse which I had loosened, almost put out of joint, for her need, because I thought of her as mediaeval and thereby connected her with the general European movement. For Deirdre and Cuchulain and all the other figures of Irish legend are still in the whale's belly.

IV. Whither?

The young English poets reject dream and personal emotion; they have thought out opinions that join them to this or that political party; they employ an intricate psychology, action in character, not as in the ballads character in action, and all consider that they have a right to the same close attention that men pay to the mathematician and the metaphysician. One of the more distinguished has just explained that man has hitherto slept but must now awake.[6] They are determined to express the factory, the metropolis, that they may be modern. Young men teaching school in some picturesque cathedral town, or settled for life in Capri or in Sicily, defend their type of metaphor by saying that it comes naturally to a man who travels to his work by Tube.[7] I am indebted to a man of this school who went through my work at my request, crossing out all conventional metaphors,[8] but they seem to me to have rejected also those dream associations which were the whole art of Mallarmé.[9] He had topped a previous wave. As they express not what the Upanishads call 'that ancient Self' but individual intellect, they have the right to choose the man in the Tube because of his objective importance. They attempt to kill the whale, push the Renaissance higher yet, out-think Leonardo;[1] their verse kills the folk ghost and yet would remain verse. I am joined to the 'Irishry' and I expect a counter-Renaissance. No doubt it is part of the game to push that Renaissance; I make no complaint; I am accustomed to the geometrical arrangement of history in *A Vision,* but I go deeper than 'custom' for my convictions. When I stand upon O'Connell Bridge[2] in the half-light and notice that discordant architecture, all those electric signs, where modern heterogeneity has taken physical form, a vague hatred comes up out of my own dark and I am certain that wherever in Europe there are

6. Perhaps W. H. Auden (1907–1973) or C. Day Lewis (1804–1972).
7. London's underground railway. Lewis taught in the spa town of Cheltenham in the early 1930s. D. H. Lawrence lived in Capri and Sicily in the early 1920s.
8. Ezra Pound did this circa 1910.
9. Stéphane Mallarmé (1842–1898), French poet.
1. Leonardo da Vinci (1452–1519), Italian Renaissance artist and inventor.
2. Over Dublin's River Liffey.

minds strong enough to lead others the same vague hatred rises; in four or five or in less generations this hatred will have issued in violence and imposed some kind of rule of kindred. I cannot know the nature of that rule, for its opposite fills the light; all I can do to bring it nearer is to intensify my hatred. I am no Nationalist, except in Ireland for passing reasons; State and Nation are the work of intellect, and when you consider what comes before and after them they are, as Victor Hugo said of something or other, not worth the blade of grass God gives for the nest of the linnet.[3]

1937 1961

3. Small finch. Victor-Marie Hugo (1802–1885), French writer.

ROMANTICISM AND CLASSICISM

Although he published only six poems during his lifetime, T. E. Hulme (1883–1917), English poet, philosopher, and critic, was one of the strongest intellectual forces behind the development of modern poetry. In this essay, probably composed in either 1911 or 1912 and probably delivered as a lecture in 1912, Hulme prophesies the development of a "dry, hard, classical verse" that exhibits precision, clarity, and freshness. He sharply repudiates the "spilt religion" of Romanticism, responsible for vagueness and gaseousness in the arts. Hulme sees human beings as limited and capable of improvement only through the influence of tradition. These ideas were an important influence on the thought and poetry of T. S. Eliot. Hulme's views of conventional language, the visual image, and verbal exactitude also influenced Ezra Pound's Imagism and Vorticism.

Hulme was born in Staffordshire, England, and attended St. John's College, Cambridge, from which he was expelled for rebellious behavior in 1904 without finishing his degree. He lived largely in London, where, befriending Pound and other poets and artists, he became a central figure of the prewar avant-garde. A critic of pacifism, Hulme enlisted as a private in the army when World War I broke out, in 1914, and was killed in battle, in 1917. First published posthumously in *Speculations* (1924), the essay is excerpted from *The Collected Writings of T. E. Hulme* (1994), ed. Karen Csengeri.

T. E. HULME

From Romanticism and Classicism

I want to maintain that after a hundred years of romanticism, we are in for a classical revival, and that the particular weapon of this new classical spirit, when it works in verse, will be fancy. And in this I imply the superiority of fancy—not superior generally or absolutely, for that would be obvious nonsense, but superior in the sense that we use the word good in empirical ethics—good for something, superior for something. I shall have to prove then two things, first that a classical revival is coming, and, secondly, for its particular purposes, fancy will be superior to imagination.

So banal have the terms Imagination and Fancy become that we imagine they must have always been in the language. Their history as two differing terms in the vocabulary of criticism is comparatively short. Originally, of course, they both mean the same thing; they first began to be differentiated by the German writers on æsthetics in the eighteenth century.

I know that in using the words 'classic' and 'romantic' I am doing a dangerous thing. They represent five or six different kinds of antitheses, and while I may be using them in one sense you may be interpreting them in another. In this present connection I am using them in a perfectly precise and limited sense. I ought really to have coined a couple of new words, but I prefer to use the ones I have used, as I then conform to the practice of the group of polemical writers who make most use of them at the present day, and have almost succeeded in making them political catchwords. I mean Maurras, Lasserre, and all the group connected with *L'Action Française.*[1]

At the present time this is the particular group with which the distinction is most vital. Because it has become a party symbol. If you asked a man of a certain set whether he preferred the classics or the romantics, you could deduce from that what his politics were.

The best way of gliding into a proper definition of my terms would be to start with a set of people who are prepared to fight about it—for in them you will have no vagueness. (Other people take the infamous attitude of the person with catholic tastes who says he likes both.)

About a year ago, a man whose name I think was Fauchois gave a lecture at the Odéon on Racine,[2] in the course of which he made some disparaging remarks about his dullness, lack of invention and the rest of it. This caused an immediate riot: fights took place all over the house; several people were arrested and imprisoned, and the rest of the series of lectures took place with hundreds of gendarmes[3] and detectives scattered all over the place. These people interrupted because the classical ideal is a living thing to them and Racine is the great classic. That is what I call a real vital interest in literature. They regard romanticism as an awful disease from which France had just recovered.

The thing is complicated in their case by the fact that it was romanticism that made the revolution.[4] They hate the revolution, so they hate romanticism.

I make no apology for dragging in politics here; romanticism both in England and France is associated with certain political views, and it is in taking a concrete example of the working out of a principle in action that you can get its best definition.

What was the positive principle behind all the other principles of '89? I am talking here of the revolution in as far as it was an idea; I leave out material causes—they only produce the forces. The barriers which could easily have resisted or guided these forces had been previously rotted away by ideas. This always seems to be the case in successful changes; the privileged class is beaten only when it has lost faith in itself, when it has itself been penetrated with the ideas which are working against it.

1. Charles Maurras (1868–1952) and Pierre Lasserre (1867–1930) were intellectuals associated with *l'Action Française,* a reactionary political movement that denigrated Romanticism and supported the Catholic Church as a force for order. (T. S. Eliot also fell under the movement's influence.)

2. Jean Racine (1639–1699), French tragic playwright associated with classicism. The riot occurred at a lecture delivered by French playwright René Fauchois (1882–1962) at the Odéon Theater, Paris, on November 3, 1910.

3. Police officers (French).

4. The French Revolution (1789–99).

It was not the rights of man—that was a good solid practical war-cry. The thing which created enthusiasm, which made the revolution practically a new religion, was something more positive than that. People of all classes, people who stood to lose by it, were in a positive ferment about the idea of liberty. There must have been some idea which enabled them to think that something positive could come out of so essentially negative a thing. There was, and here I get my definition of romanticism. They had been taught by Rousseau[5] that man was by nature good, that it was only bad laws and customs that had suppressed him. Remove all these and the infinite possibilities of man would have a chance. This is what made them think that something positive could come out of disorder, this is what created the religious enthusiasm. Here is the root of all romanticism: that man, the individual, is an infinite reservoir of possibilities; and if you can so rearrange society by the destruction of oppressive order then these possibilities will have a chance and you will get Progress.

One can define the classical quite clearly as the exact opposite to this. Man is an extraordinarily fixed and limited animal whose nature is absolutely constant. It is only by tradition and organisation that anything decent can be got out of him.

This view was a little shaken at the time of Darwin. You remember his particular hypothesis, that new species came into existence by the cumulative effect of small variations—this seems to admit the possibility of future progress. But at the present day the contrary hypothesis makes headway in the shape of De Vries's[6] mutation theory, that each new species comes into existence, not gradually by the accumulation of small steps, but suddenly in a jump, a kind of sport, and that once in existence it remains absolutely fixed. This enables me to keep the classical view with an appearance of scientific backing.

Put shortly, these are the two views, then. One, that man is intrinsically good, spoilt by circumstance; and the other that he is intrinsically limited, but disciplined by order and tradition to something fairly decent. To the one party man's nature is like a well, to the other like a bucket. The view which regards man as a well, a reservoir full of possibilities, I call the romantic; the one which regards him as a very finite and fixed creature, I call the classical.

One may note here that the Church has always taken the classical view since the defeat of the Pelagian heresy[7] and the adoption of the sane classical dogma of original sin.

It would be a mistake to identify the classical view with that of materialism. On the contrary it is absolutely identical with the normal religious attitude. I should put it in this way: That part of the fixed nature of man is the belief in the Deity. This should be as fixed and true for every man as belief in the existence of matter and in the objective world. It is parallel to appetite, the instinct of sex, and all the other fixed qualities. Now at certain times, by the use of either force or rhetoric, these instincts have been suppressed—in Florence under Savonarola, in Geneva under Calvin, and here under the Roundheads.[8] The inevi-

5. Jean-Jacques Rousseau (1712–1778), Swiss-born French writer and philosopher whose ideas greatly influenced the leaders of the French Revolution and the development of Romanticism.
6. Hugo de Vries (1848–1935), Dutch botanist.
7. Controversial Church doctrine denying the transmission of original sin, named after the theologian Pelagius (c. 354–?).
8. Puritan members of the Parliamentary Party during the English Civil War (1642–1651), named for their short haircuts. Girolamo Savonarola (1452–1498): Dominican monk who denounced the extravagance of the Renaissance. John Calvin (1509–1564): Protestant theologian who stressed the predestination and the depravity of humankind.

table result of such a process is that the repressed instinct bursts out in some abnormal direction. So with religion. By the perverted rhetoric of Rationalism, your natural instincts are suppressed and you are converted into an agnostic. Just as in the case of the other instincts, Nature has her revenge. The instincts that find their right and proper outlet in religion must come out in some other way. You don't believe in a God, so you begin to believe that man is a god. You don't believe in Heaven, so you begin to believe in a heaven on earth. In other words, you get romanticism. The concepts that are right and proper in their own sphere are spread over, and so mess up, falsify and blur the clear outlines of human experience. It is like pouring a pot of treacle[9] over the dinner table. Romanticism then, and this is the best definition I can give of it, is spilt religion.

I must now shirk the difficulty of saying exactly what I mean by romantic and classical in verse. I can only say that it means the result of these two attitudes towards the cosmos, towards man, in so far as it gets reflected in verse. The romantic, because he thinks man infinite, must always be talking about the infinite; and as there is always the bitter contrast between what you think you ought to be able to do and what man actually can, it always tends, in its later stages at any rate, to be gloomy. I really can't go any further than to say it is the reflection of these two temperaments, and point out examples of the different spirits. On the one hand I would take such diverse people as Horace, most of the Elizabethans and the writers of the Augustan age, and on the other side Lamartine, Hugo, parts of Keats, Coleridge, Byron, Shelley and Swinburne.[1]

I know quite well that when people think of classical and romantic in verse, the contrast at once comes into their mind between, say, Racine and Shakespeare. I don't mean this; the dividing line that I intend is here misplaced a little from the true middle. That Racine is on the extreme classical side I agree, but if you call Shakespeare romantic, you are using a different definition to the one I give. You are thinking of the difference between classic and romantic as being merely one between restraint and exuberance. I should say with Nietzsche[2] that there are two kinds of classicism, the static and the dynamic. Shakespeare is the classic of motion.

What I mean by classical in verse, then, is this. That even in the most imaginative flights there is always a holding back, a reservation. The classical poet never forgets this finiteness, this limit of man. He remembers always that he is mixed up with earth. He may jump; but he always returns back; he never flies away into the circumambient gas.

You might say if you wished that the whole of the romantic attitude seems to crystallise in verse round metaphors of flight. Hugo is always flying, flying over abysses, flying up into the eternal gases. The word infinite in every other line.

In the classical attitude you never seem to swing right along to the infinite nothing. If you say an extravagant thing which does exceed the limits inside which you know man to be fastened, yet there is always conveyed in some

9. Molasses (British).

1. Horace (65–8 B.C.E.): Roman poet. *The Elizabethans:* English poets and playwrights (such as Shakespeare) writing during the reign of Queen Elizabeth I (1558–1603). *The Augustan Age:* the late seventeenth and early eighteenth centuries, when English writers such as John Dryden (1631–1700) and Alexander Pope (1688–1744) embraced a classicism likened to the Augustan Age of Rome. Alphonse Lamartine (1790–1869): French poet and politician. Victor-Marie Hugo (1802–1885): French Romantic poet and novelist. John Keats (1795–1821), Samuel Taylor Coleridge (1772–1834), George Gordon (Lord) Byron (1788–1824), Percy Bysshe Shelley (1792–1822), Algernon Charles Swinburne (1837–1909): English poets.

2. Friedrich Nietzsche (1844–1900), German philosopher.

way at the end an impression of yourself standing outside it, and not quite believing it, or consciously putting it forward as a flourish. You never go blindly into an atmosphere more than the truth, an atmosphere too rarefied for man to breathe for long. You are always faithful to the conception of a limit. It is a question of pitch; in romantic verse you move at a certain pitch of rhetoric which you know, man being what he is, to be a little high-falutin. The kind of thing you get in Hugo or Swinburne. In the coming classical reaction that will feel just wrong. * * *

* * *

I object even to the best of the romantics. I object still more to the receptive attitude.[3] I object to the sloppiness which doesn't consider that a poem is a poem unless it is moaning or whining about something or other. I always think in this connection of the last line of a poem of John Webster's which ends with a request I cordially endorse:

'End your moan and come away.'[4]

The thing has got so bad now that a poem which is all dry and hard, a properly classical poem, would not be considered poetry at all. How many people now can lay their hands on their hearts and say they like either Horace or Pope? They feel a kind of chill when they read them.

The dry hardness which you get in the classics is absolutely repugnant to them. Poetry that isn't damp isn't poetry at all. They cannot see that accurate description is a legitimate object of verse. Verse to them always means a bringing in of some of the emotions that are grouped round the word infinite.

The essence of poetry to most people is that it must lead them to a beyond of some kind. Verse strictly confined to the earthly and the definite (Keats is full of it) might seem to them to be excellent writing, excellent craftsmanship, but not poetry. So much has romanticism debauched us, that, without some form of vagueness, we deny the highest.

In the classic it is always the light of ordinary day, never the light that never was on land or sea. It is always perfectly human and never exaggerated: man is always man and never a god.

But the awful result of romanticism is that, accustomed to this strange light, you can never live without it. Its effect on you is that of a drug.

* * *

* * * You have the metaphysic which in defining beauty or the nature of art always drags in the infinite. Particularly in Germany, the land where theories of æsthetics were first created, the romantic æsthetes collated all beauty to an impression of the infinite involved in the identification of our being in absolute spirit. In the least element of beauty we have a total intuition of the whole world. Every artist is a kind of pantheist.

Now it is quite obvious to anyone who holds this kind of theory that any poetry which confines itself to the finite can never be of the highest kind. It seems a contradiction in terms to them. And as in metaphysics you get the last refuge of a prejudice, so it is now necessary for me to refute this.

Here follows a tedious piece of dialectic, but it is necessary for my purpose.

3. Elsewhere in the essay, Hulme claims that every sort of verse has an accompanying receptive attitude by which readers come to expect certain qualities from poetry. These receptive attitudes, he explains, sometimes outlast the poetry from which they develop.

4. From *The Duchess of Malfi* (1623) 4.2, by English dramatist John Webster (c. 1580–c. 1625).

I must avoid two pitfalls in discussing the idea of beauty. On the one hand there is the old classical view which is supposed to define it as lying in conformity to certain standard fixed forms; and on the other hand there is the romantic view which drags in the infinite. I have got to find a metaphysic between these two which will enable me to hold consistently that a neo-classic verse of the type I have indicated involves no contradiction in terms. It is essential to prove that beauty may be in small, dry things.

The great aim is accurate, precise and definite description. The first thing is to recognise how extraordinarily difficult this is. It is no mere matter of carefulness; you have to use language, and language is by its very nature a communal thing; that is, it expresses never the exact thing but a compromise—that which is common to you, me and everybody. But each man sees a little differently, and to get out clearly and exactly what he does see, he must have a terrific struggle with language, whether it be with words or the technique of other arts. Language has its own special nature, its own conventions and communal ideas. It is only by a concentrated effort of the mind that you can hold it fixed to your own purpose. I always think that the fundamental process at the back of all the arts might be represented by the following metaphor. You know what I call architect's curves—flat pieces of wood with all different kinds of curvature. By a suitable selection from those you can draw approximately any curve you like. The artist I take to be the man who simply can't bear the idea of that 'approximately'. He will get the exact curve of what he sees whether it be an object or an idea in the mind. I shall here have to change my metaphor a little to get the process in his mind. Suppose that instead of your curved pieces of wood you have a springy piece of steel of the same types of curvature as the wood. Now the state of tension or concentration of mind, if he is doing anything really good in this struggle against the ingrained habit of the technique, may be represented by a man employing all his fingers to bend the steel out of its own curve and into the exact curve which you want. Something different to what it would assume naturally.

* * *

This is the point I aim at, then, in my argument. I prophesy that a period of dry, hard, classical verse is coming. I have met the preliminary objection founded on the bad romantic æsthetic that in such verse, from which the infinite is excluded, you cannot have the essence of poetry at all.

After attempting to sketch out what this positive quality is, I can get on to the end of my paper in this way: That where you get this quality exhibited in the realm of the emotions you get imagination, and that where you get this quality exhibited in the contemplation of finite things you get fancy.

* * * Poetry * * * is a compromise for a language of intuition which would hand over sensations bodily. It always endeavours to arrest you, and to make you continuously see a physical thing, to prevent you gliding through an abstract process. It chooses fresh epithets and fresh metaphors, not so much because they are new, and we are tired of the old, but because the old cease to convey a physical thing and become abstract counters. A poet says a ship 'coursed the seas' to get a physical image, instead of the counter word 'sailed'. Visual meanings can only be transferred by the new bowl of metaphor; prose is an old pot that lets them leak out. Images in verse are not mere decoration, but the very essence of an

intuitive language. Verse is a pedestrian taking you over the ground, prose—a train which delivers you at a destination.

* * *

I shall maintain that wherever you get an extraordinary interest in a thing, a great zest in its contemplation which carries on the contemplator to accurate description in the sense of the word accurate I have just analysed, there you have sufficient justification for poetry. It must be an intense zest which heightens a thing out of the level of prose. I am using contemplation here just in the same way that Plato used it, only applied to a different subject;[5] it is a detached interest. 'The object of æsthetic contemplation is something framed apart by itself and regarded without memory or expectation, simply as being itself, as end not means, as individual not universal.'

* * * [T]he point is that exactly the same activity is at work as in the highest verse. That is the avoidance of conventional language in order to get the exact curve of the thing.

* * *

* * * A powerfully imaginative mind seizes and combines at the same instant all the important ideas of its poem or picture, and while it works with one of them, it is at the same instant working with and modifying all in their relation to it and never losing sight of their bearings on each other—as the motion of a snake's body goes through all parts at once and its volition acts at the same instant in coils which go contrary ways.

* * *

1911–12 1924

5. The ancient Greek philosopher Plato held that the highest form of human activity was the contemplation of the Good (*Republic* 540a–c) and the Beautiful (*Symposium* 210b–212a).

BLAST

The journal *Blast* was published only twice—on June 20, 1914, though released on July 2, one month before Great Britain entered World War I, and a year later, during the war that would bring its short life to an end. But its initial preface and two-part manifesto, printed in the first pages of the first number, are among the most important documents in the history of Anglo-American modernism. They rhetorically and typographically embody the violent iconoclasm of Vorticism, an avant-garde movement in the literary and visual arts centered in London. Ezra Pound, the movement's principal literary figure, became a Vorticist after abandoning Imagism, because he felt that the *vortex,* "the point of maximum energy," offered a more dynamic model for poetry than the static image of the Imagists. The English writer and painter Wyndham Lewis (1882–1957) founded and edited *Blast,* a word he said "means the blowing away of dead ideas and worn-out notions" (it also suggests *fire, explosion,* and *damn!*). He drafted much of the Vorticist manifesto and fashioned its shocking visual design, likening *Blast* to a "battering ram." The French sculptor Henri Gaudier-Brzeska (1891–1915), killed in

World War I and memorialized both in the "War Number" of *Blast* and in a book of Pound's named for him, was another key Vorticist leader. In the pages of *Blast* 1 and 2, artwork by Lewis, Gaudier-Brzeska, and other visual artists appeared alongside the writing of Lewis, Pound, T. S. Eliot (including his "Preludes"), and other avant-garde writers. Two of *Blast*'s illustrations are reproduced here, before and after the manifesto.

The Vorticist manifesto, signed by Lewis, Pound, and Gaudier-Brzeska, among others, reflects the London modernists' competitive anxiety about European avant-gardes such as Cubism and especially Futurism, which, under the charismatic leadership of F. T. Marinetti, celebrated speed, modernization, and the machine. Futurism influenced *Blast*'s experimental layout and rhetoric of negation: Marinetti had called for a destruction of the museums, the libraries, all such bastions of the past; the Vorticists—in lists compiled at group meetings—likewise blast convention, standardization, the middle class, even the "years 1837 to 1900." And yet despite their cosmopolitan enthusiasms, the Vorticists also assert their independence, repeatedly criticizing the Futurists. For all their antipathy toward England, they also bless it, revaluing, for example, English mobility (via the sea) and inventiveness (as the engine of the Industrial Revolution). Beyond merely stating doctrine, the Vorticists fashion a manifesto that crosses poetry with poster art, creatively manipulating words on the space of the page for maximum effect. In its jagged typography, wild energy, and fire-breathing rhetoric, its radical individualism paradoxically turned to a collective purpose, the Vorticist manifesto exemplifies ingredients of avant-garde poetry through the twentieth century. The text is reprinted from *Blast: Review of the Great English Vortex*, No. 1 (1914).

Long Live the Vortex!

Long live the great art vortex sprung up in the center of this town![1]

We stand for the Reality of the Present—not for the sentimental Future, or the sacripant[2] Past.

We want to leave Nature and Men alone.

We do not want to make people wear Futurist Patches, or fuss men to take to pink and sky-blue trousers.[3]

We are not their wives or tailors.

The only way Humanity can help artists is to remain independent and work unconsciously.

WE NEED THE UNCONSCIOUSNESS OF HUMANITY—their stupidity, animalism and dreams.

We believe in no perfectibility except our own.

Intrinsic beauty is in the Interpreter and Seer, not in the object or content.

We do not want to change the appearance of the world, because we are not Naturalists, Impressionists or Futurists (the latest form of Impressionism),[4] and do not depend on the appearance of the world for our art.

WE ONLY WANT THE WORLD TO LIVE, and to feel it's crude energy flowing through us.

It may be said that great artists in England are always revolutionary, just as in France any really great artist had a strong traditional vein.

Blast sets out to be an avenue for all those vivid and violent ideas that could reach the Public in no other way.

Blast will be popular, essentially. It will not appeal to any particular class, but to the fundamental and popular instincts in every class and description of people, TO THE INDIVIDUAL. The moment a man feels or realizes himself as an artist, he ceases to belong to any milieu or time. Blast is created for this timeless, fundamental Artist that exists in everybody.

The Man in the Street and the Gentleman are equally ignored.

Popular art does not mean the art of the poor people, as it is usually supposed to. It means the art of the individuals.

Education (art education and general education) tends to destroy the creative instinct. Therefore it is in times when education has been non-existant that art chiefly flourished.

But it is nothing to do with "the People."

1. London.
2. Boastful of valor.
3. The Futurists celebrated the technology, power, and dynamism of the modern age and sought to break with the past and traditional forms.
4. Naturalism, a late nineteenth-century school of realism, claimed all human life was governed by natural laws. Impressionism emphasized the subjectivity of perspective over any inherent quality in a represented object.

It is a mere accident that this is the most favourable time for the individual to appear.

To make the rich of the community shed their education skin, to destroy politeness, standardization and academic, that is civilized, vision, is the task we have set ourselves.

We want to make in England not a popular art, not a revival of lost folk art, or a romantic fostering of such unactual conditions, but to make individuals, wherever found.

We will convert the King[5] if possible.

A VORTICIST KING! WHY NOT?

DO YOU THINK LLOYD GEORGE[6] HAS THE VORTEX IN HIM?

MAY WE HOPE FOR ART FROM LADY MOND?[7]

We are against the glorification of "the People," as we are against snobbery. It is not necessary to be an outcast bohemian, to be unkempt or poor, any more than it is necessary to be rich or handsome, to be an artist. Art is nothing to do with the coat you wear. A top-hat can well hold the Sixtine. A cheap cap could hide the image of Kephren.[8]

AUTOMOBILISM (Marinetteism)[9] bores us. We don't want to go about making a hullo-bulloo about motor cars, anymore than about knives and forks, elephants or gas-pipes.

Elephants are VERY BIG. Motor cars go quickly.

Wilde gushed twenty years ago about the beauty of machinery. Gissing,[1] in his romantic delight with modern lodging houses was futurist in this sense.

The futurist is a sensational and sentimental mixture of the aesthete of 1890 and the realist of 1870.

The "Poor" are detestable animals! They are only picturesque and amusing for the sentimentalist or the romantic! The "Rich" are bores without a single exception, *en tant que riches!*[2]

We want those simple and great people found everywhere.

Blast presents an art of Individuals.

5. George V ascended the throne in 1910 and remained the British king until 1936.
6. David Lloyd George (1863–1945), career British politician, prime minister 1916–22.
7. Wife of wealthy industrialist Sir Robert Mond, and a prominent member of fashionable London society.
8. Ancient Egyptian pharaoh buried in one of the great pyramids in Giza. *The Sixtine:* the Sistine Chapel, in the Vatican.
9. Filippo Tommaso Marinetti (1876–1944), Italian writer and founder of Futurism, he glorified war and technology, and invented a "drama of objects" in which human actors play no parts.
1. George Gissing (1857–1903), naturalist English novelist. Oscar Wilde (1854–1900), Irish writer and critic; in his 1891 essay "The Soul of Man under Socialism," he writes: "All unintellectual labour, all monotonous, dull labour, all labour that deals with dreadful things, and involves unpleasant conditions, must be done by machinery. . . . *At present machinery competes against man. Under proper conditions machinery will serve man.*"
2. Insofar as they are rich (French).

MANIFESTO.

1

BLAST First (from politeness) ENGLAND

CURSE ITS CLIMATE FOR ITS SINS AND INFECTIONS

DISMAL SYMBOL, SET round our bodies,
of effeminate lout within.

VICTORIAN VAMPIRE, the LONDON cloud sucks
the TOWN'S heart.

A 1000 MILE LONG, 2 KILOMETER Deep

BODY OF WATER even, is pushed against us

from the Floridas, TO MAKE US MILD.

OFFICIOUS MOUNTAINS keep back DRASTIC WINDS

SO MUCH VAST MACHINERY TO PRODUCE

THE CURATE of "Eltham"[3]
BRITANNIC ÆSTHETE
WILD NATURE CRANK
DOMESTICATED
POLICEMAN
LONDON COLISEUM
SOCIALIST-PLAYWRIGHT
DALY'S MUSICAL COMEDY
GAIETY[4] CHORUS GIRL
TONKS[5]

3. A character from a dirty limerick ("There was a young curate of Eltham") that appeared in the August 1879 issue of *The Pearl: Journal of Facetiae and Voluptuous Reading*.
4. The Gaiety Theatre and Daly's Theatre were both in London; the London Coliseum is the city's largest theater.
5. Henry Tonks (1862–1937), an instructor at London's Slade School of Art—where Wyndham Lewis (1882–1957) and several other Vorticists studied—who rejected the increasingly abstract innovations of Cubist and Postimpressionist artists.

CURSE

the flabby sky that can manufacture no snow, but can only drop the sea on us in a drizzle like a poem by Mr. Robert Bridges.[6]

CURSE

the lazy air that cannot stiffen the back of the SERPENTINE, or put Aquatic steel half way down the MANCHESTER CANAL.[7]

But ten years ago we saw distinctly both snow and ice here.

May some vulgarly inventive, but useful person, arise, and restore us to the necessary BLIZZARDS.

LET US ONCE MORE WEAR THE ERMINE OF THE NORTH.

WE BELIEVE IN THE EXISTENCE OF THIS USEFUL LITTLE CHEMIST IN OUR MIDST !

2

OH BLAST FRANCE

pig plagiarism
BELLY
SLIPPERS
POODLE TEMPER
BAD MUSIC

6. England's poet laureate from 1913 to 1930.

7. Artificial canal opened in 1894. *Serpentine:* a large artificial lake in London.

SENTIMENTAL GALLIC GUSH
SENSATIONALISM
FUSSINESS.

PARISIAN PAROCHIALISM. Complacent young man, so much respect for Papa and his son !—Oh !—Papa is wonderful: but all papas are !

BLAST

APERITIFS (Pernots, Amers picon)[8]
Bad change
Naively seductive Houri salon-picture Cocottes
Slouching blue porters (can carry a pantechnicon)[9]
Stupidity rapacious people at every step
Economy maniacs
Bouillon Kub[1] (for being a bad pun)

PARIS. Clap-trap Heaven of amative German professor.
Ubiquitous lines of silly little trees.
Arcs de Triomphe.
Imperturbable, endless prettiness.
Large empty cliques, higher up.
Bad air for the individual.

BLAST

MECCA OF THE AMERICAN

because it is not other side of Suez Canal,[2] instead of an afternoon's ride from London.

8. French appetizer liqueurs.
9. Place where all sorts of manufactured articles are collected for sale. *Houri:* one of the beautiful virgins of the Koranic paradise. *Cocottes:* prostitutes.
1. A brand of bouillon cube, widely advertised in France around 1912.
2. Canal linking the Red Sea and the Mediterranean.

CURSE 3

WITH EXPLETIVE OF WHIRLWIND

THE BRITANNIC ÆSTHETE

CREAM OF THE SNOBBISH EARTH
ROSE OF SHARON[3] OF GOD-PRIG
OF SIMIAN VANITY
SNEAK AND SWOT[4] OF THE SCHOOL-ROOM
IMBERB (or Berbed when in Belsize[5])-PEDANT

PRACTICAL JOKER
DANDY
CURATE

BLAST all products of phlegmatic cold
Life of **LOOKER-ON.**

CURSE

SNOBBERY
(disease of femininity)
FEAR OF RIDICULE
(arch vice of inactive, sleepy)
PLAY
STYLISM
SINS AND PLAGUES
of this **LYMPHATIC** finished
(we admit in every sense
finished)
VEGETABLE HUMANITY.

3. One of the biblical names of Jesus (Isaiah 35.1), the Sharon Rose is supposed to be the most admired in the field. The rose is also a traditional symbol of England.

4. Nerd.

5. In London. *Imberb:* beardless. *Berbed:* bearded, with pun on *suburb.*

4

BLAST

THE SPECIALIST
"PROFESSIONAL"
"GOOD WORKMAN"
"GROVE-MAN"
ONE ORGAN MAN

BLAST THE

AMATEUR
SCIOLAST[6]
ART-PIMP
JOURNALIST
SELF MAN
NO-ORGAN MAN

5

BLAST HUMOUR

Quack ENGLISH drug for stupidity and sleepiness.
Arch enemy of **REAL**, conventionalizing like
gunshot, freezing supple
REAL in ferocious chemistry
of laughter.

BLAST SPORT

HUMOUR'S FIRST COUSIN AND ACCOMPLICE.

Impossibility for Englishman to be
grave and keep his end up,
psychologically.

6. That is, *sciolist,* a person who makes a superficial show of learning.

Impossible for him to use Humour
as well and be persistently
grave.
Alas! necessity for big doll's show
in front of mouth.
Visitation of Heaven on
English Miss
gums, canines of **FIXED GRIN**
Death's Head symbol of Anti-Life.

CURSE those who will hang over this Manifesto with **SILLY CANINES** exposed.

6

BLAST

years **1837** to **1900**[7]

Curse abysmal inexcusable middle-class (also Aristocracy and Proletariat).

BLAST

pasty shadow cast by gigantic **Boehm**[8]

(Imagined at introduction of **BOURGEOIS VICTORIAN VISTAS**).

WRING THE NECK OF all sick inventions born in that progressive white wake.

BLAST their weeping whiskers—hirsute[9]
RHETORIC of EUNUCH and STYLIST—
SENTIMENTAL HYGIENICS

7. Queen Victoria reigned from 1837 to 1901.
8. Joseph Edgar Boehm (1834–1890), one of the queen's sculptors.
9. Hairy.

ROUSSEAUISMS[1] **(wild Nature cranks)**
FRATERNIZING WITH MONKEYS
DIABOLICS—raptures and roses
of the erotic bookshelves
culminating in
PURGATORY OF
PUTNEY.[2]

CHAOS OF ENOCH ARDENS
laughing Jennys
Ladies with Pains
good-for-nothing Guineveres.[3]

SNOBBISH BORROVIAN running after
GIPSY KINGS and ESPADAS[4]
bowing the knee to
wild Mother Nature,
her feminine contours,
An **Unimaginative insult to**
MAN.

DAMN

all those to-day who have taken on that Rotten Menagerie, and still crack their whips and tumble in Piccadilly Circus, as though London were a provincial town.

WE WHISPER IN YOUR EAR A GREAT SECRET.

LONDON IS <u>NOT</u> A PROVINCIAL TOWN.

1. Jean-Jacques Rousseau (1712–1778), French philosopher who argued that humans are good and noble in their natural state, before society and civilization corrupt them.
2. A middle-class London suburb.
3. In late medieval romance, King Arthur's queen in Camelot; also, the title character in two narrative poems by English poet Alfred, Lord Tennyson (1809–1892). "Enoch Arden" (1864) is another narrative poem by Tennyson, rejected here for its sentimentalism. Jenny is the title character of another sentimental poem (1870), by English poet Dante Gabriel Rossetti (1828–1882).
4. Swords (Spanish). *Borrovian*: from George Henry Borrow (1803–1881), English writer of popular gypsy romances, such as *The Zincali: Account of the Gypsies of Spain* (1843).

We will allow Wonder Zoos. But we do not want the

GLOOMY VICTORIAN CIRCUS[5] in Piccadilly Circus.

IT IS PICCADILLY'S CIRCUS!

NOT MEANT FOR MENAGERIES trundling out of Sixties DICKENSIAN CLOWNS, CORELLI LADY RIDERS,[6] TROUPS OF PERFORMING GIPSIES (who complain besides that 1/6 a night does not pay fare back to Clapham).[7]

BLAST[8]

The Post Office **Frank Brangwyn** **Robertson Nicol**

Rev. Pennyfeather (Bells) **Galloway Kyle (Cluster of Grapes)**

Bishop of London and all his posterity

Galsworthy **Dean Inge** **Croce** **Matthews**

5. *Circus:* here, traveling entertainment act with animals and acrobats; also, British traffic circle. *Wonder Zoos*: traveling exhibition of exotic animals.
6. Marie Corelli, pseudonym of Mary Mackay (1855–1924), best-selling (and royal favorite) English writer of romances and religious novels in which she aimed to reform social ills. *Dickensian clowns*: from the novels of English writer Charles Dickens (1812–1870).
7. Suburban district of London. *1/6:* 18d, or a shilling and sixpence, then equivalent to about thirty-five cents.
8. Those blasted here range from individuals, such as Charles Burgess Fry, England's star cricket player and a tireless self-promoter, to things blasted seemingly for the thrill of doing so, such as cod-liver oil. Blasted, too, are institutions or members of the national, literary, or cultural establishment (e.g., the post office, a much-lauded model of Victorian efficiency, and the British Academy, established in 1902 by Royal Charter as the national academy for humanities and social sciences), including various clergy and public leaders (e.g., Bishop of London; William Ralph Inge, dean of St. Paul's Cathedral; the Reverends Pennyfeather and Meyer; R. J. Campbell, English Congregationalist minister in the City Temple of London, and a Pantheist; Cardinal Herbert Vaughan, archbishop of Westminster and superior of the Catholic Missionary Society; Norman Angell, pacifist British economist; Arthur Christopher Benson, schoolmaster at Eton College, author of Edward VII's coronation ode). Critics unfriendly to the avant-garde are also included (e.g., William Archer, drama critic for the *Nation*; Sir William Robertson Nicoll, biblical editor and sometime literary critic; Lionel Cust, director of the National Portrait Gallery and contributor to the *Dictionary of National Biography*, etc.). Also blasted are artists and writers whom the Vorticists believed were meager talents in spite of their popularity (e.g., painter Frank Brangwyn, poet Ella Wheeler Wilcox, actors George Grossmith and Seymour Hicks, composers Joseph Holbrooke and Edward Elgar, etc.), as well as those associated with fads (e.g., Sir Abdul Baha Bahai, leader of the Bahai faith) or idealistic social reform (e.g., author Marie Corelli; Sidney Webb, a leader of the Fabian Socialist organization; Annie Besant, theosophist and suffragist). Some names (e.g., Indian poet Rabindranath Tagore) are misspelled. For a detailed discussion of the cursing and blessing in *Blast,* see William C. Wees, *Vorticism and the English Avant-Garde* (1972).

Rev Meyer Seymour Hicks
Lionel Cust C. B. Fry Bergson Abdul Bahai
Hawtrey Edward Elgar Sardlea
Filson Young Marie Corelli Geddes
Codliver Oil St. Loe Strachey Lyceum Club
Rhabindraneth Tagore Lord Glenconner of Glen
Weiniger Norman Angel Ad. Mahon
Mr. and Mrs. Dearmer Beecham Ella
A. C. Benson (Pills, Opera, Thomas) Sydney Webb
British Academy Messrs. Chapell
Countess of Warwick George Edwards
Willie Ferraro Captain Cook R. J. Campbell
Clan Thesiger Martin Harvey William Archer
George Grossmith R. H. Benson
Annie Besant Chenil Clan Meynell
Father Vaughan Joseph Holbrooke Clan Strachey

1

BLESS ENGLAND!

BLESS ENGLAND

FOR ITS SHIPS

which switchback on Blue, Green and
Red SEAS all around the PINK
EARTH-BALL,

BIG BETS ON EACH.

BLESS ALL SEAFARERS.

THEY exchange not one **LAND** for another, but one **ELEMENT** for **ANOTHER.** The **MORE** against the **LESS ABSTRACT.**

BLESS the vast planetary abstraction of the **OCEAN.**

BLESS THE ARABS OF THE **ATLANTIC.**
THIS ISLAND MUST BE CONTRASTED WITH THE BLEAK WAVES.

BLESS ALL PORTS.

PORTS, RESTLESS MACHINES of

scooped out basins
heavy Insect dredgers
monotonous cranes
stations
lighthouses, blazing
through the frosty
starlight, cutting the
storm like a cake
beaks of infant boats,
side by side,
heavy chaos of
wharves,
steep walls of
factories
womanly town

BLESS these **MACHINES** that work the little boats across clean liquid space, in beelines.

BLESS the great **PORTS**

HULL
LIVERPOOL
LONDON
NEWCASTLE-ON-TYNE
BRISTOL
GLASGOW

BLESS ENGLAND,

Industrial Island machine, pyramidal workshop, its apex at Shetland, discharging itself on the sea.

BLESS
| **cold**
| **maganimous**
| **delicate**
| **gauche**
| **fanciful**
| **stupid**

ENGLISHMEN.

2

BLESS the HAIRDRESSER.

He attacks Mother Nature for a small fee.

Hourly he ploughs heads for sixpence,

Scours chins and lips for threepence.

He makes systematic mercenary war on this WILDNESS.

He trims aimless and retrograde growths into CLEAN ARCHED SHAPES and ANGULAR PLOTS.

BLESS this HESSIAN (or SILESIAN)[9] EXPERT

correcting the grotesque anachronisms of our physique.

9. From German industrial areas Hesse and Silesia.

3

BLESS ENGLISH HUMOUR

It is the great barbarous weapon of
the genius among races.
The wild **MOUNTAIN RAILWAY** from **IDEA**
to **IDEA**, in the ancient Fair of **LIFE.**

BLESS SWIFT[1] for his solemn bleak wisdom of laughter.

SHAKESPEARE for his bitter Northern Rhetoric of humour

BLESS ALL ENGLISH EYES
that grow crows-feet with their
FANCY and **ENERGY.**

BLESS this hysterical **WALL** built round
the **EGO.**

BLESS the solitude of **LAUGHTER.**

BLESS the separating, ungregarious
BRITISH GRIN.

4

BLESS FRANCE

1. Jonathan Swift (1667–1745), Anglo-Irish poet and satirist.

for its BUSHELS of VITALITY

to the square inch.

HOME OF MANNERS (the Best, the WORST and interesting mixtures).

MASTERLY PORNOGRAPHY (great enemy of progress).

COMBATIVENESS

GREAT HUMAN SCEPTICS

DEPTHS OF ELEGANCE

FEMALE QUALITIES

FEMALES

BALLADS of its PREHISTORIC APACHE

Superb hardness and hardiesse of its

Voyou[2] type, rebellious adolescent.

Modesty and humanity of many there.

GREAT FLOOD OF LIFE pouring out

of wound of 1797.

Also bitterer stream from 1870.[3]

STAYING POWER, like a cat.

BLESS[4]

Bridget Berrwolf Bearline Cranmer Byng

Frieder Graham The Pope Maria de Tomaso

2. Hooligan.
3. Beginning of the Franco-Prussian War and end of the Second Empire, led by Napoleon Bonaparte's nephew Napoleon III. *1797:* Napoleon Bonaparte returns victorious to France from military campaigns abroad, begins his rise to power.
4. Like the blasted, the blessed generally fall into a few main groups, ranging from the same kind of seemingly arbitrary things (e.g., castor oil) to friends and sponsors of the Vorticists (e.g., sympathetic art critics Frank Rutter and P. G. Konody; Kate Lechmere, a financial backer of the magazine) and fellow avant-garde artists and supporters (e.g., James Joyce; Madame Strindberg, head of the Futurist Cabaret Club; Launcelot Cranmer-Byng, who published English translations of classical Chinese poets). Also celebrated are popular figures among typically working-class audiences (e.g., racing crook Robert Siever; boxer Jake "Young" Ahearn; actors Granville Barker and Lydia Yavorska and singer-actress Shirley Kellogg) and authors of popular fiction and poetry (e.g., Adelaide Belloc Lowndes —the misspelling in *Blast* may or may not have been intentional—author of popular thriller *The Lodger;* Sir James Matthew Barry, the Scottish playwright who created the character Peter Pan; and patriotic English poet Henry Newbolt). The blessees also include figures from various revolutionary eras, such as Charlotte Corday, an aristocrat who assassinated French Revolutionary Jean-Paul Marat in 1793, and Oliver Cromwell, lord protector of England from 1653 to 1658.

Captain Kemp Munroe Gaby Jenkins

R. B. Cuningham Grahame (not his brother) Barker (John and Granville)

Mrs. Wil Finnimore Madame Strindberg Carson

Salvation Army Lord Howard de Walden

Capt. Craig Charlotte Corday Cromwell

Mrs. Duval Mary Robertson Lillie Lenton

Frank Rutter Castor Oil James Joyce

Leveridge Lydia Yavorska Preb. Carlyle Jenny

Mon. le compte de Gabulis Smithers Dick Burge

33 Church Street Sievier Gertie Millar

Norman Wallis Miss Fowler Sir Joseph Lyons

Martin Wolff Watt Mrs. Hepburn

Alfree Tommy Captain Kendell Young Ahearn

Wilfred Walter Kate Lechmere Henry Newbolt

Lady Aberconway Frank Harris Hamel

Gilbert Canaan Sir James Mathew Barry

Mrs. Belloc Lowdnes W. L. George Rayner

George Robey George Mozart Harry Weldon

Chaliapine George Hirst Graham White

Hucks Salmet Shirley Kellogg Bandsman Rice

Petty Officer Curran Applegarth Konody

Colin Bell Lewis Hind LEFRANC

Hubert Commercial Process Co.

MANIFESTO.

I.

1 Beyond Action and Reaction we would establish ourselves.

2 We start from opposite statements of a chosen

world. Set up violent structure of adolescent clearness between two extremes.

3 **We discharge ourselves on both sides.**

4 **We fight first on one side, then on the other, but always for the SAME cause, which is neither side or both sides and ours.**

5 **Mercenaries were always the best troops.**

6 **We are Primitive Mercenaries in the Modern World.**

7 **Our <u>Cause</u> Is NO-MAN'S.**

8 **We set Humour at Humour's throat.**
Stir up Civil War among peaceful apes.

9 **We only want Humour if it has fought like Tragedy.**

10 **We only want Tragedy if it can clench its side-muscles like hands on it's belly, and bring to the surface a laugh like a bomb.**

II.

1 **We hear from America and the Continent all sorts of disagreeable things about England: "the unmusical, anti-artistic, unphilosophic country."**

2 **We quite agree.**

3 **Luxury, sport, the famous English "Humour," the thrilling ascendancy and idée fixe of Class, producing the most intense snobbery in the**

World; heavy stagnant pools of Saxon blood, incapable of anything but the song of a frog, in home-countries:—these phenomena give England a peculiar distinction in the wrong sense, among the nations.

4 This is why England produces such good artists from time to time.

5 This is also the reason why a movement towards art and imagination could burst up here, from this lump of compressed life, with more force than anywhere else.

6 To believe that it is necessary for or conducive to art, to "improve" life, for instance—make architecture, dress, ornament, in "better taste," is absurd.

7 The Art-instinct is permanently primitive.

8 In a chaos of imperfection, discord, etc., it finds the same stimulus as in Nature.

9 The artist of the modern movement is a savage (in no sense an "advanced," perfected, democratic, Futurist individual of Mr. Marinetti's limited imagination): this enormous, jangling, journalistic, fairy desert of modern life serves him as Nature did more technically primitive man.

10 As the steppes and the rigours of the Russian winter, when the peasant has to lie for weeks in his hut, produces that extraordinary acuity of feeling and intelligence we associate with the Slav; so England is just now the most

favourable country for the appearance of a great art.

III.

1 We have made it quite clear that there is nothing Chauvinistic or picturesquely patriotic about our contentions.

2 But there is violent boredom with that feeble Europeanism, abasement of the miserable "intellectual" before anything coming from Paris, Cosmopolitan sentimentality, which prevails in so many quarters.

3 Just as we believe that an Art must be organic with its Time,
So we insist that what is actual and vital for the South, is ineffectual and unactual in the North.

4 Fairies have disappeared from Ireland (despite foolish attempts to revive them)[5] and the bull-ring languishes in Spain.

5 But mysticism on the one hand, gladiatorial instincts, blood and asceticism on the other, will be always actual, and springs of Creation for these two peoples.

6 The English Character is based on the Sea.

7 The particular qualities and characteristics that the sea always engenders in men are

5. The Celtic Revival in Irish arts and letters, from the last quarter of the nineteenth century until the 1920s, emphasized the mysticism and supernatural elements in Irish legend and poetry.

those that are, among the many diagnostics of our race, the most fundamentally English.

8 That unexpected universality as well, found in the completest English artists, is due to this.

IV.

1 We assert that the art for these climates, then, must be a northern flower.

2 And we have implied what we believe should be the specific nature of the art destined to grow up in this country, and models of whose flue[6] decorate the pages of this magazine.

3 It is not a question of the characterless material climate around us.

Were that so the complication of the Jungle, dramatic Tropic growth, the vastness of American trees, would not be for us.

4 But our industries, and the Will that determined, face to face with its needs, the direction of the modern world, has reared up steel trees where the green ones were lacking; has exploded in useful growths, and found wilder intricacies than those of Nature.

V.

1 We bring clearly forward the following points, before further defining the character of this necessary native art.

6. Pipe for conveying heat; chimney duct.

2 At the freest and most vigorous period of ENGLAND's history, her literature, then chief Art, was in many ways identical with that of France.

3 Chaucer was very much cousin of Villon[7] as an artist.

4 Shakespeare and Montaigne[8] formed one literature.

5 But Shakespeare reflected in his imagination a mysticism, madness and delicacy peculiar to the North, and brought equal quantities of Comic and Tragic together.

6 Humour is a phenomenon caused by sudden pouring of culture into Barbary.[9]

7 It is intelligence electrified by flood of Naivety.

8 It is Chaos invading Concept and bursting it like nitrogen.

9 It is the individual masquerading as Humanity like a child in clothes too big for him.

10 Tragic Humour is the birthright of the North.

11 Any great Northern Art will partake of this insidious and volcanic chaos.

12 No great ENGLISH Art need be ashamed to share some glory with France, to-morrow it may be with Germany, where the Elizabethans did before it.

7. François Villon (1431–1463?): French poet (some of whose work was translated into English by Ezra Pound). Geoffrey Chaucer (c. 1343–1400): English poet.

8. Michel de Montaigne (1533–1592), French essayist.

9. Former name for the western part of North Africa, associated with barbarity.

13 But it will never be French, any more than Shakespeare was, the most catholic and subtle Englishman.

VI.

1 The Modern World is due almost entirely to Anglo-Saxon genius,—its appearance and its spirit.

2 Machinery, trains, steam-ships, all that distinguishes externally our time, came far more from here than anywhere else.

3 In dress, manners, mechanical inventions, LIFE, that is, ENGLAND, has influenced Europe in the same way that France has in Art.

4 But busy with this LIFE-EFFORT, she has been the last to become conscious of the Art that is an organism of this new Order and Will of Man.

5 Machinery is the greatest Earth-medium: incidentally it sweeps away the doctrines of a narrow and pedantic Realism at one stroke.

6 By mechanical inventiveness, too, just as Englishmen have spread themselves all over the Earth, they have brought all the hemispheres about them in their original island.

7 It cannot be said that the complication of the Jungle, dramatic tropic growths, the vastness of American trees, is not for us.

8 For, in the forms of machinery, Factories, new and vaster buildings, bridges and works, we have all that, naturally, around us.

VII.

1 Once this consciousness towards the new possibilities of expression in present life has come, however, it will be more the legitimate property of Englishmen than of any other people in Europe.

2 It should also, as it is by origin theirs, inspire them more forcibly and directly.

3 They are the inventors of this bareness and hardness, and should be the great enemies of Romance.

4 The Romance peoples will always be, at bottom, its defenders.

5 The Latins are at present, for instance, in their "discovery" of sport, their Futuristic gush over machines, aeroplanes, etc., the most romantic and sentimental "moderns" to be found.

6 It is only the second-rate people in France or Italy who are thorough revolutionaries.

7 In England, on the other hand, there is no vulgarity in revolt.

8 Or, rather, there is no revolt, it is the normal state.

9 So often rebels of the North and the South are diametrically opposed species.

10 The nearest thing in England to a great traditional French artist, is a great revolutionary English one.

Signatures for Manifesto[1]

R. Aldington

Arbuthnot

L. Atkinson

Gaudier Brzeska

J. Dismorr

C. Hamilton

E. Pound

W. Roberts

H. Sanders

E. Wadsworth

Wyndham Lewis

1914

1. The signatories are Richard Aldington, writer; Malcolm Arbuthnot, photographer and artist; Lawrence Atkinson, Vorticist artist; Henri Gaudier-Brzeska, Vorticist sculptor (whose obituary was printed in *Blast* 2, after he was killed in the trenches); Jessica Dismoor, artist and *Blast* illustrator; Cuthbert Hamilton, avant-garde artist; Ezra Pound, poet; William Roberts, painter; Helen Saunders, Vorticist designer; Edward Wadsworth, Vorticist painter; and Wyndham Lewis, avant-garde artist, playwright, and novelist.

Newcastle. **Edward Wadsworth.**

MINA LOY: FEMINIST MANIFESTO

Mina Loy composed this manifesto, which she considered a rough draft and never published, in November 1914 and sent it to her friend Mabel Dodge (1879–1962), American author and celebrated patron of the arts. The piece, which bears fruitful comparison with the iconoclasm and typographic experimentation of the virile *Blast* manifesto, published a few months earlier, was partly the result of Loy's quarrels with the Italian Futurists, with whom she was closely associated despite the movement's misogyny. In the essay, Loy tries to harness for feminism the radicalism and individualism of the avant-garde, calling for a complete revolution of gender relations. She abandons the suffragette movement's central issue of equality and insists instead on an adversarial model of gender, claiming that women should not look to men for a standard of value but should find it within themselves. First published in *The Last Lunar Baedeker* (1982), the essay is reprinted from *The Lost Lunar Baedeker* (1996); both volumes were edited by Roger L. Conover.

Feminist Manifesto

The feminist movement as at present instituted is

Inadequate

Women if you want to realise yourselves—you are on the eve of a devastating psychological upheaval—all your pet illusions must be unmasked—the lies of centuries have got to go—are you prepared for the **Wrench**—? There is no half-measure—NO scratching on the surface of the rubbish heap of tradition, will bring about **Reform**, the only method is **Absolute Demolition**

Cease to place your confidence in economic legislation, vice-crusades & uniform education—you are glossing over **Reality**.

Professional & commercial careers are opening up for you—

Is that all you want ?

And if you honestly desire to find your level without prejudice—be **Brave** & deny at the outset—that pathetic clap-trap war cry **Woman is the equal of man**—

for

She is **NOT!**

The man who lives a life in which his activities conform to a social code which is a protectorate of the feminine element——is no longer **masculine**

The women who adapt themselves to a theoretical valuation of their sex as a relative impersonality, are not yet Feminine

Leave off looking to men to find out what you are not —seek within yourselves to find out what you are

As conditions are at present constituted—you have the choice between Parasitism, & Prostitution —or Negation

Men & women are enemies, with the enmity of the exploited for the parasite, the parasite for the exploited—at present they are at the mercy of the advantage that each can take of the others sexual dependence—. The only point at which the interests of the sexes merge—is the sexual embrace.

The first illusion it is to your interest to demolish is the division of women into two classes the mistress, & the mother every well-balanced & developed woman knows that is not true, Nature has endowed the complete woman with a faculty for expressing herself through all her functions—there are no restrictions the woman who is so incompletely evolved as to be un-self-conscious in sex, will prove a restrictive influence on the temperamental expansion of the next generation; the woman who is a poor mistress will be an incompetent mother—an inferior mentality—& will enjoy an inadequate apprehension of Life.

To obtain results you must make sacrifices & the first & greatest sacrifice you have to make is of your "virtue"

The fictitious value of woman as identified with her physical purity—is too easy a stand-by——rendering her lethargic in the acquisition of intrinsic merits of character by which she could obtain a concrete value— therefore, the first self-enforced law for the female sex, as a protection against the man made bogey of virtue—which is the principle instrument of her subjection, would be the unconditional surgical destruction of virginity through-out the female population at puberty—.

The value of man is assessed entirely according to his use or interest to the community, the value of woman, depends entirely on chance, her success or insuccess in manoeuvering a man into taking the life-long responsibility of her—
The advantages of marriage of too ridiculously ample—compared to all other trades—for under modern conditions a woman can accept preposterously luxurious support from a man (with-out return of any sort—even offspring)—as a thank offering for her virginity
The woman who has not succeeded in striking that advantageous bargain—is prohibited from any but surreptitious re-action to Life-stimuli—**& entirely debarred maternity.**
Every woman has a right to maternity—
Every woman of superior intelligence should realize her race-responsibility, in producing children in adequate proportion to the unfit or degenerate members of her sex—

Each child of a superior woman should be the result of a definite period of psychic development in her life—& not necessarily of a possibly irksome & outworn continuance of an alliance—spontaneously adapted for vital creation in the beginning but not necessarily harmoniously balanced as the parties to it—follow their individual lines of personal evolution—
For the harmony of the race, each individual should be the expression of an easy & ample interpenetration of the male & female temperaments—free of stress
Woman must become more responsible for the child than man—
Women must destroy in themselves, the desire to be loved—

The feeling that it is a personal insult when a man transfers
his attentions from her to another woman
The desire for comfortable protection instead of an intelligent
curiosity & courage in meeting & resisting the pressure of life
sex or so called love must be reduced to its initial element,
honour, grief, sentimentality, pride & consequently jealousy
must be detached from it.
Woman for her happiness must retain her deceptive fragility of
appearance, combined with indomitable will, irreducible
courage, & abundant health the outcome of sound nerves—
Another great illusion that woman must use all her
introspective clear-sightedness & unbiassed bravery to
destroy—for the sake of her self respect is the impurity of sex
the realisation in defiance of superstition that there is nothing
impure in sex—except in the mental attitude to it—will
constitute an incalculable & wider social regeneration than it
is possible for our generation to imagine.

1914 1982

Preface to Some Imagist Poets

In 1914, *Des Imagistes,* an anthology edited by Ezra Pound, presented a small group of poets who aimed at clarity and compression in their work. The bulk of the book consisted of poems by the London-based poets Pound, Richard Aldington, F. S. Flint, and H. D. The next year, Amy Lowell, who had only one poem in the first Imagist anthology, edited a new, more egalitarian collection, *Some Imagist Poets,* followed in 1916 and 1917 by subsequent Imagist volumes, all published in Boston. After publication of the 1914 anthology, Pound and Lowell had clashed and Pound had formally withdrawn from the group, whose work he would derisively label "Amygism." Lowell became the chief proponent of Imagism, publishing and lecturing widely in the United States on behalf of the movement. The preface to Lowell's 1915 anthology, drafted by Aldington and revised by others, succinctly summarizes the key Imagist principles—verbal exactitude and rhythmic invention; openness to subject and reliance on the image; hardness, clarity, and concentration—all of which remained influential long after the Imagist movement was over. The text is reprinted from *Some Imagist Poets* (1915).

AMY LOWELL, ED.

Preface

In March, 1914, a volume appeared entitled "Des Imagistes." It was a collection of the work of various young poets, presented together as a school. This school has been widely discussed by those interested in new movements in the arts, and has already become a household word. Differences of taste and judgment, however, have arisen among the contributors to that book; growing tendencies are forcing them along different paths. Those of us whose work appears in this volume have therefore decided to publish our collection under a new title, and we have been joined by two or three poets who did not contribute to the first volume, our wider scope making this possible.

In this new book we have followed a slightly different arrangement to that of the former Anthology. Instead of an arbitrary selection by an editor, each poet has been permitted to represent himself by the work he considers his best, the only stipulation being that it should not yet have appeared in book form. A sort of informal committee—consisting of more than half the authors here represented—have arranged the book and decided what should be printed and what omitted, but, as a general rule, the poets have been allowed absolute freedom in this direction, limitations of space only being imposed upon them. Also, to avoid any appearance of precedence, they have been put in alphabetical order.

As it has been suggested that much of the misunderstanding of the former volume was due to the fact that we did not explain ourselves in a preface, we have thought it wise to tell the public what our aims are, and why we are banded together between one set of covers.

The poets in this volume do not represent a clique. Several of them are personally unknown to the others, but they are united by certain common principles, arrived at independently. These principles are not new; they have fallen into desuetude. They are the essentials of all great poetry, indeed of all great literature, and they are simply these:—

1. To use the language of common speech, but to employ always the *exact* word, not the nearly-exact, nor the merely decorative word.

2. To create new rhythms—as the expression of new moods—and not to copy old rhythms, which merely echo old moods. We do not insist upon "free-verse" as the only method of writing poetry. We fight for it as for a principle of liberty. We believe that the individuality of a poet may often be better expressed in free-verse than in conventional forms. In poetry, a new cadence means a new idea.

3. To allow absolute freedom in the choice of subject. It is not good art to write badly about aeroplanes and automobiles; nor is it necessarily bad art to write well about the past. We believe passionately in the artistic value of modern life, but we wish to point out that there is nothing so uninspiring nor so old-fashioned as an aeroplane of the year 1911.

4. To present an image (hence the name: "Imagist"). We are not a school of painters, but we believe that poetry should render particulars exactly and not deal in vague generalities, however magnificent and sonorous. It is for this reason that we oppose the cosmic poet, who seems to us to shirk the real difficulties of his art.

5. To produce poetry that is hard and clear, never blurred nor indefinite.

6. Finally, most of us believe that concentration is of the very essence of poetry.

The subject of free-verse is too complicated to be discussed here. We may say briefly, that we attach the term to all that increasing amount of writing whose cadence is more marked, more definite, and closer knit than that of prose, but which is not so violently nor so obviously accented as the so-called "regular verse." We refer those interested in the question to the Greek Melic[1] poets, and to the many excellent French studies on the subject by such distinguished and well-equipped authors as Remy de Gourmont, Gustave Kahn, Georges Duhamel, Charles Vildrac, Henri Ghéon, Robert de Souza, André Spire, etc.

We wish it to be clearly understood that we do not represent an exclusive artistic sect; we publish our work together because of mutual artistic sympathy, and we propose to bring out our coöperative volume each year for a short term of years, until we have made a place for ourselves and our principles such as we desire.

1915

1. Type of ancient Greek lyric poetry intended to be sung.

Preface

In May 1918, Wilfred Owen was posted in Ripon, North Yorkshire, England, and was preparing a book of his war poems. Around this time, he drafted the following preface, identifying his subject as the pity of war and offering his poetry as a warning to his generation. In September, he returned to the front in France and was killed in battle, a week before the war ended. His unfinished preface and most of his poems appeared posthumously in *Poems* (1920), edited by his friend the poet Siegfried Sassoon. The text is reprinted from *The Poems of Wilfred Owen* (1985), ed. Jon Stallworthy.

WILFRED OWEN

Preface

This book is not about heroes. English poetry is not yet fit to speak of them.

Nor is it about deeds, or lands, nor anything about glory, honour, might, majesty, dominion, or power, except War.[1]

Above all I am not concerned with Poetry.

My subject is War, and the pity of War.

The Poetry is in the pity.

Yet these elegies are to this generation in no sense consolatory. They may be to the next. All a poet can do today is warn. That is why the true Poets must be truthful.

(If I thought the letter of this book would last, I might have used proper names; but if the spirit of it survives—survives Prussia[2]—my ambition and those names will have achieved fresher fields than Flanders.[3] . . .)

1918 1920

1. Cf. Jude 1.25: "To the only wise God our Saviour, be glory and majesty, dominion and power, both now and ever."
2. Dominant region of the German Empire until the end of World War I.
3. In western Belgium, site of the front line. Canadian poet John McCrae (1872–1918) memorialized one devastating 1915 battle in his famous poem "In Flanders Fields."

A Retrospect

In 1918, Ezra Pound gathered a series of his essays and published them as "A Retrospect." He included his profoundly influential ideas about Imagism, originally published in "A Few Don'ts by an Imagiste," a companion piece to F. S. Flint's summary of an interview with an unidentified "Imagiste" (surely Pound) in the March 1913 issue of *Poetry*. There, Pound defines the image as "that which presents an intellectual and emotional complex in an instant of time." He also issues injunctions and admonitions to help poets strip their verse of unnecessary rhetoric and abstraction. Poets, he argues, should write direct, musically cadenced, image-grounded verse. Pound also included his "Prolegomena," from the *Poetry Review* of February 1912, in which he offers a sweeping view of literary history. He warns against either overestimating the freedom of free verse or underestimating the hard work essential to technical mastery as a poet, and he foretells the development of "harder and saner" verse, "like granite." He concludes with further thoughts on free verse and on the artists, musicians, and writers he considered the best of his time. The essay is reprinted from Pound's *Pavannes and Divisions* (1918).

EZRA POUND

A Retrospect

There has been so much scribbling about a new fashion in poetry, that I may perhaps be pardoned this brief recapitulation and retrospect.

In the spring or early summer of 1912, "H. D.," Richard Aldington and myself decided that we were agreed upon the three principles following:[1]

1. Direct treatment of the "thing" whether subjective or objective.
2. To use absolutely no word that does not contribute to the presentation.
3. As regarding rhythm: to compose in the sequence of the musical phrase, not in sequence of a metronome.

Upon many points of taste and of predilection we differed, but agreeing upon these three positions we thought we had as much right to a group name, at least as much right, as a number of French "schools" proclaimed by Mr. Flint in the August number of Harold Munro's magazine for 1911.[2]

This school has since been "joined" or "followed" by numerous people who, whatever their merits, do not show any signs of agreeing with the second specification. Indeed vers libre[3] has become as prolix and as verbose as any of the flaccid varieties that preceded it. It has brought faults of its own. The actual language and phrasing is often as bad as that of our elders without even the excuse that the words are shoveled in to fill a metric pattern or to complete the noise of a rhyme-sound. Whether or no the phrases followed by the followers are musical must be left to the reader's decision. At times I can find a marked metre in "vers libres," as stale and hackneyed as any pseudo-Swinburnian,[4] at times the writers seem to follow no musical structure whatever. But it is, on the whole, good that the field should be ploughed. Perhaps a few good poems have come from the new method, and if so it is justified.

• • •

Criticism is not a circumscription or a set of prohibitions. It provides fixed points of departure. It may startle a dull reader into alertness. That little of

1. In *Poetry* 1.6 (March 1913), these three principles appeared (with slightly different wording) in an article summarizing an interview with an "Imagiste" and were published under the name of F. S. Flint (1885–1960), English poet and translator. Richard Aldington (1892–1962): English poet. H. D. (1886–1961): American poet.
2. Flint's "Contemporary French Poetry" appeared in *Poetry Review* (August 1912).
3. Free verse (French).
4. Algernon Charles Swinburne (1837–1909), English poet.

it which is good is mostly in stray phrases; or if it be an older artist helping a younger it is in great measure but rules of thumb, cautions gained by experience.

I set together a few phrases on practical working about the time the first remarks on imagisme were published. The first use of the word "Imagiste" was in my note to T. E. Hulme's[5] five poems, printed at the end of my "Ripostes" in the autumn of 1912. I reprint my cautions from *Poetry* for March, 1913:

A Few Don'ts[6]

An "Image" is that which presents an intellectual and emotional complex in an instant of time. I use the term "complex" rather in the technical sense employed by the newer psychologists, such as Hart,[7] though we might not agree absolutely in our application.

It is the presentation of such a "complex" instantaneously which gives that sense of sudden liberation; that sense of freedom from time limits and space limits; that sense of sudden growth, which we experience in the presence of the greatest works of art.

It is better to present one Image in a lifetime than to produce voluminous works.

All this, however, some may consider open to debate. The immediate necessity is to tabulate A LIST OF DON'TS for those beginning to write verses. I can not put all of them into Mosaic negative.[8]

To begin with, consider the three propositions (demanding direct treatment, economy of words, and the sequence of the musical phrase), not as dogma—never consider anything as dogma—but as the result of long contemplation, which, even if it is some one else's contemplation, may be worth consideration.

Pay no attention to the criticism of men who have never themselves written a notable work. Consider the discrepancies between the actual writing of the Greek poets and dramatists, and the theories of the GraecoRoman grammarians, concocted to explain their metres.

LANGUAGE

Use no superfluous word, no adjective, which does not reveal something.

Don't use such an expression as "dim lands *of peace*." It dulls the image. It mixes an abstraction with the concrete. It comes from the writer's not realizing that the natural object is always the *adequate* symbol.

Go in fear of abstractions. Do not retell in mediocre verse what has already been done in good prose. Don't think any intelligent person is going to be deceived when you try to shirk all the difficulties of the unspeakably difficult art of good prose by chopping your composition into line lengths.

What the expert is tired of today the public will be tired of tomorrow.

Don't imagine that the art of poetry is any simpler than the art of music, or that you can please the expert before you have spent at least as much

5. English critic, poet, and philosopher (1883–1917).
6. Originally titled "A Few Don'ts by an Imagiste," this essay appeared in *Poetry* 1.6 (March 1913).
7. British psychologist Bernard Hart (1879–1966) discusses "the complex" in *The Psychology of Insanity* (1912), a book that helped popularize psychoanalysis.
8. Reference to the Ten Commandments delivered to Moses (Exodus 20).

effort on the art of verse as the average piano teacher spends on the art of music.

Be influenced by as many great artists as you can, but have the decency either to acknowledge the debt outright, or to try to conceal it.

Don't allow "influence" to mean merely that you mop up the particular decorative vocabulary of some one or two poets whom you happen to admire. A Turkish war correspondent was recently caught red-handed babbling in his dispatches of "dove-gray" hills, or else it was "pearl-pale," I can not remember.

Use either no ornament or good ornament.

RHYTHM AND RHYME

Let the candidate fill his mind with the finest cadences he can discover, preferably in a foreign language[9] so that the meaning of the words may be less likely to divert his attention from the movement; e.g., Saxon charms, Hebridean Folk Songs, the verse of Dante, and the lyrics of Shakespeare—if he can dissociate the vocabulary from the cadence. Let him dissect the lyrics of Goethe[1] coldly into their component sound values, syllables long and short, stressed and unstressed, into vowels and consonants.

It is not necessary that a poem should rely on its music, but if it does rely on its music that music must be such as will delight the expert.

Let the neophyte know assonance and alliteration, rhyme immediate and delayed, simple and polyphonic, as a musician would expect to know harmony and counterpoint and all the minutiae of his craft. No time is too great to give to these matters or to any one of them, even if the artist seldom have need of them.

Don't imagine that a thing will "go" in verse just because it's too dull to go in prose.

Don't be "viewy"—leave that to the writers of pretty little philosophic essays. Don't be descriptive; remember that the painter can describe a landscape much better than you can, and that he has to know a deal more about it.

When Shakespeare talks of the "Dawn in russet mantle clad"[2] he presents something which the painter does not present. There is in this line of his nothing that one can call description; he presents.

Consider the way of the scientists rather than the way of an advertising agent for a new soap.

The scientist does not expect to be acclaimed as a great scientist until he has *discovered* something. He begins by learning what has been discovered already. He goes from that point onward. He does not bank on being a charming fellow personally. He does not expect his friends to applaud the results of his freshman class work. Freshmen in poetry are unfortunately not confined to a definite and recognizable class room. They are "all over the shop." Is it any wonder "the public is indifferent to poetry?"

Don't chop your stuff into separate *iambs*. Don't make each line stop dead at the end, and then begin every next line with a heave. Let the beginning

9. "This is for rhythm, his vocabulary must of course be found in his native tongue" [Pound's note].

1. Johann Wolfgang von Goethe (1749–1832), German Romantic poet, playwright, and novelist.

2. From Horatio's speech in the opening scene of Shakespeare's *Hamlet*: "But look, the morn in russet mantle clad / Walks o'er the dew of yon high eastern hill."

of the next line catch the rise of the rhythm wave, unless you want a definite longish pause.

In short, behave as a musician, a good musician, when dealing with that phase of your art which has exact parallels in music. The same laws govern, and you are bound by no others.

Naturally, your rhythmic structure should not destroy the shape of your words, or their natural sound, or their meaning. It is improbable that, at the start, you will be able to get a rhythm-structure strong enough to affect them very much, though you may fall a victim to all sorts of false stopping due to line ends and cæsurae.

The musician can rely on pitch and the volume of the orchestra. You can not. The term harmony is misapplied to poetry; it refers to simultaneous sounds of different pitch. There is, however, in the best verse a sort of residue of sound which remains in the ear of the hearer and acts more or less as an organ-base.

A rhyme must have in it some slight element of surprise if it is to give pleasure; it need not be bizarre or curious, but it must be well used if used at all.

Vide further Vildrac and Duhamel's notes on rhyme in "Technique Poetique."[3]

That part of your poetry which strikes upon the imaginative *eye* of the reader will lose nothing by translation into a foreign tongue; that which appeals to the ear can reach only those who take it in the original.

Consider the definiteness of Dante's presentation, as compared with Milton's rhetoric. Read as much of Wordsworth as does not seem too unutterably dull.[4]

If you want the gist of the matter go to Sappho, Catullus, Villon, Heine when he is in the vein, Gautier when he is not too frigid; or, if you have not the tongues, seek out the leisurely Chaucer.[5] Good prose will do you no harm, and there is good discipline to be had by trying to write it.

Translation is likewise good training, if you find that your original matter "wobbles" when you try to rewrite it. The meaning of the poem to be translated can not "wobble."

If you are using a symmetrical form, don't put in what you want to say and then fill up the remaining vacuums with slush.

Don't mess up the perception of one sense by trying to define it in terms of another. This is usually only the result of being too lazy to find the exact word. To this clause there are possibly exceptions.

The first three simple proscriptions will throw out nine-tenths of all the bad poetry now accepted as standard and classic; and will prevent you from many a crime of production.

". . . *Mais d'abord il faut être un poète,*"[6] as MM. Duhamel and Vildrac have said at the end of their little book, "Notes sur la Technique Poetique."

• • •

3. Charles Vildrac (1882–1971), French poet, playwright, and critic, and Georges Duhamel (1884–1966), French novelist and critic, cowrote *Notes sur la technique poétique* (1910). *Vide*: consider.

4. "Vide infra" [Pound's note] (Latin: "See later"). John Milton (1608–1674) and William Wordsworth (1770–1850), English poets.

5. Geoffrey Chaucer (c. 1342–1400): English poet. Sappho (c. 610–c. 580 B.C.E.): Greek poet. Catullus (c. 84–c. 54 B.C.E.): Roman poet. François Villon (1431–1463?): French poet. Heinrich Heine (1797–1856): German poet. Théophile Gautier (1811–1872): French poet.

6. But first it is necessary to be a poet (French).

Since March, 1913, Ford Madox Hueffer has pointed out that Wordsworth was so intent on the ordinary or plain word that he never thought of hunting for *le mot juste*.[7]

John Butler Yeats has handled or man-handled Wordsworth and the Victorians, and his criticism, contained in letters to his son, is now printed and available.[8]

I do not like writing *about* art, my first, at least I think it was my first essay on the subject, was a protest against it.

Prolegomena[9]

Time was when the poet lay in a green field with his head against a tree and played his diversion on a ha'penny whistle, and Cæsar's predecessors conquered the earth, and the predecessors of golden Crassus embezzled,[1] and fashions had their say, and let him alone. And presumably he was fairly content in this circumstance, for I have small doubt that the occasional passerby, being attracted by curiosity to know why any one should lie under a tree and blow diversion on a ha'penny whistle, came and conversed with him, and that among these passers-by there was on occasion a person of charm or a young lady who had not read "Man and Superman";[2] and looking back upon this naïve state of affairs we call it the age of gold.

Metastasio,[3] and he should know if any one, assures us that this age endures—even though the modern poet is expected to holloa his verses down a speaking tube to the editors of cheap magazines—S. S. McClure,[4] or some one of that sort—even though hordes of authors meet in dreariness and drink healths to the "Copyright Bill";[5] even though these things be, the age of gold pertains. Imperceivably, if you like, but pertains. You meet unkempt Amyclas in a Soho[6] restaurant and chant together of dead and forgotten things—it is a manner of speech among poets to chant of dead, half-forgotten things, there seems no special harm in it; it has always been done—and it's rather better to be a clerk in the Post Office than to look after a lot of stinking, verminous sheep—and at another hour of the day one substitutes the drawing-room for the restaurant and tea is probably more palatable than mead and mare's milk, and little cakes than honey. And in this fashion one survives the resignation of Mr. Balfour,[7] and the iniquities of the American customs-house; *e quel bufera infernal*,[8] the periodical press. And then in the middle of it, there being apparently no other person at once capable and available one is stopped and asked to explain oneself.

7. The exact word (French). Hueffer was the original name of English novelist Ford Madox Ford (1873–1939).
8. *Passages from the Letters of John Butler Yeats*, by the Irish barrister and painter (1839–1922), father of the poet W. B. Yeats (1865–1939), was published in 1917.
9. From *Poetry Review* (February 1912).
1. Roman politician Crassus (c. 115 B.C.E.–53 B.C.E.) formed the First Triumvirate with Pompey (106 B.C.E.–48 B.C.E.) and Julius Caeser (100 B.C.E.–44 B.C.E.), who became dictator in 46 B.C.E. Crassus's political strength largely derived from his financial wealth, much of which he gained by selling conquered lands. *Ha'penny:* half-penny.
2. Play, by Irish playwright George Bernard Shaw (1856–1950), that popularized the term *superman* (*Übermensch*) as used by German philosopher Friedrich Nietzsche (1844–1900).
3. Pietro Metastasio (1698–1782), Italian poet and opera librettist.
4. American editor (1857–1949) and founder of the "muckraking" *McClure's Magazine*. *Halloa:* yell. *Speaking tube:* pipe through which voices traveled between rooms.
5. Copyright law had recently been amended, greatly increasing the legal rights of authors, by the Copyright Act of 1909, in the United States, and the Copyright Act of 1911, in Great Britain.
6. London neighborhood. *Amyclas:* in Greek mythology, brother of Eurydice and founder of the city of Amyclae, near Sparta.
7. Conservative English politician Arthur James Balfour (1848–1930) resigned his position as prime minister in 1905.
8. And that infernal storm (Italian).

I begin on the chord thus querulous, for I would much rather lie on what is left of Catullus' parlour floor and speculate the azure beneath it and the hills off to Salo and Riva[9] with their forgotten gods moving unhindered amongst them, than discuss any processes and theories of art whatsoever. I would rather play tennis. I shall not argue.

CREDO

Rhythm.—I believe in an "absolute rhythm," a rhythm, that is, in poetry which corresponds exactly to the emotion or shade of emotion to be expressed. A man's rhythm must be interpretative, it will be, therefore, in the end, his own, uncounterfeiting, uncounterfeitable.

Symbols.—I believe that the proper and perfect symbol is the natural object, that if a man use "symbols" he must so use them that their symbolic function does not obtrude; so that *a* sense, and the poetic quality of the passage, is not lost to those who do not understand the symbol as such, to whom, for instance, a hawk is a hawk.

Technique.—I believe in technique as the test of a man's sincerity; in law when it is ascertainable; in the trampling down of every convention that impedes or obscures the determination of the law, or the precise rendering of the impulse.

Form.—I think there is a "fluid" as well as a "solid" content, that some poems may have form as a tree has form, some as water poured into a vase. That most symmetrical forms have certain uses. That a vast number of subjects cannot be precisely, and therefore not properly rendered in symmetrical forms.

"Thinking that alone worthy wherein the whole art is employed,"[1] I think the artist should master all known forms and systems of metric, and I have with some persistence set about doing this, searching particularly into those periods wherein the systems came to birth or attained their maturity. It has been complained, with some justice, that I dump my note-books on the public. I think that only after a long struggle will poetry attain such a degree of development, of, if you will, modernity, that it will vitally concern people who are accustomed, in prose, to Henry James and Anatole France, in music to Debussy.[2] I am constantly contending that it took two centuries of Provençe and one of Tuscany to develop the media of Dante's masterwork,[3] that it took the latinists of the Renaissance, and the Pleiade,[4] and his own age of painted speech to prepare Shakespeare his tools. It is tremendously important that great poetry be written, it makes no jot of difference who writes it. The experimental demonstrations of one man may save the time of many—hence my furore over Arnaut Daniel[5]—if a man's experiments try out one new rime, or dispense conclusively with one iota of currently accepted nonsense, he is merely playing fair with his colleagues when he chalks up his result.

No man ever writes very much poetry that "matters." In bulk, that is, no

9. Towns on Lake Garda, in northern Italy.
1. "Dante, De Volgari Eloquio" [Pound's note]. Dante's Latin treatise *De Vulgari Eloquentia (On Eloquence in the Vernacular;* c. 1303) argues for the nobility of Italian as a literary language.
2. Claude Debussy (1862–1918): French composer. Henry James (1843–1916): American novelist. Anatole France (1844–1924): French fiction writer and critic.
3. That is, *The Divine Comedy* (c. 1310–14).
4. Group of sixteenth-century French writers who sought to elevate the literary prestige of the French language.
5. Provençal troubadour poet (fl. 1180–1200). *Furore:* frenzied enthusiasm.

one produces much that is final, and when a man is not doing this highest thing, this saying the thing once for all and perfectly; when he is not matching Ποικιλόθρον', ἀθάνατ' 'Αφρόδιτα,[6] or "Hist—said Kate the Queen,"[7] he had much better be making the sorts of experiment which may be of use to him in his later work, or to his successors.

"The lyf so short, the craft so long to lerne."[8] It is a foolish thing for a man to begin his work on a too narrow foundation, it is a disgraceful thing for a man's work not to show steady growth and increasing fineness from first to last.

As for "adaptations"; one finds that all the old masters of painting recommend to their pupils that they begin by copying masterwork, and proceed to their own composition.

As for "Every man his own poet." The more every man knows about poetry the better. I believe in every one writing poetry who wants to; most do. I believe in every man knowing enough of music to play "God bless our home" on the harmonicum, but I do not believe in every man giving concerts and printing his sin.

The mastery of any art is the work of a lifetime. I should not discriminate between the "amateur" and the "professional," or rather I should discriminate quite often in favour of the amateur, but I should discriminate between the amateur and the expert. It is certain that the present chaos will endure until the Art of poetry has been preached down the amateur gullet, until there is such a general understanding of the fact that poetry is an art and not a pastime; such a knowledge of technique; of technique of surface and technique of content, that the amateurs will cease to try to drown out the masters.

If a certain thing was said once for all in Atlantis or Arcadia,[9] in 450 Before Christ or in 1290 after, it is not for us moderns to go saying it over, or to go obscuring the memory of the dead by saying the same thing with less skill and less conviction.

My pawing over the ancients and semi-ancients has been one struggle to find out what has been done, once for all, better than it can ever be done again, and to find out what remains for us to do, and plenty does remain, for if we still feel the same emotions as those which launched the thousand ships,[1] it is quite certain that we come on these feelings differently, through different nuances, by different intellectual gradations. Each age has its own abounding gifts, yet only some ages transmute them into matter of duration. No good poetry is ever written in a manner twenty years old, for to write in such a manner shows conclusively that the writer thinks from books, convention and *cliché,* and not from life, yet a man feeling the divorce of life and his art may naturally try to resurrect a forgotten mode if he find in that mode some leaven, or if he think he sees in it some element lacking in contemporary art which might unite that art again to its sustenance, life.

In the art of Daniel and Cavalcanti,[2] I have seen that precision which I

6. *Poikilóthron' athánat' Aphródita:* ornately throned, deathless Aphrodite (Greek); the ancient Greek poet Sappho's invocation to the goddess of love.
7. From *Pippa Passes,* by English poet Robert Browning (1812–1889).
8. From Chaucer's "The Parlement of Foules."
9. Mountainous region of Greece portrayed as a paradise in ancient Greek, Roman, and Renaissance literature. *Atlantis:* according to a legend reported by the ancient Greek philosopher Plato, an island submerged in the Atlantic Ocean.
1. In Greek legend and Homer's *Iliad,* the beauty of Helen of Troy incites the Trojan War. The famous description of the "face that launched a thousand ships" is from the play *Doctor Faustus,* by English dramatist Christopher Marlowe (1564–1593).
2. Guido Cavalcanti (c. 1255–1300), Italian poet.

miss in the Victorians—that explicit rendering, be it of external nature, or of emotion. Their testimony is of the eyewitness, their symptoms are first hand.

As for the nineteenth century, with all respect to its achievements, I think we shall look back upon it as a rather blurry, messy sort of a period, a rather sentimentalistic, mannerish sort of a period. I say this without any self-righteousness, with no self-satisfaction.

As for there being a "movement" or my being of it, the conception of poetry as a "pure art" in the sense in which I use the term, revived with Swinburne. From the puritanical revolt to Swinburne, poetry had been merely the vehicle—yes, definitely, Arthur Symons'[3] scruples and feelings about the word not withholding—the ox-cart and post-chaise[4] for transmitting thoughts poetic or otherwise. And perhaps the "great Victorians," though it is doubtful, and assuredly the "nineties" continued the development of the art, confining their improvements, however, chiefly to sound and to refinements of manner.

Mr. Yeats has once and for all stripped English poetry of its perdamnable rhetoric. He has boiled away all that is not poetic—and a good deal that is. He has become a classic in his own lifetime and *nel mezzo del cammin.*[5] He has made our poetic idiom a thing pliable, a speech without inversions.

Robert Bridges, Maurice Hewlett and Frederic Manning are[6] in their different ways seriously concerned with overhauling the metric, in testing the language and its adaptability to certain modes. Ford Hueffer is making some sort of experiments in modernity. The Provost of Oriel continues his translation of the *Divina Commedia.*[7]

As to Twentieth century poetry, and the poetry which I expect to see written during the next decade or so, it will, I think, move against poppy-cock, it will be harder and saner, it will be what Mr. Hewlett calls "nearer the bone." It will be as much like granite as it can be, its force will lie in its truth, its interpretative power (of course, poetic force does always rest there); I mean it will not try to seem forcible by rhetorical din, and luxurious riot. We will have fewer painted adjectives impeding the shock and stroke of it. At least for myself, I want it so, austere, direct, free from emotional slither.

• • •

What is there now, in 1917, to be added?

Re Vers Libre

I think the desire for vers libre is due to the sense of quantity reasserting itself after years of starvation. But I doubt if we can take over, for English, the rules of quantity[8] laid down for greek and latin, mostly by latin grammarians.

I think one should write vers libre only when one "must," that is to say, only when the "thing" builds up a rhythm more beautiful than that of set metres, or more real, more a part of the emotion of the "thing," more ger-

3. English poet and critic (1865–1945).
4. Traveling carriage.
5. In the middle of his walk (Italian); that is, in the middle of his life; from the opening of Dante's *Divine Comedy.*
6. "(Dec., 1911)" [Pound's note]. Robert Bridges (1844–1930): English poet. Maurice Hewlett (1861–1923): English novelist. Frederic Manning (1882–1935): English novelist and author of fictional dialogues with historic figures.
7. Dante's *Divine Comedy.*
8. That is, not accentual-syllabic meters, but the patterns of long and short syllables used in classical poetry.

mane, intimate, interpretative than the measure of regular accentual verse; a rhythm which discontents one with set iambic or set anapaestic.

Eliot has said the thing very well when he said, "No *vers* is *libre* for the man who wants to do a good job."

As a matter of detail, there is vers libre with accent heavily marked as a drum-beat (as par example my "Dance Figure"), and on the other hand I think I have gone as far as can profitably be gone in the other direction (and perhaps too far). I mean I do not think one can use to any advantage rhythms much more tenuous and imperceptible than some I have used. I think progress lies rather in an attempt to approximate classical quantitative metres (NOT to copy them) than in a carelessness regarding such things.[9]

• • •

I agree with John Yeats on the relation of beauty to certitude. I prefer satire, which is due to emotion, to any sham of emotion.

I have had to write, or at least I have written a good deal about art, sculpture, painting and poetry. I have seen what seemed to me the best of contemporary work reviled and obstructed. Can any one write prose of permanent or durable interest when he is merely saying for one year what nearly every one will say at the end of three or four years? I have been battistrada[1] for a sculptor, a painter, a novelist, several poets. I wrote also of certain French writers in *The New Age*[2] in nineteen twelve or eleven.

I would much rather that people would look at Brzeska's sculpture and Lewis' drawings, and that they would read Joyce, Jules Romains, Eliot,[3] than that they should read what I have said of these men, or that I should be asked to republish argumentative essays and reviews.

All that the critic can do for the reader or audience or spectator is to focus his gaze or audition. Rightly or wrongly I think my blasts and essays have done their work, and that more people are now likely to go to the sources than are likely to read this book.

Jammes'[4] "Existences" in "La Triomphe de la Vie" is available. So are his early poems. I think we need a convenient anthology rather than descriptive criticism. Carl Sandburg[5] wrote me from Chicago, "It's hell when poets can't afford to buy each other's books." Half the people who care, only borrow. In America so few people know each other that the difficulty lies more than half in distribution. Perhaps one should make an anthology: Romains' "Un Être en Marche" and "Prières," Vildrac's "Visite." Retrospectively the fine wrought work of La Forgue, the flashes of Rimbaud, the hard-bit lines of Tristan Corbière, Tailhade's sketches in "Poèmes Aristophanesques," the "Litanies" of DeGourmont.[6]

• • •

It is difficult at all times to write of the fine arts, it is almost impossible unless one can accompany one's prose with many reproductions. Still I would

9. "Let me date this statement 20. Aug., 1917" [Pound's note].
1. Pacesetter; one who leads the way (Italian).
2. During the first half of the 1910s, Pound frequently submitted essays, including his "I Gather the Limbs of Osiris" (1911–12) and "Patria Mia" (1912), to *The New Age,* a magazine owned and edited by English writer A. R. Orage (1875–1934).
3. T. S. Eliot (1888–1965): Anglo-American poet. French sculptor Henri Gaudier-Brzeska (1891–1915) and English author and artist Wyndham Lewis (1882–1957) were central figures of Vorticism. James Joyce (1882–1941): Irish novelist. Jules Romains (1885–1972): French novelist and playwright.
4. Francis Jammes (1868–1938): French poet and novelist.
5. American poet (1878–1967).
6. Jules Laforgue (1860–1887), Arthur Rimbaud (1854–1891), Tristan Corbière (1845–1875),

seize this chance or any chance to reaffirm my belief in Wyndham Lewis' genius, both in his drawings and his writings. And I would name an out of the way prose book, the "Scenes and Portraits" of Frederic Manning, as well as James Joyce's short stories and novel, "Dubliners" and the now well known "Portrait of the Artist," as well as Lewis' "Tarr," if, that is, I may treat my strange reader as if he were a new friend come into the room, intent on ransacking my bookshelf.

Only Emotion Endures

"Only emotion endures." Surely it is better for me to name over the few beautiful poems that still ring in my head than for me to search my flat for back numbers of periodicals and rearrange all that I have said about friendly and hostile writers.

The first twelve lines of Padraic Colum's[7] "Drover"; his "O Woman shapely as a swan, on your account I shall not die"; Joyce's "I hear an army";[8] the lines of Yeats that ring in my head and in the heads of all young men of my time who care for poetry: Braseal and the Fisherman, "The fire that stirs about her when she stirs"; the later lines of "The Scholars," the faces of the Magi;[9] William Carlos Williams' "Postlude," Aldington's version of "Atthis," and "H. D.'s" waves like pine tops,[1] and her verse in "Des Imagistes" the first anthology; Hueffer's "How red your lips are" in his translation from Von der Vogelweide,[2] his "Three Ten," the general effect of his "On Heaven"; his sense of the prose values or prose qualities in poetry; his ability to write poems that will sing to music, as distinct from poems that half-chant and are spoiled by a musician's additions; beyond these a poem by Alice Corbin, "One City Only," and another ending "But sliding water over a stone."[3] These things have worn smooth in my head and I am not through with them, nor with Aldington's "In Via Sestina" nor his other poems in "Des Imagistes" though people have told me their flaws. It may be that their content is too much embedded in me for me to look back at the words.

I am almost a different person when I come to take up the argument for Eliot's poems.

• • •

1918

Laurent Tailhade (1854–1919): French poets. Rémy de Gourmont (1858–1915): French novelist, poet, and philosopher.
7. Irish-born American poet (1881–1972).
8. James Joyce's "I Hear an Army" appeared in his volume of poetry, *Chamber Music* (1907), and in slightly different form in the anthology *Des Imagistes* (1914), edited by Pound.
9. Yeats's "Breasal the Fisherman," "The Folly of Being Comforted," and "The Magi."
1. From H. D.'s "Oread." William Carlos Williams (1883–1963), American poet.
2. Walther von der Vogelweide (c. 1170–1230), German poet.
3. "Love Me at Last," by Alice Corbin (1881–1949), American poet and cofounder of the magazine *Poetry*.

How to Read

Ezra Pound's *How to Read* began as an essay, "On Criticism in General," published in the first volume of T. S. Eliot's *Criterion* in January 1923. Revised and printed as "How to Read, or Why" in three installments in the "Books" section of the *New York Herald Tribune* in January 1929, it was released as a book in 1931. In a famous passage, Pound delineates three kinds of poetry: *melopoeia,* in which words are charged with musical properties; *phanopoeia,* which works through images; and *logopoeia,* " 'the dance of the intellect among words,' " in which the words engage in ironic play with their expected contexts. Pound proffers these influential distinctions in the midst of criticizing the university's approach to literary instruction, suggesting that readers should focus their attention only on the most innovative works of each period. For Pound, the teaching of literature must preserve the clarity and efficiency of literary language to help eliminate inexact thinking. The excerpt is reprinted from *Literary Essays of Ezra Pound* (1968).

EZRA POUND

From *How to Read*

Language

* * *

Bad critics have prolonged the use of demoded terminology, usually a terminology originally invented to describe what had been done before 300 B.C., and to describe it in a rather exterior fashion. Writers of second order have often tried to produce works to fit some category or term not yet occupied in their own local literature. If we chuck out the classifications which apply to the outer shape of the work, or to its occasion, and if we look at what actually happens, in, let us say, poetry, we will find that the language is charged or energized in various manners.

That is to say, there are three 'kinds of poetry':

MELOPŒIA, wherein the words are charged, over and above their plain meaning, with some musical property, which directs the bearing or trend of that meaning.

PHANOPŒIA, which is a casting of images upon the visual imagination.

LOGOPŒIA, 'the dance of the intellect among words', that is to say, it employs words not only for their direct meaning, but it takes count in a special way of habits of usage, of the context we *expect* to find with the word, its usual concomitants, of its known acceptances, and of ironical play. It holds the aesthetic content which is peculiarly the domain of verbal manifestation, and cannot possibly be contained in plastic or in music. It is the latest come, and perhaps most tricky and undependable mode.

The *melopœia* can be appreciated by a foreigner with a sensitive ear, even though he be ignorant of the language in which the poem is written. It is practically impossible to transfer or translate it from one language to another, save perhaps by divine accident, and for half a line at a time.

Phanopœia can, on the other hand, be translated almost, or wholly, intact. When it is good enough, it is practically impossible for the translator to destroy it save by very crass bungling, and the neglect of perfectly well-known and formulative rules.

Logopœia does not translate; though the attitude of mind it expresses may pass through a paraphrase. Or one might say, you can *not* translate it 'locally', but having determined the original author's state of mind, you may or may not be able to find a derivative or an equivalent.

Prose

The language of prose is much less highly charged, that is perhaps the only availing distinction between prose and poesy. Prose permits greater factual presentation, explicitness, but a much greater amount of language is needed. During the last century or century and a half, prose has, perhaps for the first time, perhaps for the second or third time, arisen to challenge the poetic pre-eminence. That is to say, *Cœur Simple,* by Flaubert, is probably more important than Théophile Gautier's *Carmen,*[1] etc.

The total charge in certain nineteenth-century prose works possibly surpasses the total charge found in individual poems of that period; but that merely indicates that the author has been able to get his effect cumulatively, by a greater heaping up of factual data; imagined fact, if you will, but nevertheless expressed in factual manner.

By using several hundred pages of prose, Flaubert, by force of architectonics, manages to attain an intensity comparable to that in Villon's *Heaulmière,* or his prayer for his mother.[2] This does not invalidate my dissociation of the two terms: poetry, prose.

In *Phanopœia*[3] we find the greatest drive toward utter precision of word; this art exists almost exclusively by it.

In *melopœia* we find a contrary current, a force tending often to lull, or to distract the reader from the exact sense of the language. It is poetry on the borders of music and music is perhaps the bridge between consciousness and the unthinking sentient or even insentient universe.

All writing is built up of these three elements, plus 'architectonics' or 'the form of the whole', and to know anything about the relative efficiency of various works one must have some knowledge of the maximum already attained by various authors, irrespective of where and when.[4]

It is not enough to know that the Greeks attained to the greatest skill in melopœia, or even that the Provençaux added certain diverse developments and that some quite minor, nineteenth-century Frenchmen achieved certain elaborations.

It is not quite enough to have the general idea that the Chinese (more particularly Rihaku and Omakitsu)[5] attained the known maximum of

1. Poem from the collection *Émaux et camées* (*Enamels and Cameos;* 1852), by French poet Théophile Gautier (1811–1872). *Un Coeur Simple* (*A Simple Heart*): novella by French novelist Gustave Flaubert (1821–1880)
2. In *Le Grand Testament,* by French lyric poet François Villon (1431–1463?). Villon's "Heaulmière" is a ballad about a helmet-maker's wife speaking to prostitutes.
3. Pound forms his famous coinages *phanopoeia, melopoeia,* and *logopoeia* by joining the Greek terms for light (*phano*), music (*melo*), and word (*logo*) to the suffix *poeia* (Greek for making, the root of *poem* and *poetry*).
4. "Lacuna at this point to be corrected in criticism of Hindemith's 'Schwanendreher'. E.P. Sept. 1938" [Pound's note]. *Der Schwanendreher* (*The Swan-Turner*): concerto by German composer Paul Hindemith (1895–1963).
5. Japanese names of Chinese poets Li Po (701–762) and Wang Wei (699–759), respectively.

phanopœia, due perhaps to the nature of their written ideograph, or to wonder whether Rimbaud[6] is, at rare moments, their equal. One wants one's knowledge in more definite terms.

It is an error to think that vast reading will automatically produce any such knowledge or understanding. Neither Chaucer[7] with his forty books, nor Shakespeare with perhaps half a dozen, in folio, can be considered illiterate. A man can learn more music by working on a Bach fugue[8] until he can take it apart and put it together, than by playing through ten dozen heterogeneous albums.

You may say that for twenty-seven years I have thought consciously about this particular matter, and read or read at a great many books, and that with the subject never really out of my mind, I don't yet know half there is to know about *melopœia*.

* * *

1929, 1931

6. Arthur Rimbaud (1854–1891), French poet.
7. Geoffrey Chaucer (c. 1342–1400): English poet and author of *The Canterbury Tales*.
8. Musical composition in which a principle melodic line is simultaneously developed in different counterpoint voices. Johann Sebastian Bach (1685–1750), German Baroque composer.

TRADITION AND THE INDIVIDUAL TALENT

Since the first publication of T. S. Eliot's essay, one of the most influential works of twentieth-century literary criticism, poets and critics alike have grappled with its ideas. For Eliot, the poet should aspire not to Romantic self-expression, but to an ideal of aesthetic impersonality. The poet must labor assiduously to sacrifice personality and obtain tradition. Through self-surrender to the medium of literature, as Eliot describes it, the poet becomes a catalyst by which emotions are transfigured into something more significant than the individual who expresses them. Each truly innovative work transforms not only the present, but also the entire literary past. First published in the journal *The Egoist* in September and December 1919, the essay is reprinted from *Selected Prose of T. S. Eliot* (1975).

T. S. ELIOT

Tradition and the Individual Talent

I

In English writing we seldom speak of tradition, though we occasionally apply its name in deploring its absence. We cannot refer to 'the tradition' or to 'a tradition'; at most, we employ the adjective in saying that the poetry of So-and-so is 'traditional' or even 'too traditional'. Seldom, perhaps, does the word appear except in a phrase of censure. If otherwise, it is vaguely approbative, with the implication, as to the work approved, of some pleasing archaeological reconstruction. You can hardly make the word agreeable to English ears without this comfortable reference to the reassuring science of archaeology.

Certainly the word is not likely to appear in our appreciations of living or dead writers. Every nation, every race, has not only its own creative, but its own critical turn of mind; and is even more oblivious of the shortcomings and limitations of its critical habits than of those of its creative genius. We know, or think we know, from the enormous mass of critical writing that has appeared in the French language the critical method or habit of the French; we only conclude (we are such unconscious people) that the French are 'more critical' than we, and sometimes even plume ourselves a little with the fact, as if the French were the less spontaneous. Perhaps they are; but we might remind ourselves that criticism is as inevitable as breathing, and that we should be none the worse for articulating what passes in our minds when we read a book and feel an emotion about it, for criticizing our own minds in their work of criticism. One of the facts that might come to light in this process is our tendency to insist, when we praise a poet, upon those aspects of his work in which he least resembles anyone else. In these aspects or parts of his work we pretend to find what is individual, what is the peculiar essence of the man. We dwell with satisfaction upon the poet's difference from his predecessors, especially his immediate predecessors; we endeavor to find something that can be isolated in order to be enjoyed. Whereas if we approach a poet without this prejudice we shall often find that not only the best, but the most individual parts of his work may be those in which the dead poets, his ancestors, assert their immortality most vigorously. And I do not mean the impressionable period of adolescence, but the period of full maturity.

Yet if the only form of tradition, of handing down, consisted in following the ways of the immediate generation before us in a blind or timid adherence to its successes, 'tradition' should positively be discouraged. We have seen many such simple currents soon lost in the sand; and novelty is better than repetition. Tradition is a matter of much wider significance. It cannot be inherited, and if you want it you must obtain it by great labour. It involves, in the first place, the historical sense, which we may call nearly indispensable to anyone who would continue to be a poet beyond his twenty-fifth year; and the historical sense involves a perception, not only of the pastness of the past, but of its presence; the historical sense compels a man to write not merely with his own generation in his bones, but with a feeling that the whole of the literature of Europe from Homer and within it the whole of the literature of his own country has a simultaneous existence and composes a simultaneous order. This historical sense, which is a sense of the timeless as well as of the temporal and of the timeless and of the temporal together, is what makes a writer traditional. And it is at the same time what makes a writer most acutely conscious of his place in time, of his own contemporaneity.

No poet, no artist of any art, has his complete meaning alone. His significance, his appreciation is the appreciation of his relation to the dead poets and artists. You cannot value him alone; you must set him, for contrast and comparison, among the dead. I mean this as a principle of aesthetic, not merely historical, criticism. The necessity that he shall conform, that he shall cohere, is not onesided; what happens when a new work of art is created is something that happens simultaneously to all the works of art which preceded it. The existing monuments form an ideal order among themselves, which is modified by the introduction of the new (the really new) work of art among them. The existing order is complete before the new work arrives; for order to persist after the supervention of novelty, the *whole* existing order must be, if ever so slightly, altered; and so the relations, proportions, values of each work of art toward the whole are readjusted; and this is conformity between the old and the new. Whoever has approved this idea of order, of the form of European, of English literature will not find it preposterous that the past should be altered by the present as much as the present is directed by the past. And the poet who is aware of this will be aware of great difficulties and responsibilities.

In a peculiar sense he will be aware also that he must inevitably be judged by the standards of the past. I say judged, not amputated, by them; not judged to be as good as, or worse or better than, the dead; and certainly not judged by the canons of dead critics. It is a judgment, a comparison, in which two things are measured by each other. To conform merely would be for the new work not really to conform at all; it would not be new, and would therefore not be a work of art. And we do not quite say that the new is more valuable because it fits in; but its fitting in is a test of its value—a test, it is true, which can only be slowly and cautiously applied, for we are none of us infallible judges of conformity. We say: it appears to conform, and is perhaps individual, or it appears individual, and may conform; but we are hardly likely to find that it is one and not the other.

To proceed to a more intelligible exposition of the relation of the poet to the past; he can neither take the past as a lump, and indiscriminate bolus,[1] nor can he form himself wholly on one or two private admirations, nor can he form himself wholly upon one preferred period. The first course is inadmissible, the second is an important experience of youth, and the third is a pleasant and highly desirable supplement. The poet must be very conscious of the main current, which does not at all flow invariably through the most distinguished reputations. He must be quite aware of the obvious fact that art never improves, but that the material of art is never quite the same. He must be aware that the mind of Europe—the mind of his own country—a mind which he learns in time to be much more important than his own private mind—is a mind which changes, and that this change is a development which abandons nothing *en route,* which does not superannuate either Shakespeare, or Homer, or the rock drawing of the Magdalenian[2] draughtsmen. That this development, refinement perhaps, complication certainly, is not, from the point of view of the artist, any improvement. Perhaps not even an improvement from the point of view of the psychologist or not to the extent which we imagine; perhaps only in the end based upon a complication in economics and machinery. But the difference between the present and the past is that the conscious present is an awareness of the past in a way and to an extent which the past's awareness of itself cannot show.

Someone said: 'The dead writers are remote from us because we *know* so much more than they did'. Precisely, and they are that which we know.

I am alive to a usual objection to what is clearly part of my programme for the *métier*[3] of poetry. The objection is that the doctrine requires a ridiculous

1. Round mass or pill.
2. Most advanced period of Europe's Paleolithic period.
3. Vocation (French).

amount of erudition (pedantry), a claim which can be rejected by appeal to the lives of poets in any pantheon. It will even be affirmed that much learning deadens or perverts poetic sensibility. While, however, we persist in believing that a poet ought to know as much as will not encroach upon his necessary receptivity and necessary laziness, it is not desirable to confine knowledge to whatever can be put into a useful shape for examinations, drawing-rooms, or the still more pretentious modes of publicity. Some can absorb knowledge, the more tardy must sweat for it. Shakespeare acquired more essential history from Plutarch[4] than most men could from the whole British Museum. What is to be insisted upon is that the poet must develop or procure the consciousness of the past and that he should continue to develop this consciousness throughout his career.

What happens is a continual surrender of himself as he is at the moment to something which is more valuable. The progress of an artist is a continual self-sacrifice, a continual extinction of personality.

There remains to define this process of depersonalization and its relation to the sense of tradition. It is in this depersonalization that art may be said to approach the condition of science. I therefore invite you to consider, as a suggestive analogy, the action which takes place when a bit of finely filiated platinum is introduced into a chamber containing oxygen and sulphur dioxide.

II

Honest criticism and sensitive appreciation is directed not upon the poet but upon the poetry. If we attend to the confused cries of the newspaper critics and the susurrus[5] of popular repetition that follows, we shall hear the names of poets in great numbers; if we seek not Blue-book[6] knowledge but the enjoyment of poetry, and ask for a poem, we shall seldom find it. I have tried to point out the importance of the relation of the poem to other poems by other authors, and suggested the conception of poetry as a living whole of all the poetry that has ever been written. The other aspect of this Impersonal theory of poetry is the relation of the poem to its author. And I hinted, by an analogy, that the mind of the mature poet differs from that of the immature one not precisely in any valuation of 'personality', not being necessarily more interesting, or having 'more to say', but rather by being a more finely perfected medium in which special, or very varied, feelings are at liberty to enter into new combinations.

The analogy was that of the catalyst. When the two gases previously mentioned are mixed in the presence of a filament of platinum, they form sulphurous acid. This combination takes place only if the platinum is present; nevertheless the newly formed acid contains no trace of platinum, and the platinum itself is apparently unaffected: has remained inert, neutral, and unchanged. The mind of the poet is the shred of platinum. It may partly or exclusively operate upon the experience of the man himself; but, the more perfect the artist, the more completely separate in him will be the man who suffers and the mind which creates; the more perfectly will the mind digest and transmute the passions which are its material.

4. Greek writer (first century C.E.), from whose biographies of Greek and Roman figures Shakespeare culled material for his plays.
5. Whispering, murmuring.
6. Official British publication (e.g., of parliamentary reports, directories).

The experience, you will notice, the elements which enter the presence of the transforming catalyst, are of two kinds: emotions and feelings. The effect of a work of art upon the person who enjoys it is an experience different in kind from any experience not of art. It may be formed out of one emotion, or may be a combination of several; and various feelings, inhering for the writer in particular words or phrases or images, may be added to compose the final result. Or great poetry may be made without the direct use of any emotion whatever: composed out of feelings solely. Canto XV of the *Inferno* (Brunetto Latini)[7] is a working up of the emotion evident in the situation; but the effect, though single as that of any work of art, is obtained by considerable complexity of detail. The last quatrain gives an image, a feeling attaching to an image, which 'came', which did not develop simply out of what precedes, but which was probably in suspension in the poet's mind until the proper combination arrived for it to add itself to. The poet's mind is in fact a receptacle for seizing and storing up numberless feelings, phrases, images, which remain there until all the particles which can unite to form a new compound are present together.

If you compare several representative passages of the greatest poetry you see how great is the variety of types of combination, and also how completely any semi-ethical criterion of 'sublimity' misses the mark. For it is not the 'greatness', the intensity, of the emotions, the components, but the intensity of the artistic process, the pressure, so to speak, under which the fusion takes place, that counts. The episode of Paolo and Francesca[8] employs a definite emotion, but the intensity of the poetry is something quite different from whatever intensity in the supposed experience it may give the impression of. It is no more intense, furthermore, than Canto XXVI, the voyage of Ulysses,[9] which has not the direct dependence upon an emotion. Great variety is possible in the process of transmutation of emotion: the murder of Agamemnon, or the agony of Othello,[1] gives an artistic effect apparently closer to a possible original than the scenes from Dante. In the *Agamemnon*, the artistic emotion approximates to the emotion of an actual spectator; in *Othello* to the emotion of the protagonist himself. But the difference between art and the event is always absolute; the combination which is the murder of Agamemnon is probably as complex as that which is the voyage of Ulysses. In either case there has been a fusion of elements. The ode of Keats[2] contains a number of feelings which have nothing particular to do with the nightingale, but which the nightingale, partly perhaps because of its attractive name, and partly because of its reputation, served to bring together.

The point of view which I am struggling to attack is perhaps related to the metaphysical theory of the substantial unity of the soul: for my meaning is, that the poet has, not a 'personality' to express, but a particular medium, which is only a medium and not a personality, in which impressions and experiences combine in peculiar and unexpected ways. Impressions and experiences which are important for the man may take no place in the poetry,

7. In Canto 15, Dante meets Brunetto, his old master whom he greatly admires, suffering in Hell. The last quatrain of the canto reads: "Then he turned round, and seemed like one of those / Who run for the green cloth [in the footrace] at Verona / In the field; and he seemed among them / Not the loser but the winner."

8. Two lovers punished with unquenchable desire, in *Inferno* 5.

9. Homeric character who in *Inferno* tells Dante of his suffering in Hell.

1. The title character of Shakespeare's *Othello* kills himself after being duped into jealously murdering his wife. In Aeschylus's play *Agamemnon*, the title character is murdered by his wife, Clytemnestra.

2. "Ode to a Nightingale" (1819), by English poet John Keats (1795–1821).

and those which become important in the poetry may play quite a negligible part in the man, the personality.

I will quote a passage which is unfamiliar enough to be regarded with fresh attention in the light—or darkness—of these observations:

> And now methinks I could e'en chide myself
> For doating on her beauty, though her death
> Shall be revenged after no common action.
> Does the silkworm expend her yellow labours
> For thee? For thee does she undo herself?
> Are lordships sold to maintain ladyships
> For the poor benefit of a bewildering minute?
> Why does yon fellow falsify highways,
> And put his life between the judge's lips,
> To refine such a thing—keeps horse and men
> To beat their valours for her? . . . [3]

In this passage (as is evident if it is taken in its context) there is a combination of positive and negative emotions: an intensely strong attraction toward beauty and an equally intense fascination by the ugliness which is contrasted with it and which destroys it. This balance of contrasted emotion is in the dramatic situation to which the speech is pertinent, but that situation alone is inadequate to it. This is, so to speak, the structural emotion, provided by the drama. But the whole effect, the dominant tone, is due to the fact that a number of floating feelings, having an affinity to this emotion by no means superficially evident, having combined with it to give us a new art emotion.

It is not in his personal emotions, the emotions provoked by particular events in his life, that the poet is in any way remarkable or interesting. His particular emotions may be simple, or crude, or flat. The emotion in his poetry will be a very complex thing, but not with the complexity of the emotions of people who have very complex or unusual emotions in life. One error, in fact, of eccentricity in poetry is to seek for new human emotions to express; and in this search for novelty in the wrong place it discovers the perverse. The business of the poet is not to find new emotions, but to use the ordinary ones and, in working them up into poetry, to express feelings which are not in actual emotions at all. And emotions which he has never experienced will serve his turn as well as those familiar to him. Consequently, we must believe that 'emotion recollected in tranquillity'[4] is an inexact formula. For it is neither emotion, nor recollection, nor without distortion of meaning, tranquillity. It is a concentration, and a new thing resulting from the concentration, of a very great number of experiences which to the practical and active person would not seem to be experiences at all; it is a concentration which does not happen consciously or of deliberation. These experiences are not 'recollected', and they finally unite in an atmosphere which is 'tranquil' only in that it is a passive attending upon the event. Of course this is not quite the whole story. There is a great deal, in the writing of poetry, which must be conscious and deliberate. In fact, the bad poet is usually unconscious where he ought to be conscious, and conscious where he ought to be unconscious. Both errors tend to make him 'personal'. Poetry is not a turning loose of

3. From *The Revenger's Tragedy* 3.4 (1607), by English playwright Cyril Tourneur (c. 1575–1626).

4. William Wordsworth's description of poetic creation, in the preface to *Lyrical Ballads* (2nd ed., 1800).

emotion, but an escape from emotion; it is not the expression of personality, but an escape from personality. But, of course, only those who have personality and emotions know what it means to want to escape from these things.

III

ὁ δὲ νοῦς ἴσως θειότερόν τι καὶ ἀπαθές ἐστιν.[5]

This essay proposes to halt at the frontiers of metaphysics or mysticism, and confine itself to such practical conclusions as can be applied by the responsible person interested in poetry. To divert interest from the poet to the poetry is a laudable aim: for it would conduce to a juster estimation of actual poetry, good and bad. There are many people who appreciate the expression of sincere emotion in verse, and there is a smaller number of people who can appreciate technical excellence. But very few know when there is an expression of *significant* emotion, emotion which has its life in the poem and not in the history of the poet. The emotion of art is impersonal. And the poet cannot reach this impersonality without surrendering himself wholly to the work to be done. And he is not likely to know what is to be done unless he lives in what is not merely the present, but the present moment of the past, unless he is conscious, not of what is dead, but of what is already living.

1919

5. The mind is doubtless something more divine and unimpressionable (Greek); from the ancient Greek philosopher Aristotle's *De Anima* 1.4.

HAMLET

In this review, Eliot introduces his influential concept of the objective correlative—a set of objects or events that function as a formula to elicit particular emotions. Eliot claims that Shakespeare's *Hamlet* was a failure because it lacked such a formula; Hamlet's overwhelming emotions eluded Shakespeare's attempts to embody them aesthetically. Poets must be able to "drag to light, contemplate, or manipulate into art" the feelings about which they write. They should discover forms and situations that objectify inner states instead of talking about them directly. Eliot's essay is a review of two books, one by American scholar Elmer Edgar Stoll (1874–1959) and one by English scholar J. M. Robertson (1856–1933), both of which Eliot praises for moving away from the Romantic focus on Hamlet the character and emphasizing instead *Hamlet* the play. Originally published as "Hamlet and His Problems" in *Athenaeum* (September 26, 1919), the essay is excerpted from *Selected Prose of T. S. Eliot* (1975).

T. S. ELIOT

From Hamlet

* * *

The grounds of *Hamlet's* failure are not immediately obvious. Mr. Robertson is undoubtedly correct in concluding that the essential emotion of the play is the feeling of a son towards a guilty mother:

> [Hamlet's] tone is that of one who has suffered tortures on the score of his mother's degradation. . . . The guilt of a mother is an almost intolerable motive for drama, but it had to be maintained and emphasized to supply a psychological solution, or rather a hint of one.

This, however, is by no means the whole story. It is not merely the 'guilt of a mother' that cannot be handled as Shakespeare handled the suspicion of Othello, the infatuation of Antony, or the pride of Coriolanus. The subject might conceivably have expanded into a tragedy like these, intelligible, self-complete, in the sunlight. *Hamlet,* like the sonnets, is full of some stuff that the writer could not drag to light, contemplate, or manipulate into art. And when we search for this feeling, we find it, as in the sonnets, very difficult to localize. You cannot point to it in the speeches; indeed, if you examine the two famous soliloquies you see the versification of Shakespeare, but a content which might be claimed by another, perhaps by the author of the *Revenge of Bussy d'Ambois,*[1] Act V. Sc. i. We find Shakespeare's *Hamlet* not in the action, not in any quotations that we might select, so much as in an unmistakable tone which is unmistakably not in the earlier play.

The only way of expressing emotion in the form of art is by finding an 'objective correlative'; in other words, a set of objects, a situation, a chain of events which shall be the formula of that *particular* emotion; such that when the external facts, which must terminate in sensory experience, are given, the emotion is immediately evoked. If you examine any of Shakespeare's most successful tragedies, you will find this exact equivalence; you will find that the state of mind of Lady Macbeth walking in her sleep has been communicated to you by a skilful accumulation of imagined sensory impressions; the words of Macbeth on hearing of his wife's death strike us as if, given the sequence of events, these words were automatically released by the last event in the series. The artistic 'inevitability' lies in this complete adequacy of the external to the emotion; and this is precisely what is deficient in *Hamlet.* Hamlet (the man) is dominated by an emotion which is inexpressible, because it is in *excess* of the facts as they appear. And the supposed identity of Hamlet with his author is genuine to this point: that Hamlet's bafflement at the absence of objective equivalent to his feelings is a prolongation of the bafflement of his creator in the face of his artistic problem. Hamlet is up against the difficulty that his disgust is occasioned by his mother, but that his mother is not an adequate equivalent for it; his disgust envelops and exceeds her. It is thus a feeling which he cannot understand; he cannot objectify it, and it therefore remains to poison life and obstruct action. None of the possible actions can satisfy it; and nothing that Shakespeare can do

1. Revenge tragedy, by English playwright George Chapman (1559?–1634).

with the plot can express Hamlet for him. And it must be noticed that the very nature of the *données*[2] of the problem precludes objective equivalence. To have heightened the criminality of Gertrude would have been to provide the formula for a totally different emotion in Hamlet; it is just *because* her character is so negative and insignificant that she arouses in Hamlet the feeling which she is incapable of representing.

The 'madness' of Hamlet lay to Shakespeare's hand; in the earlier play a simple ruse, and to the end, we may presume, understood as a ruse by the audience. For Shakespeare it is less than madness and more than feigned. The levity of Hamlet, his repetition of phrase, his puns, are not part of a deliberate plan of dissimulation, but a form of emotional relief. In the character Hamlet it is the buffoonery of an emotion which can find no outlet in action; in the dramatist it is the buffoonery of an emotion which he cannot express in art. The intense feeling, ecstatic or terrible, without an object or exceeding its object, is something which every person of sensibility has known; it is doubtless a subject of study for pathologists. It often occurs in adolescence: the ordinary person puts these feelings to sleep, or trims down his feelings to fit the business world; the artist keeps them alive by his ability to intensify the world to his emotions. The Hamlet of Laforgue[3] is an adolescent; the Hamlet of Shakespeare is not, he has not that explanation and excuse. We must simply admit that here Shakespeare tackled a problem which proved too much for him. Why he attempted it at all is an insoluble puzzle; under compulsion of what experience he attempted to express the inexpressibly horrible, we cannot ever know. We need a great many facts in his biography; and we should like to know whether, and when, and after or at the same time as what personal experience, he read Montaigne, II. xii, *Apologie de Raimond Sebond*.[4] We should have, finally, to know something which is by hypothesis unknowable, for we assume it to be an experience which, in the manner indicated, exceeded the facts. We should have to understand things which Shakespeare did not understand himself.

1919

2. Assumptions (French).
3. French poet Jules Laforgue (1860–1887) portrayed Hamlet as a young dandy in his "Hamlet, or the Results of Filial Piety."
4. Work in which French essayist Michel de Montaigne (1533–1592) explores the problem of skepticism and human action.

THE METAPHYSICAL POETS

Eliot's critical essays produced a revaluation of the work of the seventeenth-century poet John Donne. Earlier in this essay, Eliot praises Donne and other Metaphysical writers for having "compelled into unity" much "heterogeneity of material," for their "telescoping of images and multiplied associations." Eliot argues that these writers successfully integrated thought and feeling, in contrast to the subsequent "dissociation of sensibility" that afflicted English writers after Donne. Eliot blames John Milton and John Dryden for fostering an unfortunate trend that continued through the late nineteenth century: poetic language became more refined as poetic feeling became clumsier and, consequently, thought and feeling became strictly segregated in poetry. Eliot felt that the ability to transform disparate experiences—including philosophical thought—into poetic wholes was especially crucial for the modern period, whose complexity and fragmentation required complex and difficult poetic treatment. Originally published in 1921 as a review—of *Metaphysical Lyrics and Poems of the Seventeenth Century,* by English scholar Hebert J. C. Grierson (1886–1960)—in the London *Times Literary Supplement,* the text is excerpted from *Selected Prose of T. S. Eliot* (1975).

T. S. ELIOT

From The Metaphysical Poets

* * *

If so shrewd and sensitive (though so limited) a critic as Johnson[1] failed to define metaphysical poetry by its faults, it is worth while to inquire whether we may not have more success by adopting the opposite method: by assuming that the poets of the seventeenth century (up to the Revolution[2]) were the direct and normal development of the precedent age; and, without prejudicing their case by the adjective 'metaphysical', consider whether their virtue was not something permanently valuable, which subsequently disappeared, but ought not to have disappeared. Johnson has hit, perhaps by accident, on one of their peculiarities, when he observed that 'their attempts were always analytic'; he would not agree that, after the dissociation, they put the material together again in a new unity.

It is certain that the dramatic verse of the later Elizabethan and early Jacobean poets expresses a degree of development of sensibility which is not found in any of the prose, good as it often is. If we except Marlowe, a man of prodigious intelligence, these dramatists were directly or indirectly (it is at least a tenable theory) affected by Montaigne.[3] Even if we except also Jonson and Chapman,[4] these two were notably erudite, and were notably men who incorporated their erudition into their sensibility: their mode of feeling was directly and freshly altered by their reading and thought. In Chapman especially there is a direct sensuous apprehension of thought, or a recreation of thought into feeling, which is exactly what we find in Donne:[5]

> in this one thing, all the discipline
> Of manners and of manhood is contained;
> A man to join himself with th' Universe
> In his main sway, and make in all things fit
> One with that All, and go on, round as it;
> Not plucking from the whole his wretched part
> And into straits, or into nought revert,
> Wishing the complete Universe might be

1. Samuel Johnson (1709–1784), English poet and critic.
2. The Revolution of 1688, in which William and Mary replaced James II.
3. Michel de Montaigne (1533–1592): French essayist. Christopher Marlowe (1564–1593): English playwright.
4. George Chapman (1559?–1634) and Ben Jonson (1572–1637), English playwrights and poets.
5. English poet John Donne (1572–1631).

Subject to such a rag of it as he;
But to consider great Necessity.[6]

We compare this with some modern passage:

No, when the fight begins within himself,
A man's worth something. God stoops o'er his head,
Satan looks up between his feet—both tug—
He's left, himself, i' the middle; the soul wakes
And grows. Prolong that battle through his life![7]

It is perhaps somewhat less fair, though very tempting as both poets are concerned with the perpetuation of love by offspring, to compare with the stanzas already quoted from Lord Herbert's Ode[8] the following from Tennyson:

One walked between his wife and child,
With measured footfall firm and mild,
And now and then he gravely smiled.
  The prudent partner of his blood
  Leaned on him, faithful, gentle, good
  Wearing the rose of womanhood.
And in their double love secure,
The little maiden walked demure,
Pacing with downward eyelids pure.
  These three made unity so sweet,
  My frozen heart began to beat,
  Remembering its ancient heat.[9]

The difference is not a simple difference of degree between poets. It is something which had happened to the mind of England between the time of Donne or Lord Herbert of Cherbury and the time of Tennyson and Browning; it is the difference between the intellectual poet and the reflective poet. Tennyson and Browning are poets, and they think; but they do not feel their thought as immediately as the odour of a rose. A thought to Donne was an experience; it modified his sensibility. When a poet's mind is perfectly equipped for its work, it is constantly amalgamating disparate experience; the ordinary man's experience is chaotic, irregular, fragmentary. The latter falls in love, or reads Spinoza,[1] and these two experiences have nothing to do with each other, or with the noise of the typewriter or the smell of cooking; in the mind of the poet these experiences are always forming new wholes.

We may express the difference by the following theory: The poets of the seventeenth century, the successors of the dramatists of the sixteenth, possessed a mechanism of sensibility which could devour any kind of experience. They are simple, artificial, difficult, or fantastic, as their predecessors were; no less nor more than Dante, Guido Cavalcanti, Guinicelli, or Cino.[2] In the seventeenth century a dissociation of sensibility set in, from which we have

6. *The Revenge of Bussy d'Ambois* 4.1.37–46.
7. Lines 693–97 of "Bishop Blougram's Apology," by English poet Robert Browning (1812–1889).
8. Earlier in the essay, Eliot quotes "Ode upon a Question Moved, whether Love Should Continue Forever?" by English Metaphysical poet Lord Herbert of Cherbury (1582 or 1583–1648).
9. Lines 412–23 of "The Two Voices," by English poet Alfred, Lord Tennyson (1809–1892).
1. Benedict de (or Baruch) Spinoza (1632–1677), Dutch Jewish philosopher.
2. Guido Guinicelli (Guinizelli; c. 1240–1276), Guido Cavalcanti (c. 1255–1300), Cino da Pistoia (1270–c. 1336), Italian poets associated with the "sweet new style," which greatly influenced Dante (c. 1265–1321).

never recovered; and this dissociation, as is natural, was aggravated by the influence of the two most powerful poets of the century, Milton and Dryden.[3] Each of these men performed certain poetic functions so magnificently well that the magnitude of the effect concealed the absence of others. The language went on and in some respects improved; the best verse of Collins, Gray, Johnson, and even Goldsmith satisfies some of our fastidious demands better than that of Donne or Marvell or King.[4] But while the language became more refined, the feeling became more crude. The feeling, the sensibility, expressed in the *Country Churchyard* (to say nothing of Tennyson and Browning) is cruder than that in the *Coy Mistress.*

The second effect of the influence of Milton and Dryden followed from the first, and was therefore slow in manifestation. The sentimental age began early in the eighteenth century, and continued. The poets revolted against the ratiocinative, the descriptive; they thought and felt by fits, unbalanced; they reflected. In one or two passages of Shelley's *Triumph of Life,* in the second *Hyperion* there are traces of a struggle toward unification of sensibility. But Keats and Shelley[5] died, and Tennyson and Browning ruminated.

After this brief exposition of a theory—too brief, perhaps, to carry conviction—we may ask, what would have been the fate of the 'metaphysical' had the current of poetry descended in a direct line from them, as it descended in a direct line to them? They would not, certainly, be classified as metaphysical. The possible interests of a poet are unlimited; the more intelligent he is the better; the more intelligent he is the more likely that he will have interests: our only condition is that he turn them into poetry, and not merely meditate on them poetically. A philosophical theory which has entered into poetry is established, for its truth or falsity in one sense ceases to matter, and its truth in another sense is proved. The poets in question have, like other poets, various faults. But they were, at best, engaged in the task of trying to find the verbal equivalent for states of mind and feeling. And this means both that they are more mature, and that they wear better, than later poets of certainly not less literary ability.

It is not a permanent necessity that poets should be interested in philosophy, or in any other subject. We can only say that it appears likely that poets in our civilization, as it exists at present, must be *difficult.* Our civilization comprehends great variety and complexity, and this variety and complexity, playing upon a refined sensibility, must produce various and complex results. The poet must become more and more comprehensive, more allusive, more indirect, in order to force, to dislocate if necessary, language into his meaning. (A brilliant and extreme statement of this view, with which it is not requisite to associate oneself, is that of M. Jean Epstein, *La Poésie d'aujourd-hui.*[6]) Hence we get something which looks very much like the conceit—we get, in fact, a method curiously similar to that of the 'metaphysical poets', similar also in its use of obscure words and of simple phrasing.

> O géraniums diaphanes, guerroyeurs sortilèges,
> Sacrilèges monomanes!
> Emballages, dévergondages, douches! O pressoirs

3. John Dryden (1631–1700) and John Milton (1608–1674), English poets.
4. Henry King (1592–1669) and Andrew Marvell (1621–1678): English Metaphysical poets; Marvell wrote "To His Coy Mistress." William Collins (1721–1759), Thomas Gray (1716–1771), and Oliver Goldsmith (1730–1774): English poets; Gray wrote "An Elegy Written in a Country Churchyard."
5. John Keats (1795–1821) and Percy Bysshe Shelley (1792–1822), English Romantic poets.
6. Poetry of today (French).

Des vendanges des grands soirs!
Layettes aux abois,
Thyrses au fond des bois!
Transfusions, représailles,
Relevailles, compresses et l'éternal potion,
Angélus! n'en pouvoir plus
De débâcles nuptiales! de débâcles nuptiales![7]

The same poet could write also simply:

Elle est bein loin, elle pleure,
Le grand vent se lamente aussi . . . [8]

Jules Laforgue, and Tristan Corbière[9] in many of his poems, are nearer to the 'school of Donne' than any modern English poet. But poets more classical than they have the same essential quality of transmuting ideas into sensations, of transforming an observation into a state of mind.

Pour l'enfant, amoureux de cartes et d'estampes,
L'univers est égal à son vaste appétit.
Ah, que le monde est grand à la clarté des lampes!
Aux yeux du souvenir que le monde est petit![1]

In French literature the great master of the seventeenth century—Racine[2]—and the great master of the nineteenth—Baudelaire—are in some ways more like each other than they are like anyone else. The greatest two masters of diction are also the greatest two psychologists, the most curious explorers of the soul. It is interesting to speculate whether it is not a misfortune that two of the greatest masters of diction in our language, Milton and Dryden, triumph with a dazzling disregard of the soul. If we continued to produce Miltons and Drydens it might not so much matter, but as things are it is a pity that English poetry has remained so incomplete. Those who object to the 'artificiality' of Milton or Dryden sometimes tell us to 'look into our hearts and write'.[3] But that is not looking deep enough; Racine or Donne looked into a good deal more than the heart. One must look into the cerebral cortex, the nervous system, and the digestive tracts.

1921

7. O transparent geraniums, warrior incantations, / Monomaniac sacrileges! / Packing materials, shamelessnesses, shower-baths! O presses / Great evening vintages! / Hard-pressed baby linen, / Thyrsis in the depths of the woods! / Transfusions, reprisals, / Churchings, compresses, and the eternal potion, / Angelus! No longer to be borne [are] / Catastrophic marriages! Catastrophic marriages! (French); from *Last Poems* 10, by French poet Jules Laforgue (1860–1887).
8. She is far away, she weeps, / The great wind mourns also . . . (French); from *Last Poems* 11, "On a Dead Woman."
9. French poet (1845–1875).
1. For the child, in love with maps and prints, / The universe matches his vast appetite. / Ah, how big the world is by lamplight! / How small the world is to the eyes of memory! (French); from "The Voyage," by French poet Charles Baudelaire (1821–1867).
2. Jean Racine (1639–1699), French dramatic poet.
3. Adapting the last line of the first sonnet of *Astrophil and Stella*, by English poet Sir Philip Sidney (1554–1586).

Prologue

Improvisations, the subtitle of William Carlos Williams's book *Kora in Hell,* indicates the work's experimental character, inspired in part by the ferment in avant-garde visual art, such as the Cubism and Dadaism evoked at the outset. In his fragmentary prologue, Williams turns from art to poetry, betraying varying degrees of admiration for and annoyance with H. D., Wallace Stevens, Ezra Pound, and others. He focuses his most heated criticism on T. S. Eliot, denouncing him as a "subtle conformist." Williams is irritated that the English critic Edgar Jepson, in an article in *The Little Review* entitled "The Western School," singled out Eliot's "Love Song of J. Alfred Prufrock" for praise while otherwise criticizing American poetry. In his counterattack, Williams argues that Eliot represents a version of American poetry tailor-made, in its classicism and reserve, for British taste, and that Eliot's best work merely recycles French Symbolism. Williams proposes instead an exuberant American poetry that, taking advantage of its geographic isolation, lays claim to genuine originality. "Nothing," he insists, "is good save the new." These excerpts from the essay, which was originally printed in *The Little Review* (April and May 1919), are from *Kora in Hell: Improvisations* (1920).

WILLIAM CARLOS WILLIAMS

From Prologue to *Kora in Hell*

The Return of the Sun

Her voice was like rose-fragrance waltzing in the wind.
She seemed a shadow, stained with shadow colors,
Swimming through waves of sunlight . . .

The sole precedent I can find for the broken style of my prologue is Longinus on the Sublime[1] and that one far-fetched.

* * *

Once when I was taking lunch with Walter Arensberg at a small place on 63rd St.[2] I asked him if he could state what the more modern painters were about, those roughly classed at that time as "cubists": Gleisze, Man Ray, Demuth, Du Champs[3]—all of whom were then in the city. He replied by saying that the only way man differed from every other creature was in his ability to improvise novelty and, since the pictorial artist was under discussion, anything in paint that is truly new, truly a fresh creation is good art. Thus according to Du Champs, who was Arensberg's champion at the time, a stained glass window that had fallen out and lay more or less together on the ground was of far greater interest than the thing conventionally composed *in situ.*

1. Greek critic Longinus (first century C.E.), assumed author of *On the Sublime.*
2. In New York City. Walter Arensberg (1878–1954), art collector, poet, and cofounder of the avant-garde magazine *Others.*
3. Marcel Duchamp (1887–1968): French-born iconoclastic artist associated with Dada. Albert Gleizes (1881–1953): French painter and member of the Cubist group Section d'Or. Man Ray (1890–1976): American surrealist photographer and painter. Charles Demuth (1883–1935): American painter associated with Precisionism.

We returned to Arensberg's sumptuous studio where he gave further point to his remarks by showing me what appeared to be the original of Du Champs' famous, Nude Descending a Staircase. But this, he went on to say, is a full-sized photographic print of the first picture with many new touches by Du Champs himself and so by the technique of its manufacture as by other means it is a novelty!

Led on by these enthusiasms Arensberg has been an indefatigable worker for the yearly salon of the Society of Independent Artists, Inc.[4] I remember the warmth of his description of a pilgrimage to the home of that old Boston hermit who watched over by a forbidding landlady (evidently in his pay) paints the cigar-box-cover-like nudes upon whose fingers he presses actual rings with glass jewels from the five and ten cent store.

I wish Arensberg had my opportunity for prying into jaded households where the paintings of Mama's and Papa's flowertime still hang on the walls. I propose that Arensberg be commissioned by the Independent Artists to scour the country for the abortive paintings of those men and women who without master or method have evolved perhaps two or three unusual creations in their early years. I would start the collection with a painting I have by a little English woman, A. E. Kerr, 1906, that in its unearthly gaiety of flowers and sobriety of design possesses exactly that strange freshness a spring day approaches without attaining, an expansion of April, a thing this poor woman found too costly for her possession—she could not swallow it as the niggers do diamonds in the mines.[5] Carefully selected these queer products might be housed to good effect in some unpretentious exhibition chamber across the city from the Metropolitan Museum of Art. In the anteroom could be hung perhaps photographs of prehistoric rock-paintings and etchings on horn: galloping bisons and stags, the hind feet of which have been caught by the artist in such a position that from that time until the invention of the camera obscura,[6] a matter of 6000 years or more, no one on earth had again depicted that most delicate and expressive posture of running.

The amusing controversy between Arensberg and Du Champs on one side, and the rest of the hanging committee on the other as to whether the porcelain urinal was to be admitted to the Palace Exhibition of 1917[7] as a representative piece of American Sculpture should not be allowed to slide into oblivion.

One day Du Champs decided that his composition for that day would be the first thing that struck his eye in the first hardware store he should enter. It turned out to be a pickaxe which he bought and set up in his studio. This was his composition. Together with Mina Loy and a few others Du Champs and Arensberg brought out the paper, The Blind Man, to which Robert Carlton Brown with his vision of suicide by diving from a high window of the Singer Building contributed a few poems.[8]

In contradistinction to their south, Marianne Moore's[9] statement to me at

4. Organization founded in New York in 1916 by American and European artists to sponsor exhibitions. Arensberg was its managing director.

5. Swallowing diamonds has been a common method of smuggling for centuries.

6. A predecessor of the photographic camera; a dark room into which light enters through a small hole, casting an inverted image from outside on the wall.

7. Duchamp's most notorious "ready-made" was "Fountain," a urinal he signed "R. Mutt" and submitted to the first exhibition of the Society of Independent Artists, held at New York's Grand Central Palace in 1917.

8. Along with Anglo-American poet Mina Loy (1882–1966), Arensberg, and others, Duchamp helped produce two issues of the Dadaist magazine *The Blind Man*. Robert Carlton Brown, also known as Bob Brown (1886–1959), American novelist, journalist, and avant-garde visual poet.

9. American poet (1887–1972).

the Chatham parsonage one afternoon—my wife and I were just on the point of leaving—sets up a north: My work has come to have just one quality of value in it: I will not touch or have to do with those things which I detest. In this austerity of mood she finds sufficient freedom for the play she chooses.

Of all those writing poetry in America at the time she was here Marianne Moore was the only one Mina Loy feared. By divergent virtues these two women have achieved freshness of presentation, novelty, freedom, break with banality.

* * *

Hilda Doolittle[2] before she began to write poetry or at least before she began to show it to anyone would say: "You're not satisfied with me, are you Billy? There's something lacking, isn't there?" When I was with her my feet always seemed to be sticking to the ground while she would be walking on the tips of the grass stems.

Ten years later as assistant editor of the Egoist she refers to my long poem, March, which thanks to her own and her husband's[3] friendly attentions finally appeared there in a purified form:

> 14 *Aug.* 1916
>
> Dear Bill:—
>
> * * *
>
> I don't know what you think but I consider this business of writing a very sacred thing!—I think you have the "spark"—am sure of it, and when you speak *direct* are a poet. I feel in the hey-ding-ding touch running through your poem a derivitive tendency which, to me, is not *you*—not your very self. It is as if you were *ashamed* of your Spirit, ashamed of your inspiration!—as if you mocked at your own song. It's very well to *mock* at yourself—it is a spiritual sin to mock at your inspiration—
>
> Hilda.

Oh well, all this might be very disquieting were it not that "sacred" has lately been discovered to apply to a point of arrest where stabilization has gone on past the time. There is nothing sacred about literature, it is damned from one end to the other. There is nothing in literature but change and change is mockery. I'll write whatever I damn please, whenever I damn please and as I damn please and it'll be good if the authentic spirit of change is on it.

But in any case H. D. misses the entire intent of what I am doing no matter how just her remarks concerning that particular poem happen to have been. The hey-ding-ding touch *was* derivitive but it filled a gap that I did not know how better to fill at the time. It might be said that that touch is the prototype of the improvisations.

It is to the inventive imagination we look for deliverance from every other misfortune as from the desolation of a flat Hellenic perfection of style. What good then to turn to art from the atavistic religionists, from a science doing slavey service upon gas engines, from a philosophy tangled in a miserable sort of dialect that means nothing if the full power of initiative be denied at the beginning by a lot of baying and snapping scholiasts? If the inventive

2. American poet (1886–1961), known as H. D.
3. English poet and critic Richard Aldington (1892–1962).

imagination must look, as I think, to the field of art for its richest discoveries today it will best make its way by compass and follow no path.

But before any material progress can be accomplished there must be someone to draw a discriminating line between true and false values.

The true value is that peculiarity which gives an object a character by itself. The associational or sentimental value is the false. Its imposition is due to lack of imagination, to an easy lateral sliding. The attention has been held too rigid on the one plane instead of following a more flexible, jagged resort. It is to loosen the attention, my attention since I occupy part of the field, that I write these improvisations. Here I clash with Wallace Stevens.

The imagination goes from one thing to another. Given many things of nearly totally divergent natures but possessing one-thousandth part of a quality in common, provided that be new, distinguished, these things belong in an imaginative category and not in a gross natural array. To me this is the gist of the whole matter. It is easy to fall under the spell of a certain mode, especially if it be remote of origin, leaving thus certain of its members essential to a reconstruction of its significance permanently lost in an impenetrable mist of time. But the thing that stands eternally in the way of really good writing is always one: the virtual impossibility of lifting to the imagination those things which lie under the direct scrutiny of the senses, close to the nose. It is this difficulty that sets a value upon all works of art and makes them a necessity. The senses witnessing what is immediately before them in detail see a finality which they cling to in despair, not knowing which way to turn. Thus the so-called natural or scientific array becomes fixed, the walking devil of modern life. He who even nicks the solidity of this apparition does a piece of work superior to that of Hercules when he cleaned the Augean stables.[4]

* * *

V. No. 2. By the brokeness of his composition the poet makes himself master of a certain weapon which he could possess himself of in no other way. The speed of the emotions is sometimes such that thrashing about in a thin exaltation or despair many matters are touched but not held, more often broken by the contact.

II. No. 3. The instability of these improvisations would seem such that they must inevitably crumble under the attention and become particles of a wind that falters. It would appear to the unready that the fiber of the thing is a thin jelly. It would be these same fools who would deny touch cords to the wind because they cannot split a storm endwise and wrap it upon spools. The virtue of strength lies not in the grossness of the fiber but in the fiber itself. Thus a poem is tough by no quality it borrows from a logical recital of events nor from the events themselves but solely from that attenuated power which draws perhaps many broken things into a dance giving them thus a full being.

* * *

VIII. No. 3. Those who permit their senses to be despoiled of the things under their noses by stories of all manner of things removed and unattainable are of frail imagination. Idiots, it is true nothing is possessed save by dint of

4. In Greek mythology, Hercules' sixth labor was to clean the immense stables of Augeas, a task he accomplished by redirecting a river to flow through them.

that vigorous conception of its perfections which is the imagination's special province but neither is anything possessed which is not extant. A frail imagination, unequal to the tasks before it, is easily led astray.

IV. No. 2. Although it is a quality of the imagination that it seeks to place together those things which have a common relationship, yet the coining of similes is a pastime of very low order, depending as it does upon a nearly vegetable coincidence. Much more keen is that power which discovers in things those inimitable particles of dissimilarity to all other things which are the peculiar perfections of the thing in question.

But this loose linking of one thing with another has effects of a destructive power little to be guessed at: all manner of things are thrown out of key so that it approaches the impossible to arrive at an understanding of anything. All is confusion, yet, it comes from a hidden desire for the dance, a lust of the imagination, a will to accord two instruments in a duet.

* * *

XIII. No. 3. A poet witnessing the chicory flower and realizing its virtues of form and color so constructs his praise of it as to borrow no particle from right or left. He gives his poem over to the flower and its plant themselves that they may benefit by those cooling winds of the imagination which thus returned upon them will refresh them at their task of saving the world. But what does it mean, remarked his friends?

VII. *Coda.* It would be better than depriving birds of their song to call them all nightingales. So it would be better than to have a world stript of poetry to provide men with some sort of eyeglasses by which they should be unable to read any verse but sonnets. But fortunately although there are many sorts of fools, just as there are many birds which sing and many sorts of poems, there is no need to please them.

* * *

Nothing is good save the new. If a thing have novelty it stands intrinsically beside every other work of artistic excellence. If it have not that, no loveliness or heroic proportion or grand manner will save it. It will not be saved above all by an attenuated intellectuality.

But all U. S. verse is not bad according to Mr. J.,[5] there is T. S. Eliot and his, Love Song of J. Alfred Prufrock.

But our prize poems are especially to be damned not because of superficial bad workmanship, but because they are rehash, repetition—just as Eliot's more exquisite work is rehash, repetition in another way of Verlaine, Baudelaire, Maeterlinck,—conscious or unconscious,—just as there were Pound's early paraphrases from Yeats[6] and his constant later cribbing from the renaissance, Provence and the modern French: Men content with the connotations of their masters.

It is convenient to have fixed standards of comparison: All antiquity! And there is always some everlasting Polonius[7] of Kensington forever to rate

5. English novelist and critic Edgar Jepson (1863–1938).

6. W. B. Yeats (1865–1939): Irish poet. Paul Verlaine (1844–1896), Charles Baudelaire (1821–1867): French Symbolist poets. Maurice Maeterlinck (1862–1949): Belgian Symbolist poet. Ezra Pound (1885–1972): American poet.

7. In Shakespeare's *Hamlet*, the king's councilor, given to making pronouncements.

highly his eternal Eliot. It is because Eliot is a subtle conformist. It tickles the palate of this archbishop of procurers to a lecherous antiquity to hold up Prufrock as a New World type. Prufrock, the nibbler at sophistication, endemic in every capital, the not quite (because he refuses to turn his back), is "the soul of that modern land," the United States!

> Blue undershirts,
> Upon a line,
> It is not necessary to say to you
> Anything about it—

I cannot question Eliot's observation. Prufrock is a masterly portrait of the man just below the summit, but the type is universal; the model in his case might be Mr. J.

No. The New World is Montezuma or since he was stoned to death in a parley, Guatemozin[8] who had the city of Mexico levelled over him before he was taken.

For the rest, there is no man even though he dare who can make beauty his own and "so at last live," at least there is no man better situated for that achievement than another. As Prufrock longed for his silly lady so Kensington longs for its Hardanger dairymaid. By a mere twist of the imagination, if Prufrock only knew it, the whole world can be inverted (why else are there wars?) and the mermaids be set warbling to whoever will listen to them. Seesaw and blind-man's-buff converted into a sort of football.

But the summit of United States achievement, according to Mr. J.—who can discourse on Catullus[9]—is that very beautiful poem of Eliot's, La Figlia Que Piange:[1] just the right amount of everything drained through, etc., etc., etc., etc., the rhythm delicately studied and—IT CONFORMS! ergo here we have "the very fine flower of the finest spirit of the United States."

Examined closely this poem reveals a highly refined distillation. Added to the already "faithless" formula of yesterday we have a conscious simplicity:

> Simple and faithless as a smile and shake of the hand.

The perfection of that line is beyond cavil. Yet, in the last stanza, this paradigm, this very fine flower of U. S. art is warped out of alignment, obscured in meaning even to the point of an absolute unintelligibility by the inevitable straining after a rhyme, the very cleverness with which this straining is covered being a sinister token in itself.

> And I wonder how they should have been together!

So we have no choice but to accept the work of this fumbling conjurer.

Upon the Jepson filet Eliot balances his mushroom. It is the latest touch from the literary cuisine, it adds to the pleasant outlook from the club window. If to do this, if to be a Whistler[2] at best, in the art of poetry, is to reach the height of poetic expression then Ezra and Eliot have approached it and *tant pis*[3] for the rest of us.

* * *

September 1, 1918 1919

8. Also called Cuauhtémoc (c. 1495–c. 1522); like Montezuma II (1466–1520), Aztec emperor.
9. Roman poet (c. 84–c. 54 B.C.E.).
1. The daughter who cries (Italian).
2. James McNeil Whistler (1834–1903), American-born painter who spent most of his life in Europe.
3. Too bad (French).

The Poetry of the Present

Anticipating the proponents of open form in the second half of the twentieth century, D. H. Lawrence argues in this essay for free verse in contact with the "insurgent naked throb of the instant moment," poetry unshackled from habit and traditional form. He urges that poetry be spontaneous, flexible, alive. He contrasts such "poetry of the immediate present," responsive to the flux of experience, with the "gem-like lyrics" of the Romantics. Not that Lawrence thought himself without precedent—he claims Walt Whitman as his precursor in escaping from formal symmetry and closure, in opening up new possibilities for verse. Originally published in issue 4, 5 (1919) of *Playboy*, a short-lived magazine edited by American designer Egmont Arens, the essay reappeared as the preface to Lawrence's *New Poems*, American edition (1920), from which the text below, with its original title, is reprinted.

D. H. LAWRENCE

The Poetry of the Present [Preface to the American Edition of *New Poems*]

It seems when we hear a skylark singing as if sound were running forward into the future, running so fast and utterly without consideration, straight on into futurity. And when we hear a nightingale, we hear the pause and the rich, piercing rhythm of recollection, the perfected past. The lark may sound sad, but with the lovely lapsing sadness that is almost a swoon of hope. The nightingale's triumph is a pæan, but a death-pæan.

So it is with poetry. Poetry is, as a rule, either the voice of the far future, exquisite and ethereal, or it is the voice of the past, rich, magnificent. When the Greeks heard the Iliad and the Odyssey, they heard their own past calling in their hearts, as men far inland sometimes hear the sea and fall weak with powerful, wonderful regret, nostalgia; or else their own future rippled its time-beats through their blood, as they followed the painful, glamorous progress of the Ithacan.[1] This was Homer to the Greeks: their Past, splendid with battles won and death achieved, and their Future, the magic wandering of Ulysses through the unknown.

With us it is the same. Our birds sing on the horizons. They sing out of the blue, beyond us, or out of the quenched night. They sing at dawn and sunset. Only the poor, shrill, tame canaries whistle while we talk. The wild birds begin before we are awake, or as we drop into dimness, out of waking. Our poets sit by the gateways, some by the east, some by the west. As we arrive and as we go out our hearts surge with response. But whilst we are in the midst of life, we do not hear them.

The poetry of the beginning and the poetry of the end must have that exquisite finality, perfection which belongs to all that is far off. It is in the realm of all that is perfect. It is of the nature of all that is complete and

1. From the Greek island of Ithaca; that is, Odysseus, or Ulysses.

consummate. This completeness, this consummateness, the finality and the perfection are conveyed in exquisite form: the perfect symmetry, the rhythm which returns upon itself like a dance where the hands link and loosen and link for the supreme moment of the end. Perfected bygone moments, perfected moments in the glimmering futurity, these are the treasured gem-like lyrics of Shelley and Keats.[2]

But there is another kind of poetry: the poetry of that which is at hand: the immediate present. In the immediate present there is no perfection, no consummation, nothing finished. The strands are all flying, quivering, intermingling into the web, the waters are shaking the moon. There is no round, consummate moon on the face of running water, nor on the face of the unfinished tide. There are no gems of the living plasm. The living plasm vibrates unspeakably, it inhales the future, it exhales the past, it is the quick of both, and yet it is neither. There is no plasmic finality, nothing crystal, permanent. If we try to fix the living tissue, as the biologists fix it with formation, we have only a hardened bit of the past, the bygone life under our observation.

Life, the ever-present, knows no finality, no finished crystallisation. The perfect rose is only a running flame, emerging and flowing off, and never in any sense at rest, static, finished. Herein lies its transcendent loveliness. The whole tide of all life and all time suddenly heaves, and appears before us as an apparition, a revelation. We look at the very white quick of nascent creation. A water-lily heaves herself from the flood, looks round, gleams, and is gone. We have seen the incarnation, the quick of the ever-swirling flood. We have seen the invisible. We have seen, we have touched, we have partaken of the very substance of creative change, creative mutation. If you tell me about the lotus, tell me of nothing changeless or eternal.[3] Tell me of the mystery of the inexhaustible, forever-unfolding creative spark. Tell me of the incarnate disclosure of the flux, mutation in blossom, laughter and decay perfectly open in their transit, nude in their movement before us.

Let me feel the mud and the heavens in my lotus. Let me feel the heavy, silting, sucking mud, the spinning of sky winds. Let me feel them both in purest contact, the nakedness of sucking weight, nakedly passing radiance. Give me nothing fixed, set, static. Don't give me the infinite or the eternal: nothing of infinity, nothing of eternity. Give me the still, white seething, the incandescence and the coldness of the incarnate moment: the moment, the quick of all change and haste and opposition: the moment, the immediate present, the Now. The immediate moment is not a drop of water running downstream. It is the source and issue, the bubbling up of the stream. Here, in this very instant moment, up bubbles the stream of time, out of the wells of futurity, flowing on to the oceans of the past. The source, the issue, the creative quick.

There is poetry of this immediate present, instant poetry, as well as poetry of the infinite past and the infinite future. The seething poetry of the incarnate Now is supreme, beyond even the everlasting gems of the before and after. In its quivering momentaneity it surpasses the crystalline, pearl-hard jewels, the poems of the eternities. Do not ask for the qualities of the unfading timeless gems. Ask for the whiteness which is the seethe of mud, ask for

2. Percy Bysshe Shelley (1792–1822) and John Keats (1795–1821), English Romantic poets.
3. In Hindu and Buddhist thought, the lotus flower often symbolizes the release from earthly sensuality into timeless enlightenment.

that incipient putrescence which is the skies falling, ask for the never-pausing, never-ceasing life itself. There must be mutation, swifter than iridescence, haste, not rest, come-and-go, not fixity, inconclusiveness, immediacy, the quality of life itself, without dénouement or close. There must be the rapid momentaneous association of things which meet and pass on the forever incalculable journey of creation: everything left in its own rapid, fluid relationship with the rest of things.

This is the unrestful, ungraspable poetry of the sheer present, poetry whose very permanency lies in its wind-like transit. Whitman's[4] is the best poetry of this kind. Without beginning and without end, without any base and pediment, it sweeps past forever, like a wind that is forever in passage, and unchainable. Whitman truly looked before and after. But he did not sigh for what is not. The clue to all his utterance lies in the sheer appreciation of the instant moment, life surging itself into utterance at its very well-head. Eternity is only an abstraction from the actual present. Infinity is only a great reservoir of recollection, or a reservoir of aspiration: man-made. The quivering nimble hour of the present, this is the quick of Time. This is the immanence. The quick of the universe is the *pulsating, carnal self,* mysterious and palpable. So it is always.

Because Whitman put this into his poetry, we fear him and respect him so profoundly. We should not fear him if he sang only of the "old unhappy far-off things," or of the "wings of the morning."[5] It is because his heart beats with the urgent, insurgent Now, which is even upon us all, that we dread him. He is so near the quick.

From the foregoing it is obvious that the poetry of the instant present cannot have the same body or the same motion as the poetry of the before and after. It can never submit to the same conditions. It is never finished. There is no rhythm which returns upon itself, no serpent of eternity with its tail in its own mouth. There is no static perfection, none of that finality which we find so satisfying because we are so frightened.

Much has been written about free verse. But all that can be said, first and last, is that free verse is, or should be direct utterance from the instant, whole man. It is the soul and the mind and body surging at once, nothing left out. They speak all together. There is some confusion, some discord. But the confusion and the discord only belong to the reality, as noise belongs to the plunge of water. It is no use inventing fancy laws for free verse, no use drawing a melodic line which all the feet must toe. Free verse toes no melodic line, no matter what drill-sergeant. Whitman pruned away his clichés—perhaps his clichés of rhythm as well as of phrase. And this is about all we can do, deliberately, with free verse. We can get rid of the stereotyped movements and the old hackneyed associations of sound or sense. We can break down those artificial conduits and canals through which we do so love to force our utterance. We can break the stiff neck of habit. We can be in ourselves spontaneous and flexible as flame, we can see that utterance rushes out without artificial foam or artificial smoothness. But we cannot positively prescribe any motion, any rhythm. All the laws we invent or discover—it amounts to pretty much the same—will fail to apply to free verse. They will only apply to some form of restricted, limited unfree verse.

All we can say is that free verse does *not* have the same nature as restricted

4. Walt Whitman (1819–1892), American poet.
5. Common phrase in nineteenth-century verse. The first quotation is from "The Reaper," by English poet William Wordsworth (1770–1850).

verse. It is not of the nature of reminiscence. It is not the past which we treasure in its perfection between our hands. Neither is it the crystal of the perfect future, into which we gaze. Its tide is neither the full, yearning flow of aspiration, nor the sweet, poignant ebb of remembrance and regret. The past and the future are the two great bournes of human emotion, the two great homes of the human days, the two eternities. They are both conclusive, final. Their beauty is the beauty of the goal, finished, perfected. Finished beauty and measured symmetry belong to the stable, unchanging eternities.

But in free verse we look for the insurgent naked throb of the instant moment. To break the lovely form of metrical verse, and to dish up the fragments as a new substance, called *vers libre,* this is what most of the free-versifiers accomplish. They do not know that free verse has its own *nature,* that it is neither star nor pearl, but instantaneous like plasm. It has no goal in either eternity. It has no finish. It has no satisfying stability, satisfying to those who like the immutable. None of this. It is the instant; the quick; the very jetting source of all will-be and has-been. The utterance is like a spasm, naked contact with all influences at once. It does not want to get anywhere. It just takes place.

For such utterance any externally-applied law would be mere shackles and death. The law must come new each time from within. The bird is on the wing in the winds, flexible to every breath, a living spark in the storm, its very flickering depending upon its supreme mutability and power of change. Whence such a bird came: whither it goes: from what solid earth it rose up, and upon what solid earth it will close its wings and settle, this is not the question. This is a question of before and after. Now, *now,* the bird is on the wing in the winds.

Such is the rare new poetry. One realm we have never conquered: the pure present. One great mystery of time is terra incognita to us: the instant. The most superb mystery we have hardly recognized: the immediate, instant self. The quick of all time is the instant. The quick of all the universe, of all creation, is the incarnate, carnal self. Poetry gave us the clue: free verse: Whitman. Now we know.

The ideal—what is the ideal? A figment. An abstraction. A static abstraction, abstracted from life. It is a fragment of the before or the after. It is a crystallised aspiration, or a crystallised remembrance: crystallised, set, finished. It is a thing set apart, in the great storehouse of eternity, the storehouse of finished things.

We do not speak of things crystallised and set apart. We speak of the instant, the immediate self, the very plasm of the self. We speak also of free verse.

All this should have come as a preface to "Look! We have Come Through." But is it not better to publish a preface long after the book it belongs to has appeared? For then the reader will have had his fair chance with the book, alone.

Pangbourne, 1919 1919

The Negro Artist and the Racial Mountain

Published in the same year as his first book of poetry, *The Weary Blues* (1926), Langston Hughes's essay announced his arrival as a leading poet and became a manifesto for the Harlem Renaissance that was to last through the early 1930s. In the piece, he identifies the obstacles facing African American artists, pressured from all sides to emulate white culture and reject their own. Artists of the African American middle and upper classes are, in his view, especially prone to self-division. Hughes recommends that black artists, instead of adopting white cultural norms, embrace authentic expressions of "our individual dark-skinned selves," such as jazz and the blues. In Hughes's view, these oral and musical "folk" forms provide an inexhaustible subject matter, a source of resistance to deadening standardization, and a reflection of a collective racial experience. To these themes, Hughes says, "the Negro artist can give his racial individuality, his heritage of rhythm and warmth, and his incongruous humor that so often, as in the Blues, becomes ironic laughter mixed with tears." This essay is reprinted from *The Nation* 122.3181 (June 23, 1926).

LANGSTON HUGHES

The Negro Artist and the Racial Mountain

One of the most promising of the young Negro poets said to me once, "I want to be a poet—not a Negro poet," meaning, I believe, "I want to write like a white poet"; meaning subconsciously, "I would like to be a white poet"; meaning behind that, "I would like to be white." And I was sorry the young man said that, for no great poet has ever been afraid of being himself. And I doubted then that, with his desire to run away spiritually from his race, this boy would ever be a great poet. But this is the mountain standing in the way of any true Negro art in America—this urge within the race toward whiteness, the desire to pour racial individuality into the mold of American standardization, and to be as little Negro and as much American as possible.

But let us look at the immediate background of this young poet. His family is of what I suppose one would call the Negro middle class: people who are by no means rich yet never uncomfortable nor hungry—smug, contented, respectable folk, members of the Baptist church. The father goes to work every morning. He is a chief steward at a large white club. The mother sometimes does fancy sewing or supervises parties for the rich families of the town. The children go to a mixed school. In the home they read white papers and magazines. And the mother often says "Don't be like niggers" when the children are bad. A frequent phrase from the father is, "Look how well a white man does things." And so the word white comes to be unconsciously a symbol of all the virtues. It holds for the children beauty, morality, and money. The whisper of "I want to be white" runs silently through their minds. This young poet's home is, I believe, a fairly typical home of the colored middle class. One sees immediately how difficult it would be for an artist born in such a home to interest himself in interpreting the beauty of his own people. He is never taught to see that beauty. He is taught rather not to see it, or if he does, to be ashamed of it when it is not according to Caucasian patterns.

For racial culture the home of a self-styled "high-class" Negro has nothing better to offer. Instead there will perhaps be more aping of things white than in a less cultured or less wealthy home. The father is perhaps a doctor, lawyer, landowner, or politician. The mother may be a social worker, or a teacher, or she may do nothing and have a maid. Father is often dark but he has usually married the lightest woman he could find. The family attend a fashionable church where few really colored faces are to be found. And they themselves draw a color line. In the North they go to white theaters and white movies. And in the South they have at least two cars and a house "like white folks." Nordic manners, Nordic faces, Nordic hair, Nordic art (if any), and an Episcopal heaven. A very high mountain indeed for the would-be racial artist to climb in order to discover himself and his people.

But then there are the low-down folks, the so-called common element, and they are the majority—may the Lord be praised! The people who have their nip of gin on Saturday nights and are not too important to themselves or the community, or too well fed, or too learned to watch the lazy world go round. They live on Seventh Street in Washington or State Street in Chicago and they do not particularly care whether they are like white folks or anybody else. Their joy runs, bang! into ecstasy. Their religion soars to a shout. Work maybe a little today, rest a little tomorrow. Play awhile. Sing awhile. O, let's dance! These common people are not afraid of spirituals, as for a long time their more intellectual brethren were, and jazz is their child. They furnish a wealth of colorful, distinctive material for any artist because they still hold their own individuality in the face of American standardizations. And perhaps these common people will give to the world its truly great Negro artist, the one who is not afraid to be himself. Whereas the better-class Negro would tell the artist what to do, the people at least let him alone when he does appear. And they are not ashamed of him—if they know he exists at all. And they accept what beauty is their own without question.

Certainly there is, for the American Negro artist who can escape the restrictions the more advanced among his own group would put upon him, a great field of unused material ready for his art. Without going outside his race, and even among the better classes with their "white" culture and conscious American manners, but still Negro enough to be different, there is sufficient matter to furnish a black artist with a lifetime of creative work. And when he chooses to touch on the relations between Negroes and whites in this country with their innumerable overtones and undertones, surely, and especially for literature and the drama, there is an inexaustible supply of themes at hand. To these the Negro artist can give his racial individuality, his heritage of rhythm and warmth, and his incongruous humor that so often, as in the Blues, becomes ironic laughter mixed with tears. But let us look again at the mountain.

A prominent Negro clubwoman in Philadelphia paid eleven dollars to hear Raquel Meller sing Andalusian popular songs.[1] But she told me a few weeks before she would not think of going to hear "that woman," Clara Smith,[2] a great black artist, sing Negro folksongs. And many an upper-class Negro church, even now, would not dream of employing a spiritual in its services.

1. Raquel Meller (1888–1962), Spanish singer. *Andalusia*: Mediterranean region of southern Spain.
2. American blues singer (1897–1935).

The drab melodies in white folks' hymnbooks are much to be preferred. "We want to worship the Lord correctly and quietly. We don't believe in 'shouting.' Let's be dull like the Nordics," they say, in effect.

The road for the serious black artist, then, who would produce a racial art is most certainly rocky and the mountain is high. Until recently he received almost no encouragement for his work from either white or colored people. The fine novels of Chestnutt[3] go out of print with neither race noticing their passing. The quaint charm and humor of Dunbar's[4] dialect verse brought to him, in his day, largely the same kind of encouragement one would give a sideshow freak (A colored man writing poetry! How odd!) or a clown (How amusing!).

The present vogue in things Negro, although it may do as much harm as good for the budding colored artist, has at least done this: it has brought him forcibly to the attention of his own people among whom for so long, unless the other race had noticed him beforehand, he was a prophet with little honor. I understand that Charles Gilpin[5] acted for years in Negro theaters without any special acclaim from his own, but when Broadway gave him eight curtain calls, Negroes, too, began to beat a tin pan in his honor. I know a young colored writer, a manual worker by day, who had been writing well for the colored magazines for some years, but it was not until he recently broke into the white publications and his first book was accepted by a prominent New York publisher that the "best" Negroes in his city took the trouble to discover that he lived there. Then almost immediately they decided to give a grand dinner for him. But the society ladies were careful to whisper to his mother that perhaps she'd better not come. They were not sure she would have an evening gown.

The Negro artist works against an undertow of sharp criticism and misunderstanding from his own group and unintentional bribes from the whites. "O, be respectable, write about nice people, show how good we are," say the Negroes. "Be stereotyped, don't go too far, don't shatter our illusions about you, don't amuse us too seriously. We will pay you," say the whites. Both would have told Jean Toomer not to write "Cane."[6] The colored people did not praise it. The white people did not buy it. Most of the colored people who did read "Cane" hate it. They are afraid of it. Although the critics gave it good reviews the public remained indifferent. Yet (excepting the work of DuBois[7]) "Cane" contains the finest prose written by a Negro in America. And like the singing of Robeson,[8] it is truly racial.

But in spite of the Nordicized Negro intelligentsia and the desires of some white editors we have an honest American Negro literature already with us. Now I await the rise of the Negro theater. Our folk music, having achieved world-wide fame, offers itself to the genius of the great individual American Negro composer who is to come. And within the next decade I expect to see the work of a growing school of colored artists who paint and model the beauty of dark faces and create with new technique the expressions of their own soul-world. And the Negro dancers who will dance like flame and the singers who will continue to carry our songs to all who listen—they will be with us in even greater numbers tomorrow.

3. Charles Chesnutt (1858–1932), African American novelist.
4. Paul Laurence Dunbar (1872–1906), African American poet and short-story writer.
5. African American actor and singer (1878–1930).
6. Book of modernist poetry, drama, and sketches (1923) by African American writer Jean Toomer (1894–1967).
7. W. E. B. Du Bois (1868–1963), African American author, intellectual, and protest leader.
8. Paul Robeson (1898–1976), African American singer, actor, and activist.

Most of my own poems are racial in theme and treatment, derived from the life I know. In many of them I try to grasp and hold some of the meanings and rhythms of jazz. I am sincere as I know how to be in these poems and yet after every reading I answer questions like these from my own people: Do you think Negroes should always write about Negroes? I wish you wouldn't read some of your poems to white folks. How do you find anything interesting in a place like a cabaret? Why do you write about black people? You aren't black. What makes you do so many jazz poems?

But jazz to me is one of the inherent expressions of Negro life in America: the eternal tom-tom beating in the Negro soul—the tom-tom of revolt against weariness in a white world, a world of subway trains, and work, work, work; the tom-tom of joy and laughter, and pain swallowed in a smile. Yet the Philadelphia clubwoman is ashamed to say that her race created it and she does not like me to write about it. The old subconscious "white is best" runs through her mind. Years of study under white teachers, a lifetime of white books, pictures, and papers, and white manners, morals, and Puritan standards made her dislike the spirituals. And now she turns up her nose at jazz and all its manifestations—likewise almost everything else distinctly racial. She doesn't care for the Winold Reiss[9] portraits of Negroes because they are "too Negro." She does not want a true picture of herself from anybody. She wants the artist to flatter her, to make the white world believe that all Negroes are as smug and as near white in soul as she wants to be. But, to my mind, it is the duty of the younger Negro artist, if he accepts any duties at all from outsiders, to change through the force of his art that old whispering "I want to be white," hidden in the aspirations of his people, to "Why should I want to be white? I am a Negro—and beautiful!"

So I am ashamed for the black poet who says, "I want to be a poet, not a Negro poet," as though his own racial world were not as interesting as any other world. I am ashamed, too, for the colored artist who runs from the painting of Negro faces to the painting of sunsets after the manner of the academicians because he fears the strange un-whiteness of his own features. An artist must be free to choose what he does, certainly, but he must also never be afraid to do what he might choose.

Let the blare of Negro jazz bands and the bellowing voice of Bessie Smith[1] singing Blues penetrate the closed ears of the colored near-intellectuals until they listen and perhaps understand. Let Paul Robeson singing Water Boy, and Rudolph Fisher[2] writing about the streets of Harlem, and Jean Toomer holding the heart of Georgia in his hands, and Aaron Douglas[3] drawing strange black fantasies cause the smug Negro middle class to turn from their white, respectable, ordinary books and papers to catch a glimmer of their own beauty. We younger Negro artists who create now intend to express our individual dark-skinned selves without fear or shame. If white people are pleased we are glad. If they are not, it doesn't matter. We know we are beautiful. And ugly too. The tom-tom cries and the tom-tom laughs. If colored people are pleased we are glad. If they are not, their displeasure doesn't matter either. We build our temples for tomorrow, strong as we know how, and we stand on top of the mountain, free within ourselves.

1926

9. German-born artist (1886–1953).
1. African American blues singer (1894–1937).
2. African American novelist and short-story writer (1897–1934).
3. African American artist (1899–1979).

A Letter

When Hart Crane submitted his elegy "At Melville's Tomb" to *Poetry,* in 1926, the magazine's founder and editor, Harriet Monroe (1860–1936), accepted it on the condition that Crane write a prose statement to accompany the difficult poem and to explain what she called its "succession of champion mixed metaphors." Crane reluctantly wrote the following letter, his most incisive statement of his methods, and Monroe published it alongside her initial letter, her response to his letter, and the poem. For Crane, poetry should be understood according to a "logic of metaphor" by which the connotative value of words are often more important than their denotative meanings or the rational connections between them. A portion of any poem's meaning will necessarily depend on the reader's imaginative capacity to fill in the gaps between symbols with personal experiences. To stick to rationally understood meanings and images would result in a stultifying poetry never revealing anything unexpected. Originally printed in *Poetry* 29 (October 1926), the letter is reprinted from *The Complete Poems and Selected Letters and Prose of Hart Crane* (1966), ed. Brom Weber.

HART CRANE

A Letter to Harriet Monroe

Your good nature and manifest interest in writing me about the obscurities apparent in my Melville poem[1] certainly prompt a wish to clarify my intentions in that poem as much as possible. But I realize that my explanations will not be very convincing. For a paraphrase is generally a poor substitute for any organized conception that one has fancied he has put into the more essentialized form of the poem itself.

At any rate, and though I imagine us to have considerable differences of opinion regarding the relationship of poetic metaphor to ordinary logic (I judge this from the angle of approach you use toward portions of the poem), I hope my answers will not be taken as a defense of merely certain faulty lines. I am really much more interested in certain theories of metaphor and technique involved generally in poetics, than I am concerned in vindicating any particular perpetrations of my own.

My poem may well be elliptical and actually obscure in the ordering of its content, but in your criticism of this very possible deficiency you have stated your objections in terms that allow me, at least for the moment, the privilege of claiming your ideas and ideals as theoretically, at least, quite outside the issues of my own aspirations. To put it more plainly, as a poet I may very possibly be more interested in the so-called illogical impingements of the connotations of words on the consciousness (and their combinations and interplay in metaphor on this basis) than I am interested in the preservation of their logically rigid significations at the cost of limiting my subject matter and perceptions involved in the poem.

1. "At Melville's Tomb," on p. 609 of this volume. Herman Melville (1819–1891), American novelist, author of *Moby-Dick.*

This may sound as though I merely fancied juggling words and images until I found something novel, or esoteric; but the process is much more predetermined and objectified than that. The nuances of feeling and observation in a poem may well call for certain liberties which you claim the poet has no right to take. I am simply making the claim that the poet does have that authority, and that to deny it is to limit the scope of the medium so considerably as to outlaw some of the richest genius of the past.

This argument over the dynamics of metaphor promises as active a future as has been evinced in the past. Partaking so extensively as it does of the issues involved in the propriety or non-propriety of certain attitudes toward subject matter, etc., it enters the critical distinctions usually made between "romantic" [and] "classic" as an organic factor. It is a problem that would require many pages to state adequately—merely from my own limited standpoint on the issues. Even this limited statement may prove onerous reading, and I hope you will pardon me if my own interest in the matter carries me to the point of presumption.

Its paradox, of course, is that its apparent illogic operates so logically in conjunction with its context in the poem as to establish its claim to another logic, quite independent of the original definition of the word or phrase or image thus employed. It implies (this *inflection* of language) a previous or prepared receptivity to its stimulus on the part of the reader. The reader's sensibility simply responds by identifying this inflection of experience with some event in his own history or perceptions—or rejects it altogether. The logic of metaphor is so organically entrenched in pure sensibility that it can't be thoroughly traced or explained outside of historical sciences, like philology and anthropology. This "pseudo-statement," as I. A. Richards[2] calls it in an admirable essay touching our contentions in last July's *Criterion,* demands completely other faculties of recognition than the pure rationalistic associations permit. Much fine poetry may be completely rationalistic in its use of symbols, but there is much great poetry of another order which will yield the reader very little when inspected under the limitation of such arbitrary concerns as are manifested in your judgment of the Melville poem, especially when you constitute such requirements of ordinary logical relationship between word and word as irreducible.

I don't wish to enter here defense of the particular symbols employed in my own poem, because, as I said, I may well have failed to supply the necessary emotional connectives to the content featured. But I would like to counter a question or so of yours with a similar question. Here the poem is less dubious in quality than my own, and as far as the abstract pertinacity of question and its immediate consequences are concerned the point I'm arguing about can be better demonstrated. Both quotations are familiar to you, I'm sure.

You ask me how a *portent* can possibly be wound in a *shell.* Without attempting to answer this for the moment, I ask you how Blake could possibly say that "a *sigh* is a *sword* of an Angel King."[3] You ask me how *compass, quadrant and sextant "contrive"* tides. I ask you how Eliot can possibly believe that "Every street *lamp* that I pass *beats* like a fatalistic *drum*!"[4] Both of my metaphors may fall down completely. I'm not defending their actual value in themselves; but your criticism of them in each case was leveled at an

2. English critic (1893–1979).
3. From *Jerusalem,* by English Romantic poet and artist William Blake (1757–1827).
4. From "Rhapsody on a Windy Night," by T. S Eliot (1888–1965).

illogicality of relationship between symbols, which similar fault you must have either overlooked in case you have ever admired the Blake and Eliot lines, or have there condoned them on account of some more ultimate convictions pressed on you by the impact of the poems in their entirety.

It all comes to the recognition that emotional dynamics are not to be confused with any absolute order of rationalized definitions; ergo, in poetry the *rationale* of metaphor belongs to another order of experience than science, and is not to be limited by a scientific and arbitrary code of relationships either in verbal inflections or concepts.

There are plenty of people who have never accumulated a sufficient series of reflections (and these of a rather special nature) to perceive the relation between a *drum* and a *street lamp—via* the *unmentioned* throbbing of the heart and nerves in a distraught man which *tacitly* creates the reason and "logic" of the Eliot metaphor. They will always have a perfect justification for ignoring those lines and to claim them obscure, excessive, etc., until by some experience of their own the words accumulate the necessary connotations to complete their connection. It is the same with the "patient etherized upon a table,"[5] isn't it? Surely that line must lack all eloquence to many people who, for instance, would delight in agreeing that the sky was like a dome of many-colored glass.[6]

If one can't count on some such bases in the reader now and then, I don't see how the poet has any chance to ever get beyond the simplest conceptions of emotion and thought, of sensation and lyrical sequence. If the poet is to be held completely to the already evolved and exploited sequences of imagery and logic—what field of added consciousness and increased perceptions (the actual province of poetry, if not lullabies) can be expected when one has to relatively return to the alphabet every breath or so? In the minds of people who have sensitively read, seen, and experienced a great deal, isn't there a terminology something like short-hand as compared to usual description and dialectics, which the artist ought to be right in trusting as a reasonable connective agent toward fresh concepts, more inclusive evaluations? The question is more important to me than it perhaps ought to be; but as long as poetry is written, an audience, however small, is implied, and there remains the question of an active or an inactive imagination as its characteristic.

It is of course understood that a street-lamp simply can't beat with a sound like a drum; but it often happens that images, themselves totally dissociated, when joined in the circuit of a particular emotion located with specific relation to both of them, conduce to great vividness and accuracy of statement in defining that emotion.

Not to rant on forever, I'll beg your indulgence and come at once to the explanations you requested on the Melville poem:

> "The dice of drowned men's bones he saw bequeath
> An embassy."

Dice bequeath an embassy, in the first place, by being ground (in this connection only, of course) in little cubes from the bones of drowned men by the action of the sea, and are finally thrown up on the sand, having "numbers" but no identification. These being the bones of dead men who never completed their voyage, it seems legitimate to refer to them as the only surviving evidence of certain messages undelivered, mute evidence of certain

5. From Eliot's "Love Song of J. Alfred Prufrock."

6. Adapted from line 469 of Shelley's "Adonais."

things, experiences that the dead mariners might have had to deliver. Dice as a symbol of chance and circumstance is also implied.

"The calyx of death's bounty giving back," etc.

This calyx refers in a double ironic sense both to a cornucopia and the vortex made by a sinking vessel. As soon as the water has closed over a ship, this whirlpool sends up broken spars, wreckage, etc., which can be alluded to as livid *hieroglyphs,* making a *scattered chapter* so far as any complete record of the recent ship and her crew is concerned. In fact, about as much definite knowledge might come from all this as anyone might gain from the roar of his own veins, which is easily heard (haven't you ever done it?) by holding a shell close to one's ear.

"Frosted eyes lift altars."

Refers simply to a conviction that a man, not knowing perhaps a definite god yet being endowed with a reverence for deity—such a man naturally postulates a deity somehow, and the altar of that deity by the very *action* of the eyes *lifted* in searching.

"Compass, quadrant and sextant contrive no farther tides."

Hasn't it often occurred that instruments originally invented for record and computation have inadvertently so extended the concepts of the entity they were invented to measure (concepts of space, etc.) in the mind and imagination that employed them, that they may metaphorically be said to have extended the original boundaries of the entity measured? This little bit of "relativity" ought not to be discredited in poetry now that scientists are proceeding to measure the universe on principles of pure *ratio,* quite as metaphorical, so far as previous standards of scientific methods extended, as some of the axioms in Job.[7]

I may have completely failed to provide any clear interpretation of these symbols in their context. And you will no doubt feel that I have rather heatedly explained them for anyone who professes no claims for their particular value. I hope, at any rate, that I have clarified them enough to suppress any suspicion that their obscurity derives from a lack of definite intentions in the subject-matter of the poem. The execution is another matter, and you must be accorded a superior judgment to mine in that regard.

1926

7. Book of the Bible.

APHORISMS

These selections come from the personal notebooks Wallace Stevens filled with aphorisms and maxims in the 1930s and 1940s. Exhibiting wit and pith, creative exuberance and philosophical subtlety, they both seek to define the nature of poetry and explore its role in a skeptical age. In September 1940 and October 1942, Stevens published thirty-two selections from his notebooks, as *Adagia* I and II, in the journal *View.* The aphorisms, including later selections drawn from other, miscellaneous notebooks, are excerpted from *Opus Posthumous* (1989), rev. ed., ed. Milton J. Bates.

WALLACE STEVENS

From *Adagia*

From *I*

To give a sense of the freshness or vividness of life is a valid purpose for poetry. A didactic purpose justifies itself in the mind of the teacher; a philosophical purpose justifies itself in the mind of the philosopher. It is not that one purpose is as justifiable as another but that some purposes are pure others impure. Seek those purposes that are purely the purposes of the pure poet.

The poet makes silk dresses out of worms.

It is life that we are trying to get at in poetry.

After one has abandoned a belief in god, poetry is that essence which takes its place as life's redemption.

The relation of art to life is of the first importance especially in a skeptical age since, in the absence of a belief in God, the mind turns to its own creations and examines them, not alone from the aesthetic point of view, but for what they reveal, for what they validate and invalidate, for the support that they give.

Poetry and materia poetica are interchangeable terms.

Poetry is not personal.

Poetry is a means of redemption.

Poetry is a form of melancholia. Or rather, in melancholy it is one of the "aultres choses solatieuses."[1]

In poetry at least the imagination must not detach itself from reality.

Not all objects are equal. The vice of imagism was that it did not recognize this.

All poetry is experimental poetry.

In poetry, you must love the words, the ideas and images and rhythms with all your capacity to love anything at all.

It is the belief and not the god that counts.

Poetry must be irrational.

1. Other consoling things (archaic French).

The purpose of poetry is to make life complete in itself.

Poetry increases the feeling for reality.

The mind is the most powerful thing in the world.

There is nothing in life except what one thinks of it.

Poetry is a form of melancholia.

The final belief is to believe in a fiction, which you know to be a fiction, there being nothing else. The exquisite truth is to know that it is a fiction and that you believe in it willingly.

Ethics are no more a part of poetry than they are of painting.

Poetry is the expression of the experience of poetry.

As the reason destroys, the poet must create.

We live in the mind.

To live in the world but outside of existing conceptions of it.

Money is a kind of poetry.

The death of one god is the death of all.

In the presence of extraordinary actuality, consciousness takes the place of imagination.

Every man dies his own death.

The ultimate value is reality.

Realism is a corruption of reality.

Poetry is the sum of its attributes.

I don't think we should insist that the poet is normal or, for that matter, that anybody is.

This happy creature—It is he that invented the Gods. It is he that put into their mouths the only words they have ever spoken.

Poetry is a purging of the world's poverty and change and evil and death. It is a present perfecting, a satisfaction in the irremediable poverty of life.

A poem is a pheasant.

All men are murderers.

Poetry is metaphor.

The body is the great poem.

The purpose of poetry is to contribute to man's happiness.

Metaphor creates a new reality from which the original appears to be unreal.

Description is an element, like air or water.

Poets acquire humanity.

Thought tends to collect in pools.

Poetry must resist the intelligence almost successfully.

A change of style is a change of subject.

Poetry is the statement of a relation between a man and the world.

From *II*

God is in me or else is not at all (does not exist).

Poetry is a search for the inexplicable.

Poetry is a pheasant disappearing in the brush.

The poet is a god or The young poet is a god. The old poet is a tramp.

If the mind is the most terrible force in the world, it is, also, the only force that defends us against terror. (or)

The mind is the most terrible force in the world principally in this that it is the only force that can defend us against itself. The modern world is based on this pensée.[2]

The poet represents the mind in the act of defending us against itself.

Poetry is the gaiety (joy) of language.

One cannot spend one's time in being modern when there are so many more important things to be.

Poetry is a health.

Poetry is great only as it exploits great ideas or what is often the same thing great feelings.

Imagination applied to the whole world is vapid in comparison to imagination applied to a detail.

Poetry is a cure of the mind.

2. Thought (French).

Nothing could be more inappropriate to American literature than its English source since the Americans are not British in sensibility.

Poetry is a response to the daily necessity of getting the world right.

A poem should stimulate the sense of living and of being alive.

Reality is the spirit's true centre.

A poem need not have a meaning and like most things in nature often does not have.

Newness (not novelty) may be the highest individual value in poetry. Even in the meretricious sense of newness a new poetry has value.

Poetry is often a revelation of the elements of appearance.

Poetry is a renovation of experience. Originality is an escape from repetition.

The theory of poetry is the life of poetry. Christianity is an exhausted culture.

The theory of poetry is the theory of life.

French and English constitute a single language.

Poetry is, (and should be,) for the poet, a source of pleasure and satisfaction, not a source of honors.

1934–40? 1940 and 1942

From Miscellaneous Notebooks

From *I*

Reality is a cliché
From which we escape by metaphor
It is only au pays de la métaphore
Qu'on est poète.[3]

The degrees of metaphor
The absolute object slightly turned
Is a metaphor of the object.

Some objects are less susceptible to metaphor than others. The whole world is less susceptible to metaphor than a tea-cup is.

There is no such thing as a metaphor of a metaphor. One does not progress through metaphors. Thus reality is the indispensable element of each metaphor. When I say that man is a god it is very easy to see that if I say also that a god is something else, god has become reality.

3. It is only in the country of metaphor / that one is a poet (French).

III

A poem is like a natural object.

1948–55? 1957

The Noble Rider and the Sound of Words

Originally delivered as a lecture at Princeton University in 1942, "The Noble Rider and the Sound of Words" propounds one of Wallace Stevens's persistent themes: the pressures that reality and the imagination exert on one another. In the aftermath of World War I and in the midst of World War II, Stevens counters the accusation that poetry—and his poetry in particular—is escapist. He argues that in times of violence, the imagination must abstract, evade, and resist the pressures of reality. Because it is free, noble, and beautiful, poetry can help people live their lives. Originally published in *The Language of Poetry* (1942), ed. Allen Tate, the essay is excerpted from Stevens's collection *The Necessary Angel* (1951).

WALLACE STEVENS

From *The Noble Rider and the Sound of Words*

From 3

* * * What I have said up to this point amounts to this: that the idea of nobility exists in art today only in degenerate forms or in a much diminished state, if, in fact, it exists at all or otherwise than on sufferance; that this is due to failure in the relation between the imagination and reality. I should now like to add that this failure is due, in turn, to the pressure of reality.

* * *

For more than ten years now, there has been an extraordinary pressure of news—let us say, news incomparably more pretentious than any description of it, news, at first, of the collapse of our system, or, call it, of life; then of news of a new world, but of a new world so uncertain that one did not know anything whatever of its nature, and does not know now, and could not tell whether it was to be all-English, all-German, all-Russian, all-Japanese, or all-American, and cannot tell now; and finally news of a war, which was a renewal of what, if it was not the greatest war, became such by this continuation. And for more than ten years, the consciousness of the world has concentrated on events which have made the ordinary movement of life seem to be the movement of people in the intervals of a storm. The disclosures of the impermanence of the past suggested, and suggest, an impermanence of the future. Little of what we have believed has been true. Only the prophecies are true. The present is an opportunity to repent. This is familiar enough. The war is only a part of a war-like whole. It is not possible to look backward and to see that the same thing was true in the past. It is a question of pressure, and pressure is incalculable and eludes the historian. The Napoleonic era is regarded as having had little or no effect on the poets and the novelists who lived in it. But Coleridge and Wordsworth and Sir Walter Scott and Jane Austen did not have to put up with Napoleon and Marx[1] and Europe, Asia and Africa all at one time. It seems possible to say that they knew of the events of their day much as we know of the bombings in the interior of China and not at all as we know of the bombings of London, or, rather, as we should know of the bombings of Toronto or Montreal. Another part of the war-like whole to which we do not respond quite as we do to the news of war is the income tax. The blanks are specimens of mathematical prose. They titillate the instinct of self-preservation in a class in which that instinct has been forgotten. Virginia Woolf[2] thought that the income tax, if it continued, would benefit poets by enlarging their vocabularies and I dare say that she was right.

If it is not possible to assert that the Napoleonic era was the end of one era in the history of the imagination and the beginning of another, one comes closer to the truth by making that assertion in respect to the French Revolution. The defeat or triumph of Hitler are parts of a war-like whole but the fate of an individual is different from the fate of a society. Rightly or wrongly, we feel that the fate of a society is involved in the orderly disorders of the present time. We are confronting, therefore, a set of events, not only beyond our power to tranquillize them in the mind, beyond our power to reduce them and metamorphose them, but events that stir the emotions to violence, that engage us in what is direct and immediate and real, and events that involve the concepts and sanctions that are the order of our lives and may involve our very lives; and these events are occurring persistently with increasing omen, in what may be called our presence. These are the things that I had in mind when I spoke of the pressure of reality, a pressure great enough and prolonged enough to bring about the end of one era in the history of the imagination and, if so, then great enough to bring about the beginning of another. It is one of the peculiarities of the imagination that it is always at the end of an era. What happens is that it is always attaching itself to a new reality, and adhering to it. It is not that there is a new imagination but that there is a new reality. The pressure of reality may, of course, be less than the general pressure that I have described. It exists for individuals according to the circumstances of their lives or according to the characteristics of their minds. To sum it up, the pressure of reality is, I think, the determining factor in the artistic character of an era and, as well, the determining factor in the artistic character of an individual. The resistance to this pressure or its evasion in the case of individuals of extraordinary imagination cancels the pressure so far as those individuals are concerned.

4

Suppose we try, now, to construct the figure of a poet, a possible poet. He cannot be a charioteer traversing vacant space, however ethereal. He must have lived all of the last two thousand years, and longer, and he must have

1. Karl Marx (1818–1883): German political philosopher and socialist. Samuel Taylor Coleridge (1772–1834), William Wordsworth (1770–1850): English poets. Sir Walter Scott (1771–1832): Scottish novelist. Jane Austen (1775–1817): English novelist. Napoléon Bonaparte (1769–1821): emperor of France.

2. English novelist (1882–1941).

instructed himself, as best he could, as he went along. He will have thought that Virgil, Dante, Shakespeare, Milton placed themselves in remote lands and in remote ages; that their men and women were the dead—and not the dead lying in the earth, but the dead still living in their remote lands and in their remote ages, and living in the earth or under it, or in the heavens—and he will wonder at those huge imaginations, in which what is remote becomes near, and what is dead lives with an intensity beyond any experience of life. He will consider that although he has himself witnessed, during the long period of his life, a general transition to reality, his own measure as a poet, in spite of all the passions of all the lovers of the truth, is the measure of his power to abstract himself, and to withdraw with him into his abstraction the reality on which the lovers of truth insist. He must be able to abstract himself and also to abstract reality, which he does by placing it in his imagination. He knows perfectly that he cannot be too noble a rider, that he cannot rise up loftily in helmet and armor on a horse of imposing bronze. He will think again of Milton and of what was said about him: that "the necessity of writing for one's living blunts the appreciation of writing when it bears the mark of perfection. Its quality disconcerts our hasty writers; they are ready to condemn it as preciosity and affectation. And if to them the musical and creative powers of words convey little pleasure, how out of date and irrelevant they must find the . . . music of Milton's verse." Don Quixote[3] will make it imperative for him to make a choice, to come to a decision regarding the imagination and reality; and he will find that it is not a choice of one over the other and not a decision that divides them, but something subtler, a recognition that here, too, as between these poles, the universal interdependence exists, and hence his choice and his decision must be that they are equal and inseparable. To take a single instance: When Horatio says,

> Now cracks a noble heart. Good night, sweet prince,
> And flights of angels sing thee to thy rest![4]

are not the imagination and reality equal and inseparable? Above all, he will not forget General Jackson or the picture of the *Wooden Horses*.[5]

I said of the picture that it was a work in which everything was favorable to reality. I hope that the use of that bare word has been enough. But without regard to its range of meaning in thought, it includes all its natural images, and its connotations are without limit. Bergson[6] describes the visual perception of a motionless object as the most stable of internal states. He says: "The object may remain the same, I may look at it from the same side, at the same angle, in the same light; nevertheless, the vision I now have of it differs from that which I have just had, even if only because the one is an instant later than the other. My memory is there, which conveys something of the past into the present."

Dr. Joad's[7] comment on this is: "Similarly with external things. Every body,

3. Title character of novel by Spanish writer Miguel de Cervantes (1547–1616), Quixote lives in an imaginary world of outdated chivalric codes.
4. After Hamlet's death, in Shakespeare's *Hamlet* 5.2.
5. Earlier in the essay, Stevens describes a statue of Andrew Jackson (1767–1845), American general and seventh U.S. president, as being a work neither of the imagination nor reality, but of fancy, which, according to Coleridge, involves a mental selection among alternatives already presented rather than a creative transformation of them. By contrast, he explains that *Wooden Horses*, a painting by American artist Reginald Marsh (1898–1954), is both imaginative and real.
6. Henri Bergson (1859–1941), French philosopher of memory and time.
7. C. E. M. Joad (1891–1953), English philosopher and radio personality.

every quality of a body resolves itself into an enormous number of vibrations, movements, changes. What is it that vibrates, moves, is changed? There is no answer. Philosophy has long dismissed the notion of substance and modern physics has endorsed the dismissal. . . . How, then, does the world come to appear to us as a collection of solid, static objects extended in space? Because of the intellect, which presents us with a false view of it."

The poet has his own meaning for reality, and the painter has, and the musician has; and besides what it means to the intelligence and to the senses, it means something to everyone, so to speak. Notwithstanding this, the word in its general sense, which is the sense in which I have used it, adapts itself instantly. The subject-matter of poetry is not that "collection of solid, static objects extended in space" but the life that is lived in the scene that it composes; and so reality is not that external scene but the life that is lived in it. Reality is things as they are. The general sense of the word proliferates its special senses. It is a jungle in itself. As in the case of a jungle, everything that makes it up is pretty much of one color. First, then, there is the reality that is taken for granted, that is latent and, on the whole, ignored. It is the comfortable American state of life of the eighties, the nineties and the first ten years of the present century. Next, there is the reality that has ceased to be indifferent, the years when the Victorians had been disposed of and intellectual minorities and social minorities began to take their place and to convert our state of life to something that might not be final. This much more vital reality made the life that had preceded it look like a volume of Ackermann's colored plates or one of Töpfer's books of sketches in Switzerland.[8] I am trying to give the feel of it. It was the reality of twenty or thirty years ago. I say that it was a vital reality. The phrase gives a false impression. It was vital in the sense of being tense, of being instinct with the fatal or with what might be the fatal. The minorities began to convince us that the Victorians had left nothing behind. The Russians followed the Victorians, and the Germans, in their way, followed the Russians. The British Empire, directly or indirectly, was what was left and as to that one could not be sure whether it was a shield or a target. Reality then became violent and so remains. This much ought to be said to make it a little clearer that in speaking of the pressure of reality, I am thinking of life in a state of violence, not physically violent, as yet, for us in America, but physically violent for millions of our friends and for still more millions of our enemies and spiritually violent, it may be said, for everyone alive.

A possible poet must be a poet capable of resisting or evading the pressure of the reality of this last degree, with the knowledge that the degree of today may become a deadlier degree tomorrow. There is, however, no point to dramatizing the future in advance of the fact. I confine myself to the outline of a possible poet, with only the slightest sketch of his background.

5

Here I am, well-advanced in my paper, with everything of interest that I started out to say remaining to be said. I am interested in the nature of poetry and I have stated its nature, from one of the many points of view from which it is possible to state it. It is an interdependence of the imagination and reality

8. Rudolf Ackermann (1764–1834): German art publisher. Rodolphe Töpffer (1799–1846): Swiss writer and educator who illustrated his books with his own sketches.

as equals. This is not a definition, since it is incomplete. But it states the nature of poetry. Then I am interested in the role of the poet and this is paramount. In this area of my subject I might be expected to speak of the social, that is to say sociological or political, obligation of the poet. He has none. That he must be contemporaneous is as old as Longinus[9] and I dare say older. But that he *is* contemporaneous is almost inevitable. How contemporaneous in the direct sense in which being contemporaneous is intended were the four great poets of whom I spoke a moment ago? I do not think that a poet owes any more as a social obligation than he owes as a moral obligation, and if there is anything concerning poetry about which people agree it is that the role of the poet is not to be found in morals. I cannot say what that wide agreement amounts to because the agreement (in which I do not join) that the poet is under a social obligation is equally wide. Reality is life and life is society and the imagination and reality; that is to say, the imagination and society are inseparable. That is pre-eminently true in the case of the poetic drama. The poetic drama needs a terrible genius before it is anything more than a literary relic. Besides the theater has forgotten that it could ever be terrible. It is not one of the instruments of fate, decidedly. Yes: the all-commanding subject-matter of poetry is life, the never-ceasing source. But it is not a social obligation. One does not love and go back to one's ancient mother as a social obligation. One goes back out of a suasion not to be denied. Unquestionably if a social movement moved one deeply enough, its moving poems would follow. No politician can command the imagination, directing it to do this or that. Stalin[1] might grind his teeth the whole of a Russian winter and yet all the poets in the Soviets might remain silent the following spring. He might excite their imaginations by something he said or did. He would not command them. He is singularly free from that "cult of pomp," which is the comic side of the European disaster; and that means as much as anything to us. The truth is that the social obligation so closely urged is a phase of the pressure of reality which a poet (in the absence of dramatic poets) is bound to resist or evade today. Dante in Purgatory and Paradise was still the voice of the Middle Ages but not through fulfilling any social obligation. Since that is the role most frequently urged, if that role is eliminated, and if a possible poet is left facing life without any categorical exactions upon him, what then? What is his function? Certainly it is not to lead people out of the confusion in which they find themselves. Nor is it, I think, to comfort them while they follow their readers to and fro. I think that his function is to make his imagination theirs and that he fulfills himself only as he sees his imagination become the light in the minds of others. His role in short, is to help people to live their lives. Time and time again it has been said that he may not address himself to an élite. I think he may. There is not a poet whom we prize living today that does not address himself to an élite. The poet will continue to do this: to address himself to an élite even in a classless society, unless, perhaps, this exposes him to imprisonment or exile. In that event he is likely not to address himself to anyone at all. He may, like Shostakovich,[2] content himself with pretence. He will, nevertheless, still be addressing himself to an élite, for all poets address themselves to someone and it is of the essence of that instinct, and it seems to amount to an instinct, that it should be to an élite, not to a drab but to a woman

9. Greek scholar (first century C.E.) to whom the seminal work of literary criticism, *On the Sublime*, is attributed.
1. Joseph Stalin (1879–1953), Soviet dictator.
2. Dmitry Shostakovich (1906–1975), Russian composer who wrote under the government restrictions of the Soviet Union.

with the hair of a pythoness, not to a chamber of commerce but to a gallery of one's own, if there are enough of one's own to fill a gallery. And that élite, if it responds, not out of complaisance, but because the poet has quickened it, because he has educed from it that for which it was searching in itself and in the life around it and which it had not yet quite found, will thereafter do for the poet what he cannot do for himself, that is to say, receive his poetry.

I repeat that his role is to help people to live their lives. He has had immensely to do with giving life whatever savor it possesses. He has had to do with whatever the imagination and the senses have made of the world. He has, in fact, had to do with life except as the intellect has had to do with it and, as to that, no one is needed to tell us that poetry and philosophy are akin. I want to repeat for two reasons a number of observations made by Charles Mauron.[3] The first reason is that these observations tell us what it is that a poet does to help people to live their lives and the second is that they prepare the way for a word concerning escapism. They are: that the artist transforms us into epicures; that he has to discover the possible work of art in the real world, then to extract it, when he does not himself compose it entirely; that he is *un amoureux perpétuel*[4] of the world that he contemplates and thereby enriches; that art sets out to express the human soul; and finally that everything like a firm grasp of reality is eliminated from the aesthetic field. With these aphorisms in mind, how is it possible to condemn escapism? The poetic process is psychologically an escapist process. The chatter about escapism is, to my way of thinking, merely common cant. My own remarks about resisting or evading the pressure of reality mean escapism, if analyzed. Escapism has a pejorative sense, which it cannot be supposed that I include in the sense in which I use the word. The pejorative sense applies where the poet is not attached to reality, where the imagination does not adhere to reality, which, for my part, I regard as fundamental. If we go back to the collection of solid, static objects extended in space, which Dr. Joad posited, and if we say that the space is blank space, nowhere, without color, and that the objects, though solid, have no shadows and, though static, exert a mournful power, and, without elaborating this complete poverty, if suddenly we hear a different and familiar description of the place:

> This City now doth, like a garment, wear
> The beauty of the morning, silent bare,
> Ships, towers, domes, theatres, and temples lie
> Open unto the fields, and to the sky;
> All bright and glittering in the smokeless air;[5]

if we have this experience, we know how poets help people to live their lives. This illustration must serve for all the rest. There is, in fact, a world of poetry indistinguishable from the world in which we live, or, I ought to say, no doubt, from the world in which we shall come to live, since what makes the poet the potent figure that he is, or was, or ought to be, is that he creates the world to which we turn incessantly and without knowing it and that he gives to life the supreme fictions without which we are unable to conceive of it.

And what about the sound of words? What about nobility, of which the

3. French philosopher and literary critic (1899–1966).
4. A perpetual lover (French).
5. From Wordsworth's sonnet "Composed upon Westminster Bridge, September 3, 1802."

fortunes were to be a kind of test of the value of the poet? I do not know of anything that will appear to have suffered more from the passage of time than the music of poetry and that has suffered less. The deepening need for words to express our thoughts and feelings which, we are sure, are all the truth that we shall ever experience, having no illusions, makes us listen to words when we hear them, loving them and feeling them, makes us search the sound of them, for a finality, a perfection, an unalterable vibration, which it is only within the power of the acutest poet to give them. Those of us who may have been thinking of the path of poetry, those who understand that words are thoughts and not only our own thoughts but the thoughts of men and women ignorant of what it is that they are thinking, must be conscious of this: that, above everything else, poetry is words; and that words, above everything else, are, in poetry, sounds. This being so, my time and yours might have been better spent if I had been less interested in trying to give our possible poet an identity and less interested in trying to appoint him to his place. But unless I had done these things, it might have been thought that I was rhetorical, when I was speaking in the simplest way about things of such importance that nothing is more so. A poet's words are of things that do not exist without the words. Thus, the image of the charioteer and of the winged horses,[6] which has been held to be precious for all of time that matters, was created by words of things that never existed without the words. A description of Verrocchio's statue[7] could be the integration of an illusion equal to the statue itself. Poetry is a revelation in words by means of the words. Croce[8] was not speaking of poetry in particular when he said that language is perpetual creation. About nobility I cannot be sure that the decline, not to say the disappearance of nobility is anything more than a maladjustment between the imagination and reality. We have been a little insane about the truth. We have had an obsession. In its ultimate extension, the truth about which we have been insane will lead us to look beyond the truth to something in which the imagination will be the dominant complement. It is not only that the imagination adheres to reality, but, also, that reality adheres to the imagination and that the interdependence is essential. We may emerge from our *bassesse*[9] and, if we do, how would it happen if not by the intervention of some fortune of the mind? And what would that fortune of the mind happen to be? It might be only commonsense but even that, a commonsense beyond the truth, would be a nobility of long descent.

The poet refuses to allow his task to be set for him. He denies that he has a task and considers that the organization of materia poetica is a contradiction in terms. Yet the imagination gives to everything that it touches a peculiarity, and it seems to me that the peculiarity of the imagination is nobility, of which there are many degrees. This inherent nobility is the natural source of another, which our extremely headstrong generation regards as false and decadent. I mean that nobility which is our spiritual height and depth; and while I know how difficult it is to express it, nevertheless I am bound to give a sense of it. Nothing could be more evasive and inaccessible. Nothing distorts itself and seeks disguise more quickly. There is a shame of disclosing it and in its definite presentations a horror of it. But there it is. The fact that

6. Stevens begins the essay by discussing a figure from the *Phaedrus*, by the ancient Greek philosopher Plato, of the soul as a charioteer and two winged horses, one noble and one ignoble.

7. Earlier in the essay, Stevens praises the nobility of a Venetian statue of Bartolomeo Colleoni on horseback by the Florentine painter and sculptor Andrea del Verrocchio (1435–1488).

8. Benedetto Croce (1866–1952), Italian philosopher.

9. Servility (French).

it is there is what makes it possible to invite to the reading and writing of poetry men of intelligence and desire for life. I am not thinking of the ethical or the sonorous or at all the manner of it. The manner of it is, in fact, its difficulty, which each man must feel each day differently, for himself. I am not thinking of the solemn, the portentous or demoded. On the other hand, I am evading a definition. If it is defined, it will be fixed and it must not be fixed. As in the case of an external thing, nobility resolves itself into an enormous number of vibrations, movements, changes. To fix it is to put an end to it. Let me show it to you unfixed.

Late last year Epstein[1] exhibited some of his flower paintings at the Leicester Galleries in London. A commentator in *Apollo* said: "*How with this rage can beauty hold a plea* . . . The quotation from Shakespeare's 65th sonnet prefaces the catalogue. . . . It would be apropos to any other flower paintings than Mr. Epstein's. His make no pretence of fragility. They shout, explode all over the picture space and generally oppose the rage of the world with such a rage of form and colour as no flower in nature or pigment has done since Van Gogh."

What ferocious beauty the line from Shakespeare puts on when used under such circumstances! While it has its modulation of despair, it holds its plea and its plea is noble. There is no element more conspicuously absent from contemporary poetry than nobility. There is no element that poets have sought after, more curiously and more piously, certain of its obscure existence. Its voice is one of the inarticulate voices which it is their business to overhear and to record. The nobility of rhetoric is, of course, a lifeless nobility. Pareto's[2] epigram that history is a cemetery of aristocracies easily becomes another: that poetry is a cemetery of nobilities. For the sensitive poet, conscious of negations, nothing is more difficult than the affirmations of nobility and yet there is nothing that he requires of himself more persistently, since in them and in their kind, alone, are to be found those sanctions that are the reasons for his being and for that occasional ecstasy, or ecstatic freedom of the mind, which is his special privilege.

It is hard to think of a thing more out of time than nobility. Looked at plainly it seems false and dead and ugly. To look at it all makes us realize sharply that in our present, in the presence of our reality, the past looks false and is, therefore, dead and is, therefore, ugly; and we turn away from it as from something repulsive and particularly from the characteristic that it has a way of assuming: something that was noble in its day, grandeur that was, the rhetorical once. But as a wave is a force and not the water of which it is composed, which is never the same, so nobility is a force and not the manifestations of which it is composed, which are never the same. Possibly this description of it as a force will do more than anything else I can have said about it to reconcile you to it. It is not an artifice that the mind has added to human nature. The mind has added nothing to human nature. It is a violence from within that protects us from a violence without. It is the imagination pressing back against the pressure of reality. It seems, in the last analysis, to have something to do with our self-preservation; and that, no doubt, is why the expression of it, the sound of its words, helps us to live our lives.

1942

1. Jacob Epstein (1880–1959), American-born English sculptor and painter.

2. Vilfredo Pareto (1848–1923), Italian economist and sociologist.

The Figure a Poem Makes

In this essay, originally the preface to his *Collected Poems* (1939), Robert Frost responds to modern poetry's affinity for abstraction, which he sees as only one of several factors that make poetry a vital force. A poem consists of neither sound alone nor associative juxtapositions but the tension between sound and meaning, form and wildness. With typical circumspection, Frost allots poetry an important—though limited—purpose: it creates a small space of order out of the chaotic world, "a momentary stay against confusion." Arising out of untapped memories, a poem embodies the author's surprise at its coming into being. It carries the reader from "delight to wisdom" and offers in the end a "clarification of life." The essay is reprinted from *Robert Frost: Collected Poems, Prose, and Plays* (1995).

ROBERT FROST

The Figure a Poem Makes

Abstraction is an old story with the philosophers, but it has been like a new toy in the hands of the artists of our day. Why can't we have any one quality of poetry we choose by itself? We can have in thought. Then it will go hard if we can't in practice. Our lives for it.

Granted no one but a humanist much cares how sound a poem is if it is only *a* sound. The sound is the gold in the ore. Then we will have the sound out alone and dispense with the inessential. We do till we make the discovery that the object in writing poetry is to make all poems sound as different as possible from each other, and the resources for that of vowels, consonants, punctuation, syntax, words, sentences, meter are not enough. We need the help of context—meaning—subject matter. That is the greatest help towards variety. All that can be done with words is soon told. So also with meters—particularly in our language where there are virtually but two, strict iambic and loose iambic. The ancients with many were still poor if they depended on meters for all tune. It is painful to watch our sprung-rhythmists[1] straining at the point of omitting one short from a foot for relief from monotony. The possibilities for tune from the dramatic tones of meaning struck across the rigidity of a limited meter are endless. And we are back in poetry as merely one more art of having something to say, sound or unsound. Probably better if sound, because deeper and from wider experience.

Then there is this wildness whereof it is spoken. Granted again that it has an equal claim with sound to being a poem's better half. If it is a wild tune, it is a poem. Our problem then is, as modern abstractionists, to have the wildness pure; to be wild with nothing to be wild about. We bring up as aberrationists, giving way to undirected associations and kicking ourselves from one chance suggestion to another in all directions as of a hot afternoon

1. *Sprung rhythm:* irregular meter in which each foot has one stress but varying numbers of syllables; defined by English poet Gerard Manley Hopkins (1844–1889).

in the life of a grasshopper. Theme alone can steady us down. Just as the first mystery was how a poem could have a tune in such a straightness as meter, so the second mystery is how a poem can have wildness and at the same time a subject that shall be fulfilled.

It should be of the pleasure of a poem itself to tell how it can. The figure a poem makes. It begins in delight and ends in wisdom. The figure is the same as for love. No one can really hold that the ecstasy should be static and stand still in one place. It begins in delight, it inclines to the impulse, it assumes direction with the first line laid down, it runs a course of lucky events, and ends in a clarification of life—not necessarily a great clarification, such as sects and cults are founded on, but in a momentary stay against confusion. It has denouement.[2] It has an outcome that though unforeseen was predestined from the first image of the original mood—and indeed from the very mood. It is but a trick poem and no poem at all if the best of it was thought of first and saved for the last. It finds its own name as it goes and discovers the best waiting for it in some final phrase at once wise and sad—the happy-sad blend of the drinking song.

No tears in the writer, no tears in the reader. No surprise for the writer, no surprise for the reader. For me the initial delight is in the surprise of remembering something I didn't know I knew. I am in a place, in a situation, as if I had materialized from cloud or risen out of the ground. There is a glad recognition of the long lost and the rest follows. Step by step the wonder of unexpected supply keeps growing. The impressions most useful to my purpose seem always those I was unaware of and so made no note of at the time when taken, and the conclusion is come to that like giants we are always hurling experience ahead of us to pave the future with against the day when we may want to strike a line of purpose across it for somewhere. The line will have the more charm for not being mechanically straight. We enjoy the straight crookedness of a good walking stick. Modern instruments of precision are being used to make things crooked as if by eye and hand in the old days.

I tell how there may be a better wildness of logic than of inconsequence. But the logic is backward, in retrospect, after the act. It must be more felt than seen ahead like prophecy. It must be a revelation, or a series of revelations, as much for the poet as for the reader. For it to be that there must have been the greatest freedom of the material to move about in it and to establish relations in it regardless of time and space, previous relation, and everything but affinity. We prate of freedom. We call our schools free because we are not free to stay away from them till we are sixteen years of age. I have given up my democratic prejudices and now willingly set the lower classes free to be completely taken care of by the upper classes. Political freedom is nothing to me. I bestow it right and left. All I would keep for myself is the freedom of my material—the condition of body and mind now and then to summons aptly from the vast chaos of all I have lived through.

Scholars and artists thrown together are often annoyed at the puzzle of where they differ. Both work from knowledge; but I suspect they differ most importantly in the way their knowledge is come by. Scholars get theirs with conscientious thoroughness along projected lines of logic; poets theirs cavalierly and as it happens in and out of books. They stick to nothing deliberately, but let what will stick to them like burrs where they walk in the fields.

2. Final outcome or untying of the plot of a literary work.

No acquirement is on assignment, or even self-assignment. Knowledge of the second kind is much more available in the wild free ways of wit and art. A school boy may be defined as one who can tell you what he knows in the order in which he learned it. The artist must value himself as he snatches a thing from some previous order in time and space into a new order with not so much as a ligature clinging to it of the old place where it was organic.

More than once I should have lost my soul to radicalism if it had been the originality it was mistaken for by its young converts. Originality and initiative are what I ask for my country. For myself the originality need be no more than the freshness of a poem run in the way I have described: from delight to wisdom. The figure is the same as for love. Like a piece of ice on a hot stove the poem must ride on its own melting. A poem may be worked over once it is in being, but may not be worried into being. Its most precious quality will remain its having run itself and carried away the poet with it. Read it a hundred times: it will forever keep its freshness as a metal keeps its fragrance. It can never lose its sense of a meaning that once unfolded by surprise as it went.

January 11, 1939 1939

A Transatlantic Interview

In 1946, American scholar Robert Bartlett Haas set out both to help readers understand Gertrude Stein's difficult work and to document her uniquely authoritative but elliptical conversational style. He scripted questions and then sent them overseas, and his friend William S. Sutton read them to Stein and recorded her answers. In the interview, Stein explains the notion of composition she borrows from the Postimpressionist painter Paul Cézanne, whose work revealed to her that every element of a composition is of equal value and every part is as important as the whole. She also credits the influences of Cubist painter Pablo Picasso and psychologist and philosopher William James. She traces the evolution of her work, explains the advantages and limits of abstraction, distinguishes poetry from narrative, and champions "complicated simplicity." She also discusses prose poems from her landmark early work, *Tender Buttons* (1914), explaining the aesthetic aims and compositional process that went into it. The interview, originally printed by the *UCLAN Review* (Summer 1962, Spring 1963, Winter 1964), is excerpted from *A Primer for the Gradual Understanding of Gertrude Stein* (1971), ed. Robert Bartlett Haas.

GERTRUDE STEIN

From A Transatlantic Interview

* * *

Everything I have done has been influenced by Flaubert and Cézanne,[1] and this gave me a new feeling about composition. Up to that time composition had consisted of a central idea, to which everything else was an accompaniment and separate but was not an end in itself, and Cézanne conceived the idea that in composition one thing was as important as another thing. Each part is as important as the whole, and that impressed me enormously, and it impressed me so much that I began to write *Three Lives* under this influence and this idea of composition and I was more interested in composition at that moment, this background of word-system, which had come to me from this reading that I had done. I was obsessed by this idea of composition, and the Negro story ("Melanctha" in *Three Lives*) was a quintessence of it.

You see I tried to convey the idea of each part of a composition being as important as the whole. It was the first time in any language that anyone had used that idea of composition in literature. Henry James[2] had a slight inkling of it and was in some sense a forerunner, while in my case I made it stay on the page quite composed. You see he made it sort of like an atmosphere, and it was not solely the realism of the characters but the realism of the composition which was the important thing, the realism of the composition of my thoughts.

After all, to me one human being is as important as another human being, and you might say that the landscape has the same values, a blade of grass has the same value as a tree. Because the realism of the people who did realism before was a realism of trying to make people real. I was not interested in making the people real but in the essence or, as a painter would call it, value. One cannot live without the other. This was an entirely new idea and had been done a little by the Russians but had not been conceived as a reality until I came along, but I got it largely from Cézanne. Flaubert was there as a theme. He, too, had a little of the feeling about this thing, but they none of them conceived it as an entity, no more than any painter had done other than Cézanne. They all fell down on it, because the supremacy of one interest overcame them, while the Cézanne thing I put into words came in the *Three Lives* and was followed by the *Making of Americans.*

In the *Making of Americans* I began the same thing. In trying to make a history of the world my idea here was to write the life of every individual who could possibly live on the earth. I hoped to realize that ambition. My intention was to cover every possible variety of human type in it. I made endless diagrams of every human being, watching people from windows and so on until I could put down every type of human being that could be on the earth. I wanted each one to have the same value. I was not at all interested in the little or big men but to realize absolutely every variety of human experience that it was possible to have, every type, every style and nuance. I have

1. Paul Cézanne (1839–1906): French Post-impressionist painter. Gustave Flaubert (1821–1880): French novelist.
2. American novelist (1843–1916).

always had this obsession, and that is why I enjoy talking to every GI. I must know every possible nuance.

Conception of this has to be based on a real feeling for every human being. The surprises of it are endless. Still there are the endless surprises, the combination that you don't expect, the relation of men to character that you do not expect. It never ends. All the time in it you see what I am singling out is that one thing has the same value as another. There are of course people who are more important than others in that they have more importance in the world, but this is not essential, and it ceases to be. I have no sense of difference in this respect, because every human being comprises the combination form. Just as everybody has the vote, including the women, I think children should, because as soon as a child is conscious of itself, then it has to me an existence and has a stake in what happens. Everybody who has that stake has that quality of interest, and in the *Making of Americans* that is what I tried to show.

In writing the *Three Lives* I was not particularly conscious of the question of style. The style which everybody shouted about surprised me. I was only interested in these other things. In the beginning gradually I became more conscious of the way you did this thing and I became gradually more conscious of it and at that time particularly of a need for evenness. At this time I threw away punctuation. My real objection to it was that it threw away this balance that I was trying to get, this evenness of everybody having a vote, and that is the reason I am impatient with punctuation. Finally I got obsessed with these enormously long sentences and long paragraphs. All that was an effort to get this evenness, and this went on until it sort of exhausted itself.

On the *Making of Americans* I had written about one thousand pages, and I finished the thing with a sort of rhapsody at the end. Then I started in to write *Matisse, Picasso, and Gertrude Stein*. You will see in each one of these stories that they began in the character of *Making of Americans,* and then in about the middle of it words began to be for the first time more important than the sentence structure or the paragraphs. Something happened. I mean I felt a need. I had thought this thing out and felt a need of breaking it down and forcing it into little pieces. I felt that I had lost contact with the words in building up these Beethovian[3] passages. I had lost that idea gained in my youth from the Seventeenth Century writers, and the little rhymes that used to run through my head from Shakespeare, who was always a passion, got lost from the overall pattern. I recognized and I recognize (if you look at the *Long Gay Book*) this something else I knew would guide that.

I began to play with words then. I was a little obsessed by words of equal value. Picasso[4] was painting my portrait at that time, and he and I used to talk this thing over endlessly. At this time he had just begun on cubism. And I felt that the thing I got from Cézanne was not the last composition. You had to recognize words had lost their value in the Nineteenth Century, particularly towards the end, they had lost much of their variety, and I felt that I could not go on, that I had to recapture the value of the individual word, find out what it meant and act within it.

Also the fact that as an American my mind was fresher towards language than the average English mind, as we had more or less renewed the word structure in our language. All through that middle period the interest was

3. In the style of Ludwig van Beethoven (1770–1827), German composer.

4. Pablo Picasso (1881–1973), Spanish expatriate painter, associated with Cubism.

with that largely, ending up with *Tender Buttons.* In this I think that there are some of the best uses of words that there are. The movement is simple and holds by little words. I had at the same time a new interest in portraiture. I began then to want to make a more complete picture of each word, and that is when the portrait business started. I wait until each word can intimate some part of each little mannerism. In each one of them I was not satisfied until the whole thing formed, and it is very difficult to put it down, to explain, in words.

While during that middle period I had these two things that were working back to the compositional idea, the idea of portraiture and the idea of the recreation of the word. I took individual words and thought about them until I got their weight and volume complete and put them next to another word, and at this same time I found out very soon that there is no such thing as putting them together without sense. It is impossible to put them together without sense. I made innumerable efforts to make words write without sense and found it impossible. Any human being putting down words had to make sense out of them.

All these things interested me very strongly through the middle years from about after the *Making of Americans* until 1911, leading up to *Tender Buttons,* which was the apex of that. That was the culmination. Then came the war, and through the war I was traveling a great deal.

* * *

* * * And then as a joke I began to write the *Autobiography of Alice Toklas,* and at that moment I had made a rather interesting discovery. A young French poet had begun to write, and I was asked to translate his poems, and there I made a rather startling discovery that other people's words are quite different from one's own, and that they can not be the result of your internal troubles as a writer. They have a totally different sense than when they are your own words. This solved for me the problem of Shakespeare's sonnets, which are so unlike any of his other work. These may have been his own idea, undoubtedly they were, but the words have none of the violence that exists in any of the poems, in any of the plays. They have a roughness and violence in their juxtaposition which the sonnets do not have, and this brought me to a great deal of illumination of narrative, because most narrative is based not about your opinions but upon someone else's.

Therefore narrative has a different concept than poetry or even exposition, because, you see, the narrative in itself is not what is in your mind but what is in somebody else's. Plays use it less, and so I did a tour de force with the *Autobiography of Alice Toklas,* and when I sent the first half to the agent, they sent back a telegram to see which one of us had written it! But still I had done what I saw, what you do in translation or in a narrative. I had recreated the point of view of somebody else. Therefore the words ran with a certain smoothness. Shakespeare never expressed any feelings of his own in those sonnets. They have too much smoothness. He did not feel "This is my emotion, I will write it down." If it is your own feeling, one's words have a fullness and violence.

* * *

Have there been any new developments in your attitude toward poetry?

Poetry is understandable, and the best poetry is real. The children's books and some of that in *Tender Buttons* and in some of the children's plays. There have been no new developments in poetry farther than that.

How and when are poetry and prose separate things?

I did that pretty thoroughly in that book of poetry and prose, and since then what poetry I have done has been in the children's books, and that you might call spontaneous poetry, and in *Paris, France* there is quite a bit of it, but that is mainly dealing with children. Somehow or other in war time the only thing that is spontaneously poetic is children. Children themselves are poetry. The poetry of adults in wartime is too intentional. It is too much mixed up with everything else. My poetry was children's poetry, and most of it is very good, and some of it as good as anything I have ever done. *The World is Round* is being included in a new American anthology.

The early book, Tender Buttons, *was written in Spain in 1913 and was Gertrude Stein's first attempt to "express the rhythm of the visible world."* Tender Buttons *was, therefore, to Gertrude Stein's development what the "Demoiselles d'Avignon" was to Picasso's, a key work marked with the enormous struggle of creating a new value.*

The following readings were chosen at random from Tender Buttons *and are followed by Gertrude Stein's verbatim responses.*

A DOG

A little monkey goes like a donkey that means to say that means to say that more sighs last goes. Leave with it. A little monkey goes like a donkey.

"A little monkey goes like a donkey . . ." That was an effort to illustrate the movement of a donkey going up a hill, you can see it plainly. "A little monkey goes like a donkey." An effort to make the movement of the donkey, and so the picture hangs complete.

A WHITE HUNTER

A white hunter is nearly crazy.

"A white hunter is nearly crazy." This is an abstract, I mean an abstraction of color. If a hunter is white he looks white, and that gives you a natural feeling that he is crazy, a complete portrait by suggestion, that is what I had in mind to write.

A LITTLE CALLED PAULINE[5]

"A little called anything shows shudders." This was another attempt to have only enough to describe the movement of one of those old-fashioned auto-

5. The original interview printed an excerpt from the poem, on p. 181 of this volume.

mobiles, an old Ford, the movement is like that automobile. This is an account of movement that is not always successful. For the most part it is successful and is rather interesting.

A LITTLE BIT OF A TUMBLER[6]

I have used this idea in more places. I used to take objects on a table, like a tumbler or any kind of object and try to get the picture of it clear and separate in my mind and create a word relationship between the word and the things seen. "A shining indication of yellow . . ." suggests a tumbler and something in it. ". . . when all four were bought" suggests there were four of them. I try to call to the eye the way it appears by suggestion the way a painter can do it. This is difficult and takes a lot of work and concentration to do it. I want to indicate it without calling in other things. "This was the hope which made the six and seven have no use for any more places . . ." Places bring up a reality. ". . . and this necessarily spread into nothing," which does broken tumbler which is the end of the story.

A WAIST[7]

"A star glide, a single frantic sullenness, a single financial grass greediness." This was probably an effort to express an emotion, another version of an "Ode to a Mistress's Eyebrows." "Object that is in wood. Hold the pine, hold the dark, hold in the rush, make the bottom. A piece of crystal. A change, in a change that is remarkable there is no reason to say that there was a time." This is fairly successful of what I knew up to that date. I did not have to call in other things to help. I do not like to do this, there is so much one must reject to keep the even smoothness of suggestion.

A PIECE OF COFFEE[8]

"Dirty is yellow." Dirty has an association and is a word that I would not use now. I would not use words that have definite associations. This was earlier work and none of the later things have this. This early work is not so successful. It is an effort and does not come clean. "The time to show a message is when too late and later there is no hanging in a blight." There is too much phantasy here. "A not torn rose-wood color. If it . . . is not necessary to mingle astonishment." That is the image but it is not completely successful, but it is better than the first part. You see there is too much appeal to the eye.

"The settling of stationing . . . May not be strange to." There is too much effort. If an effort that you make is successful, if you do get what you want to create, the effort must not show. It should create a satisfaction in the mind of the reader but in the same image as the creation. In this the mind is distracted and that is not satisfactory and it is therefore a failure. Here I am groping. I have not mastered my material. Insofar as creation is successful a reader realizes it as a successful entity, and in this you can see how successfully you have mastered your material.

6. On p. 181 of this volume.
7. On p. 181 of this volume.
8. On p. 180 of this volume.

A BROWN

A brown which is not liquid not more so is relaxed and yet there is a change, a news is pressing.

"A brown which is not liquid . . ." The color is held within and there you see I was groping for the color.

PEELED PENCIL, CHOKE

Rub her coke.

That is where I was beginning and went on a good deal after that period to make sound pictures but I gave that up as uninteresting.

EGGS[9]

"In white in white handkerchiefs with little dots in a white belt all shadows are singular . . ." There I used a lot of imagery and from what I was interested in it is not a success. It should allow imagery with it without troubling anybody.

SUGAR[1]

This is rather fine, looking at it dispassionately. "A violent luck . . . There is precisely that noise." I call that from my standpoint a successful poem. ". . . slight shadow and a solid fine furnace." You see a "light slight shadow" has poetical appeal, but it is not quite successful poetry.

"Water is squeezing, water is almost squeezing on lard." The imagery of that is really a perfect example of realism, there is enough there to a person looking at water that is realistic, there is enough use that is outside the image before your eyes. "A mind under is exact and so it is necessary to have a mouth and eyeglasses." That impresses any person, so to speak it is part of the water and is therefore valid. It is supposed to continue the actual realism of water, of a great body of water.

You must remember each time I took something, I said, I have got to satisfy each realistic thing I feel about it. Looking at your shoe, for instance, I would try to make a complete realistic picture of your shoe. It is devilish difficult and needs perfect concentration, you have to refuse so much and so much intrudes itself upon you that you do not want it, it is exhausting work.

MUTTON[2]

"Mouse and mountain and a quiver . . ." Here you see I was wise enough not to hesitate and still I dominated. ". . . A sign is the specimen spoken." You see also here you have a very good example. You take a paragraph like that and the values are pretty steady though this seems difficult to a normal reader's understanding. This is pretty good because it is more abstract.

9. On p. 184 of this volume.
1. The original interview printed excerpts from the poem, on p. 183 of this volume.
2. The original interview printed excerpts from the poem, on p. 182 of this volume.

You see it is the people who generally smell of the museums who are accepted, and it is the new who are not accepted. You have got to accept a complete difference. It is hard to accept that, it is much easier to have one hand in the past. That is why James Joyce[3] was accepted and I was not. He leaned toward the past, in my work the newness and difference is fundamental. Cézanne was my great influence though I never met him; he was an ailing man at that time.

This book is interesting as there is as much failure as success in it. When this was printed I did not understand this creation. I can see now, but one cannot understand a thing until it is done. With a thing in the process of doing, you do not know what you are doing until it is done, finished, and thus you cannot explain it. Until then you are struggling.

I was not interested in what people would think when they read this poetry; I was entirely taken up with my problem and if it did not tell my story it would tell some story. They might have another conception which would be their affair. It is not necessarily attached to the original idea I had when I wrote it.

Nobody enters into the mind of someone else, not even a husband and wife. You may touch, but you do not enter into each other's mind. Why should you? In a created thing it means more to the writer than it means to the reader. It can only mean something to one person and that person the one who wrote it.

* * *

Why did you answer questionnaires like those in Little Review *and* transition *cryptically, with a chip on your shoulder?*

That does not interest me; it is like the Gallup Poll. After all, my only thought is a complicated simplicity. I like a thing simple, but it must be simple through complication. Everything must come into your scheme; otherwise you cannot achieve real simplicity. A great deal of this I owe to a great teacher, William James.[4] He said, "Never reject anything. Nothing has been proved. If you reject anything, that is the beginning of the end as an intellectual." He was my big influence when I was at college. He was a man who always said, "Complicate your life as much as you please, it has got to simplify."

Nothing can be the same thing to the other person. Nobody can enter into anybody else's mind; so why try? One can only enter into it in a superficial way. You have slight contacts with other people's minds, but you cannot enter into them.

Then why did you publish manuscripts that were really written only for yourself?

There is the eternal vanity of the mind. One wants to see one's children in the world and have them admired like any fond parent, and it is a bitter blow to have them refused or mocked. It is just as bitter for me to have a thing refused as for any little writer with his first manuscript. Anything you create you want to exist, and its means of existence is in being printed.

1946 1962–64

3. Irish novelist (1882–1941).
4. American philosopher and psychologist (1842–1910).

Humility, Concentration, and Gusto

A profilic reviewer and essayist, as well as a poet, Marianne Moore illuminates in this essay the three qualities that she prizes most in poetry. Never pompous or preening, Moore likes humility in poetry, or a "quiet objectiveness" and acknowledgment of what has been done before. Hence her self-effacing, quietly witty prose abounds, like her poetry, with quotations and examples, drawn from sources ranging from poetry and criticism to a Federal Reserve of New York letter about counterfeiting. A "poem is a concentrate," she says, and both her poetry and prose display concentration in their spare, intensely particularized language, minimal in both rhetorical ornament and connective stitching. Balanced against the restraint of Moore's first two principles is the third: "gusto," or imaginative panache. A poet of both self-imposed limits and extravagant idiosyncrasies, Moore believes "gusto thrives on freedom, and freedom in art, as in life, is the result of a discipline imposed by ourselves." Originally read as a lecture at the Grolier Club in December 1948 and printed in *Grolier Club Gazette,* No. 2 (1949), the essay is reprinted from *The Complete Prose of Marianne Moore* (1986).

MARIANNE MOORE

Humility, Concentration, and Gusto

In times like these we are tempted to disregard anything that has not a direct bearing on freedom; or should I say, an obvious bearing, for what is more persuasive than poetry, though as Robert Frost[1] says, it works obliquely and delicately. Commander King-Hall, in his book *Total Victory,*[2] is really saying that the pen is the sword when he says the object of war is to persuade the enemy to change his mind.

Three foremost aids to persuasion which occur to me are humility, concentration, and gusto. Our lack of humility, together with anxiety, has perhaps stood in the way of initial liking for Caesar's *Commentaries,*[3] which now seem to me masterpieces. I was originally like the Hill School boy to whom I referred in one of my pieces of verse, who translated *summa diligentia* (with all speed): Caesar crossed the Alps on the top of a diligence.[4]

In Caxton,[5] humility seems to be a judicious modesty, which is rather different from humility. Nevertheless, could anything be more persuasive than the preface to his *Aeneid,*[6] where he says, "Some desired me to use olde and homely termes . . . and some the most curyous termes that I could fynde. And thus between playn, rude and curyous, I stand abasshed"? Daniel Berkeley Updike[7] has always seemed to me a phenomenon of eloquence because

1. American poet (1874–1963).
2. English writer and naval officer Stephen King-Hall's (1893–1966) 1941 work.
3. The war commentaries of Roman general Julius Caesar (100–44 B.C.E).
4. The Latin word *summa* is sometimes used to mean *top,* other times, such as here, *to the utmost or highest degree.* Cf. Moore's "Picking and Choosing": "*Summa Diligentia;* to the humbug whose name is so amusing—/ very young and very rushed, Caesar crossed the Alps / on the top of a 'diligence'!"
5. William Caxton (1422?–1491), translator and the first English printer.
6. His translation of the epic by Roman poet Virgil (70–19 B.C.E.).
7. An American printer and historian of typography (1860–1941), whose *In the Day's Work* (1924) Moore quotes below.

of the quiet objectiveness of his writing. And what he says of printing applies equally to poetry. It is true, is it not, that "style does not depend on decoration but on simplicity and proportion"? Nor can we dignify confusion by calling it baroque. Here, I may say, I am preaching to myself, since, when I am as complete as I like to be, I seem unable to get an effect plain enough.

We don't want war, but it does conduce to humility; as someone said in the foreword to an exhibition catalogue of his work, "With what shall the artist arm himself save with his humility?" Humility, indeed, is armor, for it realizes that it is impossible to be original, in the sense of doing something that has never been thought of before. Originality is in any case a by-product of sincerity; that is to say, of feeling that is honest and accordingly rejects anything that might cloud the impression, such as unnecessary commas, modifying clauses, or delayed predicates.

Concentration avoids adverbial intensives such as "definitely," positively," or "absolutely." As for commas, nothing can be more stultifying than needlessly overaccentuated pauses. Defoe,[8] speaking in so low a key that there is a fascination about the mere understatement, is for me one of the most persuasive of writers. For instance, in the passage about the pickpocket in *The Life of Colonel Jacque,* he has the Colonel say to the pickpocket, "Must we have it all? Must a man have none of it again, that lost it?" But persuasiveness has not died with Defoe; E. E. Cummings'[9] "little man in a hurry" (254, *No Thanks*) has not a comma in it, but by the careful ordering of the words there is not an equivocal emphasis:

little man
(in a hurry
full of an
important worry)
halt stop forget relax

wait

And James Laughlin,[1] the author of *Some Natural Things,* is eminent in this respect, his "Above the City" being an instance of inherent emphasis:

You know our office on the 18th
floor of the Salmon Tower looks
    right out on the

Empire State & it just happened
we were finishing up some
    late invoices on

a new book that Saturday morning
when a bomber roared through the
    mist and crashed

flames poured from the windows
into the drifting clouds & sirens
    screamed down in

8. Daniel Defoe (1660–1731), English novelist.
9. American poet (1894–1962).
1. American publisher and poet (1914–1997).

the streets below it was unearthly
but you know the strangest thing
we realized that

none of us were much surprised be-
cause we'd always known that those
two Paragons of

progress sooner or later would per-
form before our eyes this demon-
stration of their
true relationship.

Concentration—indispensable to persuasion—may feel to itself crystal clear, yet be through its very compression the opposite, and William Empson's attitude to ambiguity[2] does not extenuate defeat. Graham Greene once said, in reviewing a play of Gorki's,[3] "Confusion is really the plot. A meat-merchant and a miller are introduced, whom one never succeeds in identifying even in the end." I myself, however, would rather be told too little than too much. The question then arises, How obscure may one be? And I suppose one should not be consciously obscure at all. In any case, a poem is a concentrate and has, as W. H. Auden[4] says, "an immediate meaning and a possible meaning; as in the line,

Or wedg'd whole ages in a Bodkin's eye[5]

where you have forever in microscopic space; and when George Herbert says,

I gave to Hope a watch of mine,
But he an anchor gave to me,[6]

the watch suggests both the brevity of life and the longness of it; and an anchor makes you secure but holds you back."

I am prepossessed by the impassioned explicitness of the Federal Reserve Board of New York's letter regarding certain counterfeits, described by the Secret Service:

> $20 FEDERAL RESERVE NOTE . . . faint crayon marks have been used to simulate genuine fibre. . . . In the Treasury Seal, magnification reveals that a green dot immediately under the center of the arm of the balance scales blends with the arm whereas it should be distinctly separate. Also, the left end of the right-hand scale pan extends beyond the point where the left chain touches the pan. In the genuine, the pan ends where it touches the chain. The serial numbers are thicker than the genuine, and the prefix letter "G" is sufficiently defective to be mistaken for a "C" at first glance, . . . the letters "ry" in "Secretary" are joined together. In "Treasury" there is a tiny black dot just above the first downstroke in the letter "u." The back of the note, although of good work-

2. In *Seven Types of Ambiguity* (1930), British poet and critic William Empson (1906–1984) identifies different levels of ambiguity as crucial to poetry's effectiveness.
3. Maksim Gorky (1868–1936): Russian writer. Graham Greene (1904–1991): English writer.
4. Anglo-American poet (1907–1973); from an unpublished 1940 lecture.
5. From Canto II of *The Rape of the Lock* (1712–14), by English poet Alexander Pope (1688–1744).
6. From "Hope," by English poet George Herbert (1593–1633).

manship, is printed in a green much darker than that used for genuine currency.

December 13, 1948. Alfred M. Olsen, Cashier

I am tempted to dwell on the infectiousness of such matters, but shall return to verse. You remember, in Edward Lear's[7] "The Owl and the Pussy-Cat," they said:

"Dear Pig, are you willing to sell for a shilling
Your ring?" Said the Piggy, "I will."

The word "piggy" is altered from "Pig" to "Piggy" to fit the rhythm but is, even so, a virtue as contributing gusto; and I never tire of Leigh Hunt's lines about the fighting lions: "A wind went with their paws."[8] Continuing with cats, T. S. Eliot's account of "Mungojerrie and Rumpelteazer," "a very notorious couple of cats," is, like its companion pieces, a study in gusto throughout:

If a tile or two came loose on the roof,
Which presently ceased to be waterproof,
. . . .
Or after supper one of the girls
Suddenly missed her Woolworth pearls:
Then the family would say: "It's that horrible cat!
It was Mungojerrie—or Rumpleteazer!"
—And most of the time they left it at that.[9]

The words "By you" constitute a yet more persuasive instance of gusto, in T. S. Eliot's tribute to Walter de la Mare upon Mr. de la Mare's seventy-fifth birthday:

When the nocturnal traveler can arouse
No sleeper by his call; or when by chance
An empty face peers from an empty house,

By whom: and by what means, was this designed?
The whispered incantation which allows
Free passage to the phantoms of the mind?

By you; by those deceptive cadences
Wherewith the common measure is refined;
By conscious art practiced with natural ease;

By the delicate invisible web you wove—
An inexplicable mystery of sound.[1]

Dr. Maurice Bowra,[2] pausing upon the query, Can we have poetry without emotion? seemed to think not; however, suggested that it is not overperverse to regard Cowper's[3] "The Snail" as a thing of gusto although the poem has been dismissed as mere description:

7. English painter and author of limericks and nonsense verse (1812–1888).
8. From "The Glove and the Lions," by English poet and critic James Henry Leigh Hunt (1784–1859).
9. From *Old Possum's Book of Practical Cats* (1939), by Anglo-American poet T. S. Eliot (1888–1965).
1. Eliot's "To Walter de la Mare," dedicated to the British poet and novelist (1873–1956).
2. English critic and classicist (1898–1971).
3. William Cowper (1731–1800), English poet.

Give but his horns the slightest touch,
His self-collective power is such,
He shrinks into his house with much
Displeasure.

Where'er he dwells, he dwells alone.
Except himself, has chattels none,
Well satisfied to be his own
Whole treasure.

Thus hermit-like his life he leads,
Nor partner of his banquet needs,
And if he meets one, only feeds
The faster.

Who seeks him must be worse than blind,
He and his house are so combined,
If finding it, he fails to find,
Its master.

Together with the helpless sincerity which precipitates a poem, there is that domination of phrase referred to by Christopher Smart[4] as "impression." "Impression," he says, "is the gift of Almighty God, by which genius is empowered to throw an emphasis upon a word in such wise that it cannot escape any reader of good sense." Gusto, in Smart, authorized as oddities what in someone else might seem effrontery; the line in Psalm 147, for instance, about Jehovah: "He deals the beasts their food."

To everything that moves and lives,
Foot, fin, or feather, meat He gives,
He deals the beasts their food.[5]

And in "A Song to David":[6]

Strong is the lion—like a coal
His eyeball—like a bastion's mole,
His chest against the foes:
. . . .
But stronger still, in earth and air
And in the sea, the man of pray'r,
And far beneath the tide;
And in the seat to faith assign'd
Where ask is have, where seek is find,
Where knock is open wide.

With regard to emphasis in Biblical speech, there is a curious unalterableness about the statement by the Apostle James: The flower "falleth and the grace of the fashion of it perisheth."[7] Substitute, "the grace of its fashion

4. English poet (1722–1771), whose explanation of *impression,* following, is from the preface to his translation of *The Works of Horace* (1756). Smart also published *A Translation of the Psalms of David* (1765), including Psalm 147.

5. The King James version reads: "sing praise upon the harp unto our God: Who covereth the heaven with clouds, who prepareth rain for the earth, who maketh grass to grow upon the mountains. He giveth to the beast his food, and to the young ravens which cry" (Psalm 147.7–9).

6. Poem Smart wrote in 1763, while institutionalized for religious mania.

7. James 1.11.

perisheth," and overconscious correctness is weaker than the actual version, in which eloquence escapes grandiloquence by virtue of gusto.

Spenser is reprehended for coining words to suit the rhyme, but gusto in even the least felicitious of his defiances convicts the objecter of captiousness, I think, as in *The Shepheards Calender*[8] (the "Chase After Love")—the part about "the swayne with spotted winges, like Peacocks trayne"—the impulsive intimacy of the word "pumies" substituted for a repetition of pumie stones brings the whole thing to life:

I levelde againe
And shott at him with might and maine,
As thicke as it had hayled.
So long I shott, that al was spent;
Tho pumie stones I hastly hent
And threwe; but nought availed:
He was so wimble and so wight,
From bough to bough he lepped light,
And oft the pumies latched.

In any matter pertaining to writing, we should remember that major value outweighs minor defects, and have considerable patience with modifications of form, such as the embodied climax and subsiding last line. Wallace Stevens is particularly scrupulous against injuring an effect to make it fit a stated mode, and has

. . . iceberg settings satirize
. . . .
The demon that cannot be himself.[9]

Beaumarchais,[1] in saying, "A thing too silly to be said can be sung," was just being picturesque, but recordings of poetry convince one that naturalness is indispensable. One can, however, be careful that similar tones do not confuse the ear, such as "some" and "sun," "injustice" with "and justice"; the natural wording of uninhibited urgency, at its best, seeming really to write the poem in pauses, as in Walter de la Mare's lines about the beautiful lady, the epitaph:

Here lies a most beautiful lady,
Light of step and heart was she;
I think she was the most beautiful lady
That ever was in the West Country.[2]

All of which is to say that gusto thrives on freedom, and freedom in art, as in life, is the result of a discipline imposed by ourselves. Moreover, any writer overwhelmingly honest about pleasing himself is almost sure to please others. You recall Ezra Pound's[3] remark? "The great writer is always the plodder; it's the ephemeral writer that has to get on with the job." In a certain account by Padraic Colum[4] of Irish storytelling, "Hindered characters," he remarked parenthetically, "seldom have mothers in Irish stories, but they all have grandmothers"—a statement borrowed by me for something I was about

8. Series of pastoral poems (1579), by English poet Edmund Spenser (1552–1599).
9. From "The Man with the Blue Guitar" XXVII, by American poet Wallace Stevens (1879–1955).
1. Pierre-Augustin Caron de Beaumarchais (1732–1799), French dramatist.
2. From "An Epitaph."
3. American poet (1885–1972).
4. Irish-born American poet (1881–1972).

to write. The words have to come in just that order or they aren't pithy. Indeed, in Mr. Colum's telling of the story of Earl Gerald,[5] gusto as objectified made the unbelievable doings of an enchanter excitingly circumstantial.

To summarize: Humility is an indispensable ally, enabling concentration to heighten gusto. There are always objecters, but we must not be too sensitive about not being liked or not being printed. David Low,[6] the cartoonist, when carped at, said, "Ah, well—." But he has never compromised; he goes right on doing what idiosyncrasy tells him to do. The thing is to see the vision and not deny it; to care and admit that we do.

1949

5. Moore uses the phrase—and Colum's lecture on Gerald Fitzgerald, 14th (or 15th) earl of Desmond (c. 1538–1583), who led three rebellions against the English during Elizabeth I's reign—in her poem "Spenser's Ireland."

6. New Zealand–born English satirical cartoonist (1891–1963).

Writing

The Dyer's Hand, W. H. Auden's collection of essays based largely on his lectures in poetry at Oxford University, helped establish his reputation as a formidable poet-critic in the tradition of T. S. Eliot. The essays "Writing" and "Reading" form the prologue to the collection. Witheringly critical of poetic egocentricity, Auden demystifies Romantic conceptions of poetry as based in inspiration and aimed at political transformation. In witty aphorisms, he celebrates instead the hard-won craft of poetry. Auden redefines the profession of writing, dispenses advice to budding poets, reconsiders the differences between poetry and prose, reflects on problems of poetry and translation, and foregrounds the mnemonic power of poetry. Poets, in his view, must recognize that language is public property and that reason plays an important role in their art. "Poetry is not magic," he argues, but a form of truth telling that should "disenchant and disintoxicate." The essay is reprinted from *The Dyer's Hand* (1962).

W. H. AUDEN

Writing

It is the author's aim to say once and emphatically, "He said."

H. D. THOREAU[1]

The art of literature, vocal or written, is to adjust the language so that it embodies what it indicates.

A. N. WHITEHEAD[2]

All those whose success in life depends neither upon a job which satisfies some specific and unchanging social need, like a farmer's, nor, like a sur-

1. From the conclusion of *A Week on the Concord and Merrimack Rivers* (1849), by American philosopher, essayist, and poet Henry David Thoreau (1817–1862). The sentence actually reads "It should be the author's aim. . . ."

2. Alfred North Whitehead (1861–1947), English philosopher and mathematician.

geon's, upon some craft which he can be taught by others and improve by practice, but upon "inspiration," the lucky hazard of ideas, live by their wits, a phrase which carries a slightly pejorative meaning. Every "original" genius, be he an artist or a scientist, has something a bit shady about him, like a gambler or a medium.[3]

Literary gatherings, cocktail parties and the like, are a social nightmare because writers have no "shop" to talk. Lawyers and doctors can entertain each other with stories about interesting cases, about experiences, that is to say, related to their professional interests but yet impersonal and outside themselves. Writers have no impersonal professional interests. The literary equivalent of talking shop would be writers reciting their own work at each other, an unpopular procedure for which only very young writers have the nerve.

No poet or novelist wishes he were the only one who ever lived, but most of them wish they were the only one alive, and quite a number fondly believe their wish has been granted.

In theory, the author of a good book should remain anonymous, for it is to his work, not to himself, that admiration is due. In practice, this seems to be impossible. However, the praise and public attention that writers sometimes receive do not seem to be as fatal to them as one might expect. Just as a good man forgets his deed the moment he has done it, a genuine writer forgets a work as soon as he has completed it and starts to think about the next one; if he thinks about his past work at all, he is more likely to remember its faults than its virtues. Fame often makes a writer vain, but seldom makes him proud.

Writers can be guilty of every kind of human conceit but one, the conceit of the social worker: "We are all here on earth to help others; what on earth the others are here for, I don't know."

When a successful author analyzes the reasons for his success, he generally underestimates the talent he was born with, and overestimates his skill in employing it.

Every writer would rather be rich than poor, but no genuine writer cares about popularity as such. He needs approval of his work by others in order to be reassured that the vision of life he believes he has had is a true vision and not a self-delusion, but he can only be reassured by those whose judgment he respects. It would only be necessary for a writer to secure universal popularity if imagination and intelligence were equally distributed among all men.

When some obvious booby tells me he has liked a poem of mine, I feel as if I had picked his pocket.

Writers, poets especially, have an odd relation to the public because their medium, language, is not, like the paint of the painter or the notes of the composer, reserved for their use but is the common property of the linguistic

3. Person believed to be a channel for communicating with spirits.

group to which they belong. Lots of people are willing to admit that they don't understand painting or music, but very few indeed who have been to school and learned to read advertisements will admit that they don't understand English. As Karl Kraus[4] said: "The public doesn't understand German, and in Journalese I can't tell them so."

How happy the lot of the mathematician! He is judged solely by his peers, and the standard is so high that no colleague or rival can ever win a reputation he does not deserve. No cashier writes a letter to the press complaining about the incomprehensibility of Modern Mathematics and comparing it unfavorably with the good old days when mathematicians were content to paper irregularly shaped rooms and fill bathtubs without closing the waste pipe.

To say that a work is inspired means that, in the judgment of its author or his readers, it is better than they could reasonably hope it would be, and nothing else.

All works of art are commissioned in the sense that no artist can create one by a simple act of will but must wait until what he believes to be a good idea for a work "comes" to him. Among those works which are failures because their initial conceptions were false or inadequate, the number of self-commissioned works may well be greater than the number commissioned by patrons.

The degree of excitement which a writer feels during the process of composition is as much an indication of the value of the final result as the excitement felt by a worshiper is an indication of the value of his devotions, that is to say, very little indication.

The Oracle[5] claimed to make prophecies and give good advice about the future; it never pretended to be giving poetry readings.

If poems could be created in a trance without the conscious participation of the poet, the writing of poetry would be so boring or even unpleasant an operation that only a substantial reward in money or social prestige could induce a man to be a poet. From the manuscript evidence, it now appears that Coleridge's account of the composition of "Kubla Khan" was a fib.[6]

It is true that, when he is writing a poem, it seems to a poet as if there were two people involved, his conscious self and a Muse whom he has to woo or an Angel with whom he has to wrestle, but, as in an ordinary wooing or wrestling match, his role is as important as Hers. The Muse, like Beatrice in *Much Ado,*[7] is a spirited girl who has as little use for an abject suitor as she has for a vulgar brute. She appreciates chivalry and good manners, but she despises those who will not stand up to her and takes a cruel delight in telling them nonsense and lies which the poor little things obediently write down as "inspired" truth.

4. Austrian journalist, satirist, and poet (1874–1936).
5. In ancient Greece, person through whom a deity delivered messages.
6. English poet Samuel Taylor Coleridge (1772–1834) printed his poetic fragment "Kubla Khan" with an explanation of its interrupted, laudanum-influenced composition.
7. Shakespeare's *Much Ado About Nothing.*

> When I was writing the chorus in G Minor, I suddenly dipped my pen into the medicine bottle instead of the ink; I made a blot, and when I dried it with sand (blotting paper had not been invented then) it took the form of a natural, which instantly gave me the idea of the effect which the change from G minor to G major would make, and to this blot all the effect—if any—is due.
>
> (Rossini to Louis Engel.)[8]

Such an act of judgment, distinguishing between Chance and Providence, deserves, surely, to be called an inspiration.

To keep his errors down to a minimum, the internal Censor to whom a poet submits his work in progress should be a Censorate. It should include, for instance, a sensitive only child, a practical housewife, a logician, a monk, an irreverent buffoon and even, perhaps, hated by all the others and returning their dislike, a brutal, foul-mouthed drill sergeant who considers all poetry rubbish.

In the course of many centuries a few laborsaving devices have been introduced into the mental kitchen—alcohol, coffee, tobacco, Benzedrine,[9] etc.—but these are very crude, constantly breaking down, and liable to injure the cook. Literary composition in the twentieth century A.D. is pretty much what it was in the twentieth century B.C.: nearly everything has still to be done by hand.

Most people enjoy the sight of their own handwriting as they enjoy the smell of their own farts. Much as I loathe the typewriter, I must admit that it is a help in self-criticism. Typescript is so impersonal and hideous to look at that, if I type out a poem, I immediately see defects which I missed when I looked through it in manuscript. When it comes to a poem by somebody else, the severest test I know of is to write it out in longhand. The physical tedium of doing this ensures that the slightest defect will reveal itself; the hand is constantly looking for an excuse to stop.

Most artists are sincere and most art is bad, though some insincere (sincerely insincere) works can be quite good. (STRAVINSKY.[1]) Sincerity is like sleep. Normally, one should assume that, of course, one will be sincere, and not give the question a second thought. Most writers, however, suffer occasionally from bouts of insincerity as men do from bouts of insomnia. The remedy in both cases is often quite simple: in the case of the latter, to change one's diet, in the case of the former, to change one's company.

The schoolmasters of literature frown on affectations of style as silly and unhealthy. Instead of frowning, they ought to laugh indulgently. Shakespeare makes fun of the Euphuists[2] in *Love's Labour's Lost* and in *Hamlet,* but he owed them a great deal and he knew it. Nothing, on the face of it, could have been more futile than the attempt of Spenser, Harvey[3] and others to be good little humanists and write English verse in classical meters, yet, but

8. Gioacchino Rossini (1792–1868): Italian composer. Louis Engel: music critic for the English newspaper *The World* and author of a book of reminiscences about his friendships with musicians, *From Mozart to Mario* (1886).
9. Amphetamine stimulant.
1. Igor Stravinsky (1882–1971), Russian-born American composer.
2. Writers using inflated style and diction.
3. Edmund Spenser (1552–1599) and Gabriel Harvey (1550?–1631), English poets.

for their folly, many of Campion's most beautiful songs and the choruses in *Samson Agonistes*[4] would never have been written. In literature, as in life, affectation, passionately adopted and loyally persevered in, is one of the chief forms of self-discipline by which mankind has raised itself by its own boot-straps.

A mannered style, that of Góngora or Henry James,[5] for example, is like eccentric clothing: very few writers can carry it off, but one is enchanted by the rare exception who can.

When a reviewer describes a book as "sincere," one knows immediately that it is a) insincere (insincerely insincere) and b) badly written. Sincerity in the proper sense of the word, meaning authenticity, is, however, or ought to be, a writer's chief preoccupation. No writer can ever judge exactly how good or bad a work of his may be, but he can always know, not immediately perhaps, but certainly in a short while, whether something he has written is authentic—in his handwriting—or a forgery.

The most painful of all experiences to a poet is to find that a poem of his which he knows to be a forgery has pleased the public and got into the anthologies. For all he knows or cares, the poem may be quite good, but that is not the point; *he* should not have written it.

The work of a young writer—*Werther*[6] is the classic example—is sometimes a therapeutic act. He finds himself obsessed by certain ways of feeling and thinking of which his instinct tells him he must be rid before he can discover his authentic interests and sympathies, and the only way by which he can be rid of them forever is by surrendering to them. Once he has done this, he has developed the necessary antibodies which will make him immune for the rest of his life. As a rule, the disease is some spiritual malaise of his generation. If so, he may, as Goethe did, find himself in an embarrassing situation. What he wrote in order to exorcise certain feelings is enthusiastically welcomed by his contemporaries because it expresses just what they feel but, unlike him, they are perfectly happy to feel in this way; for the moment they regard him as their spokesman. Time passes. Having gotten the poison out of his system, the writer turns to his true interests which are not, and never were, those of his early admirers, who now pursue him with cries of "Traitor!"

The intellect of man is forced to choose
Perfection of the life or of the work. (YEATS.)[7]
This is untrue; perfection is possible in neither. All one can say is that a writer who, like all men, has his personal weaknesses and limitations, should be aware of them and try his best to keep them out of his work. For every writer, there are certain subjects which, because of defects in his character and his talent, he should never touch.

4. Verse tragedy by John Milton (1608–1674). Thomas Campion (1567–1620), English poet and composer.
5. American novelist (1843–1916). Luis de Góngora y Argote (1561–1627), Spanish poet noted for his baroque style.
6. *The Sorrows of Young Werther* (1774), early work by the German Romantic poet Johann Wolfgang von Goethe (1749–1832).
7. From "The Choice," by Irish poet W. B. Yeats (1865–1939).

What makes it difficult for a poet not to tell lies is that, in poetry, all facts and all beliefs cease to be true or false and become interesting possibilities. The reader does not have to share the beliefs expressed in a poem in order to enjoy it. Knowing this, a poet is constantly tempted to make use of an idea or a belief, not because he believes it to be true, but because he sees it has interesting poetic possibilities. It may not, perhaps, be absolutely necessary that he *believe* it, but it is certainly necessary that his emotions be deeply involved, and this they can never be unless, as a man, he takes it more seriously than as a mere poetic convenience.

The integrity of a writer is more threatened by appeals to his social conscience, his political or religious convictions, than by appeals to his cupidity. It is morally less confusing to be goosed[8] by a traveling salesman than by a bishop.

Some writers confuse authenticity, which they ought always to aim at, with originality, which they should never bother about. There is a certain kind of person who is so dominated by the desire to be loved for himself alone that he has constantly to test those around him by tiresome behavior; what he says and does must be admired, not because it is intrinsically admirable, but because it is *his* remark, *his* act. Does not this explain a good deal of avant-garde art?

Slavery is so intolerable a condition that the slave can hardly escape deluding himself into thinking that he is choosing to obey his master's commands when, in fact, he is obliged to. Most slaves of habit suffer from this delusion and so do some writers, enslaved by an all too "personal" style.

> *"Let me think: was I the same when I got up this morning? . . . But if I'm not the same, the next question is 'Who in the world am I?' . . . I'm sure I'm not Ada . . . for her hair goes in such long ringlets and mine doesn't go in ringlets at all; and I'm sure I can't be Mabel, for I know all sorts of things, and she, oh! she knows such a very little! Beside she's she and* I'm *I and—oh dear, how puzzling it all is! I'll try if I know all the things I used to know. . . ." Her eyes filled with tears . . . : "I must be Mabel after all, and I shall have to go and live in that poky little house, and have next to no toys to play with, and oh!—ever so many lessons to learn! No, I've made up my mind about it: if I'm Mabel, I'll stay down here!"*
>
> (*Alice in Wonderland.*)

> *At the next peg the Queen turned again and this time she said: "Speak in French when you can't think of the English for a thing—turn your toes out as you walk—and remember who you are."*
>
> (*Through the Looking-Glass.*)[9]

Most writers, except the supreme masters who transcend all systems of classification are either Alices or Mabels. For example:

8. To be poked between the buttocks.
9. *Alice's Adventures in Wonderland* (1865) and *Through the Looking-Glass* (1871): children's books by pseudonymous English writer Lewis Carroll (1832–1898).

Alice	Mabel
Montaigne	Pascal
Marvell	Donne
Burns	Shelley
Jane Austen	Dickens
Turgenev	Dostoievski
Valéry	Gide
Virginia Woolf	Joyce
E. M. Forster	Lawrence
Robert Graves[1]	Yeats

"Orthodoxy," said a real Alice of a bishop, "is reticence."

Except when used as historical labels, the terms *classical* and *romantic* are misleading terms for two poetic parties, the Aristocratic and the Democratic, which have always existed and to one of the which every writer belongs, though he may switch his party allegiance or, on some specific issue, refuse to obey his Party Whip.

The Aristocratic Principle as regards subject matter:
No subject matter shall be treated by poets which poetry cannot digest. It defends poetry against didacticism and journalism.
The Democratic Principle as regards subject matter:
No subject matter shall be excluded by poets which poetry is capable of digesting. It defends poetry against limited or stale conceptions of what is "poetic."
The Aristocratic Principle as regards treatment:
No irrelevant aspects of a given subject shall be expressed in a poem which treats it. It defends poetry against barbaric vagueness.
The Democratic Principle as regards treatment:
No relevant aspect of a given subject shall remain unexpressed in a poem which treats it. It defends poetry against decadent triviality.

Every work of a writer should be a first step, but this will be a false step unless, whether or not he realize it at the time, it is also a further step. When a writer is dead, one ought to be able to see that his various works, taken together, make one consistent *oeuvre*.

It takes little talent to see clearly what lies under one's nose, a good deal of it to know in which direction to point that organ.

The greatest writer cannot see through a brick wall but, unlike the rest of us, he does not build one.

1. English poet (1895–1985). Michel de Montaigne (1533–1592): French writer who pioneered the essay genre. Blaise Pascal (1623–1662): French mathematician and philosopher. Andrew Marvell (1621–1678) and John Donne (1572–1631): English Metaphysical poets. Robert Burns (1759–1796): Scottish poet. Percy Bysshe Shelley (1792–1822): English Romantic poet. Jane Austen (1775–1817) and Charles Dickens (1812–1870): English novelists. Ivan Sergeyevich Turgenev (1818–1883) and Fyodor Dostoyevsky (1821–1881): Russian novelists. Paul Valéry (1871–1945): French poet. André Gide (1869–1951): French novelist. Virginia Woolf (1882–1941): English novelist. James Joyce (1882–1941): Irish novelist. E. M. Forster (1879–1970) and D. H. Lawrence (1885–1930): English writers.

Only a minor talent can be a perfect gentleman; a major talent is always more than a bit of a cad. Hence the importance of minor writers—as teachers of good manners. Now and again, an exquisite minor work can make a master feel thoroughly ashamed of himself.

The poet is the father of his poem; its mother is a language: one could list poems as race horses are listed—*out of L by P.*[2]

A poet has to woo, not only his own Muse but also Dame Philology, and, for the beginner, the latter is the more important. As a rule, the sign that a beginner has a genuine original talent is that he is more interested in playing with words than in saying something original; his attitude is that of the old lady, quoted by E. M. Forster—"How can I know what I think till I see what I say?"[3] It is only later, when he has wooed and won Dame Philology, that he can give his entire devotion to his Muse.

Rhymes, meters, stanza forms, etc., are like servants. If the master is fair enough to win their affection and firm enough to command their respect, the result is an orderly happy household. If he is too tyrannical, they give notice; if he lacks authority, they become slovenly, impertinent, drunk and dishonest.

The poet who writes "free" verse is like Robinson Crusoe[4] on his desert island: he must do all his cooking, laundry and darning for himself. In a few exceptional cases, this manly independence produces something original and impressive, but more often the result is squalor—dirty sheets on the unmade bed and empty bottles on the unswept floor.

There are some poets, Kipling[5] for example, whose relation to language reminds one of a drill sergeant: the words are taught to wash behind their ears, stand properly at attention and execute complicated maneuvers, but at the cost of never being allowed to think for themselves. There are others, Swinburne, for example, who remind one more of Svengali:[6] under their hypnotic suggestion, an extraordinary performance is put on, not by raw recruits, but by feeble-minded schoolchildren.

Due to the Curse of Babel,[7] poetry is the most provincial of the arts, but today, when civilization is becoming monotonously the same all the world over, one feels inclined to regard this as a blessing rather than a curse: in poetry, at least, there cannot be an "International Style."

My language is the universal whore whom I have to make into a virgin. (KARL KRAUS.) It is both the glory and the shame of poetry that its medium is not its private property, that a poet cannot invent his words and that words are products, not of nature, but of a human society which uses them for a thou-

2. Reference to how the parentage of racehorses is indicated: out of the mother by the father.
3. An anecdote from Forster's *Aspects of the Novel* (1927).
4. Shipwrecked protagonist of the novel by English writer Daniel Defoe (1660–1731).
5. Rudyard Kipling (1865–1936), English poet and novelist.
6. Hypnotist in the novel *Trilby* (1894), by British caricaturist and writer George du Maurier (1834–1896). Algernon Charles Swinburne (1837–1909), English Pre-Raphaelite poet.
7. In Genesis 11, God punishes humankind for its attempt to build a tower to Heaven, by dividing it into different linguistic communities.

sand different purposes. In modern societies where language is continually being debased and reduced to nonspeech, the poet is in constant danger of having his ear corrupted, a danger to which the painter and the composer, whose media are their private property, are not exposed. On the other hand he is more protected than they from another modern peril, that of solipsist subjectivity; however esoteric a poem may be, the fact that all its words have meanings which can be looked up in a dictionary makes it testify to the existence of other people. Even the language of *Finnegans Wake*[8] was not created by Joyce *ex nihilo*; a purely private verbal world is not possible.

The difference between verse and prose is self-evident, but it is a sheer waste of time to look for a definition of the difference between poetry and prose. Frost's definition of poetry as the untranslatable element in language[9] looks plausible at first sight but, on closer examination, will not quite do. In the first place, even in the most rarefied poetry, there are some elements which are translatable. The sound of the words, their rhythmical relations, and all meanings and association of meanings which depend upon sound, like rhymes and puns, are, of course, untranslatable, but poetry is not, like music, pure sound. Any elements in a poem which are not based on verbal experience are, to some degree, translatable into another tongue, for example, images, similes and metaphors which are drawn from sensory experience. Moreover, because one characteristic that all men, whatever their culture, have in common is uniqueness—every man is a member of a class of one—the unique perspective on the world which every genuine poet has survives translation. If one takes a poem by Goethe and a poem by Hölderlin[1] and makes literal prose cribs of them, every reader will recognize that the two poems were written by two different people. In the second place, if speech can never become music, neither can it ever become algebra. Even in the most "prosy" language, in informative and technical prose, there is a personal element because language is a personal creation. *Ne pas se pencher au dehors* has a different feeling tone from *Nichthinauslehnen.*[2] A purely poetic language would be unlearnable, a purely prosaic not worth learning.

Valéry[3] bases his definitions of poetry and prose on the difference between the gratuitous and the useful, play and work, and uses as an analogy the difference between dancing and walking. But this will not do either. A commuter may walk to his suburban station every morning, but at the same time he may enjoy the walk for its own sake; the fact that his walk is necessary does not exclude the possibility of its also being a form of play. Vice versa, a dance does not cease to be play if it is also believed to have a useful purpose like promoting a good harvest.

If French poets have been more prone than English to fall into the heresy of thinking that poetry ought to be as much like music as possible, one reason may be that, in traditional French verse, sound effects have always played a much more important role than they have in English verse. The English-speaking peoples have always felt that the difference between poetic speech and the conversational speech of everyday should be kept small, and, when-

8. James Joyce's last work (1939), in which his extreme linguistic experimentation bordered on the invention of his own language.
9. "Poetry is what is lost in translation": Robert Frost (1874–1963), American poet, quoted in Louis Untermeyer's *Robert Frost: A Backward Look* (1964).
1. Friedrich Hölderlin (1770–1843), German lyric poet.
2. "Do not lean outside" in French and German.
3. In his essay "Poetry and Abstract Thought."

ever English poets have felt that the gap between poetic and ordinary speech was growing too wide, there has been a stylistic revolution to bring them closer again. In English verse, even in Shakespeare's grandest rhetorical passages, the ear is always aware of its relation to everyday speech. A good actor must—alas, today he too seldom does—make the audience hear Shakespeare's lines as verse not prose, but if he tries to make the verse sound like a different language, he will make himself ridiculous.

But French poetry, both in the way it is written and the way it is recited, has emphasized and gloried in the difference between itself and ordinary speech; in French drama, verse and prose *are* different languages. Valéry quotes a contemporary description of Rachel's powers of declamation; in reciting she could and did use a range of two octaves, from F below Middle C to F in alt; an actress who tried to do the same with Shakespeare as Rachel did with Racine[4] would be laughed off the stage.

One can read Shakespeare to oneself without even mentally *hearing* the lines and be very moved; indeed, one may easily find a performance disappointing because almost anyone with an understanding of English verse can speak it better than the average actor and actress. But to read Racine to oneself, even, I fancy, if one is a Frenchman, is like reading the score of an opera when one can hardly play or sing; one can no more get an adequate notion of *Phèdre* without having heard a great performance, than one can of *Tristan und Isolde* if one has never heard a great Isolde like Leider or Flagstad.[5]

(Monsieur St. John Perse[6] tells me that, when it comes to everyday speech, it is French which is the more monotonous and English which has the wider range of vocal inflection.)

I must confess that French classical tragedy strikes me as being opera for the unmusical. When I read the *Hippolytus*,[7] I can recognize, despite all differences, a kinship between the world of Euripides and the world of Shakespeare, but the world of Racine, like the world of opera, seems to be another planet altogether. Euripides' Aphrodite is as concerned with fish and fowl as she is with human beings; Racine's Venus is not only unconcerned with animals, she takes no interest in the Lower Orders. It is impossible to imagine any of Racine's characters sneezing or wanting to go to the bathroom, for in his world there is neither weather nor nature. In consequence, the passions by which his characters are consumed can only exist, as it were, on stage, the creation of the magnificent speech and the grand gestures of the actors and actresses who endow them with flesh and blood. This is also the case in opera, but no speaking voice, however magnificent, can hope to compete, in expressiveness through sound, with a great singing voice backed by an orchestra.

Whenever people talk to me about the weather, I always feel certain that they mean something else. (OSCAR WILDE.)[8] The only kind of speech which approximates to the symbolist's poetic ideal is polite tea table conversation, in which the meaning of the banalities uttered depends almost entirely upon vocal inflections.

4. Jean Racine (1639–1699): French dramatic poet. Mademoiselle Rachel (c. 1820–1858): French classical tragedienne. *Alt:* alto.

5. Kirsten Flagstad (1895–1962): Norwegian opera singer. *Phèdre:* 1677 tragedy by Racine. *Tristan und Isolde:* opera (first performed 1865) by German composer Richard Wagner (1813–1883). Frida Leider (1888–1975): German opera singer.

6. Saint-John Perse (1887–1975), pseudonymous French poet and diplomat.

7. Greek tragedy, by Euripides (c. 484–406 B.C.E.).

8. Irish writer and wit (1854–1900); from his play *The Importance of Being Earnest.*

Owing to its superior power as a mnemonic, verse is superior to prose as a medium for didactic instruction. Those who condemn didacticism must disapprove a *fortiori*[9] of didactic prose; in verse, as the Alka-Seltzer advertisements testify, the didactic message loses half its immodesty. Verse is also certainly the equal of prose as a medium for the lucid exposition of ideas; in skillful hands, the form of the verse can parallel and reinforce the steps of the logic. Indeed, contrary to what most people who have inherited the romantic conception of poetry believe, the danger of argument in verse—Pope's *Essay on Man* is an example—is that the verse may make the ideas *too* clear and distinct, more Cartesian[1] than they really are.

On the other hand, verse is unsuited to controversy, to proving some truth or belief which is not universally accepted, because its formal nature cannot but convey a certain skepticism about its conclusions.

> Thirty days hath September,
> April, June and November

is valid because nobody doubts its truth. Were there, however, a party who passionately denied it, the lines would be powerless to convince him because, formally, it would make no difference if the lines ran:

> Thirty days hath September,
> August, May and December.

Poetry is not magic. In so far as poetry, or any other of the arts, can be said to have an ulterior purpose, it is, by telling the truth, to disenchant and disintoxicate.

"The unacknowledged legislators of the world"[2] describes the secret police, not the poets.

Catharsis[3] is properly effected, not by works of art, but by religious rites. It is also effected, usually improperly, by bullfights, professional football matches, bad movies, military bands and monster rallies at which ten thousand girl guides[4] form themselves into a model of the national flag.

The condition of mankind is, and always has been, so miserable and depraved that, if anyone were to say to the poet: "For God's sake stop singing and do something useful like putting on the kettle or fetching bandages," what just reason could he give for refusing? But nobody says this. The self-appointed unqualified nurse says: "You are to sing the patient a song which will make him believe that I, and I alone, can cure him. If you can't or won't, I shall confiscate your passport and send you to the mines." And the poor patient in his delirium cries: "Please sing me a song which will give me sweet dreams instead of nightmares. If you succeed, I will give you a penthouse in New York or a ranch in Arizona."

1962

9. With stronger reason (Latin).
1. French philosopher René Descartes (1596–1650) argued that "clear and distinct" ideas, such as "I think, therefore I am," must be true. *Essay on Man:* didactic poem by English poet Alexander Pope (1688–1744).
2. "Poets are the unacknowledged legislators of the world" is the last sentence of "A Defence of Poetry," by English poet Percy Bysshe Shelley (1792–1822).
3. Purgation of emotions effected by tragedy, according to the *Poetics* of Greek philosopher Aristotle (384–322 B.C.E.).
4. British equivalent of Girl Scouts.

Selected Bibliographies

Anglo-American and Cross-National Studies

David Perkins's two-volume *A History of Modern Poetry* (1976, 1987) is an excellent overview of modern poetry in America, Great Britain, and Ireland. Other critical works that are especially helpful for the study of modern poetry are M. L. Rosenthal's *The Modern Poets* (1960); Stephen Spender's *The Struggle of the Modern* (1963); C. K. Stead's *The New Poetic: Yeats to Eliot* (1964); Irving Howe's *The Idea of the Modern* (1967); Hugh Kenner's *The Pound Era* (1971); *Modernism 1890–1930* (1976), ed. Malcolm Bradbury and James McFarlane; Robert Hughes's *The Shock of the New* (1981); M. L. Rosenthal and Sally M. Gall's *The Modern Poetic Sequence* (1983); Michael Levenson's *A Genealogy of Modernism* (1984); Lucy McDiarmid's *Saving Civilization: Yeats, Eliot, and Auden between the Wars* (1984); Marjorie Perloff's *The Dance of the Intellect: Studies in the Poetry of the Pound Tradition* (1985); Sanford Schwartz's *The Matrix of Modernism* (1985); Louis Menand's *Discovering Modernism: T. S. Eliot and His Context* (1987); James Longenbach's *Stone Cottage: Pound, Yeats, and Modernism* (1988); Sandra M. Gilbert and Susan Gubar's three-volume *No Man's Land* (1988, 1989, 1994); *The Gender of Modernism* (1990), ed. Bonnie Kime Scott and Mary Lynn Broe; Michael North's *The Political Aesthetic of Yeats, Eliot, and Pound* (1991); Stan Smith's *The Origins of Modernism* (1994); Jahan Ramazani's *Poetry of Mourning* (1994); Rainer Emig's *Modernism in Poetry* (1995); Peter Nicholls's *Modernisms* (1995); Daniel Albright's *Quantum Poetics: Yeats, Pound, Eliot, and the Science of Modernism* (1997); Lawrence Rainey's *Institutions of Modernism* (1998); Douglas Mao's *Solid Objects: Modernism and the Test of Production* (1998); *The Cambridge Companion to Modernism* (1999), ed. Levenson; Peter Childs's *The Twentieth Century in Poetry* (1999); Robert Crawford's *The Modern Poet* (2001); David Bromwich's *Skeptical Music: Essays on Modern Poetry* (2001); and Marjorie Perloff's *21st-Century Modernism* (2002). *The Modern Tradition* (1965), ed. Richard Ellmann and Charles Feidelson, and *Modernism: An Anthology of Sources and Documents* (1998), ed. Vassiliki Kolocotroni, Jane Goldman, and Olga Taxidou, are helpful collections of manifestos and other primary materials. Invaluable reference materials include *The Oxford Companion to Twentieth-Century Poetry* (1996), ed. Ian Hamilton; the essays in *A Companion to Twentieth-Century Poetry* (2001), ed. Neil Roberts; and entries in the many volumes of the *Dictionary of Literary Biography* (also available online).

American Poetry

Critical works especially helpful for the study of modern American poetry include Kenneth Rexroth's *American Poetry in the Twentieth Century* (1971); Hugh Kenner's *A Homemade World* (1974); Albert Gelpi's *A Coherent Splendor: The American Poetic Renaissance, 1910–1950* (1987); Houston A. Baker's *Modernism and the Harlem Renaissance* (1987); James Longenbach's *Modernist Poetics* (1987); Alan Shucard, Fred S. Moramarco, and William J. Sullivan's *Modern American Poetry, 1865–1950* (1989); Cary Nelson's *Repression and Recovery: Modern American Poetry and the Politics of Cultural Memory, 1910–1945* (1989); Richard Gray's *American Poetry of the Twentieth Century* (1990); Roger Gilbert's *Walks in the World* (1991); Stephen Cushman's *Fictions of Form in American Poetry* (1993); Michael North's *The Dialect of Modernism* (1994); George Hutchinson's *The Harlem Renaissance in Black and White* (1995); *Gendered Modernisms* (1996), ed. Thomas Travisano and Margaret Dickie; Paul Morrison's *The Poetics of Fascism: Ezra Pound, T. S. Eliot, Paul de Man* (1996); Elizabeth Gregory's *Quotation and Modern American Poetry* (1996); Michael Davidson's *Ghostlier Demarcations* (1997); Michael Thurston's *Making Something Happen: American Political Poetry Between the World Wars* (2000); Aldon Lynn Nielsen's *Reading Race in American Poetry* (2000); Rachel Blau DuPlessis's *Genders, Races, and Religious Cultures in Modern American Poetry 1908–1934* (2001); and Cary Nelson's *Revolutionary Memory: Recovering the Poetry of the American Left* (2001). An excellent general resource is the *Encyclopedia of American Poetry:*

The Twentieth Century (2001), ed. Eric L. Haralson. The Academy of American Poets maintains a useful website, www.poets.org, with an audio component and links to other sites on modern American poetry.

Auden Circle

For more on the Auden circle, see Derek Stanford's *Stephen Spender, Louis MacNeice, Cecil Day Lewis* (1969), Elton Edward Smith's *The Angry Young Men of the Thirties* (1975), A. T. Tolley's *The Poetry of the Thirties* (1975), Samuel Lynn Hynes's *The Auden Generation: Literature and Politics in England in the 1930s* (1976, 1992), Ronald Carter's *Thirties Poets: "The Auden Group"* (1984), B. K. Bhattacharyya's *W. H. Auden and Other Oxford Group of Poets* (1989), Michael O'Neill and Gareth Reeves's *Auden, MacNeice, Spender: The Thirties Poetry* (1992), and John Whitehead's *A Commentary on the Poetry of W. H. Auden, C. Day Lewis, Louis MacNeice, and Stephen Spender* (1992). See also **W. H. Auden, C. Day Lewis, Louis MacNeice, Stephen Spender.**

British Poetry

Works especially helpful for the study of modern British poetry include David Daiches's *Poetry and the Modern World* (1940), Lawrence Durrell's *A Key to Modern British Poetry* (1952), F. R. Leavis's *New Bearings in English Poetry* (1960), Robert H. Ross's *The Georgian Revolt, 1910–1922* (1965), John Press's *A Map of Modern English Verse* (1969), Donald Davie's *Thomas Hardy and British Poetry* (1972), Elton Edward Smith's *The Angry Young Men of the Thirties* (1975), A. T. Tolley's *The Poetry of the Thirties* (1975), Samuel Hynes's *The Auden Generation: Literature and Politics in England in the 1930s* (1976, 1992), Anthony Thwaite's *Twentieth-Century English Poetry* (1978), Philip Hobsbaum's *Tradition and Experiment in English Poetry* (1979), C. H. Sisson's *English Poetry, 1900–1950* (1981), John Williams's *Twentieth-Century British Poetry* (1987), Hugh Kenner's *A Sinking Island: The Modern English Writers* (1988), Richard Hoffpauir's *The Art of Restraint: English Poetry from Hardy to Larkin* (1991), Keith Tuma's *Fishing by Obstinate Isles: Modern and Postmodern British Poetry and American Readers* (1998), Rennie Parker's *The Georgian Poets* (1999), and James Persoon's *Modern British Poetry, 1900–1939* (1999).

The Fugitive Poets

For more on the Fugitive poets, see Louise Cowan's *The Fugitive Group* (1959), John L. Stewart's *The Burden of Time* (1965), Louis D. Rubin Jr.'s *The Wary Fugitives: Four Poets and the South* (1978), and Thomas A. Underwood's *Allen Tate: Orphan of the South* (2000). The group's magazine is collected and reprinted in *The Fugitive: A Journal of Poetry* (1966). See also **John Crowe Ransom, Laura Riding, Allen Tate, Robert Penn Warren.**

Gay and Lesbian Poetry

General studies dealing with gay and lesbian modern poetry include Robert K. Martin's *The Homosexual Tradition in Modern Poetry* (1979, 1998), Judy Grahn's *The Highest Apple: Sappho and the Lesbian Poetic Tradition* (1985), and Gregory Woods's *Articulate Flesh: Male Homo-Eroticism and Modern Poetry* (1987). Especially pertinent studies of particular poets include Thomas E. Yingling's *Hart Crane and the Homosexual Text* (1990), Diana Collecott's *H. D. and Sapphic Modernism, 1910–1950* (1999), Mary E. Galvin's *Queer Poetics: Five Modernist Women Writers* (1999), and Richard Bozorth's *Auden's Games of Knowledge: Poetry and the Meanings of Homosexuality* (2001).

Harlem Renaissance

For more on the Harlem Renaissance, see Stephen H. Bronz's *Roots of Negro Racial Consciousness* (1964); Nathan I. Huggins's *Harlem Renaissance* (1971); *The Harlem Renaissance Remembered* (1972), ed. Arna Bontemps; David Levering Lewis's *When Harlem Was in Vogue* (1981); *The Harlem Renaissance Re-Examined* (1987), ed. Victor A. Kramer; Houston A. Baker's *Modernism and the Harlem Renaissance* (1987); James De Jongh's *Vicious Modernism: Black Harlem and the Literary Imagination* (1990); George Hutchinson's *The Harlem Renaissance in Black and White* (1995); Cheryl A. Wall's *Women of the Harlem Renaissance* (1995); Richard J. Powell and David A. Bailey's *Rhapsodies in Black: Art of the Harlem Renaissance* (1997); and Lionel C. Bascom's *A Renaissance in Harlem* (1999). Alain Locke's *The New Negro* (1925) was seminal. Important anthologies include *Fire!!* (1926), ed. Wallace Thurman, and *Shadowed Dreams: Women's Poetry of the Harlem Renaissance* (1998), ed. Maureen Honey. Also useful are *The Portable Harlem Renaissance Reader* (1995), ed. Lewis, and *The Harlem Renaissance: A Historical Dictionary of the Era* (1984), ed. Bruce Kellner. See also **Sterling Brown, Countee Cullen, Langston Hughes, Claude McKay, Jean Toomer.**

Imagism

Helpful studies of Imagism include Glenn Hughes's *Imagism and the Imagists: A Study in Modern Poetry* (1931); Stanley K. Coffman's *Imagism: A Chapter for the History of Modern Poetry* (1951); *The Imagist Poem* (1963), ed. William Pratt; *Imagist Poetry*, ed. Peter Jones (1972); J. B. Harmer's *Victory in Limbo: Imagism, 1908–1917* (1975); John T. Gage's *In the*

Arresting Eye: The Rhetoric of Imagism (1981); *Homage to Imagism* (1992), ed. Pratt and Robert Richardson; and Ming Hsieh's *Ezra Pound and the Appropriation of Chinese Poetry: Cathay, Translation, and Imagism* (1999). Hugh Kenner's *The Pound Era* (1971) traces Pound's involvement in Imagism and Vorticism. An essential account of these movements in the development of early modernist doctrine is Michael Levenson's *A Genealogy of Modernism* (1984). See also **H. D., Amy Lowell, Ezra Pound.**

Irish Poetry

For more on modern Irish poetry, see Austin Clarke's *Poetry in Modern Ireland* (1951); Thomas Kinsella's *Davis, Mangan, Ferguson?: Tradition and the Irish Writer* (1970); Richard Fallis's *The Irish Renaissance* (1977); Hugh Kenner's *A Colder Eye* (1983); Seamus Deane's *Celtic Revivals* (1985) and *A Short History of Irish Literature* (1986); Robert F. Garratt's *Modern Irish Poetry* (1986); *Modernism and Ireland: The Poetry of the 1930s* (1995), ed. Patricia Coughlan and Alex Davis; Declan Kiberd's *Inventing Ireland* (1996); Neil Corcoran's *After Yeats and Joyce* (1997); A. Norman Jeffares's *The Irish Literary Movement* (1998); Gregory A. Schirmer's *Out of What Began: A History of Irish Poetry in English* (1998); Eamon Grennan's *Facing the Music: Irish Poetry in the Twentieth Century* (1999); Corcoran's *Poets of Modern Ireland: Text, Context, Intertext* (1999); Fran Brearton's *The Great War in Irish Poetry* (2000); Gregory Castle's *Modernism and the Celtic Revival* (2001); and Kiberd's *Irish Classics* (2001). See also **Austin Clarke, Patrick Kavanagh, Louis MacNeice, William Butler Yeats.**

The New Criticism and Poetry

For the original critical works in which the tenets of the New Criticism were worked out, see Laura Riding and Robert Graves's *A Survey of Modernist Poetry* (1927), John Crowe Ransom's *The New Criticism* (1941), William Empson's *Seven Types of Ambiguity* (1947), Cleanth Brooks's *The Well Wrought Urn* (1947) and his anthology *Understanding Poetry* (with Robert Penn Warren, 1938), W. K. Wimsatt and Monroe C. Beardsley's *The Verbal Icon* (1954), and Murray Krieger's *The New Apologists for Poetry* (1956). For critical discussions of the movement, see *The New Criticism and After* (1976), ed. Thomas Daniel Young; J. N. Patnaik's *The Aesthetics of the New Criticism* (1982); Robert Bechtold's *The Southern Connection* (1991); Mark Jancovich's *Cultural Politics of the New Criticism* (1993); Mark Royden Winchell's *Cleanth Brooks and the Rise of Modern Criticism* (1996); and Stephen Burt and Jennifer Lewin's "Poetry and the New Criticism," *A Companion to Twentieth-Century Poetry* (2001), ed. Neil Roberts. See also **William Empson, Robert Graves, John Crowe Ransom, Laura Riding, Allen Tate, Robert Penn Warren, Yvor Winters.**

Objectivism

Many excellent essays on Objectivism are available in the collection *The Objectivist Nexus* (1999), ed. Rachel Blau DuPlessis and Peter Quartermain. *Sagetrieb* is a journal dedicated to poetry in the Objectivist tradition. *An "Objectivists" Anthology* (1932), ed. Louis Zukofsky, is a landmark anthology. See also **Basil Bunting, Lorine Niedecker, George Oppen, Charles Reznikoff, Louis Zukofsky.**

Poets of World War I

Studies dealing with the poetry of World War I include John H. Johnston's *English Poetry of the First World War* (1964); Bernard Bergonzi's *Heroes' Twilight* (1965); Jon Silkin's *Out of Battle* (1972); Paul Fussell's *The Great War and Modern Memory* (1975); Desmond Graham's *The Truth of War: Owen, Rosenberg, and Blunden* (1984); Edna Longley's *Poetry in the Wars* (1987); Fred D. Crawford's *British Poets of the Great War* (1988); Robert Giddings's *The War Poets* (1988); Samuel Hynes's *A War Imagined* (1990); Patrick J. Quinn's *The Great War and the Missing Muse: The Early Writings of Robert Graves and Siegfried Sassoon* (1994); *War Poetry: An Introductory Reader* (1995), ed. Simon Featherstone; Allyson Booth's *Postcards from the Trenches* (1996); *British Poets of the Great War: Brooke, Rosenberg, Thomas* (2000), ed. Quinn; and Vincent Sherry's *The Great War and the Language of Modernism* (2003). A special issue of *Modernism / Modernity* 9.1 (2002) is devoted to "Men, Women and World War I." Anthologies include *Up the Line to Death: The War Poets, 1914–1918* (1964), ed. Brian Gardner; *Men Who March Away: Poems of the First World War* (1965), ed. I. M. Parsons; and *The Penguin Book of First World War Poetry* (1981), ed. Silkin. See also **Robert Graves, Ivor Gurney, David Jones, Wilfred Owen, Isaac Rosenberg, Siegfried Sassoon, Edward Thomas.**

Poets of World War II

For discussions of the poetry of World War II, see Vernon Scannell's *Not without Glory* (1976); Linda M. Shires's *British Poetry of the Second World War* (1985); Penny Pittman Merliss's *In Another Country: Three Poets of the Second World War* (1987); Edna Longley's *Poetry in the Wars* (1987); Susan Schweik's *A Gulf So Deeply Cut: American Women Poets and the Second World World War* (1991); Bernard Bergonzi's *Wartime and Aftermath* (1993); *War Poetry: An Introductory Reader* (1995), ed. Simon Featherstone; and Mark Rawlinson's *British Writing of the Second World War* (2000). Anthologies include *The Poetry of War 1939–45* (1965), ed. Ian Hamilton, and *The Terrible Rain: The War Poets, 1939–1945* (1966), ed. Brian Gardner. See also **Keith Douglas.**

San Francisco Renaissance

For discussions of the San Francisco Renaissance, see Daniel Aaron's *Writers on the Left: Episodes in American Literary Communism* (1961); Kenneth Rexroth's *American Poetry in the Twentieth Century* (1971); William Everson's *Archetype West: The Pacific Coast as a Literary Region* (1976); *Towards a New American Poetics* (1978), ed. Ekbert Faas; Lawrence Ferlinghetti and Nancy J. Peters's *Literary San Francisco* (1980); Michael McClure's *Scratching the Beat Surface* (1982); and Lee Bartlett's *The Sun Is but a Morning Star: Studies in West Coast Poetry and Poetics* (1989). See also **Kenneth Rexroth.**

Scottish Poetry

For discussions of Scottish poetry, see Duncan Glen's *Hugh MacDiarmid (Christopher Murray Grieve) and the Scottish Renaissance* (1964); *Edwin Muir: Uncollected Scottish Criticism* (1982), ed. Andrew Nobel; Glen's *The Poetry of the Scots: An Introduction and Bibliographical Guide to Poetry in Gaelic, Scots, Latin and English* (1991); and J. Derrick McClure's *Language, Poetry, and Nationhood: Scots as a Poetic Language from 1878 to the Present* (2000). Anthologies include *Modern Scottish Poetry* (1986), ed. Maurice Lindsay; *The Oxford Book of Scottish Verse* (1989), ed. John MacQueen and Tom Scott; *The Faber Book of Twentieth-Century Scottish Poetry* (1992), ed. Douglas Dunn; and *The New Penguin Book of Scottish Verse* (2000), ed. Robert Crawford and Mick Imlah. See also **Hugh MacDiarmid, Edwin Muir.**

Vorticism

For information on Vorticism, see Hugh Kenner's *The Pound Era* (1971); William Wees's *Vorticism and the English Avant-Garde* (1972); Richard Cork's *Vorticism and Abstract Art in the First Machine Age* (1976); Timothy Materer's *Vortex: Pound, Eliot, and Lewis* (1979); Michael Levenson's *A Genealogy of Modernism* (1984); Peter Nicholls's *Modernisms* (1995); *Blast: Vorticism 1914–1918* (2000), ed. Paul Edwards; and Paul Peppis's *Literature, Politics, and the English Avant-Garde* (2000). See also **Ezra Pound.**

W. H. Auden

Edward Mendelson has edited *Collected Poems* (1976, rev. 1991), *Selected Poems* (1979), and *The English Auden: Poems, Essays, and Dramatic Writings, 1927–1939* (1977). He is also the general editor of the definitive series of Auden's complete works, which includes *Plays and Other Dramatic Writings by W. H. Auden, 1928–1938* (1988); *W. H. Auden and Chester Kallman: Libretti and Other Dramatic Writings by W. H. Auden, 1939–1973* (1993); *Prose and Travel Books in Prose and Verse: Volume I, 1926–1938* (1996); and *Prose: Volume II, 1939–1948*. *Juvenilia: Poems, 1922–1928* (1994), ed. Katherine Bucknell, contains Auden's earliest work and appeared in an expanded edition in 2003. *"The Dyer's Hand" and Other Essays* (1962) is an essential collection of his lectures and essays. Other such collections include *Forewords and Afterwords* (1973) and two posthumous editions: *"In Solitude, for Company": W. H. Auden after 1940* (1995), ed. Bucknell and Nicholas Jenkins, and *Lectures on Shakespeare* (2000), ed. Arthur C. Kirsch. Auden also edited poetry anthologies, including *The Oxford Book of Light Verse* (1938) and *Poets of the English Language* (with Norman Holmes Pearson, 1950). Biographies include Humphrey Carpenter's *W. H. Auden* (1981) and R. P. T. Davenport-Hines's *Auden* (1995).

For helpful glosses on individual poems, see John Fuller's *W. H. Auden: A Commentary* (1998). Useful books of criticism include Monroe K. Spears's *The Poetry of W. H. Auden* (1963), Justin Replogle's *Auden's Poetry* (1969), Samuel Hynes's *The Auden Generation* (1976, 1992), Mendelson's *Early Auden* (1981) and *Later Auden* (1999), Edward Callan's *Auden: A Carnival of Intellect* (1983), Stan Smith's *W. H. Auden* (1985), Lucy McDiarmid's *Auden's Apologies for Poetry* (1990), John R. Boly's *Reading Auden: The Returns of Caliban* (1991), Anthony Hecht's *The Hidden Law* (1993), Marsha Bryant's *Auden and Documentary in the 1930s* (1997), Rainer Emig's *W. H. Auden: Towards a Postmodern Poetics* (2000), Richard R. Bozorth's *Auden's Games of Knowledge: Poetry and the Meanings of Homosexuality* (2001), and Peter Edgerly Firchow's *W. H. Auden: Contexts for Poetry* (2002). Useful essays are collected in *Auden: A Collection of Critical Essays* (1964), ed. Monroe K. Spears, and *Critical Essays on W. H. Auden* (1991), ed. George W. Bahlke. *W. H. Auden: The Critical Heritage* (1983), ed. John Haffenden, traces Auden's critical reception and provides contemporary reviews. The standard bibliography is B. C. Bloomfield and Mendelson's *W. H. Auden: A Bibliography 1924–1969* (1972) and is updated in *Auden Studies* (1990–95), ed. Katherine Bucknell and Nicholas Jenkins. See also the **Auden Circle.**

John Betjeman

Betjeman's *Collected Poems* was first published in 1958 and expanded in 1962 and 1970. Other volumes include *A Nip in the Air* (1974); *The Best of Betjeman* (1978), ed. John Guest; *Church Poems* (illustrations John Piper, 1981); and *Uncollected Poems* (1982). He also wrote extensively on English architecture in works including *Ghastly Good Taste; or, A Depressing Story of the Rise and Fall of English Architecture* (1933), *First and Last Loves* (1952), and *A Pictorial History of English Architecture* (1972). Candida Lycett Green has edited Betjeman's *Letters* (1994) and *Coming Home* (1997), a selection of his prose. Biographical works include Frank Delaney's *Betjeman Country* (1983), Patrick Taylor-Martin's *John Betjeman, His Life and Work* (1983), and Bevis Hillier's *John Betjeman: A Life in Pictures* (1984) and *Young Betjeman* (1988).

Studies include Derek Stanford's *John Betjeman: A Study* (1961), Jocelyn Brooke's *Ronald Firbank and John Betjeman* (1962), John Press and Ian Scott-Kilvert's *John Betjeman* (1974), Geoffrey Harvey's *The Romantic Tradition in Modern English Poetry* (1986), and Dennis Brown's *John Betjeman* (1999). A bibliography is Margaret L. Stapleton's *Sir John Betjeman: A Bibliography of Works by and about Him* (1974).

Louise Bogan

Collections of Bogan's verse include *Collected Poems, 1923–1953* (1954) and *The Blue Estuaries: Poems, 1923–1968* (1968). Other work appears in *Uncollected Poetry and Prose* (1975), ed. David Stivender and Marshall Clements. Her criticism can be found in her *Achievement in American Poetry, 1900–1950* (1951), *Selected Criticism* (1955), *Emily Dickinson: Three Views* (with Archibald MacLeish and Richard Wilbur, 1960), and *A Poet's Alphabet: Reflections on the Literary Art and Vocation* (1970). *What the Woman Lived* (1973), ed. Ruth Limmer, is a selection of letters. Limmer also edited a collection of Bogan's autobiographical writings, *Journey Around My Room: The Autobiography of Louise Bogan, A Mosaic* (1980).

Elizabeth Frank's biography, *Louise Bogan: A Portrait* (1985), analyzes the poet's life and work. *Critical Essays on Louise Bogan* (1984), ed. Martha Collins, is an extensive collection. Other studies include Jaqueline Ridgeway's *Louise Bogan* (1984), Gloria Bowles's *Louise Bogan's Aesthetic of Limitation* (1987), Elizabeth Dodd's *The Veiled Mirror and the Woman Poet* (1992), and Lee Upton's *Obsession and Release: Rereading the Poetry of Louise Bogan* (1996). Two bibliographies are Jane Couchman's "Louise Bogan: A Bibliography of Primary and Secondary Materials, 1915–1975," *Bulletin of Bibliography* 2–3 (1976), and Claire Knox's *Louise Bogan: A Reference Source* (1990).

Sterling Brown

The Collected Poems of Sterling A. Brown, ed. Michael S. Harper, was published in 1980. A selection of essays is *A Son's Return* (1996), ed. Mark A. Sanders. Brown's important critical works include *Outline for the Study of Poetry of American Negroes* (1931), *The Negro in American Fiction* (1937), and *Negro Poetry and Drama* (1937). Brown also coedited a Harlem Renaissance anthology, *The Negro Caravan* (with Arthur P. Davis and Ulysses G. Lee, 1941).

Two book-length studies are Joanne V. Gabbin's *Sterling A. Brown: Building the Black Aesthetic Tradition* (1985) and Sanders's *Afro-Modernist Aesthetics and the Poetry of Sterling A. Brown* (1999). *Callaloo* 5 (1982) and *Black American Literature Forum* 23 (1989) are special Brown issues. Other works in which Brown is discussed are Houston A. Baker's *Long Black Song* (1972); Jean Wagner's *Black Poets of the United States* (1973); Stephen Henderson's *Understanding the New Black Poetry* (1973); *Sterling A. Brown: A UMUM Tribute* (1976), ed. Black History Museum Collective; Henry Louis Gates Jr.'s *Figures in Black* (1987); and *The Harlem Renaissance Re-Examined* (1987), ed. Victor Kramer and Robert Russ. A bibliography by Robert G. O'Meally appears in *Callaloo* 5 (1982). See also **Harlem Renaissance.**

Basil Bunting

Bunting's *Complete Poems*, ed. Richard Caddel, was published in 1994. Interviews are collected in Jonathan Williams's *Descant on Rawthey's Madrigal* (1968). Bunting's critical works include *Three Essays* (1994), ed. Caddel, and *Basil Bunting on Poetry* (1999), ed. Peter Makin. Bunting also edited Ford Madox Ford's *Selected Poems* (1971) and *Selected Poems of Joseph Skipsey* (1976). Also of note is *Madeira and Toasts for Basil Bunting's 75th Birthday* (1977), ed. Jonathan Williams. Biographies include Richard Caddel and Anthony Flowers's *Basil Bunting: A Northern Life* (1997) and Keith Alldritt's *The Poet as Spy* (1998).

Critical studies include Alldritt's *Modernism in the Second World War* (1989), Victoria Forde's *The Poetry of Basil Bunting* (1991), and Peter Makin's *Bunting: The Shaping of his Verse* (1992). Many useful essays are collected in *Basil Bunting: Man and Poet* (1981), ed. Carroll F. Terrell, and *The Star You Steer By: Basil Bunting and British Modernism* (2000), ed. James McGonigal and Richard Price. *Agenda* 16.1 (1978) and *Conjunctions* 8 (1985) are special Bunting issues. Roger Guedalla's *Basil Bunting: A Bibliography of Works and Criticism* was published in 1973. See also **Objectivism.**

Austin Clarke

Clarke's *Collected Poems*, ed. Liam Miller, appeared in 1974. Clarke's works of fiction include the prose romances *The Bright Temptation* (1932), *The Singing-Men at Cashel* (1936), and *The Sun Dances at Easter* (1952). Dramatic works include *Collected Plays* (1963) and *The Impuritans* (1973). He also published works of criticism, including *Poetry in Modern Ireland* (1951) and *The Celtic Twilight and the Nineties* (1969). *Reviews and Essays of Austin Clarke*, ed. Gregory A. Schirmer, was published in 1992. Clarke's autobiographical writings include *First Visit to England and Other Memories* (1945), *Twice Round the Black Church* (1962), and *A Penny in the Clouds* (1968). Biographical information is available in Susan Halpern's *Austin Clarke: His Life and Works* (1974).

Critical studies include G. Craig Tapping's *Austin Clarke: A Study of his Writings* (1981), Gregory Schirmer's *The Poetry of Austin Clarke* (1983), and Maurice Harmon's *Austin Clarke, 1896–1974: A Critical Introduction* (1989). Also useful are the collection *A Tribute to Austin Clarke on his Seventieth Birthday* (1966), ed. John Montague and Liam Miller, and Seamus Heaney and R. Dardis Clarke's *Austin Clarke Remembered* (1996). *Irish University Review* published an Austin Clarke issue in 1974. Bibliographic information is available in Lorraine Ricigliano's *Austin Clarke: A Reference Guide* (1993). See also **Irish Poetry.**

Hart Crane

The Complete Poems of Hart Crane (1986, 2000), ed. Marc Simon, is the standard text. Also useful is *The Complete Poems and Selected Letters and Prose of Hart Crane* (1966), ed. Brom Weber. Correspondence is collected in *O My Land, My Friends: The Selected Letters of Hart Crane* (1997), ed. Langdon Hammer and Weber, which includes an illuminating introduction; *Letters, 1916–1932* (1952), ed. Weber; and *Robber Rocks: Letters and Memories of Hart Crane, 1923–1932* (1969), ed. Susan Jenkins Brown. Biographies include John Unterecker's *Voyager: A Life of Hart Crane* (1969), Paul Mariani's *The Broken Tower* (1999), and Clive Fisher's *Hart Crane* (2002).

Useful studies include Samuel Hazo's *Hart Crane* (1963), Vincent Gerard Quinn's *Hart Crane* (1963), Monroe K. Spears's *Hart Crane* (1965), Hunce Voelcker's *The Hart Crane Voyages* (1967), R. W. B. Lewis's *The Poetry of Hart Crane* (1967), R. W. Butterfield's *The Broken Arc* (1969), Samuel Hazo's *Smithereened Apart: A Critique of Hart Crane* (1977), Lee Edelman's *Transmemberment of Song* (1987), Maria F. Bennett's *Unfractioned Idiom: Hart Crane and Modernism* (1987), Warner Berthoff's *Hart Crane: A Re-Introduction* (1989), Thomas Yingling's *Hart Crane and the Homosexual Text* (1990), and Langdon Hammer's *Hart Crane and Allen Tate: Janus-Faced Modernism* (1993). Robert K. Martin's *The Homosexual Tradition in American Poetry* (1979, 1998) also contains an important discussion of Crane's work. Works helpful for studying *The Bridge* include Sherman Paul's *Hart's Bridge* (1972), Margaret Dickie's *Hart Crane: The Patterns of His Poetry* (1974), Richard P. Sugg's *Hart Crane's* The Bridge (1976), Edward Brunner's *Splendid Failure: Hart Crane and the Making of* The Bridge (1985), and Paul Giles's *Hart Crane: The Contexts of* The Bridge (1986). Collections of essays include *Critical Essays on Hart Crane* (1982), ed. David Clark; *Hart Crane: A Collection of Critical Essays* (1982), ed. Alan Trachtenberg; and *Hart Crane* (1986), ed. Harold Bloom. Also useful is Gary Lane's *A Concordance to the Poems of Hart Crane* (1972). Bibliographic information is available in *Hart Crane: An Annotated Critical Bibliography* (1970), ed. Joseph Schwartz; *Hart Crane: A Descriptive Bibliography* (1972), ed. Schwartz and Robert C. Schweik; and *Hart Crane: A Reference Guide* (1983), ed. Schwartz.

Countee Cullen

Cullen's volumes of poetry include *Color* (1925); *The Ballad of the Brown Girl* (1927); *Copper Sun* (1927); *"The Black Christ" and Other Poems* (1929); *One Way to Heaven* (1932); *"The Medea" and Some Poems* (1935); *On These I Stand: An Anthology of the Best Poems of Countee Cullen* (1947); and *My Soul's High Song: The Collected Writings of Countee Cullen, Voice of the Harlem Renaissance* (1991), ed. Gerald Early. He also wrote a novel, *One Way to Heaven* (1932); children's stories, *The Lost Zoo* (1940) and *My Lives and How I Lost Them* (1942); and plays, including *St. Louis Woman* (with Arna Bontemps, 1945). And he edited the Harlem Renaissance poetry anthology *Caroling Dusk* (1927). Biographies include Blanche E. Ferguson's *Countee Cullen and the Negro Renaissance* (1966) and Margaret Perry's *A Bio-Bibliography of Countée P. Cullen, 1903–1946* (1959).

Important book-length studies of Cullen include Houston A. Baker's *A Many-Colored Coat of Dreams* (1974) and Alan R. Shucard's *Countee Cullen* (1984). Other important discussions of his work can be found in J. Saunders Redding's *To Make A Poet Black* (1939), Stephen H. Bronz's *Roots of Negro Racial Consciousness* (1964), Darwin T. Turner's *In a Minor Chord* (1971), Jean Wagner's *Black Poets of the United States* (1973), and Arthur P. Davis's *From the Dark Tower* (1974). See also **Harlem Renaissance.**

E. E. Cummings

Cummings's *Complete Poems, 1904–1962*, ed. George J. Firmage, appeared in 1991. Firmage also edited *Three Plays and a Ballet* (1967) as well as Cummings's *Uncollected Poems* and, with Richard S. Kennedy, *The Unpublished Poems*, the latter two published together as *Etcetera* (2000). Cummings's works of fiction include *The Enormous Room* (1922) and *EIMI* (1933). Short prose works can also be found in *E. E. Cummings: A Miscellany Revisited* (1965), ed. Firmage. Cummings also published translations, including Louis Aragon's *The Red Front* (1933). In addition, Firmage has edited several editions of works in Cummings's original typescripts, including *Tulips and Chimneys* (1976), *No Thanks* (1978), *The Enormous Room* (with Cummings's illustrations, 1978), *ViVa* (1979), and *XAIPE* (1979). *Six Nonlectures* (1953) collects Cummings's 1953 Harvard talk series. *Selected Letters of E. E. Cummings* (1969) was edited by F. W. Dupee and George Stade. Also of interest is *The Correspondence of Ezra Pound and E. E. Cummings* (1996), ed. Barry Ahearn. A biography is Richard S. Kennedy's *Dreams in the Mirror* (1979).

Important studies include Norman Friedman's *E. E. Cummings: The Art of His Poetry* (1960) and his *E. E. Cummings: The Growth of a Writer* (1964), Barry A. Marks's *E. E. Cummings* (1964), Robert E. Wegner's *E. E. Cummings* (1965), Bethany K. Dumas's *E. E. Cummings: A Remembrance of Miracles* (1974), Gary Lane's *I Am: A Study of E. E. Cummings' Poems* (1976), Rushworth Kidder's *E. E. Cummings: An Introduction to the Poetry* (1979), Milton A. Cohen's *Poet and Painter: The Aesthetics of E. E. Cummings' Early Work* (1987), Richard S. Kennedy's *E. E. Cummings Revisited* (1994), Michael Webster's *Reading Visual Poetry after Futurism* (1995), and Martin Heusser's *I Am My Writing* (1997). Other useful work is available in *E. E. Cummings: A Collection of Critical Essays* (1972) and *(Re)Valuing Cummings* (1996), both edited by Norman Friedman, and *Critical Essays on E. E. Cummings* (1984), ed. Guy Rotella. *E. E. Cummings: A Bibliography*, ed. Firmage, was published in 1960.

C. Day Lewis

The Complete Poems of C. Day Lewis, ed. Jill Balcon, appeared in 1992. Under the penname Nicholas Blake, Day Lewis also wrote an immensely popular series of mystery novels, including *A Question of Proof* (1935). In addition, he translated the works of Virgil. Works of critical prose include *A Hope for Poetry* (1934) and the lectures collected in *The Poetic Image* (1947) and *The Lyric Impulse* (1965). His autobiography, *The Buried Day*, was published in 1960. Day Lewis and Auden edited and wrote a preface for the anthology *Oxford Poetry 1927* (1927). Sean Day-Lewis's biography, *C. Day-Lewis: An English Literary Life*, was published in 1980.

Albert Gelpi's book-length study *Living in Time: The Poetry of C. Day Lewis* (1998) is an excellent overview of the poet's work. See also Clifford Dyment's *C. Day Lewis* (1955) and J. N. Riddel's *C. Day Lewis* (1971). Recent critical essays include Walter Nash's "The Lyrical Game: C. Day Lewis's 'Last Words,' " *Twentieth Century Poetry: From Text to Context* (1993), ed. Peter Verdonk; and Gelpi's "Reading C. Day Lewis" and Eavan Boland's "A Lyric Voice at Bay," both in *Pn Review* 24 (1998). Much of the important work on Day Lewis occurs within discussions of the group of poets identified with Auden in the 1930s. See especially Elton Edward Smith's chapter on Day Lewis in his *The Angry Young Men of the Thirties* (1975); A. T. Tolley's *The Poetry of the Thirties* (1975); and John Whitehead's *A Commentary on the Poetry of W. H. Auden, C. Day Lewis, Louis MacNeice, and Stephen Spender* (1992). See also the **Auden Circle.**

Emily Dickinson

The three-volume *Poems of Emily Dickinson* (1955) was edited by Thomas H. Johnson. Also essential is *The Manuscript Books of Emily Dickinson* (1980), ed. R. W. Franklin, which reproduces the original, handwritten fascicles of the poems, the textual ambiguities of which can be lost in other typographic editions. Franklin also published the important *The Editing of Emily Dickinson: A Reconsideration* (1967) and edited *The Master Letters of Emily Dickinson* (1986). Other documents of biographical interest are collected in Jay Leyda's *The Years and Hours of Emily Dickinson* (1960); Vivian Pollak's *A Poet's Parents: The Courtship Letters of Emily Norcross and Edward Dickinson* (1988); Polly Longsworth's *The World of Emily Dickinson* (1990); and *Open Me Carefully: Emily Dickinson's Intimate Letters to Susan Huntington Dickinson* (1998), ed. Ellen Louise Hart and Martha Nell Smith. The standard biography is Richard B. Sewall's *The Life of Emily Dickinson* (1974). Other biographies of note are Cynthia Griffin Wolff's *Emily Dickinson* (1986) and Alfred Habegger's *My Wars Are Laid Away in Books* (2001).

Important studies include Millicent Bingham's *Ancestors' Brocades: The Literary Debut of Emily Dickinson* (1945), Charles R. Anderson's *Emily Dickinson's Poetry: Stairway to Surprise* (1960), Albert Gelpi's *Emily Dickinson: The Mind of the Poet* (1965), Jack L. Capps's *Emily Dickinson's Reading* (1966), John Cody's *After Great Pain* (1971), Joanne Feit Diehl's *Dickinson and the Romantic Imagination* (1981), Vivian R. Pollak's *Dickinson: The Anxiety of Gender* (1984), Barton Levi St. Armand's *Emily Dickinson and Her Culture* (1984), Jane Donahue Eberwein's *Dickinson: Strategies of Limitation* (1985), Susan Howe's *My Emily Dickinson* (1985), Gary Lee Stonum's *The Dickinson Sublime* (1990), Judith Farr's *The Passion of Emily*

Dickinson (1992), Martha Nell Smith's *Rowing in Eden: Rereading Emily Dickinson* (1992), Sharon Cameron's *Choosing, Not Choosing: Dickinson's Fascicles* (1993), Elizabeth Petrino's *Emily Dickinson and Her Contemporaries: Women's Verse in America, 1820–1885* (1998), James Guthrie's *Emily Dickinson's Vision: Illness and Identity in Her Poetry* (1998), Domhnall Mitchell's *Emily Dickinson: Monarch of Perception* (2000), and James McIntosh's *Nimble Believing* (2000). Collections of essays include *Critical Essays on Emily Dickinson* (1984), ed. Paul J. Ferlazzo; *Emily Dickinson: A Collection of Critical Essays* (1996), ed. Judith Farr; and *Dickinson and Audience* (1996), ed. Martin Orzeck and Robert Weisbuch.

Useful reference materials are S. P. Rosenbaum's *A Concordance to the Poems of Emily Dickinson* (1964), Joel Myerson's *Emily Dickinson: A Descriptive Bibliography* (1984), Eberwein's *An Emily Dickinson Encyclopedia* (1998), and Cynthia J. MacKenzie and Penny Gilbert's *Concordance to the Letters of Emily Dickinson* (2000).

Keith Douglas

The Complete Poems of Keith Douglas, ed. Desmond Graham, appeared in 1977. Graham also edited *A Prose Miscellany* (1985) and *The Letters* (2000). Other work includes the war narrative *Alemein to Zem Zem* (1946). Graham's biography, *Keith Douglas, 1920–1944*, was published in 1974.

Studies include Penny Pittman Merliss's *In Another Country: Three Poets of the Second World War* (1987), William Scammell's *Keith Douglas* (1988), and David Masson's *Keith Douglas's Phonetic Rhetoric and Phonetic Lyricism* (1991). Also of interest are Ted Hughes's "The Poetry of Keith Douglas," *Critical Quarterly* 5.1 (1963); Geoffrey Hill's " 'I in Another Place': Homage to Keith Douglas," *Stand* 6.4 (1964); Reginald Gibbon's "A Sharp Enquiring Blade," *Parnassus* 9 (1981); David L. Jones's "To Write True Things: The Metaphysical Realism of Keith Douglas,' *Odyssey* 11.1–2 (1989); Mark I. Goldman's "Keith Douglas: War Poetry as 'Significant Speech,' " *Durham University Journal* 51.2 (1990); and Peter Scupham's "Keith Douglas," *Pn Review* 25.1 (1998). Also of note is Vernon Scannell's *Not without Glory: Poets of the Second World War* (1976). See also **Poets of World War II.**

Richard Eberhart

Eberhart's *Collected Poems, 1930–1986* appeared in 1988. Subsequent volumes include *Maine Poems* (1989) and *New and Selected Poems, 1930–1990* (1990), ed. Jay Parini. Eberhart also wrote plays, several of which have been published together as *Collected Verse Plays* (1962). His critical works include the lecture *Poetry as a Creative Principle* (1952) and *Of Poetry and Poets* (1979). Interviews appear in *Shenandoah* 15.4 (1964) and *American Poetry Review* 6.3 (1977).

Book-length studies of Eberhart's work include Ralph J. Mills's *Richard Eberhart* (1966), Bernard F. Engel's *Richard Eberhart* (1971), and Joel Roache's *Richard Eberhart: The Progress of an American Poet* (1971). Several useful essays appear in *Richard Eberhart: A Celebration* (1980), ed. Sydney Lea, Jay Parini, and M. Robin Barone. *Negative Capability* 6.2–3 (1986) is a special Eberhart issue and includes an interview. Other critical essays include Peter Thorslev's "The Poetry of Richard Eberhart," *Poets in Progress* (1962), ed. Edward Hungerford; and Cleanth Brooks's "A Tribute to Richard Eberhart," *South Atlantic Quarterly* 50.4 (1985). Also of note is *To Eberhart from Ginsberg: A Letter about "Howl," 1956* (1976), which prints correspondence surrounding Ginsberg's poem and Eberhart's *New York Times* article "West Coast Rhythms." *Richard Eberhart: A Descriptive Bibliography, 1921–1987*, compiled by Stuart T. Wright, Charles C. Lovett, and Stephanie Lovett Stoffel, was published in 1989.

T. S. Eliot

The *Complete Poems and Plays of T. S. Eliot* was published in 1969. *Inventions of the March Hare: Poems, 1909–1917*, ed. Christopher Ricks, brought early, unpublished work to light in 1996. The fascinating manuscripts of *The Waste Land* are available as *The Waste Land: A Facsimile and Transcript of the Original Drafts Including the Annotations of Ezra Pound* (1971), ed. Valerie Eliot. Also immensely useful is the Norton Critical Edition of *The Waste Land* (2001), ed. Michael North, which contains contextual documents and criticism in addition to the poem. A selection of Eliot's most important critical writings is available in *Selected Prose of T. S. Eliot* (1975), ed. Frank Kermode. Important biographies include Peter Ackroyd's *T. S. Eliot: A Life* (1984) and Lyndall Gordon's *T. S. Eliot: An Imperfect Life* (1998). Also helpful is *The Letters of T. S. Eliot, Vol. I: 1898–1922* (1988), ed. Valerie Eliot.

Influential early studies include F. O. Matthiessen's *The Achievement of T. S. Eliot* (rev. 1947), Helen Gardner's *The Art of T. S. Eliot* (1950), Hugh Kenner's *The Invisible Poet* (1959), and Northrop Frye's *T. S. Eliot* (1963). Other important studies include Grover Smith's *T. S. Eliot's Poetry and Plays: A Study in Sources and Meanings* (1956), Bernard Bergonzi's *T. S. Eliot* (1972, 1978), Helen Gardner's *The Composition of* Four Quartets (1978), David Moody's *Thomas Stearns Eliot, Poet* (1979), Ronald Bush's *T. S. Eliot: A Study in Character and Style* (1984), Calvin Bedient's *He Do the Police in Different Voices* (1986), Louis Menand's *Dis-*

covering Modernism (1987), Maud Ellmann's *The Poetics of Impersonality* (1987), Richard Shusterman's *T. S. Eliot and the Philosophy of Criticism* (1988), Christopher Ricks's *T. S. Eliot and Prejudice* (1988), Eric Sigg's *The American T. S. Eliot: A Study of the Early Writings* (1989), Jewel Spears Brooker and Joseph Bentley's *Reading* The Waste Land (1990); Michael North's *The Political Aesthetic of Yeats, Eliot, and Pound* (1991), Brooker's *Mastery and Escape: T. S. Eliot and the Dialectic of Modernism* (1994), Anthony Julius's *T. S. Eliot, Anti-Semitism and Literary Form* (1995), Harriet Davidson's *T. S. Eliot* (1999), Ronald Schuchard's *Eliot's Dark Angel: Intersections of Life and Art* (1999), Denis Donoghue's *Words Alone* (2000), and Donald J. Childs's *From Philosophy to Poetry* (2001). Useful collection of essays are *T. S. Eliot: A Collection of Criticism* (1974), ed. Linda Wagner-Martin; *T. S. Eliot: The Modernist in History* (1991), ed. Ronald Bush; *T. S. Eliot, A Voice Descanting* (1990), ed. Shyamal Bagchee; *The Cambridge Companion to T. S. Eliot* (1994), ed. David Moody; and *T. S. Eliot and Our Turning World* (2001), ed. Jewel Spears Brooker.

T. S. Eliot: The Critical Heritage (1982), ed. Michael Grant, provides a reception history and contemporary reviews. *A Concordance to the Complete Poems and Plays of* T. S. Eliot, ed. J. L. Dawson et al., was published in 1995. A bibliography is Donald C. Gallup's *T. S. Eliot: A Bibliography* (rev. 1969).

William Empson

The Complete Poems of William Empson, ed. John Haffenden, was published in 2000. Works in which Empson made landmark contributions to the history of literary criticism include *Seven Types of Ambiguity* (1930, 1947), *Some Versions of Pastoral* (1935), *The Structure of Complex Words* (1951), and *Milton's God* (1961, 1965). Also of note are *Using Biography* (1984), *Essays on Shakespeare* (1986), *"The Royal Beasts" and Other Works* (1986), *Argufying* (1987), *Essays on Renaissance Literature* (1993), and *The Strengths of Shakespeare's Shrew* (1996).

Critical work on Empson includes J. H. Willis Jr.'s *William Empson* (1969), Philip and Averil Gardner's *The God Approached* (1978), Christopher Norris's *William Empson and the Philosophy of Literary Criticism* (1978), Paul H. Fry's *William Empson: Prophet against Sacrifice* (1991), and the collections *Modern Heroism: Essays on D. H. Lawrence, William Empson, and J. R. R. Tolkien* (1973), ed. Roger Sale; *William Empson: The Man and His Work* (1974), ed. Roma Gill; *Critical Essays on William Empson* (1993), ed. John Constable, and *William Empson: The Critical Achievement* (1993), ed. Norris and Nigel Mapp. Other critical essays include Haffenden's "The Importance of Empson (I): The Poems," *Essays in Criticism* 35.1 (1985) and Paul Dean's "The Critic as Poet: Empson's Contradictions," *New Criterion* 20.2 (2001). Frank Day's *Sir William Empson: An Annotated Bibliography* was published in 1984. See also **The New Criticism and Poetry**.

Robert Frost

The Library of America edition of Frost's *Collected Poems, Prose and Plays* (1995) contains Frost's complete poetry and selections from his drama and prose. Other important collections are *Selected Prose* (1966), ed. Hyde Cox and Edward Connery, and *Robert Frost on Writing* (1973), ed. Elaine Barry. Frost's correspondence is available in *Selected Letters of Robert Frost* (1964), ed. Lawrance Thompson; *The Letters of Robert Frost to Louis Untermeyer* (1963); and *Family Letters of Robert and Elinor Frost* (1972), ed. Arnold Grade. Interviews appear in Reginald L. Cook's *The Dimensions of Robert Frost* (1958), Daniel Smythe's *Robert Frost Speaks* (1964), Louis Mertins's *Robert Frost: Life and Talks-Walking* (1965), and Edward C. Lathem's *Interviews with Robert Frost* (1966). The first two volumes of the authorized biography, *Robert Frost: The Early Years, 1874–1915* (1966) and *Robert Frost: The Years of Triumph, 1915–1938* (1970), were written by Lawrance Thompson. Richard Winnick completed the third volume, *Robert Frost: The Later Years, 1938–1963* (1976). Other biographies include Lathem's *Robert Frost* (1981), Jeffrey Meyers's *Robert Frost* (1996), and Jay Parini's *Robert Frost: A Life* (1999).

Critical studies include Reuben Brower's *The Poetry of Robert Frost: Constellations of Intention* (1963), Frank Lentricchia's *Robert Frost: Modern Poetics and the Landscapes of Self* (1975), Richard Poirier's *Robert Frost: The Work of Knowing* (1977, 1990), John C. Kemp's *Robert Frost and New England* (1979), George Monteiro's *Robert Frost and the New England Renaissance* (1988), Mario D'Avanzo's *A Cloud of Other Poets: Robert Frost and the Romantics* (1990), Mordecai Marcus's *The Poems of Robert Frost* (1991), Judith Oster's *Toward Robert Frost* (1991), George Bagby's *Frost and the Book of Nature* (1993), Katherine Kearns's *Robert Frost and a Poetics of Appetite* (1994), Karen L. Kilcup's *Robert Frost and the Feminine Literary Tradition* (1998), Tyler Hoffman's *Robert Frost and the Politics of Poetry* (2001), and Robert Bernard Hass's *Going by Contraries: Robert Frost's Conflict with Science* (2002). Useful critical essays are available in the collections *Recognition of Robert Frost* (1937), ed. Richard Thornton; *Robert Frost: Studies of the Poetry* (1979), ed. Kathryn Gibbs Harris; *Critical Essays on Robert Frost* (1982), ed. Philip L. Gerber; *Robert Frost* (1986), ed. Harold Bloom; *On Frost* (1991), ed. Edwin Cady and Louis J. Budd;

Roads Not Taken (2000), ed. Earl J. Wilcox and Jonathan N. Barron; *The Robert Frost Encyclopedia* (2001), ed. Nancy Lewis Tuten and John Zubizarreta; and *The Cambridge Companion to Robert Frost* (2001), ed. Robert Faggen. Edward C. Lathem's *Concordance to the Poetry of Robert Frost* was published in 1971. Bibliographic information is available in Lentricchia's *Robert Frost: A Bibliography, 1913–1974* (1976) and James L. Potter's *Robert Frost Handbook* (1980).

Robert Graves

Graves's *Complete Poems*, ed. Beryl Graves and Dunstan Ward, was published in three volumes in 1995, 1997, and 1999. His *Complete Short Stories*, ed. Lucia Graves, was published in 1996. A selection of Graves's criticism is *Collected Writings on Poetry* (1995), ed. Paul O'Prey. Other important prose works include *On English Poetry* (1922), *The Meaning of Dreams* (1924), *A Survey of Modernist Poetry* (with Laura Riding, 1927), *The White Goddess* (1948), *The Common Asphodel: Collected Essays on Poetry, 1922–1949* (1949), and *On Poetry* (1969). Graves also published many historical novels, including *I, Claudius* (1934), *Wife to Mr. Milton* (1943), and *Homer's Daughter* (1955). Interviews are collected in *Conversations with Robert Graves* (1989), ed. Frank Kersnowski. Letters are selected in *In Broken Images: Selected Letters of Robert Graves, 1914–1946* (1982), ed. O'Prey; *Between Moon and Moon: Selected Letters of Robert Graves, 1946–1972* (1984), ed. O'Prey; and *Dear Robert, Dear Spike: The Graves–Milligan Correspondence* (1991), ed. Pauline Scudamore. Graves's autobiography, *Good-Bye to All That,* was published in 1929. Biographies include Martin Seymour-Smith's *Robert Graves: His Life and Work* (1982), Miranda Seymour's *Robert Graves: Life on the Edge* (1995), and Richard Perceval Graves's three-volume *Robert Graves* (1986–90).

Critical studies include Seymour-Smith's *Robert Graves* (1956), J. M. Cohen's *Robert Graves* (1960), Douglas Day's *Swifter than Reason: The Poetry and Criticism of Robert Graves* (1963), George Stade's *Robert Graves* (1967), Michael Kirkham's *The Poetry of Robert Graves* (1969), John B. Vickery's *Robert Graves and the White Goddess* (1972), James S. Mehoke's *Robert Graves: Peace-Weaver* (1975), Katherine Snipes's *Robert Graves* (1979), Patrick J. Keane's *A Wild Civility: Interactions in the Poetry and Thought of Robert Graves* (1980), D. N. G. Carter's *Robert Graves: The Lasting Poetic Achievement* (1989), Patrick J. Quinn's *The Great War and the Missing Muse* (1994), and Frank L. Kersnowski's *The Early Poetry of Robert Graves* (2002).

Collections of essays include *Robert Graves* (1987), ed. Harold Bloom, and *New Perspectives on Robert Graves* (1999), ed. Quinn. An updated version of Fred H. Higginson's *A Bibliography of the Writings of Robert Graves* was published in 1987. See also **The New Criticism and Poetry.**

Ivor Gurney

During his lifetime, Gurney published two volumes: *Severn and Somme* (1917) and *War's Embers* (1919). *Collected Poems of Ivor Gurney* (1982), ed. P. J. Kavanagh, contains the poems from these volumes as well as many of the works Gurney left unpublished at his death. Gurney was also a musical composer; of special note are his song accompaniments to *Severn and Somme.* A selection of letters has been published as *War Letters* (1983), ed. R. K. R. Thornton. A good biography is Michael Hurd's *The Ordeal of Ivor Gurney* (1978).

Work on Gurney includes Geoffrey Hill's "Gurney's 'Hobby,'" *Essays in Criticism* 34.2 (1984); Jacqueline Banerjee's "Ivor Gurney's 'Dark March'—Is It Really Over?" *English Studies* 70.2 (1989); P. J. Kavanagh's "Being Just: Ivor Gurney and the 'Poetic Sensibility,'" *Grand Street* 9.3 (1990); Piers Gery's *Marginal Men: Edward Thomas, Ivor Gurney, J. R. Ackerley* (1991); Mark William Brown's "Ivor Gurney and Edward Thomas: A Distinction," *Pn Review* 22.2 (1995); and Sally Minogue's "Displaced Poet: Location and Dislocation in Ivor Gurney's Poetry," *Critical Review* 39 (1999). Other important discussions can be found in Jon Silkin's *Out of Battle* (1972) and Paul Fussell's *The Great War and Modern Memory* (1975). The Ivor Gurney Society publishes its journal annually. Thornton's *Ivor Gurney: Towards a Bibliography* was published in 1996. See also **Poets of World War I.**

H. D. (Hilda Doolittle)

H. D.'s early poetry has been collected in *Collected Poems, 1912–1944* (1983), ed. Louis Martz. *Trilogy* (1973) includes her long poems *The Walls Do Not Fall* (1944), *Tribute to the Angels* (1945), and *The Flowering of the Rod* (1946). Other notable volumes include her tribute to the Elizabethans, *By Avon River* (1949); the dramatic monologue *Helen in Egypt* (1961); *Hermetic Definition* (1971); *Selected Poems* (1988), ed. Martz; and *Vale Ave* (1991). H. D. also wrote verse dramas, including *Hippolytus Temporizes* (1927) and a translation of Euripides' *Ion* (1937). Works of prose fiction include *Palimpsest* (1926); *Hadylus* (1928); *Bid Me to Live* (1960); and *Pilate's Wife* (2000), ed. Joan A. Burke. Autobiographical fiction includes *HERmione* (1981); *Asphodel* (1992), ed. Robert Spoo; and *Paint It Today* (1992), ed. Cassandra Laity. Also of note are the memoirs *End to Torment* (1979), ed. Norman Holmes Pearson and Michael King, and *The Gift* (1998), ed. Jane Augustine; as well as *Tribute to Freud* (1956),

H. D.'s account of her psychoanalysis with Freud. Collections of letters include two volumes of *Richard Aldington and H. D.* (1992, 1995), both edited by Caroline Zilboorg; *A Great Admiration: H. D. / Robert Duncan Correspondence* (1992), ed. Robert J. Bertholf; and *Between History and Poetry: The Letters of H. D. and Norman Holmes Pearson* (1997), ed. Donna K. Hollenberg. Barbara Guest's biography, *Herself Defined*, was published in 1984.

Important studies include Susan Stanford Friedman's *Psyche Reborn: The Emergence of H. D.* (1981), Janice S. Robinson's *H. D.: The Life and Work of an American Poet* (1982), Rachel Blau DuPlessis's *H. D.: The Career of That Struggle* (1986), Gary Dean Burnett's *H. D. between Image and Epic* (1989), Claire Buck's *H. D. and Freud: Bisexuality and a Feminine Discourse* (1991), Donna K. Hollenberg's *H. D.: The Poetics of Childbirth and Creativity* (1991), Diane Chisholm's *H. D.'s Freudian Poetics: Psychoanalysis in Translation* (1992), Susan Edmunds's *Out of Line: History, Psychoanalysis, and Montage in H. D.'s Long Poems* (1994), Raffaella Baccolini's *Tradition, Identity, Desire: Revisionist Strategies in H. D.'s Late Poetry* (1995), Hollenberg's *H. D. and Poets After* (2000), and Georgina Taylor's *H. D. and the Public Sphere of Modernist Women Writers* (2001). Lawrence Rainey provocatively argues against H. D.'s reputation in his *Institutions of Modernism* (1998). Many useful essays are collected in *H. D.: Woman and Poet* (1986), ed. Michael King, and *Signets: Reading H. D.* (1990), ed. Friedman and DuPlessis. Bibliographic information is available in Michael Boughn's *H. D.: A Bibliography, 1905–1990* (1993). See also **Imagism.**

Thomas Hardy

The five-volume *Complete Poetical Works of Thomas Hardy*, ed. Samuel Hynes, was published between 1982 and 1995. Also of note is the one-volume *The Complete Poems of Thomas Hardy* (1976, 2001), ed. James Gibson. Hardy's important novels include *The Return of the Native* (1878), *The Mayor of Casterbridge* (1886), *Tess of the d'Urbervilles* (1891), and *Jude the Obscure* (1895). Michael Millgate and Richard Purdy edited the seven-volume *Collected Letters* (1978–88), and Millgate also edited *Selected Letters* (1990). Also important are *The Personal Notebooks of Thomas Hardy* (1978), ed. Richard H. Taylor, and *Thomas Hardy's Personal Writings* (1966), ed. Harold Orel. Biographies include Florence Emily Hardy's *The Life of Thomas Hardy, 1840–1928* (1962), on which Hardy collaborated; Millgate's *Thomas Hardy: A Biography* (1982); and Gibson's *Thomas Hardy: A Literary Life* (1996).

Important studies dealing with Hardy's poetry include Douglas Brown's *Thomas Hardy* (1954), Samuel Hynes's *The Pattern of Hardy's Poetry* (1961), Irving Howe's *Thomas Hardy* (1967), Kenneth Marsden's *The Poems of Thomas Hardy* (1969), J. O. Bailey's *The Poetry of Thomas Hardy* (1970), J. Hillis Miller's *Thomas Hardy: Distance and Desire* (1970), Donald Davie's *Thomas Hardy and British Poetry* (1972), Paul Zietlow's *Moments of Vision* (1974), Tom Paulin's *Thomas Hardy: The Poetry of Perception* (1975), F. P. Pinion's *A Commentary on the Poems of Thomas Hardy* (1976), James Richardson's *Thomas Hardy: The Poetry of Necessity* (1977), John Bayley's *An Essay on Hardy* (1978), Dennis Taylor's *Hardy's Poetry, 1860–1928* (1981), W. E. Buckler's *The Poetry of Thomas Hardy* (1983), Katherine Kearney Maynard's *Thomas Hardy's Tragic Poetry* (1991), Brian Green's *Hardy's Lyrics: Pearls of Pity* (1996), Matthew Campbell's *Rhythm and Will in Victorian Poetry* (1999), A. Banerjee's *An Historical Evaluation of Thomas Hardy's Poetry* (2000), and Tim Armstrong's *Haunted Hardy: Poetry, History, Memory* (2000). Collections of essays include *Thomas Hardy, Poems: A Casebook* (1979), ed. Gibson and Trevor Johnson; *The Poetry of Thomas Hardy* (1980), ed. Patricia Clements and Juliet Grindle; *Critical Essays on Thomas Hardy's Poetry* (1995), ed. Orel; and *The Cambridge Companion to Thomas Hardy* (1999), ed. Dale Kramer. *Thomas Hardy: The Critical Heritage* (1970), ed. R. G. Cox, traces Hardy's reception and includes contemporary reviews. Bibliographic information is available in Purdy's *Thomas Hardy: A Bibliographical Study* (1954).

A. D. Hope

Hope published *Collected Poems, 1930–1970* in 1972. Subsequent volumes include *Selected Poems* (1973); *A Late Picking: Poems, 1965–1974* (1975); *A Book of Answers* (1977); *"The Drifting Continent" and Other Poems* (illustrations Arthur Boyd, 1979); *Antechinus: Poems, 1975–1980* (1981); *The Age of Reason* (1985); and *Selected Poems* (1986), ed. Ruth Morse. *A. D. Hope: Selected Poetry and Prose* (2000), ed. David Brooks, offers a good survey of Hope's work. Hope's critical work includes *Native Companions: Essays and Comments on Australian Literature, 1936–1966* (1974), *Judith Wright* (1975); *The New Cratylus: Notes on the Craft of Poetry* (1979), and *Poetry and the Art of Archery* (1980). Hope's autobiographical *Chance Encounters* was published in 1992. An interview appears in *Southerly* 47.2 (1986).

Book-length studies of Hope's work include Leonie Kramer's *A. D. Hope* (1979), Kevin Hart's *A. D. Hope* (1992), Walter Tonetto's *A. D. Hope: Questions of Poetic Strength* (1993), and Robert Darling's *A. D. Hope* (1997). Useful critical essays are collected in *The Double Looking Glass: New and Classic Essays on the Poetry of A. D. Hope* (2000), ed. Brooks. Other relevant essays include Neal Bowers's "Form as Substance in the Poetry of A. D. Hope," *Shenandoah* 44.1 (1994); Malathi Mathur's "The Music Motif in A. D. Hope's Poetry," *Literary Criterion* 30.1–2 (1997); and Xavier Pons's "A. D. Hope and the Apocalyptic Splendour of the Sexes," *Australian Literary Studies* 19.4 (2000). Two bibliographies are Patricia Anne O'Brien's *A. D. Hope: A Bibliography* (1968) and Joy Hooton's *A. D. Hope* (1979).

Gerard Manley Hopkins

Poems of Gerard Manley Hopkins, the first edition of Hopkins's poetry, was edited by Robert Bridges and published posthumously in 1918. This edition has been enlarged and revised several times, most recently as *The Poetical Works of Gerard Manley Hopkins* (1992), ed. Norman MacKenzie. Other useful collections are *The Journals and Papers of Gerard Manley Hopkins* (1959), ed. Humphry House and Graham Storey; *Sermons and Devotional Writings of Gerard Manley Hopkins* (1959), ed. Christopher Devlin; *Selected Prose* (1980), ed. Gerald Roberts; and *Poetry and Prose* (1998), ed. Walford Davies. Correspondence is available in *Letters of Gerard Manley Hopkins to Robert Bridges* and *The Correspondence of Gerard Manley Hopkins and Richard Watson Dixon* (1935), both ed. C. C. Abbott, and *Selected Letters* (1990), ed. Catherine Phillips. Two good biographies are Robert Bernard Martin's *Gerard Manley Hopkins: A Very Private Life* (1991) and Gerald Roberts's *Gerard Manley Hopkins: A Literary Life* (1994).

A good introduction to the poetry is Norman H. MacKenzie's *A Reader's Guide to Gerard Manley Hopkins* (1981). Important critical studies include W. H. Gardner's two-volume *G. M. Hopkins: A Study of Poetic Idiosyncrasy in Relation to Poetic Tradition* (1944, 1949), Paul Mariani's *A Commentary on the Complete Works of Gerard Manley Hopkins* (1970), Alison Sulloway's *Gerard Manley Hopkins and the Victorian Temper* (1972), Daniel Harris's *Inspirations Unbidden* (1982), Walter J. Ong's *Hopkins, the Self, and God* (1986), Virginia Ridley Ellis's *Gerard Manley Hopkins and the Language of Mystery* (1991), Eugene Hollahan's *Hopkins against History* (1995), Matthew Campbell's *Rhythm and Will in Victorian Poetry* (1999), Julia F. Saville's *A Queer Chivalry* (2000), and Bernadette Waterman Ward's *World as Word: Philosophical Theology in Gerard Manley Hopkins* (2002). Collections of essays include *The Authentic Cadence* (1992), ed. Anthony Robert Mortimer; *Saving Beauty: Further Studies in Hopkins* (1994), ed. Michael E. Allsopp and David Anthony Downes; and *Rereading Hopkins* (1996), ed. Francis L. Fennell. Two helpful bibliographies are Edward H. Cohen's *Works and Criticism of Gerard Manley Hopkins* (1969) and Tom Dunne's *Gerard Manley Hopkins* (1976).

A. E. Housman

The Poems of A. E. Housman, ed. Archie Burnett, was published in 1997. Also useful is *A. E. Housman: Collected Poems and Selected Prose* (1988), ed. Christopher Ricks. Much of Housman's work as a classicist is available in *The Classical Papers of A. E. Housman* (1972), ed. J. Diggle and F. R. D. Goodyear, and other essays are published in *Selected Prose* (1961), ed. John Carter. Henry Maas edited *The Letters of A. E. Housman* (1971). The best biography is Norman Page's *A. E. Housman* (1983). Also of interest is Tom Stoppard's play based on Housman's life, *The Invention of Love* (1997).

Many important essays may be found in the collections *A. E. Housman: A Collection of Critical Essays* (1968), ed. Ricks; *A. E. Housman: The Critical Heritage* (1992), ed. Philip Gardner; and *A. E. Housman: A Reassessment* (2000), ed. Alan W. Holden and J. Roy Birch. Book-length studies include B. J. Leggett's *The Poetic Art of A. E. Housman* (1978), Keith Jebb's *A. E. Housman* (1992), John Bayley's *Housman's Poems* (1992), Terence Allan Hoagwood's *A. E. Housman Revisited* (1995), and Carol Efrati's *The Road of Danger, Guilt, and Shame* (2002). Recent essays include Ruth Robbins's " 'A Very Curious Construction': Masculinity in the Poetry of A. E. Housman and Oscar Wilde," *Cultural Politics at the Fin de Siècle* (1995), ed. Sally Ledger and Scott McCracken; and Clarence Lindsay's "A. E. Housman's Silly Lad: The Loss of Romantic Consolation," *Victorian Poetry* 37.3 (1999). Also of interest is the journal published by the Housman Society. Important reference materials include John Carter, John Sparrow, and William White's *A. E. Housman: A Bibliography* (1982) and Clyde K. Hyder's *A Concordance to the Poems of A. E. Housman* (1940).

Langston Hughes

Composed of authoritative texts of Hughes's poetry, the first three volumes of the projected seventeen-volume *Collected Works of Langston Hughes,* ed. Arnold Rampersad, were published in 2001. Later volumes will contain novels, short stories, autobiography, plays, political writings, and other prose. *The Collected Poems of Langston Hughes,* ed. Rampersad and David Roessel, was published in 1994; it includes later versions of Hughes's poetry. Other important works are the novels *Not without Laughter* (1930) and *Tambourines to Glory* (1958), and the short stories, *The Ways of White Folks* (1934). Autobiographical works include *The Big Sea* (1940) and *I Wonder as I Wander* (1956). Other notable collections include *The Langston Hughes Reader* (1958); *The Best of Simple* (1961); *Five Plays by Langston Hughes* (1963), ed. Webster Smalley; and *Good Morning, Revolution: Uncollected Social Protest Writings by*

Langston Hughes (1973), ed. Faith Berry. Hughes also published many translations, including works by Federico García Lorca and Nicolás Guillén. Collections of letters include *Arna Bontemps–Langston Hughes Letters* (1980), ed. Charles Nichols, and *Remember Me to Harlem: The Letters of Langston Hughes and Carl Van Vechten* (2001), ed. Emily Bernard. Important biographies are Berry's *Langston Hughes: Before and beyond Harlem* (1983) and Rampersad's two-volume *The Life of Langston Hughes* (1986, 1988).

Helpful studies of Hughes's work include James A. Emanuel's *Langston Hughes* (1967), Onwuchekwa Jemie's *Langston Hughes: An Introduction to the Poetry* (1976), Edward J. Mullen's *Langston Hughes in the Hispanic World and Haiti* (1977), Richard Barksdale's *Langston Hughes: The Poet and His Critics* (1977), Steven C. Tracy's *Langston Hughes and the Blues* (1988), and R. Baxter Miller's *The Art and Imagination of Langston Hughes* (1989). Other discussions can be found in Nathan I. Huggins's *Harlem Renaissance* (1971), Jean Wagner's *Black Poets of the United States* (1973), and Jahan Ramazani's *Poetry of Mourning* (1994). Collections of essays include *Langston Hughes, Black Genius* (1971), ed. Therman O'Daniel; *Critical Essays on Langston Hughes* (1986), ed. Edward J. Mullen; *Langston Hughes* (1989), ed. Harold Bloom; *Langston Hughes: Critical Perspectives Past and Present* (1993), ed. Henry Louis Gates Jr. and K. Anthony Appiah; and *Langston Hughes: The Man, His Art and His Continuing Influence* (1995), ed. C. James Trotman. *Langston Hughes: The Contemporary Reviews* (1997) was edited by Letitia Dace. Also of note is the *Langston Hughes Review*. Reference material is available in Peter Mandelik and Stanley Schatt's *A Concordance to the Poetry of Langston Hughes* (1975) and Hans Ostrom's *Langston Hughes Encyclopedia* (2002). Useful bibliographies are Donald C. Dickinson's *A Bio-Bibliography of Langston Hughes* (1967) and R. Baxter Miller's *Langston Hughes and Gwendolyn Brooks: A Reference Guide* (1978). See also **Harlem Renaissance.**

Robinson Jeffers

The Collected Poetry of Robinson Jeffers, ed. Tim Hunt, was published in 2000. Jeffers also wrote plays, including an adaptation of Euripides' *Medea* (1946) and *The Tower beyond Tragedy* (1950), based on Aeschylus's *Oresteia*. Works of criticism include *Poetry, Gongorism, and a Thousand Years* (1949) and *The Last Conservative* (1977). *The Selected Letters of Robinson Jeffers, 1897–1962*, ed. Ann N. Ridgeway, was published in 1968. A biography is Melba Berry Bennett's *The Stone Mason of Tor House: The Life and Work of Robinson Jeffers* (1966) and James Karman's *Robinson Jeffers: Poet of California* (1987, 1995).

Critical studies include Frederic Ives Carpenter's *Robinson Jeffers* (1962), William Everson's *Robinson Jeffers: Fragments of an Older Fury* (1968), Arthur B. Coffin's *Robinson Jeffers: Poet of Inhumanism* (1971), Robert Brophy's *Robinson Jeffers: Myth, Ritual, and Symbol in His Narrative Poems* (1973), Marlan Beilke's *Shining Clarity* (1977), William Henry Nolte's *Rock and Hawk: Robinson Jeffers and the Romantic Agony* (1978), Robert Zaller's *The Cliffs of Solitude* (1983), Everson's *The Excesses of God: Robinson Jeffers as a Religious Figure* (1988), and Terry Beers's *A Thousand Graceful Subtleties: Rhetoric in the Poetry of Robinson Jeffers* (1995). Collections of essays include *Critical Essays on Robinson Jeffers* (1990), ed. James Karman; *Centennial Essays for Robinson Jeffers* (1991), ed. Zaller; *Robinson Jeffers: Dimensions of a Poet* (1995), ed. Brophy; and *Robinson Jeffers and a Galaxy of Writers* (1995), ed. William B. Thesing. Bibliographies include Sydney S. Alberts's *A Bibliography of the Works of Robinson Jeffers* (1933, 1968) and Jeanetta Boswell's *Robinson Jeffers and the Critics, 1912–1983* (1986).

James Weldon Johnson

Johnson's *Complete Poems*, ed. Sondra K. Wilson, was published in 2000. Wilson has also edited the two-volume *Selected Writings of James Weldon Johnson* (1995). Johnson's novel, *The Autobiography of an Ex-Coloured Man*, was originally published in 1912, and his autobiography, *Along This Way*, in 1933. Johnson also wrote the song *Lift Every Voice and Sing* (1900) and edited *The Book of American Negro Poetry* (1922, 1931). Also of note is his book on Harlem, *Black Manhattan* (1930).

Studies dealing with Johnson's life and poetry include Eugene Levy's *James Weldon Johnson: Black Leader, Black Voice* (1973) and Robert E. Fleming's *James Weldon Johnson* (1987). Other relevant studies are Houston A. Baker's *Modernism and the Harlem Renaissance* (1987), Eric Sundquist's *The Hammers of Creation: Folk Culture in African-American Fiction* (1992), and George Hutchinson's *The Harlem Renaissance in Black and White* (1995). Numerous useful essays are collected in *Critical Essays on James Weldon Johnson* (1997), ed. Kenneth M. Price and Lawrence J. Oliver. Bibliographic information is available in Fleming's *James Weldon Johnson and Arna Wendell Bontemps: A Reference Guide* (1978). See also **Harlem Renaissance.**

David Jones

Jones's two major works are the long poems *In Parenthesis* (1937) and *The Anathémata* (1952). A third volume of poetry, *"The Sleeping Lord" and Other Fragments*, was published in 1974. A useful selection of Jones's work is *Introducing David Jones* (1980), ed. John Matthias, with a preface by Stephen Spender. A collection of Jones's visual art is *The Paintings of David Jones* (1989), ed. Nicolete Grey. Important prose works can be found in *Epoch and Artist: Selected Writings* (1959) and *"The Dying Gaul" and Other Writings* (1978), both edited by Harman Grisewood. Letters are available in *David Jones: Letters to Vernon Watkins* (1976), ed. Ruth Pryor; *Dai Greatcoat: A Self-Portrait of David Jones in His Letters* (1980), ed. René Hague; *Letters to a Friend* (1980), ed. Aneirin Talfan Davies; and *Inner Necessities: The Letters of David Jones to Desmond Chute* (1984), ed. Thomas Dilworth.

Studies of Jones's poetry include David Blamires's *David Jones: Artist and Writer* (1971), Jeremy Hooker's *David Jones: An Exploratory Study of the Writings* (1975), Elizabeth Ward's *David Jones: Mythmaker* (1983), Thomas Dilworth's *The Shape of Meaning in the Poetry of David Jones* (1988), Kathleen Henderson Staudt's *At the Turn of a Civilization: David Jones and Modern Poetics* (1994), and Jonathan Miles and Derek Shiel's *David Jones: The Maker Unmade* (1995). Numerous helpful essays are collected in *David Jones: Artist and Poet* (1997), ed. Paul Hills. Other important discussions can be found in John H. Johnston's *English Poetry of the First World War* (1964), Bernard Bergonzi's *Heroes' Twilight* (1965), and Jon Silkin's *Out of Battle* (1972). *Chesterton Review* 23.1–2 (1997) is a special Jones issue. Samuel Rees published an annotated bibliography in 1977. See also **Poets of World War I.**

Patrick Kavanagh

Kavanagh's *Complete Poems*, ed. Peter Kavanagh, was published in 1972. His novels include *Tarry Flynn* (1948) and the autobiographical *The Green Fool* (1938) and *By Night Unstarred* (1977). Other important prose works are available in *Collected Pruse* [sic] (1967). *Self-Portrait* (1964) is an autobiography. Peter Kavanagh edited a collection of letters, *Lapped Furrows: Correspondence 1933–1967 between Patrick and Peter Kavanagh* (1969), and wrote the biography, *Sacred Keeper* (1980).

Studies include Darcy O'Brien's *Patrick Kavanagh* (1975), John Nemo's *Patrick Kavanagh* (1979), Antoinette Quinn's *Patrick Kavanagh* (1991), and Una Agnew's *The Mystical Imagination of Patrick Kavanagh* (1998). Michael O'Loughlin's *After Kavanagh* (1985) is an insightful study of Kavanagh's influence on contemporary Irish poetry. A useful collection of essays is *Patrick Kavanagh: Man and Poet* (1986), ed. Peter Kavanagh. Other notable discussions include Seamus Heaney's "The Placeless Heaven: Another Look at Kavanagh," *Massachusetts Review* 28.3 (1987); Declan Kiberd's "Underdeveloped Comedy—Patrick Kavanagh," *Southern Review* 31.3 (1995); and Alan A. Gillis's "Patrick Kavanagh's Poetics of the Peasant," *Critical Ireland* (2001), ed. Gillis and Aaron Kelly. Bibliographic information is available in Peter Kavanagh's bibliography, *Garden of the Golden Apples* (1972), and Jonathan Allison's *Patrick Kavanagh: A Reference Guide* (1996). See also **Irish Poetry.**

Rudyard Kipling

Kipling's poetry is available in *Rudyard Kipling's Verse: Definitive Edition* (1940) and *Early Verse by Rudyard Kipling, 1879–1889: Unpublished, Uncollected, and Rarely Collected Poems* (1986), ed. Andrew Rutherford. Also worth consulting is *A Choice of Kipling's Verse* (1941), ed. and with an introduction by T. S. Eliot. Among Kipling's major works of fiction are *The Jungle Book* (1894) and *Kim* (1901). A selection of Kipling's critical prose is *Writings on Writing* (1996), ed. Sandra Kemp and Lisa Lewis. Correspondence is available in *Letters of Rudyard Kipling* (1990), ed. Thomas Pinney. Biographies include Charles E. Carrington's *Rudyard Kipling* (1955), J. I. M. Stewart's *Rudyard Kipling* (1966), Philip Mason's *Kipling* (1975), Angus Wilson's *The Strange Ride of Rudyard Kipling* (1977), Harry Ricketts's *Rudyard Kipling* (1999), and David Gilmour's *The Long Recessional: The Imperial Life of Rudyard Kipling* (2002).

Influential earlier discussions of Kipling's work can be found in Eliot's introduction to *A Choice of Kipling's Verse* (1941); Edmund Wilson's *The Wound and the Bow* (1941); George Orwell's *Critical Essays* (1946); and Lionel Trilling's *The Liberal Imagination* (1950). Two studies of Kipling's poetry are Ann Parry's *The Poetry of Rudyard Kipling: Rousing the Nation* (1992) and P. J. Keating's *Kipling the Poet* (1994). *Kipling: The Critical Heritage* (1971), ed. Roger Lancelyn Green, traces Kipling's reception history and presents contemporary reviews. Recent critical essays include John Derbyshire's "Rudyard Kipling and the God of Things as They Are," *New Criterion* 18.7 (2000), and Peter Scupham's "Shelf Lives: Rudyard Kipling," *Pn Review* 28.2 (2001). Collections of essays include *Kipling's Mind and Art* (1964), ed. Andrew Rutherford; *Kipling and the Critics* (1965), ed. Eliot L. Gilbert; *Rudyard Kipling* (1987), ed. Harold Bloom; and *Critical Essays on Rudyard Kipling* (1989), ed. Harold Orel.

Stanley Kunitz

Kunitz published a *Collected Poems* in 2000. The author of essays and translations, he edited Keats's *Poems* (1965) and *The Essential Blake* (1987). Interviews are collected in *Interviews and Encounters with Stanley Kunitz* (1993), ed. Stanley Moss. Another interview appears in Bill Moyers's *The Language of Life* (1995). Also of note are the birthday collections *A Celebration for Stanley Kunitz* (1986) and *To Stanley Kunitz, with Love from Poet Friends* (2002), the latter edited by Moss.

Marie Henault's *Stanley Kunitz* (1980) and Gregory Orr's *Stanley Kunitz: An Introduction to the Poetry* (1985) are useful book-length studies. Helpful essays include David Yezzi's "To Turn Again," *Parnassus* 21.1–2 (1995), and David Barber's "A Visionary Poet at Ninety," *Atlantic Monthly* 277.6 (1996). *Anteus* 37 (Spring 1980), *Worcester Review* 8.2 (1985), and *American Poetry Review* 14 (September–October 1985) are special Kunitz issues.

D. H. Lawrence

Cambridge University Press began publishing the authoritative scholarly texts of Lawrence's works in 1979 and has not yet completed an edition of the poetry. The best current edition is *The Complete Poems of D. H. Lawrence* (1971), ed. Vivian de Sola Pinto and Warren Roberts. Among Lawrence's most important novels are *Sons and Lovers* (1913), *The Rainbow* (1915), and *Women in Love* (1920). Shorter fiction is collected in *The Complete Short Novels* (1982), ed. Keith Sagar and Melissa Partridge. *Plays* (1999), ed. Hans-Wilhelm Schwarze and John Worthen, is an authoritative collection. A selection of some of Lawrence's most important nonfiction is *D. H. Lawrence: Selected Critical Writings* (1998), ed. Michael Herbert. Other important works are *Studies in Classic American Literature* (1924); *Sketches of Etruscan Places* (1932, 1992); *Fantasia of the Unconscious* [1922]; *and Psychoanalysis and the Unconscious* [1921] (1960); and *Apocalypse* [1931] *and the Writings on Revelation* (1980), ed. Mara Kalnins. The eight-volume *Letters of D. H. Lawrence*, ed. James T. Boulton, was published between 1979 and 2000. A convenient *Selected Letters*, ed. Boulton, appeared in 1997. The standard biography is the Cambridge trilogy: John Worthen's *D. H. Lawrence, Volume I: The Early Years, 1885–1912* (1991); Mark Kinkead-Weekes's *D. H. Lawrence, Volume II: Triumph to Exile, 1912–1922* (1996); and David Ellis's *D. H. Lawrence, Volume III: Dying Game, 1922–1930* (1998).

Important studies focusing on Lawrence's poetry include Tom Marshall's *The Psychic Mariner* (1970), Sandra M. Gilbert's *Acts of Attention* (1972), Joyce Carol Oates's *The Hostile Sun* (1973), Jillian De Vries-Mason's *Perception in the Poetry of D. H. Lawrence* (1982), Ross C. Murfin's *The Poetry of D. H. Lawrence* (1983), Gail Porter Mandell's *The Phoenix Paradox* (1984), Charles Davey's *D. H. Lawrence: A Living Poet* (1985), Douglas A. Mackey's *D. H. Lawrence: The Poet Who Was Not Wrong* (1986), M. J. Lockwood's *A Study of the Poems of D. H. Lawrence: Thinking in Poetry* (1987), Holly Laird's *Self and Sequence* (1988), Fiona Becket's *D. H. Lawrence: The Thinker as Poet* (1997), and Rita Saldanha's *World Anew* (1997). Also of note is A. Banerjee's *D. H. Lawrence's Poetry, Demons Liberated: A Collection of Primary and Secondary Material* (1990). Helpful collections of critical essays include *D. H. Lawrence* (1986), ed. Harold Bloom, and *The Cambridge Companion to D. H. Lawrence* (2001), ed. Anne Fernihough. *D. H. Lawrence: The Critical History* (1970, 1997), ed. Ronald P. Draper, provides a valuable reception history and contains contemporary reviews. Also of note is Becket's *The Complete Critical Guide to D. H. Lawrence* (2002) and the *D. H. Lawrence Review*. Bibliographic information is available in Warren Roberts's *A Bibliography of D. H. Lawrence* (1982) and Paul Poplawski's *D. H. Lawrence: A Reference Companion* (1996).

Amy Lowell

Lowell's *Complete Poetical Works* was published in 1955. A selection of Lowell's criticism is printed in *Poetry and Poets* (1930), ed. Ferris Greenslet. Lowell also wrote plays; short stories, including *Dream Drops, or Stories from Fairy Land* (with Elizabeth Lowell and Katherine Bigelow Lowell, 1887, 1997); and a biography, *John Keats* (1925). Lowell also edited the important annual anthology *Some Imagist Poets* (1915, 1916, 1917). *The Letters of D. H. Lawrence and Amy Lowell*, ed. E. Claire Healey and Keith Cushman, appeared in 1985. Biographies include Horace Gregory's *Amy Lowell: Portrait of the Poet in Her Time* (1958), F. Cudworth Flint's *Amy Lowell* (1969), Jean Gould's *Amy: The World of Amy Lowell and the Imagist Movement* (1975), Glenn Richard Ruihley's *The Thorn of a Rose* (1975), and C. David Heymann's *American Aristocracy: The Lives and Times of James Russell, Amy, and Robert Lowell* (1980).

Richard Benvenuto's *Amy Lowell* (1985) is a good introductory study. Other relevant studies include Judy Grahn's *The Highest Apple: Sappho and the Lesbian Poetic Tradition* (1985), Cheryl Walker's *Masks Outrageous and Austere* (1991), and Mary E. Galvin's *Queer Poetics* (1999). Also of note are Lillian Faderman's "Warding Off the Watch and Ward Society: Amy Lowell's Treatment of the Lesbian Theme," *Gay Books Bulletin* 1 (Summer 1979); Andrew Thacker's "Amy Lowell and H. D.: The Other Imagists," *Women: A Cultural Review* 4.1 (1993); and Paul Lauter's "Amy Lowell and Cultural Borders," *Speaking the Other Self: American Women Writers* (1997), ed. Jeanne Campbell Reesman. See also **Imagism.**

Mina Loy

The most complete collection of Loy's work is *The Lost Lunar Baedeker* (1996), ed. Roger L.

Conover. Conover's notes and introduction are especially helpful and contain extensive bibliographic information. *Anglo-Mongrels and the Rose* was excluded from this volume but included in *The Last Lunar Baedeker* (1982), also edited by Conover. Loy's novel *Insel* was published posthumously in 1991. Carolyn Burke has published an illuminating biography, *Becoming Modern* (1996).

A good introductory study is Virginia Kouidis's *Mina Loy: American Modernist Poet* (1980). Interviews and much of the most important critical work on Loy is collected in *Mina Loy: Woman and Poet* (1998), ed. Maeera Shreiber and Keith Tuma, including valuable essays by Marjorie Perloff and Rachel Blau DuPlessis. Other studies include Miller's *Late Modernism* (1999), Janet Lyon's *Manifestoes* (1999), Mary Galvin's *Queer Poetics* (1999), and DuPlessis's *Genders, Races, and Religious Cultures in Modern American Poetry, 1908–1934* (2001).

Hugh MacDiarmid (C. M. Grieve)

The two-volume *Hugh MacDiarmid: The Complete Poems, 1920–1976* (1978) was edited by Michael Grieve and W. R. Aitken. *Selected Poetry*, ed. Grieve and Alan Riach, and *Selected Prose*, ed. Riach, were both published in 1992 and are part of Carcanet Press's projected sixteen-volume *Collected Works of Hugh MacDiarmid*. MacDiarmid's autobiography, *Lucky Poet*, was published in 1943. MacDiarmid also edited *The Golden Treasury of Scottish Poetry* (1940). Correspondence is available in *The Letters of Hugh MacDiarmid* (1984), ed. Alan Bold, and *The Hugh MacDiarmid–George Ogilvie Letters* (1988), ed. Catherine Kerrigan. Interviews appear in *Akros* 5 (April 1970) and Walter Perrie's *Metaphysics and Poetry* (1975). A good biography is Bold's *MacDiarmid* (1988).

Studies of MacDiarmid's work include Duncan Glen's *Hugh MacDiarmid (Christopher Murray Grieve) and the Scottish Renaissance* (1964), Edwin Morgan's *Hugh MacDiarmid* (1976), Kenneth Buthlay's *Hugh MacDiarmid* (1981), John Baglow's *Hugh MacDiarmid: The Poetry of Self* (1987), Peter McCarey's *Hugh MacDiarmid and the Russians* (1987), Riach's *Hugh MacDiarmid's Epic Poetry* (1991), Ruth McQuillan's *Hugh MacDiarmid: The Patrimony* (1992); and W. N. Herbert's *To Circumjack MacDiarmid* (1992). Collections of essays include *Hugh MacDiarmid: A Festschrift* (1962), ed. Kulgin D. Duval and Sydney G. Smith; *MacDiarmid: A Critical Survey* (1972), ed. Glen; *The Age of MacDiarmid* (1980), ed. P. H. Scott and A. C. Davis; and *Hugh MacDiarmid: Man and Poet* (1992), ed. Nancy Gish. *Akros* 23 (August 1977) and *Scottish Literary Journal* 5 (December 1978) are special MacDiarmid issues. A comprehensive bibliography appears in *MacDiarmid: A Critical Survey* (1972), ed. Glen. See also **Scottish Poetry.**

Archibald MacLeish

MacLeish's *Collected Poems, 1917–1982* appeared in 1985. Works of criticism include *Emily Dickinson: Three Views* (with Louise Bogan and Richard Wilbur, 1960) and *Poetry and Experience* (1960). MacLeish also published plays, including *Nobodaddy* (1926) and *The Great American Fourth of July Parade* (1975). Scott Donaldson and R. H. Winnick's biography, *Archibald MacLeish: An American Life*, was published in 1992. Winnick also edited *The Letters of Archibald MacLeish, 1907–1982* (1983). Interviews are collected in *Archibald MacLeish: Reflections* (1986), ed. Bernard A. Drabeck and Helen E. Ellis.

Grover Cleveland Smith's *Archibald MacLeish* (1971) offers a good introduction to the poetry. Also useful are the *Proceedings of the Archibald MacLeish Symposium* (1988), ed. Drabeck and Ellis. Other essays include David Barber's "In Search of an 'Image of Mankind': The Public Poetry of Archibald MacLeish," *American Poetry* 8 (Fall 1990), and Lawrence Martin's " 'To Disarm Democracy': The 1940 Hemingway–MacLeish Exchange on Modernism as Subversion," *North Dakota Quarterly* 66.2 (1999). Bibliographic information is available in Edward J. Mullaly's *Archibald MacLeish: A Checklist* (1973).

Louis MacNeice

The Collected Poems of Louis MacNeice, ed. E. R. Dodds, was published in 1966. Prose collections include *Selected Literary Criticism* (1987) and *Selected Prose* (1990), both edited by Alan Heuser. Heuser also edited *Selected Plays* (1993). A collection of MacNeice's BBC radio plays is *"The Dark Tower" and Other Radio Scripts* (1947). MacNeice's unfinished autobiography, *The Strings Are False*, ed. Dodds, was published in 1965. MacNeice and Stephen Spender edited the anthology *Oxford Poetry 1929* (1929). A fine biography is Jon Stallworthy's *Louis MacNeice* (1995).

Book-length studies of MacNeice's work include Elton Edward Smith's *Louis MacNeice* (1970), William T. McKinnon's *Apollo's Blended Dream* (1971), D. B. Moore's *The Poetry of Louis MacNeice* (1972), Terence Brown's *Louis MacNeice: Sceptical Vision* (1975), Robyn Marsack's *The Cave of Making* (1982), Edna Longley's *Louis MacNeice: A Study* (1988), and Peter McDonald's *Louis MacNeice: The Poet in His Contexts* (1991). Numerous useful essays are collected in *Time Was Away: The World of Louis MacNeice* (1974), ed. Brown and Alec Reid, and *Louis MacNeice and His Influence* (1998), ed. Kathleen Devine and Alan J. Peacock. Mac-

Neice is also often discussed in connection with the group of poets identified with Auden in the 1930s. See especially Derek Stanford's *Stephen Spender, Louis MacNeice, Cecil Day Lewis* (1969), Michael O'Neill and Gareth Reeves's *Auden, MacNeice, Spender: The Thirties Poetry* (1992), and John Whitehead's *A Commentary on the Poetry of W. H. Auden, C. Day Lewis, Louis MacNeice, and Stephen Spender* (1992). Bibliographic information is available in Christopher Armitage and Neil Clark's *A Bibliography of the Works of Louis MacNeice* (1973). See also the **Auden Circle, Irish Poetry.**

Edgar Lee Masters

An annotated edition of *Spoon River Anthology*, ed. John E. Hallwas, was published in 1992. *The Enduring River: Edgar Lee Masters' Uncollected Spoon River Poems*, ed. Herbert K. Russell, appeared in 1991. An edition of Masters's autobiography, *Across Spoon River* (1936), was published with an introduction by Ronald Primeau in 1991. Masters also wrote plays, fiction, essays, and a biography, *Mark Twain* (1938). Russell's *Edgar Lee Masters: A Biography* was published in 2001.

Studies include John T. Flanagan's *Edgar Lee Masters: The Spoon River Poet and His Critics* (1974), Primeau's *Beyond Spoon River: The Legacy of Edgar Lee Masters* (1981), and John and Margaret Wrenn's *Edgar Lee Masters* (1983). Useful essays, including Charles Burgess's "Edgar Lee Masters: The Lawyer as Writer," are collected in *The Vision of This Land: Studies of Vachel Lindsay, Edgar Lee Masters, and Carl Sandburg* (1976), ed. Hallwas and Dennis J. Reader.

Claude McKay

McKay's volumes of poetry include *Constab Ballads* (1912), *Songs of Jamaica* (1912), *"Spring in New Hampshire" and Other Poems* (1920), and *Harlem Shadows* (1922). Collections published after his death include *Selected Poems* (1953); *The Dialect Poetry* (1972); and *The Passion of Claude McKay: Selected Poetry and Prose, 1912–1948* (1973), ed. Wayne F. Cooper. McKay also published the collection of short stories *Gingertown* (1932) and three novels: *Home to Harlem* (1928), *Banjo* (1929), and *Banana Bottom* (1933). Two posthumous story collections are *Trial by Lynching* (1977), ed. A. L. MacLeod, and *My Green Hills of Jamaica* (1979), ed. Mervyn Morris. Essay collections include *Harlem: Negro Metropolis* (1940) and *The Negroes in America* (1979). McKay's autobiography, *A Long Way from Home*, was published in 1937. Biographies include James R. Giles's *Claude McKay* (1976), Wayne F. Cooper's *Claude McKay: Rebel Sojourner in the Harlem Renaissance* (1987), and Tyrone Tillery's *Claude McKay: A Black Poet's Struggle for Identity* (1992).

Relevant studies include Harold Cruse's *The Crisis of the Negro Intellectual* (1967), Addison Gayle's *Claude McKay: The Black Poet at War* (1972), Houston A. Baker's *Modernism and the Harlem Renaissance* (1987), Michael North's *The Dialect of Modernism* (1994), George Hutchinson's *The Harlem Renaissance in Black and White* (1995), Laurence Breiner's *An Introduction to West Indian Poetry* (1998), Heather Hathaway's *Caribbean Waves: Relocating Claude McKay and Paule Marshall* (1999), William Maxwell's *New Negro, Old Left* (1999), and Winston James's *A Fierce Hatred of Injustice* (2000). Numerous useful essays are collected in *Claude McKay: Centennial Studies* (1992), ed. A. L. McLeod. See also **Harlem Renaissance.**

Edna St. Vincent Millay

Millay's *Collected Poems*, ed. Norma Millay, appeared in 1956. Other work includes a collection of prose sketches, *Distressing Dialogues*, which first appeared under the pseudonym Nancy Boyd in 1924. *Three Plays* (1926) collects *Aria da Capo* (1920), *The Lamp and the Bell* (1921), and *Two Slatterns and a King* (1921). A collection of correspondence is *Letters of Edna St. Vincent Millay* (1952), ed. Allan Ross MacDougall. Nancy Milford's biography, *Savage Beauty*, was published in 2001. Other biographical studies of note are James Gray's *Edna St. Vincent Millay* (1967), Anne Cheney's *Millay in Greenwich Village* (1975), and Daniel Mark Epstein's *What Lips My Lips Have Kissed: The Loves and Love Poems of Edna St. Vincent Millay* (2001).

A helpful book-length study is Norman A. Brittin's *Edna St. Vincent Millay* (1967). Numerous useful essays may be found in the collections *Critical Essays on Edna St. Vincent Millay* (1993), ed. William B. Thesing, and *Millay at One Hundred* (1995), ed. Diane P. Freedman. Bibliographic information is available in Judith Nierman's *Edna St. Vincent Millay: A Reference Guide* (1977).

Marianne Moore

Moore's *Complete Poems* first appeared in 1967 and contains selections from Moore's translation of *The Fables of La Fontaine* (1954). Note, however, that Moore substantially revised her poetry from collection to collection. Her previous volumes include *Poems* (1921), *Observations* (1924), *Selected Poems* (1935), *"The Pangolin" and Other Verse* (1936), *What Are Years* (1941), *Nevertheless* (1944), *Collected Poems* (1951), *Like a Bulwark* (1956), *O to Be a Dragon* (1959), and *Tell Me, Tell Me* (1966). Moore's complex textual history is illuminated by Robin G. Schulze's *Becoming Marianne Moore: The Early*

Poems, 1907–1924 (2002). Patricia C. Willis edited *The Complete Prose of Marianne Moore* (1986), and Bonnie Costello edited *Selected Letters of Marianne Moore* (1997). Moore's correspondence with Robert Lowell can be found in David Kalstone's *Becoming a Poet* (1989). Moore's relationship with Wallace Stevens is the subject of Schulze's *The Web of Friendship* (1995). Charles Molesworth's biography, *Marianne Moore: A Literary Life*, was published in 1990. A helpful interview with Grace Schulman appears in *Quarterly Review of Literature* 16.1–2 (1969).

Book-length studies include Bernard F. Engel's *Marianne Moore* (1964, 1989), Donald Hall's *Marianne Moore: The Cage and the Animal* (1970), Pamela W. Hadas's *Marianne Moore, Poet of Affection* (1977), Laurence Stapleton's *Marianne Moore: The Poet's Advance* (1978), Costello's *Marianne Moore: Imaginary Possessions* (1981), Taffy Martin's *Marianne Moore: Subversive Modernist* (1986), Schulman's *Marianne Moore: The Poetry of Engagement* (1986), John M. Slatin's *The Savage's Romance* (1986), Celeste Goodridge's *Hints and Disguises: Marianne Moore and her Contemporaries* (1989), Darlene Williams Erickson's *Illusion Is More Precise than Precision* (1992), Jeanne Heuving's *Omissions Are Not Accidents: Gender in the Art of Marianne Moore* (1992), Linda Leavell's *Marianne Moore and the Visual Arts* (1995), Cristanne Miller's *Marianne Moore: Questions of Authority* (1995), Elisabeth W. Joyce's *Cultural Critique and Abstraction: Marianne Moore and the Avant-Garde* (1998), and Cynthia Stamy's *Marianne Moore and China* (1999). Collections of essays include *Marianne Moore* (1969), ed. Charles Tomlinson; *Marianne Moore: The Art of a Modernist* (1990), ed. Joseph Parisi; and *Marianne Moore: Woman and Poet* (1990), ed. Willis. Also of interest are Jeredith Merrin's *An Enabling Humility: Marianne Moore, Elizabeth Bishop, and the Uses of Tradition* (1990), Joanne Feit Diehl's *Elizabeth Bishop and Marianne Moore: The Psychodynamics of Creativity* (1993), and Elizabeth Gregory's *Quotation and Modern American Poetry* (1996). Bibliographies include Eugene P. Sheehy and Kenneth A. Lohf's *The Achievement of Marianne Moore: A Bibliography, 1907–1957* (1958) and Craig S. Abbot's *Marianne Moore: A Descriptive Bibliography* (1977). Gary Lane's concordance (1972) is another useful reference.

Edwin Muir

The Complete Poems of Edwin Muir, ed. Peter H. Butter, was published in 1991. Among Muir's important works of criticism are *We Moderns* (as Edward Moore, 1918), *Latitudes* (1924), *The Structure of the Novel* (1928), *Scott and Scotland* (1936), and *Essays on Literature and Society* (1949, 1965). Also useful are the collections *Edwin Muir: Uncollected Scottish Criticism* (1982), ed. Andrew Nobel, and *The Truth of Imagination* (1988), ed. Butter. Novels include *The Marionette* (1927), *The Three Brothers* (1931), and *Poor Tom* (1932). Muir also published translations, notably of the works of Franz Kafka. *The Story and the Fable* was published in 1940 and republished as his *Autobiography* in 1954. A *Selected Letters*, ed. Butter, appeared in 1974. Butter also wrote a biography, *Edwin Muir: Man and Poet* (1966). Biographical information is also available in Willa Muir's *Belonging* (1968).

Helpful studies include Elizabeth Huberman's *The Poetry of Edwin Muir: The Field of Good and Ill* (1971), Christopher Wiseman's *Beyond the Labyrinth* (1978), Michael J. Phillips's *Edwin Muir: A Master of Modern Poetry* (1978), Elgin W. Mellown's *Edwin Muir* (1979), Roger Knight's *Edwin Muir: An Introduction to His Work* (1980), George Marshall's *In a Distant Isle: The Orkney Background of Edwin Muir* (1987), James Aitchison's *The Golden Harvester: The Vision of Edwin Muir* (1988), and Margery McCulloch's *Edwin Muir: Poet, Critic, and Novelist* (1993). Numerous useful essays are collected in *Edwin Muir Centenary Assessments* (1990), ed. C. J. M. MacLachlan and David S. Robb. Mellown's *Bibliography of the Writings of Edwin Muir* was published in 1964. See also **Scottish Poetry.**

Lorine Niedecker

Niedecker's *Collected Works*, ed. Jenny Penberthy, was published in 2002. Letters are collected in *"Between Your House and Mine": The Letters of Lorine Niedecker to Cid Corman* (1986), ed. Lisa Pater Faranda, and Penberthy's *Niedecker and the Correspondence with Zukofsky* (1993). A biography is Jane Shaw Knox's *Lorine Niedecker* (1987).

Collections of essays on Niedecker's work include *The Full Note* (1983), ed. Peter Dent, and *Lorine Niedecker: Woman and Poet* (1996), ed. Penberthy. Other essays include Jane Augustine's "The Evolution of Matter: Lorine Niedecker's Aesthetic," *Sagetrieb* 1.1 (1982); Marjorie Perloff, "Canon and Loaded Gun" in her *Poetic License* (1990); Donald Davie's "Postmodernism and Lorine Niedecker," *Pn Review* 18.2 (1991); Douglas Crase's "On Lorine Niedecker," *Raritan* 12.2 (1992); Rae Armantrout's "Feminist Poetics and the Meaning of Clarity," *Sagetrieb* 11.3 (1992); Thom Gunn's "Weedy Speech and Tangled Bank: Lorine Niedecker" in his *Shelf Life* (1993); and Peter Middleton's "Folk Poetry and the American Avant-Garde: Placing Lorine Niedecker," *Journal of American Studies* 31.2 (1997). See also **Objectivism.**

George Oppen

The Collected Poems of George Oppen was published in 1976 and a *New Collected Poems*, ed. Michael Davidson, in 2002. Rachel Blau DuPlessis edited *Selected Letters* (1990). Biographical information can be found in Mary Oppen's autobiography, *Meaning a Life* (1978). Interviews appear in *Sagetrieb* 3.3 (1984), 5.1 (1986), and 6.1 (1987).

Collections of essays on Oppen include *George Oppen, Man and Poet* (1981), ed. Burton Hatlen, and *Not Comforts, but Vision* (1985), ed. Jonathan Griffin. Several essays on Oppen appear in *Sagetrieb* 12.3 (1993) and *Ironwood* 26 (1985), a special Oppen issue. Also of note are Michael Davidson's *Ghostlier Demarcations: Modern Poetry and the Material Word* (1997) and Burt Kimmelman's *The "Winter Mind": William Bronk and American Letters* (1998). Important essays include Norman Finkelstein's "Political Commitment and Poetic Subjectification: George Oppen's Test of Truth," *Contemporary Literature* 22.1 (1981); Hatlen's "Opening up the Text: George Oppen's 'Of Being Numerous,'" *Ironwood* 13.2 (1985); Ming-Qian Ma's "A 'Seeing' through Refraction: The Rear-View Mirror Image in George Oppen's *Collected Poems*," *Sagetrieb* 10.1–2 (1991); Paul Taggart's "Walk-Out: Rereading George Oppen," *Chicago Review* 44.2 (1998); and Peter Nicholls's "Of Being Ethical," *The Objectivist Nexus* (1999), ed. Rachel Blau DuPlessis and Peter Quartermain. See also **Objectivism.**

Wilfred Owen

Owen's *Complete Poems and Fragments*, ed. Jon Stallworthy, was published in 1983. The *Collected Letters*, ed. Harold Owen and John Bell, was published in 1967. Bell also edited a *Selected Letters* (1985). Stallworthy's excellent biography, *Wilfred Owen*, was published in 1974. Bibliographic information is also available in Harold Owen's *Journey from Obscurity: Memoirs of the Owen Family* (1963–65).

Full-length studies include Gertrude M. White's *Wilfred Owen* (1969), Arthur E. Lane's *An Adequate Response: The War Poetry of Wilfred Owen and Siegfried Sassoon* (1972), Sven Bäckman's *Tradition Transformed: Studies in the Poetry of Wilfred Owen* (1979), Desmond Graham's *The Truth of War* (1984), Dominic Hibberd's *Owen the Poet* (1986), Douglas Kerr's *Wilfred Owen's Voices* (1993), and John A. Purkis's *A Preface to Wilfred Owen* (1999). Other discussions of Owen's work can be found in Jon Silkin's *Out of Battle: The Poetry of the Great War* (1972); Jahan Ramazani's *Poetry of Mourning* (1994); Patrick J. Quinn's *Recharting the Thirties* (1996); and *The Literature of the Great War Reconsidered: Beyond Modern Memory* (2001), ed. Quinn and Steven Trout. Critical essays include Tadeusz Slawek's " 'Dark Pits of War': Wilfred Owen's Poetry and the Hermeneutics of War," *Boundary* 2 14 (1985–86); Caryn McTighe Musil's "Wilfred Owen and Abram," *Women's Studies* 13 (1986); Sandra M. Gilbert's " 'Rats' Alley': The Great War, Modernism, and the (Anti)Pastoral Elegy," *New Literary History* 30.1 (1999); and James Najarian's " 'Greater Love': Wilfred Owen, Keats, and a Tradition of Desire," *Twentieth Century Literature* 47.1 (2001). William White's bibliography was published in 1967.

Dorothy Parker

Parker's *Complete Poems*, ed. Colleen Breese, was published in 1999, and her *Complete Stories*, also edited by Breese, in 1995. Parker also wrote plays and screenplays. An interview appears in *Writers at Work* (1958), ed. Malcolm Cowley. Biographies include John Keats's *You Might as Well Live* (1970) and Marion Meade's *Dorothy Parker: What Fresh Hell Is This?* (1987). Both biographical and bibliographical information can be found in Randall Calhoun's *Dorothy Parker* (1993).

Arthur F. Kinney's *Dorothy Parker* (1978, 1998) is a good introductory study. Another book-length examination of her work is Rhonda Pettit's *A Gendered Collision: Sentimentalism and Modernism in Dorothy Parker's Poetry and Fiction* (2000). Other discussions of her work can be found in Lillian Hellman's *An Unfinished Woman* (1969); Suzanne L. Bunkers's " 'I Am Outraged Womanhood': Dorothy Parker as Feminist and Social Critic," *Regionalism and the Female Imagination* 4 (1978); Nina Miller's "Making Love Modern: Dorothy Parker and Her Public," *American Literature* 64.4 (1992); and Linda Patterson Miller's "Ernest Hemingway and Dorothy Parker: 'Nothing in Her Life Became Her Like Her Almost Leaving It,' " *North Dakota Quarterly* 66.2 (1999).

Ezra Pound

Collected Early Poems of Ezra Pound (1976), ed. Michael King, includes *A Lume Spento* (1908) through *Ripostes* (1912). *Personae: The Collected Shorter Poems* (1926) has been revised and expanded several times, most recently in 1990, and includes the early poems and a revised version of *Hugh Selwyn Mauberley* (1920) and *Homage to Sextus Propertius* (1934). The most authoritative version of *The Cantos* is the 1998 New Directions edition. Among Pound's most important works of criticism are *The Spirit of Romance* (1910, 1952), *Gaudier-Brzeska* (1916), *Instigations* (1920), *ABC of Reading* (1934), *Make It New* (1934), *Guide to Kulchur* (1938), and *Patria Mia* (1950). Also useful are *Literary Essays* (1935, 1954), ed. T. S. Eliot; *Selected Prose, 1909–1965* (1973), ed.

William Cookson; and Ezra Pound's *Poetry and Prose Contributions to Periodicals* (1991), ed. Lea Baechler, A. Walton Litz, and James Longenbach. Pound's wartime radio addresses have been published as *Ezra Pound Speaking* (1978), ed. Leonard W. Doob.

The best biographies are Humphrey Carpenter's *A Serious Character* (1988), and James J. Wilhelm's trilogy *The American Roots of Ezra Pound* (1985), *Ezra Pound in London and Paris* (1990), and *Ezra Pound: The Tragic Years* (1994). Hugh Kenner's *The Pound Era* (1971) is an influential work that combines biography and criticism of Pound and his contemporaries. Among the many collections of Pound's letters are *The Letters of Ezra Pound, 1907–1941* (1950), ed. D. D. Paige; *Ezra Pound and Dorothy Shakespear: Their Letters, 1909–1914* (1984), ed. Omar Pound and Litz; *Pound/Lewis: The Letters of Ezra Pound and Wyndham Lewis* (1985), ed. Timothy Materer; *Ezra Pound and James Loughlin* (1994), ed. David M. Gordon; *Pound/Williams: Selected Letters of Ezra Pound and William Carlos Williams* (1996), ed. Hugh Witemeyer; and *Ezra and Dorothy Pound: Letters in Captivity, 1945–1946* (1999), ed. Omar Pound and Robert Spoo.

Useful companions include Christine Brooke-Rose's *A ZBC of Ezra Pound* (1971) and James Knapp's *Ezra Pound* (1979). Christine Froula's *A Guide to Ezra Pound's Selected Poems* (1983) offers helpful glosses on individual poems, as does K. K. Ruthven's *A Guide to Ezra Pound's* Personae (1969). For extended discussions of *Hugh Selwyn Mauberley,* see John Espey's *Ezra Pound's* Mauberley: *A Study in Composition* (1955) and Jo Brantley Berryman's *Circe's Craft* (1983). For help with *The Cantos,* see Carroll F. Terrell's two-volume *A Companion to the Cantos of Ezra Pound* (1980, 1984). Also of note are Leon Surette's *A Light from Eleusis: A Study of Ezra Pound's Cantos* (1979), George Kearns's *Ezra Pound:* The Cantos (1989); and *A Poem Containing History: Textual Studies in the Cantos* (1997), ed. Lawrence Rainey.

Important general studies include Donald Davie's *Ezra Pound: Poet as Sculptor* (1964); Michael Alexander's *The Poetic Achievement of Ezra Pound* (1979); Michael André Bernstein, *The Tale of the Tribe: Ezra Pound and the Modern Verse Epic* (1980); Ian F. A. Bell's *Critic as Scientist* (1981); Marjorie Perloff's *The Dance of the Intellect* (1985); Kathryne Lindberg's *Reading Pound Reading: Modernism after Nietzsche* (1987); Robert Casillo's *The Genealogy of Demons: Anti-Semitism, Fascism, and the Myths of Ezra Pound* (1988); Lawrence Rainey's *Ezra Pound and the Monument of Culture* (1991); Vincent Sherry's *Ezra Pound, Wyndham Lewis, and Radical Modernism* (1993); Michael Coyle's *Ezra Pound, Popular Genres, and the Discourse of Culture* (1995); Zhaoming Qian's *Orientalism and Modernism: The Legacy of China in Pound and Williams* (1995); Ming Hsieh's *Ezra Pound and the Appropriation of Chinese Poetry* (1999); Leon Surette's *Pound in Purgatory: From Economic Radicalism to Anti-Semitism* (1999); and *Ezra Pound and African American Modernism,* ed. Coyle (2001).

Useful reference materials include Robert J. Dilligan, James W. Parins, and Todd K. Bender's *A Concordance to Ezra Pound's Cantos* (1981), Donald C. Gallup's *Ezra Pound: A Bibliography* (1983), and Beatrice Ricks's *Ezra Pound: A Bibliography of Secondary Works* (1986). See also **Imagism, Vorticism.**

John Crowe Ransom

Ransom's volumes of poetry include *Poems about God* (1919), *Chills and Fever* (1924), *Grace after Meat* (1924), *Two Gentlemen in Bonds* (1927), *Selected Poems* (1945), and *Poems and Essays* (1955). Since its original publication in 1945, *Selected Poems* has been enlarged several times, most recently in 1991. Ransom's influential works of criticism include *God without Thunder: An Unorthodox Defense of Orthodoxy* (1930), *The World's Body* (1938), *The New Criticism* (1941), and *Beating the Bushes: Selected Essays, 1941–1970* (1972). Thomas D. Young and George Core edited *Selected Letters of John Crowe Ransom* (1985). A good biography is Young's *Gentleman in a Dustcoat* (1976).

Studies include Karl F. Knight's *The Poetry of John Crowe Ransom* (1964), Robert Buffington's *The Equilibrist* (1967), Thornton H. Parsons's *John Crowe Ransom* (1969), James Magner Jr.'s *John Crowe Ransom* (1971), Miller Williams's *The Poetry of John Crowe Ransom* (1972), Kieran Quinlan's *John Crowe Ransom's Secular Faith* (1989), Mark Jancovich's *Cultural Politics of the New Criticism* (1993), and Mark G. Malvasi's *The Unregenerate South: The Agrarian Thought of John Crowe Ransom, Allen Tate, and Donald Davidson* (1997). Numerous useful essays and a bibliography are collected in *John Crowe Ransom: Critical Essays and a Bibliography* (1968), ed. Young. Another bibliography is Craig S. Abbott's *John Crowe Ransom: A Descriptive Bibliography* (1999). See also **The Fugitive Poets, The New Criticism and Poetry.**

Kenneth Rexroth

The Complete Poems of Kenneth Rexroth, ed. Sam Hamill and Bradford Morrow, appeared in 2002. Works of criticism include *With Eye and Ear* (1970), *American Poetry in the Twentieth Century* (1971), *The Elastic Retort* (1973), and *World outside the Window: The Selected Essays of Kenneth Rexroth* (1987), ed. Morrow. Rexroth also wrote plays and published many translations. *An Autobiographical Novel* was published in 1966. Lee Bartlett edited *Kenneth Rexroth and James Laughlin: Selected Letters* (1991). Interviews appear in *Contemporary Literature* 10 (1969), David Meltzer's *Golden Gate: Interviews with Five San Francisco Poets* (1976), and *Conjunctions* 1 (1981–82). Linda Hamalian's *A Life of Kenneth Rexroth* was published in 1991.

Book-length studies include Morgan Gibson's *Kenneth Rexroth* (1972), Gibson's *Revolutionary Rexroth: Poet of East–West Wisdom* (1986), Ken Knabb's *The Relevance of Rexroth* (1990), and Donald Gutierrez's *The Holiness of the Real: The Short Verse of Kenneth Rexroth* (1996). *Sagetrieb* 2 (1983), ed. Burton Hatlen, and *Third Rail* 8 (1987), ed. Doren Robbins, are issues devoted to Rexroth. Other important discussions of his work can be found in Sanehide Kodama's *American Poetry and Japanese Culture* (1984), Robert Hass's *Twentieth Century Pleasures* (1984, 1997), Michael Davidson's *The San Francisco Renaissance* (1989), Lee Bartlett's *The Sun Is but a Morning Star: Studies in West Coast Poetry and Poetics* (1989), and Richard Candida Smith's *Utopia and Dissent: Art, Poetry, and Politics in California* (1995). Bibliographic information is available in James Hartzell and Richard Zumwinkle's *Kenneth Rexroth: A Checklist of His Published Writings* (1967), and Morrow's "An Outline of Unpublished Rexroth Manuscripts," *Sagetrieb* 2 (1983). See also **San Francisco Renaissance.**

Charles Reznikoff

Poems 1918–1975: The Complete Poems of Charles Reznikoff, ed. Seamus Cooney, was published in 1989. Also of note are the histories in *Family Chronicle* (with Sarah and Nathan Reznikoff, 1963). Milton Hindus edited a *Selected Letters of Charles Reznikoff* (1997).

Many important essays on Reznikoff's work are included in *Charles Reznikoff: Man and Poet* (1984), ed. Hindus. *Sagetrieb* 13.1–2 (1994) is a special Reznikoff issue. Discussions of his work include Milton Hindus's *Charles Reznikoff: A Critical Essay* (1977); Robert Franciosi's " 'Detailing the Facts': Charles Reznikoff's Response to the Holocaust," *Contemporary Literature* 29.2 (1988); Benjamin Watson's "Reznikoff's Testimony," *Law Library Journal* 82.4 (1990); Michael Davidson's *Ghostlier Demarcations* (1997); Charles Bernstein's "Reznikoff's Nearness" and Norman Finkelstein's "Tradition and Modernity, Judaism and Objectivism: The Poetry of Charles Reznikoff," both in *The Objectivist Nexus* (1999), ed. Rachel Blau DuPlessis and Peter Quartermain; Stephen Fredman's *A Menorah for Athena: Charles Reznikoff and the Jewish Dilemmas of Objectivist Poetry* (2001); Ranen Omer-Sherman's *Diaspora and Zionism in Jewish American Literature* (2002). See also **Objectivism.**

Laura Riding

The Poems of Laura Riding (2001) reproduces the text of Riding's 1938 *Collected Poems* and includes both Riding's original preface and her new preface from the 1980 edition. Riding also published important works of experimental short fiction, *Progress of Stories* (1935, 1982) and *Lives of Wives* (1939, 1995), and a novel, *A Trojan Ending* (1937). Lisa Samuels has edited a new edition of Riding's important work of criticism, *Anarchism Is Not Enough* (1928, 2001). Other important critical works include *Contemporaries and Snobs* (1928, 1971); *The Telling* (1972); and *The Word "Woman" and Other Related Writings* (1993), ed. Elizabeth Friedmann and Alan J. Clark. Riding's work with Robert Graves, including *A Survey of Modernist Poetry* (1927) and *A Pamphlet against Anthologies* (1928), was extremely influential. A selection of their essays and correspondence is *Essays from "Epilogue" 1935–1937* (2001), ed. Mark Jacobs. Riding's linguistic work with Schuyler B. Jackson is published in *Rational Meaning: A New Foundation for the Definitions of Words and Supplementary Essays* (1997). An engaging biography is Deborah Baker's *In Extremis: The Life of Laura Riding* (1993).

Book-length studies include Joyce Piell Wexler's *Laura Riding's Pursuit of Truth* (1979) and Barbara Block Adams's *The Enemy Self: Poetry and Criticism of Laura Riding* (1990). Other important discussions of Riding's work can be found in M. L. Rosenthal's "Laura Riding's Poetry: A Nice Problem," *The Southern Review* 21 (1985); K. K. Ruthven's "How to Avoid Being Canonized: Laura Riding," *Textual Practice* 5 (1991); Susan M. Schultz's "Laura Riding's Essentialism and the Absent Muse," *Arizona Quarterly* 48 (1992); Jerome McGann's *Black Riders: The Visible Language of Modernism* (1993); Peter S. Temes's " 'Code of Silence': Laura (Riding) Jackson and the Refusal to Speak," *PMLA* 109 (1994); Jeanne Heuving's "Laura (Riding) Jackson's 'Really New' Poem," *Gendered Modernisms: American Women Poets and Their Readers* (1996), ed. Margaret Dickie and Thomas Travisano; Frances Wilson's *Literary Seductions* (2000); and John Ashbery's *Other Traditions* (2000). *Pn Review* 17.4 (1991) and *Chelsea* 25 (1977) and 69 (2000) are special Riding issues. Wexler's *Laura Riding: A Bibliography* appeared in 1981. See also **The Fugitive Poets, The New Criticism and Poetry.**

Edwin Arlington Robinson

An enlarged edition of the *Collected Poems of Edwin Arlington Robinson* was published in

1937. A more recent collection is *The Poetry of E. A. Robinson* (1999), ed. Robert Mezey. Robinson also wrote plays and long narrative poems, including a trilogy based on Arthurian legend: *Merlin* (1917), *Lancelot* (1920), and *Tristram* (1927). Collections of letters include *Selected Letters* (1940), ed. Ridgely Torrence; *Untriangulated Stars: Letters of Edwin Arlington Robinson to Harry de Forest Smith* (1947); and *Edwin Arlington Robinson's Letters to Edith Brower* (1968), ed. Richard Cary. Biographies include Louis Osborne Coxe's (1969) and David Henry Burton's (1987).

Studies include Yvor Winters's *Edwin Arlington Robinson* (1946, 1971); Ellsworth Barnard's *Edwin Arlington Robinson: A Critical Study* (1952); Edwin S. Fussell's *Edwin Arlington Robinson: The Literary Background of a Traditional Poet* (1954); Wallace L. Anderson's *Edwin Arlington Robinson: A Critical Introduction* (1967); Hoyt C. Franchere's *Edwin Arlington Robinson* (1968); and Richard Hoffpauir's *The Contemplative Poetry of Edwin Arlington Robinson, Robert Frost, and Yvor Winters* (2002). Collections of essays include *Edwin Arlington Robinson: A Collection of Critical Essays* (1970), ed. Francis Murphy, and *Edwin Arlington Robinson* (1988), ed. Harold Bloom. Also of note is *Early Reception of Edwin Arlington Robinson* (1974), ed. Richard Cary. Recent critical essays include Alan Trachtenberg's "Democracy and the Poet: Walt Whitman and E. A. Robinson," *Massachusetts Review* 39.2 (1998); Mark Jarman's "Robinson, Frost and Jeffers and the New Narrative Poetry," *New Expansive Poetry* (1999), ed. R. S. Gwynn; and Donald Justice's "Benign Obscurity," *Sewanee Writers on Writing* (2000), ed. Wyatt Prunty. Bibliographic information is included in Jeanetta Boswell's *Edwin Arlington Robinson and the Critics: A Bibliography of Secondary Sources with Selective Annotations* (1988).

Theodore Roethke

Roethke's *Collected Poems* appeared in 1966. A collection of Roethke's poetry for children is *Dirty Dinky and Other Creatures* (1973), ed. Beatrice Roethke and Stephen Lushington. A selection of his prose is available in *On Poetry and Craft* (2001). Also of note is *Straw for the Fire, From the Notebooks of Theodore Roethke 1943–63* (1972), ed. David Wagoner, and *Selected Letters* (1968), ed. Ralph J. Mills. A biography is Alan Seager's *The Glass House* (1968).

Helpful studies include Jenijoy La Belle's *The Echoing Wood of Theodore Roethke* (1976), Jay Parini's *Theodore Roethke: An American Romantic* (1979), George Wolff's *Theodore Roethke* (1981), Neal Bowers's *Theodore Roethke: The Journey from I to Otherwise* (1982), Randall Stiffler's *Theodore Roethke: The Poet and His Critics* (1986), Walter Kalaidjian's *Understanding Theodore Roethke* (1987), Peter Balakian's *Theodore Roethke's Far Fields: The Evolution of His Poetry* (1989), Don Bogen's *Theodore Roethke and the Writing Process* (1991), and Robert Kusch's *My Toughest Mentor: Theodore Roethke and William Carlos Williams* (1999). Numerous useful essays are collected in *Theodore Roethke* (1988), ed. Harold Bloom. Gary Lane published a concordance to Roethke's poetry in 1972. Bibliographic information is available in Keith R. Moul's *Theodore Roethke's Career: An Annotated Bibliography* (1977).

Isaac Rosenberg

The Collected Works of Isaac Rosenberg (1979), ed. I. M. Parsons, contains poetry, prose, letters, drawings, and paintings. His play, *Moses*, was published in 1916. Biographies include Jean Liddiard's *Isaac Rosenberg: The Half Used Life* (1975), Jean Moorcroft Wilson's *Isaac Rosenberg, Poet and Painter* (1975), and Joseph Cohen's *Journey to the Trenches* (1975).

Important discussions of his work can be found in John H. Johnston's *English Poetry of the First World War* (1964); Jon Silkin's *Out of Battle* (1972); Desmond Graham's *The Truth of War* (1984); and *British Poets of the Great War: Brooke, Rosenberg, Thomas* (2000), ed. Patrick Quinn. Useful essays include Diana Collecott's "Isaac Rosenberg (1890–1913): A Cross-Cultural Study," *The Jewish East End, 1840–1939* (1981), ed. Aubrey Newman; Matt Simpson's "Only a Living Thing: Some Notes toward a Reading of Isaac Rosenberg's 'Break of Day in the Trenches' " and Jennifer Breen's "Representations of the 'Feminine' in First World War Poetry," both in *Critical Survey* 2.2 (1990); and Beth Allen Roberts's "The Female God of Isaac Rosenberg," *English Literature in Transition* 39.3 (1996). See also **Poets of World War I.**

Carl Sandburg

The Complete Poems of Carl Sandburg was published in 1950 and expanded in 1970. Previously unpublished poems were collected in *Breathing Tokens* (1978), ed. Margaret Sandburg, and *"Billy Sunday" and Other Poems* (1993), ed. George and Willene Hendrick. Sandburg also wrote fiction, including the novel *Remembrance Rock* (1948), and celebrated biographies of Abraham Lincoln, *Abraham Lincoln: The Prairie Years* (1926) and *Abraham Lincoln: The War Years* (1939). He also published works of journalism, stories for children, and a book of American folk songs. Herbert Mitgang edited *The Letters of Carl Sandburg* (1968), and Margaret Sandburg edited *The Poet and the Dream Girl: The Love Letters of Lilian Steichen and Carl Sandburg* (1987). Sandburg's autobiographical

Always the Young Strangers was published in 1953, and *Ever the Winds of Chance*, ed. Margaret Sandburg and George Hendrick, in 1983. A good biography is Penelope Niven's *Carl Sandburg* (1991).

Studies include Richard Crowder's *Carl Sandburg* (1964) and Philip Yannella's *The Other Carl Sandburg* (1996). Other important discussions can be found in Bernard Duffey's *The Chicago Renaissance in American Letters* (1954); Archibald MacLeish's introduction to *Complete Poems* (1970); Carl S. Smith's *Chicago and the American Literary Imagination* (1984); Charles Kostelnick's "Sandburg, Futurism, and the Aesthetics of Urban Dynamism," *American Poetry* 8 (1990); and Mark W. Van Wienen's "Taming the Socialist: Carl Sandburg's *Chicago Poems* and Its Critics," *American Literature* 63.1 (1991). A helpful bibliography is Dale Salwak's *Carl Sandburg: A Reference Guide* (1988).

Siegfried Sassoon

The War Poems of Siegfried Sassoon, ed. Rupert Hart-Davis, was published in 1983, and *Collected Poems, 1908–1956* in 1961. Hart-Davis also edited Sassoon's *Diaries, 1920–1922* (1981), *Diaries, 1915–1918* (1983), and *Diaries, 1923–1925* (1985). Also of note are Sassoon's prose works, *Memoirs of an Infantry Officer* (1930), *Sherston's Progress* (1936), and *Siegfried's Journey* (1945). Collections of letters include *Letters to a Critic* (1976) and *Siegfried Sassoon Letters to Max Beerbohm* (1986), ed. Hart-Davis. Jean Moorcroft Wilson's biography, *Siegfried Sassoon: The Making of a War Poet*, was published in 1998.

Book-length studies of Sassoon's work include Michael Thorpe's *Siegfried Sassoon: A Critical Study* (1966), Felicitas Corrigan's *Siegfried Sassoon: Poet's Pilgrimage* (1973), and Patrick J. Quinn's *The Great War and the Missing Muse: The Early Writings of Robert Graves and Siegfried Sassoon* (1994). Other important discussions can be found in John H. Johnston's *English Poetry of the First World War* (1964), Bernard Bergonzi's *Heroes' Twilight* (1965), Arthur E. Lane's *An Adequate Response* (1972), John Silkin's *Out of Battle: The Poetry of the Great War* (1972), Paul Fussell's *The Great War and Modern Memory* (1975), and John Lehmann's *The English Poets of the First World War* (1981). Geoffrey Keynes's *A Bibliography of Siegfried Sassoon* was published in 1962. See also **Poets of World War I.**

Edith Sitwell

Collected Poems was published in 1968, and *The Early Unpublished Poems*, ed. Gerald W. Morton and Karen P. Helgeson, in 1994. Among her important works of criticism are *Alexander Pope* (1930), *The English Eccentrics* (1933, 1957), *Aspects of Modern Poetry* (1934), and *A Poet's Notebook* (1950). Richard Greene edited *Selected Letters* (1997). Her autobiography, *Taken Care Of*, was published in 1965. Biographies include Geoffrey Elborn's *Edith Sitwell* (1981) and Victoria Glendinning's *Edith Sitwell: A Unicorn Among Lions* (1981). Portraits of the Sitwell family are John Lehmann's *A Nest of Tigers* (1968), John Pearson's *Façades* (1978), and G. A. Cevasco's *The Sitwells* (1987).

For important critical discussions of her work, see Lehmann's *Edith Sitwell* (1952), Geoffrey Singleton's *Edith Sitwell: The Hymn to Life* (1960), Ralph J. Mills's *Edith Sitwell* (1966), and James Brophy's *Edith Sitwell: The Symbolist Order* (1968). Helpful essays include John B. Ower's "Cosmic Aristocracy and Cosmic Democracy in Edith Sitwell," *Contemporary Literature* 12 (1971); Blake Morrison's "Queen Edith: On Edith Sitwell," *Encounter* 57.5 (1981); Jean MacVean's "Another Look at Edith Sitwell," *Agenda* 21.3 (1983); and Holly Laird's "Laughter and Nonsense in the Making and (Postmodern) Remaking of Modernism," *The Future of Modernism* (1997), ed. Hugh Witemeyer. Bibliographic information is available in Richard Fifoot's *A Bibliography of Edith, Osbert, and Sacheverell Sitwell* (1971) and John W. Ehrstine and Douglas D. Rich's "Edith Sitwell: A Critical Bibliography 1951–1973," *Bulletin of Bibliography* 31 (1974).

Stevie Smith

The Collected Poems of Stevie Smith, arranged by Jack MacGibbon, was published in 1975 and contains many of Smith's drawings. Other work is available in *Me Again: Uncollected Writings* (1981), ed. Jack Barbera and William McBrien. Smith also published three novels, *Novel on Yellow Paper* (1936), *Over the Frontier* (1938), and *The Holiday* (1949). Short prose is collected in *A Very Pleasant Evening with Stevie Smith* (1995) and drawings in *Some Are More Human than Others* (1958). Two biographies are Barbera and McBrien's *Stevie* (1985) and Frances Spalding's *Stevie Smith* (1988). Interviews appear in *The Poet Speaks* (1966), ed. Peter Orr, and Kay Dick's *Ivy and Stevie* (1971).

Book-length studies on Smith include Arthur C. Rankin's *The Poetry of Stevie Smith: "Little Girl Lost"* (1985), Sanford Sternlicht's *Stevie Smith* (1990) and *In Search of Stevie Smith* (1991), Catherine Civello's *Patterns of Ambivalence: The Fiction and Poetry of Stevie Smith* (1997), and Laura Severin's *Stevie Smith's Resistant Antics* (1997). Other important discussions of her work can be found in Calvin Bedient's *Eight Contemporary Poets* (1974); Philip Larkin's "Frivolous and Vulnerable," in his *Required Writing* (1983); Christopher Ricks's *The Force of Poetry* (1984); Kristin Bleumel's "The Dangers of Eccentricity: Stevie Smith's Doodles and

Poetry," *Mosaic* 31.3 (1998); and Romana Huk's "Misplacing Stevie Smith," *Contemporary Literature* 40.3 (1999). A bibliography compiled by Barbera, McBrien, and Helen Bajan was published in 1987.

Stephen Spender

Spender's *Collected Poems, 1928–1985* was published in 1985. He also wrote novels, including *The Backward Son* (1940) and *The Temple* (1988); short stories, including the collection *Engaged in Writing, and the Fool and the Princess* (1958); and plays, including a translation of the *Oedipus Trilogy* (1985). Spender also published many other translations, including works by Rainer Maria Rilke and Federico García Lorca. Among Spender's important works of criticism are *The Destructive Element* (1935), *The Creative Element* (1953), *The Making of a Poem* (1955), *The Struggle of the Modern* (1963), and *Love-Hate Relations: A Study of Anglo-American Sensibilities* (1974). Among his travel writings is *China Diary* (1982). His excellent autobiography, *World within World*, was first published in 1951. *Journals, 1939–1983 / Stephen Spender*, ed. John Goldsmith, was published in 1986. Also of note is *Letters to Christopher: Stephen Spender's Letters to Christopher Isherwood, 1929–1939* (1980), ed. Lee Bartlett. Biographies include Hugh David's *Steven Spender: A Portrait with Background* (1992) and David Adams Leeming's *Stephen Spender: A Life in Modernism* (1999). Interviews appear in *American Poetry Review* 6.6 (1977) and *Partisan Review* 55.1 (1988).

For discussions of Spender's work, see Elton Edward Smith's *The "Angry Young Men" of the Thirties* (1975), A. K. Weatherhead's *Stephen Spender and the Thirties* (1975), Surya Nath Pandey's *Stephen Spender: A Study in Poetic Growth* (1982), Michael O'Neil and Gareth Reeves's *Auden, MacNeice, Spender* (1992), John Whitehead's *A Commentary on the Poetry of W. H. Auden, C. Day Lewis, Louis MacNeice, and Stephen Spender* (1992), and Sanford Sternlicht's *Stephen Spender* (1992). H. B. Kulkarni's *Stephen Spender, Works and Criticism: An Annotated Bibliography* was published in 1976. See also the **Auden Circle.**

Gertrude Stein

The Library of America published a two-volume collection of Stein's poetry and prose, *Writings 1903–1932* and *Writings 1932–1946*, in 1998. This collection contains Stein's portraits, *Tender Buttons* and "Stanzas in Meditation," as well as fiction and criticism. Stein's major works of fiction include *Three Lives* (1909), *The Making of Americans* (1925), *Lucy Church, Amiably* (1930), *Ida* (1941), and *Brewsie and Willie* (1946). Also of interest are her biographical and autobiographical works, *The Autobiography of Alice B. Toklas* (1933), *Portraits and Prayers* (1934), *Everybody's Autobiography* (1937), and *Wars I Have Seen* (1945). Critical works such as *Useful Knowledge* (1928), *How to Write* (1931), *Lectures in America* (1935), *Narration* (1935), *What Are Masterpieces* (1940), and *Four in America* (1947) offer useful insights into her work. Collections of letters include *The Flowers of Friendship* (1953), ed. Donald C. Gallup, and editions of correspondence with Mabel Dodge Luhan (1996), ed. Patricia R. Everett, and with Thornton Wilder (1996), ed. Edward Burns. *Baby Precious Always Shines* (1999), ed. Kay Turner, is an illuminating collection of Stein and Toklas's love notes. Biographies include Howard Greenfeld's *Gertrude Stein* (1973), James R. Mellow's *Charmed Circle* (1974), and Linda Wagner-Martin's *Favored Strangers: Gertrude Stein and Her Family* (1995).

Studies include Robert B. Haas's *A Primer for the Gradual Understanding of Gertrude Stein* (1971), Wendy Steiner's *Exact Resemblance to Exact Resemblance: The Literary Portraiture of Gertrude Stein* (1978), Marianne DeKoven's *A Different Language* (1983), Jayne L. Walker's *The Making of a Modernist* (1984), Harriet Scott Chessman's *The Public Is Invited to Dance: Representation, the Body, and Dialogue in Gertrude Stein* (1989), Peter Quartermain's *Disjunctive Poetics* (1992), Bob Perelman's *The Trouble with Genius* (1994), Margaret Dickie's *Stein, Bishop, and Rich: Lyrics of Love, War, and Place* (1997), M. Lynn Weiss's *Gertrude Stein and Richard Wright* (1998), Steven Watson's *Prepare for Saints: Gertrude Stein, Virgil Thomson, and the Mainstreaming of American Modernism* (1998), Jonathan Levin's *The Poetics of Transition: Emerson, Pragmatism, and American Literary Modernism* (1999), Mary E. Galvin's *Queer Poetics* (1999), Steven Meyer's *Irresistible Dictation: Gertrude Stein and the Correlations of Writing and Science* (2001), and Brad Bucknell's *Literary Modernism and Musical Aesthetics* (2001). A useful collection of essays, including contemporary reviews, is *The Critical Response to Gertrude Stein* (2000), ed. Kirk Curnutt. Other collections include *Critical Essays on Gertrude Stein* (1986), ed. Michael J. Hoffman, and *Gertrude Stein Advanced* (1990), ed. Richard Kostelanetz. Maureen R. Liston published an annotated bibliography in 1979.

Wallace Stevens

The Collected Poems of Wallace Stevens was published in 1954. *The Palm at the End of the Mind* (1971), ed. Holly Stevens, is a generous selection that contains some material not included in the earlier collection. *Opus Posthumous*, ed. Samuel French Morse, was originally published in 1957, was revised in 1989 by Milton J. Bates, and contains material left unpublished at Stevens's death. Also useful is *Collected Poetry and Prose* (1997), ed. Frank Kermode and Joan Richardson. Stevens's major work of critical prose is *The Necessary Angel* (1951). *Letters of Wallace Stevens*, ed. Holly Stevens, was published in 1966 and revised in 1996. Biographies include Joan Richardson's two-volume *Wallace Stevens* (1986, 1988) and Tony Sharpe's *Wallace Stevens: A Literary Life* (1999).

Influential earlier studies include Joseph N. Riddel's *The Clairvoyant Eye* (1965), Helen Vendler's *On Extended Wings: Wallace Stevens' Longer Poems* (1969), A. Walton Litz's *Introspective Voyager* (1972), Michel Benamou's *Wallace Stevens and the Symbolist Imagination* (1972), Harold Bloom's *Wallace Stevens: The Poems of Our Climate* (1977), Charles Berger's *Forms of Farewell: The Late Poetry of Wallace Stevens* (1985), and Milton J. Bates's *Wallace Stevens: A Mythology of Self* (1985). Vendler's *Wallace Stevens: Words Chosen out of Desire* (1984) is a brief and especially cogent look at his work. More recent studies include Mark Halliday's *Stevens and the Interpersonal* (1991), Alan Filreis's *Wallace Stevens and the Actual World* (1991) and *Modernism from Right to Left: Wallace Stevens, the Thirties and Literary Radicalism* (1994), James Longenbach's *Wallace Stevens: The Plain Sense of Things* (1991), Janet McCann's *Wallace Stevens Revisited* (1995), Anthony Whiting's *The Never-Resting Mind: Wallace Stevens' Romantic Irony* (1996), Beverly Maeder's *Wallace Stevens' Experimental Language: The Lion in the Lute* (1999), Theodore Sampson's *A Cure of the Mind* (2000), Angus Cleghorn's *Wallace Stevens' Poetics* (2000), Lee M. Jenkins's *Wallace Stevens: Rage for Order* (2000), George S. Lensing's *Wallace Stevens and the Seasons* (2001), and Justin Quinn's *Gathered beneath the Storm: Wallace Stevens, Nature and Community* (2002). Collections of essays include *Wallace Stevens: The Poetics of Modernism* (1985), ed. Albert Gelpi; *Critical Essays on Wallace Stevens* (1988), ed. Steven Gould Axelrod; and *Wallace Stevens and the Feminine* (1993), ed. Melita Schaum. Essays also appear in *The Wallace Stevens Journal*. Bibliographic information is available in J. M. Edelstein's *Wallace Stevens: A Descriptive Bibliography* (1973) and John N. Serio's *Wallace Stevens: An Annotated Secondary Bibliography* (1994).

Allen Tate

Tate's *Collected Poems, 1919–1976* was published in 1977. Among Tate's important critical works are *On the Limits of Poetry, Selected Essays: 1928–1948* (1948), and *The Poetry Reviews of Allen Tate, 1924–1944* (1983), ed. Ashley Brown and Frances Neel Cheney. Tate also wrote plays; fiction, including the novel *The Fathers* (1938); and a biography, *Jefferson Davis* (1929). *I'll Take My Stand* (1930) is a controversial celebration of southern agrarianism by Tate and eleven others. Tate also published translations and edited many collections of poetry and criticism. His *Memoirs and Opinions* was published in 1975. Collections of letters include *The Literary Correspondence of Donald Davidson and Allen Tate* (1974), ed. John Tyree Fain and Thomas Daniel Young; *The Lytle-Tate Letters: The Correspondence of Andrew Lytle and Allen Tate* (1987), ed. Young and Elizabeth Sarcone; and *Cleanth Brooks and Allen Tate: Collected Letters, 1933–1976* (1998), ed. Alphonse Vinh. Radcliffe Squires's *Allen Tate: A Literary Biography* was published in 1971. Also of note are Walter Sullivan's *Allen Tate: A Recollection* (1988), and Thomas A. Underwood's *Allen Tate: Orphan of the South* (2000).

Studies include R. K. Meiners's *The Last Alternatives: A Study of the Works of Allen Tate* (1963), Louis D. Rubin Jr.'s *The Wary Fugitives: Four Poets and the South* (1978), Robert S. Dupree's *Allen Tate and the Augustinian Imagination* (1983), William Doreski's *The Years of Our Friendship: Robert Lowell and Allen Tate* (1990), Langdon Hammer's *Hart Crane and Allen Tate: Janus-Faced Modernism* (1993), and Peter Huff's *Allen Tate and the Catholic Revival* (1996). Numerous useful essays are collected in *Allen Tate and His Work* (1972), ed. Radcliffe Squires. More recent essays include Patricia Wallace's "Warren, with Ransom and Tate," *Columbia History of American Poetry* (1993), ed. Jay Parini and Brett C. Millier, and John Burt's "On Poetic Autonomy," *Modernism/Modernity* 2.2 (1995). Marshall Fallwell, Martha Cook, and Francis Immler's *Allen Tate: A Bibliography* was published in 1969. See also **The Fugitive Poets, The New Criticism and Poetry.**

Edward Thomas

The Collected Poems of Edward Thomas, ed. R. George Thomas, was published in 1978. A selection of Thomas's prose is *A Language Not to Be Betrayed* (1981), ed. Edna Longley. *Edward Thomas: Selected Letters* (1995) was edited by R. George Thomas, as was *Letters from Edward Thomas to Gordon Bottomley* (1968). *The Diary of Edward Thomas: 1 January–8 April 1917*, with an introduction by Roland Gant, was published in 1977. Thomas also wrote works about his travels around England, including *Oxford* (1903, 1983) and *The South Country* (1909, 1984). William Cooke's *Edward Thomas: A Critical Biography* was published in 1970. Biographical information is also available in Helen Thomas's *As It Was* (1926) and *World without End* (1931), Eleanor Farjeon's *Edward Thomas: The Last Four Years* (1958), and R. George Thomas's *Edward Thomas: A Portrait* (1985). An autobiographical fragment, *The Childhood of Edward Thomas*, was published in 1983 with a preface by Roland Gant.

For important discussions of Thomas's life and work, see H. Coombes's *Edward Thomas* (1956), Jan Marsh's *Edward Thomas: A Poet for*

His Country (1978), Andrew Motion's *The Poetry of Edward Thomas* (1980), Stan Smith's *Edward Thomas* (1986), Edna Longley's *Poetry in the Wars* (1987), Piers Grey's *Marginal Men* (1990), Jeremy Hooker's *Writers in a Landscape* (1996), and Rennie Parker's *The Georgian Poets* (1999). Also useful is *British Poets of the Great War* (2000), ed. Patrick Quinn. Numerous helpful essays are collected in *The Imagination of Edward Thomas* (1986), ed. Michael Kirkham, and *The Art of Edward Thomas* (1987), ed. Jonathan Barker. Bibliographic information is available in Robert P. Eckert's *Edward Thomas: A Biography and Bibliography* (1937). See also **Poets of World War I.**

Melvin Tolson

The best collection of Tolson's work is *"Harlem Gallery" and Other Poems* (1999), ed. Raymond Nelson, with an introduction by Rita Dove. Nelson's notes to "Harlem Gallery" are invaluable. Other volumes include *Rendezvous with America* (1944), *Libretto for the Republic of Liberia* (1953), *Harlem Gallery: Book I, The Curator* (1965), and *A Gallery of Harlem Portraits* (1979). Robert M. Farnsworth edited a collection of Tolson's columns from the *Washington Tribune, Caviar and Cabbage* (1982). In 2001, Edward J. Mullen edited an edition of Tolson's *The Harlem Group of Negro Writers* (1940). An interview appears in *Anger and Beyond* (1966), ed. Herbert Hill. Biographical information, as well as critical comment, is to be found in Joy Flasch's *Melvin B. Tolson* (1972) and Farnsworth's *Melvin B. Tolson, 1898–1966: Plain Talk and Poetic Prophecy* (1984).

Book-length studies include Mariann Russell's *Melvin B. Tolson's "Harlem Gallery": A Literary Analysis* (1980) and Michael Bérubé's *Marginal Forces/Cultural Centers: Tolson, Pynchon, and the Politics of the Canon* (1992). Other important discussions include Rita Dove's "Telling It Like It Is: Narrative Techniques in Melvin Tolson's *Harlem Gallery*," *New England Review and Bread Loaf Quarterly* 8.1 (1985); Gordon E. Thompson's "Ambiguity in Tolson's *Harlem Gallery*," *Callaloo* 9.1 (1986); Craig Werner's "Blues for T. S. Eliot and Langston Hughes: The Afro-Modernist Aesthetic of *Harlem Gallery*," *Black American Literature Forum* 24 (1990); Aldon L. Nielsen's "Melvin B. Tolson and Deterritorialization of Modernism," *African American Review* 26.2 (1992); Nelson's "Harlem Gallery: An Advertisement and User's Manual," *Virginia Quarterly Review* 75.3 (1999); Russell's "Langston Hughes and Melvin Tolson: Blues People," *The Furious Flowering of African American Poetry* (1999), ed. Joanne V. Gabbin; and Gary Lenhart's "Caviar and Cabbage: The Voracious Appetite of Melvin Tolson," *American Poetry Review* 29.2 (2000).

Jean Toomer

Toomer's *Collected Poems*, ed. Robert Jones and Margery Toomer Latimer, was published in 1988. Previously uncollected materials are printed in *A Jean Toomer Reader* (1993), ed. Frederik L. Rusch. The Norton Critical Edition of Toomer's 1923 masterwork, *Cane* (1988), ed. Darwin T. Turner, contains annotations and critical essays. Also of note are the book of aphorisms, *Essentials* (1931, 1991), ed. Rudolph Byrd, and *Jean Toomer: Selected Essays and Literary Criticism* (1996), ed. Robert B. Jones. Biographies include Nellie Y. McKay's *Jean Toomer, Artist* (1984), Cynthia Earl Kerman and Richard Eldridge's *The Lives of Jean Toomer: A Hunger for Wholeness* (1987), and Byrd's *Jean Toomer's Years with Gurdjieff: Portrait of an Artist, 1923–1936* (1990).

Studies include Darwin T. Turner's *In a Minor Chord* (1971), Houston A. Baker's *Singers of Daybreak* (1974), Brian Joseph Benson and Mabel Mayle Dillard's *Jean Toomer* (1980), Donald B. Gibson's *The Politics of Literary Expression* (1981), Henry Louis Gates Jr.'s *Figures in Black* (1987), Charles R. Larson's *Invisible Darkness: Jean Toomer and Nella Larsen* (1993), Robert B. Jones's *Jean Toomer and the Prison-House of Thought* (1993), Charles Scruggs and Lee VanDemarr's *Jean Toomer and the Terrors of American History* (1998), Matthew Pratt Guterl's *The Color of Race in America, 1900–1940* (2001), and Geneviève Fabre and Michel Feith's *Jean Toomer and the Harlem Renaissance* (2001). *CLA Journal* 17 (1974) is a special Toomer issue. Other useful essays are collected in *Jean Toomer: A Critical Evaluation* (1988), ed. Therman O'Daniel. Bibliographic information is available in McKay's *Jean Toomer, Artist* and C. Lyn Munro's essay in *Black American Literature Forum* 21 (1987). See also **Harlem Renaissance.**

Robert Penn Warren

The Collected Poems of Robert Penn Warren, ed. John Burt, was published in 1998. Warren also wrote many novels, including *All the King's Men* (1946) and *World Enough and Time* (1950). Important critical works include *New and Selected Essays* (1989) and the lectures collected in *Democracy and Poetry* (1975). With Cleanth Brooks, Warren edited the influential anthology *Understanding Poetry* (1938). Correspondence is available in *Cleanth Brooks and Robert Penn Warren* (1998), ed. James A. Grimshaw Jr., and *Selected Letters of Robert Penn Warren* (2000–2001), ed. William Bedford Clark. Interviews are collected in *Robert Penn Warren Talking* (1980), ed. Floyd Watkins and John T. Hiers. John Blotner's *Robert Penn Warren: A Biography* was published in 1997.

Important book-length studies dealing with Warren's poetry include James Justus's *The*

Achievement of Robert Penn Warren (1981), Calvin Bedient's *In the Heart's Last Kingdom* (1984), Burt's *Robert Penn Warren and American Idealism* (1988), Randolph Runyon's *The Braided Dream: Robert Penn Warren's Late Poetry* (1990), Hugh Ruppersburg's *Robert Penn Warren and the American Imagination* (1990), Clark's *The American Vision of Robert Penn Warren* (1991), Robert S. Koppelman's *Robert Penn Warren's Modernist Spirituality* (1995), Lesa Carnes Corrigan's *Poems of Pure Imagination: Robert Penn Warren and the Romantic Tradition* (1999), Randy Hendricks's *Lonelier than God: Robert Penn Warren and the Southern Exile* (2000), and Grimshaw's *Understanding Robert Penn Warren* (2001). Collections of essays include *Critical Essays on Robert Penn Warren* (1981), ed. William Bedford Clark; *Robert Penn Warren* (1986), ed. Harold Bloom; and *The Legacy of Robert Penn Warren* (2000), ed. David Madden. Grimshaw's descriptive bibliography was published in 1981. See also **The Fugitive Poets, The New Criticism and Poetry.**

Walt Whitman

The various editions of *Leaves of Grass* (1855–92) are available in a *Comprehensive Reader's Edition* (1965, 1968), ed. Harold W. Blodgett and Sculley Bradley. Blodgett and Bradley also edited the Norton Critical Edition of *Leaves of Grass* (1973). Other important editions include the three-volume *"Leaves of Grass": A Textual Variorum of the Printed Poems* (1980), ed. Bradley, Blodgett, Arthur Golden, and William White; and *Blue Book* (1968), ed. Golden, a facsimile of Whitman's copy of the 1860 edition marked up with his changes for the 1867 edition. There are now over twenty volumes of *The Collected Writings of Walt Whitman* (1961–), ed. Gay Allen Wilson and others, including the six-volume *Correspondence* (1961–77) and its two-volume supplement (1990–91), ed. Edwin H. Miller; *The Early Poems and the Fiction* (1963), ed. Thomas L. Brasher; *Prose Works 1892* (1963, 1964), ed. Floyd Stovall; *Notebooks and Unpublished Prose Manuscripts* (1984), ed. Edward F. Grier; and *The Journalism* (1998–), ed. Herbert Bergman, Douglas A. Noverr, and Edward J. Recchia.

The standard biography is Allen's *The Solitary Singer* (1955). Other important accounts of Whitman's life include Justin Kaplan's *Walt Whitman* (1980), Ed Folsom's *Native Representations* (1994), David S. Reynolds's *Walt Whitman's America* (1995), and Jerome Loving's *Walt Whitman: The Song of Himself* (1999). Also of note are Brasher's *Whitman as Editor of the Brooklyn Daily Eagle* (1970); Joseph Jay Rubin's *The Historic Whitman* (1973); Stovall's *The Foreground of "Leaves of Grass"* (1974); *Whitman in His Own Time* (1991), ed. Joel Myerson; and *The Better Angel: Walt Whitman in the Civil War* (2000).

Important studies include Miller's *Walt Whitman's Poetry: A Psychological Journey* (1968), Harold Aspiz's *Walt Whitman and the Body Beautiful* (1980), M. Wynn Thomas's *The Lunar Light of Whitman's Poetry* (1987), Betsy Erkkila's *Whitman the Poetical Poet* (1989), Ezra Greenspan's *Walt Whitman and the American Reader* (1990), Kenneth M. Price's *Whitman and Tradition* (1990), Michael Moon's *The Dissemination of Whitman* (1991), Byrne R. S. Fone's *Masculine Landscapes: Walt Whitman and the Homoerotic Text* (1992), Martin Klammer's *Whitman, Slavery, and the Emergence of Leaves of Grass* (1995), Robert Leigh Davis's *Whitman and the Romance of Medicine* (1997), Vivian Pollak's *The Erotic Whitman* (2000), and Mark Maslan's *Whitman Possessed* (2001). Important collections of critical essays include *Critical Essays on Walt Whitman* (1983), ed. James Woodress; *The Continuing Presence of Walt Whitman* (1992), ed. Robert K. Martin; *Walt Whitman of Mickle Street* (1994), ed. Geoffrey M. Sill; *The Cambridge Companion to Walt Whitman* (1995), ed. Greenspan; and *Whitman East and West* (2002), ed. Folsom.

Useful companions include Allen's *A Reader's Guide to Walt Whitman* (1970) and *New Walt Whitman Handbook* (1975); and *A Historical Guide to Walt Whitman* (2000), ed. David Reynolds. Reference materials include Edwin H. Eby's *Concordance of Walt Whitman's Leaves of Grass and Selected Prose Writings* (1955) and Myerson's *Walt Whitman: A Descriptive Bibliography* (1993).

William Carlos Williams

The two-volume *Collected Poems of William Carlos Williams* (1986) was edited by A. Walton Litz and Christopher J. MacGowan. Another useful collection is *Imaginations* (1970), ed. Webster Schott, which contains the books *Kora in Hell* (1920) and *Spring and All* (1923) as well as prose works such as *The Great American Novel* (1923). The five books of *Paterson* were published together in 1963 and reprinted in a revised edition edited by MacGowan in 1992. Short stories are collected in *Make Light of It* (1950) and *The Farmers' Daughters* (1961); and plays in *Many Loves and Other Plays* (1961), ed. Robert Downing. Other important works are the essays on historical American figures, *In the American Grain* (1925) and *The Autobiography of William Carlos Williams* (1951). Other autobiographical works include *I Wanted to Write a Poem* (1958), dictated to and edited by Edith Heal; and a memoir about his mother, *Yes, Mrs. Williams* (1959). *Selected Essays* was published in 1954. *A Recognizable Image* (1978), ed. Bram Dijkstra, is a collection of Williams's writings on the visual arts.

John C. Thirwall edited *Selected Letters of William Carlos Williams* (1957). Other selections of correspondence include *William Carlos Williams and James Laughlin* (1989), ed. Hugh Witemeyer; *The Last Word: The Letters between Marcia Nardi and William Carlos Williams* (1994), ed. Elizabeth Murrie O'Neil; *Pound/Williams* (1996), ed. Witemeyer; and *The Letters of Denise Levertov and William Carlos Williams* (1998), ed. MacGowan. Two biographies are Reed Whittemore's *William Carlos Williams: Poet from Jersey* (1975) and Paul Mariani's *William Carlos Williams: A New World Naked* (1981).

Helpful introductory studies include Thomas R. Whitaker's *William Carlos Williams* (1968), James E. B. Breslin's *William Carlos Williams: An American Artist* (1970), and Kelli A. Larson's *Guide to the Poetry of William Carlos Williams* (1995). Other studies include Dijkstra's *The Hieroglyphics of a New Speech: Cubism, Stieglitz, and the Early Poetry of William Carlos Williams* (1969), Mike Weaver's *William Carlos Williams: The American Background* (1971), Jerome Mazzaro's *William Carlos Williams: The Later Poems* (1973), Joseph N. Riddel's *The Inverted Bell* (1974), Charles Doyle's *William Carlos Williams and the American Poem* (1982); Henry M. Sayre's *The Visual Text of William Carlos Williams* (1983), Stephen Cushman's *William Carlos Williams and the Meanings of Measure* (1985), Kerry Driscoll's *William Carlos Williams and the Maternal Muse* (1987), Ann W. Fisher-Wirth's *William Carlos Williams and Autobiography* (1989), Ron Callan's *William Carlos Williams and Transcendentalism* (1992), T. Hugh Crawford's *Modernism, Medicine and William Carlos Williams* (1993), Brian A. Bremen's *William Carlos Williams and the Diagnostics of Culture* (1993), Peter Halter's *The Revolution in the Visual Arts and the Poetry of William Carlos Williams* (1994), Julio Marzán's *The Spanish American Roots of William Carlos Williams* (1994), Barry Ahearn's *William Carlos Williams and Alterity* (1994), Bruce Comens's *Apocalypse and After* (1995), Robert Cirasa's *The Lost Works of William Carlos Williams* (1995), Daniel Morris's *The Writings of William Carlos Williams: Publicity for the Self* (1995), Stanley Koehler's *Countries of the Mind* (1998), and John Beck's *Writing the Radical Center: William Carlos Williams, John Dewey, and American Cultural Politics* (2001). Useful collections include *William Carlos Williams: The Critical Heritage* (1980), ed. Charles Doyle, and *Critical Essays on William Carlos Williams* (1994), ed. Steven Gould Axelrod and Helen Deese. Emily Mitchell Wallace's *A Bibliography of William Carlos Williams* was published in 1968.

Yvor Winters

The Collected Poems of Yvor Winters, with an introduction by Donald Davie, was published in 1978. Winters's critical prose works include *Edwin Arlington Robinson* (1946); *In Defense of Reason* (1947); *The Function of Criticism* (1957); *Forms of Discovery* (1967); and *Yvor Winters: Uncollected Essays and Reviews* (1973), ed. Francis Murphy. Letters are available in *Hart Crane and Yvor Winters: Their Literary Correspondence* (1978), ed. Thomas Parkinson, and *The Selected Letters of Yvor Winters* (2000), ed. R. L. Barth.

Book-length studies include Keith F. McKean's *The Moral Measure of Literature* (1961), Richard J. Sexton's *The Complex of Yvor Winters's Criticism* (1973), Grosvenor Powell's *Language as Being in the Poetry of Yvor Winters* (1980), Elizabeth Isaacs's *An Introduction to the Poetry of Yvor Winters* (1981), Dick Davis's *Wisdom and Wilderness: The Achievement of Yvor Winters* (1983), Terry Comito's *In Defense of Winters* (1986), and Richard Hoffpauir's *The Contemplative Poetry of Edwin Arlington Robinson, Robert Frost, and Yvor Winters* (2002). *Southern Review* 17 (October 1981) is a special Winters issue. Recent critical essays include David Yezzi's "The Seriousness of Yvor Winters," *New Criterion* 15.10 (1997); H. T. Kirby-Smith's "In Search of a Foot," *Southern Review* 36.3 (2000), and Neil Powell's "Winters' Talents," *Pn Review* 27 (2000). Powell's *Yvor Winters: An Annotated Bibliography, 1919–1982* was published in 1983. See also **The New Criticism and Poetry.**

Elinor Wylie

The Collected Poems of Elinor Wylie, ed. William Rose Benét, was published in 1932. Wylie also published novels, including *Jennifer Lorn* (1923), *The Venetian Glass Nephew* (1925), *The Orphan Angel* (1926), and *Mr. Hodge and Mr. Hazard* (1928). These novels are included, with Wylie's essays, in *Collected Prose* (1933). Biographies include Nancy Hoyt's *Elinor Wylie: The Portrait of an Unknown Lady* (1935), Stanley Olson's *Elinor Wylie: A Life Apart* (1979), and Judith Farr's *The Life and Art of Elinor Wylie* (1983).

A good book-length study is Thomas Gray's *Elinor Wylie* (1969). Other important discussions can be found in Benét's *The Prose and Poetry of Elinor Wylie* (1934); Julia Cluck's "Elinor Wylie's Shelley Obsession," *PMLA* 56 (September 1941); Phyllis M. Jones's "Amatory Sonnet Sequences and the Female Perspective of Elinor Wylie and Edna St. Vincent Millay," *Women's Studies* 10.1 (1983); Anna Shannon Elfenbein and Terence Allan Hoagwood's " 'Wild Peaches': Landscapes of Desire and Deprivation," *Women's Studies* 15.4 (1988); Jeanne Larsen's "Lowell, Teasdale, Wylie, Millay, and Bogan," *The Columbia History of American Poetry* (1993), ed. Jay Parini and Brett C. Millier; Margaret Barbour Gilbert's "Elinor Wylie (1885–1928)," *American Women Writers, 1900–1945: A Bio-Bibliographical Critical*

Source Book (2000), ed. Laurie Champion. Kathryn Hilt's bibliography appears in *Bulletin of Bibliography* 42.1 (1985).

William Butler Yeats

An authoritative edition of Yeats's poetry is available in the revised edition of *The Poems*, the first volume of *The Collected Works of W. B. Yeats* (1989), ed. Richard J. Finneran and George Mills Harper. Other published volumes in this series include *Later Essays* (1994), ed. William H. O'Donnell with Elizabeth Bergmann Loizeaux; *Autobiographies* (1999), ed. O'Donnell and Douglas N. Archibald; and *Later Articles and Reviews* (2000), ed. Colton Johnson. Other important scholarly editions include *The Variorum Edition of the Poems* (1957, 1966), ed. Peter Allt and Russell K. Alspach; *The Variorum Edition of the Plays* (1966), ed. Russell K. and Catherine C. Alspach; and *The Poems*, edited by Daniel Albright (1990). An excellent paperback collection is the Norton Critical Edition of *Yeats's Poetry, Drama, and Prose* (2000), ed. James Pethica, which contains a selection of secondary criticism in addition to Yeats's work. A selection of the correspondence is *The Letters of W. B. Yeats* (1954), ed. Allan Wade. John Kelly and Eric Domville are editing a multivolume series, *The Collected Letters of W. B. Yeats* (1986–). Yeats's mythological system is available in *A Vision* (1925, 1938). Also of note are *Mythologies* (1959), which contains much of Yeats's prose fiction; *Memoirs* (1972), ed. Denis Donoghue, which contains journals and the first draft of the *Autobiographies; Essays and Introductions* (1961); the miscellaneous prose in *Explorations* (1962); the two-volume *Uncollected Prose by W. B. Yeats* (1970, 1975), ed. John P. Frayne; and *Prefaces and Introductions* (1988), ed. O'Donnell.

R. F. Foster has published the first of two volumes of what will be the standard biography: *W. B. Yeats: A Life* (1997–). Also useful is A. N. Jeffares's *W. B. Yeats: A New Biography* (1989). Richard Ellmann's *Yeats: The Man and the Masks* (1948) remains one of the most important works on the poet.

In the vast body of Yeats criticism, some important book-length studies are Ellmann's *The Identity of Yeats* (1954), Frank Kermode's *Romantic Image* (1957, 2002), Jon Stallworthy's *Between the Lines: W. B. Yeats's Poetry in the Making* (1963), Helen Vendler's *Yeats's* Vision *and Later Plays* (1963), Thomas R. Whitaker's *Swan and Shadow* (1964), Harold Bloom's *Yeats* (1970), George Bornstein's *Yeats and Shelley* (1970), Donoghue's *Yeats* (1971), Thomas Parkinson's *W. B. Yeats, Self-Critic* (1973), Mary Helen Thuente's *W. B. Yeats and Irish Folklore* (1980), Elizabeth Butler Cullingford's *Yeats, Ireland and Fascism* (1981), Loizeaux's *Yeats and the Visual Arts* (1986), Paul Scott Stanfield's *Yeats and Politics in the Nineteen-Thirties* (1988), Finneran's *Editing Yeats's Poems* (1990), Stan Smith's *W. B. Yeats* (1990), Jahan Ramazani's *Yeats and the Poetry of Death* (1990), Hazard Adams's *The Book of Yeats's Poems* (1991), Michael North's *The Political Aesthetic of Yeats, Eliot, and Pound* (1991), Cullingford's *Gender and History in Yeats's Love Poetry* (1993), M. L. Rosenthal's *Running to Paradise* (1994), Marjorie Howes's *Yeats's Nations* (1996), Michael J. Sidnell's *Yeats's Poetry and Poetics* (1996), Vicki Mahaffey's *States of Desire* (1998), Bornstein's *Material Modernism* (2001), Gregory Castle's *Modernism and the Celtic Revival* (2001), and Richard Greaves's *Transition, Reception, and Modernism in W. B. Yeats* (2002). Collections of essays include *William Butler Yeats* (1986), ed. Bloom; *Yeats's Political Identities* (1996), ed. Jonathan Allison; *W. B. Yeats: Critical Assessments*, ed. David Pierce (2000); and *W. B. Yeats and Postcolonialism* (2001), ed. Deborah Fleming. *W. B. Yeats: The Critical Heritage* (1977), ed. Jeffares, provides a reception history and contemporary reviews.

Jeffares's *A New Commentary on the Poems of W. B. Yeats* (1984) and *A Commentary on the Plays of W. B. Yeats* (1975) are indispensable references. Also valuable are Sam McCready's *A William Butler Yeats Encyclopedia* (1997) and Lester I. Conner's *A Yeats Dictionary* (1998). Bibliographic information is available in Wade's *A Bibliography of the Writings of W. B. Yeats* (revised by Alspach, 1968). Many essays have appeared annually in the journals *Yeats* and *Yeats Annual*. See also **Irish Poetry.**

Louis Zukofsky

Zukofsky's *Complete Short Poetry* was published in 1991. A complete version of his long poem "A" was published in 1978. Zukofsky's critical writings are available in *Prepostitions +* (2000), ed. Mark Scroggins. *Collected Fiction* was published in 1990. Zukofsky also wrote plays, including *Arise, Arise* (1962), and translations of Latin literature, including *Catullus* (with Celia Zukofsky, 1969). He also edited collections, including *A Test of Poetry* (1948, 2000) and *The "Objectivist" Anthology* (1932). Zukofsky's correspondence with Ezra Pound is available in *Pound/Zukofsky* (1987), ed. Barry Ahearn, and with Lorine Niedecker in *Niedecker and the Correspondence with Zukofsky* (1993), ed. Jenny Penberthy.

Many useful critical essays on Zukofsky are collected in *Upper Limit Music* (1997), ed. Scroggins, and *Louis Zukofsky: Man and Poet* (1979), ed. Carroll F. Terrell. Useful book-length studies include Ahearn's *Zukofsky's "A": An Introduction* (1983), Michele J. Leggott's *Reading Zukofsky's "80 Flowers"* (1989), Sandra Kumamoto Stanley's *Louis Zukofsky and the Transformation of a Modern American Poetics* (1994), and Scroggins's *Louis Zukofsky and the Poetry of Knowledge* (1998). Studies that discuss

Zukofsky among other poets include Peter Quartermain's *Disjunctive Poetics* (1992), Alison Rieke's *The Senses of Nonsense* (1992), Bob Perelman's *The Trouble with Genius* (1994), Bruce Comens's *Apocalypse and After* (1995), Luke Carson's *Consumption and Depression in Gertrude Stein, Louis Zukofsky, and Ezra Pound* (1999), and Libbie Rifkin's *Career Moves: Olson, Creeley, Zukofsky, Berrigan, and the American Avant-Garde* (2000). Celia Zukofsky's *A Bibliography of Louis Zukofsky* was published in 1969. See also **Objectivism.**

Permissions Acknowledgments

W. H. Auden: "Writing" from THE DYER'S HAND AND OTHER ESSAYS by W. H. Auden, copyright © 1948, 1950, 1952, 1953, 1954, 1956, 1957, 1958, 1960, 1962 by W. H. Auden. "The Secret Agent," copyright © 1928 by W. H. Auden. "This Lunar Beauty" and "The Wanderer," copyright © 1930 by W. H. Auden. "Who's Who," copyright © 1937 and renewed 1965 by W. H. Auden. "On This Island," copyright © 1937 and renewed 1965 by W. H. Auden. "Lullaby" and "As I Walked Out One Evening," copyright © 1940 and renewed 1968 by W. H. Auden. "Museé des Beaux Arts," copyright © 1940 and renewed 1968 by W. H. Auden. "The Capital," copyright © 1938 by W. H. Auden. "The Unknown Citizen," copyright © 1940 and renewed 1968 by W. H. Auden. "The Shield of Achilles," copyright © 1956 by W. H. Auden. "Prologue at Sixty," copyright © 1967 by W. H. Auden. "A New Year Greeting," copyright © 1969 by W. H. Auden. "A Lullaby," copyright © 1972 by W. H. Auden. "In Memory of W. B. Yeats," copyright © 1940 and renewed 1968 by W. H. Auden. "September 1, 1939," copyright © 1940 and renewed 1968 by W. H. Auden. "In Memory of Sigmund Freud" and "In Praise of Limestone," copyright © 1951 by W. H. Auden. From "Spain 1937," copyright © 1940 and renewed 1968 by W. H. Auden. From "Sonnets from China (In Time of War)," copyright © 1976 by Edward Mendelson, William Meredith, and Monroe K. Spears, Executors of the Estate of W. H. Auden. From W. H. AUDEN: THE COLLECTED POEMS, copyright © 1976 by Edward Mendelson, William Meredith, and Monroe K. Spears, Executors of the Estate of W. H. Auden. Used by permission of Random House, Inc.

John Betjeman: From COLLECTED POEMS of John Betjeman. Copyright © 1958. Reprinted by permission of John Murray (Publishers) Ltd.

Louise Bogan: "The Alchemist," "Cassandra," "Knowledge," "Medusa," "Night," and "Women" from THE BLUE ESTUARIES by Louise Bogan. Copyright © 1968 by Louise Bogan. Copyright renewed © 1996 by Ruth Limmer. Reprinted by permission of Farrar, Straus & Giroux, LLC.

Sterling Brown: "Odyssey of Big Boy," "Southern Road," "Ma Rainey," "Strong Men," "Memphis Blues," "Slim in Atlanta," "Slim Greer," "Sporting Beasley," and "Old Lem" from THE COLLECTED POEMS OF STERLING A. BROWN, ed. Michael S. Harper. Copyright © 1980 by Sterling A. Brown. Reprinted by permission of HarperCollins Publishers, Inc.

Basil Bunting: From COMPLETE POEMS of Basil Bunting, Bloodaxe Books, 2000, reprinted by permission of the publisher.

Austin Clarke: "The Young Woman of Beare" and "The Planter's Daughter" from SELECTED POEMS of Austin Clarke. Reprinted by permission of R. Dardis Clarke.

Hart Crane: "Repose of Rivers, "At Melville's Tomb," "The Broken Tower," "Voyages" I, II, III, IV, V, VI, "Royal Palm," "The Bridge," "Black Tambourine," and "Chaplinesque" from COMPLETE POEMS OF HART CRANE by Hart Crane and by Marc Simon, editor. Copyright © 1986 by Marc Simon. Used by permission of Liveright Publishing Corporation. "A Letter to Harriet Monroe" from THE COMPLETE POEMS AND SELECTED LETTERS AND PROSE OF HART CRANE by Hart Crane, ed. Brom Weber. Copyright © 1933, 1958, 1966 by Liveright Publishing Corporation. Copyright © 1952 by Brom Weber. Used by permission of Liveright Publishing Corporation.

Countee Cullen: "For a Lady I Know," "Atlantic City Waiter," "Incident," "Yet Do I Marvel," and "Heritage" published in ON THESE I STAND by Countee Cullen, copyright © Harper & Bros NY, NY. Copyrights held by Amistad Research Center, Administered by Thompson and Thompson, New York, NY.

E. E. Cummings: "in Just-," "O sweet spontaneous," Buffalo Bill 's," "the Cambridge ladies who live in furnished souls," "i was sitting in mcsorley's. outside it was New York and beauti-," "next to of course god america i," "i sing of Olaf glad and big," "my sweet old etcetera," "anyone lived in a pretty how town," "r-p-o-p-h-e-s-s-a-g-r," "my father moved through dooms of love," "may I feel said he," and "pity this busy monster, manunkind" from COMPLETE POEMS: 1904–1962 by E. E. Cummings, ed. George J. Firmage. Copyright © 1923, 1925, 1926, 1931, 1935, 1938, 1939, 1940, 1944, 1945, 1946, 1947, 1948, 1949, 1950, 1951, 1952, 1953, 1954, 1955, 1956, 1957, 1958, 1959, 1960, 1961, 1962, 1963, 1966, 1967, 1968, 1972, 1973, 1974, 1975, 1976, 1977, 1978, 1979, 1980, 1981, 1982, 1983, 1984, 1985, 1986, 1987, 1988, 1989, 1990, 1991 by the Trustees for the E. E. Cummings Trust. Copyright © 1973, 1976, 1978, 1979, 1981, 1983, 1985, 1991 by George James Firmage. Used by permission of Liveright Publishing Corporation.

C. Day Lewis: From THE COMPLETE POEMS by C. Day Lewis, published by Sinclair-Stevenson (1992). Copyright © 1992 in this edition The Estate of C. Day Lewis. Reprinted by permission of The Random House Group Ltd.

Emily Dickinson: Reprinted by permission of the publishers and the Trustees of Amherst College from THE POEMS OF EMILY DICKINSON, ed. Thomas H. Johnson, Cambridge, Mass.: The Belknap Press of Harvard University Press, copyright © 1951, 1955, 1979 by the President and Fellows of Harvard College. Reprinted by permission of the publishers from THE LETTERS OF EMILY DICKINSON, ed. Thomas H. Johnson, Cambridge, Mass.: The Belknap Press of Harvard University Press, copyright © 1958, 1986 by the President and Fellows of Harvard College.

Keith Douglas: "Aristocrats," "Gallantry," "The Knife," "Simplify Me When I'm Dead," "Soissons," and "Vergissmeinnicht" from THE COMPLETE POEMS: THIRD EDITION by Keith Douglas. Copyright © 1998 by The Estate of Keith Douglas. Reprinted by permission of Faber and Faber, Inc., an affiliate of Farrar, Straus & Giroux, LLC.

Richard Eberhart: "The Fury of Aerial Bombardment" and "The Groundhog," from COLLECTED POEMS 1930–1986 by Richard Eberhart, copyright © 1960, 1976, 1987 by Richard Eberhart. Used by permission of Oxford University Press, Inc.

T. S. Eliot: "Little Gidding" from FOUR QUARTETS, copyright © 1942 by T. S. Eliot and renewed 1970 by Esme Valerie Eliot. "Journey of the Magi" from COLLECTED POEMS 1909–1962 by T. S. Eliot, copyright © 1936 by Harcourt, Inc., copyright © 1964, 1973 by T. S. Eliot, reprinted by permission of Harcourt, Inc. and Faber and Faber Ltd. "The Love Song of J. Alfred Prufrock," "Whispers of Immortality," "Sweeney among the Nightingales," "Gerontion," "The Waste Land," and "Preludes" from COLLECTED POEMS 1909–1962. From SELECTED PROSE by T. S. Eliot. Reprinted by permission of the publisher, Faber and Faber Ltd.

William Empson: "Villanelle," "Ignorance of Death," and "Missing Dates" from COLLECTED POEMS OF WILLIAM EMPSON, copyright © 1949 and renewed 1977 by William Empson, reprinted by permission of Harcourt, Inc. and The Random House Group Ltd. Published in Great Britain by Chatto & Windus.

Robert Frost: From THE POETRY OF ROBERT FROST, edited by Edward Connery Lathem. Copyright © 1923, 1928, 1969 by Henry Holt and Company, copyright © 1936, 1942, 1944, 1951, 1956, 1958 by Robert Frost, copyright © 1964, 1967, 1970, 1975 by Lesley Frost Ballantine. "The Figure a Poem Makes" from SELECTED PROSE OF ROBERT FROST, ed. Hyde Cox and Edward Connery Lathen. Copyright © 1939, 1967 by Henry Holt and Company. Reprinted by permission of Henry Holt and Company, LLC.

Robert Graves: From COMPLETE POEMS by Robert Graves (1995). Reprinted by permission of the publisher, Carcanet Press Ltd.

Ivor Gurney: Poems by Ivor Gurney are reprinted by permission of The Ivor Gurney Trust.

H. D.: From COLLECTED POEMS, 1912–1944, copyright © 1982 by The Estate of Hilda Doolittle. Reprinted by permission of New Directions Publishing Corp.

Thomas Hardy: "Nobody Comes" reprinted with the permission of Simon & Schuster, Inc. from THE COMPLETE POEMS OF THOMAS HARDY, ed. James Gibson. Copyright © 1925 By The

Macmillan Co. "He Never Expected Much" reprinted with the permission of Simon & Schuster, Inc. from THE COMPLETE POEMS OF THOMAS HARDY, ed. James Gibson. Copyright © 1928 by Florence E. Hardy and Sydney E. Cockerell; copyright renewed © 1956 by Lloyds Bank Ltd.

A. D. Hope: From SELECTED POEMS by A. D. Hope (1986). Reprinted by permission of the publisher, Carcanet Press Ltd.

Gerard Manley Hopkins: From SELECTED LETTERS of Gerard Manley Hopkins, ed. Catherine Phillips (1990). Reprinted by permission of Oxford University Press.

A. E. Housman: "They Say My Verse Is Sad: No Wonder" from THE COLLECTED POEMS OF A. E. HOUSMAN, copyright © 1964 by Robert E. Symons, copyright © 1936 by Barclays Bank Ltd. Reprinted by permission of Henry Holt and Company, LLC.

Langston Hughes: "The Negro Artist and the Racial Mountain" by Langston Hughes from *The Nation*, June 23, 1926. Copyright © 1926 by Langston Hughes. Reprinted by permission of Harold Ober Associates Inc. From THE COLLECTED POEMS OF LANGSTON HUGHES by Langston Hughes, copyright © 1994 by The Estate of Langston Hughes. Used by permission of Alfred A. Knopf, a division of Random House, Inc.

T. E. Hulme: From THE COLLECTED WRITINGS OF T. E. HULME, ed. Karen Csengeri. Reprinted by permission of Oxford University Press.

Robinson Jeffers: "Fawn's Foster-Mother" from THE COLLECTED POETRY OF ROBINSON JEFFERS, Vol. 1, 1920–1928, ed. Tim Hunt. "Ave Caesar" from THE COLLECTED POETRY OF ROBINSON JEFFERS, Vol. II, 1928–1938, ed. Tim Hunt Copyright © 1938 and renewed 1966 by Donnan and Garth Jeffers. Editorial matter © 1988 by the Board of Trustees of the Leland Stanford Jr. University. With the permission of Stanford University Press, www.sup.org. "Hurt Hawks," copyright © 1928 and renewed 1956 by Robinson Jeffers, "The Purse Seine," copyright © 1938 and renewed 1966 by Donnan & Garth Jeffers, from SELECTED POETRY OF ROBINSON JEFFERS, copyright © 1925, 1929 and renewed 1953, 1957 by Robinson Jeffers. Used by permission of Random House, Inc.

James Weldon Johnson: "The Creation" from GOD'S TROMBONES by James Weldon Johnson, copyright © 1927 The Viking Press, Inc., renewed 1955 by Grace Nail Johnson. From "Down by the Carib Sea" VI—"Sunset in the Tropics," and "O Black and Unknown Bards" from JAMES WELDON JOHNSON: COMPLETE POEMS, ed. Sondra Kathryn Wilson, copyright © 2000 Sondra Kathryn Wilson, Literary Executor of the Estate of James Weldon Johnson. Used by permission of Viking Penguin, a division of Penguin Putnam Inc.

David Jones: From IN PARENTHESIS and from THE ANATHÉMATA by David Jones. Reprinted by permission of the publisher, Faber and Faber Ltd.

Patrick Kavanagh: Permission granted by the publisher to reprint "Inniskeen Road: July Evening," "The Great Hunger" 1, "Epic," "Canal Bank Walk," "Come Dance with Kitty Stobling," and "In Memory of My Mother." Copyright by Devin-Adair Publishers, Inc., Old Greenwich, CT 06870. All rights reserved.

Rudyard Kipling: "We and They" from DEBITS AND CREDITS by Rudyard Kipling, copyright © 1926 by Rudyard Kipling. Used by permission of Doubleday, a division of Random House, Inc.

Stanley Kunitz: "The War against the Trees," "The Round," "Touch Me," "The Portrait," "The Magic Curtain," "Day of Foreboding," and "The Catch" from THE COLLECTED POEMS by Stanley Kunitz. Copyright © 2000 by Stanley Kunitz. Used by permission of W. W. Norton & Co., Inc.

D. H. Lawrence: "Andraitx—Pomegranate Flowers," "Bavarian Gentians," "Butterfly," "The English Are So Nice!" "Humming-Bird," "Lui et Elle," "Medlars and Sorb-Apples," "The Ship of Death," "Snake," "Sorrow," "Southern Night," "Whales Weep Not!" "You," and "Sicilian Cyclamens" from THE COMPLETE POEMS OF D. H. LAWRENCE, ed. V. de Sola Pinto and F. W. Roberts, copyright © 1964, 1971 by Angelo Ravagli and C. M. Weekley, Executors of the Estate of Frieda Lawrence Ravagli. Used by permission of Viking Penguin, a division of Penguin Putnam Inc.

Amy Lowell: "New Heavens for Old" from BALLADS FOR SALE, in THE COMPLETE POETICAL WORKS OF AMY LOWELL. Copyright © 1955 by Houghton Mifflin Company. Copyright © renewed 1983 by Houghton Mifflin Company, Brinton P. Roberts, and G. D'Andelot Belin, Esq. Reprinted by permission of Houghton Mifflin Co. All rights reserved.

Mina Loy: "English Rose" from "Anglo-Mongrels and the Rose: 1923–1925" from THE LAST LUNAR BAEDEKER by Mina Loy. Courtesy Roger L. Conover for the Estate of Mina Loy. "Brancusi's Golden Bird," "Der Blinde Junge," "Feminist Manifesto," "Gertrude Stein," from "Songs to Joannes," and "The Widow's Jazz" from THE LOST LUNAR BAEDEKER by Mina Loy. Works of Mina Loy copyright © 1996 by the Estate of Mina Loy. Introduction and edition copyright © 1996 by Roger L. Conover. Reprinted by permission of Farrar, Straus and Giroux, LLC.

Hugh MacDiarmid: "Another Epitaph on an Army of Mercenaries" and "The Sauchs in the Reuch Heuch Hauch" from SELECTED POETRY. Copyright © 1992 by Michael Grieve. Reprinted by permission of New Directions Publishing Corp. "In the Pantry," "Cloudburst and Soaring Moon," "Parley of Beasts," "O Wha's the Bride?" and "British Leftish Poetry, 1930–40" from COMPLETE POEMS of Hugh MacDiarmid (1993). Reprinted by permission of Carcanet Press Ltd.

Archibald MacLeish: "Ars Poetica," "The End of the World," and "You, Andrew Marvel" from COLLECTED POEMS, 1917–1982 by Archibald MacLeish. Copyright © 1985 by The Estate of Archibald MacLeish. Reprinted by permission of Houghton Mifflin Co. All rights reserved.

Louis MacNeice: From THE COLLECTED POEMS of Louis NacNeice, ed. E. R. Dodds. First published by Faber & Faber Ltd. Reprinted by permission of David Higham Associates Ltd.

Edna St. Vincent Millay: "I, Being Born a Woman and Distressed," Sonnet XVII of SONNETS FROM AN UNGRAFTED TREE, Sonnet XXX of FATAL INTERVIEW, "The Return," and "To a Calvinist in Bali" from COLLECTED POEMS by Edna St. Vincent Millay (HarperCollins). Copyright © 1923, 1931, 1934, 1939, 1951, 1958, 1962, 1967 by Edna St. Vincent Millay and Norma Millay Ellis. All rights reserved. Reprinted by permission of Elizabeth Barnett, literary executor.

Marianne Moore: "To a Steam Roller," "To a Snail," "The Fish," "Poetry," "England," "An Octopus," "Critics and Connoisseurs," "In the Days of Prismatic Colour," "A Grave," and "The Steeple-Jack" reprinted with the permission of Simon & Schuster, Inc. from THE COLLECTED POEMS OF MARIANNE MOORE. Copyright © 1935 by Marianne Moore; copyright renewed © 1963 by Marianne Moore and T. S. Eliot. "The Pangolin," "The Paper Nautilus," "What Are Years?" and "He Digesteth Harde Yron" reprinted with the permission of Simon & Schuster Inc. from THE COLLECTED POEMS OF MARIANNE MOORE. Copyright © 1941 by Marianne Moore; copyright renewed © 1969 by Marianne Moore. "Black Earth" by Marianne Moore is reprinted by permission of Marianne Craig Moore, Literary Executor of the Estate of Marianne Moore. "Humility, Concentration, and Gusto" from THE COMPLETE PROSE OF MARIANNE MOORE, ed. Patricia C. Willis. Used by permission of Viking Penguin, a division of Penguin Putnam Inc.

Edwin Muir: "The Horses," "The Absent," "The Wheel," "The Ballad of Hector in Hades" from COLLECTED POEMS by Edwin Muir, copyright © 1960 by Willa Muir. Used by permission of Oxford University Press, Inc. and Faber and Faber Ltd.

Lorine Niedecker: Poems from THE GRANITE PAIL by Lorine Niedecker. Copyright © 1985 by The Estate of Lorine Niedecker, Cid Corman, Executor. Published by North Point Press, a division of Farrar, Straus & Giroux, Inc. Reprinted by permission of Cid Corman.

George Oppen: From COLLECTED POEMS, copyright © 1975 by George Oppen. Reprinted by permission of New Directions Publishing Corp.

Wilfred Owen: From THE COLLECTED POEMS OF WILFRED OWEN, copyright © 1963 by Chatto & Windus, Ltd. Reprinted by permission of New Directions Publishing Corp.

Dorothy Parker: "George Sand," "Observation," "One Perfect Rose," "Oscar Wilde," and "Résumé" from THE PORTABLE DOROTHY PARKER by Dorothy Parker, ed. Brendan Gill, copyright © 1928, renewed 1956 by Dorothy Parker. Used by permission of Viking Penguin, a division of Penguin Putnam Inc.

Ezra Pound: From THE CANTOS OF EZRA POUND, copyright © 1934, 1937, 1940, 1948, 1956, 1962, 1963, 1966, and 1968 by Ezra Pound. "A Retrospect" and from "How to Read" from THE LITERARY ESSAYS OF EZRA POUND, copyright © 1935 by Ezra Pound. From PERSONAE, copyright © 1926 by Ezra Pound. Reprinted by permission of New Directions Publishing Corp.

John Crowe Ransom: From SELECTED POEMS, third ed., revised and enlarged, by John Crowe Ransom, copyright © 1924, 1927 by Alfred A. Knopf, Inc. and renewed 1952, 1955 by John Crowe Ransom. Used by permission of Alfred A. Knopf, a division of Random House, Inc.

Kenneth Rexroth: From COLLECTED SHORTER POEMS, copyright © 1944 by New Directions Publishing Corp. From THE MORNING STAR, copyright © 1979 by Kenneth Rexroth. Reprinted by permission of New Directions Publishing Corp.

Charles Reznikoff: Selections from POEMS 1918–1975: THE COMPLETE POEMS OF CHARLES REZNIKOFF. Copyright © 1977 by Marie Syrkin Reznikoff. "Entertainment" from HOLOCAUST by Charles Reznikoff. Copyright © 1975 by Charles Reznikoff. Reprinted by permission of Black Sparrow Press.

Laura Riding: "The Map of Places," "Footfalling," "Death as Death," "The Troubles of a Book," "Ding-Donging," and "With the Face" from THE POEMS OF LAURA RIDING. Copyright © 1938, 1980 by Laura (Riding) Jackson, transferred in 1991 to the Board of Literary Management of the late Laura (Riding) Jackson Reprinted by permission of Persea Books Inc. (New York). In conformity with the late author's wish, her Board of Literary Management asks us to record that, in 1940, Laura (Riding) Jackson renounced, on grounds of linguistic principal, the writing of poetry: she had come to hold that "poetry obstructs general attainment to something better in our linguistic way-of-life than we have."

Edwin Arlington Robinson: "The Sheaves" reprinted with the permission of Simon & Schuster, Inc. from THE COLLECTED POEMS OF EDWIN ARLINGTON ROBINSON, rev. Edwin Arlington Robinson. Copyright © 1925 by Edwin Arlington Robinson; copyright renewed © 1953 by Ruth Nivison and Barbara R. Holt.

Theodore Roethke: "Cuttings," copyright © 1948 by Theodore Roethke, "Cuttings (Later)," copyright © 1948 by Theodore Roethke, "Weed Puller," copyright © 1946 by Editorial Publications, Inc. "Frau Bauman, Frau Schmidt and Frau Schwartze," copyright © 1952 by Theodore Roethke, "My Papa's Waltz," copyright © 1942 by Hearst Magazines, Inc., "Dolor," copyright © 1943 by Modern Poetry Association, Inc., "The Minimal," copyright © 1942 by Theodore Roethke, "The Lost Son," copyright © 1947 by Theodore Roethke, "Elegy for Jane," copyright © 1950 by Theodore Roethke, "The Waking," copyright © 1953 by Theodore Roethke, "I Knew a Woman," copyright © 1954 by Theodore Roethke, "Wish for a Young Wife," copyright © 1963 by Beatrice Roethke, Administratrix of the Estate of Theodore Roethke, "The Far Field," copyright © 1962 by Beatrice Roethke, Administratrix of the Estate of Theodore Roethke, "In a Dark Time," copyright © 1960 by Beatrice Roethke, Administratrix of the Estate of Theodore Roethke, from THE COLLECTED POEMS OF THEODORE ROETHKE. Used by permission of Doubleday, a division of Random House, Inc.

Isaac Rosenberg: "The Mirror" from THE COLLECTED WORKS of Isaac Rosenberg, ed. I. Parsons and B. Wynick, published by Chatto & Windus. Reprinted by permission of The Random House Group Ltd.

Carl Sandburg: "Grass," "Cool Tombs," and "Gargoyle" from CORNHUSKERS by Carl Sandburg, copyright © 1918 by Holt, Rinehart and Winston and renewed 1946 by Carl Sandburg, reprinted by permission of Harcourt, Inc. "Chicago," "Subway," and "The Harbor" from CHICAGO POEMS by Carl Sandburg, copyright © 1916 by Holt, Rinehart and Winston and renewed 1944 by Carl Sandburg, reprinted by permission of Harcourt, Inc.

Siegfried Sassoon: "On Passing the New Menin Gate" from COLLECTED POEMS OF SIEGFRIED SASSOON by Siegfried Sassoon, copyright © 1918, 1920 by E. P. Dutton. Copyright © 1936, 1946, 1947, 1948 by Siegfried Sassoon. Used by permission of Viking Penguin, a division of Penguin Putnam Inc. Canadian rights to all poems administered by Barbara Levy Literary Agency. Copyright Siegfried Sassoon. Reprinted by kind permission of George Sassoon.

Edith Sitwell: From COLLECTED POEMS of Edith Sitwell, published by Sinclair Stevenson. Reprinted by permission of David Higham Associates Ltd.

Stevie Smith: From COLLECTED POEMS OF STEVIE SMITH, copyright © 1972 by Stevie Smith. Reprinted by permission of New Directions Publishing Corp.

Stephen Spender: "The Funeral" from POEMS by Stephen Spender is reprinted by permission of Faber and Faber Ltd. "The Express," "I Continually Think of Those (The Truly Great)," from "What I Expected," from "The Landscape Near an Aerodrome," and from "The Pylons," copyright © 1934 and renewed 1962 by Stephen Spender. From COLLECTED POEMS 1928–1985 by Stephen Spender, copyright © 1934 and renewed 1962 by Stephen Spender. Used by permission of Random House, Inc. and Faber and Faber Ltd.

Gertrude Stein: "Guillaume Apollinaire" and "George Hugnet" from PORTRAITS AND PRAYERS by Gertrude Stein. "Preciosilla" from COMPOSITION AND EXPLANATION by Gertrude Stein. "Stanza LXXXIII" from STANZAS IN MEDITATION by Gertrude Stein. From "A Transatlantic Interview" by Gertrude Stein. From SELECTED WRITINGS OF GERTRUDE STEIN. Reprinted by permission of the Estate of Gertrude Stein.

Wallace Stevens: From THE COLLECTED POEMS OF WALLACE STEVENS by Wallace Stevens, copyright © 1954 by Wallace Stevens and renewed 1982 by Holly Stevens. From THE NECESSARY ANGEL by Wallace Stevens, copyright © 1951 by Wallace Stevens. From OPUS POSTHUMOUS by Wallace Stevens, ed. by Samuel French Morse, copyright © 1957 by Elsie Stevens and Holly Stevens. Used by permission of Alfred A. Knopf, a division of Random House, Inc.

Allen Tate: "Mr. Pope," Ode to the Confederate Dead," and "The Swimmers" from COLLECTED POEMS 1919–1976 by Allen Tate. Copyright © 1977 by Allen Tate. Reprinted by permission of Farrar, Straus and Giroux, LLC.

Melvin Tolson: "Lambda", "Mu," "Nu," and exerpts from "Xi" by Melvin B. Tolson from HARLEM GALLERY AND OTHER POEMS by Melvin B. Tolson, ed. by Raymond Nelson (Charlottesville, VA, 1999). Reprinted with permission of the University Press of Virginia.

Jean Toomer: "Song of the Son," "Reapers," "November Cotton Flower," "Portrait in Georgia," "Georgia Dusk," and "Her Lips are Copper Wire" from CANE by Jean Toomer. Copyright © 1923 by Boni & Liveright, renewed 1951 by Jean Toomer. Used by permission of Liveright Publishing Corporation. "Gum" is reprinted from the unpublished poems of Jean Toomer in the Yale Collection of American Literature, Beinecke Rare Book and Manuscript Library, Yale University.

Robert Penn Warren: From THE COLLECTED POEMS OF ROBERT PENN WARREN. Copyright © by Robert Penn Warren. Reprinted by permission of William Morris Agency, Inc.

William Carlos Williams: From COLLECTED POEMS: 1909–1939, vol. II, copyright © 1938 by New Directions Publishing Corp. From PATERSON, copyright © 1946 by William Carlos Williams. From the Prologue to "Kora in Hell" by William Carlos Williams from IMAGINATIONS, copyright © 1970 by Florence H. Williams. Reprinted by permission of New Directions Publishing Corp.

Yvor Winters: From THE SELECTED POEMS OF YVOR WINTERS, ed. R. L. Barth. Reprinted with permission of Swallow Press/Ohio University Press, Athens, Ohio.

William Butler Yeats: "Leda and the Swan," "Sailing to Byzantium," "The Tower," and "Among School Children" reprinted with the permission of Scribner, a division of Simon & Schuster, Inc., from THE COLLECTED WORKS OF W. B. YEATS, VOL. I: THE POEMS, rev., ed. Richard J. Finneran. Copyright © 1928 by The Macmillan Co.; copyright renewed 1956 by Georgie Yeats. "In Memory of Eva Gore Booth and Con Markiewicz," "A Dialogue of Self and Soul," "Byzantium," "Vacillation," and "Crazy Jane Talks With the Bishop" reprinted with the permission of Scribner, a division of Simon & Schuster, Inc. from THE COLLECTED WORKS OF W. B. YEATS, VOL. I: THE POEMS, rev., ed. Richard J. Finneran. Copyright © 1933 by The Macmillan Co.; copyright renewed 1961 by Bertha Georgie Yeats. "Meru" reprinted with the permission of Scribner, a division of Simon & Schuster, Inc., from THE COLLECTED WORKS OF W. B. YEATS, VOL. I: THE POEMS, rev., ed. Richard J. Finneran. Copyright © 1934 by The Macmillan Co.; copyright renewed

1962 by Bertha Georgie Yeats. "The Gyres," "Lapis Lazuli," "An Acre of Grass," "The Spur," "Long-Legged Fly," "The Circus Animals' Desertion," "Under Ben Bulben," "Man and the Echo," and "Politics" reprinted with the permission of Scribner, a division of Simon & Schuster, Inc. from THE COLLECTED WORKS OF W. B. YEATS, VOL. I: THE POEMS, rev., ed. Richard J. Finneran. Copyright © 1940 by The Macmillan Co.; copyright renewed 1968 by Bertha Georgie Yeats, Michael Butler Yeats, Anne Yeats. From "Introduction" from ESSAYS AND INTRODUCTIONS by William Butler Yeats, reprinted with permission of Scribner, a division of Simon & Schuster, Inc. Copyright © 1961 by Mrs. W. B. Yeats.

Louis Zukofsky: From COMPLETE SHORT POETRY of Louis Zukofsky, pp. 8–11, 15–18, 52–53. Copyright © 1991 by Paul Zukofsky. Reprinted with permission of The John Hopkins University Press.

Every effort has been made to contact the copyright holders of each selection. Rights holders of any selection not credited should contact W. W. Norton & Co., 500 Fifth Avenue, New York, NY 10110, for a correction to be made in the next reprinting of our work.

Index

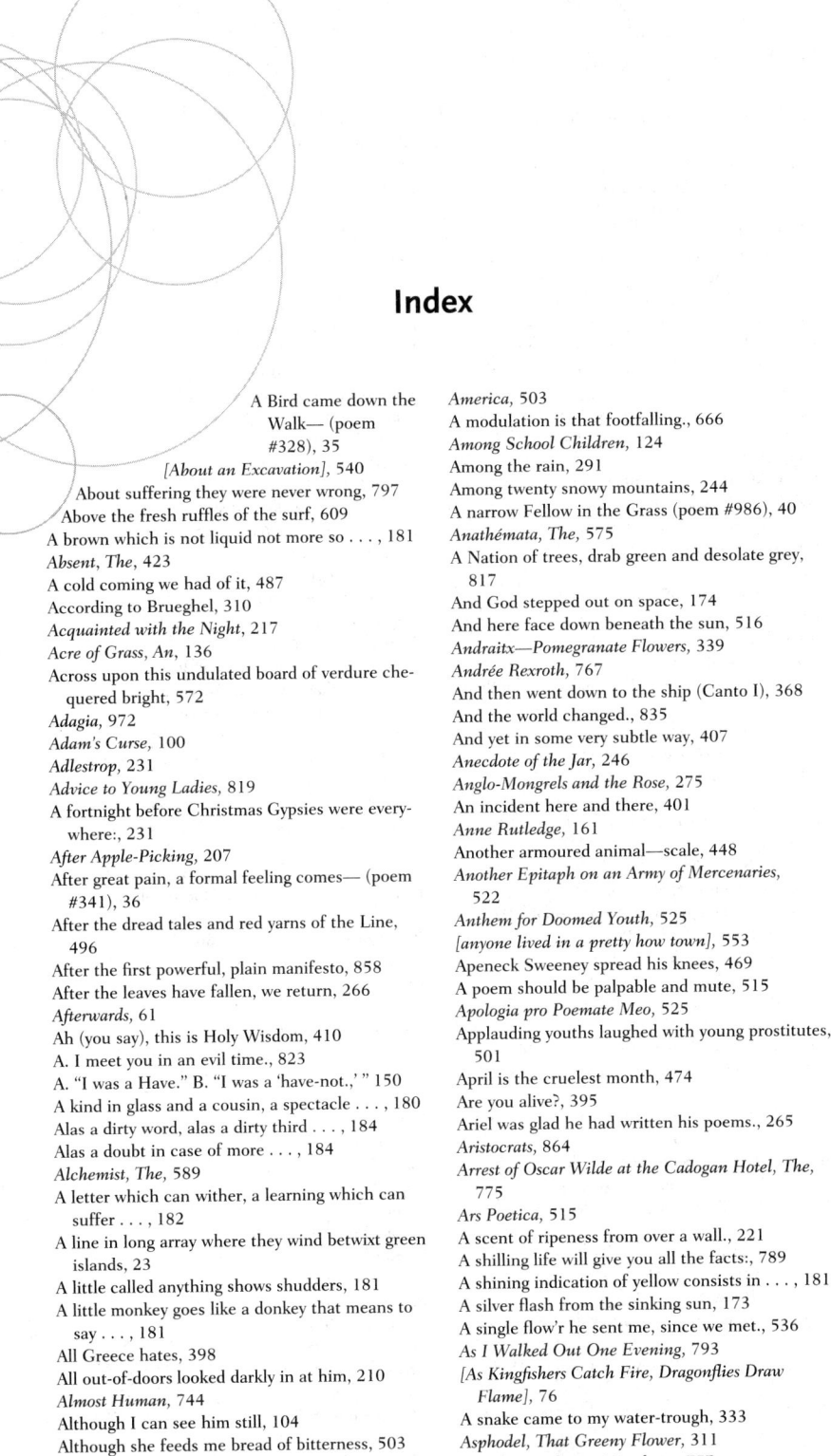